THE INTERLINEAR
LITERAL TRANSLATION OF
The GREEK
NEW TESTAMENT

With the Authorized Version

CONVENIENTLY PRESENTED IN THE MARGINS
FOR READY REFERENCE & WITH THE VARIOUS
READINGS OF THE EDITIONS OF *ELZEVIR 1624,*
GRIESBACH, LACHMANN, TISCHENDORF,
TREGELLES, ALFORD & WORDSWORTH

.TO WHICH HAS BEEN ADDED *A NEW*

Greek-English New Testament Lexicon

Supplemented by *A* Chapter Elucidating the Synonyms of the
New Testament, with A Complete Index to the Synonyms

BY THE LATE GEORGE RICKER BERRY, PH.D.

of the University of Chicago & Colgate University
Department of Semitic Languages

Editor

Chicago, WILCOX & FOLLETT Company

1952

The Value of HEBREW and GREEK to Clergymen.

1. Without *some* knowledge of Hebrew and Greek, you cannot understand the critical commentaries on the Scriptures, and a commentary that is *not* critical is of doubtful value.

2. Without *some* knowledge of Hebrew and Greek, you cannot satisfy yourself or those who look to you for help as to the changes which you will find in the Revised Old and New Testaments.

3. Without *some* knowledge of Hebrew and Greek, you cannot appreciate the critical discussions, now so frequent, relating to the books of the Old and New Testaments.

4. Without *some* knowledge of Hebrew and Greek, you cannot be certain, in a single instance, that in your sermon based on a Scripture text, you are presenting the correct teaching of that text.

5. Without *some* knowledge of Hebrew and Greek, you cannot be an independent student, or a reliable interpreter of the word of God.

6. As much knowledge of Hebrew can be secured, with the same method, under the same circumstances, by the same pupil, in *one* year, with the aid of the Interlinear Old Testament, as can be gained of Latin in three years.   Greek, though somewhat more difficult, may be readily acquired within a brief period with the aid of the Interlinear New Testament (which contains a lexicon) and an elementary Greek grammar.

7. The Hebrew language has, in all, about 7,000 words, and of these 1,000 occur in the Old Testament over 25 times each.

8. The Hebrew grammar has but *one* form for the Relative pronoun in all cases, numbers and genders; but *three* forms for the Demonstrative pronoun.   The possible verbal forms are about 300 as compared with the 1,200 found in Greek.   It has practically no declension.

9. Within ten years the average man wastes more time in fruitless reading and indifferent talk, than would be used in acquiring a good working knowledge of Hebrew and Greek that in turn would impart to his teaching that quality of independence and of reliability which so greatly enhances one's power as a teacher.

10. There is not *one* minister in *ten* who might not if he but *would*, find time and opportunity for such study of Hebrew and Greek as would enable him to make a thoroughly practical use of it in his work as a Bible-preacher and Bible-teacher.

INTRODUCTION.

THERE are many ways scarcely needing mention in which the Interlinear New Testament may prove its value, not the least of which is the facility with which it enables one, even if rusty in his Greek, to put his finger on the original Greek word or phrase, and at the same instant upon a literal rendering. To many it will repay its cost in the time saved from turning to a Greek dictionary. Of course it becomes a necessary adjunct to every complete working library.

The ever-growing interest in New Testament study makes it desirable that the general reader, who would be well informed on current topics, should have some acquaintance with the relation of the standard English version to the original text, while a still more intimate knowledge on the part of the clergyman and the Bible Class teacher would seem almost imperative. Toward this end no aid is likely to be more helpful than the Interlinear New Testament.

This work is intended therefore to help the English reader of the New Testament, who may desire to refer to the actual words used in the Greek text. It has not been framed to teach people Greek, though it may be used to good advantage for that purpose.

The Interlinear Translation brings to view certain points of interest that no other translation has ever pretended to give. Take for instance the word 'master.' This word 'master' is used in the Authorized Version to translate *six* different Greek words, all bearing different shades of meaning. The word 'judgment' in the Authorized Version stands for *eight* different Greek words in the original ; and so of many others. Of particles, 'but' represents *twelve* different words ; 'by,' *eleven ;* 'for,' *eighteen ;* 'in,' *fifteen ;* 'of,' *thirteen ;* and 'on,' *nine.*

We do not intend to imply that a given Greek word can be, or that it is desirable that it should be, translated in all places by the same English word. On the other hand, one should be able to ascertain, on occasion, just what the facts are ; and it is an interesting feature of the Interlinear New Testament that in the margin appears the English word of the Authorized Version ; in the text appears the Greek original of that particular word ; and immediately under it, the English word that is its nearest literal equivalent.

We give the Greek Text, with an interlinear translation as literal as may be to be useful ; and in the margin the Authorized Version, divided into paragraphs to correspond to the Greek text.

This work also gives in its notes not only the various readings of six different

i

INTRODUCTION.

editors of the Greek Testament, but also these variations *in English* whenever the sense is affected thereby, but without attempting to present in every case all the minute shades of meaning which a Greek scholar will attach to them. Many of these variations may be thought to be of no great importance, descending even to the different spelling of the same word ; but from this they rise to variations of the greatest importance. All are of interest, because they concern the word of God, and are here made available to the English reader, to whom we furnish in this volume all he may require both as to the *text* of the New Testament, and for its word-for-word *translation*.

THE GREEK TEXT.

The Greek Text is that of Stephens, 1550, which has long been in common use ; but as the edition of Elzevir, 1624, is the one often called the Received Text, or Textus Receptus, because of the words, "Textum . . . . ab omnibus receptum," occurring in the preface, we give the readings of this Elzevir edition in the notes, and mark them E. It is the text commonly reprinted on the Continent. In the main they are one and the same ; and either of them may be referred to as the Textus Receptus.

There are a number of minute variations between the editors which we do not attempt to present. In all these cases we have followed the majority of modern editors. With them we have also added the final ν to the third person singular and plural in σι ; third singular in ε ; in datives plural in σι, &c. For οὗτω we have given οὗτως, and αὑτοῦ where some have αὐτοῦ.

As to the *form* of the Greek text a few words are needed.

1. PARAGRAPHS.—We were disappointed in finding nothing like *authority* for where a paragraph ought to be. Ancient manuscripts were no help : they have few or no paragraphs. The editors all differed, each making paragraphs according to his own judgment. We were therefore obliged, after referring to the best examples, to form paragraphs for ourselves. We are anxious that our readers should remember that the paragraphs have *no authority*, which they might have had if the ancient manuscripts had agreed in the placing of them.

2. PARENTHESES.—Most of the editors have placed here and there parentheses in their Greek texts. These we have disregarded, seeing that there are no such things in the early Greek copies. We have placed them in the English where we deemed them necessary to preserve the sense, but not being in the Greek they also have no authority.

3. INVERTED COMMAS.—Some editors mark with inverted commas the words that are spoken, and others in a similar way mark the quotations from the Old Testament. But in some places it is doubtful where these quotations close, and it was thought best to omit them. These also, being absent from the ancient Greek copies, have no authority.

4. POINTS.—There is no authority anywhere for the punctuation. There are few or no points in the ancient copies, and editors naturally differ in their system of pointing. We have been obliged to punctuate for ourselves as we judged

best. We have not attempted to note the difference in the punctuation of the various editors, except in places where it materially alters the sense.

5. CAPITALS.—The only remark needed here is in reference to the names of God, of Christ, and of the Holy Spirit. The greatest difficulty is touching the word 'Spirit.' In some places it is very difficult to say whether the Holy Spirit as a person or the spirit of the Christian is referred to (see Rom. viii. 9); and if sometimes a small letter and sometimes a capital had been placed to the word πνεῦμα, in the Greek, persons would naturally have concluded that the question was thus indisputably settled. It was therefore judged best to put a small π everywhere. In the English we have been obliged to put a capital S when the Holy Spirit was referred to and so have retained it wherever we thought this was the case; but in some places it is really doubtful, and becomes a question for the spiritual judgment of the reader. The Greek will not help in the difficulty, because in the earliest copies every letter was a capital. In the other names we have followed the usage of modern editors; putting in the Greek a capital to Jesus but a small letter for Christ, and a small letter for Lord and for God.

6. VERSES.—In a few places it is doubtful where the verses should commence. In these cases we have followed Bruder's "Greek Concordance," though that work does not in all cases agree with itself.

THE INTERLINEAR TRANSLATION.

1. The plan. The Greek words have always been kept in their right order, and where the interlinear English would not make sense in the same order, the words have been numbered to show how they must be read. Thus, "And ⁷related ⁸to ⁹them ²also ¹those ³who ⁴had ⁵seen [⁶it]" (Luke viii. 36) are numbered so as to read "And those also who had seen [it] related to them."

To prevent this numbering, and transposition in reading, being increased unnecessarily, a few words are often made into a phrase. This has been done at the commencement of each sentence, where needed, two or more words being joined with a *low* hyphen. Thus, instead of

| Ἐγένετο δὲ | we have printed | ˙Ἐγένετο-δὲ. |
| ²It ³came ⁴to ⁵pass ¹and | | And it came to pass. |

The words in brackets [ ] are what have been added in the English to complete the sense where there is no word in the Greek to correspond to the words added.

Where a Greek word occurs which the English idiom requires should *not* be translated, the word stands alone with no English word under it: as ὅτι, 'that,' in Mark xii. 7; and οὐ in verse 14, where there are *two* negatives, which, if both were translated, would in English destroy one another; and so of μή, where it simply marks the sentence as a question.

In a few places we have been obliged to put a double translation, mostly because of the double negatives used in the Greek, where they do not immediately follow one another, and so could not be translated by such strengthened expressions as 'not at all,' 'in no wise,' &c. In such cases we have placed a *literal* translation below the one required in English. Thus—

οὐδέν.
anything.
(*lit.* nothing.)

2. Points of grammar. *The Aorist.* This tense of the Greek verb has been at all times the most difficult to deal with, being translated, in the Authorized version (and by others), sometimes by the *present*, sometimes by the *past*, sometimes by the *future*, and sometimes by the *perfect*. Grammarians say that, in the main, it is the *indefinite past*, and we have endeavored, as far as may be, to keep it to this, avoiding, except in a few places, the translation of it as a perfect. We all know what stress is often laid—and rightly so—upon the word 'have.' If I say, 'he *has* cleansed me,' it is more than saying 'he cleansed me.' The former expression indicates the *perfect*, and implies a continuance of the act, or its effects, to the present time ; whereas the latter speaks of an act at some time in the past, without anything being implied as to its continuance.

For this reason it appeared unadvisable to translate the aorist as the perfect, except in a few places where the true sense would otherwise have been destroyed. It is true that the English idiom requires it elsewhere, but it was thought best to preserve the above distinction. An extreme case will illustrate this point. In 1 Corinthians v. 9 occurs the word ἔγραψα, 'I wrote ;' and in verse 11 the same word precisely—'I wrote ;' but the Authorized Version (and others) put for the *latter* 'I have written.' It is there accompanied with the word 'now'—'now I have written.' This is needed for good English ; we have put 'I wrote' in both places, but have placed a comma after the word 'now' to make it read more smoothly. We preserve this uniformity for the sake of literalness, always remembering the fact of the Authorized Version being in proximity, which will make all plain in such instances.

In a few places we have translated the aorist as a *present* where the sense demanded it. As, for instance, ἔγνω, in 2 Timothy ii. 19 : "The Lord *knows* those that are his," instead of "the Lord knew," &c.

The Imperfect. This is mostly translated as 'I was writing,' or 'I wrote.' But there are a few places where this tense is said to have a different meaning. This will be best illustrated by the much-disputed passage in Romans ix. 3 : "For *I could wish* that myself were accursed from Christ for my brethren." Here the word for 'I could wish' is in the imperfect. If the learned were agreed as to a translation we should have kept to the same, but while some translate 'I could wish,' as a *conditional present*, others give 'I could have wished' as a *conditional past*. We have thought it best to keep the sense of the simple imperfect as referred by Winer to this passage. "*I felt a wish*, and should do so still, could it be gratified . . . . (a conditional clause being understood)." We have put "I was wishing."

The Perfect. This we have kept as uniform as we could, implying an act perfected, but continuing to the present in itself or its consequences. In a few

places we have translated it as a *present:* as in Matthew xii. 47, in the sense of
'they have stood and still *are standing.*'

The Subjunctive. In this mood perhaps we have deviated further from
ordinary practice than in any other, but we have endeavored, as far as
practicable, to keep it distinct from both the English *imperative* and the Greek
future. Thus in Romans xiii. 9 for οὐ φονεύσεις (future indicative) we have,
'thou shalt not commit murder;' but in James ii. 11, for μὴ φονεύσῃς (aorist
subjunctive) 'thou mayest not commit murder.'

THE PRONOUNS. At times it is important to know whether the pronouns
are emphatic or not. ἐγὼ γράφω and γράφω are both 'I write;' but where the
ἐγώ is put in the Greek, it makes the pronoun emphatic. This however is
somewhat due to the writer's style, and in John's Gospel and Epistles, it has
been judged that, from his peculiar style of composition, he puts in the pronouns where emphasis is not always intended. John ix. 27 gives a good example of the same verb with and without the pronoun in the Greek: "Why
again do ye wish to hear? do *ye* also wish to become his disciples?"

COMPOUND WORDS. It was found impracticable to translate these uniformly
throughout. For instance, if γνῶσις be translated 'knowledge,' it might be
thought that ἐπίγνωσις should be 'full knowledge,' &c. : but on referring to a
Concordance it will be seen that the latter word cannot be intensified in all
places, and then to translate it by 'knowledge' in some places, and 'full
knowledge' in others looks too much like interpretation. We have therefore
translated both words by 'knowledge.' In the few places however where one
of each of such words occurs in the same sentence, some distinction was imperative.

THE NOTES.

The references to the notes are marked thus in the text "αὐτοῦ" : the mark"
showing how far the variation extends. In a few places a note occurs *within* a
note. If words are to be omitted or transposed by some editors but not by
others, these latter may want to alter a word in the sentence. In such cases *one*
tick shows the termination of the *inner* note. Thus ᵃ.... ᵇ.... ⁱ.... ᵃ
See notes ᵛ and ᵚ Matthew v. 44.

This mark — stands for *omit;* and + for *add;* but in some places all the
editors do *not* actually omit, some putting the word in brackets as *doubtful.*
In that case it is put thus, "—αὐτοῦ [L] TTr"; which means that Lachmann
marks the word as *doubtful,* and Tischendorf and Tregelles *omit* it. In some
cases, *all* mark a word as doubtful, and then it could be put either thus, δὲ
[LTTr], or [δὲ] LTTr; we have adopted the latter plan. In some places the
editors mark *part* of a word as doubtful, mostly in compound words. See for
instance [ἐκ]διώξουσιν read by TrA in Luke xi. 49.

It will be seen by this that the marks [ ] *applied to the Greek or the editors*
in the notes always refer to readings which the editors point out as doubtful.
They must not be confounded with the same marks *in the English* text and
notes, which always point out that there is *no* corresponding word in the Greek.

INTRODUCTION.

In some places where a word is added by the editors, another English word is added in the note to show the *connection* of the new word. Thus in Luke xv. 2, the word 'both' is added; but it falls between the words 'the' and 'Pharisees,' therefore it is put thus in the note "+ τε both (the) LTTrA" to show that it must be read 'both the Pharisees.' Slight variations in the use of the parenthesis occur in the course of the work, but we trust the meaning intended will in all cases be plain to the student.

Where long pieces are to be omitted they are marked in the text where they commence and where they end, but in the notes the first word or two only and the last are named with . . . between. Thus in Luke ix. 55, note ⁸stands, "— καὶ εἶπεν (*verse* 55) . . . . σῶσαι (verse 56) LTTrA ;—ὁ γὰρ . . . . σῶσαι G. The four editors omit the whole twenty words; but G omits only the last twelve. In Luke xxiv. 10, note ⁷is thus, '+ ἡ the [. . .], implying that *some* word must be added.

We have endeavored to make the notes as plain as possible for the English reader. One point still needs to be explained. For instance, in Luke vii. 22 occur the words "and ²answering ¹Jesus said;" but a note omits the word 'Jesus,' and then it must be read (as stated in the note) "and answering he said." This is because the word εἶπεν (as already explained) stands for both 'he said,' and 'said.' Also in verse 27 occur the words ἐγὼ ἀποστέλλω, 'I send,' but a note omits the word ἐγὼ, 'I,' and then ἀποστέλλω is to be read 'I send,' but without emphasis on the 'I.'

The Money and Measures of the New Testament.

1. MONEY. It was deemed better not to attempt to *translate* the sums of money named in the New Testament, as we have no corresponding pieces to those then in use. We have therefore used the Greek words untranslated, and give a list of them here. It is not without interest and instruction to know the approximate value of money and the extent of the measures used. For instance, in Revelation vi. 6 we read of " a measure of wheat for a penny " in the Authorized Version; but this leaves the reader in doubt as to how far it speaks of scarcity and dearness. We want at least to know the value of the 'penny,' and the capacity of the 'measure.'

The following lists, it is hoped, will be useful; but approximate values only can now be arrived at.

GREEK.	AUTHORIZED VERSION.	IN THIS WORK.	APPROXIMATE VALUE. $
λεπτόν	mite	lepton	0.001875
κοδράντης	farthing	kodrantes	0.00375
ἀσσάριον	farthing	assarion	0.015
δηνάριον	penny	denarius	0.16
δραχμή	piece of silver	drachma	0.16
δίδραχμον	tribute money	didrachma	0.32

INTRODUCTION.

GREEK.	AUTHORIZED VERSION.	IN THIS WORK.	APPROXIMATE VALUE.
			$
στατήρ	piece of money	stater	00.64
μνάα	pound	mina	15.75
τάλαντον	talent	talent	943.66
ἀργύριον	piece of silver.		

This is the common word for silver and money, as *l'argent* in French. In different places it would represent wholly different coins.

2. MEASURES OF CAPACITY.

GREEK.	AUTHORIZED VERSION.	IN THIS WORK.	APPROXIMATE Gallon.	Pint.
ξέστης	pot (liquid measure)	vessels*	0	1
χοῖνιξ	measure (dry ")	chœnix	0	2
μόδιος	bushel (dry ")	corn measure*	2	0
σάτον	measure (dry ")	seah	2	1
βάτος	measure (liquid ")	bath	7	4
μετρητής	firkin (liquid ")	metretes	8	4
κόρος	measure (dry ")	cor	64	1

It is judged that those marked * are referred to as measures independent of their capacity : such as "washing of vessels," &c.

3. LONG MEASURE.

Here the names already in use were near enough to be retained.

GREEK.	AUTHORIZED VERSION.	IN THIS WORK.	Feet.	Inches.
πῆχυς	cubit	cubit	1	6 to 9
ὀργυιά	fathom	fathom	6	0
στάδιον	furlong	furlong	606	9
μίλιον	mile	mile	4854	0
ὁδὸς σαββάτου	sabbath day's journey	6 furlongs		

vii

LIST OF SIGNS AND EDITIONS USED.

E Elzevir, 1624.

G Griesbach, 1805.

L Lachmann, 1842–1850.

T Tischendorf, Eighth Edition, 1865–1872.

Tᵣ Tregelles, 1857–1872.

A Alford, vol. i. 1868 ; vol. ii. 1871 ; vol. iii. 1865 ; vol. iv. 1862, 1870.

W Wordsworth, 1870.

+ signifies *an addition*.

—   ,,   *an omission*.

[ ]   ,,   in the interlinear translation, that there is *no Greek word* corresponding to the English.

[ ] signifies in the notes that an editor marks the reading as *doubtful*.

‖   ,,   how far the variation in the Greek text extends.

Text. Rec. refers to *both* Stephens 1550 and E.

ΒΙΒΛΟΣ γενέσεως Ἰησοῦ χριστοῦ, υἱοῦ ᵇΔαβίδ,‖ υἱοῦ
BOOK of [the] generation of Jesus Christ; son of David, son
Ἀβραάμ.
of Abraham.

2 Ἀβραὰμ ἐγέννησεν τὸν Ἰσαάκ· Ἰσαὰκ.δὲ ἐγέννησεν τὸν
Abraham begat Isaac; and Isaac begat
Ἰακώβ· Ἰακὼβ.δὲ ἐγέννησεν τὸν Ἰούδαν καὶ τοὺς ἀδελφοὺς
Jacob; and Jacob begat Judas and ²brethren
αὐτοῦ· 3 Ἰούδας.δὲ ἐγέννησεν τὸν Φαρὲς καὶ τὸν Ζαρὰ ἐκ
¹his; and Judas begat Phares and Zara of
τῆς Θαμάρ· Φαρὲς.δὲ ἐγέννησεν τὸν Ἐσρώμ· Ἐσρὼμ.δὲ
Thamar; and Phares begat Esrom; and Esrom
ἐγέννησεν τὸν Ἀράμ· 4 Ἀράμ.δὲ ἐγέννησεν τὸν ᶜἈμιναδάβ·‖
begat Aram; and Aram begat Aminadab;
ᶜἈμιναδάβ‖.δὲ ἐγέννησεν τὸν Ναασσών· Ναασσὼν.δὲ ἐγέννη-
and Aminadab begat Naasson; and Naasson be-
σεν τὸν Σαλμών· 5 Σαλμὼν.δὲ ἐγέννησεν τὸν ᵈΒοόζ‖ ἐκ τῆς
gat Salmon; and Salmon begat Booz of
Ῥαχάβ· ᵈΒοόζ‖.δὲ ἐγέννησεν τὸν ᵉὨβήδ‖ ἐκ τῆς Ρούθ· ᵉὨβὴδ‖
Rachab; and Booz begat Obed of Ruth; and Obed
δὲ ἐγέννησεν τὸν Ἰεσσαί· 6 Ἰεσσαὶ.δὲ ἐγέννησεν τὸν ᵇΔαβὶδ‖
and begat Jesse; and Jesse begat David
τὸν βασιλέα. ᵇΔαβὶδ‖.δὲ ᶠὁ βασιλεὺς‖ ἐγέννησεν τὸν ᵍΣολο-
the king. And David the king begat Solo-
μῶντα‖ ἐκ τῆς τοῦ Οὐρίου· 7 Σολομὼν.δὲ ἐγέν-
mon of the [one who had been wife] of Urias; and Solomon be-
νησεν τὸν Ῥοβοάμ· Ῥοβοὰμ.δὲ ἐγέννησεν τὸν Ἀβιά· Ἀβιὰ
gat Roboam; and Roboam begat Abia; ²Abia
δὲ ἐγέννησεν τὸν ʰἈσά·‖ 8 ʰἈσά‖.δὲ ἐγέννησεν τὸν Ἰωσαφάτ·
¹and begat Asa; and Asa begat Josaphat;
Ἰωσαφάτ.δὲ ἐγέννησεν τὸν Ἰωράμ· Ἰωρὰμ δὲ ἐγέννησεν τὸν
and Josaphat begat Joram; and Joram begat
ⁱʲὈζίαν· 9 Ὀζίας‖.δὲ ἐγέννησεν τὸν Ἰωάθαμ· Ἰωάθαμ.δὲ
Ozias; and Ozias begat Joatham; and Joatham
ἐγέννησεν τὸν Ἄχαζ· Ἄχαζ.δὲ ἐγέννησεν τὸν ᵏἘζεκίαν·‖
begat Achaz; and Achaz begat Ezekias;
10 ˡἘζεκίας‖.δὲ ἐγέννησεν τὸν Μανασσῆ· Μανασσῆς.δὲ ἐγέν-
and Ezekias begat Manasses; and Manasses be-
νησεν τὸν ᵐἈμών·‖ ᵐἈμών‖.δὲ ἐγέννησεν τὸν ⁿἸωσίαν·
gat Amon; and Amon begat Josias;
11 ᵒἸωσίας‖.δὲ ἐγέννησεν τὸν Ἰεχονίαν καὶ τοὺς ἀδελφοὺς
and Josias begat Jechonias and ²brethren
αὐτοῦ, ἐπὶ τῆς μετοικεσίας Βαβυλῶνος. 12 Μετὰ.δὲ
¹his, at [the time] of the carrying away of Babylon. And after

THE book of the generation of Jesus Christ, the son of David, the son of Abraham.

2 Abraham begat Isaac; and Isaac begat Jacob; and Jacob begat Judas and his brethren; 3 and Judas begat Phares and Zara of Thamar; and Phares begat Esrom; and Esrom begat Aram; 4 and Aram begat Aminadab; and Aminadab begat Naasson; and Naasson begat Salmon; 5 and Salmon begat Booz of Rachab; and Booz begat Obed of Ruth; and Obed begat Jesse; 6 and Jesse begat David the king; and David the king begat Solomon of her that had been the wife of Urias; 7 and Solomon begat Roboam; and Roboam begat Abia; and Abia begat Asa; 8 and Asa begat Josaphat; and Josaphat begat Joram; and Joram begat Ozias; 9 and Ozias begat Joatham; and Joatham begat Achaz; and Achaz begat Ezekias; 10 and Ezekias begat Manasses; and Manasses begat Amon; and Amon begat Josias; 11 and Josias begat Jechonias and his brethren, about the time they were carried away to Babylon: 12 and after

---

ª Εὐαγγέλιον κατὰ Μαθθαῖον (Ματθ. GW) GLTrW ; [Εὐαγ.] κατὰ Μαθθ. Α; κατὰ Μαθθ. Τ.
ᵇ Δαυὶδ GW ; Δαυεὶδ LTTrA. ᶜ Ἀμειναδάβ Α. ᵈ Βοὸς LTr ; Βοὲς ΤΑ. ᵉ Ἰωβὴδ LTTrA·
ᶠ — ὁ βασιλεὺς LTTrA. ᵍ Σολομῶνα GTTrAW. ʰ Ἀσάφ LTTrA. ⁱ Ὀζείαν LTTrA·
ʲ Ὀζείας LTTrA. ᵏ Ἐζεκείαν L. ˡ Ἐζεκείας L. ᵐ Ἀμώς LTTrA. ⁿ Ἰωσείαν LTTrA·
ᵒ Ἰωσείας LTTrA.

they were brought to Babylon, Jechonias begat Salathiel; and Salathiel begat Zorobabel; 13 and Zorobabel begat Abiud; and Abiud begat Eliakim; and Eliakim begat Azor; 14 and Azor begat Sadoc; and Sadoc begat Achim; and Achim begat Eliud; 15 and Eliud begat Eleazar; and Eleazar begat Matthan; and Matthan begat Jacob; 16 and Jacob begat Joseph the husband of Mary, of whom was born Jesus, who is called Christ.

τὴν μετοικεσίαν Βαβυλῶνος, Ἰεχονίας ⁹ἐγέννησεν‖ τὸν Σαλα-
the carrying away of Babylon, Jechonias begat Sala-
θιήλ· Σαλαθιὴλ.δὲ ⁹ἐγέννησεν‖ τὸν Ζοροβάβελ 13 Ζοροβά-
thiel; and Salathiel begat Zorobabel; ²Zoroba-
βελ δὲ ⁹ἐγέννησεν‖ τὸν Ἀβιούδ· Ἀβιούδ.δὲ ἐγέννησεν τὸν
bel ¹and begat Abiud; and Abiud begat
Ἐλιακείμ· Ἐλιακείμ.δὲ ἐγέννησεν τὸν Ἀζώρ· 14 Ἀζώρ.δὲ
Eliakim; and Eliakim begat Azor; ²Achim and Azor
ἐγέννησεν τὸν Σαδώκ· Σαδώκ.δὲ ἐγέννησεν τὸν Ἀχείμ· Ἀχείμ
begat Sadoc; and Sadoc begat Achim; ²Achim
δὲ ἐγέννησεν τὸν Ἐλιούδ· 15 Ἐλιούδ.δὲ ἐγέννησεν τὸν Ἐλεά-
¹and begat Eliud; and Eliud begat Elea-
ζαρ· Ἐλεάζαρ.δὲ ἐγέννησεν τὸν ʳΜατθάν·‖ ʳΜατθάν‖.δὲ ἐγέν-
zar; and Eleazar begat Matthan; and Matthan be-
νησεν τὸν Ἰακώβ· 16 Ἰακώβ.δὲ ἐγέννησεν τὸν Ἰωσὴφ τὸν
gat Jacob; and Jacob begat Joseph the
ἄνδρα Μαρίας, ἐξ ἧς ἐγεννήθη Ἰησοῦς ὁ λεγόμενος χριστός.
husband of Mary, of whom was born Jesus, who is called Christ.

17 So all the generations from Abraham to David are fourteen generations; and from David until the carrying away into Babylon are fourteen generations; and from the carrying away into Babylon unto Christ are fourteen generations.

17 Πᾶσαι.οὖν αἱ γενεαὶ ἀπὸ Ἀβραὰμ ἕως ˢΔαβὶδ‖
So all the generations from Abraham to David [were]
γενεαὶ δεκατέσσαρες· καὶ ἀπὸ ˢΔαβὶδ‖ ἕως τῆς μετοικεσίας
²generations ¹fourteen; and from David until the carrying away
Βαβυλῶνος, γενεαὶ δεκατέσσαρες· καὶ ἀπὸ τῆς μετοικεσίας
of Babylon, ²generations ¹fourteen; and from the carrying away
Βαβυλῶνος ἕως τοῦ χριστοῦ, γενεαὶ δεκατέσσαρες.
of Babylon to the Christ, ²generations ¹fourteen.

18 Now the birth of Jesus Christ was on this wise: When as his mother Mary was espoused to Joseph, before they came together, she was found with child of the Holy Ghost. 19 Then Joseph her husband, being a just man, and not willing to make her a public example, was minded to put her away privily. 20 But while he thought on these things, behold, the angel of the Lord appeared unto him in a dream, saying, Joseph, thou son of David, fear not to take unto thee Mary thy wife: for that which is conceived in her is of the Holy Ghost. 21 And she shall bring forth a son, and thou shalt call his name JESUS: for he shall save his people from their sins. 22 Now all this was done, that it might be fulfilled which was spoken of the Lord by the prophet, saying, 23 Behold, a virgin shall be with child, and shall bring forth a son, and they shall

18 Τοῦ.δὲ.ᵗἸησοῦ‖ χριστοῦ ἡ ᵛγέννησις‖ οὕτως ἦν. Μνη-
Now of Jesus Christ the birth thus was. ⁶Having
στευθείσης ʷγὰρ‖ τῆς.μητρὸς.αὐτοῦ Μαρίας τῷ Ἰωσήφ, πρὶν.ἢ
⁶been ⁷betrothed ¹for ²his ²mother ²Mary to Joseph, before
συνελθεῖν αὐτοὺς εὑρέθη ἐν.γαστρὶ.ἔχουσα ἐκ πνεύματος
²came ³together ¹they she was found to be with child of [the] ²Spirit
ἁγίου. 19 Ἰωσὴφ.δὲ ὁ.ἀνὴρ.αὐτῆς, δίκαιος ὢν, καὶ μὴ θέλων
¹Holy. But Joseph her husband, ²righteous ¹being, and not willing
αὐτὴν ˣπαραδειγματίσαι,‖ ἐβουλήθη ʸλάθρα‖ ἀπολῦσαι αὐτήν.
her to make a public example, purposed secretly to put ²away ¹her.
20 ταῦτα.δὲ αὐτοῦ.ἐνθυμηθέντος, ἰδού, ἄγγελος κυρίου
And ⁵these ⁶things ¹when ²he ³had ⁴pondered, behold, an angel of [the] Lord
κατ᾽ ὄναρ ἐφάνη αὐτῷ, λέγων, Ἰωσήφ, υἱὸς ˢΔαβὶδ,‖ μὴ
in a dream appeared to him, saying, Joseph, son of David, ²not
φοβηθῇς παραλαβεῖν Μαριὰμ τ.ὴν.γυναῖκά.σου· τὸ.γὰρ ἐν
¹fear to take to [thee] Mary thy wife; for that which in
αὐτῇ γεννηθὲν ἐκ πνεύματός ἐστιν ἁγίου. 21 τέξεται.δὲ υἱόν,
her is begotten ²of [³the] ²Spirit ¹is ⁴Holy. And she shall bring forth a son,
καὶ καλέσεις τὸ.ὄνομα.αὐτοῦ Ἰησοῦν· αὐτὸς.γὰρ σώσει τὸν
and thou shalt call his name Jesus; for he shall save
λαὸν αὐτοῦ ἀπὸ τῶν.ἁμαρτιῶν.αὐτῶν. 22 Τοῦτο.δὲ ὅλον
²people ¹his from their sins. Now this all
γέγονεν, ἵνα πληρωθῇ τὸ ῥηθὲν ὑπὸ ᶻτοῦ‖ κυρίου
came to pass, that might be fulfilled that which was spoken by the Lord
διὰ τοῦ προφήτου, λέγοντος, 23 Ἰδοὺ ἡ παρθένος ἐν
through the prophet, saying, Behold, the virgin ³with
γαστρὶ.ἕξει καὶ τέξεται υἱόν, καὶ καλέσουσιν τὸ ὄνομα
⁴child ¹shall ²be, and shall bring forth a son, and they shall call ²name

---

⁹ γεννᾷ begets A. GLTTrAW. ʷ — γὰρ for LTTr[A]. ʳ Ματθάν LTTrA. ˢ Δαυὶδ GW; Δαυείδ LTTrA. ᵗ — Ἰησοῦ Tr. ᵛ γένεσις LTTrAW. ˣ δειγματίσαι LTTrA. ʸ λάθρᾳ L. ᶻ — τοῦ (read | the|) LTTrAW.

αὐτοῦ Ἐμμανουήλ, ὅ ἐστιν μεθερμηνευόμενον, Μεθ᾿ ἡμῶν
  ¹his   Emmanuel,   which is,   being interpreted,   ²With ³us
ᵃὁ‖ θεός. 24 ᵇΔιεγερθεὶς‖ δὲ ᶜὁ‖ Ἰωσὴφ ἀπὸ τοῦ ὕπνου, ἐποί-
¹God.   And ²having ³been ⁴aroused ¹Joseph from the sleep,   did
ησεν ὡς προσέταξεν αὐτῷ ὁ ἄγγελος κυρίου· καὶ παρέλαβεν
as had ordered him the angel of [the] Lord, and took to [him]
τὴν.γυναῖκα.αὐτοῦ, 25 καὶ οὐκ.ἐγίνωσκεν αὐτὴν ἕως οὗ
  his wife,   and   knew not   her   until
ἔτεκεν ᵈτὸν‖ υἱὸν ᵉαὐτῆς τὸν πρωτότοκον·‖ καὶ ἐκάλεσεν
she brought forth ²son ¹her the firstborn ;   and he called
τὸ.ὄνομα.αὐτοῦ Ἰησοῦν.
  his name   Jesus.

2 Τοῦ.δὲ.Ἰησοῦ γεννηθέντος ἐν Βηθλεὲμ τῆς Ἰουδαίας,
  Now Jesus   having been born in Bethlehem   of Judæa,
ἐν ἡμέραις Ἡρώδου τοῦ βασιλέως, ἰδού, μάγοι ἀπὸ ἀνατολῶν
in [the] days of Herod the   king, behold, magi from [the] east
παρεγένοντο εἰς Ἱεροσόλυμα, 2 λέγοντες, Ποῦ ἐστιν ὁ τεχ-
 arrived   at Jerusalem,   saying,   Where is he who has
θεὶς βασιλεὺς τῶν Ἰουδαίων; εἴδομεν γὰρ αὐτοῦ τὸν ἀστέρα
been born King of the Jews? for we saw his   star
ἐν τῇ ἀνατολῇ, καὶ ἤλθομεν προσκυνῆσαι αὐτῷ. 3 Ἀκούσας
in the east,   and are come to do homage to him.   ⁵Having ⁶heard
δὲ ᶠἩρώδης ὁ βασιλεὺς‖ ἐταράχθη, καὶ πᾶσα Ἱεροσόλυμα
·but ¹Herod ²the ⁴king he was troubled, and all   Jerusalem
μετ᾿ αὐτοῦ· 4 καὶ συναγαγὼν πάντας τοὺς ἀρχιερεῖς καὶ
with⁻ him.   And having gathered together all the chief priests and
γραμματεῖς τοῦ λαοῦ, ἐπυνθάνετο παρ᾿ αὐτῶν, ποῦ ὁ χριστὸς
scribes of the people, he inquired of them where the Christ
γεννᾶται. 5 Οἱ.δὲ ᵍεἶπον‖ αὐτῷ, Ἐν Βηθλεὲμ τῆς Ἰουδαίας.
should be born. And they said to him, In Bethlehem   of Judæa :
οὕτως.γὰρ γέγραπται διὰ τοῦ προφήτου, 6 Καὶ σὺ Βηθλεέμ,
for thus   it has been written by the prophet, And thou, Bethlehem,
γῆ Ἰούδα, οὐδαμῶς ἐλαχίστη εἶ ἐν τοῖς ἡγεμόσιν Ἰούδα· ἐκ
land of Juda, in no wise least art among the governors of Juda, ²out
σοῦ γὰρ ἐξελεύσεται ἡγούμενος, ὅστις ποιμανεῖ τὸν.λαόν.μου
³of ⁴thee ¹for shall go forth a leader,   who shall shepherd my people
τὸν Ἰσραήλ. 7 Τότε Ἡρώδης ʰλάθρα‖ καλέσας τοὺς μάγους,
 Israel.   Then   Herod, ²secretly ¹having called the magi,
ἠκρίβωσεν παρ᾿ αὐτῶν τὸν χρόνον τοῦ φαινομένου ἀστέρος·
inquired accurately of them the time of the ²appearing ¹star.
8 καὶ πέμψας αὐτοὺς εἰς Βηθλεὲμ εἶπεν, Πορευθέντες ⁱἀκρι-
And having sent them to Bethlehem he said, Having gone,   accu-
βῶς ἐξετάσατε‖ περὶ τοῦ παιδίου· ἐπὰν.δὲ εὕρητε,
rately inquire   for the little child ; and when ye shall have found [him]
ἀπαγγείλατέ μοι, ὅπως κἀγὼ ἐλθὼν προσκυνήσω αὐτῷ.
bring word back to me, that I also having come may do homage to him.
9 Οἱ.δὲ ἀκούσαντες τοῦ βασιλέως ἐπορεύθησαν· καὶ ἰδού, ὁ
And they having heard the king,   went away ; and behold, the
ἀστήρ, ὃν εἶδον ἐν τῇ ἀνατολῇ, προῆγεν αὐτοὺς ἕως ἐλθὼν
·star, which they saw in the east,   went before them, until having come
ᵏἔστη‖ ἐπάνω οὗ ἦν τὸ παιδίον. 10 ἰδόντες.δὲ τὸν ἀστέρα,
it stood over where was the little child. And having seen the star,
ἐχάρησαν χαρὰν μεγάλην σφόδρα· 11 καὶ ἐλθόντες εἰς
they rejoiced [with] joy   ²great ¹exceedingly. And having come into

call his name Emmanuel, which being interpreted is, God with us. 24 Then Joseph being raised from sleep did as the angel of the Lord had bidden him, and took unto him his wife: 25 and knew her not till she had brought forth her firstborn son : and he called his name JESUS.

II. Now when Jesus was born in Bethlehem of Judæa in the days of Herod the king, behold, there came wise men from the east to Jerusalem, 2 saying, Where is he that is born King of the Jews? for we have seen his star in the east, and are come to worship him. 3 When Herod the king had heard *these things*, he was troubled, and all Jerusalem with him. 4 And when he had gathered all the chief priests and scribes of the people together, he demanded of them where Christ should be born. 5 And they said unto him, In Bethlehem of Judæa: for thus it is written by the prophet, 6 And thou Bethlehem, *in the* land of Juda, art not the least among the princes of Juda: for out of thee shall come a Governor, that shall rule my people Israel. 7 Then Herod, when he had privily called the wise men, inquired of them diligently what time the star appeared. 8 And he sent them to Bethlehem, and said, Go and search diligently for the young child; and when ye have found *him*, bring me word again, that I may come and worship him also. 9 When they had heard the king, they departed ; and, lo, the star, which they saw in the east, went before them, till it came and stood over where the young child was. 10 When they saw the star, they rejoiced with exceeding great joy. 11 And when they

ᵃ — ὁ L.   ᵇ ἐγερθεὶς having risen LTTrA.   ᶜ — ὁ T.   ᵈ — τὸν (read a son) LTTrA.
ᵉ — αὐτῆς τὸν πρωτότοκον LTTrA.   ᶠ ὁ βασιλεὺς Ἡρώδης LTTrA.   ᵍ εἶπαν T.   ʰ λάθρα L
ⁱ ἐξετάσατε ἀκριβῶς LTTrA.   ᵏ ἐστάθη LTTrA.

were come into the house, they saw the young child with Mary his mother, and fell down, and worshipped him: and when they had opened their treasures, they presented unto him gifts; gold, and frankincense, and myrrh. 12 And being warned of God in a dream that they should not return to Herod, they departed into their own country another way.

τὴν οἰκίαν, ¹εὗρον‖ τὸ παιδίον μετὰ Μαρίας τῆς᷍μητρὸς᷍αὐτοῦ,
the house, they found the little child with Mary his mother,
καὶ πεσόντες προσεκύνησαν αὐτῷ καὶ ἀνοίξαντες τοὺς
and having fallen down did homage to him: and having opened
θησαυροὺς αὐτῶν προσήνεγκαν αὐτῷ δῶρα, χρυσὸν καὶ
²treasures ¹their they offered to him gifts; gold and
λίβανον καὶ σμύρναν. 12 καὶ χρηματισθέντες κατ'
frankincense and myrrh. And having been divinely instructed in
ὄναρ μὴ ἀνακάμψαι πρὸς Ἡρώδην, δι' ἄλλης ὁδοῦ
a dream not to return to Herod, by another way
ἀνεχώρησαν εἰς τὴν᷍χώραν᷍αὐτῶν.
they withdrew into their own country.

13 And when they were departed, behold, the angel of the Lord appeareth to Joseph in a dream, saying, Arise, and take the young child and his mother, and flee into Egypt, and be thou there until I bring thee word: for Herod will seek the young child to destroy him. 14 When he arose, he took the young child and his mother by night, and departed into Egypt: 15 and was there until the death of Herod: that it might be fulfilled which was spoken of the Lord by the prophet, saying, Out of Egypt have I called my son. 16 Then Herod, when he saw that he was mocked of the wise men, was exceeding wroth, and sent forth, and slew all the children that were in Bethlehem, and in all the coasts thereof, from two years old and under, according to the time which he had diligently inquired of the wise men. 17 Then was fulfilled that which was spoken by Jeremy the prophet, saying, 18 In Rama was there a voice heard, lamentation, and weeping, and great mourning, Rachel weeping for her children, and would not be comforted, because they are not.

13 Ἀναχωρησάντων᷍δὲ αὐτῶν, ἰδού, ἄγγελος κυρίου
Now ²having ³withdrawn ¹they, behold, an angel of [the] Lord
ᵐφαίνεται κατ' ὄναρ‖ τῷ Ἰωσήφ, λέγων, Ἐγερθεὶς παράλαβε
appears in a dream to Joseph, saying, Having risen take with [thee]
τὸ παιδίον καὶ τὴν᷍μητέρα᷍αὐτοῦ, καὶ φεῦγε εἰς Αἴγυπτον,
the little child and his mother, and flee into Egypt,
καὶ ἴσθι ἐκεῖ ἕως ἂν εἴπω σοί· μέλλει γὰρ Ἡρώδης ζητεῖν τὸ
and be there until I shall tell thee; ³is ⁴about ¹for ²Herod to seek the
παιδίον, τοῦ ἀπολέσαι αὐτό. 14 Ὁ᷍δὲ ἐγερθεὶς παρέλαβεν
little child, to destroy him. And he having risen took with [him]
τὸ παιδίον καὶ τὴν᷍μητέρα᷍αὐτοῦ νυκτός, καὶ ἀνεχώρησεν εἰς
the little child and his mother by night, and withdrew into
Αἴγυπτον, 15 καὶ ἦν ἐκεῖ ἕως τῆς τελευτῆς Ἡρώδου· ἵνα
Egypt, and was there until the death of Herod: that
πληρωθῇ τὸ ῥηθὲν ὑπὸ ⁿτοῦ‖ κυρίου διὰ τοῦ
might be fulfilled that which was spoken by the Lord through the
προφήτου, λέγοντος, Ἐξ Αἰγύπτου ἐκάλεσα τὸν᷍υἱόν᷍μου.
prophet, saying, Out of Egypt have I called my son.
16 Τότε Ἡρώδης, ἰδὼν ὅτι ἐνεπαίχθη ὑπὸ τῶν μάγων,
Then Herod, having seen that he was mocked by the magi,
ἐθυμώθη λίαν, καὶ ἀποστείλας ἀνεῖλεν πάντας τοὺς
was enraged greatly, and having sent he put to death all the
παῖδας τοὺς ἐν Βηθλεὲμ καὶ ἐν πᾶσιν τοῖς᷍ὁρίοις᷍αὐτῆς, ἀπὸ
boys that [were] in Bethlehem and in all its borders, from
διετοῦς καὶ κατωτέρω, κατὰ τὸν χρόνον ὃν ἠκρίβω-
two years old and under, according to the time which he had accurately
σεν παρὰ τῶν μάγων. 17 Τότε ἐπληρώθη τὸ ῥηθὲν
inquired from the magi. Then was fulfilled that which was spoken
ᵒὑπὸ‖ Ἱερεμίου τοῦ προφήτου, λέγοντος, 18 Φωνὴ ἐν Ῥαμᾶ
by Jeremias the prophet, saying, A voice in Rama
ἠκούσθη, ᴾθρῆνος καὶ‖ κλαυθμὸς καὶ ὀδυρμὸς πολύς, Ῥαχὴλ
was heard, lamentation and weeping and ²mourning ¹great, Rachel
κλαίουσα τὰ᷍τέκνα᷍αὐτῆς, καὶ οὐκ ᑫἤθελεν‖ παρακληθῆναι,
weeping [for] her children, and ²not ¹would be comforted,
ὅτι οὐκ᷍εἰσίν.
because they are not.

19 But when Herod was dead, behold, an angel of the Lord appeareth in a dream to Joseph in Egypt, 20 saying, Arise, and take the young child and his mother, and go

19 Τελευτήσαντος᷍δὲ τοῦ Ἡρώδου, ἰδού, ἄγγελος κυρίου
But ²having ³died ¹Herod, behold, an angel of [the] Lord
ʳκατ' ὄναρ φαίνεται‖ τῷ Ἰωσὴφ ἐν Αἰγύπτῳ, 20 λέγων, Ἐγερ-
in a dream appears to Joseph in Egypt, saying, Having
θεὶς παράλαβε τὸ παιδίον καὶ τὴν᷍μητέρα᷍αὐτοῦ, καὶ πορεύου
risen take with [thee] the little child and his mother, and go

---

¹ εἶδον they saw GLTTrAW. ᵐ κατ' ὄναρ ἐφάνη in a dream appeared L; κατ' ὄναρ φαίνεται Tr. ⁿ — τοῦ (read [the]) LTTrAW. ᵒ διὰ through LTTrAW. ᴾ — θρῆνος καὶ LTTrA. ᑫ ἠθέλησεν L. ʳ φαίνεται κατ' ὄναρ LTTrA.

εἰς   γῆν Ἰσραήλ· τεθνήκασιν.γὰρ οἱ ζητοῦντες τὴν ψυχὴν
into[the]land of Israel: for they have died who were seeking the   life

τοῦ παιδίου. 21 Ὁ.δὲ ἐγερθεὶς παρέλαβεν   τὸ παιδίον καὶ
of the little child. And he having risen took with [him] the little child and

τὴν.μητέρα.αὐτοῦ, καὶ ˢἦλθεν‖ εἰς   γῆν Ἰσραήλ. 22 ἀκούσας
his mother,   and came into[the]land of Israel. ²Having ³heard

δὲ ὅτι Ἀρχέλαος βασιλεύει ᵗἐπὶ‖ τῆς Ἰουδαίας ἀντὶ ᵛἩρώδου
¹but that Archelaus reigns over   Judæa instead of Herod

τοῦ.πατρὸς.αὐτοῦ,‖ ἐφοβήθη ἐκεῖ ἀπελθεῖν·   χρηματισ-
his father,   he was afraid there to go;   ²having ³been ¹divinely

θεὶς   δὲ κατ' ὄναρ, ἀνεχώρησεν εἰς τὰ μέρη τῆς Γαλιλαίας,
⁵instructed ⁴and in a dream, he withdrew into the parts   of Galilee:

23 καὶ   ἐλθὼν   κατῴκησεν εἰς πόλιν λεγομένην ᵂΝαζαρέτ·‖
and having come he dwelt in a city   called   Nazareth;

ὅπως   πληρωθῇ   τὸ   ῥηθὲν διὰ τῶν προφητῶν, ὅτι
so that should be fulfilled that which was spoken by the prophets, that

Ναζωραῖος κληθήσεται.
a Nazaræan shall he be called.

3 Ἐν.δὲ ταῖς.ἡμέραις.ἐκείναις παραγίνεται Ἰωάννης ὁ
Now in those days   comes   John the

βαπτιστής, κηρύσσων ἐν τῇ ἐρήμῳ τῆς Ἰουδαίας, 2 ˣκαὶ‖ λέγων,
Baptist, proclaiming in the wilderness of Judæa, and saying,

Μετανοεῖτε· ἤγγικεν.γὰρ ἡ βασιλεία τῶν οὐρανῶν. 3 Οὗτος.γάρ
Repent, for has drawn near the kingdom of the heavens. For this

ἐστιν ὁ   ῥηθεὶς ᵞὑπὸ‖ Ἡσαΐου τοῦ προφήτου, λέγοντος,
is he who was spoken of by Esaias the prophet,   saying,

Φωνὴ βοῶντος ἐν τῇ ἐρήμῳ, Ἑτοιμάσατε τὴν ὁδὸν κυ-
[The] voice of one crying in the wilderness, Prepare the way of [the]

ρίου· εὐθείας ποιεῖτε τὰς.τρίβους.αὐτοῦ. 4 Αὐτὸς.δὲ ὁ Ἰωάννης
Lord, straight make his paths.   And ²himself ¹John

εἶχεν τὸ.ἔνδυμα.αὐτοῦ ἀπὸ τριχῶν καμήλου, καὶ ζώνην δερ-
had   his raiment   of hair of a camel, and a girdle of

ματίνην περὶ τὴν.ὀσφὺν.αὐτοῦ· ἡ.δὲ τροφὴ ᶻαὐτοῦ ἦν‖ ἀκρίδες
leather about his loins,   and the food of him was locusts

καὶ μέλι ἄγριον.
and ²honey ¹wild.

5 Τότε ἐξεπορεύετο πρὸς αὐτὸν Ἱεροσόλυμα καὶ πᾶσα ἡ
Then went out   to him Jerusalem, and all

Ἰουδαία καὶ πᾶσα ἡ περίχωρος τοῦ Ἰορδάνου· 6 καὶ ἐβαπτί-
Judæa, and all the country around the Jordan, and were bap-

ζοντοª ἐν τῷ Ἰορδάνῳᵇ ὑπ' αὐτοῦ, ἐξομολογούμενοι τὰς ἁμαρ-
tized in the Jordan by him, confessing   ⁴sins

τίας αὐτῶν. 7 Ἰδὼν.δὲ πολλοὺς τῶν Φαρισαίων καὶ Σαδδου-
¹their But having seen many of the Pharisees and Saddu-

καίων ἐρχομένους ἐπὶ τὸ.βάπτισμα.ᶜαὐτοῦ,‖ εἶπεν αὐτοῖς,
cees coming   to his baptism,   he said to²them,

Γεννήματα ἐχιδνῶν, τίς ὑπέδειξεν ὑμῖν φυγεῖν ἀπὸ τῆς μελ-
Offspring of vipers, who forewarned you to flee from the com-

λούσης ὀργῆς; 8 ποιήσατε οὖν ᵈκαρποὺς ἀξίους‖ τῆς μετα-
ing wrath? Produce therefore fruits worthy of repent-

νοίας· 9 καὶ μὴ.δόξητε λέγειν ἐν ἑαυτοῖς, Πατέρα ἔχομεν
ance: and think not to say within yourselves[⁴For] ⁵father ¹we ²have

---

into the land of Israel· for they are dead which sought the young child's life. 21 And he arose, and took the young child and his mother, and came into the land of Israel. 22 But when he heard that Archelaus did reign in Judæa in the room of his father Herod, he was afraid to go thither: notwithstanding, being warned of God in a dream, he turned aside into the parts of Galilee: 23 and he came and dwelt in a city called Nazareth: that it might be fulfilled which was spoken by the prophets, He shall be called a Nazarene.

III. In those days came John the Baptist, preaching in the wilderness of Judæa, 2 and saying, Repent ye: for the kingdom of heaven is at hand. 3 For this is he that was spoken of by the prophet Esaias, saying, The voice of one crying in the wilderness, Prepare ye the way of the Lord, make his paths straight. 4 And the same John had his raiment of camel's hair, and a leathern girdle about his loins; and his meat was locusts and wild honey.

5 Then went out to him Jerusalem, and all Judæa, and all the region round about Jordan, 6 and were baptized of him in Jordan, confessing their sins. 7 But when he saw many of the Pharisees and Sadducees come to his baptism, he said unto them, O generation of vipers, who hath warned you to flee from the wrath to come? 8 Bring forth therefore fruits meet for repentance: 9 and think not to say within yourselves, We have Abraham to our fa-

---

ˢ εἰσῆλθεν entered LTTrA.   ᵗ — ἐπὶ (read τῆς Ἰου. over Judæa) LT[TrA].   ᵛ τοῦ πατρὸς αὐτοῦ Ἡρώδου LTTrA.   ᵂ Ναζαρέθ LTT W.   ˣ — καὶ LT[ ]A.   ᵞ διὰ through ETT AW.   ᶻ ἦν αὐτοῦ LTTrA.   ª + [πάντες] all L.   ᵇ + ποταμῷ river LTTrA.   ᶜ — αὐτοῦ (read the baptism) LT[TrA].   ᵈ καρπὸν ἄξιον fruit worthy GLTT. AW.

ther: for I say unto you, that God is able of these stones to raise up children unto Abraham. 10 And now also the axe is laid unto the root of the trees: therefore every tree which bringeth not forth good fruit is hewn down, and cast into the fire. 11 I indeed baptize you with water unto repentance: but he that cometh after me is mightier than I, whose shoes I am not worthy to bear: he shall baptize you with the Holy Ghost, and with fire: 12 whose fan is in his hand, and he will throughly purge his floor, and gather his wheat into the garner; but he will burn up the chaff with unquenchable fire.

τὸν Ἀβραάμ· λέγω γὰρ ὑμῖν, ὅτι δύναται ὁ θεὸς ἐκ τῶν λίθων
Abraham: for I say to you, that able is God from *stones

τούτων ἐγεῖραι τέκνα τῷ Ἀβραάμ. 10 ἤδη δὲ *καὶ* ἡ ἀξίνη
¹these to raise up children to Abraham. But already also the axe

πρὸς τὴν ῥίζαν τῶν δένδρων κεῖται· πᾶν οὖν δένδρον μὴ
to the root of the trees is applied: ²every ¹therefore tree not

ποιοῦν καρπὸν καλὸν ἐκκόπτεται καὶ εἰς πῦρ βάλλεται.
producing ²fruit ¹good is cut down and into [the] fire is cast.

11 Ἐγὼ μὲν 'βαπτίζω ὑμᾶς' ἐν ὕδατι εἰς μετάνοιαν· ὁ δὲ
I indeed baptize you with water to repentance: but he who

ὀπίσω μου ἐρχόμενος ἰσχυρότερός μου ἐστίν, οὗ οὐκ εἰμὶ
after me [is] coming mightier than I is, of whom I am not

ἱκανὸς τὰ ὑποδήματα βαστάσαι· αὐτὸς ὑμᾶς βαπτίσει ἐν
fit the sandals to bear: he ¹will ²baptize with [the]

πνεύματι ἁγίῳ καὶ πυρί. 12 οὗ τὸ πτύον ἐν τῇ χειρὶ
²Spirit ¹Holy and with fire. Of whom the winnowing fan [is] in ²hand

αὐτοῦ, καὶ διακαθαριεῖ τὴν ἅλωνα αὐτοῦ, καὶ συνάξει
¹his, and he will thoroughly purge his floor, and will gather

τὸν σῖτον αὐτοῦ εἰς τὴν ἀποθήκην,ᵍ τὸ δὲ ἄχυρον κατακαύσει
his wheat into the granary, but the chaff he will burn up

πυρὶ ἀσβέστῳ.
with fire unquenchable.

13 Then cometh Jesus from Galilee to Jordan unto John, to be baptized of him. 14 But John forbad him, saying, I have need to be baptized of thee, and comest thou to me? 15 And Jesus answering said unto him, Suffer it to be so now: for thus it becometh us to fulfil all righteousness. Then he suffered him. 16 And Jesus, when he was baptized, went up straightway out of the water: and, lo, the heavens were opened unto him, and he saw the Spirit of God descending like a dove, and lighting upon him: 17 and lo a voice from heaven, saying, This is my beloved Son, in whom I am well pleased.

13 Τότε παραγίνεται ὁ Ἰησοῦς ἀπὸ τῆς Γαλιλαίας ἐπὶ τὸν
Then comes Jesus from Galilee to the

Ἰορδάνην πρὸς τὸν Ἰωάννην, τοῦ βαπτισθῆναι ὑπ' αὐτοῦ.
Jordan to John, to be baptized by him.

14 ὁ δὲ ʰἸωάννης' διεκώλυεν αὐτόν, λέγων, Ἐγὼ χρείαν ἔχω
But John was hindering him, saying, I ²need ¹have

ὑπὸ σοῦ βαπτισθῆναι, καὶ σὺ ἔρχῃ πρός με; 15 Ἀποκριθεὶς
by thee to be baptized, and ²thou ¹comest to me? ³Answering

δὲ ὁ Ἰησοῦς εἶπεν ¹πρὸς αὐτόν,' Ἄφες ἄρτι· οὕτως γὰρ
¹but ²Jesus said to him, Suffer [it] now; for thus

πρέπον ἐστὶν ἡμῖν πληρῶσαι πᾶσαν δικαιοσύνην. Τότε
becoming it is to us to fulfil all righteousness. Then

ἀφίησιν αὐτόν. 16 ʲΚαὶ βαπτισθεὶς' ὁ Ἰησοῦς ᵏἀνέβη
he suffers him. And having been baptized Jesus went up

εὐθὺς' ἀπὸ τοῦ ὕδατος, καὶ ἰδού, ¹ἀνεῴχθησαν' ᵐαὐτῷ' οἱ
immediately from the water: and behold, were opened to him the

οὐρανοί, καὶ εἶδεν ⁿτὸ' πνεῦμα ºτοῦ' θεοῦ καταβαῖνον ὡσεὶ
heavens, and he saw the Spirit of God descending as

περιστεράν, ᵖκαὶ' ἐρχόμενον ἐπ' αὐτόν. 17 καὶ ἰδού, φωνὴ
a dove, and coming upon him: and lo, a voice

ἐκ τῶν οὐρανῶν, λέγουσα, Οὗτός ἐστιν ὁ υἱός μου ὁ ἀγα-
out of the heavens, saying, This is my Son the be-

πητός, ἐν ᾧ ᵠεὐδόκησα'.
loved, in whom I have found delight.

IV. Then was Jesus led up of the Spirit into the wilderness to be tempted of the devil. 2 And when he had fasted forty days and forty nights, he was afterward an hungred.

4 Τότε ʳὁ' Ἰησοῦς ἀνήχθη εἰς τὴν ἔρημον ὑπὸ τοῦ πνεύ-
Then Jesus was led up into the wilderness by the Spi-

ματος, πειρασθῆναι ὑπὸ τοῦ διαβόλου. 2 καὶ νηστεύσας
rit, to be tempted by the devil. And having fasted

ἡμέρας ˢτεσσαράκοντα' καὶ ᵗνύκτας τεσσαράκοντα,' ὕστερον
²days ¹forty and ²nights ¹forty, afterwards

ᵉ — καὶ LTTrAW. ᶠ ὑμᾶς βαπτίζω LTTrW. ᵍ + αὐτοῦ (read his granary) LTᵣW. ʰ — Ἰωάννης (read he was hindering) LT[TrA]W. ⁱ αὐτῷ L. ʲ βαπτισθεὶς δὲ LTTrAW. ᵏ εὐθὺς ἀνέβη LTTrW. ¹ ἠνεῴχθησαν L. ᵐ — αὐτῷ [L]T. ⁿ — τὸ (read [the]) T[Δ]. º — τοῦ T[Δ]. ᵖ — καὶ LT [TrA]. ᵠ ηὐδόκησα T. ʳ — ὁ Δ. ˢ τεσσεράκοντα TTrΔ. ᵗ τεσσεράκοντα νύκτας T ; νύκτας τεσσερ. TrΔ.

ἐπείνασεν. 3 καὶ προσελθὼν ᵛαὐτῷ‖ ὁ πειράζων εἶπεν ᵂ, Εἰ
he hungered. And having come to him the tempter said, If

υἱὸς εἶ τοῦ θεοῦ, εἰπὲ ἵνα οἱ.λίθοι.οὗτοι ἄρτοι γένωνται.
³Son ʳthou ²art of God, speak that these stones ³loaves ¹may ²become.

4 Ὁ δὲ ἀποκριθεὶς εἶπεν, Γέγραπται, Οὐκ ἐπ᾽ ἄρτῳ μόνῳ
But he answering said, It has been written, Not by bread alone

ζήσεται ˣἄνθρωπος, ἀλλ᾽ ʸἐπὶ‖ παντὶ ῥήματι ἐκπορευομένῳ διὰ
shall ¹live ¹man, but by every word going out through

στόματος θεοῦ. 5 Τότε παραλαμβάνει αὐτὸν ὁ διάβολος εἰς
[the] mouth of God. Then ²takes ⁴him ¹the ²devil to

τὴν ἁγίαν πόλιν, καὶ ᶻἵστησιν‖ αὐτὸν ἐπὶ τὸ πτερύγιον τοῦ
the holy city, and sets him upon the edge of the

ἱεροῦ, 6 καὶ ᵃλέγει‖ αὐτῷ, Εἰ υἱὸς εἶ τοῦ θεοῦ, βάλε σεαυ-
temple, and says to him, If ²Son ʳthou ²art of God, cast thy-

τὸν κάτω· γέγραπται.γάρ, Ὅτι τοῖς.ἀγγέλοις.αὐτοῦ ἐν-
self down: for it has been written, To his angels he

τελεῖται περὶ σοῦ, καὶ ἐπὶ χειρῶν ἀροῦσίν σε,
will give charge concerning thee, and in [their] hands shall they bear thee,

μήποτε προσκόψῃς πρὸς λίθον τὸν.πόδα.σου. 7 Ἔφη ²τῷ ⁴to ⁴him
lest thou strike against a stone thy foot. ²Said ²to ⁴him

ὁ Ἰησοῦς, Πάλιν γέγραπται, Οὐκ.ἐκπειράσεις κύριον τὸν
¹Jesus, Again it has been written, Thou shalt not tempt [the] Lord

θεόν.σου. 8 Πάλιν παραλαμβάνει αὐτὸν ὁ διάβολος εἰς
²God ¹thy. Again ²takes ⁴him ¹the ²devil to

ὄρος ὑψηλὸν λίαν, καὶ δείκνυσιν αὐτῷ πάσας τὰς βασι-
a mountain ²high ¹exceedingly, and shews to him all the king-

λείας τοῦ κόσμου καὶ τὴν.δόξαν.αὐτῶν, 9 καὶ ᵇλέγει‖ αὐτῷ,
doms of the world and their glory, and says to him,

ᶜΤαῦτα πάντα σοι‖ δώσω, ἐὰν πεσὼν προσκυνήσῃς
²These ³things ¹all to thee will I give if falling down thou wilt worship

μοι. 10 Τότε λέγει αὐτῷ ὁ Ἰησοῦς, Ὕπαγεᵈ, σατανᾶ·
me. Then ²says ³to ⁴him ¹Jesus, Get thee away, Satan;

γέγραπται.γάρ, Κύριον τὸν.θεόν.σου προσκυνήσεις, καὶ
for it has been written, [The] Lord thy God shalt thou worship, and

αὐτῷ μόνῳ λατρεύσεις. 11 Τότε ἀφίησιν αὐτὸν ὁ διάβολος·
him alone shalt thou serve. Then ²leaves ⁴him ¹the ²devil·

καὶ ἰδού, ἄγγελοι προσῆλθον καὶ διηκόνουν αὐτῷ.
and behold, angels came and ministered to him.

12 Ἀκούσας.δὲ ᵉὁ Ἰησοῦς‖ ὅτι Ἰωάννης παρεδόθη, ἀν-
But ²having ³heard ¹Jesus that John was delivered up, he

ἐχώρησεν εἰς τὴν Γαλιλαίαν. 13 καὶ καταλιπὼν τὴν ᶠΝαζαρέτ,‖
withdrew into Galilee: and having left Nazareth,

ἐλθὼν κατῴκησεν εἰς ᵍΚαπερναοὺμ‖ τὴν παραθαλασσίαν,
having come he dwelt at Capernaum, which [is] on the sea-side,

ἐν ὁρίοις Ζαβουλὼν καὶ Νεφθαλείμ, 14 ἵνα πληρωθῇ
in [the] borders of Zabulon and Nephthalim, that might be fulfilled

τὸ ῥηθὲν διὰ Ἡσαΐου τοῦ προφήτου, λέγοντος, 15 Γῆ
that which was spoken by Esaias the prophet, saying, Land

Ζαβουλὼν καὶ γῆ Νεφθαλείμ, ὁδὸν θαλάσσης πέραν τοῦ
of Zabulon, and land of Nephthalim, way of [the] sea, beyond the

Ἰορδάνου, Γαλιλαία τῶν ἐθνῶν, 16 ὁ λαὸς ὁ καθήμενος
Jordan, Galilee of the nations. the people which was sitting

3 And when the tempter came to him, he said, If thou be the Son of God, command that these stones be made bread. 4 But he answered and said, It is written, Man shall not live by bread alone, but by every word that proceedeth out of the mouth of God. 5 Then the devil taketh him up into the holy city, and setteth him on a pinnacle of the temple, 6 and saith unto him, If thou be the Son of God, cast thyself down: for it is written, He shall give his angels charge concerning thee: and in their hands they shall bear thee up, lest at any time thou dash thy foot against a stone. 7 Jesus said unto him, It is written again, Thou shalt not tempt the Lord thy God. 8 Again, the devil taketh him up into an exceeding high mountain, and sheweth him all the kingdoms of the world, and the glory of them; 9 and saith unto him, All these things will I give thee, if thou wilt fall down and worship me. 10 Then saith Jesus unto him, Get thee hence, Satan: for it is written, Thou shalt worship the Lord thy God, and him only shalt thou serve. 11 Then the devil leaveth him, and, behold, angels came and ministered unto him.

12 Now when Jesus had heard that John was cast into prison, he departed into Galilee; 13 and leaving Nazareth, he came and dwelt in Capernaum, which is upon the sea coast, in the borders of Zabulon and Nephthalim: 14 that it might be fulfilled which was spoken by Esaias the prophet, saying, 15 The land of Zabulon, and the land of Nephthalim, by the way of the sea, beyond Jordan, Galilee of the Gentiles; 16 the people which sat in dark-

ᵛ — αὐτῷ TTrA. ᵂ + αὐτῷ to him LTTrAW. ˣ + ὁ LTTrAW. ʸ ἐν LTrA. ᶻ ἔστησεν set LTTrA. ᵃ εἶπεν said L. ᵇ εἶπεν said LTTrA. ᶜ ταῦτά σοι πάντα TTrA. ᵈ + ὀπίσω μου behind me G[L]w. ᵉ — ὁ Ἰησοῦς TTrAW. ᶠ Ναζαράθ Nazarath L; Ναζαρὲθ w; Ναζαρὰ Nazara TTrA. ᵍ Καφαρναοὺμ LTTrAW.

ness saw great light; and to them which sat in the region and shadow of death, light is sprung up. 17 From that time Jesus began to preach, and to say, Repent: for the kingdom of heaven is at hand.

ἐν ʰσκότει εἶδε φῶςǁ μέγα, καὶ τοῖς καθημένοις ἐν
in darkness has seen aᶻlight ˡgreat, and to those which were sitting in [the]
χώρα καὶ σκιᾷ θανάτου, φῶς ἀνέτειλεν αὐτοῖς. 17 Ἀπὸ
country and shadow of death, light has sprung up to them. From
τότε ἤρξατο ὁ Ἰησοῦς κηρύσσειν καὶ λέγειν, Μετανοεῖτε·
that time began Jesus to proclaim and to say, Repent;
ἤγγικεν.γὰρ ἡ βασιλεία τῶν οὐρανῶν.
for has drawn near the kingdom of the heavens.

18 And Jesus, walking by the sea of Galilee, saw two brethren, Simon called Peter, and Andrew his brother, casting a net into the sea : for they were fishers. 19 And he saith unto them, Follow me, and I will make you fishers of men. 20 And they straightway left *their* nets, and followed him. 21 And going on from thence, he saw other two brethren, James *the son* of Zebedee, and John his brother, in a ship with Zebedee their father, mending their nets; and he called them. 22 And they immediately left the ship and their father, and followed him.

18 Περιπατῶν.δὲ ᶦὁ Ἰησοῦςǁ παρὰ τὴν θάλασσαν τῆς Γαλι-
And ʷwalking ˡJesus by the sea of Gali-
λαίας εἶδεν δύο ἀδελφούς, Σίμωνα τὸν λεγόμενον Πέτρον, καὶ
lee he saw two brothers, Simon who is called Peter, and
Ἀνδρέαν τὸν.ἀδελφὸν.αὐτοῦ, βάλλοντας ἀμφίβληστρον εἰς
Andrew his brother, casting a large net into
τὴν θάλασσαν· ἦσαν.γὰρ ἁλιεῖς. 19 καὶ λέγει αὐτοῖς,ᵏ Δεῦτε
the sea, for they were fishers: and he says to them, Come
ὀπίσω μου, καὶ ποιήσω ὑμᾶς ἁλιεῖς ἀνθρώπων. 20 Οἱ.δὲ
after me, and I will make you fishers of men. And they
εὐθέως ἀφέντες τὰ δίκτυα ἠκολούθησαν αὐτῷ. 21 Καὶ
immediately having left the nets, followed him. And
προβὰς ἐκεῖθεν, εἶδεν ἄλλους δύο ἀδελφούς, Ἰάκωβον τὸν
having gone on thence, he saw other two brothers, James the [son]
τοῦ Ζεβεδαίου καὶ Ἰωάννην τὸν.ἀδελφὸν.αὐτοῦ, ἐν τῷ πλοίῳ
of Zebedee, and John his brother, in the ship
μετὰ Ζεβεδαίου τοῦ.πατρὸς.αὐτῶν, καταρτίζοντας τὰ δίκτυα
with Zebedee their father, mending ²nets
αὐτῶν· καὶ ἐκάλεσεν αὐτούς. 22 οἱ.δὲ εὐθέως ἀφέντες τὸ
ˡtheir, and he called them; and they immediately having left the
πλοῖον καὶ τὸν.πατέρα.αὐτῶν ἠκολούθησαν αὐτῷ.
ship and their father followed him.

23 And Jesus went about all Galilee, teaching in their synagogues, and preaching the gospel of the kingdom, and healing all manner of sickness and all manner of disease among the people. 24 And his fame went throughout all Syria : and they brought unto him all sick people that were taken with divers diseases and torments, and those which were possessed with devils, and those which were lunatic, and those that had the palsy; and he healed them. 25 And there followed him great multitudes of people from Galilee, and *from* Decapolis, and *from* Jerusalem, and *from* Judæa, and *from* beyond Jordan. V. And seeing the multitudes, he went up into a mountain : and when he was set, his disciples came unto him : 2 and he

23 Καὶ περιῆγεν ˡὅλην τὴν Γαλιλαίαν ὁ Ἰησοῦς,ǁ διδάσκων
And ²went ³about ⁴all ⁵Galilee ˡJesus, teaching
ἐν ταῖς.συναγωγαῖς.αὐτῶν, καὶ κηρύσσων τὸ εὐαγγέλιον τῆς
in their synagogues, and proclaiming the glad tidings of the
βασιλείας, καὶ θεραπεύων πᾶσαν νόσον καὶ πᾶσαν μαλακίαν
kingdom, and healing every disease and every bodily weakness
ἐν τῷ λαῷ. 24 καὶ ἀπῆλθεν ἡ ἀκοὴ αὐτοῦ εἰς ὅλην τὴν Συ-
among the people. And went out the fame of him into all Sy-
ρίαν· καὶ προσήνεγκαν αὐτῷ πάντας τοὺς.κακῶς.ἔχοντας,
ria. And they brought to him all who were ill,
ποικίλαις νόσοις καὶ βασάνοις συνεχομένους, ᵐκαὶǁ δαιμονιζο-
by various diseases and torments oppressed, and · possessed by
μένους, καὶ σεληνιαζομένους, καὶ παραλυτικούς· καὶ ἐθερά-
demons, and lunatics, and paralytics; and he
πευσεν αὐτούς. 25 καὶ ἠκολούθησαν αὐτῷ ὄχλοι πολλοὶ ἀπὸ
healed them. And ³followed ⁴him ²crowds ˡgreat from
τῆς Γαλιλαίας καὶ Δεκαπόλεως καὶ Ἱεροσολύμων καὶ Ἰουδαίας
Galilee and Decapolis and Jerusalem and Judea
καὶ πέραν τοῦ Ἰορδάνου.
and beyond the Jordan.

5 Ἰδὼν.δὲ τοὺς ὄχλους, ἀνέβη εἰς τὸ ὄρος· καὶ καθίσαν-
But seeing the crowds, he went up into the mountain; and ²having ³sat
τος αὐτοῦ, ⁿπροσῆλθον ᵒαὐτῷ οἱ.μαθηταὶ.αὐτοῦ. 2 καὶ ἀνοί-
⁴down ˡhe, came to him his disciples. And having

ʰ σκοτία φῶς εἶδεν LTᵣA; σκότει φῶς εἶδεν TW. — ὁ Ἰησοῦς GLTTᵣAW. ᵏ + [ὁ Ἰησοῦς]
Jesus L. ᶦ ὁ Ἰησοῦς ὅλη τῇ Γαλιλαίᾳ L; [ὁ Ἰησοῦς] Tᵣ (— ὁ Ἰησοῦς TA) ἐν ὅλῃ τῇ Γαλιλαίᾳ
ᵃTᵣA; ὁ Ἰησοῦς ὅλην τὴν Γαλιλαίαν W. ᵐ — καὶ LTᵣA. ⁿ προσῆλθαν TTᵣ. ᵒ — αὐτῷ L

ξας τὸ.στόμα.αὐτοῦ ἐδίδασκεν αὐτούς, λέγων, 3 Μακάριοι οἱ
opened his mouth　　he taught　them,　saying,　　Blessed [are] the

πτωχοὶ τῷ πνεύματι· ὅτι αὐτῶν ἐστιν ἡ βασιλεία τῶν οὐρανῶν.
poor　　in spirit;　for theirs　is　the kingdom of the heavens.

4 Ρμακάριοι οἱ πενθοῦντες· ὅτι αὐτοὶ παρακληθήσονται.
Blessed they who mourn;　for they　　shall be comforted.

5 μακάριοι οἱ πραεῖς· ὅτι αὐτοὶ κληρονομήσουσιν τὴν γῆν.‖
Blessed the meek;　for they　shall inherit　the earth.

6 μακάριοι οἱ πεινῶντες καὶ διψῶντες τὴν δικαιοσύνην· ὅτι
Blessed they who hunger and thirst after　righteousness;　for

αὐτοὶ χορτασθήσονται. 7 μακάριοι οἱ ἐλεήμονες· ὅτι αὐτοὶ
they　shall be filled.　　Blessed the merciful;　for they

ἐλεηθήσονται. 8 μακάριοι οἱ καθαροὶ τῇ καρδίᾳ· ὅτι αὐτοὶ τὸν
shall find mercy.　Blessed the pure　in heart; for they

θεὸν ὄψονται. 9 μακάριοι οἱ εἰρηνοποιοί· ὅτι 9αὐτοὶ‖ υἱοὶ θεοῦ
3God 1shall 2see.　Blessed the peacemakers; for they　sons of God

κληθήσονται. 10 μακάριοι οἱ δεδιωγμένοι ἕνεκεν δικαιο-
shall be called.　Blessed they who have been persecuted on account of right-

σύνης· ὅτι αὐτῶν ἐστιν ἡ βασιλεία τῶν οὐρανῶν. 11 μακάριοί
eousness; for theirs　is　the kingdom of the heavens.　Blessed

ἐστε, ὅταν ὀνειδίσωσιν ὑμᾶς καὶ διώξωσιν, καὶ εἴπωσιν πᾶν
are ye when they shall reproach you, and shall persecute, and shall say every

πονηρὸν ʳῥῆμα‖ καθ᾽ ὑμῶν ˢψευδόμενοι,‖ ἕνεκεν ἐμοῦ. 12 χαί-
wicked word against you,　lying,　on account of me. Re-

ρετε καὶ ἀγαλλιᾶσθε, ὅτι ὁ.μισθὸς.ὑμῶν πολὺς ἐν τοῖς οὐρανοῖς·
joice and　exult,　for　your reward [is] great in the heavens;

οὕτως.γὰρ ἐδίωξαν τοὺς προφήτας τοὺς πρὸ ὑμῶν.
for thus　they persecuted the　prophets　who [were] before you.

13 Ὑμεῖς ἐστε τὸ ἅλας τῆς γῆς· ἐὰν.δὲ τὸ ἅλας μωρανθῇ,
Ye　are the salt of the earth: but if the salt become tasteless,

ἐν τίνι ἁλισθήσεται; εἰς οὐδὲν ἰσχύει ἔτι, εἰ.μὴ ᵗβλη-
with what shall it be salted? for nothing has it strength any longer, but to be

θῆναι‖ ἔξω, ʸκαὶ‖ καταπατεῖσθαι ὑπὸ τῶν ἀνθρώπων. 14 Ὑμεῖς
cast　out,　and to be trampled upon by　men.　　Ye

ἐστε τὸ φῶς τοῦ κόσμου· οὐ.δύναται πόλις κρυβῆναι ἐπάνω
are the light of the world,　3cannot 1a 2city be hid　on

ὄρους κειμένη· 15 οὐδὲ καίουσιν λύχνον καὶ τιθέασιν αὐτὸν
a mountain situated.　Nor do they light a lamp and put it

ὑπὸ τὸν μόδιον, ἀλλ᾽ ἐπὶ τὴν λυχνίαν, καὶ λάμπει πᾶσιν τοῖς
under the corn measure, but upon the lampstand; and it shines for all who

ἐν τῇ οἰκίᾳ. 16 οὕτως λαμψάτω τὸ.φῶς.ὑμῶν ἔμπροσθεν
[are] in the house.　Thus　let shine　your light　before

τῶν ἀνθρώπων, ὅπως ἴδωσιν ὑμῶν τὰ καλὰ ἔργα, καὶ δοξά-
men,　so that they may see your　good works, and may

σωσιν τὸν.πατέρα.ὑμῶν τὸν ἐν τοῖς οὐρανοῖς.
glorify　your Father　who [is] in the heavens.

17 Μὴ.νομίσητε ὅτι ἦλθον καταλῦσαι τὸν νόμον ἢ τοὺς προ-
Think not　that I came to abolish the　law or the pro-

φήτας· οὐκ.ἦλθον καταλῦσαι, ἀλλὰ πληρῶσαι. 18 ἀμὴν.γὰρ
phets:　I came not　to abolish,　but to fulfil.　For verily

λέγω ὑμῖν, ἕως.ἂν παρέλθῃ ὁ οὐρανὸς καὶ ἡ γῆ, ἰῶτα ἓν ἢ
I say to you, Until shall pass away the heaven　and the earth, 2iota 1one or

μία κεραία οὐ.μὴ παρέλθῃ ἀπὸ τοῦ νόμου, ἕως.ἂν πάντα
one　tittle in no wise shall pass away from the　law　until　all

ᵖ Verses 4, 5, transposed LTTr.| �q — αὐτοὶ (read κληθή. they shall be called) [L]ᵗ[Tr A].
ʳ — ῥῆμα (read [thing]) LTTrA. |ˢ — ψευδόμενοι L. | ᵗ βληθὲν having been cast LTTrA.
ʸ — καὶ LTTrA.

opened his mouth, and taught them, saying, 3 Blessed *are* the poor in spirit: for theirs is the kingdom of heaven. 4 Blessed *are* they that mourn: for they shall be comforted. 5 Blessed *are* the meek: for they shall inherit the earth. 6 Blessed *are* they which do hunger and thirst after righteousness: for they shall be filled. 7 Blessed *are* the merciful: for they shall obtain mercy. 8 Blessed *are* the pure in heart: for they shall see God. 9 Blessed *are* the peacemakers: for they shall be called the children of God. 10 Blessed *are* they which are persecuted for righteousness' sake: for theirs is the kingdom of heaven. 11 Blessed are ye, when *men* shall revile you, and persecute *you*, and shall say all manner of evil against you falsely, for my sake. 12 Rejoice, and be exceeding glad: for great is your reward in heaven: for so persecuted they the prophets which were before you.

13 Ye are the salt of the earth: but if the salt have lost his savour, wherewith shall it be salted? it is thenceforth good for nothing, but to be cast out, and to be trodden under foot of men. 14 Ye are the light of the world. A city that is set on an hill cannot be hid. 15 Neither do men light a candle, and put it under a bushel, but on a candlestick; and it giveth light unto all that are in the house. 16 Let your light so shine before men, that they may see your good works, and glorify your Father which is in heaven.

17 Think not that I am come to destroy the law, or the prophets: I am not come to destroy, but to fulfil. 18 For verily I say unto you, Till heaven and earth pass, one jot or one tittle shall in no wise pass from the law, till all be fulfilled. 19 Whosoever there-

fore shall break one of these least commandments, and shall teach men so, he shall be called the least in the kingdom of heaven: but whosoever shall do and teach *them*, the same shall be called great in the kingdom of heaven. 20 For I say unto you, That except your righteousness shall exceed *the righteousness* of the scribes and Pharisees, ye shall in no case enter into the kingdom of heaven.

21 Ye have heard that it was said by them of· old time, Thou shalt not kill; and whosoever shall kill shall be in danger of the judgment: 22 but I say unto you, That whosoever is angry with his brother without a cause shall be in danger of the judgment: and whosoever shall say to his brother, Raca, shall be in danger of the council: but whosoever shall say, Thou fool, shall be in danger of hell fire. 23 Therefore if thou bring thy gift to the altar, and there rememberest that thy brother hath ought against thee; 24 leave there thy gift before the altar, and go thy way; first be reconciled to thy brother, and then come and offer thy gift. 25 Agree with thine adversary quickly, whiles thou art in the way with him; lest at any time the adversary deliver thee to the judge, and the judge deliver thee to the officer, and thou be cast into prison. 26 Verily I say unto thee, Thou shalt by no means come out thence, till thou hast paid the uttermost farthing.

27 Ye have heard that it was said by them of old time, Thou shalt not commit adultery: 28 but I say unto you, That whosoever looketh on a woman to lust after her hath committed adultery with her already in his heart. 29 And if thy right eye offend thee, pluck it out, and cast *it* from

γένηται. 19 ὃς ἐὰν οὖν λύσῃ μίαν τῶν ἐντολῶν τούτων τῶν
come to pass.   Whoever then shall break one   of these commandments the

ἐλαχίστων, καὶ διδάξῃ οὕτως τοὺς ἀνθρώπους, ἐλάχιστος κλη-
least,   and shall teach ²so   ¹men,   least shall

θήσεται ἐν τῇ βασιλείᾳ τῶν οὐρανῶν· ὃς δ᾽ ἂν ποιήσῃ καὶ
be called in the kingdom of the heavens; but whoever shall practise and

διδάξῃ, οὗτος μέγας κληθήσεται ἐν τῇ βασιλείᾳ τῶν
shall teach [them], this [one] great shall be called in the kingdom of the

οὐρανῶν. 20 λέγω γὰρ ὑμῖν, ὅτι ἐὰν μὴ περισσεύσῃ ᵂἡ δικαιο-
heavens.   For I say to you, That unless shall abound ²right-

σύνη ὑμῶν‖ πλεῖον‖ τῶν γραμματέων καὶ Φαρισαίων, οὐ μὴ
eousness ¹your above[that]of the scribes and Pharisees, in no wise

εἰσέλθητε εἰς τὴν βασιλείαν τῶν οὐρανῶν.
shall ye enter into the kingdom of the heavens.

21 Ἠκούσατε ὅτι ˣἐρρέθη‖ τοῖς ἀρχαίοις, Οὐ φονεύσεις·
Ye have heard that it was said to the ancients, Thou shalt not commit murder;

ὃς δ᾽ ἂν φονεύσῃ, ἔνοχος ἔσται τῇ κρίσει. 22 ἐγὼ δὲ
but whoever shall commit murder, liable shall be to the judgment.   But I

λέγω ὑμῖν, ὅτι πᾶς ὁ ὀργιζόμενος τῷ ἀδελφῷ αὐτοῦ ʸεἰκῇ‖
say to you, That every one who is angry with his brother lightly.

ἔνοχος ἔσται τῇ κρίσει· ὃς δ᾽ ἂν εἴπῃ τῷ ἀδελφῷ αὐτοῦ,
liable shall be to the judgment: but whoever shall say to his brother,

ᶻ'Ρακά,‖ ἔνοχος ἔσται τῷ συνεδρίῳ· ὃς δ᾽ ἂν εἴπῃ, Μωρέ,
Raca, liable shall be to the Sanhedrim: but whoever shall say, Fool,

ἔνοχος ἔσται εἰς τὴν γέενναν τοῦ πυρός. 23 Ἐὰν οὖν προσ-
liable shall be to the Gehenna of fire.   If therefore thou

φέρῃς τὸ δῶρόν σου ἐπὶ τὸ θυσιαστήριον, κἀκεῖ μνησθῇς
shalt offer thy gift at the altar, and there shalt remember

ὅτι ὁ ἀδελφός σου ἔχει τὶ κατὰ σοῦ, 24 ἄφες ἐκεῖ τὸ δῶρόν
that thy brother has something against thee, leave there ²gift

σου ἔμπροσθεν τοῦ θυσιαστηρίου, καὶ ὕπαγε, πρῶτον διαλ-
¹thy before the altar, and go away, first be

λάγηθι τῷ ἀδελφῷ σου, καὶ τότε ἐλθὼν πρόσφερε τὸ δῶρόν
reconciled to thy brother, and then having come offer ²gift

σου. 25 Ἴσθι εὐνοῶν τῷ ἀντιδίκῳ σου ταχύ, ἕως ὅτου εἶ
¹thy.   Be agreeing with thine adverse party quickly, whilst thou art

ᵃἐν τῇ ὁδῷ μετ᾽ αὐτοῦ,‖ μήποτέ σε παραδῷ ὁ ἀντίδικος τῷ
in the way with him, lest ⁵thee ⁴deliver ¹the ²adverse ³party to the

κριτῇ, καὶ ὁ κριτής ᵇσε παραδῷ‖ τῷ ὑπηρέτῃ, καὶ εἰς φυλακὴν
judge, and the judge deliver to the officer, and into prison

βληθήσῃ. 26 ἀμὴν λέγω σοι, οὐ μὴ ἐξέλθῃς ἐκεῖθεν,
thou be cast.   Verily I say to thee, In no wise shalt thou come out thence,

ἕως ἂν ἀποδῷς τὸν ἔσχατον κοδράντην.
until thou pay the last kodrantes.

27 Ἠκούσατε ὅτι ˣἐρρέθη‖ ᶜτοῖς ἀρχαίοις,‖ Οὐ μοιχεύ-
Ye have heard that it was said to the ancients, Thou shalt not commit

σεις· 28 ἐγὼ δὲ λέγω ὑμῖν, ὅτι πᾶς ὁ βλέπων γυναῖκα πρὸς
adultery: but I say to you, that every one that looks upon a woman to

τὸ ἐπιθυμῆσαι ᵈαὐτῆς,‖ ἤδη ἐμοίχευσεν αὐτὴν ἐν τῇ
lust after her, already has committed adultery with her in

καρδίᾳ ᵉαὐτοῦ.‖ 29 εἰ δὲ ὁ ὀφθαλμός σου ὁ δεξιὸς σκανδαλίζει
²heart ¹his.   But if thine eye, the right, cause ²to ³offend

σε, ἔξελε αὐτὸν καὶ βάλε ἀπὸ σοῦ· συμφέρει γάρ σοι ἵνα
¹thee, pluck out it and cast [it] from thee: for it is profitable for thee that

---

ᵂ ὑμῶν ἡ δικαιοσύνη TA.   ˣ ἐρρήθη LT-AW.   ʸ — εἰκῆ LT[TrA].   ᶻ ῥοχά T.   ᵃ μετ᾽ αὐτοῦ ἐν τῇ ὁδῷ LTTrAW;   ᵇ — σε παραδῷ LT[Tr].   ᶜ — τοῖς ἀρχαίοις GLETrAW.   ᵈ αὐτὴν LTrAW; — αὐτῆς T.   ᵉ ἑαυτοῦ L.

ἀπόληται ἕν τῶν μελῶν σου, καὶ μὴ ὅλον τὸ σῶμά σου βληθῇ
should perish one of thy members, and not "whole ¹thy ²body be cast

εἰς γέενναν. 30 καὶ εἰ ἡ δεξιά σου χεὶρ σκανδαλίζει σε, ἔκκοψον
into Gehenna. And if thy right hand cause ²to ³offend ¹thee, cut off

αὐτὴν καὶ βάλε ἀπὸ σοῦ· συμφέρει γάρ σοι ἵνα ἀπόληται
it and cast[it] from thee: for it is profitable for thee that should perish

ἐν τῶν μελῶν σου, καὶ μὴ ὅλον τὸ σῶμά σου 'βληθῇ εἰς γέενναν.‖
one of thy members, and not "whole ¹thy ³body be cast into Gehenna.

31 ᵍἘρρέθη‖ δέ. ʰὅτι‖ ὃς ἂν ἀπολύσῃ τὴν γυναῖκα αὐτοῦ,
It was said also that whoever shall put away his wife,

δότω αὐτῇ ἀποστάσιον. 32 ἐγὼ δὲ λέγω ὑμῖν, ὅτι ¹ὃς ἂν
let him give to her a letter of divorce: but I say to you, that whoever

ἀπολύσῃ‖ τὴν γυναῖκα αὐτοῦ, παρεκτὸς λόγου πορνείας, ποιεῖ
shall put away his wife, except on account of fornication, causes

αὐτὴν ᵏμοιχᾶσθαι‖ καὶ ¹ὃς ἐὰν‖ ἀπολελυμένην ᵐγαμήσῃ,‖
her to commit adultery; and whoever her who has been put away shall marry,

μοιχᾶται.
commits adultery.

33 Πάλιν ἠκούσατε, ὅτι ᵍἐρρέθη‖ τοῖς ἀρχαίοις, Οὐκ ἐπιορ-
Again, ye have heard that it was said to the ancients, Thou shalt not

κήσεις, ἀποδώσεις δὲ τῷ κυρίῳ τοὺς ὅρκους σου· 34 ἐγὼ
forswear thyself, but thou shalt render to the Lord thine oaths.

δὲ λέγω ὑμῖν μὴ ὀμόσαι ὅλως, μήτε ἐν τῷ οὐρανῷ, ὅτι θρόνος
¹but say to you not to swear at all, neither by the heaven, because [the]throne

ἐστιν τοῦ θεοῦ· 35 μήτε ἐν τῇ γῇ, ὅτι ὑποπόδιόν ἐστιν τῶν
it is of God; nor by the earth, because[the]footstool it is

ποδῶν αὐτοῦ· μήτε εἰς Ἱεροσόλυμα, ὅτι πόλις ἐστιν τοῦ
of his feet: nor by Jerusalem, because [the] city it is of the

μεγάλου βασιλέως· 36 μήτε ἐν τῇ κεφαλῇ σου ὀμόσῃς, ὅτι
great King. Neither by thy head shalt thou swear, because

οὐ δύνασαι μίαν τρίχα λευκὴν ⁿἢ μέλαιναν ποιῆσαι.‖ 37 ᵒἔστω‖
thou art not able one hair white or black to make. ²Let ³be

δὲ ὁ λόγος ὑμῶν, ναὶ ναί, οὐ οὔ· ˉτὸ δὲ περισσὸν τούτων ἐκ
¹but ²your ⁴word, Yea, yea; Nay, nay: but what [is] more than these from

τοῦ πονηροῦ ἐστιν.
evil is.

38 Ἠκούσατε ὅτι ᵍἐρρέθη,‖ Ὀφθαλμὸν ἀντὶ ὀφθαλμοῦ, καὶ
Ye have heard that it was said, Eye for eye, and

ὀδόντα ἀντὶ ὀδόντος· 39 ἐγὼ δὲ λέγω ὑμῖν μὴ ἀντιστῆναι τῷ
tooth for tooth: but I say to you not to resist

πονηρῷ· ἀλλ᾽ ὅστις σε ᴾῥαπίσει ἐπὶ‖ τὴν δεξιάν ᑫσου σιαγόνα,‖
evil; but whosoever thee shall strike on thy right cheek,

στρέψον αὐτῷ καὶ τὴν ἄλλην· 40 καὶ τῷ θέλοντί σοι κρι-
turn to him also the other; and to him who would with thee go

θῆναι καὶ τὸν χιτῶνά σου λαβεῖν, ἄφες αὐτῷ καὶ τὸ ἱμάτιον·
to law and thy tunic take, yield to him also [thy] cloak;

41 καὶ ὅστις σε ἀγγαρεύσει μίλιον ἕν, ὕπαγε μετ᾽ αὐτοῦ δύο.
and whosoever thee will compel to go ²mile ¹one, go with him two.

42 τῷ αἰτοῦντί σε ᶜδίδου‖ καὶ τὸν θέλοντα ἀπὸ σοῦ ˢδανεί-
To him who asks of thee Give; and him that wishes from thee to bor-

σασθαι‖ μὴ ἀποστραφῇς.
row thou shalt not turn away from.

thee : for it is profitable for thee that one of thy members should perish, and not that thy whole body should be cast into hell. 30 And if thy right hand offend thee, cut it off, and cast it from thee : for it is profitable for thee that one of thy members should perish, and not that thy whole body should be cast into hell.

31 It hath been said, Whosoever shall put away his wife, let him give her a writing of divorcement : 32 but I say unto you, That whosoever shall put away his wife, saving for the cause of fornication, causeth her to commit adultery : and whosoever shall marry her that is divorced committeth adultery.

33 Again, ye have heard that it hath been said by them of old time, Thou shalt not forswear thyself, but shalt perform unto the Lord thine oaths: 34 but I say unto you, Swear not at all; neither by heaven; for it is God's throne: 35 nor by the earth; for it is his footstool: neither by Jerusalem; for it is the city of the great King. 36 Neither shalt thou swear by thy head, because thou canst not make one hair white or black. 37 But let your communication be, Yea, yea; Nay, nay: for whatsoever is more than these cometh of evil.

38 Ye have heard that it hath been said, An eye for an eye, and a tooth for a tooth: 39 but I say unto you, That ye resist not evil: but whosoever shall smite thee on thy right cheek, turn to him the other also. 40 And if any man will sue thee at the law, and take away thy coat, let him have thy cloke also. 41 And whosoever shall compel thee to go a mile, go with him twain. 42 Give to him that asketh thee, and from him that would bor-

---

ᶠ εἰς γέενναν ἀπέλθῃ into Gehenna go away LTTrA. ᵍ ἐρρήθη LTrAW. ʰ — ὅτι LTTrA. ¹ πᾶς ὁ ἀπολύων every one that puts away LTTrA. ᵏ μοιχευθῆναι LTTrA. ¹ ὁ he who L. ᵐ γαμήσας has married L. ⁿ ποιῆσαι ἢ μέλαιναν LTTrA. ᵒ ἔσται shall be LA. ᴾ ῥαπίζει εἰς strikes upon LTTrA. ᑫ σιαγόνα σου LTrA; — σου (read the right cheek) T. ʳ δός LTTrA. ˢ δανίσασθαι T.

row of thee turn not thou away.

43 Ye have heard that it hath been said, Thou shalt love thy neighbour, and hate thine enemy. 44 But I say unto you, Love your enemies, bless them that curse you, do good to them that hate you, and pray for them which despitefully use you, and persecute you; 45 that ye may be the children of your Father which is in heaven : for he maketh his sun to rise on the evil and on the good, and sendeth rain on the just and on the unjust. 46 For if ye love them which love you, what reward have ye? do not even the publicans the same ? 47 And if ye salute your brethren only, what do ye more *than others?* do not even the publicans so? 48 Be ye therefore perfect, even as your Father which is in heaven is perfect.

43 Ἠκούσατε ὅτι 'ἐῤῥέθη,'' Ἀγαπήσεις τὸν.πλησίον.σου καὶ
Ye have heard that it was said, Thou shalt love thy neighbour and

μισήσεις τὸν.ἐχθρόν.σου· 44 ἐγὼ.δὲ λέγω ὑμῖν, Ἀγαπᾶτε τοὺς
hate thine enemy. But I say to you, Love

ἐχθροὺς ὑμῶν, ⁿεὐλογεῖτε τοὺς καταρωμένους ὑμᾶς, καλῶς
ⁿenemies ¹your, bless those who curse you, ᶻwell

ποιεῖτε ʷτοὺς μισοῦντας ὑμᾶς,¹ ‖ καὶ προσεύχεσθε ὑπὲρ τῶν
¹do to those who hate you, and pray for those who

ˣἐπηρεαζόντων ὑμᾶς καὶ‖ διωκόντων ὑμᾶς· 45 ὅπως γένησθε
despitefully use you and persecute you ; so that ye may be

υἱοὶ τοῦ.πατρὸς.ὑμῶν τοῦ ἐν οὐρανοῖς· ὅτι τὸν.ἥλιον.αὐτοῦ
sons of your Father who [is] in [the] heavens: for his sun

ἀνατέλλει ἐπὶ πονηροὺς καὶ ἀγαθούς, καὶ βρέχει ἐπὶ δικαίους
he causes to rise on evil and good, and sends rain on just

καὶ ἀδίκους. 46 ἐὰν.γὰρ ἀγαπήσητε τοὺς ἀγαπῶντας ὑμᾶς,
and unjust. For if ye love those who love you,

τίνα μισθὸν ἔχετε; οὐχὶ καὶ οἱ τελῶναι ʸτὸ αὐτὸ‖ ποιοῦσιν;
what reward have ye? ²not ³also ⁴the ᵗtax ⁶gatherers ⁷the ⁸same ¹do?

47 καὶ ἐὰν ἀσπάσησθε τοὺς.ἀδελφούς.ὑμῶν μόνον, τί περισ-
and if ye salute your brethren only, what extraordi-

σὸν ποιεῖτε; οὐχὶ καὶ οἱ ᶻτελῶναι‖ ᵃοὕτως‖ ποιοῦσιν; 48 ἔσεσθε
nary do ye? ²Not ³also ⁴the ᵗtax ⁶gatherers ⁷so ¹do? ³shall ⁴be

οὖν ὑμεῖς τέλειοι, ᵇὥσπερ‖ ὁ.πατὴρ.ὑμῶν ᶜὁ ἐν τοῖς οὐρανοῖς‖
²therefore ¹ye perfect, even as your Father who [is] in the heavens

τέλειός ἐστιν.
perfect is.

VI. Take heed that ye do not your alms before men, to be seen of them : otherwise ye have no reward of your Father which is in heaven. 2 Therefore when thou doest *thine* alms, do not sound a trumpet before thee, as the hypocrites do in the synagogues and in the streets, that they may have glory of men. Verily I say unto you, They have their reward. 3 But when thou doest alms, let not thy left hand know what thy right hand doeth : 4 that thine alms may be in secret : and thy Father which seeth in secret himself shall reward thee openly.

6 Προσέχετεᵈ τὴν.ᵉἐλεημοσύνην‖.ὑμῶν μὴ ποιεῖν ἔμπροσθεν
Beware your alms not to do before

τῶν ἀνθρώπων, πρὸς.τὸ.θεαθῆναι αὐτοῖς· εἰ.δὲ.μήγε, μισθὸν
men, in order to be seen by them : otherwise reward

οὐκ.ἔχετε παρὰ τῷ.πατρὶ.ὑμῶν τῷ ἐν ᶠτοῖς‖ οὐρανοῖς. 2 ὅταν
ye have not with your Father who [is] in the heavens. When

οὖν ποιῇς ἐλεημοσύνην, μὴ.σαλπίσῃς ἔμπροσθέν σου,
therefore thou doest alms, do not sound a trumpet before thee,

ὥσπερ οἱ ὑποκριταὶ ποιοῦσιν ἐν ταῖς συναγωγαῖς καὶ ἐν ταῖς
as the hypocrites do in the synagogues and in the

ῥύμαις, ὅπως δοξασθῶσιν ὑπὸ τῶν ἀνθρώπων· ἀμὴν λέγω
streets, that they may have glory from men. Verily I say

ὑμῖν, ἀπέχουσιν τὸν.μισθὸν.αὐτῶν. 3 σοῦ.δὲ ποιοῦντος ἐλεη-
to you, they have their reward. But thou doing

μοσύνην, μὴ.γνώτω ἡ.ἀριστερά.σου τί ποιεῖ ἡ.δεξιά.σου,
alms, let not ⁴know ¹thy ²left ³hand what does thy right hand,

4 ὅπως ᵍᾖ σου ἡ.ἐλεημοσύνη ἐν τῷ κρυπτῷ· καὶ ὁ.πατήρ.σου
so that ³may ⁴be ¹thine ²alms in secret : and thy Father

ὁ βλέπων ἐν τῷ κρυπτῷ ʰαὐτὸς‖ ἀποδώσει σοι ⁱἐν.τῷ.φανερῷ.‖
who sees in secret himself shall render to thee openly.

5 And when thou prayest, thou shalt not be as the hypocrites *are:* for they love to pray standing in the synagogues and in the corners of the streets,

5 Καὶ ὅταν ᵏπροσεύχῃ, οὐκ.ἔσῃ ὥσπερ ᵈ οἱ ὑποκριταί,
And when thou prayest, thou shalt not be as the hypocrites,

ὅτι φιλοῦσιν ἐν ταῖς συναγωγαῖς καὶ ἐν ταῖς γωνίαις τῶν
for they love in the synagogues and in the corners of the

ᵗ ἐῤῥήθη LT AW.   ᵛ — εὐλογεῖτε . . . μισοῦντας ὑμᾶς LTTrA.   ʷ τοῖς μισοῦσιν ὑμᾶς GW.
ˣ — ἐπηρεαζόντων ὑμᾶς καὶ LTTrA.   ʸ οὕτως so LTrA.   ᶻ ἐθνικοὶ heathen GLTTrAW.   ᵃ τὸ αὐτὸ,
the same LTTrAW.   ᵇ ὡς as LTTrA.   ᶜ ὁ οὐράνιος the heavenly LTTrA.   ᵈ + δὲ but T[ ].
ᵉ δικαιοσύνην righteousness GLTTrAW.   ᶠ — τοῖς T.   ᵍ ᾖ σου ἐλεημοσυνη ᾖ T.   ʰ — αὐτὸς
LTTrA.   ¹ — ἐν τῷ φανερῷ LTTrAW.   ᵏ προσεύχησθε, οὐκ ἔσεσθε ὡς ye pray, ye shall not
be as LTTrA.

πλατειῶν ἑστῶτες προσεύχεσθαι, ὅπως ¹ἂν".φανῶσιν τοῖς
streets   standing   to pray,   so that they may appear

ἀνθρώποις· ἀμὴν λέγω ὑμῖν, ᵐὅτι" ἀπέχουσιν τὸν μισθὸν
to men.   Verily I say to you, that   they have   ²reward

αὐτῶν. 6 σὺ.δέ, ὅταν προσεύχῃ, εἴσελθε εἰς τὸ.ⁿταμιεῖόν".σου,
¹their. But thou, when thou prayest, . enter into thy chamber,

καὶ κλείσας τὴν.θύραν.σου, πρόσευξαι τῷ.πατρί.σου τῷ ἐν
and having shut   thy door,   pray   to thy Father who [is] in

τῷ.κρυπτῷ· καὶ ὁ.πατήρ.σου ὁ βλέπων ἐν τῷ.κρυπτῷ ἀπο-
secret;   and thy Father who sees in   secret   will

δώσει σοι °ἐν.τῷ.φανερῷ". 7 Προσευχόμενοι.δὲ μὴ.ᴾβαττολο-
render to thee   openly.   But when ye pray   do not use vain

γήσητε," ὥσπερ οἱ ἐθνικοί· δοκοῦσιν.γὰρ ὅτι ἐν τῇ.πολυλογίᾳ
repetitions, as   the heathens· for they think that in ²much ³speaking

αὐτῶν εἰσακουσθήσονται. 8 μὴ οὖν ὁμοιωθῆτε αὐτοῖς·
¹their   they shall be heard.   ²Not ³therefore ⁴be like   to them:

οἶδεν.γὰρ ὁ.πατὴρ.ὑμῶν ὧν χρείαν ἔχετε πρὸ τοῦ ὑμᾶς
for ²knows   ¹your ²Father of what things ³need ¹ye ²have before ye

αἰτῆσαι αὐτόν. 9 οὕτως οὖν προσεύχεσθε ὑμεῖς· Πάτερ.ἡμῶν
ask   him. Thus therefore pray   ye: Our Father

ὁ ἐν τοῖς οὐρανοῖς, ἁγιασθήτω τὸ.ὄνομά.σου· 10 ᵠἐλθέτω"
who [art] in the heavens,   sanctified be thy name;   let come

ἡ.βασιλεία.σου· γενηθήτω τὸ.θέλημά.σου, ὡς ἐν οὐρανῷ, καὶ
thy kingdom;   let be done   thy will   as in heaven, [so] also

ἐπὶ ʳτῆς" γῆς· 11 τὸν.ἄρτον.ἡμῶν τὸν ἐπιούσιον δὸς ἡμῖν σή-
upon the earth;   our bread   the needed   give us to-

μερον· 12 καὶ ἄφες ἡμῖν τὰ.ὀφειλήματα.ἡμῶν, ὡς καὶ ἡμεῖς
day;   and forgive us   our debts,   as also we

ˢἀφίεμεν" τοῖς.ὀφειλέταις.ἡμῶν· 13 καὶ μὴ.εἰσενέγκῃς ἡμᾶς εἰς
forgive   our debtors;   And   lead not   us into

πειρασμόν, ἀλλὰ ῥῦσαι ἡμᾶς ἀπὸ τοῦ πονηροῦ. ᵗὅτι σοῦ ἐστιν
temptation, but deliver us from   evil.   For thine is

ἡ βασιλεία καὶ ἡ δύναμις καὶ ἡ δόξα εἰς τοὺς αἰῶνας. ἀμήν."
the kingdom and the power and the glory to the ages.   Amen.

14 Ἐὰν.γὰρ ἀφῆτε τοῖς.ἀνθρώποις τὰ.παραπτώματα.αὐτῶν,
For if ye forgive   men   their offences,

ἀφήσει καὶ ὑμῖν ὁ.πατὴρ.ὑμῶν ὁ οὐράνιος· 15 ἐὰν.δὲ μὴ
ᵃwill ⁴forgive ⁸also ⁷you ¹your ²Father ³the ⁴heavenly. but if ²not

ἀφῆτε τοῖς ἀνθρώποις ᵘτὰ.παραπτώματα.αὐτῶν," οὐδὲ ὁ
¹ye ²forgive   men   their offences,   neither

πατὴρ ὑμῶν ἀφήσει τὰ.παραπτώματα.ὑμῶν.
²Father ³your ¹will forgive   your offences.

16 Ὅταν.δὲ νηστεύητε, μὴ.γίνεσθε ᵛὥσπερ" οἱ ὑποκριταὶ
And when   ye fast,   be not   as   the hypocrites,

σκυθρωποί· ἀφανίζουσιν.γὰρ τὰ.πρόσωπα.ʷαὐτῶν,"
downcast in countenance; for they disfigure   their faces,

ὅπως φανῶσιν τοῖς ἀνθρώποις νηστεύοντες· ἀμὴν λέγω
so that they may appear. to men   fasting.   Verily I say

ὑμῖν, ˣὅτι" ἀπέχουσιν τὸν.μισθὸν.αὐτῶν. 17 σὺ.δὲ νηστεύων
to you, that   they have   their reward.   But thou, fasting,

ἄλειψαί σου τὴν κεφαλήν, καὶ τὸ.πρόσωπόν.σου νίψαι· 18 ὅπως
anoint thy   head,   and thy ²face   ¹wash,   so that

μὴ.φανῇς ʸτοῖς ἀνθρώποις νηστεύων," ἀλλὰ τῷ πατρί
thou mayest not appear to men   fasting,   but to ²Father

Right column (English):

that they may be seen of men. Verily I say unto you, They have their reward. 6 But thou, when thou prayest, enter into thy closet, and when thou hast shut thy door, pray to thy Father which is in secret; and thy Father which seeth in secret shall reward thee openly. 7 But when ye pray, use not vain repetitions, as the heathen do: for they think that they shall be heard for their much speaking. 8 Be not ye therefore like unto them: for your Father knoweth what things ye have need of, before ye ask him. 9 After this manner therefore pray ye: Our Father which art in heaven, Hallowed be thy name. 10 Thy kingdom come. Thy will be done in earth, as it is in heaven. 11 Give us this day our daily bread. 12 And forgive us our debts, as we forgive our debtors. 13 And lead us not into temptation, but deliver us from evil: For thine is the kingdom, and the power, and the glory, for ever. Amen. 14 For if ye forgive men their trespasses, your heavenly Father will also forgive you: 15 but if ye forgive not men their trespasses, neither will your Father forgive your trespasses.

16 Moreover when ye fast, be not, as the hypocrites, of a sad countenance: for they disfigure their faces, that they may appear unto men to fast. Verily I say unto you, They have their reward. 17 But thou, when thou fastest, anoint thine head, and wash thy face; 18 that thou appear not unto men to fast, but unto thy Fa-

---

¹ — ἂν LTTrAW.   ᵐ — ὅτι LTTrA.   ⁿ ταμεῖόν TA.   ° — ἐν τῷ φανερῷ LTTrA.   ᴾ βατταλογήσητε TA.   ᵠ ἐλθάτω T.   ʳ — τῆς LTTrAW.   ˢ ἀφήκαμεν have forgiven LTTrA.   ᵗ — ὅτι σοῦ to end of verse GLTTrAW.   ᵘ — τὰ παραπ. αὐτῶν T.   ᵛ ὡς LTTrA.   ʷ ἑαυτῶν L.   ˣ — ὅτι LTTrA.   ʸ νησ. τοῖς ἀνθρώ. L.

ther which is in secret: and thy Father, which seeth in secret. shall reward thee openly.

19 Lay not up for yourselves treasures upon earth, where moth and rust doth corrupt, and where thieves break through and steal: 20 but lay up for yourselves treasures in heaven, where neither moth nor rust doth corrupt, and where thieves do not break through nor steal: 21 for where your treasure is, there will your heart be also. 22 The light of the body is the eye: if therefore thine eye be single, thy whole body shall be full of light. 23 But if thine eye be evil, thy whole body shall be full of darkness. If therefore the light that is in thee be darkness, how great is that darkness!

24 No man can serve two masters: for either he will hate the one, and love the other; or else he will hold to the one, and despise the other. Ye cannot serve God and mammon. 25 Therefore I say unto you, Take no thought for your life, what ye shall eat, or what ye shall drink; nor yet for your body, what ye shall put on. Is not the life more than meat, and the body than raiment? 26 Behold the fowls of the air: for they sow not, neither do they reap, nor gather into barns; yet your heavenly Father feedeth them. Are ye not much better than they? 27 Which of you by taking thought can add one cubit unto his stature? 28 And why take ye thought for raiment? Consider the lilies of the field, how they grow; they toil not, neither do they spin: 29 and yet I say unto you, That even Solomon in all his glory was not arrayed like one of these. 30 Wherefore, if God so clothe the grass of the field, which to day

---

σου τῷ ἐν τῷ ᶻκρυπτῷ·" καὶ ὁ.πατήρ.σου ὁ βλέπων ἐν τῷ
'thy who [is] in secret; and thy Father who sees in

²κρυπτῷ" ἀποδώσει σοι ᵃἐν.τῷ.φανερῷ."
secret will render to thee openly.

19 Μὴ.θησαυρίζετε ὑμῖν θησαυροὺς ἐπὶ τῆς γῆς, ὅπου
Treasure not up for yourselves treasures upon the earth, where

σὴς καὶ βρῶσις ἀφανίζει, καὶ ὅπου κλέπται διορύσσουσιν καὶ
moth and rust spoil, and where thieves dig through and

κλέπτουσιν· 20 θησαυρίζετε.δὲ ὑμῖν θησαυροὺς ἐν οὐρανῷ,
steal: but treasure up for yourselves treasures in heaven,

ὅπου οὔτε σὴς οὔτε βρῶσις ἀφανίζει, καὶ ὅπου κλέπται οὐ.δι-
where neither moth nor rust spoils and where thieves do not

ορύσσουσιν οὐδὲ κλέπτουσιν. 21 ὅπου.γάρ ἐστιν ὁ θησαυρὸς
dig through nor steal: for where ³is ²treasure

ᵇὑμῶν," ἐκεῖ ἔσται ˹καὶ˺ ἡ καρδία ᵇὑμῶν." 22 Ὁ λύχνος τοῦ
'your, there will be also ²heart 'your. The lamp of the

σώματός ἐστιν ὁ ὀφθαλμός·ᵈ ἐὰν ᶜοὖν" ⁱὁ.ὀφθαλμός.σου
body is the eye; if therefore thine eye

ἁπλοῦς ᾖ," ὅλον τὸ.σῶμά.σου φωτεινὸν ἔσται· 23 ἐὰν.δὲ ὁ
single be, ²whole ' ¹thy body light will be. But if

ὀφθαλμός.σου πονηρὸς ᾖ, ὅλον τὸ.σῶμά.σου σκοτεινὸν ἔσται.
thine eye evil be, ²whole ¹thy body dark will be.

εἰ οὖν τὸ φῶς τὸ ἐν σοὶ σκότος ἐστίν, τὸ σκότος πόσον;
If therefore the light that [is] in thee darkness is, the darkness how great;

24 Οὐδεὶς δύναται δυσὶ κυρίοις δουλεύειν· ἢ.γὰρ τὸν ἕνα
No one is able two lords to serve; for either the one

μισήσει, καὶ τὸν ἕτερον ἀγαπήσει· ἢ ἑνὸς ἀνθέξεται, καὶ
he will hate, and the other he will love; or [the] one he will hold to, and

τοῦ ἑτέρου καταφρονήσει. οὐ.δύνασθε θεῷ δουλεύειν καὶ ᵍμαμ-
the other he will despise. Ye are not able ⁵God ¹to²serve and mam-

μωνᾷ." 25 διὰ τοῦτο λέγω ὑμῖν, μὴ.μεριμνᾶτε τῇ.ψυχῇ.ὑμῶν,
mon. Because of this I say to you, be not careful as to your life,

τί φάγητε ᵇκαὶ" ⁱτί πίητε·" μηδὲ τῷ.σώματι.ὑμῶν,
what ye should eat and what ye should drink; nor as to your body

τί ἐνδύσησθε. οὐχὶ ἡ ψυχὴ πλεῖόν ἐστιν τῆς τροφῆς καὶ
what ye should put on. ²Not ³the ⁴life ⁵more ¹is than the food and

τὸ σῶμα τοῦ ἐνδύματος; 26 ἐμβλέψατε εἰς τὰ πετεινὰ τοῦ
the body than the raiment? Look at the birds of the

οὐρανοῦ, ὅτι οὐ.σπείρουσιν, οὐδὲ θερίζουσιν, οὐδὲ συνάγουσιν
heaven, that they sow not, nor do they reap, nor do they gather

εἰς ἀποθήκας, καὶ ὁ.πατήρ.ὑμῶν ὁ οὐράνιος τρέφει αὐτά· οὐχ
into granaries, and your Father the heavenly feeds them: ²not

ὑμεῖς μᾶλλον διαφέρετε αὐτῶν; 27 τίς.δὲ ἐξ ὑμῶν μερι-
¹ye ⁴much ¹are better than they? But which out of you by being

²μνῶν δύναται προσθεῖναι ἐπὶ τὴν.ἡλικίαν.αὐτοῦ πῆχυν ἕνα;
careful is able to add to his stature ²cubit ¹one?

28 καὶ περὶ ἐνδύματος τί μεριμνᾶτε; καταμάθετε τὰ κρίνα
and about raiment why are ye careful? observe the lilies

τοῦ ἀγροῦ, πῶς ᵏαὐξάνει" οὐ.ˡκοπιᾷ" οὐδὲ ᵐνήθει· 29 λέ-
of the field, how they grow: they labour not nor do they spin: ²I

γω δὲ ὑμῖν, ὅτι οὐδὲ Σολομὼν ἐν πάσῃ τῇ.δόξῃ.αὐτοῦ περιε-
say ¹but to you that not even Solomon in all his glory was

βάλετο ὡς ἓν τούτων. 30 εἰ.δὲ τὸν χόρτον τοῦ ἀγροῦ.σήμερον
clothed as one of these. But if the grass of the field, to day

---

ᶻκρυφαίῳ LTTrA. ᵃ— ἐν τῷ φανερῷ GLTTrAW. ᵇσου thy LTTrA. ᶜ— καὶ L. ᵈ+ σου thy L.
ᵉ— οὖν T. ᶠᾖ ὁ ὀφθαλμός σου ἁπλοῦς LTA. ᵍμαμωνᾷ GLTTrAW. ʰᾖ or LTr; — καὶ T.
— τί πίητε T. ᵏαὐξάνουσιν LTTrA. ˡκοπιῶσιν LT; κοπιοῦσιν TrA. ᵐνήθουσιν LTrA.

ὄντα, καὶ αὔριον εἰς κλίβανον βαλλόμενον, ὁ θεὸς οὕτως
¹which is and to-morrow into an oven is cast, God thus

ἀμφιέννυσιν. οὐ πολλῷ μᾶλλον ὑμᾶς, ὀλιγόπιστοι; 31 μὴ
arrays, [will he] not much rather you, O[ye] of little faith? ¹not

οὖν μεριμνήσητε, λέγοντες, Τί φάγωμεν. ἢ τί πίωμεν,
²therefore ¹be careful, saying, What shall we eat? or what shall we drink?

ἢ τί περιβαλώμεθα; 32 πάντα.γὰρ ταῦτα τὰ ἔθνη ⁿἐπι-
or with what shall we be clothed? For all these things the nations seek

ζητεῖ·ⁿ οἶδεν.γὰρ ὁ.πατὴρ.ὑμῶν ὁ οὐράνιος ὅτι χρῄζετε
after. For knows your Father the heavenly that ye have need

τούτων ἁπάντων· 33 ζητεῖτε.δὲ πρῶτον ᵒτὴν βασιλείαν τοῦ
ᵖᶠ ²these ³things ¹all. But seek ye first the kingdom

θεοῦ καὶ τὴν.δικαιοσύνηνᴵᴵ.αὐτοῦ, καὶ ταῦτα πάντα προσ-
of God and his righteousness, and ²these ³things ¹all shall

τεθήσεται· ὑμῖν. 34 μὴ οὖν ᴾμεριμνήσητεᴵᴵ εἰς τὴν αὔριον·
be added to you. ²Not ³therefore ¹be careful for the morrow:

ἡ.γὰρ αὔριον μεριμνήσει ᑫτὰ᎐ ʳἑαυτῆς.ᴵᴵ ἀρκετὸν τῇ
for the morrow shall be careful about the [things] of itself. Sufficient to the

ἡμέρα ἡ κακία αὐτῆς.
day [is] the evil of it.

7 Μὴ.κρίνετε, ἵνα μὴ.κριθῆτε· 2 ἐν ᾧ γὰρ.κρίματι κρίνετε,
Judge not, that ye be not judged: ²with ³what ¹for judgment ye judge,

κριθήσεσθε· καὶ ἐν ᾧ μέτρῳ μετρεῖτε, ˢἀντιμετρηθήσεταιᴵᴵ
ye shall be judged; and with what measure ye mete, it shall be measured again

ὑμῖν. 3 Τί.δὲ βλέπεις τὸ κάρφος τὸ ἐν τῷ ὀφθαλμῷ τοῦ
to you. But why lookest thou on the mote that [is] in the eye

ἀδελφοῦ.σου, τὴν.δὲ ἐν τῷ.σῷ ὀφθαλμῷ δοκὸν οὐ.κατανοεῖς;
of thy brother, but the ²in ³thine [⁴own] ⁵eye ¹beam perceivest not?

4 ἢ πῶς ἐρεῖς τῷ.ἀδελφῷ.σου, Ἄφες ἐκβάλω τὸ
Or how wilt thou say to thy brother, Suffer [that] I may cast out the

κάρφος ᵗἀπὸ ᴵᴵ τοῦ.ὀφθαλμοῦ.σου· καὶ ἰδού, ἡ δοκὸς ἐν τῷ
mote from thine eye: and behold, the beam [is] in

ὀφθαλμῷ.σου; 5 ὑποκριτά, ἔκβαλε πρῶτον ʳτὴν δοκὸν ἐκ
thine [own] eye! hypocrite, cast out first the beam out of

τοῦ.ὀφθαλμοῦ.σου,ᴵᴵ καὶ τότε διαβλέψεις ἐκβαλεῖν τὸ κάρφος
thine [own] eye, and then thou wilt see clearly to cast out the mote

ἐκ τοῦ ὀφθαλμοῦ τοῦ.ἀδελφοῦ.σου.
out of the eye of thy brother.

6 Μὴ.δῶτε τὸ ἅγιον τοῖς κυσίν· μηδὲ βάλητε τοὺς
Give not that which [is] holy to the dogs, nor cast

μαργαρίτας ὑμῶν ἔμπροσθεν τῶν χοίρων, μήποτε ʷκατα-
²pearls ¹your before the swine, lest they should

πατήσωσινᴵᴵ αὐτοὺς ἐν τοῖς.ποσὶν.αὐτῶν, καὶ στραφέντες
trample upon them with their feet, and having turned

ῥήξωσιν ὑμᾶς.
they rend you.

7 Αἰτεῖτε, καὶ δοθήσεται ὑμῖν· ζητεῖτε, καὶ εὑρήσετε·
Ask, and it shall be given to you: seek, and ye shall find:

κρούετε, καὶ ἀνοιγήσεται ὑμῖν. 8 πᾶς.γὰρ ὁ αἰτῶν λαμβάνει,
knock, and it shall be opened to you. For everyone that asks receives,

καὶ ὁ ζητῶν εὑρίσκει, καὶ τῷ κρούοντι ˣἀνοιγήσεται.ᴵᴵ
and he that seeks finds, and to him that knocks it shall be opened.

---

is, and to morrow is cast into the oven, *shall* he not much more clothe you, O ye of little faith? 31 Therefore take no thought, saying, What shall we eat? or, What shall we drink? or, Wherewithal shall we be clothed? 32 (For after all these things do the Gentiles seek:) for your heavenly Father knoweth that ye have need of all these things. 33 But seek ye first the kingdom of God, and his righteousness; and all these things shall be added unto you. 34 Take therefore no thought for the morrow: for the morrow shall take thought for the things of itself. Sufficient unto the day *is* the evil thereof.

VII. Judge not, that ye be not judged. 2 For with what judgment ye judge, ye shall be judged: and with what measure ye mete, it shall be measured to you again. 3 And why beholdest thou the mote that is in thy brother's eye, but considerest not the beam that is in thine own eye? 4 Or how wilt thou say to thy brother, Let me pull out the mote out of thine eye; and, behold, a beam is in thine own eye? 5 Thou hypocrite, first cast out the beam out of thine own eye; and then shalt thou see clearly to cast out the mote out of thy brother's eye.

6 Give not that which is holy unto the dogs, neither cast ye your pearls before swine, lest they trample them under their feet, and turn again and rend you.

7 Ask, and it shall be given you; seek, and ye shall find; knock, and it shall be opened unto you: 8 for every one that asketh receiveth; and he that seeketh findeth; and to him that knocketh it shall be opened. 9 Or

---

ᵘ ἐπιζητοῦσιν LTTrA. ᵒ τὴν δικαιοσύνην καὶ τὴν βασιλειαν L; — τοῦ θεοῦ (*read* its righteousness) LT[A] ᴾ μεριμνήσετε E. ᑫ — τὰ (*omit* the [things] of) LTTrAW. ʳ αὐτῆς A. ˢ μετρηθήσεται it shall be measured GLTTrAW. ᵗ ἐκ out of LTTr. ʳ ἐκ τοῦ ὀφθαλμοῦ σου τὴν δοκον LTTrA. ʷ καταπατήσουσιν they shall trample upon LTTrA. ˣ ἀνοίγεται it is opened LTr.

what man is there of you, whom if his son ask bread, will he give him a stone? 10 Or if he ask a fish, will he give him a serpent? 11 If ye then, being evil, know how to give good gifts unto your children, how much more shall your Father which is in heaven give good things to them that ask him?

9 ἢ τίς ⁱἐστιν‖ ἐξ ὑμῶν ἄνθρωπος, ὃν ᶻἐὰν‖ ᵃαἰτήσῃ‖ ὁ υἰὸς
Or what ¹is ³there ⁴of ²you   ¹man   who if ³should ⁴ask ²son
αὐτοῦ ἄρτον, μὴ λίθον ἐπιδώσει αὐτῷ; 10 ᵇκαὶ ἐὰν ἰχθὺν
¹his   bread,   a stone will he give him?   and if   a fish
αἰτήσῃ,‖ μὴ ὄφιν ἐπιδώσει αὐτῷ; 11 εἰ οὖν ὑμεῖς πονηροὶ
he should ask, a serpent will he give him?   If therefore ye,   ²evil
ὄντες οἴδατε   δόματα ἀγαθὰ διδόναι τοῖς.τέκνοις.ὑμῶν, πόσῳ
¹being, know [how] ²gifts ¹good to give   to your children, how much
μᾶλλον ὁ.πατὴρ.ὑμῶν ὁ ἐν τοῖς οὐρανοῖς δώσει ἀγαθὰ
more   your Father who [is] in the heavens will give good things
τοῖς αἰτοῦσιν αὐτόν;
to them that ask   him?

12 Therefore all things whatsoever ye would that men should do to you, do ye even so to them: for this is the law and the prophets.

12 Πάντα οὖν ὅσα.ᶜἂν‖ θέλητε ἵνα ποιῶσιν ὑμῖν οἱ
All things therefore whatever ye desire that ²should ³do ⁴to ⁵you
ἄνθρωποι, οὕτως καὶ ὑμεῖς ποιεῖτε αὐτοῖς· οὗτος.γάρ ἐστιν ὁ
¹men,   so also ⁶ye ¹do   to them: for this   is the
νόμος καὶ οἱ προφῆται.
law   and the prophets.

13 Enter ye in at the strait gate: for wide is the gate, and broad is the way, that leadeth to destruction, and many there be which go in thereat: 14 because strait is the gate, and narrow is the way, which leadeth unto life, and few there be that find it.

13 ᵈΕἰσέλθετε‖ διὰ τῆς στενῆς πύλης· ὅτι πλατεῖα ᵉἡ πύλη‖
Enter in through the narrow gate; for wide   the gate
καὶ εὐρύχωρος ἡ ὁδὸς ἡ ἀπάγουσα εἰς τὴν ἀπώλειαν, καὶ
and broad   the way that leads   to   destruction, and
πολλοί εἰσιν οἱ εἰσερχόμενοι δι' αὐτῆς· 14 ᶠὅτι‖ στενὴ ᵍἡ
many are they who enter   through it·   for   narrow the
πύλη‖ καὶ τεθλιμμένη ἡ ὁδὸς ἡ ἀπάγουσα εἰς τὴν ζωήν, καὶ
gate and straitened the way that leads   to   life,   and
ὀλίγοι εἰσὶν οἱ εὑρίσκοντες αὐτήν.
few   are they who find   it.

15 Beware of false prophets, which come to you in sheep's clothing, but inwardly they are ravening wolves. 16 Ye shall know them by their fruits. Do men gather grapes of thorns, or figs of thistles? 17 Even so every good tree bringeth forth good fruit; but a corrupt tree bringeth forth evil fruit. 18 A good tree cannot bring forth evil fruit, neither can a corrupt tree bring forth good fruit. 19 Every tree that bringeth not forth good fruit is hewn down, and cast into the fire. 20 Wherefore by their fruits ye shall know them.

15 Προσέχετε.ʰδὲ‖ ἀπὸ τῶν ψευδοπροφητῶν, οἵτινες ἔρχονται
But beware   of the false prophets,   who   come
πρὸς ὑμᾶς ἐν ἐνδύμασιν προβάτων, ἔσωθεν.δὲ εἰσιν λύκοι ἅρ-
to   you in raiment   of sheep, but within are ²wolves ¹ra-
παγες. 16 ἀπὸ τῶν.καρπῶν.αὐτῶν ἐπιγνώσεσθε αὐτούς· μήτι
pacious.   By   their fruits   ye shall know   them.
συλλέγουσιν ἀπὸ ἀκανθῶν ⁱσταφυλὴν ‖ ἢ ἀπὸ τριβόλων σῦκα;
Do they gather from thorns ¹a bunch of grapes, or from thistles figs?
17 οὕτως πᾶν δένδρον ἀγαθὸν καρποὺς καλοὺς ποιεῖ· τὸ.δὲ
So   every ²tree   ¹good   ⁴fruits   ²good produces, but the
σαπρὸν δένδρον καρποὺς πονηροὺς ποιεῖ. 18 οὐ.δύναται
corrupt tree   ²fruits ¹bad   produces.
δένδρον ἀγαθὸν καρποὺς πονηροὺς ʲποιεῖν,‖ οὐδὲ δένδρον σα-
¹a ³tree ²good   ⁶fruits   ⁵evil produce, nor a ²tree ¹cor-
πρὸν καρποὺς καλοὺς ʲποιεῖν.‖ 19 πᾶνᵏ δένδρον μὴ ποιοῦν
rupt ³fruits ⁴good   ²produce.   Every tree   not producing
καρπὸν καλὸν ἐκκόπτεται καὶ εἰς πῦρ βάλλεται. 20 ᶩἄραγε‖
²fruit ¹good is cut down and into fire is cast.   Then surely
ᵐἀπὸ‖ τῶν.καρπῶν.αὐτῶν ἐπιγνώσεσθε αὐτούς.
by   their fruits   ye shall know   them.

21 Not every one that saith unto me, Lord, Lord, shall enter into the kingdom of heaven; but he that doeth the will of my

21 Οὐ πᾶς ὁ λέγων μοι, Κύριε, κύριε, εἰσελεύσεται εἰς
Not every one who says to me, Lord, Lord, shall enter into
τὴν βασιλείαν τῶν οὐρανῶν· ἀλλ' ὁ ποιῶν τὸ θέλημα τοῦ
the kingdom of the heavens, but he who does the will

ʸ — ἐστιν LTr [A]. ᶻ — ἐὰν LTTrA. ᵃ αἰτήσῃ shall ask LTTrA. ᵇ ἢ καὶ ἰχθὺν αἰτήσει or
also a fish shall ask LTTrA. ᶜ ἐὰν τ. ᵈ εἰσέλθατε LTTrA. ᵉ — ἡ πύλη L[T]. ᶠ τί how GLTr.
ᵍ [ἡ πύλη] LT. ʰ — δὲ but LT [TrA]. ⁱ σταφυλὰς grapes LTTrA. ʲ ἐνεγκεῖν bear T.
ᵏ + [οὖν] now L. ᶩ ἄρα γε LTrA. ᵐ ἐκ L.

πατρός. μου τοῦ ἐν ⁿ οὐρανοῖς. 22 πολλοὶ ἐροῦσίν μοι ἐν
of my Father　who[is] in [the] heavens.　　Many　will say to me in

ἐκείνῃ τῇ ἡμέρᾳ, Κύριε, κύριε, οὐ τῷ.σῷ ὀνόματι ᵒπροεφη-
that　　day,　　Lord, Lord, ³not ⁵through ⁶thy ⁷name　　¹did ⁴we

τεύσαμεν,‖ καὶ τῷ.σῷ ὀνόματι δαιμόνια ἐξεβάλομεν, καὶ
°prophesy,　and through thy　name　demons　cast out,　and

τῷ.σῷ ὀνόματι δυνάμεις πολλὰς ἐποιήσαμεν; 23 καὶ
through thy　name　²works ³of ⁴power ¹many　perform?　　And

τότε ὁμολογήσω αὐτοῖς, ὅτι οὐδέποτε ἔγνων ὑμᾶς· ἀποχωρεῖτε
then will I confess to them,　Never　knew I　you:　depart ye

ἀπ᾽ ἐμοῦ, οἱ ἐργαζόμενοι τὴν ἀνομίαν.
from me,　who　work　　lawlessness.

24 Πᾶς οὖν ὅστις ἀκούει μου τοὺς λόγους ᵖτούτους,‖
Every one therefore whosoever hears ²my　³words ¹these,

καὶ ποιεῖ αὐτούς, ᑫὁμοιώσω αὐτὸν‖ ἀνδρὶ φρονίμῳ, ὅστις ᾠκοδό-
and does　them,　I will liken him　to a ²man ¹prudent, who　built

μησεν ʳτὴν.οἰκίαν.αὐτοῦ‖ ἐπὶ τὴν πέτραν· 25 καὶ κατέβη ἡ
his house　upon the　rock:　　and came down the

βροχὴ καὶ ˢἦλθον‖ οἱ ποταμοὶ καὶ ἔπνευσαν οἱ ἄνεμοι, καὶ
rain,　and　came　the　streams,　and blew　the winds,　and

ᵗπροσέπεσον‖ τῇ.οἰκίᾳ.ἐκείνῃ, καὶ οὐκ.ἔπεσεν· τεθεμελίωτο.γὰρ
fell upon　　that house,　and　it fell not;　for it had been founded

ἐπὶ τὴν πέτραν. 26 καὶ πᾶς ὁ ἀκούων μου τοὺς λόγους
upon　the　rock.　and everyone who hears ²my　　³words

τούτους καὶ μὴ.ποιῶν αὐτούς, ὁμοιωθήσεται ἀνδρὶ μωρῷ,
¹these　and does not do　them,　he shall be likened to a ²man foolish,

ὅστις ᾠκοδόμησεν ᵛτὴν.οἰκίαν.αὐτοῦ‖ ἐπὶ τὴν ἄμμον· 27 καὶ
who　built　　his house　upon the　sand:　　and

κατέβη ἡ βροχὴ καὶ ἦλθον οἱ ποταμοὶ καὶ ἔπνευσαν οἱ
came down the rain,　and came　the streams, and　blew　the

ἄνεμοι, καὶ προσέκοψαν τῇ.οἰκίᾳ.ἐκείνῃ, καὶ ἔπεσεν, καὶ ἦν
winds,　and　beat upon　that house,　and　it fell,　and ⁵was

ἡ πτῶσις αὐτῆς μεγάλη.
¹the　²fall ³of ⁴it　great.

28 Καὶ ἐγένετο ὅτε ʷσυνετέλεσεν‖ ὁ Ἰησοῦς τοὺς λόγους
And it came to pass when ²had ³finished ¹Jesus　³words

τούτους ἐξεπλήσσοντο οἱ ὄχλοι ἐπὶ τῇ.διδαχῇ.αὐτοῦ· 29 ἦν
⁴these　astonished were the crowds at　his teaching:　²he ³was

γὰρ διδάσκων αὐτοὺς ὡς ἐξουσίαν ἔχων, καὶ οὐχ ὡς οἱ
¹for　teaching　them　as ²authority ¹having, and　not as the

γραμματεῖςˣ.
scribes.

8 ʸΚαταβάντι.δὲ αὐτῷ‖ ἀπὸ τοῦ ὄρους, ἠκολούθησαν αὐτῷ
And when ²had ³come ⁴down ¹he　from the mountain,　³followed　⁴him

ὄχλοι πολλοί· 2 καὶ ἰδού, λεπρὸς ᶻἐλθὼν‖ προσεκύνει αὐτῷ,
²crowds ¹great.　And behold, a leper having come did homage to him,

λέγων, Κύριε, ἐὰν θέλῃς, δύνασαί με καθαρίσαι. 3 Καὶ
saying,　Lord, if thou wilt thou art able me to cleanse.　　And

ἐκτείνας τὴν.χεῖρα ἥψατο αὐτοῦ ᵃὁ Ἰησοῦς,‖ λέγων,
having stretched out [his] hand ²touched ³him　¹Jesus,　saying,

Θέλω, καθαρίσθητι. Καὶ εὐθέως ᵇἐκαθαρίσθη‖ αὐτοῦ ἡ λέπρα.
I will, be thou cleansed. And immediately .was cleansed　his　lepro y.

Father which is in heaven. 22 Many will say to me in that day. Lord, Lord, have we not prophe-ied in thy name? and in thy name have cast out devils? and in thy name done many wonderful works? 23 And then will I profess unto them, I never knew you: depart from me, ye that work iniquity.

24 Therefore whoso-ever heareth these say-ings of mine, and doeth them, I will liken him unto a wi-e man, which built his house upon a rock: 25 and the rain de-cen-ded, and the floods came, and the winds blew, and beat upon that house; and it fell not: for it was founded upon a rock. 26 And eve'y one that heareth these sayings of mine, and doeth them not, shall be likened unto a foolish man, which built his house upon the sands 27 and the rain descended, and the floods came, and the winds blew, and beat upon that house; and it fell: and great was the fall of it.

28 And it came to pass, when Jesus had ended these sayings, the people were aston-ished at his doctrine: 29 for he taught them as one having au-thority, and not as the scribes.

VIII. When he was come down from the mountain, great mul-titudes followed him. 2 And, behold, there came a'leper and wor-shipped him, saying, Lord, if thou wilt, thou canst make me clean. 3 And Jesus put forth his hand, and touched him, saying, I will; be thou clean. And im-mediately his leprosy was cleansed. 4 And

ⁿ + τοῖς the LTTrA. ᵒ ἐπροφητεύσαμεν LTTrA. ᵖ [τούτους] LTr. ᑫ ὁμοιωθήσεται he shall be likened LTTr. ʳ αὐτοῦ τὴν οἰκίαν LTTrA. ˢ ἦλθαν Tr. ᵗ προσέπαισαν struck against L; προσ-έπεσαν TTrA. ᵛ αὐτοῦ τὴν οἰκίαν LTTrA. ʷ ἐτέλεσεν LTTrA. ˣ + αὐτῶν (read their scribes) LTTrA; + καὶ οἱ Φαρισαῖοι and the Pharisees L. ʸ καὶ καταβάντος αὐτοῦ L; καταβάντος δὲ αὐτοῦ Tr. ᶻ προσελθὼν having come to [him] LTTrAW. ᵃ — ὁ Ἰησοῦς (read he touched) ʟTTrA. ᵇ ἐκαθερίσθη T.

Jesus saith unto him,
See thou tell no man;
but go thy way, shew
thyself to the priest,
and offer the gift that
Moses commanded, for
a testimony unto them.

4 Καὶ λέγει αὐτῷ ὁ Ἰησοῦς,"Ορα μηδενὶ εἴπῃς· ᶜἀλλ'� ὕπαγε,
And ²says ³to ⁴him ¹Jesus,   See   no one thou tell; but   go
σεαυτὸν δεῖξον τῷ ἱερεῖ, καὶ ᵈπροσένεγκε‖ τὸ δῶρον ὃ προσ-
thyself show to the priest, and   offer   the gift which ᶠor-
έταξεν ᵉΜωσῆς,‖ εἰς μαρτύριον αὐτοῖς.
dered ¹Moses   for a testimony to them.

5 And when Jesus
was entered into Ca-
pernaum, there came
unto him a centurion,
beseeching him, 6 and
saying, Lord, my ser-
vant lieth at home sick
of the palsy, grievously
tormented. 7 And Jesus
saith unto him, I will
come and heal him.
8 The centurion an-
swered and said, Lord,
I am not worthy that
thou shouldest come
under my roof: but
speak the word only,
and my servant shall
be healed. 9 For I am
a man under authority,
having soldiers under
me: and I say to this
man, Go, and he goeth;
and to another, Come,
and he cometh; and
to my servant, Do
this, and he doeth it.
10 When Jesus heard
it, he marvelled, and
said to them that fol-
lowed, Verily I say
unto you, I have not
found so great faith,
no, not in Israel.
11 And I say unto you,
That many shall come
from the east and west,
and shall sit down with
Abraham, and Isaac,
and Jacob, in the king-
dom of heaven. 12 But
the children of the
kingdom shall be cast
out into outer dark-
ness: there shall be
weeping and gna·hing
of teeth. 13 And Jesus
said unto the centu-
rion, Go thy way; and
as thou hast believed,
so be it done unto thee.
And his servant was
healed in the selfsame
hour.

5 ᶠΕἰσελθόντι‖ δὲ ᵍτῷ Ἰησοῦ‖ εἰς ʰΚαπερναούμ,‖ προσῆλθεν
And ²having ³entered ¹Jesus into   Capernaum,   ³came
αὐτῷ ¹ἑκατόνταρχος‖ παρακαλῶν αὐτὸν 6 καὶ λέγων, Κύριε,
⁴to ⁵him ¹a ²centurion, beseeching him and saying, Lord,
ὁ παῖς μου βέβληται ἐν τῇ οἰκίᾳ παραλυτικός, δεινῶς βασα-
my servant is laid in the house paralytic, . grievously tor-
νιζόμενος. 7 ᵏΚαὶ‖ λέγει αὐτῷ ¹ὁ Ἰησοῦς,‖ Ἐγὼ ἐλθὼν θερα-
mented.   And ²says ³to ⁴him ¹Jesus,   I having come will
πεύσω αὐτόν. 8 ᵐΚαὶ ἀποκριθεὶς‖ ὁ ¹ἑκατόνταρχος‖ ἔφη, Κύριε,
heal him.   And ²answering ¹the ²centurion   said, Lord,
οὐκ εἰμὶ ἱκανὸς ἵνα μου ὑπὸ τὴν στέγην εἰσέλθῃς· ἀλλὰ μόνον
I am not worthy that ⁴my ¹under   roof thou shouldest come, but only
εἰπὲ ⁿλόγον,‖ καὶ ἰαθήσεται ὁ παῖς μου. 9 καὶ γὰρ ἐγὼ ἄν-
speak a word, and shall be healed my servant.   For also I a
θρωπός εἰμι ὑπὸ ἐξουσίανᵒ, ἔχων ὑπ' ἐμαυτὸν στρατιώτας·
man   am under authority, having under myself soldiers;
καὶ λέγω τούτῳ, Πορεύθητι, καὶ πορεύεται· καὶ ἄλλῳ, Ἔρχου,
and I say to this [one], Go,   and he goes; and to another, Come,
καὶ ἔρχεται· καὶ τῷ δούλῳ μου, Ποίησον τοῦτο, καὶ ποιεῖ.
and he comes; and to my bondman, Do   this,   and he does [it].
10 Ἀκούσας δὲ ὁ Ἰησοῦς ἐθαύμασεν, καὶ εἶπεν τοῖς ἀκολου-
And ²having ³heard ¹Jesus   wondered,   and said to those follow-
θοῦσινᴾ, Ἀμὴν λέγω ὑμῖν, ᑫοὐδὲ ἐν τῷ Ἰσραὴλ τοσαύτην
ing,   Verily I say to you, Not even in Israel   so great
πίστιν‖ εὗρον. 11 λέγω δὲ ὑμῖν, ὅτι πολλοὶ ἀπὸ ἀνατολῶν
faith have I found. But I say to you, that many from   east
καὶ δυσμῶν ἥξουσιν, καὶ ἀνακλιθήσονται μετὰ Ἀβραὰμ καὶ
and west   shall come, and shall recline [at table] with Abraham and
Ἰσαὰκ καὶ Ἰακὼβ ἐν τῇ βασιλείᾳ τῶν οὐρανῶν· 12 οἱ δὲ υἱοὶ
Isaac and Jacob in the kingdom of the heavens; but the sons
τῆς βασιλείας ʳἐκβληθήσονται‖ εἰς τὸ σκότος τὸ ἐξώτερον· ἐκεῖ
of the kingdom shall be cast out into the darkness the outer: there
ἔσται ὁ κλαυθμὸς καὶ ὁ βρυγμὸς τῶν ὀδόντων. 13 Καὶ εἶπεν
shall be the weeping and the gnashing of the teeth.   And ²said
ὁ Ἰησοῦς τῷ ˢἑκατοντάρχῳ,‖ Ὕπαγε, ᵗκαὶ‖ ὡς ἐπίστευσας
¹Jesus to the . centurion,   Go,   and as thou hast believed
γενηθήτω σοι. Καὶ ἰάθη ὁ παῖς ᵛαὐτοῦ‖ ᵂἐν τῇ ὥρᾳ
be it to thee. And was healed his servant   in ²hour
ἐκείνῃ.‖
¹that.

14 And when Jesus
was come into Peter's
house, he saw his wife's
mother laid, and sick
of a fever. 15 And he

14 Καὶ ἐλθὼν ὁ Ἰησοῦς εἰς τὴν οἰκίαν Πέτρου, εἶδεν
And ²having ³come ¹Jesus to the house of Peter, saw
τὴν πενθερὰν αὐτοῦ βεβλημένην καὶ πυρέσσουσαν, 15 καὶ
his wife's mother   laid   and   in a fever;   and

ᶜ ἀλλὰ EGLTTᵣA. ᵈ προσένεγκον LTTᵣAW. ᵉ Μωϋσῆς LTTᵣA. ᶠ εἰσελθόντος LTTᵣA. ᵍ αὐτῷ
he GW; αὐτοῦ he LTTᵣA. ʰ Καφαρναούμ LTTᵣAW. ¹ ἑκατοντάρχης τ. ᵏ — καὶ LT[Tᵣ]A.
¹ — ὁ Ἰησοῦς (read he says) LT[Tᵣ]A. ᵐ ἀποκριθεὶς δὲ LTTᵣ. ⁿ λόγῳ by a word GLTTᵣAW.
ᵒ + τασσόμενος placed L. ᴾ + αὐτῷ him L ᑫ παρ' οὐδενὶ τοσαύτην πίστιν ἐν τῷ Ἰσραὴλ
with no one so great faith in Israel LTᵣA. ʳ ἐξελεύσονται shall go forth τ. ˢ ἑκατοντάρχη
GLTTᵣAW. ᵗ — καὶ LT[Tᵣ]A. ᵛ — αὐτοῦ (read the servant) LTT.[A]. ᵂ ἀπὸ τῆς ὥρας ἐκείνης
from that hour L.

ἥψατο τῆς χειρὸς.αὐτῆς, καὶ ἀφῆκεν αὐτὴν ὁ πυρετός· καὶ
he touched　her hand,　and　¹left　*her　¹the　²fever;　and
ἠγέρθη καὶ διηκόνει ˣαὐτοῖς.ǁ
she arose and ministered to them.

16 Ὀψίας.δὲ γενομένης προσήνεγκαν αὐτῷ δαιμονιζομένους
And evening being come,　they brought　to him ²possessed³with⁴demons
πολλούς· καὶ ἐξέβαλεν τὰ πνεύματα λόγῳ καὶ πάντας τοὺς
¹many,　and he cast out the spirits　by a word, and　all　who
κακῶς ἔχοντας ἐθεράπευσεν· 17 ὅπως πληρωθῇ τὸ
²ill　¹were　he healed :.　So that might be fulfilled that which
ῥηθὲν διὰ Ἡσαΐου τοῦ προφήτου, λέγοντος, Αὐτὸς τὰς
was spoken by Esaias the　prophet,　saying,　Himself the
ἀσθενείας ἡμῶν ἔλαβεν, καὶ τὰς νόσους ἐβάστασεν.
infirmities of us　took,　and the diseases bore.

18 Ἰδὼν.δὲ ὁ Ἰησοῦς ʸπολλοὺς ὄχλουςǁ περὶ αὐτόν, ἐκέ-
And ²seeing　¹Jesus　great　crowds around him, ¹he com-
λευσεν ἀπελθεῖν εἰς τὸ πέραν. 19 καὶ προσελθὼν εἷς
manded　to depart　to the other side.　And having come to [him] one
γραμματεὺς εἶπεν αὐτῷ, Διδάσκαλε, ἀκολουθήσω σοι ὅπου.ἐὰν
a scribe　said to him,　Teacher,　I will follow thee whithersoever
ἀπέρχῃ. 20 Καὶ λέγει αὐτῷ ὁ Ἰησοῦς, Αἱ ἀλώπεκες φωλεοὺς
thou mayest go. And ²says ³to ⁴him　¹Jesus,　The foxes　holes
ἔχουσιν καὶ τὰ πετεινὰ τοῦ οὐρανοῦ κατασκηνώσεις, ὁ.δὲ υἱὸς
¹have,　and the birds of the heaven　nests,　but the Son
τοῦ ἀνθρώπου οὐκ.ἔχει ποῦ τὴν κεφαλὴν κλίνῃ. 21 Ἕτερος
of man　has not where the head he may lay.　²Another
δὲ τῶν.μαθητῶν.ᶻαὐτοῦǁ εἶπεν αὐτῷ, Κύριε, ἐπίτρεψόν μοι
¹and　of his disciples　said to him,　Lord,　allow　me
πρῶτον ἀπελθεῖν καὶ θάψαι τὸν.πατέρα.μου. 22 Ὁ.δὲ.ᵃἸησοῦςǁ
first　to go　and bury　my father.　But Jesus
ᵇεἶπενǁ αὐτῷ, Ἀκολούθει μοι, καὶ ἄφες τοὺς νεκροὺς θάψαι
said to him,　Follow me,　and leave the　dead　to bury
τοὺς.ἑαυτῶν νεκρούς.
their own　dead.

23 Καὶ ἐμβάντι αὐτῷ εἰς ᶜτὸǁ πλοῖον, ἠκολούθησαν αὐτῷ
And ²having ³entered　¹he into the ship,　³followed　⁴him
οἱ.μαθηταὶ αὐτοῦ. 24 καὶ ἰδού, σεισμὸς μέγας ἐγένετο ἐν τῇ
¹his ²disciples.　And lo,　a ²tempest ¹great　arose　in the
θαλάσσῃ, ὥστε τὸ πλοῖον καλύπτεσθαι ὑπὸ τῶν κυμάτων·
sea,　so that the ship　was covered　by the　waves;
αὐτὸς.δὲ ἐκάθευδεν. 25 καὶ προσελθόντες ᵈοἱ μαθηταὶǁ ᵉαὐτοῦǁ
but he was sleeping.　And having come to [him] the disciples　of him
ἤγειραν αὐτόν, λέγοντες, Κύριε, σῶσον ᶠἡμᾶς,ǁ ἀπολλύμεθα.
awoke him,　saying,　Lord,　save　us;　we perish.
26 Καὶ λέγει αὐτοῖς, Τί δειλοί ἐστε, ὀλιγόπιστοι; Τότε
And he says to them, Why fearful are ye, O [ye] of little faith? Then,
ἐγερθεὶς ἐπετίμησεν τοῖς ἀνέμοις καὶ τῇ θαλάσσῃ, καὶ ἐγένετο
having arisen he rebuked the　winds　and the　sea,　and there was
γαλήνη μεγάλη. 27 οἱ.δὲ ἄνθρωποι ἐθαύμασαν, λέγοντες,
a ²calm　¹great.　And the　men　wondered,　saying,
Ποταπός ἐστιν οὗτος, ὅτι ᵍκαὶǁ οἱ ἄνεμοι καὶ ἡ θάλασσα
What kind [of man] is　this,　that even the　winds　and the　sea
ʰὑπακούουσιν αὐτῷ;ǁ
obey　him?

ˣ αὐτῷ to him LTTᵣAW. ʸ ὄχλον a crowd L. ᶻ — αὐτοῦ (*read* the disciples) LTTᵣ. ᵃ — Ἰησοῦς
(*read* he said) T. ᵇ λέγει says LTTᵣAW. ᶜ — τὸ (*read* a ship) LTᵣA. ᵈ — οἱ μαθηταὶ [L]TTᵣ.
ᵉ.— αὐτοῦ GLTTᵣAW. ᶠ — ἡμᾶς LTTᵣAW. ᵍ — καὶ L. ʰ αὐτῷ ὑπακούουσιν LTTᵣA.

28 And when he was come to the other side into the country of the Gergesenes, there met him two possessed with devils, coming out of the tombs, exceeding fierce, so that no man might pass by that way. 29 And, behold, they cried out, saying, What have we to do with thee, Jesus, thou Son of God? art thou come hither to torment us before the time? 30 And there was a good way off from them an herd of many swine feeding. 31 So the devils besought him, saying, If thou cast us out, suffer us to go away into the herd of swine. 32 And he said unto them, Go. And when they were come out, they went into the herd of swine: and, behold, the whole herd of swine ran violently down a steep place into the sea, and perished in the waters. 33 And they that kept them fled, and went their ways into the city, and told every thing, and what was befallen to the possessed of the devils. 34 And, behold, the whole city came out to meet Jesus: and when they saw him, they besought him that he would depart out of their coasts.

28 Καὶ ¹ἐλθόντι αὐτῷ‖ εἰς τὸ πέραν εἰς τὴν χώραν τῶν
And when ²had ³come ¹he   to the other side to   the   country of the
ᵏΓεργεσηνῶν‖ ὑπήντησαν αὐτῷ δύο δαιμονιζόμενοι ἐκ τῶν
Gergesenes,   ²met   ᵏhim ¹two ²possessed ³by ⁴demons out of the
μνημείων ἐξερχόμενοι, χαλεποὶ λίαν, ὥστε μὴ ἰσχύειν τινὰ
tombs   coming,   ²violent ¹very, so that not ³was ⁴able ¹any ²one
παρελθεῖν διὰ τῆς ὁδοῦ ἐκείνης· 29 καὶ ἰδού, ἔκραξαν λέγοντες,
to pass   by   that way.   And lo, they cried out, saying,
Τί ἡμῖν καὶ σοί, ᴵ'Ἰησοῦ,‖ υἱὲ τοῦ θεοῦ; ἦλθες ὧδε πρὸ
What to us and to thee, Jesus, Son   of God? art thou come here before [the]
καιροῦ βασανίσαι ἡμᾶς; 30 Ἦν δὲ μακρὰν ἀπ' αὐτῶν ἀγέλη
time   to torment   us?   Now there was far off from them   a herd
χοίρων πολλῶν βοσκομένη. 31 οἱ δὲ δαίμονες παρεκάλουν
of ²swine ¹many   feeding;   And the demons   besought
αὐτόν, λέγοντες, Εἰ ἐκβάλλεις ἡμᾶς, ᵐἐπίτρεψον ἡμῖν ἀπελθεῖν‖
him,   saying,   If thou cast out us,   allow   us   to go away
εἰς τὴν ἀγέλην τῶν χοίρων. 32 Καὶ εἶπεν αὐτοῖςⁿ, Ὑπάγετε.
into the   herd   of the   swine.   And he said to them,   Go.
Οἱ δὲ ἐξελθόντες ᵒἀπῆλθον‖ εἰς ᵖτὴν ἀγέλην τῶν χοίρων·‖
And they having gone out went away into the   herd   of the   swine:
καὶ ἰδού, ὥρμησεν πᾶσα ἡ ἀγέλη �q τῶν χοίρων‖ κατὰ τοῦ
and behold, ²rushed ¹all ²the ³herd ⁴of ⁵the ⁶swine down   the
κρημνοῦ εἰς τὴν θάλασσαν, καὶ ἀπέθανον ἐν τοῖς ὕδασιν.
steep   into the   sea,   and   died   in the   waters.
33 οἱ δὲ βόσκοντες ἔφυγον, καὶ ἀπελθόντες εἰς τὴν πόλιν
But those who fed [them] fled,   and having gone away into the   city
ἀπήγγειλαν πάντα, καὶ τὰ τῶν δαιμονιζομένων.
related   everything, and the [events] concerning those possessed by demons.
34 καὶ ἰδού, πᾶσα ἡ πόλις ἐξῆλθεν εἰς ʳσυνάντησιν‖ ˢτῷ‖ Ἰησοῦ·
And behold, all   the city   went out to   meet   Jesus;
καὶ ἰδόντες αὐτόν, παρεκάλεσαν ᵗὅπως‖ μεταβῇ ἀπὸ
and   seeing   him,   they besought [him] that   he would depart from
τῶν ὁρίων αὐτῶν. ·
their borders.

IX. And he entered into a ship, and passed over, and came into his own city. 2 And, behold, they brought to him a man sick of the palsy, lying on a bed: and Jesus seeing their faith said unto the sick of the palsy, Son, be of good cheer; thy sins be forgiven thee. 3 And, behold, certain of the scribes said within themselves, This man blasphemeth. 4 And Jesus knowing their thoughts said, Wherefore think ye evil in your hearts? 5 For whether is easier, to say, Thy sins be for-

9 Καὶ ἐμβὰς εἰς ʳτὸ‖ πλοῖον διεπέρασεν καὶ ἦλθεν εἰς
And having entered into the   ship   he passed over and came   to
τὴν ἰδίαν πόλιν. 2 καὶ ἰδού, ʷπροσέφερον‖ αὐτῷ παραλυτικὸν
his own   city.   And behold,   they brought to him a paralytic
ἐπὶ κλίνης βεβλημένον· καὶ ἰδὼν ὁ Ἰησοῦς τὴν πίστιν αὐτῶν
on a bed   lying;   and ²seeing ¹Jesus   their faith
εἶπεν τῷ παραλυτικῷ, Θάρσει, τέκνον, ˣἀφέωνταί‖
said to the paralytic,   Be of good courage, child; ²have ⁴been ¹forgiven
ʸσοι αἱ ἁμαρτίαι σου.‖ 3 Καὶ ἰδού, τινὲς τῶν γραμματέων ᶻεἶπον‖
³thee   ¹thy ²sins.   And lo, some of the   scribes   said
ἐν ἑαυτοῖς, Οὗτος βλασφημεῖ. 4 Καὶ ᵃἰδὼν‖ ὁ Ἰησοῦς τὰς
in themselves, This [man] blasphemes.   And ²perceiving ¹Jesus
ἐνθυμήσεις αὐτῶν, εἶπεν, ᵇἹνατί‖ ᶜὑμεῖς‖ ἐνθυμεῖσθε πονηρὰ
their thoughts,   said,   Why   ²ye   ¹think   evil
ἐν ταῖς καρδίαις ὑμῶν; 5 τί γάρ ἐστιν εὐκοπώτερον, εἰπεῖν,
in   your hearts?   For which is   easier,   to say,

ⁱ ἐλθόντος αὐτοῦ LTTr.   ᵏ Γερασηνῶν L; Γαδαρηνῶν Gadarenes TTrA.   ˡ — Ἰησοῦ GLTTrA.
ᵐ ἀπόστειλον ἡμᾶς send us GLTTrA.   ⁿ + [ὁ Ἰησοῦς] Jesus L.   ᵒ ἀπῆλθαν LTr.   ᵖ τοὺς
χοίρους the swine GLTTr.   q — τῶν χοίρων GLTT[A].   ʳ ὑπάντησιν LTTr.   ˢ τοῦ T.
ᵗ ἵνα L.   ᵛ — τὸ (read a ship) LTTr[A].   ʷ προσφέρουσιν they bring L.   ˣ ἀφίενταί are
forgiven LTTr.   ʸ σου αἱ ἁμαρτίαι LTTrA.   ᶻ εἶπαν LT ᵃ εἰδὼς knowing LTr.   ᵇ Ἱνατί GTW.
ᶜ — ὑμεῖς LTTrA.

d'Ἀφέωνται‖ ^eσοι‖ αἱ ἁμαρτίαι· ἢ εἰπεῖν, ^f"Ἔγειραι‖ καὶ
³Have ⁴been ⁵forgiven ⁶thee ['thy] ²sins, or to say, Arise and

περιπάτει; 6 ἵνα.δὲ εἰδῆτε ὅτι ἐξουσίαν ἔχει ὁ υἱὸς τοῦ ἀν-
walk? But that ye may know that authority has the Son of

θρώπου ἐπὶ τῆς γῆς ἀφιέναι ἁμαρτίας· τότε λέγει τῷ παρα-
man on the earth to forgive sins: then he says to the para-

λυτικῷ, ^gἘγερθεὶς‖ ἀρόν σου τὴν κλίνην, καὶ ὕπαγε εἰς τὸν
lytic, Having arisen, take up thy bed, and go to

οἶκόν σου 7 Καὶ ἐγερθεὶς ἀπῆλθεν εἰς τὸν.οἶκον.αὐτοῦ.
²house ¹thy. And having arisen he went away to his house.

8 ἰδόντες.δὲ οἱ ὄχλοι ^hἐθαύμασαν,‖ καὶ ἐδόξασαν τὸν θεόν,
And ³having ⁴seen ¹the ²crowds wondered, and glorified God,

τὸν δόντα ἐξουσίαν τοιαύτην τοῖς ἀνθρώποις.
who gave ²authority ¹such to men.

9 Καὶ παράγων ὁ Ἰησοῦς ἐκεῖθεν εἶδεν ἄνθρωπον καθήμενον
And ²passing ¹Jesus thence saw a man sitting

ἐπὶ τὸ τελώνιον, ⁱΜατθαῖον‖ λεγόμενον, καὶ λέγει αὐτῷ, Ἀκο-
at the tax-office, ²Matthew ¹called, and says to him, Fol-

λούθει μοι. Καὶ ἀναστὰς ^kἠκολούθησεν‖ αὐτῷ. 10 Καὶ ἐγένετο
low me. And having arisen he followed him. And it came to pass

^lαὐτοῦ ἀνακειμένου‖ ἐν τῇ οἰκίᾳ, ^mκαὶ‖ ἰδού, πολλοὶ τελῶναι
at his reclining [at table] in the house, that behold, many tax-gatherers

καὶ ἁμαρτωλοὶ ἐλθόντες συνανέκειντο τῷ Ἰησοῦ καὶ
and sinners having come were reclining [at table] with Jesus and

τοῖς.μαθηταῖς.αὐτοῦ. 11 καὶ ἰδόντες οἱ Φαρισαῖοι ⁿεἶπον‖
his disciples. And having seen [it] the Pharisees said

τοῖς.μαθηταῖς.αὐτοῦ, ^oΔιατί‖ μετὰ τῶν.τελωνῶν καὶ ἁμαρ-
to his disciples, Why with the tax-gatherers and sin-

τωλῶν ἐσθίει ὁ.διδάσκαλος.ὑμῶν; 12 Ὁ.δὲ.^pἸησοῦς‖ ἀκούσας
ners eats your teacher? But Jesus having heard

εἶπεν ^qαὐτοῖς,‖ Οὐ χρείαν ἔχουσιν οἱ ἰσχύοντες ἰατροῦ,
he said to them, ⁶Not ¹need ⁵have ³they ²who ⁴are ⁴strong of a physician,

^rἀλλ'‖ οἱ κακῶς ἔχοντες. 13 πορευθέντες δὲ μάθετε τί ἐστιν,
but they who ill are. But having gone learn what is,

^s"Ἔλεον‖ θέλω, καὶ οὐ θυσίαν· οὐ γὰρ ἦλθον καλέσαι δικαίους,
Mercy I desire, and not sacrifice: ⁴not ¹for ²I ³came to call righteous

^tἀλλ'‖ ἁμαρτωλοὺς ^vεἰς μετάνοιαν.‖
[ones], but sinners to repentance.

14 Τότε προσέρχονται αὐτῷ οἱ μαθηταὶ Ἰωάννου, λέγοντες,
Then come near to him the disciples of John, saying,

^wΔιατί‖ ἡμεῖς καὶ οἱ Φαρισαῖοι νηστεύομεν ^xπολλά,‖ οἱ.δὲ.μαθη-
Why ²we ³and ⁴the ⁵Pharisees ¹do fast much, but ²disci-

ταί.σου οὐ.νηστεύουσιν; 15 Καὶ εἶπεν αὐτοῖς ὁ Ἰησοῦς, Μὴ
ples ¹thy fast not? And ²said ³to ⁴them ¹Jesus,

δύνανται οἱ υἱοὶ τοῦ νυμφῶνος πενθεῖν ἐφ'.ὅσον μετ' αὐτῶν
Can the sons of the bridechamber mourn while with them

ἐστιν ὁ νυμφίος; ἐλεύσονται δὲ ἡμέραι ὅταν ἀπαρθῇ
is the bridegroom? ³will ⁴come ¹but ²days when will have been taken away

ἀπ' αὐτῶν ὁ νυμφίος, καὶ τότε νηστεύσουσιν. 16 οὐδεὶς.δὲ
from them the bridegroom, and then they will fast. But no one

ἐπιβάλλει ἐπίβλημα ῥάκους ἀγνάφου ἐπὶ ἱματίῳ.παλαιῷ·
puts a piece of ²cloth ¹unfulled on an old garment:

given thee; or to say, Arise, and walk? 6 But that ye may know that the Son of man hath power on earth to forgive sins, (then saith he to the sick of the palsy,) Arise, take up thy bed, and go unto thine house. 7 And he arose, and departed to his house, 8 But when the multitudes saw it, they marvelled, and glorified God, which had given such power unto men.

9 And as Jesus passed forth from thence, he saw a man, named Matthew, sitting at the receipt of custom: and he saith unto him, Follow me. And he arose, and followed him. 10 And it came to pass, as Jesus sat at meat in the house, behold, many publicans and sinners came and sat down with him and his disciples. 11 And when the Pharisees saw it, they said unto his disciples, Why eateth your Master with publicans and sinners? 12 But when Jesus heard that, he said unto them, They that be whole need not a physician, but they that are sick. 13 But go ye and learn what that meaneth, I will have mercy, and not sacrifice: for I am not come to call the righteous, but sinners to repentance.

14 Then came to him the disciples of John, saying, Why do we and the Pharisees fast oft, but thy disciples fast not? 15 And Jesus said unto them, Can the children of the bridechamber mourn, as long as the bridegroom is with them? but the days will come, when the bridegroom shall be taken from them, and then shall they fast. 16 No man putteth a piece of new cloth unto an old garment, for that which

---

^d ἀφίενταί are forgiven LTTr. ^e σου (read thy sins) GLTTrAW. ^f ἔγειρε LTTrAW. ^g ἔγειρε arise LTr. — ^h ἐφοβήθησαν were afraid LTTrA. ⁱ Μαθθαῖον LTTrA. ^k ἠκολούθει T. ^l ἀνακει-
μένου αὐτοῦ L. ^m — καὶ T. ⁿ ἔλεγον LTTr. ^o διὰ τί LTr. ^p — Ἰησοῦς LT[Tr]A. ^q — αὐτοῖς
LTT.A. ^r ἀλλὰ LTr. ^s Ἔλεος LTTrA. ^t ἀλλὰ TTrAW. ^v — εἰς μετάνοιαν GLTTrAW. ^w Διὰ
τί LTrA. ^x — πολλά LT.

is put into fill it up taketh from the garment, and the rent is made worse. 17 Neither do men put new wine into old bottles: else the bottles break, and the wine runneth out, and the bottles perish: but they put new wine into new bottles, and both are preserved.

αἴρει   γὰρ τὸ.πλήρωμα.αὐτοῦ ἀπὸ τοῦ ἱματίου, καὶ χεῖρον
*takes *away 'for   *its 'filling *up   from the garment, and a worse
σχίσμα γίνεται. 17 οὐδὲ βάλλουσιν οἶνον νέον εἰς ἀσκοὺς
rent   takes place.   Nor   put they   *wine 'new into *skins
παλαιούς· εἰ.δὲ.μήγε ῥήγνυνται οἱ ἀσκοί, καὶ ὁ οἶνος ἐκχεῖται,
'old,   otherwise   *are *burst 'the *skins, and the wine is poured out,
καὶ οἱ ἀσκοὶ ʸἀπολοῦνται·‖ ἀλλὰ ᶻβάλλουσιν οἶνον νέον εἰς
and the skins will be destroyed;   but   they put   *wine 'new into
ἀσκοὺς‖ καινούς, καὶ ᵃἀμφότερα‖ συντηροῦνται.
*skins 'new,   and   both   are preserved together.

18 While he spake these things unto them, behold, there came a certain ruler, and worshipped him, saying, My daughter is even now dead: but come and lay thy hand upon her, and she shall live. 19 And Jesus arose, and followed him, and so did his disciples.

18 Ταῦτα αὐτοῦ.λαλοῦντος αὐτοῖς, ἰδού, ἄρχωνᵇ ᶜἐλθὼν‖
*These *things 'as *he 'is *speaking to them, behold, a ruler having come
προσεκύνει αὐτῷ, λέγων, ᵈΟτι‖ ἡ.θυγάτηρ.μου ἄρτι ἐτελεύ-
did homage to him, saying,   My daughter just now has
τησεν· ἀλλὰ ἐλθὼν ἐπίθες τὴν.χεῖρά.σου ἐπ' αὐτήν, καὶ
died;   but having come lay   thy hand   upon her,   and
ζήσεται. 19 καὶ ἐγερθεὶς ὁ Ἰησοῦς ᵉἠκολούθησεν‖ αὐτῷ
she shall live.   And having arisen Jesus   followed   him,
καὶ οἱ.μαθηταὶ.αὐτοῦ.
and   his disciples.

20 And, behold, a woman, which was diseased with an issue of blood twelve years, came behind him, and touched the hem of his garment: 21 for she said within herself, If I may but touch his garment, I shall be whole. 22 But Jesus turned him about, and when he saw her, he said, Daughter, be of good comfort; thy faith hath made thee whole. And the woman was made whole from that hour.

20 Καὶ ἰδού, γυνὴ αἱμορροοῦσα δώδεκα ἔτη, προσελ-
And behold, a woman having had a flux of blood twelve years, having
θοῦσα ὄπισθεν ἥψατο τοῦ κρασπέδου τοῦ.ἱματίου.αὐτοῦ.
come   behind   touched the   border   of his garment.
21 ἔλεγεν.γὰρ ἐν ἑαυτῇ, Ἐὰν μόνον ἅψωμαι .τοῦ ἱματίου
For she said within herself, If only I shall touch *garment
αὐτοῦ σωθήσομαι. 22 Ὁ.δὲ.Ἰησοῦς‖ ᶠἐπιστραφεὶς‖ καὶ ἰδὼν
'his I shall be cured.   But Jesus   having turned and having seen
αὐτὴν εἶπεν,   Θάρσει,   θύγατερ· ἡ.πίστις.σου σέσωκέν σε.
her   he said, Be of good courage, daughter;   thy faith   hath cured thee.
καὶ ἐσώθη   ἡ   γυνὴ ἀπὸ τῆς.ὥρας.ἐκείνης.
And *was *cured 'the *woman from   that hour.

23 And when Jesus came into the ruler's house, and saw the minstrels and the people making a noise, 24 he said unto them, Give place: for the maid is not dead, but sleepeth. And they laughed him to scorn. 25 But when the people were put forth, he went in, and took her by the hand, and the maid arose. 26 And the fame hereof went abroad into all that land.

23 Καὶ   ἐλθὼν   ὁ Ἰησοῦς εἰς τὴν οἰκίαν τοῦ ἄρχοντος,
And *having *come 'Jesus into the house of the   ruler,
καὶ ἰδὼν τοὺς αὐλητὰς καὶ τὸν ὄχλον θορυβούμενον,
and having seen the flute-players and the crowd making a tumult,
24 �slέγει αὐτοῖς,‖ Ἀναχωρεῖτε· οὐ γὰρ ἀπέθανεν τὸ κοράσιον,
says to them,   Withdraw, *not 'for *is *dead *the *damsel,
ἀλλὰ καθεύδει. καὶ κατεγέλων αὐτοῦ. 25 ὅτε.δὲ ἐξεβλήθη
but sleeps.   And they laughed at him.   But when *had *been *put *out
ὁ ὄχλος, εἰσελθὼν ἐκράτησεν τῆς.χειρὸς.αὐτῆς, καὶ ἠγέρθη
'the *crowd, having entered he took hold   of her hand,   and *arose
τὸ κοράσιον. 26 καὶ ἐξῆλθεν ἡ.φήμη.αὔτη εἰς ὅλην τὴν
'the *damsel.   And *went *out   'this *report into   all
γῆν ἐκείνην.
land 'that.

27 And when Jesus departed thence, two blind men followed him, crying, and saying, Thou Son of David, have mercy on u. 28 And when he was come into the house, the blind men came to him: and Jesus saith

27 Καὶ παράγοντι ἐκεῖθεν τῷ Ἰησοῦ, ἠκολούθησαν ⁱαὐτῷ‖
And *passing *on *thence 'Jesus,   *followed   *him
δύο τυφλοί,   κράζοντες καὶ λέγοντες, Ἐλέησον ἡμᾶς, ᵏυἱὲ
*two *blind ['men], crying   and saying, Have pity on us, Son
Δαβίδ.‖ 28 ἐλθόντι.δὲ εἰς τὴν οἰκίαν, ˡπροσῆλθον‖ αὐτῷ οἱ
of David.   And having come into the   house,   came   to him the

---

ʸ ἀπόλλυνται are destroyed LTTr.   ᶻ οἶνον νέον εἰς ἀσκοὺς βάλλουσιν L.   ᵃ ἀμφότεροι GLTTrAW. ᵇ + εἷς (read a certain ruler) GLTr. ᶜ προσελθὼν having come to [him] L; εἰσελθὼν having entered TAW. ᵈ — ὅτι T. ᵉ ἠκολούθει LTTrA. ᶠ — Ἰησοῦς T. ᵍ στραφεὶς LTTrA. ʰ ἔλεγεν said LTTrA. ⁱ — αὐτῷ L[Tr]. ᵏ υἱὸς Δαυεὶδ LTTrA; υἱὲ Δαυὶδ GW. ˡ προσῆλθαν LTr.

τυφλοί, καὶ λέγει αὐτοῖς ὁ Ἰησοῦς, Πιστεύετε ὅτι δύναμαι
blind [men], and ²says ²to ⁴them ¹Jesus, Believe ye that I am able

ᵐτοῦτο ποιῆσαι;‖ Λέγουσιν αὐτῷ, Ναί, κύριε. 29 Τότε ἥψατο
this to do? They say to him, Yea, Lord. Then he touched

τῶν.ὀφθαλμῶν.αὐτῶν, λέγων, Κατὰ τὴν.πίστιν.ὑμῶν γενη-
their eyes, saying, According to your faith be

θήτω ὑμῖν. 30 Καὶ ⁿἀνεῴχθησαν‖ αὐτῶν οἱ ὀφθαλμοί· καὶ
it to you. And were opened their eyes; and

ᵒἐνεβριμήσατο‖ αὐτοῖς ὁ Ἰησοῦς, λέγων, Ὁρᾶτε μηδεὶς γινω-
²strictly ³charged ⁴them ¹Jesus, saying, See ²no ³one ¹let

σκέτω. 31 Οἱ.δὲ ἐξελθόντες διεφήμισαν αὐτὸν ἐν ὅλῃ τῇ
know [it]. But they having gone out made ²known ¹him in all

γῇ ἐκείνῃ.
²land ¹that.

32 Αὐτῶν.δὲ ἐξερχομένων, ἰδού, προσήνεγκαν αὐτῷ ᵖἄν-
And as they were going out, behold, they brought to him a

θρωπον‖ κωφὸν δαιμονιζόμενον. 33 καὶ ἐκβληθέντος
man dumb, possessed by a demon. And ³having ⁴been ⁵cast ⁶out

τοῦ δαιμονίου, ἐλάλησεν ὁ κωφός· καὶ ἐθαύμασαν οἱ ὄχλοι,
¹the ²demon, ⁸spake ⁷the ⁸dumb. And ³wondered ¹the ²crowds,

λέγοντες, �q″Ὅτι‖ οὐδέποτε ἐφάνη οὕτως ἐν τῷ Ἰσραήλ. 34 Οἱ.δὲ
saying, Never was it seen thus in Israel. But the

Φαρισαῖοι ἔλεγον, Ἐν τῷ ἄρχοντι τῶν δαιμονίων ἐκβάλλει
Pharisees said, By the prince of the demons he casts out

τὰ δαιμόνια.
the demons.

35 Καὶ περιῆγεν ὁ Ἰησοῦς τὰς πόλεις πάσας καὶ τὰς κώμας,
And ²went ³about ¹Jesus ⁴the ⁵cities ⁶all and the villages,

διδάσκων ἐν ταῖς.συναγωγαῖς.αὐτῶν, καὶ κηρύσσων τὸ εὐαγ-
teaching in their synagogues, and proclaiming the glad

γέλιον τῆς βασιλείας, καὶ θεραπεύων πᾶσαν νόσον καὶ πᾶσαν
tidings of the kingdom, and healing every disease and every

μαλακίαν ʳἐν τῷ λαῷ.‖ 36 ἰδὼν.δὲ τοὺς ὄχλους, ἐ-
bodily weakness among the people. And having seen the crowds he was

σπλαγχνίσθη περὶ αὐτῶν, ὅτι ἦσαν ˢἐκλελυμένοι‖ καὶ
moved with compassion for them, because they were wearied and

ᵗἐρριμμένοι‖ ᵛὡσεὶ‖ πρόβατα μὴ ἔχοντα ποιμένα. 37 τότε λέγει
cast away as sheep not having a shepherd. Then he says

τοῖς.μαθηταῖς.αὐτοῦ, Ὁ μὲν θερισμὸς πολύς, οἱ.δὲ ἐργάται
to his disciples, The ²indeed ¹harvest [is] great, but the workmen

ὀλίγοι· 38 δεήθητε οὖν τοῦ κυρίου τοῦ θερισμοῦ, ὅπως
[are] few; supplicate therefore the Lord of the harvest, that

ἐκβάλῃ ἐργάτας εἰς τὸν.θερισμὸν.αὐτοῦ.
he may send out workmen into his harvest.

10 Καὶ προσκαλεσάμενος τοὺς δώδεκα μαθητὰς αὐτοῦ,
And having called to [him] ²twelve ³disciples ¹his

ἔδωκεν αὐτοῖς ἐξουσίαν πνευμάτων ἀκαθάρτων, ὥστε
he gave to them authority over ²spirits ¹unclean, so as

ἐκβάλλειν αὐτά, καὶ θεραπεύειν πᾶσαν νόσον καὶ πᾶσαν
to cast out them, and to heal every disease and every

μαλακίαν.
bodily weakness.

2 Τῶν.δὲ δώδεκα ἀποστόλων τὰ ὀνόματά ἐστιν ταῦτα·
Now of the twelve apostles the names are these:

unto them, Believe ye that I am able to do this? They said unto him, Yea, Lord. 29 Then touched he their eyes, saying, According to your faith be it unto you. 30 And their eyes were opened; and Jesus straitly charged them, saying, See that no man know it. 31 But they, when they were departed, spread abroad his fame in all that country.

32 As they went out, behold, they brought to him a dumb man possessed with a devil. 33 And when the devil was cast out, the dumb spake: and the multitudes marvelled, saying, It was never so seen in Israel. 34 But the Pharisees said, He casteth out devils through the prince of the devils.

35 And Jesus went about all the cities and villages, teaching in their synagogues, and preaching the gospel of the kingdom, and healing every sickness and every disease among the people. 36 But when he saw the multitudes, he was moved with compassion on them, because they fainted, and were scattered abroad, as sheep having no shepherd. 37 Then saith he unto his disciples, The harvest truly is plenteous, but the labourers are few: 38 pray ye therefore the Lord of the harvest, that he will send forth labourers into his harvest.

X. And when he had called unto him his twelve disciples, he gave them power against unclean spirits, to cast them out, and to heal all manner of sickness and all manner of disease. 2 Now the names of the twelve apostles are these; The

---

ᵐ ποιῆσαι τοῦτο L. ⁿ ἠνεῴχθησαν LTTrA. ᵒ ἐνεβριμήθη LTTrA. ᵖ — ἄνθρωπον (read [one])
ᵃ[TrA]. �q — ὅτι GLTTrAW. ʳ — ἐν τῷ λαῷ GLTTrAW. ˢ ἐσκυλμένοι harassed GLTTrAW.
ᵗ ῥεριμμένοι L; ἐριμμένοι TTrA. ᵛ ὡς Tr.

first, Simon, who is called Peter, and Andrew his brother; James the son of Zebedee, and John his brother ; 3 Philip, and Bartholomew; Thomas, and Matthew the publican; James the son of Alphæus, and Lebbæus, whose surname was Thaddæus; 4 Simon the Canaanite, and Judas Iscariot, who also betrayed him.

πρῶτος Σίμων ὁ λεγόμενος Πέτρος, καὶ Ἀνδρέας ὁ ἀδελφὸς
first   Simon who is called Peter,   and Andrew the brother

αὐτοῦ· ʷἸάκωβος ὁ τοῦ Ζεβεδαίου, καὶ Ἰωάννης ὁ ἀδελφὸς
¹his;   James the[son] of Zebedee, and John   the brother

αὐτοῦ· 3 Φίλιππος, καὶ Βαρθολομαῖος· Θωμᾶς, καὶ ˣΜατθαῖος‖
¹his;   Philip,   and Bartholomew;   Thomas, and Matthew

ὁ τελώνης· Ἰάκωβος ὁ τοῦ Ἀλφαίου, καὶ ʸΛεββαῖος ὁ
the tax-gatherer; James the [son] of Alphæus, and Lebbæus who

ἐπικληθεὶς Θαδδαῖος·‖ 4 Σίμων ὁ ᶻΚανανίτης,‖ καὶ Ἰούδας
was surnamed Thaddæus; Simon the Canaanite,   and   Judas

ᵃᵇἸσκαριώτης,‖ ὁ καὶ παραδοὺς αὐτόν.
Iscariote,   who also delivered up him.

5 Τούτους τοὺς δώδεκα ἀπέστειλεν ὁ Ἰησοῦς, παραγγείλας
These   twelve ²sent ³forth ¹Jesus, having charged

αὐτοῖς, λέγων, Εἰς ὁδὸν ἐθνῶν μὴ.ἀπέλθητε, καὶ εἰς
them,   saying, Into [the] way of the Gentiles go not off, and into

5 These twelve Jesus sent forth, and commanded them, saying, Go not into the way of the Gentiles, and into any city of the Samaritans enter ye not: 6 but go rather to the lost sheep of the house of Israel. 7 And as ye go, preach, saying, The kingdom of heaven is at hand. 8 Heal the sick, cleanse the lepers, raise the dead, cast out devils: freely ye have received, freely give. 9 Provide neither gold, nor silver, nor brass in your purses, 10 nor scrip for your journey, neither two coats, neither shoes, nor yet staves : for the workman is worthy of his meat. 11 And into whatsoever city or town ye shall enter, inquire who in it is worthy; and there abide till ye go thence. 12 And when ye come into an house, salute it. 13 And if the house be worthy, let your peace come upon it: but if it be not worthy, let your peace return to you. 14 And whosoever shall not receive you, nor hear your words, when ye depart out of that house or city, shake off the dust of your feet. 15 Verily I say unto you, It shall be more tolerable for the land of Sodom and Gomorrha in the day of judgment, than for that city. 16 Behold, I send you forth

πόλιν ᶜΣαμαρειτῶν‖ μὴ.εἰσέλθητε· 6 πορεύεσθε.δὲ μᾶλλον
ᵃa city of [the] Samaritans enter not;   but go   rather

πρὸς τὰ πρόβατα τὰ ἀπολωλότα οἴκου Ἰσραήλ. 7 πο–
to the sheep the lost   of [the] house of Israel. ²Go-

ρευόμενοι δὲ κηρύσσετε, λέγοντες, Ὅτι ἤγγικεν ἡ βασιλεία
ing   ¹and proclaim,   saying, Has drawn near the kingdom

τῶν οὐρανῶν. 8 ἀσθενοῦντας θεραπεύετε, ᵈλεπροὺς καθαρί–
of the heavens. Sick   heal,   lepers   ¹cleanse,

ζετε, νεκροὺς ἐγείρετε,‖ δαιμόνια ἐκβάλλετε. δωρεὰν ἐλάβετε,
dead raise;   demons cast out: gratuitously ye received,

δωρεὰν δότε. 9 Μὴ–κτήσησθε χρυσόν, μηδὲ ἄργυρον, μηδὲ
gratuitously impart. Provide not gold,   nor   silver,   nor

χαλκὸν εἰς τὰς.ζώνας.ὑμῶν, 10 μὴ πήραν εἰς ὁδόν, μηδὲ
money in   your belts,   nor provision-bag for[the] way, nor

δύο χιτῶνας, μηδὲ ὑποδήματα, μηδὲ ᵉῥάβδον·‖ ἄξιος.γὰρ ὁ
two tunics, nor sandals,   nor   a staff: for worthy the

ἐργάτης τῆς.τροφῆς.αὐτοῦ ᶠἐστιν.‖ 11 Εἰς.ἣν.δ᾽.ἂν πόλιν ἢ
workman   of his food   is.   And into whatever city or

κώμην εἰσέλθητε, ἐξετάσατε τίς ἐν αὐτῇ ἄξιός ἐστιν· κἀκεῖ
village ye enter, inquire who in it it worthy is, and there

μείνατε, ἕως.ἂν ἐξέλθητε. 12 εἰσερχόμενοι.δὲ εἰς τὴν οἰκίαν,
remain until ye go forth. But entering   into the house,

ἀσπάσασθε αὐτήν. 13 καὶ ἐὰν μὲν ᾖ ἡ οἰκία ἀξία, ᵍἐλθέτω‖
salute   ¹it;   and if indeed ²be ¹the ²house worthy, let come

ἡ.εἰρήνη.ὑμῶν ἐπ᾽ αὐτήν· ἐὰν.δὲ μὴ.ᾖ ἀξία, ἡ.εἰρήνη.ὑμῶν
your peace   upon it;   but if it be not worthy, ²your ³peace

πρὸς ὑμᾶς ἐπιστραφήτω. 14 καὶ ὃς.ʰἐὰν‖ μὴ.δέξηται ὑμᾶς,
⁵to ⁴you   ¹let ⁴return. And whoever will not receive you,

μηδὲ ἀκούσῃ τοὺς.λόγους.ὑμῶν, ἐξερχόμενοι ⁱτῆς οἰκίας ἢ τῆς
nor will hear your words,   going forth of [that] house or the

πόλεως ἐκείνης, ἐκτινάξατε τὸν κονιορτὸν ᵏτῶν.ποδῶν.ὑμῶν.
²city ¹that,   shake off   the dust   of your feet.

15 ἀμὴν λέγω ὑμῖν, ἀνεκτότερον ἔσται γῇ Σοδόμων
Verily I say to you, More tolerable it shall be for[the] land of Sodom

καὶ ˡΓομόῤῥων‖ ἐν ἡμέρᾳ κρίσεως, ἢ τῇ.πόλει.ἐκείνῃ. 16 Ἰδού,
and of Gomorrha in   day of judgment, than for that city. Lo,

---

ʷ + καὶ and LT. ˣ Μαθθαῖος LTTᵣA. ʸ — Λεββαῖος ὁ ἐπικληθεὶς LTᵣ; — ὁ ἐπικληθεὶς Θαδδαῖος TA. ᶻ Καναναῖος Cananæan LTTᵣA. ᵃ + ὁ the EGLTAW. ᵇἸσκαριώθ L. ᶜ Σαμαριτῶν T.
ᵈ νεκροὺς ἐγείρετε, λεπροὺς καθαρίζετε GLTTᵣAW. ᵉ ῥάβδους staves W. ᶠ — ἐστιν (read [is])
LTTᵣA. ᵍ ἐλθάτω TTᵣ. ʰ ἂν LTTᵣA. ⁱ + ἔξω out LTT.A. ᵏ + ἐκ (read from your feet) I.Tᵣ.
ˡ Γομόῤῥας TᵣA.

ἐγὼ ἀποστέλλω ὑμᾶς ὡς πρόβατα ἐν μέσῳ λύκων· γίνεσθε
I send forth you. as sheep . in [the] midst of wolves: be ye

οὖν φρόνιμοι ὡς οἱ ὄφεις, καὶ ἀκέραιοι ὡς αἱ περιστεραί.
therefore prudent as the serpents, and harmless as the doves.

17 προσέχετε.δὲ ἀπὸ τῶν ἀνθρώπων· παραδώσουσιν.γὰρ ὑμᾶς
But beware of men; for they will deliver you

εἰς συνέδρια, καὶ ἐν ταῖς.συναγωγαῖς.αὐτῶν μαστιγώσουσιν
to sanhedrims, and in their synagogues they will scourge

ὑμᾶς· 18 καὶ ἐπὶ ἡγεμόνας δὲ καὶ βασιλεῖς ἀχθήσεσθε
you: and before governors also and kings ye shall be brought

ἕνεκεν ἐμοῦ, εἰς μαρτύριον αὐτοῖς καὶ τοῖς ἔθνεσιν.
on account of me, for a testimony to them and to the nations.

19 ὅταν.δὲ ¹παραδιδῶσιν‖ ὑμᾶς, μὴ.μεριμνήσητε πῶς ἢ τί
But when they deliver up you, be not careful how or what

λαλήσητε· ᵐδοθήσεται.γὰρ ὑμῖν ἐν ἐκείνῃ τῇ ὥρᾳ τί ⁿλαλή-
ye should speak: for it shall be given you in that hour what ye shall

σετε·‖ 20 οὐ.γὰρ ὑμεῖς ἐστε οἱ λαλοῦντες, ἀλλὰ τὸ πνεῦμα
speak: for not ye are they who speak, but the Spirit

τοῦ.πατρὸς.ὑμῶν τὸ λαλοῦν ἐν ὑμῖν. 21 Παραδώσει.δὲ
of your Father which speaks in you. But will deliver

ἀδελφὸς ἀδελφὸν εἰς θάνατον, καὶ πατὴρ τέκνον· καὶ ἐπανα-
brother brother to death; and father child: and will

στήσονται· τέκνα ἐπὶ γονεῖς, καὶ θανατώσουσιν αὐτούς.
rise up children against parents. and will put to death them.

22 καὶ ἔσεσθε μισούμενοι ὑπὸ πάντων διὰ τὸ.ὄνομά.μου·
And ye will be hated on account of my name;

ὁ.δὲ ὑπομείνας εἰς τέλος, οὗτος σωθήσεται. 23 ὅταν.δὲ
but he that endures to [the] end, he shall be saved. But when

διώκωσιν ὑμᾶς ἐν τῇ.πόλει.ταύτῃ, φεύγετε εἰς ᵒτὴν.ἄλλην·‖ ᴾ
they persecute you in this city, flee to another:

ἀμὴν.γὰρ λέγω ὑμῖν, οὐ.μὴ τελέσητε τὰς πόλεις
for verily I say to you, In no wise will ye have completed the cities

�۹τοῦ‖ Ἰσραὴλ ἕως.ᵣἂν‖ ἔλθῃ ὁ υἱὸς τοῦ ἀνθρώπου. 24 Οὐκ
of Israel until be come the Son of man. Not

ἔστιν μαθητὴς ὑπὲρ τὸν διδάσκαλον, οὐδὲ δοῦλος ὑπὲρ
is a disciple above the teacher, nor a bondman above

τὸν.κύριον.αὐτοῦ. 25 ἀρκετὸν τῷ μαθητῇ ἵνα γένηται ὡς
his lord. Sufficient for the disciple that he become as

ὁ.διδάσκαλος.αὐτοῦ, καὶ ὁ δοῦλος ὡς ὁ.κύριος.αὐτοῦ. εἰ ˢτὸν
his teacher, and the bondman as his lord. If the

οἰκοδεσπότην‖ Βεελζεβοὺλ ᵗἐκάλεσαν,‖ πόσῳ μᾶλλον
master of the house Beelzebul they called, how much more

ᵛτοὺς οἰκιακοὺς‖.αὐτοῦ; 26 Μὴ οὖν φοβηθῆτε αὐτούς·
those of his household? Not therefore ye should fear them;

οὐδὲν.γάρ ἐστιν κεκαλυμμένον ὃ οὐκ.ἀποκαλυφθήσεται·
for nothing is covered which shall not be uncovered,

καὶ κρυπτὸν ὃ οὐ.γνωσθήσεται. 27 ὃ λέγω ὑμῖν ἐν τῇ
and hidden which shall not be known. What I tell you in the

σκοτίᾳ εἴπατε ἐν τῷ φωτί· καὶ ὃ εἰς τὸ οὖς ἀκούετε κη-
darkness speak in the light; and what in the ear ye hear pro-

ρύξατε ἐπὶ τῶν δωμάτων. 28 καὶ ʷμὴ.φοβηθῆτε‖ ἀπὸ
claim upon the housetops. And ye should not fear because of

as sheep in the midst of wolves: be ye therefore wise as serpents, and harmless as doves. 17 But beware of men: for they will deliver you up to the councils, and they will scourge you in their synagogues; 18 and ye shall be brought before governors and kings for my sake, for a testimony against them and the Gentiles. 19 But when they deliver you up, take no thought how or what ye shall speak: for it shall be given you in that same hour what ye shall speak. 20 For it is not ye that speak, but the Spirit of your Father which speaketh in you. 21 And the brother shall deliver up the brother to death, and the father the child: and the children shall rise up against their parents, and cause them to be put to death. 22 And ye shall be hated of all men for my name's sake: but he that endureth to the end shall be saved. 23 But when they persecute you in this city, flee ye into another: for verily I say unto you, Ye shall not have gone over the cities of Israel, till the Son of man be come. 24 The disciple is not above his master, nor the servant above his lord. 25 It is enough for the disciple that he be as his master, and the servant as his lord. If they have called the master of the house Beelzebub, how much more shall they call them of his household? 26 Fear them not therefore: for there is nothing covered, that shall not be revealed; and hid, that shall not be known. 27 What I tell you in darkness, that speak ye in light: and what ye hear in the ear, that preach ye upon the housetops. 28 And fear not them

---

¹ παραδῶσιν they shall have delivered ᴸᵀᵀᵣ. ᵐ [δοθή. γὰρ ὑμῖν ἐν ἐκείνῃ τῇ ὥρᾳ τί λαλή.] ι. ⁿ λαλήσητε ye should speak ᵀᵀᵣᴬ. ᵒ τὴν ἑτέραν the next ɢʟᴛᵀᵣ. ᴾ + κἂν ἐν τῇ ἑτέρᾳ (κἂν ἐκ ταύτης ɢ) διώκωσιν ὑμᾶς, φεύγετε εἰς τὴν ἄλλην and if in the next (and if from this) they persecute you, flee to another ɢ[ʟ]. ۹—τοῦ ʟᴛᵣᴬ. ᵣ— ἂν ᴛᴬ. ˢ τῷ οἰκοδεσπότῃ ʟ. ᵗ ἐπεκά-λεσαν they have surnamed ɢʟᴛᵀᵣᴬᵂ. ᵛ τοῖς οἰκιακοῖς ʟ. ʷ μὴ φοβεῖσθε fear ye not ɢʟᴛᵀᵣᵂ

which kill the body, but are not able to kill the soul: but rather fear him which is able to destroy both soul and body in hell. 29 Are not two sparrows sold for a farthing? and one of them shall not fall on the ground without your Father. 30 But the very hairs of your head are all numbered. 31 Fear ye not therefore, ye are of more value than many sparrows. 32 Whosoever therefore shall confess me before men, him will I confess also before my Father which is in heaven. 33 But whosoever shall deny me before men, him will I also deny before my Father which is in heaven. 34 Think not that I am come to send peace on earth: I came not to send peace, but a sword. 35 For I am come to set a man at variance against his father, and the daughter against her mother, and the daughter in law against her mother in law. 36 And a man's foes *shall be* they of his own household. 37 He that loveth father or mother more than me is not worthy of me: and he that loveth son or daughter more than me is not worthy of me. 38 And he that taketh not his cross, and followeth after me, is not worthy of me. 39 He that findeth his life shall lose it: and he that loseth his life for my sake shall find it. 40 He that receiveth you receiveth me, and he that receiveth me receiveth him that sent me. 41 He that receiveth a prophet in the name of a prophet shall receive a prophet's reward; and he that receiveth a righteous man in the name of a righteous man shall receive a righteous man's reward. 42 And who-soever shall give to drink unto one of these little ones a cup of cold

τῶν ˣἀποκτεινόντων‖ τὸ σῶμα, τὴν.δὲ ψυχὴν μὴ.δυναμένων
those who   kill   the body,   but the soul   are not able
ἀποκτεῖναι· ᵞφοβήθητε.‖δὲ μᾶλλον τὸν δυνάμενον ᶻκαὶ‖
to kill;   but ye should fear rather him who is able   both
ψυχὴν καὶ σῶμα ἀπολέσαι ἐν γεέννῃ. 29 οὐχὶ δύο στρουθία
soul   and body to destroy in Gehenna. ²Not ³two ⁴sparrows
ἀσσαρίου πωλεῖται; καὶ ἓν ἐξ αὐτῶν οὐ.πεσεῖται ἐπὶ τὴν
⁶for ⁷an ⁸assarion ¹are ⁵sold? and one of them shall not fall to the
γῆν ἄνευ τοῦ.πατρὸς.ὑμῶν· 30 ὑμῶν.δὲ καὶ αἱ τρίχες τῆς
ground without   your Father.   But of you even the hairs of the
κεφαλῆς πᾶσαι ἠριθμημέναι εἰσίν. 31 μὴ οὖν ᵃφοβήθητε.‖
head   all   numbered   are.   ²Not ³therefore ¹ye ²should ⁴fear;
πολλῶν στρουθίων διαφέρετε ὑμεῖς. 32 Πᾶς οὖν ὅσ-
than many sparrows better are ye.   Every one therefore whoso-
τις ὁμολογήσει ἐν ἐμοὶ ἔμπροσθεν τῶν ἀνθρώπων, ὁμολογήσω
ever shall confess   me   before   the   men,   will ⁴confess
κἀγὼ ἐν αὐτῷ ἔμπροσθεν τοῦ.πατρός.μου τοῦ ἐν ᵇ οὐρανοῖς·
²also ¹I him   before   my Father   who[is] in [the] heavens.
33 ὅστις.ᶜδ̓ ἂν‖ ἀρνήσηταί με ἔμπροσθεν τῶν ἀνθρώπων,
But whosoever   shall deny me   before   the   men,
ἀρνήσομαι ᵈαὐτὸν κἀγὼ‖ ἔμπροσθεν τοῦ.πατρός.μου τοῦ ἐν
⁵will ⁴deny ⁵him ²also ¹I.   before   my Father   who[is]in
ᵉ οὐρανοῖς. 34 Μὴ.νομίσητε ὅτι ἦλθον βαλεῖν εἰρήνην ἐπὶ
[the] heavens.   Think not that I came to place peace on
τὴν γῆν· οὐκ.ἦλθον βαλεῖν εἰρήνην, ἀλλὰ μάχαιραν. 35 ἦλθον
the earth: I came not to place peace, but   a sword.   ²I ³came
γὰρ διχάσαι ἄνθρωπον κατὰ τοῦ.πατρὸς.αὐτοῦ, καὶ θυγα-
¹for to set at variance a man against   his father,   and a daugh-
τέρα κατὰ τῆς.μητρὸς.αὐτῆς, ʹ καὶ νύμφην κατὰ τῆς πεν-
ter against her mother,   and a daughter-in-law against ²mother-
θερᾶς αὐτῆς 36 καὶ ἐχθροὶ τοῦ.ἀνθρώπου οἱ οἰκιακοὶ
in-law ¹her. And enemies of the man [shall be] ²household
αὐτοῦ. 37 Ὁ φιλῶν πατέρα ἢ μητέρα ὑπὲρ ἐμὲ οὐκ.ἔστιν
¹his. He that loves father or mother above me is not
μου ἄξιος· καὶ ὁ φιλῶν υἱὸν ἢ θυγατέρα ὑπὲρ ἐμὲ οὐκ
of me worthy; and he that loves son or daughter above me not
ἔστιν μου ἄξιος· 38 καὶ ὃς οὐ.λαμβάνει τὸν.σταυρὸν.αὐτοῦ
¹is of me worthy. And he that takes not   his cross
καὶ ἀκολούθεῖ ὀπίσω μου οὐκ ἔστιν μου ἄξιος. 39 ὁ εὑρὼν·
and follows after me ²not ¹is of me worthy. He that has found
τὴν.ψυχὴν.αὐτοῦ ἀπολέσει αὐτήν· καὶ ὁ ἀπολέσας τὴν
his life   shall lose it; and he that has lost
ψυχὴν αὐτοῦ ἔνεκεν ἐμοῦ εὑρήσει αὐτήν. 40 Ὁ δεχόμενος
²life ¹his on account of me shall find   it. He that receives
ὑμᾶς ἐμὲ δέχεται· καὶ ὁ ἐμὲ δεχόμενος δέχεται τὸν ἀπο-
you me receives; and he that me receives receives him who sent
στείλαντά με. 41 ὁ δεχόμενος προφήτην εἰς ὄνομα προ-
me.   ᶜ He that receives a prophet in [the] name of a
φήτου μισθὸν προφήτου ᶠλήψεται.‖ καὶ ὁ δεχόμενος
prophet [the] reward of a prophet shall receive; and he that receives
δίκαιον εἰς ὄνομα δικαίου μισθὸν δικαίου
a righteous [man] in [the] name of a righteous [man] the reward of a righteous
λήψεται.‖ 42 καὶ ὃς.ᵍἐὰν‖ ποτίσῃ ἕνα τῶν μικρῶν
[man] shall receive.   And whoever shall give to drink to one ³little ⁴ones

τούτων ποτήριον ψυχροῦ　μόνον εἰς ὄνομα μαθητοῦ,
¹of ²these　a cup　of cold [water] only　in [the] name of a disciple,

ἀμὴν λέγω ὑμῖν, οὐ·μὴ ἀπολέσῃ τὸν·μισθὸν·αὐτοῦ.
verily I say to you, in nowise shall he lose　his reward.

11 Καὶ ἐγένετο ὅτε ἐτέλεσεν ὁ Ἰησοῦς διατάσσων τοῖς
And it came to pass when ²had ²finished ¹Jesus· commanding

δώδεκα μαθηταῖς αὐτοῦ, μετέβη ἐκεῖθεν τοῦ διδάσκειν καὶ
²twelve ³disciples ¹his, he departed thence　to teach　and

κηρύσσειν ἐν ταῖς·πόλεσιν·αὐτῶν.
to preach in　their cities.

2 Ὁ·δὲ·Ἰωάννης ἀκούσας ἐν τῷ δεσμωτηρίῳ τὰ ἔργα τοῦ
Now John　having heard in the　prison　the works of the

χριστοῦ, πέμψας ʰδύοʰ τῶν·μαθητῶν·αὐτοῦ, 3 εἶπεν αὐτῷ,
Christ, having sent two　of his disciples,　said　to him,

Σὺ·εἶ ὁ ἐρχόμενος, ἢ ἕτερον προσδοκῶμεν; 4 Καὶ ἀποκρι-
Art thou the coming [one], or another are we to look for? And ²answer-

θεὶς ὁ Ἰησοῦς εἶπεν αὐτοῖς, Πορευθέντες ἀπαγγείλατε Ἰωάννῃ
ing ¹Jesus said to them, Having gone　relate　to John

ἃ ἀκούετε καὶ βλέπετε· 5 τυφλοὶ ἀναβλέπουσιν, ⁱκαὶⁱ.
what ye hear and　see:　blind　receive sight, and

χωλοὶ περιπατοῦσιν· λεπροὶ καθαρίζονται, ᵏκαὶᵏ κωφοὶ
lame　walk;　lepers　are cleansed,　and　deaf

ἀκούουσιν· ˡνεκροὶ ἐγείρονται, ᵏκαὶᵏ πτωχοὶ εὐαγγελίζονται·
hear;　dead　are raised, and　poor　are evangelized.

6 καὶ μακάριός ἐστιν, ὃς·ᵐἐὰνᵐ μὴ·σκανδαλισθῇ ἐν ἐμοί.
And blessed　is,　whoever shall not be offended in me.

7 Τούτων·δὲ πορευομένων ἤρξατο ὁ Ἰησοῦς λέγειν τοῖς
But as these　were going　²began ¹Jesus　to say to the

ὄχλοις περὶ Ἰωάννου, Τί ⁿἐξήλθετεⁿ εἰς τὴν ἔρημον
crowds concerning John, What went ye out into the wilderness

θεάσασθαι; κάλαμον ὑπὸ ἀνέμου σαλευόμενον; 8 ἀλλὰ
to look at?　a reed　by [the] wind　shaken?　But

τί ⁿἐξήλθετεⁿ ἰδεῖν; ἄνθρωπον ἐν μαλακοῖς ᵒἱματίοιςᵒ ἠμφιεσ-
what went ye out to see? a man ¹in　soft　garments　ar-

μένον; ἰδού, οἱ τὰ μαλακὰ φοροῦντες ἐν τοῖς οἴκοις
rayed? Behold, those who the soft [garments] wear in the houses

τῶν βασιλέων ᵖεἰσίν·ᵖ 9 ἀλλὰ τί ⁿἐξήλθετεⁿ ⁱἰδεῖν; προ-
of kings　are.　But what went ye out to see? a pro-

φήτην;ⁱ ναί, λέγω ὑμῖν, καὶ περισσότερον προφήτου·
phet?　Yea, I say to you, and [one] more excellent than a prophet.

10 οὗτος·ᵍγάρᵍ ἐστιν περὶ οὗ γέγραπται, Ἰδού, ˢἐγὼˢ
For this　is [he] concerning whom it has been written, Behold, I

ἀποστέλλω τὸν·ἄγγελόν·μου πρὸ προσώπου·σου, ᵗὃςᵗ κατα-
send　my messenger　before thy face,　who shall

σκευάσει τὴν·ὁδόν·σου ἔμπροσθέν σου· 11 Ἀμὴν λέγω ὑμῖν,
prepare　thy way　before　thee.　Verily I say to you,

οὐκ·ἐγήγερται ἐν γεννητοῖς γυναικῶν μείζων Ἰωάννου
there has not risen among [those] born　of women a greater than John

τοῦ βαπτιστοῦ· ὁ·δὲ μικρότερος ἐν τῇ βασιλείᾳ τῶν
the Baptist. But he that [is] less　in the kingdom of the

οὐρανῶν μείζων ᵛαὐτοῦ ἐστιν.ᵛ 12 ἀπὸ·δὲ τῶν ἡμερῶν Ἰωάννου
heavens greater than he is.　But from the　days　of John

water only in the name of a disciple, verily I say unto you, he shall in no wise lose his reward.

XI. And it came to pass, when Jesus had made an end of commanding his twelve disciples, he departed thence to teach and to preach in their cities.

2 Now when John had heard in the prison the works of Christ, he sent two of his disciples, 3 and said unto him, Art thou he that should come, or do we look for another? 4 Jesus answered and said unto them, Go and shew John again those things which ye do hear and see: 5 the blind receive their sight, and the lame walk, the lepers are cleansed, and the deaf hear, the dead are raised up, and the poor have the gospel preached to them. 6 And blessed is he, whosoever shall not be offended in me.

7 And· as they departed, Jesus began to say unto the multitudes concerning John, What went ye out into the wilderness to see? A reed shaken with the wind? 8 But what went ye out for to see? A man clothed in soft raiment? behold, they that wear soft clothing are in kings' houses. 9 But what went ye out for to see? A prophet? yea, I say unto you, and more than a prophet. 10 For this is he, of whom it is written, Behold, I send my messenger before thy face, which shall prepare thy way before thee. 11 Verily I say unto you, Among them that are born of women there hath not risen a greater than John the Baptist: notwithstanding he that is least in the kingdom of heaven is greater than he. 12 And from the days of John the

---

ʰ διὰ by (his disciples) LTTrAW.　ⁱ [καὶ] LTr.　ᵏ [καὶ] L.　ˡ + καὶ and [L]TTrA.　ᵐ ἂν
LTr.　ⁿ ἐξήλθατε LTT·A.　ᵒ — ἱματίοις (read [garments]) [L]TT·A.　ᵖ — εἰσίν (read
[are]) T[A].　ᵍ προφήτην ἰδεῖν; (read But why went ye out? to see a prophet? TA.
ʳ — γάρ for T[LT·A].　ˢ [ἐγὼ] L.　ᵗ καὶ (read and he shall prepare) L.,　ᵛ ἐστιν αὐτοῦ A.

Baptist until now the kingdom of heaven suffereth violence, and the violent take it by force. 13 For all the prophets and the law prophesied until John. 14 And if ye will receive it, this is Elias, which was for to come. 15 He that hath ears to hear, let him hear. 16 But whereunto shall I liken this generation? It is like unto children sitting in the markets, and calling unto their fellows, 17 and saying, We have piped unto you, and ye have not danced; we have mourned unto you, and ye have not lamented. 18 For John came neither eating nor drinking, and they say, He hath a devil. 19 The Son of man came eating and drinking, and they say, Behold a man gluttonous, and a winebibber, a friend of publicans and sinners. But wisdom is justified of her children.

20 Then began he to upbraid the cities wherein most of his mighty works were done, because they repented not: 21 Woe unto thee, Chorazin! woe unto thee, Bethsaida! for if the mighty works, which were done in you, had been done in Tyre and Sidon, they would have repented long ago in sackcloth and ashes. 22 But I say unto you, It shall be more tolerable for Tyre and Sidon at the day of judgment, than for you. 23 And thou, Capernaum, which art exalted unto heaven, shalt be brought down to hell: for if the mighty works, which have been done in thee, had been done in Sodom, it would have remained until this day. 24 But I say unto you, That it shall be more tolerable for the land of Sodom in the day of judgment, than for thee.

τοῦ βαπτιστοῦ ἕως ἄρτι, ἡ βασιλεία τῶν οὐρανῶν βιά-
the Baptist until now, the kingdom of the heavens is taken by
ζεται, καὶ βιασταὶ ἁρπάζουσιν αὐτήν. 13 πάντες·γὰρ οἱ
violence, and [the] violent seize it. For all the
προφῆται καὶ ὁ νόμος ἕως Ἰωάννου ʷπροεφήτευσαν‖. 14 καὶ
prophets and the law until John ¹prophesied. And
εἰ θέλετε δέξασθαι, αὐτός ἐστιν ˣἨλίας‖ ὁ μέλλων ἔρχεσθαι·
if ye are willing to receive [it], he is Elias who is about to come.
15 ὁ ἔχων ὦτα ʸἀκούειν,‖ ἀκουέτω. 16 Τίνι·δὲ ὁμοιώσω
He that has ears to hear, let him hear. But to what shall I liken
τὴν·γενεὰν·ταύτην; ὁμοία ἐστὶν ᶻπαιδαρίοις‖ ᵃἐν ἀγοραῖς
this generation? like ¹it ²is to little children in [the] markets
καθημένοις,‖ ᵇκαὶ προσφωνοῦσιν·τοῖς·ἑταίροις·αὐτῶν,‖ 17 καὶ
sitting, and calling to their companions, and
λέγουσιν,‖ Ηὐλήσαμεν ὑμῖν, καὶ οὐκ·ὠρχήσασθε· ἐθρηνήσαμεν
saying, We piped to you, and ye did not dance; we mourned
ᶜὑμῖν,‖ καὶ οὐκ·ἐκόψασθε. 18 Ἠλθεν·γὰρ Ἰωάννης μήτε ἐσθίων
to you, and ye did not wail. For ²came ¹John neither eating
μήτε πίνων, καὶ λέγουσιν, Δαιμόνιον ἔχει. 19 ἦλθεν ὁ υἱὸς
nor drinking, and they say, A demon he has. ⁵Came ¹the ²Son
τοῦ ἀνθρώπου ἐσθίων καὶ πίνων, καὶ λέγουσιν, Ἰδού,
³of ⁴man eating and drinking, and they say, Behold,
ἄνθρωπος φάγος καὶ οἰνοπότης, τελωνῶν φίλος καὶ
a man a glutton and a wine bibber, of tax-gatherers a friend and
ἁμαρτωλῶν. καὶ ἐδικαιώθη ἡ σοφία ἀπὸ τῶν·ᵈτέκνων‖ αὐτῆς·
of sinners. And ²was ³justified ¹wisdom by ²children ¹her.

20 Τότε ἤρξατο ὀνειδίζειν τὰς πόλεις ἐν αἷς ἐγένοντο
Then he began to reproach the cities in which had taken place
αἱ πλεῖσται δυνάμεις·αὐτοῦ, ὅτι οὐ·μετενόησαν. 21 Οὐαί
the most of his works of power, because they repented not. Woe
σοι, ᵉΧοραζίν·‖ οὐαί σοι, ᶠΒηθσαϊδάν·‖ ὅτι εἰ ἐν Τύρῳ καὶ
to thee, Chorazin! woe to thee, Bethsaida! for if in Tyre and
Σιδῶνι ἐγένοντο αἱ δυνάμεις αἱ γενόμεναι ἐν ὑμῖν,
Sidon had taken place the works of power which have taken place in you,
πάλαι ἂν ἐν σάκκῳ καὶ σποδῷ μετενόησαν. 22 πλὴν λέγω
long ago in sackcloth and ashes they had repented. But I say
ὑμῖν, Τύρῳ καὶ Σιδῶνι ἀνεκτότερον ἔσται ἐν ἡμέρᾳ κρίσεως
to you, For Tyre and Sidon more tolerable shall it be in day of judgment
ἢ ὑμῖν. 23 Καὶ σύ, ᵍΚαπερναούμ,‖ ʰἡ‖ ἕως ⁱτοῦ‖ οὐρανοῦ
than for you. And thou, Capernaum, who to the heaven
ᵏὑψωθεῖσα,‖ ἕως ᾅδου ˡκαταβιβασθήσῃ·‖ ὅτι εἰ ἐν Σοδό-
hast been lifted up, to hades shalt be brought down: for if in Sod-
μοις, ᵐἐγένοντο‖ αἱ δυνάμεις αἱ·ⁿγενόμεναι ἐν σοί,‖
om had taken place the works of power which have taken place in thee,
ᵒἔμειναν‖·ἂν μέχρι·τῆς·σήμερον. 24 πλὴν λέγω ὑμῖν, ὅτι
it had remained until to-day. But I say to you, that
γῇ Σοδόμων ἀνεκτότερον ἔσται ἐν ἡμέρᾳ κρίσεως
for [the] land of Sodom more tolerable shall it be in day of judgment
ἢ σοί.
than for thee.

ʷ ἐπροφήτευσαν LTTrA. ˣ Ἡλείας T. ʸ — ἀκούειν T[Tr]A. ᶻ παιδίοις GLTTrAW.
ᵃ καθημένοις ἐν ἀγορᾷ (market) L; καθημένοις ἐν ταῖς ἀγοραῖς TTrA. ᵇ ἃ προσφωνοῦντα τοῖς ἑταίροις who calling to the companions (ἑτέροις read calling to the others Tr) (+ [αὐτῶν] their A) λέγουσιν say LTTrA. ᶜ — ὑμῖν LTTrA. ᵈ ἔργων works TTr. ᵉ Χοραζείν TTrA. ᶠ Βηθσαϊδά LTr. ᵍ Καφαρναούμ LTTrAW. ʰ μὴ LTTrA, ἦ W. ⁱ — τοῦ LTTrA. ᵏ ὑψωθήσῃ shalt thou be lifted up? LTTrA; ὑψώθης W. ˡ καταβήσῃ thou shalt descend LTrA. ᵐ ἐγενήθησαν LTTrA. ⁿ ἐν σοὶ γενόμεναι L. ᵒ ἔμεινεν LTTrA.

25 Ἐν ἐκείνῳ τῷ καιρῷ ἀποκριθεὶς ὁ Ἰησοῦς εἶπεν, Ἐξομο-
At that time · answering Jesus said,   I
λογοῦμαί σοι, πάτερ, κύριε τοῦ οὐρανοῦ καὶ τῆς γῆς, ὅτι
praise thee, O Father, Lord of the ·heaven and the earth, that
ᴿἀπέκρυψαςᴵᴵ ταῦτα ἀπὸ σοφῶν καὶ συνετῶν, καὶ ἀπεκάλυψας
thou didst hide these things from wise · and prudent, and didst reveal
αὐτὰ νηπίοις. 26 ναί, ὁ πατήρ, ὅτι οὕτως ᑫἐγένετο εὐδοκία ᴵᴵ
them to babes. Yea, Father, for thus · it was well-pleasing
ἔμπροσθέν σου. 27 Πάντα μοι παρεδόθη ὑπὸ τοῦ πατρός μου·
before thee. All things to me were delivered by my Father.
καὶ οὐδεὶς ἐπιγινώσκει τὸν υἱὸν εἰ μὴ ὁ πατήρ· οὐδὲ τὸν
And no one knows the Son except the Father; nor the
πατέρα τις ἐπιγινώσκει εἰ μὴ ὁ υἱός, καὶ ᾧ ἐὰν
Father ²any ³one ¹does know except the Son, and he to whomsoever
βούληται ὁ υἱὸς ἀποκαλύψαι. 28 Δεῦτε πρός με, πάντες
¹may ⁴will ¹the ²Son to reveal [him]. Come to me, all
οἱ κοπιῶντες καὶ πεφορτισμένοι, κἀγὼ ἀναπαύσω ὑμᾶς.
ye that labour and are burdened, and I will give ²rest ¹you.
29 ἄρατε τὸν ζυγόν μου ἐφ᾽ ὑμᾶς, καὶ μάθετε ἀπ᾽ ἐμοῦ, ὅτι
Take my yoke upon you, and learn from me, for
ᴿπρᾷοςᴵᴵ εἰμι καὶ ταπεινὸς τῇ καρδίᾳ· καὶ εὑρήσετε ἀνάπαυσιν
meek I am and lowly in heart; and ye shall find rest
ταῖς ψυχαῖς ὑμῶν. 30 ὁ γὰρ ζυγός μου χρηστὸς καὶ τὸ φορτίον
to your souls. For my yoke easy and ²burden
μου ἐλαφρόν ἐστιν.
¹my light is.

12 Ἐν ἐκείνῳ τῷ καιρῷ ἐπορεύθη ὁ Ἰησοῦς τοῖς ˢσάββασιν ᴵᴵ
At that time went Jesus on the Sabbath
διὰ τῶν σπορίμων· οἱ δὲ μαθηταὶ αὐτοῦ ἐπείνασαν, καὶ
through the corn-fields; and his disciples were hungry, and
ἤρξαντο τίλλειν στάχυας καὶ ἐσθίειν. 2 οἱ δὲ Φαρισαῖοι
began to pluck [the] ears and to eat. But the Pharisees
ἰδόντες ᵗεἶπον ᴵᴵ αὐτῷ, Ἰδού, οἱ μαθηταί σου ποιοῦσιν ὃ
having seen said to him, Behold, thy disciples are doing what
οὐκ ἔξεστιν ποιεῖν ἐν σαββάτῳ. 3 Ὁ δὲ εἶπεν αὐτοῖς, Οὐκ
it is not lawful to do on sabbath. But he said to them, ²Not
ἀνέγνωτε τί ἐποίησεν ᵛΔαβίδ, ᴵᴵ ὅτε ἐπείνασεν ʷαὐτὸς ᴵᴵ καὶ
²ye ¹have read what ²did ¹David, when he hungered himself and
οἱ μετ᾽ αὐτοῦ; 4 πῶς εἰσῆλθεν εἰς τὸν οἶκον τοῦ θεοῦ, καὶ
those with him? How he entered into the house of God, and
τοὺς ἄρτους τῆς προθέσεως ˣἔφαγεν, ᴵᴵ ᵞοὓς ᴵᴵ οὐκ ἐξὸν ἦν
the loaves of the presentation he ate, which ³not ⁴lawful ¹it ²was
ᵃὐτῷ φαγεῖν, οὐδὲ τοῖς μετ᾽ αὐτοῦ, εἰ μὴ τοῖς ἱερεῦσιν μόνοις;
for him to eat, nor for those with him, but for the priests only?
5 Ἢ οὐκ ἀνέγνωτε ἐν τῷ νόμῳ, ὅτι τοῖς σάββασιν οἱ ἱερεῖς
Or have ye not read in the law, that on the sabbaths the priests
ἐν τῷ ἱερῷ τὸ σάββατον βεβηλοῦσιν, καὶ ἀναίτιοί εἰσιν;
in the temple the sabbath profane, and guiltless are?
6 λέγω δὲ ὑμῖν, ὅτι τοῦ ἱεροῦ ᶻμεῖζων ᴵᴵ ἐστιν ὧδε. 7 εἰ δὲ
But I say to you, that ³than ⁴the ¹temple ¹a ²greater is here. But if
ἐγνώκειτε τί ἐστιν, ᵃἜλεον ᴵᴵ θέλω καὶ οὐ θυσίαν, οὐκ ἂν
ye had known what is, Mercy I desire and not sacrifice, ²not

25 At that time Je-
sus answered and said,
I thank thee. O Fa-
ther, Lord of heaven
and earth, because
thou hast hid these
things from the wise
and prudent, and hast
revealed them unto
babes. 26 Even so, Fa-
ther: for so it seemed
good in thy sight.
27 All things are de-
livered unto me of my
Father: and no man
knoweth the Son, but
the Father; neither
knoweth any man the
Father, save the Son,
and he to whomsoever
the Son will reveal
him. 28 Come unto
me, all ye that labour
and are heavy laden,
and I will give you
rest. 29 Take my yoke
upon you, and learn of
me; for I am meek and
lowly in heart: and ye
shall find rest unto
your souls. 30 For my
yoke is easy, and my
burden is light.

XII. At that time
Jesus went on the
sabbath day through
the corn; and his disci-
ples were an hungred,
and began to pluck the
ears of corn, and to
eat. 2 But when the
Pharisees saw it, they
said unto him, Behold,
thy disciples do that
which is not lawful to
do upon the sabbath
day. 3 But he said un-
to them, Have ye not
read what David did,
when he was an hun-
gred, and they that
were with him; 4 how
he entered into the
house of God, and did
eat the shewbread,
which was not lawful
for him to eat, neither
for them which were
with him, but only for
the priests? 5 Or have
ye not read in the law,
how that on the sab-
bath days the priests
in the temple profane
the sabbath, and are
blameless? 6 But I say
unto you, That in this
place is one greater
than the temple. 7 But
if ye had known what
this meaneth, I will
have mercy, and not
sacrifice, ye would not

ᴾ ἔκρυψας LTTrA.   ᑫ εὐδοκία ἐγένετο LT.   ʳ πραΰς LTTrA.   ˢ σαββάτοις L.   ᵗ εἶπαν LTTrA.
ᵛ Δαυείδ LTTrA ; Δαυὶδ GW.   ʷ — αὐτὸς GLTTrAW.   ˣ ἔφαγον LT.   ᵞ ὃ LTTrA.   ᶻ μεῖζόν
LTTrAW.   ᵃ Ἔλεος LTTrA.

have condemned the guiltless. 8 For the Son of man is Lord even of the sabbath day.

9 And when he was departed thence, he went into their synagogue: 10 and, behold, there was a man which had his hand withered. And they asked him, saying, Is it lawful to heal on the sabbath days? that they might accuse him. 11 And he said unto them, What man shall there be among you, that shall have one sheep, and if it fall into a pit on the sabbath day, will he not lay hold on it, and lift it out? 12 How much then is a man better than a sheep? Wherefore it is lawful to do well on the sabbath days. 13 Then saith he to the man, Stretch forth thine hand. And he stretched it forth; and it was restored whole, like as the other.

14 Then the Pharisees went out, and held a council against him, how they might destroy him. 15 But when Jesus knew it, he withdrew himself from thence: and great multitudes followed him, and he healed them all; 16 and charged them that they should not make him known: 17 that it might be fulfilled which was spoken by Esaias the prophet, saying, 18 Behold my servant whom I have chosen; my beloved, in whom my soul is well pleased: I will put my spirit upon him, and he shall shew judgment to the Gentiles. 19 He shall not strive, nor cry; neither shall any man hear his voice in the streets. 20 A bruised reed shall he not break, and smoking flax shall he not quench, till he send forth judgment unto victory. 21 And in his name shall the Gentiles trust.

κατεδικάσατε τοὺς ἀναιτίους· 8 κύριος.γάρ ἐστιν ᵇκαί‖ τοῦ
ʸe ¹had condemned the guiltless. For Lord ²is ¹also ²of ³the

σαββάτου ὁ υἱὸς τοῦ.ἀνθρώπου.
⁴sabbath the son of man.

9 Καὶ μεταβὰς ἐκεῖθεν, ἦλθεν εἰς τὴν.συναγωγὴν.αὐτῶν·
And having departed thence, he went into their synagogue.

10 καὶ ἰδού,· ἄνθρωπος ᶜῆν τὴν‖ χεῖρα ἔχων ξηράν· καὶ
And behold, a man there was ²the ³hand ¹having withered. And

ἐπηρώτησαν αὐτόν, λέγοντες, Εἰ.ἔξεστιν τοῖς σάββασιν
they asked him, saying, Is it lawful on the sabbaths

ᵈθεραπεύειν}‖ ἵνα κατηγορήσωσιν αὐτοῦ. 11 Ὁ.δὲ εἶπεν αὐτοῖς,
to heal? that they might accuse him. But he said to them,

Τίς ᵉἔσται‖ ἐξ ὑμῶν ἄνθρωπος, ὃς ἕξει πρόβατον ἕν,
What ²shall ³there ⁴be ⁵of ⁶you ¹man, who shall have ²sheep ¹one,

καὶ ἐὰν ἐμπέσῃ τοῦτο τοῖς ₋σάββασιν εἰς βόθυνον, οὐχὶ
and if ²fall ¹this on the sabbaths into a pit, will not

κρατήσει αὐτὸ καὶ ᶠἐγερεῖ·‖ 12 πόσῳ οὖν διαφέρει ἄν-
lay hold of it and will raise [it] up? How much then is ²better ¹a

θρωπος προβάτου; ὥστε ἔξεστιν τοῖς.ᵍσάββασιν‖ καλῶς
²man than a sheep? So that it is lawful on the sabbaths ³well

ποιεῖν. 13 Τότε λέγει τῷ.ἀνθρώπῳ, Ἔκτεινον ʰτὴν χεῖρά
¹to ²do. Then he says to the man, Stretch out ³hand

σου.‖ Καὶ ἐξέτεινεν, καὶ ⁱἀποκατεστάθη‖ ὑγιὴς ὡς ἡ
¹thy. And he stretched [it] out, and it was restored sound as the

ἄλλη.
other.

14 ᵏΟἱ.δὲ Φαρισαῖοι συμβούλιον ἔλαβον κατ' αὐτοῦ ἐξελ-
But the Pharisees ⁵a ⁶council ⁴held ⁷against ⁸him ¹having

θόντες,‖ ὅπως αὐτὸν ἀπολέσωσιν. 15 Ὁ.δὲ.Ἰησοῦς γνοὺς
²gone ³out how him they might destroy. But Jesus having known

ἀνεχώρησεν ἐκεῖθεν· καὶ ἠκολούθησαν αὐτῷ ˡὄχλοι‖ πολλοί,
withdrew thence, and followed him ²crowds ¹great,

καὶ ἐθεράπευσεν αὐτοὺς πάντας· 16 καὶ ἐπετίμησεν αὐτοῖς
and he healed them all, and strictly charged them

ἵνα μὴ φανερὸν αὐτὸν ποιήσωσιν· 17 ᵐὅπως‖ πλη-
that ³not ⁶publicly ¹known ⁴him ²they ⁵should ⁴make. So that ²might

ρωθῇ τὸ ῥηθὲν διὰ Ἡσαΐου τοῦ προφήτου, λέγοντος,
be fulfilled that which was spoken by Esaias the prophet, saying,

18 Ἰδοὺ ὁ.παῖς.μου ὃν ⁿῄρέτισα,‖ ὁ.ἀγαπητός.μου ᵒεἰς
Behold my servant whom I have chosen, my beloved in,

ὃν ᴾεὐδόκησεν‖ ἡ.ψυχή.μου· θήσω τὸ.πνεῦμά.μου ἐπ'
whom ³has ⁴found ⁵delight ¹my ²soul. I will put my Spirit upon

αὐτόν, καὶ κρίσιν τοῖς ἔθνεσιν ἀπαγγελεῖ· 19 οὐκ.ἐρίσει
him, and judgment to the nations he shall declare. He shall not strive

οὐδὲ κραυγάσει, οὐδὲ ἀκούσει τις ἐν ταῖς πλατείαις τὴν
nor cry out, nor shall ¹hear ²one in the streets

φωνὴν.αὐτοῦ. 20 κάλαμον συντετριμμένον οὐ.κατεάξει, καὶ
his voice. A ²reed ¹bruised he shall not break, and

λίνον τυφόμενον οὐ.σβέσει, ἕως.ἂν ἐκβάλῃ εἰς νῖκος τὴν
²flax ¹smoking he shall not quench, until he bring forth ³unto ⁴victory ¹the

κρίσιν. 21 καὶ ᵠἐν‖ τῷ.ὀνόματι.αὐτοῦ ἔθνη ἐλπιοῦσιν.
²judgment. And in his name [the] nations shall hope.

---

b — καὶ GLTTrAW. c — ῆν τὴν LTTrA. d θεραπεῦσαι; T. e — ἔσται TrA. f ἐγείρει he raises [it] up L. g σαββάτοις L. h σου τὴν χεῖρα LTTrA. i ἀπεκατεστάθη LTTrAW. k ἐξελθόντες δὲ οἱ Φαρισαῖοι συμβούλιον ἔλαβον κατ' αὐτοῦ LTTrW. l — ὄχλοι (read πολλοί many) LᵀTrA. m ἵνα that LTTrA. n ἠρέτισα Tr. o ἐν.ᾧ Tr; — εἰς LA. p ηὐδόκησεν TTr. q — ἐν (read [on]) GLTTrAW.

22 Τότε ʳπροσηνέχθη‖ αὐτῷ ˢδαιμονιζόμενος, τυφλὸς
Then was brought to him one possessed by a demon, blind

καὶ κωφός·‖ καὶ ἐθεράπευσεν αὐτόν, ὥστε τὸν ᵗτυφλὸν καὶ‖
and dumb, and he healed him, so that the blind and

κωφὸν ᵗκαὶ‖ λαλεῖν καὶ βλέπειν. 23 καὶ ἐξίσταντο πάντες
dumb both spake and saw. And ⁺were ²amazed ¹all

οἱ ὄχλοι καὶ ἔλεγον, Μήτι οὗτός ἐστιν ὁ υἱὸς ᵂΔαβίδ;‖
¹ᵗthe ²crowds and said, ²This ¹is the son of David?

24 Οἱ.δὲ Φαρισαῖοι ἀκούσαντᵗς εἶπον, Οὗτος οὐκ.ἐκβάλλει
But the Pharisees having heard said, This [man] casts not out

τὰ δαιμόνια εἰ.μὴ ἐν τῷ Βεελζεβοὺλ ἄρχοντι τῶν δαιμονίων.
the demons except by Beelzebul prince of the demons.

25 Εἰδὼς.δὲ ˣὁ Ἰησοῦς‖ τὰς.ἐνθυμήσεις.αὐτῶν εἶπεν αὐτοῖς,
But ²knowing ¹Jesus their thoughts he said to them,

Πᾶσα βασιλεία μερισθεῖσα καθ᾽ ἑαυτῆς ἐρημοῦται· καὶ
¹Every kingdom divided against itself is brought to desolation, and

πᾶσα πόλις ἢ.οἰκία μερισθεῖσα καθ᾽ ἑαυτῆς οὐ.σταθήσεται.
every city or house divided against itself will not stand.

26 καὶ εἰ ὁ σατανᾶς τὸν σατανᾶν ἐκβάλλει, ἐφ᾽ ἑαυτὸν ἐμε-
And if Satan ²Satan ¹casts ²out, against himself he was

ρίσθη· πῶς οὖν σταθήσεται ἡ.βασιλεία.αὐτοῦ; 27 καὶ εἰ ἐγὼ
divided. How then will stand his kingdom? And if I

ἐν Βεελζεβοὺλ ἐκβάλλω τὰ δαιμόνια οἱ.υἱοὶ.ὑμῶν ἐν τίνι
by Beelzebul cast out the demons, your sons by whom

ἐκβάλλουσιν; διὰ τοῦτο αὐτοὶ ᵘὑμῶν ἔσονται.κριταί.‖
do they cast out? on account of this they of you shall be ·judges.

28 εἰ.δὲ ᵛἐγὼ ἐν πνεύματι θεοῦ‖ ἐκβάλλω τὰ δαιμόνια, ἄρα
But if I by [the] Spirit of God cast out the demons, then

ἔφθασεν ἐφ᾽ ὑμᾶς ἡ βασιλεία τοῦ θεοῦ. 29 ἢ πῶς δύναταί
has come upon you the kingdom of God. Or how is able

τις εἰσελθεῖν εἰς τὴν οἰκίαν τοῦ ἰσχυροῦ καὶ τὰ σκεύη
anyone to enter into the house of the strong [man] and ²goods

αὐτοῦ ᵃδιαρπάσαι,‖ ἐὰν.μὴ πρῶτον δήσῃ τὸν ἰσχυρόν;
¹his to plunder, unless first he bind the strong [man]?

καὶ τότε τὴν.οἰκίαν.αὐτοῦ ᵇδιαρπάσει.‖ 30 ὁ μὴ.ὢν μετ᾽ ἐμοῦ
and then his house he will plunder. He who is not with me

κατ᾽ ἐμοῦ ἐστιν· καὶ ὁ μὴ.συνάγων μετ᾽ ἐμοῦ σκορπίζει.
against me is; and he who gathers not with me scatters.

31 Διὰ τοῦτο λέγω ὑμῖν, Πᾶσα ἁμαρτία καὶ βλασφημία
Because of this I say to you, Every sin and blasphemy

ἀφεθήσεταιᶜ τοῖς ἀνθρώποις· ἡ.δὲ τοῦ.πνεύματος βλασ-
shall be forgiven to men; but the ²concerning ³the ¹Spirit ¹blas-

φημία οὐκ.ἀφ·θήσεται ᵈτοῖς ἀνθρώποις.‖ 32 καὶ ὃς.ᵉἐὰν εἴπῃ
phemy shall not be forgiven to men. And whoever speaks

λόγον κατὰ τοῦ υἱοῦ τοῦ ἀνθρώπου, ἀφεθήσεται αὐτῷ·
a word against the Son of man, it shall be forgiven him;

ὃς.δ᾽.ἂν εἴπῃ κατὰ τοῦ πνεύματος τοῦ ἁγίου, ᶠοὐκ.ἀφε-
but whoever speaks against the Spirit the Holy, it shall not be

θήσεται‖ αὐτῷ, οὔτε ἐν τούτῳ τῷ αἰῶνι οὔτε ἐν τῷ μέλλον-
forgiven him, neither in this ·age nor in the coming

τι. 33 Ἢ ποιήσατε τὸ δένδρον καλὸν καὶ τὸν καρπὸν
[one]. Either make the tree good and ²fruit

ʳ προσήνεγκαν they brought L. ˢ δαιμονιζόμενον τυφλὸν καὶ κωφὸν L. ᵗ — τυφλὸν καὶ
LTTrA. ᵛ — καὶ LTTrA. ᵂ Δαυὶδ GW; Δαυεὶδ LTTrA. ˣ — ὁ Ἰησοῦς LTTrA. ʸ κριταί
ἔσονται ὑμῶν LTTrA. ᶻ ἐν πνεύματι θεοῦ ἐγὼ GLTTrAW. ᵃ ἁρπάσαι to seize upon LTTrA.
ᵇ ἁρπάσει he will seize upon L; διαρπάσῃ he might plunder T. ᶜ + [ὑμῖν] to you A.
ᵈ — τοῖς ἀνθρώποις LTTr[A]. ᵉ ἐὰν LTTrAW. ᶠ οὐ μὴ ἀφεθῇ in nowise shall it be forgiven L.

22 Then was brought unto him one possessed with a devil, blind, and dumb: and he healed him, insomuch that the blind and dumb both spake and saw. 23 And all the people were amazed, and said, Is not this the Son of David? 24 But when the Pharisees heard it, they said, This fellow doth not cast out devils, but by Beelzebub the prince of the devils. 25 And Jesus knew their thoughts, and said unto them, Every kingdom divided against itself is brought to desolation; and every city or house divided against itself shall not stand: 26 And if Satan cast out Satan, he is divided against himself; how shall then his kingdom stand? 27 And if I by Beelzebub cast out devils, by whom do your children cast them out? therefore they shall be your judges. 28 But if I cast out devils by the Spirit of God, then the kingdom of God is come unto you. 29 Or else how can one enter into a strong man's house, and spoil his goods, except he first bind the strong man? and then he will spoil his house. 30 He that is not with me is against me; and he that gathereth not with me scattereth abroad. 31 Wherefore I say unto you, All manner of sin and blasphemy shall be forgiven unto men: but the blasphemy against the Holy Ghost shall not be forgiven unto men. 32 And whosoever speaketh a word against the Son of man, it shall be forgiven him: but whosoever speaketh against the Holy Ghost, it shall not be forgiven him, neither in this world, neither in the world to come. 33 Either make the tree good, and his fruit

good; or else make the tree corrupt, and his fruit corrupt: for the tree is known by his fruit. 34 O generation of vipers, how can ye, being evil, speak good things? for out of the abundance of the heart the mouth speaketh. 35 A good man out of the good treasure of the heart bringeth forth good things: and an evil man out of the evil treasure bringeth forth evil things. 36 But I say unto you, That every idle word that men shall speak, they shall give account thereof in the day of judgment. 37 For by thy words thou shalt be justified, and by thy words thou shalt be condemned.

αὐτοῦ καλόν, ἢ ποιήσατε τὸ δένδρον σαπρον καὶ τὸν καρπὸν
[1]its good, or make the tree corrupt and [2]fruit

αὐτοῦ σαπρόν· ἐκ.γὰρ τοῦ καρποῦ τὸ.δενδρον γινώσκεται.
[1]its corrupt: for from the fruit the tree is known.

34 Γεννήματα ἐχιδνῶν, πῶς δύνασθε ἀγαθὰ λαλεῖν, πονηροὶ
Offspring of vipers, how are ye able good things to speak, [2]wicked

ὄντες; ἐκ.γὰρ τοῦ περισσεύματος τῆς καρδίας τὸ στόμα
[1]being? for out of the abundance of the heart the mouth

λαλεῖ. 35 ὁ ἀγαθὸς ἄνθρωπος ἐκ τοῦ ἀγαθοῦ θησαυροῦ
speaks. The good man out of the good treasure

ᵍτῆς καρδίας‖ ἐκβάλλει ʰτὰ‖ ἀγαθά· καὶ ὁ πονηρὸς ἄνθρω-
of the heart puts forth the good things; and the wicked man

πος ἐκ τοῦ πονηροῦ θησαυροῦ ἐκβάλλει πονηρά. 36 λέγω.δὲ
out of the wicked treasure puts forth wicked things. But I say

ὑμῖν, ὅτι πᾶν ῥῆμα ἀργὸν ὃ.ἰἐὰν‖ ᵏλαλήσωσιν‖ οἱ ἄνθρωποι,
to you, that every [2]word [1]idle whatsoever [2]may [3]speak [1]men,

ἀποδώσουσιν περὶ αὐτοῦ λόγον ἐν ἡμέρᾳ κρίσεως. 37 ἐκ
they shall render of it an account in day of judgment. [2]By

γὰρ τῶν.λόγων.σου δικαιωθήσῃ, καὶ ἐκ τῶν.λόγων.σου
[1]for thy words thou shalt be justified, and by thy words

καταδικασθήσῃ.
thou shalt be condemned.

38 Then certain of the scribes and of the Pharisees answered, saying, Master, we would see a sign from thee. 39 But he answered and said unto them, An evil and adulterous generation seeketh after a sign; and there shall no sign be given to it, but the sign of the prophet Jonas: 40 for as Jonas was three days and three nights in the whale's belly; so shall the Son of man be three days and three nights in the heart of the earth. 41 The men of Nineveh shall rise in judgment with this generation, and shall condemn it: because they repented at the preaching of Jonas; and, behold, a greater than Jonas is here. 42 The queen of the south shall rise up in the judgment with this generation, and shall condemn it: for she came from the uttermost parts of the earth to hear the wisdom of Solomon; and, behold, a greater than Solomon is here. 43 When the unclean spirit is gone out of a man, he walketh through dry places, seeking rest, and findeth none. 44 Then he saith, I will return

38 Τότε ἀπεκρίθησάνˡ τινες τῶν γραμματέων ᵐκαὶ Φαρι-
Then answered some of the scribes and Phari-

σαίων,‖ λέγοντες, Διδάσκαλε, θέλομεν ἀπὸ σοῦ σημεῖον ἰδεῖν·
sees, saying, Teacher, we wish from thee a sign to see.

39 Ὁ.δὲ ἀποκριθεὶς εἶπεν αὐτοῖς, Γενεὰ πονηρὰ καὶ μοι-
But he answering said to them, A generation wicked and adul-

χαλὶς σημεῖον ἐπιζητεῖ· καὶ σημεῖον οὐ.δοθήσεται αὐτῇ,
terous a sign seeks for, and a sign shall not be given to it,

εἰ.μὴ τὸ σημεῖον Ἰωνᾶ τοῦ προφήτου. 40 ὥσπερ.γὰρ ἦν Ἰωνᾶς
except the sign of Jonas the prophet. For even as was Jonas

ἐν τῇ κοιλίᾳ τοῦ κήτους τρεῖς ἡμέρας καὶ τρεῖς νύκτας, οὕτως
in the belly of the great fish three days and three nights, thus

ἔσται ὁ υἱὸς τοῦ ἀνθρώπου ἐν τῇ καρδίᾳ τῆς γῆς τρεῖς
shall be the Son of man in the heart of the earth three

ἡμέρας καὶ τρεῖς νύκτας. 41 Ἄνδρες ⁿΝινευῖται‖ ἀναστήσονται
days and three nights. Men Ninevites shall stand up

ἐν τῇ κρίσει μετὰ τῆς.γενεᾶς.ταύτης, καὶ κατακρινοῦσιν αὐτήν·
in the judgment with this generation, and shall condemn it;

ὅτι μετενόησαν εἰς τὸ κήρυγμα Ἰωνᾶ· καὶ ἰδού, πλεῖον
for they repented at the proclamation of Jonas; and behold, more

Ἰωνᾶ ὧδε. 42 βασίλισσα νότου ἐγερθήσεται ἐν τῇ κρίσει
than Jonas here. A queen of[the]south shall rise up in the judgment

μετὰ τῆς.γενεᾶς.ταύτης, καὶ κατακρινεῖ αὐτήν· ὅτι ἦλθεν
with this generation, and shall condemn it; for she came

ἐκ τῶν περάτων τῆς γῆς ἀκοῦσαι τὴν σοφίαν °Σολομῶντος·‖
from the ends of the earth to hear the wisdom of Solomon;

καὶ ἰδού, πλεῖον °Σολομῶντος‖ ὧδε. 43 Ὅταν.δὲ τὸ ἀκάθαρτον
and behold, more than Solomon here. But when the unclean

πνεῦμα ἐξέλθῃ ἀπὸ τοῦ ἀνθρώπου, διέρχεται δι' ἀνύδρων
spirit is gone out from the man, he goes through waterless

τόπων, ζητοῦν ἀνάπαυσιν, καὶ οὐχ.εὑρίσκει. 44 τότε λέγει,
places, seeking rest, and finds not [it]. Then he says,

ᵍ — τῆς καρδίας GLTTrAW.   ʰ — τὰ LTrW.   ⁱ — ἐὰν (read which) LTTrA.   ᵏ λαλήσωσιν
shall speak TTrA.   ˡ + αὐτῷ him LTTrA.   ᵐ — καὶ Φαρισαίων L.   ⁿ Νινευεῖται TTrA.
° Σολομῶνος GLTTrAW.

ᑫἘπιστρέψω εἰς τὸν.οἶκόν.μου,‖ ὅθεν ἐξῆλθον· καὶ ἐλθὸν
I will return to my house, whence I came out. And having come

εὑρίσκει σχολάζοντα, ʳσεσαρωμένον καὶ κεκοσμημένον. 45 τότε
he finds [it] unoccupied,. swept and adorned. Then

πορεύεται καὶ παραλαμβάνει μεθ' ἑαυτοῦ ἑπτὰ ἕτερα πνεύματα
he goes and takes with himself seven other spirits

πονηρότερα ἑαυτοῦ, καὶ εἰσελθόντα κατοικεῖ ἐκεῖ· καὶ γίνεται
more wicked than himself and entering in they dwell there; and becomes

τὰ ἔσχατα τοῦ.ἀνθρώπου.ἐκείνου χείρονα τῶν πρώτων. οὕτως
the last of that man worse than the first. Thus

ἔσται καὶ τῇ.γενεᾷ.ταύτῃ τῇ πονηρᾷ.
it shall be also to this generation the wicked.

into my house from whence I came out; and when he is come, he findeth it empty, swept, and garnished. 45 Then goeth he, and taketh with himself seven other spirits more wicked than himself, and they enter in and dwell there: and the last state of that man is worse than the first. Even so shall it be also unto this wicked generation.

46 Ἔτι.ˢδὲ‖ αὐτοῦ λαλοῦντος τοῖς ὄχλοις, ἰδού, ἡ μήτηρ
But while yet he was speaking to the crowds, behold, [his] mother

καὶ οἱ.ἀδελφοὶ.ᵗαὐτοῦ‖ εἱστήκεισαν ἔξω, ζητοῦντες αὐτῷ λα-
and his brethren were standing without, seeking to him to

λῆσαι. ᵛ47 εἶπεν.δέ τις αὐτῷ, Ἰδού, ἡ.μήτηρ.σου καὶ οἱ ἀδελφοί
speak. Then said one to him, Behold, thy mother and brethren

σου ἔξω ἑστήκασιν, ζητοῦντές σοι.λαλῆσαι.‖ 48 Ὁ.δὲ ἀπο-
thy without are standing, seeking to thee to speak. But he an-

κριθεὶς εἶπεν τῷ ʷεἰπόντι‖ αὐτῷ, Τίς ἐστιν ἡ.μήτηρ.μου;
swering said to him who spoke to him, Who is my mother?

καὶ τίνες εἰσὶν οἱ ἀδελφοί.μου; 49 Καὶ ἐκτείνας τὴν χεῖρα
and who are my brethren? And stretching out hand

ˣαὐτοῦ‖ ἐπὶ τοὺς.μαθητὰς.αὐτοῦ εἶπεν, Ἰδού, ἡ.μήτηρ.μου καὶ
his to his disciples he said, Behold, my mother and

οἱ.ἀδελφοί.μου. 50 ὅστις.γὰρ ἂν ʸποιήσῃ‖ τὸ θέλημα τοῦ
my brethren. For whosoever shall do the will of

πατρός.μου τοῦ ἐν οὐρανοῖς, αὐτός μου ἀδελφὸς καὶ
my Father who [is] in [the] heavens, he my brother and

ἀδελφὴ καὶ μήτηρ ἐστίν.
sister and mother is.

46 While he yet talked to the people, behold, his mother and his brethren stood without, desiring to speak with him. 47 Then one said unto him, Behold, thy mother and thy brethren stand without, desiring to speak with thee. 48 But he answered and said unto him that told him, Who is my mother? and who are my brethren? 49 And he stretched forth his hand toward his disciples, and said, Behold, my mother and my brethren! 50 For whosoever shall do the will of my Father which is in heaven, the same is my brother, and sister, and mother.

13 Ἐν.ˣδὲ‖ τῇ.ἡμέρᾳ.ἐκείνῃ ἐξελθὼν ὁ Ἰησοῦς ᵃἀπὸ‖
And in that day having gone forth Jesus from

τῆς οἰκίας ἐκάθητο παρὰ τὴν θάλασσαν· 2 καὶ συνήχθησαν
the house sat down by the sea. And were gathered together

πρὸς αὐτὸν ὄχλοι πολλοί, ὥστε αὐτὸν εἰς ᵇτὸ‖ πλοῖον ἐμ-
to him crowds great, so that he into the ship having

βάντα καθῆσθαι, καὶ πᾶς ὁ ὄχλος ἐπὶ τὸν αἰγιαλὸν εἱστήκει.
entered sat down, and all the crowd on the shore stood.

3 καὶ ἐλάλησεν αὐτοῖς πολλὰ ἐν παραβολαῖς, λέγων, Ἰδού,
And he spoke to them many things in parables, saying, Behold,

ἐξῆλθεν ὁ σπείρων τοῦ σπείρειν. 4 καὶ ἐν.τῷ.σπείρειν.αὐτὸν
went out the sower to sow. And as he sowed

ἃ.μὲν ἔπεσεν παρὰ τὴν ὁδόν, καὶ ᶜἦλθεν‖ τὰ πετεινὰ ᵈκαὶ‖
some fell by the way, and came the birds and

κατέφαγεν αὐτά. 5 ἄλλα.δὲ ἔπεσεν ἐπὶ τὰ πετρώδη, ὅπου
devoured them. And some fell upon the rocky places, where

οὐκ.εἶχεν γῆν πολλήν, καὶ εὐθέως ἐξανέτειλεν διὰ τὸ μὴ
they had not earth much, and immediately sprang up because of not

ἔχειν βάθος ᵉ γῆς· 6 ἡλίου.δὲ ἀνατείλαντος ἐκαυματίσθη,
having depth of earth; and [the] sun having risen they were scorched,

XIII. The same day went Jesus out of the house, and sat by the sea side. 2 And great multitudes were gathered together unto him, so that he went into a ship, and sat; and the whole multitude stood on the shore. 3 And he spake many things unto them in parables, saying, Behold, a sower went forth to sow; 4 and when he sowed, some seeds fell by the way side, and the fowls came and devoured them up: 5 some fell upon stony places, where they had not much earth: and forthwith they sprung up, because they had no deepness of earth: 6 and when the sun was up, they were scorched; and because

---

ᑫ εἰς τὸν οἶκόν μου ἐπιστρέψω LTTrA. ʳ + καὶ and [L]T. ˢ — δὲ but LTTrA. ᵗ [αὐτοῦ] L. ᵛ Verse 47 in [ ] T. ʷ λέγοντι LTTrA. ˣ — αὐτοῦ (read [his] hand) T. ʸ ποιῇ A. ᶻ — δὲ and LTTrA. ᵃ ἐκ out of LT; — ἀπὸ (read ἐξελ. having gone out of)Tr. ᵇ — τὸ (read a ship) LTTrA. ᶜ ἦλθον LTr; ἐλθόντα having come A. ᵈ — καὶ A. ᵉ + τῆς L.

44

they had no root, they withered away. 7 And some fell among thorns ; and the thorns sprung up, and choked them : 8 but other fell into good ground, and brought forth fruit, some an hundredfold, some sixtyfold, some thirtyfold. 9 Who hath ears to hear, let him hear.

10 And the disciples came, and said unto him, Why speakest thou unto them in parables ? 11 He answered and said unto them, Because it is given unto you to know the mysteries of the kingdom of heaven, but to them it is not given. 12 For whosoever hath, to him shall be given, and he shall have more abundance : but whosoever hath not, from him shall be taken away even that he hath. 13 Therefore speak I to them in parables : because they seeing see not ; and hearing they hear not, neither do they understand. 14 And in them is fulfilled the prophecy of Esaias, which saith, By hearing ye shall hear, and shall not understand ; and seeing ye shall see, and shall not perceive : 15 for this people's heart is waxed gross, and *their* ears are dull of hearing, and their eyes they have closed ; lest at any time they should see with *their* eyes, and hear with *their* ears, and should understand with *their* heart, and should be converted, and I should heal them. 16 But blessed *are* your eyes, for they see : and your ears, for they hear. 17 For verily I say unto you, That many prophets and righteous *men* have desired to see *those things* which ye see, and have not seen *them;* and to hear *those things* which ye hear, and have not heard *them.*

18 Hear ye therefore the parable of the sower. 19 When any one heareth the word of the kingdom, and

καὶ διὰ τὸ μὴ ἔχειν ῥίζαν ἐξηράνθη. 7 ἄλλα δὲ ἔπεσεν ἐπὶ
and because of not having root were dried up. And some fell upon

τὰς ἀκάνθας, καὶ ἀνέβησαν αἱ ἄκανθαι καὶ ᶠἀπέπνιξαν‖ αὐτά.
the thorns, and ³grew ⁴up ¹the ²thorns and choked them.

8 ἄλλα δὲ ἔπεσεν ἐπὶ τὴν γῆν τὴν καλήν, καὶ ἐδίδου καρπόν,
And some fell upon the ground the good, and yielded fruit,

ὃ μὲν ἑκατόν, ὃ δὲ ἑξήκοντα, ὃ δὲ τριάκοντα. 9 ὁ ἔχων
one a hundred, another sixty, another thirty. He that has

ὦτα ᵍἀκούειν‖ ἀκουέτω.
ears to hear let him hear.

10 Καὶ προσελθόντες οἱ μαθηταὶʰ ⁱεἶπονⁿ αὐτῷ, ᵏΔιατί‖
And ³having ⁴come ⁵to[ᶜhim] ¹the ²disciples said to him, Why

ἐν παραβολαῖς λαλεῖς αὐτοῖς; 11 Ὁ δὲ ἀποκριθεὶς εἶπεν
in parables speakest thou to them? And he answering said

ˡαὐτοῖς,‖ Ὅτι ὑμῖν δέδοται γνῶναι τὰ μυστήρια τῆς
to them, Because to you it has been given to know the mysteries of the

βασιλείας τῶν οὐρανῶν, ἐκείνοις δὲ οὐ δέδοται. 12 ὅστις
kingdom of the heavens, but to them it has not been given. ²Whosoever

γὰρ ἔχει, δοθήσεται αὐτῷ, καὶ περισσευθήσεται· ὅστις δὲ
¹for has, ³shall ⁴be ⁵given ¹to ²him, and he shall be in abundance ; but whosoever

οὐκ ἔχει, καὶ ὃ ἔχει ἀρθήσεται ἀπ' αὐτοῦ. 13 διὰ τοῦτο
has not, even what he has shall be taken away from him. Because of this

ἐν παραβολαῖς αὐτοῖς λαλῶ, ὅτι βλέποντες οὐ βλέπουσιν,
in parables to them I speak, because seeing they see not,

καὶ ἀκούοντες οὐκ ἀκούουσιν, οὐδὲ συνιοῦσιν. 14 καὶ ἀνα-
and hearing they hear not, nor do they understand. And ³is

πληροῦται ᵐἐπ'‖ αὐτοῖς ἡ προφητεία Ἡσαΐου, ἡ λέγουσα,
⁴filled ⁵up ¹in ²them the prophecy of Esaias, which says,

Ἀκοῇ ἀκούσετε, καὶ οὐ μὴ συνῆτε· καὶ βλέποντες βλέ-
In hearing ye shall hear, and in no wise understand ; and seeing ye shall

ψετε, καὶ οὐ μὴ ἴδητε. 15 ἐπαχύνθη γὰρ ἡ καρδία τοῦ
see, and in no wise perceive : for ⁶has ⁷grown ⁸fat the ²heart

λαοῦ τούτου, καὶ τοῖς ὠσὶνⁿ βαρέως ἤκουσαν, καὶ τοὺς
³of ⁴this ⁵people, and with the ears heavily they have heard, and

ὀφθαλμοὺς αὐτῶν ἐκάμμυσαν· μήποτε ἴδωσιν τοῖς ὀφ-
their eyes they have closed ; lest they should see with the

θαλμοῖς, καὶ τοῖς ὠσὶν ἀκούσωσιν, καὶ τῇ καρδίᾳ συν-
eyes, and with the ears they should hear, and with the heart they should

ῶσιν, καὶ ἐπιστρέψωσιν καὶ °ἰάσωμαι‖ αὐτούς. 16 Ὑμῶν δὲ
understand, and should be converted, and I should heal them. But of you

μακάριοι οἱ ὀφθαλμοί, ὅτι βλέπουσιν· καὶ τὰ ὦτα ᴾὑμῶν,‖
blessed [are] the eyes, because they see ; and the ears ᴾof you,

ὅτι ᑫἀκούει.‖ 17 ἀμὴν γὰρ‖ λέγω ὑμῖν, ὅτι πολλοὶ προφῆται
because they hear. For verily I say to you, that many prophets

καὶ δίκαιοι ἐπεθύμησαν ἰδεῖν ἃ βλέπετε, καὶ οὐκ ˢεἶδον·‖
and righteous [men] desired to see what ye see, and ²not ¹saw ;

καὶ ἀκοῦσαι ἃ ἀκούετε, καὶ οὐκ ἤκουσαν.
and to hear what ye hear, and heard not.

18 Ὑμεῖς οὖν ἀκούσατε τὴν παραβολὴν τοῦ ᵗσπείροντος‖
²Ye ³therefore ¹hear the parable of the sower.

19 Παντὸς ἀκούοντος τὸν λόγον τῆς βασιλείας καὶ μὴ
When any one hears the word of the kingdom and not [it]

ᶠ ἔπνιξαν T.   ᵍ — ἀκούειν T[Tr]A.   ʰ + αὐτοῦ (*read* his disciples) L.   ⁱ εἶπαν TTrA.
ᵏ διὰ τί LTTrA.   ˡ — αὐτοῖς T.   ᵐ — ἐπ' (*read* αὐτοῖς in them) GLTTrAW.   ⁿ + [αὐτῶν] (*read*
their ears) L.   ° ἰάσομαι I shall heal LTTrA.   ᴾ — ὑμῶν L[Tr A].   ᑫ ἀκούουσιν LTTrA.
ʳ — γὰρ for T.   ˢ εἶδαν LTr ; ἴδαν T.   ᵗ σπείραντος LTTrA.

συνιέντος, ἔρχεται ὁ πονηρὸς καὶ ἁρπάζει τὸ ἐσπαρμένον
understands,   ¹comes ¹the ²wicked³one and catches away that which was sown

ἐν τῇ καρδίᾳ αὐτοῦ· οὗτός ἐστιν ὁ παρὰ τὴν ὁδὸν σπαρείς.
in   his heart.   This is he who by   the   way was sown.

20 Ὁ δὲ ἐπὶ τὰ πετρώδη σπαρείς, οὗτός ἐστιν ὁ τὸν λόγον
And he who upon the rocky places was sown, this is he who the · word

ἀκούων καὶ εὐθὺς μετὰ χαρᾶς λαμβάνων αὐτόν· 21 οὐκ
hears and immediately with joy receives it ; ²no

ἔχει δὲ ῥίζαν ἐν ἑαυτῷ, ἀλλὰ πρόσκαιρός ἐστιν· γενομένης δὲ
²has ¹but root in himself, but temporary is ; but ⁴having ⁵risen

θλίψεως ἢ διωγμοῦ διὰ τὸν λόγον, εὐθὺς σκαν-
¹tribulation ²or ³persecution on account of the word, immediately. ‾ he is

δαλίζεται. 22 Ὁ δὲ εἰς τὰς ἀκάνθας σπαρείς, οὗτός ἐστιν
offended.   And he who among the thorns was sown, this is

ὁ τὸν λόγον ἀκούων, καὶ ἡ μέριμνα τοῦ αἰῶνος τούτου
he who the word hears, and the care of this life

καὶ ἡ ἀπάτη τοῦ πλούτου "συμπνίγει" τὸν λόγον, καὶ ἄκαρπος
and the deceit of riches choke the . word, and unfruitful

γίνεται. 23 Ὁ δὲ ἐπὶ τὴν ˣγῆν τὴν καλὴν" σπαρείς, οὗτός
it becomes. But he who on the ground the good was sown, this

ἐστιν ὁ τὸν λόγον ἀκούων καὶ ˀσυνιών· ⁱ ὃς δὴ καρ-
is he who the word hears and understands ; who indeed brings

ποφορεῖ, καὶ ποιεῖ ᶻὃ" μὲν ἑκατόν, ᶻὃ" δὲ ἑξήκοντα, ᶻὃ" δὲ
forth fruit, and produces one a hundred, another sixty, another

τριάκοντα.
thirty.

24 Ἄλλην παραβολὴν παρέθηκεν αὐτοῖς, λέγων, Ὡμοιώ-
Another parable put he before them, saying, ᵃhas ᵇbecome

θη ἡ βασιλεία τῶν οὐρανῶν ἀνθρώπῳ ᵃσπείροντι" καλὸν
ᵃlike ¹the ²kingdom ³of ⁴the ⁵heavens to a man sowing good

σπέρμα ἐν τῷ ἀγρῷ αὐτοῦ· 25 ἐν δὲ τῷ καθεύδειν τοὺς ἀνθρώ-
seed in his field ; but while ²slept ¹the   ²men

πους ἦλθεν αὐτοῦ ὁ ἐχθρὸς καὶ ᵇἔσπειρεν" ζιζάνια ἀνὰ μέσον
came his enemy and sowed darnel in[the] midst

τοῦ σίτου, καὶ ἀπῆλθεν. 26 ὅτε δὲ ἐβλάστησεν ὁ χόρτος,
of the wheat, and went away. And when ³sprouted ¹the ²blade,

καὶ καρπὸν ἐποίησεν, τότε ἐφάνη καὶ τὰ ζιζάνια. 27 προσελ-
and fruit produced, then appeared also the darnel. ²Having ³come

θόντες δὲ οἱ δοῦλοι τοῦ οἰκοδεσπότου εἶπον αὐτῷ, Κύριε,
⁴to [⁵him] ¹and the bondmen of the master of the house¹ said to him, Sir,

οὐχὶ καλὸν σπέρμα ᶜἔσπειρας" ἐν τῷ σῷ ἀγρῷ; πόθεν οὖν
²not ³good ⁴seed ¹didst ²thou ⁴sow in thy field? whence then

ἔχει ᵈτὰ" ζιζάνια; 28 Ὁ δὲ ἔφη αὐτοῖς, Ἐχθρὸς ἄνθρωπος
has it the darnel? And he said to them, ³an ⁴enemy ¹a ²man

τοῦτο ἐποίησεν. οἱ δὲ ᵉδοῦλοι" ᶠεἶπον αὐτῷ," Θέλεις οὖν
⁵this · ⁴did. And the bondmen said to him, Wilt thou then

ἀπελθόντες συλλέξωμεν αὐτά; 29 Ὁ δὲ ᵍἔφη, " Οὔ·
[that] having gone forth we should gather them? But he said, No ;

μήποτε συλλέγοντες τὰ ζιζάνια, ἐκριζώσητε ἅμα αὐτοῖς τὸν
lest gathering the darnel, ye should uproot with them the

σῖτον. 30 ἄφετε συναυξάνεσθαι ἀμφότερα ʰμέχρι" τοῦ θερισμοῦ·
wheat. Suffer to grow together both until the harvest ;

---

understandeth *it* not, then cometh the wicked *one*, and catcheth away that which was sown in his heart. This is he which received the seed by the way side. 20 But he that received the seed into stony places, the same is he that heareth the word, and anon with joy receiveth it ; 21 yet hath he not root in himself, but dureth for a while : for when tribulation or persecution ariseth because of the word, by and by he is offended. 22 He also that received seed among the thorns is he that heareth the word ; and the care of this world, and the deceitfulness of riches, choke the word, and he becometh unfruitful. 23 But he that received seed into the good ground is he that heareth the word, and understandeth *it;* which also beareth fruit, and · bringeth forth, some an hundredfold, some sixty, some thirty.

24 Another parable put he forth unto them, saying, The kingdom of heaven is likened unto a man which sowed good seed in his field : 25 but while men slept, his enemy came and sowed tares among the wheat, and went his way. 26 But when the blade was sprung up, and brought forth fruit, then appeared the tares also. 27 So the servants of the householder came and said unto him, Sir, didst not thou sow good seed in thy field? from whence then hath it tares? 28 He said unto them, An enemy hath done this. The servants said unto him, Wilt thou then that we go and gather them up? 29 But he said, Nay ; lest while ye gather up the tares, ye root up also the wheat with them. 30 Let both grow together until the harvest : and in

---

the time of harvest I will say to the reapers, Gather ye together first the tares, and bind them in bundles to burn them: but gather the wheat into my barn.

καὶ ἐν ¹τῷ‖ καιρῷ τοῦ θερισμοῦ ἐρῶ τοῖς θερισταῖς, Συλ-
and in the time of the harvest I will say to the harvest men, Ga-
λέξατε πρῶτον τὰ ζιζάνια, καὶ δήσατε αὐτὰ ²εἰς‖ δέσμας
ther first the darnel, and bind them into bundles
πρὸς.τὸ.κατακαῦσαι αὐτά· τὸν.δὲ σῖτον ᵏσυναγάγετε‖ εἰς τὴν
to burn them; but the wheat bring together into
ἀποθήκην.μου.
my granary.

31 Another parable put he forth unto them, saying, The kingdom of heaven is like to a grain of mustard seed, which a man took, and sowed in his field : 32 which indeed is the least of all seeds : but when it is grown, it is the greatest among herbs, and becometh a tree, so that the birds of the air come and lodge in the branches thereof.

31 Ἄλλην παραβολὴν παρέθηκεν αὐτοῖς, λέγων, Ὁμοία
Another parable put he before them, saying, Like
ἐστὶν ἡ βασιλεία τῶν οὐρανῶν κόκκῳ σινάπεως, ὃν λα-
is the kingdom of the heavens to a grain of mustard, which having
βὼν ἄνθρωπος ἔσπειρεν ἐν τῷ.ἀγρῷ.αὐτοῦ· 32 ὃ μικρότερον
taken, a man sowed in his field ; which less
μέν ἐστιν πάντων τῶν σπερμάτων, ὅταν.δὲ αὐξηθῇ
indeed is than all the seeds, but when it be grown,
μεῖζον τῶν λαχάνων ἐστίν. καὶ γίνεται δένδρον, ὥστε
greater than the herbs is, and becomes a tree, so that
ἐλθεῖν τὰ πετεινὰ τοῦ οὐρανοῦ καὶ ¹κατασκηνοῦν‖ ἐν τοῖς
come the birds of the heaven and roost in the
κλάδοις αὐτοῦ.
branches of it.

33 Another parable spake he unto them ; The kingdom of heaven is like unto leaven, which a woman took, and hid in three measures of meal, till the whole was leavened.

33 Ἄλλην παραβολὴν ἐλάλησεν αὐτοῖς, Ὁμοία ἐστὶν ἡ
Another parable spoke he to them, Like is the
βασιλεία τῶν οὐρανῶν ζύμῃ, ἣν λαβοῦσα γυνὴ ἐνέκρυψεν
kingdom of the heavens to leaven, which having taken, a woman hid
εἰς ἀλεύρου σάτα τρία, ἕως.οὗ ἐζυμώθη ὅλον.
in ³of ⁴meal ²seahs ¹three, until ²was ³leavened ¹all.

34 All these things spake Jesus unto the multitude in parables ; and without a parable spake he not unto them : 35 that it might be fulfilled which was spoken by the prophet, saying, I will open my mouth in parables ; I will utter things which have been kept secret from the foundation of the world.

34 Ταῦτα πάντα ἐλάλησεν ὁ Ἰησοῦς ἐν παραβολαῖς τοῖς
²These ³things ¹all spoke Jesus in parables to the
ὄχλοις, καὶ χωρὶς παραβολῆς ᵐοὐκ‖ ἐλάλει αὐτοῖς· 35 ὅπως
crowds, and without a parable ³not ¹he ²spoke to them ; so that
πληρωθῇ τὸ ῥηθὲν διὰ τοῦ προφήτουⁿ, λέγοντος,
might be fulfilled that which was spoken by the prophet, saying,
Ἀνοίξω ἐν παραβολαῖς τὸ.στόμα.μου· ἐρεύξομαι κεκρυμμένα
I will open in parables my mouth : I will utter things hidden
ἀπὸ καταβολῆς °κόσμου.‖
from [the] foundation of [the] world.

36 Τότε ἀφεὶς τοὺς ὄχλους, ἦλθεν εἰς τὴν οἰκίαν
Then having dismissed the crowds, ²went ³into ⁴the ⁵house

36 Then Jesus sent the multitude away, and went into the house : and his disciples came unto him, saying, Declare unto us the parable of the tares of the field. 37 He answered and said unto them, He that soweth the good seed is the Son of man ; 38 the field is the world ; the good seed are the children of the kingdom ; but the tares are the children of the wicked one ; 39 the enemy that sowed them is the devil ; the harvest is the end of

ᴾὁ Ἰησοῦς·‖ καὶ �qπροσῆλθον‖ αὐτῷ οἱ.μαθηταὶ.αὐτοῦ, λέγοντες,
¹Jesus ; and came to him his disciples, saying,
ʳΦράσον‖ ἡμῖν τὴν παραβολὴν τῶν ζιζανίων τοῦ ἀγροῦ.
Expound to us the parable of the darnel of the field.
37 Ὁ.δὲ ἀποκριθεὶς εἶπεν ˢαὐτοῖς,‖ Ὁ σπείρων τὸ καλὸν
And he answering said to them, He who sows the good
σπέρμα ἐστὶν ὁ υἱὸς τοῦ ἀνθρώπου· 38 ὁ.δὲ ἀγρός ἐστιν ὁ
seed is the Son of man ; and the field is the
κόσμος· τὸ.δὲ καλὸν σπέρμα, οὗτοί εἰσιν οἱ υἱοὶ τῆς βασιλείας·
world ; and the good seed, these are the sons of the kingdom ;
τὰ.δὲ ζιζάνιά εἰσιν οἱ υἱοὶ τοῦ πονηροῦ· 39 ὁ.δὲ ἐχθρὸς
but the darnel are the sons of the evil [one]; and the enemy
ᵗὁ σπείρας αὐτά ἐστιν‖ ὁ διάβολος· ὁ.δὲ θερισμὸς συν-
who sowed them is the devil ; and the harvest [the] com-

i — τῷ GLTTrAW.   j — εἰς (read [in]) [Tr]A.   ᵏ συνάγετε LTr.   ¹ κατασκηνοῖν LTTrA.   ᵐοὐδὲν
nothing LTTrA.   ⁿ + Ἡσαίου Isaiah T.   ° — κόσμου LTTrA.   ᴾ — ὁ Ἰησοῦς (read he went) LTTrA.
q προσῆλθαν LTr.   ʳ διασάφησον explain LTr.   ˢ — αὐτοῖς LTTrA.   ᵗ ἐστιν ὁ.σπείρας αὐτὰ L.

τέλεια ᵛτοῦ‖ αἰῶνός ἐστιν· οἱ.δὲ θερισταὶ ἄγγελοί εἰσιν.
pletion　of the　age　is,　and the harvest men　angels　are.

40 ὥσπερ οὖν συλλέγεται τὰ ζιζάνια, καὶ πυρὶ ʷκατα-
As　therefore　is gathered　the　darnel,　and in fire　is con-

καίεται,‖ οὕτως ἔσται· ἐν τῇ συντελείᾳ τοῦ.αἰῶνος.ˣτούτου.‖
sumed,　thus　it shall be in the　completion　of this age.

41 ἀποστελεῖ ὁ υἱὸς τοῦ ἀνθρώπου τοὺς ἀγγέλους·αὐτοῦ,
ˢshall ⁶send ⁷forth ¹the ²Son　³of ⁴man　his angels,

καὶ συλλέξουσιν ἐκ τῆς.βασιλείας.αὐτοῦ πάντα τὰ σκάνδαλα
and they shall gather out of　his kingdom　all　the　offences

καὶ τοὺς ποιοῦντας τὴν ἀνομίαν, 42 καὶ βαλοῦσιν αὐτοὺς
and those who　practise　lawlessness,　and they shall cast them

εἰς τὴν κάμινον τοῦ πυρός· ἐκεῖ ἔσται ὁ κλαυθμὸς καὶ ὁ
into the　furnace　of the fire:　there shall be the　weeping　and the

βρυγμὸς τῶν ὀδόντων. 43 τότε οἱ δίκαιοι ἐκλάμψουσιν ὡς
gnashing　of the　teeth.　Then the righteous　shall shine forth as

ὁ ἥλιος ἐν τῇ βασιλείᾳ τοῦ.πατρὸς.αὐτῶν. Ὁ ἔχων ὦτα
the sun　in the kingdom　of their Father.　He that has ears

ᵞἀκού·ιν‖ ἀκουέτω.
to hear　let him hear.

44 ᶻΠάλιν‖ ὁμοία ἐστὶν ἡ βασιλεία τῶν οὐρανῶν θησαυρῷ
Again　like　is　the kingdom of the heavens　to treasure

ᶜᶜκρυμμένῳ ἐν τῷ ἀγρῷ, ὃν εὑρὼν ἄνθρωπος ἔκρυψεν,
hid　in the　field,　which ³having ⁴found ¹a ²man　hid,

καὶ ἀπὸ τῆς χαρᾶς αὐτοῦ ὑπάγει καὶ ᵃπάντα ὅσα ἔχει
and for the　joy　of it　goes　and all things as many as he has

πωλεῖ,‖ καὶ ἀγοράζει τὸν.ἀγρὸν.ἐκεῖνον.
he sells,　and　buys　that field.

45 Πάλιν ὁμοία ἐστὶν ἡ βασιλεία τῶν οὐρανῶν ἀνθρώπῳ
Again　like　is　the kingdom of the heavens　to a man

ἐμπόρῳ, ζητοῦντι καλοὺς μαργαρίτας· 46 ᵇὃς εὑρὼν‖ ἕνα
a merchant, seeking beautiful　pearls;　who having found one

πολύτιμον μαργαρίτην, ἀπελθὼν πέπρακεν πάντα ὅσα
very precious　pearl,　having gone away has sold all things as many as

εἶχεν, καὶ ἠγόρασεν αὐτόν.
he had, and bought　it.

47 Πάλιν ὁμοία ἐστὶν ἡ βασιλεία τῶν οὐρανῶν σαγήνῃ
Again　like　is　the kingdom of the heavens　to a drag net

βληθείσῃ εἰς τὴν θάλασσαν, καὶ ἐκ παντὸς γένους συναγα-
cast　into the　sea,　and of every　kind　gathering

γούσῃ· 48 ἣν ὅτε ἐπληρώθη ἀναβιβάσαντες ᶜ δᵉπὶ τὸν
together;　which when it was filled　having drawn up　on the

αἰγιαλόν, καὶ‖ καθίσαντες συνέλεξαν τὰ καλὰ εἰς ᵉἀγγεῖα,‖
shore,　and having sat down they collected the good into vessels,

τὰ.δὲ σαπρὰ ἔξω ἔβαλον. 49 οὕτως ἔσται ἐν τῇ συντελείᾳ
and the corrupt ³out ¹they ²cast.　Thus shall it be in the completion

τοῦ αἰῶνος· ἐξελεύσονται οἱ ἄγγελοι, καὶ ἀφοριοῦσιν· τοὺς
of the age:　³shall ⁴go ⁵out ¹the ²angels,　and shall separate the

πονηροὺς ἐκ μέσου τῶν δικαίων, 50 καὶ βαλοῦσιν αὐτοὺς
wicked from [the] midst of the righteous,　and　shall cast them

εἰς τὴν κάμινον τοῦ πυρός· ἐκεῖ ἔσται ὁ κλαυθμὸς καὶ ὁ
into the　furnace　of the fire:　there shall be the　wailing　and the

βρυγμὸς τῶν ὀδόντων.
gnashing　of the　teeth.

---

the world; and the reapers are the angels. 40 As therefore the tares are gathered and burned in the fire; so shall it be in the end of this world: 41 The Son of man shall send forth his angels, and they shall gather out of his kingdom all things that offend, and them which do iniquity; 42 and shall cast them into a furnace of fire: there shall be wailing and gnashing of teeth. 43 Then shall the righteous shine forth as the sun in the kingdom of their Father. Who hath ears to hear, let him hear.

44 Again, the kingdom of heaven is like unto treasure hid in a field: the which when a man hath found, he hideth, and for joy thereof goeth and selleth all that he hath, and buyeth that field.

45 Again, the kingdom of heaven is like unto a merchant man, seeking goodly pearls: 46 who, when he had found one pearl of great price, went and sold all that he had, and bought it.

47 Again, the kingdom of heaven is like unto a net, that was cast into the sea, and gathered of every kind: 48 which, when it was full, they drew to shore, and sat down, and gathered the good into vessels, but cast the bad away. 49 so shall it be at the end of the world: the angels shall come forth, and sever the wicked from among the just, 50 and shall cast them into the furnace of fire: there shall be wailing and gnashing of teeth.

ᵛ — τοῦ (read of [the]) LTTrA. ʷ καίεται is burned GTrA. ˣ — τούτου (read the age) LTTr[A]. ʸ — ἀκούειν [L]T[Tr]A. ᶻ — πάλιν [t.]TTrA. · πωλεῖ πάντα ὅσα ἔχει LTTrA. ᵇ εὑρὼν δὲ GLTTrA. ᶜ + αὐτὴν it L[A]. ᵈ καὶ ἐπὶ τὸν αἰγιαλὸν L; ἐπὶ τὸν αἰγιαλὸν [καὶ] A. ᵉ ἄγγη TTrA.

51 Jesus saith unto them, Have ye understood all these things? They say unto him, Yea, Lord. 52 Then said he unto them, Therefore every scribe *which is* instructed unto the kingdom of heaven is like unto a man *that is* an householder, which bringeth forth out of his treasure *things* new and old.

53 And it came to pass, *that* when Jesus had finished these parables, he departed thence. 54 And when he was come into his own country, he taught them in their synagogue, insomuch that they were astonished, and said, Whence hath this *man* this wisdom, and *these* mighty works? 55 Is not this the carpenter's son? is not his mother called Mary? and his brethren, James, and Joses, and Simon, and Judas? 56 And his sisters, are they not all with us? Whence then hath this *man* all these things? 57 And they were offended in him. But Jesus said unto them, A prophet is not without honour, save in his own country, and in his own house. 58 And he did not many mighty works there because of their unbelief.

XIV. At that time Herod the tetrarch heard of the fame of Jesus, 2 and said unto his servants, This is John the Baptist; he is risen from the dead; and therefore mighty works do shew forth themselves in him. 3 For Herod had laid hold on John, and bound him, and put *him* in prison for Herodias' sake, his brother Philip's wife. 4 For John said unto him, It is not lawful for thee to have her. 5 And when he would have put him to death,

---

51 ᵍΛέγει αὐτοῖς ὁ Ἰησοῦς,‖ Συνήκατε ταῦτα πάντα;
  ²Says ³to ⁴them ¹Jesus, Have ye understood ²these ³things ¹all?
Λέγουσιν αὐτῷ, Ναί, ʰκύριε.‖ 52 Ὁ.δὲ ἰεἶπεν‖ αὐτοῖς· Διὰ
They say to him, Yea, Lord.   And he said to them, Because of
τοῦτο πᾶς γραμματεὺς μαθητευθεὶς ᵏεἰς τὴν βασιλείαν‖ τῶν
this every scribe   discipled into the kingdom of the
οὐρανῶν ὅμοιός ἐστιν ἀνθρώπῳ οἰκοδεσπότῃ, ὅστις ἐκβάλλει
heavens ²like ¹is to.a man a master of a house, who puts forth
ἐκ τοῦ.θησαυροῦ.αὐτοῦ   καινὰ καὶ παλαιά.
out of his treasure   [things] new and old.

53 Καὶ ἐγένετο ὅτε ἐτέλεσεν ὁ Ἰησοῦς τὰς παραβολὰς
  And it came to pass when ²had ³finished ¹Jesus   ²parables
ταύτας, μετῆρεν ἐκεῖθεν· 54 καὶ ἐλθὼν εἰς τὴν πατρίδα
¹these, he withdrew thence; and having come into ³country
αὐτοῦ, ἐδίδασκεν αὐτοὺς ἐν τῇ.συναγωγῇ.αὐτῶν, ὥστε ᵉἐκπλήτ-
¹his [²own], he taught them in their synagogue, so that ²were
τεσθαι‖ αὐτοὺς καὶ λέγειν, Πόθεν τούτῳ ἡ.σοφία.αὔτη καὶ
³astonished ¹they and said, Whence to this [man] this wisdom and
αἱ δυνάμεις; 55 οὐχ οὗτός ἐστιν ὁ τοῦ τέκτονος υἱός;
the works of power? ²not ³this ¹is ⁴the ⁶of ⁷the ⁸carpenter ⁵son? [Is]
ᵐοὐχὶ‖ ἡ.μήτηρ.αὐτοῦ λέγεται Μαριάμ, καὶ οἱ.ἀδελφοὶ.αὐτοῦ
not his mother called Mary, and his brethren
Ἰάκωβος καὶ ⁿἸωσῆς‖ καὶ Σίμων καὶ Ἰούδας; 56 καὶ αἱ
James and Joses and Simon and Judas?   and
ἀδελφαὶ.αὐτοῦ οὐχὶ πᾶσαι πρὸς ἡμᾶς εἰσιν; πόθεν οὖν τούτῳ
³his ⁴sisters ²not ⁵all ⁶with ⁷us ¹are? whence then to this
ταῦτα πάντα; 57 Καὶ ἐσκανδαλίζοντο ἐν αὐτῷ. Ὁ δὲ
[man] ²these ³things ¹all?   And they were offended in him. But
Ἰησοῦς εἶπεν αὐτοῖς, Οὐκ ἔστιν προφήτης ἄτιμος εἰ.μὴ
¹Jesus said to them, ²not ³is ¹a ²prophet without honour except
ἐν τῇ.ᵒπατρίδι.ᵖαὐτοῦ‖ καὶ ἐν τῇ.οἰκίᾳ.αὐτοῦ. 58 Καὶ οὐκ
in his [own] country and in his [own] house.   And ²not
ἐποίησεν ἐκεῖ δυνάμεις πολλὰς διὰ τὴν.ἀπιστίαν.αὐτῶν.
¹he.²did there ²works ³of ⁴power ¹many because of their unbelief.

14 Ἐν ἐκείνῳ τῷ καιρῷ ἤκουσεν Ἡρώδης ὁ ᑫτετράρχης‖
  At that time heard Herod the tetrarch
τὴν ἀκοὴν Ἰησοῦ, 2 καὶ εἶπεν τοῖς.παισὶν.αὐτοῦ, Οὗτός ἐστιν
the fame of Jesus, and said to his servants, This is
Ἰωάννης ὁ βαπτιστής· αὐτὸς ἠγέρθη ἀπὸ τῶν νεκρῶν, καὶ
John the Baptist: he is risen from the dead, and
διὰ τοῦτο αἱ δυνάμεις ἐνεργοῦσιν ἐν αὐτῷ. 3 Ὁ γὰρ
because of this the works of power operate in him.   For
Ἡρώδης κρατήσας τὸν Ἰωάννην ἔδησεν ʳαὐτὸν‖ καὶ ˢἔθετο
Herod having seized John bound him and put
ἐν φυλακῇ,‖ διὰ Ἡρωδιάδα τὴν γυναῖκα ᵗΦιλίππου‖
[him] in prison, on account of Herodias the wife ⁴Philip
τοῦ.ἀδελφοῦ.αὐτοῦ. 4 ἔλεγεν.γὰρ ʳαὐτῷ ὁ Ἰωάννης,‖ Οὐκ
¹of ²his ³brother.   For ²said ³to ⁴him ¹John,   ⁷Not
ἔξεστίν σοι ἔχειν αὐτήν. 5 Καὶ θέλων αὐτὸν ἀποκτεῖναι,
⁵it ⁶is lawful for thee to have her.   And wishing ³him ¹to ²kill,

---

ᵍ — Λέγει αὐτοῖς ὁ Ἰησοῦς LTTrA.   ʰ — κύριε LTTrA.   ⁱ λέγει says L.   ᵏ ἐν τῇ
βασιλείᾳ in the kingdom L; τῇ βασιλείᾳ to the kingdom GTTrA.   ˡ ἐκπλήσσεσθαι
LTTrAW.   ᵐ οὐχ LTTrA.   ⁿ Ἰωσὴφ Joseph LTTrA.   ᵒ + ἰδίᾳ own T.   ᵖ — αὐτοῦ
(read [his]) LTTrA.   ᑫ τετραάρχης T.   ʳ — αὐτὸν T.   ˢ ἐν τῇ (— τῇ T) φυλακῇ
ἀπέθετο in the prison put [him] aside LTTrA.   ᵗ — Φιλίππου [T]Δ.   ᵛ ὁ (— ὁ T)
Ἰωάννης αὐτῷ LE.

ἐφοβήθη τὸν ὄχλον, ὅτι ὡς προφήτην αὐτὸν εἶχον.
he feared the multitude, because as a prophet him they held.

6 ʷγενεσίων.δὲ ἀγομένων‖ τοῦ Ἡρώδου, ὠρχήσατο ἡ θυγάτηρ
But a birthday being celebrated of Herod, ᵃdanced ¹the ᵃdaughter

τῆς Ἡρωδιάδος ἐν τῷ μέσῳ, καὶ ἤρεσεν τῷ Ἡρώδῃ 7 ὅθεν
³of ⁴Herodias in the midst, and pleased Herod; Whereupon

μεθ' ὅρκου ὡμολόγησεν αὐτῇ δοῦναι ὃˣἐὰν‖ αἰτήσηται. 8 Ἡ.δὲ
with oath he promised to her to give whatever she should ask. But she

προβιβασθεῖσα ὑπὸ τῆς.μητρὸς.αὐτῆς, Δός μοι, φησίν, ὧδε
being urged on by her mother, Give me, she says, here

ἐπὶ πίνακι τὴν κεφαλὴν Ἰωάννου τοῦ βαπτιστοῦ. 9 Καὶ
upon a dish the head of John the Baptist. And

ᵞἐλυπήθη‖ ὁ βασιλεύς· διὰ.ᶻδὲ‖ τοὺς ὅρκους καὶ τοὺς
ᵞwas ᵞgrieved ¹the ²king; but on account of the oaths and those who

συνανακειμένους ἐκέλευσεν δοθῆναι· 10 καὶ πέμψας
reclined with [him at table] he commanded [it] to be given. And having sent

ἀπεκεφάλισεν ᵃτὸν‖ Ἰωάννην ἐν τῇ φυλακῇ. 11 καὶ ἠνέχθη
he beheaded John in the prison. And ³was ⁴brought

ἡ.κεφαλὴ.αὐτοῦ ἐπὶ πίνακι, καὶ ἐδόθη τῷ κορασίῳ· καὶ ἤν-
¹his ²head on a dish, and was given to the damsel, and she

εγκεν τῇ.μητρὶ.αὐτῆς. 12 καὶ προσελθόντες οἱ.μαθηταὶ.αὐτοῦ
brought [it] to her mother. And having come his disciples

ἦραν τὸ ᵇσῶμα,‖ καὶ ἔθαψαν ᶜαὐτό·‖ καὶ ἐλθόντες ἀπήγγειλαν
took the body, and buried it; and having come told

τῷ Ἰησοῦ. 13 ᵈκαὶ ἀκούσας‖ ὁ Ἰησοῦς ἀνεχώρησεν ἐκεῖθεν
[it] to Jesus. And ²having ³heard ¹Jesus withdrew thence

ἐν πλοίῳ εἰς ἔρημον τόπον κατ'.ἰδίαν.
by ship to a desert place apart.

Καὶ ἀκούσαντες οἱ ὄχλοι ἠκολούθησαν αὐτῷ ᵉπεζῇ‖
And having heard [of it] the crowds followed him on foot

ἀπὸ τῶν πόλεων. 14 Καὶ ἐξελθὼν ᶠὁ Ἰησοῦς‖ εἶδεν πολὺν
from the cities. And having gone out Jesus saw ²great

ὄχλον, καὶ ἐσπλαγχνίσθη ἐπ' ᵍαὐτούς,‖ καὶ ἐθεράπευσεν
¹a crowd, and was moved with compassion towards them, and healed

τοὺς.ἀρρώστους.αὐτῶν. 15 Ὀψίας.δὲ γενομένης ʰπροσῆλθον‖
their infirm. And evening having come came

αὐτῷ οἱ.μαθηταὶ.αὐτοῦ,‖ λέγοντες, Ἔρημός ἐστιν ὁ τόπος,
to him his disciples, saying, Desert is the place,

καὶ ἡ ὥρα ᵏἤδη παρῆλθεν·‖ ἀπόλυσον ˡ τοὺς ὄχλους, ἵνα
and the time already is gone by: dismiss the crowds, that

ἀπελθόντες εἰς τὰς κώμας ἀγοράσωσιν ἑαυτοῖς βρώματα.
having gone into the villages they may buy for themselves meat.

16 Ὁ.δὲ.ᵐ Ἰησοῦς‖ εἶπεν αὐτοῖς, Οὐ χρείαν ἔχουσιν ἀπελθεῖν·
But Jesus said to them, ³No ⁴need ¹they ²have to go away:

δότε αὐτοῖς ὑμεῖς φαγεῖν. 17 Οἱ.δὲ λέγουσιν αὐτῷ, Οὐκ.ἔχομεν
give ²to ³them ¹ye to eat. But they say to him, We have not

ὧδε εἰ.μὴ πέντε ἄρτους καὶ δύο ἰχθύας. 18 Ὁ.δὲ εἶπεν, Φέρετέ
here except five loaves and two fishes. And he said, Bring

μοι ᵃαὐτοὺς ὧδε.‖ 19 Καὶ κελεύσας τοὺς ὄχλους ἀνα-
²to ³me ¹them here. And having commanded the crowds to re-

κλιθῆναι ἐπὶ ᵒτοὺς χόρτους,‖ ᵖκαὶᵈ λαβὼν τοὺς πέντε ἄρτους
cline on the grass, and having taken the five loaves

he feared the multitude, because they counted him as a prophet. 6 But when Herod's birthday was kept, the daughter of Herodias danced before them, and pleased Herod. 7 Whereupon he promised with an oath to give her whatsoever she would ask. 8 And she, being before instructed of her mother, said, Give me here John Baptist's head in a charger. 9 And the king was sorry: nevertheless for the oath's sake, and them which sat with him at meat, he commanded it to be given her. 10 And he sent, and beheaded John in the prison. 11 And his head was brought in a charger, and given to the damsel: and she brought it to her mother. 12 And his disciples came, and took up the body, and buried it, and went and told Jesus. 13 When Jesus heard of it, he departed thence by ship into a desert place apart.

And when the people had heard thereof, they followed him on foot out of the cities. 14 And Jesus went forth, and saw a great multitude, and was moved with compassion toward them, and he healed their sick. 15 And when it was evening, his disciples came to him, saying, This is a desert place, and the time is now past; send the multitude away, that they may go into the villages, and buy themselves victuals. 16 But Jesus said unto them, They need not depart; give ye them to eat. 17 And they say unto him, We have here but five loaves, and two fishes. 18 He said, Bring them hither to me. 19 And he commanded the multitude to sit down on the grass, and took the five loaves, and the

---

ʷ γενεσίοις δὲ γενομένοις LTTrA. ˣ ἂν LTTrA. ʸ λυπηθεὶς being grieved LTTrA. ᶻ — δὲ but LTTrA. ᵃ — τὸν LTTrA. ᵇ πτῶμα corpse LTTr. ᶜ αὐτόν him TTrA. ᵈ ἀκούσας δὲ LTTrA. ᵉ πεζοὶ T. ᶠ — ὁ Ἰησοῦς (read he saw) LTTrA. ᵍ αὐτοῖς GLTTrAW. ʰ προσῆλθαν LTr. ⁱ — αὐτοῦ (read the disciples) LTTrA. ᵏ παρῆλθεν ἤδη T. ˡ + οὖν therefore T [A]. ᵐ — Ἰησοῦς (read he said) τ. ⁿ ὧδε αὐτούς LTTrA. ᵒ τοῦ χόρτου LTTr. ᵖ — καὶ GLTTrAW.

4

two fishes, and looking up to heaven, he blessed, and brake, and gave the loaves to *his* disciples, and the disciples to the multitude. 20 And they did all eat, and were filled: and they took up of the fragments that remained twelve baskets full. 21 And they that had eaten were about five thousand men, beside women and children

και τοὺς δύο ἰχθύας, ἀναβλέψας εἰς τὸν οὐρανὸν �·εὐλόγησε·ν·
and the two fishes, having looked up to the heaven he blessed;

καὶ κλάσας ἔδωκεν τοῖς μαθηταῖς τοὺς ἄρτους, οἱ.δὲ μα-
and having broken he gave to the disciples the loaves, and the dis-

θηταὶ τοῖς ὄχλοις. 20 καὶ ἔφαγον πάντες καὶ ἐχορτάσθησαν·
ciples to the crowds. And ²ate ¹all and were satisfied;

καὶ ἦραν τὸ περισσεῦον τῶν κλασμάτων, δώδεκα
and they took up that which was over and above of the fragments, twelve

κοφίνους πλήρεις. 21 οἱ.δὲ ἐσθίοντες ἦσαν ἄνδρες ὡσεὶ
hand-baskets full. And those who ate were men about

πεντακισχίλιοι, χωρὶς ʳγυναικῶν καὶ παιδίων.ǁ
five thousand, besides women and children.

22 Καὶ ˢεὐθέωςǁ ἠνάγκασεν ᵗὁ Ἰησοῦςǁ τοὺς.μαθητὰς.ᵛαὐτοῦǁ
And immediately ²compelled ¹Jesus his disciples

22 And straightway Jesus constrained his disciples to get into a ship, and to go before him unto the other side, while he sent the multitudes away. 23 And when he had sent the multitudes away, he went up into a mountain apart to pray: and when the evening was come, he was there alone. 24 But the ship was now in the midst of the sea, tossed with waves: for the wind was contrary. 25 And in the fourth watch of the night Jesus went unto them, walking on the sea. 26 And when the disciples saw him walking on the sea, they were troubled, saying, It is a spirit; and they cried out for fear. 27 But straightway Jesus spake unto them, saying, Be of good cheer; it is I; be not afraid. 28 And Peter answered him and said, Lord, if it be thou, bid me come unto thee on the water. 29 And he said, Come. And when Peter was come down out of the ship, he walked on the water, to go to Jesus. 30 But when he saw the wind boisterous, he was afraid; and beginning to sink, he cried, saying, Lord, save me. 31 And immediately Jesus stretched forth *his* hand, and caught him, and said unto him, O

ἐμβῆναι εἰς ʷτὸǁ πλοῖον καὶ προάγειν αὐτὸν εἰς τὸ πέραν,
to enter into the ship and to go before him to the other side,

ἕως.οῦ ἀπολύσῃ τοὺς ὄχλους. 23 καὶ ἀπολύσας τοὺς
until he should have dismissed the crowds. And having dismissed the

ὄχλους ἀνέβη εἰς τὸ ὄρος κατ'.ἰδίαν προσεύξασθαι. Ὀψί-
crowds he went up into the mountain apart to pray. ³Even-

ας δὲ γενομένης μόνος ἦν ἐκεῖ. 24 τὸ.δὲ πλοῖον ἤδη ˣμέσον
ing ¹and being come alone he was there. But the ship now in [the] midst

τῆς θαλάσσης ἦν,ǁ βασανιζόμενον ὑπὸ τῶν κυμάτων· ἦν γὰρ
of the sea was, tossed by the waves, ⁴was ⁵for

ἐναντίος ὁ ἄνεμος. 25 Τετάρτῃ.δὲ φυλακῇ τῆς νυκτὸς
ᵇcontrary ²the ³wind. But in [the] fourth watch of the night

ʸἀπῆλθενǁ πρὸς αὐτοὺς ᶻὁ Ἰησοῦς,ǁ περιπατῶν ἐπὶ ᵃτῆς θαλάσ-
²went ³to ⁴them ¹Jesus, walking on the sea.

σης.ǁ 26 ᵇκαὶ ἰδόντες αὐτὸν οἱ μαθηταὶǁ ἐπὶ ᶜτὴν θάλασσανǁ
And ³seeing ⁴him ¹the ²disciples on the sea

περιπατοῦντα ἐταράχθησαν, λέγοντες, Ὅτι φάντασμά ἐστιν·
walking were troubled, saying, An apparition it is:

καὶ ἀπὸ τοῦ φόβου ἔκραξαν. 27 ᵈεὐθέως.δὲ ἐλάλησεν ᵉαὐ-
and through fear they cried out. But immediately ¹spoke ³to

τοῖς ὁ Ἰησοῦς,ǁ λέγων, Θαρσεῖτε, ἐγώ.εἰμι, μὴ.φοβεῖσθε.
⁴them ¹Jesus, saying, Be of good courage, I am [he], fear not.

28 Ἀποκριθεὶς δὲ ᶠαὐτῷ ὁ Πέτρος εἶπεν,ǁ Κύριε, εἰ σὺ.εἶ,
And answering him Peter said, Lord, if it be thou,

κέλευσόν με ᵍπρός σε ἐλθεῖνǁ ἐπὶ τὰ ὕδατα. 29 Ὁ.δὲ εἶπεν,
bid me ³to ⁴thee ¹to ²come upon the waters. And he said,

Ἐλθέ. Καὶ καταβὰς ἀπὸ τοῦ πλοίου ʰὁ.ǁ Πέτρος περιεπά-
Come. And having descended from the ship Peter walk-

τησεν ἐπὶ τὰ ὕδατα, ⁱἐλθεῖνǁ πρὸς τὸν Ἰησοῦν. 30 βλέπων.δὲ
ed upon the waters, to go to Jesus. But seeing

τὸν ἄνεμον ᵏἰσχυρὸνǁ ἐφοβήθη, καὶ ἀρξάμενος καταπον-
the wind strong he was affrighted, and beginning to

τίζεσθαι ἔκραξεν, λέγων, Κύριε, σῶσόν με. 31 Εὐθέως.δὲ
sink he cried out, saying, Lord, save me. And immediately

ὁ Ἰησοῦς ἐκτείνας τὴν χεῖρα ἐπελάβετο αὐτοῦ, καὶ λέγει
Jesus having stretched out the hand took hold of him, and says

�q ηὐλόγησεν LTrA.   ʳ παιδίων καὶ γυναικῶν L.   ˢ — εὐθέως Τ.   ᵗ — ὁ Ἰησοῦς (*read* he compelled) GLTTrAW.   ᵛ — αὐτοῦ (*read* the disciples) GTTrAW.   ʷ — τὸ (*read* a ship) Tr.   ˣ σταδίους πολλοὺς ἀπὸ τῆς γῆς ἀπεῖχε many stadia from the land was distant Tr.   ʸ ἦλθεν LTTr.   ᶻ — ὁ Ἰησοῦς (*read* he went) GLTTrAW.   ᵃ τὴν θάλασσαν LTTrA.   ᵇ οἱ δὲ μαθηταὶ ἰδόντες αὐτὸν L; ἰδόντες δὲ αὐτὸν Τ.   ᶜ τῆς θαλάσσης LTTrA.   ᵈ εὐθὺς LTTr.   ᵉ ὁ Ἰησοῦς αὐτοῖς L, — ὁ Ἰησοῦς Τ; αὐτοῖς [ὁ Ἰησοῦς] A.   ᶠ ὁ Πέτρος εἶπεν αὐτῷ L.   ᵍ ἐλθεῖν πρός σε LTTrA.   ʰ — ὁ LTTrA.   ⁱ καὶ ἦλθεν and he went Τ.   ᵏ — ἰσχυρὸν Τ.

αὐτῷ, Ὀλιγόπιστε, εἰς.τί ἐδίστασας; 32 Καὶ ¹ἐμβάντων
to him, O [thou] of little faith, why didst thou doubt? And ²having ³entered

αὐτῶν εἰς τὸ πλοῖον ἐκόπασεν ὁ ἄνεμος· 33 οἱ.δὲ ἐν τῷ
¹they into the ship ³ceased ¹the ²wind. And those in the

πλοίῳ ᵐἐλθόντες προσεκύνησαν αὐτῷ, λέγοντες, Ἀληθῶς
ship having come worshipped him, saying, Truly

θεοῦ υἱὸς εἶ.
²of ³God ¹Son thou art!

34 Καὶ διαπεράσαντες ἦλθον ⁿεἰς τὴν γῆνᵒ ʳΓεννησαρέτ.
And having passed over they came to the land of Gennesaret.

35 καὶ ἐπιγνόντες αὐτὸν οἱ ἄνδρες τοῦ.τόπου.ἐκείνου ἀπέ-
And having recognized him the men of that place sent

στειλαν εἰς ὅλην τὴν.περίχωρον.ἐκείνην, καὶ προσήνεγκαν αὐτῷ
to all that country round, and brought to him

πάντας τοὺς κακῶς.ἔχοντας· 36 καὶ παρεκάλουν αὐτὸν ἵνα
all those who were ill; and besought him that

μόνον ἅψωνται τοῦ κρασπέδου τοῦ.ἱματίου.αὐτοῦ· καὶ
only they might touch the border of his garment; and

ὅσοι ἥψαντο διεσώθησαν.
as many as touched were cured.

15 Τότε προσέρχονται τῷ Ἰησοῦ �qοἱ ἀπὸ Ἱεροσολύμων
Then come to Jesus the ⁴from ⁵Jerusalem

ʳγραμματεῖς καὶ Φαρισαῖοι, λέγοντες, 2 ˢΔιατί οἱ μαθηταί
¹scribes ²and ³Pharisees, saying, Why ³disciples

σου παραβαίνουσιν.τὴν παράδοσιν τῶν πρεσβυτέρων; οὐ
²thy ¹transgress the tradition of the elders? ⁴not

γὰρ νίπτονται τὰς.χεῖρας.ᵗαὐτῶν ὅταν ἄρτον ἐσθίωσιν. 3 Ὁ.δὲ
¹for ²they ³wash their hands when bread they eat. But he

ἀποκριθεὶς εἶπεν αὐτοῖς, ˢΔιατί καὶ ὑμεῖς παραβαίνετε τὴν
answering said to them, Why ²also ¹ye ¹transgress the

ἐντολὴν τοῦ θεοῦ διὰ τὴν.παράδοσιν.ὑμῶν; 4 Ὁ γὰρ
commandment of God on account of your tradition? For

θεὸς ᵛἐνετείλατο, λέγων, Τίμα τὸν.πατέρα.ʷσου καὶ τὴν
God commanded, saying, Honour thy father and

μητέρα· καὶ Ὁ κακολογῶν πατέρα ἢ μητέρα, θανάτῳ τε-
mother; and, He who speaks evil of father or mother, by death let

λευτάτω. 5 ὑμεῖς.δὲ λέγετε, Ὃς.ἂν εἴπῃ τῷ πατρὶ ἢ τῇ
him die. But ye say, Whoever shall say to father or

μητρί, Δῶρον, ὃ.ἐὰν ἐξ.ἐμοῦ ὠφεληθῇς, ˣκαὶ
mother, [It is] a gift, whatever by me thou mightest be profited— and

οὐ.μὴ ʸτιμήσῃ τὸν.πατέρα.αὐτοῦ ᶻἢ τὴν.μητέρα.αὐτοῦ·
in no wise honour his father or his mother:

6 καὶ ἠκυρώσατε ᵃτὴν ἐντολὴν τοῦ θεοῦ διὰ τὴν παρά-
and ye made void the commandment of God on account of ²tra-

δοσιν ὑμῶν. 7 Ὑποκριταί, καλῶς ᵇπροεφήτευσεν περὶ ὑμῶν
dition ¹your. Hypocrites! well prophesied concerning you

Ἡσαΐας, λέγων, 8 ᶜἘγγίζει μοι ὁ.λαὸς.οὗτος ᵈτῷ στόματι
Esaias, saying, Draws near to me this people with ²mouth

αὐτῶν, καὶ τοῖς.χείλεσίν με τιμᾷ· ἡ.δὲ.καρδία.αὐτῶν πόρρω
their, and with the lips ³me ¹it ²honours; but their heart far

thou of little faith, wherefore didst thou doubt? 32 And when they were come into the ship, the wind ceased. 33 Then they that were in the ship came and worshipped him, saying, Of a truth thou art the Son of God.

34 And when they were gone over, they came into the land of Gennesaret. 35 And when the men of that place had knowledge of him, they sent out into all that country round about, and brought unto him all that were diseased; 36 and besought him that they might only touch the hem of his garment: and as many as touched were made perfectly whole.

XV. Then came to Jesus scribes and Pharisees, which were of Jerusalem, saying, 2 Why do thy disciples transgress the tradition of the elders? for they wash not their hands when they eat bread. 3 But he answered and said unto them, Why do ye also transgress the commandment of God by your tradition? 4 For God commanded, saying, Honour thy father and mother: and, He that curseth father or mother, let him die the death. 5 But ye say, Whosoever shall say to his father or his mother, It is a gift, by whatsoever thou mightest be profited by me; 6 and honour not his father or his mother, he shall be free. Thus have ye made the commandment of God of none effect by your tradition. 7 Ye hypocrites, well did Esaias prophesy of you, saying, 8 This people draweth nigh unto me with their mouth, and honoureth me with their lips; but their heart is far from me.

9 But in vain they do worship me, teaching for doctrines the commandments of men. 10 And he called the multitude, and said unto them, Hear, and understand: 11 not that which goeth into the mouth defileth a man; but that which cometh out of the mouth, this defileth a man.

12 Then came his disciples, and said unto him, Knowest thou that the Pharisees were offended, after they heard this saying? 13 But he answered and said, Every plant, which my heavenly Father hath not planted, shall be rooted up. 14 Let them alone: they be blind leaders of the blind. And if the blind lead the blind, both shall fall into the ditch. 15 Then answered Peter and said unto him, Declare unto us this parable. 16 And Jesus said, Are ye also yet without understanding? 17 Do not ye yet understand, that whatsoever entereth in at the mouth goeth into the belly, and is cast out into the draught? 18 But those things which proceed out of the mouth come forth from the heart; and they defile the man. 19 For out of the heart proceed evil thoughts, murders, adulteries, fornications, thefts, false witness, blasphemies: 20 these are the things which defile a man: but to eat with unwashen hands defileth not a man.

21 Then Jesus went thence, and departed into the coasts of Tyre and Sidon. 22 And, behold, a woman of Canaan came out of the same coasts, and cried unto him, saying, Have mercy on me, O Lord, thou son of David; my daughter is grievously vexed with a devil. 23 But he answered her not a word. And his disci-

---

ἀπέχει ἀπ' ἐμοῦ. 9 μάτην.δὲ σέβονταί με, διδάσκοντες
is away from me: But in vain they worship me, teaching [as]
διδασκαλίας ἐντάλματα ἀνθρώπων. 10 Καὶ προσκαλεσάμενος
teachings injunctions of men. And having called to [him]
τὸν ὄχλον εἶπεν αὐτοῖς, Ἀκούετε καὶ συνίετε. 11 οὐ
the crowd he said to them, Hear and understand! not
τὸ 'εἰσερχόμενον εἰς τὸ στόμα κοινοῖ τὸν ἄνθρωπον·
that which enters into the mouth defiles the man;
ἀλλὰ τὸ ἐκπορευόμενον ἐκ τοῦ στόματος, τοῦτο κοινοῖ
but that which goes forth out of the mouth, this defiles
τὸν ἄνθρωπον.
the man.

12 Τότε προσελθόντες οἱ.μαθηταὶ.ᵉαὐτοῦ‖ ᶠεῖπον‖ αὐτῷ,
Then having come to [him] his disciples said to him.
Οἶδας ὅτι οἱ Φαρισαῖοι ἀκούσαντες τὸν λόγον ἐσκανδαλί-
Knowest thou that the Pharisees having heard the saying were of-
σθησαν; 13 ὁ.δὲ ᾿ἀποκριθεὶς εἶπεν, Πᾶσα φυτεία ἣν οὐκ
fended? But he answering said, Every plant which ⁶not
ἐφύτευσεν ὁ.πατήρ.μου ὁ.οὐράνιος, ἐκριζωθήσεται. 14 ἄφετε
⁶has ⁷planted ¹my ²Father ³the ⁴heavenly, shall be rooted up. Leave
αὐτούς· ᵍὁδηγοί εἰσιν τυφλοὶ‖ τυφλῶν· τυφλὸς.δὲ τυφλὸν
them; ⁴leaders ¹they ²are ³blind of blind; ³blind ¹and ⁵blind
ἐὰν ὁδηγῇ, ἀμφότεροι εἰς βόθυνον πεσοῦνται. 15 Ἀποκριθεὶς.δὲ
²if ¹lead, both into a pit will fall. And answering
ὁ Πέτρος εἶπεν αὐτῷ, Φράσον ἡμῖν τὴν.παραβολὴν.ʰταύτην.‖
Peter said to him, Expound to us this parable.
16 Ὁ.δὲ.ⁱἸησοῦς‖ εἶπεν, Ἀκμὴν καὶ ὑμεῖς ἀσύνετοί ἐστε;
But Jesus said, ⁴Still ³also ²ye ⁵without ⁶understanding ¹are?
17 ᵏοὔπω‖ νοεῖτε ὅτι πᾶν τὸ εἰσπορευόμενον εἰς τὸ
³not ⁴yet ¹perceive ²ye that everything which enters into the
στόμα εἰς τὴν κοιλίαν χωρεῖ, καὶ εἰς ἀφεδρῶνα ἐκβάλλεται;
mouth into the belly goes, and into [the] draught is cast forth?
18 τὰ.δὲ ἐκπορευόμενα ἐκ τοῦ στόματος ἐκ τῆς
But the things which, come forth out of the mouth out of the
καρδίας ἐξέρχεται, κἀκεῖνα κοινοῖ τὸν ἄνθρωπον. 19 ἐκ.γὰρ
heart come forth, and these defile the man. For out of
τῆς καρδίας ἐξέρχονται διαλογισμοὶ πονηροί, φόνοι, μοιχεῖαι,
the heart come forth ²reasonings ¹evil, murders, adulteries,
πορνεῖαι, κλοπαί, ψευδομαρτυρίαι, βλασφημίαι. 20 ταῦτά
fornications, thefts, false-witnessings, blasphemies. These things
ἐστιν τὰ κοινοῦντα τὸν ἄνθρωπον· τὸ.δὲ ἀνίπτοις
are they which defile the man; but the ²with ³unwashed
χερσὶν φαγεῖν οὐ.κοινοῖ τὸν ἄνθρωπον.
¹hands ²eating defiles not the man.

21 Καὶ ἐξελθὼν ἐκεῖθεν ὁ Ἰησοῦς ἀνεχώρησεν εἰς τὰ μέρη
And going forth thence Jesus withdrew to the parts
Τύρου καὶ Σιδῶνος. 22 καὶ ἰδού, γυνὴ Χαναναία ἀπὸ
of Tyre and Sidon; and behold, a ²woman ¹Cananæan from
τῶν.ὁρίων.ἐκείνων ἐξελθοῦσα ᶦἐκραύγασεν‖ ᵐαὐτῷ,‖ λέγουσα,
those borders having come out cried to him, saying,
Ἐλέησόν με, κύριε, ⁿυἱὲ Δαβίδ·‖ ἡ.θυγάτηρ.μου κακῶς δαι-
Have pity on me, Lord, Son of David; my daughter miserably is pos-
μονίζεται. 23 Ὁ.δὲ οὐκ.ἀπεκρίθη αὐτῇ λόγον. καὶ προσ-
sessed by a demon. But he answered ²not ¹her a word. And having

---

ᵉ — αὐτοῦ (read the disciples) LTA. ᶠ λέγουσιν say LTTrA. ᵍ τυφλοί εἰσιν ὁδηγοὶ LTr.
ʰ — ταύτην (read the parable) LTTr[A]. ⁱ — Ἰησοῦς (read he said) LTTrA. ᵏ οὐ not LTTr.
ˡ ἔκραζεν LTr; ἔκραξεν T. ᵐ — αὐτῷ LTTrA. ⁿ υἱὲ Δαυὶδ GW; υἱὸς Δανείδ LTTrA.

ἐλθόντες οἱ μαθηταὶ αὐτοῦ °ἠρώτων‖ αὐτόν, λέγοντες,
come to [him]   his disciples   asked   him,   saying,

Ἀπόλυσον αὐτήν, ὅτι κράζει ὄπισθεν ἡμῶν· 24 Ὁ δὲ ἀποκρι-
Dismiss   her,   for she cries   after   us.   But he answer-

θεὶς εἶπεν, Οὐκ ἀπεστάλην εἰ μὴ εἰς τὰ πρόβατα τὰ ἀπολωλότα
ing said,   I was not sent except to the   sheep   the   lost

οἴκου Ἰσραήλ. 25 Ἡ δὲ ἐλθοῦσα προσεκύνει αὐτῷ,
of [the] house of Israel.   But she having come did homage to him,

λέγουσα, Κύριε, βοήθει μοι. 26 Ὁ δὲ ἀποκριθεὶς εἶπεν, Οὐκ
saying,   Lord,   help   me!   But he answering   said,   ²Not

¹ἔστιν καλὸν‖ λαβεῖν τὸν ἄρτον τῶν τέκνων, καὶ βαλεῖν
¹it ²is   good   to take the bread of the children, and to cast [it]

τοῖς κυναρίοις. 27 Ἡ δὲ εἶπεν, Ναί, κύριε· καὶ γὰρ τὰ κυνάρια
to the little dogs.   But she said, Yea, Lord: for even the little dogs

ἐσθίει ἀπὸ τῶν ψιχίων τῶν πιπτόντων ἀπὸ τῆς τραπέζης
eat   of   the crumbs   which   fall   from   the table

τῶν κυρίων αὐτῶν. 28 Τότε ἀποκριθεὶς ὁ Ἰησοῦς εἶπεν αὐτῇ,
of their masters.   Then answering   Jesus   said to her,

Ὦ γύναι, μεγάλη σου ἡ πίστις· γενηθήτω σοι ὡς θέλεις.
O woman,   great [is] thy faith: be it   to thee as thou desirest.

Καὶ ἰάθη ἡ θυγάτηρ αὐτῆς ἀπὸ τῆς ὥρας ἐκείνης.
And was healed her daughter   from   that hour.

29 Καὶ μεταβὰς ἐκεῖθεν ὁ Ἰησοῦς ἦλθεν παρὰ τὴν θάλασ-
And having departed thence   Jesus   came towards the   sea

σαν τῆς Γαλιλαίας· καὶ ἀναβὰς εἰς τὸ ὄρος ἐκάθητο
of Galilee;   and having gone up into the mountain he was sitting

ἐκεῖ. 30 καὶ προσῆλθον αὐτῷ ὄχλοι πολλοί, ἔχοντες μεθ'
there.   And   came   to him ²crowds ¹great,   having   with

ἑαυτῶν χωλούς, τυφλούς, κωφούς, κυλλούς, καὶ ἑτέρους πολ-
them   lame,   blind,   dumb,   maimed,   and ²others ¹many,

λούς, καὶ ¹ἔρριψαν‖ αὐτοὺς παρὰ τοὺς πόδας ʳτοῦ Ἰησοῦ·‖
and they cast down them   at   the   feet   of Jesus,

καὶ ἐθεράπευσεν αὐτούς· 31 ὥστε ˢτοὺς ὄχλους‖ θαυμάσαι,
and   he healed   them;   so that the   crowds   wondered,

βλέποντας κωφοὺς λαλοῦντας, κυλλοὺς ὑγιεῖς, ᵗ χωλοὺς περι-
seeing   dumb   speaking,   maimed sound,   lame   walk-

πατοῦντας, καὶ τυφλοὺς βλέποντας· καὶ ᵛἐδόξασαν‖ τὸν θεὸν
ing,   and blind   seeing;   and they glorified the God

Ἰσραήλ. 32 Ὁ δὲ Ἰησοῦς προσκαλεσάμενος τοὺς μαθητὰς
of Israel.   But Jesus   having called to [him]   ²disciples

αὐτοῦ εἶπεν, Σπλαγχνίζομαι ἐπὶ τὸν ὄχλον, ὅτι ἤδη
¹his   said,   I am moved with compassion towards the crowd, because already

ʷἡμέρας‖ τρεῖς προσμένουσίν μοι, καὶ οὐκ ἔχουσιν τί φάγω-
²days   ¹three they continue with me, and   have not   what they may

σιν· καὶ ἀπολῦσαι αὐτοὺς νήστεις οὐ θέλω, μήποτε ἐκλυθῶσιν
eat; and to send away them fasting I am not willing, lest they faint

ἐν τῇ ὁδῷ. 33 Καὶ λέγουσιν αὐτῷ οἱ μαθηταὶ ˣαὐτοῦ,‖ Πόθεν
in the way.   And ²say   ⁴to ⁵him ¹his ²disciples,   Whence

ἡμῖν ἐν ἐρημίᾳ ἄρτοι τοσοῦτοι ὥστε χορτάσαι ὄχλον τοσοῦτον;
to us in a desert loaves so many   as   to satisfy a crowd so great?

34 Καὶ λέγει αὐτοῖς ὁ Ἰησοῦς, Πόσους ἄρτους ἔχετε; Οἱ δὲ
And ²says ³to ⁴them ¹Jesus, How many loaves have ye? And they

εἶπον, Ἑπτά, καὶ ὀλίγα ἰχθύδια. 35 Καὶ ʸἐκέλευσεν τοῖς
said,   Seven, and a few small fishes.   And he commanded

ples came and be-
sought him, saying,
Send her away; for she
crieth after us. 24 But
he answered and said,
I am not sent but unto
the lost sheep of the
house of Israel. 25 Then
came she and worship-
ped him, saying, Lord,
help me. 26. But he
answered and said, It
is not meet to take the
children's bread, and
to cast it to dogs.
27 And she said, Truth,
Lord: yet the dogs eat
of the crumbs which
fall from their mas-
ters' table. 28 Then
Jesus answered and
said unto her, O wo-
man, great is thy faith:
be it unto thee even as
thou wilt. And her
daughter was made
whole from that very
hour.

29 And Jesus depart-
ed from thence, and
came nigh unto the sea
of Galilee; and went
up into a mountain,
and sat down there.
30 And great multi-
tudes came unto him,
having with them those
that were lame, blind,
dumb, maimed, and
many others, and cast
them down at Jesus'
feet; and he healed
them: 31 insomuch that
the multitude wonder-
ed, when they saw the
dumb to speak, the
maimed to be whole,
the lame to walk, and
the blind to see : and
they glorified the God
of Israel. 32 Then
Jesus called his disci-
ples unto him, and said,
I have compassion on
the multitude, because
they continue with me
now three days, and
have nothing to eat:
and I will not send
them away fasting,
lest they faint in the
way. 33 And his dis-
ciples say unto him,
Whence should we
have so much bread in
the wilderness, as to
fill so great a multi-
tude? 34 And Jesus
saith unto them, How
many loaves have ye?
And they said, Seven,
and a few little fishes.
35 And he commanded
the multitude to sit

ᵒ ἠρώτουν LTTrA. ᵖ ἔξεστιν it is allowed LTA. ۹ ἔριψαν T. ʳ αὐτοῦ of him LTTrA. ˢ τὸν
ὄχλον the crowd TA. ᵗ + καὶ and LTTrA. ᵛ ἐδόξαζον T. ʷ ἡμέραι GLTTrAW. ˣ — αὐτοῦ
(read the disciples) [L]T[Tr]A. ʸ παραγγείλας τῷ ὄχλῳ having commanded the crowd LTTr.

down on the ground.
36 And he took the
seven loaves and the
fishes, and gave thanks,
and brake *them*, and
gave to his disciples,
and the disciples to the
multitude. 37 And
they did all eat, and
were filled: and they
took up of the broken
meat that was left
seven baskets full.
38 And they that did
eat were four thousand
men, beside women
and children. 39 And
he sent away the mul-
titude, and took ship,
and came into the
coasts of Magdala.

XVI. The Pharisees
also with the Saddu-
cees came, and tempt-
ing desired him that
he would shew them a
sign from heaven.
2 He answered and
said unto them, When
it is evening, ye say,
It will be fair weather:
for the sky is red.
3 And in the morning,
It will be foul weather
to day: for the sky is
red and lowring. O *ye*
hypocrites, ye can dis-
cern the face of the
sky; but can ye not
discern the signs of the
times? 4 A wicked and
adulterous generation
seeketh after a sign;
and there shall no sign
be given unto it, but
the sign of the prophet
Jonas. And he left
them, and departed.
5 And when his dis-
ciples were come to the
other side, they had
forgotten to take
bread. 6 Then Jesus
said unto them, Take
heed and beware of
the leaven of the Pha-
risees and of the Sad-
ducees. 7 And they
reasoned among them-
selves, saying, *It is* because we have taken
no bread. 8 *Which*
when Jesus perceived,
he said unto them, O
ye of little faith, why
reason ye among your-
selves, because ye have
brought no bread?
9 Do ye not yet under-
stand, neither remem-
ber the five loaves of

ὄχλοις‖ ἀναπεσεῖν ἐπὶ τὴν γῆν· 36 ᶻκαὶ λαβὼν‖ τοὺς ἑπτά
crowds   to recline   on the ground;   and having taken the seven
ἄρτους καὶ τοὺς ἰχθύας.ᵃ εὐχαριστήσας ἔκλασεν καὶ ᵇἐδωκεν‖
loaves and the   fishes,   having given thanks he broke and   gave
τοῖς μαθηταῖς·ᶜαὐτοῦ,‖ οἱ δὲ μαθηταὶ ᵈτῷ ὄχλῳ.‖ 37 Καὶ
to his disciples,   and the disciples to the crowd.   And
ἔφαγον πάντες, καὶ ἐχορτάσθησαν καὶ ᵉἦραν τὸ περισ-
²ate   ¹all,   and were satisfied; and they took up that which was over
σεῦον τῶν κλασμάτων‖ ἑπτὰ σπυρίδας πλήρεις. 38 οἱ δὲ
and above of the fragments seven baskets   full;   and they who
ἐσθίοντες ἦσαν τετρακισχίλιοι ἄνδρες, χωρὶς ᶠγυναικῶν καὶ
ate   were   four thousand   men,   besides   women   and
παιδίων.‖ 39 Καὶ ἀπολύσας τοὺς ὄχλους ᵍἐνέβη‖ εἰς το
children.   And having dismissed the   crowds   he entered into the
πλοῖον, καὶ ἦλθεν εἰς τὰ ὅρια ʰΜαγδαλά.‖
ship,   and came to the borders of Magdala.

16 Καὶ προσελθόντες οἱ Φαρισαῖοι καὶ Σαδδουκαῖοι
   And having come to [him] the Pharisees and Sadducees
πειράζοντες   ⁱἐπηρώτησαν‖ αὐτὸν σημεῖον ἐκ τοῦ οὐρανοῦ
tempting .[him]   asked   him a sign out of the heaven
ἐπιδεῖξαι αὐτοῖς. 2 ὁ δὲ ἀποκριθεὶς εἶπεν αὐτοῖς, ᵏὈψίας
to shew   them.   But he · answering said to them, Evening
γενομένης λέγετε, Εὐδία· πυρράζει γὰρ ὁ οὐρανός. 3 καὶ
having come ye say, Fine weather;   for ³is ⁴red ¹the ²heaven.   And
πρωΐ. Σήμερον χειμών· πυρράζει γὰρ στυγνάζων ὁ οὐρανός.
at morning, To-day a storm; for ³is ⁴red   ⁵lowering ¹the ²heaven.
ˡὑποκριταί.ˡ τὸ μὲν πρόσωπον τοῦ οὐρανοῦ γινώσκετε
Hypocrites! the ⁵indeed ¹face ²of ³the ⁴heaven ye know [how]
διακρίνειν, τὰ δὲ σημεῖα τῶν καιρῶν οὐ δύνασθε;‖ 4 γενεὰ
to discern,   but the signs of the times   ye cannot !   A generation
πονηρὰ καὶ μοιχαλὶς σημεῖον ἐπιζητεῖ· καὶ σημεῖον οὐ δοθή-
wicked and adulterous a sign   seeks,   and a sign   shall not be
σεται αὐτῇ. εἰ μὴ τὸ σημεῖον Ἰωνᾶ ᵐτοῦ προφήτου.‖ Καὶ
given to it, except the sign of Jonas the   prophet.   And
καταλιπὼν αὐτοὺς ἀπῆλθεν.
leaving   them   he went away.

5 Καὶ ἐλθόντες οἱ μαθηταὶ.ⁿαὐτοῦ‖ εἰς τὸ πέραν ἐπελάθοντο
And ³having⁴ come ¹his ²disciples   to the other side they forgot
ἄρτους λαβεῖν. 6 ὁ δὲ Ἰησοῦς εἶπεν αὐτοῖς, Ὁρᾶτε καὶ προσ-
¹loaves ¹to.⁴take.   And Jesus said to them, See and be-
έχετε ἀπὸ τῆς ζύμης τῶν Φαρισαίων καὶ Σαδδουκαίων. 7 Οἱ δὲ
ware of the leaven of the Pharisees and   Sadducees.   And they
διελογίζοντο ἐν ἑαυτοῖς, λέγοντες, Ὅτι ἄρτους οὐκ ἐλά-
reasoned   among themselves, saying, Because loaves ³not ¹we
βομεν. 8 Γνοὺς δὲ   ὁ Ἰησοῦς εἶπεν ᵒαὐτοῖς,‖ Τί δια-
²took. And having known [this] ² Jesus   said to them, Why rea-
λογίζεσθε ἐν ἑαυτοῖς, ὀλιγόπιστοι, ὅτι ἄρτους οὐκ
son ye   among yourselves, O [ye] of little faith, because loaves ³not
ᵖἐλάβετε;‖ 9 οὔπω νοεῖτε, οὐδὲ μνημονεύετε τοὺς· πέντε
¹ye ²took?   Do ye not yet perceive, nor remember the five

ᶻ ἔλαβεν he took LTTr.   ᵃ + καὶ and LT.   ᵇ ἐδίδου TTr.   ᶜ — αὐτοῦ (read the disciples)
[L]T[Tr]A.   ᵈ τοῖς ὄχλοις to the crowds TTrA.   ᵉ τὸ περισσεῦον τῶν κλασμάτων ἦραν LTTrA.
ᶠ παιδίων καὶ γυναικῶν T.   ᵍ ἀνέβη he went up GTᵣAW.   ʰ Μαγαδάν \ agadan LTTrA.
ⁱ ἐπηρώτων T.   ᵏ Ὀψίας .... to end of verse 3 [TA].   ˡ — ὑποκριταί LTTrA; + καὶ
and L.   ᵐ — τοῦ προφήτου LTTrA.   ⁿ — αὐτοῦ (read the disciples) LTTrA.   ᵒ — αὐτοῖς
GLTTrA.   ᵖ ἔχετε ye have L.

ἄρτους τῶν πεντακισχιλίων, καὶ πόσους κοφίνους ἐλάβετε,
loaves of the   five thousand,   and how many hand-baskets ye took [up]?

10 οὐδὲ τοὺς ἑπτὰ ἄρτους τῶν τετρακισχιλίων, καὶ πόσας
nor   the   seven loaves of the   four thousand,   and how many

ᵠσπυρίδας‖ ἐλάβετε; 11 πῶς οὐ.νοεῖτε ὅτι οὐ περὶ
baskets   ye took [up]?   How perceive ye not that not concerning

ʳἄρτου‖ εἶπον ὑμῖν ˢπροσέχειν‖ ἀπὸ τῆς ζύμης τῶν Φαρισαίων
bread I spoke to you   to beware   of   the leaven of the   Pharisees

καὶ Σαδδουκαίων; 12 Τότε συνῆκαν ὅτι οὐκ.εἶπεν προσέχειν
and Sadducees?   Then they understood that he said not   to beware

ἀπὸ τῆς ζύμης ᵗτοῦ ἄρτου,‖ ᵛἀλλ'‖ ἀπὸ τῆς διδαχῆς τῶν
of   the leaven   of bread,   but   of   the teaching of the

Φαρισαίων καὶ Σαδδουκαίων.
Pharisees   and   Sadducees.

13 Ἐλθὼν.δὲ ὁ Ἰησοῦς εἰς τὰ μέρη Καισαρείας τῆς
And ²having ³come ¹Jesus   into the parts of Cæsarea

Φιλίππου ἠρώτα τοὺς.μαθητὰς.αὐτοῦ, λέγων, Τίνα ᵂμε‖
Philippi   he questioned   his disciples,   saying, Whom ᵂme

λέγουσιν οἱ.ἄνθρωποι εἶναι τὸν υἱὸν τοῦ ἀνθρώπου; 14 Οἱ.δὲ
¹do ²pronounce   ²men   ⁹to ¹⁰be ⁵the ⁶Son   ⁷of ⁸man?   And they

ˣεἶπον,‖ Οἱ.μὲν Ἰωάννην τὸν βαπτιστὴν ʸἄλλοι‖.δὲ ᶻἨλίαν‖
said,   Some   John   the   Baptist;   and others   Elias;

ἕτεροι.δὲ Ἱερεμίαν, ἢ ἕνα τῶν προφητῶν. 15 Λέγει αὐτοῖς,ᵃ
and others   Jeremias,   or one of the prophets.   He says to them,

Ὑμεῖς.δὲ τίνα με λέγετε εἶναι; 16 ᵇ'Ἀποκριθεὶς.δὲ‖ Σί-
But ye whom ⁴me ¹do ²ye ³pronounce to be?   And answering   Si-

μων Πέτρος εἶπεν, Σὺ εἶ ὁ χριστός, ὁ υἱὸς τοῦ θεοῦ τοῦ
mon Peter   said, Thou art the Christ,   the Son   of God the

ζῶντος. 17 ᶜΚαὶ ἀποκριθεὶς‖ ὁ Ἰησοῦς εἶπεν αὐτῷ, Μακάριος
living.   And answering   Jesus said to him, Blessed

εἶ, Σίμων ᵈΒὰρ Ἰωνᾶ,‖ ὅτι σὰρξ καὶ αἷμα οὐκ.ἀπεκάλυψέν
art thou, Simon Bar-Jonas,   for flesh and blood revealed [it] not

σοι, ἀλλ' ὁ.πατήρ.μου ὁ ἐν ᵉτοῖς‖ οὐρανοῖς. 18 Κἀγὼ.δὲ
to thee, but   my Father who [is] in   the   heavens.   And I also

σοι λέγω, ὅτι σὺ εἶ Πέτρος, καὶ ἐπὶ ταύτῃ τῇ πέτρᾳ οἰκοδο-
to thee say, That thou art Peter, and on   this   rock   I will

μήσω μου τὴν ἐκκλησίαν, καὶ πύλαι ᾅδου οὐ.κατισχύσουσιν
build my   assembly,   and gates of hades shall not prevail against

αὐτῆς. 19 ᶠκαὶ‖ δώσω σοὶ τὰς ᵍκλεῖς‖ τῆς βασιλείας τῶν
it.   And I will give to thee the keys   of the kingdom of the

οὐρανῶν· καὶ ὃ.ʰἐὰν‖ δήσῃς ἐπὶ τῆς γῆς, ἔσται δεδεμένον
heavens: and whatever thou mayest bind on the earth, shall be   bound

ἐν τοῖς οὐρανοῖς· καὶ ὃ.ⁱἐὰν‖ λύσῃς ἐπὶ τῆς γῆς, ἔσται
in the   heavens; and whatever thou mayest loose on the earth, shall be

λελυμένον ἐν τοῖς οὐρανοῖς. 20 Τότε ᵏδιεστείλατο‖ τοῖς μαθη-
loosed   in the heavens.   Then   charged he   the ²dis-

ταῖς ˡαὐτοῦ‖ ἵνα μηδενὶ εἴπωσιν ὅτι αὐτός ἐστιν ᵐ'Ἰησοῦς‖
ciples ¹his   that to no one they should say that he   is   Jesus

ὁ χριστός.
the Christ.

the five thousand, and how many baskets ye took up? 10 Neither the seven loaves of the four thousand, and how many baskets ye took up? 11 How is it that ye do not understand that I spake it not to you concerning bread, that ye should beware of the leaven of the Pharisees and of the Sadducees? 12 Then understood they how that he bade them not beware of the leaven of bread, but of the doctrine of the Pharisees and of the Sadducees.

13 When Jesus came into the coasts of Cæsarea Philippi, he asked his disciples, saying, Whom do men say that I the Son of man am? 14 And they said, Some say that thou art John the Baptist: some, Elias; and others, Jeremias, or one of the prophets. 15 He saith unto them, But whom say ye that I am? 16 And Simon Peter answered and said, Thou art the Christ, the Son of the living God. 17 And Jesus answered and said unto him, Blessed art thou, Simon Bar-jona: for flesh and blood hath not revealed it unto thee, but my Father which is in heaven. 18 And I say also unto thee, That thou art Peter, and upon this rock I will build my church; and the gates of hell shall not prevail against it. 19 And I will give unto thee the keys of the kingdom of heaven: and whatsoever thou shalt bind on earth shall be bound in heaven: and whatsoever thou shalt loose on earth shall be loosed in heaven. 20 Then charged he his disciples that they should tell no man that he was Jesus the Christ.

ᵠ σφυρίδας L.   ʳ ἄρτων loaves LTTrAW.   ˢ ; (the question ends at you) προσέχετε δὲ but beware LTTrA.   ᵗ τῶν ἄρτων of the loaves LTrA ; τῶν Φαρισαίων καὶ Σαδδουκαίων of the Pharisees and Sadducees T.   ᵛ ἀλλὰ TTrAW.   ᵂ — με [L]TTrA.   ˣ εἶπαν LTTr.   ʸ οἱ Lₒ ᶻ Ἡλείαν T.   ᵃ + [ὁ Ἰησοῦς] Jesus (says) L.   ᵇ καὶ ἀποκριθεὶς W.   ᶜ ἀποκριθεὶς δὲ LTTrA. ᵈ Βαρωνᾶ LTA.   ᵉ — τοῖς (read [the]) L[Tr].   ᶠ — καὶ T[A].   ᵍ κλεῖδας LTTrA.   ʰ ἂν LTᵗ₄. ⁱ ἂν Tr.   ᵏ ἐπετίμησεν he earnestly charged L.   ˡ — αὐτοῦ (read the disciples) LTTrA. ᵐ — Ἰησοῦς GLTTrAW.

21 From that time forth began Jesus to shew unto his disciples, how that he must go unto Jerusalem, and suffer many things of the elders and chief-priests and scribes, and be killed, and be raised again the third day. 22 Then Peter took him, and began to rebuke him, saying, Be it far from thee, Lord: this shall not be unto thee. 23 But he turned, and said unto Peter, Get thee behind me, Satan: thou art an offence unto me: for thou savourest not the things that be of God, but those that be of men. 24 Then said Jesus unto his disciples, If any *man* will come after me, let him deny himself, and take up his cross, and follow me. 25 For whosoever will save his life shall lose it: and whosoever will lose his life for my sake shall find it. 26 For what is a man profited, if he shall gain the whole world, and lose his own soul? or what shall a man give in exchange for his soul? 27 For the Son of man shall come in the glory of his Father with his angels; and then he shall reward every man according to his works. 28 Verily I say, unto you, There be some standing here, which shall not taste of death, till they see the Son of man coming in his kingdom.

XVII. And after six days Jesus taketh Peter, James, and John his brother, and bringeth them up into an high mountain apart, 2 and was transfigured before them: and his face did shine as the sun, and his raiment

---

21 Ἀπὸ τότε ἤρξατο ⁿὁ‖ Ἰησοῦς δεικνύειν τοῖς μαθηταῖς
From that time began   Jesus   to shew   to ²disciples

αὐτοῦ, ὅτι   δεῖ   αὐτὸν °ἀπελθεῖν εἰς Ἱεροσόλυμα,‖ καὶ
¹his   that it is necessary for   him   to go away to   Jerusalem,   and

πολλὰ παθεῖν ἀπὸ τῶν πρεσβυτέρων καὶ ἀρχιερέων καὶ
many things to suffer from the   elders   and chief priests and

γραμματέων, καὶ ἀποκτανθῆναι, καὶ τῇ τρίτῃ ἡμέρᾳ ἐγερθῆναι.
scribes,   and   to be killed,   and the third   day   to be raised.

22 καὶ προσλαβόμενος αὐτὸν ὁ Πέτρος ᵖἤρξατο‖ �q ἐπιτιμᾶν
And ²having ¹taken ⁴to [°him] ⁴him   ¹Peter   began   to rebuke

αὐτῷ, λέγων,‖   Ἵλεώς σοι, κύριε· οὐ.μὴ ἔσται σοι
him,   saying, [God be] favourable to thee, Lord: in no wise shall be to thee

τοῦτο. 23 Ὁ.δὲ στραφεὶς εἶπεν τῷ Πέτρῳ, Ὕπαγε ὀπίσω μου,
this.   But he having turned said   to Peter,   Get   behind me,

σατανᾶ, σκάνδαλόν ʳμου εἶ·‖ ὅτι   οὐ.φρονεῖς τὰ
Satan: an offence   to me thou art, for thy thoughts are not of the things

τοῦ θεοῦ, ἀλλὰ τὰ τῶν ἀνθρώπων. 24 Τότε ὁ Ἰησοῦς εἶπεν
of God, but the things   of men.   Then   Jesus   said

τοῖς.μαθηταῖς.αὐτοῦ, Εἴ τις θέλει ὀπίσω μου ἐλθεῖν, ἀπαρ-
to his disciples,   If any one desires after me to come,   let

νησάσθω ἑαυτόν, καὶ   ἀράτω τὸν.σταυρὸν.αὐτοῦ, καὶ ἀκο-
him deny   himself, and let him take up   his cross,   and let

λουθείτω μοι. 25 ὃς.γὰρ.ἂν‖ θέλῃ τὴν.ψυχὴν.αὐτοῦ σῶσαι,
him follow me. For whoever may desire   his life   to save,

ἀπολέσει αὐτήν· ὃς.δ'.ἂν ἀπολέσῃ τὴν.ψυχὴν.αὐτοῦ ἕνεκεν
shall lose   it;   but whoever may lose   his life   on account of

ἐμοῦ, εὑρήσει αὐτήν. 26 τί.γὰρ ˢὠφελεῖται‖ ἄνθρωπος, ἐὰν
me,   shall find it.   For what is ²profited ¹a ²man,   if

τὸν κόσμον ὅλον κερδήσῃ, τὴν.δὲ.ψυχὴν.αὐτοῦ ζημιωθῇ; ἢ
the ²world ¹whole   he gain,   and his soul   lose?   or

τί   δώσει ἄνθρωπος ἀντάλλαγμα τῆς.ψυχῆς.αὐτοῦ; 27 μέλ-
what will ³give   ¹a ²man   [as] an exchange for   his soul?   For ⁵is

λει.γὰρ ὁ υἱὸς τοῦ.ἀνθρώπου ἔρχεσθαι ἐν τῇ δόξῃ τοῦ πατρὸς
⁶about ¹the ²Son   ³of ⁴man   to come   in the glory   ³Father

αὐτοῦ μετὰ τῶν.ἀγγέλων.αὐτοῦ· καὶ τότε ἀποδώσει ἑκάστῳ
¹of ²his   with   his angels;   and then he will render   to each

κατὰ   τὴν.πρᾶξιν.αὐτοῦ. 28 Ἀμὴν λέγω ὑμῖν, ᵗ εἰσίν
according to   his doing.   Verily I say to you,   There are

τινες ᵘτῶν ὧδε ἑστηκότων,‖ οἵτινες οὐ.μὴ γεύσωνται θανάτου
some of those here   standing   who   in no wise shall taste   of death

ἕως ἂν ἴδωσιν τὸν υἱὸν τοῦ ἀνθρώπου ἐρχόμενον ἐν τῇ
until   they have seen the Son   of man   coming   in

βασιλείᾳ.αὐτοῦ.
his kingdom.

17 Καὶ μεθ' ἡμέρας ἓξ παραλαμβάνει ὁ Ἰησοῦς τὸν Πέτρον
And after ²days ¹six ⁴takes ⁵with [°him]   ³Jesus   Peter

καὶ Ἰάκωβον καὶ Ἰωάννην τὸν.ἀδελφὸν.αὐτοῦ, καὶ ἀναφέρει
and James   and John   his brother,   and brings up

αὐτοὺς εἰς ὄρος ὑψηλὸν κατ'.ἰδίαν. 2 καὶ μετεμορφώθη
them   into a ²mountain ¹high   apart.   And he was transfigured

ἔμπροσθεν αὐτῶν, καὶ ἔλαμψεν τὸ.πρόσωπον.αὐτοῦ ὡς ὁ ἥλιος,
before   them, and ³shone   ¹his ²face   as the sun,

ⁿ — ὁ L[Tr]A.   ° εἰς Ἱεροσόλυμα ἀπελθεῖν LTTrA.   ᵖ — ἤρξατο A.   q αὐτῷ ἐπιτιμᾶν
λέγων L ; λέγει αὐτῷ ἐπιτιμῶν says to him rebuking [him] A.   ʳ εἶ ἐμοὶ LTTrA.   ˢ ἐὰν
LTTrA.   ᵗ ὠφεληθήσεται shall be profited LTTrA.   ᵛ + ὅτι that LT.   ᵘ τῶν ὧδε ἑστώτων
GLTTrA ; ὧδε ἑστῶτες W.

τὰ.δὲ.ἱμάτια.αὐτοῦ ἐγένετο λευκὰ ὡς τὸ φῶς. 3 καὶ ἰδού, ˣὤφ-
and his garments became white as the light; and behold, ᵃap-
θησαν‖ αὐτοῖς ʸΜωσῆς‖ καὶ ᶻἩλίας,‖ ᵃμετ᾽ αὐτοῦ συλλαλοῦντες.‖
peared ⁴to⁵them ¹Moses ²and ³Elias ⁶with ⁵him ⁷talking.

4 ἀποκριθεὶς.δὲ ὁ Πέτρος εἶπεν τῷ Ἰησοῦ, Κύριε, καλόν ἐστιν
And answering Peter said to Jesus, Lord, good .it is

ἡμᾶς ὧδε εἶναι· εἰ θέλεις, ᵇποιήσωμεν‖ ὧδε τρεῖς σκηνάς,
for us here to be. If thou wilt, let us make here three tabernacles:

σοὶ μίαν, καὶ ᶜΜωσῇ‖ μίαν, καὶ ᵈμίαν Ἠλίᾳ.‖ 5 Ἔτι αὐτοῦ
for thee one, and for Moses one, and one for Elias. While yet he

λαλοῦντος, ἰδού, νεφέλη ᵉφωτεινὴ‖ ἐπεσκίασεν αὐτούς· καὶ
was speaking, behold, a cloud ¹bright overshadowed them: and

ἰδού, φωνὴ ἐκ τῆς νεφέλης, λέγουσα, Οὗτός ἐστιν ὁ.υἱός.μου
lo, a voice out of the cloud, saying, This is my Son

ὁ ἀγαπητός, ἐν ᾧ ᶠεὐδόκησα·‖ ᵍαὐτοῦ ἀκούετε.‖ 6 Καὶ
the beloved, in whom I have found delight: ³him ¹hear ²ye. And

ἀκούσαντες οἱ μαθηταὶ ʰἔπεσον‖ ἐπὶ πρόσωπον.αὐτῶν, καὶ
hearing [it] the ¹disciples fell upon their face, and

ἐφοβήθησαν σφόδρα. 7 καὶ ⁱπροσελθὼν‖ ὁ Ἰησοῦς ᵏἥψατο‖
were terrified greatly. And having come to [them] Jesus touched

αὐτῶν, ˡκαὶ‖ εἶπεν, Ἐγέρθητε, καὶ μὴ.φοβεῖσθε. 8 Ἐπάραντες
them, and said, Rise up, and be not terrified. 8 Having ³lifted ⁴up

δὲ τοὺς.ὀφθαλμοὺς.αὐτῶν οὐδένα εἶδον εἰ.μὴ τὸν Ἰησοῦν
¹and their eyes ²no ⁴one ¹they ²saw except Jesus

μόνον.
alone.

9 Καὶ καταβαινόντων αὐτῶν ᵐἀπὸ‖ τοῦ ὄρους ἐνετείλατο
And as ²were ³descending ¹they from the mountain ²charged

αὐτοῖς ὁ Ἰησοῦς, λέγων, Μηδενὶ εἴπητε τὸ ὅραμα, ἕως.οὗ ὁ
³them ¹Jesus, saying, To no one tell the vision, until the

υἱὸς τοῦ ἀνθρώπου ἐκ νεκρῶν ⁿἀναστῇ.‖ 10 Καὶ ἐπη-
Son of man from among [the] dead be risen. And ²ask-

ρώτησαν αὐτὸν οἱ.μαθηταὶ.ᵒαὐτοῦ,‖ λέγοντες, Τί οὖν οἱ γραμ-
ed ⁴him ¹his ²disciples, saying, Why then ²the ³scribes

ματεῖς λέγουσιν ὅτι ᵖἨλίαν‖ δεῖ ἐλθεῖν πρῶτον; 11 Ὁ.δὲ
¹say that Elias must come first? And

ᑫἸησοῦς‖ ἀποκριθεὶς εἶπεν ʳαὐτοῖς,‖ ˢἨλίας‖ μὲν ἔρχεται
Jesus answering said to them, Elias indeed comes

ᵗπρῶτον‖ καὶ ἀποκαταστήσει πάντα· 12 λέγω δὲ ὑμῖν ὅτι
first and shall restore all things. But I say to you that

ˢἨλίας‖ ἤδη ἦλθεν, καὶ οὐκ.ἐπέγνωσαν αὐτόν, ᵛἀλλ᾽‖ ἐποίη-
Elias already is come, and they knew not him, but did

σαν ἐν αὐτῷ ὅσα ἠθέλησαν· οὕτως καὶ ὁ υἱὸς τοῦ ἀνθρώπου
to him whatever they desired. Thus also the Son of man

μέλλει πάσχειν ὑπ᾽ αὐτῶν. 13 Τότε συνῆκαν οἱ μαθηταὶ ὅτι
is about to suffer from them. Then understood the disciples that

περὶ Ἰωάννου τοῦ βαπτιστοῦ εἶπεν αὐτοῖς.
concerning John the Baptist he spoke to them.

14 Καὶ ἐλθόντων ʷαὐτῶν‖ πρὸς τὸν ὄχλον προσῆλθεν
And ²having ³come ¹they to the crowd ²came

---

was white as the light.
3 And, behold, there appeared unto them Moses and Elias talking with him. 4 Then answered Peter, and said unto Jesus, Lord, it is good for us to be here: if thou wilt, let us make here three tabernacles; one for thee, and one for Moses, and one for Elias. 5 While he yet spake, behold, a bright cloud overshadowed them: and behold a voice out of the cloud, which said, This is my beloved Son, in whom I am well pleased; hear ye him. 6 And when the disciples heard it, they fell on their face, and were sore afraid. 7 And Jesus came and touched them, and said, Arise, and be not afraid. 8 And when they had lifted up their eyes, they saw no man, save Jesus only.

9 And as they came down from the mountain, Jesus charged them, saying, Tell the vision to no man, until the Son of man be risen again from the dead. 10 And his disciples asked him, saying, Why then say the scribes that Elias must first come? 11 And Jesus answered and said unto them, Elias truly shall first come, and restore all things. 12 But I say unto you, That Elias is come already, and they knew him not, but have done unto him whatsoever they listed. Likewise shall also the Son of man suffer of them. 13 Then the disciples understood that he spake unto them of John the Baptist.

14 And when they were come to the multitude, there came to

ˣ ὤφθη LTTrA. ʸ Μωϋσῆς LTTrAW. ᶻ Ἠλείας T. ᵃ συλλαλοῦντες (συνλαλ. T) μετ᾽ αὐτοῦ LTTr. ᵇ ποιήσω I will make LTA. ᶜ Μωυσεῖ LTTrA; Μωϋσῇ W. ᵈ Ἠλίᾳ (Ἠλείᾳ T) μίαν LTTrA. ᵉ φωτὸς of light G. ᶠ ηὐδόκησα LTr. ᵍ ἀκούετε αὐτοῦ LTTrA. ʰ ἔπεσαν LTTrA. ⁱ προσῆλθεν came to LTTr. ᵏ καὶ ἀψάμενος and touching LT; καὶ ἥψατο Tr. ˡ — καὶ LT. ᵐ ἐκ GLTTrAW. ⁿ ἐγερθῇ be raised LTTrA. ᵒ — αὐτοῦ (read the disciples) LTTr. ᵖ Ἠλείαν T. ᑫ — Ἰησοῦς (read he said) LTTrA. ʳ — αὐτοῖς LTTr[A]. ˢ Ἠλείας T. ᵗ — πρῶτον LTTrA. ᵛ ἀλλὰ TrA. ʷ — αὐτῶν LTTrA.

him a *certain man*, kneeling down to him, and saying, 15 Lord, have mercy on my son: for he is lunatick, and sore vexed: for ofttimes he falleth into the fire, and oft into the water. 16 And I brought him to thy disciples, and they could not cure him. 17 Then Jesus answered and said, O faithless and perverse generation, how long shall I be with you? how long shall I suffer you? bring him hither to me. 18 And Jesus rebuked the devil; and he departed out of him: and the child was cured from that very hour. 19 Then came the disciples to Jesus apart, and said, Why could not we cast him out? 20 And Jesus said unto them, Because of your unbelief: for verily I say unto you, If ye have faith as a grain of mustard seed, ye shall say unto this mountain, Remove hence to yonder place; and it shall remove; and nothing shall be impossible unto you. 21 Howbeit this kind goeth not out but by prayer and fasting.

22 And while they abode in Galilee, Jesus said unto them, The Son of man shall be betrayed into the hands of men: 23 and they shall kill him, and the third day he shall be raised again. And they were exceeding sorry.

24 And when they were come to Capernaum, they that received tribute *money* came to Peter, and said, Doth not your master pay tribute? 25 He saith, Yes. And when he was come into the house, Jesus prevented him, saying, What thinkest thou, Simon? of whom do the kings of the earth take custom or tribute? of their own children, or of strangers? 26 Pe-

αὐτῷ ἄνθρωπος γονυπετῶν ˣαὐτῷ,‖ 15 καὶ λέγων, Κύριε,
⁴to ⁵him ¹a ²man kneeling down to him, and saying, Lord,

ἐλέησόν μου τὸν υἱόν, ὅτι σεληνιάζεται καὶ ˠκακῶς πάσχει‖
have pity on my son, for he is lunatic and miserably suffers:

πολλάκις-γὰρ πίπτει εἰς τὸ πῦρ, καὶ πολλάκις εἰς τὸ ὕδωρ.
for often he falls into the fire, and often into the water.

16 καὶ προσήνεγκα αὐτὸν τοῖς-μαθηταῖς-σου, καὶ οὐκ-ἠδυνή⁴
And I brought him to thy disciples, and they were not

θησαν αὐτὸν θεραπεῦσαι. 17 Ἀποκριθεὶς-δὲ ὁ Ἰησοῦς εἶπεν,
able him to heal. And answering Jesus said,

Ὦ γενεὰ ἄπιστος καὶ διεστραμμένη, ἕως πότε ᶻἔσομαι
O generation unbelieving and perverted, until when shall I be

μεθ᾽ ὑμῶν;‖ ἕως πότε ἀνέξομαι ὑμῶν; φέρετέ μοι αὐτὸν ὧδε.
with you? until when shall I bear with you? Bring to me him here.

18 Καὶ ἐπετίμησεν αὐτῷ ὁ Ἰησοῦς, καὶ ἐξῆλθεν ἀπ᾽ αὐτοῦ τὸ
And ²rebuked ³him ¹Jesus, and went out from him the

δαιμόνιον, καὶ ἐθεραπεύθη ὁ παῖς ἀπὸ τῆς-ὥρας-ἐκείνης.
demon, and was healed the boy from that hour.

19 Τότε προσελθόντες οἱ μαθηταὶ τῷ Ἰησοῦ κατ᾽-ἰδίαν εἶπον,
Then ³having ⁴come ¹the ²disciples to Jesus apart said,

ᵃΔιατί‖ ἡμεῖς οὐκ-ἠδυνήθημεν ἐκβαλεῖν αὐτό; 20 Ὁ-δὲ-ᵇἸη‚σοῦς‖
Why ³we ¹were ²not able to cast out him? And Jesus

ᶜεἶπεν‖ αὐτοῖς, Διὰ τὴν-ᵈἀπιστίαν‖ ὑμῶν. ἀμὴν-γὰρ λέγω
said to them, Because of ²unbelief ¹your. For verily I say

ὑμῖν, ἐὰν ἔχητε πίστιν ὡς κόκκον σινάπεως, ἐρεῖτε τῷ ὄρει
to you, If ye have faith as a grain of mustard, ye shall say ²mountain

τούτῳ, ᵉΜετάβηθι ἐντεῦθεν‖ ἐκεῖ, καὶ μεταβήσεται· καὶ οὐδὲν
¹to ²this, Remove hence thither, and it shall remove; and nothing

ἀδυνατήσει ὑμῖν. 21 ᶠτοῦτο-δὲ-τὸ-γένος οὐκ-ἐκπορεύεται
shall be impossible to you. But this kind goes not out

εἰ-μὴ ἐν προσευχῇ καὶ νηστείᾳ.‖
except by prayer and fasting.

22 ᵍἈναστρεφομένων‖ δὲ αὐτῶν ἐν τῇ Γαλιλαίᾳ, εἶπεν αὐτοῖς
And while ²were ³abiding ¹they in Galilee, ³said ⁴to ⁴them

ὁ Ἰησοῦς, Μέλλει ὁ υἱὸς τοῦ ἀνθρώπου παραδίδοσθαι εἰς
¹Jesus, ⁹is ¹⁰about ⁵the ⁸Son ⁷of ⁶man to be delivered up into

χεῖρας ἀνθρώπων, 23 καὶ ἀποκτενοῦσιν αὐτόν, καὶ τῇ τρίτῃ
[the] hands of men, and they will kill him; and the third

ἡμέρᾳ ʰἐγερθήσεται.‖ Καὶ ἐλυπήθησαν σφόδρα.
day he shall be raised up. And they were grieved greatly.

24 Ἐλθόντων-δὲ αὐτῶν εἰς ⁱΚαπερναοὺμ‖ προσῆλθον οἱ
And ²having ³come ¹they to Capernaum ⁶came ¹those ²who

τὰ δίδραχμα λαμβάνοντες τῷ Πέτρῳ καὶ ᵏεἶπον,‖ Ὁ διδάσ-
⁴the ⁵didrachmas ³received to Peter and said, ²Teach-

καλος ὑμῶν οὐ-τελεῖ ˡτὰ‖ δίδραχμα; 25 Λέγει, Ναί. Καὶ
er ¹your does he not pay the didrachmas? He says, Yes. And

ᵐὅτε εἰσῆλθεν‖ εἰς τὴν οἰκίαν προέφθασεν αὐτὸν ὁ Ἰησοῦς,
when he entered into the house ²anticipated ³him ¹Jesus,

λέγων, Τί σοι-δοκεῖ, Σίμων; οἱ βασιλεῖς τῆς γῆς ἀπὸ τίνων
saying, What thinkest thou, Simon? The kings of the earth from whom

λαμβάνουσιν τέλη ἢ κῆνσον; ἀπὸ τῶν-υἱῶν-αὐτῶν, ἢ ἀπὸ
do they receive custom or tribute? from their sons, or from

ˣ αὐτόν GLTTrAW. ˠ κακῶς ἔχει is ill LTr. ᶻ μεθ᾽ ὑμῶν ἔσομαι LTTrA. ᵃ διὰ τί LTTrAW.
ᵇ Ἰησοῦς LTTrA. ᶜ λέγει he says LTTrA. ᵈ ὀλιγοπιστίαν little faith LTTrA. ᵉ Μετάβα
ἔνθεν LTTrA. ᶠ verse 21 Τ[TrA]. ᵍ Συστρεφομένων were abiding together LTTr.
ʰ ἀναστήσεται he shall rise again L. ⁱ Καφαρναοὺμ LTTrAW. ᵏ εἶπαν LTTrA. ˡ τὰ Τ.
ᵐ εἰσελθόντα entering LT; ἐλθόντα having come TrA.

τῶν ἀλλοτρίων; 26 ⁿΛέγει αὐτῷ‖ ᵒὁ Πέτρος,‖ Ἀπὸ τῶν ἀλ-
the   strangers?   ²says ³to ⁴him   ¹Peter,   From the stran-

λοτρίων. Ἔφη αὐτῷ ὁ Ἰησοῦς, ᵖἌραγε‖ ἐλεύθεροί εἰσιν οἱ
gers.   ²said ³to ⁴him ¹Jesus,   Then indeed free   are   the

υἱοί. 27 ἵνα δὲ μὴ ᵠσκανδαλίσωμεν‖ αὐτούς, πορευθεὶς εἰς
sons.   But that we may not offend   them, having gone to

ʳτὴν‖ θάλασσαν βάλε ἄγκιστρον, καὶ τὸν ἀναβάντα πρῶτον
the   sea   cast a hook,   and the ³coming ⁴up ²first

ἰχθὺν ἆρον· καὶ ἀνοίξας τὸ στόμα αὐτοῦ εὑρήσεις στα-
¹fish take, and having opened its mouth   thou shalt find a sta-

τῆρα· ἐκεῖνον λαβὼν δὸς αὐτοῖς ἀντὶ ἐμοῦ καὶ σοῦ.
ter; that   having taken give-to them for me and thee.

18 Ἐν ἐκείνῃ τῇ ˢὥρᾳ‖ προσῆλθον οἱ μαθηταὶ τῷ Ἰησοῦ,
   In that   hour   came   the disciples   to Jesus,

λέγοντες, Τίς ἄρα μείζων ἐστὶν ἐν τῇ βασιλείᾳ τῶν οὐ-
saying, Who then [²the] ³greater ¹is in the kingdom of the hea-

ρανῶν; 2 Καὶ προσκαλεσάμενος ᵗὁ Ἰησοῦς‖ παιδίον, ἔστησεν
vens?   And ²having ³called ⁴to [²him] ¹Jesus a little child, he set

αὐτὸ ἐν μέσῳ αὐτῶν, 3 καὶ εἶπεν, Ἀμὴν λέγω ὑμῖν, ἐὰν μὴ
it in their midst, and said, Verily I say to you, Unless

στραφῆτε καὶ γένησθε ὡς τὰ παιδία, οὐ μὴ εἰσέλθητε εἰς
ye are converted and become as the little children, in no wise shall ye enter into

τὴν βασιλείαν τῶν οὐρανῶν. 4 ὅστις οὖν ᵛταπεινώσῃ‖
the kingdom   of the heavens. Whosoever therefore will humble

ἑαυτὸν ὡς τὸ παιδίον τοῦτο, οὗτός ἐστιν ὁ μείζων ἐν τῇ βασι-
himself as this little child, he is the greater in the king-

λείᾳ τῶν οὐρανῶν. 5 καὶ ὃς ᵂἐὰν‖ δέξηται ˣπαιδίον τοιοῦτον
dom of the heavens; and whoever will receive ³little ⁴child ²such

ἓν‖ ἐπὶ τῷ ὀνόματί μου, ἐμὲ δέχεται· 6 ὃς δ᾽ ἂν σκανδαλίσῃ
¹one in my name,   ²me ¹receives. But whoever shall cause ⁶to ⁷offend

ἕνα τῶν μικρῶν τούτων τῶν πιστευόντων εἰς ἐμέ, συμφέρει
¹one ²of ³these ⁴little ⁵ones who believe in me, it is profitable

αὐτῷ ἵνα κρεμασθῇ μύλος ὀνικὸς ʸἐπὶ‖ τὸν
for him that should be hung ⁴a ³millstone ⁴turned ⁷by ⁸an ⁹ass ¹upon

τράχηλον αὐτοῦ, καὶ καταποντισθῇ ἐν τῷ πελάγει τῆς θαλάσ-
²his ¹neck,   and he be sunk   in the depth of the sea.

σης. 7 Οὐαὶ τῷ κόσμῳ ἀπὸ τῶν σκανδάλων· ἀνάγκη γάρ
     Woe to the world because of the offences! For necessary

ᶻἐστιν‖ ἐλθεῖν τὰ σκάνδαλα, πλὴν οὐαὶ τῷ ἀνθρώπῳ ᵃἐκείνῳ‖
it is ³to ⁴come ¹the ²offences, yet woe to that man

δι᾽ οὗ τὸ σκάνδαλον ἔρχεται. 8 Εἰ δὲ ἡ χείρ σου ἢ ὁ πούς σου
by whom the offence comes! And if thy hand or thy foot

σκανδαλίζει σε, ἔκκοψον ᵇαὐτὰ‖ καὶ βάλε ἀπὸ σοῦ· καλόν
cause ²to ³offend ¹thee, cut off them and cast [them] from thee; good

σοί ἐστιν εἰσελθεῖν εἰς τὴν ζωὴν ᶜχωλὸν ἢ κυλλόν, ἢ
for thee it is to enter into life lame or maimed, [rather] than

δύο χεῖρας ἢ δύο πόδας ἔχοντα βληθῆναι εἰς τὸ πῦρ τὸ αἰώνιον.
two hands or two feet having to be cast into the fire the eternal.

9 καὶ εἰ ὁ ὀφθαλμός σου σκανδαλίζει σε, ἔξελε αὐτὸν καὶ βάλε
And if thine eye cause ²to ³offend ¹thee, pluck out it and cast

ἀπὸ σοῦ· καλόν σοι ἐστιν μονόφθαλμον εἰς τὴν ζωὴν
[it] from thee; good for thee it is   one-eyed   into   life

---

ter saith unto him, Of
strangers. Jesus saith
unto him, Then are the
children free. 27 Not-
withstanding. lest we
should offend them,
go thou to the sea, and
cast an hook, and take
up the fish that first
cometh up; and when
thou hast opened his
mouth, thou shalt find
a piece of money: that
take, and give unto
them for me and thee\

XVIII. At the same
time came the disci-
ples unto Jesus, say-
ing, Who is the greatest
in the kingdom of
heaven? 2 And Jesus
called a little child
unto him, and set him
in the midst of them,
3 and said, Verily I say
unto you, Except ye
be converted, and be-
come as little children,
ye shall not enter into
the kingdom of hea\
ven. 4 Whosoever
therefore shall humble
himself as this little
child, the same is
greatest in the king\
dom of heaven. 5 And
whoso shall receive
one such little child in
my name receive th me.
6 But whoso shall of-
fend one of these little
ones which believe in
me, it were better for
him that a millstone
were hanged about his
neck, and that he were
drowned in the depth
of the sea. 7 Woe unto
the world because of
offences! for it must
needs be that offences
come; but woe to
that man by whom
the offence cometh!
8 Wherefore if thy
hand or thy foot of-
fend thee, cut them
off, and cast them from
thee: it is better for
thee to enter into life
halt or maimed, rather,
than having two hands
or two feet to be cast
into everlasting fire.
9 And if thine eye of-
fend thee, pluck it
out, and cast it from
thee: it is better for
thee to enter into life
with one eye, rather

ⁿ εἰπόντος δὲ and having said LTTr.   ᵒ — ὁ Πέτρος LTTrA.   ᵖ Ἄρα γε TrA.   ᵠ σκαν-
δαλίζωμεν T.   ʳ — τὴν (read [the]) LTTrAW.   ˢ ἡμέρᾳ day L.   ᵗ — ὁ Ἰησοῦς TTrA.
ᵛ ταπεινώσει LTTrAW.   ᵂ ἂν LTr.   ˣ ἐν παιδίον τοιοῦτον (— ν T) LTTrA.   ʸ περὶ about LTTr;
εἰς το A.   ᶻ — ἐστιν (read [it is]) LTrA.   ᵃ — ἐκείνῳ (read to the man) LTTr;   ᵇ αὐτὸν
it (and cast [it]) LTTrA.   ᶜ κυλλὸν ἢ χωλόν LT.

than having two eyes to be cast into hell fire. 10 Take heed that ye despise not one of these little ones; for I say unto you, That in heaven their angels do always behold the face of my Father which is in heaven. 11 For the Son of man is come to save that which was lost. 12 How think ye? if a man have an hundred sheep, and one of them be gone astray, doth he not leave the ninety and nine, and goeth into the mountains, and seeketh that which is gone astray? 13 And if so be that he find it, verily I say unto you, he rejoiceth more of that *sheep*, than of the ninety and nine which went not astray. 14 Even so it is not the will of your Father which is in heaven, that one of these little ones should perish.

εἰσελθεῖν,　　ἢ δύο ὀφθαλμοὺς ἔχοντα βληθῆναι εἰς τὴν
to enter, [rather] than two　　eyes　　having　to be cast　into the
γέενναν τοῦ πυρός. 10 Ὁρᾶτε μὴ καταφρονήσητε ἑνὸς τῶν
Gehenna of the fire.　　See ,　ye despise not　　one
μικρῶν τούτων· λέγω γὰρ ὑμῖν, ὅτι οἱ ἄγγελοι αὐτῶν [d]ἐν
of these little ones,　for I say to you, that　their angels　in [the]
οὐρανοῖς‖ διὰ παντὸς βλέπουσιν τὸ πρόσωπον τοῦ πατρός μου
heavens　continually　behold　the　face　of my Father
τοῦ ἐν οὐρανοῖς. 11 [e]ἦλθεν γὰρ ὁ υἱὸς τοῦ ἀνθρώπου
who [is] in [the] heavens.　　For is come the Son　　of man
σῶσαι τὸ ἀπολωλός.‖ 12 Τί ὑμῖν δοκεῖ; ἐὰν γένηταί
to save that which has been lost.　What think ye?　If there should be
τινι ἀνθρώπῳ ἑκατὸν πρόβατα, καὶ πλανηθῇ ἓν ἐξ αὐτῶν,
to any man　a hundred sheep,　and be gone astray one of them,
οὐχὶ [f]ἀφεὶς‖ τὰ [g]ἐννενηκονταεννέα‖ ἐπὶ τὰ ὄρη
[does he] not, having left the ninety-nine　on the mountains,
[h]πορευθεὶς ζητεῖ τὸ πλανώμενον; 13 καὶ ἐὰν γένηται
having gone　seek that which is gone astray?　and if it should be
εὑρεῖν αὐτό, ἀμὴν λέγω ὑμῖν, ὅτι χαίρει ἐπ' αὐτῷ μᾶλλον
that he find it,　verily I say to you, that he rejoices over it　more
ἢ ἐπὶ τοῖς [g]ἐννενηκονταεννέα‖ τοῖς μὴ πεπλανημένοις. 14 οὕ-
than over the　ninety-nine　which have not gone astray.　So
τως οὐκ ἔστιν θέλημα ἔμπροσθεν τοῦ πατρὸς [i]ὑμῶν‖ τοῦ
it is not [the] will　before　"Father 'your who [is]
ἐν οὐρανοῖς, ἵνα ἀπόληται [k]εἷς‖ τῶν μικρῶν τούτων.
in [the] heavens, that should perish one　of these little ones.

15 Moreover if thy brother shall trespass against thee, go and tell him his fault between thee and him alone: if he shall hear thee, thou hast gained thy brother. 16 But if he will not hear *thee*, *then* take with thee one or two more, that in the mouth of two or three witnesses every word may be established. 17 And if he shall neglect to hear them, tell *it* unto the church: but if he neglect to hear the church, let him be unto thee as an heathen man and a publican. 18 Verily I say unto you, Whatsoever ye shall bind on earth shall be bound in heaven: and whatsoever ye shall loose on earth shall be loosed in heaven. 19 Again I say unto you, That if two of you shall agree on earth as touching any thing that they shall ask, it shall be done for them of my Father which is in

15 Ἐὰν δὲ ἁμαρτήσῃ [l]εἰς σὲ‖ ὁ ἀδελφός σου, ὕπαγε [m]καὶ‖
But if　²sin　⁴against ³thee　¹thy ⁵brother,　go　and
ἔλεγξον αὐτὸν μεταξὺ σοῦ καὶ αὐτοῦ μόνου. ἐάν σου ἀκούσῃ,
reprove　him　between thee and him　alone.　If　thee he will hear,
ἐκέρδησας τὸν ἀδελφόν σου· 16 ἐὰν δὲ μὴ ἀκούσῃ, παράλαβε
thou hast gained　thy brother.　But if he will not hear,　take
[n]μετὰ σοῦ‖ ἔτι ἕνα ἢ δύο, ἵνα ἐπὶ στόματος δύο μαρτύρων
with thee besides one or two, that upon [the] mouth of two witnesses
ἢ τριῶν σταθῇ πᾶν ῥῆμα. 17 ἐὰν δὲ παρακούσῃ αὐτῶν,
or of three may stand every word.　But if he fail to listen to them,
[o]εἰπὲ‖ τῇ ἐκκλησίᾳ· ἐὰν δὲ καὶ τῆς ἐκκλησίας παρακούσῃ,
tell [it] to the assembly.　And if also the assembly he fail to listen to,
ἔστω σοι ὥσπερ ὁ ἐθνικὸς καὶ ὁ τελώνης. 18 Ἀμὴν λέγω
let him be to thee as,　the heathen and the taxgatherer.　Verily I say
ὑμῖν, ὅσα [p]ἐὰν‖ δήσητε ἐπὶ τῆς γῆς, ἔσται δεδεμένα ἐν [r]τῷ‖
to you, Whatsoever ye shall bind on the earth, shall be bound in the
οὐρανῷ· καὶ ὅσα ἐὰν λύσητε ἐπὶ τῆς γῆς, ἔσται λελυμένα
heaven;　and whatsoever ye shall loose on the earth, shall be loosed
ἐν [r]τῷ‖ οὐρανῷ. 19 [s]Πάλιν‖ λέγω ὑμῖν, ὅτι ἐὰν δύο ὑμῶν
in the heaven.　Again I say to you, that if two of you
συμφωνήσωσιν‖ ἐπὶ τῆς γῆς περὶ παντὸς πράγματος οὐ ἐὰν
may agree　on the earth concerning any matter whatever
αἰτήσωνται, γενήσεται αὐτοῖς παρὰ τοῦ πατρός μου τοῦ
they shall ask, it shall be done to them from my Father who [is]

---

[d] ἐν τῷ οὐρανῷ in the heaven [L]A. 　[e] — verse 11 LTTr[A]. 　[f] ἀφήσει (*read* will
he not leave) LTr. 　[g] ἐνενήκοντα ἐννέα LTTr; ἐνενηκονταεννέα W. 　[h] + καὶ and LTr.
[i] μου my LTr. 　[k] ἓν LTTr. 　[l] — εἰς σὲ LT[A]. 　[m] καὶ GLTTrA. 　[n] — μετὰ
σοῦ L; μετὰ σεαυτοῦ with thyself T. 　[o] + μετὰ σοῦ L. 　[p] εἰπὸν T. 　[q] ἂν LTrA.
[r] — τῷ LT[Tr]A. 　[s] ἀμὴν verily L; πάλιν ἀμὴν TrA. 　
συμφωνήσουσιν ἐξ ὑμῶν of you shall agree TTrA. 　συμφωνήσωσιν ἐξ ὑμῶν L;

ἐν οὐρανοῖς. 20 οὐ γὰρ εἰσιν δύο ἢ τρεῖς συνηγμένοι εἰς
in [the] heavens. For where are two or three gathered together unto

τὸ ἐμὸν ὄνομα, ἐκεῖ εἰμι ἐν μέσῳ αὐτῶν.
my name, there am I in [the] midst of them.

21 Τότε προσελθὼν ᵘαὐτῷ ὁ Πέτρος εἶπεν,ᵛ Κύριε, ποσάκις
Then having come to him Peter said, Lord, how often

ἁμαρτήσει εἰς ἐμὲ ὁ ἀδελφός μου καὶ ἀφήσω αὐτῷ; ἕως
shall ³sin ²against ⁵me ¹my ²brother and I forgive him? until

ἑπτάκις; 22 Λέγει αὐτῷ ὁ Ἰησοῦς, Οὐ λέγω σοι ἕως ἑπτάκις,
seven times? ²Says ³to ⁴him ¹Jesus, I say not to thee until seven times,

ᵛἀλλ'ᵛ ἕως ἑβδομηκοντάκις ἑπτά. 23 Διὰ τοῦτο ὡμοιώθη
but until seventy times seven. Because of this ⁵has ⁷become ⁸like

ἡ βασιλεία τῶν οὐρανῶν ἀνθρώπῳ βασιλεῖ, ὃς ἠθέλησεν
⁴the ¹kingdom ³of ⁴the ⁵heavens to a man a king, who would

συνᾶραι λόγον μετὰ τῶν δούλων αὐτοῦ. 24 ἀρξαμένου δὲ αὐτοῦ
take account with his bondmen. And ²having ³begun ¹he

σνναίρειν, ʷπροσηνέχθηᵛ ˣαὐτῷ εἷςᵛ ὀφειλέτης μυρίων
to reckon, there was brought to him one debtor of ten thousand

ταλάντων. 25 μὴ ἔχοντος δὲ αὐτοῦ ἀποδοῦναι, ἐ-
talents. But ²not ¹having he [wherewith] to pay, ³com-

κέλευσεν αὐτὸν ὁ κύριος ʸαὐτοῦᵛ πραθῆναι, καὶ τὴν γυναῖκα
manded ⁴him ¹his ²lord to be sold, and ³wife

ᶻαὐτοῦᵛ καὶ τὰ ᵗέκνα, καὶ πάντα ὅσα ᵃεἶχεν,ᵛ καὶ ἀποδο-
¹his and the children, and all as much as he had, and payment to

θῆναι. 26 πεσὼν οὖν ὁ δοῦλοςᵇ προσεκύνει αὐτῷ,
be made. Having fallen down therefore the bondman did homage to him,

λέγων, ᶜΚύριε,ᵛ μακροθύμησον ἐπ' ᵈἐμοί,ᵛ καὶ πάντα ᵉσοι
saying, Lord, have patience with me, and ⁶all ⁴to ⁵thee

ἀποδώσω.ᵛ 27 σπλαγχνισθεὶς δὲ ὁ κύριος τοῦ δούλου
¹I ²will ³pay. And having been moved with compassion the lord ²bondman

ᶠἐκείνουᵛ ἀπέλυσεν αὐτόν, καὶ τὸ δάνειον ἀφῆκεν αὐτῷ.
¹of ³that released him, and ³the ⁴loan forgave ²him.

28 Ἐξελθὼν δὲ ὁ δοῦλος ᵍἐκεῖνοςᵛ εὗρεν ἕνα τῶν συνδούλων
But having gone out that bondman found one ³fellow ⁴bondmen

αὐτοῦ, ὃς ὤφειλεν αὐτῷ ἑκατὸν δηνάρια, καὶ κρατήσας αὐτὸν
¹of ²his, who owed him a hundred denarii, and having seized him

ἔπνιγεν, λέγων, Ἀπόδος ʰμοι ⁱὅ τιᵛ ὀφείλεις. 29 πε-
he throttled [him], saying, Pay me what thou owest. ⁵Having ⁶fallen

σὼν οὖν ὁ σύνδουλος αὐτοῦ ᵏεἰς τοὺς πόδας αὐτοῦᵛ παρε-
⁷down ⁴therefore ¹his ²fellow ³bondman ⁴at his feet be-

κάλει αὐτόν, λέγων, Μακροθύμησον ἐπ' ¹ἐμοί,ᵛ καὶ ᵐπάντᵛ
sought him, saying, Have patience with me, and all

ἀποδώσω σοι. 30 Ὁ δὲ οὐκ ἤθελεν, ⁿἀλλὰᵛ ἀπελθὼν ἔβαλεν
I will pay thee. But he would not, but having gone he cast

αὐτὸν εἰς φυλακήν, ἕως ᵒοὗᵛ ἀποδῷ τὸ ὀφειλόμενον.
him into prison, until he should pay that which was owing.

31 ἰδόντες ᵖδὲ οἱ σύνδουλοι αὐτοῦᵛ τὰ ᵠγενόμεναᵛ
⁵Having ⁶seen ¹but ²his ³fellow ⁴bondmen what things had taken place,

ἐλυπήθησαν σφόδρα· καὶ ἐλθόντες διεσάφησαν τῷ κυρίῳ ʳαὐτῶνᵛ
were grieved greatly, and having gone narrated to their lord

ᵃ ὁ Πέτρος εἶπεν αὐτῷ LTTrA. ᵛ ἀλλὰ LTrA. ʷ προσήχθη was conducted LTrA. ˣ εἰς αὐτῷ T.
ʸ — αὐτοῦ (read [his] lord) TTrA. ᶻ — αὐτοῦ (read [his] wife) T[A]. ᵃ ἔχει he has LTrA.
ᵇ + ἐκεῖνος (read that bondman) T. ᶜ — Κύριε LTTrA. ᵈ ἐμέ Tr. ᵉ ἀποδώσω σοι ([σοὶ] A)
LTrA. ᶠ — ἐκείνου (read of the bondman) L. ᵍ — ἐκεῖνος (read the bondman) L.
ʰ — μοι LTTrAW. ⁱ εἴ τι if anything GLTTrAW. ᵏ — εἰς τοὺς πόδας αὐτοῦ GLTTr[A]. ¹ ἐμέ
LTrA. ᵐ — πάντα [L]TTrAW. ⁿ ἀλλ' EG. ᵒ — οὗ LTTrA. ᵖ οὖν (therefore) αὐτοῦ οἱ σύνδουλοι L; οὖν οἱ σύνδουλοι αὐτοῦ TTrA. ᵠ γινόμενα were taking place T. ʳ ἑαυτῶν LTrA.

that was done. 32 Then his lord, after that he had called him, said unto him, O thou wicked servant, I forgave thee all that debt, because thou desiredst me: 33 shouldest not thou also have had compassion on thy fellowservant, even as I had pity on thee? 34 And his lord was wroth, and delivered him to the tormentors, till he should pay all that was due unto him. 35 So likewise shall my heavenly Father do also unto you, if ye from your hearts forgive not every one his brother their trespasses.

πάντα τὰ γενόμενα. 32 Τότε προσκαλεσάμενος αὐτὸν ὁ
all　that had taken place.　Then　²having ⁴called ⁵to [⁷him] ⁶him

κύριος.αὐτοῦ λέγει αὐτῷ,' Δοῦλε πονηρέ, πᾶσαν τὴν ὀφειλὴν
¹his ²lord　says　to him, ²Bondman ¹wicked,　all　²debt

ἐκείνην ἀφῆκά σοι, ἐπεὶ παρεκάλεσάς με· 33 οὐκ.ἔδει καὶ
¹that　I forgave thee, since thou besoughtest me ; did it not behove ²also

σὲ ἐλεῆσαι τὸν.σύνδουλόν.σου, ὡς ⁸καὶ ἐγώ'' σε ἠλέησα;
¹thee to have pitied thy fellow bondman,　as also　I　thee had pitied?

34 καὶ ὀργισθεὶς ὁ.κύριος.αὐτοῦ παρέδωκεν αὐτὸν τοῖς βασανι-
And being angry　his lord　delivered up　him　to the tormen-

σταῖς, ἕως.'οῦ'' ἀποδῷ πᾶν τὸ ὀφειλόμενον ⱽαὐτῷ '' 35 Οὕτως
tors,　until　he should pay all that　was owing　to him.　Thus

καὶ ὁ.πατήρ.μου ὁ ʷἐπουράνιος'' ποιήσει ὑμῖν ἐὰν.μὴ ἀφῆτε
also　my Father the　heavenly　will do　to you unless ye forgive

ἕκαστος τῷ.ἀδελφῷ.αὐτοῦ ἀπὸ τῶν.καρδιῶν.ὑμῶν ˣτὰ παρα-
each　his brother　from　your hearts　²of-

πτώματα ·αὐτῶν.''
fences　¹their.

XIX. And it came to pass, that when Jesus had finished these sayings, he departed from Galilee, and came into the coasts of Judæa beyond Jordan; 2 and great multitudes followed him; and he healed them there.

19 Καὶ ἐγένετο ὅτε ἐτέλεσεν ὁ Ἰησοῦς τοὺς λόγους
And it came to pass when ²had ³finished　¹Jesus　⁵words

τούτους, μετῆρεν· ἀπὸ ˣτῆς'' Γαλιλαίας, καὶ ἦλθεν εἰς τὰ ὅρια
⁴these,　he withdrew from ·　Galilee,　and came to the borders

τῆς Ἰουδαίας πέραν τοῦ Ἰορδάνου. 2 καὶ ἠκολούθησαν αὐτῷ
of Judæa　beyond the　Jordan :　and ²followed　⁴him

ὄχλοι πολλοί, καὶ ἐθεράπευσεν αὐτοὺς ἐκεῖ.
²crowds ¹great,　and he healed　them there.

3 The Pharisees also came unto him, tempting him, and saying unto him, Is it lawful for a man to put away his wife for every cause? 4 And he answered and said unto them, Have ye not read, that he which made them at the beginning made them male and female, 5 and said, For this cause shall a man leave father and mother, and shall cleave to his wife: and they twain shall be one flesh? 6 Wherefore they are no more twain, but one flesh. What therefore God hath joined together, let not man put asunder. 7 They say unto him, Why did Moses then command to give a writing of divorcement, and to put her away? 8 He saith unto them, Moses because of the hardness of your hearts suffered you to put away your wives: but from the beginning it was not so.

3 Καὶ προσῆλθον αὐτῷ ᶻοἱ'' Φαρισαῖοι πειράζοντες αὐτόν,
And　³came　⁴to ⁵him ¹the ²Pharisees　tempting　him,

καὶ λέγοντες ᵃαὐτῷ,'' Εἰ.ἔξεστιν ᵇἀνθρώπῳ'' ἀπολῦσαι τὴν
and　saying　to him,　Is it lawful　for a man　to put away

γυναῖκα.αὐτοῦ κατὰ πᾶσαν αἰτίαν ; 4 Ὁ.δὲ ἀποκριθεὶς εἶπεν
his wife　for　every　cause ?　But he answering said

ᶜαὐτοῖς,'' Οὐκ.ἀνέγνωτε ὅτι ὁ ᵈποιήσας'' ἀπ' ἀρ-
to them,　Have ye not read that he who made [them] from [the] begin-

χῆς ἄρσεν καὶ θῆλυ ἐποίησεν αὐτούς, 5 καὶ εἶπεν, ᵉἝνεκεν''
ning male and female made·　them,　and said, On account of

τούτου καταλείψει ἄνθρωπος τὸν πατέρα καὶ τὴν μητέρα, καὶ
this　³shall ⁴leave　¹a ²man　father　and　mother,　and

ᶠπροσκολληθήσεται'' τῇ.γυναικὶ.αὐτοῦ, καὶ ἔσονται οἱ.δύο εἰς
shall be joined　to his wife,　and ²shall.⁴be ¹the ³two ⁵for

σάρκα μίαν; 6 ὥστε οὐκέτι εἰσὶν δύο, ἀλλὰ σὰρξ μία· ᶞ
⁷flesh　⁶one?　So that no longer are they two,　but ²flesh ¹one. What

οὖν ὁ θεὸς συνέζευξεν, ἄνθρωπος μὴ.χωριζέτω. 7 Λέγουσιν
therefore God united together, ²man　¹let ²not separate.　They say

αὐτῷ, Τί οὖν ᵍΜωσῆς'' ἐνετείλατο δοῦναι βιβλίον ἀπο-
to him, Why then　²Moses　¹did command to give　a bill　of di-

στασίου, καὶ ἀπολῦσαι ʰαὐτήν;'' 8 Λέγει αὐτοῖς, Ὅτι ᵍΜωσῆς''
vorce,　and to put away her?　He says to them,　Moses

πρὸς τὴν.σκληροκαρδίαν.ὑμῶν ἐπέτρεψεν ὑμῖν ἀπολῦσαι
in view of　your hard-heartedness　allowed　you　to put away

τὰς.γυναῖκας.ὑμῶν ἀπ' ἀρχῆς δὲ οὐ.γέγονεν οὕτως.
your wives ;　from [the] beginning however it was not　thus.

ˢ κἀγώ LTTrA.　ᵗ — οὗ L.　ⱽ — αὐτῷ LTrA.　ʷ οὐράνιος LTTr ; [ἐπ]ουράνιος A.
ˣ — τὰ παραπτώματα αὐτῶν GLTTrA.　ʸ — τῆς E.　ᶻ — οἱ LTrA.　ᵃ — αὐτῷ LTTrA.
ᵇ — ἀνθρώπῳ (read one's wife) LTA.　ᶜ — αὐτοῖς LTTrA.　ᵈ κτίσας created Tr.　ᵉἝνεκα
LTTrA.　ᶠ κολληθήσεται LTTrAW.　ᵍ Μωϋσῆς LTTrAW.　ʰ — αὐτήν LTTr.

9 λέγω.δὲ ὑμῖν, ᵃὅτι‖ ὃς.ἂν ἀπολύσῃ τὴν.γυναῖκα.αὐτοῦ
And I say to you, that whoever shall put away his wife

ᵏεἰ‖ ¹μὴ ἐπὶ πορνείᾳ,‖ καὶ γαμήσῃ ἄλλην, μοιχᾶται· ᵐκαὶ
if not for fornication, and shall marry another, commits adultery; and

ὁ ἀπολελυμένην γαμήσας μοιχᾶται.‖ 10 Λέγουσιν
he who ²her [²that ⁴is] ³put ⁴away ¹marries commits adultery. ³Say

αὐτῷ οἱ.μαθηταὶ.ⁿαὐτοῦ,‖ Εἰ οὕτως ἐστὶν ἡ αἰτία τοῦ ἀνθρώ-
⁴to ⁵him ¹his ²disciples, If thus is the case of the man

που μετὰ τῆς γυναικός, οὐ.συμφέρει γαμῆσαι. 11 Ὁ.δὲ εἶπεν
with the wife, it is not profitable to marry. But he said

αὐτοῖς, Οὐ πάντες χωροῦσιν τὸν.λόγον.ºτοῦτον,‖ ἀλλ'
to them, Not all receive this word, but [those]

οἷς δέδοται. 12 εἰσὶν.γὰρ εὐνοῦχοι οἵτινες ἐκ κοιλίας
to whom it has been given; for there are eunuchs who from [the] womb

μητρὸς ἐγεννήθησαν οὕτως, καὶ εἰσὶν εὐνοῦχοι οἵτινες
of [their] mother were born thus, and there are eunuchs who

εὐνουχίσθησαν ὑπὸ τῶν ἀνθρώπων, καὶ εἰσὶν εὐνοῦχοι οἵτινες
were made eunuchs by men, and there are eunuchs who

εὐνούχισαν ἑαυτοὺς διὰ τὴν βασιλείαν τῶν οὐρανῶν.
made eunuchs of themselves for the sake of the kingdom of the heavens.

ὁ δυνάμενος χωρεῖν χωρείτω.
He who is able to receive [it] let him receive [it].

13 Τότε ᴾπροσηνέχθη‖ αὐτῷ παιδία, ἵνα τὰς χεῖρας
Then were brought to him little children, that [his] hands

ἐπιθῇ αὐτοῖς, καὶ προσεύξηται· οἱ.δὲ μαθηταὶ ἐπετίμησαν
he might lay on them, and might pray; but the disciples rebuked

αὐτοῖς· 14 ὁ.δὲ.Ἰησοῦς εἶπεν ᵠ, Ἄφετε τὰ παιδία, καὶ μὴ
them. But Jesus said, Suffer the little children, and ᵘnot

κωλύετε αὐτὰ ἐλθεῖν πρός ʳμε·‖ τῶν.γὰρ.τοιούτων ἐστὶν ἡ
¹do forbid them to come to me; for of such is the

βασιλεία τῶν οὐρανῶν. 15 Καὶ ἐπιθεὶς ˢαὐτοῖς τὰς χεῖρας‖
kingdom of the heavens. And having laid upon them [his] hands

ἐπορεύθη ἐκεῖθεν.
he departed thence.

16 Καὶ ἰδού, εἷς προσελθὼν ᵗεἶπεν αὐτῷ,‖ Διδάσκαλε
And behold, one having come to [him] said to him, ²Teacher

ᵛἀγαθέ,‖ τί ἀγαθὸν ποιήσω ἵνα ʷἔχω‖ ζωὴν αἰώνιον;
¹good, what good [thing] shall I do that I may have life eternal?

17 Ὁ.δὲ εἶπεν.αὐτῷ, ˣΤί με λέγεις ἀγαθόν; οὐδεὶς ἀγαθὸς
And he said to him, Why me callest thou good? no one [is] good

εἰ.μὴ εἷς, ὁ θεός.‖ εἰ.δὲ θέλεις ʸεἰσελθεῖν εἰς τὴν ζωήν,‖
except one, God. But if thou desirest to enter into life,

ᶻτήρησον‖ τὰς ἐντολάς. 18 ᵃΛέγει αὐτῷ.‖ Ποίας; ᵇ Ὁ.δὲ.Ἰη-
keep the commandments. He says to him, Which? And Je-

σοῦς εἶπεν, Τό, οὐ.φονεύσεις· οὐ.μοιχεύσεις·
sus said, Thou shalt not commit murder; Thou shalt not commit adultery;

οὐ.κλέψεις· οὐ.ψευδομαρτυρήσεις· 19 τίμα τὸν πατέρα
Thou shalt not steal; Thou shalt not bear false witness; Honour ²father

ᶜσου‖ καὶ τὴν μητέρα· καὶ ἀγαπήσεις τὸν.πλησίον.σου ὡς
¹thy and mother; and Thou shalt love thy neighbour as

---

9 And I say unto you, Whosoever shall put away his wife, except it be for fornication, and shall marry another, committeth adultery: and whoso marrieth her which is put away doth commit adultery. 10 His disciples say unto him, If the case of the man be so with his wife, it is not good to marry. 11 But he said unto them, All men cannot receive this saying, save they to whom it is given. 12 For there are some eunuchs, which were so born from their mother's womb: and there are some eunuchs, which were made eunuchs of men: and there be eunuchs, which have made themselves eunuchs for the kingdom of heaven's sake. He that is able to receive it, let him receive it.

13 Then were there brought unto him little children, that he should put his hands on them, and pray: and the disciples rebuked them. 14 But Jesus said, Suffer little children, and forbid them not, to come unto me: for of such is the kingdom of heaven. 15 And he laid his hands on them, and departed thence.

16 And, behold, one came and said unto him, Good Master, what good thing shall I do, that I may have eternal life? 17 And he said unto him, Why callest thou me good? there is none good but one, that is, God: but if thou wilt enter into life, keep the commandments. 18 He saith unto him, Which? Jesus said, Thou shalt do no murder, Thou shalt not commit adultery, Thou shalt not steal, Thou shalt not bear false witness, 19 Honour thy father and thy mother: and, Thou shalt love thy neighbour as thyself.

ⁱ — ὅτι LTrA. ᵏ — εἰ GLTTrAW. ¹ παρεκτὸς λόγου πορνείας except for cause of fornication L. ᵐ — καὶ ὁ ἀπολελυμένην γαμήσας μοιχᾶται T[τ·]. ⁿ — αὐτοῦ (read the disciples) T[A]. º [τοῦτον] L. ᴾ προσηνέχθησαν LTTrA. ᵠ + αὐτοῖς to them T. ʳ ἐμέ T. ˢ τὰς χεῖρας αὐτοῖς LTTrA. ᵗ αὐτῷ εἶπεν LTTrA. ᵛ — ἀγαθέ LTT A. ʷ σχῶ LTTrA. ˣ Τί με ἐρωτᾷς περὶ τοῦ ἀγαθοῦ; εἷς ἐστιν ὁ ἀγαθός Why askest thou me concerning the good? One is good (+ ὁ θεός God W) GLTT-AW. ʸ εἰς.τὴν ζωὴν εἰσελθεῖν LTTrAW. ᶻ τήρει LT·A. ᵃ ἔφη αὐτῷ he said to him L; — λέγει αὐτῷ T. ᵇ + φησίν he says T. ᶜ — σου GLTTrAW.

20 The young man saith unto him, All these things have I kept from my youth up: what lack I yet? 21 Jesus said unto him, If thou wilt be perfect, go and sell that thou hast, and give to the poor, and thou shalt have treasure in heaven: and come and follow me. 22 But when the young man heard that saying, he went away sorrowful: for he had great possessions.

σεαυτόν. 20 Λέγει αὐτῷ ὁ νεανίσκος, ᵈΠάντα ταῦταᵃ
thyself.   ᵃSays ᵇto ᵇhim ¹the ²young ³man,   All   these
ἐφυλαξάμηνⁱⁱ ἐκ νεότητός.μου· ⁱⁱ τί ἔτι ὑστερῶ; 21 ᵍᴱφηⁱⁱ αὐτῷ
have I kept from my youth, what yet lack I?   ²Said ³to ⁴him
ὁ Ἰησοῦς, Εἰ θέλεις τέλειος εἶναι, ὕπαγε πώλησόν σου τὰ
¹Jesus,   If thou desirest perfect to be, go   sell   thy
ὑπάρχοντα καὶ δὸς ʰ πτωχοῖς, καὶ ἕξεις θησαυρὸν ἐν
property   and give to [the] poor, and thou shalt have treasure   in
ⁱοὐρανῷ·ⁱⁱ καὶ δεῦρο ἀκολούθει μοι. 22 Ἀκούσας.δὲ ὁ νεανίσκος
heaven;   and come   follow   me. But⁴having ⁵heard ¹the ²young ³man
ᵏτὸν λόγονⁱⁱ ˡ ἀπῆλθεν λυπούμενος, ἦν.γὰρ.ἔχων κτήματα
the   word   went away grieved,   for he had ²possessions
πολλά.
¹many.

23 Then said Jesus unto his disciples, Verily I say unto you, That a rich man shall hardly enter into the kingdom of heaven. 24 And again I say unto you, It is easier for a camel to go through the eye of a needle, than for a rich man to enter into the kingdom of God. 25 When his disciples heard it, they were exceedingly amazed, saying, Who then can be saved? 26 But Jesus beheld them, and said unto them, With men this is impossible; but with God all things are possible.

23 Ὁ.δὲ Ἰησοῦς εἶπεν τοῖς.μαθηταῖς.αὐτοῦ, Ἀμὴν λέγω
And Jesus   said   to his disciples,   Verily I say
ὑμῖν, ὅτι, ᵐδυσκόλως ᵖλούσιοςⁱⁱ εἰσελεύσεται εἰς τὴν βασι-
to you, that with difficulty a rich man shall enter   into the king-
λείαν τῶν οὐρανῶν. 24 πάλιν.δὲ λέγω ὑμῖν, ⁿ εὐκοπώτερόν ἐστιν
dom of the heavens.   And again I say to you,   easier   is it
κάμηλον διὰ τρυπήματος ῥαφίδος ᵒδιελθεῖν,ⁱⁱ ἢ πλού-
a camel through [the] eye   of a needle to pass,   than a rich
σιον ᵖ εἰς τὴν βασιλείαν ᑫτοῦ θεοῦⁱⁱ ʳεἰσελθεῖν.ⁱⁱ 25 Ἀκούσαντες
man into the   kingdom of God to enter.   ²Having ³heard
δὲ οἱ.μαθηταὶ.ˢαὐτοῦⁱⁱ ἐξεπλήσσοντο σφόδρα, λέγοντες,
¹and [this] his disciples were astonished exceedingly, saying,
Τίς ἄρα δύναται σωθῆναι; 26 Ἐμβλέψας.δὲ ὁ Ἰησοῦς
Who then is able to be saved?   But looking on [them]   Jesus
εἶπεν αὐτοῖς, Παρὰ ἀνθρώποις τοῦτο ἀδύνατόν ἐστιν, παρὰ.δὲ
said to them, With   men   this impossible is,   but with
θεῷ ᵗπάντα δυνατάⁱⁱ ᵛἐστιν.ⁱⁱ
God all things possible   are.

27 Then answered Peter and said unto him, Behold, we have forsaken all, and followed thee; what shall we have therefore? 28 And Jesus said unto them, Verily I say unto you, That ye which have followed me, in the regeneration when the Son of man shall sit in the throne of his glory, ye also shall sit upon twelve thrones, judging the twelve tribes of Israel. 29 And every one that hath forsaken houses, or brethren, or sisters, or father, or mother, or wife, or children, or lands, for my name's sake, shall receive an hundredfold, and shall

27 Τότε ἀποκριθεὶς ὁ Πέτρος εἶπεν αὐτῷ, Ἰδού, ἡμεῖς ἀφή-
Then answering Peter said to him, Lo,   we   left
καμεν πάντα καὶ ἠκολουθήσαμέν σοι· τί ἄρα ἔσται ἡμῖν;
all things and   followed   thee; what then shall be to us?
28 Ὁ.δὲ.Ἰησοῦς εἶπεν αὐτοῖς, Ἀμὴν λέγω ὑμῖν, ὅτι ὑμεῖς οἱ
And Jesus   said to them, Verily I say to you, that ye who
ἀκολουθήσαντές μοι, ἐν τῇ ʷπαλιγγενεσίᾳ·ⁱⁱ ὅταν καθίσῃ
have followed me, in the   regeneration,   when shall sit down
ὁ υἱὸς τοῦ ἀνθρώπου ἐπὶ θρόνου δόξης.αὐτοῦ, καθίσεσθε
the Son   of man   upon [the] throne of his glory, ³shall ⁴sit
καὶ ˣὑμεῖςⁱⁱ ἐπὶ δώδεκα θρόνους, κρίνοντες τὰς δώδεκα φυλὰς
²also ¹ye on twelve thrones, judging the twelve tribes
τοῦ Ἰσραήλ. 29 καὶ πᾶς ᵞὃςⁱⁱ ἀφῆκεν ᶻοἰκίας, ἢⁱⁱ ἀδελφούς,
of Israel.   And every one who has left houses, or brothers.
ἢ ἀδελφάς, ἢ πατέρα, ἢ μητέρα, ᵃἢ γυναῖκα,ⁱⁱ ἢ τέκνα, ἢ
or sisters, or father, or mother, or wife,   or children, or
ἀγρούς,ᵇ ᶜἕνεκενⁱⁱ τοῦ.ᵈᵃὀνόματός.μου,ⁱⁱ ᵉᵃἑκατονταπλασίονα
lands,   for the sake of   my name,   a hundredfold

ᵈ ταῦτα πάντα LTTr.   ᵉ ἐφύλαξα LTTrA.   ᶠ — ἐκ νεότητός μου LTTrA.   ᵍ λέγει says L.
ʰ + τοῖς to the LTrA.   ⁱ οὐρανοῖς [the] heavens TrA.   ᵏ — τὸν λόγον T.   ˡ + [τοῦτον]
(read this word) LA.   ᵐ πλούσιος δυσκόλως LTTrA.   ⁿ + ὅτι that T.   ᵒ εἰσελθεῖν to enter
GTTᴬA.   ᵖ + εἰσελθεῖν to enter L[Tr].   ᑫ τῶν οὐρανῶν of the heavens LTTrA.   ʳ — εἰσελθεῖν
LTT A.   ˢ — αὐτοῦ (read the disciples) GLTTrAW.   ᵗ δυνατὰ πάντα T.   ᵛ — ἐστιν (read [are])
GLTTʳAW.   ʷ παλιγενεσίᾳ T.   ˣ αὐτοὶ yourselves TTr.   ᵞ ὅστις LTTrAW.   ᶻ — οἰκίας ἢ TT A.
ᵃ — ἢ γυναῖκα LTTrA.   ᵇ + ἢ οἰκίας or houses TTrA.   ᶜ ἕνεκα T.   ᵈᵃ ἐμοῦ ὀνόματός ᴚ.
ᵉᵃ πολλαπλασίονα λήμψεται many times more shall receive LTTrA.

λήψεται,ʺ καὶ ζωὴν αἰώνιον κληρονομήσει.   30 πολλοὶ.δὲ
shall receive,   and   life   eternal   shall inherit ;   but many

ἔσονται πρῶτοι ἔσχατοι, καὶ ἔσχατοι πρῶτοι.   20 Ὁμοία.γάρ
²shall ³be ¹first   last,   and   last   first.   For ⁷like

ἐστιν ἡ βασιλεία τῶν οὐρανῶν ἀνθρώπῳ οἰκοδεσπότῃ, ὅστις
⁶is ¹the ²kingdom ³of ⁴the ⁵heavens   to a man   a master of a house,   who

ἐξῆλθεν ἅμα   πρωῒ μισθώσασθαι ἐργάτας εἰς τὸν ἀμπελῶνα
went out with[the] morning   to hire   workmen for   ⁸vineyard

αὑτοῦ. 2 συμφωνήσας.δὲ μετὰ τῶν ἐργατῶν ἐκ δηναρίου τὴν
¹his.   And having agreed with the   workmen for a denarius   the

ἡμέραν, ἀπέστειλεν αὐτοὺς εἰς τὸν.ἀμπελῶνα.αὑτοῦ. 3 Καὶ
day,   he sent   them   into   his vineyard.   And

ἐξελθὼν περὶ ᶠτὴνʺ τρίτην ὥραν, εἶδεν ἄλλους ἑστῶτας
having gone out about the   third   hour, he saw   others   standing

ἐν τῇ ἀγορᾷ ἀργούς· 4 ᵍκἀκείνοιςʺ εἶπεν, Ὑπάγετε καὶ
in the marketplace idle;   and to them he said,   Go   also .

ὑμεῖς εἰς τὸν ἀμπελῶνα, καὶ ὃ.ἐὰν   ᾖ δίκαιον δώσω ὑμῖν.
ye into the   vineyard,   and whatever may be just   I will give you.

5 οἱ.δὲ ἀπῆλθον. Πάλινʰ ἐξελθὼν περὶ ἕκτην καὶ
And they   went.   Again   having gone out about [the] sixth   and

ⁱἐννάτηνʲ ὥραν, ἐποίησεν ὡσαύτως. 6 Περὶ.δὲ τὴν ἐνδεκάτην
ninth   hour,   he did   likewise.   And about the   eleventh

ᵏὥρανʺ ἐξελθὼν εὗρεν ἄλλους ἑστῶτας ˡἀργούς,ʺ καὶ λέγει
hour having gone out he found others   standing   idle,   and says

αὐτοῖς, Τί ὧδε ἑστήκατε ὅλην τὴν ἡμέραν ἀργοί; 7 λέγουσιν
to them, Why here stand ye   all   the   day   idle?   They say

αὐτῷ, Ὅτι οὐδεὶς ἡμᾶς ἐμισθώσατο. λέγει αὐτοῖς, Ὑπάγετε
to him, Because no one   ²us ¹has ³hired.   He says to them,   Go

καὶ ὑμεῖς εἰς τὸν ἀμπελῶνα,ᵐ ⁿκαὶ ὃ.ἐὰν ᾖ δίκαιον λή-
also ye into the   vineyard,   and whatever may be just   ye shall

ψεσθε.ʺ 8 Ὀψίας.δὲ γενομένης λέγει ὁ κύριος τοῦ ἀμπελῶνος
receive.   But evening being come ¹says ¹the ²lord ³of ⁴the ⁵vineyard

τῷ.ἐπιτρόπῳ.αὑτοῦ, Κάλεσον τοὺς ἐργάτας, καὶ ἀπόδος ᵒαὐ-
to his steward,   Call   the   workmen, and   pay   them

τοῖςʺ τὸν μισθόν, ἀρξάμενος ἀπὸ τῶν ἐσχάτων ἕως τῶν
[their]   hire,   beginning   from   the   last   unto the

πρώτων. 9 ᵖκαὶ ἐλθόντεςʺ οἱ   περὶ τὴν ἐνδεκάτην
first.   And ⁷having ⁸come ¹those [²hired] ³about ⁴the   ⁵eleventh

ὥραν ἔλαβον ἀνὰ δηνάριον. 10 ᑫἐλθόντες.δὲʺ οἱ πρῶτοι
⁶hour   they received each a denarius.   And ³having ⁴come ¹the   ²first

ἐνόμισαν ὅτι ʳπλείονα λήψονται·ʺ καὶ ἔλαβον ˢκαὶ αὐτοὶ
they thought that   more   they would receive, and they received also themselves

ἀνὰ δηνάριον.ʺ 11 λαβόντες.δὲ   ἐγόγγυζον κατὰ τοῦ
each   a denarius.   And having received [it] they murmured against   the

οἰκοδεσπότου, 12 λέγοντες, ᵗὍτιʺ οὗτοι οἱ ἔσχατοι μίαν
master of the house,   saying,   These   last   one

ὥραν ἐποίησαν, καὶ ἴσους ᵛἡμῖν αὐτοὺςʺ ἐποίησας, τοῖς
hour   have worked,   and ⁵equal ⁶to ⁷us ⁴them ¹thou ²hast ³made, who

βαστάσασιν τὸ βάρος τῆς ἡμέρας καὶ τὸν καύσωνα.ʷ 13 ὁ.δὲ
have borne   the burden of the day   and the   heat.   But he

ἀποκριθεὶς ˣεἶπεν ἑνὶ αὐτῶν,ʺ Ἑταῖρε, οὐκ.ἀδικῶ σε· οὐχὶ
answering   said to one of them,   Friend, I do not wrong thee.   ³Not

inherit   everlasting
life. 30 But many
that are first shall be
last ; and the last *shall*
be first. XX. For the
kingdom of heaven is
like unto a man *that is*
an householder, which
went out early in the
morning to ' hire la-
bourers into his vine-
yard. 2 And when he
had agreed with the
labourers for a penny
a day, he sent them
into his vineyard.
3 And he went out
about the third hour,
and saw others stand-
ing idle in the market-
place, 4 and said unto
them ; Go ye also into
the vineyard, and
whatsoever is right I
will give you. And
they went their way.
5 Again he went out
about the sixth and
ninth hour, and did
likewise. 6 And about
the eleventh hour he
went out, and found
others standing idle,
and saith unto them,
Why stand ye here
all the day idle ? 7 They
say unto him, Because
no man hath hired us.
He saith unto them,
Go ye also into the
vineyard ; and what-
soever is right, *that*
shall ye receive. 8 So
when even was come,
the lord of the vine-
yard saith unto his
steward, Call ' the la-
bourers, and give them
their hire, beginning
from the last unto the
first. 9 And when
they came that *were*
hired about the e-
leventh hour, they re-
ceived every man a
penny. 10 But when
the first came, they
supposed that they
should have received
more ; and they like-
wise received every
man a penny. 11 And
when they had receiv-
ed *it*, they murmured
against the goodman
of the house, 12 say-
ing, These last have
wrought *but* one hour,
and thou hast made
them equal unto us,
which have borne the
burden and heat of the
day. 13 But he an-
swered one of them,
and said, Friend, I do
thee no wrong : didst

ᶠ — τὴν (read [the]) GLTTrAW.   ᵍ καὶ ἐκείνοις TA.   ʰ + δὲ and (again) TTrA.   ⁱ ἐνάτην
LTTrAW.   ᵏ — ὥραν LTTrA.   ˡ — ἀργούς GLTTrA.   ᵐ + [μου] my (vineyard) L.   ⁿ — καὶ
ὃ ἐὰν ᾖ δίκαιον λήψεσθε LTTrA.   ᵒ — αὐτοῖς T[TrA].   ᵖ ἐλθόντες δὲ L.   ᑫ καὶ ἐλθόντες TrA.
ʳ πλεῖον λήμψονται LTrA ; πλείονα λήμψονται T.   ˢ τὸ ([τὸ] A) ἀνὰ δηνάριον καὶ αὐτοί TTrA.
ᵗ — ὅτι LTTr[A].   ᵛ αὐτοὺς ἡμῖν LT.   ʷ ; (read hast thou made, &c. ?) L.   ˣ ἑνὶ αὐτῶν εἶπεν T.

not thou agree with me for a penny? 14 Take that thine is, and go thy way: I will give unto this last, even as unto thee. 15 Is it not lawful for me to do what I will with mine own? Is thine eye evil, because I am good? 16 So the last shall be first, and the first last: for many be called, but few chosen.

δηναρίου   συνεφώνησάς   μοι;   14 ἆρον τὸ.σὸν καὶ
[7]for [a][9]denarius   [1]didst [2]thou [4]agree [3]with [5]me?   Take   thine own and

ὕπαγε. θέλω.ᵞδὲ‖ τούτῳ τῷ ἐσχάτῳ δοῦναι ὡς καὶ ·σοί· 15 ᶻῂ‖
go.   But I will   to this   last   give   as also to thee: or

οὐκ.ἔξεστίν μοι ᵃποιῆσαι ὃ θέλω‖ ἐν τοῖς   ἐμοῖς; ᵇει̇‖.
is it not lawful for me   to do   what I will   in that which [is] mine?

ὁ.ὀφθαλμός.σου πονηρός ἐστιν ὅτι ἐγὼ ἀγαθός εἰμι; 16 οὕτως
[4]thine [3]eye   [2]evil   [1]is because I   good   am?   Thus

ἔσονται οἱ ἔσχατοι πρῶτοι, καὶ οἱ πρῶτοι ἔσχατοι· ᶜπολλοὶ.γάρ
shall be the · last   first,   and the first   last: for many

εἰσιν κλητοί, ὀλίγοι.δὲ ἐκλεκτοί.‖
are   called,   but few   chosen.

17 And Jesus going up to Jerusalem took the twelve disciples apart in the way, and said unto them, 18 Behold, we go up to Jerusalem; and the Son of man shall be betrayed unto the chief priests and unto the scribes, and they shall condemn him to death, 19 and shall deliver him to the Gentiles to mock, and to scourge, and to crucify· him: and the third day he shall rise again.

17 Καὶ ἀναβαίνων ὁ Ἰησοῦς εἰς Ἱεροσόλυμα παρέλαβεν,
And   [2]going [3]up   [1]Jesus   to   Jerusalem   took

τοὺς δώδεκα ᵈμαθητὰς‖ κατ᾽.ἰδίαν ᵉἐν τῇ ὁδῷ, καὶ‖ εἶπεν αὐτοῖς,
the twelve   disciples   apart   in the way, and   said to them,

18 Ἰδού, ἀναβαίνομεν εἰς Ἱεροσόλυμα, καὶ ὁ υἱὸς τοῦ ἀνθρώ-
Behold,   we go up   to   Jerusalem,   and the Son   of man

που παραδοθήσεται τοῖς ἀρχιερεῦσιν καὶ γραμματεῦσιν, καὶ
will be delivered up to the   chief priests   and   scribes,   and

κατακρινοῦσιν αὐτὸν ᶠθανάτῳ,‖ 19 καὶ παραδώσουσιν αὐτὸν
they will condemn   him   to death,   and they will deliver up   him

τοῖς ἔθνεσιν εἰς τὸ ἐμπαῖξαι καὶ μαστιγῶσαι καὶ σταυρῶσαι·
to the Gentiles to   mock   and   to scourge   and to crucify ;

καὶ τῇ τρίτῃ ἡμέρᾳ ᵍἀναστήσεται.‖
and the third   day   he will rise again.

20 Then came to him the mother of Zebedee's children with her sons, worshipping him, and desiring a certain thing of him. 21 And he said unto her, What wilt thou? She saith unto him, Grant that these my two sons may sit, the one on thy right hand, and the other on the left, in thy kingdom. 22 But Jesus answered and said, Ye know not what ye ask. Are ye able to drink of the cup that I shall drink of, and to be baptized with the baptism that I am baptized with? They say unto him, We are able. 23 And he saith unto them, Ye shall drink indeed of my cup, and be baptized with the baptism that I am baptized with: but to sit on my right hand, and on my left, is not mine to give, but it shall be given to them for whom it is prepared of my

20 Τότε προσῆλθεν αὐτῷ ἡ μήτηρ τῶν υἱῶν Ζεβεδαίου μετὰ
Then   came   to him the mother of the sons   of Zebedee   with

τῶν.υἱῶν.αὐτῆς, προσκυνοῦσα καὶ αἰτοῦσά τι ʰπαρ᾽‖ αὐτοῦ.
her sons,   doing homage and asking something from   him.

21 ὁ.δὲ εἶπεν αὐτῇ, Τί θέλεις; Λέγει αὐτῷ, Εἰπὲ ἵνα
And he said   to her, What dost thou desire? She says to him,   Say   that

καθίσωσιν ⁱοὗτοι‖ οἱ δύο υἱοί μου εἷς ᵏἐκ δεξιῶν.ᵏσου‖ καὶ εἷς
[5]may [6]sit   [1]these   [3]two [4]sons [2]my one on thy right hand and one

ἐξ   εὐωνύμωνˡ ἐν τῇ.βασιλείᾳ.σου. 22 Ἀποκριθεὶς.δὲ ὁ
on [thy]   left   in   thy kingdom.   But answering

Ἰησοῦς εἶπεν, Οὐκ.οἴδατε τί αἰτεῖσθε. δύνασθε πιεῖν τὸ
Jesus   said,   Ye know not what ye ask for. Are ye able to drink the

ποτήριον ὃ ἐγὼ μέλλω πίνειν, ᵐκαὶ τὸ βάπτισμα ὃ ἐγὼ
cup   which I   am about to drink,   and [5]the   [6]baptism   [7]which [3]I

βαπτίζομαι   βαπτισθῆναι;‖ Λέγουσιν αὐτῷ, Δυνά-
[1]am [10]baptized [11]with] [1]to [2]be [3]baptized [with]? They say to him,   We are

μεθα. 23 ⁿΚαὶ‖ λέγει αὐτοῖς, Τὸ μὲν ποτήριόν μου πίεσθε,
able.   And he says to them,   [3]Indeed   [2]cup   [1]my ye shall drink,

ᵒκαὶ τὸ βάπτισμα ὃ ἐγὼ βαπτίζομαι βαπτισθήσεσθε·‖
and the   baptism which I   am baptized [with] ye shall be baptized

τὸ.δὲ.καθίσαι ἐκ δεξιῶν.μου καὶ ἐξ εὐωνύμων.ᵖμου‖ οὐκ
[with];   but to sit   on my right hand and on   my left   [2]not

ἔστιν ἐμὸν �ۑδοῦναι, ἀλλ᾽   ·οἷς   ἡτοίμασται ὑπὸ τοῦ
[1]is   mine   to give,   but [to those] for whom · it has been prepared   by

ᵞ — δὲ but w.   ᶻ — ῂ LTr[A].   ᵃ ὁ θέλω ποιῆσαι LTTrA.   ᵇ ῂ or EGLTTrAW.   ᶜ — πολλοὶ γάρ εἰσιν κλητοί, ὀλίγοι δὲ ἐκλεκτοί Τ[TrA].   ᵈ — μαθητὰς TTr.   ᵉ καὶ ἐν τῇ ὁδῷ LTTrA.   ᶠεἰς θάνατον Τ.   ᵍ ἐγερθήσεται he shall be raised TTrA.   ʰ ἀπ᾽ LTrA.   ⁱ [οὗτοι] L.   ᵏ — σου (read [thy] right hand) LT.   ˡ + σου thy (left) GLTTrAW.   ᵐ — καὶ τὸ βάπτισμα, ὃ ἐγὼ βαπτίζομαι, βαπτισθῆναι GLTTrA.   ⁿ — καὶ LTTrA.   ᵒ — καὶ τὸ βάπτισμα ὃ ἐγὼ βαπτίζομαι βαπτισθήσεσθε GLTTrA.   ᵖ — μου (read [my] left) LTTrA.   ᵠ + τοῦτο this (is not mine) TA.

πατρός-μου. 24 ʳΚαὶ ἀκούσαντεςǁ　οἱ δέκα ἠγανάκτησαν
my Father.　　And having heard [this] the ten　were indignant

περὶ τῶν δύο ἀδελφῶν. 25 ὁ.δὲ.Ἰησοῦς προσκαλεσάμενος
about the two brothers.　　　　But Jesus　having called ²to [³him]

αὐτοὺς εἶπεν, Οἴδατε ὅτι οἱ ἄρχοντες τῶν ἐθνῶν κατακυριεύου-
¹them　said, Ye know that the　rulers　of the nations exercise lordship

σιν αὐτῶν, καὶ οἱ μεγάλοι κατεξουσιάζουσιν αὐτῶν. 26 οὐχ
over them,　and the great ones exercise authority over　them.　　Not

οὕτως ˢδὲǁ　ᵗἔσταιǁ　ἐν ὑμῖν· ἀλλ' ὃς.ᵛἐὰνǁ θέλῃ ʷἐν
thus　however　shall it be among ₋you;　but whoever would among

ὑμῖνǁ μέγας γενέσθαι, ˣἔστωǁ ὑμῶν διάκονος· 27 καὶ ὃς.ʸἐὰνǁ
you　great　become,　let him be your　servant;　　and whoever

θέλῃ ἐν ὑμῖν εἶναι πρῶτος, ᶻἔστωǁ ὑμῶν δοῦλος· 28 ὥσπερ
would among you be　first,　let him be your bondman;　　even as

ὁ υἱὸς τοῦ ἀνθρώπου οὐκ.ἦλθεν διακονηθῆναι, ἀλλὰ διακονῆ-
the Son　of man　came not　to be served,　but　to serve,

σαι καὶ δοῦναι τὴν.ψυχὴν.αὐτοῦ λύτρον ἀντὶ πολλῶν.
and to give　his life　a ransom　for　many.

29 Καὶ ἐκπορευομένων αὐτῶν ἀπὸ ᵃἹεριχὼǁ ἠκολούθησεν
And as ³were ³going ⁴out ¹they　from　Jericho　⁴followed

αὐτῷ ὄχλος πολύς. 30 καὶ ἰδού, δύο τυφλοὶ καθήμενοι
⁵him ¹a ³crowd ²great.　　And behold, two　blind [men]　sitting

παρὰ τὴν ὁδόν, ἀκούσαντες ὅτι Ἰησοῦς παράγει ἔκραξαν,
beside the way,　having heard that Jesus　is passing by　cried out,

λέγοντες, ᵇἘλέησον ἡμᾶς, κύριε,ǁ ᶜυἱὸςǁ ᵈΔαβίδ.ǁ 31 Ὁ.δὲ.ὄχλος
saying,　Have pity on us, Lord,　Son of David.　　But the crowd

ἐπετίμησεν ᵉαὐτοῖς ἵνα σιωπήσωσιν. οἱ.δὲ μεῖζον ἔκρα-
rebuked　them　that they should be silent. But they the more　cried

ζον,ǁ λέγοντες, ᶠἘλέησον ἡμᾶς, κύριε,ǁ ᵍυἱὸςǁ ᵈΔαβίδ.ǁ 32 Καὶ
out,　saying,　Have pity on us, Lord,　Son of David.　　　And

στὰς ὁ Ἰησοῦς ἐφώνησεν αὐτούς, καὶ εἶπεν, Τί　θέλετε
having stopped, Jesus　called　them,　and said, What do ye desire

ᵍ ποιήσω ὑμῖν; 33 Λέγουσιν αὐτῷ, Κύριε, ἵνα ʰἀνοιχθῶσινǁ
I should do to you?　They say to him, Lord,　that ¹may ⁴be ⁵opened

ⁱἡμῶν οἱ ὀφθαλμοί.ǁ 34 Σπλαγχνισθεὶς.δὲ ὁ Ἰησοῦς ἥψατο
²our　⁴eyes.　　And moved with compassion Jesus　touched

τῶν ᵏὀφθαλμῶνǁ αὐτῶν· καὶ εὐθέως ἀνέβλεψαν ˡαὐτῶν οἱ
their eyes;　　　and immediately ²received ⁴sight¹ ¹their

ὀφθαλμοί,ǁ καὶ ἠκολούθησαν αὐτῷ.
eyes,　　and they followed　him.

21 Καὶ ὅτε ἤγγισαν εἰς Ἱεροσόλυμα καὶ ἦλθον εἰς Βηθ-
And when they drew near to　Jerusalem　and came to　Beth-

φαγὴ ᵐπρὸςǁ τὸ ὄρος τῶν ἐλαιῶν, τότε ⁿὁǁ Ἰησοῦς ἀπέστειλεν
phage　towards the mount　of Olives,　then　　Jesus　sent

δύο μαθητάς, 2 λέγων αὐτοῖς, ᵒΠορεύθητεǁ εἰς τὴν κώμην.τὴν
two disciples,　saying to them,　Go　into the village, that

ᵖἀπέναντιǁ ὑμῶν, καὶ ᵠεὐθέωςǁ εὑρήσετε ὄνον δεδεμένην, καὶ
opposite　you,　and immediately ye will find an ass　tied,　and

πῶλον μετ' αὐτῆς· λύσαντες ʳᵃἀγάγετέǁ μοι. 3 καὶ ἐάν
a colt　with her;　having loosed [them] bring [them] to me.　And if

---

if any man say ought unto you, ye shall say, The Lord hath need of them; and straightway he will send them. 4 All this was done, that it might be fulfilled which was spoken by the prophet, saying, 5 Tell ye the daughter of Sion, Behold, thy King cometh unto thee, meek, and sitting upon an ass, and a colt the foal of an ass. 6 And the disciples went, and did as Jesus commanded them, 7 and brought the ass, and the colt, and put on them their clothes, and they set him thereon. 8 And a very great multitude spread their garments in the way; others cut down branches from the trees, and strawed them in the way. 9 And the multitudes that went before, and that followed, cried, saying, Hosanna to the son of David: Blessed is he that cometh in the name of the Lord; Hosanna in the highest. 10 And when he was come into Jerusalem, all the city was moved, saying, Who is this? 11 And the multitude said, This is Jesus the prophet of Nazareth of Galilee.

12 And Jesus went into the temple of God, and cast out all them that sold and bought in the temple, and overthrew the tables of the money changers, and the seats of them that sold doves, 13 and said unto them, It is written, My house shall be called the house of prayer; but ye have made it a den of thieves. 14 And the blind and the lame came to him in the temple; and he healed them. 15 And when the chief priests and scribes saw the won-

τις ὑμῖν εἴπῃ τι, ἐρεῖτε, "Ὅτι ὁ κύριος αὐτῶν χρείαν
any one to you say anything, ye shall say, The Lord [5]of [6]them [7]need
ἔχει· [s]εὐθέως".δὲ [t]ἀποστελεῖ[t] αὐτούς. 4 Τοῦτο.δὲ [u]ὅλον" γέ-
[1]has. And immediately he will send them. But this all came
γονεν ἵνα πληρωθῇ τὸ ῥηθὲν διὰ τοῦ προφήτου,
to pass that might be fulfilled that which was spoken by the prophet,
λέγοντος, 5 Εἴπατε τῇ θυγατρὶ Σιών, Ἰδού, ὁ.βασιλεύς.σου
saying, Say to the daughter of Sion, Behold, thy king
ἔρχεταί σοι, πραῢς [v]καὶ" ἐπιβεβηκὼς ἐπὶ ὄνον καὶ [w] πῶλον
comes to thee, meek and mounted on an ass and a colt [the]
υἱὸν ὑποζυγίου. 6 Πορευθέντες.δὲ οἱ μαθηταί, καὶ ποιήσαν-
foal of a beast of burden. And [3]having [4]gone [1]the.[2]disciples, and having
τες καθὼς [x]προσέταξεν" αὐτοῖς ὁ Ἰησοῦς, 7 ἤγαγον τὴν
done as [2]ordered [3]them [1]Jesus, they brought the
ὄνον καὶ τὸν πῶλον, καὶ ἐπέθηκαν [y]ἐπάνω" αὐτῶν τὰ ἱμάτια
ass and the colt, and put upon them [2]garments
[z]αὐτῶν," καὶ [a]ἐπεκάθισεν" ἐπάνω αὐτῶν. 8 ὁ.δὲ πλεῖστος
[1]their, and he sat on them. And the greater part [of the]
ὄχλος ἔστρωσαν ἑαυτῶν τὰ ἱμάτια ἐν τῇ ὁδῷ, ἄλλοι.δὲ ἔκοπ-
crowd strewed their garments on the way, and others were cutting
τον κλάδους ἀπὸ τῶν δένδρων καὶ [b]ἐστρώννυον" ἐν τῇ
down branches from the trees and were strewing [them] on the
ὁδῷ. 9 οἱ.δὲ ὄχλοι οἱ προάγοντες[c] καὶ οἱ ἀκολουθοῦντες
way. And the crowds those going before and those following
ἔκραζον, λέγοντες, Ὡσαννὰ τῷ υἱῷ [d]Δαβίδ·[i] εὐλογημένος
were crying out, saying, Hosanna to the Son of David; blessed
ὁ ἐρχόμενος ἐν ὀνόματι κυρίου· Ὡσαννὰ ἐν τοῖς
[be] he who comes in [the] name of [the] Lord. Hosanna in the
ὑψίστοις. 10 Καὶ εἰσελθόντος.αὐτοῦ εἰς Ἱεροσόλυμα ἐσείσθη
highest. And as he entered into Jerusalem [4]was [5]moved
πᾶσα ἡ πόλις, λέγουσα, Τίς ἐστιν οὗτος; 11 Οἱ.δὲ ὄχλοι
[1]all [2]the [3]city, saying, Who is this? And the crowds
ἔλεγον, Οὗτός ἐστιν [e]Ἰησοῦς ὁ προφήτης," ὁ ἀπὸ [f]Να-
said, This is Jesus the prophet, he who [is] from Na-
ζαρὲτ" τῆς Γαλιλαίας.
zareth of Galilee.

12 Καὶ εἰσῆλθεν [g]ὁ" Ἰησοῦς εἰς τὸ ἱερὸν [h]τοῦ θεοῦ," καὶ
And [2]entered [1]Jesus into the temple of God, and
ἐξέβαλεν πάντας τοὺς πωλοῦντας καὶ ἀγοράζοντας ἐν τῷ
cast out all those selling and buying in the
ἱερῷ, καὶ τὰς τραπέζας τῶν κολλυβιστῶν κατέστρεψεν, καὶ
temple, and the tables of the money changers he overthrew, and
τὰς καθέδρας τῶν πωλούντων τὰς περιστεράς. 13 καὶ λέγει
the seats of those selling the doves. And he says
αὐτοῖς, Γέγραπται, Ὁ.οἶκός.μου οἶκος[c] προσευχῆς κληθή-
to them, It has been written, My house, a house of prayer shall be
σεται· ὑμεῖς.δὲ αὐτὸν [i]ἐποιήσατε" σπήλαιον λῃστῶν. 14 Καὶ
called; but ye it have made a den of robbers. And
προσῆλθον αὐτῷ τυφλοὶ καὶ χωλοὶ ἐν τῷ ἱερῷ, καὶ ἐθεράπευ-
[4]came [5]to [6]him [1]blind [2]and [3]lame in the temple, and he healed
σεν αὐτούς. 15 Ἰδόντες.δὲ οἱ ἀρχιερεῖς καὶ οἱ γραμματεῖς
them. But [7]seeing [1]the [2]chief [3]priests [4]and [5]the [6]scribes

---

[s] εὐθὺς TTr.   [t] ἀποστέλλει he sends G.   [u] — ὅλον LTTrA.   [v] — καὶ A.   [w] + ἐπὶ on LTTrA.   [x] συνέταξεν did direct LTrA.   [y] ἐπ' LTTrA.   [z] — αἱ τῶν [L]TTrA.   [a] [a]ἐπεκάθισαν they set [him] E.   [b] ἔστρωσαν strewed T.   [c] + αὐτὸν him LTTrA.   [d] Δαυὶδ GW; Δαυείδ LTTrA.   [e] ὁ προφήτης Ἰησοῦς LTTrA.   [f] Ναζαρὲθ ELTTrAW.   [g] — ὁ LTTrA.   [h] — τοῦ θεοῦ LTr.   [i] ποιεῖτε make LTTrA.

τὰ θαυμάσια ἃ ἐποίησεν, καὶ τοὺς παῖδας ᵏκράζοντας ἐν τῷ
the wonders which he wrought, and the children crying in the

ἱερῷ. καὶ λέγοντας, Ὡσαννὰ τῷ υἱῷ ¹Δαβὶδ,‖ ἠγανάκτησαν,
temple, and saying, Hosanna to the Son of David, they were indignant,

16 καὶ ᵐεἶπον‖ αὐτῷ, Ἀκούεις τί οὗτοι λέγουσιν; Ὁ δὲ Ἰη-
and said to him, Hearest thou what these say? And Je-

σοῦς λέγει αὐτοῖς, Ναί· οὐδέποτε ἀνέγνωτε, Ὅτι ἐκ στόμα-
sus says to them, Yea; ²never ¹did ²ye read, Out of [the] mouth

τος νηπίων καὶ θηλαζόντων κατηρτίσω αἶνον; 17 Καὶ
of babes and sucklings thou hast perfected praise? And

καταλιπὼν αὐτοὺς ἐξῆλθεν ἔξω τῆς πόλεως εἰς Βηθανίαν, καὶ
having left them ₁he went out of the city to Bethany, and

ηὐλίσθη ἐκεῖ.
passed the night there.

18 ⁿΠρωίας‖ δὲ ⁰ἐπανάγων‖ εἰς τὴν πόλιν ἐπείνασεν,
Now early in the morning coming back into the city he hungered,

19 καὶ ἰδὼν συκῆν μίαν ἐπὶ τῆς ὁδοῦ, ἦλθεν ἐπ᾽ αὐτήν, καὶ
and seeing ²fig-tree ¹one by the way, he came to it, and

οὐδὲν εὗρεν ἐν αὐτῇ εἰ μὴ φύλλα μόνον· καὶ λέγει αὐτῇ,
nothing found on it except leaves only. And he says to it,

ᵖ Μηκέτι ἐκ σοῦ καρπὸς γένηται εἰς τὸν αἰῶνα. Καὶ ἐξηράνθη
Never more of thee fruit let there be for ever. And ⁴dried ⁵up

παραχρῆμα ἡ συκῆ. 20 Καὶ ἰδόντες οἱ μαθηταὶ ἐθαύμασαν,
₁immediately ²the ³fig-tree. And seeing [it] the disciples wondered,

λέγοντες, Πῶς παραχρῆμα ἐξηράνθη ἡ συκῆ; 21 Ἀποκριθεὶς
saying, How immediately is dried up the fig-tree! ²Answering

δὲ ὁ Ἰησοῦς εἶπεν αὐτοῖς, Ἀμὴν λέγω ὑμῖν, ἐὰν ἔχητε πίστιν,
¹and Jesus said to them, Verily, I say to you, If ye have faith,

καὶ μὴ διακριθῆτε, οὐ μόνον τὸ τῆς συκῆς ποιήσετε,
and do not doubt, not only the [miracle] of the fig-tree shall ye do,

ἀλλὰ κἂν τῷ ὄρει τούτῳ εἴπητε, Ἄρθητι καὶ βλήθητι‖
but even if to this mountain ye should say, Be thou taken away and be thou cast

εἰς τὴν θάλασσαν, γενήσεται 22 καὶ πάντα ὅσα ᑫἂν‖
into the sea, it shall come to pass. And all things whatsoever

αἰτήσητε ἐν τῇ προσευχῇ, πιστεύοντες, ʳλήψεσθε.‖
ye may ask in prayer, believing, ye shall receive.

23 Καὶ ˢἐλθόντι αὐτῷ‖ εἰς τὸ ἱερὸν προσῆλθον αὐτῷ
And on his coming into the temple there came up to him, [when]

διδάσκοντι οἱ ἀρχιερεῖς καὶ οἱ πρεσβύτεροι τοῦ λαοῦ, λέγον-
teaching, the chief priests and the elders of the people, say-

τες, Ἐν ποίᾳ ἐξουσίᾳ ταῦτα ποιεῖς; καὶ τίς σοι ἔδωκεν τὴν
ing, By what authority these things doest thou? and who to thee gave

ἐξουσίαν ταύτην; 24 Ἀποκριθεὶς ᵗδὲ‖ ὁ Ἰησοῦς εἶπεν αὐτοῖς,
this authority? And answering Jesus said to them,

Ἐρωτήσω ὑμᾶς κἀγὼ λόγον ἕνα, ὃν ἐὰν εἴπητέ μοι, κἀγὼ
ˢWill ⁴ask ⁵you ¹I ²also ⁷thing ⁶one, which if ye tell me, I also

ὑμῖν ἐρῶ ἐν ποίᾳ ἐξουσίᾳ ταῦτα ποιῶ. 25 τὸ βάπτισμα
to you will say by what authority these things I do. The baptism

ᵛ Ἰωάννου πόθεν ἦν; ἐξ οὐρανοῦ, ἢ ἐξ ἀνθρώπων;
of John, whence was it? from heaven, or from men?

Οἱ δὲ διελογίζοντο ʷπαρ᾽‖ ἑαυτοῖς, λέγοντες, Ἐὰν εἴπω-
And they reasoned with themselves, saying, If we should

μεν, Ἐξ οὐρανοῦ, ἐρεῖ ἡμῖν, ˣΔιατί‖ οὖν οὐκ ἐπιστεύσατε
say, From heaven, he will say to us, Why then did ye not believe

---

derful things that he did, and the children crying in the temple, and saying, Hosanna to the Son of David; they were sore displeased, 16 and said unto him, Hearest thou what these say? And Jesus saith unto them, Yea; have ye never read, Out of the mouth of babes and sucklings thou hast perfected praise? 17 And he left them, and went out of the city into Bethany; and he lodged there.

18 Now in the morning as he returned into the city, he hungered. 19 And when he saw a fig tree in the way, he came to it, and found nothing thereon, but leaves only, and said unto it, Let no fruit grow on thee henceforward for ever. And presently the fig tree withered away. 20 And when the disciples saw it, they marvelled, saying, How soon is the fig tree withered away! 21 Jesus answered and said unto them, Verily I say unto you, If ye have faith, and doubt not, ye shall not only do this which is done to the fig tree, but also if ye shall say unto this mountain, Be thou removed, and be thou cast into the sea; it shall be done. 22 And all things, whatsoever ye shall ask in prayer, believing, ye shall receive.

23 And when he was come into the temple, the chief priests and the elders of the people came unto him as he was teaching, and said, By what authority doest thou these things? and who gave thee this authority? 24 And Jesus answered and said unto them, I also will ask you one thing, which if ye tell me, I in like wise will tell you by what authority I do these things. 25 The baptism of John, whence was it? from heaven, or of men? And they reasoned with themselves, saying, If we shall say, From heaven; he will say unto us, Why did ye not then be-

---

ᵏ + τοὺς (read who were) LTTrA.   ˡ Δαυίδ GW; Δαυείδ LTTrA.   ᵐ εἶπαν LTTrA.
ⁿ Πρωῒ TTr.   ⁰ ἐπαναγαγὼν LTA.   ᵖ + Οὐ LT[A].   ᑫ ἐὰν Tr.   ʳ λήμψεσθε LTTrA.
ˢ ἐλθόντος αὐτοῦ LTTr.   ᵗ — δὲ and L.   ᵛ + τὸ that LTTrA.   ʷ ἐν among LTr.   ˣ διὰ τί LTTrA.

lieve him? 26 But if we shall say, Of men; we fear the people; for all hold John as a prophet. 27 And they answered Jesus, and said, We cannot tell. And he said unto them, Neither tell I you by what authority I do these things. 28 But what think ye? A *certain* man had two sons; and he came to the first, and said, Son, go work to day in my vineyard. 29 He answered and said, I will not: but afterward he repented, and went. 30 And he came to the second, and said likewise. And he answered and said, I *go*, sir: and went not. 31 Whether of them twain did the will of *his* father? They say unto him, The first. Jesus saith unto them, Verily I say unto you, That the publicans and the harlots go into the kingdom of God before you. 32 For John came unto you in the way of righteousness, and ye believed him not: but the publicans and the harlots believed him: and ye, when ye had seen *it*, repented not afterward, that ye might believe him.

αὐτῷ; 26 ἐὰν.δὲ εἴπωμεν, Ἐξ ἀνθρώπων, φοβούμεθα τὸν
him?   but if we should say, From men,   we fear   the
ὄχλον· πάντες.γὰρ ʸἔχουσιν τὸν Ἰωάννην ὡς προφήτην.‖
multitude;   for all   hold   the John   as   a prophet.
27 Καὶ ἀποκριθέντες τῷ Ἰησοῦ ᶻεἶπον,‖ Οὐκ.οἴδαμεν. Ἔφη
And answering   Jesus they said, We know not. ³Said
αὐτοῖς καὶ αὐτός, Οὐδὲ ἐγὼ λέγω ὑμῖν ἐν ποίᾳ ἐξουσίᾳ
⁴to⁵them ²also ¹he, Neither ²I ¹tell   you   by what authority
ταῦτα ποιῶ. 28 Τί.δὲ ὑμῖν.δοκεῖ; ἄνθρωπόςᵃ εἶχεν ᵇτέκνα
these things I do. But what think ye?   a man   had ²children
δύο,‖ ᶜκαὶ‖ προσελθὼν τῷ πρώτῳ εἶπεν, Τέκνον, ὕπαγε
¹two, and   having come to the first   he said, Child,   go
σήμερον ἐργάζου ἐν τῷ.ἀμπελῶνί.ᵈμου.‖ 29 Ὁ.δὲ ἀποκριθεὶς
to-day   work   in my vineyard.   And he answering
εἶπεν, Οὐ.θέλω· ὕστερον.ᵉδὲ‖ μεταμεληθεὶς ἀπῆλθεν. 30 ᶠΚαὶ
said, I will not; but afterwards having repented he went. And
προσελθὼν‖ τῷ ᵍδευτέρῳ‖ εἶπεν ὡσαύτως. ὁ.δὲ ἀποκριθεὶς
having come to the second   he said likewise. And he answering
εἶπεν, Ἐγώ, κύριε· καὶ οὐκ.ἀπῆλθεν. 31 Τίς ἐκ τῶν δύο ἐποίη-
said, I [go], sir, and went not. Which of the two did
σεν τὸ θέλημα τοῦ πατρός; Λέγουσιν ʰαὐτῷ,‖ ⁱΟ πρῶτος.‖
the will of the father? They say to him, The first.
Λέγει αὐτοῖς ὁ Ἰησοῦς, Ἀμὴν λέγω ὑμῖν, ὅτι οἱ τελῶναι καὶ
²Says ³to ⁴them ¹Jesus, Verily I say to you, that the tax-gatherers and
αἱ πόρναι προάγουσιν ὑμᾶς εἰς τὴν βασιλείαν τοῦ θεοῦ.
the harlots go before you into the kingdom of God.
32 ἦλθεν.γὰρ ᵏπρὸς ὑμᾶς Ἰωάννης‖ ἐν ὁδῷ δικαιοσύνης,
For ²came ³to ⁴you ¹John in [the] way of righteousness,
καὶ οὐκ.ἐπιστεύσατε αὐτῷ, οἱ.δὲ τελῶναι καὶ αἱ πόρναι
and ye did not believe him,· but the tax-gatherers and the harlots
ἐπίστευσαν αὐτῷ· ὑμεῖς.δὲ ἰδόντες ˡοὐ‖.μετεμελήθητε ὕστερον
believed him; but ye having seen did not repent afterwards
τοῦ πιστεῦσαι αὐτῷ.
to believe him.

33 Hear another parable: There was a certain householder, which planted a vineyard, and hedged it round about, and digged a winepress in it, and built a tower, and let it out to husbandmen, and went into a far country: 34 and when the time of the fruit drew near, he sent his servants to the husbandmen, that they might receive the fruits of it. 35 And the husbandmen took his servants, and beat one, and killed another, and stoned another. 36 Again, he sent other servants more than the first: and they did unto

33 Ἄλλην παραβολὴν ἀκούσατε. Ἄνθρωπός ᵐτις‖ ἦν
Another parable hear. A ²man ¹certain there was
οἰκοδεσπότης, ὅστις ἐφύτευσεν ἀμπελῶνα, καὶ φραγμὸν αὐτῷ
a master of a house, who planted a vineyard, and ⁴a ⁵fence ³it
περιέθηκεν, καὶ ὤρυξεν ἐν αὐτῷ ληνόν, καὶ ᾠκοδόμησεν
¹placed ²about, and dug in it a winepress, and built
πύργον, καὶ ⁿἐξέδοτο‖ αὐτὸν γεωργοῖς, καὶ ἀπεδήμησεν.
a tower, and let out it to husbandmen, and left the country.
34 ὅτε.δὲ ἤγγισεν ὁ καιρὸς τῶν καρπῶν, ἀπέστειλεν τοὺς
And when drew near the season of the fruits, he sent
δούλους.αὐτοῦ πρὸς τοὺς γεωργοὺς λαβεῖν τοὺς.καρποὺς.αὐτοῦ.
his bondmen to the husbandmen to receive his fruits.
35 καὶ λαβόντες οἱ γεωργοὶ τοὺς.δούλους.αὐτοῦ, ὃν.μὲν
And ³having ⁴taken ¹the ²husbandmen his bondmen, one
ἔδειραν, ὃν.δὲ ἀπέκτειναν, ὃν.δὲ ἐλιθοβόλησαν. 36 πάλιν
they beat, and another they killed, and another they stoned. Again
ἀπέστειλεν ἄλλους δούλους πλείονας τῶν πρώτων, καὶ ἐποίη-
he sent other bondmen more than the first, and they

ʸ ὡς προφήτην ἔχουσιν τὸν Ἰωάννην LTTrA.   ᶻ εἶπαν T.   ᵃ + τις (read a certain man) L.
ᵇ δύο τέκνα L.   ᶜ — καὶ T.   ᵈ — μου (read the vineyard) TTrA.   ᵉ — δὲ but [L]T.
ᶠ προσελθὼν δὲ LTTrA.   ᵍ ἑτέρῳ other GTAW.   ʰ — αὐτῷ LTTrA.   ⁱ ὁ ὕστερος he who
afterwards [obeyed] LTr.   ᵏ Ἰωάννης πρὸς ὑμᾶς LTTrA.   ˡ οὐδὲ (read did neither
repent) LTr; οὐ.δὲ A.   ᵐ — τις GLTTrAW.   ⁿ ἐξέδετο TA.

σαν αὐτοῖς ὡσαύτως. 37 ὕστερον.δὲ ἀπέστειλεν πρὸς αὐτοὺς
did to them in like manner. And at last he sent to them

τὸν.υἱὸν.αὐτοῦ, λέγων, Ἐντραπήσονται τὸν.υἱόν.μου.
his son, saying, They will have respect for my son.

38 Οἱ.δὲ γεωργοὶ ἰδόντες τὸν υἱὸν εἶπον ἐν ἑαυτοῖς, Οὗτός
But the husbandmen seeing the son said among themselves, This

ἐστιν ὁ κληρονόμος· δεῦτε, ἀποκτείνωμεν αὐτόν, καὶ °κατά-
is the heir; come, let us kill him, and gain pos-

σχωμεν‖ τὴν.κληρονομίαν.αὐτοῦ. 39 καὶ λαβόντες αὐτὸν
session of his inheritance. And having taken him

ἐξέβαλον ἔξω τοῦ ἀμπελῶνος καὶ ἀπέκτειναν. 40 ὅταν οὖν
they cast [him] out of the vineyard and killed [him]. When therefore

ἔλθῃ ὁ κύριος τοῦ ἀμπελῶνος, τί ποιήσει τοῖς γεωργοῖς
shall come the lord of the vineyard, what will he do ³husbandmen

ἐκείνοις; 41 Λέγουσιν αὐτῷ, Κακοὺς κακῶς ἀπολέσει
¹to ²those? They say to him, Evil [men]! miserably he will destroy

αὐτούς, καὶ τὸν ἀμπελῶνα Ρἐκδόσεται‖ ἄλλοις γεωργοῖς,
them, and the vineyard he will let out to other husbandmen,

οἵτινες ἀποδώσουσιν αὐτῷ τοὺς καρποὺς ἐν τοῖς.καιροῖς.αὐτῶν.
who will render to him the fruits in their seasons.

42 Λέγει αὐτοῖς ὁ Ἰησοῦς, Οὐδέποτε.ἀνέγνωτε ἐν ταῖς γρα-
²Says ³to ⁴them ¹Jesus, Did ye never read in the scrip-

φαῖς, Λίθον ὃν ἀπεδοκίμασαν οἱ οἰκοδομοῦντες, οὗτος
tures, [The] stone which ⁴rejected ¹those ²who ³build, this

ἐγενήθη εἰς κεφαλὴν γωνίας· παρὰ κυρίου ἐγένετο αὕτη,
is become head of [the] corner: from [the] Lord was this,

καὶ ἔστιν θαυμαστὴ ἐν ὀφθαλμοῖς.ἡμῶν; 43 Διὰ τοῦτο λέγω
and it is wonderful in our eyes? Because of this I say

ὑμῖν, ὅτι ἀρθήσεται ἀφ᾽ ὑμῶν ἡ βασιλεία τοῦ θεοῦ, καὶ
to you, that ³shall ⁴be ⁵taken ¹from ²you the kingdom of God, and

δοθήσεται ἔθνει ποιοῦντι τοὺς καρποὺς αὐτῆς. 44 ᵠκαὶ
it shall be given to a nation producing the fruits of it. And

ὁ πεσὼν ἐπὶ τὸν.λίθον.τοῦτον συνθλασθήσεται· ἐφ᾽.ὃν.δ᾽.ἂν
he who falls on this stone shall be broken; but on whomsoever

πέσῃ, λικμήσει αὐτόν.‖ 45 ʳΚαὶ ἀκούσαντες‖ οἱ
it shall fall it will grind to powder him. And ⁷hearing ¹the

ἀρχιερεῖς καὶ οἱ Φαρισαῖοι τὰς.παραβολὰς.αὐτοῦ ἔγνωσαν
²chief ³priests ⁴and ⁵the ⁶Pharisees his parables knew

ὅτι περὶ αὐτῶν λέγει. 46 καὶ ζητοῦντες αὐτὸν κρατῆσαι,
that about them he speaks. And seeking him to lay hold of,

ἐφοβήθησαν τοὺς ὄχλους, ˢἐπειδὴ‖ ᵗὡς‖ προφήτην αὐτὸν εἶχον.
they feared the crowds, because as a prophet him they held.

22 Καὶ ἀποκριθεὶς ὁ Ἰησοῦς πάλιν εἶπεν ᵛαὐτοῖς ἐν παρα-
And answering Jesus again spoke to them in para-

βολαῖς,‖ λέγων, 2 Ὡμοιώθη ἡ βασιλεία τῶν οὐρανῶν
bles, saying, ⁶Has ⁷become ⁸like ¹the ²kingdom ³of ⁴the ⁵heavens

ἀνθρώπῳ βασιλεῖ, ὅστις ἐποίησεν γάμους τῷ.υἱῷ.αὐτοῦ·
to a man a king, who made a wedding feast for his son:

3 καὶ ἀπέστειλεν τοὺς.δούλους.αὐτοῦ καλέσαι τοὺς κεκλη-
and sent his bondmen to call those who had been

μένους εἰς τοὺς γάμους, καὶ οὐκ.ἤθελον ἐλθεῖν. 4 Πάλιν
invited to the wedding feast, and they would not come. Again

ἀπέστειλεν ἄλλους δούλους, λέγων, Εἴπατε τοῖς κεκλη-
he sent other bondmen, saying, Say to those who had been

them likewise. 37 But last of all he sent unto them his son, saying, They will reverence my son. 38 But when the husbandmen saw the son, they said among themselves, This is the heir; come, let us kill him, and let us seize on his inheritance. 39 And they caught him, and cast *him* out of the vineyard, and slew *him*. 40 When the lord therefore of the vineyard cometh, what will he do unto those husbandmen? 41 They say unto him, He will miserably destroy those wicked men, and will let out *his* vineyard unto other husbandmen, which shall render him the fruits in their seasons. 42 Jesus saith unto them, Did ye never read in the scriptures, The stone which the builders rejected, the same is become the head of the corner: this is the Lord's doing, and it is marvellous in our eyes? 43 Therefore say I unto you, The kingdom of God shall be taken from you, and given to a nation bringing forth the fruits thereof. 44 And whosoever shall fall on this stone shall be broken: but on whomsoever it shall fall, it will grind him to powder. 45 And when the chief priests and Pharisees had heard his parables, they perceived that he spake of them. 46 But when they sought to lay hands on him, they feared the multitude, because they took him for a prophet.

XXII. And Jesus answered and spake unto them again by parables, and said, 2 The kingdom of heaven is like unto a certain king, which made a marriage for his son, 3 and sent forth his servants to call them that were bidden to the wedding: and they would not come. 4 Again, he sent forth other servants, saying, Tell them which are bidden, Behold, I

° σχῶμεν let us possess LTTrA. Ρ ἐκδώσεται GLTTrAW. ᵠ — verse 44 [L] T. ʳ ἀκούσαντες
δὲ T. ˢ ἐπεὶ TTrA. ᵗ εἰς for LTTrA. ᵛ ἐν παραβολαῖς αὐτοῖς LTTrA.

have prepared my din-
ner : my oxen and *my*
fatlings *are* killed, and
all things *are* ready :
come unto the mar-
riage. 5 But they
made light of *it*, and
went their ways, one
to his farm, another
to his merchandise :
6 and the remnant
took his servants, and
entreated *them* spite-
fully, and slew *them*.
7 But when the king
heard *thereof*, he was
wroth : and he sent
forth his armies, and
destroyed those mur-
derers, and burned up
their city. 8 Then saith
he to his servants, The
wedding is ready, but
they which were bid-
den were not worthy.
9 Go ye therefore into
the highways, and as
many as ye shall find,
bid to the marriage.
10 So those servants
went out into the
highways, and gather-
ed together all as many
as they found, both
bad and good : and the
wedding was furnish-
ed with guests. 11 And
when the king came in
to see the guests, he
saw there a man which
had not on a wedding
garment : 12 and he
saith unto him, Friend,
how camest thou in
hither not having
a wedding garment?
And he was speechless.
13 Then said the king
to the servants, Bind
him hand and foot, and
take him away, and
cast *him* into outer
darkness ; there shall
be weeping and gnash-
ing of teeth. 14 For
many are called, but
few *are* chosen.

15 Then went the
Pharisees, and took
counsel how they
might entangle him in
his talk. 16 And they
sent out unto him their
disciples with the He-
rodians, saying, Mas-
ter, we know that thou
art true, and teachest
the way of God in
truth, neither carest

μένοις, Ἰδού, τὸ ἄριστόν μου ᵂἡτοίμασα,ǁ οἱ ταῦροί μου καὶ
invited,   Behold,   my dinner   I prepared,   my oxen   and
τὰ σιτιστὰ τεθυμένα, καὶ πάντα ἕτοιμα· δεῦτε εἰς τοὺς
the fatted beasts. are killed, and all things [are] ready ; come to the
γάμους. 5 Οἱ δὲ ἀμελήσαντες ἀπῆλθον, ˣᵒǁ μὲν εἰς τὸν
wedding feast. But they being negligent of [it] went away,   one to
ἴδιον ἀγρόν, ᵞᵒǁ δὲ ᶻεἰςǁ τὴν ἐμπορίαν αὐτοῦ. 6 οἱ δὲ λοιποὶ
his own field, and another to   his commerce.   And the rest,
κρατήσαντες τοὺς δούλους αὐτοῦ ὕβρισαν καὶ ἀπέκτειναν.
having laid hold of his bondmen,   insulted and killed [them].
7 ᵃἈκούσας δὲ ὁ βασιλεὺς ὠργίσθη, καὶ πέμψας τὰ
And having heard [it] the   king   was wroth, . and having sent
στρατεύματα αὐτοῦ ἀπώλεσεν τοὺς φονεῖς ἐκείνους, καὶ τὴν
his forces   he destroyed   those murderers,   and
πόλιν αὐτῶν ἐνέπρησεν. 8 Τότε λέγει τοῖς δούλοις αὐτοῦ, Ὁ
their city   he burnt.   Then he says to his bondmen, The
μὲν γάμος ἕτοιμός ἐστιν, οἱ δὲ κεκλημένοι οὐκ ἦσαν
ᵃindeed ¹wedding ²feast ⁵ready ⁴is, but those who had been invited were not
ἄξιοι· 9 πορεύεσθε οὖν ἐπὶ τὰς διεξόδους τῶν ὁδῶν, καὶ
worthy ;   Go   therefore into the thoroughfares of the highways, and
ὅσους ᵇἂνǁ εὕρητε, καλέσατε εἰς τοὺς γάμους. 10 Καὶ
as many as ᵎ ye shall find,   invite to the wedding feast.   And
ἐξελθόντες οἱ δοῦλοι ἐκεῖνοι εἰς τὰς ὁδοὺς συνήγαγον πάντας
ᵃhaving ⁴gone ⁵out ¹those ²bondmen into the highways brought together all
ὅσους εὗρον, πονηρούς τε καὶ ἀγαθούς· καὶ ἐπλήσθη ὁ
as many as they found, ²evil ¹both and good ; and ⁴became ⁵full ¹the
ᶜγάμοςǁ ἀνακειμένων. 11 εἰσελθὼν δὲ ὁ βασιλεὺς θεάσα-
²wedding ᵃfeast of guests.   And ⁴coming ⁴in ¹the ²king   to see
σθαι τοὺς ἀνακειμένους εἶδεν ἐκεῖ ἄνθρωπον οὐκ ἐνδεδυμένον
the   guests   beheld there a man not clothed
ἔνδυμα γάμου· 12 καὶ λέγει αὐτῷ, Ἑταῖρε, πῶς
with a garment of [the] wedding feast ; and he says to him, Friend, how
εἰσῆλθες ὧδε μὴ ἔχων ἔνδυμα γάμου ; Ὁ δὲ
didst thou enter here not having a garment of [the] wedding feast? But he
ἐφιμώθη. 13 τότε ᵈεἶπεν ὁ βασιλεὺςǁ τοῖς διακόνοις, Δήσαν-
was speechless. Then said the king to the servants, Having
τες αὐτοῦ πόδας καὶ χεῖρας ᵉἄρατε αὐτὸν καὶǁ ἐκβάλετε ᶠ
bound his feet and hands take away him and cast out [him]
εἰς τὸ σκότος τὸ ἐξώτερον· ἐκεῖ ἔσται ὁ κλαυθμὸς καὶ ὁ
into the darkness the outer : there shall be the weeping and the
βρυγμὸς τῶν ὀδόντων. 14 πολλοὶ γάρ εἰσιν κλητοί, ὀλίγοι δὲ
gnashing of the teeth.   For many are called, but few
ἐκλεκτοί.
chosen.

15 Τότε πορευθέντες οἱ Φαρισαῖοι συμβούλιον ἔλαβον ὅπως
Then having gone the Pharisees ²counsel ¹took how
αὐτὸν παγιδεύσωσιν ἐν λόγῳ. 16 καὶ ἀποστέλλουσιν αὐτῷ
him they might ensnare in discourse. And they send to him
τοὺς μαθητὰς αὐτῶν μετὰ τῶν Ἡρωδιανῶν, ᵍ λέγοντες,ǁ Διδά-
their disciples with the Herodians,   saying, Teacher,
σκαλε, οἴδαμεν ὅτι ἀληθὴς εἶ, καὶ τὴν ὁδὸν τοῦ θεοῦ ἐν ἀληθείᾳ
we know that true thou art, and the way of God in truth

ᵂ ἡτοίμακα I have prepared LTTrA.   ˣ ὃς LTTrA.   ᵞ ὃς LTTrA.   ᶻ ἐπὶ LTTrA.
ᵃ ὁ δὲ βασιλεὺς ἀκούσας L ; ὁ δὲ βασιλεὺς TTrA ; καὶ ἀκούσας ὁ βασ. W.   ᵇ ἐὰν LTTrAW.
ᵉ νυμφῶν bridechamber T.   ᵈ ὁ βασιλεὺς εἶπεν LTTrA.   ᵉ — ἄρατε αὐτὸν καὶ LTTrA.
ᶠ + αὐτὸν him LTTrA.   ᵍ λέγοντας LTTr.

διδάσκεις, καὶ οὐ μέλει σοι περὶ οὐδενός, οὐ.γὰρ βλέπεις
teachest, and there is care to thee about no one, for ²not ¹thou ²lookest

εἰς πρόσωπον ἀνθρώπων 17 ʰεἰπὲ‖ οὖν ἡμῖν, τί ·σοι
on [the] appearance of men; tell therefore us, what ²thou

δοκεῖ; ἔξεστιν δοῦναι κῆνσον Καίσαρι ἢ οὔ; 18 Γνοὺς.δὲ
¹thinkest? Is it lawful to give tribute to Cæsar or not? But ²knowing

ὁ Ἰησοῦς τὴν.πονηρίαν.αὐτῶν εἶπεν, Τί με πειράζετε, ὑπο-
¹Jesus their wickedness said, Why me do ye tempt, hypo-

κριταί; 19 ἐπιδείξατέ μοι τὸ νόμισμα τοῦ κήνσου. Οἱ.δὲ
crites? Shew me the coin of the tribute. And they

προσήνεγκαν αὐτῷ δηνάριον. 20 καὶ λέγει αὐτοῖςⁱ, Τίνος
presented to him a denarius. And he says to them, Whose [is]

ἡ.εἰκὼν.αὕτη καὶ ἡ ἐπιγραφή; 21 Λέγουσιν ᵏαὐτῷ,‖ Καίσαρος.
this image and the inscription? They say to him, Cæsar's.

Τότε λέγει αὐτοῖς, Ἀπόδοτε οὖν τὰ Καίσαρος Καίσαρι,
Then he says to them, Render then the things of Cæsar to Cæsar,

καὶ τὰ τοῦ θεοῦ τῷ θεῷ. 22 Καὶ ἀκούσαντες ἐθαύμασαν·
and the things of God to God. And having heard they wondered;

καὶ ἀφέντες αὐτὸν ¹ἀπῆλθον.‖
and leaving him went away.

23 Ἐν ἐκείνῃ τῇ ἡμέρᾳ προσῆλθον αὐτῷ Σαδδουκαῖοι, ᵐοἱ‖
On that day came to him Sadducees, who

λέγοντες μὴ.εἶναι ἀνάστασιν, καὶ ἐπηρώτησαν αὐτόν, 24 λέ-
say there is not a resurrection, and they questioned him, say-

γοντες, Διδάσκαλε, ⁿΜωσῆς‖ εἶπεν, Ἐάν τις ἀποθάνῃ μὴ
ing, Teacher, Moses said, If any one should die not

ἔχων τέκνα, ᵒ ἐπιγαμβρεύσει ὁ.ἀδελφὸς.αὐτοῦ τὴν γυναῖκα
having children, ²shall ¹marry ¹his ·brother ·wife

αὐτοῦ, καὶ ἀναστήσει σπέρμα τῷ.ἀδελφῷ.αὐτοῦ. 25 Ἦσαν.δὲ
·his, and shall raise up seed to his brother. Now there were

παρ᾽ ἡμῖν ἑπτὰ ἀδελφοί· καὶ ὁ πρῶτος ᴾγαμήσας‖ ἐτελεύτη-
with us seven brothers; and the first having married died,

σεν, καὶ μὴ ἔχων σπέρμα ἀφῆκεν ⁴τὴν.γυναῖκα.αὐτοῦ τῷ
and not having seed left - his wife

ἀδελφῷ.αὐτοῦ. 26 ὁμοίως καὶ ὁ δεύτερος, καὶ ὁ τρίτος,
to his brother. In like manner also the second, and the third,

ἕως τῶν ἑπτά. 27 ὕστερον.δὲ πάντων ἀπέθανεν ᵍκαὶ‖ ἡ γυνή.
unto the seven. And last of all died also the woman.

28 ἐν τῇ ʳοὖν ἀναστάσει‖ τίνος τῶν ἑπτὰ ἔσται γυνή;
²In ¹the ¹therefore resurrection of which of the seven shall she be wife?

πάντες.γὰρ ἔσχον αὐτήν. 29 Ἀποκριθεὶς.δὲ ὁ Ἰησοῦς εἶπεν
for all had her. And answering Jesus said

αὐτοῖς, Πλανᾶσθε, μὴ εἰδότες τὰς γραφάς, μηδὲ τὴν δύναμιν
to them, Ye err, not knowing the scriptures, nor the power

τοῦ θεοῦ. 30 ἐν.γὰρ τῇ ἀναστάσει. οὔτε γαμοῦσιν οὔτε
of God. For in the resurrection neither do they marry nor

ˢἐκγαμίζονται,‖ ἀλλ᾽ ὡς ἄγγελοι ᵗτοῦ‖ θεοῦ‖ ἐν ʷ οὐρανῷ
are given in marriage, but as angels of God in heaven

εἰσιν. 31 περὶ.δὲ τῆς ἀναστάσεως τῶν νεκρῶν, οὐκ.ἀνέγνωτε
they are. But concerning the resurrection of the dead, have ye not read

τὸ ῥηθὲν ὑμῖν ὑπὸ τοῦ θεοῦ, λέγοντος, 32 Ἐγώ εἰμι
that which was spoken to you by God, saying, I am

---

thou for any man: for thou regardest not the person of men. 17 Tell us therefore, What thinkest thou? Is it lawful to give tribute unto Cæsar, or not? 18 But Jesus perceived their wickedness, and said, Why tempt ye me, ye hypocrites? 19 Shew me the tribute money. And they brought unto him a penny. 20 And he saith unto them, Whose is this image and superscription? 21 They say unto him, Cæsar's. Then saith he unto them, Render therefore unto Cæsar the things which are Cæsar's; and unto God the things that are God's. 22 When they had heard these words, they marvelled, and left him, and went their way.

23 The same day came to him the Sadducees, which say that there is no resurrection, 24 saying, Master, Moses said, If a man die, having no children, his brother shall marry his wife, and raise up seed unto his brother. 25 Now there were with us seven brethren: and the first, when he had married a wife, deceased, and, having no issue, left his wife unto his brother: 26 likewise the second also, and the third, unto the seventh. 27 And last of all the woman died also. 28 Therefore in the resurrection whose wife shall she be of the seven? for they all had her. 29 Jesus answered and said unto them, Ye do err, not knowing the scriptures, nor the power of God. 30 For in the resurrection they neither marry nor are given in marriage, but are as the angels of God in heaven. 31 But as touching the resurrection of the dead, have ye not read that which was spoken unto you by God, saying, 32 I am the God of

---

ʰ εἰπὸν τ.   ⁱ + ὁ Ἰησοῦς Jesus (says) LT.   ᵏ — αὐτῷ τ[A].   ¹ ἀπῆλθαν LTTrA.
ᵐ — οἱ (read saying) LTTrA.   ⁿ Μωϋσῆς LTTrAW.   ᵒ + ἵνα that L.   ᴾ γήμας LTTrA.
ᵍ — καὶ τ[Tr]A.   ʳ ἀναστάσει οὖν LTTrA.   ˢ γαμίζονται LTTrA.   ᵗ — τοῦ LTTrA.
ᵗ — θεοῦ LT:[A].   ʷ + τῷ the LTTrA.

Abraham, and the God of Isaac, and the God of Jacob? God is not the God of the dead, but of the living. 33 And when the multitude heard *this*, they were astonished at his doctrine.

ὁ θεὸς Ἀβραὰμ καὶ ὁ θεὸς Ἰσαὰκ καὶ ὁ θεὸς Ἰακώβ; οὐκ
the God of Abraham and the God of Isaac and the God of Jacob? [3]Not
ἔστιν [x]ὁ θεὸς[||] [y]θεὸς[||] νεκρῶν, ἀλλὰ ζώντων. 33 Καὶ ἀκού-
[2]is [1]God God of [the] dead, but of [the] living. And having
σαντες οἱ ὄχλοι ἐξεπλήσσοντο ἐπὶ τῇ.διδαχῇ.αὐτοῦ.
heard, the crowds were astonished at his teaching.

34 But, when the Pharisees had heard that he had put the Sadducees to silence, they were gathered together. 35 Then one of them, *which was a lawyer*, asked *him a question*, tempting him, and saying, 36 Master, which *is* the great commandment in the law? 37 Jesus said unto him, Thou shalt love the Lord thy God with all thy heart, and with all thy soul, and with all thy mind. 38 This is the first and great commandment. 39 And the second *is* like unto it, Thou shalt love thy neighbour as thyself. 40 On these two commandments hang all the law and the prophets.

34 Οἱ.δὲ Φαρισαῖοι ἀκούσαντες ὅτι ἐφίμωσεν τοὺς Σαδ-
But the Pharisees, having heard that he had silenced the Sad-
δουκαίους, συνήχθησαν ἐπὶ.τὸ.αὐτό, 35 καὶ ἐπηρώτησεν
ducees, were gathered together, and [9]questioned [[10]him]
εἷς ἐξ αὐτῶν νομικός, πειράζων αὐτόν, [z]καὶ λέγων,[||]
[1]one [2]of [3]them [4]a [5]doctor [6]of [7]the [8]law, tempting him, and saying,
36 Διδάσκαλε, ποία ἐντολὴ μεγάλη ἐν τῷ νόμῳ;
Teacher, which [4]commandment [[1]is [2]the] [3]great in the law?
37 [a]Ὁ.δὲ.Ἰησοῦς εἶπεν αὐτῷ,[||] Ἀγαπήσεις κύριον τὸν θεόν
And Jesus said to him, Thou shalt love [the] Lord [3]God
σου ἐν ὅλῃ [b]τῇ[||].καρδίᾳ σου, καὶ ἐν ὅλῃ τῇ.ψυχῇ.σου, καὶ ἐν
[1]thy with all thy heart, and with all thy soul, and with
ὅλῃ τῇ.διανοίᾳ.σου. 38 αὕτη ἐστὶν [c]πρώτη καὶ μεγάλη[||]
all thy mind. This is [the] first and great
ἐντολή. 39 δευτέρα.[d]δὲ[||] ὁμοία αὐτῇ, Ἀγαπήσεις τὸν
commandment. And [the] second [is] like it, Thou shalt love
πλησίον.σου ὡς σεαυτόν. 40 ἐν ταύταις ταῖς δυσὶν ἐντολ.αῖς
thy neighbour as thyself. On these two commandments
ὅλος ὁ νόμος [e]καὶ οἱ προφῆται κρέμανται.[||]
all the law and the prophets hang.

41 While the Pharisees were gathered together, Jesus asked them, 42 saying, What think ye of Christ? whose son is he? They say unto him, The Son of David. 43 He saith unto them, How then doth David in spirit call him Lord, saying, 44 The LORD said unto my Lord, Sit thou on my right hand, till I make thine enemies thy footstool? 45 If David then call him Lord, how is he his son? 46 And no man was able to answer him a word, neither durst any *man* from that day forth ask him any more *questions*.

41 Συνηγμένων.δὲ τῶν Φαρισαίων ἐπηρώτησεν
But [3]having [4]been [5]assembled [6]together, [1]the [2]Pharisees [8]questioned
αὐτοὺς ὁ Ἰησοῦς, 42 λέγων, Τί ὑμῖν δοκεῖ περὶ τοῦ χριστοῦ;
[7]them [9]Jesus, saying, What [2]ye [1]think concerning the Christ?
τίνος υἱός ἐστιν; Λέγουσιν αὐτῷ, Τοῦ.[f]Δαβίδ.[||] 43 Λέγει
of whom [3]son [1]is [2]he? They say to him, Of David. He says
αὐτοῖς, Πῶς οὖν [f]Δαβὶδ[||] ἐν πνεύματι [g]κύριον αὐτὸν καλεῖ;[||]
to them, How then [2]David [3]in [4]spirit [7]Lord [6]him [1]does [5]call?
λέγων, 44 Εἶπεν [h]ὁ[||] κύριος τῷ.κυρίῳ.μου, Κάθου ἐκ δεξιῶν.μου
saying, [3]Said the [2]Lord to my Lord, Sit on my right hand
ἕως.ἂν θῶ τοὺς.ἐχθρούς.σου [i]ὑποπόδιον[||] τῶν.ποδῶν.σου.
until I place thine enemies [as] a footstool for thy feet.
45 Εἰ οὖν [f]Δαβὶδ[||] καλεῖ αὐτὸν κύριον, πῶς υἱὸς.αὐτοῦ
If therefore David calls him Lord, how his son
ἐστιν; 46 Καὶ οὐδεὶς ἐδύνατο [k]αὐτῷ ἀποκριθῆναι[||] λόγον,
is he? And no one was able him to answer a word,
οὐδὲ ἐτόλμησέν τις ἀπ' ἐκείνης τῆς ἡμέρας ἐπερωτῆσαι αὐτὸν
nor dared anyone from that day to question him
οὐκέτι.
any more (*lit.* no more).

XXIII. Then spake Jesus to the multitude, and to his disciples, 2 saying, The scribes and the Pharisees sit in Moses' seat: 3 all therefore whatsoever they bid you observe,

23 Τότε ὁ Ἰησοῦς ἐλάλησεν τοῖς ὄχλοις καὶ τοῖς.μαθηταῖς
Then Jesus spoke to the crowds and to [2]disciples
αὐτοῦ, 2 λέγων, Ἐπὶ τῆς [l]Μωσέως[||] καθέδρας ἐκάθισαν οἱ
[1]his, saying, On the [2]of [3]Moses [1]seat have sat down the
γραμματεῖς καὶ οἱ Φαρισαῖοι· 3 πάντα οὖν ὅσα.[m]ἂν[||] εἴπω-
scribes and the Pharisees; all things therefore whatever they may

---

[x] — ὁ θεὸς (*read* he is not) T.   [y] — θεὸς LTr[A].   [z] — καὶ λέγων LTTr.   [a] ὁ δὲ Ἰησοῦς
ἔφη αὐτῷ G ; ὁ δὲ ἔφη αὐτῷ LTTrA; ἔφη αὐτῷ Ἰησοῦς W.   [b] [τῇ] A.   [c] ἡ μεγάλη καὶ
πρώτη LTTrAW.   [d] — δὲ and T.   [e] κρέμαται καὶ οἱ προφῆται LTTrAW.   [f] Δαυΐδ GW ; Δαυείδ
LTTrA.   [g] καλεῖ αὐτὸν κύριον LTrA ; καλεῖ κύριον αὐτὸν T.   [h] — ὁ (*read* [the]) LTTrA.
[i] ὑποκάτω under (thy feet) LTTrA.   [k] ἀποκριθῆναι αὐτῷ LTTrA.   [l] Μωϋσέως LTTrAW.   [m] ἐὰν TW.

σιν ὑμῖν ⁿτηρεῖν,‖ ᵒτηρεῖτε καὶ ποιεῖτε·‖ κατὰ.δὲ τὰ.ἔργα.αὐτῶν
tell you to keep,   keep and do.   But after   their works

μὴ.ποιεῖτε λέγουσιν.γὰρ καὶ οὐ.ποιοῦσιν. 4 δεσμεύουσιν ᵖγὰρ‖
do not;   for they say   and   do not.   ²They ³bind   ¹for

φορτία βαρέα �q καὶ δυσβάστακτα,‖ καὶ ἐπιτιθέασιν ἐπὶ τοὺς
burdens heavy · and hard to bear,   and   lay [them]   on the

ὤμους τῶν ἀνθρώπων· ʳτῷ.δὲ.δακτύλῳ.αὐτῶν‖ οὐ.θέλουσιν
shoulders   of men,   but with their own finger   they will not

κινῆσαι αὐτά. 5 πάντα.δὲ τὰ.ἔργα.αὐτῶν ποιοῦσιν πρὸς τὸ
move   them.   And all   their works   they do   to

θεαθῆναι τοῖς ἀνθρώποις. ²They ³make ⁴broad ¹and ˢδὲ‖ τὰ φυλακτήρια
be seen   by men.   ²They ³make ⁴broad ¹and   phylacteries

αὐτῶν, καὶ μεγαλύνουσιν τὰ κράσπεδα ᵗτῶν.ἱματίων.αὐτῶν·‖
⁵their,   and   enlarge   the borders   of their garments,

6 φιλοῦσίν ᵛτε‖ τὴν πρωτοκλισίαν ἐν τοῖς δείπνοις, καὶ τὰς
²love   ¹and the   first place   in the   suppers,   and the

πρωτοκαθεδρίας ἐν ταῖς συναγωγαῖς, 7 καὶ τοὺς ἀσπασμοὺς ἐν
first seats   in the   synagogues,   and the   salutations in

ταῖς ἀγοραῖς, καὶ καλεῖσθαι ὑπὸ τῶν ἀνθρώπων ʷραββί, ραββί·‖
the market-places, and to be called   by   men   Rabbi, Rabbi.

8 ὑμεῖς.δὲ μὴ.κληθῆτε ˣραββί·‖ εἷς.γάρ ἐστιν ὑμῶν ὁ ʸκαθηγητής,‖
But ²ye ¹be ²not called Rabbi;   for one is   your   leader,

ᶻὁ χριστός·‖ πάντες.δὲ ὑμεῖς ἀδελφοί ἐστε. 9 καὶ πατέρα μὴ
the Christ,   and all   ye   brethren are.   And ⁶father ²not

καλέσητε ὑμῶν   ἐπὶ τῆς γῆς· εἷς.γάρ ἐστιν ᵃὁ.πατὴρ.ὑμῶν,‖
¹call   your [³any ⁴one] on the earth; for one is   your father,

ᵇὁ   ἐν τοῖς οὐρανοῖς.‖ 10 μηδὲ κληθῆτε καθηγηταί· ᶜεἷς.γὰρ
who [is] in the   heavens.   Neither be called   leaders;   for one

ὑμῶν ἐστιν ὁ καθηγητής,‖ ὁ χριστός. 11 ὁ.δὲ μείζων ὑμῶν
⁶your   ¹is   the   Christ.   But the greater   of you

ἔσται ὑμῶν διάκονος. 12 ὅστις.δὲ ὑψώσει ἑαυτὸν ταπεινωθή-
shall be your   servant.   And whosoever will exalt himself   shall be

σεται· καὶ ὅστις ταπεινώσει ἑαυτὸν ὑψωθήσεται.
humbled; and whosoever will humble himself   shall be exalted.

13 (14) ᵈΟὐαὶ.ᵉδὲ‖ ὑμῖν, γραμματεῖς καὶ Φαρισαῖοι, ὑποκριταί,
But woe to you,   scribes   and Pharisees,   hypocrites,

ὅτι κατεσθίετε τὰς οἰκίας τῶν χηρῶν, καὶ προφάσει   μακρὰ
for ye devour   the houses   of widows, and as a pretext ²at ³great ⁴length

προσευχόμενοι· διὰ τοῦτο λήψεσθε περισσότερον κρίμα.‖
¹praying.   Because of this   ye shall receive more abundant judgment.

14 (13) Οὐαὶᶠ ὑμῖν, γραμματεῖς καὶ Φαρισαῖοι, ὑποκριταί, ὅτι
Woe to you,   scribes · and Pharisees,   hypocrites, for

κλείετε τὴν βασιλείαν τῶν οὐρανῶν ἔμπροσθεν τῶν ἀνθρώπων·
ye shut up the   kingdom   of the heavens   before   men;

ὑμεῖς.γὰρ οὐκ.εἰσέρχεσθε, οὐδὲ τοὺς εἰσερχομένους ἀφίετε
for ye   do not enter,   nor even those who   are entering   do ye suffer

εἰσελθεῖν. 15 Οὐαὶ ὑμῖν, γραμματεῖς καὶ Φαρισαῖοι, ὑποκριταί,
to enter.   Woe to you,   scribes   and Pharisees,   hypocrites,

ὅτι περιάγετε τὴν θάλασσαν καὶ τὴν ξηρὰν ποιῆσαι ἕνα
for ye go about the   sea   and the   dry [land] to make   one

that observe and do; but do not ye after their works : for they say, and do not. 4 For they bind heavy burdens and grievous to be borne, and lay them on men's shoulders; but they themselves will not move them with one of their fingers. 5 But all their works they do for to be seen of men : they make broad their phylacteries, and enlarge the borders of their garments, 6 and love the uppermost rooms at feasts, and the chief seats in the synagogues, 7 and greetings in the markets, and to be called of men, Rabbi, Rabbi. 8 But be not ye called Rabbi : for one is your Master, even Christ; and all ye are brethren. 9 And call no man your father upon the earth : for one is your Father, which is in heaven. 10 Neither be ye called masters : for one is your Master, even Christ. 11 But he that is greatest among you shall be your servant. 12 And whosoever shall exalt himself shall be abased; and he that shall humble himself shall be exalted.

13 But woe unto you, scribes and Pharisees, hypocrites! for ye shut up the kingdom of heaven against men : for ye neither go in yourselves, neither suffer ye them that are entering to go in. 14 Woe unto you, scribes and Pharisees, hypocrites! for ye devour widows' houses, and for a pretence make long prayer : therefore ye shall receive the greater damnation. 15 Woe unto you, scribes and Pharisees, hypocrites! for ye compass sea and land to make one pros-

ⁿ — τηρεῖν LTTrA.   ᵒ ποιήσατε καὶ τηρεῖτε LTTrA.   ᵖ δὲ but LTTrA.   q — καὶ δυσβάστακτα τ[Tr]A.   ʳ αὐτοὶ δὲ τῷ δακτύλῳ αὐτῶν but they themselves with their finger LTTrA.
ˢ γὰρ for LTTrA.   ᵗ — τῶν ἱματίων αὐτῶν LTTrA.   ᵛ δὲ LTTrA.   ʷ ραββί LTr; ραββεί T;
ραββὶ [ραββί] A.   ˣ ραββεί T.   ʸ διδάσκαλος teacher LTTrAW.   ᶻ — ὁ χριστός GLTTrAW.
ᵃ ὑμῶν ὁ πατὴρ LTTr.   ᵇ ὁ οὐράνιος the heavenly LTTr.   ᶜ ὅτι καθηγητὴς ὑμῶν ἐστιν εἰς LTTrA.
ᵈ Verse 13 placed after 14 E; — verse 13 LTTrA.   ᵉ — δὲ but E.   ᶠ + δὲ but (woe) ELTTrA.

elyte, and when he is made, ye make him twofold more the child of hell than yourselves. 16 Woe unto you, ye blind guides, which say, Whosoever shall swear by the temple, it is nothing; but whosoever shall swear by the gold of the temple, he is a debtor! 17 Ye fools and blind: for whether is greater, the gold, or the temple that sanctifieth the gold? 18 And, Whosoever shall swear by the altar, it is nothing; but whosoever sweareth by the gift that is upon it, he is guilty. 19 Ye fools and blind: for whether is greater, the gift, or the altar that sanctifieth the gift? 20 Whoso therefore shall swear by the altar, sweareth by it, and by all things thereon. 21 And whoso shall swear by the temple, sweareth by it, and by him that dwelleth therein. 22 And he that shall swear by heaven, sweareth by the throne of God, and by him that sitteth thereon. 23 Woe unto you, scribes and Pharisees, hypocrites! for ye pay tithe of mint and anise and cummin, and have omitted the weightier *matters* of the law, judgment, mercy, and faith: these ought ye to have done, and not to leave the other undone. 24 Ye blind guides, which strain at a gnat, and swallow a camel. 25 Woe unto you, scribes and Pharisees, hypocrites! for ye make clean the outside of the cup and of the platter, but within they are full of extortion and excess. 26 *Thou* blind Pharisee, cleanse first that *which is* within the cup and platter, that the outside of them may be clean also. ' 27 Woe unto you, scribes and Pharisees, hypocrites! for ye are like unto whited sepulchres, which indeed appear beautiful outward, but are within full of dead men's bones, and of all

προσήλυτον, καὶ ὅταν γένηται, ποιεῖτε αὐτὸν υἱὸν γε-
proselyte, and when he has become [so], ye make him a son of Ge-

έννης διπλότερον ὑμῶν. 16 Οὐαὶ ὑμῖν, ὁδηγοὶ τυφλοί, οἱ
henna twofold more than yourselves. Woe to you, "guides ¹blind, who

λέγοντες, Ὃς ἂν ὁμόσῃ ἐν τῷ ναῷ, οὐδέν ἐστιν· ὃς δ᾽ ἂν
say, Whoever shall swear by the temple, nothing it is; but whoever

ὁμόσῃ ἐν τῷ χρυσῷ τοῦ ναοῦ, ὀφείλει. 17 μωροὶ καὶ τυφλοί·
shall swear by the gold of the temple, is a debtor. Fools and ᵉ blind,

gτίς‖ γὰρ ʰμείζων‖ ἐστὶν, ὁ χρυσός, ἢ ὁ ναὸς ὁ ¹ἁγιάζων‖
for which ²greater ¹is, the gold, or the temple which sanctifies

τὸν᾽ χρυσόν; 18 καί, Ὃς ᵏἐὰν‖ ὁμόσῃ ἐν τῷ θυσιαστηρίῳ,
the gold? And, Whoever shall swear by the altar,

οὐδέν ἐστιν· ὃς δ᾽ ἂν ὁμόσῃ ἐν τῷ δώρῳ τῷ ἐπάνω αὐτοῦ,
nothing it is; but whoever shall swear by the gift that [is] upon it,

ὀφείλει. 19 ¹μωροὶ καὶ‖ τυφλοί, τί γὰρ μεῖζον, τὸ δῶρον,
is a debtor. Fools and blind, for which [is] greater, the gift,

ἢ τὸ θυσιαστήριον τὸ ἁγιάζον τὸ δῶρον; 20 ὁ οὖν ὁμόσας
or the altar which sanctifies the gift? He ᵗʰᵃᵗ ᵗherefore swears

ἐν τῷ θυσιαστηρίῳ ὀμνύει ἐν αὐτῷ καὶ ἐν πᾶσιν τοῖς ἐπάνω
by the altar swears by it and by all things that [are] upon

αὐτοῦ· 21 καὶ ὁ ὁμόσας ἐν τῷ ναῷ ὀμνύει ἐν αὐτῷ καὶ ἐν
it. And he that swears by the temple swears by it and by

τῷ ᵐκατοικοῦντι‖ αὐτόν· 22 καὶ ὁ ὁμόσας ἐν τῷ οὐρανῷ
him who dwells in it. And he that swears by the heaven

ὀμνύει ἐν τῷ θρόνῳ τοῦ θεοῦ καὶ ἐν τῷ καθημένῳ ἐπάνω
swears by the throne of God and by him who sits upon

αὐτοῦ. 23 Οὐαὶ ὑμῖν, γραμματεῖς καὶ Φαρισαῖοι, ὑποκριταί, ὅτι
it. Woe to you, scribes and Pharisees, hypocrites, for

ἀποδεκατοῦτε τὸ ἡδύοσμον καὶ τὸ ἄνηθον καὶ τὸ κύμινον, καὶ
ye pay tithes of the mint and the anise and the cummin, and

ἀφήκατε τὰ βαρύτερα τοῦ νόμου, τὴν κρίσιν καὶ ⁿτὸν
ye have left aside the weightier [matters] of the law, judgment, and

ἔλεον‖ καὶ τὴν πίστιν· ταῦτα° ἔδει ποιῆσαι, κἀκεῖνα μὴ
mercy and faith: these it behoved [you] to do, and those not

ᴾἀφιέναι.‖ 24 ὁδηγοὶ τυφλοί, ⁹οἱ‖ διϋλίζοντες τὸν κώνωπα,
to be leaving aside. ²Guides ¹blind, who filter out the gnat,

τὴν δὲ κάμηλον καταπίνοντες. 25 Οὐαὶ ὑμῖν, γραμματεῖς καὶ
but the camel swallow. Woe to you, scribes and

Φαρισαῖοι, ὑποκριταί, ὅτι καθαρίζετε τὸ ἔξωθεν τοῦ ποτηρίου
Pharisees, hypocrites, for ye cleanse the outside of the cup

καὶ τῆς παροψίδος, ἔσωθεν δὲ γέμουσιν ʳἐξ‖ ἁρπαγῆς καὶ
and of the dish, but within they are full of plunder and

ˢἀκρασίας.‖ 26 Φαρισαῖε τυφλέ, καθάρισον πρῶτον τὸ ἐντὸς
incontinence. ²Pharisee ¹blind, cleanse first the inside

τοῦ ποτηρίου ᵗκαὶ τῆς παροψίδος,‖ ᵗἵνα γένηται καὶ τὸ ἐκτὸς
of the cup and of the dish, that ⁶may ⁷become ⁸also ¹the ²outside

ᵛαὐτῶν‖ καθαρόν. 27 Οὐαὶ ὑμῖν, γραμματεῖς καὶ Φαρισαῖοι,
³of ⁴them clean. Woe to you, scribes and Pharisees,

ὑποκριταί, ὅτι ʷπαρομοιάζετε‖ τάφοις κεκονιαμένοις, οἵτινες
hypocrites, for ye are like ᵉsepulchres ¹whited, which

ἔξωθεν μὲν φαίνονται ὡραῖοι, ἔσωθεν δὲ γέμουσιν ὀστέων
outwardly indeed appear beautiful, but within are full of bones

---

g τί L.   h μείζον L.   ¹ ἁγιάσας sanctified LTTrA.   ᵏ ἂν LTTrA.   ˡ — μωροὶ καὶ [L]TTrA.
ᵐ κατοικήσαντι dwelt in GTrAW.   ⁿ τὸ ἔλεος LTTrA.   ° + δὲ but GLTrAW.   ᴾ ἀφεῖναι
to leave aside LTTrA.   ⁹ — οἱ (read filtering out.... swallowing) LTrA.   ʳ — ἐξ L [Tr]
ἀδικίας unrighteousness QW.   ˢ — καὶ τῆς παροψίδος ΤΑ.   ᵛ αὐτοῦ of it LTTrA.
ʷ ὁμοιάζετε LTr.

ν κρῶν καὶ πάσης ἀκαθαρσίας. 28 οὕτως καὶ ὑμεῖς ἔξωθεν
of [the] dead and of all　uncleanness.　Thus　also　ye outwardly

μὲν φαίνεσθε τοῖς ἀνθρώποις δίκαιοι, ἔσωθεν.δὲ ˣμεστοί ἐστε‖
indeed appear　to men　　righteous, but within　²full　¹are

ὑποκρίσεως καὶ ἀνομίας. 29 Οὐαὶ ὑμῖν, γραμματεῖς καὶ Φα-
of hypocrisy and lawlessness.　Woe to you,　scribes　and Pha-

ρισαῖοι, ὑποκριταί, ὅτι οἰκοδομεῖτε τοὺς τάφους τῶν προφητῶν,
risees,　hypocrites, for　ye build　the sepulchres of the prophets,

καὶ κοσμεῖτε τὰ μνημεῖα τῶν δικαίων, 30 καὶ λέγετε, Εἰ ˠἦμεν‖
and adorn　the tombs of the righteous,　and ye say, If we had been

ἐν ταῖς ἡμέραις τῶν.πατέρων.ἡμῶν, οὐκ.ἂν.ˠἦμεν‖ ᶻκοινωνοὶ
in the　days　. of our fathers　we would not have been partakers

αὐτῶν‖ ἐν τῷ αἵματι τῶν προφητῶν. 31 ὥστε μαρτυρεῖτε
with them . in the　blood of the　prophets.　So that ye bear witness

ἑαυτοῖς, ὅτι υἱοί ἐστε τῶν φονευσάντων τοὺς προφήτας·
to yourselves, that sons ye are of those who murdered the prophets;

32 καὶ ὑμεῖς πληρώσατε τὸ μέτρον τῶν.πατέρων.ὑμῶν. 33 ὄφεις,
and ye,　fill ye up　the measure　of your fathers.　Serpents,

γεννήματα ἐχιδνῶν, πῶς φύγητε ἀπὸ τῆς κρίσεως τῆς γε-
offspring　of vipers, how shall ye escape from the judgment　of Ge-

έννης; 34 Διὰ τοῦτο, ἰδού, ἐγὼ ἀποστέλλω πρὸς ὑμᾶς προ-
henna?　Because of this, behold, I　send　to　you　pro-

φήτας καὶ σοφοὺς καὶ γραμματεῖς· ᵃκαὶ‖ ἐξ αὐτῶν ἀπο-
phets and wise [men] and　scribes;　and [some] of them ye will

κτενεῖτε καὶ σταυρώσετε, καὶ ἐξ αὐτῶν μαστιγώσετε ἐν ταῖς
kill　and　crucify,　and [some] of them　ye will scourge in

συναγωγαῖς.ὑμῶν, καὶ διώξετε ἀπὸ πόλεως εἰς πόλιν·
your synagogues,　and will persecute from　city　to　city;

35 ὅπως ἔλθη ἐφ᾽ ὑμᾶς πᾶν αἷμα δίκαιον ᵇἐκχυνόμενον‖
so that should come upon you　all [the] ²blood ¹righteous　poured out

ἐπὶ τῆς γῆς, ἀπὸ ᶜτοῦ‖ αἵματος Ἄβελ τοῦ δικαίου, ἕως τοῦ
upon the earth from　the　blood　of Abel the righteous, to　the

αἵματος Ζαχαρίου υἱοῦ Βαραχίου, ὃν ἐφονεύσατε μεταξὺ τοῦ
blood　of Zacharias son of Barachias, whom ye murdered between the

ναοῦ καὶ τοῦ θυσιαστηρίου. 36 ἀμὴν λέγω ὑμῖν, ᵈ ἥξει
temple and the　altar.　Verily I say to you, ⁴shall ⁵come

ᵉταῦτα πάντα‖ ἐπὶ τὴν.γενεὰν.ταύτην. 37 Ἱερουσαλήμ,
³these ³things ᐧ ¹all　upon　this generation.　Jerusalem,

Ἱερουσαλήμ, ἡ ἀποκτείνουσα τοὺς προφήτας καὶ λιθοβολοῦσα
Jerusalem,　who　killest　the　prophets　and　stonest

τοὺς ἀπεσταλμένους πρὸς αὐτήν, ποσάκις ἠθέλησα ἐπισυν-
those who have been sent　to　her,　how often would I have gath-

αγαγεῖν τὰ.τέκνα.σου, ὃν.τρόπον ᶠἐπισυνάγει, ὄρνις‖ τὰ
ered together thy children, in the way ²gathers ⁴together ¹a ²hen

νοσσία.ᵍἑαυτῆς‖ ὑπὸ τὰς πτέρυγας ʰ, καὶ οὐκ.ἠθελήσατε;
her brood　under [her]　wings,　and　ye would not!

38 ἰδού, ἀφίεται ὑμῖν ὁ.οἶκος.ὑμῶν ⁱἔρημος.‖ 39 λέγω.γὰρ
Behold, is left to you　your house　desolate;　for I say

ὑμῖν, Οὐ.μή με ἴδητε ἀπ᾽.ἄρτι ἕως.ἂν εἴπητε, Εὐλογη-
to you, In no wise me shall ye see henceforth until　ye say,　Bless-

μένος ὁ ἐρχόμενος ἐν ὀνόματι κυρίου.
ed　[is] he who　comes　in [the] name of [the] Lord.

ˣ ἐστε μεστοί LTTrA. ˠ ἤμεθα GLTTrAW. ᶻ αὐτῶν κοινωνοὶ LTrA. ᵃ — καὶ LTTrA.
ᵇ ἐκχυννόμενον·LTTrA. ᶜ — τοῦ w. ᵈ + ὅτι.that G[A]w. ᵉ πάντα ταῦτα LTrA. ᶠ ὄρνις
ἐπισυνάγει LTTrA. ᵍ αὐτῆς τ[τr]AW; — ἑαυτῆς (read [her]) L. ʰ + [αὐτῆς] her (wings) L.
ⁱ — ἔρημος L.

---

uncleanness. 28 Even
so ye also outwardly
appear righteous unto
men, but within ye are
full of hypocrisy and
iniquity. 29 Woe unto
you, scribes and Pha-
risees, hypocrites! be-
cause ye build the
tombs of the prophets,
and garnish the sepul-
chres of the righteous,
30 and say, If we had
been in the days of our
fathers, we would not
have been partakers
with them in the
blood of the prophets.
31 Wherefore ye be
witnesses unto your-
selves, that ye are the
children of them which
killed the prophets.
32 Fill ye up then the
measure of your fa-
thers. 33 Ye serpents,
ye generation of vi-
pers, how can ye escape
the damnation of hell?
34 Wherefore, behold,
I send unto you pro-
phets, and wise men,
and scribes: and some
of them ye shall kill
and crucify; and some
of them shall ye
scourge in your syna-
gogues, and persecute
them from city to city:
35 that upon you may
come all the righteous
blood shed upon the
earth, from the blood
of righteous Abel unto
the blood of Zacharias
son of Barachias,
whom ye slew between
the temple and the
altar. 36 Verily I say
unto you, All these
things shall come upon
this generation. 37 O
Jerusalem, Jerusalem,
thou that killest the
prophets, and stonest
them which are sent
unto thee, how often
would I have gathered
thy children together,
even as a hen gathereth
her chickens under her
wings, and ye would
not! 38 Behold, your
house is left unto you
desolate. 39 For I say
unto you, Ye shall not
see me henceforth, till
ye shall say, Blessed is
he that cometh in the
name of the Lord.

XXIV. And Jesus went out, and departed from the temple: and his disciples came to *him* for to shew him the buildings of the temple. 2 And Jesus said unto them, See ye not all the-e things? verily I say unto you, There shall not be left here one stone upon another, that shall not be thrown down. 3 And as he sat upon the mount of Olives, the disciples came unto him privately, saying, Tell us, when shall these things be? and what *shall be* the sign of thy coming, and of the end of the world? 4 And Jesus answered and said unto them, Take heed that no man deceive you. 5 For many shall come in my name, saying, I am Christ; and shall deceive many. 6 And ye shall hear of wars and rumours of wars: see what ye be not troubled: for all *these things* must come to pass, but the end is not yet. 7 For nation shall rise against nation, and kingdom against kingdom: and there shall be famines, and pestilences, and earthquakes, in divers places. 8 All these *are* the beginning of sorrows. 9 Then shall they deliver you up to be afflicted, and shall kill you: and ye shall be hated of all nations for my name's sake. 10 And then shall many be offended, and shall betray one another, and shall hate one another. 11 And many false prophets shall rise, and shall deceive many. 12 And because iniquity shall abound, the love of many shall wax cold. 13 But he that shall endure unto the end, the same shall be saved. 14 And this gospel of the kingdom shall be preached in all the world for a witness unto all nations; and then shall the end come. 15 When ye therefore shall see the abomination of desolation, spoken of by Daniel the prophet, stand in the holy place,

24 Καὶ ἐξελθὼν ὁ Ἰησοῦς ᵏἐπορεύετο ἀπὸ τοῦ ἱεροῦ,ⁱⁱ καὶ
And going forth   Jesus   went away from the temple, and
προσῆλθον   οἱ.μαθηταὶ.αὐτοῦ ἐπιδεῖξαι αὐτῷ τὰς οἰκοδομὰς
ˢcame ⁴to [⁵him] ¹his ²disciples to point out to him the buildings
τοῦ ἱεροῦ. 2 ὁ.δὲ.ᶫἸησοῦςⁱⁱ εἶπεν αὐτοῖς, Οὐ.βλέπετε ᵐπάντα
of the temple. But Jesus   said to them, See ye not   all
ταῦτα;ⁱⁱ ἀμὴν λέγω ὑμῖν, οὐ.μὴ ἀφεθῇ ὧδε λίθος ἐπὶ λίθον
these things? Verily I say to you, not at all shall be left.here stone upon stone
ὃς οὐ.ⁿμὴ̠ⁱⁱ.καταλυθήσεται. 3 Καθημένου.δὲ αὐτοῦ ἐπὶ τοῦ
which shall not be thrown down,   And as ²was ³sitting ¹he upon the
ὄρους τῶν ἐλαιῶν προσῆλθον αὐτῷ οἱ μαθηταὶᵒ κατ'.ἰδίαν, λέ-
mount of Olives ³came ⁴to ⁵him ¹the ²disciples apart, say-
γοντες, Εἰπὲ ἡμῖν, πότε ταῦτα ἔσται; καὶ τί   τὸ σημεῖον
ing,   Tell us, when ²these ³things ¹shall be? and what [is] the sign
τῆς.σῆς παρουσίας καὶ ᴾτῆςⁱⁱ συντελείας τοῦ αἰῶνος; 4 Καὶ
of thy coming   and of the completion of the age?   And
ἀποκριθεὶς ὁ Ἰησοῦς εἶπεν αὐτοῖς, Βλέπετε, μή τις ὑμᾶς
answering   Jesus   said to them, Take heed, lest any one ²you
πλανήσῃ. 5 πολλοὶ.γὰρ ἐλεύσονται ἐπὶ τῷ.ὀνόματί.μου, λέ-
¹mislead. For many will come in   my name,
γοντες, Ἐγώ εἰμι ὁ χριστός· καὶ πολλοὺς πλανήσουσιν.
saying,   I   am the Christ; and many   they will mislead.
6 Μελλήσετε.δὲ ἀκούειν πολέμους καὶ ἀκοὰς πολέμων. ὁρᾶτε,
But ye shall be about to hear of wars and rumours of wars. See,
μὴ.θροεῖσθε· δεῖ.γὰρ ᵠπάνταⁱⁱ γενέσθαι· ἀλλ' οὔπω
be not disturbed; for it is necessary all [these] things to take place, but not yet
ἐστὶν τὸ τέλος. 7 Ἐγερθήσεται.γὰρ ἔθνος ʳἐπὶ̠ⁱⁱ ἔθνος, καὶ
is   the end.   For ²shall ⁴rise ⁴up ¹nation against nation, and
βασιλεία ἐπὶ βασιλείαν· καὶ ἔσονται λιμοὶ ˢκαὶ λοιμοὶ̠ⁱⁱ
kingdom against kingdom; and there shall be famines and pestilences
καὶ σεισμοὶ κατὰ   τόπους. 8 πάντα.δὲ ταῦτα ἀρχὴ ὠδί-
and earthquakes in [different] places. But all these [are] a beginning of
νων. 9 Τότε παραδώσουσιν ὑμᾶς εἰς θλίψιν, καὶ ἀποκτενοῦσιν
throes. Then will they deliver up you to tribulation, and will kill
ὑμᾶς· καὶ ἔσεσθε μισούμενοι ὑπὸ πάντων ᵗτῶνⁱⁱ ἐθνῶν διὰ
you; and ye will be hated   by   all   the   nations on account of
τὸ.ὄνομά.μου. 10 καὶ τότε σκανδαλισθήσονται πολλοί, καὶ
my name.   And then will be offended   many,   and
ἀλλήλους παραδώσουσιν καὶ μισήσουσιν ἀλλήλους· 11 καὶ
one another they will deliver up and will hate   one another;   and
πολλοὶ ψευδοπροφῆται ἐγερθήσονται, καὶ πλανήσουσιν πολ-
many   false prophets will arise, and   will mislead
λούς· 12 καὶ διὰ τὸ.πληθυνθῆναι τὴν ἀνομίαν, ψυγήσεται
many; and because shall have been multiplied lawlessness,⁶will ⁷grow ⁸cold
ἡ ˋἀγαπη τῶν πολλῶν· 13 ὁ.δὲ ὑπομείνας εἰς τέλος,
¹the ²love ³of ⁴the ⁵many; but he who endures to [the] end
οὗτος σωθήσεται. 14 καὶ κηρυχθήσεται τοῦτο.τὸ.εὐαγγέλιον,
he   shall be saved.   And there shall be proclaimed these glad tidings
τῆς βασιλείας ἐν ὅλῃ τῇ οἰκουμένῃ, εἰς μαρτύριον πᾶσιν τοῖς
of the kingdom in all the habitable earth, for a testimony to all the
ἔθνεσιν· καὶ τότε ἥξει τὸ τέλος. 15 Ὅταν οὖν ἴδητε τὸ
nations; and then shall come the end.   When therefore ye shall see the
βδέλυγμα τῆς ἐρημώσεως, τὸ ῥηθὲν διὰ Δανιὴλ τοῦ προ-
abomination of desolation, which was spoken of by   Daniel the pro-

ᵏ ἀπὸ (ἐκ out of L) τοῦ ἱεροῦ ἐπορεύετο LTTrA.   ⁱ ἀποκριθεὶς answering (he said) LTTrA.
ᵐ ταῦτα πάντα LTTrA.   ⁿ — μὴ GLTT:AW.   ᵒ + [αὐτοῦ] of him L.   ᴾ — τῆς LTTrA.
ᵠ — πάντα LTTr[A].   ʳ ἐπ' T.   ˢ — καὶ λοιμοὶ LTT.A.   ᵗ — τῶν ᴇ.

φήτου, ᵛἑστὸς‖ ἐν τόπῳ ἁγίῳ· ὁ ἀναγινώσκων ʷνοεί-
phet, standing in [the] ²place ¹holy (he who reads let him un-

τω·‖ 16 τότε οἱ ἐν τῇ Ἰουδαίᾳ φευγέτωσαν ˣἐπὶ‖ τὰ
derstand), then those in Judea let them flee to the

ὄρη· 17 ὁ ἐπὶ τοῦ δώματος μὴ ᵞκαταβαινέτω‖ ἆραί ᶻτι‖
mountains: he on the housetop let him not come down to take anything

ἐκ τῆς οἰκίας αὐτοῦ· 18 καὶ ὁ ἐν τῷ ἀγρῷ μὴ ἐπιστρεψάτω
out of his house; and he in the field let him not return

ὀπίσω ἆραι ᵃτὰ ἱμάτια‖ αὐτοῦ. 19 οὐαὶ δὲ ταῖς ἐν γαστρὶ ἐ-
back to take ²garments ¹his. But woe to those that are with

χούσαις καὶ ταῖς θηλαζούσαις ἐν ἐκείναις ταῖς ἡμέραις.
child and to those that give suck in those days.

20 προσεύχεσθε δὲ ἵνα μὴ γένηται ἡ φυγὴ ὑμῶν χειμῶνος, μηδὲ
And pray that ³may ⁴not ⁵be ¹your ²flight in winter, nor

ᵇἐν‖ σαββάτῳ. 21 Ἔσται γὰρ τότε θλίψις μεγάλη, οἵα ᶜοὐ
on sabbath. for there shall be then ²tribulation ¹great such as ²not

γέγονεν‖ ἀπ' ἀρχῆς κόσμου ἕως τοῦ νῦν, οὐδ' οὐ μὴ
¹has been from [the] beginning of [the] world until now, no, nor ever

γένηται. 22 καὶ εἰ μὴ ἐκολοβώθησαν αἱ ἡμέραι ἐκεῖναι, οὐκ
shall be; and unless ¹had ²been ³shortened ⁴those ⁵days, ⁶not

ἂν ἐσώθη πᾶσα σάρξ· διὰ δὲ τοὺς ἐκλεκτοὺς
⁶there ⁷would have been saved any flesh, but on account of the elect

κολοβωθήσονται αἱ ἡμέραι ἐκεῖναι. 23 Τότε ἐάν τις ὑμῖν
⁵shall ⁶be ⁶shortened ³those ⁴days. Then -if anyone to you

εἴπῃ, Ἰδού, ὧδε ὁ χριστός, ἢ ὧδε, μὴ ᵈπιστεύσητε.‖ 24 Ἐγερ-
say, Behold, here [is] the Christ, or here, believe [it] not. ²There ³will

θήσονται γὰρ ψευδόχριστοι καὶ ψευδοπροφῆται, καὶ δώσουσιν
⁴arise ¹for false Christs and false prophets, and will give

σημεῖα μεγάλα καὶ τέρατα, ὥστε ᵉπλανῆσαι‖, εἰ δυνατόν, καὶ
¹signs ²great and ¹wonders, so as to mislead, if possible, even

τοὺς ἐκλεκτούς. 25 Ἰδού, προείρηκα ὑμῖν. 26 ἐὰν οὖν εἴπωσιν
the elect. Lo, I have foretold [it] to you. If therefore they say

ὑμῖν, Ἰδού, ἐν τῇ ἐρήμῳ ἐστίν, μὴ ἐξέλθητε· Ἰδού, ἐν
to you, Behold, in the wilderness he is, go not forth: Behold, [he is] in

τοῖς ταμείοις, μὴ πιστεύσητε. 27 ὥσπερ γὰρ ἡ ἀστραπὴ ἐξέρ-
the chambers, believe [it] not. For as the lightning comes

χεται ἀπὸ ἀνατολῶν καὶ φαίνεται ἕως δυσμῶν, οὕτως
forth from [the] east and appears as far as [the] west, so

ἔσται ᶠκαὶ‖ ἡ παρουσία τοῦ υἱοῦ τοῦ ἀνθρώπου. 28 ὅπου ᵍγὰρ‖
shall be also the coming of the Son of man. For wherever

ἐὰν ᾖ τὸ πτῶμα, ἐκεῖ συναχθήσονται οἱ ἀετοί. 29 Εὐ-
may be the carcase, there will be gathered together the eagles. ²Immedi-

θέως δὲ μετὰ τὴν θλίψιν τῶν ἡμερῶν ἐκείνων ὁ ἥλιος σκοτι-
ately ¹but after the tribulation of those days the sun shall be

σθήσεται, καὶ ἡ σελήνη οὐ δώσει τὸ φέγγος αὐτῆς, καὶ οἱ
darkened, and the moon shall not give her light, and the

ἀστέρες πεσοῦνται ʰἀπὸ‖ τοῦ οὐρανοῦ, καὶ αἱ δυνάμεις τῶν
stars shall fall from the heaven, and the powers of the

οὐρανῶν σαλευθήσονται. 30 καὶ τότε φανήσεται τὸ σημεῖον
heavens shall be shaken. And then shall appear the sign

τοῦ υἱοῦ τοῦ ἀνθρώπου ἐν ⁱτῷ‖ οὐρανῷ· καὶ ᵏτότε‖ κό-
of the Son of man in the heaven; and then shall

(whoso readeth, let him
understand :) 16 then
let them which be in
Judæa flee into the
mountains : 17 let him
which is on the house-
top not come down to
take any thing out of
his house : 18 neither
let him which is in
the field return back
to take his clothes.
19 And woe unto them
that are with child,
and to them that give
suck in those days!
20 But pray ye that
your flight be not in
the winter, neither on
the sabbath day: 21 for
then shall be great
tribulation, such as
was not since the be-
ginning of the world
to this time, no, nor
ever shall be. 22 And
except those days
should be shortened,
there should no flesh
be saved: but for the
elect's sake those days
shall be shortened.
23 Then if any man
shall say unto you, Lo,
here is Christ, or there;
believe it not. 24 For
there shall arise false
Christs, and false pro-
phets, and shall shew
great signs and won-
ders; insomuch that,
if it were possible, they
shall deceive the very
elect. 25 Behold, I
have told you before.
26 Wherefore if they
shall say unto you,
Behold, he is in the
desert; go not forth :
behold, he is in the
secret chambers ; be-
lieve it not. 27 For as
the lightning cometh
out of the east, and
shineth even unto the
west ; so shall also the
coming of the Son of
man be. 28 For where-
soever the carcase is,
there will the eagles
be gathered together.
29 Immediately after
the tribulation of
those days shall the
sun be darkened, and
the moon shall not
give her light, and the
stars shall fall from
heaven, and the powers
of the heavens shall be
shaken : 30 and then
shall appear the sign
of the Son of man in
heaven: and then shall

ᵛ ἑστὼς EG. ʷ νοείτω; does he understand ? Tr. ˣ εἰς LTr. ᵞ καταβάτω LTTr.
ᶻ τὰ the things GLTTrAW. ᵃ τὸ ἱμάτιον garment LTTr. ᵇ — ἐν GLTTrAW. ᶜ οὐ
ἐγένετο T. ᵈ πιστεύετε L. ᵉ πλανηθῆναι T; πλανᾶσθαι (read so that will be misled) Tr.
ᶠ — καὶ LTTrAW. ᵍ — γὰρ for LTTrA. ʰ ἐκ out of T. ⁱ — τῷ LTTrA. ᵏ — τότε T.

all the tribes of the earth mourn, and they shall see the Son of man coming in the clouds of heaven with power and great glory. 31 And he shall send his angels with a great sound of a trumpet, and they shall gather together his elect from the four winds, from one end of heaven to the other. 32 Now learn a parable of the fig tree ; When his branch is yet tender, and putteth forth leaves, ye know that summer is nigh: 33 so likewise ye, when ye shall see all these things, know that it is near, even at the doors. 34 Verily I say unto you, This generation shall not pass, till all these things be fulfilled. 35 Heaven and earth shall pass away, but my words shall not pass away. 36 But of that day and hour knoweth no man, no, not the angels of heaven, but my Father only. 37 But as the days of Noe were, so shall also the coming of the Son of man be. 38 For as in the days that were before the flood they were eating and drinking, marrying and giving in marriage, until the day that Noe entered into the ark, 39 and knew not until the flood came, and took them all away ; so shall also the coming of the Son of man be. 40 Then shall twobe in the field; the one shall be taken, and the other left: 41 Two women shall be grinding at the mill ; the one shall be taken, and the other left. 42 Watch therefore: for ye know not what hour your Lord doth come. 43 But know this, that if the goodman of the house had

ψονται πᾶσαι αἱ φυλαὶ τῆς γῆς. καὶ ὄψονται τὸν υἱὸν τοῦ
wail　　all　the tribes of the land,　and they shall see the　Son
ἀνθρώπου, ἐρχόμενον ἐπὶ τῶν νεφελῶν τυῦ οὐρανοῦ μετὰ δυ-
of man,　　coming　　on the　clouds　　of heaven with
νάμεως καὶ δόξης πολλῆς. 31 καὶ ἀποστελεῖ τοὺς ἀγγέλους
power　and ²glory　¹great.　　And he shall send　　²angels
αὐτοῦ μετὰ σάλπιγγος ¹φωνῆς‖ μεγάλης, καὶ ἐπισυνάξουσιν
¹his　with ³of ⁴a ²trumpet ²sound　　¹great, and they shall gather together
τοὺς ἐκλεκτοὺς αὐτοῦ ἐκ τῶν τεσσάρων ἀνέμων ἀπ᾽　ἄκρων
his elect　　from the　four　　winds, from[the]extremities
οὐρανῶν ἔως ᵐ ἄκρων αὐτῶν. 32 Ἀπὸ δὲ τῆς συκῆς
of[the]heavens to [the] extremities of them.　　But from the fig-tree
μάθετε τὴν παραβολήν· ὅταν ἤ ἡ ὁ κλάδος αὐτῆς γένηται
.learn　　the　　parable :　When already　its branch　is become
ἁπαλός, καὶ τὰ φύλλα ⁿἐκφύῃ,‖ γινώσκετε ὅτι ἐγγὺς τὸ
tender,　and　the leaves it puts forth,　ye know　that　near [is] the
θέρος· 33 οὕτως καὶ ὑμεῖς, ὅταν ἴδητε ᵒπάντα ταῦτα,‖
summer.　　Thus also ye,　when ye see ⁄　all　　these things,
γινώσκετε ὅτι ἐγγύς ἐστιν ἐπὶ θύραις. 34 ἀμὴν λέγω ὑμῖν,ᵖ
know　　that near　it is, at [the] doors.　　Verily I say to you,
οὐ μὴ　παρέλθῃ ἡ γενεὰ αὕτη ἔως ἂν πάντα ταῦτα
In no wise will have passed away this generation until　all　these things
γένηται.　35 Ὁ οὐρανὸς καὶ ἡ γῆ ᑫπαρελεύσονται,‖
shall have taken place.　The heaven　and the earth　shall pass away,
οἱ δὲ λόγοι μου οὐ μὴ παρέλθωσιν. 36 Περὶ δὲ τῆς ἡμέρας
but my words　in no wise shall pass away.　But concerning　ʳday
ἐκείνης καὶ ʳτῆς‖ ὥρας οὐδεὶς οἶδεν, οὐδὲ οἱ ἄγγελοι τῶν
ᵗ¹that　and　the hour　no one knows, not even the angels of the
οὐρανῶν, ˢ εἰ μὴ ὁ πατήρ μου‖ μόνος. 37 Ὥσπερ ᵛδὲ‖ αἱ ἡμέραι
heavens,　but　my Father　only.　But as　the　days
τοῦ Νῶε, οὕτως ἔσται ᵂκαὶ‖ ἡ παρουσία τοῦ υἱοῦ τοῦ ἀνθρώ-
of Noe,　so　shall be ⁄ also the　coming of the Son　　of
που. 38 ˣὥσπερ‖ γὰρ ἦσαν ἐν ταῖς ἡμέραις ʸ ταῖς　πρὸ
man.　²As　²for they were in the　days　which [were] before
τοῦ κατακλυσμοῦ, τρώγοντες καὶ πίνοντες, γαμοῦντες καὶ
¹the　flood,　　eating　and drinking,　marrying and
ˢἐκγαμίζοντες,‖ ἄχρι ἧς ἡμέρας εἰσῆλθεν Νῶε εἰς τὴν κιβωτόν,
giving in marriage, until the day when ²entered ¹Noe into the　ark,
39 καὶ οὐκ ἔγνωσαν, ἔως ἦλθεν ὁ κατακλυσμὸς καὶ ἦρεν
and　they knew not　till　²came ¹the　²flood　and took away
ἅπαντας, οὕτως ἔσται ᵇκαὶ‖ ἡ παρουσία τοῦ υἱοῦ τοῦ ἀνθρώπου.
all;　thus shall be also the　coming of the Son　of man.
40 Τότε ᶜδύο ἔσονται‖ ἐν τῷ ἀγρῷ· ᵈὁ‖ εἷς παραλαμβάνεται,
Then two will be　in the field,　the one　is taken,
καὶ ᵈὁ‖ εἷς ἀφίεται. 41 δύο　ἀλήθουσαι ἐν τῷ ᵉμύλωνι·‖ μία
and the one is left;　two[women] grinding at the　mill,　one
παραλαμβάνεται, καὶ μία ἀφίεται. 42 Γρηγορεῖτε οὖν, ὅτι
is taken,　and one is left.　Watch　therefore, for
οὐκ οἴδατε ποίᾳ ᶠὥρᾳ‖ ὁ κύριος ὑμῶν ἔρχεται· 43 ἐκεῖνο δὲ
ye know not in what hour　your Lord　comes.　But this

ˡ — φωνῆς (read a great trumpet) T.　ᵐ + τῶν the Tr.　ⁿ ἐκφυῇ are put forth LTTrA.
ᵒ ταῦτα πάντα TTr.　ᵖ + ὅτι that LTr.　ᑫ παρελεύσεται GLTTrA.　ʳ — τῆς GLTTrA.
ˢ + οὐδὲ ὁ υἱὸς nor the son LT.　ᵗ — μου (read the Father) GLTT[A].　ᵘ γὰρ for (as) LTr.
ᵂ — καὶ LTTrA.　ˣ ὡς as LTA ; ὡς so Tr.　ʸ + ἐκείναις (read those days) L[Tr].
ˢ — ταῖς πρὸ (read of the flood) A.　ᵃ γαμίσκοντες L ; γαμίζοντες T.　ᵇ — καὶ LTTrA.
ᶜ ἔσονται δύο LT.　ᵈ — ὁ LTTrA.　ᵉ μύλῳ LTT. A.　ᶠ ἡμέρᾳ day LTTrA.

γινώσκετε, ὅτι εἰ ᾔδει ὁ οἰκοδεσπότης ποίᾳ φυλακῇ
know, that if ᵍhad ⁷known ¹the ²master ³of ⁴the ⁵house in what watch

ὁ κλέπτης ἔρχεται, ἐγρηγόρησεν.ἂν, καὶ οὐκ.ἂν.εἴασεν ᵍδιο-
the thief comes, he would have watched, and not have suffered ³to ⁴be

ρυγῆναι‖ τὴν.οἰκίαν.αὐτοῦ. 44 διὰ.τοῦτο καὶ ὑμεῖς γίνεσθε
ᵈdug ᵍthrough ¹his ²house. Wherefore also ²ye ¹be

ἕτοιμοι· ὅτι ᾗ.ʰὥρα οὐ.δοκεῖτε‖ ὁ υἱὸς τοῦ ἀνθρώπου ἔρχεται.
ready, for in what hour ye think not the Son ⁴ of man comes.

45 Τίς ἄρα ἐστὶν ὁ πιστὸς δοῦλος καὶ φρόνιμος, ὃν κατέ-
Who then is the faithful bondman and prudent, whom ³has

στησεν ὁ.κύριος.ⁱαὐτοῦ‖ ἐπὶ τῆς.ᵏθεραπείας‖.αὐτοῦ, τοῦ ¹διδόναι‖
⁴set ¹his ²lord over his household, to give

αὐτοῖς τὴν τροφὴν ἐν καιρῷ; 46 μακάριος ὁ.δοῦλος.ἐκεῖνος, ὃν,
to them the food in season? Blessed that bondman, whom

ἐλθὼν ὁ.κύριος.αὐτοῦ εὑρήσει ᵐποιοῦντα οὕτως.‖ 47 Ἀμὴν
ᵃhaving ⁴come ¹his ²lord will find doing thus. Verily

λέγω ὑμῖν, ὅτι ἐπὶ πᾶσιν τοῖς.ὑπάρχουσιν.αὐτοῦ καταστήσει
I say to you, that over all his property he will set

αὐτόν. 48 Ἐὰν.δὲ εἴπῃ ὁ.κακὸς δοῦλος ⁿἐκεῖνος‖ ἐν τῇ
him. But if ⁴should ³say ²evil ³bondman ¹that in

καρδίᾳ.αὐτοῦ, Χρονίζει ⁰ὁ.κύριός.μου‖ ᴾἐλθεῖν,‖ 49 καὶ ἄρξηται
his heart, ³Delays ¹my ²lord to come, and should begin

τύπτειν τοὺς συνδούλους۹, 'ἐσθίειν'.δὲ καὶ ˢπίνειν‖ μετὰ τῶν
to beat [his] fellow-bondmen, and to eat and to drink with the

μεθυόντων, 50 ἥξει ὁ κύριος τοῦ.δούλου.ἐκείνου ἐν ἡμέρᾳ
drunken, ⁶will ⁷come ¹the ²lord ³of ⁴that ⁵bondman in a day

ᾗ οὐ.προσδοκᾷ, καὶ ἐν ὥρᾳ ᾗ οὐ.γινώσκει, 51 καὶ
in which he does not expect, and in an hour which he knows not, and

διχοτομήσει αὐτόν, καὶ τὸ.μέρος.αὐτοῦ μετὰ τῶν ὑποκριτῶν
will cut ⁴in ²two ¹him, and his portion with the hypocrites

θήσει· ἐκεῖ ἔσται ὁ κλαυθμὸς καὶ ὁ βρυγμὸς τῶν ὀδόντων.
will appoint: there will be the weeping and the gnashing of the teeth.

25 Τότε ὁμοιωθήσεται ἡ βασιλεία τῶν οὐρανῶν δέκα
Then ⁶will ⁷be ⁸made ⁹like ¹the ²kingdom ³of ⁴the ⁵heavens [to] ten

παρθένοις, αἵτινες λαβοῦσαι τὰς.λαμπάδας.ᵗαὐτῶν‖ ἐξῆλθον
virgins, who having taken their lamps went forth

εἰς.ᵛἀπάντησιν‖ τοῦ νυμφίου. 2 πέντε.δὲ ʷῆσαν ἐξ αὐτῶν‖
to meet the bridegroom. And five ²were ¹of ²them

ˣφρόνιμοι,‖ καὶ ʸαἱ‖ πέντε ᶻμωραί.‖ 3 ᵃαἵτινες‖ μωραί, λα-
prudent, and five foolish. They who [were] foolish, hav-

βοῦσαι τὰς.λαμπάδας.ᵇἑαυτῶν,‖ οὐκ.ἔλαβον μεθ᾽ ἑαυτῶν
ing taken their lamps, did not take with themselves

ἔλαιον· 4 αἱ.δὲ φρόνιμοι ἔλαβον ἔλαιον ἐν τοῖς.ἀγγείοις
oil; but the prudent took oil in ²ve sels

ᶜαὐτῶν‖ μετὰ τῶν.λαμπάδων.ᵈαὐτῶν.‖ 5 χρονίζοντος.δὲ τοῦ
¹their with their lamps. But ³tarrying ¹the

νυμφίου, ἐνύσταξαν πᾶσαι καὶ ἐκάθευδον. 6 μέσης.δὲ
²bridegroom, they ²became ³drowsy ¹all and slept. But in [the] middle

νυκτὸς κραυγὴ γέγονεν, Ἰδού, ὁ νυμφίος ᵉἔρχεται,‖ ἐξέρ-
of [the] night ³a ⁴cry ¹there ²was, Behold, the bridegroom comes, go

known in what watch the thief would come, he would have watched, and would not have suffered his house to be broken up. 44 Therefore be ye also ready: for in such an hour as ye think not the Son of man cometh. 45 Who then is a faithful and wise servant, whom his lord hath made ruler over his household, to give them meat in due season? 46 Blessed is that servant, whom his lord when he cometh shall find so doing. 47 Verily I say unto you, That he shall make him ruler over all his goods. 48 But and if that evil servant shall say in his heart, My lord delayeth his coming; 49 and shall begin to smite his fellowservants, and to eat and drink with the drunken; 50 the lord of that servant shall come in a day when he looketh not for him, and in an hour that he is not aware of, 51 and shall cut him asunder, and appoint him his portion with the hypocrites: there shall be weeping and gnashing of teeth.

XXV. Then shall the kingdom of heaven be likened unto ten virgins, which took their lamps, and went forth to meet the bridegroom. 2 And five of them were wise, and five were foolish. 3 They that were foolish took their lamps, and took no oil with them: 4 but the wise took oil in their vessels with their lamps. 5 While the bridegroom tarried, they all slumbered and slept. 6 And at midnight there was a cry made, Behold, the bridegroom cometh;

ᵍ διορυχθῆναι TTr. ʰ οὐ δοκεῖτε ὥρᾳ LTTrA. ⁱ — αὐτοῦ (read [his]) LTT A.
ᵏ οἰκετείας LTTrA. ¹ δοῦναι GLTTrA. ᵐ οὕτως ποιοῦντα LTTrA. ⁿ — ἐκεῖνος (read the evil bondman) T. ⁰ μου ὁ κύριος LTTrA. ᴾ — ἐλθεῖν LTTr. ۹ + αὐτοῦ his (fellow bondmen) LTTrAW. ʳ ἐσθῄ should eat GLTTrAW. ˢ πίνῃ should drink GLTTrAW.
ᵗ ἑαυτῶν LTrA; αὐτῶν TW. ᵛ ὑπάντησιν LTTrA. ʷ ἐξ αὐτῶν ἦσαν LTTrA. ˣ μωραὶ foolish LTTrA. ʸ — αἱ EGLTTrA. ᶻ φρόνιμοι prudent LTTrA. ᵃ αἱ δὲ but the L; αἱ γὰρ for those who Tr; αἱ γὰρ for the TA. ᵇ αὐτῶν GW; αὐτῶν LTrA; — ἑαυτῶν T. ᶜ — αὐτῶν (read the vessels) LTTrA. ᵈ ἑαυτῶν LT; αὐτῶν TrA. ᵉ — ἔρχεται LTTrA.

go ye out to meet him. 7 Then all those virgins arose, and trimmed their lamps. 8 And the foolish said unto the wise, Give us of your oil ; for our lamps are gone out. 9 But the wise answered, saying, *Not so*; lest there be not enough for us and you : but go ye rather to them that sell, and buy for yourselves. 10 And while they went to buy, the bridegroom came ; and they that were ready went in with him to the marriage : and the door was shut. 11 Afterward came also the other virgins, saying, Lord, Lord, open to us. 12 But he answered and said, Verily I say unto you, I know you not. 13 Watch therefore, for ye know neither the day nor the hour wherein the Son of man cometh.

14 For *the kingdom of heaven is* as a man travelling into a far country, *who* called his own servants, and delivered unto them his goods. 15 And unto one he gave five talents, to another two, and to another one ; to every man according to his several ability ; and straightway took his journey. 16 Then he that had received the five talents went and traded with the same, and made *them* other five talents. 17 And likewise he that *had received* two, he also gained other two. 18 But he that had received one went and digged in the earth, and hid his lord's money. 19 After a long time the lord of those servants cometh, and reckoneth with them. 20 And so he that had received five talents came and *brought* other five talents, saying, Lord, thou deliveredst unto me five

χεσθε· εἰς.ἀπάντησιν ʰαὐτοῦ.ǁ 7 Τότε ἠγέρθησαν πᾶσαι αἱ
forth   to meet   him.   Then   arose   all

παρθένοι.ἐκεῖναι, καὶ ἐκόσμησαν τὰς.λαμπάδας.ᵍαὐτῶν.ǁ 8 αἱ.δὲ
those virgins,   and trimmed   their lamps.   And the

μωραὶ ταῖς φρονίμοις ʰεἶπον,ǁ Δότε ἡμῖν ἐκ τοῦ.ἐλαίου.ὑμῶν,
foolish to the prudent   said,ǁ Give · us of   your oil,

ὅτι αἱ.λαμπάδες.ἡμῶν σβέννυνται. 9 Ἀπεκρίθησαν.δὲ αἱ
for   our lamps   are going out.   But ³answered . ¹the

φρόνιμοι, λέγουσαι, Μήποτε ʲοὐκᵑ ἀρκέσῃ ἡμῖν καὶ ὑμῖν·
²prudent,   saying, [No,] lest   ³not ¹it ²may suffice for us and you :

πορεύεσθε.ᵏδὲǁ μᾶλλον πρὸς τοὺς πωλοῦντας, καὶ ἀγοράσατε.
but go   rather   to those who sell,   and   buy

ἑαυταῖς. 10 ἀπερχομένων.δὲ αὐτῶν ἀγοράσαι, ἦλθεν ο
for yourselves.   But as ²went ³away ¹they   to buy,   ³came ¹the

νυμφίος· καὶ αἱ ἕτοιμοι εἰσῆλθον μετ᾽ αὐτοῦ εἰς τοὺς γά-
²bridegroom, and those ready   went in with   him   to   the wedding

μους, καὶ ἐκλείσθη ἡ θύρα. 11 ὕστερον.δὲ ἔρχονται ¹καὶǁ αἱ
feast, and ³was ⁴shut ¹the ²door.   And afterwards come   also the

λοιπαὶ παρθένοι, λέγουσαι, Κύριε, κύριε, ἄνοιξον ἡμῖν. 12 Ὁ.δὲ
other   virgins,   saying,   Lord, Lord,   open   to us.   But he

ἀποκριθεὶς εἶπεν, Ἀμὴν λέγω ὑμῖν, οὐκ.οἶδα ὑμᾶς. 13 Γρη-
answering   said,   Verily I say to you, I do not know you.   Watch

γορεῖτε οὖν, ὅτι οὐκ.οἴδατε τὴν ἡμέραν οὐδὲ τὴν ὥραν ᵐἐν
therefore, for ye do not know the   day   nor   the   hour   in

ᾗ ὁ υἱὸς τοῦ ἀνθρώπου ἔρχεται.ǁ
which the Son   of man   comes.ǁ

14 Ὥσπερ.γὰρ ἄνθρωπος ἀποδημῶν ἐκάλεσεν τοὺς.ἰδίους
For [it is] as [if] a man   leaving the country called   his own

δούλους, καὶ παρέδωκεν αὐτοῖς τὰ.ὑπάρχοντα.αὐτοῦ. 15 καὶ
bondmen, and delivered to them   his property.   And

ᾧ.μὲν ἔδωκεν πέντε τάλαντα, ᾧ.δὲ δύο, ᾧ.δὲ ἕν,
to one he gave five   talents,   and to another two, and to another one,

ἑκάστῳ κατὰ τὴν.ἰδίαν δύναμιν καὶ ⁿἀπεδήμησεν εὐθέως.
to each according to his respective ability ;   and left the country immediately.

16 πορευθεὶς.°δὲǁ ὁ τὰ πέντε τάλαντα λαβὼν ᴾεἰργάσατοǁ
And ²having ³gone ¹he who the five   talents received   trafficked

ἐν αὐτοῖς, καὶ ᑫἐποίησενǁ ἄλλα πέντε ʳτάλαντα.ǁ 17 ὡσαύτως
with them, and   made   other five   talents.   In like manner

ˢκαὶǁ ὁ   τὰ δύο ἐκέρδησεν ᵗκαὶ αὐτὸςǁ ἄλλα δύο.
also he who [received] the two   ³gained   ²also ¹he   other two.

18 ὁ.δὲ τὸ ἓνᵛ λαβὼν ἀπελθὼν ὤρυξεν ʷἐν τῇ γῇ,ǁ καὶ
But he who the one received having gone away   dug   in the earth, and

ˣἀπέκρυψενǁ τὸ ἀργύριον τοῦ.κυρίου.αὐτοῦ. 19 Μετὰ.δὲ ʸχρόνον
hid   the money   of his lord.   And after a ²time

πολὺνǁ ἔρχεται ὁ κύριος τῶν.δούλων.ἐκείνων, καὶ συναίρει
¹long   comes the lord   of those bondmen,   and   takes

ᶻμετ᾽ αὐτῶν λόγον.ǁ 20 καὶ προσελθὼν ὁ τὰ πέντε τά-
²with ³them. ¹account.   And ²having ³come ¹he who the five   ta-

λαντα.λαβὼν, προσήνεγκεν· ἄλλα πέντε τάλαντα, λέγων,
lents received,   brought to [him] other five   talents,   saying,

---

ᶠ — αὐτοῦ (read [him]) TA.   ᵍ ἑαυτῶν LTTrA.   ʰ εἶπαν TTrA.   ⁱ οὐ μὴ not at all LTrAW.
ᵏ — δὲ but GLTTrAW.   ˡ — καὶ L[Tr].   ᵐ — ἐν ᾗ ὁ υἱὸς τοῦ ἀνθρώπου ἔρχεται GLTTrA.
ⁿ ἀπεδήμησεν. εὐθέως πορευθεὶς left the country. Immediately having gone T.   ° — δὲ and
[L] T [Tr].   ᴾ ἠργάσατο T.   ᑫ ἐκέρδησεν gained LTr.   ʳ — τάλαντα LTr[A].   ˢ — καὶ
[L] T.   ᵗ — καὶ αὐτὸς LTT[A].   ᵛ + τάλαντον talent ʟ.   ʷ γῆν [the] earth TTrA,
ˣ ἔκρυψεν LTTrA.   ʸ πολὺν χρόνον LTTrA.   ᶻ λόγον μετ᾽ αὐτῶν LTTrA.

Κύριε, πέντε τάλαντά μοι παρέδωκας· ἴδε, ἄλλα πέντε
Lord, five talents to me thou didst deliver; behold, other five

ᵃτάλαντα‖ ἐκέρδησα ᵇἐπ᾿ αὐτοῖς.‖ 21 Ἔφη.ᶜδὲ‖ αὐτῷ ὁ κύριος
talents ᶜhave I gained besides them. And ³said ⁴to ⁵him ²lord

αὐτοῦ, Εὖ, · δοῦλε ἀγαθὲ καὶ πιστέ, ἐπὶ ὀλίγα ἧς
¹his, Well! bondman good and faithful, over a few things thou wast

πιστός, ἐπὶ πολλῶν σε καταστήσω· εἴσελθε εἰς τὴν χαρὰν
faithful, over many things thee will I set: enter into the joy,

τοῦ.κυρίου.σου. 22 Προσελθὼν.ᵈδὲ‖ καὶ ὁ τὰ δύο τά-
of thy lord. And having c me to [him] ²also ¹he who the two ta-

λαντα ᵉλαβὼν‖ εἶπεν, Κύριε, δύο τάλαντά μοι παρέδωκας·
lents received said, Lord, two talents to me thou didst deliver;

ἴδε, ἄλλα δύο τάλαντα ἐκέρδησα ᵇἐπ᾿ αὐτοῖς.‖ 23 Ἔφη
behold, other two talents have I gained besides them. ²Said

αὐτῷ ὁ.κύριος.αὐτοῦ, Εὖ, δοῦλε ἀγαθὲ καὶ πιστέ, ἐπὶ
⁴to ⁵him ¹his ²Lord, Well! bondman good and faithful, over

ὀλίγα ἧς πιστός, ἐπὶ πολλῶν σε καταστήσω· εἴσελθε
a few things thou wast faithful, over many things thee will I set: enter

εἰς τὴν χαρὰν τοῦ.κυρίου.σου. 24 Προσελθὼν.δὲ καὶ ὁ
into the joy of thy Lord. And having come to [him] ²also ¹he who

τὸ ἓν τάλαντον εἰληφὼς εἶπεν, Κύριε, ἔγνων .σε ὅτι σκληρὸς
the one talent had received said, Lord, I knew thee that ⁴hard

εἶ ἄνθρωπος, θερίζων ὅπου οὐκ.ἔσπειρας, καὶ συνάγων
¹thou ²art ³a ⁵man, reaping where thou didst not sow, and gathering

ὅθεν ·οὐ.διεσκόρπισας· 25 καὶ φοβηθείς, ἀπελθὼν ἔκρυψα
whence thou didst not scatter, and being afraid, having gone away I hid

τὸ.τάλαντόν.σου ἐν τῇ γῇ· ἴδε, ἔχεις τὸ.σόν. 26 Ἀπο-
thy talent in the earth; behold, thou hast thine own. ⁴An-

κριθεὶς δὲ ὁ.κύριος.αὐτοῦ εἶπεν αὐτῷ, ᶠΠονηρὲ δοῦλε‖ καὶ
swering ¹and ²his ³Lord said to him, Wicked ³bondman ¹and

ὀκνηρέ, ᾔδεις ὅτι θερίζω ὅπου οὐκ.ἔσπειρα, καὶ συνάγω ὅθεν
²slothful, thou knewest that I reap where I sowed not, and gather whence

οὐ.διεσκόρπισα; 27 ἔδει ᵍοὖν σε‖ βαλεῖν ʰτὸ.ἀργύριόν‖.μου
I scattered not; it behoved ²therefore ¹thee to put my money

τοῖς ⁱτραπεζίταις·‖ καὶ ἐλθὼν ἐγὼ ἐκομισάμην.ἂν τὸ.ἐμὸν σὺν
to the money changers, and coming I should have received mine own with

τόκῳ. 28 ἄρατε οὖν ἀπ᾿ αὐτοῦ τὸ.τάλαντον, καὶ.δότε .τῷ
interest. Take therefore from him the talent, and give [it] to him who

ἔχοντι τὰ δέκα τάλαντα. 29 Τῷ.γὰρ ἔχοντι παντὶ δοθή-
has the ten talents. For ¹who ³has ²to ⁴every ³one shall

σεται, καὶ περισσευθήσεται· ᵏἀπὸ δὲ τοῦ‖ μὴ.ἔχοντος, καὶ
be given, and [he] shall be in abundance; ²from ¹but him who has not, even

ὃ ἔχει ἀρθήσεται ἀπ᾿ αὐτοῦ. 30 Καὶ τὸν ἀχρεῖον δοῦλον
that which he has shall be taken from him. And the useless bondman

ˡἐκβάλλετε‖ εἰς τὸ σκότος τὸ ἐξώτερον· ἐκεῖ ἔσται ὁ κλαυθμὸς
cast ye out into the darkness the outer: there shall be the weeping

καὶ ὁ.βρυγμὸς τῶν ὀδόντων.
and the gnashing of the teeth.

31 Ὅταν.δὲ ἔλθῃ ὁ υἱὸς τοῦ.ἀνθρώπου ἐν τῇ.δόξῃ.αὐτοῦ,
But when ⁵comes ¹the ²Son ³of ⁴man in his glory,

καὶ πάντες οἱ ᵐἅγιοι‖ ἄγγελοι μετ᾿ αὐτοῦ, τότε καθίσει ἐπὶ
and all the holy angels with him, then will he sit upon [the]

talents: behold, I have gained beside them five talents more. 21 His lord said unto him, Well done, thou good and faithful servant: thou hast been faithful over a few things, I will make thee ruler over many things: enter thou into the joy of thy lord. 22 He also that had received two talents came and said, Lord, thou deliveredst unto me two talents: behold, I have gained two other talents beside them. 23 His lord said unto him, Well done, good and faithful servant; thou hast been faithful over a few things, I will make thee ruler over many things: enter thou into the joy of thy lord. 24 Then he which had received the one talent came and said, Lord, I knew thee that thou art an hard man, reaping where thou hast not sown, and gathering where thou hast not strawed: 25 and I was afraid, and went and hid thy talent in the earth: lo, there thou hast that is thine. 26 His lord answered and said unto him, Thou wicked and slothful servant, thou knewest that I reap where I sowed not, and gather where I have not strawed: 27 thou oughtest therefore to have put my money to the exchangers, and then at my coming I should have received mine own with usury. 28 Take therefore the talent from him, and give it unto him which hath ten talents. 29 For unto every one that hath shall be given, and he shall have abundance: but from him that hath not shall be taken away even that which he hath. 30 And cast ye the unprofitable servant into outer darkness: there shall be weeping and gnashing of teeth. 31 When the Son of man shall come in his glory, and all the holy angels with him, then shall he sit upon the

---

ᵃ [τάλαντα] Tr. ᵇ — ἐπ᾿ αὐτοῖς LTTr. ᶜ — δὲ and GLTTrAW. ᵈ — δὲ and T. ᵉ — λαβὼν (read [received]) LTTrA. ᶠ Δοῦλε πονηρὲ L. ᵍ σε οὖν TTrA. ʰ τὰ ἀργύρια τ. ⁱ τραπεζείταις T. ᵏ τοῦ δὲ but of him who LTTrA. ˡ ἐκβάλετε GLTTrAW. ᵐ — ἅγιοι GLTTrA.

throne of his glory: 32 and before him shall be gathered all nations: and he shall separate them one from another, as a shepherd divideth his sheep from the goats: 33 and he shall set the sheep on his right hand, but the goats on the left. 34 Then shall the King say unto them on his right hand, Come, ye bles-ed of my Father, inherit the kingdom prepared for you from the foundation of the world: 35 for I was an hungred, and ye gave me meat: I was thirsty, and ye gave me drink: I was a stranger, and ye took me in: 36 naked, and ye clothed me: I was sick, and ye visited me: I was in prison, and ye came unto me. 37 Then shall the righteous answer him, saying, Lord, when saw we thee an hungred, and fed thee? or thirsty, and gave thee drink? 38 When saw we thee a stranger, and took thee in? or naked, and clothed thee? 39 Or when saw we thee sick, or in prison, and came unto thee? 40 And the King shall answer and say unto them, Verily I say unto you, Inasmuch as ye have done it unto one of the least of these my brethren, ye have done it unto me. 41 Then shall he say also unto them on the left hand, Depart from me, ye cursed, into everlasting fire, prepared for the devil and his angels: 42 for I was an hungred, and ye gave me no meat: I was thirsty, and ye gave me no drink: 43 I was a stranger, and ye took me not in: naked, and ye clothed me not: sick, an in prison, and ye visited me not. 44 Then shall they also answer him, saying, Lord, when saw we thee an hungred, or athirst, or a stranger, or naked, or sick, or in prison, and did not minister unto thee? 45 Then shall he answer them, saying, Verily I say unto you,

θρόνου δόξης.αὐτοῦ, 32 καὶ ⁿσυναχθήσεται‖ ἔμπροσθεν αὐτοῦ
throne of his glory,   and shall be gathered   before   him

πάντα τὰ ἔθνη, καὶ ᵒἀφοριεῖ‖ αὐτοὺς ἀπ' ἀλλήλων, ὥσπερ ὁ
all   the nations, and he will separate   them   from one another,   as   the

ποιμὴν ἀφορίζει τὰ πρόβατα ἀπὸ τῶν ἐρίφων, 33 καὶ στήσει
shepherd separates the   sheep   from the   goats;   and he will set

τὰ μὲν πρόβατα ἐκ δεξιῶν αὐτοῦ, τὰ.δὲ ἐρίφια ἐξ εὐωνύμων.
the   sheep   on ²right ³hand ¹his,   but the goats on [his]   left.

34 Τότε ἐρεῖ ὁ βασιλεὺς τοῖς ἐκ δεξιῶν αὐτοῦ, Δεῦτε, οἱ
Then ³will ⁴say ¹the ²king   to those on ²right ³hand ¹his,   Come, the

εὐλογημένοι τοῦ.πατρός.μου, κληρονομήσατε τὴν ἡτοιμασμένην
blessed   of my Father,   inherit   the ²prepared

ὑμῖν βασιλείαν ἀπὸ καταβολῆς κόσμου. 35 ἐπείνασα.γάρ,
²for ⁴you ¹kingdom from [the] foundation of [the] world.   For I hungered,

καὶ ἐδώκατέ μοι φαγεῖν· ἐδίψησα, καὶ ἐποτίσατέ με· ξένος
and ye gave ye   to eat; I thirsted,   and ye gave ²to ³drink ¹me; a stranger

ἤμην, καὶ συνηγάγετέ με· 36 γυμνός, καὶ περιεβάλετέ με· ἠσθέ-
I was, and ye took ²in ¹me;   naked,   and   ye clothed   me; I was

νησα, καὶ ἐπεσκέψασθέ με· ἐν φυλακῇ ἤμην, καὶ ᴾἤλθετε‖ πρός
sick, and   ye visited me; in prison   I was, and ye came   to

με. 37 Τότε ἀποκριθήσονται αὐτῷ οἱ δίκαιοι, λέγοντες, Κύριε,
me.   Then   will answer   him the righteous, saying, Lord,

πότε σὲ ᑫεἴδομεν‖ πεινῶντα, καὶ ἐθρέψαμεν; ἢ διψῶντα, καὶ
when ³thee ¹saw ²we hungering, and   fed [thee]? or thirsting, and

ἐποτίσαμεν; 38 πότε.δέ σε εἴδομεν ξένον, καὶ συνηγάγομεν;
gave [thee] to drink? and when ³thee ¹saw ²we a stranger, and took [thee] in?

ἢ γυμνόν, καὶ περιεβάλομεν· 39 πότε.δέ σε εἴδομεν ʳἀσθενῆ,‖
or naked, and   clothed [thee]?   And when ³thee ¹saw ²we sick,

ἢ ἐν φυλακῇ, καὶ ἤλθομεν· πρός σε; 40 Καὶ ἀποκριθεὶς ὁ
or in prison,   and   came   to thee?   And   answering the

βασιλεὺς ἐρεῖ αὐτοῖς, Ἀμὴν λέγω ὑμῖν, ἐφ'.ὅσον ἐποιήσατε
king   will say to them, Verily I say to you, Inasmuch as   ye did   [it]

ἑνὶ τούτων ˢτῶν.ἀδελφῶν.μου‖ τῶν ἐλαχίστων, ἐμοὶ ἐποιή-
to one of these   my brethren   the   least,   to me   ye

σατε. 41 Τότε ἐρεῖ καὶ τοῖς ἐξ εὐωνύμων, Πορεύεσθε ἀπ'
did [it].   Then will he say also to those on [the] left,   Go   from

ἐμοῦ, ᵗοἱ‖ κατηραμένοι, εἰς τὸ πῦρ τὸ αἰώνιον, τὸ ἡτοιμα-
me, the   cursed,   into the fire the eternal,   which has been

σμένον τῷ διαβόλῳ καὶ τοῖς.ἀγγέλοις.αὐτοῦ. 42 ἐπείνασα.γάρ,
prepared for the devil   and   his angels.   For I hungered,

καὶ οὐκ.ἐδώκατέ μοι φαγεῖν· ἐδίψησα, καὶ οὐκ.ἐποτίσατέ με·
and ye gave not to me to eat; I thirsted, and ye gave ²not ³to ⁴drink ¹me;

43 ξένος ἤμην, καὶ οὐ.συνηγάγετέ με· γυμνός, καὶ οὐ.περιεβά-
a stranger I was, and ye took ²not ³in ¹me; naked, and   ye did not

λετέ με· ἀσθενής, καὶ ἐν φυλακῇ, καὶ οὐκ.ἐπεσκέψασθέ με.
clothe me;   sick,   and in prison,   and   ye did not visit   me.

44 Τότε ἀποκριθήσονται ᵛαὐτῷ‖ καὶ αὐτοί, λέγοντες, Κύριε,
Then   ³will ⁴answer   ⁵him ²also ¹they,   saying,   Lord,

πότε σὲ εἴδομεν πεινῶντα, ἢ διψῶντα, ἢ ξένον, ἢ γυμνόν, ἢ
when ³thee ¹saw ²we hungering, or thirsting, or a stranger, or naked, or

ἀσθενῆ, ἢ ἐν φυλακῇ, καὶ οὐ.διηκονήσαμέν σοι; 45 Τότε ἀπο-
sick, or in prison,   and   did not minister to thee?   Then will

κριθήσεται αὐτοῖς, λέγων, Ἀμὴν λέγω ὑμῖν, ἐφ'.ὅσον οὐκ.ἐποι-
he answer   them,   saying, Verily I say to you, Inasmuch as ye did not

---

ⁿ συναχθήσονται LTTrA.   ᵒ ἀφορίσει T.   ᴾ ἤλθατε LTTrA.   ᑫ εἴδαμεν Tr.   ʳ ἀσθενοῦντα LTTrA.   ˢ [τῶν ἀδελφῶν μου] L.   ᵗ — οἱ T.   ᵛ — αὐτῷ GLTTrAW.

ησατε ἐνὶ τούτων τῶν ἐλαχίστων, οὐδὲ ἐμοὶ ἐποιήσατε. 46 Καὶ
[it] to one of these the   least,   neither to me did ye [it]. And

ἀπελεύσονται οὗτοι εἰς κόλασιν αἰώνιον· οἱ.δὲ δίκαιοι εἰς ζωὴν
²shall ⁵go ⁴away ¹these into punishment eternal, but the righteous into life

αἰώνιον.
eternal.

26 Καὶ   ἐγένετο   ὅτε ἐτέλεσεν ὁ Ἰησοῦς πάντας τοὺς
And it came to pass when ²had ³finished ¹Jesus   all

λόγους.τούτους, εἶπεν τοῖς.μαθηταῖς.αὐτοῦ. 2 Οἴδατε ὅτι μετὰ
these sayings   he said   to his disciples,   Ye know that after

δύο ἡμέρας τὸ πάσχα γίνεται, καὶ ὁ υἱὸς τοῦ ἀνθρώπου
two   days   the passover takes place, and the Son   of man

παραδίδοται εἰς.τὸ.σταυρωθῆναι. 3 Τότε συνήχθησαν οἱ
is delivered up   to be crucified.   Then were gathered together the

ἀρχιερεῖς ʷκαὶ οἱ γραμματεῖς∥ καὶ οἱ πρεσβύτεροι τοῦ λαοῦ
chief priests and the   scribes   and the   elders   of the people

εἰς τὴν αὐλὴν τοῦ ἀρχιερέως τοῦ λεγομένου Καϊάφα, 4 καὶ
to the   court of the high priest who was called Caiaphas,   and

συνεβουλεύσαντο ἵνα   τὸν Ἰησοῦν ˣκρατήσωσιν δόλῳ,∥
took counsel together in order that Jesus   they might seize by guile,

καὶ ἀποκτείνωσιν. 5 ἔλεγον.δέ, Μὴ ἐν τῇ ἑορτῇ, ἵνα μὴ
and   kill   [him];   but they said, Not during the feast,   that ²not

θόρυβος γένηται ἐν τῷ λαῷ.
¹a ²tumult ⁴there ³be among the people.

6 Τοῦ.δὲ.Ἰησοῦ γενομένου ἐν Βηθανίᾳ ἐν [the] οἰκίᾳ Σίμωνος
Now Jesus   being   in Bethany in [the] house of Simon

τοῦ λεπροῦ, 7 προσῆλθεν αὐτῷ γυνὴ ˟ἀλάβαστρον μύρου
the leper,   ³came   ⁴to ⁵him ¹a ²woman, an alabaster ⁶ask of ointment

ἔχουσα∥ ᶻβαρυτίμου,∥ καὶ κατέχεεν ἐπὶ ⁿτὴν.κεφαλὴν.∥αὐτοῦ
having,   very precious, and poured [it] on   his head

ἀνακειμένου. 8 ἰδόντες.δὲ οἱ.μαθηταὶ.ᵇαὐτοῦ∥ ἠγανάκ-
as he reclined [at table].   But seeing [it]   his disciples   became

τησαν, λέγοντες, Εἰς τί ἡ.ἀπώλεια.αὕτη; 9 ᶜἠδύνατο∥.γὰρ τοῦτο
indignant, saying, For what   this waste?   for ³could   ¹this

ᵈτὸ.μύρον∥ πραθῆναι πολλοῦ, καὶ δοθῆναι ᵉ πτωχοῖς.
²ointment   have been sold for much, and have been given to [the] poor.

10 Γνοὺς.δὲ   ὁ Ἰησοῦς εἶπεν αὐτοῖς, Τί κόπους παρέχετε
But knowing [this] Jesus   said to them, Why trouble do ye cause

τῇ γυναικί; ἔργον.γὰρ καλὸν ᶠεἰργάσατο∥ εἰς ἐμέ. 11 πάν-
to the woman? for a ²work ¹good she wrought towards me.   ²Al-

τοτε γὰρ τοὺς πτωχοὺς ἔχετε μεθ᾽ ἑαυτῶν, ἐμὲ.δὲ οὐ πάντοτε
ways ¹for the   poor   ye have with you, but me not always

ἔχετε. 12 βαλοῦσα.γὰρ αὕτη   τὸ.μύρον.τοῦτο ἐπὶ τοῦ
ye have. For ³in ⁴pouring ¹this [²woman] this ointment   on

σώματός.μου πρὸς τὸ.ἐνταφιάσαι.με ἐποίησεν. 13 ἀμὴν λέγω
my body   for   my burying   she did [it]. Verily I say

ὑμῖν, ὅπου.ἐὰν   κηρυχθῇ   τὸ.εὐαγγέλιον.τοῦτο ἐν ὅλῳ
to you, Wheresoever shall be proclaimed   these glad tidings   in all

τῷ κόσμῳ, λαληθήσεται καὶ ὃ ἐποίησεν αὕτη,   εἰς
the world,   shall be spoken of also that which ³did   ¹this [²woman], for

μνημόσυνον αὐτῆς.
a memorial   of her.

ʷ — καὶ οἱ γραμματεῖς LTTᵣA.   ˣ δόλῳ κρατήσωσιν GLTTᵣAW.   ˠ ἔχουσα ἀλάβαστρον
μύρου LTTᵣ.   ᶻ πολυτίμου LT.   ᵃ τῆς κεφαλῆς LTTᵣ.   ᵇ — αὐτοῦ (read the discip es)
LTTᵣA.   ᶜ ἐδύνατο TA.   ᵈ — τὸ μύρον GLTTᵣAW.   ᵉ + τοῖς (read to the poor) LW.
ᶠ ἠργάσατο T.

Inasmuch as ye did *it*
not to one of the least
of those, ye did *it* not
to me. 46 And these
shall go away into
everlasting punish-
ment: but the right-
eous into life eternal.

XXVI. And it came
to pass, when Jesus
had finished all these
sayings, he said unto
his disciples, 2 Ye know
that after two days · is
the feast of the pass-
over, and the Son of
man is betrayed to be
crucified. 3 Then as-
sembled together the
chief priests, and the
scribes, and the elders
of the people, unto the
palace of the high
priest, who was called
Caiaphas, 4 and con-
sulted that they might
take Jesus by subtilty,
and kill *him*. 5 But
they said, Not on the
feast *day*, lest there be
an uproar among the
people.

6 Now when Jesus
was in Bethany, in
the house of Simon the
leper, 7 there came
unto him a woman
having an alabaster
box of very precious
ointment, and poured
it on his head, as he
sat *at meat*. 8 But
when his disciples saw
it, they had indigna-
tion, saying, To what
purpose *is* this waste?
9 for this ointment
might have been sold
for much, and given to
the poor. 10 When Je-
sus understood *it*, he
said unto them, Why
trouble ye the woman?
for she hath wrought
a good work upon me.
11 For ye have the poor
always with you; but
me ye have not al-
ways. 12 For in that
she hath poured this
ointment on my body,
she did *it* for my burial.
13 Verily I say unto
you, Wheresoever this
gospel shall be preach-
ed in the whole world,
there shall also this,
that this woman hath
done, be told for a
memorial of her.

14 Then one of the twelve, called Judas Iscariot, went unto the chief priests, 15 and said unto them, What will ye give me, and I will deliver him unto you? And they covenanted with him for thirty pieces of silver. 16 And from that time he sought opportunity to betray him.

14 Τότε πορευθεὶς εἷς τῶν δώδεκα, ὁ λεγόμενός Ἰούδας
Then [10]having [11]gone [2]one [2]of [3]the [4]twelve, [5]who [6]was [7]called [8]Judas
Ἰσκαριώτης, πρὸς τοὺς ἀρχιερεῖς, 15 εἶπεν, Τί θέλετέ μοι
[9]Iscariote, to the chief priests, said, What are ye willing [10]me
δοῦναι, κἀγὼ ὑμῖν παραδώσω αὐτόν; Οἱ δὲ ἔστησαν αὐτῷ
[1]to [2]give, and I to you will deliver up him? And they appointed to him
τριάκοντα ἀργύρια. 16 καὶ ἀπὸ τότε ἐζήτει εὐκαιρίαν
thirty pieces of silver. And from that time he sought an opportunity
ἵνα αὐτὸν παραδῷ.
that him he might deliver up.

17 Now the first day of the feast of unleavened bread the disciples came to Jesus, saying unto him, Where wilt thou that we prepare for thee to eat the passover? 18 And he said, Go into the city to such a man, and say unto him, The Master saith, My time is at hand; I will keep the passover at thy house with my disciples. 19 And the disciples did as Jesus had appointed them; and they made ready the passover.

17 Τῇ δὲ πρώτῃ τῶν ἀζύμων προσῆλθον οἱ μαθη-
Now on the first [day] of unleavened [bread] came the disci-
ταὶ τῷ Ἰησοῦ, λέγοντες αὐτῷ, Ποῦ θέλεις ἑτοιμάσωμέν
ples to Jesus, saying to him, Where wilt thou [that] we should prepare
σοι φαγεῖν τὸ πάσχα; 18 Ὁ δὲ εἶπεν, Ὑπάγετε εἰς τὴν
for thee to eat the passover? And he said, Go into the
πόλιν πρὸς τὸν δεῖνα, καὶ εἴπατε αὐτῷ, Ὁ διδάσκαλος λέγει,
city unto such a one, and say to him, The teacher says,
Ὁ καιρός μου ἐγγύς ἐστιν· πρὸς σὲ ποιῶ τὸ πάσχα μετὰ
My time [2]near [1]is; with thee I will keep the passover with
τῶν μαθητῶν μου. 19 Καὶ ἐποίησαν οἱ μαθηταὶ ὡς συνέταξεν
my disciples. And [3]did [1]the [2]disciples [4]as [5]directed
αὐτοῖς ὁ Ἰησοῦς, καὶ ἡτοίμασαν τὸ πάσχα.
[7]them [5]Jesus, and prepared the passover.

20 Now when the even was come, he sat down with the twelve. 21 And as they did eat, he said, Verily I say unto you, that one of you shall betray me. 22 And they were exceeding sorrowful, and began every one of them to say unto him, Lord, is it I? 23 And he answered and said, He that dippeth his hand with me in the dish, the same shall betray me. 24 The Son of man goeth as it is written of him: but woe unto that man by whom the Son of man is betrayed! it had been good for that man if he had not been born. 25 Then Judas, which betrayed him, answered and said, Master, is it I? He said unto him, Thou hast said.

20 Ὀψίας δὲ γενομένης ἀνέκειτο μετὰ τῶν δώδεκα.
And evening being come he reclined [at table] with the twelve.
21 καὶ ἐσθιόντων αὐτῶν εἶπεν, Ἀμὴν λέγω ὑμῖν, ὅτι εἷς ἐξ
And as they were eating he said, Verily I say to you, that one of
ὑμῶν παραδώσει με. 22 Καὶ λυπούμενοι σφόδρα ἤρξαντο
you will deliver up me. And being grieved exceedingly they began
λέγειν αὐτῷ ἕκαστος αὐτῶν, Μήτι ἐγώ εἰμι, κύριε; 23 Ὁ δὲ
to say to him, each of them, [2]I [1]am [he], Lord? But he
ἀποκριθεὶς εἶπεν, Ὁ ἐμβάψας μετ' ἐμοῦ ἐν τῷ τρυβλίῳ
answering said, He who dipped with me in the dish
τὴν χεῖρα, οὗτός με παραδώσει. 24 ὁ μὲν υἱὸς τοῦ ἀνθρώ-
[his] hand, he me will deliver up. The [4]indeed [3]Son [2]of [1]man
που ὑπάγει, καθὼς γέγραπται περὶ αὐτοῦ, οὐαὶ δὲ τῷ
goes, as it has been written concerning him, but woe
ἀνθρώπῳ ἐκείνῳ δι' οὗ ὁ υἱὸς τοῦ ἀνθρώπου παραδίδοται·
to that man by whom the Son of man is delivered up;
καλὸν ἦν αὐτῷ εἰ οὐκ ἐγεννήθη ὁ ἄνθρωπος ἐκεῖνος.
good were it for him if [3]had [4]not [5]been [6]born that [2]man.
25 Ἀποκριθεὶς δὲ Ἰούδας ὁ παραδιδοὺς αὐτὸν εἶπεν, Μήτι
And answering Judas, who was delivering up him, said,
ἐγώ εἰμι, ῥαββί; Λέγει αὐτῷ, Σὺ εἶπας.
[2]I [1]am [he], Rabbi? He says to him, Thou hast said.

26 And as they were eating, Jesus took bread, and blessed it, and brake it, and gave it to the disciples, and said, Take, eat; this is my body. 27 And he took the cup, and gave thanks, and gave it to them, saying, Drink

26 Ἐσθιόντων δὲ αὐτῶν, λαβὼν ὁ Ἰησοῦς τὸν ἄρτον,
And as they were eating, [2]having [3]taken [1]Jesus the bread,
καὶ εὐλογήσας, ἔκλασεν καὶ ἐδίδου τοῖς μαθηταῖς, καὶ
and having blessed, broke and gave to the disciples, and
εἶπεν, Λάβετε, φάγετε· τοῦτό ἐστιν τὸ σῶμά μου. 27 Καὶ
said, Take, eat; this is my body. And
λαβὼν τὸ ποτήριον, καὶ εὐχαριστήσας, ἔδωκεν αὐτοῖς,
having taken the cup, and having given thanks, he gave [it] to them,

---

g καὶ ἐγὼ T.　　h — αὐτῷ LTTrAW.　　i + μαθητῶν disciples LT.　　k εἷς ἕκαστος each
one LTTrA.　　l τὴν χεῖρα ἐν τῷ τρυβλίῳ LTTrA.　　m ῥαββεί T.　　n — τὸν LTTr[A].　　o δοὺς
having given LTTr.　　p — καὶ LTTr.　　q — τὸ (read a cup) TTrA.　　r — καὶ L[Tr].

λέγων, Πίετε ἐξ αὐτοῦ πάντες· 28 τοῦτο.γάρ ἐστιν τὸ.αἷμά.μου,
saying, ²Drink ³of ⁴it ¹all. For this is my blood,

ᵗτὸ� τῆς ˠκαινῆς diαθήκης, τὸ περὶ πολλῶν ʷἐκχυνόμενον eἰς
that of the new covenant, which for many is poured out for

ἄφεσιν ἁμαρτιῶν. 29 λέγω.δὲ ὑμῖν, ˣὅτι οὐ.μὴ πίω ἀπ'
remission of sins. But I say to you, that not at all will I drink hence-

ἄρτι ἐκ τούτου τοῦ ˠγεννήματος τῆς ἀμπέλου, ἕως τῆς ἡμέρας
forth of this fruit of the vine, until ²day

ἐκείνης ὅταν αὐτὸ πίνω μεθ' ὑμῶν καινὸν ἐν τῇ βασιλείᾳ τοῦ
¹that when it I drink with you new in the kingdom·

πατρός.μου. 30 Καὶ ὑμνήσαντες ἐξῆλθον εἰς τὸ ὄρος τῶν
of my father. And having sung a hymn they went out to the mount

ἐλαιῶν. 31 τότε λέγει αὐτοῖς ὁ Ἰησοῦς, Πάντες ὑμεῖς σκανδα-
of Olives. Then ²says ³to⁴them ¹Jesus, All ye will be

λισθήσεσθε ἐν ἐμοὶ ἐν τῇ.νυκτὶ.ταύτῃ. γέγραπται.γάρ.
offended in me during this night. For it has been written,

Πατάξω τὸν ποιμένα, καὶ ᶻδιασκορπισθήσεται τὰ πρόβατα
I will smite the shepherd, and will be scattered abroad the sheep

τῆς ποίμνης. 32 μετὰ.δὲ τὸ.ἐγερθῆναί.με προάξω ὑμᾶς
of the flock; but after my being raised I will go before you

εἰς τὴν Γαλιλαίαν. 33 Ἀποκριθεὶς.δὲ ὁ Πέτρος εἶπεν αὐτῷ,
into Galilee. And answering Peter said to him,

Εἰ ᵃκαὶ πάντες σκανδαλισθήσονται ἐν σοί, ἐγὼ οὐδέποτε
If even all will be offended in thee, I never

σκανδαλισθήσομαι. 34 Ἔφη αὐτῷ ὁ Ἰησοῦς, Ἀμὴν λέγω σοι,
will be offended. ²Said ³to⁴him ¹Jesus, Verily I say to thee,

ὅτι ἐν ταύτῃ τῇ νυκτί, πρὶν ἀλέκτορα φωνῆσαι, τρὶς
that during this night, before [the] cock crows, thrice

ἀπαρνήσῃ με. 35 Λέγει αὐτῷ ὁ Πέτρος, Κἂν δέῃ με
thou wilt deny me. ²Says ³to⁴him ¹Peter, Even if it were needful for me

σὺν σοὶ ἀποθανεῖν, οὐ.μή σε ἀπαρνήσομαι. Ὁμοίως ᵇ καὶ
with thee to die, in nowise thee will I deny. Likewise also

πάντες οἱ μαθηταὶ εἶπον.
all the disciples said.

36 Τότε ἔρχεται μετ' αὐτῶν ὁ Ἰησοῦς εἰς χωρίον λεγόμενον
Then comes with them Jesus to a place called

ᶜΓεθσημανή, καὶ λέγει τοῖς μαθηταῖςᵈ, Καθίσατε αὐτοῦ, ἕως.οὗᵉ
Gethsemane, and he says to the disciples, Sit here, until

ἀπελθὼν ᶠπροσεύξωμαι ἐκεῖ. 37 Καὶ παραλαβὼν τὸν
having gone away I shall pray yonder. And having taken with [him]

Πέτρον καὶ τοὺς δύο υἱοὺς Ζεβεδαίου, ἤρξατο λυπεῖσθαι καὶ
Peter and the two sons of Zebedee, he began to be sorrowful and

ἀδημονεῖν. 38 τότε λέγει αὐτοῖςᵍ, Περίλυπός ἐστιν ἡ.ψυχή.μου
deeply depressed. Then he says to them, Very sorrowful is my soul

ἕως θανάτου· μείνατε ὧδε καὶ γρηγορεῖτε μετ' ἐμοῦ. 39 Καὶ
even to death; remain here and watch with me. And

ʰπροελθὼν μικρὸν ἔπεσεν ἐπὶ πρόσωπον.αὐτοῦ προσευχό-
having gone forward a little he fell upon his face pray-

μενος, καὶ λέγων, Πάτερ.ⁱμου, εἰ δυνατόν ἐστιν ᵏπαρελθέτω
ing, and saying, my Father, if possible it is let pass

ἀπ' ἐμοῦ τὸ.ποτήριον.τοῦτο· πλὴν οὐχ ὡς ἐγὼ θέλω, ἀλλ' ὡς
from me this cup; nevertheless not as I will, but as

ye all of it : 28 for this is my blood of the new testament, which is shed for many for the remission of sins. 29 But I say unto you, I will not drink henceforth of this fruit of the vine, until that day when I drink it new with you in my Father's kingdom. 30 And when they had sung an hymn, they went out into the mount of Olives. 31 Then saith Jesus unto them, All ye shall be offended because of me this night : for it is written, I will smite the shepherd, and the sheep of the flock shall be scattered abroad. 32 But after I am risen again, I will go before you into Galilee. 33 Peter answered and said unto him, Though all men shall be offended because of thee, yet will I never be offended. 34 Jesus said unto him, Verily I say unto thee, That this night, before the cock crow, thou shalt deny me thrice. 35 Peter said unto him, Though I should die with thee, yet will I not deny thee. Likewise also said all the disciples.

36 Then cometh Jesus with them unto a place called Gethsemane, and saith unto the disciples, Sit ye here, while I go and pray yonder. 37 And he took with him Peter and the two sons of Zebedee, and began to be sorrowful and very heavy. 38 Then saith he unto them, My soul is exceeding sorrowful, even unto death : tarry ye here, and watch with me. 39 And he went a little farther, and fell on his face, and prayed, saying, O my Father, if it be possible, let this cup pass from me : nevertheless not as I will, but as thou wilt.

ᵗ — τὸ LTTrA.　ᵛ — καινῆς T[A].　ʷ ἐκχυνόμενον LTTrA.　ˣ — ὅτι LTTrA.　ˠ γεννή-
ματος LTTrA.　ᶻ διασκορπισθήσονται LTT·A.　ᵃ — καὶ GLTTrAW.　ᵇ + δὲ and
(likewise) w.　ᶜ Γεθσημανεί LTrAW ; Γεθσημανεῖ T.　ᵈ + αὐτοῦ of him L.　ᵉ + ἂν L.
ᶠ ἐκεῖ προσεύξωμαι LTTrA.　ᵍ + ὁ Ἰησοῦς Jesus (says) w.　ʰ προσελθὼν having come
towards [them] TTr.　ⁱ — μου my T[Tr].　ᵏ παρελθάτω LTTrA.

40 And he cometh unto the disciples, and findeth them asleep, and saith unto Peter, What, could ye not watch with me one hour? 41 Watch and pray, that ye enter not into temptation : the spirit indeed *is* willing, but the flesh *is* weak. 42 He went away again the second time, and prayed, saying, O my Father, if this cup may not pass away from me, except I drink it, thy will be done. 43 And he came and found them asleep again : for their eyes were heavy. 44 And he left them, and went away again, and prayed the third time, saying the same words. 45 Then cometh he to his disciples, and saith unto them, Sleep on now and take *your* rest : behold, the hour is at hand, and the Son of man is betrayed into the hands of sinners. 46 Rise, let us be going : behold, he is at hand that doth betray me.

σύ. 40 Καὶ ἔρχεται πρὸς τοὺς μαθητὰς καὶ εὑρίσκει αὐτοὺς
thou.   And   he comes   to   the   disciples   and · finds   them
καθεύδοντας, καὶ λέγει τῷ Πέτρῳ, Οὕτως οὐκ.ἰσχύσατε μίαν
sleeping,   and says   to Peter,   Thus   were ye not able   one
ὥραν γρηγορῆσαι μετ' ἐμοῦ; 41 γρηγορεῖτε καὶ προσεύχεσθε,
hour   to watch   with me?   Watch   and   pray,
ἵνα μὴ.εἰσέλθητε εἰς πειρασμόν. τὸ μὲν πνεῦμα πρόθυμον,
that   ye enter not   into temptation: the ²indeed ¹spirit [is]   ready,
ἡ.δὲ σὰρξ ἀσθενής. 42 Πάλιν ἐκ.δευτέρου ἀπελθὼν προσ-
but the flesh   weak.   Again   a second time having gone away   he
ηύξατο, λέγων, Πάτερ.μου, εἰ οὐ.δύναται τοῦτο ¹τὸ ποτήριον‖
prayed,   saying,   my Father,   if   ³cannot   ¹this   ²cup
παρελθεῖν ᵐἀπ' ἐμοῦ ἐὰν.μὴ αὐτὸ πίω, γενηθήτω τὸ θέλημά
pass   from me   unless   ³it ¹I ²drink,   ⁴be ⁷done   ⁵will
σου. 43 Καὶ ἐλθὼν ⁿεὑρίσκει αὐτοὺς πάλιν καθεύδοντας,
⁴thy.   And having come   he finds   them   again   sleeping,
ἦσαν.γὰρ αὐτῶν.οἱ.ὀφθαλμοὶ βεβαρημένοι. 44 Καὶ ἀφεὶς
for ³were   ¹their ²eyes   heavy.   And . leaving
αὐτούς, ᵒἀπελθὼν πάλιν‖ προσηύξατο ᴾἐκ.τρίτου,‖ τὸν αὐτὸν
them,   having gone away again   he prayed   a third time,   ²the ³same
λόγον εἰπών٩. 45 τότε ἔρχεται πρὸς τοὺς.μαθητὰς.ᵃαὐτοῦ,‖
¹thing ¹saying.   Then he comes   to   his disciples
καὶ λέγει αὐτοῖς, Καθεύδετε ˢτὸ‖.λοιπὸν καὶ ἀναπαύεσθε·
and   says   to them,   Sleep on   now   and · take your rest;
ἰδού. ἤγγικεν ἡ ὥρα, καὶ ὁ υἱὸς τοῦ ἀνθρώπου παραδίδο-
lo,   ³has ⁴drawn ⁵near ¹the ²hour, and the Son   of man   is delivered
ται εἰς χεῖρας ἁμαρτωλῶν. 46 ἐγείρεσθε, ἄγωμεν· ἰδού,
up. into [the] hands   of sinners.   Rise up,   let us go;   behold,
ἤγγικεν ὁ παραδιδούς με.
²has ³drawn ⁴near ¹he who is delivering up me.

47 And while he yet spake, lo, Judas, one of the twelve, came, and with him a great multitude with swords and staves, from the chief priests and elders of the people. 48 Now he that betrayed him gave them a sign, saying, Whomsoever I shall kiss, that same is he : hold him fast. 49 And forthwith he came to Jesus, and said, Hail, master ; and kissed him. 50 And Jesus said unto him, Friend, wherefore art thou come ? Then came they, and laid hands on Jesus, and took him. 51 And, behold, one of them which were with Jesus stretched out *his* hand, and drew his sword, and struck a servant of the high priest's, and smote off his ear.

47 Καὶ ἔτι αὐτοῦ.λαλοῦντος, ἰδού, Ἰούδας εἷς τῶν δώδεκα
And   ⁴yet ¹as ²he ³is speaking   behold,   Judas,   one of the twelve,
ἦλθεν, καὶ μετ' αὐτοῦ ὄχλος πολὺς μετὰ μαχαιρῶν καὶ ξύλων,
came,   and with   him a ²crowd ¹great   with   swords   and staves,
ἀπὸ τῶν ἀρχιερέων καὶ πρεσβυτέρων τοῦ λαοῦ. 48 ὁ.δὲ
from the   chief priests   and   elders   of the people.   And he who
παραδιδοὺς αὐτὸν ἔδωκεν αὐτοῖς σημεῖον, λέγων, Ὃν.ἂν‖
was delivering up him   gave   them   a sign,   saying,   Whomsoever
φιλήσω, αὐτός ἐστιν· κρατήσατε αὐτόν. 49 Καὶ εὐθέως
I shall kiss,   he   it is: seize   him.   And immediately
προσελθὼν τῷ Ἰησοῦ εἶπεν, Χαῖρε, ᵛῥαββί,‖ καὶ κατεφίλησεν
having come up   to Jesus he said,   Hail,   Rabbi,   and ardently kissed
αὐτόν. 50 ὁ.δὲ Ἰησοῦς εἶπεν αὐτῷ, Ἑταῖρε, ἐφ' ʷᾧ‖
him.   But Jesus   said   to him,   Friend,   for what [purpose]
πάρει; Τότε προσελθόντες ἐπέβαλον τὰς χεῖρας ἐπὶ
art thou come? Then   having come to [him]   they laid   hands   on
τὸν Ἰησοῦν, καὶ ἐκράτησαν αὐτόν. 51 Καὶ ἰδού, εἷς τῶν
Jesus,   and   seized   him.   And behold, one of those
μετὰ Ἰησοῦ, ἐκτείνας τὴν χεῖρα ἀπέσπασεν τὴν μάχαι-
with Jesus,   having stretched out [his]   hand   drew   ²sword
ραν αὐτοῦ, καὶ πατάξας τὸν δοῦλον τοῦ ἀρχιερέως ἀφεῖλεν
¹his,   and   smiting   the bondman of the high priest   took off

---

1 — τὸ ποτήριον LTTrA.   m — ἀπ' ἐμοῦ [L]TTrA.   n πάλιν εὗρεν αὐτοὺς again he
found them LTTrA.   o πάλιν ἀπελθὼν LTTrA.   P — ἐκ τρίτου [L]A.   ٩ + πάλιν
again T.   r — αὐτοῦ (*read* the disciples) LTTrA.   s — τὸ [Tr]A.   t ἐὰν TA.
ᵛ ῥαββεί T.   ʷ ὃ GLTTrAW.

αὐτοῦ τὸ ὠτίον. 52 τότε λέγει αὐτῷ ὁ Ἰησοῦς, Ἀπόστρεψόν
his　ear.　　　Then ²says ³to ⁴him　¹Jesus,　　Return

¹σου τὴν μάχαιραν‖ εἰς τὸν.τόπον.αὐτῆς· πάντες.γὰρ οἱ λα-
thy　　sword　　to　　its place ;　　　　for all who

βόντες μάχαιραν ἐν ¹μαχαίρᾳ‖ ἀπολοῦνται. 53 ἢ δο-
take [the] sword　by [the] sword　shall perish.　　　Or think-

κεῖς ὅτι οὐ.δύναμαι ²ἄρτι‖ παρακαλέσαι τὸν.πατέρα.μου,
est thou that I am not able　now　to call upon　my Father,

καὶ παραστήσει μοι ᵃ ᵇπλείους‖ ²ἢ‖ δώδεκα ᵈλεγεῶνας‖ ἀγ-
and he will furnish to me　more　than twelve　legions　of

γέλων; 54 πῶς. οὖν πληρωθῶσιν αἱ γραφαὶ ὅτι οὕτως
angels?　　　How then should be fulfilled the scriptures that thus

δεῖ γενέσθαι;
it must　be?

55 Ἐν ἐκείνῃ τῇ ὥρᾳ εἶπεν ὁ Ἰησοῦς τοῖς ὄχλοις, Ὡς ἐπὶ
In that　hour said　Jesus to the crowds, As against

λῃστὴν ᵉἐξήλθετε¹ μετὰ μαχαιρῶν καὶ ξύλων συλλαβεῖν με;
a robber are ye come out with swords and staves to take me?

καθ᾽.ἡμέραν ᶠπρὸς ὑμᾶς‖ ᵍἐκαθεζόμην διδάσκων ἐν τῷ ἱερῷ,‖
Daily　with you　I sat　teaching　in the temple,

καὶ οὐκ.ἐκρατήσατέ.με. 56 τοῦτο.δὲ ὅλον γέγονεν ἵνα πλη-
and　ye did not seize　me.　But this all is come to pass that may

ρωθῶσιν αἱ γραφαὶ τῶν προφητῶν. Τότε οἱ μαθηταὶʰ πάντες
be fulfilled the scriptures of the prophets.　Then the disciples all

ἀφέντες αὐτὸν ἔφυγον.
forsaking him　fled.

57 Οἱ.δὲ κρατήσαντες τὸν Ἰησοῦν ἀπήγαγον πρὸς Καϊ-
But they who had seized　Jesus led [him] away to Cai-

άφαν τὸν ἀρχιερέα, ὅπου οἱ γραμματεῖς καὶ οἱ πρεσβύτεροι
aphas the high priest, where the scribes and the elders

συνήχθησαν· 58 Ὁ.δὲ.Πέτρος ἠκολούθει αὐτῷ ⁱἀπὸ‖ μακρό-
were gathered together.　And Peter　followed　him from afar

θεν, ἕως τῆς αὐλῆς τοῦ ἀρχιερέως· καὶ εἰσελθὼν ἔσω ἐκάθητο
even to the court of the high priest ; and having entered within he sat

μετὰ τῶν ὑπηρετῶν ἰδεῖν τὸ τέλος. 59 Οἱ.δὲ ἀρχιερεῖς ᵏκαὶ οἱ
with the officers to see the end.　And the chief priests and the

πρεσβύτεροι‖ καὶ τὸ συνέδριον ὅλον ἐζήτουν ψευδομαρτυρίαν
elders　and the ²sanhedrim ¹whole sought　false evidence

κατὰ τοῦ Ἰησοῦ, ὅπως ¹αὐτὸν θανατώσωσιν,‖ 60 καὶ οὐχ
against　Jesus, so that　him they might put to death,　and ²not

εὗρον· ᵐκαὶ¹ πολλῶν ⁿψευδομαρτύρων προσελθόντων⁰ ⁰οὐχ
¹found [³any]: even　many　false witnesses having come forward ³not

εὗρον.‖ 61 ὕστερον.δὲ προσελθόντες δύο ᴾψευδομάρτυρες‖
¹they ²found [any].　But at last having come forward two　false witnesses

εἶπον, Οὗτος ἔφη, Δύναμαι καταλῦσαι τὸν ναὸν τοῦ θεοῦ,
said,　This [man] said, I am able to destroy the temple of God,

καὶ διὰ τριῶν ἡμερῶν ᵠοἰκοδομῆσαι αὐτόν.‖ 62 Καὶ ἀναστὰς
and in three days　to build　it.　And having stood up

ὁ ἀρχιερ᾽ὺς εἶπεν αὐτῷ, Οὐδὲν ἀποκρίνῃ; τί οὗτοί σου
the high priest said to him, Nothing answerest thou? What ²these ⁵thee

---

52 Then said Jesus unto him, Put up again thy sword into his place: for all they that take the sword shall perish with the sword. 53 Thinkest thou that I cannot now pray to my Father, and he shall presently give me more than twelve legions of angels? 54 But how then shall the scriptures be fulfilled, that thus it must be?

55 In that same hour said Jesus to the multitudes, Are ye come out as against a thief with swords and staves for to take me? I sat daily with you teaching in the temple, and ye laid no hold on me. 56 But all this was done, that the scriptures of the prophets might be fulfilled. Then all the disciples forsook him, and fled.

57 And they that had laid hold on Jesus led him away to Caiaphas the high priest, where the scribes and the elders were assembled. 58 But Peter followed him afar off unto the high priest's palace, and went in, and sat with the servants, to see the end. 59 Now the chief priests, and elders, and all the council, sought false witness against Jesus, to put him to death; 60 but found none: yea, though many false witnesses came, yet found they none. At the last came two false witnesses, 61 and said, This fellow said, I am able to destroy the temple of God, and to build it in three days. 62 And the high priest arose, and said unto him, Answerest thou nothing? what is it which these witness against thee? 63 But

---

ˣ τὴν μάχαιράν σου LTTrA.　ʸ μαχαίρῃ LTTrA.　ᶻ – ἄρτι TTr.　ᵃ + ἄρτι now TTr.
ᵇ πλείω LTTrA.　ᶜ – ἢ (read [than]) [L] TTrA.　ᵈ λεγιώνων T.　ᵉ ἐξήλθατε LTTrA.　ᶠ – πρὸς
ὑμᾶς T[Tr]A　ᵍ ἐκαθεζόμην ἐν τῷ ἱερῷ διδάσκων L ; ἐν τῷ ἱερῷ ἐκαθεζόμην διδάσκων TTrA.
ʰ + αὐτοῦ of him [L].　ⁱ – ἀπὸ T.　ᵏ – καὶ οἱ πρεσβύτεροι LTT:A.　ˡ αὐτὸν
θανατώσουσιν LTTrA ; θανατώσωσιν αὐτὸν W.　ᵐ – καὶ GDITr.　ⁿ προσελθόντων
ψευδομαρτύρων LTT:A.　⁰ – οὐχ εὗρον G[L]TTrA.　ᴾ – ψευδομάρτυρες TTrA.　ᵠ αὐτὸν
οἰκοδομῆσαι T ; – αὐτὸν TrA.

Jesus held his peace. And the high priest answered and said unto him, I adjure thee by the living God, that thou tell us whether thou be the Christ, the Son of God. 64 Jesus saith unto him, Thou hast said: nevertheless I say unto you, Hereafter shall ye see the Son of man sitting on the right hand of power, and coming in the clouds of heaven. 65 Then the high priest rent his clothes, saying, He hath spoken blasphemy; what further need have we of witnesses? behold, now ye have heard his blasphemy. 66 What think ye? They answered and said, He is guilty of death. 67 Then did they spit in his face, and buffeted him; and others smote *him* with the palms of their hands, 68 saying, Prophesy unto us, thou Christ, Who is he that smote thee?

καταμαρτυροῦσιν; 63 Ὁ.δὲ.Ἰησοῦς ἐσιώπα. καὶ ᾽ἀποκριθεὶς‖ ὁ
¹do ³witne.s ²against?   But Jesus , was silent. And answering the
ἀρχιερεὺς εἶπεν αὐτῷ, Ἐξορκίζω σε κατὰ τοῦ θεοῦ τοῦ ζῶντος,
high priest said to him, I adjure thee by   ²God ¹the ²living,
ἵνα ἡμῖν εἴπῃς. εἰ σὺ εἶ ὁ χριστός, ὁ υἱὸς τοῦ θεοῦ. 64 Λέγει
that us . thou tell if thou art the Christ, the Son of God.   ²Says
αὐτῷ ὁ Ἰησοῦς, Σὺ εἶπας. πλὴν λέγω ὑμῖν, ἀπ᾽.ἄρτι ὄψεσθε
³to ⁴him ¹Jesus, Thou hast said. Moreover I say to you, Henceforth ye shall see
τὸν υἱὸν τοῦ ἀνθρώπου καθήμενον ἐκ δεξιῶν τῆς δυνάμεως καὶ
the Son of man sitting at[the]right hand of power, and
ἐρχόμενον ἐπὶ τῶν νεφελῶν τοῦ οὐρανοῦ. 65 Τότε ὁ ἀρχιερεὺς
coming on the clouds of heaven. Then the high priest
διέρρηξεν τὰ.ἱμάτια.αὐτοῦ, λέγων, ᵗ῾Οτι‖ ἐβλασφήμησεν· τί
rent his garments, saying, He has blasphemed; why
ἔτι· χρείαν ἔχομεν μαρτύρων; ἴδε, νῦν ἠκούσατε τὴν βλασ-
any more ¹need ¹have ²we of witnesses? lo, now ye have heard the blas-
φημίαν ᵛαὐτοῦ.‖ 66 τί ὑμῖν.δοκεῖ; Οἱ.δὲ ἀποκριθέντες εἶπον,
phemy of him. What do ye think? And they answering said,
Ἔνοχος θανάτου ἐστίν. 67 Τότε ἐνέπτυσαν εἰς τὸ πρόσωπον
Deserving of death he is. Then they spat in ²face
αὐτοῦ, καὶ ἐκολάφισαν αὐτόν, οἱ.δὲ ᵂἐρράπισαν,‖
¹his, and buffeted him, and some struck [him] with the palm of the
68 λέγοντες, Προφήτευσον ἡμῖν, χριστέ, τίς ἐστιν ὁ
hand, saying, Prophesy to us, Christ, Who is he that
παίσας σε;
struck thee?

69 Now Peter sat without in the palace: and a damsel came unto him, saying, Thou also wast with Jesus of Galilee. 70 But he denied before *them* all, saying, I know not what thou sayest. 71 And when he was gone out into the porch, another *maid* saw him, and said unto them that were there, This *fellow* was also with Jesus of Nazareth. 72 And again he denied with an oath, I do not know the man. 73 And after a while came unto *him* they that stood by, and said to Peter, Surely thou also art *one* of them; for thy speech bewrayeth thee. 74 Then began he to curse and to swear, *saying*, I know not the man. And immediately the cock crew. 75 And Peter remembered the word of Jesus, which said unto him, Before the cock crow, thou shalt deny me thrice. And he went out, and wept bitterly.

69 Ὁ.δὲ.Πέτρος ˣἔξω ἐκάθητο‖ ἐν τῇ αὐλῇ, καὶ προσῆλθεν
But Peter ³without ¹was ²sitting in the court, and ³came
αὐτῷ μία.παιδίσκη, λέγουσα, Καὶ σὺ ἦσθα μετὰ Ἰησοῦ τοῦ
⁴to ⁵him ¹a ²maid, saying, And thou wast with Jesus the
Γαλιλαίου. 70 Ὁ.δὲ ἠρνήσατο ἔμπροσθεν ᵞ πάντων, λέγων, Οὐκ
Galilæan. But he denied . before all, saying, ³Not
οἶδα τί λέγεις. 71 Ἐξελθόντα.δὲ ᶻαὐτὸν‖ εἰς τὸν πυλῶνα
¹I ²know what thou sayest. And ³having ²gone ⁴out ¹he into the porch
εἶδεν αὐτὸν ἄλλη, καὶ λέγει ᵃτοῖς‖ ἐκεῖ, ᵇΚαὶ‖ οὗτος
³saw ⁴him ¹another [²maid], and says to those there, And this [man]
ἦν μετὰ Ἰησοῦ τοῦ Ναζωραίου. 72 Καὶ πάλιν ἠρνήσατο
was with Jesus the Nazarean. And again he denied
ᶜμεθ᾽‖ ὅρκου, Ὅτι οὐκ.οἶδα τὸν ἄνθρωπον. 73 Μετὰ μικρὸν.δὲ
with an oath, I know not the man. After a little also
προσελθόντες οἱ ἑστῶτες εἶπον τῷ Πέτρῳ, Ἀληθῶς
⁵having ⁶come ⁷to [⁸him] ¹those ²who ³stood ⁴by said to Peter, Truly
καὶ σὺ ἐξ αὐτῶν εἶ· καὶ.γὰρ ἡ.λαλιά.σου δῆλόν σε ποιεῖ.
also thou of them art, for even thy speech ³manifest ²thee ¹makes.
74 Τότε ἤρξατο ᵈκαταναθεματίζειν‖ καὶ ὀμνύειν, Ὅτι οὐκ.οἶδα
Then he began to curse and to swear, I know not
τὸν ἄνθρωπον. Καὶ ᵉεὐθέως‖ ἀλέκτωρ ἐφώνησεν. 75 καὶ
the man. And immediately a cock crew. And
ἐμνήσθη ὁ Πέτρος τοῦ ῥήματος ᶠτοῦ‖ Ἰησοῦ εἰρηκότος ᵍαὐτῷ,‖
²remembered ¹Peter the word of Jesus, who had said to him,
Ὅτι πρὶν ἀλέκτορα φωνῆσαι, τρὶς ἀπαρνήσῃ με· καὶ
Before [the] cock crow, thrice thou wilt deny me. And
ἐξελθὼν ἔξω ἔκλαυσεν πικρῶς.
having gone out he wept bitterly.

ˢ — ἀποκριθεὶς Tr. ᵗ — ὅτι LTTrA. ᵛ — αὐτοῦ [L]TTrA. ᵂ ἐράπισαν LTTrA. ˣ ἐκάθητο ἔξω LTTrA. ʸ + αὐτῶν them G. ᶻ — αὐτὸν [L] Tr. ᵃ αὐτοῖς to them Aw. ᵇ — καὶ T. ᶜ μετὰ LTTrA. ᵈ καταθεματίζειν GLTTrAW. ᵉ εὐθὺς Tr. ᶠ — τοῦ LTTrA. ᵍ — αὐτῷ [L]TTrA.

27 Πρωΐας δὲ γενομένης, συμβούλιον ἔλαβον πάντες οἱ
And morning being come, ¹²counsel ¹¹took ¹all ²the
ἀρχιερεῖς καὶ οἱ πρεσβύτεροι τοῦ λαοῦ κατὰ τοῦ Ἰησοῦ,
²chief ⁴priests ⁵and ⁶the ⁷elders ⁸of ⁹the ¹⁰people against Jesus,
ὥστε θανατῶσαι αὐτόν· 2 καὶ δήσαντες αὐτὸν ἀπήγα-
so that they might put to death him; and having bound him they led
γον καὶ παρέδωκαν ᵢαὐτὸνᵏ ᵏΠοντίῳᵏ ˡΠιλάτῳᵏ τῷ
away [him] and delivered up him to Pontius Pilate the
ἡγεμόνι.
governor.

3 Τότε ἰδὼν Ἰούδας ὁ ᵐπαραδιδοὺςᵏ αὐτὸν ὅτι κατ-
Then ⁶having ⁷seen ¹Judas ²who ³delivered ⁵up ⁴him that he was
εκρίθη, μεταμεληθεὶς ⁿἀπέστρεψενᵏ τὰ τριάκοντα ἀργύ-
condemned, having regretted [it] returned the thirty pieces of
ρια τοῖς ἀρχιερεῦσιν καὶ °τοῖςᵏ πρεσβυτέροις, 4 λέγων,
silver to the chief priests and the elders, saying,
Ἥμαρτον παραδοὺς αἷμα ᴾἀθῶονᵏ. Οἱ δὲ εἶπον, Τί
I sinned delivering up ²blood ¹guiltless. But they said, What [is that]
πρὸς ἡμᾶς; σὺ �q ὄψει.ᵏ 5 Καὶ ῥίψας τὰ ἀργύρια
to us? thou wilt see [to it]. And having cast down the pieces of silver
ʳἐν τῷ ναῷᵏ ἀνεχώρησεν, καὶ ἀπελθὼν ἀπήγξατο. 6 Οἱ δὲ
in the temple he withdrew, and having gone away hanged himself. And the
ἀρχιερεῖς λαβόντες τὰ ἀργύρια ˢεἶπον,ᵏ Οὐκ ἔξεστιν βαλεῖν
chief priests having taken the pieces of silver said, It is not lawful to put
αὐτὰ εἰς τὸν κορβανᾶν, ἐπεὶ τιμὴ αἵματός ἐστιν. 7 Συμ-
them into the treasury, since [the] price of blood it is. ⁴Coun-
βούλιον δὲ λαβόντες, ἠγόρασαν ἐξ αὐτῶν τὸν ἀγρὸν τοῦ
sel ¹and ²having ³taken, they bought with them the field of the
κεραμέως, εἰς ταφὴν τοῖς ξένοις. 8 διὸ ἐκλήθη ὁ
potter, for a burying ground for strangers. Wherefore ³was ⁴called
ἀγρὸς ἐκεῖνος ἀγρὸς αἵματος ἕως τῆς σήμερον. 9 τότε
¹that ²field Field of blood to this day. Then
ἐπληρώθη τὸ ῥηθὲν διὰ Ἰερεμίου τοῦ προφήτου, λέγον-
was fulfilled that which was spoken by Jeremias the prophet, say-
τος, Καὶ ἔλαβον τὰ τριάκοντα ἀργύρια, τὴν τιμὴν τοῦ
ing, And I took the thirty pieces of silver, the price of him who
τετιμημένου, ὃν ἐτιμήσαντο ἀπὸ υἱῶν Ἰσραήλ, 10 καὶ
was set a price on, whom they ⁶set ⁷a ⁸price ⁹on ¹of [²the] ³sons ⁴of ⁵Israel, and
ἔδωκαν αὐτὰ εἰς τὸν ἀγρὸν τοῦ κεραμέως, καθὰ συνέταξέν
gave them for the field of the potter, according as ³directed
μοι κύριος.
⁴me [¹the] ²Lord.

11 Ὁ δὲ Ἰησοῦς ᵗἔστηᵏ ἔμπροσθεν τοῦ ἡγεμόνος· καὶ ἐπηρώ-
But Jesus stood before the governor; and ³ques-
τησεν αὐτὸν ὁ ἡγεμών, λέγων, Σὺ εἶ ὁ βασιλεὺς τῶν
tioned ⁴him ¹the ²governor, saying, ²Thou ¹art the king of the
Ἰουδαίων; Ὁ δὲ Ἰησοῦς ἔφη ᵛαὐτῷ,ᵏ Σὺ λέγεις. 12 Καὶ
Jews? And Jesus said to him, Thou sayest. And
ἐν τῷ κατηγορεῖσθαι αὐτὸν ὑπὸ τῶν ἀρχιερέων καὶ ʷτῶνᵏ πρεσ-
when ²was ³accused ¹he by the chief priests and the el-
βυτέρων, οὐδὲν ἀπεκρίνατο. 13 τότε λέγει αὐτῷ ὁ ˣΠιλάτος,ᵏ
ders, nothing he answered. Then ²says ³to ⁴him ¹Pilate,

XXVII. When the morning was come, all the chief priests and elders of the people took counsel against Jesus to put him to death: 2 and when they had bound him, they led him away, and delivered him to Pontius Pilate the governor.

3 Then Judas, which had betrayed him, when he saw that he was condemned, repented himself, and brought again the thirty pieces of silver to the chief priests and elders, 4 saying, I have sinned in that I have betrayed the innocent blood. And they said, What is that to us? see thou to that. 5 And he cast down the pieces of silver in the temple, and departed, and went and hanged himself. 6 And the chief priests took the silver pieces, and said, It is not lawful for to put them into the treasury, because it is the price of blood. 7 And they took counsel, and bought with them the potter's field, to bury strangers in. 8 Wherefore that field was called, The field of blood, unto this day. 9 Then was fulfilled that which was spoken by Jeremy the prophet, saying, And they took the thirty pieces of silver, the price of him that was valued, whom they of the children of Israel did value; 10 and gave them for the potter's field, as the Lord appointed me.

11 And Jesus stood before the governor: and the governor asked him, saying, Art thou the king of the Jews? And Jesus said unto him, Thou sayest. 12 And when he was accused of the chief priests and elders, he answered nothing. 13 Then said Pilate unto him, Hearest

---

ᵢ — αὐτὸν LTTrA. ᵏ — Ποντίῳ TTr. ˡ Πειλάτῳ T. ᵐ παραδοὺς had delivered up LTr.
ⁿ ἐστρεψεν TTrA. ° — τοῖς LTTrA. ᴾ ἀθῶον LTA. q ὄψῃ LTTrA. ʳ εἰς τὸν ναὸν
into the temple TTr. ˢ εἶπαν LTTr. ᵗ ἐστάθη LTTrA. ᵛ — αὐτῷ T. ʷ — τῶν T[A].
ˣ Πιλᾶτος LₜTr; Πειλᾶτος ᴛ.

thou not how many things they witness against thee? 14 And he answered him to never a word; insomuch that the governor marvelled greatly.

15 Now at *that* feast the governor was wont to release unto the people a prisoner, whom they would. 16 And they had then a notable prisoner, called Barabbas. 17 Therefore when they were gathered together, Pilate said unto them, Whom will ye that I release unto you? Barabbas, or Jesus which is called Christ? 18 For he knew that for envy they had delivered him. 19 When he was set down on the judgment seat, his wife sent unto him, saying, Have thou nothing to do with that just man: for I have suffered many things this day in a dream because of him. 20 But the chief priests and elders persuaded the multitude that they should ask Barabbas, and destroy Jesus. 21 The governor answered and said unto them, Whether of the twain will ye that I release unto you? They said, Barabbas. 22 Pilate saith unto them, What shall I do then with Jesus which is called Christ? They all say unto him, Let him be crucified. 23 And the governor said, Why, what evil hath he done? But they cried out the more, saying, Let him be crucified. 24 When Pilate saw that he could prevail nothing, but *that* rather a tumult was made, he took water, and washed *his* hands before the multitude, saying, I am innocent of the blood of this just person: see ye to *it*. 25 Then answered all the people, and said, His blood *be* on us, and on our children. 26 Then released he Barabbas unto them: and when he had scourged Jesus, he delivered *him* to be crucified.

Οὐκ.ἀκούεις　πόσα　σοῦ　καταμαρτυροῦσιν;　14 Καὶ
Hearest thou not how many things [2]thee　[1]they　[2]witness　[3]against?　And

οὐκ.ἀπεκρίθη　αὐτῷ πρὸς οὐδὲ ἓν ῥῆμα, ὥστε θαυμάζειν τὸν
he did not answer　him　to　even one word, so that [2]wondered [1]the

ἡγεμόνα　λίαν.
[2]governor exceedingly.

15 Κατὰ.δὲ　ἑορτὴν　εἰώθει　ὁ ἡγεμὼν ἀπολύειν ἕνα
Now at [the] feast [2]was [3]accustomed [1]the [2]governor to release one

τῷ　ὄχλῳ　δέσμιον, ὃν ἤθελον. 16 εἶχον.δὲ τότε δέσ-
[2]to [3]the [4]multitude [1]prisoner, whom they wished. And they had then a [2]pri-

μιον ἐπίσημον, λεγόμενον Βαραββᾶν. 17 συνηγμένων
soner [1]notable, called Barabbas. [3]Being [4]gathered [5]together

οὖν　αὐτῶν εἶπεν αὐτοῖς ὁ ʸΠιλάτος,‖ Τίνα θέλετε ἀπο-
[2]therefore [1]they [7]said [8]to [9]them [6]Pilate, Whom will ye [that] I

λύσω ὑμῖν; Βαραββᾶν, ἢ Ἰησοῦν τὸν λεγόμενον χριστόν;
release to you? Barabbas, or Jesus who is called Christ?

18 ᾔδει.γὰρ ὅτι διὰ φθόνον παρέδωκαν αὐτόν. 19 Καθη-
For he knew that through envy they delivered up him. [2]As [4]was

μένου δὲ αὐτοῦ ἐπὶ τοῦ βήματος ἀπέστειλεν πρὸς αὐτὸν ἡ
[3]sitting [1]but, [3]he · on the judgment seat [3]sent [4]to [5]him

γυνὴ.αὐτοῦ, λέγουσα,　＼Μηδέν σοι καὶ τῷ δικαίῳ
[1]his [2]wife, saying, [Let there be] nothing between thee and [2]righteous

ἐκείνῳ·　πολλὰ.γὰρ ἔπαθον σήμερον κατʼ ὄναρ διʼ
[1]that [man]; for many things I suffered to-day in a dream because of

αὐτόν. 20 Οἱ.δὲ ἀρχιερεῖς· καὶ οἱ πρεσβύτεροι ἔπεισαν τοὺς
him. But the chief priests and the elders persuaded the

ὄχλους ἵνα αἰτήσωνται τὸν Βαραββᾶν, τὸν.δὲ Ἰησοῦν ἀπολ-
crowds that they should beg for Barabbas, and [3]Jesus [1]should

έσωσιν. 21 ἀποκριθεὶς.δὲ ὁ ἡγεμὼν εἶπεν αὐτοῖς, Τίνα θέλετε
[2]destroy. And [3]answering [1]the [2]governor said to them, Which will ye

ἀπὸ τῶν δύο　ἀπολύσω ὑμῖν; Οἱ.δὲ ᶻεἶπον‖, ᵃΒαραββᾶν.
of the two [that] I release to you? And they said, Barabbas.

22 Λέγει αὐτοῖς ὁ ʸΠιλάτος,‖ Τί οὖν ποιήσω Ἰησοῦν, τὸν
[2]Says [3]to [4]them [1]Pilate, What then shall I do with Jesus, who

λεγόμενον χριστόν; Λέγουσιν ᵇαὐτῷ‖ πάντες, Σταυρωθήτω.
is called Christ? They [2]say [3]to [4]him [1]all, Let [him] be crucified.

23 Ὁ.δὲ ᶜἡγεμὼν‖ ἔφη, Τί γὰρ κακὸν ἐποίησεν; Οἱ.δὲ
And the governor said, What [2]then [1]evil did he commit? But they

περισσῶς ἔκραζον, λέγοντες, Σταυρωθήτω. 24 Ἰδὼν.δὲ ὁ
the more cried out, saying, Let [him] be crucified. [2]seeing

ʸΠιλάτος‖ ὅτι οὐδὲν ὠφελεῖ, ἀλλὰ μᾶλλον θόρυβος γίνεται,
[1]Pilate that nothing it availed, but rather a tumult is arising,

λαβὼν ὕδωρ ἀπενίψατο τὰς χεῖρας ᵈἀπέναντι‖ τοῦ ὄχλου,
having taken water he washed [his] hands before the crowd,

λέγων, ᵉἈθῷός‖ εἰμι ἀπὸ τοῦ αἵματος ᶠτοῦ.δικαίου.τούτου·‖
saying, Guiltless I am of the blood of this righteous [man];

ὑμεῖς ὄψεσθε. 25 Καὶ ἀποκριθεὶς πᾶς ὁ λαὸς .εἶπεν, Τὸ
ye .will see [to it]. And [4]answering [1]all [2]the [3]people said,

αἷμα.αὐτοῦ ἐφʼ ἡμᾶς καὶ ἐπὶ τὰ.τέκνα.ἡμῶν. 26 Τότε ἀπέλυ-
His blood [be] on us and on our children. Then he re-

σεν αὐτοῖς τὸν Βαραββᾶν· τὸν.δὲ Ἰησοῦν φραγελλώσας
leased to them Barabbas; but [2]Jesus [1]having [2]scourged

παρέδωκεν ἵνα σταυρωθῇ.
he delivered up [him] that he might be crucified.

ʸ Πιλᾶτος LTr; Πειλᾶτος T.　ᶻ εἶπαν TTr.　ᵃ + τὸν TTr.　ᵇ — αὐτῷ I.TTrA.
ᶜ — ἡγεμὼν (read and he said) TTrA.　ᵈ κατέναντι LTr.　ᵉ ἀθῷός LTA.　ᶠ τούτου [τοῦ
δικαίου] Ⱔ; — τοῦ δικαίου (read of this [man]) T[Tr]A.

27 Τότε οἱ στρατιῶται τοῦ ἡγεμόνος, παραλαβόντες
Then the soldiers of the governor, having taken with [them]
τὸν Ἰησοῦν εἰς τὸ πραιτώριον, συνήγαγον ἐπ᾽ αὐτὸν ὅλην
Jesus to the prætorium, gathered against him all
τὴν σπεῖραν· 28 καὶ ᵍἐκδύσαντες᾿᾿ αὐτὸν ʰπεριέθηκαν αὐτῷ
the band; ᾿and having stripped him they put round him
χλαμύδα κοκκίνην‖ 29 καὶ πλέξαντες στέφανον ἐξ ἀκανθῶν
a ᶻcloak ˡscarlet; And having platted a crown of thorns
ἐπέθηκαν ἐπὶ ᶦτὴν.κεφαλὴν‖.αὐτοῦ, καὶ κάλαμον ᵏἐπὶ τὴν
they put [it] on his head, and a reed in
δεξιὰν‖ αὐτοῦ· καὶ γονυπετήσαντες ἔμπροσθεν αὐτοῦ ˡἐνέ-
ᵖright ³hand ˡhis; and bowing the knees before him they
παιζον‖ αὐτῷ, λέγοντες, Χαῖρε, ᵐὁ βασιλεὺς‖ τῶν Ἰουδαίων·
mocked him, saying, Hail, king of the Jews!
30 καὶ ἐμπτύσαντες εἰς αὐτὸν ἔλαβον τὸν κάλαμον καὶ ἔτυπ-
And having spit upon him they took the reed and struck
τον εἰς τὴν.κεφαλὴν.αὐτοῦ. 31 Καὶ ὅτε ἐνέπαιξαν αὐτῷ
[him] on his head. And when they had mocked him
ⁿἐξέδυσαν‖ αὐτὸν τὴν χλαμύδα, ᵒκαὶ‖ ἐνέδυσαν αὐτὸν τὰ
they took off him the cloak, and they put on him
ἱμάτια.αὐτοῦ· καὶ ἀπήγαγον αὐτὸν εἰς τὸ.σταυρῶσαι.
his own garments; and led ᵃaway ˡhim to crucify.

32 Ἐξερχόμενοι.δὲ εὗρον ἄνθρωπον Κυρηναῖον, ὀνόματι
And going forth they found a man a Cyrenæan, by name
Σίμωνα· τοῦτον ἠγγάρευσαν ἵνα ἄρῃ τὸν.σταυρὸν.αὐτοῦ.
Simon; him they compelled that he might carry his cross.
33 Καὶ ἐλθόντες εἰς τόπον λεγόμενον ᴾΓολγοθᾶ,‖ ᵠ῿ᵗᵋ‖ ἐστιν
And having come to a place called Golgotha, which is
ʳλεγόμενος κρανίου τόπος,‖ 34 ἔδωκαν αὐτῷ ˢπιεῖν‖ ᵗὄξος‖
called ᵒ᾿ᵃ ᵃskull ˡplace, they gave him to drink vinegar
μετὰ χολῆς μεμιγμένον· καὶ γευσάμενος οὐκ.ᵛἤθελεν‖ ˢπιεῖν.‖
with gall mingled; and having tasted he would not drink.
35 Σταυρώσαντες.δὲ αὐτὸν διεμερίσαντο τὰ.ἱμάτια.αὐτοῦ,
And having crucified him they divided his garments,
ʷβάλλοντες‖ κλῆρον· ˣἵνα πληρωθῇ τὸ ῥηθὲν ὑπὸ
casting a lot; that might be fulfilled that which was spoken by
τοῦ προφήτου, Διεμερίσαντο τὰ.ἱμάτιά.μου ἑαυτοῖς, καὶ
the prophet, They divided my garments among themselves, and
ἐπὶ τὸν.ἱματισμόν.μου ἔβαλον κλῆρον.‖ 36 Καὶ καθήμενοι
for my vesture they cast a lot. And sitting down
ἐτήρουν αὐτὸν ἐκεῖ. 37 Καὶ ἐπέθηκαν ἐπάνω τῆς
they kept guard over him there. And they put up over
κεφαλῆς.αὐτοῦ τὴν.αἰτίαν.αὐτοῦ γεγραμμένην, Οὗτός ἐστιν
his head his accusation written: This is
Ἰησοῦς ὁ βασιλεὺς τῶν Ἰουδαίων. 38 Τότε σταυροῦνται σὺν
Jesus the king of the Jews. Then are crucified with
αὐτῷ δύο λῃσταί, εἷς ἐκ δεξιῶν καὶ εἷς ἐξ εὐωνύμων.
him two robbers, one at [the] right hand and one at [the] left.
39 Οἱ.δὲ παραπορευόμενοι ἐβλασφήμουν αὐτόν, κινοῦντες
But those passing by railed at him, shaking
τὰς.κεφαλὰς.αὐτῶν, 40 καὶ λέγοντες, Ὁ καταλύων τὸν ναὸν
their heads, and saying, Thou who destroyest the temple

27 Then the soldiers of the governor took Jesus into the common hall, and gathered unto him the whole band of soldiers. 28 And they stripped him, and put on him a scarlet robe. 29 And when they had platted a crown of thorns, they put it upon his head, and a reed in his right hand: and they bowed the knee before him, and mocked him, saying, Hail, King of the Jews! 30 And they spit upon him, and took the reed, and smote him on the head. 31 And after that they had mocked him, they took the robe off from him, and put his own raiment on him, and led him away to crucify him.

32 And as they came out, they found a man of Cyrene, Simon by name: him they compelled to bear his cross. 33 And when they were come unto a place called Golgotha, that is to say, a place of a skull, 34 They gave him vinegar to drink mingled with gall: and when he had tasted thereof, he would not drink. 35 And they that crucified him, and parted his garments, casting lots: that it might be fulfilled which was spoken by the prophet, They parted my garments among them, and upon my vesture did they cast lots. 36 And sitting down they watched him there; 37 and set up over his head his accusation written, THIS IS JESUS THE KING OF THE JEWS. 38 Then were there two thieves crucified with him, one on the right hand, and another on the left.

39 And they that passed by reviled him, wagging their heads, 40 and saying, Thou that destroyest the temple, and buildest

ᵍ ἐνδύσαντες having clothed L. ʰ χλαμύδα κοκκίνην περιέθηκαν αὐτῷ LTTrA. ᶦ τῆς κεφαλῆς TTrA. ᵏ ἐν τῇ δεξιᾷ LTTrA. ˡ ἐνέπαιξαν T. ᵐ βασιλεῦ O king LTr. ⁿ ἐκδύσαντες having taken off T. ᵒ — καὶ T. ᴾ Γολγοθά Tr. ᵠ ὃ GLTTrAW. ʳ κρανίου τόπος λεγόμενος LTTrA. ˢ πεῖν T. ᵗ οἶνον wine LTr. ᵛ ἠθέλησεν LTTr; ᵗθέλησεν Λ. ʷ βαλόντες having cast LTA. ˣ — ἵνα πληρωθῇ to end of verse GLTTrA.

it in three days, save thyself. If thou be the Son of God, come down from the cross. 41 Likewise also the chief priests mocking him, with the scribes and elders, said, 42 He saved others; himself he cannot save. If he be the King of Israel, let him now come down from the cross, and we will believe him. 43 He trusted in God; let him deliver him now, if he will have him: for he said, I am the Son of God. 44 The thieves also, which were crucified with him, cast the same in his teeth.

καὶ ἐν τρισὶν ἡμέραις οἰκοδομῶν,   σῶσον σεαυτόν· εἰ υἱὸς
and in · three   days   buildest [it], save thyself. If son

ᵍεἶ τοῦ θεοῦ,‖ ᶻ κατάβηθι ἀπὸ τοῦ σταυροῦ. 41 Ὁμοίως
thou art . of God, descend from the   cross.   ²In ³like ⁴manner

ᵃδὲ καὶ‖ οἱ ἀρχιερεῖς ἐμπαίζοντες μετὰ τῶν γραμματέων καὶ
¹and also the chief priests, mocking, with the scribes   and

πρεσβυτέρων ἔλεγον, 42 Ἄλλους ἔσωσεν, ἑαυτὸν οὐ δύναται
elders,   said,   Others he saved, himself he is not able

σῶσαι. ᵇεἰ‖ βασιλεὺς Ἰσραήλ ἐστιν, καταβάτω νῦν ἀπὸ τοῦ
to save. If king   of Israel he is, let him descend now from the

σταυροῦ, καὶ ᶜπιστεύσομεν‖ ᵈαὐτῷ. 43 πέποιθεν ἐπὶ ᵉτὸν θεόν·‖
cross, and we will believe him.   He trusted on God:

ῥυσάσθω νῦν ᶠαὐτόν,‖ εἰ θέλει   αὐτόν. εἶπεν γάρ, Ὅτι θεοῦ
let him deliver ²now ¹him, if he will [have] him. For he said, ⁴Of ⁵God

εἰμι υἱός. 44 Τὸ δ᾽ αὐτὸ   καὶ οἱ λῃσταὶ οἱ ᵍσυσταυρωθέν-
¹I ²am ³Son. And [with] the same thing also the robbers who were crucified to-

τες‖ ʰ αὐτῷ ὠνείδιζον ¹αὐτῷ.‖
gether with him reproached him.

---

45 Now from the sixth hour there was darkness over all the land unto the ninth hour. 46 And about the ninth hour Jesus cried with a loud voice, saying, ELI, ELI, LAMA SABACHTHANI? that is to say, My God, my God, why hast thou forsaken me? 47 Some of them that stood there, when they heard that, said, This man calleth for Elias. 48 And straightway one of them ran, and took a spunge, and filled it with vinegar, and put it on a reed, and gave him to drink. 49 The rest said, Let be, let us see whether Elias will come to save him.

45 Ἀπὸ δὲ ἕκτης   ὥρας σκότος ἐγένετο ἐπὶ πᾶσαν τὴν
Now from ²sixth [¹the] hour darkness was   over   all   the

γῆν ἕως   ὥρας ᵏἐννάτης·‖ 46 περὶ δὲ τὴν ˡἐννάτην‖ ὥραν
land until [the] ²hour ¹ninth;   and about the   ninth   hour

ᵐἀνεβόησεν‖ ὁ Ἰησοῦς   φωνῇ   μεγάλῃ, λέγων, ⁿἨλί, Ἠλί,‖
²cried ³out ¹Jesus ⁴with ⁵a ⁷voice ⁶loud, saying,   Eli,   Eli,

ᵒλαμὰ‖ ᵖσαβαχθανί;‖ τοῦτ᾽ ἔστιν, Θεέ μου, θεέ μου, �q ἱνατί‖ με
lama sabachthani? that is,   My God, my God, why me

ἐγκατέλιπες; 47 Τινὲς δὲ τῶν ἐκεῖ ʳἑστώτων‖ ἀκού-
hast thou forsaken? And some of those who there were standing having

σαντες, ἔλεγον, Ὅτι ˢἨλίαν‖ φωνεῖ οὗτος.   48 Καὶ εὐθέως
heard,   said,   Elias ³calls ¹this [²man].   And immediately

δραμὼν εἷς ἐξ αὐτῶν καὶ λαβὼν σπόγγον, πλήσας τε
⁴having ⁵run ¹one ²of ³them and taken a sponge, and filled [it]

ὄξους   καὶ περιθεὶς καλάμῳ, ἐπότιζεν αὐτόν· 49 οἱ δὲ
with vinegar and put [it] on a reed, gave ²to ³drink ¹him.   But the

λοιποὶ ᵗἔλεγον,‖ Ἄφες, ἴδωμεν εἰ ἔρχεται. ᵛἨλίας‖ σώσων
rest   said,   Let be; let us see ²comes ¹Elias to save

αὐτόν.
him.

---

50 Jesus, when he had cried again with a loud voice, yielded up the ghost. 51 And, behold, the veil of the temple was rent in twain from the top to the bottom; and the earth did quake, and the rocks rent; 52 and the graves were opened; and many bodies of the saints which slept arose, 53 and

50 Ὁ δὲ Ἰησοῦς πάλιν κράξας   φωνῇ μεγάλῃ ἀφῆκεν
And Jesus again having cried ²loud ¹voice yielded up

τὸ πνεῦμα. 51 Καὶ ἰδού, τὸ καταπέτασμα τοῦ ναοῦ ἐσχίσθη
[his] spirit. And behold, the veil   of the temple was rent

ʷεἰς δύο‖ ˣἀπὸ‖ ἄνωθεν ἕως κάτω· καὶ ἡ γῆ ἐσείσθη, καὶ
into two from top   to bottom; and the earth was shaken, and

αἱ πέτραι ἐσχίσθησαν, 52 καὶ τὰ μνημεῖα ἀνεῴχθησαν, καὶ
the rocks were rent,   and the tombs were opened, and

πολλὰ σώματα τῶν κεκοιμημένων ἁγίων ʸᵃἠγέρθη,‖ 53 καὶ
many bodies of the ᶻfallen ³asleep ¹saints   arose,   and

ʸ θεοῦ εἶ L.   ᶻ + καὶ and LT.   ᵃ [δὲ] καὶ TrA; — δὲ καὶ [L]T.   ᵇ — εἰ TTrA.
ᶜ πιστεύομεν we believe L; πιστεύσωμεν let us believe T.   ᵈ ἐπ᾽ αὐτόν on him TTr; ἐπ᾽
αὐτῷ W.   ᵉ τῷ θεῷ L.   ᶠ — αὐτόν T[Tr].   ᵍ συνσταυρωθέντες LTTrA.   ʰ + σὺν
with (him) LTTrA.   ¹ αὐτόν GLTTrAW.   ᵏ ἐνάτης LTTrA.   ˡ ἐνάτην LTTrA.   ᵐ ἐβόησεν
cried Tr.   ⁿ Ἡλὶ ἠλὶ LA; Ἠλεὶ ἠλεὶ T.   ᵒ λημᾶ L; λεμὰ TTrA.   ᵖ σαβακτανί L;
σαβαχθανεί TTr.   ᑫ ἱνα τί A.   ʳ ἑστηκότων TTr.   ˢ Ἡλείαν T.   ᵗ εἶπαν LTr.
ᵛ Ἡλείας T.   ʷ εἰς δύο placed after κάτω TTrA.   ˣ ἀπ᾽ Tr; — ἀπὸ T.   ʸᵃ ἠγέρθησαν
LTTrA.

ἐξελθόντες ἐκ τῶν μνημείων μετὰ τὴν ἐγερσιν αὐτοῦ, εἰσῆλ-
having gone forth out of the tombs after his arising, entered

θον εἰς τὴν ἁγίαν πόλιν καὶ ἐνεφανίσθησαν πολλοῖς.
into the holy city and appeared to many.

54 Ὁ δὲ ᶻἑκατόνταρχος‖ καὶ οἱ μετ' αὐτοῦ τηροῦντες
But the centurion and they who with him kept guard over

τὸν Ἰησοῦν, ἰδόντες τὸν σεισμὸν καὶ τὰ ᵃγενόμενα,‖
Jesus, having seen the earthquake and the things that took place,

ἐφοβήθησαν σφόδρα, λέγοντες, Ἀληθῶς ᵇθεοῦ υἱὸς‖ ἦν οὗτος.
feared greatly, saying, Truly ³God's ⁴Son ²was ¹this.

55 ᵀἮσαν δὲ ἐκεῖ γυναῖκες πολλαὶ ἀπὸ μακρόθεν θεωροῦ-
And there were there ²women ¹many from afar off looking

σαι, αἵτινες ἠκολούθησαν τῷ Ἰησοῦ ἀπὸ τῆς Γαλιλαίας δια-
on, who followed Jesus from Galilee min-

κονοῦσαι αὐτῷ, 56 ἐν αἷς ἦν Μαρία ἡ Μαγδαληνή, καὶ
istering to him, among whom was Mary the Magdalene, and

Μαρία ἡ τοῦ Ἰακώβου καὶ ᶜ'Ἰωσῆ‖ μήτηρ, καὶ ἡ μήτηρ τῶν
Mary the ²of ³James ⁴and ⁵Joses ¹mother; and the mother of the

υἱῶν Ζεβεδαίου.
sons of Zebedee.

57 Ὀψίας δὲ γενομένης ἦλθεν ἄνθρωπος πλούσιος ἀπὸ
And evening being come ⁴came ¹a ³man ²rich from

ᵈ'Ἀριμαθαίας,‖ τοὔνομα Ἰωσήφ. ὃς καὶ αὐτὸς ᵉἐμαθήτευσεν‖
Arimathea, by name Joseph, who also himself was discipled

τῷ Ἰησοῦ· 58 οὗτος προσελθὼν τῷ ᶠΠιλάτῳ‖ ᾐτήσατο τὸ σῶμα
to Jesus. He having gone to Pilate begged the body

τοῦ Ἰησοῦ. τότε ὁ ᵍΠιλάτος‖ ἐκέλευσεν ἀποδοθῆναι ʰτὸ σῶμα.‖
of Jesus. Then Pilate commanded to be given up the body.

59 καὶ λαβὼν τὸ σῶμα ὁ Ἰωσὴφ ἐνετύλιξεν αὐτὸ ⁱ σινδόνι
And having taken the body Joseph wrapped it in a ²linen ³cloth

καθαρᾷ, 60 καὶ ἔθηκεν αὐτὸ ἐν τῷ καινῷ αὐτοῦ μνημείῳ ὃ
¹clean, and placed it in his new tomb which

ἐλατόμησεν ἐν τῇ πέτρᾳ καὶ προσκυλίσας λίθον μέγαν
he had hewn in the rock; and having rolled a ²stone ¹great

ᵏ τῇ θύρᾳ τοῦ μνημείου ἀπῆλθεν. 61 ἦν δὲ ἐκεῖ ˡΜαρία‖
to the door of the tomb went away. And there was there Mary

ἡ Μαγδαληνὴ καὶ ἡ ἄλλη Μαρία, καθήμεναι ἀπέναντι τοῦ
the Magdalene and the other Mary, sitting opposite the

τάφου.
sepulchre.

62 Τῇ δὲ ἐπαύριον, ἥτις ἐστὶν μετὰ τὴν παρασκευήν,
Now on the morrow, which is after the preparation,

συνήχθησαν οἱ ἀρχιερεῖς καὶ οἱ Φαρισαῖοι πρὸς ᵐΠι-
were gathered together the chief priests and the Pharisees to Pi-

λάτον,‖ 63 λέγοντες, Κύριε, ἐμνήσθημεν ὅτι ἐκεῖνος
late, saying, Sir, we have called to mind that that

ὁ πλάνος εἶπεν ἔτι ζῶν, Μετὰ τρεῖς ἡμέρας ἐγείρομαι. 64 κέ-
deceiver said whilst living, After three days I arise. Com-

λευσον οὖν ἀσφαλισθῆναι τὸν τάφον ἕως τῆς τρίτης ἡμέρας·
mand therefore to be secured the sepulchre until the third day,

μήποτε ἐλθόντες οἱ μαθηταὶ ᴺαὐτοῦ‖ ᴼνυκτὸς‖ κλέψωσιν αὐτόν,
lest ²coming ¹his ²disciples by night steal ²away ¹him,

came out of the graves after his resurrection, and went into the holy city, and appeared unto many.

54 Now when the centurion, and they that were with him, watching Jesus, saw the earthquake, and those things that were done, they feared greatly, saying, Truly this was the Son of God.

55 And many women were there beholding afar off, which followed Jesus from Galilee, ministering unto him : 56 among which was Mary Magdalene, and Mary the mother of James and Joses, and the mother of Zebedee's children-

57 When the even was come, there came a rich man of Arimathæa, named Joseph, who also himself was Jesus' disciple : 58 he went to Pilate, and begged the body of Jesus. Then Pilate commanded the body to be delivered. 59 And when Joseph had taken the body, he wrapped it in a clean linen cloth, 60 and laid it in his own new tomb, which he had hewn out in the rock : and he rolled a great stone to the door of the sepulchre, and departed. 61 And there was Mary Magdalene, and the other Mary, sitting over against the sepulchre.

62 Now the next day, that followed the day of the preparation, the chief priests and Pharisees came together unto Pilate, 63 saying, Sir, we remember that that deceiver said, while he was yet alive, After three days I will rise again. 64 Command therefore that the sepulchre be made sure until the third day, lest his disciples come by night, and steal him away, and

say unto the people, He is risen from the dead : so the last error shall be worse than the first. 65 Pilate said unto them, Ye have a watch : go your way, make it as sure as ye can. 66 So they went, and made the sepulchre sure, sealing the stone, and setting a watch.

XXVIII. In the end of the sabbath, as it began to dawn toward the first day of the week, came Mary Magdalene and the other Mary to see the sepulchre.

2 And, behold, there was a great earthquake : for the angel of the Lord descended from heaven, and came and rolled back the stone from the door, and sat upon it. 3 His countenance was like lightning, and his raiment white as snow : 4 and for fear of him the keepers did shake, and became as dead men. 5 And the angel answered and said unto the women, Fear not ye : for I know that ye seek Jesus, which was crucified. 6 He is not here : for he is risen, as he said. Come, see the place where the Lord lay. 7 And go quickly, and tell his disciples that he is risen from the dead ; and, behold, he goeth before you into Galilee ; there shall ye see him : lo, I have told you. 8 And they departed quickly from the sepulchre with fear and great joy ; and did run to bring his disciples word. 9 And as they went to tell his disciples, behold, Jesus met them, saying, All hail. And they came and held him by the feet, and worshipped him. 10 Then said Jesus unto them, Be not afraid : go tell my brethren

καὶ εἴπωσιν τῷ λαῷ, Ἠγέρθη ἀπὸ τῶν νεκρῶν· καὶ ἔσται
and   say   to the people, He is risen from   the dead ;   and *shall *be
ἡ ἐσχάτη πλάνη χείρων τῆς πρώτης. 65 Ἔφη.Ρδὲ‖ αὐτοῖς
¹the ²last ³deception worse than the first.   And ²said ³to ⁴them
ὁ ⁴Πιλάτος,‖ Ἔχετε κουστωδίαν· ὑπάγετε ἀσφαλίσασθε ὡς
  ¹Pilate,   Ye have a guard :   Go   make [it as] secure as
οἴδατε. 66 Οἱ.δὲ πορευθέντες ἠσφαλίσαντο τὸν τάφον
ye know [how]. And they having gone made ¹secure ¹the ²sepulchre
σφραγίσαντες τὸν λίθον, μετὰ τῆς κουστωδίας.
⁷sealing   ⁵the ³stone, ⁴with ⁵the   ⁶guard.

28 Ὀψὲ.δὲ σαββάτων, τῇ.ἐπιφωσκούσῃ εἰς μίαν
   Now late on Sabbath, as it was getting dusk toward [the] first [day]
σαββάτων, ἦλθεν ˣΜαρία‖ ἡ Μαγδαληνὴ καὶ ἡ ἄλλη Μαρία
of [the] week, came Mary the Magdalene and-the other Mary
θεωρῆσαι τὸν τάφον.
to see   the sepulchre.

2 Καὶ ἰδού, σεισμὸς ἐγένετο μέγας· ἄγγελος.γὰρ κυρίου
And behold, ³a ⁵earthquake ¹there.²was ⁴great ; for an angel of [the] Lord
καταβὰς ἐξ οὐρανοῦ, * προσελθὼν ἀπεκύλισεν τὸν λίθον
having descended out of heaven, having come rolled away the stone
ᵗἀπὸ τῆς θύρας,‖ καὶ ἐκάθητο ἐπάνω αὐτοῦ. 3 ἦν.δὲ ἡ ᵛἰδέα‖
from the door, and was sitting upon it.   And ¹was ²look
αὐτοῦ ὡς ἀστραπή, καὶ τὸ.ἔνδυμα.αὐτοῦ λευκὸν ʷὡσεὶ‖ χιών.
¹his as lightning, and his raiment white   as snow.
4 ἀπὸ.δὲ τοῦ φόβου αὐτοῦ ἐσείσθησαν οἱ τηροῦντες, καὶ ˣἐγέ-
And from the   fear of him ⁴trembled ¹those ²keeping ³guard, and be-
νοντο ὡσεὶ‖ νεκροί. 5 Ἀποκριθεὶς.δὲ ὁ ἄγγελος εἶπεν ταῖς
came as dead [men]. But ²answering ¹the ³angel said to the
γυναιξίν, Μὴ.φοβεῖσθε ὑμεῖς· οἶδα.γὰρ ὅτι Ἰησοῦν τὸν ἐσταυ-
women, Fear not ye ; for I know that Jesus who has been
ρωμένον ζητεῖτε. 6 οὐκ.ἔστιν ὧδε· ἠγέρθη.γάρ, καθὼς εἶπεν.
crucified ye seek. He is not here, for he is risen, as he said.
δεῦτε ἴδετε τὸν τόπον ὅπου ἔκειτο ʸὁ κύριος.‖ 7 καὶ ταχὺ
Come see the place where ²was ³lying ¹the ⁴Lord.   And ²quickly
πορευθεῖσαι εἴπατε τοῖς.μαθηταῖς.αὐτοῦ, ὅτι ἠγέρθη ἀπὸ τῶν
¹going   say   to his disciples,   that he is risen from the
νεκρῶν καὶ ἰδού, προάγει ὑμᾶς εἰς τὴν Γαλιλαίαν· ἐκεῖ
dead ;   and behold, he goes before you into Galilee ;   there
αὐτὸν ὄψεσθε. ἰδού, εἶπον ὑμῖν. 8 Καὶ ᶻἐξελθοῦσαι‖ ταχὺ
him ye shall see. Lo, I have told you. And having gone out quickly
ἀπὸ τοῦ μνημείου μετὰ φόβου καὶ χαρᾶς μεγάλης, ἔδραμον
from the tomb   with fear and ²joy ¹great, they ran
ἀπαγγεῖλαι τοῖς.μαθηταῖς.αὐτοῦ. 9 ᵃὡς.δὲ ἐπορεύοντο
to tell   [it]   to his disciples.   But as they were going
ἀπαγγεῖλαι τοῖς.μαθηταῖς.αὐτοῦ,‖ καὶ ἰδού, ᵇὁ‖ Ἰησοῦς ᶜἀπήν-
to tell   [it]   to his disciples,   ²also ¹behold,   Jesus   met
τησεν‖ αὐταῖς, λέγων, Χαίρετε. Αἱ.δὲ προσελθοῦσαι ἐκρά-
them,   saying, Hail ! And they having come to [him] seized
τησαν αὐτοῦ τοὺς πόδας, καὶ προσεκύνησαν αὐτῷ. 10 τότε
hold of his feet,   and worshipped him.   Then
λέγει αὐταῖς ὁ Ἰησοῦς, Μὴ.φοβεῖσθε· ὑπάγετε, ἀπαγγείλατε
says ²to ⁴them ¹Jesus,   Fear not :   Go,   tell

P — δὲ and GLTTrAW.   ٩ Πιλᾶτος LTr ; Πειλᾶτος T.   ʳ Μαριὰμ T.   ˢ + καὶ and TTr.
ᵗ — ἀπὸ τῆς θύρας LTTrA.   ᵛ εἰδέα TTr.   ʷ ὡς LTTrA.   ˣ ἐγενήθησαν ὡς LTTrA.   ʸ — ὁ
κύριος (read he was lying) T[TrA].   ᶻ ἀπελθοῦσαι having departed TTrA.   ᵃ — ὡς δὲ
ἐπορεύοντο ἀπαγγεῖλαι τοῖς μαθηταῖς αὐτοῦ LTTrA.   ᵇ — ὁ TA.   ᶜ ὑπήντησεν TTr.

τοῖς.ἀδελφοῖς.μου ἵνα ἀπέλθωσιν εἰς τὴν Γαλιλαίαν, ᵈκἀκεῖ‖ με
my brethren   that   they go   into   Galilee,   and there me
ὄψονται·
shall they see.

11 Πορευομένων.δὲ αὐτῶν, ἰδού, τινὲς τῆς κουστωδίας ἐλ-
And as ²were ³going ¹they,   lo,   some of the   guard   hav-
θόντες εἰς τὴν πόλιν ᵉἀπήγγειλαν‖ τοῖς ἀρχιερεῦσιν ἅπαντα
ing gone into the city   reported   to the chief priests all things
τὰ γενόμενα. 12 καὶ   συναχθέντες   μετὰ τῶν πρεσ-
that were done. And having been gathered together with the   el-
βυτέρων, συμβούλιόν.τε λαβόντες, ἀργύρια ἱκανὰ ἔδωκαν
ders,   and counsel having taken,   ²money   ¹much they gave
τοῖς στρατιώταις, 13 λέγοντες, Εἴπατε ὅτι οἱ.μαθηταί.αὐτοῦ
to the   soldiers,   saying,   Say that   his disciples
νυκτὸς ἐλθόντες ἔκλεψαν αὐτὸν ἡμῶν κοιμωμένων· 14 καὶ
by night having come stole   him,   we   being asleep.   And
ἐὰν ἀκουσθῇ τοῦτο ᶠἐπὶ‖ τοῦ ἡγεμόνος, ἡμεῖς πείσομεν ᵍαὐτὸν‖
if ²be ³heard ¹this by   the governor,   we will persuade him
καὶ ὑμᾶς ἀμερίμνους ποιήσομεν. 15 Οἱ.δὲ λαβόντες τὰ
and ²you ⁴free ³from ⁵care ¹will ⁶make.   And they having taken the
ἀργύρια ἐποίησαν ὡς ἐδιδάχθησαν. καὶ ᵇδιεφημίσθη‖ ὁ λόγος
money   did   as they were taught. And ²is ¹spread ³abroad · ²report
οὗτος παρὰ Ἰουδαίοις μέχρι τῆς σήμερονⁱ.
¹this among [the] Jews   until the   present.

16 Οἱ.δὲ ἔνδεκα μαθηταὶ ἐπορεύθησαν εἰς τὴν Γαλιλαίαν,
But the eleven   disciples   went   into   Galilee,
εἰς τὸ ὄρος οὗ ἐτάξατο αὐτοῖς ὁ Ἰησοῦς. 17 καὶ ἰδόντες
to the mountain whither ²appointed ³them ¹Jesus.   And seeing
αὐτὸν προσεκύνησαν ᵏαὐτῷ·‖ οἱ.δὲ ἐδίστασαν. 18 καὶ προσ-
him   they worshipped   him: but some doubted.   And having
ελθὼν ὁ Ἰησοῦς ἐλάλησεν αὐτοῖς, λέγων, Ἐδόθη μοι
come to [them] Jesus   spoke   to them, saying, ²Has ⁴been ⁵given ⁶to ⁷me
πᾶσα ἐξουσία ἐν οὐρανῷ καὶ ἐπὶ¹ γῆς. 19 πορευθέντες ᵐοὖν‖
¹all ²authority in heaven and on earth.   Going   therefore
μαθητεύσατε πάντα τὰ ἔθνη, ⁿβαπτίζοντες‖ αὐτοὺς εἰς τὸ
disciple   all   the nations,   baptizing   them   to the
ὄνομα τοῦ πατρὸς καὶ τοῦ υἱοῦ καὶ τοῦ ἁγίου πνεύματος,
name of the Father and of the Son and of the Holy   Spirit;
20 διδάσκοντες αὐτοὺς τηρεῖν πάντα ὅσα ἐνετειλάμην
teaching   them   to observe all things whatsoever I commanded
ὑμῖν· καὶ ἰδού, ἐγὼ μεθ᾽ ὑμῶν εἰμι πάσας τὰς ἡμέρας ἕως τῆς
you. And lo,   I   with you am   all   the   days   until the
συντελείας τοῦ αἰῶνος. ᵒἈμήν.‖ ᴾ
completion of the age.   Amen.

11 Now when they were going, behold, some of the watch came into the city, and shewed unto the chief priests all the things that were done. 12 And when they were assembled with the elders, and had taken counsel, they gave large money unto the soldiers, 13 saying, Say ye, His disciples came by night, and stole him *away* while we slept. 14 And if this come to the governor's ears, we will persuade him, and secure you. 15 So they took the money, and did as they were taught: and this saying is commonly reported among the Jews until this day.

16 Then the eleven disciples went away into Galilee, into a mountain where Jesus had appointed them. 17 And when they saw him, they worshipped him: but some doubted. 18 And Jesus came and spake unto them, saying, All power is given unto me in heaven and in earth. 19 Go ye therefore, and teach all nations, baptizing them in the name of the Father, and of the Son, and of the Holy Ghost: 20 teaching them to observe all things whatsoever I have commanded you: and, lo, I am with you alway, *even* unto the end of the world. Amen.

ᵈ καὶ ἐκεῖ T.   ᵉ ἀνήγγειλαν announced T.   ᶠ ὑπὸ LTr.   ᵍ — αὐτὸν (*read* [him]) T[Tr].
ᵇ ἐφημίσθη is spoken of T.   ⁱ + ἡμέρας day LTrA.   ᵏ — αὐτῷ LTTrA.   ¹ + τῆς the LTTrA.
ᵐ — οὖν G[L]T[Tr]A.   ⁿ βαπτίσαντες having baptized Tr.   ᵒ — Ἀμήν GLTTrA.   ᴾ + κατὰ
Ματθαῖον according to Matthew TrA.

ᵃΤΟ ΚΑΤΑ ΜΑΡΚΟΝ ΑΓΙΟΝ ΕΥΑΓΓΕΛΙΟΝ.ᵇ
THE ᵃACCORDING ⁵TO ³MARK ¹HOLY ²GLAD ³TIDINGS.

THE beginning of the gospel of Jesus Christ, the Son of God; 2 as it is written in the prophets, Behold, I send my messenger before thy face, which shall prepare thy way before thee. 3 The voice of one crying in the wilderness, Prepare ye the way of the Lord, make his paths straight.

'ΑΡΧΗ τοῦ εὐαγγελίου Ἰησοῦ χριστοῦ, ᵇυἱοῦ τοῦ θεοῦ·ᴵᴵ
BEGINNING of the glad tidings of Jesus Christ, Son of God;
2 ᶜὡς‖ γέγραπται ἐν ᵈτοῖς προφήταις,‖ Ἰδού, ᵉἐγὼ‖ ἀποστέλλω
as it has been written in the prophets, Behold, I send
τὸν ἄγγελόν μου πρὸ προσώπου σου, ὃς κατασκευάσει τὴν
my messenger before thy face, who shall prepare
ὁδόν σου ᶠἔμπροσθέν σου.‖ 3 Φωνὴ βοῶντος ἐν τῇ ἐρήμῳ,
thy way before thee. [The] voice of one crying in the wilderness,
Ἑτοιμάσατε τὴν ὁδὸν κυρίου, εὐθείας ποιεῖτε τὰς τρίβους
Prepare the way of [the] Lord, straight make ²paths
αὐτοῦ.
¹his.

4 John did baptize in the wilderness, and preach the baptism of repentance for the remission of sins. 5 And there went out unto him all the land of Judæa, and they of Jerusalem, and were all baptized of him in the river of Jordan, confessing their sins. 6 And John was clothed with camel's hair, and with a girdle of a skin about his loins; and he did eat locusts and wild honey; 7 and preached, saying, There cometh one mightier than I after me, the latchet of whose shoes I am not worthy to stoop down and unloose. 8 I indeed have baptized you with water: but he shall baptize you with the Holy Ghost.

4 Ἐγένετο Ἰωάννης ᵍβαπτίζων ἐν τῇ ἐρήμῳ, ʰκαὶ‖ κηρύσ-
²Came ¹John baptizing in the wilderness, and proclaim-
σων βάπτισμα μετανοίας εἰς ἄφεσιν ἁμαρτιῶν. 5 καὶ
ing [the] baptism of repentance for remission of sins. And
ἐξεπορεύετο πρὸς αὐτὸν πᾶσα ἡ Ἰουδαία χώρα, καὶ οἱ ˡἹερο-
went out to him all the ²of ³Judæa ¹country, and they of Je-
σολυμῖται,‖ ᵏκαὶ ἐβαπτίζοντο πάντες‖ ˡἐν τῷ Ἰορδάνῃ ποταμῷ
rusalem, and were ²baptized ¹all in the ²Jordan ¹river
ὑπ᾽ αὐτοῦ,‖ ἐξομολογούμενοι τὰς ἁμαρτίας αὐτῶν. 6 ᵐἦν δὲ‖
by him, confessing their sins. And ²was
ⁿἸωάννης ἐνδεδυμένος τρίχας καμήλου, καὶ ζώνην δερματίνην
¹John clothed in hair of a camel, and a girdle of leather
περὶ τὴν ὀσφὺν αὐτοῦ, καὶ ᵒἐσθίων‖ ἀκρίδας καὶ μέλι ἄγριον.
about his loins, and eating locusts and ²honey ¹wild.
7 Καὶ ἐκήρυσσεν, λέγων, Ἔρχεται ὁ ἰσχυρότερός μου ὀπίσω
And he proclaimed, saying, He comes who [is] mightier than I after
μου, οὗ οὐκ εἰμὶ ἱκανὸς κύψας λῦσαι τὸν ἱμάντα
me, of whom I am not fit having stooped down to loose the thong
τῶν ὑποδημάτων αὐτοῦ. 8 ἐγὼ ᵖμὲν‖ ἐβάπτισα ὑμᾶς qἐν‖ ὕδατι,
of his sandals. I indeed baptized you with water,
αὐτὸς δὲ βαπτίσει ὑμᾶς ʳἐν‖ πνεύματι ἁγίῳ.
but he will baptize you with [the] ²Spirit ¹Holy.

9 And it came to pass in those days, that Jesus came from Nazareth of Galilee, and was baptized of John in Jordan. 10 And straightway coming up out of the water, he saw the heavens opened, and the Spirit like a dove descending upon him: 11 and there came a voice from

9 ˢΚαὶ‖ ἐγένετο ἐν ἐκείναις ταῖς ἡμέραις ἦλθεν Ἰησοῦς
And it came to pass in those days [that] ²came ¹Jesus
ἀπὸ ᵗΝαζαρὲτ‖ τῆς Γαλιλαίας, καὶ ἐβαπτίσθη ᵛὑπὸ Ἰωάν-
from Nazareth of Galilee, and was baptized by John
νου εἰς τὸν Ἰορδάνην.‖ 10 καὶ ʷεὐθέως‖ ἀναβαίνων ˣἀπὸ‖ τοῦ
in the Jordan. And immediately going up from the
ὕδατος, εἶδεν σχιζομένους τοὺς οὐρανούς, καὶ τὸ πνεῦμά
water, he saw parting asunder the heavens, and the Spirit
ʸὡσεὶ‖ περιστερὰν καταβαῖνον ᶻἐπ᾽‖ αὐτόν· 11 καὶ φωνὴ ᵃᵃἐγένε-
as a dove descending upon him. And a voice came

τοⁿ ἐκ τῶν οὐρανῶν, Σὺ εἶ ὁ.υἱός.μου ὁ ἀγαπητός, ἐν ^bᾧ^{ll}
out of the   heavens,   Thou art   my Son   the   beloved,   in   whom

εὐδόκησα.
I have found delight.

heaven, *saying*, Thou art my beloved Son, in whom I am well pleased.

12 Καὶ ^cεὐθὺς^{ll} τὸ πνεῦμα αὐτὸν ἐκβάλλει εἰς τὴν ἔρη-
And immediately the   Spirit   ²him   ¹drives out   into   the wilder-

μον. 13 καὶ ἦν ^dἐκεῖ^{ll} ἐν τῇ ἐρήμῳ ^eἡμέρας τεσσαράκοντα,^{ll}
ness.   And he was there in the wilderness   ²days   ¹forty,

πειραζόμενος ὑπὸ τοῦ σατανᾶ, καὶ ἦν μετὰ τῶν θηρίων· καὶ
tempted   by   Satan,   and was with the   beasts;   and

οἱ ἄγγελοι διηκόνουν αὐτῷ.
the angels   ministered to him.

12 And immediately the spirit driveth him into the wilderness. 13 And he was there in the wilderness forty days, tempted of Satan; and was with the wild beasts; and the angels ministered unto him.

14 ^fΜετὰ.δὲ^{ll} τὸ.παραδοθῆναι τὸν Ἰωάννην ἦλθεν ὁ Ἰησοῦς
And after   ²was ³delivered ⁴up   ¹John   came   Jesus

εἰς τὴν Γαλιλαίαν, κηρύσσων τὸ εὐαγγέλιον ^gτῆς βασιλείας^{ll}
into   Galilee,   proclaiming the glad tidings   of the   kingdom

τοῦ θεοῦ, 15 ^hκαὶ λέγων,^{ll}Ὅτι πεπλήρωται ὁ καιρός, καὶ ἤγ-
of God,   and saying,   ³Has ⁴been ⁵fulfilled.¹the ²time,   and has

γικεν ἡ βασιλεία τοῦ θεοῦ· μετανοεῖτε, καὶ πιστεύετε ἐν τῷ
drawn near the kingdom   of God;   repent,   and believe   in the

εὐαγγελίῳ. 16 ⁱΠεριπατῶν.δὲ^{ll} παρὰ τὴν θάλασσαν τῆς Γαλι-
glad tidings.   And walking   by   the   sea   ;   of Ga-

λαίας εἶδεν Σίμωνα καὶ Ἀνδρέαν τὸν ἀδελφὸν ^kαὐτοῦ^{ll} ^lβάλ-
lilee   he saw   Simon   and Andrew   the brother   of him   cast-

λοντας^{ll} ^mἀμφίβληστρον^{ll} ἐν τῇ θαλάσσῃ· ἦσαν.γὰρ ⁿἁλιεῖς·^{ll}
ing   a large net   in the   sea;   for they were   fishers.

17 καὶ εἶπεν αὐτοῖς ὁ Ἰησοῦς, Δεῦτε ὀπίσω μου, καὶ ποιήσω
And   ²said ³to ⁴them   ¹Jesus,   Come after   me,   and I will make

ὑμᾶς γενέσθαι ⁿἁλιεῖς^{ll} ἀνθρώπων. 18 Καὶ ^oεὐθέως^{ll} ἀφέντες
you   to become   fishers   of men.   And immediately having left

τὰ.δίκτυα.^pαὐτῶν^{ll} ἠκολούθησαν αὐτῷ. 19 Καὶ προβὰς
their nets   they followed   him.   And having gone on

^qἐκεῖθεν^{ll} ὀλίγον εἶδεν Ἰάκωβον τὸν τοῦ Ζεβεδαίου, καὶ
thence   a little   he saw   James   the [son]   of Zebedee,   and

Ἰωάννην τὸν.ἀδελφὸν.αὐτοῦ, καὶ αὐτοὺς ἐν τῷ πλοίῳ
John   his brother,   and these [were] in the   ship

καταρτίζοντας τὰ δίκτυα. 20 καὶ ^rεὐθέως^{ll} ἐκάλεσεν αὐτούς·
mending   the nets.   And immediately he called   them;

καὶ ἀφέντες τὸν πατέρα.αὐτῶν Ζεβεδαῖον ἐν τῷ πλοίῳ μετὰ
and having left   their father   Zebedee   in the   ship   with

τῶν μισθωτῶν, ἀπῆλθον ὀπίσω αὐτοῦ.
the hired servants, they went away after   him.

14 Now after that John was put in prison, Jesus came into Galilee, preaching the gospel of the kingdom of God, 15 and saying, The time is fulfilled, and the kingdom of God is at hand: repent ye, and believe the gospel. 16 Now as he walked by the sea of Galilee, he saw Simon and Andrew his brother casting a net into the sea: for they were fishers. 17 And Jesus said unto them, Come ye after me, and I will make you to become fishers of men. 18 And straightway they forsook their nets, and followed him. 19 And when he had gone a little farther thence, he saw James the *son* of Zebedee, and John his brother, who also were in the ship mending their nets. 20 And straightway he called them: and they left their father Zebedee in the ship with the hired servants, and went after him.

21 Καὶ εἰσπορεύονται εἰς ^sΚαπερναούμ·^{ll} καὶ ^tεὐθέως^{ll} τοῖς
And   they go   into   Capernaum;   and immediately on the

σάββασιν ^vεἰσελθὼν^{ll} ^wεἰς τὴν συναγωγὴν ἐδίδασκεν.^{ll} 22 καὶ
sabbaths   having entered into the   synagogue   he taught.   And

ἐξεπλήσσοντο ἐπὶ τῇ.διδαχῇ.αὐτοῦ· ἦν.γὰρ διδάσκων αὐτοὺς
they were astonished at   his teaching: for he was teaching   them

ὡς ἐξουσίαν ἔχων, καὶ οὐχ ὡς οἱ γραμματεῖς^x. 23 Καὶ ^y ἦν
as ²authority ¹having, and not as the   scribes.   And there was

21 And they went into Capernaum; and straightway on the sabbath day he entered into the synagogue, and taught. 22 And they were astonished at his doctrine: for he taught them as one that had authority, and not as the scribes. 23 And there was in

---

^b σοὶ thee LTTrA.   ^c εὐθέως LW.   ^d — ἐκεῖ GLTTrAW.   ^e τεσσεράκοντα ἡμέρας TTr ; ἡμέρας τεσσε. A.   ^f καὶ μετὰ LTrA.   ^g — τῆς βασιλείας [L]TTrA.   ^h — καὶ λέγων T ; — καὶ A.   ⁱ καὶ παράγων and passing on LTTrA.   ^k τοῦ Σίμωνος of Simon L ; Σίμωνος TTrA.   ^l ἀμφιβάλλοντας casting around GLTTrAW.   ^m — ἀμφίβληστρον (*read* [a net]) TTrA.   ⁿ ἁλεεῖς TA.   ^o εὐθὺς T.   ^p — αὐτῶν (*read* the nets) LTT[A].   ^q — ἐκεῖθεν [L]TTrA.   ^r εὐθὺς TTrA.   ^s Καφαρναούμ LTTrAW.   ^t εὐθὺς T.   ^v — εἰσελθὼν T[Tr]A.   ^w ἐδίδασκεν εἰς τὴν συναγωγὴν TA ; — τὴν E.   ^x + [αὐτῶν] (*read* their scribes) L.   ^y + εὐθὺς immediately TA.

their synagogue a man with an unclean spirit; and he cried out, 24 saying, Let us alone; what have we to do with thee, thou Jesus of Nazareth? art thou come to destroy us? I know thee who thou art, the Holy One of God. 25 And Jesus rebuked him, saying, Hold thy peace, and come out of him. 26 And when the unclean spirit had torn him, and cried with a loud voice, he came out of him. 27 And they were all amazed, insomuch that they questioned among themselves, saying, What thing is this? what new doctrine is this? for with authority commandeth he even the unclean spirits, and they do obey him. 28 And immediately his fame spread abroad throughout all the region round about Galilee.

29 And forthwith, when they were come out of the synagogue, they entered into the house of Simon and Andrew, with James and John. 30 But Simon's wife's mother lay sick of a fever, and anon they tell him of her. 31 And he came and took her by the hand, and lifted her up; and immediately the fever left her, and she ministered unto them. 32 And at even, when the sun did set, they brought unto him all that were diseased, and them that were possessed with devils. 33 And all the city was gathered together at the door. 34 And he healed many that were sick of divers diseases, and cast out many devils; and suffered not the devils to speak, because they knew him.

35 And in the morning, rising up a great while before day, he went out, and departed

ἐν τῇ.συναγωγῇ.αὐτῶν ἄνθρωπος ἐν πνεύματι.ἀκαθάρτῳ, καὶ
in   their synagogue   a man   with   an unclean spirit,   and

ἀνέκραξεν, 24 λέγων, ʳ˝Εα,‖ τί ἡμῖν καὶ σοί, Ἰησοῦ Ναζαρηνέ;
he cried out,   saying,   Ah! what to us and to thee, Jesus,   Nazarene?

ἦλθες ἀπολέσαι ἡμᾶς; ᵃοἶδά‖ σε τίς εἶ, ὁ ἅγιος
art thou come to destroy us?   I know thee who thou art, the Holy [One]

τοῦ θεοῦ. 25 Καὶ ἐπετίμησεν αὐτῷ ὁ Ἰησοῦς, ᵇλέγων,‖ Φιμώ-
of God.   And ²rebuked ³him ¹Jesus,   saying,   Be

θητι, καὶ ἔξελθε ἐξ αὐτοῦ. 26 Καὶ   σπαράξαν
silent, and come forth out of him.   And ⁵having ⁶thrown ⁸into ⁹convulsions

αὐτὸν τὸ πνεῦμα τὸ ἀκάθαρτον, καὶ ᶜκράξαν‖ φωνῇ μεγάλῃ,
⁷him ¹the ²spirit ³the ⁴unclean,   and having cried with a ²voice ¹loud,

ἐξῆλθεν ᵈἐξ‖ αὐτοῦ. 27 καὶ ἐθαμβήθησαν ᵉπάντες,‖ ὥστε
came forth out of him.   And ²were ³astonished ¹all,   so that

ᶠσυζητεῖν‖ ᵍπρὸς ʰαὐτούς,‖ λέγοντας, Τί ἐστιν τοῦτο;
they questioned together among themselves, saying, What is   this?

ᶦτίς ἡ διδαχὴ ἡ καινὴ αὕτη, ὅτι‖ κατ' ἐξουσίαν καὶ τοῖς πνεύ-
what ³teaching ²new ¹this, that with authority even the spirits

μασιν τοῖς ἀκαθάρτοις ἐπιτάσσει, καὶ ὑπακούουσιν αὐτῷ;
the   unclean   he commands, and   they obey   him!

28 ᵏἘξῆλθεν.δὲ‖ ἡ ἀκοὴ αὐτοῦ ᶦεὐθὺς‖ ᵐεἰς ὅλην τὴν περί-
And went out the fame of him immediately in all the ²around

χωρον τῆς Γαλιλαίας.
¹country   Galilee.

29 Καὶ ⁿεὐθέως‖ ἐκ τῆς συναγωγῆς ᵒἐξελθόντες ἦλθονʰ
And immediately out of the   synagogue   having gone forth they came

εἰς τὴν οἰκίαν Σίμωνος καὶ Ἀνδρέου, μετὰ Ἰακώβου καὶ Ἰωάν-
into the house of Simon and Andrew,   with   James   and   John.

νου. 30 ἡ.δὲ πενθερὰ Σίμωνος κατέκειτο πυρέσσουσα· καὶ
And the mother-in-law of Simon   was lying   in a fever.   And

ᵖεὐθέως‖ λέγουσιν αὐτῷ περὶ αὐτῆς. 31 καὶ προσελθὼν
immediately they speak to him about her.   And having come to [her]

ἤγειρεν αὐτήν, κρατήσας τῆς.χειρὸς.ᑫαὐτῆς·‖ καὶ ἀφῆκεν
he raised up her,   having taken   her hand.   And ³left

αὐτὴν ὁ πυρετὸς ʳεὐθέως,‖ καὶ διηκόνει αὐτοῖς. 32 Ὀψίας
¹her ⁴the ²fever   immediately, and she ministered to them.   ²Evening

δὲ γενομένης, ὅτε ˢἔδυ‖ ὁ ἥλιος, ἔφερον πρὸς αὐτὸν
¹and being come, when went down the sun, they brought to   him

πάντας τοὺς κακῶς ἔχοντας καὶ τοὺς δαιμονιζομένους· 33 καὶ
all   who ²ill ¹were   and those possessed by demons;   and

ᵗἡ πόλις ὅλη ἐπισυνηγμένη ἦν‖ πρὸς τὴν θύραν. 34 καὶ
the ²city ¹whole ⁴gathered ⁵together ³was   at   the   door.   And

ἐθεράπευσεν πολλοὺς κακῶς.ἔχοντας ποικίλαις νόσοις, καὶ
he healed   many   that were ill   of various diseases, and

δαιμόνια πολλὰ ἐξέβαλεν, καὶ οὐκ.ἤφιεν λαλεῖν τὰ δαιμόνια,
²demons ¹many he cast out, and suffered not ²to ⁴speak ¹the ²demons;

ὅτι ᾔδεισαν αὐτόν.
because they knew   him.

35 Καὶ πρωῒ ᵛἔννυχον‖ λίαν ἀναστὰς ἐξῆλθεν καὶ
And very early   while yet night   having risen up he went out and

---

ᶻ — ˝Εα LTTrA.   ᵃ οἴδαμέν we know τ.   ᵇ — λέγων τ.   ᶜ φωνῆσαι TTrA.   ᵈ ἀπ'
from L.   ᵉ ἅπαντες TTrA.   ᶠ συνζητεῖν LTTrA.   ᵍ — πρὸς τ.   ʰ αὐτούς E : ἑαυτοὺς
LTrAW.   ᶦ διδαχὴ καινή a new teaching LTTrA.   ᵏ καὶ ἐξῆλθεν LTTrA.   ᶦ [εὐθὺς] Tr.
ᵐ + πανταχοῦ everywhere τ[Tr]A.   ⁿ εὐθὺς LTTrA.   ᵒ ἐξελθὼν ἦλθεν having gone forth
he came LTr.   ᵖ εὐθὺς LTTrA.   ᑫ — αὐτῆς (read [her] hand) LT[Tr]A.   ʳ — εὐθέως TTr.
ˢ ἔδυσεν LTrA.   ᵗ ἦν ὅλη ἡ πόλις ἐπισυνηγμένη LTTrA.   ᵛ ἔννυχα LTTrA.

ἀπῆλθεν εἰς ἔρημον τόπον, ᵂκἀκεῖ‖ προσηύχετο. 36 καὶ
departed into ²desert ¹a place, and there was praying. And

ˣκατεδίωξαν‖ αὐτὸν ᵞὁ‖ Σίμων καὶ οἱ μετ᾽ αὐτοῦ· 37 καὶ
⁶went ⁷after ⁸him ¹Simon ²and³those ⁴with ⁵him; and

ᶻεὑρόντες αὐτόν‖ λέγουσιν αὐτῷ, "Ὅτι πάντες ᵃζητοῦσίν σε.‖
having found him they say to him, All seek thee.

38 Καὶ λέγει αὐτοῖς,᾽Ἄγωμενᵇ εἰς τὰς ἐχομένας κωμοπόλεις,
And he says to them, Let us go into the neighbouring country towns,

ἵνα ᶜκἀκεῖ‖ κηρύξω· εἰς τοῦτο γὰρ ᵈἐξελήλυθα.‖ 39 Καὶ
that there also I may preach; ²for ³this ¹because have I come forth. And

ᵉἦν‖ κηρύσσων ᶠἐν ταῖς συναγωγαῖς‖ αὐτῶν εἰς ὅλην τὴν Γαλι-
he was preaching in their synagogues in all Ga-

λαίαν, καὶ τὰ δαιμόνια ἐκβάλλων.
lilee, and the demons casting out.

40 Καὶ ἔρχεται πρὸς αὐτὸν λεπρός, παρακαλῶν αὐτὸν ᵍκαὶ
And ²comes ⁴to ⁵him ¹a ²leper, beseeching him and

γονυπετῶν αὐτόν,‖ ʰκαὶ‖ λέγων αὐτῷ, "Ὅτι ἐὰν θέλῃς δύνασαί
kneeling down to him, and saying to him, If thou wilt thou art able

με καθαρίσαι. 41 ⁱὉ δὲ Ἰησοῦς‖ σπλαγχνισθείς, ἐκ-
me to cleanse. And Jesus being moved with compassion, having

τείνας τὴν χεῖρα ᵏἥψατο αὐτοῦ,‖ καὶ λέγει ¹αὐτῷ,‖
stretched out [his] hand he touched him, and says to him,

Θέλω, καθαρίσθητι. 42 Καὶ ᵐεἰπόντος αὐτοῦ,‖ ⁿεὐθέως‖ ἀπῆλ-
I will, be thou cleansed. And he having spoken, immediately depart-

θεν ἀπ᾽ αὐτοῦ ἡ λέπρα, καὶ ᵒἐκαθαρίσθη.‖ 43 Καὶ ἐμβριμησά-
ed from him the leprosy, and he was cleansed. And having strictly

μενος αὐτῷ, ᵖεὐθέως‖ ἐξέβαλεν αὐτόν, 44 καὶ λέγει αὐτῷ,
charged him, immediately he sent away him, And says to him,

"Ὅρα μηδενὶ ᑫμηδὲν‖ εἴπῃς· ʳἀλλ᾽‖ ὕπαγε, σεαυτὸν δεῖξον
See to no one anything thou speak; but go, thyself shew
(lit. nothing)

τῷ ἱερεῖ, καὶ προσένεγκε περὶ τοῦ καθαρισμοῦ σου ἃ προσ-
to the priest, and offer for thy cleansing what ²or-

έταξεν ˢΜωσῆς,‖ εἰς μαρτύριον αὐτοῖς. 45 Ὁ δὲ ἐξελθὼν
dered ¹Moses, for a testimony to them. But he having gone out

ἤρξατο κηρύσσειν πολλὰ καὶ διαφημίζειν τὸν λόγον, ὥστε
began to proclaim [it] much and to spread abroad the matter, so that

μηκέτι αὐτὸν δύνασθαι ᵗφανερῶς εἰς πόλιν‖ εἰσελθεῖν·
no longer he was able openly into [the] city to enter;

ᵛἀλλ᾽‖ ἔξω, ᵂᵃἐν‖ ἐρήμοις τόποις ˣᵃἦν,‖ καὶ ἤρχοντο πρὸς αὐτὸν
but without in desert places was, and they came to him

ᵞᵃπανταχόθεν.‖
from every quarter.

2 Καὶ ᶻᵃπάλιν εἰσῆλθεν‖ εἰς ᵃᵃΚαπερναοὺμ‖ δι᾽ ἡμερῶν,
And again he entered into Capernaum after [some] days,

ᵇᵃκαὶ‖ ἠκούσθη ὅτι ᶜᵃεἰς οἶκόν‖ ἐστιν· 2 καὶ ᵈᵃεὐθέως‖ συνή-
and it was heard that in [the] house he is; and immediately were

χθησαν πολλοί, ὥστε μηκέτι χωρεῖν μηδὲ τὰ
gathered together many, so that there was no longer any room not even

---

into a solitary place,
and there prayed.
36 And Simon and they
that were with him
followed after him.
37 And when they had
found him, they said
unto him, All *men* seek
for thee. 38 And he
said unto them, Let us
go into the next towns,
that I may preach
there also: for there-
fore came I forth.
39 And he preached
in their synagogues
throughout all Gali-
lee, and cast out devils.
40 And there came a
leper to him, beseech-
ing him, and kneeling
down to him, and say-
ing unto him, If thou
wilt, thou canst make
me clean. 41 And Je-
sus, moved with com-
passion, put forth *his*
hand, and touched
him, and saith unto
him, I will; be thou
clean. 42 And as soon
as he had spoken, im-
mediately the leprosy
departed from him,
and he was cleansed.
43 And he straitly
charged him, and
forthwith sent him
away; 44 and saith
unto him, See thou say
nothing to any man:
but go thy way, shew
thyself to the priest,
and offer for thy
cleansing those things
which Moses com-
manded, for a testi-
mony unto them.
45 But he went out,
and began to publish
it much, and to blaze
abroad the matter, in-
somuch that Jesus
could no more openly
enter into the city, but
was without in desert
places: and they came
to him from every
quarter.
II. And again he
entered into Caperna-
um, after *some* days;
and it was noised that
he was in the house.
2 And straightway
many were gathered
together, insomuch
that there was no room
to receive *them*, no,
not so much as about

ᵂ καὶ ἐκεῖ L.   ˣ κατεδίωξεν T.   ᵞ — ὁ T[Tr]A.   ᶻ εὗρον αὐτὸν καὶ found him and TTrA.
ᵃ σὲ ζητοῦσιν LW.   ᵇ + ἀλλαχοῦ elsewhere TTrA.   ᶜ καὶ ἐκεῖ GW.   ᵈ ἐξῆλθον I came forth
TTrA.   ᵉ ἦλθεν he went TTr.   ᶠ εἰς τὰς συναγωγὰς GLTTrAW.   ᵍ — καὶ γονυπετῶν
αὐτὸν L[TrA]; — αὐτόν T.   ʰ — καὶ T[A].   ⁱ καὶ and LTTr.   ᵏ αὐτοῦ ἥψατο LTTrA.
— αὐτῷ T.   ᵐ — εἰπόντος αὐτοῦ LTTr.   ⁿ εὐθὺς TTrA.   ᵒ ἐκαθερίσθη TA.   ᵖ εὐθὺς
LTTrA.   ᑫ — μηδὲν L[Tr].   ʳ ἀλλὰ LTTrAW.   ˢ Μωϋσῆς LTTrAW.   ᵗ εἰς πόλιν φανερῶς T.
ᵛ ἀλλὰ LTrA.   ᵂᵃ ἐπ᾽ TTrA.   ˣᵃ [ἦν] L.   ᵞᵃ πανταχόθεν LTTrAW.   ᶻᵃ εἰσῆλθεν πάλιν LW;
εἰσελθὼν πάλιν he having entered again TTrA.   ᵃᵃ Καφαρναοὺμ LTTrAW.   ᵇᵃ — καὶ
[L]TTrA.   ᶜᵃ ἐν οἴκῳ LTTr.   ᵈᵃ — εὐθέως [LTr]T.

the door: and he preached the word unto them. 3 And they come unto him, bringing one sick of the palsy, which was borne of four. 4 And when they could not come nigh unto him for the press, they uncovered the roof where he was: and when they had broken it up, they let down the bed wherein the sick of the palsy lay. 5 When Jesus saw their faith, he said unto the sick of the palsy, Son, thy sins be forgiven thee. 6 But there were certain of the scribes sitting there, and reasoning in their hearts, 7 Why doth this *man* thus speak blasphemies? who can forgive sins but God only? 8 And immediately when Jesus perceived in his spirit that they so reasoned within themselves, he said unto them, Why reason ye these things in your hearts? 9 Whether is it easier to say to the sick of the palsy, *Thy* sins be forgiven thee; or to say, Arise, and take up thy bed, and walk? 10 But that ye may know that the Son of man hath power on earth to forgive sins, (he saith to the sick of the palsy,) 11 I say unto thee, Arise, and take up thy bed, and go thy way into thine house. 12 And immediately he arose, took up the bed, and went forth before them all; insomuch that they were all amazed, and glorified God, saying, We never saw it on this fashion.

πρὸς τὴν θύραν· καὶ ἐλάλει αὐτοῖς τὸν λόγον. 3 Καὶ ἔρχονται
at the door; and he spoke to them the word. And they come

ᵉπρὸς αὐτόν, παραλυτικὸν φέροντες,‖ αἰρόμενον ὑπὸ τεσσάρων.
to him, ²a ²paralytic ¹bringing, borne by four.

4 καὶ μὴ δυνάμενοι ᶠπροσεγγίσαι‖ αὐτῷ διὰ τὸν ὄχλον,
And not being able to come near to him on account of the crowd,

ἀπεστέγασαν τὴν στέγην ὅπου ἦν, καὶ ἐξορύξαντες χα-
they uncovered the roof where he was, and having broken up [it] they

λῶσιν τὸν ᵍκράββατον‖ ʰἐφ᾽ ᾧ‖ ὁ παραλυτικὸς κατέκειτο.
let down the couch on which the paralytic was lying.

5 ⁱἰδὼν δὲ‖ ὁ Ἰησοῦς τὴν πίστιν αὐτῶν λέγει τῷ παραλυτικῷ,
And ²seeing ¹Jesus their faith says to the paralytic,

Τέκνον, ᵏἀφέωνταί‖ ¹σοι αἱ ἁμαρτίαι σου.‖ 6 Ἦσαν δέ τινες
Child, ³have ²been ⁵forgiven ⁴thee ¹thy ²sins. But there were some

τῶν γραμματέων ἐκεῖ καθήμενοι, καὶ διαλογιζόμενοι ἐν ταῖς
of the scribes ²there ¹sitting, and reasoning in

καρδίαις αὐτῶν, 7 Τί οὗτος οὕτως λαλεῖ ᵐβλασφημίας‖;
their hearts, Why ²this [³man] ⁴thus ¹does ⁵speak blasphemies?

τίς δύναται ἀφιέναι ἁμαρτίας, εἰ μὴ εἷς, ὁ θεός; 8 Καὶ
who is able to forgive sins, except one, [that is] God? And

ⁿεὐθέως‖ ἐπιγνοὺς ὁ Ἰησοῦς τῷ πνεύματι αὐτοῦ ὅτι ᵒοὕτως‖ ᵖ
immediately ²knowing ¹Jesus in his spirit that thus

διαλογίζονται ἐν ἑαυτοῖς, ۹εἶπεν‖ αὐτοῖς, Τί ταῦτα δια-
they are reasoning within themselves, said to them, Why these things rea-

λογίζεσθε ἐν ταῖς καρδίαις ὑμῶν; 9 τί ἐστιν εὐκοπώτερον,
son ye in your hearts? which is easier,

εἰπεῖν τῷ παραλυτικῷ, ʳἈφέωνταί‖ ˢσοι‖ αἱ ἁμαρτίαι,
to say to the paralytic, ³Have ⁴been ²forgiven ⁶thee [¹thy] ⁵sins,

ἢ εἰπεῖν, ᵗἜγειραι,‖ ᵛκαὶ‖ ἆρόν ᵂσου τὸν κράββατον‖ καὶ
or to say, Arise, and take up ¹thy couch and

ˣπεριπάτει‖; 10 ἵνα δὲ εἰδῆτε ὅτι ἐξουσίαν ἔχει ὁ υἱὸς τοῦ
walk? but that ye may know that ⁴authority ⁵has ¹the ²Son

ἀνθρώπου ʸἀφιέναι ἐπὶ τῆς γῆς‖ ἁμαρτίας, λέγει τῷ παρα-
³of ⁴man to forgive on the earth sins,— he says to the para-

λυτικῷ, 11 Σοὶ λέγω, ᶻἔγειραι,‖ ᵃκαὶ‖ ἆρον τὸν ᵍκράββατόν‖
lytic, To thee I say, arise, and take up ²couch

σου καὶ ὕπαγε εἰς τὸν οἶκόν σου. 12 Καὶ ἠγέρθη ᵇεὐθέως, καὶ‖
¹thy and go to thy house. And he arose immediately, and

ἄρας τὸν ᵍκράββατον‖ ἐξῆλθεν ᶜἐναντίον‖ πάντων,
having taken up the couch, went forth before all,

ὥστε ἐξίστασθαι πάντας, καὶ δοξάζειν τὸν θεόν, ᵈλέγοντας,‖
so that ²were ³amazed ¹all, and glorified God, saying,

Ὅτι ᵉᵃοὐδέποτε οὕτως‖ ᶠᵃεἴδομεν.‖
Never thus did we see [it].

13 And he went forth again by the sea side; and all the multitude resorted unto him, and he taught them. 14 And as he passed

13 Καὶ ἐξῆλθεν πάλιν ᵍᵃπαρὰ‖ τὴν θάλασσαν, καὶ πᾶς ὁ
And he went forth again by the sea, and all the

ὄχλος ἤρχετο πρὸς αὐτόν, καὶ ἐδίδασκεν αὐτούς. 14 Καὶ
crowd came to him, and he taught them. And

ᵉ πρὸς αὐτὸν φέροντες παραλυτικὸν LTr; φέροντες πρὸς αὐτὸν παραλυτικὸν TA.   ᶠ προσ-
ενέγκαι to bring near T.   ᵍ κράβαττον LTTrAW.   ʰ ὅπου where LTTrA.   ⁱ καὶ ἰδὼν T.
ᵏ ἀφίενταί are forgiven LTTr.   ¹ σου αἱ ἁμαρτίαι GTT·A; σοι αἱ ἁμαρτίαι [σου] L.
ᵐ; βλασφημεῖ· (read Why does this [man] thus speak? he blasphemes.) LTTrA.   ⁿ εὐθὺς
LTTrA.   ᵒ — οὕτως L.   ᵖ + αὐτοὶ they (are reasoning) ᴳ[ᴀ]ᴡ.   ۹ λέγει says TTrA.
ʳ Ἀφίενταί are forgiven LTTr.   ˢ σου thy (sins) GTTrAW.   ᵗ Ἔγειρε GLTW; Ἐγείρου TrA.
ᵛ — καὶ ᴳ[Tr]AW.   ᵂ τὸν κράββατόν σου LTTrAW.   ˣ ὕπαγε go T.   ʸ ἐπὶ τῆς γῆς ἀφιέναι
GLTTrW.   ᶻ ἔγειρε GLTTrAW.   ᵃ — καὶ ᴳ[L]TTrAW.   ᵇ καὶ εὐθὺς TTrA.   ᶜ ἔμπροσθεν T.
ᵈ — λέγοντας [L]A.   ᵉᵃ οὕτως οὐδέποτε TTrA.   ᶠᵃ εἴδαμεν LTTrA.   ᵍᵃ εἰς τὸ T.

παράγων εἶδεν ʰΛευῒν‖ τὸν   τοῦ Ἀλφαίου καθήμενον ἐπὶ τὸ
passing on he saw Levi the [son] of Alphæus sitting at the

τελώνιον, καὶ λέγει αὐτῷ, Ἀκολούθει μοι. Καὶ ἀναστὰς
tax office, and says to him, Follow me. And having arisen

ἠκολούθησεν αὐτῷ. 15 Καὶ ⁱἐγένετο‖ ᵏἐν.τῷ‖.κατακεῖσθαι.αὐ-
he followed him. And it came to pass as he reclined

τὸν   ἐν τῇ.οἰκίᾳ.αὐτοῦ, καὶ πολλοὶ τελῶναι καὶ ἁμαρτω-
[at table] in his house, that many tax-gatherers and sin-

λοὶ   συνανέκειντο τῷ Ἰησοῦ καὶ τοῖς.μαθηταῖς.αὐτοῦ·
ners were reclining [at table] with Jesus and his disciples;

ἦσαν.γὰρ πολλοί, καὶ ˡἠκολούθησαν‖ αὐτῷ. 16 καὶ ᵐοἱ‖ γραμ-
for they were many, and they followed him. And the . scribes

ματεῖς ⁿκαὶ οἱ Φαρισαῖοι,‖ ᵒ ἰδόντες ᴾαὐτὸν ἐσθίοντα‖ μετὰ
and the Pharisees, having seen him eating with

τῶν ᑫτελωνῶν καὶ ἁμαρτωλῶν,‖ ἔλεγον τοῖς.μαθηταῖς.αὐτοῦ,
the tax-gatherers and sinners, said to his disciples,

ʳΤί‖   ὅτι μετὰ τῶν ˢτελωνῶν καὶ ἁμαρτωλῶν‖ ἐσθίει ᵗκαὶ
Why [is it] that with the tax-gatherers and sinners he eats and

πίνει;‖ 17 Καὶ ἀκούσας ὁ Ἰησοῦς λέγει αὐτοῖς, Οὐ χρείαν
drinks? And ²having ³heard ¹Jesus says to them, ⁶Not ⁷need

ἔχουσιν οἱ ἰσχύοντες ἰατροῦ, ἀλλ' οἱ κακῶς ἔχον-
⁵have ¹they ²who ³are ⁴strong of a physician, but they who ill

τες. οὐκ.ἦλθον καλέσαι δικαίους, ἀλλὰ ἁμαρτωλούς ʳεἰς
are. I came not to call righteous [ones], but sinners to

μετάνοιαν.‖
repentance.

18 Καὶ ἦσαν οἱ μαθηταὶ Ἰωάννου καὶ ʷοἱ τῶν Φαρισαίων‖
And ¹⁰were ¹the ²disciples ³of John ⁵and ⁶those ⁷of ⁸the ⁹Pharisees

νηστεύοντες· καὶ ἔρχονται καὶ λέγουσιν αὐτῷ, ˣΔιατί‖ οἱ μαθη-
fasting; and they come and say to him, Why ²the ³disci-

ταὶ Ἰωάννου καὶ οἱ ʸ τῶν Φαρισαίων νηστεύουσιν, οἱ δὲ σοὶ
ples ⁴of ⁵John ⁶and ⁷those ⁸of ⁹the ¹⁰Pharisees ⁴fast, but thy

μαθηταὶ οὐ.νηστεύουσιν; 19 Καὶ εἶπεν αὐτοῖς ὁ Ἰησοῦς, Μὴ
disciples fast not? And ²said ³to ⁴them ¹Jesus,

δύνανται οἱ υἱοὶ τοῦ νυμφῶνος. ἐν.ᾧ ὁ νυμφίος μετ' αὐτῶν
Can the sons of the bridechamber, while the bridegroom with them

ἐστιν, νηστεύειν; ὅσον.χρόνον ᶻμεθ' ἑαυτῶν ἔχουσιν τὸν νυμ-
is, fast? as long as with them they have the bride-

φίον,‖ οὐ.δύνανται νηστεύειν· 20 ἐλεύσονται.δὲ ἡμέραι ὅταν
groom, they are not able to fast. But will come days when

ἀπαρθῇ   ἀπ' αὐτῶν ὁ νυμφίος, καὶ τότε νη-
will have been taken away from them the bridegroom, and then they

στεύσουσιν ἐν ᵃἐκείναις ταῖς ἡμέραις.‖ 21 ᵇκαὶ‖ οὐδεὶς ἐπίβλημα
will fast in those days. And no one a piece

ᶜῥάκους‖ ἀγνάφου ᵈἐπιῤῥάπτει‖ ἐπὶ ἱματίῳ.παλαιῷ‖· εἰ.δὲ.μή,
of ²cloth ¹unfulled sews on an old garment; otherwise,

αἴρει ᶠ τὸ πλήρωμας ʰᵃαὐτοῦ‖ τὸ καινὸν τοῦ παλαιοῦ, καὶ
²takes ⁵away ¹the ²filling ⁴up ⁵of ⁶it ²new from the old, and

by, he saw Levi the *son* of Alphæus sitting at the receipt of custom, and said unto him, Follow me. And he arose and followed him. 15 And it came to pass, that, as Jesus sat at meat in his house, many publicans and sinners sat also together with Jesus and his disciples: for there were many, and they followed him. 16 And when the scribes and Pharisees saw him eat with publicans and sinners, they said unto his disciples, How is it that he eateth and drinketh with publicans and sinners? 17 When Jesus heard *it*, he saith unto them, They that are whole have no need of the physician, but they that are sick: I came not to call the righteous, but sinners to repentance.

18 And the disciples of John and of the Pharisees used to fast: and they come and say unto him, Why do the disciples of John and of the Pharisees fast, but thy disciples fast not? 19 And Jesus said unto them, Can the children of the bridechamber fast, while the bridegroom is with them? as long as they have the bridegroom with them, they cannot fast. 20 But the days will come, when the bridegroom shall be taken away from them, and then shall they fast in those days. 21 No man also seweth a piece of new cloth on an old garment: else the new piece that filled it up taketh away from the old, and the rent is

ʰ Λευεὶν ᴛᴀ. ⁱ γίνεται it comes to pass ᴛᴛʳᴀ. ᵏ — ἐν τῷ ᴛ[ᴛʳ.] ˡ ἠκολούθουν they were following ᴛᴛʳᴀ. ᵐ — οἱ ᴛ. ⁿ τῶν Φαρισαίων of the Pharisees ᴛᴛʳ. ᵒ + καὶ also [ʟ.]ᴛᴛʳ. ᴾ ὅτι ἐσθίει ʟ ; ὅτι ἤσθιεν that he was eating ᴛᴛʳ. ᑫ ἁμαρτωλῶν καὶ τελωνῶν ʟᴛʳᴀ. ʳ — Τί ᴛᴛʳᴀ. ˢ ἁμαρτωλῶν καὶ τῶν τελωνῶν ʟᴛʳ. ᵗ [καὶ πίνει] ʟ. ᵛ — εἰς μετάνοιαν ɢʟᴛᴛʳᴀᴡ. ʷ οἱ Φαρισαῖοι the Pharisees ɢʟᴛᴛʳᴀᴡ. ˣ Διὰ τί ʟᴛᴛʳᴀ. ʸ + μαθηταὶ (oi the) disciples ᴛᴛʳᴀ. ᶻ ἔχουσιν τὸν νυμφίον μετ' αὐτῶν (μεθ' ἑαυτῶν ʟ) ʟᴛᴛʳᴀ. ᵃ ἐκείνῃ τῇ ἡμέρᾳ that day ɢʟᴛᴛʳᴀᴡ. ᵇ — καὶ ɢʟᴛᴛʳᴀᴡ. ᶜ ῥάκκους ʟ. ᵈ ἐπιράπτει ᴛᴛʳᴀ. ᵉ ἱμάτιον παλαιόν ʟᴛᴛʳᴀ. ᶠ + ἀπ' αὐτοῦ from it ᴀ. ᵍ + ἀπ' from ʟᴛ. ʰᵃ — αὐτοῦ [ᴛʳ]ᴀ.

made worse. 22 And no man putteth new wine into old bottles: else the new wine doth burst the bottles, and the wine is spilled, and the bottles will be marred: but new wine must be put into new bottles.

χεῖρον σχίσμα γίνεται. 22 καὶ οὐδεὶς βάλλει οἶνον νέον εἰς
ʰworse ¹a rent takes place. And no one puts ²wine ʰnew into

ἀσκοὺς παλαιούς· εἰ.δὲ.μή, ᵗῥήσσει" ὁ οἶνος ᵏὸ νέος" τοὺς ἀσ-
²skins ¹old ; otherwise, ⁴bursts ¹the ³wine ²new the skins,

κούς, καὶ ὁ οἶνος ᵗἐκχεῖται καὶ οἱ ἀσκοὶ ἀπολοῦνται·" ᵐἀλλὰ
and the wine is poured out, and the skins will be destroyed ; but

οἶνον νέον εἰς ἀσκοὺς καινοὺς βλητέον."
²wine ¹new ³into ⁵skins ⁴new is to be put.

23 And it came to pass, that he went through the corn fields on the sabbath day; and his disciples began, as they went, to pluck the ears of corn. 24 And the Pharisees said unto him, Behold, why do they on the sabbath day that which is not lawful? 25 And he said unto them, Have ye never read what David did, when he had need, and was an hungred, he, and they that were with him? 26 How he went into the house of God in the days of Abiathar the high priest, and did eat the shewbread, which is not lawful to eat but for the priests, and gave also to them which were with him? 27 And he said unto them, The sabbath was made for man, and not man for the sabbath: 28 therefore the Son of man is Lord also of the sabbath.

23 Καὶ ἐγένετο ⁿπαραπορεύεσθαι.αὐτὸν ἐν τοῖς σάββασιν"
And it came to pass that he went on the sabbath

διὰ τῶν σπορίμων, καὶ ²ἤρξαντο οἱ.μαθηταὶ.αὐτοῦ" ᵖὁδὸν
through the corn-fields, and ²began ¹his ²disciples [their] way

ποιεῖν" τίλλοντες τοὺς στάχυας. 24 καὶ οἱ Φαρισαῖοι ἔλεγον
to make, plucking the ears. And the Pharisees said

αὐτῷ, Ἴδε, τί ποιοῦσιν ᵠἐν" τοῖς σάββασιν ὃ οὐκ.ἔξεστιν;
to him, Behold, why do they on the sabbath that which is not lawful?

25 Καὶ ʳαὐτὸς" ˢἔλεγεν" αὐτοῖς, Οὐδέποτε ἀνέγνωτε τί ἐποίη-
And he said to them, ³Never ¹did ²ye read what ²did

σεν ᵗΔαβίδ," ὅτε χρείαν ἔσχεν καὶ ἐπείνασεν, αὐτὸς καὶ οἱ
¹David, when need he had and hungered, he and those

μετ' αὐτοῦ; 26 ᵛπῶς" εἰσῆλθεν εἰς τὸν οἶκον τοῦ θεοῦ ἐπὶ
with him? how he entered into the house of God in

Ἀβιάθαρ ʷτοῦ" ἀρχιερέως, καὶ τοὺς ἄρτους τῆς
[the days of] Abiathar the high priest, and the loaves of the

προθέσεως ἔφαγεν, οὓς οὐκ.ἔξεστιν φαγεῖν εἰ.μὴ ˣτοῖς ἱερεῦ-
presentation ate, which it is not lawful to eat except for the priests,

σιν," καὶ ἔδωκεν καὶ τοῖς σὺν αὐτῷ οὖσιν; 27 Καὶ ἔλεγεν
and gave even to those who with him were? And he said

αὐτοῖς, Τὸ σάββατον διὰ τὸν ἄνθρωπον ἐγένετο, ʸοὐχ ὁ
to them, The sabbath on account of man was made, not

ἄνθρωπος διὰ τὸ σάββατον· 28 ὥστε κύριός ἐστιν ὁ
man on account of the sabbath: so then Lord is the

υἱὸς τοῦ ἀνθρώπου καὶ τοῦ σαββάτου.
Son of man also of the sabbath.

III. And he entered again into the synagogue; and there was a man there which had a withered hand. 2 And they watched him, whether he would heal him on the sabbath day; that they might accuse him. 3 And he saith unto the man which had the withered hand, Stand forth. 4 And he saith unto them, Is it lawful to do good on the sabbath days, or to do evil? to save life, or to kill? But they held their peace. 5 And when he had looked round about on them with anger, being grieved

3 Καὶ εἰσῆλθεν πάλιν εἰς ᶻτὴν" συναγωγήν, καὶ ᵃἦν" ἐκεῖ
And he entered again into the synagogue, and there was there

ἄνθρωπος ἐξηραμμένην ἔχων τὴν χεῖρα, 2 καὶ ᵇπαρ-
a man ⁴withered ¹having [²his] ³hand, and they

ετήρουν" αὐτὸν εἰ ᶜ τοῖς σάββασιν ᵈθεραπεύσει" αὐτόν,
were watching him whether on the sabbath he will heal him,

ἵνα ᵉκατηγορήσωσιν" αὐτοῦ. 3 καὶ λέγει τῷ ἀνθρώπῳ
in order that they might accuse him. And he says to the man

τῷ ᶠἐξηραμμένην ἔχοντι τὴν χεῖρα," ᵍΕγειραι" εἰς τὸ
who ³withered ¹had ²the hand, Arise [and come] into the

μέσον. 4 Καὶ λέγει αὐτοῖς, Ἔξεστιν τοῖς σάββασιν ʰἀγαθο-
midst. And he says to them, Is it lawful on the sabbaths to do

ποιῆσαι," ἢ κακοποιῆσαι; ψυχὴν σῶσαι, ἢ ἀποκτεῖναι; Οἱ.δὲ
good, or to do evil? ³life ¹to ²save, or to kill? But they

ἐσιώπων. 5 καὶ περιβλεψάμενος αὐτοὺς μετ' ὀργῆς, ᶦᵃσυλ-
were silent. And having looked around on them with anger, being

---

ᶦ ῥήξει will burst LTTrA. ᵏ — ὁ νέος LTTrA. ᶦ ἀπόλλυται καὶ οἱ ἀσκοὶ is destroyed
and the skins TTrA. ᵐ — ἀλλὰ....βλητέον Τ[Tr]A. ⁿ αὐτὸν ἐν τοῖς σάββασιν παρα-
πορεύεσθαι (διαπορεύεσθαι LTr) LTTrA. ᵒ οἱ μαθηταὶ αὐτοῦ ἤρξαντο LTTrA. ᵖ ὁδοποιεῖν L.
ᵠ — ἐν LTTrA. ʳ — αὐτὸς [L]TTr. ˢ λέγει he says LTTr. ᵗ Δαυείδ LTTrA; Δαυὶδ GW.
ᵛ [πῶς] TrA. ʷ — τοῦ LTTrAW. ˣ τοὺς ἱερεῖς T. ʸ + καὶ and TTrA. ᶻ — τὴν (read
[the]) Τ[Tr]A. ᵃ — ἦν (read [was]) L[Tr]. ᵇ παρετηροῦντο L. ᶜ + ἐν on (the) T. ᵈ θεραπεύει he heals T. ᵉ κατηγορήσουσιν they shall accuse LTr. ᶠ τὴν χεῖρα ἔχοντι ξηράν LTrA ;
τὴν ξηρὰν χεῖρα ἔχοντι T. ᵍ Εγειρε GLTTrA. ʰ ἀγαθὸν ποιῆσαι T. ᶦᵃ συνλυπούμενος TA.

λυπούμενος‖ ἐπὶ τῇ πωρώσει τῆς-καρδίας-αὐτῶν, λέγει τῷ
grieved   at the hardness   of their heart,   he says to the

ἀνθρώπῳ, Ἔκτεινον τὴν-χεῖρά.ᵏσου.‖ Καὶ ἐξέτεινεν, καὶ
man,   Stretch out   thy hand.   And he stretched it out [it], and

ˡἀποκατεστάθη‖ ἡ-χεὶρ.αὐτοῦ ᵐὑγιὴς ὡς ἡ ἄλλη.‖ 6 καὶ ἐξελ-
³was restored   ¹his ²hand   sound as the other.   And having

θόντες οἱ Φαρισαῖοι ⁿεὐθέως‖ μετὰ τῶν Ἡρωδιανῶν συμβούλιον
gone out the Pharisees immediately with the Herodians   °counsel

°ἐποίουν‖ κατ' αὐτοῦ, ὅπως αὐτὸν ἀπολέσωσιν.
¹took   against him, how   him they might destroy.

7 Καὶ ὁ Ἰησοῦς ᴾἀνεχώρησεν μετὰ τῶν-μαθητῶν.αὐτοῦ‖ �ۊπρὸς‖
And   Jesus   withdrew   with   his disciples   to

τὴν θάλασσαν· καὶ πολὺ πλῆθος ἀπὸ τῆς Γαλιλαίας
the   sea; '   and ²great ¹a multitude from   Galilee

ʳἠκολούθησαν‖ ˢαὐτῷ,‖ καὶ ἀπὸ τῆς Ἰουδαίας, 8 καὶ ἀπὸ Ἱε-
followed   him,   and from   Judea,   and from Je-

ροσολύμων, καὶ ἀπὸ τῆς Ἰδουμαίας, καὶ πέραν τοῦ Ἰορδάνου·
rusalem,   and from   Idumea,   and beyond the Jordan;

καὶ ᵗοἱ‖ περὶ Τύρον καὶ Σιδῶνα, πλῆθος πολύ, ᵛἀκούσαντες‖
and they around Tyre and Sidon, a ²multitude ¹great, having heard

ὅσα ᵂἐποίει.‖ ἦλθον πρὸς αὐτόν. 9 καὶ εἶπεν τοῖς.μαθη-
how much he was doing came to him.   And he spoke to his dis-

ταῖς.αὐτοῦ, ἵνα πλοιάριον προσκαρτερῇ αὐτῷ διὰ τὸν
ciples,   that a small ship might wait upon him, on account of the

ὄχλον, ἵνα μὴ.θλίβωσιν αὐτόν. 10 πολλοὺς.γὰρ ἐθερά-
crowd, that they might not press upon him   For many   he

πευσεν, ὥστε ἐπιπίπτειν αὐτῷ, ἵνα αὐτοῦ ἅψωνται, ὅσοι
healed, so that they beset him, that him they might touch, as many as

εἶχον μάστιγας· 11 καὶ τὰ πνεύματα τὰ ἀκάθαρτα, ὅταν αὐτὸν
had   scourges;   and   the spirits   the unclean,   when him

ˣἐθεώρει, προσέπιπτεν‖ αὐτῷ, καὶ ʸἔκραζεν‖, ᶻλέγοντα,‖ Ὅτι σὺ
they beheld, fell down before him, and cried,   saying,   Thou

εἶ ὁ υἱὸς τοῦ θεοῦ. 12 Καὶ πολλὰ ἐπετίμα αὐτοῖς, ἵνα μὴ
art the Son of God.   And much he rebuked them, so that ²not

ᵃαὐτὸν φανερὸν‖ ᵇποιήσωσιν‖ ᶜ.
⁵him   ⁶manifest ¹they ²should ⁴make.

13 Καὶ ἀναβαίνει εἰς τὸ ὄρος, καὶ προσκαλεῖται οὓς
And   he goes up into the mountain, and calls to [him] whom

ἤθελεν αὐτός· καὶ ἀπῆλθον πρὸς αὐτόν. 14 καὶ ἐποίησεν
²would ¹he;   and they went   to   him.   And he appointed

δώδεκα ἵνα ὦσιν μετ' αὐτοῦ, καὶ ἵνα ἀποστέλλῃ αὐτοὺς
twelve that they might be with him, and that he might send   them

κηρύσσειν, 15 καὶ ἔχειν ἐξουσίαν ᵈθεραπεύειν τὰς νόσους καὶ‖
to preach,   and to have authority   to heal   diseases   and

ἐκβάλλειν τὰ δαιμόνια. 16 ᵉκαὶ ἐπέθηκεν ᶠτῷ Σίμωνι ὄνομα‖
to cast out demons.   And he added   to Simon [the] name

Πέτρον· 17 καὶ Ἰάκωβον τὸν τοῦ Ζεβεδαίου, καὶ Ἰωάννην
Peter;   and James   the [son] of Zebedee, and   John

τὸν ἀδελφὸν τοῦ Ἰακώβου· καὶ ἐπέθηκεν αὐτοῖς ὀνόματα
the brother of James;   and he added   to them [the] names

---

for the hardness of their hearts, he saith unto the man, Stretch forth thine hand. And he stretched it out: and his hand was restored whole as the other. 6 And the Pharisees went forth, and straightway took counsel with the Herodians against him, how they might destroy him.

7 But Jesus withdrew himself with his disciples to the sea: and a great multitude from Galilee followed him, and from Judæa, 8 and from Jerusalem, and from Idumæa, and from beyond Jordan; and they about Tyre and Sidon, a great multitude, when they had heard what great things he did, came unto him. 9 And he spake to his disciples, that a small ship should wait on him because of the multitude, lest they should throng him. 10 For he had healed many; insomuch that they pressed upon him for to touch him, as many as had plagues. 11 And unclean spirits, when they saw him, fell down before him, and cried, saying, Thou art the Son of God. 12 And he straitly charged them that they should not make him known.

13 And he goeth up into a mountain, and calleth unto him whom he would: and they came unto him. 14 And he ordained twelve, that they should be with him, and that he might send them forth to preach, 15 and to have power to heal sicknesses, and to cast out devils: 16 and Simon he surnamed Peter; 17 and James the son of Zebedee, and John the brother of James; and he surnamed them Boan-

---

ᵏ — σου (read [thy]) hand ᴛ[ᴛʳ]A.   ˡ ἀπεκατεστάθη GLTTʳAW.   ᵐ—ὑγιὴς ὡς ἡ ἄλλη ᴮLTTʳAW.   ⁿ εὐθὺς TTʳA.   ° ἐποίησαν ᴛ; ἐδίδουν gave TʳA.   ᴾ μετὰ τῶν μαθητῶν αὐτοῦ ἀνεχώρησεν GLTTʳA.   ۊ εἰς GLT.   ʳ ἠκολούθησεν LTʳA; ἠκολούθησαν placed after Ἰουδαίας T.   ˢ — αὐτῷ [L]TTʳA.   ᵗ — οἱ [L]TTʳ[A].   ᵛ ἀκούοντες hearing LTTʳA.   ᵂ ποιεῖ he is doing TʳA.   ˣ ἐθεώρουν, προσέπιπτον LTTʳAW.   ʸ ἔκραζον LTTʳAW.   ᶻ λέγοντες T.   ᵃ φανερὸν αὐτὸν GW.   ᵇ ποιῶσιν TTʳA.   ᶜ + [ὅτι ᾔδεισαν τὸν χριστὸν αὐτὸν εἶναι] because they had known him to be the Christ L.   ᵈ — θεραπεύειν τὰς νόσους καὶ TTʳA.   ᵉ + καὶ ἐποίησεν τοὺς δώδεκα, and he appointed the twelve ᴛ.   ᶠ ὄνομα τῷ Σίμωνι TTʳA.

erges, which is, The sons of thunder: 18 and Andrew, and Philip, and Bartholomew, and Matthew, and Thomas, and James the *son* of Alphæus, and Thaddæus, and Simon the Cananite, 19 and Judas Iscariot, which also betrayed him:

ᵍΒοανεργές,‖ ὅ ἐστιν υἱοὶ βροντῆς· 18 καὶ Ἀνδρέαν, καὶ
Boanerges,　which　is　Sons of thunder;　　and Andrew,　and
Φίλιππον, καὶ Βαρθολομαῖον, καὶ ʰΜατθαῖον,‖ καὶ Θωμᾶν,
Philip,　and　Bartholomew,　and　Matthew,　and Thomas,
καὶ Ἰάκωβον τὸν τοῦ Ἀλφαίου, καὶ Θαδδαῖον, καὶ Σίμωνα
and James　the [son]　of Alphæus,　and Thaddæus,　and Simon
τὸν ⁱΚανανίτην,‖ 19 καὶ Ἰούδαν ᵏἸσκαριώτην,‖ ὃς καὶ παρέ-
the　Cananite,　　and Judas　Iscariote,　who also deliver-
δωκεν αὐτόν.
ed up　him.

And they went into an house. 20 And the multitude cometh together again, so that they could not so much as eat bread. 21 And when his friends heard *of it*, they went out to lay hold on him: for they said, He is beside himself. 22 And the scribes which came down from Jerusalem said, He hath Beelzebub, and by the prince of the devils casteth he out devils. 23 And he called them *unto him*, and said unto them in parables, How can Satan cast out Satan? 24 And if a kingdom be divided against itself, that kingdom cannot stand. 25 And if a house be divided against itself, that house cannot stand. 26 And if Satan rise up against himself, and be divided, he cannot stand, but hath an end. 27 No man can enter into a strong man's house, an spoil his goods, except he will first bind the strong man; and then he will spoil his house. 28 Verily I say unto you, All sins shall be forgiven unto the sons of men, and blasphemies wherewith soever they shall blaspheme : 29 but he that shall blaspheme against the Holy Ghost hath never forgiveness, but is in danger of eternal damnation : 30 because they said, He hath an unclean spirit.

Καὶ ˡἔρχονται‖ εἰς οἶκον· 20 καὶ συνέρχεται πάλιν ᵐ ὄχλος,
And they come　to a house:　and comes together again　a crowd,
ὥστε μὴ δύνασθαι αὐτούς, ⁿμήτε‖ ἄρτον φαγεῖν. 21 καὶ ἀκού-
so that　they are not able so much as　bread to eat.　　And having
σαντες οἱ παρ᾽ αὐτοῦ ἐξῆλθον κρατῆσαι αὐτόν·
heard [of it] those belonging to him　went out to lay hold of　him;
ἔλεγον γάρ, Ὅτι ἐξέστη. 22 Καὶ οἱ γραμματεῖς οἱ ἀπὸ
for they said,　He is beside himself.　And the scribes　who from
Ἱεροσολύμων καταβάντες ἔλεγον, Ὅτι Βεελζεβοὺλ ἔχει· καὶ
Jerusalem　came down　said,　Beelzebul　he has; and
Ὅτι ἐν τῷ ἄρχοντι τῶν δαιμονίων ἐκβάλλει τὰ δαιμόνια.
By the prince of the demons he casts out the demons.
23 Καὶ προσκαλεσάμενος αὐτοὺς ἐν παραβολαῖς ἔλεγεν
And　having called to [him] them in　parables　he said
αὐτοῖς, Πῶς δύναται σατανᾶς σατανᾶν ἐκβάλλειν; 24 καὶ
to them, How can Satan　Satan cast out?　and
ἐὰν βασιλεία ἐφ᾽ ἑαυτὴν μερισθῇ, οὐ δύναται σταθῆναι ἡ
if　a kingdom against itself　be divided, is not able to stand
βασιλεία ἐκείνη· 25 καὶ ἐὰν οἰκία ἐφ᾽ ἑαυτὴν μερισθῇ, ᵒοὐ
that kingdom :　and if a house against itself　be divided, not
δύναται‖ ᵖσταθῆναι ἡ οἰκία ἐκείνη· 26 καὶ εἰ ὁ σατανᾶς ἀνέστη
is able to stand　that house :　and if　Satan　has risen up
ἐφ᾽ ἑαυτὸν ᑫκαὶ μεμέρισται,‖ οὐ δύναται ʳσταθῆναι,‖ ἀλλὰ
against himself and has been divided, he is not able　to stand,　but
τέλος ἔχει. 27 ˢοὐ δύναται οὐδεὶς‖ ᵗτὰ σκεύη τοῦ ἰσχυροῦ,
an end has.　No one in any wise is able the goods of the strong man,
εἰσελθὼν εἰς τὴν οἰκίαν αὐτοῦ, διαρπάσαι, ἐὰν μὴ πρῶτον
having entered into　his house,　to plunder,　unless　first
τὸν ἰσχυρὸν δήσῃ, καὶ τότε τὴν οἰκίαν αὐτοῦ διαρπάσει. 28 ἀ-
the strong man he bind, and then　his house　he will plunder.　Ve-
μὴν λέγω ὑμῖν, ὅτι πάντα ἀφεθήσεται ʷτὰ ἁμαρτήματα τοῖς
rily I say to you, that　all　shall be forgiven the　sins　to the
υἱοῖς τῶν ἀνθρώπων,‖ καὶ ˣ βλασφημίαι ʸὅσας‖ ᶻἂν‖ βλασ-
sons　of men,　and　blasphemies　whatsoever　they shall
φημήσωσιν· 29 ὃς δ᾽ ἂν βλασφημήσῃ εἰς τὸ πνεῦμα τὸ
have blasphemed ;　but whosoever shall blaspheme against the Spirit　the
ἅγιον, οὐκ ἔχει ἄφεσιν εἰς τὸν αἰῶνα, ᵃἀλλ᾽‖ ἔνοχός ᵇἐστιν‖
Holy,　has not forgiveness to　eternity,　but　²liable ³to　¹is
αἰωνίου ᶜκρίσεως·‖ 30 ὅτι ἔλεγον, Πνεῦμα ἀκάθαρτον ἔχει
eternal　judgment;　because they said,　An unclean spirit　he has.

ᵍ βοανηργές LTTrA.　ʰ Ματθαῖον LTTrA.　ⁱ Κανανaῖον Canannæan LTTrAW.　ᵏ Ἰσκαριώθ
LTTrAW.　ˡ ἔρχεται he comes T.　ᵐ + ὁ the (crowd) LTrA.　ⁿ μηδὲ LTTrAW.　ᵒ οὐ δυνήσεται
will not be able TTrA.　ᵖ ἡ οἰκία ἐκείνη σταθῆναι (στῆναι TrA) LTTrA.　ᑫ ἐμερίσθη, καὶ he is
divided. and T.　ʳ στῆναι TTrA.　ˢ + ἀλλ᾽ but TTrA.　ᵗ οὐδεὶς δύναται GLTrW.　ᵛ εἰς τὴν
οἰκίαν τοῦ ἰσχυροῦ εἰσελθὼν τὰ σκεύη TTr.　ʷ τοῖς υἱοῖς τῶν ἀνθρώπων τὰ ἁμαρτήματα
GLTTrAW.　ˣ + αἱ the GLTTrAW.　ʸ ὅσα LTTrA.　ᶻ ἐὰν TrA.　ᵃ ἀλλὰ LTTrA.　ᵇ ἔσται
shall be T.　ᶜ ἁμαρτήματος sin (*read* guilty of eternal sin) LTTrA.

31 ᵈἜρχονται.οὖνⁿ ᵉοἱ ἀδελφοὶ καὶ ἡ.μήτηρ.αὐτοῦ,ⁿ καὶ
Then come [his] brethren and his mother, and

ἔξω ᶠἑστῶτεςⁿ ἀπέστειλαν πρὸς αὐτόν, ᵍφωνοῦντεςⁿ αὐτόν.
ᵃwithout ¹standing sent to him, calling him.

32 καὶ ἐκάθητο ʰὄχλος περὶ αὐτόν·ⁿ ⁱεἶπον.δὲⁿ αὐτῷ, Ἰδού,
And ᵃsat ¹a ²crowd around him: and they said to him, Behold,

ἡ.μήτηρ.σου καὶ οἱ.ἀδελφοί.σου ᵏ ἔξω ζητοῦσίν σε. 33 Καὶ
thy mother and thy brethren without seek thee. And

ˡἀπεκρίθη αὐτοῖς, λέγων,ⁿ Τίς ἐστιν ἡ.μήτηρ.μου ᵐἢⁿ οἱ ἀδελ-
he answered them, saying, Who is my mother or ²breth-

φοί ⁿμουⁿ; 34 Καὶ περιβλεψάμενος ᵒκύκλῳ τοὺς περὶ
ren ¹my? And having looked around on ³in ᵃa ¹circuit ¹those ²who around

αὐτὸνⁿ καθημένους, λέγει, ᵖⁿΪδε,ⁿ ἡ.μήτηρ.μου καὶ οἱ ἀδελφοί
him were sitting, he says, Behold, my mother· and ²brethren

μου· 35 ὃς.ᵟγὰρⁿ.ἂν ποιήσῃ ʳτὸ θέλημαⁿ τοῦ θεοῦ, οὗτος ἀδελ-
¹my: for whoever shall do the¹ will of God, he ²bro-

φός μου καὶ ἀδελφή.ˢμουⁿ καὶ μήτηρ ἐστίν.
ther ¹my and my sister and mother is.

4 Καὶ πάλιν ἤρξατο διδάσκειν παρὰ τὴν θάλασσαν· καὶ
And again he began to teach by the sea. And

ᵗσυνήχθηⁿ πρὸς αὐτὸν ὄχλος ᵛπολύς,ⁿ ὥστε αὐτὸν ᵂἐμ-
was gathered together to him a ²crowd ¹great, so that he having

βάντα εἰς τὸ πλοῖονⁿ καθῆσθαι ἐν τῇ θαλάσσῃ, καὶ πᾶς ὁ
entered into the ship sat in the sea, and all the

ὄχλος πρὸς τὴν θάλασσαν ἐπὶ τῆς γῆς ˣἦν.ⁿ 2 καὶ ἐδίδασκεν
crowd close to the sea on the land was. And he taught

αὐτοὺς ἐν παραβολαῖς πολλά, καὶ ἔλεγεν αὐτοῖς ἐν τῇ δι-
them in parables many things, and said to them in ²teach-

δαχῇ.αὐτοῦ, 3 Ἀκούετε· ἰδού, ἐξῆλθεν ὁ σπείρων ʸτοῦⁿ σπεῖραι
ing ¹his, Hearken: behold, went out the sower to sow.

4 καὶ ἐγένετο ἐν.τῷ.σπείρειν, ὃ.μὲν ἔπεσεν παρὰ τὴν ὁδόν,
And it came to pass as he sowed, one fell by the way,

καὶ ἦλθεν τὰ πετεινὰ ᶻτοῦ.οὐρανοῦⁿ καὶ κατέφαγεν αὐτό.
and came the birds of the heaven and devoured it.

5 ᵃἄλλο.δὲⁿ ἔπεσεν ἐπὶ τὸ πετρῶδες, ᵇὅπου οὐκ.εἶχεν γῆν
And another fell upon the rocky place, where it had not ᶜearth

πολλήνⁿ καὶ ᶜεὐθέωςⁿ ἐξανέτειλεν, διὰ τὸ.μὴ.ἔχειν βάθοςᵈᵃ
¹much, and immediately it sprang up, because of not having depth

γῆς· 6 ᵉᵃἡλίου.δὲ ἀνατείλαντοςⁿ ᶠᵃἐκαυματίσθη,ⁿ καὶ διὰ
of earth: and [the] sun having arisen it was scorched, and because of

τὸ.μὴ.ἔχειν ῥίζαν ἐξηράνθη. 7 καὶ ἄλλο ἔπεσεν εἰς ᵍᵃτὰςⁿ
not having root it withered away. And another fell among the

ἀκάνθας· καὶ ἀνέβησαν αἱ ἄκανθαι, καὶ συνέπνιξαν αὐτό, καὶ
thorns, and ³grew ᵃup ¹the ¹²thorns, and choked it, and

καρπὸν οὐκ.ἔδωκεν. 8 καὶ ʰᵃἄλλοⁿ ἔπεσεν εἰς τὴν γῆν τὴν
fruit it yielded not. And another fell into the ground the

---

31 There came then his brethren and his mother, and, standing without, sent unto him, calling him. 32 And the multitude sat about him, and they said unto him, Behold, thy mother and thy brethren without seek for thee. 33 And he answered them, saying, Who is my mother, or my brethren? 34 And he looked round about on them which sat about him, and said, Behold my mother and my brethren! 35 For whosoever shall do the will of God, the same is my brother, and my sister, and mother.

IV. And he began again to teach by the sea side: and there was gathered unto him a great multitude, so that he entered into a ship, and sat in the sea; and the whole multitude was by the sea on the land. 2 And he taught them many things by parables, and said unto them in his doctrine, 3 Hearken; Behold, there went out a sower to sow: 4 And it came to pass, as he sowed, some fell by the way side, and the fowls of the air came and devoured it up. 5 And some fell on stony ground, where it had not much earth; and immediately it sprang up, because it had no depth of earth: 6 but when the sun was up, it was scorched; and because it had no root, it withered away. 7 And some fell among thorns, and the thorns grew up, and choked it, and it yielded no fruit. 8 And other fell on good ground, and did yield

---

ᵈ καὶ ἔρχονται LTTrAW; καὶ ἔρχεται T. ᵉ ἡ μήτηρ αὐτοῦ καὶ οἱ ἀδελφοὶ αὐτοῦ GLTTrW; οἱ ἀδελφοὶ αὐτοῦ καὶ ἡ μήτηρ αὐτοῦ A. ᶠ στήκοντες TTrA. ᵍ καλοῦντες LTTrA. ʰ περὶ αὐτὸν ὄχλος LTTrAW. ⁱ καὶ λέγουσιν and they say LTTrAW. ᵏ + καὶ αἱ (— αἱ w) ἀδελφαί σου and thy sisters LT[A]w. ˡ ἀποκριθεὶς αὐτοῖς λέγει answering them he says TTrA. ᵐ καὶ and LTTr. ⁿ — μου [Tr]A. ᵒ τοὺς περὶ αὐτὸν κύκλῳ LTTr. ᵖ Ἰδοὺ L. ᵟ — γὰρ for LT [Tr]A. ʳ τὰ θελήματα (read the things God wills) A. ˢ — μου my LTTrA. ᵗ συνάγεται is gathered together LTTrAW. ᵛ πλεῖστος very great TTrAW. ᵂ εἰς τὸ (— τὸ TTrW) πλοῖον ἐμβάντα LTTrW. ˣ ἦσαν were TTrA. ʸ — τοῦ LT[Tr]A. ᶻ — τοῦ οὐρανοῦ GLTTrAW. ᵃ καὶ ἄλλο LTTrA. ᵇ + καὶ and [LTr]A. ᶜ εὐθὺς LTTrA. ᵈᵃ + τῆς L. ᵉᵃ καὶ ὅτε ἀνέτειλεν ὁ ἥλιος and when the sun was risen LTTrA. ᶠᵃ ἐκαυματίσθησαν they were scorched Tr. ᵍᵃ — τὰς G. ʰᵃ ἄλλα others TA.

fruit that sprang up and increased; and brought forth, some thirty, and some sixty, and some an hundred. 9 And he said unto them, He that hath ears to hear, let him hear. 10 And when he was alone, they that were about him with the twelve asked of him the parable. 11 And he said unto them, Unto you it is given to know the mystery of the kingdom of God: but unto them that are without, all these things are done in parables: 12 that seeing they may see, and not perceive; and hearing they may hear, and not understand; lest at any time they should be converted, and their sins should be forgiven them. 13 And he said unto them, Know ye not this parable? and how then will ye know all parables? 14 The sower soweth the word. 15 And these are they by the way side, where the word is sown; but when they have heard, Satan cometh immediately, and taketh away the word that was sown in their hearts. 16 And these are they likewise which are sown on stony ground; who, when they have heard the word, immediately receive it with gladness; 17 and have no root in themselves, and so endure but for a time: afterward, when affliction or persecution ariseth for the word's sake, immediately they are offended. 18 And these are they which are sown among thorns; such as hear the word, 19 and the cares of this world, and the deceitfulness of riches, and the lusts of other things entering in, choke the word, and it becometh unfruitful. 20 And these are they, which are sown on good ground; such as

καλήν· καὶ ἐδίδου καρπὸν ἀναβαίνοντα καὶ ¹αὐξάνοντα,‖ καὶ
good, and yielded fruit, growing up and increasing, and
ἔφερεν ᵏἐν‖ τριάκοντα, καὶ ᵏἐν‖ ἑξήκοντα, καὶ ᵏἐν‖ ἑκατόν.
bore one thirty, and one sixty, and one a hundred.
9 Καὶ ἔλεγεν ¹αὐτοῖς,‖ ᵐὉ ἔχων‖ ὦτα ἀκούειν ἀκουέτω.
And he said to them, He that has ears to hear let him hear.
10 ⁿΌτε δὲ‖ ἐγένετο ᵒκαταμόνας,‖ Ρἠρώτησαν‖ αὐτὸν οἱ · περὶ
And when he was alone, ⁷asked ⁸him ¹those ²about
αὐτὸν σὺν τοῖς δώδεκα �q τὴν παραβολήν.‖ 11 καὶ ἔλεγεν
⁴him ⁴with ⁵the ⁶twelve [as to] the parable. And he said
αὐτοῖς· Ὑμῖν ʳδέδοται γνῶναι τὸ μυστήριον‖ τῆς βασιλείας
to them, To you has been given to know the mystery of the kingdom
τοῦ θεοῦ· ἐκείνοις δὲ τοῖς ἔξω, ἐν παραβολαῖς ˢτὰ‖ πάντα
of God: but to those who are without, in parables all things
γίνεται· 12 ἵνα βλέποντες βλέπωσιν, καὶ μὴ ἴδωσιν· καὶ
are done, that seeing they may see, and not perceive; and
ἀκούοντες ἀκούωσιν, καὶ μὴ συνιῶσιν· μήποτε ἐπιστρέψω-
hearing they may hear, and not understand, lest they should be con-
σιν, καὶ ἀφεθῇ αὐτοῖς ᵗτὰ ἁμαρτήματα.‖ 13 Καὶ
verted, and ⁵should ⁶be ⁵forgiven ᵉthem [¹their] ²sins. And
λέγει αὐτοῖς, Οὐκ οἴδατε τὴν παραβολὴν ταύτην; καὶ πῶς
he says to them, Perceive ye not this parable? and how
πάσας τὰς παραβολὰς γνώσεσθε; 14 ὁ σπείρων τὸν λόγον
all the parables will ye know? The sower the word
σπείρει. 15 οὗτοι δέ εἰσιν οἱ παρὰ τὴ· ὁδόν, ὅπου σπείρεται
sows. And these are they by the way, where is sown
ὁ λόγος, καὶ ὅταν ἀκούσωσιν, ᵛεὐθέως‖ ἔρχεται ὁ σατανᾶς
the word, and when they hear, immediately comes Satan
καὶ αἴρει τὸν λόγον τὸν ἐσπαρμένον ʷἐν ταῖς καρδίαις αὐ-
and takes away the word that has been sown in their hearts.
τῶν.‖ 16 καὶ οὗτοί ˣεἰσιν ὁμοίως‖ οἱ ἐπὶ τὰ πετρώδη
And these are in like manner they who upon the rocky places
σπειρόμενοι, οἵ, ὅταν ἀκούσωσιν τὸν λόγον, ˢεὐθέως‖ μετὰ
are sown, who, when they hear the word, immediately with
χαρᾶς λαμβάνουσιν αὐτόν, 17 καὶ οὐκ ἔχουσιν ῥίζαν ἐν ἑαυ-
joy receive it, and have not root in them-
τοῖς, ἀλλὰ πρόσκαιροί εἰσιν· εἶτα γενομένης θλίψεως ἢ
selves, but temporary are; then having arisen tribulation or
διωγμοῦ διὰ τὸν λόγον, ᵛεὐθέως‖ σκανδαλίζονται. 18 καὶ
persecution on account of the word, immediately they are offended. And
ᶻοὗτοί‖ εἰσιν οἱ ᵃεἰς‖ τὰς ἀκάνθας σπειρόμενοι, οὗτοί
these are they who among the thorns are sown, these
εἰσιν οἱ τὸν λόγον ᵇἀκούοντες,‖ 19 καὶ αἱ μέριμναι τοῦ
are they who the word hear, and the cares
αἰῶνος ᶜτούτου‖ καὶ ἡ ἀπάτη τοῦ πλούτου καὶ αἱ περὶ
of this life and the deceit of riches and the ᶻof
τὰ λοιπὰ ἐπιθυμίαι εἰσπορευόμεναι ᵈσυμπνίγουσιν‖ τὸν λόγον,
⁵other ⁴things ¹desires entering in choke the word,
καὶ ἄκαρπος γίνεται. 20 καὶ ᵉοὗτοί‖ εἰσιν οἱ ἐπὶ τὴν γῆν
and unfruitful it becomes. And these are they who upon the ground

---

¹ αὐξανόμενον LTTrAW.   ᵏ εἷς A; εἰς unto TTr.   ¹ — αὐτοῖς GLTTrAW.   ᵐ ὃς ἔχει LTTrAW.
ⁿ καὶ ὅτε LTTrA.   ᵒ κατὰ μόνας LTTr.   Ρ ἠρώτων LTrA; ἠρώτουν T.   q τὰς παραβολάς
the parables TTrA.   ʳ — γνῶναι LTTrA; τὸ μυστήριον δέδοται TTrA.   ˢ — τὰ T.   ᵗ — τὰ
ἁμαρτήματα (read [their sins]) [L]TTrA.   ᵛ εὐθὺς TTrA.   ʷ ἐν αὐτοῖς in them T; εἰς αὐτούς
in them TrA.   ˣ ὁμοίως εἰσὶν T.   ʸ εὐθὺς LTTrA.   ᶻ ἄλλοι others GLTTrAW.   ᵃ ἐπὶ about T.
ᵇ ἀκούσαντες heard TTrA.   ᶜ — τούτου this GLTTrA.   ᵈ συνπνίγουσιν TA   ᵉ ἐκεῖνοί
those TTrA.

τὴν καλὴν σπαρέντες, οἵτινες ἀκούουσιν τὸν λόγον καὶ
the good have been sown, such as hear the word and

παραδέχονται, καὶ καρποφοροῦσιν, ᶠἐν᛬ τριάκοντα, καὶ ᶠἐν᛬
receive [it], and bring forth fruit, one thirty, and one

ἑξήκοντα, καὶ ᶠἐν᛬ ἑκατόν. 21 Καὶ ἔλεγεν αὐτοῖς, ᵍΜήτι ʰὁ
sixty, and one a hundred. And he said to them, ᵘThe

λύχνος ἔρχεται᛬ ἵνα ὑπὸ τὸν μόδιον τεθῇ ἢ ὑπὸ τὴν
ᵃlamp ᶜcomes that under the corn measure it may be put or under the

κλίνην; οὐχ ἵνα ἐπὶ τὴν λυχνίαν ⁱἐπιτεθῇ᛬; 22 οὐ.γάρ
couch? [Is it] not that upon the lampstand it may be put? for not

ἐστιν ᵏτι᛬ κρυπτόν, ˡὃ᛬ ἐὰν.μὴ ᵐ φανερωθῇ· οὐδὲ
ᶻis ᵃanything hidden, unless it should be made manifest, nor

ἐγένετο ἀπόκρυφον, ἀλλ᾽ ἵνα ⁿεἰς φανερὸν ἔλθη.᛬-
has taken ᵖplace ᴵᵃ ᵃsecret ᵃthing, but that to light it should come.

23 εἴτις ἔχει ὦτα ἀκούειν, ἀκουέτω. 24 Καὶ ἔλεγεν αὐτοῖς,
If anyone has ears to hear, let him hear. And he said to them,

Βλέπετε τί ἀκούετε. ἐν ᾧ μέτρῳ μετρεῖτε μετρηθήσεται
Take heed what ye hear: with what measure ye mete it shall be measured

ὑμῖν, ᵒκαὶ προστεθήσεται ὑμῖν ᵖτοῖς ἀκούουσιν.᛬ 25 ὃς.γὰρ ᑫἂν᛬
to you, and ᴵshall ᵉbe ᵃadded ᴵto ᵃyou ᵃwho ᴵhear; for whoever

ἔχῃ,᛬ δοθήσεται αὐτῷ· καὶ ὃς οὐκ.ἔχει, καὶ ὃ ἔχει
may have, ᵃshall ᵇbe ᵍgiven ᴵto ᵃhim; and he who has not, even that which he has

ἀρθήσεται ἀπ᾽ αὐτοῦ.
shall be taken from him.

26 Καὶ ἔλεγεν, Οὕτως ἐστὶν ἡ βασιλεία τοῦ θεοῦ, ὡς ʳἐὰν᛬
And he said, Thus is the kingdom of God, as᛬ if

ἄνθρωπος βάλῃ τὸν σπόρον ἐπὶ τῆς γῆς, 27 καὶ καθεύδῃ
a man should cast the seed upon the earth, and should sleep

καὶ ἐγείρηται νύκτα καὶ ἡμέραν, καὶ ὁ σπόρος ˢβλαστάνῃ᛬
and rise night and day, and the seed should sprout

καὶ μηκύνηται ὡς οὐκ.οἶδεν αὐτός· 28 αὐτομάτη ᵗγὰρ᛬ ἡ γῆ
and be lengthened how ²knows ³not ¹he; ³of ²itself ¹for the earth

καρποφορεῖ, πρῶτον χόρτον, ᵛεἶτα᛬ στάχυν, ᵛεἶτα᛬ ʷπλήρη
brings forth fruit, first a blade, then an ear, then full

σῖτον᛬ ἐν τῷ στάχυϊ. 29 ὅταν.δὲ ˣπαραδῷ᛬ ὁ καρπός,
corn in the ear. And when ³offers ²itself ¹the ²fruit,

ᵞεὐθέως᛬ ἀποστέλλει τὸ δρέπανον, ὅτι παρέστηκεν ὁ θερισμός.
ᴵimmediately he sends the sickle, for has come the harvest.

30 Καὶ ἔλεγεν, ᶻΤίνι᛬ ὁμοιώσωμεν τὴν βασιλείαν τοῦ θεοῦ;
And he said, To what shall we liken the kingdom of God?

ἢ ἐν ᵃποίᾳ παραβολῇ παραβάλωμεν αὐτήν;᛬ 31 ὡς ᵇκόκκῳ᛬
or with what parable shall we compare it? As to a grain

σινάπεως, ὅς, ὅταν σπαρῇ ἐπὶ τῆς γῆς, ᶜμικρότερος᛬
of mustard, which, when it has been sown upon the earth, less

πάντων τῶν σπερμάτων ᵈἐστὶν᛬ ᵉτῶν᛬ ἐπὶ ᵗτῆς γῆς·᛬ 32 καὶ
than all the seeds is which [are] upon the earth, and

ὅταν σπαρῇ, ἀναβαίνει, καὶ γίνεται ᶠπάντων τῶν λαχάνων
when it has been sown, it grows up, and becomes ²than ³all ⁴the ⁵herbs

μείζων,᛬ καὶ ποιεῖ κλάδους μεγάλους, ὥστε δύνασθαι ὑπὸ
ᴵgreater, and produces ²branches ¹great, so that ⁶are ⁷able ¹under

hear the word, and receive *it*, and bring forth fruit, some thirtyfold, some sixty, and some an hundred. 21 And he said unto them, Is a candle brought to be put under a bushel, or under a bed? and not to be set on a candlestick? 22 for there is nothing hid, which shall not be manifested; neither was any thing kept secret, but that it should come abroad. 23 If any man have ears to hear, let him hear. 24 And he said unto them, Take heed what ye hear: with what measure ye mete, it shall be measured to you: and unto you that hear shall more be given. 25 For he that hath, to him shall be given: and he that hath not, from him shall be taken even that which he hath.

26. And he said, So is the kingdom of God, as if a man should cast seed into the ground; 27 and should sleep, and rise night and day, and the seed should spring and grow up, he knoweth not how. 28 For the earth bringeth forth fruit of herself; first the blade, then the ear, after that the full corn in the ear. 29 But when the fruit is brought forth, immediately he putteth in the sickle, because the harvest is come.

30 And he said, Whereunto shall we liken the kingdom of God? or with what comparison shall we compare it? 31 *It is* like a grain of mustard seed, which, when it is sown in the earth, is less than all the seeds that be in the earth: 32 but when it is sown, it groweth up, and becometh greater than all herbs, and shooteth out great branches; so that the

ᶠ ἐν in TTr. ᵍ + ὅτι that TA. ʰ ἔρχεται ὁ λύχνος LTTrA. ⁱ τεθῇ LTTrAW. ᵏ — τι
(read it is not) [L]Tr[A]. ˡ — ὃ LTTrA. ᵐ + ἵνα that LT[A]. ⁿ ἔλθῃ εἰς φανερόν TTrA.
ᵒ — καὶ προσ. ὑμῖν G. ᵖ — τοῖς ἀκούουσιν GLTTrA. ᑫ ἔχει has LTTrA. ʳ — ἐὰν TTrA.
ˢ βλαστᾷ LTTrA. ᵗ — γὰρ LTTrA. ᵛ εἶτεν T. ʷ πλήρης σῖτος LTTrA. ˣ παραδοῖ LTTrA.
ᵞ εὐθὺς TTrA. ᶻ Πῶς how TTrA. ᵃ τίνι αὐτὴν παραβολῇ θῶμεν what parable shall we
represent it? LTTrA. ᵇ κόκκον a grain GLTrAW. ᶜ μικρότερον ὂν being less LTTrA.
ᵈ — ἐστὶν LTTrA. ᵉ [τῶν ἐπὶ τῆς γῆς] L. ᶠ μείζων (μεῖζον T) πάντων τῶν λαχάνων LTTrA.

fowls of the air may lodge under the shadow of it. 33 And with many such parables spake he the word unto them, as they were able to hear it. 34 But without a parable spake he not unto them : and when they were alone, he expounded all things to his disciples.

τὴν σκιὰν αὐτοῦ τὰ πετεινὰ τοῦ οὐρανοῦ κατασκηνοῦν.
²the ³shadow ⁴of ⁵it the birds of the heaven to roost.
33 Καὶ τοιαύταις παραβολαῖς πολλαῖς ἐλάλει αὐτοῖς τὸν
And with ²such ²parables ¹many he spoke to them the
λόγον, καθὼς ᵍἠδύναντο‖ ἀκούειν, 34 χωρὶς.δὲ παραβολῆς
word, as they were able to hear, but without a parable
οὐκ.ἐλάλει αὐτοῖς· κατ'.ἰδίαν.δὲ ʰτοῖς.μαθηταῖς.αὐτοῦ‖ ἐπέλυεν
spoke he not to them ; and apart to his disciples he explained
πάντα.
all things.

35 And the same day, when the even was come, he saith unto them, Let us pass over unto the other side. 36 And when they had sent away the multitude, they took him even as he was in the ship. And there were also with him other little ships. 37 And there arose a great storm of wind, and the waves beat into the ship, so that it was now full. 38 And he was in the hinder part of the ship, asleep on a pillow : and they awake him, and say unto him, Master, carest thou not that we perish? 39 And he arose, and rebuked the wind, and said unto the sea, Peace, be still. And the wind ceased, and there was a great calm. 40 And he said unto them, Why are ye so fearful? how is it that ye have no faith? 41 And they feared exceedingly, and said one to another, What manner of man is this, that even the wind and the sea obey him?

35 Καὶ λέγει αὐτοῖς ἐν ἐκείνῃ τῇ.ἡμέρᾳ, ὀψίας γενομένης,
And he says to them on that day, evening being come,
Διέλθωμεν εἰς τὸ πέραν. 36 Καὶ ἀφέντες τὸν ὄχλον,
Let us pass over to the other side. And having dismissed the crowd,
παραλαμβάνουσιν αὐτὸν ὡς ἦν ἐν τῷ πλοίῳ· καὶ ἄλλα
they take with [them] him as he was in the ship ; ²also ³other
ⁱδὲ‖ ᵏπλοιάρια‖ ˡἦν‖ μετ' αὐτοῦ. 37 καὶ γίνεται λαῖλαψ
¹but small ships were with him. And comes a ²storm
ᵐἀνέμου μεγάλη,‖ ⁿτὰ.δὲ‖ κύματα ἐπέβαλλεν εἰς τὸ πλοῖον,
³of ⁴wind ⁵violent, and the waves beat into the ship,
ὥστε ᵒαὐτὸ ἤδη γεμίζεσθαι.‖ 38 καὶ ἦν αὐτὸς ᴾἐπὶ‖ τῇ πρύ-
so that it already was filled. And ²was ¹he on the stern
μνῃ ἐπὶ τὸ προσκεφάλαιον καθεύδων· καὶ ᑫδιεγείρουσιν‖
on the cushion sleeping. And they arouse
αὐτόν, καὶ λέγουσιν αὐτῷ, Διδάσκαλε, οὐ.μέλει σοι ὅτι
him, and say to him, Teacher, is it no concern to thee that
ἀπολλύμεθα; 39 Καὶ διεγερθεὶς ἐπετίμησεν τῷ ἀνέμῳ,
we perish? And having been aroused he rebuked the wind,
καὶ εἶπεν τῇ θαλάσσῃ, Σιώπα, πεφίμωσο. Καὶ ἐκόπασεν ὁ
and said to the sea, Silence, be quiet. And ²fell ¹the
ἄνεμος, καὶ ἐγένετο γαλήνη μεγάλη. 40 καὶ εἶπεν αὐτοῖς,
²wind, and there was a ²calm ¹great. And he said to them,
Τί δειλοί ἐστε ʳοὕτως; πῶς οὐκ ἔχετε πίστιν; 41 Καὶ ἐφο-
Why fearful are ye thus? How ²not ¹have ³ye faith? And they
βήθησαν φόβον μέγαν, καὶ ἔλεγον πρὸς.ἀλλήλους, Τίς
feared [with] ²fear ¹great, and said one to another, Who
ἄρα οὗτός ἐστιν, ὅτι καὶ ὁ ἄνεμος καὶ ἡ θάλασσα ˢὑπακούου-
then ²this ¹is, that even the wind and the sea obey
σιν αὐτῷ‖;
him?

V. And they came over unto the other side of the sea, into the country of the Gadarenes. 2 And when he was come out of the ship, immediately there met him out of the tombs a man with an unclean spirit, 3 who had his dwelling among the tombs ; and no man could bind him, no, not with chains :

5 Καὶ ἦλθον εἰς τὸ πέραν τῆς θαλάσσης, εἰς τὴν χώραν
And they came to the other side of the sea, to the country
τῶν ᵗΓαδαρηνῶν.‖ 2 καὶ ᵘἐξελθόντι.αὐτῷ‖ ἐκ τοῦ πλοίου,
of the Gadarenes. And on his having gone forth out of the ship,
ᵛεὐθέως‖ ʷἀπήντησεν‖ αὐτῷ ἐκ τῶν μνημείων ἄνθρωπος
immediately met him out of the tombs a man
ἐν πνεύματι.ἀκαθάρτῳ, 3 ὃς τὴν κατοίκησιν εἶχεν ἐν τοῖς
with an unclean spirit, who [his] dwelling had in the
ˣμνημείοις·‖ καὶ ʸοὔτε‖ ᶻἀλύσεσιν‖ ᵃ οὐδεὶς ᵇἠδύνατο‖ αὐτὸν
tombs ; and not even with chains anyone was able him
(lit. no one)

ᵍ ἐδύναντο LTr.   ʰ τοῖς ἰδίοις μαθηταῖς to his own disciples TA.   ⁱ — δὲ LTr[A].   ᵏ πλοῖα ships GLTTrA.   ˡ ἦσαν T.   ᵐ μεγάλη ἀνέμου LTTrA.   ⁿ καὶ τὰ LTTrA.   ᵒ ἤδη γεμίζεσθαι τὸ πλοῖον already was filled the ship LTTrA.   ᴾ ἐν in GLTTrAW.   ᑫ ἐγείρουσιν they awake TTrA.   ʳ ; οὔπω ¹not ²yet LTr.   ˢ αὐτῷ ὑπακούει T ; ὑπακούει αὐτῷ TrA.   ᵗ Γερασηνῶν Gerasenes LTTr ; Γεργεσηνῶν Gergesenes A.   ᵘ ἐξελθόντος αὐτοῦ LTTr.   ᵛ — εὐθέως L ; εὐθὺς T[TrA].   ʷ ὑπήντησεν LTTr.   ˣ μνήμασιν (— ν GW) GLTTrAW.   ʸ οὐδὲ LTTrA.   ᶻ ἀλύσει with a chain LTTrA.   ᵃ οὐκέτι any longer (lit. no longer) LTTrAW.   ᵇ ἐδύνατο LTTrA.

δῆσαι, 4 διὰ τὸ αὐτὸν πολλάκις πέδαις καὶ ἀλύσεσιν δε-
to bind, because that he often with fetters and chains had

δέσθαι, καὶ διεσπᾶσθαι ὑπ' αὐτοῦ τὰς ἀλύσεις, καὶ
been bound, and ³had ⁴been ⁵torn ⁶asunder ⁷by ⁸him ¹the ²chains, and

τὰς πέδας συντετρίφθαι, καὶ οὐδεὶς ᶜαὐτὸν ἴσχυεν‖ δαμάσαι·
the ⁷fetters had been shattered, and no one him was able to subdue.

5 καὶ ᵈδιαπαντὸς‖ νυκτὸς καὶ ἡμέρας ἐν τοῖς ᵉὄρεσιν καὶ ἐν
And continually night and day in the mountains and in

τοῖς μνήμασιν‖ ἦν κράζων καὶ κατακόπτων ἑαυτὸν λίθοις.
the tombs he was crying and cutting himself with stones.

6 ᶠἸδὼν δὲ‖ τὸν Ἰησοῦν ἀπὸ μακρόθεν, ἔδραμεν καὶ προσ-
And having seen Jesus from afar, he ran and did

εκύνησεν ᵍαὐτῷ,‖ 7 καὶ κράξας φωνῇ μεγάλῃ ʰεῖπεν,‖ Τί ἐμοὶ
homage to him, and crying with a ²voice ¹loud he said, What to me

καὶ σοί, Ἰησοῦ, υἱὲ τοῦ θεοῦ τοῦ ὑψίστου; ὁρκίζω σε τὸν
and to thee, Jesus, Son of God the Most High? I adjure thee

θεόν, μή με βασανίσῃς. 8 ἔλεγεν.γὰρ αὐτῷ, Ἔξελθε, τὸ
by God, ²not ¹me torment. For he was saying to him, Come forth, the

πνεῦμα τὸ ἀκάθαρτον, ἐκ τοῦ ἀνθρώπου. 9 Καὶ ἐπηρώτα
spirit the unclean, out of the man. And he asked

αὐτόν, Τί ⁱσοι.ὄνομα‖; Καὶ ᵏἀπεκρίθη. λέγων,‖ ¹Λεγεὼν‖
him, What [is] thy name? And he answered, saying, Legion

ὄνομά.μοι, ᵐ ὅτι πολλοί ἐσμεν. 10 Καὶ παρεκάλει αὐτὸν
my name [is], because many we are. And he besought him

πολλά, ἵνα μὴ ⁿαὐτοὺς‖ ἀποστείλῃ ἔξω τῆς χώρας. 11 ἦν.δὲ
much, that not them he would send out of the country. Now there was

ἐκεῖ πρὸς ᵒτὰ ὄρη‖ ἀγέλη χοίρων μεγάλη βοσκομένη· 12 καὶ
there just at the mountains a ²herd ³of ⁴swine ¹great feeding; and

παρεκάλεσαν αὐτὸν ᵖπάντες οἱ δαίμονες,‖ λέγοντες, Πέμψον
⁴besought ⁵him ¹all ²the ³demons, saying, Send

ἡμᾶς εἰς τοὺς χοίρους, ἵνα εἰς αὐτοὺς εἰσέλθωμεν. 13 Καὶ
us into the swine, that into them we may enter. And

ἐπέτρεψεν αὐτοῖς ᑫεὐθέως ὁ Ἰησοῦς.‖ καὶ ἐξελθόντα τὰ
²allowed ³them ¹immediately ¹Jesus. And having gone out the

πνεύματα τὰ ἀκάθαρτα εἰσῆλθον εἰς τοὺς χοίρους· καὶ ὥρμησεν
spirits the unclean entered into the swine, and ³rushed

ἡ ἀγέλη κατὰ τοῦ κρημνοῦ εἰς τὴν θάλασσαν· ʳἦσαν δὲ‖
¹the ²herd down the steep into the sea, (now they were

ὡς δισχίλιοι· καὶ ἐπνίγοντο ἐν τῇ θαλάσσῃ. 14 ˢΟἱ.δὲ‖
about two thousand), and they were choked in the sea. And those who

βόσκοντες ᵗτοὺς χοίρους‖ ἔφυγον, καὶ ᵛἀνήγγειλαν‖ εἰς τὴν
fed the swine fled, and announced [it] to the

πόλιν καὶ εἰς τοὺς ἀγρούς. καὶ ʷἐξῆλθον‖ ἰδεῖν τί ἐστιν τὸ
city and to the country. And they went out to see what it is that

γεγονός· 15 καὶ ἔρχονται πρὸς τὸν Ἰησοῦν, καὶ θεωροῦσιν
has been done. And they come to Jesus, and see

τὸν δαιμονιζόμενον καθήμενον ˣκαὶ‖ ἱματισμένον καὶ σωφρο-
the possessed by demons sitting and clothed and of sound

νοῦντα, τὸν.ἐσχηκότα τὸν ʸλεγεῶνα·‖ καὶ ἐφοβήθησαν. 16 καὶ
mind, him who had the legion: and they were afraid. And

---

4 because that he had been often bound with fetters and chains, and the chains had been plucked asunder by him, and the fetters broken in pieces: neither could any man tame him. 5 And always, night and day, he was in the mountains, and in the tombs, crying, and cutting himself with stones. 6 But when he saw Jesus afar off, he ran and worshipped him, 7 and cried with a loud voice, and said, What have I to do with thee, Jesus, *thou* Son of the most high God? I adjure thee by God, that thou torment me not. 8 For he said unto him, Come out of the man, *thou* unclean spirit. 9 And he asked him, What *is* thy name? And he answered, saying, My name *is* Legion: for we are many. 10 And he besought him much that he would not send them away out of the country. 11 Now there was there nigh unto the mountains a great herd of swine feeding. 12 And all the devils besought him, saying, Send us into the swine, that we may enter into them. 13 And forthwith Jesus gave them leave. And the unclean spirits went out, and entered into the swine: and the herd ran violently down a steep place into the sea, (they were about two thousand;) and were choked in the sea. 14 And they that fed the swine fled, and told *it* in the city, and in the country. And they went out to see what it was that was done. 15 And they come to Jesus, and see him that was possessed with the devil, and had the legion, sitting, and clothed, and in his right mind: and they were afraid. 16 And they that saw

---

ᶜ ἴσχυεν αὐτὸν LTTrAW.   ᵈ διὰ παντὸς ALᵢ   ᵉ μνήμασιν (— ν GW) καὶ ἐν τοῖς ὄρεσιν GLTTrAW.
ᶠ καὶ ἰδὼν TTrA.   ᵍ αὐτόν A.   ʰ λέγει he says LTTrAW.   ⁱ ὄνομά σοι LTTₜA.   ᵏ λέγει
αὐτῷ he says to him GLTTrAW.   ¹ Λεγιὼν LTTrA.   ᵐ + ἐστιν is L.   ⁿ αὐτὰ TTr.
ᵒ τῷ ὄρει the mountain GLTTrAW.   ᵖ — πάντες GW[L] ; — πάντες οἱ δαίμονες (read they
besought) TTrA.   ᑫ — εὐθέως ὁ Ἰησοῦς (read he allowed) [L]TT·[A].   ʳ — ἦσαν δὲ [L]TTrA.
ˢ καὶ οἱ LTTrA.   ᵗ αὐτοὺς thom GLTTrAW.   ᵛ ἀπήγγειλαν told GLTTrAW.   ʷ ἦλθον
they went LTTrAW.   ˣ — καὶ LTTrA.   ʸ λεγιῶνα LTTrA.

it told them **how** it befell to him that was possessed with the devil, and *also* concerning the swine. 17 And they began to pray him to depart out of their coasts. 18 And when he was come into the ship, he that had been possessed with the devil prayed him that he might be with him. 19 Howbeit Jesus suffered him not, but saith unto him, Go home to thy friends, and tell them how great things the Lord hath done for thee, and hath had compassion on thee. 20 And he departed, and began to publish in Decapolis how great things Jesus had done for him: and all *men* did marvel.

διηγήσαντο αὐτοῖς οἱ ἰδόντες, πῶς ἐγένετο τῷ δαι-
⁶related   ⁷to ⁸them ¹those ²who ³had ⁴seen[⁵it] how it happened to him pos-
μονιζομένῳ, καὶ περὶ τῶν χοίρων. 17 καὶ ἤρξαντο παρα-
sessed by demons, and concerning the swine.   And they began to be-
καλεῖν αὐτὸν ἀπελθεῖν ἀπὸ τῶν ὁρίων αὐτῶν. 18 Καὶ
seech him to depart from their borders.   And
^zἐμβάντος^{||} αὐτοῦ εἰς τὸ πλοῖον, παρεκάλει αὐτὸν ὁ
²having ³entered ¹he   into the ship, ⁸besought ⁹him ¹he ²who
δαιμονισθείς,   ἵνα   ^aᾖ^{||} μετ' αὐτοῦ. ^{||} 19 ^bὁ δὲ^{||}
³had ⁴been ⁵possessed ⁶by ⁷demons that he might be with him.   But
^cἸησοῦς^{||} οὐκ ἀφῆκεν αὐτόν, ἀλλὰ λέγει αὐτῷ, Ὕπαγε εἰς τὸν
Jesus   did not suffer him, but says to him, Go to
οἶκόν σου πρὸς τοὺς σούς, καὶ ^dἀνάγγειλον^{||} αὐτοῖς ὅσα ^eσοι
thy house   to thine own, and announce to them how much for thee
ὁ κύριος^{||} ἐποίησεν,^{||} καὶ ἠλέησέν σε. 20 Καὶ ἀπῆλθεν καὶ
the Lord   did, and pitied thee.   And he departed and
ἤρξατο κηρύσσειν ἐν τῇ Δεκαπόλει, ὅσα ἐποίησεν αὐτῷ ὁ
began to proclaim in Decapolis, how much ²had ³done ⁴for ⁵him
Ἰησοῦς· καὶ πάντες ἐθαύμαζον.
¹Jesus; and all wondered.

21 And when Jesus was passed over again by ship unto the other side, much people gathered unto him: and he was nigh unto the sea. 22 And, behold, there cometh one of the rulers of the synagogue, Jairus by name; and when he saw him, he fell at his feet, 23 and besought him greatly, saying, My little daughter lieth at the point of death: *I pray thee*, come and lay thy hands on her, that she may be healed; and she shall live. 24 And *Jesus* went with him: and much people followed him, and thronged him. 25 And a certain woman, which had an issue of blood twelve years, 26 and had suffered many things of many physicians, and had spent all that she had, and was nothing bettered, but rather grew worse, 27 when she had heard of Jesus, came in the press behind, and touched his garment. 28 For she said, If I may touch but his clothes, I shall be whole. 29 And

21 Καὶ διαπεράσαντος τοῦ Ἰησοῦ ἐν τῷ πλοίῳ ^fπάλιν εἰς
And ²having ³passed ⁴over   ¹Jesus in the ship again to
τὸ πέραν,^{||} συνήχθη ὄχλος πολὺς ἐπ' αὐτόν, καὶ ἦν
the other side, ⁴was ⁵gathered ¹a ³crowd ²great to him, and he was
παρὰ τὴν θάλασσαν. 22 Καὶ ^hἰδού,^{||} ἔρχεται εἷς τῶν ἀρχι-
by the sea.   And behold, comes one of the rulers of
συναγώγων, ὀνόματι Ἰάειρος, καὶ ἰδὼν αὐτόν, πίπτει πρὸς
the synagogue, by name Jairus, and seeing him, falls at
τοὺς πόδας αὐτοῦ· 23 καὶ ⁱπαρεκάλει^{||} αὐτὸν πολλά, λέγων,
his feet;   and he besought him much, saying,
Ὅτι τὸ θυγάτριόν μου ἐσχάτως ἔχει·   ἵνα ἐλθὼν
My little daughter is at the last extremity, [I pray] that having come
ἐπιθῇς ^kαὐτῇ τὰς χεῖρας,^{||} ^lὅπως^{||} σωθῇ καὶ
thou wouldest lay on her [thy] hands, so that she may be cured, and
^mζήσεται.^{||} 24 Καὶ ἀπῆλθεν μετ' αὐτοῦ, καὶ ἠκολούθει αὐτῷ
she shall live.   And he departed with him, and ⁵him
ὄχλος πολύς, καὶ συνέθλιβον αὐτόν. 25 Καὶ γυνὴ ⁿτις^{||}
¹a ³crowd ²great, and pressed on him.   And a ²woman ¹certain
οὖσα ἐν ῥύσει αἵματος ^oἔτη δώδεκα,^{||} 26 καὶ πολλὰ παθοῦσα
being with a flux of blood ²years ¹twelve,   and much having suffered
ὑπὸ πολλῶν ἰατρῶν, καὶ δαπανήσασα τὰ παρ' ^pἑαυτῆς^{||}
under many physicians, and having spent ²her ³means
πάντα, καὶ μηδὲν ὠφεληθεῖσα ἀλλὰ μᾶλλον εἰς τὸ χεῖρον
¹all, and in no way having benefited but rather ³to ⁴worse
ἐλθοῦσα, 27 ἀκούσασα ^q περὶ τοῦ Ἰησοῦ, ἐλθοῦσα ἐν
¹having ²come, having heard concerning Jesus, having come in
τῷ ὄχλῳ ὄπισθεν, ἥψατο τοῦ ἱματίου αὐτοῦ· 28 ἔλεγεν γάρ,
the crowd behind, touched his garment;   for she said,
Ὅτι ^rκᾂν τῶν ἱματίων αὐτοῦ ἅψωμαι.^{||} σωθήσομαι. 29 Καὶ
If but his garments I shall touch, I shall be cured.   And

---

^z. ἐμβαίνοντος [was] entering LTTrAW.   ^a μετ' αὐτοῦ ᾖ LTTrAW.   ^b καὶ and GLTTrAW.
^c — Ἰησοῦς (*read* he did not suffer) G[L]TTrAW.   ^d ἀπάγγειλον tell LTTrAW.   ^e ὁ κύριός
σοι TTrA.   ^f πεποίηκεν has done GLTTrAW.   ^g εἰς τὸ πέραν πάλιν T.   ^h — ἰδού [L]TTrA.
ⁱ παρακαλεῖ he beseeches TTrA.   ^k τὰς χεῖρας αὐτῇ LTTrA.   ^l ἵνα in order that LTTrA.
^m ζήσῃ may live LTTrA.   ⁿ — τις LTTr[A].   ^o δώδεκα ἔτη T.   ^p αὐτῆς GLTTrAW.
^q + τὰ the things T[A].   ^r ἐὰν ἅψωμαι κᾂν τῶν ἱματίων αὐτοῦ TA.

ˢεὐθέως‖ ἐξηράνθη ἡ πηγὴ τοῦ.αἵματος.αὐτῆς, καὶ ἔγνω
immediately was dried up the fountain   of her blood,   and she knew

τῷ σώματι ὅτι ἴαται ἀπὸ τῆς μάστιγος. 30 καὶ ˢεὐθέως‖
in [her] body that she was healed from the   scourge.   And immediately

ὁ Ἰησοῦς, ἐπιγνοὺς ἐν ἑαυτῷ τὴν ἐξ αὐτοῦ δύναμιν
Jesus,   knowing   in himself [that] the ²out ³of ⁴him ¹power

ἐξελθοῦσαν, ἐπιστραφεὶς ἐν τῷ ὄχλῳ, ἔλεγεν, Τίς μου ἥψατο
had gone forth, having turned in the crowd,   said,   Who of me touched

τῶν ἱματίων; 31 Καὶ ἔλεγον αὐτῷ οἱ.μαθηταὶ.αὐτοῦ, Βλέπεις
the garments?   And ²said ⁴to ⁵him   ¹his ²disciples,   Thou seest

τὸν ὄχλον συνθλίβοντά σε, καὶ λέγεις, Τίς μου ἥψατο;
the crowd   pressing on   thee, and sayest thou, Who me   touched?

32 Καὶ περιεβλέπετο ἰδεῖν τὴν τοῦτο ποιήσασαν. 33 ἡ.δὲ
And he looked round to see her who this   had done.   But the

γυνὴ φοβηθεῖσα καὶ τρέμουσα, εἰδυῖα ὃ γέγονεν ᵗἐπ'‖
woman being frightened and trembling, knowing what had been done upon

αὐτῇ, ἦλθεν καὶ προσέπεσεν αὐτῷ, καὶ εἶπεν αὐτῷ πᾶσαν
her,   came and fell down before him, and told   him   all

τὴν ἀλήθειαν. 34 ὁ.δὲ ᵛ εἶπεν αὐτῇ, ʷΘύγατερ,‖ ἡ.πίστις.σου
the truth.   And he said to her, Daughter,   thy faith

σέσωκέν σε· ὕπαγε εἰς εἰρήνην, καὶ ἴσθι ὑγιὴς ἀπὸ τῆς μάστι-
has cured thee; go   in peace,   and be sound from   ²scourge

γός σου. 35 Ἔτι αὐτοῦ.λαλοῦντος, ἔρχονται ἀπὸ τοῦ ἀρχι-
¹thy.   [While] yet   he is speaking,   they come from the ruler of

συναγώγου, λέγοντες, Ὅτι ἡ.θυγάτηρ.σου ἀπέθανεν· τί ἔτι
the synagogue's [house], saying,   Thy daughter   is dead; why still

σκύλλεις τὸν διδάσκαλον; 36 Ὁ.δὲ Ἰησοῦς ˣεὐθέως‖ ʸἀκού-
troublest thou the   teacher?   But Jesus   immediately, having

σας‖ τὸν λόγον λαλούμενον λέγει τῷ ἀρχισυναγώγῳ, Μὴ
heard the   word   spoken,   says to the ruler of the synagogue, ²Not

φοβοῦ· μόνον πίστευε. 37 Καὶ οὐκ.ἀφῆκεν οὐδένα ᶻαὐτῷ‖
¹fear;   only   believe.   And he suffered no one   him

ᵃσυνακολουθῆσαι,‖ εἰ.μὴ ᵇ Πέτρον καὶ Ἰάκωβον καὶ Ἰωάννην
to accompany,   except   Peter and   James   and   John

τὸν ἀδελφὸν Ἰακώβου. 38 καὶ ᶜἔρχεται‖ εἰς τὸν οἶκον τοῦ
the brother   of James.   And he comes to the house of the

ἀρχισυναγώγου, καὶ θεωρεῖ θόρυβον, ᵈ κλαίοντας καὶ
ruler of the synagogue, and he beholds a tumult, [people] weeping and

ἀλαλάζοντας πολλά. 39 καὶ εἰσελθὼν λέγει αὐτοῖς, Τί
wailing   greatly.   And having entered he says to them, Why

θορυβεῖσθε καὶ κλαίετε; τὸ παιδίον οὐκ.ἀπέθανεν, ἀλλὰ
make ye a tumult and weep?   the child   is not dead,   but

καθεύδει. 40 Καὶ κατεγέλων αὐτοῦ. ᵉὉ‖.δὲ ἐκβαλὼν ἅπαν-
sleeps.   And they laughed at him.   But he having put out   all,

τας,‖ παραλαμβάνει τὸν πατέρα τοῦ παιδίου καὶ τὴν
  takes with [him] the   father of the child   and the

μητέρα καὶ τοὺς μετ' αὐτοῦ, καὶ εἰσπορεύεται ὅπου ἦν τὸ
mother and those with him, and   enters in   where ³was ¹the

παιδίον ᵍἀνακείμενον.‖ 41 καὶ κρατήσας τῆς χειρὸς τοῦ
²child   lying.   And having taken the   hand of the

παιδίου, λέγει αὐτῇ, Ταλιθά, ʰκοῦμι·‖ ὅ ἐστιν μεθερμηνευό-
child,   he says to her, Talitha,   koumi; which is,   being inter-

---

straightway the foun-
tain of her blood was
dried up ; and she felt
in *her* body that she
was healed of that
plague. 30 And Jesus,
immediately knowing
in himself that virtue
had gone out of him,
turned him about in
the press, and said,
Who touched my
clothes? 31 And his
disciples said unto him,
Thou seest the multi-
tude thronging thee,
and sayest thou, Who
touched me? 32 And
he looked round about
to see her that had
done this thing. 33 But
the woman fearing
and trembling, know-
ing what was done in
her, came and fell
down before him, and
told him all the truth.
34 And he said unto
her, Daughter, thy
faith hath made thee
whole; go in peace,
and be whole of thy
plague. 35 While he
yet spake, there came
from the ruler of the
synagogue's *house cer-
tain* which said, Thy
daughter is dead: why
troublest thou the
Master any further?
36 As soon as Jesus
heard the word that
was spoken, he saith
unto the ruler of the
synagogue, Be not
afraid, only believe.
37 And he suffered no
man to follow him,
save Peter, and James,
and John the brother
of James. 38 And he
cometh to the house of
the ruler of the syna-
gogue, and seeth the
tumult, and them that
wept and wailed great-
ly. 39 And when he
was come in, he saith
unto them, Why make
ye this ado, and weep?
the damsel is not dead,
but sleepeth. 40 And
they laughed him to
scorn. But when he
had put them all out,
he taketh the father
and the mother of the
damsel, and them that
were with him, and
entereth in where the
damsel was lying.
41 And he took the
damsel by the hand,
and said unto her,
Talitha cumi; which
is, being interpret-

ˢ εὐθὺς TTrA.   ᵗ — ἐπ' (*read* to-her) [L]TTrA.   ᵛ + Ἰησοῦς Jesus L.   ʷ Θυγάτηρ LTrA.
ˣ — εὐθέως [L]TTr[A].   ʸ παρακούσας having disregarded TTrA.   ᶻ μετ' αὐτοῦ with him
TTrA.   ᵃ ἀκολουθῆσαι to follow L.   ᵇ + τὸν TTrA.   ᶜ ἔρχονται they come LTTrAW.
ᵈ + καὶ and GLTTrAW.   ᵉ αὐτὸς LTTr.   ᶠ πάντας GLTTrAW.   ᵍ — ἀνακείμενον G[L]TTrA.
ʰ κοῦμ T ; κούμ TrA.

8

ed, Damsel, I say unto thee, arise. 42 And straightway the damsel arose, and walked; for she was of the age of twelve years. And they were astonished with a great astonishment. 43 And he charged them straitly that no man should know it; and commanded that something should be given her to eat.

VI. And he went out from thence, and came into his own country; and his disciples follow him. 2 And when the sabbath day was come, he began to teach in the synagogue: and many hearing him were astonished, saying, From whence hath this man these things? and what wisdom is this which is given unto him, that even such mighty works are wrought by his hands? 3 Is not this the carpenter, the son of Mary, the brother of James, and Joses, and of Juda, and Simon? and are not his sisters here with us? And they were offended at him. 4 But Jesus said unto them, A prophet is not without honour, but in his own country, and among his own kin, and in his own house. 5 And he could there do no mighty work, save that he laid his hands upon a few sick folk, and healed them. 6 And he marvelled because of their unbelief. And he went round about the villages, teaching.

7 And he called unto him the twelve, and began to send them forth by two and two; and gave them power over unclean spirits; 8 and commanded them that they should take nothing for their journey, save a staff only; no scrip, no bread, no money in their purse: 9 but be shod with sandals; and

μενον, Τὸ κοράσιον, σοὶ λέγω, ¹ʸἔγειραι.‖ 42 Καὶ ᵏεὐθέως‖
preted, Damsel, ｆto thee I ｆsay, arise. And immediately

ἀνέστη τὸ κοράσιον καὶ περιεπάτει, ἦν·γὰρ ἐτῶν δώδεκα.
arose the damsel and walked, for she was ²years ¹twelve [old].

καὶ ἐξέστησαν ¹ ἐκστάσει μεγάλῃ. 43 καὶ διεστείλατο
And they were amazed with ²amazement ¹great. And he charged

αὐτοῖς πολλὰ ἵνα μηδεὶς ᵐγνῷ‖ τοῦτο· καὶ εἶπεν
them much that no one should know this; and he said [that some-

δοθῆναι αὐτῇ φαγεῖν.
thing] should be given to her to eat.

6 Καὶ ἐξῆλθεν ἐκεῖθεν, καὶ ⁿἦλθεν‖ εἰς τὴν·πατρίδα·αὐτοῦ
And he went out thence, and came into his [own] country;

καὶ ἀκολουθοῦσιν αὐτῷ οἱ·μαθηταὶ·αὐτοῦ· 2 καὶ γενομένου
and ²follow ⁴him ¹his ²disciples. And ²being ³come

σαββάτου ἤρξατο °ἐν τῇ συναγωγῇ διδάσκειν·‖ καὶ ᴾ πολλοὶ
¹sabbath he began in the synagogue to teach; and many

ἀκούοντες ἐξεπλήσσοντο, λέγοντες, Πόθεν τούτῳ ταῦτα;
hearing were astonished, saying, Whence to this [man] these things?

καὶ τίς ἡ σοφία ἡ δοθεῖσα ᑫαὐτῷ,‖ ʳὅτι‖ καὶ δυνάμεις
and what the wisdom that has been given to him, that even ²works ³of ⁴power

τοιαῦται διὰ τῶν·χειρῶν·αὐτοῦ ˢγίνονται;‖ 3 οὐχ οὗτός ἐστιν
¹such by his hands are done? ²not ³this ¹is

ὁ τέκτων, ὁ υἱὸς ᵗΜαρίας, ˅ἀδελφὸς·δὲ‖ Ἰακώβου καὶ ʷἸωσῆ‖
the carpenter, the son of Mary, and brother of James and Joses

καὶ Ἰούδα καὶ Σίμωνος; καὶ οὐκ·εἰσὶν αἱ·ἀδελφαὶ·αὐτοῦ ὧδε
and Judas and Simon? and are not his sisters here

πρὸς ἡμᾶς; Καὶ ἐσκανδαλίζοντο ἐν αὐτῷ. 4 ˣἔλεγεν·δὲ‖ αὐτοῖς
with us? And they were offended in him. But ²said ³to ¹them

ὁ Ἰησοῦς, Ὅτι οὐκ ἔστιν προφήτης ἄτιμος, εἰ·μὴ ἐν τῇ
Jesus, ²Not ³is ⁵a ⁴prophet without honour, except in

πατρίδι·ʸαὐτοῦ‖ καὶ ἐν τοῖς ᶻσυγγενέσιν‖ ᵃ καὶ ἐν τῇ
his [own] country and among [his] kinsmen and in

οἰκίᾳ·ᵇαὐτοῦ‖. 5 Καὶ οὐκ ᶜἠδύνατο‖ ἐκεῖ ᵈοὐδεμίαν δύναμιν
his [own] house. And he was ²able ³there ¹not any work of power

ποιῆσαι,‖ εἰ·μὴ ὀλίγοις ἀρρώστοις ἐπιθεὶς τὰς χεῖρας
to do, except on a few infirm having laid [his] hands

ἐθεράπευσεν. 6 καὶ ᵉἐθαύμαζεν‖ διὰ τὴν·ἀπιστίαν·αὐ-
he healed [them]. And he wondered because of their unbelief.

τῶν· καὶ περιῆγεν τὰς κώμας κύκλῳ διδάσκων.
And he went about the villages in a circuit teaching.

7 Καὶ προσκαλεῖται τοὺς δώδεκα, καὶ ἤρξατο αὐτοὺς
And he calls to [him] the twelve, and began them

ἀποστέλλειν δύο·δύο, καὶ ἐδίδου αὐτοῖς ἐξουσίαν τῶν πνευμά-
to send forth two and two, and gave to them authority over the spirits

των τῶν ἀκαθάρτων· 8 καὶ παρήγγειλεν αὐτοῖς ἵνα μηδὲν
the unclean; and he charged them that nothing

αἴρωσιν εἰς ὁδόν, εἰ·μὴ ῥάβδον μόνον· μὴ ᶠπήραν,
they should take for [the] way, except a staff only; no provision bag,

μὴ ἄρτον,‖ μὴ εἰς τὴν ζώνην χαλκόν· 9 ᵍἀλλ᾽‖ ὑποδεδεμένους
nor bread, nor in the belt money; but be shod

ⁱ ἔγειρε GLTTrA.   ᵏ εὐθὺς TTrA.   ¹ + εὐθὺς immediately T [Tr]A.   ᵐ γνοῖ LTTrA.
ⁿ ἔρχεται comes TTrAW.   ° διδάσκειν ἐν τῇ συναγωγῇ TTr.   ᴾ + οἱ the T[A].   ᑫ τούτῳ
to this [man] TTrA.   ʳ — ὅτι GLTTrA.   ˢ γινόμεναι Tr.   ᵗ + τῆς TTrA.   ˅ καὶ
ἀδελφὸς LTTrAW.   ʷ Ἰωσῆτος LTTrA.   ˣ καὶ ἔλεγεν and ⁺·aid LTTrA.   ʸ αὐτοῦ I.TrAW,]
ἑαυτοῦ T.-   ᶻ συγγενεῦσιν TTr.   ᵃ + αὐτοῦ his (kinsmen) [L]TTrA   ᵇ αὐτοῦ LTTrAW.
ᶜ ἐδύνατο TTrA.   ᵈ ποιῆσαι οὐδεμίαν δύναμιν LTTrA.   ᵉ ἐθαύμασεν T,   ᶠ ἄρτον, μὴ
πήραν TTrA.   ᵍ ἀλλὰ LTTrAW,

σανδάλια· καὶ μὴ ʰἐνδύσησθε‖ δύο χιτῶνας. 10 Καὶ ἔλεγεν
with sandals; and   put not on   two tunics.   And he said

αὐτοῖς, Ὅπου.ἱἐὰν‖ εἰσέλθητε εἰς οἰκίαν, ἐκεῖ μένετε ἕως ἂν
to them, Wherever   ye enter into a house, there remain until

ἐξέλθητε ἐκεῖθεν. 11 καὶ ᵏὅσοι.ἂν μὴ.δέξωνται‖ ὑμᾶς, μηδὲ
ye go out thence.   And as many as will not receive you,   nor

ἀκούσωσιν ὑμῶν, ἐκπορευόμενοι ἐκεῖθεν, ἐκτινάξατε τὸν χοῦν
hear you,   departing   thence,   shake off the   dust

τὸν ὑποκάτω τῶν.ποδῶν.ὑμῶν, εἰς μαρτύριον αὐτοῖς. ˡἀμὴν
which [is] under   your feet,   for a testimony to them.   Verily

λέγω ὑμῖν, ἀνεκτότερον ἔσται Σοδόμοις ἢ Γομόρροις ἐν ἡμέρᾳ
I say to you, more tolerable it shall be for Sodom or Gomorrha in day

κρίσεως, ἢ τῇ.πόλει.ἐκείνῃ. 12 Καὶ ἐξελθόντες ᵐἐκήρυσ-
of judgment than for that city.   And having gone out they pro-

σον‖ ἵνα ⁿμετανοήσωσιν. 13 καὶ δαιμόνια πολλὰ ἐξέβαλλον,
claimed that [men] should repent. And ²demons ¹many they cast out,

καὶ ἤλειφον ἐλαίῳ πολλοὺς ἀρρώστους καὶ ἐθεράπευον [them].
and anointed with oil many   infirm   and healed [them].

14 Καὶ ἤκουσεν ὁ βασιλεὺς Ἡρώδης, .φανερὸν.γὰρ
And ⁴heard ²the ³king ¹Herod [of him], for public

ἐγένετο τὸ.ὄνομα.αὐτοῦ, καὶ °ἔλεγεν,‖ Ὅτι Ἰωάννης ὁ βαπ-
became his name, and he said, John the Bap-

τίζων ᵖἐκ νεκρῶν ἠγέρθη,‖ καὶ διὰ τοῦτο ἐνεργοῦ-
tist from among [the] dead is risen, and because of this ⁵ope-

σιν αἱ δυνάμεις ἐν αὐτῷ. 15 Ἄλλοι�q ἔλεγον, Ὅτι ʳἨλίας‖
rate ¹the ²works ³of ⁴power in him. Others said, Elias

ἐστίν· ἄλλοι.δὲ ἔλεγον, Ὅτι προφήτης ˢἐστίν,‖ ᵗἢ‖ ὡς εἷς τῶν
it is; and others said, A prophet it is, or as one of the

προφητῶν. 16 Ἀκούσας.δὲ ὁ Ἡρώδης ᵛεἶπεν,‖ ʷὍτι‖ ὃν
prophets. But having heard Herod said, ²Whom

ἐγὼ ἀπεκεφάλισα Ἰωάννην, οὗτός ˣἐστιν· αὐτὸς‖ ἠγέρθη
ᵗᴵ ⁴beheaded ¹John, he it is. He is risen

ʸἐκ νεκρῶν.‖ 17 Αὐτὸς.γὰρ ὁ Ἡρώδης ἀποστείλας
from among [the] dead. For ²himself ¹Herod having sent

ἐκράτησεν τὸν Ἰωάννην, καὶ ἔδησεν αὐτὸν ἐν ᶻτῇ‖ φυλακῇ,
seized John,   and bound him in the prison,

διὰ Ἡρωδιάδα τὴν γυναῖκα Φιλίππου τοῦ.ἀδελφοῦ.αὐτοῦ,
on account of Herodias the wife of Philip his brother,

ὅτι αὐτὴν ἐγάμησεν. 18 ἔλεγεν.γὰρ ὁ Ἰωάννης τῷ Ἡρώδῃ,
because her he had married. For ²said ¹John to Herod,

Ὅτι οὐκ.ἔξεστίν σοι ἔχειν τὴν γυναῖκα τοῦ.ἀδελφοῦ.σου.
It is not lawful for thee to have the wife of thy brother.

19 Ἡ.δὲ.Ἡρωδιὰς ἐνεῖχεν αὐτῷ, καὶ ᵃἤθελεν‖ αὐτὸν ἀπο-
But Herodias held it against him, and wished ³him ¹to

κτεῖναι· καὶ οὐκ.ἠδύνατο. 20 ὁ.γὰρ.Ἡρώδης ἐφοβεῖτο τὸν
²kill, and was not able: for Herod feared

Ἰωάννην, εἰδὼς αὐτὸν ἄνδρα.δίκαιον καὶ ἅγιον, καὶ
John, knowing him [to be] a man just and holy, and

συνετήρει αὐτόν· καὶ ἀκούσας αὐτοῦ, πολλὰ ᵇἐποίει,‖ καὶ
kept ²safe ¹him; and having heard him, many things did, and

Right column (AV text):

not put on two coats. 10 And he said unto them, In what place soever ye enter into an house, there abide till ye depart from that place. 11 And whosoever shall not receive you, nor hear you, when ye depart thence, shake off the dust under your feet for a testimony against them. Verily I say unto you, It shall be more tolerable for Sodom and Gomorrha, in the day of judgment, than for that city. 12 And they went out, and preached that men should repent. 13 And they cast out many devils, and anointed with oil many that were sick, and healed *them*.

14 And king Herod heard of him; (for his name was spread abroad:) and he said, That John the Baptist was risen from the dead, and therefore mighty works do shew forth themselves in him. 15 Others said, That it is Elias. And others said, That it is a prophet, or as one of the prophets. 16 But when Herod heard *thereof*, he said, It is John, whom I beheaded: he is risen from the dead. 17 For Herod himself had sent forth and laid hold upon John, and bound him in prison for Herodias' sake, his brother Philip's wife: for he had married her. 18 For John had said unto Herod, It is not lawful for thee to have thy brother's wife. 19 Therefore Herodias had a quarrel against him, and would have killed him; but she could not: 20 for Herod feared John, knowing that he was a just man and an holy, and observed him; and when he heard him, he did many things, and

---

ʰ ἐνδύσασθαι E.   ⁱ ἂν LTr.   ᵏ ἐὰν for ἂν L ; ὃς ἂν τόπος μὴ δέξηται whatsoever place will not receive TTrA.   ˡ — ἀμὴν λέγω .... τῇ πόλει ἐκείνῃ G[L]TTrA.   ᵐ ἐκήρυξαν TTrA. ⁿ μετανοῶσιν LTTrA.   ° ἔλεγον they said L.   ᵖ ἐγήγερται (has risen) ἐκ νεκρῶν LTTr ; ἐκ νεκρῶν ἀνέστη A.   q + δὲ also LTTrAW.   ʳ Ἠλείας T.   ˢ — ἐστίν [L]TTrA.   ᵗ — ἢ GLTTrAW. ᵛ ἔλεγεν TTrA.   ʷ — Ὅτι LTTrA.   ˣ — ἐστιν· αὐτὸς G[L]TTrA.   ʸ — ἐκ νεκρῶν T[Tr]A. ˢ — τῇ GLTTrAW.   ᵃ ἐζήτει sought L.   ᵇ ἠπόρει was at a loss [about] T.

heard him gladly.
21 And when a convenient day was come, that Herod on his birthday made a supper to his lords, high captains, and chief estates of Galilee;
22 and when the daughter of the said Herodias came in, and danced, and pleased Herod and them that sat with him, the king said unto the damsel, Ask of me whatsoever thou wilt, and I will give it thee.
23 And he sware unto her, Whatsoever thou shalt ask of me, I will give it thee, unto the half of my kingdom.
24 And she went forth, and said unto her mother, What shall I ask? And she said, The head of John the Baptist.
25 And she came in straightway with haste unto the king, and asked, saying, I will that thou give me by and by in a charger the head of John the Baptist.
26 And the king was exceeding sorry; yet for his oath's sake, and for their sakes which sat with him, he would not reject her.
27 And immediately the king sent an executioner, and commanded his head to be brought: and he went and beheaded him in the prison, 28 and brought his head in a charger, and gave it to the damsel: and the damsel gave it to her mother.
29 And when his disciples heard of it, they came and took up his corpse, and laid it in a tomb.

ἡδέως αὐτοῦ ἤκουεν. 21 καὶ γενομένης ἡμέρας.εὐκαίρου, ᶜὅτε‖
gladly　him　heard.　　And ⁴being ⁵come　¹a̱ ²opportune ³day,　when
'Ηρώδης τοῖς.γενεσίοις.αὐτοῦ δεῖπνον ᵈἐποίει‖ τοῖς μεγιστᾶσιν
Herod　　on his birthday　　a supper　made　　　to ²great ¹men
αὐτοῦ καὶ τοῖς χιλιάρχοις καὶ τοῖς πρώτοις　τῆς Γαλιλαίας,
¹his　and to the chief captains and to the　first [men]　of Galilee ;
22 καὶ εἰσελθούσης τῆς θυγατρὸς αὐτῆς τῆς 'Ηρωδιάδος, καὶ
and ⁶having ⁷come ⁸in ¹the　²daughter ³of ⁵herself　　³Herodias,　and
ὀρχησαμένης, ᵉκαὶ ἀρεσάσης‖ τῷ 'Ηρώδῃ καὶ τοῖς συνανα-
having danced,　and　pleased　　Herod　and those　reclining
κειμένοις,　　ᶠεἶπεν ὁ βασιλεὺς‖ τῷ κορασίῳ, Αἴτησόν με
[at table] with [him], ³said ²the　²king　to the damsel,　Ask　me
ὃ.ἐὰν θέλῃς, καὶ δώσω σοί· 23 καὶ ὤμοσεν αὐτῇ, "Οτι
whatever thou wilt, and I will give to thee.　And he swore　to her,
ὃ.ἐὰν με αἰτήσῃς, δώσω σοί, ἕως ἡμίσους τῆς βασιλείας
Whatever me thou mayest ask, I will give to thee, to　half　of ²kingdom
μου. 24 ᵍ'Η.δὲ‖ ἐξελθοῦσα εἶπεν τῇ.μητρὶ.αὐτῆς, Τί ʰαἰτή-
¹my.　And she having gone out said to her mother,　What shall I
σομαι;‖ 'Η.δὲ εἶπεν, Τὴν ᴿκεφαλὴν 'Ιωάννου τοῦ ⁱβαπτιστοῦ.‖
ask?　And she said,　The　head　of John　the　Baptist.
25 Καὶ εἰσελθοῦσα ᵏεὐθέως‖ μετὰ σπουδῆς πρὸς τὸν βασιλέα,
And having entered immediately with　haste　to　the　king,
ᾐτήσατο, λέγουσα, Θέλω ἵνα ¹μοι δῷς ἐξ.αὐτῆς‖ ἐπὶ πίνακι
she asked,　saying, I desire that to me thou give at once　upon a dish
τὴν κεφαλὴν 'Ιωάννου τοῦ βαπτιστοῦ. 26 Καὶ περίλυπος
the　head　of John　the　Baptist.　　And ⁵very ⁶sorrowful
γενόμενος ὁ βασιλεύς, διὰ　τοὺς ὅρκους καὶ τοὺς
[³while] ⁴made ¹the ²king, on account of the　oaths and those who
ᵐσυνανακειμένους‖ οὐκ.ἠθέλησεν ᵘαὐτὴν ἀθετῆσαι.‖ 27 καὶ
reclined [at table] with [him], would not　²her ¹reject.　And
ᵒεὐθέως‖ ἀποστείλας ὁ βασιλεὺς ᴾσπεκουλάτωρα‖ ἐπέταξεν
immediately ³having ⁴sent ¹the　²king　a guardsman　ordered
�q ἐνεχθῆναι‖ τὴν.κεφαλὴν.αὐτοῦʳ. 28 ˢὁ.δὲ‖ ἀπελθὼν ἀπεκε-
to be brought　his head.　　And he having gone　be-
φάλισεν αὐτὸν ἐν τῇ φυλακῇ, καὶ ἤνεγκεν τὴν.κεφαλὴν.αὐτοῦ
headed　him　in the prison, and brought　his head
ἐπὶ πίνακι, καὶ ἔδωκεν αὐτὴν τῷ κορασίῳ· καὶ τὸ κοράσιον
upon a dish, and　gave　it　to the damsel,　and the　damsel
ἔδωκεν αὐτὴν τῇ.μητρὶ.αὐτῆς. 29 Καὶ ἀκούσαντες οἱ μαθηταὶ
gave　it　to her mother.　And having heard [it] ²disciples
αὐτοῦ ᵗἦλθον,‖ καὶ ἦραν τὸ.πτῶμα.αὐτοῦ, καὶ ἔθηκαν ᵘαὐτὸ‖
¹his　came,　and took up　his corpse,　　and laid　it
ἐν ᵛτῷ‖ μνημείῳ.
in the　tomb.

30 And the apostles gathered themselves together unto Jesus, and told him all things, both what they had done, and what they had taught. 31 And he said unto them, Come ye yourselves apart

30 Καὶ　συνάγονται　οἱ ἀπόστολοι πρὸς τὸν 'Ιησοῦν, καὶ
And ³are ⁴gathered ⁵together ¹the ²apostles　to　Jesus,　and
ἀπήγγειλαν αὐτῷ πάντα, ʷκαὶ‖ ὅσα ἐποίησαν καὶ ˣὅσα‖
they related　to him all things,　both　what they had done and　what
ἐδίδαξαν.　31 καὶ ʸεἶπεν‖ αὐτοῖς, Δεῦτε ὑμεῖς αὐτοὶ
they had taught.　And　he said　to them,　Come ye　your-selves

ᶜ ὅτε L. ᵈ ἐποίησεν LTTrA. ᵉ ἤρεσεν she pleased LTTrA. ᶠ εἶπεν δὲ ὁ βασιλεὺς L; ὁ δὲ βασιλεὺς εἶπεν and the king said TT·A. ᵍ καὶ and TTrA. ʰ αἰτήσωμαι should I ask LTTrAW. ⁱ βαπτίζοντος TTrA. ᵏ εὐθὺς LTTrA. ˡ ἐξ αυτῆς δῷς μοι LTTrA. ᵐ ἀνακειμένους reclined [at table] TTrA. ⁿ ἀθετῆσαι αὐτὴν TTrA. ° εὐθὺς TTrA. ᴾ σπεκουλάτορα LTT·AW. q ἐνέγκαι [him] to bring TTrA. ʳ + [ἐπὶ πίνακι] on a dish L. ˢ καὶ (read and having gone he beheaded) LTTrA. ᵗ ἦλθαν TTrA. ᵘ αὐτὸν him T. ᵛ — τῷ (read a tomb) ÆGLTTrAW. ʷ — καὶ LTTrAW. ˣ — ὅσα T. ʸ λέγει he says TTrAW.

κατ᾿ ἰδίαν εἰς ἔρημον τόπον, καὶ ᶻἀναπαύεσθε‖ ὀλίγον. ᵗΗσαν
apart into ²desert ¹a place, and rest a little. ⁷Were

γὰρ οἱ ἐρχόμενοι καὶ οἱ ὑπάγοντες πολλοί, καὶ οὐδὲ φαγεῖν
for ²those ³coming ⁴and ⁵those ⁶going many, and not even to eat

ᵃηὐκαίρουν.‖ 32 καὶ ἀπῆλθον ᵇεἰς ἔρημον τόπον τῷ
had they opportunity. And they went away into ²desert · ¹a place by the

πλοίῳ‖ κατ᾿ ἰδίαν. 33 Καὶ εἶδον αὐτοὺς ὑπάγοντας ᶜοἱ ὄχλοι,‖
ship apart. And ³saw ⁴them ⁵going ¹the ²crowds,

καὶ ᵈἐπέγνωσαν‖ ᵉαὐτὸν‖ πολλοί, καὶ πεζῇ ἀπὸ πασῶν τῶν
⁶and ⁸recognized ⁹him ⁷many, and on foot from all the

πόλεων συνέδραμον ἐκεῖ, ᶠκαὶ προῆλθον αὐτούς,‖ ᵍκαὶ συνῆλ-
cities ran together there, and went before them, and came to-

θον πρὸς αὐτόν.‖ 34 καὶ ἐξελθὼν ʰεἶδεν ὁ Ἰησοῦς‖ πολὺν
gether to him. And having gone out ²saw ¹Jesus ²great

ὄχλον, καὶ ʲἐσπλαγχνίσθη ἐπ᾿ ʲαὐτοῖς,‖ ὅτι ἦσαν
¹a crowd, and was moved with compassion towards them, because they were

ὡς πρόβατα μὴ ἔχοντα ποιμένα· καὶ ἤρξατο διδάσκειν αὐτοὺς
as sheep not having a shepherd. And he began to teach them

πολλά. 35 Καὶ ἤδη ὥρας πολλῆς ᵏγενομένης,‖ προσελ-
many things. And already · a late hour [it] being, com-

θόντες ˡαὐτῷ‖ οἱ μαθηταὶ ᵐαὐτοῦ‖ ⁿλέγουσιν,‖ Ὅτι ἔρημός ἐστιν
ing to him his disciples say, Desert is

ὁ τόπος, καὶ ἤδη ὥρα πολλή· 36 ἀπόλυσον αὐτούς, ἵνα
the place, and already [it is] a late hour; dismiss them, that

ἀπελθόντες εἰς τοὺς κύκλῳ ἀγροὺς καὶ κώμας, ἀγοράσωσιν
having gone ⁴to ⁵the ¹in ²a ³circuit country and villages, they may buy

ἑαυτοῖς ᵒἄρτους‖ τί ᵖγὰρ‖ φάγωσιν ᵠοὐκ ἔχουσιν.‖
for themselves bread; ²something ¹for to eat they have not.

37 Ὁ δὲ ἀποκριθεὶς εἶπεν αὐτοῖς, Δότε αὐτοῖς ὑμεῖς φαγεῖν.
But he answering said to them, Give ²to ³them ¹ye to eat.

Καὶ λέγουσιν αὐτῷ, Ἀπελθόντες ἀγοράσωμεν ʳδιακοσίων
And they say to him, Having gone shall we buy two hundred

δηναρίων‖ ἄρτους, καὶ ˢδῶμεν‖ αὐτοῖς φαγεῖν; 38 Ὁ δὲ λέγει
denarii of bread, and give them to eat? And he says

αὐτοῖς, Πόσους ἄρτους ἔχετε; ὑπάγετε ᵗκαὶ‖ ἴδετε. Καὶ γνόν-
to them, How many loaves have ye? go and see. And having

τες λέγουσινᵛ, Πέντε, καὶ δύο ἰχθύας. 39 Καὶ πέταξεν αὐτοῖς
known they say, Five, and two fishes. And he ordered them

ʷἀνακλῖναι‖ πάντας συμπόσια συμπόσια ἐπὶ τῷ χλωρῷ χόρτῳ.
to make ²recline ¹all by companies on the green grass.

40 καὶ ˣἀνέπεσον‖ πρασιαὶ πρασιαί, ʸἀνὰ‖ ἑκατὸν καὶ ʸἀνὰ‖
And they sat down in ranks, by hundreds and by

πεντήκοντα. 41 καὶ λαβὼν τοὺς πέντε ἄρτους καὶ τοὺς δύο
fifties. And having taken the five loaves and the two

ἰχθύας, ἀναβλέψας εἰς τὸν οὐρανὸν εὐλόγησεν καὶ κατέκλα-
fishes, having looked up to the heaven he blessed and broke

σεν τοὺς ἄρτους, καὶ ἐδίδου τοῖς μαθηταῖς ᶻᵃαὐτοῦ‖ ἵνα ᵃᵃπαρα-
the loaves, and gave to his disciples that they might

into a desert place, and rest a while; for there were many coming and going, and they had no leisure so much as to eat. 32 And they departed into a desert place by ship privately. 33 And the people saw them departing, and many knew him, and ran afoot thither out of all cities, and out went them, and came together unto him. 34 And Jesus, when he came out, saw much people, and was moved with compassion toward them, because they were as sheep not having a shepherd: and he began to teach them many things. 35 And when the day was now far spent, his disciples came unto him, and said, This is a desert place, and now the time is far passed: 36 send them away, that they may go into the country round about, and into the villages, and buy themselves bread: for they have nothing to eat. 37 He answered and said unto them, Give ye them to eat. And they say unto him, Shall we go and buy two hundred pennyworth of bread, and give them to eat? 38 He saith unto them, How many loaves have ye? go and see. And when they knew, they say, Five, and two fishes. 39 And he commanded them to make all sit down by companies upon the green grass. 40 And they sat down in ranks, by hundreds and by fifties. 41 And when he had taken the five loaves and the two fishes, he looked up to heaven, and blessed, and brake the loaves, and gave them to his disciples to set before

---

ᶻ ἀναπαύσασθε TTrA. ᵃ εὐκαίρουν LTTrA. ᵇ ἐν τῷ πλοίῳ εἰς ἔρημον τόπον L. ᶜ — οἱ ὄχλοι (read they saw) GLTTrAW. ᵈ ἔγνωσαν knew LTrA. ᵉ αὐτοὺς them T; — αὐτὸν GLTrA. ᶠ — καὶ προῆλθον αὐτούς G. ᵍ — καὶ συνῆλθον πρὸς αὐτόν GLTTrAW. ʰ — ὁ Ἰησοῦς (read he saw) GTTrAW; [ὁ Ἰησοῦς] εἶδεν L. ʲ αὐτούς LTTrA. ᵏ γινομένης T. ˡ — αὐτῷ T. ᵐ [αὐτοῦ] L. ⁿ ἔλεγον said TTrA. ᵒ — ἄρτους [L]TTrA. ᵖ — γὰρ [L]TTrA. ᵠ — οὐκ ἔχουσιν (read buy for themselves something to eat) [L]TTrA. ʳ δηναρίων διακοσίων GLTTrAW. ˢ δώσομεν shall we give LTrA; δώσωμεν T. ᵗ — καὶ [L]TTrA. ᵛ + [αὐτῷ] to him L. ʷ ἀνακλιθῆναι L. ˣ ἀνέπεσαν TTrA. ᵍ κατὰ LTTrA. ᶻᵃ — αὐτοῦ (read the disciples) TTrA. ᵃᵃ παρατιθῶσιν TA.

them; and the two fishes divided he among them all. 42 And they did all eat, and were filled. 43 And they took up twelve baskets full of the fragments, and of the fishes. 44 And they that did eat of the loaves were about five thousand men. 45 And straightway he constrained his disciples to get into the ship, and to go to the other side before unto Bethsaida, while he sent away the people. 46 And when he had sent them away, he departed into a mountain to pray. 47 And when even was come, the ship was in the midst of the sea, and he alone on the land. 48 And he saw them toiling in rowing; for the wind was contrary unto them: and about the fourth watch of the night he cometh unto them, walking upon the sea, and would have passed by them. 49 But when they saw him walking upon the sea, they supposed it had been a spirit, and cried out: 50 for they all saw him, and were troubled. And immediately he talked with them, and saith unto them, Be of good cheer: it is I; be not afraid. 51 And he went up unto them into the ship; and the wind ceased: and they were sore amazed in themselves beyond measure, and wondered. 52 For they considered not *the miracle* of the loaves: for their heart was hardened.

53 And when they had passed over, they came into the land of Gennesaret, and drew to the shore. 54 And when they were come out of the ship, straightway they knew him, 55 and ran through that whole region round about, and began to carry about in beds those

θῶσιν‖ αὐτοῖς· καὶ τοὺς δύο ἰχθύας ἐμέρισεν πᾶσιν· 42 καὶ
set before them. And the two fishes he divided among all. And

ἔφαγον πάντες, καὶ ἐχορτάσθησαν· 43 καὶ ἦραν ᵇκλασμά-
ate all, and were satisfied. And they took up of frag-

των‖ δώδεκα ᶜκοφίνους‖ ᵈπλήρεις,‖ καὶ ἀπὸ τῶν ἰχθύων. 44 καὶ
ments twelve hand-baskets full, and of the fishes. And

ἦσαν οἱ φαγόντες τοὺς ἄρτους ᵉὡσεὶ‖ πεντακισχίλιοι
were those that ate of the loaves about five thousand

ἄνδρες. 45 Καὶ ᶠεὐθέως‖ ἠνάγκασεν τοὺς μαθητὰς αὐτοῦ
men. And immediately he compelled his disciples

ἐμβῆναι εἰς τὸ πλοῖον, καὶ προάγειν εἰς τὸ πέραν πρὸς Βηθ-
to enter into the ship, and to go before to the other side to Beth-

σαϊδάν, ἕως αὐτὸς ᵍἀπολύσῃ‖ τὸν ὄχλον. 46 καὶ ἀποταξάμενος
saida, until he should dismiss the crowd. And having taken leave of

αὐτοῖς, ἀπῆλθεν εἰς τὸ ὄρος προσεύξασθαι. 47 Καὶ ὀψίας
them, he departed into the mountain to pray. And evening

γενομένης, ἦν τὸ πλοῖον ἐν μέσῳ τῆς θαλάσσης, καὶ αὐτὸς
being come, was the ship in the midst of the sea, and he

μόνος ἐπὶ τῆς γῆς. 48 Καὶ ʰεἶδεν‖ αὐτοὺς βασανιζομένους
alone upon the land. And he saw them labouring

ἐν τῷ ἐλαύνειν, ἦν γὰρ ὁ ἄνεμος ἐναντίος αὐτοῖς· ⁱκαὶ‖ περὶ
in the rowing, for was the wind contrary to them; and about

τετάρτην φυλακὴν τῆς νυκτὸς ἔρχεται πρὸς αὐτούς, περιπα-
[the] fourth watch of the night he comes to them, walking

τῶν ἐπὶ τῆς θαλάσσης, καὶ ἤθελεν παρελθεῖν αὐτούς. 49 οἱ δὲ
ing on the sea, and would have passed by them. But they,

ἰδόντες αὐτὸν ᵏπεριπατοῦντα ἐπὶ τῆς θαλάσσης,‖ ἔδοξαν ˡ
seeing him walking on the sea, thought [it]

φάντασμα ᵐεἶναι,‖ καὶ ἀνέκραξαν. 50 πάντες γὰρ αὐτὸν
an apparition to be, and cried out: for all him

ⁿεἶδον,‖ καὶ ἐταράχθησαν. ᵒκαὶ εὐθέως‖ ἐλάλησεν μετ' αὐτῶν,
saw, and were troubled. And immediately he spoke with them,

καὶ λέγει αὐτοῖς, Θαρσεῖτε· ἐγώ εἰμι, μὴ φοβεῖσθε.
and says to them, Be of good courage: I am [he]; fear not.

51 Καὶ ἀνέβη πρὸς αὐτοὺς εἰς τὸ πλοῖον, καὶ ἐκόπασεν ὁ
And he went up to them into the ship, and fell the

ἄνεμος· καὶ λίαν ᴾἐκ περισσοῦ‖ ἐν ἑαυτοῖς ἐξίσταντο,
wind. And exceedingly beyond measure in themselves they were amazed,

ᵠκαὶ ἐθαύμαζον·‖ 52 οὐ γὰρ συνῆκαν ἐπὶ τοῖς ἄρτοις· ʳἦν γὰρ‖
and wondered; for they understood not by the loaves, for was

ˢἡ καρδία αὐτῶν‖ πεπωρωμένη.
their heart hardened.

53 Καὶ διαπεράσαντες ᵗἦλθον ἐπὶ τὴν γῆν‖ ⱽΓεννησαρέτ,‖
And having passed over they came to the land of Gennesaret,

καὶ προσωρμίσθησαν. 54 καὶ ἐξελθόντων αὐτῶν ἐκ τοῦ
and drew to shore. And on their coming out of the

πλοίου, ᶠεὐθέως‖ ἐπιγνόντες αὐτόνʷ, 55 ˣπεριδραμόντες‖
ship, immediately having recognized him, running through

ὅλην τὴν ʸπερίχωρον‖ ἐκείνην ᶻ ἤρξαντο ἐπὶ τοῖς ᵃκραββάτοις‖
all that country around they began on couches

ᵇ κλάσματα Λ.   ᶜ κοφίνων TΛ.   ᵈ πληρώματα TTrΛ.   ᵉ — ὡσεὶ GLTTrΛW.   ᶠ εὐθὺς TTrΛ.
ᵍ ἀπολύει dismisses LTTrΛ.   ʰ ἰδὼν seeing LTTrΛ.   ⁱ — καὶ LTTrΛ.   ᵏ ἐπὶ τῆς θαλάσσης
περιπατοῦντα T.   ˡ + ὅτι that T.   ᵐ ἔστιν it is T.   ⁿ εἶδαν TTr.   ᵒ καὶ εὐθὺς LTrΛ ;
ὁ δὲ εὐθὺς T.   ᴾ [ἐκ περισσοῦ] Tr.   ᵠ — καὶ ἐθαύμαζον [L] TTrΛ.   ʳ ἀλλ' ἦν but was TTr.
ˢ αὐτῶν ἡ καρδία LTTrΛW.   ᵗ ἐπὶ τὴν γῆν ἦλθον εἰς T.   ⱽ Γεννησαρὲτ LTTrΛW.   ʷ + [οἱ
ἄνδρες τοῦ τόπου ἐκείνου] the men of that place L.   ˣ περιέδραμον they ran through TTr.
ʸ χώραν (omit around) TTrΛ.   ᶻ + καὶ and TTr.   ᵃ κραβάττοις LTTrΛW.

τοὺς κακῶς.ἔχοντας περιφέρειν, ὅπου ἤκόνον ὅτι
those that   were ill   to carry about,   where they were hearing that

ᶜἐκεῖ‖ ἐστιν. 56 καὶ ὅπου ᵈἂν‖ εἰσεπορεύετο εἰς κώμας ἦ ᵉ
there   he was.   And wherever   he entered   into villages or
(lit. he is.)

πόλεις ἦ ᵉ ἀγρούς, ἐν ταῖς ἀγοραῖς ᶠἐτίθουν‖ τοὺς ἀσθενοῦν-
cities or   fields,   in the marketplaces they laid those who   were sick,

τας, καὶ παρεκάλουν αὐτὸν ἵνα κἂν τοῦ κρασπέδου τοῦ
and   besought   him   that if only the   border

ἱματίου.αὐτοῦ ἅψωνται· καὶ ὅσοι ἂν ᵍἤπτοντο‖ αὐτοῦ
of his garment   they might touch; and as many as   touched   him

ἐσώζοντο.
were healed.

7 Καὶ συνάγονται πρὸς αὐτὸν οἱ Φαρισαῖοι καί τινες
And are gathered together to   him   the Pharisees and some

τῶν γραμματέων, ἐλθόντες ἀπὸ Ἱεροσολύμων· 2 καὶ ἰδόντες
of the   scribes,   having come from   Jerusalem;   and having seen

τινὰς τῶν.μαθητῶν.αὐτοῦ ʰ κοιναῖς χερσίν, ⁱτοῦτ᾽ ἔστιν‖
some   of his disciples   with defiled   hands,   that   is

ἀνίπτοις, ᵏἐσθίοντας‖ ἄρτους, ᵐἐμέμψαντο·‖ 3 οἱ.γὰρ Φαρι-
unwashed,   eating   bread, they found fault;   for the Phari-

σαῖοι καὶ πάντες οἱ Ἰουδαῖοι, ἐὰν.μὴ ⁿπυγμῇ‖ νίψωνται τὰς
sees   and   all   the   Jews,   unless with the fist they wash the

χεῖρας, οὐκ.ἐσθίουσιν, κρατοῦντες τὴν παράδοσιν τῶν πρεσ-
hands,   eat not,   holding   the   tradition of the   el-

βυτέρων· 4 καὶ ᵒἀπὸ‖ ἀγορᾶς, ἐὰν.μὴ βαπτίσωνται
ders;   and [on coming] from the market, unless they wash themselves

οὐκ.ἐσθίουσιν· καὶ ἄλλα πολλά ἐστιν ἃ παρέλαβον
they eat not;   and ²other ³things ¹many there are which they received

κρατεῖν, βαπτισμοὺς ποτηρίων καὶ ξεστῶν καὶ χαλκίων ᴾκαὶ
to hold,   washings   of cups ·   and   vessels and brazen utensils and

κλινῶν·‖ 5 ᵠἔπειτα‖ ἐπερωτῶσιν αὐτὸν οἱ Φαρισαῖοι καὶ οἱ
couches: then   question   him   the Pharisees   and the

γραμματεῖς, ʳΔιατί‖ ˢοἱ.μαθηταί.σου οὐ.περιπατοῦσιν‖ κατὰ
scribes,   Why   ³thy ⁴disciples   ¹walk ²not   according to

τὴν παράδοσιν τῶν πρεσβυτέρων, ἀλλὰ ᵗἀνίπτοις‖ χερσὶν
the   tradition of the   elders,   but with unwashed hands

ἐσθίουσιν τὸν ἄρτον; 6 Ὁ.δὲ ᵛἀποκριθεὶς‖ εἶπεν αὐτοῖς, ʷ ᵛὉτι‖
eat   bread?   But he   answering   said to them,

καλῶς ˣπροεφήτευσεν‖ Ἡσαΐας περὶ ὑμῶν τῶν ὑποκριτῶν,
Well   prophesied   Esaias concerning you,   hypocrites,

ὡς γέγραπται, ʸ ᶻΟὗτος ὁ λαὸς‖ τοῖς χείλεσίν με τιμᾷ,
as   it has been written, This   people with the   lips   me honour,

ἡ.δὲ.καρδία.αὐτῶν πόρρω ἀπέχει ἀπ᾽ ἐμοῦ. 7 μάτην.δὲ σέβον-
but their heart   far   is away from me.   But in vain they wor-

ταί με, διδάσκοντες διδασκαλίας ἐντάλματα ἀνθρώπων.
ship me,   teaching [as]   teachings   injunctions   of men.

8 Ἀφέντες.ᵃγὰρ‖ τὴν ἐντολὴν τοῦ θεοῦ, κρατεῖτε τὴν παρά-
For, leaving   the commandment of God, ye hold the   tra-

δοσιν τῶν ἀνθρώπων, ᵇβαπτισμοὺς ξεστῶν καὶ ποτηρίων, καὶ
dition   of men,   washings   of vessels and   cups,   and

that were sick, where they heard he was. 56 And whithersoever he entered, into villages, or cities, or country, they laid the sick in the streets, and besought him that they might touch if it were but the border of his garment: and as many as touched him were made whole.

VII. Then came together unto him the Pharisees, and certain of the scribes, which came from Jerusalem. 2 And when they saw some of his disciples eat bread with defiled, that is to say, with unwashen, hands, they found fault. 3 For the Pharisees, and all the Jews, except they wash their hands oft, eat not, holding the tradition of the elders. 4 And when they come from the market, except they wash, they eat not. And many other things there be, which they have received to hold, as the washing of cups, and pots, brasen vessels, and of tables. 5 Then the Pharisees and scribes asked him, Why walk not thy disciples according to the tradition of the elders, but eat bread with unwashen hands? 6 He answered and said unto them, Well hath Esaias prophesied of you hypocrites, as it is written, This people honoureth me with their lips, but their heart is far from me. 7 Howbeit in vain do they worship me, teaching for doctrines the commandments of men. 8 For laying aside the commandment of God, ye hold the tradition of men, as the washing of pots and cups: and many

---

ᶜ — ἐκεῖ LT[Tr].   ᵈ ἐὰν T.   ᵉ + εἰς into [L]TTrA.   ᶠ ἐτίθεσαν TTrA.   ᵍ ἤψαντο LTTr.
ʰ + ὅτι that TTr.   ⁱ τουτέστιν LA.   ᵏ ἐσθίουσιν they eat TTr.   ˡ + τοὺς LTTrA.
ᵐ — ἐμέμψαντο (read verses 3 and 4 in parenthesis) GLTTrAW.   ⁿ πυκνὰ often T.   ᵒ ἀπ᾽ LTrA.
ᴾ — καὶ κλινῶν T.   ᵠ καὶ and LTTrA.   ʳ διὰ τί LTrA.   ˢ οὐ περιπατοῦσιν οἱ μαθηταί σου TTrA.
ᵗ κοιναῖς with defiled GLTTrAW.   ᵛ — ἀποκριθεὶς TTrA.   ʷ — Ὅτι [L]T[TrA].   ˣ ἐπροφήτευσεν
LTTrA.   ʸ + ὅτι T.   ᶻ Ὁ λαὸς οὗτος L.   ᵃ — γὰρ for LTTrA.   ᵇ — βαπτισμοὺς ....
ποιεῖτε T[TrA].

other such like things
ye do. 9 And he said
unto them, Full well
ye reject the com-
mandment of God,
that ye may keep your
own tradition. 10 For
Moses said, Honour
thy father and thy
mother; and, Whoso
curseth father or mo-
ther, let him die the
death: 11 but ye say,
If a man shall say to
his father or mother,
It is Corban, that is to
say, a gift, by whatso-
ever thou mightest be
profited by me; *he
shall be free.* 12 And
ye suffer him no more
to do ought for his fa-
ther or his mother;
13 making the word of
God of none effect
through your tradi-
tion, which ye have
delivered: and many
such like things do ye.
14 And when he had
called all the people
unto him, he said unto
them, Hearken unto
me every one *of
you,* and understand:
15 there is nothing
from without a man,
that entering into him
can defile him: but
the things which come
out of him, those are
they that defile the
man. 16 If any man
have ears to hear, let
him hear. 17 And when
he was entered into
the house from the
people, his disciples
asked him concerning
the parable. 18 And
he saith unto them,
Are ye so without un-
derstanding also? Do
ye not perceive, that
whatsoever thing from
without entereth into
the man, *it* cannot
defile him; 19 because
it entereth not into
his heart, but into the
belly, and goeth out
into the draught,
purging all meats?
20 And he said, That
which cometh out of
the man, that defileth
the man. 21 For from
within, out of the
heart of men, proceed
evil thoughts, adul-
teries, fornications,
murders, 22 thefts,
covetousness, wicked-

ἀλλὰ παρόμοια   τοιαῦτα πολλὰ ποιεῖτε.‖ 9 Καὶ ἔλεγεν
²other   ⁴like [⁵things] ³such   ¹many ye do.   And he said
αὐτοῖς, Καλῶς ἀθετεῖτε τὴν ἐντολὴν. τοῦ θεοῦ,. ἵνα τὴν
to them, Well do ye set aside the commandment of God, that
παράδοσιν. ὑμῶν τηρήσητε. 10 ᶜΜωσῆς‖. γὰρ εἶπεν, ⌐Τίμα
your tradition   ye may observe.   For Moses   said,   Honour
τὸν. πατέρα. σου καὶ τὴν. μητέρα. σου· καί, Ὁ κακολογῶν πατέρα
thy father   and the mother;   and, He who speaks evil of father
ἢ μητέρα θανάτῳ τελευτάτω. 11 Ὑμεῖς. δὲ λέγετε, Ἐὰν εἴπῃ
or mother by death let him die.   But ye say,   If ³say
ἄνθρωπος τῷ πατρὶ ἢ τῇ μητρί,   Κορβᾶν ὅ ἐστιν, δῶρον,
¹a ²man   to father or mother, [It is] a corban, (that is,   a gift,)
ὃ. ἐὰν ἐξ ἐμοῦ   ὠφεληθῇς·   12 ᵈκαὶ‖ οὐκέτι ἀφίετε
whatever from me. thou mightest be profited by :—   and no longer ye suffer
αὐτὸν οὐδὲν ποιῆσαι τῷ. πατρὶ. ᵉαὐτοῦ‖ ἢ τῇ. μητρὶ. ᵉαὐτοῦ,‖
him anything to do   for his father   or   his mother,
     (*lit.* nothing)
13 ἀκυροῦντες τὸν λόγον τοῦ θεοῦ τῇ. παραδόσει. ὑμῶν ᶠ ᾗ
    making void   the word of God   by your tradition which
παρεδώκατε· καὶ παρόμοια   τοιαῦτα πολλὰ ποιεῖτε.
ye have delivered; and ⁴like [⁵things] ²such ¹many ye do.
14 Καὶ προσκαλεσάμενος ᶠπάντα‖ τὸν ὄχλον, ἔλεγεν αὐτοῖς,
    And having called to [him] all   the crowd, he said to them,
ᵍἈκούετέ‖ μου πάντες, καὶ ʰσυνίετε.‖ 15 οὐδέν ἐστιν ἔξω-
Hear ye me, all,   and understand : Nothing there is from with-
θεν. τοῦ ἀνθρώπου εἰσπορευόμενον εἰς αὐτόν, ὃ δύναται
out the   man   entering   into him, which is able
ⁱαὐτὸν κοινῶσαι·‖ ἀλλὰ   τὰ   ᵏἐκπορευόμενα ἀπ᾽ αὐτοῦ,‖
him   to defile ; but the things which go out   from him,
ˡἐκεῖνά‖ ἐστιν   τὰ   κοινοῦντα τὸν ἄνθρωπον. 16 ᵐεἴ τις
those   are the things which defile   the   man.   If anyone
ἔχει ὦτα ἀκούειν, ἀκουέτω.‖ 17 Καὶ ὅτε εἰσῆλθεν εἰς ⁿ οἶκον
have ears to hear, let him hear.   And when he went into a house
ἀπὸ τοῦ ὄχλου, ἐπηρώτων αὐτὸν οἱ. μαθηταὶ. αὐτοῦ ᵒπερὶ τῆς
from the crowd, ³asked   ⁴him ¹his ²disciples   concerning the
παραβολῆς.‖ 18 καὶ λέγει αὐτοῖς, Οὕτως καὶ ὑμεῖς ἀσύνε-
parable.   And he says to them, ⁴Thus ³also ²ye ¹without ⁵un-
τοί   ἐστε; οὐ. νοεῖτε ὅτι πᾶν τὸ ἔξωθεν εἰσπο-
derstanding ⁶are? Perceive ye not that everything which from without en-
ρευόμενον εἰς τὸν ἄνθρωπον οὐ. δύναται αὐτὸν. κοινῶσαι;
ters   into the man   is not able   him   to defile ?
19 ὅτι οὐκ. εἰσπορεύεται αὐτοῦ εἰς τὴν καρδίαν, ἀλλ᾽ εἰς τὴν
    because it enters not ⁴of ⁵him ¹into ²the ³heart, but into the
κοιλίαν· καὶ εἰς τὸν ἀφεδρῶνα ἐκπορεύεται, ᴾκαθαρίζον‖ πάντα
belly,   and into the draught   goes out,   purifying   all
τὰ βρώματα. 20 Ἔλεγεν. δέ, Ὅτι τὸ ἐκ τοῦ ἀνθρώπου
the food.   And he said,   That which out of the   man
ἐκπορευόμενον, ἐκεῖνο κοινοῖ τὸν ἄνθρωπον. 21 ἔσωθεν. γὰρ
goes forth,   that defiles the   man.   For from within
ἐκ τῆς καρδίας τῶν ἀνθρώπων οἱ διαλογισμοὶ οἱ κακοὶ ἐκ-
out of the heart   of men   ²reasonings   ¹evil go
πορεύονται, �q μοιχεῖαι, πορνεῖαι, φόνοι, 22 κλοπαί,‖ πλεον-
forth,   adulteries, fornications, murders, thefts,   covetous

ᶜ Μωϋσῆς LTTrAW.   ᵈ — καὶ LTTr[A].   ᵉ — αὐτοῦ (*read* [his]) LTTrA.   ᶠ πάλιν again
LTTrA.   ᵍ ἀκούσατέ LTTrA.   ʰ σύνετε LTTrA.   ⁱ κοινῶσαι αὐτὸν T.   ᵏ ἐκ τοῦ ἀνθρώπου
ἐκπορευόμενα from the man go out LTTrA.   ˡ — ἐκεῖνά T[Tr].   ᵐ — verse 16 T[TrA].
ⁿ + τὸν the (house) T.   ᵒ τὴν παραβολὴν the parable LTTrA.   ᴾ καθαρίζων LTTrA.
q πορνεῖαι, κλοπαί, φόνοι, μοιχεῖαι TTrA.

εξίαι, πονηρίαι, δόλος, ἀσέλγεια, ὀφθαλμὸς πονηρός,
desires, wickednesses, guile, licentiousness, an eye wicked,

βλασφημία, ὑπερηφανία, ἀφροσύνη· 23 πάντα ταῦτα τὰ
blasphemy, haughtiness, folly: all these

πονηρὰ ἔσωθεν ἐκπορεύεται, καὶ κοινοῖ τὸν ἄνθρωπον.
evils from within go forth, and defile the man.

24 ʳΚαὶ ἐκεῖθεν‖ ἀναστὰς ἀπῆλθεν εἰς τὰ ˢμεθόρια‖
And thence having risen up he went away into the borders

Τύρου ᵗκαὶ Σιδῶνος‖. καὶ εἰσελθὼν εἰς ᵛτὴν‖ οἰκίαν, οὐδένα
of Tyre and Sidon; and having entered into the house, no one

ʷἤθελεν‖ γνῶναι, καὶ οὐκ ˣἠδυνήθη‖ λαθεῖν. 25 ʸἀκούσασα
he wished to know [it], and he could not be hid. ⁵Having ⁵heard

γὰρ‖ γυνὴ περὶ αὐτοῦ, ἧς εἶχεν τὸ.θυγάτριον.αὐτῆς πνεῦμα
¹for ²a ²woman about him, of whom ⁴had ¹her ²little ³daughter a spirit

ἀκάθαρτον, ᶻἐλθοῦσα‖ προσέπεσεν πρὸς τοὺς.πόδας.αὐτοῦ
unclean, having come fell at his feet,

26 ᵃἦν.δὲ ἡ γυνὴ‖ Ἑλληνίς, ᵇΣυροφοίνισσα‖ τῷ γένει· καὶ
(now ³was ¹the ²woman a Greek, Syrophenician by race), and

ἠρώτα αὐτὸν ἵνα τὸ δαιμόνιον ᶜἐκβάλλῃ‖ ἐκ τῆς θυγατρὸς
asked him that the demon he should cast forth out of ²daughter

αὐτῆς. 27 ᵈὁ.δὲ.Ἰησοῦς εἶπεν‖ αὐτῇ, Ἄφες πρῶτον χορτασ-
¹her. But Jesus said to her, Suffer first to be satis-

θῆναι τὰ τέκνα· οὐ.γὰρ ᵉκαλόν ἐστιν‖ λαβεῖν τὸν ἄρτον τῶν
fied the children; for not good is it to take the bread of the

τέκνων, καὶ ᶠβαλεῖν τοῖς κυναρίοις.‖ 28 Ἡ.δὲ ἀπεκρίθη καὶ
children, and cast [it] to the dogs. But she answered and

λέγει αὐτῷ, Ναί, κύριε· καὶ.ᵍγὰρ‖ τὰ κυνάρια ὑποκάτω τῆς
says to him, Yea, Lord; for even the little dogs under the

τραπέζης ʰἐσθίει‖ ἀπὸ τῶν ψιχίων τῶν παιδίων. 29 Καὶ εἶπεν
table eat of the crumbs of the children. And he said

αὐτῇ, Διὰ τοῦτον τὸν λόγον ὕπαγε· ἐξελήλυθεν ⁱτὸ δαι-
to her, Because of this word go; has gone forth the de-

μόνιον ἐκ τῆς.θυγατρός.σου.‖ 30 Καὶ ἀπελθοῦσα εἰς τὸν
mon out of thy daughter. And having gone away to

οἶκον.αὐτῆς, εὗρεν ᵏτὸ δαιμόνιον ἐξεληλυθός, καὶ τὴν θυγα-
her house, she found the demon had gone forth, and the daugh-

τέρα βεβλημένην ἐπὶ τῆς κλίνης.‖
ter laid on the bed.

31 Καὶ πάλιν ἐξελθὼν ἐκ τῶν ὁρίων Τύρου ˡκαὶ Σιδῶνος,
And again having departed from the borders of Tyre and Sidon,

ἦλθεν‖ ᵐπρὸς‖ τὴν θάλασσαν τῆς Γαλιλαίας, ἀνὰ μέσον
he came to the sea of Galilee, through [the] midst

τῶν ὁρίων Δεκαπόλεως. 32 καὶ φέρουσιν αὐτῷ κωφὸν ⁿ
of the borders of Decapolis. And they bring to him a deaf man

ᵒμογιλάλον,‖ καὶ παρακαλοῦσιν αὐτὸν ἵνα ἐπιθῇ
who spoke with difficulty, and they beseech him that he might lay

αὐτῷ τὴν χεῖρα. 33 καὶ ἀπολαβόμενος αὐτὸν ἀπὸ τοῦ
on him [his] hand. And having taken away him from the

---

ness, deceit, lasciviousness, an evil eye, blasphemy, pride, foolishness: 23 all these evil things come from within, and defile the man.

24 And from thence he arose, and went into the borders of Tyre and Sidon, and entered into an house, and would have no man know it: but he could not be hid. 25 For a certain woman, whose young daughter had an unclean spirit, heard of him, and came and fell at his feet: 26 the woman was a Greek, a Syrophenician by nation; and she besought him that he would cast forth the devil out of her daughter. 27 But Jesus said unto her, Let the children first be filled: for it is not meet to take the children's bread, and to cast it unto the dogs. 28 And she answered and said unto him, Yes, Lord: yet the dogs under the table eat of the children's crumbs. 29 And he said unto her, For this saying go thy way; the devil is gone out of thy daughter. 30 And when she was come to her house, she found the devil gone out, and her daughter laid upon the bed.

31 And again, departing from the coasts of Tyre and Sidon, he came unto the sea of Galilee, through the midst of the coasts of Decapolis. 32 And they bring unto him one that was deaf, and had an impediment in his speech; and they beseech him to put his hand upon him. 33 And he took him aside from the multitude, and

---

ʳ Ἐκεῖθεν δὲ ΤΑ. ˢ ὅρια LTTr. ᵗ — καὶ Σιδῶνος ΤΑ. ᵛ — τὴν (read a house) LTTrAW.
ʷ ἠθέλησεν Τ. ˣ ἠδυνάσθη Τ. ʸ ἀλλ᾽ εὐθὺς ἀκούσασα but immediately having heard
TTrA. ᶻ εἰσελθοῦσα·having come in T. ᵃ ἡ δὲ γυνὴ ἦν LTA ; ἡ γυνὴ δὲ ἦν Tr. ᵇ Συρα
φοινίκισσα G ; Συροφοινίκισσα LTW ; Σύρα Φοινίκισσα TrA. ᶜ ἐκβάλῃ GLTTrAW. · ᵈ και.
ἔλεγεν and he said LTTrA. ᵉ ἐστιν καλὸν LTTrA. ᶠ τοῖς κυναρίοις βαλεῖν TTrA. ᵍ και.
for [L]TTr. ʰ ἐσθίουσιν LTTrAW. ⁱ ἐκ τῆς θυγατρός σου τὸ δαιμόνιον ΤΑ. ᵏ τὸ παιδίον
(the child) βεβλημένον ἐπὶ τὴν κλίνην καὶ τὸ δαιμόνιον ἐξεληλυθός LTTrA. ˡ ἦλθεν διὰ
Σιδῶνος he came through Sidon LTTrA. ᵐ εἰς unto GLTTrA. ⁿ + καὶ and LTTr.
ᵒ μογγιλάλον Tr.

put his fingers into his ears, and he spit, and touched his tongue ; 34 and looking up to heaven, he sighed, and saith unto him, Ephphatha, that is, Be opened. 35 And straightway his ears were opened, and the string of his tongue was loosed, and he spake plain. 36 And he charged them that they should tell no man : but the more he charged them, so much the more a great deal they published *it*; 37 and were beyond measure astonished, saying, He hath done all things well: he maketh both the deaf to hear, and the dumb to speak.

ὄχλου κατ᾽.ἰδίαν, ἔβαλεν τοὺς.δακτύλους.ᵖαὐτοῦ‖ εἰς τὰ ὦτα⟩
crowd   apart,   he put   his fingers   to   ²ears
αὐτοῦ, καὶ πτύσας ἥψατο τῆς.γλώσσης.αὐτοῦ, 34 καὶ ἀνα-
'his,   and having spit he touched   his tongue,   and having
βλέψας εἰς τὸν οὐρανὸν ἐστέναξεν, καὶ λέγει αὐτῷ, Ἐφφαθά,
looked up to the heaven   he groaned, and says to him, Ephphatha,
ὅ.ἐστιν, Διανοίχθητι. 35 Καὶ ᵠεὐθέως‖ ʳδιηνοίχθησαν‖ αὐτοῦ
that is,   Be opened.   And immediately   were opened   his
αἱ ἀκοαί, καὶ ˢ ἐλύθη ὁ δεσμὸς τῆς.γλώσσης.αὐτοῦ, καὶ ἐλάλει
ears,   and was loosed the band   of his tongue,   and he spake
ὀρθῶς. 36 καὶ διεστείλατο αὐτοῖς ἵνα μηδενὶ ᵗεἴπωσιν·‖
rightly.   And   he charged   them   that   no one they should tell.
ὅσον.δὲ ᵛαὐτὸς‖ αὐτοῖς διεστέλλετο, ʷμᾶλλον πρρισσότερον
But as much as   he   them   charged,   exceeding more abundantly
ἐκήρυσσον. 37 καὶ ὑπερπερισσῶς ἐξεπλήσσοντο, λέγοντες,
they proclaimed [it]: and above measure   they were astonished,   saying,
Καλῶς πάντα πεποίηκεν· καὶ τοὺς κωφοὺς ποιεῖ ἀκούειν,
⁶Well   ⁴all ⁵things ¹he ²has ³done: both the   deaf   he makes to hear,
καὶ ˣτοὺς‖ ἀλάλους λαλεῖν.
and the   dumb   to speak.

VIII. In those days the multitude being very great, and having nothing to eat, Jesus called his disciples unto him, and saith unto them, 2 I have compassion on the multitude, because they have now been with me three days, and have nothing to eat : 3 and if I send them away fasting to their own houses, they will faint by the way : for divers of them came from far. 4 And his disciples answered him, From whence can a man satisfy these *men* with bread here in the wilderness ? 5 And he asked them, How many loaves have ye? And they said, Seven. 6 And he commanded the people to sit down on the ground : and he took the seven loaves, and gave thanks, and brake, and gave to his disciples to set before *them*; and they did set *them* before the people. 7 And they had a few small fishes: and he blessed, and commanded to set

8 Ἐν ἐκείναις.ταῖς.ἡμέραις ʸπαμπόλλου‖ ὄχλου ὄντος,
In   those days   very great [the] crowd   being,
καὶ μὴ ἐχόντων τί · φάγωσιν, προσκαλεσάμενος ᶻὁ Ἰη-
and not having what they may eat, ²having ³called ⁴to [⁵him]   ¹Je-
σοῦς‖ τοὺς.μαθητὰς.ᵃαὐτοῦ‖ λέγει αὐτοῖς, 2 Σπλαγχνίζομαι
sus   his disciples   he says to them,   I am moved with compassion
ἐπὶ τὸν ὄχλον· ὅτι ἤδη ᵇἡμέρας‖ τρεῖς προσμένουσίν ᶜμοι,‖
on   the crowd, because already ²days   ¹three   they continue   with me
καὶ οὐκ.ἔχουσιν τί φάγωσιν· 3 καὶ ἐὰν ἀπολύσω αὐτοὺς
and   have not   what they may eat;   and if I shall send away   them
ᵈνήστεις‖ εἰς οἶκον.αὐτῶν, ἐκλυθήσονται ἐν τῇ ὁδῷ· ᵉτινὲς.γὰρ‖
fasting   to   their home,   they will faint   in the way;   for some
αὐτῶν ᶠ μακρόθεν ᵍἥκασιν.‖ 4 Καὶ ἀπεκρίθησαν αὐτῷ οἱ μαθη-
of them   from afar   are come.   And   ³answered   ⁴him   ¹disci-
ταὶ αὐτοῦ, ʰΠόθεν τούτους δυνήσεταί τις ὧδε χορτάσαι
ples   'his,   Whence   ⁶these   ¹shall ³be ⁴able ²anyone ⁵here   to satisfy
ἄρτων ἐπ᾽.ἐρημίας; 5 Καὶ ⁱἐπηρώτα‖ αὐτούς, Πόσους ἔχετε
with bread   in a desert?   And he asked   them, How many ²have ³ye
ἄρτους; Οἱ.δὲ ᵏεἶπον,‖ Ἑπτά. 6 Καὶ ˡπαρήγγειλεν‖ τῷ ὄχλῳ
¹loaves? And they said,   Seven.   And   he ordered   the crowd
ἀναπεσεῖν ἐπὶ τῆς γῆς· καὶ λαβὼν τοὺς ἑπτὰ ἄρτους,
to recline   on the ground. And having taken   the seven   loaves,
ᵐεὐχαριστήσας ἔκλασεν καὶ ἐδίδου τοῖς.μαθηταῖς.αὐτοῦ, ἵνα
having given thanks   he broke   and gave   to his disciples,   that
ⁿπαραθῶσιν·‖   καὶ   παρέθηκαν   τῷ ὄχλῳ. 7 καὶ
they might set before [them]. And they set [it] before the   crowd.   And
ᵒεἶχον‖ ἰχθύδια ὀλίγα· καὶ ᵖᵃ εὐλογήσας ᵠᵃεἶπεν παρα-
they had   small fishes a few;   and   having blessed   he desired ³to ⁴be ⁵set

---

ᵖ — αὐτοῦ (*read* [his] fingers) T.   ᵠ — εὐθέως [L]TTrA.   ʳ ἠνοίγησαν LTTrA.
ˢ + εὐθὺς immediately T.   ᵗ λέγωσιν TTrA.   ᵛ — αὐτὸς (*read* he charged) LTTrAW.
ʷ + αὐτοὶ they LTTrA.   ˣ — τοὺς TTrA.   ʸ πάλιν πολλοῦ again great LTTrA.   ᶻ — ὁ Ἰησοῦς GLTTrAW.   ᵃ — αὐτοῦ (*read* the disciples) TTr.   ᵇ ἡμέραι GLTTrAW.   ᶜ — μοι
L[Tr]A.   ᵈ νήστις T.   ᵉ καί τινες and some LTTrA.   ᶠ + ἀπὸ from (afar) TTrA.
ᵍ ἥκουσί EW ; εἰσίν are A.   ʰ + ὅτι TTrA.   ⁱ ἠρώτα TTrA.   ᵏ εἶπαν TTrA.   ˡ παραγ-
γέλλει he orders LTTrA.   ᵐ + [καὶ] and L.   ⁿ παρατιθῶσιν TTrA.   ᵒ εἶχαν LTTrA.
ᵖᵃ + ταῦτα these L   ᵠᵃ εἶπεν παρατεθῆναι καὶ αὐτὰ L ; αὐτὰ εἶπεν καὶ ταῦτα παρατιθέναι Tr ;
αὐτὰ παρέθηκεν he set these before [them] TA.

θεῖναι   καὶ αὐτά.‖ 8 ᵣἔφαγον.δὲ‖ καὶ ἐχορτάσθησαν. καὶ
ᵉbefore[⁷them] ²also ¹these.   And they ate and   were satisfied. And

ἦραν   περισσεύματα κλασμάτων ἑπτὰ ˢσπυρίδας.‖ 9 ἦσαν.δὲ
they took up ³over ⁴and ⁵above ¹of²fragments seven   baskets.   And ⁵were

ᵗοἱ   φαγόντες‖ ὡς τετρακισχίλιοι· καὶ ἀπέλυσεν αὐτούς.
¹those ²who ³had ⁴eaten about four thousand; and he sent ²away ¹them.

10 Καὶ ᵛεὐθέως‖ ἐμβὰςʷ εἰς τὸ πλοῖον μετὰ τῶν μαθητῶν
And immediately having entered into the ship   with   ²disciples

αὐτοῦ, ἦλθεν εἰς.τὰ μέρη Δαλμανουθά. 11 καὶ ἐξῆλθονʸ· οἱ
¹his, he came into the parts of Dalmanutha.   And ³went ⁴out ¹the

Φαρισαῖοι καὶ ἤρξαντο ᶻσυζητεῖν‖ αὐτῷ, ζητοῦντες παρ'
²Pharisees and began to dispute with him,   seeking   from

αὐτοῦ σημεῖον ἀπὸ τοῦ οὐρανοῦ. πειράζοντες αὐτόν. 12 καὶ
him   a sign from the heaven,   tempting   him.   And

ἀναστενάξας .τῷ.πνεύματι.αὐτοῦ λέγει, Τί ἡ.γενεὰ.αὕτη
having groaned   in his spirit   he says, Why ²this ³generation

ᵛσημεῖον ἐπιζητεῖ;‖ ἀμὴν λέγω ᶻὑμῖν,‖ εἰ.δοθήσεται τῇ
⁴a ¹sign ¹seeks?   Verily I say to you, If there shall be given

γενεᾷ.ταύτῃ σημεῖον. 13 Καὶ ἀφεὶς αὐτούς, ᵃἐμβὰς
to this generation a sign.   And having left them, having entered

ᵇπάλιν‖ ᵇεἰς τὸ πλοῖον‖ ἀπῆλθεν εἰς τὸ πέραν.
again   into the ship   he went away to the other side.

14 Καὶ ἐπελάθοντο λαβεῖν ἄρτους, καὶ εἰ.μὴ ἕνα ἄρτον
And they forgot to take loaves, and except one loaf

οὐκ.εἶχον   μεθ' ἑαυτῶν ἐν τῷ πλοίῳ. 15 καὶ διεστέλλετο
they had not [any] with them in the ship.   And he charged

αὐτοῖς, λέγων, Ὁρᾶτε, ᶜβλέπετε ἀπὸ τῆς ζύμης τῶν Φαρισαίων
them, saying, See, take heed of the leaven of the · Pharisees

καὶ τῆς ζύμης Ἡρῴδου. 16 Καὶ διελογίζοντο πρὸς ἀλλήλους,
and of the leaven of Herod. And they reasoned among one another,

ᵈλέγοντες,‖ Ὅτι ἄρτους οὐκ ᵉἔχομεν.‖ 17 Καὶ γνοὺς
saying, Because loaves ³not ¹we ²have.   And knowing [it]

ᶠὁ Ἰησοῦς‖ λέγει αὐτοῖς, Τί διαλογίζεσθε ὅτι ἄρτους οὐκ.
Jesus   says to them, Why reason ye because loaves ³not

ἔχετε;   οὔπω.νοεῖτε οὐδὲ.συνίετε; ᵍἔτι‖ πεπωρωμένην
¹ye ²have? Do ye not yet perceive nor understand? Yet   hardened

ἔχετε τὴν.καρδίαν.ὑμῶν; 18 ὀφθαλμοὺς ἔχοντες οὐ.βλέπετε;
have ye your heart?   Eyes   having, · do ye not see?

καὶ ὦτα ἔχοντες οὐκ.ἀκούετε; καὶ οὐ.μνημονεύετε; 19 ὅτε
and ears having, do ye not hear? and do ye not remember? When

τοὺς πέντε ἄρτους ἔκλασα εἰς τοὺς πεντακισχιλίους, ʰ πόσους
the five loaves I broke to the five thousand,   how many

κοφίνους ⁱπλήρεις .κλασμάτων‖ ἤρατε; Λέγουσιν αὐτῷ,
hand-baskets full   of fragments took ye up? They say to him,

Δώδεκα. 20 Ὅτε.ᵏδὲ τοὺς ἑπτὰ ˡ εἰς τοὺς τετρακισχιλίους,
Twelve.   And when the seven to the four thousand,

πόσων σπυρίδων πληρώματα κλασμάτων ἤρατε; ᵐΟἱ.δὲ
of how many baskets [the] fillings of fragments took ye up? And they

εἶπον,‖ Ἑπτά. 21 Καὶ ἔλεγεν αὐτοῖς, ⁿΠῶς‖ ᵒοὐ‖ συνίετε;
said, Seven.   And he said to them, How ²not ¹do ²ye understand?

---

them also before *them.*
8 So they did eat, and
were filled: and they
took up of the broken
meat that was left
seven baskets. 9 And
they that had eaten
were about four thou-
sand: and he sent
them away.
10 And straightway
he entered into a ship
with his disciples, and
came into the parts of
Dalmanutha. 11 And
the Pharisees came
forth, and began to
question with him,
seeking of him a sign
from heaven, tempting
him. 12 And he sighed
deeply in' his spirit,
and saith, Why doth
this generation seek
after a sign? verily I
say unto you, There
shall no sign be given
unto this generation.
13 And he left them,
and entering into the
ship again departed to
the other side.
14 Now *the disciples*
had forgotten to take
bread, neither had
they in the ship with
them more than one
loaf. 15 And he charged
them, saying, Take
heed, beware of the
leaven of the Phari-
sees, and *of* the leaven
of Herod. 16 And they
reasoned among them-
selves, saying, *It is*
because we have no
bread. 17 And when
Jesus knew *it,* he saith
unto them, Why reason
ye, because ye have no
bread? perceive ye not
yet, neither under-
stand? have ye your
heart yet hardened?
18 Having eyes, see ye
not? and having ears,
hear ye not? and do
ye not remember?
19 When I brake the
five loaves among five
thousand, how many
baskets full of frag-
ments took ye up?
They say unto him,
Twelve. 20 And when
the seven among four
thousand, how many
baskets full of frag-
ments took ye up?
And they said, Seven.
21 And he said unto
them, How is it that
ye do not understand?

ᵣ καὶ ἔφαγον LTTr.   ˢ σφυρίδας L.   ᵗ — οἱ φαγόντες (*read* and they were) T[Tr]A.
ᵛ εὐθὺς LTTrA.   ʷ + [αὐτὸς] he L.   ᶻ συνζητεῖν LTTrA.   ʸ ζητεῖ σημεῖον LTTrA.   ᶻ [ὑμῖν] A.
ᵃ πάλιν ἐμβὰς LTTrA.   ᵇ — τὸ LTᵣW; [εἰς πλοῖον] Tr; — εἰς τὸ πλοῖον (*read* ἐμβὰς having
embarked) TA.   ᵉ + .[καὶ] and L.   ᵈ — λέγοντες LTTrA.   ᵉ ἔχουσιν they have LTrA.
ᶠ — ὁ Ἰησοῦς (*read* he says) T[Tr]A.   ᵍ — ἔτι LTTrA.   ʰ + καὶ T.   ⁱ κλασμάτων πλήρεις
LTTrAW.   ᵏ [δὲ] TrA; καὶ T.   ˡ + [ἄρτους] loaves L.   ᵐ καὶ λέγουσιν T; καὶ λέγουσιν
αὐτῷ and they say to him A.   ⁿ — Πῶς TA.   ᵒ οὔπω not yet LTTrA.

22 And he cometh to Bethsaida; and they bring a blind man unto him, and besought him to touch him. 23 And he took the blind man by the hand, and led him out of the town; and when he had spit on his eyes, and put his hands upon him, he asked him if he saw ought. 24 And he looked up, and said, I see men as trees, walking. 25 After that he put *his* hands again upon his eyes, and made him look up: and he was restored, and saw every man clearly. 26 And he sent him away to his house, saying, Neither go into the town, nor tell *it* to any in the town.

22 Καὶ ᵖἔρχεται‖ εἰς Βηθσαϊδάν· καὶ φέρουσιν αὐτῷ τυφλόν,
And he comes to Bethsaida; and they bring to him ⟩ a blind

καὶ παρακαλοῦσιν αὐτὸν ἵνα αὐτοῦ ἅψηται. 23 καὶ
[man], and beseech him that him he might touch. And

ἐπιλαβόμενος τῆς χειρὸς τοῦ τυφλοῦ ᑫἐξήγαγεν‖ αὐτὸν
taking hold of the hand of the blind [man] he led forth him

ἔξω τῆς ·κώμης, καὶ πτύσας εἰς τὰ.ὄμματα.αὐτοῦ, ἐπιθεὶς
out of the village, and having spit upon his eyes, having laid

τὰς χεῖρας αὐτῷ ἐπηρώτα αὐτὸν εἴ τι ʳβλέπει.‖ 24 καὶ
[his] hands upon him he asked him if anything he beholds. And

ἀναβλέψας ἔλεγεν, Βλέπω τοὺς ἀνθρώπους, ˢὅτι ὡς δένδρα
having looked up he said, I behold the men, for as trees

ὁρῶ‖ περιπατοῦντας. 25 Εἶτα. πάλιν ᵗἐπέθηκεν‖ τὰς
I see [them] walking. Then again he laid [his]

χεῖρας ἐπὶ τοὺς.ὀφθαλμοὺς.αὐτοῦ, καὶ ᵛἐποίησεν αὐτὸν ἀνα-
hands upon his eyes, and made him look

βλέψαι.‖ καὶ ʷἀποκατεστάθη,‖ καὶ ˣἐνέβλεψεν‖ ʸτηλαυγῶς‖
up. And he was restored, and looked ᵛᵛon ¹clearly

ᶻἅπαντας.‖ 26 καὶ ἀπέστειλεν αὐτὸν εἰς ᵃτὸν.ᵛοἶκον.αὐτοῦ,
all [men]. And he sent him to his house,

λέγων, ᵇΜηδὲ‖ εἰς τὴν κώμην εἰσέλθῃς. ᶜμηδὲ εἴπῃς
saying, Neither into the ⟩ village mayest thou enter, nor mayest tell [it]

τινὶ ἐν τῇ κώμῃ.ᵈ
to any one in the village.

---

27 And Jesus went out, and his disciples, into the towns of Cæsarea Philippi: and by the way he asked his disciples, saying unto them, Whom do men say that I am? 28 And they answered, John the Baptist: but some *say*, Elias; and others, One of the prophets. 29 And he saith unto them, But whom say ye that I am? And Peter answereth and saith unto him, Thou art the Christ. 30 And he charged them that they should tell no man of him. 31 And he began to teach them, that the Son of man must suffer many things, and be rejected of the elders, and *of* the chief priests, and scribes, and be killed, and after three days rise again. 32 And he spake that saying openly. And Peter took him, and began

27 Καὶ ἐξῆλθεν ὁ Ἰησοῦς καὶ οἱ.μαθηταὶ.αὐτοῦ εἰς τὰς κώ-
And ²went ³forth ¹Jesus and his disciples into the vil-

μας Καισαρείας·τῆς Φιλίππου· καὶ ἐν τῇ ὁδῷ ἐπηρώτα
lages of Cæsarea Philippi. And by the way he was questioning

τοὺς.μαθητὰς.αὐτοῦ, λέγων ᵈαὐτοῖς,‖ Τίνα με λέγουσιν οἱ
his disciples, saying to them, Whom ᵐme ¹do ²pronounce

ἄνθρωποι εἶναι; 28 Οἱ.δὲ ᶠἀπεκρίθησαν‖ ᶠ, ᵍἸωάννην τον βαπ-
²men to be? And they answered, John the Bap-

τιστήν· καὶ ἄλλοι ʰἨλίαν·‖ ἄλλοι.δὲ ᶦἕνα‖ τῶν.προφητῶν.
tist; and others, Elias; but others, one of the prophets.

29 Καὶ αὐτὸς ᵏλέγει αὐτοῖς,‖ Ὑμεῖς.δὲ τίνα με λέγετε
And he says to them, But ye, whom ᵐme ¹do ²ye ³pronounce

εἶναι; ˡἈποκριθεὶς ᵐδὲ‖ ὁ Πέτρος λέγει αὐτῷ, Σὺ.εἶ ὁ χριστός.
to be? ⁿAnswering ⟩ ¹and ² Peter says to him, Thou art the Christ.

30 Καὶ ἐπετίμησεν αὐτοῖς ἵνα μηδενὶ ⁿλέγωσιν‖ περὶ
And he strictly charged them that no one they should tell concerning

αὐτοῦ. 31 Καὶ ἤρξατο διδάσκειν αὐτοὺς ὅτι δεῖ τὸν
him. And he began to teach them that it is necessary for the

υἱὸν τοῦ ἀνθρώπου πολλὰ παθεῖν, καὶ ἀποδοκιμασθῆναι
Son of man many things to suffer, and to be rejected

ᵒἀπὸ‖ τῶν πρεσβυτέρων καὶ ᵖᵃἀρχιερέων καὶ ᵖᵃγραμματέων, καὶ
of the elders and chief priests and scribes, and

ἀποκτανθῆναι, καὶ μετὰ τρεῖς ἡμέρας ἀναστῆναι· 32 καὶ
to be killed, and after three ⟩ days to rise [again]. And

παρρησίᾳ τὸν λόγον ἐλάλει. Καὶ προσλαβόμενος ᑫᵃαὐτὸν
openly the word he spoke. And ²having ³taken ⁵to [⁶him] ⁴him

ᵖ ἔρχονται they come LTTrA.   ᑫ ἐξήνεγκεν he brought forth TTrA.   ʳ βλέπεις thou beholdest A.   ˢ ὡς δένδρα G.   ᵗ ἔθηκεν TrA.   ᵛ διέβλεψεν he saw distinctly TTrA.   ʷ ἀπεκατεστάθη L; ἀπεκατέστη TTrA.   ˣ ἐνέβλεπεν LTTrA.   ʸ δηλαυγῶς T.   ᶻ ἅπαντα all things LTTrA.   ᵃ — τὸν GLTTrA.   ᵇ μὴ not T.   ᶜ — μηδὲ .... κώμῃ T.   ᵈ [αὐτοῖς] Tr.   ᵉ εἶπαν spake TA.   ᶠ + αὐτῷ λέγοντες to him saying LTTrA.   ᵍ + ὅτι TA.   ʰ Ἠλείαν T.   ᶦ ὅτι εἷς LTTrA.   ᵏ ἐπηρώτα αὐτούς asked them LTTrA.   ˡ + καὶ and L.   ᵐ — δὲ LTTrA.   ⁿ εἴπωσιν L.   ᵒ ὑπὸ by LTTrAW.   ᵖᵃ + τῶν of the GLTTrAW.   ᑫᵃ ὁ Πέτρος αὐτὸν LTTrA.

ὁ Πέτρος‖ ἤρξατο ἐπιτιμᾶν αὐτῷ. 33 ὁ.δὲ ἐπιστραφεὶς καὶ
~ ¹Peter began to rebuke him. But he, turning and

ἰδὼν τοὺς.μαθητὰς.αὐτοῦ, ἐπετίμησεν ʳτῷ‖ Πέτρῳ, ˢλεγων,‖
seeing his disciples, rebuked Peter, saying,

Ὕπαγε ὀπίσω μου, σατανᾶ· ὅτι οὐ.φρονεῖς τὰ
Get behind me, Satan, for thy thoughts are not of the things

τοῦ θεοῦ, ἀλλὰ τὰ τῶν ἀνθρώπων.
of God, but the things of men.

34 Καὶ προσκαλεσάμενος τὸν ὄχλον σὺν τοῖς μαθηταῖς
And having called to [him] the crowd with ²disciples

αὐτοῦ εἶπεν αὐτοῖς, ᵗ Ὅστις‖ θέλει ὀπίσω μου ᵛἐλθεῖν,‖ ἀπαρ-
¹his he said to them, Whosoever desires after me to come, let

νησάσθω ἑαυτόν, καὶ ἀράτω τὸν.σταυρὸν.αὐτοῦ, καὶ
him deny himself, and let him take up his cross, and

ἀκολουθείτω μοι. 35 ὃς.γὰρ.ᵂἂν‖ θέλῃ τὴν.ψυχὴν.αὐτοῦ
let him follow me. For whoever may desire his life

σῶσαι, ἀπολέσει αὐτήν· ὃς.δ᾽.ἂν ˣἀπολέσῃ‖ τὴν.ʸψυχὴν.αὐτοῦ
to save, shall lose it, but whoever may lose his life

ἕνεκεν ἐμοῦ καὶ τοῦ εὐαγγελίου, ᶻοὗτος‖ σώσει αὐτήν.
on account of me and of the glad tidings, he shall save it.

36 τί.γὰρ ᵃὠφελήσει‖ ᵇἄνθρωπον ᶜἐὰν κερδήσῃ‖ τὸν κόσμον
For what shall it profit a man if he gain the ²world

ὅλον καὶ ᵈζημιωθῇ‖ τὴν.ψυχὴν.αὐτοῦ; 37 ᵉἢ τί δώσει
¹whole and lose his soul? or what shall ²give

ἄνθρωπος‖ ἀντάλλαγμα τῆς.ψυχῆς.αὐτοῦ; 38 ὃς.γὰρ.ᶠἂν‖
¹a ²man [as] an exchange for his soul? For whoever

ἐπαισχυνθῇ με καὶ τοὺς.ἐμοὺς.λόγους ἐν τῇ.γενεᾷ.ταύτῃ
may have been a-shamed of me and my words in this generation

τῇ μοιχαλίδι καὶ ἁμαρτωλῷ, καὶ ὁ υἱὸς τοῦ ἀνθρώπου ἐπαισ-
the adulterous and sinful, also the Son of man will be

χυνθήσεται αὐτόν. ὅταν ἔλθῃ ἐν τῇ δόξῃ τοῦ.πατρος.αὐτοῦ
ashamed of him when he shall come in the glory of his Father

μετὰ τῶν ἀγγέλων τῶν ἁγίων. 9 Καὶ ἔλεγεν αὐτοῖς, Ἀμὴν
with the angels the holy. And he said to them, Verily

λέγω ὑμῖν, ὅτι εἰσὶν τινὲς ᵍτῶν ὧδε‖ ἑστηκότων, οἵτινες
I say to you, That there are some of those here standing, who

οὐ.μὴ γεύσωνται θανάτου ἕως.ἂν ἴδωσιν τὴν βασιλείαν.τοῦ
in no wise shall taste of death until they see the kingdom

θεοῦ ἐληλυθυῖαν ἐν δυνάμει.
of God having come in power.

2 Καὶ ʰμεθ᾽‖ ἡμέρας ἓξ παραλαμβάνει ὁ Ἰησοῦς τὸν
And after ²days ¹six takes ²with [ᵉhim] ³Jesus

Πέτρον καὶ ⁱτὸν‖ Ἰάκωβον καὶ ᵏτὸν‖ Ἰωάννην, καὶ ἀναφέρει
Peter and James and John, and brings up

αὐτοὺς εἰς ὄρος ὑψηλὸν κατ᾽.ἰδίαν μόνους· καὶ μετεμορ-
them into a ²mountain ¹high apart alone. And he was trans-

φώθη ἔμπροσθεν αὐτῶν, 3 καὶ τὰ.ἱμάτια.αὐτοῦ ˡἐγένετο‖
figured before them; and his garments became

στίλβοντα, λευκὰ λίαν ᵐὡς χιών,‖ οἷα γναφεὺς ἐπὶ τῆς
shining, white exceedingly as snow, such as a fuller on the

to rebuke him. 33 But when he had turned about and looked on his disciples, he rebuked Peter, saying, Get thee behind me, Satan: for thou savourest not the things that be of God, but the things that be of men.

34 And when he had called the people unto him with his disciples also, he said unto them, Whosoever will come after me, let him deny himself, and take up his cross, and follow me. 35 For whosoever will save his life shall lose it; but whosoever shall lose his life for my sake and the gospel's, the same shall save it. 36 For what shall it profit a man, if he shall gain the whole world, and lose his own soul? 37 Or what shall a man give in exchange for his soul? 38 Whosoever therefore shall be ashamed of me and of my words in this adulterous and sinful generation; of him also shall the Son of man be ashamed, when he cometh in the glory of his Father with the holy angels. IX. And he said unto them, Verily I say unto you, That there be some of them that stand here, which shall not taste of death, till they have seen the kingdom of God come with power·

2 And after six days Jesus taketh with him Peter, and James, and John, and leadeth them up into an high mountain apart by themselves: and he was transfigured before them. 3 And his raiment became shining, exceeding white as snow; so as no fuller on earth can white

---

ʳ — τῷ LTTrA. ˢ καὶ λέγει and says TTrA. ᵗ Εἰ τις If any one LTr. ᵛ ἀκολουθεῖν to follow GTTrAW. ᵂ ἐὰν TTrA. ˣ ἀπολέσει shall lose TTrA. ʸ ἑαυτοῦ ψυχὴν GTrW. ᶻ — οὗτος GLTTrAW. ᵃ ὠφελεῖ does it profit TA. ᵇ + τὸν the (man) LTr[A]W. ᶜ κερδή-σαι to gain TA. ᵈ ζημιωθῆναι to lose TA. ᵉ τί γὰρ δοῖ ἄνθρωπος (read ¹or what, &c) TTr ; τί γὰρ [δώσει ἄνθρωπος] A. ᶠ ἐὰν LTTrA. ᵍ ὧδε τῶν ‖TTrA. ʰ μετὰ LTTrA. ⁱ — τὸν W. ᵏ — τὸν GLTrA. ˡ ἐγένοντο LTTrAW. ᵐ — ὡς χιών TT A.

them. 4 And there appeared unto them Elias with Moses: and they were talking with Jesus. 5 And Peter answered and said to Jesus, Master, it is good for us to be here: and let us make three tabernacles; one for thee, and one for Moses, and one for Elias. 6 For he wist not what to say; for they were sore afraid. 7 And there was a cloud that overshadowed them: and a voice came out of the cloud, saying, This is my beloved Son: hear him. 8 And suddenly, when they had looked round about, they saw no man any more, save Jesus only with themselves. 9 And as they came down from the mountain, he charged them that they should tell no man what things they had seen, till the Son of man were risen from the dead. 10 And they kept that saying with themselves, questioning one with another what the rising from the dead should mean. 11 And they asked him, saying, Why say the scribes that Elias must first come? 12 And he answered and told them, Elias verily cometh first, and restoreth all things; and how it is written of the Son of man, that he must suffer many things, and be set at nought. 13 But I say unto you, That Elias is indeed come, and they have done unto him whatsoever they listed, as it is written of him.

14 And when he came to his disciples, he saw a great multitude about them, and the scribes questioning with them. 15 And straightway all the people, when they beheld him, were greatly amazed, and running

γῆς οὐ.δύναται ⁿ λευκᾶναι. 4 καὶ ὤφθη αὐτοῖς °'Ηλίας‖ σὺν
earth is not able to whiten. And ⁴appeared ⁵to ⁶them ¹Elias ²with

ᴾΜωσεῖ,‖ καὶ ἦσαν ᵠσυλλαλοῦντες‖ τῷ Ἰησοῦ. 5 καὶ ἀποκριθεὶς
³Moses, and they were talking with Jesus. And ²answering

ὁ Πέτρος λέγει τῷ Ἰησοῦ, ʳΡαββί,‖ καλόν ἐστιν ἡμᾶς ὧδε
¹Peter says to Jesus, Rabbi, good it is for us here

εἶναι· καὶ ποιήσωμεν ˢσκηνὰς τρεῖς,‖ σοὶ μίαν, καὶ ᴾΜω
to be; and let us make ²tabernacles ¹three, for thee one, and for Mo-

σεῖ‖ μίαν, καὶ ᵗ'Ηλίᾳ‖ μίαν. 6 οὐ.γὰρ.ᾔδει τί ᵛλαλήσῃ·‖
ses one, and for Elias one. For he knew not what he should say;

ʷἦσαν.γὰρ ·ἔκφοβοι.‖ 7 καὶ ἐγένετο νεφέλη ἐπισκιάζουσα
for they were greatly afraid. And there came a cloud overshadowing

αὐτοῖς· καὶ ˣἦλθεν‖ φωνὴ ἐκ τῆς νεφέλης, ʸλέγουσα,‖ Οὗτός
them; and there came a voice out of the cloud, saying, This

ἐστιν ὁ.υἱός.μου ὁ ἀγαπητός· ᶻαὐτοῦ.ἀκούετε‖ 8 Καὶ ἐξάπινα
is my Son the beloved: ³him ¹hear ²ye. And suddenly

περιβλεψάμενοι οὐκέτι.οὐδένα εἶδον, ᵃἀλλὰ‖ τὸν Ἰησοῦν
having looked around no longer any one they saw, but Jesus

μόνον μεθ' ἑαυτῶν. 9 ᵇΚαταβαινόντων.δὲ‖ αὐτῶν ᶜἀπὸ‖ τοῦ
alone with themselves. And as ²were ²descending ¹they from the

ὄρους διεστείλατο αὐτοῖς ἵνα μηδενὶ ᵈδιηγήσωνται‖ ἃ εἶ-
mountain he charged them that to no one they should relate what they

δον,‖ εἰ.μὴ ὅταν ὁ υἱὸς τοῦ ἀνθρώπου ἐκ νεκρῶν
had seen except when the Son of man from among [the] dead

ἀναστῇ. 10 καὶ τὸν λόγον ἐκράτησαν πρὸς ἑαυτούς, ᵉσυζη-
be risen. And that saying they kept among themselves, ques-

τοῦντες‖ τί ἐστιν τὸ ᶠἐκ ᵍαμong [ᵗhe] ˢdead ¹rising.
tioning what is the ²from ³among ⁴[ᵗhe] ⁵dead ¹rising.

11 Καὶ ἐπηρώτων αὐτόν, λέγοντες, ᶠ'Ότι‖ λέγουσιν ᵍ οἱ γραμ-
And they asked him, saying, That ³say ᵍ ¹the ²scribes

ματεῖς ὅτι ʰ'Ηλίαν‖ δεῖ ἐλθεῖν πρῶτον; 12 Ὁ.δὲ ᶦἀποκριθεὶς
that Elias must come first? And he answering

εἶπεν αὐτοῖς, ᵏ'Ηλίας‖ ¹μὲν‖ ἐλθὼν πρῶτον, ᵐἀποκαθιστᾷ‖
said to them, Elias indeed having come first, restores

πάντα· καὶ πῶς γέγραπται ἐπὶ τὸν υἱὸν τοῦ ἀνθρώπουⁿᵃ
all things; and how it has been written of the Son of man

ἵνα πολλὰ πάθῃ καὶ °ᵃἐξουδενωθῇ.‖ 13 ἀλλὰ λέγω
that many things he should suffer and be set at nought: but I say

ὑμῖν, ὅτι καὶ ᵏ'Ηλίας‖ ἐλήλυθεν, καὶ ἐποίησαν αὐτῷ ὅσα
to you, that also Elias has come, and they did to him whatever

ᵖᵃἠθέλησαν,‖ καθὼς γέγραπται ἐπ' αὐτόν.
they desired, as it has been written of him.

14 Καὶ ᵠᵃἐλθὼν‖ πρὸς τοὺς μαθητὰς ʳᵃεἶδεν‖ ὄχλον πολὺν
And having come to the disciples he saw a ²crowd ¹great

περὶ αὐτούς, καὶ γραμματεῖς ˢᵃσυζητοῦντας‖ ᵗᵃαὐτοῖς.‖ 15 καὶ
around them, and scribes discussing with them. And

ᵛᵃεὐθέως‖ πᾶς ὁ ὄχλος ʷᵃἰδὼν‖ αὐτὸν ˣᵃἐξεθαμβήθη,‖ καὶ
immediately all the crowd seeing him were greatly amazed, and

προστρέχοντες . ἠσπάζοντο αὐτόν. 16 καὶ ἐπηρώτησεν ʸτοὺς
running to [him] saluted him. And he asked the

γραμματεῖς,‖ Τί ᶻσυζητεῖτε‖ πρὸς ªαὐτούς;‖ 17 Καὶ ᵇἀπο-
scribes, What discuss ye with them? And an-

κριθεὶς‖ εἷς ἐκ τοῦ ὄχλου ᶜεἶπεν,‖ Διδάσκαλε, ἤνεγκα τὸν υἱόν
swering one out of the crowd said, Teacher, I brought ²son

μου πρός σε, ἔχοντα πνεῦμα ἄλαλον. 18 καὶ ὅπου.ᵈἂν‖ αὐτὸν
my to thee, having a ²spirit ¹dumb; and wheresoever him

καταλάβῃ ῥήσσει ᵉαὐτόν·‖ καὶ ἀφρίζει, καὶ τρίζει τοὺς
it seizes it dashes ²down ¹him; and he foams, and gnashes

ὀδόντας.ᶠαὐτοῦ,‖ καὶ ξηραίνεται· καὶ ᵍεἶπον‖ τοῖς μαθηταῖς
his teeth, and is withering away. And I spoke to ²disciples

σου ἵνα αὐτὸ ἐκβάλωσιν, καὶ οὐκ.ἴσχυσαν. 19 Ὁ.δὲ ἀπο-
¹thy that it they might cast out, and they had not power. But he an-

κριθεὶς ʰαὐτῷ‖ λέγει,ᵀΩ γενεὰ ἄπιστος, ἕως πότε πρὸς ὑμᾶς
swering him says, O ²generation ¹unbelieving! until when with you

ἔσομαι; ἕως πότε ἀνέξομαι ὑμῶν; φέρετε αὐτὸν πρός με.
shall I be? until when shall I bear with you? Bring him to me.

20 Καὶ ἤνεγκαν αὐτὸν πρὸς αὐτόν· καὶ ἰδὼν αὐτὸν ⁱεὐθέως
And they brought him to him. And seeing him immediately

τὸ πνεῦμα‖ ᵏἐσπάραξεν‖ αὐτόν, καὶ πεσὼν ἐπὶ τῆς
the spirit threw ²into ¹convulsions ¹him, and having fallen upon the

γῆς ἐκυλίετο ἀφρίζων. 21 Καὶ ἐπηρώτησεν τὸν.πατέρα.αὐτοῦ,
earth he rolled foaming. And he asked his father,

Πόσος χρόνος ἐστὶν ὡς τοῦτο γέγονεν αὐτῷ; Ὁ.δὲ εἶπέν,
How long a time is it that this has been with him? And he said,

ˡΠαιδιόθεν. 22 καὶ πολλάκις ᵐαὐτὸν καὶ εἰς πῦρ‖ ἔβαλεν καὶ
From childhood. And often him both into fire it cast and

εἰς ὕδατα, ἵνα ἀπολέσῃ αὐτόν· ⁿἀλλ'‖ εἴ τι °δύνασαι,‖
into waters, that it might destroy him: but if anything thou art able

βοήθησον ἡμῖν, σπλαγχνισθεὶς ἐφ' ἡμᾶς. 23 Ὁ.δὲ.Ἰη-
[to do], help us, being moved with pity on us. And Je-

σοῦς εἶπεν αὐτῷ, Τὸ εἰ °δύνασαι‖ ᴾπιστεῦσαι,‖ πάντα δυνατὰ
sus said to him, If thou art able to believe, all things are possible

τῷ πιστεύοντι. 24 �qΚαὶʰ ʳεὐθέως‖ κράξας ὁ πατὴρ τοῦ
to him that believes. And immediately crying out the father of the

παιδίου ˢμετὰ δακρύων‖ ἔλεγεν, Πιστεύω, ᵗΚύριε,‖ βοήθει
little child with tears said, I believe, Lord, help

μου.τῇ.ἀπιστίᾳ. 25 Ἰδὼν.δὲ ὁ Ἰησοῦς ὅτι ἐπισυντρέχει ᵛ
mine unbelief. But ²seeing ¹Jesus that ³was ⁴running ⁵together

ὄχλος, ἐπετίμησεν τῷ πνεύματι τῷ ἀκαθάρτῳ, λέγων αὐτῷ,
¹a ¹crowd, rebuked the spirit the unclean, saying to it,

Τὸ ʷπνεῦμα τὸ ἄλαλον καὶ κωφόν,‖ ἐγώ ˣσοι ἐπιτάσσω,‖ ἔξελθε
Spirit dumb and deaf, I thee command, come

ʸªἐξ‖ αὐτοῦ, καὶ μηκέτι εἰσέλθῃς εἰς αὐτόν. 26 Καὶ ᶻªκρά-
out of him, and no more mayest thou enter into him. And having

ξαν,‖ καὶ πολλὰ ªªσπαράξαν‖ ᵇªαὐτόν,‖ ἐξῆλθεν· καὶ
cried out, and ³much ¹thrown ⁴into ⁵convulsions ²him, it came out; and

ἐγένετο ὡσεὶ νεκρός, ὥστε ᶜªπολλοὺς λέγειν ὅτι ἀπέθανεν.
he became as if dead, so that many said that he was dead.

---

to him saluted him.
16 And he asked the
scribes, What question
ye with them? 17 And
one of the multitude
answered and said,
Master, I have brought
unto thee my son,
which hath a dumb
spirit; 18 and where-
soever he taketh him,
he teareth him: and
he foameth, and gnash-
eth with his teeth, and
pineth away: and I
spake to thy disciples
that they should cast
him out; and they
could not. 19 He an-
swereth him, and saith,
O faithless generation,
how long shall I be
with you? how long
shall I suffer you?
bring him unto me.
20 And they brought
him unto him: and
when he saw him,
straightway the spirit
tare him; and he fell
on the ground, and
wallowed foaming.
21 And he asked his
father, How long is it
ago since this came
unto him? And he
said, Of a child. 22 And
ofttimes it hath cast
him into the fire, and
into the waters, to
destroy him: but if
thou canst do any
thing, have compas-
sion on us, and help
us. 23 Jesus said unto
him, If thou canst be-
lieve, all things are
possible to him that
believeth. 24 And
straightway the father
of the child cried out,
and said with tears,
Lord, I believe; help
thou mine unbelief.
25 When Jesus saw
that the people came
running together, he
rebuked the foul
spirit, saying unto
him, Thou dumb and
deaf spirit, I charge
thee, come out of him,
and enter no more
into him. 26 And the
spirit cried, and rent
him sore, and came
out of him: and he
was as one dead; in-
somuch that many
said, He is dead.

ʸ αὐτούς them GLTTrA. ᶻ συνζητεῖτε LTTrA. ª αὐτούς E. ᵇ ἀπεκρίθη αὐτῷ answered
him LTT A. ᶜ — εἶπεν LTTrA. ᵈ ἐὰν LTTrA. ᵉ — αὐτόν (read [him]) T. ᶠ — αὐτοῦ
(read [his] teeth) [L]TTrA. ᵍ εἶπα TTrA. ʰ αὐτοῖς them GLTTrAW. ⁱ τὸ πνεῦμα εὐθὺς
LTTrA. ᵏ συνεσπάραξεν LT. ˡ + ἐκ since LTTrAW. ᵐ καὶ εἰς πῦρ αὐτὸν TA. ⁿ ἀλλὰ T.
° δύνῃ LTTrA. ᴾ — πιστεῦσαι TTr[A]. q — καὶ [L]T[Tr]A. ʳ εὐθὺς TTrA. ˢ — μετὰ
δακρύων LTTrA. ᵗ — Κύριε GLTTrAW. ᵛ + ὁ the (crowd) T. ʷ ἄλαλον καὶ κωφὸν
πνεῦμα LTTrA. ˣ ἐπιτάσσω σοι TTrA. ʸª ἀπ' from L. ᶻª κράξας GLTTrAW. ªª σπαράξας
GLTTrAW. ᵇª — αὐτόν G[L]TTrA. ᶜª + τοὺς the LTTrA.

27 But Jesus took him by the hand, and lifted him up; and he arose.

27 ὁ δὲ Ἰησοῦς κρατήσας ᵈαὐτὸν τῆς χειρός‖ ἤγειρεν αὐτόν,
But Jesus,   having taken   him   by the, hand,   raised ²up   ¹him,

καὶ ἀνέστη.
and he arose.

28 And when he was come into the house, his disciples asked him privately, Why could not we cast him out? 29 And he said unto them, This kind can come forth by nothing, but by prayer and fasting.

28 Καὶ ᵉεἰσελθόντα.αὐτὸν‖ εἰς οἶκον οἱ.μαθηταὶ.αὐτοῦ
And   when he was entered   into a house   his disciples

ᶠἐπηρώτων αὐτὸν κατʼ.ἰδίαν,‖ ᵍ"Οτι‖ ἡμεῖς οὐκ.ἠδυνή-
asked   him   apart,   Because [of what] ²we   ¹were not

θημεν ἐκβαλεῖν αὐτό; 29 Καὶ εἶπεν αὐτοῖς, Τοῦτο τὸ γένος
able to cast out   it?   And he said to them,   This   kind

ἐν οὐδενὶ δύναται ἐξελθεῖν εἰ.μὴ ἐν προσευχῇ ʰκαὶ νηστείᾳ.‖
by nothing can   go out   except by prayer   and fasting.

30 And they departed thence, and passed through Galilee; and he would not that any man should know it. 31 For he taught his disciples, and said unto them, The Son of man is delivered into the hands of men, and they shall kill him; and after that he is killed, he shall rise the third day. 32 But they understood not that saying, and were afraid to ask him.

30 ⁱΚαὶ ἐκεῖθεν‖ ἐξελθόντες ᵏπαρεπορεύοντο‖ διὰ τῆς
And from thence having gone forth   they went   through

Γαλιλαίας· καὶ οὐκ.ἤθελεν ἵνα τις. ˡγνῷ·‖ 31 ἐδίδασ-
Galilee;   and he would not that anyone should know [it]; ²he ³was ⁴teach-

κεν γὰρ τοὺς.μαθητὰς.αὐτοῦ, καὶ ἔλεγεν αὐτοῖς, "Οτι ὁ υἱὸς
ing ¹for   his disciples,   and said   to them,   The Son

τοῦ ἀνθρώπου. παραδίδοται εἰς χεῖρας ἀνθρώπων, καὶ
of man   is delivered   into [the] hands   of men,   and

ἀποκτενοῦσιν αὐτόν· καὶ ἀποκτανθείς. ᵐτῇ τρίτῃ ἡμέρᾳ‖
they will kill   him;   and having been killed, on the third   day

ἀναστήσεται. 32 Οἱ.δὲ ἠγνόουν τὸ ῥῆμα, καὶ ἐφοβοῦντο
he will arise.   But they understood not the saying, and were afraid

αὐτὸν ἐπερωτῆσαι.
²him   ¹to ²ask.

33 And he came to Capernaum: and being in the house he asked them, What was it that ye disputed among yourselves by the way? 34 But they held their peace: for by the way they had disputed among themselves, who should be the greatest. 35 And he sat down, and called the twelve, and saith unto them, If any man desire to be first, the same shall be last of all, and servant of all. 36 And he took a child, and set him in the midst of them: and when he had taken him in his arms, he said unto them, 37 Whosoever shall receive one of such children in my name, receiveth me: and whosoever shall receive me, receiveth not me, but him that sent me. 38 And John answered him, saying, Master, we saw one casting out devils in thy name, and he followeth not us: and

33 Καὶ ⁿἦλθεν‖ εἰς ᵒΚαπερναούμ·‖ καὶ ἐν τῇ οἰκίᾳ γενόμενος
And he came to   Capernaum;   and ²in ³the ⁴house ¹being

ἐπηρώτα αὐτούς, Τί ἐν τῇ ὁδῷ ᴾπρὸς ἑαυτοὺς‖ διελογίζεσθε;
he asked   them,   What in the way   among yourselves were ye discussing?

34 Οἱ.δὲ ἐσιώπων· πρὸς ἀλλήλους γὰρ διελέχθησαν �q ἐν
But they were silent; ²with ³one ⁴another ¹for they had been discussing by

τῇ ὁδῷ,‖ τίς μείζων. 35 καὶ καθίσας ἐφώνησεν ʼτοὺς
the . way,   who [was] greater.   And sitting down he called   the

δώδεκα, καὶ λέγει αὐτοῖς, Εἴ τις θέλει πρῶτος εἶναι, ἔσται
twelve,   and he says to them, If anyone desires ³first ¹to ²be, he shall be

πάντων ἔσχατος καὶ πάντων διάκονος. 36 Καὶ λαβὼν
²of ³all   ¹last   and ²of ³all   ¹servant.   And having taken

παιδίον ἔστησεν αὐτὸ ἐν μέσῳ.αὐτῶν· καὶ ἐναγκαλισάμενος·
a little child he set   it   in   their midst; and having taken ²in [³his] ⁴arms

αὐτὸ εἶπεν αὐτοῖς, 37 "Ος. ἐὰν‖ ἓν τῶν ˢτοιούτων παιδίων‖
¹it   he said to them,   Whoever one   of such   little children

δέξηται ἐπὶ τῷ.ὀνόματί.μου, ἐμὲ δέχεται· καὶ ὃς.ᵗἐὰν‖ ἐμὲ
shall receive in   my name,   me receives;   and whoever   me

ᵗδέξηται,‖ οὐκ ἐμὲ δέχεται, ἀλλὰ τὸν ἀποστείλαντά με.
shall receive,   not me   receives,   but him who   sent   me.

38 ᵘἈπεκρίθη.δὲ‖ αὐτῷ.ᵒ‖ Ἰωάννης ʷλέγ ων,‖ Διδάσκαλε, εἴδομέν
And ²answered ³him   ¹John   saying,   Teacher, we saw

τινα ˣ τῷ.ὀνόματί.σου ἐκβάλλοντα δαιμόνια, ʸὃς οὐκ.ἀκολουθεῖ
some one in thy name   casting out   demons,   who follows not

---

ᵈ τῆς χειρὸς αὐτοῦ his hand LTTr.   ᵉ εἰσελθόντος αὐτοῦ LTTr.   ᶠ κατʼ ἰδίαν ἐπηρώτων αὐτὸν LTTrA.   ᵍ Ὁ τι wherefore LW.   ʰ — καὶ νηστείᾳ Τ[A].   ⁱ Κἀκεῖθεν LTTrA.   ᵏ ἐπορεύοντο LTr.   ˡ γνοῖ LTTrA.   ᵐ μετὰ τρεῖς ἡμέρας after three days LTTrA.   ⁿ ἦλθον they came LTTrA.   ᵒ Καφαρναούμ LTTrAW.   ᴾ πρὸς ἑαυτοὺς LTTrA.   q ἐν τῇ ὁδῷ] L.   ʼ ἂν LTTrA.   ˢ παιδίων τούτων of these little children T.   ᵗ δέχηται should receive TTrA.   ᵘ ἀπεκρίθη [δὲ] L; ἔφη spoke (to him) TTrA.   ᵛ — ὁ GLW.   ʷ — λέγων T.   ˣ + ἐν ELTTrAW.   ʸ — ὃς οὐκ ἀκολουθεῖ ἡμῖν G.

ἡμῖν·‖ καὶ ²ἐκωλύσαμεν‖ αὐτόν, ᵃὅτι οὐκ.ἀκολουθεῖ ἡμῖν.‖
us, and we forbade him, because he follows not us.

39 Ὁ.δὲ.Ἰησοῦς εἶπεν, Μὴ.κωλύετε αὐτόν· οὐδεὶς.γάρ ἐστιν
But Jesus said, Forbid not him; for no one there is

ὃς ποιήσει δύναμιν ἐπὶ τῷ.ὀνόματί.μου, καὶ δυνήσεται
who shall do a work of power in my name, and be able

ταχὺ κακολογῆσαί με. 40 ὃς.γὰρ οὐκ.ἔστιν καθ᾽ ᵇὑμῶν,‖ ὑπὲρ
readily to speak evil of me; for he who is not against you, for

ᵇὑμῶν‖ ἐστιν. 41 ὃς.γὰρ.ἂν ποτίσῃ ὑμᾶς ποτήριον
you is. For whoever may give ²to ³drink ¹you a cup

ὕδατος ἐν ᶜτῷ‖.ὀνόματί.ᵈμου,‖ ὅτι χριστοῦ ἐστε, ἀμὴν λέγω
or water in my name, because 'Christ's ¹ye ²are, verily I say

ὑμῖν, ᵉοὐ.μὴ ᶠἀπολέσῃ‖ τὸν.μισθὸν.αὐτοῦ. 42 Καὶ ὃς.ἂν
to you, in no wise should he lose his reward. And whoever

σκανδαλίσῃ ἕνα τῶν μικρῶν ᵍτῶν ʰπιστευόντων εἰς
may cause ⁴to ²offend ¹one ²of ³the ⁴little ⁵ones who believe in

ἐμέ,‖ καλόν ἐστιν αὐτῷ μᾶλλον εἰ περίκειται ⁱλίθος.μυλικὸς‖
me, good it is for him rather if is put a millstone

περὶ τὸν.τράχηλον.αὐτοῦ, καὶ βέβληται εἰς τὴν θάλασσαν.
about his neck, and he has been cast into the sea.

43 Καὶ ἐὰν ᵏσκανδαλίζῃ‖ σε ἡ.χείρ.σου, ἀπόκοψον αὐτήν·
And if ³should ⁴cause ⁶to ᵒoffend ⁵thee ¹thy ²hand, cut off it :

καλόν ¹σοι ἐστὶν‖ κυλλὸν ᵐεἰς τὴν ζωὴν εἰσελθεῖν,‖
good for thee it is maimed into life to enter, [rather]

ἢ τὰς δύο χεῖρας ἔχοντα ἀπελθεῖν εἰς τὴν γέενναν, εἰς τὸ
than the two hands having to go away into the Gehenna, into the

πῦρ τὸ ἄσβεστον, 44 ⁿὅπου ὁ.σκώληξ.αὐτῶν οὐ.τελευτᾷ, καὶ
fire the unquenchable, where their worm dies not, and

τὸ πῦρ οὐ.σβέννυται.‖ 45 καὶ ἐὰν ὁ.πούς.σου σκανδαλίζῃ
the fire is not quenched. And if thy foot should cause ²to ᵒoffend

σε, ἀπόκοψον αὐτόν· καλόν ᵒᴾἐστιν σοι‖ εἰσελθεῖν εἰς τὴν
¹thee, cut off it : good it is for thee to enter into

ζωὴν χωλόν, ἢ τοὺς δύο πόδας ἔχοντα βληθῆναι εἰς
life lame, [rather] than the two feet having to be cast into

τὴν γέενναν, ᑫεἰς τὸ πῦρ τὸ ἄσβεστον, 46 ʳὅπου ὁ σκώληξ
the Gehenna, into the fire the unquenchable, where ᵐworm

αὐτῶν οὐ.τελευτᾷ, καὶ τὸ πῦρ οὐ.σβέννυται.‖ 47 καὶ ἐὰν ὁ
'their dies not, and the fire is not quenched. And if

ὀφθαλμός.σου σκανδαλίζῃ σε, ἔκβαλε αὐτόν· καλόν
thine eye should cause ²to ᵒoffend ¹thee, cast out it : good

ˢσοι ἐστὶν‖ μονόφθαλμον εἰσελθεῖν εἰς τὴν βασιλείαν τοῦ
for thee it is with one eye to enter into the kingdom

θεοῦ, ἢ δύο ὀφθαλμοὺς ἔχοντα βληθῆναι εἰς τὴν γέεν-
of God, [rather] than two eyes having to be cast into the Gehen-

ναν ᵗτοῦ πυρός,‖ 48 ὅπου ὁ.σκώληξ.αὐτῶν οὐ.τελευτᾷ, καὶ τὸ
na of fire, where their worm dies not, and the

πῦρ οὐ.σβέννυται. 49 Πᾶς.γὰρ πυρὶ ἀλισθήσεται, ᵘκαὶ
fire is not quenched. For everyone with fire shall be salted, and

πᾶσα θυσία ἁλὶ ἁλισθήσεται.‖ 50 καλὸν τὸ ᵛἅλας,‖
every sacrifice with salt shall be salted. Good [is] the salt,

but if the salt have lost his saltness, wherewith will ye season it? Have salt in yourselves, and have peace one with another.

X. And he arose from thence, and cometh into the coasts of Judæa by the farther side of Jordan : and the people resort unto him again ; and, as he was wont, he taught them again. 2 And the Pharisees came to him, and asked him, Is it lawful for a man to put away *his* wife? tempting him. 3 And he answered and said unto them, What did Moses command you? 4 And they said, Moses suffered to write a bill of divorcement, and to put *her* away. 5 And Jesus answered and said unto them, For the hardness of your heart he wrote you this precept. 6 But from the beginning of the creation God made them male and female. 7 For this cause shall a man leave his father and mother, and cleave to his wife ; 8 and they twain shall be one flesh : so then they are no more twain, but one flesh. 9 What therefore God hath joined together, let not man put asunder. 10 And in the house his disciples asked him again of the same *matter.* 11 And he saith unto them, Whosoever shall put away his wife, and marry another, committeth adultery against her. 12 And if a woman shall put away her husband, and be married to another, she committeth adultery.

13 And they brought young children to him, that he should touch them : and *his* disciples rebuked those that brought *them.* 14 But when Jesus saw *it,* he was much displeased, and said unto them, Suffer the little children to come unto me,

ἐὰν.δὲ τὸ ʷἅλας⁣ⁿ ἄναλον γένηται, ἐν τίνι αὐτὸ ἀρτύσετε;
but if the salt saltless is become, with what it will ye season?

ἔχετε ἐν ἑαυτοῖς ˣἅλας,ⁿ καὶ εἰρηνεύετε ἐν ἀλλήλοις.
Have in yourselves salt, and be at peace with one another.

10 ʸΚἀκεῖθενⁿ ἀναστὰς ἔρχεται εἰς τὰ ὅρια τῆς Ἰουδαίας,
And thence rising up he comes into the borders of Judæa,

ᶻδιὰ τοῦⁿ πέραν τοῦ Ἰορδάνου· καὶ ᵃσυμπορεύονταιⁿ πάλιν
by the other side of the Jordan. And come together again

ὄχλοι πρὸς αὐτόν, καὶ ὡς εἰώθει πάλιν ἐδίδασκεν
crowds to him, and as he had been accustomed again he taught

αὐτούς. 2 Καὶ προσελθόντες ,ᵇοἱⁿ Φαρισαῖοι ᶜἐπηρώτησανⁿ
them. And coming to [him] the Pharisees asked

αὐτὸν εἰ ἔξεστιν ἀνδρὶ γυναῖκα ἀπολῦσαι, πειράζοντες
him if it is lawful for a husband a wife to put away, tempting

αὐτόν. 3 ὁ.δὲ ἀποκριθεὶς εἶπεν αὐτοῖς, Τί ὑμῖν ἐνετείλατο
him. But he answering said to them, What *you* ¹did ³command

ᵈΜωσῆς;ⁿ 4 Οἱ.δὲ ᵉεἶπον,ⁿ ᶠΜωσῆς ἐπέτρεψενⁿ βιβλίον ἀπο-
²Moses? And they said, Moses allowed a bill of di-

στασίου γράψαι, καὶ ἀπολῦσαι. 5 ᵍΚαὶ ἀποκριθεὶς ὁⁿ Ἰησοῦς
vorce to write, and to put away. And answering Jesus

εἶπεν αὐτοῖς, Πρὸς τὴν.σκληροκαρδίαν.ὑμῶν ἔγραψεν ὑμῖν
said to them, In view of your hardheartedness he wrote for you

τὴν.ἐντολὴν.ταύτην· 6 ἀπὸ.δὲ ἀρχῆς κτίσεως ἄρσεν καὶ
this commandment; but from [the] beginning of creation male and

θῆλυ ἐποίησεν αὐτούς ʰὁ θεός.ⁿ 7 ἕνεκεν τούτου καταλείψει
female, ²made ³them ¹God. On account of this shall ³leave

ἄνθρωπος τὸν.πατέρα.αὐτοῦ καὶ τὴν μητέρα, ⁱκαὶ προσκολ-
¹a ²man his father and mother, and shall be

ληθήσεταιⁿ ᵏπρὸς τὴν.γυναῖκαⁿ.αὐτοῦ, 8 καὶ ἔσονται οἱ δύο
joined to his wife, and ³shall ⁴be ¹the ²two

εἰς σάρκα μίαν· ὥστε οὐκέτι εἰσὶν δύο, ἀλλὰ μία σάρξ. 9 ὃ
²for ⁷flesh ⁶one; so that no longer are they two, but one flesh. What

οὖν ὁ θεὸς συνέζευξεν, ἄνθρωπος μὴ.χωριζέτω. 10 Καὶ ⁱἐν
therefore God united together, ²man ¹let ³not separate. And in

τῇ οἰκίᾳ πάλιν οἱ.μαθηταὶ.ᵐαὐτοῦⁿ περὶ ⁿτοῦ.αὐτοῦⁿ.ᵒἐπη-
the house again his disciples concerning the same thing

ρώτησανⁿ αὐτόν. 11 καὶ λέγει αὐτοῖς, Ὃς.ᴾἐὰνⁿ ἀπολύσῃ
asked him. And he says to them, Whoever should put away

τὴν.γυνᾶ ἰαὐτοῦ καὶ γαμήσῃ ἄλλην, μοιχᾶται ἐπʼ
his wife and should marry another, commits adultery against

αὐτήν. 12 καὶ ἐὰν ᑫγυνὴ ἀπολύσῃⁿ τὸν.ἄνδρα.αὐτῆς ʳκαὶⁿ
her. And if a woman should put away her husband and

ˢγαμηθῇ ἄλλῳ,ⁿ μοιχᾶται.
be married to another, she commits adultery.

13 Καὶ προσέφερον αὐτῷ παιδία, ἵνα ἅψηται αὐτῶν·
And they brought to him little children, that he might touch them.

οἱ.δὲ μαθηταὶ ἐπετίμων τοῖς προσφέρουσιν. 14 ἰδὼν.δὲ
But the disciples rebuked those who brought them. But having seen [it]

ὁ Ἰησοῦς ἠγανάκτησεν, καὶ εἶπεν αὐτοῖς, Ἄφετε τὰ παιδία
Jesus was indignant, and said to them, Suffer the little children

---

ʷ ἅλα τ.   ˣ ἅλα LTTrA.   ʸ καὶ ἐκεῖθεν LTTrAW.   ᶻ καὶ and LTTrA.   ᵃ συμπορεύονται ΤΑ. ᵇ — οἱ GLTrAW.   ᶜ ἐπηρώτων were asking LTTrA.   ᵈ Μωϋσῆς LTTrAW.   ᵉ εἶπαν LTTrA, ᶠ ἐπέτρεψεν Μωϋσῆς LTTrA; Μωϋσῆς ἐπέτ. W.   ᵍ ὁ δὲ but TTrA.   ʰ — ὁ θεός (read he made them) [L]TTr[A].   ⁱ — καὶ προσκολληθήσεται τ.   ᵏ τῇ γυναικὶ L ; — πρὸς τὴν γυναῖκα τ.   ⁱ εἰς τὴν οἰκίαν LTTrA.   ᵐ — αὐτοῦ (read the disciples) [L]TTr[A].   ⁿ τούτου this LTTrA.   ᵒ ἐπηρώτων were asking TA.   ᴾ ἂν LTTrA.   ᑫ αὐτὴ ἀπολύσασα she putting away TTrA.   ʳ — καὶ TTrA.   ˢ γαμήσῃ ἄλλον should marry another LTTrA.

ἔρχεσθαι πρός με, ʳκαι‖ μὴ.κωλύετε αὐτά· τῶν.γὰρ.τοιούτων
to come to me, and do not hinder them; for of such

ἐστιν ἡ βασιλεία τοῦ θεοῦ· 15 ἀμὴν λέγω ὑμῖν, ὃς.ᵛἐὰν‖
is the kingdom of God. Verily I say to you, Whoever

μὴ.δέξηται τὴν βασιλείαν τοῦ θεοῦ ὡς παιδίον, οὐ.μὴ
shall not receive the kingdom of God as a little child, in no wise

εἰσέλθῃ εἰς αὐτήν. 16 Καὶ ἐναγκαλισάμενος αὐτά, ʷ
shall enter into it. And having taken ²in [ʲhis] ⁴arms ¹them,

τιθεὶς τὰς χεῖρας ἐπ' αὐτὰ ˣηὐλόγει αὐτά.‖
having laid [his] hands on them he blessed them.

17 Καὶ ἐκπορευομένου.αὐτοῦ εἰς ὁδόν, προσδραμὼν εἷς καὶ
And as he went forth into [the] way, ²running ³up ¹one and

γονυπετήσας αὐτὸν ἐπηρώτα αὐτόν, Διδάσκαλε ἀγαθέ, τί
kneeling down to him a ked him, ²Teacher ¹good, what

ποιήσω ἵνα ζωὴν αἰώνιον κληρονομήσω; 18 Ὁ.δὲ.Ἰησοῦς
shall I do that life eternal I may inherit? But Jesus

εἶπεν αὐτῷ, Τί με λέγεις ἀγαθόν; οὐδεὶς ἀγαθὸς εἰ.μὴ
said to him, Why me callest thou good? No one [is] good except

εἷς, ὁ θεός. 19 τὰς ἐντολὰς οἶδας, ʸΜὴ.μοιχεύσῃς·
one, God. The commandments thou knowest: Thou shouldest not commit

μὴ.φονεύσῃς·‖ μὴ.κλέψῃς·
adultery; thou shouldest not commit murder; thou shouldest not steal; thou

μὴ.ψευδομαρτυρήσῃς· μὴ.ἀποστερήσῃς· τίμα τὸν
shouldest not bear false witness; thou shouldest not defraud; honour

πατέρα.σου καὶ τὴν μητέραᶻ. 20 Ὁ.δὲ ᵃἀποκριθεὶς‖ ᵇεἶπεν‖
thy father and mother. And he answering said

αὐτῷ, Διδάσκαλε, ᶜταῦτα πάντα‖ ᵈἐφυλαξάμην‖ ἐκ νεότητός
to him, Teacher, ²these ¹all have I kept from ²youth

μου. 21 Ὁ.δὲ.Ἰησοῦς ἐμβλέψας αὐτῷ ἠγάπησεν αὐτόν, καὶ
¹my. And Jesus looking upon him loved him, and

εἶπεν αὐτῷ, Ἕν ᵉσοι‖ ὑστερεῖ· ὕπαγε, ὅσα ἔχεις πώλη-
said to him, One thing to thee is lacking: go, as much as thou hast sell

σον καὶ δὸς ᶠτοῖς‖ πτωχοῖς, καὶ ἕξεις θησαυρὸν ἐν
and give to the poor, and thou shalt have treasure in

οὐρανῷ· καὶ δεῦρο, ἀκολούθει μοι, ᵍἄρας τὸν σταυρόν.‖ 22 Ὁ.δὲ
heaven; and come, follow me, taking up the cross. But he,

στυγνάσας ἐπὶ τῷ λόγῳ ἀπῆλθεν λυπούμενος· ἦν.γὰρ.ἔχων
being sad at the word, went away grieved, for he had

κτήματα πολλά. 23 Καὶ περιβλεψάμενος ὁ Ἰησοῦς λέγει τοῖς
²possessions ¹many. And looking around Jesus says

μαθηταῖς.αὐτοῦ, Πῶς δυσκόλως οἱ τὰ χρήματα ἔχοντες εἰς
to his disciples, How difficultly those ²riches ¹having into

τὴν βασιλείαν τοῦ θεοῦ εἰσελεύσονται. 24 Οἱ.δὲ μαθηταὶ ἐθαμ-
the kingdom of God shall enter! And the disciples were as-

βοῦντο ἐπὶ τοῖς.λόγοις.αὐτοῦ. Ὁ.δὲ.Ἰησοῦς πάλιν ἀποκριθεὶς
tonished at his words. And Jesus again answering

λέγει αὐτοῖς, ʰΤέκνα,‖ πῶς δύσκολόν ἐστιν ⁱτοὺς πεποιθότας
says to them, Children, how difficult it is [for] those who trust

ἐπὶ ᵏτοῖς‖ χρήμασιν‖ εἰς τὴν βασιλείαν τοῦ θεοῦ εἰσελθεῖν.
in riches into the kingdom of God to enter!

25 εὐκοπώτερόν ἐστιν κάμηλον διὰ ˡτῆς‖ τρυμαλιᾶς ˡτῆς‖
Easier it is [for] a camel through the eye of the

and forbid them not:
for of such is the king-
dom of God. 15 Verily
I say unto you, Who-
soever shall not receive
the kingdom of God as
a little child, he shall
not enter therein.
16 And he took them
up in his arms, put
his hands upon them,
and blessed them.

17 And when he was
gone forth into the
way, there came one
running, and kneeled
to him, and a ked him,
Good Master, what
shall I do that I may
inherit eternal life?
18 And Jesus said unto
him, Why callest thou
me good? *there is* none
good but one, *that is,*
God. 19 Thou knowest
the commandments,
Do not commit adul-
tery, Do not kill, Do
not steal, Do not bear
false witness, Defraud
not, Honour thy father
and mother. 20 And he
answered and said
unto him, Master, all
these have I observ-
ed from my youth.
21 Then Jesus behold-
ing him loved him,
and said unto him,
One thing thou lack-
est : go thy way, sell
whatsoever thou hast,
and give to the poor,
and thou shalt have
treasure in heaven :
and come, take up the
cross, and follow me.
22 And he was sad at
that saying, and went
away grieved : for he
had great possessions.
23 And Jesus looked
round about, and saith
unto his disciple-, How
hardly shall they that
have riches enter into
the kingdom of God !
24 And the disciples
were astonished at his
words. But Jesus an-
swereth again, and
saith unto them, Child-
ren, how hard is it for
them that trust in
riches to enter into
the kingdom of God !
25 It is easier for a
camel to go through
the eye of a needle,

ᵗ — καὶ GTTrAW ᵛ ἂν LTTrA. ʷ + κατευλόγει he blesses [them] TTrA. ˣ εὐλόγει
αὐτά he blesses them LW; - ηὐλόγει αὐτά TTrA. ʸ Μὴ φονεύσῃς, μὴ μοιχεύσῃς L.
ᶻ — σου thy (mother) LT. ᵃ — ἀπ κριθεὶς T. ᵇ ἔφη TTⁱA. ᶜ πάντα ταῦτα L.
ᵈ ἐφύλαξα ι. ᵉ σε thee TA. ᶠ — τοῖς LTrAW. ᵍ — ἄρας τὸν σταυρόν [L]TTr. ʰ τεκνία ι..
ⁱ — τοὺς πεποιθότας ἐπὶ τοῖς χρήμασιν T. ᵏ — τοῖς LTⁱAW. ˡ — τῆς (read an ⊖ e or a
needle) LTⁱW.

than for a rich man to enter into the kingdom of God. 26 And they were astonished out of measure, saying among themselves, Who then can be saved? 27 And Jesus looking upon them saith, With men it is impossible, but not with God: for with God all things are possible. 28 Then Peter began to say unto him, Lo, we have left all, and have followed thee. 29 And Jesus answered and said, Verily I say unto you, There is no man that hath left house, or brethren, or sisters, or father, or mother, or wife, or children, or lands, for my sake, and the gospel's, 30 but he shall receive an hundredfold now in this time, houses, and brethren, and sisters, and mothers, and children, and lands, with persecutions; and in the world to come eternal life. 31 But many that are first shall be last; and the last first.

ῥαφίδος ᵐεἰσελθεῖν,‖ ἢ πλούσιον εἰς τὴν βασιλείαν τοῦ θεοῦ
needle to pass, than [for] a rich man into the kingdom of God

εἰσελθεῖν. 26 Οἱ.δὲ περισσῶς ἐξεπλήσσοντο, λέγοντες πρὸς
to enter. And they exceedingly were astonished, saying among

ἑαυτούς, Καὶ τίς δύναται σωθῆναι; 27 Ἐμβλέψας.ᵃδὲ‖ αὐτοῖς
themselves, And who is able to be saved? But looking on them

ὁ Ἰησοῦς λέγει, Παρὰ ἀνθρώποις ° .ἀδύνατον, ἀλλ' οὐ παρὰ
Jesus says, With men [it is] impossible, but not with

ᴾτῷ‖ θεῷ. πάντα.γὰρ δυνατά ᑫἐστιν‖ παρὰ τῷ θεῷ. ᵣ28 ʳΚαὶ‖
God; for all things ²possible ¹are with God. And

ἤρξατο ˢὁ Πέτρος λέγειν‖ αὐτῷ, Ἰδού, ἡμεῖς ἀφήκαμεν πάντα,
²began ¹Peter to say to him, Lo, we left all,

καὶ ᵗἠκολουθήσαμεν‖ σοι. 29 ᵛἈποκριθεὶς.δὲ ὁ Ἰησοῦς εἶπεν,‖
and followed thee. But answering Jesus said,

Ἀμὴν λέγω ὑμῖν, οὐδείς ἐστιν ὃς ἀφῆκεν οἰκίαν, ἢ ἀδελφούς,
Verily I say to you, No one there is who has left house, or brothers,

ἢ ἀδελφάς, ʷἢ πατέρα, ἢ μητέρα,‖ ˣἢ γυναῖκα,‖ ἢ τέκνα, ἢ
or sisters, or father, or mother, or wife, or children, or

ἀγρούς, ἕνεκεν ἐμοῦ καὶ ʸ τοῦ εὐαγγελίου, 30 ἐὰν.μὴ.λάβῃ
lands, for the sake of me and of the glad tidings, that shall not receive

ἑκατονταπλασίονα νῦν ἐν τῷ.καιρῷ.τούτῳ, οἰκίας καὶ ἀδελ-
a hundredfold now in this time: houses and bro-

φοὺς καὶ ἀδελφὰς καὶ ᶻμητέρας‖ καὶ τέκνα καὶ ἀγρούς, μετὰ
thers and sisters and mothers and children and lands, with

διωγμῶν, καὶ ἐν τῷ αἰῶνι τῷ.ἐρχομένῳ ζωὴν αἰώνιον. 31 πολ-
persecutions, and in the age that is coming life eternal. Many

λοὶ δὲ ἔσονται πρῶτοι ἔσχατοι, καὶ ᵃοἱ‖ ἔσχατοι πρῶτοι.
¹but ⁴shall ³be ²first last, and the last first.

32 And they were in the way going up to Jerusalem; and Jesus went before them: and they were amazed; and as they followed, they were afraid. And he took again the twelve, and began to tell them what things should happen unto him, 33 saying, Behold, we go up to Jerusalem; and the Son of man shall be delivered unto the chief priests, and unto the scribes; and they shall condemn him to death, and shall deliver him to the Gentiles: 34 and they shall mock him, and shall scourge him, and shall spit upon him, and shall kill him: and the third day he shall rise again.

32 Ἦσαν.δὲ ἐν τῇ ὁδῷ ἀναβαίνοντες εἰς Ἰεροσόλυμα· καὶ
And they were in the way going up to Jerusalem, and

ἦν προάγων αὐτοὺς ὁ Ἰησοῦς, καὶ ἐθαμβοῦντο, ᵇκαὶ‖
²was ³going ⁴on ⁵before ⁶them ¹Jesus, and they were astonished, and

ἀκολουθοῦντες ἐφοβοῦντο. καὶ παραλαβὼν πάλιν τοὺς
following were afraid. And having taken to [him] again the

δώδεκα, ἤρξατο αὐτοῖς λέγειν τὰ μέλλοντα αὐτῷ
twelve, he began them to tell the things which were about ³to ⁴him

συμβαίνειν· 33 Ὅτι, ἰδού, ἀναβαίνομεν εἰς Ἰεροσόλυμα, καὶ
¹to ²happen: Behold, we go up to Jerusalem, and

ὁ υἱὸς τοῦ ἀνθρώπου παραδοθήσεται τοῖς ἀρχιερεῦσιν καὶ
the Son of man will be delivered up to the chief priests and

ᶜτοῖς‖ γραμματεῦσιν, καὶ κατακρινοῦσιν αὐτὸν θανάτῳ, καὶ
to the scribes, and they will condemn him to death, and

παραδώσουσιν αὐτὸν τοῖς ἔθνεσιν, 34 καὶ ἐμπαίξουσιν αὐτῷ,
will deliver up him to the Gentiles. And they will mock him,

ᵈκαὶ μαστιγώσουσιν αὐτόν, καὶ ἐμπτύσουσιν αὐτῷ,‖ καὶ ἀπο-
and will scourge him, and will spit upon him, and will

κτενοῦσιν ᵉαὐτόν·‖ καὶ ᶠτῇ τρίτῃ ἡμέρᾳ‖ ἀναστήσεται.
kill him; and on the third day he will rise again.

35 And James and John, the sons of Zebedee, come unto him,

35 Καὶ προσπορεύονται αὐτῷ Ἰάκωβος καὶ Ἰωάννης ᵍοἱ‖
And come up to him James and John, the

ᵐ διελθεῖν EGLTTrAW.   ⁿ — δὲ but TTrA.   ° + [τοῦτο] this [is] L.   ᴾ — τῷ TTrAW.
ᑫ — ἐστιν (read [are]) TTr.   ʳ — καὶ GLTTrAW.   ˢ λέγειν ὁ Πέτρος TA.   ᵗ ἠκολουθήκαμεν
have followed LTTrAW.   ᵛ ἀποκριθεὶς (omit but) ὁ Ἰησοῦς εἶπέν GLTrW; ἔφη ὁ Ἰησοῦς
Jesus said (— ἀποκ. δὲ) TA.   ʷ ἢ μητέρα, ἢ πατέρα LTTrA.   ˣ — ἢ γυναῖκα LTTrA.
ʸ + ἕνεκεν for the sake G[L]TTrAW.   ᶻ μητέρα mother LTr.   ᵃ — οἱ GLW.   ᵇ οἱ δὲ
and those TTr.   ᶜ — τοῖς L.   ᵈ καὶ ἐμπτύσουσιν αὐτῷ, καὶ μαστιγώσουσιν αὐτὸν LTT·A.
ᵉ — αὐτόν (read [him]) [L]T[Tr].   ᶠ μετὰ τρεῖς ἡμέρας after three days LTTrA.   ᵍ — οἱ A.

υἱοὶ Ζεβεδαίου, λέγοντες[h], Διδάσκ λε, θέλομεν ἵνα ὃ.ἐὰν
sons of Zebedee, saying, Teacher, we de re that whatever

αἰτήσωμεν [i] ποιήσῃς ἡμῖν. 36 Ὁ.δὲ εἶπεν α οῖς, Τί θέλετε
we may ask thou wouldest do for us. And he said to them, What do ye desire

[k]ποιῆσαί με[||] ὑμῖν; 37 Οἱ.δὲ [l]εἶπον[||] αὐτῷ, Δὸς ἡμῖν, ἵνα εἷς
*to *do 'me for you? And they said to him, Give to us, that one

[m]ἐκ δεξιῶν.σου[||] καὶ εἷς [n] ἐξ [o]εὐωνύμων[||] Ρσου[||] καθίσωμεν. ἐν
at thy right hand and one at thy left hand we may sit in

τῇ.δόξῃ.σου. 38 Ὁ.δὲ.Ἰησοῦς εἶπεν αὐτοῖς, Οὐκ.οἴδατε τί
thy glory. But Jesus said to them, Ye know not what

αἰτεῖσθε. δύνασθε πιεῖν τὸ ποτήριον· ὃ ἐγὼ πίνω, [q]καὶ[||] τὸ
ye ask. Are ye able to drink the cup which I drink, and *the

βάπτισμα ὃ ἐγὼ βαπτίζομαι, βαπτισθῆναι;
*baptism *which *I *am ¹⁰baptized [¹¹with], ¹to ²be ³baptized [⁴with]?

39 Οἱ.δὲ [r]εἶπον[||] αὐτῷ, Δυνάμεθα. Ὁ.δὲ.Ἰησοῦς εἶπεν αὐτοῖς,
And they said to him, We are able. But Jesus said to them,

Τὸ [s]μὲν[||] ποτήριον ὃ ἐγὼ πίνω, πίεσθε· καὶ τὸ βάπτισμα
The ²indeed ¹cup which I drink, ye shall drink; and the baptism

ὃ ἐγὼ βαπτίζομαι, βαπτισθήσεσθε· 40 τὸ.δὲ.καθί
which I am baptized [with], ye shall be baptized [with]; but to sit

σαι ἐκ δεξιῶν.μου [q]καὶ[||] ἐξ εὐωνύμων.[t]μου[||] οὐκ.ἔστιν ἐμὸν
at my right hand and at my left hand is not mine

δοῦναι, ἀλλ᾽ οἷς ἡτοίμασται. 41 Καὶ ἀκούσαν-
to give, but [to those] for whom it has been prepared. And having

τες οἱ δέκα ἤρξαντο ἀγανακτεῖν περὶ Ἰακώβου καὶ
heard [this] the ten began to be indignant about James and

Ἰωάννου. 42 [v]ὁ.δὲ.Ἰησοῦς προσκαλεσάμενος αὐτοὺς[||] λέγει
John. But Jesus having called ²to [³him] ¹them says

αὐτοῖς, Οἴδατε ὅτι οἱ δοκοῦντες ἄρχειν τῶν ἐθνῶν
to them, Ye know that those who are accounted to rule over the nations

κατακυριεύουσιν αὐτῶν· καὶ οἱ.μεγάλοι.αὐτῶν κατεξουσιάζου-
exercise lordship over them; and their great ones exercise authority

σιν αὐτῶν. 43 οὐχ οὕτως δὲ [w]ἔσται[||] ἐν ὑμῖν· ἀλλ᾽
over them; not thus however shall it be among you; but

ὃς.[x]ἐὰν[||] θέλῃ [y]γενέσθαι μέγας[||] ἐν ὑμῖν, ἔσται [z]διάκονος
whoever de ires to become great among you, shall be ²servant

ὑμῶν. 44 καὶ ὃς.[a]ἂν[||] θέλῃ [b]ὑμῶν[||] [c]γενέσθαι[||] πρῶτος, ἔσται
¹your; and whoever desires of you to become first, shall be

πάντων δοῦλος· 45 καὶ.γὰρ ὁ υἱὸς τοῦ ἀνθρώπου οὐκ.ἦλθεν
²of ³all ¹bondman. For even the Son of man came not

διακονηθῆναι, ἀλλὰ διακονῆσαι, καὶ δοῦναι τὴν.ψυχὴν.αὐτοῦ
to be served, but to serve, and to give his life

λύτρον ἀντὶ πολλῶν.
a ransom for many.

46 Καὶ [d]ἔρχονται[||] εἰς [e]Ἱεριχώ·[||] καὶ ἐκπορευομένου.αὐτοῦ
And they come to Jericho; and as he was going out

ἀπὸ [e]Ἱεριχώ,[||] καὶ τῶν.μαθητῶν.αὐτοῦ, καὶ ὄχλου ἱκανοῦ,
from Jericho, and his disciples, and a ²crowd ¹large,

[f]υἱὸς Τιμαίου Βαρτίμαιος [g]ὁ[||] τυφλὸς [ha] ἐκάθητο παρὰ τὴν
a son of Timæus, Bartimæus the blind [man], was sitting beside the

---

saying, Master, we would that thou shouldest do for us whatsoever we shall desire. 36 And he said unto them, What would ye that I should do for you? 37 They said unto him, Grant unto us that we may sit, one on thy right hand, and the other on thy left hand, in thy glory. 38 But Jesus said unto them, Ye know not what ye ask: can ye drink of the cup that I drink of? and be baptized with the baptism that I am baptized with? 39 And they said unto him, We can. And Jesus said unto them, Ye shall indeed drink of the cup that I drink of; and with the baptism that I am baptized withal shall ye be baptized: 40 but to sit on my right hand and on my left hand is not mine to give; but it shall be given to them for whom it is prepared. 41 And when the ten heard it, they began to be much displeased with James and John. 42 But Jesus called them to him, and saith unto them, Ye know that they which are accounted to rule over the Gentiles exercise lordship over them; and their great ones exercise authority upon them. 43 But so shall it not be among you: but whosoever will be great among you, shall be your minister: 44 and whosoever of you will be the chiefest, shall be servant of all. 45 For even the Son of man came not to be ministered unto, but to minister, and to give his life a ransom for many.

46 And they came to Jericho: and as he went out of Jericho with his disciples and a great number of people, blind Bartimæus, the son of Timæus, sat by the highway side begging. 47 And when

---

h + αὐτῷ to him [L]TTrA.		i + σε thee LTTrAW.		k ποιήσω I should do LTr; με
ποιήσω T.	l εἶπαν LTTrA.	m σου ἐκ δεξιῶν TTr.	n + σου thy T.	o ἀριστερῶν TTrA.
p — σου (read [thy] left hand) [L]TTrA.	q ἢ or LTTrA.	r εἶπαν LTTrA.	s — μὲν TTrA
t — μου (read [my] left hand) GLTTrAW.	v καὶ προσκαλεσάμενος αὐτοὺς ὁ Ἰησοῦς LTTrA.
w ἔστιν it is LTTrA.	x ἂν LTTr.	y μέγας γενέσθαι TTr.	z ὑμῶν διάκονος GLTTrAW.
a ἐὰν GTrA.	b ἐν ὑμῖν among you L.	c εἶναι to be LTr.	d ἔρχεται he comes L.	e Ἱεριχώ T.
f + ὁ the (son) LTTrAW.	g — ὁ (read a blind [man]) LTTrA.	ha + προσαίτης a beggar TTrA

he heard that it was
Jesus of Nazareth, he
began to cry out, and
say, Jesus, *thou* Son
of David, have mercy
on me. 48 And many
charged him that he
should hold his peace :
but he cried the more
a great deal, *Thou* Son
of David, have mercy
on me. 49 And Jesus
stood still, and com-
manded him to be
called. And they call
the blind man, saying
unto him, Be of good
comfort, rise ; he
calleth thee. 50 And
he, casting away his
garment, rose, and
came to Jesus. 51 And
Jesus answered and
said unto him, What
wilt thou that I should
do unto thee ? The
blind man said unto
him, Lord, that I
might receive my
sight. 52 And Jesus
said unto him, Go thy
way ; thy faith hath
made thee whole. And
immediately he receiv-
ed his sight, and fol-
lowed Jesus in the way.

XI. And when they
came nigh to Jerusa-
lem, unto Bethphage
and Bethany, at the
mount of Olives, he
sendeth forth two of
his disciples, 2 and
saith unto them, Go
your way into the vil-
lage over against you:
and as soon as ye be
entered into it, ye
shall find a colt : loose
wheron never man
sat ; loose him, and
bring *him*. 3 And if
any man say unto you,
Why do ye this ? say
ye that the Lord hath
need of him ; and
straightway he will
send him hither. 4 And
they went their way,
and found the colt tied
by the door without in
a place where two ways
met ; and they loose
him. 5 And certain of
them that stood there
said unto them, What
do ye, loosing the colt ?
6 And they said unto
them even as Jesus had
commanded : and they

ὁδὸν ¹προσαιτῶν.‖ 47 καὶ ἀκούσας ὅτι ᾿Ιησοῦς ὁ ᵏΝαζωραῖός‖
way,   begging .   And having heard that Jesus the Nazaræan

ἐστιν, ἤρξατο κράζειν καὶ λέγειν, ᴵ῾Ο υἱὸς ᵐΔαβίδ,‖ ᾿Ιησοῦ,
it was, he began to cry out and to say,   Son   of David,   Jesus,
(*lit.* it is)

ἐλέησόν με. 48 Καὶ ἐπετίμων αὐτῷ πολλοὶ ἵνα   σιωπήσῃ·
have pity on me.   And ²rebuked ³him. ¹many that he should be silent;

ὁ.δὲ πολλῷ μᾶλλον ἔκραζεν, Υἱὲ ᵐΔαβίδ,‖ ἐλέησόν με.
but he much   more   cried out, Son of David, have pity on me.

49 Καὶ   στὰς   ὁ ᾿Ιησοῦς ⁿεἶπεν αὐτὸν φωνηθῆναι·‖ καὶ
    And ²having ³stopped ¹Jesus asked for him   to be called.   And

φωνοῦσιν τὸν τυφλόν,   λέγοντες αὐτῷ,   Θάρσει·
they call the blind [man], saying to him, Be of good courage;

ᵒἔγειραι,‖ φωνεῖ σε. 50 ῾Ο.δὲ ἀποβαλὼν τὸ.ἱμάτιον.αὐτοῦ,
rise up,   he calls thee. And he casting away   his garment,

ᴾἀναστὰς‖ ἦλθεν πρὸς τὸν ᾿Ιησοῦν· 51 καὶ ἀποκριθεὶς ᵠλέγει
having risen up he came   to   Jesus.   And answering ²says

αὐτῷ ὁ ᾿Ιησοῦς,‖ Τί ʳθέλεις   ποιήσω σοί;‖ ῾Ο.δὲ τυφλὸς
³to ⁴him ¹Jesus, What dost thou desire I should do to thee? And the blind

εἶπεν αὐτῷ, ˢ῾Ραββονί,‖ ἵνα˜ ἀναβλέψω. 52 ῾Ο.δὲ.᾿Ιη-
[man] said to him, Rabboni, that I may receive sight.   And Je-

σοῦς εἶπεν αὐτῷ, ῞Υπαγε· ἡ.πίστις.σου σέσωκέν σε. Καὶ
sus said to him, Go,   thy faith has healed thee.   And

ᵗεὐθέως‖ ἀνέβλεψεν, καὶ ἠκολούθει ᵗτῷ ᾿Ιησοῦ‖ ἐν τῇ ὁδῷ.
immediately he received sight, and followed Jesus in the way.

11 Καὶ ὅτε ἐγγίζουσιν εἰς ᵂ᾿Ιερουσαλήμ,‖ ˣεἰς Βηθφαγὴ
    And when they drew near to   Jerusalem,   to Bethphage

καὶ Βηθανίαν,‖ πρὸς τὸ ὄρος τῶν ᾿Ελαιῶν, ʸἀποστέλλει‖ δύο
and Bethany,   towards the mount of Olives,   he sends   two

τῶν.μαθητῶν.αὐτοῦ, 2 καὶ λέγει αὐτοῖς, ῾Υπάγετε εἰς τὴν
of his disciples,   and says to them, Go   into the

κώμην τὴν.κατέναντι ὑμῶν· καὶ ᶻεὐθέως‖ εἰσπορευόμενοι εἰς
village, that opposite you, and immediately   entering   into

αὐτὴν εὑρήσετε πῶλον δεδεμένον, ἐφ᾽ ὃν οὐδεὶςᵃ ἀνθρώπωνᵇ
it   ye will find a colt tied,   upon which no one of men

κεκάθικεν· ᶜλύσαντες αὐτὸν‖ ἀγάγετε.‖ 3 καὶ ἐάν τις ὑμῖν
has sat : having loosed it   lead [it].   And if anyone to you

εἴπῃ, Τί ποιεῖτε τοῦτο ; εἴπατε, ᵉ῞Οτι ὁ κύριος αὐτοῦ χρείαν
say, Why do ye this?   say,   The Lord ³of ⁴it ²need

ἔχει· καὶ ᶠεὐθέως‖ αὐτὸν ᵍἀποστελεῖ‖ ʰ ὧδε. 4 ⁱᵃ᾿Απῆλθον.δέ,‖
¹has, and immediately   it   he will send hither.   And they departed,

καὶ εὗρον ᵏᵃτὸν‖ πῶλον δεδεμένον πρὸς ¹ᵃτὴν‖ θύραν ἔξω ἐπὶ
and found the   colt   tied   at   the   door without, by

τοῦ ἀμφόδου,.καὶ λύουσιν αὐτόν. 5 καί τινες τῶν ἐκεῖ ἑστη-
the cross way, and they loose it.   And some of those there stand-

κότων ἔλεγον αὐτοῖς, Τί ποιεῖτε λύοντες τὸν πῶλον ; 6 Οἱ.δὲ
 ing   said to them, What are ye doing loosing the colt?   And they

ᵐᵃεἶπον‖ αὐτοῖς καθὼς ⁿᵃἐνετείλατο‖ ὁ ᾿Ιησοῦς· καὶ ἀφῆκαν
said   to them as   ²commanded   ¹Jesus.   And they allowed

i — προσαιτῶν TTrA.   k Ναζαρηνός LTTrA.   l Υἱὲ LTTr.   m Δαυείδ LTTrA ; Δαυίδ GW.
n εἶπεν, φωνήσατε αὐτόν said, call ye him TTrA.   o ἔγειρε GLTTrAW.   P ἀναπηδήσας having
leaped up LTTrAW.   q αὐτῷ ὁ ᾿Ιησοῦς εἶπεν Jesus said to him TTrA.   r σοι θέλεις ποιήσω ; T.
s ῾Ραββουνί GLTTrAW.   t εὐθὺς TTrA.   v αὐτῷ him GLTTrAW.   w ῾Ιεροσόλυμα LTTrAW.
x καὶ εἰς Βηθανίαν LT.   y ἀπέστειλεν he sent L.   z εὐθὺς TTrA.   a + οὔπω not yet (read
no one yet) LTr.   b + οὔπω T.   c λύσατε αὐτὸν καὶ loose it and LTTrA.   d φέρετε
bring TTrA.   e — ῞Οτι LTTrA.   f εὐθὺς LTTrA.   g ἀποστέλλει he sends GLTTrAW.
h + πάλιν back TTr.   ia καὶ ἀπῆλθον LTTrAW.   ka — τὸν (read a colt) GLTrAW.   la — τὴν
(read a door) TrA.   ma εἶπαν T.   na εἶπεν said LTTrA.

αὐτούς. 7 καὶ °ἤγαγον‖ τὸν πῶλον πρὸς τὸν Ἰησοῦν· καὶ
them.   And   they led   the   colt   to,   Jesus.   And

Ρἐπέβαλον‖ αὐτῷ τὰ.ἱμάτια.αὐτῶν, καὶ ἐκάθισεν ἐπ᾽ � αὐτῷ·‖
they cast upon it   their garments,   and   he sat   on   it ;

8 ʳπολλοὶ.δὲ‖ τὰ.ἱμάτια.αὐτῶν ἔστρωσαν εἰς τὴν ὁδόν· ἄλλοι.δὲ
and many   their garments   strewed   on the way,   and others

ˢστοιβάδας‖ ᵗἔκοπτον‖ ἐκ τῶν ᵛδένδρων,‖ ʷκαὶ ἐστρώννυον
branches   were cutting down from   the   trees,   and were strewing

εἰς τὴν.ὁδόν.‖ 9 καὶ οἱ προάγοντες καὶ οἱ ἀκολουθοῦν-
[them] on the way.   And those going before and those   follow-

τες ἔκραζον, ˣλέγοντες,‖ Ὡσαννά· εὐλογημένος   ὁ
ing were crying out,   saying,   Hosanna !   blessed   [be] he who

ἐρχόμενος ἐν   ὀνόματι κυρίου· 10 εὐλογημένη ἡ ἐρχο-
comes   in [the]   name   of [the] Lord.   Blessed [be] the com-

μένη βασιλεία ʸἐν   ὀνόματι   κυρίου‖ τοῦ.πατρὸς.ἡμῶν
ing   kingdom   ⁶in [ᵉthe]   ⁷name   ⁸of [ᵗthe] ¹⁰Lord   ¹ ᵒof ²our ³father

ᶻΔαβίδ·‖ ᵃʼὩσαννὰ ἐν τοῖς ὑψίστοις. 11 Καὶ εἰσῆλθεν εἰς
⁴David.   Hosanna   in the   highest !   , And   ²entered ³into

Ἱεροσόλυμα ᵃὁʼἸησοῦς καὶ‖ εἰς τὸ ἱερόν· καὶ περιβλεψαμενος
⁴Jerusalem   ¹Jesus   and into the temple ; and having looked round on

πάντα, ᵇὀψίας‖ ἤδη οὔσης τῆς ὥρας, ἐξῆλθεν εἰς Βηθανίαν
all things,   late   already   being the hour,   he went out to   Bethany

μετὰ τῶν δώδεκα.
with   the   twelve.

12 Καὶ τῇ ἐπαύριον ἐξελθόντων αὐτῶν ἀπὸ Βηθανίας,
And on the   morrow   ²having ³gone ⁴out ¹they   from   Bethany,

ἐπείνασεν· 13 καὶ ἰδὼν συκῆν ᶜ μακρόθεν ἔχουσαν φύλλα,
he hungered.   And seeing a fig-tree   afar off   having   leaves,

ἦλθεν εἰ ἄρα ᵈεὑρήσει τι‖ ἐν αὐτῇ· καὶ ἐλθὼν ἐπ᾽
he went if perhaps he will find anything on   it.   , And having come to

αὐτήν, οὐδὲν εὗρεν εἰ.μὴ φύλλα·ᵉ ᶠοὐ.γὰρ.ἦν   καιρὸς‖ σύκων.
it,   nothing he found except leaves,   for it was not [the] season of figs.

14 καὶ ἀποκριθεὶς ᵍὁʼἸησοῦς‖ εἶπεν αὐτῇ, Μηκέτι ʰἐκ σοῦ εἰς
And ²answering   ¹Jesus   said to it,   No more   of thee for

τὸν αἰῶνα‖ ⁱμηδεὶς‖ καρπὸν φάγοι. Καὶ ἤκουον οἱ μαθηταὶ
ever   ²any ³one   ⁵fruit ¹let ⁴eat.   And   ³heard   ²disciples
(lit. no one)

αὐτοῦ. 15 Καὶ ἔρχονται εἰς Ἱεροσόλυμα· καὶ εἰσελθὼν
¹his.   And, they come to   Jerusalem ;   and ²having ³entered

ᵏὁʼἸησοῦς‖ εἰς τὸ ἱερὸν ἤρξατο ἐκβάλλειν τοὺς πωλοῦντας
¹Jesus   into the temple he began to cast out   those   selling

καὶ ˡ ἀγοράζοντας ἐν τῷ ἱερῷ· καὶ τὰς τραπέζας τῶν κολλυ-
and   buying   in the temple, and the   tables   of the money

βιστῶν καὶ τὰς καθέδρας τῶν πωλούντων τὰς περιστερὰς
changers and the   seats   of those   selling   the   doves

κατέστρεψεν· 16 καὶ οὐκ.ἤφιεν ἵνα τις διενέγκῃ σκεῦος
he overthrew,   and   suffered not   that anyone should carry a vessel

διὰ τοῦ ἱεροῦ. 17 καὶ ἐδίδασκεν, ᵐλέγων‖ ⁿαὐτοῖς,‖ Οὐ
through the temple.   And he taught,   saying   to them,   ³Not

let them go.   7 And
they brought the colt
to Jesus, and cast their
garments on him ;
and he sat upon him.
8 And many spread
their garments in the
way : and others cut
down branches off the
trees, and strawed
them in the way. 9 And
they that went before,
and they that fol-
lowed, cried, saying,
Hosanna ; Blessed is
he that cometh in the
name of the Lord :
10 blessed be the king-
dom of our father
David, that cometh in
the name of the Lord :
Hosanna in the high-
est. 11 And Jesus en-
tered into Jerusalem,
and into the temple :
and when he had look-
ed round about upon
all things, and now
the eventide was come,
he went out unto Beth-
any with the twelve.

12 And on the mor-
row, when they were
come from Bethany,
he was hungry : 13 and
seeing a fig tree afar
off having leaves, he
came, if haply he
might find any thing
thereon : and when he
came to it, he found
nothing but leaves ;
for the time of figs
was not yet. 14 And
Jesus answered and
said unto it, No man
eat fruit of thee here-
after for ever. And
his disciples heard it.
15 And they come to
Jerusalem : and Jesus
went into the temple,
and began to cast out
them that sold and
bought in the temple,
and overthrew the
tables of the money-
changers, and the seats
of them that sold
doves ; 16 and would
not suffer that any
man should carry any
vessel through the
temple. 17 And he
taught, saying unto

ᵒ φέρουσιν they bring TTrA.   ᵖ ἐπιβάλλουσιν they cast upon GLTTrAW.   �٩ αὐτόν LTTrA.
ʳ καὶ πολλοὶ TTrA.   ˢ στιβάδας LTTrA: ᵗ κόψαντες having cut [them] down TTrA.
ᵛ ἀγρῶν fields TTrA.   ʷ — καὶ ἐστρώννυον εἰς τὴν ὁδόν TTrA.   ˣ — λέγοντες [L]TTrA.
ʸ — ἐν ὀνόματι κυρίου GLTTrAW.   ᶻ Δαυείδ LTTrA ; Δαυὶδ GW.   ᵃ — ὁ Ἰησοῦς καὶ (read he
entered) LTTrA.   ᵇ ὀψὲ T.   ᶜ + ἀπὸ from LTTrAW.   ᵈ τι εὑρήσει LTTrAW.   ᵉ + [μόνα]
only L.   ᶠ οὐ γὰρ ἦν ὁ καιρὸς L ; ὁ γὰρ καιρὸς οὐκ ἦν TTrA.   ᵍ — ὁ Ἰησοῦς (read he said)
GLTTrAW.   ʰ εἰς τὸν αἰῶνα ἐκ σοῦ LTTrA.   ⁱ οὐδεὶς E.   ᵏ — ὁ Ἰησοῦς GLTTrAW:
ˡ + τοὺς these LTTrAW.   ᵐ καὶ ἔλεγεν and said TTrA.   ⁿ — αὐτοῖς [L]A.

them, Is it not written, My house shall be called of all nations the house of prayer? but ye have made it a den of thieves. 18 And the scribes and chief priests heard it, and sought how they might destroy him: for they feared him, because all the people was astonished at his doctrine. 19 And when even was come, he went out of the city.

20 And in the morning, as they passed by, they saw the fig tree dried up from the roots. 21 And Peter calling to remembrance saith unto him, Master, behold, the fig tree which thou cursedst is withered away. 22 And Jesus answering saith unto them, Have faith in God. 23 For verily I say unto you, That whosoever shall say unto this mountain, Be thou removed, and be thou cast into the sea; and shall not doubt in his heart, but shall believe that those things which he saith shall come to pass; he shall have whatsoever he saith. 24 Therefore I say unto you, What things soever ye desire, when ye pray, believe that ye receive them, and ye shall have them. 25 And when ye stand praying, forgive, if ye have ought against any: that your Father also which is in heaven may forgive you your trespasses. 26 But if ye do not forgive, neither will your Father which is in heaven forgive your trespasses.

27 And they come again to Jerusalem: and as he was walking in the temple, there come to him the chief priests, and the scribes, and the elders, 28 and say unto him, By what authority doest thou these things? and who gave thee this authority to do these things? 29 And Jesus

γέγραπται, ο''Ὅτι'' ὁ οἶκός μου οἶκος προσευχῆς κληθήσεται
'has ²it been written, ·   My house   a house   of prayer   shall be called

πᾶσιν τοῖς ἔθνεσιν; ὑμεῖς δὲ ᴾἐποιήσατε'' αὐτὸν σπήλαιον
for all   the   nations?   but ye   made   it   a den

λῃστῶν. 18 Καὶ ἤκουσαν οἱ �ۊγραμματεῖς καὶ οἱ ἀρχιερεῖς,''
of robbers.   And ⁷heard [⁸it] ¹the   ²scribes   ³and ⁴the ⁵chief ⁶priests,

καὶ ἐζήτουν πῶς αὐτὸν ʳἀπολέσουσιν·'' ἐφοβοῦντο γὰρ ˢαὐτόν,''
and they sought how   him   they shall destroy;   for they feared   him,

ᵗὅτι πᾶς'' ὁ ὄχλος ᵛἐξεπλήσσετο'' ἐπὶ τῇ διδαχῇ αὐτοῦ.
because all   the crowd   were astonished   at   his teaching.

19 Καὶ ʷὅτε'' ὀψὲ ἐγένετο ˣἐξεπορεύετο'' ἔξω τῆς πόλεως.
And when evening came   he went forth   out of   the   city.

20 Καὶ ʸπρωῒ παραπορευόμενοι'' εἶδον τὴν συκῆν
And in the morning   passing by   they saw the   fig-tree

ἐξηραμμένην ἐκ ῥιζῶν. 21 καὶ ἀναμνησθεὶς ὁ Πέτρος
dried up   from [the] roots.   And ²having ³remembered ¹Peter

λέγει αὐτῷ, ᶻῬαββί,'' ἴδε, ἡ συκῆ ἣν κατηράτω ἐξήρανται.
says to him   Rabbi,   see, the fig-tree which thou cursedst   is dried up.

22 Καὶ ἀποκριεὶς ᵃἸησοῦς λέγει αὐτοῖς, Ἔχετε πίστιν θεοῦ.
And ²answering ¹Jesus   says to them,   Have   faith   in God.

23 ἀμὴν ᵇγὰρ'' λέγω ὑμῖν, ὅτι ὃς ἂν εἴπῃ τῷ ὄρει τούτῳ,
For verily   I say to you, that whoever shall say   to this mountain,

Ἄρθητι καὶ βλήθητι εἰς τὴν θάλασσαν, καὶ μὴ δια-
Be thou taken away and be thou cast into the   sea,   and shall not

κριθῇ ἐν τῇ καρδίᾳ αὐτοῦ, ἀλλὰ ᶜπιστεύσῃ'' ὅτι ᵈἃ'' ἐλέγει''
doubt in   his heart,   but   shall believe that what he says

γίνεται· ἔσται αὐτῷ ᶠὃ ἐὰν εἴπῃ. 24 διὰ τοῦτο λέγω
takes place, there shall be to him whatever he shall say.   For this reason I say

ὑμῖν, Πάντα ὅσα ᵍἂν'' ʰπροσευχόμενοι'', αἰτεῖσθε, πιστεύετε
to you, All things whatsoever   praying   ye ask,   believe

ὅτι ⁱλαμβάνετε,'' καὶ ἔσται ὑμῖν. 25 Καὶ ὅταν ᵏστήκητε''
that ye receive,   and [they] shall be to you. And when ye may stand

προσευχόμενοι, ἀφίετε εἴ τι ἔχετε κατά τινος· ἵνα καὶ
praying,   forgive if anything ye have against anyone, that also

ὁ πατὴρ ὑμῶν ὁ ἐν τοῖς οὐρανοῖς ἀφῇ ὑμῖν τὰ παρα-
your Father who [is] in the heavens may forgive you   ²of-

πτώματα ὑμῶν. 26 ˡεἰ δὲ ὑμεῖς οὐκ ἀφίετε, οὐδὲ ὁ πατὴρ ὑμῶν
fences   ¹your.   But if ye   forgive not, neither   your Father

ὁ ἐν ᵐτοῖς' οὐρανοῖς ἀφήσει τὰ παραπτώματα ὑμῶν.''
who [is] in the   heavens will forgive   your offences.

27 Καὶ ἔρχονται πάλιν εἰς Ἱεροσόλυμα· καὶ ἐν τῷ ἱερῷ
And they come again to   Jerusalem   And in the temple

περιπατοῦντος αὐτοῦ ἔρχονται πρὸς αὐτὸν οἱ ἀρχιερεῖς καὶ
as he is walking   come   to   him   the chief priests and

οἱ γραμματεῖς καὶ οἱ πρεσβύτεροι, 28 καὶ ⁿλέγουσιν'' αὐτῷ,
the   scribes   and the   elders,   and   they say   to him,

Ἐν ποίᾳ ἐξουσίᾳ ταῦτα ποιεῖς; ᵒᵃκαὶ'' τίς σοι ᵖᵃτὴν ἐξουσίαν
By what authority these things doest thou? and who thee   ²authority

ταύτην ἔδωκεν,'' ἵνα ταῦτα ποιῇς; 29 Ὁ δὲ Ἰησοῦς
¹this   gave,   that these things thou shouldst do?   And Jesus

---

ο — Ὅτι L.   ᴾ πεποιήκατε have made ᴛᴛrᴀ.   ۊ ἀρχιερεῖς καὶ οἱ γραμματεῖς ʟᴛᴛrᴀᴡ.
ʳ ἀπολέσωσιν they might destroy ʟᴛᴛrᴀᴡ.   ˢ [αὐτόν] ʟ.   ᵗ πᾶς γὰρ for all ᴛᴛrᴀ.   ᵛ ἐξεπλήσσοντο ᴛ.   ʷ ὅταν ᴛᴛr.   ˣ ἐξεπορεύοντο they went forth ʟᴛr.   ʸ παραπορευόμενοι πρωῒ ʟᴛᴛrᴀ.
ᶻ Ῥαββεί ᴛᴀ.   ᵃ + ὁ ɢʟᴛᴛrᴀᴡ.   ᵇ — γὰρ for ʟᴛ[ᴛr]ᴀ.   ᶜ πιστεύῃ ᴛᴀ.   ᵈ ὃ what ᴛᴛrᴀ.
ᵉ λαλεῖ ʟᴛᴛrᴀ.   ᶠ — ὃ ἐὰν εἴπῃ ᴛᴛr[ᴀ].   ᵍ — ἂν ʟᴛᴛrᴀᴡ.   ʰ προσεύχεσθε καὶ ye pray and
ʟᴛᴛrᴀ.   ⁱ ἐλάβετε ye received ʟᴛᴛrᴀ.   ᵏ στήκετε ye stand ʟᴛᴛrᴀ.   ˡ — verse 26 ᴛᴛᴀ.
ᵐ — τοῖς ʟᴀ.   ⁿ ἔλεγον they said ᴛᴛrᴀ.   ᵒᵃ ἢ or ᴛᴀ.   ᵖᵃ ἔδωκεν τὴν ἐξουσίαν ταύτην ʟᴛr.

ʳἀποκριθεὶς‖ εἶπεν αὐτοῖς, Ἐπερωτήσω ˢὑμας κἀγὼ‖ ἕνα λόγον,
answering   said to them   ²Will ³ask   ⁴you¹ I also   one   thing,

καὶ ἀποκρίθητέ μοι, καὶ ἐρῶ ὑμῖν ἐν ποίᾳ ἐξουσίᾳ ταῦτα
and   answer   me, and I will tell you by what authority these things

ποιῶ. 30 Τὸ βάπτισμα ᵗἸωάννου ἐξ οὐρανοῦ ἦν ἢ ἐξ
I do: The baptism   of John   from heaven   was it or from

ἀνθρώπων; ἀποκρίθητέ μοι. 31 Καὶ ᵛἐλογίζοντο‖ πρὸς ἑαυ-
men?   answer   me.   And they reasoned with them

τούς, λέγοντες, Ἐὰν εἴπωμεν, Ἐξ οὐρανοῦ, ἐρεῖ, ʷΔιατί‖
selves, saying,   If we should say, From heaven,   he will say, Why

ˣοὖν‖ οὐκ ἐπιστεύσατε αὐτῷ; 32 ʸἀλλ' ἐὰν‖ εἴπωμεν, Ἐξ
then   did ye not believe   him?   but   if we should say, From

ἀνθρώπων, ἐφοβοῦντο τὸν λαόν· ᶻἅπαντες‖ γὰρ εἶχον τὸν
men,—   they feared   the people;   for all   held

Ἰωάννην ᵃὅτι ὄντως‖ προφήτης ἦν. 33 καὶ ἀποκριθέντες ᵇλέ-
John   that indeed   a prophet he was.   And answering   they

γουσιν τῷ Ἰησοῦ,‖ Οὐκ οἴδαμεν. Καὶ ᶜὁ Ἰησοῦς ἀποκριθεὶς‖ λέγει
say   to Jesus,   We know not.   And   Jesus   answering   says

αὐτοῖς, Οὐδὲ ἐγὼ λέγω ὑμῖν ἐν ποίᾳ ἐξουσίᾳ ταῦτα ποιῶ.
to them, Neither ²I   ¹tell you by what· authority these things I do.

12 Καὶ ἤρξατο αὐτοῖς ἐν παραβολαῖς ᵈλέγειν.‖ Ἀμπελῶνα
And he began to them in   parables   to say,   ⁴A ⁵vineyard

ᵉἐφύτευσεν ἄνθρωπος,‖ καὶ περιέθηκεν φραγμόν, καὶ ὤρυξεν
²planted   ¹a ²man,   and placed about [it] a fence,   and   dug

ὑπολήνιον, καὶ ᾠκοδόμησεν πύργον, καὶ ᶠἐξέδοτο‖ αὐτὸν
a wine-vat,   and   built   a tower,   and   let out   it

γεωργοῖς, καὶ ἀπεδήμησεν. 2 καὶ ἀπέστειλεν πρὸς τοὺς
to husbandmen, and left the country.   And   he sent   to   the

γεωργοὺς τῷ καιρῷ δοῦλον, ἵνα παρὰ τῶν γεωργῶν
husbandmen at the season   a bondman,   that   from   the husbandmen

λάβῃ ἀπὸ ᵍτοῦ καρποῦ‖ τοῦ ἀμπελῶνος 3 ʰοἱ δὲ‖ λα-
he might receive from the fruit   of the vineyard.   But they having

βόντες αὐτὸν ἔδειραν, καὶ ἀπέστειλαν κενόν. 4 καὶ πάλιν
taken   ²him   ¹beat,   and sent [him] away empty.   And   again

ἀπέστειλεν πρὸς αὐτοὺς ἄλλον δοῦλον· κἀκεῖνον ᵢλιθοβολή-
he sent   to them   another   bondman,   and him   having

σαντες‖ ʲἐκεφαλαίωσαν,‖ καὶ ᵏἀπέστειλαν ἠτιμωμένον.‖
stoned   they struck on the head, and sent [him] away having insulted [him].

5 καὶ ˡπάλιν‖ ἄλλον ἀπέστειλεν· κἀκεῖνον ἀπέκτειναν· καὶ
And again   another   he sent,   and him   they killed;   also

πολλοὺς ἄλλους, ᵐτοὺς‖ μὲν δέροντες, ᵐτοὺς‖ δὲ ⁿἀποκτείνον-
many   others,   ²some   ¹beating,   and ²others   ¹killing.

τες.‖ 6 ἔτι ᵒοὖν‖ ἕνα ᵖυἱὸν ἔχων‖ ἀγαπητὸν ᑫαὐτοῦ,‖
Yet therefore ²one ³son   ¹having   ⁶beloved   ⁴his ⁵own,

ἀπέστειλεν ʳᵃκαὶ‖ αὐτὸν ˢᵃπρὸς αὐτοὺς ἔσχατον,‖ λέγων, Ὅτι
he sent   also him   to them   last,   saying,

ἐντραπήσονται τὸν υἱόν μου. 7 ἐκεῖνοι δὲ οἱ γεωργοὶ ᵗᵃεἶπον
They will have respect for   my son.   But those   husbandmen   said

---

Right column (English translation):

answered and said un-
to them, I will also
ask of you one ques-
tion, and answer me,
and I will tell you by
what authority I do
these things. 30 The
baptism of John, was
it from heaven, or of
men? answer me.
31 And they reasoned
with themselves, say-
ing, If we shall say,
From heaven; he will
say, Why then did
ye not believe him?
32 But if we shall say,
Of men; they feared
the people : for all *men*
counted John, that he
was a prophet indeed.
33 And they answered
and said unto Jesus,
We cannot tell. And
Jesus answering saith
unto them, Neither do
I tell you by what
authority I do these
things.

XII. And he began
to speak unto them by
parables. A *certain*
man planted a vine-
yard, and set an hedge
about *it*, and digged a
place for the winefat,
and built a tower, and
let it out to husband-
men, and went into a
far country. 2 And at
the season he sent to
the husbandmen a ser-
vant, that he might
receive from the hus-
bandmen of the fruit
of the vineyard. 3 And
they caught *him*, and
beat him, and sent *him*
away empty. 4 And
again he sent unto
them another servant;
and at him they cast
stones, and wounded
him in the head, and
sent *him* away shame-
fully handled. 5 And
again he sent another;
and him they killed,
and many others;
beating some, and kill-
ing some. 6 Having
yet therefore one son,
his wellbeloved, ·he
sent him also last unto
them, saying, They
will reverence my son.
7 But those husband-
men said among them-

ʳ — ἀποκριθεὶς TTrA. ˢ κἀγὼ ὑμᾶς L; — κἀγὼ (*read* ἐπερ. I will ask) TTrA. ᵗ + τὸ
LTTrAW. ᵛ διελογίζοντο LTTrAW. ʷ Διὰ τί LTrA. ˣ — οὖν LTrAW. ʸ ἀλλὰ (*read* but
should we say) LTTrAW. ᶻ πάντες L. ᵃ ὄντως ὅτι TTrA. ᵇ τῷ Ἰησοῦ λέγουσιν TTrA.
ᶜ [ἀποκριθεὶς] ὁ Ἰησοῦς L; — ἀποκριθεὶς TTrA. ᵈ λαλεῖν LTTrA. ᵉ ἄνθρωπος ἐφύτευσεν T.
ᶠ ἐξέδετο TA. ᵍ τῶν καρπῶν the fruits TTrA. ʰ καὶ and LTTrA. ᵢ λιθοβολήσαντες LTTrA.
ʲ ἐκεφαλίωσαν T. ᵏ ἠτίμησαν insulted LTr; ἠτίμασαν TA. ˡ — πάλιν GLTTrA. ᵐ οὓς
LTTrA. ⁿ ἀποκτέννοντες GLTTrA. ᵒ — οὖν [L]TTrA. ᵖ ἔχων υἱὸν L; εἶχεν υἱὸν TTrA.
ᑫ — αὐτοῦ LTTrA; αὐτοῦ W. ʳᵃ — καὶ [L]TTrA. ˢᵃ ἔσχατον πρὸς αὐτοὺς LTTrA. ᵗᵃ πρὸς
ἑαυτοὺς εἶπαν TTrA; εἶπαν πρὸς ἑαυτοὺς L.

selves, This is the heir; come, let us kill him, and the inheritance shall be ours. 8 And they took him, and killed him, and cast him out of the vineyard. 9 What shall therefore the lord of the vineyard do? he will come and destroy the husbandmen, and will give the vineyard unto others. 10 And have ye not read this scripture; The stone which the builders rejected is become the head of the corner: 11 this was the Lord's doing, and it is marvellous in our eyes? 12 And they sought to lay hold on him, but feared the people: for they knew that he had spoken the parable against them: and they left him, and went their way.

πρὸς ἑαυτούς, ‖ Ὅτι οὗτός ἐστιν ὁ κληρονόμος· δεῦτε, ἀπο-
among themselves, This is the heir: come, let us
κτείνωμεν αὐτόν, καὶ ἡμῶν ἔσται ἡ κληρονομία. 8 καὶ λαβόντες
kill him, and ours will be the inheritance. And having taken
ᵛαὐτὸν ἀπέκτειναν,‖ καὶ ἐξέβαλον ʷ ἔξω τοῦ ἀμπελῶνος.
him they killed [him], and cast forth [him] outside the vineyard.
9 τί ˣοὖν‖ ποιήσει ὁ κύριος τοῦ ἀμπελῶνος; ἐλεύσεται καὶ
What therefore will do the lord of the vineyard? He will come and
ἀπολέσει τοὺς γεωργούς, καὶ δώσει τὸν ἀμπελῶνα ἄλλοις.
will destroy the husbandmen, and will give the vineyard to others.
10 Οὐδὲ τὴν γραφὴν ταύτην ἀνέγνωτε; Λίθον ὃν
³Not ⁴even ⁶this ⁷scripture ¹did ²ye ⁵read? [The] stone which
ἀπεδοκίμασαν οἱ οἰκοδομοῦντες, οὗτος ἐγενήθη εἰς κεφαλὴν
⁴rejected ¹those ²who ³build, this is become head
γωνίας. 11 παρὰ κυρίου ἐγένετο αὕτη, καὶ ἔστιν θαυ-
of [the] corner: from [the] Lord was this, and it is won-
μαστὴ ἐν ὀφθαλμοῖς ἡμῶν. 12 Καὶ ἐζήτουν αὐτὸν κρατῆσαι,
derful in our eyes. And they sought him to lay hold of,
καὶ ἐφοβήθησαν τὸν ὄχλον· ἔγνωσαν γὰρ ὅτι πρὸς αὐτοὺς
and they feared the crowd; for they knew that against them
τὴν παραβολὴν εἶπεν· καὶ ἀφέντες αὐτὸν ἀπῆλθον.
the parable he speaks. And leaving him they went away.

13 And they send unto him certain of the Pharisees and of the Herodians, to catch him in his words. 14 And when they were come, they say unto him, Master, we know that thou art true, and carest for no man: for thou regardest not the person of men, but teachest the way of God in truth: Is it lawful to give tribute to Cæsar, or not? 15 Shall we give, or shall we not give? But he, knowing their hypocrisy, said unto them, Why tempt ye me? bring me a penny, that I may see it. 16 And they brought it. And he saith unto them, Whose is this image and superscription? And they said unto him, Cæsar's. 17 And Jesus answering said unto them, Render to Cæsar the things that are Cæsar's, and to God the things that are God's. And they marvelled at him.

13 Καὶ ἀποστέλλουσιν πρὸς αὐτόν τινας τῶν Φαρισαίων
And they send to him some of the Pharisees
καὶ τῶν Ἡρωδιανῶν, ἵνα αὐτὸν ἀγρεύσωσιν λόγῳ. 14 ʸοἱ δὲ‖
and of the Herodians, that him they might catch in discourse. And they
ἐλθόντες λέγουσιν αὐτῷ, Διδάσκαλε, οἴδαμεν ὅτι ἀληθὴς εἶ,
having come say to him, Teacher, we know that true thou art,
καὶ οὐ μέλει σοι περὶ οὐδενός· οὐ γὰρ βλέπεις εἰς
and there is care to thee about no one; for ²not ¹thou ²lookest on [the]
πρόσωπον ἀνθρώπων, ἀλλ' ἐπ' ἀληθείας τὴν ὁδὸν τοῦ θεοῦ
appearance of men, but with truth the way of God
διδάσκεις. ᶻἔξεστιν ᵃκῆνσον Καίσαρι δοῦναι‖ ἢ οὔ; 15 δῶμεν
teachest: Is it lawful tribute to Cæsar to give or not? Should we give
ἢ μὴ δῶμεν; Ὁ δὲ ᵇεἰδὼς‖ αὐτῶν τὴν ὑπόκρισιν εἶπεν
or should we not give? But he knowing their hypocrisy said
αὐτοῖς, Τί με πειράζετε; φέρετέ μοι δηνάριον ἵνα ἴδω.
to them, Why me do ye tempt? Bring me a denarius that I may see [it].
16 Οἱ δὲ ἤνεγκαν. Καὶ λέγει αὐτοῖς, Τίνος ἡ εἰκὼν αὕτη καὶ
And they brought [it]. And he says to them, Whose [is] this image and
ἡ ἐπιγραφή; ᶜΟἱ δὲ‖ ᵈεἶπον‖ αὐτῷ, Καίσαρος. 17 ᵉΚαὶ
the inscription? And they said to him, Cæsar's. And
ἀποκριθεὶς ὁ‖ Ἰησοῦς εἶπεν ᶠαὐτοῖς,‖ ᵍἈπόδοτε τὰ Καί-
²answering ¹Jesus said to them, Render the things of Cæ-
σαρος‖ Καίσαρι, καὶ τὰ τοῦ θεοῦ τῷ θεῷ. Καὶ ʰἐθαύμασαν‖
sar to Cæsar, and the things of God to God. And they wondered
ἐπ' αὐτῷ,
at him.

18 Then come unto him the Sadducees, which say there is no resurrection; and they asked him, saying,

18 Καὶ ἔρχονται Σαδδουκαῖοι πρὸς αὐτόν, οἵτινες λέγουσιν
And ²come ¹Sadducees to him, who say
ἀνάστασιν μὴ εἶναι· καὶ ⁱἐπηρώτησαν‖ αὐτόν, λέγοντες·
a resurrection there is not. And they questioned him, saying,

---

ᵛ ἀπέκτειναν αὐτόν TTrA.　ʷ + αὐτὸν him LTTrAW.　ˣ — οὖν TA.　ʸ καὶ and (read
they say) LTTrA.　ᶻ + εἰπὲ οὖν ἡμῖν tell us therefore L.　ᵃ δοῦναι κῆνσον Καίσαρι LTr.
ᵇ ἰδὼν having known T.　ᶜ [οἱ δὲ] L.　ᵈ εἶπαν LTTrA.　ᵉ ὁ δὲ and (Jesus) LTTrA.
ᶠ — αὐτοῖς A.　ᵍ Τὰ Καίσαρος ἀπόδοτε TTrA.　ʰ ἐθαύμαζον LTrA; ἐξεθαύμαζον greatly
wondered T.　ⁱ ἐπηρώτων LTTrA.

19 Διδάσκαλε, ᵏΜωσῆς‖ ἔγραψεν ἡμῖν, ὅτι ἐάν τινος ἀδελ-
   Teacher,   Moses   wrote   for us, that if of anyone a bro-

φὸς ἀποθάνῃ καὶ καταλίπῃ γυναῖκα καὶ ᶥτέκνα μὴ ἀφῇ,‖
ther should die and leave behind a wife and children leave not,

ἵνα λάβῃ ὁ ἀδελφὸς αὐτοῦ τὴν γυναῖκα· ᵐαὐτοῦ‖ καὶ
that ²should ¹take ¹his ²brother   the   wife   of him and

ἐξαναστήσῃ σπέρμα τῷ ἀδελφῷ αὐτοῦ. 20 ἑπτὰ ⁿ ἀδελφοὶ
raise up   seed   to his brother.   Seven   brethren

ἦσαν· καὶ ὁ πρῶτος ἔλαβεν γυναῖκα, καὶ ἀποθνήσκων
there were ; and the first   took   a wife, and   dying

οὐκ ἀφῆκεν σπέρμα· 21 καὶ ὁ δεύτερος ἔλαβεν αὐτήν, καὶ
left no   seed· and the second   took   her,   and

ἀπέθανεν, ᵒκαὶ οὐδὲ αὐτὸς ἀφῆκεν‖ σπέρμα· καὶ ὁ τρίτος
died,   and neither he   left   seed ; and the third

ὡσαύτως· 22 καὶ ᵖἔλαβον αὐτὴν‖ οἱ ἑπτά, �q καὶ‖ οὐκ ἀφῆκαν
likewise. And   ²took ⁴her ¹the ²seven, and left no

σπέρμα. ʳἐσχάτη‖ πάντων ˢἀπέθανεν καὶ ἡ γυνή.‖ 23 ἐν τῇ
seed. Last   of all   died   also the woman.   In the

ᵗοὖν‖ ἀναστάσει, ᵛὅταν ἀναστῶσιν;‖ τίνος αὐτῶν ἔσται
²therefore ¹resurrection, when they shall arise, of which of them shall she be

γυνή ; οἱ γὰρ ἑπτὰ ἔσχον αὐτὴν γυναῖκα. 24 ʷΚαὶ ἀποκριθεὶς
wife? for the seven had   her as wife.   And ²answering

ὁ Ἰησοῦς εἶπεν αὐτοῖς,‖ Οὐ διὰ τοῦτο πλανᾶσθε, μὴ εἰδότες
¹Jesus   said to them, Not ⁴therefore ¹do ²ye err, not knowing

τὰς γραφὰς μηδὲ τὴν δύναμιν τοῦ θεοῦ; 25 ὅταν γὰρ ἐκ
the scriptures nor the power of God?   For when from among

νεκρῶν ἀναστῶσιν, οὔτε γαμοῦσιν οὔτε ˣγαμίσκονται,‖
[the] dead   they rise, neither do they marry nor are given in marriage,

ἀλλ' εἰσὶν ὡς ἄγγελοι ʸοἱ‖ ἐν τοῖς οὐρανοῖς. 26 περὶ δὲ
but 'are as angels who [are] in the heavens. But concerning

τῶν νεκρῶν, ὅτι ἐγείρονται, οὐκ ἀνέγνωτε ἐν τῇ βίβλῳ
the dead, that they rise, have ye not read in the book

ᶻΜωσέως,‖ ἐπὶ ᵃτῆς‖ βάτου, ᵇὡς‖ εἶπεν αὐτῷ ὁ θεός,
of Moses, [in the part] on the bush, how ²spoke ³to ⁴him ¹God,

λέγων, Ἐγὼ ὁ θεὸς Ἀβραὰμ καὶ ᶜὁ‖ θεὸς Ἰσαὰκ καὶ ᶜὁ‖
saying, I [am] the God of Abraham and the God of Isaac and the

θεὸς Ἰακώβ; 27 Οὐκ ἔστιν ᶜὁ‖ θεὸς νεκρῶν, ἀλλὰ ᵈθεὸς‖
God of Jacob?   He is not the God of [the] dead, but   God

ζώντων· ᵉὑμεῖς οὖν‖ πολὺ πλανᾶσθε. 28 Καὶ προσελθὼν
of [the] living. Ye therefore greatly err.   And ²having ⁶come ⁷up

εἷς τῶν γραμματέων, ἀκούσας αὐτῶν ᶠσυζητούντων,‖ εἰδὼς
¹one ²of ³the ⁴scribes, having heard them reasoning together, perceiving

ὅτι καλῶς ʰαὐτοῖς ἀπεκρίθη.‖ ἐπηρώτησεν αὐτόν, Ποία ἐστὶν
that well them he answered, questioned him, Which is-

ᶦπρώτη πασῶν ἐντολή;‖ 29 ᵏᵃὉ δὲ Ἰησοῦς ἀπεκρίθη‖
[the] first ²of ³all ¹commandment?   And Jesus   answered

ˡᵃαὐτῷ,‖ Ὅτι πρώτη ᵐᵃπασῶν τῶν ἐντολῶν,‖ Ἄκουε,
him,   [The] first of all the commandments [is], Hear,

---

19 Master, Moses wrote unto us. If a man's brother die, and leave his wife behind him, and leave no children, that his brother should take his wife, and raise up seed unto his brother. 20 Now there were seven brethren : and the first took a wife, and dying left no seed. 21 And the second took her, and died, neither left he any seed : and the third likewise. 22 And the seven had her, and left no seed : last of all the woman died also. 23 In the resurrection therefore, when they shall rise, whose wife shall she be of them? for the seven had her to wife. 24 And Jesus answering said unto them, Do ye not therefore err, because ye know not the scriptures, neither the power of God ? 25 For when they shall rise from the dead, they neither marry, nor are given in marriage ; but are as the angels which are in heaven. 26 And as touching the dead, that they rise : have ye not read in the book of Moses, how in the bush God spake unto him, saying, I am the God of Abraham, and the God of Isaac, and the God of Jacob ? 27 He is not the God of the dead, but the God of the living : ye therefore do greatly err. 28 And one of the scribes came, and having heard them reasoning together, and perceiving that he had answered them well, asked him, Which is the first commandment of all ? 29 And Jesus answered him, The first of all the commandments is, Hear, O Israel ; The

---

ᵏ Μωϋσῆς LTTrAW. ˡ μὴ ἀφῇ τέκνον leave no child TA. ᵐ — αὐτοῦ TTrA. ⁿ + οὖν therefore EW. ᵒ μὴ καταλιπὼν having left behind no TTrA. ᵖ — ἔλαβον αὐτὴν [L]TTrA. q — καὶ TTrA. ʳ ἔσχατον LTTrA. ˢ καὶ ἡ γυνὴ ἀπέθανεν LTTrA. ᵗ — οὖν TTrA. ᵛ — ὅταν ἀναστῶσιν [L]Tr. ʷ ἔφη αὐτοῖς ὁ Ἰησοῦς Jesus said to them TTrA. ˣ γαμίζονται LTTrAW. ʸ — οἱ GLT[Tr]W. ᶻ Μωϋσέως LTTrAW. ᵃ τοῦ GLTTrAW. ᵇ πῶς TTrA. ᶜ — ὁ LTrA. ᵈ θεὸς GLTTrAW. ᵉ ὑμεῖς οὖν (read πλαν. ye err) T[Tr]A. ᶠ συνζητούντων LTTrA. ᵍ ἰδὼν having seen LTTr. ʰ ἀπεκρίθη αὐτοῖς TTrA. ᶦ πρώτη πάντων ἐντολή GLW. ἐντολὴ πρώτη πάντων TTrA. ᵏᵃ ἀπεκρίθη ὁ Ἰησοῦς TTrA. ˡᵃ — αὐτῷ T[Tr]A. ᵐᵃ πάντων ἐντολή GW ; πάντων [ἐντολή ἐστιν] commandment of all is L ; ἐστὶν (read [The] first is) TTrA.

Lord our God is one
Lord: 30 and thou
shalt love the Lord thy
God with all thy heart,
and with all thy soul,
and with all thy mind,
and with all thy
strength: this *is* the
first commandment.
31 And the second *is*
like, *namely* this, Thou
shalt love thy neigh-
bour as thyself. There
is none other com-
mandment greater
than these. 32 And
the scribe said unto
him, Well, Master,
thou hast said the
truth: for there is one
God; and there is none
other but he: 33 and
to love him with all
the heart, and with
all the understanding,
and with all the soul,
and with all the
strength, and to love
his neighbour as him-
self, is more than all
whole burnt offerings
and sacrifices. 34 And
when Jesus saw that
he answered discreet-
ly, he said unto him,
Thou art not far from
the kingdom of God.
And no man after that
durst ask him *any*
question.

Ἰσραήλ· κύριος ὁ.θεὸς.ἡμῶν κύριος εἷς ἐστίν. 30 καὶ
,Israel: [the] Lord our God ³Lord ²one ¹is. And

ἀγαπήσεις κύριον τὸν.θεόν.σου ἐξ ὅλης τῆς.καρδίας.σου
thou shalt love [the] Lord thy God with all thy heart

καὶ ἐξ ὅλης τῆς.ψυχῆς.σου καὶ ἐξ ὅλης τῆς.διανοίας.σου
and with all thy soul and with all thy mind

καὶ ἐξ ὅλης τῆς.ἰσχύος.σου. ⁿαὕτη πρώτη ἐντολή.‖
and with all thy strength. This [is the] first commandment.

31 °καὶ‖ δευτέρα ᴾὁμοία‖ ᑫαὕτη,‖ Ἀγαπήσεις τὸν πλη-
And [the] second like [it is] this: Thou shalt love ²neigh-

σίον σου ὡς σεαυτόν. Μείζων τούτων ἄλλη ἐντολὴ
bour, ¹thy as thyself. Greater than these another commandment

οὐκ.ἔστιν. 32 Καὶ εἶπεν αὐτῷ ὁ γραμματεύς, Καλῶς, διδάσ-
there is not. And ³said ⁴to ⁵him ¹the ²scribe, Right, teach-

καλε, ἐπ᾽ ἀληθείας ʳεἶπας‖ ὅτι εἷς ἐστιν ˢθεός,‖ καὶ
er, according to truth thou hast said that ³one ²is ¹God, and

οὐκ.ἔστιν ἄλλος πλὴν αὐτοῦ. 33 καὶ τὸ ἀγαπᾶν αὐτὸν ἐξ
there is not another besides him: and to love him with

ὅλης τῆς καρδίας καὶ ἐξ ὅλης τῆς συνέσεως ᵗκαὶ ἐξ ὅλης
all the heart and with all the understanding and with all

τῆς ψυχῆς‖ καὶ ἐξ ὅλης τῆς ἰσχύος, καὶ τὸ ἀγαπᾶν
the soul and with all the strength, and to love [one's]

τὸν πλησίον ὡς ἑαυτόν, ᵛπλεῖόν‖ ἐστιν πάντων τῶν ὁλοκαυ-
neighbour as oneself, ²more ¹is than all the burnt

τωμάτων καὶ ᵂτῶν‖ θυσιῶν. 34 Καὶ ὁ Ἰησοῦς ἰδὼν ˣαὐτὸν‖
offerings and the sacrifices. And Jesus seeing him

ὅτι νουνεχῶς ἀπεκρίθη, εἶπεν αὐτῷ, Οὐ μακρὰν εἶ
that intelligently he answered, said to him, Not far art thou

ἀπὸ τῆς βασιλείας τοῦ θεοῦ. Καὶ οὐδεὶς.οὐκέτι ἐτόλμα αὐτὸν
from the kingdom of God. And no one any more dared ³him

ἐπερωτῆσαι.
¹to ²question.

35 And Jesus an-
swered and said, while
he taught in the tem-
ple, How say the
scribes that Christ is
the Son of David?
36 For David himself
said by the Holy Ghost,
The LORD said to my
Lord, Sit thou on my
right hand, till I make
thine enemies thy
footstool. 37 David
therefore himself call-
eth him Lord; and
whence is he *then* his
son? And the com-
mon people heard him
gladly.

35 Καὶ ἀποκριθεὶς ὁ Ἰησοῦς ἔλεγεν, διδάσκων ἐν τῷ ἱερῷ,
And ²answering ¹Jesus said, teaching in the temple,

Πῶς λέγουσιν οἱ γραμματεῖς ὅτι ὁ χριστὸς υἱός ʸἐστιν Δαβὶδ‖;
How say the scribes that the Christ ²son ¹is of David?

36 αὐτὸς ᶻγὰρ‖ ᵃΔαβὶδ‖ ᵇεἶπεν‖ ἐν ᶜτῷ‖ πνεύματι ᶜτῷ‖ ἁγίῳ,
²himself ¹for ²David said by the Spirit the Holy,

ᵈΕἶπεν‖ ᵉὁ‖ κύριος τῷ.κυρίῳ.μου, ᶠΚάθου‖ ἐκ δεξιῶν.μου ἕως.ἂν
³said ¹the ²Lord to my Lord, Sit at my right hand until

θῶ τοὺς.ἐχθρούς.σου ᵍὑποπόδιον‖ τῶν.ποδῶν.σου. 37 Αὐτὸς
I place thine enemies [as] a footstool for thy feet. ²Himself

ʰοὖν‖ ᵃΔαβὶδ‖ λέγει αὐτὸν κύριον· καὶ πόθεν ⁱυἱός.αὐτοῦ
³therefore ¹David calls him Lord, and whence his son

ἐστιν; ‖ Καὶ ὁ πολὺς ὄχλος ἤκουεν αὐτοῦ ἡδέως.
is he? And the great crowd heard him gladly.

38 And he said unto
them in his doctrine,
Beware of the scribes;
which love to go in
long clothing, and *love*

38 Καὶ ᵏἔλεγεν αὐτοῖς ἐν τῇ.διδαχῇ.αὐτοῦ,‖ Βλέπετε ἀπὸ
And he said to them in his teaching, Take heed of

τῶν γραμματέων, τῶν θελόντων ἐν στολαῖς περιπατεῖν, καὶ
the scribes, who like in robes to walk about, and

ⁿ — αὕτη πρώτη ἐντολή TA.   ᵒ — καὶ [L]TTrA.   ᴾ — ὁμοία TA.   ᑫ αὐτῇ (*read* [is] like
it) LTr. ·   ʳ εἶπες T.   ˢ — θεός (*read* he is one) GLTTrAW.   ᵗ — καὶ ἐξ ὅλης τῆς ψυχῆς [L]T.
ᵛ περισσότερόν abundantly more TTr.   ᵂ — τῶν GLTTrAW.   ˣ [αὐτὸν] Tr.   ʸ Δαυείδ
ἐστιν TTrA; ἐστιν Δαυείδ L; ἐστιν Δαυὶδ GW.   ᶻ — γὰρ [L]T[Tr]A.   ᵃ Δϲυείδ LTTrA;
Δαυὶδ GW.   ᵇ λέγει says W.   ᶜ — τῷ GW.   ᵈ λέγει says GTr.   ᵉ — ὁ (*read* [the]) LTrA.
ᶠ κάθισον TrA.   ᵍ ὑποκάτω (*read* beneath thy feet) A.   ʰ — οὖν [L]TTrA.   ⁱ αὐτοῦ ἐστιν
υἱός TTrA.   ᵏ ἐν τῇ διδαχῇ αὐτοῦ ἔλεγεν TTrA.

ἀσπασμοὺς ἐν ταῖς ἀγοραῖς 39 καὶ πρωτοκαθεδρίας ἐν ταῖς
salutations in the market-places and first seats in the

συναγωγαῖς καὶ πρωτοκλισίας ἐν τοῖς δείπνοις· 40 οἱ ¹κατεσ-
synagogues and first places at the suppers; who de-

θίοντες" τὰς οἰκίας τῶν χηρῶν, καὶ προφάσει μακρὰ
vour the houses of widows,· and as a pretext ²at ³great ⁴length

προσευχόμενοι· οὗτοι ᵐλήψονται" περισσότερον κρίμα.
¹pray. These shall receive more abundant judgment.

41 Καὶ καθίσας ⁿὁ Ἰησοῦς" ᵒκατέναντι" τοῦ γαζοφυλα-
And ²having ³sat ⁴down ¹Jesus opposite the treasury,

κίου ἐθεώρει πῶς ὁ ὄχλος βάλλει χαλκὸν εἰς τὸ γαζοφυλά-
he saw how the crowd cast money into the treasury;

κιον· καὶ πολλοὶ πλούσιοι ἔβαλλον πολλά. 42 καὶ ἐλθοῦσα
and many rich were casting [in] much. And ⁴having ⁵come

μία χήρα πτωχὴ ἔβαλεν λεπτὰ δύο, ὅ ἐστιν κοδράντης.
¹one ³widow ²poor cast [in] ²lepta ¹two, which is a kodrantes.

43 καὶ προσκαλεσάμενος τοὺς.μαθητὰς.αὐτοῦ ᵖλέγει" αὐτοῖς,
And having called to [him] his disciples he says to them,

Ἀμὴν λέγω ὑμῖν, ὅτι ἡ.χήρα.αὕτη ἡ πτωχὴ πλεῖον πάντων
Verily I say to you, that this ²widow ¹poor more than all

�q βέβληκεν" τῶν ʳβαλόντων" εἰς τὸ γαζοφυλάκιον. 44 πάν-
has cast [in] of those casting into the treasury. ²All

τες γὰρ ἐκ τοῦ περισσεύοντος αὐτοῖς ἔβαλον· αὕτη δὲ
¹for out of that which was abounding to them cast [in], but she

ἐκ τῆς.ὑστερήσεως.αὐτῆς πάντα ὅσα εἶχεν ἔβαλεν,
out of her destitution ²all ⁴as ⁵much ⁶as ⁷she ⁸had ¹cast [²in],

ὅλον τὸν.βίον.αὐτῆς.
¹⁰whole ⁹her ¹¹livelihood.

13 Καὶ ἐκπορευομένου.αὐτοῦ ἐκ τοῦ ἱεροῦ λέγει αὐτῷ
And as he was going forth out of the temple ⁵says ⁴to ⁶him

εἷς ˢ τῶν.μαθητῶν.αὐτοῦ, Διδάσκαλε, ἴδε, ποταποὶ λίθοι καὶ
¹one ²of ³his ⁴disciples, Teacher, see, what stones and

ποταπαὶ οἰκοδομαί. 2 Καὶ ᵗὁ Ἰησοῦς ἀποκριθεὶς" εἶπεν αὐτῷ,
what buildings! And Jesus answering said to him,

Βλέπεις ταύτας τὰς μεγάλας οἰκοδομάς; οὐ.μὴ ἀφεθῇᵘ
Seest thou these great buildings? not at all shall be left

λίθος ἐπὶ ʳλίθῳ" ὃς οὐ.μὴ.καταλυθῇ. 3 Καὶ καθημένου
stone upon stone which shall not be thrown down. And as ²was ³sitting

αὐτοῦ εἰς τὸ ὄρος τῶν Ἐλαιῶν κατέναντι τοῦ ἱεροῦ, ʷἐπηρώ-
¹he upon the mount of Olives opposite the temple, ²ask-

των" αὐτὸν κατ'.ἰδίαν ˣΠέτρος καὶ Ἰάκωβος καὶ Ἰωάννης καὶ
ed ⁹him ¹⁰apart ¹Peter ²and ³James ⁴and ⁵John ⁶and

Ἀνδρέας, 4 ʸΕἰπὲ" ἡμῖν πότε ταῦτα ἔσται; καὶ τί τὸ
⁷Andrew, Tell us when ²these ³things ¹shall be? and what the

σημεῖον ὅταν μέλλῃ ᶻπάντα ταῦτα συντελεῖσθαι";
sign when ²should ⁵be ⁶about ¹all ²these ³things to be accomplished?

5 Ὁ.δὲ.Ἰησοῦς ᵃἀποκριθεὶς" ᵇαὐτοῖς ἤρξατο λέγειν," Βλέπετε
And Jesus answering to them began to say, Take heed

μή τις ὑμᾶς πλανήσῃ. 6 πολλοὶ.ᶜγὰρ" ἐλεύσονται.ἐπὶ τῷ
lest anyone ²you ¹mislead. For many will come in

ὀνόματί.μου, λέγοντες, Ὅτι ἐγώ εἰμι· καὶ πολλοὺς πλανή-
my name, saying, I am [he], and many they will

---

salutations in the market-places, 39 and the chief seats in the synagogues, and the uppermost rooms at feasts: 40 which devour widows' houses, and for a pretence make long prayers: these shall receive greater damnation.

41 And Jesus sat over against the treasury, and beheld how the people cast money into the treasury: and many that were rich cast in much. 42 And there came a certain poor widow, and she threw in two mites, which make a farthing. 43 And he called unto him his disciples, and saith unto them, Verily I say unto you, That this poor widow hath cast more in, than all they which have cast into the treasury: 44 for all they did cast in of their abundance; but she of her want did cast in all that she had, even all her living.

XIII. And as he went out of the temple, one of his disciples saith unto him, Master, see what manner of stones and what buildings are here! 2 And Jesus answering said unto him, Seest thou these great buildings? there shall not be left one stone upon another, that shall not be thrown down. 3 And as he sat upon the mount of Olives over against the temple, Peter and James and John and Andrew asked him privately, 4 Tell us, when shall these things be? and what shall be the sign when all these things shall be fulfilled? 5 And Jesus answering them began to say, Take heed lest any man deceive you: 6 for many shall come in my name, saying, I am Christ; and shall deceive many. 7 And when ye shall hear of wars

---

¹ κατέσθοντες TrA.   ᵐ λήμψονται LTTrA.   ⁿ — ὁ Ἰησοῦς [L]TTrA.   ᵒ ἀπέναντι Tr.
ᵖ εἶπεν he said GLTTr.   �q ἔβαλεν did cast [in] LTr.   ʳ βαλλόντων LTTrAW.   ˢ + ἐκ of Tr[A].
ᵗ ἀποκριθεὶς ὁ Ἰησοῦς L; — ἀποκριθεὶς TTrA.   ᵘ + ὧδε here LTr.   ᵛ λίθον TTr.   ʷ ἐπηρώτα
TTrA.   ˣ + ὁ T.   ʸ εἶπον LTTrA.   ᶻ ταῦτα πάντα συντελεῖσθαι L ; ταῦτα συντελεῖσθαι πάντα
TTrA.   ᵃ — ἀποκριθεὶς TTrA.   ᵇ ἤρξατο λέγειν αὐτοῖς LTTrA.   ᶜ — γὰρ for TA.

and rumours of wars, be ye not troubled : for such things must needs be ; but the end shall not be yet. 8 For nation shall rise against nation, and kingdom against kingdom : and there shall be earthquakes in divers places, and there shall be famines and troubles : these are the beginnings of sorrows. 9 But take heed to yourselves : for they shall deliver you up to councils ; and in the synagogues ye shall be beaten : and ye shall be brought before rulers and kings for my sake, for a testimony against them. 10 And the gospel must first be published among all nations. 11 But when they shall lead you, and deliver you up, take no thought beforehand what ye shall speak, neither do ye premeditate : but whatsoever shall be given you in that hour, that speak ye : for it is not ye that speak, but the Holy Ghost. 12 Now the brother shall betray the brother to death, and the father the son ; and children shall rise up against their parents, and shall cause them to be put to death. 13 And ye shall be hated of all men for my name's sake : but he that shall endure unto the end, the same shall be saved. 14 But when ye shall see the abomination of desolation, spoken of by Daniel the prophet, standing where it ought not, (let him that readeth understand,) then let them that be in Judæa flee to the mountains : 15 and let him that is on the housetop not go down into the house, neither enter therein, to take any thing out of his house : 16 and let him that is in the field not turn back again for to take up his garment. 17 But woe to them that are

σουσιν. 7 ὅταν.δὲ ᵈἀκούσητε‖ πολέμους καὶ ἀκοὰς πολέμων,
mislead.   But when ye shall hear of   wars   and rumours   of wars,

μὴ.θροεῖσθε·   δεῖ   ᵉγὰρ‖ γενέσθαι· ἀλλ᾽ οὔπω   τὸ
be not disturbed ; ²it ³must ⁴needs ¹for come to pass, but ⁴not ⁵yet [³is] ¹the

τέλος. 8 Ἐγερθήσεται.γὰρ ἔθνος ᶠἐπὶ‖ ἔθνος καὶ βασιλεία
²end.   For ²shall ³rise ⁴up ¹nation against nation and kingdom

ἐπὶ βασιλείαν· ᵍκαὶ‖ ἔσονται σεισμοὶ κατὰ.τόπους, ʰκαὶ‖
against kingdom ;   and there shall be earthquakes in different places, and

ἔσονται λιμοὶ ⁱκαὶ ταραχαί.‖ ᵏἀρχαὶ‖ ὠδίνων ταῦτα.
there shall be famines and troubles.   Beginnings of throes [are] these.

9 Βλέπετε.δὲ ὑμεῖς ἑαυτούς. παραδώσουσιν.ˡγὰρ‖ ὑμᾶς εἰς
But take heed ye to yourselves ; for they will deliver up   you to

συνέδρια καὶ εἰς συναγωγὰς· δαρήσεσθε, καὶ ἐπὶ ἡγεμόνων
sanhedrims and to synagogues : ye will be beaten, and before governors

καὶ βασιλέων σταθήσεσθε ἕνεκεν.ἐμοῦ, εἰς μαρτύριον αὐτοῖς·
and kings ye will be brought for my sake, for a testimony to them ;

10 καὶ εἰς πάντα τὰ ἔθνη ᵐδεῖ πρῶτον‖ κηρυχθῆναι τὸ
and to all the nations must first be proclaimed the

εὐαγγέλιον. 11 ⁿὅταν.δὲ‖ °ἀγάγωσιν‖ ὑμᾶς παραδιδόντες,
glad tidings.   But whenever they may lead away you delivering [you] up,

μὴ.προμεριμνᾶτε τί λαλήσητε, ᵖμηδὲ μελετᾶτε·‖
be not careful beforehand what ye should say, nor meditate [your reply] ;

ἀλλ᾽ ὃ.�q ἐὰν‖ δοθῇ ὑμῖν ἐν ἐκείνῃ.τῇ.ὥρᾳ, τοῦτο λαλεῖτε·
but whatever may be given to you in that hour, that speak ;

οὐ.γάρ ἐστε ὑμεῖς οἱ λαλοῦντες, ἀλλὰ τὸ πνεῦμα τὸ ἅγιον.
for ³not ²are ¹ye they who speak, but the Spirit the Holy.

12 ʳπαραδώσει.δὲ‖ ἀδελφὸς ἀδελφὸν εἰς θάνατον, καὶ πατὴρ
And ²will ³deliver ⁴up ¹brother brother to death, and father

τέκνον· καὶ ἐπαναστήσονται τέκνα ἐπὶ γονεῖς, καὶ θανατώ-
child ;   and ²will ³rise ⁴up ¹children against parents, and will put to

σουσιν αὐτούς· 13 καὶ ἔσεσθε μισούμενοι ὑπὸ πάντων διὰ
death them.   And ye will be hated by all on account of

τὸ.ὄνομά.μου· ὁ.δὲ ὑπομείνας εἰς τέλος, οὗτος σωθήσε-
my name ;   but he who endures to [the] end, he shall be

ται. 14 ˢὍταν.δὲ ἴδητε τὸ βδέλυγμα τῆς ἐρημώσεως ˢτὸ
saved.   But when ye see the abomination of the desolation which

ῥηθὲν ὑπὸ Δανιὴλ τοῦ προφήτου,‖ ᵗἑστὸς‖ ὅπου οὐ.δεῖ·
was spoken of by Daniel the prophet, standing where it should not

ὁ ἀναγινώσκων νοείτω· τότε οἱ ἐν τῇ Ἰουδαίᾳ φευ-
(he who reads let him understand), then those in Judæa let

γέτωσαν εἰς.τὰ ὄρη· 15 ὁ ᵛδὲ‖ ἐπὶ τοῦ δώματος μὴ κατα-
them flee to the mountains, ²he ¹and upon the housetop ²not ⁴let ³him

βάτω ʷεἰς τὴν οἰκίαν,‖ μηδὲ ˣεἰσελθέτω‖ ʸἆραί τι‖ ἐκ
come down into the house, nor go in to take any thing out of

τῆς.οἰκίας.αὐτοῦ· 16 καὶ ὁ εἰς τὸν ἀγρὸν ᶻὢν‖ μὴ.ἐπιστρεψάτω
his house ;   and he that in the field is let him not return

εἰς τὰ ὀπίσω ἆραι τὸ.ἱμάτιον.αὐτοῦ. 17 οὐαὶ.δὲ ταῖς
to the things behind to take his garment.   But woe to those that

ἐν.γαστρὶ.ἐχούσαις καὶ ταῖς θηλαζούσαις ἐν ἐκείναις ταῖς
are with child   and to those that give suck   in   those

ᵈ ἀκούετε ye hear of Tr   ᵉ — γὰρ T[Tr]A.   ᶠ ἐπ᾽ TA.   ᵍ — καὶ TTrA.   ʰ — καὶ T[Tr]A.
ⁱ — καὶ ταραχαί LTTr[A].   ᵏ ἀρχὴ a beginning LTTr.   ˡ — γὰρ for T[Tr]A.   ᵐ πρῶτον δεῖ
LTTrA.   ⁿ καὶ ὅταν and when LTTrA.   ° ἀγωσιν GLTTrAW.   ᵖ — μηδὲ μελετᾶτε [L]TTr[A].
q ἄν L.   ʳ καὶ παραδώσει LTTrA.   ˢ — τὸ ῥηθὲν ὑπὸ Δανιὴλ τοῦ προφήτου G[L]TTrA.
ᵗ ἑστὼς EG ; ἑστηκὸς L ; ἑστηκότα TTrA.   ᵛ — δὲ L[Tr].   ʷ — εἰς τὴν οἰκίαν [L]T.
ˣ εἰσελθάτω LTTr.   ʸ τι ἆραι TrA.   ᶻ — ὢν (read [is]) LTTr.

ἡμέραις. 18 προσεύχεσθε.δὲ ἵνα μὴ.γένηται ᵃἡ.φυγὴ.ὑμῶν‖
days!   And pray   that ᵇmay ⁴not ⁵be   ¹your ²flight

χειμῶνος. 19 ἔσονται.γὰρ αἱ.ἡμέραι.ἐκεῖναι θλίψις, οἷα
in winter ;   for ⁴shall ⁵be [¹in]   ²those ³days   tribulation, such as

οὐ.γέγονεν τοιαύτη ἀπ' ἀρχῆς κτίσεως ᵇἧς‖ ἔκτισεν ὁ
has not been the like from [the] beginning of creation which ²created

θεὸς ἕως τοῦ νῦν, καὶ οὐ.μὴ γένηται. 20 καὶ εἰ.μὴ ᶜκύριος
¹God until now, and not at all shall be ; and unless [the] Lord

ἐκολόβωσεν‖ τὰς ἡμέρας, οὐκ.ἂν.ἐσώθη πᾶσα σάρξ·
had shortened the days, there would not have been saved any flesh ;

ἀλλὰ διὰ τοὺς.ἐκλεκτοὺς οὓς ἐξελέξατο. ἐκολόβωσεν τὰς
but on account of the elect whom he chose, he has shortened the

ἡμέρας. 21 Καὶ τότε ἐάν τις ὑμῖν εἴπῃ, ᵈἸδού,‖ ὧδε ὁ
days. And then if anyone to you say, Behold, here [is] the

χριστός, ᵉἤ‖ ᶠἰδού,‖ ἐκεῖ, ᵍμὴ.πιστεύσητε.‖ 22 ἐγερθήσονται
Christ, or Behold, there, ye shall not believe [it]   ²There ³will ⁴arise

ᵇγὰρ‖ ᶦψευδόχριστοι καὶ‖ ψευδοπροφῆται, καὶ ᶦδώσουσιν‖ σημεῖα
¹for false Christs and false prophets, and will give signs

καὶ τέρατα, πρὸς τὸ ἀποπλανᾷν εἰ δυνατὸν ᵏκαὶ‖ τοὺς ἐκλεκ-
and wonders, to deceive if possible even the elect.

τούς. 23 ὑμεῖς.δὲ βλέπετε· ᶦἰδού,‖ προείρηκα ὑμῖν πάντα.
But ²ye ¹take heed : lo, I have foretold to you all things.

24 ᵐἈλλ'‖ ἐν ἐκείναις ταῖς ἡμέραις, μετ' τὴν.θλίψιν.ἐκείνην,
But in those days, after that tribulation,

ὁ ἥλιος σκοτισθήσεται, καὶ ἡ σελήνη οὐ.δώσει τὸ φέγγος
the sun shall be darkened, and the moon shall not give ²light

αὐτῆς, 25 καὶ οἱ ἀστέρες ⁿτοῦ οὐρανοῦ ἔσονται ἐκπίπτοντες,‖
¹her ; and the stars of the heaven shall be falling out,

καὶ αἱ δυνάμεις αἱ ἐν τοῖς οὐρανοῖς σαλευθήσονται.
and the powers which [are] in the heavens shall be shaken ;

26 καὶ τότε ὄψονται τὸν υἱὸν τοῦ ἀνθρώπου ἐρχόμενον ἐν
and then shall they see the Son of man coming in

νεφέλαις μετὰ δυνάμεως ᵒπολλῆς καὶ δόξης.‖ 27 καὶ τότε
clouds with ²power ¹great and glory ; and then

ἀποστελεῖ τοὺς.ἀγγέλους.ᵖαὐτοῦ,‖ καὶ ἐπισυνάξει τοὺς
he will send his angels, and will gather together

ἐκλεκτοὺς.�q̄αὐτοῦ‖ ἐκ τῶν τεσσάρων ἀνέμων, ἀπ' ἄκρου
his elect from the four winds, from [the] extremity

γῆς ἕως ἄκρου οὐρανοῦ. 28 Ἀπὸ.δὲ τῆς συκῆς μάθετε
of earth to [the] extremity of heaven. But from the fig-tree learn

τὴν παραβολήν· ὅταν ʳαὐτῆς ἤδη ὁ κλάδος‖ ἀπαλὸς γένη-
the parable : when of it already the branch tender is be-

ται, καὶ ˢἐκφυῇ‖ τὰ φύλλα, ᵗγινώσκετε‖ ὅτι ἐγγὺς τὸ θέρος
come, and it puts forth the leaves, ye know that near the summer

ἐστίν· 29 οὕτως καὶ ὑμεῖς, ὅταν ᵘταῦτα ἴδητε‖ γινόμενα,
is. So also ye, when these things ye see coming to pass,

γινώσκετε ὅτι ἐγγύς ἐστιν ἐπὶ θύραις. 30 Ἀμὴν λέγω ὑμῖν,
know that near it is, at [the] doors. Verily I say to you,

ὅτι οὐ.μὴ παρέλθῃ ἡ.γενεὰ.αὕτη, μέχρις οὗ ᵛπάντα
that in no wise will have passed away this generation, until all

with child, and to
them that give suck in
those days ! 18 And
pray ye that your
flight be not in the
winter. 19 For in those
days shall be affliction,
such as was not from
the beginning of the
creation which God
created unto this
time, neither, shall be.
20 And except that the
Lord had shortened
those days, no flesh
should be saved : but
for the elect's sake,
whom he hath chosen,
he hath shortened the
days. 21 And then if
any man shall say to
you, Lo, here is Christ ;
or, lo, he is there ; be-
lieve him not : 22 for
false Christs and false
prophets shall rise,
and shall shew signs
and wonders, to se-
duce, if it were pos-
sible, even the elect.
23 But take ye heed :
behold, I have foretold
you all things. 24 But
in those days, after
that tribulation, the
sun shall be darkened,
and the moon shall
not give her light,
and the stars of
heaven shall fall, and
the powers that are
in heaven shall be
shaken. 26 And then
shall they see the Son
of man coming in
the clouds with great
power and glory.
27 And then shall he
send his angels, and
shall gather together
his elect from the four
winds, from the utter-
most part of the earth
to the uttermost part
of heaven. 28 Now
learn a parable of the
fig tree ; When her
branch is yet tender,
and putteth forth
leaves, ye know that
summer is near : 29 so
ye in like manner,
when ye shall see these
things come to pass,
know that it is nigh,
even at the doors.
30 Verily I say unto
you, that this gene-
ration shall not pass,
till all these things be

ᵃ — ἡ φυγὴ ὑμῶν (read it may not be) LTTrA.   ᵇ ἧν LTTr.   ᶜ ἐκολόβωσεν κύριος T.
ᵈ ἴδε TTrA.   ᵉ — ἢ TA.   ᶠ ἴδε LTTrA.   ᵍ μὴ πιστεύετε believe [it] not GLTTrAW.
ʰ δὲ and T.   ᶦ — ψευδόχριστοι καὶ A.   ʲ ποιήσουσιν will work TA.   ᵏ — καὶ T[Tr]A.
ˡ — ἰδού [L]TTrA.   ᵐ Ἀλλὰ LTTrA.   ⁿ ἔσονται ἐκ τοῦ οὐρανοῦ πίπτοντες LTTrA.   ᵒ καὶ
δόξης πολλῆς L.   ᵖ — αὐτοῦ (read the angels) [L]TTrA.   �q̄ — αὐτοῦ (read the elect) TTA.
ʳ ἤδη ὁ κλάδος αὐτῆς LTr.   ˢ ἐκφύῃ EGT.   ᵗ γινώσκεται it is known A.   ᵘ ἴδητε
ταῦτα LTTr.   ᵛ ταῦτα πάντα TTrA.

done. 31 Heaven and earth shall pass away: but my words shall not pass away. 32 But of that day and *that* hour knoweth no man, no, not the angels which are in heaven, neither the Son, but the Father. 33 Take ye heed, watch and pray: for ye know not when the time is. 34 *For the Son of man is* as a man taking a far journey, who left his house, and gave authority to his servants, and to every man his work, and commanded the porter to watch. 35 Watch ye therefore: for ye know not when the master of the house cometh, at even, or at midnight, or at the cockcrowing, or in the morning: 36 lest coming suddenly he find you sleeping. 37 And what I say unto you I say unto all, Watch.

ταῦτα‖ γένηται. 31 ὁ οὐρανὸς καὶ ἡ γῆ ᵂπαρε-
these things shall have taken place. The heaven and the earth shall

λεύσονται·‖ οἱ.δὲ.λόγοι.μου οὐ.ᵡμὴ‖ ʸπαρέλθωσιν.‖ 32 Περὶ.δὲ
pass away, but my words in no wise shall pass away. But concerning

τῆς.ἡμέρας.ἐκείνης ᶻκαὶ‖ τῆς ὥρας, οὐδεὶς οἶδεν, οὐδὲ ᵃοἱ ἄγ-
that day and the hour, no one knows, not even the an-

γελοι‖ ᵇοἱ‖ ἐν οὐρανῷ, οὐδὲ ὁ υἱός, εἰ.μὴ ὁ πατήρ. 33 Βλέπετε,
gels those in heaven, nor the Son, but the Father. Take heed,

ἀγρυπνεῖτε ᶜκαὶ προσεύχεσθε‖ οὐκ.οἴδατε.γὰρ πότε ὁ καιρός
watch and pray; for ye know not when the time

ἐστιν 34 ὡς ἄνθρωπος ἀπόδημος ἀφεὶς τὴν οἰκίαν
is; as a man going out of the country, leaving ²house

αὐτοῦ, καὶ δοὺς τοῖς.δούλοις.αὐτοῦ τὴν ἐξουσίαν, ᵈκαὶ‖ ἑκάστῳ
¹his, and giving to his bondmen the authority, and to each one

τὸ.ἔργον.αὐτοῦ, καὶ τῷ θυρωρῷ ἐνετείλατο ἵνα γρηγορῇ.
his work, and ²the ³door-keeper ¹commanded that he should watch.

35 γρηγορεῖτε οὖν· οὐκ.οἴδατε.γὰρ πότε ὁ.κύριος τῆς οἰκίας
Watch therefore, for ye know not when the master of the house

ἔρχεται, ᵉὀψέ, ἢ ᶠμεσονυκτίου,‖ ἢ ἀλεκτοροφωνίας, ἢ πρωΐ·
comes: at evening, or at midnight, or at cock-crowing, or morning;

36 μὴ ἐλθὼν ἐξαίφνης εὕρῃ ὑμᾶς καθεύδοντας. 37 ᵍἃ‖.δὲ
lest coming suddenly he should find you sleeping. And what

ὑμῖν λέγω, πᾶσιν λέγω, Γρηγορεῖτε.
to you I say, to all I say, Watch.

XIV. After two days was *the feast* of the passover, and of unleavened bread: and the chief priests and the scribes sought how they might take him by craft, and put *him* to death. 2 But they said, Not on the feast *day*, lest there be an uproar of the people.

14 Ἦν.δὲ τὸ πάσχα καὶ τὰ ἄζυμα μετὰ δύο
Now it was the passover and the [feast of] unleavened bread after two

ἡμέρας· καὶ ἐζήτουν οἱ ἀρχιερεῖς καὶ οἱ γραμματεῖς πῶς
days. And ⁷were ⁸seeking ¹the ²chief ³priests ⁴and ⁵the ⁶scribes how

αὐτὸν ἐν δόλῳ κρατήσαντες ἀποκτείνωσιν· 2 ἔλεγον ʰδέ,‖
him by guile getting hold of they might kill [him]. ²They ³said ¹but,

Μὴ ἐν τῇ ἑορτῇ, μήποτε ⁱθόρυβος ἔσται‖ τοῦ λαοῦ.
Not in the feast, lest a tumult there shall be of the people.

3 And being in Bethany in the house of Simon the leper, as he sat at meat, there came a woman having an alabaster box of ointment of spikenard very precious; and she brake the box, and poured *it* on his head. 4 And there were some that had indignation within themselves, and said, Why was this waste of the ointment made? 5 for it might have been sold for more than three hundred pence, and have been given to the poor. And they murmured against her. 6 And Jesus said, Let her alone; why trouble ye her? she hath

3 Καὶ ὄντος αὐτοῦ ἐν Βηθανίᾳ, ἐν τῇ οἰκίᾳ Σίμωνος τοῦ
And ²being ¹he in Bethany, in the house of Simon the

λεπροῦ, κατακειμένου.αὐτοῦ, ἦλθεν γυνὴ ἔχουσα ἀλά-
leper, as he reclined [at table], ³came ¹a ²woman having an ala-

βαστρον μύρου νάρδου πιστικῆς πολυτελοῦς· ᵏκαὶ‖ συν-
baster flask of ointment of ²nard ¹pure of great price; and having

τρίψασα ˡτὸ‖ ἀλάβαστρον, κατέχεεν αὐτοῦ ᵐκατὰ‖ τῆς
broken the alabaster flask, she poured [it] ²his ¹on the

κεφαλῆς. 4 ἦσαν.δέ τινες ἀγανακτοῦντες πρὸς.ἑαυτούς, ⁿκαὶ
head. And ²were ¹some indignant within themselves, and

λέγοντες,‖ Εἰς τί ἡ.ἀπώλεια.αὕτη τοῦ μύρου γέγονεν;
saying, For what ²this ³waste ⁴of ⁵the ⁶ointment ¹has been made?

5 ἠδύνατο.γὰρ τοῦτο ᵒ πραθῆναι ἐπάνω ᴾτριακοσίων
for it was possible [for] this to have been sold for above three hundred

δηναρίων,‖ καὶ δοθῆναι τοῖς πτωχοῖς· καὶ ᑫἐνεβριμῶντο‖
denarii, and to have been given to the poor. And they murmured

αὐτῇ. 6 Ὁ.δὲ.Ἰησοῦς εἶπεν, Ἄφετε αὐτήν· τί αὐτῇ κόπους
at her. But Jesus said, Let ²alone ¹her; why to her trouble,

ᵂ παρελεύσεται GW. ˣ — μὴ TrA. ʸ παρελεύσονται TTrA. ᶻ ἢ or GLTTrAW. ᵃ ἄγγελος an angel A. ᵇ — οἱ TTrA. ᶜ — καὶ προσεύχεσθε LT[Tr]A. ᵈ — καὶ LTTrA. ᵉ + ἢ either TTrA. ᶠ μεσονύκτιον TTrA. ᵍ ὁ LTTrA. ʰ γάρ for LTTrA. ⁱ ἔσται θόρυβος TTrA. ᵏ — καὶ TA. ˡ τὸν LTW; τὴν TⁱA. ᵐ — κατὰ (read αὐτοῦ on his) LTTrA. ⁿ — καὶ λέγοντες T[Tr]A. ᵒ + τὸ μύρον ointment GLTTrAW. ᴾ δηναρίων τριακοσίων LTTrAW. ᑫ ἐνεβριμοῦντο T.

παρέχετε; καλὸν ἔργον ʳεἰργάσατο‖ ˢεἰς ἐμέ.‖ 7 πάντοτε.γὰρ
do ye cause? a good work she wrought towards me. For always

τοὺς πτωχοὺς ἔχετε μεθ' ἑαυτῶν, καὶ ὅταν θέλητε δύνασθε
the poor ye have with you, and whenever ye desire ye are able

ᵗαὐτοὺς‖ εὖ.ποιῆσαι· ἐμὲ.δὲ οὐ πάντοτε ἔχετε. 8 ὃ ᵛεἶχεν‖
³them ¹to ²do good; but me not always ye have. What ²could

ʷαὕτη,‖ ἐποίησεν· προέλαβεν μυρίσαι ˣμου.τὸ.σῶμα‖ εἰς
¹she, she did. She came beforehand to anoint my body for

τὸν ἐνταφιασμόν. 9 ἀμὴνʸ λέγω ὑμῖν, ὅπου.ᶻἂν‖ κηρυχθῇ
the burial. Verily I say to you, Wheresoever shall be proclaimed

τὸ.εὐαγγέλιον.ᵃτοῦτο‖ εἰς ὅλον τὸν κόσμον, καὶ ὃ ἐποίησεν
this glad tidings in ²whole ¹the world, also what ³has ⁴done

αὕτη λαληθήσεται εἰς μνημόσυνον αὐτῆς.
¹this [²woman] shall be spoken of for a memorial of her.

10 Καὶ ᵇὁ‖ᵇἸούδας ᵇὁ‖ ᶜἸσκαριώτης,‖ ᵈ εἷς τῶν δώδεκα,
And Judas the Iscariote, one of the twelve,

ἀπῆλθεν πρὸς τοὺς ἀρχιερεῖς, ἵνα ᵉπαραδῷ αὐτὸν‖
went away to the chief priests, that he might deliver up him

αὐτοῖς. 11 Οἱ.δὲ ἀκούσαντες ἐχάρησαν, καὶ ἐπηγγείλαντο
to them. And they having heard rejoiced, and promised

αὐτῷ ἀργύριον δοῦναι· καὶ ἐζήτει πῶς ᶠεὐκαίρως αὐτὸν
³him ²money ¹to ²give. And he sought how ³conveniently ⁵him

παραδῷ.‖
¹he ²might ⁴deliver ⁶up.

12 Καὶ τῇ πρώτῃ ἡμέρᾳ τῶν ἀζύμων, ὅτε τὸ πάσχα
And on the first day of unleavened [bread], when the passover

ἔθυον, λέγουσιν αὐτῷ οἱ.μαθηταὶ.αὐτου, ᵍΠοῦ θέλεις
they killed, ³say ⁴to ⁵him ¹his ²disciples, Where desirest thou [that]

ἀπελθόντες ἑτοιμάσωμεν ἵνα φάγῃς τὸ πάσχα; 13 Καὶ
going we should prepare that thou mayest eat the passover? And

ἀποστέλλει δύο τῶν.μαθητῶν.αὐτοῦ, καὶ λέγει αὐτοῖς, Ὑπάγετε
he sends·forth two of his disciples, and says to them, Go

εἰς τὴν πόλιν· καὶ ἀπαντήσει ὑμῖν ἄνθρωπος κεράμιον ὕδατος
into the city, and ³will ⁴meet ⁵you ¹a ²man a pitcher of water

βαστάζων· ἀκολουθήσατε αὐτῷ, 14 καὶ ὅπου.ᵍἐὰν‖ εἰσέλθῃ,
carrying; follow him; and wherever he may enter,

εἴπατε τῷ οἰκοδεσπότῃ, Ὅτι ὁ διδάσκαλος λέγει, Ποῦ
say to the master of the house, The teacher says, Where

ἐστιν τὸ κατάλυμα ʰ ὅπου τὸ πάσχα μετὰ τῶν.μαθητῶν.μου
is the guest-chamber · where the passover with ·my disciples

φάγω; 15 καὶ αὐτὸς ὑμῖν δείξει ⁱἀνώγεον‖ μέγα ἐστρω-
I may eat? and he ³you ¹will ²shew an upper room large, fur-

μένον ᵏἕτοιμον.‖ ˡἐκεῖ‖ ἑτοιμάσατε ἡμῖν. 16 Καὶ ἐξῆλθον οἱ
nished ready. There prepare for us. And went away

μαθηταὶ.ᵐαὐτοῦ,‖ καὶ ἦλθον εἰς τὴν πόλιν, καὶ εὗρον καθὼς
his disciples, and came into the city, and found as

εἶπεν αὐτοῖς, καὶ ἡτοίμασαν τὸ πάσχα. 17 Καὶ ὀψίας
he had said to them, and they prepared the passover. And evening

γενομένης ἔρχεται μετὰ τῶν δώδεκα· 18 καὶ ἀνακειμένων
being come he comes with the twelve. And as ²were ³reclining

---

wrought a good work on me. 7 For ye have the poor with you always, and whensoever ye will ye may do them good : ·but me ye have not always. 8 She hath done what she could : she is come aforehand to anoint my body to the burying. 9 Verily I say unto you, Wheresoever this gospel shall be preached throughout the whole world, this also that she hath done shall be spoken of for a memorial of her.

10 And Judas Iscariot, one of the twelve, went unto the chief priests, to betray him unto them. 11 And when they heard it, they were glad, and promised to give him money. And he sought how he might conveniently betray him.

12 And the first day of unleavened bread, when they killed the passover, his disciples said unto him, Where wilt thou that we go and prepare that thou mayest eat the passover? 13 And he sendeth forth two of his disciples, and saith unto them, Go ye into the city, and there shall meet you a man bearing a pitcher of water : follow him. 14 And wheresoever he shall go in, say ye to the goodman of the house, The Master saith, Where is the guestchamber, where I shall eat the passover with my disciples? 15 And he will shew you a large upper room furnished and prepared : there make ready for us. 16 And his disciples went forth, and came into the city, and found as he had said unto them: and they made ready the passover. 17 And in the evening he cometh with the twelve. 18 And as they sat and did eat, Jesus said,

---

ʳ ἠργάσατο τ.　　　ˢ ἐν ἐμοί to me GLTTrAW.　　　ᵗ αὐτοῖς LTrA ; — αὐτοὺς τ.　　　ᵛ ἔσχεν
GLTTrAW.　　ʷ — αὕτη (read εἶχεν she could) [L]T[Tr]A.　　ˣ τὸ σῶμά μου LTr.　　ʸ + δὲ
and (verily) [L]TTrA.　　ᶻ ἐὰν TA.　　ᵃ — τοῦτο (read the glad tidings) [L]TTrA.　　ᵇ — ὁ
LTTrAW.　　ᶜ Ἰσκαριώθ TA.　　ᵈ + ὁ the TTrA.　　ᵉ παραδοῖ αὐτὸν L ; αὐτὸν παραδοῖ TTrA.
ᶠ αὐτὸν εὐκαίρως παραδοῖ LTTrA ; αὐτὸν εὐκ. παραδῷ W.　　ᵍ ἂν LTrA.　　ʰ + μου (read my
guest-chamber) [L]TTrA.　　ⁱ ἀνάγαιον GLTTrAW.　　ᵏ [ἕτοιμον] L.　　ˡ καὶ ἐκεῖ and
there TrA ; κἀκεῖ τ.　　ᵐ — αὐτοῦ (read the disciples) T[Tr].

Verily I say unto you, One of you which eateth with me shall betray me. 19 And they began to be sorrowful, and to say unto him one by one, *Is it* I? and another *said, Is* it I? 20 And he answered and said unto them, *It is* one of the twelve, that dippeth with me in the dish. 21 The Son of man indeed goeth, as it is written of him: but woe to that man by whom the Son of man is betrayed! good were it for that man if he had never been born.

αὐτῶν καὶ ἐσθιόντων ⁿεἶπεν ὁ Ἰησοῦς,‖ Ἀμὴν λέγω
[⁴at ⁵table] ¹they and, were eating ²said ¹Jesus, Verily I say
ὑμῖν, ὅτι εἷς ἐξ ὑμῶν παραδώσει με, ὁ ἐσθίων μετ' ἐμοῦ.
to you, that one of you will deliver up me, who is eating with me.
19 °Οἱ δὲ‖ ἤρξαντο λυπεῖσθαι, καὶ λέγειν αὐτῷ, εἷς ᴾκαθ᾽‖ εἷς,
And they began to be grieved, and to say to him, one by one,
Μή τι ἐγώ; ᑫΚαὶ ἄλλος, Μή τι ἐγώ;‖ 20 Ὁ δὲ ʳἀπο-
[Is it] I? And another, [Is it] I? But he an-
κριθεὶς‖ εἶπεν αὐτοῖς, Εἷς ˢἐκ‖ τῶν δώδεκα, ὁ ἐμβαπτό-
swering said to them, [It is] one of the twelve, who is dip-
μενος μετ' ἐμοῦ ᵗεἰς τὸ τρυβλίον. 21 ᵛὁ μὲν υἱὸς τοῦ ἀνθρώπου
ping with me in the dish. The ⁵indeed ¹Son ²of ¹man
ὑπάγει, καθὼς γέγραπται περὶ αὐτοῦ· οὐαὶ δὲ τῷ
⁴goes, as it has been written concerning him; but woe
ἀνθρώπῳ ἐκείνῳ δι᾽ οὗ ὁ υἱὸς τοῦ ἀνθρώπου παραδίδοται·
to that man by whom the Son of man, is delivered up;
καλὸν ʷἦν‖ αὐτῷ εἰ οὐκ ἐγεννήθη ὁ ἄνθρωπος ἐκεῖνος.
good were it for him if ³had ⁴not ⁵been ⁶born ¹that ²man.

22 And as they did eat, Jesus took bread, and blessed, and brake *it*, and gave to them, and said, Take, eat: this is my body. 23 And he took the cup, and when he had given thanks, he gave *it* to them: and they all drank of it. 24 And he said unto them, This is my blood of the new testament, which is shed for many. 25 Verily I say unto you, I will drink no more of the fruit of the vine, until that day that I drink it new in the kingdom of God.

22 Καὶ ἐσθιόντων αὐτῶν, λαβὼν ˣὁ Ἰησοῦς‖ ἄρτον,
And as they were eating, ²having ²taken ¹Jesus a loaf,
εὐλογήσας ἔκλασεν, καὶ ἔδωκεν αὐτοῖς, καὶ εἶπεν, Λάβετε,
having blessed he brake, and gave to them, and said, Take,
ʸφάγετε·‖ τοῦτό ἐστιν τὸ σῶμά μου. 23 Καὶ λαβὼν ᶻτὸ‖
eat; this is my body. And having taken the
ποτήριον, εὐχαριστήσας ἔδωκεν αὐτοῖς· καὶ ἔπιον ἐξ αὐτοῦ
cup, having given thanks he gave to them, and they ²drank ³of ⁴it
πάντες· 24 καὶ εἶπεν αὐτοῖς, Τοῦτό ἐστιν τὸ αἷμά μου ᵃτὸ‖
¹all And he said to them, This is my blood that
τῆς ᵇκαινῆς‖ διαθήκης, τὸ ᶜπερὶ πολλῶν ἐκχυνόμενον.‖
of the new covenant, which for many is poured out.
25 ἀμὴν λέγω ὑμῖν, ὅτι οὐκέτι οὐ μὴ πίω ἐκ τοῦ
Verily I say to you, that not any more in any wise will I drink of the
ᵈγεννήματος‖ τῆς ἀμπέλου, ἕως τῆς ἡμέρας ἐκείνης ὅταν αὐτὸ
fruit of the vine, until that day when it
πίνω καινὸν ἐν τῇ βασιλείᾳ τοῦ θεοῦ.
I drink new in the kingdom of God.

26 And when they had sung an hymn, they went out into the mount of Olives. 27 And Jesus saith unto them, All ye shall be offended because of me this night: for it is written, I will smite the shepherd, and the sheep shall be scattered. 28 But after that I am risen, I will go before you into Galilee. 29 But Peter said unto him, Although all shall be offended, yet *will* not I. 30 And Jesus saith unto him, Verily I say unto thee, That this

26 Καὶ ὑμνήσαντες ἐξῆλθον εἰς τὸ ὄρος τῶν Ἐλαιῶν.
And having sung a hymn they went out to the mount of Olives.
27 καὶ λέγει αὐτοῖς ὁ Ἰησοῦς, Ὅτι πάντες σκανδαλισθήσεσθε
And ²says ³to ⁴them ¹Jesus, All ye will be offended
ᵉἐν ἐμοὶ‖ ᶠἐν τῇ νυκτὶ ταύτῃ·‖ ὅτι γέγραπται, Πατάξω τὸν
in me in this night; for it has been written, I will smite the
ποιμένα, καὶ ᵍδιασκορπισθήσεται τὰ πρόβατα.‖ 28 Ἀλλὰ
shepherd, and will be scattered abroad the sheep. But
μετὰ τὸ ἐγερθῆναί με, προάξω ὑμᾶς εἰς τὴν Γαλιλαίαν.
after my arising, I will go before you into Galilee.
29 Ὁ δὲ Πέτρος ἔφη αὐτῷ, ʰΚαὶ εἰ‖ πάντες σκανδαλισθήσονται,
But Peter said to him, Even if all shall be offended,
ἀλλ' οὐκ ἐγώ. 30 Καὶ λέγει αὐτῷ ὁ Ἰησοῦς, Ἀμὴν λέγω σοι,
yet not I. And ²says ³to ⁴him ¹Jesus, Verily I say to thee,

ⁿ ὁ Ἰησοῦς εἶπεν TA.   ° — Οἱ δὲ (*read* ἤρξαντο they began) TA.   ᴾ κατὰ TA.   ᑫ — καὶ
ἄλλος, Μή τι ἐγώ; TTr.   ʳ — ἀποκριθεὶς LTTrA.   ˢ — ἐκ (*read* τῶν of the) T[Tr].
ᵗ + τὴν χεῖρα the hand L.   ᵛ + ὅτι for T[Tr]A.   ʷ — ἦν [L]T[Tr]A.   ˣ — ὁ Ἰησοῦς
[L] T[Tr]A.   ʸ φάγετε GLTTrAW.   ᶻ — τὸ (*read* a cup) LTTrA.   ᵃ — τὸ [L]TA.
ᵇ — καινῆς TTrA.   ᶜ ὑπὲρ πολλῶν ἐκχυννόμενον L; ἐκχυννόμενον ὑπὲρ πολλῶν LTTrA.   ᵈ γεννή-
ματος TTrAW.   ᵉ — ἐν ἐμοὶ TTrA.   ᶠ — ἐν τῇ νυκτὶ ταύτῃ [L]TTrAW.   ᵍ διασκορπισθήσονται
τὰ πρόβατα L ; τὰ πρόβατα διασκορπισθήσονται TTrA.   ʰ Εἰ καὶ TTrA.

ὅτι [1]σήμερον [j]ἐν τῇ.νυκτὶ.ταύτῃ,‖ πρὶν ἢ δὶς ἀλέκτορα
that to-day in this night, before that twice [the] cock

φωνῆσαι, τρὶς [k]ἀπαρνήσῃ με.‖ 31 Ὁ.δὲ [l]ἐκ.περισσοῦ ἔλεγεν
crow, thrice thou wilt deny me. But he [3]vehemently [4]said

μᾶλλον,‖ Ἐάν [m]με.δέῃ‖ συναποθανεῖν σοι, οὐ.μή σε
[1]the [2]more, If it were needful for me to die with thee, in no wise thee

[n]ἀπαρνήσομαι.‖ Ὡσαύτως.δὲ καὶ πάντες ἔλεγον.
will I deny. And in like manner also [3]all [2]they [1]spake.

32 Καὶ ἔρχονται εἰς χωρίον [o]οὗ τὸ‖ ὄνομα [p]Γεθσημανῆ·‖
And they come to a place of which the name [is] Gethsemane;

καὶ λέγει τοῖς.μαθηταῖς.αὐτοῦ, Καθίσατε ὧδε, ἕως προσεύξω-
and he says to his disciples, Sit here, while I shall

μαι. 33 Καὶ παραλαμβάνει τὸν Πέτρον καὶ [q]τὸν‖ Ἰάκωβον
pray. And he takes Peter and James

καὶ Ἰωάννην [r]μεθ᾽ ἑαυτοῦ.‖ Καὶ ἤρξατο ἐκθαμβεῖσθαι καὶ
and John with him; and he began to be greatly amazed and

ἀδημονεῖν. 34 καὶ λέγει αὐτοῖς, Περίλυπός ἐστιν ἡ.ψυχή.μου
deeply depressed. And he says to them, Very sorrowful is my soul

ἕως θανάτου· μείνατε ὧδε καὶ γρηγορεῖτε. 35 Καὶ [s]προελ-
even to death; remain here and watch. And having gone

θὼν‖ μικρὸν [t]ἔπεσεν‖ ἐπὶ τῆς γῆς, καὶ προσηύχετο ἵνα, εἰ
forward a little he fell upon the earth, and prayed that, if

δυνατόν ἐστιν, παρέλθῃ ἀπ᾽ αὐτοῦ ἡ ὥρα. 36 καὶ ἔλεγεν,
possible it is, might pass from him the hour. And he said,

Αββᾶ, ὁ πατήρ, πάντα δυνατά σοι· παρένεγκε τὸ ποτή-
Abba, Father, all things [are] possible to thee; take away [2]cup

ριον [u]ἀπ᾽ ἐμοῦ τοῦτο·‖ ἀλλ᾽ οὐ τί ἐγὼ θέλω, ἀλλὰ τί σύ.
[2]from [4]me [1]this; but not what I will, but what thou.

37 Καὶ ἔρχεται καὶ εὑρίσκει αὐτοὺς καθεύδοντας· καὶ λέγει τῷ
And he comes and finds them sleeping. And he says

Πέτρῳ, Σίμων, καθεύδεις; οὐκ.ἴσχυσας μίαν ὥραν γρη-
to Peter, Simon, sleepest thou? wast thou not able one hour to

γορῆσαι; 38 γρηγορεῖτε καὶ προσεύχεσθε, ἵνα μὴ [w]εἰσέλθητε‖
watch? Watch and pray, that ye enter not

εἰς πειρασμόν. τὸ μὲν πνεῦμα πρόθυμον, ἡ.δὲ σὰρξ
into temptation. The [2]indeed [1]spirit [is] ready, but the flesh

ἀσθενής. 39 Καὶ πάλιν ἀπελθὼν προσηύξατο, τὸν αὐτὸν
weak. And again having gone away he prayed, [2]the [3]same

λόγον εἰπών. 40 καὶ [x]ὑποστρέψας‖ εὗρεν αὐτοὺς [y]πάλιν‖
[4]thing [1]saying. And, having returned he found them again

καθεύδοντας· ἦσαν.γὰρ [z]οἱ.ὀφθαλμοὶ.αὐτῶν‖ [a]βεβαρημένοι,‖
sleeping; for [3]were [1]their [2]eyes heavy;

καὶ οὐκ.ᾔδεισαν τί [b]αὐτῷ ἀποκριθῶσιν.‖ 41 Καὶ ἔρχεται
and they knew not what [4]him [1]they [2]should [3]answer. And he comes

τὸ τρίτον, καὶ λέγει αὐτοῖς, Καθεύδετε [c]τὸ‖ λοιπὸν καὶ
the third time, and says to them, Sleep on now and

ἀναπαύεσθε. ἀπέχει· ἦλθεν ἡ ὥρα· ἰδού, παραδίδοται
take your rest. It is enough; has come the hour; lo, [5]is [6]delivered [7]up

ὁ υἱὸς τοῦ ἀνθρώπου εἰς τὰς χεῖρας τῶν ἁμαρτωλῶν. 42 ἐγεί-
[1]the [2]Son [3]of [4]man into the hands of sinners. Rise,

ρεσθε, ἄγωμεν· ἰδού, ὁ παραδιδούς με [d]ἤγγικεν.‖
let us go; behold, he who is delivering up me has drawn near.

i + σὺ thou GLTTrAW. j ταύτῃ τῇ νυκτὶ LTTrA. k με ἀπαρνήσῃ LTTrAW. l ἐκπερισσῶς ἐλάλει LTTrA. m δέῃ με LTr. n ἀπαρνήσωμαι T. o ᾧ L. p Γεθσημανεί LTTrAW. q — τὸν GLTTrAW. r μετ᾽ αὐτοῦ LTTrA. s προσελθὼν Tr. t ἔπιπτεν TA. u τοῦτο ἀπ᾽ ἐμοῦ LTTrAW. w ἔλθητε TA. x πάλιν ἐλθὼν again coming LA; ἐλθὼν Tr. y —πάλιν LTrA. z αὐτῶν οἱ ὀφθαλμοὶ T. a καταβαρυνόμενοι LTTrAW. b ἀποκριθῶσιν αὐτῷ LTTrAW. c —τὸ LTrAW. d ἤγγισεν T.

43 And immediately, while he yet spake, cometh Judas, one of the twelve, and with him a great multitude with swords and staves, from the chief priests and the scribes and the elders. 44 And he that betrayed him had given them a token, saying, Whomsoever I shall kiss, that same is he; take him, and lead *him* away safely. 45 And as soon as he was come, he goeth straightway to him, and saith, Master, master; and kissed him. 46 And they laid their hands on him, and took him. 47 And one of them that stood by drew a sword, and smote a servant of the high priest, and cut off his ear. 48 And Jesus answered and said unto them, Are ye come out, as against a thief, with swords and *with* staves to take me? 49 I was daily with you in the temple teaching, and ye took me not : but the scriptures must be fulfilled. 50 And they all forsook him, and fled. 51 And there followed him a certain young man, having a linen cloth cast about *his* naked *body;* and the young men laid hold on him : 52 and he left the linen cloth, and fled from them naked.

43 Καὶ ᵉεὐθέως‖ ἔτι αὐτοῦ λαλοῦντος παραγίνεται ᶠἸού-
And immediately ⁴yet ¹as ²he ³is speaking, comes up Ju-
δαςᵍ, εἷς ʰὢνⁿ τῶν δώδεκα, καὶ μετ᾿ αὐτοῦ ὄχλος ⁱπολὺς‖
das, ²one ¹being of the twelve, and with him a ²crowd ¹great,
μετὰ μαχαιρῶν καὶ ξύλων, παρὰ τῶν ἀρχιερέων καὶ τῶν
with swords and staves, from the chief priests and the
γραμματέων καὶ ᵏτῶν‖ πρεσβυτέρων. 44 δεδώκει δὲ ὁ
scribes and the elders. Now ⁷had ⁸given ¹he ²who
παραδιδοὺς αὐτὸν ¹σύσσημον‖ αὐτοῖς, λέγων, Ὃν ἂν
³was ⁴delivering ⁶up ⁵him a sign to them, saying, Whomsoever
φιλήσω αὐτός ἐστιν· κρατήσατε αὐτόν, καὶ ᵐἀπάγα /ετε‖
I shall kiss ²he ¹is; seize him, and lead [him] away
ἀσφαλῶς. 45 Καὶ ἐλθών, ᵉεὐθέως‖ προσελθὼν αὐτῷ λέγει,
safely. And being come, immediately coming up to him he says,
ⁿῬαββί, ραββί ‖ καὶ κατεφίλησεν αὐτόν. 46 Οἱ δὲ ᵒἐπέβαλον‖
Rabbi, Rabbi; and ardently kissed him. And they laid
Ρᵖἐπ᾿ αὐτὸν τὰς χεῖρας αὐτῶν,‖ καὶ ἐκράτησαν αὐτόν. 47 Εἷς δὲ
upon him ²hands ¹their, and seized him. But ³one
ᵠτις‖ τῶν παρεστηκότων σπασάμενος τὴν μάχαιραν
¹a ²certain of those standing by, having drawn the sword
ἔπαισεν τὸν δοῦλον τοῦ ἀρχιερέως καὶ ἀφεῖλεν αὐτοῦ τὸ
struck the bondman of the high priest and took off his
ʳὠτίον.‖ 48 Καὶ ἀποκριθεὶς ὁ Ἰησοῦς εἶπεν αὐτοῖς, Ὡς ἐπὶ
ear. And ²answering ¹Jesus said to them, As against
λῃστὴν ˢἐξήλθετε‖ μετὰ μαχαιρῶν καὶ ξύλων συλλαβεῖν με;
a robber are ye come out with swords and staves to take me?
49 καθ᾿ ἡμέραν ἤμην πρὸς ὑμᾶς ἐν τῷ ἱερῷ διδάσκων, καὶ
Daily I was with you in the temple teaching, and
οὐκ ἐκρατήσατέ με· ἀλλ᾿ ἵνα πληρωθῶσιν αἱ γραφαί.
ye did not seize me : but [it is] that ²may ⁴be ⁵fulfilled ¹the ²scriptures.
50 Καὶ ἀφέντες αὐτὸν ᵗπάντες ἔφυγον.‖ 51 Καὶ ᵘεἷς τις
And leaving him all fled. And one a certain
νεανίσκος‖ ᵛἠκολούθει‖ αὐτῷ, περιβεβλημένος σινδόνα ἐπὶ
young man was following him, having cast a linen cloth about
γυμνοῦ· καὶ κρατοῦσιν αὐτὸν ʷοἱ νεανίσκοι‖ 52 ὁ δὲ
[his] naked [body]; and ⁴seize ⁵him ¹the ²young ³men, but he,
καταλιπὼν τὴν σινδόνα γυμνὸς ἔφυγεν ˣἀπ᾿ αὐτῶν.ʸ
leaving behind the linen cloth, ²naked ¹fled from them.

53 And they led Jesus away to the high priest : and with him were assembled all the chief priests and the elders and the scribes. 54 And Peter followed him afar off, even into the palace of the high priest : and he sat with the servants, and warmed himself at the fire. 55 And the chief priests and all the council sought for wit-

53 Καὶ ἀπήγαγον τὸν Ἰησοῦν πρὸς τὸν ἀρχιερέα· καὶ
And they led away Jesus to the high priest. And
συνέρχονται ᶻαὐτῷ πάντες οἱ ἀρχιερεῖς καὶ οἱ ᶻπρεσβύτεροι
there come together to him all the chief priests and the elders
καὶ οἱ γραμματεῖς.‖ 54 Καὶ ὁ Πέτρος ἀπὸ μακρόθεν ἠκολού-
and the scribes. And Peter from afar off fol-
θησεν αὐτῷ· ἕως ἔσω εἰς τὴν αὐλὴν τοῦ ἀρχιερέως· καὶ ἦν
lowed him as far as within to the court of the high priest; and he was
ᵃσυγκαθήμενος‖ μετὰ τῶν ὑπηρετῶν, καὶ θερμαινόμενος πρὸς
sitting with the officers, and warming himself at
ᵇτὸ‖ φῶς. 55 Οἱ δὲ ἀρχιερεῖς καὶ ὅλον τὸ συνέδριον ἐζήτουν
the fire. And the chief priests and ²whole ¹the sanhedrim sought
(lit. light).

ᵉ εὐθὺς LTTrA.   ᶠ + ὁ LTrAW.   ᵍ + ὁ Ἰσκαριώτης Iscariote LT[Tr]A.ᵛ   ʰ — ὢν LTTr[A].
ⁱ — πολὺς [L.]TTrA.   ᵏ — τῶν T.   ˡ σύνσημον T.   ᵐ ἀπάγετε LTTrA.   ⁿ Ῥαββί LTr;
ῥαββεί T; ραββεί [ραββεί] A.   ᵒ ἐπέβαλαν T.   ᵖ τὰς χεῖρας ἐπ᾿ αὐτὸν L ; τὰς χεῖρας αὐτῷ
TTrA.   ᵠ — τις LTrAW.   ʳ ὠτάριον LTTrA.   ˢ ἐξήλθατε LTTrAW.   ᵗ ἔφυγον πάντες TTrA.
ᵘ νεανίσκος τις LTr.   ᵛ συνηκολούθει was following with LTTrA ; ἠκολούθησεν followed W.
ʷ — οἱ νεανίσκοι (read they seize) LTTrA.   ˣ — ἀπ᾿ αὐτῶν [L]TTr.   ʸ — αὐτῷ T.
ᶻ γραμματεῖς καὶ οἱ πρεσβύτεροι L.   ᵃ συνκαθήμενος T.   ᵇ — τὸ E.

κατὰ τοῦ Ἰησοῦ μαρτυρίαν, εἰς τὸ θανατῶσαι αὐτόν· καὶ οὐχ
against   Jesus   testimony,   to   put to death him,   and ²not
εὕρισκον.‖ 56 πολλοὶ.γὰρ ἐψευδομαρτύρουν κατ᾽ αὐτοῦ,
¹did find [any].   For many bore false testimony against him,
καὶ ἴσαι αἱ μαρτυρίαι οὐκ.ἦσαν. 57 καί τινες ἀναστάντες
and alike their testimonies were not.   And some · having risen up
ἐψευδομαρτύρουν κατ᾽ αὐτοῦ, λέγοντες, 58 Ὅτι ἡμεῖς ἠκούσα-
bore false testimony against him,   saying,   We   heard
μεν αὐτοῦ λέγοντος, Ὅτι ἐγὼ καταλύσω τὸν.ναὸν.τοῦτον τὸν
him   saying,   I will destroy this temple   the
χειροποίητον, καὶ διὰ τριῶν ἡμερῶν ἄλλον ἀχειροποίητον
[one] made with hands, and in three days another. not made with hands
οἰκοδομήσω. 59 Καὶ οὐδὲ οὕτως ἴση ἦν ἡ.μαρτυρία.αὐτῶν.
I will build.   And neither thus alike was   their testimony.
60 Καὶ ἀναστὰς ὁ ἀρχιερεὺς εἰς ᵉτὸ‖ μέσον ἐπηρώτησεν
And ⁴having ⁵stood ⁶up ¹the ²high ³priest in · the midst   questioned
τὸν Ἰησοῦν, λέγων, Οὐκ ἀποκρίνῃ οὐδέν; τί οὗτοί σου
Jesus,   saying,   Answerest thou nothing? What ²these ⁴thee
καταμαρτυροῦσιν; 61 Ὁ.δὲ ἐσιώπα, καὶ ᶠοὐδὲν ἀπεκρίνατο.‖
_¹testify ³against?   But he was silent, and nothing answered.
Πάλιν ὁ ἀρχιερεὺς ἐπηρώτα αὐτόν, καὶ λέγει αὐτῷ, Σὺ
Again the high priest was questioning him,   and says to him, ²Thou
εἶ ᵍὁ χριστός, ὁ υἱὸς τοῦ εὐλογητοῦ; 62 Ὁ.δὲ.Ἰησοῦς εἶπεν,
¹art the Christ, the Son of the blessed?   And Jesus said,
Ἐγώ εἰμι. καὶ ὄψεσθε τὸν υἱὸν τοῦ ἀνθρώπου ᵍκαθήμενον
I   am. And ye shall see the Son of man   sitting
ἐκ δεξιῶν‖ τῆς δυνάμεως, καὶ ἐρχόμενον μετὰ τῶν νεφελῶν
at [the] right hand of power,   and coming with the clouds
τοῦ οὐρανοῦ. 63 Ὁ.δὲ ἀρχιερεὺς διαρρήξας τοὺς.χιτῶνας.αὐτοῦ
of the heaven.   And the high priest having rent his garments
λέγει, Τί ἔτι χρείαν ἔχομεν μαρτύρων; 64 ἠκούσατε ʰτῆς
says, What any more need have we of witnesses?   Ye heard
βλασφημίας·‖ τί ὑμῖν φαίνεται; Οἱ.δὲ πάντες κατέκριναν
blasphemy: what ²to ³you ¹appears? And they   all   condemned
αὐτὸν ᶦεἶναι ἔνοχον‖ θανάτου. 65 Καὶ ἤρξαντό τινες ἐμπτύειν
him to be deserving of death.   And. ²began ¹some to spit upon
αὐτῷ, καὶ περικαλύπτειν ᵏτὸ.πρόσωπον.αὐτοῦ,‖ καὶ κολα-
him, and to cover up   his face,   and to buf-
φίζειν αὐτόν, καὶ λέγειν αὐτῷ, Προφήτευσον· καὶ οἱ ὑπηρέται
fet   him, and to say to him, Prophesy;   and the   officers
ῥαπίσμασιν αὐτὸν ᵐἔβαλλον.‖
with the palm of the hand ²him ¹struck.
66 Καὶ ὄντος τοῦ Πέτρου ⁿἐν τῇ αὐλῇ κάτω,‖ ἔρχεται μία
And ²being ¹Peter in the court below,   comes one
τῶν παιδισκῶν τοῦ ἀρχιερέως, 67 καὶ ἰδοῦσα τὸν Πέτρον
of the ᵐaids of the high priest,   and seeing   the   Peter
θερμαινόμενον, ἐμβλέψασα αὐτῷ λέγει, Καὶ σὺ μετὰ τοῦ
warming himself, having looked at him says, And thou ²with ³the
Ναζαρηνοῦ ᵒἸησοῦ ἦσθα.‖ 68 Ὁ.δὲ ἠρνήσατο, λέγων, ᴾΟὐκ
⁴Nazarene ⁵Jesus ¹wast.   But he denied,   saying, ³Not
οἶδα ᑫοὐδὲ‖ ἐπίσταμαι ʳτί σὺ λέγεις. Καὶ ἐξῆλθεν ἔξω
¹I ²know nor even understand what thou sayest. And he went forth out

ness against Jesus to put him to death; and found none. 56 For many bare false witness against him, but their witness agreed not together. 57 And there arose certain, and bare false witness against him, saying, 58 We heard him say, I will destroy this temple that is made with hands, and within three days I will build another made without hands. 59 But neither so did their witness agree together. 60 And the high priest stood up in the midst, and asked Jesus, saying, Answerest thou nothing? what is it which these witness against thee? 61 But he held his peace, and answered nothing. Again the high priest asked him, and said unto him, Art thou the Christ, the Son of the Blessed? 62 And Jesus said, I am : and ye shall see the Son of man sitting on the right hand of power, and coming in the clouds of heaven. 63 Then the high priest rent his clothes, and saith, What need we any further witnesses? 64 Ye have heard the blasphemy : what think ye? And they all condemned him to be guilty of death. 65 And some began to spit on him, and to cover his face, and to buffet him, and to say unto him, Prophesy : and the servants did strike him with the palms of their hands.

66 And as Peter was beneath in the palace, there cometh one of the maids of the high priest : 67 and, when she saw Peter warming himself, she looked upon him, and said, And thou also wast with Jesus of Nazareth. 68 But he denied, saying, I know not, neither understand I what thou sayest. And he went out into the

---

ᵈ ηὕρισκον LTTrA.   ᵉ — τὸ (read [the]) GLTTrAW.   ᶠ οὐκ ἀπεκρίνατο οὐδέν TTr.   ᵍ ἐκ
δεξιῶν καθήμενον GLTTrAW.   ʰ τὴν βλασφημίαν L.   ᶦ ἔροχον εἶναι TTrA.   ᵏ αὐτοῦ τὸ
πρόσωπον TTrA.   ᵐ ἔβαλον w ; ἔλαβον (read received him with buffets) LTTrA.   ⁿ κάτω
ἐν τῇ αὐλῇ TTrA.   ᵒ ἦσθα τοῦ Ἰησοῦ LTTrA.   ᴾ οὔτε neither (know I) LTTrA.   ᑫ οὔτε
ɴοɾ LTTrAW.   ʳ σὺ τί LTTrA.

porch; and the cock. crew. 69 And a maid saw him again, and began to say to them that stood by, This is one of them. 70 And he denied it again. And a little after, they that stood by said again to Peter, Surely thou art one of them : for thou art a Galilæan, and thy speech agreeth thereto. 71 But he began to curse and to swear, saying, I know not this man of whom ye speak. 72 And the second time the cock crew. And Peter called to mind the word that Jesus said unto him, Before the cock crow twice, thou shalt deny me thrice. And when he thought thereon, he wept.

XV. And straightway in the morning the chief priests held a consultation with the elders and scribes and the whole council, and bound Jesus, and carried him away, and delivered him to Pilate. 2 And Pilate asked him, Art thou the king of the Jews ? And he answering said unto him, Thou sayest it. 3 And the chief priests accused him of many things : but he answered nothing. 4 And Pilate asked him again, saying, Answerest thou nothing ? behold how many things they witness against thee. 5 But Jesus yet answered nothing ; so that Pilate marvelled. 6 Now at that feast he released unto them one prisoner, whomsoever they desired. 7 And there was one named Barabbas, which lay bound with them that had made insurrection with him, who had committed murder in the insurrection. 8 And the multitude crying aloud began to desire him to do as he had ever done unto them.

εἰς τὸ προαύλιον· ˢκαὶ ἀλέκτωρ εφϣ νησεν.ᵗ 69 Καὶ ἡ παιδίσκη
into the porch, and a cock crew. And the maid
ἰδοῦσα αὐτὸν ᵗπάλιν ἤρξατοᵗ λέγειν τοῖς ʷπαρεστηκόσιν,ᵘ Ὅτι
seeing him again began to say to those standing by,
οὗτος ᵉξ αὐτῶν ἐστιν. 70 Ὁ δὲ πάλιν ἠρνεῖτο. Καὶ μετὰ
This ²one ³of: ⁴them ¹is. And he again denied. And after
μικρὸν πάλιν οἱ παρεστῶτες ἔλεγον τῷ Πέτρῳ, Ἀληθῶς
a little again those standing by said to Peter, Truly
ἐξ αὐτῶν εἶ· καὶ γὰρ Γαλιλαῖος εἶ, ʷκαὶ ἡ λαλιά
from among them thou art, for both a Galilean thou art, and ²speech
σου ὁμοιάζει.ᵘ 71 Ὁ δὲ ἤρξατο ἀναθεματίζειν καὶ ˣὀμνύειν,ᵘ
¹thy agrees. But he began to curse and to swear,
Ὅτι οὐκ οἶδα τὸν ἄνθρωπον τοῦτον ὃν λέγετε. 72 Καὶ ʸ
I know not this man whom ye speak of. And
ἐκ δευτέρου ἀλέκτωρ ἐφώνησεν. Καὶ ἀνεμνήσθη ὁ Πέτρος ᶻτοῦ
the second time a cock crew. And ²remembered ¹Peter the
ῥήματος οὗᵘ εἶπεν αὐτῷ ὁ Ἰησοῦς, Ὅτι πρὶν ἀλέκτορα
word that ²said ³to ⁴him ¹Jesus, Before [the] cock
ᵃφωνῆσαι δὶςᵘ ᵇἀπαρνήσῃ με τρίς·ᵘ καὶ ἐπιβαλὼν
crow twice thou wilt deny me thrice ; and having thought thereof
ἔκλαιεν.
he wept.

15 Καὶ ᶜεὐθέωςᵘ ᵈἐπὶ τὸᵘ πρωῒ συμβούλιον ᵉποιήσαντεςᵘ
And immediately in the morning ᵉa ⁷counsel ⁴having ⁵formed
οἱ ἀρχιερεῖς μετὰ τῶν πρεσβυτέρων καὶ ᶠγραμματέων καὶ
¹the ²chief ³priests with the elders . and scribes and
ὅλον τὸ συνέδριον, δήσαντες τὸν Ἰησοῦν ἀπήνεγκαν καὶ
²whole ¹the sanhedrim, having bound Jesus carried [him] away and
παρέδωκαν ᵍτῷᵘ ʰΠιλάτῳ.ᵘ 2 καὶ ἐπηρώτησεν αὐτὸν ὁ
delivered up [him] to Pilate. And ²questioned ³him
ⁱΠιλάτος,ᵘ Σὺ εἶ ὁ βασιλεὺς τῶν Ἰουδαίων ; Ὁ δὲ ἀπο-
¹Pilate, ⁵Thou ⁴art the King of the Jews ? And he an-
κριθεὶς ʲεἶπεν αὐτῷ,ᵘ Σὺ λέγεις. 3 Καὶ κατηγόρουν αὐτοῦ οἱ
swering said to him, Thou sayest. And ²were ³accusing ⁶him ¹the
ἀρχιερεῖς πολλά· 4 ὁ δὲ ⁱΠιλάτοςᵘ πάλιν ᵏἐπηρώτησενᵘ αὐτόν,
²chief ³priests urgently. And Pilate again questioned him,
ˡλέγων,ᵘ Οὐκ ἀποκρίνῃ οὐδέν ; ἴδε, πόσα σου
saying, Answerest thou nothing ? See, of how many things ⁴thee
ᵐκαταμαρτυροῦσιν.ᵘ 5 Ὁ δὲ Ἰησοῦς οὐκέτι οὐδὲν ἀπεκρίθη,
²they ²witness ³against. But Jesus not any more any thing answered,
ὥστε θαυμάζειν τὸν ⁿΠιλάτον.ᵘ 6 Κατὰ δὲ ἑορτὴν ἀπέλυεν
so that ²wondered ¹Pilate. Now at [the] feast he released
αὐτοῖς ἕνα δέσμιον, ᵒὅνπερ ᵗᵗᵒῦντο.ᵘ 7 ἦν δὲ ὁ λεγό-
to them one prisoner, whomsoever they asked. And there was the [one] call-
μενος Βαραββᾶς μετὰ τῶν ᴾσυστασιαστῶνᵘ δεδεμένος,
ed Barabbas with the associates in insurrection bound,
οἵτινες ἐν τῇ στάσει φόνον πεποιήκεισαν. 8 καὶ ᑫἀναβοήσαςᵘ
who in the insurrection murder had committed. And crying out
ὁ ὄχλος ἤρξατο αἰτεῖσθαι καθὼς ʳἀεὶᵘ ἐποίει αὐτοῖς
the crowd began to beg [him to do] as always he did to them.

ˢ [καὶ ἀλέκτωρ ἐφώνησεν] L.　ᵗ ἤρξατο πάλιν T ; — πάλιν A.　ᵛ παρεστῶσιν TTrA.
ʷ — καὶ ἡ λαλιά σου ὁμοιάζει LTTrA.　ˣ ὀμνύναι GLTTrAW.　ʸ + εὐθὺς immediately LTTr.
ᶻ τὸ ῥῆμα ὡς LTTrA ; τὸ ῥῆμα ὃ W.　ᵃ δὶς φωνῆσαι LTrA.　ᵇ τρίς με ἀπαρνήσῃ LTTrA.
ᶜ εὐθὺς TTrA.　ᵈ — ἐπὶ τὸ (read πρωῒ early) LTTr[A].　ᵉ ἑτοιμάσαντες T.　ᶠ + τῶν the T.
ᵍ — τῷ LTTrA.　ʰ Πειλάτῳ T.　ⁱ Πειλᾶτος T.　ʲ αὐτῷ λέγει to him says TTrA.
ᵏ ἐπηρώτα TTrA.　ˡ — λέγων T.　ᵐ κατηγοροῦσιν they accuse LTTrA.　ⁿ Πειλᾶτον ᵀ
ᵒ ὃν παρῃτοῦντο T.　ᴾ στασιαστῶν LTTrA.　ᑫ ἀναβὰς coming up LTTrA.　ʳ — ἀεὶ T.

9 ὁ.δὲ.ᵃΠιλάτος‖ ἀπεκρίθη αὐτοῖς, λέγων, Θέλετε ἀπολύσω
But Pilate answered them, saying, Will ye I should release
ὑμῖν τὸν βασιλέα τῶν Ἰουδαίων; 10 Ἐγίνωσκεν.γὰρ ὅτι διὰ
to you the King of the Jews? for he knew that through
φθόνον παραδεδώκεισαν αὐτὸν οἱ ἀρχιερεῖς. 11 οἱ.δὲ ἀρχ-
envy ⁴had ⁵delivered ⁷up ⁶him ¹the ²chief ³priests. But the chief
ιερεῖς ἀνέσεισαν τὸν ὄχλον ἵνα μᾶλλον τὸν Βαραββᾶν
priests stirred up the crowd that rather Barabbas
ἀπολύσῃ αὐτοῖς· 12 ὁ.δὲ.ᵃΠιλάτος‖ ᵗἀποκριθεὶς πάλιν‖
he might release to them. And Pilate answering again
ᵛεἶπεν‖ αὐτοῖς, Τί οὖν ʷθέλετε‖ ποιήσω ˣὃν λέγετε‖
said to them, What then will ye I should do [to him] whom ye call
ʸβασιλέα τῶν Ἰουδαίων; 13 Οἱ.δὲ πάλιν ἔκραξαν,ᶻ Σταύρω-
King of the Jews? But they again cried out Cruci-
σον αὐτόν. 14 Ὁ.δὲ.ᵃΠιλάτος‖ ἔλεγεν αὐτοῖς, Τί γὰρ ᵃκακὸν
fy him. And Pilate said to them, What ²then ¹evil
ἐποίησεν‖; Οἱ.δὲ ᵇπερισσοτέρως‖ ᶜἔκραξαν,‖ Σταύρωσον αὐ-
did he commit? But they much more cried out, Crucify him.
τόν. 15 Ὁ.δὲ.ᵃΠιλάτος‖ βουλόμενος ᵈτῷ ὄχλῳ τὸ
And Pilate, desiring ⁷to ⁸the ⁹crowd ³that ⁴which [⁵was]
ἱκανὸν ποιῆσαι,‖ ἀπέλυσεν αὐτοῖς τὸν Βαραββᾶν· καὶ παρέ-
ᵉsatisfactory ¹to ²do, released to them Barabbas, and de-
δωκεν τὸν Ἰησοῦν, φραγελλώσας, ἵνα σταυρωθῇ.‖
livered up Jesus, having scourged [him], that he might be crucified.

16 Οἱ.δὲ στρατιῶται ἀπήγαγον αὐτὸν ἔσω τῆς αὐλῆς, ὅ
And the soldiers led away him within the court, which
ἐστιν πραιτώριον, καὶ ᵉσυγκαλοῦσιν‖ ὅλην τὴν σπεῖραν·
is [the] prætorium, and they call together ²whole ¹the band.
17 καὶ ᶠἐνδύουσιν‖ αὐτὸν πορφύραν, καὶ περιτιθέασιν αὐτῷ
And they put on him purple, and placed on him
πλέξαντες ἀκάνθινον στέφανον, 18 καὶ ἤρξαντο ἀσπάζε-
having platted [it] ²thorny ¹a crown, and they began to sa-
σθαι αὐτόν, Χαῖρε, ᵍβασιλεῦ‖ τῶν Ἰουδαίων· 19 καὶ ἔτυπτον
lute him, Hail, King of the Jews! And they struck
αὐτοῦ τὴν κεφαλὴν καλάμῳ, καὶ ἐνέπτυον αὐτῷ, καὶ τιθέντες
his head with a reed, and did spat on him, and bending
τὰ γόνατα προσεκύνουν αὐτῷ. 20 Καὶ ὅτε ἐνέπαιξαν αὐτῷ,
the knees did homage to him. And when they had mocked him,
ἐξέδυσαν αὐτὸν τὴν πορφύραν, καὶ ἐνέδυσαν αὐτὸν τὰ
they took off him the purple, and put on him
ʰἱμάτια.τὰ.ἴδια·‖ καὶ ⁱἐξάγουσιν‖ αὐτὸν ἵνα ᵏσταυρώσωσιν‖
his own garments; and they lead ²out ¹him that they may crucify
ˡαὐτόν.‖ 21 καὶ ἀγγαρεύουσιν παράγοντά τινα Σίμωνα Κυ-
him. And they compel ²passing ³by ¹one, Simon a Cy-
ρηναῖον, ἐρχόμενον ᵐἀπ'‖ ἀγροῦ, τὸν πατέρα Ἀλεξάνδρου καὶ
renian, coming from a field, the father of Alexander and
Ῥούφου, ἵνα ἄρῃ τὸν.σταυρὸν.αὐτοῦ.
Rufus, that he might carry his cross.

22 Καὶ φέρουσιν αὐτὸν ἐπὶ ⁿΓολγοθᾶ‖ τόπον, ὅ ἐστιν
And they bring him to ³Golgotha ¹a ²place, which is
μεθερμηνευόμενον, κρανίου τόπος. 23 Καὶ ἐδίδουν αὐτῷ
being interpreted, ²of ³a ⁴skull ¹place. And they gave him

9 But Pilate answered them, saying, Will ye that I release unto you the King of the Jews? 10 For he knew that the chief priests had delivered him for envy. 11 But the chief priests moved the people, that he should rather release Barabbas unto them. 12 And Pilate answered and said again unto them, What will ye then that I shall do unto him whom ye call the King of the Jews? 13 And they cried out again, Crucify him. 14 Then Pilate said unto them, Why, what evil hath he done? And they cried out the more exceedingly, Crucify him. 15 And so Pilate, willing to content the people, released Barabbas unto them, and delivered Jesus, when he had scourged him, to be crucified.

16 And the soldiers led him away into the hall, called Prætorium; and they call together the whole band. 17 And they clothed him with purple, and platted a crown of thorns, and put it about his head, 18 and began to salute him, Hail, King of the Jews! 19 And they smote him on the head with a reed, and did spit upon him, and bowing their knees worshipped him. 20 And when they had mocked him, they took off the purple from him, and put his own clothes on him, and led him out to crucify him. 21 And they compel one Simon a Cyrenian, who passed by, coming out of the country, the father of Alexander and Rufus, to bear his cross.

22 And they bring him unto the place Golgotha, which is, being interpreted, The place of a skull. 23 And they gave him to drink wine

---

ˢ Πειλᾶτος T. ᵗ πάλιν ἀποκριθεὶς LTTᵣA. ᵛ ἔλεγεν TT.A. ʷ [θέλετε] Tr. ˣ — ὃν
λέγετε LTr. ʸ + τὸν the LTTrAW. ᶻ + λέγοντες saying L. ᵃ ἐποίησεν κακόν TTrA.
ᵇ περισσῶς GLTTrAW. ᶜ ἔκραζον L. ᵈ ποιῆσαι τὸ ἱκανὸν τῷ ὄχλῳ T. ᵉ συγκαλοῦσιν T.
ᶠ ἐνδιδύσκουσιν LTTrA. ᵍ ὁ βασιλεὺς GAW. ʰ ἱμάτια αὐτοῦ L; ἴδια ἱμάτια αὐτοῦ T.
ⁱ ἄγουσιν they lead L. ᵏ σταυρώσουσιν they shall crucify LTTrA. ˡ — αὐτόν T.
ᵐ ἀπὸ LTr. ⁿ τὸν Γολγοθᾶν T; Γολγοθᾶν A; [τὸν] Γολγοθᾶ Tr.

mingled with myrrh : but he received it not. 24 And when they had crucified him, they parted his garments, casting lots upon them, what every man should take. 25 And it was the third hour, and they crucified him. 26 And the superscription of his accusation was written over, THE KING OF THE JEWS. 27 And with him they crucify two thieves ; the one on his right hand, and the other on his left. 28 And the scripture was fulfilled, which saith, And he was numbered with the transgressors. 29 And they that passed by railed on him, wagging their heads, and saying, Ah, thou that destroyest the temple, and buildest it in three days, 30 save thyself, and come down from the cross. 31 Likewise also the chief priests mocking said among themselves with the scribes, He saved others ; himself he cannot save. 32 Let Christ the King of Israel descend now from the cross, that we may see and believe. And they that were crucified with him reviled him. 33 And when the sixth hour was come, there was darkness over the whole land until the ninth hour. 34 And at the ninth hour Jesus cried with a loud voice, saying, ELOI, ELOI, LAMA SABACHTHANI ? which is, being interpreted, My God, my God, why hast thou forsaken me? 35 And some of them that stood by, when they heard it, said, Behold, he calleth Elias. 36 And one ran and filled a spunge full of vinegar, and put it on a reed, and gave him to drink, saying, Let alone ; let us see whether Elias will come to take him down.

ᵒπιεῖν‖ ἐσμυρνισμένον οἶνον· ᴾὁ.δὲ‖ οὐκ.ἔλαβεν. 24 Καὶ
to drink ²medicated ³with ⁴myrrh ¹wine ; but he did not take [it] And

ᵠσταυρώσαντες αὐτὸν‖ ʳδιεμέριζον‖ τὰ.ἱμάτια.αὐτοῦ, βάλλον-
having crucified him they divided his garments, cast-

τες κλῆρον ἐπ' αὐτά, τίς τί ἄρῃ. 25 ἦν.δὲ
ing a lot on them, who [and] what [each] should take. And it was [the]

ὥρα τρίτη, καὶ ἐσταύρωσαν αὐτόν. 26 Καὶ ἦν ἡ ἐπιγραφὴ
³hour ¹third, and they crucified him. And ⁶was ¹the ²inscription

τῆς.αἰτίας.αὐτοῦ ἐπιγεγραμμένη, Ὁ βασιλεὺς τῶν Ἰουδαίων.
³of ⁴his ⁵accusation written up, The King of the Jews.

27 Καὶ σὺν αὐτῷ σταυροῦσιν δύο λῃστάς, ἕνα ἐκ δεξιῶν
And with him they crucify two robbers, one at [the] right hand

καὶ ἕνα ἐξ εὐωνύμων αὐτοῦ. 28 ˢκαὶ ἐπληρώθη ἡ γραφὴ
and one at [the] left of him. And was fulfilled the scripture

ἡ λέγουσα, Καὶ μετὰ ἀνόμων ἐλογίσθη.‖ 29 Καὶ οἱ
which says, And with [the] lawless he was reckoned. And those

παραπορευόμενοι ἐβλασφήμουν αὐτόν, κινοῦντες τὰς κεφαλὰς
passing by railed at him, shaking ᵘheads

αὐτῶν, καὶ λέγοντες, Οὐά,‖ ὁ.καταλύων τὸν ναὸν καὶ ᵛἐν
¹their, and saying, Aha, thou who destroyest the temple and in

τρισὶν ἡμέραις οἰκοδομῶν,‖ 30 σῶσον σεαυτόν, ʷκαὶ κατάβα‖
three days building [it], save thyself, and descend

ἀπὸ τοῦ σταυροῦ. 31 Ὁμοίως.ˣδὲᵈ καὶ οἱ ἀρχιερεῖς, ἐμπαί-
from the cross. And in like manner also the chief priests, mock-

ζοντες πρὸς ἀλλήλους μετὰ τῶν γραμματέων, ἔλεγον, Ἄλλους
ing among one another with the scribes, said, Others

ἔσωσεν, ἑαυτὸν οὐ.δύναται σῶσαι. 32 ὁ χριστὸς ὁ βασιλεὺς
he saved, himself he is not able to save. The Christ the King

ʸτοῦ‖ Ἰσραὴλ καταβάτω νῦν ἀπὸ τοῦ σταυροῦ, ἵνα ἴδωμεν
of Israel let him descend now from the cross, that we may see

καὶ πιστεύσωμενᶻ. Καὶ οἱ συνεσταυρωμένοιᵃ αὐτῷ ὠνείδιζον
and believe. And they who were crucified with him reproached

αὐτόν. 33 ᵇΓενομένης.δὲ‖ ὥρας ἕκτης, σκότος ἐγένετο ἐφ'
him. And ⁴being ⁵come [¹the] ³hour ²sixth, darkness came over

ὅλην τὴν γῆν, ἕως ὥρας ᶜἐννάτης·‖ 34 καὶ τῇ ᵈὥρᾳ τῇ
all the land, until [the] ²hour ¹ninth ; and at the hour the

ἐννάτῃ‖ ἐβόησεν ὁ Ἰησοῦς φωνῇ μεγάλῃ, λέγων,‖ ᶠἘλωῒ,
ninth ²cried ¹Jesus with a ²voice ¹loud, saying, Eloi,

Ἐλωΐ,‖ ᵍλαμμᾶ‖ ʰσαβαχθανί ;‖ ὅ ἐστιν μεθερμηνευόμενον,
Eloi, lama sabachthani ? which is being interpreted,

Ὁ.θεός.μου, ὁ.θεός.μου, εἰς.τί ᶦμε ἐγκατέλιπες‖ ; 35 Καὶ τινὲς
My God, My God, why me hast thou forsaken ? And some

τῶν ᵏπαρεστηκότων‖ ἀκούσαντες ἔλεγον, ˡἸδού,‖ ᵐἩλίαν‖
of those standing by having heard said, Lo, Elias

φωνεῖ. 36 Δραμὼν.δὲ ⁿεἷς‖ ᵒᵃκαὶ‖ γεμίσας σπόγγον ὄξους,
he calls. And ²having ³run ¹one and filled a sponge with vinegar,

περιθεὶς ᵖᵃτε‖ καλάμῳ ἐπότιζεν αὐτόν, λέγων, Ἄφετε,
²having ³put [⁴it] ⁵on ¹and a reed gave ²to ³drink ¹him, saying, Let be,

ἴδωμεν εἰ ἔρχεται. ᵠᵃἩλίας‖ καθελεῖν αὐτόν.
let us see if ²comes ¹Elias to take down him.

ᵒ — πιεῖν TTr. ᴾ ὃς δὲ who however TTr. ᵠ σταυροῦσιν αὐτόν, καὶ they crucify him and TTrA. ʳ διαμερίζονται they divide GLTTrAW. ˢ — verse 28 T[Tr]A. ᵗ Οὐᾶ T. ᵛ οἰκοδομῶν τρισὶν ἡμέραις LTTrA. ʷ καταβὰς descending LTTrA. ˣ — δὲ and GLTTrAW. ʸ — τοῦ LTTr. ᶻ + αὐτῷ him L. ᵃ + σὺν with (read crucified along with) LT. ᵇ καὶ γενομένης LTTrA. ᶜ ἐνάτης LTTrA. ᵈ ἐνάτῃ ὥρᾳ LTTrA. ᵉ — λέγων TTrA. ᶠ Ἐλωὶ ἐλωὶ LTA. ᵍ λεμὰ LT ; λαμὰ TrAW. ʰ σαβαχθανεί TTr. ᶦ ἐγκατέλιπές με LTTrA. ᵏ παρεστώτων T. ˡ Ἴδε TTrA. ᵐ Ἡλείαν T. ⁿ τις TTrA. ᵒᵃ — καὶ L[Tr]A. ᵖᵃ — τε LTTrA. ᵠᵃ Ἡλείας T.

37 Ὁ.δὲ.Ἰησοῦς   ἀφεὶς   φωνὴν μεγάλην ἐξέπνευσεν.
And Jesus   having uttered   a ²cry   ¹loud   expired.

38 καὶ τὸ καταπέτασμα τοῦ ναοῦ ἐσχίσθη εἰς δύο, ¹ἀπὸ ἄνω
And the   veil   of the temple was rent into two, from   top

θεν ἕως κάτω.   39 Ἰδὼν.δὲ   ὁ κεντυρίων ὁ παρεστηκὼς
to bottom.   And ²having ¹seen ¹the ²centurion ³who   ⁴stood ⁵by

ἐξ.ἐναντίας αὐτοῦ ὅτι οὕτως ⁶κράξας ἐξέπνευσεν, εἶπεν,
⁶opposite   ⁷him   that thus   having cried out   he expired,   said,

Ἀληθῶς ¹ὁ.ἄνθρωπος.οὗτος vἱὸς ἦν θεοῦ. 40 Ἦσαν.δὲ καὶ
Truly   this man   ²Son ¹was of God.   And there were also

γυναῖκες ἀπὸ μακρόθεν θεωροῦσαι, ἐν αἷς ᵛἦν καὶ Μαρία
women   from   afar off   looking on, among whom was also Mary

ἡ Μαγδαληνή, καὶ Μαρία ʷἦ ˣτοῦ Ἰακώβου τοῦ μικροῦ καὶ
the Magdalene,   and   Mary the   ²of ³James ⁴the ⁵less ⁶and

ʸἸωσῆ μήτηρ, καὶ Σαλώμη, 41 αἳ ᶻκαὶ ὅτε ἦν ἐν τῇ Γαλι
⁷of ⁸Joses ¹mother, and Salome ;   who also when he was in   Gali

λαίᾳ ἠκολούθουν αὐτῷ καὶ διηκόνουν αὐτῷ, καὶ ἄλλαι πολλὰ
lee   followed   him   and ministered to him,   and ²others ¹many

αἱ συναναβᾶσαι αὐτῷ εἰς Ἱεροσόλυμα.
who came up with   him   to   Jerusalem.

42 Καὶ ἤδη ὀψίας γενομένης, ἐπεὶ ἦν   παρασκευή,
And already evening being come,   since it was [the]   preparation,

ὅ ἐστιν ᵃπροσάββατον, 43 ᵇἦλθεν Ἰωσὴφ ὁ ἀπὸ
that is [the day] before sabbath,   came   Joseph who [was] from

Ἀριμαθαίας, εὐσχήμων βουλευτής, ὃς καὶ αὐτὸς ἦν προσ
Arimathæa, [an] honourable counsellor,   who also himself was wait

δεχόμενος τὴν βασιλείαν τοῦ θεοῦ· τολμήσας εἰσῆλθεν πρὸς
ing for   the kingdom   of God, having boldness he went in   to

ᵈΠιλάτον καὶ ᾐτήσατο τὸ σῶμα τοῦ Ἰησοῦ. 44 ὁ.δὲ.ᵉΠιλάτος
Pilate   and begged the body   of Jesus.   And Pilate

ἐθαύμασεν εἰ ἤδη τέθνηκεν· καὶ προσκαλεσάμενος τὸν
wondered   if already he were dead; and   having called to   [him] the

κεντυρίωνα ἐπηρώτησεν αὐτὸν εἰ ᶠπάλαι ἀπέθανεν· 45 καὶ
centurion   he questioned   him   if   ¹long   he had died.   And

γνοὺς   ἀπὸ τοῦ κεντυρίωνος ἐδωρήσατο τὸ ᵍσῶμα τῷ
having known [it] from   the   centurion   he granted the   body   to

Ἰωσήφ. 46 καὶ ἀγοράσας σινδόνα, ʰκαὶ καθελὼν
Joseph.   And having bought a linen cloth,   and having taken ²down

αὐτὸν ἐνείλησεν τῇ σινδόνι, καὶ ⁱκατέθηκεν αὐτὸν ἐν
¹him   he wrapped [him] in the linen cloth, and   laid   him in

ᵏμνημείῳ, ὃ ἦν λελατομημένον ἐκ πέτρας· καὶ προσa tomb,   which was   cut   out of a rock.   and roll

εκύλισεν λίθον ἐπὶ τὴν θύραν τοῦ μνημείου. 47 ἡ.δὲ.Μαρία ἡ
ed a stone to   the   door of the tomb.   And Mary the

Μαγδαληνὴ καὶ Μαρία ˡἸωσῆ ἐθεώρουν ποῦ ᵐτίθεται.
Magdalene   and Mary [mother] of Joses   saw   where he is laid.

16 Καὶ διαγενομένου τοῦ σαββάτου, Μαρία ἡ Μαγδαληνὴ
And ³being ⁴past ¹the ²sabbath,   Mary the Magdalene

καὶ Μαρία ἡ ⁿτοῦ Ἰακώβου καὶ Σαλώμη ἠγόρασαν
and   Mary the [mother]   of James and Salome   bought

ἀρώματα, ἵνα ἐλθοῦσαι ἀλείψωσιν αὐτόν. 2 καὶ λίαν πρωῒ
aromatics,   that having come they might anoint   him.   And very early

---

37 And Jesus cried with a loud voice, and gave up the ghost. 38 And the veil of the temple was rent in twain from the top to the bottom. 39 And when the centurion, which stood over a-gainst him, saw that he so cried out, and gave up the ghost, he said, Truly this man was the Son of God. 40 There were also wo-men looking on afar off : among whom was Mary Magdalene, and Mary the mother of James the less and of Joses, and Salome; 41 (who also, when he was in Galilee, fol-lowed him, and minis-tered unto him ;) and many other women which came up with him unto Jerusalem.

42 And now when the even was come, because it was the preparation, that is, the day before the sabbath, 43 Joseph of Arimathæa, an ho-nourable counsellor, which also waited for the kingdom of God, came, and went in boldly unto Pilate, and craved the body of Je-sus. 44 And Pilate marvelled if he were already dead: and calling unto him the centurion, he asked him whether he had been any while dead. 45 And when he knew it of the centurion, he gave the body to Jo-seph. 46 And he bought fine linen, and took him down, and wrapped him in the linen, and laid him in a sepulchre which was hewn out of a rock, and rolled a stone unto the door of the sepulchre. 47 And Mary Magda-lene and Mary the mo-ther of Joses beheld where he was laid.

XVI. And when the sabbath was past, Ma-ry Magdalene, and Mary the mother of James, and Salome, had bought sweet spices, that they might come and anoint him. 2 And very early in the morning the first day of the week, they

---

ʳ ἀπ' LᵀʳA.   ˢ — κράξας T[Tr]A.   ᵗ οὗτος ὁ ἄνθρωπος LTTrA.   ᵛ — ἦν (read [was]) T[TrA].
ʷ [ἦ] Tr.   ˣ — τοῦ LTTrA.   ʸ Ἰωσῆτος LTTrA.   ᶻ — καὶ LT[Tr]   ᵃ πρὸς σάββατον LTr.
ᵇ ἐλθὼν having come LTTrAW.   ᶜ + τὸν TTr.   ᵈ Πειλάτον T.   ᵉ Πειλᾶτος ἐθαύμασεν T.
ᶠ ἤδη already LTr.   ᵍ πτῶμα corpse LTTrA.   ʰ — καὶ LTTrAW.   ⁱ ἔθηκεν LTr.   ᵏ μνήματι T
ˡ Ἰωσῆτος LTTrA.   ᵐ τέθειται he has been laid LTTrA.   ⁿ — τοῦ T[Tr].

came unto the sepulchre at the rising of the sun. 3 And they said among themselves, Who shall roll us away the stone from the door of the sepulchre? 4 And when they looked, they saw that the stone was rolled away: for it was very great. 5 And entering into the sepulchre, they saw a young man sitting on the right side, clothed in a long white garment; and they were affrighted. 6 And he saith unto them, Be not affrighted: Ye seek Jesus of Nazareth, which was crucified: he is risen; he is not here: behold the place where they laid him. 7 But go your way, tell his disciples and Peter that he goeth before you into Galilee: there shall ye see him, as he said unto you. 8 And they went out quickly, and fled from the sepulchre; for they trembled and were amazed: neither said they anything to any *man;* for they were afraid.

9 Now when *Jesus* was risen early the first *day* of the week, he appeared first to Mary Magdalene, out of whom he had cast seven devils. 10 *And* she went and told them that had been with him, as they mourned and wept. 11 And they, when they had heard that he was alive, and had been seen of her, believed not. 12 After that he appeared in another form unto two of them, as they walked, and went into the country. 13 And they went and told *it* unto the residue: neither believed they them. 14 Afterward he appeared unto the eleven as they sat at meat, and upbraided them with their unbelief and hardness of heart, because they believed not them which had seen him after he was risen. 15 And he

ᵒτῆς μιᾶς‖ σαββάτων ἔρχονται ἐπὶ τὸ ᴾμνημεῖον,‖ ἀνατεί-
on the first [day] of the week they come to the tomb, ³having
λαντος τοῦ ἡλίου. 3 καὶ ἔλεγον πρὸς ἑαυτάς, Τίς ἀποκυλίσει
⁴risen ¹the ²sun. And they said among themselves, Who will roll away
ἡμῖν τὸν λίθον ᑫἐκ‖ τῆς θύρας τοῦ μνημείου ; 4 Καὶ ἀνα-
for us the stone out of the ˙door of the tomb? ˙ And having
βλέψασαι θεωροῦσιν ὅτι ʳἀποκεκύλισται‖ ὁ λίθος˙ ἦν.γὰρ
looked up they see that has been rolled away the stone : for it was
μέγας σφόδρα. 5 καὶ ˢεἰσελθοῦσαι‖.εἰς τὸ μνημεῖον, εἶδον
²great ˙very. And having entered into the tomb, they saw
νεανίσκον καθήμενον ἐν τοῖς δεξιοῖς, περιβεβλημένον στολὴν
a young man sitting on the right, clothed with a ²robe
λευκήν˙ καὶ ἐξεθαμβήθησαν. 6 ὁ.δὲ λέγει αὐταῖς, Μὴ
¹white, and they were greatly amazed. But he says to them, ²Not
ἐκθαμβεῖσθε. Ἰησοῦν ζητεῖτε τὸν Ναζαρηνὸν τὸν ἐσταυ-
¹be amazed. ³Jesus ¹ye ²seek the Nazarene, who has been
ρωμένον˙ ἠγέρθη, οὐκ.ἔστιν ὧδε˙ ἴδε ὁ τόπος ὅπου ἔθηκαν
crucified. He is risen, he is not here ; behold the place where they laid
αὐτόν˙ 7 ᵗἀλλ᾽‖ ὑπάγετε, εἴπατε τοῖς.μαθηταῖς.αὐτοῦ καὶ τῷ
him. But go, say to his disciples and
Πέτρῳ, ὅτι προάγει ὑμᾶς εἰς τὴν Γαλιλαίαν˙ ἐκεῖ αὐτὸν
to Peter, that he goes before you into Galilee ; there him
ὄψεσθε, καθὼς εἶπεν ὑμῖν. 8 Καὶ ἐξελθοῦσαι ᵛταχὺ‖
shall ye see, as he said to you. And having gone out quickly
ἔφυγον ἀπὸ τοῦ μνημείου˙ εἶχεν ʷδὲ‖ αὐτὰς τρόμος καὶ
they fled from the tomb ; And ⁴possessed ⁵them ¹trembling ²and
ἔκστασις˙ καὶ οὐδενὶ ˣοὐδὲν‖.εἶπον, ἐφοβοῦντο.γάρ.⁵
³amazement, and to no one anything they spoke, for they were afraid.
(lit. nothing)

9 ʸᶻἈναστὰς.δὲ πρωῒ πρώτῃ σαββάτου ἐφάνη πρῶ-
Now having risen early [the] first [day] of the week he appeared first
τον Μαρίᾳ τῇ Μαγδαληνῇ, ᵃἀφ᾽‖ ἧς ἐκβεβλήκει ἑπτὰ δαιμό-
to Mary the Magdalene, from whom he had cast out seven demons.
νια. 10 ἐκείνηᵇ πορευθεῖσα ἀπήγγειλεν τοῖς μετ᾽ αὐτοῦ γε-
She having gone told [it] to those who with him had
νομένοις, πενθοῦσιν καὶ κλαίουσιν. 11 κἀκεῖνοι ἀκούσαντες
been, [who were] grieving and weeping. And they having heard
ὅτι ζῇ καὶ ἐθεάθη ὑπ᾽ αὐτῆς ἠπίστησαν. 12 Μετὰ.δὲ
that he is alive and has been seen by her disbelieved [it]. And after
ταῦτα δυσὶν ἐξ αὐτῶν περιπατοῦσιν ἐφανερώθη ἐν ἑτέρᾳ
these things to two of them as they walked he was manifested in another
μορφῇ, πορευομένοις εἰς ἀγρόν. 13 κἀκεῖνοι ἀπελθόντες ἀπ-
form, going into [the] country ; and they having gone
ήγγειλαν τοῖς λοιποῖς˙ οὐδὲ ἐκείνοις ἐπίστευσαν. 14 ῞Υστερονᶜ
told [it] to the rest ; neither them did they believe. Afterwards
ἀνακειμένοις αὐτοῖς τοῖς ἕνδεκα ἐφανερώθη, καὶ ὠνεί-
as ²reclined [³at ⁴table] ¹they to the eleven he was manifested, and re-
δισεν τὴν.ἀπιστίαν.αὐτῶν καὶ σκληροκαρδίαν, ὅτι τοῖς
proached their unbelief and hardness of heart, because ⁴those ⁵who
θεασαμένοις αὐτὸν ἐγηγερμένον ᵈ οὐκ.ἐπίστευσαν. 15 Καὶ εἶπεν
⁶had ⁷seen ⁸him ³arisen ¹they ²believed ³not. And he said
αὐτοῖς, Πορευθέντες εἰς τὸν κόσμον ἅπαντα κηρύξατε τὸ εὐαγ-
to them, Having gone into ²the ³world ¹all proclaim the glad

ᵒ μιᾷ τῶν LTr ; τῇ μιᾷ τῶν T　　ᴾ μνῆμα T.　ᑫ ἀπὸ from LTr.　ʳ ἀνακεκύλισται TTrA.
ˢ ἐλθούσαι having gone A.　ᵗ ἀλλὰ LTTrA.　ᵛ — ταχὺ GLTTrAW.　ʷ γὰρ for LTTr.
ˣ — οὐδὲν L.　ʸ + κατὰ Μάρκον according to Mark Tr ; [εὐαγγέλιον] κατὰ Μάρκον glad
tidings according to Mark A.　ᶻ — *verses 9 to 20* T[A].　ᵃ παρ᾽ LTr.　ᵇ + δὲ and (she) L.
ᵖ + δὲ and (afterwards) LTr.　ᵈ + ἐκ νεκρῶν from among.[the] dead L.

γέλιον πάσῃ τῇ κτίσει. 16 ὁ πιστεύσας καὶ βαπτισθεὶς σωθήσε-
tidings to all the creation. He that believes and is baptized shall be

ται· ὁ.δὲ ἀπιστήσας κατακριθήσεται. 17 σημεῖα.δὲ τοῖς
saved, and he that disbelieves shall be condemned. And ²signs ³those ⁶that

πιστεύσασιν ᵉταῦτα παρακολουθήσει‖. ἐν τῷ.ὀνόματί.μου δαι-
⁷believe ¹these ³shall ⁴follow : in my name de-

μόνια ἐκβαλοῦσιν· γλώσσαις λαλήσουσιν ᶠκαιναῖς·‖
mons ⸴ they shall cast out; with ²tongues ³they ⁴shall ⁵speak ¹new ;

18 ᵍὄφεις ἀροῦσιν· κἂν θανάσιμόν τι πίωσιν οὐ.μὴ
serpents they shall take up; and if ²deadly ¹anything they drink in no wise

ᶦαὐτοὺς ʰβλάψει‖ ἐπὶ ἀρρώστους χεῖρας ἐπιθήσουσιν, καὶ
them shall it injure; upon [the] infirm ⁴hands ¹they ²shall ³lay, and

καλῶς ἕξουσιν.
⁴well ¹they ²shall ³be.

19 Ὁ μὲν οὖν κύριος¹ μετὰ τὸ λαλῆσαι αὐτοῖς ᵏἀνελή-
The ²indeed ³therefore ¹Lord after speaking to them was taken

φθη‖ εἰς τὸν οὐρανόν, καὶ ἐκάθισεν ἐκ δεξιῶν τοῦ θεοῦ·
up into the heaven, and sat at [the] right hand of God.

20 ἐκεῖνοι.δὲ ἐξελθόντες ἐκήρυξαν πανταχοῦ, τοῦ κυρίου συνερ-
And they having gone forth preached everywhere, the Lord working

γοῦντος, καὶ τὸν λόγον βεβαιοῦντος διὰ τῶν ἐπακολουθούν-
with [them], and the word confirming by the ²following ³upon

των σημείων. ¹Ἀμήν.‖
[²it] ¹signs. Amen.

ᵐΤὸ κατὰ Μάρκον εὐαγγέλιον.‖
The ³according ⁴to ⁵Mark ¹glad ²tidings.

ᵃΤΟ ΚΑΤΑ ΛΟΥΚΑΝ ΑΓΙΟΝ ΕΥΑΓΓΕΛΙΟΝ.‖
THE ⁴ACCORDING ⁵TO ⁶LUKE ¹HOLY ²GLAD ³TIDINGS.

ΕΠΕΙΔΗΠΕΡ πολλοὶ ἐπεχείρησαν ἀνατάξασθαι διήγησιν
FORASMUCH AS many took in hand to draw up a narration

περὶ τῶν πεπληροφορημένων ἐν ἡμῖν πραγμά-
concerning the ²which ³have ⁴been ⁵fully ⁶believed ⁷among ⁸us ¹mat-

των, 2 καθὼς παρέδοσαν ἡμῖν οἱ ἀπ' ἀρχῆς
ters, as they delivered [them] to us, they ³from ⁴[the] ⁵beginning

αὐτόπται καὶ ὑπηρέται γενόμενοι τοῦ λόγου, 3 ἔδοξεν
⁶eye-witnesses ⁷and ⁸attendants ¹having ²been of the Word, it seemed good

κἀμοί, παρηκολουθηκότι ἄνωθεν πᾶσιν ἀκριβῶς, κα-
also to me, having been acquainted from the first with all things accurately, with

θεξῆς σοι γράψαι, κράτιστε Θεόφιλε, 4 ἵνα ἐπιγνῷς
method to thee to write, most excellent Theophilus, that thou mightest know

περὶ ὧν κατηχήθης λόγων τὴν ἀσφάλειαν.
⁶concerning ⁷which ⁸thou ⁹wast ¹⁰instructed ³of[⁴the] ⁵things ¹the ²certainty.

5 Ἐγένετο ἐν ταῖς·ἡμέραις Ἡρώδου ᵇτοῦ‖ βασιλέως τῆς
There was in the days of Herod the king

Ἰουδαίας ἱερεύς τις ὀνόματι Ζαχαρίας, ἐξ ἐφημερίας
of Judæa a ²priest ¹certain, by name Zacharias, ⸴ of [the] course

Ἀβιά· καὶ ᶜἡ.γυνὴ.αὐτοῦ‖ ἐκ τῶν θυγατέρων Ἀαρών, καὶ τὸ
of Abia, and his wife of the daughters of Aaron, and

said unto them, Go ye into all the world, and preach the gospel to every creature. 16 He that believeth and is baptized shall be saved; but he that believeth not shall be damned. 17 And these signs shall follow them that believe; In my name shall they cast out devils; they shall speak with new tongues; 18 they shall take up serpents; and if they drink any deadly thing, it shall not hurt them; they shall lay hands on the sick, and they shall recover.

19 So then after the Lord had spoken unto them, he was received up into heaven, and sat on the right hand of God. 20 And they went forth, and preached every where, the Lord working with *them*, and confirming the word with signs following. Amen.

FORASMUCH as many have taken in hand to set forth in order a declaration of those things which are most surely believed among us, 2 even as they delivered them unto us, which from the beginning were eyewitnesses, and ministers of the word; 3 it seemed good to me also, having had perfect understanding of all things from the very first, to write unto thee in order, most excellent Theophilus, 4 that thou mightest know the certainty of tho e things, wherein thou hast been instructed.

5 THERE was in the days of Herod, the king of Judæa, a certain priest named

---

ᵉ παρακολουθήσει ταῦτα L ; ἀκολουθήσει ταῦτα Tr. ᶠ — καιναῖς Tr. ᵍ + καὶ ἐν ταῖς χερσὶν and in the hands Tr. ʰ βλάψῃ should it injure GLTrAW. ᶦ + Ἰησοῦς Jesus Ltr. ᵏ ἀνελήμφθη LTrA. ¹ — Ἀμήν EGLTrAW. ᵐ — Τὸ κατὰ Μάρκον εὐαγγέλιον EGLTW ; Κατὰ Μάρκον Tr ; Εὐαγγέλιον κατὰ Μάρκον [A].

ᵃ Εὐαγγέλιον ([Εὐαγ.] A) κατὰ Λουκᾶν GLTrAW ; κατὰ Λουκᾶν T. ᵇ — τοῦ TTr[A].
ᶜ γυνὴ αὐτῷ LTTrA.

Zacharias, of the course of Abia: and his wife *was* of the daughters of Aaron, and her name *was* Elisabeth. 6 And they were both righteous before God, walking in all the commandments and ordinances of the Lord blameless. 7 And they had no child, because that Elisabeth was barren, and they both were now well stricken in years. 8 And it came to pass, that while he executed the priest's office before God in the order of his course, 9 according to the custom of the priest's office, his lot was to burn incense when he went into the temple of the Lord. 10 And the whole multitude of the people were praying without at the time of incense. 11 And there appeared unto him an angel of the Lord standing on the right side of the altar of incense. 12 And when Zacharias saw *him*, he was troubled, and fear fell upon him. 13 But the angel said unto him, Fear not, Zacharias: for thy prayer is heard; and thy wife Elisabeth shall bear thee a son, and thou shalt call his name John. 14 And thou shalt have joy and gladness; and many shall rejoice at his birth. 15 For he shall be great in the sight of the Lord, and shall drink neither wine nor strong drink; and he shall be filled with the Holy Ghost, even from his mother's womb. 16 And many of the children of Israel shall he turn to the Lord their God. 17 And he shall go before him in the spirit and power of Elias, to turn the hearts of the fathers to the children, and the disobedient to the wisdom of the just; to make ready a people prepared for the Lord. 18 And Zacharias said unto the angel, Whereby shall I know this? for I am an old man, and my wife well stricken in years. 19 And the angel answering said unto him,

ὄνομα αὐτῆς Ἐλισάβετ. 6 ἦσαν δὲ δίκαιοι ἀμφότεροι ᵈἐνώ-
her name   Elizabeth.   And they were ²just   ¹both   be-
πιον‖ τοῦ θεοῦ, πορευόμενοι ἐν πάσαις ταῖς ἐντολαῖς καὶ
fore   God,   walking   in   all   the commandments and
δικαιώμασιν τοῦ κυρίου ἄμεμπτοι. 7 καὶ οὐκ ἦν αὐτοῖς
ordinances   of the Lord   blameless.   And there was not to them
τέκνον, καθότι ᵉἡ Ἐλισάβετ ἦν‖ στεῖρα, καὶ ἀμφότεροι προ-
a child, inasmuch as   Elizabeth was   barren, and both   ad-
βεβηκότες ἐν ταῖς ἡμέραις αὐτῶν ἦσαν. 8 Ἐγένετο δὲ ἐν
vanced   in   their days   were.   And it came to pass in
τῷ ἱερατεύειν αὐτὸν ἐν τῇ τάξει τῆς ἐφημερίας αὐτοῦ ἔναντι
fulfilling his priestly service in the order ' of his course   before
τοῦ θεοῦ, 9 κατὰ τὸ ἔθος τῆς ἱερατείας, ἔλαχεν
God,   according to the custom of the priestly service, it fell to him by lot
τοῦ θυμιᾶσαι εἰσελθὼν εἰς τὸν ναὸν τοῦ κυρίου· 10 καὶ
to burn incense, having entered into the temple of the Lord.   And
πᾶν τὸ πλῆθος ᶠτοῦ λαοῦ ἦν‖ προσευχόμενον ἔξω τῇ ὥρᾳ
all the multitude of the people were   praying   without at the hour
τοῦ θυμιάματος. 11 ὤφθη δὲ αὐτῷ ἄγγελος κυρίου, ἑ-
of incense.   And appeared ⁷to ⁸him ¹an ²angel ³of [⁴the] ⁵Lord, stand-
στὼς ἐκ δεξιῶν τοῦ θυσιαστηρίου τοῦ θυμιάματος· 12 καὶ
ing at [the] right of the   altar   of incense.   and
ἐταράχθη Ζαχαρίας ἰδών, καὶ φόβος ἐπέπεσεν ἐπ᾽ αὐτόν.
⁴was ³troubled ¹Zacharias ²seeing [³him], and fear   fell   upon him.
13 Εἶπεν δὲ πρὸς αὐτὸν ὁ ἄγγελος, Μὴ φοβοῦ, Ζαχαρία·
But ³said   ⁴to   ⁵him   ²the   ¹angel,   Fear not,   Zacharias,
διότι εἰσηκούσθη ἡ δέησίς σου, καὶ ἡ γυνή σου Ἐλισάβετ γεν-
because has been heard thy supplication, and thy wife   Elizabeth shall
νήσει υἱόν σοι, καὶ καλέσεις τὸ ὄνομα αὐτοῦ ᵍἸωάννην.‖
bear   a son to thee, and thou shalt call his name   John.
14 καὶ ἔσται χαρά σοι καὶ ἀγαλλίασις, καὶ πολλοὶ ἐπὶ τῇ
And he shall be joy to thee and   exultation,   and   many   at
ʰγεννήσει‖ αὐτοῦ χαρήσονται. 15 ἔσται γὰρ μέγας ἐνώπιον
his birth   shall rejoice.   For he shall be great   before
ⁱτοῦ‖ κυρίου· καὶ οἶνον καὶ σίκερα οὐ μὴ πίῃ, καὶ
the   Lord;   and wine and strong drink in no wise shall he drink, and
πνεύματος ἁγίου πλησθήσεται ἔτι ἐκ κοιλίας μητρὸς
with [the] ²Spirit ¹Holy   he shall be filled even from [the] womb   ³mother
αὐτοῦ. 16 καὶ πολλοὺς τῶν υἱῶν Ἰσραὴλ ἐπιστρέψει ἐπὶ
¹of ²his.   And many   of the sons of Israel shall he turn to [the]
κύριον τὸν θεὸν αὐτῶν. 17 καὶ αὐτὸς προελεύσεται ἐνώπιον
Lord   their God.   And he   shall go forth   before
αὐτοῦ ἐν πνεύματι καὶ δυνάμει ᵏἨλίου,‖ ἐπιστρέψαι καρδίας
him in [the] spirit and   power of Elias,   to turn   hearts
πατέρων ἐπὶ τέκνα, καὶ ἀπειθεῖς ἐν φρονήσει δι-
of fathers to children, and [the] disobedient to [the] wisdom of [the]
καίων, ἑτοιμάσαι κυρίῳ λαὸν κατεσκευασμένον. 18 Καὶ
righteous, to make ready for [the] Lord a people   prepared.   And
εἶπεν Ζαχαρίας πρὸς τὸν ἄγγελον, Κατὰ τί γνώσομαι τοῦτο;
²said ¹Zacharias to the   angel,   By what shall I know this?
ἐγὼ γάρ εἰμι πρεσβύτης, καὶ ἡ γυνή μου προβεβηκυῖα ἐν ταῖς
for I   am an old man,   and my wife   advanced   in
ἡμέραις αὐτῆς. 19 Καὶ ἀποκριθεὶς ὁ ἄγγελος εἶπεν αὐτῷ,
her days.   And ³answering ¹the   ²angel   said   to him,

ᵈ ἐναντίον TTrA.   ᵉ ἦν ἡ (— ἡ L[Tr]) Ἐλισάβετ LTTrA.   ᶠ ἦν τοῦ λαοῦ GLTTrAW.
ᵍ Ἰωάνην Tr.   ʰ γενέσει GLTTrAW.   ⁱ — τοῦ (*read* [the]) GT[Tr]w.   ᵏ Ἠλεία T.

Ἐγώ εἰμι Γαβριὴλ ὁ παρεστηκὼς ἐνώπιον τοῦ θεοῦ· καὶ
I am Gabriel, who stand before God, and

ἀπεστάλην λαλῆσαι πρός σε, καὶ εὐαγγελίσασθαί σοι
I was sent to speak to thee, and to announce ²glad ³tidings ⁴to⁵thee

ταῦτα. 20 καὶ ἰδού, ἔσῃ σιωπῶν καὶ μὴ δυνάμενος λαλῆσαι
¹these; and lo, thou shalt be silent and not able to ⁶speak

ἄχρι ἧς.ἡμέρας γένηται ταῦτα· ἀνθ᾽.ὧν οὐκ.ἐπίστευσας
till the day in which shall take place these things, because thou didst not believe

τοῖς.λόγοις.μου, οἵτινες πληρωθήσονται εἰς τὸν.καιρὸν.αὐτῶν.
my words, which shall be fulfilled in their season.

21 Καὶ ἦν ὁ λαὸς προσδοκῶν τὸν Ζαχαρίαν· καὶ ἐθαύμαζον ἐν
And ³were ¹the ²people expecting Zacharias, and they wondered at

τῷ.χρονίζειν.αὐτὸν ἐν τῷ ναῷ. 22 ἐξελθὼν.δὲ .οὐκ.¹ἠδύνατο‖
his delaying in the temple. But having come out he was not able

λαλῆσαι αὐτοῖς· καὶ ἐπέγνωσαν ὅτι ὀπτασίαν ἑώρακεν ἐν
to speak to them, and they recognized that a vision he has seen - in

τῷ ναῷ· καὶ αὐτὸς ἦν .διανεύων αὐτοῖς, καὶ διέμενεν κωφός.
the temple. And he was making signs to them, and continued dumb.

23 καὶ ἐγένετο ὡς ἐπλήσθησαν αἱ ἡμέραι τῆς λειτουργίας
And it came to pass, when were fulfilled the days ³service

αὐτοῦ ἀπῆλθεν εἰς τὸν.οἶκον.αὐτοῦ.
¹of ²his he departed to his house.

24 Μετὰ.δὲ ταύτας τὰς ἡμέρας συνέλαβεν Ἐλισάβετ ἡ
Now after these days ⁴conceived ¹Elizabeth

γυνὴ.αὐτοῦ, καὶ περιέκρυβεν ἑαυτὴν μῆνας πέντε, λέγουσα,
²his ³wife, and hid herself ²months ¹five, saying,

25 Ὅτι.οὕτως μοι πεποίηκεν ᵐᵒ κύριος ἐν ἡμέραις αἷς
Thus, to me has done the Lord in [the] days in which

ἐπεῖδεν ἀφελεῖν ⁿτὸ‖.ὄνειδός.μου᾽ ἐν ἀνθρώποις.
he looked upon [me] to take away my reproach among men.

26 Ἐν.δὲ τῷ μηνὶ τῷ ἕκτῳ ἀπεστάλη ὁ ἄγγελος Γαβριὴλ
And in the month the sixth was sent the angel Gabriel .

ᵒ ὑπὸ‖ τοῦ θεοῦ εἰς πόλιν τῆς Γαλιλαίας, ᾗ ὄνομα ᴾΝα-
by God to a city of Galilee, whose name [was] Na-

ζαρέτ,‖ 27 πρὸς παρθένον �q μεμνηστευμένην‖ ἀνδρὶ ᾧ ὄνομα
zareth, to a virgin betrothed to a man whose name

Ἰωσήφ, ἐξ οἴκου ʳΔαβίδ·‖ καὶ τὸ ὄνομα τῆς παρθένου
[was] Joseph, of [the] house of David, and the name of the virgin

Μαριάμ. 28 καὶ εἰσελθὼν ˢὁ ἄγγελος‖ πρὸς αὐτὴν ᵗ εἶπεν,
[was] Mary. And ²coming ¹the ²angel to .her said,

Χαῖρε, κεχαριτωμένη· ὁ κύριος μετὰ σοῦ, ᵛεὐλογημένη
Hail, [thou] favoured one! the Lord [is] with thee, blessed [art]

σὺ ἐν γυναιξίν.‖ 29 Ἡ.δὲ ʷἰδοῦσα‖ ˣδιεταράχθη ἐπὶ
thou amongst women. But she seeing [him] was troubled at

τῷ.λόγῳ.αὐτοῦ,‖ καὶ διελογίζετο ποταπὸς εἴη ὁ ἀσπασμὸς
his word, and was reasoning of what kind might be ²salutation

οὗτος. 30 Καὶ ᵗεἶπεν ὁ ἄγγελος αὐτῇ, Μὴ.φοβοῦ, Μαριάμ·
¹this. And ³said ¹the ²angel to her, Fear not, Mary,

εὗρες.γὰρ χάριν παρὰ τῷ θεῷ· 31 καὶ ἰδού, ʸσυλλήψῃ‖
for thou hast found favour with God; and lo, thou shalt conceive

ἐν γαστρὶ καὶ τέξῃ υἱόν, καὶ καλέσεις τὸ.ὄνομα.αὐτοῦ
in [thy] womb and bring forth a son, and thou shalt call his name

I am Gabriel, that stand in the presence of God; and am sent to speak unto thee, and to shew thee these glad tidings. 20 And, behold, thou shalt be dumb, and not able to speak, until the day that these things shall be performed, because thou believest not my words, which shall be fulfilled in their season. 21 And the people waited for Zacharias, and marvelled that he tarried so long in the temple. 22 And when he came out, he could not speak unto them: and they perceived that he had seen a vision in the temple: for he beckoned unto them, and remained speechless. 23 And it came to pass, that, as soon as the days of his ministration were accomplished, he departed to his own house.

24 And after those days his wife Elisabeth conceived, and hid herself five months, saying, 25 Thus hath the Lord dealt with me in the days wherein he looked on me, to take away my reproach among men.

26 And in the sixth month the angel Gabriel was sent from God unto a city of Galilee, named Nazareth, 27 to a virgin espoused to a man whose name was Joseph, of the house of David; and the virgin's name was Mary. 28 And the angel came in unto her, and said, Hail, thou that art highly favoured, the Lord is with thee: blessed art thou among women. 29 And when she saw him, she was troubled at his saying, and cast in her mind what manner of salutation this should be. 30 And the angel said unto her, Fear not, Mary: for thou hast found favour with God. 31 And, behold, thou shalt conceive in thy womb, and bring forth a son, and shalt call his name

---

¹ ἐδύνατο LTTrA. ᵐ — ὁ (read [the]) LTTrA. ⁿ — τὸ Tr[A]. ᵒ ἀπὸ from TTrA.
ᴾ Ναζαρέθ LTW. q ἐμνηστευμένην LTTr. ʳ Δαυείδ LTTrA; Δαυίδ GW. ˢ — ὁ ἄγγελος
T[Tr]A. ᵗ + ὁ ἄγγελος the angel T. ᵛ — εὐλογημένη σὺ ἐν γυναιξίν T[Tr]A. ʷ — ἰδοῦσα
GTTrA. ˣ ἐπὶ τῷ λόγῳ διεταράχθη GTTrA. ʸ συλλήμψῃ LTTrA.

JESUS. 32 He shall be great, and shall be called the Son of the Highest: and the Lord God shall give unto him the throne of his father David : 33 and he shall reign over the house of Jacob for ever ; and of his kingdom there shall be no end. 34 Then said Mary unto the angel, How shall this be, seeing I know not a man ? 35 And the angel answered and said unto her, The Holy Ghost shall come upon thee, and the power of the Highest shall overshadow thee: therefore also that holy thing which shall be born of thee shall be called the Son of God. 36 And, behold, thy cousin Elisabeth, she hath also conceived a son in her old age: and this is the sixth month with her, who was called barren. 37 For with God nothing shall be impossible. 38 And Mary said, Behold the handmaid of the Lord ; be it unto me according to thy word. And the angel departed from her.

'Ιησοῦν. 32 οὗτος ἔσται μέγας, καὶ·υἰὸς ὑψίστου κληθήσε-
Jesus.   He shall be great,   and Son of [the] Highest shall he be
ται· καὶ δώσει αὐτῷ κύριος ὁ θεὸς τὸν θρόνον ᶻΔαβὶδ‖
called ; and ⁴shall ⁵give ⁶him [¹the] ²Lord   ³God the throne of David
τοῦ.πατρὸς.αὐτοῦ, 33 καὶ βασιλεύσει ἐπὶ τὸν οἶκον 'Ιακὼβ εἰς
   his father ;   and he shall reign over the house of Jacob to
τοὺς αἰῶνας, καὶ τῆς.βασιλείας.αὐτοῦ οὐκ.ἔσται τέλος.
the   ages,   and   of his kingdom   there shall not be an end.
34 Εἶπεν.δὲ Μαριὰμ πρὸς τὸν ἄγγελον, Πῶς ἔσται τοῦτο ἐπεὶ
But ²said ¹Mary   to   the   angel,   How shall ²be ¹this since
ἄνδρα οὐ.γινώσκω ; 35 Καὶ ἀποκριθεὶς ὁ ἄγγελος εἶπεν αὐτῇ,
a man   I know not?   And answering the angel   said to her,
Πνεῦμα ἅγιον ἐπελεύσεται ἐπὶ σέ, καὶ δύναμις ὑψίστου
[The] ²Spirit ¹Holy   shall come upon thee, and power of [the] Highest
ἐπισκιάσει σοι· διὸ καὶ τὸ γεννώμενονᵃ ἅγιον κληθή-
shall overshadow thee ; wherefore also the ³born   ¹holy ²thing shall be
σεται υἰὸς θεοῦ. 36 καὶ ἰδού, 'Ελισάβετ ἡ.ᵇσυγγενής‖.σου καὶ
called Son of God.   And lo,   Elizabeth   thy kinswoman ²also
αὐτὴ ᶜσυνειληφυῖα‖ υἱὸν ἐν ᵈγήρᾳ‖.αὐτῆς· καὶ οὗτος μὴν
¹she   has conceived a son in   her old age,   and· this [the] ²month
ἕκτος ἐστὶν αὐτῇ τῇ καλουμένῃ στείρᾳ· 37 ὅτι οὐκ ἀδυνα-
¹sixth   is   to her who [was] called   barren ;   for not ²shall ³be
τήσει παρὰ ᵉτῷ θεῷ‖ πᾶν ῥῆμα. 38 Εἶπεν.δὲ Μαριάμ,
⁵impossible ⁶with   ⁷God   ¹any ²thing.   And ²said ¹Mary,
(lit. every)
'Ιδού, ἡ δούλη κυρίου· γένοιτό μοι κατὰ τὸ.ῥῆμά.σου.
Behold, the bondmaid of [the] Lord ; ᵥ be it to me according to thy word.
Καὶ ἀπῆλθεν ἀπ' αὐτῆς ὁ ἄγγελος.
And   departed from her the angel.

39 And Mary arose in those days, and went into the hill country with haste, into a city of Juda ; 40 and entered into the house of Zacharias, and saluted Elisabeth. 41 And it came to pass, that, when Elisabeth heard the salutation of Mary, the babe leaped in her womb ; and Elisabeth was filled with the Holy Ghost : 42 and she spake out with a loud voice, and said, Blessed art thou among women, and blessed is the fruit of thy womb. 43 But whence is this to me, that the mother of my Lord should come to me ? 44 For, lo, as soon as the voice of thy salutation sounded in mine ears, the babe leaped in my womb for joy. 45 And blessed is she that believed : for there shall be a performance of those things which were told her from the Lord.

39 'Αναστᾶσα.δὲ Μαριὰμ ἐν ταῖς.ἡμέραις.ταύταις ἐπορεύθη
And ²rising ³up ¹Mary in   those days   went
εἰς τὴν ὀρεινὴν μετὰ σπουδῆς, εἰς πόλιν 'Ιούδα, 40 καὶ
into the hill-country with   haste,   to   a city of Judah,   and
εἰσῆλθεν εἰς τὸν οἶκον Ζαχαρίου καὶ ἠσπάσατο τὴν 'Ελισάβετ.
entered into the house of Zacharias and saluted   Elizabeth.
41 καὶ ἐγένετο ὡς ἤκουσεν ᶠἡ 'Ελισάβετ τὸν ἀσπασμὸν τῆς
   And it came to pass as ²heard   ¹Elizabeth the salutation
Μαρίας,‖ ἐσκίρτησεν τὸ βρέφος ἐν τῇ.κοιλίᾳ.αὐτῆς· καὶ ἐπλήσθη
of Mary, ³leaped ¹the ²babe in her womb ;   and ²was ³filled
πνεύματος ἁγίου ἡ 'Ελισάβετ, 42 καὶ ἀνεφώνησεν ᵍφωνῇ‖
⁴with [⁵the] ⁷Spirit ⁶Holy   ¹Elizabeth,   and   cried out with a ²voice
μεγάλῃ καὶ εἶπεν, Εὐλογημένη σὺ ἐν γυναιξίν, καὶ εὐλο-
¹loud   and said,   Blessed [art] thou among women,   and bless-
γημένος ὁ.καρπὸς τῆς.κοιλίας.σου. 43 καὶ πόθεν μοι τοῦτο,
ed   the fruit   of thy womb.   And whence to me this,
ἵνα ἔλθῃ ἡ μήτηρ τοῦ.κυρίου.μου πρός ʰμε‖ ; 44 ἰδοὺ.γάρ,
that should come the mother   of my Lord   to   me ?   For lo,
ὡς ἐγένετο ἡ φωνὴ τοῦ.ἀσπασμοῦ.σου εἰς τὰ.ὦτά.μου ἐσκίρ-
as   came the voice   of thy salutation into mine ears,   leap-
τησεν ⁱἐν ἀγαλλιάσει τὸ βρέφος‖ ἐν τῇ.κοιλίᾳ.μου. 45 καὶ
ed   in   exultation the babe ·in   my womb ;   and
μακαρία ἡ πιστεύσασα, ὅτι ἔσται τελείωσις τοῖς
blessed [is] she who· believed,   for there shall be a fulfilment to the things
λελαλημένοις αὐτῇ παρὰ κυρίου
spoken   to her from [the] Lord.

ᶻ Δανείδ LTTrA ; Δαυίδ GW.   ᵃ + [ἐκ σοῦ] of thee L.   ᵇ συγγενίς LTW.   ᶜ συνειλη-
φεν Tr.   ᵈ γήρει GLTTrAW.   ᵉ τοῦ θ.οῦ TTrA.   ᶠ τὸν ἀσπασμὸν τῆς Μαρίας ἡ 'Ελισάβετ
LTTrA.   ᵍ κραυγῇ with a ²cry TTrA.   ʰ ἐμέ T.   ⁱ τὸ βρέφος ἐν ἀγαλλιάσει GW.

46 Καὶ εἶπεν Μαριάμ, Μεγαλύνει ἡ.ψυχή.μου τὸν κύριον,
And said Mary, ³Magnifies ¹my ²soul the Lord,

47 καὶ ἠγαλλίασεν τὸ.πνεῦμά.μου ἐπὶ τῷ θεῷ τῷ.σωτῆρί.μου·
and ³exulted ¹my ²spirit in God my Saviour.

48 ὅτι ἐπέβλεψεν ἐπὶ τὴν ταπείνωσιν τῆς.δούλης.αὐτοῦ· ἰδοὺ
For he looked upon the humiliation of his bondmaid ; ²lo

γάρ, ἀπὸ τοῦ.νῦν μακαριοῦσίν.με πᾶσαι αἱ γενεαί. 49 ὅτι
¹for, from henceforth ³will ⁴count ⁵me ⁶blessed ¹all ²generations. For

ἐποίησέν μοι ᵏμεγαλεῖα‖ ὁ δυνατός, καὶ ἅγιον τὸ ὄνομα
⁸has ⁵done ⁶to ⁷me ⁸great ⁹things ¹the ²mighty ³one, and holy [is] ²name

αὐτοῦ· 50 καὶ τὸ.ἔλεος.αὐτοῦ εἰς γενεὰς ¹γενεῶν‖ τοῖς
¹his ; and his mercy [is] to generations of generations to those

φοβουμένοις αὐτόν. 51 ἐποίησεν κράτος ἐν βραχίονι.αὐτοῦ·
fearing him. He wrought strength with his arm,

διεσκόρπισεν ὑπερηφάνους διανοίᾳ καρδίας.αὐτῶν.
he scattered [the] haughty in [the] thought of their heart.

52 καθεῖλεν δυνάστας ἀπὸ θρόνων, καὶ ὕψωσεν ταπεινούς.
He put down rulers from thrones, and exalted [the] lowly :

53 πεινῶντας ἐνέπλησεν ἀγαθῶν, καὶ πλουτοῦντας
[the] hungry he filled with good things, and [the] rich

ἐξαπέστειλεν κενούς. 54 ἀντελάβετο Ἰσραὴλ παιδὸς αὐτοῦ,
he sent away empty. He helped Israel ²servant ¹his,

μνησθῆναι ἐλέους, 55 καθὼς ἐλάλησεν πρὸς τοὺς
[in order] to remember mercy, according as he spoke to

πατέρας.ἡμῶν, τῷ Ἀβραὰμ καὶ τῷ.σπέρματι.αὐτοῦ ᵐεἰς τὸν
our fathers, to Abraham and to his seed for

αἰῶνα.‖ 56 Ἔμεινεν.δὲ Μαριὰμ σὺν αὐτῇ ⁿὡσεὶ‖ μῆνας τρεῖς,
ever. And ²abode ¹Mary with her about ²months ¹three,

καὶ ὑπέστρεψεν εἰς τὸν.οἶκον.αὐτῆς.
and returned to her house.

57 Τῇ.δὲ.Ἐλισάβετ ἐπλήσθη ὁ χρόνος τοῦ.τεκεῖν.αὐτήν,
Now to Elizabeth was fulfilled the time that she should bring forth,

καὶ ἐγέννησεν υἱόν· 58 καὶ ἤκουσαν οἱ περίοικοι καὶ οἱ συγ-
and she bore a son. And ³heard ¹the ²neighbours and ²kins-

γενεῖς αὐτῆς ὅτι ἐμεγάλυνεν κύριος τὸ.ἔλεος.αὐτοῦ μετ'
folk ¹her that ³was ⁴magnifying [¹the] ²Lord his mercy with

αὐτῆς, καὶ συνέχαιρον αὐτῇ. 59 Καὶ ἐγένετο ἐν τῇ ᵒὀγδόῃ
her, and they rejoiced with her. And it came to pass on the eighth

ἡμέρᾳ‖ ἦλθον περιτεμεῖν τὸ παιδίον· καὶ ἐκάλουν αὐτὸ
day they came to circumcise the little child, and were calling it

ἐπὶ τῷ ὀνόματι τοῦ.πατρὸς.αὐτοῦ Ζαχαρίαν. 60 καὶ ἀπο-
after the name of his father Zacharias. And ³an-

κριθεῖσα ἡ.μήτηρ.αὐτοῦ εἶπεν, Οὐχί, ἀλλὰ κληθήσεται ᴾἸωάν-
swering ¹his ²mother said, No; but he shall be called John.

νης.‖ 61 Καὶ ᑫεἶπον‖ πρὸς αὐτήν, Ὅτι οὐδείς ἐστιν ʳἐν τῇ
And they said to her, No one is among the

συγγενείᾳ‖ σου ὃς καλεῖται τῷ.ὀνόματι.τούτῳ. 62 Ἐνένευον
kinsfolk of thee who is called by this name. ²They ³made ⁴signs

δὲ τῷ.πατρὶ.αὐτοῦ τὸ.τί ἂν.θέλοι καλεῖσθαι ˢαὐτόν.‖
¹and to his father [as to] what he might wish ²to ³be ⁴called ¹him.

63 καὶ αἰτήσας πινακίδιον ἔγραψεν, λέγων, ᴾἸωάννης‖
And having asked for a writing tablet he wrote, saying, John

ἐστὶν ᵗτὸ‖.ὄνομα.αὐτοῦ· καὶ ἐθαύμασαν πάντες. 64 Ἀνεῴχθη.δὲ
is his name. And they ²wondered ¹all. And was opened

46 And Mary said, My soul doth magnify the Lord, 47 and my spirit hath rejoiced in God my Saviour. 48 For he hath regarded the low estate of his handmaiden : for, behold, from henceforth all generations shall call me blessed. 49 For he that is mighty hath done to me great things ; and holy is his name. 50 And his mercy is on them that fear him from generation to generation. 51 He hath shewed strength with his arm; he hath scattered the proud in the imagination of their hearts. 52 He hath put down the mighty from their seats, and exalted them of low degree. 53 He hath filled the hungry with good things ; and the rich he hath sent empty away. 54 He hath holpen his servant Israel, in remembrance of his mercy ; 55 as he spake to our fathers, to Abraham, and to his seed for ever. 56 And Mary abode with her about three months, and returned to her own house.

57 Now Elisabeth's full time came that she should be delivered ; and she brought forth a son. 58 And her neighbours and her cousins heard how the Lord had shewed great mercy upon her ; and they rejoiced with her. 59 And it came to pass, that on the eighth day they came to circumcise the child ; and they called him Zacharias, after the name of his father. 60 And his mother answered and said, Not so; but he shall be called John. 61 And they said unto her, There is none of thy kindred that is called by this name. 62 And they made signs to his father, how he would have him called. 63 And he asked for a writing table, and wrote, saying, His name is John. And they marvelled all. 64 And his mouth was opened immediately,

---

ᵏ μεγάλα LTTr.   ˡ καὶ γενεὰς and generations TTrA.   ᵐ ἕως αἰῶνος G.   ⁿ ὡς LTTr.
ᵒ ἡμέρᾳ τῇ ὀγδόῃ LTTrA.   ᴾ Ἰωάνης Tr.   ᑫ εἶπαν TTr.   ʳ ἐκ τῆς συγγενείας from among
the kinsfolk LTTrA.   ˢ αὐτό it LTTrA.   ᵗ — τὸ Tr[A].

and his tongue *loosed*, and he spake, and praised God. 65 And fear came on all that dwelt round about them: and all these sayings were noised abroad throughout all the hill country of Judæa. 66 And all they that heard *them* laid *them* up in their hearts, saying, What manner of child shall this be ! And the hand of the Lord was with him.

τὸ.στόμα.αὐτοῦ παραχρῆμα καὶ ἡ.γλῶσσα.αὐτοῦ, καὶ
his mouth immediately and his tongue [loosed], and
ἐλάλει εὐλογῶν τὸν θεόν. 65 Καὶ ἐγένετο ἐπὶ πάντας φόβος
he spoke, blessing God. And ²came ³upon ⁴all ¹fear
τοὺς περιοικοῦντας αὐτούς· καὶ ἐν ²ὅλῃ τῇ ὀρεινῇ τῆς
those who dwelt around them; and in ²whole ¹the hill-country
Ἰουδαίας διελαλεῖτο πάντα τὰ.ῥήματα.ταῦτα· 66 καὶ
of Judæa ⁴were ⁵being ⁶talked ⁷of· ¹all ²these ³things. And
ἔθεντο πάντες οἱ ἀκούσαντες ἐν τῇ.καρδίᾳ.αὐτῶν, λέ-
⁴laid [²them] ⁶up ¹all ²who ³heard ·in their heart, say-
γοντες, Τί ἄρα τὸ.παιδίον.τοῦτο ἔσται; Καὶ ʷ χεὶρ
ing, What then ³this ⁴little ⁵child ¹will ²be? And [the] hand
κυρίου ἦν μετ᾽ αὐτοῦ.
of [the] Lord was with him.

67 And his father Zacharias was filled with the Holy Ghost, and prophesied, saying, 68 Blessed *be* the Lord God of Israel; for he hath visited and redeemed his people, 69 and hath rai-ed up an horn of salvation for us in the house of his servant David; 70 as he spake by the mouth of his holy prophets, which have been since the world began : 71 that we should be saved from our enemies, and from the hand of all that hate us ; 72 to perform the mercy *promised* to our fathers, and to remember his holy covenant ; 73 the oath which he sware to our father Abraham, 74 that he would grant unto us, that we being delivered out of the hand of our enemies might serve him without fear, 75 in holiness and righteousness before him, all the days of our life. 76 And thou, child, shalt be called the prophet of the Highest : for thou shalt go before the face of the Lord to prepare his ways ; 77 to give knowledge of salvation unto his people by the remission of their sins, 78 through the tender mercy of our God ; whereby the dayspring from on high hath visited us, 79 to give light to them that sit in darkness and *in* the shadow of death, to guide our feet

67 Καὶ Ζαχαρίας ὁ.πατὴρ.αὐτοῦ ἐπλήσθη πνεύματος
And Zacharias his father was filled ⁻with [the] ²Spirit
ἁγίου, καὶ ˣπροεφήτευσεν,‖ λέγων, 68 Εὐλογητὸς κύριος ὁ
¹Holy, and prophesied, saying, Blessed be [the] Lord the
θεὸς τοῦ Ἰσραήλ, ὅτι ἐπεσκέψατο καὶ ἐποίησεν λύτρωσιν
God of Israel, because he looked upon and wrought redemption
τῷ.λαῷ.αὐτοῦ· 69 καὶ ἤγειρεν κέρας σωτηρίας ἡμῖν ἐν ʸτῷ
for his people, and raised up a horn of salvation for us in the
οἴκῳ ˣΔαβὶδ‖ ᵃτοῦ‖.παιδὸς.αὐτοῦ· 70 καθὼς ἐλάλησεν διὰ
house of David his servant; according as he spoke by [the]
στόματος τῶν ἁγίων ᵇτῶν‖.ἀπ᾽.αἰῶνος προφητῶν αὐτοῦ·
mouth ³holy ⁵since ⁶time ⁷began ⁴prophets ¹of ²his ;
71 σωτηρίαν ἐξ ἐχθρῶν.ἡμῶν καὶ ἐκ χειρὸς πάντων
salvation from our enemies and from [the] hand of all
τῶν μισούντων ἡμᾶς· 72 ποιῆσαι ἔλεος μετὰ τῶν πατέρων
those who hate us; to fulfil mercy with ²fathers
ἡμῶν, καὶ μνησθῆναι διαθήκης ἁγίας αὐτοῦ, 73 ὅρκον ὃν
¹our, and to remember ³covenant ²holy ¹his, [the] oath which
ὤμοσεν πρὸς Ἀβραὰμ τὸν.πατέρα.ἡμῶν, τοῦ δοῦναι ἡμῖν
he sware to Abraham our father, to give us [that]
74 ἀφόβως ἐκ χειρὸς ᶜτῶν‖.ἐχθρῶν.ᵈἡμῶν‖ ῥυσθέντας,
without fear out of [the] hand of our enemies being saved,
λατρεύειν αὐτῷ 75 ἐν ὁσιότητι καὶ δικαιοσύνῃ ἐνώπιον αὐτοῦ
we should serve him in holiness and righteousness before him,
πάσας τὰς ἡμέρας ᵉτῆς.ζωῆς‖.ἡμῶν. 76 Καὶ σύ ᶠ, παιδίον,
all the days of our life. And thou, little child,
προφήτης ὑψίστου κληθήσῃ· προπορεύσῃ.γὰρ πρὸ
prophet of [the] Highest shalt be called ; for thou shalt go before [the]
προσώπου κυρίου ἑτοιμάσαι ὁδοὺς.αὐτοῦ· 77 τοῦ δοῦναι
·face of [the] Lord to prepare his ways ; to give
γνῶσιν σωτηρίας τῷ.λαῷ.αὐτοῦ ἐν ἀφέσει ἁμαρτιῶν.αὐτῶν,
knowledge of salvation to his people in remission of their sins,
78 διὰ σπλάγχνα ἐλέους θεοῦ.ἡμῶν, ἐν οἷς ἐπεσκέψατο
through [the] ·bowels of compassion of our God, in which has visited
ἡμᾶς ἀνατολὴ ἐξ ὕψους, 79 ἐπιφᾶναι τοῖς ἐν ·σκότει
us [the] day-spring from on high, to shine upon those ²in ³darkness
καὶ σκιᾷ θανάτου καθημένοις· τοῦ κατευθῦναι τοὺς
⁴and ⁵in [⁶the] ⁷shadow ⁸of ⁹death ¹sitting ; to direct

ʷ + γὰρ (*read* For also) LTTrA.   ˣ ἐπροφήτευσεν LTTrA.   ʸ — τῷ (*read* [the]) LTTrA.
ᶻ Δαυείδ LTTrA ; Δαυὶδ GW.   ᵃ — τοῦ LTTrA.   ᵇ — τῶν TTrA.   ᶜ — τῶν LTTrA.
ᵈ — ἡμῶν (*read* of [our] enemies) [L]TTrA.   ᵉ — τῆς ζωῆς (*read* all our days) GLTTrAW;
ᶠ + δὲ also TTrA.

πόδας.ἡμῶν εἰς ὁδὸν εἰρήνης. 80 Τὸ.δὲ παιδίον ηὔξανεν
our feet into [the] way of peace. And the little child grew

καὶ ἐκραταιοῦτο πνεύματι· καὶ ἦν ἐν ταῖς ἐρήμοις ἕως
and was strengthened in spirit; and he was in the deserts until [the]

ἡμέρας ἀναδείξεως.αὐτοῦ πρὸς τὸν Ἰσραήλ.
day of his shewing to Israel.

2 Ἐγένετο.δὲ ἐν ταῖς.ἡμέραις.ἐκείναις ἐξῆλθεν δόγμα
And it came to pass in those days ³went ⁴out ¹a ²decree

παρὰ Καίσαρος Αὐγούστου, ἀπογράφεσθαι πᾶσαν τὴν
from Cæsar Augustus, that should be registered all the

οἰκουμένην· 2 αὕτη.ᵍἡ.ἀπογραφὴ ʰπρώτη ἐγένετο" ἡγε-
habitable world; this registration first took place when

μονεύοντος τῆς Συρίας ⁱΚυρηνίου." 3 καὶ ἐπορεύοντο πάντες
²was ³governor ⁴of ⁵Syria ¹Cyrenius. And ²went ¹all

ἀπογράφεσθαι, ἕκαστος εἰς τὴν.ᵏἰδίαν".πόλιν. 4 Ἀνέβη.δὲ καὶ
to be registered, each to his own city : and ³went ⁴up ²also

Ἰωσὴφ ἀπὸ τῆς Γαλιλαίας ἐκ πόλεως ¹Ναζαρὲτ" εἰς τὴν
¹Joseph from Galilee out of [the] city Nazareth to

Ἰουδαίαν, εἰς πόλιν ᵐΔαβὶδ" ἥτις καλεῖται Βηθλεέμ, διὰ
Judæa, to a city of David which is called Bethlehem, because

τὸ.εἶναι.αὐτὸν ἐξ οἴκου. καὶ πατριᾶς ᵐΔαβίδ," 5 ⁿἀπο-
of his being . of [the] house and family of David, to re-

γράψασθαι" σὺν Μαριὰμ τῇ ᵒμεμνηστευμένῃ" αὐτῷ ᴾγυναικί,"
gister himself with Mary who was betrothed to him as wife,

οὔσῃ ἐγκύῳ. 6 Ἐγένετο.δὲ ἐν τῷ εἶναι.αὐτοὺς
she being great with child. And it came to pass in the [time] they were

ἐκεῖ ἐπλήσθησαν αἱ ἡμέραι τοῦ.τεκεῖν.αὐτήν· 7 καὶ ἔτε-
there ³were ⁴fulfilled ¹the ²days for her bringing forth, and she brought

κεν τὸν.υἱὸν.αὐτῆς τὸν πρωτότοκον, καὶ ἐσπαργάνωσεν
forth her son the first-born, and wrapped ²in ³swaddling ⁴clothes

αὐτόν, καὶ ἀνέκλινεν αὐτὸν ἐν ᑫτῇ" φάτνῃ, διότι οὐκ.ἦν
¹him, and laid him in the manger, because there was not

αὐτοῖς τόπος ἐν τῷ καταλύματι.
for them a place in the inn.

8 Καὶ ποιμένες ἦσαν ἐν τῇ χώρᾳ τῇ αὐτῇ, ἀγραυλοῦντες
And shepherds were in the ²country ¹same, lodging in the fields

καὶ φυλάσσοντες φυλακὰς τῆς νυκτὸς ἐπὶ τὴν.ποίμνην.αὐτῶν.
and keeping watch by night over their flock;

9 καὶ ʳἰδού," ἄγγελος κυρίου ἐπέστη αὐτοῖς, καὶ δόξα
and behold, an angel of [the] Lord stood by them, and [the] glory

κυρίου περιέλαμψεν αὐτούς· καὶ ἐφοβήθησαν φόβον
of [the] Lord shone around them, and they feared [with] ²fear

μέγαν. 10 καὶ εἶπεν αὐτοῖς ὁ ἄγγελος, Μὴ.φοβεῖσθε· ἰδοὺ
¹great. And ³said ⁴to ⁵them ¹the ²angel, Fear not; ²behold

γάρ, εὐαγγελίζομαι ὑμῖν χαρὰν μεγάλην, ἥτις ἔσται
³for, I announce glad tidings to you [of] ²joy ¹great, which shall be

παντὶ τῷ λαῷ· 11 ὅτι ἐτέχθη ὑμῖν σήμερον σωτήρ, ὅς ἐστιν
to all the people; for was born to you to-day a Saviour, who is

χριστὸς κύριος, ἐν πόλει ˢΔαβίδ." 12 καὶ τοῦτο ὑμῖν
Christ [the] Lord, in [the] city of David. And this [is] to you

τὸ σημεῖον· εὑρήσετε βρέφος ἐσπαργανωμένον, ᵗᵛκεί-
the sign : ye shall find a babe wrapped in swaddling clothes, ly-

---

into the way of peace.
80 And the child grew,
and waxed strong in
spirit, and was in the
deserts till the day of
his shewing unto Is-
rael.

II. And it came to
pass in those days, that
there went out a de-
cree from Cæsar Au-
gustus, that all the
world should be taxed.
2 (And this taxing was
first made when Cyre-
nius was governor of
Syria.) 3 And all went
to be taxed, every one
into his own city.
4 And Joseph also went
up from Galilee, out
of the city of Naza-
reth, into Judæa, unto
the city of David,
which is called Beth-
lehem; (because he
was of the house and
lineage of David :)
5 to be taxed with
Mary his espoused
wife, being great with
child. 6 And so it was,
that, while they were
there. the days were
accomplished that she
should be delivered.
7 And she brought
forth her firstborn son,
and wrapped him in
swaddling clothes, and
laid him in a manger;
because there was no
room for them in the
inn.

8 And there were in
the same country shep-
herds abiding in the
field, keeping watch
over their flock by
night. 9 And, lo, the
angel of the Lord came
upon them, and the
glory of the Lord shone
round about them :
and they were sore a-
fraid. 10 And the an-
gel said unto them,
Fear not : for, behold,
I bring you good ti-
dings of great joy,
which shall be to all
people. 11 For unto
you is born this day
in the city of David
a Saviour, which is
Christ the Lord. 12 And
this shall be a sign un-
to you; Ye shall find
the babe wrapped in
swaddling clothes,
lying in a manger.

ᵍ — ἡ LTTrA. ʰ ἐγένετο πρώτη T. ⁱ Κυρίνου Cyrenus L. ᵏ ἑαυτοῦ (read his city) LTTrₐ.
¹ Ναζαρὰθ L ; Ναζαρὲθ TW. ᵐ Δαυείδ LTTrA ; Δαυὶδ GW. ⁿ ἀπογράφεσθαι Lₐ
ᵒ ἐμνηστευμένῃ LTTrA. ᴾ — γυναικί LTTrₐ. ᑫ — τῇ (read a manger) LTTrA. ʳ — ἰδού
ᵀ[T.A] ˢ Δαυείδ LTTrA ; Δαυὶδ GW. ᵗ + καὶ and [LTTrA] ᵛ — κείμενον L.

11

13 And suddenly there was with the angel a multitude of the heavenly host praising God, and saying, 14 Glory to God in the highest, and on earth peace, good will toward men. 15 And it came to pass, as the angels were gone away from them into heaven, the shepherds said one to another, Let us now go even unto Bethlehem, and see this thing which is come to pass, which the Lord hath made known unto us. 16 And they came with haste, and found Mary, and Joseph, and the babe lying in a manger. 17 And when they had seen it, they made known abroad the saying which was told them concerning this child. 18 And all they that heard it wondered at those things which were told them by the shepherds. 19 But Mary kept all these things, and pondered them in her heart. 20 And the shepherds returned, glorifying and praising God for all the things that they had heard and seen, as it was told unto them.

μενον‖ ἐν ᵂτῇ‖ φάτνῃ. 13 Καὶ ἐξαίφνης ἐγένετο σὺν τῷ
ing   in   the manger.   And suddenly   there was with the

ἀγγέλῳ πλῆθος στρατιᾶς ˣοὐρανίου,‖ αἰνούντων τὸν θεόν,
angel a multitude of [the] ²host ¹heavenly,   praising   God,

καὶ λεγόντων, 14 Δόξα ἐν ὑψίστοις θεῷ, καὶ ἐπὶ γῆς
and saying,   Glory in [the] highest to God, and on earth

εἰρήνη, ἐν ἀνθρώποις ʸεὐδοκία.‖ 15 Καὶ ἐγένετο, ὡς ἀπῆλ-
peace, in   men   good pleasure. And it came to pass, as ³depart-

θον ἀπ' αὐτῶν εἰς τὸν οὐρανὸν οἱ ἄγγελοι, ᶻκαὶ οἱ ἄνθρωποι‖
ed ⁴from ⁵them ⁶into ⁷the ⁸heaven ¹the ²angels, that the   men

οἱ ποιμένες ᵃεἶπον‖ πρὸς ἀλλήλους, Διέλθωμεν δὴ ἕως
the shepherds   said   to one another, Let us go through indeed as far as

Βηθλεέμ, καὶ ἴδωμεν τὸ ῥῆμα τοῦτο τὸ γεγονὸς ὃ ὁ
Bethlehem, and let us see this thing that has come to pass which the

κύριος ἐγνώρισεν ἡμῖν. 16 Καὶ ᵇῆλθον‖ σπεύσαντες καὶ
Lord   made known to us.   And they came having hasted and

ᶜἀνεῦρον‖ τήν τε Μαριὰμ καὶ τὸν Ἰωσήφ, καὶ τὸ βρέφος κεί-
found   both Mary   and Joseph, and the babe ly-

μενον ἐν τῇ φάτνῃ. 17 ἰδόντες δὲ ᵈδιεγνώρισαν‖
ing   in the manger.   And having seen, they made known abroad

περὶ τοῦ ῥήματος τοῦ λαληθέντος αὐτοῖς περὶ τοῦ
concerning the saying which had been told them concerning

παιδίου τούτου. 18 καὶ πάντες οἱ ἀκούσαντες ἐθαύμασαν
this little child.   And   all   who   heard   wondered

περὶ τῶν λαληθέντων ὑπὸ τῶν ποιμένων πρὸς
concerning the things which had been spoken by the shepherds to

αὐτούς. 19 ἡ δὲ ᵉΜαριὰμ‖ πάντα συνετήρει τὰ ῥήματα ταῦτα,
them.   But Mary ²all ¹kept   these sayings,

ᶠσυμβάλλουσα‖ ἐν τῇ καρδίᾳ αὐτῆς. 20 καὶ ᵍἐπέστρεψαν‖
pondering [them] in her heart.   And ³returned

οἱ ποιμένες, δοξάζοντες καὶ αἰνοῦντες τὸν θεὸν ἐπὶ πᾶσιν
¹the ²shepherds, glorifying and praising   God for all things

οἷς ἤκουσαν καὶ ʰεἶδον,‖ καθὼς ἐλαλήθη πρὸς αὐτούς.
which they had heard and seen, as   it was said to   them.

21 And when eight days were accomplished for the circumcising of the child, his name was called JESUS, which was so named of the angel before he was conceived in the womb.

21 Καὶ ὅτε ἐπλήσθησαν ἡμέραι ὀκτὼ τοῦ περιτεμεῖν ¹τὸ
   And when were fulfilled ²days ¹eight for the circumcising the

παιδίον,‖ καὶ ἐκλήθη τὸ ὄνομα αὐτοῦ Ἰησοῦς, τὸ κλη-
little child, ²was ⁴called ¹his ²name   Jesus, which [he] was

θὲν ὑπὸ τοῦ ἀγγέλου πρὸ τοῦ ᵏσυλληφθῆναι‖ αὐτὸν ἐν τῇ
called by the angel   before ²was ³conceived ¹he in the

κοιλίᾳ.
womb.

22 And when the days of her purification according to the law of Moses were accomplished, they brought him to Jerusalem, to present him to the Lord; 23 (as it is written in the law of the Lord, Every male that openeth the womb shall be called holy to the Lord;) 24 and to offer a sacrifice according to that

22 Καὶ ὅτε ἐπλήσθησαν αἱ ἡμέραι τοῦ καθαρισμοῦ ¹αὐτῶν‖
   And when were fulfilled the days   for their purification

κατὰ τὸν νόμον ᵐΜωσέως,‖ ἀνήγαγον αὐτὸν εἰς Ἱεροσό-
according to the law   of Moses, they brought him to Jerusa-

λυμα παραστῆσαι τῷ κυρίῳ, 23 καθὼς γέγραπται ἐν ⁿ
lem   to present   to the Lord,   as   it has been written in [the]

νόμῳ κυρίου, Ὅτι πᾶν ἄρσεν διανοῖγον μήτραν ἅγιον
law of [the] Lord, That every male   opening a womb ⁴holy

τῷ κυρίῳ κληθήσεται· 24 καὶ τοῦ δοῦναι θυσίαν κατὰ
⁵to ⁶the ⁷Lord ¹shall ²be ³called;   and to offer a sacrifice according to

───

ᵂ — τῇ (read a manger) GLTTrAW.   ˣ οὐρανοῦ of heaven Tr.   ʸ εὐδοκίας of good
pleasure ᴇᴛᴛrᴀ.   ᶻ — καὶ οἱ ἄνθρωπι [L]ᴛ[ᴛrᴀ].   ᵃ ἐλάλουν T.   ᵇ ῆλθαν TTrᴀ.
ᶜ ἀνεῦραν TTr.   ᵈ ἐγνώρισαν they made known LTTrᴀ.   ᵉ Μαρία LTTrᴀ.   ᶠ συνβάλ-
λουσα T.   ᵍ ὑπέστρεψαν GLTTrᴀW.   ʰ ἴδον T.   ⁱ αὐτόν him GLTTrᴀW.   ᵏ συλλημφθῆναι
LTTrᴀ.   ˡ αὐτῆς (read her purification) E.   ᵐ Μωϋσέως LTTrᴀW.   ⁿ + τῷ the L.

τὸ   εἰρημένον ἐν °τῷ νόμῳ κυρίου, Ζεῦγος τρυγόνων
that which has been said in [the] law of [the] Lord, A pair of turtle doves

ἢ δύο Ρνεοσσοὺς‖ περιστερῶν.
or two young of pigeons.

25 Καὶ ἰδού, �q ἦν ἄνθρωπος‖ ἐν Ἱερουσαλὴμ ᾧ ὄνομα
And behold, there was a man in Jerusalem whose name

Συμεών, καὶ ὁ ἄνθρωπος οὗτος   δίκαιος καὶ εὐλαβής,
[was] Simeon; and this man [was] just and pious,

προσδεχόμενος   παράκλησιν τοῦ Ἰσραήλ, καὶ   πνεῦμα
waiting for [the] consolation of Israel, and [the] ²Spirit

ʳἅγιον ἦν‖ ἐπ᾽ αὐτόν· 26 καὶ ἦν αὐτῷ κεχρηματισμένον ὑπὸ
¹Holy ᵗwas upon him. And it was to him divinely communicated by

τοῦ πνεύματος τοῦ ἁγίου μὴ ἰδεῖν θάνατον πρὶν ˢἢ‖
the Spirit the Holy that he should not see death before

ἴδῃ τὸν χριστὸν κυρίου. 27 καὶ ἦλθεν ἐν τῷ πνεύματι
ᵗhe should see the Christ of [the] Lord. And he came in the Spirit

εἰς τὸ ἱερόν· καὶ ἐν τῷ εἰσαγαγεῖν τοὺς γονεῖς τὸ παιδίον Ἰη-
into the temple; and when ³brought ⁴in ¹the ²parents the little child Je-

σοῦν, τοῦ ποιῆσαι αὐτοὺς κατὰ   τὸ εἰθισμένον
sus, that they might do ³according ⁴to ⁵what ⁶had ⁷become ⁸customary

τοῦ νόμου περὶ αὐτοῦ, 28 καὶ αὐτὸς ἐδέξατο αὐτὸ εἰς τὰς ἀγκά-
⁹by ¹⁰the ¹¹law ¹for ⁶him, he also received it into ²arms,

λας ᵗαὐτοῦ,‖ καὶ εὐλόγησεν τὸν θεόν, καὶ εἶπεν, 29 Νῦν ἀπολύεις
¹his, and blessed God, and said, Now thou lettest go

τὸν δοῦλόν σου, δέσποτα, κατὰ τὸ ῥῆμά σου, ἐν εἰρήνῃ·
thy bondman, O Master, according to thy word, in peace;

30 ὅτι εἶδον οἱ ὀφθαλμοί μου τὸ σωτήριόν σου, 31 ὃ
for ³have ⁴seen ¹mine ²eyes thy salvation, which

ἡτοίμασας κατὰ   πρόσωπον πάντων τῶν λαῶν· 32 φῶς
thou hast prepared before [the] face of all the peoples; a light

εἰς ἀποκάλυψιν ἐθνῶν καὶ δόξαν λαοῦ σου Ἰσραήλ.
for revelation of [the] Gentiles and glory of thy people Israel.

33 Καὶ ᵘᵛ ἦν Ἰωσὴφ‖ καὶ ἡ μήτηρ ʷαὐτοῦ‖ θαυμάζοντες ἐπὶ
And ⁵were ¹Joseph ²and ³his ⁵mother wondering at

τοῖς   λαλουμένοις περὶ αὐτοῦ. 34 καὶ εὐλόγησεν
the things which were spoken concerning him. And ²blessed

αὐτοὺς Συμεών, καὶ εἶπεν πρὸς Μαριὰμ τὴν μητέρα αὐτοῦ,
³them ¹Simeon, and said to Mary his mother,

Ἰδού, οὗτος   κεῖται εἰς πτῶσιν καὶ ἀνάστασιν πολλῶν
Lo, this [child] is set for [the] fall and rising up of many

ἐν τῷ Ἰσραήλ, καὶ εἰς σημεῖον ἀντιλεγόμενον· 35 καὶ σοῦ ˣδὲ‖
in Israel, and for a sign spoken against; (and of thee also

αὐτῆς τὴν ψυχὴν διελεύσεται ῥομφαία· ὅπως ἂν ἀποκαλυ-
ᵗhy ⁷soul ²shall ⁶go ⁵through ¹a ²sword ;) so that may be re-

φθῶσιν ἐκ πολλῶν καρδιῶν   διαλογισμοί.
vealed of many hearts [the] reasonings.

36 Καὶ ἦν Ἄννα προφῆτις, θυγάτηρ Φανουήλ, ἐκ
And there was Anna a prophetess, daughter of Phanuel, of [the]

φυλῆς Ἀσήρ· αὕτη προβεβηκυῖα ἐν ἡμέραις πολλαῖς, ζήσασα
tribe of Asher, she was advanced in ²days ¹many, having lived

ʸἔτη μετὰ ἀνδρὸς‖ ἑπτὰ ἀπὸ τῆς ᶻπαρθενίας‖ αὐτῆς, 37 καὶ
²years ⁵with ⁴a ⁵husband ¹seven from her virginity, and

° + τῷ the LTTr.   Ρ νοσσοὺς TA.   �q ἄνθρωπος ἦν T.   ʳ ἦν ἅγιον GLTTrAW,
ˢ ἢ ἂν T; ἂν Tr.   ᵗ — αὐτοῦ (read [his] arms) [L]T[TrA].   ᵘ + ὁ L.   ᵛ ὁ πατὴρ αὐτοῦ his
father GTTrA.   ʷ — αὐτοῦ (read [his] mother) GTrA.   ˣ [δὲ] LTr.   ʸ μετὰ ἀνδρὸς
ἔτη LTTr.   ᶻ παρθενείας A.

‡ *was* a widow of about
fourscore and four
years, which departed
not from the temple,
but served *God* with
fastings and prayers
night and day. 38 And
she coming in that instant gave thanks likewise unto the Lord,
and spake of him to
all them that looked
for redemption in Jerusalem.

ᵇαὕτη‖ χήρα ᶜὡς‖ ἐτῶν ὀγδοηκοντατεσσάρων, ἣ οὐκ
she [was] a widow ²about ⁴years ¹of ³eighty-four, ⁵who ⁷not
ἀφίστατο ᵈἀπὸ‖ τοῦ ἱεροῦ, νηστείαις καὶ δεήσεσιν λατρεύουσα
⁶departed from the temple, with fastings and supplications serving
νύκτα καὶ ἡμέρας·· 38 καὶ ᵉαὕτη‖ αὐτῇ.τῇ ὥρᾳ ἐπιστᾶσα
night an day: and she at the same hour coming up
ἀνθωμολογεῖτο τῷ ᶠκυρίῳ," καὶ ἐλάλει περὶ αὐτοῦ πᾶσιν
gave praise to the Lord, and spoke concerning him to all
τοῖς προσδεχομένοις λύτρωσιν ᵍἐν‖ Ἱερουσαλήμ.
those waiting for redemption in Jerusalem.

‡ 39 And when they
had performed all
things according to
the law of the Lord,
they returned into
Galilee, to their own
city Nazareth. 40 And
the child grew, and
waxed strong in spirit,
filled with wisdom:
and the grace of God
was upon him.

39 Καὶ ὡς ἐτέλεσαν ʰἅπαντα‖ ⁱτὰ‖ κατὰ τὸν νόμον,
And when they had completed all things according to the law
κυρίου, ᵏὑπέστρεψαν‖ εἰς τὴν Γαλιλαίαν, εἰς ˡτὴν‖ πόλιν
of [the] Lord they returned to Galilee, to ³city
ᵐαὐτῶν‖ ⁿΝαζαρέτ.ᴸ 40 Τὸ.δὲ παιδίον ηὔξανεν καὶ ἐκρα-
¹their [²own], Nazareth. And the little child grew, and became
ταιοῦτο ᵒπνεύματι,‖ πληρούμενον ᵖσοφίας,‖ καὶ χάρις
strong in spirit, being filled with wisdom, and [the] grace
θεοῦ ἦν ἐπ᾽ αὐτό.
of God was upon him.

41 Now his parents
went to Jerusalem
every year at the feast
of the passover. 42 And
when he was twelve
years old, they went
up to Jerusalem after
the custom of the feast.
43 And when they had
fulfilled the days, as
they returned, the
child Jesus tarried behind in Jerusalem;
and Joseph and his
mother knew not *of it*.
44 But they, supposing
him to have been in
the company, went a
day's journey; and
they sought him among *their* kinsfolk
and acquaintance.
45 And when they
found him not, they
turned back again to
Jerusalem, seeking
him. 46 And it came to
pass, that after three
days they found him
in the temple, sitting
in the midst of the
doctors, both hearing
them, and asking them
questions. 47 And all
that heard him were
astonished at his understanding and answers. 48 And when
they saw him, they
were amazed: and his
mother said unto him,
Son, why hast thou
thus dealt with us?

41 Καὶ ἐπορεύοντο οἱ.γονεῖς.αὐτοῦ κατ᾽.ἔτος εἰς Ἱερουσαλὴμ
And ³went ¹his ²parents yearly to Jerusalem
τῇ ἑορτῇ τοῦ πάσχα. 42 καὶ ὅτε ἐγένετο ἐτῶν δώδεκα,
at the feast of the passover. And when he was ²years [³old] ¹twelve,
ᑫἀναβάντων‖ αὐτῶν ʳεἰς Ἱεροσόλυμα‖ κατὰ τὸ ἔθος τῆς
⁴having ⁵gone ⁷up ⁶they to Jerusalem according to the custom of the
ἑορτῆς, 43 καὶ τελειωσάντων τὰς ἡμέρας, ἐν.τῷ.ὑποστρέφειν
feast, and having completed the days, as ²returned
αὐτοὺς ὑπέμεινεν ˢἸησοῦς‖ ὁ παῖς ἐν Ἱερουσαλήμ, καὶ
¹they ⁴remained ⁷behind ²Jesus ³the ⁴child in Jerusalem, and
ᵗοὐκ.ἔγνω Ἰωσὴφ καὶ ἡ.μήτηρ.αὐτοῦ·‖ 44 νομίσαντες.δὲ αὐτὸν
⁵knew [⁶it] ⁷not ¹Joseph ²and ³his ⁴mother; but supposing him
ᵛἐν τῇ συνοδίᾳ εἶναι‖ ἦλθον ἡμέρας ὁδόν, καὶ ἀνεζήτουν
in the company to be they went a day's journey, and sought
αὐτὸν ἐν τοῖς συγγενέσιν καὶ ᵂἐν‖ τοῖς γνωστοῖς· 45 καὶ
him among the relations and among the acquaintances: and
μὴ εὑρόντες ˣαὐτὸν ὑπέστρεψαν εἰς Ἱερουσαλήμ, ʸζητοῦντες‖
not having found him they returned to Jerusalem, seeking
αὐτόν. 46 Καὶ ἐγένετο ᶻμεθ᾽‖ ἡμέρας τρεῖς εὗρον αὐτὸν ἐν
him. And it came to pass after ¹days ²three ¹three they found him in
τῷ ἱερῷ, καθεζόμενον ἐν μέσῳ τῶν διδασκάλων, καὶ ἀκού-
the temple, sitting in [the] midst of the teachers, both hear-
οντα.αὐτῶν καὶ ἐπερωτῶντα αὐτούς. 47 ἐξίσταντο.δὲ πάντες
ing them and questioning them. And ²were ⁶amazed ¹all
οἱ ἀκούοντες αὐτοῦ ἐπὶ τῇ συνέσει καὶ ταῖς ἀποκρίσεσιν
²those ³hearing ⁴him at [his] understanding and ²answers
αὐτοῦ. 48 Καὶ ἰδόντες αὐτὸν ἐξεπλάγησαν· καὶ ᵃπρὸς αὐτὸν
¹his. And seeing him they were astonished: and to him
ἡ.μήτηρ.αὐτοῦ εἶπεν,‖ Τέκνον, τί ἐποίησας ἡμῖν οὕτως;
his mother said, Child, why hast thou done to us thus?

ᵇ αὐτὴ herself TTrA.   ᶜ ἕως up to LTTrA.   ᵈ — ἀπὸ (*read* left not) TTrA.   ᵉ αὐτὴ W;
— αὕτη (*read* ἀνθωμολ. she gave praise) LTTrA.   ᶠ θεῷ (*read* to God) LTTrA.   ᵍ — ἐν (*read*
[in]) LTTr[A].   ʰ πάντα TTr.   ⁱ — τὰ T.   ᵏ ἐπέστρεψαν T.   ˡ — τὴν LTTrA.   ᵐ .ἑαυτῶν
LTTrAW.   ⁿ Ναζαρέθ TTrAW.   ᵒ — πνεύματι LTTrA.   ᵖ σοφία TrA.   ᑫ ἀναβαινόντων going
up LTTrA.   ʳ — εἰς Ἱεροσόλυμα T[Tr]A.   ˢ [Ἰησοῦς] A.   ᵗ οὐκ ἔγνωσαν οἱ γονεῖς αὐτοῦ his
parents knew it not LTTrA.   ᵛ εἶναι ἐν τῇ συνοδίᾳ LTTrA.   ᵂ — ἐν GLTTrAW.   ˣ — αὐτὸν
(*read* [him]) G[L]TT A.   ʸ ἀναζητοῦντες LTTrA.   ᶻ μετὰ TTrA.   ᵃ εἶπεν πρὸς αὐτὸν
ἡ μήτηρ αὐτοῦ LTTrA.

ἰδού, ὁ.πατήρ.σου κἀγὼ ὀδυνώμενοι ἐζητοῦμέν σε. 49 Καὶ
behold, thy father and I distressed were seeking thee. And

εἶπεν πρὸς αὐτούς, Τί ὅτι ἐζητεῖτέ με; οὐκ.ᾔδειτε ὅτι
he said to them, Why [is it] that ye were seeking me? knew ye.not that

ἐν τοῖς τοῦ.πατρός.μου δεῖ εἶναί με; 50 Καὶ αὐτοὶ
in the [affairs] of my Father it behoves ²to ³be ¹me? And they

οὐ.συνῆκαν τὸ ῥῆμα ὃ ἐλάλησεν αὐτοῖς. 51 Καὶ κατέβη
understood not the word which he spoke to them. And he went down

μετ᾽ αὐτῶν καὶ ἦλθεν εἰς ᵇΝαζαρέτ║ καὶ ἦν ὑποτασσόμενος
with them and came to Nazareth, and he was subject

αὐτοῖς. καὶ ἡ.μήτηρ.αὐτοῦ διετήρει ᶜπάντα τὰ.ῥήματα║.ᵈταῦτα║
to them. And his mother kept all these things

ἐν τῇ.καρδίᾳ.αὐτῆς. 52 καὶ Ἰησοῦς προέκοπτεν ᵉ ᶠσοφίᾳ καὶ
in her heart. And Jesus advanced in wisdom and

ἡλικίᾳ,║ καὶ χάριτι παρὰ θεῷ καὶ ἀνθρώποις.
stature, and in favour with God and men.

3 Ἐν ἔτει δὲ πεντεκαιδεκάτῳ τῆς ἡγεμονίας Τιβερίου
²In ⁵year ¹now [³the] ⁴fifteenth of the government of Tiberius

Καίσαρος, ἡγεμονεύοντος Ποντίου ᵍΠιλάτου║ τῆς Ἰουδαίας,
Cæsar, ³being ⁴governor ¹Pontius ²Pilate of Judæa,

καὶ ʰτετραρχοῦντος║ τῆς Γαλιλαίας Ἡρώδου, Φιλίππου.δὲ τοῦ
and ²being ³tetrarch ⁴of ⁵Galilee ¹Herod, and Philip

ἀδελφοῦ.αὐτοῦ ʰτετραρχοῦντος║ τῆς Ἰτουραίας καὶ Τραχωνί-
his brother being tetrarch of Ituræa and ³of ⁴Tracho-

τιδος χώρας, καὶ Λυσανίου τῆς Ἀβιληνῆς ʰτετραρχοῦντος,║
nitis [¹the] ²region, and Lysanias ³of ⁴Abilene ¹being ²tetrarch,

2 ⁱἐπ᾽ ἀρχιερέων║ Ἄννα καὶ ᵏΚαϊάφα,║ ἐγένετο ῥῆμα
in [the] high-priesthood of Annas and Caiaphas, came [the] word

θεοῦ ἐπὶ ˡἸωάννην║ τὸν ᵐτοῦ║ Ζαχαρίου υἱὸν ἐν τῇ ἐρήμῳ·
of God upon John the ²of ³Zacharias ¹son in the wilderness.

3 καὶ ἦλθεν εἰς πᾶσαν ⁿτὴν║ περίχωρον τοῦ Ἰορδάνου,
And he went into all the country around the Jordan,

κηρύσσων βάπτισμα μετανοίας εἰς ἄφεσιν ἁμαρτιῶν·
proclaiming [the] baptism of repentance for remission of sins;

4 ὡς γέγραπται ἐν βίβλῳ λόγων Ἡσαΐου τοῦ
as it has been written in [the] book of [the] words of Esaias the

προφήτου, ᵒλέγοντος,║ Φωνὴ βοῶντος ἐν τῇ ἐρήμῳ,
prophet, saying, [The] voice of one crying in the wilderness,

Ἑτοιμάσατε τὴν ὁδὸν κυρίου· εὐθείας ποιεῖτε τὰς τρίβους
Prepare the way of [the] Lord; ²straight ¹make ⁴paths

αὐτοῦ. 5 πᾶσα φάραγξ πληρωθήσεται, καὶ πᾶν ὄρος καὶ
³his. Every ravine shall be filled up, and every mountain and

βουνὸς ταπεινωθήσεται· καὶ ἔσται τὰ σκολιὰ εἰς
hill shall be made low; and ⁴shall ⁵become ¹the ²crooked [³places] into

ᵖεὐθεῖαν,║ καὶ αἱ τραχεῖαι εἰς ὁδοὺς λείας· 6 καὶ ὄψεται
a straight [path], and the rough into ²ways ¹smooth; and ³shall ⁴see

πᾶσα σὰρξ τὸ σωτήριον τοῦ θεοῦ. 7 Ἔλεγεν οὖν τοῖς
¹all ²flesh the salvation of God. He said therefore to the

ἐκπορευομένοις ὄχλοις βαπτισθῆναι ὑπ᾽ αὐτοῦ, Γεννήματα
²coming ³out ¹crowds to be baptized by him, Offspring

ἐχιδνῶν, τίς ὑπέδειξεν ὑμῖν φυγεῖν ἀπὸ τῆς μελλούσης ὀργῆς;
of vipers, who forewarned you to flee from the coming wrath?

behold, thy father and I have sought thee sorrowing. 49 And he said unto them, How is it that ye sought me? wist ye not that I must be about my Father's business? 50 And they understood not the saying which he spake unto them. 51 And he went down with them, and came to Nazareth, and was subject unto them: but his mother kept all these sayings in her heart. 52 And Jesus increased in wisdom and stature, and in favour with God and man.

III. Now in the fifteenth year of the reign of Tiberius Cæsar, Pontius Pilate being governor of Judæa, and Herod being tetrarch of Galilee, and his brother Philip tetrarch of Ituræa and of the region of Trachonitis, and Lysanias the tetrarch of Abilene, 2 Annas and Caiaphas being the high priests, the word of God came unto John the son of Zacharias in the wilderness. 3 And he came into all the country about Jordan, preaching the baptism of repentance for remission of sins; 4 as it is written in the book of the words of Esaias the prophet, saying, The voice of one crying in the wilderness, Prepare ye the way of the Lord, make his paths straight. 5 Every valley shall be filled, and every mountain and hill shall be brought low; and the crooked shall be made straight, and the rough ways shall be made smooth; 6 and all flesh shall see the salvation of God. 7 Then said he to the multitude that came forth to be baptized of him, O generation of vipers, who hath warned you to flee from the wrath to come? 8 Bring forth therefore fruits worthy of repentance, and begin not to say within yourselves, We have Abraham to our fa-

ᵇ Ναζαρέθ TTrAW. ᶜ τὰ ῥήματα πάντα L. ᵈ — ταῦτα these [L]T[A]. ᵉ + ἐν τῇ in
(wisdom) T. ᶠ ἡλικίᾳ καὶ σοφίᾳ Tr. ᵍ Πειλάτου T. ʰ τετρααρχοῦντος T. ⁱ ἐπὶ
ἀρχιερέως GLTTrAW. ᵏ Καϊφα L. ˡ Ἰωάνην Tr. ᵐ — τοῦ GLTTrAW. ⁿ — τὴν (read
every country around) LTrA. ᵒ — λέγοντος LTTrA. ᵖ εὐθείας straight [paths] LTTrA.

ther: for I say unto you, That God is able of these stones to raise up children unto Abraham. 9 And now also the axe is laid unto the root of the trees: every tree therefore which bringeth not forth good fruit is hewn down, and cast into the fire. 10 And the people asked him, saying, What shall we do then? 11 He answereth and saith unto them, He that hath two coats, let him impart to him that hath none; and he that hath meat, let him do likewise. 12 Then came also publicans to be baptized, and said unto him, Master, what shall we do? 13 And he said unto them, Exact no more than that which is appointed you. 14 And the soldiers likewise demanded of him, saying, And what shall we do? And he said unto them, Do violence to no man, neither accuse any falsely; and be content with your wages.

15 And as the people were in expectation, and all men mused in their hearts of John, whether he were the Christ, or not; 16 John answered, saying unto them all, I indeed baptize you with water; but one mightier than I cometh, the latchet of whose shoes I am not worthy to unloose: he shall baptize you with the Holy Ghost and with fire: 17 whose fan is in his hand, and he will throughly purge his floor, and will gather the wheat into his garner; but the chaff he will burn with fire unquenchable. 18 And many other things in his exhortation preached he unto the people. 19 But Herod the tetrarch, being reproved by him for Herodias his brother Philip's wife, and for all the evils which Herod had done, 20 added yet this above all, that he shut up John in prison.

8 ποιήσατε οὖν καρποὺς ἀξίους τῆς μετανοίας· καὶ μὴ
Produce therefore fruits worthy of repentance; and ²not
ἄρξησθε λέγειν ἐν ἑαυτοῖς, Πατέρα ἔχομεν τὸν Ἀβραάμ·
¹begin to say in yourselves, [*For] ⁵father ¹we ²have ·³Abraham,
λέγω.γὰρ ὑμῖν, ὅτι δύναται ὁ θεὸς ἐκ τῶν.λίθων.τούτων
for I say to you, that ²is ³able ¹God from these stones
ἐγεῖραι τέκνα τῷ.Ἀβραάμ. 9 ἤδη.δὲ καὶ ἡ ἀξίνη πρὸς τὴν
to raise up children to Abraham. But already also the axe to the
ῥίζαν τῶν δένδρων κεῖται· πᾶν οὖν δένδρον μὴ ποιοῦν
root of the trees is applied: ²every ¹therefore tree not producing
καρπὸν ᵣκαλὸν‖ ἐκκόπτεται καὶ εἰς πῦρ βάλλεται. 10 Καὶ
²fruit ¹good is cut down and into [the] fire is cast. And
ἐπηρώτων αὐτὸν οἱ ὄχλοι, λέγοντες, Τί οὖν ˢποιήσομεν‖;
³asked ⁴him ¹the ²crowds, saying, What then shall we do?
11 Ἀποκριθεὶς.δὲ ᵗλέγει‖ αὐτοῖς, Ὁ ἔχων δύο χιτῶνας μετα-
And answering he says to them, He that has two tunics let him
δότω τῷ μὴ.ἔχοντι· καὶ ὁ ἔχων βρώματα ὁμοίως
impart to him that has not; and he that has victuals ⁴likewise
ποιείτω. 12 Ἦλθον.δὲ καὶ τελῶναι βαπτισθῆναι, καὶ
¹let ²him ³do. And ²came ²also ¹tax-gatherers to be baptized, and
ᵛεἶπον‖ πρὸς αὐτόν, Διδάσκαλε, τί ˢποιήσομεν‖; 13 Ὁ.δὲ εἶπεν
they said to him, Teacher, what shall we do? And he said
πρὸς αὐτούς, Μηδὲν πλέον παρὰ τὸ διατεταγμένον
to them, ²Nothing ³more ⁴beyond ⁵that ⁶which ⁷is ⁸appointed
ὑμῖν πράσσετε. 14 Ἐπηρώτων.δὲ αὐτὸν καὶ στρατευόμενοι,
⁹to ¹⁰you ¹exact. And asked him also those who were soldiers,
λέγοντες, ᵂΚαὶ ἡμεῖς τί ποιήσομεν‖; Καὶ εἶπεν ˣπρὸς αὐτούς,‖
saying, And we what shall we do? And he said to them,
Μηδένα διασείσητε ʸμηδὲ‖ συκοφαντήσητε, καὶ ἀρκεῖσθε τοῖς
²No ³one ¹oppress nor accuse falsely, and be satisfied
ὀψωνίοις.ὑμῶν.
with your wages.

15 Προσδοκῶντος.δὲ τοῦ λαοῦ, καὶ διαλογιζομένων πάν-
But as ³were ⁴in ⁵expectation ¹the ²people, and ²were ²reasoning ¹all
των ἐν ταῖς.καρδίαις.αὐτῶν περὶ τοῦ ᶻἸωάννου,‖ μήποτε
in their hearts concerning the John, whether or not
αὐτὸς εἴη ὁ χριστός, 16 ἀπεκρίνατο ᵃὁ Ἰωάννης ἅπασιν,
he might be the Christ, ²answered ¹John all,
λέγων,‖ Ἐγὼ μὲν ὕδατι βαπτίζω ὑμᾶςᵇ· ἔρχεται.δὲ ὁ
saying, I indeed.with water baptize you, but he comes who[is]
ἰσχυρότερός μου, οὗ οὐκ.εἰμὶ ἱκανὸς λῦσαι τὸν ἱμάντα τῶν
mightier than I, of whom I am not fit to loose the thong
ὑποδημάτων.αὐτοῦ· αὐτὸς ὑμᾶς βαπτίσει ἐν πνεύματι
of his sandals; he ³you ¹will ²baptize with [the] ²Spirit
ἁγίῳ καὶ πυρί· 17 οὗ τὸ πτύον ἐν τῇ.χειρὶ.αὐτοῦ,
¹Holy and with fire; of whom the winnowing fan [is] in his hand,
ᶜκαὶ διακαθαριεῖ‖ τὴν.ἅλωνα.αὐτοῦ, καὶ ᵈσυνάξει‖ τὸν
and he will thoroughly purge his floor, and will gather the
σῖτον εἰς τὴν.ἀποθήκην.αὐτοῦ, τὸ.δὲ ἄχυρον κατακαύσει
wheat into his granary, but the chaff he will burn
πυρὶ ἀσβέστῳ. 18 Πολλὰ μὲν.οὖν καὶ ἕτερα παρακαλῶν
with fire unquenchable. ³Many ¹therefore ¹and other things exhorting

ᵣ [καλὸν] L. ˢ ποιήσωμεν should we do LTTrAW. ᵗ ἔλεγεν he said LTTrA. ᵛ εἶπαν
LTTr. ᵂ τί ποιήσομεν (ποιήσωμεν should we do TAW) καὶ ἡμεῖς LTTrA· ˣ αὐτοῖς to them
LTrA. ʸ μηδένα no one T. ᶻ Ἰωάνου Tr. ᵃ ὁ Ἰωάνης ἅπασιν λέγων Tr; λέγων πᾶσιν ὁ
Ἰωάννης T. ᵇ + εἰς μετάνοιαν to repentance L. ᶜ διακαθᾶραι to thoroughly purge T.
ᵈ συναγαγεῖν to gather T.

εὐηγγελίζετο   τὸν λαόν. 19 Ὁ.δὲ. Ἡρώδης ὁ ᵉτε-
he announced the glad tidings to the people.   But Herod   the te-

ρράρχης‖ ἐλεγχόμενος ὑπ' αὐτοῦ περὶ Ἡρωδιάδος τῆς
trarch   being reproved by him concerning Herodias   the

γυναικὸς ᶠΦιλίππου‖ τοῦ.ἀδελφοῦ.αὐτοῦ, καὶ περὶ πάντων
wife   of Philip   his brother,   and concerning all

ὧν ἐποίησεν   πονηρῶν ὁ Ἡρώδης, 20 προσέθηκεν ᵍκαὶ‖
ᵃwhich ᵇhad ᵈdone [¹the] ᶜevils   ⁴Herod,   added   also

τοῦτο ἐπὶ πᾶσιν ʰκαὶ‖ κατέκλεισεν τὸν Ἰωάννην‖ ἐν ᵏτῇ‖
this   to   all   that   he shut up   John   in   the

φυλακῇ.
prison.

21 Ἐγένετο.δὲ ἐν.τῷ.βαπτισθῆναι ἅπαντα τὸν λαόν, καὶ
Now it came to pass ⁴having ⁵been ⁶baptized ¹all ²the ³people, and

Ἰησοῦ βαπτισθέντος καὶ προσευχομένου, ἀνεῳχθῆναι τὸν
Jesus having been baptized and   praying, ⁷was ⁸opened ¹the

οὐρανόν, 22 καὶ καταβῆναι τὸ πνεῦμα τὸ ἅγιον σωματικῷ
²heaven,   and descended the Spirit the Holy in a bodily

εἴδει ʲὡσεὶ‖ περιστερὰν ἐπ' αὐτόν, καὶ φωνὴν ἐξ οὐρανοῦ
form   as   a dove   upon   him,   and a voice out of heaven

γενέσθαι, ᵐλέγουσαν,‖ Σὺ εἶ ὁ.υἱός.μου ὁ ἀγαπητός, ἐν σοὶ
came,   saying,   Thou art my Son the   beloved,   in thee

ⁿηὐδόκησα.‖
I have found delight.

23 Καὶ αὐτὸς ἦν °ὁ‖ Ἰησοῦς ᵖὡσεὶ ἐτῶν   τριάκοντα
And ²himself ³was ¹Jesus ⁷about ⁹years [¹⁰old] ⁸thirty

ἀρχόμενος,‖   �۩ὢν, ὡς ἐνομίζετο, υἱὸς‖ Ἰωσήφ, τοῦ ʳΗλί,‖
⁴beginning [⁵to ⁶be], being, as was supposed, son of Joseph,   of Eli,

24 τοῦ ˢΜατθάτ,‖ τοῦ ᵗΛευΐ,‖ τοῦ ᵛΜελχί,‖ τοῦ ʷϜΙαννά,‖ τοῦ
of Matthat,   of Levi,   of Melchi,   of Janna,   of

Ἰωσήφ, 25 τοῦ ˣΜατταθίου,‖ τοῦ Ἀμώς, τοῦ Ναούμ, τοῦ ʸἘσλί,‖
of Joseph,   of Mattathias,   of Amos,   of Naoum,   of Esli,

τοῦ Ναγγαί, 26 τοῦ Μαάθ, τοῦ Ματταθίου, τοῦ ᶻΣεμεΐ,‖ τοῦ
of Naggai,   of Maath,   of Mattathias,   of Semei,   of

ᵃˈἸωσήφ,‖ τοῦ ᵇἸούδα,‖ 27 τοῦ ᶜˈἸωαννᾶ,‖ τοῦ Ῥησά, τοῦ Ζορο-
of Joseph,   of Juda,   of Joannes,   of Rhesa,   of Zoro-

βάβελ, τοῦ Σαλαθιήλ, τοῦ ᵈΝηρί,‖ 28 τοῦ ᵛΜελχί,‖ τοῦ ᵉᵃἈδδί,‖
babel,   of Salathiel,   of Neri,   of Melchi,   of Addi,

τοῦ Κωσάμ, τοῦ ᶠᵃἘλμωσάμ,‖ τοῦ Ἢρ, 29 τοῦ ᵍᵃἸωσή,‖ τοῦ Ἐλι-
of Cosam,   of Elmodam,   of Er,   of Joses,   of Eli-

έζερ, τοῦ Ἰωρείμ, τοῦ ʰᵃΜατθάτ,‖ τοῦ ᶦᵃΛευΐ, 30 τοῦ Συμεών,
ezer,   of Joreim,   of Matthat,   of Levi,   of Simeon,

τοῦ Ἰούδα, τοῦ Ἰωσήφ, τοῦ ᵏᵃἸωνάν,‖ τοῦ Ἐλιακίμ, 31 τοῦ ᶦᵃΜε-
of Juda,   of Joseph,   of Jonan,   of Eliakim,   of Me-

λεᾶ,‖ ᵐᵃτοῦ Μαϊνάν,‖ τοῦ Ματταθά, τοῦ ⁿᵃΝαθάν,‖ τοῦ °ᵃΔα-
leas,   of Menna,   of Mattatha,   of Nathan,   of Da-

βίδ,‖ 32 τοῦ Ἰεσσαί, τοῦ ᵖᵃἸΩβήδ,‖ τοῦ ᑫᵃΒοόζ,‖ τοῦ ʳᵃΣαλμών,‖
vid,   of Jesse,   of Obed,   of Booz,   of Salmon,

---

21 Now when all the people were baptized, it came to pass, that Jesus also being baptized, and praying, the heaven was opened, 22 and the Holy Ghost descended in a bodily shape like a dove upon him, and a voice came from heaven, which said, Thou art my beloved Son; in thee I am well pleased.

23 And Jesus himself began to be about thirty years of age, being (as was supposed) the son of Joseph, which was the son of Heli, 24 which was the son of Matthat, which was the son of Levi, which was the son of Melchi, which was the son of Janna, which was the son of Joseph, 25 which was the son of Mattathias, which was the son of Amos, which was the son of Naum, which was the son of Esli, which was the son of Nagge, 26 which was the son of Maath, which was the son of Mattathias, which was the son of Semei, which was the son of Joseph, which was the son of Juda, 27 which was the son of Joanna, which was the son of Rhesa, which was the son of Zorobabel, which was the son of Salathiel, which was the son of Neri, 28 which was the son of Melchi, which was the son of Addi, which was the son of Cosam, which was the son of Elmodam, which was the son of Er, 29 which was the son of Jose, which was the son of Eliezer, which was the son of Jorim, which was the son of Matthat, which was the son of Levi, 30 which was the son of Simeon, which was the son of Juda, which was the son of Joseph, which was the son of Jonan, which was the son of Eliakim, 31 which was the son of Melea, which was the son of Menan, which was the son of Mattatha, which was the son of Nathan, which was the son of David, 32 which was the son of Jesse, which was the son of Obed, which was the son of Booz, which was the son of Salmon, which was the son of Naasson, 31 which was the son of Eliakim, 31 which was the son of Melea, which

---

ᵉ τετραάρχης T.   ᶠ — Φιλίππου (read of his) GLTTᵣAW.   ᵍ [καὶ] L.   ʰ — καὶ T[A].
ᶦ Ἰωάνην Tᵣ.   ᵏ — τῇ LTTᵣA.   ˡ ὡς LTTᵣA.   ᵐ — λέγουσαν LTTᵣA.   ⁿ εὐδόκησα LTTᵣA.
° — ὁ TTᵣA.   ᵖ ἀρχόμενος ὡσεὶ ἐτῶν τριάκοντα TTᵣ.   ᑫ ὢν υἱὸς ὡς ἐνομίζετο LTTᵣA.
ʳ Ἡλεί TTᵣA.   ˢ Μαθθάθ T.   ᵗ Λευεί TTᵣA.   ᵛ Μελχεί TTᵣA.   ʷ Ἰανναί LTTᵣA.
ˣ Μαθθαθίου Tᵣ.   ʸ Ἐσλεί TTᵣA.   ᶻ Σεμεείν TTᵣA.   ᵃ Ἰωσήχ Josech TTᵣA.   ᵇ Ἰωδά TTᵣA.
ᶜ Ἰωανάν LTTᵣA.   ᵈ Νηρεί TTᵣA.   ᵉᵃ Ἀδδεί TTᵣA.   ᶠᵃ Ἐλμαδάμ LTTᵣA.   ᵍᵃ Ἰησοῦ Jesus
LTTᵣA.   ʰᵃ Μαθθάθ T; Μαθθάτ TᵣA.   ᶦᵃ Λευεί TTᵣA.   ᵏᵃ Ἰωνάμ TTᵣA.   ᶦᵃ Μελεά TTᵣ.
ᵐᵃ τοῦ Μεννά [L]TTᵣA.   ⁿᵃ Ναθάμ T.   °ᵃ Δανείδ LTTᵣA; Δαυΐδ GW.   ᵖᵃ Ἰωβήδ Jobed
LTTᵣA.   ᑫᵃ Βοός LTTᵣA.   ʳᵃ Σαλά T.

was *the son* of Menan, which was *the son* of Mattatha, which was *the son* of Nathan, which was *the son* of David, 32 which was *the son of* Jesse, which was *the son* of Obed, which was *the son* of Booz, which was *the son* of Salmon, which was *the son* of Naasson, 33 which was *the son* of Aminadab, which was *the son* of Aram, which was *the son* of Esrom, which was the son of Phares, which was *the son* of Juda, 34 which was *the son of* Jacob, which was *the son of* Isaac, which was *the son* of Abraham, which was *the son of* Thara, which was *the son of* Nachor, 35 which was *the son of* Saruch, which was *the son* of Ragau, which was *the son of* Phalec, which was *the son of* Heber, which was *the son of* Sala, 36 which was *the son of* Cainan, which was *the son* of Arphaxad, which was *the son of* Sem, which was *the son of* Noe, which was *the son of* Lamech, 37 which was *the son of* Mathusala, which was *the son of* Enoch, which was *the son of* Jared, which was *the son of* Maleleel, which was *the son of* Cainan, 38 which was *the son of* Enos, which was *the son* of Seth, which was *the son of* Adam, which was *the son* of God.

IV. And Jesus being full of the Holy Ghost returned from Jordan, and was led by the Spirit into the wilderness, 2 being forty days tempted of the devil. And in those days he did eat nothing: and when they were ended, he afterward hungered. 3 And the devil said unto him, If thou be the Son of God, command this stone that it be made bread. 4 And Jesus answered him, saying, It is written, That man shall not live by bread alone, but by every word of

---

τοῦ Ναασσών, 33 τοῦ ˢ'Ἀμιναδάβ,‖ τοῦ ᵗ'Ἀράμ,‖ τοῦ ᵛ'Ἐσρωμ,ᵇ
of Naasson,   of Aminadab,   of Aram,   of Esrom,

τοῦ Φαρές, τοῦ Ἰούδα, 34 τοῦ Ἰακώβ, τοῦ Ἰσαάκ, τοῦ Ἀβραάμ,
of Phares, of Juda,   of Jacob,   of Isaac,   of Abraham,

τοῦ Θάρα, τοῦ Ναχώρ, 35 τοῦ ᵂΣαρούχ,‖ τοῦ Ῥαγαῦ, τοῦ Φαλέκ,
of Terah, of Nachor,   of Saruch,   of Ragau, of Phalek,

τοῦ ˣ'Ἔβερ,‖ τοῦ Σαλά, 36 τοῦ ʸΚαϊνάν,‖ τοῦ Ἀρφαξάδ, τοῦ
of Eber,   of Sala,   of Cainan,   of Arphaxad,

Σήμ, τοῦ Νῶε, τοῦ Λάμεχ, 37 τοῦ Μαθουσάλα, τοῦ Ἐνώχ,
of Sem, of Noe, of Lamech,   of Mathusala,   of Enoch,

τοῦ ᶻ'Ἰαρέδ,‖ τοῦ ᵃΜαλελεήλ,‖ τοῦ ᵇΚαϊνάν,‖ 38 τοῦ Ἐνώς,
of Jared,   of Maleleel,   of Cainan,   of Enos,

τοῦ Σήθ, τοῦ Ἀδάμ, τοῦ θεοῦ.
of Seth, of Adam, of God.

4 Ἰησοῦς.δὲ ᶜπνεύματος ἁγίου πλήρης‖ ὑπέστρεψεν ἀπὸ
And Jesus, ²of [³the] ⁵Spirit ⁴Holy ¹full, returned from

τοῦ Ἰορδάνου· καὶ ἤγετο ἐν τῷ πνεύματι ᵈεἰς τὴν ἔρημον‖
the Jordan, and was led by the Spirit into the wilderness

2 ἡμέρας ᵉτεσσαράκοντα,‖ πειραζόμενος ὑπὸ τοῦ διαβόλου·
²days ¹forty, being tempted by the devil;

καὶ οὐκ ἔφαγεν οὐδὲν ἐν ταῖς.ἡμέραις.ἐκείναις, καὶ συντελεσ-
and he ate nothing in those days, and ²being

θεισῶν αὐτῶν ᶠὕστερον‖ ἐπείνασεν. 3 ᵍκαὶ εἶπεν‖ αὐτῷ ὁ
²ended ¹they afterwards he hungered. And ³said ⁴to ⁵him ¹the

διάβολος, Εἰ υἱὸς εἶ τοῦ θεοῦ, εἰπὲ τῷ.λίθῳ.τούτῳ ἵνα
²devil, If Son thou art of God, speak to this stone that

γένηται ἄρτος. 4 Καὶ ἀπεκρίθη ʰἸησοῦς πρὸς αὐτόν,‖ ˡλέγων,‖
it become bread. And ²answered ¹Jesus to him, saying,

Γέγραπται,. Ὅτι οὐκ ἐπ' ἄρτῳ μόνῳ ζήσεται ὁ ἄνθρωπος,
It has been written, That not on bread alone shall ³live ¹man,

ᵏἀλλ' ἐπὶ παντὶ ῥήματι θεοῦ.‖ 5 Καὶ ἀναγαγὼν αὐτὸν ˡὁ
but on every word of God. And ³leading ⁴up ⁴him ¹the

διάβολος‖ ᵐεἰς ὄρος ὑψηλὸν‖ ἔδειξεν αὐτῷ πάσας τὰς βασι-
²devil into a ²mountain ¹high shewed him all the king-

λείας τῆς οἰκουμένης ἐν στιγμῇ χρόνου· 6 καὶ εἶπεν αὐτῷ
doms of the habitable world in a moment of time. And ³said ⁴to ⁵him

ὁ διάβολος, Σοὶ δώσω τὴν.ἐξουσίαν.ταύτην ἅπασαν καὶ
¹the ²devil, To thee will I give ³this ³authority ¹all and

τὴν.δόξαν.αὐτῶν· ὅτι ἐμοὶ παραδέδοται, καὶ ᾧ.ⁿἐὰν‖ θέλω
their glory; for to me it has been delivered, and to whomsoever I wish

δίδωμι αὐτήν· 7 σὺ οὖν ἐὰν προσκυνήσῃς ἐνώπιόν ᵒμου,‖
I give it. Thou therefore if thou wilt worship before me,

ἔσται σου ᵖπάντα.‖ 8 Καὶ ἀποκριθεὶς ᵠαὐτῷ εἶπεν ὁ Ἰησοῦς,‖
³shall ⁴be ⁵thine ¹all ²things. And answering ²said ¹Jesus,

ʳὝπαγε ὀπίσω μου, σατανᾶ·‖ γέγραπται.ˢᵃγάρ,‖ ᵗᵃΠροσκυνή-
Get thee behind me, Satan; for it has been written, Thou shalt wor-

σεις κύριον τὸν.θεόν.σου,‖ καὶ αὐτῷ μόνῳ λατρεύσεις.
ship [the] Lord thy God, and him only shalt thou serve.

9 ᵛᵃΚαὶ ἤγαγεν‖ αὐτὸν εἰς Ἱερουσαλήμ, καὶ ἔστησεν ᵂᵃαὐτὸν‖
And he led him to Jerusalem, and set him

ˢ Ἀμειναδάβ A.   ᵗ Ἀδμείν, τοῦ Ἀρνεί of Admin, of Arni, ΤΑ.   ᵛ Ἐσρών EL.   ᵂ Σερούχ
GLTTrAW.   ˣ Ἔβερ TrA.   ʸ Καϊνάμ TA.   ᶻ Ἰαρεθ L; Ἰαρετ T.   ᵃ Μελελεήλ T.   ᵇ Καϊνάμ T.
ᶜ πλήρης πνεύμ. ἁγίου LTTrA.   ᵈ ἐν τῇ ἐρήμῳ LTTrA.   ᵉ τεσσεράκοντα TTrA.   ᶠ ὕστερον LTTrA.
ᵍ εἶπεν δὲ LTTrA.   ʰ πρὸς αὐτὸν ὁ Ἰησοῦς LTTrA.   ˡ — λέγων TTrA.   ᵏ — ἀλλ' ἐπὶ παντὶ
ῥήματι θεοῦ T[Tr]A.   ˡ — ὁ διάβολος (read he shewed) TTrA.   ᵐ — εἰς ὄρος ὑψηλὸν [L]TTrA.
ⁿ ἂν LTrA.   ᵒ ἐμοῦ LTTrAW.   ᵖ πᾶσα all GLTTrAW.   ᵠ [ὁ] A; εἶπεν αὐτῷ ὁ Ἰησοῦς L; ὁ Ἰησοῦς
εἶπεν αὐτῷ T.   ʳ — ὕπαγε ὀπίσω μου, σατανᾶ G[L]TTrA.   ˢᵃ — γάρ for GLTTrAW.   ᵗᵃ κύριον
τὸν θεόν σου προσκυνήσεις LTr.   ᵛᵃ ἤγαγεν δὲ TTrA.   ᵂᵃ — αὐτὸν (read [him]) T[Tr]A.

ἐπὶ τὸ πτερύγιον τοῦ ἱεροῦ, καὶ εἶπεν αὐτῷ, Εἰ ˣὀ‖ υἱὸς εἶ
upon the edge of the temple, and said to him, If the Son thou art
τοῦ θεοῦ, βάλε σεαυτὸν ἐντεῦθεν κάτω. 10 γέγραπται.γάρ,
of God, cast thyself ²hence ¹down; for it has been written,
Ὅτι τοῖς.ἀγγέλοις.αὐτοῦ ἐντελεῖται περὶ σοῦ, τοῦ δια-
That to his angels he will give charge concerning thee, to
φυλάξαι σε· 11 καὶ ὅτι ἐπὶ χειρῶν ἀροῦσίν σε, μήποτε
keep thee; and that in [their] hands shall they bear thee, lest
προσκόψῃς πρὸς λίθον τὸν.πόδα.σου. 12 Καὶ ἀποκριθεὶς εἶπεν
thou strike against a stone thy foot. And answering ²said
αὐτῷ ὁ Ἰησοῦς, Ὅτι εἴρηται, Οὐκ.ἐκπειράσεις κύριον
¹Jesus, It has been said, Thou shalt not tempt [the] Lord
²to ⁴him
τὸν.θεόν.σου. 13 Καὶ συντελέσας πάντα πειρασμὸν ὁ διά-
thy God. And having finished every temptation the de-
βολος ἀπέστη ἀπ' αὐτοῦ ἄχρι.καιροῦ.
vil departed from him for a time.

14 Καὶ ὑπέστρεψεν ὁ Ἰησοῦς ἐν τῇ δυνάμει τοῦ πνεύματος
And ²returned ¹Jesus in the power of the Spirit
εἰς τὴν Γαλιλαίαν· καὶ φήμη ἐξῆλθεν καθ' ὅλης τῆς περι-
to Galilee; and a rumour went out into ²whole ¹the country
χώρου περὶ αὐτοῦ. 15 καὶ αὐτὸς ἐδίδασκεν ἐν ταῖς συν-
around concerning him. and he taught in ²syn-
αγωγαῖς αὐτῶν, δοξαζόμενος ὑπὸ πάντων. 16 καὶ ἦλθεν εἰς
agogues ¹their, being glorified by all. And he came to
ʸτὴν‖·ᶻΝαζαρέτ,‖ οὗ ἦν ᵃτεθραμμένος·‖ καὶ εἰσῆλθεν κατὰ
Nazareth, where he was brought up; and he entered according to
τὸ.εἰωθὸς.αὐτῷ ἐν τῇ ἡμέρᾳ τῶν σαββάτων εἰς τὴν συναγωγήν,
his custom on the day of the sabbaths into the synagogue,
καὶ.ἀνέστη ἀναγνῶναι. 17 καὶ ἐπεδόθη αὐτῷ βιβλίον
and stood up to read. And ²there was given to him [the] book
ᵇἨσαίου.τοῦ προφήτου,‖ καὶ ᶜἀναπτύξας‖ τὸ βιβλίον εὗρεν
of Esaias the prophet, and having unrolled the book he found
ᵈτὸν‖ τόπον οὗ ἦν γεγραμμένον, 18 Πνεῦμα κυρίου
the place where it was written, [The] Spirit of [the] Lord [is]
ἐπ' ἐμέ, οὗ.ᵉἕνεκεν‖ ἔχρισέν με. ᶠεὐαγγελίζεσθαι‖
upon me, on account of which he anointed me to announce the glad tidings
πτωχοῖς, ἀπέσταλκέν με ᵍἰάσασθαι τοὺς συντετριμμένους
to [the] poor, he has sent me to heal the broken
τὴν.καρδίαν,‖ κηρύξαι αἰχμαλώτοις ἄφεσιν καὶ τυφλοῖς
in heart, to proclaim to captives deliverance and to [the] blind
ἀνάβλεψιν, ἀποστεῖλαι τεθραυσμένους ἐν ἀφέσει· 19 κηρύ-
recovery of sight, to send forth [the] crushed in deliverance, to pro-
ξαι ἐνιαυτὸν κυρίου δεκτόν. 20 Καὶ πτύξας τὸ
claim [the] ²year ³of [⁴the] ⁵Lord ¹acceptable. And having rolled up the
βιβλίον, ἀποδοὺς τῷ ὑπηρέτῃ ἐκάθισεν, καὶ πάντων
book, having delivered [it] to the attendant he sat down, and ³of ⁴all
ᵇἐν τῇ συναγωγῇ οἱ ὀφθαλμοὶ ἦσαν‖ ἀτενίζοντες αὐτῷ.
²in ⁵the ⁷synagogue ¹the ²eyes were fixed upon him.
21 Ἤρξατο.δὲ λέγειν πρὸς αὐτούς, Ὅτι σήμερον πεπλήρωται
And he began to say to them, To-day is fulfilled
ἡ.γραφὴ.αὕτη ἐν τοῖς.ὠσὶν.ὑμῶν. 22 Καὶ πάντες ἐμαρτύρουν
this scripture in your ears. And all bore witness

God. 5 And the devil, taking him up into an high mountain, shewed unto him all the kingdoms of the world in a moment of time. 6 And the devil said unto him, All this power will I give thee, and the glory of them: for that is delivered unto me; and to whomsoever I will I give it. 7 If thou therefore wilt worship me, all shall be thine. 8 And Jesus answered and said unto him, Get thee behind me, Satan: for it is written, Thou shalt worship the Lord thy God, and him only shalt thou serve. 9 And he brought him to Jerusalem, and set him on a pinnacle of the temple, and said unto him, If thou be the Son of God, cast thyself down from hence: 10 for it is written, He shall give his angels charge over thee, to keep thee: 11 and in their hands they shall bear thee up, lest at any time thou dash thy foot against a stone. 12 And Jesus answering said unto him, It is said, Thou shalt not tempt the Lord thy God. 13 And when the devil had ended all the temptation, he departed from him for a season.

14 And Jesus returned in the power of the Spirit into Galilee: and there went out a fame of him through all the region round about. 15 And he taught in their synagogues, being glorified of all. 16 And he came to Nazareth, where he had been brought up: and, as his custom was, he went into the synagogue on the sabbath day, and stood up for to read. 17 And there was delivered unto him the book of the prophet Esaias. And when he had opened the book, he found the place where it was written, 18 The Spirit of the Lord is upon me, because he hath anointed me to preach the gospel to

---

ˣ — ὁ GLTTᵣAW. ʸ — τὴν LTTᵣA. ᶻ Ναζαρέθ W ; Ναζαρά Nazara T. ᵃ ἀνατεθραμμένος T. ᵇ τοῦ προφήτου Ἡσαίου LTTᵣA. ᶜ ἀνοίξας having opened LTr. ᵈ — τὸν T.
ᵉ εἵνεκεν GLTTᵣAW. ᶠ εὐαγγελίσασθαι GLTTᵣAW. ᵍ — ἰάσασθαι τοὺς συντετριμμένους
τὴν καρδίαν G[L]TTᵣA. ʰ ἐν τῇ συναγωγῇ ἦσαν οἱ ὀφθαλμοὶ L ; οἱ ὀφθαλμοὶ ἐν τῇ συναγωγῇ
ἦσαν TTᵣA.

the poor ; he hath sent me to heal the broken-hearted, to preach de-liverance to the cap-tives, and recovering of sight to the blind, to set at liberty them that are bruised, 19 to preach the acceptable year of the Lord. 20 And he closed the book, and he gave it again to the minister, and sat down. And the eyes of all them that were in the synagogue were fastened on him. 21 And he began to say unto them, This day is this scripture fulfilled in your ears. 22 And all bare him witness, and wondered at the gracious words which proceeded out of his mouth. And they said, Is not this Joseph's son? 23 And he said unto them, Ye will surely say unto me this proverb, Phy-sician, heal thyself : whatsoever we have heard done in Caper-naum, do also here in thy country. 24 And he said, Verily I say unto you, No prophet is accepted in his own country. 25 But I tell you of a truth, many widows were in Israel in the days of Elias, when the heaven was shut up three years and six months, when great famine was throughout all the land ; 26 but unto none of them was Elias sent, save unto Sa-repta, a city of Sidon, unto a woman that was a widow. 27 And many lepers were in Israel in the time of Eliseus the prophet ; and none of them was cleansed, saving Na-aman the Syrian. 28 And all they in the synagogue, when they heard these things, were filled with wrath, 29 and rose up, and thrust him out of the city, and led him unto the brow of the hill whereon their city was built, that they might cast him down head-long. 30 But he pass-ing through the midst of them went his way, 31 And came down

αὐτῷ, καὶ ἐθαύμαζον ἐπὶ τοῖς λόγοις τῆς χάριτος τοῖς ἐκπορευο-
to him, and wondered at the words of grace which pro-

μένοις ἐκ τοῦ.στόματος.αὐτοῦ, καὶ ἔλεγον, ¹Οὐχ‖ ᵏοὗτός ἐστιν
ceeded out of his mouth; and they said, ²Not ³this ¹is

ˡὁ‖ υἱὸς Ἰωσήφ‖; 23 Καὶ εἶπεν πρὸς αὐτούς, Πάντως ἐρεῖτέ
the son of Joseph? And he said to them, Surely ye will say

μοι τὴν.παραβολὴν.ταύτην, Ἰατρέ, θεράπευσον σεαυτόν·
to me this parable, Physician, heal thyself;

ὅσα ἠκούσαμεν γενόμενα ᵐἐν τῇ ‖Καπερναούμ,‖ ποίησον
whatsoever we have heard being done in Capernaum, do

καὶ ὧδε ἐν τῇ.πατρίδι.σου. 24 Εἶπεν.δέ, Ἀμὴν λέγω ὑμῖν, ὅτι
also here in thine [own] country. But he said, Verily I say to you, that

οὐδεὶς προφήτης δεκτός ἐστιν ἐν τῇ.πατρίδι.°αὐτοῦ.‖ 25 ἐπ'
no prophet acceptable is in his [own] country. ²In

ἀληθείας.δὲ λέγω ὑμῖν, ᵖ πολλαὶ χῆραι ἦσαν ἐν ταῖς ἡμέραις
¹but truth I say to you, many widows were in the days

qἨλίου‖ ἐν τῷ Ἰσραήλ, ὅτε ἐκλείσθη ὁ οὐρανὸς ʳἐπὶ‖ ἔτη
of Elias in Israel, when ³was ⁴shut ⁵up ¹the ²heaven for ²years

τρία καὶ μῆνας ἕξ, ὡς ἐγένετο λιμὸς μέγας ἐπὶ πᾶσαν τὴν
¹three and ²months ¹six, when there was a ²famine ¹great upon all the

γῆν, 26 καὶ πρὸς οὐδεμίαν αὐτῶν ἐπέμφθη sἨλίας‖ εἰ.μὴ εἰς
land, and to none of them was sent Elias except to

tΣάρεπτα‖ τῆς ᵛΣιδῶνος,‖ πρὸς γυναῖκα χήραν. 27 καὶ πολλοὶ
Sarepta of Sidonia, to a ²woman ¹widow. And many

λεπροὶ ἦσαν ʷἐπὶ Ἐλισσαίου τοῦ προφήτου ἐν τῷ Ἰσραήλ,‖
lepers were in the time of Elisha the prophet in Israel,

καὶ οὐδεὶς αὐτῶν ἐκαθαρίσθη εἰ.μὴ ˣΝεεμὰν‖ ὁ Σύρος. 28 Καὶ
and none of them was cleansed except Naaman the Syrian. And

ἐπλήσθησαν πάντες θυμοῦ ἐν τῇ συναγωγῇ, ἀκούοντες
ᵉwere ᵉfilled ¹all ⁷with ⁸indignation ²in ³the ⁴synagogue, hearing

ταῦτα. 29 καὶ ἀναστάντες ἐξέβαλον αὐτὸν ἔξω τῆς
these things; and having risen up they cast him out of [the]

πόλεως, καὶ ἤγαγον αὐτὸν ἕως ʸτῆς‖ ὀφρύος τοῦ ὄρους ἐφ'
city, and led him unto the brow of the mountain upon

οὗ ἡ.πόλις.ᶻαὐτῶν ᾠκοδόμητο,‖ ᵃεἰς τὸ‖ κατακρημνίσαι
which their city had been built, for to throw ²down ³headlong

αὐτόν· 30 αὐτὸς.δὲ διελθὼν διὰ μέσου αὐτῶν ἐπορεύετο
¹him; but he passing through [the] midst of them went away.

31 Καὶ κατῆλθεν εἰς ᵇΚαπερναούμ‖ πόλιν τῆς Γαλιλαίας·
And he went down to Capernaum a city of Galilee,

καὶ ἦν διδάσκων αὐτοὺς ἐν τοῖς σάββασιν. 32 καὶ ἐξεπλήσ-
and was teaching them on the sabbaths. And they were as-

σοντο ἐπὶ τῇ.διδαχῇ.αὐτοῦ, ὅτι ἐν ἐξουσίᾳ ἦν ὁ.λόγος.αὐτοῦ.
tonished at his teaching, for with authority was his word.

33 Καὶ ἐν τῇ συναγωγῇ ἦν ἄνθρωπος ἔχων πνεῦμα δαιμονίου
And in the synagogue was a man having a spirit of a demon

ἀκαθάρτου, καὶ ἀνέκραξεν φωνῇ μεγάλῃ, 34 ᶜλέγων,‖ Ἔα,
unclean; and he cried out with a ²voice ¹loud, saying, Ah!

τί ἡμῖν καὶ σοί, Ἰησοῦ Ναζαρηνέ; ἦλθες ἀπολέσαι ἡμᾶς;
what to us and to thee, Jesus, Nazarene? Art thou come to destroy us?

οἶδά σε τίς εἶ, ὁ ἅγιος τοῦ θεοῦ. 35 Καὶ ἐπετίμησεν
I know thee who thou art, the Holy [One] of God. And ²rebuked

---

ⁱ οὐχὶ LTTrA.   ᵏ υἱός ἐστιν Ἰωσὴφ οὗτος TA.   ˡ [ὁ] Tr.   ᵐ εἰς GLTr; εἰς τὴν TA.
ᵃ Καφαρναούμ LTTrAW.   ° ἑαυτοῦ T.   ᵖ + ὅτι that T.   q Ἡλείου T.   ʳ — ἐπὶ LTr[A].
ᵃ Ἡλείας T.   ᵗ Σάρεφθα W.   ᵛ Σιδωνίας LTTrA.   ʷ ἐν τῷ Ἰσραὴλ ἐπὶ Ἐλισαίου (Ἐλισαίου
LT) τοῦ προφήτου LTTrA.   ˣ Ναιμὰν LTTrA.   ʸ — τῆς (read a brow) GTTrA.   ᵂ ᾠκοδόμητο
αὐτῶν TTrA.   ᵃ ὥστε so as GLTTrA.   ᵇ Καφαρναοὺμ LTTrAW.   ᶜ — λέγων T[Tr]A.

αὐτῷ ὁ Ἰησοῦς, λέγων, Φιμώθητι, καὶ ἔξελθε ᵈἐξ⁸ αὐτοῦ.
³him ¹Jesus, saying, Hold thy peace, and come forth out of him.
Καὶ ῥίψαν αὐτὸν τὸ δαιμόνιον εἰς ᵉτὸ‖ μέσον ἐξῆλθεν
And ³having ⁴thrown ⁵him ¹the ²demon into the midst came out
ἀπ᾽ αὐτοῦ, μηδὲν βλάψαν αὐτόν. 36 καὶ ἐγένετο θάμβος
from him, in nothing having hurt him. And ⁴came ¹astonishment
ἐπὶ πάντας, καὶ συνελάλουν πρὸς ἀλλήλους, λέγοντες, Τίς
upon all, and they spoke to one another, saying, What
ὁ λόγος οὗτος, ὅτι ἐν ἐξουσίᾳ καὶ δυνάμει ἐπιτάσσει τοῖς
word [is] this, that with authority and power he commands the
ἀκαθάρτοις πνεύμασιν, καὶ ἐξέρχονται; 37 Καὶ ἐξεπορεύετο
unclean spirits, and they come out? And ³went ⁴out
ἦχος περὶ αὐτοῦ εἰς πάντα τόπον τῆς περιχώρου.
¹a ²rumour concerning him into every place of the country around.

38 Ἀναστὰς δὲ ᶠἐκ‖ τῆς συναγωγῆς εἰσῆλθεν εἰς τὴν οἰκίαν
And rising up out of the synagogue he entered into the house
Σίμωνος· ᵍἡ‖ πενθερὰ δὲ τοῦ Σίμωνος ἦν συνεχομένη
of Simon. ²The ³mother-in-law ¹and of Simon was oppressed with
πυρετῷ μεγάλῳ· καὶ ἠρώτησαν αὐτὸν περὶ αὐτῆς. 39 καὶ
a ²fever ¹great; and they asked him for her. And
ἐπιστὰς ἐπάνω αὐτῆς ἐπετίμησεν τῷ πυρετῷ, καὶ ἀφῆκεν αὐτήν·
standing over her he rebuked the fever, and it left her;
παραχρῆμα δὲ ἀναστᾶσα διηκόνει αὐτοῖς·
and immediately arising she served them.

40 Δύνοντος δὲ τοῦ ἡλίου πάντες ὅσοι εἶχον
And at the going down of the sun all as many as had [persons]
ἀσθενοῦντας νόσοις ποικίλαις ἤγαγον αὐτοὺς πρὸς αὐτόν·
sick with ²diseases ¹various brought them to him,
ὁ δὲ ἑνὶ ἑκάστῳ αὐτῶν τὰς χεῖρας ʰἐπιθεὶς‖ ⁱἐθεράπευ-
and he ⁴on ⁶one ⁵each ⁷of ⁸them ³hands ¹having ²laid healed
σεν‖ αὐτούς· 41 ᵏἐξήρχετο‖ δὲ καὶ δαιμόνια ἀπὸ πολλῶν,
them; and ³went ⁴out ²also ¹demons from many,
ˡκράζοντα‖ καὶ λέγοντα, Ὅτι σὺ εἶ ᵐὁ χριστὸς‖ ὁ υἱὸς τοῦ
crying out and saying, Thou art the Christ the Son
θεοῦ. Καὶ ἐπιτιμῶν οὐκ εἴα αὐτὰ λαλεῖν ὅτι ᾔδεισαν
of God. And rebuking he suffered not them to speak because they knew
τὸν χριστὸν αὐτὸν εἶναι.
⁴the ⁵Christ ¹him ²to ³be.

42 Γενομένης δὲ ἡμέρας ἐξελθὼν ἐπορεύθη εἰς ἔρημον
And ²being ³come ¹day having gone out he went into a desert
τόπον, καὶ οἱ ὄχλοι ⁿἐζήτουν‖ αὐτόν, καὶ ἦλθον ἕως αὐτοῦ
place, and the crowds sought him, and came up to him
καὶ κατεῖχον αὐτὸν τοῦ μὴ πορεύεσθαι ἀπ᾽ αὐτῶν. 43 ὁ δὲ
and were detaining him that he might not go from them. But he
εἶπεν πρὸς αὐτούς, Ὅτι καὶ ταῖς ἑτέραις πόλεσιν εὐαγ-
said to them, Also to the other cities ⁴to ⁵announce
γελίσασθαί ᵒμε δεῖ‖ τὴν βασιλείαν τοῦ θεοῦ· ὅτι
⁶the ⁷glad ⁸tidings ¹it ²behoves ³me, the kingdom of God; because
ᵖεἰς‖ τοῦτο ᑫἀπέσταλμαι.‖ 44 Καὶ ἦν κηρύσσων ʳἐν ταῖς
for this have I been sent forth. And he was preaching in the
συναγωγαῖς‖ τῆς ˢΓαλιλαίας.‖
synagogues of Galilee.

to Capernaum, a city of Galilee, and taught them on the sabbath days. 32 And they were astonished at his doctrine : for his word was with power. 33 And in the synagogue there was a man, which had a spirit of an unclean devil, and cried out with a loud voice, 34 saying, Let us alone ; what have we to do with thee, thou Jesus of Nazareth? art thou come to destroy us? I know thee who thou art; the Holy One of God. 35 And Jesus rebuked him, saying, Hold thy peace, and come out of him. And when the devil had thrown him in the midst, he came out of him, and hurt him not. 36 And they were all amazed, and spake among themselves, saying, What a word is this ! for with authority and power he commandeth the unclean spirits, and they come out. 37 And the fame of him went out into every place of the country round about.

38 And he arose out of the synagogue, and entered into Simon's house. And Simon's wife's mother was taken with a great fever; and they besought him for her. 39 And he stood over her, and rebuked the fever : and immediately she arose and ministered unto them.

40 Now when the sun was setting, all they that had any sick with divers diseases brought them unto him; and he laid his hands on every one of them, and healed them. 41 And devils also came out of many, crying out, and saying, Thou art Christ the Son of God. And he rebuking them not to speak : for they knew that he was Christ.

42 And when it was day, he departed and went into a desert place : and the people sought him, and came unto him, and stayed

ᵈ ἀπ᾽ from LTTrA. ᵉ — τὸ G. ᶠ ἀπὸ from TTrA. ᵍ — ἡ (read [the]) GLTTrAW.
ʰ ἐπιτιθεὶς laying LTTrA. ⁱ ἐθεράπευεν TTrA. ᵏ ἐξήρχοντο T. ˡ κραυγάζοντα LT.
ᵐ — ὁ χριστὸς GLTTrA. ⁿ ἐπεζήτουν sought after GLTTrAW. ᵒ δεῖ με L. ᵖ ἐπὶ LTTrA.
ᑫ ἀπεστάλην I was sent forth TTrA. ʳ εἰς τὰς συναγωγὰς TTrA. ˢ Ἰουδαίας of Judea A.

him, that he should not depart from them. 43 And he said unto them, I must preach the kingdom of God to other cities also: for therefore am I sent. 44 And he preached in the synagogues of Galilee.

V. And it came to pass, that, as the people pressed upon him to hear the word of God, he stood by the lake of Gennesaret, 2 and saw two ships standing by the lake: but the fishermen were gone out of them, and were washing *their* nets. 3 And he entered into one of the ships, which was Simon's, and prayed him that he would thrust out a little from the land. And he sat down, and taught the people out of the ship. 4 Now when he had left speaking, he said unto Simon, Launch out into the deep, and let down your nets for a draught. 5 And Simon answering said unto him, Master, we have toiled all the night, and have taken nothing: nevertheless at thy word I will let down the net. 6 And when they had this done, they inclosed a great multitude of fishes: and their net brake. 7 And they beckoned unto *their* partners, which were in the other ship, that they should come and help them. And they came, and filled both the ships, so that they began to sink. 8 When Simon Peter saw *it*, he fell down at Jesus' knees, saying, Depart from me; for I am a sinful man, O Lord. 9 For he was astonished, and all that were with him, at the draught of the fishes which they had taken: 10 and so *was* also James, and John, the sons of Zebedee, which were partners with Simon. And Jesus said unto Simon, Fear not;

5 Ἐγένετο.δὲ ἐν τῷ τὸν ὄχλον ἐπικεῖσθαι αὐτῷ
And it came to pass during the [time] the crowd pressed on him

ᵗτοῦ‖ ἀκούειν τὸν λόγον τοῦ θεοῦ, καὶ αὐτὸς ἦν ἑστὼς παρὰ
to hear the word of God, that he was standing by

τὴν λίμνην Γεννησαρέτ· 2 καὶ ᵛεἶδεχ‖ δύο ʷπλοῖα‖ ἑστῶτα
the lake of Gennesaret: and he saw two ships standing

παρὰ τὴν λίμνην· οἱ.δὲ ˣἁλιεῖς‖ ʸἀποβάντες ἀπ' αὐτῶν‖
by the lake: but the fishermen having gone out from them

ᶻἀπέπλυναν‖ τὰ δίκτυα. 3 ἐμβὰς.δὲ εἰς ἓν ' τῶν πλοίων,
washed the nets. And having entered into one of the ships,

ὃ ἦν ᵃτοῦ‖ Σίμωνος, ἠρώτησεν αὐτὸν ἀπὸ τῆς γῆς ἐπαναγα-
which was Simon's, he asked him from the land to put

γεῖν ὀλίγον· ᵇκαὶ καθίσας‖ ᶜἐδίδασκεν ἐκ τοῦ πλοίου‖ τοὺς
off a little; and having sat down he taught from the ship the

ὄχλους. 4 Ὡς.δὲ ἐπαύσατο λαλῶν εἶπεν πρὸς τὸν Σίμωνα,
crowds. And when he ceased speaking he said to Simon,

Ἐπανάγαγε εἰς τὸ βάθος καὶ χαλάσατε τὰ.δίκτυα.ὑμῶν εἰς
Put off into the deep and let down your nets for

ἄγραν. 5 Καὶ ἀποκριθεὶς ᵈὁ‖ Σίμων εἶπεν ᵉαὐτῷ,‖ Ἐπιστάτα,
a haul. And answering Simon said to him, Master,

δι' ὅλης ᶠτῆς‖ νυκτὸς κοπιάσαντες οὐδὲν ἐλάβομεν·
through ²whole ¹the night having laboured, nothing have we taken,

ἐπὶ.δὲ τῷ.ῥήματί.σου χαλάσω ᵍτὸ δίκτυον.‖ 6 Καὶ τοῦτο
but at thy word I will let down the net. And this

ποιήσαντες συνέκλεισαν ʰἰχθύων πλῆθος‖ πολύ· ⁱδιερρήγνυτο‖
having done they enclosed of fishes a ²shoal ¹great; ᵏwas ⁷breaking

δὲ ʲτὸ δίκτυον‖ αὐτῶν. 7 καὶ κατένευσαν τοῖς μετόχοις
³and ⁵net ⁴their. And they beckoned to the partners

ᵏτοῖς‖ ἐν τῷ ἑτέρῳ πλοίῳ, τοῦ.ἐλθόντας συλλαβέσθαι αὐτοῖς·
⁴those in the other ship, that coming they should help them;

καὶ ˡἦλθον,‖ καὶ ἔπλησαν ἀμφότερα τὰ πλοῖα, ὥστε βυθίζε-
and they came, and filled both the ships, so that ²were⁴sink-

σθαι.αὐτά. 8 ἰδὼν.δὲ Σίμων Πέτρος προσέπεσεν τοῖς γόνασιν
ing ¹they. And ³having ⁴seen ¹Simon ²Peter fell at the knees

ᵐτοῦ‖ Ἰησοῦ, λέγων, Ἔξελθε ἀπ' ἐμοῦ, ὅτι ἀνὴρ ἁμαρτωλός
of Jesus, saying, Depart from me, for a man a sinner

εἰμι, κύριε. 9 Θάμβος.γὰρ περιέσχεν αὐτὸν καὶ πάντας τοὺς
am I, Lord. For astonishment laid hold on him and all those

σὺν αὐτῷ, ἐπὶ τῇ ἄγρᾳ τῶν ἰχθύων ⁿῇ‖ συνέλαβον·
with him, at the haul of the fishes which they had taken;

10 ὁμοίως.δὲ καὶ Ἰάκωβον καὶ °Ἰωάννην,‖ υἱοὺς Ζεβεδαίου,
and in like manner also James and John, sons of Zebedee,

οἳ ἦσαν κοινωνοὶ τῷ Σίμωνι. Καὶ εἶπεν πρὸς τὸν Σίμωνα
who were partners with Simon. And ²said ³to ¹Simon

ᴾὁ‖ Ἰησοῦς, Μὴ.φοβοῦ· ἀπὸ τοῦ.νῦν ἀνθρώπους ἔσῃ
¹Jesus, Fear not; from henceforth men thou shalt be

ζωγρῶν. 11 Καὶ καταγαγόντες τὰ πλοῖα ἐπὶ τὴν γῆν, ἀφέντες
capturing. And having brought the ships to land, leaving

�q ἅπαντα‖ ἠκολούθησαν αὐτῷ.
all they followed him.

ᵗ καὶ also TTrA.   ᵛ ἴδεν T.   ʷ πλοιάρια small ships TA.   ˣ ἁλεεῖς T.   ʸ ἀπ' αὐτῶν ἀποβάντες TTrA.   ᶻ ἔπλυνον were washing LTrA; ἔπλυναν T.   ᵃ — τοῦ LTTrA.   ᵇ καθίσας δὲ TA.   ᶜ ἐν (in) τῷ πλοίῳ ἐδίδασκεν T; ἐκ τοῦ πλοίου ἐδίδασκεν A.   ᵈ — ὁ TTrA.   ᵉ — αὐτῷ T.   ᶠ — τῆς (read a whole night) LTTrA.   ᵍ τὰ δίκτυα the nets TTr.   ʰ πλῆθος ἰχθύων GTTrAW.   ⁱ διερρήγνυτο L; διερήσσετο TTrA.   ʲ τὰ δίκτυα nets (read διερ. were breaking) TTrA.   ᵏ — τοῖς [L]TTrA.   ˡ ἦλθαν T.   ᵐ — τοῦ LTTrAW.   ⁿ ὧν TTr.   ᵒ Ἰωάνην Tr.   ᴾ — ὁ [Tr]A.   q πάντα LTTr.

.12 Καὶ ἐγένετο ἐν.τῷ.εἶναι αὐτὸν ἐν μιᾷ τῶν πόλεων,
And it came to pass   as ²was   ¹he   in one of the   cities,
καὶ ἰδού, ἀνὴρ πλήρης λέπρας· ʳκαὶ ἰδὼνǁ τὸν Ἰησοῦν, πεσὼν
that behold, a man   full   of leprosy, and seeing   Jesus, . falling
ἐπὶ πρόσωπον ἐδεήθη αὐτοῦ, λέγων, Κύριε, ἐὰν θέλῃς·
upon [his] face he besought him, saying, Lord, if thou wilt
δύνασαί με καθαρίσαι. 13 Καὶ ἐκτείνας τὴν χεῖρα
thou art able me to cleanse. And having stretched out [his] hand
ἥψατο αὐτοῦ, ˢεἰπών,ǁ Θέλω, καθαρίσθητι. Καὶ εὐθέως ἡ
he touched him, saying, I will; be thou cleansed. And immediately the
λέπρα ἀπῆλθεν ἀπ' αὐτοῦ. 14 καὶ αὐτὸς παρήγγειλεν αὐτῷ
leprosy departed from him.   And · he   charged   him
μηδενὶ εἰπεῖν· ἀλλὰ ἀπελθὼν δεῖξον σεαυτὸν τῷ ἱερεῖ, καὶ
no one to tell; but having gone shew thyself to the priest, and
προσένεγκε περὶ τοῦ.καθαρισμοῦ.σου, καθὼς προσέταξεν ᵗΜω-
offer   for   thy cleansing, as   ²ordered   ¹Mo-
σῆς,ǁ εἰς μαρτύριον αὐτοῖς. 15 Διήρχετο.δὲ μᾶλλον ὁ
ses, for a testimony to them. But was spread abroad still more the
λόγος περὶ αὐτοῦ· καὶ συνήρχοντο ὄχλοι πολλοὶ ἀκούειν,
report concerning him; and ⁴were ⁵coming ²crowds ¹great to hear,
καὶ θεραπεύεσθαι ᵘὑπ' αὐτοῦǁ ἀπὸ τῶν.ἀσθενειῶν.αὐτῶν·
and .to be healed by   him from   their infirmities.
16 αὐτὸς.δὲ ἦν ὑποχωρῶν ἐν ταῖς ἐρήμοις καὶ προσευχό-
But he was retiring in the deserts and pray-
μενος.
ing.
17 Καὶ ἐγένετο ἐν μιᾷ τῶν ἡμερῶν καὶ αὐτὸς ἦν διδάσ-
And it came to pass on one of the days   that he was teach-
κων, καὶ ἦσαν καθήμενοι ʷΦαρισαῖοι καὶ νομοδιδάσκαλοι,
ing, and there were sitting by Pharisees and teachers of the law,
οἳ · ἦσαν ˣἐληλυθότεςǁ ἐκ πάσης κώμης τῆς Γαλιλαίας καὶ
who were come   out of every village of Galilee and
Ἰουδαίας καὶ Ἱερουσαλήμ· καὶ δύναμις κυρίου ἦν εἰς
of Judæa and of Jerusalem: and power of [the] Lord was [there] for
τὸ ἰᾶσθαι ʸαὐτούς.ǁ 18 καὶ ἰδού, ἄνδρες φέροντες ἐπὶ κλίνης
to heal them.   And behold, men   carrying upon a couch
ἄνθρωπον ὃς ἦν παραλελυμένος, καὶ ἐζήτουν αὐτὸν εἰσενεγ-
a man who was paralysed,   and they sought ³him ¹to ²bring
κεῖν καὶ θεῖναιᶻ ἐνώπιον αὐτοῦ· 19 καὶ μὴ εὑρόντες ᵃδιὰǁ
in and to place [him] .before him.   And not having found by
ποίας εἰσενέγκωσιν αὐτὸν διὰ τὸν ὄχλον, ἀναβάντες
what way they should bring in him on account of the crowd, going up
ἐπὶ τὸ δῶμα, διὰ τῶν κεράμων καθῆκαν αὐτὸν σὺν τῷ
on the housetop, through the tiles they let down him with the
κλινιδίῳ εἰς τὸ μέσον ἔμπροσθεν τοῦ Ἰησοῦ. 20 καὶ ἰδὼν τὴν
little couch into the midst before   Jesus.   And seeing
πίστιν.αὐτῶν εἶπεν ᵇαὐτῷ,ǁ Ἄνθρωπε, ἀφέωνταί σοι
their faith he said to him, Man, ³have ⁴been ⁵forgiven ¹thee
αἱ.ἁμαρτίαι.σου. 21 Καὶ ἤρξαντο διαλογίζεσθαι οἱ γραμματεῖς
thy ²sins.   And began to reason the scribes
καὶ οἱ Φαρισαῖοι, λέγοντες, Τίς ἐστιν οὗτος ὃς λαλεῖ βλασ-
and the Pharisees, saying, Who is this who speaks blas-
φημίας; τίς δύναται ᶜἀφιέναι ἁμαρτίας,ǁ εἰ.μὴ μόνος ὁ θεός;
phemies? who is able to forgive sins, except ²alone ¹God?

from henceforth thou
shalt catch men.
11 And when they had
brought their ships to
land, they forsook all,
and followed him.
12 And it came to
pass, when he was in
a certain city, behold
a man full of leprosy:
who seeing Jesus fell
on his face, and be-
sought him, saying,
Lord, if thou wilt,
thou· canst make me
clean. 13 And he put
forth · his hand, and
touched him, saying,
I will: be thou clean.
And immediately the
leprosy departed from
him. 14 And he charg-
ed him to tell no man:
but go, and shew thy-
self to the priest, and
offer for thy cleansing,
according as Moses
commanded, for a tes-
timony unto them.
15 But so much the
more went there a
fame abroad of him:
and great multitudes
came together to hear,
and to be healed by him
of their infirmities.
16 And he withdrew
himself into the wil-
derness, and prayed.

17 And it came to
pass on a certain day,
as he was teaching,
that there were Pha-
risees and doctors of
the law sitting by,
which were come out
of every town of Ga-
lilee, and Judæa, and
Jerusalem : and the
power of the Lord was
present to heal them.
18 And, behold, men
brought in a bed a
man which was taken
with a palsy: and they
sought means to bring
him in, and to lay him
before him. 19 And
when they could not
find by what way they
might bring him in
because of the multi-
tude, they went upon
the housetop, and let
him down through the
tiling with his couch
into the midst before
Jesus. 20 And when he
saw their faith, he said
unto him, Man, thy
sins are forgiven thee.
21 And the scribes and
the Pharisees began to
reason, saying, Who is
this which speaketh
blasphemies? Who can
forgive sins, but God
alone? 22 But when

ʳ ἰδὼν δὲ T.   ˢ λέγων LTr.   ᵗ Μωϋσῆς LTTrAW.   ᵛ — ὑπ' αὐτοῦ LTTrA.   ʷ + οἱ the L.
ˣ συνεληλυθότες come together L.   ʸ αὐτόν him (read was for his healing) TA.   ᶻ + αὐτὸν
him A.   ᵃ — διὰ GLTTrAW.   ᵇ — αὐτῷ GLTTrA.   ᶜ ἁμαρτίας ἀφεῖναι LTTrA.

Jesus perceived their thoughts, he answering said unto them, What reason ye in your hearts? 23 Whether is easier, to say, Thy sins be forgiven thee; or to say, Rise up and walk? 24 But that ye may know that the Son of man hath power upon earth to forgive sins, (he said unto the sick of the palsy,) I say unto thee, Arise, and take up thy couch, and go into thine house. 25 And immediately he rose up before them, and took up that whereon he lay, and departed to his own house, glorifying God. 26 And they were all amazed, and they glorified God, and were filled with fear, saying, We have seen strange things to day.

22 Ἐπιγνοὺς δὲ ὁ Ἰησοῦς τοὺς διαλογισμοὺς αὐτῶν ᵈἀπο-
But ²knowing　¹Jesus　　　their reasonings　　　　an-

κριθεὶς‖ εἶπεν πρὸς αὐτούς, Τί διαλογίζεσθε ἐν ταῖς καρδίαις
swering　said　to　them,　Why　reason ye　in　　²hearts

ὑμῶν; 23 τί ἐστιν εὐκοπώτερον, εἰπεῖν, Ἀφέωνταί σοι
¹your?　which is　　easier,　　to say, Have been forgiven thee

αἱ ἁμαρτίαι σου, ἢ εἰπεῖν, ᵉᵛἜγειραι‖ καὶ περιπάτει; 24 ἵνα δὲ
thy sins,　or to say,　Arise　and walk?　But that

εἰδῆτε ὅτι ᶠἐξουσίαν ἔχει ὁ υἱὸς τοῦ ἀνθρώπου ἐπὶ τῆς
ye may know that　authority　has the Son　　of man　　on the

γῆς ἀφιέναι ἁμαρτίας, εἶπεν τῷ ᵍπαραλελυμένῳ,‖ Σοὶ λέγω,
earth to forgive sins,　he said to the　paralysed,　To thee I say,

ʰἔγειραι,‖ καὶ ἄρας τὸ κλινίδιόν σου πορεύου εἰς τὸν οἶκόν
Arise,　and having taken up thy little couch　go　to　²house

σου. 25 Καὶ παραχρῆμα ἀναστὰς ἐνώπιον αὐτῶν, ἄρας
¹thy.　And immediately having stood up before　them, having taken up

ἐφ᾽ ⁱῷ‖ κατέκειτο, ἀπῆλθεν εἰς τὸν οἶκον αὐτοῦ, δοξάζων
[that] on which he was lying, he departed to　his house,　glorifying

τὸν θεόν. 26 καὶ ἔκστασις ἔλαβεν ἅπαντας, καὶ ἐδόξαζον
God.　And amazement seized　all,　and they glorified

τὸν θεόν, καὶ ἐπλήσθησαν φόβου, λέγοντες, Ὅτι εἴδομεν
God,　and　were filled　with fear,　saying,　We have seen

παράδοξα σήμερον.
strange things to-day.

27 Καὶ μετὰ ταῦτα ἐξῆλθεν, καὶ ἐθεάσατο τελώνην,
And after these things he went forth, and　saw　a tax-gatherer,

27 And after these things he went forth, and saw a publican, named Levi, sitting at the receipt of custom: and he said unto him, Follow me. 28 And he left all, rose up, and followed him. 29 And Levi made him a great feast in his own house: and there was a great company of publicans and of others that sat down with them. 30 But their scribes and Pharisees murmured against his disciples, saying, Why do ye eat and drink with publicans and sinners? 31 And Jesus answering said unto them, They that are whole need not a physician; but they that are sick. 32 I came not to call the righteous, but sinners to repentance. 33 And they said unto him, Why do the disciples of John fast

ὀνόματι ʲΛευΐν,‖ καθήμενον ἐπὶ τὸ τελώνιον, καὶ εἶπεν αὐτῷ,
by name　Levi,　sitting　at the tax office,　and said to him,

Ἀκολούθει μοι. 28 Καὶ καταλιπὼν ᵏἅπαντα,‖ ἀναστὰς ˡἠκο-
Follow　me.　And having left　`all,　having arisen he fol-

λούθησεν‖ αὐτῷ. 29 Καὶ ἐποίησεν δοχὴν μεγάλην ᵐὁ‖
lowed　him.　And　²made　⁵entertainment　ᵃa ⁴great

ⁿΛευῒς‖ αὐτῷ ἐν τῇ οἰκίᾳ αὐτοῦ, καὶ ἦν ὄχλος ᵒτελω-
¹Levi　for him in　his house,　and there was a ²multitude ³of ᵗtax-

νῶν πολύς‖ καὶ ἄλλων οἳ ἦσαν μετ᾽ αὐτῶν κατακείμενοι.
gatherers ¹great　and others who were with them　reclining

30 καὶ ἐγόγγυζον οἱ ᵖγραμματεῖς αὐτῶν καὶ οἱ Φαρι-
[at table].　And　murmured　their scribes　and the Phari-

σαῖοι‖ πρὸς τοὺς μαθητὰς αὐτοῦ, λέγοντες, ᑫΔιατί‖ μετὰ
sees　at　his disciples,　saying,　Why　with

ʳτελωνῶν ˢκαὶ ἁμαρτωλῶν‖ ἐσθίετε καὶ πίνετε; 31 καὶ ἀπο-
tax-gatherers and　sinners　do ye eat and drink?　And an-

κριθεὶς ὁ Ἰησοῦς εἶπεν πρὸς αὐτούς, Οὐ χρείαν ἔχουσιν οἱ
swering　Jesus　said　to　them,　No need　have　they who

ὑγιαίνοντες ἰατροῦ, ᵗἀλλ᾽‖ οἱ κακῶς ἔχοντες. 32 οὐκ
are in health of a physician, but they who ill　are.　³Not

ἐλήλυθα καλέσαι δικαίους, ἀλλὰ ἁμαρτωλοὺς εἰς μετά-
¹I ²have come to call righteous [ones], but　sinners　to repent-

νοιαν. 33 Οἱ δὲ ᵛεἶπον‖ πρὸς αὐτόν, ʷΔιατί‖ οἱ μαθηταὶ
ance.　And they said　to　him,　Why　²the ³disciples

ᵈ — ἀποκριθεὶς ʟ[ᴛʀ].　ᵉ Ἔγειρε ɢʟᴛᴛʀᴀᴡ.　ᶠ ὁ υἱὸς τοῦ ἀνθρώπου ἐξουσίαν ἔχει ᴛᴛʀᴀ.
ᵍ παραλυτικῷ paralytic ʟ.　ʰ ἔγειρε ɢʟᴛᴛʀᴀᴡ.　ⁱ ᾧ ᴛᴛʀᴀ.　ʲ Λευεὶν ᴀ; Λευείν ᴛᴛʀ.
ᵏ πάντα ʟᴛᴛʀᴀ.　ˡ ἠκολούθει ʟᴛᴛʀᴀ.　ᵐ — ὁ ɢʟᴛᴛʀᴀᴡ.　ⁿ Λευεὶς ᴀ; Λευεὶς ᴛᴛʀ.
ᵒ πολὺς τελωνῶν ʟᴛᴛʀᴀ.　ᵖ Φαρισαῖοι καὶ οἱ γραμματεῖς αὐτῶν [αὐτῶν] ᴛʀ) ʟᴛᴛʀᴀᴡ.　ᑫ Διὰ
τί ʟᴛʀᴀ.　ʳ + τῶν the ɢʟᴛᴛʀᴀᴡ.　ˢ — καὶ ἁμαρτωλῶν ᴀ.　ᵗ ἀλλὰ ʟᴛᴛʀᴀ.　ᵛ εἶπαν
ʟᴛᴛʀᴀ.　ʷ Διὰ τί ʟ[ᴛʀ]; — Διατί ᴛᴀ.

ᵍ'Ἰωάννου‖ νηστεύουσιν πυκνὰ καὶ δεήσεις ποιοῦνται, ὁ-
⁶of ⁵John ¹fast often and supplications make, in like
μοίως᾽ καὶ οἱ τῶν Φαρισαίων, οἱ.δὲ σοὶ ἐσθίουσιν καὶ
manner also those of the Pharisees, but those of thee eat and
πίνουσιν; 34 Ὁ.δὲ ʸ εἶπεν πρὸς αὐτούς, Μὴ δύνασθε τοὺς
drink? And he said to them, Are ye able ³the
υἱοὺς τοῦ νυμφῶνος, ἐν.ᾧ ὁ νυμφίος μετ᾽ αὐτῶν ἐστιν
⁴sons ⁵of ⁶the ⁷bridechamber ¹⁰while ¹¹the ¹²bridegroom ¹⁴with ¹⁵them ¹³is
ποιῆσαι ᶻνηστεύειν‖; 35 ἐλεύσονται.δὲ ἡμέραι ᵃκαὶ‖ ὅταν
¹to ²make ⁸to ⁹fast? But will come days ²also ¹when
ἀπαρθῇ ἀπ᾽ αὐτῶν ὁ νυμφίος, τότε νηστεύσουσιν ἐν
shall be taken away from them the bridegroom, then they will fast in
ἐκείναις ταῖς ἡμέραις. 36 Ἔλεγεν.δὲ καὶ παραβολὴν πρὸς
those days. And he spoke also a parable to
αὐτούς, Ὅτι οὐδεὶς ἐπίβλημα ᵇ ἱματίου καινοῦ ᶜ ἐπιβάλλει ἐπὶ
them, No one a piece of a,²garment ¹new puts on
ἱμάτιον παλαιόν· εἰ.δὲ.μήγε καὶ τὸ καινὸν ᵈσχίζει,‖ καὶ
²garment ¹an ²old, otherwise both the new he rends, and
τῷ παλαιῷ ᵉοὐ.συμφωνεῖ‖. ᶠ ἐπίβλημα τὸ ἀπὸ τοῦ
with the old does not agree [the] piece which [is] from the
καινοῦ. 37 καὶ οὐδεὶς βάλλει οἶνον νέον εἰς ἀσκοὺς παλαιούς·
new. And no one puts ²wine ¹new into ²skins ¹old,
εἰ.δὲ.μήγε ῥήξει ᵍὁ νέος οἶνος‖ τοὺς ἀσκούς, καὶ αὐτὸς
otherwise ⁴will ⁵burst ¹the ²new ³wine the skins, and it
ἐκχυθήσεται, καὶ οἱ ἀσκοὶ ἀπολοῦνται· 38 ἀλλὰ οἶνον νέον
will be poured out, and the skins will be destroyed; but ²wine ¹new
εἰς ἀσκοὺς καινοὺς βλητέον, ʰκαὶ ἀμφότεροι συντηροῦνται.‖
into ²skins ¹new is to be put, and both are preserved together.
39 καὶ οὐδεὶς πιὼν παλαιὸν ⁱεὐθέως‖ θέλει νέον·
And no one having drunk old [wine] immediately desires new;
λέγει.γάρ, Ὁ παλαιὸς ᵏχρηστότερος‖ ἐστιν.
for he says, The old ²better ¹is.

6 Ἐγένετο.δὲ ἐν σαββάτῳ ˡδευτεροπρώτῳ‖ διαπο-
And it came to pass on ⁴sabbath [¹the] ²second ¹first ⁶passed
ρεύεσθαι αὐτὸν διὰ ᵐτῶν‖ σπορίμων· καὶ ³ἔτιλλον οἱ
³along ⁵he through the corn fields; and ³were ⁴plucking the
μαθηταὶ.αὐτοῦ ⁿτοὺς στάχυας, καὶ ἤσθιον,‖ ψώχοντες
¹his ²disciples the ears, and were eating, rubbing [them]
ταῖς χερσίν°. 2 τινὲς.δὲ τῶν Φαρισαίων εἶπον ᴾαὐτοῖς,‖ Τί
in the hands. But some of the Pharisees said to them, Why
ποιεῖτε ὃ οὐκ.ἔξεστιν ᑫποιεῖν ἐν‖ τοῖς σάββασιν; 3 Καὶ
do ye that which it is not lawful to do on the sabbaths? And
ἀποκριθεὶς ʳπρὸς αὐτοὺς εἶπεν ὁ Ἰησοῦς,‖ Οὐδὲ τοῦτο ἀνέγνωτε,
answering to them ²said ¹Jesus, Not even this did ye read,
ὃ ἐποίησεν ˢΔαβίδ,‖ ᵗὁπότε‖ ἐπείνασεν αὐτὸς καὶ οἱ
that which ²did ¹David, when he hungered, himself and those who
μετ᾽ αὐτοῦ ᵛὄντες‖; 4 ᵂὡς‖ εἰσῆλθεν εἰς τὸν οἶκον τοῦ θεοῦ,
with him were? how he entered into the house of God,
καὶ τοὺς ἄρτους τῆς προθέσεως ˣᵃἔλαβεν, καὶ‖ ἔφαγεν, καὶ
and the loaves of the presentation ²took, and ate, and

often, and make pray-
ers, and likewise *the
disciples* of the Phari-
sees; but thine eat and
drink? 34 And he said
unto them, Can ye
make the children of
the bridechamber fast,
while the bridegroom
is with them? 35 But
the days will come,
when the bridegroom
shall be taken away
from them, and then
shall they fast in those
days. 36 And he spake
also a parable unto
them; No man putteth
a piece of a new gar-
ment upon an old; if
otherwise, then both
the new maketh a rent,
and the piece that was
taken out of the new
agreeth not with the
old. 37 And no man
putteth new wine into
old bottles; else the
new wine will burst
the bottles, and be
spilled, and the bottles
shall perish. 38 But
new wine must be put
into new bottles; and
both are preserved.
39 No man also hav-
ing drunk old *wine*
straightway desireth
new: for he saith, The
old is better.

VI. And it came to
pass on the second
sabbath after the first,
that he went through
the corn fields; and his
disciples plucked the
ears of corn, and did
eat, rubbing *them* in
their hands. 2 And
certain of the Phari-
sees said unto them,
Why do ye that which
is not lawful to do on
the sabbath days?
3 And Jesus answer-
ing them said, Have
ye not read so much
as this, what David
did, when himself was
an hungred, and they
which were with him;
4 how he went into
the house of God, and
did take and eat the
shewbread, and gave

ˣ Ἰωάνου Tr. ʸ + Ἰησοῦς (And) Jesus TTrA. ᶻ νηστεῦσαι TTrA. ᵃ [καὶ] L. ᵇ + ἀπὸ
from (a garment) [L]TTrA. ᶜ + σχίσας having rent (*read* puts [it]) TTrA. ᵈ σχίσει he
will rend LTTrA. ᵉ οὐ συμφωνήσει will not agree LTTrA. ᶠ + τὸ the TTrA. ᵍ ὁ οἶνος
ὁ νέος LTTrAW. ʰ — καὶ ἀμφότεροι συντηροῦνται T[Tr]A. ⁱ — εὐθέως TTrA. ᵏ χρηστός
good TTrA. ˡ — δευτεροπρώτῳ [L]Tᵢ[A]. ᵐ — τῶν LTTrA. ⁿ καὶ ἤσθιον τοὺς στάχυας TrA.
° + [αὐτῶν] of them L. ᴾ — αὐτοῖς [L]TTrA. ᑫ — ἐν T; — ποιεῖν ἐν (*read* τοῖς on the) LTrA.
ʳ ὁ Ἰησοῦς εἶπεν πρὸς αὐτοὺς L; ὁ Ἰησοῦς πρὸς αὐτοὺς εἶπεν T. ˢ Δαυὶδ GW; Δαυεὶδ LTTrA.
ᵗ ὅτε LTr. ᵛ — ὄντες LTr. ᵂ πῶς L; [ὡς] Tᵣ. ˣᵃ λαβὼν having taken LTrA.

also to them that were with him; which it is not lawful to eat but for the priests alone? 5 And he said unto them, That the Son of man is Lord also of the sabbath.

6 And it came to pass also on another sabbath, that he entered into the synagogue and taught: and there was a man whose right hand was withered. 7 And the scribes and Pharisees watched him, whether he would heal on the sabbath day; that they might find an accusation against him. 8 But he knew their thoughts, and said to the man which had the withered hand, Rise up, and stand forth in the midst. And he arose and stood forth. 9 Then said Jesus unto them, I will ask you one thing; Is it lawful on the sabbath days to do good, or to do evil? to save life, or to destroy it? 10 And looking round about upon them all, he said unto the man, Stretch forth thy hand. And he did so: and his hand was restored whole as the other. 11 And they were filled with madness; and communed one with another what they might do to Jesus.

12 And it came to pass in those days, that he went out into a mountain to pray, and continued all night in prayer to God. 13 And when it was day, he called unto him his disciples: and of them he chose twelve,' whom also he named apostles; 14 Simon, (whom he also named Peter,) and Andrew his brother, James and John, Philip and Bartholomew, 15 Matthew and Thomas, James the son

ἔδωκεν ᵞκαὶ" τοῖς μετ' αὐτοῦ, οὓς οὐκ.ἔξεστιν φαγεῖν εἰ.μὴ
gave also to those with him, which it is not lawful to eat except

μόνους τοὺς ἱερεῖς; 5 Καὶ ἔλεγεν αὐτοῖς, ᶻ"Οτι" κύριός ἐστιν
only ¹the ²priests? And he said to them, ᵉLord ⁵is

ὁ υἱὸς τοῦ ἀνθρώπου καὶ τοῦ σαββάτου:
the ²Son ³of ⁴man also of the sabbath.

6 Ἐγένετο.δὲ ᵃκαὶ" ἐν ἑτέρῳ σαββάτῳ εἰσελθεῖν αὐτὸν
And it came to pass also on another sabbath ²entered ·¹he

εἰς τὴν συναγωγὴν καὶ διδάσκειν· καὶ ἦν ᵇἐκεῖ ἄνθρωπος,"
into the synagogue and taught; and there was there a man,

καὶ ἡ.χεὶρ.αὐτοῦ ἡ δεξιὰ ἦν ξηρά. 7 ᶜπαρετήρουν".δὲ ᵈαὐτὸν"
and his hand the right was withered. And were ⁷watching ⁸him

οἱ γραμματεῖς καὶ οἱ Φαρισαῖοι, εἰ ἐν τῷ σαββάτῳ ᵉθερα-
¹the ²scribes ³and ⁴the ⁵Pharisees, whether on the sabbath he will

πεύσει," ἵνα εὕρωσιν ᶠκατηγορίαν" αὐτοῦ. 8 αὐτὸς.δὲ
heal, that they might find an accusation against him. But he

ᾔδει τοὺς.διαλογισμοὺς.αὐτῶν, ᵍκαὶ ἶπεν" τῷ ᵇἀνθρώπῳ" τῷ
knew their reasonings, and said to the man who

ξηρὰν ἔχοντι τὴν χεῖρα, ᶦΈγειραι," καὶ στῆθι εἰς τὸ μέσον.
withered ¹had ²the hand, Arise, and stand in the midst.

ᵏὉ.δὲ" ἀναστὰς ἔστη. 9 Εἶπεν ¹οὖν" ὁ Ἰησοῦς πρὸς αὐτούς,
And he having risen up stood. ²Said ·¹then ²Jesus to them,

ᵐἘπερωτήσω" ὑμᾶς, ⁿτί" ἔξεστιν ᵒτοῖς σάββασιν" ἀγαθο-
I will ask you, whether, it is lawful on the sabbaths to do

ποιῆσαι ἢ κακοποιῆσαι; ψυχὴν σῶσαι ἢ ᴾἀπολέσαι"; 10 Καὶ
good or to do evil? ³life ¹to ²save or to destroy? And

περιβλεψάμενος πάντας αὐτοὺς εἶπεν ۹τῷ ἀνθρώπῳ,"
having looked around on all them he said to the man,

Ἔκτεινον τὴν.χεῖρά.σου. Ὁ.δὲ ἐποίησεν ʳοὕτως·ᵃ καὶ ˢἀπο-
Stretch out thy hand. And he did so, and ²was

κατεστάθη" ἡ.χεὶρ.αὐτοῦ ᵗὑγιὴς" ᵛὡς ἡ ἄλλη." 11 αὐτοὶ.δὲ
¹restored ¹his ²hand sound as the other. But they

ἐπλήσθησαν ἀνοίας, καὶ διελάλουν πρὸς ἀλλήλους τί
were filled with madness, and consulted with one another [as to] what

ἂν ᵂποιήσειαν" τῷ Ἰησοῦ.
they should do to Jesus.

12 Ἐγένετο.δὲ ἐν ταῖς.ἡμέραις.ταύταις ˣἐξῆλθεν" εἰς τὸ
And it came to pass in those days he went out into the

ὄρος προσεύξασθαι· καὶ ἦν διανυκτερεύων ἐν τῇ προσευχῇ
mountain to pray, and he was spending the night in prayer

τοῦ θεοῦ. 13 καὶ ὅτε ἐγένετο ἡμέρα προσεφώνησεν τοὺς
of God. And when it became day he called to [him]

μαθητὰς.αὐτοῦ· καὶ ἐκλεξάμενος ἀπ' αὐτῶν δώδεκα, οὓς καὶ
his disciples, and chose out from them twelve, whom also

ἀποστόλους.ὠνόμασεν, 14 Σίμωνα ὃν καὶ ὠνόμασεν Πέτρον
³apostles ¹he ²named: Simon whom also he named Peter

καὶ Ἀνδρέαν τὸν.ἀδελφὸν.αὐτοῦ, ᵞᵃἸάκωβον καὶ ᶻᵃἸωάννην,"
and Andrew his brother, James and John,

ᵞᵃΦίλιππον καὶ Βαρθολομαῖον, 15 ᵞᵃ ᵃᵃΜατθαῖον" καὶ Θωμᾶν,
Philip and Bartholomew, Matthew and Thomas,

ʸ — καὶ LTTrA. ᶻ [ὅτι] Tr. ᵃ — καὶ LTTr[A]. ᵇ ἄνθρωπος ἐκεῖ TTrA. ᶜ παρετηροῦντο
LTTrAW. ᵈ — αὐτὸν LTTrAW. ᵉ θεραπεύει he heals LTTrA. ᶠ κατηγορεῖν to accuse TTrA.
ᵍ εἶπεν δὲ TTrA. ʰ ἀνδρὶ man TTrA. ᶦ Ἔγειρε GLTTrAW. ᵏ καὶ LTTrA. ˡ δὲ and LTTr.
ᵐ Ἐπερωτῶ I ask TTrA. ⁿ εἰ if LTTrA. ᵒ τῷ σαββάτῳ on the sabbath LTTrA. ᴾ ἀποκτεῖναι to kill GW. ۹ αὐτῷ to him GLTTrAW. ʳ — οὕτως GTTrAW. ˢ ἀπεκατεστάθη
GLTTrA. ᵗ — ὑγιὴς GLTTrAW. ᵛ — ὡς ἡ ἄλλη [L]T[Tr]A. ᵂ ποιήσειαν LTTrA. ˣ ἐξελθεῖν
αὐτὸν he went out TTrA. ʸᵃ + καὶ and LTTrA. ᶻᵃ Ἰωάνην Tr. ᵃᵃ Ματθαῖον LTT‹A›

ªἸάκωβον ᵇτὸν τοῦ‖ Ἀλφαίου καὶ Σίμωνα τὸν καλού-
James   the [son]   of Alphæus and Simon who [was] call-

μενον Ζηλωτήν, 16 ᶜ Ἰούδαν   Ἰακώβου, καὶ Ἰούδαν
ed   Zealot,   Judas [brother] of James, and Judas

ᵈἸσκαριώτην,‖ ὃς ᵉκαὶ‖ ἐγένετο   προδότης· 17 καὶ καταβὰς
Iscariote,   who also became [the] betrayer.   And descending

μετ' αὐτῶν ἔστη ἐπὶ τόπου πεδινοῦ, καὶ ὄχλος ᶠ μαθητῶν
with them he stood on a ²place ¹level,   and a crowd of ²disciples

αὐτοῦ καὶ πλῆθος πολὺ τοῦ λαοῦ ἀπὸ πάσης τῆς Ἰουδαίας
¹his   and a ²multitude ¹great of the people from all   Judæa

καὶ Ἱερουσαλὴμ καὶ τῆς παραλίου Τύρου καὶ Σιδῶνος, οἳ
and Jerusalem and the sea coast of Tyre and Sidon, who

ἦλθον ἀκοῦσαι αὐτοῦ, καὶ ἰαθῆναι ἀπὸ τῶν νόσων αὐτῶν,
came to hear him, and to be healed of   their diseases,

18 καὶ οἱ ᵍὀχλούμενοι‖ ʰὑπὸ‖ πνευμάτων ἀκαθάρτων, ⁱκαὶ‖
    and those   beset   by ²spirits   ¹unclean,   and

ἐθεραπεύοντο. 19 καὶ πᾶς ὁ ὄχλος ᵏἐζήτει‖ ἅπτεσθαι αὐτοῦ·
they were healed.   And all the crowd sought to touch him;

ὅτι δύναμις παρ' αὐτοῦ ἐξήρχετο καὶ ἰᾶτο πάντας.
for power from him   went out and healed all.

20 Καὶ αὐτὸς ἐπάρας τοὺς ὀφθαλμοὺς αὐτοῦ εἰς τοὺς μαθη-
    And he lifting up   his eyes   upon   ²disci-

τὰς αὐτοῦ ἔλεγεν, Μακάριοι οἱ πτωχοί, ὅτι ὑμετέρα ἐστὶν
ples ¹his said, Blessed· [are] the poor, for yours is

ἡ βασιλεία τοῦ θεοῦ. 21 μακάριοι οἱ πεινῶντες νῦν, ὅτι
the kingdom of God.   Blessed [ye] who hunger now, for

χορτασθήσεσθε. μακάριοι οἱ κλαίοντες νυν, ὅτι γελάσετε.
ye shall be filled.   Blessed· [ye] who weep   now, for ye shall laugh.

22 μακάριοί ἐστε ὅταν μισήσωσιν ὑμᾶς οἱ ἄνθρωποι, καὶ ὅταν
    Blessed are ye when ²shall ³hate ⁴you   ¹men,   and when

ἀφορίσωσιν ὑμᾶς, καὶ ὀνειδίσωσιν, καὶ ἐκβάλωσιν τὸ
they shall cut ²off ¹you, and shall reproach [you], and cast out

ὄνομα ὑμῶν ὡς πονηρόν, ˡἕνεκα‖ τοῦ υἱοῦ τοῦ ἀνθρώπου·
your name as wicked, on account of the Son of man:

23 ᵐχαίρετε‖ ἐν ἐκείνῃ τῇ ἡμέρᾳ καὶ σκιρτήσατε· ἰδοὺ γάρ, ὁ
    rejoice in that   day and leap for joy;   for lo,

μισθὸς ὑμῶν πολὺς ἐν τῷ οὐρανῷ· κατὰ ⁿταῦτα‖ γὰρ
your reward [is] great in the heaven, ²according ³to ⁴these ³things ¹for

ἐποίουν τοῖς προφήταις οἱ πατέρες αὐτῶν. 24 Πλὴν οὐαὶ
did ³to ⁴the ²prophets ¹their ²fathers.   But woe

ὑμῖν τοῖς πλουσίοις, ὅτι ἀπέχετε τὴν παράκλησιν ὑμῶν.
to you the   rich,   for ye are receiving your consolation.

25 οὐαὶ ὑμῖν οἱ ἐμπεπλησμένοιᵒ, ὅτι πεινάσετε. οὐαὶ ᵖὑμῖν‖
    Woe to you who have been filled, for ye shall hunger. Woe to you

οἱ γελῶντες νῦν, ὅτι πενθήσετε καὶ κλαύσετε. 26 οὐαὶ ᵠὑμῖν‖
who laugh now, for ye shall mourn and weep.   Woe to you

ὅταν καλῶς ʳὑμᾶς εἴπωσιν‖ ˢπάντες‖ οἱ ἄνθρωποι· κατὰ
when well of you speak   all   men,   ²according ³to

ⁿταῦτα‖ γὰρ ἐποίουν τοῖς ψευδοπροφήταις οἱ πατέρες αὐτῶν.
⁴these ³things ¹for did   ³to ⁴the ²false ¹prophets ¹their ²fathers.

27 ᵗἈλλ'‖ ὑμῖν λέγω τοῖς ἀκούουσιν, Ἀγαπᾶτε τοὺς ἐχθροὺς
    But to you I say who   hear,   Love   ²enemies

of Alphæus, and Simon called Zelotes, 16 and Judas *the brother of* James, and Judas Iscariot, which also was the traitor. 17 And he came down with them, and stood in the plain, and the company of his disciples, and a great multitude of people out of all Judæa and Jerusalem, and from the sea coast of Tyre and Sidon, which came to hear him, and to be healed of their diseases; 18 and they that were vexed with unclean spirits: and they were healed. 19 And the whole multitude sought to touch him: for there went virtue out of him, and healed *them* all.

20 And he lifted up his eyes on his disciples, and said, Blessed *be ye* poor: for yours is the kingdom of God. 21 Blessed *are ye* that hunger now: for ye shall be filled. Blessed *are ye* that weep now: for ye shall laugh. 22 Blessed are ye, when men shall hate you, and when they shall separate you *from their company,* and shall reproach *you,* and cast out your name as evil, for the Son of man's sake. 23 Rejoice ye in that day, and leap for joy: for, behold, your reward *is* great in heaven: for in the like manner did their fathers unto the prophets. 24 But woe unto you that are rich! for ye have received your consolation. 25 Woe unto you that are full! for ye shall hunger. Woe unto you that laugh now! for ye shall mourn and weep. 26 Woe unto you, when all men shall speak well of you! for so did their fathers to the false prophets. 27 But I say unto you which hear, Love your enemies, do good to them which hate you, 28 bless them, that

---

ª + καὶ and T.   ᵇ — τὸν τοῦ TTrA.   ᶜ + καὶ and LTTrA.   ᵈ Ἰσκαριώθ LTTrA.   ᵉ — καὶ
LT[Tr]A.   ᶠ + πολὺς great T.   ᵍ ἐνοχλούμενοι TTrA.   ʰ ἀπὸ GLTTrAW.   ⁱ — καὶ (omit
and they) LTTrA.   ᵏ ἐζήτουν TTrA.   ˡ ἕνεκεν L.   ᵐ χάρητε GLTTrAW.   ⁿ τὰ αὐτὰ the
same things LTTrA.   ᵒ + νῦν now T[Tr]A.   ᵖ — ὑμῖν TTrA.   ᵠ — ὑμῖν GLTTrAW.
ʳ εἴπωσιν ὑμᾶς T.   ˢ — πάντες G.   ᵗ Ἀλλὰ LTTrAW.

curse you, and pray for them which despitefully use you. 29 And unto him that smiteth thee on the one cheek offer also the other; and him that taketh away thy cloke forbid not to take thy coat also. 30 Give to every man that asketh of thee; and of him that taketh away thy goods ask them not again. 31 And as ye would that men should do to you, do ye also to them likewise. 32 For if ye love them which love you, what thank have ye? for sinners also love those that love them. 33 And if ye do good to them which do good to you, what thank have ye? for sinners also do even the same. 34 And if ye lend, to them of whom ye hope to receive, what thank have ye? for sinners also lend to sinners, to receive as much again. 35 But love ye your enemies, and do good, and lend, hoping for nothing again; and your reward shall be great, and ye shall be the children of the Highest: for he is kind unto the unthankful and to the evil. 36 Be ye therefore merciful, as your Father also is merciful. 37 Judge not, and ye shall not be judged : condemn not, and ye shall not be condemned : forgive, and ye shall be forgiven : 38 give, and it shall be given unto you; good measure, pressed down, and shaken together, and running over, shall men give into your bosom. For with the same measure that ye mete withal it shall be measured to you

ὑμῶν, καλῶς ποιεῖτε τοῖς μισοῦσιν ὑμᾶς, 28 εὐλογεῖτε
[1]your, [4]well [3]do to those who hate you, bless
τοὺς καταρωμένους ᵛὑμῖν," ʷκαὶ" προσεύχεσθε ˣὑπὲρ" τῶν
those who curse you, and pray for those who
ἐπηρεαζόντων ὑμᾶς. 29 τῷ τύπτοντί σε ʸἐπὶ" τὴν σιαγόνα,
despitefully use you. To him who strikes thee on the cheek,
πάρεχε καὶ τὴν ἄλλην· καὶ ἀπὸ τοῦ αἴροντός σου. τὸ
offer also the other; and from him who takes away thy
ἱμάτιον, καὶ τὸν χιτῶνα μὴ.κωλύσῃς. 30 παντὶ ᶻδὲ τῷ"
cloak, also the tunic do not forbid. [2]To [3]every [4]one [1]and who
αἰτοῦντί σε, δίδου· καὶ ἀπὸ τοῦ αἴροντος τὰ.σά,
asks thee, give; and from him who takes away what [is] thine,
μὴ.ἀπαίτει. 31 καὶ καθὼς θέλετε ἵνα ποιῶσιν ὑμῖν οἱ
ask [it] not back.; and according as ye desire that ²should ³do ⁴to ⁵you
ἄνθρωποι, ᵃκαὶ ὑμεῖς" ποιεῖτε αὐτοῖς ὁμοίως. 32 καὶ εἰ
¹men, also ²ye ¹do to them in like manner. And if
ἀγαπᾶτε τοὺς ἀγαπῶντας ὑμᾶς, ποία ὑμῖν χάρις ἐστίν;
ye love those who love you, what *to ⁵you·¹thank ²is ³it?
καὶ.γὰρ οἱ ἁμαρτωλοὶ τοὺς ἀγαπῶντας αὐτοὺς ἀγαπῶσιν.
for even ²those ³who ⁴love ⁵them ¹love.
33 καὶ ᵇἐὰν ἀγαθοποιῆτε τοὺς ἀγαθοποιοῦντας ὑμᾶς,
And if ye do good to those who do good to you,
ποία ὑμῖν ᶜχάρις ἐστίν"; καὶ ᵈγὰρ" οἱ ἁμαρτωλοὶ τὸ αὐτὸ
what ²to ³you ¹thank is it? ²even ¹for sinners ²the ³same
ποιοῦσιν. 34 καὶ ἐὰν ᵉδανείζητε" παρ' ὧν ἐλπίζετε
¹do. And if ye lend [to those] from whom ye hope
ᶠἀπολαβεῖν," ποία ὑμῖν χάρις ἐστίν; καὶ ᵍγὰρ" ʰοἱ" ἁμαρτωλοὶ
to receive, what ²to ³you ¹thank is it? ²even ¹for sinners
ἁμαρτωλοῖς ⁱδανείζουσιν," ἵνα ἀπολάβωσιν τὰ ᵏἴσα." 35 πλὴν
to ³sinners ¹lend, that they may receive the like. But
ἀγαπᾶτε τοὺς.ἐχθροὺς.ὑμῶν, καὶ ἀγαθοποιεῖτε, καὶ ˡδανείζετε"
love your enemies, and do good, and lend,
ᵐμηδὲν" ⁿἀπελπίζοντες·" καὶ ἔσται ὁ.μισθὸς.ὑμῶν πολύς°,
²nothing ¹⁴hoping ²for again; and ³shall ⁴be your ²reward great,
καὶ ἔσεσθε υἱοὶ ᴾτοῦ" ὑψίστου· ὅτι αὐτὸς χρηστός ἐστιν·ἐπὶ
and ye shall be sons of the Highest; for he ²good ¹is to
τοὺς ἀχαρίστους καὶ πονηρούς. 36 γίνεσθε �qοὖν" οἰκτίρμονες,
the unthankful and wicked. Be ye therefore compassionate,
καθὼς ʳκαὶ" ὁ.πατὴρ.ὑμῶν οἰκτίρμων ἐστίν. 37 καὶ μὴ.κρίνετε,
as also your father ²compassionate ¹is. And judge not,
ˢκαὶ οὐ".μὴ κριθῆτε· μὴ.καταδικάζετε, καὶ οὐ.μὴ κατα-
that in no wise ye be judged; condemn not, that in no wise ye be
δικασθῆτε. ἀπολύετε, καὶ ἀπολυθήσεσθε· 38 δίδοτε, καὶ
condemned. Release, and ye shall be released. Give, and
δοθήσεται ὑμῖν. μέτρον καλόν πεπιεσμένον ᵛᵃκαὶ" σεσαλευ-
it shall be given to you, ²measure ¹good, pressed down and shaken to-
μένον ᵛᵃκαὶ" ʷᵃὑπερεκχυνόμενον" δώσουσιν εἰς τὸν κόλπον
gether and running over shall they give into ²bosom
ὑμῶν· /ˣᵃτῷ γὰρ αὐτῷ μέτρῳ ᾧ" μετρεῖτε, ἀντιμε-
¹your: ⁴with ⁵the ³for same measure with which ye mete, it shall be

ᵛ ὑμᾶς GLTTrA. ʷ — καὶ GLTTrAW. ˣ περὶ TA. ʸ εἰς T. ᶻ [δὲ τῷ] L ; — δὲ τῷ T ; [δὲ] τῷ Tr. ᵃ [καὶ ὑμεῖς] L. ᵇ + γὰρ (read for if ye also) L. ᶜ ἐστὶν χάρις L. ᵈ — γὰρ T. ᵉ δανείσητε L ; δανίσητε T ; δανείζετε TrA. ᶠ λαβεῖν TTrA. ᵍ — γὰρ T[Tr]A. ʰ — οἱ LTTrA. ⁱ δανίζουσιν T. ᵏ ἴσα LTAW. ˡ δανίζετε T. ᵐ μηδένα T. ⁿ ἀφελπίζοντες L. ° + [ἐν τοῖς οὐρανοῖς] in the heavens L. ᴾ — τοῦ (read of [the]) GLTTrAW. q — οὖν LTTrA. ʳ — καὶ [L]T[Tr]. ˢ ἵνα (read that ye be not judged) L. ᵗ + καὶ and TA. ᵛᵃ — καὶ LTTrA. ʷᵃ ὑπερεκχυννόμενον LTTrA. ˣᵃ ᾧ γὰρ μέτρῳ LTTr.

τρηθήσεται ὑμῖν. 39 Εἶπεν.δὲ ʸ παραβολὴν αὐτοῖς, Μήτι
measured again to you.   And he spoke   a parable   to them,   Can the blind lead the

δύναται τυφλὸς   τυφλὸν ʲὁδηγεῖν; οὐχὶ ἀμφότεροι εἰς
Is ⁴able   ¹a ²blind [³man] a blind [man] to lead?   ²not   ³both   ⁴into

βόθυνον ᶻπεσοῦνται‖; 40 οὐκ ἔστιν μαθητὴς ὑπὲρ τὸν διδάσκα-
⁵a ⁵pit   ¹will fall?   ²not   ³is   ¹a ²disciple above the   teacher

λον ᵃαὐτοῦ·‖ κατηρτισμένος.δὲ   πᾶς   ἔσται ὡς ὁ διδάσκαλος
of him;   but ³perfected   ¹every ²one shall be as   ²teacher

αὐτοῦ. 41 τί.δὲ   βλέπεις τὸ κάρφος τὸ   ἐν τῷ ὀφθαλμῷ
¹his.   But why lookest thou on the mote   that [is] in the   eye

τοῦ.ἀδελφοῦ.σου,   τὴν.δὲ δοκὸν τὴν   ἐν τῷ.ἰδίῳ ὀφθαλμῷ
of thy brother,   but the   beam   that [is] in thine own   eye

οὐ.κατανοεῖς; 42 ᵇἢ‖ πῶς δύνασαι λέγειν τῷ.ἀδελφῷ.σου,
perceivest not?   or how art thou able to say   to thy brother,

Ἀδελφέ, ἄφες   ἐκβάλω τὸ κάρφος τὸ   ἐν τῷ ὀφθαλμῷ
Brother,   suffer [that] I may cast out the   mote   that [is] in   ²eye

σου, αὐτὸς τὴν ἐν τῷ.ὀφθαλμῷ.σου δοκὸν οὐ βλέπων; ʲὑπο-
¹thine, thyself the ²in ³thine [⁴own] ⁵eye   ¹beam not   seeing?   Hypo-

κριτά, ἔκβαλε πρῶτον τὴν δοκὸν ἐκ τοῦ.ὀφθαλμοῦ.σου, καὶ
crite,   cast out   first   the   beam out of   thine [own] eye,   and

τότε διαβλέψεις ᶜἐκβαλεῖν‖ τὸ κάρφος τὸ ἐν τῷ ὀφθαλμῷ
then thou wilt see clearly to cast out . the   mote   that [is] in the   eye

τοῦ.ἀδελφοῦ.σουᵈ. 43 οὐ.γάρ ἐστιν δένδρον καλὸν ποιοῦν
of thy brother.   For ²not ¹there ²is ¹a ᵃtree   ⁵good producing

καρπὸν σαπρόν· οὐδὲᵉ δένδρον σαπρὸν ποιοῦν καρπὸν καλόν·
²fruit   ¹corrupt; nor   ₐ²tree   ¹corrupt producing ²fruit   ¹good;

44 ἕκαστον.γὰρ δένδρον ἐκ τοῦ.ἰδίου καρποῦ γινώσκεται· οὐ.γὰρ
for each   tree   by its own   fruit   is known,   for not

ἐξ ἀκανθῶν συλλέγουσιν σῦκα, οὐδὲ ἐκ βάτου ᶠτρυγῶσιν
from thorns   do they gather figs,   nor from a bramble gather they

σταφυλήν.‖ 45 ὁ.ἀγαθὸς ἄνθρωπος ἐκ τοῦ ἀγαθοῦ θησαυροῦ
a bunch of grapes. The good   man   out of the   good   treasure

τῆς.καρδίας.ᵍαὐτοῦ‖ προφέρει τὸ   ἀγαθόν· καὶ ὁ πονη-
of his heart   brings forth that which [is] good;   and the   wick-

ρὸς ʰἄνθρωπος‖ ἐκ τοῦ πονηροῦ ⁱθησαυροῦ τῆς καρδίας
ed   man   out of the   wicked   treasure   of ²heart

αὐτοῦ‖ προφέρει τὸ   πονηρόν· ἐκ.γὰρ ᵏτοῦ‖ περισσεύ-
¹his   brings forth that which [is]   wicked;   for out of the   abun-

ματος ˡτῆς‖ καρδίας ᵐλαλεῖ τὸ.στόμα.αὐτοῦ.‖ 46 Τί.δὲ με
dance   of the   heart   ³speaks   ¹his ²mouth.   And why me

καλεῖτε Κύριε, κύριε, καὶ οὐ.ποιεῖτε ἃ λέγω; 47 πᾶς ὁ ἐρ-
do ye call Lord,   Lord,   and   do not   what I say?   Every one who

χόμενος πρός με καὶ ἀκούων μου.τῶν.λόγων καὶ ποιῶν αὐτούς,
is coming   to me and hearing   my words   and doing   them,

ὑποδείξω ὑμῖν τίνι ἐστὶν ὅμοιος. 48 ὅμοιός ἐστιν ἀνθρώπῳ
I will shew   you to whom he is   like.   Like   he is   to a man

οἰκοδομοῦντι οἰκίαν, ὃς ἔσκαψεν καὶ ἐβάθυνεν, καὶ ἔθηκεν
building   a house,   who dug   and deepened,   and   laid

θεμέλιον ἐπὶ τὴν πέτραν· ⁿπλημμύρας‖.δὲ γενομένης ᵒπροσέρ-
a foundation on the   rock;   and a flood   having come   ³burst

ρηξεν‖ ὁ ποταμὸς τῇ.οἰκίᾳ.ἐκείνῃ, καὶ οὐκ.ἴσχυσεν σαλεῦσαι
⁴upon ¹the ²stream   that house,   and   could not   shake

again. 39 And he spake a parable unto them, Can the blind lead the blind? shall they not both fall into the ditch? 40 The disciple is not above his master: but every one that is perfect shall be as his master. 41 And why beholdest thou the mote that is in thy brother's eye, but perceivest not the beam that is in thine own eye? 42 Either how canst thou say to thy brother, Brother, let me pull out the mote that is in thine eye, when thou thyself beholdest not the beam that is in thine own eye? Thou hypocrite, cast out first the beam out of thine own eye, and then shalt thou see clearly to pull out the mote that is in thy brother's eye. 43 For a good tree bringeth not forth corrupt fruit; neither doth a corrupt tree bring forth good fruit. 44 For every tree is known by his own fruit. For of thorns men do not gather figs, nor of a bramble bush gather they grapes. 45 A good man out of the good treasure of his heart bringeth forth that which is good; and an evil man out of the evil treasure of his heart bringeth forth that which is evil: for of the abundance of the heart his mouth speaketh. 46 And why call ye me, Lord, Lord, and do not the things which I say? 47 Whosoever cometh to me, and heareth my sayings, and doeth them, I will shew you to whom he is like: 48 he is like a man which built an house, and digged deep, and laid the foundation on a rock: and when the flood arose, the stream beat vehemently upon that house, and could not shake it: for it was founded upon a rock. 49 But he that heareth, and doeth not, is like a man that without a foundation built an house upon the earth ; against which the stream did beat vehemently, and immediately it fell ; and the ruin of that house was great.

αὐτήν· ᴾτεθεμελίωτο·γὰρ ἐπὶ τὴν πέτραν.‖ 49 ὁ.δὲ ἀκούσαι
it,   for it had been founded upon the rock.   But he who heard
καὶ μὴ.ποιήσας ὅμοιός ἐστιν ἀνθρώπῳ ᑫοἰκοδομήσαντι‖ οἰκίαι
and did not ¹like ¹is   to a man   having built   a house
ἐπὶ τὴν γῆν χωρὶς θεμελίου· ᾗ ʳπροσέρρηξεν‖ ὁ ποτα-
on the earth without a foundation ; on which ³burst   ¹the ²stream,
μός, καὶ ˢεὐθέως ἔπεσεν,‖ καὶ ἐγένετο τὸ ῥῆγμα τῆς οἰκίας
and immediately it fell, and ⁴was ¹the ²ruin ³of ⁵house
ἐκείνης μέγα.
⁴that great.

VII. Now when he had ended all his sayings in the audience of the people, he entered into Capernaum. 2 And a certain centurion's servant, who was dear unto him, was sick, and ready to die. 3 And when he heard of Jesus, he sent unto him the elders of the Jews, beseeching him that he would come and heal his servant. 4 And when they came to Jesus, they besought him instantly, saying, That he was worthy for whom he should do this: 5 for he loveth our nation, and he hath built us a synagogue. 6 Then Jesus went with them. And when he was now not far from the house, the centurion sent friends to him, saying unto him, Lord, trouble not thyself : for I am not worthy that thou shouldest enter under my roof : 7 wherefore neither thought I myself worthy to come unto thee : but say in a word, and my servant shall be healed. 8 For I also am a man set under authority, having under me soldiers, and I say unto one, Go, and he goeth ; and to another, Come, and he cometh ; and to my servant, Do this, and he doeth it. 9 When Jesus heard these things, he marvelled at him, and turned him about, and said unto the people that followed him, I say

7 ᵗἘπεὶ.δὲ‖ ἐπλήρωσεν πάντα τὰ.ῥήματα.αὐτοῦ εἰς τὰς
And when he had completed all   his words   in the
ἀκοὰς τοῦ λαοῦ εἰσῆλθεν εἰς ᵘΚαπερναούμ.‖ 2 Ἐκατοντάρχου
ears of the people he entered into Capernaum.   ⁴Of ⁵a ⁷centurion
δὲ τινος δοῦλος κακῶς ἔχων ἤμελλεν τελευτᾶν, ὃς ἦν
¹and ⁶certain ²a ³bondman ⁵ill ⁵being was about to die, who was
αὐτῷ ἔντιμος. 3 ἀκούσας.δὲ περὶ τοῦ Ἰησοῦ ἀπέστειλεν πρὸς
by him honoured. And having heard about Jesus   he sent   to
αὐτὸν πρεσβυτέρους τῶν Ἰουδαίων, ἐρωτῶν αὐτὸν ὅπως
him   elders   of the Jews,   begging him that
ἐλθὼν διασώσῃ τὸν.δοῦλον.αὐτοῦ. 4 οἱ.δὲ παραγενόμενοι
having come he might cure his bondman.   And they having come
πρὸς τὸν Ἰησοῦν ᵛπαρεκάλουν‖ αὐτὸν σπουδαίως, λέγοντες,
to   the Jesus   besought   him diligently, saying,
"Ὅτι ἄξιός ἐστιν ᾧ ᵂπαρέξει‖ τοῦτο· 5 ἀγαπᾷ.γὰρ τὸ
that ³worthy ¹he ²is to whom he shall grant this, for he loves the
ἔθνος.ἡμῶν καὶ τὴν συναγωγὴν αὐτὸς ᾠκοδόμησεν ἡμῖν.
our nation and the synagogue   he   built   for us.
6 Ὁ.δὲ.Ἰησοῦς ἐπορεύετο σὺν αὐτοῖς· ἤδη.δὲ αὐτοῦ οὐ μακρὰν
And Jesus   went with them ; but already he ²not ³far
ἀπέχοντος ˣἀπὸ‖ τῆς οἰκίας, ἔπεμψεν ʸπρὸς αὐτὸν‖ ᶻὁ ἑκατόν-
¹being distant from the house, ³sent   ⁴to ⁵him ¹the ²cen-
ταρχος φίλους,‖ λέγων ᵃαὐτῷ,‖ Κύριε, μὴ.σκύλλου· οὐ
turion friends, saying to him, Lord,   trouble not [thyself], ⁴not
γὰρ ᵇεἰμὶ ἱκανὸς‖ ἵνα ᶜὑπὸ τὴν.στέγην.μου‖ εἰσέλθῃς·
¹for ²I ³am worthy that under   my roof   thou shouldest come ;
7 διὸ οὐδὲ ἐμαυτὸν ἠξίωσα πρός σε ἐλθεῖν· ἀλλὰ
wherefore neither myself counted I worthy ³to ⁴thee ¹to ²come ; but
εἰπὲ λόγῳ, καὶ ᵈἰαθήσεται‖ ὁ.παῖς.μου. 8 καὶ.γὰρ ἐγὼ ἄν-
say by a word, and shall be healed my servant.   For also I   a
θρωπός εἰμι ὑπὸ ἐξουσίαν τασσόμενος, ἔχων ὑπ᾽ ἐμαυτὸν
man   am under authority   appointed, having under myself
στρατιώτας, καὶ λέγω τούτῳ   Πορεύθητι, καὶ πορεύεται·
soldiers, and I say to this [one] Go,   and   he goes ;
καὶ ἄλλῳ, Ἔρχου. καὶ ἔρχεται· καὶ τῷ.δούλῳ.μου, Ποίησον
and to another, Come, and he comes ; and to my bondman, Do
τοῦτο, καὶ ποιεῖ. 9 Ἀκούσας δὲ ταῦτα ὁ Ἰησοῦς ἐθαύ-
this, and he does [it]. And having heard these things Jesus   won-
μασεν αὐτόν· καὶ στραφεὶς τῷ ἀκολουθοῦντι αὐτῷ ὄχλῳ
dered at him ; and turning to the ²following   ³him ¹crowd

ᴾ διὰ τὸ καλῶς οἰκοδομεῖσθαι (οἰκοδομῆσθαι τ) αὐτήν because it was well built ᴛᴛʀᴀ.
ᑫ οἰκοδομοῦντι building ʟ.   ʳ προσέρηξεν ᴛᴛʀ.   ˢ εὐθὺς συνέπεσεν immediately it fell
together ᴛᴛʀᴀ.   ᵗ Ἐπειδὴ after that ʟᴛᴛʀᴀ.   ᵘ Καφαρναούμ ʟᴛᴛʀᴀᴡ.   ᵛ ἠρώτων asked ᴛ.
ᵂ παρέξῃ he should grant ʟᴛᴛʀᴀ.   ˣ — ἀπὸ (read τῆς from the) ᴛ.   ʸ — πρὸς αὐτὸν ᴛ.
ᶻ φίλους ὁ ἑκατόνταρχος (ἑκατοντάρχης τ) ᴛᴛʀᴀ.   ᵃ — αὐτῷ ᴛ.   ᵇ ἱκανός εἰμι ᴛᴛʀᴀ.   ᶜ μου
ὑπὸ τὴν στέγην ᴡ.   ᵈ ἰαθήτω let be healed ᴛᴛʀᴀ.

εἶπεν, Λέγω ὑμῖν, οὐδὲ ἐν τῷ Ἰσραὴλ τοσαύτην πίστιν εὗρον.
said,　I say to you, not even in　Israel　so great　faith did I find.

10 Καὶ ὑποστρέψαντες· ⁵οἱ πεμφθέντες εἰς τὸν οἶκον‖ εὗρον
And　²having ⁴returned ¹those　²sent　to the　house　found

τὸν ⁵ἀσθενοῦντα‖ δοῦλον ὑγιαίνοντα. ⁄
the　sick　　bondman in good health. ⁄

11 Καὶ ἐγένετο ἐν ᵍτῇ‖ ἑξῆς ᵸἐπορεύετο‖ εἰς πόλιν
And it came to pass on　the　next [day]　he went · into a city

καλουμένην Ναΐν, καὶ συνεπορεύοντο αὐτῷ οἱ μαθηταὶ αὐτοῦ
called　Nain, and　went with　him　his ²disciples

ⁱἱκανοὶ‖ καὶ ὄχλος πολύς. 12 ὡς δὲ ἤγγισεν τῇ πύλῃ τῆς
¹many　and a ²crowd ¹great.　And as he drew near to the gate of the

πόλεως καὶ ἰδού, ἐξεκομίζετο ᵏτεθνηκώς,‖ υἱὸς μονο-
city　²also ¹behold, was being carried out [one] who had died, an ²son　¹only

γενὴς‖ τῇ μητρὶ αὐτοῦ, καὶ ᵐαὕτη ἦν‖ χήρα· καὶ ὄχλος τῆς
to his widow, and she　was a widow, and a ²crowd ³of ⁴the

πόλεως ἱκανὸς　ⁿ σὺν αὐτῇ. 13 καὶ ἰδὼν αὐτὴν ὁ κύριος
⁵city　¹considerable [was] with her.　And seeing her　the Lord

ἐσπλαγχνίσθη ἐπ᾽ ᵒαὐτῇ‖ καὶ εἶπεν αὐτῇ, Μὴ κλαῖε.
was moved with compassion on her and said to her,　Weep not.

14 Καὶ προσελθὼν ἥψατο τῆς σοροῦ· οἱ δὲ βαστάζοντες
And　coming up he touched the bier,　and those　bearing　[it]

ἔστησαν· καὶ εἶπεν, Νεανίσκε, σοί λέγω, ἐγέρθητι. 15 Καὶ
stopped.　And he said, Young man, to thee I say,　Arise.　And

ἀνεκάθισεν ὁ νεκρὸς καὶ ἤρξατο λαλεῖν· καὶ ἔδωκεν αὐτὸν τῇ
²sat ⁴up ¹the ³dead and began　to speak,　and he gave　him

μητρὶ αὐτοῦ. 16 ἔλαβεν δὲ φόβος ᴾἅπαντας,‖ καὶ ἐδόξαζον
to his mother.　And ²seized　¹fear　all,　and they glorified

τὸν θεόν, λέγοντες, Ὅτι προφήτης μέγας ᑫἐγήγερται‖ ἐν
God,　saying,　A ²prophet ¹great　has risen up amongst

ἡμῖν, καὶ Ὅτι ἐπεσκέψατο ὁ θεὸς τὸν λαὸν αὐτοῦ. 17 Καὶ
us;　and　²Has ³visited　¹God　his people.　And

ἐξῆλθεν ὁ λόγος οὗτος ἐν ὅλῃ τῇ Ἰουδαίᾳ περὶ αὐτοῦ, καὶ
went out　this report　in all　Judæa concerning him,　and

ʳἐν‖ πάσῃ τῇ περιχώρῳ.
in　all　the country around.

18 Καὶ ἀπήγγειλαν ˢἸωάννῃ‖ οἱ μαθηταὶ αὐτοῦ περὶ
And　²brought ⁴word　¹to ²John　³his ⁴disciples　concerning

πάντων τούτων. 19 καὶ προσκαλεσάμενος δύο τινὰς τῶν
all　those things.　And　having called to [him] ²two ¹certain

μαθητῶν αὐτοῦ ὁ ᵗἸωάννης‖ ἔπεμψεν πρὸς ᵛτὸν Ἰησοῦν,‖
of his disciples　John　sent　[them] to　Jesus,

λέγων, Σὺ εἶ ὁ ἐρχόμενος ἢ ʷἄλλον‖ προσδοκῶμεν;
saying,　Art thou the　coming [one] or　another　are we to look for?

20 Παραγενόμενοι δὲ πρὸς αὐτὸν οἱ ἄνδρες ˣεἶπον,‖ ʸἸωάν-
And having come　to · him　the men　said,　John

νης‖ ὁ βαπτιστὴς ἀπέσταλκεν ἡμᾶς πρός σε, λέγων, Σὺ εἶ
the　Baptist　has sent　us　to thee, saying, Art thou

ὁ ἐρχόμενος ἢ ἄλλον προσδοκῶμεν; 21 Ἐν ᶻαὐτῇ‖ ᵃδὲ‖
the coming [one] or another are we to look for?　²In ³the ⁴same ¹and

τῇ ὥρᾳ ἐθεράπευσεν πολλοὺς ἀπὸ νόσων καὶ μαστίγων καὶ
hour　he healed　many　of　diseases and　scourges · and

Right column (Authorized Version):

unto you, I have not found so great faith, no, not in Israel. 10 And they that were sent, returning to the house, found the servant whole that had been sick.

11 And it came to pass the day after, that he went into a city called Nain; and many of his disciples went with him, and much people. 12 Now when he came nigh to the gate of the city, behold, there was a dead man carried out, the only son of his mother, and she was a widow: and much people of the city was with her. 13 And when the Lord saw her, he had compassion on her, and said unto her, Weep not. 14 And he came and touched the bier: and they that bare him stood still. And he said, Young man, I say unto thee, Arise. 15 And he that was dead sat up, and began to speak. And he delivered him to his mother. 16 And there came a fear on all: and they glorified God, saying, That a great prophet is risen up among us; and, That God hath visited his people. 17 And this rumour of him went forth throughout all Judæa, and throughout all the region round about.

18 And the disciples of John shewed him of all these things. 19 And John calling unto him two of his disciples sent them to Jesus, saying, Art thou he that should come? or look we for another? 20 When the men were come unto him, they said, John Baptist hath sent us unto thee, saying, Art thou he that should come? or look we for another? 21 And in that same hour he cured many of their infirmities and plagues, and of evil

---

ᵉ εἰς τὸν οἶκον οἱ πεμφθέντες LTTr.　ᶠ — ἀσθενοῦντα LTTr[A].　ᵍ τῷ Tr.　ᵸ ἐπορεύθη T.
ⁱ — ἱκανοὶ [L]Tr[A].　ᵏ [τεθνηκὼς] L.　ˡ μονογενὴς υἱὸς TTrA.　ᵐ αὐτὴ W; — ἦν EGW.　ⁿ + ἦν
W ᵃˢ EGT[TrA].　ᴾ πάντας GTrA.　ᑫ ἠγέρθη is risen LTTrA.　ʳ — ἐν [L]ᵀ[Tr].
ˢ Ἰωάννει T; Ἰωάνει Tr.　ᵗ Ἰωάνης Tr.　ᵛ τὸν κύριον the Lord TTrA.　ʷ ἕτερον Tr.
ˣ εἶπαν LTTrA.　ʸ Ἰωάνης Tr.　ᶻ ἐκείνῃ that TTrA.　ᵃ — δὲ LTTrA.

spirits; and unto many *that were* blind he gave sight. 22 Then Jesus answering said unto them, Go your way, and tell John what things ye have seen and heard; how that the blind see, the lame walk, the lepers are cleansed, the deaf hear, the dead are raised, to the poor the gospel is preached. 23 And blessed is *he*, whosoever shall not be offended in me.

πνευμάτων πονηρῶν, καὶ τυφλοῖς πολλοῖς ἐχαρίσατο ᵇτὸ‖
²spirits ¹evil, and to ²blind ¹many he granted

βλέπειν. 22 καὶ ἀποκριθεὶς ᶜὁ Ἰησοῦς‖.εἶπεν αὐτοῖς, Πορευθέν-
to see. And ²answering ¹Jesus said to them, Having

τες ἀπαγγείλατε ᵈἸωάννῃ‖ ἃ εἴδετε καὶ ἠκούσατε· ᵉὅτι‖
gone relate to John what ye have seen and heard; that

τυφλοὶ ἀναβλέπουσιν, χωλοὶ περιπατοῦσιν, λεπροὶ καθαρίζον-
blind receive sight, lame walk, lepers are cleansed,

ται, κωφοὶ ἀκούουσιν, νεκροὶ ἐγείρονται, πτωχοὶ εὐαγγελίζονται·
deaf hear, dead are raised, poor are evangelized;

23 καὶ μακάριός ἐστιν ὃς.ἐὰν μὴ.σκανδαλισθῇ ἐν ἐμοί.
and blessed is whoever shall not be offended in me.

24 And when the messengers of John were departed, he began to speak unto the people concerning John, What went ye out into the wilderness for to see? A reed shaken with the wind? 25 But what went ye out for to see? A man clothed in soft raiment? Behold, they which are gorgeously apparelled, and live delicately, are in kings' courts. 26 But what went ye out for to see? A prophet? Yea, I say unto you, and much more than a prophet. 27 This is *he*, of whom it is written, Behold, I send my messenger before thy face, which shall prepare thy way before thee. 28 For I say unto you, Among those that are born of women there is not a greater prophet than John the Baptist: but he that is least in the kingdom of God is greater than he. 29 And all the people that heard *him*, and the publicans, justified God, being baptized with the baptism of John. 30 But the Pharisees and lawyers rejected the counsel of God against themselves, being not baptized of him. 31 And the Lord said, Whereunto then shall I liken the men of this generation? and to what are they like? 32 They are like unto children sitting in the marketplace, and calling one to another, and say-

24 Ἀπελθόντων.δὲ τῶν ἀγγέλων ᶠἸωάννου‖ ἤρξατο λέγειν
And ⁵having ⁶departed ¹the ²messengers ³of ⁴John he began to speak

πρὸς τοὺς ὄχλους περὶ ᶠἸωάννου,‖ Τί ᵍἐξεληλύθατε‖ εἰς
to the crowds concerning John: What have ye gone out into

τὴν ἔρημον θεάσασθαι; κάλαμον ὑπὸ ἀνέμου σαλευό-
the wilderness to look at? a reed ᐧ by [the] wind shaken?

μενον; 25 ἀλλὰ τί ᵍἐξεληλύθατε‖ ἰδεῖν; ἄνθρωπον ἐν μαλα-
But what have ye gone out to see? a man in soft

κοῖς ἱματίοις ἠμφιεσμένον; ἰδού, οἱ ἐν ἱματισμῷ ἐνδόξῳ
clothing arrayed? Behold, they who in ²clothing ¹splendid

καὶ τρυφῇ ὑπάρχοντες ἐν τοῖς βασιλείοις εἰσίν. 26 ἀλλὰ τί
and in luxury are living ²in ³the ⁴palaces ¹are. But what

ᵍἐξεληλύθατε‖ ἰδεῖν; προφήτην; ναί, λέγω ὑμῖν, καὶ
have ye gone out to see? a prophet? Yea, I say to you, and [one]

περισσότερον προφήτου. 27 οὗτός ἐστιν περὶ οὗ γέ-
more excellent than a prophet. This is he concerning whom it has

γραπται, Ἰδού, ʰἐγώ‖ ἀποστέλλω τὸν.ἄγγελόν.μου πρὸ
been written, Behold, I send my messenger before

προσώπου.σου, ὃς κατασκευάσει τὴν.ὁδόν.σου ἔμπροσθέν σου.
thy face, who shall prepare thy way before thee.

28 Λέγω ⁱγὰρ‖ ὑμῖν, μείζων ἐν γεννητοῖς γυναικῶν
²I ³say ¹for to you, ⁶a ⁷greater ¹among [²those] ³born ⁴of ⁵women

ᵏπροφήτης‖ ᶠἸωάννου‖ ¹τοῦ βαπτιστοῦ‖ οὐδείς ἐστιν· ὁ.δὲ
prophet than John the Baptist no one is; but he that [is]

μικρότερος ἐν τῇ βασιλείᾳ τοῦ θεοῦ μείζων αὐτοῦ ἐστιν. 29 Καὶ
less in the kingdom of God greater than he is. And

πᾶς ὁ λαὸς ἀκούσας καὶ οἱ τελῶναι ἐδικαίωσαν τὸν θεόν,
all the people having heard and the tax-gatherers justified God,

βαπτισθέντες τὸ βάπτισμα ᶠἸωάννου·‖ 30 οἱ.δὲ Φα-
having been baptized [with] the baptism of John; but the Pha-

ρισαῖοι καὶ οἱ νομικοὶ τὴν βουλὴν τοῦ θεοῦ ἠθέτησαν
risees and the doctors of the law the counsel of God set aside

εἰς ἑαυτούς, μὴ βαπτισθέντες ὑπ' αὐτοῦ. 31 ᵐεἶπεν.δὲ ὁ
as to themselves, not having been baptized by him. And ²said ¹the

κύριος,‖ Τίνι οὖν ὁμοιώσω τοὺς ἀνθρώπους τῆς γενεᾶς
²Lord, To what therefore shall I liken the men of ²generation

ταύτης; καὶ τίνι εἰσὶν ὅμοιοι; 32 ὅμοιοί εἰσιν παιδίοις
¹this? and to what are they like? Like are they to little children

τοῖς ἐν ἀγορᾷ καθημένοις, καὶ προσφωνοῦσιν ἀλλήλοις
in a market-place sitting, and calling one to another

ᵇ — τὸ LTTrAW.　　　ᶜ — ὁ Ἰησοῦς (*read* he said) [L]TTrA.　　　ᵈ Ἰωάννει T ; Ἰωάνει Tr.
ᵉ — ὅτι L[Tr].　　ᶠ Ἰωάνου Tr.　　ᵍ ἐξήλθατε went ye out LTr.　　ʰ — ἐγὼ (*read* ἀποστ.
I send) LTTrA.　　ⁱ — γὰρ TTrA.　　ᵏ — προφήτης L[TrA].　　ˡ — τοῦ βαπτιστοῦ TTrA.
ᵐ — εἶπεν δὲ ὁ.κύριος GLTTrAW.

ⁿκαὶ λέγουσιν,‖ Ηὐλήσαμεν ὑμῖν, καὶ οὐκ.ὠρχήσασθε· ἐθρη-
and   saying,   We piped   to you, and   ye did not dance ;   we

νήσαμεν °ὑμῖν,‖ καὶ οὐκ.ἐκλαύσατε. 33 ἐλήλυθεν.γὰρ ᴾΊωάννης‖
mourned   to you, and   ye did not weep.   For ⁴has ⁵come   ¹John

ὁ βαπτιστὴς �qμήτε‖ ʳἄρτον ἐσθίων‖ sμήτε‖ ᵗοἶνον πίνων,‖
ᵃthe   ³Baptist   neither   ²bread   ¹eating   nor   ²wine   ¹drinking,

καὶ λέγετε, Δαιμόνιον ἔχει. 34 ἐλήλυθεν ὁ υἱὸς τοῦ ἀνθρώπου
and ye say,   A demon   he has.   ⁵Has ⁶come ¹the ²Son   ³of ⁴man

ἐσθίων καὶ πίνων, καὶ λέγετε, Ἰδού, ἄνθρωπος φάγος καὶ
eating   and drinking, and ye say, Behold, · a man   a glutton and

οἰνοπότης, ᵛτελωνῶν φίλος‖ καὶ ἁμαρτωλῶν. 35 καὶ ἐδι-
a wine-bibber, of tax-gatherers a friend and   of sinners ;   and ²was

καιώθη ἡ σοφία ἀπὸ ʷτῶν.τέκνων.αὐτῆς πάντων.‖
³justified ¹wisdom by   ²her ³children   ¹all. ·

36 Ἠρώτα.δὲ τις αὐτὸν τῶν Φαρισαίων ἵνα φάγῃ μετ'
And ⁵asked ¹one. ⁶him ²of ³the ⁴Pharisees   that he should eat with

αὐτοῦ· καὶ εἰσελθὼν εἰς ˣτὴν οἰκίαν‖ τοῦ Φαρισαίου ʸἀνε-
him   And having entered into   the   house of the Pharisee   he re-

κλίθη.‖   37 Καὶ ἰδού, γυνὴ ᶻἐν τῇ πόλει ἥτις.ἦν‖
clined [at table] ;   and behold, a woman in the city who was

ἁμαρτωλός, ᵃἐπιγνοῦσα ὅτι ᵇἀνάκειται‖ ἐν τῇ οἰκίᾳ
a sinner,   having known that   he had reclined [at table] in the house

τοῦ Φαρισαίου, κομίσασα ἀλάβαστρον μύρου, 38 καὶ στᾶσα
of the Pharisee, having taken an alabaster flask of ointment, and standing

ᶜπαρὰ τοὺς.πόδας.αὐτοῦ ὀπίσω‖ κλαίουσα, ᵈἤρξατο βρέχειν
at   his feet   behind   weeping,   began to bedew

τοὺς.πόδας.αὐτοῦ τοῖς.δάκρυσιν,‖ καὶ ταῖς θριξὶν τῆς κεφαλῆς
his feet   with tears,   and with the hairs   of ²head

αὐτῆς ᵉἐξέμασσεν,‖ καὶ κατεφίλει τοὺς.πόδας.αὐτοῦ,
¹her   she was wiping [them], and was ardently kissing   his feet,

καὶ ἤλειφεν τῷ μύρῳ. 39 ἰδὼν.δὲ ὁ Φαρισαῖος
and was anointing [them] with the ointment. But having seen, the   Pharisee

ὁ καλέσας αὐτὸν εἶπεν ἐν ἑαυτῷ, λέγων, Οὗτος εἰ
who invited   him   spoke within himself, saying, This [person] if

ἦν προφήτης, ἐγίνωσκεν.ἂν τίς καὶ ποταπὴ ἡ γυνὴ
he were a prophet, would have known who and what the woman [is]

ἥτις ἅπτεται αὐτοῦ, ὅτι ἁμαρτωλός ἐστιν. 40 Καὶ ἀποκριθεὶς
who touches him, for   a sinner   she is.   And ᵛ²answering

ὁ Ἰησοῦς εἶπεν πρὸς αὐτόν, Σίμων, ἔχω σοί τι εἰπεῖν.
¹Jesus   said   to   him,   Simon, I have to thee something to say.

Ὁ.δὲ ᶠφησιν, Διδάσκαλε, εἰπέ.‖ 41 Δύο ᵍχρεωφειλέται‖ ἦσαν
And he says,   Teacher,   say [it].   Two   debtors   there were

ʰδανειστῇ‖ τινι· ὁ εἷς ὤφειλεν δηνάρια πεντακόσια, ὁ.δὲ
to a ²creditor ¹certain ; the one owed   ³denarii ¹five ²hundred, and the

ἕτερος πεντήκοντα. 42 μὴ.ἐχόντων.ⁱδὲ‖ αὐτῶν ἀπο-
other   fifty.   But ²not ³having   ¹they [wherewith]   to

δοῦναι ἀμφοτέροις ἐχαρίσατο· τίς οὖν αὐτῶν, ᵏεἰπέ,‖ πλεῖον
pay,   both   he forgave : which therefore of them, say,   ⁴most

ˡαὐτὸν ἀγαπήσει‖ ; 43 Ἀποκριθεὶς.ⁱδὲ‖ ᵐὁ‖ Σίμων εἶπεν, Ὑπο-
³him   ¹will ²love ?   And ²answering   ¹Simon   said,   I

ⁿ λέγοντες ΤΤrA.   ᵒ — ὑμῖν ΤΤr.   ᴾ Ἰωάνης Τr.   q μὴ not ΤΑ.   ʳ ἐσθων ἄρτον LΤΤrA ; ἐσθίων ἄρτον Τ.   ˢ μηδὲ Τ.   ᵗ πίνων οἶνον LΤΤrA.   ᵛ φίλος τελωνῶν GLΤΤrAW.   ʷ πάντων τῶν τέκνων αὐτῆς LΤrA.   ˣ τὸν οἶκον LΤΤrA.   ʸ κατεκλίθη LΤΤrA.   ᶻ ἥτις ἦν ἐν τῇ πόλει LΤΤrA.   ᵃ + καὶ and LΤΤrAW.   ᵇ κατάκειται LΤΤrA.   ᶜ ὀπίσω παρὰ τοὺς πόδας αὐτοῦ GLΤΤrA.   ᵈ τοῖς δάκρυσιν ἤρξατο βρέχειν τοὺς πόδας αὐτοῦ LΤΤrA.   ᵉ ἐξέμαξεν Τ.   ᶠ Δι-δάσκαλε, εἰπέ, φησίν ΤΤrA.   ᵍ χρεοφειλέται LΤΤrA.   ʰ δανιστῇ Τ.   ⁱ — δὲ [L]ΤᵗrA.   ᵏ — εἰπέ LΤΤr[A].   ˡ ἀγαπήσει αὐτὸν LΤΤrA.   ᵐ — ὁ Τ[Τr].

ing, We ' have piped unto you, and ye have not danced ; we have mourned to you, and ye have not wept. 33 For John the Baptist came neither eating bread nor drinking wine ; and ye say, He hath a devil. 34 The Son of man is come eating and drinking ; and ye say, Behold a gluttonous man, and a winebibber, a friend of publicans and sinners ! 35 But wisdom is justified of all her children.

36 And one of the Pharisees desired him that he would eat with him. And he went into the Pharisee's house, and sat down to meat. 37 And, behold, a woman in the city, which was a sinner, when she knew that Jesus sat at meat in the Pharisee's house, brought an alabaster box of ointment, 38 and stood at his feet behind him weeping, and began to wash his feet with tears, and did wipe them with the hairs of her head, and kissed his feet, and anointed them with the ointment. 39 Now when the Pharisee which had bidden him saw it, he spake within himself, saying, This man, if he were a prophet, would have known who and what manner of woman this is that toucheth him : for she is a sinner. 40 And Jesus answering said unto him, Simon, I have somewhat to say unto thee. And he saith, Master, say on. 41 There was a certain creditor which had two debtors : the one owed five hundred pence, and the other fifty. 42 And when they had nothing to pay, he frankly forgave them both. Tell me therefore, which of them will love him most ? 43 Simon answered and said, I sup-

pose that *he*, to whom he forgave most. And he said unto him, Thou hast rightly judged. 44 And he turned to the woman, and said unto Simon, Seest thou this woman? I entered into thine house, thou gavest me no water for my feet: but she hath washed my feet with tears, and wiped *them* with the hairs of her head. 45 Thou gavest me no kiss: but this woman since the time I came in hath not ceased to kiss my feet. 46 My head with oil thou didst not anoint: but this woman hath anointed my feet with ointment. 47 Wherefore I say unto thee, Her sins, which are many, are forgiven; for she loved much: but to whom little is forgiven, *the same* loveth little. 48 And he said unto her, Thy sins are forgiven. 49 And they that sat at meat with him began to say within themselves, Who is this that forgiveth sins also? 50 And he said to the woman, Thy faith hath saved thee; go in peace.

λαμβάνω ὅτι   ᾧ τὸ πλεῖον ἐχαρίσατο. Ὁ.δὲ εἶπεν αὐτῷ,
take it   that [he] to whom the more he forgave. And he said to him,
Ὀρθῶς ἔκρινας. 44 Καὶ στραφεὶς πρὸς τὴν γυναῖκα, τῷ
Rightly thou hast judged. And having turned to the woman,
Σίμωνι ἔφη. Βλέπεις ταύτην τὴν γυναῖκα; εἰσῆλθόν σου εἰς
to Simon he said, Seest thou this woman? I entered ²thy ¹into
τὴν οἰκίαν, ὕδωρ ⁿἐπὶ τοὺς.πόδας.μου‖ οὐκ.ἔδωκας· αὕτη.δὲ
house, water for my feet thou gavest not, but she
τοῖς δάκρυσιν ἔβρεξέν μου τοὺς πόδας, καὶ ταῖς θριξὶν ᵒτῆς
with tears bedewed my feet, and with the hairs
κεφαλῆς‖ αὐτῆς ἐξέμαξεν. 45 φίλημά μοι οὐκ.ἔδωκας·
¹head ¹of ²her wiped [them]. A kiss to me thou gavest not,
αὕτη.δὲ ἀφ' ἧς εἰσῆλθον οὐ.ᴾδιέλιπεν‖ καταφιλοῦσά
but she from which [time] I came in ceased not ardently kissing
�q μου τοὺς πόδας.‖ 46 ἐλαίῳ τὴν.κεφαλήν.μου οὐκ.ἤλειψας·
my feet. With oil my head thou didst not anoint,
αὕτη.δὲ μύρῳ ἤλειψέν ʳμου τοὺς πόδας.‖ 47 οὗ.χάριν
but she with ointment anointed my feet. For which cause
λέγω σοι, ἀφέωνται ˢαἱ.ἁμαρτίαι.αὐτῆς‖ αἱ πολλαί, ὅτι
I say to thee, forgiven have been her ²sins ¹many; for
ἠγάπησεν πολύ· ᾧ.δὲ ὀλίγον ἀφίεται ὀλίγον ἀγαπᾷ.
she loved much; but to whom little is forgiven little he loves.
48 Εἶπεν.δὲ αὐτῇ, Ἀφέωνταί σου αἱ ἁμαρτίαι. 49 Καὶ
And he said to her, Forgiven have been thy sins. And
ἤρξαντο οἱ συνανακείμενοι λέγειν ἐν ἑαυτοῖς, Τίς ᵗοὗτός
began those reclining with [him] to say within themselves, Who ²this
ἐστιν‖ ὃς καὶ ἁμαρτίας ἀφίησιν; 50 Εἶπεν.δὲ πρὸς τὴν γυ-
¹is who even ²sins ¹forgives? But he said to the wo-
ναῖκα, Ἡ.πίστις.σου σέσωκέν σε· πορεύου εἰς εἰρήνην.
man, Thy faith has saved thee; go in peace.

8 Καὶ ἐγένετο ἐν.τῷ.καθεξῆς καὶ αὐτὸς διώδευεν
And it came to pass afterwards that he journeyed through
κατὰ.πόλιν καὶ κώμην, κηρύσσων καὶ εὐαγγελιζό-
city by city and village by village, preaching and announcing the glad
μενος τὴν βασιλείαν τοῦ.θεοῦ· καὶ οἱ δώδεκα σὺν αὐτῷ,
tidings, the kingdom of God; and the twelve [were] with him,
2 καὶ γυναῖκές τινες αἳ ἦσαν.τεθεραπευμέναι ἀπὸ πνευμάτων
and ²women ¹certain who had been cured from ²spirits
πονηρῶν καὶ ἀσθενειῶν, Μαρία ἡ καλουμένη Μαγδαληνή,
¹wicked and infirmities, Mary who is called Magdalene,
ἀφ' ἧς δαιμόνια ἑπτὰ ἐξελήλύθει, 3 καὶ ᵛἸωάννα‖ γυνὴ
from whom ²demons ¹seven had gone out; and Joanna wife
Χουζᾶ ἐπιτρόπου Ἡρώδου, καὶ Σουσάννα, καὶ ἕτεραι πολλαί,
of Chuza a steward of Herod; and Susanna, and ²others ¹many,
αἵτινες διηκόνουν ʷαὐτῷ‖ ˣἀπὸ‖ τῶν.ὑπαρχόντων.αὐταῖς.
who were ministering to him their property.
4 Συνιόντος.δὲ ὄχλου πολλοῦ, καὶ τῶν κατὰ.πόλιν ἐπι-
And ²assembling ¹a ³crowd ²great, and those who from each city were
πορευομένων πρὸς αὐτόν, εἶπεν διὰ παραβολῆς. 5 Ἐξῆλθεν
coming to him, he spoke by a parable. ²Went ¹out
ὁ σπείρων τοῦ σπεῖραι τὸν.σπόρον.αὐτοῦ· καὶ ἐν.τῷ.σπείρειν
¹the ²sower to sow his seed; and as ²sowed
αὐτὸν ὃ.μὲν ἔπεσεν παρὰ τὴν ὁδόν, καὶ κατεπατήθη, καὶ τὰ
¹he some fell by the way, and it was trampled upon, and the

VIII. And it came to pass afterward, that he went throughout every city and village, preaching and shewing the glad tidings of the kingdom of God: and the twelve *were* with him, 2 and certain women, which had been healed of evil spirits and infirmities, Mary called Magdalene, out of whom went seven devils, 3 and Joanna the wife of Chuza Herod's steward, and Susanna, and many others, which ministered unto him of their substance. 4 And when much people were gathered together, and were come to him out of every city, he spake by a parable: 5 A sower went out to sow his seed: and as he sowed, some fell by the way side; and it was trodden down, and the

ⁿ μου ἐπὶ τοὺς πόδας Τ ; μοι ἐπὶ πόδας ΤrA.   ᵒ — τῆς κεφαλῆς (*read* with her hairs)
GLᴛᴛrAW.   ᴾ διέλειπεν Τ.   �q τοὺς πόδας μου L.   ʳ τοὺς πόδας μου GLᴛrA.   ˢ αὐτῆ (αὐτῆς.Τ)
αἱ ἁμαρτίαι LT.   ᵗ ἐστιν οὗτος L.   ᵛ Ἰωάνα Τr.   ʷ αὐτοῖς to them ᴛᴛrA.   ˣ ἐκ out of LᴛᴛrA.

πετεινὰ τοῦ οὐρανοῦ κατέφαγεν αὐτό. 6 καὶ ἕτερον ⁷ἔπεσεν
birds of the heaven devoured it. And other fell

ἐπὶ τὴν πέτραν, καὶ φυὲν ἐξηράνθη, διὰ τὸ μὴ.ἔχειν.
upon the rock, and having sprung up it withered, because it had not

ἰκμάδα. 7 καὶ ἕτερον ἔπεσεν ἐν μέσῳ τῶν ἀκανθῶν, καὶ
moisture; and other fell in [the] midst of the thorns, and

ᶻσυμφυεῖσαι‖ αἱ ἄκανθαι ἀπέπνιξαν αὐτό. 8 καὶ ἕτερον
having sprung up together the thorns choked it; and other

ἔπεσεν ᵃἐπὶ‖ τὴν γῆν τὴν ἀγαθήν, καὶ φυὲν ἐποίησεν
fell upon the ground the good, and having sprung up produced

καρπὸν ἑκατονταπλασίονα. Ταῦτα λέγων ἐφώνει, Ὁ ἔχων
fruit a hundredfold. These things saying he cried, He that has

ὦτα ἀκούειν ἀκουέτω. 9 Ἐπηρώτων.δὲ αὐτὸν οἱ.μαθηταί.αὐτοῦ,
ears to hear let him hear. And ³asked ⁴him ¹his ²disciples,

ᵇλέγοντες,‖ Τίς ᶜεἴη ἡ.παραβολὴ.αὕτη; 10 Ὁ.δὲ εἶπεν,
saying, What may be this parable? And he said,

Ὑμῖν δέδοται γνῶναι τὰ μυστήρια. τῆς βασιλείας τοῦ
To you it has been given to know the mysteries of the kingdom

θεοῦ· τοῖς.δὲ λοιποῖς ἐν παραβολαῖς, ἵνα βλέποντες· μὴ
of God, but to the rest in parables, that seeing they might not

βλέπωσιν, καὶ ἀκούοντες μὴ.συνιῶσιν. 11 Ἔστιν.δὲ
they ²may see, and hearing they may not understand. Now ³is

αὕτη ἡ παραβολή· ὁ σπόρος ἐστὶν ὁ λόγος τοῦ θεοῦ· 12 οἱ.δὲ
⁴this ¹the "parable: The seed is the word of God: and those

παρὰ τὴν ὁδὸν εἰσὶν οἱ ᵈἀκούοντες,‖ εἶτα ἔρχεται ὁ διά-
by the way are those who hear; then comes the de-

βολος καὶ αἴρει τὸν λόγον ἀπὸ τῆς.καρδίας.αὐτῶν, ἵνα.μὴ
vil and takes away the word from their heart, lest

πιστεύσαντες σωθῶσιν. 13 οἱ.δὲ ἐπὶ ᵉτῆς πέτρας,‖ οἳ
having believed they should be saved. And those upon the rock, those who

ὅταν ἀκούσωσιν, μετὰ χαρᾶς δέχονται τὸν λόγον, καὶ οὗτοι
when they hear, with joy receive the word, and these

ῥίζαν οὐκ.ἔχουσιν, οἳ πρὸς καιρὸν πιστεύουσιν, καὶ ἐν καιρῷ
a root have not, who for a time believe, and in time

πειρασμοῦ ἀφίστανται. 14 τὸ.δὲ εἰς τὰς ἀκάνθας πεσόν,
of trial fall away. And that which into the thorns fell,

οὗτοί εἰσιν οἱ ἀκούσαντες, καὶ ὑπὸ μεριμνῶν καὶ πλούτου
these are they who having heard, and under cares and riches

καὶ ἡδονῶν τοῦ βίου πορευόμενοι ᶠσυμπνίγονται,‖ καὶ οὐ
and pleasures of life moving along are choked, and ²not

τελεσφοροῦσιν. 15 τὸ.δὲ ἐν τῇ καλῇ γῇ, οὗτοί εἰσιν
¹do bring to perfection. And that in the good ground, these are

οἵτινες ἐν καρδίᾳ καλῇ καὶ ἀγαθῇ ἀκούσαντες τὸν λόγον
they who in a heart right and good having heard the word

κατέχουσιν, καὶ καρποφοροῦσιν ἐν ὑπομονῇ. 16 Οὐδεὶς.δὲ
keep [it], and bring forth fruit with endurance. And no one

λύχνον ἅψας καλύπτει αὐτὸν σκεύει, ἢ ὑποκάτω κλίνης
a lamp having lighted covers it with a vessel, or under a couch

τίθησιν ᵍἀλλ᾽‖ ἐπὶ λυχνίας ʰἐπιτίθησιν,‖ ἵνα οἱ
puts [it], but on a lamp-stand puts [it], that they who

εἰσπορευόμενοι βλέπωσιν τὸ φῶς. 17 οὐ.γὰρ ἐστιν
enter in may see the light. For not [anything] is

κρυπτὸν ὃ οὐ φανερὸν γενήσεται· οὐδὲ ἀπόκρυφον ὃ
hidden which ²not ¹manifest ¹shall ³become; nor secret which

⁷ κατέπεσεν fell down TTʳA.   ˣ συνφυεῖσαι T.   ᵃ εἰς into GLTTʳAW.   ᵇ — λέγοντες
LTTʳ[A].   ᶜ αὕτη εἴη ἡ παραβολή T.   ᵈ ἀκούσαντες heard TTʳ.   ᵉ τὴν πέτραν T.
ᶠ συνπνίγονται TA.   ᵍ ἀλλὰ Tʳ.   ʰ τίθησιν LTTʳA.

fowls of the air de-
voured it. 6 And some
fell upon a rock ; and
as soon as it was sprung
up, it withered away,
because it lacked mois-
ture. 7 And some fell
among thorns; and the
thorns sprang up with
it, and choked it. 8 And
other fell' on good
ground, and sprang
up, and bare fruit
an hundredfold. And
when he had said these
things, he cried, He
that hath ears to hear,
let him hear. 9 And
his disciples asked
him, saying, What
might this parable be?
10 And he said, Unto
you it is given to know
the mysteries of the
kingdom of God: but
to others in parables;
that seeing they might
not see, and hearing
they might not under-
stand. 11 Now the pa-
rable is this: The seed
is the word of God.
12 Those by the way
side are they that hear;
then cometh the devil,
and taketh away the
word out of their
hearts, lest they should
believe and be saved.
13 They on the rock
are they, which, when
they hear, receive the
word with joy ; and
these have no root,
which for a while be-
lieve, and in time of
temptation fall away.
14 And that which fell
among thorns are they,
which, when they have
heard, go forth, and
are choked with cares
and riches and plea-
sures of this life, and
bring no fruit to per-
fection. 15 But that
on the good ground are
they, which in an ho-
nest and good heart,
having heard the word,
keep it, and bring forth
fruit with patience.
16 No man, when he
hath lighted a candle,
covereth it with a ves-
sel, or putteth it under
a bed; but setteth it on
a candlestick, that they
which enter in may see
the light. 17 For no-
thing is secret, that
shall not be made

manifest; neither *any thing* hid, that shall not be known and come abroad. 18 Take heed therefore how ye hear: for whosoever hath, to him shall be given; and whosoever hath not, from him shall be taken even that which he seemeth to have.

19 Then came to him *his* mother and his brethren, and could not come at him for the press. 20 And it was told him *by certain* which said, Thy mother and thy brethren stand without, desiring to see thee. 21 And he answered and said unto them, My mother and my brethren are these which hear the word of God, and do it.

22 Now it came to pass on a certain day, that he went into a ship with his disciples: and he said unto them, Let us go over unto the other side of the lake. And they launched forth. 23 But as they sailed he fell asleep: and there came down a storm of wind on the lake; and they were filled *with water*, and were in jeopardy. 24 And they came to him, and awoke 'him, saying, Master, master, we perish. Then he arose, and rebuked the wind and the raging of the water: and they ceased, and there was a calm. 25 And he said unto them, Where is your faith? And they being afraid wondered, saying one to another, What manner of man is this! for he commandeth even the winds and water, and they obey him.

26 And they arrived at the country of the Gadarenes, which is over against Galilee. 27 And when he went forth to land, there met him out of the city a certain man, which had

'οὐ.γνωσθήσεται" καὶ εἰς φανερὸν ἔλθῃ. 18 βλέπετε οὖν
shall not be known   and to   light   come.   Take heed therefore
πῶς ἀκούετε· ὃς-ᵏγὰρ.ἂν" ἔχῃ,   δοθήσεται αὐτῷ· καὶ
how ye hear;   for whoever may have, ³shall ⁴be ⁵given 'to ²him; and
ὃς.ˡἂν" μὴ.ἔχῃ, καὶ ὃ δοκεῖ ἔχειν ἀρθήσεται ἀπ' αὐτοῦ,
whoever may not have, even what he seems to have shall be taken from   him.

19 ᵐΠαρεγένοντο".δὲ πρὸς αὐτὸν ἡ μήτηρⁿ καὶ οἱ ἀδελ-
    And came   to   him [his] mother and ²breth-
φοὶ αὐτοῦ, καὶ οὐκ.ἠδύναντο συντυχεῖν αὐτῷ διὰ τὸν
ren 'his,   and were not able   to get   to him because of the
ὄχλον. 20 °καὶ ἀπηγγέλη" αὐτῷ, ᴾλεγόντων," ᑫ Ἡ.μήτηρ.σου
crowd.   And it was told him,   saying,   Thy mother
καὶ οἱ.ἀδελφοί.σου ἑστήκασιν ἔξω, ἰδεῖν ʳσε θέλοντες."
and thy brethren   are standing without, ²to ³see ⁴thee 'wishing.
21 Ὁ.δὲ ἀποκριθεὶς εἶπεν ˢπρὸς αὐτούς," Μήτηρ.μου καὶ
    And he answering said to   them,   My mother and
ἀδελφοί.μου οὗτοί εἰσιν οἱ τὸν λόγον τοῦ θεοῦ ἀκούοντες καὶ
my brethren ²those 'are who the word   of God are hearing and
ποιοῦντες ᵗαὐτόν."
doing   it.

22 ᵛΚαὶ ἐγένετο" ἐν μιᾷ τῶν ἡμερῶν καὶ αὐτὸς ἐνέβη
    And it came to pass on one of the   days   that   he   entered
εἰς πλοῖον καὶ οἱ.μαθηταὶ.αὐτοῦ, καὶ εἶπεν πρὸς αὐτούς,
into a ³ship,   and   his disciples,   and he said   to   them,
Διέλθωμεν εἰς τὸ πέραν τῆς λίμνης· καὶ ἀνήχθησαν.
Let us pass over to the other side of the lake;   and they put off.
23 πλεόντων.δὲ.αὐτῶν ἀφύπνωσεν· καὶ κατέβη λαῖλαψ
    And as they sailed   he fell asleep; and came down a storm
ἀνέμου εἰς τὴν λίμνην, καὶ συνεπληροῦντο, καὶ ἐκινδύνευον.
of wind on the , lake,   and they were being filled, and were in danger.
24 προσελθόντες.δὲ διήγειραν αὐτόν, λέγοντες, Ἐπιστάτα,
    And having come to [him] they aroused him, saying,   Master,
ἐπιστάτα, ἀπολλύμεθα. Ὁ.δὲ ᵂἐγερθεὶς" ἐπετίμησεν τῷ
Master,   we are perishing. And he having arisen rebuked   the
ἀνέμῳ καὶ τῷ κλύδωνι τοῦ ὕδατος· καὶ ἐπαύσαντο, καὶ ἐγένετο
wind   and the raging of the water; and they ceased, and there was
γαλήνη. 25 εἶπεν.δὲ αὐτοῖς, Ποῦ ˣἐστιν" ἡ.πίστις.ὑμῶν ;
a calm.   And he said to them, Where   is   your faith ?
Φοβηθέντες.δὲ ἐθαύμασαν, λέγοντες πρὸς ἀλλήλους, Τίς ἄρα
And being afraid they wondered, saying   to one another, Who then
οὗτός ἐστιν, ὅτι καὶ τοῖς ἀνέμοις ἐπιτάσσει καὶ τῷ ὕδατι,
²this 'is,   that even the   winds he commands and the water,
καὶ ὑπακούουσιν αὐτῷ ;
and   they obey   him ?

26 Καὶ κατέπλευσαν εἰς τὴν χώραν τῶν ʸΓαδαρηνῶν,"
    And they sailed down to the   country of the   Gadarenes,
ἥτις ἐστὶν ᶻἀντιπέραν" τῆς Γαλιλαίας. 27 ἐξελθόντι.δὲ.αὐτῷ
which is   over against   Galilee.   And on his having gone forth
ἐπὶ τὴν γῆν ὑπήντησεν ᵃαὐτῷ" ἀνήρ τις ἐκ τῆς πόλεως,
upon the land   ⁴met   ⁵him 'a ³man ²certain out of the   city,

---

ⁱ οὐ μὴ γνωσθῇ in any wise should not be known LTTrA.   ᵏ ἂν γὰρ TTr.   ˡ ἐὰν L.
ᵐ Παρεγένετο TTr.   ⁿ + αὐτοῦ his T.   ° ἀπηγγέλη δὲ LTTrA.   ᴾ — λεγόντων LTTr[A].
ᑫ + ὅτι T.   ʳ θέλοντές σε Tr.   ˢ αὐτοῖς L.   ᵗ — αὐτόν GLTTrA.   ᵛ ἐγένετο δὲ LTTrA.
ᵂ διεγερθεὶς having been aroused TTr.   ˣ — ἐστιν (*read* [is]) LTTrAW.   ʸ Γερασηνῶ?
Gerasenes LTrA ; Γεργεσηνῶν Gergesenes T.   ᶻ ἀντιπέρα LTrAW ; ἀντίπερα T.   ᵃ — αὐτῷ
(*read* [him]) T[TrA].

ᵇὃς εἶχεν‖ δαιμόνια ᶜἐκ χρόνων.ἱκανῶν, καὶ ἱμάτιον οὐκ
who had   demons   for   a long time,   and a garment ²not

ἐνεδιδύσκετο,‖ καὶ ἐν οἰκίᾳ οὐκ.ἔμενεν, ἀλλ᾽ ἐν τοῖς μνήμασιν.
¹was wearing,   and in a house did not abide,   but in the   tombs.

28 ἰδὼν.δὲ τὸν Ἰησοῦν ᵈκαὶ‖ ἀνακράξας προσέπεσεν αὐτῷ,
But having seen   Jesus   and having cried out he fell down before him,

καὶ φωνῇ μεγάλῃ εἶπεν, Τί ἐμοὶ καὶ σοί, Ἰησοῦ, υἱὲ τοῦ
and with a ²voice ¹loud   said, What to me and to thee, Jesus, Son

θεοῦ τοῦ ὑψίστου; δέομαί σου μή με βασανίσῃς.
of God the Most High? I beseech of thee ³not ⁵me ¹thou ²mayest ⁴torment.

29 ᵉΠαρήγγελλεν‖.γὰρ τῷ πνεύματι τῷ ἀκαθάρτῳ ἐξελθεῖν
For he was charging the   spirit   the unclean to come out

ἀπὸ τοῦ ἀνθρώπου· πολλοῖς.γὰρ χρόνοις συνηρπάκει αὐτόν,
from the   man.   For many   times   it had seized him;

καὶ ᶠἐδεσμεῖτο,‖ ἁλύσεσιν καὶ πέδαις φυλασσόμενος, καὶ ᵍδιαρ-
and he was bound, with chains and fetters being kept,   and break-

ρήσσων‖ τὰ δεσμὰ ἠλαύνετο ὑπὸ τοῦ ʰδαίμονος‖ εἰς τὰς
ing   the bonds he was driven by the demon   into the

ἐρήμους. 30 ἐπηρώτησεν.δὲ αὐτὸν ὁ Ἰησοῦς, ⁱλέγων,‖ Τί σοι
deserts.   And ²asked ³him   ¹Jesus, saying, What ²thy

ᵏἐστὶν ὄνομα‖; Ὁ.δὲ εἶπεν, Λεγεών·‖ ὅτι ᵐδαιμόνια πολλὰ
¹is   name? And he said, Legion, because demons many

εἰσῆλθεν‖ εἰς αὐτόν. 31 καὶ ⁿπαρεκάλει‖ αὐτὸν ἵνα μὴ ἐπι-
had entered into him.   And he besought him that ³not ¹he ²would

τάξῃ αὐτοῖς εἰς τὴν ἄβυσσον ἀπελθεῖν. 32 ἦν.δὲ ἐκεῖ
command them into the abyss   to go away. Now there was there

ἀγέλη χοίρων ἱκανῶν ᵒβοσκομένων‖ ἐν τῷ ὄρει· καὶ ᵖπαρε-
a herd of ²swine ¹many   feeding   in the mountain, and they be-

κάλουν‖ αὐτὸν ἵνα ἐπιτρέψῃ αὐτοῖς εἰς ἐκείνους εἰσελθεῖν·
sought him that he would allow them into those   to enter;

καὶ ἐπέτρεψεν αὐτοῖς. 33 ἐξελθόντα.δὲ τὰ δαιμόνια ἀπὸ τοῦ
and he allowed them.   And having gone out the demons from the

ἀνθρώπου ᑫεἰσῆλθεν‖ εἰς τοὺς χοίρους· καὶ ὥρμησεν ἡ ἀγέλη
man   they entered into the swine,   and ²rushed ¹the ²herd

κατὰ τοῦ κρημνοῦ εἰς τὴν λίμνην, καὶ ἀπεπνίγη 34 ἰδόντες.δὲ
down the steep into the lake,   and were choked. And ⁵having⁶seen

οἱ βόσκοντες τὸ ʳγεγενημένον‖ ἔφυγον, καὶ ˢἀπελ-
¹those ²who ³fed [⁴them] what had taken place fled, and having

θόντες‖ ἀπήγγειλαν εἰς τὴν πόλιν καὶ εἰς τοὺς ἀγρούς.
gone away related [it] to the city and to the country.

35 ἐξῆλθον.δὲ ἰδεῖν τὸ γεγονός· καὶ ᵗἦλθον‖ πρὸς τὸν
And they went out to see what had taken place, and came to·

Ἰησοῦν, καὶ ᵛεὗρον‖ καθήμενον τὸν ἄνθρωπον ἀφ᾽ οὗ τὰ
Jesus,   and found seated   the   man   from whom the

δαιμόνια ʷἐξεληλύθει,‖ ἱματισμένον καὶ σωφρονοῦντα, παρὰ
demons   had gone out,   clothed   and of sound mind,   at

τοὺς πόδας τοῦ Ἰησοῦ. καὶ ἐφοβήθησαν. 36 ἀπήγγειλαν.δὲ
the feet of Jesus. And they were afraid.   And ⁷related

αὐτοῖς ˣκαὶ‖ οἱ ἰδόντες πῶς ἐσώθη ὁ δαι-
²to⁸them ²also ¹those ³who ⁴had ⁵seen [⁶it] how was healed he who had been pos-

---

Right column (English)

devils long time, and ware no clothes, neither abode in any house, but in the tombs. 28 When he saw Jesus, he cried out, and fell down before him, and with a loud voice said, What have I to do with thee, Jesus, thou Son of God most high? I beseech thee, torment me not. 29(For he had commanded the unclean spirit to come out of the man. For oftentimes it had caught him: and he was kept bound with chains and in fetters; and he brake the bands, and was driven of the devil into the wilderness.) 30 And Jesus asked him, saying, What is thy name? And he said, Legion: because many devils were entered into him. 31 And they besought him that he would not command them to go out into the deep. 32 And there was there an herd of many swine feeding on the mountain: and they besought him that he would suffer them to enter into them. And he suffered them. 33 Then went the devils out of the man, and entered into the swine: and the herd ran violently down a steep place into the lake, and were choked. 34 When they that fed them saw what was done, they fled, and went and told it in the city and in the country. 35 Then they went out to see what was done; and came to Jesus, and found the man, out of whom the devils were departed, sitting at the feet of Jesus, clothed, and in his right mind: and they were afraid. 36 They also which saw it told them by what means he that was possessed of the devils

---

ᵇ ἔχων having T.   ᶜ καὶ χρόνῳ ἱκανῷ οὐκ ἐνεδύσατο ἱμάτιον and for a long time did not put on a garment TTr.   ᵈ — καὶ LTTrA.   ᵉ Παρήγγειλε he charged EG.   ᶠ ἐδεσμεύετο TTr.
ᵍ διαρήσσων LTTrA.   ʰ δαιμονίου LTTrA.   ⁱ — λέγων L.   ᵏ ὄνομα ἐστίν LTTr.   ˡ Λεγιών
TTr.   ᵐ εἰσῆλθεν δαιμόνια πολλὰ LT.   ⁿ παρεκάλουν they besought LTTrA.   ᵒ βοσ-
κομένῃ L.   ᵖ παρεκάλεσαν LTTrA.   ᑫ εἰσῆλθον LTTrAW.   ʳ γεγονὸς GLTTrAW.   ˢ — ἀπελ
θόντες GLTTrAW.   ᵗ ἦλθαν Tr.   ᵛ εὗραν Tr.   ʷ ἐξῆλθεν went out T.   ˣ — καὶ LTTr[A].

was healed. 37 Then the whole multitude of the country of the Gadarenes round about besought him to depart from them ; for they were taken with great fear: and he went up into the ship, and returned back again. 38 Now the man out of whom the devils were departed besought him that he might be with him: but Jesus sent him away, saying, 39 Return to thine own house, and shew how great things God hath done unto thee. And he went his way, and published throughout the whole city how great things Jesus had done unto him.

40 And it came to pass, that, when Jesus was returned, the people *gladly* received him: for they were all waiting for him. 41 And, behold, there came a man named Jairus, and he was a ruler of the synagogue: and he fell down at Jesus' feet, and besought him that he would come into his house: 42 for he had one only daughter, about twelve years of age, and she lay a dying. But as he went the people thronged him. 43 And a woman having an issue of blood twelve years, which had spent all her living upon physicians, neither could be healed of any, 44 came behind *him*, and touched the border of his garment: and immediately her issue of blood stanched. 45 And Jesus said, Who touched me? When all denied, Peter and they that were with him said, Master, the multitude throng thee and press *thee*, and sayest thou, Who touched me? 46 And Jesus said, Somebody hath touched me: for I perceive that virtue is gone out of me. 47 And

μονισθείς. 37 καὶ ʸἠρώτησαν‖ αὐτὸν ἅπαν τὸ πλῆθος τῆς
sessed by demons. And asked him all the multitude of the

περιχώρου τῶν ᶻΓαδαρηνῶν‖ ἀπελθεῖν ἀπ᾽ αὐτῶν, ὅτι φόβῳ
country around of the Gadarenes to depart from them, for with ²fear

μεγάλῳ συνείχοντο· αὐτὸς δὲ ἐμβὰς εἰς ᵃτὸ‖ πλοῖον
¹great they were possessed. And he having entered into the ship

ὑπέστρεψεν. 38 ᵇἐδέετο‖ δὲ αὐτοῦ ὁ ἀνὴρ ἀφ᾽ οὗ ἐξελη-
returned. And ⁹was ¹⁰begging ¹¹him ¹the ²man ³from ⁴whom ⁵had

λύθει τὰ δαιμόνια εἶναι σὺν αὐτῷ. ἀπέλυσεν δὲ αὐτὸν
⁶gone ⁷the ⁸demons to be [taken] with him. But ²sent ⁴away ³him

ᶜὁ Ἰησοῦς,‖ λέγων, 39 Ὑπόστρεφε εἰς τὸν οἶκόν σου καὶ διηγοῦ
¹Jesus, saying, Return to thy house and relate

ὅσα ᵈἐποίησέν σοι‖ ὁ θεός. Καὶ ἀπῆλθεν, καθ᾽ ὅλην τὴν
all that ²has ³done ⁴for ⁵thee ¹God. And he departed, through ²whole ¹the

πόλιν κηρύσσων ὅσα ἐποίησεν αὐτῷ ὁ Ἰησοῦς·
city proclaiming all that ²had ³done ⁴for ⁵him ¹Jesus.

40 ᵉἘγένετο δὲ ἐν‖ τῷ ᶠὑποστρέψαι‖ τὸν Ἰησοῦν ἀπ-
²It ³came ⁴to ⁵pass ¹and ⁶on ⁸returning ⁷Jesus, gladly

εδέξατο αὐτὸν ὁ ὄχλος· ἦσαν γὰρ πάντες προσδοκῶντες
received him the crowd, for they were all looking for

αὐτόν. 41 Καὶ ἰδού, ἦλθεν ἀνὴρ ᾧ ὄνομα Ἰάειρος, καὶ
him. And behold, ³came ¹a ²man whose name [was] Jairus, and

ᵍαὐτὸς‖ ἄρχων τῆς συναγωγῆς ὑπῆρχεν, καὶ πεσὼν παρὰ
he a ruler of the synagogue was, and having fallen at

τοὺς πόδας ʰτοῦ‖ Ἰησοῦ παρεκάλει αὐτὸν εἰσελθεῖν εἰς τὸν
the feet of Jesus he besought him to come to

οἶκον αὐτοῦ· 42 ὅτι θυγάτηρ μονογενὴς ἦν αὐτῷ ὡς ἐτῶν
his house, because ³daughter ¹an ²only was to him, about ²years

δώδεκα, καὶ αὕτη ἀπέθνησκεν. ⁱἘν δὲ τῷ ὑπάγειν αὐτὸν‖
[³old] ¹twelve, and she was dying. And as ²went ¹he

οἱ ὄχλοι συνέπνιγον αὐτόν. 43 Καὶ γυνὴ οὖσα ἐν ῥύσει
the crowds thronged him. And a woman being with a flux

αἵματος ἀπὸ ἐτῶν δώδεκα, ἥτις ᵏεἰς ἰατροὺς‖ προσαναλώσασα
of blood since ²years ¹twelve, who on physicians having spent

ὅλον τὸν βίον ¹ οὐκ ἴσχυσεν ᵐὑπ᾽‖ οὐδενὸς θεραπευθῆναι,
²whole ³living [¹her] could by no one be cured,

44 προσελθοῦσα ὄπισθεν ἥψατο τοῦ κρασπέδου τοῦ ἱματίου
having come behind touched the border of ²garment

αὐτοῦ, καὶ παραχρῆμα ἔστη ἡ ῥύσις τοῦ αἵματος αὐτῆς.
¹his, and immediately stopped the flux of her blood.

45 καὶ εἶπεν ὁ Ἰησοῦς, Τίς ὁ ἁψάμενός μου; Ἀρνου-
And ²said ¹Jesus, Who [is it] that was touching me? ³Deny-

μένων δὲ πάντων, εἶπεν ὁ Πέτρος καὶ οἱ ⁿμετ᾽ αὐτοῦ,‖ Ἐπι-
ing ¹and ²all, ⁹said ⁴Peter ⁵and ⁶those ⁷with ⁸him, Mas-

στάτα, ὁ ὄχλοι συνέχουσίν σε καὶ ἀποθλίβουσιν, °καὶ λέγεις,
ter, the crowds throng thee and press, and sayest thou,

Τίς ὁ ἁψάμενός μου; 46 Ὁ δὲ Ἰησοῦς εἶπεν, Ἥψατό
Who [is it] that was touching me? And Jesus said, ³Touched

μου τίς· ἐγὼ γὰρ ἔγνων δύναμιν ᵖἐξελθοῦσαν‖ ἀπ᾽
⁴me ¹some ²one, for I knew [that] power went out from

ʸ ἠρώτησαν LTrA.   ᶻ Γερασηνῶν Gerasenes LTrA ; Γεργεσηνῶν Gergesenes T.   ᵃ — τὸ
(read a ship) LTTrA.   ᵇ ἐδεῖτο L ; ἐδεῖτο TrA.   ᶜ — ἁ Ἰησοῦς (read he sent) [L]TTrA.
ᵈ σοι ἐποίησεν LTTrA.   ᵉ Ἐν δὲ Tr.   ᶠ ὑποστρέψειν T.   ᵍ οὗτος this LT.   ʰ — τοῦ T[Tr].
ⁱ καὶ ἐγένετο ἐν τῷ πορεύεσθαι αὐτὸν and it came to pass as he proceeded L.   ᵏ ἰατροῖς
GLTTrAW.   ¹ + αὐτῆς her L.   ᵐ ἀπ᾽ LTTrA.   ⁿ σὺν αὐτῷ GLTTrA.   ° — καὶ λέγεις;
Τίς ὁ ἁψάμενός μου ; T[TrA].   ᵖ ἐξεληλυθυῖαν had gone out TTrA.

μοῦ. 47 Ἰδοῦσα δὲ ἡ γυνὴ ὅτι οὐκ ἔλαθεν, τρέμουσα ἦλ-
me. And ³seeing ¹the ²woman that she was not hid, trembling she

θεν, καὶ προσπεσοῦσα αὐτῷ, δι' ἣν αἰτίαν ἥψατο
came, and having fallen down before him, for what cause she touched

αὐτοῦ ἀπήγγειλεν ⁹αὐτῷ". ἐνώπιον παντὸς τοῦ λαοῦ, καὶ ὡς
him she declared to him before all the people, and how

ἰάθη παραχρῆμα. 48 ὁ δὲ εἶπεν αὐτῇ, ʳΘάρσει,"
she was healed immediately. And he said to her, Be of good courage,

ᵛθύγατερ," ἡ πίστις σου σέσωκέν σε· πορεύου εἰς εἰρήνην.
daughter, thy faith has cured thee: go in peace.

49 Ἔτι αὐτοῦ λαλοῦντος ἔρχεταί τις ᵗπαρὰ" τοῦ ἀρχισυναγώ-
As yet he was speaking comes one from the ruler of the syna-

γου, λέγων ᵛαὐτῷ," Ὅτι τέθνηκεν ἡ θυγάτηρ σου ʷμὴ" σκύλλε
gogue, saying to him, ³Has ⁴died ¹thy ²daughter; ⁶not ⁵trouble

τὸν διδάσκαλον. 50 Ὁ δὲ Ἰησοῦς ἀκούσας ἀπεκρίθη αὐτῷ,
the teacher. But Jesus having heard answered him,

ˣλέγων," Μὴ φοβοῦ· μόνον ᵞπίστευε." καὶ σωθήσεται.
saying, Fear not; only believe, and she shall be restored.

51 ᶻΕἰσελθὼν" δὲ εἰς τὴν οἰκίαν οὐκ ἀφῆκεν εἰσελθεῖν ᵃοὐδένα"
And having entered into the house he did not suffer ²to ⁴go ⁵in ¹any ²one
(lit. no one)

εἰ μὴ Πέτρον καὶ ᵇἸάκωβον καὶ Ἰωάννην," καὶ τὸν πατέρα
except Peter and James and John, and the father

τῆς παιδὸς καὶ τὴν μητέρα. 52 ἔκλαιον δὲ πάντες καὶ
of the child and the mother. And they were ²weeping ¹all and

ἐκόπτοντο αὐτήν. ὁ δὲ εἶπεν, Μὴ κλαίετε· ᶜοὐκ ἀπέθανεν,
bewailing her. But he said, Weep not; she is not dead,

ἀλλὰ καθεύδει. 53 Καὶ κατεγέλων αὐτοῦ, εἰδότες ὅτι ἀπέ-
but sleeps. And they laughed at him, knowing that she was

θανεν. 54 αὐτὸς δὲ ᵈἐκβαλὼν ἔξω πάντας, καὶ" κρατήσας
dead. But he having put out all, and having taken hold

τῆς χειρὸς αὐτῆς, ἐφώνησεν, λέγων, Ἡ παῖς, ᵉἐγείρου." 55 Καὶ
of her hand, cried, saying, Child, arise. And

ἐπέστρεψεν τὸ πνεῦμα αὐτῆς, καὶ ἀνέστη παραχρῆμα· καὶ
²returned ¹her ²spirit, and she arose immediately; and

διέταξεν αὐτῇ δοθῆναι φαγεῖν. 56 καὶ
he directed [that] ⁵to ⁶her [¹something] ²should ³be ⁴given to eat. And

ἐξέστησαν οἱ γονεῖς αὐτῆς· ὁ δὲ παρήγγειλεν αὐτοῖς μηδενὶ
²were ⁴amazed ¹her ²parents; and he charged them to no one

εἰπεῖν τὸ γεγονός.
to tell what had happened.

9 ᶠΣυγκαλεσάμενος" δὲ τοὺς δώδεκα ᵍμαθητὰς αὐτοῦ" ἔδωκεν
And having called together the twelve disciples of him he gave

αὐτοῖς δύναμιν καὶ ἐξουσίαν ἐπὶ πάντα τὰ δαιμόνια, καὶ
to them power and authority over all the demons, and

νόσους θεραπεύειν· 2 καὶ ἀπέστειλεν αὐτοὺς κηρύσσειν τὴν
diseases to heal, and sent them to proclaim the

βασιλείαν τοῦ θεοῦ, καὶ ἰᾶσθαι ʰτοὺς ἀσθενοῦντας." 3 καὶ
kingdom of God, and to heal those being sick. And

εἶπεν πρὸς αὐτούς, Μηδὲν αἴρετε εἰς τὴν ὁδόν· μήτε ⁱῥάβδους,"
he said to them, Nothing take for the way; neither staves,

when the woman saw that she was not hid, she came trembling, and falling down before him, she declared unto him before all the people for what cause she had touched him, and how she was healed immediately. 48 And he said unto her, Daughter, be of good comfort: thy faith hath made thee whole; go in peace. 49 While he yet spake, there cometh one from the ruler of the synagogue's house, saying to him, Thy daughter is dead; trouble not the Master. 50 But when Jesus heard it, he answered him, saying, Fear not: believe only, and she shall be made whole. 51 And when he came into the house, he suffered no man to go in, save Peter, and James, and John, and the father and the mother of the maiden. 52 And all wept, and bewailed her: but he said, Weep not; she is not dead, but sleepeth. 53 And they laughed him to scorn, knowing that she was dead. 54 And he put her by the hand, and called, saying, Maid, arise. 55 And her spirit came again, and she arose straightway: and he commanded to give her meat. 56 And her parents were astonished: but he charged them that they should tell no man what was done.

IX. Then he called his twelve disciples together, and gave them power and authority over all devils, and to cure diseases. 2 And he sent them to preach the kingdom of God, and to heal the sick. 3 And he said unto them, Take nothing for your journey, neither staves, nor

---

⁹ — αὐτῷ LTTrA.   ʳ — Θάρσει LTTrA.   ˢ θυγάτηρ Tr.   ᵗ ἀπὸ L.   ᵛ — αὐτῷ T[Tr].
ʷ μηκέτι no longer LTTr.   ˣ — λέγων LTTr[A].   ᵞ πίστευσον TTrA.   ᶻ ἐλθὼν having
gone GLTTrW.   ᵃ τινὰ σὺν αὐτῷ any one with him LTTrA.   ᵇ Ἰωάννην (Ἰωάνην Tr) καὶ
Ἰάκωβον GLTTrAW.   ᶜ οὐ γὰρ (read for she is not dead) LTrA.   ᵈ — ἐκβαλὼν ἔξω πάντας
καὶ LTTrA.   ᵉ ἔγειρε LTrA.   ᶠ Συγκαλεσάμενος T.   ᵍ — μαθητὰς αὐτοῦ GTTrAW.   ʰ τοὺς
ἀσθενεῖς the sick L[Tr]; — τοὺς ἀσθενοῦντας TA.   ⁱ ῥάβδον staff GLTTrA.

scrip, neither bread, ne ther money; neither have two coats apiece. 4 And whatsoever house ye enter into, there abide, and thence depart. 5 And whosoever will not receive you, when ye go out of that city, shake off the very dust from your feet for a testimony against them. 6 And they departed, and went through the towns, preaching the gospel, and healing every where.

7 Now Herod the tetrarch heard of all that was done by him: and he was perplexed, because that it was said of some, that John was risen from the dead; 8 and of some, that Elias had appeared; and of others, that one of the old prophets was risen again. 9 And Herod said, John have I beheaded : but who is this, of whom I hear such things? And he desired to see him.

10 And the apostles, when they were returned, told him all that they had done. And he took them, and went aside privately into a desert place belonging to the city called Bethsaida. 11 And the people, when they knew it, followed him : and he received them, and spake unto them of the kingdom of God, and healed them that had need of healing. 12 And when the day began to wear away, then came the twelve, and said unto him, Send the multitude away, that they may go into the towns and country round about, and lodge, and get victuals : for we are here in a desert place. 13 But he said unto them, Give ye them to eat. And they said, We have no more but five loaves and

μήτε πήραν, μήτε ἄρτον, μήτε ἀργύριον, μήτε ᵏἀνά∥ δύο
nor provision bag, nor bread, nor money; nor each two

χιτῶνας ἔχειν. 4 καὶ εἰς ἣν.ἂν οἰκίαν εἰσέλθητε, ἐκεῖ μένετε,
tunics to have. And into whatever house ye may enter, there remain,

καὶ ἐκεῖθεν ἐξέρχεσθε. 5 καὶ ὅσοι ἂν μὴ.ˡδέξωνται∥ ὑμᾶς,
and thence go forth. And as many as may not receive you,

ἐξερχόμενοι ἀπὸ τῆς.πόλεως.ἐκείνης ᵐκαὶ∥ τὸν κονιορτὸν ἀπὸ
going forth from that city even the dust from

τῶν.ποδῶν.ὑμῶν ⁿἀποτινάξατε,∥ εἰς μαρτύριον ἐπ' αὐτούς.
your feet shake off, for a testimony against them.

6 Ἐξερχόμενοι.δὲ διήρχοντο κατὰ τὰς κώμας, εὐαγγελιζό-
And going forth they passed through the villages, announcing the

μενοι καὶ θεραπεύοντες πανταχοῦ.
glad tidings and healing everywhere.

7 Ἤκουσεν.δὲ Ἡρώδης ὁ ᵒτετράρχης∥ τὰ γινόμενα
And heard of Herod the tetrarch the things being done

ᵖὑπ' αὐτοῦ∥ πάντα· καὶ διηπόρει, διὰ τὸ λέγεσθαι ὑπὸ
by him all, and was perplexed, because it was said by

τινων, Ὅτι qΙωάννης∥ ʳἐγήγερται∥ ἐκ νεκρῶν·
some, That John has been raised from among [the] dead;

8 ὑπό τινων δὲ, Ὅτι ˢἨλίας∥ ἐφάνη· ἄλλων δὲ, Ὅτι
by some also, that Elias had appeared; by others also, that

προφήτης ᵗεἷς∥ τῶν ἀρχαίων ἀνέστη. 9 ᵛΚαὶ εἶπεν∥ ʷὁ∥
a prophet one of the ancients had arisen. And said

Ἡρώδης, ˣἸωάννην∥ ἐγὼ ἀπεκεφάλισα· τίς.δέ ἐστιν οὗτος
Herod, John I beheaded, but who is this

περὶ οὗ ʸἐγὼ∥ ἀκούω τοιαῦτα; Καὶ ἐζήτει ἰδεῖν αὐτόν.
concerning whom I hear such things? And he sought to see him.

10 Καὶ ὑποστρέψαντες οἱ ἀπόστολοι διηγήσαντο αὐτῷ
And having returned the apostles related to him

ὅσα ἐποίησαν· καὶ παραλαβὼν αὐτοὺς ὑπεχώρησεν
whatsoever they had done. And having taken them he retired

κατ'.ἰδίαν εἰς ᶻτόπον ἔρημον πόλεως καλουμένης∥ Βηθσαϊδά.
apart into a place desert of a city called Bethsaida.

11 οἱ.δὲ ὄχλοι γνόντες ἠκολούθησαν αὐτῷ· καὶ ᵃδεξά-
But the crowds having known [it] followed him; and having

μενος∥ αὐτοὺς ἐλάλει αὐτοῖς περὶ τῆς βασιλείας τοῦ θεοῦ,
received them he spoke to them concerning the kingdom of God,

καὶ τοὺς χρείαν ἔχοντας θεραπείας ἰᾶτο. 12 Ἡ.δὲ ἡμέρα
and those need having of healing he cured. But the day

ἤρξατο κλίνειν· προσελθόντες.δὲ οἱ δώδεκα εἶπον αὐτῷ, Ἀπό-
began to decline, and having come the twelve said to him, Dis-

λυσον τὸν ὄχλον, ἵνα ᵇἀπελθόντες∥ εἰς τὰς κύκλῳ κώμας καὶ
miss the crowd, that having gone into the around villages and

ᶜτοὺς∥ ἀγροὺς καταλύσωσιν, καὶ εὕρωσιν ἐπισιτισμόν· ὅτι ὧδε
the country they may find provisions; for here

ἐν ἐρήμῳ τόπῳ ἐσμέν. 13 Εἶπεν.δὲ πρὸς αὐτούς, Δότε αὐτοῖς
in desert a place we are. But he said to them, Give to them

ᵈὑμεῖς φαγεῖν.∥ Οἱ.δὲ ᵉεἶπον,∥ Οὐκ.εἰσὶν ἡμῖν πλεῖον ἢ
ye to eat. But they said, There are not to us more than

ᵏ [ἀνά] TrL. ˡ δέχωνται LTTrA. ᵐ — καὶ [L]TrA. ⁿ ἀποτινάσσετε TA. ᵒ τετραάρχης T.
ᵖ — ὑπ' αὐτοῦ [L]TTrA. q Ἰωάνης Tr. ʳ ἠγέρθη was raised LTTr. ˢ Ἡλείας T.
ᵗ τις some one TA; τὶς Tr. ᵛ εἶπεν δὲ LTTrA. ʷ — ὁ GLTTrAW. ˣ Ἰωάνην Tr.
ʸ — ἐγὼ (read ἀκούω I hear) T[Tr]. ᶻ πόλιν καλουμένην a city called TTrA. ᵃ ἀποδεξά-
μενος having gladly received LTTrA. ᵇ πορευθέντες GLTTrA. ᶜ — τοὺς T[Tr]A. ᵈ φαγειν
ὑμεῖς LTA. ᵉ εἶπαν LTTrA.

ᶠπέντε ἄρτοι‖ καὶ ᵍδύο ἰχθύες,‖ εἰ·ʰμήτι‖ πορευθέντες ἡμεῖς
five loaves and two fishes, unless indeed having gone we

ἀγοράσωμεν εἰς πάντα τὸν·λαὸν·τοῦτον βρώματα. 14 Ἦσαν
should buy for all this people victuals; ²they ³were

γὰρ‖ ὡσεὶ ἄνδρες πεντακισχίλιοι. Εἶπεν·δὲ πρὸς τοὺς μαθητὰς
¹for about ³men ¹five ²thousand. But he said to ²disciples

αὐτοῦ, Κατακλίνατε αὐτοὺς κλισίας ᵏ ἀνὰ πεντήκοντα. 15 Καὶ
¹his, Make ²recline ¹them in companies by fifties. And

ἐποίησαν οὕτως, καὶ ¹ἀνέκλιναν‖ ἅπαντας. 16 Λαβὼν·δὲ
they did so, and made ²recline ¹all. And having taken

τοὺς πέντε ἄρτους καὶ τοὺς δύο ἰχθύας, ἀναβλέψας εἰς τὸν
the five loaves and the two fishes, having looked up to the

οὐρανὸν εὐλόγησεν αὐτοὺς καὶ κατέκλασεν, καὶ ἐδίδου τοῖς
heaven he blessed them and broke, and gave to the

μαθηταῖς ᵐπαρατιθέναι‖ τῷ ὄχλῳ. 17 καὶ ἔφαγον καὶ ἐχορ-
disciples to set before the crowd. And they ate and were

τάσθησαν πάντες· καὶ ἤρθη τὸ περισσεῦσαν αὐτοῖς
²satisfied ¹all; and was taken up that which was over and above to them

κλασμάτων κόφινοι δώδεκα.
of fragments ²hand ³baskets ¹twelve.

18 Καὶ ἐγένετο ἐν·τῷ·εἶναι αὐτὸν προσευχόμενον ⁿκατα-
And it came to pass as ²was ¹he praying a-

μόνας,‖ συνῆσαν αὐτῷ οἱ μαθηταί· καὶ ἐπηρώτησεν αὐτούς,
lone, ³were ⁴with ⁵him ¹the ²disciples, and he questioned them,

λέγων, Τίνα με ᵒλέγουσιν οἱ ὄχλοι‖ εἶναι; 19 Οἱ·δὲ ἀπο-
saying, Whom ⁵me ³do ⁴pronounce ²the ³crowds to be? And they an-

κριθέντες ᴾεἶπον,‖ ᑫἸωάννην‖ τὸν βαπτιστήν· ἄλλοι·δὲ
swering said, John the Baptist; and others,

ʳἨλίαν·‖ ἄλλοι·δὲ, ὅτι προφήτης τις τῶν ἀρχαίων ἀνέστη.
Elias; and others, that ¹prophet ¹some of the ancients has arisen.

20 Εἶπεν·δὲ αὐτοῖς, Ὑμεῖς·δὲ τίνα με λέγετε εἶναι;
And he said to them, But ye whom ⁴me ¹do ²ye ³pronounce to be?

ˢἈποκριθεὶς·δὲ ὁ Πέτρος‖ εἶπεν, Τὸν χριστὸν τοῦ θεοῦ. 21 Ὁ·δὲ
And answering Peter said, The Christ of God. And he

ἐπιτιμήσας αὐτοῖς παρήγγειλεν μηδενὶ ᵗεἰπεῖν‖ τοῦτο,
strictly enjoining them charged [them] to no one to tell this,

22 εἰπών, Ὅτι δεῖ τὸν υἱὸν τοῦ ἀνθρώπου πολλὰ
saying, It is necessary for the Son of man many things

παθεῖν, καὶ ἀποδοκιμασθῆναι ἀπὸ τῶν πρεσβυτέρων καὶ ἀρχ-
to suffer, and to be rejected by the elders and chief

ιερέων καὶ γραμματέων, καὶ ἀποκτανθῆναι, καὶ τῇ τρίτῃ
priests and scribes, and to be killed, and the third

ἡμέρᾳ ᵘἐγερθῆναι.‖ 23 Ἔλεγεν·δὲ πρὸς πάντας, Εἴ τις θέλει
day to be raised. And he said to all, If any one desires

ὀπίσω μου ʷἐλθεῖν,‖ ἀπαρνησάσθω‖ ἑαυτόν, καὶ ἀράτω
after me to come, let him deny himself, and let him take up

τὸν·σταυρὸν·αὐτοῦ ˣκαθ'·ἡμέραν,‖ καὶ ἀκολουθείτω μοι.
his cross daily, and let him follow me;

24 ὃς·γὰρ·ʸἂν‖ θέλῃ τὴν·ψυχὴν·αὐτοῦ σῶσαι, ἀπολέσει αὐ-
for whoever may desire his life to save, shall lose it;

τήν· ὃς·δ'·ἂν ἀπολέσῃ τὴν·ψυχὴν·αὐτοῦ ἕνεκεν ἐμοῦ, οὗτος
but whoever may lose his life on account of me, he

two fishes; except we should go and buy meat for all this people. 14 For they were about five thousand men. And he said to his·disciples, Make them sit down by fifties in a·company. 15 And they did so, and made them all sit down. 16 Then he took the five loaves and the two fishes, and looking up to heaven, he blessed them, and brake, and gave to the disciples to set before the multitude. 17 And they did eat, and were all filled: and there was taken up of fragments that remained to them twelve baskets.

18 And it came to pass, as he was·alone praying, his disciples were with him: and he asked them, saying, Whom say the people that I am? 19 They answering said, John the Baptist; but some say, Elias; and others say, that one of the old prophets is risen again. 20 He said unto them, But whom say ye that I am? Peter answering said, The Christ of God. 21 And he straitly charged them, and commanded them to tell no man that thing; 22 saying, The Son of man must suffer many things, and be rejected of the elders and chief priests and scribes, and be slain, and be raised the third day. 23 And he said to them all, If any man will come after me, let him deny himself, and take up his cross daily, and follow me. 24 For whosoever will save his life shall·lose it: but who·oever will lo·e his life for my sake, the same shall save it.

ᶠ ἄρτοι πέντε T. ᵍ ἰχθύες δύο GLTTrAW. ʰ μή τι LTrA. ⁱ δὲ and T. ᵏ + ὡσεὶ (read about fifty each) [LTr]A. ˡ κατέκλιναν TTr. ᵐ παραθεῖναι TTrA. ⁿ κατὰ μόνας LTTr. ᵒ οἱ ὄχλοι λέγουσιν TTrA. ᴾ εἶπαν LTTrA. ᑫ Ἰωάνην Tr. ʳ Ἠλείαν T. ˢ Πέτρος δὲ ἀποκριθεὶς TTrA. ᵗ λέγειν GLTTrA. ᵘ ἀναστῆναι to arise LA. ʷ ἔρχεσθαι, ἀρνησάσθω GLTTrA. ˣ — καθ' ἡμέραν L. ʸ ἐὰν T.

25 For what is a man advantaged, if he gain the whole world, and lose himself, or be cast away? **26** For whosoever shall be ashamed of me and of my words, of him shall the Son of man be ashamed, when he shall come in his own glory, and *in his* Father's, and of the holy angels. **27** But I tell you of a truth, there be some standing here, which shall not taste of death, till they see the kingdom of God.

σώσει αὐτήν. 25 τί.γὰρ ὠφελεῖται ἄνθρωπος, κερδήσας
shall save it. For what is ²profited ¹a ²man, having gained

τὸν κόσμον ὅλον, ἑαυτὸν.δὲ ἀπολέσας ἢ ζημιωθείς;
the ²world ¹whole, but himself having destroyed or suffered the loss of?

26 ὅς.γὰρ.ἂν ἐπαισχυνθῇ με καὶ τοὺς ἐμοὺς λόγους,
For whoever may have been ashamed of me and my words,

τοῦτον ὁ υἱὸς τοῦ ἀνθρώπου ἐπαισχυνθήσεται ὅταν ἔλθῃ
him the Son of man will be ashamed of when he shall come

ἐν τῇ δόξῃ αὐτοῦ καὶ τοῦ πατρὸς καὶ τῶν ἁγίων ἀγγέλων.
in the glory of himself and of the Father and of the holy angels.

27 Λέγω.δὲ ὑμῖν ἀληθῶς, εἰσίν τινες τῶν ᶻὧδε‖ ᵃἑστηκό-
But I say to you of a truth, there are some of those here stand-

των,‖ οἳ οὐ.μὴ ᵇγεύσονται‖ θανάτου ἕως.ἂν ἴδωσιν
ing who in no wise shall taste of death until they shall have seen

τὴν βασιλείαν τοῦ θεοῦ.
the kingdom of God.

---

28 And it came to pass about an eight days after these sayings, he took Peter and John and James, and went up into a mountain to pray. **29** And as he prayed, the fashion of his countenance was altered, and his raiment *was* white *and* glistering. **30** And, behold, there talked with him two men, which were Moses and Elias; **31** who appeared in glory, and spake of his decease which he should accomplish at Jerusalem. **32** But Peter and they that were with him were heavy with sleep: and when they were awake, they saw his glory, and the two men that stood with him. **33** And it came to pass, as they departed from him, Peter said unto Jesus, Master, it is good for us to be here: and let us make three tabernacles; one for thee, and one for Moses, and one for Elias: not knowing what he said. **34** While he thus spake, there came a cloud, and overshadowed them: and they feared as they entered into the cloud. **35** And there came a voice out of the cloud, saying, This is my beloved Son: hear him. **36** And

28 Ἐγένετο.δὲ μετὰ τοὺς.λόγους.τούτους ὡσεὶ ἡμέραι ὀκτὼ
And it came to pass after these words about ²days ¹eight

ᶜκαὶ‖ παραλαβὼν ᵈτὸν‖ Πέτρον καὶ ᵉΙωάννην‖ καὶ Ἰάκωβον
that having taken Peter and John and James

ἀνέβη εἰς.τὸ ὄρος προσεύξασθαι. 29 καὶ ἐγένετο
he went up into the mountain to pray. And it came to pass

ἐν.τῷ.προσεύχεσθαι αὐτὸν τὸ εἶδος τοῦ.προσώπου.αὐτοῦ
as ²prayed ¹he the appearance of his face

ἕτερον, καὶ ὁ.ἱματισμὸς.αὐτοῦ λευκὸς ἐξαστράπτων.
[became] altered, and his clothing white effulgent.

30 Καὶ ἰδού, ἄνδρες δύο συνελάλουν αὐτῷ, οἵτινες ἦσαν
And behold, ²men ¹two talked with him, who were

ᶠΜωσῆς‖ καὶ ᵍΗλίας ‖ 31 οἳ ὀφθέντες ἐν δόξῃ ἔλεγον ᵇ τὴν
Moses and Elias, who appearing in glory spoke of the

ἔξοδον.αὐτοῦ ἣν ⁱἔμελλεν‖ πληροῦν ἐν Ἰερουσαλήμ.
his departure which he was about to accomplish in Jerusalem.

32 ὁ.δὲ.Πέτρος καὶ οἱ σὺν αὐτῷ ἦσαν βεβαρημένοι ὕπνῳ.
But Peter and those with him were oppressed with sleep.

διαγρηγορήσαντες.δὲ ᵏεἶδον‖ τὴν.δόξαν.αὐτοῦ, καὶ τοὺς δύο
and having awoke fully they saw his glory, and the two

ἄνδρας τοὺς συνεστῶτας αὐτῷ. 33 καὶ ἐγένετο ἐν.τῷ.δια-
men who stood with him. And it came to pass as ²de-

χωρίζεσθαι αὐτοὺς ἀπ' αὐτοῦ, εἶπεν ὁ Πέτρος πρὸς τὸν
parted ¹these from him, ²said ¹Peter to

Ἰησοῦν, Ἐπιστάτα, καλόν.ἐστιν ἡμᾶς ὧδε εἶναι· καὶ ποιήσωμεν
Jesus, Master, good it is for us here to be; and let us make

σκηνὰς τρεῖς, μίαν σοί, καὶ ˡΜωσεῖ μίαν,‖ καὶ μίαν
²tabernacles ¹three, one for thee, and for Moses one, and one

ᵐΗλίᾳ,‖ μὴ εἰδὼς ὃ λέγει. 34 ταῦτα.δὲ αὐτοῦ.λέγοντος
for Elias, not knowing what he is saying. But these things as he was saying

ἐγένετο νεφέλη καὶ ⁿἐπεσκίασεν‖ αὐτούς· ἐφοβήθησαν.δὲ ἐν.τῷ
²came ¹a ²cloud and overshadowed them, and they feared as

ᵒἐκείνους εἰσελθεῖν‖ εἰς τὴν νεφέλην. 35 καὶ φωνὴ ἐγένετο ἐκ
those entered into the cloud: and a voice came out of

τῆς νεφέλης, λέγουσα, Οὗτός ἐστιν ὁ.υἱός.μου ὁ ᴾἀγαπητός·‖
the cloud, saying, This is my Son the beloved;

ᶻ αὐτοῦ TTrA. ᵃ ἑστώτων GLTTrAW. ᵇ γεύσωνται should taste GLTTrAW. ᶜ [καὶ] L.
ᵈ — τὸν GLTTrAW. ᵉ Ἰωάνην Tr. ᶠ Μωϋσῆς LTTrAW. ᵍ Ἡλίας T. ᵇ + [δὲ] and L.
ⁱ ἤμελλεν T. ᵏ εἶδαν T. ˡ μίαν Μωσεῖ G; μίαν Μωϋσεῖ LTTrAW. ᵐ Ἡλείᾳ T.
ⁿ ἐπεσκίαζεν TTrA. ᵒ εἰσελθεῖν αὐτοὺς they entered TTrA. ᴾ ἐκλελεγμένος chosen TTrA.

αὐτοῦ ἀκούετε. 36 Καὶ ἐν.τῷ γενέσθαι τὴν φωνὴν εὑρέθη
[3]him [1]hear [2]ye. And as occurred the voice [2]was [3]found

ᵈὁ‖Ἰησοῦς μόνος. Καὶ αὐτοὶ ἐσίγησαν, καὶ οὐδενὶ ἀπήγγειλαν
[1]Jesus alone: and they were silent, and to no one they told

ἐν ἐκείναις ταῖς ἡμέραις οὐδὲν ὧν ʳἑωράκασιν.‖
in those days anything of what they had seen.

37 Ἐγένετο.δὲ ˢἐν‖ τῇ ἑξῆς ἡμέρᾳ, κατελθόντων.αὐτῶν
And it came to pass on the next day, on their having come down

ἀπὸ τοῦ ὄρους, συνήντησεν αὐτῷ ὄχλος πολύς. 38 Καὶ
from the mountain, [4]met [5]him [1]a [3]crowd [2]great. And

ἰδού, ἀνὴρ ἀπὸ τοῦ ὄχλου ᵗἀνεβόησεν,‖ λέγων, Διδάσκαλε;
behold, a man from the crowd cried out, saying, Teacher,

δέομαί σου ᵛἐπίβλεψον‖ ἐπὶ τὸν.υἱόν.μου, ὅτι μονογενής
I beseech thee look upon my son, for an only child

ʷἐστίν μοι·‖ 39 καὶ ἰδού, πνεῦμα λαμβάνει αὐτὸν καὶ ἐξ-
he is to me: and behold, a spirit takes him and sud-

αἴφνης κράζει, καὶ σπαράσσει αὐτὸν μετὰ ἀφροῦ,
denly he cries out, and it throws [2]into [3]convulsions [1]him with foaming,

καὶ μόγις ἀποχωρεῖ ἀπ᾽ αὐτοῦ, συντρίβον αὐτόν· 40 καὶ
and with difficulty departs from him, bruising him. And

ἐδεήθην τῶν.μαθητῶν.σου ἵνα ˣἐκβάλλωσιν‖ αὐτό, καὶ οὐκ
I besought thy disciples that they might cast out . it, and [2]not

ἠδυνήθησαν. 41 Ἀποκριθεὶς.δὲ ὁ Ἰησοῦς εἶπεν, Ὦ γενεὰ
[1]they [3]were able. And [2]answering [1]Jesus said, O generation

ἄπιστος καὶ διεστραμμένη, ἕως πότε ἔσομαι πρὸς ὑμᾶς καὶ
unbelieving and perverted, until when shall I be with you and

ἀνέξομαι ὑμῶν; προσάγαγε ᵞὧδε τὸν.υἱόν.σου.‖ 42 Ἔτι.δὲ
bear with you? Bring . hither thy son. But [4]yet

προσερχομένου.αὐτοῦ ἔρρηξεν αὐτὸν τὸ δαιμόνιον καὶ συν-
[1]as [2]he [3]was coming near [3]dashed [5]down [4]him [1]the [2]demon and threw

εσπάραξεν· ἐπετίμησεν.δὲ ὁ Ἰησοῦς τῷ πνεύματι τῷ
[him] into convulsions. And [5]rebuked [1]Jesus the spirit the

ἀκαθάρτῳ, καὶ ἰάσατο τὸν παῖδα, καὶ ἀπέδωκεν αὐτὸν τῷ
unclean, and healed the child, and gave back him to

πατρὶ.αὐτοῦ. 43 ἐξεπλήσσοντο.δὲ πάντες ἐπὶ τῇ μεγαλειότητι
his father. And [2]were [3]astonished [1]all at the majesty

τοῦ θεοῦ.
of God.

Πάντων.δὲ θαυμαζόντων ἐπὶ πᾶσιν οἷς ᶻἐποίησεν‖ ᵃὁ Ἰη-
And [as] all were wondering at all which [2]did [1]Je-

σοῦς,‖ εἶπεν πρὸς τοὺς.μαθητὰς.αὐτοῦ, 44 Θέσθε ὑμεῖς εἰς τὰ
sus, he said to his disciples, Lay [2]by [3]ye into

ὦτα.ὑμῶν τοὺς.λόγους.τούτους· ὁ.γὰρ.υἱὸς τοῦ ἀνθρώπου μέλ-
your ears these words: For the Son of man is a-

λει παραδίδοσθαι εἰς χεῖρας ἀνθρώπων. 45 Οἱ.δὲ ἠγνόουν
bout to be delivered up into [the] hands of men. But they understood not

τὸ.ῥῆμα.τοῦτο, καὶ ἦν παρακεκαλυμμένον ἀπ᾽ αὐτῶν ἵνα
this saying, and it was veiled from them that

μὴ.αἴσθωνται αὐτό· καὶ ἐφοβοῦντο ᵇἐρωτῆσαι‖ αὐτὸν
they should not perceive it. And they feared to ask him

περὶ τοῦ ῥήματος τούτου. 46 Εἰσῆλθεν.δὲ διαλογισμὸς ἐν
concerning [2]saying [1]this. But [3]came [4]up [1]a [2]reasoning among

αὐτοῖς, τό, τίς ἂν εἴη μείζων αὐτῶν. 47 ὁ.δὲ.Ἰησοῦς ᶜἰδών‖
them, this, who might be greatest of them. And Jesus having seen

�q — ὁ LTTrAW. ʳ ἑωράκαν TTrA. ˢ — ἐν T[Tr]A. ᵗ ἐβόησεν LTTrA. ᵛ ἐπιβλέψαι
GTTrAW. ʷ μοι ἐστιν LTTrAW. ˣ ἐκβάλωσιν GLTTrAW. ᵞ τὸν.υἱόν σου ὧδε GW. ᶻ ἐποίει
GLTTrA. ᵃ — ὁ Ἰησοῦς (read ἐποίει he was doing) TTrA. ᵇ ἐπερωτῆσαι L. ᶜ εἰδὼς T.

their heart, took a child, and set him by him, 48 and said unto them, Whosoever shall receive this child in my name receiveth me : and whosoever shall receive me receiveth him that sent me : for he that is least among you all, the same shall be great. 49 And John answered and said, Master, we saw one casting out devils in thy name ; and we forbad him, because he followeth not with us. 50 And Jesus said unto him, Forbid him not : for he that is not against us is for us.

τὸν διαλογισμὸν τῆς.καρδίας.αὐτῶν, ἐπιλαβόμενος ᵈπαιδίου∥
the reasoning of their heart, having taken hold of a little child
ἔστησεν αὐτὸ παρ' ἑαυτῷ, 48 καὶ. εἶπεν αὐτοῖς, "Ὃς.ᵉἐὰν∥
he set it by him, and said to them, Whoever
δέξηται τοῦτο τὸ παιδίον ἐπὶ τῷ.ὀνόματί.μου, ἐμὲ δέχεται·
shall receive this little child in my name, me receives ;
καὶ ὃς.ᶠἐὰν∥ ἐμὲ δέξηται, δέχεται τὸν ἀποστείλαντά με.
and whoever me shall receive, receives him who sent me.
ὁ.γὰρ μικρότερος ἐν πᾶσιν ὑμῖν ὑπάρχων οὗτος ᵍἔσται∥
For he who ¹less. ³among ⁵all ⁴you ¹is he sha²l be
μέγας. 49 Ἀποκριθεὶς.δὲ ʰὁ∥ ⁱἸωάννης∥ εἶπεν, Ἐπιστάτα,
great. And answering John said, Master,
εἴδομέν τινα ἐπὶ τῷ.ὀνόματί.σου ἐκβάλλοντα ᵏτὰ∥ δαιμόνια·
we saw some one in thy name casting out the demons,
καὶ ἐκωλύσαμεν αὐτόν, ὅτι οὐκ.ἀκολουθεῖ μεθ' ἡμῶν· 50 Καὶ
and we forbade him, because he follows not with us. And
εἶπεν πρὸς αὐτὸν ᵐὁ∥ Ἰησοῦς, Μὴ.κωλύετε· ὃς.γὰρ οὐκ
²said ³to ⁴him ¹Jesus, Forbid not ; for whosoever ²not
ἔστιν καθ' ⁿἡμῶν," ὑπὲρ ⁿἡμῶν∥ ἐστιν.
¹is against us, for us is.

51 And it came to pass, when the time was come that he should be received up, he stedfastly set his face to go to Jerusalem, 52 and sent messengers before his face: and they went, and entered into a village of the Samaritans, to make ready for him. 53 And they did not receive him, because his face was as though he would go to Jerusalem. 54 And when his disciples James and John saw this, they said, Lord, wilt thou that we command fire to come down from heaven, and consume them, even as Elias did? 55 But he turned, and rebuked them, and said, Ye know not what manner of spirit ye are of. 56 For the Son of man is not come to destroy men's lives, but to save them. And they went to another village.

51 Ἐγένετο.δὲ ἐν.τῷ.συμπληροῦσθαι τὰς ἡμέρας τῆς
And it came to pass when were being fulfilled the days of the
ᵒἀναλήψεως∥.αὐτοῦ, καὶ αὐτὸς τὸ.πρόσωπον.ᵖαὐτοῦ∥ �q ἐστή-
receiving him up, that he his face sted-
ριξεν∥ τοῦ πορεύεσθαι εἰς Ἱερουσαλήμ. 52 καὶ ἀπέστειλεν
fastly set to go to Jerusalem. And he sent
ἀγγέλους πρὸ προσώπου αὐτοῦ. καὶ πορευθέντες εἰσῆλθον
messengers before ²face ¹his. And having gone they entered
εἰς ʳκώμην Σαμαρειτῶν,∥ ὥστε ἑτοιμάσαι αὐτῷ. 53 καὶ οὐκ
into a village of Samaritans, so as to make ready for him. And ²not
ἐδέξαντο αὐτόν, ὅτι τὸ.πρόσωπον.αὐτοῦ ἦν πορευό-
¹they ²did receive him, because his face was [as] go-
μενον εἰς Ἱερουσαλήμ. 54 ἰδόντες.δὲ οἱ.μαθηταὶ.ˢαὐτοῦ∥
ing to Jerusalem. And seeing [it] his disciples
Ἰάκωβος καὶ ᵗἸωάννης∥ ʷεἶπον,∥ Κύριε, θέλεις εἶπω-
James and John said, Lord, wilt thou [that] we should
μεν πῦρ καταβῆναι ˣἀπὸ∥ τοῦ οὐρανοῦ, καὶ ἀναλῶσαι αὐτούς,
call fire to come down from the heaven, and consume them,
Ⱪὡς καὶ Ἠλίας ἐποίησεν∥; 55 Στραφεὶς.δὲ ἐπετίμησεν αὐτοῖς,
as also Elias did? But turning he rebuked them,
ᶻκαὶ εἶπεν, Οὐκ.οἴδατε οἵου πνεύματός ἐστε ὑμεῖς· 56 ᶻὁ.γὰρ
and said, Ye know not of what spirit ²are ¹ye. For the
υἱὸς τοῦ ἀνθρώπου οὐκ.ἦλθεν ψυχὰς ἀνθρώπων ἀπολέσαι,
Son of man did not come [the] lives of men to destroy,
ἀλλὰ σῶσαι.∥ Καὶ ἐπορεύθησαν εἰς ἑτέραν κώμην.
but to save. And they went to another village.

57 And it came to pass, that, as they went in the way, a certain man said unto him, Lord, I will follow thee whithersoever thou goest. 58 And Je-

57 ⁿἘγένετο.δὲ∥ πορευομένων.αὐτῶν ἐν τῇ ὁδῷ εἶπέν τις
And it came to pass as they were going in the way ²said ¹some ²one
πρὸς αὐτόν, Ἀκολουθήσω σοι ὅπου ᵇἂν∥ ἀπέρχῃ, ᶜκύριε."
to him, I will follow thee wherever thou mayest go, Lord.

ᵈ παιδίον TrA.   ᵉ ἂν L.   ᶠ ἂν T.   ᵍ ἐστιν is LTTrA.   ʰ — ὁ LTrA.   ⁱ Ἰωάνης Tr.
ᵏ — τὰ LTTrAW.   ˡ εἶπεν δὲ LTTrA.   ᵐ — ὁ T[A].   ⁿ ὑμῶν you GLTTrA.   ᵒ ἀναλήμψεως
LTTrA.   ᵖ [αὐτοῦ] LTrA.   �q ἐστήρισεν TTrA.   ʳ πόλιν Σαμαριτῶν a city of Samaritans T.
ˢ — αὐτοῦ (read the disciples) T[TrA]   ᵗ Ἰωάνης Tr.   ʷ εἶπαν TTrA.   ˣ ἐκ out of L.
ʸ — ὡς καὶ Ἠλίας ἐποίησεν TT[A].   ᶻ — καὶ εἶπεν (verse 55) .... σῶσαι (verse 56) LTTrA ;
— ὁ γὰρ .... σῶσαι G.   ᵃ Καὶ and TTrA.   ᵇ ἐὰν LTrA.   ᶜ — κύριε LTTr[A].

58 Καὶ εἶπεν αὐτῷ ὁ Ἰησοῦς, Αἱ ἀλώπεκες φωλεοὺς ἔχουσιν,
And ²said ³to ⁴him ¹Jesus, The foxes holes have,

sus said unto him,
Foxes have holes, and

καὶ τὰ πετεινὰ τοῦ οὐρανοῦ κατασκηνώσεις· ὁ.δὲ υἱὸς τοῦ
and the birds of the heaven nests; but the Son of

birds of the air have
nests; but the Son of
man hath not where to

ἀνθρώπου οὐκ.ἔχει ποῦ τὴν κεφαλὴν κλίνῃ. 59 Εἶπεν.δὲ
of man has not where the head he may lay. And he said

lay his head. 59 And
he said unto another,

πρὸς ἕτερον, Ἀκολούθει μοι. Ὁ.δὲ εἶπεν, ᵈΚύριε,ǁ ἐπίτρεψόν
to another, Follow me. But he said, ᵈLord, allow

Follow me. But he
said, Lord, suffer me

μοι ᵉἀπελθόντι πρῶτονǁ θάψαι τὸν.πατέρα.μου. 60 Εἶπεν.δὲ
me going away first to bury my father. But ²said

first to go and bury
my father. 60 Jesus
said unto him, Let the

αὐτῷ ᶠὁ Ἰησοῦς,ǁ Ἄφες τοὺς νεκροὺς θάψαι τοὺς ἑαυτῶν
²to ⁴him ¹Jesus, Leave the dead to bury their own

dead bury their dead:
but go thou and preach
the kingdom of God.

νεκρούς· σὺ.δὲ ἀπελθὼν διάγγελλε τὴν βασιλείαν τοῦ θεοῦ.
dead; but thou going forth declare the kingdom of God.

61 And another also
said, Lord, I will fol-
low thee; but let me

61 Εἶπεν.δὲ καὶ ἕτερος, Ἀκολουθήσω σοι, κύριε· πρῶτον.δὲ
And ²said ³also ¹another, I will follow thee, Lord, but first

first go bid them fare-
well, which are at home
at my house. 62 And

ἐπίτρεψόν μοι ἀποτάξασθαι τοῖς εἰς τὸν.οἶκόν.μου. 62 Εἶπεν.δὲ
allow me to take leave of those at my house. But ²said

Jesus said unto him,
No man, having put
his hand to the plough,

ᵍπρὸς αὐτὸν ὁ Ἰησοῦς,ǁ Οὐδεὶς ʰἐπιβαλὼνǁ τὴν.χεῖρα.ⁱαὐτοῦ ǁ
³to ⁴him ¹Jesus, No one having laid his hand

and looking back, is fit
for the kingdom of
God.

ἐπ' ἄροτρον, καὶ βλέπων εἰς τὰ ὀπίσω, εὐθετός ἐστιν
upon [the] plough, and looking ᶠon the things behind, ²fit ¹is

ᵏεἰς τὴν βασιλείανǁ τοῦ θεοῦ.
for the kingdom of God.

10 Μετὰ.δὲ ταῦτα ἀνέδειξεν ὁ κύριος ¹καὶǁ ἑτέρους ἑβδο-
Now after these things ³appointed ¹the ²Lord ⁴also ⁵others ⁶seven-

X. After these things
the Lord appointed
other seventy also, and

μήκονταᵐ, καὶ ἀπέστειλεν αὐτοὺς ἀνὰ.δύο πρὸ προσώπου
ty, and sent them two and two before ²face

sent them two and two
before his face into
every city and place,

αὐτοῦ, εἰς πᾶσαν πόλιν καὶ τόπον οὗ ⁿἔμελλενǁ αὐτὸς
¹his, into every city and place where he was about himself

whither he himself
would come. 2 There-
fore said he unto them,

ἔρχεσθαι. 2 Ἔλεγεν °οὖνǁ πρὸς αὐτούς, Ὁ μὲν θερισμὸς
to come. He said therefore to them, The ²indeed ¹harvest [is]

The harvest truly is
great, but the labour-
ers are few: pray ye

πολύς, οἱ.δὲ ἐργάται ὀλίγοι· δεήθητε οὖν τοῦ κυρίου
great, but the workmen [are] few. Supplicate therefore the Lord

therefore the Lord of
the harvest, that he
would send forth la-

τοῦ θερισμοῦ, ὅπως ᵖἐκβάλλῃ ἐργάταςǁ εἰς τὸν θερισμὸν
of the harvest, that he may send out workmen into ²harvest

bourers into his har-
vest. 3 Go your ways:

αὐτοῦ. 3 Ὑπάγετε· ἰδού, ᑫἐγὼǁ ἀποστέλλω ὑμᾶς ὡς ἄρνας ἐν
¹his. Go; lo, I send forth you as lambs in

behold, I send you
forth as lambs among

μέσῳ λύκων. 4 μὴ βαστάζετε ʳβαλάντιονǁ μὴ πήραν
[the] midst of wolves. Neither carry purse nor provision bag

wolves. 4 Carry nei-
ther purse, nor scrip,
nor shoes: and salute

ˢμηδὲǁ ὑποδήματα· ᵗκαὶǁ μηδένα κατὰ τὴν ὁδὸν ἀσπάσησθε.
nor sandals, and no one on the way salute.

no man by the way.
5 And into whatsoever
house ye enter, first

5 Εἰς.ἣν.δ'.ἂν ᵛοἰκίαν εἰσέρχησθε,ǁ πρῶτον λέγετε, Εἰρήνη τῷ
And into whatever house ye may enter, first say, Peace

say, Peace be to this
house. 6 And if the
son of peace be there,

οἴκῳ.τούτῳ. 6 καὶ ἐὰν ʷμὲνǁ ᾖ ἐκεῖ ˣυἱὸς εἰρήνης, ʸἐπανα-
to this house. And if indeed be there a son of peace,

your peace shall rest
upon it: if not, it shall
turn to you again.

παύσεται· ἐπ' αὐτὸν ἡ.εἰρήνη.ὑμῶν· εἰ.δὲ μήγε, ἐφ' ὑμᾶς
⁴rest ⁵upon ⁶it ¹your ²peace; but if not so, to you

7 And in the same
house remain, eating
and drinking such

ἀνακάμψει. 7 ἐν αὐτῇ δὲ τῇ οἰκίᾳ μένετε, ᶻἐσθίοντεςǁ καὶ
it shall return. ²In ³the ⁴same ¹and house abide, eating and

things as they give: for
the labourer is worthy

ᵈ — Κύριε τ. ᵉ πρῶτον ἀπελθεῖν first to go away L; πρῶτον ἀπελθόντι ττr. ᶠ — ὁ
Ἰησοῦς (read he said) [L]ττ A. ᵍ ὁ Ἰησοῦς πρὸς αὐτόν Lτr; — πρὸς αὐτὸν A. ʰ ἐπιβάλλων L.
ⁱ [αὐτοῦ] τr. ᵏ τῇ βασιλείᾳ LτTrA. ˡ [καὶ] τrA. ᵐ + [δύο] two L. ⁿ ἤμελλεν LττrAW.
° δὲ and (he said) LττrA. ᵖ ἐκβάλῃ ἐργάτας GLW; ἐργάτας ἐκβάλῃ ττrA. ᑫ — ἐγὼ (read
ἀπος. I send forth) LττrA. ʳ βαλλάντιον LττrAW. ˢ μὴ ττrA. ᵗ — καὶ τ. ᵛ εἰσέλθητε
οἰκίαν ττrA; οἰκίαν εἰσέλθητε L. ʷ — μὲν GLττrAW. ˣ + ὁ the (son) E. ʸ ἐπανα-
παῦσεται·τ. ᶻ ἐσθοντες LττrA.

186 ΛΟΥΚΑΣ. X

of his hire. Go not
from house to house.
8 And into whatsoever
city ye enter, and they
receive you, eat such
things as are set be-
fore you: 9 and heal
the sick that are there-
in, and say unto them,
The kingdom of God
is come nigh unto you.
10 But into whatsoever
city ye enter, and they
receive you not, go
your ways out into the
streets of the same,
and say, 11 Even the
very dust of your city,
which cleaveth on us,
we do wipe off against
you : notwithstanding
be ye sure of this, that
the kingdom of God is
come nigh unto you.
12 But I say unto you,
that it shall be more
tolerable in that day
for Sodom, than for
that city. 13 Woe unto
thee, Chorazin ! woe
unto thee, Bethsaida !
for if the mighty works
had been done in Tyre
and Sidon, which have
been done in you, they
had a great while ago
repented, sitting in
sackcloth and ashes.
14 But it shall be more
tolerable for Tyre and
Sidon at the judg-
ment, than for you.
15 And thou, Caperna-
um, which art exalted
to heaven, shalt be
thrust down to hell.
16 He that heareth
you heareth me ; and
he that despiseth you
despi-eth me ; and he
that despiseth me de-
spiseth him that sent
me.

17 And the seventy
returned again with
joy, saying, Lord, even
the devils are subject
unto us through thy
name. 18 And he said
unto them, I beheld
Satan as lightning
fall from heaven.
19 Behold, I give unto
you power to tread on
serpents and scorpions,
and over all the power
of the enemy : and
nothing shall by any
means hurt you.

πίνοντες τὰ παρ' αὐτῶν· ἄξιος·γὰρ ὁ ἐργάτης
drinking the things [supplied] by them; for worthy ²the ³workman
τοῦ.μισθοῦ.αὐτοῦ ᵃἐστιν.‖ μὴ.μεταβαίνετε ἐξ οἰκίας εἰς οἰκίαν.
⁴of ⁵his ⁶hire ¹is. Remove not from house to house.
8 καὶ εἰς ἣν.ᵇδ'‖.ἂν πόλιν εἰσέρχησθε, καὶ δέχωνται ὑμᾶς,
And into whatever ²also ¹city ye may enter, and they receive you,
ἐσθίετε τὰ παρατιθέμενα ὑμῖν, 9 καὶ θεραπεύετε τοὺς ἐν
eat the things set before you, and heal the ²in
αὐτῇ ἀσθενεῖς, καὶ λέγετε αὐτοῖς, Ἤγγικεν ἐφ' ὑμᾶς ἡ βασι-
it ¹sick, and say to them, Has drawn near to you the king-
λεία τοῦ θεοῦ. 10 εἰς.ἣν.δ'.ἂν πόλιν ᶜεἰσέρχησθε,‖ καὶ μὴ
dom of God. But into whatever city ye may enter, and ³not
δέχωνται ὑμᾶς, ἐξελθόντες εἰς τὰς.πλατείας.αὐτῆς, εἴπατε,
¹they ²do receive you, having gone out into its streets, say,
11 Καὶ τὸν κονιορτὸν τὸν κολληθέντα ἡμῖν ἐκ τῆς πόλεως
Even the dust which clung to us out of ²city
ὑμῶν ᵈ ἀπομασσόμεθα ὑμῖν· πλὴν τοῦτο γινώσκετε, ὅτι
¹your we wipe off against you; yet this know, that
ἤγγικεν ᵉἐφ' ὑμᾶς‖ ἡ βασιλεία τοῦ θεοῦ. 12 λέγω.ᶠδὲ‖ ὑμῖν,
has drawn near to you the kingdom of God. And I say to you,
ὅτι Σοδόμοις ἐν τῇ.ἡμέρᾳ.ἐκείνῃ ἀνεκτότερον ἔσται ἢ τῇ
that for Sodom in that day more tolerable it shall be than
πόλει.ἐκείνῃ. 13 Οὐαί σοι, ᵍΧωραζίν,‖ οὐαί σοι, Βηθσαϊδά·
for that city. Woe to thee, Chorazin ! woe to thee, Bethsaida !
ὅτι εἰ ἐν Τύρῳ καὶ Σιδῶνι ʰἐγένοντο‖ αἱ δυνάμεις αἱ
for if in Tyre and Sidon had taken place the works of power which
γενόμεναι ἐν ὑμῖν, πάλαι ἂν ἐν σάκκῳ καὶ σποδῷ
have been taking place in you, long ago in sackcloth and ashes
ⁱκαθήμεναι‖ μετενόησαν. 14 πλὴν Τύρῳ καὶ Σιδῶνι ἀνεκ-
sitting they had repented. But for Tyre and Sidon more
τότερον ἔσται ἐν τῇ κρίσει ἢ ὑμῖν. 15 καὶ σύ, ᵏΚαπερ-
tolerable will it be in the judgment than for you. And thou, Caper-
ναούμ, ¹ἡ‖ ἕως ᵐτοῦ‖ οὐρανοῦ ⁿὑψωθεῖσα,‖ ἕως ° ᾅδου
naum, who to the heaven hast been lifted up, to hades
καταβιβασθήσῃ. 16 Ὁ ἀκούων ὑμῶν ἐμοῦ ἀκούει· καὶ
thou shalt be brought down. He that hears you ²me ¹hears, and
ὁ ἀθετῶν ὑμᾶς ἐμὲ ἀθετεῖ· ὁ.δὲ ἐμὲ ἀθετῶν ἀθετεῖ τὸν
he that rejects you ²me ¹rejects, and he that ²me ¹rejects rejects him
ἀποστείλαντά με.
who sent me.

17 Ὑπέστρεψαν.δὲ οἱ ἑβδομήκονταᵖ μετὰ χαρᾶς, λέγοντες,
And ³returned ¹the ²seventy with joy, saying,
Κύριε, καὶ τὰ δαιμόνια ὑποτάσσεται ἡμῖν ἐν τῷ ὀνόματί
Lord, even the demons are subject to us through ²name
σου. 18 Εἶπεν.δὲ αὐτοῖς, Ἐθεώρουν τὸν σατανᾶν ὡς ἀστραπὴν
¹thy. And he said to them, I beheld Satan as lightning
ἐκ τοῦ οὐρανοῦ πεσόντα. 19 ἰδού, �q δίδωμι‖ ὑμῖν τὴν ἐξουσίαν
out of the heaven falling. Lo, I give you the authority
τοῦ πατεῖν ἐπάνω ὄφεων καὶ σκορπίων, καὶ ἐπὶ πᾶσαν τὴν
to tread upon serpents and scorpions, and upon all the
δύναμιν τοῦ ἐχθροῦ· καὶ οὐδὲν ὑμᾶς οὐ.μὴ ʳἀδικήσῃ.‖
power of the enemy, and nothing you in anywise shall injure.
(lit. in no wise)

ᵃ — ἐστιν (read [is]) LTTrA.   ᵇ — δ' also LTTrA.   ᶜ εἰσέλθητε LTTrA.   ᵈ + εἰς τοὺς
πόδας to the feet (+[ἡμῶν] of us A) LTTrA.   ᵉ — ἐφ' ὑμᾶς GLTTrA.   ᶠ — δὲ and G[L]TrAW.
ᵍ Χοραζίν EGLW ; Χοραζείν TTrA.   ʰ ἐγενήθησαν LTTrA.   ⁱ καθήμενοι LTTrA.   ᵏ Καφαρναούμ LTTrAW.   ¹ μὴ LTTrA.   ᵐ — τοῦ LTTr.   ⁿ ὑψωθήσῃ ; wilt thou be lifted up? LTTrA.
° + τοῦ the TrA.   ᵖ + [δύο] two L.   q δέδωκα I have given TTrA.   ʳ ἀδικήσει ELTTrA.

20 πλὴν ἐν τούτῳ μὴ χαίρετε, ὅτι τὰ πνεύματα ὑμῖν ὑποτάσ-
Yet   in   this   rejoice not,   that the   spirits   to you   are sub-
σεται· χαίρετε δὲ ⁵μᾶλλον‖ ὅτι τὰ ὀνόματα ὑμῶν ⁴ἐγράφη‖
jected,   but rejoice   rather   that   your names   are written
ἐν τοῖς οὐρανοῖς. 21 Ἐν αὐτῇ τῇ ὥρᾳ ἠγαλλιάσατο ᵛ τῷ
in   the   heavens.   In   the same   hour   ²rejoiced   ³in ⁴the
πνεύματιʷ ˣὁ Ἰησοῦς,‖ καὶ εἶπεν, Ἐξομολογοῦμαί σοι, πάτερ,
⁵Spirit   ¹Jesus,   and said,   I praise   thee, O Father,
κύριε τοῦ οὐρανοῦ καὶ τῆς γῆς, ὅτι ἀπέκρυψας ταῦτα ἀπὸ
Lord of   the   heaven   and of the earth,   that thou didst hide these things from
σοφῶν καὶ συνετῶν, καὶ ἀπεκάλυψας αὐτὰ νηπίοις· ναί, ὁ πα-
wise   and   prudent,   and didst reveal   them   to babes: yea,   Fa-
τήρ, ὅτι οὕτως ʸἐγένετο εὐδοκία‖ ἔμπροσθέν σου. 22 ᶻΚαὶ
ther,   for   thus   was it   well pleasing   before   thee.   And
στραφεὶς πρὸς τοὺς μαθητὰς εἶπεν,‖ Πάντα ᵃπαρεδόθη μοι‖
having turned to   the   disciples   he said,   All things were delivered to me
ὑπὸ τοῦ πατρός μου· καὶ οὐδεὶς γινώσκει τίς ἐστιν ὁ υἱὸς εἰ μὴ
by   my Father,   and no one   knows   who   is   the Son except
ὁ πατήρ, καὶ τίς ἐστιν ὁ πατήρ, εἰ μὴ ὁ υἱός, καὶ   ᵂ ᵇἐὰν‖
the Father, and who   is   the Father, except the Son, and he to whomsoever
βούληται ὁ υἱὸς ἀποκαλύψαι. 23 Καὶ στραφεὶς πρὸς
²may ⁴will ¹the ²Son   to reveal [him].   And having turned to
τοὺς μαθητὰς κατ' ἰδίαν εἶπεν, Μακάριοι οἱ ὀφθαλμοὶ
the   disciples   apart   he said,   Blessed [are] the   eyes
οἱ βλέποντες ἃ βλέπετε. 24 λέγω γὰρ ὑμῖν, ὅτι πολλοὶ
which   see   what ye see.   For I say to you,   that   many
προφῆται καὶ βασιλεῖς ἠθέλησαν ἰδεῖν ἃ ὑμεῖς βλέπετε,
prophets   and   kings   desired   to see   what ye   see,
καὶ οὐκ ᶜεἶδον‖ καὶ ἀκοῦσαι ἃ ἀκούετε, καὶ οὐκ ἤκουσαν.
and   saw not;   and to hear   what ye hear,   and   heard not.

25 Καὶ ἰδού, νομικός τις ἀνέστη, ἐκπειράζων
And   behold, a ²doctor ³of ⁴the ⁵law ¹certain stood up,   tempting
αὐτόν, ᵈκαὶ‖ λέγων, Διδάσκαλε, τί ποιήσας ζωὴν αἰώνιον
him,   and saying,   Teacher,   ²what ¹having ³done life   eternal
κληρονομήσω; 26 Ὁ δὲ εἶπεν πρὸς αὐτόν, Ἐν τῷ νόμῳ τί
shall I inherit?   And he said   to   him,   In   the   law   what
γέγραπται; πῶς ἀναγινώσκεις; 27 Ὁ δὲ ἀποκριθεὶς εἶπεν,
has been written? how   readest thou?   And he answering   said,
Ἀγαπήσεις κύριον τὸν θεόν σου ἐξ ὅλης ᵉτῆς‖ καρδίας
Thou shalt love [the] Lord   thy God   with all   ²heart
σου καὶ ᶠἐξ ὅλης τῆς ψυχῆς σου καὶ ἐξ ὅλης τῆς ἰσχύος· σου
¹thy and with all   thy soul   and with all   thy strength
καὶ ᵍἐξ ὅλης τῆς διανοίας‖ σου· καὶ τὸν πλησίον σου ὡς σεαυ-
and with all   thy mind;   and thy neighbour   as   thy-
τόν. 28 Εἶπεν δὲ αὐτῷ, Ὀρθῶς ἀπεκρίθης· τοῦτο ποίει,
self.   And he said to him,   Rightly thou hast answered: this   do,
καὶ ζήσῃ. 29 Ὁ δὲ θέλων ʰδικαιοῦν‖ ἑαυτὸν εἶπεν πρὸς
and thou shalt live.   But he desiring   to justify   himself   said   to
τὸν Ἰησοῦν, Καὶ τίς ἐστίν μου πλησίον; 30 Ὑπολαβὼν ⁱδὲ‖
Jesus,   And who   is   my   neighbour?   And taking [it] up
ὁ Ἰησοῦς εἶπεν, Ἄνθρωπός τις κατέβαινεν ἀπὸ Ἱερουσαλὴμ
Jesus   said,   A ²man   ¹certain was going down from   Jerusalem

20 Notwithstanding in
this rejoice not, that
the spirits are subject
unto you; but rather
rejoice, because your
names are written in
heaven. 21 In that
hour Jesus rejoiced in
spirit, and said, I thank
thee, O Father, Lord
of heaven and earth,
that thou hast hid
these things from the
wise and prudent, and
hast revealed them un-
to babes: even so, Fa-
ther; for so it seemed
good in thy sight.
22 All things are de-
livered to me of my
Father: and no man
knoweth who the Son
is, but the Father; and
who the Father is, but
the Son, and , he to
whom the Son will re-
veal him. 23 And he
turned him unto his
disciples, and said pri-
vately, Blessed are the
eyes which see the
things that ye see:
24 For I tell you, that
many prophets and
kings have desired to
see those things which
ye see, and have not
seen them ; and to
hear those things
which ye hear, and
have not heard them.

25 And, behold, a
certain lawyer stood
up, and tempted him,
saying, Master, what
shall I do to inherit
eternal life ? 26 He
said unto him, What
is written in the law?
how readest thou?
27 And he answering
said, Thou shalt love
the Lord thy God with
all thy heart, and with
all thy soul, and with
all thy strength, and
with all thy mind; and
thy neighbour as thy-
self. 28 And he said
unto him, Thou hast
answered right : this
do, and thou shalt live.
29 But he, willing to
justify himself, said
unto Jesus, And who
is my neighbour ?
30 And Jesus answer-
ing said, A certain man
went down from Jeru-
salem to Jericho, and

ˢ — μᾶλλον GLTTrAW.   ᵗ ἐνγέγραπται have been inscribed T ; ἐγγέ. TrA.   ᵛ + ἐν in (the) T.
ʷ + τῷ ἁγίῳ the Holy LTTrA.   ˣ — ὁ Ἰησοῦς (read ἠγαλ. he rejoiced) LTTrA.   ʸ εὐδοκία
ἐγένετο LTrA.   ᶻ — καὶ στραφεὶς πρὸς τοὺς μαθητὰς εἶπεν EGTr[A].   ᵃ μοι παρεδόθη GLTTrAW.
ᵇ ἂν LTrA.   ᶜ ἴδαν T ; εἶδαν TrA.   ᵈ — καὶ T[Tr]A.   ᵉ [τῆς] Tr.   ᶠ ἐν ὅλῃ τῇ ψυχῇ σου
καὶ ἐν ὅλῃ τῇ ἰσχύϊ LTTr.   ᵍ ἐν ὅλῃ τῇ διανοίᾳ LTTr.   ʰ δικαιῶσαι LTTrA.   ⁱ — δὲ aMd T.

fell among thieves, which stripped him of his raiment, and wounded *him*, and departed, leaving *him* half dead. 31 And by chance there came down a certain priest that way: and when he saw him, he passed by on the other side. 32 And likewise a Levite; when he was at the place, came and looked *on him*, and passed by on the other side. 33 But a certain Samaritan, as he journeyed, came where he was: and when he saw him, he had compassion *on him*, 34 and went to *him*, and bound up his wounds, pouring in oil and wine, and set him on his own beast, and brought him to an inn, and took care of him. 35 And on the morrow when he departed, he took out two pence, and gave *them* to the host, and said unto him, Take care of him; and whatsoever thou spendest more, when I come again, I will repay thee. 36 Which now of these three, thinkest thou, was neighbour unto him that fell among the thieves? 37 And he said, He that shewed mercy on him. Then said Jesus unto him, Go, and do thou likewise.

εἰς [k]Ἰεριχώ," καὶ λῃσταῖς περιέπεσεν, οἳ καὶ ἐκδύσαντες
to Jericho, and [2]robbers [1]fell [2]among, who both having stripped

αὐτὸν καὶ πληγὰς ἐπιθέντες ἀπῆλθον, ἀφέντες ἡμιθανῆ
him and wounds having inflicted went away, leaving [him], half dead

[l]τυγχάνοντα." 31 κατὰ συγκυρίαν δὲ ἱερεύς τις κατ-
being. [2]By [3]a "coincidence [1]now [5]a [6]priest [7]certain went

έβαινεν ἐν τῇ ὁδῷ ἐκείνῃ, καὶ ἰδὼν αὐτὸν ἀντιπαρῆλ-
down in that road, and having seen him he passed by on the op-

θεν. 32 ὁμοίως δὲ καὶ [m]Λευίτης," [n]γενόμενος" κατὰ τὸν
posite side; and in like manner also a Levite, being at the

τόπον, ἐλθὼν καὶ ἰδὼν [o] ἀντιπαρῆλθεν. 33 [P]Σα-
spot, having come and having seen passed by on the opposite side. [2]A [4]Sa-

μαρείτης" δέ τις ὁδεύων ἦλθεν κατ' αὐτόν, καὶ ἰδὼν
maritan [1]but [3]certain journeying, came to him, and having seen

[q]αὐτὸν" ἐσπλαγχνίσθη· 34 καὶ προσελθὼν κατέδησεν τὰ
him was moved with compassion, and having approached bound up

τραύματα αὐτοῦ, ἐπιχέων ἔλαιον καὶ οἶνον· [r]ἐπιβιβάσας δὲ
his wounds, pouring on oil and wine; and having put

αὐτὸν ἐπὶ τὸ ἴδιον κτῆνος ἤγαγεν αὐτὸν εἰς [s]πανδοχεῖον," καὶ
him on his own beast brought him to an inn, and

ἐπεμελήθη αὐτοῦ. 35 καὶ ἐπὶ τὴν αὔριον [t]ἐξελθών," ἐκβαλὼν
took care of him. And on the morrow going forth, taking out

δύο δηνάρια ἔδωκεν τῷ [v]πανδοχεῖ," καὶ εἶπεν [w]αὐτῷ,"
two denarii he gave [them] to the innkeeper, and said to him,

Ἐπιμελήθητι αὐτοῦ· καὶ ὅ,τι ἂν προσδαπανήσῃς, ἐγὼ ἐν
Take care of him, and whatsoever thou mayest expend more. I in

τῷ ἐπανέρχεσθαί με ἀποδώσω σοι. 36 Τίς [x]οὖν" τούτων
my coming back will repay thee. Which therefore of these

τῶν τριῶν [y]δοκεῖ σοι πλησίον" γεγονέναι τοῦ ἐμπεσόντος
three seems to thee [4]neighbour [1]to [2]have [3]been of him who fell

εἰς τοὺς λῃστάς; 37 Ὁ δὲ εἶπεν, Ὁ ποιήσας τὸ ἔλεος
among the robbers? And he said, He who shewed compassion

μετ' αὐτοῦ. Εἶπεν [z]οὖν" αὐτῷ ὁ Ἰησοῦς, Πορεύου, καὶ
towards him. [3]Said [2]therefore [4]to [5]him [1]Jesus, Go [2]and

σὺ ποίει ὁμοίως.
[1]thou do likewise.

38 Now it came to pass, as they went, that he entered into a certain village: and a certain woman named Martha received him into her house. 39 And she had a sister called Mary, which also sat at Jesus' feet, and heard his word. 40 But Martha was cumbered about much serving, and came to him, and said, Lord, dost thou not care that my sister hath left me to serve alone? bid her

38 [a]Ἐγένετο δὲ ἐν τῷ πορεύεσθαι αὐτοὺς [b]καὶ" αὐτὸς εἰσῆλ-
And it came to pass as [2]proceeded [1]they that he enter-

θεν εἰς κώμην τινά· γυνὴ δὲ τις ὀνόματι Μάρθα ὑπ-
ed into a [2]village [1]certain; and a [2]woman [1]certain by name Martha re-

εδέξατο αὐτὸν εἰς [c]τὸν οἶκον [d]αὐτῆς. 39 καὶ τῇδε ἦν ἀδελφὴ
ceived him into her house. And she had a sister

καλουμένη [e]Μαρία," ἣ καὶ [f]παρακαθίσασα" [g]παρὰ" τοὺς πόδας
called Mary, who also having sat down at the feet

[h]τοῦ Ἰησοῦ" ἤκουεν τὸν λόγον αὐτοῦ. 40 ἡ δὲ Μάρθα
of Jesus was listening to his word. But Martha

περιεσπᾶτο περὶ πολλὴν διακονίαν· ἐπιστᾶσα δὲ εἶπεν, Κύριε,
was distracted about much service; and coming up she said, Lord,

οὐ μέλει σοι ὅτι ἡ ἀδελφή μου μόνην με [i]κατέλιπεν" δια-
is it no concern to thee that my sister [3]alone [2]me [1]left to

---

[k] Ἱερειχώ T. [l] — τυγχάνοντα LTTr[A]. [m] Λευείτης TTrA. [n] — γενόμενος Tr. [o] + αὐτὸν him L. [P] Σαμαρίτης T. [q] — αὐτὸν [L]T[Tr]A. [r] καὶ ἐπιβιβάσας L. [s] πανδοκίον T. [t] — ἐξελθών LTTr[A]. [v] πανδοκεῖ T. [w] — αὐτῷ [L]TTr[A]. [x] — οὖν [L]T[Tr]A. [y] πλησίον δοκεῖ σοι GTTrAW. [z] δὲ [1]and ([2]Jesus) GLTTrA. [a] Ἐν δὲ And as Tr. [b] [καὶ] L. [c] τὴν οἰκίαν T. [d] αὐτῆς (read the house) T[Tr]. [e] Μαριάμ T. [f] παρακαθεσθεῖσα TTrA. [g] πρὸς against TTrA. [h] τοῦ κυρίου of the Lord LTTrAW. [i] κατέλειπεν TrA.

κονεῖν; ᵏεἶπὲ‖ οὖν αὐτῇ ἵνα μοι συναντιλάβηται. 41 Ἀπο-
serve?   Speak therefore to her that me   she may help.   ³An-

κριθεὶς δὲ εἶπεν αὐτῇ ᶦὁ Ἰησοῦς,‖ Μάρθα, Μάρθα, μεριμνᾷς
swering ¹but ⁴said ⁵to ⁶her   ²Jesus,   Martha, Martha, thou art careful

καὶ ᵐτυρβάζῃ‖ περὶ πολλά· 42 ἑνὸς δέ ἐστιν χρεία· Μαρία
and   troubled   about many things;   but of one there is need;   ¹Mary

ᴺδὲ‖ τὴν ἀγαθὴν μερίδα ἐξελέξατο, ἥτις οὐκ ἀφαιρεθήσεται
¹and   the   good   part   chose,   which   shall not be taken

ᵒἀπ'‖ αὐτῆς.
from   her.

11 Καὶ ἐγένετο ἐν τῷ εἶναι αὐτὸν ἐν τόπῳ τινὶ προσ-
And it came to pass   as ²was   ¹he   in a ²place ¹certain   pray-

ευχόμενον, ὡς ἐπαύσατο, εἶπέν τις τῶν μαθητῶν αὐτοῦ πρὸς
ing,   when he ceased,   said one   of his disciples   to

αὐτόν, Κύριε, δίδαξον ἡμᾶς προσεύχεσθαι, καθὼς καὶ ᴾΙωάν-
him, Lord,   teach   us   to pray,   as   also   John

νης‖ ἐδίδαξεν τοὺς μαθητὰς αὐτοῦ. 2 Εἶπεν δὲ αὐτοῖς, Ὅταν
taught   his disciples.   And he said to them, When

προσεύχησθε λέγετε, Πάτερ ᵠἡμῶν‖ ὁ ἐν τοῖς οὐρανοῖς,‖
ye pray   say,   ²Father ¹our, who [art] in   the heavens,

ἁγιασθήτω τὸ ὄνομά σου· ʳἐλθέτω‖ ˢἡ βασιλεία σου·‖ ᵗγενηθήτω
sanctified be   thy name;   let come   thy kingdom;   let be done

τὸ θέλημά σου,‖ ᵛὡς ἐν οὐρανῷ, καὶ ἐπὶ τῆς γῆς.‖ 3 τὸν
thy will,   as in   heaven,   [so] also upon the earth.

ἄρτον ἡμῶν τὸν ἐπιούσιον δίδου ἡμῖν τὸ καθ' ἡμέραν· 4 καὶ
Our bread   the   needed   give   us   daily;   and

ἄφες ἡμῖν τὰς ἁμαρτίας ἡμῶν, καὶ γὰρ αὐτοὶ ʷἀφίεμεν‖
forgive us   our sins,   for ²also ²ourselves ¹we forgive

παντὶ ὀφείλοντι ἡμῖν· καὶ μὴ εἰσενέγκῃς ἡμᾶς εἰς πειρασμόν,
every one indebted   to us;   and   lead not   us into temptation,

ˣἀλλὰ ῥῦσαι ἡμᾶς ἀπὸ τοῦ πονηροῦ.‖ 5 Καὶ εἶπεν πρὸς
but   deliver   us   from   evil.   And he said to

αὐτούς, Τίς ἐξ ὑμῶν ἕξει φίλον, καὶ πορεύσεται πρὸς
them,   Who among you   shall have a friend,   and   shall go to

αὐτὸν μεσονυκτίου, καὶ ʸεἴπῃ‖ αὐτῷ, Φίλε, χρῆσόν μοι τρεῖς
him   at midnight,   and   say   to him, Friend,   lend   me three

ἄρτους, 6 ἐπειδὴ φίλος μου. παρεγένετο ἐξ ὁδοῦ πρός με,
loaves,   since   a friend of mine is come   off a journey to me,

καὶ οὐκ ἔχω ὃ παραθήσω αὐτῷ· 7 κἀκεῖνος ἔσωθεν
and I have not what I shall set before him;   and he   from within

ἀποκριθεὶς εἴπῃ, Μή μοι κόπους πάρεχε· ἤδη ἡ θύρα
answering   should say, ³Not ⁴me ⁴trouble   ¹cause;   already the door

κέκλεισται, καὶ τὰ παιδία μου μετ' ἐμοῦ εἰς τὴν κοίτην εἰσίν·
has been shut, and   my children   with me in   bed   are;

οὐ δύναμαι ἀναστὰς δοῦναί σοι. 8 Λέγω ὑμῖν, εἰ καὶ οὐ
I cannot   rise up   to give to thee.   I say to you,   if even ²not

δώσει αὐτῷ ἀναστάς, διὰ τὸ εἶναι ᶻαὐτοῦ φίλον,‖
¹he ²will give to him, having risen up, because of [his]   being   his   friend,

διά γε τὴν ᵃἀναίδειαν‖ αὐτοῦ ἐγερθεὶς δώσει αὐτῷ
yet because of   his importunity   having risen he will give   him

ὅσων χρῄζει. 9 Κἀγὼ ὑμῖν λέγω, Αἰτεῖτε, καὶ δοθήσεται
as many as he needs.   And I to you say,   Ask,   and it shall be given

---

therefore that she help me. 41 And Jesus answered and said unto her, Martha, Martha, thou art careful and troubled about many things: 42 but one thing is needful: and Mary hath chosen that good part, which shall not be taken away from her.

XI. And it came to pass, that, as he was praying in a certain place, when he ceased, one of his disciples said unto him, Lord, teach us to pray, as John also taught his disciples. 2 And he said unto them, When ye pray, say, Our Father which art in heaven. Hallowed be thy name. Thy kingdom come. Thy will be done, as in heaven, so in earth. 3 Give us day by day our daily bread. 4 And forgive us our sins; for we also forgive every one that is indebted to us. And lead us not into temptation; but deliver us from evil. 5 And he said unto them, Which of you shall have a friend, and shall go unto him at midnight, and say unto him, Friend, lend me three loaves; 6 for a friend of mine in his journey is come to me, and I have nothing to set before him? 7 And he from within shall answer and say, Trouble me not: the door is now shut, and my children are with me in bed; I cannot rise and give thee. 8 I say unto you, Though he will not rise and give him, because he is his friend, yet because of his importunity he will rise and give him as many as he needeth. 9 And I say unto you, Ask, and it shall be given you.

ᵏ εἶπὸν τ.   ˡ ὁ κύριος the Lord τ.   ᵐ θορυβάζῃ agitated ʟᴛᴛʀᴀ.   ⁿ γὰρ for τ; [δὲ] ᴀ.
ᵒ — ἀπ' [ʟ]ᴛ[ᴛʀᴀ].   ᴾ Ἰωάνης ᴛʀ.   �q — ἡμῶν ὁ ἐν τοῖς οὐρανοῖς ɢᴛᴛʀᴀ.   ʳ ἐλθάτω ᴛᴛʀ.
ˢ σου ἡ βασιλεία ɢ.   ᵗ — γενηθήτω τὸ θέλημά σου ɢᴛᴛᴀ.   ᵛ — ὡς ἐν οὐρανῷ καὶ ἐπὶ τῆς
γῆς ɢ[ʟ]ᴛᴛʀᴀ.   ʷ ἀφίομεν ʟᴛᴛʀᴀ.   ˣ — ἀλλὰ ῥῦσαι ἡμᾶς ἀπὸ τοῦ πονηροῦ ɢᴛᴛʀᴀ.
ʸ ἐρεῖ ʟ.   ᶻ φίλον αὐτοῦ ᴛᴛʀᴀ.   ᵃ ἀναιδίαν τ.

seek, and ye shall find; knock, and it shall be opened unto you.
10 For every one that asketh receiveth; and he that seeketh findeth; and to him that knocketh it shall be opened. 11 If a son shall ask bread of any of you that is a father, will ho give him a stone? or if he ask a fish, will he for a fish give him a serpent? 12 Or if he shall ask an egg, will he offer him a scorpion? 13 If ye then, being evil, know how to give good gifts unto your children : how much more shall your heavenly Father give the Holy Spirit to them that ask him?

ὑμῖν· ζητεῖτε, καὶ εὑρήσετε· κρούετε, καὶ ᵇἀνοιγήσεται‖ ὑμῖν.
to you ; seek, and ye shall find ; knock, and it shall be opened to you.
10 πᾶς·γὰρ ὁ αἰτῶν λαμβάνει· καὶ ὁ ζητῶν εὑρίσκει· καὶ
For every one that asks receives ; and he that seeks finds ; and
τῷ κρούοντι ᶜἀνοιγήσεται.‖ 11 τίνα·δὲ ᵈ ὑμῶν τὸν
to him that knocks it will be opened. And which of you who [is]
πατέρα αἰτήσει ὁ υἱὸς ἄρτον, μὴ λίθον ἐπιδώσει αὐτῷ;
a father shall ³ask ⁴for ¹the ²son bread, a stone will he give to him?
ᵉεἰ‖ καὶ ἰχθύν, μὴ ἀντὶ ἰχθύος ὄφιν ᶠἐπιδώσει αὐτῷ‖; 12 ἢ
if also a fish, instead of a fish a serpent will he give to him? or
καὶ ᵍἐὰν‖ ʰαἰτήσῃ‖ ὠόν, μὴ ἐπιδώσει αὐτῷ σκορπίον; 13 εἰ
also if he should ask an egg, will he give to him a scorpion? If
οὖν ὑμεῖς πονηροὶ ὑπάρχοντες οἴδατε ¹ἀγαθὰ δόματα‖
therefore ye, ²evil ¹being, know [how] good gifts
διδόναι τοῖς·τέκνοις·ὑμῶν, πόσῳ μᾶλλον ὁ πατὴρᵏ ὁ ἐξ
to give to your children, how much more the Father who[is] of
οὐρανοῦ δώσει πνεῦμα ἅγιον τοῖς αἰτοῦσιν αὐτόν;
heaven will give [the] ²Spirit ¹Holy to those that ask him?

14 Καὶ ἦν ἐκβάλλων δαιμόνιον, ¹καὶ αὐτὸ ἦν‖ κωφόν·
And he was casting out a demon, and it was dumb;
ἐγένετο·δὲ τοῦ·δαιμονίου ᵐἐξελθόντος,‖ ἐλάλησεν ὁ κωφός·
and it came to pass on the demon having gone out, ³spoke ¹the ²dumb.
.αἰ ἐθαύμασαν οἱ ὄχλοι. 15 τινὲς·δὲ ἐξ αὐτῶν ⁿεἶπον,‖ Ἐν
And ³wondered ¹the ²crowds. But some of them said, By

14 And he was casting out a devil, and it was dumb. And it came to pass, when the devil was gone out, the dumb spake ; and the people wondered. 15 But some of them said, He casteth out devils through Beelzebub the chief of the devils. 16 And others, tempting him, sought of him a sign from heaven. 17 But he, knowing their thoughts, said unto them, Every kingdom divided against itself is brought to desolation; and a house divided against a house falleth. 18 If Satan also be divided against himself, how shall his kingdom stand? because ye say that I cast out devils through Beelzebub. 19 And if I by Beelzebub cast out devils, by whom do your sons cast them out? therefore shall they be your judges. 20 But if I with the finger of God cast out devils, no doubt the kingdom of God is come upon you. 21 When a strong man armed keepeth his palace, his goods are in peace : 22 but when a stronger than he shall

Βεελζεβοὺλ ᵒἄρχοντι τῶν δαιμονίων ἐκβάλλει τὰ δαιμόνια.
Beelzebul prince of the demons he casts out the demons.
16 ᵖἝτεροι·δὲ πειράζοντες σημεῖον ᵖπαρ᾽ αὐτοῦ ἐζήτουν ἐξ
And others, tempting, a sign from him were seeking from
οὐρανοῦ.‖ 17 Αὐτὸς·δὲ εἰδὼς �qαὐτῶν τὰ διανοήματα‖ εἶπεν
heaven. But he knowing their thoughts said
αὐτοῖς, Πᾶσα βασιλεία ʳἐφ᾽ ἑαυτὴν διαμερισθεῖσα‖ ἐρη-
to them, Every kingdom ²against ³itself ¹divided is brought to
μοῦται· καὶ οἶκος ἐπὶ οἶκον πίπτει. 18 εἰ·δὲ καὶ ὁ σατανᾶς
desolation; and a house against a house falls. And if also Satan
ἐφ᾽ ἑαυτὸν διεμερίσθη, πῶς σταθήσεται ἡ·βασιλεία·αὐτοῦ;
against himself be divided, how shall stand his kingdom?
ὅτι λέγετε, ἐν Βεελζεβοὺλ ἐκβάλλειν·με τὰ δαιμόνια. 19 εἰ·δὲ
because ye say, by Beelzebul I cast out the demons. And if
ἐγὼ ἐν Βεελζεβοὺλ ἐκβάλλω τὰ δαιμόνια, ˢοἱ‖·υἱοί·ὑμῶν ἐν
I by Beelzebul cast out the demons, your sons by
τίνι ἐκβάλλουσιν; διὰ τοῦτο ᵗκριταὶ ὑμῶν αὐτοὶ ἔσον-
whom do they cast out? on account of this judges of you they shall
ται.‖ 20 εἰ·δὲ ἐν δακτύλῳ θεοῦ ᵛἐκβάλλω τὰ δαιμόνια,
be. But if by [the] finger of God I cast out the demons,
ἄρα ἔφθασεν ἐφ᾽ ὑμᾶς ἡ βασιλεία τοῦ θεοῦ. 21 ὅταν ὁ
then is come upon you the kingdom of God. When the
ἰσχυρὸς καθωπλισμένος φυλάσσῃ τὴν·ἑαυτοῦ·αὐλήν, ἐν
strong [man] being armed may keep his own dwelling, in
εἰρήνῃ ἐστὶ τὰ·ὑπάρχοντα·αὐτοῦ· 22 ἐπὰν·δὲ ʷὁ‖ ἰσχυρό-
peace are his goods; but as soon as the stronger

ᵇ ἀνοιχθήσεται ΤΑ.   ᶜ ἀνοιχθήσεται LTAW.   ᵈ + ἐξ LTTrAW.   ᵉ ἢ or GLTTrAW.
ᶠ αὐτῷ ἐπιδώσει TTrA.   ᵍ — ἐὰν TTr[A].   ʰ αἰτήσει he shall ask ETTrA.   ¹ δόματα
ἀγαθὰ GLTTtAW.   ᵏ + ὑμῶν (read your father) ʟ.   ¹ [καὶ αὐτὸ ἦν] TrA.   ᵐ ἐκβληθέντος having been cast out ʟ.   ⁿ εἶπαν TrA.   ᵒ + τῷ the LTTrAW.   ᵖ ἐξ
οὐρανοῦ ἐζήτουν παρ᾽ αὐτοῦ LTTrAW.   �q τὰ διανοήματα αὐτῶν ʟ.   ʳ διαμερισθεῖσα ἐφ᾽
ἑαυτὴν T.   ˢ — οἱ ʟ.   ᵗ αὐτοὶ ὑμῶν κριταὶ ἔσονται LA ; αὐτοὶ κριταὶ ἔσονται ὑμῶν T ;
αὐτοὶ κριταὶ ὑμῶν ἔσονται Tr.   ᵛ + (ἐγὼ) Tr.   ʷ — ὁ (read a stronger) LTTrA.

τερος αὐτοῦ ἐπελθὼν   νικήσῃ αὐτόν, τὴν πανοπλίαν
than he coming upon [him] shall overcome him,   ²panoply

αὐτοῦ αἴρει ἐφ' ᾗ ἐπεποίθει, καὶ τὰ.σκῦλα.αὐτοῦ δια-
¹his · he takes away in which he had trusted, and   his spoils   he

δίδωσιν. 23 ὁ μὴ.ὢν μετ' ἐμοῦ κατ' ἐμοῦ ἐστιν· καὶ ὁ
divides.   He that is not with me against me is,   and he that

μὴ.συνάγων μετ' ἐμοῦ σκορπίζει. 24 Ὅταν τὸ ἀκάθαρτον
gathers not with me scatters.   When the   unclean

πνεῦμα ἐξέλθῃ ἀπὸ τοῦ ἀνθρώπου, διέρχεται δι' ἀνύδρων
spirit is gone out from the man,   he goes through waterless

τόπων, ζητοῦν ἀνάπαυσιν· καὶ μὴ εὑρίσκον ˣλέγει, Ὑπο-
places, seeking   rest;   and not finding [any] he says, I will

στρέψω εἰς τὸν.οἶκόν.μου ὅθεν ἐξῆλθον· 25 καὶ ἐλθὸν
return to my house whence I came out.   And having come

εὑρίσκει σεσαρωμένον καὶ κεκοσμημένον. 26 τότε πορεύεται
he finds [it] swept   and   adorned.   Then   he goes

καὶ παραλαμβάνει ʸἑπτὰ ἕτερα πνεύματα πονηρότερα ἑαυτοῦ,‖
and   takes   seven other spirits more wicked than himself,

καὶ εἰσελθόντα κατοικεῖ ἐκεῖ· καὶ γίνεται τὰ ἔσχατα τοῦ
and having entered they dwell there; and becomes the   last

ἀνθρώπου ἐκείνου χείρονα τῶν πρώτων. 27 Ἐγένετο.δὲ
³man   of ²that worse than the first.   And it came to pass

ἐν.τῷ.λέγειν αὐτὸν ταῦτα, ἐπάρασά τις ᶻγυνὴ φωνὴν‖
as ²spoke   ¹he these things, ⁴lifting ⁵up ²certain ¹a ²woman [her] voice

ἐκ τοῦ ὄχλου εἶπεν αὐτῷ, Μακαρία ἡ κοιλία ἡ βαστάσασά
from the crowd said to him, Blessed the womb that   bore

σε, καὶ   μαστοὶ οὓς ἐθήλασας. 28 Αὐτὸς.δὲ εἶπεν, ᵃΜεν-
thee, and [the] breasts which thou didst suck. But he said,   Yea

οῦνγε‖ μακάριοι οἱ ἀκούοντες τὸν λόγον τοῦ θεοῦ καὶ
rather   blessed they who hear   the word of God and

φυλάσσοντες ᵇαὐτόν.‖
keep   it.

29 Τῶν.δὲ ὄχλων ἐπαθροιζομένων ἤρξατο λέγειν, Ἡ γενεὰ
    But the crowds being thronged together he began to say, ²generation

αὕτη ᶜπονηρά ἐστιν· σημεῖον ᵈἐπιζητεῖ,‖ καὶ σημεῖον οὐ
¹this ⁴wicked ³is;   a sign   it seeks after, ¹and a sign ²not

δοθήσεται αὐτῇ, εἰ.μὴ τὸ σημεῖον Ἰωνᾶ ᵉτοῦ προφήτου.‖
¹shall be given to it except the sign of Jonas the   prophet.

30 καθὼς.γὰρ ἐγένετο Ἰωνᾶς ᶠσημεῖον τοῖς Νινευΐταις,‖ οὕτως
For as   was Jonas a sign to the Ninevites,   thus

ἔσται καὶ ὁ υἱὸς τοῦ ἀνθρώπου τῇ.γενεᾷ.ταύτῃ. 31 Βασίλισσα
shall be also the Son of man to this generation.   A queen

νότου ἐγερθήσεται ἐν τῇ κρίσει μετὰ τῶν ἀνδρῶν τῆς
of [the] south shall rise up in the judgment with the men

γενεᾶς.ταύτης, καὲ κατακρινεῖ αὐτούς· ὅτι ἦλθεν ἐκ τῶν
of this generation, and shall condemn them; for she came from the

περάτων τῆς γῆς ἀκοῦσαι τὴν σοφίαν ᵍΣολομῶντος,‖ καὶ ἰδού,
ends of the earth to hear the wisdom of Solomon, and behold,

πλεῖον ᵍΣολομῶντος‖ ὧδε. 32 ἄνδρες ʰΝινευῒ ἀναστήσονται
more than Solomon here. Men of Nineveh shall stand up

ἐν τῇ κρίσει μετὰ τῆς.γενεᾶς.ταύτης, καὶ κατακρινοῦσιν αὐτήν·
in the judgment with this generation, and shall condemn it,

---

come upon him, and overcome him, he taketh from him all his armour wherein he trusted, and divideth his spoils. 23 He that is not with me is against me : and he that gathereth not with me scattereth. 24 When the unclean spirit is gone out of a man, he walketh through dry places, seeking rest; and finding none, he saith, I will return unto my house whence I came out. 25 And when he cometh, he findeth *it* swept and garnished. 26 Then goeth he, and taketh *to him* seven other spirits more wicked than himself; and they enter in, and dwell there : and the last *state* of that man is worse than the first. 27 And it came to pass, as· he spake these things, a certain woman of the company lifted up her voice, and said unto him, Blessed *is* the womb that bare thee, and the paps which thou hast sucked. 28 But he said, Yea rather, blessed *are* they that hear the word of God, and keep it.

29 And when the people were gathered thick together, he began to say, This is an evil generation: they seek a sign; and there shall no sign be given it, but the sign of Jonas the prophet. 30 For as Jonas was a sign unto the Ninevites, so shall also the Son of man be to this generation. 31 The queen of the south shall rise up in the judgment with the men of this generation, and condemn them : for she came from the utmost parts of the earth to hear the wisdom of Solomon; and, behold, a greater than Solomon *is* here. 32 The men of Nineve shall rise up in the judgment with this generation, and shall condemn it: for they repented at

---

ˣ + [. τότε] then L.   ʸ ἕτερα πνεύματα πονηρότερα ἑαυτοῦ ἑπτὰ TTrA.   ᶻ φωνὴν γυνὴ LTA.
ᵃ μενοῦν TTr ; μὲν οὖν A.   ᵇ — αὐτόν (read [it]) GLTTrA.   ᶜ + γενεὰ a generation LTTrA.
ᵈ ζητεῖ it seeks TTrA.   ᵉ — τοῦ προφήτου GLTTrA.   ᶠ τοῖς Νινευείταις (Νινευΐταις TrA)
σημεῖον TTrA.   ᵍ Σολομῶνος GLTTrAW.   ʰ Νινευὴ A ; Νινευΐται Ninevites LTrW ;
Νινευείται. T.

the preaching of Jonas; and, behold, a greater than Jonas is here. 33 No man, when he hath lighted a candle, putteth it in a secret place, neither under a bushel, but on a candlestick, that they which come in may see the light. 34 The light of the body is the eye: therefore when thine eye is single, thy whole body also is full of light; but when thine eye is evil, thy body also is full of darkness. 35 Take heed therefore that the light which is in thee be not darkness. 36 If thy whole body therefore be full of light, having no part dark, the whole shall be full of light, as when the bright shining of a candle doth give thee light.

37 And as he spake, a certain Pharisee besought him to dine with him: and he went in, and sat down to meat. 38 And when the Pharisee saw it, he marvelled that he had not first washed before dinner. 39 And the Lord said unto him, Now do ye Pharisees make clean the outside of the cup and the platter; but your inward part is full of ravening and wickedness. 40 Ye fools, did not he that made that which is without make that which is within also? 41 But rather give alms of such things as ye have; and, behold, all things are clean unto you. 42 But woe unto you, Pharisees! for ye tithe mint and rue and all manner of herbs, and pass over judgment and the love of God: these ought ye to have done, and not to leave the other undone. 43 Woe unto you, Pharisees! for ye love the uppermost seats in the synagogues, and greetings in the markets. 44 Woe unto you, scribes and Pharisees, hypocrites!

ὅτι μετενόησαν εἰς τὸ κήρυγμα Ἰωνᾶ. καὶ ἰδού, πλεῖον
because they repented at the proclamation of Jonas: and behold, more

Ἰωνᾶ ὧδε. 33 Οὐδεὶς ᵢδὲ‖ λύχνον ἅψας εἰς ᵏκρυπτὸν‖
than Jonas here. But no one a lamp having lit ³in ⁴secret

τίθησιν, οὐδὲ ὑπὸ τὸν μόδιον, ¹ἀλλ'‖ ἐπὶ τὴν λυχνίαν,
¹sets ²it, nor. under the corn-measure, but upon the lampstand,

ἵνα οἱ εἰσπορευόμενοι τὸ ᵐφέγγος‖ βλέπωσιν. 34 ὁ λύχνος
that they who enter in the light, may see. The lamp

τοῦ σώματός ἐστιν ὁ ὀφθαλμός ⁿ· ὅταν °οὖν‖ ὁ ὀφθαλμός σου
of the body is the eye: when therefore thine eye

ἁπλοῦς ᾖ, ᴾκαὶ‖ ὅλον τὸ σῶμά σου φωτεινόν ἐστιν· ἐπὰν δὲ
²single ¹be, also ²whole ¹thy body light is; but when

πονηρὸς ᾖ, καὶ τὸ σῶμά σου σκοτεινόν. 35 σκόπει οὖν
evil it be, also thy body [is] dark. See therefore

μὴ τὸ φῶς τὸ ἐν σοὶ σκότος ἐστίν. 36 εἰ οὖν τὸ σῶμά
lest the light that [is] in thee ²darkness ¹is. If therefore ³body

σου ὅλον φωτεινόν, μὴ ἔχον ᑫτὶ μέρος‖ σκοτεινόν, ἔσται
¹thy ²whole [is] light, not having any part dark, it shall be

φωτεινὸν ὅλον, ὡς ὅταν ὁ λύχνος τῇ ἀστραπῇ φωτίζῃ σε.
²light ¹all, as when the lamp with [its] brightness may light thee.

37 Ἐν δὲ τῷ λαλῆσαι ʳ ˢἠρώτα‖ αὐτὸν Φαρισαῖός ᵗτις‖
Now as ²was ³speaking [¹he] asked him ¹a ³Pharisee ²certain

ὅπως ἀριστήσῃ παρ' αὐτῷ· εἰσελθὼν δὲ ἀνέπεσεν.
that he would dine with him: and having entered he reclined himself.

38 ὁ δὲ Φαρισαῖος ἰδὼν ἐθαύμασεν ὅτι οὐ πρῶτον ἐβαπτίσθη
But the Pharisee seeing [it] wondered that not first he washed

πρὸ τοῦ ἀρίστου. 39 εἶπεν δὲ ὁ κύριος πρὸς αὐτόν, Νῦν ὑμεῖς
before the dinner. But said the Lord to him, Now ye

οἱ Φαρισαῖοι τὸ ἔξωθεν τοῦ ποτηρίου καὶ τοῦ πίνακος καθαρίζετε,
Pharisees the outside of the cup and of the dish ye cleanse,

τὸ δὲ ἔσωθεν ὑμῶν γέμει ἁρπαγῆς καὶ πονηρίας. 40 ἄφρονες,
but the inside of you is full of plunder and wickedness. Fools,

οὐχ ὁ ποιήσας τὸ ἔξωθεν καὶ τὸ ἔσωθεν ἐποίησεν;
[did] not he who made the outside also the inside make?

41 πλὴν τὰ ἐνόντα δότε ἐλεημοσύνην, καὶ ἰδού,
But [of] the things which are within give alms, and lo,

πάντα καθαρὰ ὑμῖν ἐστιν. 42 ᵛἀλλ'‖ οὐαὶ ὑμῖν τοῖς Φαρισαίοις,
all things clean to you are. But woe to you Pharisees,

ὅτι ἀποδεκατοῦτε τὸ ἡδύοσμον καὶ τὸ πήγανον καὶ πᾶν
for ye pay tithes of the mint and the rue and every

λάχανον, καὶ παρέρχεσθε τὴν κρίσιν καὶ τὴν ἀγάπην τοῦ θεοῦ·
herb, and pass by the judgment and the love of God:

ταῦτα ʷ ἔδει ποιῆσαι, κἀκεῖνα μὴ ˣἀφιέναι.‖
These things it behoved [you] to do, and those not to be leaving aside.

43 οὐαὶ ὑμῖν τοῖς Φαρισαίοις, ὅτι ἀγαπᾶτε τὴν πρωτοκαθεδρίαν
Woe to you Pharisees, for ye love the first seat

ἐν ταῖς συναγωγαῖς καὶ τοὺς ἀσπασμοὺς ἐν ταῖς ἀγοραῖς ʸ.
in the synagogues and the salutations in the market-places.

44 οὐαὶ ὑμῖν, ᶻγραμματεῖς καὶ Φαρισαῖδι, ὑποκριταί,‖ ὅτι ἐστὲ
Woe to you, scribes and Pharisees, hypocrites, for ye are

ⁱ — δὲ but TTrA.   ᵏ κρυπτὴν secret place EGLTTrAW.   ˡ ἀλλὰ EW.   ᵐ φῶς LTrA.
ⁿ + σου (read thine eye) LTTrA.   ° — οὖν LTTrA.   ᴾ — καὶ L.   ᑫ μέρος τι ([τι] A)
LTrA.   ʳ + αὐτὸν he L.   ˢ ἐρωτᾷ asks LTA; ἐρώτα Tr.   ᵗ — τις TTrA.   ᵛ ἀλλὰ T.
ʷ + δὲ now [L]Tr.   ˣ παρεῖναι to pass by LTTrA.   ʸ + [καὶ τὰς πρωτοκλισίας ἐν τοῖς
δείπνοις] and the first places at the suppers L.   ᶻ — γραμματεῖς καὶ Φαρισαῖοι ὑποκριταί G[L]TTrA.

ὡς τὰ μνημεῖα τὰ ἄδηλα, καὶ οἱ ἄνθρωποι ᵃοἱ‖ περιπατοῦντες
as the ²tombs ¹unseen, and the men who walk

ἐπάνω οὐκ.οἴδασιν. 45 Ἀποκριθεὶς.δὲ τις τῶν νομι-
over [them] do not know [it]. And answering one of the doctors of the

κῶν λέγει αὐτῷ, Διδάσκαλε, ταῦτα λέγων καὶ ἡμᾶς ὑβρίζεις.
law says to him, Teacher, these things saying ²also ¹us thou insultest.

46 Ὁ.δὲ εἶπεν, Καὶ ὑμῖν τοῖς νομικοῖς οὐαί, ὅτι φορτίζετε
And he said, Also to you the doctors of the law woe, for ye burden

τοὺς ἀνθρώπους φορτία δυσβάστακτα, καὶ αὐτοὶ ἑνὶ
men [with] burdens heavy to bear, and yourselves with one

τῶν.δακτύλων.ὑμῶν οὐ.προσψαύετε τοῖς φορτίοις.᾽ 47 οὐαὶ
of your fingers do not touch the burdens. Woe

ὑμῖν, ὅτι οἰκοδομεῖτε τὰ μνημεῖα τῶν προφητῶν, ᵇοἱ δὲ‖ πα-
to you, for ye build the tombs of the prophets, and ²fa-

τέρες ὑμῶν ἀπέκτειναν· αὐτούς. 48 ἄρα ᶜμαρτυρεῖτε‖ καὶ
thers ¹your killed them. Hence ye bear witness and

συνευδοκεῖτε τοῖς ἔργοις τῶν.πατέρων.ὑμῶν· ὅτι αὐτοὶ μὲν
consent to the works of your fathers; for they indeed

ἀπέκτειναν αὐτούς, ὑμεῖς.δὲ οἰκοδομεῖτε ᵈαὐτῶν τὰ μνημεῖα.‖
killed them, and ye build their tombs.

49 διὰ τοῦτο καὶ ἡ σοφία τοῦ θεοῦ εἶπεν, Ἀποστελῶ εἰς
Because of this also the wisdom of God said, I will send to

αὐτοὺς προφήτας καὶ ἀποστόλους, καὶ ἐξ αὐτῶν ἀποκτε-
them prophets and apostles, and [some] of them they will

νοῦσιν καὶ ᵉἐκδιώξουσιν·‖ 50 ἵνα ἐκζητηθῇ τὸ αἷμα πάντων
kill and drive out, that may be required the blood of all

τῶν προφητῶν ᶠτὸ ἐκχυνόμενον‖ ἀπὸ καταβολῆς κόσμου
the · prophets poured·out from [the] foundation of [the] world,

ἀπὸ τῆς.γενεᾶς.ταύτης, 51 ἀπὸ ᵍτοῦ‖ αἵματος Ἀβελ ἕως ᵍτοῦ‖
of this generation, from the blood of Abel to the

αἵματος Ζαχαρίου τοῦ ἀπολομένου μεταξὺ τοῦ θυσιαστηρίου
blood of Zacharias, who perished between the altar

καὶ τοῦ οἴκου· ναί, λέγω ὑμῖν, ἐκζητηθήσεται ἀπὸ τῆς γενεᾶς
and the house; yea, I say to you, it shall be required of ²generation

ταύτης. 52 Οὐαὶ ὑμῖν τοῖς νομικοῖς, ὅτι ἤρατε τὴν
¹this. Woe to you the doctors of the law, for ye took away the

κλεῖδα τῆς γνώσεως· αὐτοὶ οὐκ.ʰεἰσήλθετε,‖ καὶ τοὺς εἰσερ-
key of knowledge; yourselves did not enter, and those who were

χομένους ἐκωλύσατε. 53 ⁱΛέγοντος.δὲ αὐτοῦ ταῦτα πρὸς
entering ye hindered. And as ²was ³saying ¹he these things to

αὐτούς‖ ἤρξαντο οἱ γραμματεῖς καὶ οἱ Φαρισαῖοι δεινῶς ἐν-
them began the scribes and the Pharisees urgently to press

έχειν, καὶ ἀποστοματίζειν αὐτὸν περὶ πλειόνων, 54 ἐνε-
upon [him], and to make ²speak ¹him about many things; watch-

δρεύοντες ᵏαὐτὸν‖ ⁱκαὶ‖ ᵐζητοῦντες‖ θηρεῦσαί τι ἐκ τοῦ
ing him and seeking to catch something out of

στόματος.αὐτοῦ ⁿἵνα κατηγορήσωσιν αὐτοῦ.‖
his mouth that they might accuse him.

12 Ἐν οἷς ἐπισυναχθεισῶν τῶν μυριάδων τοῦ
During which [things] being gathered together the myriads of the

ὄχλου, ὥστε καταπατεῖν ἀλλήλους, ἤρξατο λέγειν πρὸς τοὺς
crowd, so as to trample upon one another, he began to say to

---

for ye are as graves which appear not, and the men that walk over them are not aware of them. 45 Then answered one of the lawyers, and said unto him, Master, thus saying thou reproachest us also. 46 And he said, Woe unto you also, ye lawyers! for ye lade men with burdens grievous to be borne, and ye yourselves touch not the burdens with one of your fingers. 47 Woe unto you! for ye build the sepulchres of the prophets, and your fathers killed them. 48 Truly ye bear witness that ye allow the deeds of your fathers: for they indeed killed them, and ye build their sepulchres. 49 Therefore also said the wisdom of God, I will send them prophets and apostles, and some of them they shall slay and persecute: 50 That the blood of all the prophets, which was shed from the foundation of the world, may be required of this generation; 51 from the blood of Abel unto the blood of Zacharias, which perished between the altar and the temple: verily I say unto you, It shall be required of this generation. 52 Woe unto you, lawyers! for ye have taken away the key of knowledge : ye entered not in yourselves, and them that were entering in ye hindered. 53 And as he said these things unto them, the scribes and the Pharisees began to urge him vehemently, and to provoke him to speak of many things: 54 laying wait for him, and seeking to catch something out of his mouth, that they might accuse him.

XII. In the mean time, when there were gathered together an innumerable multitude of people, insomuch that they trode one upon another, he began to say unto his

---

ᵃ — οἱ (read περιπ. walking) L[A]W. ᵇ καὶ οἱ T. ᶜ μάρτυρές ἐστε witnesses ye are TTrA. ᵈ — αὐτῶν τὰ μνημεῖα [L]TTrA. ᵉ [ἐκ]διώξουσιν TrA. ᶠ τὸ ἐκχυννόμενον LTA; τὸ ἐκκεχυμένον which has been poured out Tr. ᵍ — τοῦ (read [the]) LTTrA. ʰ εἰσήλθατε GLTTrA. ⁱ Κἀκεῖθεν ἐξελθόντος αὐτοῦ and as he went out thence TTrA. ᵏ — αὐτόν T. ˡ — καὶ GLTTrAW. ᵐ — ζητοῦντες T[Tr]A. ⁿ — ἵνα κατηγορήσωσιν αὐτοῦ T[Tr]A.

disciples first of all, Beware ye of the leaven of the Pharisees, which is hypocrisy. 2 For there is nothing covered, that shall not be revealed ; neither hid, that shall not be known. 3 Therefore whatsoever ye have spoken in darkness shall be heard in the light ; and that which ye have spoken in the ear in closets shall be proclaimed upon the housetops. 4 And I say unto you my friends, Be not afraid of them that kill the body, and after that have no more that they can do. 5 But I will forewarn you whom ye shall fear : Fear him, which after he hath killed hath power to cast into hell ; yea, I say unto you, Fear him. 6 Are not five sparrows sold for two farthings, and not one of them is forgotten before God? 7 But even the very hairs of your head are all numbered. Fear not therefore : ye are of more value than many sparrows. 8 Also I say unto you, Whosoever shall confess me before men, him shall the Son of man also confess before the angels of God: 9 but he that denieth me before men shall be denied before. the angels of God. 10 And whosoever shall speak a word against the Son of man, it shall be forgiven him : but unto him that blasphemeth against the Holy Ghost it shall not be' forgiven. 11 And when they bring you unto the synagogues, and *unto* magistrates, and powers, take ye no thought how or what thing ye shall answer, or what ye shall say : 12 for the Holy Ghost shall teach you in the same hour what ye ought to say.

μαθητὰς.αὐτοῦ πρῶτον, Προσέχετε ἑαυτοῖς ἀπὸ τῆς ζύμης
his disciples   first,   Take heed   to yourselves of   the leaven

τῶν Φαρισαίων, ἥτις ἐστὶν ὑπόκρισις. 2 οὐδὲν.δὲ συγκεκαλυμ-
of the Pharisees, which is   hypocrisy ;   but nothing   [2]covered

μένον ἐστὶν ὃ οὐκ.ἀποκαλυφθήσεται, καὶ κρυπτὸν ὃ οὐ
[1]up   [1]is   which shall not be uncovered,   nor   hidden 'which [2]not

γνωσθήσεται. 3 ἀνθ'.ὧν ὅσα ἐν τῇ σκοτίᾳ εἴπατε, ἐν τῷ
[1]shall be known ;   wherefore whatever in the darkness ye said,   in the

φωτὶ ἀκουσθήσεται· καὶ ὃ πρὸς τὸ οὖς ἐλαλήσατε ἐν τοῖς
light   shall be heard ;   and the in   the ear   ye spoke   in

ταμείοις, κηρυχθήσεται ἐπὶ τῶν δωμάτων. 4 Λέγω.δὲ ὑμῖν
chambers, shall be proclaimed upon the   housetops.   But I say to you,

τοῖς.φίλοις.μου, Μὴ.φοβηθῆτε ἀπὸ τῶν Pἀποκτεινόντων||
my friends,   Ye should not fear because of those who   kill

τὸ σῶμα, καὶ μετὰ ταῦτα μὴ.ἐχόντων qπερισσότερόν||.τι
the body,   and after these things are not able   anything more

ποιῆσαι. 5 ὑποδείξω.δὲ ὑμῖν τίνα φοβηθῆτε· φοβήθητε
to do.   But I will shew you 'whom ye should fear :   Fear

τὸν μετὰ τὸ ἀποκτεῖναι rἐξουσίαν ἔχοντα|| ἐμβαλεῖν εἰς τὴν
him who after having killed, authority   has   to cast into the

γέενναν· ναί, λέγω ὑμῖν, τοῦτον φοβήθητε. 6 Οὐχὶ πέντε
gehenna ; yea, I say to you, [2]him   [1]fear.   [2]Not [3]five

στρουθία sπωλεῖται|| ἀσσαρίων δύο; καὶ ἓν ἐξ αὐτῶν οὐκ
[4]sparrows   [1]are sold   for [2]assaria [1]two?   and one of them   [2]not

ἔστιν ἐπιλελησμένον ἐνώπιον τοῦ θεοῦ· 7 ἀλλὰ.καὶ αἱ τρίχες
[1]is   forgotten   before   God.   But even the hairs

τῆς.κεφαλῆς.ὑμῶν πᾶσαι ἠρίθμηνται. μὴ tοὖν|| φοβεῖσθε·
of your head   [2]all [1]have been numbered. [2]Not [3]therefore [1]fear,

πολλῶν στρουθίων διαφέρετε. 8 Λέγω.δὲ ὑμῖν, Πᾶς ὃς.ἂν
than many sparrows   ye are better. But I say to you, Every one whoever

ὁμολογήσῃ ἐν ἐμοὶ ἔμπροσθεν τῶν ἀνθρώπων, καὶ ὁ υἱὸς τοῦ
may confess me   before   men,   also the Son

ἀνθρώπου ὁμολογήσει ἐν αὐτῷ ἔμπροσθεν τῶν ἀγγέλων τοῦ
of man   will confess him   before   the   angels

θεοῦ· 9 ὁ.δὲ ἀρνησάμενός με vἐνώπιον|| τῶν ἀνθρώπων
of God ; but he that has denied   me before   men

ἀπαρνηθήσεται ἐνώπιον τῶν ἀγγέλων τοῦ θεοῦ. 10 καὶ πᾶς
will be denied   before   the   angels   of God ;   and every one

ὃς ἐρεῖ λόγον εἰς τὸν υἱὸν τοῦ ἀνθρώπου, ἀφεθήσεται
who shall say a word against the Son of man,   it will be forgiven

αὐτῷ· τῷ.δὲ εἰς τὸ ἅγιον πνεῦμα βλασφημήσαντι
him ;   but to him who against the Holy Spirit   has blasphemed

οὐκ.ἀφεθήσεται. 11 ὅταν.δὲ wπροσφέρωσιν|| ὑμᾶς ἐπὶ τὰς
it will not be forgiven.   But when   they bring   you before the

συναγωγὰς καὶ τὰς ἀρχὰς καὶ τὰς ἐξουσίας, xμὴ.μεριμνᾶτε||
synagogues and the rulers and the authorities,   be not careful

πῶς yἢ τί|| ἀπολογήσησθε, ἢ τί εἴπητε· 12 τὸ.γὰρ
how or what ye shall reply in defence, or what ye should say ;   for the

ἅγιον πνεῦμα διδάξει ὑμᾶς ἐν αὐτῇ.τῇ ὥρᾳ ἃ δεῖ
Holy Spirit   will teach you in that same hour what it behoves [you]

εἰπεῖν.
to say.

13 And one of the company said unto him, Master, speak to

13 Εἶπεν.δὲ τις zαὐτῷ ἐκ τοῦ ὄχλου,|| Διδάσκαλε, εἰπὲ τῷ
And [2]said [1]one to him from the crowd,   Teacher,   speak

P ἀποκτενόντων G ; ἀποκτεννόντων LTTrA.   q περισσόν L.   r ἔχοντα ἐξουσίαν LTTrA.
s πωλοῦνται TTrA.   t — οὖν [L]TTrA.   v ἔμπροσθεν L.   w εἰσφέρωσιν TTrA.   x μὴ
ϕερμνήσητε ye should not be careful TTr.   y [ἢ τί] TrA.   z ἐκ τοῦ ὄχλου αὐτῷ T.

ἀδελφῷ.μου μερίσασθαι μετ᾽ ἐμοῦ τὴν κληρονομίαν. 14 Ὁ.δὲ
to my brother   to divide   with   me   the   inheritance.   But he

εἶπεν αὐτῷ, Ἄνθρωπε, τίς με κατέστησεν ᵃδικαστὴν‖ ἢ μερισ-
said to him,   Man,   who ²me ¹appointed   a judge   or   a di-

τὴν ἐφ᾽ ὑμᾶς; 15 Εἶπεν.δὲ πρὸς αὐτούς, Ὁρᾶτε καὶ φυλάσ-
vider over   you?   And he said   to   them,   See   and keep your-

σεσθε ἀπὸ ᵇτῆς‖ πλεονεξίας· ὅτι οὐκ ἐν τῷ περισσεύειν
selves from   covetousness;   for   not   in   the   abundance

τινὶ ἡ.ζωὴ.αὐτοῦ ἐστιν ἐκ τῶν ὑπαρχόντων.ᶜαὐτοῦ.‖
¹to ²anyone   ⁹his ¹⁰life   ⁶is ¹of ²that ³which   ⁴he ⁵possesses.

16 Εἶπεν.δὲ παραβολὴν πρὸς αὐτούς, λέγων, Ἀνθρώπου
And he spoke   a parable   to   them,   saying,   ³Of ⁴a ⁷man

τινὸς πλουσίου ᵈεὐφόρησεν‖ ἡ χώρα· 17 καὶ
⁵certain   ⁶rich   ⁸brought ⁹forth ¹⁰abundantly ¹the ²ground.   And

διελογίζετο ἐν. ἑαυτῷ, λέγων, Τί ποιήσω, ὅτι οὐκ.ἔχω
he was reasoning within himself,   saying,   What shall I do,   for   I have not

ποῦ συνάξω τοὺς.καρπούς.μου; 18 καὶ εἶπεν, Τοῦτο ποιήσω·
where I shall lay up   my fruit?   and he said,   This will I do:

καθελῶ μου τὰς ἀποθήκας, καὶ μείζονας οἰκοδομήσω, καὶ
I will take away my   granaries,   and   greater   will build,   and

συνάξω ἐκεῖ πάντα ᵉτὰ.γενήματά‖.ᶠμου‖ καὶ τὰ.ἀγαθά.μου,
will lay up there   all   my produce   and   my good things,

19 καὶ ἐρῶ τῇ.ψυχῇ.μου, Ψυχή, ἔχεις πολλὰ ἀγαθὰ
and I will say   to my soul,   Soul,   thou hast   many good things

κείμενα εἰς ἔτη πολλά· ἀναπαύου, φάγε, πίε, εὐφραίνου.
laid by   for ²years ¹many;   take thy rest,   eat,   drink,   be merry.

20 εἶπεν.δὲ αὐτῷ ὁ θεός, ᵍἌφρων,‖ ταύτῃ τῇ νυκτὶ τὴν ψυχὴν
But ²said ³to ⁴him   ¹God,   Fool,   this   night   ²soul

σου ʰἀπαιτοῦσιν‖ ἀπὸ σοῦ· ἃ.δὲ ἡτοίμασας τίνι
¹thy   they require   of   thee;   and ⁵what ⁶thou ⁷didst ⁴prepare ¹to ²whom

ἔσται; 21 οὕτως ὁ θησαυρίζων ⁱἑαυτῷ,‖ καὶ μὴ εἰς
³shall ⁴be?   Thus [is] he who treasures up for himself,   and not   toward

θεὸν πλουτῶν. 22 Εἶπεν.δὲ πρὸς τοὺς.μαθητὰς.ᵏαὐτοῦ,‖ Διὰ
God is rich.   And he said   to   his disciples,   Because of

τοῦτο ˡὑμῖν λέγω,‖ μὴ.μεριμνᾶτε τῇ.ψυχῇ.ᵐὑμῶν‖ τί φάγητε,
this   to you I say,   Be not careful   as to your life   what ye should eat,

μηδὲ τῷ σώματιⁿ τί ἐνδύσησθε. 23 ἡ° ψυχὴ πλεῖόν ἐστιν
nor as to the body   what ye should put on.   The life   more   is

τῆς τροφῆς, καὶ τὸ σῶμα τοῦ ἐνδύματος. 24 Κατανοήσατε
than the food,   and the body than the   raiment.   Consider

τοὺς κόρακας, ὅτι ᴾοὐ‖ σπείρουσιν ᑫοὐδὲ‖ θερίζουσιν, οἷς
the   ravens,   for ³not ¹they ²sow   nor   reap,   to which

οὐκ.ἔστιν ταμεῖον οὐδὲ ἀποθήκη, καὶ ὁ θεὸς τρέφει αὐτούς·
there is not storehouse nor   granary,   and   God   feeds   them.

πόσῳ μᾶλλον ὑμεῖς διαφέρετε τῶν πετεινῶν; 25 τίς.δὲ ἐξ
How much more   ²ye ¹are better than the   birds?   And who of

ὑμῶν ʳμεριμνῶν‖ δύναται ˢπροσθεῖναι ἐπὶ τὴν.ἡλικίαν.αὐτοῦ‖
you [by] being careful   is able   to add   to   his stature

πῆχυν ἕνα‖; 26 εἰ οὖν ᵛοὔτε‖ ἐλάχιστον δύνασθε,
²cubit   ¹one?   If therefore not even [the]   least   ye are able [to do],

τί περὶ τῶν λοιπῶν μεριμνᾶτε; 27 Κατανοήσατε τὰ κρίνα,
why about the   rest   are ye careful?   Consider   the lilies,

---

my brother, that he divide the inheritance with me. 14 And he said unto him, Man, who made me a judge or a divider over you? 15 And he said unto them, Take heed, and beware of covetousness: for a man's life consisteth not in the abundance of the things which he possesseth. 16 And he spake a parable unto them, saying, The ground of a certain rich man brought forth plentifully: 17 and he thought within himself, saying, What shall I do, because I have no room where to bestow my fruits? 18 And he said, This will I do: I will pull down my barns, and build greater; and there will I bestow all my fruits and my goods. 19 And I will say to my soul, Soul, thou hast much goods laid up for many years; take thine ease, eat, drink, and be merry. 20 But God said unto him, Thou fool, this night thy soul shall be required of thee: then whose shall those things be, which thou hast provided? 21 So is he that layeth up treasure for himself, and is not rich toward God. 22 And he said unto his disciples, Therefore I say unto you, Take no thought for your life, what ye shall eat; neither for the body, what ye shall put on. 23 The life is more than meat, and the body is more than raiment. 24 Consider the ravens: for they neither sow nor reap; which neither have storehouse nor barn; and God feedeth them: how much more are ye better than the fowls? 25 And which of you with taking thought can add to his stature one cubit? 26 If ye then be not able to do that thing which is least, why take ye thought for the rest? 27 Consider the lilies how they grow:

ᵃ κριτὴν LTTrA.   ᵇ πάσης all LTTrAW.   ᶜ αὐτῷ LTTrA.   ᵈ ηὐφόρησεν L.   ᵉ τὰ γεννήματα E ;
τὸν σῖτον the wheat Tr.   ᶠ — μου Tr[A].   ᵍ ἄφρον GW.   ʰ αἰτοῦσιν TrA.   ⁱ αὑτῷ T. .   ᵏ [αὐ-
τοῦ] L.   ˡ λέγω ὑμῖν TrA.   ᵐ — ὑμῶν (read as to the life) LTTrA.   ⁿ + [ὑμῶν] (read your
body) L.   ° + [γὰρ] (read for the) LTrA.   ᴾ οὔτε neither TA.   ᑫ οὔτε TA.   ʳ [μεριμνῶν] A.
ˢ ἐπὶ τὴν ἡλικίαν αὐτοῦ προσθεῖναι A.   ᵗ — ἕνα (read a cubit) T[Tr]A.   ᵛ οὐδὲ LTTrA.

they toil not, they spin not; and yet I say unto you, that Solomon in all his glory was not arrayed like one of these. 28 If then God so clothe the grass, which is to day in the field, and to morrow is cast into the oven; how much more *will he clothe* you, O ye of little faith? 29 And seek not ye what ye shall eat, or what ye shall drink, neither be ye of doubtful mind. 30 For all these things do the nations of the world seek after: and your Father knoweth that ye have need of these things. 31 But rather seek ye the kingdom of God ; and all these things shall be added unto you. 32 Fear not, little flock; for it is your Father's good pleasure to give you the kingdom. 33 Sell that ye have, and give alms; provide yourselves bags which wax not old, a treasure in the heavens that faileth not, where no thief approacheth, neither moth corrupteth. 34 For where your treasure is, there will your heart be also. 35 Let your loins be girded about, and *your* lights burning; 36 and ye yourselves like unto men that wait for their lord, when he will return from the wedding; that when he cometh and knocketh, they may open unto him immediately. 37 Blessed *are* those servants, whom the lord when he cometh shall find watching: verily I say unto you, that he shall gird himself, and make them to sit down to meat, and will come forth and serve them. 38 And if he shall come in the second watch, or come in the third watch, and find *them* so, blessed are those servants. 39 And this know, that if the goodman of the house had known what hour the thief would

πῶς ᵂαὐξάνει· οὐ.κοπιᾷ, οὐδὲ .νήθει·‖ λέγω.δὲ ὑμῖν,ˣ
how   they grow ;   they labour not,   nor   do they spin ; but I say   to you,

οὐδὲ Σολομὼν ἐν πάσῃ τῇ.δόξῃ.αὐτοῦ περιεβάλετο ὡς ἓν
Not even   Solomon   in   all   his glory   was clothed   as one

τούτων. 28 εἰ.δὲ ʸτὸν χόρτον ἐν τῷ ἀγρῷ σήμερον ὄντα,‖ καὶ
of these.   But if   the   grass ²in ⁴the ⁵field   ⁶to-day ¹which ³is, and

αὔριον εἰς κλίβανον βαλλόμενον, ὁ θεὸς οὕτως ᶻἀμφιέννυσιν,‖
to-morrow into an oven   is cast,   God   thus   arrays,

πόσῳ μᾶλλον ὑμᾶς, ὀλιγόπιστοι; 29 καὶ ὑμεῖς μὴ.ζητεῖτε
how much   rather   you, O [ye] of little faith?   And   ye   seek ye not

τί φάγητε ᵃἢ‖ τί πίητε, καὶ.μὴ.μετεωρίζεσθε. 30 ταῦτα
what ye may eat or what ye may drink, and   be not in anxiety ;   ²these ³things

γὰρ πάντα τὰ ἔθνη τοῦ κόσμου ᵇἐπιζητεῖ·‖ ὑμῶν.δὲ ὁ πατὴρ
¹for   all   the nations of the world   seek after;   and your   Father

οἶδεν ὅτι χρῄζετε τούτων. 31 πλὴν ζητεῖτε τὴν βασιλείαν
knows that ye have need of these things. But seek ye the kingdom

ᶜτοῦ θεοῦ,‖ καὶ ταῦτα ᵈπάντα‖ προστεθήσεται ὑμῖν. 32 μὴ
of God, and ²these ³things ¹all   shall be added   to you. ²Not

φοβοῦ, τὸ μικρὸν ποίμνιον· ὅτι εὐδόκησεν ὁ.πατὴρ.ὑμῶν
¹fear,   little   flock,   for ³took ⁴delight ¹your ²Father

δοῦναι ὑμῖν τὴν βασιλείαν. 33 πωλήσατε τὰ.ὑπάρχοντα.ὑμῶν,
in giving you   the   kingdom.   Sell   your possessions,

καὶ δότε ἐλεημοσύνην· ποιήσατε ἑαυτοῖς ᵉβαλάντια‖ μὴ
and give   alms;   make   to yourselves   purses   not

παλαιούμενα, θησαυρὸν ἀνέκλειπτον ἐν τοῖς οὐρανοῖς, ὅπου
growing old,   a treasure   unfailing   in   the   heavens,   where

κλέπτης οὐκ.ἐγγίζει, οὐδὲ σὴς διαφθείρει· 34 ὅπου.γάρ ἐστιν
thief   does not draw near, nor moth   destroy.   For where   is

ὁ.θησαυρὸς.ὑμῶν, ἐκεῖ καὶ ἡ.καρδία.ὑμῶν ἔσται. 35 Ἔστωσαν
your treasure,   there also   your heart   will be.   Let be

ᶠὑμῶν αἱ ὀσφύες‖ περιεζωσμέναι καὶ οἱ λύχνοι καιόμενοι· 36 καὶ
your   loins   girded about   and   lamps   burning ;   and

ὑμεῖς ὅμοιοι ἀνθρώποις προσδεχομένοις τὸν.κύριον.ἑαυτῶν,
ye   like   to men   waiting for   their lord,

πότε ᵍἀναλύσει‖ · ἐκ τῶν γάμων, ἵνα ἐλθόντος καὶ κρού-
whenever he shall return from the wedding feasts, that having come and having

σαντος, εὐθέως ἀνοίξωσιν αὐτῷ. 37 μακάριοι οἱ δοῦλοι
knocked, immediately they may open to him.   Blessed   ²bondmen

ἐκεῖνοι οὓς ἐλθὼν ὁ κύριος εὑρήσει γρηγοροῦντας. ἀμὴν
¹those whom coming the Lord   shall find   watching.   Verily

λέγω ὑμῖν, ὅτι περιζώσεται καὶ ἀνακλινεῖ αὐτούς, καὶ
I say to you, that he will gird himself and will make ²recline ¹them, and

παρελθὼν διακονήσει αὐτοῖς. 38 ʰκαὶ ἐὰν ἔλθῃ ἐν τῇ δευτέρᾳ
coming up   will serve   them.   And if he come in the second

φυλακῇ, καὶ‖ ἐν τῇ τρίτῃ φυλακῇ ἔλθῃ, καὶ εὕρῃ οὕτως,
watch,   and in the third   watch   he come, and find [them] thus,

μακάριοί εἰσιν ⁱοἱ δοῦλοι ἐκεῖνοι.‖ 39 τοῦτο.δὲ γινώσκετε, ὅτι
blessed   are   ²bondmen ¹those.   But this   know,   that

εἰ ᾔδει ὁ οἰκοδεσπότης ποίᾳ ὥρᾳ ὁ κλέπτης ἔρχεται,
if ⁶had ⁷known ¹the ²master ³of ⁴the ⁵house in what hour the   thief   is coming,

---

ᵂ οὔτε νήθει οὔτε ὑφαίνει they neither spin nor weave ΤΑ.   ˣ + [ὅτι] that L.   ʸ ἐν ἀγρῷ τὸν χόρτον ὄντα σήμερον ΤΑ ; τὸν χόρτον σήμερον ἐν ἀγρῷ ὄντα LTr.   ᶻ ἀμφιάζει L; ἀμφιέζει TTrA.   ᵃ καὶ and TTr.   ᵇ ἐπιζητοῦσιν TTrA.   ᶜ αὐτοῦ (*read* his kingdom) LTTrA.   ᵈ — πάντα [L]TTrA.   ᵉ βαλλάντια LTTrAW.   ᶠ αἱ ὀσφύες ὑμῶν L.   ᵍ ἀναλύσῃ he may return LTTrA.   ʰ κἂν ἐν τῇ δευτέρᾳ, κἂν and if in the second and if TTrA.   ⁱ οἱ δοῦλοι] ἐκεῖνοι TrA ; — οἱ δοῦλοι ἐκεῖνοι (*read* are they) T.

ᵏἐγρηγόρησεν ἄν, καὶ‖ οὐκ.ˡἄν‖.ἀφῆκεν ᵐδιορυγῆναι·
he would have watched,   and would not have suffered to be dug through

τὸν.οἶκον.αὐτοῦ. 40 καὶ ὑμεῖς ⁿοὖν‖ γίνεσθε ἕτοιμοι· ὅτι
his house.   And ye therefore be ye ready ; for

ᾗ ὥρᾳ οὐ.δοκεῖτε, ὁ υἱὸς τοῦ ἀνθρώπου ἔρχεται. 41 Εἶπεν.δὲ
in the hour ye think not, the Son   of man   comes.   And ²said

°αὐτῷ‖ ὁ Πέτρος, Κύριε, πρὸς ἡμᾶς τὴν.παραβολὴν.ταύτην
²to ⁴him ¹Peter, Lord, to   us   this parable

λέγεις, ἢ καὶ πρὸς πάντας; 42 ᴾΕἶπεν.δὲ‖ ὁ κύριος, Τίς
speakest thou, or also to all?   And said the Lord, Who

ἄρα ἐστὶν ὁ πιστὸς οἰκονόμος ��٩καὶ‖ φρόνιμος, ὃν καταστήσει
then is the faithful steward and prudent, whom ³will ⁴set

ὁ κύριος ἐπὶ τῆς.θεραπείας.αὐτοῦ, ʳτοῦ‖ διδόναι ἐν καιρῷ ˢτὸ‖
¹the ²Lord over his household,   to give in season the

σιτομέτριον; 43 μακάριος ὁ.δοῦλος.ἐκεῖνος ὃν ἐλθὼν
measure of corn?   Blessed   that bondman   whom ⁴having ⁵come

ὁ.κύριος.αὐτοῦ εὑρήσει ποιοῦντα οὕτως. 44 ἀληθῶς λέγω ὑμῖν,
¹his ²Lord will find doing thus.   Of a truth I say to you,

ὅτι ἐπὶ πᾶσιν τοῖς.ὑπάρχουσιν.αὐτοῦ καταστήσει αὐτόν.
that over all   his possessions   he will set   him.

45 Ἐὰν.δὲ εἴπῃ ὁ.δοῦλος.ἐκεῖνος ἐν τῇ.καρδίᾳ.αὐτοῦ, Χρο-
But if ³should ⁴say ¹that ²bondman in   his heart,   ³De-

νίζει ὁ.κύριός.μου ἔρχεσθαι· καὶ ἄρξηται τύπτειν τοὺς
lays ¹my ²Lord   to come,   and should begin to beat the

παῖδας καὶ τὰς παιδίσκας, ἐσθίειν.τε καὶ πίνειν καὶ με-
men-servants and the maid-servants, and to eat and to drink and to be

θύσκεσθαι· 46 ἥξει ὁ κύριος τοῦ.δούλου.ἐκείνου ἐν ἡμέρᾳ
drunken,   ⁶will ⁷come ¹the ²Lord ⁴of ⁵that ³bondman in a day

ᾗ οὐ.προσδοκᾷ, καὶ ἐν ὥρᾳ ᾗ οὐ.γινώσκει, καὶ
in which he does not expect, and in an hour which he knows not, and

διχοτομήσει αὐτόν, καὶ τὸ.μέρος.αὐτοῦ μετὰ τῶν ἀπίστων
will cut ²in ³two ¹him, and his portion   with the unbelievers

θήσει. 47 ἐκεῖνος.δὲ ὁ δοῦλος ὁ γνοὺς τὸ θέλημα τοῦ
will appoint. But that bondman who knew the   will

κυρίου.ˢἑαυτοῦ,‖ καὶ μὴ.ἑτοιμάσας ᵛμηδὲ‖ ποιήσας πρὸς
of his Lord, and prepared not nor   did according to

τὸ.θέλημα.αὐτοῦ, δαρήσεται πολλάς· 48 ὁ.δὲ μὴ
his will, shall be beaten with many [stripes]; but he who ²not

γνούς, ποιήσας.δὲ ἄξια πληγῶν, δαρήσεται ὀλίγας.
¹knew, and did [things] worthy of stripes, shall be beaten with few.

παντὶ.δὲ ᾧ ἐδόθη πολύ, πολὺ ζητηθήσεται παρ' αὐτοῦ·
And everyone to whom was given much, much will be required from him ;

καὶ ᾧ παρέθεντο πολύ, περισσότερον αἰτήσουσιν αὐτόν.
and to whom was committed much, the more they will ask of him.

49 Πῦρ ἦλθον βαλεῖν ʷεἰς‖ τὴν γῆν, καὶ τί θέλω εἰ ἤδη
Fire I came to cast into the earth, and what will I if already

ἀνήφθη; 50 βάπτισμα.δὲ ἔχω βαπτισθῆναι, καὶ πῶς συν-
it be kindled? But a baptism I have to be baptized [with], and how am I

ἔχομαι ἕως.ˣοὗ‖ τελεσθῇ. 51 δοκεῖτε ὅτι εἰρήνην παρε-
straitened until it be accomplished ! Think ye that peace   I

γενόμην δοῦναι ἐν τῇ γῇ; οὐχί, λέγω ὑμῖν, ἀλλ' ἢ
came to give in the earth? No, I say to you, but rather

come, he would have
watched, and not have
suffered his house to be
broken through. 40 Be
ye therefore ready al-
so : for the Son of man
cometh at an hour
when ye think not.
41 Then Peter said un-
to him, Lord, speakest
thou this parable unto
us, or even to all ?
42 And the Lord said,
Who then is that faith-
ful and wise steward,
whom his lord shall
make ruler over his
household, to give them
their portion of meat
in due season? 43 Bless-
ed is that servant,
whom his lord when he
cometh shall find so
doing. 44 Of a truth I
say unto you, that he
will make him ruler
over all that he hath.
45 But and if that ser-
vant say in his heart,
My lord delayeth his
coming; and shall be-
gin to beat the menser-
vants and maidens, and
to eat and drink, and
to be drunken ; 46 the
lord of that servant
will come in a day
when he looketh not
for him, and at an hour
when he is not aware,
and will cut him in sun-
der, and will appoint
him his portion with
the unbelievers. 47 And
that servant, which
knew his lord's will,
and prepared not him-
self, neither did accord-
ing to his will, shall be
beaten with many
stripes. 48 But he that
knew not, and did com-
mit things worthy of
stripes, shall be beat-
en with few stripes.
For unto whomsoever
much is given, of him
shall be much requir-
ed: and to whom men
have committed much,
of him they will ask
the more. 49 I am come
to send fire on the
earth; and what will
I, if it be already kin-
dled ? 50 But I have a
baptism to be baptized
with ; and how am I
straitened till it be
accomplished! 51 Sup-
pose ye that I am come
to give peace on earth?
I tell you, Nay; but ra-
ther division : 52 for

ᵏ — ἐγρηγόρησεν ἄν, καὶ (read he would not have suffered) τ.   ˡ — ἂν τrΑ.   ᵐ διορυχθῆναι τΑ.   ⁿ — οὖν ᴸᵀᵀrΑ.   ° — αὐτῷ ᴸᵀr[Α].   ᴾ καὶ εἶπεν ᵀᵀrΑ.   ٩ ὁ the ᴸᵀᵀrΑ ;
καὶ ὁ and the w.   ʳ — τοῦ ᴸ[ᵀᴾΑ].   ˢ — τὸ (read a measure of corn) τrΑ.   ᵗ αὐτοῦ
ᴸᵀᵀrΑ.   ᵛ ᾖ or τ.   ʷ ἐπὶ upon ᴸᵀᵀrΑʷ.   ˣ ὅτου ᴸᵀᵀrΑʷ.

from henceforth there shall be five in one house divided, three against two, and two against three. 53 The father shall be divided against the son, and the son against the father; the mother against the daughter, and the daughter against the mother; the mother in law against her daughter in law, and the daughter in law against her mother in law.

διαμερισμόν. 52 εσονται.γὰρ ἀπὸ τοῦ.νῦν πέντε ἐν ʸοἴκῳ
division ;   for there will be from henceforth five in ²house
ἑνὶ‖ διαμεμερισμένοι, τρεῖς ἐπὶ δυσὶν καὶ δύο ἐπὶ ᶻτρισίν.
¹one   divided,   three against two and two against three.
53 διαμερισθήσεται‖ πατὴρ ᵃἐφ'‖ υἱῷ, καὶ υἱὸς ἐπὶ πατρί·
²Will ³be ⁴divided ¹father against son, and son against father,
μήτηρ ἐπὶ ᵇθυγατρί,‖ καὶ θυγάτηρ ἐπὶ ᶜμητρί·‖ πενθερὰ
mother against daughter,   and   daughter against mother; mother-in-law
ἐπὶ τὴν νύμφην ᵈαὐτῆς,‖ καὶ νύμφη ἐπὶ τὴν
against ²daughter-in-law ¹her,   and daughter-in-law against
πενθερὰν ᵉαὐτῆς.‖
²mother-in-law ¹her.

54 And he said also to the people, When ye see a cloud rise out of the west, straightway ye say, There cometh a shower; and so it is. 55 And when ye see the south wind blow, ye say, There will be heat; and it cometh to pass. 56 Ye hypocrites, ye can discern the face of the sky and of the earth; but how is it that ye do not discern this time? 57 Yea, and why even of yourselves judge ye not what is right? 58 When thou goest with thine adversary to the magistrate, as thou art in the way, give diligence that thou mayest be delivered from him; lest he hale thee to the judge, and the judge deliver thee to the officer, and the officer cast thee into prison. 59 I tell thee, thou shalt not depart thence, till thou hast paid the very last mite.

54 Ἔλεγεν.δὲ καὶ τοῖς ὄχλοις, Ὅταν ἴδητε ᶠτὴν‖ νεφέλην
And he said also to the crowds, When ye see the cloud
ἀνατέλλουσαν ᵍἀπὸ‖ δυσμῶν, εὐθέως λέγετε, ʰ Ὄμβρος
rising up from [the] west, immediately ye say, A shower
ἔρχεται· καὶ γίνεται οὕτως. 55 καὶ ὅταν νότον πνέοντα,
is coming; and it happens so.   And when a south wind [is] blowing,
λέγετε, Ὅτι καύσων ἔσται· καὶ γίνεται. 56 ὑποκριταί, τὸ
ye say,   Heat   there will be; and it happens. Hypocrites, the
πρόσωπον τῆς γῆς καὶ τοῦ οὐρανοῦ οἴδατε δοκιμάζειν·
appearance of the earth and of the heaven ye know [how] to discern,
τὸν.δὲ.καιρὸν.τοῦτον πῶς ⁱοὐ.δοκιμάζετε‖; 57 τί.δὲ καὶ ἀφ'
but this time   how do ye not discern?   And why even of
ἑαυτῶν οὐ.κρίνετε τὸ δίκαιον; 58 ὡς.γὰρ ὑπάγεις μετὰ
yourselves judge ye not what [is] right?   For as thou goest with
τοῦ.ἀντιδίκου.σου ἐπ' ἄρχοντα, ἐν τῇ ὁδῷ δὸς ἐργασίαν
thine adverse party before a magistrate, in the way give diligence
ἀπηλλάχθαι ἀπ' αὐτοῦ· μήποτε κατασύρῃ σε πρὸς
to be set free from him,   lest he should drag away thee   to
τὸν κριτήν, καὶ ὁ κριτής σε ᵏπαραδῷ‖ τῷ πράκτορι, καὶ
the judge, and the judge thee should deliver to the officer, and
ὁ πράκτωρ σε ˡβάλλῃ‖ εἰς φυλακήν. 59 λέγω σοι, οὐ.μὴ·
the officer thee should cast into prison.   I say to thee, In no wise
ἐξέλθῃς ἐκεῖθεν ἕως.ᵐοῦ‖ καὶ τὸ ἔσχατον λεπτὸν
shalt thou come out thence until even the last lepton
ἀποδῷς.
thou shalt have paid.

XIII. There were present at that season some that told him of the Galilæans, whose blood Pilate had mingled with their sacrifices. 2 And Jesus answering said unto them, Suppose ye that these Galilæans were sinners above all the Galilæans, because they suffered such things? 3 I tell you, Nay: but, except ye repent, ye shall all likewise perish. 4 Or

13 Παρῆσαν.δέ τινες ἐν αὐτῷ.τῷ καιρῷ ἀπαγγέλλοντες
And ²were ³present ¹some at the same time telling
αὐτῷ περὶ τῶν Γαλιλαίων, ὧν τὸ αἷμα ⁿΠιλάτος‖ ἔμιξεν
him about the Galileans, of whom the blood Pilate mingled
μετὰ τῶν.θυσιῶν.αὐτῶν. 2 καὶ ἀποκριθεὶς ᵒὁ Ἰησοῦς‖ εἶπεν
with their sacrifices. 2 and answering Jesus said
αὐτοῖς, Δοκεῖτε ὅτι οἱ.Γαλιλαῖοι.οὗτοι ἁμαρτωλοὶ παρὰ πάν-
to them, Think ye that these Galileans sinners beyond all
τας τοὺς Γαλιλαίους ἐγένοντο, ὅτι ᴾτοιαῦτα‖ πεπόνθασιν;
the Galileans were, because such things they have suffered?
3 οὐχί, λέγω ὑμῖν· ἀλλ' ἐὰν μὴ.ᑫμετανοῆτε,‖ πάντες ʳὡσαύ-
No, I say to you; but if ye repent not, all ²in ³like

ʸ ἐνὶ οἴκῳ LTTrA.   ᶻ τρισὶν διαμερισθήσονται· (read three will be divided :) LTTrA.
ᵃ ἐπὶ TTrA.   ᵇ θυγατέρα LTTrA.   ᶜ μητέρα T; τὴν μητέρα LTrA.   ᵈ — αὐτῆς T.   ᵉ — αὐτῆς
TTrA.   ᶠ — τὴν (read a cloud) LTTr[A].   ᵍ ἐπὶ at T.   ʰ + ὅτι that [L]TTrA.   ⁱ οὐκ οἴδατε
δοκιμάζειν know ye not to discern? Tr.   ᵏ παραδώσει shall deliver LTTrA.   ˡ βάλῃ GW;
βαλεῖ shall cast LTTrA.   ᵐ — οὗ TTr.   ⁿ Πειλᾶτος T.   ᵒ — ὁ Ἰησοῦς (read he said)
[L]TTrA.   ᴾ ταῦτα these things TTr.   ᑫ μετανοήσητε L.   ʳ ὁμοίως LTTrA.

τως‖ ἀπολεῖσθε. 4 ἢ ἐκεῖνοι οἱ ⁵δέκα.καὶ.ὀκτώ‖ ἐφ' οὓς
⁴manner ¹ye shall perish. Or   those   eighteen   on whom

ἔπεσεν ὁ πύργος ἐν τῷ Σιλωὰμ καὶ ἀπέκτεινεν αὐτούς, δοκεῖτε
fell   the tower in   Siloam   and   killed   them, think ye

ὅτι ᵗοὗτοι‖ ὀφειλέται ἐγένοντο παρὰ πάντας ᵛἀνθρώπους
that these debtors were   beyond all   men

τοὺς κατοικοῦντας ᵂἐν‖ Ἱερουσαλήμ; 5 οὐχί, λέγω ὑμῖν· ἀλλ'
who   dwelt   in   Jerusalem?   No, I say to you ; but

ἐὰν μὴ.ˣμετανοῆτε,‖ πάντες ᵞὁμοίως‖ ἀπολεῖσθε.
if   ye repent not,   all ²in ³like ⁴manner ¹ye shall perish.

6 Ἔλεγεν.δὲ ταύτην τὴν παραβολήν· Συκῆν εἶχέν τις
And he spoke this   parable : ⁵A ⁶fig-tree ⁴had ¹a ²certain

ᶻἐν τῷ.ἀμπελῶνι.αὐτοῦ πεφυτευμένην·‖ καὶ ἦλθεν ᵃκαρπὸν
[²man] in   his vineyard   planted ;   and he came   fruit

ζητῶν‖ ἐν αὐτῇ καὶ οὐχ.εὗρεν. 7 εἶπεν.δὲ πρὸς τὸν ἀμ-
seeking on it and did not find [any]. And he said to   the vine-

πελουργόν, Ἰδού, τρία ἔτη ᵇ ἔρχομαι ζητῶν καρπὸν ἐν τῇ
dresser,   Behold, three years I come   seeking   fruit on

συκῇ ταύτῃ καὶ οὐχ.εὑρίσκω· ἔκκοψον ᶜ αὐτήν· ᵈἱνατί‖ καὶ
this fig-tree and do not find [any]: cut ²down ¹it,   why even

τὴν γῆν καταργεῖ; 8 ὁ.δὲ ἀποκριθεὶς λέγει αὐτῷ,
the ground does it render useless ? But he answering says to him,

Κύριε, ἄφες αὐτὴν καὶ τοῦτο τὸ ἔτος, ἕως.ὅτου σκάψω περὶ
Sir, let ²alone ¹it also this   year, until I shall dig about

αὐτὴν καὶ βάλω ᵉκοπρίαν·‖ 9 κἂν μὲν ποιήσῃ ᶠκαρπόν·
it   and put   manure, and if indeed it should bear fruit—;

εἰ.δὲ μήγε, εἰς.τὸ μέλλον‖. ἐκκόψεις αὐτήν.
but if not,   hereafter   thou shalt cut ²down ¹it.

10 Ἦν.δὲ διδάσκων ἐν μιᾷ τῶν συναγωγῶν ἐν τοῖς σάβ-
And he was teaching in one of the synagogues on   the   sab-

βασιν· 11 καὶ ἰδού, γυνὴ ᵍἦν‖ πνεῦμα ἔχουσα ἀσθενείας
baths.   And behold, a woman there was ²a ³spirit ¹having of infirmity

ἔτη ⁸δέκα.καὶ.ὀκτώ,‖ καὶ ἦν ʰσυγκύπτουσα‖ καὶ μὴ.δυναμένη
²years   ¹eighteen,   and she was bent together   and   ²unable

ἀνακύψαι εἰς.τὸ.παντελές. 12 ἰδὼν.δὲ αὐτὴν ὁ Ἰησοῦς
³to ⁴lift ⁵up ⁶herself ¹wholly.   And seeing her   Jesus

προσεφώνησεν καὶ εἶπεν αὐτῇ, Γύναι, ἀπολέλυσαι ⁱ
called to   [her] and said to her, Woman, thou hast been loosed from

τῆς.ἀσθενείας.σοῦ. 13 Καὶ ἐπέθηκεν αὐτῇ τὰς χεῖρας·
thine infirmity.   And   he laid upon her [his]   hands,

καὶ παραχρῆμα ᵏἀνωρθώθη,‖ καὶ ἐδόξαζεν τὸν θεόν.
and immediately she was made straight, and glorified   God.

14 Ἀποκριθεὶς.δὲ ὁ ἀρχισυνάγωγος, ἀγανακτῶν ὅτι
But ⁶answering ¹the ²ruler ³of ⁴the ⁵synagogue, indignant because

τῷ σαββάτῳ ἐθεράπευσεν ὁ Ἰησοῦς, ἔλεγεν τῷ ὄχλῳ,ˡ
on the sabbath   ²healed   ¹Jesus,   said to the crowd,

ˡἘξ ἡμέραι εἰσίν, ἐν αἷς δεῖ ἐργάζεσθαι· ἐν ᵐταύ-
Six days there are, in which it behoves [men] to work ; in   these

ταις‖ οὖν ἐρχόμενοι θεραπεύεσθε, καὶ μὴ τῇ ἡμέρᾳ τοῦ
therefore coming   be healed,   and not on the ²day

ˢ δέκα [καὶ] ὀκτὼ LTTrA ; δεκαοκτὼ T.   ᵗ αὐτοὶ they LTTrA.   ᵛ + τοὺς the LTTrA.   ᵂ — ἐν (read [in]) TrA.   ˣ μετανοήσητε LTTrA.   ᵞ ὡσαύτως TTrA.   ᶻ πεφυτευμένην ἐν τῷ ἀμπελῶνι αὐτοῦ. LTTrA.   ᵞ ζητῶν καρπὸν GLTTrAW.   ᵇ + ἀφ' οὗ since (three years) TTrA.   ᶜ + οὖν therefore (cut) L.   ᵈ ἵνα τί LTrA.   ᵉ κόπρια EGLTTrAW.   ᶠ καρπὸν εἰς τὸ μέλλον· εἰ δὲ μήγε (read bear fruit hereafter; but if not) TTrA.   ᵍ — ἦν LTTrA.   ʰ συνκύπτουσα T.   ⁱ + ἀπὸ from LT.   ᵏ ἀνορθώθη LTTrA.   ˡ + ὅτι that TA.   ᵐ αὐταῖς them LTTrA.

14

Lord then answered him, and said, *Thou* hypocrite, doth not each one of you on the sabbath loose his ox or *his* ass from the stall, and lead *him* away to watering? 16 And ought not this woman, being a daughter of Abraham, whom Satan hath bound, lo, these eighteen years, be loosed from this bond on the sabbath day? 17 And when he had said these things, all his adversaries were ashamed: and all the people rejoiced for all the glorious things that were done by him.

σαββάτου. 15 Ἀπεκρίθη °οὖν‖ αὐτῷ ὁ κύριος, καὶ εἶπεν,
¹sabbath.   ⁴Answered ¹therefore ⁵him ²the ³Lord, and said,

ᴾἙποκριτά,‖ ἕκαστος ὑμῶν τῷ σαββάτῳ οὐ.λύει τὸν
Hypocrite,   each one   of you on the   sabbath   does he not loose

βοῦν.αὐτοῦ ἢ τὸν ὄνον ἀπὸ τῆς φάτνης, καὶ ἀπαγαγὼν
his ox or   ass from the manger,   and having led [it] away

ποτίζει; 16 ταύτην.δὲ θυγατέρα Ἀβραὰμ οὖσαν,
give [it] drink?   And this [woman], ²a ³daughter ⁴of ¹Abraham ¹being,

ἣν ἔδησεν ὁ σατανᾶς, ἰδού, δέκα.καὶ.ὀκτὼ ἔτη, οὐκ.ἔδει
whom ²has ³bound ¹Satan, lo,   eighteen   years, ought [she] not

λυθῆναι ἀπὸ τοῦ.δεσμοῦ.τούτου τῇ ἡμέρᾳ τοῦ σαββάτου;
to be loosed from   this bond   on the ²day   ¹sabbath?

17 Καὶ ταῦτα λέγοντος.αὐτοῦ κατῃσχύνοντο πάντες οἱ
And ⁴these ⁵things ¹on ²his ³saying   ⁷were ⁸ashamed   ⁶all who

ἀντικείμενοι αὐτῷ· καὶ πᾶς ὁ ὄχλος ἔχαιρεν ἐπὶ πᾶσιν
were opposed to him; and all the crowd were rejoicing at   all

τοῖς ἐνδόξοις τοῖς γινομένοις ὑπ' αὐτοῦ.
the glorious things which were being done by him.

18 Then said he, Unto what is the kingdom of God like? and whereunto shall I resemble it? 19 It is like a grain of mustard seed, which a man took, and cast into his garden; and it grew, and waxed a great tree; and the fowls of the air lodged in the branches of it. 20 And again he said, Whereunto shall I liken the kingdom of God? 21 It is like leaven, which a woman took and hid in three measures of meal, till the whole was leavened.

18 Ἔλεγεν ꭓδέ,‖ Τίνι ὁμοία ἐστὶν ἡ βασιλεία τοῦ θεοῦ;
²He ³said ¹and, To what ⁴like   ¹is the kingdom of God?

καὶ τίνι ὁμοιώσω αὐτήν; 19 ὁμοία ἐστὶν κόκκῳ σινάπεως,
and to what shall I liken it?   Like it is to a grain of mustard,

ʳὃν‖ λαβὼν ἄνθρωπος ἔβαλεν εἰς κῆπον ἑαυτοῦ· καὶ
which ³having ⁴taken ¹a ²man   cast into ²garden ¹his;   and

ηὔξησεν.καὶ ἐγένετο εἰς δένδρον ˢμέγα,‖ καὶ.τὰ πετεινὰ τοῦ
it grew and came into a ²tree ¹great, and the birds of the

οὐρανοῦ κατεσκήνωσεν ἐν τοῖς.κλάδοις.αὐτοῦ. 20 ᵗΚαὶ‖ πάλιν
heaven   roosted   in   its branches.   And again

εἶπεν, Τίνι ὁμοιώσω τὴν βασιλείαν τοῦ θεοῦ; 21 ὁμοία
he said, To what shall I liken the   kingdom of God?   Like

ἐστὶν ζύμῃ, ἣν λαβοῦσα γυνὴ ᵛἐνέκρυψεν‖ εἰς ἀλεύρου
it is to leaven, which ³having ⁴taken ¹a ²woman hid   in ³of ⁴meal

σάτα τρία, ἕως.οὗ ἐζυμώθη ὅλον.
²seahs ¹three,   until ²was ³leavened ¹all.

22 And he went through the cities and villages, teaching, and journeying toward Jerusalem. 23 Then said one unto him, Lord, are there few that be saved? And he said unto them, 24 Strive to enter in at the strait gate: for many, I say unto you, will seek to enter in, and shall not be able. 25 When once the master of the house is risen up, and hath shut to the door, and ye begin to stand without, and to knock at the door, saying, Lord, Lord, open unto us; and he shall answer and say unto you, I know you not whence ye are: 26 then shall ye begin to say, We have eaten and drunk in thy presence, and thou hast taught in

22 Καὶ διεπορεύετο κατὰ πόλεις καὶ κώμας διδάσκων, καὶ
And he went through by   cities and villages teaching, and

πορείαν ποιούμενος εἰς ᵂἹερουσαλήμ.‖ 23 εἶπεν.δὲ τις αὐτῷ,
²progress ¹making   towards Jerusalem.   And said one to him,

Κύριε, εἰ ὀλίγοι οἱ σωζόμενοι; Ὁ.δὲ εἶπεν πρὸς αὐτούς,
Lord, [are] ⁴few ¹those ²being ³saved? But he said to them,

24 Ἀγωνίζεσθε εἰσελθεῖν διὰ τῆς στενῆς ˣπύλης·‖ ὅτι
Strive with earnestness to enter in through the narrow gate;   for

πολλοί, λέγω ὑμῖν, ζητήσουσιν εἰσελθεῖν, καὶ οὐκ.ἰσχύσουσιν.
many, I say to you, will seek   to enter in, and will not be able.

25 ἀφ'.οὗ.ἂν ἐγερθῇ ὁ οἰκοδεσπότης, καὶ ἀπο-
From the time ⁶shall ⁷have ⁸risen ⁹up ¹the ²master ³of ⁴the ⁵house, and shall

κλείσῃ τὴν θύραν, καὶ ἄρξησθε ἔξω ἑστάναι καὶ κρούειν τὴν
have shut the door,   and ye begin without to stand and to knock at the

θύραν, λέγοντες, Κύριε, ʸκύριε,‖ ἄνοιξον ἡμῖν· καὶ ἀποκριθεὶς
door, saying, Lord, Lord;   open to us; and he answering

ἐρεῖ ὑμῖν, Οὐκ.οἶδα ὑμᾶς πόθεν ἐστέ. 26 τότε ἄρξεσθε
will say to you, I do not know you whence ye are.   Then will ye begin

λέγειν, Ἐφάγομεν ἐνώπιόν.σου καὶ ἐπίομεν, καὶ ἐν ταῖς
to say, We ate   in thy presence and drank,   and in

° δὲ but LTTrA.   ᴾ Ὑποκριταὶ hypocrites LTTrAW.   ꭓ οὖν therefore TTrA.   ʳ ὃ E.
ˢ — μέγα [L]T[TrA].   ᵗ — καὶ W.   ᵛ ἔκρυψεν TTrA.   ᵂ Ἱεροσόλυμα T.   ˣ θύρας door.
ᴼLTTrA.   ʸ — κύριε [L]TTrA.

πλατείαις.ἡμῶν ἐδίδαξας. 27 καὶ ἐρεῖ, Λέγω ὑμῖν, οὐκ
our streets thou didst teach. And he will say, I tell you, ᵃNot

οἶδα ᶻὑμᾶςǁ πόθεν ἐστέ· ἀπόστητε ἀπ' ἐμοῦ πάντες
ᵃI ²do know you whence ye are; depart from me, all [ye]

ᵃοἱǁ ἐργάται ᵇτῆςǁ ἀδικίας. 28 ἐκεῖ ἔσται ὁ κλαυθμὸς καὶ
the workers of unrighteousness. There shall be the weeping and

ὁ βρυγμὸς τῶν ὀδόντων, ὅταν ᶜὄψησθεǁ Ἀβραὰμ καὶ Ἰσαὰκ
the gnashing of the teeth, when ye see Abraham and Isaac

καὶ Ἰακὼβ καὶ πάντας τοὺς προφήτας ἐν τῇ βασιλείᾳ τοῦ
and Jacob and all the prophets in the kingdom

θεοῦ, ὑμᾶς.δὲ ἐκβαλλομένους ἔξω. 29 καὶ ἥξουσιν ἀπὸ
of God, but yourselves being cast out. And they shall come from

ἀνατολῶν καὶ δυσμῶν, καὶ ᵈἀπὸǁ βορρᾶ καὶ νότου, καὶ ἀνα-
east and west, and from north and south, and shall

κλιθήσονται ἐν τῇ βασιλείᾳ τοῦ θεοῦ. 30 καὶ ἰδού, εἰσὶν
recline in the kingdom of God. And lo, there are

ἔσχατοι οἳ ἔσονται πρῶτοι, καί εἰσιν πρῶτοι οἳ ἔσονται
last who shall be first, and there are first who shall be

ἔσχατοι.
last.

31 Ἐν.αὐτῇ τῇ ᵉἡμέρᾳǁ ᶠπροσῆλθόνǁ τινες Φαρισαῖοι,
On the same day came to [him] certain Pharisees,

λέγοντες αὐτῷ, Ἔξελθε καὶ πορεύου ἐντεῦθεν, ὅτι Ἡρώδης
saying to him, Go out and proceed hence, for Herod

θέλει σε ἀποκτεῖναι. 32 Καὶ εἶπεν αὐτοῖς, Πορευθέντες
desires ³thee ¹to ²kill. And he said to them, Having gone

εἴπατε τῇ.ἀλώπεκι.ταύτῃ, Ἰδού, ἐκβάλλω δαιμόνια καὶ ἰάσεις
say to that fox, Lo, I cast out demons and cures

ᵍἐπιτελῶǁ σήμερον καὶ αὔριον, καὶ τῇ τρίτῃʰ τελειοῦμαι.
I complete to-day and to-morrow, and the third [day] I am perfected;

33 πλὴν δεῖ με σήμερον καὶ αὔριον καὶ τῇ ἐχομένῃ
but it behoves me to-day and to-morrow and the [day] following

πορεύεσθαι· ὅτι οὐκ.ἐνδέχεται προφήτην ἀπολέσθαι ἔξω
to proceed; for it is not possible [for] a prophet to perish out of

Ἰερουσαλήμ. 34 Ἰερουσαλήμ, Ἰερουσαλήμ, ἡ ἀποκτείνουσα
Jerusalem. Jerusalem, Jerusalem, who killest

τοὺς προφήτας, καὶ λιθοβολοῦσα τοὺς ἀπεσταλμένους πρὸς
the prophets, and stonest those who have been sent to

αὐτήν, ποσάκις ἠθέλησα ἐπισυνάξαι τὰ.τέκνα.σου, ὃν.τρόπον
her, how often would I have gathered thy children, in the way

ʲὄρνιςǁ ᵏτὴνǁ ἑαυτῆς ˡνοσσιὰνǁ ὑπὸ τὰς.πτέρυγας,
a hen [gathers] her brood under [her] wings,

καὶ οὐκ.ἠθελήσατε. 35 ἰδού, ἀφίεται ὑμῖν ὁ.οἶκος.ὑμῶν ᵐἔρη-
and ye would not. Behold, is left to you your house de-

μος·ǁ ᵃμὴν δὲ λέγωǁ ὑμῖν, ᵒὅτιǁ οὐ.μὴ ᴾμε ᵏἴδητεǁ ἔως.ˢἂνǁ
solate; ²verily ¹and I say to you, that not at all me shall ye see until

ʳἥξῃ, ˢὅτεǁ εἴπητε, Εὐλογημένος ὁ ἐρχόμενος ἐν ὀνό-
it come when ye say, Blessed [is] he who comes in [the] name

ματι κυρίου.
of [the] Lord.

14 Καὶ ἐγένετο ἐν τῷ.ἐλθεῖν.αὐτὸν εἰς οἶκόν τινος τῶν
And it came to pass on his having gone into a house of one of the

---

our streets. 27 But he
shall say, I tell you, I
know you not whence
ye are; depart from
me, all ye workers of
iniquity. 28 There shall
be weeping and gnash-
ing of teeth, when ye
shall see Abraham, and
Isaac, and Jacob, and
all the prophets, in the
kingdom of God, and
you yourselves thrust
out. 29 And they shall
come from the east,
and from the west,
and from the north,
and from the south,
and shall sit down in
the kingdom of God.
30 And, behold, there
are last which shall be
first, and there are first,
which shall be last.

31 The same day
there came certain of
the Pharisees, saying
unto him, Get thee out,
and depart hence : for
Herod will kill thee.
32 And he said unto
them, Go ye, and tell
that fox, Behold, I cast
out devils, and I do
cures to day and to
morrow, and the third
day I shall be per-
fected. 33 Nevertheless
I must walk to day,
and to morrow, and
the day following: for
it cannot be that a
prophet perish out of
Jerusalem. 34 O Je-
rusalem, Jerusalem,
which killest the pro-
phets, and stonest them
that are sent unto thee;
how often would I have
gathered thy children
together, as a hen doth
ga.her her brood un-
der her wings, and ye
would not! 35 Behold,
your house is left unto
you desolate: and veri-
ly I say unto you, Ye
shall not see me, until
the time come when ye
shall say, Blessed is he
that cometh in the
name of the Lord.

XIV. And it came to
pass, as he went into
the house of one of the

ᶻ — ὑμᾶς [L]TrA.   ᵃ — οἱ TTrA.   ᵇ — τῆς LTTrA.   ᶜ ὄψεσθε ye shall see TTr.
ᵈ — ἀπὸ [L]T[TrA.]   ᵉ ὥρᾳ hour TA.   ᶠ προσῆλθάν TTrA.   ᵍ ἀποτελῶ LTTrA.   ʰ + [ἡμέρᾳ]
day L.   ʲ ὄρνιξ T.   ᵏ τὰ L.   ˡ νοσσία L.   ᵐ — ἔρημος GLTTrAW.   ⁿ λέγω δὲ GLTrAW.
λέγω T.   ᵒ — ὅτι [L]T[A]   ᴾ ἴδητέ με LTTrA,   ᵒ — ἂν TTrA.   ʳ ἥξει it shall
come LT[TrA].   ˢ [ὅτε] TrA.

chief Pharisees to eat bread on the sabbath day, that they watched him. 2 And, behold, there was a certain man before him which had the dropsy. 3 And Jesus answering spake unto the lawyers and Pharisees, saying, Is it lawful to heal on the sabbath day? 4 And they held their peace. And he took *him*, and healed him, and let him go; 5 and answered them, saying, Which of you shall have an ass or an ox fallen into a pit, and will not straightway pull him out on the sabbath day? 6 And they could not answer him again to these things.

ἀρχόντων ʳτῶν‖ Φαρισαίων σαββάτῳ φαγεῖν ἄρτον, καὶ αὐτοὶ
rulers   of the   Pharisees   on a sabbath   to eat   bread,   that they
ἦσαν παρατηρούμενοι αὐτόν. 2 καὶ ἰδού, ἄνθρωπός τις
were   watching   him.   And behold,   a ²man   ¹certain
ἦν ὑδρωπικὸς ἔμπροσθεν αὐτοῦ. 3 καὶ ἀποκριθεὶς ὁ Ἰησοῦς
there was dropsical   before   him.   And answering   Jesus
εἶπεν πρὸς τοὺς νομικοὺς καὶ Φαρισαίους, ᵛλέγων,‖ ʷΕἰ‖
spoke   to   the   doctors of the law   and to [the] Pharisees,   saying,
ἔξεστιν τῷ σαββάτῳ ˣθεραπεύειν‖ ʸ; 4 Οἱ.δὲ ἡσύχασαν.
Is it lawful on the   sabbath   to heal?   But they were silent.
καὶ ἐπιλαβόμενος ἰάσατο αὐτόν, καὶ ἀπέλυσεν. 5 καὶ
And   taking hold [of him] he healed   him,   and let [him] go.   And
ᶻἀποκριθεὶς‖ ᵃπρὸς αὐτοὺς εἶπεν,‖ Τίνος ὑμῶν ᵇὄνος‖ ἢ βοῦς
answering   to   them he said, Of which of you ²an ³ass ⁴or ⁵an ⁶ox
εἰς φρέαρ ᶜἐμπεσεῖται,‖ καὶ οὐκ εὐθέως ἀνασπάσει αὐτὸν
¹into ⁹a ¹⁰pit   ¹shall ⁷fall,   and ³not ⁴immediately ¹he ²will pull up   him
dᵉᵛ‖ ᵉτῇ‖ ἡμέρᾳ τοῦ σαββάτου; 6 Καὶ οὐκ.ἴσχυσαν ἀνταπο-
on the   ²day   ¹sabbath?   And they were not able   to re-
κριθῆναι ʳαὐτῷ‖ πρὸς ταῦτα.
ply   to him   as to these things.

7 And he put forth a parable to those which were bidden, when he marked how they chose out the chief rooms; saying unto them, 8 When thou art bidden of any *man* to a wedding, sit not down in the highest room; lest a more honourable man than thou be bidden of him; 9 and he that bade thee and him come and say to thee, Give this man place; and thou begin with shame to take the lowest room. 10 But when thou art bidden, go and sit down in the lowest room; that when he that bade thee cometh, he may say unto thee, Friend, go up higher: then shalt thou have worship in the presence of them that sit at meat with thee. 11 For whosoever exalteth himself shall be abased; and he that humbleth himself shall be exalted.

7 Ἔλεγεν.δὲ πρὸς τοὺς κεκλημένους παραβολήν, ἐπέχων
And he spoke   to   those who were invited   a parable,   remarking
πῶς τὰς πρωτοκλισίας ἐξελέγοντο, λέγων πρὸς αὐτούς,
how the   first places   they were choosing out,   saying   to   them,
8 Ὅταν κληθῇς ὑπό τινος εἰς γάμους, μὴ.κατακλιθῇς
When thou art invited by anyone to wedding feasts,   do not recline
εἰς τὴν πρωτοκλισίαν, μήποτε ἐντιμότερός σου ᾖ.κεκλη-
in the   first place,   lest   a more honourable than thou   may have
μένος ὑπ' αὐτοῦ, 9 καὶ ἐλθὼν ὁ σὲ καὶ αὐτὸν καλέσας
been invited by him,   and having come he who thee and   him   invited
ἐρεῖ σοι, Δὸς τούτῳ τόπον· καὶ τότε ἄρξῃ ᵍμετ'‖
shall say to thee, Give ²to ³this ⁴one ¹place,   and then thou begin with
αἰσχύνης τὸν ἔσχατον τόπον κατέχειν. 10 ἀλλ' ὅταν κλη-
shame   the   last   place   to take.   But when thou art
θῇς, πορευθεὶς ʰἀνάπεσον‖ εἰς τὸν ἔσχατον τόπον· ἵνα
invited, having gone   recline   in   the   last   place,   that
ὅταν ἔλθῃ ὁ κεκληκώς σε, ⁱεἴπῃ‖ σοι, Φίλε, προσ-
when he may come who has invited thee, he may say to thee, Friend,   come
ἀνάβηθι ἀνώτερον· τότε ἔσται σοι δόξα ἐνώπιον ᵏ τῶν
up   higher.   Then shall be to thee glory   before   those who
συνανακειμένων σοι. 11 ὅτι πᾶς ὁ ὑψῶν ἑαυτὸν ταπεινω-
recline [at table] with thee;   for everyone that exalts himself   shall be
θήσεται· καὶ ὁ ταπεινῶν ἑαυτὸν ὑψωθήσεται.
humbled,   and he that humbles himself shall be exalted.

12 Then said he also to him that bade him, When thou makest a dinner or a supper, call not thy friends, nor thy brethren, neither thy kinsmen, nor *thy* rich neighbours; lest they also bid thee again, and a recompence be made thee.

12 Ἔλεγεν.δὲ καὶ τῷ κεκληκότι.αὐτόν, Ὅταν ποιῇς
And he said also to him who had invited   him,   When thou makest
ἄριστον ἢ δεῖπνον, μὴ.φώνει τοὺς.φίλους.σου μηδὲ τοὺς ἀδελ-
a dinner or a supper,   call not   thy friends   nor   ²breth-
φούς σου μηδὲ τοὺς.συγγενεῖς.σου μηδὲ γείτονας πλουσίους·
ren   ¹thy   nor   thy kinsfolk   nor   ²neighbours   ¹rich,
μήποτε καὶ αὐτοί ¹σε ἀντικαλέσωσιν,‖ καὶ γένηταί ᵐσοι
lest   also   they   thee should invite in return,   and   ³be ⁴made   ⁵thee

---

ᵗ [τῶν] A.   ᵛ [λέγων] L.   ʷ — Εἰ TTrA.   ˣ θεραπεῦσαι LTTrA.   ʸ + ἢ οὔ or not
[L]TTrA.   ᶻ — ἀποκριθεὶς LTr[A].   ᵃ εἶπεν πρὸς αὐτούς L.   ᵇ υἱὸς a son LTTrAW.
ᶜ πεσεῖται LTTrA.   ᵈ — ἐν (read τῇ on the) [L]Tr.   ᵉ — τῇ T.   ᶠ — αὐτῷ TTrA.   ᵍ μετὰ
LTTrAW.   ʰ ἀνάπεσαι G; ἀνάπεσε LTTrAW.   ⁱ ἐρεῖ he will say TTr.   ᵏ + πάντων all
LTTrA.   ˡ ἀντικαλέσωσίν σε LTTrA.   ᵐ ἀνταπόδομά σοι TTrA.

ἀνταπόδομα.‖ 13 ἀλλ᾽ ὅταν ποιῇς δοχήν, κάλει πτωχούς,
¹a ²recompense ;   but   when thou makest a feast, call   poor,

ⁿἀναπήρους,‖ χωλούς, τυφλούς· 14 καὶ μακάριος ἔσῃ·
crippled,   lame,   blind ;   and   blessed   thou shalt be ;

ὅτι οὐκ.ἔχουσιν ἀνταποδοῦναί σοι· ἀνταποδοθήσεται
for they have not [wherewith] to recompense thee ; ²it ³shall ⁴be ⁵recompensed

°γάρ‖ σοι ἐν τῇ ἀναστάσει τῶν δικαίων.
¹for   thee in the resurrection of the   just.

15 Ἀκούσας.δέ τις τῶν συνανακειμένων ταῦ-
And ⁹having ¹⁰heard ¹one ²of ³those ⁴reclining [⁵at ⁶table] ⁷with [⁸him] these

τα εἶπεν αὐτῷ, Μακάριος ᵖὃς‖ φάγεται ἄρτον ἐν τῇ
things said to him, Blessed [he] who shall eat bread in the

βασιλείᾳ τοῦ θεοῦ. 16 Ὁ.δὲ εἶπεν αὐτῷ, Ἄνθρωπός τις
kingdom of God.   But he said to him, A ²man ¹certain

ᵠᵉποίησεν‖δεῖπνον ʳμέγα,‖ καὶ.ἐκάλεσεν πολλούς· 17 καὶ ἀπέ-
made a ²supper ¹great, and invited many.   And he

στειλεν τὸν.δοῦλον.αὐτοῦ τῇ ὥρᾳ τοῦ δείπνου εἰπεῖν τοῖς
sent   his bondman   at the hour of the supper   to say to those who

κεκλημένοις, Ἔρχεσθε, ὅτι ἤδη ἕτοιμά ˢἐστιν‖ ᵗπάντα.‖ 18 Καὶ
had been invited, Come,   for now ³ready ²is   ¹all.   And

ἤρξαντο ἀπὸ μιᾶς ᵛπαραιτεῖσθαι πάντες.‖ ʷ ὁ πρῶ-
²began ³with ⁴one [⁵consent] ⁶to ⁷excuse ⁸themselves ¹all.   The first

τος εἶπεν αὐτῷ, Ἀγρὸν ἠγόρασα, καὶ ˣἔχω ἀνάγκην‖
said to him, ⁴A ⁵field ¹I ²have ³bought, and I have   need

ʸἐξελθεῖν καὶ‖ ἰδεῖν αὐτόν· ἐρωτῶ σε ἔχε με παρῃτημένον.
to go out and to see   it ; I pray thee hold me   excused.

19 καὶ ἕτερος εἶπεν, Ζεύγη βοῶν ἠγόρασα πέντε, καὶ
And another said,   ⁵Pairs ⁶of ʼoxen ¹I ²have ³bought ⁴five, and

πορεύομαι δοκιμάσαι αὐτά· ἐρωτῶ σε ἔχε με· παρῃτημένον.
I go   to prove   them ; I pray thee hold me   excused.

20 καὶ ἕτερος εἶπεν, Γυναῖκα ἔγημα, καὶ διὰ τοῦτο
And another said,   A wife I have married, and because of this

οὐ.δύναμαι ἐλθεῖν. 21 καὶ παραγενόμενος ὁ.δοῦλος.ᶻἐκεῖνος‖
I am unable to come.   And having come   that bondman

ἀπήγγειλεν τῷ.κυρίῳ.αὐτοῦ ταῦτα. Τότε ὀργισθεὶς ὁ οἰκο-
reported   to his lord   these things.   Then being angry the master

δεσπότης εἶπεν τῷ.δούλῳ.αὐτοῦ, Ἔξελθε ταχέως εἰς τὰς
of the house said   to his bondman,   Go out   quickly   into the

πλατείας καὶ ῥύμας τῆς πόλεως, καὶ τοὺς πτωχοὺς καὶ ᵃἀνα-
streets   and lanes of the   city,   and the   poor   and crip-

πήρους‖ καὶ ᵇχωλοὺς καὶ τυφλοὺς‖ εἰσάγαγε ὧδε. 22 Καὶ εἶπεν
pled   and lame   and blind   bring in here.   And said

ὁ δοῦλος, Κύριε, γέγονεν ᶜὡς‖ ἐπέταξας, καὶ ἔτι
the bondman, Sir, it has been done as thou didst command, and still

τόπος ἐστίν. 23 Καὶ εἶπεν ὁ κύριος πρὸς τὸν δοῦλον,
room there is.   And said the lord   to the bondman,

Ἔξελθε εἰς τὰς ὁδοὺς καὶ φραγμούς, καὶ ἀνάγκασον εἰσελθεῖν,
Go out into the ways and hedges,   and compel   to come in,

ἵνα γεμισθῇ ᵈὁ.οἶκός.μου.‖ 24 λέγω.γὰρ ὑμῖν, ὅτι οὐδεὶς τῶν
that may be filled my house ;   for I say to you, that not one

ἀνδρῶν.ἐκείνων τῶν κεκλημένων ·γεύσεταί μου τοῦ δείπνου.
of those men   who have been invited shall taste of my   supper.

ⁿ ἀναπείρους LTrA.   ° δέ but T.   ᵖ ὅστις whosoever TTrA.   ᵠ ἐποίει TTrA.
ʳ μέγαν L.   ˢ εἰσιν are T.   ᵗ — πάντα (read [all]) [L.]T[TrA].   ᵛ πάντες παραιτεῖσθαι
LTTrA.   ʷ + [καὶ] and L.   ˣ ἀνάγκην ἔχω L.   ʸ ἐξελθὼν having gone out TTrA.
ᶻ — ἐκεῖνος (read the bondman) LTTrA.   ᵃ ἀναπείρους LTrA.   ᵇ τυφλοὺς καὶ χωλοὺς
LTTrA.   ᶜ ὃ which TTrA.   ᵈ μου ὁ οἶκος TTrA.

---

13 But when thou makest a feast, call the poor, the maimed, the lame, the blind: 14 and thou shalt be blessed ; for they cannot recompense thee : for thou shalt be recompensed at the resurrection of the just.

15 And when one of them that sat at meat with him heard these things, he said unto him, Blessed is he that shall eat bread in the kingdom of God. 16 Then said he unto him, A certain man made a great supper, and bade many: 17 and sent his servant at supper time to say to them that were bidden, Come; for all things are now ready. 18 And they all with one consent began to make excuse. The first said unto him, I have bought a piece of ground, and I must needs go and see it: I pray thee have me excused. 19 And another said, I have bought five yoke of oxen, and I go to prove them: I pray thee have me excused. 20 And another said, I have married a wife, and therefore I cannot come. 21 So that servant came, and shewed his lord these things. Then the master of the house being angry said to his servant, Go out quickly into the streets and lanes of the city, and bring in hither the poor, and the maimed, and the halt, and the blind. 22 And the servant said, Lord, it is done as thou hast commanded, and yet there is room. 23 And the lord said unto the servant, Go out into the highways and hedges, and compel them to come in, that my house may be filled. 24 For I say unto you, That none of those men which were bidden shall taste of my supper.

25 And there went great multitudes with him: and he turned, and said unto them, 26 If any *man* come to me, and hate not his father, and mother, and wife, and children, and brethren, and sisters, yea, and his own life also, he cannot be my disciple. 27 And whosoever doth not bear his cross, and come after me, cannot be my disciple. 28 For which of you, intending to build a tower, sitteth not down first, and counteth the cost, whether he have *sufficient* to finish *it?* 29 Lest haply, after he hath laid the foundation, and is not able to finish *it*, all that behold *it* begin to mock him, 30 saying, This man began to build, and was not able to finish. 31 Or what king, going to make war against another king, sitteth not down first, and consulteth whether he be able with ten thousand to meet him that cometh against him with twenty thousand? 32 Or else, while the other is yet a great way off, he sendeth an ambassage, and desireth conditions of peace. 33 So likewise, whosoever he be of you that forsaketh not all that he hath, he cannot be my disciple. 34 Salt *is* good: but if the salt have lost his savour, wherewith shall it be seasoned? 35 It is neither fit for the land, nor yet for the dunghill; *but* men cast it out. He that hath ears to hear, let him hear.

XV. Then drew near unto him all the publicans and sinners for to hear him. 2 And the Pharisees and scribes murmured, saying,

25 Συνεπορεύοντο.δὲ αὐτῷ ὄχλοι πολλοί· καὶ στραφεὶς
And ³were ⁴going ⁵with ⁶him ²crowds ¹great; and having turned

εἶπεν πρὸς αὐτούς, 26 Εἴ τις ἔρχεται πρός με, καὶ οὐ.μισεῖ
he said to them, If any one comes to me, and hates not

τὸν.πατέρα.ᶠἑαυτοῦ‖ καὶ τὴν μητέρα καὶ τὴν γυναῖκα καὶ τὰ
his father and mother and wife and

τέκνα· καὶ τοὺς ἀδελφοὺς καὶ τὰς ἀδελφάς, ἔτι.ᵍδὲ‖ καὶ τὴν
children and brothers and sisters, and besides also

ἑαυτοῦ.ψυχήν, οὐ.δύναταί ʰμου.μαθητὴς εἶναι·‖ 27 ⁱκαὶ‖ ὅστις
his own life, he cannot my disciple be; and whosoever

οὐ.βαστάζει τὸν.σταυρὸν.ᵏαὐτοῦ,‖ καὶ ἔρχεται ὀπίσω μου,
carries not his cross, and ' comes after me,

οὐ.δύναταί ˡμου εἶναι‖ μαθητής. 28 τίς.γὰρ ἐξ ὑμῶν θέλων
cannot ²my ¹be· disciple. For which of you desiring

πύργον οἰκοδομῆσαι, οὐχὶ πρῶτον καθίσας ψηφίζει τὴν
a tower to build, ⁵not ⁶first ¹having ²sat ³down ⁴counts the

δαπάνην, εἰ ἔχει ᵐτὰ‖ ⁿπρὸς‖ ἀπαρτισμόν; 29 ἵνα μήποτε
cost, if he has the[means] for [its] completion? that lest

θέντος αὐτοῦ θεμέλιον καὶ μὴ ἰσχύοντος ἐκτελέσαι, πάντες
having laid of it a foundation and not being able to finish, all

οἱ θεωροῦντες ἄρξωνται °ἐμπαίζειν αὐτῷ,‖ 30 λέγοντες, Ὅτι
who see [it] should begin to mock at him, saying,

οὗτος ὁ ἄνθρωπος ἤρξατο οἰκοδομεῖν, καὶ οὐκ.ἴσχυσεν ἐκτελέσαι.
This man began to build, and was not able to finish.

31 Ἢ τίς βασιλεὺς πορευόμενος ᴾσυμβαλεῖν ἑτέρῳ βασι‑
Or what king proceeding to engage with another king

λεῖ‖ εἰς πόλεμον οὐχὶ καθίσας πρῶτον ᑫβουλεύεται‖
in war ⁵not ¹having ²sat ³down ⁴first ⁶takes ⁷counsel

εἰ δυνατός ἐστιν ἐν δέκα χιλιάσιν ʳἀπαντῆσαι‖ τῷ μετὰ
whether able he is with ten thousand to meet him with

εἴκοσι χιλιάδων ἐρχομένῳ ἐπ᾽ αὐτόν; 32 εἰ.δὲ μήγε, ἔτι
twenty thousand who comes against him? But if not, ²still

ˢαὐτοῦ πόρρω‖ ὄντος, πρεσβείαν ἀποστείλας ἐρωτᾷ τὰ
¹he ⁴far °off ²being, an embassy having sent he asks the[terms]

πρὸς εἰρήνην. 33 οὕτως οὖν πᾶς ἐξ ὑμῶν ὃς οὐκ ἀπο‑
for peace. Thus therefore everyone of you who ²not ¹does take

τάσσεται πᾶσιν τοῖς ἑαυτοῦ ὑπάρχουσιν, οὐ.δύναταί ᵗμου
leave of all that he himself possesses, cannot ²my

εἶναι‖ μαθητής. 34 καλὸν ᵛ τὸ ʷἅλας·‖ ἐὰν.δὲ ˣ τὸ ʷἅλας‖
¹be· disciple. Good [is] the salt, but if the salt

μωρανθῇ ἐν τίνι ἀρτυθήσεται; 35 οὔτε εἰς γῆν οὔτε
become tasteless with what shall it be seasoned? Neither for land nor

εἰς κοπρίαν εὔθετόν ἐστιν· ἔξω βάλλουσιν αὐτό. Ὁ ἔχων
for manure fit is it: ⁴out ¹they ²cast ³it. He that has

ὦτα ʸἀκούειν‖ ἀκουέτω.
ears to hear let him hear.

15 Ἦσαν.δὲ ᶻἐγγίζοντες αὐτῷ‖ πάντες οἱ τελῶναι καὶ
And were drawing near to him all the tax-gatherers and

οἱ ἁμαρτωλοὶ ἀκούειν αὐτοῦ· 2 καὶ διεγόγγυζον οἱ ᵃΦαρισαῖοι
the sinners to hear him; and murmured the Pharisees

ᶠ αὐτοῦ LTTrA.   ᵍ τε LTTrA.   ʰ εἶναί μου μαθητής TTrA.   ⁱ — καὶ T.   ᵏ ἑαυτοῦ
LTA.   ˡ εἶναί μου TTrA.   ᵐ — τὰ (*read* [the means]) GTTrA.   ⁿ εἰς to GLTTrAW.
° αὐτῷ ἐμπαίζειν LTTrA.   ᴾ ἑτέρῳ βασιλεῖ συμβαλεῖν LTTrA.   ᑫ βουλεύσεται will take
counsel T.   ʳ ὑπαντῆσαι LTTrAW.   ˢ πόρρω αὐτοῦ W.   ᵗ εἶναί μου LTTr.   ᵛ + οὖν
therefore T[Tr]A.   ʷ ἅλα T.   ˣ + καὶ also LTTrA.   ʸ ἀκούειν T.   ᶻ αὐτῷ ἐγγίζοντες
LTTrAW.   ᵃ + τε both (t)he LTTrA.

καὶ οἱ γραμματεῖς, λέγοντες, Ὅτι οὗτος ἁμαρτωλοὺς
and the scribes, saying, This [man] sinners

προσδέχεται καὶ συνεσθίει αὐτοῖς. 3 Εἶπεν δὲ πρὸς αὐτοὺς
receives and eats with them. And he spoke to them

τὴν παραβολὴν ταύτην, λέγων, 4 Τίς ἄνθρωπος ἐξ ὑμῶν
this parable, saying, What man of you

ἔχων ἑκατὸν πρόβατα, καὶ ᵇἀπολέσας‖ ᶜἐν ἐξ αὐτῶν,‖ οὐ
having a hundred sheep, and having lost one of them, ²not

καταλείπει τὰ ᵈἐννενηκονταεννέα‖ ἐν τῇ ἐρήμῳ καὶ πορεύεται
¹leaves the ninety nine in the wilderness and goes

ἐπὶ τὸ ἀπολωλός, ἕως εὕρῃ αὐτό ; 5 καὶ εὑρὼν
after that which has been lost, until he find it ? And having found [it]

ἐπιτίθησιν ἐπὶ τοὺς ὤμους ᵉἑαυτοῦ‖ χαίρων, 6 καὶ ἐλθὼν
he lays [it] on his shoulders rejoicing, and having come

εἰς τὸν οἶκον ᶠσυγκαλεῖ‖ τοὺς φίλους καὶ τοὺς γείτονας, λέ-
to the house he calls together friends and neighbours, say-

γων αὐτοῖς, ᵍΣυγχάρητέ‖ μοι, ὅτι εὗρον τὸ πρόβατόν μου
ing to them, Rejoice with me, for I have found my sheep

τὸ ἀπολωλός. 7 λέγω ὑμῖν, ὅτι οὕτως χαρὰ ʰἔσται ἐν τῷ
that was lost. I say to you, that thus joy shall be in the

οὐρανῷ‖ ἐπὶ ἑνὶ ἁμαρτωλῷ μετανοοῦντι, ἢ ἐπὶ ᵈἐννενη-
heaven over one sinner repenting, [more] than over ninety

κονταεννέα‖ δικαίοις, οἵτινες οὐ χρείαν ἔχουσιν μετανοίας.
nine righteous ones, who ²no ³need ¹have of repentance.

8 Ἢ τίς γυνὴ δραχμὰς ἔχουσα δέκα, ἐὰν ἀπολέσῃ δραχμὴν
Or what woman ³drachmas ¹having ²ten, if she should lose ²drachma

μίαν, οὐχὶ ἅπτει λύχνον καὶ σαροῖ τὴν οἰκίαν καὶ ζητεῖ ἐπι-
one, lights not a lamp and sweeps the house and seeks care-

μελῶς ἕως ὅτου‖ εὕρῃ ; 9 καὶ εὑροῦσα ᶠσυγκαλεῖται‖
fully until she find [it] ? and having found [it] she calls together

τὰς φίλας καὶ ᵏτὰς‖ γείτονας, λέγουσα, ᵍΣυγχάρητέ‖ μοι, ὅτι
friends and neighbours, saying, Rejoice with me, for

εὗρον τὴν δραχμὴν ἣν ἀπώλεσα. 10 οὕτως, λέγω ὑμῖν,
I have found the drachma which I lost. Thus, I say to you,

ˡχαρὰ γίνεται‖ ἐνώπιον τῶν ἀγγέλων τοῦ θεοῦ ἐπὶ ἑνὶ ἁμαρ-
joy there is before the angels of God over one sin-

τωλῷ μετανοοῦντι.
ner repenting.

11 Εἶπεν δέ, Ἄνθρωπός τις εἶχεν δύο υἱούς· 12 καὶ εἶπεν
And he said, A ²man ¹certain had two sons ; and said

ὁ νεώτερος αὐτῶν τῷ πατρί, Πάτερ, δός μοι τὸ ἐπιβάλ-
the younger of them to [his] father, Father, give to me that ²fall-

λον μέρος τῆς οὐσίας. ᵐκαὶ‖ διεῖλεν αὐτοῖς τὸν βίον.
ing ³to ⁴me] ¹portion of the property. And he divided to them the living.

13 καὶ μετ᾽ οὐ πολλὰς ἡμέρας συναγαγὼν ⁿἅπαντα‖
And after not many days having gathered together all

ὁ νεώτερος υἱὸς ἀπεδήμησεν εἰς χώραν μακράν, καὶ ἐκεῖ
the younger son went away into a ²country ¹distant, and there

διεσκόρπισεν τὴν οὐσίαν αὐτοῦ, ζῶν ἀσώτως. 14 δαπανή-
wasted his property, living dissolutely. ³Having

σαντος δὲ αὐτοῦ πάντα ἐγένετο λιμὸς ᵒἰσχυρὸς‖ κατὰ
⁴spent ¹but ²he all there arose a ²famine ¹violent throughout

τὴν χώραν ἐκείνην, καὶ αὐτὸς ἤρξατο ὑστερεῖσθαι. 15 καὶ
that country, and he began to be in want. And

This man receiveth sinners, and eateth with them. 3 And he spake this parable unto them, saying, 4 What man of you, having an hundred sheep, if he lose one of them, doth not leave the ninety and nine in the wilderness, and go after that which is lost, until he find it ? 5 And when he hath found it, he layeth it on his shoulders, rejoicing. 6 And when he cometh home, he calleth together his friends and neighbours, saying unto them, Rejoice with me ; for I have found my sheep which was lost. 7 I say unto you, that likewise joy shall be in heaven over one sinner that repenteth, more than over ninety and nine just persons, which need no repentance. 8 Either what woman having ten pieces of silver, if she lose one piece, doth not light a candle, and sweep the house, and seek diligently till she find it ? 9 And when she hath found it, she calleth her friends and her neighbours together, saying, Rejoice with me ; for I have found the piece which I had lost. 10 Likewise, I say unto you, there is joy in the presence of the angels of God, over one sinner that repenteth.

11 And he said, A certain man had two sons : 12 and the younger of them said to his father, Father, give me the portion of goods that falleth to me. And he divided unto them his living. 13 And not many days after the younger son gathered all together, and took his journey into a far country, and there wasted his substance with riotous living. 14 And when he had spent all, there arose a mighty famine in that land ; and he began to be in want. 15 And he went and

---

ᵇ ἀπολέσῃ should he lose Tr.   ᶜ ἐξ αὐτῶν ἕν TTrA.   ᵈ ἐνενήκοντα ἐννέα LTTr.   ᵉ αὐτοῦ
TTrA.   ᶠ συνκαλεῖ T.   ᵍ συγχάρητέ T.   ʰ ἐν τῷ οὐρανῷ ἔσται TA.   ⁱ οὗ Tr.   ᵏ — τὰς LTTrA.
ˡ γίνεται χαρὰ TTrA.   ᵐ ὁ δὲ LTTrA.   ⁿ πάντα LTTrA.   ᵒ ἰσχυρὰ LTTrAW

joined himself to a citizen of that country; and he sent him into his fields to feed swine. 16 And he would fain have filled his belly with the husks that the swine did eat: and no man gave unto him. 17 And when he came to himself, he said, How many hired servants of my father's have bread enough and to spare, and I perish with hunger! 18 I will arise and go to my father, and will say unto him, Father, I have sinned against heaven, and before thee, 19 and am no more worthy to be called thy son: make me as one of thy hired servants. 20 And he arose, and came to his father. But when he was yet a great way off, his father saw him, and had compassion, and ran, and fell on his neck, and kissed him. 21 And the son said unto him, Father, I have sinned against heaven, and in thy sight, and am no more worthy to be called thy son. 22 But the father said to his servants, Bring forth the best robe, and put *it* on him; and put a ring on his hand, and shoes on *his* feet: 23 and bring hither the fatted calf, and kill *it*; and let us eat, and be merry: 24 for this my son was dead, and is alive again; he was lost, and is found. And they began to be merry. 25 Now his elder son was in the field: and as he came and drew nigh to the house, he heard musick and dancing. 26 And he called one of the servants, and asked what these things meant. 27 And he said unto him, Thy brother is come; and thy father hath killed the fatted calf, because he hath

πορευθεὶς ἐκολλήθη ἑνὶ τῶν πολιτῶν τῆς.χώρας.ἐκείνης·
having gone he joined himself to one of the citizens of that country,
καὶ ἔπεμψεν αὐτὸν εἰς τοὺς.ἀγροὺς.αὐτοῦ βόσκειν χοίρους.
and he sent him into his fields to feed swine.
16 καὶ ἐπεθύμει γεμίσαι τὴν.κοιλίαν.αὐτοῦ ἀπὸ τῶν κερατίων
And he was longing to fill his belly from the husks'
ὧν ἤσθιον οἱ χοῖροι· καὶ οὐδεὶς ἐδίδου αὐτῷ. 17 Εἰς
which ³were ⁴eating ¹the ²swine; and no one gave to him. ⁴To
ἑαυτὸν δὲ ἐλθὼν Ρεῖπεν,‖ Πόσοι   μίσθιοι   τοῦ πατρός
⁵himself ¹but ²having ³come he said, How many hired servants ³father
μου �� περισσεύουσιν‖ ἄρτων, ἐγὼ.δὲ ʳ λιμῷ ˢ ἀπόλλυμαι;
¹of my have abundance of bread, and I with famine am perishing?
18 ἀναστὰς πορεύσομαι πρὸς τὸν.πατέρα.μου, καὶ ἐρῶ
Having risen up I will go to   my father, and I will say
αὐτῷ, Πάτερ, ἥμαρτον εἰς τὸν οὐρανὸν καὶ ἐνώπιόν σου·
to him, Father, I have sinned against heaven and before thee;
19 ᵗκαὶ‖ οὐκέτι εἰμὶ ἄξιος κληθῆναι υἱός.σου· ποίησόν με ὡς
and no longer am I worthy to be called thy son: make me as
ἕνα τῶν.μισθίων.σου. 20 καὶ ἀναστὰς ἦλθεν πρὸς τὸν πα-
one of thy hired servants. And having risen up he went to ²fa-
τέρα ᵛἑαυτοῦ.‖ Ἔτι.δὲ αὐτοῦ μακρὰν ἀπέχοντος εἶδεν αὐτὸν
ther ¹his. But ²yet ¹he ⁴far ³being distant ³saw ⁴him
ὁ.πατὴρ.αὐτοῦ καὶ   ἐσπλαγχνίσθη,   καὶ δραμὼν ἐπέπεσεν
¹his ²father   and was moved with compassion, and running fell
ἐπὶ τὸν.τράχηλον.αὐτοῦ καὶ κατεφίλησεν αὐτόν. 21 εἶπεν.δὲ
upon his neck and ardently kissed him. And ⁵said
ʷαὐτῷ ὁ υἱός,‖ Πάτερ, ἥμαρτον εἰς τὸν οὐρανὸν καὶ ἐνώ-
⁴to ⁶him ¹the ²son, Father, I have sinned against heaven and be-
πιόν σου, ˣκαὶ‖ οὐκέτι εἰμὶ ἄξιος κληθῆναι υἱός.σου. 22 Εἶπεν
fore thee, and no longer am I worthy to be called thy son. ²Said
δὲ ὁ πατὴρ πρὸς τοὺς.δούλους.αὐτοῦ, ʸ Ἐξενέγκατε ᶻτὴν‖
but the father to his bondmen, Bring out the
στολὴν τὴν πρώτην καὶ ἐνδύσατε αὐτόν, καὶ δότε δακτύλιον
robe   the best and clothe him, and give a ring
εἰς τὴν.χεῖρα.αὐτοῦ καὶ ὑποδήματα εἰς τοὺς πόδας· 23 καὶ
for his hand and sandals for the feet; and
ᵃἐνέγκαντες‖ τὸν μόσχον τὸν σιτευτὸν θύσατε, καὶ φαγόντες
having brought the ²calf ¹fattened kill [it], and eating
εὐφρανθῶμεν· 24 ὅτι οὗτος ὁ.υἱός.μου νεκρὸς ἦν, καὶ ἀνέζη-
let us be merry: for this my son ²dead ¹was, and ᵥis alive
σεν· ᵇκαὶ ἀπολωλὼς ἦν,‖ καὶ εὑρέθη. Καὶ ἤρξαντο εὐ-
again; and ²lost ¹was, and is found. And they began to
φραίνεσθαι. 25 ᷈Ἦν.δὲ ὁ.υἱός.αὐτοῦ ὁ πρεσβύτερος ἐν ἀγρῷ·
be merry.   And ⁵was ¹his ²son ³the ⁴elder in a field;
καὶ ὡς ἐρχόμενος ἤγγισεν τῇ οἰκίᾳ ἤκουσεν συμφωνίας
and as coming [up] he drew near to the house he heard music
καὶ χορῶν· 26 καὶ προσκαλεσάμενος ἕνα τῶν.παίδων.ᶜαὐτοῦ,‖
and dancing. And having called near one of his servants,
ἐπυνθάνετο τί ᵈ εἴη ταῦτα. 27 ὁ.δὲ εἶπεν αὐτῷ, Ὅτι
he inquired what might be these things. And he said to him,
ὁ.ἀδελφός.σου ἥκει· καὶ ἔθυσεν ὁ.πατήρ.σου τὸν μόσχον τὸν
Thy brother is come, and ³killed ¹thy ²father the ²calf

ᵖ ἔφη τ.   ᵠ περισσεύονται Trᴀ.   ʳ + ὧδε here GTrᴀ.   ˢ + ὧδε here Lᴛ.   ᵗ — καὶ
GLTTrᴀw.   ᵛ αὐτοῦ LTTr.   ʷ ὁ υἱὸς αὐτῷ ᴀ.   ˣ — καὶ LTTrᴀ.   ʸ + Ταχὺ Quickly
L[Tr]ᴀ.   ᶻ — τὴν (read a robe) LTTrᴀ.   ᵃ φέρετε bring TTrᴀ.   ᵇ ἦν ἀπολωλὼς LTTrᴀ;
ἀπολ. ἦν w.   ᶜ — αὐτοῦ (read the servants) EGLTTrᴀw.   ᵈ + ἂν [L]Tr[ᴀ].

σιτευτόν, ὅτι ὑγιαίνοντα αὐτὸν ἀπέλαβεν. 28 Ὠργίσθη
ᵃfattened, because safe and well ³him ¹he ²received. ²He ³was ⁴angry

δὲ καὶ οὐκ.ἤθελεν εἰσελθεῖν. ὁ ᵉοὖνᵘ πατὴρ αὐτοῦ
¹but and was not willing to go in. ²The ¹therefore father of him

ἐξελθὼν παρεκάλει αὐτόν. 29 ὁ.δὲ ἀποκριθεὶς εἶπεν τῷ.πα-
having gone besought him. But he answering said to ²fa-

τρί, Ἰδού, τοσαῦτα ἔτη δουλεύω σοι καὶ οὐδέποτε ἐντολήν
ther[¹his], Lo, so many years I serve thee and never ⁴commandment

σου παρῆλθον, καὶ ἐμοὶ οὐδέποτε ἔδωκας ἔριφον ἵνα μετὰ
³thy ¹transgressed ²I, and to me never didst thou give a kid that with

τῶν.φίλων.μου εὐφρανθῶ· 30 ὅτε.δὲ ὁ.υἱός.σου οὗτος
my friends I might make merry; but when ²thy ³son ¹this

ὁ καταφαγών σου τὸν βίον μετὰ ᵍ πορνῶν ἦλθεν, ἔθυσας
who devoured thy living with harlots came, thou didst kill

αὐτῷ τὸν ʰμόσχον τὸν σιτευτόν.ᵘ 31 ὁ.δὲ εἶπεν αὐτῷ, Τέκνον,
for him the ²calf ¹fattened. But he said to him, Child,

σὺ πάντοτε μετ᾽ ἐμοῦ εἶ, καὶ πάντα τὰ ἐμὰ σά ἐστιν.
thou always with me art, and all that [is] mine ²thine ¹is.

32 εὐφρανθῆναι.δὲ καὶ χαρῆναι ἔδει, ὅτι ὁ.ἀδελφός.σου
But to make merry and rejoice was becoming, because ²thy ³brother

οὗτος νεκρὸς ἦν, καὶ ⁱἀνέζησεν·ᵘ ᵏκαὶᵘ ἀπολωλὼς ˡἦν,ᵘ καὶ
¹this ⁵dead ⁴was, and is alive again; and ²lost ¹was, and

εὑρέθη.
is found.

16 Ἔλεγεν.δὲ καὶ πρὸς τοὺς.μαθητὰς.ᵐαὐτοῦ,ᵘ Ἄνθρωπός
And he said also to his disciples, A ³man

τις ἦν πλούσιος, ὃς εἶχεν οἰκονόμον· καὶ οὗτος διε-
¹certain ⁴there ⁵was ²rich, who had a steward, and he was

βλήθη αὐτῷ ὡς διασκορπίζων τὰ.ὑπάρχοντα.αὐτοῦ. 2 καὶ
accused to him as wasting his goods. And

φωνήσας αὐτὸν εἶπεν αὐτῷ, Τί τοῦτο ἀκούω περὶ
having called him he said to him, What [is] this I hear concerning

σοῦ; ἀπόδος τὸν λόγον τῆς.οἰκονομίας.σου· οὐ.γὰρ.ⁿδυνήσῃᵘ
thee? render the account of thy stewardship; for thou canst not

ἔτι οἰκονομεῖν. 3 Εἶπεν.δὲ ἐν ἑαυτῷ ὁ οἰκονόμος,
any longer be steward. And ³said ⁴within ⁵himself ¹the ²steward,

Τί ποιήσω, ὅτι ὁ.κύριός.μου ἀφαιρεῖται τὴν οἰκονομίαν ἀπ᾽
What shall I do, for my lord is taking away the stewardship from

ἐμοῦ; σκάπτειν οὐκ.ἰσχύω, ἐπαιτεῖν αἰσχύνομαι. 4 ἔγνων
me? To dig I am unable; to beg I am ashamed. I know

τί ποιήσω, ἵνα, ὅταν μετασταθῶ ᵒ τῆς οἰκονο-
what I will do, that, when I shall have been removed [from] the steward-

μίας, δέξωνταί με εἰς τοὺς.οἴκους.ᵖαὐτῶν.ᵘ 5 Καὶ προσ-
ship, they may receive me into their houses. And call-

καλεσάμενος ἕνα ἕκαστον τῶν ᑫχρεωφειλετῶνᵘ τοῦ κυρίου
ing to [him] ²one ¹each of the debtors ³lord

ἑαυτοῦ ἔλεγεν τῷ πρώτῳ, Πόσον ὀφείλεις τῷ.κυρίῳ.μου;
¹of ²his he said to the first, How much owest thou to my lord?

6 Ὁ.δὲ εἶπεν, Ἑκατὸν βάτους ἐλαίου. ʳΚαὶᵘ εἶπεν αὐτῷ,
And he said, A hundred baths of oil. And he said to him,

Δέξαι σου ˢτὸ γράμμαᵘ καὶ καθίσας ταχέως γράψον πεντή-
Take thy bill and sitting down quickly write fifty.

---

e δὲ but LTTrA.   f + αὐτοῦ his LTrA.   g + τῶν the LTrA.   h σιτευτὸν μόσχον TTrA.
i ἔζησεν is alive TTrA.   k — καὶ T.   l — ἦν (read ἀπολωλὼς had been lost) LTTrA.
m — αὐτοῦ (read the disciples) TTrA.   n δύνῃ TTrA.   o + ἐκ from [L]TTrA.   p ἑαυτῶν
TTrA.   q χρεοφειλετῶν LTTrA.   r ὁ δὲ LTTrA.   s τὰ γράμματα bills LTTrA.

---

received him safe and sound. 28 And he was angry, and would not go in : therefore came his father out, and intreated him. 29 And he answering said to his father, Lo, these many years do I serve thee, neither transgressed I at any time thy commandment : and yet thou never gavest me a kid, that I might make merry with my friends : 30 but as soon as this thy son was come, which hath devoured thy living with harlots, thou hast killed for him the fatted calf. 31 And he said unto him, Son, thou art ever with me, and all that I have is thine. 32 It was meet that we should make merry, and be glad : for this thy brother was dead, and is alive again ; and was lost, and is found.

XVI. And he said also unto his disciples, There was a certain rich man, which had a steward ; and the same was accused unto him that he had wasted his goods. 2 And he called him, and said unto him, How is it that I hear this of thee? give an account of thy stewardship ; for thou mayest be no longer steward. 3 Then the steward said within himself, What shall I do? for my lord taketh away from me the stewardship : I cannot dig ; to beg I am ashamed. 4 I am resolved what to do, that, when I am put out of the stewardship, they may receive me into their houses. 5 So he called every one of his lord's debtors unto him, and said unto the first, How much owest thou unto my lord? 6 And he said, An hundred measures of oil. And he said unto him, Take thy bill, and sit down quickly, and write fifty. 7 Then said he to another, And how much owest thou? And he said, An hundred measures of wheat. And he said unto him, Take thy bill, and write fourscore. 8 And the lord commended the unjust steward, because he had done wisely: for the children of this world are in their generation wiser than the children of light. 9 And I say unto you, Make to yourselves friends of the mammon of unrighteousness; that, when ye fail, they may receive you into everlasting habitations. 10 He that is faithful in that which is least is faithful also in much: and he that is unjust in the least is unjust also in much. 11 If therefore ye have not been faithful in the unrighteous mammon, who will commit to your trust the true riches? 12 And if ye have not been faithful in that which is another man's, who shall give you that which is your own? 13 No servant can serve two masters: for either he will hate the one, and love the other; or else he will hold to the one, and despise the other. Ye cannot serve God and mammon.

κοντα. 7 Ἔπειτα ἑτέρῳ εἶπεν, Σὺ δὲ πόσον ὀφείλεις;
Then   to another he said,   And thou how much owest thou?

Ὁ δὲ εἶπεν, Ἑκατὸν κόρους σίτου. ‡Καὶ‖ λέγει αὐτῷ, Δέξαι
And he said,   A hundred   cors   of wheat.   And he says to him,   Take

σου ᵘτὸ γράμμα‖ καὶ γράψον ὀγδοήκοντα. 8 Καὶ ἐπήνεσεν
thy   bill   and write   eighty.   And ᵇpraised

ὁ κύριος τὸν οἰκονόμον τῆς ἀδικίας   ὅτι φρονίμως ἐποίη-
¹the ²lord the   ²steward   ¹unrighteous because prudently   he had

σεν· ὅτι οἱ υἱοὶ τοῦ αἰῶνος τούτου φρονιμώτεροι ὑπὲρ τοὺς
done.   For the sons   of this age   ⁶more ⁷prudent ⁸than ⁹the

υἱοὺς τοῦ φωτὸς εἰς τὴν γενεὰν τὴν ἑαυτῶν εἰσιν. 9 ᵛΚἀγὼ‖
¹⁰sons ¹¹of ¹²the ¹⁴light ²in   ⁵generation ³their ⁴own   ¹are.   And I

ὑμῖν λέγω, ʷΠοιήσατε ἑαυτοῖς‖ φίλους ἐκ τοῦ μαμωνᾶ τῆς
to you say,   Make   to yourselves friends by the   mammon

ἀδικίας, ἵνα ὅταν ˣἐκλίπητε‖   δέξωνται ὑμᾶς εἰς τὰς
of unrighteousness, that when   ye fail   they may receive you into the

αἰωνίους σκηνάςʸ. 10 Ὁ   πιστὸς ἐν   ἐλαχίστῳ καὶ
eternal   dwellings.   He that [is] faithful in [the]   least   also

ἐν πολλῷ πιστός ἐστιν· καὶ ὁ ἐν   ἐλαχίστῳ   ἄδικος
in much   faithful is;   and he that in [the]   least   [is] unrighteous

καὶ ἐν πολλῷ ἄδικός ἐστιν. 11 εἰ οὖν ἐν τῷ ἀδικῳ
also in much   unrighteous is.   If therefore in the unrighteous

μαμωνᾷ πιστοὶ οὐκ ἐγένεσθε, τὸ ἀληθινὸν τίς ὑμῖν πιστεύσει;
mammon   faithful ye have not been, the   true   who to you will entrust?

12 καὶ εἰ ἐν τῷ   ἀλλοτρίῳ πιστοὶ οὐκ ἐγένεσθε, τὸ
And if in that which [is] another's   faithful ye have not been,

ὑμέτερον τίς ᶻὑμῖν δώσει;‖ 13 Οὐδεὶς οἰκέτης δύναται δυσὶ
your own who to you will give?   No   servant is able two

κυρίοις δουλεύειν· ἢ γὰρ τὸν ἕνα μισήσει, καὶ τὸν ἕτερον
lords   to serve,   for either the one he will hate, and the other

ἀγαπήσει· ἢ ἑνὸς ἀνθέξεται, καὶ τοῦ ἑτέρου καταφρονήσει.
he will love; or one he will hold to, and the other   he will despise.

οὐ δύνασθε θεῷ δουλεύειν καὶ μαμωνᾷ.
Ye are unable ²God ¹to ²serve and mammon.

14 And the Pharisees also, who were covetous, heard all these things: and they derided him. 15 And he said unto them, Ye are they which justify yourselves before men; but God knoweth your hearts: for that which is highly esteemed among men is abomination in the sight of God. 16 The law and the prophets were until John: since that time the kingdom of God is preached, and every man presseth into it. 17 And it is easier for heaven and earth to pass, than one tittle of the law to fail. 18 Whosoever putteth away his wife, and marrieth another, committeth

14 ᵃἭκουον δὲ ταῦτα πάντα ᵃκαὶ‖ οἱ Φαρισαῖοι, φιλάρ-
And ⁴heard ²these ³things ¹all   also the Pharisees,   ²covet-

γυροι ὑπάρχοντες, καὶ ἐξεμυκτήριζον αὐτόν. 15 καὶ εἶπεν
ous   ¹being,   and   they derided   him.   And he said

αὐτοῖς, Ὑμεῖς ἐστε οἱ δικαιοῦντες ἑαυτοὺς ἐνώπιον τῶν
to them,   Ye   are they who   justify   themselves   before

ἀνθρώπων, ὁ δὲ θεὸς γινώσκει τὰς καρδίας ὑμῶν· ὅτι τὸ ἐν
men,   but God   knows   your hearts;   for that ⁴among

ἀνθρώποις ὑψηλὸν   βδέλυγμα ἐνώπιον τοῦ θεοῦ ᵇἐστιν.‖
⁵men   ¹highly ²thought ³of an abomination   before   God   is.

16 Ὁ νόμος καὶ οἱ προφῆται ᶜἕως‖ ᵈἸωάννου·‖ ἀπὸ
The law   and the prophets [were] until   John: from

τότε ἡ βασιλεία τοῦ θεοῦ εὐαγγελίζεται, καὶ πᾶς εἰς
that time the kingdom   of God   is announced,   and everyone ²into

αὐτὴν βιάζεται. 17 Εὐκοπώτερον δέ ἐστιν   τὸν οὐρανὸν καὶ
³it   ¹forces.   But easier   it is [for] the heaven and

τὴν γῆν παρελθεῖν, ἢ τοῦ νόμου μίαν κεραίαν πεσεῖν.
the earth to pass away, than of the law   one   tittle   to fail.

18 Πᾶς ὁ ἀπολύων τὴν γυναῖκα αὐτοῦ καὶ γαμῶν ἑτέραν
Everyone who puts away   his wife   and marries another

ᵗ — καὶ LTTrA.   ᵘ τὰ γράμματα bills LTTrA.   ᵛ καὶ ἐγὼ TTrA.   ʷ ἑαυτοῖς ποιήσατε TA.
ˣ ἐκλίπῃ it shall fail LTTrA.   ʸ + [αὐτῶν] (read their eternal dwellings) L.   ᶻ δώσει
ὑμῖν Ttr.   ᵃ — καὶ TTr[A].   ᵇ — ἐστιν (read [is]) GLTTrAW.   ᶜ μέχρι TTiA.   ᵈ Ἰωάνου Tr.

μοιχεύει· καὶ ᵉπᾶς‖ ὁ ἀπολελυμένην ἀπὸ ἀνδρὸς
commits adultery; and everyone who ²her ³put ⁴away ⁵from ⁶a ⁷husband

γαμῶν μοιχεύει.
marries commits adultery.

19 Ἄνθρωπος.δέ τις ἦν πλούσιος, καὶ ἐνεδιδύσκετο
Now ²a ⁶man ⁴certain ¹there ²was ⁵rich, and he was clothed in

πορφύραν καὶ βύσσον, εὐφραινόμενος καθ᾽.ἡμέραν λαμπρῶς.
-purple and fine linen, making good cheer daily in splendour.

20 πτωχὸς.δέ τις ᶠἦν‖ ὀνόματι Λάζαρος, ᵍὃς‖ ἐβέβλητο
And a ²poor ³man ¹certain there was, by name Lazarus, who was laid

πρὸς τὸν.πυλῶνα.αὐτοῦ ʰἡλκωμένος,‖ 21 καὶ ἐπιθυμῶν χορ-
at his porch being full of sores, and desiring to be

‑ασθῆναι ἀπὸ ⁱτῶν ψιχίων τῶν‖ πιπτόντων ἀπὸ τῆς τραπέζης
satisfied from the crumbs which fell from the table

τοῦ πλουσίου· ἀλλὰ καὶ οἱ κύνες ἐρχόμενοι ᵏἀπέλειχον‖ τὰ
of the rich man; but even the dogs coming licked

ἕλκη.αὐτοῦ. 22 ἐγένετο.δέ ἀποθανεῖν τὸν πτωχόν, καὶ
his sores. And it came to pass ⁴died ¹the ²poor ³man, and

ἀπενεχθῆναι αὐτὸν ὑπὸ τῶν ἀγγέλων εἰς τὸν κόλπον ˡτοῦ‖
²was ³carried ⁴away ¹he by the angels into the bosom

Ἀβραάμ· ἀπέθανεν.δέ καὶ ὁ πλούσιος, καὶ ἐτάφη. 23 καὶ ἐν
of Abraham. And died also the rich man, and was buried. And in

τῷ ᾅδῃ ἐπάρας τοὺς ὀφθαλμοὺς.αὐτοῦ, ὑπάρχων ἐν βα-
the hades having lifted up his eyes, being in tor-

σάνοις, ὁρᾷ ᵐτὸν.‖ Ἀβραὰμ ἀπὸ.μακρόθεν, καὶ Λάζαρον ἐν
ments, he sees Abraham afar off, and Lazarus in

τοῖς.κόλποις.αὐτοῦ· 24 καὶ αὐτὸς φωνήσας εἶπεν, Πάτερ
his bosom. And he crying out said, Father

Ἀβραάμ, ἐλέησόν με, καὶ πέμψον Λάζαρον, ἵνα βάψῃ
Abraham, have compassion on me, and send Lazarus, that he may dip

τὸ ἄκρον τοῦ.δακτύλου.αὐτοῦ ὕδατος, καὶ καταψύξῃ τὴν γλῶσ-
the tip of his finger in water, and cool ⁴tongue

σάν μου· ὅτι ὀδυνῶμαι ἐν τῇ.φλογὶ.ταύτῃ. 25 Εἶπεν.δέ
¹my; for I am suffering in this flame. But ²said

Ἀβραάμ, Τέκνον, μνήσθητι ὅτι ἀπέλαβες ⁿσύ‖ τὰ
¹Abraham, Child, recollect that ²didst ³fully ⁴receive ¹thou

ἀγαθά.σου ἐν τῇ.ζωῇ.σου, καὶ Λάζαρος ὁμοίως τὰ.κακά·
thy good things in thy lifetime, and Lazarus likewise evil things.

νῦν.δέ ᵒὅδε‖ παρακαλεῖται, σὺ.δέ ὀδυνᾶσαι. 26 καὶ ᴾἐπὶ‖
But now he is comforted, and thou art suffering. And besides

πᾶσιν τούτοις, μεταξὺ ἡμῶν καὶ ὑμῶν χάσμα μέγα ἐστήρικ-
all these things, between us and you a ²chasm ¹great has been

ται, ὅπως οἱ θέλοντες διαβῆναι qἐντεῦθεν‖ πρὸς ὑμᾶς
fixed, so that they who desire to pass hence to you

μὴ.δύνωνται, μηδέ ʳοἱ‖ ἐκεῖθεν πρὸς ἡμᾶς διαπερῶσιν.
are unable, nor ²they ⁴thence ³us ¹can ²pass

27 Εἶπεν.δέ, Ἐρωτῶ ˢοῦν σε,‖ πάτερ, ἵνα πέμψῃς
And he said, I beseech ²then ¹thee, father, that.thou wouldest send

αὐτὸν εἰς τὸν οἶκον τοῦ.πατρός.μου, 28 ἔχω.γὰρ πέντε ἀδελ-
him to the house of my father, for I have five bro-

φούς· ὅπως διαμαρτύρηται αὐτοῖς, ἵνα μὴ καὶ αὐτοὶ
thers, so that he may earnestly testify to them, that ⁴not ²also ¹they

---

e — πᾶς LTTrA.   f — ἦν [L]TTrA.   g — ὃς [L]TTrA.   h εἱλκωμένος LTTrAW.
i — ψιχίων τῶν (read τῶν that which) [L]TA ; [τῶν ψιχίων] τῶν Tr.   k ἐπέλειχον LTTrA.
l — τοῦ GLTTrAW.   m — τὸν LTTrA.   n — σύ (read ἀπέλαβες thou didst fully receive) GTTrA.
o ὧδε here (read παρακ. he is comforted) LTTrAW.   P ἐν before τ.   q ἔνθεν GLTTrAW.
r — οἱ (read διαπ. can they pass) ᴸ[A].   s σε οὖν LTrAW.

to this place of torment. 29 Abraham saith unto him, They have Moses and the prophets ; let them hear them. 30 And he said, Nay, father Abraham : but if one went unto them from the dead, they will repent. 31 And he said unto him, If they hear not Moses and the prophets, neither will they be persuaded, though one rose from the dead.

ἔλθωσιν εἰς τὸν.τόπον.τοῦτον τῆς βασάνου· 29 λέγει· ʸαὐτῷ‖
may come to   this place   of torment.   ²Says ³to ⁴him

'Αβραάμ, Ἔχουσιν ʷΜωσέα‖ καὶ τοὺς προφήτας· ἀκουσάτωσαν
¹Abraham,   They have   Moses   and the   prophets :   let them hear

αὐτῶν.· 30 'Ο.δὲ εἶπεν, Οὐχί, πάτερ 'Αβραάμ· ἀλλ᾽ ἐάν τις
them.   But he said,   No,   father   Abraham,   but if   one

ἀπὸ νεκρῶν πορευθῇ πρὸς αὐτούς, μετανοήσουσιν.
from [the] dead   should go   to   them,   they will repent.

31 Εἶπεν.δὲ αὐτῷ, Εἰ ˣΜωσέως‖ καὶ τῶν προφητῶν οὐκ
And he said to him, If   Moses   and the   prophets   ³not

ἀκούουσιν, ʸοὐδὲ‖ ἐάν τις ἐκ νεκρῶν ἀναστῇ πεισθή-
¹they ²hear,   not even   if   one from [the] dead   should rise   will they

σονται.
be persuaded.

XVII. Then said he unto the disciples, It is impossible but that offences will come : but woe unto him, through whom they come! 2 It were better for him that a millstone were hanged about his neck, and he cast into the sea, than that he should offend one of these little ones. 3 Take heed to yourselves: If thy brother trespass against thee, rebuke him; and if he repent, forgive him. 4 And if he trespass against thee seven times in a day, and seven times in a day turn again to thee, saying, I repent ; thou shalt forgive him.

17 Εἶπεν.δὲ πρὸς τοὺς μαθητάς,ᶻ 'Ανένδεκτόν ἐστιν ᵃτοῦ‖
And he said   to   the disciples,   Impossible   it is   that

ᵇμὴ.ἐλθεῖν‖ τὰ σκάνδαλα·‖ ᶜοὐαὶ.δὲ‖ δι᾽ οὗ ἔρχεται.
²should ³not ⁴come   ¹offences,   but woe [to him] by whom they come.

2 λυσιτελεῖ αὐτῷ εἰ ᵈμύλος ὀνικὸς‖ περίκειται περὶ
It is profitable for him if   a millstone   turned by an ass   is put   about

τὸν.τράχηλον.αὐτοῦ, καὶ ἔρριπται εἰς τὴν θάλασσαν, ἢ ἵνα
his neck,   and he is cast into the   sea,   than that

σκανδαλίσῃ ᵉἕνα τῶν.μικρῶν.τούτων.‖ 3 προσέχετε
he should cause ⁶to ⁷offend ¹one   ²of ³these ⁴little ⁵ones.   Take heed

ἑαυτοῖς. ἐὰν.ᶠδὲ‖ ἁμάρτῃ ᵍεἰς σὲ‖ ὁ.ἀδελφός.σου, ἐπι-
to yourselves :   and if ⁴sin ⁵against ᵉthee   ¹thy ²brother,   re-

τίμησον αὐτῷ· καὶ ἐὰν μετανοήσῃ, ἄφες αὐτῷ. 4 καὶ ἐὰν
buke   him ;   and   if he should repent,   forgive him.   And if

ἑπτάκις τῆς ἡμέρας ʰἁμάρτῃ‖ εἰς σέ, καὶ ⁱ ἑπτάκις ᵏτῆς
seven times in the   day   he should sin against thee, and seven times in the

ἡμέρας‖ ἐπιστρέψῃ ˡἐπὶ σέ,‖ λέγων, Μετανοῶ, ἀφήσεις
day   should return to thee, saying,   I repent,   thou shalt forgive

αὐτῷ.
him.

---

5 And the apostles said unto the Lord, Increase our faith. 6 And the Lord said, If ye had faith as a grain of mustard seed, ye might say unto this sycamine tree, Be thou plucked up by the root, and be thou planted in the sea; and it should obey you. 7 But which of you, having a servant plowing or feeding cattle, will say unto him by and by, when he is come from the field, Go and sit . own to meat? 8 And will not rather say unto him, Make ready wherewith I may sup, and gird thyself, and serve me, till I have eaten and drunk-

5 Καὶ ᵐεἶπον‖ οἱ ἀπόστολοι τῷ κυρίῳ, Πρόσθες ἡμῖν
And   said ³the   apostles   to the Lord,   Give more ²to ³us

πίστιν. 6 Εἶπεν.δὲ ὁ κύριος, Εἰ ⁿεἴχετε‖ πίστιν, ὡς κόκκον
¹faith.   But ³said ¹the ²Lord,   If   ye had   faith,   as a grain

σινάπεως, ἐλέγετε.ἂν τῇ.συκαμίνῳ.ταύτῃ, 'Εκριζώθητι, καὶ
of mustard,   ye might say   to this sycamine tree,   Be thou rooted up, and

φυτεύθητι ἐν τῇ θαλάσσῃ· καὶ ὑπήκουσεν.ἂν ὑμῖν. 7 Τίς.δὲ
be thou planted in the   sea,   and it would obey   you.   But which

ᵒἐξ‖ ὑμῶν δοῦλον ἔχων ἀροτριῶντα ἢ ποιμαίνοντα, ὃς
of   you ²a ³bondman ¹having   ploughing   or   shepherding,   who

εἰσελθόντι ἐκ τοῦ ἀγροῦ ἐρεῖ ᵖ �q εὐθέως, Παρελθὼν‖
[to him] come in out of the   field will say immediately,   Having come

ʳἀνάπεσαι·‖ 8 ἀλλ᾽ οὐχὶ.ἐρεῖ αὐτῷ, 'Ετοίμασον τί
recline [at table]?   but   will he not say to him,   Prepare   what

δειπνήσω, καὶ περιζωσάμενος διακόνει μοι, ἕως φάγω καὶ
I may sup on,   and   girding thyself about   serve   me,   while   I eat   and

---

ᵗ + δὲ (read but Abraham) LTTrAW.   ᵛ — αὐτῷ T[TrA].   ʷ Μωῦσέα LTTrAW.   ˣ Μωϋσέως LTTrAW.   ʸ οὐδ᾽ LTrA.   ᶻ + αὐτοῦ (read his disciples) LTTrAW.   ᵃ — τοῦ E.
ᵇ τὰ σκάνδαλα μὴ ἐλθεῖν TTrA.   ᶜ πλὴν οὐαὶ yet woe Ltr.   ᵈ λίθος μυλικὸς a millstone
LTTrA.   ᵉ τῶν μικρῶν τούτων ἕνα TTrA.   ᶠ — δὲ and LTTrA.   ᵍ — εἰς σὲ LTTrA.
ʰ ἁμαρτήσῃ LTTrAW.   ⁱ + [ἐὰν] if L.   ᵏ — τῆς ἡμέρας LTTrA.   ˡ — ἐπὶ σέ G ; πρὸς σὲ
LTTrAW.   ᵐ εἶπαν LTTrA.   ⁿ ἔχετε ye have TTrA.   ᵒ [ἐξ] Tr.   ᵖ + αὐτῷ to him [L]TTrA.
�q Εὐθέως παρελθὼν (read Having come immediately recline) LTTrA.   ʳ ἀνάπεσε LTTrAW.

πίω· καὶ μετὰ ταῦτα φάγεσαι καὶ πίεσαι σύ; 9. Μὴ
drink; and after these things ²shalt ³eat ⁴and ⁵drink ¹thou?

ᵇχάριν.ἔχει‖ τῷ.δούλῳ.ᵗἐκείνῳ‖ ὅτι ἐποίησεν τὰ διατδ-
Is ⁹he thankful to that bondman because he did the things com-

χθέντα ᵛαὐτῷ‖; ʷοὐ.δοκῶ.‖ 10 οὕτως καὶ ὑμεῖς, ὅταν
manded him? I judge not. Thus also ye, when

ποιήσητε πάντα.τὰ διαταχθέντα ὑμῖν, λέγετε, ˣʸὍτι‖ δοῦ-
ye may have done all things commanded you, say, ²Bond-

λοι ἀχρεῖοί ἐσμεν· ᵍὍτι‖ ὃ ὠφείλομεν ποιῆσαι πεποιή-
men ¹unprofitable are we, for that which we were bound to do we have

καμεν.
done.

11 Καὶ ἐγένετο ἐν τῷ.πορεύεσθαι.ᶻαὐτὸν‖ εἰς Ἱερουσαλὴμ
And it came to pass in his going up to Jerusalem

καὶ αὐτὸς διήρχετο διὰ ᵃμέσου‖ ᵇΣαμαρείας‖ καὶ Γαλι-
that he passed through [the] midst of Samaria and Gali-

λαίας. 12 καὶ εἰσερχομένου.αὐτοῦ εἴς τινα κώμην ᶜἀπήντησαν‖
lee. And on his entering into a certain village ⁴met

ᵈαὐτῷ‖ δέκα λεπροὶ ἄνδρες, οἳ ἔστησαν πόρρωθεν· 13 καὶ
⁵him ¹ten ²leprous ³men, who stood afar off. And

αὐτοὶ ἦραν φωνὴν λέγοντες, Ἰησοῦ, ἐπιστάτα, ἐλέη-
they lifted up [their] voice saying, Jesus, Master, have compas-

σον ἡμᾶς. 14 Καὶ ἰδὼν εἶπεν αὐτοῖς, Πορευθέντες
sion on us. And seeing [them] he said to them, Having gone

ἐπιδείξατε ἑαυτοὺς τοῖς ἱερεῦσιν. Καὶ ἐγένετο ἐν τῷ ὑπά-
shew yourselves to the priests. And it came to pass in ²go-

γειν αὐτοὺς ἐκαθαρίσθησαν. 15 εἷς.δὲ ἐξ αὐτῶν, ἰδὼν ὅτι
ing ¹their they were cleansed. And one of them, seeing that

ἰάθη, ὑπέστρεψεν, μετὰ φωνῆς μεγάλης δοξάζων τὸν
he was healed, turned back, with a ²voice ¹loud glorifying

θεόν· 16 καὶ ἔπεσεν ἐπὶ πρόσωπον παρὰ τοὺς.πόδας.αὐτοῦ,
God, and fell on [his] face at his feet,

εὐχαριστῶν αὐτῷ· καὶ αὐτὸς ἦν ᵉΣαμαρείτης.‖ 17 ἀποκριθεὶς
giving thanks to him: and he was a Samaritan. ²Answering

δὲ ὁ Ἰησοῦς εἶπεν, ᶠΟὐχὶ‖ οἱ δέκα ἐκαθαρίσθησαν; οἱ.ᵍδὲ
¹and Jesus said, ²Not ³the ¹ten ¹were cleansed? but ³the

ἐννέα ποῦ; 18 οὐχ.εὑρέθησαν ὑποστρέψαντες δοῦναι
⁴nine ¹where [²are]? Were there not found [any] returning to give

δόξαν τῷ θεῷ εἰ.μὴ ὁ.ἀλλογενὴς.οὗτος; 19 Καὶ εἶπεν αὐτῷ,
glory to God except this stranger? And he said to him,

Ἀναστὰς πορεύου· ἡ.πίστις.σου σέσωκέν σε.
Having risen up go forth; thy faith has cured thee.

20 Ἐπερωτηθεὶς.δὲ ὑπὸ τῶν Φαρισαίων, πότε ἔρχεται ἡ
And having been asked by the Pharisees, when is coming the

βασιλεία τοῦ θεοῦ, ἀπεκρίθη αὐτοῖς καὶ εἶπεν, Οὐκ.ἔρχεται ἡ
kingdom of God, he answered them and said, ⁵Comes ⁶not ¹the

βασιλεία τοῦ θεοῦ μετὰ παρατηρήσεως· 21 οὐδὲ ἐροῦσιν,
²kingdom ³of ⁴God with observation; nor shall they say,

Ἰδοὺ ὧδε, ἢ ʰἰδοὺ‖ ἐκεῖ· ἰδοὺ.γάρ, ἡ βασιλεία.τοῦ.θεοῦ ἐντὸς
Lo here, or Lo there; for lo, the kingdom of God in the midst

ὑμῶν ἐστίν. 22 Εἶπεν.δὲ πρὸς τοὺς μαθητάς,ⁱ Ἐλεύσονται
of you is. And he said to the disciples, ²Will ³come

---

9 Doth he thank that
servant because he did
the things that were
commanded him? I
trow not. 10 So likewise
ye, when ye shall have
done all those things
which are commanded
you, say, We are un-
profitable servants: we
have done that which
was our duty to do.

11 And it came to
pass, as he went to Je-
rusalem, that he passed
through the midst of
Samaria and Galilee.
12 And as he entered
into a certain village,
there met him ten men
that were lepers, which
stood afar off: 13 and
they lifted up their
voices, and said, Jesus,
Master, have mercy on
us. 14 And when he saw
them, he said unto
them, Go shew your-
selves unto the priests.
And it came to pass,
that, as they went,
they were cleansed.
15 And one of them,
when he saw that he
was healed, turned
back, and with a loud
voice glorified God,
16 and fell down on
his face at his feet, giving him thanks: and
he was a Samaritan.
17 And Jesus answer-
ing said, Were there
not ten cleansed? but
where are the nine?
18 There are not found
that returned to give
glory to God, save this
stranger. 19 And he
said unto him, Arise,
go thy way: thy faith
hath made thee whole.
20 And when he was
demanded of the Pha-
risees, when the king-
dom of God should
come, he answered
them and said, The
kingdom of God com-
eth not with observa-
tion: 21 neither shall
they say, Lo here! or,
lo there! for, behold,
the kingdom of God is
within you. 22 And he
said unto the disciples,
The days will come,

ˢ — ἔχει χάριν LTTrA. ᵗ — ἐκείνῳ (read the bondman) LTTrA. ᵛ — αὐτῷ GLTTrAW.
ʷ — οὐ δοκῶ [L]TTrA. ˣ — ἢ — ὅτι L. ʸ — ὅτι LTTrAW. ᶻ — αὐτὸν (read in the going up)
T[TrA]. ᵃ μέσον LTTrA. ᵇ Σαμαρίας T. ᶜ ὑπήντησαν T. ᵈ — αὐτῷ (read [him]) L[TrA].
ᵉ Σαμαρίτης T. ᶠ οὐχ LTr. ᵍ — δὲ but LT[Tr]. ʰ — ἰδοὺ TA. ⁱ + αὐτοῦ (read his
disciples) L.

when ye shall desire to see one of the days of the Son of man, and ye shall not see it. 23 And they shall say to you, See here; or, see there: go not after them, nor follow them. 24 For as the lightning, that lighteneth out of the one part under heaven, shineth unto the other part under heaven; so shall also the Son of man be in his day. 25 But first must he suffer many things, and be rejected of this generation. 26 And as it was in the days of Noe, so shall it be also in the days of the Son of man. 27 They did eat, they drank, they married wives, they were given in marriage, until the day that Noe entered into the ark, and the flood came, and destroyed them all. 28 Likewise also as it was in the days of Lot: they did eat, they drank, they bought, they sold, they planted, they builded; 29 but the same day that Lot went out of Sodom it rained fire and brimstone from heaven, and destroyed them all. 30 Even thus shall it be in the day when the Son of man is revealed. 31 In that day, he which shall be upon the housetop, and his stuff in the house, let him not come down to take it away: and he that is in the field, let him likewise not return back. 32 Remember Lot's wife. 33 Whosoever shall seek to save his life shall lose it; and whosoever shall lose his life shall preserve it. 34 I tell you, in that night there shall be two men in one bed; the one shall be taken, and the other shall be left. 35 Two women shall be grinding together; the one shall be taken, and the other

ἡμέραι, ὅτε ἐπιθυμήσετε μίαν τῶν ἡμερῶν τοῦ υἱοῦ τοῦ ἀν-
days, when ye will desire one of the days of the Son of

θρώπου ἰδεῖν, καὶ οὐκ ὄψεσθε. 23 καὶ ἐροῦσιν ὑμῖν, Ἰδοὺ
man to see, and shall not see [it]. And they will say to you, Lo of

ᵏὧδε, ἢ ἰδοὺ ἐκεῖ·ǁ μὴ ἀπέλθητε μηδὲ διώξητε. 24 ὥσπερ γὰρ
here, or Lo there; go not forth nor follow. For as

ἡ ἀστραπὴ ˡἡǁ ἀστράπτουσα ἐκ τῆς ᵐὑπ'ǁ οὐρανὸν
the lightning which lightens from the [one end] under heaven

εἰς τὴν ὑπ' οὐρανὸν λάμπει, οὕτως ἔσται ⁿκαὶǁ ὁ
to the [other end] under heaven shines, thus will be also the

υἱὸς τοῦ ἀνθρώπου °ἐν τῇ ἡμέρᾳ αὐτοῦ.ǁ 25 πρῶτον δὲ δεῖ
Son of man in his day. But first it behoves

αὐτὸν πολλὰ παθεῖν, καὶ ἀποδοκιμασθῆναι ἀπὸ τῆς γενεᾶς
him many things to suffer, and to be rejected of ²generation

ταύτης. 26 καὶ καθὼς ἐγένετο ἐν ταῖς ἡμέραις ᴾτοῦǁ Νῶε,
¹this. And as it came to pass in the days of Noe

οὕτως ἔσται καὶ ἐν ταῖς ἡμέραις �q τοῦǁ υἱοῦ τοῦ ἀνθρώπου.
thus shall it be also in the days of the Son of man.

27 ἤσθιον, ἔπινον, ἐγάμουν, ʳἐξεγα-
They were eating, they were drinking, they were marrying, they were being

μίζοντο,ǁ ἄχρι ἧς ἡμέρας εἰσῆλθεν Νῶε εἰς τὴν κιβωτόν,
given in marriage, until the day ¹entered ¹Noe into the ark,

καὶ ἦλθεν ὁ κατακλυσμὸς καὶ ἀπώλεσεν ˢἅπαντας.ǁ 28 ὁμοίως
and came the flood and destroyed all. ²In ³like ⁴manner

ᵗκαὶ ὡς‖ ἐγένετο ἐν ταῖς ἡμέραις Λώτ· ἤσθιον, ἔπι-
¹and as it came to pass in the days of Lot; they were eating, they were

νον, ἠγόραζον, ἐπώλουν, ἐφύτευον, ᾠκοδό-
drinking, they were buying, they were selling, they were planting, they were

μουν· 29 ᾗ δὲ ἡμέρᾳ ἐξῆλθεν Λώτ ἀπὸ Σοδόμων ἔβρεξεν
building; but on the day ²went ³out ¹Lot from Sodom it rained

πῦρ καὶ θεῖον ἀπ' οὐρανοῦ καὶ ἀπώλεσεν ˢἅπαντας·ǁ 30 κα-
fire and sulphur from heaven and destroyed all. In

τὰ ᵛταῦταǁ ἔσται ᾗ ἡμέρᾳ ὁ υἱὸς τοῦ ἀνθρώπου ἀποκαλύπ-
this way shall it be in the day the Son of man is revealed.

τεται. 31 ἐν ἐκείνῃ τῇ ἡμέρᾳ ὃς ἔσται ἐπὶ τοῦ δώματος, καὶ
In that day [he] who shall be on the housetop, and

τὰ σκεύη αὐτοῦ ἐν τῇ οἰκίᾳ, μὴ καταβάτω ἆραι αὐτά·
his goods in the house, let him not come down to take away them;

καὶ ὁ ἐν ʷτῷǁ ἀγρῷ ὁμοίως μὴ ἐπιστρεψάτω εἰς τὰ ὀπίσω.
and he in the field likewise let him not return to the things behind.

32 μνημονεύετε τῆς γυναικὸς Λώτ. 33 ὃς ἐὰν ζητήσῃ τὴν
Remember the wife of Lot. Whoever may seek

ψυχὴν αὐτοῦ ˣσῶσαι,ǁ ἀπολέσει αὐτήν· καὶ ὃς ʸἐὰνǁ ᶻἀπολέσῃǁ
his life to save, shall lose it; and whoever may lose

ᵃαὐτήν,ǁ ζωογονήσει αὐτήν. 34 λέγω ὑμῖν, ταύτῃ τῇ νυκτὶ
it, shall preserve it. I say to you, In that night

ἔσονται δύο ἐπὶ κλίνης ᵇμιᾶς·ǁ ᶜὁǁ εἷς ᵈπαραληφθήσε-
there shall be two [men] upon ²bed ¹one; the one shall be ta-

ται,ǁ καὶ ὁ ἕτερος ἀφεθήσεται. 35 ᵉδύο ἔσονταιǁ ἀλή-
ken, and the other shall be left. Two [women] shall be grind-

---

ᵏ ἐκεῖ, ἢ (— ἢ TTr) ἰδοὺ ὧδε TTrA.   ˡ — ἢ T[Tr]A.   ᵐ ὑπὸ τὸν under the LTTrA.   ⁿ — καὶ
G[L]TTrAW.   ° — ἐν τῇ ἡμέρᾳ αὐτοῦ L.   ᴾ — τοῦ GLTTrAW.   q — τοῦ E.   ʳ ἐγαμίζοντο
LTTrA.   ˢ πάντας LTTA.   ᵗ καθὼς according to TTrA.   ᵛ ταὐτὰ in the same way GLW.
τὰ αὐτὰ in the same way TTrA.   ʷ — τῷ (read a field) TTrA.   ˣ περιποιήσασθαι to gain
TTrA.   ʸ ἂν TrA.   ᶻ ἀπολέσει shall lose T.   ᵃ — αὐτήν (read [it]) [L]TTrA.   ᵇ [μιᾶς] L.
ᶜ — ὁ GLTTrAW.   ᵈ παραλημφθήσεται LTTrA.   ᵉ ἔσονται δύο LTTrA.

θουσαι ἐπὶ τὸ.αὐτό· ¹μία ⁱπαραληφθήσεται,‖ ʰκαὶ ἡ‖ ἑτέρα
ing together; one shall be taken, and the other

ἀφεθήσεται. ¹ 37 Καὶ ἀποκριθέντες λέγουσιν αὐτῷ, Ποῦ,
shall be left. And answering they say to him, Where,

κύριε; Ὁ.δὲ εἶπεν αὐτοῖς, Ὅπου τὸ σῶμα ἐκεῖ ʲσυναχθή-
Lord? And he said to them, Where the body [is] there will be gathered

σονται οἱ ἀετοί.‖
together the eagles

18 Ἔλεγεν.δὲ ᵏκαὶ‖ παραβολὴν αὐτοῖς πρὸς.τὸ δεῖν
And he spoke also a parable to them to the purport that it behoves

πάντοτε προσεύχεσθαι, ¹ καὶ μὴ ᵐἐκκακεῖν,‖ 2 λέγων,
²always ³to ⁴pray ['them] and not to faint, saying,

Κριτής τις ἦν ἔν τινι πόλει, τὸν θεὸν μὴ φοβούμενος
A ²judge ¹certain there was in ²certain ¹a city, God not fearing

καὶ ἄνθρωπον μὴ ἐντρεπόμενος. 3 χήρα.δὲ ⁿ ἦν ἐν τῇ
and man not respecting. And a widow there was in

πόλει.ἐκείνῃ, καὶ ἤρχετο πρὸς αὐτόν, λέγουσα, Ἐκδίκησόν
that city, and she was coming to him, saying, Avenge

με ἀπὸ τοῦ.ἀντιδίκου.μου. 4 Καὶ οὐκ.ᵒἠθέλησεν‖ ἐπὶ χρόνον·
me of mine adverse party. And he would not for a time;

μετὰ.ᴾδὲ.ταῦτα‖ εἶπεν ἐν ἑαυτῷ, Εἰ καὶ τὸν θεὸν οὐ.φοβοῦμαι
but afterwards he said within himself, If even God I fear not

ᵠκαὶ· ἄνθρωπον οὐκ‖ ἐντρέπομαι· 5 διά.γε τὸ παρέχειν μοι
and man ²not ¹respect, yet because ²causes ⁴me

κόπον τὴν.χήραν.ταύτην ἐκδικήσω αὐτήν, ἵνα.μὴ εἰς.τέλος
³trouble ¹this ²widow I will avenge her, lest perpetually

ἐρχομένη ὑπωπιάζῃ με. 6 Εἶπεν.δὲ ὁ κύριος, Ἀκούσατε τί
coming she harass me. And said the Lord, Hear what

ὁ κριτὴς τῆς ἀδικίας λέγει· 7 ὁ.δὲ.θεὸς οὐ.μὴ ʳποιήσει‖ τὴν
the ²judge ¹unrighteous says. And ³God ²not ¹shall execute the

ἐκδίκησιν τῶν.ἐκλεκτῶν.αὐτοῦ τῶν βοώντων ˢπρὸς αὐτὸν‖
avenging of his elect who cry to him

ἡμέρας καὶ νυκτός, καὶ ᵗμακροθυμῶν‖ ἐπ' αὐτοῖς; 8 λέγω
day and night, and [is] being patient over them? I say

ὑμῖν, ὅτι ποιήσει τὴν ἐκδίκησιν αὐτῶν ἐν.τάχει. πλὴν
to you, that he will execute the avenging of them speedily. Nevertheless

ὁ υἱὸς τοῦ ἀνθρώπου ἐλθὼν ἆρα εὑρήσει τὴν πίστιν
the Son of man having come ³indeed ¹will ²he find faith

ἐπὶ τῆς γῆς;
on the earth?

9 Εἶπεν.δὲ ᵛκαὶ‖ πρός τινας τοὺς πεποιθότας ἐφ' ἑαυτοῖς
And he spoke also to some who trusted in themselves

ὅτι εἰσὶν δίκαιοι καὶ ἐξουθενοῦντας τοὺς λοιποὺς τὴν παρα-
that they are righteous and despised the rest ²para-

βολὴν ταύτην. 10 Ἄνθρωποι δύο ἀνέβησαν εἰς τὸ ἱερὸν
ble ¹this· ²Men ¹two went up into the temple

προσεύξασθαι· ʷὁ‖ εἷς Φαρισαῖος καὶ ὁ ἕτερος τελώνης· 11 ὁ
to pray; the one a Pharisee and the other a tax-gatherer. The

Φαρισαῖος σταθεὶς ˣπρὸς ἑαυτὸν ταῦτα‖ προσηύχετο, Ὁ θεός,
Pharisee standing, with himself thus was praying, God,

left. 36 Two men shall
be in the field; the one
shall be taken, and she
other left. 37 And they
answered and said un-
to him, Where, Lord?
And he said unto them,
Wheresoever the body
is, thither will the
eagles be gathered to-
gether.

XVIII. And he spake
a parable unto them
to this end, that men
ought always to pray,
and not to faint; 2 say-
ing, There was in a city
a judge, which feared
not God, neither re-
garded man: 3 and
there was a widow in
that city; and she came
unto him, saying, A-
venge me of mine
adversary. 4 And
he would not for a
while : but afterward
he said within himself,
Though I fear not God,
nor regard man; 5 yet
because this widow
troubleth me, I will a-
venge her, lest by her
continual coming she
weary me. 6 And the
Lord said, Hear what
the unjust judge saith.
7 And shall not God
avenge his own elect,
which cry day and
night unto him, though
he bear long with them?
8 I tell you that he will
avenge them speedily.
Nevertheless when the
Son of man cometh,
shall he find faith on
the earth?

9 And he spake this
parable unto them
which trusted in them-
selves that they were
righteous, and despised
others: 10 Two men
went up into the tem-
ple to pray ; the one a
Pharisee, and the other
a publican. 11 The Pha-
risee stood and prayed
thus with himself,
God, I thank thee, that

ᶠ + ἡ the EGLT[Tr]A. ᵍ παραλημφθήσεται LTTrA. ʰ ἡ δὲ TTrA. ⁱ + verse 36, Δύο
ἔσονται ἐν τῷ ἀγρῷ· ὁ εἷς παραληφθήσεται, καὶ ὁ ἕτερος ἀφεθήσεται, Two [men] shall be in the
field: the one shall be taken, and the other left E. ʲ συναχθήσονται [καὶ also] [καὶ ἀετοί L;
καὶ οἱ ἀετοὶ ἐπισυναχθήσονται TTrA. ᵏ — καὶ LT[TrA]. ¹ + αὐτοὺς them LTTrAW.
ᵐ ἐγκακεῖν LTrAW ; ἐνκακεῖν T. ⁿ + τις certain E. ᵒ ἤθελεν LTTrAW. ᴾ ταῦτα δὲ TrA.
ᵠ οὐδὲ ἄνθρωπον nor man LTTr. ʳ ποιήσῃ LTTrA. ˢ αὐτῷ TTrA. ᵗ μακροθυμεῖ is patient
LTTrA ᵛ [καὶ] L. ʷ — ὁ LTrA. ˣ ταῦτα πρὸς ἑαυτὸν Tr ; — πρὸς ἑαυτὸν T.

I am not as other men *are*, extortioners, unjust, adulterers, or even as this publican. 12 I fast twice in the week, I give tithes of all that I possess. 13 And the publican, standing afar off, would not lift up so much as *his* eyes unto heaven, but smote upon his breast, saying, God be merciful to me a sinner. 14 I tell you, this man went down to his house justified *rather* than the other: for every one that exalteth himself shall be abased; and he that humbleth himself shall be exalted.

15 And they brought unto him also infants, that he would touch them: but when *his* disciples saw *it*, they rebuked them. 16 But Jesus called them *unto him*, and said, Suffer little children to come unto me, and forbid them not: for of such is the kingdom of God. 17 Verily I say unto you, Whosoever shall not receive the kingdom of God as a little child shall in no wise enter therein.

18 And a certain ruler asked him, saying, Good Master, what shall I do to inherit eternal life? 19 And Jesus said unto him, Why callest thou me good? none is good, save one, *that is*, God. 20 Thou knowest the commandments, Do not commit adultery, Do not kill, Do not steal, Do not bear false witness, Honour thy father and thy mother. 21 And he said, All these have I kept from my youth up. 22 Now when Jesus heard these things, he said unto him, Yet lackest thou one thing: sell all that thou hast, and distribute unto the poor, and thou shalt have treasure in heaven:

εὐχαριστῶ σοι ὅτι οὐκ εἰμὶ ᵞὥσπερ‖ οἱ λοιποὶ τῶν ἀνθρώπων,
I thank thee that I am not as, the rest of men,

ἅρπαγες, ἄδικοι, μοιχοί, ἢ καὶ ὡς οὗτος ὁ τελώνης. 12 νη-
rapacious, unrighteous, adulterers, or even as this tax-gatherer. I

στεύω δὶς τοῦ σαββάτου, ᶻἀποδεκατῶ‖ πάντα ὅσα κτῶμαι.
fast twice in the week, I tithe all things as many as I gain.

13 ᵃΚαὶ ὁ‖ τελώνης μακρόθεν ἑστὼς οὐκ ἤθελεν οὐδὲ τοὺς
And the tax-gatherer afar off standing would not even the

ὀφθαλμοὺς ᵇεἰς τὸν οὐρανὸν ἐπᾶραι‖· ἀλλ' ἔτυπτεν ᶜεἰς‖ τὸ
eyes to the heaven lift up, but was striking upon

στῆθος ᵈαὐτοῦ,‖ λέγων, Ὁ θεός, ἱλάσθητί μοι τῷ ἁμαρτωλῷ.
his breast, saying, God, be propitious to me the sinner.

14 Λέγω ὑμῖν, ᵉκατέβη οὗτος δεδικαιωμένος εἰς τὸν οἶκον
I say to you, Went down this one justified to ²house

αὐτοῦ ᶠἢ ἐκεῖνος.‖ ὅτι πᾶς ὁ ὑψῶν ἑαυτὸν ταπεινω-
¹his rather than that. For everyone that exalts himself shall be

θήσεται ᵍοὐδὲ‖ ταπεινῶν ἑαυτὸν ὑψωθήσεται.
humbled; and he that humbles himself shall be exalted.

15 Προσέφερον δὲ αὐτῷ καὶ τὰ βρέφη, ἵνα αὐτῶν ἅπτη-
And they brought to him also the babes, that them he might

ται· ἰδόντες δὲ οἱ μαθηταὶ ʰἐπετίμησαν‖ αὐτοῖς. 16 ὁ δὲ
touch; but having seen [it] the disciples rebuked them. But

Ἰησοῦς ⁱπροσκαλεσάμενος αὐτὰ εἶπεν,‖ Ἄφετε τὰ παιδία
Jesus having called ²to [³him] ¹them said, Suffer the little children

ἔρχεσθαι πρός με, καὶ μὴ κωλύετε αὐτά· τῶν γὰρ τοιούτων
to come to me, and do not forbid them; for of such

ἐστὶν ἡ βασιλεία τοῦ θεοῦ. 17 ἀμὴν λέγω ὑμῖν, ὃς ᵏἐὰν‖ μὴ
is the kingdom of God. Verily I say to you, Whoever ²not

δέξηται τὴν βασιλείαν τοῦ θεοῦ ὡς παιδίον οὐ μὴ εἰσέλθῃ
¹shall receive the kingdom of God as a little child in no wise shall enter

εἰς αὐτήν.
into it.

18 Καὶ ἐπηρώτησέν τις αὐτὸν ἄρχων, λέγων, Διδάσκαλε
And ⁴asked ¹a ²certain ⁵him ³ruler, saying, ²Teacher

ἀγαθέ, τί ποιήσας ζωὴν αἰώνιον κληρονομήσω; 19 Εἶπεν
¹good, what ³having ⁴done life eternal shall I inherit? ³Said

δὲ αὐτῷ ὁ Ἰησοῦς, Τί με λέγεις ἀγαθόν; οὐδεὶς ἀγαθὸς
¹but ⁴to ⁵him ²Jesus, Why me callest thou good? No one [is] good

εἰ μὴ εἷς, ˡὁ‖ θεός. 20 τὰς ἐντολὰς οἶδας· Μὴ μοι-
except one, God. The commandments thou knowest: Thou shouldest not

χεύσῃς· μὴ φονεύσῃς· μὴ κλέψῃς·
commit adultery; thou shouldest not commit murder; thou shouldest not steal;

μὴ ψευδομαρτυρήσῃς· τίμα τὸν πατέρα σου καὶ τὴν
thou shouldest not bear false witness; honour thy father and

μητέρα ᵐσου.‖ 21 Ὁ δὲ εἶπεν, Ταῦτα πάντα ⁿἐφυλαξάμην‖ ἐκ
thy mother. And he said, ²These ¹all have I kept from

νεότητος ᵒμου.‖ 22 Ἀκούσας δὲ ᴾταῦτα‖ ὁ Ἰησοῦς εἶπεν
²youth ¹my. And having heard these things Jesus said

αὐτῷ, Ἔτι ἕν σοι λείπει· πάντα ὅσα ἔχεις πώλη-
to him, Yet one thing to thee is lacking; all as much as thou hast sell,

σον, καὶ ᑫδιάδος‖ πτωχοῖς, καὶ ἕξεις θησαυρὸν ἐν ʳοὐ-
and distribute to [the] poor, and thou shalt have treasure in hea-

---

ᵞ ὡς LTr.   ᶻ ἀποδεκατεύω T.   ᵃ ὁ δὲ T.   ᵇ ἐπᾶραι εἰς τὸν οὐρανόν TTrA.   ᶜ — εἰς LTTr[A].
ᵈ ἑαυτοῦ TrA.   ᵉ + [ὅτι] that L.   ᶠ παρ' ἐκεῖνον LTrA; ἢ γὰρ ἐκεῖνος GTW.   ᵍ καὶ ὁ L.
ʰ ἐπετίμων LTTrA.   ⁱ προσεκαλέσατο αὐτὰ λέγων called them to [him] saying TTrA.
ᵏ ἂν I.TTrA.   ˡ — ὁ TA.   ᵐ — σου thy LTrAW.   ⁿ ἐφύλαξα LTTrA.   ᵒ — μου T[Tr]A.
ᴾ — ταῦτα LTTrA.   ᑫ δὸς give L.   ʳ οὐρανοῖς T; τοῖς οὐρανοῖς the heavens LTrA.

ρανῷ·¹¹ καὶ δεῦρο ἀκολούθει μοι.ˌ 23 Ὁ.δὲ ἀκούσας ταῦτα
ven, and come follow me. But he having heard these things

περίλυπος ˢἐγένετο·¹¹ ἦν.γὰρ πλούσιος σφόδρα. 24 Ἰδὼν.δὲ
very sorrowful became, for he was ²rich ¹very. But ²seeing

αὐτὸν ὁ Ἰησοῦς ᵗπερίλυπον γενόμενον¹¹ εἶπεν, Πῶς δυσκό-
³him¹ Jesus ⁶very⁷sorrowful ⁴having ⁵become said, How diffi-

λως οἱ τὰ χρήματα ἔχοντες ᵛεἰσελεύσονται εἰς τὴν βασιλείαν
cultly those ²riches ¹having shall enter into the kingdom

τοῦ.θεοῦ.¹¹ 25 Εὐκοπώτερον.γάρ ἐστιν κάμηλον διὰ ʷτρυμαλιᾶς
of God. For easier it is a camel through an eye

ῥαφίδος¹¹ ˣεἰσελθεῖν¹¹ ἢ πλούσιον εἰς τὴν βασιλείαν τοῦ θεοῦ
of a needle to enter than a rich man into the kingdom of God

εἰσελθεῖν. 26 ʸΕἶπον¹¹.δὲ οἱ ἀκούσαντες, Καὶ τίς δύναται
to enter. And said those who heard, ²Then ¹who is able

σωθῆναι; 27 Ὁ.δὲ εἶπεν, Τὰ ἀδύνατα παρὰ ἀνθρώποις
to be saved? But he said, The things impossible with men

δυνατά ᶻἐστιν παρὰ τῷ θεῷ.¹¹ 28 Εἶπεν.δὲ ᵃὁ¹¹ Πέτρος, Ἰδού,
²possible ¹are with God. And ²said ¹Peter, Lo,

ἡμεῖς ᵇἀφήκαμεν πάντα καὶ¹¹ ἠκολουθήσαμέν σοι. 29 Ὁ.δὲ
we left all and followed thee. And he

εἶπεν αὐτοῖς, Ἀμὴν λέγω ὑμῖν, ᶜὅτι¹¹ οὐδείς ἐστιν ὃς ἀφῆκεν
said to them, Verily I say to you, That no one there is who has left

οἰκίαν ᵈἢ γονεῖς ἢ ἀδελφοὺς ἢ γυναῖκα¹¹ ἢ τέκνα ᵉἕνεκεν¹¹
house or parents or brethren or wife or children for the sake of

τῆς βασιλείας τοῦ θεοῦ, 30 ὃς ᶠοὐ¹¹ μὴ.ᵍἀπολάβῃ¹¹ πολ-
the kingdom of God, who shall not receive mani-

λαπλασίονα ἐν τῷ.καιρῷ.τούτῳ, καὶ ἐν τῷ αἰῶνι τῷ.ἐρχομένῳ
fold more in this time, and in the age that is coming

ζωὴν αἰώνιον.
life eternal.

31 Παραλαβὼν.δὲ ᵗτοὺς δώδεκα εἶπεν πρὸς αὐτούς,
And having taken to [him] the twelve he said to them,

Ἰδού, ἀναβαίνομεν εἰς ʰἹεροσόλυμα,¹¹ καὶ τελεσθήσεται
Behold, we go up to Jerusalem, and ³shall ⁴be ⁵accomplished

πάντα τὰ γεγραμμένα διὰ τῶν προφητῶν τῷ υἱῷ τοῦ
¹all ²things which have been written by the prophets about the Son

ἀνθρώπου. 32 παραδοθήσεται.γὰρ τοῖς ἔθνεσιν, καὶ ἐμπαι-
of man; for he will be delivered up to the Gentiles, and will be

χθήσεται καὶ ὑβρισθήσεται καὶ ἐμπτυσθήσεται. 33 καὶ μα-
mocked and will be insulted and will be spit upon. And having

στιγώσαντες ἀποκτενοῦσιν αὐτόν· καὶ τῇ ἡμέρᾳ τῇ τρίτῃ
scourged they will kill him; and on the ⁴day ¹the ²third

ἀναστήσεται. 34 Καὶ αὐτοὶ οὐδὲν τούτων συνῆκαν, καὶ
he will rise again. And they nothing of these things understood, and

ἦν τὸ.ῥῆμα.τοῦτο κεκρυμμένον ἀπ᾽ αὐτῶν, καὶ οὐκ.ἐγίνωσκον
³was ¹this ²saying hid from them, and they knew not

τὰ λεγόμενα.
that which was said.

35 Ἐγένετο.δὲ ἐν.τῷ.ἐγγίζειν.αὐτὸν εἰς ⁱἸεριχώ,¹¹ τυφλός
And it came to pass as he drew near to Jericho, a ²blind

τις ἐκάθητο παρὰ τὴν ὁδὸν ᵏπροσαιτῶν¹¹ 36 ἀκούσας
[³man] ¹certain sat beside the way begging. ²Having ³heard

and come, follow me.
23 And when he heard
this, he was very sor-
rowful: for he was very
rich. 24 And when Je-
sus saw that he was
very sorrowful, he said,
How hardly shall they
that have riches enter
into the kingdom of
God! 25 For it is easier
for a camel to go
through a needle's eye,
than for a rich man to
enter into the kingdom
of God. 26 And they
that heard it said,
Who then can be
saved? 27 And he said,
The things which are
impossible with men
are possible with God.
28 Then Peter said, Lo,
we have left all, and
followed thee. 29 And
he said unto them,
Verily I say unto you,
There is no man that
hath left house, or pa-
rents, or brethren, or
wife, or children, for
the kingdom of God's
sake, 30 who shall not
receive manifold more
in this present time,
and in the world to
come life everlasting.

31 Then he took unto
him the twelve, and
said unto them, Be-
hold, we go up to Jeru-
salem, and all things
that are written by
the prophets concern-
ing the Son of man
shall be accomplished.
32 For he shall be de-
livered unto the Gen-
tiles, and shall be
mocked, and spitefully
entreated, and spitted
on: 33 and they shall
scourge him, and put
him to death: and the
third day he shall rise
again. 34 And they un-
derstood none of these
things: and this saying
was hid from them,
neither knew they the
things which were spo-
ken.

35 And it came to
pass, that as he was
come nigh unto Je-
richo, a certain blind
man sat by the way
side begging: 36 and

ˢ.ἐγενήθη TTrA. ᵗ — περίλυπον γενόμενον T[Tr]A. ᵛ εἰς τὴν βασιλείαν τοῦ θεοῦ εἰσπό-
ρευονται TTrA. ʷ τρήματος βελόνης LTTrA. ˣ διελθεῖν to pass L. ʸ εἶπαν T. ᶻ παρὰ
τῷ (— τῷ L[Tr]) θεῷ ἐστιν LTTrA. ᵃ — ὁ T[A]W ᵇ ἀφέντες τὰ ἴδια having left our own
LTT A. ᶜ — ὅτι T. ᵈ ἢ γυναῖκα ἢ ἀδελφοὺς ἢ γονεῖς TA. ᵉ εινεκεν T. ᶠ οὐχὶ TA.
ᵍ λάβῃ Lₒ ʰ Ἱερουσαλήμ TTrA. ⁱ Ἱεριχώ T. ᵏ ἐπαιτῶν LTTrA.

hearing the multitude pass by, he asked what it meant. 37 And they told him, that Jesus of Nazareth passeth by. 38 And he cried, saying, Jesus, thou Son of David, have mercy on me. 39 And they which went before rebuked him, that he should hold his peace: but he cried so much the more, *Thou* Son of David, have mercy on me. 40 And Jesus stood, and commanded him to be brought unto him: and when he was come near, he asked him, 41 saying, What wilt thou that I shall do unto thee? And he said, Lord, that I may receive my sight. 42 And Jesus said unto him, Receive thy sight: thy faith hath saved thee. 43 And immediately he received his sight, and followed him, glorifying God: and all the people, when they saw *it*, gave praise unto God.

XIX. And *Jesus* entered and passed through Jericho. 2 And, behold, *there was* a man named Zacchæus, which was the chief among the publicans, and he was rich. 3 And he sought to see Jesus who he was; and could not for the press, because he was little of stature. 4 And he ran before, and climbed up into a sycomore tree to see him: for he was to pass that *way*. 5 And when Jesus came to the place, he looked up, and saw him, and said unto him, Zacchæus, make haste, and come down; for to day I must abide at thy house. 6 And he made haste, and came down, and received him joyfully. 7 And when they saw *it*, they all murmured, saying, That he was gone to be guest with a man that is a sinner. 8 And Zacchæus stood, and said unto the Lord; Behold, Lord, the half of my goods I give to the poor; and if I have

δὲ ὄχλου διαπορευομένου ἐπυνθάνετο τί¹ εἴη τοῦτο.
¹and a crowd   passing along   he asked   what ²might ³be ¹this.

37 ἀπήγγειλαν.δὲ αὐτῷ, Ὅτι Ἰησοῦς ὁ Ναζωραῖος παρέρχεται.
And they told   him,   Jesus   the Nazaræan   is passing by.

38 Καὶ ἐβόησεν λέγων, Ἰησοῦ, υἱὲ ᵐΔαβίδ,‖ ἐλέησόν με.
And he called out   saying, Jesus, Son of David, have pity on me.

39 Καὶ οἱ προάγοντες ἐπετίμων αὐτῷ ἵνα ⁿσιωπήσῃ·‖
And those going before rebuked   him   that he should be silent,

αὐτὸς.δὲ πολλῷ μᾶλλον ἔκραζεν, Υἱὲ ᵐΔαβίδ,‖ ἐλέησόν με.
but he   much   more   cried out, Son of David, have pity on me.

40 Σταθεὶς.δὲ °ὁ‖ Ἰησοῦς ἐκέλευσεν αὐτὸν ἀχθῆναι πρὸς
And ²having ³stopped ¹Jesus   commanded   him to be brought   to

αὐτόν· ἐγγίσαντος.δὲ αὐτοῦ ἐπηρώτησεν αὐτόν, 41 ᴾλέ-
him. And having drawn near   he   asked   him,   say-

γων,‖ Τί σοι θέλεις ποιήσω; Ὁ.δὲ εἶπεν, Κύριε, ἵνα
ing, What ⁶to ⁷thee ¹desirest ²thou ³I⁴shall ⁵do? And he said, Lord, that

ἀναβλέψω. 42 Καὶ ὁ Ἰησοῦς εἶπεν αὐτῷ, Ἀνάβλεψον·
I may receive sight.   And Jesus   said   to him, Receive sight:

ἡ.πίστις.σου σέσωκέν σε. 43 Καὶ παραχρῆμα ἀνέβλεψεν,
thy faith   hath healed thee. And immediately he received sight,

καὶ ἠκολούθει αὐτῷ, δοξάζων τὸν θεόν· καὶ πᾶς ὁ λαὸς
and followed   him, glorifying God. And all the people

ἰδὼν· ἔδωκεν αἶνον τῷ θεῷ.
having seen [it] gave praise to God.

19 Καὶ εἰσελθὼν διήρχετο.τὴν ᑫἸεριχώ·‖ 2 καὶ ἰδού,
And having entered he passed through Jericho. And behold,

ἀνὴρ ὀνόματι καλούμενος Ζακχαῖος, καὶ αὐτὸς ἦν ἀρχι-
a man by name   called   Zacchæus, and he was a chief

τελώνης, καὶ ʳοὗτος ἦν‖ πλούσιος· 3 καὶ ἐζήτει ἰδεῖν τὸν
tax-gatherer, and he was rich. And he was seeking to see

Ἰησοῦν τίς ἐστιν, καὶ οὐκ.ἠδύνατο ἀπὸ τοῦ ὄχλου, ὅτι τῇ
Jesus— who he is: and he was not able for the crowd, because

ἡλικίᾳ μικρὸς ἦν. 4 καὶ προδραμὼν ˢ ἔμπροσθεν ἀνέβη
in stature small he was. And having run forward before, he went up

ἐπὶ ᵗσυκομωραίαν,‖ ἵνα ἴδῃ αὐτόν· ὅτι ᵛδι'‖ ἐκείνης
into   a sycomore,   that he might see him, for by that [way]

ἤμελλεν διέρχεσθαι. 5 καὶ ὡς ἦλθεν ἐπὶ τὸν τόπον, ἀνα-
he was about to pass. And as he came to the place, look-

βλέψας ὁ Ἰησοῦς ʷεἶδεν αὐτόν, καὶ‖ εἶπεν πρὸς αὐτόν,
ing up Jesus   saw   him, and   said   to   him,

Ζακχαῖε, σπεύσας κατάβηθι· σήμερον.γὰρ ἐν τῷ.οἴκῳ.σου
Zacchæus, making haste come down, for to-day in thy house

δεῖ με μεῖναι. 6 Καὶ σπεύσας κατέβη καὶ ὑπεδέξατο
it behoveth me to remain. And making haste he came down and received

αὐτὸν χαίρων. 7 καὶ ἰδόντες ˣἅπαντες‖ διεγόγγυζον,
him rejoicing.   And having seen [it]   all   murmured,

λέγοντες, Ὅτι παρὰ ἁμαρτωλῷ ἀνδρὶ εἰσῆλθεν καταλῦσαι.
saying,   With   a sinful   man he has entered   to lodge.

8 Σταθεὶς.δὲ Ζακχαῖος εἶπεν πρὸς τὸν κύριον, Ἰδού, τὰ
But standing Zacchæus said   to   the Lord, Lo,

ἡμίση‖ ᶻτῶν.ὑπαρχόντων.μου,‖ κύριε, ᵃδίδωμι τοῖς πτωχοῖς·‖
half   of my possessions,   Lord, I give to the   poor,

---

1 + [ἂν] LTr.

ᵐ Δαυὶδ GW; Δαυείδ LTTrA.   ⁿ σιγήσῃ LTTrA.   ° [ὁ] Tr.
ᴾ — λέγων T[Tr]A.   ᑫ Ἱερειχώ T.   ʳ αὐτὸς (— ἦν [L]TrA) LTrA; — οὗτος T.   ˢ + εἰς
τὸ to the (*read* ἔμπρ. front,) T[A].   ᵗ συκομορέαν EGTTrA; συκομωρέαν L.   ᵛ — δι'
GLTTrAW.   ʷ — εἶδεν αὐτόν, καὶ TT[A].   ˣ πάντες LTTrAW.   ʸ ἡμίσεα L; ἡμίσειά TTrA.
ᶻ μου τῶν ὑπαρχόντων TTrA.   ᵃ τοῖς πτωχοῖς δίδωμι TTrA.

καὶ εἴ τινός τι ἐσυκοφάντησα, ἀποδίδωμι τετρα-
and if of anyone anything I took by false accusation, I return four-

πλοῦν. 9 Εἶπεν.δὲ πρὸς αὐτὸν ὁ Ἰησοῦς, "Ὅτι σήμερον σωτηρία
fold.   And ²said ³to ⁴him ¹Jesus,   To-day salvation

τῷ.οἴκῳ.τούτῳ ἐγένετο, καθότι καὶ αὐτὸς υἱὸς Ἀβραάμ
to this house is come, insomuch as also he a son of Abraham

ᵇἐστιν·ǁ 10 ἦλθεν.γὰρ ὁ υἱὸς τοῦ ἀνθρώπου ζητῆσαι καὶ σῶσαι
is :   for ⁵came ¹the ²Son ³of ⁴man to seek and to save

τὸ ἀπολωλός.
that which has been lost.

11 Ἀκουόντων.δὲ αὐτῶν ταῦτα, προσθεὶς εἶπεν παρα-
But as ²were ³hearing ¹they these things, adding he spoke a para-

βολήν, διὰ τὸ ἐγγὺς ᶜαὐτὸν εἶναι Ἱερουσαλήμ,ǁ καὶ δοκεῖν
ble, because ³near ¹he , ²was Jerusalem, and ²thought

αὐτοὺς ὅτι παραχρῆμα μέλλει ἡ βασιλεία τοῦ θεοῦ ἀνα-
¹they that immediately was about the kingdom of God to be

φαίνεσθαι· 12 εἶπεν οὖν, "Ἄνθρωπός τις εὐγενὴς ἐπορεύθη
manifested. He said therefore, A ²man ¹certain high born proceeded

εἰς χώραν μακράν, λαβεῖν ἑαυτῷ βασιλείαν καὶ ὑποστρέψαι.
to a ²country ¹distant, to receive for himself a kingdom and to return.

13 καλέσας.δὲ δέκα δούλους.ἑαυτοῦ ἔδωκεν αὐτοῖς δέκα μνᾶς,
And having called ten of his bondmen he gave to them ten minas,

καὶ εἶπεν πρὸς αὐτούς, Πραγματεύσασθε ᵈἕωςǁ ἔρχομαι.
and said to them, Trade until I come.

14 Οἱ.δὲ.πολῖται.αὐτοῦ ἐμίσουν αὐτόν, καὶ ἀπέστειλαν πρεσ-
But his citizens hated him and sent an em-

βείαν ὀπίσω αὐτοῦ, λέγοντες, Οὐ.θέλομεν τοῦτον
bassy after him, saying, We are unwilling [for] this [man]

βασιλεῦσαι ἐφ᾽ ἡμᾶς. 15 Καὶ ἐγένετο ἐν τῷ ἐπανελθεῖν
to reign over us. And it came to pass on ²coming ³back ⁴again

αὐτὸν λαβόντα τὴν βασιλείαν, καὶ εἶπεν φωνηθῆναι αὐτῷ.
¹his having received the kingdom, that he directed to be.called to him

τοὺς.δούλους.τούτους οἷς ᵉἔδωκενǁ τὸ ἀργύριον, ἵνα
these bondmen to whom he gave the money, in order that

ᶠγνῷǁ ᵍτίς.τί διεπραγματεύσατο.ǁ 16 παρεγένετο.δὲ ὁ
he might know what each had gained by trading. And came up the

πρῶτος, λέγων, Κύριε, ἡ.μνᾶ.σου ʰπροσειργάσατο δέκαǁ μνᾶς.
first, saying, Lord, thy mina has produced ten minas.

17 Καὶ εἶπεν αὐτῷ, ⁱΕὖ,ǁ ἀγαθὲ δοῦλε· ὅτι ἐν ἐλαχίστῳ
And he said to him, Well ! good bondman; because in a very little

πιστὸς ἐγένου, ἴσθι ἐξουσίαν ἔχων ἐπάνω δέκα πόλεων.
faithful thou wast, be thou ²authority ¹having over ten cities.

18 Καὶ ἦλθεν ὁ δεύτερος, λέγων, ᵏΚύριε, ἡ.μνᾶ.σουǁ ἐποίησεν
And came the second, saying, Lord, thy mina has made

πέντε μνᾶς. 19 Εἶπεν.δὲ καὶ τούτῳ, Καὶ σὺ ᶫγίνου ἐπάνωǁ
five minas. And he said also to this one, And ²thou ¹be over

πέντε πόλεων. 20 Καὶ ᵐ ἕτερος ἦλθεν, λέγων, Κύριε, ἰδοὺ ἡ
five cities. And another came, saying, Lord, behold

μνᾶ.σου, ἣν εἶχον ἀποκειμένην ἐν σουδαρίῳ· 21 ἐφοβούμην
thy mina, which I kept laid up in a handkerchief. ²I ³feared

γάρ σε, ὅτι ἄνθρωπος αὐστηρὸς εἶ· αἴρεις ὃ
¹for thee, because a man harsh thou art; thou takest up what

---

11 And as they heard these things, he added and spake a parable, because he was nigh to Jerusalem, and because they thought that the kingdom of God should immediately appear. 12 He said therefore, A certain nobleman went into a far country to receive for himself a kingdom, and to return. 13 And he called his ten servants, and delivered them ten pounds, and said unto them, Occupy till I come. 14 But his citizens hated him, and sent a message after him, saying, We will not have this man to reign over us. 15 And it came to pass, that when he was returned, having received the kingdom, then he commanded these servants to be called unto him, to whom he had given the money, that he might know how much every man had gained by trading. 16 Then came the first, saying, Lord, thy pound hath gained ten pounds. 17 And he said unto him, Well, thou good servant: because thou hast been faithful in a very little, have thou authority over ten cities. 18 And the second came, saying, Lord, thy pound hath gained five pounds. 19 And he said likewise to him, Be thou also over five cities. 20 And another came, saying, Lord, behold, here is thy pound, which I have kept laid up in a napkin : 21 for I feared thee, because thou art an austere man: thou takest up that

---

ᵇ — ἐστιν (read [is]) T.   ᶜ εἶναι αὐτὸν Ἱερουσαλὴμ L ; εἶναι Ἱερουσαλὴμ αὐτὸν TTrA.
ᵈ ἐν ᾧ LTTrA.   ᵉ δεδώκει he had given LTTrA.   ᶠ γνοῖ LTTrA.   ᵍ τί διεπραγματεύσαντο
what they had gained by trading TrA.   ʰ δέκα προσηργάσατο (προσειρ. Tr) LTTrA.   ⁱ εὖγε
well done LTTrA.   ᵏ ἡ μνᾶ σου, κύριε, TTrA.   ᶫ ἐπάνω γίνου TA.   ᵐ + ὁ the (ἕτερος
other) LTTrA.

thou layedst not down,
and reapest that thou
didst not sow. 22 And
he saith unto him, Out
of thine own mouth
will I judge thee, *thou*
wicked servant. Thou
knewest that I was an
austere man, taking
up that I laid not
down, and reaping
that I did not sow:
23 wherefore then gav-
est not thou my money
into the bank, that at
my coming I might
have required mine
own with usury?
24 And he said unto
them that stood by,
Take from him the
pound, and give *it* to
him that hath ten
pounds. 25 (And they
said unto him, Lord,
he hath ten pounds.)
26 For I say unto you,
That unto every one
which hath shall be
given; and from him
that hath not, even
that he hath shall be
taken away from him.
27 But those mine ene-
mies, which would not
that I should reign
over them, bring
hither, and slay *them*
before me.

28 And when he had
thus spoken, he went
before, ascending up
to Jerusalem. 29 And
it came to pass, when
he was come nigh to
Bethphage and Beth-
any, at the mount
called *the mount* of
Olives, he sent two of
his disciples, 30 say-
ing, Go ye into the
village over against
you; in the which at
your entering ye shall
find a colt tied, where-
on yet never man sat:
loose him, and bring
him hither. 31 And if
any man ask you, Why
do ye loose *him?* thus
shall ye say unto him,
Because the Lord hath
need of him. 32 And
they that were sent
went their way, and
found even as he had
said unto them. 33 And
as they were loosing
the colt, the owners
thereof said unto them,
Why loose ye the colt?
34 And they said, The
Lord hath need of him.
35 And they brought
him to Jesus: and they

οὐκ.ἔθηκας καὶ θερίζεις ὃ οὐκ.ἔσπειρας. 22 Λέγει
thou didst not lay down and thou reapest what thou didst not sow. [2]He [3]says

ⁿδὲ‖ αὐτῷ, Ἐκ τοῦ.στόματός.σου κρινῶ σε, πονηρὲ δοῦ-
¹but to him, Out of thy mouth I will judge thee, wicked bond-

λε. ἤδεις ὅτι ἐγὼ ἄνθρωπος αὐστηρός εἰμι, αἴρων ὃ
man : thou knewest that I [2]a [3]man ¹harsh ¹am, taking up what

οὐκ.ἔθηκα καὶ θερίζων ὃ οὐκ.ἔσπειρα. 23 καὶ °διατί‖
I did not lay down and reaping what I did not sow! and why

οὐκ.ἔδωκας ᴾτὸ.ἀργύριόν.μου‖ ἐπὶ �qτὴν‖.τράπεζαν, ʳκαὶ ἐγὼ‖
didst thou not give my money to the bank, that I

ἐλθὼν σὺν τόκῳ ἂν.ˢἔπραξα αὐτό‖; 24 Καὶ τοῖς παρε-
coming with interest might have required it? And to those stand-

στῶσιν εἶπεν, Ἄρατε ἀπ' αὐτοῦ τὴν μνᾶν, καὶ δότε τῷ
ing by he said, Take from him the mina, and give [it] to him who

τὰς δέκα μνᾶς ἔχοντι. 25 Καὶ ᵗεἶπον‖ αὐτῷ, Κύριε, ἔχει
the ten minas has. (And they said to him, Lord, he has

δέκα μνᾶς. 26 Λέγω.ᵛγὰρ‖ ὑμῖν, ὅτι παντὶ τῷ ἔχοντι δο-
ten minas.) For I say to you, that to everyone who has shall be-

θήσεται· ἀπὸ.δὲ τοῦ μὴ.ἔχοντος, καὶ ὃ ἔχει ἀρθήσεται
given; but from him who has not, even that which he has shall be taken

ʷἀπ' αὐτοῦ.‖ 27 Πλὴν τοὺς.ἐχθρούς.μου ˣἐκείνους‖ τοὺς
from him. Moreover ²mine ³enemies ¹those who

μὴ.θελήσαντάς με βασιλεῦσαι ἐπ' αὐτούς, ἀγάγετε ὧδε
were unwilling [for] me to reign over them, bring here

καὶ κατασφάξατε ʸ ἔμπροσθέν μου.
and slay [them] before me.

28 Καὶ εἰπὼν ταῦτα ἐπορεύετο ἔμπροσθεν, ἀναβαίνων
And having said these things he went on before, going up

εἰς Ἱεροσόλυμα· 29 Καὶ ἐγένετο ὡς ἤγγισεν εἰς Βηθ-
to Jerusalem. And it came to pass as he drew near to Beth-

φαγὴ καὶ ᶻΒηθανίαν,‖ πρὸς τὸ ὄρος τὸ καλούμενον ἐλαιῶν,
phage and Bethany, towards the mount called of Olives,

ἀπέστειλεν δύο τῶν.μαθητῶν.ᵃαὐτοῦ,‖ 30 ᵇεἰπών,‖ Ὑπάγετε εἰς
he sent two of his disciples, saying, Go into

τὴν κατέναντι κώμην· ἐν ᾗ εἰσπορευόμενοι εὑρήσετε
the ²opposite [³you] ¹village, in which entering ye will find

πῶλον δεδεμένον, ἐφ' ὃν οὐδεὶς πώποτε ἀνθρώπων ἐκάθισεν·
a colt tied, on which no one ³ever ⁴yet ¹of ²men sat:

ᶜλύσαντες αὐτὸν ἀγάγετε. 31 καὶ ἐάν τις ὑμᾶς ἐρωτᾷ,
having loosed it bring [it]. And if anyone ²you ¹ask,

ᵈΔιατί‖ λύετε; οὕτως ἐρεῖτε ᵉαὐτῷ,‖ Ὅτι ὁ κύριος
Why do ye loose [it]? thus shall ye say to him, Because the Lord

αὐτοῦ χρείαν ἔχει. 32 Ἀπελθόντες.δὲ οἱ ἀπεσταλμένοι
³of ⁴it ²need ¹has. And having departed those who had been sent

εὗρον καθὼς εἶπεν· αὐτοῖς. 33 λυόντων.δὲ.αὐτῶν τὸν πῶλον·
found as he had said to them. And on their loosing the colt

ᶠεἶπον‖ οἱ κύριοι αὐτοῦ πρὸς αὐτούς, Τί λύετε τὸν πῶλον;
⁵said ¹the ²masters ³of ⁴it to them, Why loose ye the colt?

34 Οἱ.δὲ ᶠεἶπον,‖ ᵍὉ κύριος αὐτοῦ χρείαν ἔχει. 35 Καὶ ἤγαγον
And they said, The Lord ³of ⁴it ²need ¹has. And they led

αὐτὸν πρὸς τὸν Ἰησοῦν· καὶ ʰἐπιρρίψαντες‖ ἱἑαυτῶν‖ τὰ ἱμά-
it to Jesus; and having cast their gar-

ⁿ — δὲ but ᴛᴛʀᴀ. ° διὰ τί ʟᴛᴛʀᴀ. ᴾ μου τὸ ἀργύριον ʟᴛᴛʀᴀ. q — τὴν (*read* a bank)
ʟᴛᴛʀᴀw. ʳ κἀγὼ ʟᴛᴛʀ. ˢ αὐτὸ ἔπραξα ʟᴛᴛʀᴀ. ᵗ εἶπαν ʟᴛᴛʀᴀ. ᵛ — γὰρ for [ʟ]ᴛ[ᴛʀ]ᴀ.
ʷ — ἀπ' αὐτοῦ [ʟ]ᴛᴀ. ˣ τούτους these ᴛᴛʀᴀ. ʸ + αὐτοὺς them ᴛᴛʀᴀ. ᶻ Βηθανιά ᴀ. ᵃ — αὐτοῦ (*read* the disciples) ᴛ[ᴛʀ]ᴀ. ᵇ λέγων ʟᴛʀ. ᶜ + καὶ and ᴛᴛʀᴀ. ᵈ διὰ τί ʟᴛᴛʀᴀ. ᵉ — αὐτῷ
[ʟ]ᴛᴛʀ[ᴀ]. ᶠ εἶπαν ʟᴛᴛʀᴀ. ᵍ + ὅτι because ʟᴛᴛʀᴀ. ʰ ἐπιρίψαντες ʟᴛᴛʀᴀ. ⁱ αὐτῶν ʟᴛᴛᴄᴀ.

τια· ἐπὶ τὸν πῶλον, ἐπεβίβασαν τὸν Ἰησοῦν. 36 πορευο-
ments on the　colt,　they put on [it]　Jesus.

μένου.δὲ.αὐτοῦ ὑπεστρώννυον τὰ.ἱμάτια.ᵏαὐτῶν‖ ἐν τῇ ὁδῷ.
And as he went　they were strewing　their garments　in the way.

37 Ἐγγίζοντος.δὲ.αὐτοῦ.ἤδη πρὸς τῇ καταβάσει τοῦ ὄρους
And as he drew near　already　at the　descent　of the mount

τῶν ἐλαιῶν ἤρξαντο ἅπαν τὸ πλῆθος τῶν μαθητῶν χαίρον-
of Olives　began　all　the multitude　of the. disciples,　rejoic-

τες αἰνεῖν τὸν.θεὸν φωνῇ μεγάλῃ περὶ ˡπασῶν‖ ὧν
ing, to praise　God with a ²voice ¹loud　for　all　⁵which

εἶδον　δυνάμεων. 38 λέγοντες, Εὐλογημένος ὁ
⁶they ⁷had ⁸seen [¹the] ²works ³of ⁴power,　saying,　Blessed　the

ᵐἐρχόμενος‖ βασιλεὺς ἐν ὀνόματι κυρίου· ⁿεἰρήνη ἐν
²coming　¹king ·　in [the] ₃name　of [the] Lord.　Peace　in

οὐρανῷ‖ καὶ δόξα ἐν ὑψίστοις. 39 Καί τινες τῶν Φαρισαίων
heaven　and glory in [the] highest.　And some of the Pharisees

ἀπὸ τοῦ/ὄχλου ᵒεἶπον‖ πρὸς αὐτόν, Διδάσκαλε, ἐπιτίμησον
from the crowd　said　to him,　Teacher,　rebuke

τοῖς.μαθηταῖς.σου. 40 Καὶ ἀποκριθεὶς εἶπεν ᴾαὐτοῖς,‖ Λέγω
thy disciples.　And ' answering　he said　to them,　I say

ὑμῖν, ᑫὅτι‖ ἐὰν οὗτοι ʳσιωπήσωσιν‖ οἱ λίθοι ˢκεκράξονται.‖
to you, that　if　these　should be silent　the stones　will cry out.

41 Καὶ ὡς ἤγγισεν, ἰδὼν τὴν πόλιν ἔκλαυσεν ἐπ᾽ ᵗαὐτῇ,‖
And　as he drew near, seeing the city　he wept　over ' it,

42 λέγων, Ὅτι εἰ ἔγνως καὶ σύ, ᵛκαί.γε‖ ἐν τῇ ἡμέρᾳ
saying,　If thou hadst known, even thou, even at least in　³day

ʷσου‖ ταύτῃ, τὰ πρὸς εἰρήνην ˣσου·‖ νῦν.δὲ ἐκρύβη ἀπὸ
²thy ¹this, the things for　²peace ¹thy: but now they are hid from

ὀφθαλμῶν.σου· 43 ὅτι ἥξουσιν ἡμέραι ἐπὶ σὲ καὶ ʸπεριβα-
thine eyes;　for ²shall ⁴come ¹days　upon thee that ³shall ⁴cast

λοῦσιν‖ οἱ.ἐχθροί.σου χάρακά σοι, καὶ περικυκλώσουσίν σε
⁵about　¹thine ²enemies ⁷a ⁸rampart ⁶thee, and　shall close around　thee

καὶ συνέξουσίν σε πάντοθεν, 44 καὶ ἐδαφιοῦσίν
and　keep in　thee on every side,　and shall level ²with ³the ⁴ground

σε καὶ τὰ.τέκνα.σου ἐν σοί, καὶ οὐκ.ἀφήσουσιν ᶻἐν σοὶ λίθον
¹thee and　thy children　in thee, and　shall not leave　in thee a stone

ἐπὶ λίθῳ·ᵃ‖ ἀνθ᾽.ὧν οὐκ.ἔγνως τὸν καιρὸν τῆς ἐπισκοπῆς
upon a stone, because thou knewest not the season　of ²visitation

σου.
¹thy.

45 Καὶ εἰσελθὼν εἰς τὸ ἱερὸν ἤρξατο ἐκβάλλειν τοὺς
And having entered　into the temple he began　to cast out　those

πωλοῦντας ᵇἐν αὐτῷ καὶ ἀγοράζοντας,‖ 46 λέγων αὐτοῖς,
selling　in　it　and　buying,　saying　to them,

Γέγραπται, ᵇΟ.οἶκός.μου οἶκος προσευχῆς ᶜἐστίν·‖ ὑμεῖς.δὲ
It has been written,　'My house　a house of prayer　is ;　but ye

αὐτὸν ἐποιήσατε σπήλαιον λῃστῶν. 47 Καὶ ἦν διδάσκων
it　have made　a den　of robbers.　And he was teaching

τὸ.καθ᾽.ἡμέραν ἐν τῷ ἱερῷ· οἱ.δὲ ἀρχιερεῖς καὶ οἱ γραμματεῖς
day by day　in the temple ; and the chief priests and the　scribes

cast their garments upon the colt, and they set Jesus thereon. 36 And as he went, they spread their clothes in the. way. 37 And when he was come nigh, even now at the descent of the mount of Olives, the whole multitude of the disciples began to rejoice and praise God with a loud voice for all the mighty works that they had seen ; 38 saying, Blessed be the King that cometh in the name of the Lord : peace in heaven, and glory in the highest. 39 And some of the Pharisees from among the multitude said unto him, Master, rebuke thy disciples. 40 And he answered and said unto them, I tell you that, if these should hold their peace, the stones would immediately cry out. 41 And when he was come near, he beheld the city, and wept over it, 42 saying, If thou hadst known, even thou, at least in this thy day, the things which belong unto thy peace ! but now they are hid from thine eyes. 43 For the days shall come upon thee, that thine enemies shall cast a trench about thee, and compass thee round, and keep thee in on every side, 44 and shall lay thee even with the ground, and thy children within thee ; and they shall not leave in thee one stone upon another; because thou knewest not the time of thy visitation.

45 And he went into the temple, and began to cast out them that sold therein, and them that bought; 46 saying unto them, It is written, My house is the house of prayer: but ye have made it a den of thieves. 47 And he taught daily in the temple. But the chief priests and the scribes

---

ᵏ ἑαυτῶν Tr. ˡ πάντων LTr. ᵐ — ἐρχόμενος T. ⁿ ἐν οὐρανῷ εἰρήνη TTrA. ᵒ εἶπαι LTrA. ᴾ — αὐτοῖς T[Tr]A. ᑫ [ὅτι] Tr. ʳ σιωπήσουσιν shall be silent LTrA. ˢ κράξουσιν TTrA. ᵗ αὐτήν LTrAW. ᵛ καίγε GT; — καί γε [L]Tr[A]. ʷ — σου LTr[A]. ˣ [σου] LTrA. ʸ παρεμβαλοῦσιν shall place near Tₗ ᶻ λίθον ἐπὶ λίθον (λίθῳ L) ἐν σοὶ LTrA. ᵃ — ἐν αὐτῷ καὶ ἀγοράζοντας TTrA. ᵇ + ὅτι L ; + καὶ ἔσται and shall be TTrA, ᶜ — ἐστίν TTrA.

and the chief of the people sought to destroy him, 48 and could not find what they might do: for all the people were very attentive to hear him.

ἐζήτουν αὐτὸν ἀπολέσαι, καὶ οἱ πρῶτοι τοῦ λαοῦ· 48 καὶ
[7]were [8]seeking [11]him [9]to [10]destroy, [1]and [2]the [3]first [4]of [5]the [6]people, and

οὐχ.^dεὕρισκον‖ τὸ τί ποιήσωσιν, ὁ.λαὸς.γὰρ ἅπας ^eἐξεκρέματο‖
found not   what they might do, for [2]the [3]people [1]all [5]were [6]hanging [7]on

αὐτοῦ ἀκούων.
[8]him [4]listening.

XX. And it came to pass, that on one of those days, as he taught the people in the temple, and preached the gospel, the chief priests and the scribes came upon *him* with the elders, 2 and spake unto him, saying, Tell us, by what authority doest thou these things? or who is he that gave thee this authority? 3 And he answered and said unto them, I will also ask you one thing; and answer me: 4 The baptism of John, was it from heaven, or of men? 5 And they reasoned with themselves, saying, If we shall say, From heaven; he will say, Why then believe ye him not? 6 But and if we say, Of men; all the people will stone us: for they be persuaded that John was a prophet. 7 And they answered, that they could not tell whence *it was.* 8 And Jesus said unto them, Neither tell I you by what authority I do these things.

20 Καὶ ἐγένετο ἐν μιᾷ τῶν.ἡμερῶν.^fἐκείνων,‖ διδάσκον-
And it came to pass on one   of those days,   as [2]was [3]teach-

τος αὐτοῦ τὸν λαὸν ἐν τῷ ἱερῷ καὶ εὐαγγελιζομένου,
ing [1]he   the people in the temple and announcing the glad tidings,

ἐπέστησαν οἱ ^gἀρχιερεῖς‖ καὶ οἱ γραμματεῖς σὺν τοῖς πρεσβυ-
came up the chief priests and the scribes   with the elders

τέροις, 2 καὶ ^hεἶπον‖ ⁱπρὸς αὐτόν, λέγοντες,‖ ^kΕἰπὲ‖ ἡμῖν ἐν
and spoke to him, saying,   Tell us by

ποίᾳ ἐξουσίᾳ ταῦτα ποιεῖς, ἢ τίς ἐστιν ὁ δούς σοι τὴν
what authority these things thou doest, or who it is who gave to thee

ἐξουσίαν.ταύτην; 3 Ἀποκριθεὶς.δὲ εἶπεν πρὸς αὐτούς, Ἐρω-
this authority?   And answering he said to them, [3]Will

τήσω ὑμᾶς κἀγὼ ^lἕνα‖ λόγον, καὶ εἴπατέ μοι· 4 Τὸ· βάπτισμα
[4]ask [5]you [1]I [2]also one thing, and tell me, The baptism

^m ⁿἸωάννου‖ ἐξ οὐρανοῦ ἦν ἢ ἐξ ἀνθρώπων; 5 Οἱ.δὲ
of John from heaven was it or from men?   And they

^oσυνελογίσαντο‖ πρὸς ἑαυτούς, λέγοντες, Ὅτι ἐὰν εἴπωμεν
reasoned   among themselves, saying, If we should say

Ἐξ οὐρανοῦ, ἐρεῖ ^p ^qΔιατί‖ ^rοὖν‖ οὐκ.ἐπιστεύσατε αὐτῷ;
From heaven, he will say Why then did ye not believe him?

6 ἐὰν.δὲ εἴπωμεν Ἐξ ἀνθρώπων, ^sπᾶς ὁ λαὸς‖ καταλιθάσει
But if we should say From men, all the people will stone

ἡμᾶς· πεπεισμένος.γάρ.ἐστιν ^tἸωάννην‖ προφήτην εἶναι.
us;   for they are persuaded [that] John [2]a [3]prophet [1]was.

7 Καὶ ἀπεκρίθησαν μὴ.εἰδέναι πόθεν. 8 καὶ ὁ Ἰησοῦς εἶπεν
And they answered they knew not whence. And Jesus said

αὐτοῖς, Οὐδὲ ἐγὼ λέγω ὑμῖν ἐν ποίᾳ ἐξουσίᾳ ταῦτα ποιῶ.
to them, Neither [2]I [1]tell you by what authority these things I do.

9 Then began he to speak to the people this parable; A certain man planted a vineyard, and let it forth to husbandmen, and went into a far country for a long time. 10 And at the season he sent a servant to the husbandmen, that they should give him of the fruit of the vineyard: but the husbandmen beat him, and sent *him* away empty. 11 And again he sent another servant: and they beat him also, and untreated *him* shamefully, and sent *him* away empty. 12 And again he sent a third: and

9 Ἤρξατο δὲ ^vπρὸς τὸν λαὸν λέγειν‖ τὴν.παραβολὴν.ταύτην·
And he began to the people to speak this parable:

^wἌνθρωπός ^xτις‖ ἐφύτευσεν ἀμπελῶνα,‖ καὶ ^yἐξέδοτο‖ αὐτὸν
A [2]man [1]certain planted a vineyard, and let out it

γεωργοῖς, καὶ ἀπεδήμησεν χρόνους.ἱκανούς. 10 καὶ ^zἐν‖
to husbandmen, and left the country for a long time. And in [the]

καιρῷ ἀπέστειλεν πρὸς τοὺς γεωργοὺς δοῦλον, ἵνα ἀπὸ τοῦ
season he sent to the husbandmen a bondman, that from the

καρποῦ τοῦ ἀμπελῶνος ^aδῶσιν‖ αὐτῷ· οἱ.δὲ γεωργοὶ
fruit of the vineyard they might give to him; but the husbandmen

^bδείραντες αὐτὸν ἐξαπέστειλαν‖ κενόν. 11 καὶ προσέθετο
having beat him sent [him] away empty. And he added

^cπέμψαι ἕτερον‖ δοῦλον· οἱ.δὲ κἀκεῖνον δείραντες καὶ ἀτι-
to send another bondman; but they [4]also [3]him [1]having [2]beat and dis-

μάσαντες ἐξαπέστειλαν κενόν. 12 καὶ προσέθετο ^dπέμψαι
honoured [him] sent [him] away empty. And he added to send

---

^d ηὕρισκον LTr.   ^e ἐξεκρέμετο τ.   ^f — ἐκείνων (read one of the days) LTTrA.   ^g ἱερεῖς priests TA.   ^h εἶπαν TTrA.   ⁱ λέγοντες πρὸς αὐτὸν LT ; — λέγοντες TrA.   ^k Εἰπὸν TTrA. ^l — ἕνα (read [one]) LTTrA.   ^m + τὸ T.   ⁿ Ἰωάνου Tr.   ^o συνελογίζοντο L. ^p + ἡμῖν to us L.   ^q Διὰ τί ELTrA.   ^r — οὖν [L]TTrA.   ^s ὁ λαὸς ἅπας TTrA.   ^t Ἰωάνην Tr. ^v λέγειν πρὸς τὸν λαὸν L.   ^w Ἀμπελῶνα ἐφύτευσεν ἄνθρωπος L   ^x — τις GLTTrAW. ^y ἐξέδετο TA.   ^z — ἐν (read καιρῷ at [the] season LTTrA.   ^a δώσουσιν they shall give LTTrA.   ^b ἐξαπέστειλαν αὐτὸν δείραντες TA.   ^c ἕτερον πέμψαι LTTrA.   ^d τρίτον πέμψαι LTTrA.

ρίτον·‖ οἱ.δὲ ᵉκαὶ τοῦτον‖ τραυματίσαντες ἐξέβαλον.
a third; and they ᵃalso ᵇhim ¹having ²wounded cast [him] out.

they wounded him also, and cast him out.

13 εἶπεν.δὲ ὁ κύριος τοῦ ἀμπελῶνος, Τί ποιήσω; πέμψω
And said the lord of the vineyard, What shall I do? I will send

τὸν.υἱόν.μου τὸν ἀγαπητόν· ἴσως τοῦτον ⁱἰδόντες‖ ἐντρα-
my son the beloved; perhaps him having seen they will

πήσονται. 14 Ἰδόντες.δὲ αὐτὸν οἱ γεωργοὶ ᵍδιελογίζοντο‖
respect. But having seen him the husbandmen reasoned

πρὸς ʰἑαυτούς,‖ λέγοντες, Οὗτός ἐστιν ὁ κληρονόμος· ⁱδεῦτε‖
among themselves, saying, This is the heir; come

ἀποκτείνωμεν αὐτόν, ἵνα ἡμῶν γένηται ἡ κληρονομία.
let us kill him, that ⁵ours ³may ⁴become ¹the ²inheritance.

15 Καὶ ἐκβαλόντες αὐτὸν ἔξω τοῦ ἀμπελῶνος ἀπέκτειναν.
And having cast forth him outside the vineyard they killed

Τί οὖν ποιήσει αὐτοῖς ὁ κύριος τοῦ ἀμπελῶνος;
[him]. What therefore will do to them the lord of the vineyard?

16 ἐλεύσεται καὶ ἀπολέσει τοὺς.γεωργοὺς.τούτους, καὶ δώσει
He will come and will destroy these husbandmen, and will give

τὸν ἀμπελῶνα ἄλλοις. ᵏἈκούσαντες.δὲ‖ εἶπον,‖ Μὴ
the vineyard to others. And having heard [it] they said, ³Not

γένοιτο. 17 Ὁ.δὲ ἐμβλέψας αὐτοῖς εἶπεν, Τί οὖν ἐστιν τὸ
¹may ²it be! But he looking at them said, What then is ²that

γεγραμμένον τοῦτο, Λίθον ὃν ἀπεδοκίμασαν οἱ
²has ⁴been ⁵written ¹this, [The] stone which ⁴rejected ¹they ²that

οἰκοδομοῦντες, οὗτος ἐγενήθη εἰς κεφαλὴν γωνίας; 18 Πᾶς
³build, this is become head of [the] corner? Everyone

ὁ πεσὼν ἐπ' ἐκεῖνον τὸν λίθον συνθλασθήσεται· ἐφ'.ὃν.δ'.ἂν
that falls on that stone will be broken, but on whomsoever

πέσῃ λικμήσει αὐτόν. 19 Καὶ ᵐἐζήτησαν‖ οἱ
it may fall it will grind ²to ³powder ¹him. And ⁷sought ¹the

ⁿἀρχιερεῖς καὶ οἱ γραμματεῖς‖ ἐπιβαλεῖν ἐπ' αὐτὸν τὰς χεῖρας
²chief ³priests ⁴and ⁵the ⁶scribes to lay ²on ³him ¹hands

ἐν αὐτῇ.τῇ.ὥρᾳ, καὶ ἐφοβήθησαν τὸν λαόν· ἔγνωσαν.γὰρ ὅτι
in that hour, and they feared the people; for they knew that

πρὸς αὐτοὺς ᵒτὴν.παραβολὴν.ταύτην εἶπεν.‖
against them this parable he speaks.

of the vineyard, What shall I do? I will send my beloved son: it may be they will reverence him when they see him. 14 But when the husbandmen saw him, they reasoned among themselves, saying, This is the heir: come, let us kill him, that the inheritance may be ours. 15 So they cast him out of the vineyard, and killed him. What therefore shall the lord of the vineyard do unto them? 16 He shall come and destroy these husbandmen, and shall give the vineyard to others. And when they heard it, they said, God forbid. 17 And he beheld them, and said, What is this then that is written, The stone which the builders rejected, the same is become the head of the corner? 18 Whosoever shall fall upon that stone shall be broken; but on whomsoever it shall fall, it will grind him to powder. 19 And the chief priests and the scribes the same hour sought to lay hands on him; and they feared the people: for they perceived that he had spoken this parable against them.

20 Καὶ παρατηρήσαντες ἀπέστειλαν ᵖἐγκαθέτους,‖ ὑπο-
And having watched [him] they sent secret agents, feign-

κρινομένους ἑαυτοὺς δικαίους εἶναι, ἵνα ἐπιλάβωνται
ing themselves ³righteous ¹to ²be, that they might take hold

αὐτοῦ qλόγου,‖ ʳεἰς τὸ‖ παραδοῦναι αὐτὸν τῇ ἀρχῇ καὶ
of him ⁴of his discourse, him to the [end] to deliver up to the power and

τῇ ἐξουσίᾳ τοῦ ἡγεμόνος. 21 καὶ ἐπηρώτησαν αὐτόν, λέγοῦ-
to the authority of the governor. And they questioned him, say-

τες, Διδάσκαλε, οἴδαμεν ὅτι ὀρθῶς λέγεις καὶ διδάσκεις, καὶ
ing, Teacher, we know that rightly thou sayest and teachest, and

οὐ.λαμβάνεις πρόσωπον, ἀλλ' ἐπ' ἀληθείας τὴν ὁδὸν
acceptest not [any man's] person, but with truth the way

τοῦ θεοῦ διδάσκεις. 22 ἔξεστιν ˢἡμῖν‖ Καίσαρι φόρον δοῦναι
of God teachest: is it lawful for us ⁴to ⁵Cæsar ³tribute ¹to ²give

ἢ οὔ; 23 Κατανοήσας.δὲ αὐτῶν τὴν πανουργίαν εἶπεν πρὸς
or not? But perceiving their craftiness he said to

20 And they watched him, and sent forth spies, which should feign themselves just men, that they might take hold of his words, that so they might deliver him unto the power and authority of the governor. 21 And they asked him, saying, Master, we know that thou sayest and teachest rightly, neither acceptest thou the person of any, but teachest the way of God truly: 22 is it lawful for us to give tribute unto Cæsar, or no? 23 But he perceived their craftiness, and said unto them, Why

ᵉ κἀκεῖνον L. ⌐ ἰδόντες LTTr[A]. ᵍ διελογίσαντο L. ʰ ἀλλήλους one another TTᴛA.
ⁱ — δεῦτε LTTrA. ᵏ οἱ δὲ ἀκούσαντες L. ˡ εἶπαν LTTrA. ᵐ ἐζήτουν L. ⁿ γραμματεῖς
καὶ οἱ ἀρχιερεῖς LTTrA. ᵒ εἶπεν τὴν παραβολὴν ταύτην LTTrA. ᵖ ἐνκαθέτους T. q λόγου
(read of his discourse) Tr. ʳ ὥστε so ²ˢ LTTrA. ˢ ἡμᾶς TTrA.

tempt ye me? 24 Shew me a penny. Whose image and superscription hath it? They answered and said, Cæsar's. 25 And he said unto them, Render therefore unto Cæsar the things which be Cæsar's, and unto God the things which be God's. 26 And they could not take hold of his words before the people: and they marvelled at his answer, and held their peace.

27 Then came to him certain of the Sadducees, which deny that there is any resurrection; and they asked him, 28 saying, Master, Moses wrote unto us, If any man's brother die, having a wife, and he die without children, that his brother should take his wife, and raise up seed unto his brother. 29 There were therefore seven brethren: and the first took a wife, and died without children. 30 And the second took her to wife, and he died childless. 31 And the third took her; and in like manner the seven also: and they left no children, and died. 32 Last of all the woman died also. 33 Therefore in the resurrection whose wife of them is she? for seven had her to wife. 34 And Jesus answering said unto them, The children of this world marry, and are given in marriage: 35 but they which shall be accounted worthy to obtain that world, and the resurrection from the dead, neither marry, nor are given in marriage: 36 neither can they die any more: for they are equal unto the angels; and are the children of God, being the children of the resurrection. 37 Now that the dead are raised, even Moses shewed at the bush, when he

---

αὐτούς, ᵗΤί με πειράζετε‖; 24 ᵛἐπιδείξατέ‖ μοι δηνάριον·ʷ
them, Why me do ye tempt? Shew me a denarius:

τίνος ἔχει εἰκόνα καὶ ἐπιγραφήν; ˣἈποκριθέντες‖.δὲ ᵞεἶπον,‖
whose ⁴has ⁵it ¹image ²and ³inscription? And answering they said,

Καίσαρος. 25 Ὁ.δὲ εἶπεν ᶻαὐτοῖς,‖ ᵃἈπόδοτε τοίνυν‖ τὰ
Cæsar's. And he said to them, Render therefore the things

Καίσαρος ᵇ Καίσαρι, καὶ τὰ τοῦ θεοῦ τῷ θεῷ. 26 Καὶ
of Cæsar to Cæsar, and the things of God to God. And

οὐκ.ἴσχυσαν ἐπιλαβέσθαι ᶜαὐτοῦ‖.ῥήματος ἐναντίον τοῦ
they were not able to take hold of his speech before the

λαοῦ· καὶ θαυμάσαντες ἐπὶ τῇ.ἀποκρίσει.αὐτοῦ ἐσίγησαν.
people; and wondering at his answer they were silent.

27 Προσελθόντες.δὲ τινες τῶν Σαδδουκαίων, οἱ ᵈἀντι-
And having come to [him] some of the Sadducees, who deny

λέγοντες‖ ἀνάστασιν μὴ εἶναι, ἐπηρώτησαν αὐτόν, 28 λέγον-
³a ⁴resurrection ¹there ²is, they questioned him, say-

τες, Διδάσκαλε, ᵉΜωσῆς‖ ἔγραψεν ἡμῖν, ἐάν τινος ἀδελφὸς
ing, Teacher, Moses wrote to us, If anyone's brother

ἀποθάνῃ ἔχων γυναῖκα, καὶ οὗτος ἄτεκνος ᶠἀποθάνῃ,‖ ἵνα
should die having a wife, and he childless should die, that

λάβῃ ὁ.ἀδελφὸς.αὐτοῦ τὴν γυναῖκα καὶ ἐξαναστήσῃ σπέρμα
³should ⁴take ¹his ²brother the wife and should raise up seed

τῷ.ἀδελφῷ.αὐτοῦ. 29 ἑπτὰ οὖν ἀδελφοὶ ἦσαν· καὶ ὁ πρῶτος
to his brother. ⁴Seven ³then ⁵brethren ¹there ²were; and the first

λαβὼν γυναῖκα ἀπέθανεν ἄτεκνος· 30 καὶ ᵍἔλαβεν‖ ὁ
having taken a wife died childless; and ²took ¹the

δεύτερος ʰτὴν γυναῖκα, καὶ οὗτος ἀπέθανεν ἄτεκνος·‖ 31 καὶ
²second the woman, and he died childless; and

ὁ τρίτος ἔλαβεν αὐτήνⁱ· ὡσαύτως.δὲ καὶ οἱ ἑπτὰ ᵏ οὐ.κατ-
the third took her; and likewise also the seven did not

ἔλιπον τέκνα, καὶ ἀπέθανον· 32 ὕστερον ˡδὲ πάντων‖ ᵐἀπέ-
leave children, and died; ²last ¹and of all ²also

θανεν καὶ ἡ γυνή.‖ 33 ⁿἐν.τῇ.οὖν‖ ἀναστάσει τίνος αὐτῶν
the woman. Therefore in the resurrection of which of them

γίνεται γυνή; οἱ.γὰρ ἑπτὰ ἔσχον αὐτὴν γυναῖκα. 34 Καὶ
does she become wife? for the seven had her as wife. And

ᵒἀποκριθεὶς‖ εἶπεν αὐτοῖς ὁ Ἰησοῦς, Οἱ υἱοὶ τοῦ.αἰῶνος.τούτου
answering ²said ³to ⁴them ¹Jesus, The sons of this age

γαμοῦσιν καὶ ᵖἐκγαμίσκονται·‖ 35 οἱ.δὲ καταξιωθέντες τοῦ
marry and are given in marriage; but those accounted worthy

αἰῶνος.ἐκείνου τυχεῖν καὶ τῆς ἀναστάσεως τῆς ἐκ
³that ⁴age ¹to ²obtain ²and the resurrection which [is] from among

νεκρῶν οὔτε γαμοῦσιν οὔτε ᑫἐκγαμίσκονται·‖ 36 ʳοὔτε‖
[the] dead neither marry nor are given in marriage; ²neither

γὰρ ἀποθανεῖν ἔτι δύνανται· ἰσάγγελοι.γάρ εἰσιν, καὶ
¹for ⁵die ⁶any ⁷more ⁴they ³can; for equal to angels they are, and

υἱοί εἰσιν ˢτοῦ‖ θεοῦ, τῆς ἀναστάσεως υἱοὶ ὄντες. 37 Ὅτι.δὲ
sons are of God, ³of ⁴the ³resurrection ²sons ¹being. But that

ἐγείρονται οἱ νεκροί, καὶ ᵉΜωσῆς‖ ἐμήνυσεν ἐπὶ τῆς
are raised the dead, even Moses shewed [in the part] on the

ᵗ — Τί με πειράζετε TTrA. ᵛ δείξατέ GLTTrAW. ʷ + [οἱ δὲ ἔδειξαν. καὶ εἶπεν] and
they shewed [it]. And he said L. ˣ οἱ (read and they said) T. ᵞ εἶπαν TTrA. ᶻ πρὸς
αὐτούς TTrA. ᵃ Τοίνυν ἀπόδοτε TTrA. ᵇ + τῷ Tr. ᶜ τοῦ (read [his]) A. ᵈ λέγοντες
(read who say there is not (μὴ) a resurrection) Tr. ᵉ Μωϋσῆς LTTrAW. ᶠ ῇ should be
LTTrA. ᵍ ἔλαβεν TTrA. ʰ — τὴν γυναῖκα, καὶ οὗτος ἀπέθανεν ἄτεκνος TTrA. ⁱ [ὡσαύ-
τως] likewise L. ᵏ + καὶ even E. ˡ — δὲ πάντων LTTrA. ᵐ καὶ ἡ γυνὴ ἀπέθανεν TTrA.
ⁿ ἡ γυνὴ οὖν ἐν τῇ the woman therefore in the TA. ᵒ — ἀποκριθεὶς LTTrA. ᵖ γαμίσκονται
LTTrA. ᑫ γαμίζονται LTTr; γαμίσκονται A. ʳ οὐδὲ LTrA. ˢ — τοῦ TTrA.

βάτου, ὡς λέγει κύριον τὸν θεὸν 'Αβραὰμ καὶ ᵗτὸν‖ θεὸν
bush, when he called[the] Lord the God of Abraham and the God

'Ισαὰκ καὶ ᵗτὸν‖ θεὸν 'Ιακώβ· 38 θεὸς.δὲ οὐκ.ἔστιν νεκρῶν,
of Isaac and the God of Jacob; but God he is not of [the] dead,

ἀλλὰ ζώντων. πάντες.γὰρ αὐτῷ ζῶσιν. 39 'Αποκριθέν-
but of [the] living; for all for him live. ²Answering

τες δὲ τινες τῶν γραμματέων ᵛεἶπον,‖ Διδάσκαλε, καλῶς
¹and some of the scribes said, Teacher, well

εἶπας. 40 Οὐκέτι ˣδὲ‖ ἐτόλμων ἐπερωτᾶν αὐτὸν
thou hast spoken. ²Not ³any ⁴more ¹and did they dare to ask him

οὐδέν.
anything.
(*lit.* nothing.)

41 Εἶπεν.δὲ πρὸς αὐτούς, Πῶς λέγουσιν τὸν χριστὸν ʸυἱὸν
And he said to them, How do they say the Christ ²Son

ᶻΔαβὶδ‖ εἶναι‖; 42 ᵃκαὶ αὐτὸς‖ ᶻΔαβὶδ‖ λέγει ἐν βίβλῳ
³of ⁴David ¹is? and ²himself ¹David says in [the] book

ᵇψαλμῶν, Εἶπεν ᶜὁ‖ κύριος τῷ.κυρίῳ.μου, Κάθου ἐκ δεξιῶν.μου,
of Psalms, ³Said ¹the ²Lord to my Lord, Sit on my right hand,

43 ἕως.ἂν θῶ τοὺς.ἐχθρούς.σου ὑποπόδιον τῶν.ποδῶν.σου.
until I place thine enemies [as] a footstool for thy feet.

44 ᶻΔαβὶδ‖ οὖν ᵈκύριον αὐτὸν‖ καλεῖ, καὶ πῶς ᵉυἱὸς.αὐτοῦ‖
David therefore ²Lord ²him ¹calls, and how his son

ἐστιν;
is he?

45 'Ακούοντος.δὲ παντὸς τοῦ λαοῦ εἶπεν ᶠτοῖς μαθηταῖς
And as were listening all the people he said to ²disciples

αὐτοῦ,‖ 46 Προσέχετε ἀπὸ τῶν γραμματέων τῶν θελόντων
¹his, Beware of the scribes who like

περιπατεῖν ἐν στολαῖς, καὶ φιλούντων.ἀσπασμοὺς ἐν ταῖς
to walk in robes, and love salutations in the

ἀγοραῖς· καὶ πρωτοκαθεδρίας ἐν ταῖς συναγωγαῖς καὶ πρω-
market-places and first seats in the synagogues and

τοκλισίας ἐν τοῖς δείπνοις· 47 ᵍοἳ κατεσθίουσιν‖ τὰς οἰκίας
places in the suppers; who devour the houses

τῶν χηρῶν, καὶ προφάσει μακρὰ ʰπροσεύχονται.‖ οὗτοι
of widows, and as a pretext ²at ³great ⁴length ¹pray. These

ⁱλήψονται‖ περισσότερον κρίμα.
shall receive more abundant judgment.

21 'Αναβλέψας.δὲ εἶδεν τοὺς βάλλοντας ᵏτὰ.δῶρα.αὐτῶν
And having looked up he saw the ²casting ³their ⁴gifts

εἰς τὸ γαζοφυλάκιον‖ πλουσίους· 2 εἶδεν.δὲ ¹καί τινα‖
⁵into ⁶the ⁷treasury ¹rich, and he saw also a certain

χήραν πενιχρὰν βάλλουσαν ἐκεῖ ᵐδύο λεπτά·‖ 3 καὶ εἶπεν,
²widow ¹poor casting therein two lepta. And he said,

'Αληθῶς λέγω ὑμῖν, ὅτι ἡ χήρα ⁿἡ πτωχὴ αὕτη‖ ᵒπλεῖον‖
Of a truth I say to you, that ³widow ²poor ¹this more

πάντων ἔβαλεν· 4 ᵖἅπαντες‖.γὰρ οὗτοι ἐκ τοῦ περισ-
than all cast in; for all these out of that which was

σεύοντος αὐτοῖς ἔβαλον εἰς τὰ δῶρα ᑫτοῦ.θεοῦ,‖ αὕτη.δὲ
abounding to them cast into the gifts of God; but she

Right column (KJV):

calleth the Lord the God of Abraham, and the God of Isaac, and the God of Jacob. 38 For he is not a God of the dead, but of the living : for all live unto him. 39 Then certain of the scribes answering said, Master, thou hast well said. 40 And after that they durst not ask him any *question at all.*

41 And he said unto them, How say they that Christ is David's son? 42 And David himself saith in the book of Psalms, The LORD said unto my Lord, Sit thou on my right hand, 43 till I make thine enemies thy footstool. 44 David therefore calleth him Lord, how is he then his son?

45 Then in the audience of all the people he said unto his disciples, 46 Beware of the scribes, which desire to walk in long robes, and love greetings in the markets, and the highest seats in the synagogues, and the chief rooms at feasts; 47 which devour widows' houses, and for a shew make long prayers : the same shall receive greater damnation.

XXI. And he looked up, and saw the rich men casting their gifts into the treasury. 2 And he saw also a certain poor widow casting in thither two mites. 3 And he said, Of a truth I say unto you, that this poor widow hath cast in more than they all: 4 for all these have of their abundance cast in unto the offerings of God: but she

---

ᵗ — τὸν LTTrA. ᵛ εἶπαν LTTrA. ˣ γὰρ for TTrA. ʸ εἶναι Δανεὶδ υἱόν TA.
ᶻ Δαυὶδ GW; Δανεὶδ LTTrA. ᵃ αὐτὸς γὰρ for ²himself T. ᵇ + τῶν the L. ᶜ — ὁ
(*read* [the]) LTrA. ᵈ αὐτὸν κύριον TrA. ᵉ αὐτοῦ υἱός TTrA. ᶠ — αὐτοῦ (*read* the disciples)
TTr; πρὸς αὐτούς to them A. ᵍ οἱ κατεσθίοντες those devouring L. ʰ προσευχόμενοι
praying L. ⁱ λήμψονται LTTrA. ᵏ εἰς τὸ γαζοφυλάκιον τὰ δῶρα αὐτῶν TTrA. ¹ [καὶ]
τινα L; τινα [καὶ] A; — καὶ TTr. ᵐ λεπτὰ δύο Tr. ⁿ αὕτη ἡ πτωχὴ LTr. ᵒ πλείω LTA.
ᵖ πάντες L. ᑫ — τοῦ θεοῦ T[Tr]A.

of her penury hath cast in all the living that she had.

ἐκ τοῦ.ὑστερήματος.αὐτῆς ʳἅπαντα‖ τὸν βίον ὃν εἶχεν
out of her poverty all the livelihood which she had

ἔβαλεν.
did cast.

5 And as some spake of the temple, how it was adorned with goodly stones and gifts, he said, 6 As for the e things which ye behold, the days will come, in the which there shall not be left one stone upon another, that shall not be thrown down. 7 And they asked him, saying, Master, but when shall these things be? and what sign will there be when these things shall come to pass? 8 And he said, Take heed that ye be not deceived: for many shall come in my name, saying, I am Christ; and the time draweth near: go ye not therefore after them. 9 But when ye shall hear of wars and commotions, be not terrified: for these things must first come to pass; but the end is not by and by. 10 Then said he unto them, Nation shall rise against nation, and kingdom against kingdom: 11 and great earthquakes shall be in divers places, and famines, and pestilences ; and fearful sights and great signs shall there be from heaven. 12 But before all these, they shall lay their hands on you, and persecute you, delivering you up to the synagogues, and into prisons, being brought before kings and rulers for my name's sake. 13 And it shall turn to you for a testimony. 14 Settle it therefore in your hearts, not to meditate before what ye shall answer: 15 for I will give you a mouth and wisdom, which all your adversaries shall not be able to gainsay nor resist. 16 And ye shall be betrayed both by parents, and breth-

5 Καί τινων λεγόντων περὶ τοῦ ἱεροῦ, ὅτι λίθοις καλοῖς
And as some were speaking about the temple, that with ²stones ¹goodly

καὶ ³ἀναθήμασιν‖ κεκόσμηται, εἶπεν, 6 Ταῦτα ἃ θεω-
and consecrated gifts it was adorned, he said, [As to] these things which ye are

ρεῖτε, ἐλεύσονται ἡμέραι ἐν αἷς οὐκ.ἀφεθήσεται λίθος ἐπὶ
beholding, ²will ³come ¹days in which shall not be left stone upon

λίθῳᵗ ὃς οὐ.καταλυθήσεται. 7 Ἐπηρώτησαν.δὲ αὐτόν, λέ-
stone which shall not be thrown down. And they asked him, say-

γοντες, Διδάσκαλε, ,πότε οὖν ταῦτα ἔσται; καὶ τί τὸ
ing, Teacher, when then ²these ³things ¹will be? and what the

σημεῖον ὅταν μέλλῃ ταῦτα γίνεσθαι; 8 Ὁ.δὲ εἶπεν,
sign when ³are ⁴about ¹these ²things to take place? And he said,

Βλέπετε μὴ.πλανηθῆτε· πολλοὶ.γὰρ ἐλεύσονται ἐπὶ τῷ
Take heed ye be not led astray ; for many will come in

ὀνόματί.μου, λέγοντες, ᵛΟτι‖ ἐγώ εἰμι· καί, Ὁ καιρὸς ἤγ-
my name, saying, I am [he]; and, The time is

γικεν. μὴ ʷοὖν‖ πορευθῆτε ὀπίσω αὐτῶν. 9 ὅταν.δὲ
drawn near. ³Not ⁴therefore ¹go ²ye after them. And when

ἀκούσητε πολέμους καὶ ἀκαταστασίας, μὴ.πτοηθῆτε δεῖ
ye shall hear of wars and commotions, be not terrified ; ⁴must

γὰρ ˣταῦτα γενέσθαι‖ πρῶτον, ἀλλ' οὐκ εὐθέως τὸ
¹for ²these ³things take place first, but not immediately [is] the

τέλος. 10 Τότε ἔλεγεν αὐτοῖς, Ἐγερθήσεται ἔθνος ʸἐπὶ‖
end. Then he was saying to them, ²Shall ³rise ⁴up ¹nation against

ἔθνος, καὶ βασιλεία ἐπὶ βασιλείαν· 11 σεισμοί.τε μεγάλοι
nation, and kingdom against kingdom ; also ²earthquakes ¹great

ᶻκατὰ τόπους καὶ‖ ᵃλιμοὶ καὶ λοιμοὶ‖ ἔσονται, ᵇφόβη-
in different places and famines and pestilences shall there be, ²fearful

τρά‖ τε καὶ ᶜσημεῖα ἀπ' οὐρανοῦ‖ μεγάλα ἔσται. 12 Πρὸ
³sights ¹and and ²signs ³from ⁴heaven ¹great shall there be. ²Before

δὲ τούτων ᵈἁπάντων‖ ἐπιβαλοῦσιν ἐφ' ὑμᾶς τὰς χεῖρας
¹but ⁴these ⁵things ³all they will lay upon you ²hands

αὐτῶν, καὶ διώξουσιν, παραδιδόντες εἰς ᵉ συναγωγὰς καὶ
¹their, . and will persecute [you], delivering up to synagogues and

φυλακάς, ᶠἀγομένους‖ ἐπὶ βασιλεῖς καὶ ἡγεμόνας. ἕνεκεν
prisons, bringing [you] before kings and governors, on account of

τοῦ.ὀνόματός.μου. 13 ἀποβήσεται.ᵍδὲ‖ ὑμῖν εἰς μαρτύριον·
my name ; but it shall turn out to you for a testimony.

14 ʰθέσθε‖ οὖν ¹εἰς τὰς καρδίας‖.ὑμῶν μὴ προμελετᾶν ἀπο-
Settle therefore in your hearts not to premeditate to make

λογηθῆναι· 15 ἐγὼ.γὰρ δώσω ὑμῖν στόμα καὶ σοφίαν, ᾗ
a defence ; for I will give you a mouth and wisdom, which

οὐ.δυνήσονται ᵏἀντειπεῖν ¹οὐδὲ¹ ἀντιστῆναι‖ ᵐπάντες‖ οἱ
⁵shall ⁶not ⁷be ⁸able ⁹to ⁰reply ¹¹to ¹²nor ¹³to ¹⁴resist ¹all ²those

ἀντικείμενοι ὑμῖν. 16 παραδοθήσεσθε.δὲ καὶ ὑπὸ γονέων καὶ
³opposing ⁴you. But ye will be delivered up even by parents and

---

ʳ πάντα LTr.   ˢ ἀναθέμασιν LT.   ᵗ + ὧδε here L.   ᵛ — ὅτι [L]T[TrA].   ʷ — οὖν LTTrA.
ˣ γενέσθαι ταῦτα A.   ʸ ἐπ' LTTrA.   ᶻ καὶ κατὰ τόπους TTrA.   ᵃ λοιμοὶ καὶ λιμοὶ LTrA.
ᵇ φόβηθρά LTrA.   ᶜ ἀπ' οὐρανοῦ σημεῖα L.   ᵈ πάντων GLTTrAW.   ᵉ + τὰς the TTr[A].
ᶠ ἀπαγομένους leading [you] away TT·A.   ᵍ — δὲ but T[TrA].   ʰ θέτε LTTrA.   ¹ ἐν ταῖς
καρδίαις LTTrA.   ᵏ ἀντιστῆναι οὐδὲ ἀντειπεῖν L ; ἀντιστῆναι ἢ ἀντειπεῖν (ἢ ἀντειπ.] Tr) TTrA.
¹ ἢ or G.   ᵐ ἅπαντες TTrA.

ἀδελφῶν καὶ συγγενῶν καὶ φίλων, καὶ θανατώσουσιν
brethren　and　relations　and　friends,　and they will put to death [some]

ἐξ ὑμῶν· 17 καὶ ἔσεσθε μισούμενοι ὑπὸ πάντων διὰ
from among you,　　and ye will be　hated　by　all　becau-e of

τὸ ὄνομά.μου. 18 καὶ θρὶξ ἐκ τῆς.κεφαλῆς.ὑμῶν οὐ.μὴ ἀπό-
my name.　　And a hair of　your head　in no wise may

ληται. 19 ἐν τῇ.ὑπομονῇ.ὑμῶν "κτήσασθε" τὰς.ψυχὰς.ὑμῶν.
perish.　　By your patient endurance　gain　　your souls.

20 Ὅταν.δὲ ἴδητε κυκλουμένην ὑπὸ στρατοπέδων °τὴν" Ἱερου-
But when ye see ²being ³encircled ⁴with ⁵armies　　　Jeru-

σαλήμ, τότε γνῶτε ὅτι ἤγγικεν ἡ.ἐρήμωσις.αὐτῆς. 21 τότε
salem　then　know that has drawn near　her desolation.　Then

οἱ ἐν τῇ Ἰουδαίᾳ φευγέτωσαν εἰς τὰ ὄρη· καὶ οἱ ἐν
those in　Judæa　let them flee　to the mountains; and those in

μέσῳ.αὐτῆς ἐκχωρείτωσαν· καὶ οἱ ἐν ταῖς χώραις μὴ εἰσερχέ-
her midst　let them depart out, and those in　the countries ²not ¹let ²them

σθωσαν εἰς αὐτήν. 22 ὅτι ἡμέραι ἐκδικήσεως αὗται εἰσιν, τοῦ
enter　into her;　for　days　of avenging these　are,

ᴾπληρωθῆναι" πάντα τὰ γεγραμμένα. 23 οὐαὶ.ᵈδὲ" ταῖς
that may be accomplished all things that have been written.　But woe to those

ἐν.γαστρὶ.ἐχούσαις καὶ ταῖς θηλαζούσαις ἐν ἐκείναις ταῖς ἡμέ-
with child　　and to those　giving suck in　those　　days,·

ραις· ἔσται.γὰρ ἀνάγκη μεγάλη ἐπὶ τῆς γῆς καὶ ὀργὴ ᴿἐν"
for there shall be ²distress ¹great　upon the land and wrath among

τῷ.λαῷ.τούτῳ. 24 καὶ πεσοῦνται στόματι ˢμαχαίρας," καὶ
this people.　　And they shall fall by [the] mouth of [the] sword, and

αἰχμαλωτισθήσονται εἰς ᵗπάντα τὰ ἔθνη" καὶ Ἱερουσαλὴμ
shall be led captive　into　all　the nations; and　Jerusalem

ἔσται πατουμένη ὑπὸ ἐθνῶν ᵛἄχρι " ʷπληρωθῶσιν [the]
shall be trodden down by [the] nations　until　be fulfilled　[the]

καιροὶ ἐθνῶν. 25 Καὶ ˣἔσται" σημεῖα ἐν ἡλίῳ καὶ σελήνῃ
times of [the] nations.　And there shall be　signs　in sun　and moon

καὶ ἄστροις, καὶ ἐπὶ τῆς γῆς συνοχὴ ἐθνῶν ἐν ἀπορίᾳ,
and　stars,　and upon the earth distress of nations with perplexity,

ʸἠχούσης" θαλάσσης καὶ σάλου, 26 ἀποψυχόντων ἀνθρώ-
roaring　of [the] sea and rolling surge,　²fainting ²at ⁴heart ¹men

πων ἀπὸ φόβου καὶ προσδοκίας τῶν ἐπερχομένων τῇ
from　fear　and expectation of that which　is coming　on the

οἰκουμένῃ· αἱ.γὰρ δυνάμεις τῶν οὐρανῶν σαλευθήσονται.
habitable earth; for the　powers　of the heavens　shall be shaken.

27 καὶ τότε ὄψονται τὸν υἱὸν τοῦ ἀνθρώπου ἐρχόμενον ἐν
And then shall they see the Son　of man　coming　in

νεφέλῃ μετὰ δυνάμεως καὶ δόξης πολλῆς. 28 Ἀρχομένων.δὲ
a cloud with　power　and ²glory ¹great.　　But ³beginning

τούτων γίνεσθαι ἀνακύψατε καὶ ἐπάρατε τὰς κεφαλὰς
¹these ²things to come to pass　look up　and　lift up　²heads

ὑμῶν· διότι ἐγγίζει ἡ.ἀπολύτρωσις.ὑμῶν. 29 Καὶ εἶπεν
¹your,　because draws near　your redemption.　　And he spoke

παραβολὴν αὐτοῖς, Ἴδετε τὴν συκῆν καὶ πάντα τὰ δένδρα.
a parable　to them: Behold the fig-tree and　all　the trees:

30 ὅταν προβάλωσιν ἤδη, βλέποντες ἀφ᾽ ἑαυτῶν
when　²they ³sprout ¹already,　looking　[on them] of yourselves

rep, and kinsfolks, and friends; and some of you shall they cause to be put to death. 17 And ye shall be hated of all men for my name's sake. 18 But there shall not an hair of your head perish. 19 In your patience possess ye your souls. 20 And when ye shall see Jerusalem compassed with armies, then know that the desolation thereof is nigh. 21 Then let them which are in Judæa flee to the mountains; and let them which are in the midst of it depart out; and let not them that are in the countries enter thereinto. 22 For these be the days of vengeance, that all things which are written may be fulfilled. 23 But woe unto them that are with child, and to them that give suck, in those days! for there shall be great distress in the land, and wrath upon this people. 24 And they shall fall by the edge of the sword, and shall be led away captive into all nations: and Jerusalem shall be trodden down of the Gentiles, until the times of the Gentiles be fulfilled. 25 And there shall be signs in the sun, and in the moon, and in the stars; and upon the earth distress of nations, with perplexity; the sea and the waves roaring; 26 men's hearts failing them for fear, and for looking after those things which are coming on the earth: for the powers of heaven shall be shaken. 27 And then shall they see the Son of man coming in a cloud with power and great glory. 28 And when these things begin to come to pass, then look up, and lift up your heads; for your redemption draweth nigh. 29 And he spake to them a parable; Behold the fig tree, and all the trees; 30 when they now shoot forth, ye see and

---

ⁿ κτήσεσθε ye shall gain LTTrA.　　° — τὴν LTTrA.　　ᴾ πλησθῆναι GLTTrAW.　　ᑫ — δὲ
but LTTrA.　　ᴿ — ἐν (read to this people) GLTTrAW.　　ˢ μαχαίρης TTr.　　ᵗ τὰ ἔθνη
πάντα LTTrA.　　ᵛ ἄχρις L.　　ʷ + οὗ LTTrA.　　ˣ ἔσονται LTTrA.　　ʸ ἤχους at [the]
sound GLTTrA.

know of your own selves that summer is now nigh at hand. 31 So likewise ye, when ye see these things come to pass, know ye that the kingdom of God is nigh at hand. 32 Verily I say unto you, This generation shall not pass away, till all be fulfilled. 33 Heaven and earth shall pass away: but my words shall not pass away. 34 And take heed to yourselves, lest at any time your hearts be overcharged with surfeiting, and drunkenness, and cares of this life, and so that day come upon you unawares. 35 For as a snare shall it come on all them that dwell on the face of the whole earth. 36 Watch ye therefore, and pray always, that ye may be accounted worthy to escape all these things that shall come to pass, and to stand before the Son of man.

γινώσκετε ὅτι ἤδη ἐγγὺς τὸ θέρος ἐστίν. 31 οὕτως καὶ ὑμεῖς,
ye know that already near the summer is. So also ye,
ὅταν ἴδητε ταῦτα γινόμενα γινώσκετε ὅτι ἐγγύς ἐστιν ἡ
when ye see these things coming to pass know that near is the
βασιλεία τοῦ θεοῦ. 32 ἀμὴν λέγω ὑμῖν, ὅτι οὐ μὴ παρ-
kingdom of God. Verily I say to you, that in no wise will have
έλθῃ ἡ γενεὰ αὕτη ἕως ἂν πάντα γένηται. 33 ὁ
passed away this generation until all shall have taken place. The
οὐρανὸς καὶ ἡ γῆ παρελεύσονται, οἱ δὲ λόγοι μου οὐ μὴ
heaven and the earth shall pass away, but my words in no wise
ᶻπαρέλθωσιν.‖ 34 Προσέχετε δὲ ἑαυτοῖς, μήποτε ᵃβαρυνθῶ-
may pass away. But take heed to yourselves, lest be laden
σιν‖ ᵇὑμῶν αἱ καρδίαι‖ ἐν κραιπάλῃ καὶ μέθῃ καὶ μερίμναις
your hearts with surfeiting and drinking and cares
βιωτικαῖς, καὶ ᶜαἰφνίδιος ἐφ᾽ ὑμᾶς ἐπιστῇ‖ ἡ ἡμέρα ἐκείνη·
of life, and suddenly upon you should come that day;
35 ὡς ᵈπαγὶς γὰρ ἐπελεύσεται‖ ἐπὶ πάντας τοὺς καθημένους
for as a snare shall it come upon all those sitting
ἐπὶ πρόσωπον πάσης τῆς γῆς. 36 ἀγρυπνεῖτε ᵉοὖν‖ ἐν
upon the face of all the earth. Watch therefore at
παντὶ καιρῷ δεόμενοι, ἵνα ᶠκαταξιωθῆτε‖ ἐκφυγεῖν ταῦ-
every season praying, that ye may be accounted worthy to escape ᵍthese
τα πάντα τὰ μέλλοντα γίνεσθαι, καὶ σταθῆναι ἔμπρο-
³things ¹all which are about to come to pass, and to stand before
σθεν τοῦ υἱοῦ τοῦ ἀνθρώπου.
the Son of man.

37 And in the day time he was teaching in the temple; and at night he went out, and abode in the mount that is called the mount of Olives. 38 And all the people came early in the morning to him in the temple, for to hear him.

37 Ἦν δὲ τὰς ἡμέρας ᵍἐν τῷ ἱερῷ διδάσκων·‖ τὰς δὲ νύκτας
And he was by day in the temple teaching· and by night
ἐξερχόμενος ηὐλίζετο εἰς τὸ ὄρος τὸ καλούμενον ἐλαιῶν·
going out he lodged on the mount called of Olives;
38 καὶ πᾶς ὁ λαὸς ὤρθριζεν πρὸς αὐτὸν ἐν τῷ
and all the people came early in the morning to him in the
ἱερῷ ἀκούειν αὐτοῦ.
temple to hear him.

XXII. Now the feast of unleavened bread drew nigh, which is called the Passover. 2 And the chief priests and scribes sought how they might kill him; for they feared the people. 3 Then entered Satan into Judas surnamed Iscariot, being of the number of the twelve. 4 And he went his way, and communed with the chief priests and captains, how he might betray him unto them. 5 And they were glad, and covenanted to give him money. 6 And he promised,

22 Ἤγγιζεν δὲ ἡ ἑορτὴ τῶν ἀζύμων ἡ λεγομένη
And drew near the feast of unleavened [bread] which [is] called
πάσχα· 2 καὶ ἐζήτουν οἱ ἀρχιερεῖς καὶ οἱ γραμματεῖς
passover; and ⁷were ⁸seeking ¹the ²chief ³priests ⁴and ⁵the ⁶scribes
τὸ πῶς ἀνέλωσιν αὐτόν· ἐφοβοῦντο γὰρ τὸν λαόν.
as to how they might put ²to ³death ¹him, for they feared the people.
3 Εἰσῆλθεν δὲ ᵇὁ‖ σατανᾶς εἰς ᶦἸούδαν τὸν ᶦἐπικαλούμενον‖
And ²entered ¹Satan into Judas who is surnamed
Ἰσκαριώτην, ὄντα ἐκ τοῦ ἀριθμοῦ τῶν δώδεκα· 4 καὶ ἀπελ-
Iscariote, being of the number of the twelve. And having gone
θὼν συνελάλησεν τοῖς ἀρχιερεῦσιν ᵏ καὶ ᶦτοῖς‖ στρατηγοῖς
away he spoke with the chief priests and the captains
τὸ πῶς ᵐαὐτὸν παραδῷ αὐτοῖς.‖ 5 καὶ ἐχάρησαν, καὶ
as to how him he might deliver up to them. And they rejoiced, and
συνέθεντο αὐτῷ ἀργύριον δοῦναι· 6 ⁿκαὶ ἐξωμολόγησεν,‖ καὶ
agreed ³him ²money ¹to ²give. And ⁰ he promised, and

ᶻ παρελεύσονται shall pass away LTTrA.   ᵃ βαρηθῶσιν GLTTrAW.   ᵇ αἱ καρδίαι ὑμῶν LTr.   ᶜ αἰφνίδιος ἐπιστῇ ἐφ᾽ ὑμᾶς L; ἐπιστῇ ἐφ᾽ ὑμᾶς αἰφνίδιος TTrA.   ᵈ παγὶς· ἐπεισελεύσεται γὰρ (read that day as a snare: for it shall come in) LTTrA.   ᵉ δὲ but (wa ch) LTTrA.   ᶠ κατισχύσητε ye may prevail TTrA.   ᵍ διδάσκων ἐν τῷ ἱερῷ Tr.   ʰ — ὁ GLTTrAW. ᶦ καλούμενον is called TTrA.   ᵏ + καὶ τοῖς γραμματεῦσιν and the scribes L.   ᶦ — τοῖς TTrA. ᵐ αὐτοῖς παραδῷ αὐτόν LTTrA.   ⁿ — καὶ ἐξωμολόγησεν (read he sought) L.

ἐζήτει εὐκαιρίαν τοῦ παραδοῦναι αὐτὸν °αὐτοῖς ἄτερ
sought opportunity   to deliver up   him to them away from [the]
ὄχλου.‖
crowd.

and sought opportunity to betray him unto them in the absence of the multitude.

7 Ἦλθεν.δὲ ἡ ἡμέρα τῶν.ἀζύμων Ρἐν‖ ῇ ἔδει
And came the day   of unleavened [bread] in which was needful
θύεσθαι τὸ πάσχα. 8 καὶ ἀπέστειλεν Πέτρον καὶ ᑫἸωάννην,‖
to be killed the passover. And he sent   Peter   and John,
εἰπών, Πορευθέντες ἑτοιμάσατε ἡμῖν τὸ πάσχα, ἵνα φάγω-
saying, Having gone prepare   for us the passover, that we may
μεν. 9 Οἱ.δὲ ᴿεἶπον‖ αὐτῷ, Ποῦ θέλεις ἑτοιμάσωμενˢ;
eat [it]. But they said to him, Where willest thou we should prepare?
10 Ὁ.δὲ εἶπεν αὐτοῖς, Ἰδού, εἰσελθόντων.ὑμῶν εἰς τὴν πόλιν
And he said to them, Lo, on your having entered into the city.
συναντήσει ὑμῖν ἄνθρωπος κεράμιον ὕδατος βαστάζων· ἀκο-
will ¹meet ²you   ¹a ²man, a pitcher of water carrying; fol-
λουθήσατε αὐτῷ εἰς τὴν οἰκίαν ᵗοὗ‖ εἰσπορεύεται· 11 καὶ
low him into the house where he enters;   and
ἐρεῖτε τῷ οἰκοδεσπότῃ τῆς οἰκίας, Λέγει σοι ὁ διδάσ-
ye shall say to the master of the house, ³Says ⁴to ⁵thee ¹the ²teach-
καλος, Ποῦ ἐστιν τὸ κατάλυμα ὅπου τὸ πάσχα μετὰ τῶν
er,   Where is the guest-chamber where the passover with
μαθητῶν.μου φάγω; 12 Κἀκεῖνος ὑμῖν δείξει ᵛἀνώγεον‖
my disciples I may eat? And he ³you ¹will ²shew ⁴upper ⁷room
μέγα ἐστρωμένον· ἐκεῖ ἑτοιμάσατε. 13 Ἀπελθόντες.δὲ εὗρον‖
⁴a ⁵large furnished: there prepare. And having gone they found
καθὼς ᵂεἴρηκεν‖ αὐτοῖς· καὶ ἡτοίμασαν τὸ πάσχα.
as he had said to them; and they prepared the passover.

14 Καὶ ὅτε ἐγένετο ἡ ὥρα ἀνέπεσεν,   καὶ οἱ ˣδώδεκα‖
And when was come the hour he reclined [at table], and the twelve
ἀπόστολοι σὺν αὐτῷ. 15 καὶ εἶπεν πρὸς αὐτούς, Ἐπιθυμίᾳ
apostles with him.   And he said to them, With desire
ἐπεθύμησα τοῦτο τὸ πάσχα φαγεῖν μεθ᾽ ὑμῶν πρὸ τοῦ.με.πα-
I desired   this the passover to eat with you before· I suf-
θεῖν· 16 λέγω.γὰρ ὑμῖν, ὅτι ʸοὐκέτι‖ οὐ.μὴ φάγω ᶻἐξ
fer. For I say to you, that ⁴any ⁵more ¹not ²at ³all will I eat of
              (lit. no more)
αὐτοῦ‖ ἕως.ὅτου πληρωθῇ ἐν τῇ βασιλείᾳ τοῦ θεοῦ. 17 Καὶ
it   until it be fulfilled in the kingdom of God. And
δεξάμενος ᵃποτήριον, εὐχαριστήσας εἶπεν, Λάβετε τοῦτο,
having received a cup having given thanks he said, Take this,
καὶ διαμερίσατε ᵇἑαυτοῖς·‖ 18 λέγω.γὰρ ὑμῖν, ᶜὅτι‖ οὐ.μὴ
and divide [it] among yourselves. For I say to you, that not at all
πίω ᵈἀπὸ τοῦ ᵉγεννήματος‖ τῆς ἀμπέλου ἕως.ὅτου‖ ἡ
will I drink of the fruit of the vine until the
βασιλεία τοῦ θεοῦ ἔλθῃ. 19 Καὶ λαβὼν ἄρτον, εὐχαριστή-
kingdom of God be come. And having taken a loaf, having given
σας ἔκλασεν, καὶ ἔδωκεν αὐτοῖς, λέγων, Τοῦτό ἐστιν τὸ σῶμά
thanks he broke, and gave to them, saying, This is   ²body
μου, τὸ ὑπὲρ ὑμῶν διδόμενον· τοῦτο ποιεῖτε ᵍεἰς‖ τὴν ἐμὴν
¹my, which for you is given: this do in the ²of ³me
ἀνάμνησιν. 20 ʰὩσαύτως καὶ τὸ ποτήριον‖ μετὰ τὸ.δειπνῆ-
¹remembrance. In like manner also the cup after having supped,

7 Then came the day of unleavened bread, when the passover must be killed. 8 And he sent Peter and John, saying, Go and prepare us the passover, that we may eat. 9 And they said unto him, Where wilt thou that we prepare? 10 And he said unto them, Behold, when ye are entered into the city, there shall a man meet you, bearing a pitcher of water; follow him into the house where he entereth in. 11 And ye shall say unto the goodman of the house, The Master saith unto thee, Where is the guestchamber, where I shall eat the passover with my disciples? 12 And he shall shew you a large upper room furnished: there make ready. 13 And they went, and found as he had said unto them: and they made ready the passover.

14 And when the hour was come, he sat down, and the twelve apostles with him. 15 And he said unto them, With desire I have desired to eat this passover with you before I suffer: 16 for I say unto you, I will not any more eat thereof, until it be fulfilled in the kingdom of God. 17 And he took the cup, and gave thanks, and said, Take this, and divide it among yourselves: 18 for I say unto you, I will not drink of the fruit of the vine, until the kingdom of God shall come. 19 And he took bread, and gave thanks, and brake it, and gave unto them, saying, This is my body which is given for you: this do in remembrance of me. 20 Likewise also the cup after supper, say-

---

° ἄτερ ὄχλου αὐτοῖς LTTrA.   ᴾ — ἐν (read ῇ in which) TrA.   ᑫ Ἰωάννην Tr.   ʳ εἶπαν
LTTrA.   ˢ + [σοι] for thee L.   ᵗ εἰς ἢν in which LTTrA.   ᵛ ἀνάγαιον GLTTrAW.   ᵂ εἴρηκει
LTTrA.   ˣ — δώδεκα LTTrA.   ʸ — οὐκέτι [LTrA].   ᶻ αὐτὸ it LTTrA.   ᵃ + τὸ the (cup) L.
ᵇ εἰς ἑαυτούς LTTrA.   ᶜ — ὅτι TrA.   ᵈ + ἀπὸ τοῦ νῦν henceforth T[TrA].   ᵉ γενήματος
LTTrAW.   ᶠοῦ TrA.   ᵍ [εἰς] A.   ʰ καὶ τὸ ποτήριον ὡσαύτως TTrA.

ing, This cup *is* the new testament in my blood, which is shed for you. 21 But, behold, the hand of him that betrayeth me *is* with me on the table. 22 And truly the Son of man goeth, as it was determined: but woe unto that man by whom he is betrayed! 23 And they began to inquire among themselves, which of them it was that should do this thing.

24 And there was also a strife among them, which of them should be accounted the greatest. 25 And he said unto them, The kings of the Gentiles exercise lordship over them; and they that exercise authority upon them are called benefactors. 26 But ye shall not *be* so: but he that is greatest among you, let him be as the younger; and he that is chief, as he that doth serve. 27 For whether *is* greater, he that sitteth at meat, or he that serveth? *is* not he that sitteth at meat? but I am among you as he that serveth. 28 Ye are they which have continued with me in my temptations. 29 And I appoint unto you a kingdom, as my Father hath appointed unto me; 30 that ye may eat and drink at my table in my kingdom, and sit on thrones judging the twelve tribes of Israel.

31 And the Lord said, Simon, Simon, behold, Satan hath desired *to have* you, that he may sift *you* as wheat: 32 but I have prayed for thee, that thy faith fail not: and when thou art converted, strengthen thy brethren. 33 And he said unto him, Lord, I am ready to go with thee, both into prison, and to death. 34 And he said, I tell thee, Peter.

σαι, λέγων, Τοῦτο τὸ ποτήριον ἡ καινὴ διαθήκη ἐν τῷ
saying, This cup [is] the new covenant in

αἵματί.μου, τὸ ὑπὲρ ὑμῶν ʰἐκχυνόμενον.ʰ 21 Πλὴν ἰδού,
my blood, which for you is poured out. Moreover, behold,

ἡ χεὶρ τοῦ παραδιδόντος με μετʼ ἐμοῦ ἐπὶ τῆς τραπέζης.
the hand of him delivering up ˉme [is] with me on the table;

22 ᵏκαὶ ὁ.μὲν.υἱὸςʰ τοῦ ἀνθρώπου ¹πορεύεται κατὰ ˉτὸ
and indeed the Son of man goes according as

ὡρισμένον·ʰ πλὴν οὐαὶ τῷ.ἀνθρώπῳ.ἐκείνῳ διʼ οὗ παρα-
it has been determined, but woe to that man by whom he is de-

δίδοται. 23 Καὶ αὐτοὶ ἤρξαντο ᵐσυζητεῖνʰ πρὸς ἑαυτούς,
livered up. And they began to.question together among themselves,

τό, τίς ἄρα εἴη ἐξ αὐτῶν ὁ τοῦτο μέλλων πράσσειν.
this, who then it might be of them who this was about to do.

24 Ἐγένετο.δὲ καὶ φιλονεικία ἐν αὐτοῖς, τό, τίς αὐτῶν
And there was also a strife among them, this, which of them

δοκεῖ εἶναι μείζων. 25 ὁ.δὲ εἶπεν αὐτοῖς, Οἱ βασιλεῖς
is thought to be [the] greater. And he said to them, The kings

τῶν ἐθνῶν κυριεύουσιν αὐτῶν, καὶ οἱ ἐξουσιάζοντες
of the nations rule over them, and those exercising authority over

αὐτῶν εὐεργέται καλοῦνται. 26 ὑμεῖς.δὲ οὐχ οὕτως· ἀλλʼ
them well-doers are called. But ye not thus [shall be]; but

ὁ μείζων ἐν ὑμῖν ⁿγενέσθωʰ ὡς ὁ νεώτερος· καὶ ὁ
the greater among you let him be as the younger, and he that

ἡγούμενος ὡς ὁ διακονῶν. 27 τίς.γὰρ μείζων, ὁ
leads as he that serves. For which [is] greater, he that

ἀνακείμενος ἢ ὁ διακονῶν; οὐχὶ ὁ ἀνακείμε-
reclines · [at table] or he that serves? [Is] not he that reclines

νος; ἐγὼ.δὲ °εἰμι ἐν μέσῳ ὑμῶνʰ ὡς ὁ διακονῶν.
[at table]? But I am in [the] midst of you as he that serves.

28 Ὑμεῖς.δὲ ἐστε οἱ διαμεμενηκότες μετʼ ἐμοῦ ἐν τοῖς
But ye are they who have continued with me in

πειρασμοῖς.μου· 29 κἀγὼ διατίθεμαι ὑμῖν, καθὼς διέθετό
my temptations. And I appoint to you, as ᵃappointed

μοι ὁ.πατήρ.μου, βασιλείαν, 30 ᴾἵνα ᴾἔσθίητεʰ καὶ πίνητε
ᵃto ᵇme ¹my ²father, a kingdom, that ye may eat and may drink

ἐπὶ τῆς.τραπέζης.μου ἐν τῇ.βασιλείᾳ.μου, καὶ ᑫκαθίσησθεʰ ἐπὶ
at my table in my kingdom, and may sit on

θρόνων, κρίνοντες τὰς δώδεκα φυλὰς τοῦ Ἰσραήλ.
thrones, judging the twelve tribes of Israel.

31 ʳΕἶπεν.δὲ ὁ κύριος,ʰ Σίμων, Σίμων, ἰδού, ὁ σατανᾶς
And ³said ¹the ²Lord, Simon, Simon, lo, Satan

ἐξῃτήσατο ὑμᾶς, τοῦ σινιάσαι ὡς τὸν σῖτον· 32 ἐγὼ
demanded to have you; for the sifting [you] as wheat; ²I

δὲ ἐδεήθην περὶ σοῦ, ἵνα μὴ.ˢἐκλείπῃʰ ἡ.πίστις.σου· καὶ σύ
¹but besought for thee, that may not fail thy faith; and ²thou

ποτε ἐπιστρέψας ᵗστήριξονʰ τοὺς.ἀδελφούς.σου. 33 Ὁ.δὲ
¹when hast turned back confirm thy brethren. And he

εἶπεν αὐτῷ, Κύριε, μετὰ σοῦ ἕτοιμός εἰμι καὶ εἰς φυλακὴν καὶ
said to him, Lord, with thee ready I am both to prison and

εἰς θάνατον πορεύεσθαι. 34 Ὁ.δὲ εἶπεν, Λέγω σοι, Πέτρε,
to death to go. And he said, I tell thee, Peter.

ʰ ἐκχυννόμενον LTTrA.   ᵏ ὅτι (for) ὁ υἱὸς μὲν TTrA.   ¹ κατὰ τὸ ὡρισμένον πορεύεται LTTrA.
ᵐ συνζητεῖν LTTrA.   ⁿ γινέσθω TTrA.   ° ἐν μέσῳ ὑμῶν εἰμι TTrA.   ᴾ ἔσθητε LTTrA.
ᑫ καθίσεσθε ye shall sit GLW; καθήσεσθε ye shall sit TTr; κάθησθε A.   ʳ — Εἶπεν δὲ ὁ
κύριος T[Tr]A.   ˢ ἐκλίπῃ LTTrA.   ᵗ στήρισον LTTrA.

οὐ.ᵛμὴ‖ φωνήσει σήμερον ἀλέκτωρ ᵂπρὶν.ἢ⁴ τρὶς ˣἀπαρ-
in no wise shall crow   to-day [the] cock   before that thrice thou wilt

νήσῃ ʸμὴ‖ εἰδέναι με.‖
deny   knowing me.

35 Καὶ εἶπεν αὐτοῖς, Ὅτε ἀπέστειλα ὑμᾶς ἄτερ ˣᶻβαλαν-
And he said to them, When   I sent   you without purse

τίου‖ καὶ ˉπήρας καὶ ὑποδημάτων, μή τινος ὑστερήσατε;
and provision bag and   sandals,   anything did ye lack?

Οἱ.δὲ ᵃεἶπον,‖ ᵇΟὐδενός.‖ 36 ᶜΕἶπεν οὖν‖ αὐτοῖς, Ἀλλὰ
And they said,   Nothing.   He said therefore to them, ᵃHowever

νῦν ὁ ἔχων ᵈβαλάντιον‖ ἀράτω,   ὁμοίως καὶ πήραν·
¹now he who has a purse   let him take [it], in like manner also provision bag;

καὶ ὁ μὴ.ἔχων πωλησάτω τὸ.ἱμάτιον.αὐτοῦ καὶ ἀγορασάτω
and he who has not [one] let him sell his garment and   buy

μάχαιραν· 37 λέγω.γὰρ ὑμῖν, ὅτι ᵉἔτι‖ τοῦτο τὸ γεγραμμένον
a sword;   for I say to you, that yet this that has been written

δεῖ τελεσθῆναι ἐν ἐμοί, ᶠτὸ‖ Καὶ μετὰ ἀνόμων ἐλογίσθη·
must be accomplished in me, And with [the] lawless he was reckoned:

καὶ.ᵍγὰρ‖ ʰτὰ‖ περὶ ἐμοῦ τέλος ἔχει. 38 Οἱ.δὲ ᵃεἶπον,‖
for also the things concerning me an end have.   And they said,

Κύριε, ἰδού, μάχαιραι ὧδε δύο. Ὁ.δὲ εἶπεν αὐτοῖς,
Lord, behold, ²swords ¹here [²are] ³two. And he ₌ said to them,

Ἱκανόν ἐστιν.
³Enough ¹it ²is.

39 Καὶ ἐξελθὼν ἐπορεύθη κατὰ τὸ ἔθος εἰς τὸ ὄρος
And going forth he went according to custom to the mount

τῶν ἐλαιῶν· ἠκολούθησαν.δὲ αὐτῷ καὶ οἱ.μαθηταὶ.ᵢαὐτοῦ.‖
of Olives,   and followed   him also   his disciples.

40 γενόμενος.δὲ ἐπὶ τοῦ τόπου εἶπεν αὐτοῖς, Προσεύχεσθε
And having arrived at   the place he said to them,   Pray

μὴ.εἰσελθεῖν εἰς πειρασμόν. 41 Καὶ αὐτὸς ἀπεσπάσθη ἀπ'
not to enter ⁷ into temptation. And he   was withdrawn from

αὐτῶν ὡσεὶ λίθου βολήν, καὶ θεὶς.τὰ.γόνατα προσηύχετο,
them about a stone's throw, and falling on [his] knees he prayed,

42 λέγων, Πάτερ, εἰ βούλει ᵏπαρενεγκεῖν‖ ¹τὸ ποτήριον
saying, Father, if thou art willing to take away ²cup

τοῦτο‖ ἀπ' ἐμοῦ· πλὴν μὴ τὸ.θέλημά.μου, ἀλλὰ τὸ.σὸν ᵐγε-
¹this from me—; but not my will,   but thine be

νέσθω.‖ 43 ⁿὬφθη.δὲ αὐτῷ ἄγγελος ᵒἀπ'¹ οὐρανοῦ ἐνισχύων
done.   And appeared to him an angel from heaven strengthening

αὐτόν. 44 καὶ γενόμενος ἐν ἀγωνίᾳ ἐκτενέστερον προσηύχετο.
him. And being in conflict more intently he prayed.

Ρἐγένετο.δὲ ὁ'.ἰδρὼς.αὐτοῦ ὡσεὶ θρόμβοι αἵματος ᵠκατα-
And became his sweat   as   great drops of blood falling

βαίνοντες¹ ἐπὶ τὴν γῆν.‖ 45 Καὶ ἀναστὰς ἀπὸ τῆς
down   to the earth.   And having risen up from

προσευχῆς, ἐλθὼν πρὸς τοὺς μαθητὰςʳ εὗρεν ˢαὐτοὺς κοιμω-
prayer, coming to the disciples he found them sleep-

the cock shall not crow this day, before that thou shalt thrice deny that thou knowest me.	

35 And he said unto them, When I sent you without purse, and scrip, and shoes, lacked ye any thing? And they said, Nothing. 36 Then said he unto them, But now, he that hath a purse, let him take it, and likewise his scrip: and he that hath no sword, let him sell his garment, and buy one. 37 For I say unto you, that this that is written must yet be accomplished in me, And he was reckoned among the transgressors: for the things concerning me have an end. 38 And they said, Lord, behold, here are two swords. And he said unto them, It is enough.

39 And he came out, and went, as he was wont, to the mount of Olives; and his disciples also followed him. 40 And when he was at the place, he said unto them, Pray that ye enter not into temptation. 41 And he was withdrawn from them about a stone's cast, and kneeled down, and prayed, 42 saying, Father, if thou be willing, remove this cup from me: nevertheless not my will, but thine, be done. 43 And there appeared an angel unto him from heaven, strengthening him. 44 And being in an agony he prayed more earnestly: and his sweat was as it were great drops of blood falling down to the ground. 45 And when he rose up from prayer, and was come to his disciples, he found them sleeping

---

ᵛ.— μὴ (read shall not crow) TT-A.   ᵂ ἕως until LTTrA.   ˣ με ἀπαρνήσῃ
εἰδέναι LTr.   ʸ [μὴ] A.   ᶻ βαλλαντίου LTTrAW.   ᵃ εἶπαν LTTrA.   ᵇ Οὐθενός TTrA.
ᶜ ὁ δὲ εἶπεν but he said T; εἶπεν δὲ Tr.   ᵈ βαλλάντιον LTTrAW.   ᵉ — ἔτι LTTrA.   ᶠ ὅτι L.
ᵍ [γὰρ] LTr.   ʰ τὸ that (concerning me has an end) TTrA.   ⁱ — αὐτοῦ (read the disciples) TTrA.   ᵏ παρενέγκαι T; παρένεγκε take away LTr.   ¹ τοῦτο τὸ ποτήριον TTrA.
ᵐ γινέσθω TTrAW.   ⁿ verses 43, 44 in [ ] L.   ᵒ ἀπὸ τοῦ from the LTr.   ᴾ καὶ ἐγένετο
ὁ ([ὁ] A) TA.   ᵠ καταβαίνοντος TA.   ʳ ᴴᶻαὐτοῦ (read his disciples) E.   ˢ κοιμωμένους
αὐτοὺς TTrA.

for sorrow, 46 and said unto them, Why sleep ye? rise and pray, lest ye enter into temptation.

47 And while he yet spake, behold a multitude, and he that was called Judas, one of the twelve, went before them, and drew near unto Jesus to kiss him. 48 But Jesus said unto him, Judas, betrayest thou the Son of man with a kiss? 49 When they which were about him saw what would follow, they said unto him, Lord, shall we smite with the sword? 50 And one of them smote the servant of the high priest, and cut off his right ear. 51 And Jesus answered and said, Suffer ye thus far. And he touched his ear, and healed him. 52 Then Jesus said unto the chief priests, and captains of the temple, and the elders, which were come to him, Be ye come out, as against a thief, with swords and staves? 53 When I was daily with you in the temple, ye stretched forth no hands against me: but this is your hour, and the power of darkness.

54 Then took they him, and led *him*, and brought him into the high priest's house. And Peter followed afar off. 55 And when they had kindled a fire in the midst of the hall, and were set down together, Peter sat down among them. 56 But a certain maid beheld him as he sat by the fire, and earnestly looked upon him, and said, This man was also with him. 57 And he denied him, saying, Woman, I know him not. 58 And after a little while another saw him, and said,

μένους‖ ἀπὸ τῆς λύπης, 46 καὶ εἶπεν αὐτοῖς, Τί καθεύδετε‖
ing from grief, and⸱ he said to them, Why sleep ye?
ἀναστάντες προσεύχεσθε, ἵνα μὴ εἰσέλθητε εἰς πειρασμόν.
Having risen up pray, that ye may not enter into temptation.

47 Ἔτι ᵛδὲ‖ αὐτοῦ λαλοῦντος, ἰδοὺ ὄχλος, καὶ ὁ λεγό-
  And ᵛyet. ¹as ²he ³was speaking, behold a crowd, and he who was
μενος Ἰούδας, εἷς τῶν δώδεκα, προήρχετο ʷαὐτῶν,‖ καὶ
called Judas, one of the twelve, was going before them, and
ἤγγισεν τῷ Ἰησοῦ φιλῆσαι αὐτόν. 48 ˣὁ δὲ Ἰησοῦς‖ εἶπεν
drew near to Jesus to kiss him.⸱ But Jesus said
αὐτῷ, Ἰούδα, φιλήματι τὸν υἱὸν τοῦ ἀνθρώπου παραδίδως;
to him, Judas, with a kiss the Son of man deliverest thou up?
49 Ἰδόντες δὲ οἱ περὶ αὐτὸν τὸ ἐσόμενον ʸεἶπον‖
 And ⁴seeing ¹those ²around ³him what was about to happen said
ᶻαὐτῷ,‖ Κύριε, εἰ πατάξομεν ἐν ᵃμαχαίρᾳ‖; 50 Καὶ ἐπά-
to him, Lord, shall we smite with [the] sword? And ⁶smote
ταξεν εἷς τις ἐξ αὐτῶν ᵇτὸν δοῦλον τοῦ ἀρχιερέως,‖ καὶ
 ³one ¹a ²certain ⁴of ⁵them the bondman of the high priest, and
ἀφεῖλεν ᶜαὐτοῦ τὸ οὖς‖ τὸ δεξιόν. 51 ἀποκριθεὶς δὲ ὁ Ἰησοῦς
took off his ²ear ¹right. And answering Jesus
εἶπεν, Ἐᾶτε ἕως τούτου. Καὶ ἁψάμενος τοῦ ὠτίου ᵈαὐτοῦ‖
said, Suffer thus far. And having touched the ear of him
ἰάσατο αὐτόν. 52 Εἶπεν δὲ ᵉὁ‖ Ἰησοῦς πρὸς τοὺς παρα-
he healed him. And ²said ¹Jesus to those who were
γενομένους ᶠἐπ'‖ αὐτὸν ἀρχιερεῖς καὶ στρατηγοὺς τοῦ ἱεροῦ
come against him, chief priests and captains of the temple
καὶ πρεσβυτέρους, Ὡς ἐπὶ λῃστὴν ᵍἐξεληλύθατε‖ μετὰ
and elders, 'As against a robber have ye come out with
μαχαιρῶν καὶ ξύλων; 53 καθ' ἡμέραν ὄντος μου μεθ' ὑμῶν
swords and staves? Daily when I was with you
ἐν τῷ ἱερῷ οὐκ ἐξετείνατε τὰς χεῖρας ἐπ' ἐμέ. ʰἀλλ'‖
in the temple ye stretched not out [your] hands against me; but
αὕτη ὑμῶν ἐστιν‖ ἡ ὥρα, καὶ ἡ ἐξουσία τοῦ σκότους.
this ²your ¹is hour, and the power of darkness.

54 Συλλαβόντες δὲ αὐτὸν ἤγαγον, καὶ εἰσήγαγον
 And having seized him they led [him away], and led
ᵏαὐτὸν‖ εἰς ¹τὸν οἶκον‖ τοῦ ἀρχιερέως· ὁ δὲ Πέτρος ἠκολούθει
him ⁵ into the house of the high priest. And Peter was following
μακρόθεν. ₗ55 ᵐἁψάντων‖ δὲ πῦρ ἐν μέσῳ τῆς αὐλῆς,
afar off. And having kindled a fire in [the] midst of the court,
καὶ ⁿσυγκαθισάντων‖ ᵒαὐτῶν‖ ἐκάθητο ὁ Πέτρος ᴾἐν μέσῳ‖
and ²having ³sat ⁴down ⁵together ¹they ⁷sat ⁶Peter among
αὐτῶν. 56 ἰδοῦσα δὲ αὐτὸν παιδίσκη τις καθημένην πρὸς
them. And ⁴having ⁵seen ⁶him ¹a ²maid ²certain sitting by
τὸ φῶς, καὶ ἀτενίσασα αὐτῷ, εἶπεν, Καὶ οὗτος σὺν
the light, and having looked intently on him, said, And this one with
αὐτῷ ἦν. 57 Ὁ δὲ ἠρνήσατο ᑫαὐτόν,‖ λέγων, ʳΓύναι, οὐκ
him was. But he denied him, saying, Woman, ³not
οἶδα αὐτόν.‖ 58 Καὶ μετὰ βραχὺ ἕτερος ἰδὼν αὐτὸν ἔφη,
¹I ²do know him. And after a little another seeing him said,

ᵛ — δὲ and LTTrAW. ʷ αὐτούς GLTTrAW. ˣ Ἰησοῦς δὲ TTrA. ʸ εἶπαν LTTrA.
ᶻ — αὐτῷ TTrA. ᵃ μαχαίρῃ TTrA. ᵇ τοῦ ἀρχιερέως τὸν δοῦλον TTrA ᶜ τὸ οὖς αὐτοῦ LTTrA:
ᵈ — αὐτοῦ TTrA. ᵉ ὁ LTTrA. ᶠ πρὸς T. ᵍ ἐξήλθατε came ye out LTr. ʰ ἀλλὰ TrA.
ᶦ ἐστιν ὑμῶν LTTrA. ᵏ — αὐτὸν (read [him]) LTTrA. ˡ τὴν οἰκίαν TTrA. ᵐ περιαψάντων
TTrA. ⁿ περικαθισάντων, having sat around L; συνκαθισάντων T. ᵒ — αὐτῶν LTTrA.
ᴾ μέσος TTrA. ᑫ — αὐτὸν LTr[A]. ʳ οὐκ οἶδα αὐτόν, γύναι TTrA.

Καὶ σὺ εξ αυτων εἶ. Ὁ.δὲ.Πέτρος ᵉεἶπεν, "Ἄνθρωπε, οὐκ.εἰμί.
And thou of them art. But Peter said, Man, I am not.

59 Καὶ διαστάσης ὡσεὶ ὥρας μιᾶς, ἄλλος τις διϊσχυρίζετο,
And having elapsed about ²hour ¹one, ³other ³a ᵃcertain strongly affirmed,

λέγων, Ἐπ' ἀληθείας καὶ οὗτος μετ' αὐτοῦ ἦν· καὶ.γὰρ Γαλι-
saying, In truth also this one with him was; for also a Gali-

λαῖός ἐστιν. 60 Εἶπεν.δὲ ὁ Πέτρος, Ἄνθρωπε, οὐκ.οἶδα ὃ
lean he is. And ²said ¹Peter, Man, I know not what

λέγεις. Καὶ παραχρῆμα, ἔτι λαλοῦντος.αὐτοῦ, ἐφώνησεν
thou sayest. And immediately, ²yet ¹as he was speaking, ³crew

ᵗὁ" ἀλέκτωρ· 61 καὶ στραφεὶς ὁ κύριος ἐνέβλεψεν τῷ Πέτρῳ·
¹the ²cock. And having turned, the Lord looked at Peter;

καὶ ὑπεμνήσθη ὁ Πέτρος τοῦ λόγου τοῦ κυρίου, ὡς εἶπεν αὐτῷ,
and ²remembered ¹Peter the word of the Lord, how he said to him,

Ὅτι πρὶν ἀλέκτορα φωνῆσαι ᵛ ἀπαρνήσῃ με τρίς. 62 Καὶ
Before [the] cock crow thou wilt deny me thrice. And

ἐξελθὼν ἔξω ᵂὁ Πέτρος" ἔκλαυσεν πικρῶς.
having gone forth outside Peter wept bitterly.

63 Καὶ οἱ ἄνδρες οἱ συνέχοντες ˣτὸν Ἰησοῦν" ἐνέπαιζον
And the men who ⁻were holding Jesus mocked

αὐτῷ, δέροντες· 64 καὶ περικαλύψαντες αὐτὸν ʸἔτυπτον
him, beating [him]; and having covered up him they were striking

αὐτοῦ τὸ πρόσωπον, καὶ" ἐπηρώτων ᶻαὐτόν," λέγοντες, Προ-
his face, and were asking him, saying, Pro-

φήτευσον, τίς ἐστιν ὁ παίσας σε; 65 Καὶ ἕτερα πολλὰ
phesy, who is it that struck thee? And ²other ³things ¹many

βλασφημοῦντες ἔλεγον εἰς αὐτόν.
blasphemously they said to him.

66 Καὶ ὡς ᵉ ἐγένετο ἡμέρα συνήχθη τὸ πρεσβυτέριον
And when it became day were gathered together the elderhood

τοῦ λαοῦ, ἀρχιερεῖς.τε καὶ γραμματεῖς, καὶ ᵃἀνήγαγον" αὐτὸν
of the people, both chief priests and scribes, and they led him

εἰς τὸ συνέδριον ᵇἑαυτῶν," λέγοντες, 67 Εἰ σὺ εἶ ὁ χριστός,
into ²sanhedrim ¹their, saying, If thou art the Christ,

ᶜεἰπὲ" ἡμῖν. Εἶπεν.δὲ αὐτοῖς, Ἐὰν ὑμῖν εἴπω, οὐ.μὴ
tell us. And he said to them, If you I should tell, not at all

πιστεύσητε· 68 ἐὰν.δὲ ᵈκαὶ" ἐρωτήσω, οὐ.μὴ ἀποκρι-
would ye believe; and if also I should ask [you], not at all would ye

θῆτέ ᵉμοι, ἢ ἀπολύσητε." 69 ἀπὸ.τοῦ.νῦν ᶠἔσται ὁ υἱὸς τοῦ
answer me, nor let [me] go. Henceforth shall be the Son

ἀνθρώπου καθήμενος ἐκ δεξιῶν τῆς δυνάμεως τοῦ θεοῦ.
of man sitting at [the] right hand of the power of God.

70 ᵍΕἶπον".δὲ πάντες, Σὺ οὖν εἶ ὁ υἱὸς τοῦ θεοῦ; Ὁ.δὲ
And they ²said ¹all, Thou then art the Son of God? And he

πρὸς αὐτοὺς ἔφη, Ὑμεῖς λέγετε, ὅτι ἐγώ εἰμι. 71 Οἱ.δὲ ʰεἶπον,"
to them said, Ye say, that I am. And they said,

Τί ἔτι ⁱχρείαν ἔχομεν μαρτυρίας"; αὐτοὶ.γὰρ ἠκούσαμεν
What any more need have we of witness? for ourselves have heard

ἀπὸ τοῦ.στόματος.αὐτοῦ.
from his [own] mouth.

23 Καὶ ἀναστὰν ἅπαν τὸ πλῆθος αὐτῶν ᵏἤγαγεν"
And having risen up all the multitude of them led

Thou art also of them. And Peter said, Man, I am not. 59 And about the space of one hour after another confidently affirmed, saying, Of a truth this *fellow* also was with him: for he is a Galilæan. 60 And Peter said, Man, I know not what thou sayest. And immediately, while he yet spake, the cock crew. 61 And the Lord turned, and looked upon Peter. And Peter remembered the word of the Lord, how he had said unto him, Before the cock crow, thou shalt deny me thrice. 62 And Peter went out, and wept bitterly.

63 And the men that held Jesus mocked him, and smote *him*. 64 And when they had blindfolded him, they struck him on the face, and asked him, saying, Prophesy, who is it that smote thee? 65 And many other things blasphemously spake they against him.

66 And as soon as it was day, the elders of the people and the chief priests and the scribes came together, and led him into their council, saying, 67 Art thou the Christ? tell us. And he said unto them, If I tell you ye will not believe: 68 and if I also ask *you*, ye will not answer me, nor let *me* go. 69 Hereafter shall the Son of man sit on the right hand of the power of God. 70 Then said they all, Art thou then the Son of God? And he said unto them, Ye say that I am. 71 And they said, What need we any further witness? for we ourselves have heard of his own mouth.

XXIII. And the whole multitude of them arose, and led

ˢ ἔφη TTrA.　ᵗ — ὁ (read [the]) GLTTrAW.　ᵛ + σήμερον to-day TTrA.　ᵂ — ὁ Πέτρος
(read he wept) GTTrĮA].　ˣ αὐτὸν him LTTrA.　ʸ — ἔτυπτον αὐτοῦ τὸ πρόσωπον, καὶ [L]TTrA.

ᶻ — αὐτὸν TTrA.　ᵃ ἀπήγαγον they led away TTrA.　ᵇ αὐτῶν TTrAW.　ᶜ εἰπὸν TTrA.
ᵈ — καὶ LTTrA.　ᵉ — μοι ἢ ἀπολύσητε τ[TrA].　ᶠ + δὲ however LTTrA.　ᵍ εἶπαν TTrA.
ʰ εἶπαν LTTrA.　ⁱ ἔχομεν μαρτυρίας χρείαν TTrA.　ᵏ ἤγαγον GLTTrAW.
16

him unto Pilate. 2 And they began to accuse him, saying, We found this *fellow* perverting the nation, and forbidding to give tribute to Cæsar, saying that he himself is Christ a King. 3 And Pilate asked him, saying, Art thou the King of the Jews? And he answered him and said, Thou sayest *it*. 4 Then said Pilate to the chief priests and *to* the people, I find no fault in this man. 5 And they were the more fierce, saying, He stirreth up the people, teaching throughout all Jewry, beginning from Galilee to this place. 6 When Pilate heard of Galilee, he asked whether the man were a Galilæan. 7 And as soon as he knew that he belonged unto Herod's jurisdiction, he sent him to Herod, who himself also was at Jerusalem at that time. 8 And when Herod saw Jesus, he was exceeding glad: for he was desirous to see him of a long *season*, because he had heard many things of him; and he hoped to have seen some miracle done by him. 9 Then he questioned with him in many words; but he answered him nothing. 10 And the chief priests and scribes stood and vehemently accused him. 11 And Herod with his men of war set him at nought, and mocked *him*, and arrayed him in a gorgeous robe, and sent him again to Pilate. 12 And the same day Pilate and Herod were made friends together: for before they were at enmity between themselves.

13 And Pilate, when he had called together the chief priests and the rulers and the people, 14 said unto them, Ye have brought this

αὐτὸν ἐπὶ τὸν ¹Πιλατον.‖ 2 ἤρξαντο.δὲ κατηγορεῖν αὐτοῦ,
him to Pilate. And they began to accuse him,
λέγοντες, Τοῦτον ᵐεὕρομεν‖ διαστρέφοντα τὸ ἔθνος ⁿ, καὶ
saying, This [man] we found perverting the nation, and
κωλύοντα ᵒΚαίσαρι φόρους‖ διδόναι, ᴾλέγοντα ἑαυτὸν χριστὸν
forbidding to Cæsar tribute to give, saying himself Christ
βασιλέα εἶναι. 3 Ὁ.δὲ.�q Πιλάτος‖ ʳἐπηρώτησεν‖ αὐτόν, λέγων,
a king is. And Pilate questioned him, saying,
Σὺ εἶ ὁ βασιλεὺς τῶν Ἰουδαίων; Ὁ.δὲ ἀποκριθεὶς αὐτῷ
Thou art the king of the Jews? And he answering him
ἔφη, Σὺ λέγεις. 4 Ὁ.δὲ.q Πιλάτος‖ εἶπεν πρὸς τοὺς ἀρχιερεῖς
said, Thou sayest. And Pilate said to the chief priests
καὶ τοὺς ὄχλους, Οὐδὲν εὑρίσκω αἴτιον ἐν τῷ.ἀνθρώπῳ.τούτῳ.
and the crowds, Nothing find I blamable in this man.
5 Οἱ.δὲ ἐπίσχυον, λέγοντες, Ὅτι ἀνασείει τὸν λαόν, διδάσ-
But they were insisting, saying, He stirs up the people, teach-
κων καθ᾽ ὅλης τῆς Ἰουδαίας, ˢἀρξάμενος ἀπὸ τῆς Γαλι-
ing throughout whole the of Judæa, beginning from Gali-
λαίας ἕως ὧδε. 6 qΠιλάτος‖.δὲ ἀκούσας ᵗΓαλιλαίαν‖
lee even to here. But Pilate having heard Galilee [named]
ἐπηρώτησεν εἰ ὁ ἄνθρωπος Γαλιλαῖός ἐστιν· 7 καὶ ἐπι-
asked whether the man a Galilean is; and having
γνοὺς ὅτι ἐκ τῆς ἐξουσίας Ἡρώδου ἐστίν, ἀνέπεμψεν αὐτὸν
known that from the jurisdiction of Herod he is, he sent up him
πρὸς ᵛἩρώδην, ὄντα καὶ αὐτὸν ἐν Ἱεροσολύμοις ἐν ταύταις
to Herod, being also he at Jerusalem in those
ταῖς ἡμέραις. 8 ὁ.δὲ.Ἡρώδης ἰδὼν τὸν Ἰησοῦν ἐχάρη λίαν
days. And Herod seeing Jesus rejoiced greatly,
ἦν.γὰρ ʷθέλων ἐξ.ἱκανοῦ‖ ἰδεῖν αὐτόν, διὰ τὸ ἀκούειν
for he was wishing for long to see him, because of hearing
ˣπολλὰ‖ περὶ αὐτοῦ· καὶ ἤλπιζέν τι σημεῖον ἰδεῖν ὑπ᾽
many things concerning him; and he was hoping some sign to see by
αὐτοῦ γινόμενον. 9 ἐπηρώτα.δὲ αὐτὸν ἐν λόγοις ἱκανοῖς·
him done. And he questioned him in words many,
αὐτὸς.δὲ οὐδὲν ἀπεκρίνατο αὐτῷ. 10 εἱστήκεισαν.δὲ οἱ ἀρχ-
but he nothing answered him. And had stood the chief
ιερεῖς καὶ οἱ γραμματεῖς, εὐτόνως κατηγοροῦντες αὐτοῦ.
priests and the scribes, violently accusing him.
11 ἐξουθενήσας.δὲ αὐτὸν ʸ ὁ Ἡρώδης σὺν τοῖς στρατεύμασιν
And having set at nought him Herod with troops
αὐτοῦ, καὶ ἐμπαίξας, περιβαλὼν ᶻαὐτὸν‖ ἐσθῆτα λαμ-
his, and having mocked [him], having put on him apparel splen-
πρὰν ἀνέπεμψεν αὐτὸν τῷ ᵃΠιλάτῳ.‖ 12 ἐγένοντο.δὲ φίλοι
did he sent back him to Pilate. And became friends
ὅ.τε.ᵇΠιλάτος καὶ ὁ Ἡρώδης‖ ἐν αὐτῇ.τῇ ἡμέρᾳ μετ᾽ ἀλλήλων·
both Pilate and Herod on that same day with one another;
προϋπῆρχον.γὰρ ἐν ἔχθρᾳ ὄντες πρὸς ᶜἑαυτούς.‖
for before they were at enmity between themselves.
13 qΠιλάτος‖.δὲ ᵈσυγκαλεσάμενος‖ τοὺς ἀρχιερεῖς καὶ τους
And Pilate having called together the chief priests and the
ἄρχοντας καὶ τὸν λαόν, 14 εἶπεν πρὸς αὐτούς, Προσηνέγκατέ
rulers and the people, said to them, Ye brought

---

¹ Πειλᾶτον T. ᵐ εὕραμεν TTrA. ⁿ + ἡμῶν (*read* our nation) LTTr[A]w. ᵒ φόρους Καίσαρι LTTrA. ᴾ + καὶ and [L]TTr[A]. q Πειλᾶτος T. ʳ ἠρώτησεν TTrA. ˢ + καὶ even TTr[A]. ᵗ — Γαλιλαίαν T[A]. ᵛ + τὸν L. ʷ ἐξ ἱκανῶν χρόνων θέλων many times wishing LTTrA. ˣ — πολλὰ TTrA. ʸ + καὶ also T. ᶻ — αὐτὸν (*read* [him]) [T.]T[Tr]A. ᵃ Πειλάτῳ T. ᵇ Ἡρώδης καὶ ὁ Πιλάτος (Πειλ. T) TTrA. ᶜ αὐτούς TTrA. ᵈ συγκαλεσάμενος T.

μοι τὸν.ἄνθρωπον.τοῦτον, ὡς ἀποστρέφοντα τὸν λαόν· καὶ
to me this man, as turning away the people; and

ἰδού, ἐγὼ ἐνώπιον ὑμῶν ἀνακρίνας ᵉοὐδὲν‖ εὗρον ἐν τῷ
behold, I before you having examined [him] ²nothing ¹found in

ἀνθρώπῳ.τούτῳ αἴτιον ὧν κατηγορεῖτε
this man blamable [as to the things] of which ye bring accusation

κατ' αὐτοῦ· 15 ἀλλ'.οὐδὲ Ἡρώδης· ᶠἀνέπεμψα.γὰρ ὑμᾶς πρὸς
against him; nor even Herod, for I sent ²up ¹you to

αὐτόν,‖ καὶ ἰδού, οὐδὲν ἄξιον θανάτου ἐστὶν πεπραγμένον
him, and lo, nothing worthy of death is done

αὐτῷ. 16 παιδεύσας οὖν αὐτὸν ἀπολύσω. 17 ᵍἈνάγκην
by him. Having ²chastised ¹therefore him I will release [him]. ⁴Necessity

δὲ εἶχεν ἀπολύειν αὐτοῖς κατὰ ἑορτὴν ἕνα.‖ 18 ʰἀνέ-
¹now ²he ³had to release to them at [the] feast one. ²they

κραξαν‖ δὲ ᵏπαμπληθεί,‖ λέγοντες, Αἶρε τοῦτον, ἀπόλυ-
²cried ⁴out ⁵but ³ in a mass, saying, Away with this [man], ²re-

σον δὲ ἡμῖν τὸν Βαραββᾶν· 19 ὅστις ἦν· διὰ στάσιν
lease ¹and to us Barabbas; who was on account of ³insurrection

τινὰ γενομένην ἐν τῇ πόλει καὶ φόνον ¹βεβλημένος εἰς
¹a ²certain made in the city and murder cast into

φυλακήν.‖ 20 Πάλιν ᵐοὖν‖ ὁ ⁿΠιλάτος‖ προσεφώνησενᵒ,
prison. Again therefore Pilate called to [them],

θέλων ἀπολῦσαι τὸν Ἰησοῦν. 21 οἱ.δὲ ἐπεφώνουν, λέγοντες,
wishing to release Jesus. But they were crying out, saying,

ᵖΣταύρωσον, σταύρωσον‖ αὐτόν. 22 Ὁ.δὲ τρίτον εἶπεν
Crucify, crucify him. And he a third [time] said

πρὸς αὐτούς, Τί γὰρ κακὸν ἐποίησεν οὗτος; οὐδὲν
to them, What ²then ¹evil did ³commit ¹this ['man]? No

αἴτιον θανάτου εὗρον ἐν αὐτῷ· παιδεύσας οὖν αὐτὸν
cause of death found I in him. Having ²chastised ¹therefore him

ἀπολύσω. 23 Οἱ.δὲ ἐπέκειντο φωναῖς μεγάλαις, αἰτού-
I will release [him]. But they were urgent with ²voices ¹loud, asking

μενοι αὐτὸν σταυρωθῆναι· καὶ κατίσχυον αἱ φωναὶ αὐτῶν
for him to be crucified. And prevailed the voices of them

ᵠκαὶ τῶν ἀρχιερέων.‖ 24 Ὁ.δὲ· ⁿΠιλάτος‖ ἐπέκρινεν γενέσθαι
and of the chief priests. And Pilate adjudged ²to ⁴be ⁵done

τὸ.αἴτημα.αὐτῶν. 25 ἀπέλυσεν.δὲ· ˢαὐτοῖς‖ τὸν διὰ
¹their ²request. And he released to them him who on account of

στάσιν καὶ φόνον βεβλημένον εἰς ᵗτὴν‖ φυλακήν, ὃν
insurrection and murder had been cast into the prison, whom

ᾐτοῦντο· τὸν.δὲ.Ἰησοῦν παρέδωκεν τῷ.θελήματι.αὐτῶν.
they asked for; but Jesus he delivered up to their will.

26 Καὶ ὡς ἀπήγαγον αὐτόν, ἐπιλαβόμενοι ᵛΣίμωνός
And as they led ²away ¹him, having laid hold on ³Simon

τινος Κυρηναίου ᵂτοῦ ἐρχομένου‖ ˣἀπ'‖ ἀγροῦ, ἐπέθηκαν
ᵃa ²certain a Cyrenian coming from a field, they put upon

αὐτῷ τὸν σταυρὸν φέρειν ὄπισθεν.τοῦ Ἰησοῦ. 27 Ἠκολούθει
him the cross to bear [it] behind Jesus. ²Were ³following

δὲ αὐτῷ πολὺ πλῆθος τοῦ λαοῦ καὶ γυναικῶν, αἳ ʸκαὶ‖
¹and him a great multitude of the people and of women, who also

man unto me, as one that perverteth the people: and, behold, I, having examined *him* before you, have found no fault in this man touching those things whereof ye accuse him: 15 no, nor yet Herod: for I sent you to him; and, lo, nothing worthy of death is done unto him. 16 I will therefore chastise him, and release *him*. 17 (For of necessity he must release one unto them at the feast.) 18 And they cried out all at once, saying, Away with this *man*, and release unto us Barabbas: 19 (who for a certain sedition made in the city, and for murder, was cast into prison.) 20 Pilate therefore, willing to release Jesus, spake again to them. 21 But they cried, saying, Crucify *him*, crucify him. 22 And he said unto them the third time, Why, what evil hath he done? I have found no cause of death in him: I will therefore chastise him, and let *him* go. 23 And they were instant with loud voices, requiring that he might be crucified. And the voices of them and of the chief priests prevailed. 24 And Pilate gave sentence that it should be as they required. 25 And he released unto them him that for sedition and murder was cast into prison, whom they had desired; but he delivered Jesus to their will.

26 And as they led him away, they laid hold upon one Simon, a Cyrenian, coming out of the country, and on him they laid the cross, that he might bear *it* after Jesus. 27 And there followed him a great company of people, and of women, which also be-

---

ᵉ οὐδὲν TTr. ᶠ ἀνέπεμψεν γὰρ αὐτὸν πρὸς ἡμᾶς for he sent him back to us T.
ᵍ — verse 17 [L]TTr[A]. ʰ ἀνέκραγον TTrA. ᵏ παμπληθεί T. ˡ βληθεὶς ([βληθεὶς] A)
ἐν τῇ φυλακῇ TTrA. ᵐ δὲ however LTTrA. ⁿ Πειλᾶτος T. ᵒ + αὐτοῖς them L.
ᵖ Σταύρου σταύρου LTTrA. ᵠ — καὶ τῶν ἀρχιερέων [L]T[TrA]. ʳ καὶ LTTrA. ˢ — αὐτοῖς
G[L]TTrAW. ᵗ — τὴν LTTrA. ᵛ Σίμωνά τινα Κυρηναῖον ἐρχόμενον LTTrA. ᵂ — τοῦ GW.
ˣ ἀπὸ L. ʸ — καὶ LTTrA.

wailed and lamented him. 28 But Jesus turning unto them said, Daughters of Jerusalem, weep not for me, but weep for yourselves, and for your children. 29 For, behold, the days are coming, in the which they shall say, Blessed are the barren, and the wombs that never bare, and the paps which never gave suck. 30 Then shall they begin to say to the mountains, Fall on us; and to the hills, Cover us. 31 For if they do these things in a green tree, what shall be done in the dry? 32 And there were also two other, malefactors, led with him to be put to death. 33 And when they were come to the place, which is called Calvary, there they crucified him, and the malefactors, one on the right hand, and the other on the left. 34 Then said Jesus, Father, forgive them; for they know not what they do. And they parted his raiment, and cast lots. 35 And the people stood beholding. And the rulers also with them derided *him*, saying, He saved others; let him save himself, if he be Christ, the chosen of God. 36 And the soldiers also mocked him, coming to him, and offering him vinegar, 37 and saying, If thou be the king of the Jews, save thyself. 38 And a superscription also was written over him in letters of Greek, and Latin, and Hebrew, THIS IS THE KING OF THE JEWS

39 And one of the malefactors which were hanged railed on him, saying, If thou be Christ, save thyself and us. 40 But the other answering rebuked him, saying,

ἐκόπτοντο καὶ ἐθρήνουν αὐτόν. 28 στραφεὶς.δὲ πρὸς αὐτὰς
were bewailing and lamenting him.   And turning   to   them

ᶻὁ‖ Ἰησοῦς εἶπὲν, Θυγατέρες Ἰερουσαλήμ, μὴ.κλαίετε ᶦτ᾽ ἐμέ,
Jesus   said,   Daughters   of Jerusalem,   weep not   for   me,

πλὴν ἐφ᾽ ἑαυτὰς κλαίετε καὶ ἐπὶ τὰ.τέκνα.ὑμῶν· 29 ὅτι ἰδού,
but ²for ³yourselves 'weep and for   your children: for lo,

ἔρχονται ἡμέραι ἐν αἷς ἐροῦσιν, Μακάριαι αἱ στεῖραι
are coming   days   in which they will say, Blessed [are] the barren

καὶ ᵃκοιλίαι αἳ οὐκ.ἐγέννησαν καὶ μαστοὶ οἳ ᵇοὐκ.ἐθήλασαν.‖
and   wombs which did not bear   and breasts which gave not suck.

30 τότε ἄρξονται λέγειν τοῖς ὄρεσιν, ᶜΠέσετε‖ ἐφ᾽ ἡμᾶς
Then shall they begin to say to the mountains,   Fall   upon   us ;

καὶ τοῖς βουνοῖς, Καλύψατε ἡμᾶς. 31 ὅτι εἰ ἐν ᵈτῷ‖ ὑγρῷ
and to the   hills,   Cover   us :   for if in   the   green

ξύλῳ ταῦτα ποιοῦσιν, ἐν τῷ ξηρῷ τί γένηται; 32 Ἤγοντο
tree these things they do, in the dry what may take place? ²Were ³led

δὲ καὶ ἕτεροι δύο κακοῦργοι σὺν αὐτῷ ἀναιρεθῆναι. 33 Καὶ
¹and also ²other ¹two malefactors with him to be put to death.   And

ὅτε ᵉἀπῆλθον‖ ἐπὶ τὸν τόπον τὸν καλούμενον κρανίον ἐκεῖ
when they came to   the   place   called   a Skull there

ἐσταύρωσαν αὐτόν, καὶ τοὺς κακούργους, ὃν.μὲν ἐκ δεξιῶν
they crucified   him,   and the malefactors, the one on [the] right

ὃν.δὲ ἐξ ἀριστερῶν. 34 ᶠὁ.δὲ.Ἰησοῦς ἔλεγεν, Πάτερ, ἄφες
and one on [the] left.   And Jesus   said,   Father, forgive

αὐτοῖς· οὐ.γὰρ.οἴδασιν τί ποιοῦσιν.‖ Διαμεριζόμενοι.δὲ τὰ
them,   for they know not what they do.   And dividing

ἱμάτια.αὐτοῦ ἔβαλον ᵍκλῆρον.‖ 35 καὶ εἱστήκει ὁ λαὸς θεω-
his garments   they cast a lot.   And ³stood 'the ²people behold-

ρῶν· ἐξεμυκτήριζον.δὲ ʰκαὶ‖ οἱ ἄρχοντες ᶦσὺν αὐτοῖς,‖ λέγον-
ing, and ⁴were ⁵deriding ³also 'the ²rulers   with them,   say-

τες, Ἄλλους ἔσωσεν, σωσάτω ἑαυτόν εἰ οὗτός ἐστιν ὁ χριστὸς
ing, Others he saved, let him save himself if this   is the Christ

ᵏὁ τοῦ θεοῦ‖ ἐκλεκτός. 36 ˡἘνέπαιζον‖.δὲ αὐτῷ καὶ οἱ στρα-
the ²of ³God 'chosen.   And mocked   him also the   sol-

τιῶται, προσερχόμενοι ᵐκαὶ‖ ὄξος προσφέροντες αὐτῷ, 37 καὶ
diers,   coming near   and ³vinegar 'offering ²him, and

λέγοντες, ⁿΕἰ‖ σὺ εἶ ὁ βασιλεὺς τῶν Ἰουδαίων, σῶσον σεαυ-
saying,   If thou art the king   of the Jews,   save thy-

τόν. 38 Ἦν.δὲ καὶ ἐπιγραφὴ ᵒγεγραμμένη‖ ἐπ᾽ αὐτῷ
self.   And there was also an inscription   written   over   him

ᵖγράμμασιν Ἑλληνικοῖς καὶ Ῥωμαϊκοῖς καὶ Ἑβραϊκοῖς,
in letters   Greek   and   Latin   and   Hebrew :

ᑫΟὗτός ἐστιν ὁ βασιλεὺς τῶν Ἰουδαίων.‖
This   is   the king   of the Jews.

39 Εἷς.δὲ τῶν κρεμασθέντων κακούργων ἐβλασφήμει
Now one of the ²who ³had ⁴been ⁵hanged 'malefactors   railed at

αὐτόν, ʳλέγων,‖ ˢΕἰ σὺ εἶ ὁ χριστός,‖ σῶσον σεαυτὸν καὶ
him,   saying,   If thou art the Christ,   save   thyself   and

ἡμᾶς. 40 Ἀποκριθεὶς.δὲ ὁ ἕτερος ᵗἐπετίμα αὐτῷ, λέγων,‖
us.   But answering   the other   rebuked him,   saying,

ᶻ — ὁ ᴛᴛʀᴀ.   ᵃ + αἱ the ᴛᴛʀᴀ.   ᵇ οὐκ ἔθρεψαν nourished not ʟᴛᴛʀᴀ.   ᶜ Πέσατε ᴛᴛʀᴀ.
ᵈ [τῷ] ᴛʀ.   ᵉ ἦλθον ʟᴛʀᴀ.   ᶠ [ὁ δὲ .... ποιοῦσιν] ʟ.   ᵍ κλήρους lots ᴛᴀ.   ʰ — καὶ ʟᴛ.
ᶦ — σὺν αὐτοῖς [ʟ]ᴛᴛʀᴀ.   ᵏ τοῦ θεοῦ ὁ ᴛᴀ.   ˡ ἐνέπαιξαν ᴛᴀ.   ᵐ — καὶ [ʟ]ᴛᴛʀᴀ.
ⁿ [Εἰ] ʟ.   ᵒ ἐπιγεγραμμένη ʟ[ᴛʀ] ; — γεγραμμένη ᴛᴀ.   ᵖ — γράμμασιν .... Ἑβραϊκοῖς
[ʟ]ᴛᴛʀ[ᴀ].   ᑫ ὁ βασιλεὺς τῶν Ἰουδαίων οὗτος ([οὗτος] ʟ) ʟᴛᴛʀᴀ.   ʳ — λέγων ᴛ[ᴛʀ]ᴀ.
ˢ Οὐχὶ σὺ εἶ ὁ χριστός ; Art not thou the Christ ? ᴛᴛʀᴀ.   ᵗ ἐπιτιμῶν αὐτῷ ἔφη rebuking
him said ᴛᴛʀᴀ.

Οὐδὲ   φοβῇ σὺ τὸν θεόν,   ὅτι ἐν τῷ αὐτῷ κρίματι εἶ;
²Not ⁵even ¹dost ⁵fear ⁴thou   God,·[thou] that under the same judgment art?
Dost not thou fear God, seeing thou art in the same condemnation? 41 and we in-

41 καὶ ἡμεῖς μὲν δικαίως·   ἄξια.γὰρ   ὧν   ἐπράξαμεν
And we indeed justly; for ³a ⁴due ⁵recompense ⁶of ⁷what ⁸we ⁹did
deed justly; for we receive the due reward of our deeds: but this

ἀπολαμβάνομεν οὗτος.δὲ   οὐδὲν ἄτοπον ἔπραξεν. 42 Καὶ
¹we ²receive;   but this [man] ²nothing ³amiss   did. And
man hath done nothing amiss. · 42 And he said

ἔλεγεν ᵛτῷ¹¹ Ἰησοῦ, Μνήσθητί μου, ͮκύριε,¹¹ ὅταν ἔλθῃς ἐν
he said to Jesus, Remember me, Lord, when thou comest in
unto Jesus, Lord, re-member me when thou comest into thy king-

τῇ.βασιλείᾳ.σου. 43 Καὶ εἶπεν αὐτῷ ˣὁ Ἰησοῦς,¹¹ Ἀμὴν ᵞλέγω
thy kingdom. And ²said ³to ⁴him ¹Jesus, Verily I say
dom. 43 And Jesus said unto him, Verily I say unto thee, To

σοι,¹¹ σήμερον μετ᾽ ἐμοῦ ἔσῃ   ἐν τῷ παραδείσῳ.
to thee, To-day with me thou shalt be in Paradise.
day shalt thou be with me in paradise.

44 ᶻἮν.δὲ¹¹ ὡσεὶ   ὥρα ἕκτη, καὶ σκότος ἐγένετο ἐφ᾽ ὅλην
And it was about [the] ²hour ¹sixth, and darkness came over ²whole
44 And it was about the sixth hour, and there was a darkness

τὴν γῆν ἕως   ὥρας ᵃἐννάτης·¹¹ 45 ᵇκαὶ ἐσκοτίσθη ὁ ἥλιος,¹¹
¹the land until [the] ²hour ¹ninth; and ³was ⁴darkened ¹the ²sun;
over all the earth until the ninth hour. 45 And the sun was darkened,

ᶜκαὶ ἐσχίσθη¹¹ τὸ καταπέτασμα τοῦ ναοῦ μέσον· 46 καὶ
and ⁵was ¹rent ¹the ²veil ³of ⁴the ⁵temple in [the] midst. And
and the veil of the temple was rent in the midst. 46 And when

φωνήσας φωνῇ μεγάλῃ ὁ Ἰησοῦς εἶπεν, Πάτερ, εἰς χεῖράς
having cried with a ²voice ¹loud Jesus said, Father, into ²hands
Jesus had cried with a loud voice, he said, Father, into thy hands

σου ᵈπαραθήσομαι¹¹ τὸ.πνεῦμά μου. ᵉΚαὶ ταῦτα¹¹ εἰπὼν
¹thy I will commit my spirit. And these things having said
I commend my spirit: and having said thus,

ἐξέπνευσεν. 47 Ἰδὼν.δὲ   ὁ ᶠἑκατόνταρχος¹¹ τὸ γενόμενον
he expired. Now ²having ³seen ¹the ⁴centurion that which took place
he gave up the ghost. 47 Now when the cen-turion saw what was

ᵍἐδόξασεν¹¹ τὸν θεόν, λέγων, Ὄντως ὁ.ἄνθρωπος.οὗτος δίκαιος
glorified God, saying, Indeed this man ²just
done, he glorified God, saying, Certainly this was a righteous man.

ἦν. 48 Καὶ πάντες οἱ ʰσυμπαραγενόμενοι¹¹ ὄχλοι ἐπὶ τὴν
¹was. And all the ²who ³were ⁴come ⁵together ¹crowds to
48 And all the people that came together to

θεωρίαν.ταύτην, ⁱθεωροῦντες¹¹ τὰ γενόμενα, τύπτοντες
this sight, seeing the things which took place, beating
that sight, beholding the things which were

ᵏἑαυτῶν¹¹ τὰ στήθη ὑπέστρεφον. 49 εἱστήκεισαν.δὲ πάντες
their breasts returned. And ²stood ¹all
done, smote their breasts, and returned. 49 And all his ac-quaintance, and the

οἱ γνωστοὶ ¹αὐτοῦ¹¹ ᵐμακρόθεν, καὶ γυναῖκες αἱ ⁿσυν-
²those ³who ⁴knew ⁵him afar off, also women who fol-
women that followed him from Galilee, stood afar off, behold-

ακολουθήσασαι¹¹ αὐτῷ ἀπὸ τῆς Γαλιλαίας, ὁρῶσαι ταῦτα.
lowed with him from Galilee, beholding these things.
ing these things.

50 Καὶ ἰδού, ἀνὴρ ὀνόματι Ἰωσήφ, βουλευτὴς ὑπάρχων,
And behold, a man by name Joseph, a counsellor being,
50 And, behold, there was a man named Joseph, a counseller;

ᵒ ἀνὴρ ἀγαθὸς καὶ δίκαιος, 51 οὗτος οὐκ.ἦν.ᴾσυγκατατεθειμένος¹¹
a man good and just, (he had not assented
and he was a good man, and a just: 51 (the same had not consent-

τῇ βουλῇ καὶ τῇ πράξει αὐτῶν, ἀπὸ Ἀριμαθαίας πόλεως
to the counsel and the deed of them,) from Arimathæa a city
ed to the counsel and deed of them;) he was of Arimathæa, a city

τῶν Ἰουδαίων, ὃς.ᑫκαὶ¹¹ προσεδέχετο ʳκαὶ αὐτὸς¹¹ τὴν βασι-
of the Jews, and who ³was ⁴waiting ⁵for ¹also ²himself the king-
of the Jews: who also himself waited for

λείαν τοῦ θεοῦ, 52 οὗτος προσελθὼν τῷ ˢΠιλάτῳ¹¹ ᾐτήσατο τὸ
dom of God, he having gone to Pilate begged the
the kingdom of God. 52 This man went unto Pilate, and begged the

σῶμα τοῦ Ἰησοῦ. 53 καὶ καθελὼν ᵗαὐτὸ¹¹ ἐνετύλιξεν αὐτὸ
body of Jesus. And having taken ²down ¹it he wrapped it
body of Jesus. 53 And he took it down, and wrapped it in linen,

---

ᵛ — τῷ (read he said, Jesus, remember) TTrA. ͮ — κύριε [L]TTrA. ˣ — ὁ Ἰησοῦς (read he said) ᴛ[Tr]A. ᵞ σοι λέγω TTrA. ᶻ καὶ ἦν ἤδη ([ἤδη] TrA) and it was now LTTrA. ᵃ ἐνάτης LTTrA. ᵇ τοῦ ἡλίου ἐκλιπόντος (darkness came) from the sun failing T. ᶜ ἐσχίσθη δὲ T. ᵈ παρατίθεμαι I commit LTTrAW. ᵉ καὶ τοῦτο and this ʟ; τοῦτο δὲ TTrA. ⁱ ἑκατοντάρχης TTr. ᵍ ἐδόξαζεν LTTrA. ʰ συνπαραγενόμενοι TA. ⁱ θεωρήσαντες having seen LTTrA. ᵏ — ἑαυτῶν (read the breasts) TTrA. ¹ αὐτῷ LTTrA. ᵐ + ἀπὸ from LT. ⁿ συνακολουθοῦσαι TTrA. ᵒ + καὶ and T. ᴾ συνκατατιθέμενος T; συνκατατεθειμένος A. ᑫ — καὶ and LTTrA. ʳ — καὶ αὐτὸς LTTrA. ˢ Πειλάτῳ T. ᵗ — αὐτὸ (read [it]) LTTrA.

and laid it in a sepulchre that was hewn in stone, wherein never man before was laid. 54 And that day was the preparation, and the sabbath drew on:

55 And the women also, which came with him from Galilee, followed after, and beheld the sepulchre, and how his body was laid. 56 And they returned, and prepared spices and ointments; and rested the sabbath day according to the commandment. XXIV. Now upon the first *day* of the week, very early in the morning, they came unto the sepulchre, bringing the spices which they had prepared, and certain *others* with them. 2 And they found the stone rolled away from the sepulchre. 3 And they entered in, and found not the body of the Lord Jesus. 4 And it came to pass, as they were much perplexed thereabout, behold, two men stood by them in shining garments : 5 and as they were afraid, and bowed down *their* faces to the earth, they said unto them, Why seek ye the living among the dead? 6 He is not here, but is risen: remember how he spake unto you when he was yet in Galilee, 7 saying, The Son of man must be delivered into the hands of sinful men, and be crucified, and the third day rise again. 8 And they remembered his words, 9 and returned from the sepulchre, and told all these things unto the eleven, and to all the rest. 10 It was Mary Magdalene, and Joanna, and Mary the mother of James, and other *women that were* with them, which told these things unto the apostles. 11 And their

σινδόνι καὶ ἔθηκεν ᵛαὐτὸ‖ ἐν μνήματι λαξευτῷ, οὗ
in a linen cloth and placed   it   in a tomb   hewn in a rock, in which
οὐκ ἦν ᵂοὐδέπω.οὐδεὶς‖ κείμενος. 54 καὶ ἡμέρα ἦν ˣπαρα-
²was ¹no ²one ever yet   laid.   And ⁴day ¹it ²was ₚₑ-
σκευή,‖ καὶ σάββατον ἐπέφωσκεν.
paration, and Sabbath   was coming on.

55 Κατακολουθήσασαι.δὲ ᵞκαὶ‖ ᶻ γυναῖκες, ₑαἵτινες ₑἦσαν
And ³having ⁴followed ²also ¹women, who were
συνεληλυθυῖαι ᵃαὐτῷ‖ ἐκ τῆς Γαλιλαίαςᵇ, ἐθεάσαντο τὸ
come with him out of Galilee, saw the
μνημεῖον, καὶ ὡς ἐτέθη τὸ.σῶμα.αὐτοῦ. 56 ὑποστρέψασαι.δὲ
tomb, and how was laid his body. And having returned
ἡτοίμασαν ἀρώματα καὶ μύρα. καὶ τὸ.μὲν.σάββατον ἡσύχα-
they prepared aromatics and ointments, and on the sabbath remained
σαν κατὰ τὴν ἐντολήν. 24 τῇ.δὲ μιᾷ τῶν σαβ-
quiet, according to the commandment. But on the first [day] of the week
βάτων ὄρθρου.ᶜβαθέος‖ ᵈῆλθον ἐπὶ τὸ μνῆμα,‖ φέρουσαι ἃ
at early dawn they came to the tomb, bringing ²which
ἡτοίμασαν ἀρώματα, ᵉκαί τινες σὺν αὐταῖς.‖ 2 Εὖ-
¹had ⁵prepared ¹aromatics, and some [others] with them. ²They
ρον δὲ τὸν λίθον ἀποκεκυλισμένον ἀπὸ τοῦ μνημείου, 3 ᶠκαὶ
²found ¹and the stone rolled away from the tomb; and
εἰσελθοῦσαι‖ οὐχ.εὗρον τὸ σῶμα τοῦ κυρίου Ἰησοῦ. 4 ᵍκαὶ
having entered they found not the body of the Lord Jesus. And
ἐγένετο ἐν.τῷ.ᵍδιαπορεῖσθαι‖ αὐτὰς περὶ τούτου, καὶ ἰδού,
it came to pass as ²were ³perplexed ¹they about this, that behold,
ʰδύο ἄνδρες‖ ἐπέστησαν αὐταῖς ἐν ⁱἐσθήσεσιν ἀστραπτούσαις.‖
two men stood by them in ²garments ¹shining.
5 ἐμφόβων δὲ γενομένων αὐτῶν καὶ κλινουσῶν ᵏτὸ πρόσω-
And ³filled ⁴with ⁵fear ²becoming ¹they and bowing the face
πον‖ εἰς τὴν γῆν, ˡεἶπον‖ πρὸς αὐτάς, Τί ζητεῖτε τὸν ζῶντα
to the earth, they said to them, Why seek ye the living
μετὰ τῶν νεκρῶν; 6 οὐκ.ἔστιν ὧδε, ᵐἀλλ'‖ ἠγέρθη· μνήσθητε
with the dead? He is not here, but is risen: remember
ὡς ἐλάλησεν ὑμῖν, ἔτι ὢν ἐν τῇ Γαλιλαίᾳ, 7 λέγων, ⁿὍτι
how he spoke to you, yet being in Galilee, saying,
δεῖ τὸν υἱὸν τοῦ ἀνθρώπου‖ παραδοθῆναι εἰς χεῖρας
It behoveth the Son of man to be delivered up into hands
ἀνθρώπων ἁμαρτωλῶν, καὶ σταυρωθῆναι, καὶ τῇ τρίτῃ ἡμέρᾳ
of ²men ¹sinful, and to be crucified, and the third day
ἀναστῆναι. 8 Καὶ ἐμνήσθησαν τῶν.ῥημάτων.αὐτοῦ· 9 καὶ
to arise. And they remembered his words ; and
ὑποστρέψασαι ἀπὸ τοῦ μνημείου ἀπήγγειλαν ᵒταῦτα πάντα‖
having returned from the tomb they related ²these ³things ¹all
τοῖς ἕνδεκα καὶ πᾶσιν τοῖς λοιποῖς. 10 ᴾῆσαν.δὲ‖ ἡ Μαγδαληνὴ
to the eleven and to all the rest. Now it was ²Magdalene
Μαρία καὶ ᑫΙωάννα‖ καὶ Μαρία ʳ Ἰακώβου, καὶ αἱ λοιπαὶ σὺν
¹Mary and Joanna and Mary of James, and the rest with
αὐταῖς, ˢαἳ‖ ἔλεγον πρὸς τοὺς ἀποστόλους ταῦτα. 11 Καὶ
them, who told to the apostles these things. And

ᵛ αὐτὸν him LTTrA.   ᵂ οὐδεὶς οὐδέπω T; οὐδεὶς οὔπω LTrA.   ˣ παρασκευῆς LTTrA.
ᵞ — καὶ LTTrA.   ᶻ + αἱ the LTr.   ᵃ — αὐτῷ T[TrA].   ᵇ + αὐτῷ him TA.
ᶜ βαθέως LTTrAW.   ᵈ ἐπὶ τὸ μνῆμα ἦλθον T.   ᵉ — καί τινες σὺν αὐταῖς LTTrA.   ᶠ εἰσελ-
θοῦσαι δὲ LTTrA.   ᵍ ἀπορεῖσθαι LTTrA.   ʰ ἄνδρες δύο GLTTrAW.   ⁱ ἐσθῆτι ἀστραπτούσῃ
shining raiment LTTrA.   ᵏ τὰ πρόσωπα the faces TTr.   ˡ εἶπαν LTTrA.   ᵐ ἀλλὰ TTrA.
ⁿ τὸν υἱὸν τοῦ ἀνθρώπου ὅτι δεῖ TTrA.   ᵒ πάντα ταῦτα T.   ᴾ [ἦσαν δὲ] TrA.   ᑫ Ἰωάνα Tr.
ʳ + ἡ the [...] LTTr[A]W.   ˢ — αἱ LTTr[A].

ἐφάνησάν ἐνώπιον αὐτῶν ὡσεὶ λῆρος τὰ ῥήματα ˢαὐτῶν,ᶢ
ᵃappeared ⁴before ⁵them ⁶like ⁷idle ⁸talk ²words ¹their,

words seemed to them as idle tales, and they believed them not.

καὶ ἠπίστουν αὐταῖς. 12 ᵛὁ.δὲ.Πέτρος ἀναστὰς ἔδραμεν
and they disbelieved them. But Peter having risen up ran

12 Then arose Peter, and ran unto the sepulchre; and stooping

ἐπὶ τὸ μνημεῖον, καὶ παρακύψας βλέπει τὰ ὀθόνια
to the tomb, and having stooped down he sees the linen clothes

down, he beheld the linen clothes laid by themselves, and de-

ᵂκείμενα μόνα·¹ καὶ ἀπῆλθεν πρὸς.ˣἑαυτὸν¹ θαυμάζων τὸ
lying alone, and went away home wondering at that which

parted, wondering in himself at that which was come to pass.

γεγονός.ᵂ
had come to pass.

13 Καὶ ἰδού, δύο ἐξ αὐτῶν ʸἦσαν πορευόμενοι ἐν αὐτῇ τῇ
And lo, two of them were going on ²same ¹the

ἡμέρᾳᵂ εἰς κώμην ἀπέχουσαν σταδίους ἑξήκοντα ἀπὸ Ἱερου-
day to a village being distant ²furlongs ¹sixty from Jeru-

13 And, behold, two of them went that same day to a village called Emmaus, which was from Jerusalem

σαλήμ, ᾗ ὄνομα Ἐμμαούς· 14 καὶ αὐτοὶ ὡμίλουν πρὸς
salem, whose name [is] Emmaus; and they were conversing with

about threescore fur-longs. 14 And they talked together of all

ἀλλήλους περὶ πάντων τῶν συμβεβηκότων τούτων. 15 καὶ
one another about all ²which ⁴had ⁵taken ²place ¹these ²things. And

these things which had happened. 15 And it came to pass, that,

ἐγένετο ἐν.τῷ.ὁμιλεῖν.αὐτοὺς καὶ ᶻσυζητεῖν,ᶢ καὶ αὐτὸς ᵃὁᶢ
it came to pass as they conversed and reasoned, that ²himself ¹the

while they communed together and reasoned, Jesus himself drew

Ἰησοῦς ἐγγίσας συνεπορεύετο αὐτοῖς· 16 οἱ.δὲ ὀφθαλμοὶ
¹Jesus having drawn near went with them; but the eyes

near, and went with them. 16 But their eyes were holden that they

αὐτῶν ἐκρατοῦντο τοῦ μὴ ἐπιγνῶναι αὐτόν. 17 Εἶπεν δὲ
of them were holden [so as] not to know him. And he said

should not know him. 17 And he said unto

πρὸς αὐτούς, Τίνες οἱ λόγοι οὗτοι οὓς ἀντιβάλλετε πρὸς
to them, What words [are] these which ye exchange with

them, What manner of communications are

ἀλλήλους περιπατοῦντες, ᵇκαὶ ἐστε σκυθρωποί;ᵂ
one another as ye walk, and are downcast in countenance?

these that ye have one to another, as ye walk, and are sad? 18 And

18 Ἀποκριθεὶς.δὲ ᶜὁᶢ εἷςᵈ, ᵉᾧ ὄνομαᶢ Κλεόπας, εἶπεν πρὸς
And answering the one, whose name [was] Cleopas, said to

the one of them, whose name was Cleopas, an-

αὐτόν, Σὺ μόνος παροικεῖς ᶠἐνᶢ Ἱερουσαλήμ, καὶ οὐκ.ἔγνως
him, ²Thou ³alone ¹sojournest in Jerusalem, and hast not known

swering said unto him, Art thou only a stran-ger in Jerusalem, and

τὰ γενόμενα ἐν αὐτῇ ἐν ταῖς.ἡμέραις.ταύταις;
the things which are come to pass in it in these days?

hast not known the things which are come to pass there in these

19 Καὶ εἶπεν αὐτοῖς, Ποῖα; Οἱ.δὲ ᵍεἶπονᵂ αὐτῷ, Τὰ
And he said to them, What things? And they said to him, The things

days? 19 And he said unto them, What

περὶ Ἰησοῦ τοῦ ʰΝαζωραίου,ᵂ ὃς ἐγένετο ἀνὴρ προφήτης,
concerning Jesus the Nazarǽan, who was a man a prophet,

things? And they said unto him, Concerning Jesus of Nazareth,

δυνατὸς ἐν ἔργῳ καὶ ⁱλόγῳ ἐναντίον τοῦ θεοῦ καὶ παντὸς τοῦ
mighty in deed and word before God and all the

which was a prophet mighty in deed and word before God and

λαοῦ· 20 ὅπως.τε ᵏπαρέδωκαν αὐτὸνᵂ οἱ ἀρχιερεῖς καὶ οἱ
people; and how ⁷delivered ⁸up ⁹him ¹the ²chief ³priests ⁴and

all the people: 20 and how the chief priests and our rulers deliv-

ἄρχοντες.ἡμῶν εἰς κρίμα θανάτου, καὶ ἐσταύρωσαν αὐτόν·
our ⁶rulers to judgment of death, and crucified him.

ered him to be con-demned to death, and have crucified him.

21 ἡμεῖς.δὲ ἠλπίζομεν ὅτι αὐτός ἐστιν ὁ μέλλων λυτροῦσθαι
But we were hoping he it is who is about to redeem

21 But we trusted that it had been he which should have redeemed

τὸν Ἰσραήλ. ἀλλά.γε¹ σὺν πᾶσιν τούτοις τρίτην ταύτην
Israel. But then with all these things ³third ²this

Israel: and beside all this, to day is the third

ἡμέραν ἄγει ᵐσήμερονᵂ ἀφ'.οὗ ταῦτα ἐγένετο. 22 ἀλλὰ.καὶ
⁴day ²brings ¹to-day since these things came to pass. And withal

day since these things were done. 22 Yea, and certain women

γυναῖκές τινες ἐξ ἡμῶν ἐξέστησαν ἡμᾶς, γενόμεναι
women ¹certain from amongst us astonished us, having been

also of our company made us astonished, which were early at

ᵗ ταῦτα these LTTrA.　　ᵛ — verse 12 [L]ᵀ[Tr].　　ᵂ [κείμενα μόνα] A; — κείμενα Tr.
ˣ αὐτὸν Tr.　　ʸ ἐν αὐτῇ τῇ ἡμέρᾳ ἦσαν πορευόμενοι T.　　ᶻ συνζητεῖν LTTrA.　　ᵃ — ὁ TTrA.
ᵇ ; καὶ ἐστάθησαν ([; καὶ ἐσ-ά.] A) σκυθρωποί. (question ends at walk) And they stood down-cast in countenance. TTrA.　　ᶜ — ὁ LTTrA.　　ᵈ + [ἐξ αὐτῶν] of them L.　　ᵉ ὀνόματι by name
TrA.　　— ἐν (read [in]) GTTrAW.　　ᶢ εἶπαν TTr.　　ʰ Ναζαρηνοῦ TTrA.　　ⁱ + [ἐν] in L.
ᵏ αὐτὸν.παρέδωκαν L.　　¹ + καὶ also LTTrA.　　ᵐ — σήμερον (read it brings) T[TrA].

the sepulchre ; 23 and when they found not his body, they came, saying, that they had also seen a vision of angels, which said that he was alive. 24 And certain of them which were with us went to the sepulchre, and found it even so as the women had said : but him they saw not. 25 Then he said unto them, O fools, and slow of heart to believe aH that the prophets have spoken : 26 ought not Christ to have suffered these things, and to enter into his glory ? 27 And beginning at Moses and all the prophets, he expounded unto them in all the scriptures the things concerning himself. 28 And they drew nigh unto the village, whither they went : and he made as though he would have gone further. 29 But they constrained him, saying, Abide with us : for it is toward eventing, and the day is far spent. And he went in to tarry with them. 30 And it came to pass, as he sat at meat with them, he took bread, and blessed it, and brake, and gave to them. 31 And their eyes were opened, and they knew him ; and he vanished out of their sight. 32 And they said one to another, Did not our heart burn within us, while he talked with us by the way, and while he opened to us the scriptures ? 33 And they rose up the same hour, and returned to Jerusalem, and found the eleven gathered together, and them that were with them, 34 saying, The Lord is risen indeed, and hath appeared to Simon. 35 And they told what things were done in the way, and how he was known of them in breaking of bread.

ⁿ*ὄρθριαι*‖ *ἐπὶ τὸ μνημεῖον·* 23 *καὶ μὴ* *εὑροῦσαι τὸ.σῶμα.αὐτοῦ*
early　　to the　tomb,　　and not having found　his body

ἦλθον, λέγουσαι καὶ ὀπτασίαν ἀγγέλων ἑωρακέναι, οἳ λέγουσιν
came,　declaring also　a vision　of angels　to have seen, who　say

αὐτὸν ζῆν. 24 *καὶ ἀπῆλθόν τινες τῶν σὺν ἡμῖν ἐπὶ τὸ*
he · is living.　And　⁶went　¹some ²of ³those ⁴with ⁵us　to the

μνημεῖον καὶ εὗρον οὕτως καθὼς °*καὶ*‖ *αἱ γυναῖκες εἶπον,*
tomb　and found [it]　so　as　also　the women　said,

αὐτὸν.δὲ οὐκ.εἶδον. 25 *Καὶ αὐτὸς εἶπεν πρὸς αὐτούς, Ὦ*
but him　they saw not.　And he　said　to　them,　O

ἀνόητοι καὶ βραδεῖς τῇ καρδίᾳ τοῦ πιστεύειν ἐπὶ πᾶσιν οἷς
senseless and　slow　of heart　to believe　in　all　which

ἐλάλησαν οἱ προφῆται· 26 *οὐχὶ ταῦτα* *ἔδει*
spoke　the prophets.　²Not　¹⁰these ¹¹things ¹was ²it ⁿeedful ⁵for

παθεῖν τὸν χριστόν, καὶ εἰσελθεῖν εἰς τὴν.δόξαν.αὐτοῦ ;
³to ⁹suffer ⁶the　⁷Christ,　and　to enter　into　his glory ?

27 *Καὶ ἀρξάμενος ἀπὸ* ᴾ*Μωσέως*‖ *καὶ ἀπὸ πάντων τῶν προ-*
And beginning　from　Moses　and from　all　the　pro-

φητῶν ᑫ*διηρμήνευεν*‖ *αὐτοῖς ἐν πάσαις ταῖς γραφαῖς τὰ*
phets　he interpreted　to them　in　all　the scriptures the things

περὶ ʳ*ἑαυτοῦ.*‖ 28 *Καὶ ἤγγισαν εἰς τὴν κώμην οὗ*
concerning himself.　And they drew near to　the　village　where

ἐπορεύοντο, καὶ αὐτὸς ˢ*προσεποιεῖτο*‖ ᵗ*πορρῶτέρω*‖ *πορεύεσθαι.*
they were going, and he　appeared　⁴farther　¹to ²be ³going.

29 *καὶ παρεβιάσαντο αὐτόν, λέγοντες, Μεῖνον μεθ᾽ ἡμῶν, ὅτι*
And they constrained him,　saying,　Abide　with　us,　for

πρὸς ἑσπέραν ἐστίν, καὶ κέκλικεν ᵛ *ἡ ἡμέρα. Καὶ εἰσῆλθεν*
towards evening it is,　and has declined the day.　And he entered

τοῦ μεῖναι σὺν αὐτοῖς. 30 *καὶ ἐγένετο ἐν.τῷ.κατακλιθῆναι*
to abide with them.　And it came to pass　as ²reclined

αὐτὸν μετ᾽ αὐτῶν, λαβὼν τὸν ἄρτον ʷ*εὐλόγησεν,*‖
[³at ⁴table] ¹he　with them, having taken the bread·　he blessed,

καὶ κλάσας ἐπεδίδου αὐτοῖς. 31 *αὐτῶν.δὲ διηνοίχθησαν οἱ*
and having broken he gave [it] to them.　And their　²were ³opened the

ὀφθαλμοὶ καὶ ἐπέγνωσαν αὐτόν· καὶ αὐτὸς ἄφαντος.ἐγένετο
¹eyes　and they knew　him.　And he　disappeared

ἀπ᾽ αὐτῶν. 32 *Καὶ* ˣ*εἶπον*‖ *πρὸς ἀλλήλους, Οὐχὶ ἡ καρδία*
from them.　And they said　to one another, ²Not　⁴heart

ἡμῶν καιομένη ἦν ʸ*ἐν ἡμῖν*‖ *ὡς ἐλάλει ἡμῖν ἐν τῇ ὁδῷ,*
³our　⁵burning ¹was in　us　as he was speaking to us in the way,

ᶻ*καὶ*‖ *ὡς διήνοιγεν ἡμῖν τὰς γραφάς ;* 33 *Καὶ ἀναστάντες*
and　as he was opening to us the scriptures ?　And　rising up

αὐτῇ.τῇ ὥρᾳ ὑπέστρεψαν εἰς Ἱερουσαλήμ, καὶ εὗρον ᵃ*συνη-*
the same hour they returned to　Jerusalem,　and they found gathered

θροισμένους‖ *τοὺς ἕνδεκα καὶ τοὺς σὺν αὐτοῖς,* 34 *λέγοντας,*
together　the eleven and those with them,　saying,

Ὅτι ᵇ*ἠγέρθη ὁ κύριος ὄντως,*‖ *καὶ ὤφθη Σίμωνι.* 35 *Καὶ*
³Is ⁴risen ¹the ²Lord　indeed,　and appeared to Simon.　And

αὐτοὶ ἐξηγοῦντο τὰ ἐν τῇ ὁδῷ, καὶ ὡς ἐγνώσθη αὐτοῖς
they related　the things in the way, and how he was known to them

ἐν τῇ κλάσει τοῦ ἄρτου.
in the breaking of the bread.

ⁿ *ὀρθριναὶ* LTTrAW.　　° — *καὶ* LTrA.　　ᴾ *Μωσέως* LTTrAW.　　ᑫ *διερμήνευεν* L ; *διερ-*
μήνευσεν TTrA.　ʳ *αὐτοῦ* EG ; *αὐτοῦ* LTr.　ˢ *προσεποιήσατο* LTTrA.　　ᵗ *πορρώτερον* LTrA.
ᵛ + *ἤδη* already [L]TTɪA.　　ʷ *ηὐλόγησεν* L.　　ˣ *εἶπαν* TTrA.　　ʸ [*ἐν ἡμῖν*] TɪA.　　ᶻ — *καὶ*
LTTrA.　ᵃ *ἠθροισμένους* gathered LTTɪA.　ᵇ *ὄντως ἠγέρθη ὁ κύριος* LTTrA.

36 Ταῦτα.δὲ αὐτῶν.λαλούντων, αὐτὸς °ὁ'Ἰησοῦς'' ἔστη ἐν
And these things as they were telling, ²himself ¹Jesus stood in

μέσῳ αὐτῶν ᵈκαὶ λέγει αὐτοῖς, Εἰρήνη ὑμῖν.'' ᵉ 37 Πτοηθέντες
²midst ¹their and says to them, Peace to you. ²Terrified

δὲ καὶ ἔμφοβοι γενόμενοι ἐδόκουν πνεῦμα θεωρεῖν.
¹but ⁴and ³filled ⁵with ⁷fear ⁶being they thought a spirit they beheld.

38 καὶ εἶπεν αὐτοῖς, Τί τεταραγμένοι ἐστέ; καὶ ᶠδιατί'' δια-
And he said to them, Why troubled are ye? and wherefore ²rea-

λογισμοὶ ἀναβαίνουσιν ἐν ᵍταῖς καρδίαις'' ὑμῶν; 39 ἴδετε
sonings ¹do come up in ²hearts ¹your? see

τὰς.χεῖράς.μου καὶ τοὺς.πόδας.μου, ὅτι ʰαὐτὸς ἐγώ εἰμι.''
my hands and my feet, that ³he ¹I ²am.

ψηλαφήσατέ με καὶ ἴδετε· ὅτι πνεῦμα ἰσάρκα'' καὶ ὀστέα οὐκ
Handle me and ⁵see, for a spirit flesh and bones ²not

ἔχει, καθὼς ἐμὲ θεωρεῖτε ἔχοντα. 40 ᵏΚαὶ τοῦτο εἰπὼν
¹has, as ²me ¹ye ⁵see having. And this having said

ˡἐπέδειξεν¹ αὐτοῖς τὰς χεῖρας καὶ τοὺς πόδας.'' 41 ἔτι.δὲ
he shewed to them [his] hands and feet. But yet

ἀπιστούντων.αὐτῶν ᵐἀπὸ τῆς χαρᾶς καὶ θαυμαζόντων,'' εἶπεν
while they were disbelieving for joy and were wondering, he said

αὐτοῖς, Ἔχετέ τι βρώσιμον ἐνθάδε; 42 Οἱ.δὲ ⁿἐπέδωκαν
to them, Have ye anything eatable here? And they gave

αὐτῷ ἰχθύος ὀπτοῦ μέρος ⁿκαὶ ἀπὸ μελισσίου.κηρίου.'' 43 καὶ
to him ²of ⁴a ⁵fish ³broiled ¹part and of a honeycomb. And

λαβὼν ἐνώπιον αὐτῶν ἔφαγεν. 44 Εἶπεν.δὲ °αὐτοῖς,''
having taken [it] ³before ⁴them ¹he ²ate. And he said to them,

Οὗτοι οἱ λόγοιᵖ οὓς ἐλάλησα πρὸς ὑμᾶς ἔτι ὢν σὺν ὑμῖν,
These [are] the words which I spoke to you yet being with you,

ὅτι δεῖ πληρωθῆναι πάντα τὰ γεγραμμένα ἐν τῷ.νόμῳ
that must be fulfilled all things that have been written in the law

�qΜωσέως'' καὶ ʳπροφήταις καὶ ψαλμοῖς περὶ ἐμοῦ. 45 Τότε
of Moses and prophets and psalms concerning me. Then

διήνοιξεν αὐτῶν τὸν νοῦν τοῦ συνιέναι τὰς γραφάς·
he opened their understanding to understand the scriptures,

46 καὶ εἶπεν αὐτοῖς, Ὅτι οὕτως γέγραπται, ˢκαὶ οὕτως
and said to them, Thus it has been written, and thus

ἔδει'' παθεῖν τὸν χριστὸν καὶ ἀναστῆναι ἐκ νεκρῶν
it behoved ³to ⁴suffer ¹the ²Christ and to rise from among [the] dead

τῇ τρίτῃ ἡμέρᾳ, 47 καὶ κηρυχθῆναι ἐπὶ τῷ.ὀνόματι.αὐτοῦ
the third day; and should be proclaimed in his name

μετάνοιαν ᵗκαὶ'' ἄφεσιν ἁμαρτιῶν εἰς πάντα τὰ ἔθνη, ᵘἀρξά-
repentance and remission of sins to all nations, begin-

μενον'' ἀπὸ Ἱερουσαλήμ. 48 ὑμεῖς ᵛδέ ἐστε'' μάρτυρες τούτων.
ning at Jerusalem. ²Ye ¹and are witnesses of these things.

49 ʷκαὶ ἰδού, ἐγώ'' ˣἀποστέλλω'' τὴν ἐπαγγελίαν τοῦ πατρός
And lo, I send the promise of ²Father

μου.ἐφ' ὑμᾶς· ὑμεῖς.δὲ καθίσατε ἐν τῇ πόλει ʸἹερουσαλὴμ''
¹my upon you; but ²ye ¹remain in the city of Jerusalem

ἕως.οὗ ἐνδύσησθε ᶻδύναμιν ἐξ ὕψους.''
till ye be clothed with power from on high.

---

36 And as they thus spake, Jesus himself stood in the midst of them, and saith unto them, Peace be unto you. 37 But they were terrified and affrighted, and supposed that they had seen a spirit. 38 And he said unto them, Why are ye troubled? and why do thoughts arise in your hearts? 39 Behold my hands and my feet, that it is I myself: handle me, and see; for a spirit hath not flesh and bones, as ye see me have. 40 And when he had thus spoken, he shewed them his hands and his feet. 41 And while they yet believed not for joy, and wondered, he said unto them, Have ye here any meat? 42 And they gave him a piece of a broiled fish, and of an honeycomb. 43 And he took it, and did eat before them. 44 And he said unto them, These are the words which I spake unto you, while I was yet with you, that all things must be fulfilled, which were written in the law of Moses, and in the prophets, and in the psalms, concerning me. 45 Then opened he their understanding, that they might understand the scriptures, 46 and said unto them, Thus it is written, and thus it behoved Christ to suffer, and to rise from the dead the third day: 47 and that repentance and remission of sins should be preached in his name among all nations, beginning at Jerusalem. 48 And ye are witnesses of these things. 49 And, behold, I send the promise of my Father upon you: but tarry ye in the city of Jerusalem, until ye be endued with power from on high.

ᶜ — ὁ Ἰησοῦς GLTTrA.   ᵈ — καὶ λέγει αὐτοῖς, Εἰρήνη ὑμῖν Τ.   ᵉ + [ἐγώ εἰμι, μὴ φοβεῖσθε]
I am [he], fear not L.   ᶠ διὰ τί LTrA.   ᵍ τῇ καρδίᾳ heart LTTrA.   ʰ ἐγώ εἰμι αὐτός LTTrA.
ⁱ σάρκας Τ.   ᵏ — verse 40 Τ[Tr].   ˡ ἔδειξεν LΤr; [ἐπ]έδειξεν A.   ᵐ καὶ θαυμαζόντων ἀπὸ
τῆς χαρᾶς L.   ⁿ — καὶ ἀπὸ μελισσίου κηρίου LT[TrA].   ᵒ πρὸς αὐτούς TTrA.   ᵖ + μου (read
my words) [L]TTrA.   �q Μωϋσέως LTTrAW.   ʳ + [τοῖς] the Tr.   ˢ — καὶ οὕτως ἔδει [L]TTrA.
ᵗ εἰς τὸ Τ.   ᵘ ἀρξάμενοι TTrA.   ᵛ — δέ ἐστε ([ἐστε] Tr) (read [are]) TTrA.   ʷ κἀγὼ and I T.
ˣ ἐξαποστέλλω send out TTrA.   ʸ — Ἱερουσαλήμ GLTTrA.   ᶻ ἐξ ὕψους δύναμιν TTrA.

50 And he led them out as far as to Bethany, and he lifted up his hands, and blessed them. 51 And it came to pass, while he blessed them, he was parted from them, and carried up into heaven. 52 And they worshipped him, and returned to Jerusalem with great joy: 53 and were continually in the temple, praising and blessing God. Amen.

50 Ἐξήγαγεν.δὲ αὐτοὺς ᵃἔξωⁱⁱ ἕως ᵇεἰςⁱⁱ Βηθανίαν, καὶ
And he led them out as far as to Bethany, and
ἐπάρας τὰς.χεῖρας.αὐτοῦ εὐλόγησεν αὐτούς. 51 καὶ
having lifted up his hands he blessed them. And
ἐγένετο ἐν.τῷ.εὐλογεῖν αὐτὸν αὐτοὺς διέστη ἀπ᾽ αὐτῶν
it came to pass as ²was ³blessing ¹he them he was separated from . them
ᶜκαὶ ἀνεφέρετο εἰς τὸν οὐρανόν.ⁱⁱ 52 καὶ αὐτοὶ ᵈπροσκυνή-
and was carried up into the heaven. And they having wor-
σαντες αὐτὸνⁱⁱ ὑπέστρεψαν εἰς Ἰερουσαλὴμ μετὰ χαρᾶς μεγά-
shipped him returned to Jerusalem with ²joy ¹great,
λης· 53 καὶ ἦσαν ᵉδιαπαντὸςⁱⁱ ἐν τῷ ἱερῷ, ᶠαἰνοῦντες καὶ
and were continually in the temple, praising and
εὐλογοῦντεςⁱⁱ τὸν θεόν. ᵍ᾽Ἀμήν.ⁱⁱ
blessing God. Amen.

ʰΤὸ κατὰ Λουκᾶν εὐαγγέλιον.ⁱⁱ
The ³according⁴to ⁵Luke ¹glad ²tidings..

ⁱΤΟ ᐧΚΑΤΑ ΙΩΑΝΝΗΝ ΑΓΙΟΝ ΕΥΑΓΓΕΛΙΟΝ.ⁱⁱ
THE ⁴ACCORDING ⁵TO ⁶JOHN ¹HOLY ²GLAD ³TIDINGS.

IN the beginning was the Word, and the Word was with God, and the Word was God. 2 The same was in the beginning with God. 3 All things were made by him ; and without him was not any thing made that was made. 4 In him was life ; and the life was the light of men. 5 And the light shineth in darkness ; and the darkness comprehended it not.

ἘΝ ἀρχῇ ἦν ὁ λόγος, καὶ ὁ λόγος ἦν πρὸς τὸν θεόν,
In [the] beginning was the Word, and the Word was with God,
καὶ θεὸς ἦν ὁ λόγος. 2 οὗτος ἦν ἐν ἀρχῇ πρὸς τὸν
and ⁴God ³was ¹the ²Word. He was in [the] beginning with
θεόν. 3 Πάντα δι᾽ αὐτοῦ ἐγένετο, καὶ χωρὶς αὐτοῦ
God. All things through him came into being, and without him
ἐγένετο οὐδὲ ᵏἓν ὃ γέγονεν. 4 ἐν ⁱⁱ αὐτῷ ζωὴ
came into being not even one [thing] which has come into being. In him ²life
ˡἦν,ⁱⁱ καὶ ἡ ζωὴ ἦν τὸ φῶς τῶν ἀνθρώπων· 5 καὶ τὸ φῶς ἐν
¹was, and the life was the light of men. And the light in
τῇ σκοτίᾳ φαίνει, καὶ ἡ σκοτία αὐτὸ οὐ.κατέλαβεν.
the darkness appears, and the darkness ²it ¹apprehended not.

6 There was a man sent from God, whose name was John. 7 The same came for a witness, to bear witness of the Light, that all men through him might believe. 8 He was not that Light, but was sent to bear witness of that Light. 9 That was the true Light, which lighteth every man that cometh into the world. 10 He was in the world, and the world was made by him, and the world knew him not. 11 He came unto his own, and his own received him not. 12 But as many as received him, to them gave he power

6 Ἐγένετο ἄνθρωπος ἀπεσταλμένος παρὰ θεοῦ, ὄνομα
There was a man sent from God, ²name
αὐτῷ ᵐἸωάννης.ⁱⁱ 7 οὗτος ἦλθεν εἰς μαρτυρίαν, ἵνα μαρτυ-
¹his John. He came for a witness, that he might
ρήσῃ περὶ τοῦ φωτός, ἵνα πάντες πιστεύσωσιν δι᾽ αὐτοῦ.
witness concerning the light, that all ᐧ might believe through him.
8 οὐκ.ἦν ἐκεῖνος τὸ φῶς, ἀλλ᾽ ἵνα μαρτυρήσῃ περὶ τοῦ
²Was ³not ¹he the light, but that he might witness concerning the
φωτός. 9 ἦν τὸ φῶς τὸ ἀληθινόν ὃ φωτίζει πάντα
light. ⁴Was ¹the ³light ²true that which lightens every
ἄνθρωπον ἐρχόμενον εἰς τὸν κόσμον. 10 ἐν τῷ κόσμῳ ἦν,
man coming into the world. In the world he was,
καὶ ὁ κόσμος δι᾽ αὐτοῦ ἐγένετο, καὶ ὁ κόσμος αὐτὸν
and the world through him came into being, and the world him
οὐκ.ἔγνω. 11 εἰς τὰ.ἴδια ἦλθεν, καὶ οἱ.ἴδιοι αὐτὸν οὐ.παρέλα-
knew not. To his own he came, and his own him received not;
βον· 12 ὅσοι.δὲ ⁿἔλαβονⁱⁱ αὐτὸν ἔδωκεν αὐτοῖς ἐξουσίαν
but as many as received him he gave to them authority

ᵃ — ἔξω [L]ΤΤᵣ[A].   ᵇ πρὸς LΤΤᵣA.   ᶜ — καὶ ἀνεφέρετο εἰς τὸν οὐρανόν Τ.   ᵈ — προσκυνή-
σαντες αὐτόν Τ.   ᵉ διὰ παντὸς LA.   ᶠ[αἰνοῦντες καὶ] εὐλογοῦντες ΤᵣA; — καὶ εὐλογοῦντες Τ.
ᵍ — ᾽Ἀμήν G[L]ΤΤᵣA.   ʰ Κατὰ Λουκᾶν ΤᵣA ; — Τὸ κατὰ Λουκᾶ εὐαγγέλιον EGLTW.
ⁱ — ἅγιον E ; Εὐαγγέλιον κατὰ Ἰωάννην (Ἰωάνην Τᵣ) GLΤᵣAW ; κατὰ Ἰωάννην Τ.   ᵏ ἓν. ὃ
γέγονεν ἐν (read one [thing]). That which was in him was life) LΤᵣ.   ˡ ἐστιν is LT.
ᵐ Ἰωάνης Τᵣ.   ⁿ ἔλαβαν Τᵣ.

τέκνα θεοῦ γενέσθαι, τοῖς πιστεύουσιν εἰς τὸ ὄνομα
children of God to be, to those that believe, on ²name

αὐτοῦ· 13 οἳ οὐκ ἐξ αἱμάτων οὐδὲ ἐκ θελήματος σαρκὸς οὐδὲ
'his; who not of bloods nor of will of flesh nor

ἐκ θελήματος ἀνδρὸς ἀλλ' ἐκ θεοῦ ἐγεννήθησαν·
of will of man but of God were born.

14 Καὶ ὁ λόγος σὰρξ ἐγένετο, καὶ ἐσκήνωσεν ἐν ἡμῖν,
And the Word flesh became, and tabernacled among us,

καὶ ἐθεασάμεθα τὴν δόξαν αὐτοῦ, δόξαν ὡς μονογενοῦς παρὰ
(and we discerned ˙ his glory, a glory as of an only-begotten with

πατρός, πλήρης χάριτος καὶ ἀληθείας. 15 °Ἰωάννης‖ μαρτυρεῖ
a father, full of grace and truth. John witnesses

περὶ αὐτοῦ, καὶ κέκραγεν, λέγων, Οὗτος ἦν ὃν εἶπον,
concerning him, and cried, saying, This was he of whom I said,

Ὁ ὀπίσω μου ἐρχόμενος, ἔμπροσθέν μου γέγονεν· ὅτι
He who after me comes, ²precedence ³of ⁴me ¹has, for

πρῶτός μου ἦν. 16 ᵖΚαὶ‖ ἐκ τοῦ πληρώματος αὐτοῦ ἡμεῖς
before me he was. And of his fulness we

πάντες ἐλάβομεν, καὶ χάριν ἀντὶ χάριτος· 17 ὅτι ὁ νόμος
all received, and grace upon grace. For the law

διὰ ᵠΜωσέως‖ ἐδόθη. ἡ χάρις καὶ ἡ ἀλήθεια διὰ Ἰησοῦ
through Moses was given; the grace and the truth through Jesus

χριστοῦ ἐγένετο. 18 θεὸν οὐδεὶς ἑώρακεν πώποτε· ʳὁ‖ μονο-
Christ came. ⁵God ¹no ²one ³has ⁴seen at any time; the only-

γενὴς ˢυἱός,‖ ὁ ὢν εἰς τὸν κόλπον τοῦ πατρός, ἐκεῖνος ἐξη-
begotten Son, who is in the bosom of the Father, he de-

γήσατο. 19 Καὶ αὕτη ἐστὶν ἡ μαρτυρία τοῦ ᵗἸωάννου,‖
clared [him]. And this is the witness of John,

ὅτε ἀπέστειλαν ᵛ οἱ Ἰουδαῖοι ἐξ Ἱεροσολύμων ἱερεῖς καὶ
when ²sent ¹the ²Jews from Jerusalem priests and

ʷΛευίτας,‖ ἵνα ἐρωτήσωσιν αὐτόν, Σὺ τίς εἶ; 20 Καὶ
Levites, that they might ask him, Thou who art thou? And

ὡμολόγησεν καὶ οὐκ ἠρνήσατο, καὶ ὡμολόγησεν, Ὅτι ˣοὐκ εἰμὶ
he confessed and denied not, and confessed, ³Not ⁴am

ἐγὼ‖ ὁ χριστός. 21 Καὶ ἠρώτησαν αὐτόν, ʸΤί οὖν; Ἡλίας
¹I the Christ. And they asked him, What then? Elias

εἶ σύ; ᶻΚαὶ‖ λέγει, Οὐκ εἰμί. Ὁ προφήτης εἶ σύ; Καὶ
art thou? And he says, I am not. The prophet art thou? And

ἀπεκρίθη, Οὔ. 22 ᵃΕἶπον‖ ᵇοὖν‖ αὐτῷ, Τίς εἶ; ἵνα ἀπό-
he answered, No. They said therefore to him, Who art thou? that an

κρισιν δῶμεν τοῖς πέμψασιν ἡμᾶς· τί λέγεις περὶ
answer we may give to those who ⁴sent us: what sayest thou about

σεαυτοῦ; 23 Ἔφη, Ἐγὼ φωνὴ βοῶντος ἐν τῇ ἐρήμῳ,
thyself? He said, I [am] a voice crying in the wilderness,

Εὐθύνατε τὴν ὁδὸν κυρίου· καθὼς εἶπεν Ἡσαΐας ὁ προ-
Make straight the way of [the] Lord, as said Esaias the pro-

φήτης. 24 Καὶ ᶜοἱ‖ ἀπεσταλμένοι ἦσαν ἐκ τῶν Φαρι-
phet. And those who had been sent were from among the Phari-

σαίων. 25 καὶ ἠρώτησαν αὐτὸν καὶ ᵈεἶπον‖ αὐτῷ, Τί οὖν
sees. And they asked him and said to him, Why then

βαπτίζεις, εἰ σὺ οὐκ εἶ ὁ χριστός, ᵉοὔτε‖ ᶠἨλίας,‖ ᵉοὔτε‖
baptizest thou, if thou art not the Christ, nor Elias, nor

ᵒἸωάνης Tr.   ᵖ ὅτι for GLTTrA.   ᵠ Μωϋσέως LTTrAW.   ʳ — ὁ (read [the]) Tr.   ˢ θεὸς
God Tr.   ᵗ Ἰωάνου Tr.   ᵛ + πρὸς αὐτὸν to him LTrA.   ʷ Λευείτας TTrA.   ˣ ἐγὼ οὐκ
εἰμι LTTrA.   ʸ τί οὖν; Ἡλίας εἶ; T: τί οὖν; σὺ Ἡλίας εἶ; Tr: σὺ οὖν τί; Ἡλίας εἶ; A.
ᶻ — καὶ T.   ᵃ εἶπαν LTTrA.   ᵇ — οὖν L.   ᶜ — οἱ (read [those who]) TTrA.   ᵈ εἶπαν
LTT A.   ᵉ οὐδὲ LTTrA.   ᶠ Ἡλείας T.

26 John answered them, saying, I baptize with water: but there standeth one among you, whom ye know not. 27 he it is, who coming after me is preferred before me, whose shoe's latchet I am not worthy to unloose. 28 These things were done in Bethabara beyond Jordan, where John was baptizing.

ὁ προφήτης; 26 Ἀπεκρίθη αὐτοῖς ὁ ᵍΙωάννης‖ λέγων, Ἐγὼ
the prophet?　　²Answered ³them　¹John　　saying,　I

βαπτίζω ἐν ὕδατι· μέσος.ʰδὲ‖ ὑμῶν ⁱἔστηκεν‖ ὃν ὑμεῖς
baptize with water; but in [the] midst of you　stands ' [one] whom　ye

οὐκ.οἴδατε 27 ᵏαὐτός ἐστιν‖ ¹ὁ‖ ὀπίσω μου ἐρχόμενος, ᵐὃς
know not;　　　　　'he　'it is　who after　me　comes,　who

ἔμπροσθέν μου γέγονεν·‖ οὗ ⁿἐγὼ‖ οὐκ εἰμὶ ᵒ ἄξιος ἵνα
²precedence ³of ⁴me　¹has,　of whom　I　²not ¹am　worthy that

λύσω αὐτοῦ τὸν ἱμάντα τοῦ ὑποδήματος. 28 Ταῦτα ἐν
I should loose of him ' the　thong of the　sandal.　　These things in

ᴾΒηθαβαρᾶ‖ ἐγένετο πέραν τοῦ Ἰορδάνου, ὅπου ἦν �qʳΙωάν-
Bethabara　took place across ·the　Jordan,　where ²was　¹John

νης‖ βαπτίζων.
baptizing.

29 The next day John seeth Jesus coming unto him, and saith, Behold the Lamb of God, which taketh away the sin of the world. 30 This is he of whom I said, After me cometh a man which is preferred before me. 31 And I knew him not: but that he should be made manifest to Israel, therefore am I come baptizing with water. 32 And John bare record, saying, I saw the Spirit descending from heaven like a dove, and it abode upon him. 33 And I knew him not: but he that sent me to baptize with water, the same said unto me, Upon whom thou shalt see the Spirit descending, and remaining on him, the same is he which baptizeth with the Holy Ghost. 34 And I saw, and bare record that this is the Son of God.

29 Τῇ ἐπαύριον βλέπει ˢὁ Ἰωάννης‖ τὸν Ἰησοῦν ἐρχόμενον
On the morrow　²sees　¹John　　Jesus　coming

πρὸς αὐτόν, καὶ λέγει, Ἴδε ὁ ἀμνὸς τοῦ θεοῦ, ὁ αἴρων
to　him,　and says, Behold the Lamb　of God, who takes away

τὴν ἁμαρτίαν τοῦ κόσμου. 30 οὗτός ἐστιν ᵗπερὶ‖ οὗ ἐγὼ
the　sin　of the world.　He　it is concerning whom I

εἶπον, Ὀπίσω μου ἔρχεται ἀνήρ, ὃς ἔμπροσθέν μου γέγονεν,
said,　After me comes a man, who ²precedence ³of ⁴me ¹has,

ὅτι πρῶτός μου ἦν. 31 κἀγὼ οὐκ.ᾔδειν αὐτόν· ἀλλ' ἵνα
because before me he was.　And I knew not him;　but that

φανερωθῇ τῷ Ἰσραήλ, διὰ.τοῦτο ἦλθον ἐγὼ ἐν ᵗτῷ‖
he might be manifested to Israel,　therefore came I　with

ὕδατι βαπτίζων. 32 Καὶ ἐμαρτύρησεν ʳΙωάννης‖ λέγων, Ὅτι
water baptizing.　And ²bore ³witness　¹John　saying,

τεθέαμαι τὸ πνεῦμα καταβαῖνον ʷὡσεὶ‖ περιστερὰν ἐξ οὐ-
I have beheld the Spirit　descending as　a dove　out of hea-

ρανοῦ, καὶ ἔμεινεν ἐπ' αὐτόν. 33 κἀγὼ οὐκ.ᾔδειν αὐτόν· ἀλλ'
ven,　and it abode upon him.　And I knew not him;　but

ὁ πέμψας με βαπτίζειν ἐν ὕδατι, ἐκεῖνός μοι εἶπεν, Ἐφ'
he who sent me to baptize with water,　he to me said,　Upon

ὃν ἂν ἴδῃς τὸ πνεῦμα καταβαῖνον καὶ μένον ἐπ'
whom thou shalt see the Spirit　descending　and abiding on

αὐτόν, οὗτός ἐστιν ὁ βαπτίζων ἐν πνεύματι ἁγίῳ.
him,　he　it is who baptizes with [the] ²Spirit ¹Holy.

34 κἀγὼ ἑώρακα, καὶ μεμαρτύρηκα ὅτι οὗτός ἐστιν ὁ υἱος
And I have seen, and have borne witness that　this　is the Son

τοῦ θεοῦ.
of God.

35 Again the next day after John stood, and two of his disciples; 36 and looking upon Jesus as he walked, he saith, Behold the Lamb of God! 37 And the two disciples heard him speak, and they followed Je-

35 Τῇ ἐπαύριον πάλιν εἱστήκει ˣὁ‖ ʳΙωάννης,‖ καὶ ἐκ
On the morrow　again ²was ³standing　¹John,　and ²of

τῶν.μαθητῶν.αὐτοῦ δύο. 36 καὶ ἐμβλέψας τῷ Ἰησοῦ περιπα-
³his ⁴disciples　¹two.　And looking at　Jesus　walk-

τοῦντι, λέγει, Ἴδε ὁ ἀμνὸς τοῦ θεοῦ. 37 ᶻΚαὶ‖ ἤκουσαν
ing,　he says, Behold the Lamb　of God !　And ⁴heard

ᵃαὐτοῦ οἱ δύο μαθηταὶ‖ λαλοῦντος, καὶ ἠκολούθησαν τῷ
⁵him ¹the ²two ³disciples　speaking,　and　followed

ᵍ Ἰωάνης Tr.　ʰ — δὲ but TTrA.　ⁱ στήκει †TTrA.　ᵏ — αὐτός ἐστιν G[L]TTrA.　¹ [ὁ] TrA.
ᵐ — ὃς ἔμπροσθέν μου γέγονεν G[L]TTrA.　ⁿ — ἐ.ὼ [L]TTrA.　ᵒ + ἐγὼ I T[Tʳ]A.　ᴾ Βη-
θαβαρᾶ E ; Βηθανίᾳ Bethany GLTTrAW.　q + ὁ LTTr[A].　ʳ Ἰωάνης Tr.　ˢ — ὁ Ἰωάνης
(read he sees) GLTTrAW.　ᵗ ὑπὲρ LTTrA.　ᵛ — τῷ LTT·[A].　ʷ ὡς GLTTrAW　ˣ — ὁ
LTrA.　ʸ + [ὁ αἴρων τὴν ἁμαρτίαν τοῦ κόσμου] who takes away the sin of the world L.
ᶻ — καὶ Ι.　ᵃ οἱ δύο μαθηταὶ αὐτοῦ Τ.

Ἰησοῦ. 38 στραφεὶς ᶜδὲ‖ ὁ Ἰησοῦς, ʹκαὶ θεασάμενος αὐτοὺς
Jesus. ³Having ⁴turned ¹but, ²Jesus, and beheld them

ἀκολουθοῦντας, λέγει αὐτοῖς, 39 Τί ζητεῖτε; Οἱ.δὲ ᵈεἶπον‖
following, says to them, What seek ye? And they said

αὐτῷ, ᵉʹΡαββί,‖ ὃ ˏλέγεται ᶠἑρμηνευόμενον‖ διδάσκαλε, ποῦ
to him, Rabbi, which ⁴is to say being interpreted Teacher, where

μένεις; 40 Λέγει αὐτοῖς, Ἐρχεσθε καὶ ᵍἴδετε.‖ ʰʳἨλθον‖
abidest thou? He says to them, Come and see. They went

ⁱκαὶ ᵏεἶδον‖ ποῦ μένει· καὶ παρ' αὐτῷ ἔμειναν τὴν ἡμέραν
and saw where he abides; and with him they abode ²day

ἐκείνην· ὥρα �亅δὲ‖ ἦν ὡς δεκάτη. 41 ʹἨν ᵐ Ἀνδρέας
¹that. [²The] ³hour ¹now was about [the] tenth. ⁷Was ¹Andrew

ὁ ἀδελφὸς Σίμωνος Πέτρου εἷς ἐκ τῶν δύο τῶν ἀκουσάντων
²the ³brother ⁴of ⁵Simon ⁶Peter one of the two who heard

παρὰ ⁿʹἸωάννου,‖ καὶ ἀκολουθησάντων αὐτῷ. 42 εὑρίσκει
[this] from John, and followed him. ³Finds

οὗτος ᵒπρῶτος‖ τὸν ἀδελφὸν τὸν.ἴδιον Σίμωνα, καὶ λέγει
¹he ²first ⁶brother ⁴his ⁵own Simon, and says

αὐτῷ, Εὑρήκαμεν τὸν μεσσίαν, ὅ ἐστιν μεθερμηνευόμενον
to him, We have found the Messias, which is being interpreted

Ρᵒ‖ χριστός· 43 �q καὶ‖ ἤγαγεν αὐτὸν πρὸς τὸν Ἰησοῦν.
the Christ. And he led him to Jesus.

ἐμβλέψας.ʳδὲ‖ αὐτῷ ὁ Ἰησοῦς εἶπεν, Σὺ εἶ Σίμων ὁ υἱὸς
And looking at him Jesus said, Thou art Simon the son

ˢʹἸωνᾶ·‖ σὺ κληθήσῃ Κηφᾶς, ὃ ἑρμηνεύεται Πέτρος.
of Jonas; thou shalt be called Cephas, which is interpreted Stone.

44 Τῇ ἐπαύριον ἠθέλησεν ᵗὁ Ἰησοῦς‖ ἐξελθεῖν εἰς τὴν
On the morrow ²desired ¹Jesus to go forth into

Γαλιλαίαν· καὶ εὑρίσκει Φίλιππον καὶ λέγει αὐτῷᵛ, Ἀκολούθει
Galilee, and he finds Philip and says to him, Follow

μοι. 45 ʹΗν.δὲ ὁ Φίλιππος ἀπὸ Βηθσαϊδά, ἐκ τῆς πόλεως
me. Now ²was ¹Philip from Bethsaida, of the . city

Ἀνδρέου καὶ Πέτρου. 46 Εὑρίσκει Φίλιππος τὸν Ναθαναὴλ
of Andrew and Peter. ²Finds ¹Philip Nathanael

καὶ λέγει αὐτῷ, Ὃν ἔγραψεν ʷΜωσῆς‖ ἐν τῷ νόμῳ καὶ
and says to him, [Him] whom ²wrote ³of ¹Moses in the law and

οἱ προφῆται, εὑρήκαμεν, Ἰησοῦν ˣτὸν‖ υἱὸν τοῦ Ἰωσὴφ τὸν
the prophets, we have found, Jesus the son of Joseph who

ἀπὸ ʸΝαζαρέτ.‖ 47 ᶻΚαὶ‖ εἶπεν αὐτῷ Ναθαναήλ, Ἐκ
[is] from Nazareth. And ²said ³to ⁴him ¹Nathanael, Out of

ʸΝαζαρέτ‖ δύναταί τι ἀγαθὸν εἶναι; Λέγει αὐτῷ ᵃ Φίλιππος,
Nazareth can any good thing be? ²Says ³to ⁴him ¹Philip,

Ἐρχου καὶ ἴδε. 48 Εἶδεν ᵇὁ‖ Ἰησοῦς τὸν Ναθαναὴλ ἐρχόμενον
Come and see. ²Saw ¹Jesus Nathanael coming

πρὸς αὐτόν, καὶ λέγει περὶ αὐτοῦ, Ἴδε ἀληθῶς ᶜᵃἸσραηλ-
to him, and says concerning him, Behold truly an Israel-

ίτης,‖ ἐν ᾧ δόλος οὐκ.ἔστιν. 49 Λέγει αὐτῷ Ναθαναήλ,
ite, in whom guile is not. ²Says ³to ⁴him ¹Nathanael,

Πόθεν με γινώσκεις; Ἀπεκρίθη ᵈᵃὁ‖ Ἰησοῦς καὶ εἶπεν αὐτῷ,
Whence me knowest thou? ²Answered ¹Jesus and said to him,

sus. 38 Then Jesus
turned, and saw them
following, and saith
unto them, What seek
ye? They said unto
him, Rabbi, (which is
to say, being inter-
preted, Master,) where
dwellest thou? 39 He
saith unto them, Come
and see. They came
and saw where he
dwelt, and abode with
him that day: for it
was about the tenth
hour. 40 One of the
two which heard John
speak, and followed
him, was Andrew. Si-
mon Peter's brother.
41 He first findeth his
own brother Simon,
and saith unto him,
We have found the
Messias, which is, be-
ing interpreted, the
Christ. 42 And he
brought him to Jesus.
And when Jesus be-
held him, he said, Thou
art Simon the son of
Jona: thou shalt be
called Cephas, which
is by interpretation, A
stone. 43 The day fol-
lowing Jesus would go
forth into Galilee, and
findeth Philip, and
saith unto him, Follow
me.

44 Now Philip was of
Bethsaida, the city of
Andrew and Peter.
45 Philip findeth Na-
thanael, and saith
unto him, We have
found him, of whom
Moses in the law, and
the prophets, did write,
Jesus of Nazareth, the
son of Joseph. 46 And
Nathanael said unto
him, Can there any
good thing come out
of Nazareth? Philip
saith unto him, Come
and see. 47 Jesus saw
Nathanael coming to
him, and saith of him,
Behold an Israelite in-
deed, in whom is no
guile! 48 Nathanael
saith unto him, Whence
knowest thou me? Je-
sus answered and said
unto him, Before that

ᶜ — δὲ T.   ᵈ εἶπαν LTTrA.   ᵉ Ραββεί T.   ᶠ μεθερμηνευόμενον LTTrA.   ᵍ ὄψεσθε γε
shall see TTrA.   ʰ ἠλθαν TTrA.   ⁱ οὖν therefore [L]TTrA.   ᵏ εἶδαν LTTrA.   ˡ — δὲ
GLTTrAW.   ᵐ + [δὲ] and L.   ⁿ Ἰωάνου Tr.   ᵒ πρώτον LTrA.   ᵖ — ὁ GLTTrAW.
q — καὶ [L]TTrA.   ʳ — δὲ and GTTrAW.   ˢ Ἰωάνου of John LTr ; Ἰωάννου TA.   ᵗ — ὁ
Ἰησοῦς (read he desired) GLTTrAW.   ᵛ + Ἰησοῦς Jesus (finds) LTTrAW.   ʷ Μωϋσῆς
LTTrAW.   ˣ — τὸν LT[Tr].   ʸ Ναζαρέθ EGW.   ᶻ — καὶ T.   ᵃ + ὁ LTrA.   ᵇ — ὁ
LTTrAW.   ᶜᵃ Ἰσραηλείτης TTr.   ᵈᵃ — ὁ GLTTrAW.

Philip called thee, when thou wast under the fig tree, I saw thee.
49 Nathanael answered and saith unto him, Rabbi, thou art the Son of God; thou art the King of Israel.
50 Jesus answered and said unto him, Because I said unto thee, I saw thee under the fig tree, believest thou? thou shalt see greater things than these. 51 And he saith unto him, Verily, verily, I say unto you, Hereafter ye shall see heaven open, and the angels of God ascending and descending upon the Son of man.

II. And the third day there was a marriage in Cana of Galilee; and the mother of Jesus was there: 2 and both Jesus was called, and his disciples, to the marriage. 3 And when they wanted wine, the mother of Jesus saith unto him, They have no wine. 4 Jesus saith unto her, Woman, what have I to do with thee? mine hour is not yet come. 5 His mother saith unto the servants, Whatsoever he saith unto you, do it. 6 And there were set there six waterpots of stone, after the manner of the purifying of the Jews, containing two or three firkins apiece. 7 Jesus saith unto them, Fill the waterpots with water. And they filled them up to the brim. 8 And he saith unto them, Draw out now, and bear unto the governor of the feast. And they bare it. 9 When the ruler of the feast had tasted the water that was made wine, and knew not whence it was: (but the servants which drew the water knew;) the governor of the feast called the bridegroom, 10 and saith unto him, Every man at the beginning doth set forth good wine; and when men

Πρὸ τοῦ σε Φίλιππον φωνῆσαι, ὄντα ὑπὸ τὴν συκῆν,
Before that [3]thee [1]Philip [2]called, [thou] being under the fig-tree,
εἶδόν σε. 50 Ἀπεκρίθη[e] Ναθαναὴλ [f]καὶ λέγει[g] αὐτῷ,[h] [h]Ῥαββί,[i]
I saw thee. [2]Answered [1]Nathanael and says to him, Rabbi,
σὺ εἶ ὁ υἱὸς τοῦ θεοῦ, σὺ [i]εἶ ὁ βασιλεὺς[j] τοῦ Ἰσραήλ.
thou art the Son of God, thou art the King of Israel.
51 Ἀπεκρίθη Ἰησοῦς καὶ εἶπεν αὐτῷ, Ὅτι εἶπόν σοι, [k]Εἶδόν
[2]Answered [1]Jesus and said to him, Because I said to thee, I saw
σε ὑποκάτω τῆς συκῆς, πιστεύεις; μείζω τούτων
thee under the fig-tree, believest thou? Greater things than these
[l]ὄψει.[l] 52 Καὶ λέγει αὐτῷ, Ἀμὴν ἀμὴν λέγω ὑμῖν,
thou shalt see. And he says to him, Verily verily I say to you,
[m]ἀπ᾽ ἄρτι[m] ὄψεσθε τὸν οὐρανὸν ἀνεῳγότα, καὶ τοὺς ἀγ-
Henceforth ye shall see the heaven opened, and the an-
γέλους τοῦ θεοῦ ἀναβαίνοντας καὶ καταβαίνοντας ἐπὶ τὸν
gels of God ascending and descending on the
υἱὸν τοῦ ἀνθρώπου.
Son of man.

2 Καὶ [n]τῇ ἡμέρᾳ τῇ τρίτῃ[n] γάμος ἐγένετο ἐν [o]Κανᾷ[o]
And on the [2]day [1]third a marriage took place in Cana
τῆς Γαλιλαίας· καὶ ἦν ἡ μήτηρ τοῦ Ἰησοῦ ἐκεῖ. 2 ἐκλήθη δὲ
of Galilee, and [3]was [1]the [2]mother [3]of [4]Jesus there. And [2]was [1]invited
καὶ ὁ Ἰησοῦς καὶ οἱ μαθηταὶ αὐτοῦ εἰς τὸν γάμον. 3 καὶ
[2]also [1]Jesus and his disciples to the marriage. And
[p]ὑστερήσαντος οἴνου[p] λέγει ἡ μήτηρ τοῦ Ἰησοῦ πρὸς αὐτόν,
being deficient of wine [5]says [1]the [2]mother [3]of [4]Jesus to him,
[q]Οἶνον οὐκ ἔχουσιν.[q] 4 [r]Λέγει αὐτῇ ὁ Ἰησοῦς, Τί ἐμοὶ καὶ
Wine they have not. [2]Says [3]to [4]her [1]Jesus, What to me and
σοί, γύναι; οὔπω ἥκει ἡ ὥρα μου. 5 Λέγει ἡ μήτηρ αὐτοῦ
to thee, woman? not yet is come mine hour. [2]Says [1]his [3]mother
τοῖς διακόνοις, Ὅ τι ἂν λέγῃ ὑμῖν, ποιήσατε. 6 Ἦσαν
to the servants, Whatever he may say to you, do. [2]There [3]were
δὲ ἐκεῖ [s]ὑδρίαι λίθιναι[s] ἒξ [t]κείμεναι[t] κατὰ τὸν καθα-
[1]and there [2]water-vessels [3]of [4]stone [5]six standing according to the puri-
ρισμὸν τῶν Ἰουδαίων[t], χωροῦσαι ἀνὰ μετρητὰς δύο ἢ τρεῖς.
fication of the Jews, [2]holding [1]each metretæ two or three.
7 λέγει αὐτοῖς ὁ Ἰησοῦς, Γεμίσατε τὰς ὑδρίας ὕδατος.
[2]Says [3]to [4]them [1]Jesus, Fill the water-vessels with water.
Καὶ ἐγέμισαν αὐτὰς ἕως ἄνω. 8 Καὶ λέγει αὐτοῖς, Ἀν-
And they filled them unto [the] brim. And he says to them, Draw
τλήσατε νῦν καὶ φέρετε τῷ ἀρχιτρικλίνῳ. [*]Καὶ[*] ἤνεγκαν.
out now and carry to the master of the feast. And they carried [it].
9 ὡς δὲ ἐγεύσατο ὁ ἀρχιτρίκλινος τὸ ὕδωρ οἶνον γεγενη-
But when [2]had [3]tasted [1]the [2]master [3]of [4]the [5]feast the water [4]wine [1]that [2]had
μένον, καὶ οὐκ ᾔδει πόθεν ἐστίν· οἱ δὲ διάκονοι ᾔδεισαν οἱ
[3]become, and knew not whence it is, (but the servants knew who
ἠντληκότες τὸ ὕδωρ· φωνεῖ τὸν νυμφίον ὁ ἀρχιτρίκλινος
had drawn the water,) [6]calls [7]the [8]bridegroom [1]the [2]master [3]of [4]the [5]feast
10 καὶ λέγει αὐτῷ, Πᾶς ἄνθρωπος πρῶτον τὸν καλὸν οἶνον
and says to him, Every man first the good wine

τίθησιν, καὶ ὅταν μεθυσθῶσιν ˣτότε‖ τὸν ἐλάσσω·
ˡsets on, and when they may have drunk freely then the inferior;

σὺ τετήρηκας τὸν καλὸν οἶνον ἕως ἄρτι. 11 Ταύτην ἐποίησεν
thou hast kept the good wine until now. This ˢdid

ˤτὴν‖ ἀρχὴν τῶν σημείων ὁ Ἰησοῦς ἐν ᶻΚανᾷ‖ τῆς Γαλιλαίας,
ˡbeginning ²of ³the ⁴signs Jesus in Cana of Galilee,

καὶ ἐφανέρωσεν τὴν.δόξαν.αὐτοῦ· καὶ ἐπίστευσαν εἰς αὐτὸν
and manifested his glory; and ³believed ⁴on ⁵him

οἱ.μαθηταὶ.αὐτοῦ.
ˡhis ²disciples.

12 Μετὰ τοῦτο· κατέβη εἰς ᵃΚαπερναούμ,‖ αὐτὸς καὶ ἡ
After this he went down to Capernaum, he and

μήτηρ.αὐτοῦ καὶ οἱ.ἀδελφοὶ ᵇαὐτοῦ‖ καὶ οἱ.μαθηταὶ.αὐτοῦ, καὶ
his mother and ²brethren ¹his and his disciples, and

ἐκεῖ ἔμειναν οὐ πολλὰς ἡμέρας. 13 Καὶ ἐγγὺς ἦν τὸ πάσχα
there they abode not many days. And near was the passover

τῶν Ἰουδαίων, καὶ ἀνέβη εἰς Ἱεροσόλυμα ὁ Ἰησοῦς. 14 καὶ
of the Jews, and ²went ³up ⁴to ⁵Jerusalem ¹Jesus. And

εὗρεν ἐν τῷ ἱερῷ τοὺς πωλοῦντας βόας καὶ πρόβατα καὶ
he found in the temple those who sold oxen and sheep and

περιστεράς, καὶ τοὺς κερματιστὰς καθημένους· 15 καὶ ποιή-
doves, and the money-changers sitting; and having

σας φραγέλλιον ἐκ σχοινίων πάντας ἐξέβαλεν ἐκ τοῦ
made a scourge of cords ⁴all ¹he ²drove ³out from the

ἱεροῦ, τά.τε πρόβατα καὶ τοὺς βόας. καὶ τῶν κολλυβιστῶν
temple, both the sheep and the oxen; and of the money-changers

ἐξέχεεν ᶜτὸ κέρμα‖ καὶ τὰς τραπέζας ἀνέστρεψεν. 16 καὶ
he poured out the coin and the tables overthrew. And

τοῖς τὰς.περιστερὰς πωλοῦσιν εἶπεν, Ἄρατε ταῦτα
to those who ²the ³doves ¹sold he said, Take these things

ἐντεῦθεν· ᵈμὴ.ποιεῖτε τὸν οἶκον τοῦ.πατρός.μου οἶκον ἐμ-
hence; make not the house of my father a house of mer-

πορίου. 17 Ἐμνήσθησαν.ᵉδὲ‖ οἱ.μαθηταὶ.αὐτοῦ ὅτι γε-
chandise. And ²remembered ¹his ²disciples that writ-

γραμμένον ἐστίν, Ὁ ζῆλος τοῦ.οἴκου.σου ᶠκατέφαγέν‖ με.
ten it is, The zeal of thine house has eaten ²up ¹me.

18 Ἀπεκρίθησαν οὖν οἱ Ἰουδαῖοι καὶ ᵍεἶπον‖ αὐτῷ, Τί
⁴Answered ³therefore ¹the ²Jews and said to him, What

σημεῖον δεικνύεις ἡμῖν ὅτι ταῦτα ποιεῖς; 19 Ἀπεκρίθη
sign shewest thou to us that these things thou doest? ²Answered

ʰὁ‖ Ἰησοῦς καὶ εἶπεν αὐτοῖς, Λύσατε τὸν.ναόν.τοῦτον, καὶ ⁱἐν‖
¹Jesus and said to them, Destroy this temple, and in

τρισὶν ἡμέραις ἐγερῶ αὐτόν. 20 ᵍΕἶπον‖ οὖν οἱ Ἰουδαῖοι,
three days I will raise up it. ⁴Said ³therefore ¹the ²Jews,

ᵏΤεσσαράκοντα‖ καὶ ἓξ ἔτεσιν ˡᾠκοδομήθη‖ ὁ.ναὸς.οὗτος, καὶ
Forty and six years was building this temple, and

σὺ ἐν τρισὶν ἡμέραις ἐγερεῖς αὐτόν; 21 Ἐκεῖνος.δὲ ἔλεγεν
thou in three days wilt raise up it? But he spoke

περὶ τοῦ ναοῦ τοῦ.σώματος.αὐτοῦ. 22 ὅτε οὖν ἠγέρ-
concerning the temple of his body. When therefore he was

θη ἐκ νεκρῶν ἐμνήσθησαν οἱ.μαθηταὶ.αὐτοῦ ὅτι
raised up from among [the] dead ²remembered ¹his ²disciples that

have well drunk, then that which is worse: *but* thou hast kept the good wine until now. 11 This beginning of miracles did Jesus in Cana of Galilee, and manifested forth his glory; and his disciples believed on him.

12 After this he went down to Capernaum, he, and his mother, and his brethren, and his disciples: and they continued there not many days. 13 And the Jews' passover was at hand, and Jesus went up to Jerusalem, 14 and found in the temple those that sold oxen and sheep and doves, and the changers of money sitting: 15 and when he had made a scourge of small cords, he drove them all out of the temple, and the sheep, and the oxen; and poured out the changers' money, and overthrew the tables; 16 and said unto them that sold doves, Take these things hence; make not my Father's house an house of merchandise. 17 And his disciples remembered that it was written, The zeal of thine house hath eaten me up. 18 Then answered the Jews and said unto him, What sign shewest thou unto us, seeing that thou doest these things? 19 Jesus answered and said unto them, Destroy this temple, and in three days I will raise it up. 20 Then said the Jews, Forty and six years was this temple in building, and wilt thou rear it up in three days? 21 But he spake of the temple of his body. 22 When therefore he was risen from the dead, his disciples remembered that he

---

ˣ — τότε [L]T[TrA]. ʸ — τὴν LTTrA. ᶻ Κανᾶ ELTTr. ᵃ Καφαρναούμ LTTrAw.
ᵇ — αὐτοῦ [L]Tr[A]. ᶜ τὰ κέρματα the coins TrA. ᵈ + [καὶ] and L. ᵉ — δὲ and [L]TTrA.
ᶠ καταφάγεται will eat up GLTT AW. ᵍ εἶπαν LTTrA. ʰ — ὁ LTTrAW. ⁱ [ἐν] Tr.
ᵏ Τεσσεράκοντα TTrA. ˡ οἰκοδομήθη T.

had said this unto them; and they believed the scripture, and the word which Jesus had said.

23 Now when he was in Jerusalem at the passover, in the feast day, many believed in his name. when they saw the miracles which he did. 24 But Jesus did not commit himself unto them, because he knew all men, 25 and needed not that any should testify of man: for he knew what was in man.

III. There was a man of the Pharisees, named Nicodemus, a ruler of. the Jews: 2 the same came to Jesus by night, and said unto him, Rabbi, we know that thou art a teacher come from God: for no man can do these miracles that thou doest. except God be with him. 3 Jesus answered and said unto him, Verily, verily, I say unto thee, Except a man be born again, he cannot see the kingdom of God. 4 Nicodemus saith unto him, How can a man be born when he is old? can he enter the second time into his mother's womb, and be born? 5 Jesus answered, Verily, verily, I say unto thee, Except a man be born of water and of the Spirit. he cannot enter into the kingdom of God. 6 That which is born of the flesh is flesh ; and that which is born of the Spirit is spirit. 7 Marvel not that I said unto thee, Ye must be born again. 8 The wind bloweth where it listeth, and thou hearest the sound thereof, but canst not tell whence it cometh, and whither it goeth: so is every one that is born of the Spirit. 9 Nicodemus answered

τοῦτο ἔλεγεν ᵐαὐτοῖς,‖ καὶ ἐπίστευσαν τῇ γραφῇ καὶ τῷ
this he had said to them,   and believed   the scripture and the
λόγῳ ⁿῷ‖ εἶπεν ὁ Ἰησοῦς.
word which ²had ³spoken ¹Jesus.

23 Ὡς.δὲ ἦν ἐν ᵒἹεροσολύμοις ἐν τῷ πάσχα, ᴾἐν‖ τῇ
But when he was in   Jerusalem   at the passover,   at   the
ἑορτῇ, πολλοὶ ἐπίστευσαν εἰς τὸ.ὄνομα.αὐτοῦ, θεωροῦντες αὐτοῦ
feast,   many   believed   on   his name,   beholding   his
τὰ σημεῖα ἃ ἐποίει. 24 αὐτὸς.δὲ ⁴ὁ‖ Ἰησοῦς οὐκ.ἐπίστευεν
signs which he was doing.   But ²himself ¹Jesus   did not trust
ʳἑαυτὸν‖ αὐτοῖς, διὰ τὸ.αὐτὸν.γινώσκειν πάντας, 25 καὶ
himself to them, because of   his knowing   all [men],   and
ὅτι οὐ χρείαν εἶχεν ἵνα τις μαρτυρήσῃ περὶ ˢτοῦ‖ ἀνθρώ-
that ³no ⁴need ¹he ²had that any should testify concerning   man,
που· αὐτὸς.γὰρ ἐγίνωσκεν τί ἦν ἐν τῷ ἀνθρώπῳ.
for he   knew   what was in   man.

3 Ἦν.δὲ ἄνθρωπος ἐκ τῶν Φαρισαίων, Νικόδημος ὄνομα
But there was a man of the Pharisees,   Nicodemus ²name
αὐτῷ, ἄρχων τῶν Ἰουδαίων· 2 οὗτος ἦλθεν πρὸς ᵗτὸν Ἰησοῦν‖
¹his,   a ruler of the   Jews ;   he   came to   Jesus
νυκτός, καὶ εἶπεν αὐτῷ, ᵛῬαββί.‖ οἴδαμεν ὅτι ἀπὸ θεοῦ ἐλή-
by night, and said to him,   Rabbi,   we know that from God thou
λυθας διδάσκαλος· οὐδεὶς γὰρ ʷταῦτα τὰ σημεῖα δύναται‖
hast come a teacher,   for no one   these   the signs   is able
ποιεῖν ἃ σὺ ποιεῖς ἐὰν.μὴ ᾖ ὁ θεὸς μετ' αὐτοῦ. 3 Ἀπεκρίθη
to do which thou doest unless ²be ¹God with him.   ²Answered
ˣὁ‖ Ἰησοῦς καὶ εἶπεν αὐτῷ, Ἀμὴν ἀμὴν λέγω σοι, ἐὰν.μή
¹Jesus and said to him,   Verily verily I say to thee, Unless
τις γεννηθῇ ἄνωθεν, οὐ.δύναται ἰδεῖν τὴν βασιλείαν τοῦ
anyone be born   anew,   he cannot   see   the   kingdom
θεοῦ. 4 Λέγει πρὸς αὐτὸν ʸὁ‖ Νικόδημος, Πῶς δύναται ἄν-
of God.   ²Says ³to ⁴him   ¹Nicodemus,   How can   a
θρωπος γεννηθῆναι γέρων ὤν; μὴ δύναται εἰς τὴν κοιλίαν
man   be born   ²old ¹being?   can he into the   womb
τῆς.μητρὸς.αὐτοῦ δεύτερον εἰσελθεῖν καὶ γεννηθῆναι; 5 Ἀπε-
of his mother   a second time enter   and be born?   ²An-
κρίθη ˣὁ‖ Ἰησοῦς, Ἀμὴν ἀμὴν λέγω σοι, ἐὰν.μή τις γεννηθῇ
swered   ¹Jesus,   Verily verily I say to thee, Unless anyone be born
ἐξ ὕδατος καὶ πνεύματος οὐ.δύναται εἰσελθεῖν εἰς τὴν βασιλείαν
of water   and of Spirit he cannot   enter   into the kingdom
ᵃτοῦ θεοῦ.‖ 6 τὸ ʸγεγεννημένον‖ ἐκ τῆς σαρκὸς σάρξ ἐστιν·
of God.   That which has been born of the   flesh   flesh   is ;
καὶ τὸ ᵇγεγεννημένον‖ ἐκ τοῦ πνεύματος πνεῦμά ἐστιν.
and that which has been born of the   Spirit   spirit   is.
7 μὴ.θαυμάσῃς ὅτι εἶπόν σοι, Δεῖ ὑμᾶς γεννηθῆναι
Do not wonder that I said to thee, It is needful for you   to be born
ἄνωθεν. 8 τὸ πνεῦμα ὅπου θέλει πνεῖ, καὶ τὴν.φωνὴν.αὐτοῦ
anew.   The wind ²where ³it ⁴wills ¹blows, and   its sound
ἀκούεις, ᶜἀλλ'‖ οὐκ.οἶδας πόθεν ἔρχεται ᵈκαὶ‖ ποῦ ὑπάγει
thou hearest, but knowest not whence it comes and where it goes :
οὕτως.ἐστὶν πᾶς ὁ γεγεννημένος ἐκ τοῦ πνεύματος. 9 Ἀπε-
thus   is   everyone that has been born of the   Spirit.   ²An-

---

ᵐ — αὐτοῖς GLTTrAW.   ⁿ ὃν LTTrA.   ᵒ + τοῖς GLTTrA.   ᵖ [ἐν] LTr.   ۹ — ὁ LTTrA.
ʳ αὐτὸν LTTrA.   ˢ — τοῦ L.   ᵗ αὐτὸν him GLTTrAW.   ᵛ Ῥαββεί T.   ʷ δύναται ταῦτα
τὰ σημεῖα LTTrA.   ˣ — ὁ LTTrAW.   ʸ — ὁ Tr.   ᶻ — ὁ GLT[TrA]W.   ᵃ τῶν οὐρανῶν of
the heavens. T.   ᵇ γεγεννημένον E.   ᶜ ἀλλὰ Tr.   ᵈ ᾖ or L.

κρίθη Νικόδημος καὶ εἶπεν αὐτῷ, Πῶς δύναται ταῦτα γενέ-
swered Nicodemus and said to him, How can these things be?

σθαι; 10 Ἀπεκρίθη ᵉὁ‖ Ἰησοῦς καὶ εἶπεν αὐτῷ, Σὺ εἶ ὁ
²Answered ¹Jesus and said to him, Thou art the

διδάσκαλος τοῦ Ἰσραήλ, καὶ ταῦτα οὐ.γινώσκεις; 11 ἀμὴν
teacher of Israel, and these things knowest not? Verily

ἀμὴν λέγω σοι, ὅτι ὃ οἴδαμεν λαλοῦμεν, καὶ ὃ ἑωρά-
verily I say to thee, That which we know we speak, and that which we

καμεν μαρτυροῦμεν· καὶ τὴν.μαρτυρίαν.ἡμῶν οὐ.λαμβάνετε.
have seen we bear witness of; and our witness ye receive not.

12 εἰ τὰ.ἐπίγεια εἶπον ὑμῖν, καὶ οὐ.πιστεύετε, πῶς ἐὰν εἴπω
If earthly things I said to you, and ye believe not, how if I say

ὑμῖν τὰ.ἐπουράνια πιστεύσετέ; 13 καὶ οὐδεὶς ἀναβέβηκεν
to you heavenly things will ye believe? And no one has gone up

εἰς τὸν οὐρανὸν εἰ.μὴ ὁ ἐκ τοῦ οὐρανοῦ καταβάς, ὁ υἱὸς
into the heaven except he who out of the heaven came down, tho Son

τοῦ ἀνθρώπου ὁ ὢν ἐν τῷ οὐρανῷ· 14 καὶ καθὼς ʰΜωσῆς‖
of man who is in the heaven. And even as Moses

ὕψωσεν τὸν ὄφιν ἐν τῇ ἐρήμῳ, οὕτως ὑψωθῆναι δεῖ
lifted up the serpent in the wilderness, thus to be lifted up it behoves

τὸν υἱὸν τοῦ ἀνθρώπου· 15 ἵνα πᾶς ὁ πιστεύων ᵍεἰς αὐτὸν‖
the Son of man, that everyone who believes on him

ʰμὴ.ἀπόληται, ἀλλ'‖ ἔχῃ ζωὴν αἰώνιον. 16 οὕτως.γὰρ
may not perish, but may have life eternal. For ²so

ἠγάπησεν ὁ θεὸς τὸν κόσμον ὥστε τὸν.υἱὸν.ᶦαὐτοῦ‖ τὸν μονο-
¹loved ¹God the world that his Son the only be-

γενῆ ἔδωκεν, ἵνα πᾶς ὁ πιστεύων εἰς αὐτὸν μὴ.ἀπόληται,
gotten he gave, that everyone who believes on him may not perish,

ᵏἀλλ'‖ ἔχῃ ζωὴν αἰώνιον. 17 οὐ.γὰρ.ἀπέστειλεν ὁ θεὸς τὸν
but may have life eternal. For ²sent ³not ¹God

υἱὸν.ᶦαὐτοῦ‖ εἰς τὸν κόσμον ἵνα κρίνῃ τὸν κόσμον, ἀλλ'
his Son into the world that he might judge the world, but

ἵνα σωθῇ ὁ κόσμος δι' αὐτοῦ. 18 ὁ πιστεύων εἰς
that ²might ⁴be ²saved ¹the ²world through him. He that believes on

αὐτὸν οὐ.κρίνεται· ὁ.ᵐδὲ‖ μὴ.πιστεύων ἤδη κέκριται,
him is not judged; but he that believes not already has been judged,

ὅτι μὴ.πεπίστευκεν εἰς τὸ ὄνομα τοῦ μονογενοῦς υἱοῦ τοῦ
because he has not believed on the name of the only begotten Son

θεοῦ. 19 αὕτη.δέ ἐστιν ἡ κρίσις, ὅτι τὸ φῶς ἐλήλυθεν εἰς
of God. And this is the judgment, that the light has come into

τὸν κόσμον, καὶ ἠγάπησαν οἱ ἄνθρωποι μᾶλλον τὸ σκότος
the world, and ⁴loved ²men ⁵rather ³the ⁴darkness

ἢ τὸ φῶς· ἦν.γὰρ ⁿπονηρὰ αὐτῶν‖ τὰ ἔργα. 20 πᾶς.γὰρ
than the light; for ²were ¹evil their works. For everyone

ὁ φαῦλα πράσσων μισεῖ τὸ φῶς, καὶ οὐκ.ἔρχεται πρὸς τὸ
that evil does hates the light, and comes not to the

φῶς, ἵνα μὴ.ἐλεγχθῇ τὰ.ἔργα.αὐτοῦ· 21 ὁ.δὲ ποιῶν τὴν
light, that may not be exposed his works; but he that practises the

ἀλήθειαν ἔρχεται πρὸς τὸ φῶς, ἵνα φανερωθῇ αὐτοῦ τὰ
truth comes to the light, that may be manifested his

ἔργα ὅτι ἐν θεῷ ἐστιν.εἰργασμένα.
works that in God they have been wrought.

22 Μετὰ ταῦτα ἦλθεν ὁ Ἰησοῦς καὶ οἱ.μαθηταὶ.αὐτοῦ εἰς
After these things came Jesus and his disciples into

---

and said unto him, How can these things be? 10 Jesus answered and said unto him, Art thou a master of Israel, and knowest not these things? 11 Verily, verily, I say unto thee, We speak that we do know, and testify that we have seen; and ye receive not our witness. 12 If I have told you earthly things, and ye believe not, how shall ye believe, if I tell you of heavenly things? 13 And no man hath ascended up to heaven, but he that came down from heaven, even the Son of man which is in heaven. 14 And as Moses lifted up the serpent in the wilderness, even so must the Son of man be lifted up: 15 that whosoever believeth in him should not perish, but have eternal life. 16 For God so loved the world, that he gave his only begotten Son, that whosoever believeth in him should not perish, but have everlasting life. 17 For God sent not his Son into the world to condemn the world; but that the world through him might be saved. 18 He that believeth on him is not condemned: but he that believeth not is condemned already, because he hath not believed in the name of the only begotten Son of God. 19 And this is the condemnation, that light is come into the world, and men loved darkness rather than light, because their deeds were evil. 20 For every one that doeth evil hateth the light, neither cometh to the light, lest his deeds should be reproved. 21 But he that doeth truth cometh to the light, that his deeds may be made manifest, that they are wrought in God.

22 After these things came Jesus and his disciples into the land

---

ᵉ — ὁ GLTTrAW. ᶠ Μωϋσῆς LTTrAW. ᵍ ἐπ' αὐτὸν L; ἐν αὐτῷ in him TTrA. ʰ — μὴ
ἀπόληται ἀλλ' [L]TTrA. ᶦ — αὐτοῦ (read the Son) T. ᵏ ἀλλὰ Tr. ˡ — αὐτοῦ (read the
Son) T[TrA]. ᵐ — δὲ but [L]T[Tr]A. ⁿ αὐτῶν πονηρὰ LTTrA.

of Judæa; and there he tarried with them, and baptized: 23 And John also was baptizing in Ænon near to Salim, because there was much water there: and they came, and were baptized. 24 For John was not yet cast into prison. 25 Then there arose a question between some of John's disciples and the Jews about purifying. 26 And they came unto John, and said unto him, Rabbi, he that was with thee beyond Jordan, to whom thou barest witness, behold, the same baptizeth, and all men come to him. 27 John answered and said, A man can receive nothing, except it be given him from heaven. 28 Ye yourselves bear me witness, that I said, I am not the Christ, but that I am sent before him. 29 He that hath the bride is the bridegroom: but the friend of the bridegroom, which standeth and heareth him, rejoiceth greatly because of the bridegroom's voice: this my joy therefore is fulfilled. 30 He must increase, but I must decrease. 31 He that cometh from above is above all: he that is of the earth is earthly, and speaketh of the earth: he that cometh from heaven is above all. 32 And what he hath seen and heard, that he testifieth; and no man receiveth his testimony. 33 He that hath received his testimony hath set to his seal that God is true. 34 For he whom God hath sent speaketh the words of God: for God giveth not the Spirit by measure unto him. 35 The Father loveth the Son, and hath given all things into his hand. 36 He that believeth on the Son hath everlasting life: and he that believeth not the Son shall not

τὴν Ἰουδαίαν.γῆν. καὶ ἐκεῖ διέτριβεν μετ᾽ αὐτῶν καὶ ἐβάπ-
the land of Judæa; and there he stayed with them and was bap-

τιζεν. 23 ἦν.δὲ καὶ °Ἰωάννης‖ βαπτίζων ἐν Αἰνὼν ἐγγὺς
tizing. And ³was ²also ¹John baptizing in Ænon, near

τοῦ Σαλείμ, ὅτι ὕδατα.πολλὰ ἦν ἐκεῖ· καὶ παρεγίνοντο καὶ
Salim, because ²waters ¹many were there; and they were coming and

ἐβαπτίζοντο. 24 οὔπω.γὰρ ἦν βεβλημένος εἰς τὴν φυλακὴν
being baptized. For not yet was ²cast ³into ⁴the ¹prison

ῥο‖°Ἰωάννης.‖ 25 Ἐγένετο οὖν ζήτησις ἐκ τῶν μαθητῶν
¹John. Arose then a question [on the part] of the disciples

ᾳἸωάννου‖ μετὰ ʳἸουδαίων‖ περὶ καθαρισμοῦ· 26 καὶ ˢἦλθον‖
of John with [some] Jews about purification. And they came

πρὸς τὸν ᵗἸωάννην‖ καὶ ᵛεἶπον‖ αὐτῷ, ᵂΡαββί,‖ ὃς ἦν μετὰ
to John and said to him, Rabbi, he who was with

σοῦ πέραν τοῦ Ἰορδάνου, .ᾧ σὺ μεμαρτύρηκας, ἴδε οὗτος
thee beyond the Jordan, to whom thou hast borne witness, behold · he

βαπτίζει, καὶ πάντες ἔρχονται πρὸς αὐτόν. 27 Ἀπεκρίθη
baptizes, and all come to him. ²Answered

°Ἰωάννης‖ καὶ εἶπεν. Οὐ δύναται ἄνθρωπος λαμβάνειν οὐδὲν
¹John and said, ³Is ⁴able ¹a ²man to receive nothing

ἐὰν.μὴ ᾖ δεδομένον αὐτῷ ἐκ τοῦ οὐρανοῦ. 28 αὐτοὶ.ὑμεῖς
unless it be given to him from the heaven. Ye yourselves

μοι μαρτυρεῖτε ὅτι εἶπον, ˣΟὐκ.εἰμὶ ἐγὼ‖ ὁ χριστός, ἀλλ᾽ ὅτι
to me bear witness that I said, ²Am ³not ¹I the Christ, but that

ἀπεσταλμένος εἰμὶ ἔμπροσθεν ἐκείνου. 29 ὁ ἔχων τὴν νύμ-
³sent ¹I ²am before him. He that has the bride

φην, νυμφίος ἐστίν· ὁ.δὲ φίλος τοῦ νυμφίου, ὁ ἑστηκὼς καὶ
²bridegroom ¹is; but the friend of the bridegroom, who stands and

ἀκούων αὐτοῦ, χαρᾷ χαίρει διὰ τὴν φωνὴν τοῦ νυμφίου·
hears him, with joy rejoices because of the voice of the bridegroom,

αὕτη οὖν ἡ χαρὰ ἡ ἐμὴ πεπλήρωται. 30 ἐκεῖνον δεῖ
this then ²joy ¹my is fulfilled. ³Him ¹it ²behoves

αὐξάνειν, ἐμὲ.δὲ ἐλαττοῦσθαι. 31 ὁ ἄνωθεν ἐρχόμενος ἐπάνω
to increase, but me to decrease. He who from above comes, above

πάντων ἐστίν. ὁ.ὢν ἐκ τῆς γῆς ἐκ τῆς γῆς ἐστιν, καὶ
all is. He who is from the earth from the earth is, and

ἐκ τῆς γῆς λαλεῖ· ὁ ἐκ τοῦ οὐρανοῦ ἐρχόμενος ᵞἐπάνω
from the earth speaks. He who from the heaven comes above

πάντων ἐστίν,‖ 32 ᶻκαὶ‖ ὃ ἑώρακεν καὶ ἤκουσεν ᵃτοῦτο‖
all is, and what he has seen and heard this

μαρτυρεῖ· καὶ τὴν.μαρτυρίαν.αὐτοῦ οὐδεὶς λαμβάνει. 33 ὁ
he testifies; and his testimony no one receives. He that

λαβὼν αὐτοῦ τὴν μαρτυρίαν ἐσφράγισεν ὅτι ὁ θεὸς ἀληθής
has received his testimony has set to his seal that God ²true

ἐστιν. 34 ὃν.γὰρ ἀπέστειλεν ὁ θεὸς τὰ ῥήματα τοῦ θεοῦ
¹is; for he whom ²sent ¹God the words of God

λαλεῖ· οὐ.γὰρ ἐκ μέτρου δίδωσιν ᵇὁ θεὸς‖ τὸ πνεῦμα. 35 ὁ
speaks; for not by measure ²gives ¹God the Spirit. The

πατὴρ ἀγαπᾷ τὸν υἱόν, καὶ πάντα δέδωκεν ἐν τῇ.χειρὶ.αὐ-
Father loves the Son, and all things has given into his hand,

τοῦ. 36 ὁ πιστεύων εἰς τὸν υἱὸν ἔχει ζωὴν αἰώνιον· ὁ.ᶜδὲ‖
He that believes on the Son has life eternal; and he that

ἀπειθῶν τῷ υἱῷ · οὐκ. ὄψεται ζωήν, ἀλλ' ἡ ὀργὴ τοῦ θεοῦ
is not subject to the Son shall not see life, but the wrath of God

μένει ἐπ' αὐτόν.
abides on him.

4 Ὡς οὖν ἔγνω ὁ ᵈκύριος‖ ὅτι ἤκουσαν οἱ Φαρισαῖοι,
When therefore ³knew ¹the ²Lord . that ³heard ¹the ²Phari-ees,

ὅτι Ἰησοῦς πλείονας μαθητὰς ποιεῖ καὶ βαπτίζει ἢ ᵉἸωάν-
that Jesus more disciples makes and baptizes than John

νης·‖ 2 καίτοιγε Ἰησοῦς αὐτὸς οὐκ.ἐβάπτιζεν, ἀλλ' οἱ
(although indeed Jesus himself was not baptizing but

μαθηταὶ.αὐτοῦ· 3 ἀφῆκεν τὴν Ἰουδαίαν, καὶ ἀπῆλθεν πάλιν
his disciples), he left Judæa, and went away again

εἰς τὴν Γαλιλαίαν. 4 ἔδει.δὲ αὐτὸν διέρχεσθαι διὰ τῆς
into Galilee. And it was necessary for him to pass through

ᶠΣαμαρείας.‖ 5 ἔρχεται οὖν εἰς πόλιν τῆς ᶠΣαμαρείας‖ λεγο-
Samaria. He comes therefore to a city of Samaria call-

μένην ᵍΣυχάρ,‖ πλησίον τοῦ χωρίου ʰὃ‖ ἔδωκεν Ἰακὼβ
ed Sychar, near the land which ²gave ¹Jacob

Ἰωσὴφ τῷ.υἱῷ.αὐτοῦ. 6 ἦν.δὲ ἐκεῖ πηγὴ τοῦ Ἰακώβ.
to Joseph his son. Now ³was, ⁴there ²fountain ¹Jacob's ;

ὁ.οὖν. Ἰησοῦς κεκοπιακὼς ἐκ τῆς ὁδοιπορίας ἐκαθέζετο οὕτως
Jesus therefore, being wearied from the journey, sat thus

ἐπὶ τῇ πηγῇ. ὥρα ἦν ¹ὡσεὶ‖ ἕκτη. 7 Ἔρχεται γυνὴ
at the fountain. [The] hour was about [the] sixth. Comes a woman

ἐκ τῆς ᶠΣαμαρείας‖ ἀντλῆσαι ὕδωρ. λέγει αὐτῇ ὁ Ἰησοῦς,
out of Samaria to draw water. ²Says ³to ⁴her ¹Jesus,

Δός μοι ᵏπιεῖν·‖ 8 οἱ.γὰρ.μαθηταὶ.αὐτοῦ ἀπεληλύθεισαν εἰς
Give me to drink ; for his disciples had gone away . into

τὴν πόλιν, ἵνα τροφὰς ἀγοράσωσιν. 9 Λέγει ¹οὖν‖ αὐτῷ
the city, that provisions they might buy. ⁵Says ⁴therefore ⁶to ⁷him

ἡ γυνὴ ἡ ᵐΣαμαρεῖτις,‖ Πῶς σὺ Ἰουδαῖος ὢν παρ' ἐμοῦ
¹the ³woman ²Samaritan, How ²thou ⁴a ⁵Jew ³being ⁹from ¹⁰me

ⁿπιεῖν‖ αἰτεῖς; οὔσης γυναικὸς Σαμαρείτιδος‖; Ρού.γὰρ
⁷to ⁸drink ¹dost ⁸ask, being a ²woman ¹Samaritan? For ³no

συγχρῶνται Ἰουδαῖοι Σαμαρείταις.‖ 10 Ἀπεκρίθη Ἰησοῦς
²have ⁴intercourse ¹Jews with Samaritans. ²Answered ¹Jesus

καὶ εἶπεν αὐτῇ, Εἰ ᾔδεις τὴν δωρεὰν τοῦ θεοῦ, καὶ τίς
and said to her, If thou hadst known the · gift of God, and who

ἐστιν ὁ λέγων σοι, Δός μοι ᵏπιεῖν,‖ σὺ ἂν.ᾔτησας
it is that says to thee, Give me to drink, thou wouldest have asked

αὐτόν, καὶ ἔδωκεν.ἄν σοι ὕδωρ ζῶν. 11 Λέγει αὐτῷ ᵠἡ
him, and he would have given to thee ²water ¹living. ³Says ⁴to ⁵him ¹the

γυνή,‖ Κύριε, οὔτε ἄντλημα ἔχεις, καὶ τὸ φρέαρ ἐστὶν
²woman, Sir, nothing to draw with thou hast, and the well is

βαθύ· πόθεν ¹οὖν‖ ἔχεις τὸ ὕδωρ τὸ ζῶν; 12 μὴ σὺ.μείζων.εἶ
deep; whence then hast thou the ²water ¹living? Art thou greater

τοῦ.πατρὸς.ἡμῶν Ἰακώβ, ὃς ἔδωκεν ἡμῖν τὸ φρέαρ, καὶ αὐτὸς
than our father Jacob, who gave us the well, and himself

ἐξ αὐτοῦ ἔπιεν, καὶ οἱ.υἱοὶ.αὐτοῦ καὶ τὰ.θρέμματα.αὐτοῦ;
of it drank, and his sons and his cattle?

13 Ἀπεκρίθη ʳὁ‖ Ἰησοῦς καὶ εἶπεν αὐτῇ, Πᾶς ὁ πίνων ἐκ
²Answered ¹Jesus and said to her, Everyone that drinks of

see life; but the wrath of God abideth on him.

IV. When therefore the Lord knew how the Pharisees had heard that Jesus made and baptized more disciples than John, 2 (though Jesus himself baptized not, but his disciples,) 3 he left Judæa, and departed again into Galilee. 4 And he must needs go through Samaria. 5 Then cometh he to a city of Samaria, which is called Sychar, near to the parcel of ground that Jacob gave to his son Joseph. 6 Now Jacob's well was there. Jesus therefore, being wearied with his journey, sat thus on the well: and it was about the sixth hour. 7 There cometh a woman of Samaria to draw water: Jesus saith unto her, Give me to drink. 8 (For his disciples were gone away unto the city to buy meat.) 9 Then saith the woman of Samaria unto him, How is it that thou, being a Jew, askest drink of me, which am a woman of Samaria? for the Jews have no dealings with the Samaritans. 10 Jesus answered and said unto her, If thou knewest the gift of God, and who it is that saith to thee, Give me to drink; thou wouldest have asked of him, and he would have given thee living water. 11 The woman saith unto him, Sir, thou hast nothing to draw with, and the well is deep: from whence then hast thou that living water? 12 Art thou greater than our father Jacob, which gave us the well, and drank thereof himself, and his children, and his cattle? 13 Jesus answered and said unto her, Whosoever drinketh of this water

---

ᵈ Ἰησοῦς Jesus T. ᵉ Ἰωάνης Tr. ᶠ Σαμαρίας T. ᵍ Σιχάρ E. ʰ οὗ GL. ⁱ ὡς
LTTrAW. ᵏ πεῖν TT·A. ¹ — οὖν T. ᵐ Σαμαρῖτις T. ⁿ πὶν L; πεῖν TTrA. ᵒ γυναικὸς
Σαμαρείτιδος (Σαμαρίτιδος T) οὔσης LTTrA. ᴾ — οὐ γὰρ συγχρῶνται Ἰουδαῖοι Σαμαρείταις T.
ᵠ [ἡ.γυνή] A. ʳ — ὁ GLTTrAW.

shall thirst again: 11 but whosoever drinketh of the water that I shall give him shall never thirst; but the water that I shall give him shall be in him a well of water springing up into everlasting life. 15 The woman saith unto him, Sir, give me this water, that I thirst not, neither come hither to draw. 16 Jesus saith unto her, Go, call thy husband, and come hither. 17 The woman answered and said, I have no husband. Jesus said unto her, Thou hast well said, I have no husband: 18 for thou hast had five husbands; and he whom thou now hast is not thy husband: in that saidst thou truly. 19 The woman saith unto him, Sir, I perceive that thou art a prophet. 20 Our fathers worshipped in this mountain; and ye say, that in Jerusalem is the place where men ought to worship. 21 Jesus saith unto her, Woman, believe me, the hour cometh, when ye shall neither in this mountain, nor yet at Jerusalem, worship the Father. 22 Ye worship ye know not what: we know what we worship: for salvation is of the Jews. 23 But the hour cometh, and now is, when the true worshippers shall worship the Father in spirit and in truth: for the Father seeketh such to worship him. 24 God is a Spirit: and they that worship him must worship him in spirit and in truth. 25 The woman saith unto him, I know that Messias cometh, which is called Christ: when he is come, he will tell us all things. 26 Jesus saith unto her; I that speak unto thee am he. 27 And upon this came

τοῦ.ὕδατος.τούτου διψήσει πάλιν· 14 ὃς.δ'.ἂν πίῃ ἐκ τοῦ
this water will thirst again; but whoever may drink of the

ὕδατος οὗ ἐγὼ δώσω αὐτῷ ᵛοὐ.μὴ ʷδιψήσῃ¹ εἰς τὸν.αἰῶνα·
water which I will give him in no wise shall thirst for ever,

ἀλλὰ τὸ ὕδωρ ὃ ˣ δώσω αὐτῷ¹ γενήσεται ἐν αὐτῷ πηγὴ
but the water which I will give to him shall become in him a fountain

ὕδατος ἁλλομένου εἰς ζωὴν αἰώνιον. 15 Λέγει πρὸς αὐτὸν
of water springing up into life eternal. ²Says ⁴to ⁵him

ἡ γυνή, Κύριε, δός μοι τοῦτο τὸ ὕδωρ, ἵνα μὴ.διψῶ
¹the ²woman, Sir, give me this water, that I may not thirst

μηδὲ ˠἔρχωμαι¹ ἐνθάδε ἀντλεῖν. 16 Λέγει αὐτῇ ᶻὁ¹ ᵃἸησοῦς,¹
nor come here to draw. ²Says ³to ⁴her ¹Jesus,

Ὕπαγε, φώνησον ᵇτὸν.ἄνδρα.σου¹ καὶ ἐλθὲ ἐνθάδε. 17 Ἀπε-
Go, call thy husband and come here. ³An-

κρίθη ἡ γυνὴ καὶ εἶπεν°, ᵈΟὐκ.ἔχω ἄνδρα.¹ Λέγει αὐτῇ ὁ
swered ¹the ²woman and said, I have not a husband. ²Says ³to ⁴her

Ἰησοῦς, Καλῶς °εἶπας,¹ Ὅτι ἄνδρα οὐκ.ἔχω· 18 πέντε
¹Jesus, Well didst thou say, A husband I have not; ²five

γὰρ ἄνδρας ἔσχες. καὶ νῦν ὃν ἔχεις οὐκ.ἔστιν σου
¹for husbands thou hast had, and now he whom thou hast is not thy

ἀνήρ· τοῦτο ἀληθὲς εἴρηκας. 19 Λέγει αὐτῷ ἡ γυνή,
husband: this truly thou hast spoken. ²Says ⁴to ⁵him ¹the ²woman,

Κύριε, θεωρῶ ὅτι προφήτης εἶ σύ. 20 οἱ.πατέρες.ἡμῶν ἐν
Sir, I perceive that a prophet ²art ¹thou. Our fathers in

ᶠτούτῳ τῷ ὄρει¹ προσεκύνησαν· καὶ ὑμεῖς λέγετε ὅτι ἐν Ἱε-
this mountain worshipped, and ye say that in Je-

ροσολύμοις ἐστὶν ὁ τόπος ὅπου ᵍδεῖ προσκυνεῖν.ᴸ 21 Λέγει
rusalem is the place where it is necessary to worship. ²Says

αὐτῇ ὁ Ἰησοῦς, ʰΓύναι, πίστευσόν μοι,¹ ὅτι ἔρχεται ὥρα ὅτε
³to ⁴her ¹Jesus, Woman, believe me, that is coming an hour when

οὔτε ἐν τῷ.ὄρει.τούτῳ οὔτε ἐν Ἱεροσολύμοις προσκυνήσετε
neither in this mountain nor in Jerusalem shall ye worship

τῷ πατρί. 22 ὑμεῖς προσκυνεῖτε ὃ οὐκ.οἴδατε· ἡμεῖς προσ-
the Father. Ye worship what ye know not: we wor-

κυνοῦμεν ὃ οἴδαμεν· ὅτι ἡ σωτηρία ἐκ τῶν Ἰουδαίων ἐστίν.
ship what we know; for salvation of the Jews is.

23 ἰἀλλ'¹ ἔρχεται· ὥρα καὶ νῦν ἐστιν, ὅτε οἱ ἀληθινοὶ προσ-
But is coming an hour and now is, when the true wor-

κυνηταὶ προσκυνήσουσιν τῷ πατρὶ ἐν πνεύματι καὶ ἀληθείᾳ·
shippers will worship the Father in spirit and truth;

καὶ.γὰρ ὁ πατὴρ τοιούτους ζητεῖ τοὺς προσκυνοῦντας αὐτόν.
for also the Father ²such ¹seeks who worship him.

24 Πνεῦμα ὁ θεός· καὶ τοὺς προσκυνοῦντας ᵏαὐτὸν¹ ἐν
A spirit God [is], and they that worship him in

πνεύματι καὶ ἀληθείᾳ ˡδεῖ προσκυνεῖν.¹ 25 Λέγει αὐτῷ ἡ
spirit and truth must worship. ²Says ⁴to ⁵him ¹the

γυνή, Οἶδα ὅτι μεσσίας ἔρχεται. ὁ λεγόμενος χριστός· ὅταν
²woman, I know that Messias is coming, who is called Christ; when

ἔλθῃ ἐκεῖνος ἀναγγελεῖ ἡμῖν ᵐπάντα.¹ 26 Λέγει αὐτῇ ὁ Ἰη-
²comes ¹he he will tell us all things. ²Says ³to ⁴her ¹Je-

σοῦς, Ἐγώ εἰμι, ὁ λαλῶν σοι. 27 Καὶ ἐπὶ τούτῳ
sus, I ⁶am ⁷[he], ¹who ²am ³speaking ⁴to ⁵thee. And upon this

---

ᵛ [οὐ μὴ διψήσει .... ὃ δώσω αὐτῷ] L ʷ διψήσει LTTrA. ˣ + ἐγὼ I T. ˠ ἔρχομαι Tr; διέρχωμαι TA. ᶻ — ὁ LT[Tr]A. ᵃ — Ἰησοῦς (read he says) [L]T[Tr]A. ᵇ σου τὸν ἄνδρα A. ᶜ + αὐτῷ to him [L]A. ᵈ ἄνδρα οὐκ ἔχω T. ᵉ εἶπες T. ᶠ τῷ ὄρει τούτῳ GLTTrAW. ᵍ προσκυνεῖν δεῖ LTTrAW. ʰ Γύναι, πίστευέ μοι L; Πίστευέ μοι, γύναι TTrA. ⁱ ἀλλὰ LTTrAW. ᵏ — αὐτὸν.T. ˡ προσκυνεῖν δεῖ T. ᵐ ἄπαντα TTrA.

ᵖἦλθον‖ οἱ μαθηταὶ αὐτοῦ, καὶ °ἐθαύμασαν‖ ὅτι μετὰ γυναικὸς
came   his disciples,   and   wondered   that with   a woman

ἐλάλει· οὐδεὶς μέντοι εἶπεν, Τί ζητεῖς; ἢ Τί λα-
he was speaking; no one however said, What seekest thou? or Why speakest

λεῖς μετ᾽ αὐτῆς;
thou with her?

28 Ἀφῆκεν οὖν τὴν ὑδρίαν αὐτῆς ἡ γυνὴ καὶ ἀπῆλθεν εἰς
⁴Left · ³then · ⁵her ⁶waterpot ¹the ²woman and went away into

τὴν πόλιν, καὶ λέγει τοῖς ἀνθρώποις, 29 Δεῦτε, ἴδετε ἄνθρω-
the city,   and says to the men,   Come, see   a man

πον ὃς εἶπέν μοι πάντα ᵖὅσα‖ ἐποίησα· μήτι οὗτός ἐστιν
who told   me all things whatsoever I did: ²perchance ²this ¹is

ὁ χριστός; 30 ᑫἘξῆλθον ʳοὖν‖ ἐκ τῆς πόλεως, καὶ ἤρ-
the Christ?   They went forth therefore out of the city,   and came

χοντο πρὸς αὐτόν.
unto him.

31 Ἐν ˢδὲ‖ τῷ μεταξὺ ἠρώτων αὐτὸν οἱ μαθηταί, λέ-
In, the meantime ³were ⁴asking ⁵him ¹the ²disciples, say-

γοντες, ᵗ῾Ραββὶ,‖ φάγε. 32 Ὁ δὲ εἶπεν αὐτοῖς, Ἐγὼ βρῶσιν
ing,   Rabbi,   eat.   But he said   to them,   I   meat

ἔχω φαγεῖν ἣν ὑμεῖς οὐκ οἴδατε. 33 Ἔλεγον ᵛοὖν‖ οἱ μαθη-
have to eat which ye   know not.   ⁴Said ³therefore ¹the ²disci-

ταὶ πρὸς ἀλλήλους, Μή τις ἤνεγκεν αὐτῷ   φαγεῖν;
ples to one another,   ²Anyone ¹did bring   him [anything] to eat?·

34 Λέγει αὐτοῖς ὁ Ἰησοῦς, Ἐμὸν βρῶμά ἐστιν ἵνα ˣποιῶ‖ τὸ
²Says ³to ⁴them ¹Jesus,   My   meat   is   that I should do the

θέλημα τοῦ πέμψαντός με, καὶ τελειώσω αὐτοῦ τὸ ἔργον.
will of him who   sent   me, and should finish his   work.

35 οὐχ ὑμεῖς λέγετε, ὅτι ἔτι ʸτετράμηνόν‖ ἐστιν καὶ ὁ θερισμὸς
²Not ³ye ¹say,   that yet   four months it is   and the harvest

ἔρχεται; ἰδού, λέγω ὑμῖν, Ἐπάρατε τοὺς ὀφθαλμοὺς ὑμῶν καὶ
comes? Behold, I say to you, Lift up   your eyes   ᵃand

θεάσασθε τὰς χώρας, ὅτι λευκαί εἰσιν πρὸς θερισμὸν ᶻἤδη.‖
see   the fields,   for white they are to   harvest   already.

36 ᵃκαὶ‖ ὁ θερίζων μισθὸν λαμβάνει, καὶ συνάγει καρπὸν
And he that reaps a reward receives,   and gathers   fruit

εἰς ζωὴν αἰώνιον· ἵνα ᵇκαὶ‖ ὁ σπείρων ὁμοῦ χαίρῃ
unto life eternal, that both he that sows ⁷together ⁸may ⁹rejoice

καὶ ὁ θερίζων. 37 ἐν γὰρ τούτῳ ὁ λόγος ἐστὶν ᶜὁ‖ ἀλη-
¹and ²he ³that ⁴reaps.   For in this   the saying is   true,

θινός, ὅτι ἄλλος ἐστὶν ὁ σπείρων, καὶ ἄλλος ὁ θερίζων.
That ³one ¹it ²is who   sows,   and another who reaps.

38 ἐγὼ ᵈἀπέστειλα‖ ὑμᾶς θερίζειν ὃ οὐχ ὑμεῖς κεκοπιάκατε·
I   sent   you to reap on which ²not ¹ye ²have laboured;

ἄλλοι κεκοπιάκασιν, καὶ ὑμεῖς εἰς τὸν κόπον αὐτῶν εἰσεληλύ-
others have laboured,   and ye   into   their labour   have en-

θατε.
tered.

39 Ἐκ δὲ τῆς πόλεως ἐκείνης πολλοὶ ἐπίστευσαν εἰς αὐτὸν
But out of   that city   many   believed   on him

τῶν ᵉΣαμαρειτῶν,‖ διὰ τὸν λόγον τῆς γυναικὸς μαρ-
of the Samaritans,   because of the word of the woman tes-

---

his disciples, and mar-
velled that he talked
with the woman: yet
no man said, · What
seekest thou? or, Why
talkest thou with her?

28 The woman then
left her waterpot, and
went her way into the
city, and saith to the
men, 29 Come, see a
man, which told me all
things that ever I did:
is not this the Christ?
30 Then they went out
of the city, and came
unto him.

31 In the mean while
his disciples prayed
him, saying, Master,
eat. 32 But he said
unto them, I have meat
to eat that ye know
not of. 33 Therefore
said the disciples one
to another, Hath any
man brought him *ought*
to eat? 34 Jesus saith
unto them, My meat is
to do the will of him
that sent me, and to
finish his work. 35 Say
not ye, There are yet
four months, and *then*
cometh harvest? be-
hold, I say unto you,
Lift up your eyes, and
look on the fields; for
they are white already
to harvest. 36 And he
that reapeth receiveth
wages, and gathereth
fruit unto life eternal:
that both he that sow-
eth and he that reap-
eth may rejoice to-
gether. 37 And herein
is that saying true, One
soweth, and another
reapeth. 38 I sent you
to reap that whereon
ye bestowed no labour:
other men laboured,
and ye are entered into
their labours.

39 And many of the
Samaritans of that
city believed on him
for the saying of the
woman, which testi-

ⁿ ἦλθαν TTr.   ° ἐθαύμαζον were wondering GLTTrAW.   ᵖ ἃ which T.   ᑫ + [καὶ] and L.
ʳ — οὖν GLTTrAW.   ˢ — δὲ but [L]TTrA.   ᵗ ῾Ραββεί T.   ᵛ — οὖν W.   ˣ ποιήσω LTrA.
ʸ τετράμηνός GLTTrAW.   ᶻ ἤδη (read already he that reaps) T.   ᵃ — καὶ G[L]TTrA.
ᵇ — καὶ Tr[A].   ᶜ — ὁ TTr[A].   ᵈ ἀπέσταλκα have sent T.   ᵉ Σαμαριτῶν Τ.

fied. He told me all that ever I did. 40 So when the Samaritans were come unto him, they besought him that he would tarry with them: and he abode there two days. 41 And many more believed because of his own word; 42 and said unto the woman, Now we believe, not because of thy saying: for we have heard *him* ourselves, and know that this is indeed the Christ, the Saviour of the world.

43 Now after two days he departed thence, and went into Galilee. 44 For Jesus himself testified, that a prophet hath no honour in his own country. 45 Then when he was come into Galilee, the Galilæans received him, having seen all the things that he did at Jerusalem at the feast: for they also went unto the feast.

46 So Jesus came again into Cana of Galilee, where he made the water wine. And there was a certain nobleman, whose son was sick at Capernaum. 47 When he heard that Jesus was come out of Judæa into Galilee, he went unto him, and besought him that he would come down, and heal his son: for he was at the point of death. 48 Then said Jesus unto him, Except ye see signs and wonders, ye will not believe. 49 The nobleman saith unto him, Sir, come down ere my child die. 50 Jesus saith unto him, Go thy way; thy son liveth. And the man believed the word *that* Jesus had spoken unto him, and he went his way. 51 And as he was now going down, his servants met him, and

---

τυρούσης, "Ὅτι εἶπέν μοι πάντα ˹ὅσα˺ ἐποίησα. 40 Ὡς
tifying,　He told me all things whatsoever I did.　When

οὖν ἦλθον πρὸς αὐτὸν οἱ ᵍΣαμαρεῖται,‖ ἠρώτων αὐτὸν
therefore came　to　him the Samaritans,　they asked him

μεῖναι παρ' αὐτοῖς· καὶ ἔμεινεν ἐκεῖ δύο ἡμέρας. 41 καὶ
to abide with them,　and he abode there two days.　And

πολλῷ πλείους ἐπίστευσαν διὰ τὸν λόγον αὐτοῦ· 42 τῇ τε
many more　believed because of　his word;　and to the

γυναικὶ ἔλεγον, ʰΌτι‖ οὐκέτι διὰ τὴν σὴν λαλιὰν πισ-
woman they said,　No longer because of　thy saying　we

τεύομεν· αὐτοὶ γὰρ ἀκηκόαμεν, καὶ οἴδαμεν ὅτι οὗτός ἐστιν
believe,　for ourselves have heard,　and we know that this　is

ἀληθῶς ὁ σωτὴρ τοῦ κόσμου, ⁱὁ χριστός.‖
truly the Saviour of the world,　the Christ.

43 Μετὰ δὲ τὰς δύο ἡμέρας ἐξῆλθεν ἐκεῖθεν, ᵏκαὶ ἀπῆλ-
But after the two days he went forth thence,　and went

θεν‖ εἰς τὴν Γαλιλαίαν. 44 αὐτὸς γὰρ ˡὁ‖ Ἰησοῦς ἐμαρτύρη-
away into Galilee;　for ²himself ¹Jesus　testified,

σεν, ὅτι προφήτης ἐν τῇ ἰδίᾳ πατρίδι τιμὴν οὐκ ἔχει.
that a prophet in his own country honour has not.

45 ᵐΟτε‖ οὖν ἦλθεν εἰς τὴν Γαλιλαίαν ἐδέξαντο αὐτὸν
When therefore he came into　Galilee ³received ⁴him

οἱ Γαλιλαῖοι, πάντα ἑωρακότες ⁿἅ‖ ἐποίησεν ἐν Ἱε-
¹the ²Galileans, all things having seen which he did in Je-

ροσολύμοις ἐν τῇ ἑορτῇ· καὶ αὐτοὶ γὰρ ἦλθον εἰς τὴν
rusalem during the feast,　for they also went to the

ἑορτήν.
feast.

46 Ἦλθεν οὖν ᵒὁ Ἰησοῦς‖ πάλιν ᵖεἰς τὴν Κανᾶ τῆς
²Came ³therefore ¹Jesus　again to　Cana

Γαλιλαίας, ὅπου ἐποίησεν τὸ ὕδωρ οἶνον. �q καὶ ἦν‖ τις
of Galilee,　where he made the water wine.　And there was a certain

βασιλικός, οὗ ὁ υἱὸς ἠσθένει ἐν ʳΚαπερναούμ.‖ 47 οὗτος
courtier,　whose son was sick in Capernaum.　He

ἀκούσας ὅτι Ἰησοῦς ἥκει ἐκ τῆς Ἰουδαίας εἰς τὴν Γαλι-
having heard that Jesus had come out of Judæa into Gali-

λαίαν, ἀπῆλθεν πρὸς αὐτόν, καὶ ἠρώτα ˢαὐτὸν‖ ἵνα κατα-
lee,　went to him,　and asked him that he would

βῇ καὶ ἰάσηται αὐτοῦ τὸν υἱόν· ἤμελλεν γὰρ ἀποθνήσκειν.
come down and heal his son;　for he was about to die.

48 εἶπεν οὖν ὁ Ἰησοῦς πρὸς αὐτόν, Ἐὰν μὴ σημεῖα καὶ
³Said ²therefore ¹Jesus　to　him,　Unless　signs and

τέρατα ἴδητε οὐ μὴ πιστεύσητε. 49 Λέγει πρὸς αὐτὸν ὁ
wonders ye see in no wise will ye believe. ³Says ⁴to ⁵him ¹the

βασιλικός, Κύριε, κατάβηθι πρὶν ἀποθανεῖν τὸ παιδίον μου.
²courtier,　Sir,　come down before ⁴dies　¹my ²little ³child.

50 Λέγει αὐτῷ ὁ Ἰησοῦς, Πορεύου· ὁ υἱός σου ζῇ. ᵗΚαὶ‖
²Says ³to ⁴him ¹Jesus,　Go,　thy son lives.　And

ἐπίστευσεν ὁ ἄνθρωπος τῷ λόγῳ ᵛᾧᵗ‖ εἶπεν αὐτῷ ʷ Ἰησοῦς,
³believed ¹the ²man　the word which ²said ³to ⁴him　¹Jesus,

καὶ ἐπορεύετο. 51 ἤδη δὲ αὐτοῦ καταβαίνοντος οἱ δοῦλοι ˣαὐ-
and went away.　But already as he was going down　his bondmen

ᶠ ἃ which TTrA.　ᵍ Σαμαρῖται T.　ʰ [ὅτι] L.　ⁱ — ὁ χριστός LTTrA.　ᵏ — καὶ ἀπῆλθεν
[L]TTꞏA.　ˡ — ὁ GLTTrAW.　ᵐ ὡς T.　ⁿ ὅσα whatsoever LTrA.　ᵒ — ὁ Ἰησοῦς (read he
came GLTTrAW.　ᵖ + ὁ Ἰησοῦς Jesus W.　�q Ἦν δέ T.　ʳ Καφαρναούμ LTTrAW.
ˢ — αὐτὸν [L]TTrA.　ᵗ — καὶ [L]T[Tr]A.　ᵛ ὃν LTTrA.　ʷ + ὁ LTTrAW.　ˣ — αὐτοῦ
(read the bondmen) T.

τοῦ¹ ʸἀπήντησαν¹ αὐτῷ, ᶻκαὶ ἀπήγγειλαν¹¹ ᵃλέγοντες,¹¹ "Ότι
  met him, and reported, saying,

ὁ.παῖς.ᵇσου¹¹ ζῇ. 52 Ἐπύθετο οὖν ᶜπαρ' αὐτῶν τὴν ὥραν¹¹
Thy child lives. He inquired therefore from them the hour

ἐν ᾗ κομψότερον ἔσχεν. ᵈκαὶ εἶπον¹¹ αὐτῷ, "Ότι ᵉχθὲς¹¹
in which ³better ¹he ²got. And they said to him, Yesterday

ὥραν ἑβδόμην ἀφῆκεν αὐτὸν ὁ πυρετός.. 53 "Εγνω
[at the] ²hour ¹seventh left him the fever. ³Knew

οὖν ὁ πατὴρ ὅτι ᶠἐν¹¹ ἐκείνῃ τῇ ὥρᾳ ἐν ᾗ εἶπεν
⁴therefore ¹the ²father that [it was] at that hour in which ²said

αὐτῷ ὁ Ἰησοῦς, ᵍ"Ότι¹¹ ὁ.υἱός.σου ζῇ. Καὶ ἐπίστευσεν αὐτὸς
²to ⁴him ¹Jesus, Thy son lives. And he ²believed ¹himself

καὶ ἡ.οἰκία.αὐτοῦ ὅλη. 54 τοῦτο ʰ πάλιν δεύτερον σημεῖον
and his ²house ¹whole. This again a second sign-

ἐποίησεν ὁ Ἰησοῦς, ἐλθὼν ἐκ τῆς Ἰουδαίας εἰς τὴν Γα-
did `Jesus, having come out of Judæa into Ga-
λιλαίαν.
lilee.

5 Μετὰ ταῦτα ἦν ¹ ἑορτὴ τῶν Ἰουδαίων, καὶ ἀνέβη ᵏᵒ¹¹
  After these things was a feast of the Jews, and ²went ³up

Ἰησοῦς εἰς Ἰεροσόλυμα. 2 ἔστιν.δὲ ἐν τοῖς Ἰεροσολύμοις
¹Jesus to Jerusalem. And there is in Jerusalem

ἐπὶ τῇ προβατικῇ κολυμβήθρα, ¹ᵉ ἐπιλεγομένη¹¹ Ἐβραϊστὶ
at the sheepgate a pool, which [is] called in Hebrew

ᵐΒηθεσδά,¹¹ πέντε στοὰς ἔχουσα. 3 ἐν ταύταις κατέκειτο
Bethesda, five porches having. In the e were lying

πλῆθος ⁿπολὺ¹¹ τῶν ἀσθενούντων, τυφλῶν, χωλῶν,
a ²multitude ¹great of those who were sick, blind, lame,

ξηρῶν, ᵒἐκδεχομένων‿ τὴν τοῦ ὕδατος κίνησιν. 4 ἄγγελος
withered, awaiting the ²of ³the ⁴water ¹moving. ²An ¹angel

γὰρ ᵖ κατὰ.καιρὸν κατέβαινεν ἐν τῇ κολυμβήθρᾳ, καὶ ἐτά-
¹for from time to time descended in the pool, and agi-

ρασσεν τὸ ὕδωρ· ὁ οὖν πρῶτος ἐμβὰς μετὰ τὴν ταραχὴν
tated the water. He who therefore first entered after the agitation

τοῦ ὕδατος, ὑγιὴς ἐγίνετο, �q.ᵈήποτε¹ κατείχετο νοσήματι.¹¹
of the water, ²well ¹became, whatever ²he ³was ⁴held ⁵by ¹disease.

5 Ἦν.δὲ τις ἄνθρωπος ἐκεῖ ʳτριακονταοκτὼ¹¹ ἔτη ἔχων ἐν
But ⁴was ¹a ²certain ³man there ²thirty ³eight ¹years ⁵being in

τῇ ἀσθενείᾳˢ. 6 τοῦτον ἰδὼν ὁ Ἰησοῦς κατακείμενον, καὶ
infirmity. ³Him ²seeing ¹Jesus lying, and

γνοὺς ὅτι πολὺν ἤδη χρόνον ἔχει, λέγει αὐτῷ, Θέλεις
knowing that a long ¹already ²time he has been, says to him, Desirest thou

ὑγιὴς γενέσθαι; 7 ἀπεκρίθη αὐτῷ ὁ ἀσθενῶν, Κύριε, ἄν-
well to become? ⁴Answered ⁵him ¹the ²infirm [³man], Sir, a

θρωπον οὐκ.ἔχω, ἵνα ὅταν ταραχθῇ τὸ ὕδωρ ᵗβάλλῃ¹¹
man I have not, that when ³has ⁴been ²agitated ¹the ⁵water he may put

με εἰς τὴν κολυμβήθραν· ἐν.ᾧ.δὲ ἔρχομαι ἐγὼ ἄλλος πρὸ
me into the pool; but while ²am ³coming ⁴I another before

ἐμοῦ καταβαίνει. 8 Λέγει αὐτῷ ὁ Ἰησοῦς, ᵛ"Εγειραι,¹¹ ʷ ἆρον
me descends. ²Says ³to ⁴him ¹Jesus, Arise, take up

told *him*, saying, Thy
son liveth. 52 Then in-
quired he of them the
hour when he began
to amend. And they
said unto him, Yester-
day at the seventh
hour the fever left
him. 53 So, the father
knew that *it was* at
the same hour, in the
which Jesus said unto
him, Thy son liveth:
and himself believed,
and his whole house.
54 This *is* again the
second miracle *that*
Jesus did, when he
was come out of Ju-
dæa into Galilee.

V. After this there
was a feast of the
Jews; and Jesus went
up to Jerusalem. 2 Now
there is at Jerusalem
by the sheep *market* a
pool, which is called in
the Hebrew tongue
Bethesda, having five
porches. 3 In these lay
a great multitude of
impotent folk, of blind,
halt, withered, wait-
ing for the moving of
the water. 4 For an
angel went down at
a certain season into
the pool, and troubled
the water: whosoever
then first after the
troubling of the
water stepped in
was made whole of
whatsoever disease he
had. 5 And a cer-
tain man was there,
which had an infirmity
thirty and eight years.
6 When Jesus saw him
lie, and knew that he
had been now a long
time *in that case*, he
saith unto him, Wilt
thou be made whole?
7 The impotent man
answered him, Sir, I
have no man, when the
water is troubled, to
put me into the pool:
but while I am com-
ing, another steppeth
down before me. 8 Je-
sus saith unto him,
Rise, take up thy bed,

ʸ ὑπήντησαν LTTrA. ᶻ καὶ ἤγγειλαν T; [καὶ ἀπήγγειλαν] TrA. ᵃ — λέγοντες T.
ᵇ αὐτοῦ (read that his child lives) LTTrA. ᶜ τὴν ὥραν παρ' αὐτῶν LTTrA. ᵈ εἶπον οὖν therefore they said TTrA. ᵉ ἐχθὲς LTTrAW. ᶠ — ἐν T[Tr]. ᵍ "Ότι LTTrA. ʰ + δὲ now (this)
Tr[A]. ⁱ + ἡ the (feast) T. ᵏ — ὁ LTTrAW. ˡ τὸ λεγόμενον T. ᵐ Βηθζαθά Beth-
zatha T. ⁿ — πολὺ [L]TTrA. ᵒ — ἐκδεχομένων to end of verse 4 [G]TTrA.· ᵖ + [κυρίου]
of [the] Lord L �q οἰφδηποτοῦν L. ʳ τριάκοντα καὶ (— καὶ [L]Tr) ὀκτὼ GLTTrAW. ˢ + αὐτοῦ his (infirmity) [L]TTrA. ᵗ βάλῃ GLTTrAW. ᵛ Ἔγειρε LTTrAW. ʷ + [καὶ] and L.

and walk. 9 And immediately the man was made whole, and took up his bed, and walked: and on the same day was the sabbath. 10 The Jews therefore said unto him that was cured, It is the sabbath day: it is not lawful for thee to carry *thy* bed. 11 He answered them, He that made me whole, the same said unto me, Take up thy bed, and walk. 12 Then asked they him, What man is that which said unto thee, Take up thy bed, and walk? 13 And he that was healed wist not who it was: for Jesus had conveyed himself away, a multitude being in *that* place. 14 Afterward Jesus findeth him in the temple, and said unto him, Behold, thou art made whole: sin no more, lest a worse thing come unto thee. 15 The man departed, and told the Jews that it was Jesus, which had made him whole. 16 And therefore did the Jews persecute Jesus, and sought to slay him, because he had done these things on the sabbath day. 17 But Jesus answered them, My Father worketh hitherto, and I work. 18 Therefore the Jews sought the more to kill him, because he not only had broken the sabbath, but said also that God was his Father, making himself equal with God. 19 Then answered Jesus and said unto them, Verily, verily, I say unto you, The Son can do nothing of himself, but what he seeth the Father do: for what things soever he doeth, these also doeth the Son likewise. 20 For the Father loveth the Son, and

τὸν κράββατόν σου, καὶ περιπάτει. 9 Καὶ εὐθέως ἐγένετο
thy bed, and walk. And immediately became

ὑγιὴς ὁ ἄνθρωπος, καὶ ἦρεν τὸν κράββατον αὐτοῦ, καὶ
well the man, and took up his bed, and

περιεπάτει· ἦν δὲ σάββατον ἐν ἐκείνῃ τῇ ἡμέρᾳ. 10 Ἔλεγον
walked; and it was sabbath on that day. Said

οὖν οἱ Ἰουδαῖοι τῷ τεθεραπευμένῳ, Σάββατόν ἐστιν·
therefore the Jews to him who had been healed, Sabbath it is,

οὐκ ἔξεστίν σοι ἆραι τὸν κράββατον. 11 Ἀπεκρίθη
it is not lawful for thee to take up the bed. He answered

αὐτοῖς, Ὁ ποιήσας με ὑγιῆ, ἐκεῖνός μοι εἶπεν, Ἆρον τὸν
them, He who made me well, he to me said, Take up

κράββατόν σου καὶ περιπάτει. 12 Ἠρώτησαν οὖν αὐτόν,
thy bed and walk. They asked therefore him,

Τίς ἐστιν ὁ ἄνθρωπος ὁ εἰπών σοι, Ἆρον τὸν κράββατόν
Who is the man who said to thee, Take up bed

σου καὶ περιπάτει; 13 Ὁ δὲ ἰαθεὶς οὐκ ᾔδει τίς ἐστιν·
and walk? But he who had been healed knew not who it is,

ὁ γὰρ Ἰησοῦς ἐξένευσεν, ὄχλου ὄντος ἐν τῷ τόπῳ. 14 Μετὰ
for Jesus had moved away, a crowd being in the place. After

ταῦτα εὑρίσκει αὐτὸν ὁ Ἰησοῦς ἐν τῷ ἱερῷ, καὶ εἶπεν αὐτῷ,
these things finds him Jesus in the temple, and said to him,

Ἴδε ὑγιὴς γέγονας· μηκέτι ἁμάρτανε, ἵνα μὴ χεῖρόν
Behold, well thou hast become: no more sin, that not worse

τί σοι γένηται. 15 Ἀπῆλθεν ὁ ἄνθρωπος καὶ ἀνήγ-
something to thee happens. Went away the man and told

γειλεν τοῖς Ἰουδαίοις ὅτι Ἰησοῦς ἐστιν ὁ ποιήσας αὐτὸν
the Jews that Jesus it is who made him

ὑγιῆ. 16 Καὶ διὰ τοῦτο ἐδίωκον τὸν Ἰησοῦν οἱ Ἰουδαῖοι,
well. And because of this persecuted Jesus the Jews,

καὶ ἐζήτουν αὐτὸν ἀποκτεῖναι, ὅτι ταῦτα ἐποίει ἐν σαβ-
and sought him to kill, because these things he did on a sab-

βάτῳ. 17 ὁ δὲ Ἰησοῦς ἀπεκρίνατο αὐτοῖς, Ὁ πατήρ μου
bath. But Jesus answered them, My Father

ἕως ἄρτι ἐργάζεται, κἀγὼ ἐργάζομαι. 18 Διὰ τοῦτο οὖν
until now works, and I work. Because of this therefore

μᾶλλον ἐζήτουν αὐτὸν οἱ Ἰουδαῖοι ἀποκτεῖναι, ὅτι οὐ μόνον
the more sought him the Jews to kill, because not only

ἔλυεν τὸ σάββατον, ἀλλὰ καὶ πατέρα ἴδιον ἔλεγεν τὸν
did he break the sabbath, but also Father his own called

θεόν, ἴσον ἑαυτὸν ποιῶν τῷ θεῷ. 19 ἀπεκρίνατο οὖν ὁ
God, equal himself making to God. Answered therefore

Ἰησοῦς καὶ εἶπεν αὐτοῖς, Ἀμὴν ἀμὴν λέγω ὑμῖν, οὐ δύναται
Jesus and said to them, Verily verily I say to you, is able

ὁ υἱὸς ποιεῖν ἀφ' ἑαυτοῦ οὐδέν, ἐὰν μή τι βλέπῃ
the Son to do from himself nothing, unless anything he may see

τὸν πατέρα ποιοῦντα· ἃ γὰρ ἂν ἐκεῖνος ποιῇ, ταῦτα καὶ
the Father doing: for whatever he does, these things also

ὁ υἱὸς ὁμοίως ποιεῖ. 20 ὁ γὰρ πατὴρ φιλεῖ τὸν υἱόν, καὶ
the Son in like manner does. For the Father loves the Son, and

---

x κράβαττον LTTrAW.   y — εὐθέως T.   z + καὶ and [L]T[Tr]A.   a + σου (*read* thy bed) L.   b + ὃς δὲ who however LTr.   c — οὖν [L]T[Tr]A.   d — τὸν κράββατον σου T[Tr]A.   e κράβαττόν L[Tr]w.   f ἀσθενῶν was impotent T.   g σοί τι GLTTrAW.   h + [καὶ] and L.   i εἶπεν T.   k οἱ Ἰουδαῖοι τὸν Ἰησοῦν LTTrA.   l — καὶ ἐζήτουν αὐτὸν ἀποκτεῖναι G[L]TTrA.   m — Ἰησοῦς (read he answered) T.   n — οὖν T.   o ἔλεγεν T.   p ἂν T.   q [ἂν] Tr.   r ποιεῖ ὁμοίως T.

πάντα δείκνυσιν αὐτῷ ἃ αὐτὸς ποιεῖ· καὶ μείζονα τού-
all things shews to him which ²himself ¹he does ; and greater ²than

των δείξει αὐτῷ ἔργα, ἵνα ὑμεῖς ⁸θαυμάζητε.∥ 21 ὥσπερ
²these ⁴he ⁵will ⁶shew ⁷him ¹works, that ye may wonder. ²Even ³as

γὰρ ὁ·πατὴρ ἐγείρει τοὺς νεκροὺς καὶ ζωοποιεῖ, οὕτως καὶ ὁ
¹for the Father raises up the dead and quickens, thus also the

υἱὸς οὓς θέλει ζωοποιεῖ. 22 οὐδὲ γὰρ ὁ πατὴρ κρίνει οὐδένα,
Son whom he will quickens; for the Father judges no one,

ἀλλὰ·τὴν· κρίσιν πᾶσαν δέδωκεν τῷ υἱῷ, 23 ἵνα πάντες
but ²judgment ¹all has given to the Son, that all

τιμῶσιν τὸν υἱὸν καθὼς τιμῶσιν τὸν πατέρα. ὁ μὴ·τιμῶν
may honour the Son even as they honour the Father. He that honours not

τὸν υἱὸν οὐ·τιμᾷ τὸν πατέρα τὸν πέμψαντα αὐτόν. 24 Ἀμὴν
the Son honours not the Father who sent him. Verily

ἀμὴν λέγω ὑμῖν, ὅτι ὁ τὸν·λόγον·μου ἀκούων, καὶ πιστεύων
verily I say to you, that he that my word hears, and believes

τῷ πέμψαντί με, ἔχει ζωὴν αἰώνιον, καὶ εἰς κρίσιν οὐκ
him who sent me, has life eternal, and into judgment ²not

ἔρχεται, ἀλλὰ μεταβέβηκεν ἐκ τοῦ θανάτου εἰς τὴν ζωήν.
¹comes, but has passed out of death into life.

25 Ἀμὴν ἀμὴν λέγω ὑμῖν, ὅτι ἔρχεται ὥρα καὶ νῦν ἐστιν,
Verily verily I say ⁴ you, that is coming an hour and now is,

ὅτε οἱ νεκροὶ ᵗἀκούσονται∥ τῆς φωνῆς τοῦ υἱοῦ τοῦ θεοῦ, καὶ
when the dead shall hear the voice of the Son of God, and

οἱ ἀκούσαντες ᵛζήσονται.∥ 26 ὥσπερ·γὰρ ὁ πατὴρ ἔχει
those having heard shall live. For even as the Father has

ζωὴν·ἐν ἑαυτῷ, οὕτως ʷἔδωκεν καὶ τῷ υἱῷ∥ ζωὴν ἔχειν
life in himself, so he gave also to the Son life to have

ἐν ἑαυτῷ. 27 καὶ ἐξουσίαν ἔδωκεν αὐτῷ ˣκαὶ∥ κρίσιν
in himself, and authority gave to him also judgment

ποιεῖν, ὅτι υἱὸς ἀνθρώπου ἐστίν. 28 μὴ·θαυμάζετε τοῦτο·
to execute, because Son of man he is. Wonder not at this,

ὅτι ἔρχεται ὥρα ἐν ᾗ πάντες οἱ ἐν τοῖς μνημείοις ᵗἀκού-
for ³is ¹coming ¹an ²hour in which all those in the tombs shall

σονται∥ τῆς·φωνῆς·αὐτοῦ, ·29 καὶ ἐκπορεύσονται, οἱ τὰ
hear his voice, and shall come forth, those that

ἀγαθὰ ποιήσαντες εἰς ἀνάστασιν ζωῆς, οἱ·ᵞδὲ∥ τὰ φαῦλα
good practised to a resurrection of life, and those that evil

πράξαντες εἰς ἀνάστασιν κρίσεως. 30 οὐ δύναμαι ἐγὼ ποιεῖν
did to a resurrection of judgment. ²Am ³able ¹I to do

ἀπ᾽ ἐμαυτοῦ οὐδέν· καθὼς ἀκούω κρίνω, καὶ ἡ κρίσις ἡ
from myself nothing; even as I hear I judge, and ²judgment

ἐμὴ δικαία ἐστίν· ὅτι οὐ·ζητῶ τὸ θέλημα τὸ ἐμόν, ἀλλὰ τὸ
¹my ⁴just ³is, because I seek not ²will ¹my, but the

θέλημα τοῦ πέμψαντός με ᶻπατρός.∥ 31 Ἐὰν ἐγὼ μαρτυρῶ
will of the ²who ³sent ⁴me ¹Father, If I bear witness

περὶ ἐμαυτοῦ, ἡ·μαρτυρία·μου οὐκ·ἔστιν ἀληθής. 32 ἄλλος
concerning myself, my witness is not true. Another

ἐστὶν ὁ μαρτυρῶν περὶ ἐμοῦ, καὶ ᵃοἶδα∥ ὅτι ἀληθής ἐστιν
it is who bears witness concerning me, and I know that true is

ἡ μαρτυρία ἣν μαρτυρεῖ περὶ ἐμοῦ. 33 Ὑμεῖς ἀπεστάλ-
the witness which he witnesses concerning me. Ye have

κατε πρὸς ᵇἸωάννην∥ καὶ μεμαρτύρηκεν τῇ ἀληθείᾳ· 34 ἐγὼ
sent unto John and he has borne witness to the truth. ¹I

sheweth him all things
that himself doeth
and he will shew him
greater works than
these, that ye may
marvel. 21 For as the
Father raiseth up the
dead, and quickeneth
them; even so the Son
quickeneth whom he
will. 22 For the Fa-
ther judgeth no man,
but hath committed
all judgment unto the
Son: 23 that all *men*
should honour the Son,
even as they honour
the Father. He that
honoureth not the Son
honoureth not the Fa-
ther which hath sent
him. 24 Verily, verily,
I say unto you, He
that heareth my word,
and believeth on him
that sent me, hath
everlasting life, and
shall not come into
condemnation ; but is
passed from death un-
to life. 25 Verily, ve-
rily, I say unto you,
The hour is coming,
and now is, when the
dead shall hear the
voice of the Son of
God ; and they that
hear shall live. 26 For
as the Father hath life
in himself ; so hath he
given to the Son to
have life in himself ;
27 and hath given him
authority to execute
judgment also, be-
cause he is the Son of
man. 28 Marvel not
at this : for the hour
is coming, in the which
all that are in the
graves shall hear his
voice, 29 and shall
come forth ; they that
have done good, unto
the resurrection of
life ; and they that
have done evil, unto
the resurrection of
damnation. 30, I can
of mine own self do
nothing ; as I hear, I
judge : and my judg-
ment is just ; because
I seek not mine own
will, but the will of
the Father which hath
sent me. 31 If I bear
witness of myself, my
witness is not true.
32 There is another
that beareth witness
of me ; and I know
that the witness which
he witnesseth of me is
true. 33 Ye sent unto
John, and he bare wit-
ness unto the truth.

ˢ θαυμάζετε wonder **T.** ᵗ ἀκούσουσιν **TTr.** ᵛ ζήσουσιν **LTTrA.** ʷ καὶ τῷ υἱῷ ἔδωκεν
TT A. ˣ — καὶ **LTTrA.** ᵞ — δὲ and [**L**]**T**[**Tr**]**A.** ᶻ — πατρός (*read* of him who sent me)
ᴼLTTrAW. ᵃ οἴδατε ye know **T.** ᵇ Ἰωάνην **Tr.**

34 But I receive not testimony from man: but these things I say, that ye might be saved. 35 He was a burning and a shining light: and ye were willing for a season to rejoice in his light. 36 But I have greater witness than *that* of John: for the works which the Father hath given me to finish, the same works that I do, bear witness of me, that the Father hath sent me. 37 And the Father himself, which hath sent me, hath borne witness of me. Ye have neither heard his voice at any time, nor seen his shape. 38 And ye have not his word abiding in you: for whom he hath sent, him ye believe not. 39 Search the scriptures; for in them ye think ye have eternal life: and they are they which testify of me. 40 And ye will not come to me, that ye might have life. 41 I receive not honour from men. 42 But I know you, that ye have not the love of God in you. 43 I am come in my Father's name, and ye receive me not: if another shall come in his own name, him ye will receive. 44 How can ye believe, which receive honour one of another, and seek not the honour that *cometh* from God only? 45 Do not think that I will accuse you to the Father: there is *one* that accuseth you, *even* Moses, in whom ye trust. 46 For had ye believed Moses, ye would have believed me: for he wrote of me. 47 But if ye believe not his writings, how shall ye believe my words?

δὲ οὐ παρὰ ἀνθρώπου τὴν μαρτυρίαν λαμβάνω, ἀλλὰ ταῦ-
but not from man witness receive, but these

τα λέγω ἵνα ὑμεῖς σωθῆτε. 35 ἐκεῖνος ἦν ὁ λύχνος ὁ
things I say that ye may be saved. He was the [4]lamp

καιόμενος καὶ φαίνων, ὑμεῖς δὲ ἠθελήσατε [c]ἀγαλλιασθῆναι
[1]burning [2]and [3]shining, and ye were willing to rejoice

πρὸς ὥραν ἐν τῷ φωτὶ αὐτοῦ. 36 ἐγὼ δὲ ἔχω τὴν μαρτυρίαν
for an hour in his light. But I have the witness

[d]μείζω τοῦ [e]Ἰωάννου· τὰ γὰρ ἔργα ἃ [f]ἔδωκέν μοι ὁ
greater than John's for the works which [3]gave [4]me [1]the

πατὴρ ἵνα τελειώσω αὐτά, αὐτὰ τὰ ἔργα ἃ [g]ἐγὼ
[2]Father that I should complete them, the works themselves which I

ποιῶ, μαρτυρεῖ περὶ ἐμοῦ ὅτι ὁ πατήρ με ἀπέσταλκεν,
do, bear witness concerning me that the Father me has sent.

37 καὶ ὁ πέμψας με πατήρ, [h]αὐτὸς μεμαρτύρηκεν περὶ
And the [2]who [3]sent [4]me [1]Father, himself has borne witness concerning

ἐμοῦ. οὔτε φωνὴν αὐτοῦ [i]ἀκηκόατε πώποτε, οὔτε εἶδος
me. Neither his voice have ye heard at any time, nor [2]form

αὐτοῦ ἑωράκατε. 38 καὶ τὸν λόγον αὐτοῦ οὐκ ἔχετε [k]μένοντα
[1]his have ye seen. And his word ye have not abiding

ἐν ὑμῖν, ὅτι ὃν ἀπέστειλεν ἐκεῖνος, τούτῳ ὑμεῖς οὐ πιστεύετε.
in you, for whom [2]sent [1]he, him ye believe not.

39 [l]Ἐρευνᾶτε τὰς γραφάς, ὅτι ὑμεῖς δοκεῖτε ἐν αὐταῖς ζωὴν
Ye search the scriptures, for ye think in them life

αἰώνιον ἔχειν, καὶ ἐκεῖναί εἰσιν αἱ μαρτυροῦσαι περὶ
eternal to have, and they are they which bear witness concerning

ἐμοῦ· 40 καὶ οὐ θέλετε ἐλθεῖν πρός με, ἵνα ζωὴν ἔχητε.
me; and ye are unwilling to come to me, that life ye may have.

41 Δόξαν παρὰ ἀνθρώπων οὐ λαμβάνω· 42 [m]ἀλλ᾽ ἔγνωκα
Glory from men I receive not; but I have known

ὑμᾶς ὅτι [n]τὴν ἀγάπην τοῦ θεοῦ οὐκ ἔχετε ἐν ἑαυτοῖς. 43 ἐγὼ
you that the love of God ye have not in yourselves. I

ἐλήλυθα ἐν τῷ ὀνόματι τοῦ πατρός μου, καὶ οὐ λαμβάνετέ με·
have come in the name of my Father, and ye receive not me;

ἐὰν ἄλλος ἔλθῃ ἐν τῷ ὀνόματι τῷ ἰδίῳ, ἐκεῖνον [o]λήψεσθε.
if another should come in [2]name [1]his [3]own, him ye will receive.

44 πῶς δύνασθε ὑμεῖς πιστεῦσαι, δόξαν [p]παρὰ ἀλλήλων
How are ye able to believe, [3]glory [2]from [1]one [5]another

λαμβάνοντες, καὶ τὴν δόξαν τὴν παρὰ τοῦ μόνου [q]θεοῦ
[1]who [2]receive, and the glory which [is] from the only God

οὐ ζητεῖτε; 45 μὴ δοκεῖτε ὅτι ἐγὼ κατηγορήσω ὑμῶν πρὸς τὸν
ye seek not? Think not that I will accuse you to the

πατέρα· ἔστιν ὁ κατηγορῶν ὑμῶν, [r]Μωσῆς, εἰς ὃν
Father: there is [one] who accuses you, Moses, in whom

ὑμεῖς ἠλπίκατε. 46 εἰ γὰρ ἐπιστεύετε [s]Μωσῇ, ἐπιστεύετε ἂν
ye have hoped. For if ye believed Moses, ye would have believed

ἐμοί· περὶ γὰρ ἐμοῦ ἐκεῖνος ἔγραψεν. 47 εἰ δὲ τοῖς ἐκείνου
me, for concerning me he wrote. But if his

γράμμασιν οὐ πιστεύετε, πῶς τοῖς ἐμοῖς ῥήμασιν πιστεύ-
writings ye believe not, how my words shall ye

σετε;
believe?

---

[c] ἀγαλλιαθῆναι GLTTrAW.   [d] μείζων LTrA.   [e] Ἰωάνου Tr.   [f] δέδωκέν has given TTrA.
[g] — ἐγὼ (*read* ποιῶ I do) LTTrA.   [h] ἐκεῖνος TTrA.   [i] πώποτε ἀκηκόατε LTTrAW.   [k] ἐν
ὑμῖν μένοντα TTrA.   [l] ἐρανᾶτε TTrA.   [m] ἀλλὰ LTTrAW.   [n] οὐκ ἔχετε τὴν ἀγάπην τοῦ
θεοῦ T.   [o] λήμψεσθε LTTrA.   [p] παρ᾽ Δ.   [q] [θεοῦ] L.   [r] Μωϋσῆς LTTrAW.   [s] Μωϋσεῖ
LTTrA; Μωϋσῇ W.

6 Μετὰ ταῦτα ἀπῆλθεν ὁ Ἰησοῦς πέραν τῆς θαλάσσης
After these things ²went ³away ¹Jesus over the sea

τῆς Γαλιλαίας τῆς Τιβεριάδος 2 ᵗκαὶ ἠκολούθει‖ αὐτῷ ὄχλος
of Galilee (of Tiberias), and ⁴followed ⁵him ¹ᵃ³crowd

πολύς, ὅτι ᵛἑώρων‖ ʷαὐτοῦ‖ τὰ σημεῖα ἃ ἐποίει ἐπὶ
²great, because they saw of him the signs which he wrought upon

τῶν ἀσθενούντων. 3 ἀνῆλθεν.δὲ εἰς τὸ ὄρος ˣὁ‖ Ἰησοῦς,
those who were sick. And ²went ³up ⁴into ⁵the ⁶mountain ¹Jesus,

καὶ ἐκεῖ ʸἐκάθητο‖ μετὰ τῶν.μαθητῶν.αὐτοῦ. 4 ἦν δὲ ἐγγὺς
and there sat with his disciples; and ³was ⁴near

τὸ πάσχα ἡ ἑορτὴ τῶν Ἰουδαίων. 5 ἐπάρας οὖν ²ὁ Ἰη-
¹the ²passover, the feast of the Jews. ³Having ⁴lifted ⁵up ²then ¹Je-

σοῦς τοὺς ὀφθαλμούς,‖ καὶ θεασάμενος ὅτι πολὺς ὄχλος
sus [his] eyes, and having seen that a great crowd

ἔρχεται πρὸς αὐτόν, λέγει πρὸς ᵃτὸν‖ Φίλιππον, Πόθεν
is coming to him, he says to Philip, Whence

ᵇἀγοράσωμεν‖ ἄρτους ἵνα φάγωσιν οὗτοι; 6 Τοῦτο.δὲ ἔλεγεν
shall we buy loaves that ²may ³eat ¹these? But this he said

πειράζων αὐτόν· αὐτὸς.γὰρ ᾔδει τί ἔμελλεν ποιεῖν. 7 ᶜἀπε-
trying him, for he knew what he was about to do. An-

κρίθη‖ αὐτῷ ᵈ Φίλιππος, Διακοσίων δηναρίων ἄρτοι οὐκ
swered him Philip, ²For ³two ⁴hundred ⁵denarii ¹loaves ⁷not

ἀρκοῦσιν αὐτοῖς ἵνα ἕκαστος ᵉαὐτῶν‖ βραχύ.ᶠτι‖ λάβῃ.
⁸are sufficient for them that each of them some little may receive.

8 Λέγει αὐτῷ εἷς ἐκ τῶν.μαθητῶν.αὐτοῦ, Ἀνδρέας ὁ ἀδελφὸς
Says to him one of his disciples, Andrew the brother

Σίμωνος Πέτρου, 0 Ἔστιν παιδάριον ᵍἓν‖ ὧδε, ʰὃ‖ ἔχει πέντε
of Simon Peter, ⁴Is ²little ³boy ¹a here, who has five

ἄρτους κριθίνους καὶ δύο ὀψάρια· ἀλλὰ ταῦτα τί ἐστιν εἰς
⁵loaves ⁴barley and two small fishes; but ³these ¹what ²are for

τοσούτους; 10 Εἶπεν.ⁱδὲ‖ ὁ Ἰησοῦς, Ποιήσατε τοὺς ἀνθρώπους
so many? And ²said ¹Jesus, Make the men

ἀναπεσεῖν. ἦν.δὲ χόρτος πολὺς ἐν τῷ τόπῳ. ᵏἀνέπεσον‖
to recline. Now ³was ²grass ¹much in the place: reclined

οὖν οἱ ἄνδρες τὸν ἀριθμὸν ˡὡσεὶ‖ πεντακισχίλιοι. 11 ἔλαβεν
therefore the men, the number about five thousand. ²Took

ᵐδὲ‖ τοὺς ἄρτους ὁ Ἰησοῦς, καὶ ⁿεὐχαριστήσας διέδωκεν‖ ᵒτοῖς
¹and the ⁵loaves ³Jesus, and having given thanks distributed to the

μαθηταῖς, οἱ.δὲ μαθηταὶ‖ τοῖς ἀνακειμένοις· ὁμοίως.καὶ
disciples, and the disciples to those reclining; and in like manner

ἐκ τῶν ὀψαρίων ὅσον ἤθελον. 12 ὡς.δὲ ἐνεπλήσθησαν
of the small fishes as much as they wished. And when they were filled

λέγει τοῖς.μαθηταῖς.αὐτοῦ, Συναγάγετε τὰ περισσεύσαντα
he says to his disciples, Gather together the ²over ³and ⁴above

κλάσματα, ἵνα μή.τι ἀπόληται. 13 Συνήγαγον οὖν
¹fragments, that nothing may be lost. They gathered together therefore

καὶ ἐγέμισαν δώδεκα κοφίνους κλασμάτων ἐκ τῶν πέντε
and filled twelve hand-baskets of fragments from the five

ἄρτων τῶν κριθίνων ἃ ᴾἐπερίσσευσεν‖ τοῖς βεβρω-
²loaves ¹barley which were over and above to those who had

---

over the sea of Galilee, which is the sea of Tiberias. 2. And a great multitude followed him, because they saw his miracles which he did on them that were diseased. 3 And Jesus went up into a mountain, and there he sat with his disciples. 4 And the passover, a feast of the Jews, was nigh. 5 When Jesus then lifted up his eyes, and saw a great company come unto him, he saith unto Philip, Whence shall we buy bread, that these may eat? 6 And this he said to prove him: for he himself knew what he would do. 7 Philip answered him, Two hundred pennyworth of bread is not sufficient for them, that every one of them may take a little. 8 One of his disciples, Andrew, Simon Peter's brother, saith unto him, 9 There is a lad here, which hath five barley loaves, and two small fishes! but what are they among so many? 10 And Jesus said, Make the men sit down. Now there was much grass in the place. So the men sat down, in number about five thousand. 11 And Jesus took the loaves; and when he had given thanks, he distributed to the disciples, and the disciples to them that were set down; and likewise of the fishes as much as they would. 12 When they were filled, he said unto his disciples, Gather up the fragments that remain, that nothing be lost. 13 Therefore they gathered them together, and filled twelve baskets with the fragments of the five barley loaves, which remained over and above unto them that had eaten. 14 Then

---

ᵗ ἠκολούθει δὲ LTTrA.   ᵛ ἐθεώρουν LTrA.   ʷ — αὐτοῦ GLTTrAW.   ˣ — ὁ LTTrA.
ʸ ἐκαθέζετο T.   ᶻ τοὺς ὀφθαλμοὺς ὁ Ἰησοῦς LTTrAW.   ᵃ — τὸν LTTrA.   ᵇ ἀγοράσωμεν
should we buy LTTrA.   ᶜ ἀποκρίνεται answers T.   ᵈ + ὁ T.   ᵉ — αὐτῶν LTTrA.
ᶠ — τι (read a little) [L]Tr[A].   ᵍ — ἓν (read παιδ. a little boy) [L]TTr[A].   ʰ ὃς LTTrAW.
ⁱ — δὲ and [L]TTrA.   ᵏ ἀνέπεσαν LTTrA.   ˡ ὡς TTrA.   ᵐ οὖν therefore (took) LTTrA.
ⁿ εὐχαρίστησεν καὶ ἔδωκεν gave thanks and distributed T.   ᵒ — τοῖς μαθηταῖς, οἱ δὲ μαθηταὶ LTTrA.   ᴾ ἐπερίσσευσαν LTTrA.

those men, when they had seen the miracle that Jesus did, said, This is of a truth that prophet that should come into the world. 15 When Jesus therefore perceived that they would come and take him by force, to make him a king, he departed again into a mountain himself alone

16 And when even was now come, his disciples went down unto the sea, 17 and entered into a ship, and went over the sea toward Capernaum. And it was now dark, and Jesus was not come to them. 18 And the sea arose by reason of a great wind that blew. 19 So when they had rowed about five and twenty or thirty furlongs, they see Jesus walking on the sea, and drawing nigh unto the ship: and they were afraid. 20 But he saith unto them. It is I ; be not afraid. 21 Then they willingly received him into the ship: and immediately the ship was at the land whither they went.

22 The day following, when the people which stood on the other side of the sea saw that there was none other boat there, save that one whereinto his disciples were entered, and that Jesus went not with his disciples into the boat, but that his disciples were gone away alone; 23 (howbeit there came other boats from Tiberias nigh unto the place where they did eat bread, after that the Lord had given thanks:) 24 when the people therefore saw that Jesus was not there, neither his disciples, they also took shipping, and came to Capernaum, seeking

κόσιν. 14 οἱ οὖν ἄνθρωποι ἰδόντες ὃ ἐποίησεν σημεῖον
eaten. The men therefore having seen what [3]had [4]done [1]sign
ᵠὁ Ἰησοῦς,‖ ἔλεγον, Ὅτι οὗτός ἐστιν ἀληθῶς ὁ προφήτης ὁ
[2]Jesus, said, This is truly the prophet who
ʳἐρχόμενος εἰς τὸν κόσμον.‖ 15 Ἰησοῦς οὖν γνοὺς ὅτι μέλ-
is coming into the world. Jesus therefore knowing that they
λουσιν ἔρχεσθαι καὶ ἁρπάζειν αὐτόν, ἵνα ποιήσωσιν ˢαὐτὸν‖
are about to come and seize him, that they may make him
βασιλέα, ᵗἀνεχώρησεν‖ πάλιν εἰς τὸ ὄρος αὐτὸς μόνος.
king, withdrew again to the mountain himself alone.

16 Ὡς δὲ ὀψία ἐγένετο κατέβησαν οἱ μαθηταὶ αὐτοῦ ἐπὶ
And when evening it became [3]went [4]down [1]his [2]disciples to
τὴν θάλασσαν, 17 καὶ ἐμβάντες εἰς ᵛτὸ‖ πλοῖον ἤρχοντο
the sea, and having entered into the ship they were going
πέραν τῆς θαλάσσης εἰς ᵂΚαπερναούμ.‖ ˣκαὶ σκοτία ἤδη
over the sea to Capernaum. And dark already
ἐγεγόνει;‖ καὶ ᵞοὐκ‖ ἐληλύθει ᶻπρὸς αὐτοὺς ὁ Ἰησοῦς,‖ 18 ἥ τε
it had become, and [2]not [3]had [4]come [5]to [6]them [1]Jesus, and the
θάλασσα ἀνέμου μεγάλου πνέοντος ᵃδιηγείρετο.‖ 19 ἐληλα-
sea by a [2]wind [1]strong blowing was agitated. Having
κότες οὖν ᵇὡς‖ ᶜσταδίους‖ ᵈεἰκοσιπέντε‖ ἢ τριάκοντα θεωροῦσιν
rowed then about [4]furlongs³ [1]twenty-five [2]or [3]thirty they see
τὸν Ἰησοῦν περιπατοῦντα ἐπὶ τῆς θαλάσσης, καὶ ἐγγὺς τοῦ
Jesus walking on the sea, and near the
πλοίου γινόμενον· καὶ ἐφοβήθησαν. 20 ὁ δὲ λέγει αὐτοῖς,
ship coming, and they were frightened. But he says to them,
Ἐγώ εἰμι· μὴ φοβεῖσθε. 21 Ἤθελον οὖν λαβεῖν αὐτὸν
I am [he]; fear not. They were willing then to receive him
εἰς τὸ πλοῖον, καὶ εὐθέως ᵉτὸ πλοῖον ἐγένετο‖ ἐπὶ ᶠτῆς γῆς‖
into the ship, and immediately the ship was at the land
εἰς ἣν ὑπῆγον.
to which they were going.

22 Τῇ ἐπαύριον ὁ ὄχλος ὁ ἑστηκὼς πέραν τῆς θα-
On the morrow the crowd which stood the other side of the
λάσσης, ᵍἰδὼν‖ ὅτι πλοιάριον ἄλλο οὐκ ἦν ἐκεῖ εἰ μὴ ἓν
sea, having seen that [3]small [4]ship [2]other ¹'no was there except one
ʰἐκεῖνο εἰς ὃ ἐνέβησαν οἱ μαθηταὶ αὐτοῦ,‖ καὶ ὅτι οὐ
that into which entered his disciples, and that [2]not
συνεισῆλθεν τοῖς μαθηταῖς αὐτοῦ ὁ Ἰησοῦς εἰς τὸ ⁱπλοιάριον,‖
²went ⁴with ⁵his ⁶disciples ¹Jesus into the small ship,
ἀλλὰ μόνοι οἱ μαθηταὶ αὐτοῦ ἀπῆλθον, 23 ἄλλα·ᵏδὲ‖ ἦλθεν‖,
but alone his disciples went away, (but other [2]came
ᵐπλοιάρια‖ ἐκ Τιβεριάδος ἐγγὺς τοῦ τόπου ὅπου ἔφαγον τὸν
¹small ³ships from Tiberias near the place where they ate the
ἄρτον, εὐχαριστήσαντος τοῦ κυρίου· 24 ὅτε οὖν εἶδεν ὁ
bread, ³having ⁴given ⁵thanks ¹the ²Lord;) when therefore ³saw ¹the
ὄχλος ὅτι Ἰησοῦς οὐκ ἔστιν ἐκεῖ οὐδὲ οἱ μαθηταὶ αὐτοῦ, ἐνέ-
²crowd that Jesus [2]not ¹is there nor his disciples, they
βησαν ⁿκαὶ‖ αὐτοὶ εἰς τὰ °πλοῖα‖ καὶ ἦλθον εἰς ᵖΚαπερ-
entered ¹also ²themselves into the ships and came to Caper-

ᵠ — ὁ Ἰησοῦς (*read* he had done) ΤΤΓΑ.   ʳ εἰς τὸν κόσμον ἐρχόμενος Τ.   ˢ — αὐτὸν (*read* [him]) LΤΤΓΑ.   ᵗ φεύγει escapes Τ.   ᵛ — τὸ (*read* a ship) ΤΤΓΑ.   ᵂ Καφαρναούμ LΤΤΓΑW.
ˣ κατέλαβεν δὲ αὐτοὺς ἡ σκοτία and darkness overtook them Τ.   ᵞ οὔπω not yet LΤΤΓΑ.
ᶻ Ἰησοῦς πρὸς αὐτούς Τ.   ᵃ διεγείρετο ΤΓΑ.   ᵇ ὡσεὶ L.   ᶜ στάδια Τ.   ᵈ εἴκοσι πέντε LΤΓ.
ᵉ ἐγένετο τὸ πλοῖον LΤΤΓΑ.   ᶠ τὴν γῆν Τ.   ᵍ εἶδον saw LΤΤΓΑ.   ʰ — ἐκεῖνο εἰς ὃ ἐνέβησαν οἱ
μαθηταὶ αὐτοῦ GLΤΤΓΑ.   ⁱ πλοῖον ship GLΤΓΑ.   ᵏ — δὲ but ΤΤΓ[Α].   ˡ ἦλθον Τ.   ᵐ πλοῖα
ships L.   ⁿ — καὶ GLΤΤΓΑW.   ° πλοιάρια small ships LΤΤΓΑ.   ᵖ Καφαρναούμ LΤΤΓΑW.

ναούμ," ζητοῦντες τὸν Ἰησοῦν. 25 καὶ εὑρόντες αὐτὸν
naum,   seeking   Jesus.   And having found him

πέραν · τῆς θαλάσσης, εἶπον αὐτῷ, ᵠῬαββί," πότε ὧδε
the other side of the   sea,   they said to him, Rabbi,   when here

γέγονας; 26 Ἀπεκρίθη αὐτοῖς ὁ Ἰησοῦς καὶ εἶπεν, Ἀμὴν
hast thou come?   ²Answered ³them ¹Jesus and said, Verily

ἀμὴν λέγω ὑμῖν, ζητεῖτέ με, οὐχ ὅτι εἴδετε σημεῖα, ἀλλ'
verily I say to you, Ye seek me, not because ye saw signs,   but

ὅτι ἐφάγετε ἐκ τῶν ἄρτων καὶ ἐχορτάσθητε. 27 ἐργάζεσθε
because ye ate of the loaves and were satisfied.   Work

μὴ τὴν βρῶσιν τὴν ἀπολλυμένην, ἀλλὰ τὴν βρῶσιν
not [for] the food which perishes, but [for] the food

τὴν μένουσαν εἰς ζωὴν αἰώνιον, ἣν ὁ υἱὸς τοῦ ἀνθρώπου
which abides unto life eternal, which the Son of man

ʳὑμῖν δώσει" τοῦτον·γὰρ ὁ πατὴρ ἐσφράγισεν ὁ θεός.
to you will give; for him the Father sealed, [even] God.

28 Εἶπον οὖν πρὸς αὐτόν, Τί ˢποιοῦμεν," ἵνα ἐργαζώμεθα
They said therefore to him, What do we, that we may work

τὰ ἔργα τοῦ θεοῦ; 29 Ἀπεκρίθη ᵗὁ"Ἰησοῦς καὶ εἶπεν αὐτοῖς,
the works of God?   ²Answered ¹Jesus and said to them,

Τοῦτό ἐστιν τὸ ἔργον τοῦ θεοῦ, ἵνα ᵛπιστεύσητε" εἰς ὃν
This is the work of God, that ye should believe on him whom

ἀπέστειλεν ἐκεῖνος. 30 Εἶπον οὖν αὐτῷ, Τί οὖν ποιεῖς
²sent ¹he.   They said therefore to him, What ²then ³doest

σὺ σημεῖον, ἵνα ἴδωμεν καὶ πιστεύσωμέν σοι; τί ἐργάζῃ;
¹thou ¹sign, that we may see and may believe thee? what dost thou work?

31 οἱ·πατέρες·ἡμῶν τὸ μάννα ἔφαγον ἐν τῇ ἐρήμῳ, καθώς
Our fathers the manna ate in the wilderness, as

ἐστιν γεγραμμένον, Ἄρτον ἐκ τοῦ οὐρανοῦ ἔδωκεν αὐτοῖς
it is written, Bread out of the heaven he gave them

φαγεῖν. 32 Εἶπεν οὖν αὐτοῖς ὁ Ἰησοῦς, Ἀμὴν ἀμὴν λέγω
to eat.   ²Said ³therefore ⁴to ⁵them ¹Jesus, Verily verily I say

ὑμῖν, Οὐ ʷΜωσῆς" ˣδέδωκεν" ὑμῖν τὸν ʸἄρτον ἐκ τοῦ οὐρα-
to you, ³Not ¹Moses ²has ⁴given you the bread out of the hea-

νοῦ· ἀλλ' ὁ·πατήρ·μου δίδωσιν ὑμῖν τὸν ἄρτον ἐκ τοῦ οὐ-
ven; but my Father gives you the ³out ⁴of ⁵the ⁶hea-

ρανοῦ τὸν ἀληθινόν. 33 ὁ·γὰρ ἄρτος ʸ τοῦ θεοῦ ἐστιν ὁ
ven   ¹ ²true.   For the bread of God is he who

καταβαίνων ἐκ τοῦ οὐρανοῦ, καὶ ζωὴν διδοὺς τῷ κόσμῳ.
ʸ comes down out of the heaven, and life gives to the world.

34 Εἶπον οὖν πρὸς αὐτόν, Κύριε, πάντοτε δὸς ἡμῖν τὸν
They said therefore to him, Lord, always · give to us

ἄρτον·τοῦτον. 35 Εἶπεν ᶻδὲ" αὐτοῖς ὁ Ἰησοῦς, Ἐγώ εἰμι ὁ
this bread.   ³Said ¹and ⁴to ⁵them ²Jesus,   I am the

ἄρτος τῆς ζωῆς· ὁ ἐρχόμενος πρός ᵃμε" οὐ·μὴ ᵇπεινάσῃ·"
bread of life: he that comes to me in no wise may hunger,

καὶ ὁ πιστεύων εἰς ἐμὲ οὐ·μὴ ᶜδιψήσῃ" πώποτε. 36 ἀλλ'
and he that believes on me in no wise may thirst at any time.   But

εἶπον ὑμῖν ὅτι καὶ ἑωράκατέ ᵈμε" καὶ οὐ·πιστεύετε. 37 πᾶν
I said to you that also ye have seen me and believe not.   All

ὃ δίδωσίν μοι ὁ πατὴρ πρὸς ἐμὲ ἥξει· καὶ τὸν ἐρχό-
that ³gives ⁴me ¹the ²Father to me shall come, and him that comes

---

for Jesus. 25 And when
they had found him
on the other side of
the sea, they said to
him, Rabbi, when cam-
est thou hither ? 26 Je-
sus answered them and
said, Verily, verily, I
say unto you, Ye seek
me, not because ye saw
the miracles, but be-
cause ye did eat of the
loaves, and were filled.
27 Labour not for the
meat which perisheth,
but for that meat
which endureth unto
everlasting life, which
the Son of man shall
give unto you: for him
hath God the Father
sealed. 28 Then said
they unto him, What
shall we do, that we
might work the works
of God? 29 Jesus an-
swered and said unto
them, This is the work
of God, that ye believe
on him whom he hath
sent. 30 They said
therefore unto him,
What sign shewest
thou then, that we
may see, and believe
thee? what dost thou
work? 31 Our fathers
did eat manna in the
desert; as it is written,
He gave them bread
from heaven to eat.
32 Then Jesus said un-
to them, Verily, verily,
I say unto you, Moses
gave you not that
bread from heaven;
but my Father giveth
you the true bread
from heaven. 33 For
the bread of God is he
which cometh down
from heaven, and giv-
eth life unto the world.
34 Then said they unto
him, Lord, evermore
give us this bread.
35 And Jesus said unto
them, I am the bread
of life: he that com-
eth to me shall never
hunger; and he that
believeth on me shall
never thirst. 36 But I
said unto you, That ye
also have seen me, and
believe not. 37 All
that the Father giveth
me shall come to me;
and him that cometh

ᵠ Ῥαββεί T.   ʳ δίδωσιν ὑμῖν gives to you T.   ˢ ποιῶμεν should we do EGLᴛᴛrAW.
ᵗ — ὁ T.   ᵛ πιστεύητε TTrA.   ʷ Μωϋσῆς LTTrAW.   ˣ ἔδωκεν gave LTTrA.   ʸ + ὁ T.
ᶻ οὖν therefore T ; — δὲ [L]TrA.   ᵃ ἐμὲ TTrA.   ᵇ πεινάσει shall hunger L.   ᶜ διψήσει
shall thirst LTTrA.   ᵈ — με [L]T.

to me I will in no wise
cast out. 38 For I
came down from hea-
ven, not to do mine
own will, but the will
of him that sent me.
39 And this is the Fa-
ther's will which hath
sent me, that 'of all
which he hath given
me I should lose no-
thing, but should raise
it up again at the last
day. 40 And this is
the will of him that
sent me, that every
one which seeth the
Son, and believeth on
him, may have ever-
lasting life : and I
will raise him up at
the last day. 41 The
Jews then murmured
at him, because he
said, I am the bread
which came down from
heaven. 42 And they
said, Is not this Jesus,
the son of Joseph,
whose father and mo-
ther we know ? how is
it then that he saith,
I came down from
heaven ? 43 Jesus there-
fore answered and said
unto them, Murmur
not among yourselves.
44 No man can come
to me, except the Fa-
ther which hath sent
me draw him: and I
will raise him up at
the last day. 45 It is
written in the pro-
phets, And they shall
be all taught of God.
Every man therefore
that hath heard, and
hath learned of the
Father, cometh unto
me. 46 Not that any
man hath seen the Fa-
ther, save he which is
of God, he hath seen
the Father. 47 Verily,
verily, I say unto you,
He that believeth on
me hath everlasting
life. 48 I am that
bread of life. 49 Your
Fathers did eat manna
in the wilderness, and
are dead. 50 This is
the bread which com-
eth down from hea-
ven, that a man may

μενον πρός ᵉμε‖ οὐ·μὴ ἐκβάλω ἔξω· 38 ὅτι καταβέβηκα
to   me   not at all   will I cast out.   For I have come down

ᶠἐκ‖ τοῦ οὐρανοῦ, οὐχ ἵνα ᵍποιῶ‖ τὸ θέλημα τὸ ἐμόν, ἀλλὰ
out of the   heaven,   not that I should do   ²will   ¹my,   but

τὸ θέλημα τοῦ πέμψαντός με. 39 τοῦτο.δὲ ἐστιν τὸ
the   will of him who   sent   me.   And this   is   the

θέλημα τοῦ πέμψαντός με ʰπατρός,‖ ἵνα πᾶν ὃ δέδωκέν
will of the ²who ³sent   ⁴me ¹Father,   that [of] all   that he has given

μοι, μὴ.ἀπολέσω ἐξ·αὐτοῦ, ἀλλὰ ἀναστήσω αὐτὸ ⁱἐν‖
me, I should not lose [any] of   it,   but should raise up   it   in

τῇ ἐσχάτῃ ἡμέρᾳ. 40 τοῦτο·ᵏδέ· ἐστιν τὸ θέλημα ¹τοῦ
the   last   day.   And this   is   the   will   ¹of him who

πέμψαντός με, ἵνα πᾶς ὁ θεωρῶν τὸν υἱὸν καὶ πιστεύων
sent   me, that everyone who sees   the   Son   and   believes

εἰς αὐτόν, ἔχῃ ζωὴν αἰώνιον, καὶ ἀναστήσω αὐτὸν ᵐἐγὼ‖
on   him, should have life   eternal;   and ²will ³raise ⁴up   ⁵him   ¹I

ⁿτῇ ἐσχάτῃ ἡμέρᾳ. 41 Ἐγόγγυζον οὖν οἱ Ἰουδαῖοι περὶ
at the   last   day.   Were murmuring therefore the   Jews   about

αὐτοῦ, ὅτι εἶπεν, Ἐγώ εἰμι ὁ ἄρτος ὁ καταβὰς ἐκ τοῦ
him, because he said,   I   am the bread which came down out of the

οὐρανοῦ. 42 καὶ ἔλεγον, ᴼοὐχ‖οὗτός.ἐστιν Ἰησοῦς ὁ υἱὸς
heaven.   And were saying, Is not this   Jesus   the Son

Ἰωσήφ, οὗ ἡμεῖς οἴδαμεν τὸν πατέρα καὶ τὴν μητέρα ;
of Joseph, of whom we   know   the   father   and   the   mother?

πῶς ᴾοὖν‖ λέγει ᑫοὗτος,‖Ὅτι ἐκ τοῦ οὐρανοῦ καταβέβηκὰ ;
how therefore says   he,   Out of the   heaven   I have come down?

43 Ἀπεκρίθη ʳοὖν‖ sὁ‖Ἰησοῦς καὶ εἶπεν αὐτοῖς, Μὴ·γογγύζετε
³Answered ²therefore ¹Jesus   and said to them, Murmur not

ᵗμετ᾽‖ ἀλλήλων. 44 οὐδεὶς δύναται ᵉἐλθεῖν πρός ᵛμε‖ ἐὰν·μὴ
with   one another.   No one   is able to come to   me   unless

ὁ πατὴρ ὁ πέμψας με ἑλκύσῃ αὐτόν, ʷκαὶ ἐγὼ‖ ἀναστήσω
the Father who sent   me draw   him,   and   I   will raise up

αὐτὸν ˣ τῇ ἐσχάτῃ ἡμέρᾳ. 45 ἔστιν γεγραμμένον ἐν τοῖς προ-
him   at the   last   day.   It is   written   in the   pro-

φήταις, Καὶ ἔσονται πάντες διδακτοὶ ʸτοῦ‖ θεοῦ. Πᾶς
phets,   And they shall be   all   taught   of God. Everyone

ᶻοὖν‖ ὁ ἀκούσας παρὰ τοῦ πατρὸς καὶ μαθών, ἔρχεται
therefore that has heard from   the   Father   and has learnt,   comes

πρός ᵃμε·‖ 46 οὐχ ὅτι τὸν πατέρα ᵇτις ἑώρακεν,‖ εἰ·μὴ ὁ
to   me: not that ⁴the ⁵Father ¹anyone ²has ³seen,   except he who

ὢν παρὰ τοῦ θεοῦ, οὗτος ἑώρακεν τὸν ᶜπατέρα.‖ 47 ἀμὴν
is   from   God,   he   has seen   the   Father.   Verily

ἀμὴν λέγω ὑμῖν, ὁ πιστεύων ᵈεἰς ἐμὲ‖ ἔχει ζωὴν αἰώνιον·
verily I say to you, He that believes   on   me   has   life   eternal.

48 ἐγώ εἰμι ὁ ἄρτος τῆς ζωῆς. 49 οἱ.πατέρες.ὑμῶν ἔφαγον
I   am the bread   of life.   Your Fathers   ate

ᵉτὸ μάννα ἐν τῇ ἐρήμῳ,‖ καὶ ἀπέθανον· 50 οὗτός ἐστιν ὁ
the manna   in the   desert,   and   died.   This is the

ἄρτος ὁ ἐκ τοῦ οὐρανοῦ καταβαίνων, ἵνα τις ἐξ αὐτοῦ
bread which out of   heaven   comes down,   that anyone of   it

---

ᵉ ἐμὲ τ.   ᶠ ἀπὸ from LTTrA.   ᵍ ποιήσω τ.   ʰ — πατρός (read of him who sent)
GLTTrAW.   ⁱ — ἐν (read at the) TrA.   ᵏ γάρ for (this) GLTTrAW.   ˡ τοῦ πατρός μου of
my father LTTrA.   ᵐ [ἐγὼ] L.   ⁿ + ἐν in (the) LT.   ᴼ Οὐχὶ Tr.   ᴾ νῦν now TTrA.
ᑫ — οὗτος (read λέγει says he) [L]TrA.   ʳ — οὖν G[L]TTrAW.   s — ὁ TTr.   ᵗ μετὰ Tr.
ᵛ ἐμὲ TrA.   ʷ κἀγὼ LTTrA.   ˣ + ἐν in (the) GLTTrAW.   ʸ — τοῦ GLTTrAW.   ᶻ — οὖν
GLTTrA.   ᵃ ἐμὲ TTrw.   ᵇ ἑώρακέν τις LTTrAW.   ᶜ θεόν God T.   ᵈ — εἰς ἐμέ T[TrA]
ᵉ ἐν τῇ ἐρήμῳ τὸ μάννα LTTrA.

φάγῃ καὶ μὴ ἀποθάνῃ. 51 ἐγώ εἰμι ὁ ἄρτος ὁ ζῶν, ὁ
may eat and not die. I am the ²bread ¹living, which

ἐκ τοῦ οὐρανοῦ καταβάς· ἐάν τις φάγῃ ᶠἐκ τούτου
out of the heaven came down: if anyone shall have eaten of this

τοῦ ἄρτου ζήσεται‖ εἰς.τὸν.αἰῶνα. καὶ ὁ ἄρτος δὲ ὃν ἐγὼ
bread he shall live for ever; and the bread also which I

δώσω, ᵍἡ.σάρξ.μου ἐστίν, ʰἣν ἐγὼ δώσω‖ ὑπὲρ τῆς τοῦ
will give, my flesh is, which I will give for the ²of ³the

κόσμου ζωῆς.‖ 52 Ἐμάχοντο οὖν ᶦπρὸς ἀλλήλους οἱ Ἰου-
⁴world ¹life. Were contending therefore with one another the Jews

δαῖοι,‖ λέγοντες, Πῶς δύναται ᵏοὗτος ἡμῖν‖ δοῦναι τὴν
saying, How is ²able ¹he ⁵us. ³to ⁴give

σάρκα¹ φαγεῖν; 53 Εἶπεν οὖν. αὐτοῖς ὁ Ἰησοῦς, Ἀμὴν
⁷flesh [⁶his] to eat? ³Said ²therefore ⁴to ⁵them ¹Jesus, Verily .

ἀμὴν λέγω ὑμῖν, ἐὰν.μὴ φάγητε τὴν σάρκα τοῦ υἱοῦ
verily I say to you, Unless ye shall have eaten the flesh of the Son

τοῦ ἀνθρώπου καὶ πίητε αὐτοῦ τὸ αἶμα, οὐκ.ἔχετε ζωὴν
of man and shall have drunk his blood, ye have not life

ἐν ἑαυτοῖς. 54 ὁ τρώγων μου τὴν σάρκα, καὶ πίνων μου
in yourselves. He that eats my flesh, and drinks my

τὸ αἶμα, ἔχει ζωὴν αἰώνιον, ᵐκαὶ ἐγὼ‖ ἀναστήσω αὐτὸν ⁿ τῇ
blood, has life eternal, and I will raise up him in the

ἐσχάτῃ ἡμέρᾳ· 55 ἡ.γὰρ.σάρξ.μου °ἀληθῶς‖ ἐστιν βρῶσις, καὶ
last day; for my flesh truly is food, and

τὸ.αἶμά.μου °ἀληθῶς‖ ἐστιν πόσις. 56 ὁ τρώγων μου τὴν
my blood truly is drink. He that eats my

σάρκα καὶ πίνων μου τὸ αἶμά, ἐν ἐμοὶ μένει, κἀγὼ ἐν αὐτῷ.
flesh and drinks my blood, in me abides, and I in him.

57 καθὼς ἀπέστειλέν με ὁ ζῶν πατήρ, κἀγὼ ζῶ διὰ
As ⁴sent ⁵me ¹the ²living ³Father, and I live because of

τὸν πατέρα· καὶ ὁ τρώγων με, κἀκεῖνος ᵖζήσεται‖ δι'
the Father, also he that eats me, also he shall live because of

ἐμέ. 58 οὗτός ἐστιν ὁ ἄρτος ὁ ᑫἐκ τοῦ‖ οὐρανοῦ καταβάς·
me. This is the bread which out of the heaven came down:

οὐ καθὼς ἔφαγον οἱ πατέρες ʳὑμῶν‖ ˢτὸ μάννα,‖ καὶ ἀπέθα-
Not as ⁵ate ¹the ²fathers ³of ⁴you the manna, and died;

νον· ὁ τρώγων τοῦτον τὸν ἄρτον ᵗζήσεται‖ εἰς.τὸν.αἰῶνα.
he that eats this bread shall live for ever.

59 Ταῦτα εἶπεν ἐν συναγωγῇ διδάσκων ἐν ᵛΚαπερναούμ.‖
These things he said in [the] synagogue teaching in Capernaum.

60 Πολλοὶ οὖν ἀκούσαντες ἐκ τῶν.μαθητῶν.αὐτοῦ εἶπον,
Many therefore ²having ³heard ¹of ⁴his ³disciples

Σκληρός ἐστιν ʷοὗτος ὁ λόγος·‖ τίς δύναται αὐτοῦ ἀκούειν;
Hard is this word; who is able it to hear?

61 Εἰδὼς δὲ ὁ Ἰησοῦς ἐν ἑαυτῷ ὅτι γογγύζουσιν περὶ
³Knowing ¹but ²Jesus in himself that ⁴murmur ⁴concerning

τούτου οἱ.μαθηταὶ.αὐτοῦ εἶπεν αὐτοῖς, Τοῦτο ὑμᾶς σκανδα-
⁵this ¹his ²disciples said to them, ²This ⁴you ¹does ³of-

λίζει; 62 ἐὰν οὖν θεωρῆτε τὸν υἱὸν τοῦ ἀνθρώπου ἀνα-
fend? . If then ye should see the Son of man ascend-

βαίνοντα ὅπου ἦν τὸ πρότερον; 63 τὸ πνεῦμά ἐστιν τὸ
ing up where he was before? The Spirit it is which

eat thereof, and not die. 51 I am the living bread which came down from heaven: if any man eat of this bread, he shall live for ever: and the bread that I will give is my flesh, which I will give for the life of the world. 52 The Jews therefore strove among themselves, saying, How can this man give us his flesh to eat? 53 Then Jesus said unto them, Verily, verily, I say unto you, Except ye eat the flesh of the Son of man, and drink his blood, ye have no life in you. 54 Whoso eateth my flesh, and drinketh my blood, hath eternal life; and I will raise him up at the last day. 55 For my flesh is meat indeed, and my blood is drink indeed. 56 He that eateth my flesh, and drinketh my blood, dwelleth in me, and I in him. 57 As the living Father hath sent me, and I live by the Father: so he that eateth me, even he shall live by me. 58 This is that bread which came down from heaven: not as your fathers did eat manna, and are dead: he that eateth of this bread shall live for ever. 59 These things said he in the synagogue, as he taught in Capernaum. 60 Many therefore of his disciples, when they had heard this, said, This is an hard saying; who can hear it? 61 When Jesus knew in himself that his disciples murmured at it, he said unto them, Doth this offend you? 62 What and if ye shall see the Son of man ascend up where he was before? 63 It is the spirit that

ᶠ ἐκ τοῦ ἐμοῦ ἄρτου, ζήσει of my bread, he shall live τ.   ᵍ ὑπὲρ τῆς τοῦ κόσμου ζωῆς, ἡ
σάρξ μου ἐστίν τ.   ʰ — ἣν ἐγὼ δώσω LTTrA.   ᶦ οἱ Ἰουδαῖοι πρὸς ἀλλήλους L.   ᵏ ἡμῖν
οὗτος τ.   ¹ + αὐτοῦ his L.   ᵐ κἀγὼ LTTrA.   ⁿ + [ἐν] L.   ° ἀληθής (is) true LTTrA.
ᵖ ζήσει LTTrA.   ᑫ ἐξ out of LTTrA.   ʳ — ὑμῶν LTTrA.   ˢ — τὸ μάννα GTTrA.   ᵗ ζήσει
ᵀTrA.   ᵛ Καφαρναούμ LTTrAW.   ʷ ὁ λόγος οὗτος LTTrA.

quickeneth; the flesh profiteth nothing: the words that I speak unto you, *they* are spirit, and *they* are life. 64 But there are some of you that believe not. For Jesus knew from the beginning who they were that believed not, and who should betray him. 65 And he said, Therefore said I unto you, that no man can come unto me, except it were given unto him of my Father. 66 From that *time* many of his disciples went back, and walked no more with him. 67 Then said Jesus unto the twelve, Will ye also go away? 68 Then Simon Peter answered him, Lord, to whom shall we go? thou hast the words of eternal life. 69 And we believe and are sure that thou art that Christ, the Son of the living God. 70 Jesus answered them, Have not I chosen you twelve, and one of you is a devil? 71 He spake of Judas Iscariot *the son* of Simon: for he it was that should betray him, being one of the twelve.

ζωοποιοῦν, ἡ σὰρξ οὐκ ὠφελεῖ οὐδέν· τὰ ῥήματα ἃ ²ἐγὼ
quickens, · the flesh profits nothing; the words which I

ˣλαλῶ" ὑμῖν. πνεῦμά ἐστιν καὶ ζωή ἐστιν. 64 ʸἀλλ'" εἰσὶν
speak to you, spirit are and life are; but there are

ἐξ ὑμῶν τινες οἳ οὐ·πιστεύουσιν. ᾔδει·γὰρ·ἐξ   ἀρχῆς
of · you · some, who believe not. For ³knew ³from [⁴the] ⁵beginning

ὁ Ἰησοῦς τίνες εἰσὶν οἱ μὴ·πιστεύοντες, καὶ τίς ἐστιν ὁ
¹Jesus who they are, who believe not, and who is ·he who

παραδώσων αὐτόν. 65 καὶ ἔλεγεν, Διὰ·τοῦτο εἴρηκα ὑμῖν,
shall deliver up him. And ·he said, Therefore have I said to you,

ὅτι οὐδεὶς δύναται ᵃἐλθεῖν πρός ᶻμε" ᵃἐὰν·μὴ ᾖ δεδομένον
that no one is able to come · to me ·unless it be given

αὐτῷ ἐκ τοῦ·πατρός·ᵃμου." 66 Ἐκ τούτου ᵇ πολλοὶ ꜱ
to him from my Father. From that [time] many

ᵈἀπῆλθον τῶν·μαθητῶν·αὐτοῦ" εἰς·τὰ·ὀπίσω, καὶ οὐκέτι μετ'
⁴went ⁵away ¹of ²his ³disciples back, and no more with

αὐτοῦ περιεπάτουν. 67 εἶπεν οὖν ὁ Ἰησοῦς τοῖς δώδεκα,
him walked. ²Said ³therefore ¹Jesus to the twelve,

Μὴ καὶ ὑμεῖς θέλετε ὑπάγειν; 68 Ἀπεκρίθη ᵉοὖν" αὐτῷ
³Also ²ye ¹are ⁴wishing to go away? ⁴Answered ²therefore ³him

Σίμων Πέτρος, Κύριε, πρὸς τίνα ἀπελευσόμεθα; ῥήματα ζωῆς
¹Simon ²Peter, Lord, to whom shall ³we go? words of life

αἰωνίου ἔχεις· 69 καὶ ἡμεῖς πεπιστεύκαμεν καὶ ἐγνώκαμεν
eternal thou hast; and we have believed and have known

ὅτι σὺ εἶ ᶠὁ χριστὸς ὁ υἱὸς" τοῦ θεοῦ ᵍτοῦ ζῶντος." 70 Ἀπε-
that thou art the Christ the Son of ³God ¹the ²living. An-

κρίθη αὐτοῖς ὁ Ἰησοῦς, Οὐκ ἐγὼ ὑμᾶς τοὺς δώδεκα ἐξελεξάμην,
swered them Jesus, ²Not ¹you ⁴the ²twelve ¹did ·choose,

καὶ ἐξ ὑμῶν εἷς διάβολός ἐστιν; 71 Ἔλεγεν·δὲ τὸν Ἰούδαν
and of you one a devil is? But he spoke of Judas

Σίμωνος ʰἸσκαριώτην·" οὗτος·γὰρ ⁱἤμελλεν" ᵏαὐτὸν παρα-
Simon's [son]. Iscariote, for he was about him · to de-

διδόναι," εἷς ˡὢν" ἐκ τῶν δώδεκα.
liver up, ²one ¹being of the twelve.

VII. After these things Jesus walked in Galilee: for he would not walk in Jewry, because the Jews sought · to kill him. 2 Now the Jews' feast of tabernacles was at hand. 3 His brethren therefore said unto him, Depart hence, and go into Judæa, that thy disciples also may see the works that thou doest. 4 For *there is* no man *that* doeth any thing in secret, and he himself seeketh to be known openly. If thou do these things, shew thy-

7 ᵐΚαὶ" ⁿπεριεπάτει ὁ Ἰησοῦς μετὰ ταῦτα" ἐν τῇ Γαλι-
And ²was ³walking ¹Jesus after these things in Gali-

λαίᾳ· οὐ γὰρ ἤθελεν ἐν τῇ Ἰουδαίᾳ περιπατεῖν, ὅτι
lee, ⁴not ¹for ²he ³did desire in Judæa to walk, because

ἐζήτουν αὐτὸν οἱ Ἰουδαῖοι ἀποκτεῖναι. 2 Ἦν·δὲ ἐγγὺς ἡ
³were ⁴seeking ⁵him ¹the ²Jews to kill. Now was near the

ἑορτὴ τῶν Ἰουδαίων ἡ σκηνοπηγία. 3 εἶπον οὖν πρὸς αὐτὸν
feast of the. Jews, the tabernacles. ²Said ³therefore ⁴to ⁵him

οἱ·ἀδελφοὶ·αὐτοῦ, Μετάβηθι ἐντεῦθεν, καὶ ὕπαγε εἰς τὴν Ἰου-
¹his ²brethren, Remove hence, and go into Ju-

δαίαν, ἵνα καὶ οἱ·μαθηταί·σου ᵒθεωρήσωσιν" ᴾτὰ·ἔργα·σου" ἃ
dæa, that also thy disciples may see thy works which

ποιεῖς· 4 οὐδεὶς·γὰρ ᑫἐν κρυπτῷ τι" ποιεῖ, καὶ ζητεῖ
thou doest; for no one in secret anything does, and seeks

ʳαὐτὸς" ἐν παῤῥησίᾳ εἶναι. εἰ ταῦτα ποιεῖς, φανέρωσον
himself ³in ⁴public ¹to ²be. If these things thou doest, manifest

---

ˣ λελάληκα have spoken LTTrAW.   ʸ ἀλλὰ TrW.   ᶻ ἐμὲ T.   ᵃ — μου (*read* the Father) LTTrA.   ᵇ + οὖν therefore T.   ᶜ + ἐκ [L]Tr[A].   ᵈ τῶν μαθητῶν αὐτοῦ ἀπῆλθον LTTrA.   ᵉ — οὖν GLTTrA.   ᶠ ὁ ἅγιος the holy [one] GLTTrA.   ᵍ — τοῦ ζῶντος GLTTrA.   ʰ Ἰσ-καριώτου (*read* son of Simon Iscariote) LTTrA.   ⁱ ἔμελλεν LTTrA.   ᵏ παραδιδόναι αὐτόν LTrA.   ˡ — ὢν LTrA.   ᵐ — καὶ T.   ⁿ μετὰ ταῦτα περιεπάτει ὁ ([ὁ] Tr) Ἰησοῦς LTTrAW.
ᵒ θεωρήσουσιν shall see TTrA.   ᴾ σου τὰ ἔργα Lᵣ   ᑫ ἐν κρυπτῷ LTTrA.   ʳ αὐτὸ it L.

σεαυτὸν τῷ κόσμῳ. 5 Οὐδὲ.γὰρ οἱ.ἀδελφοὶ.αὐτοῦ ἐπίστευον
thyself to the world. For neither *his *brethren ¹believed

εἰς αὐτόν. 6 Λέγει ⁸οὖν‖ αὐτοῖς ὁ Ἰησοῦς, Ὁ καιρὸς ὁ ἐμὸς
on him. ³Says ²therefore ⁴to ⁵them ¹Jesus, ⁷Time ⁶my

οὔπω πάρεστιν· ὁ.δὲ.καιρὸς ὁ ὑμέτερος πάντοτέ ἐστιν ἕτοιμος.
not yet is come, but ²time ¹your always is ready.

7 οὐ.δύναται ὁ κόσμος μισεῖν ὑμᾶς· ἐμὲ.δὲ μισεῖ, ὅτι ἐγὼ
³Is ⁴unable ¹the ²world to hate you, but me it hates, because I

μαρτυρῶ περὶ αὐτοῦ, ὅτι τὰ ἔργα αὐτοῦ πονηρά ἐστιν.
bear witness concerning it, that the works of it evil are.

8 ὑμεῖς ἀνάβητε εἰς τὴν.ἑορτὴν.ταύτην· ἐγὼ ʸοὔπω‖ ἀνα-
Ye, go ye up to this feast. I not yet am

βαίνω εἰς τὴν.ἑορτὴν.ταύτην, ὅτι ὁ ᵂκαιρὸς ὁ ἐμὸς‖ οὔπω
going up to this feast, for ²time ¹my not yet

πεπλήρωται. 9 Ταῦτα.ˣδὲ‖ εἰπὼν ʸαὐτοῖς‖ ἔμεινεν ἐν τῇ
has been fulfilled. And these things having said to them he abode in

Γαλιλαίᾳ. 10 Ὡς.δὲ ἀνέβησαν οἱ.ἀδελφοὶ.αὐτοῦ ᶻτότε καὶ
Galilee. But when were gone up his brethren then also

αὐτὸς ἀνέβη εἰς τὴν ἑορτήν,‖ οὐ φανερῶς, ᵃἀλλ᾽‖ ᵇὡς‖ ἐν
he went up to the feast, not openly, but as in

κρυπτῷ. 11 Οἱ οὖν Ἰουδαῖοι ἐζήτουν αὐτὸν ἐν τῇ ἑορτῇ,
secret. The ²therefore ¹Jews were seeking him at the feast,

καὶ ἔλεγον, Ποῦ ἐστιν ἐκεῖνος; 12 Καὶ γογγυσμὸς ᶜπολὺς
and said, Where is he? And ²murmuring ¹much

περὶ αὐτοῦ ἦν‖ ἐν ᵈτοῖς ὄχλοις‖ οἱ.μὲν ἔλεγον,
concerning him there was among the crowds. Some said,

ʸὍτι ἀγαθός ἐστιν· ἄλλοι.ᵉδὲ‖ ἔλεγον, Οὔ· ἀλλὰ πλανᾷ τὸν
⁵Good ¹he ²is; but others said, No; but he deceives the

ὄχλον. 13 Οὐδεὶς μέντοι παρρησίᾳ ἐλάλει περὶ αὐτοῦ,
crowd. No one however publicly spoke concerning him,

διὰ τὸν φόβον τῶν Ἰουδαίων.
because of the fear of the Jews.

14 Ἤδη.δὲ τῆς ἑορτῆς μεσούσης ἀνέβη ᶠὁ‖ Ἰησοῦς
But now ⁵of ⁶the ⁷feast [¹it] ²being ³the ⁴middle went up Jesus

εἰς τὸ ἱερόν, καὶ ἐδίδασκεν. 15 ᵍκαὶ ἐθαύμαζον‖ οἱ Ἰουδαῖοι
into the temple, and was teaching; and ²were ³wondering ¹the ²Jews

λέγοντες, Πῶς οὗτος γράμματα οἶδεν, μὴ μεμαθηκώς;
saying, How ²this ³one ⁴letters ¹knows, not having learned?

16 Ἀπεκρίθη ʰ αὐτοῖς ⁱὁ‖ Ἰησοῦς καὶ εἶπεν, Ἡ.ἐμὴ.διδαχὴ οὐκ
²Answered ³them ¹Jesus and said, My teaching ²not

ἔστιν ἐμή, ἀλλὰ τοῦ πέμψαντός με· 17 ἐάν τις θέλῃ τὸ
¹is mine, but his who sent me. If anyone desire

θέλημα.αὐτοῦ ποιεῖν, γνώσεται περὶ τῆς διδαχῆς πότερον
his will to practise, he shall know concerning the teaching whether

ἐκ ᵏτοῦ‖ θεοῦ ἐστιν, ἢ ἐγὼ ἀπ᾽ ἐμαυτοῦ λαλῶ. 18 ὁ ἀφ᾽
from God it is, or I from myself speak. He that from

ἑαυτοῦ λαλῶν, τὴν.δόξαν.τὴν.ἰδίαν ζητεῖ· ὁ.δὲ ζητῶν τὴν
himself speaks, his own glory seeks; but he that seeks the

δόξαν τοῦ πέμψαντος αὐτόν, οὗτος ἀληθής ἐστιν, καὶ
glory of him that sent him, he true is, and

ἀδικία ἐν αὐτῷ οὐκ.ἔστιν. 19 οὐ ⁱΜωσῆς‖ ᵐδέδωκεν‖
unrighteousness in him is not. ²Not ³Moses ¹has given

self to the world.
5 For neither did his brethren believe in him. 6 Then Jesus said unto them, My time is not yet come: but your time is alway ready. 7 The world cannot hate you; but me it hateth, because I testify of it, that the works thereof are evil. 8 Go ye up unto this feast: I go not up yet unto this feast; for my time is not yet full come. 9 When he had said these words unto them he abode still in Galilee. 10 But when his brethren were gone up, then went he also up unto the feast, not openly, but as it were in secret. 11 Then the Jews sought him at the feast, and said, Where is he? 12 And there was much murmuring among the people concerning him: for some said, He is a good man: others said, Nay; but he deceiveth the people. 13 Howbeit no man spake openly of him for fear of the Jews.

14 Now about the midst of the feast Jesus went up into the temple, and taught. 15 And the Jews marvelled, saying, How knoweth this man letters, having never learned? 16 Jesus answered them, and said, My doctrine is not mine, but his that sent me. 17 If any man will do his will, he shall know of the doctrine, whether it be of God, or whether I speak of myself. 18 He that speaketh of himself seeketh his own glory: but he that seeketh his glory that sent him, the same is true, and no unrighteousness is in him. 19 Did not Moses give you the

ᵃ — οὖν T. ᵗ — ταύτην (read the feast) LTTrAW. ᵛ οὐκ not GTTrA. ᵂ ἐμὸς καιρὸς
LTTrA. ˣ — δὲ and GTTr. ʸ αὐτὸς he (abode) T. ᶻ εἰς τὴν ἑορτήν, τότε καὶ αὐτὸς
ἀνέβη LTTrA. ᵃ ἀλλὰ LTrA. ᵇ — ὡς T. ᶜ περὶ αὐτοῦ ἦν πολὺς LTrA; ἦν περὶ αὐτοῦ
πολὺς T. ᵈ τῷ ὄχλῳ the crowd T. ᵉ — δὲ and GTW. ᶠ — ὁ LTTrA. ᵍ ἐθαύμαζον οὖν
were wondering therefore LTTrAW. ʰ + οὖν therefore LTTrAW. ⁱ — ὁ TTr. ᵏ — τοῦ T.
ˡ Μωϋσῆς LTTrAW. ᵐ ἔδωκεν gave LTrA.

18

law, and yet none of you keepeth the law? Why go ye about to kill me? 20 The people answered and said, Thou hast a devil: who goeth about to kill thee? 21 Jesus answered and said unto them, I have done one work, and ye all marvel. 22 Moses therefore gave unto you circumcision; (not because it is of Moses, but of the fathers;) and ye on the sabbath day circumcise a man. 23 If a man on the sabbath day receive circumcision, that the law of Moses should not be broken; are ye angry at me, because I have made a man every whit whole on the sabbath day? 24 Judge not according to the appearance, but judge righteous judgment. 25 Then said some of them of Jerusalem, Is not this he, whom they seek to kill? 26 But, lo, he speaketh boldly, and they say nothing unto him. Do the rulers know indeed that this is the very Christ? 27 Howbeit we know this man whence he is: but when Christ cometh, no man knoweth whence he is. 28 Then cried Jesus in the temple as he taught, saying, Ye both know me, and ye know whence I am: and I am not come of myself, but he that sent me is true, whom ye know not. 29 But I know him: for I am from him, and he hath sent me. 30 Then they sought to take him: but no man laid hands on him, because his hour was not yet come. 31 And many of the people believed on him, and said, When Christ cometh, will he do more miracles than these which this man

---

ὑμῖν τὸν νόμον, καὶ οὐδεὶς ἐξ ὑμῶν ποιεῖ τὸν νόμον; τί
you the law, and no one of you practises the law? Why

με ζητεῖτε ἀποκτεῖναι; 20 Ἀπεκρίθη ὁ ὄχλος [n]καὶ εἶπεν,[ll]
me do ye seek to kill? [3]Answered [1]the [2]crowd and said,

Δαιμόνιον ἔχεις· τίς σε ζητεῖ ἀποκτεῖναι; 21 Ἀπεκρίθη
A demon thou hast; who thee seeks to kill? [x]Answered

[o]ὁ[ll] Ἰησοῦς καὶ εἶπεν αὐτοῖς, Ἕν ἔργον ἐποίησα, καὶ πάντες
[1]Jesus and said to them, One work I did, and [2]all

[P]θαυμάζετε.[ll] 22 διὰ.τοῦτο[ll] [q]Μωσῆς[ll] δέδωκεν ὑμῖν τὴν περι-
[1]ye wonder. Therefore Moses has given you circum-

τομήν, οὐχ ὅτι ἐκ τοῦ [r]Μωσέως[ll] ἐστίν, ἀλλ' ἐκ τῶν πατέρων·
cision, not that of Moses it is, but of the fathers,

καὶ [s]ἐν[ll] σαββάτῳ περιτέμνετε ἄνθρωπον. 23 εἰ περιτομὴν
and on sabbath ye circumcise a man. If [4]circumcision

λαμβάνει ἄνθρωπος ἐν σαββάτῳ ἵνα μὴ.λυθῇ ὁ νόμος [t]
[3]receives [1]a [2]man on sabbath, that may not be broken the law

[r]Μωσέως,[ll] ἐμοὶ χολᾶτε ὅτι ὅλον ἄνθρωπον ὑγιῆ ἐποίησα
of Moses, with me are ye angry because [2]a [3]man [1]sound I made

ἐν σαββάτῳ; 24 μὴ.κρίνετε κατ' ὄψιν, ἀλλὰ τὴν δικαίαν
on sabbath? Judge not according to sight, but righteous

κρίσιν [v]κρίνατε.[ll] 25 Ἔλεγον οὖν τινες ἐκ τῶν [w]Ἱεροσο-
judgment judge. [7]Said [6]therefore [1]some [2]of [3]those [4]of [5]Jeru-

λυμιτῶν,[ll] Οὐχ.οὗτός.ἐστιν ὃν ζητοῦσιν ἀποκτεῖναι; 26 καὶ
salem, Is not this he whom they seek to kill? and

ἴδε, παῤῥησίᾳ λαλεῖ, καὶ οὐδὲν αὐτῷ λέγουσιν. μήποτε
lo, publicly he speaks, and nothing to him they say.

ἀληθῶς ἔγνωσαν οἱ ἄρχοντες, ὅτι οὗτός ἐστιν
Truly [1]have [6]recognized [2]those [3]who [4]rule, that this is

[x]ἀληθῶς[ll] ὁ χριστός; 27 ἀλλὰ τοῦτον οἴδαμεν πόθεν ἐστίν·
truly the Christ? But this one we know whence he is.

ὁ.δὲ.χριστὸς ὅταν [y]ἔρχηται,[ll] οὐδεὶς γινώσκει πόθεν ἐστίν.
But the Christ, whenever he may come, no one knows whence he is.

28 Ἔκραξεν οὖν ἐν τῷ ἱερῷ διδάσκων ὁ Ἰησοῦς καὶ λέγων,
[3]Cried [2]therefore [4]in [5]the [6]temple [7]teaching [1]Jesus and saying,

Κἀμὲ οἴδατε, καὶ οἴδατε πόθεν εἰμί· καὶ ἀπ' ἐμαυτοῦ οὐκ
Both me ye know, and ye know whence I am; and of myself [3]not

ἐλήλυθα, ἀλλ' ἔστιν ἀληθινὸς ὁ πέμψας με, ὃν ὑμεῖς
[1][2]have come, but [4]is [3]true [2]who [2]sent me, whom ye

οὐκ.οἴδατε· 29 ἐγώ.[z]δὲ[ll] οἶδα αὐτόν, ὅτι παρ' αὐτοῦ εἰμι,
know not. But I know him, because from him I am,

κἀκεῖνός με [a]ἀπέστειλεν.[ll] 30 Ἐζήτουν οὖν αὐτὸν πιά-
and he me sent. They were seeking therefore him to

σαι· καὶ οὐδεὶς ἐπέβαλεν ἐπ' αὐτὸν τὴν χεῖρα, ὅτι οὔπω
take, but no one laid upon him [his] hand, because not yet

ἐληλύθει ἡ.ὥρα.αὐτοῦ. 31 [b]Πολλοὶ.δὲ ἐκ τοῦ ὄχλου ἐπίστευ-
had come his hour. But many of the crowd believed

σαν,[ll] εἰς αὐτόν, καὶ ἔλεγον, [c]Ὅτι[ll] ὁ χριστὸς ὅταν ἔλθῃ
on him, and said, The Christ, when he comes,

[d]μήτι[ll] πλείονα σημεῖα [e]τούτων[ll] ποιήσει ὧν οὗτος
[4]more [5]signs [6]than [7]these [1]will [2]he [3]do which this [man]

---

[n] — καὶ εἶπεν LTTrA.   [o] — ὁ TTrA.   [P] θαυμάζετε διὰ τοῦτο. (read ye wonder therefore.) GLTrW; — διὰ τοῦτο, ο T.   [q] Μωϋσῆς LTTrAW.   [r] Μωϋσέως LTTrAW.   [s] [ἐν] L. [t] + ὁ T.   [v] κρίνετε LTrA.   [w] Ἱεροσολυμειτῶν T.   [x] — ἀληθῶς GLTTrAW.   [y] ἔρχεται he comes E.   [z] — δὲ but GLTTrAW.   [a] ἀπέσταλκεν has sent T.   [b] Ἐκ τοῦ ὄχλου δὲ πολλοὶ ἐπίστευσαν LTrA; πολλοὶ δὲ ἐπίστευσαν ἐκ τοῦ ὄχλου T.   [c] — Ὅτι LTTrA.   [d] μὴ LTTrA.   [e] — τούτων (read ὧν than [these] which) LTTrAW.

ἐποίησεν‖; 32 Ἤκουσαν οἱ Φαρισαῖοι τοῦ ὄχλου γογγύζοντος
did? ³Heard ¹the ²Pharisees of the crowd murmuring

περὶ αὐτοῦ ταῦτα· καὶ ἀπέστειλαν ᵍοἱ Φαρισαῖοι καὶ
²concerning ⁴him ¹those ²things, and ⁵sent ¹the ²Pharisees ³and

οἱ ἀρχιερεῖς ὑπηρέτας,‖ ἵνα πιάσωσιν αὐτόν. 33 εἶπεν
⁴the ⁵chief ⁶priests officers, that they might take him. ³Said

οὖν ᵇαὐτοῖς‖ ὁ Ἰησοῦς, Ἔτι ʲμικρὸν χρόνον‖ μεθ' ὑμῶν
¹therefore ⁴to ⁵them ¹Jesus, Yet a little time with you

εἰμι, καὶ ὑπάγω πρὸς τὸν πέμψαντά με. 34 ζητήσετέ με καὶ
I am, and I go to him who sent me. Ye will seek me and

οὐχ.εὑρήσετεᵏ· καὶ ὅπου εἰμὶ ἐγὼ ὑμεῖς οὐ.δύνασθε ἐλθεῖν.
shall not find [me], and where ²am ¹I ye are unable to come.

35 Εἶπον οὖν οἱ Ἰουδαῖοι πρὸς ἑαυτούς, Ποῦ ᵏοὗτος
⁴Said ³therefore ¹the ²Jews among themselves, Where ²he

μέλλει‖ πορεύεσθαι ὅτι ᵐⁱἡμεῖς‖ οὐχ.εὑρήσομεν αὐτόν; μὴ εἰς
¹is about to go that we shall not find him? to

τὴν διασπορὰν τῶν Ἑλλήνων μέλλει πορεύεσθαι, καὶ
the dispersion among the Greeks is he about to go, and

διδάσκειν τοὺς Ἕλληνας; 36 τίς ἐστιν ⁿοὗτος ὁ λόγος‖ ὃν
teach the Greeks? What is this word which

εἶπεν, Ζητήσετέ με, καὶ οὐχ.εὑρήσετεᵏ· καὶ Ὅπου εἰμὶ ἐγὼ
he said, Ye will seek me, and shall not find [me]; and Where ²am ¹I

ὑμεῖς οὐ.δύνασθε ἐλθεῖν;
ye are unable to come?

37 Ἐν.δὲ τῇ ἐσχάτῃ ἡμέρᾳ τῇ μεγάλῃ τῆς ἑορτῆς εἱστήκει
And in the last ¹day ¹the ²great of the feast stood

ὁ Ἰησοῦς, καὶ ᵒἔκραξεν‖ λέγων, Ἐάν τις διψᾷ, ἐρχέσθω
Jesus, and cried, saying, If anyone thirst, let him come

ᴾπρός με‖ καὶ πινέτω· 38 ὁ πιστεύων εἰς ἐμέ, καθὼς εἶπεν
to me and drink. He that believes on me, as said

ἡ γραφή, ποταμοὶ ἐκ τῆς.κοιλίας.αὐτοῦ ῥεύσουσιν ὕδατος
the scripture, rivers out of his belly shall flow of ²water

ζῶντος. 39 Τοῦτο.δὲ εἶπεν περὶ τοῦ πνεύματος οὗ ᑫἔμελ-
¹living. But this he said concerning the Spirit which ⁵were

λον‖ λαμβάνειν οἱ ᵖπιστεύοντες‖ εἰς αὐτόν· οὔπω.γὰρ ἦν
⁶about ⁷to ⁸receive ¹those ²believing ³on ⁴him; for not⁷yet was

πνεῦμα ˢἅγιον‖ᵗ· ὅτι ᵛὁ‖ Ἰησοῦς ʷοὐδέπω‖ ἐδοξάσθη.
[the] ²Spirit ¹Holy‖, because Jesus not yet was glorified.

40 ˣπολλοὶ οὖν ἐκ τοῦ ὄχλου‖ ἀκούσαντες ʸτὸν λόγον‖
Many therefore out of the crowd having heard the word

ἔλεγον, ᶻΟὗτός ἐστιν ἀληθῶς ὁ προφήτης. 41 Ἄλλοι‖ ἔλεγον,
said, This is truly the prophet. Others said,

Οὗτός ἐστιν ὁ χριστός. ᵇἌλλοι‖ ᶜδὲ‖ ἔλεγον, Μὴ γὰρ ἐκ
This is the Christ. ²Others ¹and said, ³Then ⁵out ⁶of

τῆς Γαλιλαίας ὁ χριστὸς ἔρχεται; 42 ᵈοὐχὶ‖ ἡ γραφὴ εἶπεν,
⁷Galilee ²the ³Christ ¹comes? ⁴Not ¹⁰the ¹¹scripture ⁸said,

ὅτι ἐκ τοῦ σπέρματος ᵉΔαβίδ,‖ καὶ ἀπὸ Βηθλεὲμ τῆς κώμης
that out of the seed of David, and from Bethlehem the village

ὅπου ἦν ᵉΔαβίδ,‖ ᶠᵃὁ χριστὸς ἔρχεται;‖ 43 Σχίσμα οὖν ᵍᵃἐν
where ²was ¹David, the Christ comes? A division therefore in

Right column (English translation)

hath done? 32 The Pharisees heard that the people murmured such things concerning him; and the Pharisees and the chief priests sent officers to take him. 33 Then said Jesus unto them, Yet a little while am I with you, and then I go unto him that sent me. 34 Ye shall seek me, and shall not find me: and where I am, thither ye cannot come. 35 Then said the Jews among themselves, Whither will he go, that we shall not find him? will he go unto the dispersed among the Gentiles, and teach the Gentiles? 36 What manner of saying is this that he said, Ye shall seek me, and shall not find me: and where I am, thither ye cannot come?

37 In the last day, that great day of the feast, Jesus stood and cried, saying, If any man thirst, let him come unto me, and drink. 38 He that believeth on me, as the scripture hath said, out of his belly shall flow rivers of living water. 39 (But this spake he of the Spirit, which they that believe on him should receive: for the Holy Ghost was not yet given; because that Jesus was not yet glorified.) 40 Many of the people therefore, when they heard this saying, said, Of a truth this is the prophet. 41 Others said, This is the Christ. But some said, Shall Christ come out of Galilee? 42 Hath not the scripture said, That Christ cometh of the seed of David, and out of the town of Bethlehem, where David was? 43 So there was a division among

ᶠ ποιεῖ does T. ᵍ οἱ ἀρχιερεῖς καὶ οἱ Φαρισαῖοι ὑπηρέτας LTTrAW; ὑπηρέτας οἱ ἀρχιερεῖς καὶ οἱ Φαρισαῖοι T. ʰ — αὐτοῖς GLTTrAW. ⁱ χρόνον μικρὸν LTTrA. ᵏ + με me LA. ˡ μέλλει οὗτος T. ᵐ — ἡμεῖς (read εὑρή. we shall find) T. ⁿ ὁ λόγος οὗτος LTTrA. ᵒ ἔκραξεν T. ᵖ — πρός με T. ᑫ ἤμελλον T. ʳ πιστεύσαντες having believed LTrA. ˢ — ἅγιον LT[TrA]. ᵗ + δεδομένον given L. ᵛ — ὁ LTTrAW. ʷ οὔπω LTrA. ˣ ἐκ τοῦ ὄχλου οὖν [some] out of the crowd therefore LTTrA. ʸ τῶν λόγων τούτων these words (— τούτων W) LTTrAW. ᶻ + [ὅτι] A. ᵃ + [δὲ] and L. ᵇ οἱ they LTrA. ᶜ — δὲ T. ᵈ οὐχ LTrA. ᵉ Δαυὶδ GW; Δαυεὶδ LTTrA. ᶠᵃ ἔρχεται ὁ χριστός LTrA. ᵍᵃ ἐγένετο ἐν τῷ ὄχλῳ LTTrA.

the people because of
him. 44 And some of
them would have ta-
ken him; but no man
laid hands on him.
45 Then came the offi-
cers to the chief priests
and Pharisees; and
they said unto them,
Why have ye not
brought him? 46 The
officers answered, Ne-
ver man spake like this
man. 47 Then answer-
ed them the Pharisees,
Are ye also deceived?
48 Have any of the
rulers or of the Pha-
risees believed on him?
49 But this people who
knoweth not the law
are cursed. 50 Nicode-
mus saith unto them,
(he that came to Jesus
by night, being one of
them,) 51 Doth our law
judge *any* man, before
it hear him, and know
what he doeth? 52 They
answered and said
unto him, Art thou
also of Galilee? Search,
and look: for out of
Galilee ariseth no pro-
phet. 53 And every
man went unto his
own house.

VIII. Jesus went
unto the mount of
Olives. 2 And early
in the morning, he
came again into the
temple, and all the
people came unto him;
and he sat down, and
taught them. 3 And
the scribes and Phari-
sees brought unto him
a woman taken in a-
dultery; and when
they had set her in the
midst, 4 they say unto
him, Master, this wo-
man was taken in a-
dultery, in the very
act. 5 Now Moses in
the law commanded
us, that such should
be stoned: but what
sayest thou? 6 This
they said, tempting
him, that they might
have to accuse him.

τῷ ὄχλῳ ἐγένετο‖ δι’ αὐτόν. 44 τινὲς δὲ ἤθελον ἐξ αὐτῶν
the crowd occurred because of him.   But some ⁵desired ¹of ²them

πιάσαι αὐτόν, ἀλλ’ οὐδεὶς ʰἐπέβαλεν‖ ἐπ’ αὐτὸν τὰς χεῖρας.
to take him,   but no one laid   ²on ³him ¹hands.

45 ἦλθον οὖν οἱ ὑπηρέται πρὸς τοὺς ἀρχιερεῖς καὶ Φαρι-
Came therefore the officers   to   the   chief priests   and Phari-

σαίους· καὶ εἶπον αὐτοῖς ἐκεῖνοι, ¹Διατί‖ οὐκ ἠγάγετε αὐτόν;
sees,   and ²said ³to ⁴them ¹they,   Why did ye not bring him?

46 Ἀπεκρίθησαν οἱ ὑπηρέται, Οὐδέποτε ᵏοὕτως ἐλάλησεν‖
³Answered ¹the ²officers,   Never   thus   spoke

ἄνθρωπος ¹ὡς οὗτος ᵐ ὁ ἄνθρωπος.‖ 47 Ἀπεκρίθησαν ⁿοὖν‖
man   as this   man.   ⁴Answered ³therefore

ᵒαὐτοῖς‖ οἱ Φαρισαῖοι, Μὴ καὶ ὑμεῖς πεπλάνησθε; 48 μή
⁵them ¹the ²Pharisees,   ⁴also ⁵ye ⁶have been deceived?

τις ἐκ τῶν ἀρχόντων ἐπίστευσεν εἰς αὐτόν, ἢ ἐκ τῶν
²Any ³one ⁴of ⁵the ⁶rulers ¹has believed on him, or of the

Φαρισαίων; 49 ᴾἀλλ’‖ ὁ ὄχλος οὗτος ὁ μὴ γινώσκων τὸν
Pharisees?   But   this crowd, which knows not the

νόμον �q ἐπικατάρατοί‖ εἰσιν. 50 Λέγει Νικόδημος πρὸς αὐτούς,
law, accursed are.   ²Says ¹Nicodemus to them,

ʳὁ ἐλθὼν ˢνυκτὸς‖ πρὸς αὐτόν,‖ ᵗ εἷς ὢν ἐξ αὐτῶν· 51 Μὴ
(he who came by night to him,   ²one ¹being of themselves,)

ὁ νόμος ἡμῶν κρίνει τὸν ἄνθρωπον, ἐὰν μὴ ἀκούσῃ ᵛπαρ’
²Our ³law ¹does judge the man,   unless it have heard from

αὐτοῦ πρότερον,‖ καὶ γνῷ τί ποιεῖ; 52 Ἀπεκρίθησαν καὶ
himself first,   and known what he does?   They answered and

ʷεἶπον‖ αὐτῷ, Μὴ καὶ σὺ ἐκ τῆς Γαλιλαίας εἶ; ˣἐρεύνησον‖
said to him, ³Also ²thou ⁴of ⁵Galilee ¹art?   Search

καὶ ἴδε, ὅτι ʸπροφήτης ἐκ τῆς Γαλιλαίας‖ ᶻοὐκ ἐγήγερται.‖
and look, ⁴hat a prophet out of   Galilee   has not arisen.

53 ᵃΚαὶ ἐπορεύθη ἕκαστος εἰς τὸν οἶκον αὐτοῦ.
And ²went ¹each to his house.

8 Ἰησοῦς δὲ ἐπορεύθη εἰς τὸ ὄρος τῶν ἐλαιῶν· 2 ὄρθρου δὲ
But Jesus went to the mount of Olives.   And at dawn

πάλιν παρεγένετο εἰς τὸ ἱερόν, καὶ πᾶς ὁ λαὸς ἤρχετο πρὸς
again he came into the temple, and all the people came to

αὐτόν· καὶ καθίσας ἐδίδασκεν αὐτούς. 3 ἄγουσιν δὲ οἱ
him;   and having sat down he was teaching them.   ⁷Bring ¹and ²the

γραμματεῖς καὶ οἱ Φαρισαῖοι πρὸς αὐτὸν γυναῖκα ἐν μοιχείᾳ
³scribes ⁴and ⁵the ⁶Pharisees   to   him a woman in adultery

κατειλημμένην, καὶ στήσαντες αὐτὴν ἐν μέσῳ, 4 λέγουσιν
having been taken, and having set her in [the] midst,   they say

αὐτῷ, Διδάσκαλε, αὕτη ἡ γυνὴ κατειλήφθη ᵇἐπαυτοφώρῳ‖
to him, Teacher,   this   woman was taken   in the very act

μοιχευομένη. 5 ἐν δὲ τῷ νόμῳ ᶜΜωσῆς‖ ἡμῖν ἐνετείλατο
committing adultery.   Now in the law Moses   us   commanded

τὰς τοιαύτας. ᵈλιθοβολεῖσθαι‖ σὺ οὖν τί λέγεις;ᵉ
such   to be stoned: thou therefore what sayest thou?

6 Τοῦτο δὲ ἔλεγον πειράζοντες αὐτὸν ἵνα ἔχωσιν κατη-
But this they said   tempting   him that they might have to ac-

---

ʰ ἔβαλεν LTTrA.   ¹ Διὰ τί LTrAW.   ᵏ ἐλάλησεν οὕτως LTTrA.   ˡ — ὡς οὗτος ὁ ἄνθρωπος L[TrA].   ᵐ + λαλεῖ speaks T.   ⁿ — οὖν TA.   ᵒ [αὐτοῖς] Tr.   ᴾ ἀλλὰ LTTrAW.
q ἐπάρατοί LTTrA.   ʳ — ὁ ἐλθὼν νυκτὸς πρὸς αὐτόν T.   ˢ — νυκτὸς LTrA.   ᵗ + πρότερον
formerly LTrA.   ᵛ πρῶτον παρ’ αὐτοῦ LTTrA.   ʷ εἶπαν LTTrA.   ˣ ἐραύνησον LTTrA.
ʸ ἐκ τῆς Γαλιλαίας προφήτης LT-A.   ˣ οὐκ ἐγείρεται does not arise LTTrA.   ᵃ — καὶ ἐπορεύθη . . . . ἀμάρτανε (viii. 11) [G]LTTrA.   ᵇ ἐπ’ αὐτοφώρῳ W.   ᶜ Μωϋσῆς W.   ᵈ λιθάζειν to
stone W.   ᵉ + περὶ αὐτῆς concerning her W.

γορεῖν αὐτοῦ. ὁ δὲ Ἰησοῦς κάτω κύψας, τῷ δακτύλῳ
cuse   him.   But Jesus having stooped down, with [his] finger

ἔγραφεν εἰς τὴν γῆν. 7 ὡς δὲ ἐπέμενον ἐρωτῶντες αὐτόν,
wrote   on the ground. But as they continued asking   him,

ἀνακύψας   εἶπεν πρὸς αὐτούς, Ὁ ἀναμάρτητος ὑ-
having lifted up himself he said to them,   The sinless one among

μῶν πρῶτος τὸν λίθον ἐπ᾽ αὐτῇ βαλέτω. 8 καὶ πάλιν
you ᵇfirst ⁴the ⁶stone ⁷at ⁸her ¹let ²him ³cast. And again

κάτω κύψας ἔγραφεν εἰς τὴν γῆν. 9 οἱ δὲ ἀκούσαντες,
having stooped down he wrote on the ground. But they having heard,

καὶ ὑπὸ τῆς συνειδήσεως ἐλεγχόμενοι, ἐξήρχοντο εἷς καθ᾽ εἷς,
and by the   conscience   being convicted, went out   one by one,

ἀρξάμενοι ἀπὸ τῶν πρεσβυτέρων, ἕως τῶν ἐσχάτων· καὶ
beginning from the elder ones   until the last ; and

κατελείφθη μόνος ὁ Ἰησοῦς, καὶ ἡ γυνὴ ἐν μέσῳ ἑστῶσα.
was left   alone Jesus, and the woman in [the] midst standing.

10 ἀνακύψας δὲ   ὁ Ἰησοῦς, καὶ μηδένα θεασάμενος
And ²having ³lifted ⁴up ⁵himself ¹Jesus, and ²no ³one   ¹seeing

πλὴν τῆς γυναικός, εἶπεν αὐτῇ, ᵍἩ γυνή, ποῦ εἰσιν ἐκεῖνοι
but   the woman, said to her, Woman, where are those

οἱ κατήγοροί σου, οὐδείς σε κατέκρινεν; 11 Ἡ δὲ εἶπεν,
thine accusers, ²no ³one ⁵thee ¹did ⁴condemn? And she said,

Οὐδείς, κύριε. Εἶπεν δὲ αὐτῇ ὁ Ἰησοῦς, Οὐδὲ ἐγώ σε κατα-
No one, Sir. And ²said ³to ⁴her ¹Jesus, Neither ²I ⁴thee ¹do

κρίνω· πορεύου καὶ μηκέτι ἁμάρτανε.
³condemn· go, and no more   sin.

12 Πάλιν οὖν ʰὁ Ἰησοῦς αὐτοῖς ἐλάλησεν, λέγων, Ἐγώ
Again therefore Jesus to them spoke,   saying, I

εἰμι τὸ φῶς τοῦ κόσμου· ὁ ἀκολουθῶν ⁱἐμοὶ οὐ μὴ
am the light of the world; he that follows   me   in no wise

ᵏπεριπατήσει ἐν τῇ σκοτίᾳ, ἀλλ᾽ ἕξει τὸ φῶς τῆς ζωῆς.
shall walk in the darkness, but shall have the light of the life.

13 Εἶπον οὖν αὐτῷ οἱ Φαρισαῖοι, Σὺ περὶ σεαυτοῦ
²Said ⁴therefore ⁸to ⁶him ¹the ²Pharisees, Thou concerning thyself

μαρτυρεῖς· ἡ μαρτυρία σου οὐκ ἔστιν ἀληθής. 14 Ἀπεκρίθη
bearest witness; thy witness is not   true. ²Answered

Ἰησοῦς καὶ εἶπεν αὐτοῖς, Κἂν ἐγὼ μαρτυρῶ περὶ ἐμαυτοῦ,
¹Jesus and said to them, Even if I bear witness concerning myself,

ἀληθής ἐστιν ἡ μαρτυρία μου, ὅτι οἶδα πόθεν ἦλθον καὶ
true   is   my witness, because I know whence I came and

ποῦ ὑπάγω· ὑμεῖς δὲ οὐκ οἴδατε πόθεν ἔρχομαι ᵐκαὶ ποῦ
whither I go: but ye know not whence I come and whither

ὑπάγω. 15 ὑμεῖς κατὰ τὴν σάρκα κρίνετε· ἐγὼ οὐ κρίνω
I go. Ye according to the flesh judge, I judge

οὐδένα. 16 καὶ ἐὰν κρίνω δὲ ἐγώ, ἡ κρίσις ἡ ἐμὴ ⁿἀληθής
no one. And if ²judge ³also ¹I, ⁵judgment ⁴my true

ἐστιν· ὅτι μόνος οὐκ εἰμί, ἀλλ᾽ ἐγὼ καὶ ὁ πέμψας με °πα-
is, because alone I am not, but I and the ²who ³sent ⁴me ¹Fa-

τήρ. 17 καὶ ἐν τῷ νόμῳ δὲ τῷ ὑμετέρῳ ᵖγέγραπται, ὅτι
ther. And in ²law ³also ¹your   it has been written, that

δύο ἀνθρώπων ἡ μαρτυρία ἀληθής ἐστιν. 18 ἐγώ εἰμι ὁ
of two men the witness true is. I am [one] who

But Jesus stooped down, and with his finger wrote on the ground, as though he heard them not. 7 So when they continued asking him, he lifted up himself, and said unto them, He that is without sin among you, let him first cast a stone at her. 8 And again he stooped down, and wrote on the ground. 9 And they which heard it, being convicted by their own conscience, went out one by one, beginning at the eldest, even unto the last : and Jesus was left alone, and the woman standing in the midst. 10 When Jesus had lifted up himself, and saw none but the woman, he said unto her, Woman, where are those thine accusers? hath no man condemned thee? 11 She said, No man, Lord. And Jesus said unto her, Neither do I condemn thee: go, and sin no more.

12 Then spake Jesus again unto them, saying, I am the light of the world: he that followeth me shall not walk in darkness, but shall have the light of life. 13 The Pharisees therefore said unto him, Thou bearest record of thyself; thy record is not true. 14 Jesus answered and said unto them, Though I bear record of myself, yet my record is true : for I know whence I came, and whither I go; but ye cannot tell whence I come, and whither I go. 15 Ye judge after the flesh ; I judge no man. 16 And yet if I judge, my judgment is true: for I am not alone, but I and the Father that sent me. 17 It is also written in your law, that the testimony of two men is true. 18 I am one that bear witness of

---

ᶠ οὖσα being W.   ᵍ — Ἡ γυνή W.   ʰ αὐτοῖς ἐλάλησεν ὁ ([ὁ] Tr) Ἰησοῦς LTTᵣA.
ⁱ μοι LTr.   ᵏ περιπατήσῃ should walk LTTᵣAW.   ˡ — δὲ but T.   ᵐ ἢ or GTTᵣAW.
ⁿ ἀληθινή LTTᵣA.   ° — πατήρ (read he who sent me) T.   ᵖ γεγραμμένον ἐστιν it is
written T.

myself, and the Father that sent me beareth witness of me. 19 Then said they unto him, Where is thy Father? Jesus answered, Ye neither know me, nor my Father: if ye had known me, ye should have known my Father also. 20 These words spake Jesus in the treasury, as he taught in the temple; and no man laid hands on him; for his hour was not yet come.

μαρτυρῶν περὶ ἐμαυτοῦ, καὶ μαρτυρεῖ περὶ ἐμοῦ ὁ
bears witness concerning myself, and ⁶bears ⁷witness ⁸concerning, ⁹me ¹the
πέμψας με πατήρ. 19 Ἔλεγον οὖν αὐτῷ, Ποῦ ἐστιν ὁ
³who ⁴sent ⁵me ²Father. They said therefore to him, Where is
πατήρ σου; Ἀπεκρίθη ⁹ὁ‖ Ἰησοῦς, Οὔτε ἐμὲ οἴδατε οὔτε τὸν
thy Father? ²Answered ¹Jesus, Neither me ye know nor
πατέρα μου· εἰ ἐμὲ ᾔδειτε, καὶ τὸν πατέρα μου ʳᾔδειτε ἄν.‖
my Father. If me ye had known, also my Father ye would have known.
20 Ταῦτα τὰ ῥήματα ἐλάλησεν ˢὁ Ἰησοῦς‖ ἐν τῷ γαζοφυλακίῳ,
These words spoke Jesus in the treasury,
διδάσκων ἐν τῷ ἱερῷ· καὶ οὐδεὶς ἐπίασεν αὐτόν, ὅτι οὔπω
teaching in the temple; and no one took him, for not yet
ἐληλύθει ἡ ὥρα αὐτοῦ.
had come his hour.

21 Εἶπεν οὖν πάλιν αὐτοῖς ᵗὁ Ἰησοῦς,‖ Ἐγὼ ὑπάγω,
²Said ³therefore ⁴again ⁵to ⁶them ¹Jesus, I go away,
καὶ ζητήσετέ με, καὶ ἐν τῇ ἁμαρτίᾳ ὑμῶν ἀποθανεῖσθε· ὅπου
and ye will seek me, and in your sin ye will die; where

21 Then said Jesus again unto them, I go my way, and ye shall seek me, and shall die in your sins: whither I go, ye cannot come. 22 Then said the Jews, Will he kill himself? because he saith, Whither I go, ye cannot come. 23 And he said unto them, Ye are from beneath; I am from above: ye are of this world; I am not of this world. 24 I said therefore unto you, that ye shall die in your sins: for if ye believe not that I am he, ye shall die in your sins. 25 Then said they unto him, Who art thou? And Jesus saith unto them, Even the same that I said unto you from the beginning. 26 I have many things to say and to judge of you: but he that sent me is true; and I speak to the world those things which I have heard of him. 27 They understood not that he spake to them of the Father. 28 Then said Jesus unto them, When ye have lifted up the Son of man, then shall ye know that I am he, and that I do nothing of myself; but as my Father hath taught me, I speak these things. 29 And he that sent me is with me: the Father hath not left me alone; for I do

ἐγὼ ὑπάγω ὑμεῖς οὐ δύνασθε ἐλθεῖν. 22 Ἔλεγον οὖν οἱ
I go ye are unable to come. ⁴Said ³therefore ¹the
Ἰουδαῖοι, Μήτι ἀποκτενεῖ ἑαυτόν, ὅτι λέγει, Ὅπου ἐγὼ ὑπάγω
²Jews, Will he kill himself, that he says, Where I go
ὑμεῖς οὐ δύνασθε ἐλθεῖν; 23 Καὶ ˣεἶπεν‖ αὐτοῖς, Ὑμεῖς ἐκ
ye are unable to come? And he said to them, Ye from
τῶν κάτω ἐστέ, ἐγὼ ἐκ τῶν ἄνω εἰμί· ὑμεῖς ἐκ ʷτοῦ κόσμου
beneath are, I from above am; Ye of ²world
τούτου‖ ἐστέ, ἐγὼ οὐκ εἰμὶ ἐκ τοῦ κόσμου τούτου. 24 εἶπον
¹this are, I am not of this world. I said
οὖν ὑμῖν ὅτι ἀποθανεῖσθε ἐν ταῖς ἁμαρτίαις ὑμῶν· ἐὰν γὰρ
therefore to you that ye will die in your sins; for if
μὴ πιστεύσητε ὅτι ἐγώ εἰμι, ἀποθανεῖσθε ἐν ταῖς ἁμαρτίαις
ye believe not that I am [he], ye will die in your sins
ὑμῶν. 25 Ἔλεγον οὖν αὐτῷ, Σὺ τίς εἶ; ˣΚαὶ‖ εἶπεν
your. They said therefore to him, ³Thou ¹who ²art? And ²said
αὐτοῖς ʸὁ‖ Ἰησοῦς, Τὴν ἀρχὴν ὅ τι καὶ λαλῶ ὑμῖν.
³to ⁴them ¹Jesus, Altogether that which also I say to you.
26 πολλὰ ἔχω περὶ ὑμῶν λαλεῖν καὶ κρίνειν· ἀλλ᾽ ὁ
Many things I have concerning you to say and to judge; but he who
πέμψας με ἀληθής ἐστιν, κἀγὼ ἃ ἤκουσα παρ᾽ αὐτοῦ, ταῦτα
sent me true is, and I what I heard from him, these things
ᶻλέγω‖ εἰς τὸν κόσμον. 27 Οὐκ ἔγνωσαν ὅτι τὸν πατέρα αὐτοῖς
I say to the world. They knew not that the Father to them
ἔλεγεν. 28 Εἶπεν οὖν ᵃαὐτοῖς‖ ὁ Ἰησοῦς, Ὅταν ὑψώ-
he spoke of. ³Said ²therefore ⁴to ⁵them ¹Jesus, When ye shall have
σητε τὸν υἱὸν τοῦ ἀνθρώπου, τότε γνώσεσθε ὅτι ἐγώ εἰμι·
lifted up the Son of man, then ye shall know that I am [he],
καὶ ἀπ᾽ ἐμαυτοῦ ποιῶ οὐδέν, ἀλλὰ καθὼς ἐδίδαξέν με ὁ
and from myself I do nothing, but as ³taught ⁴me the
πατήρ ᵇμου,‖ ταῦτα λαλῶ. 29 καὶ ὁ πέμψας με, μετ᾽
¹my ²Father, these things I speak. And he who sent me, with
ἐμοῦ ἐστιν· οὐκ ἀφῆκέν με μόνον ᶜὁ πατήρ,‖ ὅτι ἐγὼ τὰ
me is; ³left ⁵not ⁴me ⁶alone ¹the ²Father, because I the things

---

q — ὁ GLTTrAW.   ʳ ἂν ᾔδειτε LTTrA.   ˢ — ὁ Ἰησοῦς (read he spoke) GLTTrAW.
ᵗ — ὁ Ἰησοῦς (read he said) LTTrAW.   ᵛ ἔλεγεν LTTrA.   ʷ τούτου τοῦ κόσμου LTrA.
ˣ — καὶ LTTrAW.   ʸ [ὁ] Tr.   ᶻ λαλῶ LTTrA.   ᵃ — αὐτοῖς LTTrA.   ᵇ — μου (read the
Father) LTTrA.   ᶜ — ὁ πατήρ (read he left not) LTTrA.

ἀρεστὰ αὐτῷ ποιῶ πάντοτε. 30 Ταῦτα αὐτοῦ.λαλοῦντος
pleasing to him do always. ⁴These ⁵things ¹as ²he ³spoke

πολλοὶ ἐπίστευσαν εἰς αὐτόν.
many believed on him.

31 Ἔλεγεν οὖν ὁ Ἰησοῦς πρὸς τοὺς πεπιστευκότας αὐτῷ
³Said ₁ ²therefore ¹Jesus to the ²who ³had ⁴believed ⁵on ⁶him

Ἰουδαίους, Ἐὰν ὑμεῖς μείνητε ἐν τῷ λόγῳ τῷ ἐμῷ, ἀληθῶς
¹Jews, If ye abide in ²word ¹my, truly

μαθηταί μου ἐστέ· 32 καὶ γνώσεσθε τὴν ἀλήθειαν, καὶ ἡ
²disciples ¹my ye are. And ye shall know the truth, and the

ἀλήθεια ἐλευθερώσει ὑμᾶς. 33 Ἀπεκρίθησαν ᵈαὐτῷ,ᵇ Σπέρμα
truth shall set free you. They answered him, ²Seed

Ἀβραάμ ἐσμεν, καὶ οὐδενὶ δεδουλεύκαμεν πώποτε· πῶς
¹Abraham's we are, and to anyone have been under bondage never; how
                  (lit. to no one)

σὺ λέγεις, Ὅτι ἐλεύθεροι γενήσεσθε; 34 Ἀπεκρίθη αὐτοῖς
²thou ¹sayest, Free ye shall become? ²Answered ³them

ᵉὁ Ἰησοῦς, Ἀμὴν ἀμὴν λέγω ὑμῖν, ὅτι πᾶς ὁ ποιῶν
¹Jesus, Verily verily I say to you, that everyone that practises

τὴν ἁμαρτίαν δοῦλός ἐστιν τῆς ἁμαρτίας. 35 ὁ.δὲ δοῦλος
sin a bondman is of sin. Now the bondman

οὐ.μένει ἐν τῇ οἰκίᾳ εἰς.τὸν.αἰῶνα· ὁ υἱὸς μένει εἰς.τὸν.αἰῶνα.
abides not in the house for ever; the Son abides for ever.

36 ἐὰν οὖν ὁ υἱὸς ὑμᾶς ἐλευθερώσῃ, ὄντως ἐλεύθεροι ἔσ-
If therefore the Son ³you ¹shall ²set free, really free ye

εσθε. 37 οἶδα ὅτι σπέρμα Ἀβραάμ ἐστε· ἀλλὰ ζητεῖτέ με
shall be. I know that ²seed ¹Abraham's ye are; but ye seek me

ἀποκτεῖναι, ὅτι ὁ λόγος ὁ ἐμὸς οὐ.χωρεῖ ἐν ὑμῖν. 38 ᶠἐγὼ
to kill, because ²word ¹my has no entrance in you. I

ᵍὁ ἑώρακα παρὰ τῷ.πατρί.ᵍμου λαλῶ· καὶ ὑμεῖς οὖν ʰὁ
what I have seen with my Father speak; and ye therefore what

ἑωράκατε παρὰ ᶦτῷ.πατρὶ.ὑμῶν ποιεῖτε. 39 Ἀπεκρίθησαν
ye have seen with your father do., They answered

καὶ ᵏεἶπον αὐτῷ, Ὁ.πατὴρ.ἡμῶν Ἀβραάμ ἐστιν. Λέγει αὐτοῖς
and said to him, ³Our ⁴Father ¹Abraham ²is. ⁶Says ⁷to ⁸them

ᶦὁ Ἰησοῦς, Εἰ τέκνα τοῦ Ἀβραὰμ ᵐἦτε, τὰ ἔργα τοῦ.Ἀβραὰμ
⁵Jesus, If children of Abraham ye were, the works of Abraham

ἐποιεῖτε.ⁿἄν· ᵖ 40 νῦν.δὲ ζητεῖτέ με ἀποκτεῖναι, ἄνθρωπον ὃς
ye would do; but now ye seek me to kill, a man who

τὴν ἀλήθειαν ὑμῖν λελάληκα, ἣν ἤκουσα παρὰ τοῦ θεοῦ·
the truth to you has spoken, which I heard from God:

τοῦτο Ἀβραὰμ οὐκ.ἐποίησεν. 41 ὑμεῖς ποιεῖτε τὰ ἔργα τοῦ
this Abraham did not. Ye do the works

πατρὸς.ὑμῶν. ᵒΕἶπον ᵖοὖν αὐτῷ, Ἡμεῖς ἐκ πορνείας ᑫοὐ
of your father. They said therefore to him, We of fornication ²not

γεγεννήμεθα. ἕνα πατέρα ἔχομεν, τὸν θεόν. 42 Εἶπεν ʳοὖν
¹have been born; one Father we have, God. ³Said ²therefore

αὐτοῖς ˢὁ Ἰησοῦς, Εἰ ὁ θεὸς ᵗ πατὴρ ὑμῶν ἦν, ἠγαπᾶτε.ἂν
⁴to ⁵them ¹Jesus, If God Father of you were, ye would have loved

ἐμέ· ἐγὼ.γὰρ ἐκ τοῦ θεοῦ ἐξῆλθον καὶ ἥκω· οὐδὲ.γὰρ ἀπ'
me, for I from God came forth and am come; for neither of

ἐμαυτοῦ ἐλήλυθα, ἀλλ' ἐκεῖνός με ἀπέστειλεν. 43 ᵛδιατί τὴν
myself have I come, but he ²me ¹sent. Why

ᵈ πρὸς αὐτόν to him LTTrA.   ᵉ — ὁ L[Tr].   ᶠ ἃ ἐγὼ LTTr; ἐγὼ ἃ Λ.   ᵍ — μου (read
the Father) LTTrA.   ʰ ἃ ἠκούσατε what ye have heard LTTrA.   ᶦ τοῦ πατρὸς the father
LTTrA.   ᵏ εἶπαν LTTrA.   ᶦ [ὁ] Tr.   ᵐ ἐστε ye are GLTTrA.   ᵖ — ἂν GTTrA.   ᵒ εἶπαν T.
ᵖ — οὖν LTTrA.   ᑫ οὐκ ἐγεννήθημεν were not born LTrA.   ᵛ̶ — οὖν GLTTrA..   ˢ — ὁ L[Tr]
ᵗ + ὁ the ι.   ᵛ διὰ τί LTrA.

do ye not understand my speech? *even because ye cannot hear my word. 44 Ye are of *your* father the devil, and the lusts of your father ye will do. He was a murderer from the beginning, and abode not in the truth, because there is no truth in him. When he speaketh a lie, he speaketh of his own: for he is a liar, and the father of it. 45 And because I tell *you* the truth, ye believe me not. 46 Which of you convinceth me of sin? And if I say the truth, why do ye not believe me? 47 He that is of God heareth God's words: ye therefore hear *them* not, because ye are not of God. 48 Then answered the Jews, and said unto him, Say we not well that thou art a Samaritan, and hast a devil? 49 Jesus answered, I have not a devil; but I honour my Father, and ye do dishonour me. 50 And I seek not mine own glory: there is one that seeketh and judgeth. 51 Verily, verily, I say unto you, If a man keep my saying, he shall never see death. 52 Then said the Jews unto him, Now we know that thou hast a devil. Abraham is dead, and the prophets; and thou sayest, If a man keep my saying, he shall never taste of death. 53 Art thou greater than our father Abraham, which is dead? and the prophets are dead: whom makest thou thyself? 54 Jesus answered, If I honour myself, my honour is nothing: it is my Father that honoureth me; of whom ye say, that he is your God: 55 yet ye have not known him; but I know him: and if I

λαλιὰν τὴν ἐμὴν οὐ‿γινώσκετε; ὅτι οὐ‿δύνασθε ἀκούειν τὸν
²speech ‵my ′my do ye not know? Because ye are unable to hear

λόγον τὸν ἐμόν. 44 ὑμεῖς ἐκʷ πατρὸς τοῦ διαβόλου ἐστέ,
²word ‵my.   Ye of [the] father ,the devil are,

καὶ τὰς ἐπιθυμίας τοῦ‿πατρὸς‿ὑμῶν θέλετε ποιεῖν. ἐκεῖνος
and the lusts   of your father   ye desire to do.   He

ἀνθρωποκτόνος ἦν ἀπ' ἀρχῆς, καὶ ἐν τῇ ἀληθείᾳ ˣοὐχ‖
a murderer   was from [the] beginning, and in the truth   ²not

ἕστηκεν· ὅτι οὐκ.ἔστιν ἀλήθεια ἐν αὐτῷ. ὅταν λαλῇ
¹has stood, because there is not truth in him. Whenever he may speak

τὸ ψεῦδος, ἐκ τῶν.ἰδίων λαλεῖ· ὅτι ψεύστης ἐστὶν καὶ ὁ
falsehood, from his own he speaks; for a liar he is and the

πατὴρ αὐτοῦ. 45 ἐγὼ δὲ ὅτι τὴν ἀλήθειαν λέγωʸ, οὐ
father of it.   ³I ¹and ²because the truth speak, ³not

πιστεύετέ μοι. 46 τίς ἐξ ὑμῶν ἐλέγχει με περὶ ἁμαρτίας;
¹ye ²do believe me. Which of you convinces me concerning sin?

εἰ.ᶻδὲ‖ ἀλήθειαν λέγω, ᵃδιατί‖ ὑμεῖς οὐ.πιστεύετέ μοι; 47 ὁ
But if truth I speak, why ²ye ¹do ³not believe me? He that

ὢν ἐκ τοῦ θεοῦ τὰ ῥήματα τοῦ θεοῦ ἀκούει· διὰ.τοῦτο ὑμεῖς
is of God the words of God hears: therefore ye

οὐκ.ἀκούετε, ὅτι ἐκ τοῦ θεοῦ οὐκ.ἐστέ. 48 Ἀπεκρίθησαν
hear not, because of God ye are not.   Answered

ᵇοὖν‖ οἱ Ἰουδαῖοι καὶ ᶜεἶπον‖ αὐτῷ, Οὐ καλῶς λέγομεν ἡμεῖς
therefore the Jews and said to him, ³Not ⁴well ¹say ²we

ὅτι ᵈΣαμαρείτης‖ εἶ σύ, καὶ δαιμόνιον ἔχεις; 49 ²Ἀπεκρίθη
that a Samaritan ²art ¹thou, and a demon hast?   ²Answered

Ἰησοῦς, Ἐγὼ δαιμόνιον οὐκ.ἔχω, ἀλλὰ τιμῶ τὸν.πατέρα.μου,
¹Jesus, I a demon have not; but I honour my Father,

καὶ ὑμεῖς ἀτιμάζετέ με. 50 ἐγὼ.δὲ οὐ.ζητῶ τὴν.δόξαν.μου·
and ye dishonour me.   But I seek not my glory:

ἔστιν ὁ ζητῶν καὶ κρίνων. 51 ἀμὴν ἀμὴν λέγω ὑμῖν, ἐάν
there is he who seeks and judges. Verily verily I say to you, If

τις τὸν ᵉλόγον τὸν ἐμὸν‖ τηρήσῃ, θάνατον οὐ.μὴ θεωρήσῃ
anyone ³word ²my ¹keep, death in 2o wise shall he see

εἰς.τὸν.αἰῶνα. 52 ᶠΕἶπον‖ ᵍοὖν‖ αὐτῷ οἱ Ἰουδαῖοι, Νῦν
for ever.   ⁴Said ³therefore ⁵to ⁶him ¹the ²Jews, Now

ἐγνώκαμεν ὅτι δαιμόνιον ἔχεις. Ἀβραὰμ ἀπέθανεν καὶ οἱ
we know that a demon thou hast. Abraham died and the

προφῆται, καὶ σὺ λέγεις, Ἐάν τις τὸν.λόγον.μου τηρήσῃ,
prophets, and thou sayest, If anyone ²my ¹word ¹keep,

οὐ.μὴ ʰγεύσεται‖ θανάτου εἰς.τὸν.αἰῶνα. 53 μὴ σὺ μείζων
in no wise shall he taste of death for ever.   ²Thou ³greater

εἶ τοῦ.πατρὸς.ἡμῶν Ἀβραάμ, ὅστις ἀπέθανεν; καὶ οἱ προ
¹art than our father Abraham, who died? and the pro

φῆται ἀπέθανον· τίνα σεαυτὸν ᶦσὺ‖ ποιεῖς; 54 Ἀπεκρίθη
phets died! whom ³thyself ²thou ¹makest?   ¹Answered

Ἰησοῦς, Ἐὰν ἐγὼ ᵏδοξάζω‖ ἐμαυτόν, ἡ.δόξα.μου οὐδέν ἐστιν·
¹Jesus, If I glorify myself, my glory nothing is;

ἔστιν ὁ.πατήρ.μου ὁ δοξάζων με, ὃν ὑμεῖς λέγετε, ὅτι
it is my Father who glorifies me, [of] whom ye say, that

θεὸς ¹ὑμῶν‖ ἐστιν, 55 καὶ οὐκ.ἐγνώκατε αὐτόν, ἐγὼ.δὲ οἶδα
²God ¹your he is.   And ye have not known him, but I know

ʷ + τοῦ the GLTTrA.   ˣ οὐκ T.   ʸ + [ὑμῖν] to thee L.   ᶻ — δὲ but GLTTrA.
ᵃ διὰ τί LTrA.   ᵇ — οὖν GLTTrA.   ᶜ εἶπαν LTTrA.   ᵈ Σαμαρίτης T.   ᵉ ἐμὸν λόγον LTTrA.
ᶠ εἶπαν T.   ᵍ — οὖν LTTrA.   ʰ γεύσηται should he taste GLTTrAW.   ᶦ — σὺ (read
ποιεῖς makest thou) GLTTrA.   ᵏ δοξάσω shall glorify LTTrA.   ¹ ἡμῶν our TTrAW.

αὐτόν· ᵐκαὶ ἐὰνⁿ εἴπω ὅτι οὐκ.οἶδα αὐτόν, ἔσομαι ὅμοιος
him;　　and if　　I say　that I know not　him,　I shall be　like

ⁿὑμῶν,ⁿ ψεύστης· °ἀλλ'ⁿ οἶδα αὐτόν, καὶ τὸν.λόγον.αὐτοῦ
you,　　a liar.　　But I know him,　and　　his word

τηρῶ. 56 Ἀβραὰμ ὁ.πατὴρ.ὑμῶν ἠγαλλιάσατο ἵνα ᴾἴδῃⁿ
I keep.　　Abraham　your Father　　exulted　in that he should see

τὴν ἡμέραν τὴν ἐμήν· καὶ εἶδεν καὶ ἐχάρη. 57 ᑫΕἶπονⁿ οὖν
²day　　ˡmy,　ˡand he saw and rejoiced.　　Said　　therefore

οἱ Ἰουδαῖοι πρὸς αὐτόν, Πεντήκοντα ἔτη οὔπω ἔχεις,
the Jews　　to　him,　　Fifty　years [old] not yet art thou,

καὶ Ἀβραὰμ ἑώρακας; 58 Εἶπεν αὐτοῖς ʳὁⁿ Ἰησοῦς, Ἀμὴν
and Abraham hast thou seen?　²Said　³to ⁴them　　ˡJesus,　Verily

ἀμὴν λέγω ὑμῖν, πρὶν Ἀβραὰμ γενέσθαι ἐγώ εἰμι. 59 Ἦραν
verily I say to you, Before　Abraham　was　　I am.　They took up

οὖν λίθους ἵνα βάλωσιν ἐπ' αὐτόν· Ἰησοῦς.δὲ ἐκρύβη,
therefore stones that they might cast at　him;　but Jesus hid himself,

καὶ ἐξῆλθεν ἐκ τοῦ ἱεροῦ, ˢδιελθὼν διὰ μέσου αὐτῶν·
and went forth out of the temple,　going　through the midst of them,

καὶ παρῆγεν οὕτως.ⁿ
and ²passed ³on ˡthus.

9 Καὶ παράγων εἶδεν ἄνθρωπον τυφλὸν ἐκ γενετῆς. 2 καὶ
And passing on he saw　a man　blind from birth.　And

ἠρώτησαν αὐτὸν οἱ.μαθηταὶ.αὐτοῦ λέγοντες, ᵗῬαββί,ⁿ τίς
³asked　⁴him　ˡhis ²disciples　　saying,　　Rabbi,　who

ἥμαρτεν, οὗτος ἢ οἱ.γονεῖς.αὐτοῦ, ἵνα τυφλὸς γεννηθῇ;
sinned,　this [man] or　his parents,　that blind he should be born?

3 Ἀπεκρίθη ᵘὁⁿ Ἰησοῦς, Οὔτε οὗτος ἥμαρτεν οὔτε οἱ.γονεῖς
²Answered　ˡJesus,　Neither this [man] sinned　nor　²parents

αὐτοῦ ἀλλ' ἵνα φανερωθῇ τὰ ἔργα τοῦ θεοῦ ἐν αὐτῷ.
ˡhis;　but that should be manifested the works of God in him.

4 ᵛἐμὲⁿ δεῖ ἐργάζεσθαι τὰ ἔργα τοῦ πέμψαντός ʷμε
²Me ⁱit ²behoves　to work　the works of him who sent　me

ἕως ἡμέρα ἐστίν· ἔρχεται νύξ, ὅτε οὐδεὶς δύναται ἐργάζεσθαι.
while day　it is;　²comes ˡnight, when no one　is able　to work.

5 ὅταν ἐν τῷ κόσμῳ ὦ, φῶς εἰμι τοῦ κόσμου. 6 Ταῦ-
While in the world I may be, [the] light I am of the world.　These

τα εἰπών, ἔπτυσεν χαμαί, καὶ ἐποίησεν πηλὸν ἐκ
things having said, he spat on [the] ground, and made　clay　of

τοῦ πτύσματος, καὶ ἐπέχρισεν ˣ τὸν πηλὸν ἐπὶ τοὺς ὀφθαλμοὺς
the　spittle,　and · applied　the clay　to the　eyes

ʸτοῦ τυφλοῦ·ⁿ 7 καὶ εἶπεν αὐτῷ, Ὕπαγε, ᶻνίψαιⁿ εἰς τὴν
of the blind [man]. And he said to him,　Go,　wash　in the

κολυμβήθραν τοῦ Σιλωάμ, ὃ ἑρμηνεύεται, ἀπεσταλμένος.
pool　　of Siloam, which is interpreted,　　Sent.

ἀπῆλθεν οὖν καὶ ἐνίψατο, καὶ ἦλθεν βλέπων. 8 Οἱ οὖν
He went therefore and washed, and came seeing.　The ²therefore

γείτονες καὶ οἱ θεωροῦντες αὐτὸν τὸ πρότερον ὅτι ᵃτυφλὸςⁿ
ˡneighbours and those who　saw　him　before　that blind

ἦν, ἔλεγον, Οὐχ οὗτός ἐστιν ὁ καθήμενος καὶ προσαιτῶν;
he was, said, ²Not ³this　ˡis he who was sitting and　begging?

9 Ἄλλοι ἔλεγον, Ὅτι οὗτός ἐστιν ἄλλοι.ᵇδέ,ⁿ ᶜᵈΟτιⁿ ὅμοιος
Some　said,　³He　ⁱit ²is,　but others,　　ⁱLike

should say, I know
him not, I shall be a
liar like unto you: but
I know him, and keep
his saying. 56 Your
father Abraham re-
joiced to see my day:
and he saw *it*, and was
glad. 57 Then said the
Jews unto him, Thou
art not yet fifty years
old, and hast thou seen
Abraham? 58 Jesus
said unto them, Verily,
verily, I say unto you,
Before Abraham was,
I am. 59 Then took
they up stones to cast
at him: but Jesus hid
himself, and went out
of the temple, going
through the midst of
them, and so passed
by.

IX. And as *Jesus*
passed by, he saw a
man which was blind
from *his* birth. 2 And
his disciples asked
him, saying, Master,
or his parents, that he
was born blind? 3 Je-
sus answered, Neither
hath this man sinned,
nor his parents : but
that the works of God
should be made mani-
fest in him. 4 I must
work the works of
him that sent me,
while it is day : the
night cometh, when no
man can work. 5 As
long as I am in the
world, I am the light
of the world. 6 When
he had thus spoken, he
spat on the ground,
and made clay of the
spittle, and he anoint-
ed the eyes of the blind
man with the clay,
7 and said unto him,
Go, wash in the pool
of Siloam, (which is by
interpretation, Sent.)
He went his way there-
fore, and washed, and
came seeing. 8 The
neighbours therefore,
and they which before
had seen him that he
was blind, said, Is not
this he that sat and
begged? 9 Some said,
This is he: others *said*,
He is like him : *but he*

ᵐ κἂν LTTr. ⁿ ὑμῖν LTr. ° ἀλλὰ LTTrAW. ᴾ εἴδῃ T. ᑫ Εἶπαν T. ʳ — ὁ TTr. ˢ — διελθὼν
.... οὕτως GLTTrA. ᵗ Ῥαββεί T. ᵘ — ὁ GLTTrAW. ᵛ ἡμᾶς us TTr. ʷ ἡμᾶς us ᴱ.
ˣ + αὐτοῦ on him LTTrA. ʸ — τοῦ τυφλοῦ [L]TTrA. ᶻ [νίψαι] L. ᵃ προσαίτης a beggar
GLTTrAW. ᵇ — δέ but [L]TTrA. ᶜ ἔλεγον, Οὐχί, ἀλλ' (ἀλλὰ T) said, No, but TTrA ;
ἔλεγον [Οὐχί, ἀλλ'] L.

said, I am he. 10 There-
fore said they unto
him, How were thine
eyes opened? 11 He
answered and said, A
man that is called Je-
sus made clay, and an-
ointed mine eyes, and
said unto me, Go to
the pool of Siloam,
and wash: and I went
and washed, and I re-
ceived sight. 12 Then
said they unto him,
Where is he? He said,
I know not.

αὐτῷ ἐστιν. Ἐκεῖνος[d] ἔλεγεν, Ὅτι ἐγώ εἰμι. 10 Ἔλεγον
*him   [1]he   [2]is.   He   said,   I   am [he].   They said

οὖν αὐτῷ, Πῶς[e] [f]ἀνεῴχθησάν[||] [g]σου[||] οἱ ὀφθαλμοί; 11 Ἀπ-
therefore to him, How   were opened   thine   eyes?   [2]An-

εκρίθη ἐκεῖνος [h]καὶ εἶπεν,[||] [i] Ἄνθρωπος [i] λεγόμενος Ἰησοῦς
swered [1]he   and said,   A man   called   Jesus

πηλὸν ἐποίησεν καὶ ἐπέχρισέν μου τοὺς ὀφθαλμούς, καὶ εἶπέν
clay   made   and applied to   mine   eyes,   and said

μοι,[k] Ὕπαγε εἰς [l]τὴν κολυμβήθραν τοῦ[||] Σιλωὰμ καὶ νίψαι.
to me,   Go to   the   pool   of Siloam and wash:

ἀπελθὼν [m]δὲ[||] καὶ νιψάμενος ἀνέβλεψα. 12 [n]Εἶπον[||] [o]οὖν[||]
[2]having [3]gone [1]and and   washed   I received sight.   They said therefore

αὐτῷ, Ποῦ ἐστιν ἐκεῖνος; Λέγει, Οὐκ.οἶδα.
to him, Where   is   he?   He says,   I know not.

13 Ἄγουσιν αὐτὸν πρὸς τοὺς Φαρισαίους, τόν ποτε
They bring *him   [1]to   [2]the   [3]Pharisees,   who once [was]

13 They brought to
the Pharisees him that
aforetime was blind.
14 And it was the
sabbath day when
Jesus made the clay,
and opened his eyes.
15 Then again the Pha-
risees also asked him
how he had received
his sight. He said un-
to them, He put clay
upon mine eyes, and I
washed, and do see.
16 Therefore said some
of the Pharisees, This
man is not of God, be-
cause he keepeth not
the sabbath day.
Others said, How can
a man that is a sinner
do such miracles? And
there was a division
among them. 17 They
say unto the blind man
again, What sayest
thou of him, that he
hath opened thine
eyes? He said, He is
a prophet. 18 But the
Jews did not believe
concerning him, that
he had been blind, and
received his sight, un-
til they called the pa-
rents of him that had
received his sight.
19 And they asked
them, saying, Is this
your son, who ye say
was born blind? how
then doth he now see?
20 His parents answer-
ed them and said, We
know that this is our
son, and that he was
born blind: 21 but by
what means he now

τυφλόν. 14 ἦν.δὲ σάββατον [q]ὅτε[||] τὸν πηλὸν ἐποίησεν ὁ
blind.   Now it was sabbath   when [3]the   [4]clay   [2]made

Ἰησοῦς καὶ ἀνέῳξεν αὐτοῦ τοὺς ὀφθαλμούς. 15 πάλιν οὖν
[1]Jesus and opened   his   eyes.   Again therefore

ἠρώτων αὐτὸν καὶ οἱ Φαρισαῖοι πῶς ἀνέβλεψεν. ὁ.δὲ εἶπεν
asked   him   also the Pharisees   how he received sight. And he said

αὐτοῖς, Πηλὸν ἐπέθηκεν [r]ἐπὶ τοὺς.ὀφθαλμούς.μου,[||] καὶ ἐνι-
to them, Clay   he put on   mine eyes,   and   I

ψάμην, καὶ βλέπω. 16 Ἔλεγον οὖν ἐκ τῶν Φαρισαίων τινές,
washed, and I see.   Said therefore [2]of [3]the   [4]Pharisees [1]some,

[s]Οὗτος ὁ ἄνθρωπος οὐκ.ἐστιν παρὰ τοῦ θεοῦ,[||] ὅτι τὸ σάββατον
This   man   is not   from   God,   for the sabbath

οὐ.τηρεῖ. Ἄλλοι ἔλεγον, Πῶς δύναται ἄνθρωπος ἁμαρτωλὸς
he does not keep. Others said,   How can   a man   a sinner

τοιαῦτα σημεῖα ποιεῖν; Καὶ σχίσμα ἦν ἐν αὐτοῖς. 17 Λέ-
such   signs   do?   And a division was among them.   They

γουσιν[t] τῷ τυφλῷ πάλιν, [v]Σὺ τί[||] λέγεις περὶ αὐτοῦ,
say   to the blind [man] again, [3]Thou [1]what [2]sayest concerning him,

ὅτι [w]ἤνοιξέν[||] σου τοὺς ὀφθαλμούς; Ὁ.δὲ εἶπεν, Ὅτι προ-
for he opened   thine   eyes?   And he said,   A pro-

φήτης ἐστίν. 18 Οὐκ.ἐπίστευσαν οὖν οἱ Ἰουδαῖοι περὶ
phet   he is.   [4]Did [5]not [6]believe [3]therefore [1]the [2]Jews   concerning

αὐτοῦ, ὅτι [x]τυφλὸς ἦν[||] καὶ ἀνέβλεψεν, ἕως.ὅτου ἐφώνησαν
him,   that [3]blind [1]he [2]was and received sight,   until   they called

τοὺς γονεῖς αὐτοῦ τοῦ ἀναβλέψαντος· 19 καὶ ἠρώτησαν
the parents of him who had received sight.   And they asked

αὐτοὺς λέγοντες, Οὗτός ἐστιν ὁ.υἱὸς.ὑμῶν ὃν ὑμεῖς λέγετε
them   saying,   [2]This [1]is   your son,   of whom ye   say

ὅτι τυφλὸς ἐγεννήθη; πῶς οὖν [y]ἄρτι βλέπει[||]; 20 Ἀπεκρίθη-
that blind   he was born? how then now does he see?   [3]Answered

σαν[z] [a]αὐτοῖς[||] οἱ.γονεῖς.αὐτοῦ καὶ [b]εἶπον,[||] Οἴδαμεν ὅτι οὗτός
*them   [1]his [2]parents   and said,   We know that this

ἐστιν ὁ.υἱὸς.ἡμῶν, καὶ ὅτι τυφλὸς ἐγεννήθη· 21 πῶς.δὲ νῦν
is   our son,   and that blind   he was born;   but how now

---

[d] + δὲ however L.   [e] + οὖν then [L]T[A].   [f] ἠνεῴχθησάν LTTrA.   [g] σοι E.   [h] — καὶ εἶπεν
[L]TTrA.   [i] + ὁ (read the man that is called) TTr[A].   [k] + ὅτι TTr.   [l] τὸν (read Go to Siloam) GLTTrA.   [m] οὖν therefore LTTrA.   [n] + [καὶ] and Tr.   [o] εἶπαν LTTrA.   [p] — οὖν LTTrA.
[q] ἐν ᾗ ἡμέρᾳ in which day LTTrA.   [r] μου ἐπὶ τοὺς ὀφθαλμούς GLTTrAW.   [s] Οὐκ ἔστιν οὗτος
παρὰ θεοῦ ὁ ἄνθρωπος LTTrA.   [t] + οὖν therefore LTTrAW.   [v] Τί σὺ TrA.   [w] ἠνέῳξέν TrA.
[x] ἦν τυφλὸς TTrA.   [y] βλέπει ἄρτι LTTrA.   [z] + οὖν therefore LT.   [a] — αὐτοῖς [L]TTrA.
[b] εἶπαν TTrA.

βλέπει οὐκ.οἴδαμεν, ἢ τίς ἤνοιξεν αὐτοῦ τοὺς ὀφθαλμοὺς
he sees   we know not,   or who opened   his   eyes

ἡμεῖς οὐκ.οἴδαμεν· ᵈαὐτὸς ἡλικίαν.ἔχει, αὐτὸν ἐρωτήσατε,‖
we   know not;   he   is of age,   ²him   ¹ask,

αὐτὸς περὶ ᵉαὐτοῦ‖ λαλήσει.   22 Ταῦτα εἶπον οἱ γονεῖς
he concerning himself shall speak.   These things said   ²parents

αὐτοῦ, ὅτι ἐφοβοῦντο τοὺς Ἰουδαίους· ἤδη.γὰρ συνε-
¹his,   because they feared   the   Jews;   for already had agreed

τέθειντο οἱ Ἰουδαῖοι, ἵνα ἐάν τις αὐτὸν ὁμολογήσῃ
together the Jews,   that if anyone him should confess [to be the]

χριστόν, ἀποσυνάγωγος γένηται.   23 διὰ τοῦτο οἱ γονεῖς
Christ, put out of the synagogue he should be.   Because of this   ²parents

αὐτοῦ ᶠεἶπον,‖ Ὅτι ἡλικίαν.ἔχει, αὐτὸν ᵍἐρωτήσατε·‖ 24 Ἐφώ-
¹his   said,   He is of age,   ²him   ¹ask.   They

νησαν οὖν ʰἐκ.δευτέρου τὸν ἄνθρωπον‖ ὃς ἦν τυφλός, καὶ
called therefore a second time the   man   who was blind,   and

ᶠεἶπον‖ αὐτῷ, Δὸς δόξαν τῷ θεῷ· ἡμεῖς οἴδαμεν ὅτι ⁱὁ ἄνθρω-
said to him, Give glory to God; we   know that   ²man

πος οὗτος‖ ἁμαρτωλός ἐστιν.   25 Ἀπεκρίθη οὖν ἐκεῖνος
¹this   a sinner   is.   ³Answered ²therefore ¹he

ᵏκαὶ εἶπεν,‖ Εἰ ἁμαρτωλός ἐστιν οὐκ.οἶδα· ἓν   οἶδα, ὅτι
and said,   If   a sinner   he is I know not.   One [thing] I know, that

τυφλὸς ὢν ἄρτι βλέπω.   26 Εἶπον.ˡδὲ‖ αὐτῷ ᵐπάλιν,‖ Τί
²blind ¹being now I see.   And they said to him   again,   What

ἐποίησέν σοι; πῶς ἤνοιξέν σου τοὺς ὀφθαλμούς; 27 Ἀπε-
did he to thee? how opened he thine eyes?   He an-

κρίθη αὐτοῖς, Εἶπον ὑμῖν ἤδη, καὶ οὐκ.ἠκούσατε· τί πάλιν
swered them,   I told you already, and ye did not hear: why again

θέλετε ἀκούειν; μὴ καὶ ὑμεῖς.θέλετε αὐτοῦ μαθηταὶ γενέσθαι;
do ye wish to hear?   ²also ¹do ²ye wish   his   disciples   to become?

28 ⁿ Ἐλοιδόρησαν ᵒοὖν‖ αὐτόν, καὶ ᵖεἶπον,‖ Σὺ �q εἶ μαθητὴς‖
They ²railed ³at ¹therefore him,   and   said,   Thou art ³disciple

ἐκείνου· ἡμεῖς.δὲ τοῦ ʳΜωσέως‖ ἐσμὲν μαθηταί. 29 ἡμεῖς οἴδα-
¹his,   but we   of Moses   are disciples.   We know

μεν ὅτι ˢΜωσῇ‖ λελάληκεν ὁ θεός· τοῦτον.δὲ οὐκ.οἴδαμεν
that to Moses ²has ¹spoken   God;   but this [man] we know not

πόθεν ἐστίν. 30 Ἀπεκρίθη ὁ ἄνθρωπος καὶ εἶπεν αὐτοῖς, Ἐν
whence he is.   ²Answered ¹the   ²man   and said to them,   ²In

ᵗγὰρ τούτῳ‖ ᵛθαυμαστόν ἐστιν, ὅτι ὑμεῖς οὐκ.οἴδατε πόθεν
¹indeed this   a wonderful thing is,   that ye   know not   whence

ἐστίν, καὶ ᵂἀνέῳξέν‖ μου τοὺς ὀφθαλμούς. 31 οἴδαμεν.ˣδὲ‖ ὅτι
he is, and   he opened   mine   eyes.   But we know that

ʸἁμαρτωλῶν ὁ θεὸς‖ οὐκ.ἀκούει· ἀλλ᾽ ἐάν τις θεοσεβὴς ᾖ,
sinners   God   does not hear;   but   if anyone God-fearing be,

καὶ τὸ θέλημα αὐτοῦ ποιῇ, τούτου ἀκούει. 32 ἐκ.τοῦ.αἰῶνος
and the   will   of him   do,   him   he hears.   ⁴Ever

οὐκ.ἠκούσθη, ὅτι ᶻἤνοιξέν‖ τις   ὀφθαλμοὺς τυφλοῦ
¹it ²was ³not heard that   ²opened   ¹anyone [the]   eyes   of [one] ⁴blind

γεγεννημένου. 33 εἰ μὴ ἦν οὗτος   παρὰ θεοῦ οὐκ ἠ-
¹having ²been ³born.   If ²not ³were ¹this [²man] from God   he

δύνατο ποιεῖν οὐδέν. 34 Ἀπεκρίθησαν καὶ ᵃεἶπον‖ αὐτῷ, Ἐν
could   do   nothing.   They answered and   said   to him,   In

---

seeth, we know not; or who hath opened his eyes, we know not: he is of age; ask him: he shall speak for himself. 22 These *words* spake his parents, because they feared the Jews: for the Jews had agreed already, that if any man did confess that he was Christ, he should be put out of the synagogue. 23 Therefore said his parents, He is of age; ask him. 24 Then again called they the man that was blind, and said unto him, Give God the praise: we know that this man is a sinner. 25 He answered and said, Whether he be a sinner *or no*, I know not: one thing I know, that, whereas I was blind, now I see. 26 Then said they to him again, What did he to thee? how opened he thine eyes? 27 He answered them, I have told you already, and ye did not hear: wherefore would ye hear it again? will ye also be his disciples? 28 Then they reviled him, and said, Thou art his disciple; but we are Moses' disciples. 29 We know that God spake unto Moses: *as for* this *fellow*, we know not from whence he is. 30 The man answered and said unto them, Why herein is a marvellous thing, that ye know not from whence he is, and *yet* he hath opened mine eyes. 31 Now we know that God heareth not sinners: but if any man be a worshipper of God, and doeth his will, him he heareth. 32 Since the world began was it not heard that any man opened the eyes of one that was born blind. 33 If this man were not of God, he could do nothing. 34 They answered and said unto him, Thou wast alto-

---

ᵈ αὐτὸν ἐρωτήσατε, αὐτὸς (— αὐτὸς TTrA) ἡλικίαν ἔχει LTTrA.   ᵉ ἑαυτοῦ TTr.   ᶠ εἶπαν LTTrA.
ᵍ ἐπερωτήσατε T.   ʰ τὸν ἄνθρωπον ἐκ δευτέρου LTTrA.   ⁱ οὗτος ὁ ἄνθρωπος L.   ᵏ — καὶ εἶπεν
LTTrAW.   ˡ οὖν therefore (they said) LTTrA.   ᵐ — πάλιν LTTrA.   ⁿ + οἱ δὲ (read But they
railed) Tr.   ᵒ — οὖν GLTTrAW.   ᵖ εἶπαν T.   q μαθητὴς εἶ LTTrA.   ʳ Μωϋσέως LTTrAW.
ˢ Μωϋσεῖ LTTrA ; Μωυσῇ W   ᵗ τούτῳ γὰρ TTrA.   ᵛ + τὸ the (wonderful thing) TTr.
ᵂ ἠνοῖξέν LTTr.   ˣ — δὲ but LTTrA.   ʸ ὁ θεὸς ἁμαρτωλῶν LTrA.   ᶻ ἠνεῳξέν Tr.   ᵃ εἶπαν LTTrA.

gether born in sins, and dost thou teach us? And they cast him out. 35 Jesus heard that they had cast him out; and when he had found him, he said unto him, Dost thou believe on the Son of God? 36 He answered and said, Who is he, Lord, that I might believe on him? 37 And Jesus said unto him, Thou hast both seen him, and it is he that talketh with thee. 38 And he said, Lord, I believe. And he worshipped him. 39 And Jesus said, For judgment I am come into this world, that they which see not might see; and that they which see might be made blind. 40 And some of the Pharisees which were with him heard these words, and said unto him, Are we blind also? 41 Jesus said unto them, If ye were blind, ye should have no sin: but now ye say, We see; therefore your sin remaineth.

X. Verily, verily, I say unto you, He that entereth not by the door into the sheepfold; but climbeth up some other way, the same is a thief and a robber. 2 But he that entereth in by the door is the shepherd of the sheep. 3 To him the porter openeth; and the sheep hear his voice: and he calleth his own sheep by name, and leadeth them out. 4 And when he putteth forth his own sheep, he goeth before them, and the sheep follow him: for they know his voice. 5 And a stranger will they not follow, but will flee from him: for they know not the voice of strangers. 6 This parable spake Jesus unto them: but they understood not what things they were which he spake unto them.

ἁμαρτίαις σὺ ἐγεννήθης ὅλος, καὶ σὺ διδάσκεις ἡμᾶς; Καὶ
sins thou wast born wholly, and ²thou ¹teachest us? And

ἐξέβαλον αὐτὸν ἔξω. 35 Ἤκουσεν ᵇὁ‖ Ἰησοῦς ὅτι ἐξέβαλον
they cast him out. ²Heard ¹Jesus that they cast

αὐτὸν ἔξω· καὶ εὑρὼν αὐτὸν εἶπεν ᶜαὐτῷ,‖ Σὺ πιστεύεις
him out, and having found him said to him, ²Thou ¹believest

εἰς τὸν υἱὸν τοῦ ᵈθεοῦ;‖ 36 Ἀπεκρίθη ἐκεῖνος ᵉκαὶ εἶπεν,‖ ᶠΤίς
on the Son of God? ²Answered ¹he and said, Who

ἐστιν, κύριε, ἵνα πιστεύσω εἰς αὐτόν; 37 Εἶπεν ᵍδὲ‖ αὐτῷ
is he, Lord, that I may believe on him? And ²said ³to ⁴him

ὁ Ἰησοῦς, Καὶ ἑώρακας αὐτόν, καὶ ὁ λαλῶν μετὰ σοῦ
¹Jesus, ²Both ⁵thou ⁶hast seen him, and he who speaks with thee

ἐκεῖνός ἐστιν. 38 Ὁ δὲ ἔφη, Πιστεύω, κύριε· καὶ προσεκύνη-
²he ¹is. And he said, I believe, Lord: and he worshipped

σεν αὐτῷ. 39 καὶ εἶπεν ὁ Ἰησοῦς, Εἰς κρίμα ἐγὼ εἰς τὸν
him. And ²said ¹Jesus, For judgment I into

κόσμον τοῦτον ἦλθον, ἵνα οἱ μὴ βλέποντες βλέπωσιν, καὶ
this world came, that they that see not might see, and

οἱ βλέποντες τυφλοὶ γένωνται. 40 ʰΚαὶ‖ ἤκουσαν ἐκ τῶν
they that see blind might become. And ⁹heard ²of ³the

Φαρισαίων ⁱταῦτα‖ οἱ ᵏὄντες μετ᾽ αὐτοῦ,‖ καὶ ¹εἶ-
⁴Pharisees ¹⁰these¹¹things ¹those⁵who ⁶were ⁷with ⁸him, and they

πον‖ αὐτῷ, Μὴ καὶ ἡμεῖς τυφλοί ἐσμεν; 41 Εἶπεν αὐτοῖς ὁ
said to him, ³Also ²we ⁴blind ¹are? Said to them

Ἰησοῦς, Εἰ τυφλοὶ ἦτε, οὐκ ἂν εἴχετε ἁμαρτίαν· νῦν δὲ λέ-
Jesus, If blind ye were, ye would not have sin; but now ye

γετε, Ὅτι βλέπομεν· ἡ ᵐοὖν‖ ἁμαρτία ὑμῶν μένει.
say, We see; the ²therefore ¹sin of you remains.

10 Ἀμὴν ἀμὴν λέγω ὑμῖν, ὁ μὴ εἰσερχόμενος διὰ τῆς
Verily verily I say to you, He that enters not in by the

θύρας εἰς τὴν αὐλὴν τῶν προβάτων, ἀλλὰ ἀναβαίνων ἀλ-
door to the fold of the sheep, but mounts up else-

λαχόθεν, ἐκεῖνος κλέπτης ἐστὶν καὶ λῃστής· 2 ὁ δὲ εἰσερ-
where, he a thief is and a robber; but he that en-

χόμενος διὰ τῆς θύρας ποιμήν ἐστιν τῶν προβάτων. 3 τούτῳ
ters in by the door shepherd ¹ is of the sheep. To him

ὁ θυρωρὸς ἀνοίγει, καὶ τὰ πρόβατα τῆς φωνῆς αὐτοῦ ἀκούει,
the door-keeper opens, and the sheep his voice hear,

καὶ τὰ ἴδια πρόβατα ⁿκαλεῖ‖ κατ᾽ ὄνομα, καὶ ἐξάγει αὐτά.
and his own sheep he calls by name, and leads ²out ¹them.

4 °καὶ‖ ὅταν τὰ ἴδια ᵖπρόβατα‖ ἐκβάλῃ ἔμπροσθεν αὐτῶν
And when his own sheep he puts forth before them

πορεύεται· καὶ τὰ πρόβατα αὐτῷ ἀκολουθεῖ, ὅτι οἴδασιν
he goes; and the sheep him follow, because they know

τὴν φωνὴν αὐτοῦ. 5 ἀλλοτρίῳ δὲ οὐ μὴ ⁹ἀκολουθήσωσιν,‖
his voice. But a stranger in no wise they should follow,

ἀλλὰ φεύξονται ἀπ᾽ αὐτοῦ· ὅτι οὐκ οἴδασιν τῶν ἀλλοτρίων
but will flee from him, because they know not of strangers

τὴν φωνήν. 6 Ταύτην τὴν παροιμίαν εἶπεν αὐτοῖς ὁ Ἰησοῦς,
the voice. This allegory ²spoke ³to ⁴them ¹Jesus,

ἐκεῖνοι δὲ οὐκ ἔγνωσαν τίνα ʳἦν‖ ἃ ἐλάλει αὐτοῖς.
but they knew not what it was which he spoke to them.

ᵇ — ὁ τ[Τr]. ᶜ — αὐτῷ τ[ΤrΑ]. ᵈ ἀνθρώπου of man τ. ᵉ — καὶ εἶπεν L[Α].
ᶠ + καὶ and GTΤrΑW. ᵍ — δὲ and LTΤrΑ. ʰ — καὶ ΤΤrΑ. ⁱ — ταῦτα τ. ᵏ μετ᾽
αὐτοῦ ὄντες LTΤrΑ. ˡ εἶπαν τ. ᵐ — οὖν [L]ΤΤrΑ. ⁿ φωνεῖ he calls LTΤrΑ. ° — καὶ
ΤΤrΑ. ᵖ πάντα all (his own) LTΤrΑ. ⁹ ἀκολουθήσουσιν will they follow LTΤrΑW. ʳ ᾖ
it might be Τr.

7 Εἶπεν οὖν ˢπάλιν αὐτοῖς‖ ὁ Ἰησοῦς, Ἀμὴν ἀμὴν λέγω
²Said ³therefore ⁴again ⁵to ⁶them   ¹Jesus,   Verily verily I say

ὑμῖν, ᵗὅτι‖ ἐγώ εἰμι ἡ θύρα τῶν προβάτων. 8 πάντες ὅσοι
to you, that I am the door of the   sheep.   All   whoever

ᵛπρὸ ἐμοῦ ἦλθον‖ κλέπται εἰσὶν καὶ λῃσταί· ἀλλ᾽ οὐκ.ἤκουσαν
before me came   thieves are ᶜand robbers; but ³did ⁴not ⁵hear

αὐτῶν τὰ πρόβατα. 9 ἐγώ εἰμι ἡ θύρα· δι᾽ ἐμοῦ ἐάν τις
⁶them ¹the ²sheep.   I am the door: by me   if anyone

εἰσέλθῃ σωθήσεται, καὶ εἰσελεύσεται καὶ ἐξελεύσεται, καὶ
enter in he shall be saved, and shall go in and shall go out, and

νομὴν εὑρήσει. 10 ὁ κλέπτης οὐκ.ἔρχεται εἰ.μὴ ἵνα κλέψῃ
pasture shall find.   The thief comes not except that he may steal

καὶ θύσῃ καὶ ἀπολέσῃ· ἐγὼ ἦλθον ἵνα ζωὴν .ἔχωσιν,
and may kill and may destroy: I came that life they might have,

καὶ περισσὸν ἔχωσιν. 11 Ἐγώ εἰμι ὁ ποιμὴν ὁ καλός· ὁ
and abundantly might have [it].   I am the ²shepherd ¹good. The

ποιμὴν ὁ καλὸς τὴν.ψυχὴν.αὐτοῦ τίθησιν ὑπὲρ τῶν προβά-
²shepherd ¹good   his life   lays down for the sheep:

των. 12 ὁ.μισθωτὸς.ʷδὲ,‖ καὶ οὐκ.ὢν ποιμήν, οὗ οὐκ
but the hired servant, and who is not [the] shepherd, whose ⁴not

ˣεἰσὶν‖ τὰ πρόβατα ἴδια, θεωρεῖ τὸν λύκον ἐρχόμενον, καὶ
⁴are ²the ³sheep ¹own, sees the wolf coming, and

ἀφίησιν τὰ πρόβατα ᵏαὶ φεύγει· καὶ ὁ λύκος ἁρπάζει αὐτὰ
leaves the sheep, and flees; and the wolf seizes them

καὶ σκορπίζει ʸτὰ πρόβατα. 13 ὁ.δὲ μισθωτὸς φεύγει‖ ὅτι
and scatters the sheep.   Now the hired servant flees because

μισθωτός ἐστιν, καὶ οὐ.μέλει.αὐτῷ περὶ τῶν προβάτων.
a hired servant he is, and is not himself concerned about the sheep.

14 ἐγώ εἰμι ὁ ποιμὴν ὁ καλός· καὶ γινώσκω τὰ ἐμά,
I am the ²shepherd ¹good; and I know those that [are] mine,

καὶ ᶻγινώσκομαι ὑπὸ τῶν ἐμῶν.‖ 15 καθὼς γινώσκει
and am known of those that [are] mine. As ³knows

με ὁ πατήρ, κἀγὼ γινώσκω τὸν πατέρα· καὶ τὴν.ψυχήν.μου
⁴me ¹the ²Father, I also know the Father; and my life

τίθημι ὑπὲρ τῶν προβάτων. 16 καὶ ἄλλα πρόβατα ἔχω,
I lay down for the sheep.   And other sheep I have,

ἃ οὐκ.ἔστιν ἐκ τῆς.αὐλῆς.ταύτης· κἀκεῖνά ᵃμε δεῖ‖
which are not of this fold; those also ¹me ²it ²behoves

ἀγαγεῖν, καὶ τῆς.φωνῆς.μου ἀκούσουσιν· καὶ ᵇγενήσεται‖ μία
to bring, and my voice they will hear; and there shall be one

ποίμνη, εἷς ποιμήν. 17 διὰ.τοῦτο ᶜὁ πατήρ με‖ ἀγαπᾷ,
flock, one shepherd.   On this account the Father me loves,

ὅτι ἐγὼ τίθημι τὴν.ψυχήν.μου, ἵνα πάλιν λάβω αὐτήν.
because I lay down my life, that again I may take it.

18 οὐδεὶς αἴρει αὐτὴν ἀπ᾽ ἐμοῦ, ἀλλ᾽ ἐγὼ τίθημι αὐτὴν ἀπ᾽
No one takes it from me, but I lay down it of

ἐμαυτοῦ. ἐξουσίαν ἔχω θεῖναι αὐτήν, καὶ ἐξουσίαν ἔχω
myself. Authority I have to lay down it, and authority I have

πάλιν λαβεῖν αὐτήν· ταύτην τὴν ἐντολὴν ἔλαβον παρὰ
again to take it. This commandment I received from

τοῦ.πατρός.μου. 19 Σχίσμα ᵈοὖν‖ πάλιν ἐγένετο ἐν τοῖς
my Father.   A division therefore again there was among the

Right column (KJV):

7 Then said Jesus unto them again, Verily, verily, I say unto you, I am the door of the sheep. 8 All that ever came before me are thieves and robbers: but the sheep did not hear them. 9 I am the door: by me if any man enter in, he shall be saved, and shall go in and out, and find pasture. 10 The thief cometh not, but for to steal, and to kill, and to destroy: I am come that they might have life, and that they might have it more abundantly. 11 I am the good shepherd: the good shepherd giveth his life for the sheep. 12 But he that is an hireling, and not the shepherd, whose own the sheep are not, seeth the wolf coming, and leaveth the sheep, and fleeth: and the wolf catcheth them, and scattereth the sheep. 13 The hireling fleeth, because he is an hireling, and careth not for the sheep. 14 I am the good shepherd, and know my sheep, and am known of mine. 15 As the Father knoweth me, even so know I the Father: and I lay down my life for the sheep. 16 And other sheep I have, which are not of this fold: them also I must bring, and they shall hear my voice; and there shall be one fold, and one shepherd. 17 Therefore doth my Father love me, because I lay down my life, that I might take it again. 18 No man taketh it from me, but I lay it down of myself. I have power to lay it down, and I have power to take it again. This commandment have I received of my Father. 19 There was a division therefore again among the Jews for these

---

ˢ αὐτοῖς πάλιν L; — πάλιν αὐτοῖς T; — αὐτοῖς A.   ᵗ — ὅτι [L]Tr[A].   ᵛ ἦλθον πρὸ
ἐμοῦ GLTrA; — πρὸ ἐμοῦ T.   ʷ — δὲ but T[Tr].   ˣ ἔστιν LTTrA.   ʸ — τὰ πρόβατα
([τὰ πρόβατα] A) ὁ δὲ μισθωτὸς φεύγει [L]TTrA.   ᶻ γινώσκουσίν με τὰ ἐμά those that [are]
mine know me LTTrA.   ᵃ δεῖ με LTTrA.   ᵇ γενήσονται TrA.   ᶜ με ὁ πατὴρ LTTrA.
ᵈ — οὖν LTTrA.

sayings. 20 And many of them said, He hath a devil, and is mad; why hear ye him? 21 Others said, These are not the words of him that hath a devil. Can a devil open the eyes of the blind?

Ἰουδαίοις διὰ τοὺς λόγους τούτους. 20 ἔλεγον δὲ
Jews on account of these words; ²said ¹but

πολλοὶ ἐξ αὐτῶν, Δαιμόνιον ἔχει καὶ μαίνεται· τί αὐτοῦ
many of them, A demon he has and is mad; why him

ἀκούετε; 21 Ἄλλοι ἔλεγον, Ταῦτα τὰ ῥήματα οὐκ ἔστιν
do ye hear? Others said, These sayings are not [those]

δαιμονιζομένου· μὴ δαιμόνιον δύναται τυφλῶν
of one possessed by a demon. ²A ³demon ¹is able of [the] blind [the]

ὀφθαλμοὺς ἀνοίγειν;
eyes to open?

22 Ἐγένετο δὲ τὰ ἐγκαίνια ἐν τοῖς Ἱεροσολύμοις,
And took place the feast of dedication at Jerusalem,

καὶ χειμὼν ἦν· 23 καὶ περιεπάτει ὁ Ἰησοῦς ἐν τῷ ἱερῷ
and winter it was. And ²was ³walking ¹Jesus in the temple

ἐν τῇ στοᾷ τοῦ Σολομῶντος. 24 ἐκύκλωσαν οὖν αὐτὸν
in the porch of Solomon. ⁴Encircled ³therefore ⁵him

22 And it was at Jerusalem the feast of the dedication, and it was winter. 23 And Jesus walked in the temple in Solomon's porch. 24 Then came the Jews round about him, and said unto him, How long dost thou make us to doubt? If thou be the Christ, tell us plainly. 25 Jesus answered them, I told you, and ye believed not: the works that I do in my Father's name, they bear witness of me. 26 But ye believe not, because ye are not of my sheep, as I said unto you. 27 My sheep hear my voice, and I know them, and they follow me: 28 and I give unto them eternal life; and they shall never perish, neither shall any man pluck them out of my hand. 29 My Father, which gave them me, is greater than all; and no man is able to pluck them out of my Father's hand. 30 I and my Father are one. 31 Then the Jews took up stones again to stone him. 32 Jesus answered them, Many good works have I shewed you from my Father; for which of those works do ye stone me? 33 The Jews answered him, saying, For a good work we

οἱ Ἰουδαῖοι, καὶ ἔλεγον αὐτῷ, Ἕως πότε τὴν ψυχὴν ἡμῶν
¹the ²Jews, and said to him, Until when our soul

αἴρεις; εἰ σὺ εἶ ὁ χριστός, εἰπὲ ἡμῖν παρ-
holdest thou in suspense? If thou art the Christ, tell us plain-

ρησίᾳ. 25 Ἀπεκρίθη αὐτοῖς ὁ Ἰησοῦς, Εἶπον ὑμῖν, καὶ
ly. ²Answered ³them ¹Jesus, I told you, and

οὐ πιστεύετε. τὰ ἔργα ἃ ἐγὼ ποιῶ ἐν τῷ ὀνόματι τοῦ πατρός
ye believe not. The works which I do in the name of ²Father

μου, ταῦτα μαρτυρεῖ περὶ ἐμοῦ· 26 ἀλλ᾽ ὑμεῖς οὐ
¹my, these bear witness concerning me: but ye ²not

πιστεύετε· οὐ γάρ ἐστε ἐκ τῶν προβάτων τῶν ἐμῶν, καθὼς
¹believe, for ye are not of ²sheep ¹my, as

εἶπον ὑμῖν. 27 τὰ πρόβατα τὰ ἐμὰ τῆς φωνῆς μου ἀκούει,
I said to you. ²Sheep ¹my my voice hear,

κἀγὼ γινώσκω αὐτά· καὶ ἀκολουθοῦσίν μοι, 28 κἀγὼ ζωὴν
and I know them, and they follow me; and I life

αἰώνιον δίδωμι αὐτοῖς· καὶ οὐ μὴ ἀπόλωνται εἰς τὸν
eternal give them; and in no wise shall they perish for

αἰῶνα, καὶ οὐχ ἁρπάσει τις αὐτὰ ἐκ τῆς χειρός μου. 29 ὁ
ever, and ³shall ¹not ⁴seize ²anyone them out of my hand.

πατήρ μου ὃς δέδωκέν μοι μείζων πάντων ἐστίν· καὶ
My Father who has given [them] to me greater than all is, and

οὐδεὶς δύναται ἁρπάζειν ἐκ τῆς χειρὸς τοῦ πατρός μου.
no one is able to seize out of the hand tell my Father.

30 ἐγὼ καὶ ὁ πατὴρ ἕν ἐσμεν. 31 Ἐβάστασαν οὖν πάλιν
I and the Father one are. ⁵Took ⁶up ³therefore ⁴again

λίθους οἱ Ἰουδαῖοι ἵνα λιθάσωσιν αὐτόν. 32 ἀπεκρίθη
⁷stones ¹the ²Jews that they might stone him. ²Answered

αὐτοῖς ὁ Ἰησοῦς, Πολλὰ καλὰ ἔργα ἔδειξα ὑμῖν ἐκ τοῦ
²them ¹Jesus, Many good works I shewed you from

πατρός μου· διὰ ποῖον αὐτῶν ἔργον λιθάζετέ με;
my Father; because of which ²of ³them ¹work do ye stone me?

33 Ἀπεκρίθησαν αὐτῷ οἱ Ἰουδαῖοι λέγοντες, Περὶ καλοῦ
³Answered ⁴him ¹the ²Jews, saying, For a good

ᵉ οὖν then T. ᶠ ἀνοῖξαι to have opened TTrA. ᵍ ἐνκαίνια T. ʰ — τοῖς T. ⁱ — καὶ TTrA. ᵏ [ὁ] Tr. ˡ Σολομῶνος GLTAW; τοῦ Σολομῶνος Tr. ᵐ εἰπὸν T. ⁿ — αὐ- τοῖς T. ᵒ ἀλλὰ LTTrAW. ᵖ ὅτι οὐκ TTr. �q — καθὼς εἶπον ὑμῖν [L]TTr[A]. ʳ ἀκούουσιν [are] hearing TTrA. ˢ δίδωμι αὐτοῖς ζωὴν αἰώνιον TTrA. ᵗ — μου (read The Father) T. ᵘ ὃ what (he has given) TTrA. ʷ πάντων μεῖζόν TTrA. ˣ — μου (read the Father) T[Tr]A. ʸ οὖν T[Tr]. ᶻ ἔργα καλὰ LT. ᵃ — μου (read the Father) [L]T[Tr]A. ᵇ ἐμὲ λιθάζετε TTrA. ᶜ — λέγοντες LTTrAW.

ἔργου οὐ.λιθάζομέν σε, ἀλλὰ περὶ βλασφημίας, καὶ ὅτι
work we do not stone thee, but for blasphemy, and because

σὺ ἄνθρωπος ὢν ποιεῖς σεαυτὸν θεόν. 34 Ἀπεκρίθη αὐτοῖς
thou ªaªman ¹being makest thyself God. ²Answered ³them

dό‖ Ἰησοῦς, Οὐκ.ἔστιν γεγραμμένον ἐν τῷ.νόμῳ.ὑμῶν, eἘγὼ
¹Jesus, Is it not written in your law, I

fεἶπα,‖ θεοί ἐστε; 35 Εἰ ἐκείνους εἶπεν θεούς, πρὸς οὓς ὁ
said, ³gods ¹ye ²are? If them he called gods, to whom the

λόγος gτοῦ θεοῦ ἐγένετο,‖ καὶ οὐ.δύναται λυθῆναι ἡ γραφή·
word of God came, (and ³cannot ⁴be ⁵broken ¹the ²scripture,)

36 ὃν ὁ πατὴρ ἡγίασεν καὶ ἀπέστειλεν εἰς τὸν κόσμον,
[of him] whom the Father sanctified and sent into the world,

ὑμεῖς.λέγετε, Ὅτι βλασφημεῖς, ὅτι εἶπον, Υἱὸς hτοῦ‖ θεοῦ
do ye say, Thou blasphemest, because I said, Son of God

εἰμι; 37 εἰ οὐ.ποιῶ τὰ ἔργα τοῦ.πατρός.μου, μὴ.πιστεύετέ
I am? If I do not the works of my Father, believe not

μοι· 38 εἰ.δὲ ποιῶ, κἂν ἐμοὶ μὴ.¹πιστεύητε,‖ τοῖς ἔργοις
me; but if I do, even if me ye believe not, the works

kπιστεύσατε,‖ ἵνα γνῶτε καὶ ¹πιστεύσητε‖ ὅτι ἐν ἐμοὶ
believe, that ye may perceive and may believe that in me [is]

ὁ πατήρ, κἀγὼ ἐν mαὐτῷ.‖ 39 Ἐζήτουν nοῦν‖ oπάλιν‖
the Father, and I in him. They sought therefore again

αὐτὸν πιάσαι· καὶ ἐξῆλθεν ἐκ τῆς.χειρὸς.αὐτῶν. 40 Καὶ
him to take, and he went forth out of their hand; and

ἀπῆλθεν πάλιν πέραν τοῦ Ἰορδάνου, εἰς τὸν τόπον ὅπου ἦν
departed again beyond the Jordan, to the place where was

pἸωάννης‖ τὸ πρῶτον βαπτίζων· καὶ qἔμεινεν‖ ἐκεῖ. 41 καὶ
John first baptizing; and he abode there. And

πολλοὶ ἦλθον πρὸς αὐτόν, καὶ ἔλεγον, Ὅτι pἸωάννης‖ μὲν
many came to him, and said, John indeed

σημεῖον ἐποίησεν οὐδέν· πάντα.δὲ ὅσα εἶπεν pἸωάννης‖
³sign ¹did ²no; but all whatsoever ²said ¹John

περὶ τούτου, ἀληθῆ ἦν· 42 Καὶ rἐπίστευσαν πολλοὶ
concerning this [man], true were. And ²believed ¹many

ἐκεῖ εἰς αὐτόν.‖
there on him.

11 ᾽Ην.δὲ τις ἀσθενῶν Λάζαρος ἀπὸ Βηθανίας,
Now there was a certain [man] sick, Lazarus of Bethany,

ἐκ τῆς κώμης sΜαρίας καὶ Μάρθας τῆς.ἀδελφῆς.αὐτῆς. 2 ἦν
of the village of Mary and Martha her sister. ²It ³was

δὲ tΜαρία‖ ἡ ἀλείψασα τὸν κύριον μύρῳ καὶ ἐκμάξασα
¹and Mary who anointed the Lord with ointment and wiped

τοὺς.πόδας.αὐτοῦ ταῖς.θριξὶν.αὐτῆς, ἧς ὁ ἀδελφὸς Λάζαρος
his feet with her hair, whose brother Lazarus

ἠσθένει. 3 ἀπέστειλαν οὖν αἱ.ἀδελφαὶ πρὸς αὐτὸν λέγου-
was sick. ⁴Sent ³therefore ¹the ²sisters to him, say-

σαι, Κύριε, ἴδε ὃν φιλεῖς ἀσθενεῖ. 4 Ἀκούσας.δὲ ὁ Ἰησοῦς
ing, Lord, lo, he whom thou lovest is sick. But ²having ³heard ¹Jesus

εἶπεν, Αὕτη ἡ ἀσθένεια οὐκ.ἔστιν πρὸς θάνατον, ἀλλ᾽ ὑπὲρ
said, . This sickness is not unto death, but for

τῆς δόξης τοῦ θεοῦ, ἵνα δοξασθῇ ὁ υἱὸς τοῦ θεοῦ δι᾽
the glory of God, that may be glorified the Son of God by

stone thee not; but for blasphemy ; and because that thou, being a man, makest thyself God. 34 Jesus answered them, Is it not written in your law, I said, Ye are gods ? 35 If he called them gods, unto whom the word of God came, and the scripture cannot be broken ; 36 say ye of him, whom the Father hath sanctified, and sent into the world, Thou blasphemest; because I said, I.am the Son of God ? 37 If I do not the works of my Father, believe me not. 38 But if I do, though ye believe not me, believe the works: that ye may know, and believe, that the Father is in me, and I in him. 39 Therefore they sought again to take him: but he escaped out of their hand, 40 and went away again beyond Jordan into the place where John at first baptized; and there he abode. 41 And many resorted unto him, and said, John did no miracle : but all things that John spake of this man were true. 42 And many believed on him there.

XI. Now a certain man was sick, named Lazarus, of Bethany, the town of Mary and her sister Martha. 2 (It was that Mary which anointed the Lord with ointment, and wiped his feet with her hair, whose brother Lazarus was sick.) 3 Therefore his sisters sent unto him, saying, Lord. behold, he whom thou lovest is sick. 4 When Jesus heard that, he said, This sickness is not unto death, but for the glory of God, that the Son of God might be glorified

d [ὁ] .Tr. e + ὅτι that LTTrA. f εἶπον L. g ἐγένετο τοῦ θεοῦ T. h — τοῦ T.
i πιστεύητε T. k πιστεύετε LTTr. l γινώσκητε may know LTTrA. m τῷ πατρί the
Father LTTrA. n [οὖν] TrA. o — πάλιν T. p Ἰωάνης Tr. q ἔμενεν L. r πολλοὶ
ἐπίστευσαν εἰς αὐτὸν ἐκεῖ LTTrA. s + τῆς T. t Μαριάμ Tr.

thereby. 5 Now Jesus loved Martha, and her sister, and Lazarus. 6 When he had heard therefore that he was sick, he abode two days still in the same place where he was. 7 Then after that saith he to *his* disciples, Let us go into Judæa again. 8 *His* disciples say unto him, Master, the Jews of late sought to stone thee; and goest thou thither again? 9 Jesus answered, Are there not twelve hours in the day? If any man walk in the day, he stumbleth not, because he seeth the light of this world. 10 But if a man walk in the night, he stumbleth, because there is no light in him. 11 These things said he : and after that he saith unto them, Our friend Lazarus sleepeth ; but I go, that I may awake him out of sleep. 12 Then said his disciples, Lord, if he sleep, he shall do well. 13 Howbeit Jesus spake of his death: but they thought that he had spoken of taking of rest in sleep. 14 Then said Jesus unto them plainly, Lazarus is dead. 15 And I am glad for your sakes that I was not there, to the intent ye may believe ; nevertheless let us go unto him. 16 Then said Thomas, which is called Didymus, unto his fellow-disciples, Let us also go, that we may die with him.

αὐτῆς. 5 Ἠγάπα δὲ ὁ Ἰησοῦς τὴν Μάρθαν καὶ τὴν ἀδελφὴν
it.   ³Loved ¹now ²Jesus   Martha and   ²sister
αὐτῆς καὶ τὸν Λάζαρον. 6 ὡς οὖν ἤκουσεν ὅτι ἀσθενεῖ,
¹her and Lazarus.   When therefore he heard that he is sick,
τότε μὲν ἔμεινεν ἐν ᾧ ἦν τόπῳ δύο ἡμέρας. 7 Ἔπειτα
then indeed he remained in which ²he ³was ¹place two days.   Then
μετὰ τοῦτο λέγει τοῖς μαθηταῖς,ʷ Ἄγωμεν εἰς τὴν Ἰουδαίαν
after this he says to the disciples, Let us go into   Judæa
πάλιν. 8 Λέγουσιν αὐτῷ οἱ μαθηταί, ˣῬαββί,‖ νῦν ἐζή-
again.   ³Say   ⁴to ⁵him ¹the ²disciples, Rabbi, just now ³were
τουν σε λιθάσαι οἱ Ἰουδαῖοι, καὶ πάλιν ὑπάγεις ἐκεῖ;
⁴seeking ⁷thee ⁵to ⁶stone ¹the   ²Jews, and again goest thou thither?
9 Ἀπεκρίθη ʸὁ‖ Ἰησοῦς, Οὐχὶ δώδεκά ᶻεἰσιν ὧραι‖ τῆς
²Answered ¹Jesus, ⁵Not ⁴twelve ³are ⁴there hours in the
ἡμέρας ; ἐάν τις περιπατῇ ἐν τῇ ἡμέρᾳ, οὐ προσκόπτει,
day?   If anyone walk   in the day,   he stumbles not,
ὅτι τὸ φῶς τοῦ κόσμου τούτου βλέπει· 10 ἐὰν δὲ τις
because the⁸ light of this world he sees ;   but if anyone
περιπατῇ ἐν τῇ νυκτί, προσκόπτει, ὅτι τὸ φῶς οὐκ ἔστιν ἐν
walk   in the night, he stumbles, because the light is not   in
αὐτῷ. 11 Ταῦτα εἶπεν, καὶ μετὰ τοῦτο λέγει αὐτοῖς, Λά-
him.   These things he said ; and after this he says to them, La-
ζαρος ὁ φίλος ἡμῶν κεκοίμηται· ἀλλὰ πορεύομαι ἵνα ἐξ-
zarus our friend has fallen asleep ; but I go   that I may
ὑπνίσω αὐτόν. 12 Εἶπον οὖνᵃ ᵇοἱ μαθηταὶ‖ αὐτοῦ,‖ Κύριε,
awake him.   ²Said ¹therefore his disciples, Lord,
εἰ κεκοίμηται σωθήσεται. 13 Εἰρήκει δὲ ὁ Ἰησοῦς περὶ
if he has fallen asleep he will get well. But ²had ³spoken ¹Jesus of
τοῦ θανάτου αὐτοῦ· ἐκεῖνοι δὲ ἔδοξαν ὅτι περὶ τῆς κοιμήσεως
his death, but they thought that of   the rest
τοῦ ὕπνου λέγει. 14 τότε ᵈοὖν‖ εἶπεν αὐτοῖς ὁ Ἰησοῦς
of sleep he speaks. Then therefore ²said ¹to ⁴them ³Jesus
παρρησίᾳ, Λάζαρος ἀπέθανεν· 15 καὶ χαίρω δι᾽ ὑμᾶς,
plainly, Lazarus   died.   And I rejoice on your account,
ἵνα πιστεύσητε, ὅτι οὐκ ἤμην ἐκεῖ· ᵉἀλλ᾽‖ ἄγωμεν πρὸς
in order that ye may believe, that I was not there. But let us go to
αὐτόν. 16 Εἶπεν οὖν Θωμᾶς, ὁ λεγόμενος Δίδυμος, τοῖς
him.   ²Said ¹therefore Thomas,   called   Didymus, to the
ᶠσυμμαθηταῖς,‖ Ἄγωμεν καὶ ἡμεῖς, ἵνα ἀποθάνωμεν μετ᾽
fellow-disciples, Let ³go ²also ¹us,   that we may die with
αὐτοῦ.
him.

17 ᵍἘλθὼν‖ οὖν ὁ Ἰησοῦς ʰ εὗρεν αὐτὸν τέσσαρας
³Having ⁴come ²therefore ¹Jesus found him   four

17 Then when Jesus came, he found that he had *lain* in the grave four days already. 18 Now Bethany was nigh unto Jerusalem, about fifteen furlongs off: 19 and many of the Jews came to Martha and Mary, to comfort them concerning their

ἡμέρας ἤδη. ἔχοντα ἐν τῷ μνημείῳ. 18 ἦν δὲ ᵏἡ‖ Βηθανία
days already having been in the   tomb.   Now ²was ¹Bethany
ἐγγὺς τῶν Ἱεροσολύμων, ὡς ἀπὸ σταδίων δεκαπέντε 19 ᵏκαὶ
near   to Jerusalem, about ³off ²furlongs ¹fifteen,   and
πολλοὶ‖ ἐκ τῶν Ἰουδαίων ἐληλύθεισαν πρὸς ᵐτὰς περὶ‖
many   of the Jews   had come unto those around
Μάρθαν καὶ ⁿΜαρίαν,‖ ἵνα παραμυθήσωνται αὐτὰς περὶ
Martha and   Mary,   that they might console them concerning

ʷ + [αὐτοῦ] (*read* his disciples) L.   ˣ Ῥαββεί τ.   ʸ — ὁ GLTTrAW.   ᶻ ὧραί εἰσιν
LTTrAW.   ᵃ + αὐτῷ to him LT.   ᵇ [οἱ μαθηταί] A.   ᶜ — αὐτοῦ (*read* the disciples) LT;
αὐτῷ to him TrA.   ᵈ [οὖν] L.   ᵉ ἀλλὰ LTTrA.   ᶠ συνμαθηταῖς T.   ᵍ Ἦλθεν came L.
ʰ + καὶ and L.   ⁱ ἤδη ἡμέρας TrA ; — ἤδη T.   ᵏ — ἡ T.   ˡ πολλοὶ δὲ LTTrA.   ᵐ τὴν
(*read* had come to Martha) LTrA.   ⁿ Μαριάμ LTTrA.

τοῦ ἀδελφοῦ ᵒαὐτῶν.ʰ 20 ἡ οὖν Μάρθα ὡς ἤκουσεν ὅτι ρᵒ‖
their brother.   Martha therefore when she heard that

'Ιησοῦς ἔρχεται, ὑπήντησεν αὐτῷ· Μαρία δὲ ἐν τῷ οἴκῳ ἐκα-
Jesus   is coming,   met   him;   but Mary   in the house   was

θέζετο. 21 εἶπεν οὖν ᧇἡ‖ Μάρθα πρὸς ʳτὸν‖ 'Ιησοῦν, Κύριε, εἰ
sitting.   Then said   Martha   to   Jesus,   Lord,   if

ἦς ὧδε, ˢὁ ἀδελφός μου οὐκ ἂν ἐτεθνήκει.‖ 22 ᵗἀλλὰ‖
thou hadst been here,   my brother   had not died;   but

καὶ νῦν οἶδα ὅτι ὅσα ἂν αἰτήσῃ τὸν θεόν, δώσει
even now I know that whatsoever thou mayest ask of   God, ²will ³give

σοι ὁ θεός. 23 Λέγει αὐτῇ ὁ 'Ιησοῦς, 'Αναστήσεται ὁ ἀδελφός
⁴thee ¹God.   Says to her   Jesus,   ³Will ⁴rise ⁵again   ²brother

σου. 24 Λέγει αὐτῷ ᵛΜάρθα, Οἶδα ὅτι ἀναστήσεται ἐν τῇ
¹thy.   Says to him   Martha,   I know that he will rise again in the

ἀναστάσει ἐν τῇ ἐσχάτῃ ἡμέρᾳ 25 Εἶπεν αὐτῇ ὁ 'Ιησοῦς,
resurrection in the   last   day.   ²Said ³to ⁴her   ¹Jesus,

'Εγώ εἰμι ἡ ἀνάστασις καὶ ἡ ζωή. ὁ πιστεύων εἰς ἐμέ,
I   am the resurrection and the life: he that believeth   on me,

κἂν ἀποθάνῃ ζήσεται· 26 καὶ πᾶς ὁ ζῶν καὶ ᴨιστεύων
though he die   he shall live;   and everyone who lives and believes

εἰς ἐμέ, οὐ μὴ ἀποθάνῃ εἰς τὸν αἰῶνα. πιστεύεις τοῦτο;
on me,   in no wise shall die   for ever.   Believest thou this?

27 Λέγει αὐτῷ, Ναί, κύριε· ἐγὼ πεπίστευκα ὅτι σὺ εἶ ὁ
She says to him; Yea,   Lord;   I   have believed that thou art the

χριστός, ὁ υἱὸς τοῦ θεοῦ, ὁ εἰς τὸν κόσμον ἐρχόμενος.
Christ,   the Son   of God, who into the   world   coming.

28 Καὶ ᵂταῦτα‖ εἰποῦσα ἀπῆλθεν, καὶ ἐφώνησεν ˣΜαρίαν‖
And these things having said she went away, and called   Mary

τὴν ἀδελφὴν αὐτῆς ʸλάθρα,‖ ᶻεἰποῦσα,‖ 'Ο διδάσκαλος πάρ-
her sister   secretly,   saying,   The teacher   is

εστιν καὶ φωνεῖ σε. 29 'Εκείνη ᵃ ὡς ἤκουσεν ᵇἐγείρεται‖ ταχὺ
come and calls thee.   She   when she heard   rises up quickly

καὶ ᶜἔρχεται‖ πρὸς αὐτόν. 30 οὔπω δὲ ἐληλύθει ὁ 'Ιησοῦς
and comes   to   him.   Now not yet had ²come   ¹Jesus

εἰς τὴν κώμην, ἀλλ' ἦν ᵈ ἐν τῷ τόπῳ ὅπου ὑπήντησεν αὐτῷ
into the village, but was in the place where   ²met   ³him

ἡ Μάρθα. 31 οἱ οὖν 'Ιουδαῖοι οἱ ὄντες μετ' αὐτῆς ἐν τῇ οἰκίᾳ
¹Martha.   The Jews therefore who were with her in the house

καὶ παραμυθούμενοι αὐτήν, ἰδόντες τὴν ᵉΜαρίαν‖ ὅτι ταχέως
and consoling   her, having seen   Mary   that quickly

ἀνέστη καὶ ἐξῆλθεν, ἠκολούθησαν αὐτῇ, ⸤λέγοντες,‖ "Οτι
she rose up and went out,   followed   her,   saying,

ὑπάγει εἰς τὸ μνημεῖον ἵνα κλαύσῃ ἐκεῖ. 32 'Η οὖν ᵍΜαρία‖
She is going to the   tomb   that she may weep there.   Mary therefore

ὡς ἦλθεν ὅπου ἦν ʰὁ‖ 'Ιησοῦς, ἰδοῦσα αὐτὸν ἔπεσεν ⁱεἰς‖
when she came where ²was   ¹Jesus,   seeing him,   fell   at

τοὺς πόδας αὐτοῦ,‖ λέγουσα αὐτῷ, Κύριε, εἰ ἦς ὧδε
his feet,   saying   to him,   Lord,   if thou hadst been here

οὐκ ἂν ᵏἀπέθανέν μου‖ ὁ ἀδελφός. 33 'Ιησοῦς οὖν ὡς εἶδεν
³had ⁴not ⁵died   ¹my   ²brother.   Jesus therefore when he saw

---

brother. 20 Then Martha, as soon as she heard that Jesus was coming, went and met him : but Mary sat still in the house. 21 Then said Martha unto Jesus, Lord, if thou hadst been here, my brother had not died. 22 But I know, that even now, whatsoever thou wilt ask of God, God will give it thee. 23 Jesus saith unto her, Thy brother shall rise again. 24 Martha saith unto him, I know that he shall rise again in the resurrection at the last day. 25 Jesus said unto her, I am the resurrection, and the life : he that believeth in me, though he were dead, yet shall he live : 26 and whosoever liveth and believeth in me shall never die. Believest thou this? 27 She saith unto him, Yea, Lord : I believe that thou art the Christ, the Son of God, which should come into the world. 28 And when she had so said, she went her way, and called Mary her sister secretly, saying, The Master is come, and calleth for thee. 29 As soon as she heard that, she arose quickly, and came unto him. 30 Now Jesus was not yet come into the town, but was in that place where Martha met him. 31 The Jews then which were with her in the house, and comforted her, when they saw Mary, that she rose up hastily and went out, followed her, saying, She goeth unto the grave to weep there. 32 Then when Mary was come where Jesus was, and saw him, she fell down at his feet, saying unto him, Lord, if thou hadst been here, my brother had not died. 33 When Jesus therefore saw her weeping,

---

ᵒ — αὐτῶν (read [their] brother) TTrA.   ᴾ — ὁ GLTTrAW.   ᑫ — ἡ GL.   ʳ — τὸν T[Tr].
ˢ οὐκ ἂν ἀπέθανεν (ἐτεθνήκει A) ὁ ἀδελφός μου LTTrA.   ᵗ — ἀλλὰ [L]TTrA.   ᵛ + ἡ LTTrA.
ᵂ τοῦτο this TTrA.   ˣ Μαριάμ. LTTrA.   ʸ λάθρα L.   ᶻ εἴπασα Tr.   ᵃ + δὲ and (she) Tr[A].
ᵇ ἠγέρθη rose up LTrA.   ᶜ ἤρχετο came TrA.   ᵈ + ἔτι yet LTr[A].   ᵉ Μαριὰμ LTTrA.
ᶠ δόξαντες thinking TTrA.   ᵍ Μαριὰμ TTrA.   ʰ — ὁ LTTrA.   ⁱ αὐτοῦ εἰς (πρὸς TTrA)
⸤ τοὺς πόδας GTTrAW.   ᵏ μου ἀπέθανεν TTrA.

and the Jews also weeping which came with her, he groaned in the spirit, and was troubled, 34 and said, Where have ye laid him? They said unto him, Lord, come and see. 35 Jesus wept. 36 Then said the Jews, Behold how he loved him! 37 And some of them said, Could not this man, which opened the eyes of the blind, have caused that even this man should not have died? 38 Jesus therefore again groaning in himself cometh to the grave. It was a cave, and a stone lay upon it. 39 Jesus said, Take ye away the stone. Martha, the sister of him that was dead, saith unto him, Lord, by this time he stinketh: for he hath been *dead* four days. 40 Jesus saith unto her, Said I not unto thee, that, if thou wouldest believe, thou shouldest see the glory of God? 41 Then they took away the stone *from the place* where the dead was laid. And Jesus lifted up *his* eyes, and said, Father, I thank thee that thou hast heard me. 42 And I knew that thou hearest me always: but because of the people which stand by I said *it*, that they may believe that thou hast sent me. 43 And when he thus had spoken, he cried with a loud voice, Lazarus, come forth. 44 And he that was dead came forth, bound hand and foot with graveclothes: and his face was bound about with a napkin. Jesus saith unto them, Loose him, and let him go.

45 Then many of the Jews which came to Mary, and had seen the things which Jesus did, believed on him. 46 But some of them went their ways to the Pharisees, and told

αὐτὴν κλαίουσαν, καὶ τοὺς συνελθόντας αὐτῇ Ἰουδαίους
her weeping, and the ²who ³came ⁴with ⁵her ¹Jews

κλαίοντας, ἐνεβριμήσατο τῷ πνεύματι, καὶ ἐτάραξεν ἑαυτόν,
weeping, he groaned in spirit, and troubled himself,

34 καὶ εἶπεν, Ποῦ τεθείκατε αὐτόν; Λέγουσιν αὐτῷ, Κύριε,
and said, Where have ye laid him; They say to him, Lord,

ἔρχου καὶ ἴδε. 35 Ἐδάκρυσεν ὁ Ἰησοῦς. 36 ἔλεγον οὖν οἱ
come and see. ²Wept ¹Jesus. ³Said ⁴therefore ¹the

Ἰουδαῖοι, Ἴδε πῶς ἐφίλει αὐτόν. 37 Τινὲς δὲ ἐξ αὐτῶν
²Jews, Behold how he loved him! But some of them

εἶπον, Οὐκ ἠδύνατο οὗτος ὁ ἀνοίξας τοὺς ὀφθαλμοὺς
said, Was not ³able ¹this [²man] who opened the eyes

τοῦ τυφλοῦ, ποιῆσαι ἵνα καὶ οὗτος μὴ ἀποθάνῃ;
of the blind [man], to have caused that also this one should not have died?

38 Ἰησοῦς οὖν πάλιν ᵐἐμβριμώμενος ἐν ἑαυτῷ ἔρχεται
Jesus therefore again groaning in himself comes

εἰς τὸ μνημεῖον. ἦν δὲ σπήλαιον, καὶ λίθος ἐπέκειτο ἐπ'
to the tomb. Now it was a cave, and a stone was lying upon

αὐτῷ. 39 λέγει ⁿὁ Ἰησοῦς, Ἄρατε τὸν λίθον. Λέγει αὐτῷ
it. ²Says ¹Jesus, Take away the stone. ²Says ¹to ²him

ἡ ἀδελφὴ τοῦ ᵒτεθνηκότος Μάρθα, Κύριε, ἤδη ὄζει·
⁵the ⁶sister ⁷of ⁸him ⁹who ¹⁰has ¹¹died, ⁴Martha, Lord, already he stinks,

τεταρταῖος γάρ ἐστιν. 40 Λέγει αὐτῇ ὁ Ἰησοῦς, Οὐκ εἶπόν
⁴four ⁵days ¹for ²it ³is. ²Says ³to ⁴her ¹Jesus, Said I not

σοι, ὅτι ἐὰν πιστεύσῃς, Pὄψει τὴν δόξαν τοῦ θεοῦ;
to thee, that if thou shouldest believe, thou shalt see the glory of God?

41 Ἦραν οὖν τὸν λίθον ᑫοὗ ἦν ὁ τεθνηκὼς κείμενος.
They took away therefore the stone where ³was ¹the ²dead laid.

Ὁ δὲ Ἰησοῦς ἦρεν τοὺς ὀφθαλμοὺς ἄνω, καὶ εἶπεν, Πά-
And Jesus lifted [his] eyes upwards, and said, Fa-

τερ, εὐχαριστῶ σοι ὅτι ἤκουσάς μου. 42 ἐγὼ δὲ ᾔδειν ὅτι
ther, I thank thee that thou heardest me; and I knew that

πάντοτέ μου ἀκούεις· ἀλλὰ διὰ τὸν ὄχλον τὸν περι-
always me thou hearest; but on account of the crowd who stand

εστῶτα εἶπον ἵνα πιστεύσωσιν ὅτι σύ με ἀπέστειλας.
around I said [it], that they might believe that thou me didst send.

43 Καὶ ταῦτα εἰπών, φωνῇ μεγάλῃ ἐκραύγασεν, Λά-
And these things having said, with a ²voice ¹loud he cried, La-

ζαρε, δεῦρο ἔξω. 44 ʳΚαὶ ἐξῆλθεν ὁ τεθνηκώς, δεδεμένος
zarus, come forth. And came forth he who had been dead, bound

τοὺς πόδας καὶ τὰς χεῖρας κειρίαις, καὶ ἡ ὄψις αὐτοῦ
feet and hands with grave clothes, and his face

σουδαρίῳ περιεδέδετο. Λέγει αὐτοῖς ὁ Ἰησοῦς, Λύσατε
with a handkerchief bound about. ²Says ³to ⁴them ¹Jesus, Loose

αὐτὸν καὶ ἄφετε ˢ ὑπάγειν.
him and let [him] go.

45 Πολλοὶ οὖν ἐκ τῶν Ἰουδαίων οἱ ἐλθόντες πρὸς τὴν
Many therefore of the Jews who came to

ᵗΜαρίαν καὶ θεασάμενοι ᵛἃ ἐποίησεν ʷὁ Ἰησοῦς, ἐπίστευσαν
Mary and saw what ²did ¹Jesus, believed

εἰς αὐτόν. 46 τινὲς δὲ ἐξ αὐτῶν ἀπῆλθον πρὸς τοὺς Φαρι-
on him; but some of them went to the Phari-

ˡ ἐδύνατο LTTrA.   ᵐ ἐμβριμούμενος T.   ⁿ — ὁ L[Tr].   ᵒ τετελευτηκότος LTTrAW.
ᑫ ὄψῃ thou shouldest see LTTrAW.   ᑫ — οὗ ἦν ὁ τεθνηκὼς κείμενος GLTTrA.   ʳ — καὶ
GTTrA.   ˢ + αὐτὸν him T[Tr]A.   ᵗ Μαριὰμ LTTrA.   ᵛ ὁ TrA.   ʷ — ὁ Ἰησοῦς
(read he did) GLTTrAW.

σαίους καὶ ˣεἶπον‖ αὐτοῖς ʸἃ‖ ἐποίησεν ᶻὁ‖ Ἰησοῦς. 47 συνήγα-
sees   and   told   them what ²did   ¹Jesus.   Gathered

γον οὖν οἱ ἀρχιερεῖς καὶ οἱ Φαρισαῖοι συνέδριον, καὶ ἔλεγον,
therefore the chief priests and the Pharisees   a council, and   said,

Τί ποιοῦμεν; ὅτι οὗτος ὁ ἄνθρωπος πολλὰ ⁿσημεῖα ποιεῖ.‖
What   do we? for   this   man   many   signs   does.

48 ἐὰν ἀφῶμεν αὐτὸν οὕτως, πάντες πιστεύσουσιν εἰς αὐτόν·
If   we let alone him   thus,   all   will believe   on him,

καὶ ἐλεύσονται οἱ Ῥωμαῖοι καὶ ἀροῦσιν ἡμῶν καὶ τὸν τόπον
and   will come   the Romans and will take away from us both the   place

καὶ τὸ ἔθνος. 49 Εἷς δέ τις ἐξ αὐτῶν, Καϊάφας, ἀρχιερεὺς
and the nation.   But a certain one of   them,   Caiaphas,   high priest

ὢν τοῦ ἐνιαυτοῦ ἐκείνου, εἶπεν αὐτοῖς, Ὑμεῖς οὐκ οἴδατε
being   of that year,   said   to them,   Ye   know

οὐδέν, 50 οὐδὲ ᵇδιαλογίζεσθε‖ ὅτι συμφέρει ᶜἡμῖν‖ ἵνα εἷς
nothing,   nor   consider   that it is profitable for us that one

ἄνθρωπος ἀποθάνῃ ὑπὲρ τοῦ λαοῦ, καὶ μὴ ὅλον τὸ ἔθνος
man   should die   for   the people, and not ²whole ¹the nation

ἀπόληται. 51 Τοῦτο δὲ ἀφ' ἑαυτοῦ οὐκ εἶπεν, ἀλλὰ ἀρχ-
should perish.   But this from himself he said not, but   high

ιερεὺς ὢν τοῦ ἐνιαυτοῦ ἐκείνου, ᵈπροεφήτευσεν‖ ὅτι ᵉἔμελλεν‖
priest being   of that year,   prophesied that   ²was ³about

ᶠὁ‖ Ἰησοῦς ἀποθνήσκειν ὑπὲρ τοῦ ἔθνους, 52 καὶ οὐχ ὑπὲρ
¹Jesus   to die   for   the   nation;   and not for

τοῦ ἔθνους μόνον, ἀλλ' ἵνα καὶ τὰ τέκνα τοῦ θεοῦ τὰ διεσκορ-
the nation   only,   but that also the children   of God who have been

πισμένα   συναγάγῃ   εἰς ἕν. 53 ἀπ' ἐκείνης οὖν
scattered abroad he might gather together into one.   From that ²therefore

τῆς ἡμέρας ᵍσυνεβουλεύσαντο‖ ἵνα ἀποκτείνωσιν αὐτόν.
¹day   they took counsel together   that   they might kill   him.

54 ʰἸησοῦς οὖν‖ ⁱοὐκ ἔτι‖ παρρησίᾳ περιεπάτει ἐν τοῖς
Jesus therefore no longer publicly   walked   among the

Ἰουδαίοις, ἀλλὰ ἀπῆλθεν ἐκεῖθεν εἰς τὴν χώραν ἐγγὺς τῆς
Jews,   but went away thence into the country near the

ἐρήμου, εἰς Ἐφραὶμ λεγομένην πόλιν, κἀκεῖ ᵏδιέτριβεν‖
desert,   to ⁴Ephraim ³called   ¹a ²city,   and there   he stayed

μετὰ τῶν μαθητῶν ˡαὐτοῦ.‖
with   his disciples.

55 Ἦν δὲ ἐγγὺς τὸ πάσχα τῶν Ἰουδαίων, καὶ ἀνέβησαν
Now ⁶was ⁷near ¹the ²passover ³of ⁴the   ⁵Jews,   and   went up

πολλοὶ εἰς Ἱεροσόλυμα ἐκ τῆς χώρας πρὸ τοῦ πάσχα, ἵνα
many to   Jerusalem out of the country before the passover, that

ἁγνίσωσιν ἑαυτούς. 56 ἐζήτουν οὖν τὸν Ἰησοῦν, καὶ
they might purify themselves. They were seeking therefore Jesus,   and

ᵐἔλεγον‖ μετ' ἀλλήλων ἐν τῷ ἱερῷ ἑστηκότες, Τί δοκεῖ
were saying among one another in the temple standing, What does it seem

ὑμῖν, ὅτι οὐ μὴ ἔλθῃ εἰς τὴν ἑορτήν; 57 Δεδώκεισαν δὲ
to you, that in no wise he will come to the   feast?   Now had given

ⁿκαὶ‖ οἱ ἀρχιερεῖς καὶ οἱ Φαρισαῖοι ᵒἐντολήν,‖ ἵνα ἐάν τις
both the chief priests and the Pharisees a command, that if anyone

γνῷ ποῦ ἐστιν μηνύσῃ, ὅπως πιάσωσιν αὐτόν.
should know where he is he should shew [it], that they might take him.

---

them what things Jesus had done. 47 Then gathered the chief priests and the Pharisees a council, and said, What do we? for this man doeth many miracles. 48 If we let him thus alone, all *men* will believe on him: and the Romans shall come and take away both our place and nation. 49 And one of them, *named* Caiaphas, being the high priest that same year, said unto them, Ye know nothing at all, 50 nor consider that it is expedient for us, that one man should die for the people, and that the whole nation perish not. 51 And this spake he not of himself: but being high priest that year, he prophesied that Jesus should die for that nation; 52 and not for that nation only, but that also he should gather together in one the children of God that were scattered abroad. 53 Then from that day forth they took counsel together for to put him to death. 54 Jesus therefore walked no more openly among the Jews; but went thence unto a country near to the wilderness, into a city called Ephraim, and there continued with his disciples.

55 And the Jews' passover was nigh at hand: and many went out of the country up to Jerusalem before the passover, to purify themselves. 56 Then sought they for Jesus, and spake among themselves, as they stood in the temple, What think ye, that he will not come to the feast? 57 Now both the chief priests and the Pharisees had given a commandment, that, if any man knew where, he were he should shew *it*, that they might take him.

ˣ εἶπαν T.   ʸ ὃ L.   ᶻ — ὁ LTTrA.   ᵃ ποιεῖ σημεῖα LTTrAW.   ᵇ λογίζεσθε LTTrAW.
ᶜ ὑμῖν for you TTrA.   ᵈ ἐπροφήτευσεν LTTrAW.   ᵉ ἤμελλεν LTTrAW.   ᶠ — ὁ GLTTrAW.
ᵍ ἐβουλεύσαντο they took counsel LTTr.   ʰ ὁ οὖν Ἰησοῦς TrA.   ⁱ οὐκέτι GLTTr.
ᵏ ἔμεινεν TrA.   ˡ — αὐτοῦ (*read* the disciples) TTrA.   ᵐ ἔλεγαν T.   ⁿ — καὶ LTTrAW.
ᵒ ἐντολὰς commands TTrA.

　　　　ΙΩΑΝΝΗΣ.　　　　XII

XII. Then Jesus six days before the passover came to Bethany, where Lazarus was which had been dead, whom he raised from the dead. 2 There they made him a supper; and Martha served: but Lazarus was one of them that sat at the table with him. 3 Then took Mary a pound of ointment of spikenard, very costly, and anointed the feet of Jesus, and wiped his feet with her hair: and the house was filled with the odour of the ointment. 4 Then saith one of his disciples, Judas Iscariot, Simon's son, which should betray him, 5 Why was not this ointment sold for three hundred pence, and given to the poor? 6 This he said, not that he cared for the poor; but because he was a thief, and had the bag, and bare what was put therein. 7 Then said Jesus, Let her alone: against the day of my burying hath she kept this. 8 For the poor always ye have with you; but me ye have not always.

1‍2 Ο.οὖν.'Ιησοῦς πρὸ ἓξ ἡμερῶν τοῦ πάσχα ἦλθεν εἰς
　Jesus therefore ³before ¹six ²days the passover came to
Βηθανίαν, ὅπου ἦν Λάζαρος Pὁ τεθνηκώς,‖ ὃν ἤγειρεν
Bethany, where was Lazarus who had died, whom he raised
ἐκ νεκρῶνq. 2 ἐποίησαν οὖν αὐτῷ δεῖπνον ἐκεῖ,
from among [the] dead. They made therefore him a supper there,
καὶ ἡ Μάρθα διηκόνει· ὁ.δὲ.Λάζαρος εἷς ἦν r τῶν ˢσυνανα-
and Martha served, but Lazarus one was of.those re-
κειμένων‖ αὐτῷ. 3 Ἡ.οὖν.ᵗΜαρία‖ λαβοῦσα λίτραν μύρου
clining with him. Mary therefore having taken a pound of ointment
νάρδου πιστικῆς πολυτίμου, ἤλειψεν τοὺς πόδας ᵛτοῦ‖ 'Ιησοῦ,
of ¹hard ¹pure of great price, anointed the feet of Jesus,
καὶ ἐξέμαξεν ταῖς.θριξὶν.αὐτῆς τοὺς.πόδας.αὐτοῦ· ἡ.δὲ οἰκία
and wiped with her hair his feet; and the house
ἐπληρώθη ἐκ τῆς ὀσμῆς τοῦ μύρου. 4 λέγει ʷοὖν‖ ˣεἷς ἐκ
was filled with the odour of the ointment. Says therefore one of
τῶν.μαθητῶν.αὐτοῦ, 'Ιούδας, Σίμωνος 'Ισκαριώτης,‖ ὁ
his disciples, Judas, Simon's [son] Iscariote, who
μέλλων αὐτὸν παραδιδόναι, 5 ʸΔιατί‖ τοῦτο τὸ μύρον οὐκ
was about him to deliver up, Why ²this ⁴ointment ²not
ἐπράθη τριακοσίων δηναρίων, καὶ ἐδόθη πτωχοῖς; 6 Εἶπεν
¹was sold for three hundred denarii, and given to [the] poor? ²he ¹said
δὲ τοῦτο, οὐχ ὅτι περὶ τῶν πτωχῶν ἔμελεν.αὐτῷ, ἀλλ' ὅτι
¹but this, not that for the poor he was caring, but because
κλέπτης ἦν, καὶ τὸ γλωσσόκομον ᶻεἶχεν, καὶ‖ τὰ βαλλόμενα
a thief he was, and the bag had, and what was put into
ἐβάσταζεν. 7 Εἶπεν οὖν ὁ 'Ιησοῦς, "Αφες αὐτήν· ᵃ εἰς
[it] carried. ³Said ²therefore 'Jesus, Let 'alone 'her: for
τὴν ἡμέραν τοῦ.ἐνταφιασμοῦ.μου ᵇτετήρηκεν‖ αὐτό. 8 τοὺς
the day of my burial has she kept it: ²the
πτωχοὺς γὰρ πάντοτε ἔχετε μεθ' ἑαυτῶν, ἐμὲ.δὲ οὐ πάντοτε
³poor ⁴for always ye have with you, but me not always
ἔχετε.
ye have.

9 Much people of the Jews therefore knew that he was there: and they came not for Jesus' sake only, but that they might see Lazarus also, whom he had raised from the dead. 10 But the chief priests consulted that they might put Lazarus also to death; 11 because that by reason of him many of the Jews went away, and believed on Jesus.

9 "Εγνω οὖν ᶜὄχλος πολὺς ἐκ τῶν 'Ιουδαίων ὅτι ἐκεῖ
'Knew ²therefore ¹a ³crowd ²great ⁴of ⁵the ⁶Jews that there
ἐστιν, καὶ ἦλθον, οὐ διὰ τὸν 'Ιησοῦν μόνον, ἀλλ' ἵνα
he is; and they came, not because of Jesus only, but that
καὶ τὸν Λάζαρον ἴδωσιν ὃν ἤγειρεν ἐκ νεκρῶν.
also Lazarus they might see whom he raised from among [the] dead.
10 ἐβουλεύσαντο.δὲ οἱ ἀρχιερεῖς ἵνα καὶ τὸν Λάζαρον ἀπο-
But ⁴took ⁵counsel ¹the ²chief ³priests that also Lazarus they
κτείνωσιν, 11 ὅτι πολλοὶ δι' αὐτὸν ὑπῆγον
might kill, because many ⁴by ⁵reason ⁶of ⁷him ⁸were ⁹going ¹⁰away
τῶν 'Ιουδαίων καὶ ἐπίστευον εἰς τὸν 'Ιησοῦν.
¹of ²the ³Jews and were believing on Jesus.

12 On the next day much people that were come to the feast, when they heard that Jesus was coming to Jerusalem, 13 took branches of palm trees, and went forth to meet him, and

12 Τῇ.ἐπαύριον ὄχλος πολὺς ὁ ἐλθὼν εἰς τὴν ἑορτήν,
On the morrow a ²crowd ¹great who came to the feast,
ἀκούσαντες ὅτι ἔρχεται ᵈὁ‖ 'Ιησοῦς εἰς 'Ιεροσόλυμα, 13 ἔλα-
having heard that ²is ³coming ¹Jesus into Jerusalem, took
βον.τὰ βαΐα τῶν φοινίκων καὶ ἐξῆλθον εἰς ὑπάντησιν ᵉαὐτῷ,‖
branches of the palms and went out to meet him,

P — ὁ τεθνηκὼς [L]τ[TrA].　　q + ὁ (— ὁ T)'Ιησοῦς Jesus (raised) LTTrAW.　　ʳ + ἐκ of
(those) TA.　ˢ ἀνακειμένων σὺν GLTTrAW.　ᵗ Μαριὰμ Tr.　ᵛ [τοῦ] Tr.　ʷ δὲ but (says) T.
ˣ 'Ιούδας ὁ 'Ισκαριώτης εἷς ἐκ (— ἐκ Tr) τῶν μαθητῶν αὐτοῦ TTrA.　ʸ Διὰ τί LTrA.　ᶻ ἔχων
having TTrA.　ᵃ + ἵνα that LTTrAW.　ᵇ τηρήσῃ she may keep LTTrAW.　ᶜ + ὁ the
(crowd) T.　ᵈ — ὁ GLTTrAW.　ᵉ αὐτῶν them W

καὶ ᶠἔκραζον,ⁱⁱ ᵍ᾿Ωσαννά, εὐλογημένος   ὁ ἐρχόμενος ἐν
and   were crying,   Hosanna, , blessed [is] he who comes   in [the]

ὀνόματι κυρίου, ʰ ὁ βασιλεὺς τοῦ ᾿Ισραήλ. 14 Εὑρὼν   δὲ
name of [the] Lord, the   king   of Israel. ³Having ⁴found ¹and

ὁ ᾿Ιησοῦς ὀνάριον ἐκάθισεν ἐπ᾽ αὐτό, καθώς ἐστιν γεγραμ-
²Jesus   a young ass sat upon it,   as   it is   writ-

μένον, 15 Μὴ.φοβοῦ, ⁱθύγατερⁱⁱ Σιών· ἰδού, ὁ.βασιλεύς.σου
ten,   Fear not, daughter of Sion : behold,   thy king

ἔρχεται, καθήμενος ἐπὶ πῶλον ὄνου 16 ταῦτα ᵏδὲⁱⁱ οὐκ
comes,   sitting   on a colt of an ass. ²These ³things ¹now ⁷not

ἔγνωσαν ᶦοἱ.μαθηταὶ.αὐτοῦⁱⁱ τὸ.πρῶτον, ἀλλ᾽ ὅτε ἐδοξάσθη
⁸knew   ⁴his ⁵disciples at the first,   but when was glorified

ᵐὁⁱⁱ ᾿Ιησοῦς τότε ἐμνήσθησαν ὅτι ταῦτα ἦν ἐπ᾽ αὐτῷ
Jesus   then · they remembered that these things were of him

γεγραμμένα, ᾽καὶ ταῦτα ἐποίησαν αὐτῷ. 17 ἐμαρτύρει οὖν
written, and these things they did to him. Bore witness therefore

ὁ ὄχλος ὁ ὢν μετ᾽ αὐτοῦ, ⁿὅτεⁱⁱ τὸν Λάζαρον ἐφώνησεν ἐκ
the crowd that was with him,   when Lazarus he called out of

τοῦ μνημείου, καὶ ἤγειρεν αὐτὸν ἐκ   νεκρῶν. 18 διὰ
the tomb,   and raised him from among [the] dead. On account of

τοῦτο ᵒκαὶⁱⁱ ὑπήντησεν αὐτῷ ὁ ὄχλος, ὅτι ᴾἤκουσενⁱⁱ τοῦτο
this also met   him the crowd, because it heard ⁵this

αὐτὸν.πεποιηκέναι τὸ σημεῖον. 19 οἱ οὖν Φαρισαῖοι ᑫεῖπονⁱⁱ
¹of ²his ³having ⁴done sign. The ²therefore ¹Pharisees said

πρὸς ἑαυτούς, Θεωρεῖτε ὅτι οὐκ ὠφελεῖτε οὐδέν; ἴδε, ὁ κόσμος
among themselves, Do ye see that ye gain nothing? lo, the world

ὀπίσω αὐτοῦ ἀπῆλθεν.
after him is gone.

20 ᾿Ησαν.δὲ ʳτινες ῞Ελληνεςⁱⁱ ἐκ τῶν ἀναβαινόντων ἵνα
And there were certain Greeks   among those coming up that

ˢπροσκυνήσωσινⁱⁱ ἐν τῇ ἑορτῇ· 21 οὗτοι οὖν προσῆλθον
they might worship in the feast; these therefore came

Φιλίππῳ, τῷ ἀπὸ Βηθσαϊδὰ τῆς Γαλιλαίας, καὶ ἠρώτων
to Philip, who was from Bethsaida of Galilee,   and they asked

αὐτὸν λέγοντες, Κύριε, θέλομεν τὸν ᾿Ιησοῦν ἰδεῖν. 22 ῎Ερχε-
him saying, Sir, we desire ³Jesus ¹to ²see. ⁵Comes

ται ᵗ Φίλιππος καὶ λέγει τῷ ᾿Ανδρέᾳ· ᵛκαὶ πάλινⁱⁱ ᾿Ανδρέας
⁴Philip   and tells Andrew,   and again   Andrew

καὶ Φίλιππος ʷ λέγουσιν τῷ ᾿Ιησοῦ. 23 ὁ.δὲ.᾿Ιησοῦς ˣἀπε-
and Philip   tell   Jesus.   But Jesus an-

κρίνατοⁱⁱ αὐτοῖς λέγων, ᾿Ελήλυθεν ἡ ὥρα ἵνα δοξασθῇ
swered   them saying, ³Has ⁴come ¹the ²hour that should be glorified

ὁ υἱὸς τοῦ ἀνθρώπου. 24 ἀμὴν ἀμὴν λέγω ὑμῖν, ἐὰν.μὴ ὁ
the Son of man.   Verily verily I say to you, Unless the

κόκκος τοῦ σίτου πεσὼν εἰς τὴν γῆν ἀποθάνῃ, αὐτὸς μόνος
grain of wheat falling into the ground should die, it   alone

μένει· ἐὰν.δὲ ἀποθάνῃ, πολὺν καρπὸν φέρει. 25 ὁ φιλῶν
abides ; but if it should die, much fruit it bears. He that loves

τὴν.ψυχὴν.αὐτοῦ ʸἀπολέσειⁱⁱ αὐτήν, καὶ ὁ μισῶν τὴν
his life   shall lose it,   and he that hates

ψυχὴν αὐτοῦ ἐν τῷ.κόσμῳ.τούτῳ εἰς ζωὴν αἰώνιον φυλάξει
²life ¹his in   this world   to life eternal shall keep

cried, Hosanna: Blessed is the King of Israel that cometh in the name of the Lord. 14 And Jesus, when he had found a young ass, sat thereon ; as it, is written, 15 Fear not, daughter of Sion : behold, thy King cometh, sitting on an ass's colt. 16 These things understood not his disciples at the first: but when Jesus was glorified, then remembered they that these things were written of him, and that they had done these things unto him. 17 The people therefore that was with him when he called Lazarus out of his grave, and raised him from the dead, bare record. 18 For this cause the people also met him, for that they heard that he had done this miracle. 19 The Pharisees therefore said among themselves, Perceive ye how ye prevail nothing? behold, the world is gone after him.

20 And there were certain Greeks among them that came up to worship at the feast: 21 the same came therefore to Philip, which was of Bethsaida of Galilee, and desired him, saying, Sir, we would see Jesus. 22 Philip cometh and telleth Andrew: and again Andrew and Philip tell Jesus. 23 And Jesus answered them, saying, The hour is come, that the Son of man should be glorified. 24 Verily, verily, I say unto you, Except a corn of wheat fall into the ground and die, it abideth alone : but if it' die, it bringeth forth much fruit. 25 He that loveth his life shall lose it ; and he that hateth his life in this world shall keep it unto life eternal. 26 If

---

ᶠ ἐκραύγαζον LTTrA.   ᵍ + [λέγοντες] saying L.   ʰ + καὶ and TTrA.   ⁱ θυγάτηρ LTTrA.
ᵏ — δὲ [L]TTrA.   ˡ αὐτοῦ οἱ μαθηταὶ T.   ᵐ — ὁ TTrAW.   ⁿ ὅτι because EGLTW.
ᵒ — καὶ Tr.   ᴾ ἤκουσαν they heard GLTTrAW.   ᑫ εἶπαν TTr.   ʳ ᾽Ελληνές τινες LTTrA.
ˢ προσκυνήσουσιν they shall worship LTrA.   ᵗ + ὁ TrA.   ᵛ ἔρχεται (Andrew) comes LTTrA.
ʷ + καὶ and LTTrA.   ˣ ἀποκρίνεται answers TTr.   ʸ ἀπολλύει loses TTr.

any man serve me, let him follow me; and where I am, there shall also my servant be: if any man serve me, him will my Father honour.

27 Now is my soul troubled; and what shall I say? Father, save me from this hour: but for this cause came I unto this hour. 28 Father, glorify thy name. Then came there a voice from heaven, saying, I have both glorified it, and will glorify it again. 29 The people therefore, that stood by, and heard it, said that it thundered: others said, An angel spake to him. 30 Jesus answered and said, This voice came not because of me, but for your sakes. 31 Now is the judgment of this world : now shall the prince of this world be cast out. 32 And I, if I be lifted up from the earth, will draw all men unto me. 33 This he said, signifying what death he should die. 34 The people answered him, We have heard out of the law that Christ abideth for ever: and how sayest thou, The Son of man must be lifted up? who is this Son of man? 35 Then Jesus said unto them, Yet a little while is the light with you. Walk while ye have the light, lest darkness come upon you : for he that walketh in darkness knoweth not whither he goeth. 36 While ye have light, believe in the light, that ye may be the children of light. These things spake Jesus, and departed, and did hide himself from them. 37 But though he had done so many miracles before them, yet they believed not on him: 38 that the saying of Esaias the prophet might be ful-

αὐτήν. 26 ἐὰν ἐμοὶ ᵈδιακονῇ τις,‖ ἐμοὶ ἀκολουθείτω· καὶ
it.   If   ²me   ²serve ¹anyone, me   let him follow ;. and
ὅπου εἰμὶ ἐγὼ ἐκεῖ καὶ ὁ διάκονος ὁ ἐμὸς ἔσται· ᵃκαὶ‖ ἐάν
where ²am ¹I there also ²servant ¹my shall be.   And if
τις ἐμοὶ διακονῇ, τιμήσει αὐτὸν ὁ πατήρ.
anyone me   serve, ²will ⁵honour ¹him ³the ⁴Father.

27 Νῦν ἡ.ψυχή.μου τετάρακται, καὶ τί εἴπω; Πάτερ,
   Now my soul   has been troubled, and what shall I say? Father,
σῶσόν με ἐκ τῆς.ὥρας.ταύτης.ᵇ ἀλλὰ διὰ τοῦτο ἦλθον
save me from   this hour.   But on account of this I came
εἰς τὴν.ὥραν.ταύτην. 28 Πάτερ, δόξασόν σου τὸ ὄνομα.
to   this hour.   Father, glorify thy   name.
ᵉΗλθεν.οὖν φωνὴ ἐκ τοῦ οὐρανοῦ, Καὶ ἐδόξασα καὶ πάλιν
Therefore came a voice out of   heaven, ²Both ¹I glorified and again
δοξάσω. 29 Ὁ.ᶜοὖν‖.ὄχλος ὁ ᵈἐστὼς‖ ᵉκαὶ‖ ἀκούσας
will glorify [it]. Therefore the crowd which stood [there] and heard
ἔλεγεν βροντὴν.γεγονέναι. ἄλλοι ἔλεγον, Ἄγγελος⸋ αὐτῷ‖
said, Thunder there has been : others said,   An angel ; to him
λελάληκεν. 30 Ἀπεκρίθη ᶠὁ‖ Ἰησοῦς καὶ εἶπεν, Οὐ δι᾽ ἐμὲ
has spoken. ²Answered ¹Jesus and said, Not because of me
ᵍαὕτη ἡ φωνὴ‖ γέγονεν, ἀλλὰ δι᾽ ὑμᾶς. 31 νῦν κρίσις
this   voice   has come, but because of you. Now judgment
ἐστιν τοῦ.κόσμου.τούτου· νῦν ὁ ἄρχων τοῦ.κόσμου.τούτου
is   of.this world ;   now the prince of this world
ἐκβληθήσεται ἔξω· 32 κἀγὼ ἐὰν ὑψωθῶ ἐκ τῆς γῆς, πάν-
shall be cast out :   and I if I be lifted up from the earth, ²all
τας ἑλκύσω πρὸς ἐμαυτόν. 33 Τοῦτο.δὲ ἔλεγεν, σημαίνων
¹will ²draw to myself.   But this   he said, signifying
ποίῳ θανάτῳ ἤμελλεν ἀποθνήσκειν. 34 ἀπεκρίθη ʰ αὐτῷ
by what death he was about to die.   ³Answered ⁴him
ὁ ὄχλος, Ἡμεῖς ἠκούσαμεν ἐκ τοῦ νόμου ὅτι ὁ χριστὸς
¹the ²crowd, We   heard   out of the law that the Christ
μένει εἰς.τὸν.αἰῶνα, καὶ πῶς ¹σὺ λέγεις,‖ Ὅτι δεῖ ὑψωθῆναι
abides for ever,   and how ²thou ¹sayest, that must be lifted up
τὸν υἱὸν τοῦ ἀνθρώπου; τίς ἐστιν οὗτος ὁ υἱὸς τοῦ ἀνθρώπου;
the Son of man?   Who is this   the Son of man?
35 Εἶπεν οὖν αὐτοῖς ὁ Ἰησοῦς, Ἔτι μικρὸν χρόνον τὸ
   ³Said ²therefore ⁴to ⁵them ¹Jesus, Yet a little while the
φῶς ᵏμεθ᾽ ὑμῶν‖ ἐστιν. περιπατεῖτε ˡἕως‖ τὸ φῶς ἔχετε, ἵνα
light with you   is.   Walk   while the light ye have, that
μὴ σκοτία ὑμᾶς καταλάβῃ· καὶ ὁ περιπατῶν ἐν τῇ
²not ¹darkness ¹you ²may ⁴overtake. And he who walks in the
σκοτίᾳ οὐκ.οἶδεν ποῦ ὑπάγει. 36 ˡἕως‖ τὸ φῶς ἔχετε, πισ-
darkness knows not where he goes. While the light ye have, be-
τεύετε εἰς τὸ φῶς, ἵνα υἱοὶ φωτὸς γένησθε. Ταῦτα
lieve in the light, that sons of light ye may become. These things
ἐλάλησεν ᵐὁ‖ Ἰησοῦς, καὶ ἀπελθὼν ἐκρύβη ἀπ᾽ αὐτῶν.
spoke   Jesus,   and going away was hid from   them.
37 Τοσαῦτα.δὲ αὐτοῦ σημεῖα πεποιηκότος ἔμπροσθεν αὐτῶν
   But [though] so many ²he ¹signs had done   before   them
οὐκ.ἐπίστευον εἰς αὐτόν, 38 ἵνα ὁ λόγος Ἡσαΐου τοῦ προ-
they believed not on him,   that the word of Esaias the pro-

ᶻ τις διακονῇ LTTrAW. ᵃ— καὶ GLTTrA. ᵇ ταυτης; (continue the question to the word hour) GLTr. ᶜ [οὖν] LTr. ᵈ ἐστηκὼς L. ᵉ — καὶ T. ᶠ — ὁ TTrA. ᵍ ἡ φωνὴ αὕτη LTTrAW. ʰ + οὖν therefore TA. ¹ λέγεις σύ TTrA. ᵏ ἐν ὑμῖν among you GLTTrA. ˡ ἕως LTTrA. ᵐ — ὁ LTTrA.

φήτου πληρωθῇ, ὃν εἶπεν, Κύριε, τίς ἐπίστευσεν τῇ
phet might be fulfilled, which he said, Lord, who believed

ἀκοῇ.ἡμῶν; καὶ ὁ βραχίων κυρίου τίνι ἀπεκαλύφθη;
our report? and the arm of [the] Lord to whom was it revealed?

39 Διὰ.τοῦτο οὐκ.ἠδύναντο πιστεύειν, ὅτι πάλιν εἶπεν
On this account they could not believe, because again said

Ἡσαΐας, 40 Τετύφλωκεν αὐτῶν τοὺς ὀφθαλμοὺς καὶ ⁿπε-
Esaias, He has blinded their eyes and has

πώρωκεν‖ αὐτῶν τὴν καρδίαν· ἵνα μὴ.ἴδωσιν τοῖς ὀφ-
hardened their heart, that they should not see with the

θαλμοῖς καὶ νοήσωσιν τῇ καρδίᾳ καὶ °ἐπιστραφῶσιν,‖ καὶ
eyes and understand with the heart and be converted, and

ᴾἰάσωμαι‖ αὐτούς. 41 Ταῦτα εἶπεν Ἡσαΐας, �q ὅτε‖ εἶδεν
I should heal them. These things said Esaias, when he saw

τὴν.δόξαν.αὐτοῦ, καὶ ἐλάλησεν περὶ αὐτοῦ. 42 ὅμως μέντοι
his glory, and spoke concerning him. Although indeed

καὶ ἐκ τῶν ἀρχόντων πολλοὶ ἐπίστευσαν εἰς αὐτόν·
even from among the rulers many believed on him,

ἀλλὰ διὰ τοὺς Φαρισαίους οὐχ.ὡμολόγουν, ἵνα μὴ
but on account of the Pharisees they confessed not, that not

ἀποσυνάγωγοι γένωνται. 43 ἠγάπησαν.γὰρ τὴν δόξαν
put out of the synagogue they might be; for they loved the glory

τῶν ἀνθρώπων μᾶλλον ἤπερ τὴν δόξαν τοῦ θεοῦ. 44 ²Ἰησοῦς
of men more than the glory of God. ²Jesus

δὲ ἔκραξεν καὶ εἶπεν, Ὁ πιστεύων εἰς ἐμέ, οὐ.πιστεύει εἰς
¹but cried and said, He that believes on me, believes not on

ἐμέ, ᵗἀλλ᾽‖ εἰς τὸν πέμψαντά με· 45 καὶ ὁ θεωρῶν ἐμέ,
me, but on him who sent me; and he that beholds me,

θεωρεῖ τὸν πέμψαντά με. 46 ἐγὼ φῶς εἰς τὸν κόσμον
beholds him who sent me. I a light into the world

ἐλήλυθα, ἵνα πᾶς ὁ πιστεύων εἰς ἐμὲ ἐν τῇ σκοτίᾳ μὴ
have come, that everyone that believes on me in the darkness ²not

μείνῃ. 47 καὶ ἐάν τις μου ἀκούσῃ τῶν ῥημάτων καὶ μὴ
¹may abide. And if anyone ⁴of ⁵me ¹hear ²the ³words and ²not

ˢπιστεύσῃ,‖ ἐγὼ οὐ.κρίνω αὐτόν· οὐ.γὰρ.ἦλθον ἵνα κρίνω
¹believe, I do not judge him, for I came not that I might judge

τὸν κόσμον, ἀλλ᾽ ἵνα σώσω τὸν κόσμον. 48 ὁ ἀθετῶν
the world, but that I might save the world. He that rejects

ἐμὲ καὶ μὴ.λαμβάνων τὰ.ῥήματά.μου, ἔχει τὸν κρίνοντα
me and does not receive my words, has him who judges

αὐτόν· ὁ λόγος ὃν ἐλάλησα, ἐκεῖνος κρινεῖ αὐτὸν ἐν τῇ
him: the word which I spoke, that shall judge him in the

ἐσχάτῃ ἡμέρᾳ. 49 ὅτι ἐγὼ ἐξ ἐμαυτοῦ οὐκ.ἐλάλησα· ἀλλ᾽
last day; for I from myself spoke not, but

ὁ πέμψας με πατήρ, αὐτός μοι ἐντολὴν ᵗἔδωκεν‖ τί
the ²who ³sent ⁴me ¹Father, himself me commandment gave what

εἴπω καὶ τί λαλήσω· 50 καὶ οἶδα ὅτι ἡ.ἐντολὴ.αὐτοῦ
I should say and what I should speak; and I know that his commandment

ζωὴ αἰώνιός ἐστιν· ἃ οὖν ᵛλαλῶ ἐγώ,‖ καθὼς εἴρηκέν μοι
life eternal is. What therefore ²speak ¹I, as has said to me

ὁ πατήρ, οὕτως λαλῶ.
the Father, so I speak.

13 Πρὸ.δὲ τῆς ἑορτῆς του πάσχα, εἰδὼς ὁ Ἰησοῦς ὅτι
Now before the feast of the passover, ²knowing ¹Jesus that

---

filled, which he spake,
Lord, who hath be-
lieved our report? and
to whom hath the arm
of the Lord been re-
vealed? 39 Therefore
they could not believe,
because that Esaias
said again, 40 He hath
blinded their eyes, and
hardened their heart;
that they should not
see with *their* eyes, nor
understand with *their*
heart, and be convert-
ed, and I should heal
them. 41 These things
said Esaias, when he
saw his glory, and
spake of him. 42 Never-
theless among the chief
rulers also many be-
lieved on him; but be-
cause of the Pharisees
they did not confess
him, lest they should
be put out of the syna-
gogue: 43 for they
loved the praise of men
more than the praise of
God. 44 Jesus cried and
said, He that believeth
on me, believeth not on
me, but on him that
sent me. 45 And he that
seeth me seeth him
that sent me. 46 I am
come a light into the
world, that whosoever
believeth on me should
not abide in darkness.
47 And if any man
hear my words, and be-
lieve not, I judge him
not: for I came not to
judge the world, but to
save the world. 48 He
that rejecteth me, and
receiveth not my
words, hath one that
judgeth him: the word
that I have spoken, the
same shall judge him
in the last day. 49 For
I have not spoken of
myself; but the Father
which sent me, he gave
me a commandment,
what I should say, and
what I should speak.
50 And I know that
his commandment is
life everlasting: what-
soever I speak there-
fore, even as the Father
said unto me, so I
speak.

XIII. Now before the
feast of the passover,
when Jesus knew that

ⁿ ἐπώρωσεν hardened TTrA. ° στραφῶσιν LTTrA. ᴾ ἰάσομαι I shall heal LTTrA.
q ὅτι because GLTTrA. ʳ ἀλλὰ LTTrA. ˢ φυλάξῃ keep [them] LTTrAW. ᵗ δέδωκεν has
given LTTrAW. ᵛ ἐγὼ λαλῶ LTTrA.

his hour was come that he should depart out of ·this world unto the Father, having loved his own which were in the world, he loved them unto the end. 2 And supper being ended, the devil having now put into the heart of Judas Iscariot, Simon's *son*, to betray him; 3 Jesus knowing that the Father had given all things into his hands, and that he was come from God, and went to God; 4 he riseth from supper, and laid aside his garments ; and took a towel, and girded himself. 5 After that he poureth water into a bason, and began to wash the disciples' feet, and to wipe *them* with the towel wherewith he was girded. 6 Then cometh he to Simon Peter: and Peter saith unto him, Lord, dost thou wash my feet? 7 Jesus answered and said unto him, What I do thou knowest not now ; but thou shalt know hereafter. 8 Peter saith unto him, Thou shalt never wash my feet. Jesus answered him, If I wash thee not, thou hast no part with me. 9 Simon Peter saith unto him, Lord, not my feet only, but also my hands and *my* head. 10 Jesus saith to him, He that is washed needeth not save to wash *his* feet, but is clean every whit : and ye are clean, but not all. 11 For he knew who should betray him; therefore said he, Ye are not all clean. 12 So after he had washed their feet, and had taken his garments, and was set down again, he said unto them, Know ye what I have done to you? 13 Ye call me

ᵂἐλήλυθεν‖ αὐτοῦ ἡ ὥρα ἵνα μεταβῇ ἐκ τοῦ.κόσμου.τού-
has come his hour that he should depart out of this world

του πρὸς τὸν πατέρα, ἀγαπήσας τοὺς.ἰδίους τοὺς ἐν τῷ
to the Father, having loved his own which [were] in the

κόσμῳ εἰς τέλος ἠγάπησεν αὐτούς. 2 καὶ δείπνου ˣγενο-
world to [the] end , he loved them. And supper taking

μένου,‖ τοῦ διαβόλου ἤδη βεβληκότος εἰς τὴν καρδίαν
place, the devil already having put . into the heart

ʸἸούδα Σίμωνος Ἰσκαριώτου, ἵνα αὐτὸν παραδῷ,‖
of Judas, Simon's [son] Iscariote, that him he should deliver up,

3 εἰδὼς ᶻὁ Ἰησοῦς‖ ὅτι πάντα ᵃδέδωκεν‖ αὐτῷ ὁ πατὴρ
²knowing ¹Jesus ³that ⁹all ¹⁰things ⁸has ⁷given ⁸him ⁴the ⁵Father

εἰς ·τὰς χεῖρας, καὶ ὅτι ἀπὸ θεοῦ ἐξῆλθεν καὶ πρὸς τὸν
into [his] hands, and that from God he came out and to

θεὸν ὑπάγει, 4 ἐγείρεται ·ἐκ τοῦ δείπνου καὶ τίθησιν τὰ
God goes, he rises from the supper and lays aside [his]

ἱμάτια, καὶ λαβὼν λέντιον διέζωσεν ἑαυτόν· 5. εἶτα βάλ-
garments and having taken a towel he girded himself : afterwards he

λει ὕδωρ εἰς τὸν νιπτῆρα, καὶ ἤρξατο νίπτειν τοὺς πόδας
pours water into. the washing-basin, and began to wash the feet

τῶν μαθητῶν, καὶ ἐκμάσσειν τῷ λεντίῳ ᾧ ἦν
of the disciples, and to wipe [them] with the towel with which he was

διεζωσμένος. 6 ἔρχεται οὖν πρὸς Σίμωνα Πέτρον· ᵇκαὶ‖
girded. He comes therefore to Simon Peter, and

λέγει αὐτῷ ᶜἐκεῖνος,‖ Κύριε, σύ μου νίπτεις τοὺς πόδας;
²says ³to ⁴him ⁵ ¹he, Lord, ²thou ³of ⁴me ¹dost wash the feet?

7 Ἀπεκρίθη Ἰησοῦς καὶ εἶπεν αὐτῷ, Ὃ ἐγὼ ποιῶ σὺ οὐκ
²Answered ¹Jesus and said to him, What I do thou ²not

οἶδας ἄρτι, γνώσῃ.δὲ μετὰ.ταῦτα. 8 Λέγει αὐτῷ Πέ-
¹knowest now, but thou shalt know hereafter. ²Says ³to ⁴him ¹Pe-

τρος, Οὐ.μὴ νίψῃς ᵈτοὺς.πόδας.μου‖ εἰς.τὸν.αἰῶνα.
ter, In no wise mayest thou wash my feet for ever.

Ἀπεκρίθη ᵉαὐτῷ ὁ Ἰησοῦς,‖ Ἐὰν.μὴ νίψω σε, οὐκ.ἔχεις
²Answered ³him ¹Jesus, Unless I wash thee, thou hast not

μέρος μετ᾽ ἐμοῦ. 9 Λέγει αὐτῷ Σίμων Πέτρος, Κύριε, μὴ
part with me. ³Says ⁴to ⁵him ¹Simon ²Peter, Lord, not

τοὺς.πόδας.μου μόνον, ἀλλὰ καὶ τὰς χεῖρας καὶ τὴν κεφαλήν.
my feet only, but also the hands and the head.

10 Λέγει αὐτῷ ᶠὁ‖ Ἰησοῦς, Ὁ λελουμένος ᵍοὐ χρείαν
²Says ³to ⁴him ¹Jesus, He that has been laved ²not ³need

ἔχει ʰἢ‖ ⁱτοὺς πόδας‖ νίψασθαι, ἀλλ᾽ ἔστιν καθαρὸς
¹has [other] than the feet to wash, but is clean

ὅλος· καὶ ὑμεῖς καθαροί ἐστε, ἀλλ᾽ οὐχὶ πάντες. 11 ᾔδει.γὰρ
wholly; and ye clean are, but not all. For he knew

τὸν παραδιδόντα αὐτόν· διὰ τοῦτο εἶπεν, ᵏΟὐχὶ πάν-
him who was delivering up ·him : on account of this· he said, ³Not ⁴all

τες καθαροί ἐστε. 12 Ὅτε οὖν ἔνιψεν τοὺς.πόδας.αὐτῶν,
⁵clean ¹ye ²are. When therefore he had washed. their feet,

ˡκαὶ‖ ἔλαβεν τὰ.ἱμάτια.αὐτοῦ, ᵐ ⁿἀναπεσὼν‖ πάλιν, εἶπεν
and taken his garments, having reclined again, he said

αὐτοῖς, Γινώσκετε τί πεποίηκα ὑμῖν; 13 ὑμεῖς φωνεῖτέ με
to them, . Do ye know what I have done to you? Ye call me

ᵂ ἦλθεν was come LTTrA. ˣ γινομένου TTr. ʸ ἵνα παραδοῖ αὐτὸν Ἰούδας Σίμωνος Ἰσκαριώτης TTrA ; Ἰούδα Σίμ. Ἰσκ. ἵνα παραδοῖ αὐτὸν L. ᶻ — ὁ Ἰησοῦς (*read* [Jesus] [L]TTrA. ᵃ ἔδωκεν gave TTr. ᵇ — καὶ TTrA. ᶜ — ἐκεῖνος (*read* λέγει he says) LT[Tr]A. ᵈ μου τοὺς πόδας LTTrA. ᵉ Ἰησοῦς αὐτῷ LTTrA. ᶠ — ὁ T[Tr]. ᵍ οὐκ ἔχει χρείαν LTTrAW. ʰ εἰ μὴ except LTrA ; — ἢ T. ⁱ — τοὺς πόδας T. ᵏ + ὅτι LTTrA. ˡ — καὶ L. ᵐ + καὶ LTTrA. ⁿ ἀνέπεσεν reclined TTrA.

ὁ διδάσκαλος καὶ ὁ κύριος, καὶ καλῶς λέγετε, εἰμὶ γάρ.
the Teacher and the Lord, and well ye say, "I "am ['so] 'for.

14 εἰ οὖν ἐγὼ ἔνιψα ὑμῶν τοὺς πόδας, ὁ κύριος καὶ ὁ
If therefore I washed your feet, the Lord and the

διδάσκαλος, καὶ ὑμεῖς ὀφείλετε ἀλλήλων νίπτειν τοὺς πόδας.
Teacher, also ye ought of one another to wash the feet;

15 ὑπόδειγμα.γὰρ °ἔδωκα" ὑμῖν, ἵνα καθὼς ἐγὼ ἐποίησα ὑμῖν,
for an example I gave you, that as I did to you,

καὶ ὑμεῖς ποιῆτε. 16 ἀμὴν ἀμὴν λέγω ὑμῖν, οὐκ.ἔστιν δοῦλος
also ye should do. Verily verily I say to you, ²Is ⁴not ¹a ²bondman

μείζων τοῦ.κυρίου.αὐτοῦ, οὐδὲ ἀπόστολος μείζων τοῦ.πέμψαν-
greater than his lord, nor a messenger greater than he who sent

τος αὐτόν. 17 εἰ ταῦτα οἴδατε, μακάριοί ἐστε ἐὰν ποιῆτε
him. If these things ye know, blessed are ye if ye do

αὐτά. 18 οὐ περὶ πάντων ὑμῶν λέγω· ἐγὼᵖ οἶδα ᵠοὓς"
them. Not of ²all ¹you I speak. I know whom

ἐξελεξάμην· ἀλλ᾽ ἵνα ἡ γραφὴ πληρωθῇ, Ὁ τρώγων
I chose, but that the scripture might be fulfilled, He that eats

ʳμετ᾽ ἐμοῦ" τὸν ἄρτον ˢἐπῆρεν" ἐπ᾽ ἐμὲ τ.ην.πτέρναν.αὐτοῦ.
²with ¹me ¹bread lifted up against me his heel.

19 ᵗἀπ᾽.ἄρτι" λέγω ὑμῖν πρὸ τοῦ.γενέσθαι, ἵνα ᵛὅταν γένη-
From this time I tell you, before it comes to pass, that when it come

ται, πιστεύσητε" ὅτι ἐγώ εἰμι. 20 ἀμὴν ἀμὴν λέγω ὑμῖν,
to pass, ye may believe that I am [he]. Verily verily I say to you,

Ὁ λαμβάνων ᵂἐάν".τινα πέμψω, ἐμὲ λαμβάνει· ὁ.δὲ
He that receives whomsoever I shall send, me receives; and he that

ἐμὲ λαμβάνων, λαμβάνει τὸν πέμψαντά με. 21 Ταῦτα
me receives, receives him who sent me. These things

εἰπὼν ˣὁ" Ἰησοῦς ἐταράχθη τῷ πνεύματι, καὶ ἐμαρτύρησεν
saying Jesus was troubled in spirit, and testified

καὶ εἶπεν, Ἀμὴν ἀμὴν λέγω ὑμῖν, ὅτι εἷς ἐξ ὑμῶν παραδώσει
and said, Verily verily I say to you, that one of you will deliver up

με. 22 ˣΈβλεπον ᵞοὖν" εἰς ἀλλήλους οἱ μαθηταί, ἀπορού-
me. ⁴Looked ³therefore ⁵upon ⁶one ⁷another ¹the ²disciples, doubt-

μενοι περὶ τίνος λέγει. 23 ἦν.ᶻδὲ" ἀνακείμενος εἷς ᵃ τῶν
ing of whom he speaks. But there was reclining one of the

μαθητῶν.αὐτοῦ ἐν τῷ κόλπῳ τοῦ.Ἰησοῦ, ὃν ἠγάπα ὁ Ἰησοῦς·
of his disciples in the bosom of Jesus, whom ²loved ¹Jesus.

24 νεύει οὖν τούτῳ Σίμων Πέτρος ᵇπυθέσθαι τίς
⁵Makes ⁷a ⁸sign ³therefore ⁹to ¹⁰him ³Simon ⁴Peter to ask who

ἂν.εἴη" περὶ οὗ λέγει. 25 ᶜἐπιπεσὼν" ᵈδὲ" ἐκεῖνοςᵉ ἐπὶ τὸ
it might be of whom he speaks. ³Having ⁴leaned ¹and ²he on the

στῆθος τοῦ Ἰησοῦ, λέγει αὐτῷ, Κύριε, τίς ἐστιν; 26 Ἀπο-
breast of Jesus, says to him, Lord, who is it? ²An-

κρίνεταιᶠ ᵍὁ" Ἰησοῦς, Ἐκεῖνός ἐστιν ᾧ ἐγὼ ʰβάψας" τὸ
swers ¹Jesus, He it is to whom I, having dipped the

ψωμίον ⁱἐπιδώσω." ᵏΚαὶ ἐμβάψας" τὸ ψωμίον ˡ δίδωσιν
morsel, shall give [it]. And having dipped the morsel he gives [it]

Ἰούδα Σίμωνος ᵐΙσκαριώτῃ." 27 καὶ μετὰ τὸ ψωμίον,
to Judas, Simon's [son] Iscariote. And after the morsel,

Master and Lord: and ye say well; for so I am. 14 If I then, your Lord and Master, have washed your feet; ye also ought to wash one another's feet. 15 For I have given you an example, that ye should do as I have done to you. 16 Verily, verily, I say unto you, The servant is not greater than his lord; neither he that is sent greater than he that sent him. 17 If ye know these things, happy are ye if ye do them. 18 I speak not of you all: I know whom I have chosen: but that the scripture may be fulfilled, He that eateth bread with me hath lifted up his heel against me. 19 Now I tell you before it come, that, when it is come to pass, ye may believe that I am he. 20 Verily, verily, I say unto you, He that receiveth whomsoever I send receiveth me; and he that receiveth me receiveth him that sent me. 21 When Jesus had thus said, he was troubled in spirit, and testified, and said, Verily, verily, I say unto you, that one of you shall betray me. 22 Then the disciples looked one on another, doubting of whom he spake. 23 Now there was leaning on Jesus' bosom one of his disciples, whom Jesus loved. 24 Simon Peter therefore beckoned to him, that he should ask who it should be of whom he spake. 25 He then lying on Jesus' breast saith unto him, Lord, who is it? 26 Jesus answered, He is it, to whom I shall give a sop, when I have dipped it. And when he had dipped the sop, he gave it to Judas Iscariot, the son of Simon. 27 And after the sop

ᵒ δέδωκα I have given τ. ᵖ + [γὰρ] for (I) L. ᵠ τίνας TTrA. ʳ μου my TrA.
ˢ ἐπῆρκεν has lifted up τ. ᵗ ἀπάρτι τ. ᵛ πιστεύσητε (πιστεύητε Tr) ὅταν γένηται TTrA.
ᵂ ἂν LTTrA. ˣ — ὁ TTrA. ᵞ — οὖν T[Tr]A. ᶻ — δὲ but TTrA. ᵃ + ἐκ of (his) GLTTrAW.
ᵇ καὶ λέγει αὐτῷ Εἰπὲ τίς ἐστιν and says to him, Say who it is LTTrA. ᶜ ἀναπεσὼν having
leaned back LTrA. ᵈ — δὲ TrA ; οὖν therefore τ. ᵉ + οὕτως thus T[Tr]AW. ᶠ + οὖν
therefore [L].A. ᵍ [ὁ] Tr. ʰ ἐμβάψας L ; βάψω shall dip TTrA. ⁱ καὶ δώσω αὐτῷ and
sh.ll give to him TTrA. ᵏ βάψας οὖν having dipped therefore TTrA. ˡ + λαμβάνει
καὶ he takes and TTrA. ᶠ ᵐ Ἰσκαριώτου (read son of Simon Iscariote.) TTrA.

Satan entered into him. Then said Jesus unto him, That thou doest, do quickly. 28 Now no man at the table knew for what intent he spake this unto him. 29 For some of them thought, because Judas had the bag, that Jesus had said unto him, Buy those things that we have need of against the feast; or, that he should give something to the poor. 30 He then having received the sop went immediately out: and it was night.

τότε εἰσῆλθεν εἰς ἐκεῖνον ὁ σατανᾶς. λέγει οὖν αὐτῷ ⁿὁ‖
then entered into him Satan. ²Says ²therefore ⁴to ⁵him
Ἰησοῦς, Ὁ ποιεῖς, ποίησον τάχιον. 28 Τοῦτο.δὲ οὐδεὶς
¹Jesus, What thou doest, do quickly. But this no one
ἔγνω τῶν ἀνακειμένων πρὸς.τί εἶπεν αὐτῷ. 29 τινὲς.γὰρ
knew of those reclining wherefore he spoke to him; for some
ἐδόκουν, ἐπεὶ τὸ γλωσσόκομον εἶχεν °ὁ‖ Ἰούδας, ὅτι λέγει
thought, since ²the ⁴bag ²had ¹Judas, that ²is ³saying
αὐτῷ ᴾὁ‖ Ἰησοῦς, Ἀγόρασον ὧν χρείαν ἔχομεν εἰς
⁴to ⁵him ¹Jesus, Buy what things need [of] we have for
τὴν ἑορτήν· ἢ τοῖς πτωχοῖς ἵνα τι δῷ. 30 λα-
the feast; or to the poor that something he should give. Having
βὼν οὖν τὸ ψωμίον ἐκεῖνος ᑫεὐθέως ἐξῆλθεν·‖ ἦν.δὲ
received therefore the morsel he immediately. went out; and it was
νύξ.
night.

31 Therefore, when he was gone out, Jesus said, Now is the Son of man glorified, and God is glorified in him.. 32, If God be glorified in him, God shall also glorify him in himself, and shall straightway glorify him. 33 Little children, yet a little while I am with you. Ye shall seek me: and as I said unto the Jews, Whither I go, ye cannot come; so now I say to you. 34 A new commandment I give unto you, That ye love one another; as I have loved you, that ye also love one another. 35 By this shall all men know that ye are my disciples, if ye have love one to another. 36 Simon Peter said unto him, Lord, whither goest thou? Jesus answered him, Whither I go, thou canst not follow me now; but thou shalt follow me afterwards. 37 Peter said unto him, Lord, why cannot I follow thee now? I will lay down my life for thy sake. 38 Jesus answered him, Wilt thou lay down thy life for my sake? Verily, verily, I say unto thee, The cock shall not crow, till thou hast denied me thrice.

31 Ὅτε ʳ ἐξῆλθεν λέγει ˢὁ‖ Ἰησοῦς, Νῦν ἐδοξάσθη
When he was gone out ²says ¹Jesus, Now has been glorified
ὁ υἱὸς τοῦ ἀνθρώπου, καὶ ὁ θεὸς ἐδοξάσθη ἐν αὐτῷ. 32 ᵗεἰ
the Son of man, and God has been glorified in him. If
ὁ θεὸς ἐδοξάσθη ἐν αὐτῷ,‖ καὶ ὁ θεὸς δοξάσει. αὐτὸν ἐν
God has been glorified in him, also God shall glorify him in
ᵛἑαυτῷ,‖ καὶ εὐθὺς δοξάσει αὐτόν. 33 Τεκνία, ἔτι
himself, and immediately shall glorify him. Little children, yet
μικρὸν μεθ' ὑμῶν εἰμι. ζητήσετέ με, καὶ καθὼς εἶπον τοῖς
a little while with you I am. Ye will seek me; and, as I said to the
Ἰουδαίοις, Ὅτι ὅπου ʷὑπάγω ἐγώ,‖ ὑμεῖς οὐ.δύνασθε ἐλθεῖν,
Jews, That where ²go ¹I, ye are not able to come,
καὶ ὑμῖν λέγω ἄρτι. 34 Ἐντολὴν καινὴν δίδωμι ὑμῖν, ἵνα
also to you I say now. A ²commandment ¹new I give to you, that
ἀγαπᾶτε ἀλλήλους· καθὼς ἠγάπησα ὑμᾶς, ἵνα καὶ ὑμεῖς
ye should love one another; according as I loved you, that ²also ¹ye
ἀγαπᾶτε ἀλλήλους. 35 ἐν τούτῳ γνώσονται πάντες ὅτι ἐμοὶ
should love one another. By this shall ¹know ²all that to me
μαθηταί ἐστε, ἐὰν ἀγάπην ἔχητε ἐν ἀλλήλοις. 36 Λέγει
disciples ye are, if love ye have among one another. ²Says
αὐτῷ Σίμων Πέτρος, Κύριε, ποῦ ὑπάγεις; ἀπεκρίθη ˣαὐτῷ
⁴to ⁵him ¹Simon ²Peter, Lord, where goest thou? ²Answered ³him
ὁ‖ Ἰησοῦς, Ὅπου ʸ ὑπάγω οὐ.δύνασαί μοι νῦν ἀκολουθῆσαι·
¹Jesus, Where I go thou art not able me now to follow,
ᶻὕστερον.δὲ ἀκολουθήσεις μοι.‖ 37 Λέγει αὐτῷ ᵃὁ‖ Πέτρος,
but afterwards thou shalt follow me. ²Says ³to ⁴him ¹Peter,
Κύριε, ᵇδιατί‖ οὐ.δύναμαί σοι ᶜἀκολουθῆσαι‖ ἄρτι; τὴν ψυχήν
Lord, why am I not able thee to follow now? ²life
μου ὑπὲρ σοῦ θήσω. 38 ᵈἈπεκρίθη αὐτῷ ὁ‖ Ἰησοῦς,
¹my for thee I will lay down. ²Answered ³him ¹Jesus,
Τὴν.ψυχήν.σου ὑπὲρ ἐμοῦ θήσεις; ἀμὴν ἀμὴν λέγω
Thy life for me thou wilt lay down? Verily verily I say
σοι, οὐ.μὴ ἀλέκτωρ ᵉφωνήσει‖ ἕως.οὖ ᶠἀπαρνήσῃ‖ με
to thee, in no wise [the] cock will crow until thou wilt deny me
τρίς.
thrice.

ⁿ — ὁ ΤΤΓΑ. ° — ὁ LΤΤΓΑ. ᵖ — ὁ Τ[Τʳ]Α. ᑫ ἐξῆλθεν εὐθύς LΤΤΓΑ. ʳ + οὖν therefore
ELΤΤΓΑ. ˢ — ὁ ΤΤΓΑ. ᵗ [εἰ ὁ θεὸς ἐδοξάσθη ἐν αὐτῷ] LΤΓΑ. ᵛ αὐτῷ ΤΤΓ. ᵛ ἐγὼ
ὑπάγω GLΤΤΓΑW. ˣ — αὐτῷ ὁ LΤΤΓΑ. ʸ + ἐγὼ Ι (go) Τ. ᶻ ἀκολουθήσεις δὲ ὕστερον LΤΤΓΑ.
ᵃ — ὁ GLΤΤΓΑW. ᵇ διὰ τί LΤΓΑ. ᶜ ἀκολουθεῖν Τʳ. ᵈ ἀποκρίνεται answers LΤΤΓΑW.
ᵉ φωνήσῃ LΤΤΓΑ. ᶠ ἀρνήσῃ LΤΤΓΑ.

14 Μὴ.ταρασσέσθω ὑμῶν ἡ καρδία· πιστεύετε εἰς τὸν Θεόν,
   Let not be troubled   your   heart; ye believe on   God,

καὶ εἰς ἐμὲ πιστεύετε. 2 ἐν τῇ οἰκίᾳ τοῦ.πατρός.μου μοναὶ
also on me believe.   In the house   of my Father   ᵃabodes

πολλαί εἰσιν· εἰ.δὲ.μή,   εἶπον.ἂν ὑμῖν· ᵍ πορεύομαι ἑτοι-
¹many there are; otherwise I would have told you;   I go   to pre-

μάσαι τόπον ὑμῖν. 3 καὶ ἐὰν.πορευθῶ ʰκαὶ‖ ἑτοιμάσω ⁱὑμῖν
pare a place for you; and if I go   and   prepare   for you

τόπον,‖ πάλιν ἔρχομαι καὶ ᵏπαραλήψομαι‖ ὑμᾶς πρὸς ἐμαυ-
a place, again I am coming and   will receive   you   to   my-

τόν· ἵνα ὅπου εἰμὶ ἐγώ, καὶ ὑμεῖς ἦτε. 4 καὶ ὅπου ˡἐγὼ‖
self, that where ²am I ⁴also ³ye may be. And where I

ὑπάγω οἴδατε ᵐκαὶ‖ τὴν ὁδὸν ⁿοἴδατε.‖ 5 Λέγει αὐτῷ Θωμᾶς,
go   ye know and   the way   ye know.   ²Says ³to ⁴him ¹Thomas,

Κύριε, οὐκ.οἴδαμεν ποῦ ὑπάγεις, ᵒκαὶ‖ πῶς ᵖδυνάμεθα τὴν
Lord,   we know not where thou goest, and how   can we the

ὁδὸν εἰδέναι;‖ 6 Λέγει αὐτῷ ᑫὁ‖ Ἰησοῦς, Ἐγώ εἰμι ἡ ὁδὸς
way   know?   ²Says ³to ⁴him   ¹Jesus,   I   am the way

καὶ ἡ ἀλήθεια καὶ ἡ ζωή· οὐδεὶς ἔρχεται πρὸς τὸν πατέρα
and the truth and the life. No one comes   to   the Father

εἰ.μὴ δι' ἐμοῦ. 7 εἰ ʳἐγνώκειτέ με,‖ καὶ τὸν.πατέρα.μου
but by me.   If ye had known me, also my Father

ˢἐγνώκειτε.ἂν‖ ᵗκαὶ‖ ᵛἀπ'.ἄρτι‖ γινώσκετε αὐτόν, καὶ ἑωρά-
ye would have known; and   henceforth   ye know   him,   and have

κατε ʷαὐτόν‖ 8 Λέ.ει αὐτῷ Φίλιππος, Κύριε, δεῖξον ἡμῖν
seen   him.   ²Says ³to ⁴him   ¹Philip,   Lord,   shew   us

τὸν πατέρα, καὶ ἀρκεῖ ἡμῖν. 9 Λέγει αὐτῷ ὁ Ἰησοῦς,
the Father, and it suffices us.   ²Says ³to ⁴him   ¹Jesus,

ˣΤοσοῦτον χρόνον‖ μεθ' ὑμῶν εἰμι, καὶ οὐκ.ἔγνωκάς με,
So long   a time   with you   am I, and thou hast not known me,

Φίλιππε; ὁ ἑωρακὼς ἐμέ, ἑώρακεν τὸν πατέρα· ʸκαὶ‖ πῶς
Philip? He that has seen   me, has seen the Father;   and how

σὺ λέγεις, Δεῖξον ἡμῖν τὸν πατέρα; 10 οὐ.πιστεύεις ὅτι
²thou ¹sayest, Shew   us   the Father?   Believest thou not that

ἐγὼ ἐν τῷ πατρί, καὶ ὁ πατὴρ ἐν ἐμοί ἐστιν; τὰ ῥήματα
I [am] in the Father, and the Father ²in ³me ¹is?   The words

ἃ ἐγὼ ᶻλαλῶ‖ ὑμῖν, ἀπ' ἐμαυτοῦ οὐ.λαλῶ· ὁ.δὲ πατὴρ
which I   speak   to you, from myself I speak not; but the Father

ᵃὃ‖ ἐν ἐμοὶ μένων ᵇαὐτὸς ποιεῖ τὰ ἔργα‖ ᶜ. 11 πιστεύετέ μοι
who in me abides   he   does the works.   Believe   me

ὅτι ἐγὼ ἐν τῷ πατρί, καὶ ὁ πατὴρ ἐν ἐμοί· εἰ.δὲ μή,
that I [am] in the Father, and the Father in me; but if not,

διὰ τὰ ἔργα αὐτὰ πιστεύετέ ᵉμοι.‖ 12 Ἀμὴν ἀμὴν λέγω
because of the works themselves believe   me.   Verily verily I say

ὑμῖν, ὁ πιστεύων εἰς ἐμέ, τὰ ἔργα ἃ ἐγὼ ποιῶ, κἀκεῖνος
to you, He that believes on me, the works which I   do,   also he

ποιήσει, καὶ μείζονα τούτων ποιήσει, ὅτι ἐγὼ πρὸς τὸν
shall do, and greater than these he shall do, because I   to

πατέρα.ᶠμου‖ πορεύομαι. 13 καὶ ὅ.τι.ἂν αἰτήσητε ἐν τῷ
my Father   go.   And whatsoever ye may ask in

XIV. Let not your heart be troubled: ye believe in God, believe also in me. 2 In my Father's house are many mansions: if *it* were not *so*, I would have told you. I go to prepare a place for you. 3 And if I go and prepare a place for you, I will come again, and receive you unto myself; that where I am, *there* ye may be also. 4 And whither I go ye know, and the way ye know. 5 Thomas saith unto him, Lord, we know not whither thou goest; and how can we know the way? 6 Jesus saith unto him, I am the way, the truth, and the life: no man cometh unto the Father, but by me. 7 If ye had known me, ye should have known my Father also: and from henceforth ye know him, and have seen him. 8 Philip saith unto him, Lord, shew us the Father, and it sufficeth us. 9 Jesus saith unto him, Have I been so long time with you, and yet hast thou not known me, Philip? he that hath seen me hath seen the Father; and how sayest thou *then*, Shew us the Father? 10 Believest thou not that I am in the Father, and the Father in me? the words that I speak unto you I speak not of myself: but the Father that dwelleth in me, he doeth the works. 11 Believe me that I *am* in the Father, and the Father in me: or else believe me for the very works' sake. 12 Verily, verily, I say unto you, He that believeth on me, the works that I do shall he do also; and greater *works* than these shall he do; because I go unto my Father. 13 And whatsoever ye shall ask in

ᵍ + ὅτι for LTTrAW.   ʰ — καὶ L.   ⁱ τόπον ὑμῖν TTrA.   ᵏ παραλήμψομαι LTTrA.
ˡ [ἐγὼ] L.   ᵐ — καὶ [L]TTrA.   ⁿ — οἴδατε [L]TTrA.   ᵒ — καὶ LTr.   ᵖ οἴδαμεν τὴν ὁδὸν
know we the way LTTrA.   ᑫ — ὁ T.   ʳ ἐγνώκατε ἐμέ ye have known me T.   ˢ ἂν ἤδειτε
TrA; γνώσεσθε ye will know T.   ᵗ — καὶ [L]TrA.   ᵛ ἀπάρτι T.   ʷ [αὐτόν] LTrA.
ᶻ τοσούτῳ χρόνῳ LT.   ʸ — καὶ LT[Tr].   ᶻ λέγω TTrA.   ᵃ [ὁ] LTrA.   ᵇ ποιεῖ τὰ ἔργα
αὐτοῦ does his works TTrA.   ᶜ + [αὐτοῦ] (read his works) L.   ᵈ + ἐστίν is E.
ᵉ — μοι T[Tr].   ᶠ — μου (read the father) LTTrA.

U

my name, that will I do, that the Father may be glorified in the Son. 14 If ye shall ask any thing in my name, I will do it. 15 If ye love me, keep my commandments. 16 And I will pray the Father, and he shall give you another Comforter, that he may abide with you for ever; 17 even the Spirit of truth; whom the world cannot receive, because it seeth him not, neither knoweth him: but ye know him; for he dwelleth with you, and shall be in you. 18 I will not leave you comfortless: I will come to you. 19 Yet a little while, and the world seeth me no more; but ye see me: because I live, ye shall live also. 20 At that day ye shall know that I *am* in my Father, and ye in me, and I in you. 21 He that hath my commandments, and keepeth them, he it is that loveth me: and he that loveth me shall be loved of my Father, and I will love him, and will manifest myself to him. 22 Judas saith unto him, not Iscariot, Lord, how is it that thou wilt manifest thyself unto us, and not unto the world? 23 Jesus answered and said unto him, If a man love me, he will keep my words: and my Father will love him, and we will come unto him, and make our abode with him. 24 He that loveth me not keepeth not my sayings: and the word which ye hear is not mine, but the Father's which sent me. 25 These things have I spoken unto you, being *yet* present with you. 26 But the Comforter, *which is* the Holy Ghost, whom the Father will send in my name, he shall teach you all things, and bring all things to your remembrance,

ὀνόματί.μου, τοῦτο ποιήσω, ἵνα δοξασθῇ ὁ πατὴρ ἐν τῷ
my name, this will I do, that may be glorified the Father in the

υἱῷ. 14 ἐάν τι αἰτήσητε [g] ἐν τῷ.ὀνόματί.μου, ἐγὼ ποιήσω.
Son. If anything ye ask in my name, I will do [it].

15 ἐὰν ἀγαπᾶτέ με, τὰς ἐντολὰς τὰς ἐμὰς [h] τηρήσατε.
If ye love me, commandments my keep.

16 [i] καὶ ἐγὼ ἐρωτήσω τὸν πατέρα, καὶ ἄλλον παράκλητον
And I will ask the Father, and another Paraclete

δώσει ὑμῖν, ἵνα [k] μένῃ μεθ᾽ ὑμῶν εἰς.τὸν.αἰῶνα, 17 τὸ
he will give you, that he may remain with you for ever, the

πνεῦμα τῆς ἀληθείας, ὃ ὁ κόσμος οὐ.δύναται λαβεῖν, ὅτι
Spirit of truth, whom the world cannot receive, because

οὐ.θεωρεῖ αὐτό, οὐδὲ γινώσκει [l] αὐτό. ὑμεῖς [m] δὲ γινώσκετε
it does not see him, nor know him; but ye know

αὐτό, ὅτι παρ᾽ ὑμῖν μένει, καὶ ἐν ὑμῖν [n] ἔσται. 18 οὐκ.ἀφήσω
him, for with you he abides, and in you shall be. I will not leave

ὑμᾶς ὀρφανούς· ἔρχομαι πρὸς ὑμᾶς. 19 ἔτι μικρὸν καὶ ὁ
you orphans; I am coming to you. Yet a little while and the

κόσμος με [o] οὐκ ἔτι θεωρεῖ, ὑμεῖς.δὲ θεωρεῖτέ με· ὅτι ἐγὼ
world me no longer sees, but ye see me: because I

ζῶ, καὶ ὑμεῖς [p] ζήσεσθε. 20 ἐν ἐκείνῃ τῇ ἡμέρᾳ [q] γνώσεσθε
live, also ye shall live. In that day shall know

ὑμεῖς ὅτι ἐγὼ ἐν τῷ.πατρί.μου, καὶ ὑμεῖς ἐν ἐμοί, κἀγὼ
ye that I [am] in my Father, and ye in me, and I

ἐν ὑμῖν. 21 ὁ ἔχων τὰς.ἐντολάς.μου καὶ τηρῶν αὐτάς,
in you. He that has my commandments and keeps them,

ἐκεῖνός ἐστιν ὁ ἀγαπῶν με· ὁ.δὲ ἀγαπῶν με, ἀγαπηθήσε-
he it is that loves me; but he that loves me, shall be loved

ται ὑπὸ τοῦ.πατρός.μου· [r] καὶ ἐγὼ ἀγαπήσω αὐτόν, καὶ
by my Father; and I will love him, and

ἐμφανίσω αὐτῷ ἐμαυτόν. 22 Λέγει αὐτῷ Ἰούδας οὐχ
will manifest to him myself. Says to him Judas, (not

ὁ Ἰσκαριώτης, Κύριε, [s] τί γέγονεν ὅτι ἡμῖν μέλλεις
the Iscariote,) Lord, what has occurred that to us thou art about

ἐμφανίζειν σεαυτόν, καὶ οὐχὶ τῷ κόσμῳ; 23 Ἀπεκρίθη [t] ὁ
to manifest thyself, and not to the world? Answered

Ἰησοῦς καὶ εἶπεν αὐτῷ, Ἐάν τις ἀγαπᾷ με, τὸν.λόγον.μου
Jesus and said to him, If anyone love me, my word

τηρήσει, καὶ ὁ.πατήρ.μου ἀγαπήσει αὐτόν, καὶ πρὸς αὐτὸν
he will keep, and my Father will love him, and to him

ἐλευσόμεθα, καὶ μονὴν παρ᾽ αὐτῷ [v] ποιήσομεν. 24 ὁ μὴ
we will come, and an abode with him will make. He that not

ἀγαπῶν με, τοὺς.λόγους.μου οὐ.τηρεῖ· καὶ ὁ λόγος ὃν
loves me, my words does not keep; and the word which

ἀκούετε οὐκ.ἔστιν ἐμός, ἀλλὰ τοῦ πέμψαντός με πατρός.
ye hear is not mine, but of the who sent me Father.

25 Ταῦτα λελάληκα ὑμῖν παρ᾽ ὑμῖν μένων· 26 ὁ.δὲ παρά-
These things I have said to you, with you abiding; but the Para-

κλητος, τὸ πνεῦμα τὸ ἅγιον, ὃ πέμψει ὁ πατὴρ ἐν τῷ
clete, the Spirit the Holy, whom will send the Father in

ὀνόματί.μου, ἐκεῖνος ὑμᾶς διδάξει πάντα, καὶ ὑπο-
my name, he you will teach all things, and will bring to re-

---

[g] + με me [L]T.   [h] τηρήσετε ye will keep TTr.   [i] κἀγὼ LTTrA.   [k] μεθ᾽ ὑμῶν εἰς τὸν αἰῶνα ᾖ he may be with you for ever L; μεθ᾽ ὑμῶν ᾖ εἰς τὸν αἰῶνα T; ᾖ μεθ᾽ ὑμῶν εἰς τὸν αἰῶνα TrA.   [l] [αὐτό] L.   [m] — δὲ but [L]T[Tr]A.   [n] ἐστίν is LTrA.   [o] οὐκέτι GLT.   [p] ζήσετε TTrA.   [q] ὑμεῖς (ὑμεῖς) L) γνώσεσθε LTrA.   [r] κἀγὼ LTTrAW.   [s] + καὶ then GT[A]W.   [t] — ὁ GLTTrA.   [v] ποιησόμεθα LTTrA.

μνήσει ὑμᾶς πάντα ἃ εἶπον ὑμῖν. 27 εἰρήνην ἀφίημι
membrance ¹your all things which I said to you.   Peace   I leave

ὑμῖν, εἰρήνην τὴν ἐμὴν δίδωμι ὑμῖν· οὐ καθὼς ὁ κόσμος
with you; ²peace .   ¹my   I give to you; not as the world

δίδωσιν, ἐγὼ δίδωμι ὑμῖν· μὴ.ταρασσέσθω ὑμῶν ἡ καρδία, μηδὲ
gives, ²I ¹give to you. Let not be troubled your heart, nor

δειλιάτω. 28 ἠκούσατε ὅτι ἐγὼ εἶπον ὑμῖν, Ὑπάγω καὶ
let it fear.   Ye heard that I said to you, I am going away and

ἔρχομαι πρὸς ὑμᾶς. εἰ ἠγαπᾶτέ με, ἐχάρητε.ἂν ὅτι
I am coming to you. If ye loved me, ye would have rejoiced that

ʷεἶπον,ǁ Πορεύομαι πρὸς τὸν πατέρα· ὅτι ὁ.πατήρ·ˣμουǁ
I said,   I am going to the Father, for . my Father

μείζων μου ἐστίν. 29 καὶ νῦν εἴρηκα ὑμῖν πρὶν γενέ-
²greater ³than ⁴I ¹is.   And now I have told you before it comes to

σθαι, ἵνα ὅταν γένηται πιστεύσητε. 30 ʸοὐκ ἔτιǁ
pass, that when it shall have come to pass ye may believe.   No longer

πολλὰ λαλήσω μεθ᾽ ᶻὑμῶν·ǁ ἔρχεται.γὰρ ὁ τοῦ κόσμου
much I will speak with you,   for comes the ²of ⁴world

ᵃτούτουǁ ἄρχων, καὶ ἐν ἐμοὶ οὐκ ἔχει οὐδέν· 31 ἀλλ᾽ ἵνα
³this ¹ruler, and in me he has nothing; but that

γνῷ ὁ κόσμος ὅτι ἀγαπῶ τὸν πατέρα, ᵇκαὶǁ καθὼς
may ᵏknow ¹the ²world that I love the Father, and as

ᶜἐνετείλατόǁ μοι ὁ πατήρ, οὕτως ποιῶ· ἐγείρεσθε, ἄγωμεν
³commanded ⁴me ¹the ²Father, thus I do. Rise up, let us go

ἐντεῦθεν.
hence.

15 Ἐγώ εἰμι ἡ ἄμπελος ἡ ἀληθινή, καὶ ὁ.πατήρ.μου ὁ
I am the ᵛvine ¹true, and my Father the

γεωργός ἐστιν. 2 πᾶν κλῆμα ἐν ἐμοὶ μὴ φέρον καρπόν,
husbandman is.   Every branch in me not bearing fruit,

αἴρει αὐτό· καὶ πᾶν τὸ καρπὸν φέρον, καθαίρει αὐτὸ
he takes away it; and everyone that fruit bears, he cleanses it

ἵνα ᵈπλείονα καρπὸνǁ φέρῃ. 3 ἤδη ὑμεῖς καθαροί ἐστε
that more fruit it may bear. Already ye clean are

διὰ τὸν λόγον ὃν λελάληκα ὑμῖν. 4 μείνατε ἐν ἐμοί,
by reason of the word which I have spoken to you. Abide in me,

κἀγὼ ἐν ὑμῖν. Ἃς τὸ κλῆμα οὐ.δύναται καρπὸν φέρειν ἀφ᾽
and I in you. As the branch is not able fruit to bear of

ἑαυτοῦ ἐὰν.μὴ ᵉμείνῃǁ ἐν τῇ ἀμπέλῳ, οὕτως οὐδὲ ὑμεῖς
itself unless it abide in the vine, so neither [can] ye

ἐὰν.μὴ ἐν ἐμοὶ ᶠμείνητε.ǁ 5 ἐγώ εἰμι ἡ ἄμπελος, ὑμεῖς τὰ
unless in me ye abide. I am the vine, ye [are] the

κλήματα. ὁ μένων ἐν ἐμοί, κἀγὼ ἐν αὐτῷ, οὗτος φέρει
branches. He that abides in me, and I in him, he bears

καρπὸν πολύν· ὅτι χωρὶς ἐμοῦ οὐ.δύνασθε ποιεῖν οὐδέν.
²fruit ¹much; for apart from me ye are able to do nothing.

6 ἐὰν.μή τις ᵍμείνῃǁ ἐν ἐμοί, ἐβλήθη ἔξω ὡς τὸ κλῆμα, καὶ
Unless anyone abide in me, he is cast out as the branch, and

ἐξηράνθη, καὶ συνάγουσιν ʰαὐτὰǁ καὶ εἰς ⁱ πῦρ βάλλουσιν, καὶ
is dried up, and they gather them and into a fire cast, and

καίεται. 7 ἐὰν μείνητε ἐν ἐμοί, καὶ τὰ.ῥήματά.μου ἐν ὑμῖν
it is burned. If ye abide in me, and my words in you

whatsoever I have said unto you. 27 Peace I leave with you, my peace I give unto you: not as the world giveth, give I unto you. Let not your heart be troubled, neither let it be afraid. 28 Ye have heard how I said unto you, I go away, and come *again* unto you. If ye loved me, ye would rejoice, because I said, I go unto the Father: for my Father is greater than I. 29 And now I have told you before it come to pass, that, when it is come to pass, ye might believe. 30 Hereafter I will not talk much with you: for the prince of this world cometh, and hath nothing in me. 31 But that the world may know that I love the Father; and as the Father gave me commandment, even so I do. Arise, let us go hence.

XV. I am the true vine, and my Father is the husbandman. 2 Every branch in me that beareth not fruit he taketh away: and every *branch* that beareth fruit, he purgeth it, that it may bring forth more fruit. 3 Now ye are clean through the word which I have spoken unto you. 4 Abide in me, and I in you. As the branch cannot bear fruit of itself, except it abide in the vine; no more can ye, except ye abide in me. 5 I am the vine, ye *are* the branches: he that abideth in me, and I in him, the same bringeth forth much fruit: for without me ye can do nothing. 6 If a man abide not in me, he is cast forth as a branch, and is withered; and men gather them, and cast *them* into the fire, and they are burned. 7 If ye abide in me, and my words abide in you;

ʷ — εἶπον GLTTrAW.   ˣ — μου (*read* the Father) [L]TTrA.   ʸ οὐκέτι GLT.   ᶻ ὑμῖν W.
ᵃ — τούτου (*read* of the world) GLTTrAW.   ᵇ [καὶ] L.   ᶜ ἐντολὴν ἔδωκέν gave (me) commandment LTr.   ᵈ καρπὸν πλείονα LTTrA.   ᵉ μένῃ T.   ᶠ μένητε LTTrA.   ᵍ μένῃ Lᵀʳ·
ʰ αὐτὸ it .   ⁱ + τὸ the (fire) TTrAW.

ye shall ask what ye will, and it shall be done unto you. 8 Herein is my Father glorified, that ye bear much fruit; so shall ye be my disciples. 9 As the Father hath loved me, so have I loved you: continue ye in my love. 10 If ye keep my commandments, ye shall abide in my love; even as I have kept my Father's commandments, and abide in his love. 11 These things have I spoken unto you, that my joy might remain in you, and *that* your joy might be full. 12 This is my commandment, That ye love one another, as I have loved you. 13 Greater love hath no man than this, that a man lay down his life for his friends. 14 Ye are my friends, if ye do whatsoever I command you. 15 Henceforth I call you not servants; for the servant knoweth not what his lord doeth: but I have called you friends; for all things that I have heard of my Father I have made known unto you. 16 Ye have not chosen me, but I have chosen you, and ordained you, that ye should go and bring forth fruit, and *that* your fruit should remain: that whatsoever ye shall ask of the Father in my name, he may give it you. 17 These things I command you, that ye love one another. 18 If the world hate you, ye know that it hated me before *it hated* you. 19 If ye were of the world, the world would love his own: but because ye are not of the world, but I have chosen you out of the world, therefore the world hateth you. 20 Remember the word that I said unto you, The servant is not greater than his lord. If they have persecuted me, they will also persecute you; if they

μείνῃ, ὃ.ᵏ¹ἐὰν‖ θέλητε ¹αἰτήσεσθε,‖ καὶ γενήσεται ὑμῖν.
abide,   whatever ye will ye shall ask,   and it shall come to pass to you.

8 ἐν τούτῳ ἐδοξάσθη ὁ.πατήρ.μου, ἵνα καρπὸν πολὺν φέρητε,
In this   is glorified my Father,   that ²fruit ¹much ye should bear,

καὶ ᵐγενήσεσθε‖ ἐμοὶ μαθηταί. 9 καθὼς ἠγάπησέν με ὁ
and ye shall become ²to ³me ¹disciples.   As   loved me the

πατήρ, κἀγὼ ⁿἠγάπησα ὑμᾶς·‖ μείνατε ἐν τῇ ἀγάπῃ τῇ ἐμῇ.
Father, I also   loved   you: abide in ²love ¹my.

10 ἐὰν τὰς.ἐντολάς.μου τηρήσητε, μενεῖτε ἐν τῇ.ἀγάπῃ.μου·
If my commandments   ye keep, ye shall abide in my love,

καθὼς ᵒἐγὼ‖ ᴾτὰς ἐντολὰς τοῦ.πατρός‖.⁹μου τετήρηκα, καὶ
as   I   the commandments of my Father have kept, and

μένω αὐτοῦ ἐν τῇ ἀγάπῃ. 11 ταῦτα λελάληκα ὑμῖν, ἵνα
abide ²his ¹in love.   These things I have spoken to you, that

ἡ χαρὰ ἡ ἐμὴ ἐν ὑμῖν ʳμείνῃ,‖ καὶ ἡ.χαρὰ.ὑμῶν πληρωθῇ.
²joy ¹my in you may abide, and   your joy   may be full.

12 αὕτη ἐστὶν ἡ ἐντολὴ ἡ ἐμή, ἵνα ἀγαπᾶτε ἀλλήλους,
This is ²commandment ¹my, that ye love   one another,

καθὼς ἠγάπησα ὑμᾶς. 13 μείζονα ταύτης ἀγάπην οὐδεὶς
as I loved you.   Greater than this love no one

ἔχει, ἵνα ˢτις‖ τὴν.ψυχὴν.αὐτοῦ θῇ ὑπὲρ τῶν φίλων
has, that one his life   should lay down for ¹friends

αὐτοῦ. 14 ὑμεῖς φίλοι μου ἐστὲ ἐὰν ποιῆτε ᵗὅσα‖ ἐγὼ
¹his.   Ye ²friends ¹my are if ye practise whatsoever I

ἐντέλλομαι ὑμῖν. 15 οὐκέτι ᵛὑμᾶς λέγω‖ δούλους, ὅτι ὁ δοῦ-
command   you. No longer you ¹call bondmen, for the bond-

λος οὐκ.οἶδεν τί ποιεῖ αὐτοῦ ὁ κύριος· ὑμᾶς.δὲ εἴρηκα
man knows not what ³is ⁴doing ¹his   ²master. But you I have called

φίλους, ὅτι πάντα ἃ ἤκουσα παρὰ τοῦ.πατρός.μου ἐγνώ-
friends, for all things which I heard   of   my Father I made

ρισα ὑμῖν. 16 οὐχ ὑμεῖς με ἐξελέξασθε, ἀλλ' ἐγὼ ἐξελεξάμην
known to you. ²Not ¹ye ⁴me ³chose,   but I   chose

ὑμᾶς, καὶ ἔθηκα ὑμᾶς ἵνα ὑμεῖς ὑπάγητε καὶ καρπὸν φέ-
you, and appointed you that ye   should go and fruit ye should

ρητε, καὶ ὁ.καρπὸς.ὑμῶν μένῃ· ἵνα ὅ.τι.ἂν αἰτήσητε τὸν
bear, and your fruit should abide; that whatsoever ye may ask the

πατέρα ἐν τῷ.ὀνόματί.μου δῷ ὑμῖν. 17 ταῦτα ἐντέλ-
Father in my name he may give you. These things I com-

λομαι ὑμῖν, ἵνα ἀγαπᾶτε ἀλλήλους. 18 Εἰ ὁ κόσμος ὑμᾶς
mand you, that ye love   one another.   If the world you

μισεῖ, γινώσκετε ὅτι ἐμὲ πρῶτον ᵂὑμῶν‖ μεμίσηκεν. 19 εἰ ἐκ
hates, ye know that me before   you it has hated. If of

τοῦ κόσμου ἦτε, ὁ κόσμος ἂν.τὸ.ἴδιον.ἐφίλει· ὅτι.δὲ ἐκ τοῦ
the world ye were, the world would love its own; but because of the

κόσμου οὐκ.ἐστέ, ἀλλ' ἐγὼ ἐξελεξάμην ὑμᾶς ἐκ τοῦ κόσμου,
world ye are not, but I   chose   you out of the world,

διὰ τοῦτο μισεῖ ὑμᾶς ὁ κόσμος. 20 μνημονεύετε τοῦ
on account of this ³hates ⁴you ¹the ²world.   Remember the

λόγου οὗ ἐγὼ εἶπον ὑμῖν, Οὐκ.ἔστιν δοῦλος μείζων τοῦ
word which I said to you, ²Is ⁴not ¹a ²bondman greater

κυρίου.αὐτοῦ. εἰ ἐμὲ ἐδίωξαν, καὶ ὑμᾶς διώξουσιν· εἰ
than his master. If me they persecuted, also you they will persecute; if

---

ᵏ ἂν L. ¹ αἰτήσασθε ask ye LTTrAW. ᵐ γένησθε ye should become LTrA. ⁿ ὑμᾶς
ἠγάπησα LTrA. ᵒ κἀγὼ I also T. ᴾ τοῦ πατρὸς (+ μου T) τὰς ἐντολὰς TA. ⁹ — μου
(read the Father) LTA. ʳ ᾖ may be LTTrA. ˢ — τις T. ᵗ ἃ what LTTrA. ᵛ λεγω
ὑμᾶς LTTrA. ᵂ — ὑμῶν.T.

τον.λόγον.μου ἐτήρησαν, καὶ τὸν ὑμέτερον τηρήσουσιν. 21 ἀλλὰ
my word they kept, also yours they will keep. But

ταῦτα πάντα ποιήσουσιν ˣὑμῖν‖ διὰ τὸ.ὄνομά.μου,
these ³things ¹all they will do to you on account of my name,

ὅτι οὐκ.οἴδασιν τὸν πέμψαντά με. 22 εἰ μὴ.ἦλθον καὶ
because they know not him who sent me. If I had not come and

ἐλάλησα αὐτοῖς, ἁμαρτίαν οὐκ.ʸεῖχον‖ νῦν.δὲ πρόφασιν
spoken to them, sin they had not had; but now a pretext

οὐκ.ἔχουσιν περὶ τῆς.ἁμαρτίας.αὐτῶν. 23 ὁ ἐμὲ μισῶν, καὶ
they have not for their sin. He that ²me ¹hates, ³also

τον.πατέρα.μου μισεῖ. 24 εἰ τὰ ἔργα μὴ.ἐποίησα ἐν
¹my ⁶Father ⁷hates. If ⁷the ⁸works ¹¹ ²had ³not ⁴done ⁵among

αὐτοῖς ἃ οὐδεὶς.ἄλλος ᶻπεποίηκεν,‖ ἁμαρτίαν οὐκ.ᵃεῖχον‖
⁶them which no other one has done, sin they had not had,

νῦν.δὲ καὶ ἑωράκασιν καὶ μεμισήκασιν καὶ ἐμὲ.καὶ τὸν πατέρα
but now both they have seen and have hated both me and ²Father

μου. 25 ἀλλ᾽ ἵνα πληρωθῇ ὁ λόγος ὁ ᵇγεγραμμένος ἐν
¹my. But that might be fulfilled the word that has been written in

τῷ.νόμῳ.αὐτῶν,‖ Ὅτι ἐμίσησάν με δωρεάν. 26 Ὅταν.ᶜδὲ‖
their law, They hated me without cause. But when

ἔλθῃ ὁ παράκλητος, ὃν ἐγὼ.πέμψω ὑμῖν παρὰ τοῦ πατρός,
is come the Paraclete, whom I will send to you from the Father,

τὸ πνεῦμα τῆς ἀληθείας, ὃ παρὰ τοῦ πατρὸς ἐκπορεύεται,
the Spirit of truth, who from the Father goes forth,

ἐκεῖνος μαρτυρήσει περὶ ἐμοῦ. 27 καὶ ὑμεῖς δὲ μαρ-
he will bear witness concerning me; ³also ²ye ¹and bear

τυρεῖτε, ὅτι ἀπ᾽ ἀρχῆς.μετ᾽ ἐμοῦ ἐστε.
witness, because from [the] beginning with me ye are.

16 Ταῦτα λελάληκα ὑμῖν ἵνα μὴ.σκανδαλισθῆτε. 2 ἀπο-
These things I have spoken to you that ye may not be offended. Out of

συναγώγους ποιήσουσιν ὑμᾶς· ἀλλ᾽ ἔρχεται ὥρα ἵνα πᾶς
the synagogues they will put you; but is coming an hour that everyone

ὁ ἀποκτείνας ὑμᾶς δόξῃ λατρείαν προσφέρειν τῷ θεῷ.
who kills you will think service to render to God;

3 καὶ ταῦτα ποιήσουσιν ᵈὑμῖν‖ ὅτι οὐκ.ἔγνωσαν τὸν πα-
and these things they will do, to you because they know not the Fa-

τέρα οὐδὲ ἐμέ. 4 ἀλλὰ ταῦτα λελάληκα ὑμῖν, ἵνα ὅταν
ther nor me. But these things I have said to you, that when

ἔλθῃ ἡ ὥρα ᵉ μνημονεύητε ᶠαὐτῶν‖ ὅτι ἐγὼ εἶπον
may have come the hour ye may remember them that ¹I said [them]

ὑμῖν ταῦτα.δὲ ὑμῖν ἐξ ἀρχῆς οὐκ.εἶπον ὅτι
to you. But these things to you from [the] beginning I did not say because

μεθ᾽ ὑμῶν ἤμην. 5 νῦν.δὲ ὑπάγω πρὸς τὸν πέμψαντά με,
with you I was. But now I go to him who sent me,

καὶ οὐδεὶς ἐξ ὑμῶν ἐρωτᾷ με, Ποῦ ὑπάγεις; 6 ἀλλ᾽ ὅτι
and none of you asks me, Where goest thou? But because

ταῦτα λελάληκα ὑμῖν ἡ λύπη πεπλήρωκεν ὑμῶν τὴν
these things I have said to you grief has filled your

καρδίαν. 7 ἀλλ᾽ ἐγὼ τὴν ἀλήθειαν λέγω ὑμῖν, συμφέρει
heart. But I the truth say to you, It is profitable

ὑμῖν ἵνα ἐγὼ ἀπέλθω· ἐὰν.γὰρ ᵍ μὴ.ἀπέλθω ὁ παράκλη-
for you that I should go away; for if I go not away the Paraclete

τος ʰοὐκ.ἐλεύσεται‖ πρὸς ὑμᾶς· ἐὰν.δὲ πορευθῶ, πέμψω
will not come to you; but if I go, I will send

have kept my saying,
they will keep yours
also. 21 But all these
things will they do un-
to you for my name's
sake, because they
know not him that
sent me. 22 If I had
not come and spoken
unto them, they had
not had sin: but now
they have no cloke for
their sin. 23 He that
hateth me hateth my
Father also. 24 If I had
not done among them
the works which none
other man did, they
had not had sin: but
now have they both
seen and hated both
me and my Father.
25 But *this cometh to
pass,* that the word
might be fulfilled that
is written in their law,
They hated me with-
out a cause. 26 But
when the Comforter is
come, whom I will
send unto you from the
Father, *even* the Spirit
of truth, which pro-
ceedeth from the Fa-
ther, he shall testify of
me: 27 and ye also
shall bear witness, be-
cause ye have been
with me from the be-
ginning.

XVI. These things
have I spoken unto
you, that ye should not
be offended. 2 They
shall put you out of
the synagogues: yea,
the time cometh, that
whosoever killeth you
will think that he do-
eth God service. 3 And
these things will they
do unto you, because
they have not known
the Father, nor me.
4 But these things have
I told you, that when
the time shall come, ye
may remember that I
told you of them. And
these things I said not
unto you at the begin-
ning, because I was
with you. 5 But now I
go my way to him that
sent me; and none of
you asketh me, Whi-
ther goest thou? 6 But
because I have said
these things unto you,
sorrow hath filled your
heart. 7 Nevertheless
I tell you the truth;
It is expedient for you
that I go away: for
if I go not away, the
Comforter will not
come unto you; but if
I depart I will send

ˣ εἰς ὑμᾶς to you LTTʳA. ʸ εἴχοσαν LTTʳA. ᶻ ἐποίησεν did LTTʳA. ᵃ εἴχοσαν LTTʳA. ᵇ ἐν
τῷ νόμῳ αὐτῶν γεγραμμένος LTTʳA. ᶜ — δὲ T[TʳA]. ᵈ — ὑμῖν GLTTʳAW. ᵉ + αὐτῶν (read
their hour) LTTʳA ᶠ [αὐτῶν] Tr. ᵍ + ἐγὼ L[A]W. ʰ οὐ μὴ ἔλθῃ in no wise should come Tr.

him unto you. 8 And
when he is come, he
will reprove the world
of sin, and of righte-
ousness, and of judg-
ment: 9 of sin, because
they believe not on me;
10 of righteousness, be-
cause I go to my Fa-
ther, and ye see me no
more; 11 of judgment,
because the prince of
this world is judged.
12 I ha· yet many
things to· unto you,
but ye cannot bear
them now. 13 Howbeit
when he, the Spirit of
truth, is come, he will
guide you into all
truth: for he shall not
speak of himself; but
whatsoever he shall
hear, that shall he
speak: and he will shew
you things to come.
14 He shall glorify me;
for he shall receive of
mine, and shall shew
it unto you. 15 All
things that the Father
hath are mine: there-
fore said I, that he
shall take of mine, and
shall shew it unto you.
16 A little while, and
ye shall not see me:
and again, a little
while, and ye shall see
me, because I go to the
Father. 17 Then said
some of his disciples
among themselves,
What is this that he
saith unto us, A little
while, and ye shall not
see me: and again, a
little while, and ye
shall see me: and, Be-
cause I go to the Fa-
ther? 18 They said
therefore, What is this
that he saith, A little
while? we cannot tell
what he saith. 19 Now
Jesus knew that they
were desirous to ask
him, and said unto
them, Do ye inquire
among yourselves of
that I said, A little
while, and ye shall not
see me: and again, a
little while, and ye
shall see me? 20 Verily,
verily, I say unto you,
That ye shall weep and
lament, but the world
shall rejoice: and ye

αὐτὸν πρὸς ὑμᾶς· 8 καὶ ἐλθὼν ἐκεῖνος ἐλέγξει τὸν κόσμον
him   to   you.   And having come   he   will convict the world
περὶ ἁμαρτίας καὶ περὶ δικαιοσύνης καὶ περὶ κρίσεως.
concerning sin   and concerning righteousness and concerning judgment.
9 περὶ ἁμαρτίας μέν, ὅτι οὐ.πιστεύουσιν εἰς ἐμέ· 10 περὶ
Concerning sin,   because they believe not on me; concerning
δικαιοσύνης δέ, ὅτι πρὸς τὸν.πατέρα.ᵢμου‖ ὑπάγω, καὶ ᵏοὐκ
righteousness because to my Father   I go away, and   no
ἔτι‖ θεωρεῖτέ με· 11 περὶ.δὲ κρίσεως, ὅτι ὁ ἄρχων τοῦ
longer ye behold me; and concerning judgment, because the ruler
κόσμου.τούτου κέκριται. 12 Ἔτι πολλὰ ἔχω ˡλέγειν
of this world has been judged.   Yet many things I have to say
ὑμῖν,‖ ἀλλ᾽ οὐ.δύνασθε βαστάζειν ἄρτι· 13 ὅταν.δὲ ἔλθῃ
to you, but ye are not able to bear them now.   But when ²may ³have ⁴come
ἐκεῖνος, τὸ πνεῦμα τῆς ἀληθείας, ὁδηγήσει ὑμᾶς ᵐεἰς πᾶσαν
ᵎhe,   the Spirit   of truth,   he will guide you   into all
τὴν ἀλήθειαν·‖ οὐ γὰρ λαλήσει ἀφ᾽ ἑαυτοῦ, ἀλλ᾽ ὅσα.ⁿἂν‖
the   truth;   ⁴not ˡfor ²he ³will speak from himself, but whatsoever
ᵒἀκούσῃ‖ λαλήσει, καὶ τὰ ἐρχόμενα ἀναγγελεῖ ὑμῖν.
he may hear he will speak; and the things coming he will announce to you.
14 ἐκεῖνος ἐμὲ δοξάσει, ὅτι ἐκ τοῦ ἐμοῦ ᴾλήψεται,‖ καὶ ἀναγ-
He   me will glorify, for of   .mine he will receive, and will an-
γελεῖ ὑμῖν. 15 πάντα ὅσα ἔχει ὁ πατὴρ ἐμά ἐστιν·
nounce to you.   All things whatsoever ³has ᵎthe ²Father ⁵mine ⁴are;
διὰ τοῦτο εἶπον, ὅτι ἐκ τοῦ ἐμοῦ ᵠλήψεται,‖ καὶ ἀναγ-
because of this I said,   that of .mine he will receive, and will an-
γελεῖ ὑμῖν. 16 Μικρὸν καὶ ʳοὐ.θεωρεῖτέ με, καὶ πάλιν
nounce to you.   A little [while] and ye do not behold me; and again
μικρὸν, καὶ ὄψεσθέ με, ˢὅτι ἐγὼ ὑπάγω πρὸς τὸν πα-
a little [while] and ye shall see me, because I go away to the Fa-
τέρα.‖ 17 Εἶπον οὖν ἐκ τῶν.μαθητῶν.αὐτοῦ πρὸς
ther.   Said therefore [some] of   his disciples to
ἀλλήλους, Τί ἐστιν τοῦτο ὃ λέγει ἡμῖν, Μικρὸν καὶ
one another, What is this which he says to us, A little [while] and
οὐ.θεωρεῖτέ με, καὶ πάλιν μικρὸν καὶ ὄψεσθέ με; καὶ
ye do not behold me; and again a little [while] and ye shall see me? and
Ὅτι ᵗἐγὼ‖ ὑπάγω πρὸς τὸν πατέρα; 18 Ἔλεγον οὖν,
Because I   go away to   the Father?   They said therefore,
ᵛΤοῦτο τί ἐστιν‖ ὃ λέγει, ᵂτὸ‖ μικρόν; οὐκ.οἴδαμεν
³This ˡwhat ²is which he says, the little [while]? We do not know
τί λαλεῖ. 19 Ἔγνω ˣοὖν‖ ʸὁ‖ Ἰησοῦς ὅτι ἤθελον αὐτὸν
what he speaks. ²Knew ³therefore ˡJesus that they desired ³him
ἐρωτᾶν, καὶ εἶπεν αὐτοῖς, Περὶ τούτου ζητεῖτε μετ᾽
ˡto ²ask, and said to them, Concerning this do ye inquire among
ἀλλήλων, ὅτι εἶπον, Μικρὸν καὶ οὐ.θεωρεῖτέ με, καὶ
one another, that I said, A little [while] and ye do not behold me; and
πάλιν μικρὸν καὶ ὄψεσθέ με; 20 ἀμὴν ἀμὴν λέγω ὑμῖν,
again a little [while] and ye shall see me?   Verily verily I say to you,
ὅτι κλαύσετε καὶ θρηνήσετε ὑμεῖς, ὁ.δὲ κόσμος χαρήσεται·
that ²will ³weep ⁴and ⁵will ⁶lament ˡye,   but the world   will rejoice;

ᵢ — μου (read the.Father) ΤΤ_ᵣ[A]. ᵏ οὐκέτι GLT. ˡ ὑμῖν λέγειν ΤΤ_ᵣA. ᵐ εἰς τὴν
ἀλήθειαν πᾶσαν LΤ_ᵣA; ἐν τῇ ἀληθείᾳ πάσῃ Τ. ⁿ — ἂν LΤΤ_ᵣA. ᵒ ἀκούσει he shall
hear Τ_ᵣA; ἀκούει he hears Τ. ᴾ λήμψεται LΤΤ_ᵣA. ᵠ λαμβάνει receives GLΤΤ_ᵣAW.
ʳ οὐκέτι no longer (do ye behold) LΤA; οὐκ ἔτι Τ. ˢ — ὅτι ἐγὼ ὑπάγω πρὸς τὸν πατέρα
ΤΤ_ᵣA; ὅτι ὑπάγω πρὸς τὸν πατέρα G[L]W. ᵗ — ἐγὼ (read ὑπάγω I go away) LΤΤ_ᵣAW.. ᵛ Τί
ἐστιν τοῦτο LΤ_ᵣ. ᵂ — τὸ (read a little [while]) Τ_ᵣA. ˣ —; οὖν GΤΤ.AW. ʸ — ὁ ΤΤ_ᵣA.

ὑμεῖς *δὲ‖ λυπηθήσεσθε, ᵃἀλλ'‖ ἡ.λύπη.ὑμῶν εἰς χαρὰν ᵐ γενή-
but ye   will be grieved,   but   your grief   to   joy   shall be-

σεται. 21 ἡ γυνὴ ὅταν τίκτῃ, λύπην ἔχει, ὅτι ἦλθεν
come.   21 the woman when she gives birth,   grief   has,   because is come

ἡ.ὥρα.αὐτῆς· ὅταν.δὲ γεννήσῃ τὸ παιδίον, ᵇοὐκ ἔτι‖
her hour;   but when she brings forth the child,   no longer

μνημονεύει τῆς θλίψεως, διὰ τὴν χαρὰν ὅτι ἐγεννήθη
she remembers the tribulation, on account of the   joy   that has been born

ἄνθρωπος εἰς τὸν κόσμον. 22 καὶ ὑμεῖς οὖν ᶜλύπην μὲν
a man   into the world.   And ye therefore grief indeed

νῦν ᵈἔχετε·‖ πάλιν.δὲ ὄψομαι ὑμᾶς, καὶ χαρήσεται ὑμῶν
now have;   but again I will see you, and ʰshall ᵉrejoice ¹your

ἡ καρδία, καὶ τὴν.χαρὰν.ὑμῶν οὐδεὶς ᵉαἴρει ἀφ᾽ ὑμῶν. 23 καὶ
heart,   and   your joy   no one takes from you.   And

ᵍἐν ἐκείνῃ τῇ ἡμέρᾳ ἐμὲ οὐκ ἐρωτήσετε οὐδέν. Ἀμὴν ἀμὴν
in   that   day of me   ye shall ask nothing. Verily verily

λέγω ὑμῖν, ᶠὅτι‖ ᵍὅσα.ἂν‖ αἰτήσητε τὸν πατέρα ʰἐν τῷ
I say to you, That whatsoever ye may ask the Father in

ὀνόματί.μου· δώσει ὑμῖν.‖ 24 ἕως.ἄρτι οὐκ ᾐτήσατε οὐδὲν
my name   he will give you.   Hitherto   ye asked nothing

ἐν.τῷ.ὀνόματί.μου· αἰτεῖτε, καὶ ⁱλήψεσθε,‖ ἵνα ἡ.χαρὰ.ὑμῶν
in   my name;   ask,   and ye shall receive, that   your joy

ᾖ πεπληρωμένη. 25 ταῦτα ἐν παροιμίαις λελάληκα ὑμῖν·
may be   full.   These things in allegories I have spoken to you;

ᵏἀλλ'‖ ἔρχεται ὥρα ὅτε ˡοὐκ ἔτι‖ ἐν παροιμίαις λαλήσω
but   is coming an hour when no longer in allegories I will speak

ὑμῖν, ἀλλὰ παρρησίᾳ περὶ τοῦ πατρὸς ᵐἀναγγελῶ ὑμῖν.
to you, but plainly concerning the Father I will announce to you.

26 ἐν ἐκείνῃ τῇ ἡμέρᾳ ἐν τῷ.ὀνόματί.μου αἰτήσεσθε· καὶ οὐ
In   that   day in   my name   ye shall ask; and ³not

λέγω ὑμῖν ὅτι ἐγὼ ἐρωτήσω τὸν πατέρα περὶ ὑμῶν· 27 αὐ-
¹ ²say to you that I   will beseech the Father for you,   27 ⁴him-

τὸς γὰρ ὁ πατὴρ φιλεῖ ὑμᾶς, ὅτι ὑμεῖς ἐμὲ πεφιλήκατε, καὶ
self ¹for ⁴the ³Father loves you, because ye   me have loved, and

πεπιστεύκατε ὅτι ἐγὼ παρὰ ⁿτοῦ θεοῦ‖ ἐξῆλθον. 28 ἐξῆλθον
have believed that I   from   God   came out.   I came out

ᵒπαρὰ‖ τοῦ πατρὸς καὶ ἐλήλυθα εἰς τὸν κόσμον· πάλιν ἀφίημι
from   the Father and have come into the world; again I leave

τὸν κόσμον καὶ πορεύομαι πρὸς τὸν πατέρα. 29 Λέγουσιν
the world   and   go   to   the Father.   29 ¹Say

ᵖαὐτῷ‖ οἱ.μαθηταὶ.αὐτοῦ. Ἴδε, νῦν ᵠπαρρησίᾳ λαλεῖς, καὶ
²to ²him   ¹his ⁴disciples, Lo, now plainly thou speakest, and

παροιμίαν οὐδεμίαν λέγεις. 30 νῦν οἴδαμεν ὅτι οἶδας
²allegory ¹no   speakest.   Now we know that thou knowest

πάντα, καὶ οὐ χρείαν ἔχεις ἵνα τίς σε ἐρωτᾷ. ἐν τούτῳ
all things, and ²not ³need ¹hast that anyone thee should ask. By this

πιστεύομεν ὅτι ἀπὸ θεοῦ ἐξῆλθες. 31 Ἀπεκρίθη αὐτοῖς
we believe that from God thou camest forth.   ²Answered ³them

ᵣὁ‖ Ἰησοῦς, Ἄρτι πιστεύετε; 32 ἰδού, ἔρχεται ὥρα καὶ ˢνῦν‖
¹Jesus,   Now ⁴do ³ye ⁷believe?   Lo,   is coming an hour and now

ἐλήλυθεν, ἵνα σκορπισθῆτε ἕκαστος εἰς τὰ.ἴδια, ᵗκαὶ ἐμὲ‖
has come,   that ye will be scattered each   to his own, and me

---

Second column (English):

shall be sorrowful, but
your sorrow shall be
turned into joy. 21 A
woman when she is in
travail hath sorrow,
because her hour is
come: but as soon as
she is delivered of the
child, she remembereth
no more the anguish,
for joy that a man is
born into the world.
22 And ye now there-
fore have sorrow: but
I will see you again,
and your heart shall
rejoice, and your joy
no man taketh from
you. 23 And in that
day ye shall ask me no-
thing. Verily, verily,
I say unto you, What-
soever ye shall ask the
Father in my name,
he will give it you.
24 Hitherto have ye
asked nothing in my
name: ask, and ye shall
receive, that your joy
may be full. 25 These
things have I spoken
unto you in proverbs:
but the time cometh,
when I shall no more
speak unto you in pro-
verbs, but I shall shew
you plainly of the Fa-
ther. 26 At that day ye
shall ask in my name:
and I say not unto
you, that I will pray
the Father for you:
27 for the Father him-
self loveth you, because
ye have loved me, and
have believed that I
came out from God.
28 I came forth from
the Father, and am
come into the world:
again, I leave the
world, and go to the
Father. 29 His disci-
ples said unto him, Lo,
now speakest thou
plainly, and speakest
no proverb. 30 Now
are we sure that thou
knowest all things,
and needest not that
any man should ask
thee: by this we be-
lieve that thou camest
forth from God. 31 Je-
sus answered them, Do
ye now believe? 32 Be-
hold, the hour cometh,
yea, is now come, that
ye shall be scattered,
every man to his own,
and shall leave me a-

ᶻ — δὲ but LTTrA.   ᵃ ἀλλὰ T‚A.   ᵇ οὐκέτι GLT.   ᶜ νῦν μὲν λυπην LTTrA.   ᵈ ἔξετε shall
have L.   ᵉ ἀρεῖ shall take LTrA.   ᶠ — ὅτι [L]TTrA.   ᵍ ἄν τι if anything LTTrA.
ʰ δώσει ὑμῖν
ἐν τῷ ὀνόματί μου TTrA.   ⁱ λήμψεσθε LTTrA.   ᵏ — ἀλλ G[L]TT AW.   ˡ οὐκέτι GLT.
ᵐ ἀπαγγελῶ LTTrAW.   ⁿ — τοῦ L; τοῦ πατρὸς the Father TrA.   ᵒ ἐκ LTTrA.   ᵖ — αὐτῷ
[L]TTrA.   ᵠ + ἐν LTTrA.   ʳ — ὁ TTrA.   ˢ — νῦν LTTrA.   ᵗ κἀμὲ TTrA.
20

lone: and yet I am not alone, because the Father is with me. 33 These things I have spoken unto you, that in me ye might have peace. In the world ye shall have tribulation: but be of good cheer; I have overcome the world.

μόνον ἀφῆτε· καὶ οὐκ.εἰμὶ μόνος, ὅτι ὁ πατὴρ μετ'
alone ye.will leave; and [yet] I am not alone, for the Father with

ἐμοῦ ἐστιν. 33 ταῦτα λελάληκα ὑμῖν ἵνα ἐν ἐμοὶ εἰρήνην
me is. These things I have spoken to you that in me peace

ἔχητε. ἐν τῷ κόσμῳ θλίψιν ἕχετε· ἀλλὰ θαρσεῖτε,
ye may have. In the world tribulation ye have; but be of good courage,

ἐγὼ νενίκηκα τὸν κόσμον.
I have overcome the world.

XVII. These words spake Jesus, and lifted up his eyes to heaven, and said, Father, the hour is come; glorify thy Son, that thy Son also may glorify thee: 2 as thou hast given him power over all flesh, that he should give eternal life to as many as thou hast given him. 3 And this is life eternal, that they might know thee the only true God, and Jesus Christ, whom thou hast sent. 4 I have glorified thee on the earth: I have finished the work which thou gavest me to do. 5 And now, O Father, glorify thou me with thine own self with the glory which I had with thee before the world was. 6 I have manifested thy name unto the men which thou gavest me out of the world: thine they were, and thou gavest them me; and they have kept thy word. 7 Now they have known that all things whatsoever thou hast given me are of thee. 8 For I have given unto them the words which thou gavest me; and they have received them, and have known surely that I came out from thee, and they have believed that thou didst send me. 9 I pray for them: I pray not for the world, but for them which thou hast given me; for they are thine. 10 And all mine are thine, and thine are mine: and I am glorified in them. 11 And now I am no more in the world, but these are in the world,

17 Ταῦτα ἐλάλησεν ὁ Ἰησοῦς, καὶ ἐπῆρεν τοὺς ὀφθαλ-
These things spoke Jesus, and lifted up eyes

μοὺς αὐτοῦ εἰς τὸν οὐρανὸν καὶ εἶπεν, Πάτερ, ἐλήλυθεν ἡ
his to the heaven and said, Father, has come the

ὥρα· δόξασόν σου τὸν υἱόν, ἵνα καὶ ὁ υἱός.σου δοξάσῃ
hour; glorify thy Son, that also thy Son may glorify

σε· 2 καθὼς ἔδωκας αὐτῷ ἐξουσίαν πάσης σαρκός, ἵνα
thee; as thou gavest him authority over all flesh, that [of]

πᾶν ὃ δέδωκας αὐτῷ, δώσῃ αὐτοῖς ζωὴν αἰώνιον.
all which thou hast given him, he should give to them life eternal.

3 αὕτη.δέ ἐστιν ἡ αἰώνιος ζωή, ἵνα γινώσκωσίν σε τὸν
And this is the eternal life, that they should know thee the

μόνον ἀληθινὸν θεόν, καὶ ὃν ἀπέστειλας Ἰησοῦν χριστόν.
only true God, and whom thou didst send Jesus Christ.

4 ἐγώ σε ἐδόξασα ἐπὶ τῆς γῆς· τὸ ἔργον ἐτελείωσα ὃ
I thee glorified on the earth; the work I completed which

δέδωκάς μοι ἵνα ποιήσω· 5 καὶ νῦν δόξασόν με σύ· πά-
thou hast given me that I should do; and now glorify thou me, Fa-

τερ, παρὰ σεαυτῷ, τῇ δόξῃ ᾗ εἶχον πρὸ τοῦ τὸν κόσμον
ther, with thyself, with the glory which I had before the world

εἶναι παρὰ σοί. 6 Ἐφανέρωσά σου τὸ ὄνομα τοῖς ἀνθρώποις
was with thee. I manifested thy name to the men

οὓς δέδωκάς μοι ἐκ τοῦ κόσμου· σοὶ ἦσαν, καὶ ἐμοὶ
whom thou hast given me out of the world. Thine they were, and to me

αὐτοὺς δέδωκας· καὶ τὸν.λόγον.σου τετηρήκασιν. 7 νῦν
them thou hast given, and thy word they have kept. Now

ἔγνωκαν ὅτι πάντα ὅσα δέδωκάς μοι, παρὰ σοῦ
they have known that all things whatsoever thou hast given me, of thee

ἐστιν· 8 ὅτι τὰ ῥήματα ἃ δέδωκάς μοι δέδωκα αὐτοῖς·
are; for the words which thou hast given me I have given them,

καὶ αὐτοὶ ἔλαβον, καὶ ἔγνωσαν ἀληθῶς ὅτι παρὰ σοῦ
and they received [them], and knew truly that from thee

ἐξῆλθον, καὶ ἐπίστευσαν ὅτι σύ με ἀπέστειλας. 9 ἐγὼ περὶ
I came out, and they believed that thou me didst send. I concerning

αὐτῶν ἐρωτῶ· οὐ περὶ τοῦ κόσμου ἐρωτῶ, ἀλλὰ
them make request; not concerning the world make I request, but

περὶ ὧν δέδωκάς μοι, ὅτι σοί εἰσιν. 10 καὶ τὰ
concerning whom thou hast given me, for thine they are; (and things

ἐμὰ πάντα σά ἐστιν, καὶ τὰ.σὰ ἐμά· καὶ δεδόξασμαι
my all thine are, and thine [are] mine,) and I have been glorified

ἐν αὐτοῖς. 11 καὶ οὐκ ἔτι εἰμὶ ἐν τῷ κόσμῳ, καὶ οὗτοι ἐν
in them. And no longer I am in the world, and these in

ᵗ ἕξετε ye will have EL.   ʷ — ὁ T.   ˣ ἐπάρας having lifted up LTTrA.   ʸ — καὶ LTTrA.
ᶻ — καὶ LTTrAW.   ᵃ — σου (read the Son) TTr[A].   ᵇ δώσει he shall give A.   ᶜ γινώ-
σκουσιν they know TTr.   ᵈ τελειώσας having completed LTTrA.   ᵉ ἔδωκάς thou
gavest LTTr.   ᶠ κἀμοὶ Tr.   ᵍ τετήρηκαν LTTrA.   ʰ ἔδωκάς thou gavest L.
ⁱ εἰσίν TTrA.   ᵏ ἔδωκάς thou gavest LTTrA.   ˡ [καὶ ἔγνωσαν] L.   ᵐ οὐκέτι LTW.
ⁿ αὐτοὶ they·T.

τῷ κόσμῳ εἰσίν, °καὶ ἐγὼ‖ πρός σε ἔρχομαι. ²πάτερ ἅγιε, τήρη-
the world are, and I to thee come. ²Father ¹Holy, keep

σον αὐτοὺς ἐν τῷ ὀνόματί σου Ροὺς‖ δέδωκάς μοι. ἵνα
them in thy name whom thou hast given me, that

ὦσιν ἕν, καθὼς �۹ ἡμεῖς. 12 ὅτε ἤμην μετ' αὐτῶν ʳἐν τῷ
they may be one, as we. When I was with them in the

κόσμῳ ἐγὼ ἐτήρουν αὐτοὺς ἐν τῷ ὀνόματί σου ˢοὓς‖ δέ-
world I was keeping them in thy name: whom thou

δωκάς μοι ᵗ ἐφύλαξα, καὶ οὐδεὶς ἐξ αὐτῶν ἀπώλετο, εἰ μὴ ὁ
hast given me I guarded, and no one of them perished, except the

υἱὸς τῆς ἀπωλείας, ἵνα ἡ γραφὴ πληρωθῇ. 13 νῦν δὲ
son of perdition, that the scripture might be fulfilled. And now

πρός σε ἔρχομαι, καὶ ταῦτα λαλῶ ἐν τῷ κόσμῳ ἵνα ἔχω-
to thee I come; and these things I speak in the world that they may

σιν τὴν χαρὰν τὴν ἐμὴν πεπληρωμένην ἐν ᵘαὐτοῖς.‖ 14 ἐγὼ
have ¹my ²joy fulfilled in them. I

δέδωκα αὐτοῖς τὸν λόγον σου, καὶ ὁ κόσμος ἐμίσησεν αὐτούς,
have given them thy word, and the world hated them,

ὅτι οὐκ εἰσὶν ἐκ τοῦ κόσμου, καθὼς ἐγὼ οὐκ εἰμὶ ἐκ τοῦ
because they are not of the world, as I am not of the

κόσμου. 15 οὐκ ἐρωτῶ ἵνα ἄρῃς αὐτοὺς ἐκ τοῦ
world. I do not make request that thou shouldest take them out of the

κόσμου, ἀλλ' ἵνα τηρήσῃς αὐτοὺς ἐκ τοῦ πονηροῦ.
world, but that thou shouldest keep them out of the evil.

16 ἐκ τοῦ κόσμου οὐκ εἰσίν, καθὼς ἐγὼ ᵛἐκ τοῦ κόσμου οὐκ
Of the world they are not, as I ¹not ²of ³the ⁴world

εἰμί. 17 ἁγίασον αὐτοὺς ἐν τῇ ἀληθείᾳ ᵂσου·‖ ὁ λόγος ὁ σὸς
¹am. Sanctify them by thy truth: ²word ¹thy

ἀλήθειά ἐστιν. 18 καθὼς ἐμὲ ἀπέστειλας εἰς τὸν κόσμον,
truth is. As me thou didst send into the world,

κἀγὼ ἀπέστειλα αὐτοὺς εἰς τὸν κόσμον· 19 καὶ ὑπὲρ αὐτῶν
I also sent them into the world; and for them

ˣἐγὼ‖ ἁγιάζω ἐμαυτόν, ἵνα ʸκαὶ αὐτοὶ ὦσιν‖ ἡγιασμένοι ἐν
I sanctify myself, that also they may be sanctified in

ἀληθείᾳ. 20 Οὐ περὶ τούτων δὲ ἐρωτῶ μόνον, ἀλλὰ
truth. ²Not ³for ⁴these ¹and ⁷make ⁶I ⁵request ⁸only, but

καὶ περὶ τῶν ᶻπιστευσόντων‖ διὰ τοῦ λόγου αὐτῶν εἰς
also for those who shall believe through their word on

ἐμέ· 21 ἵνα πάντες ἓν ὦσιν, καθὼς σύ, ᵃπάτερ,‖ ἐν ἐμοί,
me; that all may be one, as thou, Father, [art] in me,

κἀγὼ ἐν σοί, ἵνα καὶ αὐτοὶ ἐν ἡμῖν ᵇἓν‖ ὦσιν· ἵνα ὁ κόσμος
and I in thee, that also they in us one may be, that the world

ᶜπιστεύσῃ‖ ὅτι σύ με ἀπέστειλας. 22 ᵈκαὶ ἐγὼ‖ τὴν δόξαν
may believe that thou me didst send. And I the glory

ἣν ᵉδέδωκάς‖ μοι δέδωκα αὐτοῖς, ἵνα ὦσιν ἕν, καθὼς
which thou hast given me have given them, that they may be one, as

ἡμεῖς ἕν ᶠἐσμεν·‖ 23 ἐγὼ ἐν αὐτοῖς, καὶ σὺ ἐν ἐμοί, ἵνα
we one are: I in them, and thou in me, that

ὦσιν τετελειωμένοι εἰς ἕν, ᵍκαὶ‖ ἵνα γινώσκῃ ὁ κόσμος
they may be perfected into one, and that ³may ⁴know ¹the ²world

and I come to thee.
Holy Father, keep
through thine own
name those whom
thou hast given me,
that they may be
one, as we are.
12 While I was with
them in the world, I
kept them in thy name:
those that thou gavest
me I have kept, and
none of them is lost,
but the son of perdi-
tion; that the scrip-
ture might be fulfilled.
13 And now come I to
thee; and these things
I speak in the world,
that they might have
my joy fulfilled in
themselves. 14 I have
given them thy word;
and the world hath
hated them, because
they are not of the
world, even as I am
not of the world. 15 I
pray not that thou
shouldest take them
out of the world, but
that thou shouldest
keep them from the
evil. 16 They are not
of the world, even as
I am not of the world.
17 Sanctify them
through thy truth:
thy word is truth.
18 As thou hast sent
me into the world, even
so have I also sent
them into the world.
19 And for their sakes
I sanctify myself, that
they also might be
sanctified through the
truth. 20 Neither pray
I for these alone, but
for them also which
shall believe on me
through their word;
21 that they all may be
one; as thou, Father,
art in me, and I in
thee, that they also
may be one in us: that
the world may believe
that thou hast sent
me. 22 And the glory
which thou gavest me
I have given them;
that they may be one,
even as we are one:
23 I in them, and thou
in me, that they may
be made perfect in one;
and that the world
may know that thou

ᵘ κἀγὼ LTTrA. Ρ ᾧ which GLTTrAW. ۹ + καὶ also Tr. ʳ — ἐν τῷ κόσμῳ LTTrA. ˢ ᾧ which TTrA. ᵗ + καὶ and (read I was keeping them in thy name which thou hast given me, and I guarded [them]) [L]TTrA. ᵘ ἑαυτοῖς TTrA. ᵛ οὐκ εἰμὶ ἐκ τοῦ κόσμου LTTrAW. ᵂ — σου (read the truth) LTTrA. ˣ — ἐγὼ (read ἅγ. I sanctify) [L]T. ʸ ὦσιν καὶ αὐτοὶ LTTrAW. ᶻ πιστευόντων believe GLTTrAW. ᵃ πατὴρ TTrA. ᵇ — ἐν [L]TTrA. ᶜ πιστεύῃ TTr. ᵈ κἀγὼ LTTrA. ᵉ ἔδωκας thou gavest L. ᶠ — ἐσμεν (read [are]) TTrA. ᵍ — καὶ LTTrA.

hast sent me, and hast loved them, as thou hast loved me. 24 Father, I will that they also, whom thou hast given me, be with me where I am; that they may behold my glory, which thou hast given me: for thou lovedst me before the foundation of the world. 25 O righteous Father, the world hath not known thee: but I have known thee, and these have known that thou hast sent me. 26 And I have declared unto them thy name, and will declare it: that the love wherewith thou hast loved me may be in them, and I in them.

ὅτι σύ με ἀπέστειλας, καὶ ἠγάπησας αὐτοὺς καθὼς ἐμὲ ἠγά-
that thou me didst send, and lovedst them as me thou

πησας. 24 hΠάτερ,ǁ iοὕςǁ jδέδωκάςǁ μοι θέλω ἵνα ὅπου εἰμὶ
lovedst. Father, whom thou hast given me I desire that where ²am

ἐγὼ κἀκεῖνοι ὦσιν μετ' ἐμοῦ, ἵνα θεωρῶσιν τὴν δόξαν τὴν
¹I they also may be with me, that they may behold ²glory

ἐμὴν ἣν kἔδωκάςǁ μοι, ὅτι ἠγάπησάς με πρὸ καταβολῆς
¹my which thou gavest me, for thou lovedst me before [the] foundation

κόσμου 25 lΠάτερǁ δίκαιε, καὶ ὁ κόσμος σε οὐκ ἔγνω,
of [the] world. ²Father ¹righteous, and the world thee knew not,

ἐγὼ δὲ σε ἔγνων, καὶ οὗτοι ἔγνωσαν ὅτι σύ με ἀπέστειλας·
but I thee knew, and these knew that thou me didst send.

26 καὶ ἐγνώρισα αὐτοῖς τὸ ὄνομά σου, καὶ γνωρίσω·
And I made known to them thy name, and will make [it] known;

ἵνα ἡ ἀγάπη ἣν ἠγάπησάς με ἐν αὐτοῖς ᾖ, κἀγὼ
that the love with which thou lovedst me in them may be; and I

ἐν αὐτοῖς.
in them.

XVIII. When Jesus had spoken these words, he went forth with his disciples over the brook Cedron, where was a garden, into the which he entered, and his disciples. 2 And Judas also, which betrayed him, knew the place: for Jesus ofttimes resorted thither with his disciples. 3 Judas then, having received a band of men and officers from the chief priests and Pharisees, cometh thither with lanterns and torches and weapons. 4 Jesus therefore, knowing all things that should come upon him, went forth, and said unto them, Whom seek ye? 5 They answered him, Jesus of Nazareth. Jesus saith unto them, I am he. And Judas also, which betrayed him, stood with them. 6 As soon then as he had said unto them, I am he, they went backward, and fell to the ground. 7 Then asked he them again, Whom seek ye? And they said, Jesus of Nazareth. 8 Jesus answered, I have told you that I am he: if therefore ye seek me, let these go their way:

18 Ταῦτα εἰπὼν mὁǁ Ἰησοῦς ἐξῆλθεν σὺν τοῖς μαθηταῖς
²These ⁵things ³having ⁴said ¹Jesus went out with ²disciples

αὐτοῦ πέραν τοῦ χειμάρρου nτῶν Κέδρων,ǁ ὅπου ἦν κῆπος,
¹his beyond the winter stream of Kedron, where was a garden,

εἰς ὃν εἰσῆλθεν αὐτὸς καὶ οἱ μαθηταὶ αὐτοῦ. 2 ᾔδει δὲ καὶ
into which ²entered ¹he and his disciples. And ³knew ²also

Ἰούδας ὁ παραδιδοὺς αὐτὸν τὸν τόπον· ὅτι πολλάκις
¹Judas who ⁴was ⁵delivering ⁶up ⁷him the place, because ¹often

συνήχθη oὁǁ Ἰησοῦς ἐκεῖ μετὰ τῶν μαθητῶν αὐτοῦ. 3 ὁ οὖν
²was ³gathered ¹Jesus there with his disciples. ²Therefore

Ἰούδας λαβὼν τὴν σπεῖραν, καὶ ἐκ τῶν ἀρχιερέων καὶ p
¹Judas having received the band, and ²from ³the ⁴chief ⁵priests ⁶and

Φαρισαίων ὑπηρέτας, ἔρχεται ἐκεῖ μετὰ φανῶν καὶ λαμπάδων
⁷Pharisees ¹officers, comes there with torches and lamps

καὶ ὅπλων. 4 Ἰησοῦς qοὖνǁ εἰδὼς πάντα τὰ ἐρχόμενα
and weapons. Jesus therefore knowing all things that were coming

ἐπ' αὐτόν, rἐξελθὼν εἶπενǁ αὐτοῖς, Τίνα ζητεῖτε; 5 Ἀπε-
upon him, having gone forth said to them. Whom seek ye? They

κρίθησαν αὐτῷ, Ἰησοῦν τὸν Ναζωραῖον. Λέγει αὐτοῖς sὁ
answered him, Jesus the Nazarœan. ²Says ³to ⁴them

Ἰησοῦς,ǁ Ἐγώ εἰμι. Εἱστήκει δὲ καὶ Ἰούδας ὁ παρα-
¹Jesus, I am [he]. And ⁸was ⁹standing ²also ¹Judas ³who ⁴was ⁵de-

διδοὺς αὐτὸν μετ' αὐτῶν. 6 Ὡς οὖν εἶπεν αὐτοῖς, tὍτι
livering ⁷up ⁶him with them. When therefore he said to them,

ἐγώ εἰμι, vἀπῆλθονǁ εἰς τὰ ὀπίσω καὶ wἔπεσονǁ χαμαί.
I am [he], they went backward and fell to [the] ground.

7 πάλιν οὖν xαὐτοὺς ἐπηρώτησεν,ǁ Τίνα ζητεῖτε; Οἱ δὲ
Again therefore ³them ¹he ²questioned, Whom seek ye? And they

εἶπον, Ἰησοῦν τὸν Ναζωραῖον. 8 Ἀπεκρίθη yὁǁ Ἰησοῦς, Εἶπον
said, Jesus the Nazarœan. ²Answered ¹Jesus, I told

ὑμῖν ὅτι ἐγώ εἰμι. εἰ οὖν ἐμὲ ζητεῖτε, ἄφετε τούτους ὑπά-
you that I am [he]. If therefore me ye seek, suffer these to go

---

h πατήρ LTTrA. i ὁ what TTr. j ἐδωκάς thou gavest L. . k δέδωκάς thou hast
given LTTrAW. l πατὴρ LTTrA. ' m — ὁ TTr. n τοῦ Κεδρών GL; τοῦ κέδρου T.
o — ὁ TTrA. p + τῶν LTr[A]; + ἐκ τῶν from the T. q δὲ and (Jesus) Tr. r ἐξῆλθεν
καὶ λέγει went forth and says LTTrA. s — ὁ T; — ὁ Ἰησοῦς (read he says) TrA. t — ὅτι
LTTr. v ἀπῆλθαν LTTrA. w ἔπεσαν LTTrA. x ἐπηρώτησεν αὐτούς LTrA; αὐτὸς ἐπηρώτησεν W. y — ὁ GLTTrAW.

γειν· 9 ἵνα πληρωθῇ ὁ λόγος ὃν εἶπεν. Ὅτι οὓς δέ-
away;　　that might be fulfilled the word which he said,　Whom thou

δωκάς μοι οὐκ ἀπώλεσα ἐξ αὐτῶν οὐδένα. 10 Σίμων οὖν
hast given me　I lost　of them not one.　　Simon ²therefore

Πέτρος ἔχων μάχαιραν, εἵλκυσεν αὐτήν, καὶ ἔπαισεν τὸν
¹Peter having a sword,　drew　it,　and smote the

τοῦ ἀρχιερέως δοῦλον, καὶ ἀπέκοψεν αὐτοῦ τὸ ᶻὠτίον‖ τὸ
²of ³the ⁴high ¹priest ¹bondman, and　cut off　his ᶻ ear　the

δεξιόν. ἦν δὲ ὄνομα τῷ δούλῳ Μάλχος. 11 εἶπεν οὖν
¹right. And ⁴was ³name ¹the ²bondman's Malchus.　²Said ³therefore

ὁ Ἰησοῦς τῷ Πέτρῳ, Βάλε τὴν μάχαιράν ªσου‖ εἰς τὴν θήκην.
¹Jesus　to Peter, Put　thy sword　　into the sheath;

τὸ ποτήριον ὃ δέδωκέν μοι ὁ πατὴρ οὐ μὴ πίω αὐτό;
the　cup　which ³has ⁴given ⁵me ¹the ²Father should I not drink it?

12 Ἡ οὖν σπεῖρα καὶ ὁ χιλίαρχος καὶ οἱ ὑπηρέται τῶν
The ²therefore ¹band and the chief captain and the　officers of the

Ἰουδαίων συνέλαβον τὸν Ἰησοῦν, καὶ ἔδησαν αὐτόν, 13 καὶ
Jews　took hold of　the Jesus,　and bound　him;　and

ᵇἀπήγαγον αὐτὸν‖ πρὸς Ἅνναν πρῶτον· ἦν γὰρ πενθερὸς
they led away him　to　Annas　first;　for he was father-in-law

τοῦ Καϊάφα, ὃς ἦν ἀρχιερεὺς τοῦ ἐνιαυτοῦ ἐκείνου. 14 ἦν δὲ
of Caiaphas, who was high priest　that that year.　Now was

Καϊάφας ὁ συμβουλεύσας τοῖς Ἰουδαίοις, ὅτι συμφέρει
Caiaphas who gave counsel to the Jews,　that it is profitable

ἕνα ἄνθρωπον ᶜἀπολέσθαι‖ ὑπὲρ τοῦ λαοῦ. 15 Ἠκολούθει δὲ
for one man　to perish　for the people. Now there followed

τῷ Ἰησοῦ Σίμων Πέτρος καὶ ᵈὁ‖ ἄλλος μαθητής. ὁ δὲ μαθητὴς
Jesus　Simon Peter and the other disciple. And ²disciple

ἐκεῖνος ἦν γνωστὸς τῷ ἀρχιερεῖ, καὶ συνεισῆλθεν τῷ Ἰησοῦ
¹that was known to the high priest, and entered with Jesus

εἰς τὴν αὐλὴν τοῦ ἀρχιερέως· 16 ὁ δὲ Πέτρος εἱστήκει πρὸς
into the court of the high priest;　but Peter stood　at

τῇ θύρᾳ ἔξω. ἐξῆλθεν οὖν ὁ μαθητὴς ὁ ἄλλος ᵉὃς ἦν‖
the door without. Went out therefore the ²disciple ¹other who was

γνωστὸς ᶠτῷ ἀρχιερεῖ,‖ καὶ εἶπεν τῇ θυρωρῷ καὶ εἰσήγα-
known to the high priest, and spoke to the door-keeper and brought

γεν τὸν Πέτρον. 17 λέγει οὖν ᵍἡ παιδίσκη ἡ θυρωρὸς τῷ
in　Peter.　⁶Says ⁵therefore ¹the ²maid ³the ⁴door-keeper

Πέτρῳ, Μὴ καὶ σὺ ἐκ τῶν μαθητῶν εἶ τοῦ ἀνθρώπου
to Peter, ²not ¹also ³thou ⁵of ⁶the ⁷disciples ⁴art ²of ²man

τούτου; Λέγει ἐκεῖνος, Οὐκ εἰμί. 18 Εἱστήκεισαν δὲ οἱ δοῦλοι
¹this?　⁴Says ³he,　I am not. But ⁶were ⁷standing ¹the ²bondmen

καὶ οἱ ὑπηρέται ἀνθρακιὰν πεποιηκότες, ὅτι ψῦχος ἦν,
³and ⁴the ⁵officers,　a fire of coals having made, for cold　it was,

καὶ ἐθερμαίνοντο· ἦν δὲ ʰμετ᾽ αὐτῶν ὁ Πέτρος‖ ἑστὼς
and were warming themselves; and ²was ³with ⁴them ¹Peter standing

καὶ θερμαινόμενος. 19 Ὁ οὖν ἀρχιερεὺς ἠρώτησεν τὸν Ἰη-
and warming himself.　The high priest therefore questioned Je-

σοῦν περὶ τῶν μαθητῶν αὐτοῦ, καὶ περὶ τῆς διδαχῆς
sus concerning his disciples, and concerning ²teaching

αὐτοῦ. 20 ἀπεκρίθη ⁱαὐτῷ‖ ᵏὁ‖ Ἰησοῦς, Ἐγὼ παρρησίᾳ
¹his.　²Answered ³him　¹Jesus,　I　openly

---

9 that the saying might be fulfilled, which he spake, Of them which thou gavest me have I lost none. 10 Then Simon Peter having a sword drew it, and smote the high priest's servant, and cut off his right ear. The servant's name was Malchus. 11 Then said Jesus unto Peter, Put up thy sword into the sheath: the cup which my Fath r hath given me, shall I not drink it?

12 Then the band and the captain and officers of the Jews took Jesus, and bound him, 13 and led him away to Anuas first; for he was father in law to Caiaphas, which was the high priest that same year. 14 Now Caiaphas was he, which gave counsel to the Jews, that it was expedient that one man should die for the people. 15 And Simon Peter followed Jesus, and so did another disciple: that disciple was known unto the high pri st, and went in with Jesus into the palace of the high priest. 16 But Peter stood at the door without. Then went out that other disciple, which was known unto the high priest, and spake unto her that kept the door, and brought in Peter. 17 Then saith the damsel that kept the door unto Peter, Art not thou also one of this man's disciples? He saith, I am not. 18 And the servants and officers stood there, who had made a fire of coals; for it was cold: and they warmed themselves: and Peter stood with them, and warmed himself. 19 The high priest then asked Jesus of his disciples, and of his doctrine. 20 Jesus answered him, I spake openly to the

---

ʲ ⁺ ὠτάριον TTrA.　ª — σου (read the sword) GLTTrAW.　ᵇ ἤγαγον [αὐτὸν] they led him
L; ἤγαγον TTr: [ἀπ]ήγαγον αὐτὸν A.　ᶜ ἀποθανεῖν to die LTTrA.　ᵈ — ὁ (read another
LT[r A].　ᵉ ὁ TTrA.　ᶠ τοῦ ἀρχιερέως of the high priest TTrA.　ᵍ τῷ Πέτρῳ ἡ παιδίσκη
ἡ θυρωρός LTTrA.　ʰ καὶ [also] ὁ Πέτρος μετ᾽ αὐτῶν LTTrA.　ⁱ [αὐτῷ] L.　ᵏ — ὁ TTr.

world; I ever taught in the synagogue, and in the temple, whither the Jews always resort; and in secret have I said nothing. 21 Why askest me? ask them which heard me, what I have said unto them: behold, they know what I said. 22 And when he had thus spoken, one of the officers which stood by struck Jesus with the palm of his hand, saying, Answerest thou the high priest so? 23 Jesus answered him, If I have spoken evil, bear witness of the evil: but if well, why smitest thou me? 24 Now Annas had sent him bound unto Caiaphas the high priest.

25 And Simon Peter stood and warmed himself. They said therefore unto him, Art not thou also one of his disciples? He denied it, and said, I am not. 26 One of the servants of the high priest, being his kinsman whose ear Peter cut off, saith, Did not I see thee in the garden with him? 27 Peter then denied again: and immediately the cock crew.

28 Then led they Jesus from Caiaphas unto the hall of judgment: and it was early; and they themselves went not into the judgment hall, lest they should be defiled: but that they might eat the passover. 29 Pilate then went out unto them, and said, What accusation bring ye against this man? 30 They answered and said unto him, If he were not a malefactor, we would not have delivered him up unto thee. 31 Then said Pilate unto them, Take ye him, and judge him according to your law. The Jews therefore said unto him, It is not

---

ἐλάλησα‖ τῷ κόσμῳ· ἐγὼ πάντοτε ἐδίδαξα ἐν ᵐτῇ‖ συνα-
spoke to the world; I always taught in the syna-

γωγῇ καὶ ἐν τῷ ἱερῷ, ὅπου ⁿπάντοτε‖ οἱ Ἰουδαῖοι συνέρχον-
gogue and in the temple, where always the Jews come to-

ται, καὶ ἐν κρυπτῷ ἐλάλησα οὐδέν. 21 τί με °ἐπερωτᾷς;
gether, and in secret I spoke nothing. Why me dost thou question?

ἐπερώτησον‖ τοὺς ἀκηκοότας τί ἐλάλησα αὐτοῖς· ἴδε οὗτοι
question those who have heard what I spoke to them; lo, they

οἴδασιν ἃ εἶπον ἐγώ. 22 Ταῦτα δὲ αὐτοῦ εἰπόντος εἷς ᴾτῶν
know what ²said ¹I. But ⁴these ⁵things ¹on ²his ³saying one of the

ὑπηρετῶν παρεστηκὼς‖ ἔδωκεν ῥάπισμα τῷ
officers standing by gave a blow with the palm of the hand the

Ἰησοῦ, εἰπών, Οὕτως ἀποκρίνῃ τῷ ἀρχιερεῖ; 23 Ἀπεκρίθη
to Jesus, saying, Thus answerest thou the high priest? ²Answered

αὐτῷ ᑫᵒ‖ Ἰησοῦς, Εἰ κακῶς ἐλάλησα, μαρτύρησον περὶ τοῦ
³him ¹Jesus, If evil ¹spoke, bear witness concerning the

κακοῦ· εἰ δὲ καλῶς, τί με δέρεις; 24 Ἀπέστειλεν ʳ αὐτὸν
evil; but if well, why me strikest thou? ²Sent ³him

ὁ Ἄννας δεδεμένον πρὸς Καϊάφαν τὸν ἀρχιερέα.
¹Annas bound to Caiaphas the high priest.

25 Ἦν δὲ Σίμων Πέτρος ἑστὼς καὶ θερμαινόμενος·
Now ³was ¹Simon ²Peter standing and warming himself.

εἶπον οὖν αὐτῷ, Μὴ καὶ σὺ ἐκ τῶν μαθητῶν αὐτοῦ
They said therefore to him, ²Not ⁴al-o ³thou ⁵of ⁶his ⁷disciples

εἶ; Ἠρνήσατο ἐκεῖνος, καὶ εἶπεν, Οὐκ εἰμί. 26 Λέγει εἷς
¹art? He denied, and said, I am not. Says one

ἐκ τῶν δούλων τοῦ ἀρχιερέως, συγγενὴς ὢν οὗ
of the bondmen of the high priest, kinsman being [of him] of whom

ἀπέκοψεν Πέτρος τὸ ὠτίον, Οὐκ ἐγώ σε εἶδον ἐν τῷ κήπῳ
²cut ³off ¹Peter the ear, ²I ¹not ⁴thee ¹saw in the garden

μετ᾽ αὐτοῦ; 27 Πάλιν οὖν ἠρνήσατο ˢὅ‖ Πέτρος, καὶ εὐθέως
with him? Again therefore ²denied ¹Peter, and immediately

ἀλέκτωρ ἐφώνησεν.
a cock crew.

28 Ἄγουσιν οὖν τὸν Ἰησοῦν ἀπὸ τοῦ Καϊάφα εἰς τὸ
They lead therefore Jesus from Caiaphas into the

πραιτώριον· ἦν δὲ ᵗπρωΐα·‖ καὶ αὐτοὶ οὐκ εἰσῆλθον εἰς τὸ
prætorium, and it was early. And they entered not into the

πραιτώριον, ἵνα μὴ μιανθῶσιν, ᵛἀλλ᾽ ἵνα‖ φάγωσιν τὸ
prætorium, that they might not be defiled, but that they might eat the

πάσχα. 29 ἐξῆλθεν οὖν ὁ ʷΠιλᾶτος‖ ˣ πρὸς αὐτούς, καὶ
passover. ³Went ⁴forth ²therefore ¹Pilate to them, and

ʸεἶπεν,‖ Τίνα κατηγορίαν φέρετε ᶻκατὰ‖ τοῦ ἀνθρώπου τούτου;
said, What accusation bring ye against this man?

30 Ἀπεκρίθησαν καὶ ᵃεἶπον‖ αὐτῷ, Εἰ μὴ ἦν οὗτος ᵇκακο-
They answered and said to him, If ²were ³not ¹he an evil

ποιός,‖ οὐκ ἄν σοι παρεδώκαμεν αὐτόν. 31 Εἶπεν
doer, ²not ⁴to ⁵thee ¹we ²would have delivered up him. ³Said

ᶜοὖν‖ αὐτοῖς ᵈὅ‖ ʷΠιλᾶτος,‖ Λάβετε αὐτὸν ὑμεῖς, καὶ
²therefore ⁴to ⁵them ¹Pilate, Take him ye, and

κατὰ τὸν νόμον ὑμῶν κρίνατε ᵉαὐτόν.‖ Εἶπον ᶠοὖν‖
according to your law judge him. ⁴Said ³therefore

---

l λελάληκα have spoken LTTrAW. m — τῇ (read a) GLTTrAW. n πάντοθεν E; πάντες all GLTTrAW₁. o ἐρωτᾷς; ἐρώτησον (ἐπερ. W) LTTrAW. P παρεστηκὼς τῶν ὑπηρετῶν LTTrA. q — ὁ LTTrA. r + οὖν therefore ELT[Tr]A. s — ὁ LTTrAW. t πρωΐ GLTTrAW. v ἀλλὰ LTTrA. w Πειλᾶτος T. x + ἔξω out LTTrA. y φησίν says TTrA. z — κατὰ T. a εἶπαν LTTrA. b κακὸν ποιῶν TTrA. c [οὖν] L. d — ὁ TrA. e — αὐτόν T. f — οὖν LTrA.

αὐτῷ οἱ Ἰουδαῖοι, Ἡμῖν οὐκ ἔξεστιν ἀποκτεῖναι οὐδένα·
ᵃto ᵇhim ᶜthe ·²Jews, To us   it is permitted to put ³to ⁴death ¹no²one ;

32 ἵνα ὁ λόγος τοῦ Ἰησοῦ πληρωθῇ ὃν εἶπεν σημαίνων
that the word   of Jesus might be fulfilled which he spoke signifying

ποίῳ θανάτῳ ἤμελλεν ἀποθνήσκειν. 33 Εἰσῆλθεν οὖν
by what death   he was about   to die.·   ²Entered ³therefore

ᵍεἰς τὸ πραιτώριον πάλιν‖ ὁ ʰΠιλάτος,‖ καὶ ἐφώνησεν τὸν
⁴into ⁵the ᵉprætorium ⁷again   ¹Pilate,   and , called

Ἰησοῦν, καὶ εἶπεν αὐτῷ, Σὺ εἶ ὁ βασιλεὺς τῶν Ἰουδαίων ;
Jesus,   and said   to him, ²Thou ¹art the   king   of the   Jews?

34 Ἀπεκρίθη ⁱαὐτῷ ὁ‖ Ἰησοῦς, ᵏἈφ᾽ ἑαυτοῦ‖ σὺ τοῦτο
²Answered ³him ¹Jesus,   From   thyself ²thou ³this

λέγεις, ἢ ἄλλοι ¹σοι εἶπον‖ περὶ ἐμοῦ ; 35 Ἀπεκρίθη
¹sayest, ⁴or ⁶others ⁷to ⁸thee ⁵did say [it] concerning me?   ²Answered

ὁ ʰΠιλάτος,‖ Μήτι ἐγὼ Ἰουδαῖός εἰμι ; τὸ ἔθνος τὸ σὸν καὶ
¹Pilate,   ⁴I   ⁵a ⁶Jew   ³am ?   ⁸Nation ⁷thy and

οἱ ἀρχιερεῖς παρέδωκάν σε ἐμοί· τί ἐποίησας ; 36 Ἀπεκρίθη
the chief priests delivered up thee to me: what didst thou?   ²Answered

ᵐὁ‖ Ἰησοῦς, Ἡ βασιλεία ἡ ἐμὴ οὐκ ἔστιν ἐκ τοῦ κόσμου τούτου·
¹Jesus,   ⁴kingdom ³my   is not   of   this world ;

εἰ ἐκ τοῦ κόσμου τούτου ἦν ἡ βασιλεία ἡ ἐμή, οἱ ὑπηρέται ⁿἂν
if of   this world   were ²kingdom ¹my,   ⁴attendants

οἱ ἐμοὶ ἠγωνίζοντο‖ ἵνα μὴ παραδοθῶ τοῖς Ἰουδαίοις·
³my   would fight   that I might not be delivered up to the   Jews ;

νῦν δὲ ἡ βασιλεία ἡ ἐμὴ οὐκ ἔστιν ἐντεῦθεν. 37 Εἶπεν οὖν
but now ²kingdom ¹my   is not   from hence.   ³Said ²therefore

αὐτῷ ὁ ʰΠιλάτος,‖ Οὐκοῦν βασιλεὺς εἶ σύ ; Ἀπεκρίθη ᵒὁ‖
⁴to ⁵him ¹/¹Pilate,   Then   a king   art thou? ²Answered

Ἰησοῦς, Σὺ λέγεις, ὅτι βασιλεύς εἰμι ᴾἐγώ.‖ ᵠἐγὼ‖ εἰς τοῦτο
¹Jesus, Thou sayest [it], for   a king   ²am ¹I.   I   for this

γεγέννημαι, καὶ εἰς τοῦτο ἐλήλυθα εἰς τὸν κόσμον, ἵνα
have been born, and for   this   I have come into the   world,   that

μαρτυρήσω τῇ ἀληθείᾳ. πᾶς ὁ ὢν ἐκ τῆς ἀληθείας
I may bear witness to the   truth.   Everyone that is of   the   truth

ἀκούει μου τῆς φωνῆς. 38 Λέγει αὐτῷ ὁ ʰΠιλάτος,‖ Τί ἐστιν
hears   my   voice.   ²Says ³to ⁴him ¹Pilate,   What is

ἀλήθεια ; Καὶ τοῦτο εἰπών, πάλιν ἐξῆλθεν πρὸς τοὺς
truth?   And   this having said, again   he went out to   the

Ἰουδαίους, καὶ λέγει αὐτοῖς, Ἐγὼ οὐδεμίαν ʳαἰτίαν εὑρίσκω ἐν
Jews,   and says to them,   I   not any   fault   find   in

αὐτῷ.‖ 39 ἔστιν δὲ συνήθεια ὑμῖν ἵνα ἕνα ˢὑμῖν ἀπολύσω‖
him.   But it is   a custom with you that one to you I should release

ἐν τῷ πάσχα· βούλεσθε οὖν ᵗὑμῖν ἀπολύσω‖ τὸν βασιλέα
at the passover ;   will ye   therefore to you I should release the   king

τῶν Ἰουδαίων ; 40 Ἐκραύγασαν οὖν πάλιν ⁿπάντες,‖ λέ-
of the   Jews?   They ²cried ⁴out ²therefore ⁵again   ¹all,   say-

γοντες, Μὴ τοῦτον, ἀλλὰ τὸν Βαραββᾶν· ἦν δὲ ὁ Βαραβ-
ing,   Not   this one, but   the   Barabbas.   Now ²was ¹Barab-

βᾶς λῃστής. 19 Τότε οὖν ἔλαβεν ὁ ʰΠιλάτος‖ τὸν Ἰησοῦν
bas   a robber.   Then therefore ²took   ¹Pilate   Jesus

καὶ ἐμαστίγωσεν. 2 καὶ οἱ στρατιῶται πλέξαντες στέφανον
and   scourged [him]. And the   soldiers   having platted   a crown

---

lawful for us to put any man to death: 32 that the saying of Jesus might be fulfilled, which he spake, signifying what death he should die. 33 Then Pilate entered into the judgment hall again, and called Jesus, and said unto him, Art thou the King of the Jews? 34 Jesus answered him, Sayest thou this thing of thyself, or did others tell it thee of me? 35 Pilate answered, Am I a Jew? Thine own nation and the chief priests have delivered thee unto me: what hast thou done? 36 Jesus answered, My kingdom is not of this world: if my kingdom were of this world, then would my servants fight, that I should not be delivered to the Jews: but now is my kingdom not from hence. 37 Pilate therefore said unto him, Art thou a king then? Jesus answered, Thou sayest that I am a king. To this end was I born, and for this cause came I into the world, that I should bear witness unto the truth. Every one that is of the truth heareth my voice. 38 Pilate saith unto him, What is truth? And when he had said this, he went out again unto the Jews, and saith unto them, I find in him no fault at all. 39 But ye have a custom, that I should release unto you one at the passover: will ye therefore that I release unto you the King of the Jews? 40 Then cried they all again, saying, Not this man, but Barabbas. Now Barabbas was a robber. XIX. Then Pilate therefore took Jesus, and scourged him. 2 And the soldiers platted a crown

---

ᵍ πάλιν εἰς τὸ πραιτώριον LTTrAW.   ʰ Πειλᾶτος T.   ⁱ — αὐτῷ ὁ LTTrA ; — αὐτῷ W.
ᵏ ἀπ᾽ ἐμαυτοῦ LTrA.   ¹ εἶπόν σοι TrA.   ᵐ — ὁ GLTTrAW.   ⁿ οἱ ἐμοὶ ἠγωνίζοντο ἂν Tr.
ᵒ — ὁ [A]W.   ᴾ — ἐγώ (read εἰμι I am) TTr[A].   ᵠ [ἐγὼ] L.   ʳ εὑρίσκω ἐν αὐτῷ αἰτίαν
LTTrA.   ˢ ἀπολύσω ὑμῖν LTTr.   ᵗ ἀπολύσω ὑμῖν LTTrW.   ⁿ — πάντες T.

of thorns, and put it
on his head, and they
put on him a purple
robe, 3 and said, Hail,
King of the Jews! and
they smote him with
their hands. 4 Pilate
therefore went forth
again, and saith unto
them, Behold, I bring
him forth to you, that
ye may know that I
find no fault in him.
5 Then came Jesus
forth, wearing the
crown of thorns, and
the purple robe. And
Pilate saith unto
them, Behold the
man! 6 When the chief
priests therefore and
officers saw him, they
cried out, saying, Cru-
cify *him*, crucify *him*.
Pilate saith unto
them, Take ye him,
and crucify *him*: for I
find no fault in him.
7 The Jews answered
him, We have a law,
and by our law, he
ought to die, because
he made himself the
Son of God. 8 When
Pilate therefore heard
that saying, he was
the more afraid; 9 and
went again into the
judgment hall, and
saith unto Jesus,
Whence art thou? But
Jesus gave him no an-
swer. 10 Then saith
Pilate unto him,
Speakest thou not un-
to me? knowest thou
not that I have power
to crucify thee, and
have power to release
thee? 11 Jesus an-
swered, Thou couldest
have no power *at all*
against me, except it
were given thee from
above: therefore he
that delivered me un-
to thee hath the great-
er sin. 12 And from
thenceforth Pilate
sought to release him:
but the Jews cried out,
saying, If thou let
this man go, thou art

ἐξ ᾿ ἀκανθῶν ἐπέθηκαν αὐτοῦ τῇ κεφαλῇ, καὶ ἱμάτιον πορ-
of thorns put [it] on · his head, and a ²cloak ¹pur-
φυροῦν περιέβαλον αὐτόν, 3 ᵛ καὶ ἔλεγον, Χαῖρε, ὁ βασιλεὺς
ple cast around him, and said, Hail, king
τῶν Ἰουδαίων· καὶ ʷἐδίδουν‖ αὐτῷ ῥαπίσματα.
of the Jews! and they gave him blows with the palm of the hand.
4 ˣ ᾿Εξῆλθεν ʸοῦν‖ πάλιν ᶻἔξω ὁ Πιλάτος,‖ καὶ ·λέγει αὐτοῖς,
⁴Went ²therefore ³again ⁵out ¹Pilate, and says to them,
Ἴδε, ἄγω ὑμῖν αὐτὸν ἔξω, ἵνα γνῶτε ὅτι ᵃἐν αὐτῷ
Behold, I bring ⁵to ⁴you ¹him ²out, that ye may know that in him
οὐδεμίαν αἰτίαν εὑρίσκω.‖ 5 ᾿Εξῆλθεν οὖν ᵇὁ‖ Ἰησοῦς ἔξω,
not any fault I find. Went therefore Jesus out,
φορῶν τὸν ἀκάνθινον στέφανον καὶ τὸ πορφυροῦν ἱμάτιον.
wearing the thorny crown and the purple cloak;
καὶ λέγει αὐτοῖς, ᶜʺΙδε,‖ ὁ ἄνθρωπος. 6 ʺΟτέ οὖν ᵈεἶδον‖
and he says to them, Behold the man! When therefore saw
αὐτὸν οἱ ἀρχιερεῖς καὶ οἱ ὑπηρέται ἐκραύγασαν ᵉλέγοντες,‖
him the chief priests and the officers they cried out saying,
Σταύρωσον, σταύρωσον·. Λέγει αὐτοῖς ὁ Πιλάτος,‖ Λάβετε
Crucify, crucify [him]. ²Says ³to ⁴them ¹Pilate, Take
αὐτὸν ὑμεῖς καὶ σταυρώσατε· ἐγὼ γὰρ οὐχ εὑρίσκω ἐν αὐτῷ
him ye and crucify [him], for I find not in him
αἰτίαν. 7 ᾿Απεκρίθησαν ʰαὐτῷ‖ οἱ Ἰουδαῖοι, Ἡμεῖς νόμον
a fault. ²Answered ⁴him ¹the ²Jews, We a law
ἔχομεν, καὶ κατὰ τὸν νόμον ʰμῶν‖ ὀφείλει ἀποθανεῖν,
have, and according to our law he ought to die,
ὅτι ᵏἑαυτὸν υἱὸν θεοῦ‖ ἐποίησεν. 8 ʺΟτε οὖν ἤκουσεν
because himself Son of God he made. . When therefore ²heard
ὁ ᵍΠιλάτος‖ τοῦτον τὸν λόγον μᾶλλον ἐφοβήθη, 9 καὶ
¹Pilate this word [the] more he was afraid, and
εἰσῆλθεν εἰς τὸ πραιτώριον πάλιν, καὶ λέγει τῷ Ἰησοῦ, Πόθεν
went into the prætorium again, and says to Jesus, Whence
εἶ σύ; ῾Ο δὲ Ἰησοῦς ἀπόκρισιν οὐκ ἔδωκεν αὐτῷ. 10 λέγει
art thou? But Jesus an answer did not give him. ²Says
ᵒοῦν‖ αὐτῷ ὁ ᵍΠιλάτος,‖ ᾿Εμοὶ οὐ λαλεῖς; · οὐκ οἶδας
³therefore ⁴to ⁵him ¹Pilate, To me speakest thou not? Knowest not thou
ὅτι ἐξουσίαν ἔχω ᵐσταυρῶσαί σε, καὶ ἐξουσίαν ἔχω ἀπο-
that authority I have to crucify thee, and authority I have to re-
λῦσαί σε‖; 11 ᾿Απεκρίθη‖ ᵒὁ‖ Ἰησοῦς, Οὐκ ᴾεἶχες‖ ἐξουσίαν
lease thee? ²Answered ¹Jesus, Thou hadst ³authority
ᑫοὐδεμίαν κατ' ἐμοῦ‖ εἰ μὴ ἦν ʳσοι δεδομένον‖ ἄνωθεν·
¹not ²any against me if it were not to thee given ₊from above.
διὰ τοῦτο ὁ ˢπαραδιδούς‖ μέ σοι μείζονα ἁμαρτίαν
On this account he who delivers up me to thee greater sin
ἔχει. 12 ᾿Εκ τούτου ᵗἐζήτει ὁ Πιλάτος‖ ἀπολῦσαι αὐτόν·
has. From this sought Pilate to release him;
οἱ δὲ Ἰουδαῖοι ᵛᵃἔκραζον,‖ λέγοντες, ᾿Εὰν τοῦτον ἀπο-
but the Jews cried out, saying, ·If this [man] thou re-

ᵛ + καὶ ἤρχοντο πρὸς αὐτὸν and came to him LTTrA.   ʷ ἐδίδοσαν LTTrA.   ˣ + καὶ
and LTrA. .   ʸ — οὖν GLTTrA.   ᶻ ὁ Πειλᾶτος ἔξω T.   ᵃ οὐδεμίαν αἰτίαν εὑρίσκω ἐν
αὐτῷ LTr; αἰτίαν ἐν αὐτῷ οὐδεμίαν εὑρίσκω A; αἰτίαν οὐχ εὑρίσκω T.   ᵇ [ὁ] Tr.   ᶜ ᾿Ιδοὺ
TTrA.   ᵈ ἴδον T.   ᵉ — λέγοντες T.   ᶠ + αὐτὸν him GLW.   ᵍ Πειλᾶτος T.   ʰ — αὐτῷ T.
ⁱ — ἡμῶν (read the law) LTTrA.   ᵏ ἑαυτὸν υἱὸν τοῦ θεοῦ E; υἱὸν θεοῦ ἑαυτὸν LTTrA.
ˡ — οὖν T[A].   ᵐ ἀπολῦσαί σε, καὶ ἐξουσίαν ἔχω σταυρῶσαί σε LTTrA.   ⁿ + αὐτῷ him
[L]Tr[A].   ᵒ — ὁ GLTTrAW.   ᴾ ἔχεις thou hast T.   ᑫ κατ' ἐμοῦ οὐδεμίαν LTTrAW.   ʳ δεδομένον σοι LTTrA.   ˢ παραδούς delivered up LT.   ᵗ ὁ Πιλᾶτος (Πειλᾶτος T) ἐζήτει LTTrA.
ᵛᵃ ἐκραύγαζον LT; ἐκραύγασαν Tr.

λύσῃς οὐκ εἶ φίλος τοῦ Καίσαρος. πᾶς ὁ βασιλέα
lease thou art not a friend of Cæsar. Everyone ³the ⁴king

ʷαὐτὸν॥ ποιῶν ἀντιλέγει τῷ Καίσαρι. 13 Ὁ οὖν ˣΠιλᾶτος॥
²himself ¹making speaks against Cæsar. Pilate therefore

ἀκούσας ʸτοῦτον τὸν λόγον,॥ ἤγαγεν ἔξω τὸν Ἰησοῦν, καὶ
having heard this word, led out Jesus, and

ἐκάθισεν ἐπὶ ᶻτοῦ॥ βήματος, εἰς τόπον λεγόμενον Λιθό-
sat down upon the judgment-seat, at a place called Pave-

στρωτον, Ἑβραϊστὶ δὲ Γαββαθά· 14 ἦν δὲ παρασκευὴ
ment, but in Hebrew Gabbatha: (and it was [the] preparation

τοῦ πάσχα, ὥρα ªδὲ ὡσεὶ॥ ἕκτη· καὶ λέγει τοῖς Ἰου-
of the passover, [²the] ³hour ¹and about the sixth;) and he says to the Jews,

δαίοις, Ἴδε ὁ βασιλεὺς ὑμῶν. 15 ᵇΟἱ δὲ ἐκραύγασαν,॥ ᵀΑρον
Behold your king! But they cried out, Away,

ἆρον, σταύρωσον αὐτόν. Λέγει αὐτοῖς ὁ ˣΠιλᾶτος,॥ Τὸν
away, crucify him. ²Says ³to ⁴them ¹Pilate,

βασιλέα ὑμῶν σταυρώσω; Ἀπεκρίθησαν οἱ ἀρχιερεῖς, Οὐκ
Your king shall I crucify? ⁴Answered ¹the ²chief ³priests, ⁷Not

ἔχομεν βασιλέα εἰ μὴ Καίσαρα. 16 Τότε οὖν παρέδωκεν
⁵we ⁶have a king except Cæsar. Then therefore he delivered up

αὐτὸν αὐτοῖς ἵνα σταυρωθῇ. Παρέλαβον ᶜδὲ॥ τὸν Ἰη-
him to them that he might be crucified. ²They ³took ¹and Je-

σοῦν ᵈκαὶ ἀπήγαγον·॥ 17 καὶ βαστάζων ᵉτὸν σταυρὸν αὐτοῦ॥
sus and led [him] away. And bearing his cross

ἐξῆλθεν εἰς τὸν λεγόμενον κρανίου τοπον, ᶠὃς॥ λέγεται
he went out to the ²called ³of ⁴a ⁵skull ¹place, which ʳs called

Ἑβραϊστὶ Γολγοθᾶ. 18 ὅπου αὐτὸν ἐσταύρωσαν, καὶ μετ'
in Hebrew Golgotha: where him they crucified, and with

αὐτοῦ ἄλλους δύο ἐντεῦθεν καὶ ἐντεῦθεν, μέσον δὲ
him ²others ¹two on this side and on that side [one], and in the middle

τὸν Ἰησοῦν. 19 Ἔγραψεν δὲ καὶ τίτλον ὁ ˣΠιλᾶτος॥ καὶ
Jesus. And ²wrote ²also ⁴a ⁵title ¹Pilate and

ἔθηκέν ἐπὶ τοῦ σταυροῦ· ἦν δὲ γεγραμμένον. Ἰησοῦς ὁ
put on the cross. And it was written, Jesus the

Ναζωραῖος, ὁ βασιλεὺς τῶν Ἰουδαίων. 20 Τοῦτον οὖν
Nazarean, the king of the Jews. This ²therefore

τὸν τίτλον πολλοὶ ἀνέγνωσαν τῶν Ἰουδαίων, ὅτι ἐγγὺς ἦν
¹title ⁴many ³read of the Jews, for near ¹was

ᵍτῆς πόλεως ὁ τόπος,॥ ὅπου ἐσταυρώθη ὁ Ἰησοῦς· καὶ ἦν
¹the ²city the place, where was crucified Jesus; and it was

γεγραμμένον Ἑβραϊστί, ʰἙλληνιστί, Ῥωμαϊστί.॥ 21 ἔλεγον
written in Hebrew, in Greek, in Latin. ⁷Said

οὖν τῷ ⁱΠιλάτῳ οἱ ἀρχιερεῖς τῶν Ἰουδαίων, Μὴ γράφε,
²therefore ²to ¹⁰Pilate ¹the ²chief ³priests ⁴of ⁵the ⁶Jews, Write not,

Ὁ βασιλεὺς τῶν Ἰουδαίων· ἀλλ' ὅτι ἐκεῖνος εἶπεν, Βασιλεύς
The king of the Jews, but that he said, King

ᵏεἰμι τῶν Ἰουδαίων.॥ 22 Ἀπεκρίθη ὁ ˣΠιλᾶτος,॥ Ὁ γέ-
I am of the Jews. ²Answered ¹Pilate, What I have

γραφα γέγραφα. 23 Οἱ οὖν στρατιῶται, ὅτε ἐσταύρωσαν
written I have written. The ²therefore ¹soldiers, when they crucified

τὸν Ἰησοῦν ἔλαβον τὰ ἱμάτια αὐτοῦ, καὶ ἐποίησαν ¹τέσσαρα॥
Jesus took his garments, and made four

not Cæsar's friend : whosoever maketh himself a king speaketh against Cæsar. 13 When Pilate therefore heard that saying, he brought Jesus forth, and sat down in the judgment seat in a place that is called the Pavement, but in the Hebrew, Gabbatha. 14 And it was the preparation of the passover, and about the sixth hour: and he saith unto the Jews, Behold your King ! 15 But they cried out, Away with him, away with him, crucify him. Pilate saith unto them, Shall I crucify your King? The chief priests answered, We have no king but Cæsar. 16 Then delivered he him therefore unto them to be crucified. And they took Jesus, and led him away. 17 And he bearing his cross went forth into a place called the place of a skull, which is called in the Hebrew Golgotha : 18 where they crucified him, and two other with him, on either side one, and Jesus in the midst. 19 And Pilate wrote a title, and put it on the cross. And the writing was, JESUS OF NAZARETH, THE KING OF THE JEWS. 20 This title then read many of the Jews: for the place where Jesus was crucified was nigh to the city: and it was written in Hebrew, and Greek, and Latin. 21 Then said the chief priests of the Jews to Pilate, Write not, The King of the Jews; but that he said, I am King of the Jews. 22 Pilate answered, What I have written I have written. 23 Then the soldiers, when they had crucified Jesus, took his garments, and made four parts, to

---

ʷ ἑαυτὸν GLTTrAW. ˣ Πειλᾶτος Τ. ʸ τῶν λόγων τούτων these words LTTrAW. ᶻ — τοῦ (read a judgment seat) LTTrAW. ª ἦν ὡς was about LTTrAW. ᵇ ἐκραύγασαν οὖν ἐκεῖνοι they therefore cried out TTrA. ᶜ οὖν therefore LTTrA. ᵈ καὶ ἤγαγον G ; — καὶ ἀπήγαγον LTTrA. ᵉ αὐτῷ (ἑαυτῷ Τ) τὸν σταυρὸν LTTrA. ᶠ ὃ LTTrA. ᵍ ὁ τόπος τῆς πόλεως GLTTrAW. ʰ Ῥωμαιστί, Ἑλληνιστί TTrA. ⁱ Πειλάτῳ Τ. ᵏ τῶν Ἰουδαίων εἰμί TrA. ¹ τέσσερα TTrA every soldier a part; and also *his* coat: now the coat was without seam, woven from the top throughout. 24 They said therefore among themselves, Let us not rend it, but cast lots for it, whose it shall be: that the scripture might be fulfilled, which saith, They parted my raiment among them, and for my vesture they did cast lots. These things therefore the soldiers did.

25 Now there stood by the cross of Jesus his mother, and his mother's sister, Mary the *wife* of Cleophas, and Mary Magdalene. 26 When Jesus therefore saw his mother, and the disciple standing by, whom he loved, he saith unto his mother, Woman, behold thy son! 27 Then saith he to the disciple, Behold thy mother! And from that hour that disciple took her unto his own *home*. 28 After this, Jesus knowing that all things were now accomplished, that the scripture might be fulfilled, saith, I thirst. 29 Now there was set a vessel full of vinegar: and they filled a spunge with vinegar, and put *it* upon hyssop, and put *it* to his mouth. 30 When Jesus therefore had received the vinegar, he said, It is finished: and he bowed his head, and gave up the ghost. 31 The Jews therefore, because it was the preparation, that the bodies should not remain upon the cross on the sabbath day, (for that sabbath day was an high day,) besought Pilate that their legs might be broken, and *that* they might be taken away. 32 Then came the soldiers, and brake the legs of the first, and of the other which was crucified with him. 33 But when they came to Je-

μέρη, ἑκάστῳ στρατιώτῃ μέρος, καὶ τὸν χιτῶνα. ἦν.δὲ ὁ
parts, to each soldier a part, and the tunic; but ³was ¹the

χιτὼν ᵐἄῤῥαφος,ᵐ ἐκ τῶν ἄνωθεν ὑφαντὸς δι'.ὅλου. 24 ⁿεἶ-
²tunic seamless, from the top woven throughout. They

πον¹ οὖν πρὸς ἀλλήλους, Μὴ.σχίσωμεν αὐτόν, ἀλλὰ
said therefore to one another, Let us not rend it, but

λάχωμεν περὶ αὐτοῦ τίνος ἔσται· ἵνα ἡ γραφὴ πλη-
let us cast lots for it whose it shall be; that the scripture ·might be

ρωθῇ ᵒἡ λέγουσα,ᵒ Διεμερίσαντο τὰ.ἱμάτιά.μου ἑαυτοῖς.
fulfilled which says, They divided my garments among them,

καὶ ἐπὶ τὸν.ἱματισμόν.μου ἔβαλον κλῆρον. Οἱ μὲν οὖν
and for my vesture they cast a lot. The ²therefore

στρατιῶται ταῦτα ἐποίησαν.
¹soldiers these things did.

25 Εἱστήκεισαν.δὲ παρὰ τῷ σταυρῷ τοῦ Ἰησοῦ ἡ.μήτηρ.αὐ-
And stood by the cross of Jesus his mother,

τοῦ, καὶ ἡ ἀδελφὴ τῆς.μητρὸς.αὐτοῦ, ᴾΜαρία‖ ἡ τοῦ
and the sister of his mother, Mary the [wife]

Κλωπᾶ, καὶ ᴾΜαρία‖ ἡ Μαγδαληνή. 26 Ἰησοῦς οὖν ἰδὼν
of Clopas, and Mary· the Magdalene. Jesus therefore seeing

·τὴν μητέρα, καὶ τὸν μαθητὴν παρεστῶτα ὃν ἠγάπα, λέγει
[his] mother, and the disciple standing by whom he loved, says

τῇ.μητρὶ.ᵠαὑτοῦ,‖ Γύναι, ʳἰδού‖ ὁ.υἱός.σου. 27 Εἶτα λέγει τῷ
to his mother, Woman, behold thy son. Then he says to the

μαθητῇ, ʳἸδού‖ ἡ.μήτηρ.σου. Καὶ ἀπ' ἐκείνης τῆς ὥρας
disciple, Behold thy mother. And from that hour

ἔλαβεν ˢαὐτὴν ὁ μαθητὴς‖ εἰς τὰ.ἴδια. 28 Μετὰ τοῦτο
³took ⁴her ¹the ²disciple to his own [home]. After this,

.εἰδὼς ὁ Ἰησοῦς ὅτι ᵗπάντα.ἤδη‖ τετέλεσται, ἵνα τελειωθῇ
²knowing ¹Jesus that all things now have been finished, that might be fulfilled

ἡ γραφὴ λέγει, Διψῶ. 29 Σκεῦος ᵛοὖν‖ ἔκειτο ὄξους·
the scripture he says, I thirst. A vessel therefore was set ²of ³vinegar

μεστόν· ʷοἱ.δὲ πλήσαντες σπόγγον ὄξους, καὶ ὑσσώπῳ‖
¹full, and they having filled a sponge with vinegar, and ⁵hyssop

περιθέντες προσήνεγκαν αὐτοῦ τῷ.στόματι. 30 ὅτε
¹having ²put [³it] ⁴on they brought it to [his] mouth. When

οὖν ἔλαβεν τὸ ὄξος ˣὁ Ἰησοῦς‖ εἶπεν, Τετέλεσται· καὶ
therefore ²took ³the ⁴vinegar ¹Jesus he said, It has been finished; and

κλίνας τὴν κεφαλὴν παρέδωκεν τὸ πνεῦμα. 31 Οἱ
having bowed the head he yielded up [his] spirit. The

οὖν Ἰουδαῖοι, ʸἵνα μὴ.μείνῃ ἐπὶ τοῦ σταυροῦ τὰ
²therefore ¹Jews, that might not remain on the cross the

σώματα ἐν τῷ σαββάτῳ, ʸἐπεὶ παρασκευὴ ἦν,‖ ἦν.γὰρ
bodies on the sabbath, because [the] preparation it was, (for ᵂwas

μεγάλη ἡ ἡμέρα ᶻἐκείνου‖ τοῦ σαββάτου, ἠρώτησαν τὸν ᵃΠι-
²great ³day ¹that ²sabbath,) requested Pi-

λάτον‖ ἵνα κατεαγῶσιν αὐτῶν τὰ σκέλη, καὶ ἀρθῶσιν.
late that ³might ⁴be ⁵broken ¹their ²legs, and taken away.

32 ἦλθον οὖν οἱ στρατιῶται, καὶ τοῦ μὲν πρώτου κατέαξαν
Came therefore the soldiers, and of the first broke

τὰ σκέλη καὶ τοῦ ἄλλου τοῦ ᵇσυσταυρωθέντος‖ αὐτῷ· 33 ἐπὶ.δὲ
the legs and of the other who was crucified with him; but to

ᵐ ἄραφος TTrA. ⁿ εἶπαν T. ᵒ — ἡ λέγουσα LT. ᴾ Μαριάμ T. ᵠ — αὐτοῦ (*read*
[his]) [L]TTr[A]. ʳ ἴδε GLTTrA. ˢ ὁ μαθητὴς αὐτὴν GTrAW. ᵗ ἤδη πάντα LTTrAW.
ᵛ — οὖν LTTrAW. ʷ.σπόγγον οὖν μεστὸν τοῦ (— τοῦ T) ὄξους ὑσσώπῳ (ὑσώπῳ L) a sponge
therefore full of the vinegar, ᵃhyssop LTT·A. ˣ [ὁ] Tr; - ὁ Ἰησοῦς T. ʸ ἐπεὶ παρασκευὴ ἦν *placed after* Ἰουδαῖοι TTrA. ᶻ ἐκείνη E. ᵃ Πειλᾶτον T. ᵇ συσταυρωθέντος LTTrA.

τὸν Ἰησοῦν ἐλθόντες, ὡς εἶδον ᶜαὐτὸν ἤδη‖ τεθνηκότα,
Jesus　　having come, when they saw　he　already　was dead,

οὐ.κατέαξαν αὐτοῦ τὰ σκέλη· 34 ἀλλ' εἷς.τῶν στρατιωτῶν
they did not break his　　legs,　　but　one of the　　soldiers

λόγχῃ αὐτοῦ τὴν πλευρὰν ἔνυξεν, καὶ ᵈεὐθὺς ἐξῆλθεν‖
with a spear　his　　　side　　pierced, and immediately came out

αἷμα καὶ ὕδωρ.　35 καὶ ὁ ᵉἑωρακὼς μεμαρτύρηκεν, καὶ
blood and water.　　　And he who has seen　has borne witness, and

ἀληθινὴ αὐτοῦ ἐστιν ἡ μαρτυρία, ᵉκἀκεῖνος‖ οἶδεν ὅτι ἀληθῆ
true　²his　¹is　　witness,　　and he　knows that true

λέγει, ἵνα ᶠὑμεῖς ᵍπιστεύσητε.‖ 36 ἐγένετο.γὰρ ταῦτα ἵνα
he says, that　ye　may believe.　For ³took ⁴place ¹these ²things that

ἡ γραφὴ πληρωθῇ, Ὀστοῦν.οὐ συντριβήσεται αὐτοῦ.
the scripture might be fulfilled, Not a bone　shall be broken　of him.

37 καὶ πάλιν ἑτέρα γραφὴ λέγει, Ὄψονται εἰς ὃν
And　again　another scripture says, They shall look on him whom

ἐξεκέντησαν.
they pierced.

38 Μετὰ.δὲ ταῦτα ἠρώτησεν τὸν ʰΠιλάτον‖ ⁱὁ‖ Ἰωσὴφ
And after these things　asked　the　Pilate　　　Joseph

ᵏὁ‖ ἀπὸ Ἀριμαθαίας, ὢν μαθητὴς τοῦ Ἰησοῦ, κεκρυμμένος.δὲ
(from　Arimathæa, being a disciple of Jesus,　but concealed

διὰ τὸν φόβον τῶν Ἰουδαίων, ἵνα ἄρῃ τὸ σῶμα
through　fear　of the Jews,)　that he might take away the body

τοῦ Ἰησοῦ· καὶ ἐπέτρεψεν ὁ ¹Πιλάτος.‖ ᵐἦλθεν‖ οὖν καὶ
·　of Jesus: and　²gave ³leave　¹Pilate.　He came therefore and

ⁿἦρεν‖ ᵒτὸ σῶμα‖ ᵖτοῦ Ἰησοῦ.‖ 39 ἦλθεν.δὲ καὶ Νικόδημος,
took away the body　of Jesus.　　And came also Nicodemus,

ὁ ἐλθὼν πρὸς �q τὸν Ἰησοῦν‖ νυκτὸς τὸ.πρῶτον, φέρων μίγμα
who came　to　Jesus by night　at first,　bearing a mixture

σμύρνης καὶ ἀλόης ʳὡσεὶ‖ λίτρας ἑκατόν. 40 ἔλαβον οὖν
of myrrh and aloes　about ³pounds ¹a ²hundred.　They took therefore

τὸ σῶμα τοῦ Ἰησοῦ, καὶ ἔδησαν αὐτὸ ˢ ὀθονίοις μετὰ τῶν
the body　of Jesus, and bound it　in linen cloths with the

ἀρωμάτων, καθὼς ἔθος ἐστὶν τοῖς Ἰουδαίοις ἐντα-
aromatics,　as　a custom is　among the　Jews　to prepare for

φιάζειν. 41 ἦν.δὲ ἐν τῷ τόπῳ ὅπου ἐσταυρώθη κῆπος,
burial.　Now there was in the place where he was crucified a garden,

καὶ ἐν τῷ κήπῳ μνημεῖον καινόν, ἐν ᾧ οὐδέπω.οὐδεὶς ἐτέθη.
and in the garden a ²tomb ¹new, in which no one ever was laid.

42 ἐκεῖ οὖν διὰ τὴν παρασκευὴν τῶν Ἰουδαίων, ὅτι
There therefore on account of the，preparation of the　Jews, because

ἐγγὺς ἦν τὸ μνημεῖον, ἔθηκαν τὸν Ἰησοῦν.
near was the tomb,　they laid　Jesus.

20 Τῇ.δὲ μιᾷ τῶν σαββάτων ᵗΜαρία‖ ἡ Μαγδαληνὴ
But on the first [day] of the　week　Mary the Magdalene

ἔρχεται πρωῒ σκοτίας ἔτι οὔσης.εἰς τὸ.μνημεῖον, καὶ βλέπει
comes　early ⁴dark ³still ¹it ²being to the　tomb,　and　sees

τὸν λίθον ἠρμένον ἐκ τοῦ μνημείου. 2 τρέχει οὖν καὶ
the stone taken away from the　tomb.　She runs therefore and

ἔρχεται πρὸς Σίμωνα Πέτρον καὶ πρὸς τὸν ἄλλον μαθητὴν
comes　to　Simon Peter and·　to the　other　disciple

---

sus, and saw that he was dead already, they brake not his legs: 34 but one of the soldiers with a spear pierced his side, and forthwith came there out blood and water. 35 And he that saw it bare record, and his record is true: and he knoweth that he saith true, that ye might believe. 36 For these things were done; that the scripture should be fulfilled, A bone of him shall not be broken. 37 And again another scripture saith, They shall look on him whom they pierced.

38 And after this Joseph of Arimathæa, being a disciple of Jesus, but secretly for fear of the Jews, besought Pilate that he might take away the body of Jesus: and Pilate gave him leave. He came therefore, and took the body of Jesus. 39 And there came also Nicodemus, which at the first came to Jesus by night, and brought a mixture of myrrh and aloes, about an hundred pound weight. 40 Then took they the body of Jesus, and wound it in linen clothes with the spices, as the manner of. the Jews is to bury. 41 Now in the place where he was crucified there was a garden; and in the garden a new sepulchre, wherein was never man yet laid. 42 There laid they Jesus therefore because of the Jews' preparation day; for the sepulchre was nigh at hand.

XX. The first day of the week cometh Mary Magdalene early, when it was yet dark, unto the sepulchre, and seeth the stone taken away from the sepulchre. 2 Then she runneth, and cometh to Simon Peter, and to the other disciple,

---

ᶜ ἤδη αὐτὸν TTrA.　ᵈ ἐξῆλθεν εὐθὺς TTrA.　ᵉ καὶ ἐκεῖνος LTr.　ᶠ + καὶ also.GLTTrAW.
ᵍ πιστεύητε T.　ʰ Πειλάτον T.　ⁱ — ὁ LTTrAW.　ᵏ — ὁ LTrA.　¹ Πειλάτος T.
ᵐ ἦλθον they came T.　ⁿ ἦραν T.　ᵒ — τὸ σῶμα T.　ᵖ αὐτοῦ of him LTrA ; αὐτοῦ
ʰim T.　q αὐτὸν him LTTrAW.　ʳ ὡς GLTTrAW.　ˢ + ἐν W.　ᵗ Μαριάμ T.

X

whom Jesus loved, and saith unto them, They have taken away the Lord out of the sepulchre, and we know not where they have laid him. 3 Peter therefore went forth, and that other disciple, and came to the sepulchre. 4 So they ran both together : and the other disciple did outrun Peter, and came first to the sepulchre. 5 And he stooping down, *and looking in*, saw the linen clothes lying ; yet went he not in. 6 Then cometh Simon Peter following him, and went into the sepulchre, and seeth the linen clothes lie, 7 and the napkin, that was about his head, not lying with the linen clothes, but wrapped together in a place by itself. 8 Then went in also that other disciple, which came first to the sepulchre, and he saw, and believed. 9 For as yet they knew not the scripture, that he must rise again from the dead. 10 Then the disciples went away again unto their own home. 11 But Mary stood without at the sepulchre weeping: and as she wept, she stooped down, *and looked* into the sepulchre, 12 and seeth two angels in white sitting, the one at the head, and the other at the feet, where the body of Jesus had lain. 13 And they say unto her, Woman, why weepest thou ? She saith unto them, Because they have taken away my Lord, and I know not where they have laid him. 14 And when she had thus said, she turned herself back, and saw Jesus standing, and knew not that it was Jesus. 15 Jesus saith unto her, Woman, why weepest thou ? whom seekest thou ? She, supposing him to be the gardener, saith unto him, Sir, if thou have borne him hence, tell me where thou hast laid him, and I will take him away. 16 Jesus saith unto her, Mary. She turned her-

ὃν ἐφίλει ὁ Ἰησοῦς, καὶ λέγει αὐτοῖς,   Ἦραν   τὸν κύριον
whom ²loved   ¹Jesus,   and says   to them, They took away the   Lord

ἐκ τοῦ μνημείου, καὶ οὐκ.οἴδαμεν ποῦ ἔθηκαν αὐτόν.
out of the   tomb,   and   we know not   where they laid   him.

3 Ἐξῆλθεν   οὖν   ὁ Πέτρος καὶ ὁ ἄλλος μαθητής, καὶ ἤρχοντο
³Went ⁴forth ²therefore   ¹Peter   and the other   disciple,   and   came

εἰς τὸ μνημεῖον.   4 ἔτρεχον.δὲ οἱ δύο ὁμοῦ· ᵛκαὶ ὁ‖ ἄλλος
to the   tomb.   And ³ran   ¹the ²two together,   and the   other

μαθητὴς προέδραμεν τάχιον τοῦ Πέτρου, καὶ ἦλθεν πρῶτος
disciple   ran forward   faster   than Peter,   and   came   first

εἰς τὸ μνημεῖον, 5 καὶ παρακύψας βλέπει ʷκείμενα τὰ ὀθόνια,‖
to the   tomb,   and stooping down   he sees   lying   the linen cloths ;

οὐ μέντοι εἰσῆλθεν. 6 ἔρχεται οὖν ˣ Σίμων Πέτρος ἀκολου-
³not ⁴however ¹he ²entered.   Comes   then   Simon   Peter   follow-

θῶν αὐτῷ, καὶ εἰσῆλθεν εἰς τὸ μνημεῖον, καὶ θεωρεῖ τὰ
ing   him,   and   entered   into the   tomb,   and   sees   the

ὀθόνια κείμενα, 7 καὶ τὸ σουδάριον ὃ ἦν ἐπὶ τῆς κεφαλῆς
linen cloths   lying,   and the handkerchief which was upon   ²head

αὐτοῦ, οὐ μετὰ τῶν ὀθονίων κείμενον, ἀλλὰ χωρὶς ἐν-
¹his,   not   with   the   linen cloths   lying,   but   ⁶by ⁷itself

τετυλιγμένον εἰς ἕνα τόπον. 8 τότε   οὖν   εἰσῆλθεν καὶ ὁ
¹folded ⁵up   ³in   ⁴a   ⁵place.   Then therefore entered   also the

ἄλλος μαθητὴς ὁ ἐλθὼν πρῶτος εἰς τὸ μνημεῖον, καὶ εἶδεν
other   disciple   who came   first   to   the   tomb,   and saw

καὶ ἐπίστευσεν· 9 οὐδέπω.γὰρ ᾔδεισαν τὴν γραφήν, ὅτι
and   believed ;   for not yet   knew they   the   scripture,   that

δεῖ   αὐτὸν   ἐκ   νεκρῶν ἀναστῆναι. 10 ἀπῆλθον
it behoves   him   from among [the] dead   to rise.   Went away

οὖν πάλιν πρὸς ᵞἑαυτοὺς‖   οἱ μαθηταί. 11 ᶻΜαρία‖.δὲ
therefore again   to   their   [home] the ¹ disciples.   But Mary

εἰστήκει πρὸς ᵃτὸ μνημεῖον‖ ᵇκλαίουσα ἔξω.‖ ὡς οὖν
stood   at   the   tomb   ²weeping ¹outside.   As therefore

ἔκλαιεν, παρέκυψεν εἰς τὸ μνημεῖον, 12 καὶ θεωρεῖ δύο ἀγ-
she wept, she stooped down into the   tomb,   and beholds two an-

γέλους ἐν λευκοῖς καθεζομένους, ἕνα πρὸς τῇ κεφαλῇ καὶ ἕνα
gels   in   white   sitting,   one   at   the   head   and   one

πρὸς τοῖς ποσίν, ὅπου ἔκειτο τὸ σῶμα τοῦ Ἰησοῦ. 13 ᶜκαὶ‖
at   the   feet,   where was laid the   body   of Jesus.   And

λέγουσιν αὐτῇ ἐκεῖνοι, Γύναι, τί κλαίεις ;   Λέγει αὐτοῖς,
²say   ³to ⁴her   ¹they,   Woman, why weepest thou ? She says to them,

Ὅτι   ἦραν   τὸν.κύριόν.μου, καὶ οὐκ.οἶδα ποῦ ἔθηκαν
Because they took away   my Lord,   and I know not where they laid

αὐτόν. 14 ᵈΚαὶ‖   ταῦτα   εἰποῦσα ἐστράφη εἰς.τὰ.ὀπίσω, καὶ
him.   And   these things having said she turned   backward,   and

θεωρεῖ τὸν Ἰησοῦν ἑστῶτα· καὶ οὐκ.ᾔδει ὅτι ᵉὁ‖ Ἰησοῦς ἐστιν.
beholds   Jesus   standing,   and knew not that   Jesus   it is.

15 λέγει αὐτῇ *ᵒ‖ Ἰησοῦς, Γύναι, τί κλαίεις ; τίνα ζητεῖς ;
²Says ³to ⁴her   ¹Jesus,   Woman, why weepest thou ? Whom seekest thou ?

Ἐκείνη δοκοῦσα ὅτι ὁ κηπουρός ἐστιν, λέγει αὐτῷ, Κύριε, εἰ
She   thinking   that the gardener   it is,   says to him,   Sir,   if

σὺ ἐβάστασας αὐτόν, εἰπέ μοι ποῦ ᶠαὐτὸν ἔθηκας‖ κἀγὼ
thou didst carry off   him,   tell me where   him   thou didst lay, and I

αὐτὸν   ἀρῶ.   16 Λέγει αὐτῇ ᵍᵒ‖ Ἰησοῦς, ʰΜαρία.‖ Στρα-
him   will take away.   ²Says ³to ⁴her   ¹Jesus,   Mary.   Turn-

ᵛ ὁ δὲ L.   ʷ τὰ ὀθόνια κείμενα L.   ˣ + καὶ also TrA.   ᵞ αὐτοὺς TTr.   ᶻ Μαριάμ T.
ᵃ τῷ μνημείῳ GLTTᵣAW   ᵇ ἔξω κλαίουσα TTrA ; — ἔξω L.   ᶜ — καὶ T.   ᵈ — καὶ GLTTᵣAW,
ᵉ — ὁ GLTTᵣAW.   * — ὁ LTTᵣAW.   ᶠ ἔθηκας αὐτόν GLTTᵣAW.   ᵍ — ὁ LTTᵣA.   ʰ Μαριάμ TTᵣA,

φεῖσα ἐκείνη λέγει αὐτῷ¹, 'Ραββουνί· ὃ λέγεται, διδάσκαλε.
ing round she says to him, Rabboni, that is to say, Teacher.

17 λέγει αὐτῇ ᵏὁ‖'Ιησοῦς, Μή μου ἅπτου, οὔπω.γὰρ ἀναβέ-
²Says ³to ⁴her ¹Jesus, ⁷Not ⁶me ⁸touch, for not yet have I

βηκα πρὸς τὸν.πατέρα.¹μου·‖ πορεύου.δὲ πρὸς τοὺς ἀδελφούς
ascended to my Father; but go to ²brethren

μου, καὶ εἰπὲ αὐτοῖς, 'Αναβαίνω πρὸς τὸν.πατέρα.μου καὶ
¹my, and say to them, I ascend to my Father and

πατέρα.ὑμῶν, καὶ θεόν.μου καὶ θεὸν.ὑμῶν. 18 Ἔρχεται
your Father, and my God and your God. ⁴Comes

ᵐΜαρία‖ ἡ Μαγδαληνὴ ⁿἀπαγγέλλουσα‖ τοῖς μαθηταῖς ὅτι
¹Mary ²the ³Magdalene bringing word to the disciples

ᵒἑώρακεν‖ τὸν κύριον, καὶ ταῦτα εἶπεν αὐτῇ. 19 Οὔσης.οὖν
she has seen the Lord, and these things he said to her. It being therefore

ὀψίας τῇ.ἡμέρα.ἐκείνῃ, τῇ μιᾷ ᴾτῶν‖.σαββάτων, καὶ τῶν
evening on that day, the first [day] of the week, and the

θυρῶν κεκλεισμένων ὅπου ἦσαν οἱ μαθηταὶ ᑫσυνηγμένοι,‖ διὰ
doors having been shut where ³were ¹the ²disciples assembled, through

τὸν φόβον τῶν 'Ιουδαίων, ἦλθεν ὁ 'Ιησοῦς καὶ ἔστη εἰς τὸ
fear of the Jews, ²came ¹Jesus and stood ⁸in the

μέσον, καὶ λέγει αὐτοῖς, Εἰρήνη ὑμῖν. 20 Καὶ τοῦτο εἰπὼν
midst, and says to them, Peace to you. And this having said

ἔδειξεν ʳαὐτοῖς τὰς χεῖρας καὶ τὴν πλευρὰν αὐτοῦ.‖ ἐχάρη-
he shewed to them the hands and the side of himself. ³Rejoiced

σαν οὖν οἱ μαθηταὶ ἰδόντες τὸν κύριον. 21 εἶπεν οὖν
⁴therefore ¹the ²disciples having seen the Lord. ³Said ²therefore

αὐτοῖς ˢὁ 'Ιησοῦς‖ πάλιν, Εἰρήνη ὑμῖν· καθὼς ἀπέσταλκέν
⁴to ⁵them ¹Jesus again, Peace to you: as ²has ⁴sent ⁵forth

με ὁ πατήρ, κἀγὼ πέμπω.ὑμᾶς. 22 Καὶ τοῦτο εἰπὼν
³me ὁ ²Father, I also send you. And this having said

ἐνεφύσησεν, καὶ λέγει αὐτοῖς, Λάβετε πνεῦμα ἅγιον.
he breathed into [them], and says to them, Receive [the] ²Spirit ¹Holy:

23 ᵗἄν‖.τινων ἀφῆτε τὰς ἁμαρτίας, ʳἀφίενται‖ αὐτοῖς·
of whomsoever ye may remit the sins, they are remitted to them;

ᵗἄν‖.τινων κρατῆτε, κεκράτηνται. 24 Θωμᾶς.δὲ, εἷς ἐκ
of whomsoever ye may retain, they have been retained. But Thomas, one of

τῶν δώδεκα ὁ λεγόμενος Δίδυμος, οὐκ.ἦν μετ' αὐτῶν ὅτε
the twelve called Didymus, was not with them when

ἦλθεν ʷὁ‖'Ιησοῦς. 25 ἔλεγον οὖν αὐτῷ οἱ ἄλλοι μαθηταί,
²came ¹Jesus. ²Said ³therefore ⁴to ⁵him ¹the ²other ³disciples,

'Εωράκαμεν τὸν κύριον. Ὁ.δὲ εἶπεν αὐτοῖς, 'Εὰν.μὴ ἴδω ἐν
We have seen the Lord. But he said to them, Unless I see in

ταῖς.χερσὶν.αὐτοῦ τὸν τύπον τῶν ἥλων, καὶ βάλω ˣτὸν δάκτυ-
his hands the mark of the nails, and put ⁵finger

λόν μου‖ εἰς τὸν ʸτύπον‖ τῶν ἥλων, καὶ βάλω ᶻτὴν.χεῖρά.μου‖
¹my into the mark of the nails, and put my hand

εἰς τὴν.πλευρὰν.αὐτοῦ, οὐ.μὴ πιστεύσω. 26 Καὶ μεθ' ἡμέρας
into his side, not at all will I believe. And after ²days

ὀκτὼ πάλιν ἦσαν ἔσω οἱ.μαθηταὶ.αὐτοῦ, καὶ Θωμᾶς μετ'
¹eight again were ²within ¹his ³disciples, and Thomas with

αὐτῶν. ἔρχεται ὁ 'Ιησοῦς, τῶν θυρῶν κεκλεισμένων, καὶ ἔστη
them. Comes Jesus, the doors having been shut, and stood

self, and saith unto him, Rabboni ; which is to say, Master. 17 Jesus saith unto her, Touch me not; for I am not yet ascended to my Father: but go to my brethren, and say unto them, I ascend unto my Father, and your Father ; and to my God, and your God. 18 Mary Magdalene came and told the disciples that she had seen the Lord, and that he had spoken these things unto her. 19 Then the same day at evening, being the first day of the week, when the doors were shut where the disciples were assembled for fear of the Jews, came Jesus and stood in the midst, and saith unto them, Peace be unto you. 20 And when he had so said, he shewed unto them his hands and his side. Then were the disciples glad, when they saw the Lord. 21 Then said Jesus to them again, Peace be unto you: as my Father hath sent me, even so send I you. 22 And when he had said this, he breathed on them, and saith unto them, Receive ye the Holy Ghost: 23 whose soever sins ye remit, they are remitted unto them; and whose soever sins ye retain, they are retained. 24 But Thomas, one of the twelve, called Didymus, was not with them when Jesus came. 25 The other disciples therefore said unto him, We have seen the Lord. But he said unto them, Except I shall see in his hands the print of the nails, and put my finger into the print of the nails, and thrust my hand into his side, I will not believe. 26 And after eight days again his disciples were within, and Thomas with them: then came Jesus, the doors being shut, and stood in the

ⁱ + 'Εβραϊστί in Hebrew [L]TTrA.   ᵏ — ὁ LTTrA.   ˡ — μου (read the Father) [L]TTrA.
ᵐ Μαριὰμ TTrA.   ⁿ ἀγγέλλουσα LTTrA.   ᵒ ἑώρακα I have seen TTrA.   ᴾ — τῶν LTTrAW.
ᑫ — συνηγμένοι LTTrA.   ʳ καὶ (— καὶ T) τὰς χεῖρας καὶ τὴν πλευρὰν αὐτοῖς LTTrA.   ˢ — ὁ
'Ιησοῦς (read he said) TTr[A].   ᵗ ἐὰν L.   ᵛ ἀφέωνται they have been remitted LTTr.
ʷ — ὁ LTTrA.   ˣ μου τὸν δάκτυλον T.   ʸ τόπον place LT.   ᶻ μου τὴν χεῖρα TTrA.

midst, and said, Peace be unto you. 27 Then saith he to Thomas, Reach hither thy finger, and behold my hands ; and reach hither thy hand, and thrust *it* into my side: and be not faithless, but believing. 28 And Thomas answered and said unto him, My Lord and my God. 29 Jesus saith unto him, Thomas, because thou hast seen me, thou hast believed: blessed *are* they that have not seen, and *yet* have believed.

30 And many other signs truly did Jesus in the presence of his disciples, which are not written in this book: 31 but these are written, that ye might believe that Jesus is the Christ, the Son of God ; and that believing ye might have life through his name.

XXI. After these things Jesus shewed himself again to the disciples at the sea of Tiberias ; and on this wise shewed he *himself.* 2 There were together Simon Peter, and Thomas called Didymus, and Nathanael of Cana in Galilee, and the *sons* of Zebedee, and two other of his disciples. 3 Simon Peter saith unto them, I go a fishing. They say unto him, We also go with thee. They went forth, and entered into a ship immediately ; and that night they caught nothing. 4 But when the morning was now come, Jesus stood on the shore : but the disciples knew not that it was Jesus. 5 Then Jesus saith unto them, Children, have ye any meat ? They answered him, No. 6 And he said unto them, Cast the net on the right side of the ship, and

εἰς τὸ μέσον καὶ εἶπεν, Εἰρήνη ὑμῖν. 27 Εἶτα λέγει τῷ Θωμᾷ,
in the midst and said, Peace to you. Then he says to Thomas,
Φέρε τὸν.δάκτυλόν.σου ὧδε, καὶ ἴδε τὰς.χεῖράς.μου· καὶ
Bring thy finger here, and see my hands; and
φέρε τὴν.χεῖρά.σου, καὶ βάλε εἰς τὴν.πλευράν.μου· καὶ
bring thy hand, and put [it] into my side; and
μὴ.γίνου ἄπιστος, ἀλλὰ πιστός. 28 [a]Καὶ ἀπεκρίθη [b]ὁ
be not unbelieving, but believing. And [2]answered
Θωμᾶς καὶ εἶπεν αὐτῷ, Ὁ.κύριός.μου καὶ ὁ.θεός.μου. 29 Λέγει
[1]Thomas and said to him, My Lord and my God. [2]Says
αὐτῷ [c]ὁ Ἰησοῦς, Ὅτι ἑώρακάς με, [d]Θωμᾶ, πεπίστευκας·
to him [1]Jesus, Because thou hast seen me, Thomas, thou hast believed :
μακάριοι οἱ μὴ.ἰδόντες καὶ πιστεύσαντες.
blessed they who have not seen and have believed.

30 Πολλὰ μὲν οὖν καὶ ἄλλα σημεῖα ἐποίησεν ὁ Ἰη-
Many [3]therefore [4]also [1]other [2]signs did Je-
σοῦς ἐνώπιον τῶν.μαθητῶν.[e]αὐτοῦ, ἃ οὐκ.ἔστιν γεγραμ-
sus in presence of his disciples, which are not written
μένα ἐν τῷ.βιβλίῳ.τούτῳ. 31 ταῦτα.δὲ γέγραπται ἵνα
in this book ; but these have been written that
[f]πιστεύσητε ὅτι [g]ὁ Ἰησοῦς ἐστιν ὁ χριστὸς ὁ υἱὸς τοῦ
ye may believe that Jesus is the Christ the Son
θεοῦ, καὶ ἵνα πιστεύοντες ζωὴν [h] ἔχητε ἐν τῷ ὀνόματι
of God, and that believing life ye may have in [2]name
αὐτοῦ.
[1]his.

21 Μετὰ ταῦτα ἐφανέρωσεν ἑαυτὸν πάλιν [i]ὁ Ἰησοῦς
After these things [2]manifested [4]himself [3]again [1]Jesus
τοῖς μαθηταῖς ἐπὶ τῆς θαλάσσης τῆς Τιβεριάδος· ἐφανέρωσεν.δὲ
to the disciples at the sea of Tiberias. And he manifested
οὕτως· 2 ἦσαν ὁμοῦ Σίμων Πέτρος, καὶ Θωμᾶς ὁ
[himself] thus : There were together Simon Peter, and Thomas
λεγόμενος Δίδυμος, καὶ Ναθαναὴλ ὁ ἀπὸ Κανᾶ τῆς Γαλι-
called Didymus, and Nathanael from Cana of Gali-
λαίας, καὶ οἱ τοῦ Ζεβεδαίου, καὶ ἄλλοι ἐκ τῶν μαθητῶν
lee, and the [sons] of Zebedee, and [2]others [3]of [4]disciples
αὐτοῦ δύο. 3 λέγει αὐτοῖς Σίμων Πέτρος, Ὑπάγω ἁλιεύειν.
[1]his [1]two. [8]Says [9]to [10]them [6]Simon [7]Peter, I go to fish.
Λέγουσιν αὐτῷ, Ἐρχόμεθα καὶ ἡμεῖς σὺν σοί. [k]Ἐξῆλθον
They say to him, [2]Come [3]also [1]we with thee. They went forth
καὶ [l]ἀνέβησαν εἰς τὸ πλοῖον [m]εὐθύς, καὶ ἐν ἐκείνῃ τῇ
and went up into the ship immediately, and during that
νυκτὶ ἐπίασαν οὐδέν. 4 πρωΐας.δὲ ἤδη [n]γενομένης ἔστη [o]ὁ
night they took nothing. And morning already being come [2]stood
Ἰησοῦς [p]εἰς τὸν αἰγιαλόν· οὐ μέντοι ᾔδεισαν οἱ μαθηταὶ ὅτι
[1]Jesus on the shore ; [5]not [6]however [4]knew [1]the [2]disciples that
Ἰησοῦς ἐστιν. 5 λέγει οὖν αὐτοῖς [q]ὁ Ἰησοῦς, Παιδία,
Jesus it is. [3]Says [2]therefore [4]to [5]them [1]Jesus, Little children,
μή τι προσφάγιον ἔχετε; Ἀπεκρίθησαν αὐτῷ, Οὔ. 6 ὁ.δὲ
any food have ye ? They answered him, No. And he
εἶπεν αὐτοῖς, Βάλετε εἰς τὰ δεξιὰ μέρη τοῦ πλοίου τὸ δίκτυον,
said to them, Cast to the right side of the ship the net,

---

[a] — καὶ GLTTrAW.   [b] — ὁ GLTTrAW.   [c] [ὁ] Tr.   [d] — Θωμᾶ GLTTrAW.   [e] — αὐτοῦ (*read* the disciples) LTTrA.   [f] πιστεύητε T.   [g] — ὁ GLTTrAW.   [h] + [αἰώνιον] eternal L.   [i] — ὁ Ἰησοῦς (*read* he manifested) A ; — ὁ TTr.   [k] + [καὶ] and L.   [l] ἐνέβησαν entered GLTTrAW.   [m] — εὐθύς LTTrA.   [n] γινομένης breaking TTrw.   [o] — ὁ LTTrA.   [p] ἐπὶ LT.
[q] [ὁ Ἰησοῦς] L ; [ὁ] Ἰησοῦς Tr ; — ὁ TA.   [r] λέγει he says T.

καὶ εὑρήσετε. Ἔβαλον οὖν, καὶ ᵛοὐκ ἔτι‖ αὐτὸ ἑλκῦσαι
and ye shall find. They cast therefore, and no longer it to draw

ᵗἴσχυσαν‖ ἀπὸ τοῦ πλήθους τῶν ἰχθύων. 7 λέγει οὖν
were they able from the multitude of the fishes. Says therefore

ὁ μαθητὴς ἐκεῖνος ὃν ἠγάπα ὁ Ἰησοῦς τῷ Πέτρῳ, Ὁ κύριός
that disciple whom ²loved ¹Jesus to Peter, The Lord

ἐστιν. Σίμων οὖν Πέτρος, ἀκούσας ὅτι ὁ κύριός ἐστιν,
it is. Simon ²therefore ¹Peter, having heard that the Lord it is,

τὸν ἐπενδύτην διεζώσατο· ἦν γὰρ γυμνός· καὶ ἔβαλεν
[his] upper garment he girded on, for he was naked, and cast

ἑαυτὸν εἰς τὴν θάλασσαν. 8 οἱ δὲ ἄλλοι μαθηταὶ τῷ
himself into the sea. And the other disciples in the

πλοιαρίῳ ἦλθον· οὐ γὰρ ἦσαν μακρὰν ἀπὸ τῆς γῆς, ᵛἀλλ'‖
small ship came, for not were they far from the land, but

ὡς ἀπὸ πηχῶν᾽ διακοσίων, σύροντες τὸ δίκτυον τῶν
somewhere about ³cubits ¹two ²hundred, dragging the net

ἰχθύων. ᵗ⁹ Ὡς οὖν ἀπέβησαν εἰς τὴν γῆν βλέπουσιν
of fishes. When therefore they went up on the land they see

ἀνθρακιὰν κειμένην καὶ ὀψάριον ἐπικείμενον, καὶ ἄρτον.
a fire of coals lying and fish lying on [it], and bread.

10 λέγει αὐτοῖς ʷὁ‖ Ἰησοῦς, Ἐνέγκατε ἀπὸ τῶν ὀψαρίων ὧν
²Says ³to ⁴them ¹Jesus, Bring of the fishes which

ἐπιάσατε νῦν. 11. Ἀνέβη ˣ Σίμων Πέτρος, καὶ εἵλκυσεν τὸ
ye took just now. Went up Simon Peter, and drew the

δίκτυον ʸἐπὶ τῆς γῆς,‖ μεστὸν ᶻἰχθύων μεγάλων‖ ἑκατὸν
net ¹to the land, full of ²fishes ¹large a hundred [and]

ᵃπεντηκοντατριῶν·‖ καὶ τοσούτων ὄντων οὐκ ἐσχίσθη τὸ
fifty three; and [though] so many there were was not rent the

δίκτυον. 12 Λέγει αὐτοῖς ᵇὁ‖ Ἰησοῦς, Δεῦτε ἀριστήσατε.
net. ²Says ³to ⁴them ¹Jesus, Come ye, dine.

οὐδεὶς ᶜδὲ‖ ἐτόλμα τῶν μαθητῶν ἐξετάσαι αὐτόν, Σὺ τίς
But none ᵛ ventured ¹of ²the ³disciples to ask him, ³Thou ¹who

εἶ; εἰδότες ὅτι ὁ κύριός ἐστιν· 13 ἔρχεται ᵈοὖν ᵈὁ‖ Ἰησοῦς
ᵇart? knowing that the Lord it is. ²Comes ²therefore ¹Jesus

καὶ λαμβάνει τὸν ἄρτον καὶ δίδωσιν αὐτοῖς, καὶ τὸ ὀψάριον
and takes the bread and gives to them, and the fish

ὁμοίως. 14 τοῦτο ἤδη τρίτον ἐφανερώθη ᵉὁ‖ Ἰησοῦς
in like manner. This [is] now the third time ²was ³manifested ¹Jesus

τοῖς μαθηταῖς ᶠαὐτοῦ‖ ἐγερθεὶς ἐκ νεκρῶν.
to his disciples having been raised from among [the] dead.

15 Ὅτε οὖν ἠρίστησαν, λέγει τῷ Σίμωνι Πέτρῳ ὁ Ἰησοῦς,
When therefore they had dined, ²says ³to ⁴Simon ⁵Peter ¹Jesus,

Σίμων ᵍἸωνᾶ,‖ ἀγαπᾷς με ʰπλεῖον‖ τούτων; Λέγει αὐτῷ,
Simon [son] of Jonas, lovest thou me more than these? He says to him,

Ναί, κύριε· σὺ οἶδας ὅτι φιλῶ σε. Λέγει αὐτῷ,
Yea, Lord; thou knowest that I have affection for thee. He says to him,

Βόσκε τὰ ἀρνία μου. 16 Λέγει αὐτῷ πάλιν δεύτερον, Σίμων
Feed my lambs. He says to him again a second time, Simon

ᵍἸωνᾶ,‖ ἀγαπᾷς με; Λέγει αὐτῷ, Ναί κύριε· σὺ οἶδας
[son] of Jonas, lovest thou me? He says to him, Yea, Lord; thou knowest

ὅτι φιλῶ σε. Λέγει αὐτῷ, Ποίμαινε τὰ ¹προβατά‖
that I have affection for thee. He says to him, Shepherd ²sheep

---

ye shall find. They cast therefore, and now they were not able to draw it for the multitude of fishes. 7 Therefore that disciple whom Jesus loved saith unto Peter, It is the Lord. Now when Simon Peter heard that it was the Lord, he girt his fisher's coat unto him, (for he was naked,) and did cast himself into the sea. 8 And the other disciples came in a little ship; (for they were not far from land, but as it were two hundred cubits,) dragging the net with fishes. 9 As soon then as they were come to land, they saw a fire of coals there, and fish laid thereon, and bread. 10 Jesus saith unto them, Bring of the fish which ye have now caught. 11 Simon Peter went up, and drew the net to land full of great fishes, an hundred and fifty and three: and for all there were so many, yet was not the net broken. 12 Jesus saith unto them, Come and dine. And none of the disciples durst ask him, Who art thou? knowing that it was the Lord. 13 Jesus then cometh, and taketh bread, and giveth them, and fish likewise. 14 This is now the third time that Jesus shewed himself to his disciples, after that he was risen from the dead. 15 So when they had dined, Jesus saith to Simon Peter, Simon, son of Jonas, lovest thou me more than these? He saith unto him, Yea, Lord: thou knowest that I love thee. He saith unto him, Feed my lambs. 16 He saith to him again the second time, Simon, son of Jonas, lovest thou me? He saith unto him, Yea, Lord; thou knowest that I love thee. He saith unto him, Feed my sheep. 17 He saith

---

ᵛ οὐκέτι GLTW. ᵗ ἴσχυον LTTrA. ᵛ ἀλλὰ TTrA. ʷ [ὁ] Tr. ˣ + οὖν therefore TrA.
ʸ εἰς τὴν γῆν LTTrA. ᶻ μεγάλων ἰχθύων L. ᵃ πεντήκοντα τριῶν LTTr. ᵇ [ὁ] Tr.
ᶜ — δὲ but [Tr]A. ᵈ — οὖν G; — οὐν ὁ LTTrA. ᵉ — ὁ LTTrA. ᶠ — αὐτοῦ (read the
disciples) LTTrAW. ᵍ Ἰωάνου John LTr; Ἰωάννου TA. ʰ πλέον LTTrA. ¹ προβατιά
little sheep A.

unto him the third time, Simon, *son* of Jonas, lovest thou me? Peter was grieved because he said unto him the third time, Lovest thou me? And he said unto him, Lord, thou knowest all things; thou knowest that I love thee. Jesus saith unto him, Feed my sheep. 18 Verily, verily, I say unto thee, When thou wast young, thou girdedst thyself, and walkedst whither thou wouldest: but when thou shalt be old, thou shalt stretch forth thy hands, and another shall gird thee, and carry *thee* whither thou wouldest not. 19 This spake he, signifying by what death he should glorify God. And when he had spoken this, he saith unto him, Follow me. 20 Then Peter, turning about, seeth the disciple whom Jesus loved following; which also leaned on his breast at supper, and said, Lord, which is he that betrayeth thee? 21 Peter seeing him saith to Jesus, Lord, and what *shall* this man *do?* 22 Jesus saith unto him, If I will that he tarry till I come, what *is that* to thee? follow thou me. 23 Then went this saying abroad among the brethren, that disciple should not die: yet Jesus said not unto him, He shall not die; but, If I will that he tarry till I come, what *is that* to thee?

24 This is the disciple which testifieth of these things, and wrote these things: and we know that his testimony is true. 25 And there are also many other things which Jesus did, the which, if they should be written every one, I suppose that even the world itself could not contain the books that should be written. Amen.

μου. 17 Λέγει αὐτῷ τὸ τρίτον, Σίμων ᵏἸωνᾶ,ˡˡ φι-
'my.   He says to him the third time, Simon [son] of Jonas, hast thou
λεῖς με; Ἐλυπήθη ὁ Πέτρος ὅτι εἶπεν αὐτῷ τὸ
affection for me?   ²Was ³grieved .¹Peter because he said to him the
τρίτον, Φιλεῖς με; ¹καὶˡˡ ᵐεἶπενˡˡ αὐτῷ, Κύριε, ⁿσὺ
third time, Hast thou affection for me? and said to him, Lord, thou
πάνταˡˡ οἶδας· σὺ γινώσκεις ὅτι φιλῶ σε. Λέγει
all things knowest; thou knowest that I have affection for thee. ²Says
αὐτῷ ᵒὁ Ἰησοῦς,ˡˡ Βόσκε τὰ ᵖπρόβατάˡˡ μου. 18 ἀμὴν ἀμὴν
³to ⁴him ¹Jesus, Feed my sheep. Verily verily
λέγω σοι, ὅτε ἧς νεώτερος ἐζώννυες σεαυτόν, καὶ
I say to thee, When thou wast younger thou girdedst thyself, and
περιεπάτεις ὅπου ἤθελες· ὅταν δὲ γηράσῃς ἐκ-
walkedst where thou didst desire; but when thou shalt be old thou shalt
τενεῖς τὰς χεῖράς σου, καὶ ἄλλος �q σε ζώσει,ˡˡ καὶ οἴσει ʳ
stretch forth thy hands, and another thee shall gird, and bring [thee]
ὅπου οὐ θέλεις. 19 Τοῦτο δὲ εἶπεν σημαίνων ποίῳ
where thou dost not desire. But this he said signifying by what
θανάτῳ δοξάσει τὸν θεόν. καὶ τοῦτο εἰπὼν λέγει αὐτῷ,
death he should glorify God. And this having said he says to him,
Ἀκολούθει μοι. 20 Ἐπιστραφεὶς ˢδὲˡˡ ὁ Πέτρος βλέπει τὸν
Follow me. But having turned Peter sees the
μαθητὴν ὃν ἠγάπα ὁ Ἰησοῦς ἀκολουθοῦντα, ὃς καὶ ἀνέπεσεν
disciple whom ²loved ¹Jesus following, who also reclined
ἐν τῷ δείπνῳ ἐπὶ τὸ στῆθος αὐτοῦ καὶ εἶπεν, Κύριε, τίς ἐστιν
at the supper on his breast and said, Lord, who is it
ὁ παραδιδούς σε; 21 Τοῦτον ᵗ ἰδὼν ὁ Πέτρος λέγει τῷ Ἰη-
who is delivering up thee? ³Him ²seeing ¹Peter says to Je-
σοῦ, Κύριε, οὗτος δὲ τί; 22 Λέγει αὐτῷ ὁ Ἰησοῦς, Ἐὰν
sus, Lord, but of this one what; ²Says ³to ⁴him ¹Jesus, If
αὐτὸν θέλω μένειν ἕως ἔρχομαι, τί πρός σε; σὺ
³him ¹I ²desire to abide till I come, what [is it] to thee? ²Thou
ᵛἀκολούθει μοι.ˡˡ 23 Ἐξῆλθεν οὖν ʷὁ λόγος οὗτοςˡˡ εἰς
¹follow me. Went out therefore this word among
τοὺς ἀδελφούς, Ὅτι ὁ μαθητὴς ἐκεῖνος οὐκ ἀποθνήσκει· ˣκαὶ
the brethren, That that disciple does not die. However
οὐκ εἶπενˡˡ αὐτῷ ὁ Ἰησοῦς, ὅτι οὐκ ἀποθνήσκει· ἀλλ', Ἐὰν
³not ²said ⁴to ⁵him ¹Jesus, That he does not die; but, If
αὐτὸν θέλω μένειν ἕως ἔρχομαι, ʸτί πρός σε;ˡˡ
³him ¹I ²desire to abide till I come, what [is it] to thee?

24 Οὗτός ἐστιν ὁ μαθητὴς ὁ μαρτυρῶν περὶ τούτων,
This is the disciple who bears witness concerning these things,
καὶ ᶻγράψας ταῦτα· καὶ οἴδαμεν ὅτι ἀληθής ᵃἐστιν ἡ
and [who] wrote these things: and we know that true is
μαρτυρία αὐτοῦ.ˡˡ 25 ᵇἔστιν δὲ καὶ ἄλλα πολλὰ ᶜὅσα¹
his witness. And there are also ²other ³things ¹many whatsoever
ἐποίησεν ὁ Ἰησοῦς, ἅτινα ἐὰν γράφηται καθ' ἕν, ᵈοὐδὲ¹
²did ¹Jesus, which if they should be written one by one, ³not ⁴even
αὐτὸν οἶμαι τὸν κόσμον ᵉχωρῆσαι¹ τὰ γραφόμενα βιβλία.
²itself ¹I ²suppose ⁵the ⁶world would contain the ⁷written ¹books.
ᶠἈμήν.ˡˡ ᵍ
Amen.

ᵏ Ἰωάνου John LTr ; Ἰωάνιου TA.   ˡ [καὶ] L.   ᵐ λέγει says T.   ⁿ πάντα σὺ LTTrA.   ᵒ — ὁ
LTTrA ; — Ἰησοῦς (*read* he says) T[Tr].   ᵖ προβάρια little sheep TTrA.   �q ζώσει σε TrA.
ʳ + [σε] thee L.   ˢ — δὲ but LTTrAW.   ᵗ + οὖν therefore LTTrA.   ᵛ μοι ἀκολούθει LTTrAW.
ʷ οὗτος ὁ λόγος LTTrA.   ˣ οὐκ εἶπεν δὲ Tr.   ʸ — τί πρός σε T.   ᶻ + ὁ who LTr[A].   ᵃ αὐτοῦ
ἡ μαρτυρία ἐστίν TTrA.   ᵇ — verse 25 T.   ᶜ ἃ which LTrA.   ᵈ οὐδ᾽ LTrA.   ᵉ χωρήσειν Tr.
ᶠ — Ἀμήν GLTrA.   ᵍ + κατὰ Ἰωάνην (Ἰωάννην A) according to John TrA.

ΠΡΑΞΕΙΣ ʰΤΩΝ ΑΓΙΩΝ‖ ⁱΑΠΟΣΤΟΛΩΝ.‖
ACTS OF THE HOLY APOSTLES.

ΤΟΝ μὲν πρῶτον λόγον ἐποιησάμην περὶ πάντων, ὦ
The ³indeed ¹first ²account I made concerning all things, O

Θεόφιλε, ὦν ἤρξατο ʲὸ‖ Ἰησοῦς ποιεῖν.τε καὶ διδάσκειν,
Theophilus, which ²began ¹Jesus both to do and to teach,

2 ἄχρι ἧς.ἡμέρας ἐντειλάμενος τοῖς ἀποστόλοις διὰ
until the day in which, having given command ⁵to ⁶the ⁷apostles ¹by

πνεύματος ἁγίου οὓς ἐξελέξατο, ᵏἀνελήφθη.‖ 3 οἷς
[²the] ⁴Spirit ³Holy whom he chose, he was taken up: to whom

καὶ παρέστησεν ἑαυτὸν ζῶντα μετὰ τὸ.παθεῖν.αὐτόν, ἐν
also he presented himself living after he had suffered, with

πολλοῖς τεκμηρίοις, δι᾽ ἡμερῶν ˡτεσσαράκοντα‖ ὀπτανόμενος
many proofs, during ²days ¹forty being seen

αὐτοῖς, καὶ λέγων τὰ περὶ τῆς βασιλείας τοῦ θεοῦ.
by them, and speaking the things concerning the kingdom of God:

4 καὶ συναλιζόμενος ᵐπαρήγγειλεν αὐτοῖς‖ ἀπὸ Ἱερο-
and being assembled with [him] he charged them from Jeru-

σολύμων μὴ χωρίζεσθαι, ἀλλὰ περιμένειν τὴν ἐπαγγελίαν
salem not to depart, but to await the promise

τοῦ πατρός, ἣν ἠκούσατέ μου· 5 ὅτι ⁿἸωάννης‖ μὲν
of the Father, which [said he] ye heard of me. For John indeed

ἐβάπτισεν ὕδατι, ὑμεῖς.δὲ ᵒβαπτισθήσεσθε ἐν πνεύμα-
baptized with water, but ye shall be baptized with [the] ²Spirit

τι‖ ἁγίῳ οὐ μετὰ πολλὰς ταύτας ἡμέρας. 6 Οἱ μὲν οὖν
¹Holy ⁴not ³after many days. They indeed therefore

συνελθόντες ᵖἐπηρώτων‖ αὐτὸν λέγοντες, Κύριε, εἰ ἐν
having come together asked him, saying, Lord, ³at

τῷ.χρόνῳ.τούτῳ ἀποκαθιστάνεις τὴν βασιλείαν τῷ Ἰσραήλ;
⁴this ⁵time ¹restorest ²thou the kingdom to Israel?

7 Εἶπεν.ᑫδὲ‖ πρὸς αὐτούς, Οὐχ ὑμῶν ἐστι γνῶναι χρόνους
And he said to them, ³Not ⁴yours ¹it ²is to know times

ἢ καιροὺς οὓς ὁ πατὴρ ἔθετο ἐν τῇ.ἰδίᾳ ἐξουσίᾳ· 8 ἀλλὰ
or seasons which the Father placed in his own authority; but

ʳλήψεσθε‖ δύναμιν, ἐπελθόντος τοῦ ἁγίου πνεύματος ἐφ᾽
ye will receive power, ⁴having ⁵come ¹the ²Holy ³Spirit upon

ὑμᾶς, καὶ ἔσεσθέ ˢμοι‖ μάρτυρες ἔν.τε Ἱερουσαλὴμ καὶ ᵗἐν‖
you, and ye shall be to me witnesses both in Jerusalem and in

πάσῃ ᵛτῇ‖ Ἰουδαίᾳ καὶ ᵂΣαμαρείᾳ‖ καὶ ἕως ἐσχάτου
all Judæa and Samaria and to [the] uttermost part

τῆς γῆς. 9 Καὶ ταῦτα εἰπών, βλεπόντων αὐτῶν
of the earth. And these things having said, ²beholding [³him] ¹they

ἐπήρθη, καὶ νεφέλη ὑπέλαβεν αὐτὸν ἀπὸ τῶν ὀφθαλμῶν
he was taken up, and a cloud withdrew him from ²eyes

αὐτῶν.
¹their.

10 Καὶ ὡς ἀτενίζοντες ἦσαν εἰς τὸν οὐρανὸν πορευομένου
And as ³looking ⁴intently ¹they ²were into the heaven as ²was ⁴going

THE former treatise have I made, O Theophilus, of all that Jesus began both to do and teach, 2 until the day in which he was taken up, after that he through the Holy Ghost had given commandments unto the apostles whom he had chosen: 3 to whom also he shewed himself alive after his passion by many infallible proofs, being seen of them forty days, and speaking of the things pertaining to the kingdom of God: 4 and, being assembled together with them, commanded them that they should not depart from Jerusalem, but wait for the promise of the Father, which, saith he, ye have heard of me. 5 For John truly baptized with water; but ye shall be baptized with the Holy Ghost not many days hence. 6 When they therefore were come together, they asked of him, saying, Lord, wilt thou at this time restore again the kingdom to Israel? 7 And he said unto them, It is not for you to know the times or the seasons, which the Father hath put in his own power. 8 But ye shall receive power, after that the Holy Ghost is come upon you: and ye shall be witnesses unto me both in Jerusalem, and in all Judæa, and in Samaria, and unto the uttermost part of the earth. 9 And when he had spoken these things, while they beheld, he was taken up; and a cloud received him out of their sight.

10 And while they looked stedfastly toward heaven as he

ʰ — ἁγίων G ; — τῶν ἁγίων (read of [the]) LTTrAW. ⁱ — ἀποστόλων T. ʲ — ὁ LTrAW.
ᵏ ἀνελήμφθη LTTrA. ˡ τεσσεράκοντα LTTrA. ᵐ αὐτοῖς παρήγγειλεν AW. ⁿ Ἰωάνης Tr.
ᵒ ἐν πνεύματι βαπτισθήσεσθε LTTrA. ᵖ ἠρώτων LTTrA. ᑫ — δὲ and TTr. ʳ λήμψεσθε
LTTrA. ˢ μου of me LTTrAW. ᵗ — ἐν L[TrA]. ᵛ — τῇ A. ᵂ Σαμαρίᾳ T.

went up, behold, two men stood by them in white apparel; 11 which also said, Ye men of Galilee, why stand ye gazing up into heaven? this same Jesus, which is taken up from you into heaven, shall so come in like manner as ye have seen him go into heaven. 12 Then returned they unto Jerusalem from the mount called Olivet, which is from Jerusalem a sabbath day's journey. 13 And when they were come in, they went up into an upper room, where abode both Peter, and James, and John, and Andrew, Philip, and Thomas, Bartholomew, and Matthew, James the son of Alphæus, and Simon Zelotes, and Judas the brother of James. 14 These all continued with one accord in prayer and supplication, with the women, and Mary the mother of Jesus, and with his brethren.

15 And in those days Peter stood up in the midst of the disciples, and said, (the number of names together were about an hundred and twenty,) 16 Men and brethren, this scripture must needs have been fulfilled, which the Holy Ghost by the mouth of David spake before concerning Judas, which was guide to them that took Jesus. 17 For he was numbered with us, and had obtained part of this ministry. 18 Now this man purchased a field with the reward of iniquity; and falling headlong, he burst asunder in the midst, and all his bowels gushed out. 19 And it

αὐτοῦ, καὶ ἰδοὺ ἄνδρες δύο παρειστήκεισαν αὐτοῖς ἐν ˣἐσθῆτι
¹he, ⁵also.⁴behold ⁷men ⁶two stood by them in ²apparel

λευκῇ,‖ 11 οἳ καὶ ˠεἶπον,‖ "Ανδρες Γαλιλαῖοι, τί ἑστήκατε ᶻἐμ-
¹white, who also said, Men Galileans, why do ye stand look-

βλέποντες‖ εἰς τὸν οὐρανόν; οὗτος ὁ Ἰησοῦς ὁ ᵃἀναληφθεὶς‖
ing into the heaven? This Jesus who was taken up

ἀφ᾽ ὑμῶν εἰς τὸν οὐρανὸν οὕτως ἐλεύσεται ὃν.τρόπον
from you into the heaven thus will come in the manner

ἐθεάσασθε αὐτὸν πορευόμενον εἰς τὸν οὐρανόν. 12 Τότε
ye beheld him going into the' heaven. Then

ὑπέστρεψαν εἰς Ἰερουσαλὴμ ἀπὸ ὄρους τοῦ καλουμένου
they returned to Jerusalem from [the] mount called

ἐλαιῶνος, ὅ ἐστιν ἐγγὺς Ἰερουσαλήμ, σαββάτου ἔχον
of Olives, which is near Jerusalem, ²a ⁴sabbath's ¹being ²distant

ὁδόν. 13 Καὶ ὅτε εἰσῆλθον ᵇἀνέβησαν εἰς τὸ ὑπερῷον,‖
journey. And when they had entered they went up to the upper chamber,

οὗ ἦσαν καταμένοντες ὅ.τε.Πέτρος καὶ ᶜἸάκωβος καὶ Ἰωάν-
where were staying both Peter and James and John

νης‖ καὶ Ἀνδρέας, Φίλιππος καὶ Θωμᾶς, Βαρθολομαῖος καὶ
and Andrew, • Philip and Thomas, Bartholomew and

ᵈΜατθαῖος,‖ Ἰάκωβος Ἀλφαίου καὶ Σίμων ὁ Ζηλωτής,
Matthew, James [son] of Alphæus and Simon the Zealot,

καὶ Ἰούδας Ἰακώβου. 14 οὗτοι πάντες ἦσαν προσκαρ-
and Jude [brother] of James. These all were ⁴steadfastly

τεροῦντες ὁμοθυμαδὸν τῇ προσευχῇ ᵉκαὶ τῇ δεήσει,‖ σὺν
continuing ¹with ²one ³accord in prayer and supplication, with [the]

γυναιξὶν καὶ ᶠΜαρίᾳ‖ τῇ μητρὶ τοῦ Ἰησοῦ, καὶ ᵍσὺν‖ τοῖς
women and Mary the mother of Jesus, and with

ἀδελφοῖς.αὐτοῦ.
his brethren.

15 Καὶ ἐν ταῖς.ἡμέραις.ταύταις ἀναστὰς Πέτρος ἐν
And in those days ²having ³stood ⁴up ¹Peter in

μέσῳ τῶν ʰμαθητῶν‖ εἶπεν· ἦν τε ὄχλος ὀνομάτων
[the] midst of the disciples said, (¹was ¹and [²the] ³number ⁴of ⁵names

ἐπὶ.τὸ.αὐτὸ ¹ὡς‖ ἑκατὸν.ˣεἴκοσιν· 16 "Ανδρες ἀδελφοί, ἔδει
⁶together about a hundred and twenty,) Men brethren, it was neces-

πληρωθῆναι τὴν.γραφὴν.¹ταύτην,‖ ἣν προεῖπεν τὸ
sary ²to ⁴have ⁵been ⁶fulfilled ¹this ³scripture, which ⁵spoke ⁶before ¹the

πνεῦμα τὸ ἅγιον διὰ στόματος ᵐΔαβὶδ‖ περὶ Ἰούδα τοῦ
²Spirit ³the ⁴Holy by [the] mouth of David concerning Judas who

γενομένου ὁδηγοῦ τοῖς συλλαβοῦσιν ⁿτὸν‖ Ἰησοῦν‖ 17 ὅτι
became guide to those who took Jesus; for

κατηριθμημένος ἦν ᵒσὺν‖ ἡμῖν, καὶ ἔλαχεν τὸν κλῆρον τῆς
numbered he was with us, and obtained a part

διακονίας.ταύτης. 18 Οὗτος μὲν οὖν ἐκτήσατο χωρίον
in this service. This [man] indeed then got a field

ἐκ ᴾτοῦ‖ μισθοῦ τῆς ἀδικίας, καὶ πρηνὴς γενόμενος
out of the reward of unrighteousness, and ³headlong ¹having ²fallen

ἐλάκησεν μέσος, καὶ ἐξεχύθη πάντα τὰ.σπλάγχνα.αὐτοῦ.
burst in [the] midst, and ⁴gushed ⁵out ¹all '²his ³bowels.

ˣ ἐσθήσεσι(ν Α) λευκαῖς LTTrA.   ˠ εἶπαν LTTrA.   ᶻ βλέποντες TTr.   ᵃ ἀναλημφθεὶς LTTrA.   ᵇ εἰς τὸ ὑπερῷον ἀνέβησαν LTTrA.   ᶜ Ἰωάνης (Ἰωάνης Tr) καὶ Ἰάκωβος LTTrAW.   ᵈ Ματθαῖος LTTrA.   ᵉ — καὶ τῇ δεήσει GLTTrAW.   ᶠ Μαριὰμ TTr.   ᵍ — σὺν LT[Tr]AW.   ʰ ἀδελφῶν brethren LTTrAW.   ¹ ὡσεὶ T.   ᵏ εἴκοσι LTA.   ¹ — ταύτην (read the scripture) LTTr[A]W.   ᵐ Δανεὶδ LTTrA; Δαυὶδ GW.   ⁿ — τὸν LTTrA   ᵒ ἐν among GLTTrAW.   ᴾ — τοῦ (read a reward) GLTTrAW.

19 �q καὶ γνωστὸν ἐγένετο πᾶσιν τοῖς κατοικοῦσιν Ἰερουσαλήμ,
And known it became to all those dwelling in Jerusalem,
ὥστε κληθῆναι τὸ.χωρίον.ἐκεῖνο τῇ.ᶦἰδίᾳ‖.διαλέκτῳ.αὐτῶν
so that was called that field in their own language
ˢἈκελδαμά,‖ ᵗτουτέστιν‖ χωρίον αἵματος. 20 γέγραπται.γὰρ
Aceldama ; that is, field of blood. For it has been written
ἐν βίβλῳ ψαλμῶν, Γενηθήτω ἡ.ἔπαυλις.αὐτοῦ ἔρημος,
in [the] book of Psalms, Let ³become ¹his ²habitation desolate,
καὶ μὴ.ἔστω ὁ κατοικῶν ἐν αὐτῇ. καί, Τὴν ἐπισκοπὴν
and let there not be [one] dwelling in it; and, ⁵Overseership
αὐτοῦ ᵛλάβοι‖ ἕτερος. 21 Δεῖ οὖν τῶν συνελθόντων
⁴his ¹let ²take ²another. It behoves therefore of those ²consorting
ἡμῖν ἀνδρῶν ἐν παντὶ χρόνῳ ᵂἐν‖ ᵂ εἰσῆλθεν καὶ
²with ⁴us ¹men during all [the] time ¹in which came in and
ἐξῆλθεν ἐφ' ἡμᾶς ὁ κύριος Ἰησοῦς, 22 ἀρξάμενος ἀπὸ τοῦ
went out among us the Lord Jesus, beginning from the
βαπτίσματος ˣἸωάννου‖ ᵞἕως‖ τῆς ἡμέρας ἧς ᶻἀνελήφθη‖
baptism of John until the day in which he was taken up
ἀφ' ἡμῶν, μάρτυρα τῆς.ἀναστάσεως.αὐτοῦ ᵃγενέσθαι σὺν
from us, ⁸a ⁹witness ¹⁰of ¹¹his ¹²resurrection ⁴to ⁵become ⁶with
ἡμῖν ἕνα τούτων. 23 Καὶ ἔστησαν δύο, Ἰωσὴφ τὸν καλού-
us ¹one ²of ³these. And they set forth two, Joseph call-
μενον ᵇΒαρσαβᾶν,‖ ὃς ἐπεκλήθη Ἰοῦστος, καὶ ᶜΜατθίαν.‖
ed Barsabas, who was surnamed Justus, and Matthias.
24 καὶ προσευξάμενοι ᵈεἶπον,‖ Σὺ κύριε, καρδιογνῶστα
And praying they said, Thou Lord, knower of the hearts
πάντων, ἀνάδειξον ᵉἐκ τούτων τῶν δύο ἕνα ὃν ἐξελέξω‖
of all, shew of these two ²one ¹which thou didst choose
25 λαβεῖν τὸν ᶠκλῆρον‖ τῆς.διακονίας.ταύτης καὶ ἀποστολῆς,
to receive the part of this service and apostleship,
ᵍἐξ‖ ἧς παρέβη Ἰούδας, πορευθῆναι εἰς τὸν τόπον
from which ²transgressing ³fell ¹Judas, to go to his ²place
τὸν ἴδιον. 26 Καὶ ἔδωκαν κλήρους ʰαὐτῶν,‖ καὶ ἔπεσεν ὁ
¹own. And they gave ²lots ¹their, and ²fell ¹the
κλῆρος ἐπὶ ᶜΜατθίαν,‖ καὶ ᶦσυγκατεψηφίσθη‖ μετὰ τῶν ἕνδεκα
²lot on Matthias, and he was numbered with the eleven
ἀποστόλων.
apostles.

2 Καὶ ἐν τῷ ᵏσυμπληροῦσθαι‖ τὴν ἡμέραν τῆς πεντη-
And during the accomplishing of the day of Pente-
κοστῆς ἦσαν ¹ἅπαντες ὁμοθυμαδὸν‖ ἐπὶ.τὸ.αὐτό. 2 καὶ
cost they were all with one accord in the same place. And
ἐγένετο ἄφνω ἐκ τοῦ οὐρανοῦ ἦχος ὥσπερ φερομένης
²came ¹suddenly out of the heaven a sound as ²rushing
πνοῆς βιαίας, καὶ ἐπλήρωσεν ὅλον τὸν οἶκον οὗ ἦσαν
¹of ²a ⁴breath ³violent, and filled ¹whole ¹the house where they were
ᵐκαθήμενοι‖ 3 καὶ ὤφθησαν αὐτοῖς διαμεριζόμεναι γλῶσσαι
sitting. And there appeared to them divided tongues
ὡσεὶ πυρός, ⁿἐκάθισέν.τε‖ ἐφ' ἕνα ἕκαστον αὐτῶν· 4 καὶ
as of fire, and sat upon ²one ¹each of them. And

was known unto all the dwellers at Jerusalem ; insomuch as that field is called in their proper tongue, Aceldama, that is to say, The field of blood. 20 For it is written in the book of Psalms, Let his habitation be desolate, and let no man dwell therein : and his bishoprick let another take. 21 Wherefore of these men which have companied with us all the time that the Lord Jesus went in and out among us, 22 beginning from the baptism, of John, unto that same day that he was taken up from us, must one be ordained to be a witness with us of his resurrection. 23 And they appointed two, Joseph called Barsabas, who was surnamed Justus, and Matthias. 24 And they prayed, and said, Thou, Lord, which knowest the hearts of all men, shew whether of these two thou hast chosen, 25 that he may take part of this ministry and apostleship, from which Judas by transgression fell, that he might go to his own place. 26 And they gave forth their lots; and the lot fell upon Matthias; and he was numbered with the eleven apostles.

II. And when the day of Pentecost was fully come, they were all with one accord in one place. 2 And suddenly there came a sound from heaven as of a rushing mighty wind, and it filled all the house where they were sitting. 3 And there appeared unto them cloven tongues like as of fire, and it sat upon each of them. 4 And they were all

�q + ὁ T. ʳ [ἰδίᾳ] TrA. ˢἈκελδαμάχ Acᵉldamach LA ; Ἀχελδαμάχ Acheldamach TTr. ᵗ τοῦτ' ἔστιν GTTr. ᵛ λαβέτω LTTrAW. ᵂ — ἐν (read ᾧ in which) LTTrA. ˣἸωάνου T. ᵞ ἄχρι T. ᶻ ἀνελήμφθη LTTrA. ᵃ σὺν ἡμῖν γενέσθαι LTTrAW. ᵇ Βαρσαββᾶν LTTrA. ᶜ Μαθθίαν TTrA. ᵈ εἶπαν LTTrAW. ᵉ ὃν ἐξελέξω ἐκ τούτων τῶν δύο ἕνα GLTTrAW. ᶠ τόπον place LTTrA. ᵍ ἀφ' LTTrAW. ʰ αὐτοῖς on them LTTrA. ᶦ συν- T. ᵏ συν- TA. ¹ πάντες ὁμοῦ all together LTTrA. ᵐ καθεζόμενοι L. ⁿ καὶ ἐκάθισεν LTTr.

filled with the Holy Ghost, and began to speak with other tongues, as the Spirit gave them utterance. 5 And there were dwelling at Jerusalem Jews, devout men, out of every nation under heaven. 6 Now when this was noised abroad, the multitude came together, and were confounded, because that every man heard them speak in his own language. 7 And they were all amazed and marvelled, saying one to another, Behold, are not all these which speak Galilæans? 8 And how hear we every man in our own tongue, wherein we were born? 9 Parthians, and Medes, and Elamites, and the dwellers in Mesopotamia, and in Judæa, and Cappadocia, in Pontus, and Asia, 10 Phrygia, and Pamphylia, in Egypt, and in the parts of Libya about Cyrene, and strangers of Rome, Jews and proselytes, 11 Cretes and Arabians, we do hear them speak in our tongues the wonderful works of God. 12 And they were all amazed, and were in doubt, saying one to another, What meaneth this? 13 Others mocking said, These men are full of new wine. 14 But Peter, standing up with the eleven, lifted up his voice, and said unto them, Ye men of Judæa, and all ye that dwell at Jerusalem, be this known unto you, and hearken to my words : 15 for these are not drunken, as ye suppose, seeing it is but the third hour of the day. 16 But this is that which was spoken by the prophet Joel ; 17 And it shall come to pass in the last days, saith God, I

ἐπλήσθησαν °ἅπαντες‖ πνεύματος ἁγίου, καὶ ἤρξαντο λαλεῖν
they were ²filled   ¹all   with [the] ²Spirit ¹Holy, and   began to speak

ἑτέραις γλώσσαις, καθὼς τὸ πνεῦμα ἐδίδου Ραὐτοῖς ἀποφθέγ-
with other tongues, · as the Spirit gave to them   to utter

γεσθαι.‖ 5 ᵀΗσαν.δὲ ᵠἐν‖ Ἰερουσαλὴμ κατοικοῦντες Ἰουδαῖοι,
forth.   Now ³were ¹in   ²Jerusalem dwelling   Jews,

ἄνδρες εὐλαβεῖς ἀπὸ παντὸς ἔθνους τῶν ὑπὸ τὸν οὐρανόν.
²men   ¹pious from every nation of those under the heaven.

6 γενομένης.δὲ τῆς φωνῆς ταύτης, συνῆλθεν τὸ πλῆθος
But ⁵having ⁶arisen ¹the ²rumour ³of ⁴this, ⁹came ¹⁰together the ⁸multitude

καὶ συνεχύθη·   ὅτι ἤκουον εἷς ἕκαστος τῇ.ἰδίᾳ διαλέκτῳ
and were confounded, because ²heard ²one ¹each in his own language

λαλούντων αὐτῶν. 7 ἐξίσταντο.δὲ ʳπάντες‖ καὶ ἐθαύμαζον,
²speaking ¹them. And ²were ³amazed ¹all   and wondered,

λέγοντες ˢπρὸς ἀλλήλους,‖ ᵗΟὐκ‖ ἰδοὺ ᵛπάντες‖ οὗτοί εἰσιν οἱ
saying   to one another, ³Not ¹lo ⁴all ⁵these ²are who

λαλοῦντες Γαλιλαῖοι; 8 καὶ πῶς ἡμεῖς ἀκούομεν ἕκαστος
are speaking Galileans?   and how ²we ¹hear   each

τῇ.ἰδίᾳ.διαλέκτῳ.ἡμῶν ἐν ᾗ ἐγεννήθημεν, 9 Πάρθοι καὶ
in our own language in which ² we were born, Parthians and

Μῆδοι καὶ ʷἘλαμῖται,‖ καὶ οἱ κατοικοῦντες τὴν Μεσοπο-
Medes and Elamites, and those who inhabit   Mesopo-

ταμίαν, Ἰουδαίαν.τε καὶ Καππαδοκίαν, Πόντον καὶ τὴν Ἀσίαν,
tamia,   and Judæa and Cappadocia, Pontus and Asia,

10 Φρυγίαν.τε καὶ Παμφυλίαν, Αἴγυπτον καὶ τὰ μέρη τῆς
both Phrygia and Pamphylia, Egypt   and the parts

Λιβύης τῆς   κατὰ Κυρήνην, καὶ οἱ ἐπιδημοῦντες
of Libya which [is] about Cyrene,   and the ²sojourning [³here]

Ῥωμαῖοι, Ἰουδαῖοί.τε καὶ προσήλυτοι, 11 Κρῆτες καὶ Ἄραβες,
¹Romans, both Jews and proselytes,   Cretans and Arabians,

ἀκούομεν λαλούντων αὐτῶν ταῖς.ἡμετέραις γλώσσαις τὰ
we hear   ²speaking ¹them   in our own tongues the

μεγαλεῖα τοῦ θεοῦ; 12 Ἐξίσταντο.δὲ πάντες καὶ ˣδιηπόρουν,‖
great things of God? And ²were ³amazed ¹all   and were in perplexity,

ἄλλος.πρὸς.ἄλλον λέγοντες, Τί ʸἂν.θέλοι‖ τοῦτο εἶναι;
one to another saying, What ³would this   be?

13 Ἕτεροι.δὲ ᶻχλευάζοντες‖ ἔλεγον, Ὅτι γλεύκους μεμεστω-
But others mocking   said,   Of new wine ³full

μένοι εἰσίν. 14 Σταθεὶς.δὲ ᵃΠέτρος σὺν τοῖς ἕνδεκα ἐπῆρεν
¹they ²are. But ²standing ³up ¹Peter with the eleven lifted up

τὴν.φωνὴν.αὐτοῦ καὶ ἀπεφθέγξατο αὐτοῖς, Ἄνδρες Ἰουδαῖοι,
his voice   and spoke forth   to them, Men   Jews,

καὶ οἱ κατοικοῦντες Ἰερουσαλὴμ ᵇἅπαντες,‖ τοῦτο ὑμῖν
and ²ye ³who ⁴inhabit ⁵Jerusalem ¹all,   ⁷this ¹⁰to ¹¹you

γνωστὸν ἔστω, καὶ ἐνωτίσασθε τὰ.ῥήματά.μου. 15 οὐ.γὰρ ὡς
⁹known ⁶let ⁸be, and give heed to my words: for not as

ὑμεῖς ὑπολαμβάνετε, οὗτοι μεθύουσιν· ἔστιν.γὰρ ὥρα
ye   take it, ²these ¹are drunken, for it is [the] ²hour

τρίτη τῆς ἡμέρας· 16 ἀλλὰ τοῦτό ἐστιν τὸ εἰρημένον
¹third of the day;   but this is that which has been spoken

διὰ τοῦ προφήτου ᵇἸωήλ,‖ 17 ᶜΚαὶ‖ ἔσται ἐν ταῖς ἐσχάταις
by the prophet   Joel,   And it shall be in the last

ᵒ πάντες LTTr.   ᴾ ἀποφθέγγεσθαι αὐτοῖς LTTrAW.   ᵠ εἰς T.   ʳ — πάντες (read they were amazed) L[Tr]A.   ˢ — πρὸς ἀλλήλους LTTrA.   ᵗ Οὐχ LT; Οὐχὶ TrA.   ᵛ ἅπαντες LTA.
ʷ Ἐλαμεῖται T.   ˣ διηπορούντο TTrA.   ʸ θέλει LTTr.   ᶻ διαχλευάζοντες GLTTrAW.
ᵃ + ὁ LTTrA.   ᵇ — Ἰωήλ A.   ᶜ — καὶ A.

ἡμέραις, λέγει ὁ θεός, ἐκχεῶ ἀπὸ τοῦ.πνεύματός.μου ἐπὶ
days, says God, I will pour out of my Spirit upon

πᾶσαν σάρκα, καὶ προφητεύσουσιν οἱ.υἱοὶ.ὑμῶν καὶ αἱ θυγα-
all flesh; and shall prophesy your sons and ²daugh-

τέρες ὑμῶν· καὶ οἱ.νεανίσκοι.ὑμῶν ὁράσεις ὄψονται, καὶ οἱ
ters ¹your; and your young men visions shall see, and

πρεσβύτεροι.ὑμῶν ᵉἐνύπνια‖ ἐνυπνιασθήσονται· 18 ᶠκαί γε‖
your elders dreams shall dream; and even

ἐπὶ τοὺς.δούλους.μου καὶ ἐπὶ τὰς.δούλας.μου ἐν ταῖς ἡμέραις
upon my bondmen and upon my bondwomen in ²days

ἐκείναις ἐκχεῶ ἀπὸ τοῦ.πνεύματός.μου, καὶ προφητεύ-
¹those will I pour out of my Spirit, and they shall pro-

σουσιν. 19 καὶ δώσω τέρατα ἐν τῷ οὐρανῷ ἄνω καὶ σημεῖα
phesy. and I will give wonders in the heaven above and signs

ἐπὶ τῆς γῆς κάτω, αἷμα καὶ πῦρ καὶ ἀτμίδα καπνοῦ. ᵗ 20 ὁ
on the earth below, blood and fire and vapour of smoke. The

ἥλιος μεταστραφήσεται εἰς σκότος καὶ ἡ σελήνη εἰς αἷμα,
sun shall be turned into darkness and the moon into blood,

πρὶν ᵍἢ‖ ἐλθεῖν ʰτὴν‖ ἡμέραν κυρίου τὴν μεγάλην ⁱκαὶ
before come ⁵day ⁶of [⁷the] ⁸Lord ¹the ²great ³and

ἐπιφανῆ.‖ 21 καὶ ἔσται,· πᾶς ὃς.ᵏἂν‖ ἐπικαλέσηται τὸ
⁴manifest. And it shall be, everyone whoever shall call upon the

ὄνομα κυρίου σωθήσεται. 22 Ἄνδρες ¹Ἰσραηλῖται,‖ ἀκούσατε
name of [the] Lord shall be saved. Men Israelites, hear

τοὺς.λόγους.τούτους· Ἰησοῦν τὸν Ναζωραῖον, ἄνδρα ᵐἀπὸ
these words: Jesus the Nazaræan, a man by

τοῦ θεοῦ ἀποδεδειγμένον‖ εἰς ὑμᾶς δυνάμεσιν· καὶ τέρασιν
God set forth to you by works of power and wonders

καὶ σημείοις, οἷς ἐποίησεν δι᾽ αὐτοῦ ὁ θεὸς ἐν μέσῳ ὑμῶν,
and signs, which ²wrought ³by ⁴him ¹God in ²midst ¹your,

καθὼς ⁿκαὶ‖ αὐτοὶ οἴδατε, 23 τοῦτον τῇ ὡρισμένῃ βουλῇ
as also yourselves know: him, ³by ⁴the ⁵determinate ⁶counsel

καὶ προγνώσει τοῦ θεοῦ ἔκδοτον ᵒλαβόντες‖ διὰ ᴾχειρῶν‖
⁷and ⁸foreknowledge ⁹of ¹⁰God ¹given ²up, having taken by ²hands

ἀνόμων προσπήξαντες ᑫἀνείλετε·‖ 24 ὃν ὁ θεὸς ἀνέστησεν,
¹lawless, having crucified ye put to death. Whom God raised up,

λύσας τὰς ὠδῖνας τοῦ θανάτου, καθότι οὐκ.ἦν δυνατὸν
having loosed the throes of death, inasmuch as it was not possible

κρατεῖσθαι αὐτὸν ὑπ᾽ αὐτοῦ. 25 ʳΔαβὶδ‖.γὰρ λέγει εἰς
[for] ²to ³be ⁴held ¹him by it; for David says as to

αὐτόν, ˢΠροορώμην‖ τὸν κύριον ᵗἐνώπιόν μου ᵛδιὰ.παντός,‖
him, I foresaw the Lord before me continually,

ὅτι ἐκ δεξιῶν.μου ἐστίν, ἵνα μὴ.σαλευθῶ. 26 διὰ.τοῦτο
because at my right hand he is, that I may not be shaken. Therefore

ʷεὐφράνθη‖ ˣἡ.καρδία.μου‖ καὶ ἠγαλλιάσατο ἡ.γλῶσσά.μου·
³rejoiced ¹my ²heart and ³exulted ¹my ²tongue;

ἔτι.δὲ καὶ ἡ.σάρξ.μου κατασκηνώσει ᵞἐπ᾽‖ ἐλπίδι· 27 ὅτι οὐκ
yea more, also my flesh shall rest in hope, for ³not

ᶻἐγκαταλείψεις‖ τὴν.ψυχήν.μου εἰς ªᾅδου,‖ οὐδὲ δώσεις τὸν
¹thou ²wilt leave my soul in hades, nor wilt thou give

will pour out of my Spirit upon all flesh: and your sons and your daughters shall prophesy, and your young men shall see visions, and your old men shall dream dreams: 18 and on my servants and on my handmaidens I will pour out in those days of my Spirit; and they shall prophesy: 19 and I will shew wonders in heaven above, and signs in the earth beneath; blood, and fire, and vapour of smoke: 20 the sun shall be turned into darkness, and the moon into blood, before that great and notable day of the Lord come: 21 and it shall come to pass, that whosoever shall call on the name of the Lord shall be saved. 22 Ye men of Israel, hear these words; Jesus of Nazareth, a man approved of God among you by miracles and wonders and signs, which God did by him in the midst of you, as ye yourselves also know: 23 him, being delivered by the determinate counsel and foreknowledge of God, ye have taken, and by wicked hands have crucified and slain: 24 whom God hath raised up, having loosed the pains of death: because it was not possible that he should be holden of it. 25 For David speaketh concerning him, I foresaw the Lord always before my face, for he is on my right hand, that I should not be moved: 26 therefore did my heart rejoice, and my tongue was glad; moreover also my flesh shall rest in hope: 27 because thou wilt not leave my soul in hell, neither wilt

---

ᵉ ἐνυπνίοις with dreams GLTTrAW. ᶠ καίγε GT. ᵍ — ἢ LTTr.   ʰ — τὴν LTTrA.
ⁱ — καὶ ἐπιφανῆ T. ᵏ ἐὰν TrA. ˡ Ἰσραηλεῖται T. ᵐ ἀποδεδειγμένον ἀπὸ τοῦ θεοῦ TTr.
ⁿ — καὶ LTTrA. ᵒ — λαβόντες LTTrA. ᴾ χειρὸς hand (read by [the] hand of lawless
[ones]) LTTrA. ᑫ ἀνείλατε GLTTrAW. ʳ Δαυείδ LTTrA ; Δαυὶδ GW. ˢ Προορώμην LTTrA.
ᵗ + μου (read my Lord) T. ᵛ διαπαντός GT. ʷ ηὐφράνθη LTTrAW. ˣ μου ἡ καρδία TTrA.
ʸ ἐφ᾽ LT. ᶻ ἐνκαταλείψεις T. ª ᾅδην LTTrAW.

thou suffer thine Holy
One to see corruption.
28 Thou hast made
known to me the ways
of life; thou shalt
make me full of joy
with thy countenance.
29 Men and brethren,
let me freely speak
unto you of the patri-
arch David, that he is
both dead and buried,
and his sepulchre is
with us unto this day.
30 Therefore being a
prophet, and knowing
that God had sworn
with an oath to him,
that of the fruit of his
loins, according to the
flesh, he would raise
up Christ to sit on his
throne : 31 he seeing
this before spake of
the resurrection of
Christ, that his soul
was not left in hell,
neither his flesh did
see corruption. 32 This
Jesus hath God raised
up, whereof we all are
witnesses. 33 There-
fore being by the right
hand of God exalted,
and having received
of the Father the pro-
mise of the Holy
Ghost, he hath shed
forth this, which ye
now see and hear.
34 For David is not
ascended into the hea-
vens: but he saith him-
self, The LORD said
unto my Lord, Sit
thou on my right
hand, 35 until I make
thy foes thy footstool.
36 Therefore let all the
house of Israel know
assuredly, that God
hath made that same
Jesus, whom ye have
crucified, both Lord
and Christ.

ὅσιόν σου ἰδεῖν διαφθοράν. 28 ἐγνώρισάς μοι ὁδοὺς
²holy ³one ¹thy to see corruption. Thou didst make known to me paths
ζωῆς· πληρώσεις με εὐφροσύνης μετὰ τοῦ.προσώπου.σου.
of life, thou wilt fill me with joy with thy countenance.
29 Ἄνδρες ἀδελφοί, ἐξὸν εἰπεῖν μετὰ παρρησίας
Men brethren, it is permitted [me] to speak with freedom
πρὸς ὑμᾶς περὶ τοῦ πατριάρχου ᵇΔαβίδ,ǁ ὅτι καὶ ἐτελεύτη-
to you concerning the patriarch David, that both he died
σεν καὶ ἐτάφη, καὶ τὸ.μνῆμα.αὐτοῦ ἐστιν ἐν ἡμῖν ἄχρι
and was buried, and his tomb is amongst us unto
τῆς.ἡμέρας.ταύτης. 30 προφήτης οὖν ὑπάρχων, καὶ εἰδὼς
this day. A prophet therefore being, and knowing
ὅτι ὅρκῳ ὤμοσεν αὐτῷ ὁ θεός, ἐκ καρποῦ τῆς ὀσφύος
that with an oath ²swore ³to ⁴him ¹God, of [the] fruit of ²loins
αὐτοῦ ᶜτὸ.κατὰ σάρκα ἀναστήσειν τὸν χριστόν,ǁ καθίσαι ἐπὶ
¹his as concerning flesh to raise up the Christ, to sit upon
ᵈτοῦ.θρόνου ǁ.αὐτοῦ, 31 προϊδὼν ἐλάλησεν περὶ τῆς ἀνα-
his throne, foreseeing he spoke concerning the resur-
στάσεως τοῦ χριστοῦ, ὅτι ᵉοὐ ǀ.ᶠκατελείφθη ǁ ᵍἡ.ψυχὴ.αὐτοῦ ǁ εἰς
rection of the Christ, that was not left his soul in
ʰᾅδου,ǁ ¹οὐδὲǁ ἡ.σὰρξ.αὐτοῦ εἶδεν διαφθοράν. 32 τοῦτον τὸν
hades, nor his flesh saw corruption. This
Ἰησοῦν ἀνέστησεν ὁ θεός οὗ πάντες ἡμεῖς ἐσμεν μάρτυρες.
Jesus ²raised ³up ¹God whereof all we are witnesses.
33 τῇ δεξιᾷ οὖν τοῦ θεοῦ ὑψωθείς, τήν.τε ἐπαγ-
By the right hand therefore of God having been exalted, and the pro-
γελίαν τοῦ ᵏἁγίου πνεύματοςǁ λαβὼν παρὰ τοῦ πατρός,
mise of the Holy Spirit having received from the Father,
ἐξέχεεν τοῦτο ὃ ¹νῦνǁ ὑμεῖς ᵐβλέπετε καὶ ἀκούετε. 34 οὐ
he poured out this which now ye behold and hear. ⁴Not
γὰρ ᵇΔαβὶδ ǁ ἀνέβη εἰς τοὺς οὐρανούς, λέγει.δὲ αὐτός,
¹for ²David ³ascended into the heavens, but he says himself,
Εἶπεν ⁿὁǁ κύριος τῷ.κυρίῳ.μου, Κάθου ἐκ δεξιῶν.μου· 35 ἕως
Said the Lord to my Lord, Sit at my right hand, until
ἂν θῶ τοὺς.ἐχθρούς.σου ὑποπόδιον τῶν.ποδῶν.σου. 36 Ἀ-
I place thine enemies a footstool of thy feet. As-
σφαλῶς οὖν γινωσκέτω πᾶς ᵒ οἶκος Ἰσραήλ, ὅτι ᵖκαὶǁ
suredly therefore let know all [the] house of Israel, that both
κύριον �q καὶ χριστὸν αὐτὸνǁ ʳὁ θεὸς ἐποίησεν,ǁ τοῦτον τὸν
Lord and Christ him God made, this
Ἰησοῦν ὃν ὑμεῖς ἐσταυρώσατε.
Jesus whom ye crucified.

37 Now when they
heard this, they were
pricked in their heart,
and said unto Peter
and to the rest of the
apostles, Men and
brethren, what shall
we do ? 38 Then Peter
said unto them, Re-
pent, and be baptized
every one of you in the
name of Jesus Christ

37 Ἀκούσαντες.δὲ κατενύγησαν ˢτῇ.καρδίᾳ,ǁ εἶπόν.τε πρὸς
And having heard they were pricked in heart, and said to
τὸν Πέτρον καὶ τοὺς λοιποὺς ἀποστόλους, Τί ᵗποιήσομεν,ǁ
Peter and the other apostles, What shall we do,
ἄνδρες ἀδελφοί; 38 Πέτρος.δὲ ᵛἔφηǁ πρὸς αὐτούς, Μετανοή-
men brethren? And Peter said to them, Repent,
σατεᵂ, καὶ βαπτισθήτω ἕκαστος ὑμῶν ˣἐπὶǁ τῷ ὀνόματι Ἰησοῦ
and be baptized each of you in the name of Jesus

ᵇ Δαυεὶδ LTTrA; Δαυίδ GW.   ᶜ — τὸ κατὰ σάρκα ἀναστήσειν τὸν χριστόν GLTTrA.   ᵈ τὸν
θρόνον LTTrA.   ᵉ οὔτε LTTrAW.   ᶠ ἐγκατελείφθη LTrA; ἐνκ- T.   ᵍ — ἡ ψυχὴ αὐτοῦ
GLTTrA.   ʰ ᾅδην T.   ¹ οὔτε LTTrAW.   ᵏ πνεύματος τοῦ ἁγίου LTTrA.   ¹ — νῦν GLTTrA.
ᵐ + καὶ also T[A].   ⁿ — ὁ (read [the]) TTrA.   ᵒ + ὁ the L.   ᵖ — καὶ E.   q αὐτὸν καὶ
χριστὸν GLTTrAW.   ʳ ἐποίησεν ὁ θεός T.   ˢ τὴν καρδίαν LTTrA.   ᵗ ποιήσωμεν should we
do TTrA.   ᵛ — ἔφη LTTrA.   ᵂ + φησίν says T.   ˣ ἐν LTr.

χριστοῦ, εἰς ἄφεσιν ʸἁμαρτιῶν,‖ καὶ ᶻλήψεσθε‖ τὴν δωρεὰν
Christ, for remission of sins, and ye will receive the gift
τοῦ ἁγίου πνεύματος. 39 ὑμῖν.γάρ ἐστιν ἡ ἐπαγγελία καὶ
of the Holy Spirit. For to you is the promise and
τοῖς.τέκνοις.ὑμῶν, καὶ πᾶσιν τοῖς εἰς μακράν, ᵃὅσους‖ ἂν
to your children, and to all those at a distance, as many as
προσκαλέσηται κύριος ὁ.θεὸς.ἡμῶν. 40 Ἑτέροις.τε λόγοις
 ⁵may ⁶call [¹the] ²Lord ³our ⁴God. And with ²other ³words
πλείοσιν ᵇδιεμαρτύρετο‖ καὶ παρεκάλει ᶜ λέγων, Σώθητε ἀπὸ
¹many he earnestly testified and exhorted, saying, Be saved from
τῆς γενεᾶς τῆς.σκολιᾶς.ταύτης. 41 Οἱ.μὲν.οὖν ᵈἀσμένως‖
³generation ¹this ²crooked. Those therefore who gladly
ἀποδεξάμενοι τὸν.λόγον.αὐτοῦ ἐβαπτίσθησαν· καὶ προσετέθη-
had welcomed his word were baptized ; and were added
σαν ᵉ τῇ.ἡμέρᾳ.ἐκείνῃ ψυχαὶ ὡσεὶ τρισχίλ:αι. 42 Ἦσαν.δὲ
that day ⁴souls ¹about ²three ³thousand. And they were
προσκαρτεροῦντες ᶠ τῇ διδαχῇ .τῶν ἀποστόλων καὶ τῇ κοινωνίᾳ
steadfastly continuing in the teaching of the apostles and in fellowship,
ᵍκαὶ‖ τῇ κλάσει τοῦ ἄρτου καὶ ταῖς προσευχαῖς. 43 ʰἐγένετο‖
and the breaking of bread and prayers. ²There ³came
δὲ πάσῃ ψυχῇ φόβος, πολλά.ⁱτε‖ τέρατα καὶ σημεῖα διὰ
¹and upon every soul fear, and many wonders and signs through
τῶν ἀποστόλων ἐγίνετο.ʲ 44 ᵏ πάντες.δὲ οἱ ˡπιστεύοντες‖ ἦσαν
the apostles took place. And all who believed were
ἐπὶ.τὸ.αὐτὸ καὶ εἶχον ἅπαντα κοινά, 45 καὶ τὰ κτήματα
together and · had all things common, and [their] possessions
καὶ τὰς.ὑπάρξεις ἐπίπρασκον, καὶ διεμέριζον αὐτὰ πᾶσιν,
and goods they sold, and ⁴divided them to all,
καθότι ἄν τις χρείαν εἶχεν. 46 καθ'.ἡμέραν.τε προσκαρ-
according as anyone ¹need ¹had. And every day steadfastly
τεροῦντες ὁμοθυμαδὸν ἐν τῷ ἱερῷ, κλῶντές.τε κατ'.οἶκον
continuing with one accord in the temple, and breaking ²in [²their] ⁴houses
ἄρτον, μετελάμβανον τροφῆς ἐν ἀγαλλιάσει καὶ ἀφελότητι
¹bread, they partook of food with gladness and simplicity
καρδίας, 47 αἰνοῦντες τὸν θεὸν, καὶ ἔχοντες χάριν πρὸς ὅλον
of heart, praising God, and having favour with ²whole
τὸν λαόν. ὁ.δὲ κύριος προσετίθει τοὺς σωζομένους
¹the people ; and the Lord added ²those ³who ⁴were ⁵being ⁶saved
καθ'.ἡμέραν ᵐτῇ ἐκκλησίᾳ.‖
¹daily to the assembly.

3 ⁿἘπὶ.τὸ.αὐτὸ‖ ᵒδὲ Πέτρος‖ καὶ ᴾἸωάννης‖ ἀνέβαινον
 ⁵Together ¹and ²Peter ³and ⁴John went up
εἰς τὸ ἱερὸν ἐπὶ τὴν ὥραν τῆς προσευχῆς τὴν ᵠἐννάτην.‖
into the temple at the hour of prayer, the ninth ;
2 καί τις ἀνὴρ χωλὸς ἐκ κοιλίας μητρὸς αὐτοῦ ὑπάρχων
and a certain man ²lame ³from ⁶womb ⁵mother's ⁴his ¹being
ἐβαστάζετο· ὃν ἐτίθουν καθ'.ἡμέραν πρὸς τὴν θύραν τοῦ
was being carried, whom they placed daily at the door of the
ἱεροῦ τὴν λεγομένην Ὡραίαν, τοῦ αἰτεῖν ἐλεημοσύνην παρὰ
temple called Beautiful, to ask alms from

for the remission of sins, and ye shall receive the gift of the Holy Ghost. 39 For the promise is unto you, and to your children and to all that are afar off, *even* as many as the Lord our God shall call. 40 And with many other words did he testify and exhort, saying, Save yourselves from this untoward generation. 41 Then they that gladly received his word were baptized : and ʼ the same day there were added *unto them* about three thousand souls. 42 And they continued stedfastly in the apostles' doctrine and fellowship, and in breaking of bread, and in prayers. 43 And fear came upon every soul: and many wonders and signs were done by the apostles. 44 And all that believed were together, and had all things common ; 45 and sold their possessions and goods, and parted them to all *men*, as every man had need. 46 And they, continuing daily with one accord in the temple, and breaking bread from house to house, did eat their meat with gladness and singleness of heart, 47 praising God, and having favour with all the people. And the Lord added to the church daily such as should be saved.

III. Now Peter and John went up together into the temple at the hour of prayer, *being* the ninth *hour*. 2 And a certain man lame from his mother's womb was carried, whom they laid daily at the gate of the temple which is called Beautiful, to ask alms of them that entered

---

ʸ τῶν ἁμαρτιῶν ὑμῶν of your sins LTTr. ᶻ λήμψεσθε LTTrA. ᵃ οὓς whom L. ᵇ διεμαρτύρατο LTTrAW. ᶜ + αὐτοὺς them LTTrAW. ᵈ – ἀσμένως LTTrA. ᵉ + ἐν in LTTr[A].
ᶠ + [ἐν] L. ᵍ – καὶ LTTrA. ʰ ἐγίνετο LTTrA. ⁱ δὲ T. ʲ + ἐν Ἰερουσαλήμ, φόβος τε ἦν μέγας ἐπὶ πάντας. in Jerusalem, and great fear was upon all. T. ᵏ + καὶ (read And all also) T. ˡ πιστεύσαντες T. . ᵐ – τῇ ἐκκλησίᾳ LTTrA. ⁿ ἐπὶ τὸ αὐτό joined to chapter ii. LTTrA. ᵒ Πέτρος δὲ LTTrA. ᴾ Ἰωάνης Tr. ᵠ ἐνάτην LTTrAW.

into the temple: 3 who seeing Peter and John about to go into the temple asked an alms. 4 And Peter, fastening his eyes upon him with John, said, Look on us. 5 And he gave heed unto them, expecting to receive something of them. 6 Then Peter said, Silver and gold have I none; but such as I have give I thee: In the name of Jesus Christ of Nazareth rise up and walk. 7 And he took him by the right hand, and lifted *him* up: and immediately his feet and ancle bones received strength. 8 And he leaping up stood, and walked, and entered with them into the temple, walking, and leaping, and praising God. 9 And all the people saw him walking and praising God: 10 and they knew that it was he which sat for alms at the Beautiful gate of the temple: and they were filled with wonder and amazement at that which had happened unto him. 11 And as the lame man which was healed held Peter and John, all the people ran together unto them in the porch that is called Solomon's, greatly wondering. 12 And when Peter saw *it*, he answered unto the people, Ye men of Israel, why marvel ye at this? or why look ye so earnestly on us, as though by our own power or holiness we had made this man to walk? 13 The God of Abraham, and of Isaac, and of Jacob, the God of our fathers, hath glorified his Son Jesus; whom ye delivered up, and denied him in the presence of Pilate, when he was determined to let *him*

τῶν εἰσπορευομένων εἰς τὸ ἱερόν. 3 ὃς ἰδὼν Πέτρον καὶ
those who were going into the temple; who seeing Peter and
ʳἸωάννην‖ μέλλοντας εἰσιέναι εἰς τὸ ἱερόν, ἠρώτα ἐλεημοσύ-
John being about to enter into the temple, asked ³alms
νην λαβεῖν. 4 ἀτενίσας.δὲ Πέτρος εἰς αὐτὸν σὺν τῷ ˢἸωάν-
¹to ²receive. And ²looking ³intently ¹Peter upon him with John
νῃ‖ εἶπεν, Βλέψον εἰς ἡμᾶς. 5 Ὁ.δὲ ἐπεῖχεν αὐτοῖς, προσδοκῶν
said, Look on us. And he gave heed to them, expecting
τι παρ' αὐτῶν λαβεῖν. 6 εἶπεν.δὲ Πέτρος, Ἀργύριον καὶ
something from them to receive. But said Peter, Silver and
χρυσίον οὐχ.ὑπάρχει μοι· ὃ.δὲ ἔχω, τοῦτό σοι δίδωμι.
gold there is not to me, but what I have, this to thee I give:
ἐν τῷ ὀνόματι Ἰησοῦ χριστοῦ τοῦ Ναζωραίου ᵗἔγειραι καὶ‖
In the name of Jesus Christ the Nazaræan rise up and
περιπάτει. 7 Καὶ πιάσας αὐτὸν τῆς δεξιᾶς χειρὸς ἤγειρεν·ᵛ
walk. And having taken him by the right hand he raised up
παραχρῆμα.δὲ ἐστερεώθησαν ʷαὐτοῦ αἱ βάσεις‖ καὶ τὰ
[him], and immediately were strengthened his feet and
ˣσφυρά·‖ 8 καὶ ἐξαλλόμενος ἔστη καὶ περιεπάτει, καὶ εἰσῆλ-
ankle bones. And leaping up he stood and walked, and entered
θεν σὺν αὐτοῖς εἰς τὸ ἱερόν, περιπατῶν καὶ ἀλλόμενος ʸκαὶ‖
with them into the temple, walking and leaping and
αἰνῶν τὸν θεόν. 9 καὶ εἶδεν ᶻαὐτὸν πᾶς ὁ λαὸς‖ περιπα-
praising God. And ⁴saw ⁵him ¹all ²the ³people walk-
τοῦντα καὶ αἰνοῦντα τὸν θεόν· 10 ἐπεγίνωσκόν.ᵃτε‖ αὐτὸν
ing and praising God. And they recognized him
ὅτι ᵇοὗτος‖ ἦν ὁ πρὸς τὴν ἐλεημοσύνην καθήμενος ἐπὶ
that he it was who for alms [was] sitting at
τῇ Ὡραίᾳ πύλῃ τοῦ ἱεροῦ· καὶ ἐπλήσθησαν θάμβους καὶ
the Beautiful gate of the temple, and they were filled with wonder and
ἐκστάσεως ἐπὶ τῷ συμβεβηκότι αὐτῷ. 11 Κρατοῦντος.δὲ
amazement at that which had happened to him. And ²as ³held
ᶜτοῦ ἰαθέντος χωλοῦ‖ τὸν Πέτρον καὶᵈ ᵉἸωάννην,‖
¹the ⁴who ⁵had ⁶been ⁷healed ³lame [³man] the Peter and John,
συνέδραμεν ᶠπρὸς αὐτοὺς πᾶς ὁ λαὸς‖ ἐπὶ τῇ στοᾷ τῇ
ran together to them all the people in the porch
καλουμένῃ ᵍΣολομῶντος,‖ ἔκθαμβοι. 12 ἰδὼν.δὲ ʰ Πέτρος
called Solomon's, greatly amazed. And seeing [it] Peter
ἀπεκρίνατο πρὸς τὸν λαόν, Ἄνδρες ⁱἸσραηλῖται,‖ τί. θαυ-
answered to the people, Men Israelites, why won-
μάζετε ἐπὶ τούτῳ, ἢ ἡμῖν τί ἀτενίζετε ὡς ἰδίᾳ δυνάμει
der ye at this? or on us why look intently as if by [our] own power
ἢ εὐσεβείᾳ πεποιηκόσιν τοῦ περιπατεῖν αὐτόν; 13 ὁ θεὸς
or piety [we] had made ²to ³walk ¹him? The God
Ἀβραὰμ καὶᵏ Ἰσαὰκ καὶᵏ Ἰακώβ, ὁ θεὸς τῶν.πατέρων.ἡμῶν,
of Abraham and Isaac and Jacob, the God of our fathers,
ἐδόξασεν τὸν.παῖδα.αὐτοῦ Ἰησοῦν· ὃν ὑμεῖς ˡ παρεδώκατε,
glorified his servant Jesus, whom ye delivered up,
καὶ ἠρνήσασθε ᵐαὐτὸν‖ κατὰ.πρόσωπον ⁿΠιλάτου,‖ κρίναντος
and denied him in the presence of Pilate, ⁿhaving ³adjudged

ʳ Ἰωάνην Tr.   ˢ Ἰωάῃ Tr.   ᵗ ἔγειρε καὶ L[Tr] ; — ἔγειραι καὶ T[A].   ᵛ + αὐτόν him LTTrA.   ʷ αἱ βάσεις αὐτοῦ LTTrA.   ˣ σφυδρά T.   ʸ [καὶ] L.   ᶻ πᾶς ὁ λαὸς αὐτὸν LTTrAW.   ᵃ δὲ LTTrA.   ᵇ αὐτὸς LT.   ᶜ αὐτοῦ he (held) GLTTrAW.   ᵈ + τὸν LTTr.   ᵉ Ἰωάνην Tr.   ᶠ πᾶς ὁ λαὸς πρὸς αὐτοὺς LTTrA.   ᵍ Σολομῶνος GTrW.   ʰ ὁ LTTrA.   ⁱ Ἰσραηλεῖται T.   ᵏ + θεὸς God L ; + ὁ θεὸς T.   ˡ + μὲν indeed GLTTrAW.   ᵐ — αὐτὸν Λ𝔗[TrA].   ⁿ Πειλάτου T.

ἐκείνου ἀπολύειν.   14 ὑμεῖς.δὲ τὸν ἅγιον καὶ δίκαιον
ʰhe   to release [him].   But ye   the   holy   and righteous one

ἠρνήσασθε, καὶ ἠτήσασθε ἄνδρα φονέα χαρισθῆναι ὑμῖν,
denied,   and requested   a man   a murderer   to be granted to you,

15 τὸν.δὲ ἀρχηγὸν τῆς ζωῆς ἀπεκτείνατε· ὃν ὁ θεὸς ἤγειρεν
but the   Author   of life   ye killed,   whom   God raised up

ἐκ νεκρῶν, οὗ ἡμεῖς μάρτυρές ἐσμεν. 16 καὶ ἐπὶ
from among [the] dead, whereof   we   witnesses   are :   and by

τῇ πίστει τοῦ.ὀνόματος.αὐτοῦ τοῦτον ὃν θεωρεῖτε καὶ
faith   in his name   this [man] whom ye behold and

οἴδατε ἐστερέωσεν τὸ.ὄνομα.αὐτοῦ· καὶ ἡ πίστις ἡ δι'
know ³made ⁴strong ¹his ²name ;   and the faith which [is] by

αὐτοῦ ἔδωκεν αὐτῷ τὴν.ὁλοκληρίαν.ταύτην ἀπέναντι πάντων
him   gave   to him   this complete soundness   before   all

ὑμῶν. 17 καὶ νῦν, ἀδελφοί, οἶδα ὅτι κατὰ ἄγνοιαν ἐπράξατε,
of you.   And now, brethren, I know that in   ignorance ye acted,

ὥσπερ καὶ οἱ.ἄρχοντες.ὑμῶν· 18 ὁ.δὲ.θεὸς ἃ προκατήγγειλεν
as   also   your rulers ;   but ²God ¹what before announced

διὰ στόματος πάντων τῶν.προφητῶν.ᵒαὐτοῦ‖ παθεῖν
by [the] mouth of all   his prophets   [that] ³should ⁴suffer

τὸν χριστόνᵖ, ἐπλήρωσεν οὕτως. 19 μετανοήσατε οὖν καὶ
¹the ²Christ,   he fulfilled thus.   Repent   therefore and

ἐπιστρέψατε, ᵠεἰς‖ τὸ ἐξαλειφθῆναι ὑμῶν τὰς ἁμαρτίας, ὅπως
be converted,   for the   blotting out   of your   sins,   so that

ἂν.ἔλθωσιν καιροὶ ἀναψύξεως ἀπὸ προσώπου τοῦ κυρίου,
may come   times   of refreshing from [the] presence   of the Lord,

20 καὶ ἀποστείλῃ τὸν ʳπροκεκηρυγμένον‖ ὑμῖν, ˢΙησοῦν
and [that] he may send him who was before proclaimed to you,   Jesus

χριστόν,‖ 21 ὃν δεῖ οὐρανὸν μὲν δέξασθαι ἄχρι χρόνων
Christ,   whom ²must ¹heaven indeed receive   till   times

ἀποκαταστάσεως πάντων, ὧν ἐλάλησεν ὁ θεὸς διὰ
of restoration   of all things, of which ²spoke ¹God by [the]

στόματος ᵗπάντων‖ ἁγίων ᵛαὐτοῦ προφητῶν ἀπ' αἰῶνος.‖
mouth   of all   ²holy ¹his   prophets from of old.

22 ᵂΜωσῆς‖ μὲν ˣγὰρ‖ ʸπρὸς τοὺς πατέρας‖ εἶπεν, Ὅτι
²Moses ³indeed ¹for   to   the   fathers   said,   A

προφήτην ὑμῖν ἀναστήσει κύριος ὁ θεὸς ᶻὑμῶν‖ ἐκ
A prophet to you will ⁵raise ⁶up [¹the] ²Lord   ⁴God   ³your from among

τῶν.ἀδελφῶν.ὑμῶν, ὡς ἐμέ· αὐτοῦ ἀκούσεσθε κατὰ πάντα
your brethren,   like me :   him shall ye hear in all things

ὅσα.ἂν λαλήσῃ πρὸς ὑμᾶς. 23 ἔσται.δὲ πᾶσα ψυχὴ
whatsoever he may say to   you.   And it shall be [that] every soul

ἥτις ᵃἂν‖.μὴ.ἀκούσῃ τοῦ.προφήτου.ἐκείνου ᵇἐξολοθρευθήσεται‖
which   may not hear   that prophet   shall be destroyed

ἐκ τοῦ λαοῦ. 24 Καὶ πάντες.δὲ οἱ προφῆται ἀπὸ
from among the people.   And indeed all the prophets from

Σαμουὴλ καὶ τῶν καθεξῆς, ὅσοι ἐλάλησαν καὶ ᶜπροκατήγ-
Samuel and those subsequent, as many as spoke   also   before an-

γειλαν‖ τὰς.ἡμέρας.ταύτας. 25 ὑμεῖς ἐστε ᵈυἱοὶ τῶν προφητῶν
nounced   these days.   Ye   are sons of the   prophets

καὶ τῆς διαθήκης ἧς ᵉδιέθετο ὁ θεὸς‖ πρὸς τοὺς πατέρας
and of the covenant which ²appointed ¹God   to   ²fathers

---

go. 14 But ye denied the Holy One and the Just, and desired a murderer to be granted unto you ; 15 and killed the Prince of life, whom God hath raised from the dead ; whereof we are witnesses. 16 And his name through faith in his name hath made this man strong, whom ye see and know: yea, the faith which is by him hath given him this perfect soundness in the presence of you all. 17 And now, brethren, I wot that through ignorance ye did it, as *did* also your rulers. 18 But those things, which God before had shewed by the mouth of all his prophets, that Christ should suffer, he hath so fulfilled. 19 Repent ye therefore, and be converted, that your sins may be blotted out, when the times of refreshing shall come from the presence of the Lord ; 20 and he shall send Jesus Christ, which before was preached unto you : 21 whom the heaven must receive until the times of restitution of all things, which God hath spoken by the mouth of all his holy prophets since the world began. 22 For Moses truly said unto the fathers, A prophet shall the Lord your God raise up unto you of your brethren, like unto me ; him shall ye hear in all things whatsoever he shall say unto you. 23 And it shall come to pass, *that* every soul, which will not hear that prophet, shall be destroyed from among the people. 24 Yea, and all the prophets from Samuel and those that follow after, as many as have spoken, have likewise foretold of these days. 25 Ye are the children of the prophets, and of the covenant which God made with our fathers, saying unto

---

ᵒ — αὐτοῦ (*read* the prophets) LTTrA.   ᵖ + αὐτοῦ (*read* his Christ) LTTrAW.   ᵠ πρὸς ᴛ.
ʳ προκεχειρισμένον was foreordained GLTTrAW.   ˢ χριστὸν Ἰησοῦν LTTrA.   ᵗ τῶν (*omit* all)
GLTTrAW.   ᵛ ἀπ' αἰῶνος αὐτοῦ προφητῶν LTTrA.   ᵂ Μωϋσῆς GLTTrAW.   ˣ — γὰρ GLTTrAW.
ʸ — πρὸς τοὺς πατέρας LTTrA.   ᶻ ἡμῶν our ᴛ.   ᵃ ἐὰν ᴛᴀ.   ᵇ ἐξολεθρευθήσεται LTTrA.
ᶜ κατήγγειλαν announced GLTTrAW.   ᵈ + οἱ the GLTTrAW.   ᵉ ὁ θεὸς διέθετο ʟ.

Abraham, And in thy seed shall all the kindreds of the earth be blessed. 26 Unto you first God, having raised up his Son Jesus, sent him to bless you, in turning away every one of you from his iniquities.

[f]ἡμῶν,[n] λέγων πρὸς Ἀβραάμ, Καὶ [g] τῷ.σπέρματί.σου ἐνευλο-
[f]our, saying to Abraham, And in thy seed shall be

γηθήσονται πᾶσαι αἱ πατριαὶ τῆς γῆς. 26 ὑμῖν πρῶτον
blessed all the families of the earth. To you first

[h]ὁ θεὸς ἀναστήσας[n] τὸν.παῖδα.αὐτοῦ [i]Ἰησοῦν,[n] ἀπέστειλεν
God, having raised up his servant Jesus, sent

αὐτὸν εὐλογοῦντα ὑμᾶς ἐν τῷ ἀποστρέφειν ἕκαστον ἀπὸ
him, blessing you in turning each, from

τῶν πονηριῶν [k]ὑμῶν.[n]
[2]wickedness [1]your.

IV. And as they spake unto the people, the priests, and the captain of the temple, and the Sadducees, came upon them, 2 being grieved that they taught the people, and preached through Jesus the resurrection from the dead. 3 And they laid hands on them, and put them in hold unto the next day : for it was now eventide. 4 Howbeit many of them which heard the word believed; and the number of the men was about five thousand.

4 Λαλούντων.δὲ αὐτῶν πρὸς τὸν λαόν, ἐπέστησαν[m] αὐτοῖς
And as [2]were [3]speaking [1]they to the people, came upon them

οἱ ἱερεῖς καὶ ὁ στρατηγὸς τοῦ ἱεροῦ καὶ οἱ Σαδδουκαῖοι,
the priests and captain of the temple and the Sadducees,

2 διαπονούμενοι διὰ τὸ διδάσκειν αὐτοὺς τὸν λαόν, καὶ
being distressed because [2]teach [1]they the people, and

καταγγέλλειν ἐν τῷ Ἰησοῦ τὴν ἀνάστασιν τὴν ἐκ
announce in Jesus the resurrection which [is] from among

νεκρῶν· 3 καὶ ἐπέβαλον αὐτοῖς τὰς χεῖρας καὶ ἔθεντο[l]
[the] dead;. and they laid [2]on [3]them [1]hands and put

εἰς τήρησιν εἰς τὴν αὔριον· ἦν.γὰρ ἑσπέρα ἤδη.
[them] in hold till the morrow; for it was evening already.

4 πολλοὶ.δὲ τῶν ἀκουσάντων τὸν λόγον ἐπίστευσαν,
But many of those who had heard the word believed,

καὶ ἐγενήθη [m]ὁ[n] ἀριθμὸς τῶν ἀνδρῶν [n]ὡσεὶ[n] χιλιάδες πέντε.
and [6]became [1]the [2]number [3]of [4]the [5]men about [4]thousand [1]five.

---

5 And it came to pass on the morrow, that their rulers, and elders, and scribes, 6 and Annas the high priest, and Caiaphas, and John, and Alexander, and as many as were of the kindred of the high priest, were gathered together at Jerusalem. 7 And when they had set them in the midst, they asked, By what power, or by what name, have ye done this? 8 Then Peter, filled with the Holy Ghost, said unto them, Ye rulers of the people, and elders of Israel, 9 if we this day be examined of the good deed done to the impotent man, by what means he is made whole; 10 be it known unto you all, and to all the people of Israel, that by the name of Jesus Christ of Nazareth, whom ye crucified, whom God raised from the dead, even by him doth this

5 Ἐγένετο.δὲ ἐπὶ τὴν αὔριον συναχθῆναι αὐτῶν
And it came to pass on the morrow were gathered together their

τοὺς ἄρχοντας καὶ [o] πρεσβυτέρους καὶ [o] γραμματεῖς [p]εἰς[n] Ἰε-
rulers and elders and scribes at Je-

ρουσαλήμ, 6 καὶ [q]Ἄνναν τὸν ἀρχιερέα καὶ Καϊάφαν καὶ
rusalem, and Annas the high priest and Caiaphas and

Ἰωάννην καὶ Ἀλέξανδρον,[n] καὶ ὅσοι ἦσαν ἐκ γένους
John and Alexander, and as many as were of [4]family

ἀρχιερατικοῦ. 7 καὶ στήσαντες αὐτοὺς ἐν [r]τῷ[n] μέσῳ ἐπυν-
[3]high-priestly. And having placed them in the midst they

θάνοντο, Ἐν ποίᾳ δυνάμει ἢ ἐν ποίῳ ὀνόματι [s]ἐποιήσατε
inquired, In what power or in what name [4]did

τοῦτο[n] ὑμεῖς; 8 Τότε Πέτρος πλησθεὶς πνεύματος ἁγίου
[2]this [1]ye? Then Peter, filled with [the] [2]Spirit [1]Holy,

εἶπεν πρὸς αὐτούς, Ἄρχοντες τοῦ λαοῦ καὶ πρεσβύτεροι
said to them, Rulers of the people and elders

[t]τοῦ Ἰσραήλ,[n] 9 εἰ ἡμεῖς σήμερον ἀνακρινόμεθα ἐπὶ εὐεργεσίᾳ
of Israel, If we this day are examined as to a good work

ἀνθρώπου.ἀσθενοῦς, ἐν τίνι οὗτος [v]σέσωσται,[n] 10 γνωστὸν
[to the] infirm man, by what he has been cured, [3]known

ἔστω πᾶσιν ὑμῖν καὶ παντὶ τῷ λαῷ Ἰσραήλ, ὅτι ἐν τῷ
[1]be [2]it to all you and to all the people of Israel, that in the

ὀνόματι Ἰησοῦ χριστοῦ τοῦ Ναζωραίου, ὃν ὑμεῖς ἐσταυ-
name of Jesus Christ the Nazaræan, whom ye cruci-

ρώσατε, ὃν ὁ θεὸς ἤγειρεν ἐκ νεκρῶν, ἐν τούτῳ
fied, whom God raised from among [the] dead, by him

---

[f] ὑμῶν your TrA.
[k] αὐτῶν their L.
[o] + τοὺς the LTTrA.
Ἀλέξανδρος LTTrA.
[v] σέσωται T.

[g] + ἐν GLTTrAW.
[l] + αὐτοὺς them W.
[p] ἐν LTrAW.
[r] — τῷ G[A].

[h] ἀναστήσας ὁ θεὸς TA.
[m] — ὁ LT[Tr]A.
[q] Ἄννας ὁ ἀρχιερεὺς καὶ Καϊάφας καὶ Ἰωάννης καὶ
[s] τοῦτο ἐποιήσατε T.

[i] — Ἰησοῦν GLTTrA.
[n] [ὡς] LTrA ; — ὡσεὶ T.
[t] — τοῦ Ἰσραήλ LTTr[A].

οὗτος　παρέστηκεν ἐνώπιον ὑμῶν ὑγιής. 11.οὗτός ἐστιν ὁ
this [man]　stands　before　you　sound.　This　is　the

λίθος ὁ　ἐξουθενηθεὶς　ὑφ' ὑμῶν τῶν ᵂοἰκοδομούντων,�00
stone which has been set at nought by　you　the　builders,

ὁ γενόμενος εἰς κεφαλὴν γωνίας.　12 καὶ οὐκ ἔστιν
which is become　　head　of [the] corner.　And　　there is

ἐν ἄλλῳ οὐδενὶ ἡ σωτηρία·　ˣοὔτε‖.γὰρ ὄνομά ἐστιν ἕτερον
in ²other　¹no one　salvation,　for neither ⁴name ¹is ²there ²another

ὑπὸ τὸν οὐρανὸν ͺτὸ δεδομένον ἐν ἀνθρώποις, ἐν ᾦ
under the　heaven　which has been given among　men,　by which

δεῖ σωθῆναι ἡμᾶς.
³must ³be ⁴saved　¹we.

13 Θεωροῦντες.δὲ τὴν τοῦ Πέτρου παρρησίαν καὶ ʸ'Ἰωάν-
But seeing　the　²of ³Peter　¹boldness　and　of John,

νου,‖ καὶ καταλαβόμενοι ὅτι ἄνθρωποι ἀγράμματοί εἰσιν
and ͺhaving perceived　that　¹men　⁴unlettered　¹they ²are

καὶ ἰδιῶται, ἐθαύμαζον, ἐπεγίνωσκόν.τε αὐτοὺς ὅτι σὺν τῷ
and uninstructed, they wondered, and they recognized　them　that with

Ἰησοῦ ἦσαν.　14 τὸν.ᶻδὲ‖ ἄνθρωπον βλέποντες σὺν αὐτοῖς
Jesus they were.　But ²the　³man　¹beholding　⁵with　⁶them

ἑστῶτα ͺτὸν τεθεραπευμένον, οὐδὲν εἶχον ἀντειπεῖν. 15 κελεύ-
⁴standing who　had been healed,　nothing they had to gainsay.　²Having

σαντες　δὲ αὐτοὺς ἔξω τοῦ συνεδρίου ἀπελθεῖν ᵃσυνέβαλον‖
³commanded ¹but them　outside the sanhedrim　to go　they conferred

πρὸς ἀλλήλους, 16 λέγοντες, Τί ᵇποιήσομεν‖ τοῖς ἀνθρώ-
with one another,　saying,　What shall we do　to ²men

ποις τούτοις ; ὅτι.μὲν.γὰρ γνωστὸν σημεῖον γέγονεν
¹these ;　for that indeed ¹a known　²sign　has come to pass

δι' αὐτῶν, πᾶσιν τοῖς κατοικοῦσιν Ἰερουσαλὴμ φανερόν,
through them,　³to ⁴all ⁵those ⁶inhabiting　⁷Jerusalem ['is] ²manifest,

καὶ οὐ.δυνάμεθα ᶜἀρνήσασθαι·‖　17 ἀλλ' ἵνα μὴ ἐπὶ.πλεῖον
and we are unable　to deny　[it].　But that not　further

διανεμηθῇ εἰς τὸν λαόν, ᵈἀπειλῇ‖ ἀπειλησώμεθα αὐτοῖς
it may spread among the people,　with a threat　let us threaten　them

μηκέτι λαλεῖν ἐπὶ τῷ.ὀνόματι.τούτῳ μηδενὶ ἀνθρώπων.
no longer to speak in　this name　to any　man.
　　　　　　　　　　　(lit. to no)

18 Καὶ καλέσαντες αὐτοὺς παρήγγειλαν ᵉαὐτοῖς‖ ᶠτὸ‖ καθόλου
And having called them　they charged　them　²at ³all

μὴ φθέγγεσθαι μηδὲ διδάσκειν ἐπὶ τῷ ὀνόματι τοῦ Ἰησοῦ.
ͺnot to speak　nor　to teach　in the　name　of Jesus.

19 .ὁ.δὲ.Πέτρος καὶ ᵍ'Ἰωάννης‖ ἀποκριθέντες ʰπρὸς αὐτοὺς
But Peter　and　John　answering　to them

εἶπον,‖　Εἰ δίκαιόν ἐστιν ἐνώπιον τοῦ θεοῦ ὑμῶν ἀκούειν
said,　Whether right　it is　before　God　³to ⁴you ¹to ²listen

μᾶλλον ἢ τοῦ θεοῦ κρίνατε. 20 οὐ.δυνάμεθα γὰρ ἡμεῖς ἃ
rather than　God,　judge ye ;　²cannot　¹for　⁴we　⁵what

ᶦεἴδομεν‖ καὶ ἠκούσαμεν μὴ.λαλεῖν. 21 Οἱ.δὲ προσαπειλη-
⁷we ⁶saw　³and　¹⁰heard　⁴but ⁵speak.　But they　having further

σάμενοι ἀπέλυσαν αὐτούς, μηδὲν εὑρίσκοντες τὸ.πῶς κολά-
threatened let ²go　¹them, nothing ͺ finding　as to how they might

σωνται αὐτούς διὰ τὸν λαόν, ὅτι πάντες ἐδόξαζον
punish　them　on account of the people, because　all　were glorifying

man stand here before you whole. ⁽11 This is the stone which was set at nought of you builders, which is become the head of the corner. 12 Neither is there salvation in any other: for there is none other name under heaven given among men, whereby we must be saved.

13 Now when they saw the boldness of Peter and John, and perceived that they were unlearned and ignorant men, they marvelled; and they took knowledge of them, that they had been with Jesus. 14And beholding the man which was healed standing with them, they could say nothing against it. 15 But when they had commanded them to go aside out of the council, they conferred among themselves, 16 saying, What shall we do to these men? for that indeed a notable miracle hath been done by them is manifest to all them that dwell in Jerusalem ; and we cannot deny it. 17 But that it spread no further among the people, let us straitly threaten them, that they speak henceforth to no man in this name. 18 And they called them, and commanded them not to speak at all nor teach in the name of Jesus. 19 But Peter and John answered and said unto them, Whether it be right in the sight of God to hearken unto you more than unto God, judge ye. 20 For we cannot but speak the things which we have seen and heard. 21 So when they had further threatened them, they let them go, finding nothing how they might punish them, because of the people: for all men glorified God for that

---

ᵂ οἰκοδόμων LTTrA.　　ˣ οὐδὲ LTTrW.　　ʸ·Ἰωάνου Tr.　　ᶻ τε and LTTr A. ᵃ συνέβαλλον
LTTrA.　　ᵇ ποιήσωμεν should we do TTrA.　　ᶜ ἀρνεῖσθαι LTTrA.　　ᵈ — ἀπειλῇ LTT [A].
ᵉ — αὐτοῖς (read [them]) LTTrA.　　ᶠ — τὸ LT.　　ᵍ Ἰωάνης Tr.　　ʰ εἶπον (εἶπαν Tr) πρὸς
αὐτούς LTTrAW.　　ᶦ εἴδαμεν LTTrA.

which was done. 22 For the man was above forty years old, on whom this miracle of healing was shewed.

τὸν θεὸν ἐπὶ τῷ γεγονότι. 22 ἐτῶν.γὰρ ἦν
God for that which has taken place; for ⁶years [⁷old] ³was

πλειόνων ᵏτεσσαράκοντα‖ ὁ ἄνθρωπος ἐφ᾽ ὃν ᴸἐγεγόνει‖
⁴above ⁵forty ¹the ²man on whom had taken place

τὸ.σημεῖον.τοῦτο τῆς ἰάσεως.
this sign of healing.

23 And being let go, they went to their own company, and reported all that the chief priests and elders had said unto them. 24 And when they heard that, they lifted up their voice to God with one accord, and said, Lord, thou *art* God, which hast made heaven, and earth, and the sea, and all that in them is: 25 who by the mouth of thy servant David hast said, Why did the heathen rage, and the people imagine vain things? 26 The kings of the earth stood up, and the rulers were gathered together against the Lord, and against his Christ. 27 For of a truth against thy holy child Jesus, whom thou hast anointed, both Herod, and Pontius Pilate, with the Gentiles, and the people of Israel, were gathered together, 28 for to do whatsoever thy hand and thy counsel determined before to be done. 29 And now, Lord, behold their threatenings: and grant unto thy servants, that with all boldness they may speak thy word, 30 by stretching forth thine hand to heal; and that signs and wonders may be done by the name of thy holy child Jesus. 31 And when they had prayed, the place was shaken where they were assembled together; and they were all filled with the Holy Ghost, and they spake the word of God with boldness.

23 Ἀπολυθέντες.δὲ ἦλθον πρὸς τοὺς.ἰδίους, καὶ
And having been let go they came to their own [company], and

ἀπήγγειλαν ὅσα πρὸς αὐτοὺς οἱ ἀρχιερεῖς καὶ οἱ πρεσ-
reported whatever to them the chief priests and the el-

βύτεροι ᵐεἶπον.‖ 24 οἱ.δὲ ἀκούσαντες, ὁμοθυμαδὸν ἦραν
ders said. And they having heard, with one accord lifted up

φωνὴν πρὸς τὸν θεόν, καὶ ᵐεἶπον,‖ Δέσποτα, σὺ ⁿὁ
[their] voice to God, and said, O master, thou [art] the

θεὸς‖ ὁ ποιήσας τον οὐρανὸν καὶ τὴν γῆν καὶ τὴν θάλασσαν
God who made the heaven and the earth and the sea

καὶ πάντα τὰ ἐν αὐτοῖς, 25 ᵒὁ διὰ στόματος‖ ᴾΔαβὶδ‖
and all that[are]in them, who by [the] mouth of David

⁹τοῦ‖.παιδός.σου εἰπών, ʳἹνατί‖ ἐφρύαξαν ἔθνη, καὶ
thy servant didst say, Why did ²rage ³haughtily ¹nations, and

λαοὶ ἐμελέτησαν κενά; 26 παρέστησαν οἱ βασιλεῖς τῆς
²peoples ¹did meditate vain things? Stood up the kings of the

γῆς, καὶ οἱ ἄρχοντες συνήχθησαν ἐπὶ.τὸ.αὐτὸ κατὰ τοῦ
earth, and the rulers were gathered together against the

κυρίου καὶ κατὰ τοῦ.χριστοῦ.αὐτοῦ. 27 Συνήχθησαν.γὰρ
Lord and against his Christ. For were gathered together

ἐπ᾽.ἀληθείας ˢ ἐπὶ τὸν ἅγιον παῖδά σου Ἰησοῦν, ὃν
of a truth against ²holy ³servant ¹thy Jesus, whom

ἔχρισας, Ἡρώδης.τε καὶ Πόντιος ᵗΠιλάτος,‖ σὺν ἔθνεσιν
thou didst anoint, both Herod and Pontius Pilate, with nations

καὶ λαοῖς Ἰσραήλ, 28 ποιῆσαι ὅσα ἡ.χείρ.σου καὶ ἡ βουλή
and peoples of Israel, to do whatever thy hand and ²counsel

ᵘσου‖ προώρισεν γενέσθαι. 29 καὶ τὰ νῦν, κύριε, ⱽἔπιδε‖
¹thy predetermined to come to pass. And now, Lord, look

ἐπὶ τὰς.ἀπειλὰς.αὐτῶν, καὶ δὸς τοῖς.δούλοις.σου μετὰ παρ-
upon their threatenings, and give to thy bondmen with ²bold-

ρησίας πάσης λαλεῖν τὸν.λόγον.σου, 30 ἐν τῷ τὴν.χεῖρά.ʷσου‖
ness ¹all to speak thy word, in that thy hand

ἐκτείνειν ˣσε‖ εἰς ἴασιν, καὶ.σημεῖα καὶ τέρατα γίνεσθαι
²stretchest ³out ¹thou for healing, and signs and wonders take place

διὰ τοῦ ὀνόματος τοῦ ἁγίου παιδός σου Ἰησοῦ. 31 Καὶ
through the name ³holy ⁴servant ¹of ²thy Jesus. And

δεηθέντων αὐτῶν ἐσαλεύθη ὁ τόπος ἐν ᾧ ἦσαν συνηγ-
²having ³prayed ¹they ⁶was ⁷shaken ⁴the ⁵place in which they were assem-

μένοι, καὶ ἐπλήσθησαν ἅπαντες ʸπνεύματος ἁγίου,‖ καὶ
bled, and they were ²filled ¹all with [the] ²Spirit ¹Holy, and

ἐλάλουν τὸν λόγον τοῦ θεοῦ μετὰ παρρησίας.
spoke the word of God with boldness.

32 And the multitude of them that believed were of one

32 Τοῦ.δὲ πλήθους τῶν πιστευσάντων ἦν ᶻἡ‖ καρδία
And of the multitude of those that believed ⁶were ¹the ²heart

---

καὶ ᵃἡ‖ ψυχὴ μία· καὶ ᵇοὐδὲ‖ εἷς τι τῶν ὑπαρ-
²and ⁴the ⁵soul one, and not one ²anything ³of ⁴that ⁵which ⁷pos-

χόντων αὐτῷ ἔλεγεν ἴδιον εἶναι, ἀλλ' ἦν αὐτοῖς ᶜἅπαντα‖
sessed ⁶he ¹said ⁹his ¹⁰own ⁸was, ¹¹but ¹⁴were ¹⁵to ¹⁶them ¹²all ¹³things

κοινά. 33 καὶ ᵈμεγάλῃ δυνάμει‖ ἀπεδίδουν τὸ μαρτύριον
common. And with great power ³gave ⁴testimony

οἱ ἀπόστολοι ᵉτῆς ἀναστάσεως τοῦ κυρίου Ἰησοῦ,‖ χάρις.τε
¹the ²apostles of the resurrection of the Lord Jesus, and ²grace

μεγάλη ἦν ἐπὶ πάντας αὐτούς. 34 οὐδὲ.γὰρ ἐνδεής τις
¹great was upon all them. For neither in want ²anyone

ᶠὑπῆρχεν‖ ἐν αὐτοῖς· ὅσοι.γὰρ κτήτορες χωρίων ἢ οἰκιῶν
¹was among them; for as many as owners of estates or houses

ὑπῆρχον, πωλοῦντες ἔφερον τὰς τιμὰς τῶν πιπρα-
were, selling [them] brought the values of those sold,

σκομένων, 35 καὶ ἐτίθουν παρὰ τοὺς πόδας τῶν ἀπο-
and laid [them] at the feet of the apos-

στόλων· ᵍδιεδίδοτο‖.δὲ ἑκάστῳ καθότι.ἄν τις χρείαν
tles; and distribution was made to each according as anyone ²need

εἶχεν.
¹had.

36 ʰἸωσῆς‖.δὲ ὁ ἐπικληθεὶς Βαρνάβας ⁱὑπὸ‖ τῶν απο-
And Joses who was surnamed Barnabas by the apos-

στόλων, ὅ ἐστιν μεθερμηνευόμενον, υἱὸς παρακλήσεως,
tles, (which is, being interpreted, Son of consolation,)

ᵏΛευίτης,‖ Κύπριος τῷ.γένει, 37 ὑπάρχοντος αὐτῷ ἀγροῦ,
a Levite, a Cypriot by birth, having land,

πωλήσας ἤνεγκεν τὸ χρῆμα καὶ ἔθηκεν ˡπαρὰ‖ τοὺς πόδας
having sold [it] brought the money and laid [it] at the feet

τῶν ἀποστόλων 5 Ἀνὴρ.δέ τις ᵐἈνανίας ὀνόματι,‖
of the apostles. But ³man ¹a ²certain, Ananias by name,

σὺν ⁿΣαπφείρῃ‖ τῇ.γυναικί.αὐτοῦ, ἐπώλησεν κτῆμα, 2 καὶ
with Sapphira his wife, sold a possession, and

ἐνοσφίσατο ἀπὸ τῆς τιμῆς, ᵒσυνειδυίας‖ καὶ τῆς γυναικὸς
kept back from the value, being aware of [it] also ²wife

ᵖαὐτοῦ,‖ καὶ ἐνέγκας μέρος.τι παρὰ τοὺς πόδας τῶν
¹his, and having brought a certain part ³at ⁴the ⁵feet ⁶of ⁷the

ἀποστόλων ἔθηκεν. 3 εἶπεν.δὲ �q Πέτρος, Ἀνανία, ʳδιατί‖
⁸apostles ¹laid [²it]. But said Peter, Ananias, why

ἐπλήρωσεν ὁ σατανᾶς τὴν.καρδίαν.σου, ψεύσασθαί σε τὸ
did ²fill ¹Satan thy heart, ³to ⁴lie ⁵to [¹for] ²thee the

πνεῦμα τὸ ἅγιον, καὶ νοσφίσασθαι ˢ ἀπὸ τῆς τιμῆς τοῦ
Spirit the Holy, and to keep back from the value of the

χωρίου; 4 οὐχὶ μένον σοὶ ἔμενεν; καὶ πραθὲν
estate? ⁵Not ¹remaining ²to ³thee ⁴did ⁶it remain? and having been sold,

ἐν τῇ.σῇ ἐξουσίᾳ ὑπῆρχεν; τί ὅτι ἔθου ἐν τῇ
in thine own authority was it [not]? why didst thou purpose in

καρδίᾳ.σου τὸ.πρᾶγμα.τοῦτο; οὐκ.ἐψεύσω ἀνθρώποις, ἀλλὰ
thy heart this thing? Thou didst not lie to men, but

τῷ.θεῷ. 5 Ἀκούων.δὲ ᵗ Ἀνανίας τοὺς.λόγους.τούτους, πεσὼν
to God. And ²hearing ¹Ananias these words, falling down

---

heart and of one soul: neither said any of them that ought of the things which he possessed was his own; but they had all things common. 33 And with great power gave the apostles witness of the resurrection of the Lord Jesus: and great grace was upon them all. 34 Neither was there any among them that lacked: for as many as were possessors of lands or houses sold them, and brought the prices of the things that were sold, 35 and laid them down at the apostles' feet: and distribution was made unto every man according as he had need.

36 And Joses, who by the apostles was surnamed Barnabas, (which is, being interpreted, The son of consolation,) a Levite, and of the country of Cyprus, 37 having land, sold it, and brought the money, and laid it at the apostles' feet. V. But a certain man named Ananias, with Sapphira his wife, sold a possession, 2 and kept back part of the price, his wife also being privy to it, and brought a certain part, and laid it at the apostles' feet. 3 But Peter said, Ananias, why hath Satan filled thine heart to lie to the Holy Ghost, and to keep back part of the price of the land? 4 Whiles it remained, was it not thine own? and after it was sold, was it not in thine own power? why hast thou conceived this thing in thine heart? thou hast not lied unto men, but unto God. 5 And Ananias hearing these words fell down, and gave up the

---

ᵃ — ἡ LTTrA. ᵇ οὐδ᾽ E. ᶜ πάντα L. ᵈ δυνάμει μεγάλῃ LTTrA. ᵉ τοῦ κυρίου Ἰησοῦ [χριστοῦ Christ] τῆς ἀναστάσεως L ; τῆς ἀναστάσεως Ἰησοῦ χριστοῦ τοῦ κυρίου T. ᶠ ἦν LTTr. ᵍ διεδίδετο LTTrA. ʰ Ἰωσὴφ Joseph LTTrAW. ⁱ ἀπὸ LTTrAW. ᵏ Λευείτης T \. ˡ πρὸς T. ᵐ ὀνόματι Ἀνανίας L. ⁿ Σαπφείρα LTr. ᵒ συνειδυίης LTTrA. ᵖ — αὐτοῦ (read [his]) LTTrA. �q + ὁ LTTrA. ʳ διὰ τί LTrA. ˢ + [σε] thee (to keep back) A. ᵗ + ὁ GLTTrAW.

ghost : and great fear came on all them that heard these things. 6 And the young men arose, wound him up, and carried him out, and buried him. 7 And it was about the space of three hours after, when his wife, not knowing what was done, came in. 8 And Peter answered unto her, Tell me whether ye sold the land for so much? And she said, Yea, for so much. 9 Then Peter said unto her, How is it that ye have agreed together to tempt the Spirit of the Lord? behold, the feet of them which have buried thy husband are at the door, and shall carry thee out. 10 Then fell she down straightway at his feet, and yielded up the ghost : and the young men came in, and found her dead, and, carrying her forth, buried her by her husband. 11 And great fear came upon all the church, and upon as many as heard these things. 12 And by the hands of the apostles were many signs and wonders wrought among the people; (and they were all with one accord in Solomon's porch. 13 And of the rest durst no man join himself to them: but the people magnified them. 14 And believers were the more added to the Lord, multitudes both of men and women.) 15 Insomuch that they brought forth the sick into the streets, and laid them on beds and couches, that at the least the shadow of Peter passing by might overshadow some of them. 16 There came also a multitude out of the cities round about unto Jerusalem, bringing sick folks, and them which were vexed with unclean spirits : and they were healed every one.

ἐξέψυξεν· καὶ ἐγένετο φόβος μέγας ἐπὶ πάντας τοὺς
expired. And came fear great upon all who

ἀκούοντας [v]ταῦτα.‖ 6 ἀναστάντες.δὲ οἱ νεώτεροι συνέ-
heard these things. And having risen the younger [men] swathed

στειλαν αὐτόν, καὶ ἐξενέγκαντες ἔθαψαν. 7 Ἐγένετο.δὲ
him, and having carried out buried [him]. And it came to pass

ὡς ὡρῶν τριῶν διάστημα καὶ ἡ.γυνὴ.αὐτοῦ μὴ εἰδυῖα τὸ
about hours three afterwards also his wife, not knowing what

γεγονὸς εἰσῆλθεν. 8 ἀπεκρίθη.δὲ [w]αὐτῇ‖ [x]ὁ‖ Πέτρος,
had come to pass, came in. And answered her Peter,

Εἰπέ μοι εἰ τοσούτου τὸ χωρίον ἀπέδοσθε; Ἡ.δὲ εἶπεν,
Tell me if for so much the estate ye sold? And she said,

Ναί, τοσούτου. 9 Ὁ.δὲ.Πέτρος [y]εἶπεν‖ πρὸς αὐτήν, Τί
Yes, for so much. And Peter said to her, Why [is it]

ὅτι συνεφωνήθη.ὑμῖν πειράσαι τὸ πνεῦμα κυρίου; ἰδού, οἱ
that ye agreed together to tempt the Spirit of [the] Lord? Lo, the

πόδες τῶν θαψάντων τὸν.ἄνδρα.σου ἐπὶ τῇ θύρᾳ, καὶ
feet of those who buried thy husband [are] at the door, and

ἐξοίσουσίν σε. 10 Ἔπεσεν.δὲ παραχρῆμα [z]παρὰ‖ τοὺς
they shall carry out thee. And she fell down immediately at

πόδας.αὐτοῦ καὶ ἐξέψυξεν· εἰσελθόντες.δὲ οἱ.νεανίσκοι
his feet and expired. And having come in the young [men]

[a]εὗρον‖ αὐτὴν νεκράν, καὶ ἐξενέγκαντες ἔθαψαν πρὸς
found her dead; and having carried out they buried [her] by

τὸν.ἄνδρα.αὐτῆς. 11 καὶ ἐγένετο φόβος μέγας ἐφ᾽ ὅλην τὴν
her husband. And came fear great upon whole the

ἐκκλησίαν, καὶ ἐπὶ πάντας τοὺς ἀκούοντας ταῦτα. 12 Διὰ.δὲ
assembly, and upon all who heard these things. And by

τῶν χειρῶν τῶν ἀποστόλων [b]ἐγένετο‖ σημεῖα καὶ τέρατα
the hands of the apostles came to pass signs and wonders

[c]ἐν τῷ λαῷ πολλά·‖ καὶ ἦσαν ὁμοθυμαδὸν [d]ἅπαντες‖
among the people many; (and they were with one accord all

ἐν τῇ στοᾷ [e]Σολομῶντος·‖ 13 τῶν.δὲ λοιπῶν οὐδεὶς ἐτόλμα
in the porch of Solomon, but of the rest no one durst

κολλᾶσθαι αὐτοῖς, ἀλλ᾽ ἐμεγάλυνεν αὐτοὺς ὁ λαός· 14 μᾶλλον
join them, but magnified them the people; the more

δὲ προσετίθεντο πιστεύοντες τῷ κυρίῳ, πλήθη ἀνδρῶν.τε
and were added believers to the Lord, multitudes both of men

καὶ γυναικῶν· 15 ὥστε [f]κατὰ‖ τὰς πλατείας ἐκφέρειν τοὺς
and women;) so as in the streets to bring out the

ἀσθενεῖς καὶ τιθέναι ἐπὶ [g]κλινῶν‖ καὶ [h]κραββάτων,‖ ἵνα
sick, and to put [them] on beds and couches, that

ἐρχομένου Πέτρου κἂν ἡ σκιὰ [i]ἐπισκιάσῃ‖ τινὶ
coming of Peter at least the shadow might overshadow some one

αὐτῶν. 16 συνήρχετο.δὲ καὶ τὸ πλῆθος τῶν πέριξ
of them. And came together also the multitude of the round about

πόλεων [k]εἰς‖ Ἰερουσαλήμ, φέροντες ἀσθενεῖς καὶ ὀχλου-
cities to Jerusalem, bringing sick ones and those

μένους ὑπὸ πνευμάτων ἀκαθάρτων, οἵτινες ἐθεραπεύοντο
beset by spirits unclean, who were healed

ἅπαντες.
all.

---

[v] — ταῦτα LTTrA. [w] πρὸς αὐτὴν to her LTTrA. [x] — ὁ LTTrA. [y] — εἶπεν (read [said] LTTrA. [z] πρὸς LTTrA. [a] εὗραν Tr. [b] ἐγένετο EGLTTrAW. [c] πολλὰ ἐν τῷ λαῷ LTTrAW. [d] πάντες LTr. [e] Σολομῶνος GTrAW. [f] καὶ εἰς even into LTr. [g] κλιναρίων LTTrA. [h] κραβάττων LTTrAW. [i] ἐπισκιάσει shall overshadow Tr. [k] — εἰς LTTrA.

17 Ἀναστὰς.δὲ ὁ ἀρχιερευς καὶ πάντες οἱ σὺν αὐτῷ,
And having risen up the high priest and all those with him,

ἡ οὖσα αἵρεσις τῶν Σαδδουκαίων, ἐπλήσθησαν ζήλου,
which is [the] sect of the Sadducees, were filled with anger,

18 καὶ ἐπέβαλον τὰς χεῖρας ¹αὐτῶν‖ ἐπὶ τοὺς ἀποστόλους καὶ
and laid ²hands ¹their on the apostles and

ἔθεντο αὐτοὺς ἐν τηρήσει δημοσίᾳ. 19 ἄγγελος.δὲ κυρίου
put them in [the] ²hold ¹public. But an angel of [the] Lord

διὰ ᵐτῆς‖ νυκτὸς ⁿἤνοιξεν‖ τὰς θύρας τῆς φυλακῆς,
during the night opened the doors of the prison,

ἐξαγαγών.τε αὐτοὺς εἶπεν, 20 Πορεύεσθε, καὶ σταθέντες
and having brought ²out ¹them said, Go ye, and standing

λαλεῖτε ἐν τῷ ἱερῷ τῷ λαῷ 'πάντα τὰ ῥήματα τῆς ζωῆς
speak in the temple to the people all the words of ²life

ταύτης. 21 Ἀκούσαντες.δὲ εἰσῆλθον ὑπὸ τὸν ὄρθρον εἰς τὸ
¹this. And having heard they entered at the dawn into the

ἱερόν, καὶ ἐδίδασκον. παραγενόμενος.δὲ ὁ ἀρχιερεὺς καὶ οἱ
temple, and were teaching. But having come the high priest and those

σὺν αὐτῷ, συνεκάλεσαν τὸ συνέδριον καὶ πᾶσαν τὴν γερου-
with him, they called together the sanhedrim and all the elder-

σίαν τῶν υἱῶν Ἰσραήλ, καὶ ἀπέστειλαν εἰς τὸ δεσμωτήριον
hood of the sons of Israel, and sent to the prison

ἀχθῆναι.αὐτούς. 22 οἱ.δὲ ᵒὑπηρέται παραγενόμενοι‖ οὐχ
to have them brought. But the officers having come ²not

εὗρον αὐτοὺς ἐν τῇ φυλακῇ· ἀναστρέψαντες.δὲ ἀπήγγειλαν,
¹did find them in the prison; and having returned they reported,

23 λέγοντες, ῞Οτι τὸ ᵖμὲν‖ δεσμωτήριον εὕρομεν κεκλεισ-
saying, The ²indeed ¹prison we found shut

μένον ἐν πάσῃ ἀσφαλείᾳ, καὶ τοὺς φύλακας ᑫἔξω‖ ἑστῶτας
with all security, and the keepers without standing

ʳπρὸ‖ τῶν θυρῶν· ἀνοίξαντες.δέ, ἔσω οὐδένα εὕρομεν.
before the doors; but having opened, within no one we found.

24 Ὡς.δὲ ἤκουσαν τοὺς.λόγους.τούτους ὅ.τε ˢἱερεὺς καὶ
And when they heard these words both the priest and

ὅ‖ στρατηγὸς τοῦ ἱεροῦ καὶ οἱ ἀρχιερεῖς διηπόρουν περὶ
the captain of the temple and the chief priests were perplexed concerning

αὐτῶν, τί ἂν.γένοιτο τοῦτο. 25 παραγενόμενος.δὲ τις
them, what ²might ³be ¹this. But having come a certain one

ἀπήγγειλεν αὐτοῖς ᵗλέγων,‖ ῞Οτι ἰδοὺ οἱ ἄνδρες οὓς ἔθεσθε
reported to them, saying, Lo, the men whom ye put

ἐν τῇ φυλακῇ εἰσὶν ἐν τῷ ἱερῷ ἑστῶτες καὶ διδάσκοντες τὸν
in the prison are in the temple standing and teaching the

λαόν. 26 Τότε ἀπελθὼν ὁ στρατηγὸς σὺν τοῖς ὑπηρέταις
people. Then ³having ⁴gone ¹the ²captain with the officers

ᵛἤγαγεν‖ αὐτούς, οὐ μετὰ βίας, ἐφοβοῦντο.γὰρ τὸν λαόν,
brought them, not with violence, for they feared the people,

ʷἵνα‖ μὴ.λιθασθῶσιν. 27 ἀγαγόντες.δὲ αὐτοὺς.ἔστησαν
that they might not be stoned. And having brought them they set

ἐν τῷ συνεδρίῳ· καὶ.ἐπηρώτησεν.αὐτοὺς ὁ ἀρχιερεύς,
[them] in the sanhedrim. And ⁴asked ⁵them ¹the ²high ³priest,

28 λέγων, ˣΟὐ‖ παραγγελίᾳ παρηγγείλαμεν ὑμῖν μὴ διδάσ-
saying, ³Not ⁴by ⁵a ⁶charge ¹did ²we charge you not to teach

17 Then the high priest rose up, and all they that were with him, (which is the sect of the Sadducees,) and were filled with indignation, 18 and laid their hands on the apostles, and put them in the common prison. 19 But the angel of the Lord by night opened the prison doors, and brought them forth, and said, 20 Go, stand and speak in the temple to the people all the words of this life. 21 And when they heard that, they entered into the temple early in the morning, and taught. But the high priest came, and they that were with him, and called the council together, and all the senate of the children of Israel, and sent to the prison to have them brought. 22 But when the officers came, and found them not in the prison, they returned, and told, 23 saying, The prison truly found we shut with all safety, and the keepers standing without before the doors : but when we had opened, we found no man within. 24 Now when the high priest and the captain of the temple and the chief priests heard these things, they doubted of them whereunto this would grow. 25 Then came one and told them, saying, Behold, the men whom ye put in prison are standing in the temple, and teaching the people. 26 Then went the captain with the officers, and brought them without violence: for they feared the people, lest they should have been stoned. 27 And when they had brought them, they set them before the council: and the high priest asked them, 28 saying, Did not we straitly command you that ye should not teach in

---

¹ — αὐτῶν LTTrAW. ᵐ — τῆς LTTrA. ⁿ ἀνοίξας having opened T. ᵒ παραγενόμενοι ὑπηρέται LTTrA. ᵖ — μὲν LTTrAW. ᑫ — ἔξω GLTTrAW. ʳ ἐπὶ LTTrA. ˢ — ἱερεὺς καὶ ὁ LTTrA. ᵗ — λέγων GLTTrAW. ᵛ ἤγεν T. ʷ — ἵνα (read lest they should be stoned) LTTr[A]. ˣ — Οὐ (read We did charge you by a charge, &c.) LTTrA.

this name? and, be
hold, ye have filled
Jerusalem with your
doctrine, and intend to
bring this man's blood
upon us. 29 Then Pe-
ter and the *other* apos-
tles answered and said,
We ought to obey
God rather than men.
30 The God of our fa-
thers raised up Jesus,
whom ye slew and
hanged on a tree.
31 Him hath God
exalted with his right
hand *to be* a Prince
and a Saviour, for to
give repentance to Is-
rael, and forgiveness
of sins. 32 And we are
his witnesses of these
things; and *so is* also
.he Holy Ghost, whom
God hath given to
them that obey him.
33 When they heard
that, they were cut *to
the heart,* and took
counsel to slay them.
34 Then stood there up
one in the council, a
Pharisee, named Ga-
maliel, a doctor of the
law, had in reputation
among all the people,
and commanded to put
the apostles forth a
little space; 35 and
said unto them, Ye
men of Israel, take
heed to yourselves
what ye intend to do
as touching these men.
36 For before these
days rose up Theudas,
boasting himself to be
somebody; to whom a
number of men, about
four hundred, joined
themselves: who was
slain; and all, as many
as obeyed him, were
scattered, and brought
to nought. 37 After
this man rose up Ju-
das of Galilee in the
days of the taxing,
and drew away much
people after him: he
also perished; and all,
even as many as obeyed
him, were dispersed.
38 And now I say unto
you, Refrain from
these men, and let
them alone: for if
this counsel or this

κειν επι τῷ.ὀνόματι.τούτῳ ˣ; ‖ καὶ ἰδοὺ πεπληρώκατε τὴν 'Ιε-
in   this name?   and lo,   ye have filled   Je-
ρουσαλὴμ τῆς.διδαχῆς.ὑμῶν, καὶ βούλεσθε ἐπαγαγεῖν ἐφ
rusalem   with your teaching,   and purpose   to bring   upon
ἡμᾶς τὸ αἷμα τοῦ.ἀνθρώπου.τούτου. 29 'Αποκριθεὶς.δὲ ᵞὁ ‖
us   the blood   of this man.   But ⁵answering
Πέτρος καὶ οἱ ἀπόστολοι ᶻεἶπον, ‖ Πειθαρχεῖν   δεῖ
¹Peter ²and ³the ⁴apostles   said,   ⁴To ⁵obey ¹it ²is ³necessary
θεῷ μᾶλλον ἢ ἀνθρώποις. 30 ὁ θεὸς τῶν.πατέρων.ἡμῶν
God rather than men.   The God   of our fathers
ἤγειρεν 'Ιησοῦν, ὃν ὑμεῖς διεχειρίσασθε κρεμάσαντες.ἐπὶ
raised up Jesus, whom ye   killed,   having hanged . on
ξύλου· 31 τοῦτον ὁ θεὸς ἀρχηγὸν καὶ σωτῆρα ὕψωσεν τῇ
a tree.   Him   God   a chief   and Saviour exalted by the
δεξιᾷ αὐτοῦ, ᵃδοῦναι μετάνοιαν τῷ 'Ισραὴλ καὶ ἄφεσιν
right hand of him, to give repentance ⁴to Israel and remission
ἁμαρτιῶν. 32 καὶ ἡμεῖς ᵇἐσμεν αὐτοῦ μάρτυρες ‖ τῶν ῥημάτων
of sins.   And we   are of him witnesses   of ¹things
τούτων, καὶ τὸ πνεῦμα ᶜδὲ τὸ ἅγιον, ὃ ἔδωκεν ὁ θεὸς
¹these, and ²the ¹Spirit ¹also the Holy, which ²gave ¹God
τοῖς πειθαρχοῦσιν αὐτῷ. 33 Οἱ.δὲ ἀκούσαντες διεπρίοντο,
to those that obey   him.   But they having heard were cut
καὶ ᵈἐβουλεύοντο ‖ ἀνελεῖν αὐτούς. 34 ἀναστὰς
[to the heart], and took counsel to put to death them. ⁵Having ⁶risen ⁷up
δέ τις   ἐν τῷ συνεδρίῳ Φαρισαῖος, ὀνόματι Γα-
¹but ²a ³certain [⁴man] in the sanhedrim a Pharisee, by name Ga-
μαλιήλ, νομοδιδάσκαλος, τίμιος παντὶ τῷ λαῷ, ἐκέλευσεν
maliel, a teacher of the law, honoured by all the people, commanded
ἔξω βραχύ.ᵉτι ‖ ᶠτοὺς ἀποστόλους ‖ ποιῆσαι, 35 εἶπέν.τε
³out ⁴for ⁵a ⁶short ⁷while ⁸the   ⁹apostles   ¹to ²put, and said
πρὸς αὐτούς, Ἄνδρες ᵍ'Ισραηλῖται, ‖ προσέχετε ἑαυτοῖς
to them,   Men   Israelites,   take heed to yourselves
ἐπὶ τοῖς.ἀνθρώποις.τούτοις τί ¹μέλλετε πράσσειν. 36 πρὸ
as regards   these men   what ye are about to do;   ²before
γὰρ τούτων τῶν ἡμερῶν ἀνέστη Θευδᾶς, λέγων εἶναί τινα
¹for   these   days   rose up Theudas, affirming ²to ³be ⁴somebody
ἑαυτόν, ᾧ ʰπροσεκολλήθη ἀριθμὸς ἀνδρῶν, ὡσεὶ ‖ τετρα-
¹himself, to whom were joined a number of men, about four
κοσίων· ὃς ἀνῃρέθη, καὶ πάντες ὅσοι ἐπείθοντο αὐτῷ
hundred; who was put to death, and all as many as were persuaded by him
διελύθησαν καὶ ἐγένοντο εἰς οὐδέν. 37 μετὰ τοῦτον ἀνέστη
were dispersed and came to nothing.   After   this one rose up
'Ιούδας ὁ Γαλιλαῖος ἐν ταῖς ἡμέραις τῆς ἀπογραφῆς, καὶ
Judas the Galilean in the days   of the registration, and
ἀπέστησεν λαὸν ⁱἱκανὸν ‖ ὀπίσω αὐτοῦ· κἀκεῖνος ἀπώλετο,
drew away ²people ¹much after . him;   and he   perished,
καὶ πάντες ὅσοι ἐπείθοντο αὐτῷ διεσκορπίσθησαν. 38 καὶ
and   all as many as were persuaded by him were scattered abroad. And
τὰ νῦν λέγω ὑμῖν, ἀπόστητε ἀπὸ τῶν.ἀνθρώπων.τούτων, καὶ
¹²now I say to you, Withdraw from   these men,   and
ᵏἐάσατε ‖ αὐτούς· ὅτι ἐὰν ᾖ ἐξ ἀνθρώπων ἡ.βουλὴ.αὕτη ἢ
let ²alone ¹them, for if ⁶be ⁷from ⁸men ¹this ²counsel ³or

ˣ —; LTTrA.   ᵞ — ὁ LTTrA.   ᶻ εἶπαν LTTrA.   ᵃ + τοῦ T.   ᵇ ἐν αὐτῷ μάρτυρές ἐσμεν L;
— αὐτοῦ TTr.   ᶜ — δὲ LTTr[A].   ᵈ ἐβούλοντο resolved LTr.   ᵉ — τι LTTrAW.   ᶠ τοὺς
ἀνθρώπους the men LTTrA.   ᵍ 'Ισραηλεῖται T.   ʰ προσεκλίθη ἀνδρῶν ἀριθμὸς ὡς LTTrAW.
ⁱ — ἱκανὸν LTTrA.   ᵏ ἄφετε LTTrA.

τὸ.ἔργον.τοῦτο, καταλυθήσεται· 39 εἰ.δὲ ἐκ θεοῦ ἐστιν,
*this ⁵work,   it will be overthrown ; ⁻ but if from God it be,

¹οὐ.δύνασθε‖ καταλῦσαι ᵐαὐτό,‖ μήποτε καὶ θεομάχοι
ye are not able to overthrow it, lest also fighters against God

εὑρεθῆτε. 40 Ἐπείσθησαν.δὲ αὐτῷ· καὶ προσκαλεσάμενοι
ye be found. And they were persuaded by him ; and having called to

τοὺς ἀποστόλους, δείραντες παρήγγειλαν μὴ λαλεῖν
[them] the apostles, having beaten they enjoined [them] not to speak

ἐπὶ τῷ ὀνόματι τοῦ Ἰησοῦ, καὶ ἀπέλυσαν ⁿαὐτούς.‖ 41 Οἱ
in the name of Jesus, and released them. They

μὲν οὖν ἐπορεύοντο χαίροντες ἀπὸ προσώπου τοῦ
therefore departed rejoicing from [the] presence of the

συνεδρίου ὅτι ᵒὑπὲρ τοῦ ὀνόματος αὐτοῦ κατηξιώθησαν‖
sanhedrim that for the name of him they were accounted worthy

ἀτιμασθῆναι· 42 πᾶσάν.τε ἡμέραν ἐν τῷ ἱερῷ καὶ κατ'.οἶκον
to be dishonoured. And every day in the temple and in the houses

οὐκ.ἐπαύοντο διδάσκοντες καὶ εὐαγγελιζόμενοι ᴾἸησοῦν
they ceased not teaching and announcing the glad tidings— Jesus

τὸν χριστόν.‖
the Christ.

6 Ἐν.δὲ ταῖς.ἡμέραις.ταύταις πληθυνόντων τῶν μαθητῶν
But in those days ³multiplying ¹the ²disciples

ἐγένετο γογγυσμὸς τῶν Ἑλληνιστῶν πρὸς τοὺς Ἑβραίους,
there arose a murmuring of the Hellenists against the Hebrews,

ὅτι παρεθεωροῦντο ἐν τῇ διακονίᾳ τῇ καθημερινῇ αἱ
because were overlooked in the ²ministration ¹daily

χῆραι.αὐτῶν. 2 προσκαλεσάμενοι.δὲ οἱ δώδεκα τὸ πλῆθος
their widows. And ³having ⁴called ⁵to [⁶them] ¹the ²twelve the multitude

τῶν μαθητῶν, �q εἶπον,‖ Οὐκ ἀρεστόν ἐστιν ἡμᾶς, καταλείψαν-
of the disciples, said, Not seemly it is [for] us, leaving

τας τὸν λόγον τοῦ θεοῦ, διακονεῖν τραπέζαις. 3 ἐπισκέψασθε
the word of God, to attend tables. Look out

ʳοὖν,‖ ˢἀδελφοί,‖ ἄνδρας ἐξ ὑμῶν μαρτυρουμένους
therefore, brethren, ²men ³from ⁴among ⁵yourselves, ⁶borne ⁷witness ⁸to

ἑπτά, πλήρεις πνεύματος ᵗἁγίου‖ καὶ σοφίας, οὓς ᵛκατα-
¹seven, full of [the] ²Spirit ¹Holy and wisdom, whom we will

στήσομεν‖ ἐπὶ τῆς.χρείας.ταύτης· 4 ἡμεῖς.δὲ τῇ προσευχῇ
appoint over this business ; but we to prayer

καὶ τῇ διακονίᾳ τοῦ λόγου προσκαρτερήσομεν. 5 Καὶ
and the ministry of the word will steadfastly continue. And

ἤρεσεν ὁ λόγος ἐνώπιον παντὸς τοῦ πλήθους· καὶ
¹was ²pleasing ¹the ²saying before all the multitude ; and

ἐξελέξαντο Στέφανον, ἄνδρα ʷπλήρη‖ πίστεως καὶ πνεύ-
they chose Stephen, a man full of faith and [the] ²Spi-

ματος ἁγίου, καὶ Φίλιππον, καὶ Πρόχορον, καὶ Νικάνορα, καὶ
rit ¹Holy, and Philip, and Prochorus, and Nicanor, and

Τίμωνα, καὶ Παρμενᾶν, καὶ Νικόλαον προσήλυτον Ἀντιοχέα,
Timon, and Parmenas, and Nicolas a proselyte of Antioch,

6 οὓς ἔστησαν ἐνώπιον τῶν ἀποστόλων· καὶ προσευξάμενοι
whom they set before the apostles ; and having prayed

ἐπέθηκαν αὐτοῖς τὰς χεῖρας. 7 καὶ ὁ λόγος τοῦ θεοῦ
they laid ²on ³them ¹hands. And the word of God

work be of men, it will come to nought : 39 but if it be of God, ye cannot overthrow it ; lest haply ye be found even to fight against God. 40 And to him they agreed: and when they had called the apostles, and beaten them, they commanded that they should not speak in the name of Jesus, and let them go. 41 And they departed from the presence of the council, rejoicing that they were counted worthy to suffer shame for his name. 42 And daily in the temple, and in every house, they ceased not to teach and preach Jesus Christ.

VI. And in those days, when the number of the disciples was multiplied, there arose a murmuring of the Grecians against the Hebrews, because their widows were neglected in the daily ministration. 2 Then the twelve called the multitude of the disciples unto them, and said, It is not reason that we should leave the word of God, and serve tables. 3 Wherefore, brethren, look ye out among you seven men of honest report, full of the Holy Ghost and wisdom, whom we may appoint over this business. 4 But we will give ourselves continually to prayer, and to the ministry of the word. 5 And the saying pleased the whole multitude : and they chose Stephen, a man full of faith and of the Holy Ghost, and Philip, and Prochorus, and Nicanor, and Timon, and Parmenas, and Nicolas a proselyte of Antioch : 6 whom they set before the apostles : and when they had prayed, they laid their hands on them. 7 And the word of God increased ;

---

¹ οὐ δυνήσεσθε ye will not be able LTTr.   ᵐ αὐτούς them GLTTrA.   ⁿ — αὐτούς (read [them]) TTrA.   ᵒ — αὐτοῦ GLTTrAW ; κατηξιώθησαν ὑπὲρ τοῦ ὀνόματος LTTrA.   ᴾ τὸν χριστὸν Ἰησοῦν LTTrA.   q εἶπαν LTTrA.   ʳ δή indeed L ; δέ but T.   ˢ — ἀδελφοί L ᵗ ἁγίου GLTTrA.   ᵛ καταστήσωμεν we may appoint EW.   ʷ πλήρης L.

and the number of the disciples multiplied in Jerusalem greatly; and a great company of the priests were obedient to the faith.

ηὔξανεν, καὶ ἐπληθύνετο ὁ ἀριθμὸς τῶν μαθητῶν ἐν Ἱε-
increased, and [7]multiplied [1]the [2]number [3]of [4]the [5]disciples in Je-
ρουσαλὴμ σφόδρα, πολύς.τε ὄχλος τῶν ἱερέων ὑπήκουον
rusalem exceedingly, and a great multitude of the priests were obedient
τῇ πίστει.
to the faith.

8 And Stephen, full of faith and power, did great wonders and miracles among the people. 9 Then there arose certain of the synagogue, which is called the synagogue of the Libertines, and Cyrenians, and Alexandrians, and of them of Cilicia and of Asia, disputing with Stephen. 10 And they were not able to resist the wisdom and the spirit by which he spake. 11 Then they suborned men, which said, We have heard him speak blasphemous words against Moses, and against God. 12 And they stirred up the people, and the elders, and the scribes, and came upon him, and caught him, and brought him to the council, 13 and set up false witnesses, which said, This man ceaseth not to speak blasphemous words against this holy place, and the law: 14 for we have heard him say, that this Jesus of Nazareth shall destroy this place, and shall change the customs which Moses delivered us. 15 And all that sat in the council, looking stedfastly on him, saw his face as it had been the face of an angel.

8 Στέφανος.δὲ πλήρης *πίστεως* καὶ δυνάμεως ἐποίει
And Stephen, full of faith and power, wrought
τέρατα καὶ σημεῖα μεγάλα ἐν τῷ λαῷ. 9 ἀνέστησαν.δέ
wonders and [2]signs [1]great among the people. And arose
τινες τῶν ἐκ τῆς συναγωγῆς ʸτῆς λεγομένης* Λιβερτίνων,
certain of those of the synagogue called Libertines,
καὶ Κυρηναίων, καὶ Ἀλεξανδρέων, καὶ τῶν.ἀπὸ Κιλικίας
and of Cyrenians, and of Alexandrians, and of those from Cilicia
ᶻκαὶ Ἀσίας,* ᶦ·ᵃσυζητοῦντες* τῷ Στεφάνῳ· 10 καὶ οὐκ.ἴσχυον
and Asia, disputing with Stephen. And they were not able
ἀντιστῆναι τῇ σοφίᾳ καὶ τῷ πνεύματι ᾧ ἐλάλει. 11 τότε
to resist the wisdom and the spirit by which he spoke. Then
ὑπέβαλον ἄνδρας, λέγοντας, Ὅτι ἀκηκόαμεν αὐτοῦ.λαλοῦν-
they suborned men, saying, We have heard him speaking
τος ῥήματα βλάσφημα εἰς ᵇΜωσῆν* καὶ τὸν θεόν. 12 Συν-
[2]words [1]blasphemous against Moses and God. [2]They
ἐκίνησάν τε τὸν λαὸν καὶ τοὺς πρεσβυτέρους καὶ τοὺς
[3]stirred [4]up [1]and the people and the elders and the
γραμματεῖς, καὶ ἐπιστάντες συνήρπασαν αὐτόν, καὶ ἤγαγον
scribes, and coming upon they seized him, and brought
εἰς τὸ συνέδριον, 13 ἔστησάν.τε μάρτυρας ψευδεῖς,
[him] to the sanhedrim, And they set [2]witnesses [1]false,
λέγοντας, Ὁ.ἄνθρωπος.οὗτος οὐ.παύεται ᶜῥήματα βλάσφημα
saying, This man does not cease [3]words [2]blasphemous
λαλῶν* κατὰ τοῦ τόπου τοῦ ἁγίου ᵈτούτου* καὶ τοῦ νόμου·
[1]speaking against [3]place [2]holy ¹this and the law;
14 ἀκηκόαμεν.γὰρ αὐτοῦ λέγοντος, Ὅτι Ἰησοῦς ὁ Ναζω-
for we have heard him saying, That [2]Jesus [3]the [4]Naza-
ραῖος οὗτος καταλύσει τὸν.τόπον.τοῦτον, καὶ ἀλλάξει τὰ
ræan ¹this will destroy this place, and will change the
ἔθη ἃ παρέδωκεν ἡμῖν Μωϋσῆς. 15 Καὶ ἀτενίσαντες εἰς
customs which [2]delivered [3]to [4]us ¹Moses. And looking intently on
αὐτὸν ᵉἅπαντες* οἱ καθεζόμενοι ἐν τῷ συνεδρίῳ ᶠεἶδον* τὸ
him all who sat in the sanhedrim saw the
πρόσωπον.αὐτοῦ ὡσεὶ πρόσωπον ἀγγέλου.
his face as [the] face of an angel.

VII. Then said the high priest, Are these things so? 2 And he said, Men, brethren, and fathers, hearken; The God of glory appeared unto our father Abraham, when he was in Mesopotamia, before he dwelt in Charran, 3 and said unto him, Get thee out of thy country, and from thy kindred, and

7 Εἶπεν.δὲ ὁ ἀρχιερεύς, Εἰ ᵍἄρα* ταῦτα οὕτως ʰἔχει*;
And [2]said ¹the [2]high [3]priest, [6]Then [7]these [8]things [9]so [5]are?
2 Ὁ.δὲ ἔφη, Ἄνδρες ἀδελφοὶ καὶ πατέρες, ἀκούσατε. ὁ θεὸς
And he said, Men brethren and fathers, hearken. The God
τῆς δόξης ὤφθη τῷ.πατρὶ.ἡμῶν Ἀβραὰμ ὄντι ἐν τῇ Μεσο-
of glory appeared to our father Abraham being in Meso-
ποταμίᾳ, πρὶν ἢ κατοικῆσαι αὐτὸν ἐν Χαρράν, 3 καὶ εἶπεν
potamia, before ²dwelt ¹he in Charran, and said
πρὸς αὐτόν, Ἔξελθε ἐκ τῆς.γῆς.σου καὶ ᶦἐκ* τῆς συγγενείας
to him, Go out from thy land and from ²kindred

ˣ χάριτος of grace GLTTrAW.   ʸ τῶν λεγομένων T.   ᶻ — καὶ Ἀσίας L.   ᵃ συνζητοῦντες
LTTrA.   ᵇ Μωϋσῆν GLTTrAW.   ᶜ βλάσφημα GLTTrAW ; λαλῶν ῥήματα TTr.   ᵈ — τούτου
(read the holy place) GLTTrAW.   ᵉ πάντες LTTr.   ᶠ εἶδαν Tr.   ᵍ — ἄρα LTTr[A].
ʰ — ἔχει (read [are]) W.   ᶦ — ἐκ ᴸᴸ]Tr[A].

σου, καὶ δεῦρο εἰς^k γῆν ἣν ἄν σοι δείξω. 4 Τότε ἐξελθὼν
¹thy and come into land which to thee I will shew. Then ·going out

ἐκ γῆς Χαλδαίων, κατῴκησεν ἐν Χαρράν, κἀκεῖθεν
from [the] land of Chaldeans, he dwelt in Charran, and thence

μετὰ τὸ ἀποθανεῖν τὸν.πατέρα.αὐτοῦ, μετῴκισεν αὐτὸν εἰς
after ³died ¹his ²father, he removed him into

τὴν.γῆν.ταύτην εἰς ἣν ὑμεῖς νῦν κατοικεῖτε· 5 καὶ οὐκ
this land in which ye now dwell. And ²not

ἔδωκεν αὐτῷ κληρονομίαν ἐν αὐτῇ, οὐδὲ βῆμα.ποδός·
¹he ²did give to him an inheritance in it, not even a foot's tread;

καὶ ἐπηγγείλατο ¹αὐτῷ δοῦναι‖ εἰς κατάσχεσιν ᵐαὐτήν,‖ καὶ
and promised to him to give ²for ³a ⁴possession ¹it, and

τῷ.σπέρματι.αὐτοῦ μετ' αὐτόν, οὐκ.ὄντος αὐτῷ τέκνου.
to his seed after him, there not being to him a child.

6 ἐλάλησεν.δὲ οὕτως ὁ θεός, Ὅτι ἔσται τὸ.σπέρμα.αὐτοῦ
And ²spoke ²thus ¹God: That ³shall ⁴be ¹his ²seed

πάροικον ἐν γῇ ἀλλοτρίᾳ, καὶ δουλώσουσιν αὐτὸ καὶ
a sojourner in a ²land ¹strange, and they will enslave it and

κακώσουσιν ἔτη τετρακόσια. 7 καὶ τὸ ἔθνος ᾧ ⁿἐὰν‖
ill-treat [it] ³years ¹four ²hundred; and the nation to which

ᵒδουλεύσωσιν,‖ κρινῶ ἐγώ, ᴾεἶπεν ὁ θεός·‖ καὶ μετὰ
they may be in bondage will ²judge ¹I, said God; and after

ταῦτα ἐξελεύσονται καὶ λατρεύσουσίν μοι ἐν τῷ τόπῳ
these things they shall come forth and serve me in ²place

τούτῳ. 8 Καὶ ἔδωκεν αὐτῷ διαθήκην περιτομῆς· καὶ οὕτως
¹this. And he gave to him a covenant of circumcision; and thus

ἐγέννησεν τὸν Ἰσαάκ, καὶ περιέτεμεν αὐτὸν τῇ ἡμέρᾳ τῇ
he begat Isaac, and circumcised him the ²day

ὀγδόῃ· καὶ ᑫᵒ‖Ἰσαὰκ τὸν Ἰακώβ, καὶ ᑫᵒ‖Ἰακὼβ τοὺς
¹eighth; and Isaac [begat] Jacob, and Jacob the

δώδεκα πατριάρχας. 9 καὶ οἱ πατριάρχαι ζηλώσαντες τὸν
twelve patriarchs. And the patriarchs, envying

Ἰωσὴφ ἀπέδοντο εἰς Αἴγυπτον· καὶ ἦν ὁ θεὸς μετ'
Joseph, sold [him] into Egypt. And ²was ¹God with

αὐτοῦ, 10 καὶ ʳἐξείλετο‖ αὐτὸν ἐκ πασῶν τῶν.θλίψεων.αὐτοῦ,
him, and delivered him out of all his tribulations,

καὶ ἔδωκεν αὐτῷ χάριν καὶ σοφίαν ˢἐναντίον‖ Φαραὼ βασι-
and gave him favour and wisdom before Pharaoh king

λέως Αἰγύπτου, καὶ κατέστησεν αὐτὸν ἡγούμενον ἐπ' Αἴγυπ-
of Egypt, and he appointed him ruler over Egypt

τον καὶ ᵗ ὅλον τὸν.οἶκον.αὐτοῦ. 11 ἦλθεν.δὲ λιμὸς ἐφ' ὅλην
and ²whole ¹his house. But came ¹a ²famine upon ²whole

τὴν.γῆν ᵛΑἰγύπτου‖ καὶ Χανάαν, καὶ θλίψις μεγάλη· καὶ
¹the land of Egypt and Canaan, and ²tribulation ¹great, and

οὐχ.ʷεὕρισκον‖ χορτάσματα οἱ.πατέρες.ἡμῶν. 12 ἀκούσας.δὲ
³did ²not ¹find ⁶sustenance ¹our ⁴fathers. But ²having ³heard

Ἰακὼβ ὄντα ˣσῖτα ἐν Αἰγύπτῳ,‖ ἐξαπέστειλεν τοὺς πατέρας
¹Jacob ⁵was ⁴corn in Egypt, sent forth ⁶fathers

ἡμῶν πρῶτον· 13 καὶ ἐν τῷ δευτέρῳ ʸἀνεγνωρίσθη‖ Ἰωσὴφ
¹our first; and at the second time was made known Joseph

τοῖς.ἀδελφοῖς.αὐτοῦ, καὶ φανερὸν ἐγένετο τῷ Φαραὼ τὸ γένος
to his brethren, and ²known ¹became to Pharaoh the family

come into the land which I shall shew thee. 4 Then came he out of the land of the Chaldæans, and dwelt in Charran: and from thence, when his father was dead, he removed him into this land, wherein ye now dwell. 5 And he gave him none inheritance in it, no, not so much as to set his foot on: yet he promised that he would give it to him for a possession, and to his seed after him, when as yet he had no child. 6 And God spake on this wise, That his seed should sojourn in a strange land; and that they should bring them into bondage, and entreat them evil four hundred years. 7 And the nation to whom they shall be in bondage will I judge, said God: and after that shall they come forth, and serve me in this place. 8 And he gave him the covenant of circumcision: and so Abraham begat Isaac, and circumcised him the eighth day; and Isaac begat Jacob; and Jacob begat the twelve patriarchs. 9 And the patriarchs, moved with envy, sold Joseph into Egypt: but God was with him, 10 and delivered him out of all his afflictions, and gave him favour and wisdom in the sight of Pharaoh king of Egypt; and he made him governor over Egypt and all his house. 11 Now there came a dearth over all the land of Egypt and Chanaan, and great affliction: and our fathers found no sustenance. 12 But when Jacob heard that there was corn in Egypt, he sent out our fathers first. 13 And at the second time Joseph was made known to his brethren; and Joseph's kindred was made known unto Pha-

---

k + τὴν the LTTrAW.   l δοῦναι αὐτῷ LTTrA ; δοῦναι αὐτὴν to give it w.   m αὐτῷ to
him w.   n ἂν LTr.   o δουλεύσουσιν they will be in bondage TTrA.   P ὁ θεὸς εἶπεν
LTTrAW.   q — ὁ LTTrA.   r ἐξείλατο GLTTrAW.   s ἔναντι T.   t + ἐφ' over T.
v Αἴγυπτον (read over all Egypt) LTTrAW.   w ηὕρισκον TrA.   x σιτία εἰς Αἴγυπτον LTTrAW.
y ἐγνωρίσθη Tr.

raoh. 14 Then sent Joseph, and called his father Jacob to *him*, and all his kindred, threescore and fifteen souls. 15 So Jacob went down into Egypt and died, he, and our fathers, 16 and were carried over into Sychem, and laid in the sepulchre that Abraham bought for a sum of money of the sons of Emmor *the father* of Sychem. 17 But when the time of the promise drew nigh, which God had sworn to Abraham, the people grew, and multiplied in Egypt, 18 till another king arose, which knew not Joseph. 19 The same dealt subtilly with our kindred, and evil entreated our fathers, so that they cast out their young children, to the end they might not live. 20 In which time Moses was born, and was exceeding fair, and nourished up in his father's house three months: 21 and when he was cast out, Pharaoh's daughter took him up, and nourished him for her own son. 22 And Moses was learned in all the wisdom of the Egyptians, and was mighty in words and in deeds. 23 And when he was full forty years old, it came into his heart to visit his brethren the children of Israel. 24 And seeing one *of them* suffer wrong, he defended *him*, and avenged him that was oppressed, and smote the Egyptian: 25 for he supposed his brethren would have understood how that God by his hand would deliver them: but they understood not. .26 And the

ᶻτοῦ‖ ᵃ'Ιωσήφ.‖ 14 ἀποστείλας.δὲ 'Ιωσήφ μετεκαλέσατο ᵇτὸν
of Joseph.   And having sent   Joseph   he called for

πατέρα.αὐτοῦ 'Ιακώβ,‖ καὶ πᾶσαν τὴν.συγγένειαν.ᶜαῦτοῦ,‖ ἐν
his father   Jacob,   and all   his kindred,   in

ψυχαῖς ἑβδομήκοντα πέντε. 15 ᵈκατέβη.δὲ‖ 'Ιακὼβ εἰς Αἴγυπ-
³souls   ¹seventy   ²five.   And went down   Jacob   into   Egypt

τον, καὶ ἐτελεύτησεν αὐτὸς καὶ οἱ.πατέρες.ἡμῶν· 16 καὶ
and   died,   he   and   our fathers,   and

μετετέθησαν εἰς Συχέμ, .καὶ ἐτέθησαν ἐν τῷ μνήματι ᵉὅ‖
were carried over to Sychem,   and were placed in the   tomb   which

ὠνήσατο 'Αβραὰμ τιμῆς ἀργυρίου παρὰ τῶν υἱῶν ᶠ'Εμμὸρ‖
²bought   ¹Abraham for a sum of money from the sons of Emmor

ᵍτοῦ‖ ʰ Συχέμ. 17 Καθὼς.δὲ ἤγγιζεν ὁ χρόνος τῆς ἐπαγ-
of Sychem.   But as   drew near the time of the   pro-

γελίας ἧς ⁱὤμοσεν‖ ὁ θεὸς τῷ 'Αβραάμ, ηὔξησεν ὁ λαὸς καὶ
mise   which ²swore   ¹God   to Abraham, ³increased ¹the ²people and

ἐπληθύνθη ἐν Αἰγύπτῳ, 18 ᵏἄχρις‖ οὗ ἀνέστη βασιλεὺς
multiplied in   Egypt,   until   arose   ²king

ἕτερος,ˡ ὃς οὐκ.ᾔδει τὸν 'Ιωσήφ. 19 οὗτος κατασοφισάμενος
¹another, who knew not   Joseph.   He having dealt subtilly with

τὸ.γένος.ἡμῶν, ἐκάκωσεν τοὺς.πατέρας.ᵐἡμῶν,‖ τοῦ ποιεῖν
our race,   ill-treated   our fathers,   making

ⁿἔκθετα τὰ.βρέφη‖.αὐτῶν εἰς.τὸ μὴ.ζωογονεῖσθαι. 20 'Εν ᾧ
²exposed   ¹their   ²babes   that   they might not live.   In which

καιρῷ ἐγεννήθη ᵒΜωσῆς,‖ καὶ ἦν ἀστεῖος τῷ θεῷ· ὃς ἀνε-
time   was born   Moses,   and was beautiful   to God; who was

τράφη μῆνας τρεῖς ἐν τῷ οἴκῳ τοῦ.πατρὸς.ᴾαὐτοῦ.‖
brought up ²months ¹three in the   house   of his father.

21 �qἐκτεθέντα.δὲ αὐτόν,‖ ʳἀνείλετο αὐτὸν ἡ θυγάτηρ Φαραώ,
And ²being ³exposed ¹he,   took up   him   the daughter of Pharaoh,

καὶ ἀνεθρέψατο αὐτὸν ἑαυτῇ εἰς υἱόν. 22 καὶ ἐπαιδεύθη
and brought up   him   for herself for a son.   And ²was ³instructed

ᵒΜωσῆς‖ ˢ πάσῃ σοφίᾳ Αἰγυπτίων· ἦν.δὲ δυνατὸς ἐν
¹Moses   in all [the] wisdom of [the] Egyptians, and he was mighty   in

λόγοις καὶ ᵗἐν‖ ἔργοιςᵛ. 23 'Ως.δὲ ἐπληροῦτο αὐτῷ ʷτεσ-
words and   in   deeds.   And when was fulfilled to him   ²of

σαρακονταετὴς‖ χρόνος, ἀνέβη ἐπὶ τὴν.καρδίαν.αὐτοῦ ἐπι-
⁴forty ⁵years   ¹a ²period, it came into   his heart   to

σκέψασθαι τοὺς.ἀδελφοὺς.αὐτοῦ τοὺς υἱοὺς 'Ισραήλ. 24 καὶ
look upon   his brethren   the   sons of Israel;   and

ἰδών τινα ἀδικούμενον, ἠμύνατο καὶ ἐποίησεν.ἐκδίκησιν
seeing a certain one being wronged, he defended [him] and   avenged

τῷ καταπονουμένῳ, πατάξας τὸν Αἰγύπτιον. 25 ἐνόμιζεν.δὲ
him being oppressed,   having smitten the   Egyptian.   For he thought

συνιέναι τοὺς.ἀδελφοὺς.ˣαὐτοῦ‖ ὅτι ὁ θεὸς διὰ χειρὸς
³would ⁴understand ¹his ²brethren   that   God   by   ⁷hand

αὐτοῦ δίδωσιν ʸαὐτοῖς σωτηρίαν.‖ οἱ.δὲ οὐ.συνῆκαν.
¹his   is giving   them   salvation.   But they   understood not.

ᶻ — τοῦ LTTrA.   ᵃ αὐτοῦ (*read* his family) T.   ᵇ 'Ιακὼβ τὸν πατέρα αὐτοῦ LTTrA.
ᶜ — αὐτοῦ (*read* [his]) GLTTrA.   ᵈ καὶ κατέβη LTTrAW.   ᵉ ᾧ GLTTrAW   ᶠ'Εμμὼρ LTTrAW.
ᵍ — τοῦ TTr.   ʰ + ἐν in LTTr.   ⁱ ὡμολόγησεν promised LTTrAW.   ᵏ ἄχρι LTTrA.
ˡ + ἐπ' Αἴγυπτον over Egypt LTTr.   ᵐ — ἡμῶν (*read* the fathers) LTTrA.   ⁿ τὰ βρέφη
ἔκθετα LTTrA.   ᵒ Μωϋσῆς GLTTrAW.   ᴾ — αὐτοῦ (*read* [his]) GLTTrA.   q ἐκτεθέντος δὲ
αὐτοῦ LTTrA.   ʳ ἀνείλατο GLTTrAW.   ˢ + ἐν (*read* πάσῃ all) TTrAW.   ᵗ — ἐν LTTrA.
ᵛ + αὐτοῦ (*read* his deeds) GLTTrAW.   ʷ τεσσερακονταετὴς TTrA.   ˣ — αὐτοῦ (*read*
[his]) TTr[A].   ʸ σωτηρίαν αὐτοῖς LTTrAW.

26 τῇ.²τε∥ ἐπιούσῃ ἡμέρᾳ ὤφθη αὐτοῖς μαχομένοις, καὶ
And on the following day he appeared to those who were contending, and

ᵃσυνήλασεν∥ αὐτοὺς εἰς εἰρήνην, εἰπών, Ἄνδρες ἀδελφοί ἐστε
urged them to peace, saying, Men ³brethren ²are

ᵇὑμεῖς·∥ ᶜἱνατί∥ ἀδικεῖτε ἀλλήλους; 27 Ὁ.δὲ ἀδικῶν
¹ye, why wrong ye one another? But he who was wronging [his]

τὸν πλησίον ἀπώσατο αὐτόν, εἰπών, Τίς σε κατέστησεν
neighbour thrust away him, saying, Who ²thee ¹appointed

ἄρχοντα καὶ δικαστὴν ἐφ' ᵈἡμᾶς∥; 28 μὴ ἀνελεῖν με
ruler and judge over us? To put to death me

σὺ θέλεις, ὃν.τρόπον ἀνεῖλες ᵉχθὲς∥ τὸν Αἰγύπτιον;
²thou ¹wishest, in the way thou puttest to death yesterday the Egyptian?

29 Ἔφυγεν.δὲ ᶠΜωσῆς∥ ἐν τῷ.λόγῳ.τούτῳ, καὶ ἐγένετο
And ²fled ¹Moses at this saying, and became

πάροικος ἐν γῇ Μαδιάμ, οὗ ἐγέννησεν υἱοὺς δύο.
a sojourner in [the] land of Madiam, where he begat ²sons ¹two.

30 Καὶ πληρωθέντων ἐτῶν ᵍτεσσαράκοντα∥ ὤφθη αὐτῷ ἐν
And ³being ⁴fulfilled ²years ¹forty appeared to him in

τῇ ἐρήμῳ τοῦ ὄρους Σινᾶ ἄγγελος ʰκυρίου∥ ἐν φλογὶ
the desert of the Mount Sina an angel of [the] Lord in a flame

πυρὸς βάτου. 31 Ὁ.δὲ ᶠΜωσῆς∥ ἰδὼν ⁱἐθαύμασεν∥ τὸ
of fire of a bush. And Moses seeing [it] wondered at the

ὅραμα· προσερχομένου.δὲ αὐτοῦ κατανοῆσαι, ἐγένετο φωνὴ
vision; and ²coming ³near ¹he to consider [it], there was a voice

κυρίου ᵏπρὸς αὐτόν,∥ 32 Ἐγὼ ὁ θεὸς τῶν.πατέρων.σου,
of [the] Lord to him, I [am] the God of thy fathers,

ὁ θεὸς Ἀβραὰμ καὶ ˡὁ θεὸς∥ Ἰσαὰκ καὶ ˡὁ θεὸς∥ Ἰακώβ.
the God of Abraham and the God of Isaac and the God of Jacob.

Ἔντρομος.δὲ γενόμενος ᶠΜωσῆς∥ οὐκ.ἐτόλμα κατανοῆσαι.
And ⁴trembling ²having ³become ¹Moses he durst not consider [it].

33 εἶπεν.δὲ αὐτῷ ὁ κύριος, Λῦσον τὸ ὑπόδημα τῶν ποδῶν
And ³said ⁴to ⁵him ¹the ²Lord, Loose the sandal of ²feet

σου· ὁ.γὰρ τόπος ᵐἐν' ᾧ ἕστηκας, γῆ ἁγία ἐστίν. 34 ἰδὼν
¹thy, for the place on which thou standest, ²ground ³holy ¹is. Seeing,

εἶδον τὴν κάκωσιν τοῦ.λαοῦ.μου τοῦ ἐν Αἰγύπτῳ, καὶ τοῦ
I.saw the ill-treatment of my people of in Egypt, and the

στεναγμοῦ.ⁿαὐτῶν∥ ἤκουσα· καὶ κατέβην ἐξελέσθαι αὐτούς·
their groaning heard, and came down to take ²out ¹them;

καὶ νῦν δεῦρο, °ἀποστελῶ∥ σε εἰς Αἴγυπτον. 35 Τοῦτον τὸν
and now come, I will send thee to Egypt. This

Μωϋσῆν ὃν ἠρνήσαντο εἰπόντες, Τίς σε κατέστησεν ἄρ-
Moses, whom they refused, saying, Who ²thee ¹appointed ru-

χοντα καὶ δικαστήν; τοῦτον ὁ θεὸς ᵖ ἄρχοντα καὶ λυτρωτὴν
ler and judge? him God [²as] ³ruler ⁴and ⁵deliverer

ᑫἀπέστειλεν ἐν∥ χειρὶ ἀγγέλου τοῦ ὀφθέντος αὐτῷ ἐν τῇ
¹sent by [the] hand of [the] angel who appeared to him in the

βάτῳ.. 36 οὗτος ἐξήγαγεν αὐτούς, ποιήσας τέρατα καὶ
bush. This one led out them, having wrought wonders and

σημεῖα ἐν ʳγῇ∥ ˢΑἰγύπτου∥ καὶ ἐν ἐρυθρᾷ θαλάσσῃ,
signs in [the] land of Egypt and in [the] Red Sea,

next day he shewed himself unto them as they strove, and would have set them at one again, saying, Sirs, ye are brethren; why do ye wrong one to another? 27 But he that did his neighbour wrong thrust him away, saying, Who made thee a ruler and a judge over us? 28 Wilt thou kill me, as thou diddest the Egyptian yesterday? 29 Then fled Moses at this saying, and was a stranger in the land of Madian, where he begat two sons. 30 And when forty years were expired, there appeared to him in the wilderness of mount Sina an angel of the Lord in a flame of fire in a bush. 31 When Moses saw it, he wondered at the sight: and as he drew near to behold it, the voice of the Lord came unto him, 32 saying, I am the God of thy fathers, the God of Abraham, and the God of Isaac, and the God of Jacob. Then Moses trembled, and durst not behold. 33 Then said the Lord to him, Put off thy shoes from thy feet: for the place where thou standest is holy ground. 34 I have seen, I have seen the affliction of my people which is in Egypt, and I have heard their groaning, and am come down to deliver them. And now come, I will send thee into Egypt. 35 This Moses whom they refused, saying, Who made thee a ruler and a judge? the same did God send to be a ruler and a deliverer by the hand of the angel which appeared to him in the bush. 36 He brought them out, after that he had shewed wonders and signs in the land of Egypt, and in the Red sea, and in the wil-

¹ δὲ EGW. ᵃ συνήλλασσεν LTTᵣW. ᵇ — ὑμεῖς (read ἐστε ye are) LTTᵣ[A]W. ᶜ ἵνα τί LᴛᴛᵣA. ᵈ ἡμῶν LTTᵣW. ᵉ ἐχθὲς LTTᵣA. ᶠ Μωϋσῆς GLTTᵣAW. ᵍ τεσσεράκοντα TTᵣA. ʰ — κυρίου LTTᵣA. ⁱ ἐθαύμαζεν GTAW. ᵏ — πρὸς αὐτόν LTTᵣA. ˡ ὁ θεὸς LTTᵣA. ᵐ ἐφ' LTTᵣA. ⁿ αὐτοῦ (read [their]) Lᴛᵣ. ° ἀποστελῶ LTTᵣAW. ᵖ + καὶ both Lᴛ[Tᵣ]A. ᑫ ἀπέσταλκεν σὺν has sent with LTTᵣAW. ʳ τῇ (read in Egypt) Lᴛᵣ. ˢ Αἰγύπτῳ GLTTᵣA.

Left column (Authorized Version):

derness forty years. 37 This is that Moses, which said unto the children of Israel, A prophet shall the Lord your God raise up unto you of your brethren, like unto me; him shall ye hear. 38 This is he, that was in the church in the wilderness with the angel which spake to him in the mount Sina, and with our fathers: who received the lively oracles to give unto us: 39 to whom our fathers would not obey, but thrust him from them, and in their hearts turned back again into Egypt, 40 saying unto Aaron, Make us gods to go before us: for as for this Moses, which brought us out of the land of Egypt, we wot not what is become of him. 41 And they made a calf in those days, and offered sacrifice unto the idol, and rejoiced in the works of their own hands. 42 Then God turned, and gave them up to worship the host of heaven; as it is written in the book of the prophets, O ye house of Israel, have ye offered to me slain beasts and sacrifices by the space of forty years in the wilderness? 43 Yea, ye took up the tabernacle of Moloch, and the star of your god Remphan, figures which ye made to worship them: and I will carry you away beyond Babylon. 44 Our fathers had the tabernacle of witness in the wilderness, as he had appointed, speaking unto Moses, that he should make it according to the fashion that he had seen. 45 Which also our fathers that came after brought in with Jesus into the possession of the Gentiles, whom God drave out before the face of our fathers,

Interlinear Greek with English gloss:

καὶ ἐν τῇ ἐρήμῳ ἔτη τεσσαράκοντα· 37 Οὗτός ἐστιν ὁ
and in the wilderness years forty. This is the

Μωϋσῆς ὁ εἰπὼν· τοῖς υἱοῖς Ἰσραήλ, Προφήτην ὑμῖν
Moses who said to the sons of Israel, A prophet to you

ἀναστήσει κύριος ὁ θεὸς ὑμῶν ἐκ τῶν ἀδελφῶν
will raise up the Lord God your from among brethren

ὑμῶν ὡς ἐμέ· αὐτοῦ ἀκούσεσθε. 38 Οὗτός ἐστιν ὁ γενό-
your like me, him ye shall hear. This is he who was

μενος ἐν τῇ ἐκκλησίᾳ ἐν τῇ ἐρήμῳ μετὰ τοῦ ἀγγέλου τοῦ
in the assembly in the wilderness with the angel who

λαλοῦντος αὐτῷ ἐν τῷ ὄρει Σινᾶ, καὶ τῶν πατέρων ἡμῶν,
spoke to him in the mount Sina, and with our fathers;

ὃς ἐδέξατο λόγια ζῶντα δοῦναι ἡμῖν· 39 ᾧ οὐκ ἠθέλησαν
who received oracles living to give to us: to whom would not

ὑπήκοοι γενέσθαι οἱ πατέρες ἡμῶν, ἀλλ᾽ ἀπώσαντο, καὶ
subject be our fathers, but thrust [him] away, and

ἐστράφησαν ταῖς καρδίαις αὐτῶν εἰς Αἴγυπτον, 40 εἰπόντες
turned back their hearts to Egypt, saying

τῷ Ἀαρών, Ποίησον ἡμῖν θεοὺς οἳ προπορεύσονται ἡμῶν·
to Aaron, Make us gods who shall go before us;

ὁ γὰρ Μωσῆς οὗτος ὃς ἐξήγαγεν ἡμᾶς ἐκ γῆς Αἰγύπ-
for Moses that who brought out us from [the] land of Egypt,

του, οὐκ οἴδαμεν τί γέγονεν αὐτῷ. 41 Καὶ ἐμοσχοποίησαν
we know not what has happened to him. And they made a calf

ἐν ταῖς ἡμέραις ἐκείναις, καὶ ἀνήγαγον θυσίαν τῷ εἰδώλῳ,
in those days, and offered sacrifice to the idol,

καὶ εὐφραίνοντο ἐν τοῖς ἔργοις τῶν χειρῶν αὐτῶν. 42 Ἔστρεψεν
and rejoiced in the works of their hands. Turned

δὲ ὁ θεὸς καὶ παρέδωκεν αὐτοὺς λατρεύειν τῇ στρατιᾷ τοῦ
but God and delivered up them to serve the host of the

οὐρανοῦ· καθὼς γέγραπται ἐν βίβλῳ τῶν προφητῶν,
heaven; as it has been written in [the] book of the prophets,

Μὴ σφάγια καὶ θυσίας προσηνέγκατέ μοι ἔτη τεσσαρά-
Slain beasts and sacrifices did ye offer to me years forty

κοντα ἐν τῇ ἐρήμῳ, οἶκος Ἰσραήλ; 43 καὶ ἀνελάβετε τὴν
in the wilderness, O house of Israel? And ye took up the

σκηνὴν τοῦ Μολόχ, καὶ τὸ ἄστρον τοῦ θεοῦ ὑμῶν Ῥεμφάν,
tabernacle of Moloch, and the star of your god Remphan,

τοὺς τύπους οὓς ἐποιήσατε προσκυνεῖν αὐτοῖς· καὶ μετοικιῶ
the models which ye made to worship them; and I will remove

ὑμᾶς ἐπέκεινα Βαβυλῶνος. 44 Ἡ σκηνὴ τοῦ μαρτυρίου ἦν
you beyond Babylon. The tabernacle of the testimony was

ἐν τοῖς πατράσιν ἡμῶν ἐν τῇ ἐρήμῳ, καθὼς διετάξατο
among our fathers in the wilderness, as commanded

ὁ λαλῶν τῷ Μωσῇ, ποιῆσαι αὐτὴν κατὰ τὸν τύπον
he who spoke to Moses, to make it according to the model

ὃν ἑωράκει· 45 ἣν καὶ εἰσήγαγον διαδεξάμενοι
which he had seen; which also brought in having received by succession

οἱ πατέρες ἡμῶν μετὰ Ἰησοῦ ἐν τῇ κατασχέσει τῶν ἐθνῶν,
our fathers with Joshua in the taking possession of the nations,

ὧν ἐξῶσεν ὁ θεὸς ἀπὸ προσώπου τῶν πατέρων ἡμῶν,
whom drove out God from [the] face of our fathers,

τεσσεράκοντα TTrA.   εἶπας LTTrA.   — κύριος LTTrA.   — ὑμῶν GLTTrA.
— αὐτοῦ ἀκούσεσθε LTTrA.   ἀλλὰ LTTrA.   + ἐν LTTrA.   Μωσῆς GLTTrAW.
ἐγένετο happened LTTrA.   — ὑμῶν (read the God) LTTrA.   Ῥεφάν Rephan LTrAW;
Ῥομφάν Romphan T.   — ἐν (read to our) LTTrA.   Μωϋσῇ GLTTrAW.   ἐξωσεν T.

ἕως τῶν ἡμερῶν ¹Δαβίδ·‖ 46 ὃς εὗρεν χάριν ἐνώπιον τοῦ
until the   days   of David;   who found   favour   before

θεοῦ, καὶ ᾐτήσατο εὑρεῖν σκήνωμα τῷ ᵐθεῷ‖ Ἰακώβ.
God, and   asked   to find a tabernacle for the   God   of Jacob;

47 ⁿΣολομῶν‖.δὲ ᵒᾠκοδόμησεν‖ αὐτῷ οἶκον. 48 Ἀλλ᾽ οὐχ ὁ
but Solomon   built   him   a house.   But ⁴not ¹the

ὕψιστος ἐν χειροποιήτοις ᴾναοῖς‖ κατοικεῖ, καθὼς ὁ προ-
²Most ³High in   hand-made   temples   dwells;   as the pro-

φήτης λέγει, 49 Ὁ οὐρανός μοι θρόνος ἡ.δὲ γῆ ὑπο-
phet says,   The heaven [is] to me a throne and the earth a foot-

πόδιον τῶν.ποδῶν.μου· ποῖον οἶκον οἰκοδομήσετέ μοι; λέγει
stool   of my feet: what house will ye build me? says

κύριος· ἢ τίς τόπος τῆς.καταπαύσεώς.μου; 50 οὐχὶ
[the] Lord, or what [the] place   of my rest?   ²not

ἡ.χείρ.μου ἐποίησεν ταῦτα πάντα; 51 σκληροτράχηλοι καὶ
³my ⁴hand ¹made ⁶these ⁷things ⁵all?   O stiffnecked   and

ἀπερίτμητοι �ۣτῇ καρδίᾳ‖ καὶ τοῖς ὠσίν, ὑμεῖς ἀεὶ τῷ πνεύματι
uncircumcised   in heart and   ears, ye always the Spirit

τῷ ἁγίῳ ἀντιπίπτετε, ʳὡς‖ οἱ.πατέρες.ὑμῶν, καὶ ὑμεῖς. 52 τίνα
the Holy resist;   as   your fathers, also ye.   Which

τῶν προφητῶν οὐκ.ἐδίωξαν οἱ.πατέρες.ὑμῶν; καὶ ἀπέ-
of the prophets did not ³persecute ¹your ²fathers? and they

κτειναν. τοὺς προκαταγγείλαντας περὶ τῆς ἐλεύσεως τοῦ
killed those who before announced concerning the coming of the

δικαίου, οὗ νῦν ὑμεῖς προδόται καὶ φονεῖς ˢγεγένησθε·‖
Just One, of whom now ye   betrayers and murderers have become!

53 οἵτινες ἐλάβετε τὸν νόμον εἰς διαταγὰς ἀγγέλων, καὶ
who   received the law by [the] disposition of angels, and

οὐκ.ἐφυλάξατε.
kept [it] not.

54 Ἀκούοντες.δὲ ταῦτα διεπρίοντο ταῖς.καρδίαις.αὐτῶν,
And hearing these things they were cut   to their hearts,

καὶ ἔβρυχον τοὺς ὀδόντας ἐπ᾽ αὐτόν. 55 Ὑπάρχων.δὲ πλήρης
and gnashed the   teeth at him.   But being full

πνεύματος ἁγίου, ἀτενίσας εἰς τὸν οὐρανόν, εἶδεν
of [the] ²Spirit ¹Holy, having looked intently into heaven, he saw

δόξαν θεοῦ, καὶ Ἰησοῦν ἑστῶτα ἐκ δεξιῶν τοῦ θεοῦ,
[the] glory of God, and Jesus standing at the right hand of God,

56 καὶ εἶπεν, Ἰδού, θεωρῶ τοὺς οὐρανοὺς ᵗἀνεῳγμένους,‖ καὶ
and said,   Lo, I behold the heavens opened,   and

τὸν υἱὸν τοῦ ἀνθρώπου ἐκ δεξιῶν ἑστῶτα τοῦ θεοῦ.
the Son of man ²at ³the ⁴right [⁵hand] ¹standing of God.

57 Κράξαντες.δὲ φωνῇ μεγάλῃ συνέσχον τὰ.ὦτα.αὐτῶν
And crying out with a ²voice ¹loud they held   their ears

καὶ ὥρμησαν ὁμοθυμαδὸν ἐπ᾽ αὐτόν, 58 καὶ ἐκβαλόντες
and rushed with one accord upon him,   and having cast [him]

ἔξω τῆς πόλεως ἐλιθοβόλουν. καὶ οἱ μάρτυρες ἀπέθεντο
out of the city   they stoned [him]. And the witnesses laid aside

τὰ.ἱμάτια.αὐτῶν παρὰ τοὺς πόδας νεανίου καλουμένου
their garments at   the   feet of a young man called

Σαύλον. 59 καὶ ἐλιθοβόλουν τὸν Στέφανον, ἐπικαλούμενον
Saul.   And they stoned the Stephen,   invoking

καὶ λέγοντα, Κύριε Ἰησοῦ, δέξαι τὸ.πνεῦμά.μου. 60 θεὶς.δὲ
and saying, Lord Jesus, receive my spirit. And having bowed

unto the days of Da-
vid; 46 who found fa
vour before God, and
desired to find a taber-
nacle for the God of
Jacob. 47 But Solo-
mon built him an
house. 48 Howbeit the
most High dwelleth
not in temples made
with hands; as saith
the prophet, 49 Heaven
is my throne, and earth
is my footstool: what
house will ye build me?
saith the Lord: or what
is the place of my rest?
50 Hath not my hand
made all these things?
51 Ye stiffnecked and
uncircumcised in heart
and ears, ye do always
resist the Holy Ghost:
as your fathers did, so
do ye. 52 Which of the
prophets have not your
fathers persecuted?
and they have slain
them which showed be-
fore of the coming of
the Just One; of whom
ye have been now the
betrayers and murder-
ers: 53 who have re-
ceived the law by the
disposition of angels,
and have not kept it.

54 When they heard
these things, they were
cut to the heart, and
they gnashed on him
with their teeth. 55 But
he, being full of the
Holy Ghost, looked up
stedfastly into heaven,
and saw the glory of
God, and Jesus stand-
ing on the right hand
of God, 56 and said,
Behold, I see the
heavens opened, and
the Son of man stand-
ing on the right hand
of God. 57 Then they
cried out with a loud
voice, and stopped their
ears, and ran upon
him with one accord,
58 and cast him out of
the city, and stoned
him: and the witnesses
laid down their clothes
at a young man's feet,
whose name was Saul.
59 And they stoned
Stephen, calling upon
God, and saying, Lord
Jesus, receive my spi-
rit. 60 And he kneeled

¹ Δανεὶδ LTTrA ; Δαυΐδ GW.   ᵐ οἴκῳ house LT.   ⁿ Σαλωμὼν T.   ᵒ οἰκοδόμησεν Tr.
ᴾ — ναοῖς (read [places]) GLTTrAW.   �ۣ καρδίαις hearts LTTr ; ταῖς καρδίαις W.   ʳ καθὼς Lᴇ
ˢ ἐγένεσθε became LTTrAW.   ᵗ διηνοιγμένους LTTrAW.

down, and cried with a loud voice, Lord, lay not this sin to their charge. And when he had said this, he fell asleep. VIII. And Saul was consenting unto his death.

And at that time there was a great persecution against the church which was at Jerusalem; and they were all scattered abroad throughout the regions of Judæa and Samaria, except the apostles. 2 And devout men carried Stephen to his burial, and made great lamentation over him. 3 As for Saul, he made havock of the church, entering into every house, and haling men and women committed them to prison.

4 Therefore they that were scattered abroad went every where preaching the word. 5 Then Philip went down to the city of Samaria, and preached Christ unto them. 6 And the people with one accord gave heed unto those things which Philip spake, hearing and seeing the miracles which he did. 7 For unclean spirits, crying with loud voice, came out of many that were possessed with them: and many taken with palsies, and that were lame, were healed. 8 And there was great joy in that city.

9 But there was a certain man, called Simon, which beforetime in the same city used sorcery, and bewitched the people of Samaria, giving out that himself was some great one: 10 to whom they all gave heed, from the least to the greatest, saying, This man is the great power of God. 11 And to him they had regard, because that of long time he had bewitched them with sorceries. 12 But when they believed Philip preaching the things concerning the

---

τὰ γόνατα ἔκραξεν φωνῇ μεγάλῃ, Κύριε, μὴ στήσῃς αὐτοῖς
the knees he cried with a voice loud, Lord, lay not to them
τὴν ἁμαρτίαν ταύτην. Καὶ τοῦτο εἰπὼν ἐκοιμήθη.
this sin. And this having said he fell asleep.

8 Σαῦλος δὲ ἦν συνευδοκῶν τῇ ἀναιρέσει αὐτοῦ.
And Saul was consenting to the killing of him.

Ἐγένετο δὲ ἐν ἐκείνῃ τῇ ἡμέρᾳ διωγμὸς μέγας ἐπὶ τὴν
And took place on that day a persecution great against the
ἐκκλησίαν τὴν ἐν Ἱεροσολύμοις· πάντες τε διεσπάρησαν
assembly which in Jerusalem, and all were scattered
κατὰ τὰς χώρας τῆς Ἰουδαίας καὶ Σαμαρείας· πλὴν τῶν
throughout the countries of Judæa and Samaria except the
ἀποστόλων. 2 συνεκόμισαν δὲ τὸν Στέφανον ἄνδρες εὐλαβεῖς,
apostles. And buried Stephen men pious,
καὶ ἐποιήσαντο κοπετὸν μέγαν ἐπ' αὐτῷ. 3 Σαῦλος δὲ
and made lamentation great over him. But Saul
ἐλυμαίνετο τὴν ἐκκλησίαν, κατὰ τοὺς οἴκους εἰσπορευόμενος,
was ravaging the assembly, house by house entering,
σύρων τε ἄνδρας καὶ γυναῖκας παρεδίδου εἰς φυλακήν.
and dragging men and women delivered [them] up to prison.

4 Οἱ μὲν οὖν διασπαρέντες διῆλθον, εὐαγγελιζό-
They who therefore had been scattered passed through, announcing the
μενοι τὸν λόγον. 5 Φίλιππος δὲ κατελθὼν εἰς πόλιν
glad tidings— the word. And Philip, going down to a city
τῆς Σαμαρείας ἐκήρυσσεν αὐτοῖς τὸν χριστόν. 6 προσεῖχόν
of Samaria, proclaimed to them the Christ; gave heed
τε οἱ ὄχλοι τοῖς λεγομένοις ὑπὸ τοῦ Φιλίππου ὁμο-
and the crowds to the things spoken by Philip with
θυμαδόν, ἐν τῷ ἀκούειν αὐτοὺς καὶ βλέπειν τὰ σημεῖα ἃ
one accord, when they heard and saw the signs which
ἐποίει. 7 πολλῶν γὰρ τῶν ἐχόντων πνεύματα ἀκά-
he did. For of many of those who had spirits un-
θαρτα, βοῶντα μεγάλῃ φωνῇ ἐξήρχετο· πολλοὶ δὲ
clean, crying with a loud voice they went out; and many
παραλελυμένοι καὶ χωλοὶ ἐθεραπεύθησαν. 8 καὶ ἐγένετο
having been paralysed and lame were healed. And was
χαρὰ μεγάλη ἐν τῇ πόλει ἐκείνῃ.
joy great in that city.

9 Ἀνὴρ δέ τις ὀνόματι Σίμων προϋπῆρχεν ἐν τῇ πόλει
But a certain man, by name Simon, was formerly in the city
μαγεύων καὶ ἐξιστῶν τὸ ἔθνος τῆς Σαμαρείας, λέγων
using magic arts and amazing the nation of Samaria, saying
εἶναί τινα ἑαυτὸν μέγαν· 10 ᾧ προσεῖχον πάντες
to be some himself great one. To whom they were giving heed all
ἀπὸ μικροῦ ἕως μεγάλου, λέγοντες, Οὗτός ἐστιν ἡ δύναμις
from small to great, saying, This one is the power
τοῦ θεοῦ ἡ μεγάλη. 11 Προσεῖχον δὲ αὐτῷ, διὰ
of God which [is] great. And they were giving heed to him, because
τὸ ἱκανῷ χρόνῳ ταῖς μαγείαις ἐξεστακέναι αὐτούς.
that for a long time with the magic arts [he] had amazed them.
12 Ὅτε δὲ ἐπίστευσαν τῷ Φιλίππῳ εὐαγγελιζομένῳ
But when they believed Philip announcing the glad tidings—

---

v ταύτην τὴν ἁμαρτίαν LTrAW. LTTrAW.   z + τὴν the (city) LT. ἐξήρχοντο (ἐξήρχετο G) GLTTrAW.   f + καλουμένη called GLTTrAW.

w δὲ LTrA; — τε T.   a δὲ LTTrAW.   d ἐγένετο δὲ πολλὴ χαρὰ LTTrA.

x Σαμαρίας T.   b πολλοὶ LTTrA.   e ἐξιστάνων LTTrA.

y ἐποίησαν LTTrAW.   c φωνῇ μεγάλῃ LTTrA.   g μαγίαις T.

[h]τὰ[||] περὶ τῆς βασιλείας τοῦ θεοῦ καὶ τοῦ ὀνόματος
the things concerning the kingdom of God and the name

[i]τοῦ[||] Ἰησοῦ χριστοῦ, ἐβαπτίζοντο ἄνδρες.τε καὶ γυναῖκες.
of Jesus Christ, they were baptized both men and women.

13 ὁ.δὲ.Σίμων καὶ αὐτὸς ἐπίστευσεν, καὶ βαπτισθεὶς ἦν
And Simon also himself believed, and having been baptized was

προσκαρτερῶν τῷ Φιλίππῳ· θεωρῶν τε [k]σημεῖα καὶ δυνά-
steadfastly continuing with Philip; ²beholding ¹and signs and ²works ³of

μεις μεγάλας γινομένας,[||] ἐξίστατο. 14 Ἀκούσαντες.δὲ οἱ
⁴power ¹great being done, was amazed. And ⁵having ⁶heard ¹the

ἐν Ἱεροσολύμοις ἀπόστολοι ὅτι δέδεκται ἡ [l]Σαμάρεια[||] τὸν
²in ¹Jerusalem ²apostles that ²had ³received ¹Samaria the

λόγον τοῦ θεοῦ, ἀπέστειλαν πρὸς αὐτοὺς [m]τὸν[||] Πέτρον καὶ
word of God, they sent to them Peter and

[n]Ἰωάννην·[||] 15 οἵτινες καταβάντες προσηύξαντο περὶ
John; who having come down prayed for

αὐτῶν, ὅπως λάβωσιν πνεῦμα ἅγιον. 16 [o]οὔπω[||].γὰρ
them, that they might receive [the] ²Spirit ¹Holy; for not yet

ἦν ἐπ᾽ οὐδενὶ· αὐτῶν ἐπιπεπτωκός, μόνον.δὲ βεβαπ-
was he upon any of them fallen, but only ³bap-
(lit. no one)

τισμένοι ὑπῆρχον εἰς τὸ ὄνομα τοῦ κυρίου Ἰησοῦ. 17 τότε
tized ¹they ²were to the name of the Lord Jesus. Then

[p]ἐπετίθουν[||] τὰς χεῖρας ἐπ᾽ αὐτούς, καὶ ἐλάμβανον πνεῦμα
they laid hands upon them, and they received [the] ²Spirit

ἅγιον. 18 [q]Θεασάμενος[||].δὲ ὁ Σίμων ὅτι διὰ τῆς ἐπιθέσεως
¹Holy. But ²having ³seen ¹Simon that by the laying on

τῶν χειρῶν τῶν ἀποστόλων δίδοται τὸ πνεῦμα [r]τὸ ἅγιον,[||]
of the hands of the apostles was given the Spirit the Holy,

προσήνεγκεν αὐτοῖς χρήματα, 19 λέγων, Δότε.καμοὶ τὴν
he offered to them riches, saying, Give also to me

ἐξουσίαν.ταύτην, ἵνα ᾧ.[s]ἄν[||] ἐπιθῶ τὰς χεῖρας, λαμ-
this authority, that on whomsoever I may lay hands, he may re-

βάνῃ πνεῦμα ἅγιον. 20 Πέτρος.δὲ εἶπεν πρὸς αὐτόν,
ceive [the] ²Spirit ¹Holy. But Peter said to him,

Τὸ.ἀργύριόν.σου σὺν σοὶ εἴη εἰς ἀπώλειαν· ὅτι τὴν
Thy money with thee may it be to destruction, because the

δωρεὰν τοῦ θεοῦ ἐνόμισας διὰ χρημάτων κτᾶσθαι. 21 οὐκ
gift of God thou didst think by riches to be obtained. ²Not

ἔστιν σοι μερὶς οὐδὲ κλῆρος ἐν τῷ.λόγῳ.τούτῳ· ἡ.γὰρ
⁴there ²is to thee part nor lot in this matter; for the

καρδία σου οὐκ.ἔστιν εὐθεῖα [t]ἐνώπιον[||] τοῦ θεοῦ. 22 μετανόη-
heart of thee is not right before God. Repent

σον οὖν ἀπὸ τῆς.κακίας.σου ταύτης, καὶ δεήθητι [v]τοῦ θεοῦ,[||]
therefore of ²thy ³wickedness ¹this, and supplicate God,

εἰ ἄρα· ἀφεθήσεταί σοι ἡ ἐπίνοια τῆς.καρδίας.σου. 23 εἰς
if indeed may be forgiven to thee the thought of thy heart; ²in

γὰρ χολὴν πικρίας καὶ σύνδεσμον ἀδικίας ὁρῶ σε
¹for a gall of bitterness and a bond of unrighteousness I see thee

ὄντα. 24 Ἀποκριθεὶς.δὲ ὁ Σίμων εἶπεν, Δεήθητε ὑμεῖς ὑπὲρ
to be. And ²answering ¹Simon said, Supplicate ye on behalf

ἐμοῦ πρὸς τὸν κύριον, ὅπως μηδὲν ἐπέλθῃ ἐπ᾽ ἐμὲ ὧν
of me to the Lord, so that nothing may come upon me of which

kingdom of God, and the name of Jesus Christ, they were baptized, both men and women. 13 Then Simon himself believed also: and when he was baptized, he continued with Philip, and wondered, beholding the miracles and signs which were done. 14 Now when the apostles which were at Jerusalem heard that Samaria had received the word of God, they sent unto them Peter and John: 15 who, when they were come down, prayed for them, that they might receive the Holy Ghost: 16 (for as yet he was fallen upon none of them: only they were baptized in the name of the Lord Jesus.) 17 Then laid they their hands on them, and they received the Holy Ghost. 18 And when Simon saw that through laying on of the apostles' hands the Holy Ghost was given, he offered them money, 19 saying, Give me also this power, that on whomsoever I lay hands, he may receive the Holy Ghost. 20 But Peter said unto him, Thy money perish with thee, because thou hast thought that the gift of God may be purchased with money. 21 Thou hast neither part nor lot in this matter: for thy heart is not right in the sight of God. 22 Repent therefore of this thy wickedness, and pray God, if perhaps the thought of thine heart may be forgiven thee. 23 For I perceive that thou art in the gall of bitterness, and in the bond of iniquity. 24 Then answered Simon, and said, Pray ye to the Lord for me, that none of these things which ye have spoken come upon me.

---

[h] — τὰ LTTrAW.   [i] — τοῦ GLTTrAW.   [k] δυνάμεις καὶ σημεῖα μεγάλα γινόμενα GW.
[l] Σαμαρία T.   [m] — τὸν LTTrAW.   [n] Ἰωάνην Tr.   [o] οὐδέπω LTTrAW.   [p] ἐπετίθεσαν
LTTrA   [q] ἰδὼν GLTTrAW.   [r] — τὸ ἅγιον T[Tr]A.   [s] ἐὰν BGLTTrAW.   [t] ἔναντι GLTTrAW.
[v] τοῦ κυρίου the Lord LTTrAW.

25 And they, when they had testified and preached the word of the Lord, returned to Jerusalem, and preached the gospel in many villages of the Samaritans.

26 And the angel of the Lord spake unto Philip, saying, Arise, and go toward the south unto the way that goeth down from Jerusalem unto Gaza, which is desert. 27 And he arose and went: and, behold, a man of Ethiopia, an eunuch of great authority under Candace queen of the Ethiopians, who had the charge of all her treasure, and had come to Jerusalem for to worship, 28 was returning, and sitting in his chariot read Esaias the prophet. 29 Then the Spirit said unto Philip, Go near, and join thyself to this chariot. 30 And Philip ran thither to him, and heard him read the prophet Esaias, and said, Understandest thou what thou readest? 31 And he said, How can I, except some man should guide me? And he desired Philip that he would come up and sit with him. 32 The place of the scripture which he read was this, He was led as a sheep to the slaughter; and like a lamb dumb before his shearer, so opened he not his mouth: 33 in his humiliation his judgment was taken away: and who shall declare his generation? for his life is taken from the earth. 34 And the eunuch answered Philip, and said, I pray thee, of whom speaketh the prophet this? of himself, or of some other man? 35 Then Philip opened his mouth, and began at the same

εἰρήκατε.   25 Οἱ μὲν οὖν   διαμαρτυράμενοι καὶ λαλή-
ye have spoken.   They   therefore having earnestly testified and having

σαντες τὸν λόγον τοῦ κυρίου, ʷὑπέστρεψαν‖ εἰς ˣἸερουσαλήμ,‖
spoken the word of the Lord,   returned   to   Jerusalem,

πολλάς.τε κώμας τῶν ʸΣαμαρειτῶν‖ ᶻεὐηγγελίσαντο.‖
and [to] many villages of the   Samaritans   announced the.glad tidings.

26 Ἄγγελος.δὲ κυρίου ἐλάλησεν πρὸς Φίλιππον, λέγων,
But an angel of [the] Lord- spoke   to   Philip,   saying,

Ἀνάστηθι καὶ ᵃπορεύου‖ κατὰ   μεσημβρίαν, ἐπὶ τὴν ὁδὸν
Rise up   and   go   towards [the]   south,   on the way

τὴν καταβαίνουσαν ἀπὸ Ἰερουσαλὴμ εἰς Γάζαν· αὕτη
which   goes down.   from Jerusalem to Gaza: the same

ἐστὶν ἔρημος. 27 καὶ ἀναστὰς ἐπορεύθη· καὶ ἰδού, ἀνὴρ
is   desert.   And having risen up he went. And lo,   a man

Αἰθίοψ εὐνοῦχος δυνάστης Κανδάκης ᵇτῆς‖ βασιλίσσης
an Ethiopian, a eunuch, one in power under Candace the   queen

Αἰθιόπων, ὃς ἦν ἐπὶ πάσης τῆς.γάζης.αὐτῆς, ᶜὃς‖
of [the] Ethiopians, who was over all   her treasure,   who

ἐληλύθει προσκυνήσων εἰς Ἰερουσαλήμ, 28 ἦν.τε ὑποστρέφων
had come   ³to ⁴worship   ¹to   ²Jerusalem,   and was returning

καὶ καθήμενος ἐπὶ τοῦ.ἅρματος.αὐτοῦ, ᵈκαὶ‖ ἀνεγίνωσκεν
and   sitting   in   his chariot,   and   he was reading

τὸν προφήτην Ἠσαΐαν. 29 εἶπεν.δὲ τὸ πνεῦμα τῷ Φιλίππῳ,
the   prophet   Esaias.   And said the Spirit   to Philip,

Πρόσελθε καὶ κολλήθητι τῷ.ἅρματι.τούτῳ. 30 Προσδραμὼν.δὲ
Go near   and join thyself   to this chariot.   And running up

ὁ Φίλιππος ἤκουσεν αὐτοῦ ἀναγινώσκοντος ᶠτὸν προφήτην
Philip   heard   him   reading   the   prophet

Ἠσαΐαν,‖ καὶ εἶπεν, ᵍἈρά.γε‖ γινώσκεις ἃ ἀναγινώσκεις;
Esaias,   and said, ³Then ¹dost ²thou   know   what   thou readest?

31 Ὁ.δὲ εἶπεν, Πῶς.γὰρ ἂν.δυναίμην ἐὰν.μή τις ʰὁδη-
But he said, [No,] for how   should I be able   unless   some one should

γήσῃ‖ με; Παρεκάλεσέν.τε τὸν Φίλιππον ἀναβάντα καθίσαι
guide me? And he besought   Philip   having come up to sit

σὺν αὐτῷ. 32 ἡ.δὲ περιοχὴ τῆς γραφῆς ἣν ἀνεγίνωσκεν
with him.   And the   passage of the scripture which he was reading

ἦν αὕτη, Ὡς πρόβατον ἐπὶ σφαγὴν ἤχθη, καὶ ὡς ἀμνὸς
was this, As   a sheep   to slaughter he was led, and as a lamb

ἐναντίον τοῦ ⁱκείροντος‖ αὐτὸν ἄφωνος, οὕτως οὐκ.ἀνοίγει
before him who shears   him [is] dumb,   thus   he opens not

τὸ.στόμα.αὐτοῦ. 33 ἐν τῇ.ταπεινώσει.ᵏαὐτοῦ‖ ἡ.κρίσις.αὐτοῦ
his mouth.   In   his humiliation   his judgment

ἤρθη, τὴν.ˡδὲ‖ γενεὰν αὐτοῦ τίς διηγήσεται; ὅτι
was taken away, and the generation of him who shall declare?   for

αἴρεται ἀπὸ τῆς γῆς ἡ.ζωὴ.αὐτοῦ. 34 Ἀποκριθεὶς.δὲ ὁ εὐνοῦχος
is taken from the earth   his life.   And answering the eunuch

τῷ Φιλίππῳ εἶπεν, Δέομαί σου, περὶ τίνος ὁ προφήτης
²to ³Philip ¹said,   I pray thee, concerning whom ²the   ³prophet

λέγει τοῦτο; περὶ ἑαυτοῦ, ἢ περὶ ἑτέρου.τινός;
¹says   this?   concerning himself, or concerning some other?

35 Ἀνοίξας.δὲ ὁ Φίλιππος τὸ.στόμα.αὐτοῦ, καὶ ἀρξάμενος
And ²having ³opened ¹Philip   his mouth,   and having begun

ʷ ὑπέστρεφον were returning LTTrAW.   ˣ Ἱεροσόλυμα LTTrA.   ʸ Σαμαριτῶν T.
ᶻ εὐηγγελίζοντο were announcing the glad tidings LTTrAW.   ᵃ πορεύθητι L.   ᵇ — τῆς
LTTrAW.   ᶜ — ὃς LT[Tr].   ᵈ — καὶ LT[Tr]W.   ᵉ +.τε, and L.   ᶠ Ἠσαΐαν τὸν προφήτην
LTTrA.   ᵍ ἄραγε GT.   ʰ ὁδηγήσει shall guide TTr.   ʲ κείραντος TA.   ᵏ αὐτοῦ
(read the humiliation) LTTr.   ˡ — δὲ and LTTr[A].

ἀπὸ τῆς.γραφῆς.ταύτης, εὐηγγελίσατο.αὐτῷ τὸν Ἰη-
from this scripture, announced to him the glad tidings— Je-
σοῦν. 36 ὡς.δὲ ἐπορεύοντο κατὰ τὴν ὁδόν, ἦλθον ἐπί
sus. And as they were going along the way, they came upon
τι ὕδωρ· καί φησιν ὁ εὐνοῦχος, Ἰδοὺ ὕδωρ· τί κωλύει
a certain water, and ³says ¹the ²eunuch, Behold water; what hinders
με βαπτισθῆναι; 37 ᵖΕἶπεν δὲ ὁ Φίλιππος, Εἰ πιστεύεις ἐξ
me to be baptized? And ²said ¹Philip, If thou believest from
ὅλης τῆς καρδίας, ἔξεστιν. Ἀποκριθεὶς.δὲ εἶπεν, Πιστεύω
²whole ¹the heart, it is lawful. And answering he said, I believe
τὸν υἱὸν τοῦ θεοῦ εἶναι τὸν Ἰησοῦν χριστόν.ǁ 38 Καὶ ἐκέλευ-
²the ⁶Son ⁷of ⁸God ³to ⁴be ¹Jesus ²Christ. And he com-
σεν στῆναι τὸ ἅρμα· καὶ κατέβησαν ἀμφότεροι εἰς
manded ³to ²stand ⁵still ¹the ²chariot. And they went down both to
τὸ ὕδωρ, ὅ.τε.Φίλιππος καὶ ὁ εὐνοῦχος· καὶ ἐβάπτισεν αὐτόν.
the water, both Philip and the eunuch, and he baptized him.
39 ὅτε.δὲ ἀνέβησαν ἐκ τοῦ ὕδατος πνεῦμα κυρίου
But when they came up out of the water [the] Spirit of [the] Lord
ἥρπασεν τὸν Φίλιππον· καὶ οὐκ εἶδεν αὐτὸν οὐκέτι ὁ
caught away Philip, and ³saw ⁴him ⁵no ⁶longer ¹the
εὐνοῦχος, ἐπορεύετο.γὰρ τὴν.ὁδὸν.αὐτοῦ χαίρων. 40 Φίλιππος
²eunuch, for he went his way rejoicing. ²Philip
δὲ εὑρέθη εἰς Ἄζωτον· καὶ διερχόμενος εὐηγ-
¹but was found at Azotus, and passing through he announced the
γελίζετο τὰς πόλεις πάσας, ἕως τοῦ.ἐλθεῖν.αὐτὸν εἰς
glad tidings [to] ²the ³cities ¹all, till he came to
ᵒΚαισάρειαν.ǁ
Cæsarea.

9 Ὁ.δὲ.Σαῦλος ἔτι ᵖἐμπνέωνǁ ἀπειλῆς καὶ φόνου εἰς
, But Saul, still breathing out threatenings and slaughter towards
τοὺς μαθητὰς τοῦ κυρίου, προσελθὼν τῷ ἀρχιερεῖ 2 ᾐτήσατο
the disciples of the Lord, having come to the high priest asked
παρ' αὐτοῦ ἐπιστολὰς εἰς Δαμασκὸν πρὸς τὰς συναγωγάς,
from him letters to Damascus, to the synagogues,
ὅπως ᑫἐάνǁ τινας εὕρῃ ʳτῆς ὁδοῦ ὄνταςǁ ἄνδρας.τε καὶ
so that if any he found ²of ³the ⁴way ¹being both men and
γυναῖκας, δεδεμένους ἀγάγῃ εἰς Ἱερουσαλήμ. 3 ἐν.δὲ
women, having bound he might bring [them] to Jerusalem. But in
τῷ πορεύεσθαι ἐγένετο αὐτὸν ἐγγίζειν τῇ Δαμασκῷ, ˢκαὶ
proceeding it came to pass he drew near to Damascus, and
ἐξαίφνηςǁ ᵗπεριήστραψεν αὐτὸνǂ φῶς ᵘἀπόǁ τοῦ οὐρανοῦ·
suddenly shone round about him a light from the heaven,
4 καὶ πεσὼν ἐπὶ τὴν γῆν ἤκουσεν φωνὴν λέγουσαν αὐτῷ,
and having fallen on the earth he heard a voice saying to him,
Σαούλ, Σαούλ, τί με διώκεις; 5 Εἶπεν.δέ, Τίς εἶʷ,
Saul, Saul, why me dost thou persecute? And he said, Who art thou,
κύριε; Ὁ.δὲ ˣκύριος εἶπεν,ǁ Ἐγώ εἰμι Ἰησοῦς ʸ ὃν σὺ
Lord? And the Lord said, I am Jesus whom thou
διώκεις· ᶻσκληρόν σοι πρὸς κέντρα λακτίζειν.
persecutest. [It is] hard for thee against [the] goads to kick.
6 Τρέμων.τε καὶ θαμβῶν εἶπεν, Κύριε, τί με θέλεις
And trembling and astonished he said, Lord, What me desirest thou

scripture,and preached unto him Jesus. 36 And as they went on *their* way, they came unto a certain water : and the eunuch said, See, *here is* water ; what doth hinder me to be baptized ? 37 And Philip said, If thou believest with all thine heart, thou mayest. And he answered and said, I believe that Jesus Christ is the Son of God. 38 And he commanded the chariot to stand still : and they went down both into the water, both Philip and the eunuch; and he baptized him. 39 And when they were come up out of the water, the Spirit of the Lord caught away Philip, that the eunuch saw him no more : and he went on his way rejoicing. 40 But Philip was found at Azotus : and passing through he preached in all the cities, till he came to Cæsarea.

IX. And Saul, yet breathing out threatenings and slaughter against the disciples of the Lord, went unto the high priest, 2 and desired of him letters to Damascus to the synagogues, that if he found any of this way, whether they were men or women, he might bring them bound unto Jerusalem. 3 And as he journeyed, he came near Damascus : and suddenly there shined round about him a light from heaven : 4 and he fell to the earth, and heard a voice saying unto him, Saul, Saul, why persecutest thou me ? 5 And he said, Who art thou, Lord ? And the Lord said, I am Jesus whom thou persecutest : *it is* hard for thee to kick against the pricks. 6 And he trembling and astonished said, Lord, what wilt thou have me to

---

ⁿ — *verse* 37 GLTTᵣA. ᵒ Καισαρίαν T. ᵖ ἐνπνέων T. ᑫ ἄν T. ʳ ὄντας τῆς ὁδοῦ, T.
ˢ ἐξαίφνης τε LTTᵣAW. ᵗ περιέστραψεν αὐτὸν E ; αὐτὸν περιέ- L ; αὐτὸν περιή- TTᵣAW.
ᵛ ἐκ out of LTTᵣW. ʷ + [σύ] A. ˣ — κύριος εἶπεν (read he [said]) LTTᵣAW. ʸ + ὁ
Ναζωραῖος the Nazarene [L]W. ᶻ — σκληρόν .... πρὸς αὐτόν (*verse* 6) GLTTᵣAW.

do? And the Lord said unto him, Arise, and go into the city, and it shall be told thee what thou must do. 7 And the men which journeyed with him stood speechless, hearing a voice, but seeing no man. 8 And Saul arose from the earth; and when his eyes were opened, he saw no man: but they led him by the hand, and brought him into Damascus. 9 And he was three days without sight, and neither did eat nor drink. 10 And there was a certain disciple at Damascus, named Ananias; and to him said the Lord in a vision, Ananias. And he said, Behold, I am here, Lord. 11 And the Lord said unto him, Arise, and go into the street which is called Straight, and inquire in the house of Judas for one called Saul, of Tarsus: for, behold, he prayeth, 12 and hath seen in a vision a man named Ananias coming in, and putting his hand on him, that he might receive his sight. 13 Then Ananias answered, Lord, I have heard by many of this man, how much evil he hath done to thy saints at Jerusalem: 14 and here he hath authority from the chief priests to bind all that call on thy name. 15 But the Lord said unto him, Go thy way: for he is a chosen vessel unto me, to bear my name before the Gentiles, and kings, and the children of Israel: 16 for I will shew him how great things he must suffer for my name's sake. 17 And Ananias went his way, and entered into the house; and putting his hands on him said, Brother Saul, the Lord,

ποιῆσαι; Καὶ ὁ κύριος πρὸς αὐτόν,‖ ª Ἀνάστηθι καὶ
to do? And the Lord [said] to him, Rise up and

εἴσελθε εἰς τὴν πόλιν, καὶ λαληθήσεταί σοι ᵇτί‖ σε δεῖ
enter into the city, and it shall be told thee what thee it behoves

ποιεῖν. 7 Οἱ δὲ ἄνδρες οἱ συνοδεύοντες αὐτῷ εἱστήκεισαν
to do. But the men who were travelling with him stood

ᶜἐννεοί,‖ ἀκούοντες μὲν τῆς φωνῆς μηδένα δὲ θεωροῦντες·
speechless, hearing indeed the voice but no one seeing.

8 ἠγέρθη δὲ ᵈὁ‖ Σαῦλος ἀπὸ τῆς γῆς· ᵉἀνεῳγμένων‖ δὲ τῶν
And rose up Saul from the earth, and having been opened

ὀφθαλμῶν αὐτοῦ ᶠοὐδένα‖ ἔβλεπεν. χειραγωγοῦντες δὲ αὐτὸν
his eyes no one he saw. But leading ²by ³the ⁴hand ¹him

εἰσήγαγον εἰς Δαμασκόν. 9 καὶ ἦν ἡμέρας τρεῖς μὴ βλέ-
they brought [him] to Damascus. And he was ²days ¹three ³not⁴ see-

πων, καὶ οὐκ ἔφαγεν οὐδὲ ἔπιεν. 10 Ἦν δέ τις μαθητὴς
ing, and did not eat nor drink. And there was a certain disciple

ἐν Δαμασκῷ ὀνόματι Ἀνανίας· καὶ εἶπεν πρὸς αὐτὸν ᵍὁ κύριος
in Damascus by name Ananias. And ³said ⁴to ⁵him ¹the ²Lord

ἐν ὁράματι,‖ Ἀνανία. Ὁ δὲ εἶπεν, Ἰδοὺ ἐγώ, κύριε.
in a vision, Ananias. And he said, Behold [here am] I, Lord.

11 Ὁ δὲ κύριος πρὸς αὐτόν, ʰ Ἀναστὰς‖ πορεύθητι ἐπὶ
And the Lord to him [said], Having risen up go into

τὴν ῥύμην τὴν καλουμένην Εὐθεῖαν, καὶ ζήτησον ἐν [the] house
the street which is called Straight, and seek in [the] house

Ἰούδα Σαῦλον ὀνόματι, Ταρσέα. ἰδοὺ γὰρ προσεύχεται,
of Judas [one] Saul by name, of Tarsus: for lo he prays,

12 καὶ εἶδεν ⁱἐν ὁράματι ἄνδρα ᵏὀνόματι Ἀνανίαν‖ εἰσελθόντα
and he saw in a vision a man by name Ananias coming

καὶ ἐπιθέντα αὐτῷ ˡχεῖρα,‖ ὅπως ἀναβλέψῃ. 13 Ἀπε-
and putting on him a hand, so that he should receive sight. An-

κρίθη δὲ ᵐὁ‖ Ἀνανίας, Κύριε, ⁿἀκήκοα‖ ἀπὸ πολλῶν περὶ
swered ¹and Ananias, Lord, I have heard from many concerning

τοῦ ἀνδρὸς τούτου, ὅσα κακὰ ᵒἐποίησεν τοῖς ἁγίοις σου‖ ἐν
this man, how many evils he did to thy saints in

Ἰερουσαλήμ· 14 καὶ ὧδε ἔχει ἐξουσίαν παρὰ τῶν ἀρχιερέων
Jerusalem; and here he has authority from the chief priests

δῆσαι πάντας τοὺς ἐπικαλουμένους τὸ ὄνομά σου. 15 Εἶπεν δὲ
to bind all who call on thy name. And ³said

πρὸς αὐτὸν ὁ κύριος, Πορεύου, ὅτι σκεῦος ἐκλογῆς ᴾμοι
⁴to ⁵him ¹the ²Lord, Go, for a vessel of election to me

ἐστιν‖ οὗτος, τοῦ βαστάσαι τὸ ὄνομά μου ἐνώπιον ᑫἐθνῶνʳ
is this [man], to bear my name before Gentiles

καὶ βασιλέων, υἱῶν τε Ἰσραήλ. 16 ἐγὼ γὰρ ὑποδείξω
and kings, and [the] sons of Israel: for I will shew

αὐτῷ ὅσα δεῖ αὐτὸν ὑπὲρ τοῦ ὀνόματός μου παθεῖν.
to him how much it behoves him for my name to suffer.

17 Ἀπῆλθεν δὲ Ἀνανίας καὶ εἰσῆλθεν εἰς τὴν οἰκίαν, καὶ
And ²went ³away ¹Ananias and entered into the house; and

ἐπιθεὶς ἐπ᾽ αὐτὸν τὰς χεῖρας εἶπεν, Σαοὺλ ἀδελφέ, ὁ
having laid upon him [his] hands he said, ²Saul ¹brother, the

ª + ἀλλὰ but GLTTrAW.   ᵇ ὅ τι LTTrA.   ᶜ ἐνεοί LTTrAW.   ᵈ - ὁ LTTrAW.   ᵉ ἠνεῳγ-
μένων LA; ἠνοιγμένων T.   ᶠ οὐδὲν nothing LTTrW.   ᵍ ἐν ὁράματι ὁ κύριος LTTrAW.
ʰ Ἀνάστα Rise up L.   ⁱ - ἐν ὁράματι ETrA; ἄνδρα [ἐν ὁράματι] Tr.   ᵏ Ἀνανίαν ὀνόματι
LTTrA.   ˡ τὰς (— τὰς TTr) χεῖρας the hands LTTr.   ᵐ - ὁ GLTTrAW.   ⁿ ἤκουσα I
heard LTTrA.   ᵒ τοῖς ἁγίοις σου ἐποίησεν LTTrA.   ᴾ ἐστίν μοι LTTrAW.   ᑫ + τῶν the L.
ʳ + τε both (Gentiles) LTTrAW.

κύριος ἀπέσταλκέν με, Ἰησοῦς ὁ ὀφθείς σοι ἐν τῇ ὁδῷ
Lord   has sent   me,   Jesus   who appeared to thee in   the   way

ᾗ ἤρχου, ὅπως ἀναβλέψῃς καὶ πλησθῇς πνεύ-
in which thou camest, that thou mightest receive sight and   be filled   with [the]

ματος ἁγίου. 18 Καὶ εὐθέως ˢἀπέπεσον ἀπὸ τῶν ὀφθαλμῶν
ˢSpirit ¹Holy.   And immediately   fell   from   ²eyes

αὐτοῦ‖ ᵗὡσεὶ‖ λεπίδες, ἀνέβλεψέν.τε ᵛπαραχρῆμα,‖ καὶ
¹his   as it were   scales,   and he received sight   instantly,   and

ἀναστὰς ἐβαπτίσθη, 19 καὶ λαβὼν τροφὴν ἐνίσχυσεν·
having risen up was baptized ;   and having taken   food   he was strengthened.

Ἐγένετο.δὲ ʷὁ Σαῦλος‖ μετὰ τῶν ἐν Δαμασκῷ μαθητῶν ἡμέρας
And ²was   ¹Saul   with the   ²in ³Damascus   ¹disciples   ⁵days

τινάς· 20 καὶ εὐθέως ἐν ταῖς συναγωγαῖς ἐκήρυσσεν
⁴certain.   And immediately in   the   synagogues   he was proclaiming

τὸν ˣχριστόν,‖ ὅτι οὗτός ἐστιν ὁ υἱὸς τοῦ θεοῦ. 21 ἐξίσταντο.δὲ
Christ,   that   he   is   the Son   of God.   And ²were ³amazed

πάντες οἱ ἀκούοντες, καὶ ἔλεγον, Οὐχ οὗτός ἐστιν ὁ πορθήσας
¹all   who   heard,   and said,   ²Not ³this   ¹is he who destroyed

ᵉ́ἐν‖ Ἱερουσαλὴμ τοὺς ἐπικαλουμένους τὸ.ὄνομα.τοῦτο, καὶ
in   Jerusalem   those who   called on   this name,   and

ὧδε εἰς τοῦτο ἐληλύθει ἵνα δεδεμένους αὐτοὺς ἀγάγῃ
here for   this   had come   that   ¹he ²might ³bring   them

ἐπὶ τοὺς ἀρχιερεῖς; 22 Σαῦλος.δὲ μᾶλλον ἐνεδυναμοῦτο, καὶ
to   the   chief priests ?   But Saul   more   increased in power, and

ᶻσυνέχυνεν‖ ᵃτοὺς‖ Ἰουδαίους τοὺς κατοικοῦντας ἐν Δαμασκῷ,
confounded   the   Jews   who   dwelt   in   Damascus,

συμβιβάζων ὅτι οὗτός ἐστιν ὁ χριστός. 23 ὡς.δὲ ἐπληροῦντο
proving   that   this   is   the   Christ.   Now when were fulfilled

ἡμέραι ἱκαναί, συνεβουλεύσαντο οἱ Ἰουδαῖοι ἀνελεῖν αὐ-
²days   ¹many,   ⁵consulted ⁶together   ³the   ⁴Jews   to put to death him.

τόν· 24 ἐγνώσθη.δὲ τῷ Σαύλῳ ἡ.ἐπιβουλὴ.αὐτῶν. ᵇπαρε-
But became known   to Saul   their plot.   ²They ³were

τήρουν‖ ᶜτε‖ τὰς πύλας ἡμέρας.τε καὶ νυκτός, ὅπως αὐτὸν
⁴watching ¹and the   gates   both day   and night,   that   him

ἀνέλωσιν· 25 λαβόντες.δὲ ᵈαὐτὸν οἱ μαθηταὶ‖ νυκτὸς
they might put to death ;   but taking   him   the disciples   by night

ᵉκαθῆκαν διὰ τοῦ τείχους‖ ᶠ, χαλάσαντες ἐν σπυρίδι.
let down ²through ³the   ⁴wall [¹him],   lowering   [him] in   a basket.

26 Παραγενόμενος.δὲ ᵍὁ Σαῦλος‖ ʰεἰς‖ Ἱερουσαλήμ, ⁱἐπει-
And ²having ³arrived   ¹Saul   at   Jerusalem,   he at-

ράτο‖ κολλᾶσθαι τοῖς μαθηταῖς· καὶ πάντες ἐφοβοῦντο
tempted to join himself to the   disciples,   and   all   were afraid of

αὐτόν, μὴ πιστεύοντες ὅτι ἐστὶν μαθητής. 27 Βαρνάβας.δὲ
him,   not   believing   that   he is   a disciple.   But Barnabas

ἐπιλαβόμενος αὐτόν, ἤγαγεν πρὸς τοὺς ἀποστόλους, καὶ
having taken   him,   brought [him] to   the   apostles,   and

διηγήσατο αὐτοῖς πῶς ἐν τῇ ὁδῷ εἶδεν τὸν κύριον, καὶ ὅτι
related   to them how   in the   way he saw the   Lord,   and that

ἐλάλησεν αὐτῷ, καὶ πῶς ἐν Δαμασκῷ ἐπαρρησιάσατο ἐν τῷ
he spoke   to him, and how in   Damascus   he spoke boldly   in   the

ὀνόματι ᵏτοῦ‖ Ἰησοῦ. 28 καὶ ἦν μετ᾽ αὐτῶν εἰσπορευόμενος
name   of Jesus.   And he was with   them   coming in

even Jesus, that appeared unto thee in the way as thou camest, hath sent me, that thou mightest receive thy sight, and be filled with the Holy Ghost. 18 And immediately there fell from his eyes as it had been scales : and he received sight forthwith, and arose, and was baptized. 19 And when he had received meat, he was strengthened. Then was Saul certain days with the disciples which were at Damascus. 20 And straightway he preached Christ in the synagogues, that he is the Son of God. 21 But all that heard *him* were amazed, and said ; Is not this he that destroyed them which called on this name in Jerusalem, and came hither for that intent, that he might bring them bound unto the chief priests ? 22 But Saul increased the more in strength, and confounded the Jews which dwelt at Damascus, proving that this is very Christ. 23 And after that many days were fulfilled, the Jews took counsel to kill him : 24 but their laying await was known of Saul. And they watched the gates day and night to kill him. 25 Then the disciples took him by night, and let *him* down by the wall in a basket.

26 And when Saul was come to Jerusalem, he assayed to join himself to the disciples : but they were all afraid of him, and believed not that he was a disciple. 27 But Barnabas took him, and brought *him* to the apostles, and declared unto them how he had seen the Lord in the way, and that he had spoken to him, and how he had preached boldly at Damascus in the name of Jesus. 28 And he was with them coming in and going out

---

ˢ ἀπέπεσαν αὐτοῦ ἀπὸ τῶν ὀφθαλμῶν LTTrA.   ᵗ ὡς LTTr.   ᵛ — παραχρῆμα GLTTrA.
ʷ — ὁ Σαῦλος (*read* he was) GLTTrAW.   ˣ Ἰησοῦν Jesus GLTTrAW.   ʸ εἰς at T.   ᶻ συν-
έχυννεν TA.   ᵃ — τοὺς T.   ᵇ παρετηροῦντο LTTrAW.   ᶜ δὲ καὶ and also LTTrA.   ᵈ —
μαθηταὶ αὐτοῦ his disciples LTTrA.   ᵉ διὰ τοῦ τείχους καθῆκαν LTTrA.   ᶠ + αὐτὸν him LTTrA.
ᵍ — ὁ Σαῦλος GLTTrAW.   ʰ ἐν in L.   ⁱ ἐπείραζεν LTTr.   ᵏ — τοῦ LTTrA.

at Jerusalem. 29 And he spake boldly in the name of the Lord Jesus, and disputed against the Grecians: but they went about to slay him. 30 Which when the brethren knew, they brought him down to Cæsarea, and sent him forth to Tarsus. 31 Then had the churches rest throughout all Judæa and Galilee and Samaria, and were edified; and walking in the fear of the Lord, and in the comfort of the Holy Ghost, were multiplied.

καὶ ἐκπορευόμενος ¹ἐν¹¹ Ἱερουσαλήμ. ᵐκαὶ¹¹ παῤῥησιαζόμενος
and   going out   in   Jerusalem,   and   speaking boldly
ἐν τῷ ὀνόματι τοῦ κυρίου ⁿἸησοῦ·¹¹ 29 ἐλάλει.τε καὶ συνεζήτει
in the name   of the Lord   Jesus.   And he spoke and discussed
πρὸς τοὺς Ἑλληνιστάς· οἱ.δὲ ἐπεχείρουν °αὐτὸν   ἀνε-
with the   Hellenists ;   but they took in hand ³him   ¹to ²put to
λεῖν.¹¹ 30 ἐπιγνόντες.δὲ οἱ ἀδελφοὶ κατήγαγον αὐτὸν εἰς
death.   But having known [it] the brethren brought down him to
ᴾΚαισάρειαν,¹¹ καὶ ἐξαπέστειλαν ᑫαὐτὸν¹¹ εἰς Ταρσόν. 31 ʳΑἱ¹
Cæsarea,   and   sent away   him   to Tarsus.   The
μὲν οὖν ˢἐκκλησίαι¹¹ καθ᾽ ὅλης τῆς Ἰουδαίας καὶ Γαλι-
²indeed ³then ¹assemblies throughout ²whole ¹the of Judæa and Gali-
λαίας καὶ ᵗΣαμαρείας¹¹ ᵛεἶχον¹¹ εἰρήνην, ʷοἰκοδομούμεναι καὶ
lee and Samaria   had   peace,   being built up and
πορευόμεναι¹¹ τῷ φόβῳ τοῦ κυρίου, καὶ τῇ παρακλήσει τοῦ
going on   in the fear of the Lord, and in the comfort of the
ἁγίου πνεύματος ˣἐπληθύνοντο.¹¹
Holy   Spirit   were increased.

32 And it came to pass, as Peter passed throughout all quarters, he came down also to the saints which dwelt at Lydda. 33 And there he found a certain man named Æneas, which had kept his bed eight years, and was sick of the palsy. 34 And Peter said unto him, Æneas, Jesus Christ maketh thee whole: arise, and make thy bed. And he arose immediately. 35 And all that dwelt at Lydda and Saron saw him, and turned to the Lord.

32 Ἐγένετο.δὲ   Πέτρον διερχόμενον διὰ πάντων,
Now it came to pass [that] Peter, passing   through all
κατελθεῖν καὶ πρὸς τοὺς ἁγίους τοὺς κατοικοῦντας
[quarters], went down also to the saints that   inhabited
ʸΛύδδαν.¹¹ 33 εὗρεν.δὲ ἐκεῖ ἄνθρωπόν.τινα ᶻΑἰνέα ὀνόματι,¹¹
Lydda,   And he found there a certain man,   Æneas by name,
ἐξ ἐτῶν ὀκτὼ κατακείμενον ἐπὶ ᵃκραββάτῳ,¹¹ ὃς ἦν παρα-
for ²years ¹eight lying   on   a couch, who was para-
λελυμένος. 34 καὶ εἶπεν αὐτῷ ὁ Πέτρος, Αἰνέα, ἰαταί σε
lysed.   And ²said ³to ¹him ¹Peter, Æneas, ⁴heals ⁵thee
Ἰησοῦς ᵇὁ¹¹ χριστός· ἀνάστηθι καὶ στρῶσον   σεαυτῷ.
¹Jesus ²the ³Christ ; rise up,   and spread [a couch] for thyself.
Καὶ εὐθέως ἀνέστη· 35 καὶ ᶜεἶδον¹¹ αὐτὸν πάντες οἱ
And immediately he rose up. And ⁵saw   him   all those
κατοικοῦντες ʸΛύδδαν¹¹ καὶ τὸν ᵈΣαρωνᾶν,¹¹ οἵτινες ἐπέστρεψαν
inhabiting   Lydda   and the Saron,   who   turned
ἐπὶ τὸν κύριον.
to the Lord.

36 Now there was at Joppa a certain disciple named Tabitha, which by interpretation is called Dorcas: this woman was full of good works and almsdeeds which she did. 37 And it came to pass in those days, that she was sick, and died: whom when they had washed, they laid her in an upper chamber. 38 And forasmuch as Lydda was nigh to Joppa, and the disciples had heard that Peter was there, they sent unto him two men, desiring him that he

36 Ἐν.Ἰόππῃ.δὲ τις   ἦν μαθήτρια ὀνόματι Ταβιθά,
And in Joppa ²a ³certain ¹was disciple, by name   Tabitha,
ἣ διερμηνευομένη λέγεται Δορκάς· αὕτη ἦν πλήρης ᵉἀγαθῶν
which being interpreted is called Dorcas, She was full   of good
ἔργων¹¹ καὶ ἐλεημοσυνῶν ὧν ἐποίει· 37 ἐγένετο.δὲ ἐν ταῖς
works and of alms   which she did. And it came to pass in
ἡμέραις.ἐκείναις ἀσθενήσασαν αὐτὴν ἀποθανεῖν· λούσαν-
those days   [that] having sickened she died ;   ²having
τες δὲ ᶠαὐτὴν ἔθηκαν¹¹ ἐν ᵍ ὑπερῴῳ. 38 ἐγγὺς.δὲ
³washed ¹and her they put [her] in an upper room. And ²near
οὔσης ʰΛύδδης¹¹ τῇ Ἰόππῃ, οἱ μαθηταὶ ἀκούσαντες ὅτι Πέτρος
¹being ¹Lydda to Joppa, the disciples having heard that Peter
ἐστὶν ἐν αὐτῇ ἀπέστειλαν δύο ἄνδρας πρὸς αὐτόν, παρα-
is   in it   sent   two men   to him,   beseech-

---

¹ εἰς at LTTrAW.   ᵐ — καὶ LTTrA.   ⁿ — Ἰησοῦ LTTrAW.   ° ἀνελεῖν αὐτόν LTTrAW.
ᴾ Καισαρίαν T.   ᑫ — αὐτὸν L.   ʳ Ἡ LTTrAW.   ˢ ἐκκλησία assembly LTTrAW.
ᵗ Σαμαρίας T.   ᵛ εἶχεν LTTrAW.   ʷ οἰκοδομουμένη καὶ πορευομένη LTTrAW.   ˣ ἐπλη-
θίνετο was increased LTTrAW.   ʸ Λύδδα LTTrA.   ᶻ ὀνόματι Αἰνέαν LTTrAW.   ᵃ κραβάττου
LTTrAW.   ᵇ — ὁ LTTrW.   ᶜ εἶδαν LTTrA.   ᵈ Σάρωνα EGLTTrAW.   ᵉ ἔργων ἀγαθῶν LTrW;
ᶠ ἔθηκαν αὐτὴν TTr.   ᵍ + τῷ the L.   ʰ Λύδδας TTrA.

καλοῦντες ¹μὴ ὀκνῆσαι‖ διελθεῖν ἕως ᵏαὐτῶν.‖ 39 ἀναστὰς
ing   [him] not to delay   to come to them. ²Having ³risen ⁴up

δὲ Πέτρος συνῆλθεν αὐτοῖς· ὃν παραγενόμενον ἀνήγαγον
¹and· Peter went with them, whom, having arrived they brought

εἰς τὸ ὑπερῷον, καὶ παρέστησαν αὐτῷ πᾶσαι αἱ χῆραι
into the upper room, and   stood by   him   all   the widows

κλαίουσαι καὶ ἐπιδεικνύμεναι χιτῶνας καὶ ἱμάτια ὅσα ἐ-
weeping   and   shewing   tunics   and garments which ²was

ποίει μετ' αὐτῶν οὖσα ἡ Δορκάς. 40 ἐκβαλὼν δὲ ἔξω πάντας
³making ⁶with ⁶them ⁴being ¹Dorcas. But ²having ³put ⁵out ⁴all

ὁ Πέτρος, ¹ θεὶς τὰ γόνατα προσηύξατο· καὶ ἐπιστρέψας
¹Peter, having bowed the knees   he prayed.   And having turned

πρὸς τὸ σῶμα εἶπεν, Ταβιθά, ἀνάστηθι. Ἡ δὲ ἤνοιξεν
to the body he said, Tabitha, Arise.   And she opened

τοὺς ὀφθαλμοὺς αὐτῆς· καὶ ἰδοῦσα τὸν Πέτρον ἀνεκάθισεν·
her eyes,   and seeing   Peter   she sat up.

41 δοὺς δὲ αὐτῇ χεῖρα ἀνέστησεν αὐτήν, φωνήσας δὲ
And having given her [his] hand he raised up her,   and having called

τοὺς ἁγίους καὶ τὰς χήρας παρέστησεν αὐτὴν ζῶσαν. 42 γνω-
the saints and the widows he presented her living.   ⁴Known

στὸν δὲ ἐγένετο καθ' ὅλης ᵐτῆς‖ Ἰόππης, καὶ ⁿπολλοὶ
¹and ²it ³became throughout ⁴whole ¹the of Joppa, and   many

ἐπίστευσαν‖ ἐπὶ τὸν κύριον· 43 ἐγένετο δὲ ᵒἡμέρας
believed   on the Lord. And it came to pass [that] ⁴days

ἱκανὰς μεῖναι αὐτὸν‖ ἐν Ἰόππῃ παρά τινι Σίμωνι βυρσεῖ.
³many ²abode ¹he in Joppa with a certain Simon a tanner.

10 Ἀνὴρ δέ τις ᵖἦν‖ ἐν ᑫΚαισαρείᾳ‖ ὀνόματι Κορνήλιος,
But a certain man was in Cæsarea   by name   Cornelius,

ἑκατοντάρχης ἐκ σπείρης τῆς καλουμένης Ἰταλικῆς, 2 εὐ-
a centurion of a band which is called   Italic,   ²pious

σεβὴς καὶ φοβούμενος τὸν θεὸν σὺν παντὶ τῷ οἴκῳ αὐτοῦ,
and   fearing   God with all   his house,

ποιῶν ʳτε‖ ἐλεημοσύνας πολλὰς τῷ λαῷ, καὶ δεόμενος
both doing ²alms   ¹much to the people, and supplicating

τοῦ θεοῦ ˢδιαπαντός.‖ 3 εἶδεν ἐν ὁράματι φανερῶς, ὡσεὶ·
God   continually, He saw in a vision plainly, about

ὥραν ᵗἐννάτην‖ τῆς ἡμέρας, ἄγγελον τοῦ θεοῦ εἰσελθόντα
³hour ⁴the ²ninth of the day, an angel of God coming

πρὸς αὐτόν, καὶ εἰπόντα αὐτῷ, Κορνήλιε. 4 Ὁ δὲ ἀτε-
to him, and saying to him, Cornelius. But he having looked

νίσας αὐτῷ καὶ ἔμφοβος γενόμενος εἶπεν, Τί ἐστιν, κύριε;
intently on him and ²afraid ¹becoming said, What is it, Lord?

εἶπεν δὲ αὐτῷ, Αἱ προσευχαί σου καὶ αἱ ἐλεημοσύναι σου
And he said to him, Thy prayers   and   thine alms

ἀνέβησαν εἰς μνημόσυνον ʷἐνώπιον‖ τοῦ θεοῦ. 5 καὶ νῦν
are gone up for a memorial   before   God.   And now

πέμψον ˣεἰς Ἰόππην ἄνδρας,‖ καὶ μετάπεμψαι Σίμωνα ʸ ὃς
send ²to ³Joppa ¹men,   and send for   Simon who

ἐπικαλεῖται Πέτρος· 6 οὗτος ξενίζεται παρά τινι Σίμωνι
is surnamed   Peter. He lodges   with ¹a certain Simon

βυρσεῖ, ᾧ ἐστιν οἰκία παρὰ θάλασσαν· ᶻοὗτος λαλήσει σοι
³tanner, whose ²is ¹house by [the] sea;   he shall tell thee

ⁱ μὴ ὀκνήσῃς delay not LTTrAW. ᵏ ἡμῶν us LTTrAW. ¹ + καὶ and LTTrAW. ᵐ [τῆς] Tr.
ⁿ ἐπίστευσαν πολλοὶ LTTrAW. ᵒ αὐτὸν ἡμέρας ἱκανὰς μεῖναι LTr; — αὐτὸν T. ᵖ — ἦν
GLTTrAW. ᑫ Καισαρίᾳ T. ʳ — τε LTTrA. ˢ διὰ παντός LTrA. · ᵗ + περὶ LTTrAW.
ᵛ ἐνάτην LTTrAW. ʷ ἔμπροσθεν LTTrA. ˣ ἄνδρας εἰς Ἰόππην LTTrAW. ʸ + τινα a certain
(Simon) LTTrA. ᶻ — οὗτος λαλήσει σοι τί σε δεῖ ποιεῖν GLTTrAW.

would not delay to come to them. 39 Then Peter arose and went with them. When he was come, they brought him into the upper chamber: and all the widows stood by him weeping, and shewing the coats and garments which Dorcas made, while she was with them. 40 But Peter put them all forth, and kneeled down, and prayed; and turning him to the body said, Tabitha, arise. And she opened her eyes: and when she saw Peter, she sat up. 41 And he gave her his hand, and lifted her up, and when he had called the saints and widows, presented her alive. 42 And it was known throughout all Joppa; and many believed in the Lord. 43 And it came to pass, that he tarried many days in Joppa with one Simon a tanner.

X. There was a certain man in Cæsarea called Cornelius, a centurion of the band called the Italian band, 2 a devout man, and one that feared God with all his house, which gave much alms to the people, and prayed to God alway. 3 He saw in a vision evidently about the ninth hour of the day an angel of God coming in to him, and saying unto him, Cornelius. 4 And when he looked on him, he was afraid, and said, What is it, Lord? And he said unto him, Thy prayers and thine alms are come up for a memorial before God. 5 And now send men to Joppa, and call for one Simon, whose surname is Peter: 6 he lodgeth with one Simon a tanner, whose house is by the sea side: he shall tell thee what thou. oughtest to do. 7 And when the angel which spake unto Cornelius was departed, he called two of his household servants, and a devout soldier of them that waited on him continually; 8 and when he had declared all *these* things unto them, he sent them to Joppa. 9 On the morrow, as they went on their journey, and drew nigh unto the city, Peter went up upon the housetop to pray about the sixth hour: 10 and he became very hungry, and would have eaten : but while they made ready, he fell into a trance, 11 and saw heaven opened, and a certain vessel descending unto him, as it had been a great sheet knit at the four corners, and let down to the earth : 12 wherein were all manner of fourfooted beasts of the earth, and wild beasts, and creeping things, and fowls of the air. 13 And there came a voice to him, Rise, Peter; kill, and eat. 14 But Peter said, Not so, Lord ; for I have never eaten any thing that is common or unclean. 15 And the voice *spake* unto him again the second time, What God hath cleansed, *that* call not thou common. 16 This was done thrice : and the vessel was received up again into heaven. 17 Now while Peter doubted in himself what this vision which he had seen should mean, behold, the men which were sent from Cornelius had made inquiry for Simon's house, and stood before the gate, 18 and called, and asked whether Simon, which was surnamed Peter, were lodged there. 19 While Peter thought on the vision, the Spirit said unto him, Be-

---

τί σε δεῖ ποιεῖν.‖ 7 Ὡς.δὲ ἀπῆλθεν ὁ ἄγγελος ὁ
what ³thee ¹it ²behoves to do.   And when ²departed ¹the ²angel who

λαλῶν ªτῷ Κορνηλίῳ,‖ φωνήσας δύο τῶν.οἰκετῶν.ᵇαὐτοῦ,‖
spoke   to Cornelius, having called two   of his servants,

καὶ στρατιώτην εὐσεβῆ τῶν προσκαρτερούντων αὐτῷ, 8 καὶ
and a ²soldier ¹pious of those continually waiting on him, and

ἐξηγησάμενος ᶜαὐτοῖς ἅπαντα‖ ἀπέστειλεν αὐτοὺς· εἰς τὴν
having related to them all things he sent them to

Ἰόππην. 9 Τῇ.δὲ ἐπαύριον ὁδοιπορούντων ᵈἐκείνων‖ καὶ
Joppa. And on the morrow, as ²are ³journeying ¹these and

τῇ πόλει ἐγγιζόντων, ἀνέβη Πέτρος ἐπὶ τὸ δῶμα προσ-
to the city drawing near, ²went ³up ¹Peter ⸍ on the housetop to

εὔξασθαι, περὶ ὥραν ἕκτην. 10 ἐγένετο.δὲ πρόσπεινος,
pray,   about ³hour ¹the ²sixth.   And he became very hungry,

καὶ ἤθελεν γεύσασθαι· παρασκευαζόντων.δὲ ᵉἐκείνων‖ ἐπέ-
and wished to eat. But as ²were ³making ⁴ready ¹they ⁷fell

πεσεν‖ ἐπ᾽ αὐτὸν ἔκστασις, 11 καὶ θεωρεῖ τὸν οὐρανὸν ἀνεῳγ-
⁵upon ⁹him ⁵a ⁶trance, and he beholds the heaven opened,

μένον, καὶ καταβαῖνον ᵍἐπ᾽ αὐτὸν‖ σκεῦός τι ὡς ὀθόνην
and descending upon him a ²vessel ¹certain, as a ²sheet

μεγάλην, τέσσαρσιν ἀρχαῖς ʰδεδεμένον,. καὶ‖ καθιέμενον ἐπὶ
¹great, by four corners bound, and let down upon

τῆς γῆς· 12 ἐν ᾧ ὑπῆρχεν πάντα τὰ τετράποδα ⁱτῆς γῆς
the earth ; in which were all the quadrupeds of the earth

καὶ τὰ θηρία καὶ τὰ ἑρπετὰ‖ καὶ ᵏτὰ‖ πετεινὰ τοῦ οὐ-
and the wild beasts and the creeping things and the birds of the hea-

ρανοῦ. 13 καὶ ἐγένετο φωνὴ πρὸς αὐτόν, Ἀναστάς, Πέτρε,
ven. And came a voice to him, Having risen up, Peter,

θῦσον καὶ φάγε. 14 Ὁ.δὲ.Πέτρος εἶπεν, Μηδαμῶς, κύριε· ὅτι
kill and eat. But Peter said, In no wise, Lord; for

οὐδέποτε ἔφαγον πᾶν κοινὸν ˡἢ‖ ἀκάθαρτον. 15 Καὶ φωνὴ
never did I eat anything common or unclean.   And a voice

πάλιν ἐκ.δευτέρου πρὸς αὐτόν, Ἃ ὁ θεὸς ᵐἐκαθάρισεν,‖
[came] again the second time to him, What God cleansed,

σὺ μὴ κοίνου. 16 Τοῦτο.δὲ ἐγένετο ἐπὶ.τρίς· καὶ ⁿπάλιν‖
²thou ²not ¹make common. And this took place thrice, and again

ᵒἀνελήφθη‖ τὸ σκεῦος εἰς τὸν οὐρανόν. 17 Ὡς.δὲ ἐν ἑαυτῷ
was taken up the vessel into the heaven.   And as ⁴in ⁵himself

διηπόρει ὁ Πέτρος τί ἂν.εἴη τὸ ὅραμα ὃ εἶδεν, ᴾκαὶ‖
²was ³perplexed ¹Peter what might be the vision which he saw, ²also

ἰδού, οἱ ἄνδρες οἱ ἀπεσταλμένοι �q ἀπὸ‖ τοῦ Κορνηλίου, διε-
¹behold, the men who were sent from Cornelius, having

ρωτήσαντες τὴν οἰκίαν ʳ Σίμωνος, ἐπέστησαν ἐπὶ τὸν πυλῶνα·
inquired for the house of Simon, stood at the porch ;

18 καὶ φωνήσαντες ἐπυνθάνοντο εἰ Σίμων ὁ ἐπικαλού-
and having called out they asked if Simon who [is] surnamed

μενος Πέτρος ἐνθάδε ξενίζεται. 19 Τοῦ.δὲ.Πέτρου ˢἐνθυμου-
Peter ²here ¹lodges.   But as Peter was think-

μένου‖ περὶ τοῦ ὁράματος, εἶπεν ᵗαὐτῷ τὸ πνεῦμα,‖ Ἰδού,
ing over the vision, ³said ⁴to ⁵him ¹the ²Spirit, Behold,

ª αὐτῷ to him GLTTrAW.   ᵇ — αὐτοῦ (*read* of the servants) LTTrAW.   ᶜ ἅπαντα αὐτοῖς LTTrA.   ᵈ αὐτῶν they T.   ᵉ αὐτῶν LTTrA.   ᶠ ἐγένετο came LTTrAW.   ᵍ — ἐπ᾽ αὐτὸν GLTTrAW.   ʰ — δεδεμένον καὶ LTTr[A].   ⁱ καὶ τὰ (— τὰ LTTrA) ἑρπετὰ τῆς γῆς LTTrAW.   ᵏ — τὰ LTTrA.   ˡ καὶ and LTTrA.   ᵐ ἐκαθάρισεν Tr.   ⁿ εὐθὺς immediately LTTrAW.   ᵒ ἀνελήμφθη LTTrA.   ᴾ — καὶ LTTr[A].   �q ὑπὸ T.   ʳ + τοῦ LTTrAW.   ˢ διενθυμουμένου was pondering GLTTrAW.   ᵗ τὸ πνεῦμα αὐτῷ LTTrA.

ἄνδρες ᵛτρεῖς‖ ʷζητοῦσίν‖ σε· 20 ἀλλὰ ἀναστὰς κατάβηθι,
ˢmen ¹three seek thee; but having risen go down,

καὶ πορεύου σὺν αὐτοῖς, μηδὲν διακρινόμενος· ˣδιότι‖ ἐγὼ
and proceed with them, nothing doubting, because I

ἀπέσταλκα αὐτούς. 21 Καταβὰς.δὲ Πέτρος πρὸς τοὺς
have sent them. And ²having ³gone ⁴down ¹Peter to the

ἄνδρας ʸτοὺς ἀπεσταλμένους ἀπὸ τοῦ Κορνηλίου πρὸς αὐτόν,‖
men who were sent from Cornelius to him,

εἶπεν, Ἰδού, ἐγώ εἰμι ὃν ζητεῖτε· τίς ἡ αἰτία δι᾽ ἣν
said, Behold, I am whom ye seek; what [is] the cause for which

πάρεστε; 22 οἱ.δὲ ᶻεἶπον,‖ Κορνήλιος ἑκατοντάρχης, ἀνὴρ
ye are come? And they said, Cornelius a centurion, a ²man

δίκαιος καὶ φοβούμενος τὸν θεόν, μαρτυρούμενός.τε ὑπὸ ὅλου
¹righteous and fearing God, and borne witness to by ²whole

τοῦ ἔθνους τῶν Ἰουδαίων, ἐχρηματίσθη ὑπὸ ἀγγέλου
¹the nation of the Jews, was divinely instructed by ³angel

ἁγίου, μεταπέμψασθαί σε εἰς τὸν.οἶκον.αὐτοῦ, καὶ ἀκοῦσαι
¹a ²holy, to send for thee to his house, and to hear

ῥήματα παρὰ σοῦ. 23 Εἰσκαλεσάμενος οὖν αὐτοὺς ἐξένισεν.
words from thee. Having called ²in ³therefore ¹them he lodged

Τῇ.δὲ ἐπαύριον ᵃὁ Πέτρος‖ ἐξῆλθεν σὺν αὐτοῖς, καί
[them]. And on the morrow Peter went forth with them, and

τινες τῶν ἀδελφῶν τῶν ἀπὸ ᵇτῆς‖ Ἰόππης συνῆλθον αὐτῷ.
certain of the brethren those from Joppa went with him.

24 ᶜκαὶ τῇ‖ ἐπαύριον ᵈεἰσῆλθον‖ εἰς τὴν ᵉΚαισάρειαν·‖
And on the morrow they entered into Cæsarea.

ὁ.δὲ.Κορνήλιος ἦν προσδοκῶν αὐτούς, ᶠσυγκαλεσάμενος‖ τοὺς
And Cornelius was expecting them, having called together

συγγενεῖς.αὐτοῦ καὶ τοὺς ἀναγκαίους φίλους. 25 Ὡς.δὲ
his kinsmen and intimate friends. And as

ἐγένετο ᵍ εἰσελθεῖν τὸν Πέτρον, συναντήσας αὐτῷ ὁ Κορνήλιος,
²was ³coming ⁴in ¹Peter, having ⁷met ⁸him ⁵Cornelius,

πεσὼν ἐπὶ τοὺς πόδας προσεκύνησεν. 26 ὁ.δὲ.Πέτρος
having fallen at [his] feet did homage. But Peter

ᵇαὐτὸν ἤγειρεν,‖ λέγων, Ἀνάστηθι· ¹κἀγὼ‖ αὐτὸς ἄνθρωπός
²him ¹raised, saying, Rise up: I also myself a man

εἰμι. 27 Καὶ συνομιλῶν αὐτῷ εἰσῆλθεν, καὶ εὑρίσκει συνελη-
am. And talking with him he went in, and finds gathered to-

λυθότας πολλούς. 28 ἔφη.τε πρὸς αὐτούς, Ὑμεῖς ἐπίστασθε
gether many. And he said to them, Ye know

ὡς ἀθέμιτόν ἐστιν ἀνδρὶ Ἰουδαίῳ κολλᾶσθαι ἢ προσέρ-
how unlawful it is for a man a Jew to unite himself or come

χεσθαι ἀλλοφύλῳ· ᵏκαὶ ἐμοὶ‖ ¹ὁ θεὸς ἔδειξεν‖ μηδένα
near to one of another race. And to me God shewed ²no

κοινὸν ἢ ἀκάθαρτον λέγειν ἄνθρωπον· 29 διὸ καὶ ἀναν-
¹common ⁶or ⁷unclean ¹to ²call ⁸man. Wherefore also without

τιρρήτως ἦλθον μεταπεμφθείς. πυνθάνομαι οὖν, τίνι
gainsaying I came, having been sent for. I inquire therefore, for what

λόγῳ ᵐμετεπέμψασθέ‖ με; 30 Καὶ ὁ Κορνήλιος ἔφη, Ἀπὸ
reason did ye send for me? And Cornelius said, ³Ago

τετάρτης ἡμέρας μέχρι ταύτης τῆς ὥρας ἤμην ⁿνηστεύων, καὶ‖
¹four ²days until this hour I was fasting, and

---

hold, three men seek thee. 20 Arise therefore, and get thee down, and go with them, doubting nothing: for I have sent them. 21 Then Peter went down to the men which were sent unto him from Cornelius; and said, Behold, I am he whom ye seek: what is the cause wherefore ye are come? 22 And they said, Cornelius the centurion, a just man, and one that feareth God, and of good report among all the nation of the Jews, was warned from God by an holy angel to send for thee into his house, and to hear words of thee. 23 Then called he them in, and lodged them. And on the morrow Peter went away with them, and certain brethren from Joppa accompanied him. 24 And the morrow after they entered into Cæsarea. And Cornelius waited for them, and had called together his kinsmen and near friends. 25 And as Peter was coming in, Cornelius met him, and fell down at his feet, and worshipped him. 26 But Peter took him up saying, Stand up; I myself also am a man. 27 And as he talked with him, he went in, and found many that were come together. 28 And he said unto them, Ye know how that it is an unlawful thing for a man that is a Jew to keep company, or come unto one of another nation; but God hath shewed me that I should not call any man common or unclean. 29 Therefore came I unto you without gainsaying, as soon as I was sent for: I ask therefore for what intent ye have sent for me? 30 And Cornelius said, Four days ago I was fasting until this hour; and at the ninth hour I prayed in my

---

ᵛ — τρεῖς TA. ʷ ζητοῦντές TA. ˣ ὅτι GLTTrAW. ʸ — τοὺς ἀπεσταλμένους ἀπὸ τοῦ Κορνηλίου πρὸς αὐτόν GLTTrAW. ᶻ εἶπαν LTTrA. ᵃ ἀναστὰς having arisen (he went forth) GLTTrAW. ᵇ — τῆς GLTTrAW. ᶜ τῇ δὲ LTTrAW. ᵈ εἰσῆλθεν he entered LT; εἰσηλθαν T. ᵉ Καισαρίαν T. ᶠ συν- T ᵍ + τοῦ GLTTrAW. ᵇ ἤγειρεν αὐτὸν LTTrAW. ¹ καὶ ἐγὼ TTrA. ᵏ κἀμοῦ LTTrA. ¹ ἔδειξεν ὁ θεὸς T. ᵐ μεταπέμψασθέ Δ. ⁿ — νηστεύων καὶ LTTr[A].

23

house, and, behold, a man stood before me in bright clothing, 31 and said, Cornelius, thy prayer is heard, and thine alms are had in remembrance in the sight of God. 32 Send therefore to Joppa, and call hither Simon, whose surname is Peter; he is lodged in the house of one Simon a tanner by the sea side: who, when he cometh, shall speak unto thee. 33 Immediately therefore I sent to thee; and thou hast well done that thou art come. Now therefore are we all here present before God, to hear all things that are commanded thee of God. 34 Then Peter opened his mouth, and said, Of a truth I perceive that God is no respecter of persons: 35 but in every nation he that feareth him, and worketh righteousness, is accepted with him. 36 The word which God sent unto the children of Israel, preaching peace by Jesus Christ: (he is Lord of all:) 37 that word, I say, ye know, which was published throughout all Judæa, and began from Galilee, after the baptism which John preached; 38 how God anointed Jesus of Nazareth with the Holy Ghost and with power: who went about doing good, and healing all that were oppressed of the devil; for God was with him. 39 And we are witnesses of all things which he did both in the land of the Jews, and in Jerusalem; whom they slew and hanged on a tree: 40 him God raised up the third day, and shewed him openly; 41 not to all the people, but unto witnesses

τὴν °ἐννάτην‖ Pὥραν‖ προσευχόμενος ἐν τῷ οἴκῳ μου· καὶ ἰδού,
the ninth hour praying in my house; and behold,

ἀνὴρ ἔστη ἐνώπιόν μου ἐν ἐσθῆτι λαμπρᾷ, 31 καί φησιν,
a man stood before me in ²apparel ¹bright, and said,

Κορνήλιε, εἰσηκούσθη σου ἡ προσευχὴ καὶ αἱ ἐλεημοσύναι σου
Cornelius, ³was ⁴heard ¹thy ²prayer and ⁵thine alms

ἐμνήσθησαν ἐνώπιον τοῦ θεοῦ. 32 πέμψον οὖν εἰς Ἰόππην,
were remembered before. God. Send therefore to Joppa,

καὶ μετακάλεσαι Σίμωνα ὃς ἐπικαλεῖται Πέτρος· οὗτος ξενίζε-
and call for Simon who is surnamed Petcr; he lodges

ται ἐν οἰκίᾳ Σίμωνος βυρσέως παρὰ θάλασσαν· ᵠὃς
in [the] house of Simon a tanner by [the] sea; who,

παραγενόμενος λαλήσει σοι.‖ 33 ʳἘξαυτῆς‖ οὖν ἔπεμψα
having come will speak to thee. At once therefore I sent

πρός σε· σύ τε καλῶς ἐποίησας παραγενόμενος. νῦν οὖν
to thee; and thou ²well ¹didst having come. Now therefore

πάντες ἡμεῖς ἐνώπιον τοῦ θεοῦ πάρεσμεν ἀκοῦσαι πάντα τὰ
all we before God are present to hear all things that

προστεταγμένα σοι ˢὑπὸ‖ ᵗτοῦ θεοῦ.‖ 34 Ἀνοίξας δὲ Πέτρος
have been ordered, thee by God. And ²opening ¹Peter

τὸ στόμα εἶπεν, Ἐπ᾽ ἀληθείας καταλαμβάνομαι ὅτι οὐκ
[his] mouth said, Of a truth I perceive that ²not

ἔστιν ᵛπροσωπολήπτης‖ ὁ θεός, 35 ἀλλ᾽ ἐν παντὶ ἔθνει ὁ
¹is ⁴a ²respecter ⁶of ¹person· ³God, but in every nation he that

φοβούμενος αὐτὸν καὶ ἐργαζόμενος δικαιοσύνην, δεκτὸς αὐτῷ
fears him and works righteousness, acceptable to him

ἐστιν. 36 τὸν λόγον ʷὃν‖ ἀπέστειλεν τοῖς υἱοῖς Ἰσραήλ,
is. The word which he sent to the sons of Israel,

εὐαγγελιζόμενος εἰρήνην διὰ Ἰησοῦ χριστοῦ, οὗτός ἐστιν
announcing the glad tidings— peace by Jesus Christ, (he is

πάντων κύριος, 37 ὑμεῖς οἴδατε· τὸ γενόμενον ῥῆμα
²of ³all ¹Lord), ye know; the ²which ³came ¹declaration

καθ᾽ ὅλης τῆς Ἰουδαίας, ˣἀρξάμενον‖ ʸ ἀπὸ τῆς Γαλιλαίας,
through ²whole ¹the of Judæa, beginning from Galilee,

μετὰ τὸ βάπτισμα ὃ ἐκήρυξεν ᶻἸωάννης·‖ 38 Ἰησοῦν τὸν
after the baptism which ²proclaimed ¹John: Jesus who

ἀπὸ ªΝαζαρέτ,‖ ὡς ἔχρισεν αὐτὸν ὁ θεὸς πνεύματι
[was] from Nazareth, how ²anointed ³him ¹God with [the] ²Spirit

ἁγίῳ καὶ δυνάμει, ὃς διῆλθεν εὐεργετῶν καὶ ἰώμενος
¹Holy and with power, who went through, doing good and healing

πάντας τοὺς καταδυναστευομένους ὑπὸ τοῦ διαβόλου, ὅτι
all that were being oppressed by the devil, because

ὁ θεὸς ἦν μετ᾽ αὐτοῦ· 39 καὶ ἡμεῖς ᵇἐσμεν‖ μάρτυρες πάντων
God was with him. And we are witnesses of all things

ὧν ἐποίησεν ἔν τε τῇ χώρᾳ τῶν Ἰουδαίων καὶ ᶜἐν‖ Ἰε-
which he did both in the country of the Jews and in Je-

ρουσαλήμ· ὃν ᵈ ᵉἀνεῖλον‖ κρεμάσαντες ἐπὶ ξύλου.
rusalem; whom they put to death having hanged [him] on a tree.

40 τοῦτον ὁ θεὸς ἤγειρεν ᶠ τῇ τρίτῃ ἡμέρᾳ, καὶ ἔδωκεν αὐτὸν
This one God raised up on the third day, and gave him

ἐμφανῆ γενέσθαι, 41 οὐ παντὶ τῷ λαῷ, ἀλλὰ μάρτυσιν τοῖς
²manifest ¹to ³become, not to all the people, but to witnesses who

---

º ἐνάτην LTTrA.   ᴾ — ὥραν LTTrA.   �q — ὃς παραγενόμενος λαλήσει σοι LTTr[A].
ʳ ἐξ αὐτῆς A.   ˢ ἀπὸ from LA.   ᵗ τοῦ κυρίου the Lord LTTr.   ᵛ προσωπολήμπτης LTTrA.
ʷ — ὃν L[Tr].   ˣ ἀρξάμενος TTrA.   ʸ + [γὰρ] L.   ᶻ Ἰωάνης Tr.   ª Ναζαρέθ ELTTrA.
ᵇ ἐσμεν (read [are]) GLTTrAW.   ᶜ — ἐν L[Tr.   ᵈ + καὶ also GLTTrAW.   ᵉ ἀνεῖλαν
LTTrA.   ᶠ + ἐν T.

προκεχειροτονημένοις ὑπὸ τοῦ θεοῦ, ἡμῖν, οἵτινες συνεφάγομεν
had been chosen before   by   God, to us,   who   did eat with

καὶ συνεπίομεν αὐτῷ μετὰ τὸ.ἀναστῆναι.αὐτὸν   ἐκ
and did drink with him   after   he had risen   from among [the]

νεκρῶν· 42 καὶ παρήγγειλεν ἡμῖν κηρύξαι τῷ λαῷ, καὶ
dead.   And   he charged   us   to proclaim to the people, and

διαμαρτύρασθαι ὅτι ᵍαὐτός‖ ἐστιν ὁ ὡρισμένος ὑπὸ τοῦ
to testify fully   that   he   it is who has been appointed by

θεοῦ κριτὴς ζώντων καὶ νεκρῶν. 43 τούτῳ πάντες οἱ προφῆται
God   judge   of living   and   dead.   To him   all   the   prophets

μαρτυροῦσιν, ἄφεσιν ἁμαρτιῶν λαβεῖν διὰ τοῦ ὀνόματος
bear witness, [that] ⁸remission ⁶of ¹⁰sins ⁷receives ¹¹through   ¹³name

αὐτοῦ πάντα τὸν πιστεύοντα εἰς αὐτόν.
¹²his   ¹every ²one ³that   ⁴believes   ⁵on   ⁶him.

44 Ἔτι λαλοῦντος τοῦ Πέτρου τὰ.ῥήματα.ταῦτα, ʰἐπέπεσεν‖
    ⁴Yet ¹as ³is ²speaking   ²Peter   these words,   ⁵fell

τὸ πνεῦμα τὸ ἅγιον ἐπὶ πάντας τοὺς ἀκούοντας τὸν λόγον.
¹the ²Spirit ³the ⁴Holy   upon   all   those   hearing   the   word.

45 καὶ ἐξέστησαν οἱ ἐκ περιτομῆς πιστοὶ ⁱὅσοι ᵏσυνῆλ-
    And were amazed the ²of ³the ⁴circumcision ¹believers as many as   came

θον‖ τῷ Πέτρῳ, ὅτι καὶ ἐπὶ τὰ ἔθνη ἡ δωρεὰ τοῦ ¹ἁγίου
with   Peter,   that also upon the Gentiles the gift   of the Holy

πνεύματος‖ ἐκκέχυται, 46 ἤκουον.γὰρ αὐτῶν λαλούν-
Spirit   had been poured out;   for they heard them   speak-

των γλώσσαις καὶ μεγαλυνόντων τὸν θεόν. τότε ἀπεκρίθη
ing with tongues and   magnifying   God, Then   answered

ᵐὁ‖ Πέτρος, 47 Μήτι τὸ ὕδωρ ⁿκωλῦσαι δύναταί‖ τις
Peter,   ⁵The ⁶water   ⁴forbid   ¹can   ²any ³one

τοῦ μὴ.βαπτισθῆναι τούτους, οἵτινες τὸ πνεῦμα· τὸ ἅγιον
that should not be baptized these, who the Spirit the Holy

ἔλαβον ᵒκαθὼς‖ καὶ ἡμεῖς; 48 προσέταξεν ᴾτε‖ �q αὐτοὺς‖ ʳβαπ-
received   as   also we?   And he ordered   them   to be

τισθῆναι ἐν τῷ ὀνόματι τοῦ κυρίου.‖ τότε ἠρώτησαν αὐτὸν
baptized   in the name   of the Lord.   Then they begged   him

ἐπιμεῖναι ἡμέρας τινάς.
to remain ¹days ¹some.

11 Ἤκουσαν.δὲ οἱ ἀπόστολοι καὶ οἱ ἀδελφοὶ οἱ ὄντες κατὰ
    And ³heard ¹the ²apostles   and the brethren who were in

τὴν Ἰουδαίαν, ὅτι καὶ τὰ ἔθνη ἐδέξαντο τὸν λόγον τοῦ θεοῦ.
Judæa,   that also the Gentiles received   the word   of God;

2 ˢκαὶ ὅτε‖ ἀνέβη Πέτρος εἰς ᵗἹεροσόλυμα,‖ διεκρίνοντο πρὸς
and when ²went ³up ¹Peter to   Jerusalem,   ⁵contended   ⁴with

αὐτὸν οἱ ἐκ περιτομῆς, 3 λέγοντες, Ὅτι ᵛ πρὸς ἄνδρας
²him ¹those ²of [³the] ⁴circumcision, saying,   To men

ἀκροβυστίαν.ἔχοντας ᵛεἰσῆλθες,‖ καὶ ᵂσυνέφαγες‖ αὐτοῖς.
uncircumcised   thou wentest in, and   didst eat with   them.

4 Ἀρξάμενος.δὲ ˣὁ‖ Πέτρος ἐξετίθετο αὐτοῖς καθεξῆς λέ-
   But ²having ³begun   ¹Peter   he set [it] forth to them in order   say-

γων, 5 Ἐγὼ ἤμην ἐν πόλει Ἰόππῃ προσευχόμενος, καὶ
ing,   I   was in [the] city of Joppa   praying,   and

εἶδον ἐν ἐκστάσει ὅραμα, καταβαῖνον σκεῦός τι ὡς ὀθόνην
I saw in a trance a vision, ⁴descending ¹a ²vessel ²certain like a ²sheet

chosen before of God, even to us, who did eat and drink with him after he rose from the dead. 42 And he commanded us to preach unto the people, and to testify that it is he which was ordained of God to be the Judge of quick and dead. 43 To him give all the prophets witness, that through his name whosoever believeth in him shall receive remission of sins.

44 While Peter yet spake these words, the Holy Ghost fell on all them which heard the word. 45 And they of the circumcision which believed were astonished, as many as came with Peter, because that on the Gentiles also was poured out the gift of the Holy Ghost. 46 For they heard them speak with tongues, and magnify God. Then answered Peter, 47 Can any man forbid water, that these should not be baptized, which have received the Holy Ghost as well as we? 48 And he commanded them to be baptized in the name of the Lord. Then prayed they him to tarry certain days.

XI. And the apostles and brethren that were in Judæa heard that the Gentiles had also received the word of God. 2 And when Peter was come up to Jerusalem, they that were of the circumcision contended with him, 3 saying, Thou wentest in to men uncircumcised, and didst eat with them. 4 But Peter rehearsed the matter from the beginning, and expounded it by order unto them, saying, 5 I was in the city of Joppa praying: and in a trance I saw a vision, A certain vessel descend, as it had been a great sheet, let down

ᵍ οὗτός LTTr.   ʰ ἔπεσε L.   ⁱ οἱ who L.   ᵏ συνῆλθαν TTr.   ˡ πνεύματος τοῦ
ἁγίου L.   ᵐ — ὁ LTTrA.   ⁿ δύναται κωλῦσαί LTTrA.   ᵒ ὡς LTTrA.   ᴾ δὲ TTr.
q αὐτοῖς T.   ʳ ἐν τῷ ὀνόματι Ἰησοῦ χριστοῦ (Jesus Christ) βαπτισθῆναι LTTr; ἐν τῷ ὀνόματι
τοῦ κυρίου βαπ. A.   ˢ ὅτε δὲ LTTrA.   ᵗ Ἱερουσαλήμ LTTrA.   ᵛ εἰσῆλθες (εἰσῆλθεν he went
in Tr) placed before πρὸς LTTrAW.   ᵂ συνέφαγεν did eat with Tr.   ˣ — ὁ LTTrAW.

from heaven by four corners ; and it came even to me : 6 upon the which when I had fastened mine eyes, I considered, and saw fourfooted beasts of the earth, and wild beasts, and creeping things; and fowls of the air. 7 And I heard a voice saying unto me, Arise, Peter ; slay and eat. 8 But I said, Not so, Lord ; for nothing common or unclean hath at any time entered into my mouth. 9 But the voice answered me again from heaven, What God hath cleansed, that call not thou common. 10 And this was done three times : and all were drawn up again into heaven. 11 And, behold, immediately there were three men already come unto the house where I was, sent from Cæsarea unto me. 12 And the spirit bade me go with them, nothing doubting. Moreover these six brethren accompanied me, and we entered into the man's house: 13 and he shewed us how he had seen an angel in his house, which stood and said unto him, Send men to Joppa, and call for Simon, whose surname is Peter ; 14 who shall tell thee words, whereby thou and all thy house shall be saved. 15 And as I began to speak, the Holy Ghost fell on them, as on us at the beginning. 16 Then remembered I the word of the Lord, how that he said; John indeed baptized with water; but ye shall be baptized with the Holy Ghost. 17 Forasmuch then as God gave them the like gift as he did unto us, who believed on the Lord Jesus Christ; what was I, that I could withstand God? 18 When they heard these things, they held their peace, and

μεγάλην, τέσσαρσιν ἀρχαῖς καθιεμένην ἐκ τοῦ οὐρανοῦ. καὶ
'great,ᵃ   by four   corners   let down   out of the   heaven, and
ἦλθεν ᵞἄχρις‖ ἐμοῦ. 6 εἰς ἣν   ἀτενίσας   κατενόουν,
it came as far as   me: on which having looked intently I considered,
καὶ εἶδον τὰ τετράποδα τῆς γῆς καὶ τὰ θηρία καὶ τὰ ἑρ-
and saw the quadrupeds of the earth and the wild beasts and the creeping
πετὰ καὶ τὰ πετεινὰ τοῦ οὐρανοῦ. 7 ἤκουσα δὲ ᶻ φωνῆς λε-
things and the birds of the heaven.   And I heard a voice say-
γούσης μοι, Ἀναστάς, Πέτρε, θῦσον καὶ φάγε. 8 εἶπον δέ.
ing to me, Having risen up, Peter,   kill and eat.   But I said,
Μηδαμῶς, κύριε· ὅτι ᵃπᾶν‖ κοινὸν ἢ ἀκάθαρτον οὐδέποτε
In no wise, Lord, for anything common or ·unclean   never
εἰσῆλθεν εἰς τὸ στόμα μου. 9 ἀπεκρίθη δὲ ᵇμοι‖ φωνὴ ἐκ δευ-
entered into my mouth.   But ³answered ᵇme ¹a ²voice the second
τέρου ἐκ τοῦ οὐρανοῦ, Ἃ ὁ θεὸς ᶜἐκαθάρισεν,‖ σὺ μὴ
time out of the heaven, What God   cleansed, · ³thou ²not
κοίνου.   10 τοῦτο δὲ ἐγένετο ἐπὶ τρίς, καὶ ᵈπάλιν ἀνε-
¹make common.   And this took place thrice,   and   again   was
σπάσθη‖ ἅπαντα εἰς τὸν οὐρανόν. 11 καὶ ἰδού, ᵉἐξαυτῆς‖ τρεῖς
drawn up   all into the heaven.   And lo,   at once   three
ἄνδρες ἐπέστησαν ἐπὶ τὴν οἰκίαν ἐν ᾗ ᶠἤμην,‖ ἀπεσταλμένοι
men   stood   at the house in which I was,   sent
ἀπὸ ᵍΚαισαρείας‖ πρός με. 12 εἶπεν δὲ ʰμοι τὸ πνεῦμα,
from   Cæsarea   to me.   And ³said ᵗto ⁵me ¹the ²Spirit, ,
συνελθεῖν αὐτοῖς, ¹μηδὲν διακρινόμενον·‖ ἦλθον δὲ σὺν ἐμοὶ
to go with them, nothing doubting.   And went with me
καὶ οἱ ἓξ ἀδελφοὶ οὗτοι, καὶ εἰσήλθομεν εἰς τὸν οἶκον τοῦ
also ²six ³brethren ¹these, and we entered . into the house of the
ἀνδρός, 13 ἀπήγγειλέν ᵏτε‖ ἡμῖν πῶς εἶδεν τὸν ἄγγελον ἐν
man,   and he related to us how he saw the angel in
τῷ οἴκῳ αὐτοῦ σταθέντα καὶ εἰπόντα ¹αὐτῷ,‖ Ἀπόστειλον εἰς
his house   standing and saying to him,   Send   ²to
Ἰόππην ᵐἄνδρας,‖ καὶ μετάπεμψαι Σίμωνα τὸν ἐπικαλούμενον
³Joppa ¹men, and send for Simon who is surnamed ᶠ
Πέτρον, 14 ὃς λαλήσει ῥήματα πρός σε ἐν οἷς σωθήσῃ
Peter,   who shall speak words to thee whereby shalt be saved
σὺ καὶ πᾶς ὁ οἶκός σου. 15 ἐν δὲ τῷ ἄρξασθαί με λαλεῖν
thou and . all   thy house.   And in   my beginning   to speak
ἐπέπεσεν τὸ πνεῦμα τὸ ἅγιον ἐπ᾽ αὐτούς, ὥσπερ καὶ ἐφ᾽
⁵fell ¹the ²Spirit ³the ⁴Holy upon them, even as also upon
ἡμᾶς ἐν   ἀρχῇ 16 ἐμνήσθην δὲ τοῦ ῥήματος ⁿ κυρίου,
us in [the] beginning. And I remembered the word of [the] Lord,
ὡς ἔλεγεν, ᵒἸωάννης‖ μὲν ἐβάπτισεν ὕδατι, ὑμεῖς δὲ
how he said,   John   indeed baptized with water, but ye
βαπτισθήσεσθε ἐν   πνεύματι ἁγίῳ. 17 Εἰ οὖν τὴν ἴσην
shall be baptized with [the] ²Spirit ¹Holy.   If then . the like
δωρεὰν ἔδωκεν αὐτοῖς ὁ θεὸς ὡς καὶ ἡμῖν, πιστεύσασιν ἐπὶ
gift ²gave ³to ⁴them ¹God as also to us, having believed on .
τὸν κύριον Ἰησοῦν χριστόν, ἐγώ ᴾδὲ‖ τίς ἤμην   δυνατὸς
the Lord Jesus Christ, and I, who was I, [to be] able
κωλῦσαι τὸν θεόν ; 18 Ἀκούσαντες δὲ ταῦτα ἡσύχασαν,
to forbid   God ?   And having heard these things they were silent,

---

ᵞ ἄχρι TTrA.   ᶻ + καὶ also LTTrA.   ᵃ — πᾶν GLTTrAW.   ᵇ — μοι LTTrA.   ᶜ ἐκαθέρι-
σεν Tr.   ᵈ ἀνεσπάσθη πάλιν LTTrA.   ᵉ ἐξ αὐτῆς A.   ᶠ ἤμεν we were LTTr.   ᵍ Καισαρίας T.   ʰ τὸ πνεῦμά μοι LTTrA.   ¹ μηδὲν διακρίναντα LTTr ; — μηδὲν διακρινόμενον A.
ᵏ δὲ LTTr.   ¹ — αὐτῷ LTTr.   ᵐ — ἄνδρας GLTTrAW.   ᴾ + τοῦ of the GLTTrAW.
ᵒ Ἰωάνης Tr.   ᴾ — δὲ and LTTr[A].

καὶ ᵟἐδόξαζον‖ τὸν θεόν, λέγοντες, ʳ″Αραγε‖ καὶ τοῖς ἔθνεσιν
and   glorified   God,   saying,   Then indeed also to the Gentiles

ὁ θεὸς τὴν μετάνοιαν ˢἔδωκεν εἰς ζωήν.ⁱ
God   ²repentance ¹gave unto life.

19 Οἱ μὲν οὖν διασπαρέντες ἀπὸ τῆς θλίψεως τῆς
They indeed therefore who were scattered by   the   tribulation that

γενομένης ἐπὶ ʹΣτεφάνῳ,‖ διῆλθον ἕως Φοινίκης καὶ Κύπρου
took place   upon   Stephen,   passed through to Phœnicia and Cyprus

καὶ Ἀντιοχείας, μηδενὶ λαλοῦντες τὸν λόγον εἰ.μὴ μόνον
and   Antioch,   to no one speaking   the   word except ³only

Ἰουδαίοις. 20 ἦσαν.δὲ τινες ἐξ αὐτῶν ἄνδρες Κύπριοι καὶ
¹to ²Jews.   But were certain ²of ³them ¹men Cypriots and

Κυρηναῖοι, οἵτινες ʳεἰσελθόντες‖ εἰς Ἀντιόχειαν, ἐλάλουν ʷ
Cyrenians,   who   having come into Antioch,   spoke

πρὸς τοὺς ˣἙλληνιστὰς‖ εὐαγγελιζόμενοι τὸν κύριον
to   the   Hellenists   announcing the glad tidings— the   Lord

Ἰησοῦν. 21 καὶ ἦν χεὶρ κυρίου μετ᾽ αὐτῶν· πολύς.τε
Jesus.   And ⁶was [¹the] ²hand ³of [⁴the] ⁵Lord with them,   and a great

ἀριθμὸς ʸ πιστεύσας ἐπέστρεψεν ἐπὶ τὸν κύριον. 22 Ἠκούσθη
number   having believed turned   to   the Lord.   ⁴Was ⁵heard

δὲ ὁ λόγος εἰς τὰ ὦτα τῆς ἐκκλησίας τῆς ᶻ ἐν ᵃἹερο-
¹and ²the ³report in   the ears of the assembly which [was] in   Jeru-

σολύμοις‖ περὶ αὐτῶν· καὶ ἐξαπέστειλαν Βαρνάβαν ᵇδιελ-
salem   concerning them; and they sent forth Barnabas   to go

θεῖν‖ ἕως Ἀντιοχείας. 23 ὃς παραγενόμενος καὶ ἰδὼν
through as far as Antioch: who   having come   and having seen

τὴν χάριν ᶜ τοῦ θεοῦ ἐχάρη, καὶ παρεκάλει πάντας τῇ.προθέσει
the grace   of God rejoiced, and exhorted   all   with purpose

τῆς καρδίας προσμένειν τῷ κυρίῳ· 24 ὅτι ἦν ἀνὴρ ἀγαθὸς
of heart   to abide with the Lord;   for he was a ²man ¹good

καὶ πλήρης πνεύματος ἁγίου καὶ πίστεως. καὶ προσετέθη
and   full   of [the] ²Spirit ¹Holy and of faith.   And was added

ὄχλος ἱκανὸς τῷ κυρίῳ. 25 Ἐξῆλθεν.δὲ εἰς Ταρσὸν ᵈὁ Βαρ-
a ²crowd ¹large to the Lord.   And ²went ³forth ⁴to ⁵Tarsus   ¹Bar-

νάβας‖ ἀναζητῆσαι Σαῦλον, 26 καὶ εὑρὼν ᵉαὐτὸν‖ ἤγαγεν
nabas   to seek   Saul;   and having found him he brought

ᵉαὐτὸν‖ εἰς Ἀντιόχειαν. ἐγένετο.δὲ ᶠαὐτοὺς‖ ἐνιαυτὸν
him   to Antioch.   And it came to pass they   a ²year

ὅλον συναχθῆναι ἐν τῇ ἐκκλησίᾳ, καὶ διδάξαι ὄχλον
¹whole were gathered together in the assembly,   and   taught a ²crowd

ἱκανόν, χρηματίσαι.τε ᵍπρῶτον‖ ἐν Ἀντιοχείᾳ τοὺς μαθητὰς
¹large: and ³were ⁵called   ⁴first   ⁷in   ⁸Antioch   ¹the   ²disciples

Χριστιανούς.
⁶Christians.

27 Ἐν.ταύταις.δὲ ταῖς ἡμέραις κατῆλθον ἀπὸ Ἱεροσολύμων
And in these   days   came down from   Jerusalem

προφῆται εἰς Ἀντιόχειαν. 28 ἀναστὰς.δὲ εἷς ἐξ
prophets   to   Antioch;   and ⁵having ⁶risen ⁴up ¹one ²from ³among

αὐτῶν ὀνόματι Ἄγαβος, ʰἐσήμανεν‖ διὰ τοῦ πνεύματος,
⁴them,   by name   Agabus,   he signified   by   the   Spirit,

Λιμὸν ⁱμέγαν‖ μέλλειν ἔσεσθαι ἐφ᾽ ὅλην τὴν οἰκουμένην·
A ²famine ¹great   is about   to be   over ²whole ¹the habitable world;

ᵠ ἐδόξασαν LTTr.   ʳ″Αρα then LTTr; ″Αρα [γε] A.   ˢ εἰς ζωὴν ἔδωκεν LTTrAW.   ᵗ Στεφάνου L.   ᵛ ἐλθόντες GLTTrAW.   ʷ + καὶ also LTTrA.   ˣἙλληνας Greeks GLTTrA.   ʸ + ὁ
LTTrA.   ᶻ + οὔσης was TTr.   ᵃ Ἱερουσαλὴμ LTTrAW.   ᵇ — διελθεῖν LTTr.   ᶜ + τὴν which
[was] LTTrA.   ᵈ — ὁ Βαρνάβας (read he went forth) LTTrA.   ᵉ — αὐτὸν (read [him]) LTTrA.
αὐτοὶς καὶ to them even LTTrA.   ᵍ πρώτως TTrA.   ʰ ἐσήμαινεν L.   ⁱ μεγάλην LTTrAW.

Right column (Authorised Version):

glorified God, saying, Then hath God also to the Gentiles granted repentance unto life.

19 Now they which were scattered abroad upon the persecution that arose about Stephen travelled as far as Phenice, and Cyprus, and Antioch, preaching the word to none but unto the Jews only. 20 And some of them were men of Cyprus and Cyrene, which, when they were come to Antioch, spake unto the Grecians, preaching the Lord Jesus. 21 And the hand of the Lord was with them: and a great number believed, and turned unto the Lord. 22 Then tidings of these things came unto the ears of the church which was in Jerusalem: and they sent forth Barnabas, that he should go as far as Antioch. 23 Who, when he came, and had seen the grace of God, was glad, and exhorted them all, that with purpose of heart they would cleave unto the Lord. 24 For he was a good man, and full of the Holy Ghost and of faith: and much people was added unto the Lord. 25 Then departed Barnabas to Tarsus, for to seek Saul: 26 and when he had found him, he brought him unto Antioch. And it came to pass, that a whole year they assembled themselves with the church, and taught much people. And the disciples were called Christians first in Antioch.

27 And in these days came prophets from Jerusalem unto Antioch. 28 And there stood up one of them named Agabus, and signified by the spirit that there should be great dearth throughout all the world:

which came to pass in the days of Claudius Cæsar. 29 .Then the disciples, every man according to his ability, determined to send relief unto the brethren which dwelt in Judæa : 30 which also they did, and sent it to the elders by the hands of Barnabas and Saul.

XII. Now about that time Herod the king stretched forth his hands to vex certain of the church. 2 And he killed James the brother of John with the sword. 3 And because he saw it pleased the Jews, he proceeded further to take Peter also. (Then were the days of unleavened bread.) 4 And when he had apprehended him, he put him in prison, and delivered him to four quaternions of soldiers to keep him ; intending after Easter to bring him forth to the people. 5 Peter therefore was kept in prison: but prayer was made without ceasing of the church unto God for him. 6 And when Herod would have brought him forth, the same night Peter was sleeping between two soldiers, bound with two chains : and the keepers before the door kept the prison. 7 And, behold, the angel of the Lord came upon him, and a light shined in the prison : and he smote Peter on the side, and raised him up, saying, Arise up quickly. And his chains fell off from his hands. 8 And the angel said unto him, Gird thyself, and bind on thy sandals. And so he did. And he saith unto him, Cast thy garment about thee, and follow me. 9 And he went out, and followed him ; and wist not that it was true which was done by the angel ; but thought he saw a vision.

κ'όστις‖ ¹καὶ‖ ἐγένετο · ἐπὶ Κλαυδίου ᵐΚαίσαρος·‖ 29 τῶν.δὲ
which   also   came to pass under Claudius   Cæsar.   And the

μαθητῶν καθὼς ⁿηὐπορεῖτό‖ τις, ὥρισαν ἕκαστος αὐ-
disciples according as ³was ⁴prospered ¹any ²one, determined, each   of

τῶν εἰς διακονίαν πέμψαι τοῖς κατοικοῦσιν ἐν τῇ Ἰουδαίᾳ
them, for ministration to send to the ²dwelling ³in ⁴Judæa

ἀδελφοῖς· 30 ὃ καὶ ἐποίησαν, ἀποστείλαντες πρὸς τοὺς
¹brethren ;   which also they did,   sending   [it] to the,

πρεσβυτέρους διὰ χειρὸς Βαρνάβα καὶ Σαύλου.
elders   by [the] hand of Barnabas and Saul.

12 Κατ᾽.ἐκεῖνον.δὲ τὸν.καιρὸν ἐπέβαλεν ᵒ'Ηρώδης ὁ βασι-'
And at 'that   time   ⁴put ⁵forth ¹Herod ²the ³king

λεὺς‖ τὰς χεῖρας κακῶσαί τινας τῶν ἀπὸ τῆς ἐκκλησίας.
[his]   hands to ill-treat some of those of the assembly ;

2 ἀνεῖλεν.δὲ Ἰάκωβον τὸν ἀδελφὸν ᴾΙωάννου‖ ᑫμαχαίρᾳ.‖
and he put to death James the brother of John with a sword,

3 ʳκαὶ ἰδὼν‖ ὅτι ἀρεστόν ἐστιν τοῖς Ἰουδαίοις προσέθετο
And having seen that pleasing it is to the Jews he added

συλλαβεῖν καὶ Πέτρον· ἦσαν.δὲ ˢ ἡμέραι τῶν.ἀζύμων‖·
to take   also Peter : (and they were days of unleavened bread :)

4 ὃν καὶ πιάσας ἔθετο εἰς φυλακήν, παραδοὺς τέσσαρ-
whom also having seized he put in prison, having delivered to four

σιν τετραδίοις στρατιωτῶν φυλάσσειν αὐτόν, βουλόμενος μετὰ
sets of four soldiers to guard him, purposing after

τὸ πάσχα ἀναγαγεῖν αὐτὸν τῷ λαῷ. 5 ὁ.μὲν.οὖν.Πέτρος
the passover to bring out him to the people. Peter therefore indeed

ἐτηρεῖτο ἐν τῇ φυλακῇ· προσευχὴ.δὲ ἦν ᵗἐκτενὴς‖ γινομένη
was kept in the prison : but ²prayer ¹was ⁴fervent   ³made

ὑπὸ τῆς ἐκκλησίας πρὸς τὸν θεὸν ᵛὑπὲρ‖ αὐτοῦ. 6 Ὅτε.δὲ
by the assembly   to the God concerning him. But when

ᵂἔμελλεν‖ ˣαὐτὸν προάγειν‖ ὁ Ἡρώδης, τῇ.νυκτὶ.ἐκείνῃ ἦν
²was ³about ⁶him ;⁴to ⁵bring ⁷forth ¹Herod, in that night was

ὁ Πέτρος κοιμώμενος μεταξὺ δύο στρατιωτῶν, δεδεμένος ἁλύ-
Peter   sleeping   between two soldiers,   bound   with

σεσιν δυσίν, φύλακές τε πρὸ τῆς θύρας ἐτήρουν τὴν φυλακήν.
²chains ¹two, guards also before the .door kept the prison.

7 καὶ ἰδού, ἄγγελος κυρίου ἐπέστη, καὶ φῶς ἔλαμψεν ἐν
And behold, an angel of [the] Lord stood by, and a light shone in,

τῷ οἰκήματι. πατάξας.δὲ τὴν πλευρὰν τοῦ Πέτρου ἤγειρεν
the building. And having smitten the side of Peter he roused up

αὐτὸν λέγων, Ἀνάστα ἐν τάχει. Καὶ ʸἐξέπεσον‖ αὐτοῦ αἱ
him, saying, Rise up in haste. And fell off   of him the

ἁλύσεις ἐκ τῶν χειρῶν. 8 εἶπέν.ᶻτε‖ ὁ ἄγγελος πρὸς
chains from [his] .hands. And ³said ¹the ²angel to

αὐτόν, ᵃΠερίζωσαι,‖ καὶ ὑπόδησαι τὰ.σανδάλιά.σου. ²He ³did
him, .Gird thyself about, and bind on thy sandals.   ²He ³did

σεν δὲ οὕτως. καὶ λέγει αὐτῷ, Περιβαλοῦ τὸ.ἱμάτιόν.σου,
and so.   And he says to him, Cast about [thee] thy garment,

καὶ ἀκολούθει μοι. 9 Καὶ ἐξελθὼν ἠκολούθει ᵇαὐτῷ.‖ καὶ
and follow   me. And going forth he followed   him,   and

οὐκ.ᾔδει ὅτι ἀληθές ἐστιν τὸ γινόμενον διὰ τοῦ ἀγ-
did not know that ⁑ is which is happening by means of the an-

---

ᵏ ἥτις LTTrAW.   ¹ — καὶ LTTr[A].   ᵐ — Καίσαρος GLTTrAW.   ⁿ εὐπορεῖτο LTTrA.
ᵒ ὁ βασιλεὺς Ἡρώδης T.   ᴾ Ἰωάνου Tr.   ᑫ μαχαίρῃ TTrA.   ʳ ἰδὼν δὲ LTTrA.   ˢ + αἱ
the GL[A]W.   ᵗ ἐκτενῶς fervently LTTrA.   ᵛ περὶ LTTr.   ᵂ ἤμελλεν TTrA.   ˣ προαγαγεῖν
αὐτὸν LTA ; προάγειν αὐτὸν Tr.   ʸ ἐξέπεσαν LTTrAʃ   ᶻ δὲ LTr.   ᵃ Ζῶσαι gird thyself
LTTrA.   ᵇ — αὐτῷ LTTrA.

γέλου, ἐδόκει.δὲ ὅραμα βλέπειν. 10 διελθόντες.δὲ πρώτην
gel, but thought a vision he saw. And having passed through a first

φυλακὴν καὶ δευτέραν, ᶜἦλθον‖ ἐπὶ τὴν πύλην τὴν σιδηρᾶν
guard and a second, they came to the ²gate ¹iron

τὴν φέρουσαν εἰς τὴν πόλιν, ἥτις αὐτομάτη ᵈἠνοίχθη‖ αὐτοῖς,
that leads into the city, which of itself opened to them;

καὶ ἐξελθόντες προῆλθον ῥύμην μίαν, καὶ εὐθέως
and having gone out they went on through ²street ¹one, and immediately

ἀπέστη ὁ ἄγγελος ἀπ᾽ αὐτοῦ. 11 καὶ ὁ Πέτρος ᵉγενόμενος
departed the angel from him. And Peter having come

ἐν.ἑαυτῷ‖ εἶπεν, Νῦν οἶδα ἀληθῶς ὅτι ἐξαπέστειλεν
to himself said, Now I know of a truth that ³sent ⁴forth [¹the]

κύριος τὸν.ἄγγελον.αὐτοῦ, καὶ ᶠἐξείλετό‖ με ἐκ χειρὸς
²Lord his angel, and delivered me out of [the] hand

Ἡρώδου καὶ πάσης τῆς προσδοκίας τοῦ λαοῦ τῶν Ἰουδαίων.
of Herod and all the expectation of the people of the Jews.

12 συνιδών.τε ἦλθεν ἐπὶ τὴν οἰκίαν ᵍ Μαρίας τῆς μητρὸς
And considering [it] he came to the house of Mary the mother

ʰἸωάννου‖ τοῦ ἐπικαλουμένου Μάρκου, οὗ ἦσαν ἱκανοὶ
of John who is surnamed Mark, where were many

συνηθροισμένοι καὶ προσευχόμενοι. 13 Κρούσαντος.δὲ ⁱτοῦ
gathered together and praying. And ²having ³knocked

Πέτρου‖ τὴν θύραν τοῦ πυλῶνος, προσῆλθεν παιδίσκη ὑπα-
¹Peter [at] the door of the porch, ³came ¹a ²damsel to

κοῦσαι, ὀνόματι Ῥόδη· 14 καὶ ἐπιγνοῦσα τὴν φωνὴν τοῦ
listen, by name Rhoda; and having recognized the voice

Πέτρου, ἀπὸ τῆς χαρᾶς οὐκ.ἤνοιξεν τὸν πυλῶνα, εἰσδρα-
of Peter, from joy she opened not the porch, ⁿhaving

μοῦσα δὲ ἀπήγγειλεν ἑστάναι τὸν Πέτρον πρὸ τοῦ
⁵run ⁴in ¹but she reported ²to ³be ⁴standing ¹Peter before the

πυλῶνος. 15 οἱ.δὲ πρὸς αὐτὴν ᵏεἶπον,‖ Μαίνῃ. Ἡ.δὲ
porch. But they to her said, Thou art mad. But she

διϊσχυρίζετο οὕτως ἔχειν. οἱ.ᴵδ᾽ ἔλεγον,‖ Ὁ ἄγγελος ᵐαὐ-
strongly affirmed thus it was. And they said, The angel of

τοῦ ἐστιν.‖ 16 Ὁ.δὲ Πέτρος ἐπέμενεν κρούων· ἀνοίξαντες.δὲ
him it is. But Peter continued knocking: and having opened

ⁿεἶδον‖ αὐτόν, καὶ ἐξέστησαν. 17 κατασείσας.δὲ αὐτοῖς
they saw him, and were amazed. And having made a sign to them

τῇ χειρὶ σιγᾶν διηγήσατο °αὐτοῖς‖ πῶς ὁ κύριος αὐτὸν
with the hand to be silent he related ⅰ to them how the Lord him

ἐξήγαγεν ἐκ τῆς φυλακῆς. εἶπεν.ᴾδέ,‖ Ἀπαγγείλατε Ἰακώβῳ
brought out of the prison. And he said, Report to James

καὶ τοῖς ἀδελφοῖς ταῦτα. Καὶ ἐξελθὼν ἐπορεύθη εἰς ἕτερον
and to the brethren these things. And having gone out he went to another

τόπον. 18 γενομένης.δὲ ἡμέρας ἦν τάραχος οὐκ ὀλίγος
place. And ²having ³come ¹day there was ³disturbance ¹no ²small

ἐν τοῖς στρατιώταις, τί ἄρα ὁ Πέτρος ἐγένετο. 19 Ἡρώδης
among the soldiers, what then [²of] ⁴Peter ¹was ²become. ⁶Herod

δὲ ἐπιζητήσας αὐτὸν καὶ μὴ εὑρών, ἀνακρίνας τοὺς
⁵and having sought after ⁵him ¹and ²not ³having ⁴found, having examined the

φύλακας ἐκέλευσεν ἀπαχθῆναι· καὶ κατελθὼν
guards he commanded [them] to be led away [to death]. And having gone down

10 When they were past the first and the second ward, they came unto the iron gate that leadeth unto the city; which opened to them of his own accord: and they went out, and passed on through one street; and forthwith the angel departed from him. 11 And when Peter was come to himself, he said, Now I know of a surety, that the Lord hath sent his angel, and hath delivered me out of the hand of Herod, and from all the expectation of the people of the Jews. 12 And when he had considered the thing, he came to the house of Mary the mother of John, whose surname was Mark; where many were gathered together praying. 13 And as Peter knocked at the door of the gate, a damsel came to hearken, named Rhoda. 14 And when she knew Peter's voice, she opened not the gate for gladness, but ran in, and told how Peter stood before the gate. 15 And they said unto her, Thou art mad. But she constantly affirmed that it was even so. Then said they, It is his angel. 16 But Peter continued knocking: and when they had opened the door, and saw him, they were astonished. 17 But he, beckoning unto them with the hand to hold their peace, declared unto them how the Lord had brought him out of the prison. And he said, Go shew these things unto James, and to the brethren. And he departed, and went into another place. 18 Now as soon as it was day, there was no small stir among the soldiers, what was become of Peter. 19 And when Herod had sought for him, and found him not, he examined the keepers, and commanded that they should be put to

---

ᶜ ἦλθαν LTTrA. ᵈ ἠνοίγη LTTrA. ᵉ ἐν ἑαυτῷ γενόμενος LTTrAW. ᶠ ἐξείλατό GLTTrAW.
ᵍ + τῆς LTTrAW. ʰ Ἰωάνου Tr. ⁱ αὐτοῦ hθ GLTTrAW. ᵏ εἶπαν LTTrA. ᴵ δὲ
εἶπαν L; δὲ ἔλεγον GTTrAW. ᵐ ἐστιν αὐτοῦ LTTr. ⁿ εἶδαν LTTrA. ° — αὐτοῖς T[Tr],
ᴾ τε LTTrA.

ᵉath. And he went
down from Judæa to
Cæsarea, and there a-
bode. 20 And Herod
was highly displeased
with them of Tyre and
Sidon : but they came
with one accord to
him, and, having made
Blastus the king's
chamberlain their
friend, desired peace ;
because their coun-
try was nourished by
the king's *country*.
21 And upon a set
day Herod, arrayed in
royal apparel, sat up-
on his throne, and
made an oration un-
to them. 22 And
the people gave a
shout, *saying, It is* the
voice of a god, and not
of a man. 23 And im-
mediately the angel of
the Lord smote him,
because he gave not
God the glory : and he
was eaten of worms,
and gave up the ghost.
24 But the word of God
grew and multiplied.
25 And Barnabas and
Saul returned from
Jerusalem, when they
had fulfilled *their* ministry, and took with
them John, whose sur-
name was Mark.

XIII. Now there
were in the church
that was at Antioch
certain prophets and
teachers ; as Barna-
bas, and Simeon that
was called Niger, and
Lucius of Cyrene, and
Manaen, which had
been brought up with
Herod the tetrarch,
and Saul. 2 As they
ministered to the Lord,
and fasted, the Holy
Ghost said, Separate
me Barnabas and Saul
for the work where-
unto I have called
them. 3 And when
they had fasted and
prayed, and laid *their*
hands on them, they
sent *them* away. 4 So
they, being sent forth
by the Holy Ghost, de-
parted unto Seleucia ;
and from thence they
sailed to Cyprus. 5 And
when they were at Sa-
lamis, they preached
the word of God in
the synagogues of the

ἀπὸ τῆς Ἰουδαίας εἰς �qτὴν‖ ʳΚαισάρειαν‖ διέτριβεν.　20 ᵀΗν
from　Judæa　to　　Cæsarea　he stayed [there].　³Was
δὲ ˢὁ Ἡρώδης‖ θυμομαχῶν Τυρίοις καὶ Σιδωνίοις·
¹and　²Herod　in bitter hostility with [the] Tyrians and　Sidonians ;
ὁμοθυμαδὸν.δὲ παρῆσαν πρὸς αὐτόν, καὶ πείσαντες Βλάστον
but with one accord they came　to　him, and having gained Blastus
τὸν ἐπὶ τοῦ κοιτῶνος τοῦ βασιλέως, ᾐτοῦντο εἰρήνην,
who [was] over the bedchamber of the　king,　sought　peace,
διὰ τὸ τρέφεσθαι αὐτῶν τὴν χώραν ἀπὸ τῆς βασιλικῆς.
because was nourished their　country　by　the　king's.
21 Τακτῇ.δὲ ἡμέρᾳ ὁ Ἡρώδης ἐνδυσάμενος ἐσθῆτα βασιλικήν,
And on a set day　Herod　having put on ²apparel ¹royal,
ᵗκαὶ‖ καθίσας ἐπὶ τοῦ βήματος, ἐδημηγόρει πρὸς αὐ-
and having sat on the tribunal, was making an oration to them.
τούς. 22 ὁ.δὲ δῆμος ἐπεφώνει, Θεοῦ φωνὴ καὶ οὐκ
And the people were crying out, ³Of ⁴a ⁵god [¹the] ²voice and not
ἀνθρώπου. 23 παραχρῆμα.δὲ ἐπάταξεν αὐτὸν ἄγγελος κυ-
of a man !　And immediately ⁶smote ⁷him ¹an ²angel ³of [⁴the]
ρίου, ἀνθ'.ὧν οὐκ ἔδωκεν ᵛτὴν‖ δόξαν τῷ θεῷ· καὶ γενόμενος
⁵Lord, because he gave not the　glory　to God, and having been
σκωληκόβρωτος ἐξέψυξεν. 24 ὁ.δὲ λόγος τοῦ θεοῦ ηὔξανεν
eaten of worms　he expired. But the word of God　grew
καὶ ἐπληθύνετο. 25 Βαρνάβας.δὲ καὶ Σαῦλος ὑπέστρεψαν ἐξ
and　multiplied.　And Barnabas and　Saul　returned from
Ἰερουσαλήμ, πληρώσαντες τὴν διακονίαν, ʷσυμπαραλαβόν-
Jerusalem,　having fulfilled the ministration,　having taken with
τες‖ ˣκαὶ‖ ʸἸωάννην‖ τὸν ἐπικληθέντα Μάρκον.
[them] also　John　who was surnamed Mark.

13 ᵀΗσαν.δὲ ᶻτινες‖ ἐν Ἀντιοχείᾳ κατὰ τὴν οὖσαν
Now there were certain in　Antioch　in the ²which ³was [⁴there]
ἐκκλησίαν προφῆται καὶ διδάσκαλοι, ὅ.τε.Βαρνάβας καὶ Συμεὼν
¹assembly　prophets and　teachers,　both Barnabas and Simeon
ὁ καλούμενος Νίγερ, καὶ Λούκιος ὁ Κυρηναῖος, Μαναήν.τε
who was called Niger, and Lucius the Cyrenian, and Manaen,
Ἡρώδου τοῦ ᵃτετράρχου‖ σύντροφος, καὶ Σαῦλος. 2 λειτουρ-
of Herod the tetrarch　a foster-brother, and Saul. ²As ⁴were ⁵min-
γούντων δὲ αὐτῶν τῷ κυρίῳ καὶ νηστευόντων, εἶπεν τὸ
istering ¹and ³they to the Lord and　fasting,　⁵said ¹the
πνεῦμα τὸ ἅγιον, Ἀφορίσατε δή μοι τόν.ᵇτε‖.Βαρνάβαν καὶ
²Spirit ³the ⁴Holy,　Separate indeed to me　both Barnabas and
ᶜτὸν‖ Σαῦλον εἰς τὸ ἔργον ὃ προσκέκλημαι αὐτούς. 3 Τότε
Saul　for the work to which I have called them. Then
νηστεύσαντες καὶ προσευξάμενοι, καὶ ἐπιθέντες τὰς χεῖρας
having fasted and　prayed,　and having laid　hands
αὐτοῖς, ἀπέλυσαν. 4 ᵈΟὗτοι‖ μὲν οὖν ἐκπεμφθέντες
on them, they let [them] go. They indeed therefore having been sent forth
ὑπὸ τοῦ ᵉπνεύματος τοῦ ἁγίου,‖.κατῆλθον εἰς ᶠτὴν‖ ᵍΣελεύ-
by the　Spirit　the Holy,　went down to　Seleu-
κειαν,‖ ἐκεῖθέν.τε ἀπέπλευσαν εἰς ᶠτὴν‖ Κύπρον. 5 καὶ γενό-
cia,　and thence　sailed away　to　Cyprus.　And having
μενοι ἐν Σαλαμῖνι κατήγγελλον τὸν λόγον.τοῦ θεοῦ ἐν ταῖς
come into Salamis they announced the　word　of God in the

---

q — τὴν LTTrAW.　　ʳ Καισαρίαν T.　　ˢ — ὁ Ἡρώδης (*read* he was) GLTTrAW.　　ᵗ — καὶ
[L]T[Tr].　　ᵛ — τὴν GL.　　ʷ συν- T.　　ˣ — καὶ LTTr[A].　　ʸ Ἰωάνην Tr.　　ᶻ — τινες LTTrA.
ᵃ τετραάρχου T.　　ᵇ — τε GLTTrAW.　　ᶜ — τὸν LTTrAW.　　ᵈ αὐτοὶ LTTrA.　　ᵉ ἁγίου πνεύματος LTTrA.　　ᶠ — τὴν LTTrA.　　ᵍ Σελευκίαν T.

συναγωγαῖς τῶν Ἰουδαίων· εἶχον.δὲ καὶ ʰἸωάννην‖
synagogues of the Jews. And they had also John [as]

ὑπηρέτην. 6 διελθόντες.δὲ ⁱ τὴν νῆσον ἄχρι Πάφου
an attendant. And having passed through the island as far as Paphos

εὗρόν ʲ τινα μάγον ψευδοπροφήτην Ἰουδαῖον, ᾧ ὄνομα
they found a certain magician, a false prophet a Jew, whose name

ᵏΒαριησοῦς,‖ 7 ὃς ἦν σὺν τῷ ἀνθυπάτῳ Σεργίῳ Παύλῳ,
[was] Barjesus, who was with the proconsul Sergius Paulus,

ἀνδρὶ συνετῷ. οὗτος προσκαλεσάμενος Βαρνάβαν καὶ
³man ¹an ²intelligent. He having called to [him] Barnabas and

Σαῦλον ἐπεζήτησεν ἀκοῦσαι τὸν λόγον τοῦ θεοῦ· 8 ἀνθίστατο.δὲ
Saul desired to hear the word of God. But there withstood

αὐτοῖς Ἐλύμας ὁ μάγος· οὕτως.γὰρ μεθερμηνεύεται τὸ ὄνομα
them Elymas the magician, (for so is interpreted ²name

αὐτοῦ· ζητῶν διαστρέψαι τὸν ἀνθύπατον ἀπὸ τῆς πίστεως.
¹his), seeking to pervert the proconsul from the faith.

9 Σαῦλος.δὲ, ὁ καὶ Παῦλος, πλησθεὶς πνεύματος ἁγίου,
But Saul, who also [is] Paul, being filled with [the] ²Spirit ¹Holy,

ˡκαὶ‖ ἀτενίσας εἰς αὐτὸν 10 εἶπεν, Ὦ πλήρης παν-
and having looked steadfastly upon him said, O full of

τὸς δόλου καὶ πάσης ῥᾳδιουργίας, υἱὲ διαβόλου, ἐχθρὲ πάσης
all guile and all craft, son of [the] devil, enemy of all

δικαιοσύνης, οὐ.παύσῃ διαστρέφων τὰς ὁδοὺς κυρίου
righteousness, wilt thou not cease perverting the ᵐways ᵐ᷀of [ᵐthe] ²Lord

τὰς εὐθείας; 11 καὶ νῦν ἰδού, χεὶρ ᵐτοῦ‖ κυρίου ἐπὶ σέ,
¹straight? And now lo, [the] hand of the Lord [is] upon thee,

καὶ ἔσῃ τυφλός, μὴ βλέπων τὸν ἥλιον ἄχρι καιροῦ.
and thou shalt be blind, not seeing the sun for a season.

Παραχρῆμα.ⁿδὲ‖ ᵒἐπέπεσεν‖ ἐπ᾽ αὐτὸν ἀχλὺς καὶ σκότος, καὶ
And immediately fell upon him a mist and darkness, and

περιάγων ἐζήτει χειραγωγούς. 12 τότε ἰδὼν
going about he sought some to lead [him] by the hand. Then ⁴having ⁴seen

ὁ ἀνθύπατος τὸ γεγονὸς ἐπίστευσεν, ᴾἐκπλησσόμενος‖ ἐπὶ
¹the ²proconsul what had happened believed, being astonished at

τῇ διδαχῇ τοῦ κυρίου.
the teaching of the Lord.

13 Ἀναχθέντες.δὲ ἀπὸ τῆς Πάφου οἱ περὶ ᵠτὸν‖
And having sailed from Paphos [²with] ³those ⁴about [⁵him]

Παῦλον ἦλθον εἰς Πέργην τῆς Παμφυλίας. ʳἸωάννης‖.δὲ
¹Paul came to Perga of Pamphylia; and John

ἀποχωρήσας ἀπ᾽ αὐτῶν ὑπέστρεψεν εἰς Ἱεροσόλυμα. 14 αὐ-
having departed from them returned to Jerusalem. ²They

τοὶ δὲ διελθόντες ἀπὸ τῆς Πέργης παρεγένοντο εἰς Ἀν-
¹but, having passed through from Perga, came to An-

τιόχειαν ˢτῆς Πισιδίας,‖ καὶ ᵗεἰσελθόντες‖ εἰς τὴν συναγωγὴν
tioch of Pisidia, and having gone into the synagogue

τῇ ἡμέρᾳ τῶν σαββάτων ἐκάθισαν. 15 Μετὰ.δὲ τὴν ἀνά-
on the ²day ¹sabbath they sat down. And after the read-

γνωσιν τοῦ νόμου καὶ τῶν προφητῶν ἀπέστειλαν οἱ ἀρχισυνά-
ing of the law and of the prophets ⁶sent ¹the ²rulers ³of

γωγοι πρὸς αὐτούς, λέγοντες, Ἄνδρες ἀδελφοί, εἰ ᵛ ἔστιν
the ⁵synagogue to them, saying, Men brethren, if there is

ʰ Ἰωάνην Tr.   ⁱ + ὅλην (the) whole GLTTrAW.   ʲ + ἄνδρα a man LTTrAW.   ᵏ Βαρ-
ιησοῦ T.   ˡ — καὶ LTTrAW.   ᵐ — τοῦ (read of [the]) GLTTrAW.   ⁿ τε T.   ᵒ ἔπεσεν LTTr.
ᴾ ἐκπληττόμενος Tr.   ᵠ — τὸν LTTrAW.   ʳ Ἰωάνης Tr.   ˢ τὴν Πισιδίαν LTTrA.
ᵗ ἐλθόντες TTr.   ᵛ + τις any (word) LTTrAW.

any word of exhortation for the people, say on. 16 Then Paul stood up, and beckoning with *his* hand said, Men of Israel, and ye that fear God, give audience. 17 The God of this people of Israel chose our fathers, and exalted the people when they dwelt as strangers in the land of Egypt, and with an high arm brought he them out of it. 18 And about the time of forty years suffered he their manners in the wilderness. 19 And when he had destroyed seven nations in the land of Chanaan, he divided their land to them by lot. 20 And after that he gave *unto them* judges about the space of four hundred and fifty years, until Samuel the prophet. 21 And afterward they desired a king: and God gave unto them Saul the son of Cis, a man of the tribe of Benjamin, by the space of forty years. 22 And when he had removed him, he raised up unto them David to be their king; to whom also he gave testimony, and said, I have found David the *son* of Jesse, a man after mine own heart, which shall fulfil all my will. 23 Of this man's seed hath God according to *his* promise raised unto Israel a Saviour, Jesus: 24 when John had first preached before his coming the baptism of repentance to all the people of Israel. 25 And as John fulfilled his course, he said, Whom think ye that I am? I am not *he*. But, behold, there cometh one after me, whose shoes of *his* feet I am not worthy to loose. 26 Men *and* brethren, children of the stock of Abraham, and whosoever among you feareth God, to

ʷλόγος ἐν ὑμῖνǁ παρακλήσεως πρὸς τὸν λαόν, λέγετε.
a word among you   of exhortation   to   the people, speak.

16 Ἀναστὰς.δὲ Παῦλος, καὶ κατασείσας τῇ χειρί, εἰπεν,
And ²having ³risen ⁴up ¹Paul,   and making a sign with the hand, said,

Ἄνδρες ˣἸσραηλῖται,ǁ καὶ οἱ φοβούμενοι τὸν θεόν, ἀκούσατε.
Men   Israelites, · and those fearing   God, hearken.

17 ὁ θεὸς τοῦ.λαοῦ.τούτου ʸἸσραὴλǁ ἐξελέξατο τοὺς πατέρας
The God of this people   Israel   chose   ²fathers

ἡμῶν· καὶ τὸν λαὸν ὕψωσεν ἐν τῇ παροικίᾳ ἐν   γῇ
¹our,   and ²the ³people ¹exalted in the sojourning in [the] land

ᶻΑἰγύπτῳ,ǁ καὶ μετὰ βραχίονος ὑψηλοῦ ἐξήγαγεν αὐτοὺς ἐξ
of Egypt,   and with ³arm ¹a ²high   brought   them   out of

αὐτῆς· 18 καὶ ὡς ªτεσσαρακονταετῇǁ χρόνον ᵇἐτροπο-
it,   and about ³forty ⁴years ¹[the] ²time he bore

φόρησεν αὐτοὺς ἐν τῇ ἐρήμῳ. 19 καὶ καθελὼν ἔθνη ἑπτὰ
²manners ¹their in the desert. And having destroyed ²nations ¹seven

ἐν γῇ Χαναάν, ᶜκατεκληροδότησενǁ ᵈαὐτοῖςǁ τὴν.γῆν.αὐ-
in [the] land of Canaan, he gave by lot   to them   their land.

τῶν. 20 ᵉκαὶ μετὰ ταῦτα, ὡς ἔτεσιν τετρακοσίοις καὶ
     And after these things about ⁵years ¹four ²hundred ³and

πεντήκονταǁ ἔδωκεν κριτὰς ἕως Σαμουὴλ ᶠτοῦǁ προφήτου·
⁴fifty   he gave judges until Samuel the   prophet.

21 κἀκεῖθεν ᾐτήσαντο βασιλέα, καὶ ἔδωκεν αὐτοῖς ὁ θεὸς
And then they asked for a king, and ²gave ³to ⁴them ¹God

τὸν Σαοὺλ υἱὸν ᵍΚίς,ǁ ἄνδρα ἐκ   φυλῆς ʰΒενιαμίν,ǁ ἔτη
Saul son of Cis, a man of [the] tribe of Benjamin, ²years

ⁱτεσσαράκοντα.ǁ 22 καὶ μεταστήσας αὐτὸν ἤγειρεν ᵏαὐτοῖς
¹forty.   And having removed him he raised up to them

τὸν Δαβὶδǁ εἰς βασιλέα, ᾧ καὶ εἶπεν   μαρτυρήσας·
David for king, to whom also ⁴he ⁵said ¹having ²borne ³witness,

Εὗρον ˡΔαβὶδǁ τὸν τοῦ Ἰεσσαί, ἄνδρα κατὰ τὴν καρδίαν
I found David the [son] of Jesse, a man according to ²heart

μου, ὃς ποιήσει πάντα τὰ.θελήματά.μου. 23 Τούτου
¹my, who will do all   my will.   ⁴Of ⁵this [⁶man,]

ὁ θεὸς ἀπὸ τοῦ σπέρματος κατ᾽ ἐπαγγελίαν ᵐἤγειρενǁ τῷ
³God ¹of ²the ³seed   according to promise raised up

Ἰσραὴλ σωτῆρα Ἰησοῦν, 24 προκηρύξαντος ⁿἸωάννουǁ
to Israel a Saviour Jesus, ²having ³before ⁴proclaimed ¹John

πρὸ προσώπου τῆς.εἰσόδου.αὐτοῦ βάπτισμα μετανοίας
before [the] face   of his entrance a baptism of repentance

παντὶ τῷ λαῷ Ἰσραήλ. 25 ὡς.δὲ ἐπλήρου °ὁǁ ᴾἸωάννηςǁ
to all the people of Israel. And as ²was ³fulfilling ¹John

τὸν δρόμον, ἔλεγεν, �q Τίνα μεǁ ὑπονοεῖτε εἶναι; οὐκ εἰμὶ
[his] course, he said, Whom me do ye suppose to be? ³Not ²am

ἐγώ, ἀλλ᾽ ἰδού, ἔρχεται μετ᾽ ἐμέ, οὗ οὐκ.εἰμὶ ἄξιος τὸ ὑπό-
¹I [he], but lo, he comes after me, of whom I am not worthy the san-

δημα τῶν ποδῶν λῦσαι. 26 Ἄνδρες ἀδελφοί, υἱοὶ γένους
dal of the feet to loose. Men   brethren, sons of [the] race

Ἀβραάμ, καὶ οἱ ἐν ὑμῖν φοβούμενοι τὸν θεόν, ʳὑμῖνⁿ ὁ
of Abraham, and those among you fearing   God, to you the

ʷ ἐν ὑμῖν λόγος LTTrW.   ˣ Ἰσραηλεῖται T.   ʸ — Ἰσραὴλ G.   ᶻ Αἰγύπτου LTr.   ª τεσσερα-
κονταέτη TTrA.   ᵇ ἐτροφοφόρησεν αὐτοὺς he nourished them GLTAW.   ᶜ κατεκληρονόμησεν
GLTTrAW.   ᵈ — αὐτοῖς TTr[A].   ᵉ ὡς ἔτεσιν τετρακοσίοις καὶ πεντήκοντα· καὶ μετὰ ταῦτα (read
their land about four hundred and fifty years. And after these things he gave, &c.)
LTTrW.   ᶠ — τοῦ TTr[A].   ᵍ Κείς Keis LTTrA.   ʰ Βενιαμείν LTTrA.   ⁱ τεσσεράκοντα TTrA.
ᵏ τὸν Δαυεὶδ αὐτοῖς LTTrA; Δαυὶδ GW.   ˡ Δαυεὶδ LTTrA; Δαυὶδ GW.   ᵐ ἤγαγεν brought
GLTTrAW.   ⁿ Ἰωάνου Tr.   ° — ὁ LTTrA.   ᴾ Ἰωάνης Tr   q Τί ἐμὲ LTTrA.   ʳ ἡμῖν to us TA.

λόγος τῆς σωτηρίας ταύτης ^sἀπεστάλη·‖ 27 οἱ γὰρ κατοικοῦν-
word   of this salvation   was sent :   for those   dwelling

τες ἐν Ἰερουσαλὴμ καὶ οἱ ἄρχοντες αὐτῶν, τοῦτον ἀγνοήσαντες
in   Jerusalem   and   their rulers,   him   not having known

καὶ τὰς φωνὰς τῶν προφητῶν τὰς κατὰ πᾶν σάββατον ἀνα-
and the   voices of the prophets   who on   every   sabbath   are

γινωσκομένας, κρίναντες   ἐπλήρωσαν· 28 καὶ μηδεμίαν
read,   ³having ⁴judged [⁵him] ¹they ²fulfilled.   And   no one

αἰτίαν θανάτου εὑρόντες ᾐτήσαντο Πιλάτον‖ ἀναιρεθῆναι
cause   of death having found   they begged   Pilate   to put ²to ³death

αὐτόν. 29 ὡς δὲ ἐτέλεσαν ^vἅπαντα‖ τὰ   περὶ αὐτοῦ γε-
¹him.   And when they finished all things   that concerning him had

γραμμένα,   καθελόντες   ἀπὸ τοῦ ξύλου, ἔθηκαν εἰς
been written, having taken [him] down from the   tree,   they put [him] in

μνημεῖον· 30 ὁ δὲ θεὸς ἤγειρεν αὐτὸν ἐκ   νεκρῶν,
a tomb ;   but God   raised   him from among [the] dead,

31 ὃς ὤφθη ἐπὶ ἡμέρας πλείους τοῖς συναναβᾶσιν αὐτῷ
who appeared for   ²days   ¹many to those who   came up with   him

ἀπὸ τῆς Γαλιλαίας εἰς Ἰερουσαλήμ, οἵτινές ^w εἰσιν μάρτυρες
from   Galilee   to   Jerusalem,   who   are   ²witnesses

αὐτοῦ πρὸς τὸν λαόν. 32 καὶ ἡμεῖς ^x ὑμᾶς εὐαγγελιζόμεθα
¹his   to the people.   And we   to you announce the glad tidings—

τὴν πρὸς τοὺς πατέρας ἐπαγγελίαν γενομένην, ὅτι ταύτην
the ³to ⁴the ⁵fathers ¹promise   ²made,   that   this

ὁ θεὸς ἐκπεπλήρωκεν τοῖς τέκνοις ^yαὐτῶν ἡμῖν,‖ ἀναστήσας
God   has fulfilled   ⁴children ³their ¹to ²us, having raised up

Ἰησοῦν· 33 ὡς καὶ ἐν ^zτῷ ψαλμῷ τῷ δευτέρῳ γέγραπται,‖
Jesus;   as also in the   ²psalm   ¹second it has been written,

Υἱός μου εἶ σύ, ἐγὼ σήμερον γεγέννηκά σε. 34 Ὅτι δὲ
⁴Son ³my ¹thou ²art,   I   to-day   have begotten thee.   And that

ἀνέστησεν αὐτὸν ἐκ   νεκρῶν, μηκέτι μέλλοντα ὑπο-
he raised   him from among [the] dead,   no more to be about   to

στρέφειν εἰς διαφθοράν, οὕτως εἴρηκεν, Ὅτι δώσω ὑμῖν τὰ
return   to   corruption,   thus   he spoke :   I will give to you the

ὅσια ^aΔαβὶδ‖ τὰ πιστά. 35 ^bδιὸ‖ καὶ ἐν ἑτέρῳ λέγει,
²mercies ³of ⁴David   ¹faithful.   Wherefore also in another he says,

Οὐ δώσεις   τὸν ὅσιόν σου ἰδεῖν διαφθοράν. 36 ^aΔαβὶδ‖
Thou wilt not suffer   thy Holy One   to see   corruption.   36   ²David

μὲν γὰρ ἰδίᾳ γενεᾷ ὑπηρετήσας τῇ τοῦ θεοῦ βουλῇ
³indeed ¹for to his own generation having ministered by the   ²of ³God ¹counsel

ἐκοιμήθη, καὶ προσετέθη πρὸς τοὺς πατέρας αὐτοῦ, καὶ εἶδεν
fell asleep,   and   was added   to   his fathers,   and   saw

διαφθοράν. 37 ὃν δὲ ὁ θεὸς ἤγειρεν οὐκ εἶδεν διαφθοράν.
corruption.   37 But he whom   God   raised up   did not see   corruption.

38 Γνωστὸν οὖν ἔστω ὑμῖν, ἄνδρες ἀδελφοί, ὅτι διὰ τού-
⁴Known ³therefore ¹be ²it to you,   men   brethren,   that through this

του ὑμῖν ἄφεσις ἁμαρτιῶν καταγγέλλεται· 39 ^cκαὶ‖ ἀπὸ
one   to you remission   of sins   is announced;   and   from

πάντων ὧν   οὐκ ἠδυνήθητε ἐν ^dτῷ‖ νόμῳ ^eΜωσέως‖ δι-
all things from which   ye could not   in   the   law   of Moses   be

καιωθῆναι, ἐν τούτῳ πᾶς ὁ πιστεύων δικαιοῦται. 40 βλέ-
justified,   in him   everyone that   believes   is justified.   Take

you is the word of this
salvation sent. 27 For
they that dwell at Je-
rusalem, and their ru-
lers, because they knew
him not, nor yet the
voices of the prophets
which are read every
sabbath day, they have
fulfilled them in con-
demning him. 28 And
though they found no
cause of death in him,
yet desired they Pilate
that he should be slain.
29 And when they had
fulfilled all that was
written of him, they
took him down from
the tree, and laid him
in a sepulchre. 30 But
God raised him from
the dead : 31 and he
was seen many days of
them which came up
with him from Galilee
to Jerusalem, who are
his witnesses unto the
people. 32 And we de-
clare unto you glad
tidings, how that the
promise which was
made unto the fathers,
33 God hath fulfilled
the same unto us their
children, in that he
hath raised up Jesus
again ; as it is also
written in the second
psalm, Thou art my
Son, this day have I
begotten thee. 34 And
as concerning that he
raised him up from
the dead, now no more
to return to corrup-
tion, he said on this
wise, I will give you
the sure mercies of
David. 35 Wherefore
he saith also in an-
other psalm, Thou
shalt not suffer thine
Holy One to see cor-
ruption. 36 For David,
after he had served his
own generation by the
will of God, fell on
sleep, and was laid un-
to his fathers, and saw
corruption : 37 but he,
whom God raised a-
gain, saw no corrup-
tion. 38 Be it known
unto you therefore,
men and brethren,
that through this man
is preached unto you
the forgiveness of
sins : 39 and by him
all that believe are
justified from all
things, from which ye
could not be justified
by the law of Moses.

---

^s ἐξαπεστάλη was sent forth LTTrAW.   ^t Πειλᾶτον T.   ^v πάντα GLTTrAW.   ^w + νῦν
now LTTrAW.   ^x + νῦν now W.   ^y ἡμῶν to our LTTr ; αὐτῶν ἡμῶν W.   ^z τῷ πρώτῳ
(first) ψαλμῷ γέγραπται GTTr ; τῷ ψαλμῷ γέγ. τῷ πρώτῳ (δευτέρῳ AW) LAW.   ^a Δαυείδ LTT A ;
Δαυὶδ GW.   ^b διότι LTTrA.   ^c — καὶ LT[TrA].   ^d — τῷ LTTrA.   ^e Μωϋσέως GLTTrAW.

40 Beware therefore, lest that come upon you, which is spoken of in the prophets; 41 Behold, ye despisers, and wonder, and perish : for I work a work in your days, a work which ye shall in no wise believe, though a man declare it unto you. 42 And when the Jews were gone out of the synagogue, the Gentiles besought that these words might be preached to them the next sabbath. 43 Now when the congregation was broken up, many of the Jews and religious proselytes followed Paul and Barnabas : who, speaking to them, persuaded them to continue in the grace of God.

πετε. οὖν μὴ.ἐπέλθῃ ᶠἐφ᾽ ὑμᾶς‖ τὸ εἰρημένον ἐν
heed therefore that it may not come upon you that which has been said in
τοῖς προφήταις, 41 Ἴδετε, οἱ.καταφρονηταί, καὶ θαυμάσατε
the prophets, Behold, ye despisers, and wonder
καὶ ἀφανίσθητε· ὅτι ἔργον ᵍἐγὼ ἐργάζομαι‖ ἐν ταῖς ἡμέραις
and perish; for a work I work in ²days
ὑμῶν, ἔργον ʰᾧ‖ οὐ.μὴ πιστεύσητε ἐάν τις ἐκδιηγῆται
¹your, a work which in no wise ye would believe if one should declare it
ὑμῖν. 42 Ἐξιόντων.δὲ ⁱἐκ τῆς συναγωγῆς τῶν Ἰουδαίων,‖
to you. But ³having ⁴departed ⁵from ⁶the ⁷synagogue ¹the ²Jews,
παρεκάλουν ᵏτὰ ἔθνη‖ εἰς τὸ μεταξὺ σάββατον λαληθῆναι
¹⁰besought ⁸the ⁹Gentiles on the next sabbath ³to ⁴be spoken
αὐτοῖς τὰ.ῥήματα.ταῦτα. 43 λυθείσης.δὲ τῆς συναγωγῆς,
⁶to ⁷them ¹these ²words. And ³having ⁴broken ⁵up ¹the ²synagogue,
ἠκολούθησαν πολλοὶ τῶν Ἰουδαίων καὶ τῶν σεβομένων
¹⁵followed ⁶many ⁷of ⁸the ⁹Jews ¹⁰and ¹¹of ¹²the ¹³worshipping
προσηλύτων τῷ Παύλῳ καὶ τῷ Βαρνάβᾳ· οἵτινες προσλα-
¹⁴proselytes Paul and Barnabas, who ·speak-
λοῦντες αὐτοῖς ἔπειθον αὐτοὺς ˡἐπιμένειν‖ τῇ χάριτι τοῦ
ing to them persuaded them to continue in the grace
θεοῦ.
of God.

44 And the next sabbath day came almost the whole city together to hear the word of God. 45 But when the Jews saw the multitudes, they were filled with envy, and spake against those things which were spoken by Paul, contradicting and blaspheming. 46 Then Paul and Barnabas waxed bold, and said, It was necessary that the word of God should first have been spoken to you : but seeing ye put it from you, and judge yourselves unworthy of everlasting life, lo, we turn to the Gentiles. 47 For so hath the Lord commanded us, saying, I have set thee to be a light of the Gentiles, that thou shouldest be for salvation unto the ends of the earth. 48 And when the Gentiles heard this, they were glad, and glorified the word of the Lord : and as many as were ordained to eternal life believed. 49 And the word of the Lord was published throughout all the region. 50 But the Jews stirred up the devout and honourable women, and the chief

44 Τῷ ᵐδὲ‖ ⁿἐρχομένῳ‖ σαββάτῳ σχεδὸν πᾶσα ἡ πόλις
And on the coming sabbath almost all the city
συνήχθη ἀκοῦσαι τὸν λόγον ᵒτοῦ θεοῦ.‖ 45 ἰδόντες.δὲ
was gathered together to hear the word of God. But ³having ⁵seen
οἱ Ἰουδαῖοι τοὺς ὄχλους, ἐπλήσθησαν ζήλου, καὶ ἀντέλεγον
¹the ²Jews the crowds, were filled with envy, and contradicted
τοῖς ὑπὸ ᴾτοῦ‖ Παύλου ᑫλεγομένοις,‖ ʳἀντιλέγοντες καὶ‖
the things ²by ³Paul ¹spoken, contradicting and
βλασφημοῦντες. 46 παῤῥησιασάμενοι.ˢδὲ‖ ὁ Παῦλος καὶ ὁ Βαρ-
blaspheming. But ⁴speaking ⁵boldly ¹Paul ²and ³Bar-
νάβας ᵗεἶπον,‖ Ὑμῖν ἦν ἀναγκαῖον πρῶτον λαληθῆναι τὸν
nabas said, To you was necessary first to be spoken the
λόγον τοῦ θεοῦ· ἐπειδὴ.ᵛδὲ‖ ἀπωθεῖσθε αὐτόν, καὶ οὐκ ἀξίους
word of God; but since ye thrust away it, and not worthy
κρίνετε ἑαυτοὺς τῆς αἰωνίου ζωῆς, ἰδοὺ στρεφόμεθα εἰς τὰ
ye judge yourselves of eternal life, lo, ᾽ we turn to the
ἔθνη· 47 οὕτως.γαρ ἐντέταλται ἡμῖν ὁ κύριος, Τέθεικά σε
Gentiles; for thus has enjoined us the Lord, I have set thee
εἰς φῶς ἐθνῶν. τοῦ.εἶναί.σε εἰς σωτηρίαν ἕως ἐσχά-
for ᾽a light of [the] Gentiles, that thou be for salvation to [the] uttermost
του τῆς γῆς. 48 Ἀκούοντα.δὲ τὰ ἔθνη ἔχαιρον, καὶ ἐδόξα-
part of the earth. And hearing [it] the Gentiles rejoiced, and glori-
ζον τὸν λόγον τοῦ κυρίου, καὶ ἐπίστευσαν ὅσοι ἦσαν
fied the word of the Lord, and believed as many as were
τεταγμένοι εἰς ζωὴν αἰώνιον. 49 διεφέρετο.δὲ ὁ λόγος τοῦ
appointed to life eternal. And was carried the word of the
κυρίου ʷδι᾽‖ ὅλης τῆς χώρας. 50 οἱ.δὲ Ἰουδαῖοι παρώτρυναν
Lord through ²whole ¹the country. But the Jews excited
τὰς σεβομένας γυναῖκας ˣκαὶ‖ τὰς εὐσχήμονας καὶ τοὺς πρώ-
the worshipping ²women ¹and ²honourable and the principal

ᶠ — ἐφ᾽ ὑμᾶς LTTr[A].　ᵍ ἐργάζομαι ἐγὼ LTTrAW.　ʰ ὁ LTTrAW.　ⁱ αὐτῶν they (having
departed) GLTTrAW.　ᵏ — τὰ ἔθνη (read they besought) GLTTrAW.　ˡ προσμένειν GLTTrAW.
ᵐ τε GA.　ⁿ ἐρχομένῳ following GLAW.　ᵒ τοῦ κυρίου of the Lord LTTr.　ᴾ — τοῦ LTTr[A].
ᑫ λαλουμένοις LTTr.　ʳ — ἀντιλέγοντες καὶ LTr[A].　ˢ τε LTTrA.　ᵗ εἶπαν LTTrA.
ᵛ — δὲ but LTTr.　ʷ καθ᾽ T.　ˣ — καὶ GLTTrAW.

τοὺς τῆς πόλεως, καὶ ἐπήγειραν διωγμὸν ἐπὶ τὸν Παῦλον
men of the city,   and   stirred up   a persecution against   Paul

καὶ ʸτὸν‖ Βαρνάβαν, καὶ ἐξέβαλον αὐτοὺς ἀπὸ τῶν.ὁρίων.αὐ-
and   Barnabas,   and   cast out   them   from   their borders.

τῶν. 51 οἱ.δὲ ἐκτιναξάμενοι τὸν κονιορτὸν τῶν.ποδῶν.ᶻαὐτῶν‖
But they having shaken off   the   dust   of their feet

ἐπ᾽ αὐτούς, ἦλθον εἰς Ἰκόνιον. 52 οἱ.ᵃδὲ‖ μαθηταὶ ἐπλη-
against them,   came   to   Iconium.   And the   disciples   were

ροῦντο χαρᾶς καὶ πνεύματος ἁγίου.
filled   with joy and [the]   ²Spirit   ¹Holy.

14 Ἐγένετο.δὲ ἐν Ἰκονίῳ κατὰ.τὸ.αὐτὸ εἰσελθεῖν αὐτοὺς
And it came to pass in Iconium   ²together   ³entered   ¹they

εἰς τὴν συναγωγὴν τῶν Ἰουδαίων, καὶ λαλῆσαι οὕτως ὥστε
into   the   synagogue   of the   Jews,   and   spoke   so   that

πιστεῦσαι Ἰουδαίων.τε καὶ Ἑλλήνων πολὺ πλῆθος. 2 οἱ.δὲ
⁹believed   ¹both ²of ³Jews ⁴and   ⁵Hellenists   ⁶a ⁷great   ⁸number.   But the

ᵇἀπειθοῦντες‖ Ἰουδαῖοι ἐπήγειραν καὶ ἐκάκωσαν τὰς ψυχὰς
disobeying   Jews   stirred up   and made evil-affected the   souls

τῶν ἐθνῶν κατὰ τῶν ἀδελφῶν. 3 ἱκανὸν μὲν οὖν χρόνον
of the Gentiles against the   brethren.   A long   ²therefore ¹time

διέτριψαν παρρησιαζόμενοι ἐπὶ τῷ κυρίῳ, τῷ μαρτυ-
they stayed,   speaking boldly, [confiding] in   the   Lord,   who bore wit-

ροῦντι ᶜτῷ λόγῳ τῆς.χάριτος.αὐτοῦ, ᵈκαὶ‖ ἐδιδόντι‖ σημεῖα καὶ
ness   to the word   of his grace,   and   giving   signs   and

τέρατα γίνεσθαι διὰ τῶν.χειρῶν.αὐτῶν. 4 ἐσχίσθη.δὲ τὸ
wonders · to be done through   their hands.   And was divided the

πλῆθος τῆς πόλεως· καὶ οἱ.μὲν ἦσαν σὺν τοῖς Ἰουδαίοις,
multitude of the city,   and   some   were   with the   Jews

οἱ.δὲ σὺν τοῖς ἀποστόλοις. 5 Ὡς.δὲ ἐγένετο ὁρμὴ τῶν
and some with the   apostles.   And when there was a rush ²of ³the

ἐθνῶν τε καὶ Ἰουδαίων σὺν τοῖς.ἄρχουσιν.αὐτῶν, ὑβρίσαι
⁴Gentiles ¹both and   Jews   with   their rulers,   to insult

καὶ λιθοβολῆσαι αὐτούς, 6 συνιδόντες κατέφυγον εἰς τὰς
and to stone   them,   being aware   they fled   to the

πόλεις τῆς Λυκαονίας, ᶠΛύστραν, καὶ Δέρβην, καὶ τὴν περί-
cities   of Lycaonia,   Lystra,   and   Derbe,   and   the country

χωρον, 7 κἀκεῖ ᵍἦσαν εὐαγγελιζόμενοι.‖
around,   and there they were announcing the glad tidings.

8 Καί τις ἀνὴρ ʰἐν Λύστροις ἀδύνατος‖ τοῖς ποσὶν ἐκά-
And a certain man   in   Lystra,   impotent   in the feet,   sat,

θητο, χωλὸς ἐκ κοιλίας μητρὸς.αὐτοῦ ᵎὑπάρχων,‖ ὃς
lame   from [the] womb   of his mother   being,   who

οὐδέποτε ᵏπεριπεπατήκει.‖ 9 οὗτος ᶦἤκουεν‖ τοῦ Παύλου
never   had walked.   This [man]   heard   Paul

λαλοῦντος· ὃς ἀτενίσας αὐτῷ, καὶ ἰδὼν ὅτι ᵐπίστιν
speaking,   who, having looked intently on him, and seeing that   faith

ἔχει‖ τοῦ σωθῆναι, 10 εἶπεν μεγάλῃ ⁿτῇ‖ φωνῇ, ᵒἈνάστηθι
he has   to be healed,   said   with a loud   voice,   Stand up

ἐπὶ τοὺς.πόδας.σου ὀρθός. Καὶ ᵖἥλλετο‖ καὶ περιεπάτει.
on   thy feet   upright.   And he sprang up and   walked.

men of the city, and raised persecution against Paul and Barnabas, and expelled them out of their coasts. , 51 But they shook off the dust of their feet against them, and came unto Iconium. 52 And the disciples were filled with joy, and with the Holy Ghost.

XIV. And it came to pass in Iconium, that they went both together into the synagogue of the Jews, and so spake, that a great multitude both of the Jews and also of the Greeks believed. 2 But the unbelieving Jews stirred up the Gentiles, and made their minds evil affected against the brethren. 3 Long time therefore abode they speaking boldly in the Lord, which gave testimony unto the word of his grace, and granted signs and wonders to be done by their hands. 4 But the multitude of the city was divided: and part held with the Jews, and part with the apostles. 5 And when there was an assault made both of the Gentiles, and also of the Jews with their rulers, to use them despitefully, and to stone them, 6 they were ware of it, and fled unto Lystra and Derbe, cities of Lycaonia, and unto the region that lieth round about: 7 and there they preached the gospel.

8 And there sat a certain man at Lystra, impotent in his feet, being a cripple from his mother's womb, who never had walked: 9 the same heard Paul speak: who stedfastly beholding him, and perceiving that he had faith to be healed, 10 said with a loud voice, Stand upright on thy feet. And he leaped and walked.

ʸ — τὸν LTTrA.   ᶻ — αὐτῶν (read of the feet) LTTrA.   ᵃ τε LTrA.   ᵇ ἀπειθήσαντες LTTrA.   ᶜ + ἐπὶ to (the) T.   ᵈ — καὶ GLTTrAW.   ᵉ διδόντος T.   ᶠ + εἰς to L.   ᵍ εὐαγγελιζόμενοι ἦσαν LTTrA.   ʰ ἀδύνατος ἐν Λύστροις T.   ᵎ ὑπάρχων GLTTrAW.   ᵏ περιεπεπατήκει E ; περιεπάτησεν walked LTTrA.   ᶦ ἤκουσεν LTTr.   ᵐ ἔχει πίστιν LTTrA.   ⁿ — τῇ LTTr.   ᵒ + Σοὶ λέγω ἐν τῷ ὀνόματι τοῦ κυρίου Ἰησοῦ χριστοῦ To thee I say in the name of the Lord Jesus Christ L.   ᵖ ἥλατο GLTTrAW.

11 And when the people saw what Paul had done, they lifted up their voices, saying in the speech of Lycaonia, The gods are come down to us in the likeness of men. 12 And they called Barnabas, Jupiter; and Paul, Mercurius, because he was the chief speaker. 13 Then the priest of Jupiter, which was before their city, brought oxen and garlands unto the gates, and would have done sacrifice with the people. 14 *Which* when the apostles, Barnabas and Paul, heard *of*, they rent their clothes, and ran in among the people, crying out, 15 and saying, Sirs, why do ye these things? We also are men of like passions with you, and preach unto you that ye should turn from these vanities unto the living God, which made heaven, and earth, and the sea, and all things that are therein: 16 who in times past suffered all nations to walk in their own ways. 17 Nevertheless he left not himself without witness, in that he did good, and gave us rain from heaven, and fruitful seasons, filling our hearts with food and gladness. 18 And with these sayings scarce restrained they the people, that they had not done sacrifice unto them. 19 And there came thither *certain* Jews from Antioch and Iconium, who persuaded the people, and, having stoned Paul, drew *him* out of the city, supposing he had been dead. 20 Howbeit, as the disciples stood 'round about him, he rose up, and came into the city: and the next day he departed with Barnabas to Derbe. 21 And when they had preached the gospel to that city, and had taught many, they returned again to Lys-

11 Οἱ δὲ ᵁ ὄχλοι ἰδόντες ὃ ἐποίησεν ˢ ὁ ᵁ Παῦλος, ἐπῆραν
And the crowds having seen what ²did ¹Paul, lifted up

τὴν φωνὴν αὐτῶν Λυκαονιστὶ λέγοντες, Οἱ θεοὶ ὁμοιωθέντες
their voice in Lycaonian saying, The gods, having become like

ἀνθρώποις κατέβησαν πρὸς ἡμᾶς· 12 ἐκάλουν τε τὸν ᵗμὲνᵁ
men, are come down to us. And they called

Βαρνάβαν Δία· τὸν δὲ Παῦλον Ἑρμῆν, ἐπειδὴ αὐτὸς ἦν ὁ
Barnabas Zeus; and Paul Hermes, because he was the

ἡγούμενος τοῦ λόγου. 13 ᵛὁ δὲᵁ ἱερεὺς τοῦ Διὸς τοῦ ὄντος
leader in speaking. And the priest of Zeus who was

πρὸ τῆς πόλεως ʷαὐτῶν,ᵁ ταύρους καὶ στέμματα ἐπὶ τοὺς
before their city, oxen and garlands to the

πυλῶνας ἐνέγκας, σὺν τοῖς ὄχλοις ἤθελεν θύειν. 14 Ἀκού-
gates having brought, with the crowds wished to sacrifice. ⁷Having

σαντες δὲ οἱ ἀπόστολοι Βαρνάβας καὶ Παῦλος, διαρρήξαντες
⁸heard ¹but ²the ³apostles ⁴Barnabas ⁵and, ⁶Paul, having rent

τὰ ἱμάτια αὐτῶν ˣεἰσεπήδησανᵁ εἰς τὸν ὄχλον, κράζοντες
their garments, rushed in to the crowd, crying

15 καὶ λέγοντες, Ἄνδρες, τί ταῦτα ποιεῖτε; καὶ ἡμεῖς
and saying, Men, why these things do ye? also we

ὁμοιοπαθεῖς ἐσμεν ὑμῖν ἄνθρωποι, εὐαγγελιζόμενοι
³of ⁴like ⁵feelings ¹are ⁶with ⁷you ²men, announcing the glad tidings to

ὑμᾶς ἀπὸ τούτων τῶν ματαίων ἐπιστρέφειν ἐπὶ ʸτὸνᵁ θεὸν
you from these vanities to turn to God

ʸτὸνᵁ ζῶντα, ὃς ἐποίησεν τὸν οὐρανὸν καὶ τὴν γῆν καὶ τὴν
the living, who made the heaven and the earth and the

θάλασσαν καὶ πάντα τὰ ἐν αὐτοῖς· 16 ὃς ἐν ταῖς παρ-
sea and all the things in them; who in the

ῳχημέναις γενεαῖς εἴασεν πάντα τὰ ἔθνη πορεύεσθαι ταῖς
past generations suffered all the nations to go

ὁδοῖς αὐτῶν· 17 ᶻκαί τοι γεᵁ οὐκ ἀμάρτυρον ªἑαυτὸνᵁ ἀφῆ-
in their [own] ways, though indeed not without witness himself he

κεν ᵇἀγαθοποιῶν,ᵁ οὐρανόθεν ᶜἡμῖνᵁ ὑετοὺς διδοὺς καὶ καιροὺς
left, doing good, from heaven to us ²rains ¹giving and ²seasons

καρποφόρους, ἐμπιπλῶν τροφῆς καὶ εὐφροσύνης τὰς καρδίας
¹fruitful, filling with food and gladness the hearts

ᵈἡμῶν.ᵁ 18 Καὶ ταῦτα λέγοντες μόλις κατέπαυσαν τοὺς
of us. And these things saying hardly they stopped the

ὄχλους τοῦ μὴ θύειν αὐτοῖς. 19 ᵉἘπῆλθονᵁ δὲ ἀπὸ Ἀντιοχείας
crowds from sacrificing to them. But thither came from Antioch

καὶ Ἰκονίου Ἰουδαῖοι, καὶ πείσαντες τοὺς ὄχλους, καὶ λιθά-
and Iconium Jews, and having persuaded the crowds, and having

σαντες τὸν Παῦλον, ἔσυρον ἔξω τῆς πόλεως, ᶠνομίσαντεςᵁ
stoned Paul, drew [him] outside the city, supposing

αὐτὸν ᵍτεθνάναι.ᵁ 20 κυκλωσάντων δὲ ʰαὐτὸν τῶν μαθητῶν,ᵁ
him to have died. But ³having ⁴surrounded ⁵him ¹the ²disciples,

ἀναστὰς εἰσῆλθεν εἰς τὴν πόλιν· καὶ τῇ ἐπαύριον ἐξῆλ-
having risen up he entered into the city. And on the morrow he went

θεν σὺν τῷ Βαρνάβᾳ εἰς Δέρβην. 21 ⁱεὐαγγελισάμενοίᵁ τε
away with Barnabas to Derbe. And having announced the glad tidings to

τὴν πόλιν ἐκείνην, καὶ μαθητεύσαντες ἱκανοὺς ὑπέστρεψαν εἰς
that city, and having discipled many they returned to

ʳ τε LTA.   ˢ — ὁ LTTrAW.   ᵗ — μὲν LTTrAW.   ᵛ ὅ τε LTTrA.   ʷ — αὐτῶν (read the city) GLTTrAW.   ˣ ἐξεπήδησαν rushed out GLTTrAW.   ʸ — τὸν LTTrAW.   ᶻ καίτοι LT; καιτοιγε GAW; — γε LTTr.   ª αὐτὸν LTTr.   ᵇ ἀγαθουργῶν LTTrAW.   ᶜ ὑμῖν to you GLT[Tr]A.   ᵈ ὑμῶν of you GLTTrA.   ᵉ ἐπῆλθαν LTTrA.   ᶠ νομίζοντες LTTrA.   ᵍ τεθνηκέναι LTTrA.   ʰ τῶν μαθητῶν αὐτὸν LTTr.   ⁱ εὐαγγελιζόμενοί announcing &c. LT.

τὴν Λύστραν καὶ [k] Ἰκόνιον καὶ [k] Ἀντιόχειαν· 22 ἐπιστηρίζοντες
Lystra   and   Iconium   and   Antioch,   establishing

τὰς ψυχὰς τῶν μαθητῶν, παρακαλοῦντες ἐμμένειν τῇ
the souls   of the disciples,   exhorting   [them] to continue in the

πίστει, καὶ ὅτι διὰ πολλῶν θλίψε.ων δεῖ ἡμᾶς εἰσελθεῖν εἰς
faith,   and that through many   tribulations must   we   enter   into

τὴν βασιλείαν τοῦ θεοῦ. 23 χειροτονήσαντες.δὲ αὐτοῖς [1]πρεσ-
the   kingdom   of God.   And having chosen   for them   el-

βυτέρους κατ᾽.ἐκκλησίαν,[ll] προσευξάμενοι μετὰ νηστειῶν πα-
ders   in every assembly,   having prayed   with fastings   they

ρέθεντο αὐτοὺς τῷ κυρίῳ εἰς ὃν πεπιστεύκεισαν. 24 καὶ
committed   them   to the Lord,   on whom they had believed.   And

διελθόντες τὴν Πισιδίαν ἦλθον εἰς [m] Παμφυλίαν· 25 καὶ
having passed through   Pisidia   they came to   Pamphylia,   and

λαλήσαντες [n]ἐν Πέργῃ[ll] τὸν λόγον κατέβησαν εἰς [o]Ἀττάλειαν·[ll]
having spoken   in Perga   the   word they came down to   Attalia;

26 κἀκεῖθεν ἀπέπλευσαν εἰς Ἀντιόχειαν, ὅθεν ἦσαν παρα-
and thence   they sailed   to   Antioch,   whence they had been

δεδομένοι τῇ χάριτι τοῦ θεοῦ εἰς τὸ ἔργον ὃ ἐπλήρωσαν.
committed   to the grace   of God for   the   work which they fulfilled.

27 παραγενόμενοι.δὲ καὶ συναγαγόντες τὴν ἐκκλησίαν
And having arrived   and having gathered together   the   assembly

[p]ἀνήγγειλαν[ll] ὅσα ἐποίησεν ὁ θεὸς μετ᾽ αὐτῶν, καὶ ὅτι ἤνοιξεν
they declared   all that [2]did   God with them,   and that he opened

τοῖς ἔθνεσιν θύραν πίστεως. 28 διέτριβον.δὲ [q]ἐκεῖ[ll] χρόνον
to the nations   a door   of faith.   And they stayed there [4]time

οὐκ ὀλίγον σὺν τοῖς μαθηταῖς.
[1]not [2]a [3]little with the disciples.

15 Καί τινες κατελθόντες ἀπὸ τῆς Ἰουδαίας ἐδίδασκον
And certain having come down from   Judæa   were teaching

τοὺς ἀδελφούς, Ὅτι ἐὰν.μὴ [r]περιτέμνησθε[ll] τῷ ἔθει [s] Μωϋ-
the brethren,   Unless   ye be circumcised after the custom of Mo-

σέως οὐ.δύνασθε σωθῆναι. 2 Γενομένης [t]οῦν[ll] στάσεως
ses   ye cannot   be saved.   Having taken place therefore a commotion

καὶ [v]συζητήσεως[ll] οὐκ ὀλίγης τῷ Παύλῳ καὶ τῷ Βαρνάβᾳ πρὸς
and   discussion   not a little   by Paul and   Barnabas with

αὐτούς, ἔταξαν ἀναβαίνειν Παῦλον καὶ Βαρνάβαν καί
them,   they appointed [4]to [5]go [6]up   [1]Paul [2]and [3]Barnabas   and

τινας ἄλλους ἐξ αὐτῶν πρὸς τοὺς ἀποστόλους καὶ
certain others   from amongst them   to   the   apostles   and

πρεσβυτέρους εἰς Ἱερουσαλήμ, περὶ τοῦ.ζητήματος.τούτου.
elders   to   Jerusalem,   about   this question.

3 οἱ μὲν οὖν προπεμφθέντες ὑπὸ τῆς ἐκκλησίας διήρ-
They indeed therefore having been sent forward by   the   assembly   passed

χοντο τὴν [w] Φοινίκην καὶ [x]Σαμάρειαν,[ll] ἐκδιηγούμενοι τὴν
through   Phœnicia   and   Samaria,   relating   the

ἐπιστροφὴν τῶν ἐθνῶν· καὶ ἐποίουν χαρὰν μεγάλην πᾶσιν
conversion   of the nations. And they caused [2]joy [1]great   to all

τοῖς ἀδελφοῖς. 4 παραγενόμενοι.δὲ εἰς [y]Ἱερουσαλὴμ[ll] [z]ἀπε-
the brethren.   And having come   to   Jerusalem   they were

δέχθησαν[ll] [a]ὑπὸ[ll] τῆς ἐκκλησίας καὶ τῶν ἀποστόλων καὶ τῶν
welcomed   by   the   assembly   and   the   apostles   and the

tra, and to Iconium, and Antioch, 22 confirming the souls of the disciples, and exhorting them to continue in the faith, and that we must through much tribulation enter into the kingdom of God. 23 And when they had ordained them elders in every church, and had prayed with fasting, they commended them to the Lord, on whom they believed. 24 And after they had passed throughout Pisidia, they came to Pamphylia. 25 And when they had preached the word in Perga, they went down into Attalia: 26 and thence sailed to Antioch, from whence they had been recommended to the grace of God for the work which they fulfilled. 27 And when they were come, and had gathered the church together, they rehearsed all that God had done with them, and how he had opened the door of faith unto the Gentiles. 28 And there they abode long time with the disciples.

XV. And certain men which came down from Judæa taught the brethren, and said, Except ye be circumcised after the manner of Moses, ye cannot be saved. 2 When therefore Paul and Barnabas had no small dissension and disputation with them, they determined that Paul and Barnabas, and certain other of them, should go up to Jerusalem unto the apostles and elders about this question. 3 And being brought on their way by the church, they passed through Phenice and Samaria, declaring the conversion of the Gentiles: and they caused great joy unto all the brethren. 4 And when they were come to Jerusalem, they were received of the church, and of

---

[k] + εἰς to LTTrA.   [l] κατ᾽ ἐκκλησίαν πρεσβυτέρους LTTrAW.   [m] + τὴν TTr.   [n] εἰς
τὴν Πέργην T.   [o] Ἀτταλίαν TA.   [p] ἀνήγγελλον LTTrA.   [q] — ἐκεῖ GLTTrAW.   [r] περι-
τμηθῆτε ye have been circumcised LTTrA.   [s] + τῷ LTTrA.   [t] δὲ but (having taken
place) TTr.   [v] ζητήσεως GLTTrAW.   [w] + τε both LTTrA.   [x] Σαμαρίαν T.   [y] Ἱεροσόλυμα Tr.   [z] παρεδέχθησαν they were received LTTrAW.   [a] ἀπὸ Tr.

the apostles and elders, and they declared all things that God had done with them. 5 But there rose up certain of the sect of the Pharisees which believed, saying, That it was needful to circumcise them, and to command them to keep the law of Moses. 6 And the apostles and elders came together for to consider of this matter. 7 And when there had been much disputing, Peter rose up, and said unto them, Men *and* brethren, ye know how that a good while ago God made choice among us, that the Gentiles by my mouth should hear the word of the gospel, and believe. 8 And God, which knoweth the hearts, bare them witness, giving them the Holy Ghost, even as *he did* unto us; 9 And put no difference between us and them, purifying their hearts by faith. 10 Now therefore why tempt ye God, to put a yoke upon the neck of the disciples, which neither our fathers nor we were able to bear? 11 But we believe that through the grace of the Lord Jesus Christ we shall be saved, even as they. 12 Then all the multitude kept silence, and gave audience to Barnabas and Paul, declaring what miracles and wonders God had wrought among the Gentiles by them. 13 And after they had held their peace, James answered, saying, Men *and* brethren, hearken unto me: 14 Simeon hath declared how God at the first did visit the Gentiles, to take out of them a people for his name. 15 And to this agree the words of the prophets; as it is written, 16 After this I will return, and will build again the tabernacle of David, which is fallen down; and I will build again the ruins thereof, and

πρεσβυτέρων, ἀνήγγειλάν.τε ὅσα ὁ θεὸς ἐποίησεν μετ' αὐτῶν.
elders,   and they declared all that God did   with them.

5 ἐξανέστησαν.δέ τινες τῶν ἀπὸ τῆς αἱρέσεως τῶν Φαρισαίων
And rose up   certain of those of   the   sect   of the Pharisees

πεπιστευκότες, λέγοντες, "Οτι δεῖ περιτέμνειν αὐτούς,
who believed,   saying,   It is necessary to circumcise   them,

παραγγέλλειν.τε τηρεῖν τὸν νόμον Μωϋσέως. 6 Συνήχ-
and charge   [them] to keep the   law   of Moses.   ²Were ³gathered

θησαν ᵇδὲ‖ οἱ ἀπόστολοι καὶ οἱ πρεσβύτεροι ἰδεῖν περὶ τοῦ
⁴together ¹and the   apostles   and the   elders   to see about

λόγου.τούτου. 7 πολλῆς.δὲ ᶜσυζητήσεως‖ γενομένης, ἀνα-
this matter.   And much   discussion   having taken place, ²having

στὰς Πέτρος εἶπεν πρὸς αὐτούς, "Ανδρες ἀδελφοί, ὑμεῖς
³risen ⁴up ¹Peter said   to   them,   Men   brethren,   ye

ἐπίστασθε ὅτι ἀφ' ἡμερῶν ἀρχαίων ᵈὁ θεὸς ἐν ἡμῖν ἐξελέξατο‖
know   that from ²days ¹early   God among us   chose

διὰ τοῦ.στόματός.μου ἀκοῦσαι τὰ ἔθνη τὸν λόγον τοῦ
by   my mouth   [for] ³to ⁴hear ¹the ²nations the   word of the

εὐαγγελίου, καὶ πιστεῦσαι. 8 καὶ ὁ καρδιογνώστης θεὸς ἐμαρ-
glad tidings, and to believe.   And the heart-knowing   God   bore

τύρησεν αὐτοῖς, δοὺς ᵉαὐτοῖς‖ τὸ πνεῦμα τὸ ἅγιον, καθὼς καὶ
witness to them, giving to them the   Spirit the Holy,   as   also

ἡμῖν· 9 καὶ ᶠοὐδὲν‖ διέκρινεν μεταξὺ ἡμῶν ᵍτε‖ καὶ αὐτῶν,
to us,   and   put no difference between   ²us ¹both and them,

τῇ πίστει καθαρίσας τὰς.καρδίας.αὐτῶν. 10 νῦν οὖν τί
by the faith having purified   their hearts.   Now therefore why

πειράζετε τὸν θεόν, ἐπιθεῖναι ζυγὸν ἐπὶ τὸν τράχηλον τῶν
tempt ye   God,   to put   a yoke upon the   neck   of the

μαθητῶν, ὃν οὔτε οἱ.πατέρες.ἡμῶν οὔτε ἡμεῖς ἰσχύσαμεν
disciples, which neither   our fathers   nor   we   were able

βαστάσαι; 11 ἀλλὰ διὰ τῆς χάριτος ʰ κυρίου Ἰησοῦ ⁱχριστοῦ‖
to bear?   But   by the   grace   of [the] Lord Jesus   Christ

πιστεύομεν σωθῆναι, καθ' ὃν.τρόπον κἀκεῖνοι. 12 Ἐσίγησεν
we believe to be saved, in the same manner as they also.   ²Kept ¹silence

δὲ πᾶν τὸ πλῆθος, καὶ ἤκουον Βαρνάβα καὶ Παύλου ἐξη-
¹and all the multitude, and heard Barnabas   and   Paul   re-

γουμένων ὅσα ἐποίησεν ὁ θεὸς σημεῖα καὶ τέρατα ἐν τοῖς
lating   what ⁵did   ⁴God   ¹signs ²and ³wonders among the

ἔθνεσιν δι' αὐτῶν. 13 Μετὰ.δὲ τὸ.σιγῆσαι αὐτοὺς ἀπεκρίθη
nations   by   them.   And after ²were ³silent ¹they   ²answered

Ἰάκωβος λέγων, "Ανδρες ἀδελφοί, ἀκούσατέ μου. 14 Συμεὼν
⁴James,   saying,   Men   brethren,   hear   me.   Simeon

ἐξηγήσατο καθὼς πρῶτον ὁ θεὸς ἐπεσκέψατο λαβεῖν ἐξ
related   how   first   God   visited   to take out of

ἐθνῶν λαὸν ᵏἐπὶ‖ τῷ.ὀνόματι.αὐτοῦ. 15 καὶ τούτῳ συμφω-
nations a people for   his name.   And with this   agree

νοῦσιν οἱ λόγοι τῶν προφητῶν, καθὼς γέγραπται, 16 Μετὰ
the words of the prophets: as   it has been written,   After

ταῦτα ἀναστρέψω καὶ ἀνοικοδομήσω τὴν σκηνὴν ¹Δαβὶδ‖
these things I will return and will build again the   tabernacle of David

τὴν πεπτωκυῖαν· καὶ τὰ ᵐκατεσκαμμένα‖ αὐτῆς ἀνοικοδομήσω,
which is fallen;   and the   ruins   of it   I will build again,

---

ᵇ τε TrA.   ᶜ συνζητήσεως LA ; ζητήσεως TTr.   ᵈ ἐν ὑμῖν you (ἡμῖν W) ἐξελέξατο ὁ θεὸς
LTTrAW.   ᵉ — αὐτοῖς TTrA.   ᶠ οὐθὲν TTrA.   ᵍ — τε W.   ʰ + τοῦ of the GLTTrAW.
ⁱ — χριστοῦ GTTrAW.   ᵏ — ἐπὶ (read τῷ ὀν. αὐτοῦ for his name) LTTrAW.   ¹ Δαυείδ
ᶫTTrA ; Δαυὶδ GW.   ᵐ.κατεστραμμένα T ; κατεστρεμμένα Tr.

καὶ ἀνορθώσω αὐτήν, 17 ὅπως ἂν.ἐκζητήσωσιν οἱ κατάλοιποι
and will set up it, so that ⁵may ⁶seek ⁷out ¹the ²residue

τῶν ἀνθρώπων τὸν κύριον, καὶ πάντα τὰ ἔθνη ἐφ᾽ οὓς ἐπι-
³of ⁴men the Lord, and all the nations upon whom has

κέκληται τὸ.ὄνομά.μου ἐπ᾽ αὐτούς· λέγει κύριος ⁿὁ‖ ποιῶν
been called my name upon them, says [the] Lord who does

ταῦτα °πάντα.‖ 18 ᴾΓνωστὰ‖ ἀπ᾽ αἰῶνός �pἐστιν τῷ θεῷ
"these ³things ¹all: known from eternity are to God

πάντα τὰ.ἔργα.αὐτοῦ.‖ 19 διὸ ἐγὼ κρίνω μὴ παρενοχλεῖν
all his works. Wherefore I judge not to trouble

τοῖς ἀπὸ τῶν ἐθνῶν ἐπιστρέφουσιν ἐπὶ τὸν θεόν· 20 ἀλλὰ
those who from the nations turn to God; but

ἐπιστεῖλαι αὐτοῖς τοῦ ἀπέχεσθαι ʳἀπὸ‖ τῶν ἀλισγημάτων τῶν
to write to them to abstain from the pollutions of the

εἰδώλων καὶ τῆς πορνείας καὶ ˢτοῦ‖ πνικτοῦ καὶ τοῦ αἵματος.
idols and fornication and what is strangled and blood.

21 ᵗΜωσῆς‖.γὰρ ἐκ γενεῶν ἀρχαίων κατὰ.πόλιν τοὺς κη-
For Moses from generations of old in every city ²those ³pro-

ρύσσοντας αὐτὸν ἔχει ἐν ταῖς συναγωγαῖς κατὰ.πᾶν σάββατον
claiming ⁴him ¹has in the synagogues, every sabbath

ἀναγινωσκόμενος.
being read.

22 Τότε ἔδοξεν τοῖς ἀποστόλοις καὶ τοῖς πρεσβυτέροις
Then it seemed good to the apostles and to the elders

σὺν ὅλῃ τῇ ἐκκλησίᾳ, ἐκλεξαμένους ἄνδρας ἐξ αὐτῶν
with ²whole ¹the assembly, chosen men from among them

πέμψαι εἰς Ἀντιόχειαν σὺν τῷ Παύλῳ καὶ Βαρνάβᾳ, Ἰούδαν
to send to Antioch with Paul and Barnabas, Judas

τὸν ᵛἐπικαλούμενον‖ ʷΒαρσαβᾶν,‖ καὶ Σίλαν, ἄνδρας ἡγου-
surnamed Barsabas, and Silas, ²men ¹lead-

μένους ἐν τοῖς ἀδελφοῖς, 23 γράψαντες διὰ χειρὸς.αὐτῶν
ing among the brethren, having written by their hand

ˣτάδε,‖ Οἱ ἀπόστολοι καὶ οἱ πρεσβύτεροι ʸκαὶ οἱ‖ ἀδελφοί,
thus: The ᵗapostles and the elders and the brethren,

τοῖς κατὰ τὴν Ἀντιόχειαν καὶ Συρίαν καὶ Κιλικίαν ἀδελφοῖς
to those in Antioch and Syria and Cilicia, brethren

τοῖς ἐξ ἐθνῶν, χαίρειν. 24 Ἐπειδὴ ἠκούσαμεν ὅτι
ᶻfrom among [the] nations, greeting. Inasmuch as we have heard that

τινὲς ἐξ ἡμῶν ἐξελθόντες ἐτάραξαν ὑμᾶς λόγοις,
certain from amongst us having gone out troubled you by words,

ἀνασκευάζοντες τὰς.ψυχὰς.ὑμῶν, ᶻλέγοντες περιτέμνεσθαι
upsetting your souls, saying [ye must] be circumcised

καὶ τηρεῖν τὸν νόμον,‖ οἷς οὐ.διεστειλάμεθα· 25 ἔδοξεν
and keep the law; to whom we gave no [such] command; it seemed good

ἡμῖν γενομένοις ὁμοθυμαδόν, ᵃἐκλεξαμένους‖ ἄνδρας πέμψαι
to us having come with one accord, chosen men to send

πρὸς ὑμᾶς, σὺν τοῖς.ἀγαπητοῖς.ἡμῶν Βαρνάβᾳ καὶ Παύλῳ,
to you, with our beloved Barnabas and Paul,

26 ἀνθρώποις παραδεδωκόσιν τὰς.ψυχὰς.αὐτῶν ὑπὲρ τοῦ
men who have given up their lives for the

ὀνόματος τοῦ.κυρίου.ἡμῶν Ἰησοῦ χριστοῦ. 27 ἀπεστάλκαμεν
name of our Lord Jesus Christ. We have sent

I will set it up: 17 that the residue of men might seek after the Lord, and all the Gentiles, upon whom my name is called, saith the Lord, who doeth all these things. 18 Known unto God are all his works from the beginning of the world. 19 Wherefore my sentence is, that we trouble not them, which from among the Gentiles are turned to God: 20 but that we write unto them, that they abstain from pollutions of idols, and from fornication, and from things strangled, and from blood. 21 For Moses of old time hath in every city them that preach him, being read in the synagogues every sabbath day.

22 Then pleased it the apostles and elders, with the whole church, to send chosen men of their own company to Antioch with Paul and Barnabas; namely, Judas surnamed Barsabas, and Silas, chief men among the brethren: 23 and they wrote letters by them after this manner; The apostles and elders and brethren send greeting unto the brethren which are of the Gentiles in Antioch and Syria and Cilicia: 24 forasmuch as we have heard, that certain which went out from us have troubled you with words, subverting your souls, saying, Ye must be circumcised, and keep the law: to whom we gave no such commandment: 25 it seemed good unto us, being assembled with one accord, to send chosen men unto you with our beloved Barnabas and Paul, 26 men that have hazarded their lives for the name of our Lord Jesus Christ. 27 We have sent there-

---

ᵘ — ὁ LTTr.   ° —.πάντα GLTTrAW.   ᴾ γνωστὸν LW.   �q τῷ κυρίῳ τὸ ἔργον αὐτοῦ to the Lord his work L; ἐστιν τῷ θεῷ τὸ ἔργον αὐτοῦ W; — ἐστιν τῷ θεῷ παντα τὰ εργα αυτου GTTrA.   ʳ — ἀπὸ (read τῶν from the) LTTr[A].   ˢ — τοῦ LTr.   ᵗ Μωσῆς GLTTrAW.   ᵛ καλουμενον called LTTrAW.   ʷ Βαρσαββᾶν LTTrA.   ˣ — τάδε LTTrA.   ʸ — καὶ οἱ (read elder brethren) LTTrA.   ᶻ — λέγοντες περιτέμνεσθαι καὶ τηρειν τὸν νόμον LTTrA.   ᵃ ἐκλεξαμένοις having chosen LTrW.

24

fore Judas and Silas, who shall also tell *you* the same things by mouth. 28 For it seemed good to the Holy Ghost, and to us, to lay upon you no greater burden than these necessary things; 29 that ye abstain from meats offered to idols, and from blood, and from things strangled, and from fornication: from which if ye keep yourselves, ye shall do well. Fare ye well. 30 So when they were dismissed, they came to Antioch: and when they had gathered the multitude together, they delivered the epistle: 31 which when they had read, they rejoiced for the consolation. 32 And Judas and Silas, being prophets also themselves, exhorted the brethren with many words, and confirmed *them*. 33 And after they had tarried *there* a space, they were let go in peace from the brethren unto the apostles. 34 Notwithstanding it pleased Silas to abide there still. 35 Paul also and Barnabas continued in Antioch, teaching and preaching the word of the Lord, with many others also.

οὖν Ἰούδαν καὶ Σίλαν, καὶ αὐτοὺς διὰ λόγου ἀπαγγέλ-
therefore Judas and Silas, [2]also [1]themselves by word telling
λοντας τὰ αὐτά. 28 ἔδοξεν.γὰρ [b]τῷ ἁγίῳ πνεύματι[ll]
[you] the same things. For it seemed good to the Holy Spirit
καὶ ἡμῖν, μηδὲν πλέον ἐπιτίθεσθαι ὑμῖν βάρος πλὴν [c]τῶν
and to us, no further [2]to [3]lay [4]upon [5]you [1]burden than
ἐπάναγκες.τούτων,[ll] 29 ἀπέχεσθαι εἰδωλοθύτων καὶ
these necessary things : to abstain from things sacrificed to idols, and
αἵματος καὶ [d]πνικτοῦ[ll] καὶ πορνείας· ἐξ ὧν
from blood and from what is strangled, and from fornication ; from which
διατηροῦντες ἑαυτούς, εὖ πράξετε· ἔρρωσθε. 30 Οἱ μὲν
keeping yourselves, well ye will do. Farewell. They
οὖν ἀπολυθέντες [e]ἦλθον[ll] εἰς Ἀντιόχειαν· καὶ συναγαγόντες
therefore, being let go went to Antioch, and having gathered
τὸ πλῆθος ἐπέδωκαν τὴν ἐπιστολήν. 31 ἀναγνόντες.δὲ ἐχά-
the multitude delivered the epistle. And having read they
ρησαν ἐπὶ τῇ παρακλήσει. 32 Ἰούδας.[f]τε[ll] καὶ Σίλας, καὶ αὐ-
rejoiced at the consolation. And Judas and Silas, [2]also [1]them-
τοὶ προφῆται ὄντες, διὰ λόγου πολλοῦ παρεκάλεσαν τοὺς
selves [4]prophets [3]being, by [2]discourse [1]much exhorted the
ἀδελφούς, καὶ ἐπεστήριξαν. 33 Ποιήσαντες.δὲ χρόνον ἀπε-
brethren, and established [them]. And having continued a time they
λύθησαν μετ᾽ εἰρήνης ἀπὸ τῶν ἀδελφῶν πρὸς [g]τοὺς ἀποστό-
were let go in peace from the brethren to the apostles;
λους.[ll] 34 [h]ἔδοξεν.δὲ τῷ Σίλᾳ ἐπιμεῖναι αὐτοῦ.[ll] 35 Παῦλος.δὲ
but it seemed good to Silas to remain there. And Paul
καὶ Βαρνάβας διέτριβον ἐν Ἀντιοχείᾳ, διδάσκοντες καὶ εὐαγ-
and Barnabas stayed in Antioch, teaching and [5]an-
γελιζόμενοι μετὰ καὶ ἑτέρων πολλῶν, τὸν λόγον τοῦ
nouncing [6]the [7]glad [8]tidings [1]with [4]also [3]others [2]many— the word of the
κυρίου.
Lord.

36 And some days after Paul said unto Barnabas, Let us go again and visit our brethren in every city where we have preached the word of the Lord, *and see* how they do. 37 And Barnabas determined to take with them John, whose surname was Mark. 38 But Paul thought not good to take him with them, who departed from them from Pamphylia, and went not with them to the work. 39 And the contention was so sharp between them, that they departed asunder one from the other : and so Barnabas took Mark, and

36 Μετὰ.δὲ τινας ἡμέρας εἶπεν [i]Παῦλος πρὸς Βαρνάβαν,[ll]
But after certain days said Paul to Barnabas,
Ἐπιστρέψαντες δὴ ἐπισκεψώμεθα τοὺς.ἀδελφοὺς.[k]ἡμῶν[ll] κατὰ
Having turned back [3]indeed [1]let [2]us look after our brethren in
[l]πᾶσαν πόλιν[ll] ἐν αἷς κατηγγείλαμεν τὸν λόγον τοῦ κυρίου,
every city in which we have announced the word of the Lord,
πῶς ἔχουσιν. 37 Βαρνάβας.δὲ [m]ἐβουλεύσατο[ll] [n]συμπαρα-
how they are. And Barnabas purposed to take
λαβεῖν[ll] [o][p]τὸν[ll] [q]Ἰωάννην[ll] τὸν καλούμενον Μάρκον· 38 Παῦ-
with [them] John called Mark; [2]Paul
λος δὲ ἠξίου τὸν ἀποστάντα ἀπ᾽ αὐτῶν ἀπὸ Παμ-
[1]but thought it well him who withdrew from them from Pam-
φυλίας, καὶ μὴ.συνελθόντα αὐτοῖς εἰς τὸ ἔργον, μὴ [r]συμπαρα-
phylia, and went not with them to the work, not to take
λαβεῖν[ll] τοῦτον. 39 ἐγένετο [s]οὖν[ll] παροξυσμός. ὥστε
[2]with [3][them] [1]him. Arose therefore a[3]sharp contention so that
ἀποχωρισθῆναι αὐτοὺς ἀπ᾽ ἀλλήλων, τόν.τε.Βαρνάβαν παρα-
[2]departed [1]they from one another, and Barnabas having

---

[b] τῷ πνεύματι τῷ ἁγίῳ TTrW.   [c] τούτων τῶν ἐπάναγκες LTTr; — τούτων A.   [d] πνικτῶν LTTrA.   [e] κατῆλθον LTTrA.   [f] δὲ E.   [g] τοὺς ἀποστείλαντας αὐτούς, those who sent them GLTTrAW.   [h] — *verse* 34 LTTrAW.   [i] πρὸς Βαρνάβαν Παῦλος, LTTrA.   [k] — ἡμῶν (*read* the brethren) GLTTrAW.   [l] πόλιν πᾶσαν LTTrA.   [m] ἐβούλετο LTTrAW.   [n] συν- TA.   [o] + καὶ also GLTTrA.   [p] — τὸν GLA.   [q] Ἰωάνην Tr.   [r] συμ-(συν- TA)παραλαμβάνειν LTTrA.   [s] δὲ and (arose) LTTrA.

λαβόντα τὸν Μάρκον ἐκπλεῦσαι εἰς Κύπρον· 40 Παῦλος.δὲ
taken　　the Mark　　sailed　　to　Cyprus;　　　but Paul

ἐπιλεξάμενος Σίλαν ἐξῆλθεν, παραδοθεὶς τῇ χάριτι
having chosen　Silas　went forth, having been committed to the　grace

ᵗτοῦ θεοῦ‖ ὑπὸ τῶν ἀδελφῶν. 41 διήρχετο.δὲ τὴν Συρίαν
of God　by　the　brethren.　And he passed through　　Syria

καὶ ʷ Κιλικίαν, ἐπιστηρίζων τὰς ἐκκλησίας. 16 Κατήντησεν.δὲ ˣ
and　Cilicia,　establishing　the assemblies.　And he arrived

εἰς Δέρβην καὶ ʸ Λύστραν· καὶ ἰδού, μαθητής τις ἦν ἐκεῖ,
at　Derbe　and　Lystra:　and behold, a ²disciple ¹certain was there,

ὀνόματι Τιμόθεος, υἱὸς γυναικός ᶻτινος‖ Ἰουδαίας πιστῆς
by name Timotheus,　son　of a ⁴woman ¹certain　²Jewish ³believing

πατρὸς.δὲ Ἕλληνος· 2 ὃς ἐμαρτυρεῖτο ὑπὸ τῶν ἐν Λύσ-
but [the] father a Greek,　who was borne witness to by　the ²in ³Lys-

τροις καὶ Ἰκονίῳ ἀδελφῶν. 3 τοῦτον ἠθέλησεν ὁ Παῦλος σὺν
tra　⁴and ⁵Iconium ¹brethren.　This one　²wished　¹Paul　with

αὐτῷ ἐξελθεῖν, καὶ λαβὼν περιέτεμεν αὐτὸν διὰ τοὺς
him　to go forth,　and having taken he circumcised him　on account of the

Ἰουδαίους τοὺς ὄντας ἐν τοῖς.τόποις.ἐκείνοις· ᾔδεισαν.γὰρ
Jews　who were in　those places,　　for they ²knew

ᵖἅπαντες τὸν.πατέρα.αὐτοῦ ὅτι Ἕλλην‖ ὑπῆρχεν. 4 ὡς.δὲ
¹all　　his father　　that a Greek　he was.　And as

διεπορεύοντο τὰς πόλεις ᵇπαρεδίδουν‖ αὐτοῖς φυλάσσειν
they passed through the cities　they delivered　to them　to keep

τὰ δόγματα τὰ κεκριμένα ὑπὸ τῶν ἀποστόλων καὶ ᶜτῶν‖
the decrees　decided on　by　the　apostles　and the

πρεσβυτέρων⟩ τῶν ἐν ᵈἹερουσαλήμ.‖ 5 αἱ μὲν οὖν ἐκ-
elders　　of those in　Jerusalem.　The　²therefore ¹as-

κλησίαι ἐστερεοῦντο τῇ πίστει, καὶ ἐπερίσσευον τῷ ἀριθμῷ
semblies were strengthened in the faith, ˙ and　abounded　　in number

καθ'.ἡμέραν.
every day.

6 ᵉΔιελθόντες‖ δὲ τὴν Φρυγίαν καὶ ᶠτὴν‖ Γαλατικὴν
²Having ³passed ⁴through ¹and　Phrygia　and　the　Galatian

χώραν, κωλυθέντες ὑπὸ τοῦ ἁγίου πνεύματος λαλῆσαι
country, having been forbidden by　the　Holy　Spirit　to speak

τὸν λόγον ἐν τῇ Ἀσίᾳ, 7 ἐλθόντες ᵍ κατὰ τὴν Μυσίαν ἐπείρα-
the　word　in　Asia,　having come down to　　Mysia　they at-

ζον ʰκατὰ‖ ⁱτὴν‖ Βιθυνίαν ᵏπορεύεσθαι·‖ καὶ οὐκ.εἴασεν
tempted to　　Bithynia　to go;　and ³did ⁴not ⁵suffer

αὐτοὺς τὸ πνεῦμα¹. 8 παρελθόντες.δὲ τὴν Μυσίαν κατέβη-
⁶them　¹the　²Spirit;　and having passed by　Mysia　they came

σαν εἰς Τρωάδα. 9 καὶ ὅραμα διὰ ᵐτῆς‖ νυκτὸς ⁿὤφθη τῷ
down to　Troas.　And a vision during　the　night　appeared

Παύλῳ·‖ Ἀνήρ ᵒτις ἦν Μακεδὼν‖ ἑστώς, ᵖ παρακαλῶν
to Paul:　A ²man ¹certain ³was ³of ⁴Macedonia standing,　beseeching

αὐτὸν καὶ λέγων, Διαβὰς εἰς Μακεδονίαν. βοήθησον
him　and saying, Having passed over into　Macedonia　help

ἡμῖν. 10 Ὡς.δὲ τὸ ὅραμα εἶδεν, εὐθέως ἐζητήσαμεν ἐξελθεῖν
us.　And when　the vision he saw, immediately　we sought　to go forth

---

sailed unto Cyprus;
40 and Paul chose Si-
las, and departed, be-
ing recommended by
the brethren unto the
grace of God. 41 And
he went through Sy-
ria and Cilicia, con-
firming the churches.
XVI. Then came he
to Derbe and Lystra:
and, behold, a certain
disciple was there,
named Timotheus, the
son of a certain wo-
man, which was a
Jewess, and believed;
but his father was a
Greek: 2 which was
well reported of by the
brethren that were at
Lystra and Iconium.
3 Him would Paul
have to go forth with
him; and took and
circumcised him be-
cause of the Jews
which were in those
quarters: for they
knew all that his fa-
ther was a Greek:
4 And as they went
through the cities,
they delivered them
the decrees for to keep,
that were ordained of
the apostles and elders
which were at Jerusa-
lem, 5 And so were the
churches established
in the faith, and in-
creased in number
daily.

6 Now when they
had gone throughout
Phrygia and the re-
gion of Galatia, and
were forbidden of the
Holy Ghost to preach
the word in Asia, 7 af-
ter they were come to
Mysia, they assayed to
go into Bithynia: but
the Spirit suffered
them not. 8 And they
passing by Mysia came
down to Troas. 9 And
a vision appeared to
Paul in the night;
There stood a man of
Macedonia, and pray-
ed him, saying, Come
over into Macedonia,
and help us. 10 And
after he had seen the
vision, immediately
we endeavoured to go

ᵛ τοῦ κυρίου of the Lord LTTrAW.　ʷ + τὴν L.　ˣ + καὶ also L[Tr].　ʸ + εἰς at LTTr.
ᶻ — τινος GLTTrAW.　ᵃ πάντες (ἅπαντες Tr) ὅτι Ἕλλην ὁ πατὴρ αὐτοῦ LTr.　ᵇ παρεδίδοσαν
LTTrAW.　ᶜ — τῶν LTTrAW.　ᵈ Ἱεροσολύμοις LTTrAW.　ᵉ διῆλθον they passed through
LTTrAW.　ᶠ — τὴν LTTrA.　ᵍ + δὲ and (having come) LTTrAW.　ʰ εἰς GLTTrAW.
ⁱ — τὴν W.　ᵏ πορευθῆναι LTTrA.　¹ + Ἰησοῦ of Jesus GLTTrAW.　ᵐ — τῆς LTTr[A]W.
ⁿ τῷ Παύλῳ ὤφθη TTrA.　ᵒ Μακεδών τις ἦν (— ἦν A) LTTrAW.　ᵖ καὶ and LTTr.

into Macedonia, assuredly gathering that the Lord had called us for to preach the gospel unto them. 11 Therefore loosing from Troas, we came with a straight course to Samothracia, and the next *day* to Neapolis ; 12 and from thence to Philippi, which is the chief city of that part of Macedonia, *and* a colony : and we were in that city abiding certain days. 13 And on the sabbath we went out of the city by a river side, where prayer was wont to be made ; and we sat down, and spake unto the women which resorted *thither.* 14 And a certain woman named Lydia, a seller of purple, of the city of Thyatira, which worshipped God, heard *us:* whose heart the Lord opened, that she attended unto the things which were spoken of Paul. 15 And when she was baptized, and her houshold, she besought *us,* saying, If ye have judged me to be faithful to the Lord, come into my house, and abide *there.* And she constrained us. 16 And it came to pass, as we went to prayer, a certain damsel possessed with a spirit of divination met us, which brought her masters much gain by soothsaying: 17 the same followed Paul and us, and cried, saying, These men are the servants of the most high God, which shew unto us the way of salvation. 18 And this did she many days. But Paul, being grieved, turned and said to the spirit, I command thee in the name of Jesus Christ to come out of her. And he came out the same hour. 19 And when her masters saw that the hope of their gains was gone, they caught

εἰς ᵠτὴν‖ Μακεδονίαν, συμβιβάζοντες ὅτι προσκέκληται ἡμᾶς
to　　　Macedonia,　　concluding　　that　³had ⁴called　　ᵘus

ʳὁ κύριος‖ εὐαγγελίσασθαι αὐτούς. 11 Ἀναχθέντες
¹the　²Lord　to announce the glad tidings to　them.　　Having sailed

ˢοῦν‖ ἀπὸ ˡτῆς‖ Τρωάδος εὐθυδρομήσαμεν εἰς Σαμο-
therefore from　Troas　we came with a straight course to　Samo-

θράκην, τῇ.ʸτε‖ ἐπιούσῃ εἰς ᵂΝεάπολιν,‖ 12 ˣἐκεῖθέν.τε‖
thracia,　and on the following day to　Neapolis,　　and thence

εἰς Φιλίππους, ἥτις ἐστὶν πρώτη τῆς μερίδος ʸτῆς‖
to　Philippi,　which is [the] first　²of [³that] ⁴part

Μακεδονίας πόλις, κολωνία. Ἦμεν.δὲ ἐν ταύτῃ τῇ πόλει δια-
⁵of ⁶Macedonia ¹city,　a colony. And we were in　this　　city stay-

τρίβοντες ἡμέρας τινάς, 13 τῇ.τε ἡμέρᾳ τῶν σαββάτων
ing　　²days　¹certain.　And on the day of the　sabbath

ἐξήλθομεν ᶻἔξω‖ τῆς ᵃπόλεως‖ παρὰ ποταμόν, οὗ ᵇἐνομίζετο
we went forth outside the　city　　by　a river,　where was customary

προσευχὴ‖ εἶναι, καὶ καθίσαντες ἐλαλοῦμεν ταῖς συνελ-
prayer　　to be,　and having sat down we spake　to the ²who ³came

θούσαις γυναιξίν. 14 Καί τις γυνὴ ὀνόματι Λυδία, πορ-
⁴together ¹women.　　And a certain woman, by name　Lydia,　a seller

φυρόπωλις πόλεως Θυατείρων, σεβομένη τὸν θεόν, ἤκουεν·
of purple of [the] city of Thyatira, who worshipped　God, was hearing;

ἧς ὁ κύριος διήνοιξεν τὴν καρδίαν προσέχειν τοῖς
of whom the Lord　opened　the　heart　to attend to the things

λαλουμένοις ὑπὸ ᶜτοῦ‖ Παύλου. 15 ὡς.δὲ ἐβαπτίσθη καὶ
spoken·　by　　'Paul.　　And when she was baptized and

ὁ.οἶκος.αὐτῆς παρεκάλεσεν λέγουσα, Εἰ κεκρίκατέ με πιστὴν
her house　she besought　saying,　If ye have judged me faithful

τῷ κυρίῳ εἶναι, εἰσελθόντες εἰς τὸν.οἶκόν.μου, ᵈμείνατε·‖
to the Lord　to be, having entered into　my house,　　abide.

καὶ παρεβιάσατο ἡμᾶς. 16 Ἐγένετο.δὲ πορευομένων.ἡμῶν
And she constrained us.　　And it came to pass　as we were going

εἰς ᵉ προσευχήν, παιδίσκην τινὰ ἔχουσαν πνεῦμα ᶠΠύθωνος‖
to　prayer,　a ²damsel ¹certain, having　a spirit of Python,

ᵍἀπαντῆσαι‖ ἡμῖν, ἥτις ἐργασίαν πολλὴν παρεῖχεν τοῖς
met　us,　who　²gain　¹much　brought

κυρίοις.αὐτῆς μαντευομένη. 17 αὕτη ʰκατακολουθήσασα‖ τῷ
to her masters　by divining.　　She　　having followed

Παύλῳ καὶ ἡμῖν ἔκραζεν λέγουσα, Οὗτοι οἱ ἄνθρωποι δοῦλοι
Paul　and ᵤus　cried　saying,　These　men　bondmen

τοῦ θεοῦ τοῦ ὑψίστου εἰσίν, οἵτινες καταγγέλλουσιν ἡμῖν‖
of the ³God　¹Most ²High are,　who　announce　to us [the]

ὁδὸν σωτηρίας. 18 Τοῦτο.δὲ ἐποίει ἐπὶ πολλὰς ἡμέρας· δια-
way of salvation.　And this she did for many　days.　³Being

πονηθεὶς δὲ ᵏὁ‖ Παῦλος, καὶ ἐπιστρέψας τῷ πνεύματι εἶπεν,
⁴distressed ¹but　²Paul,　and having turned to the　spirit　said,

Παραγγέλλω σοι ἐν ˡτῷ‖ ὀνόματι Ἰησοῦ χριστοῦ ἐξελθεῖν
I charge　thee in the　name　of Jesus　Christ to come out

ἀπ' αὐτῆς. Καὶ ἐξῆλθεν αὐτῇ.τῇ ὥρᾳ. 19 Ἰδόντες.δὲ οἱ κύριοι
from her.　And it came out the same hour.　　And ³seeing　²masters

αὐτῆς ὅτι ἐξῆλθεν ἡ ἐλπὶς τῆς.ἐργασίας.αὐτῶν, ἐπιλαβόμενοι
¹her　that was gone the hope　of their gain,　　having taken hold of

ᵠ — τὴν LTTr.　　ʳ ὁ θεὸς God LTTrA.　　ˢ δὲ and (having sailed) TA.　　ᵗ — τῆς LTTrA.
ᵛ δὲ LTTrA.　ᵂ Νέαν πόλιν TTr.　ˣ κἀκεῖθεν LTTrAW.　ʸ — τῆς LTTr.　ᶻ — ἔξω W.
ᵃ πύλης gate LTTrAW.　ᵇ ἐνομίζομεν προσευχὴν we supposed prayer LTTr.　ᶜ — τοῦ TTr.
ᵈ μένετε LTTrW.　ᵉ + τὴν the [place] for] LTTrAW.　ᶠ Πύθωνα LTTrA.　ᵍ ὑπαντῆσαι TTrA.
ʰ κατακολουθοῦσα following TTr.　ⁱ ὑμῖν to you ETTr.　ᵏ — ὁ TTr.　ˡ — τῷ LTTrA.

τὸν Παῦλον καὶ ᵐτὸν‖ Σίλαν εἵλκυσαν εἰς τὴν ἀγοράν
Paul and Silas they dragged [them] into the market

ἐπὶ τοὺς ἄρχοντας· 20 καὶ προσαγαγόντες αὐτοὺς τοῖς
before the magistrates; and having brought up them to the

στρατηγοῖς ⁿεῖπον,‖ Οὗτοι οἱ ἄνθρωποι ἐκταράσσουσιν ἡμῶν
captains said, These men ³exceedingly ⁴trouble ⁵our

τὴν πόλιν, Ἰουδαῖοι ὑπάρχοντες· 21 καὶ καταγγέλλουσιν ἔθη
⁶city, ¹Jews ¹being, and announce customs

ἃ οὐκ.ἔξεστιν ἡμῖν παραδέχεσθαι οὐδὲ ποιεῖν, Ῥωμαίοις
which it is not lawful for us to receive nor to do, ²Romans

οὖσιν. 22 Καὶ συνεπέστη ὁ ὄχλος κατ’ αὐτῶν, καὶ οἱ στρα-
¹being. And rose up together the crowd against them, and the cap-

τηγοὶ ᵒπεριρρήξαντες‖ αὐτῶν τὰ ἱμάτια ἐκέλευον ῥαβδί-
tains having torn off of them the garments commanded to beat [them]

ζειν· 23 πολλάς.τε ἐπιθέντες αὐτοῖς πληγὰς ἔβαλον
with rods. And ³many ¹having ²laid ⁵on ⁶them ⁴stripes they cast [them]

εἰς φυλακήν, παραγγείλαντες τῷ δεσμοφύλακι ἀσφαλῶς τηρεῖν
into prison, charging the jailor safely to keep

αὐτούς· 24 ὃς παραγγελίαν τοιαύτην ᴾεἴληφὼς‖ ἔβαλεν αὐτοὺς
them; who ²a ³charge ¹such having received thrust them

εἰς τὴν ἐσωτέραν φυλακήν, καὶ τοὺς.πόδας.ᑫαὐτῶν ἠσφαλί-
into the inner prison, and their foot secured

σατο‖ εἰς τὸ ξύλον. 25 Κατὰ.δὲ τὸ μεσονύκτιον Παῦλος καὶ
to the stocks. And towards midnight Paul and

Σίλας προσευχόμενοι ὕμνουν τὸν θεόν· ἐπηκροῶντο
Silas praying were singing praises to God, ⁴listened ⁵to

δὲ αὐτῶν οἱ δέσμιοι. 26 ἄφνω.δὲ σεισμὸς ἐγένετο μέγας,
¹and ⁶them ³the ²prisoners. And suddenly ⁵earthquake ¹there ²was ³a ⁴great,

ὥστε σαλευθῆναι τὰ θεμέλια τοῦ δεσμωτηρίου· ʳἀνεῴχθησάν‖
so that were shaken the foundations of the prison, ⁵were ⁹opened

ˢτε‖ παραχρῆμα αἱ θύραι πᾶσαι, καὶ πάντων τὰ δεσμὰ ἀνέθη.
¹and immediately ²the ³doors ¹all, and ³of ⁴all ¹the ²bonds were loosed.

27 ἔξυπνος.δὲ γενόμενος ὁ δεσμοφύλαξ, καὶ ἰδὼν ἀνεῳγ-
And ⁴awoke ⁵out ⁶of ⁷sleep ³being ¹the ²jailor, and seeing opened

μένας τὰς θύρας τῆς φυλακῆς, σπασάμενος ᵗ μάχαιραν ᵛἔμελ-
the doors of the prison, having drawn a sword was

λεν‖ ἑαυτὸν ἀναιρεῖν, νομίζων ἐκπεφευγέναι τοὺς δεσμίους.
about himself to put to death, supposing had escaped the prisoners.

28 ἐφώνησεν.δὲ ʷφωνῇ μεγάλῃ ὁ Παῦλος‖ λέγων, Μηδὲν
But ²called ⁷out ⁴with ⁵a ³voice ⁶loud ¹Paul saying, ⁴No

πράξῃς σεαυτῷ κακόν· ἅπαντες.γάρ ἐσμεν ἐνθάδε. 29 Αἰ-
¹do ²to ³thyself injury; for ²all ¹we ³are here. ¹Having

τήσας δὲ φῶτα εἰσεπήδησεν, καὶ.ἔντρομος.γενόμενος προσ-
³asked ⁴for ¹and lights he rushed in, and trembling fell

έπεσεν τῷ Παύλῳ καὶ ˣτῷ‖ Σίλᾳ· 30 καὶ προαγαγὼν αὐτοὺς
down before Paul and Silas. And having brought them

ἔξω ἔφη, Κύριοι, τί με.δεῖ ποιεῖν ἵνα σωθῶ;
out he said, Sirs, what is necessary for me to do that I may be saved?

31 Οἱ.δὲ ʸεἶπον,‖ Πίστευσον ἐπὶ τὸν κύριον Ἰησοῦν ᶻχριστόν,‖
And they said, Believe on the Lord Jesus Christ,

καὶ σωθήσῃ, σὺ καὶ ὁ.οἶκός.σου. 32 Καὶ ἐλάλησαν αὐτῷ
and thou shalt be saved, thou and thy house. And they spoke to him

Paul and Silas, and drew *them* into the marketplace unto the rulers, 20 and brought them to the magistrates, saying, These men, being Jews, do exceedingly trouble our city, 21 and teach customs, which are not lawful for us to receive, neither to observe, being Romans. 22 And the multitude rose up together against them: and the magistrates rent off their clothes, and commanded to beat *them*. 23 And when they had laid many stripes upon them, they cast *them* into prison, charging the jailor to keep them safely: 24 who, having received such a charge, thrust them into the inner prison, and made their feet fast in the stocks. 25 And at midnight Paul and Silas prayed, and sang praises unto God: and the prisoners heard them. 26 And suddenly there was a great earthquake, so that the foundations of the prison were shaken: and immediately all the doors were opened, and every one's bands were loosed. 27 And the keeper of the prison awaking out of his sleep, and seeing the prison doors open, he drew out his sword, and would have killed himself, supposing that the prisoners had been fled. 28 But Paul cried with a loud voice, saying, Do thyself no harm: for we are all here. 29 Then he called for a light, and sprang in, and came trembling, and fell down before Paul and Silas, and brought them out, and said, Sirs, what must I do to be saved? 31 And they said, Believe on the Lord Jesus Christ, and thou shalt be saved, and thy house. 32 And they spake unto him the word of the Lord, and to all that were in his house. 33 And he took them the same hour of the night, and washed *their* stripes; and was baptized, he and all his, straightway. 34 And when he had brought them into his house, he set meat before them, and rejoiced, believing in God with all his house. 35 And when it was day, the magistrates sent the serjeants, saying, Let those men go. 36 And the keeper of the prison told this saying to Paul, The magistrates have sent to let you go: now therefore depart, and go in peace. 37 But Paul said unto them, They have beaten us openly uncondemned, being Romans, and have cast *us* into prison; and now do they thrust us out privily? nay verily; but let them come themselves and fetch us out. 38 And the serjeants told these words unto the magistrates: and they feared, when they heard that they were Romans. 39 And they came and besought them, and brought *them* out, and desired *them* to depart out of the city. 40 And they went out of the prison, and entered into *the house of* Lydia: and when they had seen the brethren, they comforted them, and departed.

XVII. Now when they had passed through Amphipolis and Apollonia, they came to Thessalonica, where was a synagogue of the Jews: 2 and Paul, as his manner was, went in unto them, and three sabbath days reasoned with them out of the scriptures, 3 opening and alleging, that Christ must needs have suffered,

τὸν λόγον τοῦ κυρίου, ᵃκαὶ πᾶσιν∥ τοῖς ἐν τῇ.οἰκίᾳ.αὐτοῦ
the   word   of the Lord,   and   to all   those   in   his house.
33 καὶ παραλαβὼν αὐτοὺς ἐν ἐκείνῃ τῇ ὥρᾳ τῆς νυκτὸς ἔλου-
   And   having taken   them   in   that   hour of the night   he wash-
σεν   ἀπὸ τῶν πληγῶν, καὶ ἐβαπτίσθη αὐτὸς καὶ οἱ αὐτοῦ
ed [them] from the   stripes;   and ²was ³baptized   ¹he   and   ²his
ᵇπάντες∥ παραχρῆμα. 34 ἀναγαγών.τε αὐτοὺς εἰς τὸν οἶκον
¹all   immediately.   And having brought   them   into   the   ²house
ᶜαὐτοῦ∥ παρέθηκεν τράπεζαν, καὶ ᵈἠγαλλιάσατο∥ ᵉπαν-
¹his   he laid   a table   [for them], and   exulted   with all
οἰκὶ∥. πεπιστευκὼς τῷ θεῷ. 35 Ἡμέρας.δὲ γενομένης ἀπέ-
[his] house, having believed   in God.   And day   having come
στειλαν οἱ στρατηγοὶ τοὺς ῥαβδούχους λέγοντες, Ἀπόλυσον
³sent   ¹the   ²captains   the   serjeants,   saying,   Let ²go
τοὺς.ἀνθρώπους.ἐκείνους. 36 ᶠἈπήγγειλεν.δὲ ὁ δεσμοφύλαξ
¹those   ²men.   And ²reported   ¹the   ²jailor
τοὺς.λόγους.ᶠτούτους∥ πρὸς τὸν Παῦλον, Ὅτι ᵍἀπεστάλκασιν∥
   these words   to   Paul,   ³Have ⁴sent
οἱ στρατηγοὶ ἵνα ἀπολυθῆτε· νῦν οὖν ἐξελθόντες πο-
¹the   ²captains   that ye may be let go. Now therefore having gone out de-
ρεύεσθε ἐν εἰρήνῃ. 37 Ὁ.δὲ.Παῦλος ἔφη πρὸς αὐτούς, Δείραντες
part   in peace.   But Paul   said   to   them, Having beaten
ἡμᾶς δημοσίᾳ ἀκατακρίτους, ἀνθρώπους Ῥωμαίους ὑπάρχον-
us   publicly   uncondemned,   men   Romans   being,
τας, ʰἔβαλον∥ εἰς φυλακήν, καὶ νῦν λάθρα ἡμᾶς ἐκβάλλου-
they cast [us] into   prison,   and now secretly   us   do they thrust
σιν; οὐ γάρ· ἀλλὰ ἐλθόντες αὐτοὶ ἡμᾶς ἐξαγαγέτωσαν.
out?   no indeed,   but having come themselves   us   let them bring out.
38 ⁱἈνήγγειλαν∥.ᵏδὲ∥ τοῖς στρατηγοῖς οἱ ῥαβδοῦχοι τὰ ῥήματα
   And ³reported   ⁴to ⁵the   ⁶captains ¹the   ²serjeants   ⁶words
ταῦτα· ¹καὶ ἐφοβήθησαν∥ ἀκούσαντες ὅτι Ῥωμαῖοί εἰσιν.
⁷these.   And they were afraid   having heard   that   Romans they are.
39 καὶ ἐλθόντες παρεκάλεσαν αὐτούς, καὶ ἐξαγαγόντες
   And having come they besought   them,   and having brought out
ἠρώτων   ᵐἐξελθεῖν∥ τῆς πόλεως. 40 ἐξελθόντες.δὲ ⁿἐκ∥
they asked [them] to go out   of the   city.   And having gone forth out of
τῆς φυλακῆς εἰσῆλθον ᵒεἰς∥ τὴν Λυδίαν· καὶ ἰδόντες ᵖτοὺς
the   prison   they came to   Lydia;   and having seen   the
ἀδελφούς παρεκάλεσαν αὐτούς,∥ καὶ �qἐξῆλθον.∥
brethren   they exhorted   them,   and went away.

17 Διοδεύσαντες.δὲ   τὴν Ἀμφίπολιν καὶ ʳ Ἀπολλωνίαν
   And having journeyed through   Amphipolis   and   Apollonia
ἦλθον εἰς Θεσσαλονίκην, ὅπου ἦν ˢἡ∥ συναγωγὴ τῶν Ἰου-
they came to   Thessalonica,   where was the   synagogue of the Jews.
δαίων. 2 κατὰ.δὲ τὸ εἰωθὸς τῷ Παύλῳ εἰσῆλθεν πρὸς αὐτούς,
   And according to the custom   with Paul he went in   to   them,
καὶ ἐπὶ σάββατα τρία ᵗδιελέγετο∥ αὐτοῖς ἀπὸ τῶν γραφῶν,
and for ²sabbaths ¹three   reasoned   with them from the   scriptures,
3 διανοίγων καὶ παρατιθέμενος ὅτι τὸν χριστὸν ἔδει πα-
   opening   and   setting forth   that ³the   ⁴Christ ¹it ²behoved to have

---

ᵃ σὺν πᾶσιν with all GLTTrAW.   ᵇ ἄπαντες T.   ᶜ — αὐτοῦ (*read* the house) LT[Tr]A.
ᵈ ἠγαλλιᾶτο A.   ᵉ πανοικεὶ TA.   ᶠ — τούτους (*read* the words) LTr.   ᵍ ἀπέσταλκαν LTTrA.
ʰ ἔβαλαν LTTrA.   ⁱ ἀπήγγειλαν LTTrAW.   ᵏ τε T.   ¹ ἐφοβήθησαν δὲ LTTrA.   ᵐ ἀπελθεῖν
ἀπὸ to depart from (the) LTTrA.   ⁿ ἀπὸ from T.   ᵒ πρὸς GLTTrAW.   ᵖ παρεκάλεσαν τοὺς
ἀδελφούς LTTrA.   q ἐξῆλθαν TTr.   ʳ + τὴν LTTr.   ˢ — ἡ (*read* a synagogue) LTTr[A].
ᵗ διελέξατο LTTr.

θεῖν καὶ ἀναστῆναι ἐκ 'νεκρῶν, καὶ ὅτι οὗτός ἐστιν
suffered and to have risen from among [the] dead, and that this is

ʷὁ‖ χριστὸς ˣ Ἰησοῦς, ὃν ἐγὼ καταγγέλλω ὑμῖν. 4 Καί τινες
the Christ Jesus, whom I announce to you. And some

ἐξ αὐτῶν ἐπείσθησαν, καὶ προσεκληρώθησαν τῷ Παύλῳ καὶ
of them were obedient, and joined themselves to Paul and

τῷ Σίλᾳ, τῶν.τε σεβομένων ʸ Ἑλλήνων ᶻπολὺ πλῆθος,‖
to Silas, and of the worshipping Greeks a great multitude,

γυναικῶν.τε τῶν πρώτων οὐκ ὀλίγαι. 5 ᵃζηλώσαντες.δὲ
and of ²women ¹the ⁴chief not a few. But ⁴having ⁵become ⁶envious

οἱ ἀπειθοῦντες Ἰουδαῖοι, καὶ προσλαβόμενοι‖ τῶν
¹the ²disobeying ³Jews, and having taken to [them] ²of ³the

ἀγοραίων ᵇτινὰς ἄνδρας‖ πονηρούς, καὶ ὀχλοποιήσαντες
⁴market-loungers ¹certain ⁶men ⁵evil, and having collected a crowd

ἐθορύβουν τὴν πόλιν· ᶜἐπιστάντες.τε‖ τῇ οἰκίᾳ Ἰάσονος
roused ²in ¹tumult ⁴the ²city; and having assaulted the house of Jason

ἐζήτουν αὐτοὺς ᵈἀγαγεῖν‖ εἰς τὸν δῆμον· 6 μὴ.εὑρόντες.δὲ
they sought ³them ¹to ²bring out to the people; but not having found

αὐτοὺς ἔσυρον ᵉτὸν‖ Ἰάσονα καί τινας ἀδελφοὺς ἐπὶ τοὺς
them they dragged Jason and certain brethren before the

πολιτάρχας, βοῶντες, Ὅτι οἱ τὴν οἰκουμένην ἀνα-
city magistrates, crying out, Those who ⁶the ⁵habitable ⁷world ¹have ²set

στατώσαντες οὗτοι καὶ ἐνθάδε πάρεισιν, 7 οὓς ὑποδέδεκται
³in ⁴confusion these ⁴also ³here ¹are ²come, whom ²has ³received

Ἰάσων· καὶ οὗτοι πάντες ἀπέναντι τῶν δογμάτων Καίσαρος
¹Jason; and these all contrary to the decrees of Cæsar

ᶠπράττουσιν,‖ βασιλέα ᵍλέγοντες ἕτερον‖ εἶναι, Ἰησοῦν.
do, ³king ¹saying ²another there is— Jesus.

8 Ἐτάραξαν.δὲ τὸν ὄχλον καὶ τοὺς πολιτάρχας ἀκούοντας
And they troubled the crowd and the city magistrates hearing

ταῦτα. 9 καὶ λαβόντες τὸ ἱκανὸν παρὰ τοῦ Ἰάσονος καὶ
these things. And having taken security from Jason and

τῶν λοιπῶν ἀπέλυσαν αὐτούς. 10 Οἱ.δὲ ἀδελφοὶ εὐθέως διὰ
the rest they let ²go ¹them. But the brethren immediately by

ʰτῆς‖ νυκτὸς ἐξέπεμψαν τόν.τε.Παῦλον καὶ τὸν Σιλαν εἰς Βέ-
night sent away both Paul and Silas to Be-

ροιαν· οἵτινες παραγενόμενοι, εἰς τὴν συναγωγὴν ⁱτῶν Ἰου-
rœa; who, being arrived, into the synagogue of the Jews

δαίων ἀπῇεσαν.‖ 11 οὗτοι.δὲ ἦσαν εὐγενέστεροι τῶν ἐν
went. And these were more noble than those in

Θεσσαλονίκῃ, οἵτινες ἐδέξαντο τὸν λόγον μετὰ πάσης προθυ-
Thessalonica, who received the word with all readi-

μίας, ᵏτὸ‖ καθ'.ἡμέραν ἀνακρίνοντες τὰς γραφὰς εἰ ἔχοι
ness, daily examining the scriptures if were

ταῦτα οὕτως. 12 πολλοὶ μὲν οὖν ἐξ αὐτῶν ἐπί-
these things so. Many indeed therefore from among them be-

στευσαν, καὶ τῶν Ἑλληνίδων γυναικῶν τῶν εὐσχημόνων καὶ
lieved, and of the ²Grecian ³women ¹honourable and

ἀνδρῶν οὐκ ὀλίγοι. 13 ὡς.δὲ ἔγνωσαν οἱ ἀπὸ τῆς Θεσσαλο-
men not a few. But when ⁵knew ¹the ³from ⁴Thessalo-

νίκης Ἰουδαῖοι ὅτι καὶ ἐν τῇ Βεροίᾳ κατηγγέλη ὑπὸ τοῦ
nica ²Jews that also in Berœa was announced by

And risen again from the dead; and that this Jesus, whom I preach unto you, is Christ. 4 And some of them believed, and consorted with Paul and Silas; and of the devout Greeks a great multitude, and of the chief women not a few. 5 But the Jews which believed not, moved with envy, took unto them certain lewd fellows of the baser sort, and gathered a company, and set all the city on an uproar, and assaulted the house of Jason, and sought to bring them out to the people. 6 And when they found them not, they drew Jason and certain brethren unto the rulers of the city, crying, These that have turned the world upside down are come hither also; 7 whom Jason hath received: and these all do contrary to the decrees of Cæsar, saying that there is another king, one Jesus. 8 And they troubled the people and the rulers of the city, when they heard these things. 9 And when they had taken security of Jason, and of the other, they let them go. 10 And the brethren immediately sent away Paul and Silas by night unto Berea: who coming thither went into the synagogue of the Jews. 11 These were more noble than those in Thessalonica, in that they received the word with all readiness of mind, and searched the scriptures daily, whether those things were so. 12 Therefore many of them believed; also of honourable women which were Greeks, and of men, not a few. 13 But when the Jews of Thessalonica had knowledge that the word of God was preached of Paul at Berea, they came thither also, and stirred up the people. 14 And then immediately the brethren sent away Paul to go as it were to the sea: but Silas and Timotheus abode there still. 15 And they that conducted Paul brought him unto Athens: and receiving a commandment unto Silas and Timotheus for to come to him with all speed, they departed.

Παύλου ὁ λόγος τοῦ θεοῦ, ἦλθον κἀκεῖ σαλεύοντες [1] τοὺς
Paul the word of God, they came also there stirring up the

ὄχλους. 14 εὐθέως δὲ τότε τὸν Παῦλον ἐξαπέστειλαν οἱ
crowds. And immediately then [5]Paul [3]sent [4]away [1]the

ἀδελφοὶ πορεύεσθαι [m]ὡς[||] ἐπὶ τὴν θάλασσαν· [n]ὑπέμενον δὲ[||]
[2]brethren to go as to the sea; but remained

ὅ τε Σίλας καὶ ὁ Τιμόθεος ἐκεῖ. 15 Οἱ δὲ [o]καθιστῶντες[||] τὸν
both Silas and Timotheus there. But those conducting

Παῦλον ἤγαγον [p]αὐτὸν[||] ἕως Ἀθηνῶν καὶ λαβόντες ἐντολὴν
Paul brought him unto Athens; and having received a command

πρὸς τὸν Σίλαν καὶ [q]Τιμόθεον, ἵνα ὡς τάχιστα ἔλθω-
to Silas and Timotheus, that as quickly as possible they should

σιν πρὸς αὐτόν, ἐξῄεσαν.
come to him, they departed.

16 Ἐν δὲ ταῖς Ἀθήναις ἐκδεχομένου αὐτοὺς τοῦ Παύλου,
But in Athens [2]waiting [3]for [4]them [1]Paul,

16 Now while Paul waited for them at Athens, his spirit was stirred in him, when he saw the city wholly given to idolatry. 17 Therefore disputed he in the synagogue with the Jews, and with the devout persons, and in the market daily with them that met with him. 18 Then certain philosophers of the Epicureans, and of the Stoicks, encountered him. And some said, What will this babbler say? Other some, He seemeth to be a setter forth of strange gods: because he preached unto them Jesus, and the resurrection. 19 And they took him, and brought him unto Areopagus, saying, May we know what this new doctrine, whereof thou speakest, is? 20 For thou bringest certain strange things to our ears: we would know therefore what these things mean. 21 For all the Athenians and strangers which were there spent their time in nothing else, but either to tell, or to hear some new thing.) 22 Then Paul stood in the midst of Mars' hill, and said, Ye men of Athens, I perceive that in all things ye

παρωξύνετο τὸ πνεῦμα αὐτοῦ ἐν αὐτῷ [r]θεωροῦντι[||] κατ-
[7]was [8]painfully [9]excited [5]his [6]spirit in him seeing [4]full

είδωλον οὖσαν τὴν πόλιν. 17 διελέγετο μὲν οὖν ἐν τῇ
[3]of [1]idols [2]being [1]the [2]city. He reasoned indeed therefore in the

συναγωγῇ τοῖς Ἰουδαίοις καὶ τοῖς σεβομένοις, καὶ ἐν τῇ
synagogue with the Jews and those who worshipped, and in the

ἀγορᾷ κατὰ πᾶσαν ἡμέραν πρὸς τοὺς παρατυγχάνον-
market-place every day with those who met with

τας. 18 τινὲς δὲ [s] τῶν [t]Ἐπικουρείων[||] καὶ [t]τῶν[||] [w]Στωϊκῶν[||]
[him]. But some of the Epicureans and the Stoics,

φιλοσόφων συνέβαλλον αὐτῷ· καί τινες ἔλεγον, Τί ἂν θέλοι
philosophers, encountered him. And some said, What may [3]desire

ὁ σπερμολόγος οὗτος λέγειν; Οἱ δέ, Ξένων δαιμονίων δοκεῖ
[1]this [2]chatterer to say? And some, Of foreign gods he seems
(lit. demons)

καταγγελεὺς εἶναι· ὅτι τὸν Ἰησοῦν καὶ τὴν ἀνάστασιν
a proclaimer to be, because [of] Jesus and the resurrection

[x]αὐτοῖς εὐηγγελίζετο.[||] 19 ἐπιλαβόμενοί [y]τε[||] αὐτοῦ,
to them he announced the glad tidings. And having taken hold of him,

ἐπὶ τὸν [z]Ἄρειον[||] πάγον ἤγαγον λέγοντες, Δυνάμεθα
to the Mars' hill they brought [him], saying, Are we able

γνῶναι τίς ἡ καινὴ αὕτη [a]ἡ[||] ὑπὸ σοῦ λαλουμένη διδαχή;
to know what [is] this new [2]which [3]by [4]thee [5]is [6]spoken [1]teaching?

20 ξενίζοντα γάρ τινα εἰσφέρεις εἰς τὰς ἀκοὰς ἡμῶν. βου-
For [2]strange [3]things [1]certain thou bringest to our ears. We

λόμεθα οὖν γνῶναι [b]τί ἂν θέλοι[||] ταῦτα εἶναι. 21 Ἀθη-
wish therefore to know what [3]may [4]mean [1]these [2]things. [7]Athe-

ναῖοι δὲ πάντες καὶ οἱ ἐπιδημοῦντες ξένοι εἰς οὐδὲν ἕτερον
nians [5]now [6]all and the sojourning strangers in nothing else

[c]εὐκαίρουν[||] ἢ λέγειν τι [d]καὶ[||] ἀκούειν [e] καινότερον.
spent their leisure than to tell [4]something [1]and [2]to [3]hear newer.

22 Σταθεὶς δὲ [f]ὁ[||] Παῦλος ἐν μέσῳ τοῦ [g]Ἀρείου[||] πάγου
And [2]having [3]stood [1]Paul in [the] midst of Mars' hill

ἔφη, Ἄνδρες Ἀθηναῖοι, κατὰ πάντα ὡς δεισιδαιμονεστέρους
said, Men Athenians, in all things very religious
(lit. very reverent to demons)

---

[1] + καὶ ταράσσοντες and troubling LTTrA. [m] ἕως as far as LTTr. [n] ὑπέμενεν (-νάν TTr)
τε LTTrA. [o] καθιστάνοντες LTTrA. [p] — αὐτὸν (read [him]) LTTrA. [q] + τὸν TTr.
[r] θεωροῦντος LTTrAW. [s] + καὶ also LTTrAW. [t] Ἐπικουρίων T. [t] — τῶν LTTrA.
[w] Στοϊκῶν LTA. [x] εὐηγγελίζετο αὐτοῖς ([αὐτοῖς] A) LA; — αὐτοῖς TTr. [y] δὲ Tr. [z] Ἄριον T.
[a] — ἢ L[Tr]. [b] τίνα θέλει what mean LTTr. [c] ηὐκαίρουν LTTrA. [d] ἢ OI' LTTrA.
[e] + τι something LT[Tr]. [f] — ὁ LTTr. [g] Ἀρίου T.

ὑμᾶς θεωρῶ. 23 διερχόμενος.γὰρ καὶ ἀναθεωρῶν τὰ σεβάσ-
you I behold ;   for, passing through and   beholding   ²objects ³of

ματα ὑμῶν, εὗρον καὶ βωμὸν ἐν ᾧ ἐπεγέγραπτο,
veneration ¹your, I found also an altar on which had been inscribed,

Ἀγνώστῳ θεῷ ⁱⁱὃν‖ οὖν ἀγνοοῦντες εὐσεβεῖτε, ᵗτοῦτον‖
To an unknown God. Whom therefore not knowing ye reverence,   him

ἐγὼ καταγγέλλω ὑμῖν. 24 ὁ θεὸς ὁ ποιήσας τὸν κόσμον καὶ
I   announce   to you. The God who made   the   world and

πάντα τὰ ἐν αὐτῷ, οὗτος οὐρανοῦ καὶ γῆς ᵏκύριος
all things that [are] in it,   he of heaven and earth Lord

ὑπάρχων,‖ οὐκ ἐν χειροποιήτοις ναοῖς κατοικεῖ, 25 οὐδὲ ὑπὸ
being,   not in hand-made temples dwells,   nor by

χειρῶν ˡἀνθρώπων‖ θεραπεύεται προσδεόμενός τινος, αὐτὸς
hands of men   is served   as needing anything, himself

διδοὺς πᾶσιν ζωὴν καὶ πνοὴν ᵐκατὰ.πάντα·‖ 26 ἐποίησέν.τε
giving to all life and breath in every [respect];   and he made

ἐξ ἑνὸς ⁿαἵματος·‖ πᾶν ἔθνος ἀνθρώπων, κατοικεῖν ἐπὶ °πᾶν
of one blood   every nation of men,   to dwell upon all

τὸ πρόσωπον‖ τῆς γῆς, ὁρίσας ᴾπροτεταγμένους‖ και-
the face of the earth, having determined fore-arranged times

ρούς καὶ τὰς ὁροθεσίας τῆς.κατοικίας.αὐτῶν· 27 ζητεῖν ᵠτὸν
and the boundaries of their dwelling—   to seek the

κύριον,‖ εἰ ἄρα.γε ψηλαφήσειαν αὐτὸν ʳκαὶ‖ εὕροιεν,
Lord; if perhaps they might feel after him and might find him,

ˢκαίτοιγε‖ οὐ μακρὰν ἀπὸ ἑνὸς.ἑκάστου.ἡμῶν ὑπάρχοντα.
though indeed ²not ³far ⁴from ⁵one ⁶each ⁷of ⁸us   ¹being ;

28 ἐν.αὐτῷ.γὰρ ζῶμεν καὶ κινούμεθα καί ἐσμεν· ὡς καί τινες
for in him we live and move and are ; as also some

τῶν καθ᾽.ὑμᾶς ποιητῶν εἰρήκασιν, Τοῦ.γὰρ καὶ γένος
of the ²among ³you ¹poets have said, For of him ²also ¹offspring

ἐσμέν. 29 Γένος οὖν ὑπάρχοντες τοῦ θεοῦ, οὐκ.ὀφείλομεν
we are. Offspring therefore being of God, we ought not

νομίζειν χρυσῷ ἢ ἀργύρῳ ἢ λίθῳ, χαράγματι τέχνης καὶ
to think to gold or to silver or to stone, a graven thing of art and

ἐνθυμήσεως ἀνθρώπου, τὸ θεῖον εἶναι ὅμοιον. 30 Τοὺς
imagination of man, that which [is] divine to be like.   The

μὲν οὖν χρόνους τῆς ἀγνοίας ὑπεριδὼν ὁ θεός, ᵗτὰ
²indeed ³therefore ¹times of ignorance ²having overlooked ¹God,

νῦν‖ ᵛπαραγγέλλει‖ τοῖς ἀνθρώποις ʷπᾶσιν‖ πανταχοῦ μετα-
now   charges   men   all everywhere to re-

νοεῖν· 31 ˣδιότι‖ ἔστησεν ἡμέραν ἐν ᾗ μέλλει κρίνειν τὴν
pent,   because he set a day in which he is about to judge the

οἰκουμένην ἐν δικαιοσύνῃ, ἐν ἀνδρὶ ᾧ ὥρισεν, πίστιν
habitable world in righteousness, by a man whom he appointed ; ³proof

παρασχὼν πᾶσιν ἀναστήσας αὐτὸν ἐκ νεκρῶν.
¹having ²given to all [in] having raised him from among [the] dead.

32 Ἀκούσαντες.δὲ ἀνάστασιν νεκρῶν, οἱ μὲν ἐχλεύαζον·
And having heard a resurrection of [the] dead, some   mocked,

οἱ.δὲ ʸεἶπον,‖ Ἀκουσόμεθά σου ᶻπάλιν περὶ τούτου.‖
and some said,   We will hear thee again concerning this.

---

are too superstitious.
23 For as I passed by,
and beheld your devo-
tions, I found an altar
with this inscription,
TO THE UNKNOWN
GOD. Whom therefore
ye ignorantly worship,
him declare I unto you.
24 God that made the
world and all things
therein, seeing that he
is Lord of heaven and
earth, dwelleth not in
temples made with
hands ; 25 neither is
worshipped with men's
hands, as though he
needed any thing, see-
ing he giveth to all
life, and breath, and
all things ; 26 and hath
made of one blood all
nations of men for to
dwell on all the face of
the earth, and hath
determined the times
before appointed, and
the bounds of their ha-
bitation ; 27 that they
should seek the Lord,
if haply they might
feel after him, and find
him, though he be not
far from every one of
us : 28 for in him we
live, and move, and
have our being ; as
certain also of your
own poets have said,
For we are also his off-
spring. 29 Forasmuch
then as we are the
offspring of God, we
ought not to think
that the Godhead is
like unto gold, or sil-
ver, or stone, graven
by art and man's de-
vice. 30 And the times
of this ignorance God
winked at ; but now
commandeth all men
every where to repent :
31 because he hath ap-
pointed a day, in the
which he will judge
the world in right-
eousness by that man
whom he hath ordain-
ed ; whereof he hath
given assurance unto
all men, in that he
hath raised him from
the dead. 32 And when
they heard of the re-
surrection of the dead,
some mocked : and
others said, We will
hear thee again of this

ʰ ὃ what LTTrAW.   ⁱ τοῦτο this LTTrAW.   ᵏ ὑπάρχων κύριος LTTrA.   ˡ ἀνθρωπίνων
(read human hands) LTTrA.   ᵐ καὶ τὰ πάντα and all things EGLTTrAW.   ⁿ — αἵματος
(read made from one) LTTr[A].   ° παντὸς προσώπου LTTrA.   ᴾ προστεταγμένους arranged
GTTrAW ; πρὸς τεταγμένους L.   ᵠ τὸν θεόν God GLTTrA.   ʳ ἢ or L.   ˢ καὶ γε LTrA ;
καίγε T.   ᵗ τανῦν FGW.   ᵛ ἀπαγγέλλει sends word (to all) T.   ʷ πάντας LTTrA.
ˣ καθότι inasmuch as LTTrAW.   ʸ εἶπαν TT.A.   ᶻ περὶ τούτου καὶ (also) πάλιν LTTrA.

matter. 33 So Paul departed from among them. 34 Howbeit certain men clave unto him, and believed: among the which *was* Dionysius the Areopagite, and a woman named Damaris, and others with them.

33 ᵃΚαὶ‖ οὕτως ὁ Παῦλος ἐξῆλθεν ἐκ μέσου αὐτῶν.
And thus Paul went out from [the] midst of them.

34 τινὲς δὲ ἄνδρες κολληθέντες αὐτῷ ἐπίστευσαν· ἐν οἷς
But some men joining themselves to him believed ; among whom

καὶ Διονύσιος ᵇὁ‖ ᶜἈρεοπαγίτης,‖ καὶ γυνὴ ὀνόματι Δά-
also [was] Dionysius the Areopagite, and a woman by name Da-

μαρις, καὶ ἕτεροι σὺν αὐτοῖς.
maris, and others with them.

18 Μετὰ ᵈδὲ‖ ταῦτα χωρισθεὶς ᵉὁ Παῦλος‖ ἐκ τῶν
And after these things ²having ³departed ¹Paul from

Ἀθηνῶν ἦλθεν εἰς Κόρινθον· 2 καὶ εὑρών τινα Ἰουδαῖον
Athens, came to Corinth ; and having found a certain Jew

ὀνόματι Ἀκύλαν, Ποντικὸν τῷ γένει, προσφάτως ἐληλυθότα
by name Aquila, of Pontus by race, lately come

ἀπὸ τῆς Ἰταλίας, καὶ Πρίσκιλλαν γυναῖκα αὐτοῦ, διὰ τὸ
from Italy, and Priscilla his wife, because

ᶠδιατεταχέναι‖ Κλαύδιον χωρίζεσθαι πάντας τοὺς Ἰουδαίους
²had ³ordered ¹Claudius to depart all the Jews

ᵍἐκ‖ τῆς Ῥώμης, προσῆλθεν αὐτοῖς· 3 καὶ διὰ τὸ ὁμό-
out of Rome, he came to them, and because of ²the ³same

τεχνον εἶναι, ἔμενεν παρ᾽ αὐτοῖς καὶ ʰεἰργάζετο·‖ ἦσαν γὰρ
⁴trade ¹being, he abode with them and worked ; for th.y were

σκηνοποιοὶ ⁱτὴν τέχνην.‖ 4 διελέγετο δὲ ἐν τῇ συναγωγῇ
tent makers by trade. And he reasoned in the synagogue

κατὰ πᾶν σάββατον, ἔπειθέν τε Ἰουδαίους καὶ Ἕλληνας.
every sabbath, and persuaded Jews and Greeks.

5 Ὡς δὲ κατῆλθον ἀπὸ τῆς Μακεδονίας ὅ τε Σίλας καὶ ὁ Τι-
And when came down from Macedonia both Silas and Ti-

μόθεος ᵏσυνείχετο τῷ πνεύματι‖ ὁ Παῦλος διαμαρτυρόμενος
motheus ²was ³pressed ⁴in ⁵spirit ¹Paul earnestly testifying

τοῖς Ἰουδαίοις¹ τὸν χριστὸν Ἰησοῦν. 6 ἀντιτασ-
to the Jews [²to ³be] ⁴the ⁵Christ ¹Jesus. ⁷As ⁹set ¹⁰themselves ¹¹in

σομένων δὲ αὐτῶν καὶ βλασφημούντων, ἐκτιναξάμενος
¹²opposition ⁶but ⁸they and were blaspheming, having shaken [his]

τὰ ἱμάτια, εἶπεν πρὸς αὐτούς, Τὸ αἷμα ὑμῶν ἐπὶ τὴν
garments, he said to them, Your blood [be] upon

κεφαλὴν ὑμῶν· καθαρὸς ἐγὼ ἀπὸ τοῦ νῦν εἰς τὰ ἔθνη
your head : ²pure [³from ⁴it] ¹I from henceforth to the nations

πορεύσομαι. 7 Καὶ μεταβὰς ἐκεῖθεν ᵐἦλθεν‖ εἰς οἰκίαν
will go. And having departed thence he came to [the] house

τινὸς ὀνόματι ⁿἸούστου, σεβομένου τὸν θεόν, οὗ
of a certain one by name Justus, who worshipped God, of whom

ἡ οἰκία ἦν συνομοροῦσα τῇ συναγωγῇ. 8 Κρίσπος δὲ ὁ
the house was adjoining the synagogue. But Crispus the

ἀρχισυνάγωγος ἐπίστευσεν τῷ κυρίῳ σὺν ὅλῳ τῷ οἴκῳ αὐ-
ruler of the synagogue believed in the Lord with ²whole ¹his house;

τοῦ· καὶ πολλοὶ τῶν Κορινθίων ἀκούοντες ἐπίστευον καὶ
and many of the Corinthians hearing believed and

ἐβαπτίζοντο. 9 Εἶπεν δὲ ὁ κύριος ᵒδι᾽ ὁράματος ἐν νυκτὶ‖
were baptized. And said the Lord by a vision in [the] night

τῷ Παύλῳ, Μὴ φοβοῦ, ἀλλὰ λάλει καὶ μὴ σιωπήσῃς· 10 διότι
to Paul, Fear not, but speak and be not silent ; because

XVIII. After these things Paul departed from Athens, and came to Corinth; 2 and found a certain Jew named Aquila, born in Pontus, lately come from Italy, with his wife Priscilla; (because that Claudius had commanded all Jews to depart from Rome:) and came unto them. 3 And because he was of the same craft, he abode with them, and wrought: for by their occupation they were tentmakers. 4 And he reasoned in the synagogue every sabbath, and persuaded the Jews and the Greeks. 5 And when Silas and Timotheus were come from Macedonia, Paul was pressed in the spirit and testified to the Jews *that* Jesus *was* Christ. 6 And when they opposed themselves, and blasphemed, he shook *his* raiment, and said unto them, Your blood *be* upon your own head; I *am* clean: from henceforth I will go unto the Gentiles. 7 And he departed thence, and entered into a certain man's house, named Justus, *one* that worshipped God, whose house joined hard to the synagogue. 8 And Crispus, the chief ruler of the synagogue, believed on the Lord with all his house; and many of the Corinthians hearing believed, and were baptized. 9 Then spake the Lord to Paul in the night by a vision, Be not afraid, but speak, and hold not thy peace: 10 for. I am with thee,

---

ᵃ — καὶ LTTrA.   ᵇ — ὁ L[Tr].   ᶜ Ἀρεοπαγείτης T ; Ἀρειοπαγίτης W.   ᵈ — δὲ and LTTr[A].   ᵉ — ὁ Παῦλος (*read* he having departed) LTTrA.   ᶠ τεταχέναι T.   ᵍ ἀπὸ from LTTrAW.   ʰ ἠργάζετο LTrA : ἠργάζοντο they worked T.   ⁱ τῇ τέχνῃ LTTrAW.   ᵏ συνείχετο τῷ λόγῳ ᶻwas ᵉengrossed ⁴with ᵉthe ᵉword GLTTrAW.   + εἶναι to be LTTr.   ᵐ εἰσῆλθεν LT.   ⁿ + Τιτίου Titius T[Tr].   ᵒ ἐν νυκτὶ δι᾽ ὁράματος LTTrA.

ἐγώ εἰμι μετὰ σοῦ, καὶ οὐδεὶς ἐπιθήσεταί σοι τοῦ κακῶσαί σε·
I am with thee, and no one shall set on thee to ill-treat thee ;

διότι λαός ἐστίν μοι πολὺς ἐν τῇ.πόλει.ταύτῃ. 11 Ἐκάθισέν
●because people there is to me much in this city. ²He ³remained

Ρτε‖ ἐνιαυτὸν καὶ μῆνας ἐξ διδάσκων ἐν αὐτοῖς τὸν λόγον
'and a year and ²months ¹six, teaching among them the. word.

τοῦ θεοῦ.
of God.

12 Γαλλίωνος.δὲ ᑫἀνθυπατεύοντος‖ τῆς Ἀχαίας, κατεπ-
But Gallio being proconsul of Achaia, ⁶rose

έστησαν ὁμοθυμαδὸν οἱ Ἰουδαῖοι τῷ Παύλῳ, καὶ ἤγαγον
'against ³with ⁴one ⁵accord ¹the ²Jews Paul, and led

αὐτὸν ἐπὶ τὸ βῆμα, 13 λέγοντες, Ὅτι παρὰ τὸν νόμον
him to the judgment seat, saying, That contrary to the law

Ροὗτος ἀναπείθει‖ τοὺς ἀνθρώπους σέβεσθαι τὸν θεόν.
this [man] persuades men to worship God.

14 Μέλλοντος.δὲ τοῦ Παύλου ἀνοίγειν τὸ στόμα, εἶπεν ὁ
But ²being ³about ¹Paul to open [his] mouth, ²said

Γαλλίων πρὸς τοὺς Ἰουδαίους, Εἰ μὲν ˢοῦν‖ ἦν ἀδί-
¹Gallio to the Jews, If indeed therefore it was ²unrighteous-

κημά τι ἢ ῥᾳδιούργημα πονηρόν, ὦ Ἰουδαῖοι, κατὰ λόγον
ness ¹some or ²criminality ¹wicked, O Jews, according to reason

ἂν ᵗἠνεσχόμην‖ ὑμῶν, 15 εἰ.δὲ ᵛΖήτημά‖ ἐστιν περὶ
I should have borne ᵛith you, but if a question is about

λόγου καὶ ὀνομάτων καὶ νόμου τοῦ καθ' ὑμᾶς, ὄψεσθε
a word and names and a law which [is] among you, ye will see

αὐτοί· κριτὴς.ᵂγὰρ‖ ἐγὼ τούτων οὐ.βούλομαι εἶναι.
[to it] yourselves ; for a judge I of these things do not wish to be.

16 Καὶ ἀπήλασεν αὐτοὺς ἀπὸ τοῦ βήματος· 17 ἐπιλαβό-
And he drove them from the judgment seat. ⁵Having ⁶laid

μενοι δὲ πάντες ˣοἱ Ἕλληνες‖ Σωσθένην τὸν ἀρχισυνάγωγον
'hold ⁸on ¹and ²all ³the ⁴Greeks Sosthenes the ruler of the synagogue,

ἔτυπτον ἔμπροσθεν τοῦ βήματος· καὶ οὐδὲν τού-
they beat [him] before the judgment seat. And ²nothing ⁶about ⁷these

των τῷ Γαλλίωνι ἔμελεν.
³things ¹to ⁵Gallio ¹it ⁴mattered.

18 Ὁ.δὲ.Παῦλος ἔτι προσμείνας ἡμέρας ἱκανάς, τοῖς ἀδελ-
But Paul yet having remained ²days ¹many, ¹the ³breth-

φοῖς ἀποταξάμενος, ἐξέπλει εἰς τὴν Συρίαν, καὶ σὺν αὐτῷ
ren ³having ⁴taken ⁵leave ⁶of sailed away to Syria, and with him

Πρίσκιλλα καὶ Ἀκύλας, κειράμενος ᵀτὴν κεφαλὴν ἐν Κεγ-
Priscilla and Aquila, having shorn [his] head in Cen-

χρεαῖς·‖ εἶχεν.γὰρ εὐχήν. 19 ᶻκατήντησεν‖.δὲ εἰς Ἔφεσον, κἀ-
chrea, for he had a vow: and he came to Ephesus, and

κείνους κατέλιπεν ᵃαὐτοῦ·‖ αὐτὸς.δὲ εἰσελθὼν εἰς τὴν
⁶them ¹left there. But he himself having entered into the

συναγωγὴν ᵇδιελέχθη‖ τοῖς Ἰουδαίοις. 20 ἐρωτώντων.δὲ
synagogue reasoned with the Jews. And ²asking ³[him]

αὐτῶν ἐπὶ πλείονα χρόνον μεῖναι ᶜπαρ' αὐτοῖς‖ οὐκ.ἐπένευσεν·
¹they for a longer time to remain with them he did not accede,

21 ᵈἀλλ' ἀπετάξατο αὐτοῖς, εἰπών, ᵉΔεῖ με πάντως τὴν
but took leave of them, saying, It behoves me by all means the

and no man shall set on thee to hurt thee : for I have much people in this city. 11 And he continued there a year and six months, teaching the word of God among them.

12 And when Gallio was the deputy of Achaia, the Jews made insurrection with one accord against Paul, and brought him to the judgment seat, 13 saying, This *fellow* persuadeth men to worship God contrary to the law. 14 And when Paul was now about to open *his* mouth, Gallio said unto the Jews, If it were a matter of wrong or, wicked lewdness, O *ye* Jews, reason would that I should bear with you : 15 but if it be a question of words and names, and *of* your law, look *ye to it;* for I will be no judge of such *matters.* 16 And he drave them from the judgment seat. 17 Then all the Greeks took Sosthenes, the chief ruler of the synagogue, and beat *him* before the judgment seat. And Gallio cared for none of those things.

18 And Paul *after* , *this* tarried *there* yet a good while, and then took his leave of the brethren, and sailed thence into Syria, and with him Priscilla and Aquila ; having shorn *his* head in Cenchrea : for he had a vow. 19 And he came to Ephesus, and left them there : but he himself entered into the synagogue, and reasoned with the Jews. 20 When they desired *him* to tarry longer time with them, he consented not ; 21 but bade them farewell, saying, I must by all means keep this

---

P δὲ LTTrA. ᑫ ἀνθυπάτου ὄντος LTTrA. ʳ ἀναπείθει οὗτος LTTrAW. ˢ — οὖν LTTr[A]W.
ᵗ ἀνεσχόμην LTTr. ᵛ ζητήματά questions LTTrA. ᵂ — γὰρ LTTrAW. ˣ — οἱ Ἕλληνες
LTTrAW. ʸ ἐν Κεγχρεαῖς (Κενχρεαῖς T) τὴν κεφαλὴν LTTrA. ᶻ κατήντησαν they came
LTTrA. ᵃ ἐκεῖ L. ᵇ διελέξατο LTTr. ᶜ — παρ' αὐτοῖς LᵀTrA. ᵈ ἀλλὰ ἀποταξάμενος
καὶ but taking leave and LTTrA. ᵉ — Δεῖ με .... Ἱεροσόλυμα LTTrA.

feast that cometh in Jerusalem: but I will return again unto you, if God will. And he sailed from Ephesus. 22 And when he had landed at Cæsarea, and gone up, and saluted the church, he went down to Antioch. 23 And after he had spent some time *there*, he departed, and went over *all* the country of Galatia and Phrygia in order, strengthening all the disciples.

ἑορτὴν τὴν ἐρχομένην ποιῆσαι εἰς Ἱεροσόλυμα·ᵃ πάλιν δὲ
feast ¹coming to keep at Jerusalem, but again

ἀνακάμψω πρὸς ὑμᾶς, τοῦ θεοῦ θέλοντος. ᵍΚαὶᵇ ἀνήχθη ἀπὸ
I will return to you, God willing. And he sailed from

τῆς Ἐφέσου· 22 καὶ κατελθὼν εἰς ʰΚαισάρειαν,‖ ἀναβὰς
Ephesus. And having landed at Cæsarea, having gone up

καὶ ἀσπασάμενος τὴν ἐκκλησίαν κατέβη εἰς Ἀντιόχειαν·
and having saluted the assembly he went down to Antioch.

23 καὶ ποιήσας χρόνον τινὰ ἐξῆλθεν, διερχόμενος καθεξῆς
And having stayed ²time ¹some he went forth, passing through ⁸in ⁷order

τὴν Γαλατικὴν χώραν καὶ Φρυγίαν, ⁱἐπιστηρίζων‖ πάντας
¹the ²Galatian ⁵country ³and ⁴Phrygian, establishing all

τοὺς μαθητάς.
the disciples.

24 And a certain Jew named Apollos, born at Alexandria, an eloquent man, *and* mighty in the scriptures, came to Ephesus. 25 This man was instructed in the way of the Lord; and being fervent in the spirit, he spake and taught diligently the things of the Lord, knowing only the baptism of John. 26 And he began to speak boldly in the synagogue: whom when Aquila and Priscilla had heard, they took him unto *them*, and expounded unto him the way of God more perfectly. 27 And when he was disposed to pass into Achaia, the brethren wrote, exhorting the disciples to receive him: who, when he was come, helped them much which had believed through grace: 28 for he mightily convinced the Jews, *and* that publicly, shewing by the scriptures that Jesus was Christ.

24 Ἰουδαῖος δέ τις Ἀπολλὼς ὀνόματι, Ἀλεξανδρεὺς τῷ
But a ²Jew ¹certain, Apollos by name, an Alexandrian

γένει, ἀνὴρ λόγιος, κατήντησεν εἰς Ἔφεσον, δυνατὸς ὢν
by birth, ³man ¹an ²eloquent, came to Ephesus, ²mighty ¹being

ἐν ταῖς γραφαῖς. 25 οὗτος ἦν κατηχημένος τὴν ὁδὸν τοῦ
in the scriptures. He was instructed in the way of the

κυρίου, καὶ ζέων τῷ πνεύματι, ἐλάλει καὶ ἐδίδασκεν
Lord, and being fervent in spirit, he spoke and taught

ἀκριβῶς τὰ περὶ ᵏτοῦ κυρίου,‖ ἐπιστάμενος μόνον τὸ
accurately the things concerning the Lord, knowing only the

βάπτισμα ˡἸωάννου·‖ 26 οὗτός τε ἤρξατο παρρησιάζεσθαι ἐν
baptism of John. And he began to speak boldly in

τῇ συναγωγῇ. ἀκούσαντες δὲ αὐτοῦ ᵐἈκύλας καὶ Πρίσκιλλα‖
the synagogue. And ⁴having ⁵heard ⁶him ¹Aquila ²and ³Priscilla

προσελάβοντο αὐτόν, καὶ ἀκριβέστερον αὐτῷ ἐξέθεντο τὴν
they took ²to [³them] ¹him, and more accurately to him expounded the

ⁿτοῦ θεοῦ ὁδόν.‖ 27 βουλομένου δὲ αὐτοῦ διελθεῖν εἰς τὴν
²of ³God ¹way. And ²being ³minded ¹he to pass through into

Ἀχαΐαν, προτρεψάμενοι οἱ ἀδελφοὶ ἔγραψαν τοῖς μαθηταῖς
Achaia, ⁷exhorting [⁸them] ¹the ²brethren ³wrote ⁴to ⁵the ⁶disciples

ἀποδέξασθαι αὐτόν· ὃς παραγενόμενος συνεβάλετο πολὺ τοῖς
to welcome him; who having arrived helped much those who

πεπιστευκόσιν διὰ τῆς χάριτος· 28 εὐτόνως γὰρ τοῖς Ἰου-
believed through grace. For powerfully the Jews

δαίοις διακατηλέγχετο δημοσίᾳ, ἐπιδεικνὺς διὰ τῶν γραφῶν,
he confuted publicly, shewing by the scriptures

εἶναι τὸν χριστὸν Ἰησοῦν.
²to ³be ⁴the ⁵Christ ¹Jesus.

XIX. And it came to pass, that, while Apollos was at Corinth, Paul having passed through the upper coasts came to Ephesus: and finding certain disciples, 2 he said unto them, Have ye received the Holy Ghost since ye believed? And they said unto him, We have not so much as heard whether there be any Holy Ghost. 3 And he said

19 Ἐγένετο δὲ ἐν τῷ τὸν Ἀπολλὼ εἶναι ἐν Κορίνθῳ, Παῦ-
And it came to pass, while Apollos was in Corinth, Paul,

λον διελθόντα τὰ ἀνωτερικὰ μέρη, °ἐλθεῖν‖ εἰς Ἔφεσον·
having passed through the upper parts, came to Ephesus;

καὶ ᵖεὑρὼν‖ τινας μαθητὰς 2 εἶπεν ᑫ πρὸς αὐτούς, Εἰ
and having found certain disciples he said to them, [The]

πνεῦμα ἅγιον ἐλάβετε πιστεύσαντες; Οἱ δὲ ʳεἶπον‖ πρὸς
²Spirit ¹Holy did ye receive, having believed? And they said to

αὐτόν, Ἀλλ᾽ ˢοὐδὲ‖ εἰ πνεῦμα ἅγιόν ἐστιν, ἠκούσαμεν.
him, Not even if [the] ²Spirit ¹Holy is, did we hear.

---

f — δὲ but LTTrA.   g — καὶ LTTrA.   h Καισαρίαν T.   i στηρίζων LTTrA.   k τοῦ Ἰησοῦ Jesus LTTrAW.   l Ἰωάνου Tr.   m Πρίσκιλλα καὶ Ἀκύλας LTTrA.   n ὁδὸν τοῦ θεοῦ LTTr; — τοῦ θεοῦ A.   o κατελθεῖν T.   p εὑρεῖν found LTTrA.   q + τε and (he said) LTTrA.   r — εἶπον (read [said]) LTTrAW.   s οὐδ᾽ LTA.

3 ᾿Εἶπέν.τε πρὸς αὐτούς, Εἰς τί οὖν ἐβαπτίσθητε; Οἱ.δὲ
And he said to them, To what then were ye baptized? And they

εἶπον, Εἰς τὸ Ἰωάννου βάπτισμα. **4** Εἶπεν.δὲ Παῦλος,
said, To the of John baptism. And said Paul,

Ἰωάννης μὲν ἐβάπτισεν βάπτισμα μετανοίας, τῷ
John indeed baptized [with] a baptism of repentance, to the

λαῷ λέγων, εἰς τ... ἐρχόμενον μετ' αὐτὸν ἵνα πιστεύσωσιν,
people saying, On him coming after him that they should believe,

τουτέστιν εἰς τὸν χριστὸν Ἰησοῦν. **5** Ἀκούσαντες.δὲ ἐβαπ-
that is, on the Christ Jesus. And having heard they

τίσθησαν εἰς τὸ ὄνομα τοῦ κυρίου Ἰησοῦ. **6** καὶ ἐπιθέντος
were baptized to the name of the Lord Jesus. And having laid

αὐτοῖς τοῦ Παύλου τὰς χεῖρας ἦλθεν τὸ πνεῦμα τὸ ἅγιον
on them Paul hands came the Spirit the Holy

ἐπ' αὐτούς, ἐλάλουν.τε γλώσσαις καὶ προεφήτευον.
upon them, and they were speaking with tongues and prophesying.

7 ἦσαν.δὲ οἱ πάντες ἄνδρες ὡσεὶ δεκαδύο. **8** Εἰσελθὼν.δὲ
And were the all men about twelve. And having entered

εἰς τὴν συναγωγὴν ἐπαρρησιάζετο, ἐπὶ μῆνας τρεῖς διαλεγό-
into the synagogue he spoke boldly, for months three reason-

μενος καὶ πείθων τὰ περὶ τῆς βασιλείας τοῦ θεοῦ.
ing and persuading the things concerning the kingdom of God.

9 Ὡς.δὲ τινες ἐσκληρύνοντο καὶ ἠπείθουν, κακολογοῦντες τὴν
But when some were hardened and disobeyed, speaking evil of the

ὁδὸν ἐνώπιον τοῦ πλήθους, ἀποστὰς ἀπ' αὐτῶν ἀφώρισεν
way before the multitude, having departed from them he separated

τοὺς μαθητάς, καθ'.ἡμέραν διαλεγόμενος ἐν τῇ σχολῇ Τυράν-
the disciples, daily reasoning in the school of Tyran-

νου τινός. **10** Τοῦτο.δὲ ἐγένετο ἐπὶ ἔτη δύο, ὥστε πάντας
nus a certain. And this was for years two, so that all

τοὺς κατοικοῦντας τὴν Ἀσίαν ἀκοῦσαι τὸν λόγον τοῦ κυρίου
those who inhabited Asia heard the word of the Lord

Ἰησοῦ, Ἰουδαίους.τε καὶ Ἕλληνας· **11** Δυνάμεις.τε οὐ τὰς
Jesus, both Jews and Greeks. And works of power not

τυχούσας ἐποίει ὁ θεὸς διὰ τῶν χειρῶν Παύλου, **12** ὥστε καὶ
common wrought God by the hands of Paul, so that even

ἐπὶ τοὺς ἀσθενοῦντας ἐπιφέρεσθαι ἀπὸ τοῦ.χρωτὸς.αὐτοῦ
to those being sick were brought from his skin

σουδάρια ἢ σιμικίνθια, καὶ ἀπαλλάσσεσθαι ἀπ' αὐτῶν τὰς
handkerchiefs or aprons, and departed from them the

νόσους, τά.τε πνεύματα τὰ πονηρὰ ἐξέρχεσθαι ἀπ' αὐτῶν.
diseases, and the spirits wicked went out from them.

13 Ἐπεχείρησαν.δὲ τινες ἀπὸ τῶν περιερχομένων Ἰουδαίων
But took in hand certain from the wandering Jews,

ἐξορκιστῶν ὀνομάζειν ἐπὶ τοὺς ἔχοντας τὰ πνεύματα τὰ
exorcists, to name over those who had the spirits

πονηρὰ τὸ ὄνομα τοῦ κυρίου Ἰησοῦ, λέγοντες, Ὁρκίζομεν
wicked the name of the Lord Jesus, saying, We adjure

ὑμᾶς τὸν Ἰησοῦν ὃν Παῦλος κηρύσσει. **14** Ἦσαν.δὲ
you [by] Jesus whom Paul proclaims. And there were

unto them, Unto what then were ye baptized? And they said, Unto John's baptism. 4 Then said Paul, John verily baptized with the baptism of repentance, saying unto the people, that they should believe on him which should come after him, that is, on Christ Jesus. 5 When they heard this, they were baptized in the name of the Lord Jesus. 6 And when Paul had laid his hands upon them, the Holy Ghost came on them; and they spake with tongues, and prophesied. 7 And all the men were about twelve. 8 And he went into the synagogue, and spake boldly for the space of three months, disputing and persuading the things concerning the kingdom of God. 9 But when divers were hardened, and believed not, but spake evil of that way before the multitude, he departed from them, and separated the disciples, disputing daily in the school of one Tyrannus. 10 And this continued by the space of two years; so that all they which dwelt in Asia heard the word of the Lord Jesus, both Jews and Greeks. 11 And God wrought special miracles by the hands of Paul: 12 so that from his body were brought unto the sick handkerchiefs or aprons, and the diseases departed from them, and the evil spirits went out of them. 13 Then certain of the vagabond Jews, exorcists, took upon them to call over them which had evil spirits the name of the Lord Jesus, saying, We adjure you by Jesus whom Paul preacheth. 14 And there were seven sons

---

t ὁ δὲ εἶπεν T.   v — πρὸς αὐτούς LTTrAW.   w εἶπαν LTTrA.   x Ἰωάνου Tr.
y Ἰωάνης Tr.   z — μὲν GLTTrA.   a τοῦτ' ἔστιν GT.   b — χριστὸν GLTTrA.   c — τὰς LTTrA.   d ἐπροφήτευον LTTrA.   e δώδεκα LTTrAW.   f — τὰ LTr.   g — τινός LTTrA.   h — Ἰησοῦ GLTTrAW.   i ὁ θεὸς ἐποίει LTTrAW.   k ἀποφέρεσθαι LTTrA.   l ἐκ-πορεύεσθαι (— ἀπ' αὐτῶν) GLTTrAW.   m καὶ τῶν also of the LTTrA.   n Ὁρκίζω I adjure GLTTrAW.   o — ὁ LTTrA.

of one Sceva, a Jew, and chief of the priests, which did so. 15 And the evil spirit answered and said, Jesus I know, and Paul I know; but who are ye? 16 And the man in whom the evil spirit was leaped on them, and overcame them, and prevailed against them, so that they fled out of that house naked and wounded. 17 And this was known to all the Jews and Greeks also dwelling at Ephesus; and fear fell on them all, and the name of the Lord Jesus was magnified. 18 And many that believed came, and confessed, and shewed their deeds. 19 Many of them also which used curious arts brought their books together, and burned them before all men: and they counted the price of them, and found it fifty thousand pieces of silver. 20 So mightily grew the word of God and prevailed.

P_{τινες}‖ ^qυἱοὶ‖ Σκευᾶ Ἰουδαίου ἀρχιερέως ἑπτὰ ^{q r}‖ τοῦτο
certain [men] ²sons ³of *Sceva ⁵a ⁶Jew, ⁷a ⁸high ⁹priest ¹seven who this
ποιοῦντες. 15 ἀποκριθὲν.δὲ τὸ πνεῦμα τὸ πονηρὸν εἶπεν³,
were doing.   But answering the ²spirit ¹wicked said,
Τὸν Ἰησοῦν γινώσκω, καὶ τὸν Παῦλον ἐπίσταμαι· ὑμεῖς
Jesus   I know,   and   Paul   I am acquainted with; ²ye
δὲ τίνες ἐστέ; 16 Καὶ ʰἐφαλλόμενος‖ ᵛἐπ᾽ αὐτοὺς ὁ ἄνθρω-
¹but, who are ye?   And   leaping   on   them ¹the   man
πος‖ ἐν ᾧ ἦν τὸ πνεῦμα τὸ πονηρόν, ʷκαὶ‖ κατακυριεύσας
in whom was the ²spirit ¹wicked,   and   having mastered
ˣαὐτῶν‖ ἴσχυσεν κατ᾽ αὐτῶν, ὥστε γυμνοὺς καὶ τετραυματισ-
them   prevailed against them, so that   naked   and   wounded
μένους ἐκφυγεῖν ἐκ τοῦ.οἴκου.ἐκείνου. 17 τοῦτο.δὲ ἐγένετο
they escaped out of   that house.   And this   became
γνωστὸν πᾶσιν Ἰουδαίοις.τε καὶ Ἕλλησιν τοῖς κατοικοῦσιν τὴν
known   to all both Jews   and   Greeks, these   inhabiting
Ἔφεσον, καὶ ʸἐπέπεσεν‖ φόβος ἐπὶ πάντας αὐτούς, καὶ ἐμεγα-
Ephesus, and ¹fell   ¹fear upon ²all   ¹them,   and was mag-
λύνετο τὸ ὄνομα τοῦ κυρίου Ἰησοῦ. 18 Πολλοί.τε τῶν
nified   the name of the Lord Jesus.   And many of those who
πεπιστευκότων ἤρχοντο ἐξομολογούμενοι καὶ ἀναγγέλλοντες
believed   came   confessing   and   declaring
τὰς.πράξεις.αὐτῶν. 19 ἱκανοὶ.δὲ τῶν τὰ περίεργα πρα-
their deeds.   And many of those who the curious arts prac-
ξάντων συνενέγκαντες τὰς βίβλους κατέκαιον ἐνώπιον
tised   having brought the   books   burnt [them] before
πάντων· καὶ συνεψήφισαν τὰς τιμὰς αὐτῶν, καὶ εὗρον
all.   And they reckoned up the   prices of them,   and found [it]
ἀργυρίου μυριάδας πέντε. 20 οὕτως κατὰ κράτος ᶻὁ λόγος τοῦ
²of *silver ³myriads ¹five.   Thus with might ²the word of
κυρίου‖ ηὔξανεν καὶ ἴσχυεν.
Lord   increased and prevailed.

21 After these things were ended, Paul purposed in the spirit, when he had passed through Macedonia and Achaia, to go to Jerusalem, saying, After I have been there, I must also see Rome. 22 So he sent into Macedonia two of them that ministered unto him, Timotheus and Erastus; but he himself stayed in Asia for a season. 23 And the same time there arose no small stir about that way. 24 For a certain man named Demetrius, a silversmith, which made silver shrines for Diana, brought no small gain unto the craftsmen; 25 whom he called together with the work-

21 Ὡς.δὲ ἐπληρώθη ταῦτα ἔθετο ὁ Παῦλος ἐν τῷ πνεύ-
And when were fulfilled these things ²purposed ¹Paul in the spirit,
ματι, ªδιελθὼν‖ τὴν Μακεδονίαν καὶ ᵇἈχαΐαν πορεύε-
having passed through   Macedonia and   Achaia,   to
σθαι εἰς ᶜʳἹερουσαλήμ, εἰπών, Ὅτι μετὰ τὸ γενέσθαι με ἐκεῖ
go to Jerusalem,   saying, After ²having ⁴been ⁵my there
δεῖ με καὶ Ῥώμην ἰδεῖν. 22 Ἀποστείλας.δὲ εἰς ᵈτὴν‖
it behoves me also Rome   to see.   And having sent into
Μακεδονίαν δύο τῶν διακονούντων αὐτῷ, Τιμόθεον καὶ
Macedonia two of those who ministered to him, Timotheus and
Ἔραστον, αὐτὸς ἐπέσχεν χρόνον εἰς τὴν Ἀσίαν. 23 Ἐγένετο
Erastus,   he remained a time in   Asia.   ²Came ³to ⁴pass
δὲ κατὰ τὸν.καιρὸν.ἐκεῖνον τάραχος οὐκ ὀλίγος περὶ τῆς
¹and at   that time   ³disturbance ¹no   ²small about the
ὁδοῦ. 24 Δημήτριος.γάρ τις ὀνόματι, ἀργυροκόπος,
way.   For *Demetrius ¹a ²certain[²man] by name,   a silversmith,
ποιῶν ναοὺς ἀργυροῦς Ἀρτέμιδος, ᵉπαρείχετο‖ τοῖς τεχνίταις
making ²temples ¹silver   of Artemis,   brought   to the artificers
ᶠἐργασίαν οὐκ ὀλίγην·‖ 25 οὓς συναθροίσας, καὶ τοὺς
³gain ¹no   ²little;   whom having brought together, and the

P τινος (read seven sons of a certain one) LTr. q υἱοὶ placed after ἑπτὰ LTTrA. r — οἱ
LTTr[A]. s + αὐτοῖς to them LTTrAW. t ἐφαλόμενος LTTrA. v ὁ ἄνθρωπος ἐπ᾽ αὐτοὺς
LTTrA. w — καὶ LTTrAW. x ἀμφοτέρων both LTTrA. y ἔπεσεν LTr. z τοῦ κυρίου ὁ
λόγος LTTrA. a διελθεῖν to have passed through L. b + τὴν L. c Ἱεροσόλυμα
LTTrAW. d — τὴν T. e παρεῖχε L. f οὐκ ὀλίγην ἐργασίαν LTTrA.

περὶ τὰ.τοιαῦτα ἐργάτας, εἶπεν, Ἄνδρες, ἐπίστασθε ὅτι ἐκ
²in ³such ⁴things ¹workmen, he said, Men, ye know that from

ταύτης τῆς ἐργασίας ἡ εὐπορία ᵍἡμῶν‖ ἐστιν· 26 καὶ θεωρεῖτε
this gain the wealth of us is; and ye see

καὶ ἀκούετε ὅτι οὐ μόνον Ἐφέσου ἀλλὰ ʰ σχεδὸν πάσης τῆς
and hear that not only of Ephesus but almost of all

Ἀσίας ὁ.Παῦλος.οὗτος πείσας μετέστησεν ἱκανὸν ὄχλον,
Asia this Paul having persuaded turned away a great multitude,

λέγων ὅτι οὐκ.εἰσὶν θεοὶ οἱ διὰ χειρῶν γινόμενοι. 27 οὐ
saying that they are not gods which by hands are made. ²Not

μόνον δὲ τοῦτο κινδυνεύει ἡμῖν τὸ μέρος εἰς ἀπελεγμὸν
³only ¹now ⁵this ⁴is dangerous to us [lest] the business ²into ³disrepute

ἐλθεῖν, ἀλλὰ καὶ τὸ τῆς μεγάλης θεᾶς ⁱ'Ἀρτέμιδος ἱερὸν‖ εἰς
¹come, but also the ²of ³the ⁴great ⁵goddess ⁶Artemis ¹temple for

ᵏοὐδὲν‖ ¹λογισθῆναι, μέλλειν‖.ᵐδὲ‖ καὶ καθαιρεῖσθαι ⁿτὴν μεγα-
nothing be reckoned, and be about also to be destroyed the ma-

λειότητα‖ αὐτῆς, ἣν ὅλη °ᵋἡ‖ Ἀσία καὶ ἡ οἰκουμένη σέβεται.
jesty of her, whom all Asia and the habitable world worships.

28 Ἀκούσαντες.δὲ καὶ γενόμενοι πλήρεις θυμοῦ, ἔκρα-
And having heard, and having become full of indignation, they cried

ζον λέγοντες, Μεγάλη ἡ Ἄρτεμις Ἐφεσίων. 29 Καὶ
out saying, Great the Artemis of [the] Ephesians. And

ἐπλήσθη ἡ πόλις ᴾὅλη‖ ᑫ συγχύσεως· ὥρμησάν.τε ὁμοθυ-
was ⁶filled ¹the ³city ²whole with confusion, and they rushed with one

μαδὸν εἰς τὸ θέατρον, συναρπάσαντες Γάϊον καὶ Ἀρί-
accord to the theatre, having seized with [them] Gaius and Ari-

σταρχον Μακεδόνας, συνεκδήμους ʳτοῦ‖ Παύλου. 30 ʳτοῦ‖ ˢδὲ‖
starchus, Macedonians, fellow-travellers of Paul. But

Παύλου‖ βουλομένου εἰσελθεῖν εἰς τὸν δῆμον, οὐκ.εἴων αὐτὸν
Paul intending to go in to the people, ²did ⁴not ⁵suffer ⁶him

οἱ μαθηταί· 31 τινὲς.δὲ καὶ τῶν Ἀσιαρχῶν ὄντες αὐτῷ
¹the ²disciples, and some also of the chiefs of Asia being ²to ³him

φίλοι, πέμψαντες πρὸς αὐτόν, παρεκάλουν μὴ δοῦναι ἑαυτὸν
¹friends, having sent to him, urged [him] not to venture himself

εἰς τὸ θέατρον. 32 ἄλλοι.μὲν.οὖν.ἄλλο.τι ἔκραζον.
into the theatre. Some therefore one thing and some another were crying out;

ἦν.γὰρ ἡ ἐκκλησία ˢσυγκεχυμένη,‖ καὶ οἱ πλείους οὐκ.ᾔδεισαν
for ³was ¹the ²assembly confused, and the most did not know

τίνος ᵛἕνεκεν‖ συνεληλύθεισαν. 33 ἐκ.δὲ τοῦ ὄχλου
for what cause they had come together. But from among the crowd

ʷπροεβίβασαν‖ Ἀλέξανδρον, ˣπροβαλόντων‖ αὐτὸν τῶν
they put forward Alexander, ³thrusting ⁵forward ⁴him ¹the

Ἰουδαίων‖ ὁ.δὲ.Ἀλέξανδρος κατασείσας τὴν χεῖρα,
²Jews. And Alexander, having made a sign with the hand,

ἤθελεν ᵞἀπολογεῖσθαι τῷ δήμῳ. 34 ᶻἐπιγνόντων‖.δὲ ὅτι
wished to make a defence to the people. But having recognized that

Ἰουδαῖός ἐστιν, φωνὴ ἐγένετο μία ἐκ πάντων, ὡς.ἐπὶ ὥρας
a Jew he is, ⁴cry ¹there ²was ³one from all, for about ⁵hours

δύο ᵃκραζόντων,‖ Μεγάλη ἡ Ἄρτεμις Ἐφεσίων. 35 Κατα-
²two crying out, Great the Artemis of [the] Ephesians. ⁴Having

στείλας δὲ ὁ γραμματεὺς τὸν ὄχλον φησίν, Ἄνδρες Ἐφέσιοι,
⁶calmed ¹and ²the ³recorder the crowd says, Men Ephesians,

men of like occupa-
tion, and said, Sirs, ye
know that by this craft
we have our wealth.
26 Moreover ye see and
hear, that not alone at
Ephesus, but almost
throughout all Asia,
this Paul hath per-
suaded and turned a-
way much people, say-
ing that they be no
gods, which are made
with hands : 27 so that
not only this our craft
is in danger to be set
at nought ; but also
that the temple of the
great goddess Diana
should be despised,
and her magnificence
should be destroyed,
whom all Asia and
the world worshippeth.
28 And when they
heard these sayings,
they were full of wrath,
and cried out, saying,
Great is Diana of the
Ephesians. 29 And the
whole city was filled
with confusion : and
having caught Gaius
and Aristarchus, men
of Macedonia, Paul's
companions in travel,
they rushed with one
accord into the thea-
tre. 30 And when Paul
would have entered in
unto the people, the
disciples suffered him
not. 31 And certain of
the chief of Asia, which
were his friends, sent
unto him, desiring him
that he would not ad-
venture himself into
the theatre. 32 Some
therefore cried one
thing, and some an-
other : for the as-
sembly was confused ;
and the more part
knew not wherefore
they were come to-
gether. 33 And they
drew Alexander out
of the multitude, the
Jews putting him for-
ward. And Alexander
beckoned with the
hand, and would have
made his defence unto
the people. 34 But
when they knew that
he was a Jew, all with
one voice about the
space of two hours
cried out, Great is
Diana of the Ephe-
sians. 35 And when the
townclerk had ap-
peased the people, he
said, Ye men of Ephe-

ᵍ ἡμῖν to us LTTrA.   ʰ + καὶ also L.   ⁱ ἱερὸν Ἀρτέμιδος TA.   ᵏ οὐθὲν LTTrA.
ˡ λογισθήσεται (shall be counted), μέλλει L.   ᵐ τε EGLTTrA.   ⁿ τῆς μεγαλειότητος LTTrA.
ᵒ [ἡ] Tr.   ᴾ — ὅλη LTTrA.   ᑫ + τῆς GTTrAW.   ʳ — τοῦ GLTTrAW.   ˢ Παύλου δὲ LTTrAW.
ᵗ συν- T.   ᵛ ἕνεκα LTTrA.   ʷ συνεβίβασαν they instructed LTTr.   ˣ προβαλλόντων EGL.
ᵞ ἐπιγνόντες GLTTrAW.   ᶻ κράζοντες T.

sus, what man is there that knoweth not how that the city of the Ephesians is a worshipper of the great goddess Diana, and of the *image* which fell down from Jupiter? 36 Seeing then that these things cannot be spoken against, ye ought to be quiet, and to do nothing rashly. 37 For ye have brought hither these men, which are neither robbers of churches, nor yet blasphemers of your goddess. 38 Wherefore if Demetrius, and the craftsmen which are with him, have a matter against any man, the law is open, and there are deputies : let them implead one another. 39 But if ye inquire any thing concerning other matters, it shall be determined in a lawful assembly. 40 For we are in danger to be called in question for this day's uproar, there being no cause whereby we may give an account of this concourse. 41 And when he had thus spoken, he dismissed the assembly.

τίς γὰρ ἐστιν ᵃἄνθρωπος‖ ὃς οὐ.γινώσκει τὴν Ἐφεσίων
²what ¹for ⁴is ⁵there ³man who knows not the ²of [³the] ⁴Ephesians

πόλιν νεωκόρον οὖσαν τῆς μεγάλης ᵇθεᾶς‖ Ἀρτέμιδος καὶ
¹city ⁷temple-keepers ⁵as ⁶being of the great goddess Artemis, and

τοῦ Διοπετοῦς; 36 ἀναντιῤῥήτων οὖν ὄντων τούτων,
of that fallen from Zeus? Undeniable therefore being these things

δέον ἐστὶν ὑμᾶς κατεσταλμένους ὑπάρχειν, καὶ μηδὲν προ-
necessary it is for you calm to be, and ²nothing ⁴head-

πετὲς ᶜπράττειν.‖ 37 ἠγάγετε.γὰρ τοὺς.ἄνδρας.τούτους,
long ¹to ²do. For ye brought these men, [who are]

οὔτε ἱεροσύλους οὔτε βλασφημοῦντας τὴν ᵈθεὰν‖ ᵉὑμῶν.‖
neither temple plunderers nor are defaming ²goddess ¹your.

38 εἰ μὲν οὖν Δημήτριος καὶ οἱ σὺν αὐτῷ τεχνῖται ᶠπρός
If indeed therefore Demetrius and the ²with ³him ¹artificers against

τινα λόγον ἔχουσιν,‖ ἀγοραῖοι ἄγονται, καὶ ἀνθύπατοί εἰσιν·
anyone a matter have, courts are held, and proconsuls there are:

ἐγκαλείτωσαν ἀλλήλοις. 39 εἰ.δέ τι ᵍπερὶ ἑτέρων‖
let them accuse one another. But if anything concerning other matters

ἐπιζητεῖτε, ἐν τῇ ἐννόμῳ ἐκκλησίᾳ ἐπιλυθήσεται. 40 καὶ.γὰρ
ye inquire, in the lawful assembly it shall be solved. For also

κινδυνεύομεν ἐγκαλεῖσθαι στάσεως περὶ τῆς.σήμερον,
we are in danger to be accused of insurrection in regard to this day,

μηδενὸς αἰτίου ὑπάρχοντος περὶ οὗ ʰ δυνησόμεθα ἀπο-
not one cause existing concerning which we shall be able to

δοῦναι λόγον ⁱ τῆς.συστροφῆς.ταύτης. 41 Καὶ ταῦτα εἰπών,
give a reason for this concourse. And these things having said,

ἀπέλυσεν τὴν ἐκκλησίαν.
he dismissed the assembly.

XX. And after the uproar was ceased, Paul called unto *him* the disciples, and embraced *them*, and departed for to go into Macedonia. 2 And when he had gone over those parts, and had given them much exhortation, he came into Greece. 3 And *there* abode three months. And when the Jews laid wait for him, as he was about to sail into Syria, he purposed to return through Macedonia. 4 And there accompanied him into Asia Sopater of Berea ; and of the Thessalonians, Aristarchus and Secundus ; and Gaius of Derbe, and Timotheus ; and of Asia, Tychicus and Trophimus. 5 These going before tarried for us at

20 Μετὰ.δὲ τὸ παύσασθαι τὸν θόρυβον, ᵏπροσκαλεσάμενος‖
But after ³ceased ¹the ²tumult, ⁵having ⁶called ⁷to

ὁ Παῦλος τοὺς μαθητάς, καὶ ⁱ ἀσπασάμενος, ἐξῆλθεν
[⁸him] ⁴Paul the disciples, and saluted [them], went away

ᵐπορευθῆναι‖ εἰς ⁿτὴν‖ Μακεδονίαν. 2 διελθὼν.δὲ τὰ
to go to Macedonia. And having passed through

μέρη.ἐκεῖνα, καὶ παρακαλέσας αὐτοὺς λόγῳ πολλῷ, ἦλ-
those parts, and having exhorted them with ²discourse ¹much, he

θεν εἰς τὴν Ἑλλάδα· 3 ποιήσας.τε μῆνας τρεῖς, γενο-
came to Greece. And having continued ²months ¹three, having been

μένης ᵒαὐτῷ ἐπιβουλῆς‖ ὑπὸ τῶν Ἰουδαίων μέλλοντι
made against them a plot by the Jews being about

ἀνάγεσθαι εἰς τὴν Συρίαν, ἐγένετο ᵖγνώμη‖ τοῦ ὑποστρέφειν
to sail into Syria, ²arose ¹a ²purpose to return

διὰ Μακεδονίας. 4 συνείπετο.δὲ αὐτῷ ᑫἄχρι τῆς Ἀσίαςᵘ
through Macedonia. And accompanied him as far as Asia

Σώπατρος ʳ Βεροιαῖος· Θεσσαλονικέων.δὲ Ἀρίσταρχος · καὶ
Sopater a Beroean, and of Thessalonians Aristarchus and

Σεκοῦνδος, καὶ Γάϊος Δερβαῖος καὶ Τιμόθεος· Ἀσιανοὶ.δὲ
Secundus, and Gaius of Derbe and Timotheus, and of Asia

Τυχικὸς καὶ Τρόφιμος. 5 οὗτοι ˢ ᵗπροελθόντες‖ ἔμενον ἡμᾶς
Tychicus and Trophimus. These having gone before waited for us

---

ᵃ ἀνθρώπων (*read* τις who) of men LTTrA. ᵇ — θεᾶς GLTTrAW. ᶜ πράσσειν LTTrA.
ᵈ θεὸν GLTTrAW. ᵉ ἡμῶν our LTTrA. ᶠ ἔχουσιν πρός τινα λόγον GLTTrAW.
ᵍ περαιτέρω further LTr. ʰ + οὐ TTr[A]. ⁱ + περὶ concerning (this concourse) LTTr.
ᵏ μεταπεμψάμενος having sent for TTr. ˡ + παρακαλέσας having exhorted [and] LTTrA.
ᵐ πορεύεσθαι LTTr. ⁿ — τὴν LTTr[A]. ᵒ ἐπιβουλῆς αὐτῷ LTTr. ᵖ γνώμης TTrA.
ᑫ — ἄχρι τῆς Ἀσίας T[Tr]. ʳ + Πύῤῥου of Pyrrhus GLTTrAW. ˢ + δὲ and (these) LTTr[A].
ᵗ προσελθόντες having gone Tr.

ἐν Τρωάδι." 6 ἡμεῖς.δὲ ἐξεπλεύσαμεν μετὰ τὰς ἡμέρας τῶν
in Troas; but we sailed away after the days of the

ἀζύμων ἀπὸ Φιλίππων, καὶ ἤλθομεν πρὸς αὐτοὺς εἰς
unleavened bread from Philippi, and came to them at

τὴν Τρωάδα" ἄχρις" ἡμερῶν πέντε, οὗ" διετρίψαμεν ἡμέρας
Troas in days five, where we stayed days

ἑπτά. 7 Ἐν.δὲ τῇ μιᾷ τῶν σαββάτων, συνηγμένων
seven. And on the first [day] of the week, having been assembled

τῶν μαθητῶν τοῦ" κλάσαι ἄρτον, ὁ Παῦλος διελέγετο αὐτοῖς,
the disciples to break bread, Paul discoursed to them,

μέλλων ἐξιέναι τῇ ἐπαύριον, παρέτεινέν.τε τὸν λόγον μέχρι
about to depart on the morrow; and he continued the discourse till

μεσονυκτίου. 8 ἦσαν.δὲ λαμπάδες ἱκαναὶ ἐν τῷ ὑπερῴῳ οὗ
midnight. And were lamps many in the upper room where

ἦσαν" συνηγμένοι. 9 καθήμενος".δὲ τις νεανίας ὀνόματι
they were assembled. And was sitting a certain youth, by name

Εὔτυχος ἐπὶ τῆς θυρίδος, καταφερόμενος ὕπνῳ βαθεῖ, δια-
Eutychus, by the window, overpowered by sleep deep, as

λεγομένου τοῦ Παύλου ἐπὶ.πλεῖον, κατενεχθεὶς ἀπὸ
discoursed Paul for a longer time, having been overpowered by

τοῦ ὕπνου ἔπεσεν ἀπὸ τοῦ τριστέγου κάτω, καὶ ἤρθη
the sleep he fell from the third story down, and was taken up

νεκρός. 10 καταβὰς.δὲ ὁ Παῦλος ἐπέπεσεν αὐτῷ, καὶ συμ-
dead. But having descended Paul fell upon him, and em-

περιλαβὼν" εἶπεν, Μὴ.θορυβεῖσθε· ἡ.γὰρ ψυχὴ αὐτοῦ ἐν
bracing [him] said, Do not make a tumult, for the life of him is

αὐτῷ ἐστιν. 11 Ἀναβὰς.δὲ καὶ κλάσας ἄρτον καὶ γευσά-
him is. And having gone up and having broken bread and having

μενος, ἐφ'.ἱκανόν.τε ὁμιλήσας ἄχρις" αὐγῆς, οὕτως ἐξῆλ-
eaten, and for long having conversed until day-break, so he de-

θεν. 12 ἤγαγον.δὲ τὸν παῖδα ζῶντα, καὶ παρεκλήθησαν οὐ
parted. And they brought the boy alive, and were comforted not

μετρίως. 13 Ἡμεῖς.δὲ προελθόντες" ἐπὶ τὸ πλοῖον ἀνήχθημεν
a little. But we having gone before to the ship sailed

εἰς" τὴν Ἄσσον, ἐκεῖθεν μέλλοντες ἀναλαμβάνειν τὸν Παῦ-
to Assos, there being about to take in Paul;

λον· οὕτως.γὰρ ἦν.διατεταγμένος," μέλλων αὐτὸς πεζεύειν.
for so he had appointed, being about himself to go on foot.

14 ὡς.δὲ συνέβαλεν" ἡμῖν εἰς τὴν Ἄσσον, ἀναλαβόντες αὐτὸν
And when he met with us at Assos, having taken in him

ἤλθομεν εἰς Μιτυλήνην· 15 κἀκεῖθεν ἀποπλεύσαντες τῇ
we came to Mitylene; and thence having sailed away, on the

ἐπιούσῃ κατηντήσαμεν ἀντικρὺ" Χίου· τῇ.δὲ ἑτέρᾳ
following [day] arrived opposite Chios, and the next [day]

παρεβάλομεν εἰς Σάμον· καὶ μείναντες ἐν Τρωγυλλίῳ," τῇ
we arrived at Samos; and having remained at Trogyllium, the

ἐχομένῃ ἤλθομεν εἰς Μίλητον. 16 ἔκρινεν".γὰρ ὁ Παῦλος
next [day] we came to Miletus: for had decided Paul

παραπλεῦσαι τὴν Ἔφεσον, ὅπως μὴ.γένηται αὐτῷ χρονο-
to sail by Ephesus, so that it might not happen to him to spend

τριβῆσαι ἐν τῇ Ἀσίᾳ· ἔσπευδεν.γὰρ εἰ δυνατὸν ἦν" αὐτῷ
time in Asia; for he hastened if possible it was for him

Troas. 6 And we sailed away from Philippi after the days of unleavened bread, and came unto them to Troas in five days; where we abode seven days. 7 And upon the first day of the week, when the disciples came together to break bread, Paul preached unto them, ready to depart on the morrow; and continued his speech until midnight. 8 And there were many lights in the upper chamber, where they were gathered together. 9 And there sat in a window a certain young man named Eutychus, being fallen into a deep sleep: and as Paul was long preaching, he sunk down with sleep, and fell down from the third loft, and was taken up dead. 10 And Paul went down, and fell on him, and embracing him said, Trouble not yourselves; for his life is in him. 11 When he therefore was come up again, and had broken bread, and eaten, and talked a long while, even till break of day, so he departed. 12 And they brought the young man alive, and were not a little comforted. 13 And we went before to ship, and sailed unto Assos, there intending to take in Paul: for so had he appointed, minding himself to go afoot. 14 And when he met with us at Assos, we took him in, and came to Mitylene. 15 And we sailed thence, and came the next day over against Chios; and the next day we arrived at Samos, and tarried at Trogyllium; and the next day we came to Miletus. 16 For Paul had determined to sail by Ephesus, because he would not spend the time in Asia: for he hasted, if it were possible for him, to be at

᷍ Τρωάδι LT. ᷍ Τρωάδα LT. ᷍ ἄχρι LTTrA. ᷍ ὅπου T. ᷍ ἡμῶν we (having been assembled) GLTTrAW. ᷍ ἡμεν we were GLTTrAW. ᷍ καθεζόμενος LTTrAW. ᷍ συν- T. ᷍ τὸν the LTTrAW. ᷍ ἄχρι TTrA. ᷍ προσελθόντες having gone Tr. ᷍ ἐπὶ LTTrA. ᷍ διατεταγμένος ἦν LTTrA. ᷍ συνέβαλλεν LTTrA. ᷍ ἄντικρυς LTTrA. ᷍ Τρωγυλίῳ A ; — καὶ μείναντες ἐν Τρω. LTTr. ᷍ + δὲ and (the) LTTr. ᷍ κεκρίκει GLTTrAW. ᷍ εἴη it might be LTTrA.
25

Jerusalem the day of Pentecost. 17And from Miletus he sent to Ephesus, and called the elders of the church. 18 And when they were come to him, he said unto them, Ye know, from the first day that I came into Asia, after what manner I have been with you at all seasons, 19 serving the Lord with all humility of mind, and with many tears, and temptations, which befell me by the lying in wait of the Jews : 20 and how I kept back· nothing that was profitable unto you, but have shewed you, and have taught you publickly, and from house to house, 21 testifying both to the Jews, and also to the Greeks, repentance toward God, and faith toward our Lord Jesus Christ. 22 And now, behold, I go bound in the spirit unto Jerusalem, not knowing the things that shall befall me there : 23 save that the Holy Ghost witnesseth in every city, saying that bonds and afflictions abide me. 24 But none of these things move me, neither count I my life dear unto myself, so that I might finish my course with joy, and the ministry, which I have received of the Lord Jesus, to testify the gospel of the grace of God. 25 And now, behold, I know that ye all, among whom I have gone preaching the kingdom of God, shall see my face no more. 26 Wherefore I take you to record this day, that I am pure from the blood of all men. 27 For I have not shunned to declare unto you all the coun-

τὴν ἡμέραν τῆς πεντηκοστῆς γενέσθαι εἰς ᵖἸεροσόλυμα.‖
the   day   of Pentecost   to be   in   Jerusalem.

17 Ἀπὸ.δὲ τῆς Μιλήτου πέμψας εἰς Ἔφεσον μετεκαλέσατο
And from   Miletus   having sent to   Ephesus   he called for

τοὺς πρεσβυτέρους τῆς°ἐκκλησίας. 18 ὡς.δὲ παρεγένοντο πρὸς
the   elders   of the assembly.   And when they were come to

αὐτὸν ᑫ εἶπεν αὐτοῖς, Ὑμεῖς ἐπίστασθε, ἀπὸ πρώτης ἡμέρας
him   he said to them,   Ye   know,   from the first   day

ἀφ' ἧς ἐπέβην εἰς τὴν Ἀσίαν, πῶς μεθ' ὑμῶν τὸν.πάντα
on which I arrived in   Asia,   how with   you   all the

χρόνον ἐγενόμην, 19 δουλεύων τῷ κυρίῳ μετὰ πάσης ταπεινο-
time   I was,   serving   the Lord with   all   humi-

φροσύνης καὶ ʳπολλῶν‖ δακρύων καὶ πειρασμῶν, τῶν-συμ-
lity   and   many   tears   and temptations,   which hap-

βάντων μοι ἐν ταῖς ἐπιβουλαῖς τῶν Ἰουδαίων· 20 ὡς
pened   to me through the   plots   of the   Jews ;   how

οὐδὲν ὑπεστειλάμην τῶν συμφερόντων τοῦ.μὴ ἀναγγεῖλαι
nothing   I kept back   of what   is profitable   so as not   to announce [it]

ὑμῖν, καὶ διδάξαι ὑμᾶς δημοσίᾳ καὶ κατ'.οἴκους, 21 διαμαρ-
to you, and to teach   you   publicly   and from house to house,   earnestly

τυρόμενος Ἰουδαίοις.τε καὶ ᵗἝλλησιν τὴν εἰς ˢτὸν‖ θεὸν
testifying   both to Jews   and   Greeks   ²toward   ³God

μετάνοιαν καὶ πίστιν ᵗτὴν‖ εἰς τὸν.κύριον.ἡμῶν Ἰησοῦν
¹repentance   and   faith   toward   our Lord   Jesus

ᵛχριστόν.‖ 22 καὶ νῦν ἰδοὺ ʷἐγὼ δεδεμένος‖ τῷ πνεύματι
Christ.   And now, lo,   I,   bound   in the   spirit,

πορεύομαι εἰς Ἰερουσαλήμ, τὰ ἐν αὐτῇ συναντήσοντά
go   to   Jerusalem,   the things which in   it   shall happen

ˣμοι‖ μὴ εἰδώς, 23 πλὴν ὅτι τὸ πνεῦμα τὸ ἅγιον κατὰ.πόλιν
to me not knowing ;   except that the Spirit the Holy   in every city

διαμαρτύρεταιʸ ᶻλέγον‖ ὅτι δεσμά ᵃμε καὶ θλίψεις‖ μένουσιν.
fully testifies,   saying that bonds   ⁴me ¹and ²tribulations   ³await.

24 ἀλλ' οὐδενὸς ᵇλόγον‖ ᶜποιοῦμαι, οὐδὲ ἔχω‖ τὴν ψυχήν
But   ⁴of ⁵nothing   ³account   ¹I ²make,   nor   hold I   ²life

ᵈμου‖ τιμίαν ἐμαυτῷ, ὡς τελειῶσαι τὸν.δρόμον.μου ᵉμετὰ
¹my   dear   to myself, so as to finish   my course   with

χαρᾶς,‖ καὶ τὴν διακονίαν ἣν ἔλαβον παρὰ τοῦ κυρίου Ἰη-
joy,   and the   ministry   which I received   from   the Lord   Je-

σοῦ, διαμαρτύρασθαι τὸ εὐαγγέλιον τῆς χάριτος τοῦ θεοῦ.
sus,   to testify fully   the   glad tidings   of the   grace   of God.

25 καὶ νῦν ἰδοὺ ἐγὼ οἶδα ὅτι οὐκέτι ὄψεσθε τὸ.πρόσωπόν.μου
And now,   lo,   I   know that no more ³will ⁴see   ⁵my ⁶face

ὑμεῖς πάντες, ἐν οἷς διῆλθον κηρύσσων τὴν βασιλείαν
¹ye   ²all,   among whom I have gone about proclaiming the   kingdom

ᶠτοῦ θεοῦ.‖ 26 ᵍδιὸ‖ μαρτύρομαι ὑμῖν ἐν τῇ.σήμερον.ἡμέρᾳ,
of God.   Wherefore   I testify   to you in   this day

ὅτι καθαρὸς ʰἐγὼ‖ ἀπὸ τοῦ αἵματος πάντων· 27 οὐ.γὰρ
that   pure   I [am] from   the   blood   of all,   for ²not

ὑπεστειλάμην τοῦ μὴ ἀναγγεῖλαι ⁱὑμῖν‖ πᾶσαν τὴν βουλὴν
¹I ²kept back   from announcing to you   all   the   counsel

ᵖἸερουσαλήμ T.   ᑫ + ὁμοῦ ὄντων αὐτῶν they being together L.   ʳ — πολλῶν GLTTrAW.
ˢ — τὸν TTrA.   ᵗ — τὴν LTTrA.   ᵛ — χριστόν L[Tr]A.   ʷ δεδεμένος ἐγὼ GLTTrAW.
ˣ ἐμοὶ T.   ʸ + μοι to me GLTT:AW.   ᶻ λέγων A.   ᵃ καὶ‌θλίψεις με LTTrA.   ᵇ λόγου
TTrA.   ᶜ ἔχω, οὐδὲ ποιοῦμαι L ;   — οὐδὲ ἔχω TTrA.   ᵈ — μου LTTrA.   ᵉ — μετὰ χαρᾶς
ΛTTrA.   ᶠ — τοῦ θεοῦ LTTrAW.   ᵍ διότι TA.   ʰ εἰμι am LTTrA.   ⁱ — ὑμῖν
LTTrA.

τοῦ. θεοῦ ʲ. 28 προσέχετε ᵏοὖνⁿ ἑαυτοῖς καὶ παντὶ τῷ
of God.   Take heed therefore to yourselves and to all the

ποιμνίῳ. ἐν.ᾧ ὑμᾶς τὸ πνεῦμα τὸ ἅγιον ἔθετο ἐπισκόπους,
flock, wherein you the Spirit the Holy did set overseers,

ποιμαίνειν τὴν ἐκκλησίαν ˡτοῦ θεοῦ,ⁿ ἣν περιεποιήσατο διὰ
to shepherd the assembly of God, which he purchased with

τοῦ ᵐἰδίου αἵματος.ⁿ 29 ἐγὼ.ⁿγὰρⁿ οἶδα ᵒτοῦτο,ⁿ ὅτι εἰσελεύ-
the of his own blood. For I know this, that will

σονται μετὰ τὴν.ἄφιξίν.μου λύκοι βαρεῖς εἰς ὑμᾶς, μὴ
come in after my departure wolves grievous amongst you, not

φειδόμενοι τοῦ ποιμνίου· 30 καὶ ἐξ ὑμῶν.αὐτῶν ἀνα-
sparing the flock; and from amongst your own selves will

στήσονται ἄνδρες λαλοῦντες διεστραμμένα, τοῦ ἀποσπᾶν τοὺς
rise up men speaking perverted things, to draw away the

μαθητὰς ὀπίσω ᴾαὐτῶν.ⁿ 31 διὸ γρηγορεῖτε, μνημονεύοντες
disciples after themselves. Wherefore watch, remembering

ὅτι τριετίαν νύκτα καὶ ἡμέραν οὐκ.ἐπαυσάμην μετὰ δακρύων
that three years night and day I ceased not with tears

νουθετῶν ἕνα ἕκαστον. 32 καὶ ᑫτανῦνⁿ παρατίθεμαι ὑμᾶς,
admonishing one each. And now I commit you,

ʳἀδελφοί,ⁿ τῷ θεῷ καὶ τῷ λόγῳ τῆς.χάριτος.αὐτοῦ, τῷ δυνα-
brethren, to God and to the word of his grace, which is

μένῳ ˢἐποικοδομῆσαιⁿ καὶ δοῦναι ᵗὑμῖνⁿ ᵛ κληρονομίαν ἐν
able to build up and to give you an inheritance among

τοῖς ἡγιασμένοις πᾶσιν. 33 ἀργυρίου ἢ χρυσίου ἢ ἱματισμοῦ
the sanctified all. Silver or gold or clothing

ʷοὐδενὸςⁿ ἐπεθύμησα· 34 αὐτοὶ.ˣδὲⁿ γινώσκετε ὅτι ταῖς
of no one I desired. But yourselves know that

χρείαις.μου καὶ τοῖς οὖσιν μετ' ἐμοῦ ὑπηρέτησαν αἱ
to my needs and to those who were with me did minister

χεῖρες.αὗται. 35 πάντα ὑπέδειξα ὑμῖν ὅτι οὕτως κοπιῶντας
these hands. All things I shewed you that thus labouring

δεῖ ἀντιλαμβάνεσθαι τῶν ἀσθενούντων, μνημονεύειν.τε
it behoves [us] to aid those being weak, and to remember

τῶν λόγων τοῦ κυρίου Ἰησοῦ ὅτι αὐτὸς εἶπεν, Μακάριόν ἐστιν
the words of the Lord Jesus that himself said, Blessed it is

ʸδιδόναι μᾶλλονⁿ ἢ λαμβάνειν. 36 Καὶ ταῦτα εἰπών,
to give more than to receive. And these things having said

θεὶς τὰ.γόνατα.αὐτοῦ σὺν πᾶσιν αὐτοῖς προσηύξατο.
having bowed his knees with all them he prayed.

37 Ἱκανὸς.δὲ ᶻἐγένετο κλανθμὸςⁿ πάντων· καὶ ἐπιπεσόντες
And much there was weeping of all: and falling

ἐπὶ τὸν τράχηλον τοῦ Παύλου κατεφίλουν αὐτόν· 38 ὀδυνώ-
upon the neck of Paul they ardently kissed him, dis-

μενοι μάλιστα ἐπὶ τῷ λόγῳ ᾧ εἰρήκει, ὅτι οὐκέτι μέλ-
tressed most of all for the word which he had said, that no more they

λουσιν τὸ.πρόσωπον.αὐτοῦ θεωρεῖν. προέπεμπον.δὲ αὐτὸν
are about his face to see. And they accompanied him

εἰς τὸ πλοῖον.
to the ship.

21 Ὡς.δὲ ἐγένετο ἀναχθῆναι ἡμᾶς ἀποσπασθέντας ἀπ'
And when it was sailed we, having drawn away from

sel of God. 28 Take heed therefore unto yourselves, and to all the flock, over the which the Holy Ghost hath made you overseers, to feed the church of God, which he hath purchased with his own blood. 29 For I know this, that after my departing shall grievous wolves enter in among you, not sparing the flock. 30 Also of your own selves shall men arise, speaking perverse things, to draw away disciples after them. 31 Therefore watch, and remember, that by the space of three years I ceased not to warn every one night and day with tears. 32 And now, brethren, I commend you to God, and to the word of his grace, which is able to build you up, and to give you an inheritance among all them which are sanctified. 33 I have coveted no man's silver, or gold, or apparel. 34 Yea, ye yourselves know, that these hands have ministered unto my necessities, and to them that were with me. 35 I have shewed you all things, how that so labouring ye ought to support the weak, and to remember the words of the Lord Jesus, how he said, It is more blessed to give than to receive. 36 And when he had thus spoken, he kneeled down, and prayed with them all. 37 And they all wept sore, and fell on Paul's neck, and kissed him, 38 sorrowing most of all for the words which he spake, that they should see his face no more. And they accompanied him unto the ship.

XXI. And it came to pass, that after we were gotten from

ʲ + ὑμῖν to you LTTrA. ᵏ — οὖν [L]TTr. ˡ τοῦ κυρίου of the Lord GLTTr. ᵐ αἵματος τοῦ ἰδίου GLTTrAW. ⁿ — γὰρ for LTTrAW. ᵒ — τοῦτο LTTrAW. ᴾ ἑαυτῶν TTrA. ᑫ τὰ νῦν LTTrA. ʳ — ἀδελφοί LTTrA. ˢ οἰκοδομῆσαι to build LTTrAW. ᵗ — ὑμῖν LTTrA. ᵛ + τὴν (read the inheritance) TTrA. ʷ οὐθενός T. ˣ — δὲ but GLTTrAW. ʸ μᾶλλον διδόναι GLTTrAW. ᶻ κλανθμὸς ἐγένετο LTTrAW.

them, and had launched, we came with a straight course unto Coos, and the *day* following unto Rhodes, and from thence unto Patara : 2 and finding a ship sailing over unto Phenicia, we went aboard, and set forth. 3 Now when we had discovered Cyprus, we left it on the left hand, and sailed into Syria, and landed at Tyre : for there the ship was to unlade her burden. 4 And finding disciples, we tarried there seven days : who said to Paul through the Spirit, that he should not go up to Jerusalem. 5 And when we had accomplished those days, we departed and went our way ; and they all brought us on our way, with wives and children, till *we were* out of the city : and we kneeled down on the shore, and prayed. 6 And when we had taken our leave one of another, we took ship ; and they returned home again. 7 And when we had finished *our* course from Tyre, we came to Ptolemais, and saluted the brethren, and abode with them one day. 8 And the next *day* we that were of Paul's company departed, and came unto Cæsarea : and we entered into the house of Philip the evangelist, which was *one* of the seven ; and abode with him. 9 And the same man had four daughters, virgins, which did prophesy. 10 And as we tarried *there* many days, there came down from Judæa a certain prophet, named Agabus. 11 And when he was come unto us, he took Paul's girdle, and bound his own hands and feet, and said, Thus saith the Holy Ghost, So shall the Jews at Jerusalem bind the man that

αὐτῶν, εὐθυδρομήσαντες ἤλθομεν εἰς τὴν ᵃΚῶν,ᶥᶥ τῇ.δὲ ἑξῆς
them, having run direct we came to Cos, and on the next

εἰς τὴν Ῥόδον, κἀκεῖθεν εἰς Πάταρα. 2 καὶ εὑρόντες
[day] to Rhodes, and thence to Patara. And having found

πλοῖον διαπερῶν.εἰς Φοινίκην, ἐπιβάντες ἀνήχθημεν.
a ship passing over into Phœnicia, having gone on board we sailed ;

3 ᵇἀναφάναντεςᶥᶥ.δὲ τὴν Κύπρον, καὶ καταλιπόντες αὐτὴν
and having sighted Cyprus, and having left it

εὐώνυμον ἐπλέομεν εἰς Συρίαν, καὶ ᶜκατήχθημενᶥᶥ εἰς Τύρονᵛ
on the left we sailed to Syria, and brought to at Tyre,

ἐκεῖσε.γὰρ ᵈἦν τὸ πλοῖονᶥᶥ ἀποφορτιζόμενον τὸν γόμον. 4 ᵉκαὶ
for there was the ship discharging the lading. And

ἀνευρόντεςᶥᶥ τοὺς μαθητάς, ἐπεμείναμεν ᶠαὐτοῦᶥ ἡμέρας ἑπτά·
having found out the ʌ disciples, we remained there ²days ¹seven ;

οἵτινες τῷ Παύλῳ ἔλεγον διὰ τοῦ πνεύματος, μὴ ᵍἀναβαίνεινᶥᶥ
who to Paul said by the Spirit, not to go up

εἰς ʰἹερουσαλήμ.ᶥᶥ 5 ὅτε.δὲ ἐγένετο ⁱἡμᾶς ἐξαρτίσαιᶥᶥ τὰς ἡμέ-
to Jerusalem. But when it was we completed the days,

ρας, ἐξελθόντες ἐπορευόμεθα, προπεμπόντων ἡμᾶς πάντων
having set out we journeyed, ¹accompanying ⁴us ¹all

σὺν γυναιξὶν καὶ τέκνοις ἕως ἔξω τῆς πόλεως· καὶ θέντες
with wives and children as far as outside the city. And having bowed

τὰ γόνατα ἐπὶ τὸν αἰγιαλὸν ᵏπροσηυξάμεθα. 6 καὶ ἀσπασά-
the knees on the shore we prayed. And having

μενοιᶥᶥ ἀλλήλους ˡ ᵐἐπέβημενᶥᶥ εἰς τὸ πλοῖον, ἐκεῖνοι.δὲ ὑπέ-
saluted one·another we went up into the ship, and they re-

στρεψαν εἰς τὰ.ἴδια. 7 Ἡμεῖς.δὲ τὸν πλοῦν διανύσαντες
turned to their own [homes]. And we, the voyage having completed

ἀπὸ Τύρου κατηντήσαμεν εἰς Πτολεμαΐδα, καὶ ἀσπασάμενοι
from Tyre, arrived at Ptolemais, and having saluted

τοὺς ἀδελφοὺς ἐμείναμεν ἡμέραν μίαν παρ' αὐτοῖς. 8 τῇ.δὲ
the brethren we abode ²day ¹one with them. And on the

ἐπαύριον ἐξελθόντες ⁿοἱ.περὶ.τὸν.Παῦλονᶥ ᵒἦλθονᶥᶥ εἰς
morrow ⁶having ⁷gone ⁸forth ¹Paul ²and ³those ⁴with ⁵him they came to

ᴾΚαισάρειαν·ᶥᶥ καὶ εἰσελθόντες εἰς τὸν οἶκον Φιλίππου τοῦ
Cæsarea ; and having entered into the house of Philip the

εὐαγγελιστοῦ, ᑫτοῦᶥᶥ ὄντος ἐκ τῶν ἑπτά, ἐμείναμεν παρ' αὐτῷ.
evangelist, being of the seven, we abode with him.

9 τούτῳ.δὲ ἦσαν θυγατέρες ʳπαρθένοι τέσσαρεςᶥᶥ προφη-
Now to this [man] there were ¹daughters ³virgins ²four proph-

τεύουσαι. 10 ἐπιμενόντων.δὲ ˢἡμῶν.ᶥᶥ ἡμέρας πλείους κατῆλθέν
phesied. And ²remaining ¹we ⁴days ³many ⁵came ⁶down

τις ἀπὸ τῆς Ἰουδαίας προφήτης ὀνόματι Ἄγαβος·
⁵a ⁶certain ⁷one from Judæa, a prophet, by name Agabus ;

11 καὶ ἐλθὼν πρὸς ἡμᾶς, καὶ ἄρας τὴν ζώνην τοῦ
and having come to us, and having taken the girdle

Παύλου, δήσας.ᵗεᶥᶥ ᵛαὐτοῦ τὰς χεῖρας καὶ τοὺς πόδαςᶥᶥ
of Paul, and having bound of himself the hands and the feet

εἶπεν, Τάδε λέγει τὸ πνεῦμα τὸ ἅγιον, Τὸν ἄνδρα οὗ ἐστιν
said, Thus says the Spirit the Holy, The man of whom is

ᵃ Κῶ GLTTrAW. ᵇ ἀναφανέντες EGLTrAW. ᶜ κατήλθομεν landed LTTrA. ᵈ τὸ
πλοῖον ἦν LTTrAW. ᵉ ἀνευρόντες δὲ LTTrAW. ᶠ αὐτοῖς with them L. ᵍ ἐπιβαίνειν LTTrA.
ʰ Ἱεροσόλυμα GLTTrAW. ⁱ ἐξαρτίσαι ἡμᾶς LTrA. ᵏ προσευξάμενοι ἀπησπασάμεθα
having prayed we took our leave LTTrAW. ˡ + καὶ and LTTrAW. ᵐ ἐνέβημεν LTr ;
ἀνέβημεν TAW. ⁿ — οἱ περὶ τὸν Παῦλον GLTTrAW. ᵒ ἤλθομεν we came EGLTAW ; ἠλ-
ϑαμεν Tr. ᴾ Καισαρίαν T. ᑫ — τοῦ GLTTrAW. ʳ τέσσαρες παρθένοι LTTrA. ˢ — ἡμῶν
LTTrAW. ᵗ — τε and LTTrAW. ᵛ ἑαυτοῦ τοὺς πόδας καὶ τὰς χεῖρας LTTrAW.

ἡ.ζώνη.αὕτη οὕτως δήσουσιν ἐν Ἱερουσαλὴμ οἱ Ἰουδαῖοι, καὶ
this girdle   thus   shall ³bind ⁴in ⁵Jerusalem ¹the ²Jews, and

παραδώσουσιν εἰς χεῖρας ἐθνῶν. 12 Ὡς.δὲ ἠκούσαμεν
deliver up   into [the] hands of [the] nations.   And when we heard

ταῦτα, παρεκαλοῦμεν ἡμεῖς.τε καὶ οἱ ἐντόπιοι τοῦ
these things,   ⁸besought   ¹both ²we ³and ⁴those ⁵of [⁶the] ⁷place

μὴ ἀναβαίνειν αὐτὸν εἰς Ἱερουσαλήμ. 13 ʷ ἀπεκρίθη.ˣδὲ‖ ὁ
¹⁰not ¹¹to ¹²go ¹³up ⁹him to Jerusalem.   But ²answered

Παῦλος, ʸ Τί ποιεῖτε κλαίοντες καὶ συνθρύπτοντές μου τὴν
¹Paul,   What do ye   weeping   and   breaking   my

καρδίαν; ἐγὼ.γὰρ οὐ μόνον δεθῆναι ἀλλὰ καὶ ἀποθανεῖν εἰς
heart?   for I   not only to be bound but also   to die   at

Ἱερουσαλὴμ ἑτοίμως.ἔχω ὑπὲρ τοῦ ὀνόματος τοῦ κυρίου Ἰησοῦ.
Jerusalem am ready for the   name   of the Lord   Jesus.

14 Μὴ.πειθομένου.δὲ αὐτοῦ ἡσυχάσαμεν εἰπόντες, ᶻΤὸ θέλημα
And ²not ³being ⁴persuaded ¹he   we were silent, saying, The will

τοῦ κυρίου.γενέσθω.‖
of the Lord   be done.

15 Μετὰ.δὲ τὰς.ἡμέρας ταύτας ᵃἀποσκευασάμενοι‖ ἀνε-
And after these days,   having packed the baggage we

βαίνομεν εἰς ᵇἹερουσαλήμ.‖ 16 συνῆλθον.δὲ καὶ τῶν
went up to   Jerusalem.   And went   ᵃlso [some] of the

μαθητῶν ἀπὸ ᶜΚαισαρείας‖ σὺν ἡμῖν, ἄγοντες παρ᾿ ᾧ
disciples from   Cæsarea   with us, bringing [one] with whom

ξενισθῶμεν, Μνάσωνί.τινι Κυπρίῳ, ἀρχαίῳ μαθητῇ. 17 Γενο-
we might lodge, a certain Mnason, a Cypriot, an old disciple.   ³Having

μένων δὲ ἡμῶν εἰς Ἱεροσόλυμα ἀσμένως ᵈἐδέξαντο‖ ἡμᾶς οἱ
⁴arrived ¹and ²we at Jerusalem ³gladly ⁴received ⁵us ¹the

ἀδελφοί. 18 τῇ.ᵉδὲ‖ ἐπιούσῃ εἰσῄει ὁ Παῦλος σὺν ἡμῖν
²brethren.   And on the following [day]²went ³in ¹Paul with us

πρὸς Ἰάκωβον, πάντες.τε παρεγένοντο οἱ πρεσβύτεροι. 19 καὶ
to   James,   and all ³assembled ¹the ²elders.   And

ἀσπασάμενος αὐτοὺς ἐξηγεῖτο καθ᾿.ἓν.ἕκαστον ὧν ἐποίησεν
having saluted them he related   one by one   what things ²wrought

ὁ θεὸς ἐν τοῖς ἔθνεσιν διὰ τῆς.διακονίας.αὐτοῦ. 20 οἱ.δὲ
¹God among the nations by   his ministry.   And they

ἀκούσαντες ἐδόξαζον ᶠτὸν κύριον.‖ ᵍεἶπόν.τε‖ αὐτῷ, Θεωρεῖς,
having heard glorified the Lord.   And they said to him, Thou seest,

ἀδελφέ, πόσαι μυριάδες εἰσὶν ʰἸουδαίων‖ τῶν πεπι-
brother, how many myriads there are of Jews   who have be-

στευκότων, καὶ πάντες ζηλωταὶ τοῦ νόμου ὑπάρχουσιν.
lieved,   and   all zealous ones of the law   are.

21 κατηχήθησαν.δὲ περὶ σοῦ, ὅτι ἀποστασίαν διδάσκεις
And they were informed concerning thee, that ⁹apostasy ¹thou ²teachest

ἀπὸ ¹Μωσέως‖ τοὺς κατὰ τὰ ἔθνη ᵏπάντας‖ Ἰουδαίους,
¹⁰from ¹¹Moses ⁴the ⁶among ⁷the ⁸nations ³all   ⁵Jews,

λέγων μὴ περιτέμνειν αὐτοὺς τὰ τέκνα, μηδὲ τοῖς ἔθεσιν
telling ²not ³to ⁴circumcise ¹them the children, nor in the customs

περιπατεῖν. 22 τί οὖν ἐστιν; πάντως ¹δεῖ πλῆθος
to walk.   What then is it?   certainly ³must ¹a ²multitude

---

owneth this girdle, and shall deliver *him* into the hands of the Gentiles. 12 And when we heard these things, both we, and they of that place, besought him not to go up to Jerusalem. 13 Then Paul answered, What mean ye to weep and to break mine heart? for I am ready. not to be bound only, but also to die at Jerusalem for the name of the Lord Jesus. 14 And when he would not be persuaded, we ceased, saying, The will of the Lord be done.

15 And after those days we took up our carriages, and went up to Jerusalem. 16 There went with us also *certain* of the disciples of Cæsarea, and brought with them one Mnason of Cyprus, an old disciple, with whom we should lodge. 17 And when we were come to Jerusalem, the brethren received us gladly. 18 And the *day* following Paul went in with us unto James; and all the elders were present. 19 And when he had saluted them, he declared particularly what things God had wrought among the Gentiles by his ministry. 20 And when they heard *it*, they glorified the Lord, and said unto him, Thou seest, brother, how many thousands of Jews there are which believe; and they are all zealous of the law: 21 and they are informed of thee, that thou teachest all the Jews which are among the Gentiles to forsake Moses, saying that they ought not to circumcise *their* children, neither to walk after the customs. 22 What is it therefore? the multitude must

---

ʷ + τότε then LTTrAW.   ˣ — δὲ but LTTrAW.   ʸ + καὶ εἶπεν and said τ.   ᶻ Τοῦ κυρίου
τὸ θέλημα γινέσθω LTTrAW.   ᵃ ἐπισκευασάμενοι LTTrAW.   ᵇ Ἱεροσόλυμα LTTrAW.
ᶜ Καισαρίας T.   ᵈ ἀπεδέξαντο welcomed LTTrAW.   ᵉ τε T.   ᶠ τὸν θεόν God GLTTrAW.
ᵍ εἰπόντες saying L; εἶπάν τε TTr.   ʰ ἐν τοῖς Ἰουδαίοις among the Jews LTrAW; — Ἰουδαίων T.   ¹ Μωϋσέως GLTTrAW.   ᵏ — πάντας L[Tr].   ¹ δεῖ συνελθεῖν πλῆθος LTA ; — δεῖ
πλῆθος συνελθεῖν Tr.

needs come together: for they will hear that thou art come. 23 Do therefore this that we say to thee : We have four men which have a vow on them ; 24 them take, and purify thyself with them, and be at charges with them, that they may shave *their* heads : and all may know that those things, whereof they were informed concerning thee, are nothing ; but *that* thou thyself also walkest orderly, and keepest the law. 25 As touching the Gentiles which believe, we have written *and* concluded that they observe no such thing, save only that they keep themselves from *things* offered to idols, and from blood, and from strangled, and from fornication. 26 Then Paul took the men, and the next day purifying himself with them entered into the temple, to signify the accomplishment of the days of purification, until that an offering should be offered for every one of them. 27 And when the seven days were almost ended, the Jews which were of Asia, when they saw him in the temple, stirred up all the people, and laid hands on him, 28 crying out, Men of Israel, help : This is the man, that teacheth all *men* every where against the people, and the law, and this place: and further brought Greeks also into the temple, and hath polluted this holy place. 29 (For they had seen before with him in the city Trophimus an Ephesian, whom they supposed that Paul had brought into the temple.) 30 And all the city was moved, and the people ran together : and they took Paul, and drew him out of the temple: and forthwith the doors were shut. 31 And as they went about to kill him, tidings came un-

συνελθεῖν·‖ ἀκούσονται.ᵐγὰρ‖ ὅτι ἐλήλυθας. 23 τοῦτο οὖν
come together ; for they will hear that thou hast come. This therefore

ποίησον ὅ σοι λέγομεν· εἰσὶν ἡμῖν ἄνδρες τέσσαρες εὐχὴν
do thou what ³to ⁴thee ¹we ²say : There are with us ²men ¹four a vow

ἔχοντες ἐφ' ἑαυτῶν· 24 τούτους παραλαβὼν ἁγνίσθητι σὺν
having on themselves ; these having taken be purified with

αὐτοῖς, καὶ δαπάνησον ἐπ' αὐτοῖς, ἵνα ⁿξυρήσωνται‖ τὴν
them, and be at expense for them, that they may shave the

κεφαλήν, καὶ °γνῶσιν‖ πάντες ὅτι ὧν κατήχηνται
head ; and ²may ³know ¹all that of which they have been informed

περὶ σοῦ οὐδέν ἐστιν, ἀλλὰ στοιχεῖς καὶ αὐτὸς
about thee ²nothing ¹is, but thou ³walkest ⁴orderly ²also ¹thyself

Pτὸν νόμον φυλάσσων.‖ 25 περὶ.δὲ τῶν πεπιστευκότων
⁶the ⁷law ⁵keeping. But concerning those who have believed

ἐθνῶν ἡμεῖς qἐπεστείλαμεν.‖ κρίναντες ʳμηδὲν.τοιοῦτον
of the nations we wrote, judging ⁴no ⁵such ⁶thing

τηρεῖν αὐτούς, εἰ.μὴ‖ φυλάσσεσθαι αὐτοὺς τό τε εἰδωλό-
²to ³observe ¹them, except to keep ²from ¹themselves things offered

θυτον καὶ ˢτὸ‖ αἷμα καὶ πνικτὸν καὶ πορνείαν. 26 Τότε
to idols, and blood, and what is strangled, and fornication. Then

ὁ Παῦλος παραλαβὼν τοὺς ἄνδρας, τῇ ἐχομένῃ ἡμέρᾳ σὺν
Paul having taken the men, on the next day with

αὐτοῖς ἁγνισθεὶς εἰσῄει εἰς τὸ ἱερόν, διαγγέλλων τὴν
them having been purified entered into the temple, declaring the

ἐκπλήρωσιν τῶν ἡμερῶν τοῦ ἁγνισμοῦ, ἕως οὗ προσηνέχθη
fulfilment of the days of the purification, until was offered

ὑπὲρ ἑνὸς ἑκάστου αὐτῶν ἡ προσφορά. 27 ὡς.δὲ. ἔμελλον
for ²one ¹each of them the offering. But when ⁴were ³about

αἱ ἑπτὰ ἡμέραι συντελεῖσθαι οἱ ἀπὸ τῆς Ἀσίας Ἰουδαῖοι
¹the ²seven ³days to be completed the ²from ³Asia ¹Jews

θεασάμενοι αὐτὸν ἐν τῷ ἱερῷ, ᵗσυνέχεον‖ πάντα τὸν ὄχλον,
having seen him in the temple, stirred up all the crowd,

καὶ ᵛἐπέβαλον‖ ʷτὰς χεῖρας ἐπ' αὐτόν,‖ 28 κράζοντες, Ἄνδρες
and laid hands upon him, crying, Men

ˣἸσραηλῖται,‖ βοηθεῖτε· οὗτός ἐστιν ὁ ἄνθρωπος ὁ κατὰ
Israelites, help ! this is the man who against

τοῦ λαοῦ καὶ τοῦ νόμου καὶ τοῦ.τόπου.τούτου πάντας ʸπαν-
the people and the law and this place all every-

ταχοῦ‖ διδάσκων· ἔτι.τε καὶ Ἕλληνας εἰσήγαγεν εἰς τὸ ἱερόν,
where teaches, and further also Greeks he brought into the temple,

καὶ κεκοίνωκεν τὸν ἅγιον τόπον τοῦτον. 29 Ἦσαν.γὰρ.προ-
and defiled ²holy ³place ¹this. For they had before

ἑωρακότες Τρόφιμον τὸν Ἐφέσιον ἐν τῇ πόλει σὺν αὐτῷ, ὃν
seen Trophimus the Ephesian in the city with him, whom

ἐνόμιζον ὅτι εἰς τὸ ἱερὸν εἰσήγαγεν ὁ Παῦλος. 30 ἐκινήθη
they supposed that into the temple ²brought ¹Paul. ⁴Was ⁵moved

τε ἡ πόλις ὅλη, καὶ ἐγένετο συνδρομὴ τοῦ λαοῦ· καὶ ἐπι-
³and ⁶the ⁸city ⁷whole, and there was a concourse of the people ; and having

λαβόμενοι τοῦ Παύλου, εἷλκον αὐτὸν ἔξω τοῦ ἱεροῦ· καὶ
laid hold of Paul, they drew him outside the temple, and

εὐθέως ἐκλείσθησαν αἱ θύραι. 31 ζητούντων.ᶻδὲ‖ αὐτὸν
immediately were shut the - doors. But as they were seeking him

---

m — γὰρ for Tr. n ξυρήσονται they shall shave ΤΤrA. o γνώσονται will know GLTTrAW. P φυλάσσων τὸν νόμον LTTrAW. q ἀπεστείλαμεν LTr. r — μηδὲν τοιοῦτον τηρεῖν αὐτούς, εἰ μὴ LTTr. s — τὸ LTTr[A]w. t συνέχεαν L. v ἐπέβαλαν TTr. w ἐπ' αὐτὸν τὰς χεῖρας GLTTrAW. x Ἰσραηλεῖται T. y πανταχῇ LTr; πανταχῆ TAW. z τε And LTTrA.

ἀποκτεῖναι ἀνέβη   φάσις   τῷ χιλιάρχῳ τῆς σπείρης,
to kill   there came a representation to the chief captain of the   band,

ὅτι ὅλη ^aσυγκέχυται" Ἱερουσαλήμ. 32 ὃς ^bἐξαυτῆς" ^cπαρα-
that all ²was ³in ⁴a ⁵tumult ¹Jerusalem ;   who   at once   having

λαβὼν"   στρατιώτας καὶ ^dἑκατοντάρχους" κατέδραμεν ἐπ'
taken with [him] soldiers   and   centurions   ran down   upon

αὐτούς. οἱ.δὲ ἰδόντες ^eτὸν" χιλίαρχον καὶ τοὺς στρατιώτας
them.   And they having seen the chief captain and the   soldiers

ἀπαύσαντο τύπτοντες τὸν Παῦλον. 33 τότε   ἐγγίσας
ceased   beating   Paul.   Then ⁴having ⁵drawn ⁶near

ὁ χιλίαρχος ἐπελάβετο αὐτοῦ, καὶ ἐκέλευσεν   δεθῆναι
¹the ²chief ³captain laid hold of him, and commanded [him] to be bound

ἀλύσεσιν δυσίν· καὶ ἐπυνθάνετο τίς ^fἂν".εἴη, καὶ τί
with ²chains ¹two, and   inquired   who he might be, and what

ἐστιν.πεποιηκώς.   34 ἄλλοι.δὲ.ἄλλο.τι   ^gἐβόων"
he had been doing. But some ³one ⁴thing ⁵and ⁶some ⁷another ¹were ²crying

ἐν τῷ ὄχλῳ· ^hμὴ.δυνάμενος.δὲ" γνῶναι τὸ ἀσφαλὲς   διὰ
in the crowd.   And not being able to know the certainty on account of

τὸν θόρυβον, ἐκέλευσεν   ἄγεσθαι αὐτὸν εἰς τὴν παρεμ-
the   tumult,   he commanded ²to ³be ⁴brought ¹him into the   for-

βολήν. 35 ὅτε.δὲ ἐγένετο ἐπὶ τοὺς ἀναβαθμοὺς συνέβη
tress.   But when he came on the   stairs   it happened

βαστάζεσθαι αὐτὸν ὑπὸ τῶν στρατιωτῶν διὰ τὴν βίαν
²was ³borne   ¹he   by the   soldiers because of the violence

τοῦ ὄχλου. 36 ἠκολούθει.γὰρ τὸ πλῆθος τοῦ λαοῦ ¹κράζον,"
of the crowd.   For followed   the multitude of the people,   crying,

Αἶρε αὐτόν. 37 Μέλλων.τε εἰσάγεσθαι εἰς τὴν παρεμβολὴν
Away with him.   But being about to be brought into the   fortress

ὁ Παῦλος λέγει τῷ χιλιάρχῳ, Εἰ ἔξεστίν μοι εἰπεῖν τι
Paul   says to the chief captain, Is it permitted to me to say something

πρὸς σε; Ὁ.δὲ ἔφη, Ἑλληνιστὶ γινώσκεις; 38 οὐκ ἄρα
to   thee? And he said,   Greek   dost thou know ?   ³Not ⁴then

σὺ εἶ ὁ Αἰγύπτιος ὁ πρὸ τούτων τῶν ἡμερῶν ἀναστα-
²thou ¹art the Egyptian who before   these   days   caused a

τώσας καὶ ἐξαγαγὼν εἰς τὴν ἔρημον τοὺς τετρακισχιλίους
confusion and   led out   into the   desert   the   four thousand

ἄνδρας τῶν σικαρίων; 39 Εἶπεν.δὲ ὁ Παῦλος, Ἐγὼ ἄνθρωπος
men of the assassins ?   But ²said   ¹Paul,   I   a man

μέν εἰμι Ἰουδαῖος Ταρσεύς, τῆς Κιλικίας οὐκ ἀσήμου πόλεως
indeed am   a Jew   of Tarsus, ⁷of ⁸Cilicia ⁴no ³of ⁵insignificant ⁶city

πολίτης· δέομαι.δέ σου, ἐπίτρεψόν.μοι λαλῆσαι πρὸς τὸν
¹a ²citizen, and I beseech thee,   allow   me to speak   to   the

λαόν. 40 Ἐπιτρέψαντος.δὲ   αὐτοῦ, ὁ Παῦλος ἑστὼς ἐπὶ
people.   And ²having ³allowed [⁴him] ¹he,   Paul   standing on

τῶν ἀναβαθμῶν κατέσεισεν τῇ χειρὶ τῷ λαῷ· πολλῆς.δὲ
the   stairs   made a sign with the hand to the people;   and great

σιγῆς γενομένης προσεφώνησεν   τῇ Ἑβραΐδι διαλέκτῳ
silence having taken place   he spoke to   [them] in the Hebrew   language

λέγων, 22 Ἄνδρες ἀδελφοὶ καὶ πατέρες, ἀκούσατέ μου τῆς
saying,   Men,   brethren and fathers,   hear   my

πρὸς ὑμᾶς ^kνῦν" ἀπολογίας. 2 Ἀκούσαντες.δὲ ὅτι τῇ Ἑβραΐδι·
²to ³you ⁴now ¹defence.   And having heard that in the Hebrew

to the chief captain of the band, that all Jerusalem was in an uproar. 32 Who immediately took soldiers and centurions, and ran down unto them : and when they saw the chief captain and the soldiers, they left beating of Paul. 33 Then the chief captain came near, and took him, and commanded him to be bound with two chains ; and demanded who he was, and what he had done. 34 And some cried one thing, some another, among the multitude : and when he could not know the certainty for the tumult, he commanded him to be carried into the castle. 35 And when he came upon the stairs, so it was, that he was borne of the soldiers for the violence of the people. 36 For the multitude of the people followed after, crying, Away with him. 37 And as Paul was to be led into the castle, he said unto the chief captain, May I speak unto thee? who said, Canst thou speak Greek ? 38 Art not thou that Egyptian, which before these days madest an uproar, and leddest out into the wilderness four thousand men that were murderers ? 39 But Paul said, I am a man which am a Jew of Tarsus, a city in Cilicia, a citizen of no mean city : and, I beseech thee, suffer me to speak unto the people. 40 And when he had given him licence, Paul stood on the stairs, and beckoned with the hand unto the people. And when there was made a great silence, he spake unto them in the Hebrew tongue, saying, XXII. Men, brethren, and fathers, hear ye my defence which I make now unto you. 2 (And when they heard that he spake in the Hebrew tongue to

^a συγ(συν- T)χύννεται LTTrA ; συγχύνεται W.   ^b ἐξ αὐτῆς A.   ^c λαβὼν having taken L.
^d ἑκατοντάρχας LTTrAW.   ^e — τὸν W.   ^f — ἂν LTTr[A]w.   ^g ἐπεφώνουν LTTrAW.
^h μὴ δυναμένου δὲ αὐτοῦ he not being able LTTrAW.   ⁱ κράζοντες LTTrAW.   ^k νυνὶ
GLTT ᵥW.

them, they kept the more silence: and he saith,) 3 I am verily a man *which am* a Jew, born in Tarsus, *a city* in Cilicia, yet brought up in this city at the feet of Gamaliel, *and* taught according to the perfect manner of the law of the fathers, and was zealous toward God, as ye all are this day. 4 And I persecuted this way unto the death, binding and delivering into prisons both men and women. 5 As also the high priest doth bear me witness, and all the estate of the elders: from whom also I received letters unto the brethren, and went to Damascus, to bring them which were there bound unto Jerusalem, for to be punished. 6 And it came to pass, that, as I made my journey, and was come nigh unto Damascus about noon, suddenly there shone from heaven a great light round about me. 7 And I fell unto the ground, and heard a voice saying unto me, Saul, Saul, why persecutest thou me? 8 And I answered, Who art thou, Lord? And he said unto me, I am Jesus of Nazareth, whom thou persecutest. 9 And they that were with me saw indeed the light, and were afraid; but they heard not the voice of him that spake to me, 10 And I said, What shall I do, Lord? And the Lord said unto me, Arise, and go into Damascus; and there it shall be told thee of all things which are appointed for thee to do. 11 And when I could not see for the glory of that light, being led by the hand of them that were with me, I came into Damascus. 12 And one Ananias, a devout man according to the law, having a good report of all the Jews which dwelt *there*, 13 came unto me, and stood, and said unto me, Brother Saul, receive thy sight. And the

διαλέκτῳ προσεφώνει αὐτοῖς, μᾶλλον παρέσχον ἡσυχίαν. καί
language   he spoke to   them,   ²the ⁴more ¹they ²kept   quiet ;   and

φησιν, 3 Ἐγὼ ¹μέν‖ εἰμι ἀνὴρ Ἰουδαῖος, γεγεννημένος ἐν
he says,   I indeed am a man   a Jew,   born   in

Ταρσῷ τῆς Κιλικίας, ἀνατεθραμμένος δὲ ἐν τῇ πόλει ταύτῃ
Tarsus   of Cilicia,   but brought up   in   this city

παρὰ τοὺς πόδας Γαμαλιήλ, πεπαιδευμένος κατὰ
at   the   feet   of Gamaliel,   having been instructed according to [the]

ἀκρίβειαν τοῦ πατρῴου νόμου, ζηλωτὴς ὑπάρχων τοῦ θεοῦ,
exactness   of the ancestral   law,   ²a ³zealous ⁴one   ¹being   for God,

καθὼς πάντες ὑμεῖς ἐστε σήμερον· 4 ὃς ταύτην τὴν ὁδὸν
even as   all   ye   are   this day ;   who   this   , way

ἐδίωξα ἄχρι θανάτου, δεσμεύων καὶ παραδιδοὺς εἰς φυλακὰς
persecuted unto   death,   binding   and   delivering up to   prisons

ἄνδρας τε καὶ γυναῖκας, 5 ὡς καὶ ὁ ἀρχιερεὺς μαρτυρεῖ μοι,
both men   and   women ;   as also the high priest bears witness to me,

καὶ πᾶν τὸ πρεσβυτέριον· παρ᾽ ὧν καὶ ἐπιστολὰς δεξάμενος
and all the   elderhood ;   from whom also   letters   having received

πρὸς τοὺς ἀδελφούς, εἰς Δαμασκὸν ἐπορευόμην, ἄξων καὶ τοὺς
to   the   brethren,   to Damascus   I went,   to bring also those

ἐκεῖσε ὄντας, δεδεμένους εἰς Ἱερουσαλήμ, ἵνα τιμωρη-
there who were,   bound   to Jerusalem,   in order that they might

θῶσιν. 6 ἐγένετο δέ μοι πορευομένῳ καὶ ἐγγίζοντι τῇ
be punished. And it came to pass to me   journeying   and drawing near

Δαμασκῷ περὶ μεσημβρίαν ἐξαίφνης ἐκ τοῦ οὐρανοῦ περι-
to Damascus, about   mid-day   suddenly out of the   heaven

ἀστράψαι φῶς ἱκανὸν περὶ ἐμέ· 7 ᵐἔπεσόν‖ τε εἰς τὸ ἔδαφος,
shone   a ²light ¹great about me.   And I fell   to the ground,

καὶ ἤκουσα φωνῆς λεγούσης μοι, Σαούλ, Σαούλ, τί με διώ-
and   heard   a voice   saying   to me,   Saul,   Saul,   why me perse-

κεις ; 8 Ἐγὼ δὲ ἀπεκρίθην, Τίς εἶ, κύριε ; Εἶπέν τε
cutest thou ?   And I   answered,   Who art thou, Lord ?   And he said

πρός ⁿμε,‖ Ἐγώ εἰμι Ἰησοῦς ὁ Ναζωραῖος ὃν σὺ διώκεις.
to   me,   I   am Jesus the Nazaræan,   whom thou persecutest.

9 Οἱ δὲ σὺν ἐμοὶ ὄντες τὸ μὲν φῶς ἐθεάσαντο, °καὶ ἔμ-
But those ²with ³me ¹being the ²indeed ¹light ,beheld,   and   af-

φοβοι ἐγένοντο·‖ τὴν δὲ φωνὴν οὐκ ἤκουσαν τοῦ λαλοῦντός
larmed   were,   but the   voice   did not hear of him   speaking

μοι. 10 εἶπον δέ, Τί ποιήσω κύριε ; Ὁ δὲ κύριος εἶπεν
to me.   And I said, What shall I do, Lord ?   And the   Lord   said

πρός με, Ἀναστὰς πορεύου εἰς Δαμασκόν, κἀκεῖ σοι λα-
to me, Having risen up   go   to   Damascus, and there thee   it

ληθήσεται περὶ πάντων ὧν τέτακταί σοι ποιῆσαι.
shall be told concerning all things which it has been appointed thee   to do.

11 Ὡς δὲ οὐκ ἐνέβλεπον ἀπὸ τῆς δόξης τοῦ φωτὸς ἐκείνου,
And as   I did not see   from the   glory   of that light,

χειραγωγούμενος ὑπὸ τῶν συνόντων μοι, ἦλθον εἰς Δαμασ-
being led by the hand   by those being with   me, I came   to   Damas-

κόν. 12 Ἀνανίας δέ τις, ἀνὴρ ᴾεὐσεβὴς‖ κατὰ τὸν νόμον,
cus.   And a certain Ananias, a ²man.   ¹pious   according to the   law,

μαρτυρούμενος ὑπὸ πάντων τῶν κατοικούντων Ἰουδαίων,
borne witness to   by   all   the   ²dwelling [³there]   ¹Jews,

13 ἐλθὼν πρός ᑫμε‖ καὶ ἐπιστὰς εἶπέν μοι, Σαοὺλ ἀδελφέ,
coming   to   me   and standing by said to me, ²Saul   ¹brother,

---

¹ — μέν LTTrAW.   ᵐ ἔπεσά LTTrA.   ᶰ ἐμέ LTTr.   ° — καὶ ἔμφοβοι ἐγένοντο LTTr[A].
ᴾ εὐλαβὴς LTTrA.   ᑫ ἐμὲ LTTr.

ἀνάβλεψον. Κἀγὼ αὐτῇ.τῇ.ὥρᾳ ἀνέβλεψα εἰς αὐτόν. 14 ὁ.δὲ
look up.   And I   in the same hour   looked up   on him.   And he

εἶπεν, Ὁ θεὸς τῶν.πατέρων.ἡμῶν προεχειρίσατό σε γνῶναι
said,   The God   of our fathers   appointed   thee to know

τὸ.θέλημα.αὐτοῦ, καὶ ἰδεῖν τὸν δίκαιον καὶ ἀκοῦσαι φωνὴν
his will,   and to see the Just One, and to hear a voice

ἐκ ˟ τοῦ.στόματος.αὐτοῦ· 15 ὅτι ἔσῃ μάρτυς αὐτῷ
out of   his mouth ;   for thou shalt be a witness for him

πρὸς πάντας ἀνθρώπους ὧν ἑώρακας καὶ ἤκουσας. 16 καὶ
to all   men of what thou hast seen and heard.   And

νῦν τί μέλλεις; ἀναστὰς ˟βάπτισαι καὶ ἀπόλουσαι τὰς
now why delayest thou? Having arisen be baptized and   wash away

ἁμαρτίας.σου, ἐπικαλεσάμενος τὸ ὄνομα ʳτοῦ κυρίου.‖ 17 Ἐ-
thy sins,   calling on   the name of the Lord.   ²It ²came

γένετο δέ μοι ὑποστρέψαντι εἰς Ἱερουσαλήμ, καὶ προσευ-
to ³pass ¹and to me having returned to Jerusalem,   and on ²pray-

χομένου μου ἐν τῷ ἱερῷ, γενέσθαι.με ἐν ἐκστάσει, 18 καὶ ˢἰδεῖν‖
ing   ¹my in the temple, I became   in a trance,   and saw

αὐτὸν λέγοντά μοι, Σπεῦσον καὶ ἔξελθε ἐν.τάχει ἐξ Ἰε-
him   saying to me, Make haste and go away with speed out of Je-

ρουσαλήμ, διότι οὐ.παραδέξονταί σου.ʼτὴν‖ μαρτυρίαν
rusalem,   because they will not receive thy   testimony

περὶ ἐμοῦ. 19 Κἀγὼ εἶπον, Κύριε, αὐτοὶ ἐπίστανται,
concerning me.   And I said,   Lord, themselves   know

ὅτι ἐγὼ ἤμην φυλακίζων καὶ δέρων κατὰ.τὰς.συναγωγὰς τοὺς
that I   was imprisoning and beating in every synagogue those

πιστεύοντας ἐπὶ σέ· 20 καὶ ὅτε ˣἐξεχεῖτο‖ τὸ αἷμα Στεφάνου
believing   on thee ;   and when was poured out the blood of Stephen

τοῦ.μάρτυρός.σου, καὶ αὐτὸς ἤμην ἐφεστὼς καὶ συνευδοκῶν
thy witness,   also myself   was standing by and   consenting

ʷτῇ ἀναιρέσει αὐτοῦ,‖ καὶ φυλάσσων τὰ ἱμάτια τῶν
to the putting to death of him,   and   keeping the garments of those who

ἀναιρούντων αὐτόν. 21 Καὶ εἶπεν πρός με, Πορεύου, ὅτι ἐγὼ
killed   him.   And he said to me, Go,   for 1

εἰς ἔθνη μακρὰν ἐξαποστελῶ σε. 22 Ἤκουον.δὲ αὐτοῦ ἄχρι
to nations afar off will send forth thee.   And they heard him   until

τούτου, τοῦ λόγου, καὶ ἐπῆραν τὴν.φωνὴν.αὐτῶν λέγοντες,
this   word,   and lifted up   their voice,   saying,

Αἶρε ἀπὸ τῆς γῆς τὸν.τοιοῦτον· οὐ.γὰρ ˣκαθῆκον‖ αὐτὸν
Away with ⁵from ⁶the ⁶earth ¹such ²a ³one,   for ³not ¹it ²is fit he

ζῆν. 23 Κραυγαζόντων.ʸδὲ‖ αὐτῶν, καὶ ῥιπτούντων
should live. And as ²were ³crying ⁴out ¹they, and casting off [their]

τὰ ἱμάτια, καὶ κονιορτὸν βαλλόντων εἰς τὸν ἀέρα, 24 ἐκέλευσεν
garments, and   ²dust   ¹throwing into the air,   ⁴commanded

ᶻαὐτὸν ὁ χιλίαρχος ἄγεσθαι‖ εἰς τὴν παρεμβολήν, ᵃεἰπὼν‖
⁵him ¹the ²chief.³captain to be brought into the   fortress,   bidding

μάστιξιν ἀνετάζεσθαι αὐτόν, ἵνα ἐπιγνῷ δι᾽ ἣν αἰτίαν
⁶by ⁷scourges ²to ³be ⁴examined ¹him, that he might know for what cause

οὕτως ἐπεφώνουν αὐτῷ. 25 ὡς.δὲ ᵇπροέτεινεν‖ αὐτὸν
thus   they cried out against him.   But as he stretched forward him

τοῖς ἱμᾶσιν εἶπεν πρὸς τὸν ἑστῶτα ἑκατόνταρχον ᶜὁ
with the thongs ²said ³to ⁴the ⁶who ⁷stood ⁸by   ⁵centurion

same hour I looked
up upon him. 14 And
he said, The God of our
fathers hath chosen
thee, that thou shouldest know his will,
and see that Just
One, and shouldest
hear the voice of
his mouth. 15 For
thou shalt be his witness unto all men of
what thou hast seen
and heard. 16 And
now why tarriest thou?
arise, and be baptized,
and wash away thy
sins, calling on the
name of the Lord.
17 And it came to pass,
that, when I was come
again to Jerusalem,
even while I prayed in
the temple, I was in a
trance ; 18 and saw
him saying unto me,
Make haste, and get
thee quickly out of
Jerusalem : for they
will not receive thy
testimony concerning
me. 19 And I said,
Lord, they know that
I imprisoned and beat
in every synagogue
them that believed on
thee : 20 and when
the blood of thy martyr Stephen was shed,
I also was standing
by, and consenting
unto his death, and
kept the raiment of
them that slew him.
21 And he said unto me,
Depart : for I will send
thee far hence unto
the Gentiles. 22 And
they gave him audience unto this word,
and then lifted up
their voices, and said,
Away with such a
fellow from the earth :
for it is not fit that he
should live. 23 And
as they cried out, and
cast off their clothes,
and threw dust into the
air, 24 the chief captain commanded him
to be brought into the
castle, and bade that
he should be examined
by scourging ; that he
might know wherefore
they cried so against
him. 25 And as they
bound him with
thongs, Paul said unto the centurion that

ʳ αὐτοῦ (read his name) GLTTrAW.   ˢ ἰδού T.   ᵗ — τὴν LTTr[A].   ᵛ ἐξεχύννετο LTTrA.
ʷ — τῇ ἀναιρέσει αὐτοῦ GLTTrAW.   ˣ καθῆκεν GLTTrAW.   ʸ τε LTrAW.   ᶻ ὁ χιλίαρχος
εἰσάγεσθαι αὐτὸν GLTTrAW.   ᵃ εἶπας LTTrAW.   ᵇ προέτειναν they stretched forward
GLTTrAW.   ᶜ [ὁ Παῦλος] Α.

stood by, Is it lawful
for you to scourge a
man that is a Roman,
and uncondemned?
26 When the centurion
heard *that*, he went
and told the chief cap-
tain, saying, Take
heed what thou doest:
for this man is a Ro-
man. 27 Then the chief
captain came, and said
unto him, Tell me, art
thou a Roman? He
said, Yea. 28 And the
chief captain answer-
ed, With a great sum
obtained I this free-
dom. And Paul said,
But I was *free* born.
29 Then straightway
they departed from
him which should
have examined him:
and the chief captain
also was afraid, after
he knew that he was
a Roman, and because
he had bound him.
30 On the morrow, be-
cause he would have
known the certainty
wherefore he was ac-
cused of the Jews, he
loosed him from *his*
bands, and command-
ed the chief priests
and all their council
to appear, and brought
Paul down, and set
him before them.

XXIII. And Paul,
earnestly beholding
the council, said, Men
and brethren, I have
lived in all good con-
science before God un-
til this day. 2 And the
high priest Ananias
commanded them that
stood by him to smite
him on the mouth.
3 Then said Paul unto
him, God shall smite
thee, *thou* whited wall:
for sittest thou to
judge me after the law,
and commandest me
to be smitten contrary
to the law? 4 And
they that stood by
said, Revilest thou
God's high priest?
5 Then said Paul, I
wist not, brethren, that
he was the high priest:
for it is written, Thou
shalt not speak evil of
the ruler of thy peo-
ple. 6 But when Paul
perceived that the one
part were Sadducees,

Παῦλος,‖ Εἰ ἄνθρωπον Ῥωμαῖον καὶ ἀκατάκριτον ἔξεστιν
¹Paul, A man a Roman and uncondemned is it lawful
ὑμῖν μαστίζειν; 26 Ἀκούσας.δὲ ὁ ᵈἑκατόνταρχος,‖ προσ-
for you to scourge? And ³having ⁴heard [⁵it] ¹the ²centurion, having
ελθὼν ᵉἀπήγγειλεν τῷ χιλιάρχῳ‖ λέγων, ᶠῬ Ὅρα‖ τί μέλ-
gone he reported [it] to the chief captain saying, See what art
λεις ποιεῖν; ὁ.γὰρ.ἄνθρωπος.οὗτος Ῥωμαῖός ἐστιν.
thou about to do? For this man a Roman is.
27 Προσελθὼν.δὲ ὁ χιλίαρχος εἶπεν αὐτῷ, Λέγε μοι, ᵍεἰ‖ σὺ
And having come up the chief captain said to him, Tell me, ²thou
Ῥωμαῖος εἶ; Ὁ.δὲ ἔφη, Ναί. 28 Ἀπεκρίθη.ʰτε‖ ὁ χιλίαρχος,
³a ⁴Roman ¹art? And he said, Yes. And ⁴answered ¹the ²chief ³captain,
Ἐγὼ πολλοῦ κεφαλαίου τὴν.πολιτείαν.ταύτην ἐκτησάμην.
I with a great sum this citizenship ᵗ bought.
Ὁ.δὲ.Παῦλος ἔφη, Ἐγὼ.δὲ καὶ γεγέννημαι. 29 Εὐθέως οὖν
And Paul said, But I also was [free] born. Immediately therefore
ἀπέστησαν ἀπ' αὐτοῦ οἱ μέλλοντες αὐτὸν ἀνετάζειν· καὶ
departed from him those being about ³him ¹to ²examine, and
ὁ χιλίαρχος δὲ ἐφοβήθη, ἐπιγνοὺς ὅτι Ῥωμαῖός ἐστιν,
the chief captain also was afraid, having ascertained that a Roman he is,
καὶ ὅτι ⁱἦν.αὐτὸν‖.δεδεκώς. 30 Τῇ.δὲ ἐπαύριον βουλόμενος
and because he had bound him. And on the morrow, desiring
γνῶναι τὸ ἀσφαλὲς τὸ.τί κατηγορεῖται ᵏπαρὰ‖ τῶν Ἰουδαίων,
to know the certainty wherefore he is accused by the Jews,
ἔλυσεν αὐτὸν ˡἀπὸ τῶν δεσμῶν,‖ καὶ ἐκέλευσεν ᵐἐλθεῖν‖ τους
he loosed him from the bonds, and commanded to come the
ἀρχιερεῖς καὶ ⁿὅλον‖ τὸ.συνέδριον.ᵒαὐτῶν·‖ καὶ καταγαγὼν
chief priests and ²whole ¹their sanhedrim, and having brought down
τὸν Παῦλον ἔστησεν εἰς αὐτούς.
Paul he set [him] among them.

23 Ἀτενίσας.δὲ Ρὁ Παῦλος τῷ συνεδρίῳ‖ εἶπεν,
And ²having ³looked ⁴intently ¹Paul on the sanhedrim said,
Ἄνδρες ἀδελφοί, ἐγὼ πάσῃ συνειδήσει ἀγαθῇ πεπολίτευμαι
Men brethren, I in all ²conscience ¹good have conducted myself
τῷ θεῷ ἄχρι ταύτης τῆς ἡμέρας. 2 Ὁ.δὲ ἀρχιερεὺς Ἀνα-
towards God unto this day. But the high priest Ana-
νίας ἐπέταξεν τοῖς παρεστῶσιν αὐτῷ τύπτειν αὐτοῦ τὸ στόμα.
nias ordered those standing by him to smite his mouth.
3 τότε ὁ Παῦλος πρὸς αὐτὸν εἶπεν, Τύπτειν σε μέλλει ὁ
Then Paul to him said, ⁴To ⁵smite ⁶thee ²is ³about
θεός, τοῖχε κεκονιαμένε· καὶ σὺ κάθῃ κρίνων με κατὰ
¹God, ⁸wall ⁷whited. And thou dost thou sit judging me according to
τὸν νόμον, καὶ παρανομῶν κελεύεις με τύπτεσθαι; 4 Οἱ.δὲ
the law, and contrary to law commandest me to be smitten? And those who
παρεστῶτες �۹εἶπον,‖ Τὸν ἀρχιερέα τοῦ θεοῦ λοιδορεῖς;
stood by said, ⁴The ⁵high ⁶priest ⁷of ⁸God ¹railest ²thou ³at?
5 Ἔφη.τε ὁ Παῦλος, Οὐκ.ᾔδειν, ἀδελφοί, ὅτι ἐστὶν ἀρχ-
And ²said ¹Paul, I was not conscious, brethren, that he is a high
ιερεύς· γέγραπται.γάρ, ʳἌρχοντα τοῦ.λαοῦ.σου οὐκ ἐ-
priest; for it has been written, A ruler of thy people ³not ¹thou ²shalt
ρεῖς κακῶς. 6 Γνοὺς.δὲ ὁ Παῦλος ὅτι τὸ ἓν μέρος ἐστὶν
speak ²of ¹evil. But ²having ³known ¹Paul that the one part consists

ᵈ ἑκατοντάρχης LT.   ᵉ τῷ χιλιάρχῳ ἀπήγγειλεν GLTTrA.   ᶠ — Ὅρα GLTTrAW.   ᵍ — εἰ
GLTTrAW.   ʰ δὲ LTTr; — τε A.   ⁱ αὐτὸν ἦν LTTrAW.   ᵏ ἀπὸ τῶν
δεσμῶν GLTTrAW.   ᵐ συνελθεῖν to come together GLTTrAW.   ⁿ πᾶν all GLTTrAW.
ᵒ — αὐτῶν (*read* the sanhedrim) GLTTrAW.   ᵖ τῷ συνεδρίῳ ὁ Παῦλος LTTr.   ۹ εἶπαν TTr.
ʳ + ὅτι TTr[A].

Σαδδουκαίων τὸ.δὲ ἕτερον Φαρισαίων ˢἔκραξεν‖ ἐν τῷ συν-
of Sadducees and the other of Pharisees cried out in the sanhe-

εδρίῳ, Ἄνδρες ἀδελφοί, ἐγὼ Φαρισαῖός εἰμι, υἱὸς ᵗΦαρισαίου·‖
drim, Men brethren, I a Pharisee am, son of a Pharisee:

περὶ ἐλπίδος καὶ ἀναστάσεως νεκρῶν ἐγὼ κρίνομαι.
concerning a hope and resurrection of [the] dead I am judged.

7 Τοῦτο.δὲ αὐτοῦ ᵛλαλήσαντος‖ ἐγένετο στάσις τῶν Φαρι-
And this he having spoken there was a dissension of the Phari-

σαίων καὶ ʷτῶν‖ Σαδδουκαίων, καὶ ἐσχίσθη ˣ τὸ πλῆθος·
sees and the Sadducees, and was divided the multitude.

8 Σαδδουκαῖοι ʸμὲν‖ γὰρ λέγουσιν μὴ.εἶναι ἀνάστασιν ᶻμηδὲ‖
²Sadducees ³indeed ¹for say there is no resurrection nor

ἄγγελον μήτε πνεῦμα· Φαρισαῖοι.δὲ ὁμολογοῦσιν τὰ ἀμφότερα.
angel nor spirit; but Pharisees confess both.

9 ἐγένετο.δὲ κραυγὴ μεγάλη· καὶ ἀναστάντες ᵃοἵ‖ ᵇγραμ-
And there was a ²clamour ¹great, and having risen up the ¹scribes

ματεῖς τοῦ μέρους‖ τῶν Φαρισαίων διεμάχοντο λέγοντες,
of the part of the Pharisees they were contending, saying,

Οὐδὲν κακὸν εὑρίσκομεν ἐν τῷ.ἀνθρώπῳ.τούτῳ· εἰ.δὲ πνεῦμα
Nothing evil we find in this man; and if a spirit

ἐλάλησεν αὐτῷ ἢ ἄγγελοςᶜ, μὴ.θεομαχῶμεν.‖ 10 Πολλῆς.δὲ
spoke to him or an angel, let us not fight against God. And a great

ᵈγενομένης στάσεως, εὐλαβηθεὶς‖ ὁ χιλίαρχος μὴ δια-
²arising ¹dissension, ⁶fearing ³the ⁴chief ⁵captain lest ²should ³be

σπασθῇ ὁ Παῦλος ὑπ' αὐτῶν, ἐκέλευσεν τὸ στράτευμα
⁴torn ⁵in ⁶pieces ¹Paul by them, commanded the troop

καταβὰν ἁρπάσαι αὐτὸν ἐκ μέσου αὐτῶν, ἄγειν.τε
having gone down to take by force him from ²midst ¹their, and to bring

εἰς τὴν παρεμβολήν. 11 Τῇ.δὲ ἐπιούσῃ νυκτὶ ἐπιστὰς
ⁱhim‖into the fortress. But the following night ³standing ᵇby

αὐτῷ ὁ κύριος εἶπεν, Θάρσει ᵉΠαῦλε·‖ ὡς.γὰρ διε-
⁵him ¹the ²Lord said, Be of good courage, Paul; for as thou didst

μαρτύρω τὰ περὶ ἐμοῦ εἰς Ἰερουσαλήμ, οὕτως σε.δεῖ
fully testify the things concerning me at Jerusalem, so thou must

καὶ εἰς Ῥώμην μαρτυρῆσαι. 12 Γενομένης.δὲ ἡμέρας, ποιή-
also at Rome bear witness. And it being day, ³having

σαντές ᶠτινες τῶν Ἰουδαίων συστροφὴν‖ ἀνεθεμάτισαν
⁶made ¹some ²of ³the ⁴Jews a combination put ²under ³a ⁴curse

ἑαυτούς, λέγοντες μήτε φαγεῖν μήτε πιεῖν ἕως.οὗ ἀποκτεί-
¹themselves, declaring neither to eat nor to drink till they should

νωσιν τὸν Παῦλον· 13 ἦσαν.δὲ πλείους ᵍτεσσαράκοντα‖ οἱ
kill Paul. And they were more than forty who

ταύτην τὴν συνωμοσίαν ʰπεποιηκότες·‖ 14 οἵτινες προσελ-
this con-piracy had made; who having

θόντες τοῖς ἀρχιερεῦσιν καὶ τοῖς πρεσβυτέροις ⁱεἶπον,‖ Ἀνα-
come to the chief priests and the elders said, With a

θέματι ἀνεθεματίσαμεν ἑαυτούς, ᵏμηδενὸς‖ γεύσασθαι ἕως.οὗ
curse we have cursed ourselves, nothing to taste until

ἀποκτείνωμεν τὸν Παῦλον. 15 νῦν οὖν ὑμεῖς ἐμφανίσατε
we should kill Paul. Now therefore ye make a representation

---

and the other Phari-
sees, he cried out in
the council, Men *and*
brethren, I am a Pha-
risee, the son of a Pha-
risee: of the hope and
resurrection of the
dead I am called in
question. 7 And when
he had so said, there
arose a dissension be-
tween the Pharisees
and the Sadducees:
and the multitude was
divided. 8 For the
Sadducees say that
there is no resurrec-
tion, neither angel,
nor spirit: but the
Pharisees confess both.
9 And there arose a
great cry: and the
scribes *that were* of
the Pharisees' part a-
rose, and strove, say-
ing, We find no evil in
this man: but if a
spirit or an angel hath
spoken to him, let us
not fight against God.
10 And when there a-
rose a great dissen-
sion, the chief cap-
tain, fearing lest Paul
should have been pull-
ed in pieces of them,
commanded the sol-
diers to go down, and
to take him by force
from among them, and
to bring *him* into the
castle. 11 And the
night following the
Lord stood by him,
and said, Be of good
cheer, Paul: for as
thou hast testified of
me in Jerusalem, so
must thou bear wit-
ness also at Rome.
12 And when it was
day, certain of the
Jews banded together,
and bound themselves
under a curse, saying
that they would nei-
ther eat nor drink till
they had killed Paul.
13 And they were more
than forty which had
made this conspiracy.
14 And they came to
the chief priests and
elders, and said, We
have bound ourselves
under a great curse,
that we will eat no-
thing until we have
slain Paul. 15 Now
therefore ye with the

ˢ ἔκραζεν TTrA. ᵗ Φαρισαίων of Pharisees LTTrAW. ᵛ εἰπόντος LTrW. ʷ — τῶν
I.TTrAW. ˣ + μὲν indeed L. ʸ — μὲν L[Tr]. ᶻ μήτε LTTrAW. ᵃ τινὲς some LTTrA.
ᵇ τῶν γραμματέων τοῦ μέρους TTrA; — γραμ. τοῦ μέρους L. ᶜ ; — μὴ θεομαχῶμεν (*leaving
the sentence incomplete*) GLTTrAW. ᵈ στάσεως γινομένης φοβηθεὶς L; γενομένης (γιν- T)
στάσεως φοβηθεὶς TTrA. ᵉ — Παῦλε GLTTrAW. ᶠ συστροφὴν οἱ Ἰουδαῖοι GLTTrAW.
ᵍ τεσσεράκοντα TTrA. ʰ ποιησάμενοι LTTrAW. ⁱ εἶπαν LTTrA. ᵏ μηθενὸς A.

council signify to the chief captain that he bring him down unto you to morrow, as though ye would inquire something more perfectly concerning him : and we, or ever he come near, are ready to kill him. 16 And when Paul's sister's son heard of their lying in wait, he went and entered into the castle, and told Paul. 17 Then Paul called one of the centurions unto *him*, and said, Bring this young man unto the chief captain : for he hath a certain thing to tell him. 18 So he took him, and brought *him* to the chief captain, and said, Paul the prisoner called me unto *him*, and prayed me to bring this young man unto thee, who hath something to say unto thee. 19 Then the chief captain took him by the hand, and went *with him* aside privately, and asked *him*, What is that thou hast to tell me? 20 And he said, The Jews have agreed to desire thee that thou wouldest bring down Paul to morrow into the council, as though they would inquire somewhat of him more perfectly. 21 But do not thou yield unto them : for there lie in wait for him of them more than forty men, which have bound themselves with an oath, that they will neither eat nor drink till they have killed him : and now are they ready, looking for a promise from thee. 22 So the chief captain *then* let the young man depart, and charged *him*, See *thou* tell no man that thou hast shewed these things to me. 23 And he called unto *him* two centurions, saying, Make ready two hundred soldiers to go to Cæsarea, and

τῷ χιλιάρχῳ σὺν τῷ συνεδρίῳ, ὅπως [1]αὔριον[m] [m]αὐτὸν
to the chief captain with the sanhedrim, so that to-morrow him

καταγάγῃ πρὸς[||] ὑμᾶς, ὡς μέλλοντας διαγινώσκειν ἀκρι-
he may bring down to you, as being about to examine more

βέστερον τὰ περὶ αὐτοῦ· ἡμεῖς δέ, πρὸ τοῦ ἐγγίσαι
accurately the things concerning him, and we, before ²drawing ³near

αὐτὸν ἕτοιμοί ἐσμεν τοῦ ἀνελεῖν αὐτόν. 16 Ἀκούσας δὲ
¹his ⁵ready ⁴are ' to put to death him. But ⁸having ⁹heard ¹⁰of

ὁ υἱὸς τῆς ἀδελφῆς Παύλου [n]τὸ ἔνεδρον,[||] παραγενόμενος
¹the ²son ³of ⁴the ⁵sister ⁶of ⁷Paul the lying in wait, having come near

καὶ εἰσελθὼν εἰς τὴν παρεμβολὴν ἀπήγγειλεν τῷ Παύλῳ.
and entered into the fortress he reported [it] to Paul.

17 προσκαλεσάμενος δὲ ὁ Παῦλος ἕνα τῶν ἑκατοντάρχων,
And ²having ³called ⁴to [⁵him] ¹Paul one of the centurions,

ἔφη, Τὸν νεανίαν τοῦτον [o]ἀπάγαγε[||] πρὸς τὸν χιλίαρχον· ἔχει
said, ²This ³young ⁴man ¹take to the chief captain, ²he ¹has

γάρ [p]τι ἀπαγγεῖλαι[||] αὐτῷ. 18 Ὁ μὲν οὖν παραλαβὼν
¹for something to report to him. He indeed therefore having taken

αὐτὸν ἤγαγεν πρὸς τὸν χιλίαρχον, καί φησιν, Ὁ δέσμιος
him brought [him] to the chief captain, and says, The prisoner

Παῦλος προσκαλεσάμενός με ἠρώτησεν τοῦτον, τὸν
Paul having called ²to [³him] ¹me asked [me] this

[q]νεανίαν[||] ἀγαγεῖν πρός σε, ἔχοντά τι λαλῆσαί σοι.
young man to lead to thee, having something to say to thee.

19 Ἐπιλαβόμενος δὲ τῆς χειρὸς αὐτοῦ ὁ χιλίαρχος, καὶ
And ⁴having ⁵taken ⁶hold ⁷of ⁸his ⁹hand ¹the ²chief ³captain, and

ἀναχωρήσας κατ᾽ ἰδίαν ἐπυνθάνετο, Τί ἐστιν ὃ ἔχεις
having withdrawn apart inquired, What is it which thou hast

ἀπαγγεῖλαί μοι; 20 Εἶπεν δέ, Ὅτι οἱ Ἰουδαῖοι συνέθεντο
to report to me? And he said, The Jews agreed

τοῦ ἐρωτῆσαί σε, ὅπως αὔριον [r]εἰς τὸ συνέδριον κατα-
to request thee, that to-morrow into the sanhedrim thou mayest

γάγῃς τὸν Παῦλον, ὡς μέλλοντές[||] τι ἀκριβέστερον
bring down Paul, · as being about ²something ⁴more ³accurately

πυνθάνεσθαι περὶ αὐτοῦ. 21 σὺ οὖν μὴ πεισθῇς αὐτοῖς·
¹to ²inquire concerning him. Thou therefore be not persuaded by them,

ἐνεδρεύουσιν γὰρ αὐτὸν ἐξ αὐτῶν ἄνδρες πλείους [s]τεσσαρά-
for lie in wait for him, of them ⁴men ¹more ²than ³forty

κοντα,[||] οἵτινες ἀνεθεμάτισαν ἑαυτοὺς μήτε φαγεῖν μήτε
who put ²under ³a ⁴curse ¹themselves neither to eat nor

πιεῖν ἕως οὗ ἀνέλωσιν αὐτόν· καὶ νῦν [t]ἕτοιμοί εἰσιν[||]
to drink till they put to death him; and now ready they are

προσδεχόμενοι τὴν ἀπὸ σοῦ ἐπαγγελίαν. 22 Ὁ μὲν οὖν
waiting the ²from ³thee ¹promise. The ²therefore

χιλίαρχος ἀπέλυσεν τὸν [q]νεανίαν,[||] παραγγείλας μηδενὶ
¹chief ²captain dismissed the young man, having charged [him] to no one

ἐκλαλῆσαι ὅτι ταῦτα ἐνεφάνισας πρός [v]με.[||] 23 Καὶ
to utter that these things thou didst represent to me. And

προσκαλεσάμενος [w]δύο τινὰς[||] τῶν ἑκατοντάρχων εἶπεν,
having called to [him] ²two ¹certain of the centurions he said,

Ἑτοιμάσατε στρατιώτας διακοσίους ὅπως πορευθῶσιν ἕως
Prepare soldiers two hundred, that they may go as far as

---

1 — αὔριον GLTTrAW.   m καταγάγῃ αὐτὸν εἰς LTTrAW.   n τὴν ἐνέδραν EGLTTrA.
o ἄπαγε TTr.   p ἀπαγγεῖλαί τι LTrAW.   q νεανίσκον LTTrA.   r τὸν Παῦλον καταγάγῃς
εἰς τὸ συνέδριον ὡς μέλλων LTTrAW.   s τεσσεράκοντα TTrA.   t εἰσὶν ἕτοιμοι LTTrAW.
v ἐμέ TTr.   w τινας δυο TTr.

ˣΚαισαρείας,‖ καὶ ἱππεῖς ἐβδομήκοντα, καὶ δεξιολάβους δια-
Cæsarea,   and horsemen   seventy,   and spearmen   two

κοσίους, ἀπὸ τρίτης ὥρας τῆς νυκτός· 24 κτήνη.τε παραστῆ-
hundred,   for the third hour of the night.   And ᵇbeasts ¹to ²have ³pro-

σαι, ἵνα ἐπιβιβάσαντες τὸν Παῦλον   διασώσωσιν
vided, that   having set ²on   ¹Paul   they may carry [him] safe through

πρὸς Φήλικα τὸν ἡγεμόνα· 25 γράψας ἐπιστολὴν ʸπερι-
to   Felix   the governor,   having written   a letter   hav-

ἔχουσαν‖ τὸν.τύπον.τοῦτον· 26 Κλαύδιος Λυσίας τῷ κρατίστῳ
ing   this form :   Claudius Lysias to the most excellent

ἡγεμόνι Φήλικι χαίρειν. 27 Τὸν.ἄνδρα.τοῦτον ᶻσυλληφθέντα‖
governor, ·Felix,   greeting.   This man,   having been seized

ὑπὸ τῶν Ἰουδαίων, καὶ μέλλοντα ἀναιρεῖσθαι ὑπ᾽ αὐτῶν,
by   the   Jews,   and being about to be put to death by   them,

ἐπιστὰς σὺν τῷ στρατεύματι ᵃἐξειλόμην‖,ᵇαὐτόν,‖ μαθὼν
having come up with the   troop   I rescued   him, having learnt

ὅτι Ῥωμαῖός ἐστιν. 28 βουλόμενος.ᶜδὲ γνῶναι‖ τὴν αἰτίαν
that a Roman he is.   And desiring   to know   the charge

δι᾽ ἣν ἐνεκάλουν αὐτῷ κατήγαγον ᵈαὐτὸν‖ εἰς τὸ
on account of which they accused him I brought down   him   to

συνέδριον.αὐτῶν· 29 ὃν εὗρον ἐγκαλούμενον περὶ ζητη-
their sanhedrim :   whom I found   to be accused   concerning ques-

μάτων τοῦ.νόμου.αὐτῶν, μηδὲν.δὲ ἄξιον θανάτου ἢ δεσμῶν
tions   of their law,   but ²no   ᵉworthy ⁵of ⁴death ⁷or ⁸of ⁹bonds

ᵉἔγκλημα ἔχοντα.‖ 30 μηνυθείσης.δὲ μοι ἐπιβουλῆς εἰς
³accusation ¹having. And it having been intimated to me of a plot against

τὸν ἄνδρα ᶠμέλλειν‖ ἔσεσθαι ᵍὑπὸ τῶν Ἰουδαίων ‖
the   man   about   to be [carried out] by   the ᾽   Jews

ʰἐξαυτῆς‖ ἔπεμψα πρός σε, παραγγείλας καὶ τοῖς κα-
at once   I sent [him] to   thee,· having charged also the ac-

τηγόροις λέγειν ⁱτὰ‖ ᵏπρὸς αὐτὸν‖ ἐπὶ σοῦ. ˡἜρρωσο.‖
cusers   to say the things against him before thee.   Farewell.

31 Οἱ μὲν οὖν στρατιῶται, κατὰ τὸ διατεταγμένον
The ²therefore ¹soldiers,   according to   the   orders given

αὐτοῖς, ἀναλαβόντες τὸν Παῦλον ἤγαγον διὰ ᵐτῆς‖ νυκτὸς
to them,   having taken   Paul   brought [him] by   night

εἰς τὴν Ἀντιπατρίδα. 32 τῇ.δὲ ἐπαύριον ἐάσαντες τοὺς
to   Antipatris,   and on the   morrow   having left   the

ἱππεῖς ⁿπορεύεσθαι‖ σὺν αὐτῷ, ὑπέστρεψαν εἰς τὴν παρεμ-
horsemen   to go   with him, they returned to the   for-

βολήν· 33 οἵτινες εἰσελθόντες εἰς τὴν ᵒΚαισάρειαν,‖ καὶ
tress·   33 Who   having entered into   Cæsarea,   and

ἀναδόντες τὴν ἐπιστολὴν τῷ ἡγεμόνι, παρέστησαν καὶ τὸν
given up   the   letter   to the governor,   presented   also

Παῦλον αὐτῷ. 34 ἀναγνοὺς.δὲ ᵖὁ ἡγεμών,‖ καὶ ἐπερω-
Paul   to him.   And ³having ⁴read [⁵it] ¹the ²governor,   and having

τήσας ἐκ ποίας �q ἐπαρχίας‖ ἐστί, καὶ πυθόμενος ὅτι ἀπὸ
asked   of   what   province   he is,   and having learnt that from

Κιλικίας,. 35 Διακούσομαί σου, ἔφη, ὅταν καὶ οἱ κατήγοροί
Cilicia   [he is],   I will ²hear ¹fully thee, he said, when also   ²accusers

---

horsemen threescore
and ten, and spearmen
two hundred, at the
third hour of the
night ; 24 and provide
them beasts, that they
may set Paul on, and
bring *him* safe unto
Felix the governor.
25 And he wrote a let-
ter after this manner:
26 Claudius Lysias un-
to the most excellent
governor Felix *send-
eth* greeting. 27 This
man was taken of the
Jews, and should have
been killed of them :
then came I with an
army, and rescued him,
having understood
that he was a Roman.
28 And when I would
have known the cause
wherefore they ac-
cused him, I brought
him forth into their
council : 29 whom I
perceived to be accused
of questions of their
law, but to have no-
thing laid to his charge
worthy of death or of
bonds. 30 And when
it was told me how
that the Jews laid
wait for the man, I
sent straightway to
thee, and gave com-
mandment to his ac-
cusers also to say be-
fore thee what *they
had* against him.
Farewell. 31 Then the
soldiers, as ᵗit was com-
manded them, took
Paul, and brought
him by night to Anti-
patris. 32 On the mor-
row they left the
horsemen to go with
him, and returned to
the castle : 33 who,
when they came to
Cæsarea, and delivered
the epistle to the go-
vernor, presented Paul
also before him. 34 And
when the governor
had read *the letter*, he
asked of what pro-
vince he was. And
when he understood
that he was of Cilicia;
35 I will hear thee,
said he, when thine ac-

ˣ Καισαρίας Τ.   ʸ ἔχουσαν LTTr ; [περι]έχουσαν Α.   ᶻ συλλημφθέντα LTTrA.
ᵃ ἐξειλάμην LTTrAW.   ᵇ — αὐτόν LTTr[A]W.   ᶜ τε (δὲ W) ἐπιγνῶναι LTTrAW.   ᵈ — αὐτὸν (read [him]) Τ[Tr].   ᵉ ἔχοντα ἔγκλημα LTTrAW.   ᶠ — μέλλειν LTTr.   ᵍ — ὑπὸ
τῶν Ἰουδαίων LTTrA.   ʰ ἐξ αὐτῶν by them LTTr ; ἐξ αὐτῆς Α.   ⁱ — τὰ LTTr.   ᵏ αὐτοὺς
ᶠᵒʳ ᵗʰᵉᵐ (to speak) LT.   ˡ — Ἔρρωσο LTTrA.   ᵐ — τῆς LTTrAW.   ⁿ ἀπέρχεσθαι to go
ᵃʷᵃʸ LTTrA.   ᵒ Καισαρίαν Τ.   ᵖ — ὁ ἡγεμών GLTTrAW   �q ἐπαρχείας Τ.

cusers are also come. And he commanded him to be kept in Herod's judgment hall.

σου παραγένωνται^r. Ἐκέλευσέν.τε αὐτὸν[∥] ἐν τῷ πραιτωρίῳ
'thine may have arrived. And he commanded him in the prætorium

τοῦ Ἡρώδου φυλάσσεσθαι^s.
of Herod to be kept.

XXIV. And after five days Ananias the high priest descended with the elders, and with a certain orator named Tertullus, who informed the governor against Paul. 2 And when he was called forth, Tertullus began to accuse him, saying, Seeing that by thee we enjoy great quietness, and that very worthy deeds are done unto this nation by thy providence, 3 we accept it always, and in all places, most noble Felix, with all thankfulness. 4 Notwithstanding, that I be not further tedious unto thee, I pray thee that thou wouldest hear us of thy clemency a few words. 5 For we have found this man a pestilent fellow, and a mover of sedition among all the Jews throughout the world, and a ringleader of the sect of the Nazarenes : 6 who also hath gone about to profane the temple: whom we took, and would have judged according to our law. 7 But the chief captain Lysias came upon us, and with great violence took him away out of our hands, 8 commanding his accusers to come unto thee : by examining of whom thyself mayest take knowledge of all these things, whereof we accuse him. 9 And the Jews also assented, saying that these things were so. 10 Then Paul, after that the governor had beckoned unto him to speak, answered, Forasmuch as I know that thou hast been of many years a judge unto this nation, I do the more cheerfully answer for myself: 11 because that thou mayest understand, that there are yet but twelve days since I

24 Μετὰ.δὲ πέντε ἡμέρας κατέβη ὁ ἀρχιερεὺς Ἀνανίας
And after five days came down the high priest Ananias

μετὰ ^tτῶν πρεσβυτέρων[∥] καὶ ῥήτορος Τερτύλλου τινός, οἵτινες
with the elders and an orator ³Tertullus ¹ª ²certain, who

ἐνεφάνισαν τῷ ἡγεμόνι κατὰ τοῦ Παύλου. 2 κληθέν-
made a representation to the governor against Paul. ³Having ⁴been

τος δὲ αὐτοῦ ἤρξατο κατηγορεῖν ὁ Τέρτυλλος λέγων,
⁵called ¹and ²he ⁷began ⁸to ⁹accuse ⁶Tertullus, saying,

3 Πολλῆς εἰρήνης τυγχάνοντες διὰ σοῦ, καὶ ^vκατορθωμάτων[∥]
²Great ³peace ¹obtaining through thee, and excellent measures

γινομένων τῷ.ἔθνει.τούτῳ διὰ τῆς.σῆς.προνοίας, πάντῃ.τε
being done for this nation through thy forethought, both in every way

καὶ πανταχοῦ ἀποδεχόμεθα, κράτιστε Φῆλιξ, μετὰ πάσης
and everywhere we gladly accept [it], most excellent Felix, with all

εὐχαριστίας. 4 ἵνα.δὲ μὴ ἐπὶ πλεῖόν σε ^wἐγκόπτω[∥]
thankfulne-s. But that ¹not ⁷to ⁹longer ⁸thee ¹I ²may ⁴be ⁵a ⁶hindrance

παρακαλῶ ἀκοῦσαί σε ἡμῶν συντόμως τῇ.σῇ.ἐπιεικείᾳ. 5 εὑ-
I beseech ²to ¹hear 'thee us briefly in thy clemency. ²Having

ρόντες γὰρ τὸν.ἄνδρα.τοῦτον λοιμόν, καὶ κινοῦντα ^xστάσιν[∥]
²found ¹for this man a pest, and moving insurrection

πᾶσιν τοῖς Ἰουδαίοις τοῖς κατὰ τὴν οἰκουμένην, πρωτοστάτην
among all the Jews in the habitable world, ²a ³leader

τε τῆς τῶν Ναζωραίων αἱρέσεως· 6 ὃς καὶ τὸ ἱερὸν
¹and of the ²of ³the ⁴Nazarœans ¹sect; who also the temple

ἐπείρασεν βεβηλῶσαι, ὃν καὶ ἐκρατήσαμεν ^yκαὶ κατὰ
attempted to profane, whom also we seized, and according to

τὸν.ἡμέτερον νόμον ἠθελήσαμεν ^zκρίνειν.[|] 7 παρελθὼν.δὲ
our law wished to judge; but ⁵having ⁶come ⁷up

Λυσίας ὁ χιλίαρχος μετὰ πολλῆς βίας ἐκ τῶν.χειρῶν.ἡμῶν
¹Lysias ²the ³chief ⁴captain with great force out of our hands

ἀπήγαγεν, 8 κελεύσας τοὺς.κατηγόρους.αὐτοῦ ἔρχεσθαι
took away [him], having commanded his accusers to come

^aἐπὶ σέ·[∥] παρ' οὗ δυνήσῃ αὐτὸς ἀνακρίνας περὶ
to thee, from whom thou wilt be able thyself, having examined concerning

πάντων τούτων ἐπιγνῶναι ὧν ἡμεῖς κατηγοροῦμεν
all these things ⁶to ⁷know ¹of ²which ⁴we ⁵accuse

αὐτοῦ. 9 ^bΣυνέθεντο[∥].δὲ καὶ οἱ Ἰουδαῖοι, φάσκοντες ταῦτα
⁵him. And ⁴agreed ³also ¹the .²Jews, declaring these things

οὕτως ἔχειν. 10 Ἀπεκρίθη.^cδὲ[∥] ὁ Παῦλος, νεύσαντος
³thus ¹to ²be. But ²answered ¹Paul, ³having ⁴made ⁷a ⁸sign

αὐτῷ τοῦ ἡγεμόνος λέγειν, Ἐκ·πολλῶν ἐτῶν ὄντα σε
⁵to ¹⁰him ³the ⁴governor to speak, ⁵For ⁶many ⁷years ³as ⁴being ²thee

κριτὴν τῷ.ἔθνει.τούτῳ ἐπιστάμενος, ^dεὐθυμότερον[∥] τὰ
³judge ⁹to ¹⁰this ¹¹nation ¹knowing, more cheerfully [as to] the things

περὶ ἐμαυτοῦ ἀπολογοῦμαι. 11 δυναμένου σου ^eγνῶναι[∥]
concerning myself I make defence. ²Being ³able ¹thou to know

ὅτι οὐ πλείους εἰσίν μοι ἡμέραι ^fἢ[∥] ^gδεκαδύο[∥] ἀφ'.ἧς
that ³not ⁴more ⁵than ¹there ²are ⁸to ⁹me ³days ⁶twelve since

---

^r, κελεύσας having commanded LTTrA.　　^s + αὐτόν him LTTrA.　　^t πρεσβυτέρων τινῶν certain elders LTTrA.　　^v διορθωμάτων reforms LTTrA.　　^w ἐγκόπτω T.　　^x στάσεις insurrections LTTrW.　　^y — καὶ κατὰ . . . . ἐπὶ σέ (verse 8) LTTr[A].　　^z κρίναι A.　　^a πρὸς A.
^b συνεπέθεντο joined in attack GLTTrAW.　　^c τε and LTTrA.　　^d εὐθύμως cheerfully LTTrA.
^e ἐπιγνῶναι LTTrA.　　^f — ἢ GLTTrAW.　　^g δώδεκα LTTrA.

ἀνέβην προσκυνήσων hἐν‖ Ἱερουσαλήμ 12 καὶ οὖτε ἐν τῷ
I went up to worship   at   Jerusalem,   and neither in the

ἱερῷ εὗρόν με πρός τινα διαλεγόμενον ἢ iἐπισύστασιν‖
temple did they find me with anyone reasoning, or a tumultuous gathering

ποιοῦντα ὄχλου οὖτε ἐν ταῖς συναγωγαῖς οὖτε κατὰ τὴν
making of a crowd neither in the synagogues nor in the

πόλιν· 13 kοὖτε‖ παραστῆσαί lμε‖ δύνανταί m περὶ
city;   neither ⁴to ⁵prove ¹are ²they ³able [the things] concerning

ὧν ⁿνῦν‖ κατηγοροῦσίν μου. 14 ὁμολογῶ.δὲ τοῦτό σοι,
which now they accuse me. But I confess this to thee,

ὅτι κατὰ τὴν ὁδὸν ἢν λέγουσιν αἵρεσιν, οὕτως λατρεύω τῷ
that in the way which they call sect, so I serve the

πατρῴῳ θεῷ, πιστεύων πᾶσιν τοῖς κατὰ τὸν νόμον καὶ ᵒ
ancestral God, believing all things which throughout the law and

τοῖς προφήταις γεγραμμένοις, 15 ἐλπίδα ἔχων Pεἰς‖ τὸν θεόν,
the prophets have been written, a hope having in God,

ἢν καὶ αὐτοὶ οὗτοι προσδέχονται, ἀνάστασιν μέλλειν
which also they themselves receive, [that] a resurrection is about

ἔσεσθαι qνεκρῶν,‖ δικαίων.τε καὶ ἀδίκων· 16 ἐν.τούτῳ.ʳδὲ‖
to be of [the] dead, both of just and of unjust. And in this

αὐτὸς ἀσκῶ, ἀπρόσκοπον συνείδησιν ἔχειν πρὸς τὸν θεὸν
myself I exercise, ⁵without ⁶offence ³a ⁴conscience ¹to ²have towards God

καὶ τοὺς ἀνθρώπους ˢδιαπαντός.‖ 17 δι'.ἐτῶν.δὲ πλειόνων
and men continually. And after ⁸years ¹many

ᵗπαρεγενόμην‖ ἐλεημοσύνας ποιήσων εἰς τὸ.ἔθνος.μου ᵗ.καὶ
I arrived ²alms ¹bringing to my nation , and

προσφοράς· 18 ἐν ᵛοἷς‖ εὗρόν με ἡγνισμένον ἐν τῷ ἱερῷ,
offerings. Amidst which they found me purified in the temple,

οὐ μετὰ ὄχλου οὐδὲ μετὰ θορύβου, τινὲς.ʷδὲ‖ ἀπὸ τῆς
not with crowd nor with tumult. But [it was] certain ²from

Ἀσίας Ἰουδαῖοι, 19 οὓς ˣδεῖ‖ ἐπὶ σοῦ παρεῖναι καὶ κατηγορεῖν
³Asia ¹Jews, who ought before thee to appear and to accuse

εἴ τι ἔχοιεν πρός ᵞμε·‖ 20 ἢ αὐτοὶ.οὗτοι εἰπάτωσαν,
if anything they may have against me; or these themselves let them say,

ᶻεἴ‖ τι εὗρον ᵃἐν ἐμοὶ‖ ἀδίκημα, στάντος.μου ἐπὶ τοῦ
if any ²they ³found ⁴in me ¹unrighteousness, when I stood before the

συνεδρίου, 21 ἢ περὶ μιᾶς.ταύτης φωνῆς, ἧς ᵇἔκραξα‖
sanhedrim, [other] than concerning this one voice, which I cried out

ᶜἐστὼς ἐν αὐτοῖς,‖ Ὅτι περὶ ἀναστάσεως νεκρῶν ἐγὼ
standing among them: Concerning a resurrection of [the] dead I

κρίνομαι σήμερον ᵈὑφ'‖ ὑμῶν. 22 ᵉἈκούσας.δὲ ταῦτα ὁ
am judged this day by you. And ²having ³heard ⁴these ⁵things

Φῆλιξ ἀνεβάλετο αὐτούς,‖ ἀκριβέστερον εἰδὼς τὰ περὶ
¹Felix he put ⁶off ⁵them, more accurately knowing the things concerning

τῆς ὁδοῦ, ᶠεἰπών,‖ Ὅταν Λυσίας.ὁ χιλίαρχος καταβῇ,
the way, saying, When Lysias the chief captain may have come down,

διαγνώσομαι τὰ καθ'.ὑμᾶς· 23 διαταξάμενός ᵍτε‖ τῷ ἑκα-
I will examine the things as to you; having ordered the

τοντάρχῃ τηρεῖσθαι ʰᵃτὸν Παῦλον,‖ ἔχειν.τε ἄνεσιν, καὶ
centurion to keep Paul, and to [let him] have ease, and

---

went up to Jerusalem for to worship. 12 And they neither found me in the temple disputing with any man, neither raising up the people, neither in the synagogues, nor in the city: 13 neither can they prove the things whereof they now accuse me. 14 But this I confess unto thee, that after the way which they call heresy, so worship I the God of my fathers, believing all things which are written in the law and in the prophets: 15 and have hope toward God, which they themselves also allow, that there shall be a resurrection of the dead, both of the just and unjust. 16 And herein do I exercise myself, to have always a conscience void of offence toward God, and toward men. 17 Now after many years I came to bring alms to my nation, and offerings. 18 Whereupon certain Jews from Asia found me purified in the temple, neither with multitude, nor with tumult. 19 Who ought to have been here before thee, and object, if they had ought against me. 20 Or else let these same here say, if they have found any evil doing in me, while I stood before the council, 21 except it be for this one voice, that I cried standing among them, Touching the resurrection of the dead I am called in question by you this day. 22 And when Felix heard these things, having more perfect knowledge of that way, he deferred them, and said, When Lysias the chief captain shall come down, I will know the uttermost of your matter. 23 And he commanded a centurion to keep Paul, and to let him have liberty, and that

---

ʰ εἰς LTTrAW.   ⁱ ἐπίστασιν LTTrA.   ᵏ οὐδὲ LT.   ˡ — με EGLTTrAW.   ᵐ + σοι to
thee LTTrAW.   ⁿ νυνὶ LTTrA.   ᵒ + ἐν in ELW; + τοῖς ἐν GTTr[A].   ᵖ πρὸς towards T.
q — νεκρῶν LTTrA.   ʳ καὶ LTTrA.   ˢ διὰ παντός LTrA.   ᵗ παρεγενόμην placed after μου
LTTrA.   ᵛ αἷς LTTrA.   ʷ — δὲ but E.   ˣ ἔδει EGLTTrAW.   ʸ ἐμέ LTTrA.   ᶻ — εἴ (read
τι what) GLTTrAW.   ᵃ — ἐν ἐμοὶ LT[TrA].   ᵇ ἐκέκραξα TTrA.   ᶜ ἐν αὐτοῖς ἑστὼς LTTrAW.
ᵈ ἐφ' LTTrAW.   ᵉ Ἀνεβάλετο δὲ αὐτοὺς ὁ Φῆλιξ GLTTrAW.   ᶠ εἴπας LTTrAW.   ᵍ — τε
ᵀTrAW.   ʰᵃ αὐτὸν him GLTTrAW.

he should forbid none of his acquaintance to minister or come unto him. 24 And after certain days, when Felix came with his wife Drusilla, which was a Jewess, he sent for Paul, and heard him concerning the faith in Christ. 25 And as he reasoned of righteousness, temperance, and judgment to come, Felix trembled, and answered, Go thy way for this time; when I have a convenient season. I will call for thee. 26 He hoped also that money should have been given him of Paul, that he might loose him: wherefore he sent for him the oftener, · and communed with him. 27 But after two years Porcius Festus came into Felix' room: and Felix, willing to shew the Jews a pleasure, **left Paul bound.**

μηδένα κωλύειν τῶν ἰδίων αὐτοῦ ὑπηρετεῖν [i]ἢ προσέρχεσθαι[ll]
¹none   ¹to ²forbid   of his own   to minister or   to come

αὐτῷ. 24 Μετὰ δὲ [k]ἡμέρας τινὰς[ll] παραγενόμενος ὁ Φῆλιξ
to him.   And after ²days ¹certain ⁴having ⁵arrived ³Felix

οὖν Δρουσίλλῃ τῇ γυναικὶ [m]αὐτοῦ[ll] οὔσῃ Ἰουδαίᾳ, μετε-
with Drusilla   his wife,   who was a Jewess,   he

πέμψατο τὸν Παῦλον, καὶ ἤκουσεν αὐτοῦ περὶ τῆς εἰς
sent for   Paul,   and   heard   him   concerning the ²in

χριστὸν [n] πίστεως. 25 διαλεγομένου δὲ αὐτοῦ περὶ δικαιο-
³Christ   ¹faith.   And as ²reasoned   ¹he   concerning right-

σύνης καὶ ἐγκρατείας καὶ τοῦ κρίματος τοῦ μέλλοντος [o]ἔσεσθαι,[ll]
eousness and self-control and the judgment   about   to be,

ἔμφοβος γενόμενος ὁ Φῆλιξ ἀπεκρίθη, Τὸ νῦν ἔχον πορεύου·
²afraid ¹becoming   Felix   answered,   For the present   go,

καιρὸν δὲ μεταλαβὼν μετακαλέσομαί σε· 26 ἅμα [p]δὲ[ll]
and an opportunity having found   I will call for   thee ;   withal too

καὶ ἐλπίζων ὅτι χρήματα δοθήσεται αὐτῷ ὑπὸ τοῦ Παύλου,
also   hoping   that ⁴riches   will be given   him   by   Paul,

[q]ὅπως λύσῃ αὐτόν·[ll] διὸ καὶ πυκνότερον αὐτὸν μετα-
that he might loose him :   wherefore also   oftener   him   send-

πεμπόμενος ὡμίλει αὐτῷ. 27 Διετίας δὲ πληρωθείσης
ing for   he conversed with him.   But two years being completed

ἔλαβεν διάδοχον ὁ Φῆλιξ Πόρκιον Φῆστον· θέλων τε
²received [³as] ⁴successor ¹Felix   Porcius   Festus ;   and wishing

[r]χάριτας[ll] καταθέσθαι τοῖς Ἰουδαίοις ὁ Φῆλιξ κατέλιπεν
favours to acquire for himself with the Jews   Felix   left

τὸν Παῦλον δεδεμένον.
· Paul   bound.

XXV. Now when Festus was come into the province, after three days he ascended from Cæsarea to Jerusalem. 2 Then the high priest and the chief of the Jews informed him against Paul, and besought him, 3 and desired favour against him, that he would send for him to Jerusalem, laying wait in the way to kill him. 4 But Festus answered, that Paul should be kept at Cæsarea, and that he himself would depart shortly *thither.* 5 Let them therefore, said he, which among you are able, go down with *me,* and accuse this man, if there be any wickedness in him. 6 And when he had tarried among them more than ten days, he went down

25 Φῆστος οὖν ἐπιβὰς τῇ [s]ἐπαρχίᾳ,[ll] μετὰ τρεῖς
Festus therefore being come into the province,   after three

ἡμέρας ἀνέβη εἰς Ἱεροσόλυμα ἀπὸ [t]Καισαρείας.[ll] 2 ἐνε-
days went up to Jerusalem from   Cæsarea.   ²Made ³a ⁴re-

φάνισαν [v]δὲ[ll] αὐτῷ [w]ὁ ἀρχιερεὺς[ll] καὶ οἱ πρῶτοι τῶν
presentation ⁵before ¹and him   the high priest and   the   chief   of the

Ἰουδαίων κατὰ τοῦ Παύλου, καὶ παρεκάλουν αὐτόν, 3 αἰτού-
Jews   against   Paul,   and besought   him,   ask-

μενοι χάριν κατ᾽ αὐτοῦ, ὅπως μεταπέμψηται αὐτὸν εἰς
ing   a favour against him,   that   he would send for   him   to

Ἱερουσαλήμ, ἐνέδραν ποιοῦντες ἀνελεῖν αὐτὸν κατὰ τὴν
Jerusalem,   an ambush   forming to put to death him   on   the

ὁδόν. 4 ὁ μὲν οὖν Φῆστος ἀπεκρίθη, τηρεῖσθαι τὸν Παῦλον
way.   Festus therefore   answered,   ²should ³be ⁴kept   ¹Paul

[x]ἐν Καισαρείᾳ,[ll] ἑαυτὸν δὲ μέλλειν ἐν τάχει ἐκπορεύεσθαι.
at   Cæsarea,   and himself   was about shortly   to set out.

5 Οἱ οὖν [y]δυνατοὶ ἐν ὑμῖν, φησίν,[ll] [z]συγκαταβάντες,[ll]
Those therefore in-power among you, says he,   having gone down too,

εἴ τι ἐστὶν ἐν τῷ ἀνδρὶ [a]τούτῳ,[ll] κατηγορείτωσαν αὐτοῦ.
if anything is   in   ²man   ¹this,   let them accuse   him.

6 Διατρίψας δὲ ἐν αὐτοῖς ἡμέρας [b]πλείους ἢ[ll] δέκα, κατα-
And having spent among them   ⁴days   ¹more ²than ³ten,   having

βὰς εἰς ᶜΚαισάρειαν,‖ τῇ ἐπαύριον καθίσας ἐπὶ τοῦ
gone down to Cæsarea, on the morrow having sat on - the

βήματος ἐκέλευσεν τὸν Παῦλον ἀχθῆναι. 7 παραγενομένου
judgment seat he commanded Paul to be brought. ³Being ⁴come

δὲ αὐτοῦ, περιέστησαν ᵈ οἱ ἀπὸ Ἱεροσολύμων καταβε-
¹and ²he, stood round the ²from ³Jerusalem ⁴who ⁵had ⁶come

βηκότες Ἰουδαῖοι, πολλὰ καὶ βαρέα ᵉαἰτιάματα‖ ᶠφέροντες
⁷down ¹Jews, many and weighty charges bringing

κατὰ τοῦ Παύλου,‖ ἃ οὐκ ἴσχυον ἀποδεῖξαι, 8 ᵍἀπο-
against Paul, which they were not able to prove: ²said ³in

λογουμένου αὐτοῦ,‖ Ὅτι οὔτε εἰς τὸν νόμον τῶν Ἰουδαίων
⁴defence ¹he, Neither against the law of the Jews

οὔτε εἰς τὸ ἱερὸν οὔτε εἰς Καίσαρά τι ἥμαρτον.
nor against the temple nor against Cæsar [in] anything sinned I.

9 Ὁ Φῆστος δὲ ᵇτοῖς Ἰουδαίοις θέλων‖ χάριν κατα-
But Festus, ⁷with ⁸the ⁹Jews ¹wishing ⁶favour ²to ³acquire ⁴for

θέσθαι ἀποκριθεὶς τῷ Παύλῳ εἶπεν, Θέλεις εἰς Ἱεροσόλυμα
⁵himself answering Paul said, Art thou willing to Jerusalem

ἀναβάς, ἐκεῖ περὶ τούτων ⁱκρίνεσθαι‖ ἐπ' ἐμοῦ;
naving gone up there concerning these things to be judged before me?

10 Εἶπεν δὲ ὁ Παῦλος, ᵏ Ἐπὶ τοῦ βήματος Καίσαρος ᵏἑ-
But ²said ¹Paul, Before the judgment seat of Cæsar stand-

στώς‖ εἰμι, οὗ με δεῖ κρίνεσθαι. Ἰουδαίους οὐδὲν ˡἠδί-
ing I am, where it behoves me to be judged. To Jews ²nothing ¹I ³did

κησα,‖ ὡς καὶ σὺ κάλλιον ἐπιγινώσκεις· 11 εἰ μὲν ᵐγὰρ‖
wrong, as also thou very well knowest. ²If ³indeed ¹for

ἀδικῶ καὶ ἄξιον θανάτου πέπραχά τι, οὐ παραιτοῦμαι
I do wrong and worthy of death have done anything, I do not deprecate

τὸ ἀποθανεῖν· εἰ δὲ οὐδέν ἐστιν ὧν οὗτοι κατηγοροῦσίν
to die; but if nothing there is of which they accuse

μου, οὐδείς με δύναται αὐτοῖς χαρίσασθαι. Καίσαρα ἐπι-
me, no one me can to them give up. To Cæsar I ap-

καλοῦμαι. 12 Τότε ὁ Φῆστος ⁿσυλλαλήσας‖ μετὰ τοῦ συμ-
peal. Then Festus, having conferred with the coun-

βουλίου, ἀπεκρίθη, Καίσαρα ἐπικέκλησαι, ἐπὶ Καίσαρα
cil, answered, To Cæsar thou hast appealed, to Cæsar

πορεύσῃ.
thou shalt go.

13 Ἡμερῶν δὲ διαγενομένων τινῶν, Ἀγρίππας ὁ βασιλεὺς
And ²days ³having ⁴passed ¹certain, Agrippa the king

καὶ Βερνίκη κατήντησαν εἰς °Καισάρειαν,‖ ᴾἀσπασόμενοι‖ τὸν
and Bernice came down to Cæsarea, saluting

Φῆστον. 14 ὡς δὲ πλείους ἡμέρας διέτριβον ἐκεῖ ὁ Φῆστος
Festus. And when many days they stayed there Festus

τῷ βασιλεῖ ἀνέθετο τὰ κατὰ τὸν Παῦλον λέγων,
²the ¹king ¹laid ²before the things relating to Paul, saying,

Ἀνήρ τις ἐστὶν καταλελειμμένος ὑπὸ Φήλικος δέσμιος,
A ²man ¹certain there is left by Felix a prisoner,

15 περὶ οὗ, γενομένου μου εἰς Ἱεροσόλυμα, ἐνε-
concerning whom, ³being ¹on ²my in Jerusalem, ⁴made ⁵a ⁶re-

φάνισαν οἱ ἀρχιερεῖς καὶ οἱ πρεσβύτεροι τῶν Ἰουδαίων,
presentation ¹the ²chief ³priests and the elders of the Jews,

unto Cæsarea; and the next day sitting on the judgment seat commanded Paul to be brought. 7 And when he was come, the Jews which came down from Jerusalem stood round about, and laid many and grievous complaints against Paul, which they could not prove. 8 While he answered for himself, Neither against the law of the Jews, neither against the temple, nor yet against Cæsar, have I offended any thing at all. 9 But Festus, willing to do the Jews a pleasure, answered Paul, and said, Wilt thou go up to Jerusalem, and there be judged of these things before me? 10 Then said Paul, I stand at Cæsar's judgment seat, where I ought to be judged: to the Jews have I done no wrong, as thou very well knowest. 11 For if I be an offender, or have committed any thing worthy of death, I refuse not to die: but if there be none of these things whereof these accuse me, no man may deliver me unto them. I appeal unto Cæsar. 12 Then Festus, when he had conferred with the council, answered, Hast thou appealed unto Cæsar? unto Cæsar shalt thou go.

13 And after certain days king Agrippa and Bernice came unto Cæsarea to salute Festus. 14 And when they had been there many days, Festus declared Paul's cause unto the king, saying, There is a certain man left in bonds by Felix: 15 about whom, when I was at Jerusalem, the chief priests and the elders of the Jews informed me, desiring to

---

ᶜ Καισαρίαν ᴛ. ᵈ + αὐτὸν him ʟᴛᴛʀᴀᴡ. ᵉ αἰτιώματα ɢʟᴛᴛʀᴀᴡ. ᶠ καταφέροντες
(— κατὰ τοῦ Παύλου) ʟᴛᴛʀᴀ. ᵍ τοῦ Παύλου ἀπολογουμένου Paul said in defence ʟᴛᴛʀᴀ.
ᵇ θέλων τοῖς Ἰουδαίοις ʟᴛᴛʀᴀᴡ. ⁱ κριθῆναι ʟᴛᴛʀᴀ. ᵏ ἐστὼς placed before Ἐπί ᴛ.
ˡ ἠδίκηκα I have done wrong ᴛᴛʀ. ᵐ οὖν therefore ʟᴛᴛʀᴀᴡ. ⁿ συνλαλήσας ᴛ.
° Καισαρίαν ᴛ. ᴾ ἀσπασάμενοι ᴛᴛʀᴀ.
26

have judgment against him. 16 To whom I answered, It is not the manner of the Romans to deliver any man to die, before that he which is accused have the accusers face to face, and have licence to answer for himself concerning the crime laid against him. 17 Therefore, when they were come hither, without any delay on the morrow I sat on the judgment seat, and commanded the man to be brought forth. 18 Against whom when the accusers stood up, they brought none accusation of such things as I supposed : 19 but had certain questions against him of their own superstition, and of one Jesus, which was dead, whom Paul affirmed to be alive. 20 And because I doubted of such manner of questions, I asked *him* whether he would go to Jerusalem, and there be judged of these matters. 21 But when Paul had appealed to be reserved unto the hearing of Augustus, I commanded him to be kept till I might send him to Cæsar. 22 Then Agrippa said unto Festus, I would also hear the man myself. To morrow, said he, thou shalt hear him.

αἰτούμενοι κατ᾽ αὐτοῦ ᵠδίκην·‖ 16 πρὸς οὓς ἀπεκρίθην,
asking   ²against ³him ¹judgment: to   whom I answered,

ὅτι οὐκ.ἔστιν ἔθος Ῥωμαίοις χαρίζεσθαί τινα ἄνθρωπον
It is not a custom with Romans to give up   any   man

ʳεἰς ἀπώλειαν,‖ πρὶν ἢ ὁ κατηγορούμενος κατὰ.πρόσωπον
to destruction, before he· being accused   face to face

ἔχοι τοὺς κατηγόρους, τόπον.τε ἀπολογίας λάβοι
may have the accusers, and opportunity of defence he may get

περὶ τοῦ ἐγκλήματος. 17 συνελθόντων οὖν ˢαὐτῶν‖
concerning the accusation. ²Having ³come ⁴together ⁵therefore ¹they

ἐνθάδε, ἀναβολὴν μηδεμίαν ποιησάμενος, τῇ ἑξῆς καθίσας,
here,   delay   none   having made, the next [day] having sat

ἐπὶ τοῦ βήματος ἐκέλευσα ἀχθῆναι τὸν ἄνδρα· 18 περὶ
on the judgment seat I commanded to be brought the man; concerning

οὗ σταθέντες οἱ κατήγοροι οὐδεμίαν αἰτίαν ᵗἐπέφερον‖ ὧν
whom standing up the accusers ²no ³charge ¹brought of which

ᵛὑπενόουν ἐγώ‖ ʷ· 19 ζητήματα.δὲ τινα περὶ τῆς.ἰδίας
²supposed ¹I ;   but ²questions ¹certain concerning their own

δεισιδαιμονίας εἶχον πρὸς αὐτόν, καὶ περὶ τινος Ἰησοῦ
system of religion they had against him, and concerning a certain Jesus
(*lit.* demon-worship)

τεθνηκότος, ὃν ἔφασκεν ὁ Παῦλος ζῆν. 20 ἀπορούμενος.δὲ
who is dead, whom ²affirmed ¹Paul to be alive. And ²being ³perplexed

ἐγὼ ˣεἰς‖ τὴν περὶ ʸτούτου‖ ζήτησιν ἔλεγον, εἰ.βούλοιτο
¹I as to the ²concerning ³this ¹inquiry said, Would he be willing

πορεύεσθαι εἰς ᶻἹερουσαλήμ,‖ κἀκεῖ κρίνεσθαι περὶ
to go   to   Jerusalem,   and there to be judged concerning

τούτων. 21 τοῦ.δὲ.Παύλου ἐπικαλεσαμένου τηρηθῆναι αὐ-
these things. But Paul having appealed for ²to ³be ⁴kept ¹him-

τὸν εἰς τὴν τοῦ Σεβαστοῦ διάγνωσιν, ἐκέλευσα τηρεῖσθαι
self for the ²of ³Augustus ¹cognizance, I commanded ²to ³be ⁴kept

αὐτὸν ἕως.οὗ ᵃπέμψω‖ αὐτὸν πρὸς Καίσαρα. 22 Ἀγρίππας
¹him till I might send him to   Cæsar.   ²Agrippa

δὲ πρὸς τὸν Φῆστον ᵇἔφη,‖ Ἐβουλόμην καὶ αὐτὸς τοῦ
¹and to   Festus   said, I was desiring also myself the

ἀνθρώπου ἀκοῦσαι· ᶜΟ.δέ,‖ Αὔριον, φησίν, ἀκούσῃ αὐτοῦ.
man   to hear. And he ²To-morrow ¹says, thou shalt hear him.

---

23 And on the morrow, when Agrippa was come, and Bernice, with great pomp, and was entered into the place of hearing, with the chief captains, and principal men of the city, at Festus' commandment Paul was brought forth. 24 And Festus said, King Agrippa, and all men, which are here present with us, ye see this man, about whom all the multitude of the Jews have dealt with me, both at Jerusalem, and *also* here, crying that he ought

23 Τῇ οὖν ἐπαύριον ἐλθόντος τοῦ Ἀγρίππα καὶ τῆς
On the ²therefore ¹morrow ⁴having ⁵come ³Agrippa and

Βερνίκης μετὰ πολλῆς φαντασίας, καὶ εἰσελθόντων εἰς τὸ
Bernice, with great pomp,   and having entered into the

ἀκροατήριον, σύν τε ᵈτοῖς‖ χιλιάρχοις καὶ ἀνδράσιν τοῖς
hall of audience, with both the chief captains and men

κατ᾽.ἐξοχὴν ᵉοὖσιν‖ τῆς πόλεως, καὶ κελεύσαντος τοῦ Φήστου
of eminence being of the city, and ²having ³commanded ¹Festus

ἤχθη ὁ Παῦλος. 24 καί φησιν ὁ Φῆστος, Ἀγρίππα βασι-
²was ⁶brought ⁴Paul. And ²says ¹Festus, ²Agrippa ³king

λεῦ, καὶ πάντες οἱ ʳσυμπαρόντες‖ ἡμῖν ἄνδρες, θεωρεῖτε τοῦ-
and all   the ²being ³present ⁴with ⁵us ¹men, ye see this

τον περὶ οὗ ᵍπᾶν‖ τὸ πλῆθος τῶν Ἰουδαίων ἐνέτυχόν
one concerning whom all the multitude of the Jews pleaded

μοι ἔν τε Ἱεροσολύμοις καὶ ἐνθάδε, ʰἐπιβοῶντες‖ μὴ
with me in both Jerusalem   and here, crying out [that]

ᵠ καταδίκην LTTrAW.   ʳ — εἰς ἀπώλειαν GLTTrAW.   ˢ [αὐτῶν] A.   ᵗ ἔφερον LTTrAW.
ᵛ ἐγὼ ὑπενόουν LTTrAW.   ʷ + πονηράν (*read* evil charge) LT[A]w ; πονηρῶν of evils Tr.
ˣ — εἰς TTr[A].   ʸ τούτων these things LTTrAW.   ᶻ Ἱεροσόλυμα LTTrAW.   ᵃ ἀναπέμψω
I might send up LTTrAW.   ᵇ — ἔφη (*read* [said]) LTTrA.   ᶜ — Ὁ δέ (*read* φησίν says
he) LTTrA.   ᵈ — τοῖς LTTrA.   ᵉ — οὖσιν LTTrAW.   ᶠ συν- T.   ᵍ ἅπαν LTTrAW.
ʰ βοῶντες crying LTTr ; [ἐπι]βοῶντες A.

δεῖν ¹ζῆν αὐτὸν‖ μηκέτι 25 ἐγὼ.δὲ ᵏκαταλαβόμενος‖ μηδὲν
ᶻought ᵃto ⁴live ¹he   no longer. But I   ʰaving perceived   nothing

ἄξιον ¹θανάτου αὐτὸν‖ πεπραχέναι, ᵐκαὶ‖ αὐτοῦ δὲ τούτου
worthy of death   he   had done,   ˢalso ⁴himself ¹and ²this ³one

ἐπικαλεσαμένου τὸν Σεβαστόν, ἔκρινα πέμπειν ⁿαὐτόν·‖
ʰaving appealed to   Augu-tus, I determined to send   him,

26 περὶ οὗ ἀσφαλές τι γράψαι τῷ.κυρίῳ οὐκ.ἔχω·
concerning whom ᵘcertain ¹anything to write to [my] lord I have not.

διὸ προήγαγον αὐτὸν ἐφ᾽ ὑμῶν, καὶ μάλιστα ἐπὶ σοῦ,
Wherefore I brought ²forth ¹him before you, and ᵍspecially before thee,

βασιλεῦ Ἀγρίππα, ὅπως τῆς ἀνακρίσεως γενομένης
king   Agrippa, so that the examination having taken place

σχῶ τι ᵒγράψαι.‖ 27 ἄλογον.γάρ μοι δοκεῖ πέμ-
I may have something to write ;   for irrational to me it seems send-

ποντα δέσμιον, μὴ καὶ τὰς κατ᾽ αὐτοῦ αἰτίας σημᾶναι.
ing a prisoner, not also the ²against ³him ¹charges to signify.

26 Ἀγρίππας.δὲ πρὸς τὸν Παῦλον ἔφη, Ἐπιτρέπεταί σοι
   And Agrippa to   Paul   said,   It is allowed thee

ᴾὑπὲρ‖ σεαυτοῦ λέγειν. Τότε ὁ Παῦλος ᑫἀπελογεῖτο,‖ ἐκτείνας
for   thyself to speak. Then   Paul   made a defence, stretching out

τὴν χεῖρα, ᑫ 2 Περὶ πάντων ὧν ἐγκαλοῦμαι ὑπὸ Ἰου-
the hand :   Concerning all of which I am accused by Jews,

δαίων, βασιλεῦ Ἀγρίππα, ἥγημαι ἐμαυτὸν μακάριον ʳμέλλων
king   Agrippa, I esteem myself   happy being about

ἀπολογεῖσθαι ἐπὶ σοῦ σήμερον·‖ 3 μάλιστα γνώστην ˢὄντα
to make defence before thee to-day, especially ³acquainted ²being

σε‖ πάντων τῶν κατὰ Ἰουδαίους ἐθῶν τε καὶ ζητημάτων·
¹thou of all   the ⁴among ⁶Jews· ⁵customs ²and ³also ⁷questions ;

διὸ δέομαί ᵗσου‖ μακροθύμως ἀκοῦσαί μου. 4 τὴν μὲν οὖν
wherefore I beseech thee patiently to hear me. The ⁵then

βίωσίν μου ᵛτὴν‖ ἐκ νεότητος, τὴν ἀπ᾽ ἀρχῆς
ᵐanner ²of ⁴life ¹my   from youth,   which from [its] commencement

γενομένην ἐν τῷ.ἔθνει.μου ἐν ʷ Ἱεροσολύμοις, ἴσασιν πάντες
was   among my nation in   Jerusalem,   know all

ˣοἱ‖ Ἰουδαῖοι, 5 προγινώσκοντές με ἄνωθεν, ἐὰν θέλωσιν
the Jews, who before knew me from the first, if they would

μαρτυρεῖν, ὅτι κατὰ τὴν ἀκριβεστάτην αἵρεσιν τῆς
bear witness, that according to the strictest   sect

ἡμετέρας ʸθρησκείας.‖ ἔζησα Φαρισαῖος· 6 καὶ νῦν ἐπ᾽
of our religion I lived a Pharisee. And now for [the]

ἐλπίδι τῆς ᶻπρὸς‖ τοὺς πατέρας ᵃἐπαγγελίας γενομένης ὑπὸ
hope of the ²to ⁴the· ⁵fathers ¹promise   ²made .by

τοῦ θεοῦ ἕστηκα κρινόμενος, 7 εἰς ἣν τὸ.δωδεκάφυλον.ἡμῶν
God, I stand being judged,   to which   our twelve tribes

ἐν.ἐκτενείᾳ νύκτα καὶ ἡμέραν λατρεῦον ἐλπίζει καταντῆσαι·
intently ⁻night and day serving hope to arrive;

περὶ ἧς ἐλπίδος ἐγκαλοῦμαι, ᵇβασιλεῦ Ἀγρίππα,‖ ὑπὸ
concerning which hope I am accused, O king   Agrippa, by

ᶜτῶν‖ Ἰουδαίωνᵈ. 8 τί ἄπιστον κρίνεται παρ᾽ ὑμῖν εἰ ὁ θεὸς
the Jews. Why incredible is it judged by you if God

νεκροὺς ἐγείρει; 9 ἐγὼ·μὲν οὖν ἔδοξα ἐμαυτῷ πρὸς
[the] dead raises?   I indeed therefore thought in myself ⁸to

not to live any longer.
25 But when I found
that he had committed
nothing worthy of
death, and that he
himself hath appealed
to Augustus, I have
determined to send
him. 26 Of whom I
have no certain thing
to write unto my lord.
Wherefore I have
brought him forth be-
fore you, and specially
before thee, O king
Agrippa, that, after
examination had, I
might have somewhat
to write. 27 For it
seemeth to me unrea-
sonable to send a pri-
soner, and not withal
to signify the crimes
laid against him.

XXVI. Then Agrip-
pa said unto Paul,
Thou art permitted to
speak for thyself. Then
Paul stretched forth
the hand, and an-
swered for himself :
2 I think myself happy,
king Agrippa, because
I shall answer for my-
self this day before
thee touching all the
things whereof I am
accu-ed of the Jews :
3 especially because I
know thee to be expert
in all customs and
questions which are
among the Jews :
wherefore I beseech
thee to hear me pa-
tiently. 4 My manner
of life from my youth,
which was at the first
among mine own na-
tion at Jerusalem,
know all the Jews ;
5 which knew me from
the beginning, if they
would testify, that
after the most strait-
est sect of our religion
I lived a Pharisee.
6 And now I stand and
am judged for the
hope of the promise
made of God unto
our fathers : 7 unto
which promise our
twelve tribes, in tant-
ly serving God day
and night, hope to
come. For ₋ which
hope's sake, king A-
grippa, I am accused
of the Jews. 8 Why
should it be thought a
thing incredible with
you, that God should
raise the dead? 9 I
verily thought with

¹ αὐτὸν ζῆν LTTrAW. ᵏ κατελαβόμην LTTrAW. ˡ αὐτὸν θανάτου LTTrAW. ᵐ — καὶ LTTrAW.
ⁿ — αὐτὸν (read [him]) LTTrA. ᵒ γράψω I shall write LTTrAW. ᴾ περὶ LTTrA. ᑫ ἀπε-
λογεῖτο placed after χεῖρα LTTrAW; ʳ ἐπὶ σοῦ μέλλων σήμερον ἀπολογεῖσθαι GLTTrA. ˢ σε
ὄντα T. ᵗ — σου LTTrA. ᵛ — τὴν Tr[A]. ʷ + τε and (in) LTTrAW. ˣ — οἱ LTrA.
ʸ θρησκίας T. ᶻ εἰς LTTrAW. ᵃ + ἡμῶν (read our fathers) LTTrAW. ᵇ — βασιλεῦ
Ἀγρίππα LTTrA ; — Ἀγρίππα W. ᶜ — τῶν GLTTrAW. ᵈ + βασιλεῦ O king LTTrA.

myself, that I ought to do many things contrary to the name of Jesus of Nazareth. 10 Which thing I also did in Jerusalem: and many of the saints did I shut up in prison, having received authority from the chief priests; and when they were put to death, I gave my voice against them. 11 And I punished them oft in every synagogue, and compelled them to blaspheme; and being exceedingly mad against them, I persecuted them even unto strange cities. 12 Whereupon as I went to Damascus with authority and commission from the chief priests, 13 at midday, O king, I saw in the way a light from heaven, above the brightness of the sun, shining round about me and them which journeyed with me. 14 And when we were all fallen to the earth, I heard a voice speaking unto me, and saying in the Hebrew tongue, Saul, Saul, why persecutest thou me? It is hard for thee to kick against the pricks. 15 And I said, Who art thou, Lord? And he said, I am Jesus whom thou persecutest. 16 But rise, and stand upon thy feet: for I have appeared unto thee for this purpose, to make thee a minister and a witness both of these things which thou hast seen, and of those things in the which I will appear unto thee; 17 delivering thee from the people, and from the Gentiles, unto whom now I send thee, 18 to open their eyes, and to turn them from darkness to light, and from the power of Satan unto God, that they may receive forgiveness of sins, and inheritance among them which are sanctified by faith that is in me. 19 Whereupon, O king Agrippa,

τὸ ὄνομα Ἰησοῦ τοῦ Ναζωραίου δεῖν πολλὰ ἐναντία
[7]the [8]name [9]of [10]Jesus [11]the [12]Nazarœan [1]I [2]ought [3]many [4]things [5]contrary

πρᾶξαι· 10 ὃ καὶ ἐποίησα ἐν Ἱεροσολύμοις, καὶ πολλοὺς [e]
to do. Which also I did in Jerusalem; and many

τῶν ἁγίων ἐγὼ [f]φυλακαῖς κατέκλεισα, τὴν παρὰ τῶν ἀρχ-
of the saints I in prisons shut up, the [2]from [3]the [4]chief

ιερέων ἐξουσίαν λαβών· ἀναιρουμένων·τε αὐτῶν
[5]priests [1]authority having received; and [2]being [3]put [4]to [5]death [1]they

κατήνεγκα.ψῆφον. 11 καὶ κατὰ πάσας τὰς συναγωγὰς
I gave [my] vote against [them]. And in all the synagogues

πολλάκις τιμωρῶν αὐτούς, ἠνάγκαζον βλασφημεῖν· περισ-
often punishing them, I compelled [them] to blaspheme. [4]Exceed-

σῶς τε ἐμμαινόμενος αὐτοῖς ἐδίωκον ἕως·καὶ εἰς
ingly [1]and [2]being [3]furious against them I persecuted [them] even as far as to

τὰς ἔξω πόλεις. 12 ἐν οἷς [g]καὶ[11] πορευόμενος εἰς τὴν Δα-
foreign cities. During which also journeying to Da-

μασκὸν μετ' ἐξουσίας καὶ ἐπιτροπῆς [h]τῆς παρὰ[11] τῶν ἀρχ-
mascus, with authority and a commission from the chief

ιερέων, 13 ἡμέρας.μέσης κατὰ τὴν ὁδὸν εἶδον, βασιλεῦ,
priests, at mid-day in the way I saw, O king,

οὐρανόθεν ὑπὲρ τὴν λαμπρότητα τοῦ ἡλίου περιλάμψαν
from heaven above the brightness of the sun [shining [2]round [3]about

με φῶς καὶ τοὺς σὺν ἐμοὶ πορευομένους. 14 πάντων.[i]δὲ[11]
[6]me [1]a [2]light and those with me journeying. And all

καταπεσόντων ἡμῶν εἰς τὴν γῆν ἤκουσα φωνὴν [k]λαλοῦσαν[11]
[3]having [4]fallen [5]down [1]of [2]us to the ground I heard a voice speaking

πρός με [1]καὶ λέγουσαν[11] τῇ Ἑβραΐδι διαλέκτῳ, Σαούλ, Σαούλ,
to me and saying in the Hebrew language, Saul, Saul,

τί με διώκεις; σκληρόν σοι πρὸς κέντρα λακτίζειν.
why me persecutest thou? [it is] hard for thee against goads to kick.

15 Ἐγὼ.δὲ [m]εἶπον,[11] Τίς εἶ κύριε; Ὁ.δὲ [n]εἶπεν, Ἐγώ εἰμι
And I said, Who art thou, Lord? And he said, I am

Ἰησοῦς ὃν σὺ διώκεις. 16 ἀλλὰ ἀνάστηθι, καὶ στῆθι ἐπὶ
Jesus whom thou persecutest: but rise up, and stand on

τοὺς.πόδας.σου· εἰς.τοῦτο.γὰρ ὤφθην σοι, προχειρίσασθαί
thy feet; for, for this purpose I appeared to thee, to appoint

σε ὑπηρέτην καὶ μάρτυρα ὧν.τε εἶδες ὧν.τε
thee an attendant and a witness both of what thou did-t see and in what

ὀφθήσομαί σοι, 17 ἐξαιρούμενός σε ἐκ τοῦ λαοῦ καὶ [o]
I shall appear to thee, taking out thee from among the people and

τῶν ἐθνῶν, εἰς οὓς [p]νῦν σε ἀποστέλλω,[11] 18 ἀνοῖξαι ὀφθαλμοὺς
the nations, to whom now thee I send, to open [2]eyes

αὐτῶν, τοῦ.ἐπιστρέψαι ἀπὸ σκότους εἰς φῶς καὶ τῆς ἐξουσίας
[1]their, that [they] may turn from darkness to light and the authority

τοῦ σατανᾶ ἐπὶ τὸν θεόν, τοῦ.λαβεῖν αὐτοὺς ἄφεσιν ἁμαρ-
of Satan to God, that [may] receive [1]they remission of sins

τιῶν καὶ κλῆρον ἐν τοῖς ἡγιασμένοις πίστει τῇ
and inheritance among those that have been sanctified by faith that [is]

εἰς ἐμέ. 19 Ὅθεν, βασιλεῦ Ἀγρίππα, οὐκ.ἐγενόμην ἀπειθὴς
in me. Whereupon, O king Agrippa, I was not disobedient

τῇ οὐρανίῳ ὀπτασίᾳ, 20 ἀλλὰ τοῖς ἐν Δαμασκῷ πρῶτον
to the heavenly vision; but to those in Damascus first

---

[e] + τε also LTTrA.　　　[f] + ἐν in (prisons) GLTTrAW. 　[g] — καὶ LTTrA. 　[h] — τῆς παρὰ
(read τῶν from the) L; — τῆς [Tr]w; — παρὰ TTr. 　[i] τε LTTrAW. 　[k] λέγουσαν LTTrA.
[l] — καὶ λέγουσαν LTTrA. 　[m] εἶπα LTTrA. 　[n] + κύριος (read the Lord said) LTTrAW.
[o] + ἐκ from among LTTrA. 　[p] ἐγὼ ἀποστέλλω σε (omit now) LTTrA; ἐγὼ σε ἀποστ. GW.
[q] + τε (read and also) LTTrA.

καὶ ʳ Ἱεροσολύμοις, ˢεἰς" πᾶσάν τε τὴν χώραν τῆς Ἰουδαίας
and Jerusalem, ²to ³all ¹and the region of Judæa

καὶ τοῖς ἔθνεσιν, ʰἀπαγγέλλων" μετανοεῖν καὶ ἐπιστρέφειν
and to the nations. declaring [to them] to repent and to turn

ἐπὶ τὸν θεόν, ἄξια τῆς μετανοίας ἔργα πράσσοντας. 21 ἕνεκα
to God, ³worthy ⁴of ⁵repentance ²works ¹doing. On account of

τούτων με ᵛοἱ" Ἰουδαῖοι συλλαβόμενοι ᵂἐν τῷ ἱερῷ, ἐπει-
these things me the Jews having seized in the temple, at-

ρῶντο διαχειρίσασθαι. 22 ἐπικουρίας οὖν τυχὼν τῆς
tempted to kill. Aid therefore having obtained

ˣπαρὰ" τοῦ θεοῦ ἄχρι τῆς ἡμέρας ταύτης ἔστηκα, ʸμαρτυρού-
from God unto this day I have stood, bearing wit-

ᵐενος" μικρῷ τε καὶ μεγάλῳ, οὐδὲν ἐκτὸς λέγων ὧν τε
ness both to small and to great, nothing else saying than what both

οἱ προφῆται ἐλάλησαν μελλόντων γίνεσθαι καὶ ᶻΜωσῆς,"
the prophets ³said ⁴was ⁵about ⁶to ⁷happen ¹and ²Moses,

23 εἰ παθητὸς ὁ χριστός, εἰ πρῶτος ἐξ ἀναστά-
whether ²should ³suffer ¹Christ; whether [he] first through resurrec-

σεως νεκρῶν φῶς μέλλει καταγγέλλειν τῷ ᵃ λαῷ καὶ τοῖς
tion of [the] dead ⁵light ¹is ²about ³to ⁴announce to the people and to the

ἔθνεσιν. 24 Ταῦτα δὲ αὐτοῦ ἀπολογουμένου, ὁ Φῆστος με-
nations. And ²these ³things ¹uttering in his defence, Festus

γάλῃ τῇ φωνῇ ᵇἔφη," Μαίνῃ Παῦλε· τὰ πολλά σε γράμ-
loud voice said, Thou art mad, Paul; much ²thee ¹learn-

ματα εἰς μανίαν περιτρέπει. 25 Ὁ δὲ ᶜ, Οὐ μαίνομαι, φησίν,
ing ⁴to ⁵madness ²turns. But he, ²I ³am ⁴not ⁵mad, ¹says,

κράτιστε Φῆστε, ᵈἀλλ'" ἀληθείας καὶ σωφροσύνης ῥήματα
most noble Festus, but of truth and discreetness words

ἀποφθέγγομαι· 26 ἐπίσταται γὰρ περὶ τούτων ὁ βασι-
I utter; for ³is ⁴informed ⁵concerning ⁶these ⁷things ¹the ²king

λεύς, πρὸς ὃν καὶ παῤῥησιαζόμενος λαλῶ· λανθάνειν γὰρ
to whom also using boldness I speak. For hidden from

αὐτόν τι τούτων οὐ πείθομαι ᵉοὐδέν·" οὐ γάρ
him any of these things [are] not I am persuaded; ⁴not ¹for

ἐστιν ἐν γωνίᾳ πεπραγμένον τοῦτο. 27 πιστεύεις βασιλεῦ
²in ³a ⁴corner ³has ⁵been ¹done ²this. Believest thou, king

Ἀγρίππα τοῖς προφήταις; οἶδα ὅτι πιστεύεις. 28 Ὁ δὲ
Agrippa, the prophets? I know that thou believest. And

Ἀγρίππας πρὸς τὸν Παῦλον ἔφη," Ἐν ὀλίγῳ με ᵍπείθεις"
Agrippa to Paul said, In a little ³me ¹thou ²persuadest

χριστιανὸν ʰγενέσθαι." 29 Ὁ δὲ Παῦλος ἰεἶπεν," ᵏΕὐξαίμην" ἂν
a Christian to become. And Paul said, I would wish

τῷ θεῷ, καὶ ἐν ὀλίγῳ καὶ ἐν ˡπολλῷ" οὐ μόνον σε ἀλλὰ καὶ
to God, both in a little and in much not only thou but also

πάντας τοὺς ἀκούοντάς μου σήμερον γενέσθαι τοιούτους
all those hearing me this day should become such

ᵒποῖος κἀγώ εἰμι, παρεκτὸς τῶν δεσμῶν τούτων. 30 ᵐΚαὶ"
as I also am, except these bonds. And

ταῦτα εἰπόντος αὐτοῦ," ἀνέστη ⁿ ὁ βασιλεὺς καὶ ὁ ἡγεμὼν
these things ²having ³said ¹he, ⁴rose ⁷up ⁴the ⁵king and the governor

ἥ τε Βερνίκη καὶ οἱ ᵒσυγκαθήμενοι" αὐτοῖς· 31 καὶ ἀνα-
also Bernice and those who sat with them, and having

I was not disobedient unto the heavenly vision: 20 but shewed first unto them of Damascus, and at Jerusalem, and throughout all the coasts of Judæa, and *then* to the Gentiles, that they should repent and turn to God, and do works meet for repentance. 21 For these causes the Jews caught me in the temple, and went about to kill *me*. 22 Having therefore obtained help of God, I continue unto this day, witnessing both to small and great, saying none other things than those which the prophets and Moses did say should come: 23 that Christ should suffer, *and* that he should be the first that should rise from the dead, and should shew light unto the people, and to the Gentiles. 24 And as he thus spake for himself, Festus said with a loud voice, Paul, thou art beside thyself; much learning doth make thee mad. 25 But he said, I am not mad, most noble Festus; but speak forth the words of truth and soberness. 26 For the king knoweth of these things, before whom also I speak freely: for I am persuaded that none of these things are hidden from him; for this thing was not done in a corner. 27 King Agrippa, believest thou the prophets? I know that thou believest. 28 Then Agrippa said unto Paul, Almost thou persuadest me to be a Christian. 29 And Paul said, I would to God, that not only thou, but also all that hear me this day, were both almost, and altogether such as I am, except these bonds. 30 And when he had thus spoken, the king rose up, and the governor, and Bernice, and they that sat with them: 31 and when they were gone

---

ʳ + ἐν 111 L.   ˢ — εἰς LTTɪ[A].   ᵗ ἀπήγγελλον I was declaring EGLTTɾAW.   ᵛ — οἱ TTr.
ᵂ + ὄντα being T.   ˣ ἀπὸ LTTɾAW.   ʸ μαρτυρόμενος LTTɾAW.   ᶻ Μωϋσῆς GLTTɾAW.   ᵃ + τε (*read* both to the) LTTɾA.   ᵇ φησίν says LTTɾA.   ᶜ + Παῦλος (*read* Paul says) LTTɾW.   ᵈ ἀλλὰ LTTɾA.
ᵉ — οὐδέν L; οὐθέν T[Tɾ]A.   ᶠ — ἔφη (*read* [said]) LTTɾAW.   ᵍ πείθῃ thou persuadest thyself A.
ʰ ποιῆσαι to make (me a Christian) LTTɾA.   ⁱ — εἶπεν (*read* [said]) LTTɾA.   ᵏ εὐξάμην T.   ˡ μεγάλῳ LTTɾA.   ᵐ — καὶ ταῦτα εἰπόντος αὐτοῦ GLTTɾAW.   ⁿ + τε both GLTTɾAW.   ᵒ συν- T.

aside, they talked between themselves, saying, This man doeth nothing worthy of death or of bonds. 32 Then said Agrippa unto Festus, This man might have been set at liberty, if he had not appealed unto Cæsar.

χωρήσαντες ἐλάλουν πρὸς ἀλλήλους λέγοντες, Ὅτι οὐδὲν
withdrawn   they spoke   to   one another   saying,   Nothing
θανάτου ρ ἄξιον ἢ δεσμῶν‖ ۹ πράσσει ὁ ἄνθρωπος οὗτος,
²of ³death   ¹worthy   or   of bonds   does   this man.
32 Ἀγρίππας δὲ τῷ Φήστῳ ἔφη, Ἀπολελύσθαι ʳἐδύνατο‖ ὁ
And Agrippa   to Festus   said,   ⁴Have ⁵been ⁶let ⁷go   ³might
ἄνθρωπος οὗτος εἰ μὴ ˢἐπεκέκλητο‖ Καίσαρα.
¹this ²man   if he had not appealed to   Cæsar.

XXVII. And when it was determined that we should sail into Italy, they delivered Paul and certain other prisoners unto one named Julius, a centurion of Augustus' band. 2 And entering into a ship of Adramyttium, we launched, meaning to sail by the coasts of Asia; one Aristarchus, a Macedonian of Thessalonica, being with us. 3 And the next day we touched at Sidon. And Julius courteously entreated Paul, and gave him liberty to go unto his friends to refresh himself. 4 And when we had launched from thence, we sailed under Cyprus, because the winds were contrary. 5 And when we had sailed over the sea of Cilicia and Pamphylia, we came to Myra, a city of Lycia. 6 And there the centurion found a ship of Alexandria sailing into Italy; and he put us therein. 7 And when we had sailed slowly many days, and scarce were come over against Cnidus, the wind not suffering us, we sailed under Crete, over against Salmone; 8 and, hardly passing it, came unto a place which is called The fair havens; nigh whereunto was the city of Lasea. 9 Now when much time was spent, and when sailing was now dangerous, because the fast was now already past, Paul admonished them, 10 and said unto them, Sirs, I perceive that this voyage will be with hurt and much damage, not only of

27 Ὡς δὲ ἐκρίθη τοῦ ἀποπλεῖν ἡμᾶς εἰς τὴν Ἰταλίαν
But when it was decided that ²should ³sail ¹we   to   Italy
παρεδίδουν τόν τε Παῦλον καί τινας ἑτέρους δεσμώτας ἑκα-
they delivered up   both Paul   and certain   other   prisoners   ²to a
τοντάρχῃ, ὀνόματι Ἰουλίῳ, σπείρης Σεβαστῆς. 2 ἐπιβάν-
centurion,   by name   Julius,   of the band of Augustus. ²Having ³gone ⁴on
τες δὲ πλοίῳ Ἀδραμυττηνῷ ᵗμέλλοντες‖ πλεῖν ᵘ τοὺς κατὰ
⁵board ¹and a ship   of Adramyttium   about   to navigate the   ²along
τὴν Ἀσίαν τόπους ἀνήχθημεν, ὄντος σὺν ἡμῖν Ἀριστάρχου,
³Asia   ¹places   we set sail,   being with us   Aristarchus
Μακεδόνος Θεσσαλονικέως. 3 τῇ τε ἑτέρᾳ κατήχθημεν εἰς
a Macedonian   of Thessalonica.   And the next [day]   we landed   at
Σιδῶνα· φιλανθρώπως τε ὁ Ἰούλιος τῷ Παύλῳ χρησάμενος
Sidon.   And ⁵kindly   ⁴Julius   ²Paul   ²having ³treated
ἐπέτρεψεν πρὸς ᵛ φίλους ᵂπορευθέντα‖ ἐπιμελείας
allowed   [him] ²to [³his] ⁴friends   ¹going   [⁷their]   ⁸care
τυχεῖν. 4 κἀκεῖθεν ἀναχθέντες ὑπεπλεύσαμεν τὴν Κύπρον
⁵to ⁶receive.   And thence setting sail   we sailed under   Cyprus
διὰ τὸ τοὺς ἀνέμους εἶναι ἐναντίους. 5 τό τε πέλαγος τὸ
because   the   winds   were   contrary.   And the sea   the
κατὰ τὴν Κιλικίαν καὶ Παμφυλίαν διαπλεύσαντες ˣκατήλθομενˢ
along   Cilicia   and Pamphylia   having sailed over   we came
εἰς ʸΜύρα‖ τῆς Λυκίας. 6 Κἀκεῖ εὑρὼν ὁ ᶻἑκατοντάρχοςˢ
to   Myra   of Lycia.   And there ³having ⁴found ¹the   ²centurion
πλοῖον Ἀλεξανδρῖνον πλέον εἰς τὴν Ἰταλίαν ἐνεβίβασεν
a ship   of Alexandria   sailing   to   Italy   he caused ²to ³enter
ἡμᾶς εἰς αὐτό. 7 ἐν ἱκαναῖς δὲ ἡμέραις βραδυπλοοῦντες καὶ
¹us   into   it.   And for many   days   sailing slowly   and
μόλις γενόμενοι κατὰ τὴν Κνίδον, μὴ προσεῶντος ἡμᾶς
hardly having come over against   Cnidus,   ³not   ⁴suffering   ⁵us
τοῦ ἀνέμου, ὑπεπλεύσαμεν τὴν Κρήτην κατὰ Σαλμώνην·
¹the   ²wind,   we sailed under   Crete   over against   Salmone;
8 μόλις τε παραλεγόμενοι αὐτὴν ἤλθομεν εἰς τόπον τινὰ
and hardly   coasting along   it   we came   to a   ²place ¹certain
καλούμενον Καλοὺς Λιμένας, ᾧ ἐγγὺς ᵃἦν πόλις‖ ᵇΛασαία.ᵃ
called   Fair   Havens,   near which   was   a city   of Lasæa.
9 Ἱκανοῦ δὲ χρόνου διαγενομένου καὶ ὄντος ἤδη ἐπισφαλοῦς
And much   time   having passed   and being   already   dangerous
τοῦ πλοός, διὰ τὸ καὶ τὴν νηστείαν ἤδη παρεληλυθέναι,
the voyage,   because   also   the   fast   already   had past,
παρῄνει ὁ Παῦλος 10 λέγων αὐτοῖς, Ἄνδρες, θεωρῶ ὅτι μετὰ
²exhorted   ¹Paul   ⁴saying ³them,   Men,   I perceive that with
ὕβρεως καὶ πολλῆς ζημίας οὐ μόνον τοῦ ᶜφόρτου‖ καὶ τοῦ
disaster   and   much   loss   not only   of the   cargo   and of the

---

ᵖ ἢ δεσμῶν ἄξιον LTTr.   ۹ + τι T.   ʳ ἠδύνατο LW.   ˢ ἐπικέκλητο L.   ᵗ μέλλοντι
LTTrAW.   ᵘ + εἰς in LTTr[A].   ᵛ + τοὺς the GLTTrAW.   ᵂ πορευθέντι LTTrA.
ˣ κατήλθαμεν TTr.   ʸ Μύρρα LTTrA.   ᶻ ἑκατοντάρχης LTTrA.   ᵃ πόλις ἦν Τ.
ᵇ Ἀλασσα Alassa L; Λασέα Lasea TrA.   ᶜ φορτίου GLTTrAW

πλοίου ἀλλὰ καὶ τῶν ψυχῶν ἡμῶν μέλλειν ἔσεσθαι τον πλοῦν.
ship but also of our lives is about to be the voyage.

11 Ὁ δὲ ᵈἑκατόνταρχος‖ τῷ κυβερνήτῃ καὶ τῷ ναυκλήρῳ
But the centurion by the steersman and the ship-owner

ᵉἐπείθετο μᾶλλον‖ ἢ τοῖς ὑπὸ ᶠτοῦ‖ Παύλου λεγο-
was persuaded rather than by the things ²by ³Paul ¹spoken.

μένοις. 12 ἀνευθέτου δὲ τοῦ λιμένος ὑπάρχοντος πρὸς παρα-
And ill-adapted the port being to winter

χειμασίαν, οἱ ᵍπλείους‖ ἔθεντο βουλὴν ἀναχθῆναι ʰκἀκεῖθεν,‖
in, the most counselled to set sail thence also,

ⁱεἴπως‖ δύναιντο καταντήσαντες εἰς Φοίνικα παρα-
if by any means they might be able having arrived at Phœnice to

χειμάσαι, λιμένα τῆς Κρήτης βλέποντα κατὰ ᾿λίβα
winter [there], a port of Crete looking towards south-west

καὶ κατὰ χῶρον. 13 ὑποπνεύσαντος δὲ νότου, δόξαν-
and towards north-west. And ³blowing ⁵gently ¹a ²south ³wind, think-

τες τῆς προθέσεως κεκρατηκέναι, ἄραντες ἆσσον
ing the purpose to have gained, having weighed [anchor] ⁴close ⁵by

παρελέγοντο τὴν Κρήτην. 14 μετ᾿ οὐ πολὺ δὲ ἔβαλεν
¹they ²coasted ³along Crete. ⁴After ²not ³long ¹but there came

κατ᾿ αὐτῆς ἄνεμος τυφωνικός, ὁ καλούμενος ᵏεὐροκλύδων.‖
down it a ²wind ¹tempestuous, ²called Euroclydon.

15 συναρπασθέντος δὲ τοῦ πλοίου, καὶ μὴ δυναμένου ἀντ-
And ³having ⁴been ⁵caught ¹the ²ship, and not able to bring

οφθαλμεῖν τῷ ἀνέμῳ, ἐπιδόντες ἐφερόμεθα. 16 νησίον
[her] head to the wind, giving [her] up we were driven along. ²Small ¹island

δὲ τι ὑποδραμόντες καλούμενον ˡΚλαύδην‖ ᵐμόλις
¹but ²a ⁵certain ³running ⁴under called Clauda ²hardly

ἰσχύσαμεν‖ περικρατεῖς γενέσθαι τῆς σκάφης· 17 ἣν ἄραν-
¹we were able masters to become of the boat; which having taken

τες βοηθείαις ἐχρῶντο, ὑποζωννύντες τὸ πλοῖον· φοβούμενοί
up ¹helps they used, undergirding the ship; ²fearing

τε μὴ εἰς τὴν σύρτιν ἐκπέσωσιν, χαλάσαντες τὸ σκεῦος
¹and lest into the quicksand they should fall, having lowered the gear

οὕτως ἐφέροντο. 18 Σφοδρῶς δὲ χειμαζομένων ἡμῶν
so they were driven. But ³violently ²being ⁴tempest-tossed ¹we

τῇ ἑξῆς ἐκβολὴν ἐποιοῦντο· 19 καὶ τῇ
on the next [day] ³a ⁴casting ⁵out [²of ⁷cargo] ¹they ²made, and on the

τρίτῃ αὐτόχειρες τὴν σκευὴν τοῦ πλοίου ⁿἐρρίψαμεν·‖
third [day] with [our] own hands the equipment of the ship we cast away.

20 μήτε δὲ ἡλίου μήτε ἄστρων ἐπιφαινόντων ἐπὶ πλείονας
And neither sun nor stars appearing for many

ἡμέρας, χειμῶνός τε οὐκ ὀλίγου ἐπικειμένου, λοιπὸν περιῃ-
days, and ²tempest ¹no ²small lying on [us], henceforth was taken

ρεῖτο ᵒπᾶσα ἐλπὶς‖ τοῦ σώζεσθαι ἡμᾶς. 21 πολλῆς ᴾδὲ‖ ἀσιτίας
away all hope of our being saved. And ³a ⁴long ³abstinence

ὑπαρχούσης, τότε σταθεὶς ὁ Παῦλος ἐν μέσῳ αὐτῶν εἶπεν,
¹there ²being, then ²standing ³up ¹Paul in their midst said,

Ἔδει μέν, ὦ ἄνδρες, πειθαρχήσαντάς μοι μὴ ἀνά-
It behoved [you] indeed, O men, having been obedient to me not to have

γεσθαι ἀπὸ τῆς Κρήτης κερδῆσαί τε τὴν ὕβριν ταύτην καὶ
set sail from Crete and to have gained this disaster and

---

the lading and ship, but also of our lives. 11 Nevertheless the centurion believed the master and the owner of the ship, more than those things which were spoken by Paul. 12 And because the haven was not commodious to winter in, the more part advised to depart thence also, if by any means they might attain to Phenice, *and there* to winter; *which is* an haven of Crete, and lieth toward the south west and north west. 13 And when the south wind blew softly, supposing that they had obtained *their* purpose, loosing *thence*, they sailed close by Crete. 14 But not long after there arose against it a tempestuous wind, called Euroclydon. 15 And when the ship was caught, and could not bear up into the wind, we let *her* drive. 16 And running under a certain island which is called Clauda, we had much work to come by the boat: 17 which when they had taken up, they used helps, undergirding the ship; and, fearing lest they should fall into the quicksands, strake sail, and so were driven. 18 And we being exceedingly tossed with a tempest, the next *day* they lightened the ship; 19 and the third *day* we cast out with our own hands the tackling of the ship. 20 And when neither sun nor stars in many days appeared, and no small tempest lay on *us*, all hope that we should be saved was then taken away. 21 But after long abstinence Paul stood forth in the midst of them, and said, Sirs, ye should have hearkened unto me, and not have loosed from Crete, and to have gained this harm and loss.

---

22 And now I exhort you to be of good cheer: for there shall be no loss of any man's life among you, but of the ship. 23 For there stood by me this night the angel of God, whose I am, and whom I serve, 24 saying, Fear not, Paul; thou must be brought before Cæsar: and, lo, God hath given thee all them that sail with thee. 25 Wherefore, sirs, be of good cheer: for I believe God, that it shall be even as it was told me. 26 Howbeit we must be cast upon a certain island. 27 But when the fourteenth night was come, as we were driven up and down in Adria, about midnight the shipmen deemed that they drew near to some country; 28 and sounded, and found it twenty fathoms: and when they had gone a little further, they sounded again, and found it fifteen fathoms. 29 Then fearing lest we should have fallen upon rocks, they cast four anchors out of the stern, and wished for the day. 30 And as the shipmen were about to flee out of the ship, when they had let down the boat into the sea, under colour as though they would have cast anchors out of the foreship, 31 Paul said to the centurion and to the soldiers, Except these abide in the ship, ye cannot be saved. 32 Then the soldiers cut off the ropes of the boat, and let her fall off. 33 And while the day was coming on, Paul besought them all to take meat, saying, This day is the fourteenth day that ye have tarried and continued fasting, having taken nothing. 34 Wherefore I pray you to take some meat: for this is for your

τὴν ζημίαν. 22 καὶ ᵠτανῦν‖ παραινῶ ὑμᾶς εὐθυμεῖν·
loss.   and now   I exhort you   to be of good cheer,

ἀποβολὴ-γὰρ ψυχῆς οὐδεμία ἔσται ἐξ ὑμῶν, πλὴν τοῦ
for ³loss   ⁴of ⁵life ¹not ²any shall be from among you,   only of the

πλοίου. 23 παρέστη-γάρ μοι ʳτῇ-νυκτὶ-ταύτῃ‖ ˣἄγγελος‖ τοῦ
ship.   For stood by me   this night   an angel

θεοῦ, οὗ εἰμὶᵗ ᾧ-καὶ λατρεύω,ˢ 24 λέγων, Μὴ-φοβοῦ Παῦλε,
of God, whose I am and whom I serve,   saying, Fear not,   Paul;

Καίσαρί σε δεῖ παραστῆναι· καὶ ἰδοὺ κεχάρισταί σοι ὁ θεὸς
Cæsar thou must stand before;   and lo ²has ³granted ⁴to ⁵thee ¹God

πάντας τοὺς πλέοντας μετὰ σοῦ. 25 Διὸ εὐθυμεῖτε ἄνδρες·
all those sailing with thee.   Wherefore be of good cheer, men,

πιστεύω-γὰρ τῷ θεῷ ὅτι οὕτως ἔσται καθ᾽ ὃν-τρόπον
for I believe   God   that thus it shall be according to   the way

λελάληταί μοι. 26 εἰς-νῆσον-δὲ τινα δεῖ-ἡμᾶς ἐκπεσεῖν.
it has been said to me.   But on ²island ¹a ²certain we must fall.

27 Ὡς-δὲ τεσσαρεσκαιδεκάτη νὺξ ἐγένετο διαφερομένων
And when the fourteenth   night was come ²being ³driven ⁴about

ἡμῶν ἐν τῷ Ἀδρίᾳ, κατὰ μέσον τῆς νυκτὸς ὑπενόουν
¹we in the Adriatic, towards [the] middle of the night   ²supposed

οἱ ναῦται προσάγειν τινὰ αὐτοῖς χώραν· 28 καὶ βολίσαντες
¹the ²sailors ⁴neared ⁴some ³them ²country,   and having sounded

εὗρον ὀργυιὰς εἴκοσι· βραχὺ-δὲ διαστήσαντες καὶ πάλιν
they found ²fathoms ¹twenty, and ²a ⁴little ¹having ³gone ⁴farther and again

βολίσαντες εὗρον ὀργυιὰς δεκαπέντε· 29 φοβούμενοί-τε
having sounded they found ²fathoms ¹fifteen;   and fearing

ᵛμήπως‖ ʷεἰς‖ τραχεῖς τόπους ˣἐκπέσωσιν,‖ ἐκ πρύμνης
lest on rocky places they should fall, out of [the] stern

ῥίψαντες ἀγκύρας τέσσαρας ʸηὔχοντο‖ ἡμέραν γενέσθαι.
having cast ²anchors ¹four they wished   day to come.

30 τῶν-δὲ ναυτῶν ζητούντων φυγεῖν ἐκ τοῦ πλοίου, καὶ
But the sailors seeking   to flee out of the ship,   and

χαλασάντων τὴν σκάφην εἰς τὴν θάλασσαν, προφάσει ὡς ἐκ
having let down the boat into the sea,   with pretext as from

ᶻπρώρας‖ ᵃμελλόντων ἀγκύρας‖ ἐκτείνειν, 31 εἶπεν ὁ Παῦ-
[the] prow being about ²anchors ¹to ²cast ³out, said ¹Paul

λος τῷ ἑκατοντάρχῃ καὶ τοῖς στρατιώταις, Ἐὰν-μὴ οὗτοι
to the centurion and to the soldiers,   Unless these

μείνωσιν ἐν τῷ πλοίῳ, ὑμεῖς σωθῆναι οὐ-δύνασθε. 32 Τότε ᵇοἱ
abide in the ship ye ²be ³saved ¹cannot.   Then the

στρατιῶται ἀπέκοψαν‖ τὰ σχοινία τῆς σκάφης καὶ εἴασαν
soldiers cut away the ropes of the boat and let

αὐτὴν ἐκπεσεῖν. 33 ἄχρι-δὲ-οὗ ᶜἔμελλεν ἡμέρα‖ γίνεσθαι,
her fall.   And until ²was ³about ¹day ⁴to ⁵come,

παρεκάλει ὁ Παῦλος ἅπαντας μεταλαβεῖν τροφῆς, λέγων,
⁷exhorted ⁶Paul all   to partake of food, saying,

Τεσσαρεσκαιδεκάτην σήμερον ἡμέραν προσδοκῶντες ἄσι-
⁴The ⁵fourteenth ¹to-²day [³is] day watching without

τοι διατελεῖτε, ᵈμηδὲν‖ ᵉπροσλαβόμενοι. 34 διὸ παρα-
taking food ye continue, nothing having taken.   Wherefore I ex-

καλῶ ὑμᾶς ᶠπροσλαβεῖν‖ τροφῆς· τοῦτο-γὰρ πρὸς τῆς
hort you to take food,   for this for

ᵠ τὰ νῦν LTTrA. 　ʳ ταύτῃ τῇ νυκτὶ GLTTrAW. 　ˣ ἄγγελος placed after λατρεύω LTTrAW. 　ʷ κατὰ against LTTrAW. 　ˣ ἐκ-
ᵗ + ἐγώ LT[A]. 　ᵛ μήπω L; μήπου TTr; μή που A. 　ᵗπέσωμεν we should fall GLTTrA. 　ʸ εὔχοντο TTrA. 　ᶻ πρώρης LT. 　ᵃ ἀγκύρας μελλόντων
LTTrA. 　ᵇ ἀπέκοψαν οἱ στρατιῶται LTTrA. 　ᶜ ἡμέρα ἤμελλεν (ἔμελλεν T) LTTrA. 　ᵈ μηδὲν
LTTrA. 　ᵉ προσλαμβανόμενοι taking L 　ᶠ μεταλαβεῖν to partake of GLTTrAW.

ὑμετέρας.σωτηρίας ὑπάρχει· ᵍοὐδενὸς‖.γὰρ ὑμῶν θρὶξ ʰἐκ‖
your safety   is ;   for of no one   of you   a hair   of

τῆς κεφαλῆς ⁱπεσεῖται.‖ 35 ᵏΕἰπὼν‖.δὲ ταῦτα καὶ λαβὼν
the   head   shall fall.   And having said these things and having taken

ἄρτον εὐχαρίστησεν τῷ θεῷ ἐνώπιον πάντων, καὶ κλάσας
a loaf   he gave thanks   to God before   all,   and having broken [it]

ἤρξατο ἐσθίειν. 36 εὔθυμοι.δὲ γενόμενοι πάντες καὶ αὐ-
began   to eat.   And ⁴of ⁵good ⁶cheer ²having ³become ¹all   also them-

τοὶ προσελάβοντο τροφῆς· 37 ᵐἦμεν.δὲ ᵐἐν τῷ πλοίῳ αἱ
selves   took   food.   And we were in the   ship· ²the

πᾶσαι ψυχαὶ‖ διακόσιαι ⁿἑβδομηκονταἑξ.‖ 38 κορεσθέντες.δὲ
¹all   souls   two hundred [and]   seventy six.   And being satisfied

τροφῆς ἐκούφιζον τὸ πλοῖον, ἐκβαλλόμενοι τὸν σῖτον εἰς τὴν
with food they lightened the   ship,   casting out   the wheat into the

θάλασσαν. 39 Ὅτε.δὲ ἡμέρα ἐγένετο τὴν γῆν οὐκ.ἐπεγίνωσκον·
sea.   And when ³day   ¹it ²was   the land they did not recognize ;

κόλπον.δὲ τινα κατενόουν ἔχοντα αἰγιαλόν, εἰς ὃν °ἐβού-
but a ²bay   ¹certain they perceived having   a shore,   on which · they

λεύσαντο‖ εἰ δύναιντο ἐξῶσαι τὸ πλοῖον. 40 καὶ τὰς
purposed   if they should be able to drive the   ship ;   and ⁴the

ἀγκύρας περιελόντες εἴων εἰς τὴν θάλασσαν, ἅμα
⁵anchors ¹having ²cut ³away they left in the   sea,   at the same time

ἀνέντες τὰς ζευκτηρίας τῶν πηδαλίων· καὶ ἐπάραντες τὸν
having loosened the   bands · of the rudders,   and having hoisted the

ᴾἀρτέμονα‖ τῇ πνεούσῃ κατεῖχον εἰς τὸν αἰγιαλόν. 41 περι-
foresail   to the   wind   they made for the   shore.   ²Having

πεσόντες δὲ εἰς τόπον διθάλασσον ᑫἐπώκειλαν‖ τὴν ναῦν·
³fallen   ¹and into a place where two seas-met they ran aground the vessel ;

καὶ ἡ μὲν πρῶρα ἐρείσασα ἔμεινεν ἀσάλευτος, ἡ.δὲ
and the   prow   having stuck fast remained   immovable,   but the

πρύμνα ἐλύετο ὑπὸ τῆς βίας ʳτῶν κυμάτων.‖ 42 τῶν.δὲ
stern   was broken by the violence of the waves.   And of the

στρατιωτῶν βουλὴ ἐγένετο ἵνα τοὺς δεσμώτας ἀποκτείνωσιν,
soldiers   [the] counsel · was that the prisoners they should kill,

μήτις ἐκκολυμβήσας ˢδιαφύγοι·‖ 43 ὁ.δὲ ᵗἑκατόνταρχος‖
lest anyone having swum out should escape.   But the   centurion

βουλόμενος διασῶσαι τὸν Παῦλον ἐκώλυσεν αὐτοὺς τοῦ
desiring   to save   Paul   hindered   them   of [their]

βουλήματος, ἐκέλευσέν.τε τοὺς δυναμένους κολυμβᾷν, ᵛἀπορ-
purpose,   and commanded those being able to swim,   having

ῥίψαντας‖ -πρώτους, ἐπὶ τὴν γῆν ἐξιέναι, 44 καὶ τοὺς
cast [themselves] off   first,   on the land to go out ;   and the

λοιπούς, οὓς μὲν ἐπὶ σανίσιν οὓς.δὲ ἐπί τινων.τῶν ἀπὸ τοῦ
rest,   some indeed on boards and others on some things ⸱ from the

πλοίου· καὶ οὕτως ἐγένετο πάντας διασωθῆναι ἐπὶ τὴν γῆν.
ship ;   and thus it came to pass all   were brought safely to the land.

28 Καὶ διασωθέντες τότε ʷἐπέγνωσαν‖ ὅτι Μελίτη ἡ
And having been saved then they knew   that Melita the

νῆσος .καλεῖται. 2 Οἱ.ˣδὲ‖ βάρβαροι ʸπαρεῖχον‖ οὐ τὴν
island   is called.   And the barbarians   shewed   no   the

τυχοῦσαν φιλανθρωπίαν ἡμῖν· ᶻἀνάψαντες‖.γὰρ πυρὰν προσ-
common   philanthropy to us ;   for having kindled   a fire   they

health : for there shall
not an hair fall from
the head of any of you.
35 And when he had
thus spoken, he took
bread, and gave thanks
to God in presence of
them all : and when
he had broken it, he be-
gan to eat. 36 Then
were they all of good
cheer, and they also
took some meat. 37 And
we were in all in
the ship two hundred
threescore and sixteen
souls. 38 And when
they had eaten enough,
they lightened the
ship, and cast out the
wheat into the sea.
39 And when it was
day, they knew not
the land : but they
discovered a certain
creek with a shore,
into the which they
were minded, if it were
possible, to thrust in
the ship. 40 And when
they had taken up the
anchors, they commit-
ted themselves unto
the sea, and loosed the
rudder bands, and
hoised up the mainsail
to the wind, and made
toward shore. 41 And
falling into a place
where two seas met,
they ran the ship a-
ground ; and the fore-
part stuck fast, and
remained unmoveable,
but the hinder part
was broken with the
violence of the waves.
42 And the soldiers'
counsel was to kill
the prisoners, lest any
of them should swim
out, and escape. 43 But
the centurion, willing
to save Paul, kept
them from their pur-
pose ; and command-
ed that they which
could swim should
cast themselves first
into the sea, and get
to land : 44 and the
rest, some on boards,
and some on broken
pieces of the ship. And
so it came to pass,
that they escaped all
safe to land.

XXVIII. And when
they were escaped,then
they knew that the
island was called Me-
lita. 2 And the barbar-
ous people shewed us
no little kindness : for
they kindled a fire,

ᵍ οὐ.θεὸς L.   ʰ ἀπὸ LTTrA.   ⁱ ἀπολεῖται shall perish GLTTrAW.   ᵏ εἶπας LTTrA.
ˡ ἤμεθα LTTrAW.   ᵐ αἱ πᾶσαι ψυχαὶ ἐν τῷ πλοίῳ LTTrAW.   ⁿ ἑβδομήκοντα ἕξ GLTTrW.
° ἐβουλεύοντο LTTrAW.   ᴾ ἀρτέμωνα LTTrAW.   ᑫ ἐπέκειλαν LTTrA.   ʳ — τῶν κυμάτων
LTTr-A].   ˢ διαφύγῃ GLTTrAW.   ᵗ ἑκατοντάρχης LTTrA.   ᵛ ἀπορίψαντας T.   ʷ ἐπέγνωμεν
we knew LTTrAW.   ˣ τε LTTrAW.   ʸ παρειχαν LTTrA.   ᶻ ἅψαντες LTTrAW.

and received us every one, because of the present rain, and because of the cold. 3 And when Paul had gathered a bundle of sticks, and laid *them* on the fire, there came a viper out of the heat, and fastened on his hand. 4 And when the barbarians saw the *venomous* beast hang on his hand, they said among themselves, No doubt this man is a murderer, whom, though he hath escaped the sea, yet vengeance suffereth not to live. 5 And he shook off the beast into the fire, and felt no harm. 6 Howbeit they looked when he should have swollen, or fallen down dead suddenly: but after they had looked a great while, and saw no harm come to him, they changed their minds, and said that he was a god. 7 In the same quarters were possessions of the chief man of the island, whose name was Publius; who received us, and lodged us three days courteously. 8 And it came to pass, that the father of Publius lay sick of a fever and of a bloody flux: to whom Paul entered in, and prayed, and laid his hands on him, and healed him. 9 So when this was done, others also, which had diseases in the island, came, and were healed: 10 who also honoured us with many honours; and when we departed, they laded *us* with such things as were necessary.

11 And after three months we departed in a ship of Alexandria, which had wintered in the isle, whose sign was Castor and Pollux. 12 And landing at Syracuse, we tarried *there* three days. 13 And from thence we fetched a compass, and came to Rhegium: and

ελάβοντο πάντας ἡμᾶς, διὰ ⁻ τὸν ὑετὸν τὸν ἐφεστῶτα καὶ
received all of us, because of the rain that was present and

διὰ τὸ ψύχος. 3 Συστρέψαντος.δὲ τοῦ Παύλου φρυγάνων ᵃ
because of the cold. And ²having ³gathered ¹Paul ᵒᶠ ²sticks

πλῆθος, καὶ ἐπιθέντος ἐπὶ τὴν πυρὰν ἔχιδνα ⁻ᵇἐκ⁻ τῆς
⁴a ⁵quantity, and having laid [them] on the fire a viper out of the

θέρμης ᶜἐξελθοῦσα⁻ καθῆψεν τῆς.χειρὸς.αὐτοῦ. 4 ὡς.δὲ ᵈεἶδον⁻
heat having come wound about his hand. And when ³saw

οἱ βάρβαροι κρεμάμενον τὸ θηρίον ἐκ τῆς.χειρὸς.αὐτοῦ
¹the ²barbarians ⁶hanging ⁴the ⁵beast from his hand

ᵉἔλεγον πρὸς ἀλλήλους,⁻ Πάντως φονεύς ἐστιν ὁ ἄνθρωπος
they said to one another, By all means a murderer is ²man

οὗτος, ὃν διασωθέντα ἐκ τῆς.θαλάσσης ἡ δίκη ζῆν οὐκ
¹this, whom having been saved from the sea justice ³to ¹live ²not

εἴασεν. 5 Ὁ μὲν οὖν ᶠἀποτινάξας⁻ τὸ θηρίον εἰς τὸ πῦρ
¹permitted. He indeed then having shaken off the beast in.o the fire

ἔπαθεν οὐδὲν κακόν. 6 οἱ.δὲ προσεδόκων αὐτὸν μέλλειν
suffered no injury. But they were expecting him to be about

ᵍπίμπρασθαι⁻ ἢ καταπίπτειν ἄφνω νεκρόν· ἐπὶ.πολὺ.δὲ
to become inflamed or to fall down suddenly dead. But for a long time

αὐτῶν προσδοκώντων καὶ θεωρούντων μηδὲν ἄτοπον εἰς αὐτὸν
they expecting and seeing nothing amiss to him

γινόμενον, ʰμεταβαλλόμενοι⁻ ἔλεγον ⁱθεὸν αὐτὸν εἶναι.⁻
happening, changing their opinion said a god he was.

7 Ἐν.δὲ τοῖς περὶ τὸν.τόπον.ἐκεῖνον ὑπῆρχεν χωρία
Now in the [parts] about that place were lands

τῷ πρώτῳ τῆς νήσου, ὀνόματι Ποπλίῳ, ὃς ἀνα-
belonging to the chief of the island, by name Publius, who having

δεξάμενος ἡμᾶς ᵏτρεῖς ἡμέρας⁻ φιλοφρόνως ἐξένισεν.
received us three days in a friendly way lodged [us].

8 ἐγένετο.δὲ τὸν πατέρα τοῦ Ποπλίου πυρετοῖς καὶ ˡδυσεν-
And it happened the father of Publius ⁴fevers ⁵and ⁶dyscu-

τερίᾳ⁻ συνεχόμενον κατακεῖσθαι· πρὸς ὃν ὁ Παῦλος εἰσελ-
tery ²oppressed ³with ¹lay, to whom Paul having en-

θὼν καὶ προσευξάμενος, ἐπιθεὶς τὰς χεῖρας αὐτῷ ἰάσατο
tered and having prayed, having laid on [²his] ³hands ¹him cured

αὐτόν. 9 τούτου ᵐοὖν⁻ γενομένου καὶ οἱ λοιποὶ οἱ ⁿἔχον-
him. This therefore having taken place also the rest who had

τες ἀσθενείας ἐν τῇ νήσῳ⁻ προσήρχοντο καὶ ἐθεραπεύοντο·
infirmities in the island came and were healed:

10 οἳ καὶ πολλαῖς τιμαῖς ἐτίμησαν ἡμᾶς, καὶ ἀναγομένοις
who also with many honours honoured us, and on setting sail

ἐπέθεντο τὰ πρὸς ᵒτὴν χρείαν.⁻
they laid on [us] the things for [our]

11 Μετὰ.δὲ τρεῖς μῆνας ἀνήχθημεν ἐν πλοίῳ παρακεχει-
And after three months we sailed in a ship which had

μακότι ἐν τῇ νήσῳ, Ἀλεξανδρίνῳ, παρασήμῳ Διοσκούροις·
wintered in the island, an Alexandrian, with an ensign [the] Dioscuri.

12 καὶ καταχθέντες εἰς Συρακούσας ἐπεμείναμεν ᵖἡμέρας
And having been brought to at Syracuse we remained ²days

τρεῖς·⁻ 13 ὅθεν περιελθόντες κατηντήσαμεν εἰς Ῥήγιον, καὶ
¹three. Whence having gone round we arrived at Rhegium; and

ᵃ + τι (*read* a certain quantity) LTTrAW.   ᵇ ἀπὸ from LTTrAW.   ᶜ διεξελθοῦσα AW.
ᵈ εἶδαν Tr.   ᵉ πρὸς ἀλλήλους ἔλεγον LTTrA.   ᶠ ἀποτιναξάμενος W.   ᵍ ἐμπιπρᾶσθαι T.
ʰ μεταβαλόμενοι TrA.   ⁱ αὐτὸν εἶναι θεόν LTTrAW.   ᵏ ἡμέρας τρεῖς A.   ˡ δυσεντερίῳ
LTTrAW.   ᵐ δὲ and (this) LTTrA.   ⁿ ἐν τῇ νήσῳ ἔχοντες ἀσθενείας LTTrA.   ᵒ τὰς
χρείας needs LTTrAW.   ᵖ ἡμέραις τρισίν L.

μετὰ μίαν ἡμέραν ἐπιγενομένου νότου δευτεραῖοι
after one day, ⁴having °come °on ¹a ²south ³wind. on the second day

ἤλθομεν εἰς Ποτιόλους 14 οὗ εὑρόντες ἀδελφοὺς παρε-
we came to Puteoli; where having found brethren we were

κλήθημεν ᵃἐπ᾽ᴵᴵ αὐτοῖς ἐπιμεῖναι ἡμέρας ἑπτά· καὶ οὕτως ʳεἰς
entreated ³with ⁴them ¹to °remain ⁵days ⁶seven. And thus to

τὴν Ῥώμην ἤλθομεν.ᴵᴵ 15 κἀκεῖθεν οἱ ἀδελφοὶ ἀκούσαντες
Rome we came. And thence the brethren having heard

τὰ περὶ ἡμῶν ˢἐξῆλθον⁴ᴵ εἰς ἀπάντησιν ἡμῖν ᵗἄχρις⁴ᴵ
the things concerning us came out to meet us as far as

Ἀππίου.Φόρου καὶ Τριῶν Ταβερνῶν· οὓς ἰδὼν ὁ Παῦ-
[the] market-place of Appius and Three Taverns; whom ²seeing ¹Paul,

λος, εὐχαριστήσας.τῷ θεῷ ἔλαβεν θάρσος.
having given thanks to God he took courage.

16 Ὅτε.δὲ ᵛἤλθομενᴵᴵ εἰς ᵂῬώμην ˣὁ ἑκατόνταρχος παρέ-
And when we came to Rome the centurion de-

δωκεν τοὺς δεσμίους τῷ στρατοπεδάρχῃ·ᴵᴵ ʸτῷ.δὲ.Παύλῳ
livered the prisoners to the commander of the camp, but Paul

ἐπετράπηᴵᴵ μένειν καθ᾽.ἑαυτόν, σὺν.τῷ φυλάσσοντι αὐτὸν
was allowed to remain by himself, with the ²who ³kept ⁴him

στρατιώτῃ. 17 Ἐγένετο.δὲ μετὰ ἡμέρας τρεῖς ᶻσυγκαλέσασ-
¹soldier. And it came to pass after ²days ³three ⁴called ⁵to-

θαιᴵᴵ ᵃτὸν Παῦλονᴵᴵ τοὺς ὄντας τῶν Ἰουδαίων ᵖρώτους·
gether ³Paul those who were ³of ⁴the ⁵Jews ¹chief ²ones.

συνελθόντων.δὲ αὐτῶν ἔλεγεν πρὸς αὐτούς, ᵇἌνδρες
And ²having ³come ⁴together ¹they he said to them, Men

ἀδελφοί, ἐγώᴵᴵ οὐδὲν ἐναντίον ποιήσας τῷ λαῷ ἢ τοῖς
brethren, I ²nothing ⁴against ¹having ²done the people or the

ἔθεσιν τοῖς πατρῴοις δέσμιος ἐξ Ἱεροσολύμων παρεδόθην
²customs ¹ancestral a prisoner from Jerusalem was delivered

εἰς τὰς χεῖρας τῶν Ῥωμαίων· 18 οἵτινες ἀνακρίναντές με
into the hands of the Romans, who having examined me

ἐβούλοντο ἀπολῦσαι, διὰ τὸ μηδεμίαν αἰτίαν θανάτου
wished to let [me] go, because not one cause of death

ὑπάρχειν ἐν ἐμοί. 19 ἀντιλεγόντων.δὲ τῶν Ἰουδαίων
was there in me. But ³speaking ⁴against [⁵it] ¹the ²Jews

ἠναγκάσθην ἐπικαλέσασθαι Καίσαρα, οὐχ ὡς τοῦ.ἔθνους.μου
I was compelled to appeal to Cæsar, not as °my ⁷nation

ἔχων τι ᶜκατηγορῆσαι.ᴵᴵ 20 διὰ ταύτην οὖν τὴν αἰτίαν
¹having ²anything ³to ⁴lay ⁵against. For this ²therefore ¹cause

παρεκάλεσα ὑμᾶς ἰδεῖν καὶ προσλαλῆσαι· ᵈἕνεκενᴵᴵ.γὰρ
I called for you to see and to speak to [you]; for on account of

τῆς ἐλπίδος τοῦ Ἰσραὴλ τὴν.ἅλυσιν.ταύτην περίκειμαι.
the hope of Israel this chain I have around [me].

21 Οἱ.δὲ πρὸς αὐτὸν ᵉεἶπον,ᴵᴵ Ἡμεῖς οὔτε γράμματα ᶠπερὶ
And they to him said, We neither letters concerning

σοῦ ἐδεξάμεθαᴵᴵ ἀπὸ τῆς Ἰουδαίας οὔτε παραγενόμενός τις
thee received from Judæa, nor having arrived any one

τῶν ἀδελφῶν ἀπήγγειλεν ἢ ἐλάλησέν τι περὶ σοῦ
of the brethren reported or said anything ²concerning ³thee

πονηρόν. 22 ἀξιοῦμεν.δὲ παρὰ σοῦ ἀκοῦσαι ἃ φρονεῖς·
¹evil. But we think well from thee to hear what thou thinkest,

after one day the south wind blew, and we came the next day to Puteoli: 14 where we found brethren, and were desired to tarry with them seven days: and so we went toward Rome. 15 And from thence, when the brethren heard of us, they came to meet us as far as Appii forum, and The three taverns: whom when Paul saw, he thanked God, and took courage.

16 And when we came to Rome, the centurion delivered the prisoners to the captain of the guard: but Paul was suffered to dwell by himself with a soldier that kept him. 17 And it came to pass, that after three days Paul called the chief of the Jews together: and when they were come together, he said unto them, Men and brethren, though I have committed nothing against the people, or customs of our fathers, yet was I delivered prisoner from Jerusalem into the hands of the Romans. 18 Who, when they had examined me, would have let me go, because there was no cause of death in me. 19 But when the Jews spake against it, I was constrained to appeal unto Cæsar; not that I had ought to accuse my nation of. 20 For this cause therefore have I called for you, to see you, and to speak with you: because that for the hope of Israel I am bound with this chain. 21 And they said unto him, We neither received letters out of Judæa concerning thee, neither any of the brethren that came shewed or spake any harm of thee. 22 But we desire to hear of thee what thou thinkest:

ᵠ παρ᾽ LTTrA.   ʳ ἤλθαμεν εἰς Ῥώμην L ; εἰς τὴν Ῥώμην ἤλθαμεν TTrA.   ˢ ἦλθαν came TTrA ;
ἦλθον L.   ᵗ ἄχρι TTrA.   ᵛ εἰσήλθομεν we came in LTA ; εἰσήλθαμεν Tr.   ᵂ + τὴν T.
ˣ — ὁ ἑκατόνταρχος .... στρατοπεδάρχῃ LTTrA.   ʸ ἐπετράπη τῷ Παύλῳ (omit but) LTTrA.
ᶻ συν- T.   ᵃ αὐτὸν he GLTTrAW.   ᵇ Ἐγώ, ἄνδρες ἀδελφοί, LTTrA.   ᶜ κατηγορεῖν LTTrA.
ᵈ εἵνεκεν T.   ᵉ εἶπαν LTTrA.   ᶠ ἐδεξάμεθα περὶ σοῦ L.

for as concerning this
sect, we know that
every where it is spo-
ken against. 23 And
when they had ap-
pointed him a day,
there came many to
him into *his* lodging ;
to whom he expounded
and testified the king-
dom of God, persuad-
ing them concerning
Jesus, both out of the
law of Moses, and *out
of* the prophets, from
morning till evening.
24 And some believed
the things which were
spoken, and some be-
lieved not. 25 And
when they agreed not
among themselves,
th y departed, after
that Paul had spoken
one word, Well spake
the Holy Ghost by
Esaias the prophet un-
to our fathers, 26 say-
ing, Go unto this peo-
ple, and say, Hearing
ye shall hear, and shall
not understand ; and
seeing ye shall see, and
not perceive : 27 for
the heart of this peo-
ple is waxed gross,
and their ears are
dull of hearing, and
their eyes have they
closed; lest they should
see with *their* eyes,
and hear with *their*
ears, and understand
with *their* heart, and
should be converted,
and I should heal
them. 28 Be it known
therefore unto you,
that the salvation of
God is sent unto the
Gentiles, and *that* they
will hear it. 29 And
when he had said
these words, the Jews
departed, and had
great reasoning among
themselves.

περὶ.μὲν.γὰρ τῆς.αἱρέσεως.ταύτης γνωστόν ᵍἔστιν ἡμῖν‖
for indeed as concerning this sect known it is to us
ὅτι πανταχοῦ ἀντιλέγεται. 23 Ταξάμενοι.δὲ αὐτῷ ἡμέραν
that everywhere it is spoken against. And having appointed him a day
ʰἧκον‖ πρὸς αὐτὸν εἰς τὴν ξενίαν πλείονες· οἷς· ἐξετίθετο
came to him to the lodging many, to whom he expounded
διαμαρτυρόμενος τὴν βασιλείαν τοῦ θεοῦ, πείθων.τε αὐτοὺς
fully testifying the kingdom of God, and persuading them
ⁱτὰ‖ περὶ τοῦ Ἰησοῦ, ἀπό.τε τοῦ νόμου ᵏΜωσέως·
the things concerning Jesus, both from the law of Moses
καὶ τῶν προφητῶν, ἀπὸ πρωῒ ἕως ἑσπέρας. 24 καὶ οἱ
and the prophets, ˙ from morning to evening. And some
μὲν ἐπείθοντο τοῖς ∾ λεγομένοις, οἱ.δὲ ἠπίστουν.
indeed were persuaded of the things spoken, but some disbelieved.
25 ἀσύμφωνοι.ᶦδὲ‖.ὄντες πρὸς ἀλλήλους ἀπελύοντο, εἰπόν-
And disagreeing with one another they departed; ²having
τος τοῦ Παύλου ῥῆμα ἕν, Ὅτι καλῶς τὸ πνεῦμα τὸ ἅγιον
³spoken ¹Paul – ⁵word ⁴one, Well the Spirit the Holy
ἐλάλησεν διὰ Ἡσαΐου τοῦ προφήτου πρὸς τοὺς πατέρας
spoke by Esaias the prophet to ²fathers
ᵐἡμῶν,‖ 26 ⁿλέγον,‖ Πορεύθητι ᵖπρὸς τὸν.λαὸν.τοῦτον καὶ
¹our, saying, Go to this people, and
°εἰπέ,‖ Ἀκοῇ ἀκούσετε, καὶ οὐ.μὴ συνῆτε· καὶ βλέποντες
say, In hearing ye shall hear, and in no wise understand, and seeing
βλέψετε, καὶ οὐ.μὴ ἴδητε· 27 ἐπαχύνθη.γὰρ ἡ καρδία
ye shall see, and in no wise perceive. For has grown fat the heart
τοῦ.λαοῦ.τούτου, καὶ τοῖς ὠσὶν βαρέως ἤκουσαν, καὶ
of this people, and with the ears heavily they have heard, and
τοὺς.ὀφθαλμοὺς.αὐτῶν ἐκάμμυσαν· μήποτε ἴδωσιν τοῖς
their eyes they have closed, lest they should see with the
ὀφθαλμοῖς, καὶ τοῖς ὠσὶν ἀκούσωσιν, καὶ τῇ καρδίᾳ
eyes, and with the ears they should hear, and with the heart
συνῶσιν, καὶ ἐπιστρέψωσιν, καὶ ᵖἰάσωμαι‖ αὐτούς.
they should understand, and should be converted, and I should heal them.
28 Γνωστὸν οὖν ᵠἔστω ὑμῖν,‖ ὅτι τοῖς ἔθνεσιν ἀπεστάλη ʳ
Known therefore be it to you, that to the nations is sent
τὸ σωτήριον τοῦ θεοῦ, αὐτοὶ.καὶ ἀκούσονται. 29 ˢΚαὶ ταῦτα
the salvation of God; and they will hear. And these things
αὐτοῦ εἰπόντος ἀπῆλθον οἱ Ἰουδαῖοι, πολλὴν ἔχοντες ἐν
he having said ³went ⁴away ¹the ²Jews, ⁶much ⁵having ⁸among
ἑαυτοῖς, συζήτησιν.‖
⁹themselves ⁷discussion.

30 ᵗἜμεινεν .δὲ ᵛὁ Παῦλος‖ διετίαν ὅλην ἐν ἰδίῳ μισ-
And ²abode ¹Paul two ²years ¹whole in his own hired

30 And Paul dwelt
two whole years in his
own hired house, and
received all that came
in unto him, 31 preach-
ing the kingdom of
God,and teaching those
things which concern
the Lord Jesus Christ,
with all confidence,
no man forbidding
him.

θώματι, καὶ ἀπεδέχετο πάντας τοὺς εἰσπορευομένους πρὸς
house, and welcomed all who came in to
αὐτόν, 31 κηρύσσων τὴν βασιλείαν τοῦ θεοῦ, καὶ διδάσκων
him, proclaiming the kingdom of God, and teaching
τὰ περὶ τοῦ κυρίου Ἰησοῦ ʷχριστοῦ,‖ μετὰ πάσης
the things concerning the Lord Jesus Christ, with all
παῤῥησίας ἀκωλύτως. ˣ
freedom unhinderedly.

ᵍ ἡμῖν ἐστιν LTTrA.   ʰ ἧλθον LTTrA.   ⁱ — τὰ LTTrA.   ᵏ Μωϋσέως GLTTrAW.   ˡ τε T.
ᵐ ὑμῶν your LTTrA.   ⁿ λέγων TTrA.   ° εἰπόν GLTTrAW.   ᵖ ἰάσομαι I shall heal TTrA.
ᵠ ὑμῖν ἔστω A.   ʳ + τοῦτο (*read* this salvation) LTTrA.   ˢ — *verse* 29 LTTrA.
ᵗ Ἐνέμειναν TTrA.   ᵛ — ὁ Παῦλος (*read* he abode) GLTTrAW.   ʷ — χριστοῦ T.
ˣ + Πράξεις Ἀποστόλων TrA.

ᵃΠΑΥΛΟΥ ΤΟΥ ΑΠΟΣΤΟΛΟΥ Η ΠΡΟΣ ΡΩΜΑΙΟΥΣ
³OF ⁴PAUL ⁵THE ⁶APOSTLE ¹THE ⁷TO [⁸THE] ⁹ROMANS

ΕΠΙΣΤΟΛΗ.ᵇ
²EPISTLE:

ΠΑΥΛΟΣ δοῦλος ᵇ'Ιησοῦ χριστοῦ,ᵇ κλητὸς ἀπόστολος, ἀφω-
Paul, bondman of Jesus Christ, a called apostle, sepa-
ρισμένος εἰς εὐαγγέλιον θεοῦ, 2 ὃ προεπηγγείλατο διὰ
rated to glad tidings of God, which he before promised through
τῶν προφητῶν αὐτοῦ ἐν γραφαῖς ἁγίαις, 3 περὶ τοῦ υἱοῦ
his prophets in ²writings ¹holy, concerning ²Son
αὐτοῦ, τοῦ γενομένου ἐκ σπέρματος ᶜΔαβὶδ‖ κατὰ
¹his, who came of [the] seed of David according to
σάρκα, 4 τοῦ ὁρισθέντος υἱοῦ θεοῦ ἐν δυνάμει, κατὰ
flesh, who was marked out Son of God in power, according to [the]
πνεῦμα ἁγιωσύνης, ἐξ ἀναστάσεως νεκρῶν, 'Ιησοῦ χριστοῦ
Spirit of holiness, by resurrection of [the] dead— Jesus Christ
τοῦ κυρίου ἡμῶν, 5 δι' οὗ ἐλάβομεν χάριν καὶ ἀποστολὴν
our Lord; by whom we received grace and apostleship
εἰς ὑπακοὴν πίστεως ἐν πᾶσιν τοῖς ἔθνεσιν, ὑπὲρ τοῦ
unto obedience of faith among all the nations, in behalf of
ὀνόματος αὐτοῦ, 6 ἐν οἷς ἐστε καὶ ὑμεῖς, κλητοὶ 'Ιησοῦ
his name, among whom are also ye, called of Jesus
χριστοῦ· 7 πᾶσιν τοῖς οὖσιν ἐν 'Ρώμῃ ἀγαπητοῖς θεοῦ,
hrist: to all those who are in Rome beloved of God,
κλητοῖς ἁγίοις· χάρις ὑμῖν καὶ εἰρήνη ἀπὸ θεοῦ πατρὸς ἡμῶν
called saints: grace to you and peace from God our Father
καὶ κυρίου 'Ιησοῦ χριστοῦ.
and Lord Jesus Christ.

8 Πρῶτον μὲν εὐχαριστῶ τῷ θεῷ μου διὰ 'Ιησοῦ χριστοῦ
First, I thank my God through Jesus Christ
ᵈὑπὲρ‖ πάντων ὑμῶν, ὅτι ἡ πίστις ὑμῶν καταγγέλλεται ἐν
for ²all ¹you, that your faith is announced in
ὅλῳ τῷ κόσμῳ· 9 μάρτυς γάρ μου ἐστὶν ὁ θεός, ᾧ λατρεύω
²whole ¹the world; for ⁴witness ⁵my ²is ¹God, whom I serve
ἐν τῷ πνεύματί μου ἐν τῷ εὐαγγελίῳ τοῦ υἱοῦ αὐτοῦ, ὡς
in my spirit in the glad tidings of his Son, how
ἀδιαλείπτως μνείαν ὑμῶν ποιοῦμαι, 10 πάντοτε ἐπὶ τῶν
unceasingly mention of you I make, always at
προσευχῶν μου δεόμενος, ᵉεἴπως‖ ἤδη ποτὲ εὐοδωθήσομαι
my prayers beseeching, if by any means now at length I shall be prospered
ἐν τῷ θελήματι τοῦ θεοῦ ἐλθεῖν πρὸς ὑμᾶς· 11 ἐπιποθῶ γὰρ
by the will of God to come to you. For I long
ἰδεῖν ὑμᾶς, ἵνα τι μεταδῶ χάρισμα ὑμῖν πνευματικόν,
to see you, that some ³I ¹may ²impart ²gift ⁴to ⁵you ¹spiritual,
εἰς τὸ στηριχθῆναι ὑμᾶς, 12 τοῦτο δέ ἐστιν, ᶠσυμπαρα-
to the [end] ²be ³established ¹ye, that is, to be comforted

PAUL, a servant of Jesus Christ, called to be an apostle, separated unto the gospel of God, 2 (which he had promised afore by his prophets in the holy scriptures,) 3 concerning his Son Jesus Christ our Lord, which was made of the seed of David according to the flesh; 4 and declared to be the Son of God with power, according to the spirit of holiness, by the resurrection from the dead: 5 by whom we have received grace and apostleship, for obedience to the faith among all nations, for his name: 6 among whom are ye also the called of Jesus Christ: 7 to all that be in Rome, beloved of God, called to be saints: Grace to you and peace from God our Father, and the Lord Jesus Christ.

8 First, I thank my God through Jesus Christ for you all, that your faith is spoken of throughout the whole world. 9 For God is my witness, whom I serve with my spirit in the gospel of his Son, that without ceasing I make mention of you always in my prayers; 10 making request, if by any means now at length I might have a prosperous journey by the will of God to come unto you. 11 For I long to see you, that I may impart unto you some spiritual gift, to the end ye may be established; 12 that is, that I may be comforted together with

---

you by the mutual faith both of you and me. 13 Now I would not have you ignorant, brethren, that oftentimes I purposed to come unto you, (but was let hitherto,) that I might have some fruit among you also, even as among other Gentiles. 14 I am debtor both to the Greeks, and to the Barbarians; both to the wise, and to the unwise. 15 So, as much as in me is, I am ready to preach the gospel to you that are at Rome also. 16 For I am not ashamed of the gospel of Christ : for it is the power of God unto salvation to every one that believeth ; to the Jew first, and also to the Greek. 17 For therein is the righteousness of God revealed from faith to faith : as it is written, The just shall live by faith.

18 For the wrath of God is revealed from heaven against all ungodliness and unrighteousness of men, who hold the truth in unrighteousness ; 19 because that which may be known of God is manifest in them ; for God hath shewed it unto them. 20 For the invisible things of him from the creation of the world are clearly seen, being understood by the things that are made, even his eternal power and Godhead ; so that they are without excuse : 21 because that, when they knew God, they glorified him not as God, neither were thankful ; but became vain in their imaginations, and their foolish heart was darkened. 22 Professing themselves to be wise, they became fools, 23 and changed the glory of the uncorruptible God into an image made like to corruptible man, and to birds, and fourfooted beasts, and creeping things. 24 Wherefore God also gave them up to uncleanness through the lusts of their own hearts, to

κληθῆναι‖ ἐν ὑμῖν διὰ τῆς ἐν ἀλλήλοις πίστεως ὑμῶν.τε
together among you, through the ²in ³one ⁴another ¹faith, both yours
καὶ ἐμοῦ· 13 οὐ.θέλω.δὲ ὑμᾶς ἀγνοεῖν, ἀδελφοί, ὅτι πολ-
and mine.   But I do not wish you to be ignorant, brethren, that many
λάκις προεθέμην ἐλθεῖν πρὸς ὑμᾶς, καὶ ἐκωλύθην ἄχρι τοῦ
times I proposed to come to you, and was hindered until the
δεῦρο, ἵνα ᵍκαρπόν τινα‖ σχῶ καὶ ἐν ὑμῖν, καθὼς
present, that ²fruit ¹some I might have also among you, according as
καὶ ἐν τοῖς λοιποῖς ἔθνεσιν. 14 Ἕλλησίν.τε καὶ βαρβάροις,
also among the other nations.   Both to Greeks and barbarians,
σοφοῖς.τε καὶ ἀνοήτοις, ὀφειλέτης εἰμί· 15 οὕτως τὸ κατ' ἐμὲ
both to wise and unintelligent, a debtor I am :   so   as to me
    πρόθυμον καὶ ὑμῖν τοῖς ἐν Ῥώμῃ εὐαγ-
[there is] readiness ³also ⁴to ⁵you ⁶who [⁷are] ⁸in⁀ ⁹Rome ¹to ²announce
γελίσασθαι. 16 οὐ.γὰρ.ἐπαισχύνομαι τὸ εὐαγγέλιον ʰτοῦ
the glad tidings.   For I am not ashamed of the glad tidings of the
χριστοῦ·‖ δύναμις.γὰρ θεοῦ ἐστιν εἰς σωτηρίαν παντὶ τῷ
Christ :   for power of God it is unto salvation to every one that
πιστεύοντι, Ἰουδαίῳ.τε ⁱπρῶτον‖ καὶ Ἕλληνι. 17 δικαιοσύνη
believes,   both to Jew first and to Greek :   ²righteousness
γὰρ θεοῦ ἐν αὐτῷ ἀποκαλύπτεται ἐκ πίστεως εἰς πίστιν,
¹for of God in it is revealed by faith to faith ;
καθὼς γέγραπται, Ὁ.δὲ δίκαιος ἐκ πίστεως ζήσεται.
according as it has been written, But the just by faith shall live.

18 Ἀποκαλύπτεται.γὰρ ὀργὴ θεοῦ ἀπ' οὐρανοῦ ἐπὶ πᾶσαν
For there is revealed wrath of God from heaven upon all
ἀσέβειαν καὶ ἀδικίαν ἀνθρώπων τῶν τὴν ἀλήθειαν ἐν
ungodliness and unrighteousness of men who the truth in
ἀδικίᾳ κατεχόντων. 19 διότι τὸ.γνωστὸν τοῦ θεοῦ
unrighteousness hold.   Because that which is known of God
φανερόν ἐστιν ἐν αὐτοῖς, ὁ.ᵏγὰρ.θεὸς‖ αὐτοῖς ἐφανέρωσεν·
²manifest ¹is among them,   for God to them manifested [it];
20 τὰ.γὰρ ἀόρατα αὐτοῦ ἀπὸ κτίσεως κόσμου τοῖς
for the invisible things of him from creation of [the] world by the
ποιήμασιν νοούμενα καθορᾶται, ἥ.τε ἀΐδιος αὐτοῦ δύνα-
things made being understood are perceived, both ²eternal ¹his power
μις καὶ θειότης, εἰς τὸ εἶναι αὐτοὺς ἀναπολογήτους. 21 διότι
and divinity; for ²to ³be ¹them without excuse.   Because
γνόντες τὸν θεόν, οὐχ ὡς θεὸν ἐδόξασαν ἢ ¹εὐχαρίσ-
having known God, not as God they glorified [him] or were thank-
τησαν,‖ ᵐἀλλ'‖ ἐματαιώθησαν ἐν τοῖς.διαλογισμοῖς.αὐτῶν, καὶ
ful ;   but became vain in their reasonings, and
ἐσκοτίσθη ἡ ἀσύνετος αὐτῶν καρδία· 22 φάσκοντες
was darkened the ⁴without ⁵understanding ²of ³them ¹heart :   professing
εἶναι σοφοὶ ἐμωράνθησαν, 23 καὶ ἤλλαξαν τὴν δόξαν τοῦ
to be wise they became fools,   and changed the glory of the
ἀφθάρτου θεοῦ ἐν ὁμοιώματι εἰκόνος φθαρτοῦ ἀνθρώπου
incorruptible God into a likeness of an image of corruptible man
καὶ πετεινῶν καὶ τετραπόδων καὶ ἑρπετῶν. 24 διὸ ⁿκαὶ‖
and of birds and quadrupeds and creeping things.   Wherefore also
παρέδωκεν αὐτοὺς ὁ θεὸς ἐν ταῖς ἐπιθυμίαις τῶν.καρδιῶν.αὐ-
²gave ⁴up ³them ¹God in the desires of their hearts
τῶν εἰς ἀκαθαρσίαν, τοῦ ἀτιμάζεσθαι τα.σώματα.αὐτῶν ἐν
to uncleanness, ³to ⁴be ⁵dishonoured ¹their ²bodies between

ᵍ τινὰ καρπόν GLTTrAW.   ʰ — τοῦ χριστοῦ GLTTrAW.   ⁱ [πρῶτον] L.   ᵏ θεὸς γὰρ GLTTrAW.
ⁿὐχαρίστησαν GLTTrA.   ᵐ ἀλλὰ Tr.   ⁿ — καὶ LTTr[A].

ºἑαυτοῖς·‖ 25 οἵτινες μετήλλαξαν τὴν ἀλήθειαν τοῦ θεοῦ ἐν
themselves :   who   changed   the   truth   of God into

τῷ ψεύδει, καὶ ἐσεβάσθησαν καὶ ἐλάτρευσαν τῇ κτίσει
falsehood, and   reverenced   and   served   the created thing

παρὰ τὸν κτίσαντα, ὅς ἐστιν εὐλογητὸς εἰς τοὺς αἰῶνας.
beyond him who created [it], who is   blessed   to the   ages.

ἀμήν. 26 διὰ.τοῦτο παρέδωκεν αὐτοὺς ὁ θεὸς εἰς πάθη
Amen.   For this reason   ²gave ⁴up   ³them   ¹God   to passions

ἀτιμίας· αἵ τε · γὰρ θήλειαι αὐτῶν μετήλλαξαν τὴν φυσικὴν
of dishonour, ²both ¹for ⁴females ³their   changed   the   natural

χρῆσιν εἰς τὴν παρὰ φύσιν· 27 ὁμοίως.ᵖτε‖ καὶ οἱ ᵠἄῤῥενες‖
use   into that contrary to nature ; and in like manner also the   males

ἀφέντες τὴν φυσικὴν χρῆσιν τῆς θηλείας, ἐξεκαύθησαν ἐν τῇ
having left the   natural   use   of the female,   were inflamed in

ὀρέξει.αὐτῶν εἰς ἀλλήλους, ʳἄρσενες‖ ἐν ˢἄρσεσιν‖ τὴν
their lust   towards one another,   males   with   males

ἀσχημοσύνην κατεργαζόμενοι, καὶ τὴν ἀντιμισθίαν ἣν ἔδει
²shame   ¹working ²out,   and the   recompense   which was fit

τῆς.πλάνης.αὐτῶν ἐν ἑαυτοῖς ἀπολαμβάνοντες. 28 καὶ
of their error   in themselves   receiving.   And

καθὼς οὐκ.ἐδοκίμασαν τὸν θεὸν ἔχειν ἐν ἐπιγνώσει,
according as they did not approve ³God ¹to ²have in [their] knowledge,

παρέδωκεν αὐτοὺς ὁ θεὸς εἰς ἀδόκιμον νοῦν, ποιεῖν τὰ μὴ
²gave ⁴up   ³them   ¹God to an unapproving mind, to do things not

καθήκοντα, 29 πεπληρωμένους πάσῃ ἀδικίᾳ, ᵗπορνείᾳ,‖
fitting ;   being filled with   all   unrighteousness, fornication,

ᵛπονηρίᾳ, πλεονεξίᾳ, κακίᾳ·‖ μεστοὺς φθόνου, φόνου, ἔριδος,
wickedness, covetousness, malice ;   full   of envy, murder, strife,

δόλου, κακοηθείας· ψιθυριστάς, 30 καταλάλους, θεοστυγεῖς,
guile, evil dispositions ; whisperers,   slanderers,   hateful to God,

ὑβριστάς, ὑπερηφάνους, ἀλαζόνας, ἐφευρετὰς κακῶν,
insolent,   proud,   vaunting,   inventors of evil things,

γονεῦσιν ἀπειθεῖς, 31 ἀσυνέτους, ἀσυνθέτους, ἀ-
to parents disobedient, without understanding,   perfidious,   without

στόργους, ʷἀσπόνδους,‖ ἀνελεήμονας· 32 οἵτινες τὸ
natural affection, implacable,   unmerciful ;   who   the

δικαίωμα τοῦ θεοῦ ἐπιγνόντες, ὅτι οἱ τὰ.τοιαῦτα
righteous judgment of God having known, that those   such things

πράσσοντες ἄξιοι θανάτου εἰσίν, οὐ μόνον αὐτὰ ποιοῦσιν,
doing   worthy of death are, not only ²them ¹practise,

ἀλλὰ καὶ συνευδοκοῦσιν τοῖς πράσσουσιν.
but also are consenting to those that   do   [them].

2 Διὸ ἀναπολόγητος εἶ, ὦ ἄνθρωπε, πᾶς ὁ κρίνων·
Wherefore inexcusable thou art, O   man,   every one who judgest,

ἐν.ᾧ.γὰρ κρίνεις τὸν ἕτερον, σεαυτὸν κατακρίνεις·
for in that in which thou judgest the   other,   thyself   thou condemnest :

τὰ.γὰρ αὐτὰ πράσσεις ὁ κρίνων. 2 οἴδαμεν ˣδὲ‖ ὅτι τὸ
for the   same things thou doest who judgest. ²We ³know ¹but that the

κρίμα τοῦ θεοῦ ἐστιν κατὰ ἀλήθειαν ἐπὶ τοὺς τὰ τοιαῦτα
judgment of God is according to truth upon those that such things

πράσσοντας. 3 λογίζῃ.δὲ τοῦτο, ὦ ἄνθρωπε, ὁ κρίνων
do.   And reckonest thou this, O   man,   who judgest

τοὺς τὰ.τοιαῦτα πράσσοντας καὶ ποιῶν αὐτά, ὅτι
those that such things   do,   and practisest them [thyself], that

---

dishonour their own bodies between themselves: 25 who changed the truth of God into a lie, and worshipped and served the creature more than the Creator, who is blessed for ever. Amen. 26 For this cause God gave them up unto vile affections: for even their women did change the natural use into that which is against nature : 27 and likewise also the men, leaving the natural use of the woman, burned in their lust one toward another ; men with men working that which is unseemly, and receiving in themselves that recompence of their error which was meet. 28 And even as they did not like to retain God in *their* knowledge, God gave them over to a reprobate mind, to do those things which are not convenient ; 29 being filled with all unrighteousness, fornication, wickedness, covetousness, maliciousness ; full of envy, murder, debate, deceit, malignity ; whisperers, 30 backbiters, haters of God, despiteful, proud, boasters, inventors of evil things, disobedient to parents, 31 without understanding, covenantbreakers, without natural affection, implacable, unmerciful: 32 who knowing the judgment of God, that they which commit such things are worthy of death, not only do the same, but have pleasure in them that do them.

II. Therefore thou art inexcusable, O man, whosoever thou art that judgest : for wherein thou judgest another, thou condemnest thyself ; for thou that judgest doest the same things. 2 But we are sure that the judgment of God is according to truth against them which commit such things. 3 And thinkest thou this, O man, that judgest them which do such things, and doest the same, that thou

---

º αὐτοῖς LTTrA.   ᵖ δὲ L.   ᵠ ἄρσενες ELTTrAW.   ʳ ἄῤῥενες T.   ˢ ἄῤῥεσιν T.
ᵗ — πορνείᾳ GLTTrAW.   ᵛ κακίᾳ πονηρίᾳ πλεονεξίᾳ, L ; πονηρίᾳ κακίᾳ πλε. T.   ʷ — ἀ-
σπόνδους LTTrAW.   ˣ γὰρ for T.

shalt escape the judg-
ment of God? 4 or
despisest thou the
riches of his good-
ness and forbearance
and longsuffering; not
knowing that the
goodness of God lead-
eth thee to repentance?
5 But after thy hard-
ness and impenitent
heart treasurest up un-
to thyself wrath a-
gainst the day of
wrath and revelation
of the righteous judg-
ment of God; 6 who
will render to every
man according to his
deeds : 7 to them who
by patient continu-
ance in well doing
seek for glory and
honour and immortal-
ity, eternal life : 8 but
unto them that are
contentious, and do
not obey the truth, but
obey unrighteousness,
indignation and wrath,
9 tribulation and an-
guish, upon every soul
of man that doeth evil,
of the Jew first, and
also of the Gentile;
10 but glory, honour,
and peace, to every
man that worketh
good, to the Jew first,
and also to the Gen-
tile : 11 for there is no
respect of persons with
God. 12 For as many
as have sinned with-
out law shall also
perish without law :
and as many as have
sinned in the law shall
be judged by the law ;
13 (for not the hearers
of the law are just
before God, but the
doers of the law shall
be justified. 14 For
when the Gentiles,
which have not the
law, do by nature the
things contained in
the law, these, having
not the law, are a
law unto themselves :
15 which shew the
work of the law writ-
ten in their hearts,
their conscience also
bearing witness, and
their thoughts the
mean while accusing
or else excusing one
another ;) 16 in the
day when God shall
judge the secrets of
men by Jesus Christ
according to my gos-
pel.
17 Behold, thou art
called a Jew, and
restest in the law, and

σὺ ἐκφεύξῃ τὸ κρίμα τοῦ θεοῦ; 4 ἢ τοῦ πλούτου τῆς χρη-
thou shalt escape the judgment of God? or the riches of the kind-
στότητος αὐτοῦ καὶ τῆς ἀνοχῆς καὶ τῆς μακροθυμίας κατα-
ness of him and the forbearance and the long-suffering despisest
φρονεῖς, ἀγνοῶν ὅτι τὸ χρηστὸν τοῦ θεοῦ εἰς μετάνοιάν σε
thou, not knowing that the kindness of God to repentance thee
ἄγει ; 5 κατὰ.δὲ τὴν.σκληρότητά.σου καὶ ἀμετανόητον
leads? but according to thy hardness and impenitent
καρδίαν θησαυρίζεις σεαυτῷ ὀργὴν ἐν ἡμέρᾳ ὀργῆς καὶ ἀπο-
heart treasurest up to thyself wrath in a day of wrath and re-
καλύψεως δικαιοκρισίας τοῦ θεοῦ. 6 ὃς ἀποδώσει ἑκάστῳ
velation of righteous judgment of God, who will render to each
κατὰ τὰ.ἔργα.αὐτοῦ. 7 τοῖς μὲν καθ' ὑπομονὴν ἔργου,
according to his works : to those that with endurance in [2]work
ἀγαθοῦ, δόξαν καὶ τιμὴν καὶ ἀφθαρσίαν ζητοῦσιν, ζωὴν
[1]good, glory and honour and incorruptibility are seeking— life
αἰώνιον. 8 τοῖς.δὲ ἐξ ἐριθείας, καὶ ἀπειθοῦσιν [3]μὲν[4] τῇ
eternal. But to those of contention, and who disobey the
ἀληθείᾳ, πειθομένοις.δὲ τῇ ἀδικίᾳ, [2]θυμὸς καὶ ὀργή,[1]
truth, but obey unrighteousness— indignation and wrath,
9 θλίψις καὶ στενοχωρία, ἐπὶ πᾶσαν ψυχὴν ἀνθρώπου τοῦ
tribulation and strait, on every soul of man that
κατεργαζομένου τὸ κακόν, Ἰουδαίου.τε πρῶτον καὶ Ἕλληνος·
works out evil, both of Jew first and of Greek;
10 δόξα.δὲ καὶ τιμὴ καὶ εἰρήνη παντὶ τῷ ἐργαζομένῳ τὸ
but glory and honour and peace to every one that works
ἀγαθόν, Ἰουδαίῳ.τε πρῶτον καὶ Ἕλληνι· 11 οὐ.γάρ.ἐστιν
good, both to Jew first, and to Greek: for there is not
[a]προσωπολήψία[a] παρὰ τῷ θεῷ. 12 ὅσοι.γὰρ ἀνόμως ἥμαρτον,
respect of persons with God. For as many as without law sinned,
ἀνόμως καὶ ἀπολοῦνται· καὶ ὅσοι ἐν νόμῳ ἥμαρτον, διὰ
without law also shall perish ; and as many as in law sinned, by
νόμου κριθήσονται, 13 οὐ.γὰρ οἱ ἀκροαταὶ [b]τοῦ[b] νόμου δίκαιοι
law shall be judged, (for not the hearers of the law [are] just
παρὰ [c]τῷ[c] θεῷ, ἀλλ' οἱ ποιηταὶ [b]τοῦ[b] νόμου δικαιωθήσονται.
with God, but the doers of the law shall be justified.
14 Ὅταν.γὰρ ἔθνη , τὰ μὴ νόμον ἔχοντα φύσει τὰ
For when nations which [2]not [3]law [1]have by nature the things
τοῦ νόμου [d]ποιῇ,[d] οὗτοι νόμον μὴ ἔχοντες, ἑαυτοῖς εἰσιν
of the law practise, these, law not having, to themselves are
νόμος· 15 οἵτινες ἐνδείκνυνται τὸ ἔργον τοῦ νόμου γραπτὸν
a law; who shew the work of the law written
ἐν ταῖς.καρδίαις.αὐτῶν, [e]συμμαρτυρούσης[e] αὐτῶν τῆς συνει-
in their hearts, bearing [4]witness [5]with [1]their [2]con-
δήσεως, καὶ μεταξὺ ἀλλήλων τῶν λογισμῶν κατηγορούντων
[3]science, and between one another the reasonings accusing
ἢ καὶ ἀπολογουμένων, 16 ἐν ἡμέρᾳ [f]ὅτε[f] κρινεῖ ὁ θεὸς
or also defending ;) in a day when [2]shall [3]judge [1]God
τὰ κρυπτὰ τῶν ἀνθρώπων, κατὰ τὸ.εὐαγγέλιόν.μου, διὰ
the secrets of men, according to my glad tidings, by
[g]Ἰησοῦ χριστοῦ.[g]
Jesus Christ.
17 [h]Ἴδε[h] σὺ Ἰουδαῖος ἐπονομάζῃ, καὶ ἐπαναπαύῃ [i]τῷ[i]
Lo, thou a Jew art named, and restest in the

γ — μὲν LTTr.　　　　　ᶻ ὀργὴ καὶ θυμός GLTTrAW.　　ᵃ προσωπολημψία LTTrA.　　ᵇ — τοῦ the
LTTrAW.　　　ᶜ — τῷ [L]Tr.　　ᵈ ποιῶσιν LTTrA.　　ᵉ συν- T.　　ᶠ ᾗ in which LA.
ᵍ χριστοῦ Ἰησοῦ T.　　ʰ εἰ δὲ but if GLTTrAW.　　ⁱ — τῷ the LTTrAW.

νόμῳ, καὶ καυχᾶσαι ἐν θεῷ, 18 καὶ γινώσκεις τὸ θέλημα, καὶ
law, and boastest in God, and knowest the will, and

δοκιμάζεις τὰ διαφέροντα, κατηχούμενος ἐκ τοῦ
approvest the things that are more excellent, being instructed out of the

νόμου· 19 πέποιθάς.τε σεαυτὸν ὁδηγὸν εἶναι τυφλῶν,
law; and art persuaded [that] thyself a guide art of [the] blind,

φῶς · τῶν ἐν σκότει, 20 παιδευτὴν ἀφρόνων, διδάσκαλον
a light of those in darkness, an instructor of [the] foolish, a teacher

νηπίων, ἔχοντα τὴν μόρφωσιν τῆς γνώσεως καὶ τῆς ἀληθείας
of infants, having the form of knowledge and of the truth

ἐν τῷ νόμῳ· 21 ὁ.οῦν διδάσκων ἕτερον, σεαυτὸν οὐ δι-
in the law: thou then that teachest another, thyself not [1]dost

δάσκεις; ὁ κηρύσσων μὴ κλέπτειν, κλέπτεις; 22 ὁ
[2]thou teach? thou that proclaimest not to steal, dost thou steal? thou that

λέγων μὴ μοιχεύειν, μοιχεύεις; ὁ
sayest not to commit adultery, dost thou commit adultery? thou that

βδελυσσόμενος τὰ εἴδωλα, ἱεροσυλεῖς; 23 ὃς ἐν
abhorrest idols, dost thou commit sacrilege? thou who in

νόμῳ καυχᾶσαι, διὰ τῆς παραβάσεως τοῦ νόμου τὸν θεὸν
law boastest, through the transgression of the law . [3]God

ἀτιμάζεις; 24 Τὸ.γὰρ ὄνομα τοῦ θεοῦ δι' ὑμᾶς βλασ-
dishonourest [4]thou? For the name of God through you is blas-

φημεῖται ἐν τοῖς ἔθνεσιν, καθὼς γέγραπται. 25 Περι-
phemed among the nations, according as it has been written. [2]Circum-

τομὴ μὲν · γὰρ ὠφελεῖ ἐὰν νόμον πράσσῃς· ἐὰν.δὲ
cision [3]indeed [1]for profits if [the] law thou doest; but if

παραβάτης νόμου ᾖς, ἡ.περιτομή.σου ἀκροβυστία γέγονεν.
a transgressor of law thou art, thy circumcision uncircumcision has become.

26 ἐὰν οὖν ἡ ἀκροβυστία τὰ δικαιώματα τοῦ νόμου φυλάσ-
If therefore the uncircumcision the requirements of the law keep,

σῃ, [k]οὐχὶ[||] ἡ.ἀκροβυστία.αὐτοῦ εἰς περιτομὴν λογισθήσεται;
[1]not [3]his [4]uncircumcision [5]for [6]circumcision [1]shall be reckoned?

27 καὶ κρινεῖ ἡ ἐκ φύσεως ἀκροβυστία, τὸν νόμον τελοῦσα,
and [8]shall [9]judge [1]the [3]by [4]nature [2]uncircumcision, [6]the [7]law [5]fulfilling,

σὲ τὸν διὰ γράμματος καὶ περιτομῆς παραβάτην νόμου;
thee who with letter and circumcision [art] a transgressor of law?

28 οὐ.γὰρ ὁ ἐν.τῷ.φανερῷ Ἰουδαῖός ἐστιν, οὐδὲ
For not he that [is one] outwardly [2]a [3]Jew [1]is, neither

ἡ ἐν.τῷ.φανερῷ ἐν σαρκὶ περιτομή· 29 [1]ἀλλ'[||] ὁ
that outwardly in flesh [is] circumcision; but he that [is]

ἐν.τῷ.κρυπτῷ Ἰουδαῖος, καὶ περιτομὴ καρδίας ἐν πνεύ-
hiddenly a Jew [is one]; and circumcision [is] of heart, in spi-

ματι, οὐ.γράμματι· οὗ ὁ ἔπαινος οὐκ ἐξ ἀνθρώπων,
rit, not in letter; of whom the praise [is] not of men,

[m]ἀλλ'[||] ἐκ τοῦ θεοῦ.
but of God.

3 Τί οὖν τὸ περισσὸν τοῦ Ἰουδαίου, ἢ τίς ἡ ὠφέλεια
What then [is] the superiority of the Jew? or what the profit

τῆς περιτομῆς; 2 πολὺ κατὰ πάντα τρόπον. πρῶτον μὲν
of the circumcision? Much in every way: [2]first

[n]γὰρ[||] ὅτι ἐπιστεύθησαν τὰ λόγια τοῦ θεοῦ. 3 τί.γάρ, εἰ
[1]for that they were entrusted with the oracles of God. For what, if

ἠπίστησάν.τινες; μὴ ἡ.ἀπιστία.αὐτῶν τὴν πίστιν τοῦ θεοῦ
[2]not [?]believed [1]some? [3]their [6]unbelief [11]the [12]faith [13]of [14]God

makest thy boast of
God, 18 and knowest
his will, and approv-
est the things that are
more excellent, being
instructed out of the
law; 19 and art con-
fident that thou thy-
self art a guide of the
blind, a light of them
which are in darkness,
20 an instructor of the
foolish, a teacher of
babes, which hast the
form of knowledge
and of the truth in the
law. 21 Thou there-
fore which teachest
another, teachest thou
not thyself? thou that
preachest a man should
not steal, dost thou
steal? 22 thou that
sayest a man should
not commit adultery,
dost thou commit a-
dultery? thou that
abhorrest idols, dost
thou commit sacrilege?
23 thou that makest
thy boast of the law,
through breaking the
law dishonourest thou
God? 24 For the name
of God is blasphemed
among the Gentiles
through you, as it is
written. 25 For circum-
cision verily profiteth,
if thou keep the law:
but if thou be a break-
er of the law, thy cir-
cumcision is made un-
circumcision. 26 There-
fore if the uncircum-
cision keep the right-
eousness of the law,
shall not his uncir-
cumcision be count-
ed for circumcision?
27 And shall not un-
circumcision which is
by nature, if it fulfil
the law, judge thee,
who by the letter
and circumcision dost
transgress the law?
28 For he is not a Jew,
which is one outward-
ly; neither is that
circumcision, which is
outward in the flesh:
29 but he is a Jew,
which is one inward-
ly; and circumcision
is that of the heart, in
the spirit, and not in
the letter, and whose
praise is not of men,
but of God.

III. What advan-
tage then hath the
Jew? or what profit
is there of circumci-
sion? 2 Much every
way: chiefly, because
that unto them were
committed the oracles

---

of God. 3 For what if some did not believe? shall their unbelief make the faith of God without effect? 4 God forbid: yea, let God be true, but every man a liar; as it is written, That thou mightest be justified in thy sayings, and mightest overcome when thou art judged. 5 But if our unrighteousness commend the righteousness of God, what shall we say? Is God unrighteous who taketh vengeance? (I speak as a man) 6 God forbid: for then how shall God judge the world? 7 For if the truth of God hath more abounded through my lie unto his glory; why yet am I also judged as a sinner? 8 And not *rather*, (as we be slanderously reported, and as some affirm that we say,) Let us do evil, that good may come? whose damnation is just.

9 What then? are we better *than they?* No, in no wise: for we have before proved both Jews and Gentiles, that they are all under sin; 10 as it is written, There is none righteous, no, not one: 11 there is none that understandeth, there is none that seeketh after God. 12 They are all gone out of the way, they are together become unprofitable; there is none that doeth good, no, not one. 13 Their throat *is* an open sepulchre; with their tongues they have used deceit; the poison of asps *is* under their lips: 14 whose mouth *is* full of cursing and bitterness: 15 their feet *are* swift to shed blood: 16 destruction and misery *are* in their ways: 17 and the way of peace have they not known: 18 there is no fear of God before their eyes. 19 Now we know that what things soever the law saith, it saith to them who are under the law: that every mouth may be stopped, and all the world may become guilty before God.

καταργήσει; 4 μὴ.γένοιτο· γινέσθω.δὲ ὁ θεὸς ἀληθής,
shall ⁷make ⁸of ⁹no ¹⁰effect? may it not be! but let ²be ¹God ᵧtrue,

πᾶς.δὲ ἄνθρωπος ψεύστης, °καθὼς‖ γέγραπται, Ὅπως
and every man false, according as it has been written, That

ἀν.δικαιωθῇς ἐν τοῖς.λόγοις.σου, καὶ ᴾνικήσῃς‖ ἐν τῷ
thou shouldest be justified in thy words, and overcome in

κρίνεσθαί.σε. 5 Εἰ.δὲ ἡ.ἀδικία.ἡμῶν θεοῦ δικαιοσύνην συνί-
thy being judged. But if our unrighteousness ²God's ³righteousness ¹com-

στησιν, τί ἐροῦμεν; μὴ ἄδικος ὁ θεὸς ὁ ἐπιφέρων τὴν
mend, what shall we say? [is] ²unrighteous ¹God who inflicts

ὀργήν; κατὰ ἄνθρωπον λέγω. 6 μὴ.γένοιτο· ἐπεὶ πῶς
wrath? According to man I speak. May it not be! since how

κρινεῖ ὁ θεὸς τὸν κόσμον; 7 εἰ ᑫγὰρ‖ ἡ ἀλήθεια τοῦ θεοῦ
shall ²judge ¹God the world? ²If ¹for the truth of God

ἐν τῷ.ἐμῷ.ψεύσματι ἐπερίσσευσεν εἰς τὴν.δόξαν.αὐτοῦ, τί ἔτι
in my lie abounded to his glory, why yet

κἀγὼ ὡς ἁμαρτωλὸς κρίνομαι; 8 καὶ μὴ καθὼς βλασ-
²also ²I ⁴as ³a ⁶sinner, ¹am judged? and not, according as we are

φημούμεθα, καὶ καθώς φασίν τινες ἡμᾶς λέγειν, Ὅτι
injuriously charged and according as ²affirm ¹some [that] we say,

ποιήσωμεν τὰ.κακὰ ἵνα ἔλθῃ τὰ.ἀγαθά; ὧν τὸ κρίμα
Let us practise evil things that ³may ⁴come ¹good ²things? whose judgment

ἔνδικόν ἐστιν.
²just ¹is.

9 Τί οὖν; προεχόμεθα; οὐ.πάντως· προῃτιασάμεθα.γὰρ
What then? are we better? not at all: for we before charged

Ἰουδαίους.τε καὶ Ἕλληνας πάντας ὑφ᾽ ἁμαρτίαν εἶναι,
both Jews and Greeks all ³under ⁴sin [¹with] ²being:

10 καθὼς γέγραπται, Ὅτι οὐκ.ἔστιν δίκαιος οὐδὲ
according as it has been written, There is not a righteous one, not even

εἷς· 11 οὐκ.ἔστιν ʳο‖ συνιῶν, οὐκ.ἔστιν ˢο‖ ἐκζητῶν
one: there is not [one] that understands, there is not [one] that seeks after

τὸν θεόν. 12 πάντες ἐξέκλιναν, ἅμα ᵗἠχρειώθη-
God. All did go out of the way, together they became unprofit-

σαν·‖ οὐκ.ἔστιν ⱽ ποιῶν χρηστότητα, οὐκ.ἔστιν ἕως
able; there is not [one] practising kindness, there is not so much as

ἑνός. 13 τάφος ἀνεῳγμένος ὁ.λάρυγξ.αὐτῶν, ταῖς γλώσσαις
one; ³sepulchre ¹an ²opened [is] their throat, with ²tongues

αὐτῶν ἐδολιοῦσαν· ἰὸς ἀσπίδων ὑπὸ τὰ.χείλη.αὐτῶν·
¹their they used deceit: poison of asps [is] under their lips:

14 ὧν τὸ στόμα ʷ ἀρᾶς καὶ πικρίας γέμει· 15 ὀξεῖς οἱ
of whom the mouth of cursing and of bitterness is full; swift

πόδες.αὐτῶν ἐκχέαι αἷμα· 16 σύντριμμα καὶ ταλαιπωρία
their feet to shed blood; ruin and misery [are]

ἐν ταῖς.ὁδοῖς.αὐτῶν· 17 καὶ ὁδὸν εἰρήνης οὐκ.ἔγνωσαν.
in their ways; and a way of peace they did not know;

18 οὐκ.ἔστιν φόβος θεοῦ ἀπέναντι τῶν.ὀφθαλμῶν.αὐτῶν.
there is no fear of God before their eyes.

19 Οἴδαμεν.δὲ ὅτι ὅσα ὁ νόμος λέγει, τοῖς ἐν τῷ νόμῳ
Now we know that whatsoever the law says, to those in the law

λαλεῖ· ἵνα πᾶν στόμα φραγῇ, καὶ ὑπόδικος γένηται
it speaks, that every mouth may be stopped, and under judgment be

πᾶς ὁ κόσμος τῷ θεῷ. 20 διότι ἐξ ἔργων νόμου οὐ δικαιω-
all the world to God. Wherefore by works of law ²not ¹shall be

---

° καθάπερ ΤΤr. ᴾ νικήσεις shalt overcome τ. ᑫ δὲ but τ. ʳ — ὁ L[Τr]. ˢ [ὁ] L.
ᵗ ἠχρεώθησαν ΤΤr. ⱽ + ὁ (read that practises) τ. ʷ + [αὐτῶν] (read their mouth) L.

θήσεται πᾶσα σὰρξ ἐνώπιον αὐτοῦ· διὰ.γὰρ νόμου ἐπί-
justified   any   flesh   before   him;   for through · law [is] know-
        (lit. all)
γνῶσις ἁμαρτίας.
ledge   of sin.

21 Νυνὶ.δὲ χωρὶς νόμου δικαιοσύνη θεοῦ πεφανέρωται,
   But now apart from   law   righteousness of God has been manifested,

μαρτυρουμένη ὑπὸ τοῦ νόμου καὶ τῶν προφητῶν· 22 δι-
being borne witness to by the law and the   prophets: ²right-

καιοσύνη δὲ θεοῦ διὰ πίστεως Ἰησοῦ χριστοῦ, εἰς πάντας
eousness ¹even of God through faith of Jesus   Christ,   towards   all

ˣκαὶ ἐπὶ πάντας‖ τοὺς πιστεύοντας· οὐ.γάρ.ἐστιν διαστολή·
and upon   all   those that believe: for there is no   difference:

23 πάντες.γὰρ ἥμαρτον καὶ ὑστεροῦνται τῆς δόξης τοῦ θεοῦ,
   for all   sinned   and   come short of the glory   of God;

24 δικαιούμενοι δωρεὰν ·τῇ.αὐτοῦ.χάριτι, διὰ τῆς ἀπολυ-
   being justified gratuitously by his grace,   through the   re-

τρώσεως τῆς ἐν χριστῷ Ἰησοῦ, 25 ὃν προέθετο ὁ θεὸς
demption which [is] in Christ   Jesus;   whom ²set ³forth   ¹God

ἱλαστήριον διὰ ʸτῆς‖ πίστεως ἐν τῷ.αὐτοῦ.αἵματι, εἰς ἔν-
a mercy seat through   faith   in   his blood,   for a shew-

δειξιν τῆς.δικαιοσύνης.αὐτοῦ, διὰ τὴν πάρεσιν τῶν
ing forth of his righteousness, in respect of the passing by the

   προγεγονότων ἁμαρτημάτων 26 ἐν τῇ ἀνοχῇ τοῦ
²that ³had ⁴before ⁵taken ⁶place   ¹sins   in the forbearance

θεοῦ, πρὸς ᶻ ἔνδειξιν τῆς.δικαιοσύνης.αὐτοῦ ἐν τῷ νῦν
of God; for [the] shewing forth of his righteousness in the present

καιρῷ, εἰς τὸ εἶναι.αὐτὸν δίκαιον καὶ δικαιοῦντα τὸν ἐκ
time,   for his being just and justifying him that [is] of [the]

πίστεως Ἰησοῦ. 27 Ποῦ οὖν ἡ καύχησις; ἐξεκλείσθη.
faith   of Jesus.   Where then [is] the boasting?   It was excluded.

διὰ ποίου νόμου; τῶν ἔργων; οὐχί, ἀλλὰ διὰ νόμου
Through what   law?   of works? No, but through a law

πίστεως. 28 λογιζόμεθα ªοὖν‖ ᵇπίστει δικαιοῦσθαι‖ ἄνθρω-
of faith.   ²We ¹reckon ¹therefore ⁹by ¹⁰faith ⁶to ⁷be ⁸justified ⁴a ⁵man

πον, χωρὶς ἔργων νόμου. 29 ἢ Ἰουδαίων ὁ θεὸς μόνον;
apart from works of law.   Of Jews [is he] the God only?

οὐχὶ.ᶜδὲ‖ καὶ ἐθνῶν; ναὶ καὶ ἐθνῶν· 30 ᵈἐπείπερ‖ εἷς
and not   also of Gentiles? Yea, also of Gentiles: since indeed one

ὁ θεὸς ὃς δικαιώσει περιτομὴν ἐκ πίστεως, καὶ
God [it is] who will justify [the] circumcision by   faith,   and

ἀκροβυστίαν διὰ τῆς πίστεως. 31 νόμον οὖν καταργοῦ-
uncircumcision through   faith.   ⁵Law   ⁵then ¹do ²we ⁴make of no

μεν διὰ τῆς πίστεως; μὴ.γένοιτο· ἀλλὰ νόμον ᵉἱστῶμεν.‖
effect through   faith?   May it not be! but ³law ¹we ²establish.

4 Τί οὖν ἐροῦμεν ᶠἈβραὰμ τὸν.πατέρα.ἡμῶν εὑρηκέναι‖
  What then shall we say Abraham   our father   has found

κατὰ σάρκα; 2 εἰ.γὰρ Ἀβραὰμ ἐξ ἔργων ἐδικαιώθη, ἔχει
according to flesh?   For if Abraham by works was justified, he has

καύχημα, ἀλλ᾽ οὐ πρὸς ᵍτὸν‖ θεόν. 3 τί.γὰρ ἡ γραφὴ
ground of boasting, but not towards   God.   For what ²the ³scripture

λέγει; Ἐπίστευσεν.δὲ Ἀβραὰμ τῷ θεῷ, καὶ ἐλογίσθη αὐτῷ
¹says?   And ²believed ¹Abraham   God, and it was reckoned to him

20 Therefore by the
deeds of the law there
shall no flesh be justi-
fied in his sight : for
by the law is the know-
ledge of sin.
21 But now the right-
eousness of God with-
out the law is mani-
fested, being witness-
ed by the law and the
prophets ; 22 even the
righteousness of God
which is by faith of
Jesus Christ unto all
and upon all them that
believe : for there is
no difference : 23 for
all have sinned, and
come short of the glory
of God ; 24 being justi-
fied freely by his grace
through the redemp-
tion that is in Christ Jesus: 25 whom God hath
set forth to be a pro-
pitiation through faith
in his blood, to declare
his righteousness for
the remission of sins
that are past, through
the forbearance of
God ; 26 to declare, I
say, at this time his
righteousness : that he
might be just, and the
justifier of him which
believeth in Jesus.
27 Where is boasting
then ? It is excluded.
By what law ? of
works? Nay : but by
the law of faith.
28 Therefore we con-
clude that a man is
justified by faith with-
out the deeds of the
law. 29 Is he the God
of the Jews only ? is
he not also of the
Gentiles ? Yes, of the
Gentiles also : 30 see-
ing it is one God, which
shall justify the cir-
cumcision by faith,
and uncircumcision
through faith. 31 Do
we then make void
the law through faith?
God forbid : yea, we
establish the law.
IV. What shall we
say then that Abraham
our father, as pertain-
ing to the flesh, hath
found ? 2 For if Abra-
ham were justified by
works, he hath whereof
to glory ; but not be-
fore God. 3 For what
saith the scripture ? A-
braham believed God,
and it was counted
unto him for right-
eousness. 4 Now to him
that worketh is the

ˣ — καὶ ἐπὶ πάντας LTTr[A].   ʸ — τῆς LTTrA.   ᶻ + τὴν the LTTrA.   ª γὰρ ¹for GLTTrAW.
ᵇ δικαιοῦσθαι πίστει GLTTrA.   ᶜ — δὲ and GLTTrA.   ᵈ εἴ περ LTTrA.   ᵉ ἱστάνομεν
LTTrA.   ᶠ εὑρηκέναι ([εὑρηκέναι] Α) Ἀβραὰμ τὸν προπάτορα (forefather) ἡμῶν LTTrA.
ᵍ — τὸν LTTrAW.

reward not reckoned of grace, but of debt. 5 But to him that worketh not, but believeth on him that justifieth the ungodly, his faith is counted for righteousness. 6 Even as David also describeth the blessedness of the man, unto whom God imputeth righteousness without works, 7 *saying*, Blessed *are* they whose iniquities are forgiven, and whose sins are covered. 8 Blessed *is* the man to whom the Lord will not impute sin.

9 *Cometh* this blessedness then upon the circumcision *only*, or upon the uncircumcision also? for we say that faith was reckoned to Abraham for righteousness. 10 How was it then reckoned? when he was in circumcision, or in uncircumcision? Not in circumcision, but in uncircumcision. 11 And he received the sign of circumcision, a seal of the righteousness of the faith which *he had* yet being uncircumcised: that he might be the father of all them that believe, though they be not circumcised; that righteousness might be imputed unto them also: 12 and the father of circumcision to them who are not of the circumcision only, but who also walk in the steps of that faith of our father Abraham, which *he had* being *yet* uncircumcised.

13 For the promise, that he should be the heir of the world, *was* not to Abraham, or to his seed, through the law, but through the righteousness of faith. 14 For if they which are of the law *be* heirs, faith is made void, and the promise made of none effect: 15 because the law worketh wrath: for where no law is, *there is* no transgression. 16 Therefore *it is* of faith, that *it* might be by grace ; to the end the promise might be sure to all the seed ; not to that only which is of the

εἰς δικαιοσύνην. 4 Τῷ.δὲ ἐργαζομένῳ ὁ μισθὸς οὐ.λογίζεται
for righteousness. Now to him that works the reward is not reckoned
κατὰ χάριν, ἀλλὰ κατὰ ¹τὸ‖ ὀφείλημα· 5 τῷ.δὲ
according to grace, but according to debt : but to him that
μὴ.ἐργαζομένῳ, πιστεύοντι.δὲ ἐπὶ τὸν δικαιοῦντα τὸν ᵏἀ-
does not work, but believes on him that justifies the un-
σεβῆ,‖ λογίζεται ἡ.πίστις.αὐτοῦ εἰς δικαιοσύνην. 6 καθάπερ
godly, ³is ⁴reckoned ¹his ²faith for righteousness. Even as
καὶ ¹Δαβὶδ‖ λέγει τὸν μακαρισμὸν τοῦ ἀνθρώπου ᾧ ὁ θεὸς
also David declares the blessedness of the man to whom God
λογίζεται δικαιοσύνην χωρὶς ἔργων, 7 Μακάριοι ὧν
reckons righteousness apart from works : Blessed [they] of whom
ἀφέθησαν αἱ ἀνομίαι, καὶ ὧν ἐπεκαλύφθησαν αἱ ἁμαρτιαι.
are forgiven the lawlessnesses, and of whom are covered. the sins :
8 μακάριος ἀνὴρ ᵐῷ‖ οὐ.μὴ λογίσηται κύριος ἁμαρτίαν.
blessed [the] man to whom in no wise ³will ⁴reckon [¹the] ²Lord sin.

9 Ὁ.μακαρισμὸς.οὖν.οὗτος ἐπὶ τὴν περιτομήν, ἢ καὶ ἐπὶ
[Is] this blessedness then on the circumcision, or also on
τὴν ἀκροβυστίαν; λέγομεν.γὰρ ⁿὅτι‖ ἐλογίσθη τῷ Ἀβραὰμ
the uncircumcision ? For we say that was reckoned to Abraham
ἡ πίστις εἰς δικαιοσύνην. 10 πῶς οὖν ἐλογίσθη; ἐν περι-
faith for righteousness. How then was it reckoned? ²in ³circum-
τομῇ ὄντι, ἢ ἐν ἀκροβυστίᾳ; οὐκ ἐν περιτομῇ, ἀλλ᾽ ἐν ἀκρο-
cision ¹being, or in uncircumcision ? Not in circumcision, but in uncir-
βυστίᾳ· 11 καὶ σημεῖον ἔλαβεν περιτομῆς, σφραγῖδα
cumcision. And [the] sign he received of circumcision, [as] seal
τῆς δικαιοσύνης τῆς πίστεως τῆς ἐν τῇ ἀκροβυστια,
of the righteousness of the faith which [he had] in the uncircumcision,
εἰς τὸ.εἶναι.αὐτὸν πατέρα πάντων τῶν πιστευόντων ᵒδι᾽‖
for him to be father of all those that believe in
ἀκροβυστίας, εἰς τὸ λογισθῆναι ᴾκαὶ‖ αὐτοῖς ᑫτὴν‖ δικαιο-
uncircumcision, for ⁴to ⁵be ⁶reckoned ³also ⁷to ⁶them ¹the ²righteous-
σύνην· 12 καὶ πατέρα περιτομῆς τοῖς οὐκ ἐκ περιτομῆς
ness ; and father of circumcision to those not of circumcision
μόνον, ἀλλὰ καὶ τοῖς στοιχοῦσιν τοῖς ἴχνεσιν τῆς ἐν
only, but also to those that walk in the steps of the ²during
ʳτῇ ἀκροβυστίᾳ πίστεως τοῦ.πατρὸς.ἡμῶν Ἀβραάμ.
³uncircumcision ¹faith of our father Abraham.

13 Οὐ.γὰρ διὰ νόμου ἡ ἐπαγγελία τῷ Ἀβραὰμ ἢ τῷ
For not by law the promise [was] to Abraham or
σπέρματι.αὐτοῦ, τὸ κληρονόμον αὐτὸν εἶναι ˢτοῦ‖ κόσμου,
to his seed, that heir he should be of the world,
ἀλλὰ διὰ δικαιοσύνης πίστεως. 14 εἰ.γὰρ οἱ ἐκ νόμου
but by righteousness of faith. For if those of law [be]
κληρονόμοι, κεκένωται ἡ πίστις.καὶ κατήργηται ἡ ἐ-
heirs, ²has ³been ⁴made ⁵void ¹faith, and ²made ³of ²no ⁵effect ¹the ²pro-
παγγελία· 15 ὁ.γὰρ.νόμος ὀργὴν κατεργάζεται· οὗ ᵗγὰρ‖ οὐκ
mise. For the law ¹wrath ²works ³out ; where ²for ⁴not
ἔστιν νόμος, οὐδὲ παράβασις. 16 διὰ.τοῦτο ἐκ πίστεως,
⁵is ⁶law, neither [is] transgression. Wherefore of faith
ἵνα κατὰ χάριν, εἰς τὸ εἶναι βεβαίαν τὴν
[it is], that according to grace [it might be], for ³to ⁴be ⁵sure ¹the
ἐπαγγελίαν παντὶ τῷ σπέρματι, οὐ τῷ ἐκ τοῦ νόμου μόνον,
²promise to all the seed, not to that of the law only,

---

i — τὸ GLTTrAW.   ᵏ ἀσεβῆν T.   ˡ Δανεὶδ LTTrA ; Δαυὶδ GW.   ᵐ οὗ whose (sin) TTr.
ⁿ — ὅτι [L]TTr.   ᵒ διὰ L.   ᴾ — καὶ ᵀᵀr[A].   ᑫ — τὴν T.   ʳ — τῇ GLTTrAW.
ˢ — τοῦ (read [the]) GLTTrAW.   ᵗ δὲ but LTTrAW.

ἀλλὰ καὶ τῷ ἐκ πίστεως Ἀβραάμ, ὅς ἐστιν πατὴρ
but also to that of [the] faith of Abraham, who is father

πάντων.ἡμῶν, 17 καθὼς γέγραπται. Ὅτι πατέρα πολ-
of us all, (according as it has been written, A father of

λῶν ἐθνῶν τέθεικά σε, κατέναντι οὗ ἐπίστευσεν θεοῦ,
many nations I have made thee,) before ²whom ³he ⁴believed, ¹God,

τοῦ ζωοποιοῦντος τοὺς νεκρούς, καὶ καλοῦντος τὰ μὴ
who quickens the dead, and calls the things not

ὄντα ὡς ὄντα. 18 Ὃς παρ᾽ ἐλπίδα ᵛἐπ᾽ᴵᴵ ἐλπίδι ἐπίστευσεν,
being as being; who against hope in hope believed,

εἰς τὸ γενέσθαι αὐτὸν πατέρα πολλῶν ἐθνῶν, κατὰ τὸ
for ²to ³become ¹him father of many nations, according to that which

εἰρημένον, Οὕτως ἔσται τὸ.σπέρμα.σου· 19 καὶ μὴ ἀσθενήσας
had been said, ·So shall be thy seed: and not being weak

τῇ πίστει, ʷοὐᴵᴵ κατενόησεν τὸ.ἑαυτοῦ σῶμα ˣἤδηᴵᴵ νενεκρω-
in the faith, ³not ¹he ²considered his own body already become

μένον, ἑκατονταέτης που ὑπάρχων, καὶ τὴν νέκρωσιν
dead, ·³a ⁴hundred ⁵years ⁶old ²about ¹being, and .the deadening

τῆς μήτρας Σάρρας· 20 εἰς.δὲ τὴν ἐπαγγελίαν τοῦ θεοῦ οὐ
of the womb of Sarah, and at the promise of God ²not

διεκρίθη τῇ ἀπιστίᾳ, ʸἀλλ᾽ᴵᴵ ἐνεδυναμώθη τῇ πίστει,
¹doubted through unbelief; but was strengthened in faith,

δοὺς δόξαν τῷ θεῷ, 21 καὶ πληροφορηθεὶς ὅτι ὃ ἐπήγ-
giving glory to God, and being fully assured that what he has

γελται, δυνατός ἐστιν καὶ ποιῆσαι. 22 διὸ ᶻκαὶᴵᴵ ἐλογίσθη
promised, able he is also to do; wherefore also it was reckoned

αὐτῷ εἰς δικαιοσύνην. 23 Οὐκ.ἐγράφη δὲ δι᾽ αὐτὸν
to him for righteousness. ²It ³was ⁴not ⁵written ¹but on account of him

μόνον, ὅτι ἐλογίσθη αὐτῷ· 24 ἀλλὰ καὶ δι᾽ ἡμᾶς,
only, that it was reckoned to him, but also on account of us,

οἷς μέλλει λογίζεσθαι, τοῖς πιστεύουσιν ἐπὶ τὸν
to whom it is about to be reckoned, to those that believe on him who

ἐγείραντα.Ἰησοῦν τὸν.κύριον.ἡμῶν ἐκ νεκρῶν, 25 ὃς
raised Jesus our Lord from among [the] dead, who

παρεδόθη διὰ τὰ.παραπτώματα.ἡμῶν, καὶ ἠγέρθη διὰ τὴν
was delivered for our offences, and was raised for

δικαίωσιν.ἡμῶν.
our justification.

5 Δικαιωθέντες οὖν ἐκ πίστεως, εἰρήνην ᵃἔχομενᴵᴵ
Having been justified therefore by faith, peace we have

πρὸς τὸν θεὸν διὰ τοῦ.κυρίου.ἡμῶν Ἰησοῦ χριστοῦ, 2 δι᾽
toward God through our Lord Jesus Christ, through

οὗ καὶ τὴν προσαγωγὴν ἐσχήκαμεν ᵇτῇ πίστειᴵᴵ εἰς τὴν χάριν
whom also access we have by faith into ²grace

ταύτην ἐν ᾗ ἑστήκαμεν· καὶ καυχώμεθα ἐπ᾽ ἐλπίδι τῆς δόξης
¹this in which we stand, and· we boast in hope of the glory

τοῦ θεοῦ. 3 οὐ.μόνον.δέ, ἀλλὰ καὶ ᶜκαυχώμεθαᴵᴵ ἐν ταῖς
of God. And not only [so], but also we boast in

θλίψεσιν, εἰδότες ὅτι ἡ θλίψις ὑπομονὴν κατεργάζεται,
tribulations, knowing that the tribulation ³endurance ¹works ²out;

4 ἡ.δὲ ὑπομονὴ δοκιμήν, ἡ.δὲ δοκιμὴ ἐλπίδα, 5 ἡ.δὲ ἐλπὶς
and the endurance proof; and the proof hope; and the hope

οὐ.καταισχύνει· ὅτι ἡ ἀγάπη τοῦ θεοῦ ἐκκέχυται ἐν
does not make ashamed, because the love of God has been poured out in

(right column English)

law, but to that also which is of the faith of Abraham; who is the father of us all, 17 (as it is written, I have made thee a father of many nations,) before him whom he believed, even God, who quickeneth the dead, and calleth those things which be not as though they were. 18 Who against hope believed in hope, that he might become the father of many nations, according to that which was spoken, So shall thy seed be. 19 And being not weak in faith, he considered not his own body now dead, when he was about an hundred years old, neither yet the deadness of Sarah's womb: 20 he staggered not at the promise of God through unbelief; but was strong in faith, giving glory to God; 21 and being fully persuaded that, what he had promised, he was able also to perform. 22 And therefore it was imputed to him for righteousness. 23 Now it was not written for his sake alone, that it was imputed to him; 24 but for us also, to whom it shall be imputed, if we believe on him that raised up Jesus our Lord from the dead; 25 who was delivered for our offences, and was raised again for our justification.

V. Therefore being justified by faith, we have peace with God through our Lord Jesus Christ: 2 by whom also we have access by faith into this grace wherein we stand, and rejoice in hope of the glory of God. 3 And not only so, but we glory in tribulations also: knowing that tribulation worketh patience; 4 and patience, experience; and experience, hope: 5 and hope maketh not ashamed; because the love of God is shed abroad in our hearts by the Holy Ghost which is given unto us. 6 For when we were yet without strength, in due time Christ died for the ungodly. 7 For scarcely for a righteous man will one die : yet peradventure for a good man some would even dare to die. 8 But God commendeth his love toward us, in that, while we were yet sinners, Christ died for us. 9 Much more then, being now justified by his blood, we shall be saved from wrath through him. 10 For if, when we were enemies, we were reconciled to God by the death of his Son, much more, being reconciled, we shall be saved by his life. 11 And not only so, but we also joy in God through our Lord Jesus Christ, by whom we have now received the atonement.

ταῖς καρδίαις ἡμῶν διὰ πνεύματος ἁγίου τοῦ δοθέντος ἡμῖν.
our hearts   by   the ²Spirit ¹Holy   which was given to us :

6 d″Ετι γὰρ‖ χριστὸς ὄντων ἡμῶν ἀσθενῶν e κατὰ καιρὸν
For still   ⁵Christ ²being ¹we ³without ⁴strength   in due time

ὑπὲρ ἀσεβῶν ἀπέθανεν. 7 μόλις γὰρ ὑπὲρ δικαίου
for [the] ungodly   died.   For hardly   for   a just [man]

τις ἀποθανεῖται· ὑπὲρ γὰρ τοῦ ἀγαθοῦ τάχα τις
²any ³one ¹will die ;   for on behalf of the   good [man] perhaps some one

καὶ τολμᾷ ἀποθανεῖν· 8 συνίστησιν δὲ τὴν ἑαυτοῦ ἀγάπην
even might dare to die ;   but ²commends   ³his ⁴own   ⁵love

εἰς ἡμᾶς fὁ θεός,‖ ὅτι ἔτι ἁμαρτωλῶν ὄντων ἡμῶν χριστὸς
⁴to ⁷us ¹God,   that ²still   ⁴sinners   ²being ¹we   Christ

ὑπὲρ ἡμῶν ἀπέθανεν. 9 πολλῷ οὖν μᾶλλον, δικαιωθέντες
²for ³us ¹died.   Much therefore more, having been justified

νῦν ἐν τῷ αἵματι αὐτοῦ, σωθησόμεθα δι' αὐτοῦ ἀπὸ τῆς
now by   his blood,   we shall be saved   by   him   from

ὀργῆς. 10 εἰ γὰρ ἐχθροὶ ὄντες κατηλλάγημεν τῷ θεῷ διὰ
wrath.   For if, ²enemies ¹being we were reconciled to God through

τοῦ θανάτου τοῦ υἱοῦ αὐτοῦ, πολλῷ μᾶλλον καταλλαγέντες
the death   of his Son,   much more,   having been reconciled

σωθησόμεθα ἐν τῇ ζωῇ αὐτοῦ· 11 οὐ μόνον δέ, ἀλλὰ καὶ
we shall be saved by   his life.   And not only [so], but   also

καυχώμενοι ἐν τῷ θεῷ διὰ τοῦ κυρίου ἡμῶν Ἰησοῦ χριστοῦ,
boasting   in   God through   our Lord   Jesus   Christ,

δι' οὗ νῦν τὴν καταλλαγὴν ἐλάβομεν.
through whom now the   reconciliation   we received.

12 Wherefore, as by one man sin entered into the world, and death by sin ; and so death passed upon all men, for that all have sinned : 13 (for until the law sin was in the world : but sin is not imputed when there is no law. 14 Nevertheless death reigned from Adam to Moses, even over them that had not sinned after the similitude of Adam's transgression, who is the figure of him that was to come. 15 But not as the offence, so also is the free gift. For if through the offence of one many be dead, much more the grace of God, and the gift by grace, which is by one man, Jesus Christ, hath abounded unto many. 16 And not as it was by one that sinned, so is the gift : for the judgment was

12 Διὰ τοῦτο ὥσπερ δι' ἑνὸς ἀνθρώπου ἡ ἁμαρτία εἰς τὸν
On this account, as   by one   man   sin   into the

κόσμον εἰσῆλθεν, καὶ διὰ τῆς ἁμαρτίας ὁ θάνατος, καὶ οὕτως
world   entered, and by   sin   death,   and thus

εἰς πάντας ἀνθρώπους gὁ θάνατος‖ διῆλθεν, ἐφ' ᾧ πάντες
to   all   men   death   passed,   for that   all

ἥμαρτον. 13 ἄχρι γὰρ νόμου ἁμαρτία ἦν ἐν κόσμῳ·
sinned :   (for until   law   sin   was in [the] world ;

ἁμαρτία δὲ οὐκ ἐλλογεῖται, μὴ ὄντος νόμου· 14 hἀλλ'‖
but sin   is not put to account, there not being law ;   but

ἐβασίλευσεν ὁ θάνατος ἀπὸ Ἀδὰμ μέχρι iΜωσέως‖ καὶ ἐπὶ
²reigned   ¹death   from   Adam until   Moses   even upon

τοὺς μὴ ἁμαρτήσαντας ἐπὶ τῷ ὁμοιώματι τῆς παραβάσεως
those who   had not sinned   in   the   likeness   of the transgression

Ἀδάμ, ὅς ἐστιν τύπος τοῦ μέλλοντος. 15 Ἀλλ' οὐχ
of Adam, who is   a figure of the   coming [one].   But [shall] not

ὡς τὸ παράπτωμα, οὕτως καὶ τὸ χάρισμα.k εἰ γὰρ τῷ
as the   offence,   so   also [be] the free gift ?   For if by the

τοῦ ἑνὸς παραπτώματι οἱ πολλοὶ ἀπέθανον, πολλῷ μᾶλλον
²of ³the ⁴one   ¹offence   the many   died,   much more

ἡ χάρις τοῦ θεοῦ καὶ ἡ δωρεὰ ἐν χάριτι τῇ τοῦ ἑνὸς
the grace of God, and the gift   in   grace, which [is] of the one

ἀνθρώπου Ἰησοῦ χριστοῦ εἰς τοὺς πολλοὺς ἐπερίσσευσεν.
man   Jesus   Christ, to the   many   did abound.

16 καὶ οὐχ ὡς δι' ἑνὸς ἁμαρτήσαντος τὸ δώρημα·k
And [shall] not as   by one   having sinned   [be] the   gift ?

---

d εἴ γε if indeed A.   e + ἔτι still' GLTTrAW.   f — ὁ θεός (read συνίστησιν he commends) A.   g [ὁ θάνατος] A.   h ἀλλὰ TTrAW.   i Μωσέως GLſTrAW.   k The various Editors do not mark this as a question : to read it as pointed in the Greek omit [shall] and substitute [is] for [be].

τὸ.μὲν.γὰρ κρῖμα ἐξ ἑνὸς εἰς κατάκριμα, τὸ.δὲ χάρισμα
For the ²indeed ¹judgment [was] of one to condemnation, but the free gift

ἐκ πολλῶν παραπτωμάτων εἰς δικαίωμα. 17 εἰ.γὰρ τῷ
[is] of many offences to justification. For if by the

τοῦ ἑνὸς παραπτώματι ὁ θάνατος ἐβασίλευσεν διὰ τοῦ ἑνός,
²of ³the ⁴one ¹offence death reigned by the one,

πολλῷ μᾶλλον οἱ τὴν περισσείαν τῆς χάριτος καὶ ᵐτῆς
much more those the abundance of grace, and of the

δωρεᾶς‖ τῆς δικαιοσύνης λαμβάνοντες, ἐν ζωῇ βασιλεύσουσιν
gift of righteousness receiving, in life shall reign

διὰ τοῦ ἑνὸς Ἰησοῦ χριστοῦ. 18 Ἄρα οὖν ὡς δι' ἑνὸς παρα-
by the one Jesus Christ :) so then as by one of-

πτώματος εἰς πάντας ἀνθρώπους εἰς κατάκριμα,
fence [it was] towards all men to condemnation,

οὕτως καὶ δι' ἑνὸς δικαιώματος εἰς πάντας ἀνθρώ-
so also by one accomplished righteousness towards all men

πους εἰς δικαίωσιν ζωῆς. 19 ὥσπερ.γὰρ διὰ τῆς παρακοῆς
to justification of life. For as by the disobedience

τοῦ ἑνὸς ἀνθρώπου ἁμαρτωλοὶ κατεστάθησαν οἱ πολλοί,
of the one man ⁵sinners ³were ⁴constituted ¹the ²many,

οὕτως καὶ διὰ τῆς ὑπακοῆς τοῦ ἑνὸς δίκαιοι κατασταθήσονται
so also by the obedience of the one ²righteous ³shall ⁴be ⁵constituted

οἱ πολλοί. 20 Νόμος.δὲ παρεισῆλθεν, ἵνα πλεονάσῃ τὸ
¹the ²many. But law came in by the bye, that might abound the

παράπτωμα. οὖ.δὲ ἐπλεόνασεν ἡ ἁμαρτία, ὑπερεπερίσσευσεν
offence; but where abounded sin, overabounded

ἡ χάρις· 21 ἵνα ὥσπερ ἐβασίλευεν‖ ἡ ἁμαρτία ἐν τῷ θανάτῳ,
grace, that as ²reigned ¹sin in death,

οὕτως καὶ ἡ χάρις βασιλεύσῃ διὰ δικαιοσύνης εἰς ζωὴν
so also grace might reign through righteousness to life

αἰώνιον, διὰ Ἰησοῦ χριστοῦ τοῦ.κυρίου ἡμῶν.
eternal, through Jesus Christ our Lord.

6 Τί οὖν ἐροῦμεν; ⁿἐπιμενοῦμεν‖ τῇ ἁμαρτίᾳ ἵνα ἡ χάρις
What then shall we say? Shall we continue in sin that grace

πλεονάσῃ; 2 μὴ.γένοιτο. οἵτινες.ἀπεθάνομεν τῇ ἁμαρτίᾳ,
may abound? May it not be! We who died to sin,

πῶς ἔτι ζήσομεν ἐν αὐτῇ; 3 ἢ ἀγνοεῖτε ὅτι ὅσοι
how still shall we live in it? Or are ye ignorant that ²as ³many ⁴as

ἐβαπτίσθημεν εἰς χριστὸν Ἰησοῦν, εἰς τὸν.θάνατον.αὐτοῦ
¹we were baptized unto Christ Jesus, unto his death

ἐβαπτίσθημεν; 4 συνετάφημεν οὖν αὐτῷ διὰ τοῦ βαπ-
we were baptized? We were buried therefore with him by bap-

τίσματος εἰς τὸν θάνατον· ἵνα ὥσπερ ἠγέρθη χριστὸς
tism unto death, that as ²was ³raised ⁴up ¹Christ

ἐκ νεκρῶν διὰ τῆς δόξης τοῦ πατρός, οὕτως καὶ
from among [the] dead by the glory of the Father, so also

ἡμεῖς ἐν καινότητι ζωῆς περιπατήσωμεν. 5 Εἰ.γὰρ σύμφυτοι
we in newness of life should walk. For if conjoined

γεγόναμεν τῷ ὁμοιώματι τοῦ.θανάτου.αὐτοῦ, ἀλλὰ.καὶ
we have become in the likeness of his death, so also

τῆς.ἀναστάσεως ἐσόμεθα· 6 τοῦτο γινώσκοντες, ὅτι ὁ παλαιὸς
of [his] resurrection we shall be; this knowing, that ²old

ἡμῶν ἄνθρωπος συνεσταυρώθη, ἵνα καταργηθῇ τὸ σῶμα
¹our man was crucified with [him], that might be annulled the body

---

by one to condemnation, but the free gift is of many offences unto justification. 17 For if by one man's offence death reigned by one; much more they which receive abundance of grace and of the gift of righteousness shall reign in life by one, Jesus Christ.) 18 Therefore as by the offence of one *judgment came* upon all men to condemnation; even so by the righteousness of one *the free gift came* upon all men unto justification of life. 19 For as by one man's disobedience many were made sinners, so by the obedience of one shall many be made righteous. 20 Moreover the law entered, that the offence might abound. But where sin abounded, grace did much more abound: 21 that as sin hath reigned unto death, even so might grace reign through righteousness unto eternal life by Jesus Christ our Lord.

VI. What shall we say then? Shall we continue in sin, that grace may abound? 2 God forbid. How shall we, that are dead to sin, live any longer therein? 3 Know ye not, that so many of us as were baptized into Jesus Christ were baptized into his death? 4 Therefore we are buried with him by baptism into death: that like as Christ was raised up from the dead by the glory of the Father, even so we also should walk in newness of life. 5 For if we have been planted together in the likeness of his death, we shall be also *in the likeness of his* resurrection: 6 knowing this, that our old man is crucified with *him,* that the body of sin might be destroyed,

---

ᵐ [τῆς δωρεᾶς] L.   ⁿ ἐπιμένωμεν should we continue GLTTrAW.

that henceforth we should not serve sin. 7 For he that is dead is freed from sin. 8 Now if we be dead with Christ, we believe that we shall also live with him: 9 knowing that Christ being raised from the dead dieth no more; death hath no more dominion over him. 10 For in that he died, he died unto sin once: but in that he liveth, he liveth unto God. 11 Likewise reckon ye also yourselves to be dead indeed unto sin, but alive unto God through Jesus Christ our Lord. 12 Let not sin therefore reign in your mortal body, that ye should obey it in the lusts thereof. 13 Neither yield ye your members as instruments of unrighteousness unto sin: but yield yourselves unto God, as those that are alive from the dead, and your members as instruments of righteousness unto God. 14 For sin shall not have dominion over you: for ye are not under the law, but under grace.

15 What then? shall we sin, because we are not under the law, but under grace? God forbid. 16 Know ye not, that to whom ye yield yourselves servants to obey, his servants ye are to whom ye obey; whether of sin unto death, or of obedience unto righteousness? 17 But God be thanked, that ye were the servants of sin, but ye have obeyed from the heart that form of doctrine which was delivered you. 18 Being then made free from sin, ye became the servants of righteousness. 19 I speak after the manner of men because of the infirmity of your flesh: for as ye have yielded your members servants to uncleanness and to iniquity unto iniquity; even so now yield your members servants to righteousness unto holiness. 20 For when ye were

τῆς ἁμαρτίας, τοῦ μηκέτι δουλεύειν ἡμᾶς τῇ ἁμαρτίᾳ.
of sin,　that [2]no [3]longer [4]be [5]subservient [1]we　to sin.

7 ὁ.γὰρ ἀποθανὼν δεδικαίωται ἀπὸ τῆς ἁμαρτίας. 8 Εἰ.δὲ
For he that died　has been justified from　sin.　Now if

ἀπεθάνομεν σὺν χριστῷ, πιστεύομεν ὅτι καὶ °συζήσομεν⁰
we died　with　Christ,　we believe　that also we shall live with

αὐτῷ, 9 εἰδότες ὅτι χριστὸς ἐγερθεὶς ἐκ
him,　knowing that　Christ　having been raised up from among [the]

νεκρῶν, οὐκέτι ἀποθνήσκει· θάνατος αὐτοῦ οὐκέτι κυριεύει.
dead,　no more　dies:　death [5]him [1]no [2]more [3]rules [4]over.

10 Pὃ⁰ γὰρ ἀπέθανεν, τῇ ἁμαρτίᾳ ἀπέθανεν ἐφάπαξ. Pὃ⁰.δὲ
For in that he died,　to sin　he died once for all ; but in that

ζῇ, ζῇ τῷ θεῷ. 11 οὕτως καὶ ὑμεῖς λογίζεσθε ἑαυτοὺς
he lives, he lives to God.　So also ye　reckon　yourselves

νεκροὺς μὲν ʳεἶναι⁰ τῇ ἁμαρτίᾳ, ζῶντας.δὲ τῷ θεῷ, ἐν χριστῷ
[3]dead [4]indeed [1]to [2]be　to sin,　but alive　to God, in　Christ

Ἰησοῦ ˢτῷ.κυρίῳ.ἡμῶν.⁰ 12 Μὴ οὖν βασιλευέτω ἡ ἁμαρτία
Jesus　our Lord.　[2]Not [4]therefore [1]let [5]reign　[3]sin

ἐν τῷ.θνητῷ.ὑμῶν· σώματι, εἰς τὸ ὑπακούειν ᵗαὐτῇ ἐν ᵛταῖς
in　your mortal　body,　for　to obey　it　in

ἐπιθυμίαις.αὐτοῦ·⁰ 13 μηδὲ παριστάνετε τὰ.μέλη.ὑμῶν ὅπλα
its desires.　Neither　be yielding　your members instruments

ἀδικίας τῇ ἁμαρτίᾳ· ἀλλὰ παραστήσατε ἑαυτοὺς τῷ
of unrighteousness　to sin,　but　yield　yourselves

θεῷ ʷὡς⁰ ἐκ νεκρῶν ζῶντας, καὶ τὰ.μέλη.ὑμῶν
to God as　[2]from [3]among [4]the] [5]dead　[1]alive,　and　your members

ὅπλα δικαιοσύνης τῷ θεῷ. 14 ἁμαρτία.γὰρ ὑμῶν οὐ
instruments of righteousness　to God.　For sin　[1]you [2]not

κυριεύσει· οὐ.γὰρ ἐστε ὑπὸ νόμον, ˣἀλλ⁰ ὑπὸ χάριν.
[1]shall [3]rule [4]over, for [3]not [2]are [1]ye under law,　but　under grace.

15 Τί οὖν; ʸἁμαρτήσομεν⁰ ὅτι οὐκ.ἐσμὲν ὑπὸ νόμον,
What then?　shall we sin　because we are not　under　law

ˣἀλλ⁰ ὑπὸ χάριν; μὴ.γένοιτο. 16 οὐκ.οἴδατε ὅτι ᾧ
but　under grace?　May it not be !　Know ye not that to whom

παριστάνετε ἑαυτοὺς δούλους εἰς ὑπακοήν, δοῦλοί ἐστε
ye yield　yourselves bondmen　for　obedience,　bondmen ye are

ᾧ ὑπακούετε, ἤτοι ἁμαρτίας εἰς θάνατον, ἢ ὑπακοῆς
to him whom ye obey,　whether of sin to　death,　or of obedience

εἰς δικαιοσύνην; 17 χάρις.δὲ τῷ.θεῷ, ὅτι ἦτε δοῦλοι τῆς
to righteousness?　But thanks [be]　to God, that ye were bondmen

ἁμαρτίας, ὑπηκούσατε.δὲ ἐκ καρδίας εἰς ὃν παρεδόθητε
of sin,　but ye obeyed　from [the] heart [5]to [6]which [7]ye [8]were [9]delivered

τύπον διδαχῆς. 18 ἐλευθερωθέντες.δὲ ἀπὸ τῆς ἁμαρτίας,
[1]a [2]form [3]of [4]teaching.　And having been set free from　sin,

ἐδουλώθητε τῇ δικαιοσύνῃ. 19 Ἀνθρώπινον λέγω διὰ
ye became bondmen　to righteousness.　Humanly　I speak on account of

τὴν ἀσθένειαν τῆς.σαρκὸς.ὑμῶν. ὥσπερ.γὰρ παρεστήσατε
the　weakness　of your flesh.　For as　ye yielded

τὰ.μέλη.ὑμῶν δοῦλα τῇ ἀκαθαρσίᾳ καὶ τῇ ἀνομίᾳ εἰς τὴν
your members in bondage　to uncleanness and　to lawlessness unto

ἀνομίαν, οὕτως νῦν παραστήσατε τὰ.μέλη.ὑμῶν δοῦλα τῇ
lawlessness,　so　now　yield　your members　in bondage

δικαιοσύνῃ εἰς ἁγιασμόν. 20 ὅτε.γὰρ δοῦλοι ἦτε τῆς
to righteousness unto sanctification.　For when bondmen ye were

---

° συνζ- LTTrA.　P ὃ E.　�q + εἶναι to be T[Tr].　ʳ — εἶναι GLTTrAW.　ˢ — τῷ
κυρίῳ ἡμῶν GLTTrAW.　ᵗ — αὐτῇ ἐν GLTTrAW.　ᵛ — ταῖς ἐπιθυμίαις αὐτοῦ G.　ʷ ὡσεὶ
LTTrA.　ˣ ἀλλὰ LTTrAW.　ʸ ἁμαρτήσωμεν should we sin LTTrAW.

ἁμαρτίας, ἐλεύθεροι ἦτε τῇ δικαιοσύνῃ. 21 τίνα οὖν
of sin, free ye were as to righteousness. What ²therefore

καρπὸν εἴχετε τότε,ᶻ ἐφ᾽.οἷς νῦν ἐπαισχύνεσθε;
¹fruit had ye then, in the [things] of which now ye are ashamed?

τὸ·ª.γὰρ τέλος ἐκείνων θάνατος. 22 νυνὶ.δὲ ἐλευθερω-
for the end of those things [is] death. But now having been

θέντες ἀπὸ τῆς ἁμαρτίας, δουλωθέντες.δὲ τῷ θεῷ, ἔχετε
set free from sin, and having become bondmen to God, ye have

τὸν.καρπὸν.ὑμῶν εἰς ἁγιασμόν, τὸ.δὲ τέλος ζωὴν αἰώνιον.
your fruit unto sanctification, and the end life eternal.

23 τὰ.γὰρ ὀψώνια τῆς ἁμαρτίας θάνατος· τὸ.δὲ χάρισμα
For the wages of sin [is] death; but the free gift

τοῦ θεοῦ ζωὴ αἰώνιος ἐν χριστῷ Ἰησοῦ τῷ.κυρίῳ.ἡμῶν.
of God life eternal in Christ Jesus our Lord.

7 Ἤ.ἀγνοεῖτε, ἀδελφοί, γινώσκουσιν.γὰρ νόμον λαλῶ, ὅτι
Are ye ignorant, brethren, for to those knowing law I speak, that

ὁ νόμος κυριεύει τοῦ ἀνθρώπου ἐφ᾽ ὅσον χρόνον ζῇ;
the law rules over the man for as long ²as ¹time he may live?

2 ἡ.γὰρ ὕπανδρος γυνὴ τῷ ζῶντι ἀνδρὶ δέδεται νόμῳ·
For the married woman to the living husband is bound by law;

ἐὰν.δὲ ἀποθάνῃ ὁ ἀνὴρ κατήργηται ἀπὸ ᵇτοῦ νόμου‖ τοῦ
but if should die the husband, she is cleared from the law of the

ἀνδρός. 3 ἄρα.οὖν ζῶντος τοῦ ἀνδρὸς μοιχαλὶς χρηματίσει,
husband: so then, ³living ¹the ²husband, an adulteress she shall be called,

ἐὰν γένηται ἀνδρὶ ἑτέρῳ· ἐὰν.δὲ ἀποθάνῃ ὁ ἀνήρ, ἐλευθέρα
if she be to ²man ¹another; but if should die the husband, free

ἐστὶν ἀπὸ τοῦ νόμου, τοῦ.μὴ.εἶναι.αὐτὴν μοιχαλίδα, γενο-
she is from the law, so as for her not to be an adulteress, having

μένην ἀνδρὶ ἑτέρῳ. 4 ὥστε, ἀδελφοί.μου, καὶ ὑμεῖς ἐθανατώ-
become to ²man ¹another. So that, my brethren, also ye were made

θητε τῷ νόμῳ διὰ τοῦ σώματος τοῦ χριστοῦ, εἰς τὸ γενέσθαι
dead to the law by the body of the Christ, for ²to ³be

ὑμᾶς ἑτέρῳ, τῷ ἐκ νεκρῶν ἐγερθέντι, ἵνα καρπο-
¹you to another, who from among [the] dead was raised, that we should

φορήσωμεν τῷ θεῷ. 5 ὅτε.γὰρ ἦμεν ἐν τῇ σαρκί, τὰ παθή-
bring forth fruit to God. For when we were in the flesh, the pas-

ματα τῶν ἁμαρτιῶν τὰ διὰ τοῦ νόμου ἐνηργεῖτο ἐν
sions of sins, which [were] through the law, wrought in

τοῖς.μέλεσιν.ἡμῶν εἰς τὸ καρποφορῆσαι τῷ θανάτῳ· 6 νυνὶ.δὲ
our members to the bringing forth fruit to death; but now

κατηργήθημεν ἀπὸ τοῦ νόμου, ᶜἀποθανόντες‖ ἐν ᾧ κατει-
we were cleared from the law, having died [in that] in which we were

χόμεθα, ὥστε δουλεύειν ᵈἡμᾶς‖ ἐν καινότητι πνεύματος, καὶ
held, so that ²should ³serve ¹we in newness of spirit, and

οὐ παλαιότητι γράμματος.
not in oldness of letter.

7 Τί οὖν ἐροῦμεν; ὁ νόμος ἁμαρτία; μὴ.γένοιτο·
What then shall we say? [Is] the law sin? May it not be!

ἀλλὰ τὴν ἁμαρτίαν οὐκ.ἔγνων εἰ.μὴ διὰ νόμου· τήν.τε.γὰρ
But sin I knew not unless by law: for also

ἐπιθυμίαν οὐκ.ᾔδειν εἰ.μὴ ὁ νόμος ἔλεγεν, Οὐκ
lust I had not been conscious of unless the law said, ³Not

ἐπιθυμήσεις· 8 ἀφορμὴν.δὲ λαβοῦσα ἡ ἁμαρτία διὰ τῆς
¹thou ²shalt lust; but ⁴an ⁵occasion ²having ³taken ¹sin by the

---

the servants of sin, ye were free from right-eousness. 21 What fruit had ye then in those things whereof ye are now ashamed? for the end of those things is death. 22 But now being made free from sin, and become servants to God, ye have your fruit unto holiness, and the end everlasting life. 23 For the wages of sin is death; but the gift of God is eternal life through Jesus Christ our Lord.

VII. Know ye not, brethren, (for I speak to them that know the law,) how that the law hath domi-nion over a man as long as he liveth? 2 For the woman which hath an hus-band is bound by the law to her husband so long as he liveth; but if the husband be dead, she is loosed from the law of her husband. 3 So then if, while her husband liveth, she be married to another man, she shall be called an a-dulteress: but if her husband be dead, she is free from that law; so that she is no adul-teress, though she be married to another man. 4 Wherefore, my brethren, ye also are become dead to the law by the body of Christ; that ye should be married to another, even to him who is raised from the dead, that we should bring forth fruit unto God. 5 For when we were in the flesh, the motions of sins, which were by the law, did work in our members to bring forth fruit unto death. 6 But now we are de-livered from the law, that being dead where-in we were held; that we should serve in newness of spirit, and not in the oldness of the letter.

7 What shall we say then? Is the law sin? God forbid. Nay, I had not known sin, but by the law: for I had not known lust, except the law had said, Thou shalt not covet. 8 But sin,

taking occasion by the commandment, wrought in me all manner of concupiscence. For without the law sin was dead. 9 For I was alive without the law once: but when the commandment came, sin revived, and I died. 10 And the commandment, which was ordained to life, I found to be unto death. 11 For sin, taking occasion by the commandment, deceived me, and by it slew me. 12 Wherefore the law is holy, and the commandment holy, and just, and good. 13 Was then that which is good made death unto me? God forbid. But sin, that it might appear sin, working death in me by that which is good; that sin by the commandment might become exceeding sinful. 14 For we know that the law is spiritual: but I am carnal, sold under sin. 15 For that which I do I allow not: for what I would, that do I not; but what I hate, that do I. 16 If then I do that which I would not, I consent unto the law that it is good. 17 Now then it is no more I that do it, but sin that dwelleth in me. 18 For I know that in me (that is, in my flesh,) dwelleth no good thing: for to will is present with me; but how to perform that which is good I find not. 19 For the good that I would I do not: but the evil which I would not, that I do. 20 Now if I do that I would not, it is no more I that do it, but sin that dwelleth in me. 21 I find then a law, that, when I would do good, evil is present with me. 22 For I delight in the law of God after the inward man: 23 but I see another law in my

ἐντολῆς ᵉκατειργάσατο‖ ἐν ἐμοὶ πᾶσαν ἐπιθυμίαν. χωρὶς·γὰρ
commandment, worked out in me every lust; for apart from

νόμου ἁμαρτία νεκρά· 9 ἐγὼ·δὲ ἔζων χωρὶς νόμου
law sin [was] dead. But I was alive apart from law

ποτέ ἐλθούσης·δὲ τῆς ἐντολῆς, ἡ ἁμαρτία ἀνέζησεν, ἐγὼ·δὲ
once; but having come the commandment, sin revived, but I

ἀπέθανον· 10 καὶ εὑρέθη μοι ἡ ἐντολὴ ἡ
died. And was found to me [that] the commandment which [was]

εἰς ζωήν, ᶠαὕτη‖ εἰς θάνατον. 11 ἡ·γὰρ·ἁμαρτία ἀφορμὴν
to life, this [to be] to death: for sin ³an ⁴occasion

λαβοῦσα διὰ τῆς ἐντολῆς ἐξηπάτησέν με, καὶ δι' αὐτῆς
¹having ²taken by the commandment, deceived me, and by it

ἀπέκτεινεν. 12 ὥστε ὁ·μὲν·νόμος ἅγιος, καὶ ἡ ἐντολὴ
slew [me]. So that the law indeed [is] holy, and the commandment

ἁγία καὶ δικαία καὶ ἀγαθή. 13 Τὸ οὖν ἀγαθὸν ἐμοὶ
holy and just and good. That which then [is] good, to me

ᵍγέγονεν‖ θάνατος; μὴ·γένοιτο· ʰἀλλὰ‖ ἡ ἁμαρτία, ἵνα
has it become death? May it not be! But sin, that

φανῇ ἁμαρτία, διὰ τοῦ ἀγαθοῦ μοι κατεργαζζμένη
it might appear sin, by that which [is] good to me working out

θάνατον, ἵνα γένηται καθ'·ὑπερβολὴν ἁμαρτωλὸς ἡ·ἁμαρτία
death; that ²might ³become ⁴excessively ⁵sinful ¹sin

διὰ τῆς ἐντολῆς. 14 Οἴδαμεν·γὰρ ὅτι ὁ νόμος πνευματικός
by the commandment. For we know that the law spiritual

ἐστιν· ἐγὼ·δὲ ¹σαρκικός‖ εἰμι, πεπραμένος ὑπὸ τὴν ἁμαρτίαν.
is; but I ²fleshly ¹am, having been sold under sin.

15 ὃ·γὰρ κατεργάζομαι, οὐ·γινώσκω· οὐ·γὰρ ὃ θέλω, τοῦτο
For what I work out, I do not own: for not what I will, this

πράσσω· ἀλλ' ὃ μισῶ, τοῦτο ποιῶ. 16 εἰ·δὲ ὃ οὐ·θέλω,
I do; but what I hate, this I practise. But if what I do not will,

τοῦτο ποιῶ, ᵏσύμφημι‖ τῷ νόμῳ ὅτι καλός. 17 νυνὶ·δὲ
this I practise, I consent to the law that [it is] right. Now then

οὐκέτι ἐγὼ κατεργάζομαι αὐτό, ¹ἀλλ'‖ ἡ ᵐοἰκοῦσα‖ ἐν ἐμοὶ
no longer ²I ¹am working ²out ¹it; but the ²dwelling ³in ⁴me

ἁμαρτία. 18 Οἶδα·γὰρ ὅτι οὐκ·οἰκεῖ ἐν ἐμοί, ⁿτουτέστιν‖ ἐν
¹sin. For I know that there dwells not in me, that is in

τῇ·σαρκί·μου, ἀγαθόν· τὸ·γὰρ·θέλειν παράκειταί μοι, τὸ δὲ
my flesh, good: for to will is present with me, but

κατεργάζεσθαι τὸ καλὸν ᵒοὐχ·εὑρίσκω.‖ 19 οὐ·γὰρ ὃ θέλω
to work out the right I find not. For not what ²I ³will

ποιῶ ἀγαθόν· ᴾἀλλ'‖ ὃ οὐ·θέλω κακόν, τοῦτο πράσ-
I do good; but what ²I ³do ⁴not ⁵will ¹evil, this I do.

σω. 20 εἰ·δὲ ὃ οὐ·θέλω �q ἐγώ,‖ τοῦτο ποιῶ, οὐκέτι
But if what ²do ³not ⁴will ¹I, this I practise, [it is] no longer

ἐγὼ κατεργάζομαι αὐτό, ᴾἀλλ'‖ ἡ οἰκοῦσα ἐν ἐμοὶ ἁμαρτία.
I [who] work ²out ¹it, but the ²dwelling ³in ⁴me ¹sin.

21 Εὑρίσκω ἄρα τὸν νόμον τῷ θέλοντι ἐμοὶ ποιεῖν τὸ καλόν,
I find then the law ³who ⁴will ¹to ²me to practise the right,

ὅτι ἐμοὶ τὸ κακὸν παράκειται. 22 συνήδομαι·γὰρ τῷ νόμῳ
that me evil is present with. For I delight in the law

τοῦ θεοῦ κατὰ τὸν ἔσω ἄνθρωπον· 23 βλέπω·δὲ ἕτερον
of God according to the inward man: but I see another

ᵉ κατηργάσατο TTrA.   ᶠ αὐτὴ GW.   ᵍ ἐγένετο did it become LTTrAW.   ʰ ἀλλ' LA.
ⁱ σάρκινός fleshly GLTTrAW.   ᵏ σύν- T.   ¹ ἀλλὰ LTTrA.   ᵐ ἐνοικοῦσα T.   ⁿ τοῦτ'
ἔστιν GT.   ᵒ οὐ [is] not LTTrA.   ᴾ ἀλλὰ TTrA.   q — ἐγώ (read οὐ θέλω I do not will)
ᴸᵀᵣ[A]W.

νόμον ἐν τοῖς.μέλεσίν.μου ἀντιστρατευόμενον τῷ νόμῳ τοῦ
law　in　my members　　warring against　　the　law
νοός.μου, καὶ αἰχμαλωτίζοντά με ʳ τῷ νόμῳ τῆς ἁμαρτίας
of my mind, and　leading ²captive　¹me to the law　　　of sin
τῷ ὄντι ἐν τοῖς.μέλεσίν.μου. 24 ταλαίπωρος ἐγὼ ἄνθρωπος·
which　is　in　my members.　　O wretched　⁴I　¹man !
τίς με ῥύσεται ἐκ τοῦ σώματος τοῦ.θανάτου.τούτου ;
who ³me ¹shall ²deliver out of the　body　　of this death ?
25 ˢεὐχαριστῶ‖ τῷ θεῷ διὰ Ἰησοῦ χριστοῦ τοῦ.κυρίου.ἡμῶν·
I thank　　God through Jesus　Christ　　our Lord.
ἄρα.οὖν αὐτὸς ἐγὼ τῷ ¹μὲν‖ νοῒ δουλεύω νόμῳ θεοῦ·
So then ²myself ¹I with the ²indeed ¹mind　serve　²law ¹God's ;
τῇ.δὲ σαρκὶ νόμῳ ἁμαρτίας.
but with the flesh　²law　　¹sin's.

8 Οὐδὲν.ἄρα.νῦν κατάκριμα τοῖς ἐν χριστῷ Ἰηι οῦ, ᵘμὴ
[There is] then now no　condemnation to those in　Christ　Jesus,　³not
κατὰ σάρκα περιπατοῦσιν, ἀλλὰ κατὰ πνεῦμα.‖ 2 ὁ.γὰρ
⁴according ⁵to ⁶flesh　¹who ²walk,　　but according to Spirit.　For the
νόμος τοῦ πνεύματος τῆς ζωῆς ἐν χριστῷ Ἰησοῦ ἠλευθέρωσέν
law of the Spirit　of life in　Christ Jesus　set ²free
ᵛμε‖ ἀπὸ τοῦ νόμου τῆς ἁμαρτίας καὶ τοῦ θανάτου. 3 Τὸ γὰρ
¹me from the law　of sin and　of death.　　For
ἀδύνατον τοῦ νόμου, ἐν.ᾧ ἠσθένει διὰ τῆς σαρκός,
⁴powerless [³being] ¹the ²law,　in that it was weak through the　flesh,
ὁ θεὸς τὸν.ἑαυτοῦ υἱὸν πέμψας ἐν ὁμοιώματι σαρκὸς ἁμαρτίας
God,　³his ¹own　⁴Son ²having ²sent, in　likeness　of flesh　of sin,
καὶ περὶ.ἁμαρτίας κατέκρινεν τὴν ἁμαρτίαν ἐν τῇ σαρκί, 4 ἵνα
and　for　sin,　condemned　sin　in the flesh,　that
τὸ δικαίωμα τοῦ νόμου πληρωθῇ ἐν ἡμῖν, τοῖς μὴ κατὰ
the requirement of the law should be fulfilled in us,　who not according to
σάρκα περιπατοῦσιν, ἀλλὰ κατὰ πνεῦμα. 5 Οἱ.γὰρ
flesh　walk,　　but　according to　Spirit.　For they that
κατὰ σάρκα ὄντες, τὰ τῆς σαρκὸς φρονοῦσιν· οἱ.δὲ
according to flesh　are, the things of the flesh　mind ;　and they
κατὰ πνεῦμα, τὰ τοῦ πνεύματος. 6 τὸ.γὰρ φρόνημα
according to Spirit, the things of the Spirit.　For the　mind
τῆς σαρκὸς θάνατος· τὸ.δὲ φρόνημα τοῦ πνεύματος, ζωὴ
of the flesh [is] death ; but the　mind　of the　Spirit,　life
καὶ εἰρήνη. 7 Διότι τὸ φρόνημα τῆς σαρκὸς ἔχθρα εἰς
and　peace.　Because the　mind　of the flesh [is] enmity towards
θεόν· τῷ.γὰρ νόμῳ τοῦ θεοῦ οὐχ.ὑποτάσσεται, οὐδὲ.γὰρ δύνα-
God : for to the　law　of God it is not subject ;　for neither　can
ται· 8 οἱ.δὲ ἐν σαρκὶ ὄντες, θεῷ.ἀρέσαι οὐ.δύνανται.
it [be] ; and they that ²in　³flesh　¹are,　⁶God ⁵please　⁴cannot.
9 Ὑμεῖς.δὲ οὐκ ἐστὲ ἐν σαρκί, ʷἀλλ᾽‖ ἐν πνεύματι, εἴπερ
But ye ²not ¹are in flesh,　but　in　Spirit,　if indeed [the]
πνεῦμα θεοῦ οἰκεῖ ἐν ὑμῖν. εἰ.δέ τις πνεῦμα χριστοῦ
Spirit　of God dwells in　you ;　but if anyone [the] Spirit　of Christ
οὐκ.ἔχει, οὗτος οὐκ.ἔστιν αὐτοῦ. 10 εἰ.δὲ χριστὸς ἐν ὑμῖν, τὸ
has not,　he　is not of him : but if　Christ [be] in you, the
μὲν σῶμα νεκρὸν ˣδι᾽‖ ἁμαρτίαν, τὸ.δὲ πνεῦμα ζωὴ
²indeed ¹body [is] dead on account of　sin,　but the　Spirit　life
διὰ δικαιοσύνην. 11 εἰ.δὲ τὸ πνεῦμα τοῦ ἐγείραντος ʸ
on account of righteousness.　But if the. Spirit　of him who　raised up

members, warring a-
gainst the law of my
mind, and bringing
me into captivity to
the law of sin which
is in my members.
24 O wretched man
that I am ! who shall
deliver me from the
body of this death ?
25 I thank God
through Jesus Christ
our Lord. So then
with the mind I my-
self serve the law of
God ; but with the
flesh the law of sin.

VIII. There is there-
fore now no condem-
nation to them which
are in Christ Jesus,
who walk not after
the flesh, but after the
Spirit. 2 For the law
of the Spirit of life
in Christ Jesus hath
made me free from
the law of sin and
death. 3 For what the
law could not do,
in that it was weak
through the flesh, God
sending his own Son
in the likeness of sin-
ful flesh, and for sin,
condemned sin in the
flesh : 4 that the right-
eousness of the law
might be fulfilled in
us, who walk not after
the flesh, but after the
Spirit. 5 For they that
are after the flesh do
mind the things of
the flesh ; but they
that are after the
Spirit the things of
the Spirit. 6 For to be
carnally minded is
death ; but. to be spi-
ritually minded is life
and peace. 7 Because
the carnal mind is
enmity against God :
for it is not subject to
the law of God, nei-
ther indeed can be.
8 So then they that
are in the flesh can-
not please God. 9 But
ye are not in the flesh,
but in the Spirit, if so
be that the Spirit of
God dwell in you.
Now if any man have
not the Spirit of
Christ, he is none of
his. 10 And if Christ
be in you, the body is
dead because of sin ;
but the Spirit is life
because of righteous-
ness. 11 But if the
Spirit of him that
raised up Jesus from
the dead dwell in
you, he that rais-
ed up Christ from

ʳ + ἐν in (the) ΤΤr[Α].　　ˢ χάρις thanks (to God) LTTrA.　　ᵗ — μὲν Τ.　　ᵘ — μὴ κατὰ τὸ
end of verse GLTTrAW.　　ᵛ σε thee Τ.　　ʷ ἀλλὰ ΤΤrΑ.　　ˣ διὰ LTTrΑ.　　ʸ + τὸν ΤΤr[Α].

the dead shall also quicken your mortal bodies by his Spirit that dwelleth in you. 12 Therefore, brethren, we are debtors, not to the flesh, to live after the flesh. 13 For if ye live after the flesh, ye shall die: but if ye through the Spirit do mortify the deeds of the body, ye shall live. 14 For as many as are led by the Spirit of God, they are the sons of God. 15 For ye have not received the spirit of bondage again to fear; but ye have received the Spirit of adoption, whereby we cry, Abba, Father. 16 The Spirit itself beareth witness with our spirit, that we are the children of God: 17 And if children, then heirs; heirs of God, and joint-heirs with Christ; if so be that we suffer with him, that we may be also glorified together.

18 For I reckon that the sufferings of this present time are not worthy to be compared with the glory which shall be revealed in us. 19 For the earnest expectation of the creature waiteth for the manifestation of the sons of God. 20 For the creature was made subject to vanity, not willingly, but by reason of him who hath subjected the same in hope, 21 because the creature itself also shall be delivered from the bondage of corruption into the glorious liberty of the children of God. 22 For we know that the whole creation groaneth and travaileth in pain together until now. 23 And not only they, but ourselves also, which have the firstfruits of the Spirit, even we ourselves groan within ourselves, waiting for the adoption, to wit, the redemption of our body. 24 For we are saved by hope: but hope that is seen is not hope: for what a

'Ιησοῦν ἐκ νεκρῶν οἰκεῖ ἐν ὑμῖν, ὁ ἐγείρας ᶻτὸν‖
Jesus from among [the] dead dwells in you, he who raised up the
ᵃχριστὸν ἐκ νεκρῶν‖ ζωοποιήσει καὶ τὰ θνητὰ σώματα
Christ from among [the] dead will quicken also ²mortal ³bodies
ὑμῶν διὰ ᵇτὸ ἐνοικοῦν αὐτοῦ πνεῦμα‖ ἐν ὑμῖν. 12 Ἄρα
¹your on account of ³that ⁴dwells ¹his ²Spirit in you. So
οὖν, ἀδελφοί, ὀφειλέται ἐσμέν οὐ τῇ σαρκί, τοῦ κατὰ σάρκα
then, brethren, debtors we are, not to the flesh, ³according ⁴to ⁵flesh
ζῆν· 13 εἰ.γὰρ κατὰ σάρκα ζῆτε, μέλλετε ἀποθνήσκειν·
¹to ²live; for if according to flesh ye live, ye are about to die;
εἰ.δὲ πνεύματι τὰς πράξεις τοῦ σώματος θανατοῦτε, ζήσεσθε.
but if by [the] Spirit the deeds of the body ye put to death, ye will live:
14 Ὅσοι.γὰρ πνεύματι θεοῦ ἄγονται, οὗτοί ᶜεἰσιν υἱοὶ θεοῦ.‖
for as many as by [the] Spirit of God are led, these are sons of God.
15 οὐ.γὰρ ἐλάβετε πνεῦμα ᵈδουλείας‖ πάλιν εἰς φόβον, ᵉἀλλ'‖
For ³not ¹ye ²received a spirit of bondage again unto fear, but
ἐλάβετε πνεῦμα υἱοθεσίας, ἐν.ᾧ κράζομεν, Ἀββᾶ, ὁ πατήρ.
ye received a Spirit of adoption, whereby we cry, Abba, Father.
16 Αὐτὸ τὸ πνεῦμα ᶠσυμμαρτυρεῖ‖ τῷ.πνεύματι.ἡμῶν, ὅτι
³Itself ¹the ²Spirit bears witness with our spirit, that
ἐσμὲν τέκνα θεοῦ. 17 εἰ.δὲ τέκνα, καὶ κληρονόμοι· κληρονόμοι
we are children of God. And if children, also heirs: heirs
μὲν θεοῦ, ᵍσυγκληρονόμοι‖.δὲ χριστοῦ· εἴπερ ᵍσυμπάσχομεν,‖
indeed of God, and joint-heirs of Christ; if indeed we suffer together,
ἵνα καὶ συνδοξασθῶμεν.
that also we may be glorified together.

18 Λογίζομαι.γὰρ ὅτι οὐκ ἄξια τὰ παθήματα τοῦ νῦν
For I reckon that not worthy [are] the sufferings of the present
καιροῦ πρὸς τὴν μέλλουσαν δόξαν ἀποκαλυφθῆναι
time [to be compared] with the ²about ¹glory to be revealed
εἰς ἡμᾶς. 19 Ἡ.γὰρ ἀποκαραδοκία τῆς κτίσεως τὴν ἀποκά-
to us. For the earnest expectation of the creation ²the ³reve-
λυψιν τῶν υἱῶν τοῦ θεοῦ ἀπεκδέχεται. 20 τῇ.γὰρ.ματαιότητι
lation ⁴of ⁵the ⁶sons ⁷of ⁸God ¹awaits; for to vanity
ἡ κτίσις ὑπετάγη, οὐχ ἑκοῦσα, ἀλλὰ διὰ τὸν ὑπο-
the creation was subjected, not willingly, but by reason of him who sub-
τάξαντα, ʰἐπ'‖ ἐλπίδι 21 ᶦὅτι‖ καὶ αὐτὴ ἡ κτίσις ἐλευθερω-
jected [it], in hope that also ¹the ²creation shall be
θήσεται ἀπὸ τῆς ʲδουλείας‖ τῆς φθορᾶς εἰς τὴν ἐλευθερίαν
freed from the bondage of corruption into the freedom
τῆς δόξης τῶν τέκνων τοῦ θεοῦ. 22 οἴδαμεν.γὰρ ὅτι πᾶσα ἡ
of the glory of the children of God. For we know that all the
κτίσις ᵍσυστενάζει‖ καὶ συνωδίνει ἄχρι τοῦ νῦν· 23 οὐ
creation groans together and travails together until now. ²Not
μόνον δέ, ἀλλὰ καὶ αὐτοὶ τὴν ἀπαρχὴν τοῦ πνεύματος
³only ¹and [so], but even ourselves the first-fruit of the Spirit
ἔχοντες, ᵏκαὶ ἡμεῖς‖ αὐτοὶ ἐν ἑαυτοῖς στενάζομεν, υἱοθεσίαν
having, also we ourselves ²in ³ourselves ¹groan, ⁴adoption
ἀπεκδεχόμενοι, τὴν ἀπολύτρωσιν τοῦ.σώματος.ἡμῶν. 24 τῇ
⁵awaiting— the redemption of our body.
γὰρ.ἐλπίδι ἐσώθημεν· ἐλπὶς.δὲ βλεπομένη οὐκ.ἐστιν ἐλπίς·
For in hope we were saved; but hope seen is not hope;

ᶻ — τὸν LTTrA. ᵃ χριστὸν ['Ιησοῦν] (Jesus) ἐκ νεκρῶν L; ἐκ νεκρῶν χριστὸν 'Ιησοῦν T.
ᵇ τοῦ ἐνοικοῦντος αὐτοῦ πνεύματος (read as A. V.) ET. ᶜ υἱοί εἰσιν θεοῦ LTTrAW. ᵈ δουλίας T. ᵉ ἀλλὰ LTTrA. ᶠ συν- T. ᵍ συν- TA. ʰ ἐφ' T. ᶦ διότι T. ʲ δουλίας T.
ᵏ ἡμεῖς καὶ TA; [ἡμεῖς] καὶ LTr.

ὅ.γὰρ βλέπει τις τί ᵐκαὶᴵᴵ ἐλπίζει; 25 εἰ.δὲ ὃ οὐ
for what　²sees　¹anyone　why　also　does he hope for?　But if what ³not

βλέπομεν ἐλπίζομεν, δι' ὑπομονῆς ἀπεκδεχόμεθα. 26 Ὡσαύτως
¹we ²see　we hope for, in endurance ¹　we await.　²In ¹like ⁴manner

δὲ καὶ τὸ πνεῦμα συναντιλαμβάνεται ⁿταῖς.ἀσθενείαιςᴵᴵ.ἡμῶν·
¹and also the　Spirit　jointly helps　our weaknesses ;

τὸ.γὰρ τί προσευξώμεθα καθὸ δεῖ, οὐκ.οἴδαμεν, °ἀλλ'ᴵᴵ
for that which we should pray for according as it behoves, we know not,　but

αὐτὸ τὸ πνεῦμα ὑπερεντυγχάνει ᴾὑπὲρ ἡμῶνᴵᴵ στεναγμοῖς
³itself ⁴the　²Spirit　makes intercession　for　us　with groanings

ἀλαλήτοις· 27 ὁ.δὲ ᵠἐρευνῶνᴵᴵ τὰς καρδίας οἶδεν τί τὸ
inexpressible　But he who searches　the　hearts　knows what [is] the

φρόνημα τοῦ πνεύματος, ὅτι κατὰ θεὸν ἐντυγχάνει ὑπὲρ
mind　of the Spirit,　because according to God　he intercedes　for

ἁγίων. 28 Οἴδαμεν.δὲ ὅτι τοῖς ἀγαπῶσιν τὸν θεὸν πάντα
saints.　But we know that to those who love　God　all things

ʳσυνεργεῖᴵᴵ εἰς ἀγαθόν, τοῖς κατὰ πρόθεσιν κλητοῖς
work together for　good, to those who according to purpose ²called

οὖσιν. 29 ὅτι οὓς προέγνω, καὶ προώρισεν συμμόρ-
¹are.　Because whom he foreknew, also he predestinated [to be] conformed

φους τῆς εἰκόνος τοῦ.υἱοῦ.αὐτοῦ, εἰς τὸ εἶναι αὐτὸν πρω-
to the　image　of his Son,　for　²to ³be ¹him [the] first-

τότοκον ἐν πολλοῖς ἀδελφοῖς· 30 οὓς.δὲ προώρισεν. τούτους
born among　many　brethren.　But whom he predestinated, these

καὶ ἐκάλεσεν· καὶ οὓς ἐκάλεσεν, τούτους καὶ ἐδικαίωσεν· οὓς
also he called ; and whom he called, these also he justified ; ²whom

δὲ ἐδικαίωσεν, τούτους καὶ ἐδόξασεν.
¹but he justified,　these also he glorified.

31 Τί οὖν ἐροῦμεν πρὸς ταῦτα; εἰ ὁ θεὸς ὑπὲρ ἡμῶν,
What then shall we say to these things? If God [be] for　us,

τίς καθ' ἡμῶν; 32 ὅς γε τοῦ.ἰδίου.υἱοῦ οὐκ.ἐφείσατο, ˢἀλλ'ᴵᴵ
who against us?　Who indeed　his own Son　spared not,　but

ὑπὲρ ἡμῶν πάντων παρέδωκεν αὐτόν, πῶς οὐχὶ καὶ σὺν αὐτῷ
¹for　us　all　gave up　him,　how ³not ⁴also ⁵with ⁶him

τὰ.πάντα ἡμῖν χαρίσεται; 33 τίς ἐγκαλέσει κατὰ
²all ¹⁰things　⁸us ¹will ²he ⁷grant?　Who shall bring an accusation against

ἐκλεκτῶν θεοῦ; θεὸς ὁ δικαιῶν. 34 τίς ὁ κατα-
[the]　elect　of God ? [It is] God who justifies :　who he that con-

κρίνων; χριστὸς ᵗ ὁ ἀποθανών, μᾶλλον.δὲ ⱽκαὶᴵᴵ ἐγερθείς,
demns?　[It is] Christ who died,　but rather　also is raised up;

ὃς ʷκαὶᴵᴵ ἔστιν ἐν δεξιᾷ τοῦ θεοῦ, ὃς καὶ ἐντυγχάνει ὑπὲρ
who also is　at [the] right hand of God ; who also intercedes for

ἡμῶν. 35 τίς ἡμᾶς χωρίσει ἀπὸ τῆς ἀγάπης τοῦ χριστοῦ;
us :　who us shall separate from the　love　of Christ?

θλῖψις, ἢ στενοχωρία, ἢ διωγμός, ἢ λιμός, ἢ γυμνότης, ἢ
tribulation, or　strait,　or persecution, or famine, or nakedness, or

κίνδυνος, ἢ μάχαιρα; 36 καθὼς γέγραπται, "Ὅτι ˣἕνεκά".σου
danger, · or　sword?　According as it has been written,　For thy sake

θανατούμεθα ὅλην τὴν ἡμέραν· ἐλογίσθημεν ὡς πρόβατα
we are put to death ²whole ¹the　day ;　we were reckoned as　sheep

σφαγῆς. 37 Ἀλλ' ἐν τούτοις πᾶσιν ὑπερνικῶμεν διὰ
of slaughter.　But in ²these ³things ¹all we more than overcome through

man seeth, why doth he yet hope for? 25 But if we hope for that we see not, _then_ do we with patience wait for _it_. 26 Likewise the Spirit also helpeth our infirmities: for we know not what we should pray for as we ought: but the Spirit itself maketh intercession for us with groanings which cannot be uttered. 27 And he that searcheth the hearts knoweth what _is_ the mind· of the Spirit, because he maketh intercession for the saints according to _the will of_ God. 28 And we know that all things work together for good to them that love God, to them who are the called according to _his_ purpose. 29 For whom he did foreknow, he also did predestinate _to be_ conformed to the image of his Son, that he might be the firstborn among many brethren. 30 Moreover whom he did predestinate, them he also called: and whom he called, them he also justified: and whom he justified, them he also glorified.

31 What shall we then say to these things? If God _be_ for us, who _can be_ against us? 32 He that spared not his own Son, but delivered him up for us all, how shall he not with him also freely give us all things? 33 Who shall lay any thing to the charge of God's elect? _It is_ God that justifieth. 34 Who _is_ he that condemneth? _It is_ Christ that died, yea rather, that is risen again, who is even at the right hand of God, who also maketh intercession for us. 35 Who shall separate us from the love of Christ? _shall_ tribulation, or distress, or persecution, or famine, or nakedness, or peril, or sword ? 36 As it is written, For thy sake we are killed all the day long ; we are

---

m — καὶ LTⱼ[A].　ⁿ τῇ ἀσθενείᾳ (read our weakness) LTTⱼAW.　° ἀλλὰ TTⱼW.
ᴾ — ὑπὲρ ἡμῶν LTTⱼAW.　ᵠ ἐραννῶν TTⱼ.　ʳ συνεργεῖ ὁ θεὸς God works together Lₐ
ˢ ἀλλὰ LTTⱼA.　ᵗ ⊥ Ἰησοῦς Jesus [L]T.　ⱽ — καὶ LTTⱼ[A].　ʷ — καὶ [L]T.　ˣ ἕνεκαⱼ
GLTTⱼAW.

accounted as sheep for the slaughter. 37 Nay, in all these things we are more than conquerors through him that loved us. 38 For I am persuaded, that neither death, nor life, nor angels, nor principalities, nor powers, nor things present, nor things to come, 39 nor height, nor depth, nor any other creature, shall be able to separate us from the love of God, which is in Christ Jesus our Lord.

IX. I say the truth in Christ, I lie not, my conscience also bearing me witness in the Holy Ghost, 2 that I have great heaviness and continual sorrow in my heart. 3 For I could wish that myself were accursed from Christ for my brethren, my kinsmen according to the flesh: 4 who are Israelites; to whom *pertaineth* the adoption, and the glory, and the covenants, and the giving of the law, and the service *of God*, and the promises; 5 whose *are* the fathers, and of whom as concerning the flesh Christ *came*, who is over all, God blessed for ever. A-men. 6 Not as though the word of God hath taken none effect. For they *are* not all Israel, which are of Israel: 7 Neither, because they are the seed of Abraham, *are they* all children: but, In Isaac shall thy seed be called. 8 That is, They which are the children of the flesh, these *are* not the children of God: but the children of the promise are counted for the seed. 9 For this *is* the word of promise, At this time will I come, and Sarah shall have a son. 10 And not only *this;* but when Rebecca also had conceived by one, *even* by our father Isaac; 11 (for *the children* being not yet born, neither having done any good or evil, that the purpose of God according to election might stand, not of works, but of him that

τοῦ ἀγαπήσαντος ἡμᾶς. 38 πέπεισμαι.γὰρ ὅτι οὔτε
him who　loved　us.　For I am persuaded that neither
θάνατος, οὔτε ζωή, οὔτε ἄγγελοι, οὔτε ἀρχαί, ⁷οὔτε δυ-
death,　nor life,　nor angels,　nor principalities,　nor
νάμεις,‖ οὔτε ἐνεστῶτα, οὔτε μέλλοντα,⁷ 39 οὔτε ὕψωμα, οὔτε
powers,　nor things present,　nor things to be,　nor height,　nor
βάθος, οὔτε τις κτίσις ἑτέρα δυνήσεται ἡμᾶς χωρίσαι
depth,　nor any ²created ³thing ¹other will be able　us　to separate
ἀπὸ τῆς ἀγάπης τοῦ θεοῦ, τῆς ἐν χριστῷ Ἰησοῦ τῷ κυρίῳ
from the　love　of God, which [is] in　Christ　Jesus　²Lord
ἡμῶν.
¹our.

9 Ἀλήθειαν λέγω ἐν χριστῷ, οὐ.ψεύδομαι, ²συμμαρτυρούσης‖
　Truth　I say in Christ,　I lie not,　bearing witness with
μοι τῆς.συνειδήσεώς.μου ἐν πνεύματι ἁγίῳ, 2 ὅτι λύπη
me　my conscience　in [the] ²Spirit ¹Holy,　that ²grief
μοί ἐστιν μεγάλη, καὶ ἀδιάλειπτος ὀδύνη τῇ.καρδίᾳ.μου·
³to ⁴me ¹is ¹great,　and　unceasing　sorrow　in my heart,
3 ηὐχόμην.γὰρ ᵃαὐτὸς ἐγὼ ἀνάθεμα εἶναι‖ ἀπὸ τοῦ χριστοῦ
for I was wishing ²myself ¹I　a curse　to be　from　the　Christ
ὑπὲρ τῶν.ἀδελφῶν.μου, τῶν.συγγενῶν.μου κατὰ σάρκα·
for　my brethren,　my kinsmen　according to flesh;
4 οἵτινές εἰσιν ᵇἸσραηλῖται,‖ ὧν ἡ υἱοθεσία καὶ ἡ δόξα,
who　are　Israelites,　whose [is] the adoption and the glory,
καὶ ᶜαἱ διαθῆκαι‖ καὶ ἡ νομοθεσία, καὶ ἡ λατρεία καὶ αἱ
and the covenants and the lawgiving,　and the service and the
ἐπαγγελίαι, 5 ὧν οἱ πατέρες, καὶ ἐξ ὧν ὁ χριστὸς τὸ
promises;　whose [are] the fathers; and of whom [is] the Christ
κατὰ σάρκα, ὁ ὢν ἐπὶ πάντων θεὸς εὐλογητὸς εἰς τοὺς
according to flesh, who is over　all　God blessed　to the
αἰῶνας. ἀμήν. 6 Οὐχ οἷον.δὲ ὅτι ἐκπέπτωκεν ὁ λόγος τοῦ
ages.　Amen.　Not however that has failed　the word
θεοῦ. οὐ.γὰρ πάντες οἱ ἐξ Ἰσραήλ, οὗτοι Ἰσραήλ·
of God; for not　all ⁴which [⁵are] ⁶of ⁷Israel ¹those [²are] ³Israel:
7 οὐδ᾽ ὅτι εἰσὶν σπέρμα Ἀβραάμ, πάντες τέκνα, ἀλλ᾽
nor because they are seed of Abraham [are] all children: but,
ἐν Ἰσαὰκ κληθήσεταί σοι σπέρμα. 8 ᵈΤουτέστιν,‖ οὐ τὰ
In Isaac shall be called to thee a seed.　That is, ²not ¹the
τέκνα τῆς σαρκός, ταῦτα τέκνα τοῦ θεοῦ· ἀλλὰ τὰ τέκνα
²children ³of ⁴the ⁵flesh, ⁶these [⁷are] children of God; but the children
τῆς ἐπαγγελίας λογίζεται εἰς σπέρμα. 9 ἐπαγγελίας.γὰρ
of the promise　are reckoned for　seed.　For of promise
ὁ.λόγος.οὗτος, Κατὰ τὸν.καιρὸν.τοῦτον ἐλεύσομαι, καὶ
this word [is], According to　this time　I will come, and
ἔσται τῇ Σάρρᾳ υἱός. 10 Οὐ.μόνον.δέ, ἀλλὰ καὶ ᾽Ρε-
there shall be to Sarah a son.　And not only [that], but also Re-
βέκκα ἐξ ἑνὸς κοίτην ἔχουσα, Ἰσαὰκ τοῦ.πατρὸς.ἡμῶν·
becca. ³by ⁴one ²conception ¹having,　Isaac　our father,
11 ᵉμήπω‖ γὰρ γεννηθέντων, μηδὲ πραξάντων
⁴not ⁵yet [²the ³children] ¹for　being born,　nor　having done
τι ἀγαθὸν ἢ ᶠκακόν,‖ ἵνα ἡ κατ᾽ ἐκλογὴν ᵍτοῦ θεοῦ
anything good or evil,　(that the ⁴according ⁵to ⁶election ²of ³God
πρόθεσις‖ μένῃ, οὐκ ἐξ ἔργων, ἀλλ᾽ ἐκ τοῦ καλοῦντος,
¹purpose might abide, not of works,　but of him who calls),

---

⁷ οὔτε δυνάμεις *placed after* μέλλοντα GLTTrAW.　ᶻ συνμ- T.　ᵃ ἀνάθεμα εἶναι αὐτὸς ἐγὼ LTTrAW.　ᵇ Ἰσραηλεῖται T.　ᶜ ἡ διαθήκη the covenant L.　ᵈ τοῦτ᾽ ἔστιν GTTrA.　ᵉ μὴ ᵖⁿ LTr.　ᶠ φαῦλον LTTrA.　ᵍ πρόθεσις τοῦ θεοῦ GLTTrAW.

12 ^hἐρρήθη^{ll} αὐτῇ, "Οτι ὁ μείζων δουλεύσει τῷ ἐλάσσονι·
it was said to her, The greater shall serve the lesser :

13 καθὼς γέγραπται, Τὸν Ἰακὼβ ἠγάπησα, τὸν.δὲ.Ησαῦ
according as it has been written, Jacob I loved, and Esau

ἐμίσησα.
I hated.

14 Τί οὖν ἐροῦμεν; μὴ ἀδικία παρὰ τῷ θεῷ;
What then shall we say? Unrighteousness with God [is there]?

μὴ.γένοιτο· 15 τῷ.ⁱγὰρ.Μωσῇ^{ll} λέγει, Ἐλεήσω ὃν.ἂν
May it not be! For to Moses he says, I will shew mercy to whomsoever

ἐλεῶ, καὶ οἰκτειρήσω ὃν.ἂν οἰκτείρω.
I shew mercy, and I will feel compassion on whomsoever I feel compassion.

16 Ἄρα οὖν οὐ τοῦ θέλοντος, οὐδὲ τοῦ τρέχοντος,
So then [it is] not of him that wills, nor of him that runs,

ἀλλὰ τοῦ ^kἐλεοῦντος^{ll} θεοῦ. 17 λέγει.γὰρ ἡ γραφὴ τῷ Φαραώ,
but ³who ⁴shews ⁵mercy ¹of ²God. For says the scripture to Pharaoh,

'Οτι εἰς αὐτὸ.τοῦτο ἐξήγειρά σε, ὅπως ἐνδείξωμαι ἐν σοὶ
For this same thing I raised out thee, so that I might shew in thee

τὴν.δύναμίν.μου, καὶ ὅπως διαγγελῇ τὸ.ὄνομά.μου ἐν πάσῃ
my power, and so that should be declared my name in all

τῇ γῇ. 18 Ἄρα οὖν ὃν θέλει ἐλεεῖ· ὃν.δὲ θέλει
the earth. So then to whom he will he shews mercy, and whom he will

σκληρύνει.
he hardens.

19 Ἐρεῖς ^lοὖν μοι,^{ll} Τί^m ἔτι · μέμφεται; τῷ.ⁿγὰρ^{ll} βου-
Thou wilt say then to me, Why yet does he find fault? for ⁴the ⁵pur-

λήματι αὐτοῦ τίς ἀνθέστηκεν; 20 ^{ll}Μενοῦνγε, ὦ ἄνθρωπε,^{ll}
pose ⁶of ⁷him ¹who ²has ³resisted? Yea, rather, O man,

σὺ τίς εἶ ὁ ἀνταποκρινόμενος τῷ θεῷ; μὴ ἐρεῖ τὸ
³thou ¹who ²art that answerest against God? Shall ⁴say ¹the

πλάσμα τῷ πλάσαντι, Τί με ἐποίησας οὕτως;
²thing ³formed to him who formed [it], Why me madest thou thus?

21 ^{ll}Ἡ οὐκ.ἔχει ἐξουσίαν ὁ κεραμεὺς τοῦ πηλοῦ, ἐκ τοῦ
Or has not authority the potter over the clay, out of the

αὐτοῦ φυράματος ποιῆσαι ὃ.μὲν εἰς τιμὴν σκεῦος, ὃ.δὲ
same lump to make one ²to ³honour ¹vessel, and another

εἰς ἀτιμίαν; 22 εἰ.δὲ θέλων ὁ θεὸς ἐνδείξασθαι τὴν ὀργήν,
to dishonour? And if ²willing ¹God to shew wrath,

καὶ γνωρίσαι τὸ.δυνατὸν.αὐτοῦ, ἤνεγκεν ἐν πολλῇ μακρο-
and to make known his power, bore in much long-

θυμίᾳ σκεύη ὀργῆς κατηρτισμένα εἰς ἀπώλειαν· 23 καὶ ἵνα
suffering vessels of wrath fitted for destruction; and that

γνωρίσῃ τὸν πλοῦτον τῆς.δόξης.αὐτοῦ ἐπὶ σκεύη
he might make known the riches of his glory upon vessels

ἐλέους, ἃ προητοίμασεν εἰς δόξαν; 24 οὓς καὶ ἐκάλεσεν
of mercy, which he before prepared for glory, ²whom ³also ⁴he ⁵called

ἡμᾶς οὐ μόνον ἐξ Ἰουδαίων, ἀλλὰ καὶ ἐξ
¹us not only from among [the] Jews, but also from among [the]

ἐθνῶν; 25 ὡς καὶ ἐν τῷ Ὡσηὲ λέγει, Καλέσω τὸν οὐ
nations? As also in Hosea he says, I will call that which [is] not

λαόν.μου, λαόν.μου· καὶ τὴν οὐκ ἠγαπημένην, ἠγαπημένην.
my people, My People; and that not beloved, Beloved.

26 Καὶ ἔσται, ἐν τῷ τόπῳ οὗ ^hἐρρήθη^{ll} Ραὐτοῖς,^{ll} Οὐ λαός
And it shall be, in the place where it was said to them, Not ²people

---

^h ἐρρέθη LTTrA. ⁱ γὰρ Μωσῇ G ; Μωσῇ γὰρ LA ; Μωϋσεῖ γὰρ TTr ; Μωϋσῇ γὰρ W.
^k ἐλεῶντος LTTrA. ^l μοι οὖν LTTrAW. ^m + οὖν then L[A]W. ⁿ — γὰρ for E.
^o ὦ ἄνθρωπε, μενοῦνγε (μενοῦν γε LTr) LTTrA. ^p — αὐτοῖς [L]Tr.

---

calleth ;) 12 it was said unto her, The elder shall serve the younger. 13 As it is written, Jacob have I loved, but Esau have I hated.

14 What shall we say then? *Is there* unrighteousness with God? God forbid. 15 For he saith to Moses, I will have mercy on whom I will have mercy, and I will have compassion on whom I will have compassion. 16 So then *it is* not of him that willeth, nor of him that runneth, but of God that sheweth mercy. 17 For the scripture saith unto Pharaoh, Even for this same purpose have I raised thee up, that I might shew my power in thee, and that my name might be declared throughout all the earth. 18 Therefore hath he mercy on whom he will *have* mercy, and whom he will he hardeneth.

19 Thou wilt say then unto me, Why doth he yet find fault? For who hath resisted his will? 20 Nay but, O man, who art thou that repliest against God? Shall the thing formed say to him that formed *it*, Why hast thou made me thus? 21 Hath not the potter power over the clay, of the same lump to make one vessel unto honour, and another unto dishonour? 22 *What* if God, willing to shew *his* wrath, and to make his power known, endured with much longsuffering the vessels of wrath fitted to destruction : 23 and that he might make known the riches of his glory on the vessels of mercy, which he had afore prepared unto glory, 24 even us, whom he hath called, not of the Jews only, but also of the Gentiles? 25 As he saith also in Osee, I will call them my people, which were not my people ; and her beloved, which was not beloved. 26 And it shall come

to pass, that in the place where it was said unto them, Ye are not my people ; there shall they be called the children of the living God. 27 Esaias also crieth concerning Israel, Though the number of the children of Israel be as the sand of the sea, a remnant shall be saved: 28 for he will finish the work, and cut it short in righteousness: because a short work will the Lord make upon the earth. 29 And as Esaias said before, Except the Lord of Sabaoth had left us a seed, we had been as Sodoma, and been made like unto Gomorrha.

30 What shall we say then ? That the Gentiles, which followed not after righteousness, have attained to righteousness, even the righteousness which is of faith. 31 But Israel, which followed after the law of righteousness, hath not attained to the law of righteousness. 32 Wherefore ? Because they sought it not by faith, but as it were by the works of the law. For they stumbled at that stumblingstone ; 33 as it is written, Behold, I lay in Sion a stumblingstone and rock of offence : and whosoever believeth on him shall not be ashamed.

X. Brethren, my heart's desire and prayer to God for Israel is, that they might be saved. 2 For I bear them record that they have a zeal of God, but not according to knowledge. 3 For they being ignorant of God's righteousness, and going about to establish their own righteousness, have not submitted themselves unto the righteousness of God. 4 For Christ is the end of the law for righteousness to every one that believeth.

5 For Moses describ-

μου ὑμεῖς, ἐκεῖ κληθήσονται υἱοὶ θεοῦ ζῶντος. 27 Ἡ-
my [are] ye, there they shall be called sons of ²God [¹the]²living. ²Ε-

σαΐας δὲ κράζει ὑπὲρ τοῦ Ἰσραήλ, Ἐὰν.ᾖ ὁ ἀριθμὸς
saias ¹but cries concerning Israel, If ³should ⁰be ¹the ²number

τῶν υἱῶν Ἰσραὴλ ὡς ἡ ἄμμος τῆς θαλάσσης, τὸ ˣκατάλειμ-
³of ⁴the ⁵sons ⁶of ⁷Israel as the sand of the sea, the remnant

μα‖ σωθήσεται· 28 λόγον γὰρ συντελῶν καὶ συντέμνων
shall be saved.: for [the] matter [he is] concluding and cutting short

ᵇἐν δικαιοσύνῃ· ὅτι λόγον συντετμημένον‖ ποιήσει
in righteousness: because a matter cut short will ³do [¹the]

κύριος ἐπὶ τῆς γῆς. 29 Καὶ καθὼς προείρηκεν Ἡσαΐας,
²Lord upon the earth. And according as said before Esaias,

Εἰ.μὴ κύριος Σαβαὼθ ᵗἐγκατέλιπεν‖ ἡμῖν σπέρμα, ὡς Σόδομα
Unless [the] Lord of Hosts had left us a seed, as Sodom

ἂν.ἐγενήθημεν, καὶ ὡς Γόμορρα ἂν.ὡμοιώθημεν.
we should have become, and as Gomorrha we should have been made like.

30 Τί οὖν ἐροῦμεν; ὅτι ἔθνη τὰ μὴ.διώκοντα δικαιο-
What then shall we say? That Gentiles that follow not after right-

σύνην, κατέλαβεν δικαιοσύνην, δικαιοσύνην.δὲ τὴν ἐκ πίστεως·
eousness, attained righteousness, but righteousness that [is] by faith.

31 Ἰσραὴλ.δὲ διώκων νόμον δικαιοσύνης, εἰς νόμον ᵛδι-
But Israel, following after a law of righteousness, to a law of

καιοσύνης‖ οὐκ.ἔφθασεν. 32 ʷδιατί;‖ ὅτι οὐκ ἐκ πίσ-
righteousness did not attain. Why? Because [it was] not by faith,

τεως, ἀλλ᾽ ὡς ἐξ ἔργων ˣνόμου·‖ προσέκοψαν.ʸγὰρ‖ τῷ λίθῳ
but as by works of law. For they stumbled at the stone

τοῦ προσκόμματος; 33 καθὼς γέγραπται, Ἰδοὺ τίθημι ἐν
of stumbling, according as it has been written, Behold I place in

Σιὼν λίθον προσκόμματος καὶ πέτραν σκανδάλου· καὶ ᶻπᾶς‖
Sion a stone of stumbling and rock of offence: and every one

ὁ πιστεύων ἐπ᾽ αὐτῷ οὐ.καταισχυνθήσεται.
that believes on him shall not be ashamed.

10 Ἀδελφοί, ἡ μὲν εὐδοκία τῆς.ἐμῆς καρδίας, καὶ ἡ
Brethren, the good pleasure of my own heart, and

δέησις ªἡ‖ πρὸς τὸν θεὸν ὑπὲρ ᵇτοῦ Ἰσραήλ ἐστιν‖ εἰς
supplication to God on behalf of Israel is for

σωτηρίαν. 2 μαρτυρῶ.γὰρ αὐτοῖς ὅτι ζῆλον θεοῦ ἔχουσιν,
salvation. For I bear witness to them that zeal for God they have,

ἀλλ᾽ οὐ κατ᾽ ἐπίγνωσιν. 3 ἀγνοοῦντες.γὰρ τὴν τοῦ θεοῦ
but not according to knowledge. For being ignorant of the ²of ³God

δικαιοσύνην, καὶ τὴν.ἰδίαν ᶜδικαιοσύνην‖ ζητοῦντες στῆσαι,
¹righteousness, and their own righteousness seeking to establish,

τῇ δικαιοσύνῃ τοῦ θεοῦ οὐχ.ὑπετάγησαν. 4 τέλος.γὰρ
to the righteousness of God they submitted not. For ⁴end

νόμου χριστὸς εἰς δικαιοσύνην παντὶ τῷ πιστεύοντι.
⁵of ⁶law ¹Christ [²is] for righteousness to every one that believes.

5 ᵈΜωσῆς‖.γὰρ γράφει ᵉ τὴν δικαιοσύνην τὴν ἐκ ᶠτοῦ‖
For Moses writes [of] the righteousness which [is] of the

νόμου, ᵍὍτι‖ ὁ ποιήσας ʰαὐτὰ‖ ἄνθρωπος ζήσεται
law, That the ²having ³practised ⁴those ⁵things ¹man shall live

ἐν ⁱαὐτοῖς.‖ 6 Ἡ.δὲ ἐκ πίστεως δικαιοσύνη οὕτως λέγει,
by them. But the ²of ³faith ¹righteousness thus speaks:

ʳ ὑπόλειμμα LTTrA.   ˢ — ἐν δικαιοσύνῃ ὅτι λόγον συντετμημένον LTTr[A].   ᵗ ἐν- T.
ᵛ — δικαιοσύνης (read to [that] law) LTTrAW.   ʷ διὰ τί LTTrA.   ˣ — νόμου LTTr[A]W.
ʸ — γὰρ for LTTrA.   ᶻ — πᾶς (read ὁ he that) LTTrAW.   ª — ἡ LTTrAW.   ᵇ αὐτῶν them
[is] GLTTrAW.   ᶜ — δικαιοσύνην GLTr[A]W.   ᵈ Μωϋσῆς GLTTrAW.   ᵉ + ὅτι that T.
ᶠ — τοῦ TTrA.   ᵍ — ὅτι T.   ʰ — αὐτὰ [L]T.   ⁱ αὐτῇ it LTTrA.

Μὴ.εἴπῃς ἐν ᵏτῇ".καρδίᾳ.σου, Τίς ἀναβήσεται εἰς τὸν
Thou mayest not say in   thy heart,   Who shall ascend to the

οὐρανόν; τοῦτ' ἔστιν χριστὸν καταγαγεῖν· 7 ἤ, Τίς κατα-
heaven? that is,   Christ to bring down. Or, Who shall

βήσεται εἰς τὴν ἄβυσσον; τοῦτ' ἔστιν χριστὸν ἐκ
descend into the abyss?   that is,   Christ from among [the]

νεκρῶν ἀναγαγεῖν. 8 ἀλλὰ τί λέγει; Ἐγγύς σου τὸ ῥῆμά
dead   to bring up. But what says it? Near thee the word

ἐστιν, ἐν τῷ.στόματί.σου καὶ ἐν τῇ.καρδίᾳ.σου. τοῦτ' ἔστιν τὸ
is,   in thy mouth   and in thy heart: that is the

ῥῆμα τῆς πίστεως ὃ κηρύσσομεν· 9 ὅτι ἐὰν ὁμολογήσῃς
word of faith which we proclaim, that if thou confess

ἐν τῷ.στόματί.σου κύριον Ἰησοῦν, καὶ πιστεύσῃς ἐν τῇ
with thy mouth   [the] Lord Jesus, and believe in

καρδίᾳ.σου ὅτι ὁ θεὸς αὐτὸν ἤγειρεν ἐκ νεκρῶν,
thy heart that God him   raised from among [the] dead,

σωθήσῃ· 10 καρδίᾳ.γὰρ πιστεύεται εἰς δικαιοσύνην.
thou shalt be saved. For with [the] heart is belief to righteousness;

στόματι.δὲ ὁμολογεῖται εἰς σωτηρίαν. 11 Λέγει.γὰρ ἡ
and with [the] mouth is confession to salvation. For says the

γραφή, Πᾶς ὁ πιστεύων ἐπ' αὐτῷ οὐ.καταισχυνθήσεται.
scripture, Everyone that believes on him   shall not be ashamed.

12 Οὐ.γάρ.ἐστιν διαστολὴ Ἰουδαίου τε καὶ Ἕλληνος· ὁ.γὰρ
For there is not a difference of Jew and Greek; for the

αὐτὸς κύριος πάντων πλουτῶν εἰς πάντας τοὺς ἐπικαλου-
same Lord of all [is] rich toward all that call

μένους αὐτόν. 13 Πᾶς.γὰρ ὃς.ἂν ἐπικαλέσηται τὸ ὄνομα
upon him.   For everyone, whoever may call on the name

κυρίου, σωθήσεται. 14 Πῶς οὖν ˡἐπικαλέσονται" εἰς
of [the] Lord, shall be saved. How then shall they call on [him]

ὃν οὐκ.ἐπίστευσαν; πῶς.δὲ ᵐπιστεύσουσιν" οὗ
whom they believed not? and how shall they believe on [him] of whom

οὐκ.ἤκουσαν; πῶς.δὲ ⁿἀκούσουσιν" χωρὶς κηρύσσοντος;
they heard not? and how shall they hear apart from [one] preaching?

15 πῶς.δὲ ᵒκηρύξουσιν," ἐὰν.μὴ ἀποσταλῶσιν; καθὼς
and how shall they preach, unless they be sent? according as

γέγραπται, Ὡς ὡραῖοι οἱ πόδες τῶν ᴾεὐαγγελιζο-
it has been written, How beautiful the feet of those announcing the glad

μένων εἰρήνην, τῶν" εὐαγγελιζομένων ᑫτὰ" ἀγαθά.
tidings of peace, of those announcing the glad tidings of good things!

16 Ἀλλ' οὐ πάντες ὑπήκουσαν τῷ εὐαγγελίῳ· Ἡσαΐας.γὰρ
But not all. obeyed the glad tidings. For Esaias

λέγει, Κύριε, τίς ἐπίστευσεν τῇ.ἀκοῇ.ἡμῶν; 17 Ἄρα ἡ πίστις
says, Lord, who believed our report? So faith [is]

ἐξ ἀκοῆς, ἡ.δὲ ἀκοὴ διὰ ῥήματος ʳθεοῦ." 18 ἀλλὰ λέγω,
by report, but the report by [the] word of God. But I say,

Μὴ οὐκ.ἤκουσαν; ˢμενοῦνγε" εἰς πᾶσαν τὴν γῆν ἐξῆλθεν
Did they not hear? Yea, rather, Into all the earth went out

ὁ.φθόγγος.αὐτῶν, καὶ εἰς τὰ πέρατα τῆς οἰκουμένης τὰ ῥήματα
their voice, and to the ends of the habitable world ²words

αὐτῶν. 19 Ἀλλὰ λέγω, Μὴ.²οὐκ.ἔγνω Ἰσραήλ"; πρῶτος
¹their.   But I say, Did not ²know ¹Israel? First,

eth the righteousness
which is of the law,
That the man which
doeth those things
shall live by them,
6 But the righteous-
ness which is of faith
speaketh on this wise,
Say not in thine heart,
Who shall ascend into
heaven? (that is, to
bring Christ down
from above:) 7 or,
Who shall descend in-
to the deep? (that is, to
bring up Christ again
from the dead.) 8 But
what saith it? The
word is nigh thee,
even in thy mouth, and
in thy heart: that is,
the word of faith,
which we preach;
9 That if thou shalt
confess with thy
mouth the Lord Je-
sus, and shalt believe
in thine heart that
God hath raised him
from the dead, thou
shalt be saved. 10 For
with the heart man
believeth unto right-
eousness; and with
the mouth confession
is made unto salva-
tion. 11 For the scrip-
ture saith, Whosoever
believeth on him shall
not be ashamed. 12 For
there is no difference
between the Jew and
the Greek: for the
same Lord over all is
rich unto all that
call upon him. 13 For
whosoever shall call
upon the name of the
Lord shall be saved.
14 How then shall
they call on him in
whom they have not
believed? and how
shall they believe in
him of whom they
have not heard? and
how shall they hear
without a preacher?
15 And how shall they
preach, except they be
sent? as it is written,
How beautiful are
the feet of them that
preach the gospel of
peace, and bring glad
tidings of good things!
16 But they have not
all obeyed the gospel.
For Esaias saith,
Lord, who hath be-
lieved our report?
17 So then faith com-
eth by hearing, and
hearing by the word
of God. 18 But I say,

ᵏ — τῇ E. ˡ ἐπικαλέσωνται should they call LTTrAW. ᵐ πιστεύσωσιν should they
believe LTTrAW. ⁿ ἀκούσονται T; ἀκούσωσιν should they hear LTrAW. ᵒ κηρύξωσιν
should they preach LTTrAW. ᴾ — εὐαγγελιζομένων εἰρήνην τῶν LTTr[A]. ᑫ — τὰ LTrAW.
ʳ χριστοῦ or Christ LTTrA. ˢ μενοῦν γε LTrW. ᵗ Ἰσραὴλ οὐκ ἔγνω GLTTrAW.
2R

Have they not heard? Yes verily, their sound went into all the earth, and their words unto the ends of the world. 19 But I say, Did not Israel know? First Moses saith, I will provoke you to jealousy by *them that are* no people, *and* by a foolish nation I will anger you. 20 But Esaias is very bold, and saith, I was found of them that sought me not; I was made manifest unto them that asked not after me. 21 But to Israel he saith, All day long I have stretched forth my hands unto a disobedient and gainsaying people.

XI. I say then, Hath God cast away his people? God forbid. For I also am an Israelite, of the seed of Abraham, *of* the tribe of Benjamin. 2 God hath not cast away his people which he foreknew. Wot ye not what the scripture saith of Elias? how he maketh intercession to God against Israel, saying, 3 Lord, they have killed thy prophets, and digged down thine altars; and I am left alone, and they seek my life. 4 But what saith the answer of God unto him? I have reserved to myself seven thousand men, who have not bowed the knee to the image of Baal. 5 Even so then at this present time also there is a remnant according to the election of grace. 6 And if by grace, then *is it* no more of works: otherwise grace is no more grace. But if *it be* of works, then is it no more grace: otherwise work is no more work.

7 What then? Israel hath not obtained that which he seeketh for; but the election hath obtained it, and the rest were blinded 8 (according as it is written, God hath given them the spirit

^uΜωσῆς^{||} λέγει, Ἐγὼ παραζηλώσω[|] ὑμᾶς ἐπ'[|] οὐκ
Moses says, I will provoke to jealousy you through [those] not

ἔθνει, ^vἐπὶ^{||} ἔθνει ἀσυνέτῳ παροργιῶ ὑμᾶς. 20 Ἡ-
a nation, through a nation without understanding I will anger you. E-

σαΐας δὲ ἀποτολμᾷ καὶ λέγει, Εὑρέθην ^w τοῖς ἐμὲ μὴ ζη-
saias ¹but is very bold and says, I was found by those ³me ¹not ²seek-

τοῦσιν, ἐμφανὴς ἐγενόμην ^x τοῖς ἐμὲ μὴ ἐπερωτῶσιν. 21 πρὸς
ing; manifested I became to those ⁴me ¹not ²enquiring ³after. To

δὲ τὸν Ἰσραὴλ λέγει, Ὅλην τὴν ἡμέραν ἐξεπέτασα τὰς
²but Israel he says, ²Whole ¹the day I stretched out

χεῖράς μου πρὸς λαὸν ἀπειθοῦντα καὶ ἀντιλέγοντα.
my hands to a people disobeying and contradicting.

11 Λέγω οὖν, Μὴ ἀπώσατο ὁ θεὸς τὸν λαὸν αὐτοῦ^y;
I say then, Did ²thrust ³away ¹God his people?

μὴ γένοιτο· καὶ γὰρ ἐγὼ ^zἸσραηλίτης^{||} εἰμί, ἐκ σπέρματος
May it not be! For also I an Israelite am, of [the] seed

Ἀβραάμ, φυλῆς ^aΒενιαμίν.^{||} 2 οὐκ ἀπώσατο ὁ θεὸς
of Abraham, of [the] tribe of Benjamin. ²Did ³not ⁴thrust ⁵away ¹God

τὸν λαὸν αὐτοῦ, ὃν προέγνω. ἢ οὐκ οἴδατε ἐν
his people, whom he foreknew. Know ye not in [the history of]

^bἨλίᾳ^{||} τί λέγει ἡ γραφή; ὡς ἐντυγχάνει τῷ θεῷ κατὰ
Elias what says the scripture? how he pleads with God against

τοῦ Ἰσραήλ, ^cλέγων,^{||} 3 Κύριε, τοὺς προφήτας σου ἀπέκτειναν,
Israel, saying, Lord, thy prophets they killed,

^dκαὶ^{||} τὰ θυσιαστήριά σου κατέσκαψαν· κἀγὼ ὑπελείφθην μό-
and thine altars they dug down; and I was left a-

νος, καὶ ζητοῦσιν τὴν ψυχήν μου. 4 Ἀλλὰ τί λέγει αὐτῷ ὁ
lone, and they seek my life. But what says to him the

χρηματισμός; Κατέλιπον ἐμαυτῷ ἑπτακισχιλίους ἄνδρας
divine answer? I left to myself seven thousand men

οἵτινες οὐκ ἔκαμψαν γόνυ τῇ Βάαλ. 5 Οὕτως οὖν καὶ ἐν τῷ
who bowed not a knee to Baal. Thus then also in the

νῦν καιρῷ λεῖμμα κατ' ἐκλογὴν χάριτος γέγονεν.
present time a remnant according to election of grace there has been.

6 εἰ δὲ χάριτι, οὐκέτι ἐξ ἔργων· ἐπεὶ ἡ χάρις οὐκέτι γίνεται
But if by grace, no longer of works; else grace no longer becomes

χάρις. ^eεἰ δὲ ἐξ ἔργων, οὐκέτι ^fἐστὶν[|] χάρις· ἐπεὶ τὸ ἔργον[|]
grace; but if of works, no longer is it grace; else work

οὐκέτι ἐστὶν ἔργον.^{||}
no longer is work.

7 Τί οὖν; ὃ ἐπιζητεῖ Ἰσραήλ, ^gτούτου^{||} οὐκ ἐπέτυχεν,
What then? What ²seeks ³for ¹Israel, this it did not obtain;

ἡ δὲ ἐκλογὴ ἐπέτυχεν· οἱ δὲ λοιποὶ ἐπωρώθησαν, 8 ^hκαθὼς^{||}
but the election obtained [it], and the rest were hardened, according as

γέγραπται, Ἔδωκεν αὐτοῖς ὁ θεὸς πνεῦμα κατανύξεως,
it has been written, ²Gave ³them ¹God a spirit of slumber,

ὀφθαλμοὺς τοῦ μὴ βλέπειν, καὶ ὦτα τοῦ μὴ ἀκούειν, ἕως
eyes so as not to see, and ears so as not to hear, unto

τῆς σήμερον ἡμέρας. 9 καὶ ⁱΔαβὶδ^{||} λέγει, Γενηθήτω ἡ τράπεζα
this day. And David says, Let be ²table

αὐτῶν εἰς παγίδα, καὶ εἰς θήραν, καὶ εἰς σκάνδαλον, καὶ εἰς
¹their for a snare, and for a trap, and for cause of offence, and for

---

^u Μωϋσῆς GLTTrAW.   ^v ἐπ' TTr.   ^w + [ἐν] by (those) LTrA.   ^x + [ἐν] by (those) LTr.
^y + [, ὃν προέγνω] whom he foreknew L.   ^z Ἰσραηλείτης T.   ^a Βενιαμείν LTTrA.
^b Ἠλείᾳ T.   ^c — λέγων GLTTrAW.   ^d — καὶ LTTrAW.   ^e — εἰ δὲ ἐξ to end of verse
GLTTr[A].   ^f — ἐστὶν A.   ^g τοῦτο GLTTrAW.   ^h καθάπερ even as TTr.   ⁱ Δαυείδ
LTTrA; Δαυὶδ GW.

ἀνταπόδομα αὐτοῖς· 10 σκοτισθήτωσαν οἱ.ὀφθαλμοὶ.αὐτῶν
a recompense   to them: let be darkened   their eyes

τοῦ.μὴ βλέπειν, καὶ τὸν.νῶτον.αὐτῶν ᵏδιαπαντὸς‖ ¹σύγ-
so as not   to see,   and   their back   continually   bow thou

καμψον.‖
down.

11 Λέγω οὖν, μὴ ἔπταισαν ἵνα πέσωσιν; μὴ.γένοιτο·
I say then,   Did they stumble that they might fall? May it not be!

ἀλλὰ τῷ.αὐτῶν παραπτώματι ἡ σωτηρία τοῖς ἔθνεσιν, εἰς
but   by their   offence   salvation [is] to the nations, for

τὸ παραζηλῶσαι αὐτούς. 12 εἰ.δὲ τὸ.παράπτωμα.αὐτῶν
to provoke to jealousy them.   But if   their offence   [be the]

πλοῦτος κόσμου, καὶ.τὸ.ἥττημα.αὐτῶν πλοῦτος ἐθνῶν,
wealth of[the] world, and   their default   [the] wealth of[the] nations,

πόσῳ μᾶλλον τὸ.πλήρωμα.αὐτῶν; 13 Ὑμῖν ᵐγὰρ‖ λέγω
how much   more   their fulness?   ²To ³you   ¹for I speak,

τοῖς ἔθνεσιν· ἐφ'.ὅσον μὲν ⁿ εἰμι ἐγὼ ἐθνῶν ἀπόστολος,
the nations, inasmuch as   ²am   ¹I ⁴of [⁵the] ⁶nations   ³apostle,

τὴν.διακονίαν.μου δοξάζω, 14 εἴ.πως παραζηλώσω
my service   I glorify,   if by any means I shall provoke to jealousy

μου τὴν.σάρκα, καὶ σώσω τινὰς ἐξ αὐτῶν. 15 εἰ.γὰρ
my   flesh,   and shall save some from among them.   For if

ἡ.ἀποβολὴ.αὐτῶν καταλλαγὴ κόσμου, τίς ἡ °πρόσ-
their casting away [be the] reconciliation of [the] world, what the recep-

ληψις,‖ εἰ.μὴ ζωὴ ἐκ νεκρῶν;
tion,   except life from among [the] dead?

16 εἰ.δὲ ἡ ἀπαρχὴ ἁγία, καὶ τὸ φύραμα· καὶ εἰ ἡ ῥίζα
Now if the first-fruit [be] holy, also the   lump;   and if the root

ἁγία, καὶ οἱ κλάδοι. 17 εἰ.δέ τινες τῶν κλάδων ἐξεκλάσθη-
[be] holy, also the branches.   But if some of the branches   were broken

σαν, σὺ.δὲ ἀγριέλαιος ὢν ἐνεκεντρίσθης ἐν αὐτοῖς, καὶ
off,   and thou, a wild olive tree being, wast grafted in amongst them, and

¹συγκοινωνὸς‖ τῆς ῥίζης ᴾκαὶ‖ τῆς πιότητος τῆς ἐλαίας
a fellow-partaker of the root   and of the   fatness   of the olive tree

ἐγένου, 18 μὴ.κατακαυχῶ τῶν κλάδων· εἰ.δὲ κατακαυχᾶσαι,
became,   boast not against   the branches; but if thou boastest against

οὐ σὺ τὴν ῥίζαν βαστάζεις, ᑫἀλλ'‖ ἡ ῥίζα σέ. 19 Ἐ-
[them], ³not ¹thou ⁴the   ⁵root   ²bearest,   but the root thee.   Thou

ρεῖς οὖν, Ἐξεκλάσθησαν ʳοἱ‖ κλάδοι, ἵνα ἐγὼ ˢἐγκεντρισθῶ.‖
wilt say then, Were broken out the branches, that I might be grafted in.

20 Καλῶς· τῇ ἀπιστίᾳ ᵗἐξεκλάσθησαν,‖ σὺ.δὲ τῇ πίστει
Well: by unbelief they were broken out, and thou   by faith

ἕστηκας. μὴ.ὑψηλοφρόνει,‖ ἀλλὰ φοβοῦ· 21 εἰ.γὰρ ὁ θεὸς
standest.   Be not high-minded,   but   fear: for if   God

τῶν κατὰ φύσιν κλάδων οὐκ.ἐφείσατο, ʷμήπως‖ οὐδέ σου
the ²according ³to ⁴nature ¹branches spared not—   lest neither thee

ˣφείσηται.‖ 22 Ἴδε οὖν χρηστότητα καὶ ἀποτομίαν θεοῦ·
he should spare.   Behold then [the] kindness and   severity of God:

ἐπὶ μὲν τοὺς πεσόντας, ʸἀποτομίαν·‖ ἐπὶ.δὲ σε, ᶻχρηστό-
upon   those that   fell,   severity;   and upon thee,   kind-

τητα,‖ ἐὰν ˢᵉἐπιμείνῃς‖ τῇ χρηστότητι· ἐπεὶ καὶ σὺ ἐκ-
ness,   if   thou continue in [his]   kindness,   else also thou wilt

of slumber, eyes that they should not see, and ears that they should not hear;) unto this day. 9 And David saith, Let their table be made a snare, and a trap, and a stumbling-block, and a recompence unto them : 10 let their eyes be darkened, that they may not see, and bow down their back alway.

11 I say then, Have they stumbled that they should fall? God forbid : but *rather* through their fall salvation *is come* unto the Gentiles, for to provoke them to jealousy. 12 Now if the fall of them *be* the riches of the world, and the diminishing of them the riches of the Gentiles ; how much more their fulness? 13 For I speak to you Gentiles, inasmuch as I am the apostle of the Gentiles, I magnify mine office : 14 if by any means I may provoke to emulation *them which are* my flesh, and might save some of them. 15 For if the casting away of them *be* the reconciling of the world, what *shall* the receiving *of them be*, but life from the dead?

16 For if the first-fruit *be* holy, the lump *is* also *holy*. and if the root *be* holy, so *are* the branches. 17 And if some of the branches be broken off, and thou, being a wild olive tree, wert grafted in among them, and with them partakest of the root and fatness of the olive tree; 18 boast not against the branches. But if thou boast, thou bearest not the root, but the root thee. 19 Thou wilt say then, The branches were broken off, that I might be graffed in. 20 Well; because of unbelief they were broken off, and thou standest by faith. Be not highminded, but fear : 21 for if God spared not the natural

ᵏ διὰ παντὸς LTᴛA.   ¹ συν– T.   ᵐ δὲ and LTTᴛA.   ⁿ + οὖν then LT[Tr]AW.
° πρόσληψις LTTᴛA.   ᴾ — καὶ T[Tr]A.   ᑫ ἀλλὰ TTᴛA.   ʳ — οἱ GLTTᴛAW.   ˢ ἐν– T.
ᵗ ἐκλάσθησαν broken off LTr.   ᵛ ὑψηλὰ φρόνει TTr.   ʷ — μήπως LTTr[A].   ˣ φείσεται
he will spare GLTTᴛAW.   ʸ ἀποτομία LTTᴛA.   ᶻ χρηστότης θεοῦ kindness of God LTTᴛA,
ˢᵉ ἐπιμένῃς TTr–

branches, *take heed* lest he also spare not thee. 22 Behold therefore the goodness and severity of God : on them which fell, severity ; but toward thee, goodness, if thou continue in *his* goodness : otherwise thou also shalt be cut off. 23 And they also, if they abide not still in unbelief, shall be graffed in : for God is able to graff them in again. 24 For if thou wert cut out of the olive tree which is wild by nature, and wert graffed contrary to nature into a good olive tree : how much more shall these, which be the natural *branches*, be graffed into their own olive tree? 25 For I would not, brethren, that ye should be ignorant of this mystery, lest ye should be wise in your own conceits ; that blindness in part is happened to Israel, until the fulness of the Gentiles be come in. 26 And so all Israel shall be saved: as it is written, There shall come out of Sion the Deliverer, and shall turn away ungodliness from Jacob : 27 For this *is* my covenant unto them, when I shall take away their sins. 28 As concerning the gospel, *they are* enemies for your sakes : but as touching the election, *they are* beloved for the fathers' sakes. 29 For the gifts and calling of God *are* without repentance. 30 For as ye in times past have not believed God, yet have now obtained mercy through their unbelief: 31 Even so have these also now not believed, that through *your* mercy they also may obtain mercy. 32 For God hath concluded them all in unbelief, that he might have mercy upon all. 33 O the depth of the riches both of the wisdom and knowledge of God ! how unsearchable *are* his judgments, and his ways past finding out ! 34 For who hath known the mind of the Lord?

κοπήσῃ. 23 ᵇκαὶ ἐκεῖνοι‖ δέ, ἐὰν μὴ.ᶜἐπιμείνωσιν‖ τῇ ἀπιστίᾳ,
be cut off.   ²Also   ²they   ¹and, if   they continue not   in unbelief,

ᵈἐγκεντρισθήσονται‖ δυνατὸς.γάρ ἐστιν ὁ θεὸς πάλιν ᵈἐγκεν-
shall be grafted in ;   for able   is   God   again   to graft

τρίσαι‖ αὐτούς. 24 εἰ.γὰρ σὺ ἐκ τῆς κατὰ φύσιν ἐξε-
.in   them.   For if   thou out of the ⁴according ⁵to ⁶nature ⁷wast

κόπης ἀγριελαίου, καὶ παρὰ φύσιν ἐνεκεντρίσθης εἰς
cut ⁹off ¹wild ²olive ³tree,   and, contrary to nature,   wast grafted in   to

καλλιέλαιον, πόσῳ μᾶλλον οὗτοι οἱ κατὰ φύσιν,
a good olive tree, how much more   these who according to nature [are],

ᵈἐγκεντρισθήσονται‖ τῇ.ἰδίᾳ ἐλαίᾳ ; 25 Οὐ.γὰρ θέλω ὑμᾶς
shall be grafted into   their own olive tree?   For ²not ²do ¹I wish you

ἀγνοεῖν, ἀδελφοί, τὸ.μυστήριον.τοῦτο, ἵνα μὴ.ῆτε ᵉπαρ᾿‖
to be ignorant, brethren,   of this mystery,   that ye may not be   in

ἑαυτοῖς φρόνιμοι, ὅτι πώρωσις ἀπὸ μέρους τῷ.Ἰσραὴλ γέ-
yourselves wise,   that hardness   in   part   to Israel has

γονεν, ἄχρις.οὗ τὸ πλήρωμα τῶν ἐθνῶν εἰσέλθῃ· 26 καὶ
happened, until   the fulness   of the nations be come in ;   and

οὕτως πᾶς Ἰσραὴλ σωθήσεται, καθὼς γέγραπται,
so   all   Israel   shall be saved, according as it has been written,

"Ἥξει ἐκ Σιὼν ὁ ῥυόμενος, ᶠκαὶ‖ ἀποστρέψει ἀσεβείας
Shall come out of Sion the deliverer, and he shall turn away ungodliness

ἀπὸ Ἰακώβ· 27 καὶ αὕτη αὐτοῖς ἡ παρ᾿ ἐμοῦ διαθήκη,
from Jacob.   And this [is] ⁵to ⁶them ¹the ³from ⁴me ²covenant,

ὅταν ἀφέλωμαι τὰς.ἁμαρτίας.αὐτῶν. 28 Κατὰ μὲν
when I may have taken away   their sins.   As regards indeed

τὸ εὐαγγέλιον, ἐχθροὶ δι᾿.ὑμᾶς· κατὰ.δὲ τὴν
the glad tidings, [they are] enemies on your account ; but as regards the

ἐκλογήν, ἀγαπητοὶ διὰ τοὺς πατέρας. 29 ἀμεταμέλητα
election,   beloved   on account of the fathers.   ²Not ³to ⁴be ⁵repented ⁶of

γὰρ τὰ χαρίσματα καὶ ἡ κλῆσις τοῦ θεοῦ. 30 ὥσπερ.γὰρ
¹for [are] the   gifts   and the calling of God.   For as

ᵍκαὶ ὑμεῖς ποτε ἠπειθήσατε τῷ θεῷ, νῦν.δὲ ἠλεήθητε
also   ye   once were disobedient   to God, but now have been shewn mercy

τῇ.τούτων ἀπειθείᾳ· 31 οὕτως καὶ οὗτοι νῦν ἠπείθησαν
through their disobedience ;   so   also these now were disobedient

τῷ.ʰὑμετέρῳ‖ ἐλέει, ἵνα καὶ αὐτοὶ ⁱ ἐλεηθῶσιν.
to your mercy,   that also they   may have mercy shewn [them].

32 συνέκλεισεν.γὰρ ὁ θεὸς τοὺς πάντας εἰς ἀπείθειαν, ἵνα τοὺς
For ²shut ³up ⁴together ¹God   all   in disobedience, that

πάντας ἐλεήσῃ. 33 Ὦ βάθος πλούτου καὶ σοφίας
all   he might shew mercy to.   O depth of riches both of wisdom

καὶ γνώσεως θεοῦ. ὡς ᵏἀνεξερεύνητα‖ τὰ.κρίματα.αὐτοῦ, καὶ
and knowledge of God ! How unsearchable   his judgments,   and

ἀνεξιχνίαστοι αἱ.ὁδοὶ.αὐτοῦ. 34 τίς.γὰρ ἔγνω νοῦν
untraceable   his ways ǃ   For who did know [the] mind

κυρίου ; ἢ τίς σύμβουλος.αὐτοῦ ἐγένετο ; 35 ἢ τίς προέ-
of [the] Lord, or who   his counsellor   became ?   Or who   first

δωκεν αὐτῷ, καὶ ἀνταποδοθήσεται αὐτῷ; 36 ὅτι ἐξ αὐτοῦ
gave   to him, and it shall be recompensed to him ?   For of   him

καὶ δι᾿ αὐτοῦ καὶ εἰς αὐτὸν τὰ.πάντα· αὐτῷ ἡ δόξα
and through him   and unto him [are] all things :   to him [be] the glory

εἰς τοὺς αἰῶνας. ἀμήν.
to the   ages.   Amen.

ᵇ κἀκεῖνοι GLTTrAW.   ᶜᵉ ἐπιμένωσιν TTr.   ᵈ ἐν- T.   ᵉ ἐν TrA.   ᶠ — καὶ LTTrAV
ᵍ — καὶ GLTTrAW.   ʰ ἡμετέρῳ (read to our mercy) E.   ⁱ + νῦν now [L]Tr.   ᵏ ἀνεξεραύνητα TT.

12 Παρακαλῶ οὖν ὑμᾶς, ἀδελφοί, διὰ τῶν οἰκτιρμῶν τοῦ
I exhort   therefore you,   brethren,   by the compassions

θεοῦ, παραστῆσαι τὰ σώματα ὑμῶν θυσίαν ζῶσαν, ἁγίαν,
of God, to present   your bodies   a ²sacrifice ¹living,   holy,

εὐάρεστον τῷ θεῷ, τὴν λογικὴν λατρείαν ὑμῶν· 2 καὶ μὴ
well-pleasing to God, ²intelligent ³service ¹your.   And ²not

ᵐσυσχηματίζεσθε τῷ αἰῶνι τούτῳ, ἀλλὰ ⁿμεταμορφοῦσθε τῇ
¹fashion yourselves to this age,   but   be transformed by the

ἀνακαινώσει τοῦ νοὸς °ὑμῶν, εἰς τὸ δοκιμάζειν ὑμᾶς τί
renewing   of your mind,   for   to prove by you what [is]

τὸ θέλημα τοῦ θεοῦ τὸ ἀγαθὸν καὶ εὐάρεστον καὶ τέλειον.
⁷will   ⁸of ⁹God ¹the ²good ³and ⁴well-pleasing⁵and ⁶perfect.

3 λέγω γὰρ διὰ τῆς χάριτος τῆς δοθείσης μοι, παντὶ
For I say through the   grace which is given to me, to everyone

τῷ ὄντι ἐν ὑμῖν, μὴ ὑπερφρονεῖν παρ' ὃ δεῖ
that is among you, not to be high-minded above what it behoves [you]

φρονεῖν, ἀλλὰ φρονεῖν εἰς τὸ σωφρονεῖν, ἑκάστῳ ὡς ὁ
to be minded ; but to be minded so as to be sober-minded to each as

θεὸς ἐμέρισεν μέτρον πίστεως. 4 Καθάπερ γὰρ ἐν ἑνὶ σώματι
God divided a measure of faith. For even as in one body

ᴾμέλη πολλὰ ἔχομεν, τὰ δὲ μέλη πάντα οὐ τὴν αὐτὴν
²members ¹many we have, but the members all ²not ³the ⁴same

ἔχει πρᾶξιν· 5 οὕτως οἱ πολλοὶ ἓν σῶμά ἐσμεν ἐν χριστῷ,
¹have function ; thus ³the ²many ¹one ⁴body ¹we ⁴are in Christ,

ᵍ0 δὲ καθ' εἷς ἀλλήλων μέλη. 6 ἔχοντες δὲ χαρίσματα
and each one ²of ³each ⁴other ¹members. But having   ²gifts

κατὰ τὴν χάριν τὴν δοθεῖσαν ἡμῖν διάφορα· εἴτε
²according ⁴to ⁵the ⁶grace ⁷which ⁸is ⁹given ¹⁰to ¹¹us ¹different, whether

προφητείαν, κατὰ τὴν ἀναλογίαν τῆς πίστεως· 7 εἴτε δια-
prophecy— according to the proportion   of faith ; or ser-

κονίαν, ἐν τῇ διακονίᾳ· εἴτε ὁ διδάσκων, ἐν τῇ διδασκαλίᾳ·
vice— in service ; or he that teaches— in teaching ;

8 εἴτε ὁ παρακαλῶν, ἐν τῇ παρακλήσει· ὁ μεταδιδούς, ἐν
or that exhorts— in the exhortation ; he that imparts— in

ἁπλότητι· ὁ προϊστάμενος, ἐν σπουδῇ· ὁ ἐλεῶν,
simplicity, he that takes the lead— with diligence ; he that shews mercy—

ἐν ἱλαρότητι. 9 Ἡ ἀγάπη ἀνυπόκριτος· ἀποστυγοῦντες τὸ
with cheerfulness. [Let] love [be] unfeigned ; abhorring

πονηρόν, κολλώμενοι τῷ ἀγαθῷ· 10 τῇ φιλαδελφίᾳ εἰς ἀλ-
evil,   cleaving   to good ; in brotherly love towards one

λήλους φιλόστοργοι· τῇ τιμῇ ἀλλήλους προηγούμενοι·
another kindly affectioned ; in [giving] honour ²one ⁴another ¹going ²before ;

11 τῇ σπουδῇ μὴ ὀκνηροί, τῷ πνεύματι ζέοντες, ʳτῷ καιρῷ
in diligence, not slothful ; in spirit, fervent ; in ³season

δουλεύοντες· 12 τῇ ἐλπίδι χαίροντες, τῇ θλίψει ὑπομένον-
¹serving. In hope, rejoicing ; in tribulation, endur-

τες, τῇ προσευχῇ προσκαρτεροῦντες· 13 ταῖς χρείαις τῶν
ing ; in prayer, stedfastly continuing ; to the needs of the

ἁγίων κοινωνοῦντες, τὴν φιλοξενίαν διώκοντες· 14 εὐλογεῖτε
saints communicating ; hospitality pursuing ; Bless

τοὺς διώκοντας ὑμᾶς· εὐλογεῖτε, καὶ μὴ καταρᾶσθε. 15 χαί-
those that persecute you ; bless,   and curse not.   Re-

ρειν μετὰ χαιρόντων, ˢκαὶ κλαίειν μετὰ κλαιόντων. 16 τὸ
joice with rejoicing ones, and weep with weeping ones ; the

---

or who hath been his
counseller ? 35 or who
hath first given to him,
and it shall be recom-
pensed unto him again?
36 For of him, and
through him, and to
him, are all things : to
whom be glory for
ever. Amen.

XII. I beseech you
therefore, brethren, by
the mercies of God,
that ye present your
bodies a living sacri-
fice, holy, acceptable
unto God, which is
your reasonable ser-
vice. 2 And be not
conformed to this
world : but be ye trans-
formed by the renew-
ing of your mind, that
ye may prove what is
that good, and accept-
able, and perfect, will
of God. 3 For I say,
through the grace
given unto me, to
every man that is a-
mong you, not to think
of himself more highly
than he ought to think;
but to think soberly,
according as God hath
dealt to every man the
measure of faith. 4 For
as we have many mem-
bers in one body, and
all members have not
the same office : 5 so we,
being many, are one
body in Christ, and
every one members one
of another. 6 Having
then gifts differing ac-
cording to the grace
that is given to us,
whether prophecy, let
us prophesy according
to the proportion of
faith ; 7 or ministry,
let us wait on our
ministering : or he
that teacheth, on
teaching ; 8 or he that
exhorteth, on exhor-
tation : he that giveth,
let him do it with sim-
plicity ; he that ruleth,
with diligence ; he that
sheweth mercy, with
cheerfulness. 9 Let
love be without dissi-
mulation. Abhor that
which is evil ; cleave
to that which is good.
10 Be kindly affec-
tioned one to another
with brotherly love ;
in honour preferring
one another ; 11 not
slothful in business ;
fervent in spirit ; serv-
ing the Lord ; 12 re-
joicing in hope ; pa-
tient in tribulation ;
continuing instant in

ˡ τῷ θεῷ εὐάρεστον T.   ᵐ συν(συν- A)σχηματίζεσθαι to fashion yourselves) LA ; συνσχη-
ματίζεσθε T, ⁿ μεταμορφοῦσθαι to be transformed LA.   ° — ὑμῶν (read the mind) LTTrAW.
ᴾ πολλὰ μέλη LTTrAW.   ᵍ τὸ LTTrAW.   ʳ τῷ κυρίῳ the Lord ELTTrAW.   ˢ — καὶ LTTrAW.

prayer; 13 distributing to the necessity of saints; given to hospitality. 14 Bless them which persecute you: bless, and curse not. 15 Rejoice with them that do rejoice, and weep with them that weep. 16 *Be* of the same mind one toward another. Mind not high things, but condescend to men of low estate. Be not wise in your own conceits. 17 Recompense to no man evil for evil. Provide things honest in the sight of all men. 18 If it be possible, as much as lieth in you, live peaceably with all men. 19 Dearly beloved, avenge not yourselves, but *rather* give place unto wrath: for it is written, Vengeance *is* mine; I will repay, saith the Lord. 20 Therefore if thine enemy hunger, feed him; if he thirst, give him drink: for in so doing thou shalt heap coals of fire on his head. 21 Be not overcome of evil, but overcome evil with good.

XIII. Let every soul be subject unto the higher powers. For there is no power but of God: the powers that be are ordained of God. 2 Whosoever therefore resisteth the power, resisteth the ordinance of God: and they that resist shall receive to themselves damnation. 3 For ru-
.ers are not a terror to good works, but to the evil. Wilt thou then not be afraid of the power? do that which is good, and thou shalt have praise of the same: 4 for he is the minister of God to thee for good. But if thou do that which is evil, be afraid; for he beareth not the sword in vain: for he is the minister of God, a revenger to *execute* wrath upon him that doeth evil. 5 Wherefore ye must needs be subject, not only for wrath, but also for conscience sake. 6 For for this cause pay ye tribute also: for they are God's ministers, attending continually

αὐτὸ　εἰς　ἀλλήλους　φρονοῦντες· μὴ τὰ ὑψηλὰ φρο-
same thing　toward　one another　minding,　not high things mind-
νοῦντες, ἀλλὰ τοῖς ταπεινοῖς συναπαγόμενοι. μὴ γίνεσθε
ing,　but with the　lowly ∕　going along:　be not
φρόνιμοι παρ᾽ ἑαυτοῖς. 17 μηδενὶ κακὸν ἀντὶ κακοῦ ἀποδι-
wise　in yourselves:　to no one evil for evil ren-
δόντες· προνοούμενοι καλὰ ᵗ　ἐνώπιον ⱽπάντων‖ ἀνθρώπων·
dering:　providing　right [things] before　all　men:
18 εἰ δυνατόν, τὸ ἐξ ὑμῶν, μετὰ πάντων ἀνθρώπων εἰρη-
if possible, as to yourselves, with　all　men　being
νεύοντες. 19 μὴ ἑαυτοὺς ἐκδικοῦντες, ἀγαπητοί, ἀλλὰ δότε
at peace;　not yourselves avenging,　beloved,　but give
τόπον τῇ ὀργῇ· γέγραπται γάρ, Ἐμοὶ ἐκδίκησις, ἐγὼ ἀντα-
place　to wrath; for it has been written, To me vengeance! I　will
ποδώσω, λέγει κύριος. 20 ʷ Ἐὰν οὖν‖　πεινᾷ ὁ ἐχθρός
recompense, says [the] Lord.　If therefore should hunger ²enemy
σου, ψώμιζε αὐτόν· ἐὰν διψᾷ,　πότιζε αὐτόν· τοῦτο
¹thine, feed　him;　if he should thirst, give ²drink ¹him;　⁴this
γὰρ ποιῶν, ἄνθρακας πυρὸς σωρεύσεις ἐπὶ τὴν κεφαλὴν
²for　doing,　coals of fire thou wilt heap upon　²head
αὐτοῦ. 21 μὴ νικῶ ὑπὸ τοῦ κακοῦ, ἀλλὰ νίκα ἐν τῷ
¹his.　Be not overcome by　evil,　but overcome ²with
ἀγαθῷ τὸ κακόν.
³good　¹evil.

13 Πᾶσα ψυχὴ ἐξουσίαις ὑπερεχούσαις ὑποτασσέσθω.
²Every ³soul ⁶to ⁷authorities　⁸above　[⁹him] ¹let ⁴be ⁵subject.
οὐ γάρ ἐστιν ἐξουσία εἰ μὴ ˣἀπὸ‖ θεοῦ· αἱ δὲ οὖσαι
For there is no　authority except　from　God; and those that are
ʸἐξουσίαι‖ ὑπὸ ᶻτοῦ‖ θεοῦ τεταγμέναι εἰσίν. 2 ὥστε ὁ
authorities,　by　᾽God have been appointed. So that he that
ἀντιτασσόμενος τῇ ἐξουσίᾳ, τῇ τοῦ θεοῦ διαταγῇ ἀνθέστηκεν·
sets himself against the authority, the　²of ³God ¹ordinance resists;
οἱ δὲ ἀνθεστηκότες, ἑαυτοῖς κρῖμα ᵃλήψονται.‖ 3 οἱ
and they that　resist,　to themselves judgment shall receive.　²The
γὰρ ἄρχοντες οὐκ εἰσὶν φόβος ᵇτῶν ἀγαθῶν ἔργων,‖ ἀλλὰ
¹for　rulers　are not　a terror　to good　works,　but
ᶜτῶν κακῶν.‖　θέλεις δὲ μὴ φοβεῖσθαι τὴν ἐξουσίαν; τὸ
to evil [ones].　Dost thou desire not to be afraid of the　authority? ²the
ἀγαθὸν ποίει, καὶ ἕξεις ἔπαινον ἐξ αὐτῆς· 4 θεοῦ γὰρ
³good　¹practise, and thou shalt have praise from it;　for ²f God
διάκονός ἐστίν σοι εἰς τὸ ἀγαθόν. ἐὰν δὲ τὸ κακὸν ποιῇς,
a servant　it is to thee for　good.　But if　evil thou practisest,
φοβοῦ· οὐ γὰρ εἰκῇ τὴν μάχαιραν φορεῖ· θεοῦ γὰρ διάκονός
fear;　for not in vain the　sword　it wears; for of God a servant
ἐστιν, ἔκδικος εἰς ὀργὴν τῷ　τὸ κακὸν πράσσοντι. 5 διὸ
it is,　an avenger for wrath to him that ²evil　¹does.　Wherefore
ἀνάγκη　ὑποτάσσεσθαι, οὐ μόνον διὰ τὴν ὀργήν,
necessary [it is]　to be subject,　not　only on account of wrath.
ἀλλὰ καὶ διὰ τὴν συνείδησιν. 6 διὰ τοῦτο γὰρ καὶ
but　also on account of　conscience.　For on this account also
φόρους τελεῖτε· λειτουργοὶ γὰρ θεοῦ εἰσιν, εἰς αὐτὸ τοῦτο
tribute pay ye;　for ministers　of God they are, on this same thing
προσκαρτεροῦντες. 7 ἀπόδοτε ᵈοὖν‖ πᾶσιν τὰς ὀφειλάς·
attending continually.　Render　therefore to all　their　dues:

ᵗ + [ἐνώπιον τοῦ θεοῦ καὶ] before God and L.　ᵛ τῶν L.　ʷ ἀλλὰ ἐὰν But if LTTrA.
ˣ ὑπὸ LTTr.　ʸ — ἐξουσίαι GLTTrAW.　ᶻ — τοῦ GLTTrAW.　ᵃ λήμψονται LTTrA.　ᵇ τῷ ἀγαθῷ
ἔργῳ to a good work LTTrAW.　ᶜ τῷ κακῷ to an evil [one] LTTrAW.　ᵈ — οὖν LTTrAW.

τῷ τὸν φόρον, τὸν φόρον· τῷ τὸ τέλος, τὸ τέλος· τῷ
to whom tribute, tribute; to whom custom, custom; to whom

τὸν φόβον, τὸν φόβον· τῷ. τὴν τιμήν, τὴν τιμήν. 8 Μηδενὶ
fear, fear; to whom honour, honour. To no one

μηδὲν ὀφείλετε, εἰ.μὴ τὸ ᵉἀγαπᾶν ἀλλήλους·‖ ὁ.γὰρ
anything owe ye, unless to love one another: for he that
(lit. nothing)

ἀγαπῶν τὸν ἕτερον, νόμον πεπλήρωκεν. 9 τὸ γάρ, Οὐ
loves the other, law has fulfilled. For, ³Not

μοιχεύσεις, οὐ.φονεύσεις, οὐ.κλέψεις,
¹thou ²shalt commit adultery, Thou shalt not commit murder, Thou shalt not steal,

ᶠοὐ.ψευδομαρτυρήσεις,‖ οὐκ.ἐπιθυμήσεις, καὶ εἴ τις ἑτέρα
Thou shalt not bear false witness, Thou shalt not lust; and if any other com-

ἐντολή, ἐν ᵍτούτῳ τῷ λόγῳ‖ ἀνακεφαλαιοῦται, ʰἐν τῷ,‖ Ἀγα-
mandment, in this word it is summed up, in this, Thou

πήσεις τὸν.πλησίον.σου ὡς ¹ἑαυτόν.‖ 10 Ἡ ἀγάπη τῷ πλη-
shalt love thy neighbour as thyself. Love to the neigh-

σίον κακὸν οὐκ.ἐργάζεται· πλήρωμα οὖν νόμου ἡ ἀγάπη.
bour, evil does not work: ³fulness ⁴therefore ⁵of [⁶the] ⁷law ¹love[²is].

11 Καὶ τοῦτο, εἰδότες τὸν καιρόν, ὅτι ὥρα ᵏἡμᾶς
Also this, knowing the time, that [the] hour ⁴we [¹it ²is]

ἤδη‖ ἐξ ὕπνου ἐγερθῆναι· νῦν.γὰρ ἐγγύτερον ἡμῶν ἡ
³already out of sleep should be roused; for now nearer [is] of us the

σωτηρία, ἢ ὅτε ἐπιστεύσαμεν. 12 ἡ νὺξ προέκοψεν, ἡ.δὲ
salvation, than when we believed. The night is advanced, and the

ἡμέρα ἤγγικεν. ἀποθώμεθα οὖν τὰ ἔργα τοῦ σκότους,
day has drawn near; we should cast off therefore the works of darkness,

¹καὶ ἐνδυσώμεθα‖ τὰ ὅπλα τοῦ φωτός. 13 ὡς ἐν ἡμέρᾳ,
and should put on the armour of light. As in [the] day,

εὐσχημόνως περιπατήσωμεν, μὴ κώμοις καὶ μέθαις, μὴ κοί-
becomingly we should walk; not in revels and drinking, not in cham-

ταις καὶ ἀσελγείαις, μὴ ἔριδι καὶ ζήλῳ· 14 ᵐἀλλ'‖ ἐνδύσασθε
bering and wantonness, not in strife and emulation. But put on

τὸν κύριον Ἰησοῦν χριστόν, καὶ ⁷τῆς σαρκὸς πρόνοιαν μὴ
the Lord Jesus Christ, and ⁷of ⁸the ⁹flesh ⁴forethought ²not

ποιεῖσθε εἰς ἐπιθυμίας.
¹do ³take ⁵for ⁶desire.

14 Τὸν.δὲ ἀσθενοῦντα τῇ πίστει προσλαμβάνεσθε, μὴ εἰς
But him being weak in the faith receive not for

διακρίσεις διαλογισμῶν. 2 Ὃς.μὲν πιστεύει φαγεῖν πάντα,
decisions of reasonings. One believes to eat all things;

ὁ.δὲ ἀσθενῶν λάχανα ἐσθίει. 3 ὁ ἐσθίων, τὸν μὴ
another being weak ²herbs ¹eats. He that eats, ⁵him ⁶that ⁷not

ἐσθίοντα μὴ.ἐξουθενείτω· ⁿκαὶ ὁ‖ μὴ.ἐσθίων, τὸν ἐ-
⁴eats ¹let ²him ³not ⁴despise; and he that eats not, ⁵him ⁶that

σθίοντα μὴ.κρινέτω· ὁ.θεὸς.γὰρ αὐτὸν προσελάβετο. 4 σὺ
⁴eats ¹let ²him ³not ⁴judge: for God him received. ²Thou

τίς εἶ ὁ κρίνων ἀλλότριον οἰκέτην; τῷ.ἰδίῳ κυρίῳ στήκει
¹who ³art judging another's servant? to his own master he stands

ἢ πίπτει. σταθήσεται.δέ· ᵒδυνατὸς.γάρ ἐστιν ὁ θεὸς‖
or falls. And he shall be made to stand; for able is God

στῆσαι αὐτόν. 5 Ὃς.μὲν ᵖ κρίνει ἡμέραν παρ' ἡμέραν,
to make ²stand ¹him. One judges a day [to be] above a day;

---

upon this very thing. 7 Render therefore to all their dues: tribute to whom tribute *is due*; custom to whom custom; fear to whom fear; honour to whom honour. 8 Owe no man any thing, but to love one another: for he that loveth another hath fulfilled the law. 9 For this, Thou shalt not commit adultery, Thou shalt not kill, Thou shalt not steal, Thou shalt not bear false witness, Thou shalt not covet; and if *there be* any other commandment, it is briefly comprehended in this saying, namely, Thou shalt love thy neighbour as thyself. 10 Love worketh no ill to his neighbour: therefore love *is* the fulfilling of the law. 11 And that, knowing the time, that now *it is* high time to a-wake out of sleep: for now *is* our salvation nearer than when we believed. 12 The night is far spent, the day is at hand: let us therefore cast off the works of darkness, and let us put on the armour of light. 13 Let us walk honestly, as in the day; not in rioting and drunkenness, not in chambering and wantonness, not in strife and envying. 14 But put ye on the Lord Jesus Christ, and make not provision for the flesh, to *fulfil* the lusts *thereof*.

XIV. Him that is weak in the faith receive ye, *but* not to doubtful disputations. 2 For one believeth that he may eat all things: another, who is weak, eateth herbs. 3 Let not him that eateth despise him that eateth not; and let not him which eat-eth not judge him that eateth: for God hath received him. 4 Who art thou that judgest another man's servant? To his own master he standeth or falleth. Yea, he shall be holden up: for God is able to make him stand. 5 One man es-

---

ᵉ ἀλλήλους ἀγαπᾶν GLTTrAW. ᶠ — οὐ ψευδομαρτυρήσεις GLTTrAW. ᵍ τῷ λόγῳ τούτῳ
LTTrAW. ʰ [ἐν τῷ] LTTrA. ⁱ σεαυτόν LTTrA. ᵏ ἤδη ἡμᾶς LTTrW; ἤδη ὑμᾶς already
you TrA. ¹ ἐνδυσώμεθα δὲ LTTrAW. ᵐ ἀλλὰ TTrAW. ⁿ ὁ δὲ LTTrA. ᵒ δυνατεῖ γὰρ ὁ
κύριος for able is the Lord LTTrA; δυνατεῖ γὰρ ὁ θεὸς W. ᵖ + γὰρ for (one) [L]T.

teemeth one day above another : another esteemeth every day alike. Let every man be fully persuaded in his own mind. 6 He that regardeth the day, regardeth it unto the Lord ; and he that regardeth not the day, to the Lord he doth not regard it. He that eateth, eateth to the Lord, for he giveth God thanks ; and he that eateth not, to the Lord he eateth not, and giveth God thanks. 7 For none of us liveth to himself, and no man dieth to himself. 8 For whether we live, we live unto the Lord ; and whether we die, we die unto the Lord : whether we live therefore, or die, we are the Lord's. 9 For to this end Christ both died, and rose, and revived, that he might be Lord both of the dead and living. 10 But why dost thou judge thy brother? or why dost thou set at nought thy brother? for we shall all stand before the judgment seat of Christ. 11 For it is written, As I live, saith the Lord, every knee shall bow to me, and every tongue shall confess to God. 12 So then every one of us shall give account of himself to God. 13 Let us not therefore judge one another any more: but judge this rather, that no man put a stumbling block or an occasion to fall in his brother's way. 14 I know, and am persuaded by the Lord Jesus, that there is nothing unclean of itself : but to him that esteemeth any thing to be unclean, to him it is unclean. 15 But if thy brother be grieved with thy meat, now walkest thou not charitably. Destroy not him with thy meat, for whom Christ died. 16 Let not then your good be evil spoken of : 17 for the kingdom of God is not meat and drink ; but righteousness, and

---

ὃς δὲ κρίνει πᾶσαν ἡμέραν.   ἕκαστος ἐν τῷ ἰδίῳ νοΐ
another judges every day [to be alike]. Each in his own mind

πληροφορείσθω. ὁ φρονῶν τὴν ἡμέραν, κυρίῳ φρονεῖ·
let be fully assured. He that regards the day, to [the] Lord regards [it];

q καὶ ὁ μὴ φρονῶν τὴν ἡμέραν, κυρίῳ οὐ φρονεῖ." r ὁ
and he that regards not the day, to [the] Lord regards [it] not. He that

ἐσθίων, κυρίῳ ἐσθίει, εὐχαριστεῖ γὰρ τῷ θεῷ· καὶ ὁ μὴ
eats, to [the] Lord eats, for he gives thanks to God ; and he that not

ἐσθίων, κυρίῳ οὐκ ἐσθίει, καὶ εὐχαριστεῖ τῷ θεῷ. 7 οὐδεὶς
eats, to [the] Lord he eats not, and gives thanks to God. 7 No one

γὰρ ἡμῶν ἑαυτῷ ζῇ, καὶ οὐδεὶς ἑαυτῷ ἀποθνήσκει. 8 ἐάν τε
for of us to himself lives, and no one to himself dies. 8 Both if

γὰρ ζῶμεν, τῷ κυρίῳ ζῶμεν· ἐάν τε s ἀποθνήσκωμεν,||
for we should live, to the Lord we should live; and if we should die,

τῷ κυρίῳ ἀποθνήσκομεν. ἐάν τε οὖν ζῶμεν, ἐάν τε s ἀπο-
to the Lord we die: both if then we should live, and if we should

θνήσκωμεν,|| τοῦ κυρίου ἐσμέν. 9 εἰς τοῦτο γὰρ χριστὸς t καὶ||
die, the Lord's we are. For, for this Christ both

ἀπέθανεν καὶ v ἀνέστη καὶ ἀνέζησεν,|| ἵνα καὶ νεκρῶν καὶ
died and rose and lived again, that both [the] dead and

ζώντων κυριεύσῃ. 10 Σὺ δὲ τί κρίνεις τὸν ἀδελφόν
living he might rule over. But thou why judgest thou brother

σου; ἢ καὶ σὺ τί ἐξουθενεῖς τὸν ἀδελφόν σου; πάντες γὰρ
thy? or also thou why dost thou despise thy brother? For all

παραστησόμεθα τῷ βήματι w τοῦ χριστοῦ.|| 11 γέγραπται
we shall stand before the judgment seat of the Christ. It has been written

γάρ, Ζῶ ἐγώ, λέγει κύριος· ὅτι ἐμοὶ κάμψει πᾶν γόνυ,
for, Live I, says [the] Lord, that to me shall bow every knee,

καὶ x πᾶσα γλῶσσα ἐξομολογήσεται|| τῷ θεῷ. 12 Ἄρα y οὖν||
and every tongue shall confess to God. So then

ἕκαστος ἡμῶν περὶ ἑαυτοῦ λόγον z δώσει|| a τῷ θεῷ.|| 13 Μη-
each of us concerning himself account shall give to God. No

κέτι οὖν ἀλλήλους κρίνωμεν· ἀλλὰ τοῦτο κρίνατε μᾶλλον,
longer therefore one another should we judge ; but this judge ye rather,

τὸ μὴ τιθέναι πρόσκομμα τῷ ἀδελφῷ ἢ σκάνδαλον.
not to put an occasion of stumbling to the brother or a cause of offence.

14 οἶδα καὶ πέπεισμαι ἐν κυρίῳ Ἰησοῦ, ὅτι οὐδὲν
I know and am persuaded in [the] Lord Jesus, that nothing [is]

κοινὸν δι' b ἑαυτοῦ·|| εἰ μὴ τῷ λογιζομένῳ τι κοινὸν
unclean of itself : except to him who reckons anything unclean

εἶναι, ἐκείνῳ κοινόν· 15 εἰ c δὲ|| διὰ βρῶμα ὁ
to be, to that one unclean [it is]. If but on account of meat the

ἀδελφός σου λυπεῖται, οὐκέτι κατὰ ἀγάπην περιπατεῖς.
brother is grieved, no longer according to love thou walkest.

μὴ τῷ βρώματί σου ἐκεῖνον ἀπόλλυε ὑπὲρ οὗ χριστὸς ἀπέ-
Not with thy meat him destroy for whom Christ died.

θανεν. 16 Μὴ βλασφημείσθω οὖν ὑμῶν τὸ ἀγαθόν. 17 οὐ
Let not be evil spoken of therefore your good ; not

γάρ ἐστιν ἡ βασιλεία τοῦ θεοῦ βρῶσις καὶ πόσις, ἀλλὰ
for is the kingdom of God eating and drinking ; but

δικαιοσύνη καὶ εἰρήνη καὶ χαρὰ ἐν πνεύματι ἁγίῳ· 18 ὁ
righteousness and peace and joy in [the] Spirit Holy. He that

---

q — καὶ ὁ μὴ φρονῶν τὴν ἡμέραν, κυρίῳ οὐ φρονεῖ LTTr[A].   r + καὶ and GLTTrAW.   s ἀποθνήσκομεν we die L.   t — καὶ LTTrAW.   v ἔζησεν lived GLTTrAW.   w τοῦ θεοῦ of God LTTrAW.   x ἐξομολογήσεται πᾶσα γλῶσσα LTr.   y — οὖν LTr[A].   z ἀποδώσει LTr [ἀποδώσει A].   a [τῷ θεῷ] L.   b αὐτοῦ GLTrW.   c γὰρ for LTTrAW.

γὰρ ἐν ᵈτούτοις∥ δουλεύων ᵉτῷ∥ χριστῷ εὐάρεστος τῷ θεῷ,
ᶠfor in these things　serves　the　Christ [is] well-pleasing　to God,

καὶ δόκιμος τοῖς ἀνθρώποις. 19 ἄρα οὖν τὰ τῆς εἰρήνης
and approved　by men.　So then the things　of peace

ᶠδιώκωμεν,∥ καὶ τὰ τῆς οἰκοδομῆς τῆς.εἰς.ἀλλήλους.
we should pursue, and the things　for building up　one another.

20 Μὴ ἕνεκεν βρώματος κατάλυε τὸ ἔργον τοῦ θεοῦ.
Not for the sake of　meat　destroy　the work·　of God.

πάντα μὲν καθαρά, ἀλλὰ κακὸν τῷ ἀνθρώπῳ τῷ
All things indeed [are] pure ;　but [it is] evil to the man　who

διὰ προσκόμματος ἐσθίοντι. 21 καλὸν τὸ μὴ φαγεῖν κρέα,
through stumbling　eats.　[It is] right　not to eat flesh,

μηδὲ πιεῖν οἶνον, μηδὲ ἐν ᾧ ὁ.ἀδελφός.σου προσκόπτει ᵍἢ
nor drink wine, nor in what thy brother stumbles,　or

σκανδαλίζεται ἢ ἀσθενεῖ.∥ 22 Σὺ πίστιν ʰἔχεις; κατὰ∥ ⁱσαυτὸν∥
is offended,　or is weak.　²Thou ³faith ¹hast? To thyself

ἔχε ἐνώπιον τοῦ θεοῦ· μακάριος ὁ μὴ.κρίνων ἑαυτὸν
have [it] before　God. Blessed [is] he that judges not himself

ἐν ᾧ δοκιμάζει. 23 ὁ.δὲ διακρινόμενος, ἐὰν φάγῃ, κατα-
in what he approves.　But he that doubts,　if he eat, has been

κέκριται, ὅτι οὐκ ἐκ πίστεως· πᾶν.δὲ ὃ οὐκ ἐκ
condemned, because [it is] not of faith ;　and everything which [is] not of

πίστεως, ἁμαρτία ἐστίν. ᵏ
faith,　²sin　¹is.

15 Ὀφείλομεν.δὲ ἡμεῖς οἱ δυνατοὶ τὰ ἀσθενήματα τῶν
But we ought,　we who [are] strong,　the infirmities of the

ἀδυνάτων βαστάζειν, καὶ μὴ ἑαυτοῖς ἀρέσκειν· 2 ἕκαστος.ⁱγὰρ∥
weak　to bear,　and not ourselves to please.　For ²each

ἡμῶν τῷ πλησίον ἀρεσκέτω εἰς τὸ ἀγαθὸν·πρὸς οἰκοδομήν.
³of ⁴us ᵉthe ⁷neighbour　¹let ⁵please unto　good　for building up.

3 καὶ.γὰρ ὁ χριστὸς οὐχ ἑαυτῷ ἤρεσεν, ἀλλά, καθὼς γέ-
For also the　Christ ²not ³himself ¹pleased ; but, according as it has

γραπται, Οἱ ὀνειδισμοὶ τῶν ὀνειδιζόντων σε ᵐἐπέπεσον∥
been written, The reproaches of those reproaching thee　fell

ἐπ' ἐμέ. 4 Ὅσα.γὰρ προεγράφη, εἰς τὴν ἡμετέραν
on me.　For as many things as were written before for　our

διδασκαλίαν ⁿπροεγράφη,∥ ἵνα διὰ τῆς ὑπομονῆς καὶ ᵒ τῆς
instruction　were written before, that through　endurance and

παρακλήσεως τῶν γραφῶν τὴν ἐλπίδα ἔχωμεν. 5 ὁ.δὲ
encouragement of the scriptures　hope we might have.· Now the

θεὸς τῆς ὑπομονῆς καὶ.τῆς παρακλήσεως δῴη ὑμῖν τὸ αὐτὸ
God　of endurance and　encouragement give you ³the⁴same⁵thing

φρονεῖν ἐν ἀλλήλοις κατὰ ᴾχριστὸν Ἰησοῦν·∥ 6 ἵνα
¹to ²mind with one another according to Christ Jesus ;　that

ὁμοθυμαδὸν ἐν ἑνὶ στόματι δοξάζητε τὴν θεὸν καὶ πατέρα
with one accord with ' one　mouth ye may glorify the God and Father

τοῦ.κυρίου.ἡμῶν Ἰησοῦ χριστοῦ. 7 Διὸ προσλαμβάνεσθε
of our Lord　Jesus　Christ.　Wherefore　receive ye

ἀλλήλους, καθὼς καὶ ὁ χριστὸς προσελάβετο ᑫἡμᾶς∥ εἰς
one another, according as also· the Christ　received　us　to

δόξαν ʳ θεοῦ.
[the] glory of God.

ᵈ τούτῳ this GLTTrAW. ᵉ — τῷ L[Tr]. ᶠ διώκομεν we pursue T. ᵍ — ἢ σκανδαλίζεται ἢ ἀσθενεῖ T. ʰ ἢν ([ἢν] A) ἔχεις κατὰ (read faith which thou hast, to &c.) LTTrA. ⁱ σεαυτὸν GLTTrAW. ᵏ Place here verses 25—27 of chapter xvi. G. ˡ — γὰρ for GLTTrAW. ᵐ ἐπέπεσαν LTTrA. ⁿ ἐγράφη were written LTTrAW. ᵒ + διὰ through LTTrAW. ᴾ Ἰησοῦν Tr. ᑫ ὑμᾶς you GLTTrAW. ʳ + τοῦ LTTrA.

peace, and joy in the Holy Ghost. 18 For he that in these things serveth Christ is acceptable to God, and approved of men. 19 Let us therefore follow after the things which make for peace, and things wherewith one may edify another. 20 For meat destroy not the work of God. All things indeed are pure; but it is evil for that man who eateth with offence. 21 It is good neither to eat flesh, nor to drink wine, nor any thing whereby thy brother stumbleth, or is offended, or is made weak. 22 Hast thou faith ? have it to thyself before God. Happy is he that condemneth not himself in that thing which he alloweth. 23 And he that doubteth is damned if he eat, because he eateth not of faith : for whatsoever is not of faith is sin.

XV. We then that are strong ought to bear the infirmities of the weak, and not to please ourselves. 2 Let every one of us please his neighbour for his good to edification. 3 For even Christ pleased not himself ; but, as it is written, The reproaches of them that reproached thee fell on me. 4 For whatsoever things were written aforetime were written for our learning, that we through patience and comfort of the scriptures might have hope. 5 Now the God of patience and consolation grant you to be likeminded one toward another according to Christ Jesus : 6 that ye may with one mind and one mouth glorify God, even the Father of our Lord Jesus Christ. 7 Wherefore receive ye one another, as Christ also received us to the glory of God.

8 Now I say that Jesus Christ was a minister of the circumcision for the truth of God, to confirm the promises *made* unto the fathers: 9 and that, the Gentiles might glorify God for *his* mercy; as it is written, For this cause I will confess to thee among the Gentiles, and sing unto thy name. 10 And again he saith, Rejoice, ye Gentiles, with his people. 11 And again, Praise the Lord, all ye Gentiles; and laud him, all ye people. 12 And again, Esaias saith, There shall be a root of Jesse, and he that shall rise to reign over the Gentiles; in him shall the Gentiles trust. 13 Now the God of hope fill you with all joy and peace in believing, that ye may abound in hope, through the power of the Holy Ghost.

8 Λέγω *δὲ,* *Ἰησοῦν* χριστὸν διάκονον *γεγενῆσθαι* περι-
²I ³say ¹but, Jesus Christ a servant has become of cir-
τομῆς ὑπὲρ ἀληθείας θεοῦ, εἰς τὸ βεβαιῶσαι τὰς ἐπαγ-
cumcision for [the] truth of God, for to confirm the pro-
γελίας τῶν πατέρων· 9 τὰ δὲ ἔθνη ὑπὲρ ἐλέους δοξάσαι τὸν
mises of the fathers; and the nations for mercy to glorify
θεόν, καθὼς γέγραπται, Διὰ τοῦτο ἐξομολογήσομαί
God; according as it has been written, Because of this I will confess
σοι ἐν ἔθνεσιν, καὶ τῷ ὀνόματί σου ψαλῶ. 10 Καὶ
to thee among [the] nations, and thy name will I praise. And
πάλιν λέγει, Εὐφράνθητε, ἔθνη, μετὰ τοῦ λαοῦ αὐτοῦ. 11 Καὶ
again it says, Rejoice ye, nations, with his people. And
πάλιν*, Αἰνεῖτε *τὸν κύριον πάντα τὰ ἔθνη,* καὶ *ἐπαινέσατε*
again, Praise the Lord, all the nations, and praise
αὐτὸν πάντες οἱ λαοί. 12 Καὶ πάλιν, Ἡσαΐας λέγει, Ἔ-
him, all the peoples. And again, Esaias says, There
σται ἡ ῥίζα τοῦ Ἰεσσαί, καὶ ὁ ἀνιστάμενος ἄρχειν
shall be the root of Jesse, and he that arises to rule [the]
ἐθνῶν, ἐπ' αὐτῷ ἔθνη ἐλπιοῦσιν. 13 Ὁ δὲ θεὸς τῆς
nations: in him [the] nations shall hope. Now ²the ³God
ἐλπίδος πληρώσαι ὑμᾶς πάσης χαρᾶς καὶ εἰρήνης ἐν τῷ
⁴of ⁵hope ¹may fill you with all joy and peace in
πιστεύειν, εἰς τὸ περισσεύειν ὑμᾶς ἐν τῇ ἐλπίδι, ἐν δυνάμει
believing, for ²to ³abound ¹you in hope, in power
πνεύματος ἁγίου.
of [the] ²Spirit ¹Holy.

14 And I myself also am persuaded of you, my brethren, that ye also are full of goodness, filled with all knowledge, able also to admonish one another. 15 Nevertheless, brethren, I have written the more boldly unto you in some sort, as putting you in mind, because of the grace that is given to me of God, 16 that I should be the minister of Jesus Christ to the Gentiles, ministering the gospel of God, that the offering up of the Gentiles might be acceptable, being sanctified by the Holy Ghost. 17 I have therefore whereof I may glory through Jesus Christ in those things which pertain to God. 18 For I will not dare to speak of any of those things which Christ hath not wrought by me, to make the Gentiles obedient, by word and deed, 19 through mighty signs and wonders, by the power of the Spirit of God; so that

14 Πέπεισμαι δέ, ἀδελφοί μου, καὶ αὐτὸς ἐγὼ περὶ
But ⁴am ⁵persuaded, ⁶my ⁷brethren, ²also ³myself ¹I concerning
ὑμῶν, ὅτι καὶ αὐτοὶ μεστοί ἐστε ἀγαθωσύνης, πεπληρωμένοι
you, that also yourselves full are of goodness, being filled
πάσης ᵍνώσεως, δυνάμενοι καὶ ἀλλήλους νουθετεῖν. 15 *τολ-
with all knowledge, being able also one another to admonish. ²More
μηρότερον* δὲ ἔγραψα ὑμῖν, *ἀδελφοί,* ἀπὸ μέρους, ὡς
³boldly ¹but I did write to you, brethren, in part, as
ἐπαναμιμνήσκων ὑμᾶς, διὰ τὴν χάριν τὴν δοθεῖσάν μοι
reminding you, because of the grace which was given to me
ὑπὸ τοῦ θεοῦ, 16 εἰς τὸ εἶναί με λειτουργὸν *Ἰησοῦ χριστοῦ*
by God, for ²to ³be me a minister of Jesus Christ
εἰς τὰ ἔθνη, ἱερουργοῦντα τὸ εὐαγγέλιον τοῦ θεοῦ,
to the nations, administering in sacred service the glad tidings of God,
ἵνα γένηται ἡ προσφορὰ τῶν ἐθνῶν εὐπρόσδεκτος, ἡγιασμένη
that might be the offering up of the nations acceptable, sanctified
ἐν πνεύματι ἁγίῳ. 17 ἔχω οὖν ᵉκαύχησιν ἐν χριστῷ
by [the] ²Spirit ¹Holy. I have therefore boasting in Christ
Ἰησοῦ τὰ πρὸς ᶠθεόν· 18 οὐ γὰρ τολμήσω ᵍλα-
Jesus [as to] the things pertaining to God. For not will I dare to
λεῖν τι* ὧν οὐ κατειργάσατο χριστὸς δι' ἐμοῦ, εἰς
speak anything of what ³not ²worked ⁴out ¹Christ by me, for [the]
ὑπακοὴν ἐθνῶν, λόγῳ καὶ ἔργῳ, 19 ἐν δυνάμει ση-
obedience of [the] nations, by word and work, in [the] power of
μείων καὶ τεράτων, ἐν δυνάμει πνεύματος *θεοῦ·* ὥστε με
signs and wonders, in [the] power of [the] Spirit of God; so a for me

---

ˢ γὰρ for LTTrAW.   ᵗ — Ἰησοῦν LTTrA.   ᵛ γενέσθαι became LTr.   ʷ + λέγει it
says L[A].   ˣ πάντα τὰ ἔθνη τὸν κύριον LTTrA.   ʸ ἐπαινεσάτωσαν LTTrA.   ᶻ + τηςT[A]
ᵃ τολμηροτέρως Tr.   ᵇ — ἀδελφοί LTTr[A].   ᶜ ἀπὸ TTr.   ᵈ χριστοῦ Ἰησοῦ LTTrAW.
ᵉ + τὴν LTTrAW.   ᶠ + τὸν GLTTrAW.   ᵍ τι λαλεῖν LTTrAW.   ʰ ἁγίου Holy (Spirit)
GLT[A]W.

ἀπὸ Ἱερουσαλὴμ καὶ κύκλῳ μέχρι τοῦ Ἰλλυρικοῦ πεπληρω-
from Jerusalem, and in a circuit unto Illyricum, to have fully

κέναι τὸ εὐαγγέλιον τοῦ χριστοῦ· 20 οὕτως δὲ [1]φιλοτιμού-
preached the glad tidings of the Christ; and so being am-

μενον[2] εὐαγγελίζεσθαι, οὐχ ὅπου ὠνομάσθη χριστός,
bitious to announce the glad tidings, not where [2]was [3]named [1]Christ,

ἵνα μὴ ἐπ᾽ ἀλλότριον θεμέλιον οἰκοδομῶ· 21 ἀλλὰ καθὼς
that not upon another's foundation I might build; but according as

γέγραπται, Οἷς οὐκ ἀνηγγέλη περὶ αὐτοῦ, ὄψον-
it has been written, To whom it was not announced concerning him, they shall

ται· καὶ οἳ οὐκ ἀκηκόασιν, συνήσουσιν. 22 Διὸ καὶ ἐνε-
see; and those that have not heard, shall understand. Wherefore also I was

κοπτόμην [k]τὰ πολλὰ[||] τοῦ ἐλθεῖν πρὸς ὑμᾶς. 23 νυνὶ δὲ
hindered many times from coming to you. But now,

μηκέτι τόπον ἔχων ἐν τοῖς κλίμασιν τούτοις, ἐπιποθίαν δὲ
no longer [2]place [1]having in these regions, and [2]a [3]longing

ἔχων [l]τοῦ[||] ἐλθεῖν πρὸς ὑμᾶς ἀπὸ [m]πολλῶν[||] ἐτῶν, 24 ὡς [n]ἐὰν[||]
[1]having to come to you for many years, whenever

πορεύωμαι εἰς τὴν Σπανίαν, [o]ἐλεύσομαι πρὸς ὑμᾶς·[||] ἐλπίζω
I may go to Spain, I will come to you; [2]I [3]hope

γὰρ διαπορευόμενος θεάσασθαι ὑμᾶς, καὶ [p]ὑφ᾽[||] ὑμῶν προπεμ-
[1]for going through to see you, and by you to be set

φθῆναι ἐκεῖ, ἐὰν ὑμῶν πρῶτον ἀπὸ μέρους ἐμπλησθῶ.
forward thither, if of you first in part I should be filled.

25 Νυνὶ δὲ πορεύομαι εἰς Ἱερουσαλήμ, διακονῶν τοῖς ἁγίοις.
But now I go to Jerusalem, doing service to the saints;

26 [q]εὐδόκησαν[||] γὰρ Μακεδονία καὶ Ἀχαΐα κοινωνίαν τινὰ
for [4]were [5]pleased [1]Macedonia [2]and [3]Achaia [6]a [3]contribution [4]certain

ποιήσασθαι εἰς τοὺς πτωχοὺς τῶν ἁγίων τῶν ἐν Ἱερουσα-
to make for the poor of the saints who [are] in Jerusa-

λήμ· 27 [q]εὐδόκησαν[||] γὰρ καὶ ὀφειλέται [r]αὐτῶν εἰσίν.[||] εἰ γὰρ
lem. For they were pleased and debtors [1]their they are; for if

τοῖς πνευματικοῖς αὐτῶν ἐκοινώνησαν τὰ ἔθνη, ὀφείλουσιν
in their spiritual things [3]participated [1]the [2]nations, they ought

καὶ ἐν τοῖς σαρκικοῖς λειτουργῆσαι αὐτοῖς. 28 τοῦτο οὖν
also in the fleshly things to minister to them. This therefore

ἐπιτελέσας, καὶ σφραγισάμενος αὐτοῖς τὸν καρπὸν τοῦτον,
having finished, and having sealed to them this fruit,

ἀπελεύσομαι δι᾽ ὑμῶν εἰς [s]τὴν[||] Σπανίαν. 29 οἶδα δὲ ὅτι
I will set off by you into Spain. And I know that

ἐρχόμενος πρὸς ὑμᾶς, ἐν πληρώματι εὐλογίας [t]τοῦ εὐαγγελίου
coming to you, in fulness of blessing of the glad tidings

τοῦ[||] χριστοῦ ἐλεύσομαι. 30 Παρακαλῶ δὲ ὑμᾶς, [v]ἀδελφοί,[||] διὰ
of Christ I shall come. But I exhort you, brethren, by

[t]τοῦ κυρίου ἡμῶν[||] Ἰησοῦ χριστοῦ, καὶ διὰ τῆς ἀγάπης τοῦ
our Lord Jesus Christ, and by the love of the

πνεύματος, συναγωνίσασθαί μοι ἐν ταῖς προσευχαῖς ὑπὲρ
Spirit, to strive together with me in prayers for

ἐμοῦ πρὸς τὸν θεόν· 31 ἵνα ῥυσθῶ ἀπὸ τῶν ἀπει-
me to God, that I may be delivered from those being

θούντων ἐν τῇ Ἰουδαίᾳ, καὶ [w]ἵνα[||] ἡ [x]διακονία[||] μου ἡ
disobedient in Judæa; and that [2]service [1]my which [is]

from Jerusalem, and round about unto Illyricum, I have fully preached the gospel of Christ. 20 Yea, so have I strived to preach the gospel, not where Christ was named, lest I should build upon another man's foundation: 21 but as it is written, To whom he was not spoken of, they shall see: and they that have not heard shall understand. 22 For which cause also I have been much hindered from coming to you. 23 But now having no more place in these parts, and having a great desire these many years to come unto you; 24 whensoever I take my journey into Spain, I will come to you: for I trust to see you in my journey, and to be brought on my way thitherward by you, if first I be somewhat filled with your *company*. 25 But now I go unto Jerusalem to minister unto the saints. 26 For it hath pleased them of Macedonia and Achaia to make a certain contribution for the poor saints which are at Jerusalem. 27 It hath pleased them verily; and their debtors they are. For if the Gentiles have been made partakers of their spiritual things, their duty is also to minister unto them in carnal things. 28 When therefore I have performed this, and have sealed to them this fruit, I will come by you into Spain. 29 And I am sure that, when I come unto you, I shall come in the fulness of the blessing of the gospel of Christ. 30 Now I beseech you, brethren, for the Lord Jesus Christ's sake, and for the love of the Spirit, that ye strive together with me in *your* prayers to God for me; 31 that I may be delivered from them that do not believe in Judæa; and that my service which

---

[i] φιλοτιμοῦμαι I am ambitibus LTr.   [k] πολλάκις L.   [l] [τοῦ] L.   [m] ἱκανῶν TrA.
[n] ἂν LTTrAW.   [o] — ἐλεύσομαι πρὸς ὑμᾶς GLTT·AW.   [p] ἀφ᾽ LA.   [q] ηὐδόκησαν TTr.
[r] εἰσὶν αὐτῶν LTTrAW.   [s] — τὴν LTTrA.   [t] — τοῦ εὐαγγελίου τοῦ GLTTrAW.   [v] [ἀδελφοί] A.
[w] — ἵνα LTTrA.   [x] δωροφορία offering of gifts L.

I have for Jerusalem may be accepted of the saints; 32 that I may come unto you with joy by the will of God, and may with you be refreshed. 33 Now the God of peace be with you all. Amen.

γείς[c] 'Ιερουσαλὴμ εὐπρόσδεκτος ᵗγένηται τοῖς ἁγίοις·[||] 32 ἵνα
for   Jerusalem   acceptable   may be   to the saints ;   that

ᵃἐν χαρᾷ ἔλθω[||] πρὸς ὑμᾶς διὰ θελήματος ᵇθεοῦ,[||] ᶜκαὶ
in   joy   I may come   to   you   by [the]   will   of God,   and

συναναπαύσωμαι ὑμῖν.[||] 33 ὁ.δὲ θεὸς τῆς εἰρήνης μετὰ
I may be refreshed with you.   And the God   of peace [be] with

πάντων ὑμῶν. ᵈἀμήν.[||]
ᶻall ⁱyou.   Amen.

16 Συνίστημι.δὲ ὑμῖν Φοίβην τὴν.ἀδελφὴν.ἡμῶν, οὖσαν·
But I commend   to you   Phœbe,   our sister,   being

διάκονον τῆς ἐκκλησίας τῆς ἐν ᵉΚεγχρεαῖς·[||] 2 ἵνα ᶠαὐτὴν προσ-
servant   of the assembly   in   Cenchrea;   that   her   ye may

δέξησθε[||] ἐν κυρίῳ ἀξίως τῶν ἁγίων, καὶ παραστῆτε αὐτῇ
receive   in [the] Lord   worthily   of saints, and   ye may assist   her

ἐν ᾧ.ἂν ὑμῶν χρῄζῃ πράγματι· καὶ.γὰρ ᵍαὐτη[||] προ-
in whatever ²of ³you ⁴she ⁵may ⁶need ¹matter ;   for also   she   a suc-

στάτις πολλῶν ἐγενήθη, καὶ ʰαὐτοῦ ἐμοῦ.[||] 3 Ἀσπάσασθε
courer   of many   has been, and   ³myself ¹of ²me.   Salute

ⁱΠρίσκιλλαν[||] καὶ Ἀκύλαν τοὺς.συνεργούς.μου ἐν χριστῷ Ἰη-
Priscilla   and   Aquila   my fellow-workers   in   Christ   Je-

σοῦ· 4 οἵτινες ὑπὲρ τῆς.ψυχῆς.μου τὸν.ἑαυτῶν τράχηλον
sus,   (who   for   my life   their own   neck

ὑπέθηκαν, οἷς οὐκ ἐγὼ μόνος εὐχαριστῶ, ἀλλὰ καὶ πᾶσαι αἱ
laid down : whom not ²I ¹only   thank,   but also   all   the

ἐκκλησίαι τῶν ἐθνῶν· 5 καὶ τὴν κατ' οἶκον αὐτῶν ἐκκλησίαν.
assemblies of the nations,)   and the ²at ⁴house ³their ¹assembly.

ἀσπάσασθε Ἐπαίνετον τὸν.ἀγαπητόν.μου, ὅς ἐστιν ἀπαρχὴ
Salute   Epænetus   my beloved,   who is   a first-fruit

τῆς ᵏἈχαίας[||] εἰς χριστόν. 6 ἀσπάσασθε ˡΜαριάμ,[||] ἥτις πολλὰ
of Achaia   for   Christ.   Salute   Mary,   who ²much

ἐκοπίασεν εἰς ᵐἡμᾶς.[||] 7 ἀσπάσασθε Ἀνδρόνικον καὶ Ἰουνίαν
¹laboured   for us.   Salute   Andronicus   and   Junias

τοὺς.συγγενεῖς.μου καὶ συναιχμαλώτους μου· οἵτινές εἰσιν
my kinsmen   and   ²fellow-prisoners ¹my,   who   are

ἐπίσημοι ἐν τοῖς ἀποστόλοις, οἳ καὶ πρὸ ἐμοῦ ⁿγεγόνασιν[||]
of note   among the   apostles ;   who also before   me   were

ἐν χριστῷ. 8 ἀσπάσασθε ᵒἈμπλίαν[||] τὸν.ἀγαπητόν.μου ἐν
in   Christ.   Salute   Amplias   my beloved   in [the]

κυρίῳ. 9 ἀσπάσασθε Οὐρβανὸν τὸν.συνεργὸν.ἡμῶν ἐν ᴾχριστῷ,[||]
Lord.   Salute   Urbanus   our fellow-worker   in   Christ,

καὶ Στάχυν τὸν.ἀγαπητόν.μου. 10 ἀσπάσασθε Ἀπελλῆν τὸν
and Stachys   my beloved.   Salute   Apelles   the

δόκιμον ἐν χριστῷ. ἀσπάσασθε τοὺς ἐκ τῶν   Ἀρι-
approved in   Christ.   Salute   those of the [household] of Ari-

στοβούλου. 11 ἀσπάσασθε qἩροδίωνα[||] τὸν.ʳσυγγενῆ[||].μου.
stobulus.   Salute   Herodion   my kinsman.

ἀσπάσασθε τοὺς ἐκ τῶν   Ναρκίσσου, τοὺς ὄντας ἐν
Salute   those of the [household] of Narcissus,   who are   in [the

κυρίῳ. 12 ἀσπάσασθε Τρύφαιναν καὶ Τρυφῶσαν τὰς κοπιώσας
Lord.   Salute   Tryphæna   and   Tryphosa,   who   labour

ἐν κυρίῳ. ˢἀσπάσασθε Περσίδα τὴν ἀγαπητήν, ἥτις πολλὰ
in [the] Lord.   Salute   Persis   the beloved,   who   much

XVI. I commend unto you Phebe our sister, which is a servant of the church which is at Cenchrea: 2 that ye receive her in the Lord, as becometh saints, and that ye assist her in whatsoever business she hath need of you: for she hath been a succourer of many, and of myself also. 3 Greet Priscilla and Aquila my helpers in Christ Jesus: 4 who have for my life laid down their own necks: unto whom not only I give thanks, but also all the churches of the Gentiles. 5 Likewise *greet* the church that is in their house. Salute my wellbeloved Epænetus, who is the firstfruits of Achaia unto Christ. 6 Greet Mary, who bestowed much labour on us. 7 Salute Andronicus and Junia my kinsmen, and my fellowprisoners, who are of note among the apostles, who also were in Christ before me. 8 Greet Amplias my beloved in the Lord. 9 Salute Urbane, our helper in Christ, and Stachys my beloved. 10 Salute Apelles approved in Christ. Salute them which are of Aristobulus' *household*. 11 Salute Herodion my kinsman. Greet them that be of the *household* of Narcissus, which are in the Lord. 12 Salute Tryphena and Tryphosa, who labour in the Lord. Salute the beloved Persis, which laboured

---

γ ἐν at L, ᵗ τοῖς ἁγίοις γένηται LTTrA.   ᵃ ἐλθὼν (having come) ἐν χαρᾷ T.   ᵇ κυρίου Ἰησοῦ of [the] Lord Jesus L.   ᶜ — καὶ T ; — καὶ συναναπαύσωμαι ὑμῖν L[A].   ᵈ [ἀμήν] LTr.   ᵉ Κεν- T ᶠ προσδέξησθε αὐτὴν LTrA.   ᵍ αὐτὴ GLTAW.   ʰ ἐμοῦ αὐτοῦ LTTrA.   ⁱ Πρίσκαν Prisca GLTTrAW.   ᵏ Ἀσίας Asia GLTTrAW.   ˡ Μαρίαν LTrA.   ᵐ ὑμᾶς you LTTrA.   ⁿ γέγοναν LTTrA.   ᵒ Ἀμπλίατον Ampliatus TTrA.   ᴾ κυρίῳ [the] Lord L.   q Ἡρωδίωνα GLTTrAW. ʳ συγγενὴν Tr.   ˢ [ἀσπάσασθε .... κυρίῳ] L.

ἐκοπίασεν ἐν κυρίῳ.‖ 13 ἀσπάσασθε Ῥοῦφον τὸν ἐκλεκτὸν
laboured in [the] Lord. Salute Rufus the chosen

ἐν κυρίῳ, καὶ τὴν.μητέρα.αὐτοῦ καὶ ἐμοῦ. 14 ἀσπάσασθε
in [the] Lord, and his mother and mine. Salute

ᵗ Ἀσύγκριτον,‖ Φλέγοντα, ᵛ Ἑρμᾶν,‖ Πατρόβαν, ʷ Ἑρμῆν,‖ καὶ
Asyncritus, Phlegon, Hermas, Patrobas, Hermes, and

τοὺς σὺν αὐτοῖς ἀδελφούς. 15 ἀσπάσασθε Φιλόλογον καὶ
the ²with ³them ¹brethren, Salute Philologus and

Ἰουλίαν, Νηρέα καὶ τὴν.ἀδελφὴν.αὐτοῦ, καὶ Ὀλυμπᾶν, καὶ
Julias, Nereus and his sister, and Olympas, and

τοὺς σὺν αὐτοῖς πάντας ἁγίους. 16 ἀσπάσασθε ἀλλήλους
²the ⁴with ⁵them ¹all ³saints. Salute one another

ἐν φιλήματι ἁγίῳ. ἀσπάζονται ὑμᾶς αἱ ἐκκλησίαι ˣ τοῦ
with a ²kiss ¹holy. ⁷Salute ⁸you ³the ⁴assemblies

χριστοῦ.
⁵of ⁶Christ.

17 Παρακαλῶ.δὲ ὑμᾶς, ἀδελφοί, σκοπεῖν τοὺς τὰς διχο-
But I exhort you, brethren to consider those who ⁵divi-

στασίας καὶ τὰ σκάνδαλα, παρὰ τὴν διδαχὴν ἣν ὑμεῖς
sions ¹and ⁴causes ⁵of ⁶offence ⁷contrary ⁸to ⁹the ¹⁰teaching ¹¹which ¹²ye

ἐμάθετε, ποιοῦντας· καὶ ʸἐκκλίνατε‖ ἀπ᾽ αὐτῶν. 18 οἱ γὰρ
¹³learnt, ¹make, and turn away from them. For

τοιοῦτοι τῷ.κυρίῳ.ἡμῶν ᶻἸησοῦ‖ χριστῷ οὐ.δουλεύουσιν, ἀλλὰ
such ³our ⁴Lord ⁵Jesus ⁶Christ ¹serve ²not, but

τῇ.ἑαυτῶν κοιλίᾳ· καὶ διὰ τῆς χρηστολογίας καὶ εὐλογίας
their own belly, and by kind speaking and praise

ἐξαπατῶσιν τὰς καρδίας τῶν ἀκάκων. 19 ἡ.γὰρ ὑμῶν ὑπακοὴ
deceive the hearts of the innocent. For the ²of ³you ¹obedience

εἰς πάντας ἀφίκετο· ᵃχαίρω οὖν τὸ.ἐφ᾽ ὑμῖν.‖ θέλω.δὲ
²to ⁴all ¹reached. I rejoice therefore concerning you; but I wish

ὑμᾶς σοφοὺς ᵇμὲν‖ εἶναι εἰς τὸ ἀγαθόν, ἀκεραίους.δὲ εἰς τὸ
¹you wise to be [as] to good, and simple to

κακόν. 20 ὁ.δὲ θεὸς τῆς εἰρήνης συντρίψει τὸν σατανᾶν ὑπὸ
evil. But the God of peace will bruise Satan under

τοὺς.πόδας.ὑμῶν ἐν τάχει. ἡ χάρις τοῦ.κυρίου.ἡμῶν Ἰησοῦ
your feet shortly. The grace of our Lord Jesus

ᶜχριστοῦ‖ μεθ᾽ ὑμῶν. ᵈ
Christ [be] with you.

21 ᵉἈσπάζονται‖ ὑμᾶς Τιμόθεος ὁ.συνεργός.μου καὶ Λούκιος
¹²Salute ¹³you ¹Timotheus ²my ³fellow-worker ⁴and ⁵Lucius

καὶ Ἰάσων καὶ Σωσίπατρος οἱ.συγγενεῖς.μου. 22 ἀσπάζομαι
⁶and ⁷Jason ⁸and ⁹Sosipater ¹⁰my ¹¹kinsmen. ²⁰Salute

ὑμᾶς ἐγὼ Τέρτιος ὁ γράψας τὴν ἐπιστολὴν ἐν κυρίῳ.
²¹you ¹⁴I ¹⁵Tertius ¹⁶who ¹⁷wrote ¹⁸the ¹⁹epistle in [the] Lord.

23 ἀσπάζεται ὑμᾶς Γάϊος ὁ ξένος μου καὶ ᶠτῆς ἐκκλησίας
²Salutes ³you ¹Gaius, the host of me ⁶and of the ²assembly

ὅλης.‖ ἀσπάζεται ὑμᾶς Ἔραστος ὁ οἰκονόμος τῆς πόλεως,
¹whole. ¹³Salutes ¹⁴you ³Erastus ⁴the ⁵steward ⁶of ⁷the ⁸city,

καὶ Κούαρτος ὁ ἀδελφός. 24 ᵍΗ χάρις τοῦ.κυρίου.ἡμῶν
⁹and ¹⁰Quartus ¹¹the ¹²brother. The grace of our Lord

Ἰησοῦ χριστοῦ μετὰ πάντων ὑμῶν. ἀμήν.‖
Jesus Christ [be] with ²all ¹you. Amen.

much in the Lord.
13 Salute Rufus chosen
in the Lord, and his
mother and mine.
14 Salute Asyncritus,
Phlegon, Hermas, Pa-
trobas, Hermes, and
the brethren which are
with them. 15 Salute
Philologus, and Julia,
Nereus, and his sister,
and Olympas, and all
the saints which are
with them. 16 Salute
one another with an
holy kiss. The churches
of Christ salute you.

17 Now I beseech
you, brethren, mark
them which cause di-
visions and offences
contrary to the doc-
trine which ye have
learned; and avoid
them. 18 For they that
are such serve not our
Lord Jesus Christ, but
their own belly; and
by good words and
fair speeches deceive
the hearts of the sim-
ple. 19 For your obe-
dience is come abroad
unto all men. I am
glad therefore on your
behalf: but yet I would
have you wise unto
that which is good,
and simple concerning
evil. 20 And the God
of peace shall bruise
Satan under your feet
shortly. The grace of
our Lord Jesus Christ
be with you. Amen.

21 Timotheus my
workfellow, and Lu-
cius, and Jason, and
Sosipater, my kins-
men, salute you. 22 I
Tertius, who wrote
this epistle, salute you
in the Lord. 23 Gaius
mine host, and of the
whole church, saluteth
you. Erastus the
chamberlain of the
city saluteth you, and
Quartus a brother.
24 The grace of our
Lord Jesus Christ be
with you all. Amen.

ᵗ Ἀσύν- T. ᵛ Ἑρμῆν LTTrAW. ʷ Ἑρμᾶν LTTrAW. ˣ + πᾶσαι all (the assemblies)
GLTTrAW. ʸ ἐκκλίνετε TTr. ᶻ — Ἰησοῦ GLTTrAW. ᵃ ἐφ᾽ ὑμῖν οὖν χαίρω LTTrAW.
ᵇ — μὲν LTTrA. ᶜ — χριστοῦ T[TrA]. ᵈ + ἀμήν Amen E. ᵉ Ἀσπάζεται Salutes
LTTrAW. ᶠ ὅλης τῆς ἐκκλησίας LTTrA. ᵍ — verse 24 LTTr[AL.

25 Now to him that is of power to stablish you according to my gospel, and the preaching of Jesus Christ, according to the revelation of the mystery, which was kept secret since the world began, 26 but now is made manifest, and by the scriptures of the prophets, according to the commandment of the everlasting God, made known to all nations for the obedience of faith : 27 to God only wise, be glory through Jesus Christ for ever. Amen.

25 h Τῷ.δὲ δυναμενῳ ὑμᾶς στηρίξαι κατὰ τὸ εὐαγ-
Now to him who is able you to establish according to the glad

γέλιόν μου καὶ τὸ κήρυγμα Ἰησοῦ χριστοῦ, κατὰ ἀπο-
tidings my and the proclamation of Jesus Christ, according to a reve-

κάλυψιν μυστηρίου χρόνοις αἰωνίοις σεσιγημένου,
lation of [the] mystery in times of the ages having been kept secret,

26 φανερωθέντος.δὲ νῦν, διά.τε γραφῶν προφητικῶν, κατ
but made manifest now, and by scriptures prophetic, according to

ἐπιταγὴν τοῦ αἰωνίου θεοῦ, εἰς ὑπακοὴν πίστεως εἰς παντα
commandment of the eternal God, for obedience of faith to all

τὰ ἔθνη γνωρισθέντος. 27 μόνῳ σοφῷ θεῷ, διὰ Ἰη-
the nations having been made known— [the] only wise God, through Je-

σοῦ χριστοῦ, ᾧ ἡ δόξα εἰς τοὺς αἰῶνας[i]. ἀμήν.
sus Christ, to whom be glory to the ages. Amen.

kΠρὸς Ῥωμαίους ἐγράφη ἀπὸ Κορίνθου, διὰ Φοίβης τῆς
To [the] Romans written from Corinth. by Phœbe

διακόνου τῆς ἐν Κεγχρεαῖς ἐκκλησίας.‖
servant of the ²in ³Cenchrea ¹assembly.

Ἡ ΠΡΟΣ ΤΟΥΣ ΚΟΡΙΝΘΙΟΥΣ ΕΠΙΣΤΟΛΗ ΠΡΩΤΗ.‖
¹THE ⁴TO ⁵THE ⁶CORINTHIANS ³EPISTLE ²FIRST.

PAUL, called to be an apostle of Jesus Christ through the will of God, and Sosthenes our brother, 2 unto the church of God which is at Corinth, to them that are sanctified in Christ Jesus, called to be saints, with all that in every place call upon the name of Jesus Christ our Lord, both theirs and ours: 3 Grace be unto you, and peace, from God our Father, and from the Lord Jesus Christ.

ΠΑΥΛΟΣ bκλητὸς‖ ἀπόστολος c᾽Ιησοῦ χριστοῦ,‖ διὰ θελή-
Paul a called apostle of Jesus Christ, by [the] will

ματος θεοῦ, καὶ Σωσθένης ὁ ἀδελφός, 2 τῇ ἐκκλησίᾳ τοῦ
of God, and Sosthenes the brother, to the assembly

θεοῦ dτῇ οὔσῃ ἐν Κορίνθῳ,‖ ἡγιασμένοις ἐν χριστῷ Ἰη-
of God which is in Corinth, having been sanctified in Christ Je-

σοῦ,d κλητοῖς ἁγίοις, σὺν πᾶσιν τοῖς ἐπικαλουμένοις τὸ ὄνομα
sus, called saints, with all those ⁴calling ⁵on ⁶the ⁷name

τοῦ.κυρίου.ἡμῶν Ἰησοῦ χριστοῦ ἐν παντὶ τόπῳ, αὐτῶν.εͅτε‖
⁸of ⁹our ¹⁰Lord ¹¹Jesus ¹²Christ ¹in ²every ³place, both theirs

καὶ ἡμῶν· 3 χάρις ὑμῖν καὶ εἰρήνη ἀπὸ θεοῦ πατρὸς.ἡμῶν
and ours: grace to you and peace from God our Father

καὶ κυρίου Ἰησοῦ χριστοῦ.
and [the] Lord Jesus Christ.

4 I thank my God always on your behalf, for the grace of God which is given you by Jesus Christ ; 5 that in every thing ye are enriched by him, in all utterance, and in all knowledge; 6 even as the testimony of Christ was confirmed in you : 7 so that ye come behind in no gift ; waiting for the coming of our Lord Jesus Christ: 8 who

4 Εὐχαριστῶ τῷ.θεῷ.μου πάντοτε περὶ ὑμῶν, ἐπὶ τῇ
I thank my God always concerning you, for the

χάριτι τοῦ θεοῦ τῇ δοθείσῃ ὑμῖν ἐν χριστῷ Ἰησοῦ, 5 ὅτι ἐν
grace of God that was given to you in Christ Jesus, that in

παντὶ ἐπλουτίσθητε ἐν αὐτῷ, ἐν παντὶ λόγῳ καὶ πάσῃ
everything ye were enriched in him, in all discourse and all

γνώσει, 6 καθὼς τὸ μαρτύριον τοῦ χριστοῦ ἐβεβαιώθη ἐν
knowledge, according as the testimony of the Christ was confirmed in

ὑμῖν· 7 ὥστε ὑμᾶς μὴ ὑστερεῖσθαι ἐν μηδενὶ χαρίσματι, ἀπεκ-
you, so that ye are behind in not one gift,

δεχομένους τὴν ἀποκάλυψιν τοῦ.κυρίου.ἡμῶν Ἰησοῦ χριστοῦ·
awaiting the revelation of our Lord Jesus Christ ;

---

h Verses 25—27 placed at end of chapter xiv. G.   i + τῶν αἰώνων of ages LT.   k — the subscription GLTW ; Πρὸς Ῥωμαίους TᵣA.
a + Παύλου τοῦ Ἀποστόλου of Paul the Apostle E ; + Παύλου G; — τοὺς EG ; Πρὸς Κορινθίους ά LTTᵣAW.   b [κλητὸς] LA.   c χριστοῦ Ἰησοῦ LTTᵣAW.   d τῇ οὔσῃ ἐν Κορίνθῳ placed after Ἰησοῦ LTᵣA.   e — τε both LTTᵣ[A].

8 ὃς καὶ βεβαιώσει ὑμᾶς ἕως τέλους, ἀνεγκλήτους ἐν τῇ
who also will confirm you to [the] end, unimpeachable in the

ἡμέρᾳ τοῦ κυρίου ἡμῶν Ἰησοῦ χριστοῦ. 9 πιστὸς ὁ θεός, δι'
day of our Lord Jesus Christ. Faithful [is] God, by

οὗ ἐκλήθητε εἰς κοινωνίαν τοῦ υἱοῦ αὐτοῦ Ἰησοῦ χριστοῦ
whom ye were called into fellowship of his Son Jesus Christ

τοῦ κυρίου ἡμῶν.
our Lord.

10 Παρακαλῶ δὲ ὑμᾶς, ἀδελφοί, διὰ τοῦ ὀνόματος τοῦ
Now I exhort you, brethren, by the name

κυρίου ἡμῶν Ἰησοῦ χριστοῦ, ἵνα τὸ αὐτὸ λέγητε πάντες,
of our Lord Jesus Christ, that ⁴the ⁵same ⁶thing ¹ye ²say ²all,

καὶ μὴ ᾖ ἐν ὑμῖν σχίσματα, ἦτε δὲ κατηρτισμένοι
and ²no ¹there ²be ⁵among ⁶you ⁴divisions; but ye be knit together

ἐν τῷ αὐτῷ νοΐ. καὶ ἐν τῇ αὐτῇ γνώμῃ. 11 ἐδηλώθη γάρ
in the same mind and in the same judgment. For it was shewn

μοι περὶ ὑμῶν, ἀδελφοί μου, ὑπὸ τῶν Χλόης,
to me concerning you, my brethren, by those of [the house of] Chloe,

ὅτι ἔριδες ἐν ὑμῖν εἰσιν· 12 λέγω δὲ τοῦτο, ὅτι ἕκαστος
that strifes among you there are. But I say this, that each

ὑμῶν λέγει, Ἐγὼ μέν εἰμι Παύλου, ἐγὼ δὲ Ἀπολλώ, ἐγὼ δὲ
of you says, I am of Paul, and I of Apollos, and I

Κηφᾶ, ἐγὼ δὲ χριστοῦ. 10 Μεμέρισται ὁ χριστός; μὴ Παῦ-
of Cephas, and I of Christ. Has ³been ⁴divided ¹the ²Christ? ⁵Paul

λος ἐσταυρώθη ὑπὲρ ὑμῶν; ἢ εἰς τὸ ὄνομα Παύλου ἐβαπ-
⁴was crucified for you? or to the name of Paul were ye

τίσθητε; 14 εὐχαριστῶ τῷ θεῷ ὅτι οὐδένα ὑμῶν ἐβάπτισα,
baptized? I thank God that no one of you I baptized,

εἰ μὴ Κρίσπον καὶ Γάϊον· 15 ἵνα μή τις εἴπῃ ὅτι εἰς τὸ
except Crispus and Gaius, that not anyone should say that unto

ἐμὸν ὄνομα ἐβάπτισα. 16 ἐβάπτισα δὲ καὶ τὸν Στεφανᾶ
my name I baptized. And I baptized also the ²of ³Stephanas

οἶκον· λοιπὸν οὐκ οἶδα εἴ τινα ἄλλον ἐβάπτισα. 17 Οὐ γὰρ
¹house; as to the rest I know not if any other I baptized. For ²not

ἀπέστειλέν με χριστὸς βαπτίζειν, ἀλλ' εὐαγγελίζεσθαι·
²sent ³me ¹Christ to baptize, but to announce the glad tidings;

οὐκ ἐν σοφίᾳ λόγου, ἵνα μὴ κενωθῇ ὁ σταυρὸς τοῦ χριστοῦ.
not in wisdom of word, that ²not ¹be made void the cross of the Christ.

18 ὁ λόγος γὰρ ὁ τοῦ σταυροῦ τοῖς μὲν ἀπολλυμένοις μωρία
For the word of the cross to those perishing ²foolishness

ἐστίν, τοῖς δὲ σωζομένοις ἡμῖν δύναμις θεοῦ ἐστιν. 19 γέ-
¹is, but ²who ⁴are ⁵being ⁶saved ¹to ²us ⁹power ¹⁰of ¹¹God ⁷it ⁸is. ¹³It ¹⁴has

γραπται γάρ, Ἀπολῶ τὴν σοφίαν τῶν σοφῶν, καὶ τὴν
¹been ¹⁶written ¹⁵for, I will destroy the wisdom of the wise, and the

σύνεσιν τῶν συνετῶν ἀθετήσω. 20 Ποῦ σοφός;
understanding of the understanding ones I will set aside. Where [is the] wise?

ποῦ γραμματεύς; ποῦ συζητητὴς τοῦ αἰῶνος τούτου;
where [the] scribe? where [the] disputer of this age?

οὐχὶ ἐμώρανεν ὁ θεὸς τὴν σοφίαν τοῦ κόσμου τούτου;
did not ²make ³foolish ¹God the wisdom of this world?

21 Ἐπειδὴ γὰρ ἐν τῇ σοφίᾳ τοῦ θεοῦ οὐκ ἔγνω ὁ κόσμος διὰ
For since, in the wisdom of God, ⁵knew ⁶not ¹the ²world ³by

τῆς σοφίας τὸν θεόν, εὐδόκησεν ὁ θεὸς διὰ τῆς μωρίας τοῦ
⁴wisdom God, ²was ³pleased ¹God by the foolishness of the

---

shall also confirm you unto the end, *that ye may be* blameless in the day of our Lord Jesus Christ. 9 God is faithful, by whom ye were called unto the fellowship of his Son Jesus Christ our Lord.

10 Now I beseech you, brethren, by the name of our Lord Jesus Christ, that ye all speak the same thing, and *that* there be no divisions among you; but *that* ye be perfectly joined together in the same mind and in the same judgment. 11 For it hath been declared unto me of you, my brethren, by them *which are of the house* of Chloe, that there are contentions among you. 12 Now this I say, that every one of you saith, I am of Paul; and I of Apollos; and I of Cephas; and I of Christ. 13 Is Christ divided? was Paul crucified for you? or were ye baptized in the name of Paul? 14 I thank God that I baptized none of you, but Crispus and Gaius; 15 lest any should say that I had baptized in mine own name. 16 And I baptized also the household of Stephanas: besides, I know not whether I baptized any other. 17 For Christ sent me not to baptize, but to preach the gospel: not with wisdom of words, lest the cross of Christ should be made of none effect. 18 For the preaching of the cross is to them that perish foolishness; but unto us which are saved it is the power of God. 19 For it is written, I will destroy the wisdom of the wise, and will bring to nothing the understanding of the prudent. 20 Where is the wise? where is the scribe? where is the disputer of this world? hath not God made foolish the wisdom of this world? 21 For after that in the wisdom of God the world by wisdom knew not God, it pleased God by the

---

f περὶ L.   g — τῷ θεῷ (*read* εὐχαριστῶ I give thanks) τ.   h ἐβαπτίσθητε ye were
baptized LTTrAW.   i + [ὁ] L.   k ἀλλὰ TTrA.   l συνζητητὴς LTTrA.   m — τούτου (r·ad
the world) LTTrAW.

foolishness of preaching to save them that believe. 22 For the Jews require a sign, and the Greeks seek after wisdom: 23 but we preach Christ crucified, unto the Jews a stumbling-block, and unto the Greeks foolishness; 24 but unto them which are called, both Jews and Greeks, Christ the power of God, and the wisdom of God. 25 Because the foolishness of God is wiser than men; and the weakness of God is stronger than men. 26 For ye see your calling, brethren, how that not many wise men after the flesh, not many mighty, not many noble, are called: 27 but God hath chosen the foolish things of the world to confound the wise; and God hath chosen the weak things of the world to confound the things which are mighty; 28 and base things of the world, and things which are despised, hath God chosen, yea, and things which are not, to bring to nought things that are: 29 that no flesh should glory in his presence. 30 But of him are ye in Christ Jesus, who of God is made unto us wisdom, and righteousness, and sanctification, and redemption: 31 that, according as it is written, He that glorieth, let him glory in the Lord.

II. And I, brethren, when I came to you, came not with excellency of speech or of wisdom, declaring unto you the testimony of God. 2 For I determined not to know any thing among you, save Jesus Christ, and him crucified. 3 And I was with you in weakness, and in fear, and in much trembling. 4 And my speech and my preaching was not with enticing words of man's wisdom, but in demon-

κηρύγματος σῶσαι τοὺς πιστεύοντας· 22 ἐπειδὴ καὶ Ἰου-
proclamation to save those that believe. Since both Jews

δαῖοι ⁿσημεῖον∥ αἰτοῦσιν, καὶ Ἕλληνες σοφίαν ζητοῦσιν.
²a ⁴sign ¹ask ²for, and Greeks ²wisdom ¹seek;

23 ἡμεῖς δὲ κηρύσσομεν χριστὸν ἐσταυρωμένον, Ἰουδαίοις
but we proclaim Christ crucified, to Jews

μὲν σκάνδαλον, ᵒἝλλησιν∥ δὲ μωρίαν· 24 αὐτοῖς δὲ τοῖς
indeed a cause of offence, ²to ³Greeks ¹and foolishness; but to those the

κλητοῖς, Ἰουδαίοις τε καὶ Ἕλλησιν, χριστὸν θεοῦ δύναμιν καὶ
called, both Jews and Greeks, Christ God's power and

θεοῦ σοφίαν. 25 ὅτι τὸ μωρὸν τοῦ θεοῦ σοφώτερον τῶν
God's wisdom. Because the foolishness of God wiser

ἀνθρώπων ἐστίν· καὶ τὸ ἀσθενὲς τοῦ θεοῦ ἰσχυρότερον τῶν
than men is, and the weakness of God stronger

ἀνθρώπων ᴾἐστίν.∥ 26 Βλέπετε γὰρ τὴν κλῆσιν ὑμῶν, ἀδελφοί,
than men is. For ye see your calling, brethren,

ὅτι οὐ πολλοὶ σοφοὶ κατὰ σάρκα, οὐ πολλοὶ δυνα-
that not many wise according to flesh [there are], not many power-

τοί, οὐ πολλοὶ εὐγενεῖς· 27 ἀλλὰ τὰ μωρὰ τοῦ κόσμου
ful, not many high-born. But the foolish things of the world

ἐξελέξατο ὁ θεός, �q ἵνα τοὺς σοφοὺς καταισχύνῃ∥ ʳκαὶ τὰ
²chose ¹God, that the wise he might put to shame; and the

ἀσθενῆ τοῦ κόσμου ἐξελέξατο ὁ θεός,∥ ἵνα καταισχύνῃ
weak things of the world ²chose ¹God, that he might put to shame

τὰ ἰσχυρά· 28 καὶ τὰ ἀγενῆ τοῦ κόσμου καὶ τὰ ἐξουθενη-
the strong things; and the low-born of the world, and the de-

μένα ἐξελέξατο ὁ θεός, ˢκαὶ∥ τὰ μὴ ὄντα, ἵνα τὰ
spised ²chose ¹God, and the things that are not, that the things that

ὄντα καταργήσῃ· 29 ὅπως μὴ ᵗκαυχήσηται∥ πᾶσα σὰρξ
are he may annul; so that ²not ³might ⁵boast ¹all ²flesh

ἐνώπιον ᵛαὐτοῦ.∥ 30 ἐξ αὐτοῦ δὲ ὑμεῖς ἐστε ἐν χριστῷ Ἰησοῦ,
before him. But of him are ye in Christ Jesus,

ὃς ἐγενήθη ʷἡμῖν σοφία∥ ἀπὸ θεοῦ δικαιοσύνη τε καὶ ἁγιασ-
who was made to us wisdom from God and righteousness and sancti-

μὸς καὶ ἀπολύτρωσις· 31 ἵνα, καθὼς γέγραπται,
fication and redemption; that, according as it has been written,

Ὁ καυχώμενος, ἐν κυρίῳ καυχάσθω.
He that boasts, in [the] Lord let him boast.

2 Κἀγὼ ἐλθὼν πρὸς ὑμᾶς, ἀδελφοί, ἦλθον οὐ καθ'
And I having come to you, brethren, came not according to

ὑπεροχὴν λόγου ἢ σοφίας καταγγέλλων ὑμῖν τὸ μαρτύριον
excellency of word or wisdom, announcing to you the testimony

τοῦ θεοῦ. 2 οὐ γὰρ ἔκρινα ˣτοῦ∥ ʸεἰδέναι τι∥ ἐν ὑμῖν,
of God. For ²not ¹I ²decided to know anything among you,

εἰ μὴ Ἰησοῦν χριστόν, καὶ τοῦτον ἐσταυρωμένον. 3 ᶻκαὶ ἐγὼ∥
except Jesus Christ, and him crucified. And I

ἐν ἀσθενείᾳ καὶ ἐν φόβῳ καὶ ἐν τρόμῳ πολλῷ ἐγενόμην πρὸς
in weakness and in fear and in trembling ¹much was with

ὑμᾶς· 4 καὶ ὁ λόγος μου καὶ τὸ κήρυγμά μου οὐκ ἐν πειθοῖς
you; and my word and my preaching [was] not in persuasive

ᵃἀνθρωπίνης∥ σοφίας λόγοις, ᵇἀλλ'∥ ἐν ἀποδείξει πνεύματος
³human ²of ⁴wisdom ¹words, but in demonstration of [the] Spirit

---

ⁿ σημεῖα signs GLTTrAW.   �q ἔθνεσιν to nations GLTTrAW.   ᴾ — ἐστίν TTr.   ᑫ ἵνα
καταισχύνῃ τοὺς σοφούς [L]TTrA.   ʳ [καὶ τὰ .... ὁ θεός] L.   ˢ — καὶ LTTrA.   ᵗ καυχή-
σεται E.   ᵛ τοῦ θεοῦ God GLTTrAW.   ʷ σοφία ἡμῖν LTTrA.   ˣ — τοῦ GLTTrAW.   ʸ τι
εἰδέναι GLTTrAW.   ᶻ κἀγὼ LTTrA.   ᵃ — ἀνθρωπίνης GLTTrAW.   ᵇ ἀλλὰ Tr.

καὶ δυνάμεως· 5 ἵνα ἡ.πίστις.ὑμῶν μὴ.ᾖ ἐν σοφίᾳ ἀνθρώ-
and of power ;　　that　　your faith　　might not be in wisdom　of men,
πων, ᵇἀλλ'ⁿ ἐν δυνάμει θεοῦ.
but　　in power of God.

6 Σοφίαν.δὲ λαλοῦμεν ἐν τοῖς τελείοις· σοφίαν.δὲ οὐ τοῦ
But wisdom　we speak among the　　perfect ;　but wisdom, not

αἰῶνος.τούτου, οὐδὲ τῶν ἀρχόντων τοῦ.αἰῶνος.τούτου. τῶν
of this age,　　nor of the　　rulers　　of this age,　　who

καταργουμένων· 7 ἀλλὰ λαλοῦμεν ᶜσοφίαν θεοῦⁿ ἐν μυστηρίῳ,
are coming to nought.　But · we speak　　wisdom of God in　a mystery,

τὴν ἀποκεκρυμμένην　　ἣν προώρισεν ὁ θεὸς πρὸ τῶν
the　　hidden　　[wisdom] which ²predetermined　¹God before the

αἰώνων εἰς δόξαν.ἡμῶν, 8 ἣν οὐδεὶς τῶν ἀρχόντων τοῦ
ages　for　　our glory,　　which no one of the　　rulers

αἰῶνος.τούτου ἔγνωκεν· εἰ.γὰρ ἔγνωσαν, οὐκ.ἂν τὸν κύριον
of this age　　has known, (for if they had known, ⁸not　　¹the ²Lord

τῆς δόξης　ἐσταύρωσαν· 9 ἀλλὰ καθὼς γέγραπ-
³of ⁴the ⁵glory ⁶they ⁷would have crucified,)　but according as it has been

ται, ῭Α ὀφθαλμὸς οὐκ.εἶδεν, καὶ οὖς οὐκ.ἤκουσεν, καὶ
written, Things which　eye　　saw not,　and ear　heard not,　and

ἐπὶ καρδίαν ἀνθρώπου οὐκ.ἀνέβη, ᵈἃⁿ ἡτοίμασεν ὁ θεὸς
into　heart　of man　　came not, which ²prepared　¹God

τοῖς　ἀγαπῶσιν αὐτόν· 10 ἡμῖν.δὲ ᵉὁ θεὸς ἀπεκάλυψενⁿ
for those that　love　　him,　but to us　God　revealed [them]

διὰ τοῦ.πνεύματος.ᶠαὐτοῦ·ⁿ τὸ.γὰρ πνεῦμα πάντα ᵍἐρευνᾷ,ⁿ
by　　his Spirit ;　　for the　Spirit all things searches,

καὶ τὰ βάθη τοῦ θεοῦ. 11 τίς.γὰρ οἶδεν ἀνθρώπων τὰ
even the depths　of God.　For who　³knows　¹of ²men the things

τοῦ ἀνθρώπου, εἰ.μὴ τὸ πνεῦμα τοῦ ἀνθρώπου τὸ ἐν
of man,　except　the　spirit　　of man　　which [is] in

αὐτῷ; οὕτως καὶ τὰ τοῦ.θεοῦ οὐδεὶς· ʰοἶδεν,ⁿ εἰ.μὴ τὸ
him ?　so　also the things of God no one　knows,　except the

πνεῦμα τοῦ θεοῦ. 12 ἡμεῖς.δὲ οὐ τὸ πνεῦμα τοῦ κόσμου ἐλά-
Spirit　of God.　But we not the　spirit of the world　re-

βομεν, ἀλλὰ τὸ πνεῦμα τὸ ἐκ τοῦ.θεοῦ, ἵνα εἰδῶμεν
ceived,　but the　Spirit which [is] from　God,　that we might.know

τὰ ὑπὸ τοῦ θεοῦ χαρισθέντα ἡμῖν. 13 ῭Α καὶ λαλοῦμεν,
the things by　God　granted　to us :　which also we speak,

οὐκ ἐν διδακτοῖς ἀνθρωπίνης σοφίας λόγοις, ἀλλ' ἐν δι-
not in ²taught　³of ⁴human ⁵wisdom ¹words,　but in [those]

δακτοῖς πνεύματος ⁱἁγίου,ⁿ πνευματικοῖς πνευματικὰ
taught　of [the] ²Spirit ¹Holy,　　ᵉby ⁷spiritual [⁸means] ⁵spiritual ⁵things

ᵏσυγκρίνοντες.ⁿ 14 ψυχικὸς.δὲ ἄνθρωπος οὐ.δέχεται τὰ
³communicating.　But [the] natural　man　receives not the things

τοῦ πνεύματος τοῦ θεοῦ· μωρία.γὰρ αὐτῷ ἐστιν, καὶ
of the　Spirit　　of God, for foolishness to him they are ; and

οὐ.δύναται γνῶναι, ὅτι πνευματικῶς ἀνακρίνεται.
he cannot　know　[them], because　spiritually　they are discerned ;

15 ὁ.δὲ πνευματικὸς ἀνακρίνει ¹μὲνⁿ πάντα, αὐτὸς.δὲ ὑπ'
· but the　spiritual　discerns　all things,　but he　by

οὐδενὸς ἀνακρίνεται. 16 τίς.γὰρ ἔγνω νοῦν κυρίου,
no one　is discerned.　For who did know [the] mind of [the] Lord ?

ὃς συμβιβάσει αὐτόν; ἡμεῖς.δὲ νοῦν ᵐχριστοῦⁿ ἔχομεν.
who shall.instruct　him ?　But we [the] mind　of Christ　have.

stration of the Spirit and of power : 5 that your faith should not stand in the wisdom of men, but in the power of God.

6 Howbeit we speak wisdom among them that are perfect : yet not the wisdom of this world, nor of the princes of this world, that come to nought : 7 but we speak the wisdom of God in a mystery, even the hidden wisdom, which God ordained before the world unto our glory : 8 which none of the princes of this world knew : for had they known it, they would not have crucified the Lord of glory. 9 But as it is written, Eye hath not seen, nor ear heard, neither have entered into the heart of man, the things which God hath prepared for them that love him. 10 But God hath revealed them unto us by his Spirit : for the Spirit searcheth all things, yea, the deep things of God. 11 For what man knoweth the things of a man, save the spirit of man which is in him ? even so the things of God knoweth no man, but the Spirit of God. 12 Now we have received, not the spirit of the world, but the spirit which is of God; that we might know the things that are freely given to us of God. 13 Which things also we speak, not in the words which man's wisdom teacheth, but which the Holy Ghost teacheth ; comparing spiritual things with spiritual. 14 But the natural man receiveth not the things of the Spirit of God : for they are foolishness unto him : neither can he know them, because they are spiritually discerned. 15 But he that is spiritual judgeth all things, yet he himself is judged of no man. 16 For who hath known the mind of the Lord, that he may instruct him ? But we have the mind of Christ.

ᵇ ἀλλὰ Tr.　　ᶜ θεοῦ σοφίαν GLTTrAW.　ᵈ ὅσα whatsoever LTrA.　ᵉ ἀπεκάλυψεν ὁ θεὸς
LTTrAW.　ᶠ — αὐτοῦ (read the Spirit) LTTr[A].　ᵍ ἐραυνᾷ TTrA.　ʰ ἔγνωκεν has known LTTrAWⱼ
ⁱ — Ἁγίου GLTTrAW.　ᵏ συν- T.　¹ [ταὶ] L : — μὲν.T[TrA].　ᵐ κυρίου of [the] Lord L.

III. And I, brethren, could not speak unto you as unto spiritual, but as unto carnal, even as unto babes in Christ. 2 I have fed you with milk, and not with meat: for hitherto ye were not able *to bear it*, neither yet now are ye able. 3 For ye are yet carnal: for whereas *there is* among you envying, and strife, and divisions, are ye not carnal, and walk as men? 4 For while one saith, I am of Paul; and another, I *am* of Apollos; are ye not carnal? 5 Who then is Paul, and who *is* Apollos, but ministers by whom ye believed, even as the Lord gave to every man? 6 I have planted, Apollos watered; but God gave the increase. 7 So then neither is he that planteth any-thing, neither he that watereth; but God that giveth the in-crease. 8 Now he that planteth and he that watereth are one: and every man shall re-ceive his own reward according to his own labour. 9 For we are labourers together with God: ye are God's husbandry, *ye are* God's building. 10 Ac-cording to the grace of God which is given unto me, as a wise masterbuilder, I have laid the foundation, and another buildeth thereon. But let every man take heed how he buildeth thereupon. 11 For other foun-dation can no man lay than that is laid, which is Jesus Christ. 12 Now if any man build upon this foundation gold, sil-ver, precious stones, wood, hay, stubble, 13 every man's work shall be made mani-fest: for the day shall declare it, because it shall be revealed by fire ; and the fire shall try every man's work of what sort it is. 14 If any man's

3 ⁿΚαὶ ἐγώ,‖ ἀδελφοί, οὐκ_ἠδυνήθην λαλῆσαι ὑμῖν ὡς
   And   I,   brethren,   was not able   to speak   to you as

πνευματικοῖς, ἀλλ' ὡς °σαρκικοῖς,‖ ὡς νηπίοις ἐν χριστῷ.
to spiritual,   but as   to fleshly ;   as   to babes   in   Christ.

2 γάλα ὑμᾶς ἐπότισα, ᵖκαὶ‖ οὐ βρῶμα· οὔπω_γὰρ ᑫἠδύνασθε,‖
   Milk ³you ¹I ²gave to drink ; and not   meat,   for not yet   were ye able,

ἀλλ' ʳοὔτε‖ ˢἔτι‖ νῦν δύνασθε· 3 ἔτι_γὰρ σαρκικοί ἐστε.
   but   neither   yet   now are ye able ;   for yet   fleshly   ye are.

ὅπου_γὰρ ἐν ὑμῖν ζῆλος καὶ ἔρις ᵗκαὶ διχοστασίαι,‖
For where   among you   emulation and strife and   divisions   [there are],

οὐχὶ σαρκικοί ἐστε. καὶ κατὰ ἄνθρωπον περιπατεῖτε ;
³not   ⁴fleshly ¹are ²ye, and ²according ³to   ⁴man   ¹walk ?

4 ὅταν_γὰρ λέγῃ τις, Ἐγὼ μέν εἰμι Παύλου, ἕτερος_δέ, Ἐγὼ
For when ²may ³say ¹one,   I   am   of Paul,   and another,   I

Ἀπολλώ, ʳοὐχὶ σαρκικοί‖ ἐστε ; 5 ʷΤίς‖ οὖν ἐστιν ˣΠαῦλος,‖
of Apollos,   ³not   ⁴fleshly ¹are ²ye ?   Who then is   Paul,

ʷτίς‖ δὲ ʸ ˣ'Ἀπολλώς,‖ ᶻἀλλ' ἢ‖ διάκονοι δι' ὧν ἐπιστεύ-
²who ¹and   Apollos ?   but   servants through whom   ye be-

σατε, καὶ ἑκάστῳ ὡς ὁ κύριος ἔδωκεν ; 6 ἐγὼ ἐφύτευσα,
lieved, and   to each   as the   Lord   gave ?   I   planted,

Ἀπολλὼς ἐπότισεν, ᵃἀλλ'‖ ὁ θεὸς ηὔξανεν· 7 ὥστε οὔτε
Apollos   watered ;   but   God gave growth. So that neither

ὁ φυτεύων ἐστίν τι, οὔτε ὁ ποτίζων, ἀλλ' ὁ αὐξά-
he that   plants   is   anything, nor he that waters ;   but ²who ³gives

νων θεός. 8 ὁ_φυτεύων_δὲ καὶ ὁ ποτίζων ἕν εἰσιν· ἕκαστος
⁴growth ¹God.   But he that plants and he that waters   ²one ¹are ;   ⁴each

δὲ τὸν_ἴδιον μισθὸν ᵇλήψεται‖ κατὰ τὸν_ἴδιον κόπον.
³but his own   reward   shall receive according to   his own   labour.

9 θεοῦ_γὰρ ἐσμεν συνεργοί· θεοῦ γεώργιον, θεοῦ οἰκοδομὴ
For God's ²we ³are ¹fellow-workers ; God's   husbandry,   God's   building

ἐστε. 10 Κατὰ τὴν χάριν τοῦ θεοῦ τὴν δοθεῖσάν μοι, ὡς
ye are.   According to the   grace   of God which was given to me, as

σοφὸς ἀρχιτέκτων θεμέλιον ᶜτέθεικα,‖ ἄλλος_δὲ ἐποικοδομεῖ·
a wise   architect   [the] foundation I have laid, and another   builds up.

ἕκαστος_δὲ βλεπέτω πῶς ἐποικοδομεῖ· 11 θεμέλιον_γὰρ ἄλλον
But ²each   ¹let take heed how   he builds up.   For ²foundation ¹other

οὐδεὶς δύναται θεῖναι παρὰ τὸν κείμενον, ὅς ἐστιν ᵈἸη-
no one   is able   to lay   besides that which is laid, which is   Je-

σοῦς ὁ χριστός.‖ 12 εἰ_δὲ τις ἐποικοδομεῖ ἐπὶ τὸν θεμέλιον
sus the Christ.   Now if anyone   build up   on   ²foundation

ᵉτοῦτον‖ ᶠχρυσόν, ἄργυρον,‖ λίθους τιμίους, ξύλα, χόρτον,
¹this   gold,   silver,   ²stones ¹precious,   wood,   grass,

καλάμην, 13 ἑκάστου τὸ ἔργον φανερὸν γενήσεται· ἡ_γὰρ
straw,   of each the   work   manifest   will become ·   for the

ἡμέρα δηλώσει· ὅτι ἐν πυρὶ ἀποκαλύπτεται· καὶ ἑκάστου
day   will declare [it], because in   fire   it is revealed ;   and of each

τὸ ἔργον ὁποῖόν ἐστιν, τὸ πῦρ ᵍ δοκιμάσει. 14 εἴ τινος τὸ
the work   what sort   it is, the fire   will prove.   If of anyone the

ἔργον ʰμένει‖ ὃ ⁱἐπῳκοδόμησεν,‖ μισθὸν ᵏλήψεται.‖ 15 εἴ
work   abides which   he built up,   a reward he shall receive.   If

---

ⁿ κἀγώ GLTTrAW.   ° σαρκίνοις to fleshy GLTTrAW.   ᵖ — καὶ GLTTrAW.   ᑫ ἐδύνασθε GLTTrA.   ʳ οὐδὲ GLTTrAW.   ˢ [ἔτι] L.   ᵗ — καὶ διχοστασίαι LTTrA.   ᵛ οὐκ (οὐχὶ W) ἄνθρωποί not men LTTrAW.   ʷ τί what LTTr ; τί[ς] A.   ˣ Ἀπολλώς and Παῦλος transposed LTTrAW.   ʸ + ἐστιν is LTTrA.   ᶻ — ἀλλ' ἢ GLTTrAW.   ᵃ ἀλλὰ LTTrA.   ᵇ λήμψεται LTTrA.   ᶜ ἔθηκα I laid LTTrA.   ᵈ χριστὸς Ἰησοῦς L ; — ὁ GTTrAW.   ᵉ — τοῦτον read the foundation) LTTr[A].   ᶠ χρυσίον, ἀργύριον TTr.   ᵍ + αὐτὸ itself LTTrAW.   ʰ μενεῖ shall abide GLTAW.   ⁱ ἐποικοδόμησεν TTrA.   ᵏ λήμψεται LTTrA.

τινὸς τὸ ἔργον κατακαήσεται. ζημιωθήσεται· αὐτὸς.δὲ
of anyone the　work　shall be consumed,　he shall suffer loss,　but Himself

σωθήσεται, οὕτως.δὲ ὡς διὰ πυρός. 16 Οὐκ.οἴδατε ὅτι ναὸς
shall be saved,　but so　as through fire.　Know ye not that [2]temple

θεοῦ ἐστε, καὶ τὸ πνεῦμα τοῦ θεοῦ οἰκεῖ ἐν ὑμῖν; 17 εἴ τις
[1]God's ye are, and the Spirit　of God dwells in you?　If anyone

τὸν ναὸν τοῦ θεοῦ φθείρει,　　φθερεῖ　　[1]τοῦτον[ll] ὁ
the temple　of God corrupt,　[2]shall [4]bring [5]to [6]corruption　[1]him

θεός· ὁ.γὰρ ναὸς τοῦ θεοῦ ἅγιός ἐστιν, οἵτινές ἐστε ὑμεῖς.
[3]God; for the temple　of God [2]holy [1]is,　which [2]are [1]ye.

18 μηδεὶς ἑαυτὸν ἐξαπατάτω· εἴ τις δοκεῖ　　σοφὸς
[4]No [5]one [1]himself [3]let [6]deceive:　if anyone [3]thinks [[4]himself] [7]wise

εἶναι ἐν ὑμῖν ἐν τῷ.αἰῶνι.τούτῳ, μωρὸς γενέσθω, ἵνα
[2]to [6]be, [1]among [2]you in　this age,　foolish let him become, that

γένηται σοφός. 19 ἡ.γὰρ σοφία τοῦ.κόσμου.τούτου μωρία
he may be wise.　For the wisdom　of this world　foolishness

παρὰ [m]τῷ θεῷ ἐστιν· γέγραπται.γάρ, Ὁ δρασσόμενος τοὺς
with　God is;　for it has been written, He　takes　the

σοφοὺς ἐν τῇ.πανουργίᾳ.αὐτῶν. 20 καὶ πάλιν,　Κύριος
wise　in　their craftiness.　And again, [The] Lord

γινώσκει τοὺς διαλογισμοὺς τῶν σοφῶν, ὅτι εἰσὶν μάταιοι.
knows　the　reasonings　of the wise,　that they are vain.

21 Ὥστε μηδεὶς καυχάσθω ἐν ἀνθρώποις· πάντα.γὰρ ὑμῶν
So that [2]no [3]one [1]let boast　in　men;　for all things [2]yours

ἐστιν, 22 εἴτε Παῦλος, εἴτε Ἀπολλώς, εἴτε Κηφᾶς, εἴτε
[1]are.　Whether Paul,　or Apollos,　or Cephas,　or [the]

κόσμος, εἴτε ζωή, εἴτε θάνατος, εἴτε ἐνεστῶτα, εἴτε μέλλοντα·
world,　or life, or death,　or present things, or coming things,

πάντα ὑμῶν [n]ἐστιν·[ll] 23 ὑμεῖς.δὲ χριστοῦ· χριστὸς.δὲ θεοῦ.
all　yours [1]are·　and ye Christ's,　and Christ God's.

4 Οὕτως ἡμᾶς λογιζέσθω ἄνθρωπος ὡς ὑπηρέτας χριστοῦ
So [5]of [6]us [1]let [4]reckon [2]a [3]man　as attendants of Christ

καὶ οἰκονόμους μυστηρίων θεοῦ. 2 ὃ δὲ[ll] λοιπόν, ζητεῖται
and stewards [3]mysteries [1]of [2]God's.　But as to the rest, it is required

ἐν τοῖς οἰκονόμοις ἵνα πιστός τις εὑρεθῇ. 3 ἐμοὶ.δὲ εἰς ἐλά-
in　stewards　that faithful one be found.　But to me　the small-

χιστόν ἐστιν ἵνα ὑφ' ὑμῶν ἀνακριθῶ, ἢ ὑπὸ ἀνθρωπίνης
est matter it is that by　you I be examined, or　by　man's

ἡμέρας· ἀλλ' οὐδὲ ἐμαυτὸν ἀνακρίνω. 4 οὐδὲν.γὰρ ἐμαυτῷ
day.　But neither myself do I examine.　For of nothing in myself

σύνοιδα· ἀλλ' οὐκ ἐν τούτῳ δεδικαίωμαι· ὁ.δὲ ἀνα-
I am conscious; but not by this　have I been justified : but he who ex-

κρίνων με κύριός ἐστιν. 5 ὥστε μὴ πρὸ καιροῦ τι
amines me [the] Lord　is.　So that not before [the] time anything

κρίνετε, ἕως ἂν ἔλθῃ ὁ κύριος, ὃς καὶ φωτίσει τὰ
judge,　until　may have come the Lord,　who both will bring to light the

κρυπτὰ τοῦ σκότους, καὶ φανερώσει τὰς βουλὰς τῶν
hidden things　of darkness, and will make manifest the counsels

καρδιῶν· καὶ τότε ὁ ἔπαινος γενήσεται ἑκάστῳ ἀπὸ τοῦ θεοῦ.
of hearts; and then praise　shall be to each from　God.

6 Ταῦτα.δέ, ἀδελφοί, μετεσχημάτισα εἰς ἐμαυτὸν καὶ [P]Ἀ-
Now these things, brethren,　I transferred　to myself and A-

πολλώ[ll] δι' ὑμᾶς, ἵνα ἐν ἡμῖν μάθητε τὸ μὴ ὑπὲρ
pollos　on account of you,　that in us　ye may learn　not [3]above

---

work abide which he hath built thereupon, he shall receive a reward. 15 If any man's work shall be burned, he shall suffer loss : but he himself shall be saved ; yet so as by fire. 16 Know ye not that ye are the temple of God, and that the Spirit of God dwelleth in you? 17 If any man defile the temple of God, him shall God destroy ; for the temple of God is holy, which temple ye are. 18 Let no man deceive himself. If any man among you seemeth to be wise in this world, let him become a fool, that he may be wise. 19 For the wisdom of this world is foolishness with God. For it is written, He taketh the wise in their own craftiness. 20 And again, The Lord knoweth the thoughts of the wise, that they are vain. 21 Therefore let no man glory in men. For all things are yours ; 22 whether Paul, or Apollos, or Cephas, or the world, or life, or death, or things present, or things to come ; all are yours ; 23 and ye are Christ's ; and Christ is God's.

IV. Let a man so account of us, as of the ministers of Christ, and stewards of the mysteries of God. 2 Moreover it is required in stewards, that a man be found faithful. 3 But with me it is a very small thing that I should be judged of you, or of man's judgment: yea, I judge not mine own self. 4 For I know nothing by myself ; yet am I not hereby justified : but he that judgeth me is the Lord. 5 Therefore judge nothing before the time, until the Lord come, who both will bring to light the hidden things of darkness, and will make manifest the counsels of the hearts : and then shall every man have praise of God.

6 And these things, brethren, I have in a figure transferred to myself and to Apollos for your sakes ; that

---

[1] αὐτὸν L.　　[m] — τῷ L[A].　　[n] — ἐστιν (read [are]) LTTrA.　　[o] ὧδε here LTTrA.
[P] Ἀπολλὼν TTr.

ye might learn in us not to think *of men* above that which is written, that no one of you be puffed up for one against another. 7 For who maketh thee to differ *from another?* and what hast thou that thou didst not receive? now if thou didst receive *it,* why dost thou glory, as if thou hadst not received *it?* 8 Now ye are full, now ye are rich, ye have reigned as kings without us : and I would to God ye did reign, that we also might reign with you. 9 For I think that God hath set forth us the apostles last, as it were appointed to death : for we are made a spectacle unto the world, and to angels, and to men. 10 We *are* fools for Christ's sake, but ye *are* wise in Christ; we *are* weak, but ye *are* strong ; ye *are* honourable, but we *are* despised. 11 Even unto this present hour we both hunger, and thirst, and are naked, and are buffeted, and have no certain dwellingplace ; 12 and labour, working with our own hands : being reviled, we bless; being persecuted, we suffer it :13 being defamed, we intreat : we are made as the filth of the world, *and are* the offscouring of all things unto this day. 14 I write not these things to shame you, but as my beloved sons I warn *you.* 15 For though ye have ten thousand instructors in Christ, yet *have ye* not many fathers; for in Christ Jesus I have begotten you through the gospel. 16 Wherefore I beseech you, be ye followers of me.

17 For this cause have I sent unto you Timotheus, who is my beloved son, and faithful in the Lord, who shall bring you into remembrance of my ways which be in Christ, as I teach every where in every church. 18 Now some are puffed up, as

ᵠὅ‖ γέγραπται ʳφρονεῖν,‖ ἵνα μὴ εἷς ὑπὲρ τοῦ ἑνὸς
⁴what ⁵has ⁶been ⁷written ¹to ²think,   that not one for   one

φυσιοῦσθε κατὰ τοῦ ἑτέρου. 7 τίς.γάρ σε διακρίνει ;
ye be puffed up against the other.   For who thee makes to differ?

τί.δὲ ἔχεις ὃ οὐκ.ἔλαβες ; εἰ.δὲ καὶ ἔλαβες,
and what hast thou which thou didst not receive? but if also thou didst receive,

τί καυχᾶσαι ὡς μὴ λαβών ; 8 ἤδη κεκορεσμένοι ἐστέ,
why boastest thou as not having received? Already satiated   ye are;

ἤδη ἐπλουτήσατε, χωρὶς ἡμῶν ἐβασιλεύσατε· καὶ ὄφελόν
already ye were enriched; apart from us   ye reigned ; and I would

γε ἐβασιλεύσατε, ἵνα καὶ ἡμεῖς ὑμῖν ˢσυμβασιλεύσωμεν.‖
surely ye did reign, that also we ⁴you ¹might ²reign ³with.

9 δοκῶ.γὰρ ᵗὅτι‖ ὁ θεὸς ἡμᾶς τοὺς ἀποστόλους ἐσχάτους ἀπέ-
For I think that God us the   apostles   last   set

δειξεν ὡς ἐπιθανατίους· ὅτι θέατρον ἐγενήθημεν τῷ κόσμῳ,
forth as appointed to death. For a spectacle we became to the world,

καὶ ἀγγέλοις καὶ ἀνθρώποις. 10 ἡμεῖς μωροὶ διὰ
both to angels and to men.   We [are] fools on account of

χριστόν, ὑμεῖς.δὲ φρόνιμοι ἐν χριστῷ· ἡμεῖς ἀσθενεῖς, ὑμεῖς.δὲ
Christ,   but ye prudent in Christ ; we   weak,   but ye

ἰσχυροί· ὑμεῖς ἔνδοξοι, ἡμεῖς.δὲ ἄτιμοι. 11 ἄχρι τῆς ἄρτι
strong ; ye glorious, but we without honour.   To the present

ὥρας καὶ πεινῶμεν καὶ διψῶμεν, καὶ ᵛγυμνητεύομεν,‖ καὶ
hour both we hunger and thirst   and are naked,   and

κολαφιζόμεθα, καὶ ἀστατοῦμεν, 12 καὶ κοπιῶμεν, ἐργα-
are buffeted,   and wander without a home, and   labour,   work-

ζόμενοι ταῖς.ἰδίαις χερσίν· λοιδορούμενοι, εὐλογοῦμεν· διω-
ing   with our own hands.   Railed at,   we bless;   per-

κόμενοι, ἀνεχόμεθα· 13 ʷβλασφημούμενοι,‖ παρακαλοῦμεν·
secuted, we bear ;   evilly spoken to,   we beseech :

ὡς περικαθάρματα τοῦ κόσμου ἐγενήθημεν, πάντων
as [the] refuse   of the world we are become, of all [the]

περίψημα ἕως ἄρτι. 14 Οὐκ ἐντρέπων ὑμᾶς γράφω ταῦτα,
off-scouring until now. Not shaming you do I write these things,

ˣἀλλ'‖ ὡς τέκνα μου ἀγαπητὰ ʸνουθετῶ.‖ 15 ἐὰν.γὰρ
but as ³children ¹my ²beloved I admonish [you].   For if

μυρίους παιδαγωγοὺς ἔχητε ἐν χριστῷ, ἀλλ' οὐ πολ-
ten thousand tutors   ye should have in Christ, yet not 'many

λοὺς πατέρας· ἐν.γὰρ χριστῷ Ἰησοῦ διὰ τοῦ εὐαγγελίου
fathers ;   for in Christ Jesus through the glad tidings

ἐγὼ ὑμᾶς ἐγέννησα. 16 παρακαλῶ οὖν ὑμᾶς, μιμηταί μου
I   you did beget.   I exhort therefore you, ²imitators ³of ⁴me

γίνεσθε.
¹become.

17 Διὰ   τοῦτο ᶻἔπεμψα ὑμῖν Τιμόθεον, ὅς ἐστιν ᵃτέκνον
On account of this I sent to you Timotheus, who is   ³child

μου‖ ἀγαπητὸν καὶ πιστὸν ἐν κυρίῳ, ὃς ὑμᾶς ἀναμνήσει
¹my ²beloved and faithful in [the] Lord, who ³you ¹will ²remind of

τὰς.ὁδούς.μου τὰς ἐν χριστῷ,ᵇ καθὼς πανταχοῦ ἐν πάσῃ
my ways   that [are] in Christ, according as everywhere in every

ἐκκλησίᾳ διδάσκω. 18 ὡς μὴ.ἐρχομένου δέ μου πρὸς ὑμᾶς
assembly I teach.   ²As ³to ⁵not ⁶coming ¹now ⁴my to you

ἐφυσιώθησάν τινες· 19 ἐλεύσομαι.δὲ ταχέως πρὸς ὑμᾶς, ἐὰν
²were ³puffed ⁴up ¹some;   but I shall come shortly to you,   if

---

ᵠ ἃ LTTrAW.   ʳ — φρονεῖν (*read* μὴ nothing) LTTrAW.   ˢ συν- T.   ᵗ — ὅτι LTTrAW.
ᵛ γυμνιτεύομεν LTTrAW.   ʷ δυσφημούμενοι defamed TA.   ˣ ἀλλὰ Tr.   ʸ νουθετῶν
admonishing T.   ᶻ + αὐτὸ very [thing] T.   ᵃ μου τέκνον LTTrA.   ᵇ + Ἰησοῦ Jesus LT.

ὁ κύριος θελήσῃ, καὶ γνώσομαι, οὐ τὸν λόγον τῶν
the Lord will, and I will know, not the word of those who

πεφυσιωμένων, ἀλλὰ τὴν δύναμιν. 20 οὐ γὰρ ἐν λόγῳ ἡ
are puffed up, but the power. For not in word the

βασιλεία τοῦ θεοῦ, ἀλλ' ἐν δυνάμει. 21 τί θέλετε; ἐν
kingdom of God [is], but in power. What will ye? with

ῥάβδῳ ἔλθω πρὸς ὑμᾶς, ἢ ἐν ἀγάπῃ πνεύματί.τε ᶜπραό-
a rod I should come to you, or in love and a spirit of meek-

τητος‖;
ness?

5 Ὅλως ἀκούεται ᵈἐν ὑμῖν πορνεία, καὶ τοιαύτη πορνεία
Commonly ²is ³reported ⁴among ⁵you ¹fornication, and such fornication

ἥτις οὐδὲ ἐν τοῖς ἔθνεσιν ᵈὀνομάζεται,‖ ὥστε γυναῖκά
which not even among the nations is named, so as ⁶wife

τινα τοῦ πατρὸς ἔχειν. 2 καὶ ὑμεῖς πεφυσιωμένοι ἐστέ,
¹one [⁴his] ⁵father's ²to ³have. And ye ²puffed ³up ¹are,

καὶ οὐχὶ μᾶλλον ἐπενθήσατε, ἵνα ᵉἐξαρθῇ‖ ἐκ μέσου.ὑμῶν
and not rather did mourn, that might be taken out of your midst

ᵍὁ τὸ.ἔργον.τοῦτο ᶠποιήσας;‖ 3 ἐγὼ μὲν γὰρ ᵍὡς‖ ἀπὼν τῷ
he who this deed did! ²I ¹for as being absent in the

σώματι, παρὼν.δὲ τῷ πνεύματι, ἤδη κέκρικα ὡς παρών,
in body, but being present in spirit, already have judged as being present,

τὸν οὕτως τοῦτο κατεργασάμενον, 4 ἐν τῷ ὀνόματι τοῦ
him who so ³this ¹worked ²out, in the name of

κυρίου.ʰἡμῶν‖ Ἰησοῦ ¹χριστοῦ,‖ συναχθέντων ὑμῶν καὶ
our Lord Jesus Christ, being gathered together ye and

τοῦ ἐμοῦ πνεύματος, σὺν τῇ δυνάμει τοῦ.κυρίου.ʰἡμῶν‖ Ἰησοῦ
my spirit, with the power of our Lord Jesus

ⁱχριστοῦ,‖ 5 παραδοῦναι τὸν.τοιοῦτον τῷ σατανᾷ εἰς ὄλεθρον
Christ, to deliver such a one to Satan for destruction

τῆς σαρκός, ἵνα τὸ πνεῦμα σωθῇ ἐν τῇ ἡμέρᾳ τοῦ κυρίου
of the flesh, that the spirit may be saved in the day of the Lord

ˡἸησοῦ.‖ 6 Οὐ καλὸν τὸ.καύχημα.ὑμῶν· οὐκ.οἴδατε ὅτι μικρὰ
Jesus. Not good [is] your boasting. Know ye not that a little

ζύμη ὅλον τὸ φύραμα ζυμοῖ; 7 ἐκκαθάρατε ᵐοὖν‖ τὴν πα-
leaven ³whole ²the ⁴lump ¹leavens? Purge out therefore the

λαιὰν ζύμην,ἵνα ἦτε νέον φύραμα, καθὼς ἐστε ἄζυμοι·
old leaven, that ye may be a new lump, according as ye are unleavened.

καὶ.γὰρ τὸ.πάσχα.ἡμῶν ⁿὑπὲρ ἡμῶν‖ ᵒἐτύθη‖ χριστός.
For also ²our ³passover ⁶for ⁷us ⁴was ⁵sacrificed ¹Christ.

8 ὥστε ἑορτάζωμεν, μὴ ἐν ζύμῃ παλαιᾷ, μηδὲ ἐν
So that we should celebrate the feast, not with ²leaven ¹old, nor with

ζύμῃ κακίας καὶ πονηρίας, ἀλλ' ἐν ἀζύμοις Ρεἰλι-
leaven of malice and wickedness, but with unleavened [bread] of

κρινείας‖ καὶ ἀληθείας.
sincerity and of truth.

9 Ἔγραψα ὑμῖν ἐν τῇ ἐπιστολῇ, μὴ συναναμίγνυσθαι
I wrote to you in the epistle, not to associate with

πόρνοις· 10 ᑫκαὶ‖ οὐ πάντως τοῖς πόρνοις τοῦ.κόσμου.τού-
fornicators; and not altogether with the fornicators of this world,

του, ἢ τοῖς πλεονέκταις, ʳἢ‖ ἅρπαξιν, ἢ εἰδωλολάτραις· ἐπεὶ
or with the covetous, or rapacious, or idolaters, since

---

though. I would not come to you. 19 But I will come to you shortly, if the Lord will, and will know not the speech of them which are puffed up, but the power. 20 For the kingdom of God is not in word, but in power. 21 What will ye? shall I come unto you with a rod, or in love, and in the spirit of meekness?

V. It is reported commonly that there is fornication among you, and such fornication as is not so much as named among the Gentiles, that one should have his father's wife. 2 And ye are puffed up, and have not rather mourned, that he that hath done this deed might be taken away from among you. 3 For I verily, as absent in body, but present in spirit, have judged already, as though I were present, concerning him that hath so done this deed, 4 in the name of our Lord Jesus Christ, when ye are gathered together, and my spirit, with the power of our Lord Jesus Christ, 5 to deliver such a one unto Satan for the destruction of the flesh, that the spirit may be saved in the day of the Lord Jesus. 6 Your glorying is not good. Know ye not that a little leaven leaveneth the whole lump? 7 Purge out therefore the old leaven, that ye may be a new lump, as ye are unleavened. For even Christ our passover is sacrificed for us: 8 therefore let us keep the feast, not with old leaven, neither with the leaven of malice and wickedness; but with the unleavened bread of sincerity and truth.

9 I wrote unto you in an epistle not to company with fornicators: 10 yet not altogether with the fornicators of this world, or with the covetous, or extortioners, or

---

ᶜ πραύτητος LTTrA.　　ᵈ — ὀνομάζεται (read [is]) GLTTrAW.　　ᵉ ἀρθῇ GLTTrAW.　　ᶠ πράξας; T.
ᵍ — ὡς LTTrAW.　　ʰ — ἡμῶν (read the Lord) [L]T.　　ⁱ — χριστοῦ LTTrA.　　ᵏ [ἡμῶν] L.
ˡ [ἡμῶν Ἰησοῦ χριστοῦ] (read our Lord Jesus Christ) L;　— Ἰησοῦ A;　ἡμῶν Ἰησοῦ W.
ᵐ — οὖν GLTTrAW.　　ⁿ — ὑπὲρ ἡμῶν LTTrAW.　　ᵒ ἐθύθη E.　　Ρ εἰλικρινίας T.　　ᑫ — καὶ
LTTrAW.　　ʳ καὶ and LTTrAW.

with idolaters; for then must ye needs go out of the world. 11 But now I have written unto you not to keep company, if any man that is called a brother be a fornicator, or covetous, or an idolater, or a railer, or a drunkard, or an extortioner; with such an one no not to eat. 12 For what have I to do to judge them also that are without? do not ye judge them that are within? 13 But them that are without God judgeth. Therefore put away from among yourselves that wicked person.

VI. Dare any of you, having a matter against another, go to law before the unjust, and not before the saints? 2 Do ye not know that the saints shall judge the world? and if the world shall be judged by you, are ye unworthy to judge the smallest matters? 3 Know ye not that we shall judge angels? how much more things that pertain to this life? 4 If then ye have judgments of things pertaining to this life, set them to judge who are least esteemed in the church. 5 I speak to your shame. Is it so, that there is not a wise man among you? no, not one that shall be able to judge between his brethren? 6 But brother goeth to law with brother, and that before the unbelievers. 7 Now therefore there is utterly a fault among you, because ye go to law one with another. Why do ye not rather take wrong? why do ye not rather *suffer yourselves* to be defrauded? 8 Nay, ye do wrong, and defraud, and that *your* brethren. 9 Know ye not that the unrighteous shall not inherit the kingdom of God? Be not deceived: neither fornicators, nor idolaters, nor adulterers, nor effemin-

ᵃὀφείλετε‖ ἄρα ἐκ τοῦ κόσμου ἐξελθεῖν. 11 ᵗνυνὶ‖.δὲ ἔγραψα
ye ought   then out of the   world   to go.   But now, I wrote
ὑμῖν μὴ συναναμίγνυσθαι,   ἐάν τις ἀδελφὸς ὀνομαζόμενος
.to you not   to associate with   [him], if anyone ²brother   ¹designated
ᵛῇ‖ πόρνος, ἢ πλεονέκτης, ἢ εἰδωλολάτρης, ἢ λοίδορος,
[be] either a fornicator, or   covetous,   or   idolater,   or   railer,
ἢ μέθυσος, ἢ ἅρπαξ· τῷ.τοιούτῳ · μηδὲ συνεσθίειν. 12 τί
or a drunkard, or rapacious; with such a one not even   to eat.   ²What
γάρ   μοι ʷκαὶ‖ τοὺς ἔξω κρίνειν; οὐχὶ τοὺς ἔσω ὑμεῖς
¹for [is it] to me also those outside to judge,   ⁴not ⁵those ⁷within   ³ye
κρίνετε; 13 τοὺς.δὲ ἔξω ὁ θεὸς ˣκρίνει.‖ ʸκαὶ ἐξαρεῖτε‖
²do ³ye ⁶judge?   But those outside God judges.   And ye shall put out
τὸν πονηρὸν ἐξ ὑμῶν.αὐτῶν.
the wicked person from among yourselves.

6 Τολμᾷ τις ὑμῶν, πρᾶγμα ἔχων πρὸς τὸν ἕτερον,
   Dare anyone of you,   a matter having against the   other,
κρίνεσθαι ἐπὶ τῶν ἀδίκων, καὶ οὐχὶ ἐπὶ τῶν ἁγίων; 2 ᶻοὐκ
go to law before the unrighteous, and not before the saints?   ²Not
οἴδατε ὅτι οἱ ἅγιοι τὸν κόσμον κρινοῦσιν; καὶ εἰ ἐν ὑμῖν
¹know ²ye that the saints ³the   ⁴world   ¹will ²judge? and if by you
κρίνεται ὁ κόσμος, ἀνάξιοί ἐστε κριτηρίων ἐλαχίστων; 3 οὐκ
is judged the world,   ³unworthy ¹are ²ye of judgments the smallest?   ³Not
οἴδατε ὅτι ἀγγέλους κρινοῦμεν; ᵃμήτι.γε‖ βιωτικά;
¹know ²ye that   angels   we shall judge? much more then things of this life?
4 βιωτικὰ μὲν οὖν κριτήρια ἐὰν ἔχητε, τοὺς
⁸Things ⁹of ¹⁰this ¹¹life   ⁴then ⁵judgment [⁶as ⁷to] ¹if ²ye ³have, who
ἐξουθενημένους ἐν τῇ ἐκκλησίᾳ, τούτους ᵇκαθίζετε.‖ 5 πρὸς
are least esteemed in the   assembly,   ⁴those   ¹set ²ye ³up.   For
ἐντροπὴν ὑμῖν ᶜλέγω.‖ οὕτως οὐκ.ᵈἔστιν‖ ἐν ὑμῖν ᵉσοφὸς
shame   to you I speak.   Thus is there not among you   a wise [man]
οὐδὲ εἷς,‖ ὃς δυνήσεται διακρῖναι ἀνὰ.μέσον τοῦ ἀδελφοῦ
not even one, who shall be able to decide   between   ²brother
αὐτοῦ;   6 ἀλλὰ ἀδελφὸς μετὰ ἀδελφοῦ κρίνεται, καὶ
¹his [and brother]?   But   brother with brother goes to law, and
τοῦτο ἐπὶ ἀπίστων; 7 ἤδη μὲν ᶠοὖν‖ ὅλως ἥττημα
this before unbelievers!   Already indeed therefore altogether a default
ᵍἐν‖ ὑμῖν ἐστιν, ὅτι κρίματα ἔχετε μεθ᾽ ἑαυτῶν. ʰδιατί‖ οὐχὶ
among you   is,   that law-suits ye have among yourselves. Why not
μᾶλλον ἀδικεῖσθε; ʰδιατί‖ οὐχὶ μᾶλλον ἀποστερεῖσθε; 8 ἀλλὰ
rather suffer wrong? why   not   rather   be defrauded?   But
ὑμεῖς ἀδικεῖτε καὶ ἀποστερεῖτε, καὶ ⁱταῦτα‖   ἀδελφούς.
ye   do wrong and   defraud,   and these things [to your] brethren.
9 ἢ οὐκ.οἴδατε ὅτι ἄδικοι ᵏβασιλείαν θεοῦ‖ οὐ κληρονο-
Or know ye not that unjust ones [the]   kingdom of God.²not   ¹shall in-
μήσουσιν; Μὴ.πλανᾶσθε· οὔτε πόρνοι, οὔτε εἰδωλολάτραι,
herit?   Be not misled;   neither fornicators, nor   idolaters,
οὔτε μοιχοί, οὔτε   μαλακοί,   οὔτε   ἀρσενο-
nor adulterers, nor abusers of themselves as women, nor abusers of them-
κοῖται,   10 οὔτε κλέπται, οὔτε πλεονέκται, ¹οὔτε‖ μέθυσοι,
selves with men, nor thieves, nor covetous, nor drunkards,
οὐ λοίδοροι, οὐχ ἅρπαγες, βασιλείαν θεοῦ ᵐοὐ‖ κληρονο-
nor railers, nor rapacious, [the] kingdom of God   shall

ᵃ ὠφείλετε LTTrA.   ᵗ νῦν LTrA.   ᵛ ῇ be EGLTTrAW.   ʷ — καὶ LTTrA.   ˣ κρινεῖ (; LTr) will judge GLT.   ʸ ἐξάρατε put ye out GLTTrAW.   ᶻ + ἢ or GLTTrAW.   ᵃ μήτιγε GT.   ᵇ καθίζετε; (read do ye set up those, &c.) GTW.   ᶜ λαλῶ L.   ᵈ ἔνι GLTTrA.   ᵉ οὐδεὶς σοφὸς LTTrA.   ᶠ — οὖν T[Tr].   ᵍ — ἐν (read ὑμῖν with you) GLTTrAW.   ʰ διὰ τί LTrA.   ⁱ τοῦτο this LTTrAW.   ᵏ θεοῦ βασιλείαν GLTTrAW.   ¹ οὐ TA.   ᵐ — οὐ LTTrA.

μήσουσιν. 11 καὶ ταῦτά τινες.ἦτε· ⁿἀλλὰ‖ ἀπελού-
inherit. And these things some of you were; but ye were

σασθε, ἀλλὰ ἡγιάσθητε, °ἀλλ'‖ ἐδικαιώθητε, ἐν τῷ ὀνόματι
washed, but ye were sanctified, but ye were justified, in the name

τοῦ κυρίου ᴾ Ἰησοῦ, ᑫ καὶ ἐν τῷ πνεύματι τοῦ.θεοῦ.ἡμῶν.
of the Lord Jesus, and by the Spirit of our God.

12 Πάντα μοι ἔξεστιν, ἀλλ' οὐ πάντα συμφέρει· πάντα
All things to me are lawful, but not all things do profit; all things

μοι ἔξεστιν, ἀλλ' οὐκ.ἐγὼ ἐξουσιασθήσομαι ὑπό τινος.
to me are lawful, but ²not ¹I ²will be brought under the power of any.

13 Τὰ βρώματα τῇ κοιλίᾳ, καὶ ἡ κοιλία τοῖς βρώμασιν·
Meats for the belly, and the belly for meats:

ὁ.δὲ.θεὸς καὶ ταύτην καὶ ταῦτα ʹ καταργήσει. τὸ.δὲ σῶμα
but God both this and these will bring to nought: but the body [is]

οὐ τῇ πορνείᾳ, ἀλλὰ τῷ κυρίῳ, καὶ ὁ κύριος τῷ σώματι·
not for fornication, but for the Lord, and the Lord for the body.

14 ὁ.δὲ.θεὸς καὶ τὸν κύριον ἤγειρεν, καὶ ʳἡμᾶς‖ ˢἐξεγερῶ̈‖ διὰ
And God both the Lord raised up, and us will raise out by

τῆς.δυνάμεως.αὐτοῦ. 15 οὐκ.οἴδατε ὅτι τὰ.σώματα.ὑμῶν μέλη
his power, Know ye not that your bodies members

χριστοῦ ἐστίν; ἄρας οὖν τὰ μέλη τοῦ.χριστοῦ, ποιήσω
of Christ are? Having taken then the members of the Christ, shall I make

πόρνης μέλη; μὴ.γένοιτο. 16 ἢ οὐκ.οἴδατε ὅτι ὁ
[them] ²of ᵃa ¹harlot ¹members? May it not be! Or know ye not that he that

κολλώμενος τῇ πόρνῃ, ἐν σῶμά ἐστιν; Ἔσονται.γάρ, ᵗφησίν,‖
is joined to the harlot, ²one ³body ¹is? For shall be, he says,

οἱ δύο εἰς σάρκα μίαν· 17 ὁ.δὲ κολλώμενος τῷ κυρίῳ, ἓν
the two for ²flesh ¹one. But he that is joined to the Lord, ²one

πνεῦμά ἐστιν. 18 Φεύγετε τὴν πορνείαν. πᾶν ἁμάρτημα ὃ
²spirit ¹is. Flee fornication. Every sin which

ἐὰν ποιήσῃ ἄνθρωπος, ἐκτὸς τοῦ σώματός ἐστιν· ὁ.δὲ
³may ⁴practise ¹aᵃ²man, without the body is, but he that

πορνεύων, εἰς τὸ.ἴδιον σῶμα ἁμαρτάνει. 19 ἢ οὐκ
commits fornication, against his own body sins. Or ³not

οἴδατε ὅτι τὸ.σῶμα.ὑμῶν ναὸς τοῦ ἐν ὑμῖν ἁγίου πνεύματός
¹know ²ye that your body a temple of the ²in ⁴you ¹Holy ³Spirit

ἐστιν, οὗ ἔχετε ἀπὸ θεοῦ, καὶ οὐκ ἐστὲ ἑαυτῶν; 20 ἠγορά-
is, which ye have from God; and ²not ²are ¹ye your own? ²ye ³were

σθητε γὰρ τιμῆς· δοξάσατε δὴ τὸν θεὸν ἐν τῷ σώματι
⁵bought ¹for with a price; glorify ²indeed ¹God in ²body

ὑμῶν, ᵛκαὶ ἐν τῷ.πνεύματι.ὑμῶν, ἅτινά ἐστιν τοῦ θεοῦ.‖
¹your, and in your spirit, which are God's.

7 Περὶ.δὲ ὧν ἐγράψατέ ᵂμοι,‖ καλὸν ἀνθρώπῳ
But concerning what things ye wrote to me: [It is] good for a man

γυναικὸς μὴ ἅπτεσθαι· 2 διὰ.δὲ τὰς πορνείας ἕκαστος
ᵃ¹woman ¹not ²to ³touch; but on account of fornication ²each

τὴν.ἑαυτοῦ.γυναῖκα ἐχέτω, καὶ ἑκάστη τὸν.ἴδιον ἄνδρα ἐχέτω.
ᐧ⁴his ⁵own ⁶wife ¹let ³have, and ²each ⁴her ⁵own ⁶husband ¹let ³have.

3 τῇ γυναικὶ ὁ ἀνὴρ τὴν ˣὀφειλομένην εὔνοιαν‖ ἀπο-
To the wife ²the ³husband ⁵due ⁵benevolence ¹let

διδότω· ὁμοίως.ʸδὲ‖ καὶ ἡ γυνὴ τῷ ἀνδρί. 4 ἡ γυνὴ τοῦ.ἰδίου
⁴render, and likewise also the wife to the husband. The wife her own

σώματος οὐκ.ἐξουσιάζει, ᶻἀλλ'‖ ὁ ἀνήρ· ὁμοίως.δὲ καὶ ὁ
body has not authority over, but the husband; and likewise also the

---

ate, nor abusers of themselves with mankind, 10 nor thieves, nor covetous, nor drunkards, nor revilers, nor extortioners, shall inherit the kingdom of God. 11 And such were some of you : but ye are washed, but ye are sanctified, but ye are justified in the name of the Lord Jesus, and by the Spirit of our God.

12 All things are lawful unto me, but all things are not expedient : all things are lawful for me, but I will not be brought under the power of any. 13 Meats for the belly, and the belly for meats : but God shall destroy both it and them. Now the body is not for fornication, but for the Lord ; and the Lord for the body. 14 And God hath both raised up the Lord, and will also raise up us by his own power. 15 Know ye not that your bodies are the members of Christ? shall I then take the members of Christ, and make them the members of an harlot? God forbid. 16 What? know ye not that he which is joined to an harlot is one body? for two, saith he, shall be one flesh. 17 But he that is joined unto the Lord is one spirit. 18 Flee fornication. Every sin that a man doeth is without the body ; but he that committeth fornication sinneth against his own body. 19 What! know ye not that your body is the temple of the Holy Ghost which is in you, which ye have of God, and ye are not your own ? 20 For ye are bought with a price : therefore glorify God in your body, and in your spirit, which are God's.

VII. Now concerning the things whereof ye wrote unto me : It is good for a man not to touch a woman. 2 Nevertheless, to avoid fornication, let every man have

---

ⁿ ἀλλ' L. ° ἀλλὰ TTrA. ᴾ + [ἡμῶν] (read our Lord) L. ᑫ + χριστοῦ Christ LTTr.
ʳ ὑμᾶς you E. ˢ ἐξεγείρει raises out L. ᵗ [φησίν] L. ᵛ — καὶ ἐν to end of verse
GLTTrAW. ᵂ — μοι T[Tr]A. ˣ ὀφειλὴν [her] due GLTTrAW. ʸ [δὲ] L. ᶻ ἀλλὰ LTTrA.

his own wife, and let every woman have her own husband. 3 Let the husband render unto the wife due benevolence : and likewise also the wife unto the husband. 4 The wife hath not power of her own body, but the husband: and likewise also the husband hath not power of his own body, but the wife. 5 Defraud ye not one the other, except *it be* with consent for a time, that ye may give yourselves to fasting and prayer; and come together again, that Satan tempt you not for your incontinency. 6 But I speak this by permission, *and* not of commandment. 7 For I would that all men were even as I myself. But every man hath his proper gift of God, one after this manner, and another after that. 8 I say therefore to the . unmarried and widows, It is good for them , if they abide even as I. 9 But if they cannot contain, let them marry: for it is better to marry than to burn. 10 And unto the married I command, *yet* not I, but the Lord, Let not the wife depart from *her* husband: 11 but and if she depart, let her remain unmarried, or be reconciled to *her* husband: and let not the husband put away *his* wife. 12 But to the rest speak I, not the Lord: If any brother hath a wife that believeth not, and she be pleased to dwell with him, let him not put her away. 13 And the woman which hath an husband that believeth not, and if he be pleased to dwell with her, let her not leave him. 14 For the unbelieving husband is sanctified by the wife, and the unbelieving wife is sanctified by the husband: else were your children unclean; but now are they holy. 15 But if the unbelieving de-

ἀνὴρ τοῦ.ἰδίου σώματος οὐκ.ἐξουσιάζει, ᶻἀλλ'ǁ ἡ γυνή. 5 μὴ
husband his own   body   has not authority over, but the wife. ᵃNot

ἀποστερεῖτε ἀλλήλους, εἰ.μή τι ἂν ἐκ συμφώνου πρὸς καιρόν,
 ¹defraud   one another, unless   by   consent   for a season,

ἵνα ᵃσχολάζητεǁ ᵇτῇ νηστείᾳ καὶǁ τῇ προσευχῇ, καὶ πάλιν
that ye may be at leisure   for fasting and   for prayer,   and again

ᶜἐπὶ.τὸ.αὐτὸ ,συνέρχησθε,ǁ ἵνα μὴ πειράζῃ ὑμᾶς ὁ σατανᾶς
into one place come together,   that ³not ²may ⁴tempt ⁵you   ¹Satan

διὰ   τὴν.ἀκρασίαν.ὑμῶν. 6 τοῦτο.δὲ λέγω κατὰ ᵈσυγ-
because of your incontinence. But this I say by way of   per-

γνώμην,ǁ οὐ κατ' ἐπιταγήν. 7 θέλω ᵉγὰρǁ πάντας ἀνθρώ-
mission,   not by way of command. ²I ³wish ¹but   all   men

πους εἶναι ὡς.καὶ ἐμαυτόν· ᶻἀλλ'ǁ ἕκαστος ἴδιον ᶠχάρισμα
    to be even as   myself: but   each   his own   gift

ἔχειǁ ἐκ θεοῦ, ᵍὃςǁ μὲν οὕτως, ᵍὃς.ǁδὲ οὕτως. 8 Λέγω.δὲ
has from God; one   so,   and another so.   But I say

τοῖς ἀγάμοις καὶ ταῖς χήραις, καλὸν αὐτοῖς ʰἐστινǁ ἐὰν ⁱ
to the unmarried and to the widows, good for them   it is   if

μείνωσιν ὡς κἀγώ. 9 εἰ.δὲ οὐκ.ἐγκρατεύονται, γαμησά-
they should remain as even I. But if they have not self-control, let them

τωσαν· ᵏκρεῖσσονǁ.γὰρ ⁱἐστινǁ⁻ ᵐγαμῆσαιǁ ἢ πυροῦσθαι.
marry ;   for better   it is   to marry than to burn.

10 Τοῖς.δὲ γεγαμηκόσιν παραγγέλλω, οὐκ ἐγώ, ᶻἀλλ'ǁ ὁ
But to the married   I charge,   not I,   but the

κύριος, γυναῖκα ἀπὸ ἀνδρὸς μὴ ⁿχωρισθῆναι·ǁ 11 ἐὰν.δὲ καὶ
Lord,   wife   from husband not to be separated; (but if also

χωρισθῇ,   μενέτω ἄγαμος, ἢ τῷ ἀνδρὶ καταλλαγήτω·
she be separated, let her remain unmarried, or to the husband be reconciled ;)

καὶ ἄνδρα γυναῖκα μὴ ἀφιέναι. 12 Τοῖς.δὲ λοιποῖς ᵒἐγὼ λέγω,ǁ
and husband ⁴wife ³not ²to ³leave. But to the rest   I say,

οὐχ ὁ κύριος, εἴ τις ἀδελφὸς γυναῖκα ἔχει ἄπιστον, καὶ
not the Lord, If any brother ⁴wife ¹has ²an ³unbelieving, and

ᴾαὐτὴǁ συνευδοκεῖ οἰκεῖν μετ' αὐτοῦ, μὴ.ἀφιέτω αὐτήν·
 she consents to dwell with him, let him not leave   her.

13 καὶ γυνὴ ᑫἥτιςǁ ἔχει ἄνδρα ἄπιστον, καὶ ʳαὐτὸςǁ
And a woman who   has ¹husband ²an ³unbelieving, and he

συνευδοκεῖ οἰκεῖν μετ' αὐτῆς, μὴ.ἀφιέτω ˢαὐτόν.ǁ 14 ἡγίασται
consents to dwell with¹ her, let her not leave ⁵him.   ²Is ³sanctified

γὰρ ὁ ἀνὴρ ὁ ἄπιστος ἐν τῇ γυναικί, καὶ ἡγίασται ἡ γυνὴ
¹for the ²husband ¹unbelieving in the wife,   and is sanctified the ²wife

ἡ ἄπιστος ἐν τῷ ᵗἀνδρί·ǁ ἐπεὶ ἄρα τὰ.τέκνα.ὑμῶν ἀκάθαρτά
¹unbelieving in the husband; else then your children   unclean

ἐστιν, νῦν.δὲ ἅγιά ἐστιν. 15 εἰ.δὲ ὁ ἄπιστος χωρίζεται,
are, but now ²holy ¹are.   But if the unbeliever separates himself,

χωριζέσθω.   οὐ.δεδούλωται ὁ ἀδελφὸς ἢ ἡ ἀδελφὴ ἐν
let him separate himself ; is not under bondage the brother or the sister in

τοῖς τοιούτοις· ἐν.δὲ εἰρήνῃ κέκληκεν ᵛἡμᾶςǁ ὁ θεός. 16 τί
such [cases], but in peace ²has ³called ⁴us   ¹God. ⁶What

γὰρ οἶδας, γύναι, εἰ τὸν ἄνδρα σώσεις; ἢ τί οἶδας,⁷
⁵for knowest thou, O wife, if the husband thou shalt save? or what knowest thou,

---

ᶻ ἀλλὰ LTTrA.   ᵃ σχολάσητε GLTTrAW.   ᵇ — τῇ νηστείᾳ καὶ GLTTrAW.   ᶜ ἐπὶ τὸ αὐτο συνέρχεσθε E; ἐπὶ τὸ αὐτὸ ἦτε together may be GLTTrAW.   ᵈ συν- T.   ᵉ.δὲ but LTTrAW.   ᶠ ἔχει χάρισμα GLTTrAW.   ᵍ ὁ LTTrAW.   ʰ — ἐστιν (read [it is]) GLTTrAW.   ⁱ + [οὕτως] L.   ᵏ κρεῖττον LTTr.   ˡ — ἐστιν W.   ᵐ γαμεῖν T.   ⁿ χωρίζεσθαι L.   ᵒ λέγω ἐγώ LTTrAW.   ᴾ αὕτη LTAW.   ᑫ εἴ τις if any T.   ʳ οὗτος LTTrAW.   ˢ τὸν ἄνδρα the husband LTTrAW.   ᵗ ἀδελφῷ brother LTTrAW.   ᵛ ὑμᾶς you T.

ἄνερ, εἰ τὴν γυναῖκα σώσεις; 17 εἰ μὴ ἑκάστῳ ὡς
O husband, if the wife thou shalt save? Only to each as

ʷἐμέρισεν‖ ˣὁ θεός,‖ ἕκαστον ὡς κέκληκεν ˣὁ κύριος,‖ οὕτως
²divided ¹God, each as ³has ⁴called ¹the ²Lord, so

περιπατείτω· καὶ οὕτως ἐν ταῖς ἐκκλησίαις πάσαις διατάσ-
let him walk; and thus in ²the ³assemblies ¹all I order.

σομαι. ·18 Περιτετμημένος τις ἐκλήθη; μὴ ἐπι-
Having been circumcised ²any ³one ¹was called? let him not be

σπάσθω. ἐν ἀκροβυστίᾳ ˢτις ἐκλήθη;‖ μὴ περι-
uncircumcised: in uncircumcision ²any ³one ¹was called? let him not be

τεμνέσθω. 19 ἡ περιτομὴ οὐδέν ἐστιν, καὶ ἡ ἀκροβυστία οὐδέν
circumcised. Circumcision ¹nothing ¹is, and uncircumcision ²nothing

ἐστιν, ἀλλὰ τήρησις ἐντολῶν θεοῦ. 20 ἕκαστος ἐν τῇ κλήσει
¹is, but keeping ²commandments ¹God's. Each in the calling

ᾗ ἐκλήθη, ἐν ταύτῃ μενέτω. 21 δοῦλος ἐκλή-
in which he was called, in this let him abide. Bondman [being] wast

θης; μή σοι μελέτω· ἀλλ᾽ εἰ καὶ δύνασαι ἐλεύθερος
thou called, not to thee let it be a care; but and if thou art able ³free

γενέσθαι, μᾶλλον χρῆσαι. 22 ὁ γὰρ ἐν κυρίῳ κληθεὶς
¹to ²become, ⁶rather ⁴use [⁵it]. For he ³in [⁴the] ⁵Lord ¹being ²called

δοῦλος, ἀπελεύθερος κυρίου ἐστίν· ὁμοίως ˣκαὶ‖ ὁ
[being] a bondman, a freedman of [the] Lord is; likewise also he

ἐλεύθερος κληθείς, δοῦλός ἐστιν χριστοῦ. 23 τιμῆς ἠγορά-
free being called, a bondman is of Christ. With a price ye were

σθητε· μὴ γίνεσθε δοῦλοι ἀνθρώπων. 24 ἕκαστος ἐν ᾧ ἐκλή-
bought; become not bondmen of men. Each wherein he was

θη, ἀδελφοί, ἐν τούτῳ μενέτω παρὰ ˣτῷ‖ θεῷ.
called, brethren, in that let him abide with God.

25 Περὶ δὲ τῶν παρθένων ἐπιταγὴν κυρίου οὐκ ἔχω·
But concerning virgins, commandment of [the] Lord I have not;

γνώμην δὲ δίδωμι, ὡς ἠλεημένος ὑπὸ κυρίου πιστὸς
but judgment I give, as having received mercy from [the] Lord ³faithful

εἶναι. 26 νομίζω οὖν τοῦτο καλὸν ὑπάρχειν διὰ τὴν ἐν-
¹to ²be. I think then this ²good ¹is because of the pre-

εστῶσαν ἀνάγκην, ὅτι καλὸν ἀνθρώπῳ τὸ οὕτως εἶναι.
sent necessity, that [it is] good for a man so to be.

27 δέδεσαι γυναικί; μὴ ζήτει λύσιν. λέλυσαι ἀπὸ
Hast thou been bound to a wife? seek not to be loosed. Hast thou been loosed from

γυναικός; μὴ ζήτει γυναῖκα. 28 ἐὰν δὲ καὶ ᵇγήμῃς,‖
a wife? seek not a wife. But if also thou mayest have married,

οὐχ ἥμαρτες· καὶ ἐὰν γήμῃ ᶜἡ‖ παρθένος, οὐχ
thou didst not sin; and if ³may ⁴have ⁵married ¹the ²virgin, ⁶not

ἥμαρτεν· θλίψιν δὲ τῇ σαρκὶ ἕξουσιν οἱ τοιοῦτοι· ἐγὼ δὲ
⁶she ⁷did sin: but tribulation in the flesh ²shall ³have ¹such; but I

ὑμῶν φείδομαι. 29 Τοῦτο δὲ φημι, ἀδελφοί, ᵈ ὁ καιρὸς συν-
²you ¹spare. But this I say, brethren, the season strait-

εσταλμένος· ᵉτὸ λοιπόν ἐστιν,‖ ἵνα καὶ ᶠοἱ‖ ἔχοντες γυναῖκας,
ened [is]. For the rest is, that even those having wives,

ὡς μὴ ἔχοντες ὦσιν· 30 καὶ οἱ κλαίοντες, ὡς μὴ κλαίοντες· καὶ
²as ³not ⁴having ¹be; and those weeping, as not weeping; and

οἱ χαίροντες, ὡς μὴ χαίροντες· καὶ οἱ ἀγοράζοντες, ὡς μὴ
those rejoicing, as not rejoicing; and those buying, as not

part, let him depart. A brother or a sister is not under bondage in such *cases:* but God hath called us to peace. 16 For what knowest thou, O wife, whether thou shalt save *thy* husband? or how knowest thou, O man, whether thou shalt save *thy* wife? 17 But as God hath distributed to every *man, as the Lord hath called *every one, so let him walk. And so ordain I in all churches. 18 Is any man called being circumcised? let him not become uncircumcised. Is any called in uncircumcision? let him not be circumcised. 19 Circumcision is nothing, and uncircumcision is nothing, but the keeping of the commandments of God. 20 Let every man abide in the same calling wherein he was called. 21 Art thou called *being* a servant? care not for it: but if thou mayest be made free, use *it* rather. 22 For he that is called in the Lord, *being* a servant, is the Lord's freeman: likewise also he that is called, *being* free, is Christ's servant. 23 Ye are bought with a price ; be not ye the servants of men. 24 Brethren, let every man, wherein he is called, therein abide with God.

25 Now concerning virgins I have no commandment of the Lord: yet I give my judgment, as one that hath obtained mercy of the Lord to be faithful. 26 I suppose therefore that this is good for the present distress, *I* say, that *it is* good for a man so to be. 27 Art thou bound unto a wife? seek not to be loosed. Art thou loosed from a wife? seek not a wife. 28 But and if thou marry, thou hast not sinned ; and if a virgin marry, she hath not sinned. Nevertheless such shall have trouble in the flesh: but I spare you. 29 But this I say,

---

ʷ μεμέρικεν has divided ᴛᴛʀ.   ˣ ὁ θεός and ὁ κύριος *transposed* ɢʟᴛᴛʀᴀᴡ.   ʸ κέκληταί
τις has any one been called ʟᴛᴛʀᴀᴡ.   ᶻ — καὶ ʟᴛᴛʀᴀᴡ.   ᵃ — τῷ ɢʟᴛᴛʀᴀᴡ.   ᵇ γαμήσῃς
ʟᴛᴛʀᴀ.   ᶜ [ἡ] ʟᴛʀᴀ.   ᵈ + ὅτι ᴇ.   ᵉ ἐστὶν τὸ λοιπόν, (τὸ λοιπόν ἐστιν· ᴇ) (*read* is *for*
the rest *joined to* straitened) ᴇᴛʀᴀᴡ ; ἐστίν· τὸ λοιπὸν ʟᴛ.   ᶠ - οἱ ᴇ.

brethren. the time *is*
short: it remaineth,
that both they that
have wives be as
though they had none;
30 and they that weep,
as though they wept
not; and they that re-
joice. as though they
rejoiced not ; and they
that buy, as though
they possessed not ;
31 and they that use
this world, as not a-
busing *it :* for the
fashion of this world
passeth away. 32 But
I would have you
without carefulness.
He that is unmarried
careth for the things
that belong to the
Lord, how he may
please the Lord: 33 but
he that is married
careth for the things
that are of the world,
how he may please *his*
wife. 34 There is dif-
ference *also* between a
wife and a virgin. The
unmarried woman car-
eth for the things of
the Lord, that she may
be holy both in body
and in spirit: but she
that is married careth
for the things of the
world, how she may
please *her* husband.
35 And this I speak
for your own profit ;
not that I may cast
a snare upon you, but
for that which is
comely, and that ye
may attend upon the
Lord without distrac-
tion. 36 But if any
man think that he
behaveth himself un-
comely toward his vir-
gin, if she pass the
flower of *her* age, and
need so require, let
him do what he will,
he sinneth not: let
them marry. 37 Ne-
vertheless he that
standeth stedfast in
his heart, having no
necessity, but hath
power over his own
will, and hath so de-
creed in his heart that
he will keep his virgin,
doeth well. 38 So then
he that giveth *her* in
marriage doeth well;
but he that giveth *her*

κατέχοντες 31 καὶ οἱ χρώμενοι ᵍτῷ.κόσμῳ.τούτῳ,ᴵᴵ ὡς μὴ
possessing ; and those using this world, as not

καταχρώμενοι. παράγει.γὰρ τὸ σχῆμα τοῦ.κόσμου.τούτου.
using [it] as their own ; for passes away the fashion of this world.

32 θέλω.δὲ ὑμᾶς ἀμερίμνους εἶναι. ὁ ἄγαμος μεριμνᾷ τὰ
But I wish you without care to be. The unmarried cares for the things

τοῦ κυρίου, πῶς ʰἀρέσειᴵᴵ τῷ κυρίῳ· 33 ὁ.δὲ γαμήσας
of the Lord, how he shall please the Lord; but he that is married

μεριμνᾷ τὰ τοῦ κόσμου, πῶς ʰἀρέσειᴵᴵ τῇ γυναικί.
cares for the things of the world, how he shall please the wife.

34 ᶦμεμέρισταιᴵᴵ ἡ ᵏγυνὴᴵᴵ καὶ ἡ παρθένος. ᶦἡ ἄγαμοςᴵᴵ μεριμνᾷ
Divided are the wife and the virgin. The unmarried cares for

τὰ τοῦ κυρίου, ἵνα ᾖ ἁγία ᵐκαὶᴵᴵ ⁿ σώματι καὶ ⁿ
the things of the Lord, that she may be holy both in body and

πνεύματι· ἡ.δὲ γαμήσασα μεριμνᾷ τὰ τοῦ κόσμου,
spirit ; but she that is married cares for the things of the world,

πῶς ᵒἀρέσειᴵᴵ τῷ ἀνδρί. 35 τοῦτο.δὲ πρὸς το.ὑμῶν.αὐτῶν
how she shall please the husband. But this for your own

ᴾσυμφέρονᴵᴵ λέγω· οὐχ ἵνα βρόχον ὑμῖν ἐπιβάλω, ἀλλὰ
profit I say ; not that a noose ˢyou ¹I ²may ³cast ⁴before. but

πρὸς τὸ εὔσχημον καὶ ᑫεὐπρόσεδρονᴵᴵ τῷ κυρίῳ ἀπερι-
for what [is] seemly, and waiting on the Lord without

σπάστως. 36 εἰ.δέ τις ἀσχημονεῖν ἐπὶ τὴν παρθένον
distraction. But if anyone [²he] ³behaves ⁴un-seemly ⁵to ⁷virginity

αὐτοῦ νομίζει, ἐὰν ᾖ ὑπέρακμος, καὶ οὕτως ὀφείλει γίνε-
⁶his ¹thinks, if he be beyond [his] prime, and so it ought to

σθαι. ὃ θέλει ποιείτω, οὐχ.ἁμαρτάνει· γαμείτωσαν. 37 ὃς.δὲ
be, what he wills let him do, he does not sin : let them marry. But he who

ἕστηκεν ʳἑδραῖος ἐν τῇ καρδίᾳ,ᴵᴵ μὴ ἔχων ἀνάγκην, ἐξουσίαν.δὲ
stands firm in heart, not having necessity, but authority

ἔχει περὶ τοῦ.ἰδίου θελήματος, καὶ τοῦτο κέκρικεν ἐν τῇ ˢ
has over his own will, and this has judged in

καρδίᾳ.ᵗαὐτοῦᴵᴵ ᵛτοῦᴵᴵ τηρεῖν τὴν.ἑαυτοῦ παρθένον, καλῶς
his heart to keep his own virginity, well

ʷποιεῖ.ᴵᴵ 38 ὥστε καὶ ὁ ˣἐκγαμίζων καλῶς ποιεῖ· ᵞὁ.δὲᴵᴵ
he does. So that also he that gives in marriage ²well ¹does ; and he that

μὴ ᶻἐκγαμίζωνᴵᴵ κρεῖσσον ʷποιεῖ.ᴵᴵ 39 Γυνὴ δέδεται ᵃνόμῳᴵᴵ
²not ¹gives in marriage ²better ¹does. A wife is bound by law

ἐφ' ὅσον χρόνον ζῇ ὁ.ἀνὴρ.αὐτῆς· ἐὰν.δὲ κοι-
for as long ²as ¹time ⁵may ⁶live ³her ⁴husband ; but if may have fallen

μηθῇ ὁ ἀνὴρ ᵇαὐτῆς,ᴵᴵ ἐλευθέρα ἐστὶν ᾧ θέλει γαμη-
asleep the husband of her, free she is to whom she wills to be

θῆναι, μόνον ἐν κυρίῳ. 40 μακαριωτέρα.δέ ἐστιν ἐὰν οὕτως
married, only in [the] Lord. But happier she is if so

μείνῃ, κατὰ τὴν ἐμὴν γνώμην· δοκῶ.δὲ κἀγὼ
she should remain, according to my judgment ; and I think I also

πνεῦμα θεοῦ ἔχειν.
³Spirit ²God's ¹have.

ᵍ τὸν κόσμον the world LTTrA. ʰ ἀρέσῃ be should please LTTrA. ᶦ , καὶ μεμέρισται. καὶ and has become divided. Also LTr; καὶ (— καὶ w) μεμέρισται καὶ And
divided are also ᴛᴀw. ᵏ γυνὴ ἡ ἄγαμος unmarried woman LTr. ᶦ — . ἡ ἄγαμος
(read the virgin cares for) Tr. ᵐ [καὶ] LTr. ⁿ + τῷ the LTTrA. ᵒ ἀρέσῃ she should
please LTTrA. ᴾ σύμφορον LTTrA. ᑫ εὐπάρεδρον GLTTrAW. ʳ ἐν τῇ καρδίᾳ αὐτοῦ
(in his heart) ἑδραῖος LTTrA. ˢ + ἰδίᾳ (read his own) TTrA. ᵗ — αὐτοῦ LTTrA.
ᵛ — τοῦ LTTrA. ʷ ποιήσει he shall do LTTrA. ˣ γαμίζων τὴν παρθένον ἑαυτοῦ (ἑαυτοῦ
παρθένον Τ) marries his own virginity LTTr ; [ἐκ]γαμίζων (τὴν ἑαυτοῦ παρθένον) A. ᵞ καὶ ὁ
GLTTrAW. ᶻ γαμίζων marries GLTTr ; [ἐκ]γαμίζων A. ᵃ — νόμῳ GLTTrAW. ᵇ — αὐτῆς
LTTrA.

8 Περὶ.δὲ τῶν.εἰδωλοθύτων, οἴδαμεν, ὅτι πάντες γνῶσιν
But concerning things sacrificed to idols, we know, (for   ²all ⁴knowledge

ἔχομεν. ἡ γνῶσις φυσιοῖ, ἡ δὲ ἀγάπη οἰκοδομεῖ. 2 εἰ.ᶜδέ‖
¹we ³have :   knowledge puffs up,   but   love   builds up.   But if

τις δοκεῖ ᵈεἰδέναι‖ τι, ᵉοὐδέπω.οὐδὲν ἔγνωκεν‖
anyone thinks to have known anything,   nothing yet   he has known

καθὼς δεῖ γνῶναι. 3 εἰ.δέ τις ἀγαπᾷ τὸν θεόν,
according as it is necessary to know.   But if anyone love   God,

οὗτος ἔγνωσται ὑπ᾽ αὐτοῦ. 4 περὶ τῆς βρώσεως οὖν τῶν
he   is known   by him:) concerning the   eating   then

εἰδωλοθύτων, οἴδαμεν ὅτι οὐδὲν εἴδωλον ἐν κόσμῳ,
of things sacrificed to idols, we know that nothing   an idol [is] in [the] world,

καὶ ὅτι οὐδεὶς θεὸς ᶠἕτερος‖ εἰ.μὴ εἷς. 5 καὶ.γὰρ εἴπερ
and that [there is] no   ²God   ¹other   except one.   For even if indeed

εἰσὶν λεγόμενοι θεοί, εἴτε ἐν οὐρανῷ εἴτε ἐπὶ ᵍτῆς‖
there are [those]   called   gods, whether in heaven   or   on   the

γῆς· ὥσπερ εἰσὶν θεοὶ πολλοὶ καὶ κύριοι πολλοί· 6 ʰἀλλ᾽‖
earth,   as   there are gods many and lords many,   but

ἡμῖν εἷς θεὸς ὁ πατήρ, ἐξ οὗ τὰ.πάντα, καὶ ἡμεῖς
to us [there is] one God the Father, of whom [are] all things,- and we

εἰς αὐτόν· καὶ εἷς κύριος Ἰησοῦς χριστός, δι᾽ οὗ τὰ.πάντα,
for him; and one Lord Jesus   Christ, by whom [are] all things,

καὶ ἡμεῖς δι᾽ αὐτοῦ. 7 ἀλλ᾽ οὐκ ἐν πᾶσιν ἡ γνῶσις· τινὲς
and we by him.   But not in all [is] the knowledge : ²some

δὲ τῇ ⁱσυνειδήσει‖ ᵏτοῦ εἰδώλου ἕως ἄρτι‖ ὡς εἰδωλό-
¹but   with conscience of the idol,   until now ²as ³of ⁴a ⁵thing ⁶sacrificed

θυτον ἐσθίουσιν, καὶ ἡ.συνείδησις.αὐτῶν ἀσθενὴς οὖσα
⁷to ⁸an ⁹idol   ¹eat,   and   their conscience,   ²weak   ¹being,

μολύνεται. 8 βρῶμα.δὲ ἡμᾶς οὐ.ˡπαρίστησιν‖ τῷ θεῷ· οὔτε
is defiled.   But meat us   does not commend   to God ; ²neither

ᵐγὰρ‖ ἐὰν ⁿφάγωμεν περισσεύομεν· οὔτε ἐὰν μὴ.φάγωμεν
¹for   if   we eat   have we an advantage; neither if   we eat not

ὑστερούμεθα.‖ 9 βλέπετε.δὲ μήπως ἡ ἐξουσία ὑμῶν αὕτη
do we come short.   But take heed   lest   ³power   ²your ¹this

πρόσκομμα γένηται °τοῖς ἀσθενοῦσιν.‖ 10 ἐὰν.γάρ
an occasion of stumbling become to those being weak.   For if

τις ἴδῃ ᴾσε,‖ τὸν ἔχοντα γνῶσιν, ἐν �qεἰδωλείῳ‖ κατακείμενον,
anyone see thee, who hast knowledge, in an idol-temple   reclining

οὐχὶ ἡ συνείδησις αὐτοῦ ἀσθενοῦς ὄντος οἰκοδο-
[at table], ²not ³the ⁴conscience ⁵of ⁶him ⁸weak ⁷being ¹will be

μηθήσεται εἰς.τὸ τὰ.εἰδωλόθυτα ἐσθίειν; 11 ʳκαὶ ἀπο-
built up   so as ³things ⁴sacrificed ⁵to ⁶idols ¹to ²eat?   and will

λεῖται‖ ὁ ἀσθενῶν ˢἀδελφὸς ἐπὶ τῇ.σῇ.γνώσει,‖ δι᾽ ὃν χριστὸς
perish   the weak   brother on thy knowledge, for whom Christ

ἀπέθανεν. ᵗ 12 οὕτως.δὲ ἁμαρτάνοντες εἰς τοὺς ἀδελφούς,
died.   Now thus   sinning   against the brethren,

καὶ τύπτοντες αὐτῶν τὴν συνείδησιν ἀσθενοῦσαν, εἰς χριστὸν
and wounding their   ²conscience \ ¹weak,.   against Christ

ἁμαρτάνετε. 13 ᵛδιόπερ‖ εἰ βρῶμα σκανδαλίζει τὸν ἀδελφόν
ye sin.   Wherefore if meat   cause ³to ⁴offend   ²brother

ᶜ — δὲ but LTTrAW.   ᵈ ἐγνωκέναι LTTrAW.   ᵉ οὔπω ἔγνω not yet did he know LTTrA.
ᶠ — ἕτερος LTTrA.   ᵍ — τῆς GLTTrAW.   ʰ [ἀλλ᾽] L.   ⁱ συνηθείᾳ from custom (with
respect to the idol) LTTr.   ᵏ ἕως ἄρτι τοῦ εἰδώλου LTTrAW.   ˡ παραστήσει shall not
commend LTTrA.   ᵐ — γὰρ for LTTrA.   ⁿ μὴ φάγωμεν ὑστερούμεθα (περισσεύομεν L)·
οὔτε ἐὰν φάγωμεν περισσεύομεν (ὑστερούμεθα L περισσεύομεθα Tr) LTrA.   ° τοῖς ἀσθενέσιν
to the weak LTTrAW.   ᴾ [σὲ] L.   q εἰδωλίῳ T.   ʳ ἀπόλλυται γὰρ for perishes LTTr; καὶ
ἀπόλλυται AW.   ˢ ἐν τῇ σῇ γνώσει, ὁ ἀδελφὸς LTTrAW.   ᵗ ; (read verse 11 as a question) A.
ᵛ διό περ Tr.

not in marriage doeth
better. 39 The wife
is bound by the law
as long as her hus-
band liveth; but if
her husband be dead,
she is at liberty to be
married to whom she
will; only in the
Lord. 40 But she is
happier if she so abide,
after my judgment :
and I think also that I
have the Spirit of God.

VIII. Now as touch-
ing things offered un-
to idols, we know that
we all have know-
ledge.   Knowledge
puffeth up, but cha-
rity edifieth. 2 And
if any man think that
he knoweth any thing,
he knoweth nothing
yet as he ought to
know. 3 But if any
man love God, the
same is known of him.
4 As concerning there-
fore the eating of
those things that are
offered in sacrifice
unto idols, we know
that an idol is nothing
in the world, and
that there is none other
God but one 5 For
though there be that
are called gods, whe-
ther in heaven or in
earth, (as there be
gods many, and lords
many,) 6 but to us
there is but one God,
the Father, of whom
are all things, and we
in him ; and one Lord
Jesus Christ, by whom
are all things, and we
by him. 7 Howbeit
there is not in every
man that knowledge :
for some with con-
science of the idol un-
to this hour eat it as
a thing offered unto
an idol ; and their con-
science being weak is
defiled. 8 But meat
commendeth us not to
God : for neither, if
we eat, are we the bet-
ter ; neither, if we eat
not, are we the worse.
9 But take heed lest
by any means this li-
berty of yours become
a stumblingblock to
them that are weak.
10 For if any man see
thee which hast know-
ledge sit at meat in

the idol's temple, shall not the conscience of him which is weak be emboldened to eat those things which are offered to idols; 11 and through thy knowledge shall the weak brother perish, for whom Christ died? 12 But when ye sin so against the brethren, and wound their weak conscience, ye sin against Christ. 13 Wherefore, if meat make my brother to offend, I will eat no flesh while the world standeth, lest I make my brother to offend.

IX. Am I not an apostle? am I not free? have I not seen Jesus Christ our Lord? are not ye my work in the Lord? 2 If I be not an apostle unto others, yet doubtless I am to you: for the seal of mine apostleship are ye in the Lord. 3 Mine answer to them that do examine me is this, 4 have we not power to eat and to drink? 5 have we not power to lead about a sister, a wife, as well as other apostles, and as the brethren of the Lord, and Cephas? 6 or I only and Barnabas, have not we power to forbear working? 7 Who goeth a warfare any time at his own charges? who planteth a vineyard, and eateth not of the fruit thereof? or who feedeth a flock, and eateth not of the milk of the flock? 8 Say I these things as a man? or saith not the law the same also? 9 for it is written in the law of Moses, Thou shalt not muzzle the mouth of the ox that treadeth out the corn. Doth God take care for oxen? 10 or saith he it altogether for our sakes? For our sakes, no doubt, this is written: that he that ploweth should plow in hope; and that he that thresheth in hope should be partaker of his hope. 11 If we have sown unto you spiritual things, is it a great thing if we

μου, οὐ·μὴ φάγω κρέα εἰς·τὸν·αἰῶνα, ἵνα μὴ τὸν ἀδελφόν.
my, not at all should I eat flesh for ever, that ¹not ⁶brother

μου σκανδαλίσω.
my ¹I ²may ⁴cause to offend.

9 Οὐκ·εἰμὶ ˣἀπόστολος‖; οὐκ·εἰμὶ ˣἐλεύθερος‖; οὐχὶ Ἰησοῦν
Am I not an apostle? am I not free? ²not ⁵Jesus

ᵡριστὸν‖ τὸν·κύριον·ἡμῶν ᶻἑώρακα‖; οὐ τὸ·ἔργον·μου ὑμεῖς
⁶Christ ⁷our ⁸Lord ¹have ²I ⁴seen? ¹⁰not ¹²my ¹³work ¹¹ye

ἐστε ἐν κυρίῳ; 2 εἰ ἄλλοις οὐκ·εἰμὶ ἀπόστολος, ἀλλά
⁹are in [the] Lord? If to others I am not an apostle, yet

γε ὑμῖν εἰμι· ἡ·γὰρ σφραγὶς ᵃτῆς·ἐμῆς·ἀποστολῆς‖ ὑμεῖς
at any rate to you I am; for the seal of my apostleship ye

ἐστε ἐν κυρίῳ. 3 ἡ·ἐμὴ·ἀπολογία τοῖς ἐμὲ ἀνακρίνουσιν
are in [the] Lord. My defence to those ³me ¹who ²examine

ᵇαὕτη ἐστίν,‖ 4 Μὴ οὐκ·ἔχομεν ἐξουσίαν φαγεῖν καὶ ᶜπιεῖν‖;
⁵this ⁴is: Have we not authority to eat and to drink?

5 μὴ οὐκ·ἔχομεν ἐξουσίαν ἀδελφὴν γυναῖκα περιάγειν, ὡς καὶ
have we not authority a sister, a wife, to take about, as also

οἱ λοιποὶ ἀπόστολοι, καὶ οἱ ἀδελφοὶ τοῦ κυρίου, καὶ Κηφᾶς;
the other apostles, - and the brethren of the Lord, and Cephas?

6 ἢ μόνος ἐγὼ καὶ Βαρνάβας οὐκ·ἔχομεν ἐξουσίαν ᵈτοῦ‖ μὴ
Or only I and Barnabas have we not authority not

ἐργάζεσθαι; 7 Τίς στρατεύεται ἰδίοις ὀψωνίοις ποτέ;
to work? Who serves as a soldier at his own charges at any time?

τίς φυτεύει ἀμπελῶνα, καὶ ᵉἐκ τοῦ καρποῦ‖ αὐτοῦ οὐκ·ἐσθίει;
who plants a vineyard, and of the fruit of it does not eat?

ᶠἢ‖ τίς ποιμαίνει ποίμνην, καὶ ἐκ τοῦ γάλακτος τῆς ποίμνης
or who shepherds a flock, and of the milk of the flock

οὐκ·ἐσθίει; 8 μὴ κατὰ ἄνθρωπον ταῦτα λαλῶ; ἢ ᵍοὐχὶ
does not eat? according to a man these things do I speak, or ⁷not

καὶ ὁ νόμος ταῦτα‖ λέγει; 9 ἐν·γὰρ τῷ ʰΜωσέως‖ νόμῳ
³also ⁴the ⁵law ⁶these ⁷things ¹says? For in the ²of ²Moses ¹law

γέγραπται, Οὐ·ⁱφιμώσεις‖ βοῦν ἀλοῶντα. μὴ τῶν
it has been written, Thou shalt not muzzle an ox treading out corn. ⁴For ³the

βοῶν μέλει τῷ θεῷ; 10 ἢ δι' ἡμᾶς πάντως λέγει;
⁶oxen ¹is ²there ³care with God? or because of us altogether says he [it]?

δι'·ἡμᾶς·γὰρ ἐγράφη, ὅτι ʲἐπ'·ἐλπίδι ὀφείλει‖ ὁ ἀροτριῶν
For because of us it was written, that in hope ought he that ploughs

ἀροτριᾷν, καὶ ὁ ἀλοῶν ᵏτῆς·ἐλπίδος·αὐτοῦ μετέχειν
to plough, and he that treads out corn, ⁵of ⁶his ⁷hope ³io ⁴partake

ἐπ'·ἐλπίδι.‖ 11 Εἰ ἡμεῖς ὑμῖν τὰ πνευματικὰ ἐσπείραμεν,
¹in ²hope. If we to you spiritual things did sow, [is it]

μέγα εἰ ἡμεῖς ὑμῶν τὰ σαρκικὰ θερίσομεν; 12 εἰ ἄλλοι
a great thing if we your fleshly things shall reap? If others

τῆς ˡἐξουσίας ὑμῶν‖ μετέχουσιν, οὐ μᾶλλον ἡμεῖς;
²of the ³authority ⁵over ⁶you ¹partake, [should] not rather we?

ἀλλ' οὐκ·ἐχρησάμεθα τῇ·ἐξουσίᾳ·ταύτῃ· ἀλλὰ πάντα στέ-
But we did not use this authority; but all things we

γομεν, ἵνα μὴ ᵐἐγκοπήν τινα‖ δῶμεν τῷ εὐαγγελίῳ τοῦ
bear, that not ²hindrance ¹any we should give to the glad tidings of the

χριστοῦ. 13 οὐκ·οἴδατε ὅτι οἱ τὰ·ἱερὰ ἐργαζόμενοι, ⁿ
Christ. Know ye not that those [²at] ³sacred ⁴things ¹labouring, [the

---

ˣ ἀπόστολος and ἐλεύθερος transposed GLTTrAW. ʸ — χριστὸν LTTrA. ᶻ ἑόρακα T.
ᵃ μου τῆς ἀποστολῆς LTTrA. ᵇ ἐστιν αὕτη LTTrA. ᶜ πεῖν TA. ᵈ — τοῦ LTTr[A]. ᵉ τὸν
καρπὸν the fruit LTTrAW. ᶠ — ἢ L[Tr]AW. ᵍ καὶ ὁ νόμος ταῦτα οὐ LTTrAW. ʰ Μωϋσέως
GLTTrAW. ⁱ κημώσεις TTrA. ʲ ὀφείλει ἐπ' ἐλπίδι LTTrA. ᵏ ἐπ' ἐλπίδι τοῦ μετέχειν GLTTrAW.
ˡ ὑμῶν ἐξουσίας GLTTrAW. ᵐ τινα ἐγκοπὴν (ἐκκ- T) LTTrAW. ⁿ + τὰ the things TTr[A].

ἐκ τοῦ ἱεροῦ ἐσθίουσιν· οἱ τῷ θυσιαστηρίῳ °προσεδ-
things]of the temple eat; those ²at ³the ⁴altar attend-
ρεύοντες,‖ τῷ θυσιαστηρίῳ συμμερίζονται; 14 οὕτως καὶ ὁ
ing, with the altar partake? So also the
κύριος διέταξεν τοῖς τὸ εὐαγγέλιον καταγγέλλουσιν, ἐκ τοῦ
Lord did order to those the glad tidings announcing, of the
εὐαγγελίου ζῆν. 15 ἐγὼ.δὲ Pοὐδενὶ ἐχρησάμην‖ τούτων·
glad tidings to live. But I ¹none ¹used of these things.
οὐκ.ἔγραψα.δὲ ταῦτα ἵνα οὕτως γένηται ἐν ἐμοί·
Now I did not write these things that thus it should be with me; [²it ³were]
καλὸν γάρ μοι μᾶλλον ἀποθανεῖν, ἢ τὸ.καύχημά.μου �qἵνα
¹good ²for for ¹me rather to die, than ³my ⁴boasting ¹that
τις‖ ʳκενώσῃ.‖ 16 ἐὰν.γὰρ εὐαγγελίζωμαι, οὐκ.ἔστιν
²anyone should make void. For if I announce the glad tidings, there is not
μοι καύχημα· ἀνάγκη.γάρ μοι ἐπίκειται· οὐαὶ.ˢδέ‖ μοι
²to ³me ¹boasting; for necessity ⁴me ¹is ²laid ³upon; ⁶woe ⁵but to me
ἐστὶν ἐὰν μὴ.ᵗεὐαγγελίζωμαι.‖ 17 εἰ.γὰρ ἑκὼν τοῦτο
it is if I should not announce the glad tidings. For if willingly this
πράσσω, μισθὸν ἔχω· εἰ.δὲ ἄκων οἰκονομίαν πεπί-
I do, a reward I have; but if unwillingly an administration I am en-
στευμαι. 18 τίς οὖν ᵛμοι‖ ἐστὶν ὁ μισθός; ἵνα εὐαγ-
trusted with. What then ²my ¹is reward? That in announcing
γελιζόμενος ἀδάπανον θήσω τὸ εὐαγγέλιον· ʷτοῦ
the glad tidings ⁴without ⁵expense ⁶I ⁷should ⁸make ⁹the ¹⁰glad ¹¹tidings ¹of ²the
χριστοῦ,‖ εἰς.τὸ μὴ καταχρήσασθαι τῇ.ἐξουσία.μου ἐν τῷ
³Christ, so as not using as my own my authority in the
εὐαγγελίῳ. 19 Ἐλεύθερος.γὰρ ὢν ἐκ πάντων, πᾶσιν ἐμαυτὸν
glad tidings. For free being from all, to all myself
ἐδούλωσα, ἵνα τοὺς πλείονας κερδήσω· 20 καὶ ἐγενόμην
I became bondman, that the more I might gain. And I became
τοῖς Ἰουδαίοις ὡς Ἰουδαῖος, ἵνα Ἰουδαίους κερδήσω· τοῖς
to the Jews as a Jew, that Jews I might gain : to those
ὑπὸ νόμον ὡς ὑπὸ νόμον, ˣ ἵνα τοὺς ὑπὸ νόμον κερδήσω·
under law as under law, that those under· law I might gain :
21 τοῖς ἀνόμοις ὡς ἄνομος, μὴ ὢν ἄνομος ᵞθεῷ,‖ ἀλλ᾽
to those without law as without law, (not being without law to God, but
ἔννομος ᶻχριστῷ,‖ ἵνα ᵃκερδήσω‖ ἀνόμους. 22 ἐγενόμην
within law to Christ,) that I might gain those without law. I became
τοῖς ἀσθενέσιν ᵇὡς‖ ἀσθενής, ἵνα τοὺς ἀσθενεῖς κερδήσω.
to the weak as weak, that the weak I might gain.
τοῖς.πᾶσιν γέγονα ᶜτὰ‖.πάντα, ἵνα πάντως τινὰς σώσω.
To all these I have become all things, that by all means some I might save.
23 ᵈτοῦτο‖ δὲ ποιῶ διὰ τὸ εὐαγγέλιον, ἵνα ᵉσυγκοινωνὸς‖
ᵈThis ¹and I do on account of the glad tidings, that a fellow-partaker
αὐτοῦ.γένωμαι.
with it I might be.
24 Οὐκ.οἴδατε ὅτι οἱ ἐν σταδίῳ τρέχοντες πάντες μὲν
Know ye not that those who in a·race-course run all
ꝼρέχουσιν, εἰς.δὲ λαμβάνει τὸ βραβεῖον; οὕτως τρέχετε, ἵνα
run, but one receives the prize? Thus run, ˙that
καταλάβητε. 25 πᾶς.δὲ ὁ ἀγωνιζόμενος, πάντα ἐγκρα-
ye may obtain. But everyone that ˍstrives, in all things controls

shall reap your carnal things? 12 If others be partakers of this power over you, are not we rather? Nevertheless we have not used this power; but suffer all things, lest we should hinder the gospel of Christ. 13 Do ye not know that they which minister about holy things live of the things of the temple? and they which wait at the altar are partakers with the altar? 14 Even so hath the Lord ordained that they which preach the gospel should live of the gospel. 15 But I have used none of these things : neither have I written these things, that it should be so done unto me : for it were better for me to die, than that any man should make my glorying void. 16 For though I preach the gospel, I have nothing to glory of : for necessity is laid upon me; yea, woe is unto me, if I preach not the gospel ! 17 For if I do this thing willingly, I have a reward : but if against my will, a dispensation of the gospel is committed unto me. 18 What is my reward then? Verily that, when I preach the gospel, I may make the gospel of Christ without charge, that I abuse not my power in the gospel. 19 For though I be free from all men, yet have I made myself servant unto all, that I might gain the more. 20 And unto the Jews I became as a Jew, that I might gain the Jews; to them that are under the law, as under the law, that I might gain them that are under the law; 21 to them that are without law, as without law, (being not without law to God, but under the law to Christ,) that I might gain them that are without law. 22 To the weak became I as weak, that I might gain the weak : I am made all things to all men, that I might by

---

° παρεδρεύοντες LTTrAW.   P οὐ κέχρημαι οὐδενὶ have not used any GLTTrAW.   q οὐδεὶς
LTTr.   ʳ κενώσει shall make vain LTTrA.   ˢ γάρ for GLTTrAW.   ᵗ εὐαγγελίσωμαι LTTrAW.
ᵛ μου TTrA.   ʷ — τοῦ χριστοῦ LTTrAW.   ˣ + μὴ ὢν αὐτὸς ὑπὸ νόμον not being myself
under law GLTTrAW.   ᵞ θεοῦ of God LTTrAW.   ᶻ χριστοῦ of Christ LTTrAW.   ᵃ κερδάνω
τοὺς LTTrAW.   ᵇ — ὡς [L]TTrAW.   ᶜ — τὰ LTTrAW.   ᵈ πάντα all things LTTrAW.   ᵉ συν- T.

all means save some. 23 And this I do for the gospel's sake, that I might be partaker thereof with *you*. 24 Know ye not that they which run in a race run all, but one receiveth the prize? So run, that ye may obtain. 25 And every man that striveth for the mastery is temperate in all things. Now they *do it* to obtain a corruptible crown; but we an incorruptible. 26 I therefore so run, not as uncertainly; so fight I, not as one that beateth the air: 27 but I keep under my body, and bring *it* into subjection: lest that by any means, when I have preached to others, I myself should be a castaway.

X. Moreover, brethren, I would not that ye should be ignorant, how that all our fathers were under the cloud, and all passed through the sea; 2 and were all baptized unto Moses in the cloud and in the sea; 3 and did all eat the same spiritual meat; 4 and did all drink the same spiritual drink: for they drank of that spiritual Rock that followed them: and that Rock was Christ. 5 But with many of them God was not well pleased: for they were overthrown in the wilderness. 6 Now these things were our examples, to the intent we should not lust after evil things, as they also lusted. 7 Neither be ye idolaters, as *were* some of them; as it is written, The people sat down to eat and drink, and rose up to play. 8 Neither let us commit fornication, as some of them committed, and fell in one day three and twenty thousand. 9 Neither let us tempt Christ, as some of them also tempted, and were destroyed of serpents. 10 Neither murmur ye, as some of them also murmured, and were

τεύεται· ἐκεῖνοι μὲν οὖν ἵνα φθαρτὸν στέφανον λάβωσιν,
himself: they indeed then that a corruptible   crown   they may receive,

ἡμεῖς δὲ ἄφθαρτον. 26 ἐγὼ τοίνυν οὕτως τρέχω, ὡς 'οὐκ
but we   an incorruptible.   I   therefore   so   run,   as   not

ἀδήλως· οὕτως πυκτεύω, ὡς οὐκ ἀέρα δέρων· 27 ᵍἀλλ'ⁱⁱ
uncertainly;   so   I combat,   as   not [the] air   beating.   But

ὑπωπιάζω μου τὸ σῶμα, καὶ δουλαγωγῶ, μήπως ἄλλοις
I buffet   my   body,   and bring [it] into servitude, lest   to others

κηρύξας αὐτὸς ἀδόκιμος γένωμαι.
having preached ²myself   ⁵rejected   ¹I ³might ⁴be.

10 Οὐ θέλω ʰδὲⁱⁱ ὑμᾶς ἀγνοεῖν, ἀδελφοί, ὅτι οἱ πατέρες
²I ³wish ⁴not ¹now   you   to be ignorant, brethren, that   ⁴fathers

ἡμῶν πάντες ὑπὸ τὴν νεφέλην ἦσαν, καὶ πάντες διὰ τῆς
¹our   all   under the   cloud   were,   and   all   through the

θαλάσσης διῆλθον, 2 καὶ πάντες εἰς τὸν ¹Μωσῆνⁱⁱ ᵏἐβαπτίσαντοⁱⁱ
sea   · passed,   and all   to   Moses   were baptized

ἐν τῇ νεφέλῃ καὶ ἐν τῇ θαλάσσῃ, 3 καὶ πάντες τὸ αὐτὸ ¹βρῶμα
in the cloud   and in the   sea,   and   all   the same   ²meat

πνευματικὸν ἔφαγον,ᵏ 4 καὶ πάντες τὸ αὐτὸ ᵐπόμα πνευ-
¹spiritual   ate,   and   all   the same   ²drink ¹spi-

ματικὸν ἔπιον·ⁱⁱ ἔπινον γὰρ ἐκ πνευματικῆς ἀκολουθούσης
ritual   drank;   for they drank of a spiritual   ²following

πέτρας· ἡ ⁿδὲ πέτρα ἦν ὁ χριστός. 5 ἀλλ' οὐκ ἐν τοῖς
¹rock,   and the rock   was the Christ: yet   not with the

πλείοσιν αὐτῶν °εὐδόκησενⁱⁱ ὁ θεός· κατεστρώθησαν γὰρ ἐν
most   of them was ²well ³pleased   ¹God;   for they were strewed   in

τῇ ἐρήμῳ. 6 ταῦτα δὲ τύποι ἡμῶν ἐγενήθησαν, εἰς τὸ μὴ
the desert.   But these things types   for us   became,   for   ²not

εἶναι ἡμᾶς ἐπιθυμητὰς κακῶν, καθὼς κἀκεῖνοι ἐπεθύμη-
¹to ⁴be   us   desirers   of evil things, according as they also   desired,

σαν. 7 μηδὲ εἰδωλολάτραι γίνεσθε, καθώς τινες αὐτῶν· ᴾὡςⁱⁱ
  Neither   idolaters   be ye,   according as some of them;   as

γέγραπται, Ἐκάθισεν ὁ λαὸς φαγεῖν καὶ ᵠπιεῖν,ⁱⁱ καὶ ἀν-
it has been written, ³Sat ⁴down ¹the ²people to eat   and to drink,   and   rose

έστησαν παίζειν. 8 μηδὲ πορνεύωμεν, καθώς τινες
up   to play.   Neither should we commit fornication, according as some

αὐτῶν ἐπόρνευσαν, καὶ ἔπεσονⁱⁱ ˢἐνⁱⁱ μιᾷ ἡμέρᾳ εἰκοσιτρεῖς
of them committed fornication, and   fell   in   one   day   twenty-three

χιλιάδες. 9 μηδὲ ἐκπειράζωμεν τὸν ᵗχριστόν,ⁱⁱ καθὼς ᵛκαίⁱⁱ
thousand.   Neither should we tempt the '   Christ,   according as also

τινες αὐτῶν ʷἐπείρασαν,ⁱⁱ καὶ ὑπὸ τῶν ὄφεων ˣἀπώλοντο.ⁱⁱ
some of them   tempted,   and by the   serpents   perished.

10 μηδὲ γογγύζετε, ʸκαθὼςⁱⁱ ᵛκαίⁱⁱ τινες αὐτῶν ἐγόγγυσαν,
  Neither murmur ye, according as also   some of them   murmured,

καὶ ἀπώλοντο ὑπὸ τοῦ ὀλοθρευτοῦ. 11 ταῦτα δὲ ᶻπάνταⁱⁱ
and perished   by the   destroyer.   Now these things   all   [as]

ᵃτύποιⁱⁱ ᵇσυνέβαινονⁱⁱ ἐκείνοις· ἐγράφη δὲ πρὸς νουθεσίαν
types   happened   to them, and were written for   ²admonition

ἡμῶν εἰς οὓς τὰ τέλη τῶν αἰώνων ᶜκατήντησεν.ⁱⁱ 12 ὥστε
¹our   on whom the ends of the   ages   are arrived.   So that

---

ᵍ ἀλλὰ Tr.   ʰ γὰρ for GLTTrAW.   ⁱ Μωϋσῆν GLTTrAW.   ᵏ ἐβαπτίσθησαν LT.   ˡ πνευματικὸν ἔφαγον βρῶμα (βρῶμα ἔφαγον TTr) LTTr.   ᵐ πνευματικὸν ἔπιον πόμα LTTrAW.   ⁿ πέτρα δὲ LTTrA.   ° ηὐδόκησεν LTrAW.   ᴾ ὥσπερ LTTrA.   ᵠ πεῖν TA.   ʳ ἔπεσαν LTTrAW.   ˢ — ἐν LTTr[A].   ᵗ κύριον Lord LTTrA.   ᵛ — καὶ LTTrAW.   ʷ ἐξεπείρασαν T.   ˣ ἀπώλλυντο TTr.   ʸ καθάπερ TTr.   ᶻ — πάντα [L]TTr[A].   ᵃ τυπικῶς typically LTTrAW.   ᵇ συνέβαινεν TTr.   ᶜ κατήντηκεν have come LTTrAW.

ὁ δοκῶν ἑστάναι, βλεπέτω μὴ πέσῃ. 13 Πειρασμὸς
he that thinks   to stand,   let him take heed lest   he fall.   Temptation

ὑμᾶς οὐκ.εἴληφεν εἰ.μὴ ἀνθρώπινος· πιστὸς.δὲ ὁ θεός, ὃς
you   has not taken except what belongs to man; and faithful [is] God, who

οὐκ.ἐάσει ὑμᾶς πειρασθῆναι ὑπὲρ ὃ δύνασθε, ἀλλὰ ποιήσει
will not suffer you   to be tempted above what ye are able,   but will make

σὺν τῷ πειρασμῷ καὶ τὴν ἔκβασιν, τοῦ.δύνασθαι ᵉὑμᾶς‖
with the temptation   also   the   issue,   for ²to ³be ⁴able   ¹you

ὑπενεγκεῖν. 14 Διόπερ, ἀγαπητοί.μου, φεύγετε ἀπὸ τῆς
to bear   [it].   Wherefore, · my beloved,   flee   from

εἰδωλολατρείας. 15 ὡς φρονίμοις λέγω· κρίνατε ὑμεῖς ὅ
idolatry.   As to intelligent ones I speak: judge   ye   what

φημι. 16 τὸ ποτήριον τῆς εὐλογίας ὃ εὐλογοῦμεν, οὐχὶ
I say.   The   cup   of blessing which we bless,   ²not

κοινωνία ᶠτοῦ αἵματος τοῦ χριστοῦ ἐστιν;‖ τὸν ἄρτον ὃν
⁴fellowship ⁵of ⁶the ⁷blood ⁸of ⁹the ¹⁰Christ   ¹is ²it ?   The bread which

κλῶμεν, οὐχὶ κοινωνία τοῦ σώματος τοῦ χριστοῦ ἐστιν;
we break,   ²not   ⁴fellowship ⁵of ⁶the   ⁷body   ⁸of ⁹the ¹⁰Christ   ¹is ²it ?

17 ὅτι εἷς ἄρτος, ἓν σῶμα οἱ πολλοί ἐσμεν· οἱ γὰρ πάντες
Because ⁵one ⁶loaf, ⁷one ⁸body ²the   ³many ¹we ⁴are ;   for   ²all

ἐκ τοῦ ἑνὸς ἄρτου μετέχομεν. 18 βλέπετε τὸν Ἰσραὴλ κατὰ
³of ⁴the ⁵one   ⁶loaf ¹we partake.   See   Israel according to

σάρκα· ᵍοὐχὶ‖ οἱ ἐσθίοντες τὰς θυσίας, κοινωνοὶ
flesh :   ²not   ³those ⁴eating   ⁵the ⁶sacrifices, ⁷fellow-partakers

τοῦ θυσιαστηρίου εἰσίν; 19 τί οὖν φημι; ὅτι ʰεἴδωλον‖ τί
⁸with ⁹the ¹⁰altar   ¹are ?   What then say I ? that   an idol anything

ἐστιν, ἢ ὅτι ʰεἰδωλόθυτον‖ τί ἐστιν; 20 ἀλλ' ὅτι
is, - or that what is sacrificed to an idol anything is ?   but that

ἃ ᶦθύει‖ ᵏτὰ ἔθνη,‖ δαιμονίοις ᶦθύει,‖ καὶ οὐ θεῷᵐ·
what ²sacrifice ¹the ²nations, to demons   they sacrifice, and not to God.

οὐ.θέλω.δὲ ὑμᾶς κοινωνοὺς τῶν δαιμονίων γίνεσθαι.
But I do not wish you   fellow-partakers   with demons   to be.

21 οὐ.δύνασθε ποτήριον κυρίου πίνειν, καὶ ποτήριον
Ye cannot [the]   cup   of [the] Lord drink,   and [the]   cup

δαιμονίων· οὐ.δύνασθε τραπέζης κυρίου μετέχειν καὶ
of demons :   ye cannot   of [the] table of [the] Lord partake and

τραπέζης δαιμονίων.. 22 ἢ παραζηλοῦμεν τὸν κύριον;
of [the] table   of demons.   Or, do we provoke to jealousy the Lord ?

μὴ ἰσχυρότεροι αὐτοῦ ἐσμεν;
stronger   than he   are we ?

23 Πάντα ⁿμοι‖ ἔξεστιν, ἀλλ' οὐ πάντα συμφέρει·
All things for me are lawful, but   ⁴not ¹all ²things ³are profitable ;

ἱπάντα ⁿμοι‖ ἔξεστιν, ἀλλ' οὐ πάντα οἰκοδομεῖ. 24 μηδεὶς
all things for me are lawful, but   ³not ¹all   ²do build up.   ⁴No ³one

τὸ ἑαυτοῦ ζητείτω, ἀλλὰ τὸ τοῦ ἑτέρου ᵒἕκαστος.‖
³that ⁶of ⁷himself ¹let ⁴seek, ''   but   ³that ⁴of ⁵the ⁶other   ¹each ²one.

25 Πᾶν τὸ ἐν μακέλλῳ πωλούμενον ἐσθίετε, μηδὲν ἀνα-
Everything that in ' a market   is sold   eat,   nothing in-

κρίνοντες διὰ τὴν συνείδησιν· 26 τοῦ.ᵖγὰρ. κυρίου‖
quiring   on account of   conscience.   For ⁴the   ⁵Lord's [²is]

ἡ γῆ καὶ τὸ πλήρωμα αὐτῆς. 27 εἰ.ᑫδὲ‖ τις καλεῖ ὑμᾶς
¹the ²earth and the   fulness   of it.   But if   anyone ⁴invite ⁵you

---

destroyed of the destroyer. 11 Now all these things happened unto them for ensamples : and they are written for our admonition, upon whom the ends of the world are come. 12 Wherefore let him that thinketh he standeth take heed lest he fall. 13 There hath no temptation taken you but such as is common to man : but God is faithful, who will not suffer you to be tempted above that ye are able ; but will with the temptation also make a way to escape, that ye may be able to bear it. 14 Wherefore, my dearly beloved, flee from idolatry. 15 I speak as to wise men ; judge ye what I say. 16 The cup of blessing which we bless, is it not the communion of the blood of Christ ? The bread which we break, is it not the communion of the body of Christ ? 17 For we being many are one bread, and one body, for we are all partakers of that one bread. 18 Behold Israel after the flesh : are not they which eat of the sacrifices partakers of the altar ? 19 What say I then ? that the idol is any thing, or that which is offered in sacrifice to idols is any thing ? 20 But I say, that the things which the Gentiles sacrifice, they sacrifice to devils, and not to God : and I would not that ye should have fellowship with devils. 21 Ye cannot drink the cup of the Lord, and the cup of devils : ye cannot be partakers of the Lord's table, and of the table of devils. 22 Do we provoke the Lord to jealousy ? are we stronger than he ? 23 All things are lawful for me, but all things are not expedient : all things are lawful for me, but all things edify not. 24 Let no man seek his own, but every man another's wealth. 25 Whatsoever is sold in the

---

ᵉ — ὑμᾶς (read [you]) GLTTrAW.   ᶠ ἐστὶν τοῦ αἵματος τοῦ χριστοῦ Tr.   ᵍ οὐχ LTAW.
ʰ εἴδωλον and εἰδωλόθυτον transposed LTTrAW.   ᶦ θύουσιν they sacrifice LTTrAW.   ᵏ — τὰ
ἔθνη LTA.   ˡ — θύει LTTrA.   ᵐ + θύουσιν they sacrifice LTTrA.   ⁿ — μοι GLTTrAW.
ᵒ — ἕκαστος GLTTrAW.   ᵖ κυρίου γὰρ LTTrAW.   ᑫ — δὲ but LTTrAW.

shambles, *that* eat, asking no question for conscience sake : 26 for the earth *is* the Lord's, and the fulness thereof. 27 If any of them that believe not bid you *to a feast,* and ye be disposed to go ; whatsoever is set before you, eat, asking no question for conscience sake. 28 But if any man say unto you, This is offered in sacrifice unto idols, eat not for his sake that shewed it, and for conscience sake : for the earth *is* the Lord's, and the fulness thereof : 29 conscience, I say, not thine own, but of the other : for why is my liberty judged of another *man's* conscience ? 30 For if I by grace be a partaker, why am I evil spoken of for that for which I give thanks ? 31 Whether therefore ye eat, or drink, or whatsoever ye do, do all to the glory of God. 32 Give none offence, neither to the Jews, nor to the Gentiles, nor to the church of God : 33 even as I please all *men* in all *things,* not seeking mine own profit, but the *profit* of many, that they may be saved. XI. Be ye followers of me, even as I also am of Christ.

2 Now I praise you, brethren, that ye remember me in all things, and keep the ordinances, as I delivered *them* to you. 3 But I would have you know, that the head of every man is Christ ; and the head of the woman *is* the man ; and the head of Christ *is* God. 4 Every man praying or prophesying, having *his* head covered, dishonoureth his head. 5 But every woman that prayeth or prophesieth with *her* head uncovered dishonoureth her head : for that is even all one as if she were shaven. 6 For if the woman be not covered, let her also be shorn : but if it be a shame for a woman to be shorn or shaven, let her be covered.

τῶν ἀπίστων, καὶ θέλετε πορεύεσθαι, πᾶν τὸ παρατιθέμενον
[1]of [2]the [3]unbelieving, and ye wish   to go,   all that   is set before
ὑμῖν ἐσθίετε, μηδὲν ἀνακρίνοντες διὰ τὴν συνείδησιν.
you,   eat,   nothing   inquiring   on account of   conscience.
28 ἐὰν.δέ τις ὑμῖν εἴπῃ, Τοῦτο ᵣεἰδωλόθυτόν‖ ἐστιν· μὴ
But if   anyone to you say,   This   [2]offered [3]to [4]an [5]idol   [1]is,   [7]not
ἐσθίετε, δι' ἐκεῖνον τὸν μηνύσαντα καὶ τὴν συνείδησιν·
[6]do eat, on account of him that   shewed [it], and the conscience ;
ˢτοῦ.γὰρ κυρίου ἡ γῆ καὶ τὸ πλήρωμα αὐτῆς.‖ 29 συνεί-
for [1]the   [5]Lord's [[3]is] [1]the [2]earth and the ₂ fulness   of it.   [2]Con-
δησιν δὲ λέγω, οὐχὶ τὴν ἑαυτοῦ, ἀλλὰ τὴν τοῦ ἑτέρου.
science [1]but, I say,   not that of thyself,   but   that of the other ;
ἵνα.τί.γὰρ ἡ.ἐλευθερία.μου κρίνεται ὑπὸ ἄλλης συνειδήσεως ;
for why   [2]my [3]freedom   [1]is judged by another's   conscience ?
30 εἰ.ᵗδὲ‖ ἐγὼ χάριτι μετέχω, τί βλασφημοῦμαι ὑπὲρ οὗ
But if   I   with thanks partake, why am I evil spoken of   for what
ἐγὼ εὐχαριστῶ ; 31 Εἴτε οὖν ἐσθίετε, εἴτε πίνετε, εἴτε
I   give thanks ?   Whether therefore ye eat,   or   ye drink   or
τι ποιεῖτε, πάντα εἰς δόξαν θεοῦ ποιεῖτε. 32 ἀπρόσκοποι
anything ye do, all things to [2]glory [1]God's   do.   Without offence
ᵛγίνεσθε καὶ Ἰουδαίοις‖ καὶ Ἕλλησιν καὶ τῇ ἐκκλησίᾳ.τοῦ
be ye both   to Jews   and   Greeks   and to the assembly
θεοῦ· 33 καθὼς κἀγὼ πάντα πᾶσιν ἀρέσκω, μὴ ζητῶν
of God.   According as I also   all   in all things please ;   not seeking
τὸ ἐμαυτοῦ ᵂσυμφέρον,‖ ἀλλὰ τὸ τῶν πολλῶν, ἵνα σωθῶ-
the [2]of [3]myself   [1]profit,   but that of the   many,   that they may
σιν. 11. μιμηταί μου γίνεσθε, καθὼς κἀγὼ χριστοῦ.
be saved.   Imitators of me   be,   according as I also [am] of Christ.

2 Ἐπαινῶ.δὲ ὑμᾶς, ˣἀδελφοί,‖ ὅτι πάντα μου μέ-
Now I praise   you,   brethren,   that in all things me ye have
μνησθε, καὶ καθὼς παρέδωκα ὑμῖν, τὰς παραδόσεις κατ-
remembered ; and according as I delivered to you,   the   traditions   ye
έχετε. 3 θέλω.δὲ ὑμᾶς εἰδέναι, ὅτι παντὸς ἀνδρὸς ἡ κεφαλὴ
keep.   But I wish you to know, that of every man [4]the [5]head
ὁ χριστός ἐστιν· κεφαλὴ.δὲ γυναικὸς ὁ ἀνήρ· κεφαλὴ.δὲ
[1]the [2]Christ [3]is,   but head of [the] woman [is] the man,   and head
ʸχριστοῦ, ὁ θεός. 4 πᾶς ἀνὴρ προσευχόμενος ἢ προφητεύων,
of Christ,   God.   Every man   praying   or prophesying, /
κατὰ κεφαλῆς ἔχων, καταισχύνει τὴν.κεφαλὴν.αὐτοῦ.
[anything] on [his] head having, puts to shame   his head.
5 πᾶσα.δὲ γυνὴ προσευχομένη ἢ προφητεύουσα ἀκατακαλύπτῳ
But every woman   praying   or   prophesying   [4]uncovered
τῇ κεφαλῇ, καταισχύνει τὴν.κεφαλὴν.ᶻἑαυτῆς·‖ ἓν.γὰρ
[1]with [2]the [3]head,   puts to shame   her head ;   for one
ἐστιν καὶ τὸ αὐτὸ τῇ.ἐξυρημένῃ. 6 εἰ.γὰρ οὐ.κατακαλύπ-
it is   and the same with having been shaven.   For if   be not covered
τεται γυνή, καὶ κειράσθω· εἰ.δὲ αἰσχρὸν γυναικὶ τὸ
a woman, also let her be shorn. But if [it be] shameful to a woman
κείρασθαι ἢ ξυρᾶσθαι, κατακαλυπτέσθω. 7 ἀνὴρ.μὲν.γὰρ οὐκ
to be shorn or to be shaven, let her be covered.   For man indeed ˣnot
ὀφείλει κατακαλύπτεσθαι τὴν κεφαλήν, εἰκὼν καὶ δόξα θεοῦ
[1]ought   to have [2]covered   [1]the   [2]head,   image and glory of God
ὑπάρχων· ᵃ γυνὴ.δὲ δόξα ἀνδρός ἐστιν· 8 οὐ.γάρ ἐστιν ἀνὴρ
[3]being ;   but woman glory of man   is.   For not   is   man

---

ʳ ἱερόθυτόν offered in sacrifice LTTrA.   ˢ — τοῦ γὰρ to end of verse GLTTrAW.   ᵗ — δὲ but GLTTrAW.   ᵛ καὶ Ἰουδαίοις γίνεσθε LTTrA.   ᵂ σύμφορον LTTrA.   ˣ — ἀδελφοί LTTrAW, ʸ + τοῦ (*read* of the Christ) [L]TTrA.   ᶻ αὐτῆς LTTrA.   ᵃ + ἡ the (woman) LTTrAW.

ἐκ γυναικός, ἀλλὰ γυνὴ ἐξ ἀνδρός· 9 καὶ·γὰρ οὐκ ἐκτίσθη
of woman,   but woman of   man.   For also   not was created

ἀνὴρ διὰ τὴν γυναῖκα, ἀλλὰ γυνὴ διὰ τὸν ἄνδρα·
man on account of the ˍ woman,   but. woman on account of the man.

10 διὰ τοῦτο ὀφείλει ἡ γυνὴ ἐξουσίαν ἔχειν ἐπὶ τῆς κε-
Because of this   ought the woman authority to have on the

φαλῆς, διὰ τοὺς ἀγγέλους. 11 πλὴν οὔτε ᵇἀνὴρ
head,   on account of the   angels.   However neither [is] man

χωρὶς γυναικός, οὔτε γυνὴ χωρὶς ἀνδρός,‖ ἐν κυρίῳ·
apart from woman,   nor woman apart from man,   in [the] Lord.

12 ὥσπερ·γὰρ ἡ γυνὴ ἐκ·τοῦ ἀνδρός, οὕτως καὶ ὁ ἀνὴρ
For as   the woman of the   man [is],   so   also the man

διὰ τῆς γυναικός, τὰ·δὲ·πάντα ἐκ τοῦ θεοῦ. 13 ἐν ὑμῖν·αὐτοῖς
by the   woman [is]; but all things of   God.   In yourselves

κρίνατε· πρέπον ἐστὶν γυναῖκα ἀκατακάλυπτον τῷ θεῷ
judge: becoming is it   for a woman   uncovered   to God

προσεύχεσθαι; 14 ᶜἢ‖ οὐδὲ ᵈαὐτὴ ἡ φύσις‖ διδάσκει ὑμᾶς,
to pray?   Or ²not ⁵even ⁵itself ⁴nature ¹does teach you,

ὅτι ἀνὴρ μὲν ἐὰν κομᾷ, ἀτιμία αὐτῷ ἐστιν· 15 γυνὴ
that ²a ³man   ¹if have long hair a dishonour to him it is?   ⁵A ⁴woman

δὲ ἐὰν κομᾷ, δόξα αὐτῇ ἐστιν; ὅτι ἡ .κόμη ἀντὶ
¹but ²if have long hair; glory to her it is;   for the long hair instead

περιβολαίου δέδοται ᵉαὐτῇ·‖ 16 εἰ·δέ τις δοκεῖ φιλόνεικος
of a covering   is given to her.   But if anyone thinks ³contentious

εἶναι, ἡμεῖς τοιαύτην συνήθειαν οὐκ·ἔχομεν, οὐδὲ αἱ ἐκκλησίαι
¹to ²be, we   ³such   ⁴custom   ¹have ²not,   nor the assemblies

τοῦ θεοῦ.
of God.

17 Τοῦτο·δὲ ᶠπαραγγέλλων οὐκ·ἐπαινῶ,‖ ὅτι οὐκ
But [²as ⁴to] ³this   ¹charging [²you] I do not praise [you], that not

εἰς τὸ ᵍκρεῖττον,‖ ʰἀλλ᾽‖ εἰς τὸ ⁱἧττον‖ συνέρχεσθε. 18 πρῶτον
for the better,   but   for the worse ye come together.   ²First

μὲν γὰρ συνερχομένων ὑμῶν ἐν ᵏτῇ‖ ἐκκλησίᾳ, ἀκούω σχίσ-
⁵indeed ¹for   coming together ³ye ⁴in the assembly,   I hear di-

ματα ἐν ὑμῖν ὑπάρχειν, καὶ μέρος·τι πιστεύω· 19 δεῖ·γὰρ
visions among you   to be,   and partly   I believe [it]. For there must

καὶ αἱρέσεις ἐν ὑμῖν εἶναι, ἵνα ˡ οἱ δόκιμοι φανεροὶ γένωνται
also   sects   among you be,   that the approved manifest may become

ἐν ὑμῖν. 20 συνερχομένων οὖν ὑμῶν ἐπὶ·τὸ·αὐτό, οὐκ
among you.   Coming together therefore ye   into one place,   ²not

ἔστιν κυριακὸν δεῖπνον φαγεῖν· 21 ἕκαστος·γὰρ τὸ·ἴδιον
¹it ²is [the] Lord's   supper   to eat.   For each one   his own

δεῖπνον προλαμβάνει ἐν τῷ φαγεῖν, καὶ ὃς·μὲν πεινᾷ ὃς·δὲ
supper   takes first   in   eating, and one ¹is hungry and another

μεθύει. 22 μὴ γὰρ οἰκίας οὐκ·ἔχετε εἰς τὸ ἐσθίειν·καὶ πίνειν;
is drunken.   For houses have ye not for   eating and drinking?

ἢ τῆς ἐκκλησίας τοῦ θεοῦ καταφρονεῖτε, καὶ καταισχύνετε
or the   assembly   of God do ye despise,   and   put to shame

τοὺς μὴ·ἔχοντας; τί ᵐὑμῖν εἴπω; ⁿἐπαινέσω‖ὑμᾶς °ἐν
them that have not? What to you should I say? shall ¹ praise you   in

τούτῳ; οὐκ·ἐπαινῶ. 23 Ἐγὼ·γὰρ παρέλαβον ἀπὸ τοῦ κυρίου,
this?   I do not praise.   For I   received   from the Lord

7 For a man indeed ought not to cover *his* head, forasmuch as he is the image and glory of God : but the woman is the glory of the man. 8 For the man is not of the woman ; but the woman of the man. 9 Neither was the man created for the woman ; but the woman for the man. 10 For this cause ought the woman to have power on *er* head because of the angels. 11 Nevertheless neither is the man without the woman, neither the woman without the man, in the Lord. 12 For as the woman *is* of the man, even so *is* the man also by the woman ; but all things of God. 13 Judge in yourselves: is it comely that a woman pray unto God uncovered? 14 Doth not even nature itself teach you, that, if a man have long hair, it is a shame unto him? 15 But if a woman have long hair, it is a glory to her : for *her* hair is given her for a covering. 16 But if any man seem to be contentious, we have no such custom, neither the churches of God.

17 Now in this that I declare unto you I praise *you* not, that ye come together not for the better, but for the worse. 18 For first of all, when ye come together in the church, I hear that there be divisions among you ; and I partly believe it. 19 For there must be also heresies among you, that they which are approved may be made manifest among you. 20 When ye come together therefore into one place, *this* is not to eat the Lord's supper. 21 For in eating every one taketh before *other* his own supper: and one is hungry, and another is drunken: 22 What? have ye not houses to eat and to drink in? or despise ye the church of God, and shame them that have not? What shall I say to

---

ᵇ γυνὴ χωρὶς ἀνδρὸς οὔτε ἀνὴρ χωρὶς γυναικὸς GLTTrAW. .   ᶜ — ἢ LTTrAW.   ᵈ ἡ φύσις αὐτὴ LTTrAW.   ᵉ [αὐτῇ] A.   ᶠ παραγγέλλω οὐκ·ἐπαινῶν LTrAW.   ᵍ κρεῖσσον LTTʳA. ʰ ἀλλὰ TTrA.   ⁱ ἧσσον LTTrA.   ᵏ τῇ GLTTrAW.   ˡ + καὶ also [L]Tr[A].   ᵐ εἴπω ὑμῖν LTTrAW.   ⁿ ἐπαινῶ praise I L.   ° ; ἐν τούτῳ οὐκ (read In this I do not praise) ET.

30

you ? shall I praise you in this? I praise *you* not. 23 For I have received of the Lord that which also I delivered unto you, That. the Lord Jesus the *same* night in which he was betrayed took bread : 24 and when he had given thanks, he brake *it*, and said, Take, eat : this is my body, which is broken for you : this do in remembrance of me. 25 After the same manner also *he took* the cup, when he had supped, saying, This cup is the new testament in my blood: this do ye, as oft as ye drink *it*, in remembrance of me. 26 For as often as ye eat this bread, and drink this cup, ye do shew the Lord's death till he come. 27 Wherefore whosoever shall eat this bread, and drink *this* cup of the Lord, unworthily, shall be guilty of the body and blood of the Lord. 28 But let a man examine himself, and so let him eat of *that* bread, and drink of *that* cup. 29 For he that eateth and drinketh unworthily, eateth and drinketh damnation to himself, not discerning the Lord's body. 30 For this cause many *are* weak and sickly among you, and many sleep. 31 For if we would judge ourselves, we should not be judged. 32 But when we are judged, we are chastened of the Lord, that we should not be condemned with the world. 33 Wherefore, my brethren, when ye come together to eat, tarry one for another. 34 And if any man hunger, let him eat at home ; that ye come not together unto condemnation. And the rest will I set in order when I come.

XII. Now concerning spiritual *gifts*, brethren, I would not have you ignorant. 2 Ye know that ye were Gentiles, carried away unto these dumb idols, even as ye were led. 3 Wherefore I give you to understand, that

---

ὃ καὶ παρέδωκα ὑμῖν, ὅτι ὁ κύριος Ἰησοῦς ἐν τῇ νυκτὶ
that which also I delivered to you, that the Lord Jesus in the night

ᾗ ᴾπαρεδίδοτο,ⁱⁱ ἔλαβεν ἄρτον, 24 καὶ εὐχαριστήσας
in which he was delivered up took bread, and having given thanks

ἔκλασεν, καὶ εἶπεν, ᑫΛάβετε, φάγετε·ⁱⁱ τοῦτό μου ἐστὶν τὸ
he broke [it], and said, Take, eat, this of me is the

σῶμα τὸ ὑπὲρ ὑμῶν ʳκλώμενον·ⁱⁱ. τοῦτο ποιεῖτε εἰς τὴν
body which for you [is] being broken: this do in

ἐμὴν ἀνάμνησιν. 25 Ὡσαύτως καὶ τὸ ποτήριον, μετὰ τὸ
remembrance of me. In like manner also the cup, after

δειπνῆσαι, λέγων, Τοῦτο τὸ ποτήριον ἡ καινὴ διαθήκη ἐστὶν
having supped, saying, This cup the new covenant is

ἐν τῷ ἐμῷ αἵματι· τοῦτο ποιεῖτε, ὁσάκις ˢἂνⁱⁱ πίνητε,
in my blood: this do, as often as ye may drink [it],

εἰς τὴν ἐμὴν ἀνάμνησιν. 26 Ὁσάκις γὰρ ˢἂνⁱⁱ ἐσθίητε τὸν
in remembrance of me. For as often as ye may eat

ἄρτον τοῦτον, καὶ τὸ ποτήριον τοῦτοⁱⁱ πίνητε, τὸν θάνατον
this bread, and this cup may drink, the death

τοῦ κυρίου καταγγέλλετε, ᵛἄχριςⁱⁱ οὗ ʷἂνⁱⁱ ἔλθῃ. 27 Ὥστε
of the Lord ye announce, until he may come. So that

ὃς ἂν ἐσθίῃ τὸν ἄρτον ˣτοῦτονⁱⁱ ἢ πίνῃ τὸ ποτήριον
whosoever should eat this bread or should drink the cup

τοῦ κυρίου ἀναξίως, ἔνοχος ἔσται τοῦ σώματος καὶʸ αἵματος
of the Lord unworthily, guilty shall be of the body and blood

τοῦ κυρίου. 28 δοκιμαζέτω δὲ ᶻἄνθρωπος ἑαυτόν,ⁱⁱ καὶ οὕτως
of the Lord. But let ᶻprove ²man himself, and thus

ἐκ τοῦ ἄρτου ἐσθιέτω, καὶ ἐκ τοῦ ποτηρίου πινέτω· 29 ὁ γὰρ
of the bread let him eat, and of the cup let him drink. For he that

ἐσθίων καὶ πίνων ᵃἀναξίως,ⁱⁱ κρίμα ἑαυτῷ ἐσθίει καὶ πίνει,
eats and drinks unworthily, judgment to himself eats and drinks,

μὴ διακρίνων τὸ σῶμα ᵇτοῦ κυρίου.ⁱⁱ 30 διὰ τοῦτο ἐν ὑμῖν
not discerning the body of the Lord. Because of this among you

πολλοὶ ἀσθενεῖς καὶ ἄρρωστοι, καὶ κοιμῶνται ἱκανοί.
many [are] weak and infirm, and are fallen asleep many.

31 εἰ ᶜγὰρⁱⁱ ἑαυτοὺς διεκρίνομεν, οὐκ ἂν ἐκρινόμεθα· 32 κρινό-
²If ¹for ourselves. we scrutinized, we should not be judged. ᴸBeing

μενοι δέ, ὑπὸ ᵈ κυρίου παιδευόμεθα, ἵνα μὴ σὺν τῷ
³judged ⁴but, by [the] Lord we are disciplined, that not with the

κόσμῳ κατακριθῶμεν. 33 Ὥστε, ἀδελφοί μου, συνερχόμενοι
world we should be condemned. So that, my brethren, coming together

εἰς τὸ φαγεῖν, ἀλλήλους ἐκδέχεσθε· 34 εἰ ᵉδέⁱⁱ τις πεινᾷ,
for to eat, one another wait for. But if anyone be hungry,

ἐν οἴκῳ ἐσθιέτω· ἵνα μὴ εἰς κρίμα συνέρχησθε. τὰ δὲ
at home let him eat, that not for judgment ye may come together ; and the

λοιπά, ὡς ἂν ἔλθω, διατάξομαι.
other things whenever I may come, I will set in order.

12 Περὶ δὲ τῶν πνευματικῶν, ἀδελφοί, οὐ θέλω ὑμᾶς
But concerning spirituals,. brethren, I do not wish you

ἀγνοεῖν. 2 οἴδατε ὅτιᶠ ἔθνη ἦτε, πρὸς τὰ εἴδωλα τὰ ἄφωνα
to be ignorant. Ye know that Gentiles ye were, ³to ⁵idols ⁴dumb

ὡς ἂν ἤγεσθε, ἀπαγόμενοι· 3 διὸ γνωρίζω ὑμῖν, ὅτι
⁶as ⁷ye ⁸might ⁹be ¹⁰led, ¹led ²away. Therefore I give ²to ³know ¹you, that

---

ᴾ παρεδίδετο LTTrA. ᑫ — Λάβετε, φάγετε GLTTrA. ʳ — κλώμενον LTTrA. ˢ ἐὰν LTTrA.
ᵗ — τοῦτο (*read* the cup) LTTrAW. ᵛ ἄχρι T. ʷ — ἂν GLTTrA. ˣ — τοῦτον (*read* the bread) GLTTrAW. ʸ + τοῦ of the GLTTrAW. ᶻ ἑαυτὸν ἄνθρωπος W. ᵃ — ἀναξίως LTTrA.
ᵇ — τοῦ κυρίου LTTrA. ᶜ δὲ but LTTrAW. ᵈ + τοῦ the TTr[A]W. ᵉ — δὲ but GLTTrAW.
ᶠ + ὅτε when [L]TTrA.

οὐδεὶς ἐν   πνεύματι θεοῦ λαλῶν λέγει ἀνάθεμα   ʰἸησοῦν·ǁ
no one in [the]   Spirit   of God speaking says accursed [is]   Jesus ;

καὶ οὐδεὶς δύναται εἰπεῖν ⁱΚύριον Ἰησοῦν,ǁ εἰ.μὴ ἐν   πνεύ-
and no one   can   say   Lord   Jesus,   except in [the] ²Spirit

ματι ἁγίῳ. 4 διαιρέσεις.δὲ χαρισμάτων εἰσίν. τὸ.δὲ αὐτὸ
¹Holy.   But diversities   of gifts   there are, but the same

πνεῦμα· 5 καὶ διαιρέσεις διακονιῶν εἰσίν, καὶ ὁ αὐτὸς κύριος·
Spirit ;   and diversities of services there are, and the same Lord ;

6 καὶ διαιρέσεις ἐνεργημάτων εἰσίν, ᵏὸ.δὲǁ αὐτός ¹ἐστινǁ θεός,
and diversities   of operations   there are, but the same ²it ³is ¹God,

ὁ ἐνεργῶν τὰ.πάντα ἐν πᾶσιν. 7 ἑκάστῳ.δὲ δίδοται ἡ φανέ-
who operates   all things   in all.   But to each   is given the mani-

ρωσις τοῦ πνεύματος πρὸς τὸ συμφέρον. 8 ᾧ.μὲν.γὰρ διὰ
festation of the   Spirit   for   profit.   For to one   by

τοῦ πνεύματος δίδοται λόγος σοφίας, ἄλλῳ.δὲ λόγος
the   Spirit   is given a word of wisdom ; and to another a word

γνώσεως,   κατὰ τὸ αὐτὸ πνεῦμα· 9 ἑτέρῳ.ᵐδὲǁ   πίστις,ⁿ
of knowledge, according to the same Spirit ;   and to a different one faith,

ἐν τῷ αὐτῷ πνεύματι· ἄλλῳ.δὲ χαρίσματα ἰαμάτων, ἐν τῷ
in the same   Spirit ;   and to another   gifts   of healing, in the

ⁿαὐτῷǁ πνεύματι· 10 ἄλλῳ.δὲ ἐνεργήματα δυνάμεων,
same   Spirit ;   and to another   operations of works of power ;

ἄλλῳ.ᵒδὲǁ προφητεία, ἄλλῳ.ᵖδὲǁ ᵠδιακρίσειςǁ πνευμάτων,·
and to another prophecy ; and to another   discerning   of spirits ;

ἑτέρῳ.ʳδὲǁ γένη γλωσσῶν, ἄλλῳ.δὲ ˢἑρμηνείαǁ γλωσ-
and to a different one kinds of tongues ; and to another interpretation of

σῶν· 11 πάντα.δὲ ταῦτα ἐνεργεῖ τὸ ἓν καὶ τὸ αὐτὸ πνεῦ-
tongues.   But all these things ⁷operates ¹the ²one ³and ⁴the ⁵same ⁶Spirit,

μα, διαιροῦν ἰδίᾳ ἑκάστῳ καθὼς βούλεται. 12 Καθάπερ
dividing   separately to each according as   he wills.   ²Even ³as

γὰρ τὸ σῶμα ἕν ἐστιν καὶ μέλη ᵗἔχει πολλά,ǁ πάντα.δὲ τὰ
¹for the body ²one ¹is   and ³members ¹has ²many,   but all   the

μέλη τοῦ σώματος ᵛτοῦ ἑνός,ǁ πολλὰ ὄντα, ἕν ἐστιν σῶμα·
members of the ⁰body   ¹one, ⁴many ³being, ⁶one ⁵are   body:

οὕτως καὶ ὁ χριστός. 13 καὶ.γὰρ ἐν ἑνὶ πνεύματι ἡμεῖς
so   also [is] the Christ.   For also by one   Spirit   we

πάντες εἰς ἓν σῶμα ἐβαπτίσθημεν, εἴτε Ἰουδαῖοι εἴτε Ἕλ-
all   into one body   were baptized,   whether   Jews   or

ληνες, εἴτε δοῦλοι εἴτε ἐλεύθεροι· καὶ πάντες ʷεἰςǁ ἓν πνεῦμα
Greeks, whether bondmen or   free   and all   into one Spirit

ἐποτίσθημεν. 14 Καὶ.γὰρ τὸ σῶμα οὐκ.ἔστιν ἓν μέλος, ἀλλὰ
were made to drink.   For also the body   is not one member, but

πολλά. 15 ἐὰν εἴπῃ ὁ πούς, Ὅτι οὐκ.εἰμὶ χείρ, οὐκ.εἰμὶ
many.   If should say the foot, Because I am not a hand, I am not

ἐκ τοῦ σώματος· οὐ παρὰ τοῦτο οὐκ.ἔστιν ἐκ τοῦ σώματοςˣ;
of the   body: on account of this is it not of the body?

16 καὶ ἐὰν εἴπῃ τὸ οὖς, Ὅτι οὐκ.εἰμὶ ὀφθαλμὸς οὐκ.εἰμὶ ἐκ
And   if should say the ear, Because I am not   an eye   I am not of

τοῦ σώματος· οὐ παρὰ τοῦτο οὐκ.ἔστιν ἐκ τοῦ σώματοςˣ;
the   body: on account of this is it not of the body?

17 εἰ ὅλον τὸ σῶμα   ὀφθαλμός, ποῦ ἡ ἀκοή; εἰ ὅλον
If ²whole ¹the body [were]   an eye,   where the hearing? if [the] whole

---

no man speaking by the Spirit of God calleth Jesus accursed : and *that* no man can say that Jesus is the Lord, but by the Holy Ghost. 4 Now there are diversities of gifts, but the same Spirit. 5 And there are differences of administrations, but the same Lord. 6 And there are diversities of operations, but it is the same God which worketh all in all. 7 But the manifestation of the Spirit is given to every man to profit withal. 8 For to one is given by the Spirit the word of wisdom ; to another the word of knowledge by the same Spirit ; 9 to another faith by the same Spirit ; to another the gifts of healing by the same Spirit ; 10 to another the working of miracles ; to another prophecy ; to another discerning of spirits ; to another *divers* kinds of tongues ; to another the interpretation of tongues : 11 but all these worketh that one and the selfsame Spirit, dividing to every man severally as he will. 12 For as the body is one, and hath many members, and all the members of that one body, being many, are one body : so also *is* Christ. 13 For by one Spirit are we all baptized into one body, whether *we* be Jews or Gentiles, whether *we* be bond or free ; and have been all made to drink into one Spirit. 14 For the body is not one member, but many. 15 If the foot shall say, Because I am not the hand, I am not of the body ; is it therefore not of the body ? 16 And if the ear shall say, Because I am not the eye, I am not of the body ; is it therefore not of the body ? 17 If the whole body were an eye, where *were* the hearing ? If the whole *were* hear-

---

ʰ Ἰησοῦς LTTrAW. .   ⁱ Κύριος Ἰησοῦς LTTrAW.   ᵏ καὶ ὁ and the A.   ¹ — ἐστιν GLTTrAW.
ᵐ — δὲ and [L]TTr[A].   ⁿ ἑνὶ one LTTrA.   ᵒ — δὲ and LTr.   ᵖ — δὲ and LTr.   ᵠ διά-
κρισις T.   ʳ — δὲ and LTTr.   ˢ διερμηνεία L.   ᵗ πολλὰ ἔχει LTTrA.   ᵛ — τοῦ ἑνός
LTTrAW.   ʷ — εἰς LTTrAW.   ˣ — ; (*read* it is not on account of this not of the body.) LT.

ing, where *were*. the smelling? 18 But now hath God set the members every one of them in the body, as it hath pleased him. 19 And if they were all one member, where *were* the body? 20 But now *are they* many members, yet but one body. 21 And the eye cannot say unto the hand, I have no need of thee: nor again the head to the feet, I have no need of you. 22 Nay, much more those members of the body, which seem to be more feeble, are necessary: 23 and those *members* of the body, which we think to be less honourable, upon these we bestow more abundant honour; and our uncomely *parts* have more abundant comeliness. 24 For our comely *parts* have no need: but God hath tempered the body together, having given more abundant honour to that *part* which lacked: 25 that there should be no schism in the body; but *that* the members should have the same care one for another. 26 And whether one member suffer, all the members suffer with it; or one member be honoured, all the members rejoice with it. 27 Now ye are the body of Christ, and members in particular. 28 And God hath set some in the church, first apostles, secondarily prophets, thirdly teachers, after that miracles, then gifts of healings, helps, governments, diversities of tongues. 29 *Are* all apostles? *are* all prophets? *are* all teachers? *are* all workers of miracles? 30 have all the gifts of healing? do all speak with tongues? do all interpret? 31 But covet earnestly the best gifts: and yet shew I unto you a more excellent way.

XIII. Though I speak with the tongues of

ἀκοή, ποῦ ἡ ὄσφρησις; 18 ᵞνυνὶ‖ δὲ ὁ θεὸς ἔθετο τὰ μέλη,
hearing, where the smelling? But now God set the members,

ἓν ἕκαστον αὐτῶν ἐν τῷ σώματι, καθὼς ἠθέλησεν. 19 εἰ δὲ
²one ¹each of them in the body, according as he would. But if

ἦν. ᶻτὰ‖ πάντα ἓν μέλος, ποῦ τὸ σῶμα; 20 νῦν δὲ πολλὰ
²were ¹all one member, where the body? But now many

ᵃμὲν‖ μέλη, ἓν δὲ σῶμα. 21 οὐ δύναται ᵇδὲ‖ ᶜ ὀφ-
[are the] members, but one body. And is not able [the]

θαλμὸς εἰπεῖν τῇ χειρί, Χρείαν σου οὐκ ἔχω· ἢ πάλιν ἡ
eye to say to the hand, Need of thee I have not; or again the

κεφαλὴ τοῖς ποσίν, Χρείαν ὑμῶν οὐκ ἔχω. 22 ἀλλὰ πολλῷ
head to the feet, Need of you I have not. But much

μᾶλλον τὰ δοκοῦντα μέλη τοῦ σώματος ἀσθενέστερα ὑπάρ-
rather the ⁵which ⁶seem ¹members ²of ³the ⁴body ⁸weaker ⁷to

χειν, ἀναγκαῖά ἐστιν· 23 καὶ ἃ δοκοῦμεν ᵈἀτιμότερα‖
⁶be, necessary are; and those which we think more void of honour

εἶναι τοῦ σώματος, τούτοις τιμὴν περισσοτέραν περιτίθεμεν·
to be of the body, ⁴these ⁷honour ⁵more ⁶abundant ¹we ²put ³about;

καὶ τὰ ἀσχήμονα ἡμῶν εὐσχημοσύνην περισσοτέραν ἔχει·
and the ·uncomely [parts] of us comeliness more abundant have;

24 τὰ δὲ εὐσχήμονα ἡμῶν οὐ χρείαν ἔχει. ᵉἀλλ‖ ὁ θεὸς
but the comely [parts] of us ²no ¹need ¹have. But God

συνεκέρασεν τὸ σῶμα, τῷ ᶠὑστεροῦντι‖ περισσοτέραν
tempered together the body, to that being deficient more abundant

δοὺς τιμήν, 25 ἵνα μὴ ᾖ ᵍσχίσμα‖ ἐν τῷ
²having ³given ¹honour, 'that there might not be division in the

σώματι, ἀλλὰ τὸ αὐτὸ ὑπὲρ ἀλλήλων μεριμνῶσιν τὰ
body, but ⁴the ⁵same ⁶for ⁹one ¹⁰another ³might ⁴have ⁷concern ¹the

μέλη· 26 καὶ ʰεἴτε‖ πάσχει ἓν μέλος, ¹συμπάσχει‖ πάντα
²members. And if suffers one member, suffers with [it] all

τὰ μέλη· εἴτε δοξάζεται ᵏἓν‖ μέλος, ¹συγχαίρει‖ πάντα τὰ
the members; if be glorified one member, rejoice with [it] ¹all the

μέλη. 27 ὑμεῖς δὲ ἐστε σῶμα χριστοῦ, καὶ μέλη ἐκ
members. Now ye are [the] body of Christ, and members in

μέρους. 28 Καὶ οὓς μὲν ἔθετο ὁ θεὸς ἐν τῇ ἐκκλησίᾳ πρῶ-
particular. And ⁴certain ²did ³set ¹God in the assembly: first,

τον ἀποστόλους, δεύτερον προφήτας, τρίτον διδασκάλους,
apostles; secondly prophets; thirdly teachers;

ἔπειτα δυνάμεις, ᵐεἶτα‖ χαρίσματα ἰαμάτων, ⁿἀντιλήψεις,‖
then works of power; then gifts of healings; helps;

κυβερνήσεις, γένη γλωσσῶν. 29 μὴ πάντες ἀπόστολοι; μὴ
governments; kinds of tongues. [Are] all apostles?

πάντες προφῆται; μὴ πάντες διδάσκαλοι; μὴ πάντες δυνά-
all prophets? all teachers? [have] all works of

μεις; 30 μὴ πάντες χαρίσματα ἔχουσιν ἰαμάτων; μὴ πάντες
power? ²all ³gifts ¹have of healings?

γλώσσαις λαλοῦσιν; μὴ πάντες διερμηνεύουσιν; 31 Ζηλοῦτε
¹do speak with tongues? ²all ¹do interpret? ²Be ³emulous ⁴of

δὲ τὰ χαρίσματα τὰ ᵒκρείττονα·‖ καὶ ἔτι καθ᾽ ὑπερβολὴν
¹but the ³gifts ¹better, and yet ²more ³surpassing

ὁδὸν ὑμῖν δείκνυμι.
¹a ⁴way to you I shew.

ʸ νῦν LTrA.   ᶻ [τὰ] LTrA.   ᵃ [μὲν] LTr.   ᵇ — δὲ and G[L].   ᶜ + ὁ the GLTTrAW.
ᵈ ἀτιμώτερα E.   ᵉ ἀλλὰ LTTrA.   ᶠ ὑστερουμένῳ LTTrA.   ᵍ σχίσματα divisions T.
ʰ εἴ τι if anything LTr.   ¹ συν- TA.   ᵏ — ἓν (read a member) TTr[A].   ¹ συν- T.
ᵐ ἔπειτα LTTrA.   ⁿ ἀντιλήμψεις LTTrA.   ᵒ μείζονα greater LTTrA.

13 Ἐὰν ταῖς γλώσσαις τῶν ἀνθρώπων λαλῶ καὶ τῶν
If   with the   tongues   of men   I speak and ‑

ἀγγέλων, ἀγάπην.δὲ μὴ.ἔχω, γέγονα χαλκὸς ἠχῶν ἢ
of angels,   but love   have not, I have become ᵃbrass ¹sounding or

κύμβαλον ἀλαλάζον· **2** ᴾκαὶ ἐὰν‖ ἔχω προφητείαν, καὶ εἰδῶ
a ²cymbal ¹clanging.   And if I have   prophecy,   and know

τὰ μυστήρια πάντα καὶ πᾶσαν τὴν γνῶσιν, ᑫκαὶ ἐὰν‖ ἔχω
²mysteries ¹all   and   all   knowledge, and if   I have

πᾶσαν τὴν πίστιν, ὥστε ὄρη ʳμεθιστάνειν,‖ ἀγάπην.δὲ
all   the   faith,   so as mountains   to remove,   but love

μὴ.ἔχω, ˢοὐθέν‖ εἰμι. **3** ᵗκαὶ ἐὰν‖ ᵛψωμίσω‖ πάντα τὰ
have not,   nothing I am.   And if   I give away in food   all

ὑπάρχοντά.μου, ᵂκαὶ ἐὰν‖ παραδῶ τὸ.σῶμά.μου ἵνα ˣκαυθή‑
my goods,   and if   I deliver up   my body   that   I may be

σωμαι,‖ ἀγάπην.δὲ μὴ.ἔχω, ʸοὐδὲν‖ ὠφελοῦμαι. **4** Ἡ ἀγάπη
burned,   but love   have not, nothing I am profited.   Love

μακροθυμεῖ, χρηστεύεται· ἡ ἀγάπη οὐ.ζηλοῖ· ᶻἡ ἀγάπη‖ οὐ
has patience,   is kind;   love   is not envious;   love ²not

περπερεύεται, οὐ.φυσιοῦται, **5** οὐκ.ἀσχημονεῖ, οὐ.ζητεῖ τὰ
¹is vain-glorious,   is not puffed up,   acts not unseemly,   seeks not the things

ἑαυτῆς, οὐ.παροξύνεται, οὐ.λογίζεται τὸ κακόν· **6** οὐ.χαίρει
of its own, is not quickly provoked,   reckons not   evil,   rejoices not

ἐπὶ τῇ ἀδικίᾳ, ᵃσυγχαίρει‖.δὲ τῇ ἀληθείᾳ, **7** πάντα στέγει,
at   unrighteousness, but rejoices with the truth ;   all things covers,

πάντα πιστεύει, πάντα ἐλπίζει, πάντα ὑπομένει. **8** Ἡ ἀγάπη
all things believes, all things hopes,   all things endures.   Love

οὐδέποτε ᵇἐκπίπτει.‖ εἴτε.ᶜδὲ‖ προφητεῖαι, καταργηθήσονται·
never   fails;   but whether   prophecies, they shall be done away ;

εἴτε γλῶσσαι, παύσονται· εἴτε γνῶσις, καταργηθήσεται.
whether tongues,   they shall cease ; whether knowledge it shall be done away.

9 ἐκ.μέρους.γὰρ γινώσκομεν, καὶ ἐκ μέρους προφητεύομεν·
For in part   we know,   and in part   we prophesy ;

10 ὅταν.δὲ ἔλθῃ τὸ τέλειον, ᵈτότε‖ τὸ ἐκ μέρους κατ‑
but when may come that which is perfect,   then   that in   part   shall be

αργηθήσεται. **11** ὅτε ἤμην νήπιος, ᵉὡς νήπιος ἐλάλουν,‖.ᶠὡς
done away.   When I was an infant, as an infant   I spoke,   as

νήπιος ἐφρόνουν, ὡς νήπιος ἐλογιζόμην· ὅτε.ᵍδὲ‖ γέγονα
an infant I thought, as an infant I reasoned;   but when I became

ἀνήρ, κατήργηκα τὰ τοῦ νηπίου. **12** βλέπομεν.γὰρ
a man, I did away with the things of the   infant.   For we see

ἄρτι δι᾽ ἐσόπτρου ἐν αἰνίγματι, τότε.δὲ πρόσωπον πρὸς
now through   a glass   obscurely,   but then   face   to

πρόσωπον· ἄρτι γινώσκω.ἐκ μέρους, τότε.δὲ ἐπιγνώσομαι
face;   now   I know   in part,   but then   I shall know

καθὼς καὶ ἐπεγνώσθην. **13** νυνὶ.δὲ μένει πίστις, ἐλπίς,
according as also I have been known.   And now abides   faith,   hope,

ἀγάπη, τὰ.τρία.ταῦτα· μείζων.δὲ τούτων ἡ ἀγάπη.
love;   these three things;   but the greater of these [is]   love.

14 Διώκετε τὴν ἀγάπην· ζηλοῦτε.δὲ τὰ πνευματικά,
Pursue   love,   and be emulous of   spirituals,

μᾶλλον.δὲ ἵνα προφητεύητε. **2** ὁ.γὰρ λαλῶν γλώσσῃ, οὐκ
but rather that ye may prophesy.   For he that speaks with a tongue, not

---

men and of angels, and have not charity, I am become as sounding brass, or a tinkling cymbal. 2 And though I have the gift of prophecy, and understand all mysteries, and all knowledge ; and though I have all faith, so that I could remove mountains, and have not charity, I am nothing. 3 And though I bestow all my goods to feed the poor, and though I give my body to be burned, and have not charity, it profiteth me nothing. 4 Charity suffereth long, and is kind ; charity envieth not ; charity vaunteth not itself, is not puffed up, 5 doth not behave itself unseemly, seeketh not her own, is not easily provoked, thinketh no evil ; 6 rejoiceth not in iniquity, but rejoiceth in the truth ; 7 beareth all things, believeth all things, hopeth all things, endureth all things. 8 Charity never faileth : but whether there be prophecies, they shall fail ; whether there be tongues, they shall cease : whether there be knowledge, it shall vanish away. 9 For we know in part, and we prophesy in part. 10 But when that which is perfect is come, then that which is in part shall be done away. 11 When I was a child, I spake as a child, I understood as a child, I thought as a child : but when I became a man, I put away childish things. 12 For now we see through a glass, darkly ; but then face to face : now I know in part ; but then shall I know even as also I am known. 13 And now abideth faith, hope, charity, these three ; but the greatest of these is charity.

XIV. Follow after charity, and desire spiritual gifts, but rather that ye may prophesy. 2 For he that speaketh in an unknown tongue speaketh not unto men, but

---

ᴾ κἂν LA.   ᑫ κἂν TτA.   ʳ μεθιστάναι LTTr.   ˢ οὐδὲν EGW.   ᵗ κἂν LTτA.   ᵛ ψωμίζω E.
ᵂ κἂν LA.   ˣ καυθήσομαι I shall be burned T.   ʸ οὐθὲν T.   ᶻ [ἡ ἀγάπη] I.TτA.   ᵃ συν‑ T.
ᵇ πίπτει LTTrA.   ᶜ [δὲ] Tr.   ᵈ ‑ τότε LTTrAW.   ᵉ ἐλάλουν ὡς νήπιος I TTrAW.   ᶠ ἐφρόνουν
ὡς νήπιος, ἐλογιζόμην ὡς νήπιος LTTrA.   ᵍ — δὲ but LTTrA.

unto God: for no man understandeth *him;* howbeit in the spirit he speaketh mysteries. 3 But he that prophesieth speaketh unto men *to* edification, and exhortation, and comfort. 4 He that speaketh in an *unknown* tongue edifieth himself; but he that prophesieth edifieth the church. 5 I would that ye all spake with tongues, but rather that ye prophesied: for greater *is* he that prophesieth than he that speaketh with tongues, except he interpret, that the church may receive edifying. 6 Now, brethren, if I come unto you speaking with tongues, what shall I profit you, except I shall speak to you either by revelation, or by knowledge, or by prophesying, or by doctrine? 7 And even things without life giving sound, whether pipe or harp, except they give a distinction in the sounds, how shall it be known what is piped or harped? 8 For if the trumpet give an uncertain sound, who shall prepare himself to the battle? 9 So likewise ye, except ye utter by the tongue words easy to be understood, how shall it be known what is spoken? for ye shall speak into the air. 10 There are, it may be, so many kinds of voices in the world, and none of them *is* without signification. 11 Therefore if I know not the meaning of the voice, I shall be unto him that speaketh a barbarian, and he that speaketh *shall be* a barbarian unto me. 12 Even so ye, forasmuch as ye are zealous of spiritual *gifts,* seek that ye may excel to the edifying of the church. 13 Wherefore let him that speaketh in an *unknown* tongue pray that he may interpret. 14 For if I pray in an *unknown* tongue, my spirit prayeth, but my understanding is unfruitful. 15 What is it then? I

ἀνθρώποις λαλεῖ, ἀλλὰ ʰτῷʱ θεῷ· οὐδεὶς.γὰρ ἀκούει, πνεύματι
to men speaks, but to God: for no one hears; ²in ³spirit

δὲ λαλεῖ μυστήρια· 3 ὁ.δὲ προφητεύων, ἀνθρώποις λαλεῖ
¹but he speaks mysteries. But he that prophesies, to men speaks

οἰκοδομὴν καὶ παράκλησιν καὶ παραμυθίαν. 4 ὁ λαλῶν
[for] building up and encouragement and consolation. He that speaks

γλώσσῃ, ἑαυτὸν οἰκοδομεῖ· ὁ.δὲ προφητεύων, ἐκκλησίαν
with a tongue, himself builds up; but he that prophesies, [the] assembly

οἰκοδομεῖ. 5 θέλω.δὲ πάντας ὑμᾶς λαλεῖν γλώσσαις, μᾶλλον
builds up. Now I desire all you to speak with tongues, ²rather

δὲ ἵνα προφητεύητε· μείζων ⁱγὰρʱ ὁ προφητεύων ἢ
¹but that ye should prophesy· ²greater ¹for [is] he that prophesies than

ὁ λαλῶν γλώσσαις, ἐκτὸς εἰ.μὴ διερμηνεύῃ, ἵνα ἡ ἐκ-
he that speaks with tongues, unless he should interpret, that the as-

κλησία οἰκοδομὴν λάβῃ· 6 ᵏΝυνὶʱ.δὲ, ἀδελφοί, ἐὰν ἔλθω
sembly building up may receive. And now, brethren, if I come

πρὸς ὑμᾶς γλώσσαις λαλῶν, τί ὑμᾶς ὠφελήσω, ἐὰν.μὴ
to you with tongues speaking, what you shall I profit, unless

ὑμῖν λαλήσω ἢ ἐν ἀποκαλύψει, ἢ ἐν γνώσει, ἢ ἐν προ-
to you I shall speak either in revelation, or in knowledge, or in pro-

φητείᾳ, ἢ ᶦἐνʱ διδαχῇ; 7 ὅμως τὰ ἄψυχα φωνὴν διδόντα,
phecy, or in teaching? Even lifeless things a sound giving,

εἴτε αὐλὸς εἴτε κιθάρα, ἐὰν διαστολὴν ᵐτοῖς φθόγγοιςʱ
whether pipe or harp, if distinction to the sounds

μὴ.δῷ, πῶς γνωσθήσεται τὸ αὐλούμενον ἢ τὸ κιθαρι-
they give not, how shall be known that being piped or being

ζόμενον; 8 καὶ.γὰρ ἐὰν ἄδηλον ⁿφωνὴν σάλπιγξʱ δῷ, τίς
harped? For also if an uncertain sound a trumpet ʼ give, who

παρασκευάσεται εἰς πόλεμον; 9 οὕτως καὶ ὑμεῖς διὰ τῆς
shall prepare himself for war? So also ye, by means of the

γλώσσης ἐὰν.μὴ εὔσημον λόγον δῶτε, πῶς γνωσθήσεται τὸ
tongue unless an intelligible speech ye give, how shall be known that

λαλούμενον; ἔσεσθε.γὰρ εἰς ἀέρα λαλοῦντες. 10 Τοσαῦτα
being spoken? for ye will be ²into[³the] ⁴air ¹speaking. So many,

εἰ τύχοι, γένη φωνῶν ᵒἐστινʱ ἐν κόσμῳ, καὶ οὐδὲν ᴾαὐ-
it may be, kinds of sounds there are in [the] world, and none of

τῶνʱ. ἄφωνον· 11 ἐὰν οὖν μὴ.εἰδῶ τὴν δύναμιν
them without [distinct] sound. If therefore I know not the power

τῆς φωνῆς, ἔσομαι τῷ λαλοῦντι βάρβαρος· καὶ ὁ
of the sound, I shall be to him that speaks a barbarian; and he that

λαλῶν, ἐν ἐμοὶ βάρβαρος· 12 οὕτως καὶ ὑμεῖς, ἐπεὶ ζηλωταί
speaks, ³for ⁴me ¹a ²barbarian. So also ye, since emulous

ἐστε πνευμάτων, πρὸς τὴν οἰκοδομὴν τῆς ἐκκλησίας ζητεῖτε
ye are of spirits, for the building up of the assembly seek

ἵνα περισσεύητε. 13 �q Διόπερʱ ὁ λαλῶν γλώσσῃ, προσευ-
that ye may abound. Wherefore he that speaks with a tongue, let him

χέσθω ἵνα διερμηνεύῃ. 14 ἐὰν.ʳγὰρʱ προσεύχωμαι γλώσσῃ,
pray that he may interpret. For if I pray with a tongue,

τὸ.πνεῦμά.μου προσεύχεται, ὁ.δὲ.νοῦς.μου ἄκαρπός ἐστιν.
my spirit prays, but my understanding unfruitful is.

15 τί οὖν ἐστιν; προσεύξομαι τῷ πνεύματι, προσεύξομαι
What then is it? I will pray with the Spirit, ²I ³will ¹pray

δὲ καὶ τῷ νοΐ· ψαλῶ τῷ πνεύματι, ψαλῶ
¹but also with the understanding. I will praise with the Spirit, ²I ³will ¹praise

---

ʰ — τῷ LTTr[A].　　　ⁱ δὲ and LTTrA.　　ᵏ νῦν LTTrAW.　　ˡ — ἐν T[Tr].　　ᵐ τοῦ φθόγγου of
the sound L.　　ⁿ σάλπιγξ φωνὴν T.　　ᵒ εἰσὶν LTTrAW.　　ᴾ — αὐτῶν LTTrAW.　　q διὸ LTTrA.
ʳ [γὰρ] LTr.

ˢδὲˢ καὶ ᵗτῷˡˡ νοΐ. 16 ἐπεὶ ἐὰν ᵛεὐλογήσῃςˡˡ ʷτῷˡˡ
¹but also with the understanding.   Else if thou bless with the

πνεύματι, ὁ ἀναπληρῶν τὸν τόπον τοῦ ἰδιώτου πῶς
spirit, he that fills the place of the uninstructed how

ἐρεῖ τὸ ἀμὴν ἐπὶ τῇ.σῇ.εὐχαριστίᾳ, ἐπειδὴ τί λέγεις
shall he say the Amen at thy giving of thanks, since what thou sayest

οὐκ.οἶδεν; 17 σὺ.μὲν.γὰρ καλῶς εὐχαριστεῖς, ˣἀλλʼˡˡ ὁ ἕτερος
he knows not?   For thou indeed well givest thanks, but the other

οὐκ.οἰκοδομεῖται. 18 εὐχαριστῶ τῷ θεῷ ʸμου,ˡˡ πάντων ὑμῶν
is not built up.   I thank ²God ¹my, ⁷than ⁸all ⁹of ¹⁰you

μᾶλλον ᶻγλώσσαις λαλῶν·ˡˡ 19 ᵃἀλλʼˡˡ ἐν ἐκκλησίᾳ θέλω πέντε
⁶more ⁴with ⁵tongues ³speaking; but in [the] assembly I desire five

λόγους ᵇδιὰ τοῦ νοόςˡˡ μου λαλῆσαι, ἵνα καὶ ἄλλους
words with ²understanding ¹my to speak, that also others

κατηχήσω, ἢ μυρίους λόγους ἐν γλώσσῃ. 20 Ἀδελφοί, μὴ
I may·instruct, than ten thousand words in a tongue. Brethren, ²not

παιδία γίνεσθε ταῖς.φρεσίν· ἀλλὰ τῇ κακίᾳ νηπιάζετε,
³children ¹be in [your] minds, but in malice be babes;

ταῖς.δὲ φρεσὶν τέλειοι γίνεσθε. 21 ἐν τῷ νόμῳ γέγρα-
but in [your] minds ²full ³grown ¹be. In the law it has been

πται, "Ὅτι ἐν ἑτερογλώσσοις, καὶ ἐν χείλεσιν ᶜἑτέροις,ˡˡ λα-
written, By other tongues, and by ²lips ¹other I will

λήσω τῷ.λαῷ.τούτῳ, καὶ οὐδʼ οὕτως εἰσακούσονταί μου,
speak to this people, and not even thus will they hear me,

λέγει κύριος. 22 Ὥστε αἱ γλῶσσαι εἰς σημεῖόν εἰσιν, οὐ
saith [the] Lord. So that the tongues for a sign are, not

τοῖς πιστεύουσιν, ἀλλὰ τοῖς ἀπίστοις· ἡ.δὲ.προφητεία,
to those that believe, but to the unbelievers; but prophecy,

οὐ τοῖς ἀπίστοις, ἀλλὰ τοῖς πιστεύουσιν. 23 ἐὰν οὖν
not to the unbelievers, but to those that believe. If therefore

ᵈσυνέλθῃˡˡ ἡ ἐκκλησία ὅλη ἐπὶ.τὸ.αὐτό, καὶ πάντες ᵉγλώσ-
⁴come ²together ¹the ³assembly ²whole in one place, and all with

σαις λαλῶσιν,ˡˡ εἰσέλθωσιν.δὲ ἰδιῶται ἢ ἄπιστοι,
tongues should speak, and come in uninstructed ones or unbelievers,

οὐκ.ἐροῦσιν ὅτι μαίνεσθε; 24 ἐὰν.δὲ πάντες προφητεύωσιν,
will they not say that ye are mad? But if all prophesy,

εἰσέλθῃ.δὲ τις ἄπιστος ἢ ἰδιώτης, ἐλέγχεται ὑπὸ πάν-
and should come in some unbeliever or uninstructed, he is convicted by all,

των, ἀνακρίνεται ὑπὸ πάντων, 25 ᶠκαὶ οὕτωςˡˡ τὰ κρυπτὰ
he is examined by all; and thus the secrets

τῆς.καρδίας.αὐτοῦ φανερὰ γίνεται· καὶ οὕτως πεσὼν ἐπὶ
of his heart manifest become; and thus,ˎ falling upon

πρόσωπον, προσκυνήσει τῷ θεῷ, ἀπαγγέλλων ὅτι ᵍὁ θεὸς
[his] face, he will do homage to God, declaring that God

ὄντωςˡˡ ἐν ὑμῖν ἐστιν.
indeed amongst you is.

26 Τί οὖν ἐστιν, ἀδελφοί; ὅταν συνέρχησθε, ἕκαστος
What then is it, brethren? when ye may come together, each

ʰὑμῶνˡˡ ψαλμὸν ἔχει, διδαχὴν ἔχει, ⁱγλῶσσαν ἔχει, ἀποκά-
of you a psalm has, a teaching has, a tongue . has, a reve-

λυψιν ἔχει,ˡˡ ἑρμηνείαν ἔχει· πάντα πρὸς οἰκοδομὴν ᵏγε-
lation has, an interpretation has. All things for building up let be

---

will pray with the spirit, and I will pray with the understanding also: I will sing with the spirit, and I will sing with the understanding also. 16 Else when thou shalt bless with the spirit, how shall he that occupieth the room of the unlearned say Amen at thy giving of thanks, seeing he understandeth not what thou sayest? 17 For thou verily givest thanks well, but the other is not edified. 18 I thank my God, I speak with tongues more than ye all: 19 yet in the church I had rather speak five words with my understanding, that by my voice I might teach others also, than ten thousand words in an *unknown* tongue. 20 Brethren, be not children in understanding: howbeit in malice be ye children, but in understanding be men. 21 In the law it is written, With *men of* other tongues and other lips will I speak unto this people; and yet for all that will they not hear me, saith the Lord. 22 Wherefore tongues are for a sign, not to them that believe, but to them that believe not: but prophesying *serveth* not for them that believe not, but for them which believe. 23 If therefore the whole church be come together into one place, and all speak with tongues, and there come in *those that are* unlearned, or unbelievers, will they not say that ye are mad? 24 But if all prophesy, and there come in one that believeth not, or *one* unlearned, he is convinced of all, he is judged of all: 25 and thus are the secrets of his heart made manifest; and so falling down on *his* face he' will worship God, and report that God is in you of a truth. 26 How is it then, brethren? when ye come together, every

---

ˢ — δὲ L[Tr]. ᵗ — τῷ the E. ᵛ εὐλογῇς LTTrA. ʷ — τῷ (*read* πνευ. with [the] Spirit)
LTTrA. ˣ ἀλλὰ Tr. ʸ — μου GLTTrAW. ᶻ γλώσσῃ λαλῶ I speak with a tongue LTTrA.
ᵃ ἀλλὰ LTTrA. ᵇ τῷ νοΐ LTTrAW. ᶜ ἑτέρων 'others' LTTrA. ᵈ ἔλθῃ come L. ᵉ λαλῶσιν
γλώσσαις LTTrA. ᶠ - καὶ οὕτως GLTTrAW. ᵍ ὄντως ὁ (— ὁ T) θεὸς LTTrAW. ʰ — ὑμῶν
LTTr[A]. ⁱ ἀποκάλυψιν ἔχει, γλῶσσαν ἔχει LTTrAW. ᵏ γινέσθω GLTTrAW.

one of you hath a psalm, hath a doctrine, hath a tongue, hath a revelation, hath an interpretation. Let all things be done unto edifying. 27 If any man speak in an unknown tongue, let it be by two, or at the most by three, and that by course; and let one interpret. 28 But if there be no interpreter, let him keep silence in the church; and let him speak to himself, and to God. 29 Let the prophets speak two or three, and let the other judge. 30 If any thing be revealed to another that sitteth by, let the first hold his peace. 31 For ye may all prophesy one by one, that all may learn, and all may be comforted. 32 And the spirits of the prophets are subject to the prophets. 33 For God is not the author of confusion, but of peace, as in all churches of the saints.

34 Let your women keep silence in the churches: for it is not permitted unto them to speak; but they are commanded to be under obedience, as also saith the law. 35 And if they will learn any thing, let them ask their husbands at home: for it is a shame for women to speak in the church. 36 What? came the word of God out from you? or came it unto you only? 37 If any man think himself to be a prophet, or spiritual, let him acknowledge that the things that I write unto you are the commandments of the Lord. 38 But if any man be ignorant, let him be ignorant. 39 Wherefore, brethren, covet to prophesy, and forbid not to speak with tongues. 40 Let all things be done decently and in order.

XV. Moreover, brethren, I declare unto you the gospel which I preached unto you,

νέσθω.‖ 27 εἴτε γλώσσῃ τις λαλεῖ, κατὰ δύο ἢ τὸ
done. If with a tongue anyone speak, [let it be] by two or the
πλεῖστον τρεῖς, καὶ ἀνὰ.μέρος, καὶ εἷς διερμηνευέτω. 28 ἐὰν.δὲ
most three, and in succession, and ²one ¹let interpret; and if
μὴ.ῇ ¹διερμηνευτής,‖ σιγάτω ἐν ἐκκλησίᾳ· ἑαυτῷ.δὲ
there be not an interpreter, let him be silent in an assembly; and to himself
λαλείτω καὶ τῷ θεῷ· 29 προφῆται.δὲ δύο ἢ τρεῖς λαλεί-
let him speak and to God. And prophets ²two ³or ⁴three ¹let
τωσαν, καὶ οἱ ἄλλοι διακρινέτωσαν· 30 ἐὰν.δὲ ἄλλῳ
speak, and ²the ³others ¹let discern. But if to another
ἀποκαλυφθῇ καθημένῳ, ὁ πρῶτος σιγάτω. 31 δύ-
³should ⁴be ⁵a ⁶revelation ¹sitting ²by, ⁸the ⁹first ⁷let be silent. ²Ye
νασθε γὰρ καθ'.ἕνα πάντες προφητεύειν, ἵνα πάντες μαν-
²can ¹for one by one all prophesy, that all may
θάνωσιν, καὶ πάντες παρακαλῶνται· 32 καὶ πνεύματα
learn, and all may be exhorted. And spirits
προφητῶν προφήταις ὑποτάσσεται· 33 οὐ.γάρ ἐστιν ἀκατα-
of prophets to prophets are subject. For ²not ¹he ²is ⁶of ⁷dis-
στασίας ὁ θεός, ᵐἀλλ'‖ εἰρήνης, ὡς ἐν πάσαις ταῖς ἐκκλησίαις
order ⁴the ⁵God, but of peace, as in all the assemblies
τῶν ⁿἁγίων.
of the saints.
34 Αἱ‖ γυναῖκες ᵒὑμῶν‖ ἐν ταῖς ἐκκλησίαις σιγάτωσαν·
²Women ¹your in the assemblies let them be silent,
οὐ.γὰρ.ᴾἐπιτέτραπται‖ αὐταῖς λαλεῖν, ᵐἀλλ'‖ ⁹ὑποτάσσεσθαι,‖
for it is not allowed to them to speak; but to be in subjection,
καθὼς καὶ ὁ νόμος λέγει. 35 εἰ.δέ τι μαθεῖν θέλουσιν,
according as also the law says. But if anything to learn they wish,
ἐν.οἴκῳ τοὺς.ἰδίους ἄνδρας ἐπερωτάτωσαν· αἰσχρὸν.γάρ ἐστιν
at home their own husbands let them ask; for a shame it is
ʳγυναιξὶν ἐν ἐκκλησίᾳ λαλεῖν.‖
for women in assembly to speak.
36 Ἢ ἀφ' ὑμῶν ὁ λόγος τοῦ θεοῦ ἐξῆλθεν; ἢ εἰς ὑμᾶς
Or ³from ⁴you ⁵the ⁶word ⁷of ⁸God ¹went ²out, or to you
μόνους κατήντησεν; 37 εἴ τις δοκεῖ προφήτης εἶναι ἢ
only did it arrive? If anyone thinks a prophet to be or
πνευματικός, ἐπιγινωσκέτω ἃ γράφω ὑμῖν, ὅτι ˢτοῦ‖
spiritual, let him recognize the things I write to you, that of the
κυρίου ᵗεἰσὶν‖ ᵛἐντολαί·‖ 38 εἰ.δέ τις ἀγνοεῖ, ᵂἀγνοείτω.‖
Lord they are commands. But if any be ignorant, let him be ignorant.
39 Ὥστε, ἀδελφοί,ˣ ζηλοῦτε τὸ προφητεύειν, καὶ τὸ λαλεῖν
So that, brethren, be emulous to prophesy, and to speak
ʸγλώσσαις μὴ.κωλύετε.‖ 40 πάντα ᶻ εὐσχημόνως καὶ κατὰ
with tongues do not forbid. All things becomingly and with
τάξιν γινέσθω.
order let be done.
15 Γνωρίζω.δὲ ὑμῖν, ἀδελφοί, τὸ εὐαγγέλιον ὃ εὐηγ-
But I make known to you, brethren, the glad tidings which I an-
γελισάμην ὑμῖν, ὃ καὶ παρελάβετε, ἐν ᾧ καὶ ἑστήκατε,
nounced to you; which also ye received, in which also ye stand,

¹ ἑρμηνευτής LTr. ᵐ ἀλλὰ LTTrAW. ⁿ ἁγίων, αἱ (read verse 33 joined to verse 34) GLT. ᵒ — ὑμῶν LTTrA. ᴾ ἐπιτρέπεται LTTrAW. ⁹ ὑποτασσέσθωσαν let them be in subjection LTTr. ʳ γυναικὶ (a woman) λαλεῖν ἐν ἐκκλησίᾳ LTTrA. ˢ — τοῦ (read of [the]) GLTTrAW. ᵗ ἐστὶν it is LTTrAW. ᵛ ἐντολή a command LTr[A]W; — ἐντολαί T. ᵂ ἀγνοεῖται he is ignored LT. ˣ + μου my (brethren) [L]TTr[A]. ʸ μὴ κωλύετε (+ ἐν [L]A) γλώσσαις LTTrA. ᶻ + δὲ But (all things) GLTTrAW.

2 δι' οὗ καὶ σώζεσθε. τίνι λόγῳ ᵇεὐηγγελισάμην‖ ὑμῖν
by which also ye are being saved, ⁵what ⁶word ⁷I ⁸announced ⁹to ¹⁰you

εἰ κατέχετε, ἐκτὸς εἰ.μὴ εἰκῇ ἐπιστεύσατε. 3 Παρέδωκα.γὰρ
¹if ²ye ³hold ⁴fast, unless in vain ye believed. For I delivered

ὑμῖν ἐν πρώτοις, ὃ καὶ παρέλαβον, ὅτι χριστὸς ἀπέθανεν
to you in the first place, what also I received, that Christ died

ὑπὲρ τῶν.ἁμαρτιῶν.ἡμῶν, ' κατὰ τὰς γραφάς· 4 καὶ ὅτι
for our sins, according to the scriptures; and that

ἐτάφη, καὶ ὅτι ἐγήγερται τῇ ᶜτρίτῃ ἡμέρᾳ,‖ κατὰ τὰς
he was buried; and that he was raised the third day, according to the

γραφάς· 5 καὶ ὅτι ὤφθη Κηφᾷ, ᵈεἶτα‖ τοῖς δώδεκα. 6 ἔπειτα
scriptures; and that he appeared to Cephas, then to the twelve. Then

ὤφθη ἐπάνω πεντακοσίοις ἀδελφοῖς ἐφάπαξ, ἐξ ὧν οἱ
he appeared to above five hundred brethren at once, of whom the

ᵉπλείους‖ μένουσιν ἕως ἄρτι, τινὲς.δὲ ᶠκαὶ‖ ἐκοιμήθησαν.
greater part remain until now, but some also are fallen asleep.

7 ἔπειτα ὤφθη Ἰακώβῳ, *εἶτα‖ τοῖς ἀποστόλοις πᾶσιν·
Then he appeared to James; then to ᵍthe ³apostles ¹all;

8 ἔσχατον.δὲ πάντων, ὡσπερεὶ τῷ.ἐκτρώματι. ὤφθη κἀμοί.
and last of all, as to an abortion, he appeared also to me.

9 ἐγὼ.γὰρ εἰμι ὁ ἐλάχιστος τῶν ἀποστόλων, ὃς οὐκ.εἰμὶ
For I am the least of the apostles, who am not

ἱκανὸς · καλεῖσθαι ἀπόστολος, διότι ἐδίωξα τὴν ἐκκλησίαν
fit to be called apostle, because I persecuted the assembly

τοῦ θεοῦ. 10 χάριτι.δὲ θεοῦ εἰμι ὅ εἰμι, καὶ ἡ.χάρις.αὐτοῦ
of God. But by grace of God I am what I am, and his grace

ἡ εἰς ἐμὲ οὐ κενὴ ἐγενήθη, ἀλλὰ περισσότερον αὐ-
which [was] towards me not void has been, but more abundantly than

τῶν πάντων ἐκοπίασα· οὐκ.ἐγὼ.δὲ, ᵍἀλλ'‖ ἡ χάρις τοῦ θεοῦ
them all I laboured, but not I, but the grace of God

ʰἡ‖ σὺν ἐμοί. 11 εἴτε οὖν ἐγὼ εἴτε ἐκεῖνοι, οὕτως κηρύσ-
with me. Whether therefore I or they, so we preach,

σομεν, καὶ οὕτως ἐπιστεύσατε. 12 Εἰ.δὲ χριστὸς κηρύσσεται,
and so ye believed. Now if Christ is preached,

ⁱὅτι‖ ἐκ νεκρῶν‖ ἐγήγερται, πῶς λέγουσίν ᵏτινες
that from among [the] dead he has been raised, how say some

ἐν ὑμῖν‖ ὅτι ἀνάστασις νεκρῶν οὐκ.ἔστιν; 13 εἰ.δὲ ἀνά-
among you that a resurrection of [the] dead there is not? But if a resur-

στασις νεκρῶν οὐκ.ἔστιν, οὐδὲ χριστὸς ἐγήγερται· 14 εἰ.δὲ
rection of [the] dead there is not, neither Christ has been raised: but if

χριστὸς οὐκ.ἐγήγερται, κενὸν.ἄρα ¹ τὸ.κήρυγμα.ἡμῶν, κενὴ
Christ has not been raised, then void [is] our proclamation, ²void

ᵐδὲ‖ καὶ ἡ.πίστις.ὑμῶν. 15 εὑρισκόμεθα.δὲ καὶ ψευδομάρτυρες
¹and also your faith. And we are found also false witnesses

τοῦ θεοῦ, ὅτι ἐμαρτυρήσαμεν κατὰ τοῦ θεοῦ ὅτι ἤγειρεν
of God; for we witnessed concerning God that he raised up

τὸν χριστόν, ὃν οὐκ.ἤγειρεν εἴπερ ἄρα νεκροὶ οὐκ
the Christ, whom he raised not if then [the] dead ²not

ἐγείρονται· 16 εἰ.γὰρ νεκροὶ οὐκ.ἐγείρονται, οὐδὲ χριστὸς
¹are raised. For if [the] dead are not raised, neither Christ

ἐγήγερται· 17 εἰ.δὲ χριστὸς οὐκ.ἐγήγερται, ματαία ἡ πίστις
has been raised: but if Christ has not been raised, vain ²faith

which also ye have received, and wherein ye stand; 2 by which also ye are saved, if ye keep in memory what I preached unto you, unless ye have believed in vain. 3 For I delivered unto you first of all that which I also received, how that Christ died for our sins according to the scriptures; 4 and that he was buried, and that he rose again the third day according to the scriptures : 5 and that he was seen of Cephas, then of the twelve : 6 after that, he was seen of above five hundred brethren at once ; of whom the greater part remain unto this present, but some are fallen asleep. 7 After that, he was seen of James ; then of all the apostles. 8 And last of all he was seen of me also, as of one born out of due time. 9 For I am the least of the apostles, that am not meet to be called an apostle, because I persecuted the church of God. 10 But by the grace of God I am what I am : and his grace which was bestowed upon me was not in vain ; but I laboured more abundantly than they all : yet not I, but the grace of God which was with me. 11 Therefore whether it were I or they, so we preach, and so ye believed. 12 Now if Christ be preached that he rose from the dead, how say some among you that there is no resurrection of the dead ? 13 But if there be no resurrection of the dead, then is Christ not risen:14 and if Christ be not risen, then is our preaching vain, and your faith is also vain. 15 Yea, and we are found false witnesses of God; because we have testified of God that he raised up Christ : whom he raised not up, if so be that the dead rise not. 16 For if the dead rise not, then is not Christ raised: 17 and if Christ

ᵇ εὐαγγελισάμην· L.   ᶜ ἡμέρᾳ τῇ τρίτῃ LTTrAW.   ᵈ ἔπειτα T.   ᵉ πλείονες
LTTrAW.   ᶠ — καὶ LTTr[A].   * ἔπειτα TA   ᵍ ἀλλὰ LTTrAW.   ʰ — ἡ LTTrA.   ⁱ ἐκ
νεκρῶν ὅτι A.   ᵏ ἐν ὑμῖν τινὲς LTTrAW.   ˡ + καὶ also [L]TrAW.   ᵐ — δὲ LTTrAW.

be not raised, your faith *is* vain; ye are yet in your sins. 18 Then they also which are fallen asleep in Christ are perished. 19 If in this life only we have hope in Christ, we are of all men most miserable.

ὑμῶν°· ἔτι ἐστὲ ἐν ταῖς ἁμαρτίαις ὑμῶν· 18 ἄρα καὶ οἱ
your [is] ; still ye are in　　your sins.　　And then those that

κοιμηθέντες ἐν χριστῷ ἀπώλοντο. 19 εἰ ἐν τῇ ζωῇ ταύτῃ
fell asleep in Christ perished. If in this life

ᵖἠλπικότες ἐσμὲν ἐν χριστῷ‖ μόνον, ἐλεεινότεροι πάντων ἀν-
²we ³have ⁴hope ⁵in ⁶Christ ¹only, more miserable than all

θρώπων ἐσμέν.
men　　we are.

20 But now is Christ risen from the dead, *and* become the first-fruits of them that slept. 21 For since by man *came* death, by man *came* also the resurrection of the dead. 22 For as in Adam all die, even so in Christ shall all be made alive. 23 But every man in his own order: Christ the firstfruits; afterward they that are Christ's at his coming. 24 Then *cometh* the end, when he shall have delivered up the kingdom to God, even the Father; when he shall have put down all rule and all authority and power. 25 For he must reign, till he hath put all enemies under his feet. 26 The last enemy *that* shall be destroyed *is* death. 27 For he hath put all things under his feet. But when he saith, all things are put under *him, it is* manifest that he is excepted, which did put all things under him. 28 And when all things shall be subdued unto him, then shall the Son also himself be subject unto him that put all things under him, that God may be all in all.

20 Νυνὶ δὲ χριστὸς ἐγήγερται ἐκ νεκρῶν, ἀπαρχὴ
But now Christ has been raised from among [the] dead, first-fruit

τῶν κεκοιμημένων ᑫἐγένετο.ʰ 21 ἐπειδὴ γὰρ δι᾽ ἀνθρώπου
of those fallen asleep he became. For since by man [is]

ʳὁ‖ θάνατος, καὶ δι᾽ ἀνθρώπου ἀνάστασις νεκρῶν. 22 ὥσπερ
death, also by man resurrection of [the] dead. ²As

γὰρ ἐν τῷ Ἀδὰμ πάντες ἀποθνήσκουσιν, οὕτως καὶ ἐν τῷ
¹for in Adam all die, so also in the

χριστῷ πάντες ζωοποιηθήσονται. 23 ἕκαστος δὲ ἐν τῷ ἰδίῳ
Christ all shall be made alive. But each in his own

τάγματι· ἀπαρχὴ χριστός, ἔπειτα οἱ ˢ χριστοῦ ἐν τῇ
rank: [²the] ³first-fruit ¹Christ, then those of Christ at

παρουσίᾳ αὐτοῦ· 24 εἶτα τὸ τέλος, ὅταν ᵗπαραδῷ‖ τὴν
his coming. Then the end, when he shall have given up the

βασιλείαν τῷ θεῷ καὶ πατρί, ὅταν καταργήσῃ
kingdom to him who [is] God and Father ; when he shall have annulled

πᾶσαν ἀρχὴν καὶ πᾶσαν ἐξουσίαν καὶ δύναμιν. 25 δεῖ γὰρ
all rule and all authority and power. For it behoves

αὐτὸν βασιλεύειν, ᵛἄχρις‖ οὗ ᵂἂν‖ θῇ πάντας τοὺς
him to reign, until he shall have put all

ἐχθροὺς ˣ ὑπὸ τοὺς πόδας αὐτοῦ. 26 ἔσχατος ἐχθρὸς καταρ-
enemies under his feet. [The] last enemy an-

γεῖται ὁ θάνατος. 27 Πάντα γὰρ ὑπέταξεν ὑπὸ τοὺς
nulled [is] death. For all things he put in subjection under

πόδας αὐτοῦ· ὅταν δὲ εἴπῃ ʸὅτι‖ πάντα ὑποτέτακται,
his feet. But when it be said that all things have been put in subjection,

δῆλον ὅτι ἐκτὸς τοῦ ὑποτάξαντος αὐτῷ τὰ πάντα·
[it is] manifest that [it is] except him who put in subjection to him all things.

28 ὅταν δὲ ὑποταγῇ αὐτῷ τὰ πάντα, τότε
But when shall have been put in subjection to him all things, then

ᶻκαὶ‖ αὐτὸς ὁ υἱὸς ὑποταγήσεται τῷ ὑποτάξαντι
also ³himself ¹the ²Son will be put in subjection to him who put in subjection

αὐτῷ τὰ πάντα, ἵνα ᾖ ὁ θεὸς ᵃτὰ‖ πάντα ἐν πᾶσιν.
to him all things, that ²may ³be ¹God all in all.

29 Else what shall they do which are baptized for the dead, if the dead rise not at all? why are they then baptized for the dead? 30 and why stand we in jeopardy every hour? 31 I protest by your rejoicing which I have in Christ Jesus our Lord, I die daily. 32 If after the manner of men I have

29 Ἐπεὶ τί ποιήσουσιν οἱ βαπτιζόμενοι ὑπὲρ τῶν νεκρῶν
Since what shall they do who are baptized for the dead

εἰ ὅλως νεκροὶ οὐκ ἐγείρονται; τί καὶ βαπτίζονται ὑπὲρ
if ⁴at ⁵all [¹the] ²dead ³not are raised ? why also are they baptized for

ᵇτῶν νεκρῶν‖ ; 30 τί καὶ ἡμεῖς κινδυνεύομεν πᾶσαν ὥραν ;
the dead ? Why also ²we ¹are in danger every hour ?

31 καθ᾽ ἡμέραν ἀποθνήσκω, νὴ τὴν ᶜἡμετέραν‖ καύχησιν, ᵈ
Daily I die, by our boasting,

ἣν ἔχω ἐν χριστῷ Ἰησοῦ τῷ κυρίῳ ἡμῶν. 32 εἰ κατὰ
which I have in Christ Jesus our Lord. If according to

.° + [ἐστίν] is L.　　　ᵖ ἐν χριστῷ ἠλπικότες ἐσμὲν LTTrAW.　　　ᑫ — ἐγένετο GLTTrAW.
ʳ — ὁ LTTr[A]W.　　ˢ + τοῦ (*read* of the Christ) GLTTrAW.　　ᵗ παραδιδοῖ he may give up
LTTrA.　　ᵛ ἄχρι TA.　　ᵂ — ἂν LTTrAW.　　ˣ + [αὐτοῦ] his (enemies) L.　　ʸ [ὅτι] L.
ᶻ — καὶ [L]Tr[A].　　ᵃ — τὰ LTTrA.　　ᵇ αὐτῶν them GLTTrAW.　　ᶜ ὑμετέραν your EGLTTrAW.
ᵈ + ἀδελφοί brethren LTTrA.

ἄνθρωπον ἐθηριομάχησα ἐν Ἐφέσῳ,. τί μοι τὸ ⁶ὄφελος,
man   I fought with beasts in Ephesus, what to me the   profit,

εἰ νεκροὶ οὐκ.ἐγείρονται ;ᶠ φάγωμεν καὶ πίωμεν,
if [the] dead are not raised ?   We may eat and we may drink;

αὔριον.γὰρ ἀποθνήσκομεν. 33 μὴ.πλανᾶσθε· φθείρουσιν ἤδη
for to-morrow we die.   Be not misled: ³corrupt ⁵manners

ᶠχρήσθ᾽ᵍ ὁμιλίαι κακαί. 34 ἐκνήψατε δικαίως, καὶ μὴ
⁴good   ²companionships ¹evil.   Awake up righteously, and ²not

ἁμαρτάνετε· ἀγνωσίαν.γὰρ θεοῦ τινες ἔχουσιν· πρὸς ἐντροπὴν
¹sin ;   for ignorance of God some have :   to   ²shame

ὑμῖν ᵍλέγω.ᴴ
¹your I speak.

35 ʰἈλλ᾽ᴴ ἐρεῖ τις, Πῶς ἐγείρονται οἱ νεκροί ; ποίῳ
But will say some one, How are raised the dead ? ²with ³what

δὲ σώματι ἔρχονται ; 36 ᶦἄφρον,ᴴ σὺ ὃ σπείρεις, οὐ
¹and body do they come ?   Fool ; ²thou ¹what sowest, ²not

ζωοποιεῖται ἐὰν.μὴ ἀποθάνῃ· 37 καὶ ὃ σπείρεις, οὐ τὸ σῶμα
¹is quickened unless it die.   And what thou sowest, not the body

τὸ γενησόμενον σπείρεις, ἀλλὰ γυμνὸν κόκκον, εἰ τύχοι,
that ⁴ shall be thou sowest, but a bare grain, it may be

σίτου ἤ τινος τῶν λοιπῶν· 38 ὁ.δὲ.θεὸς ʲαὐτῷ δίδωσινᴴ
of wheat or of some one of the rest ;   and God to it gives

σῶμα καθὼς ἠθέλησεν, καὶ ἑκάστῳ τῶν σπερμάτων ᵏτὸ.ᴴἴδιον
a body according as he willed, and to each of the seeds   its own

σῶμα. 39 οὐ πᾶσα σὰρξ ἡ αὐτὴ σάρξ· ἀλλὰ ἄλλη μὲν
body.   Not every flesh [is] the same flesh, but one

ᶫσὰρξᴴ ἀνθρώπων, ἄλλη.δὲ σὰρξ κτηνῶν, ἄλλη.δὲ ᵐⁿἰχθύων,
flesh   of men, and another flesh of beasts, and another of fishes,

ἄλλη.δὲ πτηνῶν.ᴴ 40 καὶ σώματα ἐπουράνια, καὶ
and another of birds.   And bodies [there are] heavenly, and

σώματα ἐπίγεια· ᵒἀλλ᾽ᴴ ἑτέρα μὲν ἡ τῶν ἐπουρανίων
bodies earthly :   but different [is]   the ²of ³the ⁴heavenly

δόξα, ἑτέρα.δὲ ἡ τῶν ἐπιγείων. 41 ἄλλη δόξα ἡλίου,
¹glory, and different that of the earthly :   one glory of [the] sun,

καὶ ἄλλη δόξα σελήνης, καὶ ἄλλη δόξα ἀστέρων· ἀστὴρ
and another glory of [the] moon, and another glory of [the] stars ; ²star

γὰρ ἀστέρος διαφέρει ἐν δόξῃ. 42 οὕτως καὶ ἡ ἀνάστασις
¹for ⁴from ⁵star ³differs in glory.   So also [is] the resurrection

τῶν νεκρῶν. σπείρεται ἐν φθορᾷ, ἐγείρεται ἐν ἀφθαρσίᾳ·
of the dead.   It is sown in corruption, it is raised in incorruptibility.

43 σπείρεται ἐν ἀτιμίᾳ, ἐγείρεται ἐν δόξῃ· σπείρεται ἐν ἀ-
It is sown in dishonour, it is raised in glory.   It is sown in weak-

σθενείᾳ, ἐγείρεται ἐν δυνάμει· 44 σπείρεται σῶμα ψυχικόν,
ness,   it is raised in   power.   It is sown a ²body ¹natural,

ἐγείρεται σῶμα πνευματικόν. ᴾἔστιν σῶμα ψυχικόν, ᵠκαὶ
it is raised a ²body ¹spiritual :   there is a ²body ¹natural, and

ἔστινᴴ ʳσῶμαᴴ πνευματικόν. 45 οὕτως καὶ γέγραπται,
there is a ²body ¹spiritual.   So   also it has been written,

Ἐγένετο ὁ πρῶτος ˢἄνθρωποςᴴ Ἀδὰμ εἰς ψυχὴν ζῶσαν· ὁ
⁵Became ¹the ²first ³man ⁴Adam a ²soul ¹living ; the

ἔσχατος Ἀδὰμ εἰς πνεῦμα ζωοποιοῦν. 46 ἀλλ᾽ οὐ πρῶτον
last Adam a ²spirit ¹quickening.   But not first [was]

fought with beasts at Ephesus, what advantageth it me, if the dead rise not *'let us eat and drink ; for to morrow we die. 33 Be not deceived : evil communications corrupt good manners. 34 Awake to righteousness, and sin not ; for some have not the knowledge of God : I speak *this* to your shame.

35 But some *man* will say, How are the dead raised up? and with what body do they come ? 36 *Thou* fool, that which thou sowest is not quickened, except it die : 37 and that which thou sowest, thou sowest not that body that shall be, but bare grain, it may chance of wheat, or of some other *grain*: 38 but God giveth it a body as it hath pleased him, and to every seed his own body. 39 All flesh *is* not the same flesh : but *there is* one *kind of* flesh of men, another flesh of beasts, another of fishes, *and* another of birds. 40 *There are* also celestial bodies, and bodies terrestrial : but the glory of the celestial *is* one, and the glory of the terrestrial *is* another. 41 *There* is one glory of the sun and another glory of the moon, and another glory of the stars : for *one* star differeth from *another* star in glory. 42 So also *is* the resurrection of the dead. It is sown in corruption ; it is raised in incorruption : 43 it is sown in dishonour ; it is raised in glory : it is sown in weakness ; it is raised in power : 44 it is sown a natural body ; it is raised a spiritual body. There is a natural body, and there is a spiritual body. 45 And so it is written, The first man Adam was made a living soul ; the last Adam *was made* a quickening spirit. 46 Howbeit that *was* not first which is spiritual,

---

· e ὄφελος ; .... ἐγείρονται, (*end the question at profit*) GLTTrA.   f χρηστὰ GTTrAW.   g λαλῶ LTTrA.   h ἀλλὰ TTr.   i ἄφρων LTTrA.   j δίδωσιν αὐτῷ LTTrAW.   k — τὸ LTTrA.   l — σὰρξ GLTT.AW.   m + σὰρξ flesh [L]TTrA.   n πτηνῶν, ἄλλη δὲ ἰχθύων LTTrAW.   o ἀλλὰ LTTrAW.   p + εἰ if LTTrAW.   q ἔστιν καὶ there is also LTTrAW.   r — σῶμα LTTrAW.   s [ἄνθρωπος] L.

but that which is natural: and afterward that which is spiritual. 47 The first man is of the earth, earthy : the second man is the Lord from heaven. 48 As is the earthy, such are they also that are earthy : and as is the heavenly, such are they also that are heavenly. 49 And as we have borne the image of the earthy, we shall also bear the image of the heavenly. 50 Now this I say, brethren, that flesh and blood cannot inherit the kingdom of God ; neither doth corruption inherit incorruption.

τὸ πνευματικόν, ἀλλὰ τὸ ψυχικόν, ἔπειτα τὸ πνευματικόν.
the　spiritual,　but the　natural,　then the　spiritual :
47 ὁ πρῶτος ἄνθρωπος ἐκ γῆς, χοϊκός· ὁ δεύτερος ἄν-
　the first　man　out of earth, made of dust ; the second
θρωπος, ᵗὁ κύριος‖ ἐξ οὐρανοῦ. 48 οἷος ὁ χοϊκός, τοιοῦτοι
man,　the Lord　out of heaven.　Such as he made of dust,　such
καὶ οἱ χοϊκοί· καὶ οἷος ὁ ἐπουράνιος, τοιοῦτοι καὶ οἱ
also [are] those made of dust ; and such as the heavenly [one], such　also the
ἐπουράνιοι· 49 καὶ καθὼς ἐφορέσαμεν τὴν εἰκόνα τοῦ
heavenly [ones].　And according as　we bore　the image of the [one]
χοϊκοῦ, ᵛφορέσομεν‖ καὶ τὴν εἰκόνα τοῦ ἐπουρανίου.
made of dust,　we shall bear also　the　image of the [²one]　¹heavenly.
50 Τοῦτο.δὲ φημι, ἀδελφοί, ὅτι σὰρξ καὶ αἷμα βασιλείαν
　But this　I say,　brethren,　that　flesh and blood [the] kingdom
θεοῦ κληρονομῆσαι οὐ.ʷδύνανται,‖ οὐδὲ ἡ φθορὰ τὴν ἀ-
of God　²inherit　¹cannot,　nor　²corruption　⁴incor-
φθαρσίαν ˣκληρονομεῖ.‖
ruptibility　¹does ³inherit.

51 Behold, I shew you a mystery ; We shall not all sleep, but we shall all be changed, 52 in a moment, in the twinkling of an eye, at the last trump : for the trumpet shall sound, and the dead shall be raised incorruptible, and we shall be changed. 53 For this corruptible must put on incorruption, and this mortal must put on immortality. 54 So when this corruptible shall have put on incorruption, and this mortal shall have put on immortality, then shall be brought to pass the saying that is written, Death is swallowed up in victory. 50 O death, where is thy sting ? O grave, where is thy victory ? 56 The sting of death is sin ; and the strength of sin is the law. 57 But thanks be to God, which giveth us the victory through our Lord Jesus Christ. 58 Therefore, my beloved brethren, be ye stedfast, unmoveable, always abounding in the work of the Lord, forasmuch as ye know that your labour is not in vain in the Lord.

XVI. Now concerning the collection for the saints, as I have

51 Ἰδοὺ μυστήριον ὑμῖν λέγω· Πάντες ʸμὲν‖ ᶻοὐ κοιμηθη-
　Lo　a mystery　to you I tell :　All　³not ¹we ³shall
σόμεθα·‖ πάντες.δὲ ἀλλαγησόμεθα, 52 ἐν ἀτόμῳ, ἐν
fall asleep,　but all　we shall be changed,　in an instant, in [the]
ῥιπῇ ὀφθαλμοῦ, ἐν τῇ ἐσχάτῃ σάλπιγγι· σαλπίσει.γάρ,
twinkling of an eye,　at the　last　trumpet ; for a trumpet shall sound,
καὶ οἱ νεκροὶ ᵃἐγερθήσονται‖ ἄφθαρτοι, καὶ ἡμεῖς ἀλλαγησό-
and the dead　shall be raised　incorruptible, and we　shall be
μεθα. 53 δεῖ.γὰρ τὸ.φθαρτὸν.τοῦτο ἐνδύσασθαι ἀφθαρσίαν,
changed.　For it behoves　this corruption　to put on　incorruptibility,
καὶ τὸ.θνητὸν.τοῦτο ἐνδύσασθαι ἀθανασίαν. 54 ὅταν.δὲ τὸ
and　this mortal　to put on　immortality.　But when
φθαρτὸν.τοῦτο ἐνδύσηται ἀφθαρσίαν, καὶ τὸ.θνητὸν.τοῦτο
this corruptible　shall have put on incorruptibility, and　this mortal
ἐνδύσηται ἀθανασίαν, τότε γενήσεται ὁ λόγος ὁ γε-
shall have put on　immortality,　then shall come to pass the word that has
γραμμένος, Κατεπόθη ὁ θάνατος εἰς νῖκος. 55 Ποῦ σου,
been written, ²Was ³swallowed ⁴up　¹death　in victory.　Where of thee,
θάνατε, τὸ ᵇκέντρον‖ ; ποῦ σου, ᶜᾅδη,‖ τὸ ᵇνῖκος‖ ; 56 Τὸ.δὲ
O death,　the sting ?　where of thee, O hades, the victory ?　Now the
κέντρον τοῦ θανάτου ἡ ἁμαρτία· ἡ.δὲ δύναμις τῆς ἁμαρ-
sting　of death [is]　sin ;　and the power　of sin
τίας ὁ νόμος· 57 τῷ.δὲ.θεῷ χάρις τῷ διδόντι ἡμῖν τὸ νῖκος
the law ;　but to God [be] thanks, who gives　us the victory
διὰ τοῦ.κυρίου.ἡμῶν Ἰησοῦ χριστοῦ. 58 Ὥστε, ἀδελφοί.μου
by　our Lord　Jesus　Christ.　So that,　my brethren
ἀγαπητοί, ἑδραῖοι γίνεσθε, ἀμετακίνητοι, περισσεύοντες ἐν τῷ
beloved,　²firm　¹be,　immovable,　abounding　in the
ἔργῳ τοῦ κυρίου πάντοτε, εἰδότες ὅτι ὁ.κόπος.ὑμῶν οὐκ.ἔστιν
work of the Lord　always,　knowing that　your toil　is not
κενὸς ἐν κυρίῳ.
void　in [the] Lord.

16 Περὶ.δὲ τῆς λογίας τῆς εἰς τοὺς ἁγίους, ὥσπερ
　Now concerning the　collection which [is] for the　saints,　as

ᵗ — ὁ κύριος LTTrA. 　 ᵛ φορέσωμεν we should bear LTTr. 　 ʷ δύναται TTr. 　 ˣ κληρονομήσει shall inherit L. 　 ʸ — μὲν [L]TTrA. 　 ᶻ κοιμηθησόμεθα, οὐ (read we shall all
sleep, but not all &c.) L. 　 ᵃ ἀναστήσονται L. 　 ᵇ νῖκος and κέντρον transposed LTTr.
ᶜ θάνατε O death LTTrA.

διέταξα ταῖς ἐκκλησίαις τῆς Γαλατίας, οὕτως καὶ ὑμεῖς
I directed   the   assemblies   ʲof Galatia,   so   also   ye

ποιήσατε. 2 κατὰ.μίαν ᵈσαββάτων‖ ἕκαστος ὑμῶν παρ'
do.   Every first [day]   of the week   ²each   ³of ⁴you   ⁶₁y

ἑαυτῷ τιθέτω, θησαυρίζων ὅ.τι ᵉἂν‖ εὐοδῶται· ἵνα μὴ
⁷him   ¹let ⁵put,   treasuring up   whatever   he may be prospered in,   that not

ὅταν ἔλθω τότε λογίαι γίνωνται. 3 ὅταν.δὲ παραγένω-
when I may come then   collections there should be.   And when   I shall have

μαι, οὓς.ᵉ̓ὰν‖ δοκιμάσητε δι' ἐπιστολῶν τούτους πέμψω
arrived,   whomsoever ye may approve by   epistles   these   I will send

ἀπενεγκεῖν τὴν.χάριν.ὑμῶν εἰς Ἱερουσαλήμ· 4 ἐὰν.δὲ ᵍῇ
to carry   your bounty   to   Jerusalem: and if   it be

ἄξιον‖ τοῦ.κἀμὲ πορεύεσθαι, σὺν ἐμοὶ πορεύσονται. 5 Ἐλεύ-
suitable for me also   to go,   with me   they shall go.   ²I ³will

σομαι δὲ πρὸς ὑμᾶς ὅταν Μακεδονίαν διέλθω·
⁴come ¹but to   you   when   Macedonia   I shall have gone through;

Μακεδονίαν.γὰρ διέρχομαι. 6 πρὸς.ὑμᾶς.δὲ τυχὸν παραμενῶ,
for Macedonia   I do go through.   And with you   it may be   I shall stay,

ἢ καὶ παραχειμάσω, ἵνα ὑμεῖς με προπέμψητε οὗ.ἐὰν
or even   I shall winter,   that   ye   me   may set forward   wheresoever

πορεύωμαι. 7 οὐ.θέλω.γὰρ ὑμᾶς ἄρτι ἐν παρόδῳ ἰδεῖν· ἐλπίζω
I may go.   For I will not   ³you   ⁴now ⁵in ⁶passing ¹to ²see,   ⁸I ⁹hope

ʰδὲ‖ χρόνον τινὰ ἐπιμεῖναι πρὸς ὑμᾶς, ἐὰν ὁ κύριος ¹ἱ̓πι-
⁷but   a ²time   ¹certain to remain   with   you,   if   the Lord   per-

τρέπῃ.‖ 8 ἐπιμενῶ.δὲ ἐν Ἐφέσῳ ἕως τῆς πεντηκοστῆς·
mit.   But I shall remain   in   Ephesus   till   the   Pentecost.

9 θύρα.γάρ μοι ἀνέῳγεν μεγάλη καὶ ἐνεργής, καὶ ἀντι-
For a door   to me has been opened   great   and   efficient,   and   op-

κείμενοι πολλοί.
posers   [are]   many.

10 Ἐὰν.δὲ ἔλθῃ Τιμόθεος, βλέπετε ἵνα ἀφόβως γένηται
Now if   ²come ¹Timotheus,   see   that   without fear   he may be

πρὸς ὑμᾶς· τὸ.γὰρ ἔργον κυρίου ἐργάζεται, ὡς ᵏκαὶ ἐγώ.‖
with   you;   for the   work   of [the] Lord   he works,   as   even   I.

11 μή τις οὖν αὐτὸν ἐξουθενήσῃ· προπέμψατε.δὲ αὐτὸν
ᶻNot ³anyone ¹therefore   him   should despise;   but ²et forward   him

ἐν εἰρήνῃ, ἵνα ἔλθῃ πρός ¹με·‖ ἐκδέχομαι.γὰρ αὐτὸν μετὰ
in   peace,   that he may come to   me;   for I await   him   with

τῶν ἀδελφῶν. 12 Περὶ.δὲ Ἀπολλὼ τοῦ ἀδελφοῦ, πολλὰ
the   brethren.   And concerning   Apollos   the   brother,   much

παρεκάλεσα αὐτὸν ἵνα ἔλθῃ πρὸς ὑμᾶς μετὰ τῶν
I exhorted   him   that he should go   to   you   with   the

ἀδελφῶν· καὶ πάντως.οὐκ ἦν θέλημα ἵνα νῦν ἔλθῃ,
brethren;   and   not at all   was [his]   will   that now he should come;

ἐλεύσεται.δὲ ὅταν εὐκαιρήσῃ. 13 Γρηγορεῖτε, στήκετε
but he will come when he shall have opportunity.   Watch ye;   stand fast

ἐν τῇ πίστει, ἀνδρίζεσθε, ᵐκραταιοῦσθε. 14 πάντα
in the   faith,   quit yourselves like men,   be strong.   ²All ⁴things

ὑμῶν ἐν ἀγάπῃ γινέσθω.
³your ⁵in ⁶love   ¹let be done.

15 Παρακαλῶ.δὲ ὑμᾶς, ἀδελφοί· οἴδατε τὴν οἰκίαν Στεφανᾶ,
But I exhort   you,   brethren, (ye know   the   house of Stephanas,

ὅτι ἐστὶν ἀπαρχὴ τῆς Ἀχαΐας, καὶ εἰς διακονίαν τοῖς ἁγίοις
that it is   ²first-fruit   ¹Achaia's,   and ⁷for ⁸service   ⁴to ⁵the ⁶saints

given order to the churches of Galatia, even so do ye. 2 Upon the first *day* of the week let every one of you lay by him in store, as *God* hath prospered him, that there be no gatherings when I come. 3 And when I come, whomsoever ye shall approve by *your* letters, them will I send to bring your liberality unto Jerusalem. 4 And if it be meet that I go also, they shall go with me. 5 Now I will come unto you, when I shall pass through Macedonia: for I do pass through Macedonia. 6 And it may be that I will abide, yea, and winter with you, that ye may bring me on my journey whithersoever I go. 7 For I will not see you now by the way; but I trust to tarry awhile with you, if the Lord permit. 8 But I will tarry at Ephesus until Pentecost. 9 For a great door and effectual is opened unto me, and *there are* many adversaries.

10 Now if Timotheus come, see that he may be with you without fear: for he worketh the work of the Lord, as I also *do*. 11 Let no man therefore despise him: but conduct him forth in peace, that he may come unto me: for I look for him with the brethren. 12 As touching *our* brother Apollos, I greatly desired him to come unto you with the brethren: but his will was not at all to come at this time; but he will come when he shall have convenient time. 13 Watch ye, stand fast in the faith, quit you like men, be strong. 14 Let all your things be done with charity.

15 I beseech you, brethren, (ye know the house of Stephanas, that it is the first-fruits of Achaia, and *that* they have addicted themselves to the ministry of the

ᵈ σαββάτου LTTrAW.   ᵉ ἐὰν Tr.   ᶠ ἂν LTr.   ᵍ ἄξιον ᾖ LTrA.   ʰ γὰρ for GLTTrAW.
¹ ἐπιτρέψῃ LTTrAW.   ᵏ κἀγώ LTTrA.   ˡ ἐμέ LTr.   ᵐ + [καὶ] and L.

saints,) 16 that ye submit yourselves unto such, and to every one that helpeth with us, and laboureth. 17 I am glad of the coming of Stephanas and Fortunatus and Achaicus : for that which was lacking on your part they have supplied. 18 For they have refreshed my spirit and yours : therefore acknowledge ye them that are such. 19 The churches of Asia salute you. Aquila and Priscilla salute you much in the Lord, with the church that is in their house. 20 All the brethren greet you. Greet ye one another with an holy kiss.

ἔταξαν ἑαυτούς· 16 ἵνα καὶ ὑμεῖς ὑποτάσσησθε τοῖς
¹they ²appointed ³themselves,)   that also   ye   be subject

τοιούτοις, καὶ παντὶ τῷ συνεργοῦντι καὶ κοπιῶντι. 17 Χαίρω
to such,   and to everyone   working with [us] and labouring.   ²I ³rejoice

δὲ ἐπὶ τῇ παρουσίᾳ Στεφανᾶ καὶ ⁿΦουρτουνάτου‖ καὶ Ἀχαϊκοῦ,
¹but at the coming of Stephanas and   Fortunatus   and Achaicus ;

ὅτι τὸ °ὑμῶν‖ ὑστέρημα Ροῦτοι‖ ἀνεπλήρωσαν· 18 ἀνέπαυ-
because   your   deficiency these   filled up.   ²They ³re-

σαν γὰρ τὸ ἐμὸν πνεῦμα καὶ τὸ ὑμῶν, ἐπιγινώσκετε οὖν
freshed ¹for   my   spirit and   yours ;   · recognize therefore

τοὺς τοιούτους. 19 Ἀσπάζονται ὑμᾶς αἱ ἐκκλησίαι τῆς Ἀσίας·
such.   ⁵Salute   ⁶you ¹the ²assemblies   ³of ⁴Asia.

ᵠἀσπάζονται‖ ὑμᾶς ἐν   κυρίῳ πολλὰ Ἀκύλας καὶ ¹Πρίσ-
¹⁰Salute   ¹¹you ¹³in [¹⁴the] ¹⁵Lord ¹²much ·⁷Aquila ⁸and ⁹Pris-

κιλλα,‖ σὺν τῇ κατ᾽ οἶκον αὐτῶν ἐκκλησίᾳ· 20 ἀσπάζονται
cilla,   with the ²in ³their ⁴house ¹assembly.   ⁴Salute

ὑμᾶς οἱ ἀδελφοὶ πάντες. ἀσπάσασθε ἀλλήλους ἐν φιλήματι
⁵you ²the ³brethren ¹all.   Salute ye   one another with a ²kiss

ἁγίῳ.
¹holy.

21 The salutation of me Paul with mine own hand. 22 If any man love not the Lord Jesus Christ, let him be Anathema Maranatha. 23 The grace of our Lord Jesus Christ be with you. 24 My love be with you all in Christ Jesus. Amen.

21 Ὁ ἀσπασμὸς τῇ ἐμῇ   χειρὶ Παύλου· 22 εἴ τις οὐ φιλεῖ
The salutation ³by ⁴my [⁵own] ⁶hand ¹of ²Paul.   If anyone love not

τὸν κύριον ˢἸησοῦν χριστόν,‖ ἤτω ἀνάθεμα· μαρὰν ἀθά.
the Lord Jesus Christ,‖ let him be accursed : Maran   atha.

23 ἡ χάρις τοῦ κυρίου Ἰησοῦ ᵗχριστοῦ‖ μεθ᾽ ὑμῶν. 24 ἡ
The grace of the Lord Jesus   Christ [be] with you.

ἀγάπη μου μετὰ πάντων ὑμῶν ἐν χριστῷ Ἰησοῦ. ᵛἀμήν.‖
My love [be] with ²all   ¹you in Christ Jesus.   Amen.

ᵂΠρὸς   Κορινθίους πρώτη ἐγράφη ἀπὸ Φιλίππων, διὰ
²To [³the] ⁴Corinthians ¹first written from Philippi, by

Στεφανᾶ καὶ Φουρτουνάτου καὶ Ἀχαϊκοῦ καὶ Τιμοθέου.‖
Stephanas and Fortunatus and Achaicus and Timotheus.

ᵃΗ ΠΡΟΣ ΤΟΥΣ ΚΟΡΙΝΘΙΟΥΣ ΕΠΙΣΤΟΛΗ ΔΕΥΤΕΡΑ.‖
THE ³TO ⁴THE ⁵CORINTHIANS ²EPISTLE ¹SECOND.

PAUL, an apostle of Jesus Christ by the will of God, and Timothy our brother, unto the church of God which is at Corinth, with all the saints which are in all Achaia : 2 Grace be to you and peace from God our Father, and from the Lord Jesus Christ.

ΠΑΥΛΟΣ ἀπόστολος ᵇἸησοῦ χριστοῦ‖ διὰ θελήματος θεοῦ,
Paul,   apostle   of Jesus Christ   by   will   of God,

καὶ Τιμόθεος ὁ ἀδελφός, τῇ ἐκκλησίᾳ τοῦ θεοῦ τῇ οὔσῃ ἐν
and Timotheus the brother, to the assembly of God which is in

Κορίνθῳ, σὺν τοῖς ἁγίοις πᾶσιν τοῖς οὖσιν ἐν ὅλῃ τῇ Ἀ-
Corinth, with ²the ³saints ¹all who are in ²whole ¹the [of] A-

χαΐᾳ· 2 χάρις ὑμῖν καὶ εἰρήνη ἀπὸ ᶜθεοῦ‖ πατρὸς ἡμῶν καὶ
chaia.   Grace to you and peace from God   our Father   and

κυρίου Ἰησοῦ χριστοῦ.
[the] Lord Jesus Christ.

3 Blessed be God, even the Father of our Lord Jesus Christ, the

3 Εὐλογητὸς   ὁ θεὸς καὶ πατὴρ τοῦ κυρίου ἡμῶν Ἰησοῦ
Blessed [be] the God and Father of our Lord   Jesus

ᵃ Φορτουνάτου LTTrAW.   ° ὑμέτερον LTTrAW.   ᴾ αὐτοὶ they LAW.   ᵠ ἀσπάζεται ΤΑ.
ʳ Πρίσκα Prisca TTr.   ˢ — Ἰησοῦν χριστόν LTTrA.   ᵗ — χριστοῦ TTrA.   ᵛ — ἀμήν
[L]TTr[A].   ᵂ — the subscription GLTTrW ; Πρὸς Κορινθίους ά Α.
ᵃ + Παύλου τοῦ Ἀποστόλου of Paul the Apostle E ; + Παύλου of Paul ᴳ ; — τοὺς ΕΘ ;
Πρὸς Κορινθίους β´ LTTrAW.   ᵇ χριστοῦ Ἰησοῦ TTrA.   ᶜ — θεοῦ W.

χριστοῦ, ὁ πατὴρ τῶν οἰκτιρμῶν καὶ θεὸς πάσης παρακλή-
Christ, the Father of compassions, and God of all encourage-

σεως, 4 ὁ παρακαλῶν ἡμᾶς ἐπὶ πάσῃ τῇ θλίψει ἡμῶν, εἰς
ment; who encourages us in all our tribulation, for

τὸ δύνασθαι ἡμᾶς παρακαλεῖν τοὺς ἐν πάσῃ θλίψει, διὰ
²to ³be ⁴able ¹us to encourage those in every tribulation, through

τῆς παρακλήσεως ἧς παρακαλούμεθα αὐτοὶ ὑπὸ τοῦ
the encouragement with which we are encouraged ourselves by

θεοῦ· 5 ὅτι καθὼς περισσεύει τὰ παθήματα τοῦ χριστοῦ
God. Because according as abound the sufferings of the Christ

εἰς ἡμᾶς, οὕτως διὰ ᵈ χριστοῦ περισσεύει καὶ ἡ παράκλησις
toward us, so through Christ abounds also ²encouragement

ἡμῶν. 6 εἴτε δὲ θλιβόμεθα, ὑπὲρ τῆς ὑμῶν παρακλήσεως
¹our. But whether we are troubled, [it is] for your encouragement

καὶ σωτηρίας, ᵉτῆς ἐνεργουμένης ἐν ὑπομονῇ τῶν αὐτῶν
and salvation, being wrought in [the] endurance of the same

παθημάτων ὧν καὶ ἡμεῖς πάσχομεν···‖ ᶠεἴτε παρακαλούμεθα,
sufferings which ²also ¹we suffer, whether we are encouraged,

ὑπὲρ τῆς ὑμῶν παρακλήσεωςᵉ ᵍκαὶ σωτηρίας·‖·‖ καὶ ἡ ἐλπὶς
[it is] for your encouragement and salvation; (and ²hope

ἡμῶν βεβαία ὑπὲρ ὑμῶνᶠ· 7 εἰδότες ὅτι ʰὥσπερ‖ κοινωνοί
¹our [is] sure for you;) knowing that as partners

ἐστε τῶν παθημάτων, οὕτως καὶ τῆς παρακλήσεως. 8 Οὐ γὰρ
ye are of the sufferings, so also of the encouragement. For ²not

θέλομεν ὑμᾶς ἀγνοεῖν, ἀδελφοί, ⁱὑπὲρ‖ τῆς θλίψεως ἡμῶν
²do ¹we wish you to be ignorant, brethren, as to our tribulation

τῆς γενομένης ᵏἡμῖν‖ ἐν τῇ Ἀσίᾳ, ὅτι καθ᾽ ὑπερβολὴν ˡἐβαρή-
which happened to us in Asia, that excessively we were

θημεν ὑπὲρ δύναμιν,‖ ὥστε ἐξαπορηθῆναι ἡμᾶς καὶ τοῦ ζῆν·
burdened beyond [our] power, so as for us to despair even of living.

9 ᵐἀλλ᾽‖ αὐτοὶ ἐν ἑαυτοῖς τὸ ἀπόκριμα τοῦ θανάτου ἐσχή-
But ourselves in ourselves the sentence of death we have

καμεν, ἵνα μὴ πεποιθότες ὦμεν ἐφ᾽ ἑαυτοῖς, ἀλλ᾽ ἐπὶ τῷ
had, that we should not have trust in ourselves, but in

θεῷ τῷ ἐγείροντι τοὺς νεκρούς· 10 ὃς ἐκ τηλικούτου θανάτου
God who raises the dead; who from so great a death

ⁿἐρρύσατο‖ ἡμᾶς ᵒκαὶ ῥύεται,‖ εἰς ὃν ἠλπίκαμεν ᴾὅτι καὶ
delivered us and does deliver; in whom we have hope that also

ἔτι ῥύσεται, 11 συνυπουργούντων καὶ ὑμῶν ὑπὲρ ἡμῶν
still he will deliver; labouring together ²also ¹ye for us

τῇ δεήσει, ἵνα ἐκ πολλῶν προσώπων τὸ εἰς ἡμᾶς χάρισμα
by supplication, that by many persons the ²towards ³us ¹gift

διὰ πολλῶν εὐχαριστηθῇ ὑπὲρ ἡμῶν. 12 Ἡ
³through ¹⁰many ⁴might ⁵be ⁶subject ⁷of ⁸thanksgiving for us.

γὰρ καύχησις ἡμῶν αὕτη ἐστίν, τὸ μαρτύριον τῆς συνειδήσεως
For our boasting this is, the testimony of ²conscience

ἡμῶν, ὅτι ἐν ᑫἀπλότητι‖ καὶ ʳεἰλικρινείᾳ‖ ˢθεοῦ, οὐκ ἐν σοφίᾳ
¹our, that in simplicity and sincerity of God, (not in ²wisdom

σαρκικῇ, ἀλλ᾽ ἐν χάριτι θεοῦ, ἀνεστράφημεν ἐν τῷ κόσμῳ,
¹fleshly, but in grace of God,) we had our conduct in the world,

περισσοτέρως δὲ πρὸς ὑμᾶς. 13 οὐ γὰρ ἄλλα γράφομεν
and more abundantly towards you. For not other things do we write

Father of mercies, and the God of all comfort; 4 who comforteth us in all our tribulation, that we may be able to comfort them which are in any trouble, by the comfort wherewith we ourselves are comforted of God. 5 For as the sufferings of Christ abound in us, so our consolation also aboundeth by Christ. 6 And whether we be afflicted, it is for your consolation and salvation, which is effectual in the enduring of the same sufferings which we also suffer: or whether we be comforted, it is for your consolation and salvation. 7 And our hope of you is stedfast, knowing, that as ye are partakers of the sufferings, so shall ye be also of the consolation. 8 For we would not, brethren, have you ignorant of our trouble which came to us in Asia, that we were pressed out of measure, above strength, insomuch that we despaired even of life: 9 but we had the sentence of death in ourselves, that we should not trust in ourselves, but in God which raiseth the dead: 10 who delivered us from so great a death, and doth deliver: in whom we trust that he will yet deliver us; 11 ye also helping together by prayer for us, that for the gift bestowed upon us by the means of many persons thanks may be given by many on our behalf. 12 For our rejoicing is this, the testimony of our conscience, that in simplicity and godly sincerity, not with fleshly wisdom, but by the grace of God, we have had our conversation in the world, and more abundantly to you-ward. 13 For we write none other things unto you, than

---

+ τοῦ GLTTrAW.   ᵉ τῆς ἐνεργουμένης .... πάσχομεν placed after παρακλήσεως GT.
ᶠ ειτε παρακαλούμεθα .... σωτηρίας placed after ὑπὲρ ὑμῶν LTrAW.   ᵍ — καὶ σωτηρίας GT.
ʰ ὡς LTTrAW.   ⁱ περὶ LTTr.   ᵏ — ἡμῖν LTTrAW.   ˡ ὑπὲρ δύναμιν ἐβαρήθημεν LTTrA.
ᵐ ἀλλ᾽ L   ⁿ ἐρύσατο Tr.   ᵒ καὶ ῥύσεται and will deliver [L]TTrA.   ᴾ [ὅτι] LTr.
ᑫ ἁγιότητι holiness LTTrA.   ʳ εἰλικρινίᾳ T.   ˢ + τοῦ LTTrAW.

what ye read or acknowledge; and I trust ye shall acknowledge even to the end; 14 as also ye have acknowledged us in part, that we are your rejoicing, even as ye also *are* ours in the day of the Lord Jesus. 15 And in this confidence I was minded to come unto you before, that ye might have a second benefit; 16 and to pass by you into Macedonia, and to come again out of Macedonia unto you, and of you to be brought on my way toward Judæa. 17 When I therefore was thus minded, did I use lightness? or the things that I purpose, do I purpose according to the flesh, that with me there should be yea yea, and nay nay? 18 But *as* God *is* true, our word toward you was not yea and nay. 19 For the Son of God, Jesus Christ, who was preached among you by us, *even* by me and Silvanus and Timotheus, was not yea and nay, but in him was yea. 20 For all the promises of God in him *are* yea, and in him Amen, unto the glory of God by us. 21 Now he which stablisheth us with you in Christ, and hath anointed us, *is* God; 22 who hath also sealed us, and given the earnest of the Spirit in our hearts.

ὑμῖν [t]ἀλλ᾽[u] ἢ ἃ ἀναγινώσκετε, ἢ καὶ ἐπιγινώσκετε, ἐλπίζω.δὲ
to you but what ye read, or even recognize; and I hope
ὅτι [v]καὶ[u] ἕως τέλους ἐπιγνώσεσθε, 14 καθὼς καὶ ἐπέ-
that even to [the] end ye will recognize, according as also ye did
γνωτε ἡμᾶς ἀπὸ μέρους, ὅτι καύχημα.ὑμῶν ἐσμεν, καθάπερ
recognize us in part, that [3]your [4]boasting [1]we [2]are, even as
καὶ ὑμεῖς ἡμῶν ἐν τῇ ἡμέρᾳ τοῦ κυρίου [w]᾿Ιησοῦ. 15 Καὶ
also ye [are] ours in the day of the Lord Jesus. And
ταύτῃ τῇ πεποιθήσει ἐβουλόμην [x]πρὸς ὑμᾶς ἐλθεῖν πρότερον,[u]
with this confidence I purposed [3]to [4]you [1]to [2]come previously,
ἵνα δευτέραν χάριν [y]ἔχητε·[u] 16 καὶ δι᾽ ὑμῶν [z]διελθεῖν[u]
that a second favour ye might have; and by you to pass through
εἰς Μακεδονίαν, καὶ πάλιν ἀπὸ Μακεδονίας ἐλθεῖν πρὸς ὑμᾶς,
to Macedonia, and again from Macedonia to come to you,
καὶ ὑφ᾽·ὑμῶν προπεμφθῆναι εἰς τὴν Ἰουδαίαν. 17 τοῦτο.οὖν
and by you to be set forward to Judæa. This therefore
[a]βουλευόμενος,[u] μή τι ἄρα τῇ ἐλαφρίᾳ ἐχρησάμην; ἢ ἃ
purposing, [3]indeed [5]lightness [4]did [2]I [1]use? or what
βουλεύομαι, κατὰ σάρκα βουλεύομαι, ἵνα ᾖ παρ᾽
I purpose, according to flesh do I purpose, that there should be with
ἐμοὶ τὸ ναὶ ναί, καὶ τὸ οὒ οὔ; 18 πιστὸς.δὲ ὁ θεός, ὅτι ὁ
me yea yea, and nay nay? Now faithful God [is], that
λόγος.ἡμῶν ὁ πρὸς ὑμᾶς οὐκ [b]ἐγένετο[u] ναὶ καὶ οὔ· 19 ὁ.[c]γὰρ
our word to you [2]not [1]was yea and nay. For the
τοῦ θεοῦ[u] υἱὸς [d]Ἰησοῦς χριστὸς[u] ὁ ἐν ὑμῖν δι᾽ ἡμῶν κη-
[2]of [3]God [1]Son, Jesus Christ, who among you by us was
ρυχθείς, δι᾽ ἐμοῦ καὶ Σιλουανοῦ καὶ Τιμοθέου, οὐκ.ἐγένετο ναὶ
proclaimed, (by me and Silvanus and Timotheus,) was not yea
καὶ οὔ, ἀλλὰ ναὶ ἐν αὐτῷ γέγονεν· 20 ὅσαι.γὰρ ἐπαγγελίαι
and nay, but yea in him has been. For whatever promises
θεοῦ, ἐν αὐτῷ τὸ ναί, [e]καὶ ἐν αὐτῷ[u] τὸ ἀμήν,
of God [there are], in him [is] the yea, and in him the Amen,
τῷ θεῷ πρὸς δόξαν δι᾽ ἡμῶν. 21 ὁ.δὲ βεβαιῶν ἡμᾶς σὺν
[3]to [4]God [1]for [2]glory by us. Now he who confirms us with
ὑμῖν εἰς χριστόν, καὶ χρίσας ἡμᾶς, θεός· 22 ὁ καὶ σφραγι-
you unto Christ, and anointed us, [is] God, who also sealed
σάμενος ἡμᾶς, καὶ δοὺς τὸν [f]ἀρραβῶνα[u] τοῦ πνεύματος ἐν
us, and gave the earnest of the Spirit in
ταῖς.καρδίαις.ἡμῶν.
our hearts.

23 Moreover I call God for a record upon my soul, that to spare you I came not as yet unto Corinth. 24 Not for that we have dominion over your faith, but are helpers of your joy: for by faith ye stand. II. But I determined this with myself, that I would not come again to you in heaviness. 2 For if I make you sorry, who is he then that maketh me glad, but the same

23 Ἐγὼ.δὲ μάρτυρα τὸν θεὸν ἐπικαλοῦμαι ἐπὶ τὴν ἐμὴν
But I [3]as [4]witness [2]God [1]call upon my
ψυχήν, ὅτι φειδόμενος ὑμῶν οὐκέτι ἦλθον εἰς Κόρινθον·
soul, that sparing you not yet did I come to Corinth.
24 οὐχ ὅτι κυριεύομεν ὑμῶν τῆς πίστεως, ἀλλὰ συνεργοί
Not that we rule over your faith, but fellow-workers
ἐσμεν τῆς.χαρᾶς.ὑμῶν, τῇ.γὰρ.πίστει ἑστήκατε. 2 ἔκρινα.δὲ
are of your joy: for by faith ye stand. But I judged
ἐμαυτῷ τοῦτο, τὸ μὴ πάλιν [g]ἐλθεῖν ἐν λύπῃ πρὸς ὑμᾶς.[u]
with myself this, not again to come in grief to you.
2 εἰ.γὰρ ἐγὼ λυπῶ ὑμᾶς, καὶ τίς [h]ἐστιν[u] ὁ εὐφραίνων με, εἰ.μὴ
For if I grieve you, [2]also [1]who is it that gladdens me, except

---

[t] [ἀλλ᾽] L; ἀλλὰ W.　　　[v] — καὶ LTTrA.　　[w] + ἡμῶν (read our Lord) [L]TA.　　[x] πρότερον
πρὸς ὑμᾶς ἐλθεῖν LTTrA; πρό.ἐλθ. πρὸς ὑμᾶς W.　　[y] σχῆτε TTrA.　　[z] ἀπελθεῖν to pass on L.
[a] βουλόμενος LTTrAW.　　[b] ἔστιν is LTTrAW.　　[c] τοῦ θεοῦ γὰρ LTTrAW.　　[d] χριστὸς
᾿Ιησοῦς T.　　[e] διὸ καὶ δι᾽ αὐτοῦ wherefore also through him LTTrAW.　　[f] ἀραβῶνα LT.
[g] ἐν λύπῃ πρὸς ὑμᾶς ἐλθεῖν GLTTrAW.　　[h] — ἐστιν LTTrAW.

ὁ λυπούμενος ἐξ ἐμοῦ; 3 καὶ ἔγραψα ¹ὑμῖν'' τοῦτο αὐτό,
he who is grieved by me?   And I wrote to you this   same,

ἵνα.μὴ ἐλθὼν λύπην ᵏἔχω'' ἀφ' ὧν ἔδει με
lest having come grief I might have from [those] of whom it behoves me

χαίρειν· πεποιθὼς ἐπὶ πάντας ὑμᾶς, ὅτι ἡ.ἐμὴ.χαρὰ
to rejoice; trusting in ²all ¹you, that my joy [²that]

πάντων ὑμῶν ἐστιν. 4 ἐκ.γὰρ πολλῆς θλίψεως καὶ συνοχῆς
³of ⁵all ⁴you ¹is.   For out of much tribulation and distress

καρδίας ἔγραψα ὑμῖν διὰ πολλῶν δακρύων, οὐχ ἵνα λυπη-
of heart I wrote to you through many tears;   not that ye might

θῆτε, ἀλλὰ τὴν ἀγάπην ἵνα γνῶτε ἣν ἔχω περισ-
be grieved, but ²the ³love ¹that ye might know which I have more

σοτέρως εἰς ὑμᾶς. 5 Εἰ.δέ τις λελύπηκεν, οὐκ ἐμὲ
abundantly towards you.   But if anyone has grieved, ²not ¹me

λελύπηκεν, ¹ἀλλ'' ἀπὸ.μέρους, ἵνα μὴ.ἐπιβαρῶ, πάντας
¹he ²has ⁴grieved, but in part, that I may not overcharge) ²all

ὑμᾶς. 6 ἱκανὸν τῷ.τοιούτῳ ἡ.ἐπιτιμία.αὕτη ἡ ὑπὸ τῶν
¹you. Sufficient to such a one [is] this rebuke   which [is] by the

πλειόνων· 7 ὥστε τοὐναντίον ᵐμᾶλλον'' ὑμᾶς χαρίσασθαι
greater part; so that on the contrary rather ye should forgive

καὶ παρακαλέσαι, μήπως τῇ.περισσοτέρᾳ λύπῃ κατα-
and encourage, lest with more abundant grief should be swal-

ποθῇ ὁ.τοιοῦτος. 8 διὸ παρακαλῶ ὑμᾶς κυρῶσαι εἰς
lowed up such a one. Wherefore I exhort you to confirm ²towards

αὐτὸν ἀγάπην. 9 εἰς.τοῦτο.γὰρ καὶ ἔγραψα, ἵνα γνῶ
³him ¹love.   For, for this   also did I write, that I might know

τὴν δοκιμὴν ὑμῶν, εἰ εἰς πάντα ὑπήκοοί ἐστε. 10 ᾧ.δέ
the proof of you, if to everything obedient ye are. But to whom

τι χαρίζεσθε, ⁿκαὶ.ἐγώ·'' καὶ.γὰρ ἐγὼ °εἴ τι κεχάρισ-
anything ye forgive, also I;   for also I if anything I have for-

μαι, ᾧ κεχάρισμαι, δι' ὑμᾶς.ἐν προσώπῳ χριστοῦ,
given, of whom I have forgiven, [is] for sake of you, in [the] person of Christ;

11 ἵνα μὴ.πλεονεκτηθῶμεν ὑπὸ τοῦ σατανᾶ· οὐ.γὰρ αὐτοῦ
that we should not be overreached by   Satan,   for not of his

τὰ νοήματα ἀγνοοῦμεν.
thoughts are we ignorant.

12 Ἐλθὼν.δὲ εἰς τὴν ᵖΤρωάδα'' εἰς τὸ εὐαγγέλιον τοῦ
Now having come to Troas for the glad tidings of the

χριστοῦ, καὶ θύρας μοι ἀνεῳγμένης ἐν κυρίῳ, 13 οὐκ
Christ, also a door to me having been opened in [the] Lord, ²not

ἔσχηκα ἄνεσιν τῷ.πνεύματί.μου τῷ.μὴ.εὑρεῖν.με Τίτον τὸν
¹I had ease in my spirit at my not finding Titus the

ἀδελφόν.μου· ἀλλὰ ἀποταξάμενος αὐτοῖς, ἐξῆλθον εἰς Μακε-
my brother; but having taken leave of them, I went out to Mace-

δονίαν. 14 Τῷ.δὲ.θεῷ χάρις τῷ πάντοτε θριαμβεύοντι
donia. But to God [be] thanks, who always leads in triumph

ἡμᾶς ἐν τῷ χριστῷ, καὶ τὴν ὀσμὴν τῆς γνώσεως αὐτοῦ
us in the Christ, and the odour of the knowledge of him

φανεροῦντι δι' ἡμῶν ἐν παντὶ τόπῳ. 15 ὅτι χριστοῦ
makes manifest through us in every place. For of Christ

εὐωδία ἐσμὲν τῷ θεῷ ἐν τοῖς σωζομένοις καὶ ἐν τοῖς ἀπολ-
a sweet perfume we are to God in those being saved and in those perish-

λυμένοις· 16 οἷς.μὲν, ὀσμὴ ᑫθανάτου εἰς θάνατον· οἷς.δὲ,
ing;   to the ones, an odour of death to death, but to the others,

which is made sorry by me? 3 And I wrote this same unto you, lest, when I came, I should have sorrow from them of whom I ought to rejoice; having confidence in you all, that my joy is the joy of you all. 4 For out of much affliction and anguish of heart I wrote unto you with many tears; not that ye should be grieved, but that ye might know the love which I have more abundantly unto you. 5 But if any have caused grief, he hath not grieved me, but in part: that I may not overcharge you all. 6 Sufficient to such a man is this punishment, which was inflicted of many. 7 So that contrariwise ye ought rather to forgive him, and comfort him, lest perhaps such a one should be swallowed up with overmuch sorrow. 8 Wherefore I beseech you that ye would confirm your love toward him. 9 For to this end also did I write, that I might know the proof of you, whether ye be obedient in all things. 10 To whom ye forgive any thing, I forgive also: for if I forgave any thing, to whom I forgave it, for your sakes forgave I it in the person of Christ; 11 lest Satan should get an advantage of us: for we are not ignorant of his devices.

12 Furthermore, when I came to Troas to preach Christ's gospel, and a door was opened unto me of the Lord, 13 I had no rest in my spirit, because I found not Titus my brother: but taking my leave of them, I went from thence into Macedonia. 14 Now thanks be unto God, which always causeth us to triumph in Christ, and maketh manifest the savour of his knowledge by us in every place. 15 For we are unto God a sweet savour of Christ, in them that are saved, and in them that perish: 16 to the one we

i — ὑμῖν LTTrAW.   ᵏ σχῶ TTrA.   ¹ ἀλλὰ LTTrAW.   ᵐ [μᾶλλον] ᵀᵗA.   ⁿ κἀγὼ
LTTrAW.   ° ὁ κεχάρισμαι, εἴ τι κεχάρισμαι GLTTrAW.   ᵖ Τρῳάδα LT.   ᑫ + ἔκ (read
from death) LTTrA.
3·

are the savour of death unto death ; and to the other the savour of life unto life. And who *is* sufficient for these things ? 17 For we are not as many, which corrupt the word of God : but as of sincerity, but as of God, in the sight of God speak we in Christ.

III. Do we begin again to commend ourselves ? or need we, as some *others*, epistles of commendation to you, or *letters* of commendation from you ? 2 Ye are our epistle written in our hearts, known and read of all men: 3 *for-asmuch as ye are* manifestly declared to be the epistle of Christ ministered by us, written not with ink, but with the Spirit of the living God ; not in tables of stone, but in fleshy tables of the heart. 4 And such trust have we through Christ to God-ward : 5 not that we are sufficient of ourselves to think any thing as of ourselves; but our sufficiency *is* of God ; 6 who also hath made us able ministers of the new testament ; not of the letter, but of the spirit: for the letter killeth, but the spirit giveth life. 7 But if the ministration of death, written *and* engraven in stones, was glorious, so that the children of Israel could not stedfastly behold the face of Moses for the glory of his countenance ; which *glory* was to be done away : 8 how shall not the ministration of the spirit be rather glorious ? 9 For if the ministration of condemnation *be* glory, much more doth the ministration of righteousness exceed in glory. 10 For even that which was made glorious had no glory

ὀσμὴ ᵠ ζωῆς εἰς ζωήν. καὶ πρὸς ˎταῦτα τίς ἱκανός;
an odour of life to life; and for these things who [is] competent?

17 οὐ.γάρ ἐσμεν ὡς οἱ πολλοί, καπηλεύοντες τὸν λόγον
For ³not ¹we ²are as the many, making gain by corrupting the word

τοῦ θεοῦ, ʳἀλλ'ᴵᴵ ὡς ἐξ ˢεἰλικρινείας,ᴵᴵ ἀλλ' ὡς ἐκ θεοῦ, ᵗκατ-
of God, but · as of sincerity, but as of God. be-

ενώπιον ᵘτοῦᴵᴵ θεοῦ, ἐν χριστῷ λαλοῦμεν.
fore God, in Christ we speak.

3 Ἀρχόμεθα πάλιν ἑαυτοὺς ᵛσυνιστάνεινᴵᴵ; ʷεἰᴵᴵ.μὴ χρῄ-
Do we begin again ourselves to commend? unless we

ζομεν, ὥς ˣτινες, ʸσυστατικῶν,ᴵᴵ ἐπιστολῶν πρὸς ὑμᾶς, ἢ ἐξ
need, as some, commendatory epistles to you, or ³from

ὑμῶν ᶻσυστατικῶνᴵᴵ; 2 ἡ.ἐπιστολὴ.ἡμῶν ὑμεῖς ἐστε, ᵃἐγγεγραμ-
⁴you ¹commendatory [²ones]? Our epistle ye are, having been

μένηᴵᴵ ἐν ταῖς.καρδίαις.ἡμῶν, γινωσκομένη καὶ ἀναγινω-
inscribed in our hearts, being known and being

σκομένη ὑπὸ πάντων ἀνθρώπων· 3 φανερούμενοι ὅτι ἐστὲ
read by all men, being manifested that ye are

ἐπιστολὴ χριστοῦ διακονηθεῖσα ὑφ' ἡμῶν, ᵃἐγγεγραμμένηᴵᴵ
²epistle ¹Christ's, ministered by us; having been inscribed,

οὐ μέλανι, ἀλλὰ πνεύματι θεοῦ ζῶντος, οὐκ ἐν πλαξὶν
not with ink, but with [the] Spirit of ²God [¹the] ²living; not on tablets

λιθίναις, ᵇἀλλ'ᴵᴵ ἐν πλαξὶν ᶜκαρδίαςᴵᴵ σαρκίναις. 4 Πεποί-
of stone, but on ²tablets ³of [⁴the] ⁵heart ¹fleshy. ⁷Confi-

θησιν δὲ τοιαύτην ἔχομεν διὰ τοῦ χριστοῦ πρὸς τὸν θεόν·
dence ⁶and such have we through the Christ towards God:

5 οὐχ ὅτι ᵈἱκανοί ἐσμεν ἀφ' ἑαυτῶν λογίσασθαί τι ὡς ἐξ
not that competent we are from ourselves to reckon anything as of

ἑαυτῶν,ᴵᴵ ἀλλ' ἡ.ἱκανότης.ἡμῶν ἐκ τοῦ θεοῦ· 6 ὃς καὶ
ourselves, but our competency [is] of God; who also

ἱκάνωσεν ἡμᾶς διακόνους καινῆς διαθήκης, οὐ γράμ-
made ²competent ¹us [as] servants of a new covenant; not of let-

ματος, ἀλλὰ πνεύματος· τὸ.γὰρ γράμμα ᶠἀποκτείνει,ᴵᴵ τὸ.δὲ
ter, but of Spirit; for the letter kills, but the

πνεῦμα ζωοποιεῖ. 7 Εἰ.δὲ ἡ διακονία τοῦ θανάτου ἐν ᵍγράμ-
Spirit quickens. But if the service of death in let-

μασιν,ᴵᴵ ἐντετυπωμένη ʰἐνᴵᴵ λίθοις, ἐγενήθη ἐν δόξῃ, ὥστε
ters, having been engraven in stones, was produced with glory, so as

μὴ.ὁύνασθαι ἀτενίσαι τοὺς υἱοὺς Ἰσραὴλ εἰς τὸ πρόσω-
⁵not ᶜto ⁷be ᵃable ⁸to ¹⁰look ¹¹intently ¹the ²children ³of ⁴Israel into the face

πον ⁱΜωσέως,ᴵᴵ διὰ τὴν δόξαν τοῦ.προσώπου.αὐτοῦ, τὴν
of Moses, on account of the glory of his face, which

καταργουμένην· 8 πῶς οὐχὶ μᾶλλον ἡ διακονία τοῦ πνεύμα-
is being annulled; how not rather the service of the Spirit

τος ἔσται ἐν δόξῃ; 9 εἰ.γὰρ ᵏἡ διακονίαᴵᴵ τῆς κατακρίσεως
shall be in glory? For if the service of condemnation [be]

δόξα, πολλῷ μᾶλλον περισσεύει ἡ διακονία τῆς δικαιοσύνης
glory, much rather abounds the service of righteousness

ˡἐνᴵᴵ δόξῃ. 10 καὶ.γὰρ ᵐοὐδὲᴵᴵ δεδόξασται τὸ
in glory. For even neither ⁷has ⁸been ⁹made ¹⁰glorious ¹that ²which

---

ᵠ + ἐκ (*read* from life) LTTᵣA.   ʳ ἀλλὰ Tr.   ˢ εἰλικρινίας T.   ᵗ κατέναντι LTTᵣA.
ᵘ — τοῦ LTT·[A].   ᵛ συνιστᾶν LTr.   ʷ ἢ (*read* or need we) GLTTᵣA.   ˣ + [πέρ] L.   ʸ συνσ- Tr.
ᶻ — συστατικῶν LTTᵣAW.   ᵃ ἐν- T.   ᵇ ἀλλὰ EGW.   ᶜ καρδίαις hearts LTTᵣA.   ᵈ ἱκανοί
ἐσμεν λογίζεσθαί (λογίσασθαί AW) τι ἀφ' ἑαυτῶν LAW ; ἀφ' ἑαυτῶν ἱκανοί ἐσμεν λογίσασθαί
τι TTr.   ᵉ αὐτῶν them LTr.   ᶠ ἀποκταίνει L ; ἀποκτέννει TTᵣA.   ᵍ γράμματι writing LTᵣA.
ʰ — ἐν (*read* λίθοις on stones) LTT·AW.   ⁱ Μωϋσέως GLTT·AW.   ᵏ τῇ διακονίᾳ with the
service LTTr.   ˡ — ἐν (*read* δόξῃ in glory) LTTᵣA.   ᵐ οὐ not GLTTᵣAW.

δεδοξασμένον   ἐν τούτῳ τῷ μέρει.   ⁿἕνεκεν⁽¹⁾ τῆς ὑπερ-
ⁿhas ¹been ⁵made ⁶glorious in   this   respect, on account of the   sur-

βαλλούσης δόξης.   11 εἰ.γὰρ   τὸ   καταργούμενον   διὰ
passing   glory.   For if that which is being annulled [was] through

δόξης, πολλῷ μᾶλλον   τὸ   μένον   ἐν δόξῃ.   12 Ἔχοντες
glory,   much   rather   that which remains [is] in glory.   Having

οὖν   τοιαύτην ἐλπίδα, πολλῇ παῤῥησίᾳ χρώμεθα·   13 καὶ
therefore   such   hope,   much   boldness   we use: and

οὐ καθάπερ ᵒΜωσῆς⁽²⁾ ἐτίθει κάλυμμα ἐπὶ τὸ πρόσωπον ᴾἑαυ-
not according as   Moses   put   a veil   on the   face   of him-

τοῦ,⁽²⁾ πρὸς.τὸ μὴ   ἀτενίσαι   τοὺς υἱοὺς Ἰσραὴλ εἰς τὸ τέλος
self,   for   ⁵not ⁶to ⁷look ⁸intently ¹the   ²sons   ³of ⁴Israel to the end

τοῦ καταργουμένου·   14 ᑫἀλλ'⁽²⁾ ἐπωρώθη τὰ.νοήματα.αὐτῶν.
of that   being annulled.   But   were hardened   their thoughts,

ἄχρι.γὰρ τῆς σήμερον ʳτὸ αὐτὸ κάλυμμα ἐπὶ τῇ ἀναγνώσει
for unto   the   present the same   veil   at the   reading

τῆς παλαιᾶς διαθήκης μένει, μὴ ἀνακαλυπτόμενον, ˢὅ τι⁽¹⁾
of the   old   covenant   remains, not   uncovered,   which

ἐν χριστῷ καταργεῖται·   15 ἀλλ' ἕως σήμερον, ἡνίκα ᵗἀνα-
in Christ   is being annulled.   But   unto this day,   when   is

γινώσκεται⁽¹⁾ ᵒΜωσῆς,⁽²⁾ κάλυμμα ἐπὶ τὴν.καρδίαν.αὐτῶν κεῖται·
read   Moses,   a veil   upon   their heart   lies.

16 ἡνίκα.ᵛδ' ἂν⁽²⁾ ἐπιστρέψῃ   πρὸς   κύριον, περιαιρεῖται τὸ
But when   it shall have turned   to [the] Lord,   is taken away the

κάλυμμα.   17 Ὁ.δὲ κύριος τὸ πνεῦμά ἐστιν· οὗ.δὲ τὸ πνεῦμα
veil.   Now the Lord   the Spirit   is; and where the Spirit

κυρίου,   ʷἐκεῖ⁽¹⁾ ἐλευθερία.   18 ἡμεῖς.δὲ πάντες ἀνακεκα-
of [the] Lord [is], there [is]   freedom.   But we   all   with un-

λυμμένῳ προσώπῳ τὴν δόξαν κυρίου   κατοπτριζόμενοι,
covered   face   the   glory of [the] Lord beholding as in a mirror, [to]

τὴν αὐτὴν εἰκόνα μεταμορφούμεθα ἀπὸ δόξης εἰς δόξαν,
the   same   image   are being transformed   from glory to glory,

καθάπερ ἀπὸ   κυρίου   πνεύματος.
even as   from [the] Lord   [the]   Spirit.

4 Διὰ.τοῦτο ἔχοντες τὴν.διακονίαν.ταύτην, καθὼς ἠλεή-
Therefore,   having   this service,   according as we re-

θημεν,   οὐκ.ˣἐκκακοῦμεν·⁽¹⁾ 2 ʸἀλλ'⁽¹⁾ ἀπειπάμεθα τὰ κρυπτὰ
ceived mercy,   we faint not.   But   we renounced the hidden things

τῆς αἰσχύνης, μὴ περιπατοῦντες ἐν πανουργίᾳ μηδὲ δολοῦν-
of shame,   not   walking   in   craftiness,   nor   falsify-

τες τὸν λόγον τοῦ θεοῦ, ἀλλὰ τῇ φανερώσει τῆς ἀληθείας
ing the   word   of God,   but   by manifestation of the   truth

ᶻσυνιστῶντες⁽¹⁾ ἑαυτοὺς πρὸς πᾶσαν συνείδησιν ἀνθρώπων
commending   ourselves   to   every   conscience   of men

ἐνώπιον τοῦ θεοῦ.   3 Εἰ.δὲ καὶ ἔστιν κεκαλυμμένον τὸ εὐαγ-
before   God.   But if also   is   covered   ²glad

γέλιον ἡμῶν, ἐν τοῖς ἀπολλυμένοις ἐστὶν κεκαλυμμένον·   4 ἐν
¹tidings ⁰our,   in those   perishing   it is   covered;   in

οἷς ὁ θεὸς τοῦ.αἰῶνος.τούτου ἐτύφλωσεν τὰ νοήματα τῶν
whom the god   of this age   blinded   the thoughts of the

ἀπίστων, εἰς.τὸ μὴ   αὐγάσαι ᵃαὐτοῖς⁽¹⁾ τὸν φωτισμὸν τοῦ
unbelieving,   so as   not to beam forth to them   the   radiancy of the

In this respect, by rea-
son of the glory that
excelleth. 11 For if
that which is done a-
way *was* glorious,
much more that which
remaineth *is* glorious.
12 Seeing then that we
have such hope, we
use great plainness of
speech : 13 and not as
Moses, *which* put a vail
over his face, that
the children of Israel
could not stedfastly
look to the end of that
which is abolished :
14 but their minds
were blinded : for un-
til this day remaineth
the same vail untaken
away in the reading
of the old testament ;
which *vail* is done a-
way in Christ. 15 But
even unto this day,
when Moses is read,
the vail is upon their
heart. 16 Nevertheless
when it shall turn to
the Lord, the vail shall
be taken away. 17 Now
the Lord is that Spirit:
and where the Spirit of
the Lord *is*, there *is*
liberty. 18 But we all,
with open face behold-
ing as in a glass the
glory of the Lord, are
changed into the same
image from glory to
glory, *even* as by the
Spirit of the Lord.

IV. Therefore see-
ing we have this min-
istry, as we have re-
ceived mercy, we faint
not ; 2 but have re-
nounced the hidden
things of dishonesty,
not walking in crafti-
ness, nor handling the
word of God deceit-
fully ; but by mani-
festation of the truth
commending ourselves
to every man's con-
science in the sight of
God. 3 But if our gos-
pel be hid, it is hid to
them that are lost : 4 in
whom the god of this
world hath blinded the
minds of them which
believe not, le-t the
light of the glorious
gospel of Christ, who
is the image of
God, should shine

ⁿ εἵνεκεν LTTrA.   ᵒ Μωϋσῆς GLTTrAW.   ᴾ αὐτοῦ (read his face) LTrAW.   ᑫ ἀλλὰ Tr.
ʳ + ἡμέρας day LTTrAW.   ˢ ὅτι that [it] GLTTrAW.   ᵗ ἂν ἀναγινώσκηται may be read LTTrA.
ᵛ δὲ ἂν Tr ; δὲ ἐὰν T.   ʷ — ἐκεῖ LTTrAW.   ˣ ἐγκ- LTTrAW.   ʸ ἀλλὰ LTTrA.   ᶻ συνιστανтες
LTTrAW.   ᵃ — αὐτοῖς GLTTrAW.

unto them. 5 For we preach not ourselves, but Christ Jesus the Lord; and ourselves your servants for Jesus' sake. 6 For God, who commanded the light to shine out of darkness, hath shined in our hearts, to *give* the light of the knowledge of the glory of God in the face of Jesus Christ. 7 But we have this treasure in earthen vessels, that the excellency of the power may be of God, and not of us. 8 *We are* troubled on every side, yet not distressed ; *we are* perplexed, but not in despair ; 9 persecuted, but not forsaken; cast down, but not destroyed ; 10 always bearing about in the body the dying of the Lord Jesus, that the life also of Jesus might be made manifest in our body. 11 For we which live are alway delivered unto death for Jesus' sake, that the life also of Jesus might be made manifest in our mortal flesh. 12 So then death worketh in us, but life in you. 13 We having the same spirit of faith, according as it is written, I believed, and therefore have I spoken; we also believe, and therefore speak; 14 knowing that he which raised up the Lord Jesus shall raise up us also by Jesus, and shall present *us* with you. 15 For all things *are* for your sakes, that the abundant grace might through the thanksgiving of many redound to the glory of God.

16 For which cause we faint not; but though our outward man perish, yet the inward *man* is renewed day by day. 17 For

εὐαγγελίου ᶜτῆς‖ δόξης τοῦ χριστοῦ, ὅς ἐστιν εἰκὼν τοῦ
glad tidings   of the   glory   of the Christ,   who is [the] image

θεοῦ. 5 οὐ γὰρ ἑαυτοὺς κηρύσσομεν, ἀλλὰ ᵈχριστὸν Ἰη-
of God.   For not ourselves do we proclaim, but   Christ   Je-

σοῦν‖ κύριον· ἑαυτοὺς δὲ δούλους ὑμῶν διὰ Ἰησοῦν.
sus   Lord, and ourselves   your bondmen for the sake of Jesus.

6 ὅτι   ὁ θεὸς ὁ εἰπὼν ἐκ σκότους φῶς ᵉλάμψαι,‖ ὅς
Because [it is] God who spoke out of darkness light to shine, who

ἔλαμψεν ἐν ταῖς καρδίαις ἡμῶν, πρὸς   φωτισμὸν τῆς γνώ-
shone   in   our hearts,   for [the] radiancy of the know-

σεως τῆς δόξης ᶠτοῦ θεοῦ‖ ἐν   ·προσώπῳ ᵍἸησοῦ‖ χριστοῦ.
ledge of the glory of God in [the]   face   of Jesus   Christ.

7 Ἔχομεν δὲ τὸν θησαυρὸν τοῦτον ἐν ὀστρακίνοις σκεύεσιν,
But we have   this treasure   in   earthen   vessels,

ἵνα ἡ ὑπερβολὴ τῆς δυνάμεως ᾖ τοῦ θεοῦ, καὶ μὴ ἐξ
that the surpassingness of the power may be of God, and not from

ἡμῶν· 8 ἐν παντὶ   θλιβόμενοι, ἀλλ' οὐ στενοχωρούμενοι·
us :   in every [way] oppressed, but not   straitened ;

ἀπορούμενοι, ἀλλ' οὐκ ἐξαπορούμενοι· 9 διωκόμενοι, ἀλλ' οὐκ
perplexed,   but not utterly at a loss; persecuted, but not

ἐγκαταλειπόμενοι· καταβαλλόμενοι, ἀλλ' οὐκ ἀπολλύμενοι·
forsaken;   cast down,   but not   destroyed;

10 πάντοτε τὴν νέκρωσιν τοῦ ʰκυρίου‖ Ἰησοῦ ἐν τῷ σώματι
always   the dying   of the Lord   Jesus in the body

περιφέροντες, ἵνα καὶ ἡ ζωὴ τοῦ Ἰησοῦ ἐν ⁱτῷ σώματι‖ ἡμῶν
bearing about, that also the life   of Jesus in ᵏbody ¹our

φανερωθῇ. 11 ἀεὶ γὰρ ἡμεῖς οἱ ζῶντες εἰς θάνατον παρα-
may be manifested ; for always we who live   to death   are de-

διδόμεθα διὰ   Ἰησοῦν, ἵνα καὶ ἡ ζωὴ τοῦ Ἰησοῦ φανε-
livered   on account of Jesus, that also the life of Jesus may be

ρωθῇ ἐν τῇ θνητῇ σαρκὶ ἡμῶν. 12 Ὥστε ὁ ᵏμὲν‖ θάνατος
manifested in ²mortal ³flesh ¹our ;   so that   death

ἐν ἡμῖν ἐνεργεῖται, ἡ δὲ ζωὴ ἐν ὑμῖν· 13 ἔχοντες δὲ τὸ αὐτὸ
in us works,   and life in you.   And having the same

πνεῦμα τῆς πίστεως, κατὰ   τὸ γεγραμμένον, Ἐπίστευσα,
spirit   of faith, according to what has been written, I believed,

διὸ ¹ἐλάλησα, καὶ ἡμεῖς πιστεύομεν, διὸ καὶ λαλοῦμεν·
therefore I spoke ; ²also ¹we   believe,   therefore also we speak ;

14 εἰδότες ὅτι ὁ ἐγείρας τὸν ᵐκύριον‖ Ἰησοῦν, καὶ ἡμᾶς
knowing that he who raised up the Lord   Jesus, also us

ⁿδιὰ‖ Ἰησοῦ ἐγερεῖ, καὶ παραστήσει σὺν ὑμῖν. 15 τὰ
through Jesus will raise up, and will present. with you.

γὰρ πάντα   δι' ὑμᾶς, ἵνα ἡ χάρις πλεονάσασα
For all things [are] for the sake of you, that the grace   abounding

διὰ τῶν πλειόνων τὴν εὐχαριστίαν περισσεύσῃ εἰς τὴν
through the   most,   ³thanksgiving ¹may ²cause to exceed to the

δόξαν τοῦ θεοῦ.
glory of God.

16 Διὸ οὐκ ᵒἐκκακοῦμεν·‖ ἀλλ' εἰ καὶ ὁ ἔξω ἡμῶν ἄν-
Wherefore we faint not;   but if indeed ²outward ¹our

θρωπος   διαφθείρεται,   ἀλλ' ὁ ᴾἔσωθεν‖ ἀνακαινοῦται
man   is being brought to decay, yet the inward   is being renewed

---

ᶜ τὸν the ᴇ. ᵈ Ἰησοῦν χριστὸν L. ᵉ λάμψει shall shine LTTrA. ᶠ αὐτοῦ (*read*
his glory) L. ᵍ - Ἰησοῦ LTTrA. ʰ - κυρίου GLTTrAW. ⁱ τοῖς σώμασιν bodies ᴛ.
ᵏ - μὲν GLTTrAW. ¹ + καὶ also ᴛ. ᵐ [κύριον] TrA. ⁿ σὺν with LTTrAW. ᵒ ἐγκ-
ᴌᴛᴛʳᴀᴡ. ᴾ ἔσω ἡμῶν (*read* our inward [man]) LTTr ; ἔσω[θεν] ἡμῶν A.

ἡμέρα.καὶ.ἡμέρᾳ. 17 τὸ.γὰρ παραυτίκα ἐλαφρὸν τῆς θλίψεως
day by day.   For the momentary lightness of ²tribulation

ἡμῶν καθ'.ὑπερβολὴν.εἰς.ὑπερβολὴν αἰώνιον βάρος δόξης
¹our   ⁴excessively ⁵surpassing   ³an eternal weight of glory

κατεργάζεται ἡμῖν, 18 μὴ σκοπούντων ἡμῶν τὰ βλεπό-
works out   for us ; ²not ³considering ¹we the things seen,

μενα, ἀλλὰ τὰ μὴ βλεπόμενα· τὰ.γὰρ βλεπόμενα
but the things not   seen ; for the things seen   [are]

πρόσκαιρα· ⸆ τὰ.δὲ μὴ βλεπόμενα αἰώνια. 5 οἴδαμεν.γὰρ
temporary, but the things not seen   eternal.   For we know

ὅτι ἐὰν ἡ ἐπίγειος ἡμῶν οἰκία τοῦ σκήνους καταλυθῇ, οἰκο-
that ¹if ²earthly ¹our house of the tabernacle ¸be destroyed, a build-

δομὴν ἐκ θεοῦ ἔχομεν, οἰκίαν ἀχειροποίητον, αἰώνιον ἐν τοῖς
ing from God we have, a house not made with hands, eternal in the

οὐρανοῖς. 2 καὶ.γὰρ ἐν τούτῳ στενάζομεν, τὸ.οἰκητήριον.ἡμῶν
heavens.   For indeed in this we groan, our dwelling

τὸ ἐξ οὐρανοῦ ἐπενδύσασθαι ἐπιποθοῦντες· 3 ᵠεἴγε‖
which [is] from heaven ²to ³be ⁴clothed ⁵with ¹longing ;   if indeed

καὶ ἐνδυσάμενοι, οὐ γυμνοὶ εὑρεθησόμεθα. 4 καὶ.γὰρ οἱ
also being clothed, not naked we shall be found.   For indeed ²who

ὄντες ἐν τῷ σκήνει στενάζομεν βαρούμενοι· ʳἐπειδὴ‖ οὐ
¹are in ⁵the ⁶tabernacle ⁴we groan being burdened; since ²not

θέλομεν ἐκδύσασθαι, ˢἀλλ'ᵗ ἐπενδύσασθαι, ἵνα καταπωθῇ
⁴we ³do wish to be unclothed, but to be clothed upon, that may be swallowed up

τὸ θνητὸν ὑπὸ τῆς ζωῆς. 5 ὁ.δὲ κατεργασάμενος ἡμᾶς εἰς
the mortal by   life. Now he who wrought out   us for

αὐτὸ.τοῦτο θεός, ὁ ᵗκαὶ‖ δοὺς ἡμῖν τὸν ᵛἀῤῥαβῶνα‖ τοῦ
this same thing [is] God, who also gave to us the   earnest   of the

πνεύματος. 6 θαῤῥοῦντες οὖν πάντοτε, καὶ εἰδότες ὅτι
Spirit.   Being ²confident ³therefore ¹always, and knowing that

ἐνδημοῦντες ἐν τῷ σώματι ἐκδημοῦμεν ἀπὸ τοῦ κυρίου·
being at home in the body we are from home away from the Lord,·

7 διὰ.πίστεως.γὰρ περιπατοῦμεν, οὐ διὰ εἴδους· 8 θαῤῥοῦμεν δέ,
(for by faith we walk,   not by sight ;) we are confident,

καὶ εὐδοκοῦμεν μᾶλλον ἐκδημῆσαι ἐκ τοῦ σώματος καὶ
and are pleased rather to be from home out of the body   and

ἐνδημῆσαι πρὸς τὸν κύριον. 9 Διὸ καὶ φιλοτιμούμεθα,
to be at home with the Lord.   Wherefore also we are ambitious,

εἴτε ἐνδημοῦντες εἴτε ἐκδημοῦντες, εὐάρεστοι αὐτῷ εἶναι.
whether being at home or being from home, well-pleasing to him to be.

10 τοὺς.γὰρ.πάντας ἡμᾶς φανερωθῆναι δεῖ ἔμπροσθεν τοῦ
For ²all   ¹we ⁴be ⁵manifested ³must before   the

βήματος τοῦ χριστοῦ, ἵνα κομίσηται ἕκαστος τὰ
judgment seat of the Christ, that ²may ³receive ¹each the things [done]

διὰ τοῦ σώματος, πρὸς ἃ ἔπραξεν, εἴτε ἀγαθὸν εἴτε
in the body, according to what he did, whether good or

ʷκακόν.‖ 11 Εἰδότες οὖν τὸν φόβον τοῦ κυρίου, ἀνθρώπους
evil.   Knowing therefore the terror of the Lord, ²men

πείθομεν, θεῷ.δὲ πεφανερώμεθα· ἐλπίζω.δὲ καὶ ἐν ταῖς
¹we ²persuade, but to God we have been manifested, and I hope also in

συνειδήσεσιν.ὑμῶν πεφανερῶσθαι. 12 οὐ.ˣγὰρ‖ πάλιν ἑαυτοὺς
your consciences to have been manifested. For not again ourselves

συνιστάνομεν ὑμῖν, ἀλλὰ ἀφορμὴν διδόντες ὑμῖν καυχήματος
do we commend to you, but occasion are giving to you of boasting

our light affliction,
which is but for a
moment, worketh for
us a far more exceed-
ing and eternal weight
of glory; 18 while we
look not at the things
which are seen, but at
the things which are
not seen: for the things
which are seen are
temporal ; but the
things which are not
seen are eternal.
V. For we know that
if our earthly house
of this tabernacle
were dissolved, we
have a building of
God, an house not
made with hands, e-
ternal in the heavens.
2 For in this we groan,
earnestly desiring to
be clothed upon with
our house which is
from heaven : 3 if so
be that being clothed
we shall not be found
naked. 4 For we that
are in this tabernacle
do groan, being bur-
dened : not for that we
would be unclothed,
but clothed upon, that
mortality might be
swallowed up of life.
5 Now he that hath
wrought us for the
selfsame thing is
God, who also hath
given unto us the
earnest of the Spirit.
6 Therefore we are al-
ways confident, know-
ing that, whilst we
are at home in the bo-
dy, we are absent from
the Lord : 7 (for we
walk by faith, not by
sight :) 8 we are con-
fident, I say, and will-
ing rather to be absent
from the body, and to
be present with the
Lord. 9 Wherefore we
labour, that, whether
present or absent, we
may be accepted of
him. 10 For we must
all appear before the
judgment seat of
Christ ; that every
one may receive the
things done in his bo-
dy, according to that
he hath done, whether
it be good or bad.
11 Knowing therefore
the terror of the Lord,
we persuade men ; but
we are made manifest
unto God ; and I trust
also are made mani-
fest in your con-
sciences. 12 For not ourselves
commend not our-
selves again unto you,

but give you occasion to glory on our behalf, that ye may have somewhat to *answer* them which glory in appearance, and not in heart. 13 For whether we be beside ourselves, *it is* to God: or whether we be sober, *it is* for your cause. 14 For the love of Christ constraineth us; because we thus judge, that if one died for all, then were all dead: 15 and *that* he died for all, that they which live should not henceforth live unto themselves, but unto him which died for them, and rose again. 16 Wherefore henceforth know we no man after the flesh: yea, though we have known Christ after the flesh, yet now henceforth know we *him* no more. 17 Therefore if any man *be* in Christ, *he is* a new creature: old things are passed away; behold, all things are become new. 18 And all things *are* of God, who hath reconciled us to himself by Jesus Christ, and hath given to us the ministry of reconciliation; 19 to wit, that God was in Christ, reconciling the world unto himself, not imputing their trespasses unto them; and hath committed unto us the word of reconciliation. 20 Now then we are ambassadors for Christ, as though God did beseech *you* by us: we pray *you* in Christ's stead, be ye reconciled to God. 21 For he hath made him *to be* sin for us, who knew no sin; that we might be made the righteousness of God in him.

VI. We then, *as workers together with him*, beseech *you* also that ye receive not the grace of God in vain. 2 (For he saith, I have heard thee in a time accepted, and in the day of salvation have I succoured thee: behold, now *is* the accepted time; behold, now *is* the day of salvation.) 3 Giving no offence in anything, that the ministry be

ὑπὲρ ἡμῶν, ἵνα ἔχητε   πρὸς τοὺς ἐν προσωπίῳ
in behalf of us,   that ye may have [such] towards those ˤin ³appearance
καυχωμένους καὶ ʸοὐ‖ καρδίᾳ. 13 εἴτε γὰρ   ἐξέστημεν,
¹boasting   and not in heart.   For whether we were beside ourselves,
θεῷ· εἴτε σωφρονοῦμεν,   ὑμῖν. 14 ἡ γὰρ ἀγάπη
[it was] to God;   or   are sober-minded [it is] for you.   For the love
τοῦ χριστοῦ συνέχει ἡμᾶς, κρίναντας τοῦτο, ὅτι ²εἰ‖ εἷς ὑπὲρ
of the Christ constrains us,   having judged this,   that if one ²for
πάντων ἀπέθανεν, ἄρα οἱ πάντες ἀπέθανον· 15 καὶ ὑπὲρ
³all   ¹died,   then   all   died;   and for
πάντων ἀπέθανεν, ἵνα οἱ. ζῶντες μηκέτι ἑαυτοῖς ζῶ-
all   he died,   that they who live no longer to themselves should
σιν, ἀλλὰ τῷ ὑπὲρ αὐτῶν ἀποθανόντι καὶ ἐγερθέντι.
live, but to him who for them died   and was raised again.
16 ὥστε ἡμεῖς ἀπὸ τοῦ νῦν οὐδένα οἴδαμεν κατὰ σάρκα·
So that we from now no one know according to flesh;
εἰ ᵃδὲ‖ καὶ ἐγνώκαμεν κατὰ σάρκα χριστόν, ἀλλὰ νῦν
but if even we have known according to flesh Christ, yet now
οὐκέτι γινώσκομεν 17 ὥστε εἴ τις ἐν χριστῷ,
no longer we know [him]. So that if anyone [be] in Christ [there is]
καινὴ κτίσις· τὰ ἀρχαῖα παρῆλθεν, ἰδοὺ γέγονεν καινὰ
a new creation: the old things passed away; lo, have become new
ᵇτὰ πάντα.‖ 18 τὰ δὲ πάντα   ἐκ τοῦ θεοῦ, τοῦ καταλλάξαν-
all things: and all things [are] of God, who reconciled
τος ἡμᾶς ἑαυτῷ διὰ ᶜἸησοῦ‖ χριστοῦ, καὶ δόντος ἡμῖν τὴν
us to himself by Jesus Christ, and gave to us the
διακονίαν τῆς καταλλαγῆς· 19 ὡς ὅτι θεὸς ἦν ἐν χριστῷ
service of reconciliation: how that God was in Christ [the]
κόσμον καταλλάσσων ἑαυτῷ, μὴ λογιζόμενος αὐτοῖς τὰ
world reconciling to himself, not reckoning to them
παραπτώματα αὐτῶν, καὶ θέμενος ἐν ἡμῖν τὸν λόγον τῆς
their offences, and having put in us the word of
καταλλαγῆς. 20 ὑπὲρ χριστοῦ οὖν πρεσβεύομεν, ὡς
reconciliation. For Christ therefore we are ambassadors, as it were
τοῦ θεοῦ παρακαλοῦντος δι᾽ ἡμῶν· δεόμεθα ὑπὲρ χριστοῦ,
God exhorting by us, we beseech for Christ,
καταλλάγητε τῷ θεῷ· 21 τὸν ᵈγὰρ‖ μὴ γνόντα ἁμαρτίαν
Be reconciled to God. For him who knew not sin
ὑπὲρ ἡμῶν ἁμαρτίαν ἐποίησεν, ἵνα ἡμεῖς ᵉγινώμεθα‖ δι-
⁴for ᵘus ³sin ¹he ²made, that we might become right-
καιοσύνη θεοῦ ἐν αὐτῷ.
eousness of God in him.

6 Συνεργοῦντες δὲ καὶ παρακαλοῦμεν μὴ εἰς κενὸν τὴν
But working together ²also ¹we exhort ²not ³in ⁴vain ⁵the
χάριν τοῦ θεοῦ δέξασθαι ὑμᾶς· 2 λέγει γάρ, Καιρῷ δεκτῷ
⁶grace ⁷of ⁸God ⁹to ¹⁰receive ¹you: (for he says, In a time accepted
ἐπήκουσά σου, καὶ ἐν ἡμέρα σωτηρίας ἐβοήθησά σοι· ἰδοὺ νῦν
I listened to thee, and in a day of salvation I helped thee: lo, now
καιρὸς εὐπρόσδεκτος, ἰδοὺ νῦν ἡμέρα σωτηρίας· 3 μηδεμίαν
[the] time well-accepted; behold, now [the] day of salvation:) not one
ἐν μηδενὶ διδόντες προσκοπήν, ἵνα μὴ μωμηθῇ ἡ διακονία·
³in ⁴anything ²giving ¹offence, that be not blamed the service;
           (*lit.* nothing)
4 ἀλλ᾽ ἐν παντὶ ᶠσυνιστῶντες‖ ἑαυτοὺς ὡς θεοῦ διάκονοι,
but in everything commending ourselves as God's servants,

ʸ μὴ ἐν LTTr.   ᶻ — εἰ LTTrAW.   ᵃ — δὲ but LTTrA.   ᵇ — τὰ πάντα LTTrA.   ᶜ — Ἰησοῦ LTTrAW.   ᵈ — γὰρ for LTTrAW.   ᵉ γεινώμεθα LTTrAW.   ᶠ συνιστάντες LTTrAW.

ἐν ὑπομονῇ πολλῇ, ἐν θλίψεσιν, ἐν ἀνάγκαις, ἐν στενο-
in ²endurance ¹much, in tribulations, in necessities, in straits,

χωρίαις, 5 ἐν πληγαῖς, ἐν φυλακαῖς, ἐν ἀκαταστασίαις, ἐν
in stripes, in imprisonments, in commotions, in

κόποις, ἐν ἀγρυπνίαις, ἐν νηστείαις, 6 ἐν ἁγνότητι, ἐν γνώσει,
labours, in watchings, in fastings, in pureness, in knowledge,

ἐν μακροθυμίᾳ, ἐν χρηστότητι, ἐν πνεύματι ἁγίῳ, ἐν ἀγάπῃ
in long-suffering, in kindness, in [the] ²Spirit ¹Holy, in love

ἀνυποκρίτῳ, 7 ἐν λόγῳ ἀληθείας, ἐν δυνάμει θεοῦ,
unfeigned, in [the] word of truth, in [the] power of God;

διὰ τῶν ὅπλων τῆς δικαιοσύνης τῶν δεξιῶν καὶ ἀριστερῶν,
through the arms of righteousness on the right hand and left,

8 διὰ δόξης καὶ ἀτιμίας, διὰ δυσφημίας καὶ εὐφημίας· ὡς
through glory and dishonour, through evil report and good report: as

πλάνοι, καὶ ἀληθεῖς· 9 ὡς ἀγνοούμενοι, καὶ ἐπιγινωσκόμενοι·
deceivers, and true; as being unknown, and well-known;

ὡς ἀποθνήσκοντες, καὶ ἰδοὺ ζῶμεν· ὡς παιδευόμενοι, καὶ
as dying, and lo we live; as disciplined, and

μὴ θανατούμενοι· 10 ὡς λυπούμενοι, ἀεὶ δὲ χαίροντες· ὡς
not put to death; as sorrowful, but always rejoicing; as

πτωχοί, πολλοὺς δὲ πλουτίζοντες· ὡς μηδὲν ἔχοντες, καὶ
poor, but many enriching; as nothing having, and

πάντα κατέχοντες.
all things possessing.

11 Τὸ στόμα ἡμῶν ἀνέῳγεν πρὸς ὑμᾶς, Κορίνθιοι, ἡ
Our mouth has been opened to you, Corinthians, the

καρδία ἡμῶν πεπλάτυνται 12 οὐ στενοχωρεῖσθε ἐν ἡμῖν,
our heart has been expanded. Ye are not straitened in us,

στενοχωρεῖσθε δὲ ἐν τοῖς σπλάγχνοις ὑμῶν. 13 τὴν δὲ αὐτὴν
but ye are straitened in your bowels; but the same

ἀντιμισθίαν, ὡς τέκνοις λέγω, πλατύνθητε καὶ ὑμεῖς.
[as] recompense, (as to children I speak,) be expanded also ye.

14 Μὴ γίνεσθε ἑτεροζυγοῦντες ἀπίστοις· τίς γὰρ με-
Be not diversely yoked with unbelievers; for what par-

τοχη δικαιοσύνῃ καὶ ἀνομίᾳ; ʰτίς δὲ ᵏ κοινωνία φωτὶ
ticipation [has] righteousness and lawlessness? and what fellowship light

πρὸς σκότος; 15 τίς δὲ συμφώνησις ⁱχριστῷ ᵏ πρὸς ᵏΒελίαρ;
with darkness? and what concord Christ with Beliar,

ἢ τίς μερὶς πιστῷ μετὰ ἀπίστου; 16 τίς δὲ ˡσυγκατά-
or what part to a believer with an unbeliever? and what agree-

θεσις ᵏ ναῷ θεοῦ μετὰ εἰδώλων; ᵐὑμεῖς ᵏ γὰρ ναὸς θεοῦ
ment a temple of God with idols? ²ye ¹for a temple of ³God

ⁿἐστε ᵏ ζῶντος, καθὼς εἶπεν ὁ θεός, Ὅτι ἐνοικήσω ἐν
⁴are [¹the] ²living, according as ²said ¹God, I will dwell among

αὐτοῖς, καὶ ᵒἐμπεριπατήσω· ᵏ καὶ ἔσομαι αὐτῶν θεός, καὶ
them, and walk among [them]; and I will be their God, and

αὐτοὶ ἔσονταί ᴾμοι ᵏ λαός. 17 διὸ ᑫἐξέλθετε ᵏ ἐκ μέσου
they shall be to me a people. Wherefore come out from the midst

αὐτῶν καὶ ἀφορίσθητε, λέγει κύριος, καὶ ἀκαθάρτου
of them and be separated, says [the] Lord, and [the] unclean

μὴ ἅπτεσθε· κἀγὼ εἰσδέξομαι ὑμᾶς, 18 καὶ ἔσομαι ὑμῖν εἰς
touch not. and I will receive you; and I will be to you for

πατέρα, καὶ ὑμεῖς ἔσεσθέ μοι εἰς υἱοὺς καὶ θυγατέρας, λέγει
a father, and ye shall be to me for sons and daughters, says

not blamed : 4 but in all *things* approving ourselves as the ministers of God, in much patience, in afflictions, in necessities, in distresses, 5 in stripes, in imprisonments, in tumults, in labours, in watchings, in fastings ; 6 by pureness, by knowledge, by long-suffering, by kindness, by the Holy Ghost, by love unfeigned, 7 by the word of truth, by the power of God, by the armour of righteousness on the right hand and on the left, 8 by honour and dishonour, by evil report and good report : as deceivers, and *yet* true ; 9 as unknown, and *yet* well known ; as dying, and, behold, we live ; as chastened, and not killed ; 10 as sorrowful, yet alway rejoicing ; as poor, yet making many rich ; as having nothing, and *yet* possessing all things.

11 O *ye* Corinthians, our mouth is open unto you, our heart is enlarged. 12 Ye are not straitened in us, but ye are straitened in your own bowels. 13 Now for a recompence in the same, (I speak as unto *my* children,) be ye also enlarged.

14 Be ye not unequally yoked together with unbelievers : for what fellowship hath righteousness with unrighteousness ? and what communion hath light with darkness ? 15 and what concord hath Christ with Belial ? or what part hath he that believeth with an infidel ? 16 And what agreement hath the temple of God with idols ? for ye are the temple of the living God ; as God hath said, I will dwell in them, and walk in *them* ; and I will be their God, and they shall be my people. 17 Wherefore come out from among them, and be ye separate, saith the Lord, and touch not the unclean *thing* ; and I will receive you, 18 and will be a

ʰ ἢ τίς or what LTTrAw. ⁱ χριστοῦ of Christ LTTrA. ᵏ Βελίαλ Belial EL. ˡ συν- Ͳ ᵐ ἡμεῖς we LTTr. ⁿ ἐσμὲν LTTr. ᵒ ἐν- T. ᴾ μου of me LTTr. ᑫ ἐξέλθατε LTTrA.

Father unto you, and ye shall be my sons and daughters, saith the Lord Almighty. VII. Having therefore these promises, dearly beloved, let us cleanse ourselves from all filthiness of the flesh and spirit, perfecting holiness in the fear of God.

2 Receive us; we have wronged no man, we have corrupted no man, we have defrauded no man. 3 I speak not *this* to condemn *you*: for I have said before, that ye are in our hearts to die and live with *you*. 4 Great *is* my boldness of speech toward you, great *is* my glorying of you : I am filled with comfort, I am exceeding joyful in all our tribulation. 5 For, when we were come into Macedonia, our flesh had no rest, but we were troubled on every side; without *were* fightings, within *were* fears. 6 Nevertheless God, that comforteth those that are cast down, comforted us by the coming of Titus ; 7 and not by his coming only, but by the consolation wherewith he was comforted in you, when he told us your earnest desire, your mourning, your fervent mind toward me ; so that I rejoiced the more. 8 For though I made you sorry with a letter, I do not repent, though I did repent: for I perceive that the same epistle hath made you sorry, though *it were* but for a season. 9 Now I rejoice, not that ye were made sorry, but that ye sorrowed to repentance: for ye were made sorry after a godly manner, that ye might receive damage by us in nothing. 10 For godly sorrow worketh repentance to salvation not to be repented of : but the sorrow of the world worketh death. 11 For behold this selfsame thing, that ye sorrowed after a godly sort, what carefulness it wrought in you, yea, *what* clear-

κύριος παντοκράτωρ. 7 Ταύτας οὖν ἔχοντες τὰς
[the] Lord Almighty. ³These ²therefore ¹having
ἐπαγγελίας, ἀγαπητοί, καθαρίσωμεν ἑαυτοὺς ἀπὸ παντὸς
promises, beloved, we should cleanse ourselves from every
μολυσμοῦ σαρκὸς καὶ πνεύματος, ἐπιτελοῦντες ἁγιωσύνην ἐν
defilement of flesh and spirit, perfecting holiness in
φόβῳ θεοῦ.
fear of God.

2 Χωρήσατε ἡμᾶς· οὐδένα ἠδικήσαμεν, οὐδένα ἐφθείραμεν,
Receive us: no one did we wrong, no one did we corrupt,
οὐδένα ἐπλεονεκτήσαμεν. 3 ᵀοὐ πρὸς κατάκρισιν‖ λέγω·
no one did we overreach. Not for condemnation I speak,
προείρηκα.γὰρ ὅτι ἐν ταῖς.καρδίαις.ἡμῶν ἐστε εἰς τὸ συν-
for I have before-said that in our hearts ye are, for to die
αποθανεῖν καὶ ˢσυζῆν.‖ 4 πολλή μοι παρρησία πρὸς
together and to live together. Great [is] to me boldness towards
ὑμᾶς, πολλή μοι καύχησις ὑπὲρ ὑμῶν· πεπλήρωμαι
you, great to me boasting in respect of you ; I have been filled
τῇ παρακλήσει, ὑπερπερισσεύομαι τῇ χαρᾷ ἐπὶ πάσῃ τῇ
with encouragement; I overabound with joy at all
θλίψει.ἡμῶν. 5 Καὶ.γὰρ ἐλθόντων ἡμῶν εἰς Μακεδονίαν,
our tribulation. For indeed, ²having ³come ¹we into. Macedonia,
οὐδεμίαν ᵗἔσχηκεν‖ ἄνεσιν ἡ.σὰρξ.ἡμῶν, ἀλλ᾽ ἐν παντὶ
⁴not ⁵any ³had ⁶ease ¹our ²flesh, but in every [way]
θλιβόμενοι· ἔξωθεν μάχαι, ἔσωθεν φόβοι. 6 ἀλλ᾽ ὁ
being oppressed ; without contentions, within fears. But he who
παρακαλῶν τοὺς ταπεινοὺς παρεκάλεσεν ἡμᾶς ὁ θεὸς ἐν τῇ
encourages those brought low encouraged us— God— by the
παρουσίᾳ Τίτου· 7 οὐ.μόνον.δὲ ἐν τῇ παρουσίᾳ.αὐτοῦ, ἀλλὰ
coming of Titus ; and not only by his coming, but
καὶ ἐν τῇ παρακλήσει ᾗ παρεκλήθη ἐφ᾽ ὑμῖν,
also by the encouragement with which he was encouraged as to you ;
ἀναγγέλλων ἡμῖν τὴν.ὑμῶν.ἐπιπόθησιν, τὸν.ὑμῶν.ὀδυρμόν,
relating to us your longing, your mourning,
τὸν.ὑμῶν.ζῆλον ὑπὲρ ἐμοῦ, ὥστε.με μᾶλλον χαρῆναι. 8 Ὅτι
your zeal for me; so as for me the more to be rejoiced. For
εἰ καὶ ἐλύπησα ὑμᾶς ἐν τῇ ἐπιστολῇ, οὐ.μεταμέλομαι, εἰ καὶ
if also I grieved you in the epistle, I do not regret [it], if even
μετεμελόμην· βλέπω.ᵛγὰρ‖ ὅτι ἡ.ἐπιστολὴ ἐκείνη εἰ καὶ πρὸς
I did regret; for I see that that epistle, if even for
ὥραν ἐλύπησεν ὑμᾶς. 9 νῦν χαίρω, οὐχ ὅτι ἐλυπήθητε, ἀλλ᾽
an hour, grieved you. Now I rejoice, not that ye were grieved, but
ὅτι ἐλυπήθητε εἰς μετάνοιαν· ἐλυπήθητε.γὰρ κατὰ θεόν,
that ye were grieved to repentance; for ye were grieved according to God,
ἵνα ἐν μηδενὶ ζημιωθῆτε ἐξ ἡμῶν. 10 ἡ.γὰρ κατὰ
that in nothing ye might suffer loss by us. For the ²according ³to
θεὸν λύπη μετάνοιαν εἰς σωτηρίαν ἀμεταμέλητον ʷκατερ-
⁴God ¹grief repentance to salvation not to be regretted works
γάζεται·‖ ἡ.δὲ τοῦ κόσμου λύπη θάνατον κατεργάζεται.
out ; but the ²of ³the ⁴world ¹grief death works out.
11 ἰδοὺ.γὰρ αὐτὸ.τοῦτο τὸ κατὰ θεὸν λυπηθῆναι ˣὑμᾶς,‖
For lo, this same thing, according to God ²to ³have ⁴been ⁵grieved ¹you,
πόσην ʸκατειργάσατο‖ ᶻ ὑμῖν σπουδήν, ἀλλὰ ἀπολογίαν,
how much ²it ⁴worked ⁴out ⁵in ⁶you ¹diligence, but [what] defence,

---

ᵀ πρὸς κατάκρισιν οὐ LTTrA.   ˢ συνζῆν LTTrA.   ᵗ ἔσχεν LTr.   ᵛ — γὰρ for [L]Tr.
ʷ ἐργάζεται works LTTrAW.   ˣ — ὑμᾶς LTTᵢ[A].   ʸ κατηργάσατο T.   ᶻ + [ἐν] L.

ἀλλὰ ἀγανάκτησιν, ἀλλὰ φόβον, ἀλλὰ ἐπιπόθησιν, ἀλλὰ
but   indignation,   but   fear,   but   longing,   but

ζῆλον, *ἀλλ' ἐκδίκησιν; ἐν παντὶ συνεστήσατε ἑαυτοὺς
zeal,   but   vengeance! in every [way] ye proved yourselves

ἁγνοὺς εἶναι ᵇἐν τῷ πράγματι. 12 ἄρα εἰ καὶ ἔγραψα ὑμῖν,
pure   'to ²bo in the   matter.   Then if also I wrote to you,

οὐχ ᶜεἵνεκεν τοῦ ἀδικήσαντος, οὐδὲ ᶜεἵνεκεν τοῦ
not for the sake of him who did wrong, nor for the sake of him who

ἀδικηθέντος· ᵈἀλλ' ᶜεἵνεκεν τοῦ φανερωθῆναι τὴν σπουδὴν
suffered wrong, but for the sake of ⁷being ⁸manifested ⁹diligence

ᵉὑμῶν τὴν ὑπὲρ ᶠἡμῶν πρὸς ὑμᾶς ἐνώπιον τοῦ θεοῦ.
'your ³which [⁴is] ²for ⁶us   to you   before   God.

13 Διὰ τοῦτο παρακεκλήμεθα ἐπὶ ᵍ τῇ παρακλήσει
On account of this we have been encouraged in ²encouragement

ʰὑμῶν περισσοτέρως.ⁱδὲ μᾶλλον ἐχάρημεν ἐπὶ τῇ χαρᾷ
'your, and the more abundantly rather we rejoiced at the joy

Τίτου, ὅτι ἀναπέπαυται τὸ.πνεῦμα.αὐτοῦ ἀπὸ πάντων
of Titus, because has been refreshed   his spirit   by   all

ὑμῶν· 14 ὅτι εἴ τι αὐτῷ ὑπὲρ ὑμῶν κεκαύχημαι, οὐ
of you. Because if anything to him about you I have boasted, ³not

κατῃσχύνθην· ἀλλ' ὡς πάντα ἐν ἀληθείᾳ ἐλαλήσαμεν
'I ²was put to shame; but   as all things in truth   we spoke

ὑμῖν, οὕτως καὶ ἡ καύχησις ᵏἡμῶν ˡᵃ ἐπὶ Τίτου
to you, so also the boasting of us which [was] to Titus

ἀλήθεια ἐγενήθη· 15 καὶ τὰ.σπλάγχνα.αὐτοῦ περισσοτέρως
truth became;   and   his bowels   more abundantly

εἰς ὑμᾶς ἐστιν, ἀναμιμνῃσκομένου τὴν πάντων ὑμῶν
towards you   are,   remembering   the ²of ³all ⁴of ⁵you

ὑπακοήν, ὡς μετὰ φόβου καὶ τρόμου ἐδέξασθε αὐτόν.
'obedience, how with fear   and trembling ye received him.

16 χαίρω ᵐ ὅτι ἐν παντὶ θαρρῶ ἐν ὑμῖν.
I rejoice that in everything I am confident in you.

8 Γνωρίζομεν.δὲ ὑμῖν, ἀδελφοί, τὴν χάριν τοῦ θεοῦ τὴν
But we make known to you, brethren, the grace   of God which

δεδομένην ἐν ταῖς ἐκκλησίαις τῆς Μακεδονίας· 2 ὅτι ἐν πολλῇ
has been given in the assemblies   of Macedonia;   that in much

δοκιμῇ θλίψεως ἡ περισσεία τῆς.χαρᾶς.αὐτῶν καὶ ἡ κατὰ
proof of tribulation the abundance of their joy   and

βάθους πτωχεία αὐτῶν ἐπερίσσευσεν εἰς ⁿτὸν πλοῦτον τῆς
²deep   ³poverty 'their   abounded   to the riches

ἁπλότητος.αὐτῶν· 3 ὅτι κατὰ δύναμιν, μαρτυρῶ,
of their liberality. For according to [their] power, I bear witness,

καὶ ᵒὑπὲρ δύναμιν αὐθαίρετοι, 4 μετὰ πολ-
and beyond [their] power [they were] willing of themselves, with much

λῆς παρακλήσεως δεόμενοι ἡμῶν τὴν χάριν καὶ τὴν κοινωνίαν
entreaty beseeching of us, ⁵the ⁶grace ⁷and ⁸the ⁹fellowship

τῆς διακονίας τῆς εἰς τοὺς ἁγίους ᴾδέξασθαι.ἡμᾶς·
⁴of ¹¹the ¹²service ¹³which [¹⁴was] ¹⁵for ¹⁶the ¹⁷saints 'for ²us ⁴to 'receive.

5 καὶ οὐ καθὼς ἠλπίσαμεν, ᑫἀλλ' ἑαυτοὺς ἔδωκαν πρῶ-
And not [only] according as we hoped, but themselves they gave first

τον τῷ κυρίῳ, καὶ ἡμῖν διὰ θελήματος θεοῦ 6 εἰς.τὸ παρα-
to the Lord, and to us by [the] will   of God. So that ²ex-

ing of yourselves, yea,
what indignation, yea,
what fear, yea, what
vehement desire, yea,
what zeal, yea, what
revenge! In all things
ye have approved your-
selves to be clear in
this matter. 12 Where-
fore, though I wrote
unto you, I did it not
for his cause that had
done the wrong, nor
for his cause that suf-
fered wrong, but that
our care for you in the
sight of God might
appear unto you.
13 Therefore we were
comforted in your
comfort : yea, and ex-
ceedingly the more
joyed we for the joy of
Titus, because his spi-
rit was refreshed by
you all. 14 For if I
have boasted anything
to him of you, I am
not ashamed ; but as
we spake all things to
you in truth, even so
our boasting, which I
made before Titus, is
found a truth. 15 And
his inward affection is
more abundant toward
you, whilst he remem-
bereth the obedience
of you all, how with
fear and trembling ye
received him. 16 I re-
joice therefore that I
have confidence in you
in all things.

VIII.   Moreover,
brethren, we do you to
wit of the grace of
God bestowed on the
churches of Macedo-
nia ; 2 how that in a
great trial of affliction
the abundance of their
joy and their deep po-
verty abounded unto
the riches of their li-
berality. 3 For to
their power, I bear re-
cord, yea, and beyond
their power they were
willing of themselves;
4 praying us with much
intreaty that we would
receive the gift, and
take upon us the fel-
lowship of the mini-
stering to the saints.
5 And this they did,
not as we hoped, but
first gave their own
selves to the Lord, and
unto us by the will of
God. 6 Insomuch that
we desired Titus, that

ᵃ ἀλλὰ LTTrAW. ᵇ — ἐν (read τῷ in the) [L]TTrAW. ᶜ ἕνεκεν LTTrA. ᵈ ἀλλὰ Tr.
ᵉ ἡμῶν our EG. ᶠ ὑμῶν you EG ᵍ + δὲ and (in) commencing a sentence at ἐπὶ LTTrAW.
ʰ ἡμῶν our LTTrAW. ⁱ — δὲ and LTTrAW. ᵏ ὑμῶν of you LA. ˡ — ἡ T[r].
ᵐ + οὖν before E. ⁿ τὸ πλοῦτος LTTrA, ᵒ παρὰ LTTrAW. ᴾ — δέξασθαι ἡμᾶς
GLTTrAW. ᑫ ἀλλὰ TTr.

as he had begun, so he would also finish in you the same grace also. 7 Therefore, as ye abound in every *thing, in* faith, and utterance, and knowledge, and *in* all diligence, and *in* your love to us, *see* that ye abound in this grace also. 8 I speak not by commandment, but by occasion of the forwardness of others, and to prove the sincerity of your love. 9 For ye know the grace of our Lord Jesus Christ, that, though he was rich, yet for your sakes he became poor, that ye through his poverty might be rich. 10 And herein I give *my* advice: for this is expedient for you, who have begun before, not only to do, but also to be forward a year ago. 11 Now therefore perform the doing *of it;* that as *there was* a readiness to will, so *there may* be a performance also out of that which ye have. 12 For if there be first a willing mind, *it is* accepted according to that a man hath, *and* not according to that he hath not. 13 For *I mean* not that other men be eased, and ye be burdened : 14 but by an equality, *that* now at this time your abundance *may be a supply* for their want, that their abundance also may be *a supply* for your want: that there may be equality : 15 as it is written, He that *had gathered* much had nothing over ; and he that *had gathered* little had no lack.

16 But thanks *be* to God, which put the same earnest care into the heart of Titus for you. 17 For indeed he accepted the exhortation ; but being more forward, of his own accord he went unto you. 18 And we have sent with him the brother, whose praise *is* in the gospel throughout all the churches ; 19 and not *that* only, but who was also chosen of the

καλέσαι ἡμᾶς Τίτον, ἵνα καθὼς προενήρξατο, οὕτως καὶ
horted 	¹we 	Titus, 	that according as he before began, 	so 	also

ἐπιτελέσῃ εἰς ὑμᾶς καὶ τὴν χάριν ταύτην. 7 Ἀλλ' ὥσπερ
he might complete with you 	also 	this grace. 	But 	even as

ἐν παντὶ περισσεύετε, πίστει, καὶ λόγῳ, καὶ γνώσει, καὶ
in every [way] ye abound, in faith, and word, and knowledge, and

πάσῃ σπουδῇ, καὶ τῇ ἐξ ὑμῶν ἐν ἡμῖν ἀγάπῃ, ἵνα καὶ ἐν
all 	diligence, and in the ²from ³you ⁴to ⁵us 	¹love, 	that also in

ταύτῃ τῇ χάριτι περισσεύητε· 8 οὐ κατ' ἐπιταγὴν λέγω,
this 	grace ye should abound. 	Not according to a command do I speak,

ἀλλὰ διὰ τῆς ἑτέρων σπουδῆς καὶ τὸ τῆς ʳὑμετέρας‖ ἀγάπης
but through the ²of ³others ¹diligence and the ²of ³your ⁴love

γνήσιον δοκιμάζων· 9 γινώσκετε γὰρ τὴν χάριν τοῦ κυρίου
¹genuineness proving. 	For ye know the grace of ²Lord

ἡμῶν Ἰησοῦ χριστοῦ, ὅτι δι' ὑμᾶς ἐπτώχευσεν
¹our 	Jesus 	Christ, 	that ²for ⁴the ⁵sake ⁶of ⁷you ⁸he ⁹became ¹⁰poor,

πλούσιος ὤν, ἵνα ὑμεῖς τῇ ἐκείνου πτωχείᾳ πλουτήσητε.
¹rich 	¹being; that that ye 	by his poverty 	might be enriched.

10 καὶ γνώμην ἐν τούτῳ δίδωμι· τοῦτο γὰρ ὑμῖν συμφέρει,
And a judgment in 	this 	I give, 	for this for you is profitable,

οἵτινες οὐ μόνον τὸ ποιῆσαι, ἀλλὰ καὶ τὸ θέλειν προενήρ-
who not only the doing, 	but also the being willing 	began

ξασθε ἀπὸ πέρυσι· 11 νυνὶ δὲ καὶ τὸ ποιῆσαι ἐπιτελέσατε,
before 	a year ago. 	But now also ²the 	³doing 	¹complete;

ὅπως καθάπερ ἡ προθυμία τοῦ θέλειν, οὕτως καὶ
so that even as [there was] the readiness of the being willing, so, also

τὸ ἐπιτελέσαι ἐκ τοῦ ἔχειν. 12 Εἰ γὰρ ἡ προθυμία πρό-
the completing out of that [ye] have. 	For if the readiness is pre-

κειται, καθὸ ˢἐὰν‖ ἔχῃ ᵗτις‖ εὐπρόσδεκτος, οὐ καθὸ
sent, according as ²may ³have ¹anyone [he is] accepted, 	not according as

οὐκ ἔχει. 13 οὐ γὰρ ἵνα ἄλλοις ἄνεσις, ὑμῖν δὲᵂ
he has not. 	For [it is] not that to others [there may be] 	ease, 	but for you

θλίψις· ἀλλ' ἐξ ἰσότητος, ἐν τῷ νῦν καιρῷ τὸ ὑμῶν περίσ-
pressure, but of equality, in the present time 	your 	abun-

σευμα εἰς τὸ ἐκείνων ὑστέρημα, 14 ἵνα καὶ τὸ ἐκείνων περίσ-
dance for 	their deficiency, 	that also 	their 	abun-

σευμα γένηται εἰς τὸ ὑμῶν ὑστέρημα· ὅπως γένηται
dance 	may be for 	your deficiency, 	so that there should be

ἰσότης· 15 καθὼς γέγραπται, Ὁ τὸ πολὺ οὐκ
equality. 	According as it has been written, He that [gathered] 	much ⁴not

ἐπλεόνασεν· καὶ ὁ τὸ ὀλίγον οὐκ ἠλαττόνησεν.
¹had over, 	and he that [gathered] 	little 	did not lack.

16 Χάρις δὲ τῷ θεῷ, τῷ ᵂδιδόντι‖ τὴν αὐτὴν σπουδὴν ὑπὲρ
But thanks to God, who gives 	the same diligence for

ὑμῶν ἐν τῇ καρδίᾳ Τίτου· 17 ὅτι τὴν μὲν παράκλησιν
you in the heart of Titus. 	For the ²indeed ¹exhortation he

δέξατο, σπουδαιότερος δὲ ὑπάρχων, αὐθαίρετος ἐξῆλθεν
received, 	but more diligent 	being, 	of his own accord he went out

πρὸς ὑμᾶς. 18 συνεπέμψαμεν δὲ ˣμετ' αὐτοῦ τὸν ἀδελφὸν‖
to you. 	But we sent 	with him 	the brother

οὗ ὁ ἔπαινος ἐν τῷ εὐαγγελίῳ διὰ πασῶν τῶν ἐκ-
of whom the praise [is] in the glad tidings through all 	the as-

κλησιῶν· 19 οὐ μόνον δέ, ἀλλὰ καὶ χειροτονηθεὶς ὑπὸ τῶν
semblies; 	and not only [so], but also having been chosen by the

---

ʳ ἡμετέρας of our E.　　ˢ ἂν τ.　　ᵗ — τις (read ἔχῃ he may have) LTTrAW.　　ᵛ — δὲ
but LTTr[A].　　ᵂ δόντι gave W.　　ˣ — τὸν ἀδελφὸν μετ' αὐτοῦ τ.

ἐκκλησιῶν　συνέκδημος.ἡμῶν　 ʸσὺν‖　τῇ.χάριτι.ταύτῃ　τῇ
assemblies [is]　our fellow-traveller　with　　this grace,　　　which [is]

διακονουμένῃ　ὑφ᾽ ἡμῶν　πρὸς　τὴν　ᶻαὐτοῦ‖　τοῦ　κυρίου　δόξαν
served　　　by　us　　to　the　ᵃhimself　²of ³the　⁴Lord　¹glory

καὶ　　　προθυμίαν　ᵃὑμῶν.‖　20 στελλόμενοι　τοῦτο,　μή
and [a witness of]　²readiness　¹your;　　　avoiding　this,　lest

τις　ἡμᾶς　μωμήσηται　ἐν　τῇ.ἁδρότητι.ταύτῃ　τῇ　　διακονου-
anyone　us　should blame　in　this abundance　which [is]　served

μένῃ　ὑφ᾽ ἡμῶν·　21 ᵇπρονοούμενοι‖　καλὰ　οὐ　μόνον　ἐνώπιον
by　us;　　　providing　　things right not ¹only　　before

κυρίου,　ἀλλὰ καὶ ἐνώπιον　ἀνθρώπων. 22 Συνεπέμψαμεν.δὲ
[the] Lord,　but also before　　men.　　And we sent with

αὐτοῖς　τὸν.ἀδελφὸν.ἡμῶν　ὃν　ἐδοκιμάσαμεν　ἐν　πολλοῖς　πολ-
them　　our brother　　whom　we proved　　in　many things often

λάκις　σπουδαῖον ὄντα,　νυνὶ.δὲ πολὺ σπουδαιότερον πεποι-
diligent　to be,　and now　much　more diligent　by the ²con-

θήσει　πολλῇ　τῇ　εἰς　ὑμᾶς.　23 εἴτε　　ὑπὲρ　Τίτου,
fidence　¹great　which [is] towards　you.　Whether as regards　Titus,

κοινωνὸς ἐμὸς καὶ εἰς ὑμᾶς　συνεργός·　εἴτε　ἀδελφοὶ
[he is]　²partner　¹my and for you a fellow-worker;　∕or　²brethren

ἡμῶν,　　ἀπόστολοι ἐκκλησιῶν,　δόξα. χριστοῦ.　24 Τὴν
¹our,　[they are] messengers of assemblies,　²glory ¹Christ's.　　The

οὖν　ἔνδειξιν τῆς.ἀγάπης.ὑμῶν,　καὶ ἡμῶν καυχήσεως ὑπὲρ
²therefore ¹proof　of your love,　　and of our　boasting　about

ὑμῶν, εἰς αὐτοὺς ᶜἐνδείξασθε‖　ᵈκαὶ‖ εἰς πρόσωπον τῶν ἐκκλησιῶν.
you,　²to ⁴them　　¹shew ²ye　and　in　face　of the assemblies.

9 Περὶ.μὲν.γὰρ　τῆς　διακονίας τῆς　εἰς τοὺς ἁγίους
For concerning the　　service　which [is] for　the　saints

περισσόν	μοι ἐστὶν τὸ γράφειν ὑμῖν.　2 ᵉοἶδα.γὰρ τὴν προθυ-
superfluous for me it is　writing to you.　For I know　²readi-

μίαν ὑμῶν　ἣν　ὑπὲρ ὑμῶν καυχῶμαι Μακεδόσιν,　ὅτι
ness　¹your which concerning you　I boast of　to Macedonians;　that

Ἀχαΐα παρεσκεύασται ἀπὸ.πέρυσι·　καὶ　ᵉᵒ‖ ᶠἐξ‖ ὑμῶν ζῆλος
Achaia　has been prepared　a year ago,　and the ²of　³you　¹zeal

ἠρέθισεν τοὺς πλείονας.　3 ἔπεμψα.δὲ τοὺς ἀδελφούς, ἵνα.μὴ
provoke　the greater number.　But I sent　the brethren,　lest

τὸ.καύχημα.ἡμῶν　τὸ　　ὑπὲρ ὑμῶν　κενωθῇ　ἐν τῷ
our boasting　　which [is] about　you　should be made void in the

μέρει.τούτῳ·　ἵνα καθὼς ἔλεγον,　παρεσκευασμένοι　ἦτε,
this respect,　that according as I said,　prepared　　　ye may be ;

4 μήπως ἐὰν ἔλθωσιν σὺν ἐμοὶ Μακεδόνες, καὶ εὕρωσιν ὑμᾶς
lest perhaps if should come with me Macedonians, and find　you

ἀπαρασκευάστους,　καταισχυνθῶμεν　ἡμεῖς, ἵνα μὴ.λέγωμεν
unprepared,　　²should ³be ⁴put ⁵to ⁶shame ¹we, (that we may not say

ὑμεῖς, ἐν τῇ.ὑποστάσει.ταύτῃ ᵍτῆς καυχήσεως.‖　5 ἀναγκαῖον
ye,)　in　this confidence　　of boasting.　　Necessary

οὖν　ἡγησάμην　παρακαλέσαι τοὺς ἀδελφούς ἵνα προέλ-
²therefore ¹I esteemed [it]　to exhort　the brethren that they should

θωσιν ʰεἰς‖ ὑμᾶς, καὶ προκαταρτίσωσιν τὴν ⁱπροκατηγ-
go before to　you,　and should complete beforehand　　²fore-

γελμένην‖ εὐλογίαν ὑμῶν ταύτην ἑτοίμην εἶναι οὕτως ὡς
announced　⁴blessing ²your ¹this　⁷ready ⁵to ⁶be　thus as

ʸ ἐν in LTᵣAW.　　ᶻ — αὐτοῦ LTᵣAW.　　ᵃ ἡμῶν our GLTTᵣAW.　　ᵇ προνοοῦμεν γὰρ for
we provide LTTᵣA ; προνοούμενοι γὰρ G.　ᶜ ἐνδεικνύμενοι shewing LTTᵣA.　　ᵈ — καὶ
GLTTᵣAW.　　ᵉ τὸ TTr.　　ᶠ — ἐξ (read ὑμῶν of you) LTTr[A].　　ᵍ — τῆς καυχήσεως GLTTᵣAW.
ʰ πρὸς LTᵣW.　　ⁱ προεπηγγελμένην before promised LTTᵣAW.

---

churches to travel with us with this grace, which is administered by us to the glory of the same Lord, and declaration of your ready mind: 20 avoiding this, that no man should blame us in this abundance which is administered by us: 21 providing for honest things, not only in the sight of the Lord, but also in the sight of men. 22 And we have sent with them our brother, whom we have oftentimes proved diligent in many things, but now much more diligent, upon the great confidence which I have in you. 23 Whether any do inquire of Titus, he is my partner and fellowhelper concerning you : or our brethren be inquired of, they are the messengers of the churches, and the glory of Christ. 24 Wherefore shew ye to them, and before the churches, the proof of your love, and of our boasting on your behalf.

IX. For as touching the ministering to the saints, it is superfluous for me to write to you: 2 for I know the forwardness of your mind, for which I boast of you to them of Macedonia, that Achaia was ready a year ago; and your zeal hath provoked very many. 3 Yet have I sent the brethren, lest our boasting of you should be in vain in this behalf; that, as I said, ye may be ready : 4 lest haply if they of Macedonia come with me, and find you unprepared, we (that we say not, ye) should be ashamed in this same confident boasting. 5 Therefore I thought it necessary to exhort the brethren, that they would go before unto you, and make up beforehand your bounty, whereof ye had notice before, that the same might be ready, as a matter of bounty, and not as *of covetousness.* 6 But this *I say*, He which soweth sparingly shall reap also sparingly; and he which soweth bountifully shall reap also bountifully. 7 Every man according as he purposeth in his heart, *so let him give;* not grudgingly, or of necessity: for God loveth a cheerful giver. 8 And God *is* able to make all grace abound toward you; that ye, always having all sufficiency in all *things,* may abound to every good work: 9 (as it is written, He hath dispersed abroad; he hath given to the poor: his righteousness remaineth for ever. 10 Now he that ministereth seed to the sower both minister bread for *your* food, and multiply your seed sown, and increase the fruits of your righteousness;) 11 being enriched in every thing to all bountifulness, which causeth through us thanksgiving to God. 12 For the administration of this service not only supplieth the want of the saints, but is abundant also by many thanksgivings unto God; 13 whiles by the experiment of this ministration they glorify God for your professed subjection unto the gospel of Christ, and for *your* liberal distribution unto them, and unto all *men;* 14 and by their prayer for you, which long after you for the exceeding grace of God in you. 15 Thanks *be* unto God for his unspeakable gift.

X. Now I Paul myself beseech you by the meekness and gentleness of Christ, who in presence *am* base among you, but being absent am bold toward you: 2 but I beseech *you,* that I may not be bold when I am present with that confidence, wherewith I think to be bold against some, which

εὐλογίαν, ᵏκαὶ‖ μὴ ¹ὥσπερ‖ πλεονεξίαν. 6 Τοῦτο.δὲ,   ὁ
a blessing, and not as [of] covetousness.   But this[I say], he that

σπείρων φειδομένως, φειδομένως καὶ θερίσει· καὶ ὁ σπείρων
sows   sparingly,   sparingly   also shall reap; and he that sows

ἐπ' εὐλογίαις, ἐπ' εὐλογίαις καὶ θερίσει. 7 ἕκαστος καθὼς
on blessings, on blessings also shall reap: each   according as

ᵐπροαιρεῖται‖ τῇ καρδίᾳ· μὴ ἐκ.λύπης ἢ ἐξ ἀνάγκης· ἱλαρὸν
he purposes in the heart; not grievingly, or of necessity; ²a ³cheerful

γὰρ δότην ἀγαπᾷ ὁ θεός. 8 ᵒδυνατὸς.δὲ‖ ὁ θεὸς πᾶσαν χάριν
¹for giver ²loves ¹God.   For able [is] God every grace

περισσεῦσαι εἰς ὑμᾶς, ἵνα ἐν παντὶ πάντοτε πᾶσαν
to make abound towards you, that in every [way] always   all

αὐτάρκειαν ἔχοντες, περισσεύητε εἰς πᾶν ἔργον ἀγαθόν·
sufficiency having, ye may abound to every ²work   ¹good:

9 καθὼς γέγραπται,   Ἐσκόρπισεν, ἔδωκεν τοῖς πένησιν·
according as it has been written, He scattered abroad, he gave to the poor,

ἡ.δικαιοσύνη.αὐτοῦ μένει εἰς.τὸν.αἰῶνα. 10 Ὁ.δὲ ἐπιχορηγῶν
his righteousness abides for ever.   Now he that supplies

ᵒσπέρμα‖ τῷ σπείροντι καὶ ἄρτον εἰς βρῶσιν ᴾχορηγήσαι‖
seed   to him that sows and bread for eating   may he supply

καὶ ᑫπληθύναι‖ τὸν.σπόρον.ὑμῶν, καὶ ʳαὐξήσαι‖ τὰ ˢγεννή-
and may he multiply   your sowing,   and may he increase the fruits

ματα‖ τῆς.δικαιοσύνης.ὑμῶν. 11 ἐν παντὶ   πλουτιζόμενοι
of your righteousness: in every [way] being enriched

εἰς πᾶσαν ἁπλότητα, ἥτις κατεργάζεται δι' ἡμῶν εὐχαρισ-
to all liberality, which works out   through us thanks-

τίαν ᵗτῷ‖ θεῷ· 12 ὅτι ἡ διακονία. τῆς.λειτουργίας.ταύτης
giving to God.   Because the service   of this ministration

οὐ μόνον ἐστὶν προσαναπληροῦσα τὰ ὑστερήματα τῶν ἁγίων,
not only   is   completely filling up the deficiencies of the saints,

ἀλλὰ καὶ περισσεύουσα διὰ πολλῶν εὐχαριστιῶν τῷ θεῷ·
but also   abounding   through many thanksgivings   to God;

13 διὰ τῆς δοκιμῆς τῆς.διακονίας.ταύτης   δοξάζοντες τὸν
through the proof   of this service   [they] glorifying

θεὸν ἐπὶ τῇ ὑποταγῇ τῆς.ὁμολογίας.ὑμῶν εἰς τὸ εὐαγγέλιον
God at the subjection, by your confession, to the glad tidings

τοῦ χριστοῦ, καὶ ἁπλότητι τῆς κοινωνίας εἰς αὐτοὺς καὶ
of the Christ, and liberality of the communication towards them and

εἰς πάντας, 14 καὶ αὐτῶν.δεήσει ὑπὲρ ὑμῶν, ἐπιποθούν-
towards all;   and in their supplication for you,   a longing

των ὑμᾶς   διὰ   τὴν ὑπερβάλλουσαν χάριν τοῦ θεοῦ ἐφ'
for you, on account of the   surpassing   grace of God upon

ὑμῖν. 15 χάρις. ᵛδὲ‖ τῷ θεῷ ἐπὶ τῇ ἀνεκδιηγήτῳ αὐτοῦ δωρεᾷ.
you.   Now thanks [be] to God for ²indescribable ¹his free gift.

10 Αὐτὸς.δὲ ἐγὼ Παῦλος παρακαλῶ ὑμᾶς διὰ τῆς ʷπραό-
Now ²myself ¹I Paul   exhort   you . by the meek-

τητος‖ καὶ ἐπιεικείας τοῦ χριστοῦ, ὃς κατὰ πρόσωπον μὲν
ness and gentleness of the Christ, who as to appearance [am]

ταπεινὸς ἐν ὑμῖν, ἀπὼν.δὲ θαρρῶ εἰς ὑμᾶς· 2 δέομαι.δὲ
mean   among you, but absent am bold towards you; but I beseech

τὸ μὴ παρὼν   θαρρῆσαι τῇ · πεποιθήσει   ᾗ
that ²not ¹being ²present ³I ⁴should be bold with the confidence   with which

---

ᵏ — καὶ T.   ¹ ὡς GLTTrAW.   ᵐ προῄρηται he has purposed LTTrAW.   ⁿ δυνατεῖ δὲ
For is able LTTrA.   ᵒ σπόρον LTr.   ᴾ χορηγήσει will supply GLTTrAW.   ᑫ πληθυνεῖ
will multiply GLTAW; πληθύνει multiplies Tr.   ʳαὐξήσει will increase GLTTrAW.   ˢγεννή-
ματα GLTTrAW.   ᵗ [τῷ] L.   ᵛ — δὲ now LTTrA.   ʷ πραΰτητος LTTrAW.

λογίζομαι τολμῆσαι ἐπί τινας τοὺς λογιζομένους ἡμᾶς ὡς
I reckon to be daring towards some who reckon of us as

κατὰ σάρκα περιπατοῦντας. 3 ἐν.σαρκὶ.γὰρ περιπατοῦντες,
²according ²to ⁴flesh ¹walking.. For in flesh walking,

οὐ κατὰ σάρκα στρατευόμεθα· 4 τὰ.γὰρ ὅπλα τῆς ˣστρα-
not according to flesh do we war. For the arms of ᵃwar-

τείας". ἡμῶν - οὐ σαρκικά, ἀλλὰ δυνατὰ τῷ θεῷ πρὸς
fare ¹our [are] not fleshly, but powerful through God to [the]

καθαίρεσιν ὀχυρωμάτων· 5 λογισμοὺς καθαιροῦντες καὶ πᾶν
overthrow of strong-holds; ²reasonings ¹overthrowing and every

ὕψωμα ἐπαιρόμενον κατὰ τῆς γνώσεως τοῦ θεοῦ, καὶ αἰχμα-
high thing lifting itself up against the knowledge of God, and leading

λωτίζοντες πᾶν νόημα εἰς τὴν ὑπακοὴν τοῦ χριστοῦ, 6 καὶ
captive every thought into the obedience of the Christ; and

ἐν ἑτοίμῳ ἔχοντες ἐκδικῆσαι πᾶσαν παρακοήν, ὅταν πλη-
²in ³readiness ¹having to avenge all disobedience, when may have

ρωθῇ ὑμῶν ἡ ὑπακοή. 7 Τὰ κατὰ πρόσωπον
been fulfilled your obedience. The things according to appearance

βλέπετε; εἰ τις πέποιθεν ἑαυτῷ χριστοῦ εἶναι, τοῦτο
do ye look at? If anyone is persuaded in himself of Christ to be, this

λογιζέσθω πάλιν ˢἀφ'".ἑαυτοῦ, ὅτι καθὼς αὐτὸς χριστοῦ,
let him reckon again of himself, that according as he [is] of Christ,

οὕτως καὶ ἡμεῖς ᶻχριστοῦ." 8 ἐάν.ᵃτε".γὰρ ᵇκαὶ" περισ-
so also [are] we of Christ. For and if even more a-

σότερόν τι ᶜκαυχήσωμαι" περὶ τῆς.ἐξουσίας.ἡμῶν, ἧς
bundantly somewhat I should boast concerning our authority, which

ἔδωκεν ὁ κύριος ᵈἡμῖν" εἰς οἰκοδομὴν καὶ οὐκ εἰς καθαίρεσιν
²gave ¹the ²Lord to us for building up and not for overthrowing

ὑμῶν, οὐκ.αἰσχυνθήσομαι 9 ἵνα μὴ.δόξω ὡς ἂν ἐκφοβεῖν
you, I shall not be put to shame; that I may not seem as if frightening

ὑμᾶς διὰ τῶν ἐπιστολῶν. 10 ὅτι αἱ ᵉμὲν ἐπιστολαί,
you by means of epistles: because the epistles,

φησίν," βαρεῖαι καὶ ἰσχυραί· ἡ.δὲ παρουσία τοῦ σώματος
says he, [are] weighty and strong, but the presence of the body

ἀσθενής, καὶ ὁ λόγος ᶠἐξουθενημένος." 11 τοῦτο λογιζέσθω
weak, and the speech naught. This let ʳreckon

ὁ τοιοῦτος, ὅτι οἷοί ἐσμεν τῷ λόγῳ δι' ἐπιστολῶν ἀπόντες,
¹such ²a ³one, that such as we are in word by epistles being absent,

τοιοῦτοι καὶ παρόντες τῷ ἔργῳ. 12 Οὐ.γὰρ τολμῶμεν
such [we are] also being present in deed. For ²not ³dare ¹we

ᵍἐγκρῖναι" ἢ ʰσυγκρῖναι" ἑαυτούς τισιν τῶν ἑαυτοὺς συν-
rank among or compare ²with ¹ourselves some who themselves com-

ιστανόντων, ἀλλὰ αὐτοὶ ἐν ἑαυτοῖς ἑαυτοὺς μετροῦντες, καὶ
mend, but these by themselves themselves measuring, and

ʰσυγκρίνοντες" ἑαυτοὺς ἑαυτοῖς, οὐ.ᶦσυνιοῦσιν." 13 ἡμεῖς
comparing themselves with themselves, do not understand. ²We

δὲ ᵏοὐχὶ" εἰς τὰ ἄμετρα καυχησόμεθα, ἀλλὰ κατὰ
¹now not to the things beyond measure will boast, but according to

τὸ μέτρον τοῦ κανόνος οὗ ἐμέρισεν ἡμῖν ὁ θεὸς μέτρου
the measure of the rule which ⁵divided ⁶to ⁷us ¹the ²God ³of ⁴measure

ἐφικέσθαι ἄχρι καὶ ὑμῶν. 14 οὐ γὰρ ὡς" μὴ ἐφικνούμενοι εἰς
to reach ²to ¹also you. ²Not ¹for as not reaching to

think of us as if we walked according to the flesh. 3 For though we walk in the flesh, we do not war after the flesh: 4 (for the weapons of our warfare are not carnal, but mighty through God to the pulling down of strong holds;) 5 casting down imaginations, and every high thing that exalteth itself against the knowledge of God, and bringing into captivity every thought to the obedience of Christ; 6 and having in a readiness to revenge all disobedience, when your obedience is fulfilled. 7 Do ye look on things after the outward appearance? If any man trust to himself that he is Christ's, let him of himself think this again, that, as he is Christ's, even so are we Christ's. 8 For though I should boast somewhat more of our authority, which the Lord hath given us for edification, and not for your destruction, I should not be ashamed: 9 that I may not seem as if I would terrify you by letters. 10 For his letters, say they, are weighty and powerful; but his bodily presence is weak, and his speech contemptible. 11 Let such an one think this, that, such as we are in word by letters when we are absent, such will we be also in deed when we are present. 12 For we dare not make ourselves of the number, or compare ourselves with some that commend themselves: but they measuring themselves by themselves, and comparing themselves among themselves, are not wise. 13 But we will not boast of things without our measure, but according to the measure of the rule which God hath distributed to us, a measure to reach even unto you. 14 For we stretch not ourselves beyond our measure, as though we

---

ˣ στρατιᾶς T.   ʸ ἐφ' TTr.   ᶻ — χριστοῦ GLTTrAW.   ᵃ — τε and [L]Tr[A].   ᵇ — καὶ
LTTrA.   ᶜ καυχήσομαι I shall boast T.   ᵈ — ἡμῖν LTTrA.   ᵉ ἐπιστολαὶ μὲν φησιν
(φασιν say they L) LTTr.   ᶠ ἐξουδενημένος L.   ᵍ ἐν- T.   ʰ συν- T.   ᶦ συνιᾶσιν LTTrA.
ᵏ οὐκ LTTrAW.   ˡ ὡς γὰρ (reading the sentence as a question) L.

reached not unto you:
for we are come as
far as to you also
in *preaching* the gos-
pel of Christ : 15 not
boasting of things
without *our* measure,
that is, of other men's
labours ; but having
hope, when your faith
is increased, that we
shall be enlarged by
you according to our
rule abundantly, 16 to
preach the gospel in
the *regions* beyond
you, *and* not to boast
in another man's line
of things made ready
to our hand. 17 But
he that glorieth, let
him glory in the
Lord. 18 For not he
that commendeth him-
self is approved, but
whom the Lord com-
mendeth.

XI. Would to God
ye could bear with me
a little in *my* folly:
and indeed bear with
me. 2 For I am jea-
lous over you with
godly jealousy : for I
have espoused you to
one husband, that I
may present *you as*
a chaste virgin to
Christ. 3 But I fear,
lest by any means, as
the serpent beguiled
Eve through his sub-
tilty, so your minds
should be corrupted
from the simplicity
that is in Christ. 4 For
if he that cometh
preacheth another Je-
sus, whom we have
not preached, or *if* ye
receive another spirit,
which ye have not re-
ceived, or another gos-
pel, which ye have
not accepted, ye
might well bear with
him. 5 For I suppose
I was not a whit be-
hind the very chiefest
apostles. 6 But though
I be rude in speech,
yet not in knowledge ;
but we have been
throughly made mani-
fest among you in all
things. 7 Have I com-
mitted an offence in
abasing myself that
ye might be exalted,
because I have preach-
ed to you the gospel of
God freely ? 8 I robbed
other churches, taking
wages *of them*, to do
you service. 9 And

ὑμᾶς ὑπερεκτείνομεν ἑαυτούς· ἄχρι.γὰρ καὶ ὑμῶν ἐφθάσαμεν
you   do we overstretch ourselves,   (for to ²also ¹you   we came

ἐν τῷ εὐαγγελίῳ τοῦ χριστοῦ· 15 οὐκ εἰς   τὰ   ἄμετρα
in the glad tidings of the Christ ;)   not ²to ³the ⁴things ⁵beyond ⁶measure

καυχώμενοι ἐν ἀλλοτρίοις κόποις, ἐλπίδα.δὲ ἔχοντες, αὐξανο-
¹boasting   in   others'   labours,   but hope   having,   ³increas-

μένης τῆς.πίστεως.ὑμῶν, ἐν ὑμῖν μεγαλυνθῆναι κατὰ
ing   ¹your ²faith,   among you   to be enlarged   according to

τὸν.κανόνα.ἡμῶν εἰς περισσείαν, 16 εἰς τὰ ὑπερέκεινα ὑμῶν
our rule   to abundance,   to that beyond   you

εὐαγγελίσασθαι, οὐκ ἐν ἀλλοτρίῳ κανόνι εἰς τὰ
to announce the glad tidings, not ³in ⁴another's   ⁵rule ⁶as ⁷to ⁸things

ἕτοιμα καυχήσασθαι. 17 Ὁ.δὲ   καυχώμενος, ἐν   κυρίῳ
⁹ready ¹to ²boast.   But he that   boasts,   in [the] Lord

καυχάσθω· 18 οὐ.γὰρ ὁ ἑαυτὸν ⁿσυνιστῶν,‖ ἐκεῖνός ἐστιν
let him boast,   For not he that himself   commends,   this [one]   is

δόκιμος, ᵒἀλλ'‖ ὃν ὁ κύριος συνίστησιν.
approved,   but whom the Lord   commends.

11 Ὄφελον ᴾἀνείχεσθέ‖ μου μικρὸν �ۼ ʳτῇ ἀφροσύνῃ·‖
- I would   ye were bearing with me   a little   in folly ;

ἀλλὰ καὶ ἀνέχεσθέ μου. 2 ζηλῶ.γὰρ ὑμᾶς θεοῦ ζή-
but indeed bear with me.   For I am jealous as to you ²of ³God ¹with ⁴[the]

λῳ· ἡρμοσάμην.γὰρ ὑμᾶς ἑνὶ ἀνδρὶ παρθένον ἀγνὴν
³jealousy, for I have espoused you to one man   ⁴a ²virgin   ³chaste

παραστῆσαι τῷ χριστῷ· 3 φοβοῦμαι.δὲ μήπως ὡς ὁ
¹to ²present [³you] to the Christ.   But I fear   lest by any means as the

ὄφις ˢΕὔαν ἐξηπάτησεν‖ ἐν τῇ.πανουργίᾳ.αὐτοῦ, ᵗοὕτως‖
serpent ²Eve   ¹deceived   'n   his craftiness,   so

φθαρῇ τὰ.νοήματα.ὑμ ν ἀπὸ τῆς ἁπλότητος ʳτῆς
should be corrupted   your thoughts   from   simplicity   which [is]

εἰς ᵂτὸν‖ χριστόν. 4 εἰ.μὲν.γὰρ ὁ ἐρχόμενος ἄλλον Ἰησοῦν
as to the   Christ.   For if indeed he that   comes   another Jesus

κηρύσσει ὃν οὐκ.ἐκηρύξαμεν, ἢ πνεῦμα ἕτερον λαμβάνετε
proclaims whom we did not proclaim, or a ²spirit   ¹different ye receive

ὃ οὐκ.ἐλάβετε, ἢ εὐαγγέλιον ἕτερον ὃ οὐκ.ἐδέξασθε,
which ye did not receive, or ²glad ³tidings ¹different which ye did not accept,

καλῶς ˣἠνείχεσθε.‖ 5 Λογίζομαι ʸγὰρ‖ μηδὲν ὑστερη-
well   were ye bearing with [it].   ²I ³reckon   ¹for in nothing to have been

κέναι τῶν ᶻὑπὲρ.λίαν‖ ἀποστόλων. 6 εἰ.δὲ καὶ ἰδιώτης
behind those in a surpassing degree apostles.   But if even unpolished

τῷ λόγῳ, ἀλλ' οὐ τῇ γνώσει· ἀλλ' ἐν παντὶ ᵃφανε-
in speech [I am], yet not   in knowledge ; but   in   every [way] made

ρωθέντες‖ ἐν πᾶσιν εἰς ὑμᾶς. 7 ἢ ἁμαρτίαν.ἐποίησα, ἐμαυτὸν
manifest   in all things to you.   Or   did I commit sin,   ²myself

ταπεινῶν ἵνα ὑμεῖς ὑψωθῆτε, ὅτι δωρεὰν τὸ τοῦ θεοῦ
¹humbling that ye   might be exalted, because gratuitously the ³of ⁴God

εὐαγγέλιον εὐηγγελισάμην ὑμῖν ; 8 ἄλλας ἐκκλησίας ἐσύλησα,
¹glad ²tidings I announced   to you?   Other assemblies I despoiled,

λαβὼν ὀψώνιον πρὸς τὴν ὑμῶν διακονίαν· 9 καὶ
having received wages   for   ²towards ³you ¹service.   And

παρὼν πρὸς ὑμᾶς καὶ ὑστερηθείς, οὐ κατενάρκησα
being present with   you   and having been deficient,   I did lazily burden

---

ⁿ συνιστάνων LTTrAW.   ᵒ ἀλλὰ LTr.   ᴾ ἠνείχεσθέ E.   ᵠ + τι some (little) ELTTrAW.
ʳ τῆς E ; ἀφροσύνης ELTTrAW.   ˢ ἐξηπάτησεν Εὔαν LTTrAW.   ᵗ — οὕτως LTTrA.   ᵛ + καὶ
τῆς ἀγνότητος and the purity LTrAW.   ᵂ — τὸν T.   ˣ ἀνείχεσθε GTTrW ; ἀνέχεσθε ye
bear with LA.   ʸ δὲ but L.   ᶻ ὑπερλίαν GLTAW,   ᵃ φανερώσαντες having made [it]
manifest LTTrA.

bοὐδενός·‖ τὸ.γὰρ ὑστέρημά μου προσανεπλήρωσαν οἱ ἀδελ-
no one, (for the deficiency of me ³completely ⁴filled ⁵up ¹the ²breth-

φοὶ ἐλθόντες ἀπὸ Μακεδονίας· καὶ ἐν παντὶ ἀβαρῆ
ren who came from Macedonia,) and in everything not burdensome

cὑμῖν ἐμαυτὸν‖ ἐτήρησα ᾽καὶ τηρήσω. 10 ἔστιν ἀλήθεια
to you myself I kept and will keep. ⁵Is [¹the] ²truth

χριστοῦ ἐν ἐμοὶ ὅτι ἡ.καύχησις.αὕτη dοὐ.σφραγίσεται‖ εἰς ἐμὲ
³of ⁴Christ in me that this boasting shall not be sealed up as to me

ἐν τοῖς κλίμασιν τῆς Ἀχαίας. 11 eδιατί‖; ὅτι οὐκ.ἀγαπῶ
in the regions of Achaia. Why? because I do.not love

ὑμᾶς; ὁ θεὸς οἶδεν· 12 ὃ.δὲ ποιῶ, καὶ ποιήσω, ἵνα ἐκ-
you? God knows. But what I do, also I will do, that I may

κόψω τὴν ἀφορμὴν τῶν θελόντων ἀφορμήν, ἵνα ἐν.ᾧ͂ καυ-
cut off the occasion of those wishing an occasion, that wherein they

χῶνται εὑρεθῶσιν καθὼς καὶ ἡμεῖς. 13 οἱ.γὰρ.τοιοῦτοι
boast they may be found according as also we. For such [are]

ψευδαπόστολοι, ἐργάται δόλιοι, μετασχηματιζόμενοι εἰς ἀπο-
false apostles, ²workers ¹deceitful, transforming themselves into apo-

στόλους χριστοῦ· 14 καὶ fοὐ θαυμαστόν·‖ αὐτὸς.γὰρ ὁ
stles of Christ. And not wonderful [is it], for ⁶himself

σατανᾶς μετασχηματίζεται εἰς ἄγγελον φωτός· 15 οὐ
¹Satan transforms himself into an angel of light. [It is] not

μέγα οὖν εἰ καὶ οἱ.διάκονοι αὐτοῦ μετασχηματίζον-
a great thing therefore if also his servants transform themselves

ται ὡς διάκονοι δικαιοσύνης, ὧν τὸ τέλος ἔσται κατὰ
as servants of righteousness; of whom the end shall be according to

τὰ.ἔργα.αὐτῶν.
their works.

16 Πάλιν λέγω, μή τίς με δόξῃ ἄφρονα εἶναι· εἰ.δὲ
Again I say, Not anyone ²me ¹should ³think a fool to be; but if

μήγε, κἂν ὡς ἄφρονα δέξασθέ με, ἵνα gμικρόν τι κἀγὼ‖
otherwise, even as a fool receive me, that ²little ¹some I also

καυχήσωμαι. 17 ὃ λαλῶ, οὐ hλαλῶ κατὰ κύριον,‖
may boast. What I speak, ³not ²do ¹I speak according to [the] Lord,

ἀλλ᾽ ὡς ἐν ἀφροσύνῃ, ἐν ταύτῃ τῇ ὑποστάσει τῆς καυχήσεως.
but as in folly, in this confidence of boasting.

18 ἐπεὶ πολλοὶ καυχῶνται κατὰ iτὴν‖ σάρκα, κἀγὼ καυ-
Since many boast according to flesh, I also will

χήσομαι. 19 ἡδέως.γὰρ ἀνέχεσθε τῶν ἀφρόνων, φρόνιμοι
boast. For ⁴gladly ¹ye ⁵bear ⁶with ⁷fools ³intelligent

ὄντες· 20 ἀνέχεσθε.γὰρ εἴ τις ὑμᾶς καταδουλοῖ, εἴ τις
²being. For ye bear [it] if anyone ²you ¹bring into bondage, if anyone

κατεσθίει, εἴ τις λαμβάνει, εἴ τις ἐπαίρεται,
devour [you], if anyone take [from you], if anyone exalt himself,

εἴ τις kὑμᾶς εἰς πρόσωπον‖ δέρει. 21 κατὰ ἀτιμίαν λέγω,
if anyone ²you ³on ⁴the ⁵face ¹beat. As to dishonour I speak,

ὡς ὅτι ἡμεῖς lἠσθενήσαμεν.‖ ἐν.ᾧ.δ᾽ ἄν τις τολμᾷ, ἐν
as that we were weak; but wherein anyone may be daring, (in

ἀφροσύνῃ λέγω, τολμῶ κἀγώ. 22 Ἑβραῖοί εἰσιν; κἀγώ·
folly I speak,) ²am ³daring ¹I also. Hebrews are they? I also.

mἸσραηλῖταί‖ εἰσιν; κἀγώ· σπέρμα Ἀβραάμ εἰσιν; κἀγώ·
Israelites are they? I also. Seed of Abraham are they? I also.

when I was present with you, and wanted, I was chargeable to no man: for that which was lacking to me the brethren which came from Macedonia supplied: and in all *things* I have kept myself from being burdensome unto you, and *so* will I keep *myself*. 10 As the truth of Christ is in me, no man shall stop me of this boasting in the regions of Achaia. 11 Wherefore? *because* I love you not? God knoweth. 12 But what I do, that I will do, that I may cut off occasion from them which desire occasion; that wherein they glory, they may be found even as we. 13 For such *are* false apostles, deceitful workers, transforming themselves into the apostles of Christ. 14 And no marvel; for Satan himself is transformed into an angel of light. 15 Therefore *it is* no great thing if his ministers also be transformed as the ministers of righteousness; whose end shall be according to their works.

16 I say again, Let no man think me a fool; if otherwise, yet as a fool receive me, that I may boast myself a little. 17 That which I speak, I speak *it* not after the Lord, but as it were foolishly, in this confidence of boasting. 18 Seeing that many glory after the flesh, I will glory also. 19 For ye suffer fools gladly, seeing ye *yourselves* are wise. 20 For ye suffer, if a man bring you into bondage, if a man devour *you,* if a man take *of you,* if a man exalt himself, if a man smite you on the face. 21 I speak as concerning reproach, as though we had been weak. Howbeit whereinsoever any is bold, (I speak foolishly,) I am bold also. 22 Are they Hebrews? so *am* I. Are they Israelites? so *am* I. Are they the seed of

---

b οὐθενός LTTrA. c ἐμαυτὸν ὑμῖν LTTrA. d οὐ φραγήσεται shall not be stopped EGLTTrAW. e διὰ τί LTTrA. f οὐ θαῦμα no wonder LTTrA. g κἀγὼ μικρόν τι GLTTrAW. h κατὰ κύριον λαλῶ LTTrAW. i — τὴν TTr. k εἰς πρόσωπον ὑμᾶς LTTrAW. l ἠσθενή-καμεν have been weak LTTr. m Ἰσραηλεῖταί T.

Abraham? so am I.
23 Are they mini-ters
of Christ? (I speak as
a fool) I am more;
in labours more abun-
dant, in stripes above
measure. iu prisons
more frequent, in
deaths oft. 24 Of the
Jews five times re-
ceived I forty stripes
save one. 25 Thrice
was I beaten with
rods,once was I stoned,
thrice I suffered ship-
wreck, a night and
a day I have been
in the deep; 26 in
journeyings often, in
perils of waters, in
perils of robbers, in
perils by mine own
countrymen, in perils
by the heathen, in pe-
rils in the city, in pe-
rils in the wilderness,
in perils in the sea, in
perils among false
brethren ; 27 in weari-
ness and painfulness,
in watchings often, in
hunger and thirst, in
fastings often, in cold
and nakedness. 28 Be-
side those things that
are without, that
which cometh upon
me daily, the care
of all the churches.
29 Who is weak, and I
am not weak? who is
offended, and I burn
not? 30 If I must
needs glory, I will
glory of the things
which concern mine
infirmities. 31 The God
and Father of our
Lord Jesus Christ,
which is blessed for
evermore, knoweth
that I lie not. 32 In
Damascus the govern-
or under Aretas the
king kept the city of
the Damascenes with
a garrison, desirous to
apprehend me : 33 and
through a window in a
basket was I let down
by the wall, and escap-
ed his hands.

XII. It is not expe-
dient for me doubt-
less to glory. I will
come to visions and
revelations of the
Lord. 2 I knew a man
in Christ above four-
teen years ago, (whe-
ther in the body, I can-
not tell ; or whether
out of the body, I can-
not tell: God know-
eth ;) such an one

23 διάκονοι χριστοῦ εἰσιν; παραφρονῶν λαλῶ, ⁿὑπὲρ
Servants of Christ are they? (as being beside myself I speak,) above

ἐγώ·‖ ἐν °κόποις περισσοτέρως, °ἐν πληγαῖς ὑπερ-
[measure] I [too];·in labours more abundantly, in stripes above

βαλλόντως, ἐν φυλακαῖς περισσοτέρως,‖ ἐν θανάτοις πολ-
measure, in imprisonments more abundantly, in deaths often.

λάκις. 24 ὑπὸ Ἰουδαίων πεντάκις ᴾτεσσαράκοντα‖
From Jews five times forty [stripes]

παρὰ μίαν ἔλαβον, 25 τρὶς ᑫἐῤῥαβδίσθην.‖ ἅπαξ ἐλιθάσθην,
except one I received. Thrice I was beaten with rods, once I was stoned,

τρὶς ἐναυάγησα, νυχθήμερον ἐν τῷ βυθῷ πεποίηκα·
three times I was shipwrecked, a night and a day in the deep I have passed:

26 ὁδοιπορίαις πολλάκις· κινδύνοις ποταμῶν, κινδύνοις
in journeyings often, in perils of rivers, in perils

λῃστῶν, κινδύνοις ἐκ γένους, κινδύνοις ἐξ ἐθνῶν,
of robbers, in perils from [my own] race, in perils from [the] nations,

κινδύνοις ἐν πόλει, κινδύνοις ἐν ἐρημίᾳ, κινδύνοις ἐν
in perils in [the] city, in perils in [the] desert, in perils on

θαλάσσῃ, κινδύνοις ἐν ψευδαδέλφοις· 27 ʳἐν‖ κόπῳ καὶ
[the] sea, in perils among false brethren ; in labour and

μόχθῳ, ἐν ἀγρυπνίαις πολλάκις, ἐν λιμῷ καὶ δίψει, ἐν νη-
toil, in watchings often, in hunger and thirst, in fast-

στείαις πολλάκις, ἐν ψύχει καὶ γυμνότητι· 28 χωρὶς τῶν
ings often, in cold and nakedness. Besides the things

παρεκτός, ˢἡ ἐπισύστασίς μου‖ ἡ καθ᾽ ἡμέραν, ἡ μέριμνα
without, the crowding on me daily, the care

πασῶν τῶν ἐκκλησιῶν. 29 τίς ἀσθενεῖ, καὶ οὐκ ἀσθενῶ ; τίς
concerning all the assemblies. Who is weak, and I am not weak? who

σκανδαλίζεται, καὶ οὐκ ἐγὼ πυροῦμαι; 30 εἰ καυχᾶσθαι
is offended, and ³not ¹I ²do burn? If ²to ¹boast

δεῖ, τὰ τῆς ἀσθενείας μου καυχήσομαι. 31 Ὁ
¹it ²behoves, [in] the things concerning my infirmity I will boast. The

θεὸς καὶ πατὴρ τοῦ κυρίου·ᵗἡμῶν‖ Ἰησοῦ ᵛχριστοῦ‖ οἶδεν, ὁ
God and Father of our Lord Jesus Christ knows, he who

ὢν εὐλογητὸς εἰς τοὺς αἰῶνας, ὅτι οὐ ψεύδομαι. 32 ἐν Δα-
is blessed to the ages, that I do not lie. In Da-

μασκῷ ὁ ἐθνάρχης Ἀρέτα τοῦ βασιλέως ἐφρούρει τὴν
mascus the ethnarch of Aretas the king was guarding the

ʷΔαμασκηνῶν πόλιν,‖ πιάσαι με ˣθέλων·‖ 33 καὶ διὰ
²of ³the ⁴Damascenes ¹city, ⁵to ⁷take ⁶me ³wishing. And through

θυρίδος ἐν σαργάνῃ ἐχαλάσθην διὰ τοῦ τείχους, καὶ
a window in a basket I was let down through the wall, and

ἐξέφυγον τὰς χεῖρας αὐτοῦ.
escaped his hands.

12 Καυχᾶσθαι ʸδὴ οὐ συμφέρει μοι· ἐλεύσομαι γὰρ‖ ᶻ εἰς
To boast indeed is not profitable to me; for I will come to

ὀπτασίας καὶ ἀποκαλύψεις κυρίου· 2 οἶδα ἄνθρωπον ἐν
visions and revelations of [the] Lord. I know a man in

χριστῷ πρὸ ἐτῶν δεκατεσσάρων, εἴτε ἐν σώματι οὐκ οἶδα,
Christ ²years ³ago ¹fourteen, (whether in [the] body I know not,

εἴτε ἐκτὸς ᵃτοῦ‖ σώματος οὐκ οἶδα· ὁ θεὸς οἶδεν· ἁρπαγέντα
or out of the body I know not, God knows,) ⁴caught ⁵away

ᵖ ὑπερεγὼ L. ° ἐν φυλακαῖς περισσοτέρως, ἐν πληγαῖς ὑπερβαλλόντως LTTrA ; ἐν πλη. περισσ.
ἐν φυλ. ὑπερβ. T. ᴾ τεσσεράκοντα LTTrA. ᑫ ἐραβδίσθην LTTrA. ʳ — ἐν LTTrAW. ˢ ἡ ἐπί-
στασίς μοι my anxiety LTTrAW. ᵗ — ἡμῶν (read the Lord) LTTrAW. ᵛ — χριστοῦ LTTrA.
ʷ πόλιν Δαμασκηνῶν LTTrA. ˣ — θέλων LTTr[A]W. ʸ δεῖ, οὐ συμφέρον μέν, ἐλεύσομαι δὲ
it behoves [me], not profitable [is it], but I will come LTTr. ᶻ + καὶ also L. ᵃ — τοῦ L.

τὸν.τοιοῦτον ἕως τρίτου οὐρανοῦ. 3 καὶ οἶδα τὸν τοιοῦτον
¹such ²a ³one   to [the] third   heaven.   And I know   such

ἄνθρωπον, εἴτε ἐν ·σώματι εἴτε ᵇἐκτὸς‖ τοῦ σώματος ᶜοὐκ
a man,   (whether in [the] body   or   out of   the   body   ²not

οἶδα·‖ ὁ Θεὸς οἶδεν· 4 ὅτι   ἡρπάγη   εἰς τὸν παράδεισον,
¹I ²know,   God knows:)   that he was caught away to   Paradise,

καὶ ἤκουσεν ἄρρητα ·ῥήμα:α, ἃ οὐκ.ἐξὸν ἀνθρώπῳ
and   heard   unutterable sayings,   which it is not permitted   to man

λαλῆσαι. 5 ὑπὲρ τοῦ.τοιούτου καυχήσομαι· ὑπὲρ.δὲ ἐμαυτοῦ
to speak.   Concerning   such a one   I will boast,   but concerning· myself

οὐ.καυχήσομαι, εἰ.μὴ ἐν ταῖς.ἀσθενείαις.ᵈμου·‖ 6 ἐὰν.γὰρ
I will not boast,   unless   in   ·my weaknesses.   For if

θελήσω καυχήσασθαι, οὐκ.ἔσομαι ἄφρων·᷈ ἀλήθειαν.γὰρ
I should desire   to boast,   I shall not be   a fool;   for truth

ἐρῶ· φείδομαι.δὲ, μή τις· εἰς ἐμὲ λογίσηται ὑπὲρ ὃ
I will say;· but I forbear,   lest anyone as to me   should reckon   above what

βλέπει με, ἢ ·ἀκούει ᵉτι‖ ἐξ ἐμοῦ. 7 Καὶ τῇ ὑπερβολῇ
he sees me, or   hears   anything of me.   And by the surpassingness

ᶠτῶν ἀποκαλύψεων ᶠἵνα μὴ.ὑπεραίρωμαι, ἐδόθη μοι σκόλοψ
of the   revelations   that I might not be exalted, was given to me a thorn

τῇ σαρκί, ἄγγελος ᵍσατᾶν‖ ἵνα με κολαφίζῃ, ʰἵνα ²not
for the flesh,   a messenger   of Satan,   that me he might buffet,   that ²not

ὑπεραίρωμαι.‖ 8 ὑπὲρ τούτου τρὶς τὸν κύριον παρεκάλεσα,
¹I ²might be exalted.   For this thrice the Lord   I besought

ἵνα ἀποστῇ ἀπ᾽ ἐμοῦ· 9 καὶ εἴρηκέν μοι, Ἀρκεῖ σοι ἡ
that it might depart from me,   And   he said to me,   Suffices thee

χάρις.μου· ἡ.γὰρ δύναμίς ᵏμου‖ ἐν ἀσθενείᾳ ᶫτελειοῦται.‖
my grace;   for the   power   of me in   weakness   is perfected.

ἥδιστα   οὖν   μᾶλλον καυχήσομαι ἐν ταῖς.ἀσθενείαις.ᵐμου·‖
Most gladly therefore   rather   will I boast in   my weaknesses

ἵνα ἐπισκηνώσῃ ἐπ᾽ ἐμὲ ἡ δύναμις τοῦ χριστοῦ. 10 διὸ
that may dwell   upon me the power   of the   Christ.   Wherefore

εὐδοκῶ   ἐν ἀσθενείαις, ἐν ὕβρεσιν, ἐν ἀνάγκαις, ἐν διωγ-
I take pleasure in weaknesses,   in insults,   in necessities,   in perse-

μοῖς, ⁿἐν‖ στενοχωρίαις, ὑπὲρ χριστοῦ· ὅταν.γὰρ ἀσθενῶ,
cutions,   in   straits,   for   Christ: for when   I may be weak,

τότε· δυνατός εἰμι.
then   powerful I am.

11 Γέγονα ἄφρων ᵒκαυχώμενος·‖ ὑμεῖς μὲ ἠναγκάσατε.
I have become a fool   boasting;   ye   me   compelled;

ἐγὼ.γὰρ ὤφειλον ὑφ᾽ ὑμῶν   συνίστασθαι· οὐδὲν.γὰρ
for I   ought ᵛ by   you   to have been commended;   for nothing

ὑστέρησα τῶν ᵖὑπὲρ.λίαν‖ ἀποστόλων, εἰ καὶ οὐδέν εἰμι.
I was behind   those in a surpassing degree   apostles,   if also nothing I am.

12 Τὰ μὲν σημεῖα τοῦ ἀποστόλου ᵠκατειργάσθη‖ ἐν ὑμῖν
The ²indeed ¹signs of the   apostle   were worked out   among you

ᶠἐν πάσῃ ὑπομονῇ, ᶠἐν‖ σημείοις ˢκαὶ‖ τέρασιν καὶ δυνάμεσιν.
in all   endurance,   in   signs   and   wonders and works of power.

13 τί.γὰρ ἐστιν ὃ ᵗἡττήθητε‖ ὑπὲρ τὰς λοιπὰς ἐκ-
For in what is it that ye were inferior beyond the   rest   [of the] as-

κλησίας, εἰ.μὴ ὅτι αὐτὸς ἐγὼ οὐ.κατενάρκησα ὑμῶν; χαρί-
semblies,   unless that ²myself ¹I   did not lazily burden   you?   For-

caught up to the third
heaven. 3 And I know
such a man, (whether
in the body, or out of
the body, I cannot tell:
God knoweth;) 4 how
that he was caught up
into paradise, and
heard unspeakable
words, which it is not
lawful for a man to
utter. 5 Of such an
one will I glory: yet
of myself I will not
glory, but in mine in-
firmities. 6 For though
I would desire to glo-
ry, I shall not be a
fool; for I will say the
truth: but now I for-
bear, lest any man
should think of me
above that which he
seeth me to be, or.that
he heareth of me.
7 And lest I should be
exalted above mea-
sure through the a-
bundance of the re-
velations, there was
given to me a thorn in
the flesh, the messen-
ger of Satan to buffet
me, lest I should be
exalted above mea-
sure. 8 For this thing
I besought the Lord
thrice, that it might
depart from me.
9 And he said unto me,
My grace is sufficient
for thee: for my
strength is made per-
fect in weakness.
Most gladly therefore
will I rather glory in
my infirmities, · that
the power of Christ
may rest upon me.
10 Therefore I take
pleasure in infirmities,
in reproaches, in ne-
cessities, in persecu-
tions, in distresses for
Christ's sake: for when
I am weak, then am I
strong.

11 I am become a
fool in glorying; ye
have compelled me :
for I ought to have
been commended of
you : for in nothing
am I behind the
very chiefest apostles,
though I be nothing.
12 Truly the signs
of an apostle were
wrought among you
in all patience, in
signs, and wonders,
and mighty deeds.
13 For what is it
wherein ye were infe-
rior to other churches,

ᵇ χωρὶς apart from LTTrA.   ᶜ — οὐκ οἶδα L.   ᵈ — μου my LTr[A].   ᵉ — τι LTTr[A].
ᶠ + διὸ therefore LTr[A].   ᵍ σατανᾶ LTTtA.   ʰ — ἵνα μὴ ὑπεραίρωμαι [L]Tr[A].   ⁱ + [καὶ]
and L.   ᵏ — μου LTTrA.   ᶫ τελεῖται LTTrA.   ᵐ [μου] Tr.   ⁿ καὶ and T.   ᵒ — καυχώμενος GLTTrAW.   ᵖ ὑπερλίαν GLTAW.   ᵠ κατηργάσθη T.   ʳ — ἐν LTTrAW.   ˢ τε καὶ
and also TA.   ᵗ ἡσσώθητε LTTrA.

except *it be* that I myself was not burdensome to you ? forgive me this wrong. 14 Behold, the third time I am ready to come to you ; and I will not be burdensome to you : for I seek not yours, but you : for the children ought not to lay up for the parents, but the parents for the children. 15 And I will very gladly spend and be spent for you; though the more abundantly I love you, the less I be loved. 16 But be it so, I did not burden you: nevertheless, being crafty, I caught you with guile. 17 Did I make a gain of you by any of them whom I sent unto you? 18 I desired Titus, and with *him* I sent a brother. Did Titus make a gain of you ? *walked* we not in the same spirit ?

19 Again, think ye that we excuse ourselves unto you ? we speak before God in Christ : but *we do* all things, dearly beloved, for your edifying. 20 For I fear, lest,when I come,I shall not find you such as I would, and *that* I shall be found unto you such as ye would not : lest *there* be debates, envyings, wraths, strifes, backbitings, whisperings, swellings, tumults : 21 *and* lest, when I come again, my God will humble me among you, and *that* I shall bewail many which have sinned already, and have not repented of the uncleanness and fornication and lasciviousness which they have committed.

XIII. This *is* the third *time* I am coming to you. In the mouth of two or three witnesses shall every word be established. 2 I told you before, and foretell you, as if I were present, the second time ; and being absent now I write

σασθέ μοι τὴν.ἀδικίαν.ταύτην. 14 ἰδοὺ τρίτον ᵘ ἑτοίμως ἔχω
give me this injustice.   Lo, a third time ready I am

ἐλθεῖν πρὸς ὑμᾶς, καὶ οὐ καταναρκήσω ᵛὑμῶν·� ού.γὰρ.ζητῶ
to come to you, and I will not lazily burden you ; for I do not seek

τὰ ὑμῶν, ᵂἀλλ'�\|| ὑμᾶς. ού.γὰρ ὀφείλει τὰ τέκνα τοῖς
the things of you, but you ; for ⁴not ³ought ¹the ²children for the

γονεῦσιν θησαυρίζειν, ˣἀλλ'�\|| οἱ γονεῖς τοῖς τέκνοις. 15 ἐγὼ.δὲ
parents to treasure up, but the parents for the children. Now I

ἥδιστα δαπανήσω καὶ ἐκδαπανηθήσομαι ὑπὲρ τῶν ψυχῶν
most gladly will spend and will be utterly spent for ²souls

ὑμῶν· εἰ ʸκαὶ\|| περισσοτέρως ὑμᾶς ᶻἀγαπῶν,\|| ᵃἧττον\|| ᵇἀγαπῶ-
¹your, if even more abundantly ²you ¹loving, less I am loved.

μαι.\|| 16 Ἔστω.δέ, ἐγὼ ού.κατεβάρησα ὑμᾶς· ᵂἀλλ'ᴵᴵ ὑπάρχων
But be it so, I did not burden you ; but being

πανοῦργος δόλῳ ὑμᾶς ἔλαβον. 17 μή τινα ὧν ἀπέσταλκα
crafty with guile you I took. Any of whom I have sent

πρὸς ὑμᾶς, δι' αὐτοῦ ἐπλεονέκτησα ὑμᾶς ; 18 παρεκάλεσα
to you, by him did I overreach you ? I besought

Τίτον, καὶ συναπέστειλα τὸν ἀδελφόν· μή τι ἐπλεονέκτησεν
Titus, and sent with [him] the brother :   Did ²overreach

ὑμᾶς Τίτος ; ού τῷ αὐτῷ πνεύματι περιεπατήσαμεν ; ού
¹you ¹Titus ? Not by the same spirit walked we ? Not

τοῖς αὐτοῖς ἴχνεσιν ;
in the same steps ?

19 ᶜΠάλιν\|| δοκεῖτε ὅτι ὑμῖν ἀπολογούμεθα ; ᶜ ᵈκατενώ-
Again do ye think that to you we are making a defence ? be-

πιον\|| ᵉτοῦ\|| θεοῦ ἐν χριστῷ λαλοῦμεν· τὰ.δὲ.πάντα, ἀγαπητοί,
fore   God in Christ we speak ; and all things, beloved,

ὑπὲρ τῆς.ὑμῶν.οἰκοδομῆς. 20 φοβοῦμαι.γάρ, μήπως ἐλθὼν
for your building up.   For I fear, lest perhaps having come

ούχ οἵους θέλω εὕρω ὑμᾶς, κἀγὼ εὑρεθῶ ὑμῖν οἷον\||
not such as I wish I should find you, and I be found by you such as

ού.θέλετε· μήπως ᶠἔρεις,\|| ᵍζῆλοι,\|| θυμοί, ἐριθεῖαι,
ye do not wish: lest perhaps [there be] strifes, jealousies, indignations, contentions,

καταλαλιαί, ψιθυρισμοί, φυσιώσεις, ἀκαταστασίαι· 21 μὴ
evil speakings, whisperings, puffings up, commotions ; lest

πάλιν ʰἐλθόντα με\|| ⁱταπεινώσῃ\|| ᵏ ὁ θεός μου πρὸς ὑμᾶς,
again. having come ²me ³should ⁴humble ²God ¹my as to you,

καὶ πενθήσω πολλοὺς τῶν προημαρτηκότων, καὶ
and I should mourn over many of those who have before sinned, and

μὴ.μετανοησάντων ἐπὶ τῇ ἀκαθαρσίᾳ καὶ πορνείᾳ καὶ ἀσελ-
have not repented upon the uncleanness and fornication and licen-

γείᾳ ᾗ ἔπραξαν.
tiousness which they practised.

13 Τρίτον.τοῦτο ἔρχομαι πρὸς ὑμᾶς. ἐπὶ στόματος
This third time I am coming to you. In [the] mouth

δύο μαρτύρων καὶ τριῶν σταθήσεται πᾶν ῥῆμα. 2 προεί-
of two witnesses or of three shall be established every matter. I have be-

ρηκα καὶ προλέγω, ὡς παρὼν τὸ δεύτερον, καὶ
fore declared and I say beforehand, as being present the second time, and

ἀπὼν νῦν ¹γράφω\|| τοῖς προημαρτηκόσιν, καὶ τοῖς
being absent now I write to those who have before sinned, and to ²the

---

ᵘ + τοῦτο this (third time) GLTTr[A]W. ᵛ — ὑμῶν LTTrA. ᵂ ἀλλὰ LTTrAW. ˣ ἀλλὰ TTr.
ʸ — καὶ LTTrA. ᶻ ἀγαπῶ I love T. ᵃ ἧσσον LTTrA. ᵇ ἀγαπῶμαι; am I loved ? T. ᶜ Πάλαι
and — ; (*read* Long ago ye are thinking, &c.) LTTrA. ᵈ κατέναντι LTTrA. ᵉ — τοῦ
LTTrAW. ᶠ ἔρις strife LT. ᵍ ζῆλος jealousy LTTrAW. ʰ ἐλθόντος μου I having come
LTTrAW. ⁱ ταπεινώσει shall humble LTTrA. ᵏ + με ᵇme LTTrAW. ˡ — γράφω GLTTrAW.

λοιποῖς πᾶσιν, ὅτι ἐὰν ἔλθω εἰς τὸ πάλιν οὐ.φείσομαι. 3 ἐπεὶ
²rest   ¹all,   that if   I come   again   I will not spare.   Since

δοκιμὴν ζητεῖτε τοῦ ἐν ἐμοὶ λαλοῦντος χριστοῦ, ὃς εἰς
a proof ye seek ⁴in ⁵me ³speaking ¹of ²Christ, (who towards

ὑμᾶς οὐκ.ἀσθενεῖ, ἀλλὰ δυνατεῖ ἐν ὑμῖν· 4 καὶ.γὰρ ᵐεἰˡˡ
you   is not weak, but is powerful in you,   for indeed if

ἐσταυρώθη ἐξ ἀσθενείας, ἀλλὰ ζῇ ἐκ δυνάμεως θεοῦ·
he was crucified in   weakness,   yet he lives by ·²power ¹God's;

καὶ.γὰρ ⁿ ἡμεῖς ἀσθενοῦμεν ἐν αὐτῷ, ἀλλὰ °ζησόμεθαˡˡ σὺν
for indeed we   are weak   in him,   but   we shall live with

αὐτῷ ἐκ δυνάμεως θεοῦ ᴾεἰς ὑμᾶς·ˡˡ 5 ἑαυτοὺς πειράζετε
him by ²power ¹God's towards ²you,) yourselves try ye

εἰ ἐστὲ ἐν τῇ πίστει, ἑαυτοὺς δοκιμάζετε. ἢ οὐκ.ἐπιγινώσκετε
if ye are in the faith; yourselves prove: or do ye not recognize

ἑαυτούς, ὅτι ᑫἸησοῦς χριστὸςˡˡ ἐν ὑμῖν ʳἐστιν·ˡˡ εἰ.μή τι ἀδό-
yourselves, that Jesus Christ   in you is,   unless re-

κιμοί ἐστε. 6 ἐλπίζω.δὲ ὅτι γνώσεσθε ὅτι ἡμεῖς οὐκ.ἐσμὲν
jected ye are?   Now I hope that ye will know that we   are not

ἀδόκιμοι. 7 ˢεὔχομαι·ˡˡ.δὲ πρὸς τὸν θεὸν μὴ ποιῆσαι ὑμᾶς
rejected.   But I pray   to   God [that] ²may ³do ye

κακὸν μηδέν, οὐχ ἵνα ἡμεῖς δόκιμοι φανῶμεν, ἀλλ᾽ ἵνα ὑμεῖς
⁵evil ⁴nothing; not that we   approved may appear, but that ye

τὸ καλὸν ποιῆτε, ἡμεῖς.δὲ ὡς ἀδόκιμοι ὦμεν. 8 οὐ.γὰρ
what [is] right may do, and we as rejected   be.   For not

δυνάμεθά τι κατὰ τῆς ἀληθείας, ᵗἀλλ᾽ˡˡ ὑπὲρ τῆς ἀληθείας.
have we ²power ¹any against the truth,   but for the truth.

9 χαίρομεν.γὰρ ὅταν ἡμεῖς ἀσθενῶμεν, ὑμεῖς.δὲ δυνατοὶ ἦτε·
For we rejoice when we may be weak, and ye powerful may be.

τοῦτο.ᵛδὲˡˡ καὶ εὐχόμεθα, τὴν.ὑμῶν.κατάρτισιν. 10 διὰ.τοῦτο
But this   also we pray for,   your perfecting.   On this account

ταῦτα ἀπὼν γράφω, ἵνα παρὼν μὴ ἀποτόμως χρή-
these things being absent I write, that being present not with severity I may

σωμαι, κατὰ τὴν ἐξουσίαν ἣν ʷἔδωκέν μοι ὁ κύριοςˡˡ εἰς
treat [you], according to the authority which ¹³gave ¹me ¹the ²Lord for

οἰκοδομὴν καὶ οὐκ εἰς καθαίρεσιν.
building up and not for overthrowing.

11 Λοιπόν, ἀδελφοί, χαίρετε, καταρτίζεσθε, παρακαλεῖσθε,
For the rest, brethren, rejoice;   be perfected;   be encouraged;

τὸ.αὐτὸ φρονεῖτε, εἰρηνεύετε· καὶ ὁ θεὸς τῆς ἀγάπης καὶ
²the ³same ⁴thing ¹mind; be at peace; and the God of love and

εἰρήνης ἔσται μεθ᾽ ὑμῶν. 12 Ἀσπάσασθε ἀλλήλους ἐν ἁγίῳ
peace shall be with you.   Salute   one another with a holy

φιλήματι. ἀσπάζονται ὑμᾶς οἱ ἅγιοι πάντες. 13 Ἡ χάρις
kiss.   ⁴Salute ⁵you ²the ³saints ¹all.   The grace

τοῦ κυρίου Ἰησοῦ χριστοῦ, καὶ ἡ ἀγάπη τοῦ θεοῦ, καὶ ἡ
of the Lord   Jesus Christ,   and the love of God,   and the

κοινωνία τοῦ ἁγίου πνεύματος μετὰ πάντων ὑμῶν. ˣἀμήν.ˡˡ
fellowship of the Holy Spirit   [be] with ²all ¹you. Amen.

ʸΠρὸς Κορινθίους δευτέρα ἐγράφη ἀπὸ Φιλίππων τῆς
²To [³the] ⁴Corinthians ¹second written from Philippi

Μακεδονίας, διὰ Τίτου καὶ Λουκᾶ.ˡˡ
of Macedonia, by Titus and Lucas.

[right column — KJV]

to them which hereto-
fore have sinned, and
to all other, that, if I
come again, I will not
spare: 3 since ye seek
a proof of Christ
speaking in me, which
to you-ward is not
weak, but is mighty
in you. 4 For though he
was crucified through
weakness, yet he liveth
by the power of God.
For we also are weak
in him, but we shall
live with him by the
power of God toward
you. 5 Examine your-
selves, whether ye be
in the faith; prove
your own selves. Know
ye not your own selves,
how that Jesus Christ
is in you, except ye be
reprobates? 6 But I
trust that ye shall
know that we are not
reprobates. 7 Now I
pray to God that ye do
no evil; not that we
should appear approv-
ed, but that ye should
do that which is ho-
nest, though we be as
reprobates. 8 For we
can do nothing against
the truth, but for the
truth. 9 For we are
glad, when we are
weak, and ye are
strong: and this also
we wish, even your
perfection. 10 There-
fore I write these
things being absent,
lest being present I
should use sharpness,
according to the power
which the Lord hath
given me to edifica-
tion, and not to de-
struction.

11 Finally, brethren,
farewell. Be perfect,
be of good comfort,
be of one mind, live
in peace; and the God
of love and peace shall
be with you. 12 Greet
one another with an
holy kiss. 13 All the
saints salute you.
14 The grace of the
Lord Jesus Christ, and
the love of God, and
the communion of the
Holy Ghost, be with
you all. Amen.

ᵐ — εἰ [L]TTrA.   ⁿ + καὶ also E.   ° ζήσομεν LTTrAW.   ᴾ [εἰς ὑμᾶς] A.   ᑫ χριστὸς
Ἰησοῦς TTr.   ʳ — ἐστιν (read [is]) [L]TTr[A].   ˢ εὐχόμεθα we pray LTTrAW.   ᵗ ἀλλὰ TTrA.
ᵛ — δὲ but LTTrAW.   ʷ ὁ κύριος ἔδωκέν μοι LTTrA.   ˣ — ἀμήν GLTTrAW.   ʸ — the
subscription GLTW; Πρὸς Κορινθίους β′ TrA.

PAUL, an apostle, (not of men, neither by man, but by Jesus Christ, and God the Father, who raised him from the dead ;) 2 and all the brethren which are with me, unto the churches of Galatia : 3 Grace be to you and peace from God the Father, and from our Lord Jesus Christ, 4 who gave himself for our sins, that he might deliver us from this present evil world, according to the will of God and our Father: 5 to whom be glory for ever and ever. Amen.

ΠΑΥΛΟΣ ἀπόστολος, οὐκ ἀπ' ἀνθρώπων οὐδὲ δι' ἀν-
Paul   apostle,   not from   men   nor through
θρώπου, ἀλλὰ διὰ Ἰησοῦ χριστοῦ, καὶ θεοῦ   πατρὸς τοῦ
man,   but through Jesus   Christ, and God [the] Father, who
ἐγείραντος αὐτὸν   ἐκ   νεκρῶν, 2 καὶ οἱ σὺν ἐμοὶ
raised   him from among [the] dead,   and '²the ⁴with ⁵me
πάντες ἀδελφοί, ταῖς ἐκκλησίαις τῆς Γαλατίας· 3 χάρις ὑμῖν
¹all ³brethren, to the assemblies   ' of Galatia. Grace to you
καὶ εἰρήνη ἀπὸ θεοῦ   πατρὸς καὶ κυρίου ἡμῶν Ἰησοῦ χρισ-
and peace from God [the] Father and ²Lord ¹our Jesus Christ,
τοῦ, 4 τοῦ δόντος ἑαυτὸν ^bὑπὲρ‖ τῶν.ἁμαρτιῶν.ἡμῶν, ὅπως
who gave himself for   our sins,   so that
ἐξέληται ἡμᾶς ' ἐκ τοῦ ^cἐνεστῶτος αἰῶνος‖ πονηροῦ,
he might deliver us out of the present   ²age   ¹evil,
κατὰ τὸ θέλημα τοῦ θεοῦ καὶ πατρὸς ἡμῶν, 5 ᾧ
according to the will of ²God ³and ⁴Father ¹our ; to whom [be]
ἡ δόξα εἰς τοὺς αἰῶνας τῶν αἰώνων. ἀμήν.
the glory to the ages of the ages. Amen.

6 I marvel that ye are so soon removed from him that called you into the grace of Christ unto another gospel : 7 which is not another ; but there be some that trouble you, and would pervert the gospel of Christ. 8 But though we, or an angel from heaven, preach any other gospel unto you than that which we have preached unto you, let him be accursed. 9 As we said before, so say I now again, If any man preach any other gospel unto you than that ye have received, let him be accursed. 10 For do I now persuade men, or God ? or do I seek to please men ? for if I yet pleased men, I should not be the servant of Christ.

6 Θαυμάζω ὅτι οὕτως ταχέως μετατίθεσθε ἀπὸ τοῦ
I wonder that thus quickly ye are being changed from him who
καλέσαντος ὑμᾶς ἐν χάριτι . χριστοῦ, εἰς ἕτερον εὐαγ-
called   you in ²grace 'Christ's, to a different glad
γέλιον· 7 ὃ ' οὐκ.ἔστιν ἄλλο, εἰ.μή τινές εἰσιν οἱ ταράσ-
tidings, which is not another ; but ³some ¹there ²are who trou-
σοντες ὑμᾶς, καὶ θέλοντες μεταστρέψαι τὸ εὐαγγέλιον τοῦ
ble   you,   and desire to pervert the glad tidings of the
χριστοῦ. 8 ἀλλὰ καὶ ἐὰν ἡμεῖς ἢ ἄγγελος ἐξ οὐρανοῦ ^dεὐαγ-
Christ :   but even if we or an angel out of heaven should an-
γελίζηται‖ ^eὑμῖν‖ παρ' ὃ εὐηγγελισάμεθα ὑμῖν, ἀνάθεμα
nounce glad tidings to you contrary to what we announced to you, accursed
ἔστω. 9 ὡς προειρήκαμεν, καὶ ἄρτι πάλιν λέγω, εἴ τις
let him be. As we have said before, ²also ¹now again I say, If anyone
ὑμᾶς εὐαγγελίζεται   παρ' ὃ παρελάβετε, ἀνάθεμα
[to] you announces glad tidings contrary to what ye received, accursed
ἔστω. 10 ἄρτι.γὰρ ἀνθρώπους πείθω ἢ τὸν θεόν ; ἢ
let him be. For now men   do I persuade or God ? or
ζητῶ ἀνθρώποις ἀρέσκειν ; εἰ.^fγὰρ‖ ἔτι ἀνθρώποις ἤρεσκον,
do I seek men   to please ? For if yet   men   I were pleasing,
χριστοῦ δοῦλος οὐκ.ἂν.ἤμην.
Christ's bondman I should not be.

11 But I certify you, brethren, that the gospel which was preached of me is not after man. 12 For I nei-

11 Γνωρίζω ^gδὲ‖ ὑμῖν, ἀδελφοί, τὸ εὐαγγέλιον τὸ εὐαγ-
²I ³make ⁴known ¹but to you, brethren, the glad tidings which was
γελισθὲν ὑπ' ἐμοῦ, ὅτι οὐκ.ἔστιν κατὰ ἄνθρωπον· 12 οὐδὲ
announced by me, that it is not according to man.   ²Neither

^a + τοῦ ἀποστόλου the apostle E ; Πρὸς Γαλάτας LTTrAW.   ^b περὶ GLTTrAW.   ^c αἰῶνος τοῦ ἐνεστῶτος LTTrA.   ^d εὐαγγελίσηται T.   ^e — ὑμῖν T.   ^f — γὰρ for LTTrAW.   ^g γὰρ for TrA.

γὰρ ἐγὼ παρὰ ἀνθρώπου παρέλαβον αὐτό, ʰοὔτε‖ ἐδιδάχθην,
for I from man received it, nor was I taught [it],

ἀλλὰ δι᾽ ἀποκαλύψεως Ἰησοῦ χριστοῦ. 13 Ἠκούσατε.γὰρ τὴν
but by a revelation of Jesus Christ. For ye heard of

ἐμὴν.ἀναστροφήν ποτε ἐν τῷ Ἰουδαϊσμῷ, ὅτι καθ᾽.ὑπερβολὴν
my conduct once in Judaism, that excessively

ἐδίωκον τὴν ἐκκλησίαν τοῦ θεοῦ καὶ ἐπόρθουν αὐτὴν·
I was persecuting the assembly of God and was ravaging it;

14 καὶ προέκοπτον ἐν τῷ Ἰουδαϊσμῷ ὑπὲρ πολλοὺς συνηλικιώτας
and was advancing in Judaism beyond many contemporaries

ἐν τῷ.γένει.μου, περισσοτέρως ζηλωτὴς ὑπάρχων τῶν πατρι-
in my [own] race, more abundantly zealous being ⁴of ⁵fathers

κῶν μου παραδόσεων. 15 ὅτε.δὲ εὐδόκησεν ⁱὁ θεός‖ ὁ
¹my ²for [²the] ³traditions. But when ²was ³pleased ¹God, who

ἀφορίσας με ἐκ κοιλίας μητρός.μου, καὶ καλέσας διὰ τῆς
selected me from ³womb ¹my ²mother's, and called [me] by

χάριτος.αὐτοῦ, 16 ἀποκαλύψαι τὸν.υἱὸν.αὐτοῦ ἐν ἐμοί, ἵνα
his grace, to reveal his Son in me, that

εὐαγγελίζωμαι.αὐτὸν ἐν τοῖς ἔθνεσιν· εὐθέως
I should announce him as the glad tidings among the nations, immediately

οὐ.προσανεθέμην σαρκὶ καὶ αἵματι, 17 οὐδὲ ᵏἀνῆλθον‖ εἰς
I conferred not with flesh and blood, nor went I up to

Ἱεροσόλυμα πρὸς τοὺς πρὸ ἐμοῦ ἀποστόλους, ⁱἀλλ᾽‖
Jerusalem to those [who were] ᵐbefore ᵐme ¹apostles, but

ἀπῆλθον εἰς Ἀραβίαν, καὶ πάλιν ὑπέστρεψα εἰς Δαμασκόν.
I went away into Arabia, and again returned to Damascus.

18 Ἔπειτα μετὰ ᵐἔτη τρία‖ ἀνῆλθον εἰς Ἱεροσόλυμα ἱσ-
Then after ²years ¹three I went up to Jerusalem to make

τορῆσαι ⁿΠέτρον,‖ καὶ ἐπέμεινα πρὸς αὐτὸν ἡμέρας
acquaintance with Peter, and I remained with him ²days

δεκαπέντε· 19 ἕτερον.δὲ τῶν ἀποστόλων οὐκ.εἶδον, εἰ.μὴ
¹fifteen; but other of the apostles I saw not, except

Ἰάκωβον τὸν ἀδελφὸν τοῦ κυρίου. 20 ἃ.δὲ γράφω ὑμῖν,
James the brother of the Lord. Now what [things] I write to you,

ἰδοὺ ἐνώπιον τοῦ θεοῦ, ὅτι οὐ.ψεύδομαι. 21 Ἔπειτα ἦλθον εἰς
lo, before God, I lie not. Then I came into

τὰ κλίματα τῆς Συρίας καὶ τῆς Κιλικίας· 22 ἤμην.δὲ ἀ-
the regions of Syria and Cilicia; but I was un-

γνοούμενος τῷ.προσώπῳ ταῖς ἐκκλησίαις τῆς Ἰουδαίας ταῖς
known by face to the assemblies of Judæa which

ἐν χριστῷ· 23 μόνον.δὲ ἀκούοντες ἦσαν, Ὅτι ὁ
[are] in Christ, only ³hearing ¹they ²were, That he who

διώκων ἡμᾶς ποτε, νῦν εὐαγγελίζεται τὴν πίστιν
²persecuted ³us ¹once, now announces the glad tidings— the faith,

ἣν ποτε ἐπόρθει. 24 καὶ ἐδόξαζον ἐν ἐμοὶ τὸν θεόν.
which once he ravaged: and they were glorifying ²in ³me ¹God.

2 Ἔπειτα διὰ δεκατεσσάρων ἐτῶν πάλιν ἀνέβην εἰς Ἱε-
Then after fourteen years again I went up to Je-

ροσόλυμα μετὰ Βαρνάβα, ᵒσυμπαραλαβὼν‖ καὶ Τίτον·
rusalem with Barnabas, taking with [me] also Titus;

2 ἀνέβην.δὲ κατὰ ἀποκάλυψιν, καὶ ἀνεθέμην αὐτοῖς τὸ
but I went up according to revelation, and laid before them the

εὐαγγέλιον· ὃ κηρύσσω ἐν τοῖς ἔθνεσιν, κατ᾽.ἰδίαν.δὲ τοῖς
glad tidings which I proclaim among the nations, but privately to those

ther received it of man, neither was I taught it, but by the revelation of Jesus Christ. 13 For ye have heard of my conversation in time past in the Jews' religion, how that beyond measure I persecuted the church of God, and wasted it: 14 and profited in the Jews' religion above many my equals in mine own nation, being more exceedingly zealous of the traditions of my fathers. 15 But when it pleased God, who separated me from my mother's womb, and called me by his grace, 16 to reveal his Son in me, that I might preach him among the heathen; immediately I conferred not with flesh and blood: 17 neither went I up to Jerusalem to them which were apostles before me; but I went into Arabia, and returned again unto Damascus. 18 Then after three years I went up to Jerusalem to see Peter, and abode with him fifteen days. 19 But other of the apostles saw I none, save James the Lord's brother. 20 Now the things which I write unto you, behold, before God, I lie not. 21 Afterwards I came into the regions of Syria and Cilicia; 22 and was unknown by face unto the churches of Judæa which were in Christ: 23 but they had heard only, That he which persecuted us in times past now preacheth the faith which once he destroyed. 24 And they glorified God in me.

II. Then fourteen years after I went up again to Jerusalem with Barnabas, and took Titus with me also. 2 And I went up by revelation, and communicated unto them that gospel which I preach among the Gentiles, but privately to them which were of reputation, lest by any means I should run, or had run, in vain. 3 But neither Titus, who

---

ᵇ οὐδὲ LTr.   ⁱ — ὁ θεὸς (read he was pleased) [L]TA.   ᵏ ἀπῆλθον went I away LA.
ἀλλὰ LTTrA.   ᵐ τρία ἔτη T.   ⁿ Κηφᾶν Cephas LTTrAW.   ᵒ συν- TA.

was with me, being a Greek, was compelled to be circumcised : 4 and that because of false brethren unawares brought in, who came in privily to spy out our liberty which we have in Christ Jesus, that they might bring us into bondage : 5 to whom we gave place by subjection, no, not for an hour ; that the truth of the gospel might continue with you. 6 But of these who seemed to be somewhat, (whatsoever they were, it maketh no matter to me : God accepteth no man's person :) for they who seemed *to be somewhat* in conference added nothing to me : 7 but contrariwise, when they saw that the gospel of the uncircumcision was committed unto me, as *the gospel* of the circumcision *was* unto Peter ; 8 (for he that wrought effectually in Peter to the apostleship of the circumcision, the same was mighty in me toward the Gentiles :) 9 and when James, Cephas, and John, who seemed to be pillars, perceived the grace that was given unto me, they gave to me and Barnabas the right hands of fellowship ; that we *should go* unto the heathen and they unto the circumcision. 10 Only *they would* that we should remember the poor ; the same which I also was forward to do.

11 But when Peter was come to Antioch, I withstood him to the face, because he was to be blamed. 12 For before that certain came from James, he did eat with the Gentiles : but when they were come, he withdrew and separated himself, fearing them which were of the circumcision. 13 And the other Jews dissembled likewise with him ; insomuch that Barnabas also was carried away with their dissimulation. 14 But when I saw that they walked

δοκοῦσιν, μήπως εἰς κενὸν τρέχω ἢ ἔδραμον· 3 ἀλλ'
of repute, lest somehow in vain I should be running or had run ;   (but
οὐδὲ Τίτος ὁ σὺν ἐμοί, Ἕλλην· ὤν, ἠναγκάσθη περι-
not even Titus who[was]with me, [2]a [3]Greek [1]being, was compelled   to be
τμηθῆναι. 4 διὰ.δὲ τοὺς παρεισάκτους ψευδ-
circumcised ;) and [this] on account of the [3]brought [4]in [2]stealthily [1]false
ἀδέλφους, οἵτινες παρεισῆλθον κατασκοπῆσαι τὴν ἐλευθερίαν
[2]brethren, who came in by stealth to spy out [2]freedom
ἡμῶν ἣν ἔχομεν ἐν χριστῷ Ἰησοῦ, ἵνα ἡμᾶς [P]καταδουλώ-
[1]our which we have in Christ Jesus, that us they might bring
σωνται·ǁ 5 οἷς οὐδὲ πρὸς ὥραν εἴξαμεν τῇ ὑποταγῇ,
into bondage ; to whom not even for an hour did we yield in subjection,
ἵνα ἡ ἀλήθεια τοῦ εὐαγγελίου διαμείνῃ πρὸς ὑμᾶς. 6 Ἀπὸ
that the truth of the glad tidings might continue with you.   [2]From
δὲ τῶν δοκούντων εἶναί τι, ὁποῖοί.ποτε ἦσαν οὐδέν
[1]but those reputed to be something, whatsoever they were   [2]no
μοι διαφέρει· πρόσωπον [9]θεὸς ἀνθρώπου οὐ λαμ-
[4]to [5]me [1]makes [3]difference : [the] person [3]God [1]of [2]man [1]not [4]does
βάνει· ἐμοὶ.γὰρ οἱ δοκοῦντες οὐδὲν προσανέθεντο, 7 ἀλλὰ
accept ; for to me those of repute nothing conferred ;   but
τοὐναντίον, ἰδόντες ὅτι πεπίστευμαι τὸ εὐαγγέλιον
on the contrary, having seen that I have been entrusted with the glad tidings
τῆς ἀκροβυστίας, καθὼς Πέτρος τῆς περιτομῆς· 8 ὁ
of the uncircumcision, according as Peter [that] of the circumcision, (the [3]who
γὰρ ἐνεργήσας Πέτρῳ εἰς ἀποστολὴν τῆς περιτομῆς, ἐνήργη-
[1]for wrought in Peter for apostleship of the circumcision, wrought
σεν [r]καὶ ἐμοὶǁ εἰς τὰ ἔθνη· 9 καὶ γνόντες τὴν χάριν τὴν
also in me towards the nations,) and having known the grace which
δοθεῖσάν μοι, Ἰάκωβος καὶ Κηφᾶς καὶ [s]Ἰωάννης,ǁ οἱ δο-
was given to me, James and Cephas and John, those re-
κοῦντες στῦλοι εἶναι, δεξιὰς ἔδωκαν ἐμοὶ καὶ Βαρνάβᾳ
puted [3]pillars [1]to [2]be, [the] right hands [3]they [4]gave [5]to [6]me [7]and [8]Barnabas
κοινωνίας, ἵνα ἡμεῖς [t] εἰς τὰ ἔθνη, αὐτοὶ.δὲ εἰς τὴν
[1]of [2]fellowship, that we [should go] to the nations, and they to the
περιτομήν· 10 μόνον τῶν πτωχῶν ἵνα μνημονεύωμεν, ὃ
circumcision : only the poor that we should remember, which
καὶ ἐσπούδασα αὐτὸ.τοῦτο ποιῆσαι.
[2]also [4]I [3]was [5]diligent [1]very [2]thing to do.

11 Ὅτε.δὲ ἦλθεν [v]Πέτροςǁ εἰς Ἀντιόχειαν, κατὰ.πρόσωπον
But when [2]came [1]Peter to Antioch, to [the] face
αὐτῷ ἀντέστην, ὅτι κατεγνωσμένος ἦν. 12 πρὸ.τοῦ.γὰρ
him I withstood, because . to be condemned he was :   for before that
ἐλθεῖν τινας ἀπὸ Ἰακώβου, μετὰ τῶν ἐθνῶν συνήσθιεν· ὅτε.δὲ
[2]came [1]some from James, with the nations he was eating ; but when
[w]ἦλθον,ǁ ὑπέστελλεν καὶ ἀφώριζεν ἑαυτόν, φοβούμενος
they came, he was drawing back and was separating himself, being afraid of
τοὺς ἐκ περιτομῆς· 13 καὶ συνυπεκρίθησαν αὐτῷ καὶ οἱ
those of [the] circumcision ; and conjointly dissembled with him also the
λοιποὶ Ἰουδαῖοι, ὥστε καὶ Βαρνάβας συναπήχθη αὐτῶν
rest of [the] Jews, so that even Barnabas was carried away [2]their
τῇ ὑποκρίσει. 14 Ἀλλ' ὅτε εἶδον· ὅτι οὐκ.ὀρθοποδοῦσιν
[1]by dissimulation.' But when I saw that they walk not uprightly
πρὸς τὴν ἀλήθειαν τοῦ εὐαγγελίου, εἶπον τῷ [x]Πέτρῳǁ
according to the truth of the glad tidings, I said to Peter

[P] καταδουλώσουσιν they shall bring into bondage LTTrAW.   [q] + ὁ T.   [r] κἀμοὶ LTrW.
[s] Ἰωάνης Tr.   [t] + μὲν G[L].   [v] Κηφᾶς Cephas LTTrAW.   [w] ἦλθεν he came LTr.
[x] Κηφᾶ Cephas LTTrAW.

ἔμπροσθεν πάντων, Εἰ σύ, Ἰουδαῖος ὑπάρχων, ἐθνικῶς
before   all,   If thou, ²a ¹Jew   ¹being,   nation-like

ʲζῇς καὶ οὐκ Ἰουδαϊκῶς,‖ ᶻτί‖ τὰ ἔθνη ἀναγκάζεις Ἰου-
livest and not   Jewishly,   why the nations dost thou compel to ju-

δαΐζειν; 15 Ἡμεῖς φύσει Ἰουδαῖοι, καὶ οὐκ ἐξ ἐθνῶν
daize?   We, ²by ³nature ¹Jews,   and not ²of [³the] ⁴nations

ἁμαρτωλοί, 16 εἰδότες ᵃ ὅτι οὐ.δικαιοῦται ἄνθρωπος ἐξ ἔργων
¹sinners,   knowing that ³is ⁴not ⁵justified ¹a ²man   by works

νόμου, ἐὰν.μὴ διὰ πίστεως ᵇΙησοῦ χριστοῦ,‖ καὶ ἡμεῖς εἰς
of law,   but through faith of Jesus Christ,   also we   on

χριστὸν Ἰησοῦν ἐπιστεύσαμεν, ἵνα δικαιωθῶμεν ἐκ πίστεως
Christ   Jesus   believed,   that we might be justified by   faith

χριστοῦ, καὶ οὐκ ἐξ ἔργων νόμου· ᶜδιότι‖ ᵈοὐ.δικαιωθήσεται
of Christ, and not by works of law;   because   shall not be justified

ἐξ ἔργων νόμου‖ πᾶσα σάρξ. 17 εἰ.δὲ ζητοῦντες δικαιωθῆναι
by works of law   any flesh.   Now if seeking to be justified
        (lit. all)

ἐν χριστῷ εὑρέθημεν καὶ αὐτοὶ ἁμάρτωλοί, ᵉἆρα‖ χριστὸς
in Christ we ⁴were ⁵found ²also ¹ourselves sinners,   [is] then Christ

ἁμαρτίας διάκονος;ᶠ μὴ.γένοιτο. 18 εἰ.γὰρ ἃ κατέλυσα
ᶻof ³sin   ¹minister?   May it not be!   For if what I threw down

ταῦτα πάλιν οἰκοδομῶ, παραβάτην ἐμαυτὸν ᵍσυνίστημι.‖
these things again   I build,   a transgressor myself   I constitute.

19 Ἐγὼ.γὰρ διὰ νόμου νόμῳ ἀπέθανον, ἵνα θεῷ ζήσω.
For I   through law to law   died,   that to God I may live.

20 χριστῷ συνεσταύρωμαι· ζῶ.δὲ, οὐκέτι ἐγώ, ζῇ.δὲ
ᶜChrist ⁴I ²have ³been ⁴crucified ⁵with, yet I live, no longer   I,   but ⁵lives

ἐν ἐμοὶ χριστός· ὃ.δὲ νῦν ζῶ ἐν σαρκί, ἐν πίστει
⁵in ⁴me   Christ;   but that which now I live in flesh, in   faith

ζῶ τῇ ᵇτοῦ υἱοῦ τοῦ θεοῦ,‖ τοῦ ἀγαπήσαντός με καὶ παρα-
I live, that of the Son   of God,   who   loved   me and gave

δόντος ἑαυτὸν ὑπὲρ ἐμοῦ. 21 οὐκ.ἀθετῶ τὴν χάριν τοῦ θεοῦ·
up himself for me.   I do not set aside the grace of God;

εἰ.γὰρ διὰ νόμου δικαιοσύνη, ἄρα χριστὸς δωρεὰν
for if through law righteousness [is], then   Christ   ²for ³nought

ἀπέθανεν.
¹died.

3 ᵗΩ ἀνόητοι Γαλάται, τίς ὑμᾶς ἐβάσκανεν ⁱτῇ ἀληθείᾳ
O senseless Galatians, who you bewitched, ⁴the ⁵truth

μὴ πείθεσθαι;‖ οἷς κατ' ὀφθαλμοὺς Ἰησοῦς χριστὸς προε-
not ²to ³obey?   ⁷whose ⁶before eyes   Jesus   Christ was openly

γράφη ᵏἐν ὑμῖν‖ ἐσταυρωμένος; 2 τοῦτο μόνον θέλω μαθεῖν
set forth among you—   crucified?   This only I wish to learn

ἀφ' ὑμῶν, ἐξ ἔργων νόμου τὸ πνεῦμα ἐλάβετε, ἢ ἐξ ἀκοῆς
from you, by works of law the Spirit receive ye, or by report

πίστεως; 3 οὕτως ἀνόητοί ἐστε; ἐναρξάμενοι πνεύματι, νῦν
of faith?   So senseless are ye?   Having begun   in Spirit,   now

σαρκὶ ἐπιτελεῖσθε; 4 τοσαῦτα ἐπάθετε εἰκῇ; εἴγε
in flesh are ye being perfected? So many things did ye suffer in vain? if indeed

καὶ εἰκῇ. 5 ὁ οὖν ἐπιχορηγῶν ὑμῖν τὸ πνεῦμα, καὶ
also in vain.   He who therefore supplies to you the Spirit,   and

ἐνεργῶν δυνάμεις ἐν ὑμῖν, ἐξ ἔργων νόμου ἢ ἐξ ἀκοῆς
works   works of power among you, [is it] by works of law or by report

---

not uprightly accord-
ing to the truth of the
gospel, I said unto Pe-
ter before them all, If
thou, being a Jew,
livest after the man-
ner of Gentiles, and
not as do the Jews,
why compellest thou
the Gentiles to live as
do the Jews? 15 We
who are Jews by na-
ture, and not sinners
of the Gentiles,
16 knowing that a
man is not justified by
the works of the law,
but by the faith of
Jesus Christ, even we
have believed in Jesus
Christ, that we might
be justified by the
faith of Christ, and
not by the works of
the law: for by the
works of the law shall
no flesh be justified.
17 But if, while we
seek to be justified by
Christ, we ourselves
also are found sinners,
is therefore Christ the
minister of sin? God
forbid. 18 For if I
build again the things
which I destroyed, I
make myself a trans-
gressor. 19 For I
through the law am
dead to the law, that
I might live unto God.
20 I am crucified with
Christ : nevertheless I
live; yet not I, but
Christ liveth in me:
and the life which I
now live in the flesh I
live by the faith of
the Son of God, who
loved me, and gave
himself for me. 21 I
do not frustrate the
grace of God : for if
righteousness come by
the law, then Christ is
dead in vain.

III. O foolish Gala-
tians, who hath be-
witched you, that ye
should not obey the
truth, before whose
eyes Jesus Christ hath
been evidently set
forth, crucified among
you? 2 This only
would I learn of you,
Received ye the Spirit
by the works of the
law, or by the hearing
of faith? 3 Are ye so
foolish? having be-
gun in the Spirit, are
ye now made perfect
by the flesh. 4 Have
ye suffered so many
things in vain? if it

ʲ καὶ οὐχ (οὐκ ΤᴿA) Ἰουδαϊκῶς ζῇς LTTrA.   ᶻ πῶς how GLTTrAW.   ᵃ + δὲ but (knowing)
GLTTrAW.   ᵇ χριστοῦ Ἰησοῦ ΤΤr.   ᶜ ὅτι LTTrA.   ᵈ ἐξ ἔργων νόμου οὐ δικαιωθήσεται
GLTTrAW.   ᵉ ἆρα L.   ᶠ —; (read Christ [is] then &c.) L.   ᵍ συνιστάνω GLTTrAW.   ᵇ τοῦ
θεοῦ καὶ χριστοῦ of God and Christ LTr.   ⁱ — τῇ ἀληθείᾳ μὴ πείθεσθαι GLTTrAW.   — ἐν
ὑμῖν LTTrA.

be yet in vain. –5 He therefore that ministereth to you the Spirit, and worketh miracles among you, *doeth he it* by the works of the law, or by the hearing of faith? 6 Even as Abraham believed God, and it was accounted to him for righteousness. 7 Know ye therefore that they which are of faith, the same are the children of Abraham. 8 And the scripture, foreseeing that God would justify the heathen through faith, preached before the gospel unto Abraham, *saying*, In thee shall all nations be blessed. 9 So then they which be of faith are blessed with faithful Abraham. 10 For as many as are of the works of the law are under the curse: for it is written, Cursed *is* every one that continueth not in all things which are written in the book of the law to do them. 11 But that no man is justified by the law in the sight of God, *it is* evident: for, The just shall live by faith. 12 And the law is not of faith: but, The man that doeth them shall live in them. 13 Christ hath redeemed us from the curse of the law, being made a curse for us: for it is written, Cursed *is* every one that hangeth on a tree: 14 that the blessing of Abraham might come on the Gentiles through Jesus Christ; that we might receive the promise of the Spirit through faith.

15 Brethren, I speak after the manner of men; Though *it be* but a man's covenant, yet *if it be* confirmed, no man disannulleth, or addeth thereto. 16 Now to Abraham and his seed were the promises made. He saith not, And to seeds, as of many; but as of one, And to thy seed, which is Christ. 17 And this I say, *that* the covenant, that was confirmed before of God in Christ, the law, which was four hun-

πίστεως; 6 καθὼς Ἀβραὰμ ἐπίστευσεν τῷ θεῷ, καὶ ἐλογίσθη
of faith?   Even as   Abraham   believed   God, and it was reckoned
αὐτῷ εἰς δικαιοσύνην. 7 γινώσκετε ἄρα ὅτι οἱ ἐκ πίστεως,
to him for   righteousness.   Know   then that they that of   faith
οὗτοί ᵏεἰσιν υἱοὶ‖ Ἀβραάμ. 8 προϊδοῦσα.δὲ ἡ γραφὴ
[are], these   are   sons of Abraham;   and ²foreseeing ¹the ²scripture
ὅτι ἐκ πίστεως δικαιοῖ τὰ ἔθνη ὁ θεός,   προευηγγελί-
that by   faith   ²justifies ³the ⁴nations ¹God, before announced glad
σατο τῷ Ἀβραάμ, "Ὅτι ¹ἐνευλογηθήσονται‖ ἐν σοὶ πάντα τὰ
tidings   to Abraham: Shall be blessed   in thee   all   the
ἔθνη. 9 ὥστε οἱ ἐκ πίστεως εὐλογοῦνται σὺν τῷ πιστῷ
nations.   So that those of   faith   are being blessed with the believing
Ἀβραάμ. 10 ὅσοι.γὰρ ἐξ ἔργων νόμου εἰσίν, ὑπὸ κατάραν
Abraham.   For as many as of   works   of law   are,   under a curse
εἰσίν· γέγραπται.γάρ. ᵐ Ἐπικατάρατος πᾶς ὃς οὐκ ἐμ-
are.   For it has been written, Cursed   [is] everyone who ²not ¹does
μένει ⁿἐν‖ πᾶσιν τοῖς γεγραμμένοις ἐν τῷ βιβλίῳ τοῦ νόμου,
continue   in all things which have been written in the   book   of the   law
τοῦ ποιῆσαι αὐτά. 11 Ὅτι.δὲ ἐν νόμῳ οὐδεὶς δικαιοῦται·
to do   them.   But that in virtue of law   no one is being justified
παρὰ τῷ θεῷ δῆλον· ὅτι ὁ δίκαιος ἐκ πίστεως ζήσεται·
with   God [is] manifest; because the just   by   faith   shall live;
12 ὁ.δὲ νόμος οὐκ.ἔστιν ἐκ πίστεως, °ἀλλ᾽‖ ὁ ποιήσας
but the   law   is not   of   faith;   but, the ²who ³did
αὐτὰ ᴾἄνθρωπος‖ ζήσεται ἐν αὐτοῖς. 13 χριστὸς ἡμᾶς
⁴these ⁵things ¹man   shall live in virtue of them.   Christ   us
ἐξηγόρασεν ἐκ τῆς κατάρας τοῦ νόμου, γενόμενος ὑπὲρ ἡμῶν
ransomed   from the   curse   of the   law,   having become for   us
κατάρα· ᑫγέγραπται.γάρ,‖ Ἐπικατάρατος πᾶς ὁ κρεμά-
a curse,   (for it has been written,)   Cursed   [is] everyone who   hangs
μενος ἐπὶ ξύλου· 14 ἵνα εἰς τὰ ἔθνη ἡ εὐλογία τοῦ Ἀβραὰμ
on   a tree,)   that to the nations the blessing   of Abraham
γένηται ἐν ʳχριστῷ Ἰησοῦ,‖ ἵνα τὴν ἐπαγγελίαν τοῦ πνεύμα-
might come in   Christ   Jesus,   that the   promise   of the   Spirit
τος λάβωμεν διὰ τῆς πίστεως.
we might receive through   faith.

15 Ἀδελφοί, κατὰ ἄνθρωπον λέγω, ὅμως ἀνθρώπου
Brethren, (according to   man   I am speaking,) even   of man
κεκυρωμένην διαθήκην οὐδεὶς ἀθετεῖ ἢ ἐπιδιατάσσεται.
a confirmed   covenant   no one sets aside, or   adds thereto.
16 τῷ.δὲ Ἀβραὰμ ˢἐρρήθησαν‖ αἱ ἐπαγγελίαι, καὶ τῷ σπέρματι
But to Abraham   were spoken   the promises, and   to ²seed
αὐτοῦ. οὐ.λέγει, Καὶ τοῖς σπέρμασιν. ὡς ἐπὶ πολλῶν, ᵗἀλλ᾽‖
¹his: he does not say, And   to seeds,   as of   many;   but
ὡς ἐφ᾽ ἑνός, Καὶ τῷ.σπέρματί.σου, ὅς ἐστιν χριστός. 17 τοῦτο
as of one,   And   to thy seed;   ¹which is   Christ.   ²This
δὲ λέγω, διαθήκην προκεκυρωμένην ὑπὸ τοῦ θεοῦ ᵛεἰς χρισ-
¹now I say, [the] covenant   confirmed beforehand by   God   to Christ,
τὸν‖ ὁ μετὰ ʷἔτη τετρακόσια καὶ τριάκοντα‖ γεγονὼς
the ⁵after ¹⁰years ⁶four ⁷hundred ⁸and   ⁹thirty ²which ⁵took ⁴place
νόμος οὐκ.ἀκυροῖ, εἰς.τὸ καταργῆσαι τὴν ἐπαγγελίαν. 18 εἰ
¹law   does not annul   so as to make of no effect the   promise.   ²If

---

ᵏ υἱοί εἰσιν LTTr.   ˡ εὐλογηθήσονται E.   ᵐ + ὅτι that GLTTrAW.   ⁿ — ἐν (read
πᾶσιν in all things) TTr.   ° ἀλλὰ TTr.   ᴾ — ἄνθρωπος (read ὁ ποιήσας he who did)
GLTTrAW.   ᑫ ὅτι γέγραπται LTTrAW.   ʳ Ἰησοῦ χριστῷ Tr.   ˢ ἐρρέθησαν LTTrA.
ᵗ ἀλλὰ Tr.   ᵛ — εἰς χριστὸν LTTrA.   ʷ τετρακόσια καὶ τριάκοντα ἔτη GLTTrAW.

γὰρ ἐκ νόμου ἡ κληρονομία,   οὐκέτι ἐξ ἐπαγγελίας·
for by law [be] the inheritance, [it is] no longer by   promise;

τῷ.δὲ.Ἀβραὰμ δι' ἐπαγγελίας κεχάρισται ὁ θεός. 19 Τί
but to Abraham through promise ²granted [³it] ¹God. Why

οὖν ὁ νόμος; τῶν παραβάσεων χάριν ˣπροσετέθη,‖
then the law? ⁵transgressions ¹for ²the ²sake ⁴of it was added,

ἄχρις οὗ ἔλθῃ τὸ σπέρμα ᾧ ἐπήγγελται,
until should have come the seed to whom promise has been made,

διαταγεὶς δι' ἀγγέλων ἐν χειρὶ μεσίτου. 20 ὁ.δὲ
having been ordained through angels in ³hand ¹a ²mediator's. But the

μεσίτης ἑνὸς οὐκ.ἔστιν, ὁ.δὲ.θεὸς εἷς ἐστιν.
mediator ³of ⁴one ¹is ²not, but God ²one ¹is.

21 Ὁ.οὖν.νόμος κατὰ τῶν ἐπαγγελιῶν ⸆τοῦ θεοῦ‖;
The law then [is it] against the promises of God?

μὴ.γένοιτο· εἰ.γὰρ ἐδόθη νόμος ὁ δυνάμενος ζωοποιῆσαι,
May it not be! For if was given a law which was able to quicken,

ὄντως ²ἂν ἐκ νόμου ἦν‖ ἡ δικαιοσύνη· 22 ἀλλὰ συνέ-
indeed by law would have been rigtheousness; but ²shut

κλεισεν ἡ γραφὴ τὰ.πάντα ⁴ὑπὸ ἁμαρτίαν, ἵνα ἡ ἐπαγγελία
¹up ¹the ²scripture all things under sin, that the promise

ἐκ πίστεως Ἰησοῦ χριστοῦ δοθῇ τοῖς πιστεύουσιν.
by faith of Jesus Christ might be given to those that believe.

23 Πρὸ.τοῦ.δὲ ἐλθεῖν τὴν πίστιν, ὑπὸ νόμον ἐφρουρούμεθα,
But before ²came ¹faith, under law we were guarded,

ᵇσυγκεκλεισμένοι‖ εἰς τὴν μέλλουσαν πίστιν ἀποκαλυφθῆναι·
having been shut up to the ²being ³about ¹faith to be revealed.

24 ὥστε ὁ νόμος παιδαγωγὸς ἡμῶν γέγονεν εἰς χριστόν, ἵνα
So that the law ²tutor ¹our has been [up] to Christ, that

ἐκ πίστεως δικαιωθῶμεν· 25 ἐλθούσης.δὲ τῆς πίστεως,
by faith we might be justified. But ²having ³come ¹faith,

οὐκέτι ὑπὸ παιδαγωγόν ἐσμεν. 26 πάντες.γὰρ υἱοὶ θεοῦ
no longer under a tutor we are; for all sons of God

ἐστε διὰ τῆς πίστεως ἐν χριστῷ Ἰησοῦ· 27 ὅσοι.γὰρ εἰς
ye are through faith in Christ Jesus. For as many as to

χριστὸν ἐβαπτίσθητε, χριστὸν ἐνεδύσασθε. 28 οὐκ.ἔνι Ἰου-
Christ were baptized, ³Christ ¹ye ²did ³put ⁴on. There is not Jew

δαῖος οὐδὲ Ἕλλην· οὐκ.ἔνι δοῦλος οὐδὲ ἐλεύθερος· οὐκ.ἔνι
nor Greek; there is not bondman nor free; there is not

ἄρσεν καὶ θῆλυ· ᶜπάντες‖.γὰρ ὑμεῖς εἷς ἐστε ἐν.χριστῷ Ἰησοῦ·
male and female; for all ye one are in Christ Jesus:

29 εἰ.δὲ ὑμεῖς χριστοῦ, ἄρα τοῦ Ἀβραὰμ σπέρμα ἐστέ,
but if ye [are] Christ's, then Abraham's seed ye are,

ᵈκαὶ‖ ᵉκατ'‖ ἐπαγγελίαν κληρονόμοι.
and according to promise heirs.

4 Λέγω.δέ, ἐφ' ὅσον χρόνον ὁ κληρονόμος νήπιός ἐστιν,
Now I say, for as long ²as ¹time the heir an infant is,

οὐδὲν διαφέρει δούλου, κύριος πάντων ὤν· 2 ἀλλὰ
nothing he differs from a bondman, [though] ²lord ³of ⁴all ¹being; but

ὑπὸ ἐπιτρόπους ἐστὶν καὶ οἰκονόμους ἄχρι τῆς προθεσμίας
under guardians he is and stewards until the time before appointed

τοῦ πατρός. 3 οὕτως καὶ ἡμεῖς, ὅτε ἦμεν νήπιοι, ὑπὸ τὰ
of the father. So also we, when we were infants, under the

στοιχεῖα τοῦ κόσμου ᶠἦμεν‖ δεδουλωμένοι· 4 ὅτε.δὲ ἦλθεν τὸ
elements of the world were held in bondage; but when came the

---

dred and thirty years after, cannot disannul, that it should make the promise of none effect. 18 For if the inheritance be of the law, it is no more of promise: but God gave it to Abraham by promise. 19 Wherefore then serveth the law? It was added because of transgressions, till the seed should come to whom the promise was made; and it was ordained by angels in the hand of a mediator. 20 Now a mediator is not a mediator of one, but God is one.

21 Is the law then against the promises of God? God forbid: for if there had been a law given which could have given life, verily righteousness should have been by the law. 22 But the scripture hath concluded all under sin, that the promise by faith of Jesus Christ might be given to them that believe. 23 But before faith came, we were kept under the law, shut up unto the faith which should afterwards be revealed. 24 Wherefore the law was our schoolmaster to bring us unto Christ, that we might be justified by faith. 25 But after that faith is come, we are no longer under a schoolmaster. 26 For ye are all the children of God by faith in Christ Jesus. 27 For as many of you as have been baptized into Christ have put on Christ. 28 There is neither Jew nor Greek, there is neither bond nor free, there is neither male nor female: for ye are all one in Christ Jesus. 29 And if ye be Christ's, then are ye Abraham's seed, and heirs according to the promise.

IV. Now I say, That the heir, as long as he is a child, differeth nothing from a servant, though he be lord of all; 2 but is under tutors and governors until the time appointed of the father. 3 Even so we, when

---

ˣ ἐτέθη it was appointed G.   ⸆ [τοῦ θεοῦ] L.   ² ἐκ νόμου ἂν ἦν (ἦν ἂν T) LTTrA.   ᵃ ὑφ' L.
ᵇ συγ(συν- T)κλειόμενοι being shut up LTTrA.   ᶜ ἅπαντες TTrA.   ᵈ — καὶ LTTrA.
ᵉ κατὰ T.   ᶠ ἤμεθα T.

we were children, were in bondage under the elements of the world: 4 but when the fulness of the time was come, God sent forth his Son, made of a woman, made under the law, 5 to redeem them that were under the law, that we might receive the adoption of sons. 6 And because ye are sons, God hath sent forth the Spirit of his Son into your hearts, crying, Abba, Father. 7 Wherefore thou art no more a servant, but a son; and if a son, then an heir of God through Christ. 8 Howbeit then, when ye knew not God, ye did service unto them which by nature are no gods. 9 But now, after that ye have known God, or rather are known of God, how turn ye again to the weak and beggarly elements, whereunto ye desire again to be in bondage? 10 Ye observe days, and months, and times, and years. 11 I am afraid of you, lest I have bestowed upon you labour in vain.

12 Brethren, I beseech you, be as I am; for I am as ye are: ye have not injured me at all. 13 Ye know how through infirmity of the flesh I preached the gospel unto you at the first. 14 And my temptation which was in my flesh ye despised not, nor rejected; but received me as an angel of God, even as Christ Jesus. 15 Where is then the blessedness ye spake of? for I bear you record, that, if it had been possible, ye would have plucked out your own eyes, and have given them to me. 16 Am I therefore become your enemy, because I tell you the truth? 17 They zealously affect you, but not well; yea, they would exclude you, that ye might affect them. 18 But it is good to be zealously affected always in a good thing, and not only when I am pre-

πλήρωμα τοῦ χρόνου, ἐξαπέστειλεν ὁ θεὸς τὸν.υἱὸν.αὐτοῦ,
fulness　of the　time,　²sent ³forth　¹God　his Son,

γενόμενον ἐκ γυναικός, γενόμενον ὑπὸ νόμον, 5 ἵνα τοὺς
come　of woman,　come　under law,　that those

ὑπὸ νόμον ἐξαγοράσῃ, ἵνα τὴν υἱοθεσίαν ἀπολάβωμεν.
under law he might ransom, that　adoption　we might receive.

6 ὅτι.δὲ ἐστε υἱοί, ἐξαπέστειλεν ὁ θεὸς τὸ πνεῦμα τοῦ
But because ye are sons,　²sent ³forth　¹God　the Spirit

υἱοῦ.αὐτοῦ εἰς τὰς καρδίας ᵍὑμῶν,�‖ κρᾶζον, Ἀββᾶ ὁ πατήρ.
of his Son into ²hearts　¹your,　crying,　Abba,　Father.

7 ὥστε οὐκέτι εἶ δοῦλος, ʰἀλλʼᵃ υἱός· εἰ.δὲ υἱός, καὶ
So　no longer thou art bondman,　but　son; and if son, also

κληρονόμος ⁱθεοῦ διὰ χριστοῦ.‖ 8 Ἀλλὰ τότε μὲν οὐκ
heir　of God through Christ.　But　then indeed not

εἰδότες θεόν, ἐδουλεύσατε ⸀τοῖς ᵏμὴ φύσειᵏ οὖσιν
knowing God, ye were in bondage to those who not by nature are

θεοῖς· 9 νῦν.δέ, γνόντες θεόν, μᾶλλον.δὲ γνωσθέντες
gods;　but now, having known God, but rather having been known

ὑπὸ θεοῦ, πῶς ἐπιστρέφετε πάλιν ἐπὶ τὰ ἀσθενῆ καὶ πτωχὰ
by God, how do ye turn again to the weak and beggarly

στοιχεῖα οἷς πάλιν ἄνωθεν ⁱδουλεύειν‖ θέλετε; 10 ἡμέρας
elements to which again anew to be in bondage ye desire?　Days

παρατηρεῖσθε, καὶ μῆνας, καὶ καιρούς, καὶ ἐνιαυτούς.ᵐ 11 φο-
ye observe, and months, and times, and years.　I am

βοῦμαι ὑμᾶς, μήπως εἰκῆ κεκοπίακα εἰς ὑμᾶς.
afraid of you, lest somehow in vain I have laboured as to you.

12 Γίνεσθε ὡς ἐγώ, ὅτι.κἀγὼ ὡς ὑμεῖς, ἀδελφοί, δέο-
Be　as　I [am], for I also [am] as　ye,　brethren, I be-

μαι ὑμῶν· οὐδέν με ἠδικήσατε. 13 οἴδατε.δὲ ὅτι δι'
seech you: in nothing me ye wronged.　But ye know that in

ἀσθένειαν τῆς σαρκὸς εὐηγγελισάμην ὑμῖν τὸ.πρότερον,
weakness of the flesh I announced the glad tidings to you at the first;

14 καὶ τὸν πειρασμόν ⁿμου τὸν‖ ἐν τῇ.σαρκί.μου οὐκ ἐξου-
and　²temptation　¹my　in　my flesh　³not ¹ye ²de-

θενήσατε οὐδὲ ἐξεπτύσατε, ʰἀλλʼ‖ ὡς ἄγγελον θεοῦ ἐ-
spised　nor rejected with contempt; but　as　an angel of God ye

δέξασθέ με, ὡς χριστὸν Ἰησοῦν. 15 ⸀τίς‖ οὖν ᴾἦν‖ ὁ μακαρισμὸς
received me, as Christ Jesus.　What then was　²blessedness

ὑμῶν; μαρτυρῶ.γὰρ ὑμῖν ὅτι, εἰ δυνατόν, τοὺς ὀφθαλμοὺς
¹your?　for I bear ²witness ¹you that, if possible,　²eyes

ὑμῶν ἐξορύξαντες ᑫἄν‖ ἐδώκατέ μοι. 16 ὥστε ἐχθρὸς
¹your having plucked out ye would have given [them] to me.　So　²enemy

ὑμῶν γέγονα ἀληθεύων ὑμῖν; 17 Ζηλοῦσιν ὑμᾶς
¹your have I become speaking truth to you? They are zealous after you

οὐ καλῶς, ἀλλὰ ἐκκλεῖσαι ʳὑμᾶς‖ θέλουσιν, ἵνα αὐτοὺς
not rightly, but to exclude you [from us] they desire, that them

ζηλοῦτε. 18 καλὸν.δὲ ˢτὸ‖ ζηλοῦσθαι ἐν καλῷ
ye may be zealous after.　But right [it is]　to be zealous in a right [thing]

πάντοτε, καὶ μὴ μόνον ἐν τῷ.παρεῖναί.με πρὸς ὑμᾶς, 19 ᵗτεκ-
at all times, and not only in my being present with you—　²little

νία‖ μου, οὓς πάλιν ὠδίνω ᵛἄχρις‖ οὗ μορφωθῇ
³children ¹my, of whom again I travail until　shall have been formed

---

χριστὸς ἐν ὑμῖν· 20 ἤθελον.δὲ   παρεῖναι πρὸς ὑμᾶς ἄρτι, καὶ
Christ   in you :   and I was wishing to be present with   you   now, and
ἀλλάξαι τὴν.φωνήν.μου, ὅτι ἀποροῦμαι ἐν ὑμῖν.
to change   my voice,   for I am perplexed as to you.

21 Λέγετέ μοι, οἱ ὑπὸ νόμον θέλοντες εἶναι, τὸν νόμον
Tell   me, ye who under law   wish   to be,   the law
οὐκ.ἀκούετε;   22 γέγραπται.γάρ, ὅτι Ἀβραὰμ δύο υἱοὺς
do ye not hear?   For it has been written, that Abraham two sons
ἔσχεν· ἕνα ἐκ τῆς παιδίσκης, καὶ ἕνα ἐκ τῆς ἐλευθέρας·
had ;   one of the maid-servant, and one of the   free   [woman].
23 ʷἀλλ'ᵚ ὁ ˣμὲνᵚ ἐκ τῆς παιδίσκης, ·κατὰ σάρκα ʸγε-
But he   of the maid-servant, according to flesh has
γέννηταιᵚ ὁ.δὲ ἐκ τῆς ἐλευθέρας, ᶻδιὰ τῆςᵚ ἐπαγγελίας.
born,   and he of the   free [woman], through the   promise.
24 ἅτινά ἐστιν ἀλληγορούμενα· αὗται.γάρ εἰσιν ᵃαἱᵚ δύο
Which things are   allegorized ;   for these   are the two
διαθῆκαι· μία μὲν ἀπὸ ὄρους Σινᾶ, εἰς ᵇδουλείανᵚ γεννῶσα,
covenants ; one   from mount Sina,   to   bondage bringing forth,
ἥτις ἐστὶν Ἄγαρ. 25 τὸ γὰρ ᶜˣἌγαρᵚ Σινᾶ ὄρος ἐστὶν ἐν τῇ
which is   Agar.   For Agar Sina mount is in
Ἀραβίᾳ, ᵈσυστοιχεῖᵚ.δὲ τῇ νῦν Ἱερουσαλήμ, δουλεύει
Arabia,   and corresponds to the now Jerusalem,   she is in bondage
ᵉδὲᵚ μετὰ τῶν.τέκνων αὐτῆς. 26 ἡ.δὲ ἄνω Ἱερουσαλήμ, ἐλευ-
and with   her children ;   but the above Jerusalem,   free
θέρα ἐστίν, ἥτις ἐστὶ μήτηρ ᶠπάντωνᵚ ἡμῶν. 27 γέγραπται
is,   which is   mother of all   of us.   It has been written
γάρ, Εὐφράνθητι στεῖρα ἡ οὐ.τίκτουσα· ῥῆξον καὶ βόησον
for,   Rejoice,   O barren that bearest not · break forth and   cry,
ἡ οὐκ.ὠδίνουσα· ὅτι πολλὰ τὰ τέκνα τῆς ἐρήμου μᾶλλον ἢ
that travailest not ; because many the children of the desolate   more than
τῆς ἐχούσης τὸν ἄνδρα. 28 ᵍἩμεῖςᵚ.δέ, ἀδελφοί, κατὰ Ἰσαάκ,
of her that   has the husband.   But we,   brethren, like   Isaac,
ἐπαγγελίας τέκνα ʰἐσμέν·ᵚ 29 ἀλλ' ὥσπερ τότε ὁ κατὰ
of promise children are.   But as   then he who according to
σάρκα γεννηθεὶς ἐδίωκεν τὸν   κατὰ πνεῦμα, οὕτως καὶ
flesh   was born persecuted him [born] according to Spirit,   so also
νῦν. 30 ἀλλὰ τί λέγει ἡ γραφή; Ἔκβαλε τὴν παιδίσκην
now.   But what says the scripture? Cast out the maid-servant
καὶ τὸν.υἱὸν.αὐτῆς, οὐ.γὰρ.μὴ ⁱκληρονομήσῃᵚ ὁ υἱὸς τῆς
and   her son,   for in no wise may inherit   the son of the
παιδίσκης μετὰ τοῦ υἱοῦ τῆς ἐλευθέρας. 31 ᵏἌρα,ᵚ ἀδελ-
maid-servant with the son of the free [woman].   So then, breth-
φοί, οὐκ.ἐσμὲν παιδίσκης τέκνα, ἀλλὰ τῆς ἐλευθέρας.
ren,   we are not of a maid-servant children, but of the   free [woman].

5 Τῇ ἐλευθερίᾳ ˡοὖνᵚ ᵐῇᵚ ⁿχριστὸς ἡμᾶςᵚ ἠλευθέρω-
In the freedom therefore wherewith Christ   us   made free,
σεν, ᵒστήκετε,ᵚ ᵖκαὶ μὴ πάλιν ζυγῷ �qδουλείαςᵚ ἐνέχεσθε. 2 ἴδε
stand fast,   and not again in a yoke of bondage   be held.   Lo,
ἐγὼ Παῦλος λέγω ὑμῖν, ὅτι ἐὰν περιτέμνησθε, χριστὸς ὑμᾶς
I   Paul   say   to you, that if   ye be circumcised, Christ   you
οὐδὲν ὠφελήσει· 3 μαρτύρομαι.δὲ πάλιν παντὶ ἀνθρώπῳ
nothing shall profit.   And I testify   again to every   man

**Right margin:**
sent with you. 19 My little children, of whom I travail in birth again until Christ be formed in you, 20 I desire to be present with you now, and to change my voice ; for I stand in doubt of you.
21 Tell me, ye that desire to be under the law, do ye not hear the law ? 22 For it is written, that Abraham had two sons, the one by a bondmaid, the other by a freewoman. 23 But he who was of the bondwoman was born after the flesh ; but he of the freewoman was by promise. 24 Which things are an allegory : for these are the two covenants ; the one from the mount Sinai, which gendereth to bondage, which is Agar. 25 For this Agar is mount Sinai in Arabia, and answereth to Jerusalem which now is, and is in bondage with her children. 26 But Jerusalem which is above is free, which is the mother of us all. 27 For it is written, Rejoice, thou barren that bearest not ; break forth and cry, thou that travailest not : for the desolate hath many more children than she which hath an husband. 28 Now we, brethren, as Isaac was, are the children of promise. 29 But as then he that was born after the flesh persecuted him that was born after the Spirit, even so it is now. 30 Nevertheless what saith the scripture? Cast out the bondwoman and her son : for the son of the bondwoman shall not be heir with the son of the freewoman. 31 So then, brethren, we are not children of the bondwoman, but of the free.
V. Stand fast therefore in the liberty wherewith Christ hath made us free, and be not entangled again with the yoke of bondage. 2 Behold, I Paul

ʷ ἀλλὰ Tr.   ˣ [μὲν] L.   ʸ γεγένηται W.   ᶻ δι' Tr.   ᵃ — αἱ GLTTrAW.   ᵇ δουλίαν Tr.
ᶜ —Ἄγαρ Lᴛ[Tr].   ᵈ συνσ- T.   ᵉ γὰρ for GLTTrAW.   ᶠ — πάντων G[L]TTrA.   ᵍ ὑμεῖς you LTTrA.
ʰ ἐστέ LTTrA.   ⁱ κληρονομήσει shall inherit LTTr.   ᵏ διό wherefore LTTrA.   ˡ — οὖν
GLTTrAW.   ᵐ — ῇ (read With freedom &c.) LTTrA.   ⁿ ἡμᾶς χριστὸς GLTTᴀW.   ᵒ στήκετε
(commencing a sentence at Stand fast) LTTrA.   ᵖ + οὖν therefore LTTrAW.   q δουλίας T.

say unto you, that if ye be circumcised, Christ shall profit you nothing. 3 For I testify again to every man that is circumcised, that he is a debtor to do the whole law. 4 Christ is become of no effect unto you, whosoever of you are justified by the law ; ye are fallen from grace. 5 For we through the Spirit wait for the hope of righteousness by faith. 6 For in Jesus Christ neither circumcision availeth any thing, nor uncircumcision ; but faith which worketh by love. 7 Ye did run well ; who did hinder you that ye should not obey the truth ? 8 This persuasion *cometh* not of him that calleth you. 9 A little leaven leaveneth the whole lump. 10 I have confidence in you through the Lord, that ye will be none otherwise minded : but he that troubleth you shall bear his - judgment, whosoever he be.

11 And I, brethren, if I yet preach circumcision, why do I yet suffer persecution? then is the offence of the cross ceased. 12 I would they were even cut off which trouble you. 13 For, brethren, ye have been called unto liberty ; only *use* not liberty for an occasion to the flesh, but by love serve one another. 14 For all the law is fulfilled in one word, *even* in this ; Thou shalt love thy neighbour as thyself. 15 But if ye bite and devour one another, take heed that ye be not consumed one of another. 16 *This* I say then, Walk in the Spirit, and ye shall not fulfil the lust of the flesh. 17 For the flesh lusteth against the Spirit, and the Spirit against the flesh : and these are contrary the one to the other: so that ye cannot do the things that ye would. 18 But if ye be led of the Spirit, ye are not under the law. 19 Now

περιτεμνομένῳ, ὅτι ὀφειλέτης ἐστὶν ὅλον τὸν νόμον ποιῆσαι.
being circumcised, that a debtor he is *whole ¹the law to do.
4 κατηργήθητε ἀπὸ ˣτοῦ‖ χριστοῦ, οἵτινες ἐν νόμῳ δι-
Ye are deprived of all effect from the Christ, whosoever in law are
καιοῦσθε, . τῆς χάριτος. ἐξεπέσατε. 5 ἡμεῖς.γὰρ πνεύματι
being justified ; grace ye fell from. For we, by [the] Spirit
ἐκ πίστεως ἐλπίδα δικαιοσύνης ἀπεκδεχόμεθα. 6 ἐν.γὰρ
by faith [the] hope of righteousness await. For in
χριστῷ Ἰησοῦ οὔτε περιτομή τι ἰσχύει. οὔτε ἀκροβυστία‚
Christ Jesus neither circumcision ²any ¹is ²of force, nor uncircumcision ;
ἀλλὰ πίστις δι᾽ ἀγάπης ἐνεργουμένη. 7 Ἐτρέχετε καλῶς.
but faith ²by ³love ¹ ⁴working. Ye were running well :
τίς ὑμᾶς ᵃἀνέκοψεν‖ ᵗτῇ‖ ἀληθείᾳ μὴ πείθεσθαι; 8 ἡ πεισ-
who ²you ¹hindered ⁴the ⁷truth ²not ⁶to ⁵obey ? The persua-
μονὴ οὐκ ἐκ τοῦ καλοῦντος ὑμᾶς. 9 Μικρὰ ζύμη ὅλον
sion [is] not of him who calls you. A little leaven ²whole
τὸ φύραμα ζυμοῖ. 10 ἐγὼᵛ πέποιθα εἰς ὑμᾶς ἐν κυρίῳ,
²the ⁴lump ¹leavens. I am persuaded as to you in [the] Lord,
ὅτι οὐδὲν.ἄλλο.φρονήσετε, ὁ.δὲ ταράσσων ὑμᾶς βαστάσει τὸ
that ye will have no other mind, and he troubling you shall bear the
κρίμα, ὅστις ʷἂν‖ ᾖ.
judgment, whosoever he may be.
11 Ἐγὼ.δὲ, ἀδελφοί, εἰ περιτομὴν ἔτι κηρύσσω, τί ἔτι διώ-
But I, brethren, if circumcision yet I proclaim, why yet am I
κομαι; ἄρα κατήργηται· τὸ σκάνδαλον τοῦ σταυροῦ.
persecuted ? Then has been done away the offence of the cross.
12 ὄφελον καὶ ἀποκόψονται οἱ ἀναστατοῦντες
I would ²even ¹they ²would cut themselves off who throw ²into ³confusion
ὑμᾶς. 13 Ὑμεῖς.γὰρ ἐπ᾽ ἐλευθερίᾳ ἐκλήθητε, ἀδελφοί· μόνον
¹you. For ye for freedom were called, brethren ; only
μὴ τὴν ἐλευθερίαν εἰς ἀφορμὴν τῇ σαρκί, ἀλλὰ διὰ τῆς
[use] not the freedom for an occasion to the flesh, but by
ἀγάπης δουλεύετε ἀλλήλοις. 14 ὁ.γὰρ.πᾶς νόμος ἐν ἑνὶ
love serve ye one another. For the whole law in one
λόγῳ ˣπληροῦται,‖ ἐν τῷ, Ἀγαπήσεις τὸν.πλησίον.σου ὡς
word is fulfilled, in Thou shalt love thy neighbour as
ἑαυτόν.‖ 15 εἰ.δὲ ἀλλήλους δάκνετε καὶ κατεσθίετε, βλέπετε
thyself ; but if one another ye bite and devour, take heed
μὴ ᶻὑπὸ‖ ἀλλήλων ἀναλωθῆτε.
²not ⁵by ⁶one ⁷another ¹ye ²be ⁴consumed.
16 Λέγω.δὲ, Πνεύματι περιπατεῖτε, καὶ ἐπιθυμίαν σαρκὸς
But I say, By [the] Spirit walk ye, and ²desire ¹flesh's
οὐ.μὴ τελέσητε. 17 ἡ.γὰρ σὰρξ ἐπιθυμεῖ κατὰ τοῦ πνεύ-
in no wise should ye fulfil. For the flesh desires against the Spirit,
ματος, τὸ.δὲ πνεῦμα κατὰ τῆς σαρκός· ταῦτα ᵃδὲ‖ ᵇἀντί-
and the Spirit against the flesh ; ²these ²things ¹and are op-
κειται ἀλλήλοις,‖ ἵνα μὴ ἃ.ᶜἂν‖ θέλητε ταῦτα ποιῆτε.
posed to one another, that not whatsoever ye may wish those things ye should do ;
18 εἰ.δὲ πνεύματι ἄγεσθε, οὐκ.ἐστὲ ὑπὸ νόμον. 19 φανερὰ
but if by [the] Spirit ye are led, ye are ²no ¹under law. ²Manifest
δέ ἐστιν τὰ ἔργα τῆς σαρκός, ἅτινά ἐστιν ᵈμοιχεία,‖ πορνεία,
¹now are the works of the flesh, which are adultery, fornication,
ἀκαθαρσία, ἀσέλγεια, 20 εἰδωλολατρεία, φαρμακεία, ἔχθραι,
uncleanness, licentiousness, idolatry, sorcery, enmities,

ʳ — τοῦ LTTr[A].ⁱ ˢ ἐνέκοψεν GLTTrAW. ᵗ — τῇ TTr[A]. ᵛ + [δὲ] but L. ʷ ἐὰν TTrA.
ˣ πεπλήρωται has been fulfilled LTTrAW. ʸ σεαυτόν GLTTrAW. ᶻ ὑπ᾽ LTTr. ᵃ γὰρ for‚
LTTrAW. ᵇ ἀλλήλοις ἀντίκειται GLTTrAW. ᶜ ἐὰν [L]TTrA.. ᵈ — μοιχεία GLTTrAW.

ᵉἔρεις, ζῆλοι,ⁱⁱ θυμοί, ἐριθεῖαι, διχοστασίαι, αἱρέσεις,
strifes,   jealousies,   indignations,   contentions,   divisions,   sects,

21 φθόνοι, ᶠφόνοι,ⁱⁱ μέθαι, κῶμοι, καὶ τὰ ὅμοια τούτοις·
envyings,   murders, drunkennesses, revels,   and things like   these;

ἃ   προλέγω ὑμῖν, καθὼς ᵍκαὶⁱⁱ προεῖπον, ὅτι οἱ
as to which I tell ²beforehand ¹you, even as   also I said before, that they who

τὰ.τοιαῦτα πράσσοντες βασιλείαν θεοῦ οὐ.κληρονομήσουσιν.
such things   do   ²kingdom ¹God's   shall not inherit.

22 ὁ.δὲ καρπὸς τοῦ πνεύματός ἐστιν ἀγάπη, χαρά, εἰρήνη,
But the fruit of the Spirit   is   love, -   joy,   peace,

μακροθυμία, χρηστότης, ἀγαθωσύνη, πίστις, 23 ʰπραότης,ⁱⁱ
long-suffering,   kindness,   goodness,   faith,   meekness,

ἐγκράτεια· κατὰ τῶν.τοιούτων οὐκ.ἔστιν νόμος. 24 οἱ.δὲ
self-control: against such things   there is no law.   But they that [are]

τοῦ χριστοῦⁱ τὴν σάρκα ἐσταύρωσαν σὺν τοῖς παθήμασιν καὶ
of the Christ ²the ³flesh ¹crucified   with the   passions   and

ταῖς ἐπιθυμίαις. 25 εἰ ζῶμεν πνεύματι, πνεύματι· καὶ
the   desires.   If we live by [the] Spirit, by [the] Spirit also

στοιχῶμεν. 26 μὴ.γινώμεθα κενόδοξοι, ἀλλήλους προκα-
we should walk. We should not become vain-glorious, one another   provok-

λούμενοι, ᵏἀλλήλοιςⁱⁱ φθονοῦντες.
ing,   one another   envying.

6 Ἀδελφοί, ἐὰν καὶ ¹προληφθῇⁱⁱ ἄνθρωπος ἔν τινι παρα-
Brethren, if even be taken a man   in some   of-

πτώματι, ὑμεῖς οἱ πνευματικοὶ καταρτίζετε τὸν.τοιοῦτον ἐν
fence,   ye, the spiritual [ones], restore   such a one   in

πνεύματι ᵐπραΰτητος,ⁱⁱ σκοπῶν σεαυτὸν μὴ καὶ σὺ πει-
a spirit   of meekness,   considering thyself lest also thou be

ρασθῇς. 2 ἀλλήλων τὰ βάρη βαστάζετε, καὶ οὕτως ⁿἀνα-
tempted.   One another's burdens bear ye,   and thus   ful-

πληρώσατεⁱⁱ τὸν νόμον τοῦ χριστοῦ. 3 εἰ.γὰρ δοκεῖ τις
fil   the law of the Christ.   For if ²thinks ¹anyone

εἶναί τι, μηδὲν ὤν, ᵒἑαυτὸν φρεναπατᾷ·ⁱⁱ 4 τὸ.δὲ ἔργον
to be something, ²nothing ¹being, himself he deceives: but the work

ἑαυτοῦ δοκιμαζέτω ἕκαστος, καὶ τότε εἰς ἑαυτὸν μόνον τὸ
of himself let ²prove   ¹each,   and then as to himself   alone   the

καύχημα ἕξει, καὶ οὐκ εἰς τὸν.ἕτερον· 5 ἕκαστος.γὰρ τὸ
boasting he will have, and not as to   another.   For each

ἴδιον φορτίον βαστάσει.
his own   load   shall bear.

6 Κοινωνείτω.δὲ ὁ κατηχούμενος τὸν λόγον τῷ
Let ⁷share   ¹him ²being ⁴taught ⁴in ⁵the ⁶word with him that

κατηχοῦντι ἐν πᾶσιν ἀγαθοῖς. 7 μὴ.πλανᾶσθε, θεὸς οὐ μυκ-
teaches   in all   good things.   Be not misled;   God   ³not ¹is

τηρίζεται· ὃ.γὰρ.ᴾἐὰνⁱⁱ σπείρῃ ἄνθρωπος, τοῦτο καὶ θερί-
mocked;   for whatsoever ²may ³sow ¹a ²man,   that also he shall

σει· 8 ὅτι ὁ σπείρων εἰς τὴν.σάρκα.ἑαυτοῦ, ἐκ τῆς σαρκὸς
reap.   For he that sows to   his own flesh,   from the   flesh

θερίσει φθοράν· ὁ.δὲ σπείρων εἰς τὸ πνεῦμα, ἐκ τοῦ
shall reap corruption; but he that sows   to the Spirit,   from the

πνεύματος θερίσει ζωὴν αἰώνιον. 9 τὸ.δὲ   καλὸν ποιοῦντες
Spirit   shall reap life   eternal: but [in] well   doing

---

the works of the flesh are manifest, which are *these;* Adultery, fornication, uncleanness, lasciviousness, 20 idolatry, witchcraft, hatred, variance, emulations, wrath, strife, seditions, heresies, 21 envyings, murders, drunkenness, revellings, and such like: of the which I tell you before, as I have also told *you* in time past, that they which do such things shall not inherit the kingdom of God. 22 But the fruit of the Spirit is love, joy, peace, longsuffering, gentleness, goodness, faith, 23 meekness, temperance: against such there is no law. 24 And they that are Christ's have crucified the flesh with the affections and lusts. 25 If we live in the Spirit, let us also walk in the Spirit. 26 Let us not be desirous of vain glory, provoking one another, envying one another.

VI. Brethren if a man be overtaken in a fault, ye which are spiritual, restore such an one in the spirit of meekness; considering thyself, lest thou also be tempted. 2 Bear ye one another's burdens, and so fulfil the law of Christ. 3 For if a man think himself to be something, when he is nothing, he deceiveth himself. 4 But let every man prove his own work, and then shall he have rejoicing in himself alone, and not in another. 5 For every man shall bear his own burden.

6 Let him that is taught in the word communicate unto him that teacheth in all good things. 7 Be not deceived; God is not mocked: for whatsoever a man soweth, that shall he also reap. 8 For he that soweth to his flesh shall of the flesh reap corruption; but he that soweth to the Spirit shall of the Spirit reap life everlasting. 9 And let us

---

ᵉ ἔρις, ζῆλος strife, jealousy LTTrAW.   ᶠ — φόνοι [L]T[TrA].   ᵍ — καὶ [L]TTr.   ʰ πραΰτης LTTrAW.   ⁱ + Ἰησοῦ Jesus [L]TTrA.   ᵏ ἀλλήλους L.   ˡ προλημφθῇ LTT A.   ᵐ πραΰτητος TTrAW.   ⁿ ἀναπληρώσετε ye shall fulfil LT.   ᵒ φρεναπατᾷ ἑαυτόν LTTrA.   ᴾ ἄν LTr.

not be weary in well doing : for in due season we shall reap, if we faint not. 10 As we have therefore opportunity, let us do good unto all men, especially unto them who are of the household of faith.

11 Ye see how large a letter I have written unto you with mine own hand. 12 As many as desire to make a fair shew.in the flesh, they constrain you to be circumcised ; only lest they should suffer persecution for the cross of Christ. 13 For neither they themselves who are circumcised keep the law ; but desire to have you circumcised, that they may glory in your flesh. 14 But God forbid that I should glory, save in the cross of our Lord Jesus Christ, by whom the world is crucified unto me, and I unto the world. 15 For in Christ Jesus neither circumcision availeth any thing, nor uncircumcision, but a new creature. 16 And as many as walk according to this rule, peace be on them, and mercy, and upon the Israel of God.

17 From henceforth let no man trouble me : for I bear in my body the marks of the Lord Jesus. 18 Brethren, the grace of our Lord Jesus Christ be with your spirit. Amen.

μὴ.ᵠἐκκακῶμεν·‖ καιρῷ.γὰρ ἰδίῳ θερίσομεν, μὴ ἐκλυόμενοι.
we should not lose heart; for in ²time ¹due ⁵we ⁶shall ⁷reap ⁴not ³fainting.

10 ἄρα οὖν ὡς καιρὸν ʳἔχομεν‖ ἐργαζώμεθα τὸ ἀγαθὸν πρὸς
So then as occasion we have we should work good towards

πάντας, μάλιστα.δὲ πρὸς τοὺς οἰκείους τῆς πίστεως.
all, and specially towards those of the household of faith.

11 Ἴδετε πηλίκοις ὑμῖν γράμμασιν ἔγραψα τῇ.ἐμῇ.χειρι.
See in how large ⁴to ⁵you ¹letters ²I ³wrote with my [own] hand.

12 ὅσοι θέλουσιν εὐπροσωπῆσαι ἐν σαρκί, οὗτοι
As many as wish to have a fair appearance in [the] flesh, these

ἀναγκάζουσιν ὑμᾶς περιτέμνεσθαι, μόνον ἵνα ˢμὴ‖ τῷ
compel you to be circumcised, only that not for the

σταυρῷ τοῦ χριστοῦˢ ᵗδιώκωνται.‖ 13 οὐδὲ.γὰρ οἱ
cross of the Christ they may be persecuted. .For neither they who

ᵘπεριτεμνόμενοι‖ αὐτοὶ νόμον φυλάσσουσιν· ἀλλὰ θέ-
are being circumcised themselves [the] law keep ; but they

λουσιν ὑμᾶς περιτέμνεσθαι, ἵνα ἐν τῇ.ὑμετέρᾳ.σαρκὶ καυ-
wish you to be circumcised, that in your flesh they

χήσωνται. 14 ἐμοὶ.δὲ μὴ.γένοιτο καυχᾶσθαι εἰ.μὴ. ἐν τῷ
might boast. But for me may it not be to boast except in the

σταυρῷ τοῦ κυρίου.ἡμῶν Ἰησοῦ χριστοῦ· δι᾽ οὗ ἐμοὶ
cross of our Lord Jesus Christ; through whom to me [the]

κόσμος ἐσταύρωται, κἀγὼ ᵛτῷ‖ κόσμῳ. 15 ʷἐν γὰρ χριστῷ
world has been crucified, and I to the world. ²In ¹for Christ

Ἰησοῦ οὔτε‖ περιτομή ˣτι ἰσχύει,‖ οὔτε ἀκροβυστία,
Jesus neither circumcision ³any ¹is ²of force, nor uncircumcision,

ἀλλὰ καινὴ κτίσις. 16 καὶ ὅσοι τῷ.κανόνι.τούτῳ στοι-
but a new creation. And as many as by this rule shall

χήσουσιν, εἰρήνη ἐπ᾽ αὐτοὺς καὶ ἔλεος, καὶ ἐπὶ τὸν Ἰσραὴλ
walk, peace [be] upon them and mercy, and upon the Israel

τοῦ θεοῦ.
of God.

17 Τοῦ.λοιποῦ, κόπους μοι μηδεὶς παρεχέτω· ἐγὼ.γὰρ τὰ
For the rest, ³troubles ⁶to ⁷me ²no ³one ¹let ⁴give, for I the

στίγματα τοῦ ʸκυρίου‖ Ἰησοῦ ἐν τῷ.σώματί.μου βαστάζω.
brands of the Lord Jesus in my body bear.

18 Ἡ χάρις τοῦ.κυρίου.ἡμῶν Ἰησοῦ χριστοῦ μετὰ τοῦ πνεύ-
The grace of our Lord Jesus Christ [be] with ²spi-

ματος ὑμῶν, ἀδελφοί. ἀμήν.
rit ¹your, brethren. Amen.

ᶻΠρὸς Γαλάτας ἐγράφη ἀπὸ Ῥώμης.‖
To [the] Galatians written from Rome.

ᵃΠΡΟΣ ΕΦΕΣΙΟΥΣ ΕΠΙΣΤΟΛΗ ΠΑΥΛΟΥ.‖
ᵇTO [ᵇTHE] ᶜEPHESIANS ¹EPISTLE ²OF ³PAUL.

PAUL, an apostle of Jesus Christ by the will of God, to the saints which are at Ephesus, and to the

ΠΑΥΛΟΣ ἀπόστολος ᵇ᾽Ιησοῦ χριστοῦ‖ διὰ θελήματος θεοῦ,
Paul, apostle of Jesus Christ by will of God,

τοῖς ἁγίοις τοῖς οὖσιν ᶜἐν Ἐφέσῳ‖ καὶ πιστοῖς. ἐν χριστῷ
to the saints who are at Ephesus and faithful in Christ

ᵠ ἐγ- LTTrAW ; ἐν- T.   ʳ ἔχωμεν we may have T.   ˢ μὴ placed after χριστοῦ LTTrA.
ᵗ διώκονται are being persecuted T   ᵘ περιτετμημένοι have been circumcised L.   ᵛ — τῷ (read to [the]) LTTrA.   ʷ οὔτε γὰρ For neither TTrA.   ˣ τι ἐστὶν is anything GLTTrAW.
ʸ — κυρίου LTTrAW.   ᶻ — the subscription GLTW ; Πρὸς Γαλάτας TrA.
ᵃ + τοῦ Ἀποστόλου of the Apostle E ; Πρὸς Ἐφεσίους LTTrAW.   ᵇ χριστοῦ Ἰησοῦ LTTrA.
ᶜ [ἐν Ἐφέσῳ] TA.

'Ιησοῦ· 2 χάρις ὑμῖν καὶ εἰρήνη ἀπὸ θεοῦ πατρὸς.ἡμῶν καὶ
Jesus.   Grace to you and peace from God   our Father and

κυρίου Ἰησοῦ χριστοῦ.
[the] Lord Jesus Christ.

3 Εὐλογητὸς ὁ θεὸς καὶ πατὴρ τοῦ.κυρίου.ἡμῶν Ἰησοῦ
Blessed [be] the God and Father of our Lord   Jesus

χριστοῦ, ὁ εὐλογήσας ἡμᾶς ἐν πάσῃ εὐλογίᾳ πνευματικῇ ἐν
Christ, who blessed   us with every ²blessing ¹spiritual in

τοῖς ἐπουρανίοις ᵈ χριστῷ, 4 καθὼς ἐξελέξατο ἡμᾶς ἐν αὐτῷ
the heavenlies   with Christ; according as he chose us in him

πρὸ καταβολῆς κόσμου, εἶναι.ἡμᾶς ἁγίους καὶ ἀμώ-
before [the] foundation of [the] world, for us to be holy and blame-

μους κατενώπιον αὐτοῦ ᶜἐν ἀγάπῃ,∥ 5 προορίσας ἡμᾶς εἰς
less before   him in love;   having predestinated us for

υἱοθεσίαν διὰ Ἰησοῦ χριστοῦ εἰς αὐτόν, κατὰ τὴν εὐδο-
adoption through Jesus Christ to himself, according to the good

κίαν τοῦ.θελήματος.αὐτοῦ, 6 εἰς ἔπαινον δόξης τῆς.χάρι-
pleasure of his will,   to [the] praise of [the] glory of ²grace

τος αὐτοῦ, ᶠἐν.ᾗ∥ ἐχαρίτωσεν ἡμᾶς ἐν τῷ ἠγαπημένῳ·
¹his,   wherein he made ²objects ³of ⁴grace ¹us in the Beloved:

7 ἐν ᾧ ἔχομεν τὴν ἀπολύτρωσιν διὰ τοῦ.αἵματος.αὐτοῦ,
in whom we have redemption through his blood,

τὴν ἄφεσιν τῶν παραπτωμάτων, κατὰ ᵍτὸν πλοῦτονʰ τῆς
the remission of offences, according to the riches

χάριτος.αὐτοῦ· 8 ἧς ἐπερίσσευσεν εἰς ἡμᾶς ἐν πάσῃ
of his grace; which he caused to abound toward us in all

σοφίᾳ καὶ φρονήσει, 9 γνωρίσας ἡμῖν τὸ μυστήριον τοῦ
wisdom and intelligence, having made known to us the mystery

θελήματος.αὐτοῦ, κατὰ τὴν.εὐδοκίαν.αὐτοῦ, ἣν προέθετο
of his will,   according to his good pleasure, which he purposed

ἐν αὐτῷ 10 εἰς οἰκονομίαν τοῦ πληρώματος τῶν καιρῶν,
in himself for [the] administration of the fulness of times;

ἀνακεφαλαιώσασθαι τὰ.πάντα ἐν τῷ χριστῷ, τά.ʰτε∥ ἰ ἐνʰ
to head up   all things in the Christ, both the things in

τοῖς οὐρανοῖς καὶ τὰ ἐπὶ τῆς γῆς· 11 ἐν αὐτῷ, ἐν ᾧ
the heavens and the things upon the earth; in him, in whom

καὶ ᵏἐκληρώθημεν,∥ προορισθέντες κατὰ πρό-
also we obtained an inheritance, being predestinated according to [the] pur-

θεσιν τοῦ τὰ.πάντα ἐνεργοῦντος κατὰ τὴν βουλὴν
pose of him who ²all ³things ¹works according to the counsel

τοῦ.θελήματος.αὐτοῦ, 12 εἰς τὸ εἶναι ἡμᾶς εἰς ἔπαινον
of his will, for ²to ³be ¹us to [the] praise

τῆς∥.δόξης.αὐτοῦ, τοὺς προηλπικότας ἐν τῷ χριστῷ· 13 ἐν
of his glory; who have fore-trusted in the Christ: in

ᾧ καὶ ὑμεῖς, ἀκούσαντες τὸν λόγον τῆς ἀληθείας, τὸ εὐαγ-
whom also ye, having heard the word of the truth, the glad

γέλιον τῆς.σωτηρίας.ὑμῶν, ἐν ᾧ καὶ πιστεύσαντες ἐσφρα-
tidings of your salvation— in whom also, having believed, ye were

γίσθητε τῷ πνεύματι τῆς ἐπαγγελίας τῷ ἁγίῳ, 14 ᵐὅς∥ ἐστιν
sealed with the Spirit of promise the Holy, who is

ἀρραβὼν τῆς.κληρονομίας.ἡμῶν, εἰς ἀπολύτρωσιν τῆς
[the] earnest of our inheritance, to [the] redemption of the

περιποιήσεως, εἰς ἔπαινον τῆς.δόξης.αὐτοῦ.
acquired possession, to   praise   of his glory.

faithful in Christ Je-
sus : 2 Grace be to you
and peace, from God
our Father, and from
the Lord Jesus Christ,

3 Blessed be the God
and Father of our
Lord Jesus Christ, who
hath blessed us with
all spiritual blessings
in heavenly places in
Christ : 4 according as
he hath chosen us in
him before the founda-
tion of the world, that
we should be holy and
without blame before
him in love : 5 having
predestinated us unto
the adoption of chil-
dren by Jesus Christ
to himself, according
to the good pleasure of
his will, 6 to the praise
of the glory of his
grace, wherein he hath
made us accepted in
the beloved. 7 In whom
we have redemption
through his blood, the
forgiveness of sins, ac-
cording to the riches
of his grace ; 8 where-
in he hath abounded
toward us in all wis-
dom and prudence;
9 having made known
unto us the mystery
of his will, according
to his good pleasure
which he hath purpos-
ed in himself : 10 that
in the dispensation of
the fulness of times
he might gather to-
gether in one all things
in Christ, both which
are in heaven, and
which are on earth ;
even in him : 11 in
whom also we have
obtained an inherit-
ance, being predesti-
nated according to the
purpose of him who
worketh all things
after the counsel of
his own will : 12 that
we should be to the
praise of his glory, who
first trusted in Christ.
13 In whom ye also
trusted, after that ye
heard the word of
truth, the gospel of
your salvation : in
whom also after that
ye believed, ye were
sealed with that holy
Spirit of promise,
14 which is the earnest
of our inheritance un-
til the redemption of
the purchased posses-
sion, unto the praise
of his glory.

ᵈ + ἐν in (Christ) EGLTTrAW.   ᵉ. ἐν ἀγάπῃ (read in love having predestinated us) GLT.
ᶠ.ἧς which (read ἔχα. he freely bestowed on) LTTrA.   ᵍ τὸ πλοῦτος LTTrAW.   ʰ — τε both
LTTrAW.   ⁱ ἐπὶ upon LTTrA.   ᵏ ἐκλήθημεν we were called L.   ˡ — τῆς LTTrA.   ᵐ ὃ which LA.

15 Wherefore I also, after I heard of your faith in the Lord Jesus, and love unto all the saints, 16 cease not to give thanks for you, making mention of you in my prayers; 17 that the God of our Lord Jesus Christ, the Father of glory, may give unto you the spirit of wisdom and revelation in the knowledge of him: 18 the eyes of your understanding being enlightened; that ye may know what is the hope of his calling, and what the riches of the glory of his inheritance in the saints, 19 and what is the exceeding greatness of his power to us-ward who believe, according to the working of his mighty power, 20 which he wrought in Christ, when he raised him from the dead, and set him at his own right hand in the heavenly places, 21 far above all principality, and power, and might, and dominion, and every name that is named, not only in this world, but also in that which is to come: 22 and hath put all things under his feet, and gave him to be the head over all things to the church, 23 which is his body, the fulness of him that filleth all in all. II. And you hath he quickened, who were dead in trespasses and sins; 2 wherein in time past ye walked according to the course of this world, according to the prince of the power of the air, the spirit that now worketh in the children of disobedience: 3 among whom also we all had our conversation in times past in the lusts of our flesh, fulfilling the desires of the flesh and of the mind; and were by nature the children of

15 Διὰ τοῦτο κἀγὼ ἀκούσας ¹ τὴν καθ᾽ ὑμᾶς πίστιν ἐν
Because of this　I also having heard of the ²among ³you ¹faith in

τῷ κυρίῳ Ἰησοῦ, καὶ ⁿτὴν ἀγάπην‖ τὴν εἰς ᾿πάντας τοὺς
the Lord　Jesus, and the love ᾿ which [is] toward all the

ἁγίους, 16 οὐ.παύομαι εὐχαριστῶν ὑπὲρ ὑμῶν, μνείαν ᵒὑμῶν‖
saints,　do not cease giving thanks for you,　mention of you

ποιούμενος ἐπὶ τῶν.προσευχῶν.μου· 17 ἵνα ὁ θεὸς τοῦ κυρίου
making　in　my prayers,　that the God　of ²Lord

ἡμῶν Ἰησοῦ χριστοῦ, ὁ πατὴρ τῆς δόξης, δῴη ὑμῖν πνεῦμα
᾿our　Jesus　Christ,　the Father of glory, may give to you [the] spirit

᾿σοφίας καὶ ἀποκαλύψεως ἐν ᾿ ἐπιγνώσει αὐτοῦ, 18 πεφω-
of wisdom　and revelation in [the] knowledge of him,　ᵇbeing

τισμένους τοὺς ὀφθαλμοὺς τῆς ᴾδιανοίας‖ ὑμῶν, εἰς τὸ εἰδέναι
⁷enlightened ¹the ²eyes ⁵mind ³of ⁴your, for ²to ³know

ὑμᾶς τίς ἐστιν ἡ ἐλπὶς τῆς.κλήσεως.αὐτοῦ, ᑫκαὶ‖ τίς ὁ πλοῦ-
¹you what is the hope of his calling,　and what the riches

τος τῆς δόξης τῆς.κληρονομίας.αὐτοῦ ἐν τοῖς ἁγίοις, 19 καὶ
of the glory of his inheritance in the saints,　19 and

τί τὸ ὑπερβάλλον μέγεθος τῆς.δυνάμεως.αὐτοῦ εἰς ἡμᾶς
what the surpassing greatness of his power towards us

τοὺς πιστεύοντας κατὰ τὴν ἐνέργειαν τοῦ κράτους τῆς
who believe　according to the working of the might

ἰσχύος.αὐτοῦ, 20 ἣν ᶠἐνήργησεν‖ ἐν τῷ χριστῷ ἐγείρας
of his strength,　which he wrought in the Christ, having raised

αὐτὸν ἐκ ˢ νεκρῶν, καὶ ᵗἐκάθισεν‖ ᵛ ἐν δεξιᾷ
him from among [the] dead, and he set [him] at ᵗright ᵗhand

αὐτοῦ ἐν τοῖς.ᵂἐπουρανίοις,‖ 21 ὑπεράνω πάσης ἀρχῆς ᾿
¹his　in the heavenlies,　above every principality

καὶ ἐξουσίας καὶ δυνάμεως καὶ κυριότητος, καὶ παντὸς ὀνό-
and authority and power and lordship, and every name

ματος ὀνομαζομένου οὐ μόνον ἐν τῷ.αἰῶνι.τούτῳ, ἀλλὰ καὶ
named,　not only in this age,　but also

ἐν τῷ μέλλοντι· 22 καὶ ˣ πάντα ὑπέταξεν ὑπὸ τοὺς πόδας
in the coming [one]; and all things he put under ²feet

αὐτοῦ· καὶ αὐτὸν ἔδωκεν κεφαλὴν ὑπὲρ πάντα τῇ ἐκ-
¹his,　and ²him ¹gave [to be] head over all things to the as-

κλησίᾳ, 23 ἥτις ἐστὶν τὸ.σῶμα.αὐτοῦ, τὸ πλήρωμα τοῦ
sembly,　which is his body,　the fulness of him who

ʸ πάντα ἐν πᾶσιν πληρουμένου 2 καὶ ὑμᾶς ὄντας νεκροὺς
all things in all fills—　and you being dead

τοῖς παραπτώμασιν καὶ ταῖς ἁμαρτίαιςᶻ, 2 ἐν αἷς ποτε
in offences　and　sins,　in which once

περιεπατήσατε κατὰ τὸν αἰῶνα τοῦ.κόσμου.τούτου, κατὰ
ye walked　according to the age of this world,　according to

τὸν ἄρχοντα τῆς ἐξουσίας τοῦ ἀέρος, τοῦ πνεύματος τοῦ νῦν
the ruler of the authority of the air, the spirit that now

ἐνεργοῦντος ἐν τοῖς υἱοῖς τῆς ἀπειθείας· 3 ἐν οἷς καὶ ἡμεῖς
works　in the sons of disobedience: among whom also we

πάντες ἀνεστράφημέν ποτε ἐν ταῖς ἐπιθυμίαις τῆς σαρκὸς
all　had our conduct once in the desires of ²flesh

ἡμῶν, ποιοῦντες τὰ θελήματα τῆς σαρκὸς καὶ τῶν διανοιῶν,
¹our,　doing the things willed of the flesh and of the thoughts,

---

ⁿ — τὴν ἀγάπην L[A].　ᵒ — ὑμῶν LTTrA.　ᴾ καρδίας heart GLTTrAW.　ᑫ — καὶ LTTrA.
ᶠ ἐνήργηκεν he has wrought LTA.　ˢ + τῶν the w.　ᵗ καθίσας having set LTTrA.
ᵛ + αὐτὸν him T.　ᵂ οὐρανοῖς heavens L.　ˣ + τὰ w.　ʸ + τὰ GLTTrAW.　ᶻ + ὑμῶν
(read your offences and sins) LTTr[A].

καὶ ^aἦμεν^ⁿ ^bτέκνα φύσει^ⁿ ὀργῆς, ὡς καὶ οἱ λοιποί· 4 ὁ.δὲ.θεός,
and were children, by nature, of wrath, as even the rest : but God,

πλούσιος ὢν ἐν ἐλέει, διὰ τὴν πολλὴν ἀγάπην αὐτοῦ
²rich ¹being in mercy, because of ²great ³love ¹his

ἣν ἠγάπησεν ἡμᾶς, 5 καὶ ὄντας ἡμᾶς νεκροὺς τοῖς
wherewith he loved us, ²also ³being ¹we dead

παραπτώμασιν, συνεζωοποίησεν ^c τῷ χριστῷ· χάριτί ἐστε
in offences, quickened [us] with the Christ, (by grace ye are

σεσωσμένοι· 6 καὶ συνήγειρεν, καὶ συνεκάθισεν ἐν τοῖς
saved,) and raised [us] up together, and seated [us] together in the

ἐπουρανίοις ἐν χριστῷ Ἰησοῦ· 7 ἵνα ἐνδείξηται ἐν τοῖς
heavenlies in Christ Jesus, that he might shew in the

αἰῶσιν τοῖς ἐπερχομένοις ^dτὸν· ὑπερβάλλοντα πλοῦτον^ⁿ
ages that [are] coming the surpassing riches

τῆς.χάριτος.αὐτοῦ ἐν χρηστότητι ἐφ᾽ ἡμᾶς ἐν χριστῷ Ἰησοῦ·
of his grace in kindness toward us in Christ Jesus.

8 τῇ γὰρ ·χάριτί ἐστε σεσωσμένοι διὰ ^eτῆς^ⁿ πίστεως· καὶ
For by grace ye are saved through faith; and

τοῦτο οὐκ ἐξ ὑμῶν, θεοῦ τὸ δῶρον· 9 οὐκ ἐξ ἔργων, ἵνα
this not of yourselves; [it is] God's gift: not of works, that

μή τις καυχήσηται. 10 αὐτοῦ.γάρ ἐσμεν ποίημα, κτισθέν-
not anyone might boast. For his ²we ³are ¹workmanship, created

τες ἐν χριστῷ Ἰησοῦ ἐπὶ ἔργοις ἀγαθοῖς, οἷς προητοίμασεν ὁ
in Christ Jesus for ²works ¹good, which ²before ³prepared

θεὸς ἵνα ἐν αὐτοῖς περιπατήσωμεν.
¹God that in them we should walk.

11 Διὸ μνημονεύετε ὅτι ^fὑμεῖς ποτε^ⁿ τὰ ἔθνη ἐν
Wherefore remember that ye once the nations in [the]

σαρκί, οἱ λεγόμενοι ἀκροβυστία ὑπὸ τῆς λεγομένης περιτο-
flesh, who are called uncircumcision by that called circum-

μῆς ἐν σαρκὶ χειροποιήτου, 12 ὅτι ἦτε ^gἐν^ⁿ τῷ.καιρῷ.ἐκείνῳ
cision in [the] flesh made by hand— that ye were at that time

χωρὶς χριστοῦ, ἀπηλλοτριωμένοι τῆς πολιτείας τοῦ Ἰσραήλ,
apart from Christ, alienated from the commonwealth of Israel,

καὶ ξένοι τῶν διαθηκῶν τῆς ἐπαγγελίας, ἐλπίδα μὴ ἔχον-
and strangers from the covenants of promise, hope not hav-

τες, καὶ ἄθεοι ἐν τῷ κόσμῳ 13 νυνὶ.δὲ ἐν χριστῷ Ἰησοῦ,
ing, and without God in the world : but now in Christ Jesus,

ὑμεῖς οἱ ποτε ὄντες μακρὰν ^hἐγγὺς ἐγενήθητε^ⁿ ἐν τῷ αἵματι
ye who once were afar off near are become by the blood

τοῦ χριστοῦ. 14 αὐτὸς.γάρ ἐστιν ἡ.εἰρήνη.ἡμῶν, ὁ ποιήσας
of the Christ. For he is our peace, who made

τὰ ἀμφότερα ἕν, καὶ τὸ μεσότοιχον τοῦ φραγμοῦ λύσας·
both one, and the middle wall of the fence broke down,

15 τὴν ἔχθραν ³in ^hhis ⁵flesh, ⁸the ⁹law ¹⁰of ¹¹commandments
ᵉthe ⁷enmity ³in his ⁵flesh, the law of commandments

ἐν δόγμασιν καταργήσας· ἵνα τοὺς δύο κτίσῃ ἐν ⁱἑαυ-
¹²in ¹³decrees ¹having ²annulled, that the two he might create in him-

τῷ^ⁿ εἰς ἕνα καινὸν ἄνθρωπον, ποιῶν εἰρήνην· 16 καὶ ἀπο-
self into one new man, making peace ; and might

καταλλάξῃ τοὺς ἀμφοτέρους ἐν ἑνὶ σώματι τῷ θεῷ διὰ τοῦ
reconcile both in one body to God through the

σταυροῦ, ἀποκτείνας τὴν ἔχθραν ἐν αὐτῷ· 17 καὶ ἐλθὼν
cross, having slain the enmity by it; and having come

---

wrath, even as others. 4 But God, who is rich in mercy, for his great love wherewith he loved us, 5 even when we were dead in sins, hath quickened us together with Christ, (by grace ye are saved ;) 6 and hath raised us up together, and made us sit together in heavenly *places* in Christ Jesus : 7 that in the ages to come he might shew the exceeding riches of his grace in *his* kindness toward us through Christ Jesus. 8 For by grace are ye saved through faith ; and that not of yourselves : *it is* the gift of God : 9 not of works, lest any man should boast. 10 For we are his workmanship, created in Christ Jesus unto good works, which God hath before ordained that we should walk in them.

11 Wherefore remember, that ye *being* in time past Gentiles in the flesh, who are called Uncircumcision by that which is called the Circumcision in the flesh made by hands ; 12 that at that time ye were without Christ, being aliens from the commonwealth of Israel, and strangers from the covenants of promise, having no hope, and without God in the world : 13 but now in Christ Jesus ye who sometimes were far off are made nigh by the blood of Christ. 14 For he is our peace, who hath made both one, and hath broken down the middle wall of partition *between us* ; 15 having abolished in his flesh the enmity, *even* the law of commandments *contained* in ordinances ; for to make in himself of twain one new man, so making peace ; 16 and that he might reconcile both unto God in one body by the cross, having slain the enmity thereby : 17 and came and preached

---

^a ἤμεθα ΤΤrA. ^b φύσει τέκνα L. ^c + [ἐν] L. ^d τὸ ὑπερβάλλον πλοῦτος LTTrAW.
^e — τῆς LTT[A]. ^f ποτὲ ὑμεῖς LTTrA. ^g — ἐν (read τῷ κ. ἐν, at that time) LTTrAW.
^h ἐγενήθητε ἐγγὺς LTTrA. ⁱ αὐτῷ LTTrA.

peace to you which
were afar off, and to
them that were nigh.
18 For through him
we both have access by
one Spirit unto the Fa-
ther. 19 Now there-
fore ye are no more
strangers and foreign-
ers, but fellowcitizens
with the saints, and
of the household of
God ; 20 and are built
upon the foundation
of the apostles and
prophets, Jesus Christ
himself being the
chief corner *stone*;
21 in whom all the
building fitly framed
together groweth unto
an holy temple in the
Lord : 22 in whom ye
also are builded toge-
ther for an habitation
of God through the
Spirit.

εὐηγγελίσατο　　εἰρήνην ὑμῖν τοῖς　　μακρὰν· καὶ[k]
he announced the glad tidings— peace　to you who [were] afar off　and

τοῖς ἐγγύς, 18 ὅτι.δι'　αὐτοῦ ἔχομεν τὴν προσαγωγὴν οἱ
to those near.　For through him　we have　　access

ἀμφότεροι ἐν ἑνὶ πνεύματι πρὸς τὸν πατέρα. 19 ἄρα οὖν
both　by one　Spirit　to the　Father.　　So then

οὐκέτι ἐστὲ ξένοι καὶ πάροικοι, [l]ἀλλὰ[l] [m n]συμπολῖται[l] τῶν
no longer are ye strangers and sojourners,　but　fellow-citizens of the

ἁγίων καὶ οἰκεῖοι τοῦ θεοῦ, 20 ἐποικοδομηθέντες ἐπὶ τῷ
saints and of the household of God,　being built up　on the

θεμελίῳ τῶν ἀποστόλων καὶ προφητῶν, ὄντος ἀκρο-
foundation of the　apostles　and　prophets,　[s]being [the] [o]corner-

γωνιαίου αὐτοῦ [o]'Ιησοῦ χριστοῦ,[l] 21 ἐν ᾧ πᾶσα [p]ἡ[l] οἰκοδομὴ
stone　[3]himself [1]Jesus [2]Christ,　in whom all　the building

συναρμολογουμένη αὔξει εἰς ναὸν ἅγιον ἐν　κυρίῳ, 22 ἐν
fitted together　increases to a [z]temple [1]holy in [the] Lord ;　in

ᾧ καὶ ὑμεῖς συνοικοδομεῖσθε εἰς κατοικητήριον τοῦ θεοῦ
whom also　ye are being built together for　a habitation　of God

ἐν　πνεύματι.
in [the] Spirit.

III. For this cause
I Paul, the prisoner
of Jesus Christ for you
Gentiles, 2 if ye have
heard of the dispensa-
tion of the grace of
God which is given me
to you-ward : 3 how
that by revelation he
made known unto me
the mystery; (as I
wrote afore in few
words, 4 whereby,
when ye read, ye may
understand my know-
ledge in the mystery
of Christ) 5 which in
other ages was not
made known unto the
sons of men, as it is
now revealed unto his
holy apostles and pro-
phets by the Spirit ;
6 that the Gentiles
should be fellowheirs,
and of the same body,
and partakers of his
promise in Christ by
the gospel : 7 whereof
I was made a minister,
according to the gift
of the grace of God
given unto me by the
effectual working of
his power. 8 Unto me,
who am less than the
least of all saints, is
this grace given, that
I should preach among
the Gentiles the un-
searchable riches of

3 Τούτου.χάριν ἐγὼ Παῦλος ὁ δέσμιος τοῦ χριστοῦ [q]Ἰη-
For this cause I.　Paul　prisoner of the Christ　Je-

σοῦ[l] ὑπὲρ ὑμῶν τῶν ἐθνῶν· 2 εἴγε ἠκούσατε τὴν οἰκονομίαν
sus　for　you　nations,　if indeed ye heard of the administration

τῆς χάριτος τοῦ θεοῦ τῆς δοθείσης μοι εἰς ὑμᾶς, 3 [r]ὅτι[l]
of the grace　of God which was given to me towards you,　that

κατὰ ἀποκάλυψιν [s]ἐγνώρισέν[l] μοι τὸ μυστήριον, καθὼς
by　revelation　he made known to me the　mystery,　(according as

προέγραψα ἐν.ὀλίγῳ, 4 πρὸς ὃ δύνασθε ἀναγινώσκοντες
I wrote before briefly,　by which ye are able,　reading　[it],

νοῆσαι τὴν.σύνεσίν.μου ἐν τῷ μυστηρίῳ τοῦ.χριστοῦ· 5 ὃ
to perceive my understanding in the mystery of the Christ,)　which

[t]ἐν[l] ἑτέραις γενεαῖς οὐκ.ἐγνωρίσθη τοῖς υἱοῖς τῶν ἀνθρώ-
in　other generations was not made known to the sons　of men,

πων, ὡς νῦν ἀπεκαλύφθη τοῖς ἁγίοις ἀποστόλοις αὐτοῦ καὶ
as now　it was revealed to [2]holy [3]apostles [1]his and

προφήταις ἐν　πνεύματι· 6 εἶναι τὰ ἔθνη [v]συγκληρονόμα[l]
prophets　in [the] Spirit,　[3]to [4]be [1]the [2]nations　joint-heirs

καὶ [w]σύσσωμα[l] καὶ [v]συμμέτοχα[l] τῆς.ἐπαγγελίας.[x]αὐτοῦ[l] ἐν
and　a joint-body　and　joint-partakers　of his promise　in

[y]τῷ[l] χριστῷ[z], διὰ τοῦ εὐαγγελίου, 7 οὗ [a]ἐγενόμην[l] διάκονος
the　Christ through the glad tidings ; of which　I became　servant

κατὰ τὴν δωρεὰν τῆς χάριτος τοῦ θεοῦ [b]τὴν δοθεῖσάν[l]
according to the gift　of the grace　of God　given

μοι κατὰ τὴν ἐνέργειαν τῆς.δυνάμεως.αὐτοῦ· 8 ἐμοὶ
to me, according to the　working　of his power.　To me,

τῷ ἐλαχιστοτέρῳ πάντων [c]τῶν[l] ἁγίων ἐδόθη ἡ.χάρις.αὕτη,
the less than the least of all　the saints, was given　this grace,

[d]ἐν[l] τοῖς ἔθνεσιν　εὐαγγελίσασθαι　[e]τὸν[l] ἀνεξιχνίαστον
among the nations to announce the glad tidings—　the　unsearchable

---

[k] + εἰρήνην peace LTTrAW.　[l] ἀλλ' L.　[m] + ἐστὲ ye are LTTrA.　[n] συν- TA.　[o] χριστοῦ
Ἰησοῦ LTTrA.　[p] — ἡ (*read* [the]) LTTrAW.　[q] — Ἰησοῦ T[A].　[r] [ὅτι] L.　[s] ἐγνωρίσθη
was made known GLTTrAW.　[t] — ἐν (*read* ἑτέραις to other) GLTTrAW.　[v] συν- T.　[w] σύν-
LTTrA.　[x] — αὐτοῦ (*read* of the promise) LTTrA.　[y] — τῷ LTTrA.　[z] + Ἰησοῦ Jesus LTTrA.
[a] ἐγενήθην LTTrAW.　[b] τῆς δοθείσης GLTTrA.　[c] — τῶν GLTTrAW.　[d] — ἐν (*read* τοῖς
to the) LTTrA.　[e] τὸ LTTrAW.

ᶠπλοῦτον‖ τοῦ χριστοῦ, 9 καὶ φωτίσαι ᵍπάντας‖ τίς
riches   of the Christ,   and to enlighten all   [as to] what [is]

ἡ ʰκοινωνία‖ τοῦ μυστηρίου τοῦ ἀποκεκρυμμένου ἀπὸ τῶν
the fellowship of the mystery which has been hidden from the

αἰώ,νων ἐν τῷ θεῷ, τῷ τὰ.πάντα κτίσαντι ⁱδιὰ Ἰησοῦ χριστοῦ,‖
ages   in God, who all things created by Jesus Christ,

10 ἵνα γνωρισθῇ νῦν ταῖς ἀρχαῖς καὶ ταῖς ἐξουσίαις ἐν
that might be known now to the principalities and the authorities in

τοῖς ἐπουρανίοις διὰ τῆς ἐκκλησίας ἡ πολυποίκιλος σοφία
the heavenlies through the assembly the multifarious wisdom

τοῦ θεοῦ, 11 κατὰ   πρόθεσιν τῶν αἰώνων, ἣν ἐποίησεν
of God, according to [the] purpose of the ages, which he made

ἐν ᵏχριστῷ Ἰησοῦ τῷ.κυρίῳ.ἡμῶν, 12 ἐν ᾧ ἔχομεν τὴν παρ-
in Christ Jesus   our Lord,   in whom we have bold-

ρησίαν καὶ ˡτὴν‖ προσαγωγὴν ἐν πεποιθήσει διὰ τῆς πίστεως
ness and access   in confidence by the faith

αὐτοῦ. 13 διὸ αἰτοῦμαι μὴ ᵐἐκκακεῖν‖ ἐν ταῖς θλίψεσίν
of him. Wherefore I beseech [you] not to faint at   ²tribulations

μου ὑπὲρ ὑμῶν, ἥτις ἐστὶν δόξα.ὑμῶν. 14 τούτου.χάριν
¹my for you, which is   your glory.   For this cause

κάμπτω τὰ.γόνατά.μου πρὸς τὸν πατέρα ⁿτοῦ.κυρίου.ἡμῶν
I bow   my knees   to the Father   f our Lord

Ἰησοῦ χριστοῦ,‖ 15 ἐξ οὗ πᾶσα πατριὰ ἐν οὐρανοῖς καὶ
Jesus Christ,   of whom every family in [the] heavens and

ἐπὶ γῆς ὀνομάζεται, 16 ἵνα ᵒδῴη‖ ὑμῖν κατὰ ᴾτὸν
on earth is named,   that he may give you according to the

πλοῦτον‖ τῆς.δόξης.αὐτοῦ, δυνάμει κραταιωθῆναι διὰ τοῦ
riches   of his glory, with power to be strengthened by

πνεύματος.αὐτοῦ εἰς τὸν ἔσω ἄνθρωπον, 17 κατοικῆσαι τὸν
his Spirit   in the inner man ; [for] ᵃto ᵇdwell ¹the

χριστὸν διὰ τῆς πίστεως ἐν ταῖς.καρδίαις.ὑμῶν· 18 ἐν ἀγάπῃ
²Christ, through faith, in your hearts, in love

ἐρριζωμένοι καὶ τεθεμελιωμένοι ἵνα ἐξισχύσητε κατα-
being rooted and founded, that ye may be fully able to ap-

λαβέσθαι σὺν πᾶσιν τοῖς ἁγίοις τί   τὸ πλάτος καὶ μῆκος
prehend with all the saints what [is] the breadth and length

καὶ �۹βάθος καὶ ὕψος,‖ 19 γνῶναί.τε τὴν ὑπερβάλλουσαν
and depth and height ; and to know the   surpassing

τῆς γνώσεως ἀγάπην τοῦ χριστοῦ, ἵνα πληρωθῆτε εἰς πᾶν
knowledge love of the Christ ; that ye may be filled unto all

τὸ πλήρωμα τοῦ θεοῦ. 20 τῷ.δὲ δυναμένῳ ὑπὲρ πάντα
the fulness of God. But to him who is able above all things

ποιῆσαι ʳὑπὲρ.ἐκ.περισσοῦ‖ ὧν αἰτούμεθα ἢ νοοῦμεν,. κατὰ
to do   exceedingly above what we ask or think, according to

τὴν δύναμιν τὴν ἐνεργουμένην ἐν ἡμῖν, 21 αὐτῷ ἡ δόξα
the power which works in us,   to him [be] glory

ἐν τῇ ἐκκλησίᾳˢ ἐν χριστῷ Ἰησοῦ, εἰς πάσας τὰς γενεὰς τοῦ
in the assemblyˢ in Christ Jesus, to all the generations of the

αἰῶνος τῶν αἰώνων. ἀμήν. 4 Παρακαλῶ οὖν ὑμᾶς ἐγὼ
age of the ages. Amen. I exhort therefore you, I

ὁ δέσμιος ἐν κυρίῳ, ἀξίως περιπατῆσαι τῆς κλήσεως
the prisoner in [the] Lord, ³worthily ¹to ²walk of the calling

Christ ; 9 and to make all *men* see what *is* the fellowship of the mystery, which from the beginning of the world hath been hid in God, who created all things by Jesus Christ: 10 to the intent that now unto the principalities and powers in heavenly *places* might be known by the church the manifold wisdom of God, 11 according to the eternal purpose which he purposed in Christ Jesus our Lord : 12 in whom we have boldness and access with confidence by the faith of him. 13 Wherefore I desire that ye faint not at my tribulations for you, which is your glory. 14 For this cause I bow my knees unto the Father of our Lord Jesus Christ, 15 of whom the whole family in heaven and earth is named, 16 that he would grant you, according to the riches of his glory, to be strengthened with might by his Spirit in the inner man ; 17 that Christ may dwell in your hearts by faith ; that ye, being rooted and grounded in love, 18 may be able to comprehend with all saints what *is* the breadth, and length, and depth, and height ; 19 and to know the love of Christ, which passeth knowledge, that ye might be filled with all the fulness of God. 20 Now unto him that is able to do exceeding abundantly above all that we ask or think, according to the power that worketh in us, 21 unto him *be* glory in the church by Christ Jesus throughout all ages, world without end. Amen. IV. I therefore, the prisoner of the Lord, beseech you that ye walk worthy of the vocation wherewith ye are call-

---

ᶠ πλοῦτος LTTrAW. ᵍ — πάντας [L]T. ʰ οἰκονομία administration GLTTrAW.
ⁱ — διὰ Ἰησοῦ χριστοῦ GLTTrAW. ᵏ + τῷ LTTrA. ˡ — τὴν LTTr[A]. ᵐ ἐγ- LTrAW;
ἐν- T. ⁿ — τοῦ κυρίου ἡμῶν Ἰησοῦ χριστοῦ LTTrAW. ᵒ δῷ LTTrA. ᴾ τὸ πλοῦτος
LTTrAW. ۹ ὕψος καὶ βάθος LTrA. ʳ ὑπερεκπερισσοῦ GLTTrAW. ˢ + καὶ and LTTr[A].

ed, 2 with all lowliness and meekness, with longsuffering, forbearing one another in love; 3 endeavouring to keep the unity of the Spirit in the bond of peace. 4 *There is* one body, and one Spirit, even as ye are called in one hope of your calling; 5 one Lord, one faith, one baptism, 6 one God and Father of all, who *is* above all, and through all, and in you all. 7 But unto every one of us is given grace according to the measure of the gift of Christ. 8 Wherefore he saith, When he ascended up on high, he led captivity captive, and gave gifts unto men. 9 (Now that he ascended, what is it but that he also descended first into the lower parts of the earth? 10 He that descended is the same also that ascended up far above all heavens, that he might fill all things.) 11 And he gave some, apostles; and some, prophets; and some, evangelists; and some, pastors and teachers; 12 for the perfecting of the saints, for the work of the ministry, for the edifying of the body of Christ: 13 till we all come in the unity of the faith, and of the knowledge of the Son of God, unto a perfect man, unto the measure of the stature of the fulness of Christ: 14 that we *henceforth* be no more children, tossed to and fro, and carried about with every wind of doctrine, by the sleight of men, *and* cunning craftiness, whereby they lie in wait to deceive; 15 but speaking the truth in love, may grow up into him in all things, which is the head, *even* Christ: 16 from whom the whole body fitly joined together and compacted by that which every joint supplieth, according to the effectual working in the measure of every part,

ἧς ἐκλήθητε, 2 μετὰ πάσης ταπεινοφροσύνης καὶ ᵗπραό-
wherewith ye were called, with all humility and meek-
τητος,‖ μετὰ μακροθυμίας, ἀνεχόμενοι ἀλλήλων ἐν ἀγάπῃ,
ness, with longsuffering, bearing with one another in love;
3 σπουδάζοντες τηρεῖν τὴν ἑνότητα τοῦ πνεύματος ἐν τῷ
being diligent to keep the unity of the Spirit in the
συνδέσμῳ τῆς εἰρήνης. 4 ῞Εν σῶμα καὶ ἓν πνεῦμα, καθὼς καὶ
bond of peace. One body and one Spirit, even as also
ἐκλήθητε ἐν μιᾷ ἐλπίδι τῆς κλήσεως ὑμῶν· 5 εἷς κύριος, μία
ye were called in one hope of your calling; one Lord, one
πίστις, ἓν βάπτισμα· 6 εἷς θεὸς καὶ πατὴρ πάντων, ὁ
faith, one baptism; one God and Father of all, who [is]
ἐπὶ πάντων, καὶ διὰ πάντων, καὶ ἐκ πᾶσιν ᵘὑμῖν.‖
over all, and through all, and in ²all ¹you.
7 ἑνὶ δὲ ἑκάστῳ ἡμῶν ἐδόθη ʷἡ‖ χάρις κατὰ τὸ μέτρον
But to each one of us was given grace according to the measure
τῆς δωρεᾶς τοῦ χριστοῦ. 8 διὸ λέγει, Ἀναβὰς εἰς
of the gift of the Christ. Wherefore he says, Having ascended up on
ὕψος ᾐχμαλώτευσεν αἰχμαλωσίαν, ˣκαὶ‖ ἔδωκεν δόματα τοῖς
high he led ²captive ¹captivity, and gave gifts
ἀνθρώποις. 9 Τὸ δὲ ἀνέβη, τί ἐστιν εἰ μὴ ὅτι καὶ κατέβη
to men. But that he ascended, what is it but that also he descended
ʸπρῶτον⸾‖ εἰς τὰ κατώτερα ᶻμέρη‖ τῆς γῆς; 10 ὁ καταβὰς
first into the lower parts of the earth? He that descended
ᵃαὐτός ἐστιν καὶ ὁ ἀναβὰς ὑπεράνω πάντων τῶν οὐρανῶν,
ᵃthe ³same ¹is also who ascended above all the heavens,
ἵνα πληρώσῃ τὰ πάντα. 11 καὶ αὐτὸς ἔδωκεν τοὺς μὲν ἀπο-
that he might fill all things; and he gave some apo-
στόλους, τοὺς δὲ προφήτας, τοὺς δὲ εὐαγγελιστάς, τοὺς δὲ
stles, and some prophets, and some evangelists, and some
ποιμένας καὶ διδασκάλους, 12 πρὸς τὸν καταρτισμὸν τῶν
shepherds and teachers, with a view to the perfecting of the
ἁγίων, εἰς ἔργον διακονίας, εἰς οἰκοδομὴν τοῦ σώματος τοῦ
saints; for work of [the] service, for building up of the body of the
χριστοῦ· 13 μέχρι καταντήσωμεν οἱ πάντες εἰς τὴν ἑνότητα
Christ; until we ²may ³arrive ¹all at the unity
τῆς πίστεως καὶ τῆς ἐπιγνώσεως τοῦ υἱοῦ τοῦ θεοῦ, εἰς ἄνδρα
of the faith and of the knowledge of the Son of God, at a ²man
τέλειον, εἰς μέτρον ἡλικίας τοῦ πληρώματος τοῦ
¹full-grown, at [the] measure of [the] stature of the fulness of the
χριστοῦ· 14 ἵνα μηκέτι ὦμεν νήπιοι, κλυδωνιζόμενοι καὶ
Christ; that no longer we may be infants, being tossed and
περιφερόμενοι παντὶ ἀνέμῳ τῆς διδασκαλίας ἐν τῇ ᵃκυβείᾳᵘ
carried about by every wind of the teaching in the sleight
τῶν ἀνθρώπων, ἐν πανουργίᾳ πρὸς τὴν ᵇμεθοδείαν‖ τῆς
of men, in craftiness with a view to the systematizing
πλάνης· 15 ἀληθεύοντες δὲ ἐν ἀγάπῃ αὐξήσωμεν εἰς αὐτὸν
of error; but holding the truth in love we may grow up into him
τὰ πάντα, ὅς ἐστιν ἡ κεφαλή, ᶜὁ‖ χριστός, 16 ἐξ οὗ πᾶν
in all things, who is the head, the Christ; from whom all
τὸ σῶμα συναρμολογούμενον καὶ ᵈσυμβιβαζόμενον‖ διὰ πάσης
the body, fitted together and compacted by every
ἁφῆς τῆς ἐπιχορηγίας κατ' ἐνέργειαν ἐν μέτρῳ
joint of supply according to [the] working in [its] measure

ᵗ πραΰτητος TTrA.   ᵛ — ὑμῖν LTTrA; ἡμῖν us GW.   ʷ — ἡ LTr[A].   ˣ — καὶ LTW.
ʸ — πρῶτον GLTTrAW.   ᶻ — μέρη (*read* [parts]) W.   ᵃ κυβίᾳ T.   ᵇ μεθοδίαν T.
ᶜ — ὁ LTTrAW.   ᵈ συν- T.

ἑνὸς.ἑκάστου μέρους, τὴν αὔξησιν τοῦ σώματος ποιεῖται εἰς
of each one   part,   the increase of the body   makes for itself to

οἰκοδομὴν ᵉἑαυτοῦ‖ ἐν ἀγάπῃ.
[the] building up of itself in love.

17 Τοῦτο οὖν λέγω καὶ μαρτύρομαι ἐν κυρίῳ, μηκέτι
This therefore I say, and testify in [the] Lord, ³no ⁴longer

ὑμᾶς.περιπατεῖν, καθὼς καὶ τὰ ᶠλοιπὰ‖ ἔθνη περιπατεῖ ἐν
¹that ²ye walk   even as also the rest, [the] nations, are walking in

ματαιότητι τοῦ.νοὸς.αὐτῶν, 18 ᵍἐσκοτισμένοι‖ τῇ δια-
[the] vanity of their mind,   being darkened in the under-

νοίᾳ, ὄντες ἀπηλλοτριωμένοι τῆς ζωῆς τοῦ θεοῦ, ·διὰ
standing, being alienated from   the life of God, on account of

τὴν ἄγνοιαν τὴν οὖσαν ἐν αὐτοῖς, διὰ τὴν πώρωσιν
the ignorance which is in them, on account of the hardness

τῆς.καρδίας.αὐτῶν· 19 οἵτινες ἀπηλγηκότες ἑαυτοὺς
of their heart,   who having cast off all feeling, themselves

παρέδωκαν τῇ ἀσελγείᾳ εἰς ἐργασίαν ἀκαθαρσίας πάσης
gave up to licentiousness, for [the] working of ²uncleanness ¹all

ἐν πλεονεξίᾳ· 20 ὑμεῖς.δὲ οὐχ οὕτως ἐμάθετε τὸν χριστόν,
with craving. But ye ²not ³thus ¹learned the Christ,

21 εἴγε αὐτὸν ἠκούσατε καὶ ἐν αὐτῷ ἐδιδάχθητε, καθὼς
if indeed him ye heard and in him were taught, according as

ἐστιν ἀλήθεια ἐν τῷ Ἰησοῦ· 22 ἀποθέσθαι.ὑμᾶς κατὰ
is [the] truth in Jesus; for you to have put off according to

τὴν προτέραν ἀναστροφήν τὸν παλαιὸν ἄνθρωπον, τὸν
the former conduct   the   old   man,   which

φθειρόμενον κατὰ τὰς ἐπιθυμίας τῆς ἀπάτης· 23 ἀνα-
is corrupt according to the desires of deceit; ' ²to ³be ⁴re-

νεοῦσθαι ʰδὲ‖ τῷ πνεύματι τοῦ.νοὸς ὑμῶν· 24 καὶ ἐνδύσασθαι
newed ¹and in the spirit of your mind;   and to have put on

τὸν καινὸν ἄνθρωπον, τὸν κατὰ θεὸν κτισθέντα ἐν δι-
the new   man,   which according to God was created in right-

καιοσύνῃ καὶ ὁσιότητι τῆς ἀληθείας. 25 Διὸ ἀποθέμενοι τὸ
eousness and holiness of truth.   Wherefore having put off

ψεῦδος, λαλεῖτε ἀλήθειαν ἕκαστος μετὰ τοῦ.πλησίον.αὐτοῦ·
falsehood, speak truth each with his neighbour,

ὅτι ἐσμὲν ἀλλήλων μέλη. 26 Ὀργίζεσθε καὶ μὴ ἁμαρ-
because we are of one another members. Be angry, and ²not ¹sin;

τάνετε· ὁ ἥλιος μὴ.ἐπιδυέτω ἐπὶ ⁱτῷ‖.παροργισμῷ.ὑμῶν,
³the ⁶sun ³let ⁴not set upon your provocation,

27 ᵏμήτε‖ δίδοτε τόπον τῷ διαβόλῳ. 28 ὁ κλέπτων μηκέτι
neither give place to the devil.   He that steals ⁴no ⁵more

κλεπτέτω, μᾶλλον.δὲ κοπιάτω, ἐργαζόμενος ᶫτὸ ἀγαθὸν
¹let ²him ³steal, but rather ' let him labour, working what [is] good

ταῖς.χερσίν,‖ ἵνα ἔχῃ μεταδιδόναι τῷ χρείαν ἔχοντι.
with [his] hands, that he may have to impart to him that ²need ¹has.

29 πᾶς λόγος σαπρὸς ἐκ τοῦ.στόματος.ὑμῶν μὴ ἐκ-
⁵Any ⁷word ⁶corrupt ¹⁰out ¹¹of ¹²your ¹³mouth ⁴not ³let
(kt. every)

πορευέσθω, ᵐἀλλ'‖ εἴ τις ἀγαθὸς πρὸς οἰκοδομὴν τῆς.χρείας,
²go ³forth, but if any good for building up in respect of need,

ἵνα δῷ χάριν τοῖς ἀκούουσιν. 30 καὶ μὴ.λυπεῖτε τὸ
that it may give grace to them that hear.   And grieve not the

πνεῦμα τὸ ἅγιον τοῦ θεοῦ, ἐν ᾧ ἐσφραγίσθητε εἰς ἡμέραν
Spirit the Holy of God, by which ye were sealed for [the] day

---

maketh increase of the body unto the edifying of itself in love.

17 This I say there-fore, and testify in the Lord, that ye hence-forth walk not as other Gentiles walk, in the vanity of their mind, 18 having the under-standing darkened, being alienated from the life of God through the ignorance that is in them, because of the blindness of their heart: 19 who being past feeling have given themselves over unto lasciviousness, to work all uncleanness with greediness. 20 But ye have not so learned Christ; 21 if so be that ye have heard him, and have been taught by him, as the truth is in Jesus: 22 that ye put off concerning the former conversation the old man, which is corrupt according to the deceitful lusts; 23 and be renewed in the spirit of your mind; 24 and that ye put on the new man, which after God is created in righteous-ness and true holiness. 25 Wherefore putting away lying, speak every man truth with his neighbour: for we are members one of another. 26 Be ye an-gry, and sin not: let not the sun go down upon your wrath: 27 neither give place to the devil. 28 Let him that stole steal no more: but rather let him labour, working with his hands the thing which is good, that he may have to give to him that need-eth. 29 Let no corrupt communication pro-ceed out of your mouth, but that which is good to the use of edifying, that it may minister grace unto the hearers. 30 And grieve not the holy Spirit of God, where-by ye are sealed unto the day of redemption.

---

31 Let all bitterness, and wrath, and anger, and clamour, and evil speaking, be put away from you, with all malice : 32 and be ye kind one to another, tenderhearted, forgiving one another, even as God for Christ's sake hath forgiven you. V. Be ye therefore followers of God, as dear children ; 2 and walk in love, as Christ also hath loved us, and hath given himself for us an offering and a sacrifice to God for a sweetsmelling savour.

ἀπολυτρώσεως. 31 πᾶσα πικρία καὶ θυμὸς καὶ ὀργὴ καὶ
of redemption.   All   bitterness, and indignation, and wrath, and

κραυγὴ καὶ βλασφημία ἀρθήτω ἀφ' ὑμῶν, σὺν πάσῃ
clamour,   and   evil speaking let be removed from   you,   with   all

κακίᾳ· 32 γίνεσθε.ⁿδὲ|| εἰς ἀλλήλους χρηστοί, εὔσπλαγχνοι,
malice ;   and be   to one another kind,   tender-hearted,

χαριζόμενοι ἑαυτοῖς, .καθὼς καὶ ὁ θεὸς ἐν χριστῷ ἐχαρί-
forgiving   each other, according as also God in Christ   for-

σατο ᵒὑμῖν.|| 5 Γίνεσθε οὖν μιμηταὶ τοῦ θεοῦ, ὡς τέκνα
gave you.   Be ye   therefore imitators   of God, as children

ἀγαπητά· 2 καὶ περιπατεῖτε ἐν ἀγάπῃ, καθὼς καὶ ὁ χριστὸς
beloved,   and   walk   in   love, even as also the Christ

ἠγάπησεν ᴾἡμᾶς,|| καὶ παρέδωκεν ἑαυτὸν ὑπὲρ �๑ἡμῶν|| προσ-
loved   us,   and   gave up himself for   us,   an of-

φορὰν καὶ θυσίαν τῷ θεῷ εἰς ὀσμὴν εὐωδίας.
fering and a sacrifice to God for an odour of a sweet smell.

3 But fornication, and all uncleanness, or covetousness, let it not be once named among you, as becometh saints ; 4 neither filthiness, nor foolish talking, nor jesting, which are not convenient : but rather giving of thanks. 5 For this ye know, that no whoremonger, nor unclean person, nor covetous man, who is an idolater, hath any inheritance in the kingdom of Christ and of God. 6 Let no man deceive you with vain words : for because of these things cometh the wrath of God upon the children of disobedience. 7 Be not ye therefore partakers with them. 8 For ye were sometimes darkness, but now are ye light in the Lord : walk as children of light : 9 (for the fruit of the Spirit is in all goodness and righteousness and truth;) 10 proving what is acceptable unto the Lord. 11 And have no fellowship with the unfruitful works of darkness, but rather reprove them : 12 For it is a shame even to speak of those things which are done of them in secret. 13 But all things that are reproved are made manifest by the light : for whatsoever doth make manifest is light. 14 Wherefore he saith, Awake thou that sleepest, and arise from the dead, and Christ shall

3 Πορνεία.δὲ καὶ ʳπᾶσα ἀκαθαρσία|| ἢ πλεονεξία μηδὲ
But fornication and all   uncleanness or covetousness not even

ὀνομαζέσθω ἐν ὑμῖν, καθὼς πρέπει ἁγίοις· 4 ˢκαὶ|| αἰσχρό-
let it be named among you, even as is becoming to saints ;   and   filthi-

της ᵗκαὶ|| μωρολογία ἢ εὐτραπελία, ᵛτὰ οὐκ.ἀνήκοντα,|| ἀλλὰ
ness and foolish talking or   jesting,   which are not becoming ; but

μᾶλλον εὐχαριστία. 5 τοῦτο.γὰρ ʷἔστε.γινώσκοντες|| ὅτι πᾶς
rather thanksgiving. For this   ye know   that any
                                                (lit. every)

πόρνος, ἢ ἀκάθαρτος, ἢ πλεονέκτης, ˣὅς|| ἐστιν εἰδωλολά-
fornicator, or unclean person, or ·covetous,   who is   an idola-

τρης, οὐκ.ἔχει κληρονομίαν ἐν τῇ βασιλείᾳ τοῦ χριστοῦ καὶ
ter, has not   inheritance in the kingdom of the Christ and

θεοῦ. 6 μηδεὶς ὑμᾶς ἀπατάτω κενοῖς λόγοις·   διὰ
of God. ᵃNo ³one ⁵you ¹let ⁴deceive with empty words ; ²on ³account ⁴of

ταῦτα γὰρ ἔρχεται ἡ ὀργὴ τοῦ θεοῦ ἐπὶ τοὺς υἱοὺς τῆς
ᵇthese ⁶things ⁷for comes the wrath ᵇf God upon the sons

ἀπειθείας. 7 μὴ οὖν γίνεσθε ʸσυμμέτοχοι|| αὐτῶν. 8 ἦτε
of disobedience. ²Not ³therefore ¹be joint-partakers with them ; ²ye ³were

γὰρ ποτε σκότος, νῦν.δὲ φῶς ἐν κυρίῳ· ὡς τέκνα φωτὸς
ⁱfor once darkness, but now light in [the] Lord ; as children of light

περιπατεῖτε· 9 ὁ.γὰρ καρπὸς τοῦ ᶻπνεύματος|| ἐν πάσῃ
walk,   (for the fruit of the Spirit   [is] in all

ἀγαθωσύνῃ καὶ δικαιοσύνῃ καὶ ἀληθείᾳ· 10 δοκιμάζοντες τί
goodness and righteousness and truth,)   proving   what

ἐστιν εὐάρεστον τῷ κυρίῳ. 11 καὶ μὴ;ᵃσυγκοινωνεῖτε|| τοῖς
is   well-pleasing to the Lord;   and   have no fellowship with the

ἔργοις τοῖς ἀκάρποις τοῦ σκότους, μᾶλλον.δὲ καὶ ἐλέγχετε·
ᵃworks ¹unfruitful of darkness, · but rather also reprove ;

12 τὰ.γὰρ ᵇκρυφῆ||·γινόμενα ὑπ' αὐτῶν αἰσχρόν ἐστιν καὶ
for the things in secret being done by them shameful ᶦt is even

λέγειν. 13 τὰ.δὲ.πάντα ἐλεγχόμενα ὑπὸ τοῦ φωτὸς φανεροῦ-
to say.   But all of them being reproved by the light are made mani-

ται· πᾶν.γὰρ τὸ φανερούμενον φῶς ἐστιν 14 διὸ
fest ; for ⁴everything ¹that ²which ³makes ⁵manifest ⁷light ⁶is.   Wherefore

λέγει, cᵛἜγειραι|| ὁ καθεύδων, καὶ ἀνάστα ἐκ τῶν
he says, Arouse, [thou] that sleepest, and rise up from among the

ⁿ — δὲ and L.   ᵒἡμῖν us L.   ᴾὑμᾶς you ᴛᴛⱃA.   ๑ὑμῶν you A.   ʳἀκαθαρσία
πᾶσα ʟᴛᴛⱃA.   ˢἢ or L.   ᵗἢ or ʟᴛ.   ᵛἃ οὐκ ἀνῆκεν ʟᴛᴛⱃA.   ʷἴστε γινώσκοντες
ye are aware of, knowing ɢʟᴛᴛⱃAW.   ˣὅ that ʟᴛᴛⱃA.   ʸσυν- TA.   ᶻφωτὸς light
ɢʟᴛᴛⱃAW.   ᵃσυν- T.   ᵇκρυφῇ L.   cᵛἜγειρε ɢʟᴛᴛⱃAW.

νεκρῶν, καὶ ἐπιφαύσει σοι ὁ χριστός. 15 Βλέπετε οὖν
dead, and shall shine upon thee the Christ. Take heed therefore

ᵈπῶς ἀκριβῶς‖ περιπατεῖτε, μὴ ὡς ἄσοφοι, ἀλλ᾽ ὡς σοφοί,
how accurately ye walk, not as unwise, but as wise,

16 ἐξαγοραζόμενοι τὸν καιρόν, ὅτι αἱ ἡμέραι πονηραί εἰσιν.
ransoming the time, because the days ᵉevil ¹are.

17 διὰ.τοῦτο μὴ.γίνεσθε ἄφρονες, ἀλλὰ ᵉσυνιέντες‖ τί τὸ
On this account be not foolish, but understanding what the

θέλημα τοῦ κυρίου. 18 καὶ μὴ.μεθύσκεσθε οἴνῳ, ἐν ᾧ
will of the Lord [is]. And be not drunk with wine, in which

ἐστιν ἀσωτία· ἀλλὰ πληροῦσθε ἐν πνεύματι, 19 λα-
is dissoluteness; but be filled with [the] Spirit, speak-

λοῦντες ἑαυτοῖς ᶠ ψαλμοῖς καὶ ὕμνοις καὶ ᵍᾠδαῖς ᵍπνευματι-
ing to each other in psalms and hymns and ²songs ¹spiritual,

καῖς,‖ ᾄδοντες καὶ ψάλλοντες ʰἐν‖ ⁱτῇ καρδίᾳ‖ ὑμῶν τῷ κυρίῳ,
singing and praising with ²heart ¹your to the Lord;

20 εὐχαριστοῦντες πάντοτε ὑπὲρ πάντων ἐν ὀνόματι τοῦ
giving thanks at all times for all things in [the] name

κυρίου.ἡμῶν Ἰησοῦ χριστοῦ τῷ θεῷ καὶ πατρί· 21 ὑπο-
of our Lord Jesus Christ to him who [is] God and Father, submit-

τασσόμενοι ἀλλήλοις ἐν φόβῳ ᵏθεοῦ.‖
ting yourselves to one another in [the] fear of God.

22 Αἱ γυναῖκες, τοῖς.ἰδίοις ἀνδράσιν ˡὑποτάσσεσθε,‖ ὡς τῷ
Wives, to your own husbands submit yourselves, as to the

κυρίῳ· 23 ὅτι ᵐὁ‖ ἀνήρ ἐστιν κεφαλὴ τῆς γυναικός, ὡς καὶ
Lord, for the husband is head of the wife, as also

ὁ χριστὸς κεφαλὴ τῆς ἐκκλησίας, ⁿκαὶ‖ αὐτός ᵒἐστιν‖ σωτὴρ
the Christ [is] head of the assembly, and he is Saviour

τοῦ σώματος· 24 ᴾἀλλ᾽‖ �q̓ὥσπερ‖ ἡ ἐκκλησία ὑποτάσσεται τῷ
of the body. But even as the assembly is subjected to the

χριστῷ, οὕτως καὶ αἱ γυναῖκες τοῖς.ʳἰδίοις‖ ἀνδράσιν ἐν παντί.
Christ, so also wives to their own husbands in everything.

25 Οἱ ἄνδρες, ἀγαπᾶτε τὰς.γυναῖκας.ˢἑαυτῶν,‖ καθὼς καὶ ὁ
Husbands, love your own wives, even as also the

χριστὸς ἠγάπησεν τὴν ἐκκλησίαν, καὶ ἑαυτὸν παρέδωκεν ὑπὲρ
Christ loved the assembly, and himself gave up for

αὐτῆς· 26 ἵνα αὐτὴν ἁγιάσῃ, καθαρίσας τῷ λουτρῷ
it, that it he might sanctify, having cleansed [it] by the washing

τοῦ ὕδατος ἐν ῥήματι, 27 ἵνα παραστήσῃ ᵗαὐτὴν‖ ἑαυτῷ
of water by [the] word, that he might present it to himself

ἔνδοξον τὴν ἐκκλησίαν μὴ ἔχουσαν σπίλον ἢ ῥυτίδα ἤ τι
²glorious ¹the ²assembly, not having spot, or wrinkle, or any

τῶν.τοιούτων, ἀλλ᾽ ἵνα ᾖ ἁγία καὶ ἄμωμος. 28 οὕτως
of such things; but that it might be holy and blameless. So

ᵛὀφείλουσιν ʷ οἱ ἄνδρες‖ ἀγαπᾶν τὰς.ἑαυτῶν.γυναῖκας ὡς
ought husbands to love their own wives as

τὰ.ἑαυτῶν σώματα· ὁ ἀγαπῶν τὴν ἑαυτοῦ γυναῖκα ἑαυτὸν
their own bodies: he that loves his own wife ²himself

ἀγαπᾷ· 29 οὐδεὶς.γάρ ποτε τὴν.ἑαυτοῦ σάρκα ἐμίσησεν,
¹loves. For no one at any time his own flesh hated,

---

give thee light. 15 See then that ye walk circumspectly, not as fools, but as wise, 16 redeeming the time, because the days are evil. 17 Wherefore be ye not unwise, but understanding what the will of the Lord is. 18 And be not drunk with wine, wherein is excess; but be filled with the Spirit; 19 speaking to yourselves in psalms and hymns and spiritual songs, singing and making melody in your heart to the Lord; 20 giving thanks always for all things unto God and the Father in the name of our Lord Jesus Christ; 21 submitting yourselves one to another in the fear of God.

22 Wives, submit yourselves unto your own husbands, as unto the Lord. 23 For the husband is the head of the wife, even as Christ is the head of the church: and he is the saviour of the body. 24 Therefore as the church is subject unto Christ, so let the wives be to their own husbands in every thing. 25 Husbands, love your wives, even as Christ also loved the church, and gave himself for it; 26 that he might sanctify and cleanse it with the washing of water by the word, 27 that he might present it to himself a glorious church, not having spot, or wrinkle, or any such thing; but that it should be holy and without blemish. 28 So ought men to love their wives as their own bodies. He that loveth his wife loveth himself. 29 For no man ever yet hated his own flesh; but

---

ᵈ ἀκριβῶς πῶς T. ᵉ συνίετε understand LTTʳA. ᶠ + [ἐν] LA. ᵍ [πνευματικαῖς] LA.
ʰ — ἐν (read with your heart) T[TʳA]. ⁱ ταῖς καρδίαις hearts L. ᵏ χριστοῦ of Christ
GLTTʳAW. ˡ — ὑποτάσσεσθε TA; ὑποτασσέσθωσαν (read to their own husbands let them
submit themselves) LTʳ. ᵐ — ὁ (read a husband) GLTTʳAW. ⁿ — καὶ GLTTʳAW.
ᵒ — ἐστιν LTTʳAW. ᴾ ἀλλὰ LTTʳA. q̓ ὡς as LTTʳA. ʳ — ἰδίοις.(read to the husbands)
LTTʳA. ˢ — ἑαυτῶν (read the wives) LTTʳA. ᵗ αὐτὸς (read he might himself present)
GLTTʳAW. ᵛ καὶ (also) οἱ ἄνδρες ὀφείλουσιν LW. ʷ + καὶ also TʳA.

nourisheth and cherisheth it, even as the Lord the church: 30 for we are members of his body, of his flesh, and of his bones. 31 For this cause shall a man leave his father and mother, and shall be joined unto his wife, and they two shall be one flesh. 32 This is a great mystery : but I speak concerning Christ and the church. 33 Nevertheless let every one of you in particular so love his wife even as himself ; and the wife *see* that she reverence *her* husband.

ˣἀλλ'‖ ἐκτρέφει καὶ θάλπει αὐτήν, καθὼς καὶ ὁ ˣκύριος‖ τὴν
but　　nourishes and cherishes　it,　even as　also the　Lord　the
ἐκκλησίαν. 30 ὅτι μέλη ἐσμὲν τοῦ.σώματος.αὐτοῦ, ᶻἐκ τῆς
assembly :　　for members we are　　of his body,　　　of
σαρκὸς.αὐτοῦ, καὶ ἐκ τῶν.ὀστέων.αὐτοῦ.‖ 31 Ἀντὶ τούτου
his flesh,　　and of　　his bones.　　Because of this
καταλείψει ἄνθρωπος ᵃτὸν‖ πατέρα ᵇαὐτοῦ‖ καὶ ᶜτὴν‖ μητέρα,
³shall ⁴leave ¹a ²man　　ᵉfather ⁵his　　and　　mother,
καὶ προσκολληθήσεται ᵈπρὸς τὴν γυναῖκα‖ ᵉαὐτοῦ,‖·καὶ ἔσον-
and　　shall be joined　　to　　　²wife　　¹his,　　and ³shall
ται οἱ δύο εἰς σάρκα μίαν. 32 Τὸ.μυστήριον.τοῦτο μέγα ἐστίν·
⁴be ¹the ²two for ²flesh　¹one.　　This mystery　　²great ¹is,
ἐγὼ.δὲ λέγω εἰς χριστὸν καὶ ᶠεἰς‖ τὴν ἐκκλησίαν. 33 πλὴν
but I　speak as to Christ　and as to　the　assembly.　However
καὶ ὑμεῖς οἱ.καθ'.ἕνα, ἕκαστος τὴν.ἑαυτοῦ γυναῖκα οὕτως ἀγα-
also ye everyone,　²each ⁴his ⁵own　ᵉwife　⁷so　　⁰let
πάτω ὡς ἑαυτόν· ἡ.δὲ γυνὴ ἵνα φοβῆται τὸν ἄνδρα.
³love as himself ; and the wife　that she may fear the husband.

VI. Children, obey your parents in the Lord : for this is right. 2 Honour thy father and mother ; which is the first commandment with promise ; 3 that it may be well with thee, and thou mayest live long on the earth. 4 And, ye fathers, provoke not your children to wrath : but bring them up in the nurture and admonition of the Lord,

6 Τὰ τέκνα, ὑπακούετε τοῖς.γονεῦσιν.ὑμῶν ᵍἐν κυρίῳ·‖
Children,　obey　　　your parents　in [the] Lord,
τοῦτο.γάρ ἐστιν δίκαιον. 2 Τίμα τὸν.πατέρα.σου καὶ τὴν
for this　is　just.　　Honour　thy father　　and
μητέρα· ἥτις ἐστὶν ἐντολὴ πρώτη ἐν ἐπαγγελίᾳ· 3 ἵνα
mother, which　is　³commandment ¹the ²first with a promise,　that
εὖ σοι γένηται, καὶ ἔσῃ μακροχρόνιος ἐπὶ τῆς γῆς.
well with thee it may be, and thou mayest be　long-lived　on the earth.
4 Καὶ οἱ πατέρες, μὴ.παροργίζετε τὰ.τέκνα.ὑμῶν, ˣἀλλ'‖ ἐκ-
And　　fathers,　do not provoke　your children,　but bring
τρέφετε αὐτὰ ἐν παιδείᾳ καὶ νουθεσίᾳ κυρίου.
up　them in [the] discipline and admonition of [the] Lord.

5 Servants, be obedient to them that are *your* masters according to the flesh, with fear and trembling, in singleness of your heart, as unto Christ ; 6 not with eyeservice, as menpleasers ; but as the servants of Christ, doing the will of God from the heart ; 7 with good will doing service, as to the Lord, and not to men : 8 knowing that whatsoever good thing any man doeth, the same shall he receive of the Lord, whether *he be* bond or free. 9 And, ye masters, do the same things unto them, forbearing threatening : knowing that your Master also is in heaven ; neither is there respect of persons with him.

5 Οἱ δοῦλοι, ὑπακούετε τοῖς ʰκυρίοις κατὰ σάρκα‖
Bondmen,　obey　[your]　masters according to flesh
μετὰ φόβου καὶ τρόμου, ἐν ἁπλότητι ⁱτῆς.καρδίας.ὑμῶν, ὡς
with　fear　and trembling, in simplicity　of your heart,　as
τῷ χριστῷ· 6 μὴ κατ' ᵏὀφθαλμοδουλείαν‖ ὡς ἀνθρωπάρεσκοι,
to the Christ ;　not with　eye-service　as　men-pleasers ;
ἀλλ' ὡς δοῦλοι ˡτοῦ‖ χριστοῦ, ποιοῦντες τὸ θέλημα τοῦ θεοῦ
but as bondmen of the Christ,　doing the .will　of God
ἐκ ψυχῆς, 7 μετ' εὐνοίας δουλεύοντες ᵐ τῷ κυρίῳ καὶ
from [the] soul,　with good will　doing service　to the Lord and
οὐκ ἀνθρώποις· 8 εἰδότες ὅτι ⁿὃ.ἐάν.τι ἕκαστος ποιήσῃ
not　to men ;　knowing that whatsoever　²each　³may ⁴have ⁵done
ἀγαθόν, τοῦτο ᵒκομιεῖται‖ παρὰ ᵖτοῦ‖ κυρίου, εἴτε δοῦλος
¹good,　this he shall receive from　the　Lord,　whether bondman
εἴτε ἐλεύθερος. 9 Καὶ οἱ κύριοι, τὰ.αὐτὰ ποιεῖτε πρὸς
or　free.　And　masters, the same things　do　towards
αὐτούς, ἀνιέντες τὴν ἀπειλήν· εἰδότες ὅτι καὶ ᑫὑμῶν.αὐτῶν
them,　giving up　threatening, knowing that also　your own
ὁ‖ κύριός ἐστιν ἐν οὐρανοῖς, καὶ ʳπροσωποληψία‖ οὐκ.ἔστιν
master　is　in [the] heavens,　and　respect of persons　there is.not
παρ' αὐτῷ.
with　him.

ˣ ἀλλὰ LTTrAW.　ʸ χριστὸς Christ GLTTrAW.　ᶻ — ἐκ τῆς to end of verse LTTr[A].　ᵃ — τὸν
LTTrA.　ᵇ — αὐτοῦ LTTrA.　ᶜ — τὴν LT·A.　ᵈ τῇ γυναικὶ to the wife LTTr.　ᵉ — αὐτοῦ T.
ᶠ [εἰς] LA.　ᵍ — ἐν κυρίῳ L[TrA].　ʰ κατὰ σάρκα κυρίοις LTTr.　ⁱ — τῆς T.　ᵏ ὀφθαλμο-
δουλίαν T.　ˡ — τοῦ the LTTrAW.　ᵐ + ὡς as GLTTrAW.　ⁿ ἕκαστος ὃ — ὃ (*read* if anything) TA) ἐάν (ἂν Tr) τι (— τι LTr) LTTrAW.　ᵒ κομίσεται LTTrA.　ᵖ — τοῦ (*read* [the])
GLTTrAW.　ᑫ αὐτῶν κὰι ὑμῶν ὁ of them and of you the LTTrAW.　ʳ προσωπολημψία LTTrA.

10 ᵗΤὸ.λοιπόν,‖ ᵛἀδελφοί.μου,‖ ἐνδυναμοῦσθε ἐν κυρίῳ,
For the rest,   my brethren,   be empowered   in [the] Lord,

καὶ ἐν τῷ κράτει τῆς.ἰσχύος.αὐτοῦ. 11 ἐνδύσασθε τὴν παν-
and in the might   of his strength.   Put on   the pan-

οπλίαν τοῦ θεοῦ, πρὸς τὸ δύνασθαι ὑμᾶς στῆναι πρὸς τὰς
oply   of God, for ²to ³be ⁴able ¹you · to stand against the

ʷμεθοδείας‖ τοῦ διαβόλου· 12 ὅτι οὐκ.ἔστιν ˣἡμῖν‖ ἡ πάλη
artifices of the devil : because ³is ⁴not ⁵to ⁶us ¹the ²wrestling

πρὸς αἷμα καὶ σάρκα, ἀλλὰ πρὸς τὰς ἀρχάς, πρὸς τὰς
against blood and flesh, but against principalities, against

ἐξουσίας, πρὸς τοὺς κοσμοκράτορας τοῦ σκότους ʸτοῦ αἰῶνος‖
authorities, against the world-rulers of the darkness   of ᵃage

ᶻτούτου,‖ πρὸς τὰ πνευματικὰ τῆς πονηρίας ἐν τοῖς ἐπου-
¹this, against the spiritual [powers] of wickedness in the hea-

ρανίοις. 13 διὰ τοῦτο ἀναλάβετε τὴν πανοπλίαν τοῦ θεοῦ,
venlies. Because of this take up the panoply of God,

ἵνα δυνηθῆτε ἀντιστῆναι ἐν τῇ ἡμέρᾳ τῇ πονηρᾷ. καὶ ἅπαντα
that ye may be able to withstand in the ²day ¹evil, and all things

κατεργασάμενοι στῆναι. 14 στῆτε οὖν περιζωσάμενοι τὴν
having worked out to stand. Stand-therefore, having girt about

ὀσφὺν.ὑμῶν ἐν ἀληθείᾳ, καὶ ἐνδυσάμενοι τὸν θώρακα τῆς
your loins with truth, and having put on the breastplate

δικαιοσύνης, 15 καὶ ὑποδησάμενοι τοὺς πόδας ἐν ἑτοι-
of righteousness, and having shod the feet with [the] pre-

μασίᾳ τοῦ εὐαγγελίου τῆς εἰρήνης· 16 ᵃἐπὶ‖ πᾶσιν ἀναλα-
paration of the glad tidings of peace :   besides   all   having

βόντες τὸν θυρεὸν τῆς πίστεως, ἐν ᾧ δυνήσεσθε πάντα
taken up the shield of faith, · with which ye will be able all

τὰ βέλη τοῦ πονηροῦ ᵇτὰ‖ πεπυρωμένα σβέσαι· 17 καὶ
the ²darts ³of ⁴the ⁵wicked ⁶one ¹burning to quench. Also

τὴν περικεφαλαίαν τοῦ σωτηρίου δέξασθε, καὶ τὴν μάχαιραν
the helmet of salvation receive, and the sword

τοῦ πνεύματος, ὅ ἐστιν ῥῆμα θεοῦ· 18 διὰ πάσης προσευχῆς
of the Spirit, which is ²word ¹God's; by all prayer

καὶ δεήσεως προσευχόμενοι ἐν παντὶ καιρῷ ἐν πνεύματι,
and supplication praying in every season in [the] Spirit,

καὶ εἰς αὐτὸ ᶜτοῦτο‖ ἀγρυπνοῦντες ἐν πάσῃ προσκαρτερήσει
and unto this very thing watching with all perseverance

καὶ δεήσει περὶ πάντων τῶν ἁγίων, 19 καὶ ὑπὲρ ἐμοῦ ἵνα
and supplication for all saints; and for me that

μοι ᵈδοθείη‖ λόγος ἐν ἀνοίξει τοῦ.στόματός.μου ἐν
to me may be given utterance in [the] opening of my mouth · with

παρρησίᾳ, γνωρίσαι τὸ μυστήριον ᵉτοῦ εὐαγγελίου,‖ 20 ὑπὲρ
boldness to make known the mystery of the glad tidings, for

οὗ πρεσβεύω ἐν ἁλύσει, ἵνα ἐν αὐτῷ παρρησιάσωμαι
which I am an ambassador in a chain, that in it I may be bold

ὡς δεῖ με λαλῆσαι.
as it behoves me to speak.

21 Ἵνα.δὲ ᶠεἰδῆτε καὶ ὑμεῖς‖ τὰ, κατ᾽ ἐμέ, τί
But that,³may ⁴know ²also ¹ye the things concerning me, what

πράσσω, πάντα ᵍὑμῖν γνωρίσει‖ Τυχικὸς ὁ ἀγαπητὸς
I am doing, all things to you will make known Tychicus the beloved

ᵗ τοῦ λοιποῦ LTTrA.   ᵛ — ἀδελφοί μου LTTrA.   ʷ μεθοδίας Τ.   ˣ ὑμῖν to you L.
ʸ — τοῦ αἰῶνος (read of this darkness) GLTTrAW.   ᶻ — τούτου (read of darkness) w.   ᵃ ἐν
in LTTr.   ᵇ — τὰ L[TrA].   ᶜ — τοῦτο very thing LTTrA.   ᵈ δοθῇ GLTTrAW.   ᵉ [τοῦ εὐαγ
γελίου] L.   ᶠ καὶ ὑμεῖς εἰδῆτε LTTr.   ᵍ γνωρίσει ὑμῖν LTTr.

10 Finally, my bre-
thren, be strong in
the Lord, and in the
power of his might.
11 Put on the whole
armour of God, that
ye may be able to
stand against the
wiles of the devil.
12 For we wrestle
not against flesh and
blood, but against
principalities, against
powers, against the
rulers of the dark-
ness of this world, a-
gainst spiritual wick-
edness in high *places*.
13 Wherefore take un-
to you the whole ar-
mour of God, that ye
may be able to with-
stand in the evil day,
and having done all,
to stand. 14. Stand
therefore, having your
loins girt about with
truth, and having on
the breastplate of
righteousness; 15 and
your feet shod with
the preparation of the
gospel of peace; 16 a-
bove all, taking the
shield of faith, where-
with ye shall be able
to quench all the fiery
darts of the wicked.
17 And take the helmet
of salvation, and the
sword of the Spirit,
which is the word of
God: 18 praying al-
ways with all prayer
and supplication in
the Spirit, and watch-
ing thereunto with
all perseverance and
supplication for all
saints; 19 and for me,
that utterance may
be given unto me,
that I may open my
mouth boldly, to make
known the mystery of
the gospel, 20 for
which I am an ambas-
sador in bonds : that
therein I may speak
boldly, as I ought to
speak.

21 But that ye also
may know my affairs,
and how I do, Tychi-
cus, a beloved brother

and faithful minister in the Lord, shall make known to you all things : 22 whom I have sent unto you for the same purpose, that ye might know our affairs, and *that* le might comfort your hearts.

ἀδελφὸς καὶ πιστὸς διάκονος ἐν κυρίῳ· 22 ὃν ἔπεμψα
brother and faithful servant in [the] Lord ; whom I sent
πρὸς ὑμᾶς εἰς αὐτὸ.τοῦτο, ἵνα γνῶτε τὰ περὶ
to you for this very thing, that ye might know the things concerning
ἡμῶν καὶ παρακαλέσῃ τὰς.καρδίας.ὑμῶν.
us and he might encourage your hearts.

23 Peace be to the brethren, and love with faith, from God the Father and the Lord Jesus Christ. 24 Grace be with all them that love our Lord Jesus Christ in sincerity. Amen.

23 Εἰρήνη τοῖς ἀδελφοῖς καὶ ἀγάπη μετὰ πίστεως ἀπὸ
Peace to the brethren, and love with faith from
θεοῦ πατρὸς καὶ κυρίου Ἰησοῦ χριστοῦ. 24 Ἡ.χάρις μετὰ
God [the] Father and Lord Jesus Christ. Grace with
πάντων τῶν ἀγαπώντων τὸν.κύριον.ἡμῶν Ἰησοῦν χριστὸν
all those that love our Lord Jesus Christ
ἐν ἀφθαρσίᾳ.. ʰἀμήν.ⁱⁱ
in incorruption. Amen.

ⁱΠρὸς Ἐφεσίους ἐγράφη ἀπὸ Ῥώμης, διὰ Τυχικοῦ.ⁱⁱ
To [the] Ephesians written from Rome, by Tychicus.

ᵏἩ ΠΡΟΣ ΤΟΥΣ ΦΙΛΙΠΠΗΣΙΟΥΣ ΕΠΙΣΤΟΛΗ.ⁱⁱ
THE ²TO ³THE ⁴PHILIPPIANS ¹EPISTLE.

PAUL and Timotheus, the servants of Jesus Christ, to all the saints in Christ Jesus which are at Philippi, with the bishops and deacons : 2 Grace be unto you, and peace, from God our Father, and *from* the Lord Jesus Christ.

ΠΑΥΛΟΣ καὶ Τιμόθεος δοῦλοι ˡἸησοῦ χριστοῦ,ⁱⁱ πᾶσιν τοῖς
Paul and Timotheus, bondmen of Jesus Christ, to all the
ἁγίοις ἐν χριστῷ Ἰησοῦ τοῖς οὖσιν ἐν Φιλίπποις, σὺν
saints in Christ Jesus who are in Philippi, with [the]
ἐπισκόποις καὶ διακόνοις· 2 χάρις ὑμῖν καὶ· εἰρήνη ἀπὸ θεοῦ
overseers and those who serve. Grace to you and peace from God
πατρὸς.ἡμῶν καὶ κυρίου ᵐἸησοῦ χριστοῦ.ⁱⁱ
our Father and [the] Lord Jesus Christ.

3 I thank my God upon every remembrance of you, 4 always in every prayer of mine for you all making request with joy, 5 for your fellowship in the gospel from the first day until now ; 6 being confident of this very thing, that he which hath begun a good work in you· will perform *it* until the day of Jesus Christ : 7 even as it is meet for me to think this of you all, because I have you in my heart ; inasmuch as both in my bonds, and in the defence and confirmation of the gospel, ye all are partakers of my grace, 8 For God is my re-

3 Εὐχαριστῶ τῷ.θεῷ.μου ἐπὶ πάσῃ.τῇ μνείᾳ ὑμῶν,
I thank my God on the whole remembrance of you,
4 πάντοτε ἐν πάσῃ δεήσει μου ὑπὲρ πάντων ὑμῶν μετὰ
always in ²every ³supplication ¹my for ²all ¹you with
χαρᾶς τὴν δέησιν ποιούμενος, 5 ἐπὶ τῇ.κοινωνίᾳ.ὑμῶν εἰς
joy ²supplication ¹making, for your fellowship in
τὸ εὐαγγέλιον, ἀπὸ ⁿ πρώτης ἡμέρας ἄχρι τοῦ νῦν· 6 πε-
the glad tidings, from [the] first day until now ; being
ποιθὼς αὐτὸ.τοῦτο, ὅτι ὁ ἐναρξάμενος ἐν ὑμῖν ἔργον
persuaded of this very thing, that he who began in you a ²work
ἀγαθὸν ἐπιτελέσει ᵒἄχριⁱⁱ ἡμέρας ˡἸησοῦ χριστοῦ·ⁱⁱ
¹good will complete [it] until [the] day of Jesus Christ :
7 καθὼς ἐστιν δίκαιον ἐμοὶ τοῦτο φρονεῖν ὑπὲρ πάντων ὑμῶν,
as it is righteous for me this to think as to ²all ¹you,
διὰ τὸ ἔχειν με ἐν τῇ καρδίᾳ ὑμᾶς, ἔν.τε τοῖς.δεσμοῖς.μου
because ²have ³me ⁴in ⁵the ⁶heart ¹ye, both in my bonds
καὶ ᵖ τῇ ἀπολογίᾳ καὶ βεβαιώσει τοῦ εὐαγγελίου, qσυγ-
and in the defence and confirmation of the glad tidings, fellow-
κοινωνούςⁱⁱ μου.τῆς.χάριτος πάντας ὑμᾶς ὄντας. 8 μάρτυς.γάρ
partakers of my grace all ye are. For ²witness

ʰ — ἀμήν GLTTrA.   ⁱ — *the subscription* GLTW ; Πρὸς Ἐφεσίους TrA.
ᵏ + Παύλου τοῦ Ἀποστόλου of Paul the Apostle E ; + Παύλου G ; — τοὺς FG · Πρὸς
Φιλιππησίους LTTrA.   ˡ χριστοῦ Ἰησοῦ LTTrAW.   ᵐ χριστοῦ Ἰησοῦ W.   - + τῆς
the LTTrA.   ᵒ ἄχρι LTA.   ᵖ + ἐν in (*read* τῇ the) [L]TTrAW.   q συν- T.

μου ʳἐστὶν‖ ὁ θεός, ὡς ἐπιποθῶ πάντας ὑμᾶς ἐν · σπλάγ-
'my   ²is   ¹God, how I long after ²all ¹you in [the] bowels

χνοις ˢἸησοῦ χριστοῦ.‖ 9 καὶ τοῦτο προσεύχομαι, ἵνα ἡ ἀγάπη
of Jesus Christ.   And this   I pray, that ²love

ὑμῶν ἔτι μᾶλλον καὶ μᾶλλον ᵗπερισσεύῃ‖ ἐν ἐπιγνώσει καὶ
¹your yet more and more may abound in knowledge and

πάσῃ αἰσθήσει, 10 εἰς τὸ δοκιμάζειν ὑμᾶς τὰ δια-
all intelligence, for ²to ³approve ¹you the things that are

φέροντα, ἵνα ἦτε εἰλικρινεῖς καὶ ἀπρόσκοποι εἰς ἡμέραν
excellent, that ye may be pure and without offence for [the] day

χριστοῦ, 11 πεπληρωμένοι ᵛκαρπῶν‖ δικαιοσύνης ʷτῶν‖
of Christ,   being filled with fruits of righteousness which [are]

διὰ Ἰησοῦ χριστοῦ, εἰς δόξαν καὶ ἔπαινον θεοῦ.
by Jesus Christ, to ²glory ³and ⁴praise ¹God's.

12 Γινώσκειν δὲ ὑμᾶς βούλομαι, ἀδελφοί, ὅτι τὰ κατ'
But ⁴to ⁵know ³you ¹I ²wish, brethren, that the things concerning

ἐμὲ μᾶλλον εἰς προκοπὴν τοῦ εὐαγγελίου ἐλήλυθεν·
me rather to [the] advancement of the glad tidings have turned out,

13 ὥστε τοὺς δεσμούς μου φανεροὺς ἐν χριστῷ γενέσθαι
so as my bonds ¹manifest ²in ⁴Christ ¹to ³have ⁵become

ἐν ὅλῳ τῷ πραιτωρίῳ καὶ τοῖς λοιποῖς πᾶσιν· 14 καὶ τοὺς
in ²whole ¹the praetorium and to ⁴the ³rest ¹all; and the

πλείονας τῶν ἀδελφῶν ἐν κυρίῳ πεποιθότας τοῖς δεσμοῖς
most of the brethren ²in [³the] ⁴Lord ¹trusting by ²bonds

μου περισσοτέρως τολμᾶν ἀφόβως τὸν λόγον ˣλαλεῖν. 15 Τινὲς
¹my ⁴more ⁵abundantly ³dare ¹⁰fearlessly ⁸the ⁹word ⁶to ⁷speak. Some

μὲν καὶ διὰ φθόνον καὶ ἔριν, τινὲς δὲ καὶ δι' εὐδοκίαν τὸν
indeed even from envy and strife, but some also from good-will the

χριστὸν κηρύσσουσιν. 16 οἱ μὲν ʸἐξ ἐριθείας ᶻτὸν‖ χριστὸν
Christ are proclaiming. Those indeed out of contention the Christ

καταγγέλλουσιν οὐχ ἁγνῶς, οἰόμενοι θλίψιν ᵃἐπιφέρειν‖
are announcing, not purely, supposing tribulation to add

τοῖς δεσμοῖς μου· 17 οἱ δὲ ʸἐξ ἀγάπης, εἰδότες ὅτι εἰς ἀπο-
to my bonds, but these out of love, knowing that for de-

λογίαν τοῦ εὐαγγελίου κεῖμαι.‖ 18 τί γάρ; πλὴν ᵇ παντὶ
fence of the glad tidings I am set. What then? nevertheless in every

τρόπῳ, εἴτε προφάσει εἴτε ἀληθείᾳ, χριστὸς καταγγέλλεται·
way, whether in pretext or in truth, Christ is announced;

καὶ ἐν τούτῳ χαίρω, ἀλλὰ καὶ χαρήσομαι. 19 οἶδα γὰρ ὅτι
and in this I rejoice, yea, also I will rejoice: for I know that

τοῦτό μοι ἀποβήσεται εἰς σωτηρίαν διὰ τῆς ὑμῶν δεήσεως,
this for me shall turn out to salvation through your supplication,

καὶ ἐπιχορηγίας τοῦ πνεύματος Ἰησοῦ χριστοῦ, 20 κατὰ
and [the] supply of the Spirit of Jesus Christ: according to

τὴν ἀποκαραδοκίαν καὶ ἐλπίδα μου, ὅτι ἐν οὐδενὶ αἰσχυνθή-
²earnest ³expectation ⁴and ⁵hope ¹my, that in nothing I shall be

σομαι, ἀλλ' ἐν πάσῃ παρρησίᾳ, ὡς πάντοτε, καὶ νῦν μεγα-
ashamed, but in all boldness, as always, also now shall be

λυνθήσεται χριστὸς ἐν τῷ σώματί μου εἴτε διὰ ζωῆς εἴτε διὰ
magnified Christ in my body whether by life or by

θανάτου. 21 Ἐμοὶ γὰρ τὸ ζῇν χριστός, καὶ τὸ ἀποθανεῖν
death. For to me to live [is] Christ, and to die

cord, how greatly I long after you all in the bowels of Jesus Christ. 9 And this I pray, that your love may abound yet more and more in knowledge and in all judgment ; 10 that ye may approve things that are excellent ; that ye may be sincere and without offence till the day of Christ ; 11 being filled with the fruits of righteousness, which are by Jesus Christ, unto the glory and praise of God.

12 But I would ye should understand, brethren, that the things which happened unto me have fallen out rather unto the furtherance of the gospel ; 13 so that my bonds in Christ are manifest in all the palace, and in all other places ; 14 and many of the brethren in the Lord, waxing confident by my bonds, are much more bold to speak the word without fear. 15 Some indeed preach Christ even of envy and strife ; and some also of good will: 16 the one preach Christ of contention, not sincerely, supposing to add affliction to my bonds : 17 but the other of love, knowing that I am set for the defence of the gospel. 18 What then ? notwithstanding, every way, whether in pretence, or in truth, Christ is preached ; and I therein do rejoice, yea, and will rejoice. 19 For I know that this shall turn to my salvation through your prayer, and the supply of the Spirit of Jesus Christ, 20 according to my earnest expectation and my hope, that in nothing I shall be ashamed, but that with all boldness, as always, so now also Christ shall be magnified in my body, whether it be by life, or by death. 21 For to me to live is Christ, and to die is

ʳ — ἐστὶν (read [is]) [L]TTrA.   ˢ χριστοῦ Ἰησοῦ GLTTrAW.   ᵗ περισσεύσῃ L.   ᵛ καρπὸν (with) fruit GLTTrAW.   ʷ τὸν (read which [is]) G[L]TTrAW.   ˣ + τοῦ θεοῦ of God LTTrA.
ʸ verses 16 and 17 transposed, except οἱ μὲν and οἱ δὲ GLTTrAW.   ᶻ [τὸν] LTrA.   ᵃ ἐγείρειν
to arouse LTTrAW.   ᵇ + ὅτι that (read πλὴν except) LTTrA.

gain. 22 But if I live in the flesh, this *is* the fruit of my labour: yet what I shall choose I wot not. 23 For I am in a strait betwixt two, having a desire to depart, and to be with Christ; which is far better: 24 nevertheless to abide in the flesh *is* more needful for you. 25 And having this confidence, I know that I shall abide and continue with you all for your furtherance and joy of faith; 26 that your rejoicing may be more abundant in Jesus Christ for me by my coming to you again. 27 Only let your conversation be as it becometh the gospel of Christ: that whether I come and see you, or else be absent, I may hear of your affairs, that ye stand fast in one spirit, with one mind striving together for the faith of the gospel; 28 and in nothing terrified by your adversaries, which is to them an evident token of perdition, but to you of salvation, and that of God. 29 For unto you it is given in the behalf of Christ, not only to believe on him, but also to suffer for his sake; 30 having the same conflict which ye saw in me, and now hear *to be* in me.

II. If *there* be therefore any consolation in Christ, if any comfort of love, if any fellowship of the Spirit, if any bowels and mercies, 2 fulfil ye my joy, that ye be likeminded, having the same love, *being* of one accord, of one mind. 3 *Let* nothing *be done* through strife or vainglory; but in lowliness of mind let each esteem other better than themselves. 4 Look not every man on his own things, but

κέρδος. 22 εἰ.δὲ τὸ ζῆν ἐν σαρκί, τοῦτό μοι καρπὸς ἔργου·
gain;   but if to live in flesh, this for me [is] fruit of labour:
καὶ τί αἱρήσομαι οὐ.γνωρίζω· 23 συνέχομαι ᶜγὰρ‖ ἐκ τῶν
and what I shall choose I know not. ²I ³am ⁴pressed ¹for by the
δύο, τὴν ἐπιθυμίαν ἔχων εἰς τὸ ἀναλῦσαι, καὶ σὺν χριστῷ
two, ²the ³desire ¹having for to depart, and with Christ
εἶναι, πολλῷ ᵈ μᾶλλον κρεῖσσον· 24 τὸ.δὲ.ἐπιμένειν ᵉἐν‖
to be, [for it is] very much better; but to remain in
τῇ σαρκὶ ἀναγκαιότερον δι᾽ ὑμᾶς· 25 καὶ τοῦτο
the flesh [is] more necessary for the sake of you; and this
πεποιθὼς οἶδα ὅτι μενῶ καὶ ᶠσυμπαραμενῶ‖ πᾶσιν
being persuaded of, I know that I shall abide and continue with ²all
ὑμῖν εἰς τὴν.ὑμῶν.προκοπὴν καὶ χαρὰν τῆς πίστεως, 26 ἵνα
¹you; for your advancement and joy of faith; that
τὸ.καύχημα.ὑμῶν περισσεύῃ ἐν χριστῷ Ἰησοῦ ἐν ἐμοὶ διὰ
your boasting may abound in Christ Jesus in me through
τῆς.ἐμῆς.παρουσίας πάλιν πρὸς ὑμᾶς. 27 Μόνον ἀξίως τοῦ
my presence again with you. Only worthily of the
εὐαγγελίου τοῦ χριστοῦ πολιτεύεσθε, ἵνα εἴτε ἐλθὼν καὶ
glad tidings of the Christ conduct yourselves, that whether having come and
ἰδὼν ὑμᾶς, εἴτε ἀπὼν ᵍἀκούσω‖ τὰ περὶ ὑμῶν,
having seen you, or being absent I might hear the things concerning you,
ὅτι στήκετε ἐν ἑνὶ πνεύματι, μιᾷ ψυχῇ συναθλοῦντες
that ye stand fast in one spirit, with one soul striving together
τῇ πίστει τοῦ εὐαγγελίου, 28 καὶ μὴ πτυρόμενοι ἐν μη-
with the faith of the glad tidings; and being frightened in no-
δενὶ ὑπὸ τῶν ἀντικειμένων· ἥτις ʰαὐτοῖς μέν ἐστιν‖ ἐν-
thing by those who oppose; which to them is a demon-
δειξις ἀπωλείας, ⁱὑμῖν‖ δὲ σωτηρίας, καὶ τοῦτο ἀπὸ θεοῦ·
stration of destruction, ²to ¹you but of salvation, and this from God;
29 ὅτι ὑμῖν ἐχαρίσθη τὸ ὑπὲρ χριστοῦ, οὐ μόνον τὸ
because to you it was granted concerning Christ, not only
εἰς αὐτὸν πιστεύειν, ἀλλὰ καὶ τὸ ὑπὲρ αὐτοῦ πάσχειν·
³on ⁴him ¹to ²believe, but also concerning him to suffer,
30 τὸν αὐτὸν ἀγῶνα ἔχοντες οἷον ᵏἴδετε‖ ἐν ἐμοί, καὶ νῦν
the same conflict having such as ye saw in me, and now
ἀκούετε ἐν ἐμοί.
hear of in me.

2 Εἴ τις οὖν παράκλησις ἐν χριστῷ, εἴ τι παρα-
If ²any ¹then encouragement [there be] in Christ, if any conso-
μύθιον ἀγάπης, εἴ τις κοινωνία πνεύματος, εἴ ˡτινα‖ σπλάγ-
lation of love, if any fellowship of [the] Spirit, if any bowels
χνα καὶ οἰκτιρμοί, 2 πληρώσατέ μου τὴν χαράν, ἵνα
and compassions, fulfil my joy, that
τὸ.αὐτὸ.φρονῆτε, τὴν αὐτὴν ἀγάπην ἔχοντες, ᵐσύμψυχοι,‖
ye may be of the same mind, the same love having, joined in soul,
τὸ ἓν φρονοῦντες· 3 μηδὲν ⁿκατὰ‖ ἐριθείαν ᵒἢ‖ κενο-
the one thing minding— nothing according to contention or vain-
δοξίαν, ἀλλὰ τῇ ταπεινοφροσύνῃ ἀλλήλους ἡγούμενοι ὑπερ-
glory, but in humility one another esteeming a-
έχοντας ἑαυτῶν. 4 μὴ τὰ ἑαυτῶν ᴾἕκαστος‖
bove themselves, ²not ⁴the ⁵things ⁶of ⁷themselves ³each

ᶜ δὲ but GLTTᵣAW.   ᵈ + γὰρ for EGLTTᵣAW.   ᵉ — ἐν (read τῇ in the) τ.   ᶠ παραμενῶ continue (read πᾶσιν with all) LTTᵣA.   ᵍ ἀκούω LTTᵣ.   ʰ ἐστὶν αὐτοῖς GLTTᵣAW.
ⁱ ὑμῶν (read but of your salvation) LTTᵣAW.   ᵏ εἴδετε LTTᵣAW.   ˡ τις GLTTᵣA.   ᵐ σύν τ.
ⁿ κατ᾽ TTᵣAW.   ᵒ μηδὲ κατὰ nor according to LTTᵣA.   ᴾ ἕκαστοι LTTᵣA.

ᵠσκοπεῖτε,‖ ἀλλὰ καὶ τὰ ἑτέρων ʳἕκαστος.‖ 5 Τοῦτο
¹consider, but ²also ³the ⁴things ⁵of ⁶others ¹each. ⁹This

ˢγὰρ φρονείσθω‖ ἐν ὑμῖν ὃ καὶ ἐν χριστῷ Ἰησοῦ, 6 ὃς
⁷for ⁸let mind be in you which also in Christ Jesus [was]; who,

ἐν μορφῇ θεοῦ ὑπάρχων, οὐχ ἁρπαγμὸν ἡγήσατο τὸ εἶναι
in [the] form of God subsisting, ²not ⁴rapine ¹esteemed ²it to be

ᵗἴσα‖ θεῷ, 7 ᵛἀλλ'‖ ἑαυτὸν ἐκένωσεν, μορφὴν δούλου
equal with God; but ³himself ¹emptied, ⁷form ⁵a ⁶bondman's

λαβών, ἐν ὁμοιώματι ἀνθρώπων γενόμενος· 8 καὶ σχή-
³having ⁴taken, in [the] likeness of men having become; and in

ματι εὑρεθεὶς ὡς ἄνθρωπος, ἐταπείνωσεν ἑαυτόν, γενό-
figure having been found as a man, he humbled himself, having

μενος ὑπήκοος μέχρι θανάτου, θανάτου.δὲ σταυροῦ. 9 διὸ
become obedient unto death, even death of [the] cross. Wherefore

καὶ ὁ θεὸς αὐτὸν ὑπερύψωσεν καὶ ἐχαρίσατο αὐτῷ ʷ ὄνομα
also God him highly exalted and granted to him a name

τὸ ὑπὲρ πᾶν ὄνομα· 10 ἵνα ἐν τῷ ὀνόματι Ἰησοῦ πᾶν
which [is] above every name, that at the name of Jesus every

γόνυ κάμψῃ ἐπουρανίων καὶ ἐπιγείων καὶ καταχθονίων·
knee should bow of [beings] in heaven and on earth and under the earth,

11 καὶ πᾶσα γλῶσσα ˣἐξομολογήσηται‖ ὅτι κύριος Ἰησοῦς
and every tongue should confess that [³is] ⁴Lord ¹Jesus

χριστὸς εἰς δόξαν θεοῦ πατρός.
²Christ to [the] glory of God [the] Father.

12 Ὥστε, ἀγαπητοί.μου, καθὼς πάντοτε ὑπηκούσατε, μὴ
So that, my beloved, even as always ye obeyed, not

ὡς ἐν τῇ.παρουσίᾳ.μου μόνον, ἀλλὰ νῦν πολλῷ μᾶλλον ἐν
as in my presence only, but now much rather in

τῇ.ἀπουσίᾳ.μου, μετὰ φόβου καὶ τρόμου·τὴν.ἑαυτῶν σωτηρίαν
my absence, with fear and trembling your own salvation

κατεργάζεσθε· 13 ʸὁ.θεὸς.γάρ ἐστιν ὁ ἐνεργῶν ἐν ὑμῖν καὶ τὸ
work out; for God it is who works in you both

θέλειν καὶ τὸ ἐνεργεῖν ὑπὲρ τῆς εὐδοκίας. 14 πάντα
to will and to work according to [his] good pleasure. ²All ³things

ποιεῖτε χωρὶς γογγυσμῶν καὶ διαλογισμῶν, 15 ἵνα ᶻγένησθε‖
¹do apart from murmurings and reasonings, ⁴that ye may be

ἄμεμπτοι καὶ ἀκέραιοι, τέκνα θεοῦ ᵃἀμώμητα‖ ᵇἐν μέσῳ‖
faultless and simple, children of God unblamable in [the] midst

γενεᾶς σκολιᾶς καὶ διεστραμμένης, ἐν οἷς φαίνεσθε ὡς
of a generation crooked and perverted; among whom ye appear as

φωστῆρες ἐν κόσμῳ, 16 λόγον ζωῆς ἐπέχοντες, εἰς καύχημα
luminaries in [the] world, [the] word of life holding forth, for a boast

ἐμοὶ εἰς ἡμέραν χριστοῦ, ὅτι οὐκ εἰς·κενὸν ἔδραμον οὐδὲ εἰς
to me in ²day ¹Christ's, that not in vain I ran nor in

κενὸν ἐκοπίασα. 17 ᶜἀλλ'‖ εἰ καὶ σπένδομαι ἐπὶ τῇ θυσίᾳ καὶ
vain laboured. But if also I am poured out on the sacrifice and

λειτουργίᾳ τῆς.πίστεως.ὑμῶν, χαίρω καὶ ᵈσυγχαίρω‖ πᾶσιν
ministration of your faith, I rejoice and rejoice with all

ὑμῖν· 18 τὸ.ᵈδ'‖.αὐτὸ καὶ ὑμεῖς χαίρετε καὶ ᵈσυγχαίρετέ‖ μοι.
you. And in the same also ²ye ¹rejoice and rejoice with me.

19 Ἐλπίζω.δὲ ἐν ᶠκυρίῳ‖ Ἰησοῦ Τιμόθεον ταχέως πέμψαι
But I hope in [the] Lord Jesus ³Timotheus ⁴soon ¹to ²send

every man also on the things of others. 5 Let this mind be in you, which was also in Christ Jesus : 6 who, being in the form of God, thought it not robbery to be equal with God : 7 but made himself of no reputation, and took upon him the form of a servant, and was made in the likeness of men: 8 and being found in fashion as a man, he humbled himself, and became obedient unto death, even the death of the cross. 9 Wherefore God also hath highly exalted him, and given him a name which is above every name : 10 that at the name of Jesus every knee should bow, of things in heaven, and things in earth, and things under the earth; 11 and that every tongue should confess that Jesus Christ is Lord, to the glory of God the Father.

12 Wherefore, my beloved, as ye have always obeyed, not as in my presence only, but now much more in my absence, work out your own salvation with fear and trembling. 13 For it is God which worketh in you both to will and to do of his good pleasure. 14 Do all things without murmurings and disputings : 15 that ye may be blameless and harmless, the sons of God, without rebuke, in the midst of a crooked and perverse nation, among whom ye shine as lights in the world ; 16 holding forth the word of life; that I may rejoice in the day of Christ, that I have not run in vain, neither laboured in vain. 17 Yea, and if I be offered upon the sacrifice and service of your faith, I joy, and rejoice with you all. 18 For the same cause also do ye joy, and rejoice with me. 19 But I trust in the Lord Jesus to send Timotheus shortly unto

---

ᵠ σκοποῦντες considering GLTTrAW. ʳ ἕκαστοι GLTTrAW. ˢ φρονεῖτε (omit for) LTTrA.
ᵗ ἴσα LTAW. ᵛ ἀλλὰ LTTrAW. ʷ + τὸ (the (name) LTTr[A]W. ˣ ἐξομολογήσεται
shall confess TAW. ʸ — ὁ LTTrAW. ᶻ ἦτε L. ᵃ ἄμωμα LTTrA. ᵇ μέσον [in the]
midst LTTrAW. ᶜ ἀλλὰ LTTrAW. ᵈ συν- T. ᵉ δὲ TTr. ᶠ χριστῷ Christ L.

you, that I also may be of good comfort, when I know your state. 20 For I have no man likeminded, who will naturally care for your state. 21 For all seek their own, not the things which are Jesus Christ's. 22 But ye know the proof of him, that, as a son with the father, he hath served with me in the gospel. 23 Him therefore I hope to send presently, so soon as I shall see how it will go with me. 24 But I trust in the Lord that I also myself shall come shortly. 25 Yet I supposed it necessary to send to you Epaphroditus, my brother, and companion in labour, and fellowsoldier, but your messenger, and he that ministered to my wants. 26 For he longed after you all, and was full of heaviness, because that ye had heard that he had been sick. 27 For indeed he was sick nigh unto death : but God had mercy on him ; and not on him only, but on me also, lest I should have sorrow upon sorrow. 28 I sent him therefore the more carefully, that, when ye see him again, ye may rejoice, and that I may be the less sorrowful. 29 Receive him therefore in the Lord with all gladness ; and hold such in reputation : 30 because for the work of Christ he was nigh unto death, not regarding his life, to supply your lack of service toward me.

III. Finally, my brethren, rejoice in the Lord. To write the same things to you, to me indeed *is* not grievous, but for you *it is* safe. 2 Beware of dogs, beware of evil workers, beware of the concision. 3 For we are the circumcision, which worship God in the spirit, and rejoice in Christ Jesus, and have no confidence in the flesh. 4 Though I might also have confidence in

ὑμῖν, ἵνα κἀγὼ εὐψυχῶ, γνοὺς τὰ περὶ
to you, that I also may be of good courage, having known the things concerning
ὑμῶν· 20 οὐδένα.γὰρ ἔχω ἰσόψυχον, ὅστις γνησίως τὰ
you. For no one have I like-minded, who genuinely the things
περὶ ὑμῶν μεριμνήσει· 21 οἱ.πάντες.γὰρ τὰ ἑαυτῶν
relative to you will care for. For all the things of themselves
ζητοῦσιν, οὐ τὰ ʰτοῦ‖ ⁱχριστοῦ Ἰησοῦ·‖ 22 τὴν.δὲ δοκιμὴν
are seeking, not the things of Christ Jesus. But the proof
αὐτοῦ γινώσκετε, ὅτι ὡς πατρὶ τέκνον, σὺν ἐμοὶ ἐδούλευσεν
of him ye know, that, as ³to ⁴a ⁵father ¹a ²child, with me he served
εἰς τὸ εὐαγγέλιον. 23 τοῦτον μὲν οὖν ἐλπίζω πέμψαι ὡς
for the glad tidings. Him therefore I hope to send ³when
ἂν ᵏἀπίδω‖ τὰ περὶ ἐμέ, ἐξαυτῆς· 24 πέ-
⁴I ⁵shall ⁶have ⁷seen ⁸the ⁹things ¹⁰concerning ¹¹me ¹at ²once : ¹³I ¹⁴am
ποιθα δὲ ἐν κυρίῳ ὅτι καὶ αὐτὸς ταχέως ἐλεύσομαι.
¹⁵persuaded ¹²but in [the] Lord that also ²myself ³soon ¹I ³shall come :
25 Ἀναγκαῖον.δὲ ἡγησάμην Ἐπαφρόδιτον τὸν ἀδελφὸν καὶ
but necessary I esteemed [it] ⁵Epaphroditus, ⁷brother ⁸and
συνεργὸν καὶ ¹συστρατιώτην‖ μου, ὑμῶν.δὲ ἀπόστολον καὶ
⁹fellow-worker ¹⁰and ¹¹fellow-soldier ⁶my, ¹²but ¹³your ¹⁴messenger ¹⁵and
λειτουργὸν τῆς.χρείας.μου, πέμψαι πρὸς ὑμᾶς· 26 ἐπειδὴ
¹⁶minister ¹⁷of ¹⁸my ¹⁹need, ¹to ²send ³to ⁴you, since
ἐπιποθῶν ἦν πάντας ὑμᾶςᵐ, καὶ ἀδημονῶν διότι
³longing ⁴after ¹he ²was ⁶all ⁵you, and [was] deeply depressed because
ἠκούσατε ὅτι ἠσθένησεν· 27 καὶ.γὰρ ἠσθένησεν παραπλήσιον
ye heard that he was sick ; for indeed he was sick like
θανάτῳ· ⁿἀλλ’‖ ὁ θεὸς °αὐτὸν ἠλέησεν,‖ οὐκ.αὐτὸν.δὲ μόνον,
to death, but God him had mercy on, and not him alone,
ἀλλὰ καὶ ἐμέ, ἵνα μὴ λύπην ἐπὶ ᵖλύπῃ‖ σχῶ. 28 σπου-
but also me, that not sorrow upon sorrow I might have. The more
δαιοτέρως οὖν ἔπεμψα αὐτόν, ἵνα ἰδόντες αὐτὸν πάλιν
diligently therefore I sent him, that seeing him again
χαρῆτε, κἀγὼ ἀλυπότερος ὦ. 29 προσδέχεσθε οὖν
ye might rejoice, and I the less sorrowful might be. Receive therefore
αὐτὸν ἐν κυρίῳ μετὰ πάσης χαρᾶς, καὶ τοὺς τοιούτους
him in [the] Lord with all joy, and such
ἐντίμους ἔχετε· 30 ὅτι διὰ τὸ ἔργον �۹τοῦ‖ ʳχριστοῦ‖
in honour hold ; because for the sake of the work of the Christ
μέχρι θανάτου ἤγγισεν, ˢπαραβουλευσάμενος‖ τῇ ψυχῇ,
unto death he went near, having disregarded [his] life,
ἵνα ἀναπληρώσῃ τὸ.ὑμῶν.ὑστέρημα τῆς πρός με λειτουργίας.
that he might fill up your deficiency ·of the ²towards ³me ¹ministration.
3 Τὸ.λοιπόν, ἀδελφοί.μου, χαίρετε ἐν κυρίῳ· τὰ αὐτὰ
For the rest, my brethren, rejoice in [the] Lord : the same things
γράφειν ὑμῖν, ἐμοὶ μὲν οὐκ ὀκνηρόν, ὑμῖν.δὲ ἀσφαλές.
to write to you, to me [is] not irksome, and for you safe.
2 βλέπετε τοὺς κύνας, βλέπετε τοὺς κακοὺς ἐργάτας, βλέπετε
See to dogs, see to evil workers, see to
τὴν κατατομήν· 3 ἡμεῖς.γὰρ ἐσμεν ἡ περιτομή, οἱ πνεύματι
the concision. For we are the circumcision, who ³in ⁴spirit
ᵗθεῷ‖ λατρεύοντες, καὶ καυχώμενοι ἐν χριστῷ Ἰησοῦ, καὶ οὐκ
²God ¹serve, and boast in Christ Jesus, and not

ʰ — τοῦ GLTTrAW.   ⁱ Ἰησοῦ χριστοῦ GLTrAW.   ᵏ ἀφίδω LTTrA.   ˡ συνσ- LTTrA.
ᵐ + [ἰδεῖν] to see L.   ⁿ ἀλλὰ LTTrAW.   ° ἠλέησεν αὐτὸν LTTrAW.   ᵖ λύπῃ GLTTrAW.
۹ — τοῦ the LTTrA.   ʳ — χριστοῦ A.   ˢ παραβολευσάμενος having hazarded GLTTrAW.
ᵗ θεοῦ (*read* serve in [the] Spirit of God) LTTrAW.

ἐν σαρκὶ πεποιθότες,ᵛ 4 καίπερ ἐγὼ ἔχων πεποίθησιν καὶ ἐν
in   flesh   trust.   Though   I   have   trust   even in

σαρκί· ᵛ εἴ τις δοκεῖ ἄλλος πεποιθέναι ἐν σαρκί, ἐγὼ μᾶλλον·
flesh;   if any ²thinks ¹other   to trust   in flesh,   I   rather:

5 ʷπεριτομῇ ὀκταήμερος, ἐκ γένους Ἰσραήλ, φυλῆς
[as to] circumcision. on [the] eighth day ; of [the] race of Israel, of [the] tribe

ˣΒενιαμίν,‖ Ἑβραῖος ἐξ Ἑβραίων, κατὰ νόμον Φαρισαῖος,
of Benjamin,   Hebrew of Hebrews; according to [the] law   a Pharisee ;

6 κατὰ ʸζῆλον‖ διώκων τὴν ἐκκλησίαν, κατὰ δικαιοσύ-
according to zeal,   persecuting the assembly ;   according to righteous-

νην τὴν ἐν νόμῳ γενόμενος ἄμεμπτος. 7 ᶻἀλλ'‖ -ἅτινα
ness which [is] in [the] law, having become blameless;   but what things

ᵃἦν μοι‖ κέρδη, ταῦτα ἥγημαι διὰ τὸν χριστὸν
were to me gain,   these I have esteemed, on account of   Christ,

ζημίαν· 8 ἀλλὰ ᵇμενοῦνγε‖ καὶ ἡγοῦμαι πάντα ζημίαν
loss.   But   yea rather,   also I am esteeming all things loss

εἶναι διὰ τὸ ὑπερέχον τῆς γνώσεως ᶜ χριστοῦ Ἰησοῦ
to be on account of the . excellency of the knowledge of Christ Jesus

τοῦ κυρίου μου, δι' ὃν τὰ πάντα ἐζημιώθην, καὶ ἡγοῦ-
my Lord,   on account of whom all things I suffered loss of, and esteem

μαι σκύβαλα ᵈεἶναι,‖ ἵνα χριστὸν κερδήσω, 9 καὶ εὑρεθῶ
[them] refuse   to be,   that   Christ I may gain;   and be found

ἐν αὐτῷ, μὴ ἔχων ἐμὴν δικαιοσύνην τὴν ἐκ νόμου, ἀλλὰ
in him,   not having my righteousness   which [is] of law,   but

τὴν διὰ πίστεως χριστοῦ, τὴν ἐκ θεοῦ δικαιοσύνην ἐπὶ
that which by faith of Christ [is], the ²of ³God ¹righteousness on

τῇ πίστει, 10 τοῦ γνῶναι αὐτὸν καὶ τὴν δύναμιν τῆς ἀνα-
faith,   to know him   and the power of ²resur-

στάσεως αὐτοῦ, καὶ ᵉτὴν‖ κοινωνίαν ᶠτῶν‖ παθημάτων αὐτοῦ,
rection ¹his,   and the fellowship   of his sufferings,

ᵍσυμμορφούμενος‖ τῷ θανάτῳ αὐτοῦ, 11 εἴ πως καταντήσω
being conformed   to his death,   if by any means I may arrive

εἰς τὴν ἐξανάστασιν ʰτῶν‖ νεκρῶν. 12 οὐχ ὅτι ἤδη ἔλαβον,
at the resurrection of the dead.   Not that ²already ¹I received,

ἢ ἤδη τετελείωμαι· διώκω δὲ εἰ ⁱκαὶ‖ καταλάβω
or already have been perfected; but I am pursuing, if also I may lay hold,

ἐφ' ᾧ καὶ ᵏκατελήφθην‖ ὑπὸ ˡτοῦ‖ χριστοῦ ᵐἸησοῦ.‖ 13 ἀδελ-
for that also I was laid hold of by the   Christ Jesus.   Bre-

φοί, ἐγὼ ἐμαυτὸν ⁿοὐ‖ λογίζομαι κατειληφέναι· ἓν δέ,
thren,   I   myself   ²not ¹do reckon to have laid hold; but one thing—

τὰ μὲν ὀπίσω ἐπιλανθανόμενος, τοῖς δὲ ἔμπροσθεν
the things behind   forgetting,   and to the things before

ἐπεκτεινόμενος, 14 κατὰ σκοπὸν διώκω ᵒἐπὶ‖ τὸ βραβεῖον
stretching out,   towards [the] goal I pursue for the prize

τῆς ἄνω κλήσεως τοῦ θεοῦ ἐν χριστῷ Ἰησοῦ. 15 Ὅσοι
of the ²on ³high ¹calling   of God in   Christ Jesus.   As many as

οὖν τέλειοι τοῦτο φρονῶμεν· καὶ εἴ τι ἑτέρως
therefore [are] perfect should be of this mind; and if [in] anything differently

φρονεῖτε, καὶ τοῦτο ὁ θεὸς ὑμῖν ἀποκαλύψει. 16 πλὴν εἰς ὃ
ye are minded, ²also ¹this God to you will reveal.   But whereto

---

the flesh. If any other man thinketh that he hath whereof he might trust in the flesh, I more: 5 circumcised the eighth day, of the stock of Israel, of the tribe of Benjamin, an Hebrew of the Hebrews; as touching the law, a Pharisee; 6 concerning zeal, persecuting the church; touching the righteousness which is in the law, blameless. 7 But what things were gain to me, those I counted loss for Christ. 8 Yea doubtless, and I count all things but loss for the excellency of the knowledge of Christ Jesus my Lord: for whom I have suffered the loss of all things, and do count them but dung, that I may win Christ. 9 and be found in him, not having mine own righteousness, which is of the law, but that which is through the faith of Christ, the righteousness which is of God by faith: 10 that I may know him, and the power of his resurrection, and the fellowship of his sufferings, being made conformable unto his death; 11 if by any means I might attain unto the resurrection of the dead. 12 Not as though I had already attained, either were already perfect: but I follow after, if that I may apprehend that for which also I am apprehended of Christ Jesus. 13 Brethren, I count not myself to have apprehended: but this one thing I do, forgetting those things which are behind, and reaching forth unto those things which are before, 14 I press toward the mark for the prize of the high calling of God in Christ Jesus. 15 Let us therefore, as many as be perfect, be thus minded: and if in any thing ye be otherwise

---

ᵛ To read as pointed in the Greek join though I have &c. to what precedes, commencing a sentence at εἴ τις. ʷ περιτομῇ GLTTrAW. ˣ Βενιαμείν LTTr. ʸ ζῆλος LTTrAW. · ᶻ ἀλλὰ [L]Tr[A] ; — ἀλλ' T. ᵃ μοι ἦν L. ᵇ μὲν οὖν then indeed GLTrAW. ᶜ + τοῦ (read of the Christ) L. ᵈ εἶναι LTTr. ᵉ — τὴν LTTr[A]. ᶠ — τῶν TTr. ᵍ συμμορφιζόμενος (συν- T) LTTrAW. ʰ τὴν ἐκ from among [the] LTTrAW. ⁱ — καὶ T. ᵏ κατελήμφθην LTTrA. ˡ — τοῦ GLTTrAW. ᵐ — Ἰησοῦ GLTιAW. ⁿ οὔπω not yet T. ᵒ εἰς LTTrA.

minded, God shall reveal even this unto you. 16 Nevertheless, whereto we have already attained, let us walk by the same rule, let us mind the same thing. 17 Brethren, be followers together of me, and mark them which walk so as ye have us for an ensample. 18 (For many walk, of whom I have told you often, and now tell you even weeping, *that they are* the enemies of the cross of Christ: 19 whose end *is* destruction, whose God *is their* belly, and *whose* glory *is* in their shame, who mind earthly things.) 20 For our conversation is in heaven; from whence also we look for the Saviour, the Lord Jesus Christ: 21 who shall change our vile body, that it may be fashioned like unto his glorious body, according to the working whereby he is able even to subdue all things unto himself.

IV. Therefore, my brethren dearly beloved and longed for, my joy and crown, so stand fast in the Lord, *my* dearly beloved. 2 I beseech Euodias, and beseech Syntyche, that they be of the same mind in the Lord. 3 And I entreat thee also, true yokefellow, help, those women which laboured with me in the gospel, with Clement also, and *with* other my fellowlabourers, whose names *are* in the book of life.

4 Rejoice in the Lord alway: *and* again I say, Rejoice. 5 Let your moderation be known unto all men. The Lord *is* at hand. 6 Be careful for nothing; but in every thing by prayer and supplication with thanksgiving let your requests be made known unto God. 7 And the peace of God, which passeth all understanding, shall keep your hearts and minds through Christ Jesus. 8 Finally, brethren, whatsoever things

ἐφθάσαμεν, τῷ αὐτῷ στοιχεῖν Ρκανόνι, †ὸ.αὐτὸ.φρονεῖν.ǁ
we attained,   by the same   ²to ³walk   ¹rule,-   to be of the same mind.

17 ᵠΣυμμιμηταίǁ μου γίνεσθε, ἀδελφοί, καὶ σκοπεῖτε τοὺς
    ²Imitators ³together ⁴of ⁵me   ¹be,   brethren,   and   consider   'those

οὕτως περιπατοῦντας καθὼς ἔχετε τύπον ἡμᾶς. 18 πολ-
thus   walking   as   ye have [²for] ³a ⁴pattern ¹us;   ᶜmany

λοὶ γὰρ περιπατοῦσιν οὓς πολλάκις ἔλεγον ὑμῖν, νῦν.δὲ
ᵃfor   are walking [of] whom often   I told   you,   and now

καὶ κλαίων λέγω,   τοὺς ἐχθροὺς τοῦ σταυροῦ τοῦ
even weeping I tell [you, they are] the   enemies   of the   cross

χριστοῦ· 19 ὧν τὸ τέλος ἀπώλεια, ὧν ὁ θεὸς ἡ κοιλία,
of Christ: whose end [is] destruction, whose God [is] the belly,

καὶ ἡ δόξα ἐν τῇ.αἰσχύνῃ.αὐτῶν, οἱ τὰ.ἐπίγεια φρονοῦντες.
and the glory in   their shame,   who earthly things   mind:

20 ἡμῶν.γὰρ τὸ πολίτευμα ἐν οὐρανοῖς ὑπάρχει, ἐξ οὗ
for of us   the commonwealth in [the] heavens   exists,   from which

καὶ σωτῆρα ἀπεκδεχόμεθα κύριον Ἰησοῦν χριστόν, 21 ὃς
also [as] Saviour   we are awaiting [the] Lord   Jesus   Christ,   who

μετασχηματίσει τὸ σῶμα.τῆς ταπεινώσεως ἡμῶν, ʳεἰς τὸ γε-
will transform   ²body   ³of ⁴humiliation 'our,   for   ²to

νέσθαι αὐτὸǁ ᵠσύμμορφονǁ τῷ σώματι τῆς.δόξης.αὐτοῦ, κατὰ
³become ¹it   conformed   to ²body   ³of ¹his ⁴glory, according to

τὴν ἐνέργειαν τοῦ.δύνασθαι.αὐτὸν καὶ ὑποτάξαι ˢἑαυτῷǁ
the   working   of his power   even   to subdue   to himself

τὰ.πάντα.
all things.

4 Ὥστε, ἀδελφοί.μου ἀγαπητοὶ καὶ ἐπιπόθητοι, χαρὰ καὶ
So that,   my brethren   beloved   and longed for,   ²joy ³and

στέφανός μου, οὕτως στήκετε ἐν κυρίῳ, ἀγαπητοί. 2 ᵗΕὐω-
⁴crown 'my,   thus   stand fast in [the] Lord,   beloved.   Eno-

δίανǁ παρακαλῶ, καὶ Συντύχην παρακαλῶ, τὸ.αὐτὸ.φρονεῖν
dia   I exhort,   and° Syntyche   I exhort,   to be of the same mind

ἐν κυρίῳ· 3 ᵛκαὶǁ ἐρωτῶ καί σε, ʷσύζυγε γνήσιε,ǁ ˣσυλ-
in [the] Lord.   And I ask also thee, ²yoke-fellow 'true,   as-

λαμβάνουǁ αὐταῖς,   ᵃ αἵτινες ἐν τῷ εὐαγγελίῳ συνήθλησάν
·sist   these [women], who   in the glad tidings strove together.

μοι, μετὰ καὶ Κλήμεντος, καὶ τῶν λοιπῶν συνεργῶν.μου,
with me; with also   Clement,   and the rest of my fellow-workers,

ὧν τὰ ὀνόματα ἐν βίβλῳ ζωῆς.
whose   names [are] in [the] book   of life.

4 Χαίρετε ἐν κυρίῳ πάντοτε· πάλιν ἐρῶ, χαίρετε.
Rejoice   in [the] Lord   always: again I will say, rejoice.

5 τὸ.ἐπιεικὲς.ὑμῶν γνωσθήτω πᾶσιν ἀνθρώποις. ὁ κύριος
²Your ³gentleness ¹let be known to all   men.   The Lord [is]

ἐγγύς. 6 Μηδὲν μεριμνᾶτε, ἀλλ' ἐν παντὶ τῇ.προσευχῇ
near.   Nothing be careful about, but   in everything   by prayer

καὶ τῇ.δεήσει μετὰ εὐχαριστίας τὰ.αἰτήματα.ὑμῶν γνωρι-
and by supplication with   thanksgiving   ²your ³requests 'let be made

ζέσθω πρὸς τὸν θεόν· 7 καὶ ἡ εἰρήνη τοῦ θεοῦ ἡ ὑπερέχουσα
known to   God;   and the peace   of God which   surpasses

πάντα νοῦν φρουρήσει τὰς.καρδίας.ὑμῶν καὶ τὰ νοήματα
every understanding shall guard   your hearts   and   ²thoughts

ὑμῶν ἐν χριστῷ Ἰησοῦ. 8 Τὸ.λοιπόν, ἀδελφοί, ὅσα
¹your   in Christ   Jesus.   For the rest, brethren, whatsoever [things]

P — κανόνι, τὸ αὐτὸ φρονεῖν GLTTrA.   ᵠ συν- T.   ʳ — εἰς τὸ γενέυθαι αὐτὸ GLTTrAW.
ˢ αὐτῷ LTTrA.   ᵗ Εὐοδίαν EGLTTrAW.   ᵛ ναὶ yea GLTTrAW.   ʷ γνήσιε σύνζυγε LTTrA.
ˣ συν- ITrA.

ἐστὶν ἀληθῆ, ὅσα σεμνά, ὅσα δίκαια. ὅσα ἁγνά,
are true, what-oever venerable, whatsoever just, whatsoever pure,

ὅσα προσφιλῆ, ὅσα εὔφημα, εἴ τις ἀρετὴ καὶ εἴ τις
whatsoever lovely, whatsoever of good report; if any virtue and if any

ἔπαινος, ταῦτα λογίζεσθε· 9 ἃ καὶ ἐμάθετε καὶ παρελάβετε
praise, these things consider. What also ye learned and received

καὶ ἠκούσατε καὶ εἴδετε ἐν ἐμοί, ταῦτα πράσσετε· καὶ ὁ θεὸς
and heard and saw in me, these things do; and the God

τῆς εἰρήνης ἔσται μεθ' ὑμῶν. 10 Ἐχάρην.δὲ ἐν κυρίῳ
of peace shall be with you.   But I rejoiced in [the] Lord

μεγάλως, ὅτι ἤδη.ποτὲ ἀνεθάλετε τὸ ὑπὲρ ἐμοῦ φρονεῖν·
greatly, that now at length ye revived [your] ²of ⁵me ¹thinking;

ἐφ'.ᾧ καὶ ἐφρονεῖτε, ἠκαιρεῖσθε.δὲ. 11 οὐχ ὅτι
although ye were thinking, but ye were lacking opportunity. Not that

καθ' ὑστέρησιν λέγω· ἐγὼ.γὰρ ἔμαθον ἐν οἷς εἰμι,
as to destitution I speak; for I learned in what [circumstances] I am,

αὐτάρκης εἶναι. 12 οἶδα.ʸδὲ‖ ταπεινοῦσθαι, οἶδα.καὶ
content to be. And I know [how] to be brought low, and I know [how]

περισσεύειν· ἐν παντὶ καὶ ἐν πᾶσιν μεμύημαι καὶ χορτά-
to abound. In everything and in all things I am initiated both to be

ζεσθαι καὶ πεινᾶν, καὶ περισσεύειν καὶ ὑστερεῖσθαι· 13 πάντα
full and to hunger, both to abound and to be deficient. ⁵All ⁶things

ἰσχύω ἐν τῷ ἐνδυναμοῦντί με ˣχριστῷ.‖ 14 πλὴν
¹I ²am ³strong ⁴for in the ⁷who ⁸empowers ⁴me ⁹Christ. But

καλῶς ἐποιήσατε, ᵃσυγκοινωνήσαντές‖ μου τῇ θλίψει. 15 οἴδατε
well ye did, having fellowship in my tribulation. ²Know

δὲ καὶ ὑμεῖς, Φιλιππήσιοι, ὅτι ἐν ἀρχῇ τοῦ εὐαγγελίου,
¹and also ye, O Philippians, that in [the] beginning of the glad tidings,

ὅτε ἐξῆλθον ἀπὸ Μακεδονίας, οὐδεμία μοι ἐκκλησία ἐκοι-
when I came out from Macedonia, not any ⁴with ⁵me ¹assembly ²had

νώνησεν εἰς λόγον δόσεως καὶ ᵇλήψεως,‖ εἰ.μὴ ὑμεῖς
³fellowship with regard to an account of giving and receiving, except ye

μόνοι· 16 ὅτι καὶ ἐν Θεσσαλονίκῃ καὶ ἅπαξ καὶ δὶς ᶜεἰς‖ τὴν
alone; because also in Thessalonica both once and twice for

χρείαν.μοι ἐπέμψατε. 17 οὐχ ὅτι ἐπιζητῶ τὸ δόμα, ᵈἀλλ'‖
my need ye sent. Not that I seek after gift, but

ἐπιζητῶ τὸν καρπὸν τὸν πλεονάζοντα εἰς λόγον.ὑμῶν·
I seek after fruit that abounds to your account.

18 ἀπέχω.δὲ πάντα καὶ περισσεύω· πεπλήρωμαι, δεξάμενος
But I have all things and abound· I am full, having received

παρὰ Ἐπαφροδίτου τὰ παρ' ὑμῶν, ὀσμὴν εὐωδίας,
from Epaphroditus the things from you, an odour of a sweet smell,

θυσίαν δεκτήν, εὐάρεστον τῷ.θεῷ. 19 ὁ δὲ θεός.μου πληρώσει
a sacrifice acceptable, well-pleasing to God. But my God will fill up

πᾶσαν χρείαν.ὑμῶν κατὰ ᵉτὸν.πλοῦτον‖.αὐτοῦ ἐν δόξῃ ἐν
all your need according to his riches in glory in

χριστῷ Ἰησοῦ. 20 τῷ.δὲ θεῷ καὶ πατρὶ ἡμῶν ἡ δόξα εἰς
Christ Jesus. But to the God and Father of us [be] glory to

τοὺς αἰῶνας τῶν αἰώνων. ἀμήν.
the ages of the ages. Amen.

21 Ἀσπάσασθε πάντα ἅγιον ἐν χριστῷ Ἰησοῦ. ἀσπάζον-
Salute every saint in Christ Jesus. ⁵Sa-

ται ὑμᾶς οἱ σὺν ἐμοὶ ἀδελφοί. 22 ἀσπάζονται ὑμᾶς πάν-
lute ⁴you ¹the ³with ⁴me ²brethren. ¹⁰Salute ¹¹you ⁷all

are true, whatsoever things are honest, whatsoever things are just, whatsoever things are pure, whatsoever things are lovely, whatsoever things are of good report; if there be any virtue, and if there be any praise, think on these things. 9 Those things, which ye have both learned, and received, and heard, and seen in me, do: and the God of peace shall be with you. 10 But I rejoiced in the Lord greatly, that now at the last your care of me hath flourished again; wherein ye were also careful, but ye lacked opportunity. 11 Not that I speak in respect of want: for I have learned, in whatsoever state I am, therewith to be content. 12 I know both how to be abased, and I know how to abound: every where and in all things I am instructed both to be full and to be hungry, both to abound and to suffer need. 13 I can do all things through Christ which strengtheneth me. 14 Notwithstanding ye have well done, that ye did communicate with my affliction. 15 Now ye Philippians know also, that in the beginning of the gospel, when I departed from Macedonia, no church communicated with me as concerning giving and receiving, but ye only. 16 For even in Thessalonica ye sent once and again unto my necessity. 17 Not because I desire a gift: but I desire fruit that may abound to your account. 18 But I have all, and abound: I am full, having received of Epaphroditus the things which were sent from you, an odour of a sweet smell, a sacrifice acceptable, wellpleasing to God. 19 But my God shall supply all your need according to his riches in glory by Christ Jesus. 20 Now unto God and our Father be glory for ever and ever. Amen. 21 Salute every saint

ʸ καὶ GLTTrAW.   ˣ.— χριστῷ (read τῷ him) GLTTrAW.   ᵃ συν- T.   ᵇ λήμψεως LTTrA.
ᵉ [εἰς] L.   ᵈ ἀλλὰ LTTrAW.   ᵉ τὸ πλοῦτος LTTrAW.
34

in Christ Jesus. The
brethren which are
with me greet you.
22 All the saints salute
you, chiefly they thảt
are of Cæsar's house-
hold. 23 The grace of
our Lord Jesus Christ
be with you all. A-
men.

τες οἱ ἅγιοι, μάλιστα. δὲ οἱ ἐκ τῆς Καίσαρος οἰκίας. 23 Ἡ
    *the   °saints, and especially those of the   ²of ªCæsar ¹household.   The

χάρις τοῦ.κυρίου.¹ἡμῶν‖ Ἰησοῦ χριστοῦ μετὰ ᵍπάντων
grace   of our Lord   Jeₔus   Christ [be] with   ²all

ὑμῶν.‖ ʰἀμήν.ᵇ
¹you.   Amen.

ⁱΠρὸς   Φιλιππησίους ἐγράφη ἀπὸ Ῥώμης, δι' Ἐπα-
   To [the]   Philippians   written   from   Rome,   by   Epa-

φροδίτου.‖
phroditus.

ᵏΗ ΠΡΟΣ   ΚΟΛΑΣΣΑΕΙΣ ΕΠΙΣΤΟΛΗ ΠΑΥΛΟΥ.ˡ
THE   ⁴TO [⁵THE]   ⁶COLOSSIANS   ¹EPISTLE   ²OF ³PAUL.

PAUL, an apostle of
Jesus Christ by the
will of God, and Ti-
motheus our brother,
2 to the saints and
faithful brethren in
Christ which are at
Colosse: Grace be un-
to you, and peace,
from God our Father
and the Lord Jesus
Christ.

ΠΑΥΛΟΣ ἀπόστολος ˡ¹Ἰησοῦ χριστοῦ‖. διὰ θελήματος θεοῦ, καὶ
Paul   apostle   of Jesus Christ   by   ²will   ¹God's, and

Τιμόθεος ὁ ἀδελφός, 2 τοῖς ἐν ᵐΚολασσαῖς‖ ἁγίοις καὶ πισ-
Timotheus the brother,   to the ⁷in   ⁸Colosse   ¹saints ²and ³faith-

τοῖς ἀδελφοῖς ἐν χριστῷ.ⁿ χάρις ὑμῖν καὶ εἰρήνη ἀπὸ θεοῦ
ful   ⁴brethren   ⁵in   ⁶Christ.   Grace to you and · peace   from God

πατρὸς.ἡμῶν ᵒκαὶ   κυρίου Ἰησοῦ χριστοῦ.‖
our Father   and [the] Lord   Jesus   Christ.

3 Εὐχαριστοῦμεν τῷ θεῷ ᵖκαὶ‖ πατρὶ τοῦ.κυρίου.ἡμῶν Ἰη-
   We give thanks to the God and   Father   of our Lord   Je-

3 We give thanks to
God and the Father of
our Lord Jesus Christ,
praying always for
you, 4 since we heard
of your faith in Christ
Jesus, and of the love
which ye have to all
the saints, 5 for the
hope which is laid up
for you in heaven,
whereof ye heard be-
fore in the word of
the truth of the gos-
pel ; 6 which is come
unto you, as it is in all
the world ; and bring-
eth forth fruit, as it
doth also in you, since
the day ye heard of it,
and knew the grace of
God in truth : 7 as ye
also learned of Epa-
phras our dear fellow-
servant, who is for you
a faithful minister of
Christ ; 8 who also
declared unto us your
love in the Spirit.

σοῦ χριστοῦ, πάντοτε �q περὶ‖ ὑμῶν προσευχόμενοι· 4 ακού-
sus   Christ,   continually   ²for   ¹you   ¹praying,   having

σαντες τὴν.πίστιν.ὑμῶν ἐν χριστῷ Ἰησοῦ, καὶ τὴν ἀγάπην
heard   of your faith   in   Christ   Jesus, and the   love

ʳτὴν‖   εἰς πάντας τοὺς ἁγίους, 5 διὰ   τὴν ἐλπίδα
which [ye have] towards   all   the   saints, on account of the   hope

τὴν ἀποκειμένην ὑμῖν ἐν τοῖς οὐρανοῖς, ἣν προηκούσατε
which [is]   laid up   for you in the   heavens ; which ye heard of before

ἐν τῷ λόγῳ τῆς ἀληθείας τοῦ εὐαγγελίου, 6 τοῦ παρόντος εἰς
in the   word   of the truth   of the glad tidings,   which are come   to

ὑμᾶς, καθὼς καὶ ἐν παντὶ τῷ κόσμῳ, ˢκαὶ‖ ἔστιν καρποφορού-
you,   even as   also in   all   the   world, · and   are   bringing forth

μενονᵗ, καθὼς καὶ ἐν ὑμῖν, ἀφ' ἧς.ἡμέρας ἠκούσατε καὶ
fruit,   even as   also among you,   from the day in which   ye heard   and

ἐπέγνωτε τὴν χάριν τοῦ θεοῦ ἐν ἀληθείᾳ· 7 καθὼς ᵘκαὶ‖
knew   the   grace   of God in   truth :   even as   also

ἐμάθετε ἀπὸ Ἐπαφρᾶ τοῦ ἀγαπητοῦ συνδούλου ἡμῶν, ὅς
ye learned from   Epaphras   ²beloved   ³fellow-bondman   ¹our,   who

ἐστιν πιστὸς ὑπὲρ ᵛὑμῶν‖ διάκονος τοῦ χριστοῦ, 8 ὁ καὶ
is   ⁶faithful ⁵for   ¹you   ¹a ³servant   ⁴of ⁵Christ,   who also

δηλώσας ἡμῖν τὴν.ὑμῶν.ἀγάπην ἐν   πνεύματι.
signified   to us   your love   in [the] Spirit.

---

f — ἡμῶν (read of the Lord) LTTrAW.   g τοῦ πνεύματος ὑμῶν your spirit LTTrAW.
h — ἀμήν [L]TTr[A].   i — the subscription GLTW ; Πρὸς Φιλιππησίους TrA.
k + τοῦ Ἀποστόλου of the Apostle E ; Πρὸς Κολοσσαεῖς ET ; Παύλου ἐπιστολὴ πρὸς
Κολοσσαεῖς G ; Πρὸς Κολοσσαεῖς I.TrAW.   ˡ χριστοῦ Ἰησοῦ LTTrAW.   m Κολοσσαῖς
EᴜᴛᴀW.   n + Ἰησοῦ Jesus L.   o — καὶ κυρίου Ἰησοῦ χριστοῦ G[L]TTrAW.   p — καὶ (read
to God [the] Father) LA.   q ὑπὲρ LTr.   r ἣν ἔχετε which ye have LTTrAW.   s — καὶ
LTTrAW.   t + καὶ αὐξανόμενον and growing GLTTrAW.   u — καὶ LTTrAW.   v ἡμῶν
us LTrA.

9 Διὰ τοῦτο καὶ ἡμεῖς ἀφ᾽ ἧς.ἡμέρας ἠκούσαμεν,
On account of this also we from the day in which we heard [of it],

οὐ.παυόμεθα ὑπὲρ ὑμῶν προσευχόμενοι καὶ αἰτούμενοι ἵνα
do not cease ²for ³you ¹praying and asking that

πληρωθῆτε τὴν ἐπίγνωσιν τοῦ.θελήματος.αὐτοῦ ἐν πάσῃ
ye may be filled with the knowledge of his will in all

σοφίᾳ καὶ συνέσει πνευματικῇ, 10 περιπατῆσαι ʷὑμᾶςǁ
wisdom and ²understanding ¹spiritual, ⁵to ⁶walk [²for] ⁴you

ἀξίως τοῦ κυρίου εἰς πᾶσαν ˣἀρέσκειαν·ǁ ἐν παντὶ ἔργῳ ἀγαθῷ
worthily of the Lord to all pleasing, in every ²work ¹good

καρποφοροῦντες καὶ αὐξανόμενοι ʸεἰς τὴν ἐπίγνωσινǁ τοῦ
bringing forth fruit and growing into the knowledge

θεοῦ· 11 ἐν πάσῃ δυνάμει δυναμούμενοι κατὰ τὸ κράτος
of God; with all power being strengthened according to the might

τῆς.δόξης.αὐτοῦ εἰς πᾶσαν ὑπομονὴν καὶ μακροθυμίαν μετὰ
of his glory to all endurance and longsuffering with

χαρᾶς· 12 εὐχαριστοῦντες τῷ πατρί, τῷ ᶻ ἱκανώσαντι ᵃἡμᾶςǁ
joy; giving thanks to the Father, who made ²competent ¹us

εἰς τὴν μερίδα τοῦ κλήρου τῶν ἁγίων ἐν τῷ φωτί, 13 ὃς
for the share of the inheritance of the saints in the light, who

ᵇἐῤῥύσατοǁ ἡμᾶς ἐκ τῆς ἐξουσίας τοῦ σκότους, καὶ μετέστη-
delivered us from the authority of darkness, and trans-

σεν εἰς τὴν βασιλείαν τοῦ υἱοῦ τῆς.ἀγάπης.αὐτοῦ, 14 ἐν
lated [us] into the kingdom of the Son of his love: in

ᾧ ἔχομεν τὴν ἀπολύτρωσιν ᶜδιὰ τοῦ.αἵματος.αὐτοῦ,ǁ τὴν
whom we have redemption ³by ¹his ²blood, the

ἄφεσιν τῶν ἁμαρτιῶν· 15 ὅς ἐστιν εἰκὼν τοῦ θεοῦ τοῦ
remission of sins; who is [the] image of God the

ἀοράτου, πρωτότοκος πάσης κτίσεως· 16 ὅτι ἐν αὐτῷ ἐ-
invisible, firstborn of all creation; because by him were

κτίσθη τὰ.πάντα, ᵈτὰǁ ἐν τοῖς οὐρανοῖς καὶ ᵉτὰǁ ἐπὶ τῆς
created all things, the things in the heavens and the things upon the

γῆς, τὰ ὁρατὰ καὶ τὰ ἀόρατα, εἴτε θρόνοι εἴτε κυριότητες
earth, the visible and the invisible, whether thrones, or lordships,

εἴτε ἀρχαὶ εἴτε ἐξουσίαι· τὰ.πάντα δι᾽ αὐτοῦ καὶ εἰς αὐτὸν
or principalities, or authorities: all things by him and for him

ἔκτισται· 17 καὶ αὐτός ἐστιν πρὸ πάντων, καὶ τὰ.πάντα
have been created. And he is before all, and all things

ἐν αὐτῷ συνέστηκεν· 18 καὶ αὐτός ἐστιν ἡ κεφαλὴ τοῦ σώμα-
in him subsist. And he is the head of the body,

τος τῆς ἐκκλησίας· ὅς ἐστιν ἀρχή, πρωτότοκος ἐκ
the assembly; who is [the] beginning, firstborn from among

τῶν νεκρῶν, ἵνα γένηται ἐν πᾶσιν αὐτὸς πρωτεύων·
the dead, that ²might ³be ⁴in ⁵all ⁶things ¹he holding the first place;

19 ὅτι ἐν αὐτῷ εὐδόκησεν πᾶν τὸ πλήρωμα κατοικῆσαι,
because in him ⁴was ⁵pleased ¹all ²the ³fulness to dwell,

20 καὶ δι᾽ αὐτοῦ ἀποκαταλλάξαι τὰ.πάντα εἰς αὐτόν, εἰρη-
and by him to reconcile all things to itself, having

νοποιήσας διὰ τοῦ αἵματος τοῦ.σταυροῦ.αὐτοῦ, ᶠδι᾽ αὐτοῦ,ǁ
made peace by the blood of his cross, by him,

εἴτε τὰ ἐπὶ τῆς γῆς, εἴτε τὰ ἐν τοῖς οὐρανοῖς. 21 καὶ
whether the things on the earth, or the things in the heavens. And

ὑμᾶς ποτε ὄντας ἀπηλλοτριωμένους καὶ ἐχθροὺς τῇ διανοίᾳ
you once being alienated and enemies in mind

---

9 For this cause we also, since the day we heard it, do not cease to pray for you, and to desire that ye might be filled with the knowledge of his will in all wisdom and spiritual understanding ; 10 that ye might walk worthy of the Lord unto all pleasing, being fruitful in every good work, and increasing in the knowledge of God ; 11 strengthened with all might, according to his glorious power, unto all patience and longsuffering with joyfulness ; 12 giving thanks unto the Father, which hath made us meet to be partakers of the inheritance of the saints in light : 13 who hath delivered us from the power of darkness, and hath translated us into the kingdom of his dear Son : 14 in whom we have redemption through his blood, even the forgiveness of sins : 15 who is the image of the invisible God, the firstborn of every creature : 16 for by him were all things created, that are in heaven, and that are in earth, visible and invisible, whether they be thrones, or dominions, or principalities, or powers : all things were created by him, and for him : 17 and he is before all things, and by him all things consist. 18 And he is the head of the body, the church : who is the beginning, the firstborn from the dead ; that in all things he might have the pre-eminence. 19 For it pleased the Father that in him should all fulness dwell ; 20 and, having made peace through the blood of his cross, by him to reconcile all things unto himself ; by him, I say, whether they be things in earth, or things in heaven. 21 And you, that were sometime alienated and enemies in your mind by wicked works,

---

ʷ — ὑμᾶς GLTTrA. ˣ ἀρεσκίαν T. ʸ τῇ ἐπιγνώσει by the knowledge GLTTrAW. ᶻ + καλέσαντι καὶ called and L. ᵃ ὑμᾶς you T. ᵇ ἐρύσατο TTr. ᶜ — διὰ τοῦ αἵματος αὐτοῦ GLTTrAW. ᵈ — τὰ LTTr. ᵉ — τὰ [L]T[Tr]. ᶠ — δι᾽ αὐτοῦ LTTr.

yet now hath he re-
conciled 22 in the body
of his flesh through
death, to present you
holy and unblameable
and unreproveable in
his sight : 23 if ye con-
tinue in the faith
grounded and settled,
and be not moved a-
way from the hope of
the gospel, which ye
have heard, and which
was preached to every
creature which is un-
der heaven ; whereof
I Paul am made a
minister ;

ἐν τοῖς ἔργοις τοῖς πονηροῖς. νυνὶ.δὲ ᵍἀποκατήλλαξεν· 22 ἐν
by　²works　¹wicked,　yet now　he reconciled　　in

τῷ σώματι τῆς.σαρκὸς.αὐτοῦ διὰ τοῦ θανάτουʰ, παρα-
the body　of his flesh　through　death,　to pre-

στῆσαι ὑμᾶς ἁγίους καὶ ἀμώμους καὶ ἀνεγκλήτους κατενώ-
sent　you　holy　and unblamable and unimpeachable　before

πιον αὐτοῦ· 23 εἴγε ἐπιμένετε τῇ πίστει τεθεμελιωμένοι
him,　if indeed ye continue　in the faith　founded

καὶ ἑδραῖοι, καὶ μὴ μετακινούμενοι ἀπὸ τῆς ἐλπίδος τοῦ
and　firm,　and not being moved away　from the　hope of the

εὐαγγελίου οὗ ἠκούσατε, τοῦ κηρυχθέντος ἐν πάσῃ ⁱτῇ
glad tidings,　which ye heard,　which were proclaimed in　all　the

κτίσει τῇ ὑπὸ τὸν οὐρανόν, · οὗ ἐγενόμην ἐγὼ Παῦλος
creation which [is] under　heaven,　of which ³became ¹I ²Paul

διάκονος.
servant.

24 who now rejoice
in my sufferings for
you, and fill up that
which is behind of the
afflictions of Christ in
my flesh for his body's
sake, which is the
church : 25 whereof I
am made a minister,
according to the dis-
pensation of God
which is given to me
for you, to fulfil the
word of God ; 26 even
the mystery which
hath been hid from
ages and from gene-
rations, but now is
made manifest to his
saints : 27 to whom God
would make known
what is the riches of
the glory of this mys-
tery among the Gen-
tiles ; which is Christ
in you, the hope of
glory : 28 whom we
preach, warning every
man, and teaching
every man in all
wisdom ; that we
may present every
man perfect in Christ
Jesus : 29 whereunto
I also labour, striv-
ing according to his
working, which work-
eth in me mightily.

24 Νῦν χαίρω ἐν τοῖς.παθήμασίν.ᵏμου‖ ὑπὲρ ὑμῶν, καὶ
Now, I am rejoicing in　my sufferings　for you,　and

ἀνταναπληρῶ τὰ ὑστερήματα τῶν θλίψεων τοῦ χριστοῦ
I am filling up　that which is behind　of the tribulations of the　Christ

ἐν τῇ.σαρκί.μου ὑπὲρ τοῦ.σώματος.αὐτοῦ, ὅ ἐστιν ἡ ἐκ-
in　my flesh　for　his body,　which is　the as-

κλησία· 25 ἧς ἐγενόμην ἐγὼ διάκονος · κατὰ τὴν οἰκονο-
sembly ;　of which ²became ¹I　servant,　according to the adminis-

μίαν τοῦ θεοῦ τὴν δοθεῖσάν μοι εἰς ὑμᾶς πληρῶσαι τὸν
tration　of God which [is] given　me towards you to complete the

λόγον τοῦ θεοῦ, 26 τὸ μυστήριον τὸ ἀποκεκρυμμένον ἀπὸ
word　of God,　the　mystery　which　has been hidden　from

τῶν αἰώνων καὶ ἀπὸ τῶν γενεῶν, ¹νυκὶ.δὲ ἐφανερώθη
ages　and from　the generations, but now was made manifest

τοῖς.ἁγίοις.αὐτοῦ· 27 οἷς ἠθέλησεν ὁ θεὸς γνωρίσαι ᵐτίς
to his saints ;　to whom ²did ³will ¹God to make known what

ὁ‖ πλοῦτος τῆς δόξης τοῦ.μυστηρίου.τούτου ἐν τοῖς ἔ-
the riches of the glory of this mystery　[are] among the na-

θνεσιν, ⁿὅς‖ ἐστιν χριστὸς ἐν ὑμῖν ἡ ἐλπὶς τῆς δόξης· 28 ὃν
tions,　which is　Christ　in you　the hope　of glory : whom

ἡμεῖς καταγγέλλομεν, νουθετοῦντες πάντα ἄνθρωπον, καὶ
we　announce,　admonishing　every　man,　and

διδάσκοντες πάντα ἄνθρωπον ἐν πάσῃ σοφίᾳ, ἵνα παρα-
teaching　every　man　in all　wisdom, that we may

στήσωμεν πάντα ἄνθρωπον τέλειον ἐν χριστῷ °Ἰησοῦ.‖
present　every　man　perfect　in　Christ　Jesus.

29 εἰς.ὃ καὶ κοπιῶ, ἀγωνιζόμενος κατὰ τὴν ἐνέργειαν
Whereunto also I labour, ·　striving　according to　²working

αὐτοῦ τὴν ἐνεργουμένην ἐν ἐμοὶ ἐν δυνάμει.
¹his　which works　in me　in power.

II. For I would that
ye knew what great
conflict I have for you,
and for them at Lao-
dicea, and for as many
as have not seen my
face in the flesh ; 2 that
their hearts might be
comforted, being knit

2 Θέλω.γὰρ ὑμᾶς εἰδέναι ἡλίκον ἀγῶνα ἔχω ᴾπερὶ‖ ὑμῶν
For I wish　you to know how great conflict I have for　you,

καὶ τῶν ἐν �q Λαοδικείᾳ,‖ καὶ ὅσοι οὐχ.ʳἑωράκασιν‖ τὸ πρόσω-
and those in　Laodicea,　and as many as　have not seen　²face

πόν μου ἐν σαρκί, 2 ἵνα παρακληθῶσιν αἱ.καρδίαι.αὐτῶν,
¹my　in flesh ;　that may be encouraged　their hearts,

ᵍ ἀποκατηλλάγητε were ye reconciled L.　ʰ + [αὐτοῦ] (read his death) L.　ⁱ — τῇ
LTTrAW.　ᵏ — μου (read the sufferings) GLTTrAW.　ˡ νῦν LTTrA.　ᵐ τί τὸ LTTrAW.
ⁿ ὅ LTrA.　° — Ἰησοῦ GLTTrAW.　ᴾ ὑπὲρ LTTrA.　q Λαοδικίᾳ T.　ʳ ἑώρακαν LTrAW ;
ἑόρακαν T.

ᵃσυμβιβασθέντων‖ ἐν ἀγάπῃ, καὶ εἰς ᵗπάντα πλοῦτον᾽ τῆς
being knit together   in   love,   and to   all   riches   of the

πληροφορίας τῆς συνέσεως᾽ εἰς ἐπίγνωσιν τοῦ μυστηρίου
full assurance   of understanding; to [the] knowledge of the   mystery

τοῦ θεοῦ ᵛκαὶ πατρὸς καὶ τοῦ‖ ʷχριστοῦ,‖ 3 ἐν ᾧ εἰσιν
of God   and of [the] Father and of the   Christ;   in which are

πάντες οἱ θησαυροὶ τῆς σοφίας καὶ ˣτῆς‖ γνώσεως ἀπόκρυ-
all   the treasures   of wisdom and   of knowledge   hid.

φοι. 4 τοῦτο.ʸδὲ‖ λέγω, ἵνα ᶻμὴ τις‖ ὑμᾶς παραλογίζηται ἐν
And this   I say, that not anyone you   may beguile   by

πιθανολογίᾳ· 5 εἰ.γὰρ καὶ τῇ σαρκὶ ἄπειμι, ἀλλὰ τῷ
persuasive speech.   For if indeed in the flesh I am absent,   yet

πνεύματι σὺν ὑμῖν εἰμί, χαίρων καὶ βλέπων ὑμῶν τὴν τάξιν,
in spirit   with you I am, rejoicing and seeing   your   order,

καὶ τὸ στερέωμα τῆς εἰς χριστὸν πίστεως.ὑμῶν. 6 ὡς οὖν
and the firmness   ⁴in   ⁵Christ   ¹of ²your ³faith.   As therefore

παρελάβετε τὸν χριστὸν Ἰησοῦν τὸν κύριον, ἐν αὐτῷ περιπα-
ye received   the   Christ,   Jesus   the   Lord, . in° him   walk,

τεῖτε, 7 ἐρριζωμένοι καὶ ἐποικοδομούμενοι ἐν αὐτῷ, καὶ
having been rooted and   being built up   in   him,   and

βεβαιούμενοι ᵃἐν‖ τῇ πίστει, καθὼς ἐδιδάχθητε, περισσεύοντες
being confirmed   in the faith,   even as ye were taught,   abounding

ᵇἐν αὐτῇ᾽ ἐν εὐχαριστίᾳ.
in   it   with thanksgiving.

8 Βλέπετε μή τις ᶜὑμᾶς ἔσται‖ ὁ συλαγωγῶν
Take ʰeed lest ⁴anyone ¹⁰you ¹there ²shall ³be ⁸who ⁶makes ⁷a ³prey ⁵of

διὰ τῆς φιλοσοφίας καὶ κενῆς ἀπάτης, κατὰ τὴν παρά-
through   philosophy   and empty   deceit,   according to the   tra-

δοσιν τῶν ἀνθρώπων, κατὰ τὰ στοιχεῖα τοῦ κόσμου, καὶ
dition   of men,   according to the elements of the world, and

οὐ κατὰ χριστόν· 9 ὅτι ἐν αὐτῷ κατοικεῖ πᾶν τὸ πλήρωμα
not according to Christ.   For in him   dwells   all   the   fulness

τῆς θεότητος σωματικῶς,᾽10 καί ἐστε ἐν αὐτῷ πεπληρωμένοι·
of the Godhead   bodily;   and ye are ²in ³him   ¹complete,

ᵈὅς‖ ἐστιν ἡ κεφαλὴ πάσης ἀρχῆς καὶ ἐξουσίας· 11 ἐν ᾧ
who   is   the head   of all principality and authority,   in whom

καὶ περιετμήθητε περιτομῇ ἀχειροποιήτῳ, ἐν τῇ ἀπ-
also ye were circumcised with circumcision not made by hand, in the put-

εκδύσει τοῦ σώματος ᵉτῶν ἁμαρτιῶν‖ τῆς σαρκός, ἐν τῇ περι-
ting off of the   body   of the sins   of the flesh,   in the circum-

τομῇ τοῦ χριστοῦ, 12 συνταφέντες αὐτῷ ἐν τῷ ᶠβαπτίσματι·‖
cision of the Christ;   having been buried with him   in   baptism,

ἐν ᾧ καὶ συνηγέρθητε διὰ τῆς πίστεως τῆς ἐνερ-
in which also ye were raised with [him] through the   faith   of the work-

γείας τοῦ θεοῦ τοῦ ἐγείραντος αὐτὸν ἐκ ᵍτῶν‖ νεκρῶν.
ing   of God who   raised   him from among the   dead.

13 καὶ ὑμᾶς νεκροὺς ὄντας ʰἐν‖ τοῖς παραπτώμασιν καὶ τῇ
And you,   ²dead ¹being in   offences   and in the

ἀκροβυστίᾳ τῆς.σαρκὸς.ὑμῶν, ⁱσυνεζωποίησεν‖ ᵏ σὺν αὐτῷ,
uncircumcision   of your flesh,   he quickened together   with him,

together in love, and unto all riches of the full assurance of understanding, to the acknowledgement of the mystery of God, and of the Father, and of Christ ; 3 in whom are hid all the treasures of wisdom and knowledge. 4 And this I say, lest any man should beguile you with enticing words. 5 For though I be absent in the flesh, yet am I with you in the spirit, joying and beholding your order, and the stedfastness of your faith in Christ. 6 As ye have therefore received Christ Jesus the Lord, so walk ye in him : 7 rooted and built up in him, and stablished in the faith, as ye have been taught, abounding therein with thanksgiving.

8 Beware lest any man spoil you through philosophy and vain deceit, after the tradition of men, after the rudiments of the world, and not after Christ. 9 For in him dwelleth all the fulness of the Godhead bodily. 10 And ye are complete in him, which is the head of all principality and power : 11 in whom also ye are circumcised with the circumcision made without hands, in putting off the body of the sins of the flesh by the circumcision of Christ : 12 buried with him in baptism, wherein also ye are risen with him through the faith of the operation of God, who hath raised him from the dead. 13 And you, being dead in your sins and the uncircumcision of your flesh, hath he quickened together with him, having for-

---

ᵃ συμβιβασθέντες GLTTrAW.   ᵗ πᾶν (+ τὸ the l.[Tr]w) πλοῦτος LTTrAW.   ᵛ — καὶ πατρὸς καὶ τοῦ (read [even] Christ) GLTTrAW.   ʷ — χριστοῦ GA.   ˣ — τῆς LTTr.   ʸ — δὲ and T[Tr A].   ᶻ μηδεὶς LTTrAW.   ᵃ — ἐν (read τῇ in the) LTTr[A].   ᵇ — ἐν αὐτῇ TTr[A].   ᶜ ἔσται ὑμᾶς L.   ᵈ ὅ L.   ᵉ — τῶν ἁμαρτιῶν GLTTrAW.   ᶠ βαπτισμῷ TrA.   ᵍ — τῶν (read [the]) UT[A]w.   ʰ — ἐν (read παραπ. in offences) TTr.   ⁱ συνεζωοποίησεν GLTTrAW.   ᵏ + ὑμᾶς you LTTrAW.

given you all trespasses ; 14 blotting out the handwriting of ordinances that was against us, which was contrary to us, and took it out of the way, nailing it to his cross ; 15 *and* having spoiled principalities and powers, he made a shew of them openly, triumphing over them in it.

χαρισάμενος ¹ἡμῖν‖ πάντα τὰ παραπτώματα· 14 ἐξαλείψας
having forgiven us all the offences ; having blotted out
τὸ καθ᾽ ἡμῶν χειρόγραφον τοῖς δόγμασιν, ὃ ἦν ὑπεναν-
the ᵍagainst ⁶us ¹handwriting ²in ³the ⁴decrees, which was adverse
τίον ἡμῖν, καὶ αὐτὸ ἦρκεν ἐκ τοῦ μέσου, προσηλώσας
to us, also it he has taken out of the midst, having nailed
αὐτὸ τῷ σταυρῷ, 15 ἀπεκδυσάμενος τὰς ἀρχὰς καὶ τὰς
it to the cross ; having stripped the principalities and the
ἐξουσίας ἐδειγμάτισεν ἐν.παῤῥησίᾳ, θριαμβεύσας
authorities, he made a show [of them] publicly, leading in triumph
αὐτοὺς ἐν αὐτῷ.
them in it.

16 Let no man therefore judge you in meat, or in drink, or in respect of an holyday, or of the new moon, or of the sabbath *days*: 17 which are a shadow of things to come ; but the body *is* of Christ. 18 Let no man beguile you of your reward in a voluntary humility and worshipping of angels, intruding into those things which he hath not seen, vainly puffed up by his fleshly mind, 19 and not holding the Head, from which all the body by joints and bands having nourishment ministered, and knit together, increaseth with the increase of God.

16 Μὴ οὖν τις ὑμᾶς κρινέτω ἐν βρώσει ᵐἢ‖ ἐν πόσει,
²Not ³therefore ⁴anyone ⁵you ¹let ⁵judge in meat or in drink,
ἢ ἐν μέρει ἑορτῆς ἢ ⁿνουμηνίας‖ ἢ σαββάτων· 17 °ἅ‖ ἐστιν
or in respect of feast, or new moon, or sabbaths· which are
σκιὰ τῶν.μελλόντων, τὸ.δὲ σῶμα ᴾτοῦ‖ χριστοῦ. 18 μη-
a shadow of things to come ; but the body [is] of the Christ. ²No
δεὶς ὑμᾶς καταβραβευέτω θέλων ἐν ταπεινοφροσύνῃ καὶ
³one ⁵you ¹let ⁴defraud of the prize, doing [his] will in humility and
ᵠθρησκείᾳ‖ τῶν ἀγγέλων, ἃ ˢμὴ‖ ˢἑώρακεν‖ ἐμβατεύων,
worship of the angels, ³things ⁴which ⁷not ⁶he ⁸has ⁸seen ¹intruding ²into,
εἰκῇ φυσιούμενος ὑπὸ τοῦ νοὸς τῆς.σαρκὸς.αὐτοῦ, 19 καὶ οὐ
vainly puffed up ' by the mind of his flesh, and not
κρατῶν τὴν κεφαλήν, ἐξ οὗ πᾶν τὸ σῶμα διὰ τῶν ἁφῶν
holding fast the head, from whom all the body by the joints
καὶ συνδέσμων ἐπιχορηγούμενον καὶ ᵗσυμβιβαζόμενον,‖ αὔξει
and bands being supplied and knit together, increases
τὴν αὔξησιν τοῦ θεοῦ.
[with] the increase of God.

20 Wherefore if ye be dead with Christ from the rudiments of the world, why, as though living in the world, are ye subject to ordinances, 21 (Touch not ; taste not ; handle not ; 22 which all are to perish with the using ;) after the commandments and doctrines of men ? 23 which things have indeed a shew of wisdom in will worship, and humility, and neglecting of the body ; not in any honour to the satisfying of the flesh.

20 Εἰ ᵛοὖν‖ ἀπεθάνετε σὺν ʷτῷ‖ χριστῷ ἀπὸ τῶν στοιχείων
If then ye died with the Christ from the elements
τοῦ κόσμου, τί ὡς ζῶντες ἐν κόσμῳ δογματί-
of the world, why as if alive in [the] world do ye subject yourselves
ζεσθε ; ˣ 21 Μὴ.ἅψῃ, μηδὲ.γεύσῃ, μηδὲ.θίγῃς·
to decrees ? Thou mayest not handle, Thou mayest not taste, Thou mayest not touch,
22 ἅ ἐστιν πάντα εἰς φθορὰν τῇ ἀποχρήσει· κατὰ
(which things are all unto corruption in the using,) according to
τὰ ἐντάλματα καὶ διδασκαλίας τῶν ἀνθρώπων· ˣ 23 ἅτινά
the injunctions and teachings of men, which
ἐστιν λόγον μὲν ἔχοντα σοφίας ἐν ʸἐθελοθρησκείᾳ‖
are ²an ³appearance ⁴indeed ¹having of wisdom in • voluntary worship
καὶ ταπεινοφροσύνῃ ᶻκαὶ‖ ᵃἀφειδίᾳ‖ σώματος, οὐκ ἐν
and humility and unsparing treatment of [the] body, not in
τιμῇ τινι πρὸς πλησμονὴν τῆς σαρκός.ˣ
³honour ¹a ²certain for satisfaction of the flesh.

III. If ye then be risen with Christ, seek those things which are above, where Christ sitteth on the right hand of God. 2 Set your affection on things above, not on things on the earth. 3 For ye are dead, and

3 Εἰ οὖν συνηγέρθητε τῷ.χριστῷ, τὰ ἄνω ζητεῖτε,
If therefore ye were raised with Christ, ²the ³things ⁴above ¹seek,
οὗ ὁ χριστός ἐστιν ἐν δεξιᾷ τοῦ θεοῦ καθήμενος·
where the Christ is ²at [³the] ⁴right ⁵hand ⁶of ⁷God ¹sitting :
2 τὰ ἄνω φρονεῖτε, μὴ τὰ ἐπὶ τῆς γῆς. 3 ἀπεθάνετε
⁹the ¹⁰things ¹¹above ⁸mind, not the things on the earth ; ²ye ³died

---

¹ ὑμῖν you E. ᵐ καὶ and A. ⁿ νεομηνίας LTr. ° ὅ LA. ᴾ — τοῦ (*read of* Christ) GW.
ᵠ θρησκίᾳ T. ʳ — μὴ (*read* ἐμβ. ¹standing ²on) [L]TTɪA. ˢ ἑόρακεν TA. ᵗ συν- TA.
ᵛ — οὖν GLTTɪAW. ʷ — τῷ GLTTɪAW. ˣ *Continue question to end of verse* 21 GW ; *to end
of verse* 22LT ; *to end of verse* 23 A. ʸ ἐθελοθρησκίᾳ T. ᶻ [καὶ] L. ᵃ ἀφειδείᾳ L.

γάρ, καὶ ἡ.ζωὴ.ὑμῶν κέκρυπται σὺν τῷ χριστῷ ἐν τῷ θεῷ·
for, and your life has been hid with the Christ in   God.

4 ὅταν ὁ χριστὸς φανερωθῇ ἡ.ζωὴ.ᵇἡμῶν,‖ τότε καὶ
When the Christ ²may ⁴be ⁵manifested ¹our ²life, then also

ὑμεῖς σὺν αὐτῷ φανερωθήσεσθε ἐν δόξῃ.
ye with him shall be manifested in glory.

5 Νεκρώσατε οὖν τὰ μέλη ᶜὑμῶν‖ τὰ ἐπὶ τῆς γῆς,
Put to death therefore ²members ¹your which [are] on the earth,

πορνείαν, ἀκαθαρσίαν, πάθος, ἐπιθυμίαν κακήν, καὶ τὴν
fornication, uncleanness, passion, ²desire ¹evil, and

πλεονεξίαν, ἥτις ἐστὶν εἰδωλολατρεία, 6 δι'   ᵈἃ‖
covetousness, which is idolatry. On account of which things

ἔρχεται ᵉἡ‖ ὀργὴ τοῦ θεοῦ ᶠἐπὶ τοὺς υἱοὺς τῆς ἀπειθείας·‖
comes the wrath of God upon the sons of disobedience.

7 ἐν οἷς καὶ ὑμεῖς περιεπατήσατέ ποτε ὅτε ἐζῆτε ἐν
Among whom also ye walked once when ye were living in

ᵍαὐτοῖς·‖ 8 νυνὶ.δὲ ἀπόθεσθε καὶ ὑμεῖς τὰ.πάντα, ὀργήν,
these things. But now, put off also ye, all [these] things, wrath,

θυμόν, κακίαν, βλασφημίαν, αἰσχρολογίαν ἐκ τοῦ στόμα-
indignation, malice, blasphemy, foul language - out of ²mouth

τος ὑμῶν. 9 Μὴ.ψεύδεσθε εἰς ἀλλήλους, ἀπεκδυσάμενοι τὸν
¹your. Do not lie to one another, having put off the

παλαιὸν ἄνθρωπον σὺν ταῖς.πράξεσιν.αὐτοῦ, 10 καὶ ἐνδυσά-
old man with his deeds, and having

μενοι τὸν νέον τὸν ἀνακαινούμενον εἰς ἐπίγνωσιν κατ'
put on the new that [is] being renewed into knowledge according to

εἰκόνα τοῦ κτίσαντος αὐτόν· 11 ὅπου οὐκ.ἔνι
[the] image of him who created him; where there is not

Ἕλλην καὶ Ἰουδαῖος, περιτομὴ καὶ ἀκροβυστία, βάρβαρος,
Greek and Jew, circumcision and uncircumcision, barbarian,

Σκύθης, δοῦλος, ʰἐλεύθερος· ἀλλὰ ¹τὰ‖.πάντα καὶ ἐν πᾶσιν
Scythian, bondman, free; but ³all ⁴things ⁵and ⁶in ⁷all

χριστός.
[²is] ¹Christ.

12 Ἐνδύσασθε οὖν, ὡς ἐκλεκτοὶ ᵏτοῦ‖ θεοῦ, ἅγιοι καὶ
Put on therefore, as elect of God, holy and

ἠγαπημένοι, σπλάγχνα ¹οἰκτιρμῶν,‖ χρηστότητα, ταπεινο-
beloved, bowels of compassions, kindness, -humi-

φροσύνην, ᵐπρᾳότητα,‖ μακροθυμίαν· 13 ἀνεχόμενοι ἀλ-
lity, meekness, long-suffering; bearing with one

λήλων, καὶ χαριζόμενοι ἑαυτοῖς, ἐάν τις πρός τινα ἔχῃ
another, and forgiving each other, if any against any should have

μομφήν· καθὼς καὶ ὁ ⁿχριστὸς‖ ἐχαρίσατο ὑμῖν, οὕτως καὶ
a complaint; even as also the Christ forgave you, so also [do]

ὑμεῖς· 14 ἐπὶ.πᾶσιν.δὲ τούτοις τὴν ἀγάπην, ᵒἥτις‖ ἐστὶν
ye. And to all these [add] love, which is [the]

σύνδεσμος τῆς τελειότητος· 15 καὶ ἡ εἰρήνη ᴾτοῦ θεοῦ‖ βρα-
bond of perfectness. And the peace of God let

βευέτω ἐν ταῖς.καρδίαις.ὑμῶν, εἰς ἣν καὶ ἐκλήθητε ἐν ἑνὶ σώ-
preside in your hearts, to which also ye were called in one

ματι· καὶ εὐχάριστοι γίνεσθε. 16 ὁ λόγος τοῦ χριστοῦ ἐνοικείτω
body, and thankful be. The word of the Christ let dwell

your life is hid with Christ in God. 4 When Christ, *who is* our life, shall appear, then shall ye also appear with him in glory.

5 Mortify therefore your members which are upon the earth; fornication, uncleanness, inordinate affection, evil concupiscence, and covetousness, which is idolatry: 6 for which things' sake the wrath of God cometh on the children of disobedience : 7 in the which ye also walked some time, when ye lived in them. 8 But now ye also put off all these ; anger, wrath, malice, blasphemy, filthy communication out of your mouth. 9 Lie not one to another, seeing that ye have put off the old man with his deeds ; 10 and have put on the new *man*, which is renewed in knowledge after the image of him that created him . 11 where there is neither Greek nor Jew, circumcision nor uncircumcision, Barbarian, Scythian, bond *nor* free : but Christ *is* all, and in all.

12 Put on therefore, as the elect of God, holy and beloved, bowels of mercies, kindness, humbleness of mind, meekness, longsuffering ; 13 forbearing one another, and forgiving one another, if any man have a quarrel against any : even as Christ forgave you, so also do ye. 14 And above all these things *put on* charity, which is the bond of perfectness. 15 And let the peace of God rule in your hearts, to the which also ye are called in one body ; and be ye thankful. 16 Let the word of Christ dwell in you richly in all

ᵇ ὑμῶν (*read* your life) ᴛᴛʀ.   ᶜ — ὑμῶν (*read* the members) ᴛᴛʀᴀ.   ᵈ ὃ which ᴀ.
ᵉ [ἡ] ʟ.   ᶠ — ἐπὶ τοὺς υἱοὺς τῆς ἀπειθείας (*read* ἐν οἷς In which things) [ʟ]ᴛᴛʀᴀ.   ᵍ τούτοις ʟᴛᴛʀᴀᴡ.   ʰ + καὶ and ʟ.   ⁱ — τὰ ᴛ.   ᵏ — τοῦ ʟ.   ¹ οἰκτιρμοῦ of compassion
ɢʟᴛᴛʀᴀᴡ.   ᵐ πραΰτητα ʟᴛᴛʀᴀᴡ.   ⁿ κύριος Lord ʟᴛʀᴀ.   ᵒ ὅ ʟᴛᴛʀᴀᴡ.   ᴾ τοῦ χριστοῦ
of the Christ ɢʟᴛᴛʀᴀᴡ.

wisdom; teaching and admonishing one another in psalms and hymns and spiritual songs, singing with grace in your hearts to the Lord. 17 And whatsoever ye do in word or deed, *do* all in the name of the Lord Jesus, giving thanks to God and the Father by him.

ἐν ὑμῖν πλουσίως, ἐν πάσῃ σοφίᾳ· διδάσκοντες καὶ νουθε-
in you   richly,   in all wisdom;   teaching   and admon-
τοῦντες ἑαυτοὺς ψαλμοῖς ᵠκαὶ‖ ὕμνοις ʳκαὶ‖ ᾠδαῖς, πνευματι-
ishing   each other   in psalms   and   hymns   and   ᵇsongs   ¹spiritual
καῖς ἐν ˢχάριτι ᾄδοντες ἐν ᵗτῇ καρδίᾳ‖ ὑμῶν ᵛτῷ κυρίῳ·‖
  with grace singing in   ᶻheart   ¹your to the Lord.
17 καὶ   πᾶν   ὅ.τι.ʷἂν‖ ποιῆτε ἐν λόγῳ ἢ ἐν ἔργῳ,   πάντα
And everything, whatsoever ye may do in word or in work, [do]   all
ἐν ὀνόματι ˣκυρίου Ἰησοῦ,‖ εὐχαριστοῦντες τῷ θεῷ ʸκαὶ‖
in [the] name   of [the] Lord Jesus,   giving thanks   to God and
πατρὶ δι' αὐτοῦ.
[the] Father by   him.

18 Wives, submit yourselves unto your own husbands, as it is fit in the Lord. 19 Husbands, love *your* wives, and be not bitter against them. 20 Children, obey *your* parents in all things: for this is well pleasing unto the Lord. 21 Fathers, provoke not your children *to anger*, lest they be discouraged. 22 Servants, obey in all things *your* masters according to the flesh; not with eyeservice, as menpleasers; but in singleness of heart, fearing God: 23 and whatsoever ye do, do *it* heartily, as to the Lord, and not unto men; 24 knowing that of the Lord ye shall receive the reward of the inheritance: for ye serve the Lord Christ. 25 But he that doeth wrong shall receive for the wrong which he hath done: and there is no respect of persons. IV. Masters, give unto *your* servants that which is just and equal; knowing that ye also have a Master in heaven.

18 Αἱ γυναῖκες, ὑποτάσσεσθε τοῖς·ᶻἰδίοις‖ ἀνδράσιν, ὡς
   Wives,   subject yourselves to your own   husbands,   as
ἀνῆκεν ἐν κυρίῳ. 19 Οἱ ἄνδρες, ἀγαπᾶτε τὰς γυναῖκαςᵃ
is becoming in [the] Lord.   Husbands,. love   the   wives,
καὶ μὴ.πικραίνεσθε πρὸς αὐτάς. 20 Τὰ τέκνα, ὑπακούετε
and   be not bitter   against them.   Children,   obey
τοῖς γονεῦσιν κατὰ.πάντα· τοῦτο.γὰρ ᵇἐστιν εὐάρεστον‖ ᶜτῷ‖
the parents /in all things;   for this   is well-pleasing to the
κυρίῳ. 21 Οἱ πατέρες, μὴ.ᵈἐρεθίζετε‖ τὰ.τέκνα.ὑμῶν, ἵνα μὴ
Lord.   Fathers,   do not provoke   your children,   that ᶻnot
ἀθυμῶσιν. 22 Οἱ δοῦλοι, ὑπακούετε. κατὰ.πάντα τοῖς
¹they ᶻbe disheartened.   Bondmen,   obey   in all things   the
κατὰ   σάρκα κυρίοις, μὴ ἐν ᵉὀφθαλμοδουλείαις‖ ὡς ἀν-
²according ³to ⁴flesh   ¹masters, not with   eye-services,   as
θρωπάρεσκοι, ᶠἀλλ'‖ ἐν ἁπλότητι καρδίας, φοβούμενοι ᵍτὸν
men-pleasers,   but   in simplicity of heart,   fearing
θεόν.‖ 23 ʰκαὶ πᾶν.ὅ.τι‖ ἐὰν ποιῆτε, ἐκ.ψυχῆς ἐργάζεσθε, ὡς
God.   And whatsoever   ye may do, ᶻheartily   ᵗwork,   aᶻ
τῷ κυρίῳ καὶ οὐκ ἀνθρώποις· 24 εἰδότες ὅτι ἀπὸ κυρίου
to the Lord and not   to men;   knowing that from [the] Lord
ⁱἀπολήψεσθε‖ τὴν ἀνταπόδοσιν τῆς·κληρονομίας· τῷ.ᵏγὰρ‖
ye shall receive   the recompense   of the inheritance,   for the
κυρίῳ χριστῷ δουλεύετε. 25 ὁ.ᵈδὲ‖   ἀδικῶν ᵐκομιεῖται·
Lord Christ   ye serve.   But he that does wrong shall receive [for]
ὃ ἠδίκησεν, καὶ οὐκ.ἔστιν ⁿπροσωποληψία.‖ 4 Οἱ κύριοι,
what he did wrong, and there is no   respect of persons.   Masters,
τὸ   δίκαιον καὶ τὴν   ἰσότητα τοῖς δούλοις
that which [is] just and that which [is] equal   to bondmen
παρέχεσθε, εἰδότες ὅτι καὶ ὑμεῖς ἔχετε κύριον ἐν   οὐρανοῖς.‖
give,   knowing that also ye   have a Master in [the] heavens.

2 Continue in prayer, and watch in the same with thanksgiving; 3 withal praying also for us, that God would open unto us a door of utterance, to speak the mystery of Christ, for which I am also in bonds: 4 that I may make it manifest,

2 Τῇ προσευχῇ προσκαρτερεῖτε, γρηγοροῦντες ἐν αὐτῇ ἐν
  In prayer stedfastly continue,   watching   in it   with
εὐχαριστίᾳ· 3 προσευχόμενοι ἅμα .καὶ περὶ ἡμῶν, ἵνα ὁ θεὸς
thanksgiving;   praying   withal also for us, that God
ἀνοίξῃ ἡμῖν θύραν τοῦ λόγου λαλῆσαι τὸ μυστήριον τοῦ
may open to us   a door of the word   to speak   the   mystery   of the
χριστοῦ,   δι'   ρᵒ‖ καὶ   δέδεμαι,   4 ἵνα   φανε-
Christ,   on account of which also I have been bound,   that   I may make

ᵠ — καὶ LTTrAW.   ʳ — καὶ LTTrAW.   ˢ + τῇ LTTrAW.   ᵗ ταῖς καρδίαις hearts GLTTrAW.   ᵛ τῷ θεῷ to God GLTTrAW.   ʷ ἐὰν LTr.   ˣ Ἰησοῦ χριστοῦ of Jesus Christ LW.   ʸ — καὶ LTTrAW.   ᶻ — ἰδίοις (*read* to the husbands) GLTTrAW.   ᵃ + ὑμῶν (*read* your wives) L.   ᵇ εὐάρεστόν ἐστιν LTTrA.   ᶜ ἐν in [the] GLTTrAW.   ᵈ παροργίζετε L.   ᵉ ὀφθαλμοδουλεία eye-service LW; ὀφθαλμοδουλίαις T.   ᶠ ἀλλὰ Tr.   ᵍ τὸν κύριον the Lord GLTTrAW.   ʰ ὃ (*read* whatever) LTTrAW   ⁱ ἀπολήμψεσθε LTTrA. ·   ᵏ — γὰρ for LTTrAW.   ˡ γὰρ (*read* for he that) LTTrAW.   ᵐ κομίσεται L.   ⁿ προσωπολημψία LTTrA.   ᵒ οὐρανῷ heaven LTTrAW.   ᵖ ὃν whom L.

ρώσω αὐτὸ ὡς δεῖ με λαλῆσαι. 5 Ἐν σοφίᾳ περιπατεῖτε
manifest it as it behoves me to speak. In wisdom walk

πρὸς τοὺς ἔξω, τὸν καιρὸν ἐξαγοραζόμενοι. 6 ὁ λόγος
towards those without, ²the ³time ¹ransoming. [Let] ²word

ὑμῶν πάντοτε ἐν χάριτι, ἅλατι ἠρτυμένος, εἰδέναι πῶς
¹your [be] always with grace, ²with ³salt ¹seasoned, to know how

δεῖ ὑμᾶς ἑνὶ.ἑκάστῳ ἀποκρίνεσθαι.
it behoves you ³each ⁴one ¹to ²answer.

7 Τὰ κατ' ἐμὲ πάντα γνωρίσει ὑμῖν Τυχικὸς
²The ³things ⁴concerning ⁵me ¹all ⁷will ⁵make ⁹known ¹⁰to ¹¹you ⁶Tychicus

ὁ ἀγαπητὸς ἀδελφὸς καὶ πιστὸς διάκονος καὶ ·σύνδουλος
the beloved ,brother and faithful servant and fellow-bondman

ἐν κυρίῳ, 8 ὃν ἔπεμψα πρὸς ὑμᾶς εἰς αὐτὸ.τοῦτο, ἵνα
in [the] Lord; whom I sent to you for this very thing, that

ᵖγνῷ‖ τὰ περὶ ʳὑμῶν‖ καὶ παρακαλέσῃ τὰς
he might know the things concerning you, and might encourage

καρδίας.ὑμῶν, 9 σὺν Ὀνησίμῳ, τῷ πιστῷ καὶ ἀγαπητῷ
your hearts; with Onesimus, the faithful and beloved

ἀδελφῷ, ὅς ἐστιν ἐξ ὑμῶν· πάντα ·ὑμῖν ˢγνωριοῦσιν‖
brother, who is of you. All things ²to ³you ⁴they ⁵will ⁶make ⁷known

τὰ ὧδε.
¹here.

10 Ἀσπάζεται ὑμᾶς Ἀρίσταρχος ὁ.συναιχμάλωτός.μου, καὶ
⁴Salutes ⁵you ¹Aristarchus ²my ³fellow-prisoner, and

Μάρκος ὁ ἀνεψιὸς Βαρνάβα, περὶ οὗ ἐλάβετε ἐντολάς·
Mark, the cousin of Barnabas, concerning whom ye received orders,

ἐὰν ἔλθῃ ᵗπρὸς ὑμᾶς, δέξασθε αὐτόν· 11 καὶ Ἰησοῦς ὁ λεγό-
(if he come to you, receive him,) and Jesus called

μενος Ἰοῦστος, οἱ ὄντες ἐκ περιτομῆς· ᵗ οὗτοι μόνοι
Justus, who are of [the] circumcision. These [are the] only

συνεργοὶ εἰς τὴν βασιλείαν τοῦ θεοῦ, οἵτινες ἐγενήθησάν
fellow-workers for the kingdom of God, who were

μοι παρηγορία. 12 ἀσπάζεται ὑμᾶς Ἐπαφρᾶς ὁ ἐξ ὑμῶν
to me a consolation. ²Salutes ³you ¹Epaphras who [is] of you,

δοῦλος χριστοῦᵘ, πάντοτε ἀγωνιζόμενος ὑπὲρ ὑμῶν ἐν ταῖς
a bondman of Christ, always striving for you in

προσευχαῖς, ἵνα ᵛστῆτε‖ τέλειοι καὶ ʷπεπληρωμένοι‖ ἐν
prayers, that ye may stand perfect and complete in

παντὶ θελήματι τοῦ θεοῦ. 13 μαρτυρῶ.γὰρ αὐτῷ ὅτι ἔχει
every will of God. For I bear witness to him that he has

ˣζῆλον πολὺν‖ ὑπὲρ ὑμῶν καὶ τῶν ἐν ʸΛαοδικείᾳ‖ καὶ τῶν
²zeal ¹much for you and them in Laodicea and them

ἐν Ἱεραπόλει. 14 ἀσπάζεται ὑμᾶς Λουκᾶς ὁ ἰατρὸς ὁ ἀγα-
in Hierapolis. ⁵Salutes ⁶you ¹Luke ²the ³physician ³be-

πητός, καὶ Δημᾶς. 15 ἀσπάσασθε τοὺς ἐν ʸΛαοδικείᾳ‖ ἀδελ-
loved, and Demas. Salute the ²in ³Laodicea ¹breth-

φούς, καὶ ᶻΝυμφᾶν‖ καὶ τὴν κατ'.οἶκον.ᵃαὐτοῦ‖ ἐκκλησίαν·
ren, and· Nymphas, and the ⁴in ⁵his ⁶house ¹assembly.

16 καὶ ὅταν ἀναγνωσθῇ παρ' ὑμῖν ἡ ἐπιστολή, ποιήσατε
And when may be read among you , the epistle, cause

ἵνα καὶ ἐν τῇ Λαοδικέων ἐκκλησίᾳ ἀναγνωσθῇ, καὶ
that also in the ²of [³the] ⁴Laodiceans ¹assembly it may be read, and

---

as I ought to speak. 5 Walk in wisdom toward them that are without, redeeming the time. 6 Let your speech be alway with grace, seasoned with salt, that ye may know how ye ought to answer every man.

7 All my state shall Tychicus declare unto you, who is a beloved brother, and a faithful minister and fellowservant in the Lord : 8 whom I have sent unto you for the same purpose, that he might know your estate, and comfort your hearts ; 9 with Onesimus, a faithful and beloved brother, who is one of you. They shall make known unto you all things which are done here.

10 Aristarchus my fellowprisoner saluteth you, and Marcus, sister's son to Barnabas, (touching whom ye received commandments : if he come unto you, receive him ;) 11 and Jesus, which is called Justus, who are of the circumcision. These only are my fellowworkers unto the kingdom of God, which have been a comfort unto me. 12 Epaphras, who is one of you, a servant of Christ, saluteth you, always labouring fervently for you in prayers, that ye may stand perfect and complete in all the will of God. 13 For I bear him record, that he hath a great zeal for you, and them that are in Laodicea, and them in Hierapolis. 14 Luke, the beloved physician, and Demas, greet you. 15 Salute the brethren which are in Laodicea, and Nymphas, and the church which is in his house. 16 And when this epistle is read among you, cause that it be read also in the church of the Laodiceans ; and that ye

---

ᵖ γνῶτε ye might know LTTr. ʳ ἡμῶν us LTTr. ˢ γνωρίσουσιν L. ᵗ Punctuate so as to
read These only who are of the circumcision [are the] &c. LTA. ᵘ + Ἰησοῦ Jesus LTTrA.
ᵛ σταθῆτε TTr. ʷ πεπληροφορημένοι fully assured LTTrAW. ˣ πολὺν πόνον much labour
GLTTrA ; πόνον πολὺν W. ʸ Λαοδικία T. ᶻ Νύμφαν Nympha L. ᵃ αὐτῆς (read her
house) Lₑ αὐτῶν (read their house) TTrA.

likewise read the e-
pistle from Laodicea.
17 And say to Archip-
pus, Take heed to the
ministry which thou
hast received in the
Lord, that thou fulfil
it. 18 The salutation
by the hand of me
Paul. Remember my
bonds. Grace be with
you. Amen.

τὴν ἐκ ᵇΛαοδικείας‖ ἵνα καὶ ὑμεῖς ἀναγνῶτε· 17 καὶ εἴπατε
that from Laodicea that also ye may read. And say

Ἀρχίππῳ, Βλέπε τὴν διακονίαν ἣν παρέλαβες ἐν
to Archippus, Take heed to the ، service which thou didst receive in [the]

κυρίῳ, ἵνα αὐτὴν πληροῖς. 18 Ὁ ἀσπασμὸς τῇ.ἐμῇ.χειρὶ
Lord, that it thou fulfil. The salutation ³by ⁴my [⁵own] ⁶hand

Παύλου. μνημονεύετέ μου τῶν δεσμῶν. ἡ χάρις μεθ'
¹of ²Paul. Remember my bonds. Grace [be] with

ὑμῶν. ᶜἀμήν.‖
you. Amen.

ᵈΠρὸς Κολασσαεῖς ἐγράφη ἀπὸ Ῥώμης, διὰ Τυχικοῦ καὶ
To [the] Colossians written from Rome, by ، Tychicus and

Ὀνησίμου.‖
Onesimus.

ᵉΗ ΠΡΟΣ   ΘΕΣΣΑΛΟΝΙΚΕΙΣ ΕΠΙΣΤΟΛΗ ΠΑΥΛΟΥ
THE ⁵TO [⁶THE] ⁷THESSALONIANS   ²EPISTLE   ³OF ⁴PAUL

ΠΡΩΤΗ.⁰
¹FIRST.

PAUL, and Silvanus,
and Timotheus, unto
the church of the
Thessalonians which is
in God the Father and
in the Lord Jesus
Christ: Grace be unto
you, and peace, from
God our Father, and
the Lord Jesus Christ.

ΠΑΥΛΟΣ καὶ Σιλουανὸς καὶ Τιμόθεος, τῇ ἐκκλησίᾳ Θεσ-
Paul and Silvanus and Timotheus, to the assembly of Thes-

σαλονικέων ἐν θεῷ πατρὶ καὶ κυρίῳ Ἰησοῦ χριστῷ·
salonians in God [the] Father and [the] Lord Jesus Christ.

χάρις ὑμῖν καὶ εἰρήνη ᶠἀπὸ θεοῦ ᵖπατρὸς.ἡμῶν καὶ κυρίου
Grace to you and peace from God our Father and [the] Lord

Ἰησοῦ χριστοῦ.‖
Jesus Christ.

2 We give thanks to
God always for you
all, making mention
of you in our prayers;
3 remembering with-
out ceasing your work
of faith, and labour of
love, and patience of
hope in our Lord Je-
sus Christ, in the sight
of God and our Fa-
ther ; 4 knowing, bre-
thren beloved, your
election of God. 5 For
our gospel came not
unto you in word only,
but also in power, and
in the Holy Ghost, and
in much assurance; as
ye know what manner
of men we were a-
mong you for your
sake. 6 And ye be-
came followers of us,

2 Εὐχαριστοῦμεν τῷ θεῷ πάντοτε περὶ πάντων ὑμῶν,
We give thanks to God always concerning all you,

μνείαν ᵍὑμῶν‖ ποιούμενοι ἐπὶ τῶν.προσευχῶν.ἡμῶν, 3 ἀδια-
¹mention ²of ⁴you ¹making at our prayers, un-

λείπτως μνημονεύοντες ὑμῶν τοῦ ἔργου τῆς πίστεως καὶ τοῦ
ceasingly remembering your work of faith and

κόπου τῆς ἀγάπης καὶ τῆς ὑπομονῆς τῆς ἐλπίδος τοῦ κυρίου
labour of love and endurance of hope of ¹Lord

ἡμῶν Ἰησοῦ χριστοῦ, ἔμπροσθεν τοῦ θεοῦ καὶ πατρὸς ἡμῶν·
¹our Jesus Christ, before ²God ³and ⁴Father our ;

4 εἰδότες, ἀδελφοὶ ἠγαπημένοι ὑπὸ ʰ θεοῦ, τὴν.ἐκλογὴν.ὑμῶν·
knowing, brethren beloved by God, your election.

5 ὅτι τὸ.εὐαγγέλιον.ἡμῶν οὐκ.ἐγενήθη ⁱεἰς‖ ὑμᾶς ἐν λόγῳ
Because our glad tidings came not to you in word

μόνον, ἀλλὰ καὶ ἐν δυνάμει καὶ ἐν πνεύματι ἁγίῳ, καὶ ᵏἐν‖
only, but also in power and in [the] ²Spirit ¹Holy, and in

πληροφορίᾳ πολλῇ, καθὼς οἴδατε οἷοι ἐγενήθημεν ˡἐν‖
²full ³assurance ¹much, even as ye know what we were among

ὑμῖν δι' ὑμᾶς. 6 καὶ ὑμεῖς μιμηταὶ ἡμῶν ἐγενήθητε
you for the sake of you: and ye imitators of us became

ᵇ Λαοδικίας T.   ᶜ — ἀμήν GLTTrAW.   ᵈ Πρὸς Κολοσσαεῖς &c. E; — the subscription
GLTW ; Πρὸς Κολασσαεῖς TrA.
 ᵉ + τοῦ Ἀποστόλου the apostle E ; Πρὸς Θεσσαλονικεις α΄ LTTrAW.   ᶠ — ἀπὸ θεοῦ to end
of verse [L]ᴛᴛrA.   ᵍ — ὑμῶν LTTr[A].   ʰ + τοῦ T.   ⁱ πρὸς L.   ᵏ — ἐν T[Tr].
ˡ ['ν] Tr.

καὶ - τοῦ κυρίου, δεξάμενοι τὸν λόγον ἐν θλίψει πολλῇ
and of the Lord, having accepted the word in ²tribulation ¹much

μετὰ χαρᾶς πνεύματος ἁγίου, 7 ὥστε γενέσθαι ὑμᾶς ᵐτύπους‖
with joy of [the] ²Spirit ¹Holy, so that ²became ¹ye patterns

πᾶσιν τοῖς πιστεύουσιν ἐν τῇ Μακεδονίᾳ καὶ ⁿ τῇ Ἀχαΐᾳ.
to all those believing in Macedonia and Achaia :

8 ἀφ᾽.ὑμῶν.γὰρ ἐξήχηται ὁ λόγος τοῦ κυρίου οὐ μόνον ἐν
for from you has sounded out the word of the Lord not only in

τῇ Μακεδονίᾳ καὶ º Ἀχαΐᾳ, ᴾἀλλὰ‖ �qκαὶ‖ ἐν παντὶ τόπῳ ἡ
Macedonia and Achaia, but also in every place

ⁱπίστις.ὑμῶν ἡ πρὸς τὸν θεὸν ἐξελήλυθεν, ὥστε μὴ
your faith which [is] towards God has gone abroad, so as ²no

χρείαν ʳἡμᾶς.ἔχειν‖ λαλεῖν τι· 9 αὐτοὶ.γὰρ περὶ
⁶need ¹for ²us ³to ⁴have to say anything ; for themselves concerning

ἡμῶν ἀπαγγέλλουσιν ὁποίαν εἴσοδον ˢἔχομεν‖ πρὸς ὑμᾶς,
us relate what entrance in we have to you,

καὶ πῶς ἐπεστρέψατε πρὸς τὸν θεὸν ἀπὸ τῶν εἰδώλων, δου-
and how ye turned to God from idols, to

λεύειν θεῷ ζῶντι καὶ ἀληθινῷ, 10 καὶ ἀναμένειν τὸν υἱὸν
serve a ⁴God ¹living ²and ³true, and to await ²Son

αὐτοῦ ἐκ τῶν οὐρανῶν, ὃν ἤγειρεν .ἐκ ᵗ νεκρῶν, Ἰη-
¹his from the heavens, whom he raised from among [the] dead— Je-

σοῦν τὸν ῥυόμενον ἡμᾶς ᵛἀπὸ‖ τῆς ὀργῆς τῆς ἐρχομένης.
sus, who delivers us from the ²wrath ¹coming.

2 Αὐτοὶ.γὰρ οἴδατε, ἀδελφοί, τὴν.εἴσοδον.ἡμῶν τὴν
For ²yourselves ¹ye know, brethren, our entrance in which [we had]

πρὸς ὑμᾶς, ὅτι οὐ κενὴ γέγονεν. 2 ἀλλὰ ʷκαὶ‖ προπαθόν-
to you, that not void it has been ; but also having before suf-

τες καὶ ὑβρισθέντες, καθὼς οἴδατε, ἐν Φιλίπποις, ἐπαρ-
fered and having been insulted, even as ye know, at Philippi, we

ρησιασάμεθα ἐν τῷ.θεῷ.ἡμῶν λαλῆσαι πρὸς ὑμᾶς τὸ εὐαγγέλιον
were bold in our God to speak to you the glad tidings

τοῦ θεοῦ ἐν πολλῷ ἀγῶνι. 3 Ἡ γὰρ παράκλησις ἡμῶν οὐκ
of God in much conflict. For ²exhortation ¹our [was] not

ἐκ πλάνης, οὐδὲ ἐξ ἀκαθαρσίας, ˣοὔτε‖ ἐν δόλῳ, 4 ἀλλὰ καθὼς
of error, nor of uncleanness, nor in guile ; but even as

δεδοκιμάσμεθα ὑπὸ τοῦ θεοῦ πιστευθῆναι τὸ εὐαγγέλιον,
we have been approved by God to be entrusted with the glad tidings,

οὕτως λαλοῦμεν, οὐχ ὡς ἀνθρώποις ἀρέσκοντες, ἀλλὰ ʸτῷ‖
so we speak ; not as ²men ¹pleasing, but

θεῷ, τῷ δοκιμάζοντι τὰς καρδίας ᶻἡμῶν.‖ 5 Οὔτε.γὰρ ποτε
God, who proves the hearts of us. For neither at any time

ἐν λόγῳ ᵃκολακείας‖ ἐγενήθημεν, καθὼς οἴδατε, οὔτε
with word of flattery were we [with you], even as ye know, nor

ἐν προφάσει πλεονεξίας, θεὸς μάρτυς, 6 οὔτε ζητοῦντες
with a pretext of covetousness, God [is] witness ; nor seeking

ἐξ ἀνθρώπων δόξαν, οὔτε ἀφ᾽ ὑμῶν οὔτε ἀπ᾽ ἄλλων,
from men glory, neither from you nor from others, [though]

δυνάμενοι ἐν.βάρει εἶναι ὡς χριστοῦ ἀπόστολοι· 7 ᵇἀλλ᾽‖
having power ³burdensome ¹to ²be as Christ's apostles ; but

ἐγενήθημεν ᶜἤπιοι‖ ἐν μέσῳ.ὑμῶν, ὡς ᵈἂν‖ τροφὸς θάλπῃ
we were gentle in your midst, as a nurse would cherish

and of the Lord, hav-
ing received the word
in much affliction,
with joy of the Holy
Ghost : 7 so that ye
were ensamples to all
that believe in Mace-
donia and Achaia.
8 For from you sound-
ed out the word of the
Lord not only in Ma-
cedonia and Achaia,
but also in every place
your faith to God-
ward is spread abroad ;
so that we need not
to speak any thing.
9 For they themselves
shew of us what man-
ner of entering in we
had unto you, and how
ye turned to God from
idols to serve the liv-
ing and true God ;
10 and to wait for
his Son from heaven,
whom he raised from
the dead, even Jesus,
which delivered us
from the wrath to
come.

II. For yourselves,
brethren, know our
entrance in unto you,
that it was not in
vain : 2 but even after
that we had suffered
before, and were
shamefully entreated,
as ye know, at Phi-
lippi, we were bold in
our God to speak unto
you the gospel of God
with much contention.
3 For our exhortation
was not of deceit, nor
of uncleanness, nor in
guile : 4 but as we
were allowed of God
to be put in trust with
the gospel, even so we
speak ; not as pleasing
men, but God, which
trieth our hearts. 5 For
neither at any time
used we flattering
words, as ye know,
nor a cloke of covet-
ousness ; God is wit-
ness : 6 nor of men
sought we glory, nei-
ther of you, nor yet of
others, when we might
have been burden-
some, as the apostles
of Christ. 7 But we
were gentle among
you, even as a nurse
cherisheth her chil-

ᵐ τύπον a pattern LTTrAW.   ⁿ + ἐν in LTTrAW.   º + ἐν (in) τῇ LT.   ᴾ ἀλλ᾽ LA.
q — καὶ LTTrAW.   ʳ ἔχειν ἡμᾶς LTTrAW.   ˢ ἔσχομεν we had GLTTrAW.   ᵗ + τῶν the
GLTT:A.   ᵛ ἐκ out of TTr.   ʷ — καὶ GLTTrAW.   ˣ οὐδὲ LTTrAW.   ʸ — τῷ [L]TTrA.
ὑμῶν of you W.   ᵃ κολακίας T.   ᵇ ἀλλὰ TTr.   ᶜ νήπιοι simple L.   ᵈ ἐὰν LTTιA.

dren : 8 so being affectionately desirous of you, we were willing to have imparted unto you, not the gospel of God only, but also our own souls, because ye were dear unto us. 9 For ye remember, brethren, our labour and travail : for labouring night and day, because we would not be chargeable unto any of you, we preached unto you the gospel of God. 10 Ye *are* witnesses, and God *also*, how holily and justly and unblameably we behaved ourselves among you that believe : 11 as ye know how we exhorted and comforted and charged every one of you, as a father *doth* his children, 12 that ye would walk worthy of God, who hath called you unto his kingdom and glory. 13 For this cause also thank we God without ceasing, because, when ye received the word of God which ye heard of us, ye received *it* not *as* the word of men, but as it is in truth, the word of God, which effectually worketh also in you that believe. 14 For ye, brethren, became followers of the churches of God which in Judæa are in Christ Jesus : for ye also have suffered like things of your own countrymen, even as they *have* of the Jews: 15 who both killed the Lord Jesus, and their own prophets, and have persecuted us ; and they please. n** God, and are contrary ' to all 'men : 16 forbidding us to speak to the Gentiles that they might be saved, to fill up their sins alway : for the wrath is come upon them to the uttermost.

17 But we, brethren, being taken from you for a short time in

τὰ.ἑαυτῆς τέκνα. 8 οὕτως ᵉἱμειρόμενοι‖ ὑμῶν, εὐδοκοῦμεν
her own   children.   Thus   yearning over   you,   we were pleased

μεταδοῦναι ὑμῖν οὐ μόνον τὸ εὐαγγέλιον τοῦ θεοῦ, ἀλλὰ
to have imparted to you not   only   the   glad tidings   of God,   but

καὶ τὰς ἑαυτῶν ψυχάς, διότι ἀγαπητοὶ ἡμῖν ᶠγεγένησθε.‖
also our   own   lives,   because   beloved   to us ye have become.

9 μνημονεύετε.γάρ, ἀδελφοί, τὸν.κόπον.ἡμῶν καὶ τὸν μόχθον·
For ye remember,   brethren,   our labour   and the   'toil,

νυκτὸς.ᵍγὰρ‖ καὶ ἡμέρας ἐργαζόμενοι, πρὸς τὸ μὴ ἐπιβαρῆσαί
for night   and   day   working,   for   not   to burden

τινα ὑμῶν, ἐκηρύξαμεν εἰς ὑμᾶς τὸ εὐαγγέλιον τοῦ θεοῦ.
anyone of you, we proclaimed to   you   the   glad tidings   of God.

10 ὑμεῖς   μάρτυρες καὶ ὁ θεός, ὡς ὁσίως καὶ δικαίως καὶ
Ye [are]   witnesses, and   God, how   holily and righteously and

ἀμέμπτως ὑμῖν τοῖς πιστεύουσιν ἐγενήθημεν, 11 καθάπερ
blamelessly   with you that   believe   we were :   even as

οἴδατε, ὡς ἕνα.ἕκαστον ὑμῶν, ὡς πατὴρ τέκνα ἑαυτοῦ, παρα-
ye know, how   each one   of you, as a father ³children ¹his ²own,   ex-

καλοῦντες ὑμᾶς καὶ παραμυθούμενοι 12 καὶ ʰμαρτυρούμενοι,‖
horting   you   and   consoling   and   testifying,

εἰς τὸ ¹περιπατῆσαι‖ ὑμᾶς ἀξίως τοῦ θεοῦ τοῦ καλοῦντος
for   ²to ³have ⁴walked   ¹you worthily   of God,   who   calls

ὑμᾶς εἰς τὴν.ἑαυτοῦ βασιλείαν καὶ δόξαν. 13 ᵏ Διὰ   τοῦτο
you to   his own   kingdom   and   glory.   Because of this

καὶ ἡμεῖς εὐχαριστοῦμεν τῷ θεῷ ἀδιαλείπτως, ὅτι παραλα-
also we   give thanks   to God unceasingly,   that,   having re-

βόντες   λόγον ἀκοῆς παρ' ἡμῶν τοῦ θεοῦ ἐδέξασθε οὐ
ceived [the] word of [the] report ³by   ⁴us   ¹of ²God, ye accepted not

λόγον ἀνθρώπων, ἀλλὰ καθώς ἐστιν ἀληθῶς, λόγον θεοῦ, ὃς
²word   ¹men's,   but even as it is truly,   ²word ¹God's, which

καὶ ἐνεργεῖται ἐν ὑμῖν τοῖς πιστεύουσιν. 14 ὑμεῖς.γὰρ μιμηταὶ
also   works   in you who   believe.   For ye   imitators

ἐγενήθητε, ἀδελφοί, τῶν ἐκκλησιῶν τοῦ θεοῦ τῶν οὐσῶν ἐν τῇ
became,   brethren, of the assemblies   of God which are in

Ἰουδαίᾳ ἐν χριστῷ Ἰησοῦ, ὅτι ¹ταὐτὰ‖ ἐπάθετε καὶ ὑμεῖς
Judæa in Christ Jesus ; because the same things ³suffered ²also ¹ye

ὑπὸ τῶν.ἰδίων συμφυλετῶν καθὼς καὶ αὐτοὶ ὑπὸ τῶν Ἰου-
from your own   countrymen   as   also   they   from the Jews,

δαίων, 15 τῶν καὶ τὸν κύριον ἀποκτεινάντων Ἰησοῦν καὶ
who ²both ³the ⁴Lord   ¹killed   Jesus   and

τοὺς.ᵐἰδίους‖ προφήτας, καὶ ⁿὑμᾶς‖ ἐκδιωξάντων, καὶ θεῷ
their own   prophets,   and   ²you   ¹drove out,   and ⁴God

μὴ.ἀρεσκόντων, καὶ πᾶσιν ἀνθρώποις ἐναντίων, 16 κω-
¹do ⁵not ³please,   and   ⁴all   ³to ⁵men   [¹are] ²contrary,   for-

λυόντων ἡμᾶς τοῖς ἔθνεσιν λαλῆσαι ἵνα σωθῶσιν, εἰς
bidding   us   to the nations to speak that they may be saved, for

τὸ ἀναπληρῶσαι αὐτῶν τὰς ἁμαρτίας πάντοτε· ᵒἔφθασεν‖.δὲ
to fill up   their   sins   always :   but is come

ἐπ' αὐτοὺς ἡ ὀργὴ εἰς.τέλος.
upon them the wrath to the uttermost.

17 Ἡμεῖς.δὲ, ἀδελφοί, ἀπορφανισθέντες ἀφ' ὑμῶν πρὸς
But we,   brethren,   having been bereaved   of   you   for

ᵉ ὁμειρόμενοι GLTTrAW.   ᶠ ἐγενήθητε ye became LTTrAW.   ᵍ — γὰρ for GLTTrAW.
ʰ μαρτυρόμενοι TTrAW.   ¹ περιπατεῖν 'to 'walk LTTrAW.   ᵏ + καὶ and LTTᵢA.   ¹ τὰ
αὐτὰ ᴳLTTrAW.   ᵐ — ἰδίους (*read* the prophets) GLTTrAW   ⁿ ἡμᾶς us EGLTTrAW.
ᵒ ἔφθακεν has come L.

καιρὸν   ὥρας   προσώπῳ   οὐ καρδίᾳ,   περισσοτέρως   ἐσπου-
time   of an hour   in face,   not in heart,   more abundantly   were

δάσαμεν τὸ.πρόσωπον.ὑμῶν ἰδεῖν ἐν πολλῇ ἐπιθυμίᾳ· 18 ⁹διὸ‖
diligent   your face   to see with much   desire ;   wherefore

ἠθελήσαμεν ἐλθεῖν πρὸς ὑμᾶς, ἐγὼ μὲν Παῦλος καὶ ἅπαξ
we wished   to come to   you,   I indeed Paul,   both once

καὶ δίς, καὶ ἐνέκοψεν ἡμᾶς ὁ σατανᾶς. 19 τίς.γὰρ   ἡμῶν
and twice, and ²hindered   ·¹us   ¹Satan ;   for what [is] our

ἐλπὶς ἢ χαρὰ ἢ στέφανος καυχήσεως; ἢ   οὐχὶ καὶ ὑμεῖς
hope or joy or   crown   of boasting?   or [are] not even   ye

ἔμπροσθεν τοῦ.κυρίου.ἡμῶν Ἰησοῦ ˣχριστοῦ‖ ἐν τῇ αὐτοῦ
before   our Lord   Jesus   Christ   at   his

παρουσίᾳ ; 20 ὑμεῖς.γὰρ ἐστε ἡ.δόξα.ἡμῶν καὶ ἡ χαρά.
coming ?   for ye   are   our glory·   and   joy.

3 Διὸ   μηκέτι στέγοντες, ˢεὐδοκήσαμεν‖ καταλειφθῆναι
Wherefore no longer enduring,   we thought good   to be left

ἐν Ἀθήναις μόνοι, 2 καὶ ἐπέμψαμεν Τιμόθεον τὸν ἀδελφὸν
in Athens   alone,   and   sent   Timotheus   ²brother

ἡμῶν καὶ ᵗδιάκονον‖ τοῦ θεοῦ ᵛκαὶ συνεργὸν ἡμῶν‖ ἐν τῷ
¹our   and   servant   of God and ²fellow-worker ¹our   in the

εὐαγγελίῳ τοῦ χριστοῦ, εἰς τὸ στηρίξαι ὑμᾶς καὶ παρακαλέσαι
glad tidings of the Christ,   for   to establish you and to encourage

ʷὑμᾶς‖ ˣπερὶ‖ τῆς.πίστεως.ὑμῶν 3 ʸτῷ‖ ᶻμηδένα σαίνεσθαι‖
you   concerning   your faith   that   no one   be moved

ἐν ταῖς.θλίψεσιν ταύταις· αὐτοὶ.γὰρ οἴδατε ὅτι εἰς τοῦτο
by   these tribulations.   (For yourselves know that for this

κείμεθα· 4 καὶ.γὰρ ὅτε πρὸς ὑμᾶς ἦμεν, προελέγομεν ὑμῖν
we are set ;   for also, when with you we were, we told ²beforehand ¹you

ὅτι μέλλομεν   θλίβεσθαι,   καθὼς καὶ ἐγένετο καὶ οἴ-
we are about to suffer tribulation, even as also it came to pass, and ye

δατε· 5 διὰ τοῦτο κἀγὼ μηκέτι στέγων, ἔπεμψα εἰς τὸ
know.) Because of this·   I also no longer enduring,   sent   for

γνῶναι τὴν.πίστιν.ὑμῶν, μήπως ἐπείρασεν ὑμᾶς ὁ
to know   your faith,   lest perhaps ⁴did ⁵tempt ⁶you ¹he ²who

πειράζων, καὶ εἰς κενὸν γένηται ὁ.κόπος.ἡμῶν. 6 ἄρτι.δὲ
³tempts,   and   void should become   our labour.   But now

ἐλθόντος Τιμοθέου πρὸς ἡμᾶς ἀφ' ὑμῶν, καὶ εὐαγγελισα-
²having ³come ¹Timotheus to   us from you,   and having announced

μένου ἡμῖν τὴν πίστιν καὶ τὴν ἀγάπην ὑμῶν, καὶ ὅτι
glad tidings to us [of] ²faith ³and   ⁴love ¹your,   and that

ἔχετε μνείαν ἡμῶν ἀγαθὴν πάντοτε, ἐπιποθοῦντες ἡμᾶς
ye have ³remembrance ⁴of ⁵us ²good   ¹always,   longing   ⁶us

ἰδεῖν, καθάπερ καὶ ἡμεῖς ὑμᾶς, 7 διὰ τοῦτο παρεκλή-
¹to ²see,   even as also we   you : because of this   we were encou-

θημεν, ἀδελφοί, ἐφ' ὑμῖν, ἐπὶ πάσῃ τῇ ᵃθλίψει καὶ ἀνάγκῃ‖
raged,   brethren, as to you,   in all   ²tribulation ³and ⁴necessity

ἡμῶν, διὰ τῆς.ὑμῶν.πίστεως· 8 ὅτι νῦν ζῶμεν ἐὰν ὑμεῖς
¹our,   through   your faith,   because now we live if   ye

ᵇστήκητε‖ ἐν κυρίῳ. 9 τίνα.γὰρ εὐχαριστίαν δυνάμεθα
should stand fast in [the] Lord.   For what   thanksgiving   are we able

τῷ θεῷ ἀνταποδοῦναι περὶ ὑμῶν, ἐπὶ πάσῃ τῇ χαρᾷ
³to ⁴God ¹to ²render   concerning you,   for   all   the joy

presence, not in heart,
endeavoured the more
abundantly to see your
face with great desire.
18 Wherefore we would
have come unto you,
even I Paul, once
and again ; but Satan
hindered us. 19 For
what is our hope, or
joy, or crown of re-
joicing ? Are not even
ye in the presence of
our Lord Jesus Christ
at his coming ? 20 for
ye are our glory and
joy.

III. Wherefore when
we could no longer
forbear, we thought
it good to be left at
Athens alone ; 2 and
sent Timotheus, our
brother, and minister
of God, and our fellow-
labourer in the gospel
of Christ, to establish
you, and to comfort
you concerning your
faith : 3 that no man
should be moved by
these afflictions : for
yourselves know that
we are appointed there-
unto. 4 For verily,
when we were with
you, we told you be-
fore that we should
suffer   tribulation ;
even as it came to pass,
and ye know. 5 For
this cause, when I
could no longer for-
bear, I sent to know
your faith, lest by
some means the temp-
ter have tempted you,
and our labour be in
vain. 6 But now when
Timotheus came from
you unto ' us, and
brought us good tid-
ings of your faith and
charity, and that ye
have good remem-
brance of us always,
desiring greatly to see
us, as we also to see
you : 7 therefore, bre-
thren, we were com-
forted over you in all
our affliction and dis-
tress by your faith :
8 for now we live, if
ye stand fast in the
Lord. 9 For what
thanks can we render
to God again for you,
for all the joy where-

ᑫ διότι because LTTrAW.   ʳ — χριστοῦ LTTrA.   ˢ ηὐδοκήσαμεν TTr.   ᵗ συνεργὸν
fellow-worker (read τοῦ θεοῦ under God) GLAW.   ᵛ — καὶ συνεργὸν ἡμῶν GLTTrAW.
ʷ — ὑμᾶς LTTrAW.   ˣ ὑπὲρ GLTTrAW.   ʸ τὸ LTTrAW.   ᶻ μηδὲν (nothing [ye]) ἀσαίνεσ-
θαι L.   ᵃ ἀνάγκῃ καὶ θλίψει LTTrAW.   ᵇ στήκετε stand fast TTrA.

with we joy for your sakes before our God ; 10 night and day praying exceedingly that we might see your face, and might perfect that which is lacking in your faith? 11 Now God himself and our Father, and our Lord Jesus Christ, direct our way unto you. 12 And the Lord make you to increase and abound in love one toward another, and toward all *men*, even as we *do* toward you : 13 to the end he may stablish your hearts unblameable in holiness before God, even our Father, at the coming of our Lord Jesus Christ with all his saints.

ᾗ χαίρομεν δι᾽ ὑμᾶς ἔμπροσθεν τοῦ.θεοῦ.ἡμῶν,[c]
wherewith we rejoice on account of you before our God,
10 νυκτὸς καὶ ἡμέρας [d]ὑπὲρ.ἐκπερισσοῦ‖ δεόμενοι εἰς τὸ ἰδεῖν
night and day exceedingly beseeching for to see
ὑμῶν τὸ πρόσωπον, καὶ καταρτίσαι τὰ.ὑστερήματα τῆς πίστεως
your face, and to perfect the things lacking in [2]faith
ὑμῶν; 11 Αὐτὸς.δὲ ὁ θεὸς καὶ πατὴρ.ἡμῶν καὶ ὁ.κύριος.ἡμῶν
[1]your? But [e]himself [3]God [4]and [2]our [5]Father [7]and [6]our [8]Lord
Ἰησοῦς [e]χριστὸς‖ κατευθύναι τὴν.ὁδὸν.ἡμῶν πρὸς ὑμᾶς.
[10]Jesus [11]Christ [1]may direct our way to you.
12 ὑμᾶς.δὲ ὁ κύριος πλεονάσαι καὶ περισσεύσαι τῇ
But [3]you [2]the [3]Lord [1]may [4]make to exceed and to abound
ἀγάπῃ εἰς ἀλλήλους καὶ εἰς πάντας, καθάπερ καὶ ἡμεῖς
in love toward one another and toward all, even as also we
εἰς ὑμᾶς, 13 εἰς τὸ στηρίξαι ὑμῶν τὰς καρδίας ἀμέμπτους
toward you, for to establish your hearts blameless
ἐν ἁγιωσύνῃ ἔμπροσθεν τοῦ θεοῦ καὶ πατρὸς ἡμῶν, ἐν τῇ
in holiness before [2]God [3]and [4]Father. [1]our, at the
παρουσίᾳ τοῦ.κυρίου.ἡμῶν Ἰησοῦ [f]χριστοῦ‖ μετὰ πάντων τῶν
coming of our Lord Jesus Christ with all
ἁγίων.αὐτοῦ. [g]
his saints.

IV. Furthermore then we beseech you, brethren, and exhort *you* by the Lord Jesus, that as ye have received of us how ye ought to walk and to please God, *so* ye would abound more and more. 2 For ye know what commandments we gave you by the Lord Jesus. 3 For this is the will of God, *even* your sanctification, that ye should abstain from fornication : 4 that every one of you should know how to possess his vessel in sanctification and honour ; 5 not in the lust of concupiscence, even as the Gentiles which know not God : 6 that no *man* go beyond and defraud his brother in *any* matter : because that the Lord *is* the avenger of all such, as we also have forewarned you and testified. 7 For God hath not called us unto uncleanness, but unto holiness. 8 He therefore that despiseth, despiseth not man, but God, who hath also given unto us his holy Spirit.

4 [h]Τὸ‖.λοιπὸν οὖν, ἀδελφοί, ἐρωτῶμεν ὑμᾶς καὶ παρα-
For the rest then, brethren, we beseech you and we
καλοῦμεν ἐν κυρίῳ Ἰησοῦ, [i]καθὼς παρελάβετε παρ᾽ ἡμῶν
exhort in [the] Lord Jesus, even as ye received from us
τὸ πῶς δεῖ ὑμᾶς περιπατεῖν καὶ ἀρέσκειν θεῷ, [k]ἵνα περισ-
how it behoves you to walk and please God, that ye should
σεύητε μᾶλλον. 2 οἴδατε.γὰρ τίνας παραγγελίας ἐδώκαμεν.
abound more. For ye know what injunctions we gave
ὑμῖν διὰ τοῦ κυρίου Ἰησοῦ. 3 τοῦτο.γάρ ἐστιν [l]θέλημα τοῦ
you through the Lord Jesus. For this is [2]will
θεοῦ, ὁ.ἁγιασμὸς.ὑμῶν, ἀπέχεσθαι ὑμᾶς ἀπὸ τῆς πορνείας,
[1]God's, your sanctification, [3]to [4]abstain [1]for] [2]you from fornication,
4 εἰδέναι ἕκαστον ὑμῶν τὸ.ἑαυτοῦ σκεῦος κτᾶσθαι ἐν
[4]to [5]know [1]each [2]of [3]you [how] [5]his [4]own [6]vessel [1]to [2]possess in
ἁγιασμῷ καὶ τιμῇ, 5 μὴ ἐν πάθει ἐπιθυμίας καθάπερ καὶ
sanctification and honour, (not in passion of lust even as also
τὰ ἔθνη τὰ μὴ.εἰδότα τὸν θεόν· 6 τὸ μὴ ὑπερβαίνειν καὶ
the nations who know not God,) not to go beyond and
πλεονεκτεῖν ἐν τῷ πράγματι τὸν.ἀδελφὸν.αὐτοῦ, διότι ἔκ-
to overreach in the , matter his brother ; because [the] a-
δικος [m]ὁ‖ κύριος περὶ πάντων τούτων, καθὼς καὶ
venger [is] the Lord concerning all these things, even as also
[n]προείπαμεν‖ ὑμῖν καὶ διεμαρτυράμεθα. 7 οὐ.γὰρ ἐκάλεσεν
we told [2]before [1]you and fully testified. For [4]not [2]called
ἡμᾶς ὁ θεὸς ἐπὶ ἀκαθαρσίᾳ, [o]ἀλλ᾽‖ ἐν ἁγιασμῷ. 8 τοιγαροῦν
[3]us [1]God to uncleanness, but in sanctification. So then
ὁ ἀθετῶν, οὐκ ἄνθρωπον ἀθετεῖ, ἀλλὰ τὸν θεόν, τὸν
he that sets aside, [2]not [3]man [1]sets aside, but God, who
[p]καὶ‖.[q]δόντα‖ [r]τὸ.πνεῦμα.αὐτοῦ‖ τὸ ἅγιον εἰς [s]ἡμᾶς.‖
also gave his [2]Spirit [1]Holy to us.

---

[c] ; (*ending the question at* ἡμῶν) GA.   [d] ὑπερεκπερισσοῦ GLTTrAW.   [e] — χριστὸς LTTrA.
[f] — χριστοῦ LTTrAW.   [g] + ἀμήν Amen [L]T.   [h] — Τὸ GLTTrAW.   [i] + ἵνα that LTTrA.
[k] + καθὼς καὶ περιπατεῖτε even as also ye are walking LTTrAW.   [l] + [τὸ] (*read* the will of God) L.   [m] — ὁ (*read* [the]) I.TTrA.   [n] προείπομεν G.   [o] ἀλλὰ TTr.   [p] — καὶ LTr[A].
[q] διδόντα gives LTTr.   [r] αὐτοῦ τὸ πνεῦμα L.   [s] ὑμᾶς you LTTrAW.

9 Περὶ.δὲ   τῆς φιλαδελφίας οὐ χρείαν ⸀ἔχετε⸀   γρά-
Now concerning   brotherly love ³no ⁴need ¹ye ²have [for me]   to

φειν ὑμῖν, αὐτοὶ.γὰρ ὑμεῖς θεοδίδακτοί ἐστε εἰς τὸ ἀγαπᾷν
write to you, for ²yourselves ¹ye ⁴taught ⁵of ⁶God ³are for   to love

ἀλλήλους· 10 καὶ.γὰρ ποιεῖτε αὐτὸ εἰς πάντας τοὺς ἀδελ-
one another.   For also   ye do this towards all   the   bre-

φοὺς ⸀τοὺς⸀ ἐν ὅλῃ.τῇ.Μακεδονίᾳ. παρακαλοῦμεν.δὲ ὑμᾶς,
thren who [are] in the whole of Macedonia;   but we exhort   you,

ἀδελφοί, περισσεύειν μᾶλλον, 11 καὶ φιλοτιμεῖσθαι ἡσυχάζειν
brethren, to abound   more,   and endeavour earnestly to be quiet

καὶ πράσσειν τὰ.ἴδια,   καὶ ἐργάζεσθαι ταῖς.ʷἰδίαις⸀.χερσὶν
and   to do your own things, and   to work   with ²own ³hands

ὑμῶν, καθὼς ὑμῖν παρηγγείλαμεν, 12 ἵνα περιπατῆτε εὐ-
¹your, even as on you   we enjoined,   that ye may walk   be-

σχημόνως πρὸς τοὺς ἔξω, καὶ μηδενὸς χρείαν ἔχητε.
comingly towards those without, and of no one ²need ¹may ³have.

13 Οὐ ˣθέλω⸀ δὲ ὑμᾶς ἀγνοεῖν, ἀδελφοί, περὶ
⁴Not ²I ³do ⁵wish ¹but you to be ignorant, brethren, concerning

⸀τῶν ʸκεκοιμημένων,⸀ ἵνα μὴ.λυπῆσθε, καθὼς καὶ οἱ λοιποὶ
those who have fallen asleep, that ye be not grieved, even as also the rest

οἱ μὴ.ἔχοντες ἐλπίδα. 14 εἰ.γὰρ πιστεύομεν ὅτι Ἰησοῦς ἀπέ-
who have no hope.   For if we believe that Jesus died

θανεν· καὶ ἀνέστη, οὕτως καὶ ὁ θεὸς τοὺς κοιμηθέντας
and rose again, so also   God those who are fallen asleep

διὰ τοῦ Ἰησοῦ ἄξει σὺν αὐτῷ. 15 τοῦτο.γὰρ ὑμῖν λέ-
through   Jesus will bring with him.   For this to you we

γομεν ἐν   λόγῳ κυρίου,   ὅτι ἡμεῖς οἱ ζῶντες, οἱ περι-
say   in [the] word of [the] Lord, that we the living who re-

λειπόμενοι εἰς τὴν παρουσίαν τοῦ κυρίου, οὐ.μὴ φθάσωμεν
main   to the   coming of the Lord, in no wise may anticipate

τοὺς κοιμηθέντας· 16 ὅτι αὐτὸς ὁ κύριος ἐν   κελεύσ-
those who are fallen asleep; because ³himself ¹the ²Lord with a shout of com-

ματι, ἐν φωνῇ ἀρχαγγέλου καὶ ἐν σάλπιγγι θεοῦ κατα-
mand, with ²voice ³archangel's and with trumpet of God   shall

βήσεται.ἀπ' οὐρανοῦ, καὶ οἱ νεκροὶ ἐν χριστῷ ἀναστήσονται
descend from heaven, and the dead in Christ   shall rise

πρῶτον· 17 ἔπειτα ἡμεῖς οἱ ζῶντες οἱ περιλειπόμενοι, ἅμα
first·   then we the living who   remain,   together

σὺν αὐτοῖς ἁρπαγησόμεθα ἐν νεφέλαις εἰς ἀπάντησιν
with   them shall be caught away in [the] clouds for [the] meeting

τοῦ κυρίου εἰς ἀέρα, καὶ οὕτως πάντοτε σὺν · κυρίῳ ἐσό-
of the Lord in [the] air ; and thus   always   with [the] Lord we shall

μεθα. 18 ὥστε παρακαλεῖτε ἀλλήλους ἐν τοῖς.λόγοις.τούτοις.
be.   So encourage   one another with these words.

5 Περὶ.δὲ τῶν χρόνων καὶ τῶν καιρῶν, ἀδελφοί, οὐ χρείαν
But concerning the times and the seasons, brethren, ³no ⁴need

ἔχετε ὑμῖν γράφεσθαι· 2 αὐτοὶ.γὰρ ἀκριβῶς οἴδατε ὅτι
¹ye ²have for you to be written [to], for ²yourselves ⁴accurately ¹ye ³know that

ᶻἡ⸀ ἡμέρα κυρίου ὡς κλέπτης ἐν νυκτὶ οὕτως ἔρχεται·
the day of [the] Lord as a thief by night so   comes.

3 ὅταν.ᵃγὰρ⸀ λέγωσιν, Εἰρήνη καὶ ἀσφάλεια, τότε αἰφνί-
For when they may say, Peace and security, then   sud-

διος αὐτοῖς ᵇἐφίσταται⸀ ὄλεθρος, ὥσπερ ἡ.ὠδὶν τῇ
den ³upon ⁴them ²comes ¹destruction, as   travail to her

ᵗ ἔχομεν we have L.   ᵛ — τοὺς LT[Tr].   ʷ — ἰδίαις own LTTrAW.   ˣ θέλομεν ²we
ᵃdo ³wish GLTTrAW.   ʸ κοιμωμένων are falling asleep LTTrA.   ᶻ — ἡ (read [the]) LTTr[A]w.
ᵃ — γὰρ for GTTrA ; [δὲ] but L.   ᵇ ἐπίσταται TTr.

9 But as touching
brotherly love ye need
not that I write unto
you : for ye yourselves
are taught of God
to love one another.
10 And indeed ye do
it toward all the bre-
thren which are in all
Macedonia : but we
beseech you, brethren,
that ye increase more
and more ; 11 and that
ye study to be quiet, and
to do your own busi-
ness, and to work with
your own hands, as
we commanded you ;
12 that ye may walk
honestly toward them
that are without, and
that ye may have lack
of nothing.

13 But I would not
have you to be igno-
rant, brethren, con-
cerning them which
are asleep, that ye sor-
row not, even as others
which have no hope.
14 For if we believe
that Jesus died and
rose again, even so
them also which sleep
in Jesus will God bring
with him. 15 For this
we say unto you by
the word of the Lord,
that we which are a-
live and remain unto
the coming of the Lord
shall not prevent them
which are asleep.
16 For the Lord him-
self shall descend from
heaven with a shout,
with the voice of the
archangel, and with
the trump of God :
and the dead in Christ
shall rise first : 17 then
we which are alive and
remain shall be caught
up together with them
in the clouds, to meet
the Lord in the air :
and so shall we ever
be with the Lord.
18 Wherefore comfort
one another with these
words.

V. But of the times
and the seasons, bre-
thren, ye have no need
that I write unto you.
2 For yourselves know
perfectly that the day
of the Lord so com-
eth as a thief in the
night. 3 For when
they shall say, Peace
and safety ; then sud-
den destruction com-
eth upon them, as
travail upon a woman

with child; and they shall not escape. 4 But ye, brethren, are not in darkness, that that day should overtake you as a thief. 5 Ye are all the children of light, and the children of the day: we are not of the night, nor of darkness. 6 Therefore let us not sleep, as do others; but let us watch and be sober. 7 For they that sleep sleep in the night; and they that be drunken are drunken in the night. 8 But let us, who are of the day, be sober, putting on the breastplate of faith and love; and for an helmet, the hope of salvation. 9 For God hath not appointed us to wrath, but to obtain salvation by our Lord Jesus Christ, 10 who died for us, that, whether we wake or sleep, we should live together with him. 11 Wherefore comfort yourselves together, and edify one another, even as also ye do.

12 And we beseech you, brethren, to know them which labour among you, and are over you in the Lord, and admonish you; 13 and to esteem them very highly in love for their work's sake. And be at peace among yourselves. 14 Now we exhort you, brethren, warn them that are unruly, comfort the feebleminded, support the weak, be patient toward all men. 15 See that none render evil for evil unto any man; but ever follow that which is good, both among yourselves, and to all men. 16 Rejoice evermore. 17 Pray without ceasing. 18 In every thing give thanks: for this is the will of God in Christ Jesus concerning you. 19 Quench not the Spirit. 20 Despise not prophesyings. 21 Prove all things; hold fast that

ἐν.γαστρὶ.ἐχούσῃ, καὶ οὐ.μὴ ἐκφύγωσιν. 4 ὑμεῖς.δὲ, ἀδελ-
that is with child; and in no wise shall they escape. But ye, bre-
φοί, οὐκ.ἐστὲ ἐν σκότει, ἵνα ᶜἡ ἡμέρα ὑμᾶς‖ ὡς ᵈκλέπτης‖
thren, are not in darkness, that the day you as a thief
καταλάβῃ· 5 πάντες ᵉὑμεῖς υἱοὶ φωτός ἐστε καὶ υἱοὶ ἡμέρας·
should overtake: all ye sons of light are and sons of day;
οὐκ.ἐσμὲν νυκτὸς οὐδὲ σκότους. 6 ἄρα οὖν μὴ.καθεύδωμεν
we are not of night nor of darkness. So then we should not sleep
ὡς ᶠκαὶ‖ οἱ λοιποί, ἀλλὰ γρηγορῶμεν καὶ νήφωμεν.
as also the rest, but we should watch and we should be sober;
7 οἱ.γὰρ καθεύδοντες νυκτὸς καθεύδουσιν, καὶ οἱ μεθυ-
for they that sleep ²by ³night ¹sleep, and they that are
σκόμενοι νυκτὸς μεθύουσιν· 8 ἡμεῖς.δὲ ἡμέρας ὄντες νήφω-
drunken ³by ⁴night ¹get ²drunk; but we ²of ³day ¹being should be
μεν, ·ἐνδυσάμενοι θώρακα πίστεως καὶ ἀγάπης, καὶ
sober, having put on [the] breastplate of faith and love, and [as]
περικεφαλαίαν ἐλπίδα σωτηρίας· 9 ὅτι οὐκ ἔθετο ἡμᾶς
helmet ²hope ¹salvation's; because ³not ²has ⁴set ¹us
ὁ θεὸς εἰς ὀργήν, ᵍἀλλ'‖ εἰς περιποίησιν σωτηρίας διὰ τοῦ
¹God for wrath, but for obtaining salvation through
κυρίου.ἡμῶν Ἰησοῦ χριστοῦ, 10 τοῦ ἀποθανόντος ʰὑπὲρ‖ ἡμῶν,
our Lord Jesus Christ, who died for us,
ἵνα εἴτε γρηγορῶμεν εἴτε καθεύδωμεν, ἅμα σὺν αὐτῷ
that whether we may watch or we may sleep, together with him
ζήσωμεν. 11 διὸ παρακαλεῖτε ἀλλήλους, καὶ οἰκοδομεῖτε εἷς
we may live. Wherefore encourage one another, and build up one
τὸν ἕνα, καθὼς καὶ ποιεῖτε.
the other, even as also ye are doing.

12 Ἐρωτῶμεν.δὲ ὑμᾶς, ἀδελφοί, εἰδέναι τοὺς κοπιῶντας
But we beseech you, brethren, to know those who labour
ἐν ὑμῖν, καὶ προϊσταμένους ὑμῶν ἐν κυρίῳ, καὶ νουθε-
among you, and take the lead of you in [the] Lord, and admo-
τοῦντας ὑμᾶς, 13 καὶ ἡγεῖσθαι αὐτοὺς ⁱὑπὲρ.ἐκπερισσοῦ‖ ἐν
nish you, and to esteem them exceedingly in
ἀγάπῃ διὰ τὸ.ἔργον.αὐτῶν. εἰρηνεύετε ἐν ᵏἑαυτοῖς.‖
love on account of their work. Be at peace among yourselves.
14 παρακαλοῦμεν.δὲ ὑμᾶς, ἀδελφοί, νουθετεῖτε τοὺς ἀτάκτους,
But we exhort you, brethren, admonish the disorderly,
παραμυθεῖσθε τοὺς ὀλιγοψύχους, ἀντέχεσθε τῶν ἀσθενῶν, μα-
console 'the faint-hearted, sustain the weak, be
κροθυμεῖτε πρὸς πάντας. 15 ὁρᾶτε μή τις κακὸν ἀντὶ κακοῦ
patient towards all. See that not anyone evil for evil
τινὶ ˡἀποδῷ·‖ ἀλλὰ πάντοτε τὸ ἀγαθὸν διώκετε ᵐκαὶ‖ εἰς
to anyone render, but always the good pursue both towards
ἀλλήλους καὶ εἰς πάντας. 16 πάντοτε χαίρετε. 17 ἀδια-
one another and towards all; always rejoice; unceas-
λείπτως προσεύχεσθε. 18 ἐν παντὶ εὐχαριστεῖτε· τοῦτο.γὰρ ⁿ
ingly pray; in everything give thanks, for this
θέλημα θεοῦ ἐν χριστῷ Ἰησοῦ εἰς ὑμᾶς. 19 τὸ πνεῦμα
[is the] will of God in Christ Jesus towards you; the Spirit
μὴ.ᵒσβέννυτε.‖ 20 προφητείας μὴ.ἐξουθενεῖτε. 21 πάντα ᵖ
do not quench; prophecies do not set at naught; all things

ᶜ ὑμᾶς ἡ ἡμέρα LW.   ᵈ κλέπτας thieves L.   ᵉ + γὰρ for (all) GLTTrAW.   ᶠ — καὶ
LTTr[A].   ᵍ ἀλλὰ TTrA.   ʰ περὶ TTr.   ⁱ ὑπερεκπερισσῶς LTTrA; ὑπερεκπερισσοῦ GW.
ᵏ αὐτοῖς (read with them) TTr.   ˡ ἀποδοῖ T.   ᵐ — καὶ LTTr.   ⁿ + ἐστιν is L.   ᵒ ζβέν-
νυτε T.   ᵖ — δὲ but (all things) GLTTrAW.

δοκιμάζετε· τὸ καλὸν κατέχετε. 22 ἀπὸ παντὸς εἴδους πονη-
prove,   the right hold fast ;   from every   form of wicked-
ροῦ ἀπέχεσθε. 23 Αὐτὸς.δὲ ὁ θεὸς τῆς εἰρήνης   ἁγιάσαι
ness abstain.   Now ⁶himself ²the ³God   ⁴of ⁵peace ¹may sanctify
ὑμᾶς ὁλοτελεῖς· καὶ ὁλόκληρον ὑμῶν τὸ πνεῦμα καὶ ἡ ψυχὴ
you   wholly ;   and   ²entire   ²your   ⁴spirit ⁵and   ⁶soul
καὶ τὸ σῶμα ἀμέμπτως ἐν τῇ παρουσίᾳ τοῦ.κυρίου.ἡμῶν
⁷and   ⁸body ¹¹blameless ¹²at ¹³the ¹⁴coming   ·¹⁵of ¹⁶our ¹⁷Lord
Ἰησοῦ χριστοῦ   τηρηθείη.   24 πιστὸς ὁ καλῶν ὑμᾶς,
¹⁸Jesus ¹⁹Christ ¹may ⁹be ¹⁰preserved. [He is] faithful who calls   you,
ὃς καὶ ποιήσει.   25 Ἀδελφοί, προσεύχεσθε ᵠ περὶ ἡμῶν.
who. also will perform [it].   Brethren,   pray   for   us.
26 ἀσπάσασθε τοὺς ἀδελφοὺς πάντας ἐν φιλήματι ἁγίῳ.
Salute   ²the· ³brethren ¹all with a ²kiss ¹holy.
27 ʳὁρκίζω‖ ὑμᾶς τὸν κύριον   ἀναγνωσθῆναι τὴν ἐπιστο-
I adjure   you [by] the Lord [that]   be read   the   epistle
λὴν πᾶσιν τοῖς ˢἁγίοις‖ ἀδελφοῖς· 28 ἡ χάρις τοῦ.κυρίου.ἡμῶν
to all   the   holy brethren.   The grace   of our Lord
Ἰησοῦ χριστοῦ   μεθ᾽ ὑμῶν. ᵗἀμήν.‖
Jesus Christ [be] with you.   Amen.

ᵛ Πρὸς   Θεσσαλονικεῖς πρώτη ἐγράφη ἀπὸ Ἀθηνῶν.‖
²To [⁴the] ⁴Thessalonians ¹first written from Athens.

ᵃΗ ΠΡΟΣ   ΘΕΣΣΑΛΟΝΙΚΕΙΣ ΕΠΙΣΤΟΛΗ ΔΕΥΤΕΡΑ.‖
THE ³TO [⁴THE] ⁵THESSALONIANS   ²EPISTLE   ¹SECOND.

ΠΑΥΛΟΣ καὶ Σιλουανὸς καὶ Τιμόθεος, τῇ ἐκκλησίᾳ Θεσ-
Paul   and Silvanus and Timotheus, to the assembly of Thes-
σαλονικέων ἐν θεῷ πατρὶ ἡμῶν καὶ κυρίῳ Ἰησοῦ χριστῷ·
salonians in God ²Father ¹our and Lord Jesus   Christ.
2 χάρις ὑμῖν καὶ εἰρήνη ἀπὸ θεοῦ πατρὸς ᵇἡμῶν‖ καὶ κυρίου
Grace to you and peace from God ²Father ¹our   and Lord
Ἰησοῦ χριστοῦ.
Jesus   Christ.

3 Εὐχαριστεῖν ὀφείλομεν τῷ θεῷ πάντοτε περὶ ὑμῶν,
³To ¹thank   ¹we ²ought God always concerning ¹you,
ἀδελφοί, καθὼς ἄξιόν ἐστιν, ὅτι   ὑπεραυξάνει ἡ πίστις
brethren, even as meet it is, because increases exceedingly ²faith
ὑμῶν, καὶ πλεονάζει ἡ ἀγάπη ἑνὸς ἑκάστου πάντων ὑμῶν
¹your, and abounds the love of ²one ¹each of ²all ¹you
εἰς ἀλλήλους· 4 ὥστε ᶜἡμᾶς αὐτοὺς‖ ἐν ὑμῖν ᵈκαυχᾶσθαι‖ ἐν
to one another ; so as for us ourselves ³in ⁴you ¹to ²boast in
ταῖς ἐκκλησίαις τοῦ θεοῦ ὑπὲρ τῆς.ὑπομονῆς.ὑμῶν καὶ πίστεως
the assemblies of God for   your endurance and faith
ἐν πᾶσιν τοῖς.διωγμοῖς.ὑμῶν καὶ ταῖς θλίψεσιν αἷς ἀνέ-
in all   your persecutions and the tribulations which ye are
χεσθε, 5 ἔνδειγμα τῆς δικαίας κρίσεως τοῦ θεοῦ, εἰς τὸ
bearing ; a manifest token of the righteous judgment of God, for

which is good. 22 Ab-
stain from all appear-
ance of evil. 23 And the
very God of peace
sanctify you wholly ;
and *I pray God* your
whole spirit and soul
and body be preserved
blameless unto the
coming of our Lord
Jesus Christ. 24 Faith-
ful *is* he that calleth
you, who also will do
it. 25 Brethren, pray
for us. 26 Greet all the
brethren with an holy
kiss. 27 I charge you
by the Lord that this
epistle be read unto all
the holy brethren.
28 The grace of our
Lord Jesus Christ *be*
with you. Amen.

PAUL, and Silvanus,
and Timotheus, unto
the church of the
Thessalonians in God
our Father and the
Lord Jesus Christ :
2 Grace unto you, and
peace, from God our
Father and the Lord
Jesus Christ.

3 We are bound to
thank God always for
you, brethren, as it is
meet, because that
your faith groweth
exceedingly, and the
charity of every one
of you all toward each
other aboundeth ; 4 so
that we ourselves glory
in you in the churches
of God for your pa-
tience and faith in all
your persecutions and
tribulations that ye
endure : 5 *which* is a
manifest token of the
righteous judgment of
God, that ye may be

ᵠ + [καὶ] also L.   ʳ ἐνορκίζω LTTrAW.   ˢ — ἁγίοις LTTrA.   ᵗ — ἀμήν GLTTrAW.
ᵛ — *the subscription* GLTW ; Πρὸς Θεσσαλονικεῖς αʹ.TrA. .
ᵃ + Παύλου τοῦ Ἀποστόλου of the Apostle Paul E ; + Παύλου G ; Πρὸς Θεσσαλονικεῖς βʹ
LTTrAW.   ᵇ — ἡμῶν (*read* [the]) [LTr]A   ᶜ αὐτοὺς ἡμᾶς TTrA.   ᵈ ἐγκαυχᾶσθαι
(ἐν- T) LTTrA.

counted worthy of the kingdom of God, for which ye also suffer: 6 seeing it is a righteous thing with God to recompense tribulation to them that trouble you; 7 and to you who are troubled rest with us, when the Lord Jesus shall be revealed from heaven with his mighty angels, 8 in flaming fire taking vengeance on them that know not God, and that obey not the gospel of our Lord Jesus Christ: 9 who shall be punished with everlasting destruction from the presence of the Lord, and from the glory of his power; 10 when he shall come to be glorified in his saints, and to be admired in all them that believe (because our testimony among you was believed) in that day. 11 Wherefore also we pray always for you, that our God would count you worthy of this calling, and fulfil all the good pleasure of his goodness, and the work of faith with power: 12 that the name of our Lord Jesus Christ may be glorified in you, and ye in him, according to the grace of our God and the Lord Jesus Christ.

II. Now we beseech you, brethren, by the coming of our Lord Jesus Christ, and by our gathering together unto him, 2 that ye be not soon shaken in mind, or be troubled, neither by spirit, nor by word, nor by letter as from us, as that the day of Christ is at hand. 3 Let no man deceive you by any means: for that day shall not come, except there come a falling away first, and that man of sin be revealed, the son of perdition; 4 who opposeth and exalteth himself above all that is called

καταξιωθῆναι　ὑμᾶς τῆς βασιλείας τοῦ θεοῦ, ὑπὲρ ἧς
[2]to [3]be [4]accounted [5]worthy [1]you of the kingdom　of God, for which

καὶ πάσχετε· 6 εἴπερ δίκαιον　παρὰ θεῷ ἀνταποδοῦναι
also ye suffer ;　if at least righteous [it is] with　God　to recompense

τοῖς　θλίβουσιν ὑμᾶς θλίψιν, 7 καὶ ὑμῖν τοῖς θλιβο-
to those who　oppress　you tribulation,　and to you that　are op-

μένοις ἄνεσιν μεθ' ἡμῶν, ἐν τῇ ἀποκαλύψει τοῦ κυρίου Ἰησοῦ
pressed repose with us,　at the　revelation　of the Lord　Jesus

ἀπ' οὐρανοῦ μετ' ἀγγέλων δυνάμεως.αὐτοῦ, 8 ἐν ᵉπυρὶ φλογός,ǁ
from heaven with [the] angels　of his power,　　in ℩ fire　of flame,

διδόντος ἐκδίκησιν　τοῖς　μὴ εἰδόσιν θεόν, καὶ　τοῖς　μὴ
awarding vengeance on those that ᵗnot ¹know　God, and those that ²not

ὑπακούουσιν τῷ εὐαγγελίῳ τοῦ.κυρίου.ἡμῶν Ἰησοῦ ᶠχριστοῦ·ǁ
¹obey　the glad tidings　of our Lord　Jesus　Christ,

9 οἵτινες　δίκην τίσουσιν, ᵍὄλεθρονǁ αἰώνιον, ἀπὸ
who [the] penalty shall suffer, ²destruction ᵗeternal,　from [the]

προσώπου τοῦ κυρίου, καὶ ἀπὸ τῆς δόξης τῆς.ἰσχύος.αὐτοῦ,
presence of the Lord,　and from the　glory　of his strength,

10 ὅταν　ἔλθῃ　ἐνδοξασθῆναι ἐν τοῖς.ἁγίοις.αὐτοῦ καὶ
when he shall have come　to be glorified　in　his saints　and

θαυμασθῆναι ἐν πᾶσιν τοῖς ᵇπιστεύουσιν,ǁ ὅτι ᵉπιστεύθη
to be wondered at in all　them that　believe, (because ⁵was ⁶believed

τὸ.μαρτύριον.ἡμῶν ἐφ' ὑμᾶς, ἐν τῇ.ἡμέρᾳ.ἐκείνῃ. 11 εἰς ὃ
¹our ²testimony　³to ⁴you,)　in　that day.　For which

καὶ προσευχόμεθα πάντοτε περὶ ὑμῶν, ἵνα ὑμᾶς　ἀξιώσῃ
also　we pray　always for you, that ⁵you ³may ⁴count ⁶worthy

τῆς κλήσεως ὁ.θεὸς.ἡμῶν, καὶ πληρώσῃ πᾶσαν εὐδοκίαν
⁷of ⁸the ⁹calling　¹our ²God,　and may fulfil　every good pleasure

ἀγαθωσύνης καὶ ἔργον πίστεως ἐν δυνάμει· 12 ὅπως ἐν-
of goodness　and work of faith with power;　so that may

δοξασθῇ τὸ ὄνομα τοῦ.κυρίου.ἡμῶν Ἰησοῦ ᶦχριστοῦǁ ἐν ὑμῖν,
be glorified the name　of our Lord　Jesus　Christ　in you,

καὶ ὑμεῖς ἐν αὐτῷ,　κατὰ τὴν χάριν τοῦ.θεοῦ.ἡμῶν καὶ
and ye　in him,　according to the　grace　of our God　and

κυρίου Ἰησοῦ χριστοῦ.
of [the] Lord Jesus Christ.

2 Ἐρωτῶμεν.δὲ ὑμᾶς, ἀδελφοί, ὑπὲρ τῆς παρουσίας τοῦ
Now we beseech you,　brethren,　by　the　coming

κυρίου.ἡμῶν Ἰησοῦ χριστοῦ καὶ ἡμῶν ἐπισυναγωγῆς ἐπ'
of our Lord　Jesus　Christ　and our　gathering together to

αὐτόν, 2 εἰς τὸ μὴ ταχέως σαλευθῆναι ὑμᾶς ἀπὸ τοῦ νοός,
him,　for ⁷not ⁵quickly ³to ⁴be ⁶shaken ¹you in　mind,

ᵏμήτεǁ θροεῖσθαι, μήτε διὰ πνεύματος, μήτε διὰ λόγου, μήτε
nor　to be troubled, neither by　spirit,　nor　by word,　nor

δι' ἐπιστολῆς ὡς δι' ἡμῶν, ὡς ὅτι ἐνέστηκεν ἡ ἡμέρα τοῦ
by' epistle,　as if by us,　as　that is present the day of

χριστοῦ.ǁ 3 Μή τις ὑμᾶς ἐξαπατήσῃ κατὰ μηδένα τρόπον·
Christ.　Not anyone ²you ¹should ²deceive in　any　way,

(lit. no)

ὅτι　ἐὰν.μὴ　ἔλθῃ ἡ ἀποστασία πρῶτον
because [it will not be] unless shall have come the apostasy　first,

καὶ ἀποκαλυφθῇ ὁ ἄνθρωπος τῆς ᵐἁμαρτίας,ǁ ὁ υἱὸς
and shall have been revealed the　man　of sin,　the son

τῆς ἀπωλείας, 4 ὁ ἀντικείμενος καὶ ὑπεραιρόμενος ἐπὶ πάντα
of perdition,　he who　opposes　and　exalts himself　above　all

ᵉ φλογὶ πυρὸς a flame of fire LTrw.　ᶠ — χριστου [L]TTrA.　ᵍ ὀλέθριον, (read fatal, eternal) L.　ᵇ πιστεύσασιν believed GLTTrAW.　ᶦ — χριστοῦ [L]TTrAW.　ᵏ μηδὲ LTTrAW.
ᶦ κυρίου Lord GLTTrAW.　ᵐ ἀνομίας of lawlessness TTr.

λεγόμενον θεὸν ἢ   σέβασμα,   ὥστε.αὐτὸν εἰς τὸν ναὸν
called   God   or object of veneration : so as for him   in   the temple

τοῦ θεοῦ ⁿὡς θεὸν‖ καθίσαι, ἀποδεικνύντα ἑαυτὸν ὅτι ἐστὶν
of God   as   God   to sit down,   setting forth   himself   that he is

θεός. 5 οὐ.μνημονεύετε ὅτι ἔτι ὢν πρὸς ὑμᾶς, ταῦτα
God.   Do ye not remember that,   yet being with   you,   these things

ἔλεγον ὑμῖν; 6 καὶ νῦν   τὸ   κατέχον οἴδατε, εἰς τὸ ἀπο-
I said   to you?   And now that which restrains ye know, for   ²to ³be

καλυφθῆναι αὐτὸν ἐν τῷ.ᵒἑαυτοῦ‖ καιρῷ. 7 τὸ.γὰρ μυστήριον
¹revealed   ¹him   in   his own   time.   For the   mystery

ἤδη ἐνεργεῖται τῆς ἀνομίας, μόνον   ὁ κατέχων
¹already ⁴is ⁵working   ¹of ²lawlessness ; only   [there is] he who restrains

ἄρτι ἕως ἐκ   μέσου γένηται· 8 καὶ τότε ἀποκαλυ-
at present until out of [the] midst   he be [gone],   and then   will be re-

φθήσεται ὁ ἄνομος,   ὃν ὁ κύριος ᵖ ᑫἀναλώσει‖ τῷ
vealed   the lawless [one], whom the Lord   will consume with the

πνεύματι τοῦ.στόματος.αὐτοῦ, καὶ καταργήσει τῇ ἐπιφανείᾳ
breath   of his mouth,   and   annul   by the appearing

τῆς.παρουσίας.αὐτοῦ· 9 οὗ ἐστιν ἡ παρουσία κατ'
of his coming ;   whose ²is   ¹coming according to [the]

ἐνέργειαν τοῦ σατανᾶ ἐν πάσῃ δυνάμει καὶ σημείοις.καὶ τέρασιν
working   of Satan in   every   power   and   signs   and wonders

ψεύδους, 10 καὶ ἐν πάσῃ ἀπάτῃ ʳτῆς‖ ἀδικίας ˢἐν‖ τοῖς
of falsehood,   and in   every   deceit   of unrighteousness in them that

ἀπολλυμένοις, ἀνθ'.ὧν τὴν ἀγάπην τῆς ἀληθείας οὐκ.ἐδέξαντο
perish,   because the   love   of the   truth   they received not

εἰς τὸ σωθῆναι αὐτούς· 11 καὶ   διὰ   τοῦτο ᵗπέμψει‖
for   ²to ³be ⁴saved ¹them.   And on account of   this   ²will ³send

αὐτοῖς ὁ θεὸς ἐνέργειαν πλάνης, εἰς τὸ πιστεῦσαι αὐτοὺς
⁴to ⁵them   ¹God   a working   of error,   for   ²to ³believe ¹them

τῷ   ψεύδει· 12 ἵνα κριθῶσιν ᵛπάντες‖ οἱ μὴ.πιστεύσαντες
what [is] false,   that may be judged   all   who   believed not

τῇ ἀληθείᾳ, ʷἀλλ'‖ εὐδοκήσαντες ˣἐν‖ τῇ ἀδικίᾳ.
the truth,   but   delighted   in   unrighteousness.

13 Ἡμεῖς.δὲ ὀφείλομεν εὐχαριστεῖν τῷ θεῷ πάντοτε περὶ
But we   ought   to give thanks   to God always concerning

ὑμῶν, ἀδελφοὶ ἠγαπημένοι ὑπὸ   κυρίου, ὅτι ʸεἵλετο‖ ὑμᾶς
you,   brethren   beloved   by [the] Lord, that ²chose ⁵you

ὁ θεὸς ᶻἀπ'‖   ἀρχῆς‖ εἰς σωτηρίαν ἐν ἁγιασμῷ πνεύματος
¹God   from [the] beginning to   salvation in   sanctification of [the] Spirit

καὶ πίστει ἀληθείας, 14 εἰς.ὃ ᵃ ἐκάλεσεν ᵇὑμᾶς‖ διὰ τοῦ
and belief of [the] truth ;   whereto   he called   you   by

εὐαγγελίου.ἡμῶν, εἰς   περιποίησιν   δόξης   τοῦ κυρίου
our glad tidings,   to [the]   obtaining   of [the] glory   of ²Lord

ἡμῶν Ἰησοῦ χριστοῦ. 15 ἄρα οὖν, ἀδελφοί, στήκετε, καὶ
¹our   Jesus   Christ.   So then,   brethren, stand firm, and

κρατεῖτε τὰς παραδόσεις ἃς ἐδιδάχθητε, εἴτε διὰ λόγου
hold fast   the   traditions which ye were taught, whether by word

εἴτε δι' ἐπιστολῆς.ἡμῶν. 16 αὐτὸς.δὲ ὁ κύριος ἡμῶν Ἰησοῦς
or by   our epistle.   But ⁵himself   ²Lord   ¹our   ³Jesus

ᶜχριστός, καὶ ᵈὁ‖ θεὸς ᵉκαὶ‖ πατὴρ ἡμῶν, ὁ ἀγαπήσας ἡμᾶς
⁴Christ, and   ²God ³and   ⁴Father ¹our,   who   loved   us,

God, or that is wor-shipped ; so that he as God sitteth in the temple of God, shew-ing himself that he is God. 5 Remember ye not, that, when I was yet with you, I told you these things? 6 and now ye know what withholdeth that he might be revealed in his time. 7 For the mystery of iniquity doth already work : only he who now let-teth *will let*, until he be taken out of the way. 8 And then shall that Wicked be reveal-ed, whom the Lord shall consume with the spirit of his mouth, and shall destroy with the brightness of his coming : 9 *even him*, whose coming is after the working of Satan with all power and signs and lying won-ders, 10 and with all deceivableness of un-righteousness in them that perish ; because they received not the love of the truth, that they might be saved. 11 And for this cause God shall send them strong delusion, that they should believe a lie : 12 that they all might be damned who believed not the truth, but had pleasure in unrighteousness.

13 But we are bound to give thanks alway to God for you, bre-thren beloved of the Lord, because God hath from the begin-ning chosen you to sal-vation through sanc-tification of the Spirit and belief of the truth : 14 whereunto he called you by our gospel, to the obtain-ing of the glory of our Lord Jesus Christ. 15 Therefore, brethren, stand fast, and hold the traditions which ye have been taught, whether by word, or our epistle. 16 Now our Lord Jesus Christ himself, and God, even our Father, which hath loved us, and hath

---

ⁿ — ὡς θεὸν GLTTrAW.   ᵒ αὐτοῦ (*read* his time) TTr.   ᵖ + Ἰησοῦς Jesus GLTTrAW.
ᑫ ἀνελεῖ will slay LTTrA.   ʳ — τῆς LTTrAW.   ˢ — ἐν (*read* τοῖς to them that) LTTrAW.
ᵗ πέμπει sends LTTrAW.   ᵛ ἅπαντες TTrA.   ʷ ἀλλὰ TTr.   ˣ — ἐν (*read* ἀδικίᾳ in
..iteousness) [L]TTr[A].   ʸ εἵλατο GLTTrAW.   ᶻ ἀπαρχὴν L.   ᵃ + καὶ also T.
   ις us L.   ᶜ + ὁ the L.   ᵈ — ὁ [L]Tr.   ᵉ LTTrA.

given *us* everlasting consolation and good hope through grace, 17 comfort your hearts, and stablish you in every good word and work.

καὶ δοὺς παράκλησιν αἰωνίαν καὶ. ἐλπίδα ἀγαθὴν ἐν χάριτι,
and gave [us] ²encouragement ¹eternal and ²hope ¹good by grace,
17 παρακαλέσαι ὑμῶν τὰς καρδίας, καὶ στηρίξαι ᶠὑμᾶς∥
may he encourage your hearts, and may he establish you
ἐν παντὶ ᵍλόγῳ καὶ ἔργῳ∥ ἀγαθῷ.
in every ²word ³and ⁴work ¹good.

III. Finally, brethren, pray for us, that the word of the Lord may have *free* course, and be glorified, even as *it is* with you : 2 and that we may be delivered from unreasonable and wicked men : for all *men* have not faith. 3 But the Lord is faithful, who shall stablish you, and keep *you* from evil. 4 And we have confidence in the Lord touching you, that ye both do and will do the things which we command you. 5 And the Lord direct your hearts into the love of God, and into the patient waiting for Christ.

3 Τὸ.λοιπόν, προσεύχεσθε, ἀδελφοί, περὶ ἡμῶν, ἵνα ὁ
For the rest, pray, brethren, for us, that the
λόγος τοῦ κυρίου τρέχῃ καὶ δοξάζηται, καθὼς καὶ πρὸς
word of the Lord may run and may be glorified, even as also with
ὑμᾶς, 2 καὶ ἵνα ῥυσθῶμεν ἀπὸ τῶν ἀτόπων καὶ πονηρῶν
you ; ³ and that we may be delivered from perverse and wicked
ἀνθρώπων· οὐ.γὰρ πάντων ἡ πίστις. 3 πιστὸς
men, for ²not ⁶of ⁷all [²is] ¹faith [⁴the ⁵portion]. ³Faithful
δὲ ἐστιν ᵇὁ κύριος,∥ ὃς στηρίξει ὑμᾶς καὶ φυλάξει
ᵇbut is the Lord, who will establish you and will keep.[you]
ἀπὸ τοῦ πονηροῦ. 4 πεποίθαμεν.δὲ ἐν κυρίῳ ἐφ' ὑμᾶς,
from evil. But we trust in [the] Lord as to you,
ὅτι ἃ παραγγέλλομεν ᶦὑμῖν,∥ ᵏκαὶ∥ ποιεῖτε καὶ
that the things which we charge you, both ye are doing and
ποιήσετε. 5 ὁ.δὲ κύριος κατευθύναι ὑμῶν τὰς καρδίας εἰς
will do. But ²the ³Lord ¹may direct your hearts into
τὴν ἀγάπην τοῦ θεοῦ, καὶ εἰς ᵐ ὑπομονὴν τοῦ χριστοῦ.
the love of God, and into [the] endurance of the Christ.

6 Now we command you, brethren, in the name of our Lord Jesus Christ, that ye withdraw yourselves from every brother that walketh disorderly, and not after the tradition which he received of us. 7 For yourselves know how ye ought to follow us : for we behaved not ourselves disorderly among you ; 8 neither did we eat any man's bread for nought ; but wrought with labour and travail night and day, that we might not be chargeable to any of you : 9 not because we have not power, but to make ourselves an ensample unto you to follow us. 10 For even when we were with you, this we commanded you, that if any would not work, neither should he eat. 11 For we hear that there are some which walk among you disorderly, working not at all, but are busybodies. 12 Now them that are such we command and exhort by our Lord Je-

6 Παραγγέλλομεν.δὲ ὑμῖν, ἀδελφοί, ἐν ὀνόματι τοῦ
Now we charge you, brethren, in [the] name
κυρίου.ⁿἡμῶν∥ Ἰησοῦ χριστοῦ, στέλλεσθαι ὑμᾶς ἀπὸ παν-
of our Lord Jesus Christ, [that] ²withdraw ¹ye from every
τὸς ἀδελφοῦ ἀτάκτως περιπατοῦντος, καὶ μὴ κατὰ τὴν
brother ²disorderly ¹walking, and not according to the
παράδοσιν ἣν °παρέλαβεν∥ παρ' ἡμῶν. 7 αὐτοὶ.γὰρ οἴδατε
tradition which he received from us. For ²yourselves ¹ye know
πῶς δεῖ μιμεῖσθαι ἡμᾶς· ὅτι οὐκ.ἠτακτήσαμεν
how it behoves [you] to imitate us, because we behaved not disorderly
ἐν ὑμῖν, 8 οὐδὲ δωρεὰν ἄρτον ἐφάγομεν παρά τινος, ᴾἀλλ'∥
among you ; nor for nought bread did we eat from anyone ; but
ἐν κόπῳ καὶ μόχθῳ, ᑫνύκτα καὶ ἡμέραν∥ ἐργαζόμενοι, πρὸς τὸ
in labour and toil, night and day working, for
μὴ ἐπιβαρῆσαί τινα ὑμῶν· 9 οὐχ ὅτι οὐκ.ἔχομεν ἐξουσίαν,
not to be burdensome to anyone of you. Not that we have not authority,
ἀλλ' ἵνα ἑαυτοὺς τύπον δῶμεν ὑμῖν εἰς τὸ μιμεῖσθαι ἡμᾶς.
but that ourselves a pattern we might give to you for to imitate us.
10 καὶ.γὰρ ὅτε ἦμεν πρὸς ὑμᾶς τοῦτο παρηγγέλλομεν ὑμῖν,
For also when we were with you this we charged you,
ὅτι εἴ τις οὐ.θέλει ἐργάζεσθαι, μηδὲ ἐσθιέτω. 11 ἀκούομεν
that if anyone does not wish to work, neither let him eat. ²We ³hear
γάρ τινας περιπατοῦντας ἐν ὑμῖν ἀτάκτως, μηδὲν ἐργαζο-
¹for some are walking among you disorderly, not at all work-
μένους, ἀλλὰ περιεργαζομένους. 12 τοῖς.δὲ.τοιούτοις παραγ-
ing, but being busy bodies. Now such we
γέλλομεν καὶ παρακαλοῦμεν ᵣδιὰ τοῦ.κυρίου.ἡμῶν Ἰησοῦ
charge and exhort by our Lord Jesus

ᶠ — ὑμᾶς (*read* [you]) LTTrAW.   ᵍ ἔργῳ καὶ λόγῳ LTTrAW.   ʰ ὁ θεός God L.   ᶦ — ὑμῖν [L]TTrA.   ᵏ + [καὶ ἐποιήσατε] ye did L.   ˡ — καὶ [L]T[Tr].   ᵐ + τὴν the GLTTrAW.   ⁿ — ἡμῶν (*read* the Lord) [L]A.   ° παρελάβοσαν they received.ᴳᴬᵀᵂ ; παρελάβετε ye received LTr.   ᴾ ἀλλὰ Tr.   ᑫ νυκτὸς καὶ ἡμέρας LTTr.   ᵣ ἐν κυρίῳ Ἰησοῦ χριστῷ in [the] Lord Jesus Christ LTTrA.

χριστοῦ,‖ ἵνα μετὰ ἡσυχίας ἐργαζόμενοι, τὸν ἑαυτῶν ἄρτον
Christ, that with quietness working, their own bread

ἐσθίωσιν. 13 ὑμεῖς δέ, ἀδελφοί, μὴ ᵗἐκκακήσητε‖ καλοποιοῦν-
they may eat. But ye, brethren, do not lose heart [in] well-doing.

τες. 14 εἰ δέ τις οὐχ ὑπακούει τῷ λόγῳ ἡμῶν διὰ τῆς ἐπι-
But if anyone obey not our word by the epis-

στολῆς, τοῦτον σημειοῦσθε ᵗκαὶ‖ ᵛμὴ συναναμίγνυσθε‖ αὐτῷ,
tle, ²that [³man] ¹mark and associate not with him,

ἵνα ἐντραπῇ· 15 καὶ μὴ ὡς ἐχθρὸν ἡγεῖσθε, ἀλλὰ
that he may be ashamed; and not as an enemy esteem [him], but

νουθετεῖτε ὡς ἀδελφόν. 16 αὐτὸς δὲ ὁ κύριος τῆς εἰρήνης
admonish [him] as a brother. But ᵉhimself ²the ³Lord ⁴of ⁵peace

δῴη ὑμῖν τὴν εἰρήνην διὰ παντὸς ἐν παντὶ ᵂτρόπῳ.‖ ὁ
¹may give you peace continually in every way. The

κύριος μετὰ πάντων ὑμῶν.
Lord [be] with all you.

17 Ὁ ἀσπασμὸς τῇ ἐμῇ χειρὶ Παύλου, ὅ ἐστιν σημεῖον
The salutation ³by ⁴my [⁵own] ⁶hand ¹of ²Paul, which is [the] sign

ἐν πάσῃ ἐπιστολῇ· οὕτως γράφω. 18 ἡ χάρις τοῦ κυρίου ἡμῶν
in every epistle; so I write. The grace of our Lord

Ἰησοῦ χριστοῦ μετὰ πάντων ὑμῶν. ˣἀμήν.‖
Jesus Christ [be] with ²all ¹you. Amen.

ʸΠρὸς Θεσσαλονικεῖς δευτέρα ἐγράφη ἀπὸ Ἀθηνῶν.‖
²Το [³the] ⁴Thessalonians ¹second written from Athens.

ᵃΗ ΠΡΟΣ ΤΙΜΟΘΕΟΝ ΕΠΙΣΤΟΛΗ ΠΡΩΤΗ.ᵇ
THE ³TO ⁴TIMOTHY ²EPISTLE ¹FIRST.

ΠΑΥΛΟΣ ἀπόστολος ᵇ᾽Ιησοῦ χριστοῦ‖ κατ᾽ ἐπιταγὴν
Paul, apostle of Jesus Christ according to [the] command

θεοῦ σωτῆρος ἡμῶν, καὶ ᶜκυρίου‖ ᵈἸησοῦ χριστοῦ‖ τῆς
of God our Saviour, and of [the] Lord Jesus Christ

ἐλπίδος ἡμῶν, 2 Τιμοθέῳ γνησίῳ τέκνῳ ἐν πίστει· χάρις,
our hope, to Timotheus, [my] true child in faith; grace,

ἔλεος, εἰρήνη ἀπὸ θεοῦ πατρὸς ᵉἡμῶν‖ καὶ χριστοῦ Ἰησοῦ
mercy, peace, from God our Father and Christ Jesus

τοῦ κυρίου ἡμῶν.
our Lord.

3 Καθὼς παρεκάλεσά σε προσμεῖναι ἐν Ἐφέσῳ,
Even as I besought thee to remain in Ephesus, [when I was]

πορευόμενος εἰς Μακεδονίαν, ἵνα παραγγείλῃς τισὶν μὴ
going to Macedonia, that thou mightest charge some not

ἑτεροδιδασκαλεῖν, 4 μηδὲ προσέχειν μύθοις καὶ γενεαλογίαις
to teach other doctrines, nor to give heed to fables and ²genealogies

ἀπεράντοις, αἵτινες ᶠζητήσεις‖ παρέχουσιν μᾶλλον ἢ ᵍοἰκονο-
¹interminable, which ²questionings ¹bring rather than ²adminis-

μίαν‖ θεοῦ τὴν ἐν πίστει· 5 τὸ δὲ τέλος τῆς παραγγελίας
tration ¹God's which [is] in faith. But the end of the charge

sus Christ, that, with
quietness they work,
and eat their own
bread. 13 But ye, bre-
thren, be not weary in
well doing. 14 And if
any man obey not our
word by this epistle,
note that man, and
have no company with
him, that he may be
ashamed. 15 Yet count
him not as an enemy,
but admonish *him* as a
brother. 16 Now the
Lord of peace himself
give you peace always
by all means. The
Lord *be* with you all.

17 The salutation of
Paul with mine own
hand, which is the to-
ken in every epistle:
so I write. 18 The
grace of our Lord Je-
sus Christ *be* with you
all. Amen.

PAUL, an apostle of
Jesus Christ by the
commandment of God
our Saviour, and
Lord Jesus Christ,
which is our hope;
2 unto Timothy, *my*
own son in the faith:
Grace, mercy, *and*
peace, from God our
Father and Jesus
Christ our Lord.

3 As I besought thee
to abide still at Ephe-
sus, when I went into
Macedonia, that thou
mightest charge some
that they teach no
other doctrine, 4 nei-
ther give heed to fables
and endless genealo-
gies, which minister
questions, rather than
godly edifying which
is in faith: *so do.*
5 Now the end of the
commandment is cha-

ˢ ἐγ- LTTrAW,   ᵗ — καὶ LTTrA.   ᵛ μὴ συναναμίγνυσθαι not to associate yourselves
with LTrA.   ᵂ τόπῳ place L.   ˣ — ἀμήν TTrA.   ʸ — *the subscription* GLTW ; Πρὸς Θεσσαλονικεῖς β´ TrA.

ᵃ + Παύλου τοῦ Ἀποστόλου of the Apostle Paul E ; + Παύλου G ; Πρὸς Τιμόθεον α´ LTTrAW.
ᵇ χριστοῦ Ἰησοῦ TTrAW.   ᶜ — κυρίου GLTTrAW.   ᵈ χριστοῦ Ἰησοῦ GLTTrAW.   ᵉ — ἡμῶν
(*read* [the]) LTTrAW.   ᶠ ἐκζητήσεις TTr.   ᵍ οἰκοδομίαν building up E.

rity out of a pure heart, and of a good conscience, and of faith unfeigned:6 from which some having swerved have turned aside unto vain jangling; 7 desiring to be teachers of the law; understanding neither what they say, nor whereof they affirm. 8 But we know that the law *is* good, if a man use it lawfully; 9 knowing this, that the law is not made for a righteous man, but for the lawless and disobedient, for the ungodly and for sinners, for unholy and profane, for murderers of fathers and murderers of mothers, for manslayers, 10 for whoremongers, for them that defile themselves with mankind, for menstealers, for liars, for perjured persons, and if there be any other thing that is contrary to sound doctrine; 11 according to the glorious gospel of the blessed God, which was committed to my trust. 12 And I thank Christ Jesus our Lord, who hath enabled me, for that he counted me faithful, putting me into the ministry; 13 who was before a blasphemer, and a persecutor, and injurious: but I obtained mercy, because I did it ignorantly in unbelief. 14 And the grace of our Lord was exceeding abundant with faith and love which is in Christ Jesus. 15 This *is* a faithful saying, and worthy of all acceptation, that Christ Jesus came into the world to save sinners; of whom I am chief. 16 Howbeit for this cause I obtained mercy, that in me first Jesus Christ might shew forth all longsuffering, for a pattern to them which should hereafter believe on him to life everlasting. 17 Now unto the King eternal, immortal, invisible, the only wise God, *be* honour and glory for ever and ever. Amen. 18 This charge I com-

ἐστὶν ἀγάπη ἐκ καθαρᾶς καρδίας καὶ συνειδήσεως ἀγαθῆς
is love out of ²pure ¹a heart and a "conscience ¹good

καὶ πίστεως ἀνυποκρίτου· 6 ὧν τινες ἀστοχήσαντες,
and faith unfeigned; from which some, having missed the mark,

ἐξετράπησαν εἰς ματαιολογίαν, 7 θέλοντες εἶναι νομοδιδάσ-
turned aside to vain talking, wishing to be law-teachers,

καλοι, μὴ νοοῦντες μήτε ἃ λέγουσιν, μήτε περὶ τίνων
understanding neither what they say, nor concerning what

διαβεβαιοῦνται. 8 οἴδαμεν.δὲ ὅτι καλὸς ὁ νόμος, ἐάν τις
they strongly affirm. Now we know that good [is] the law, if anyone

αὐτῷ νομίμως ʰχρῆται,‖ 9 εἰδὼς τοῦτο, ὅτι δικαίῳ
²it ³lawfully ¹use, knowing this, that for a righteous [one]

νόμος οὐ.κεῖται, ἀνόμοις.δὲ καὶ ἀνυποτάκτοις, ἀσεβέσιν
law is not enacted, but for lawless and insubordinate[ones], for[the]ungodly

καὶ ἁμαρτωλοῖς, ἀνοσίοις καὶ βεβήλοις, ⁱπατραλῴαις‖
and ¹sinful, for[the]unholy and profane, ₍for smiters of fathers

καὶ ᵏμητραλῴαις,‖ ἀνδροφόνοις, 10 πόρνοις, ἀρσενο-
and smiters of mothers; for slayers of man, fornicators, abusers of them-

κοίταις, ἀνδραποδισταῖς, ψεύσταις, ἐπιόρκοις, καὶ εἴ
selves with men, men-stealers, liars, perjurers, and if

τι ἕτερον τῇ ὑγιαινούσῃ διδασκαλίᾳ ἀντίκειται, 11 κατὰ
any ²thing ¹other to sound teaching is opposed, according to

τὸ εὐαγγέλιον τῆς δόξης τοῦ μακαρίου θεοῦ, ὃ ἐπιστεύ-
the glad tidings of the glory of the blessed God, which ²was ³entrusted

θην ἐγώ. 12 ˡκαὶ‖ χάριν.ἔχω τῷ ἐνδυναμώσαντί με χριστῷ
⁴with ¹I. And I thank him who strengthened me, Christ

Ἰησοῦ τῷ.κυρίῳ.ἡμῶν, ὅτι πιστόν με ἡγήσατο, θέμενος εἰς
Jesus our Lord, that faithful me he esteemed, appointing [me] to

διακονίαν, 13 ᵐτὸν‖ πρότερον ὄντα ⁿβλάσφημον καὶ διώκτην
service, ²previously ¹being a blasphemer and persecutor

καὶ ὑβριστήν· ᵒἀλλ'‖ ἠλεήθην, ὅτι ἀγνοῶν ἐποίησα
and insolent; but I was shewn mercy, because being ignorant I did

ἐν ἀπιστίᾳ· 14 ὑπερεπλεόνασεν.δὲ ἡ χάρις τοῦ.κυρίου.ἡμῶν
[it] in unbelief. But superabounded the grace of our Lord

μετὰ πίστεως καὶ ἀγάπης τῆς ἐν χριστῷ Ἰησοῦ. 15 πιστὸς
with faith and love which [is] in Christ Jesus. Faithful

ὁ λόγος καὶ πάσης ἀποδοχῆς ἄξιος, ὅτι χριστὸς Ἰησοῦς
[is] the word, and of all acceptation worthy, that Christ Jesus

ἦλθεν εἰς τὸν κόσμον ἁμαρτωλοὺς σῶσαι, ὧν πρῶτός
came into the world sinners to save, of whom [the] first

εἰμι ἐγώ. 16 ἀλλὰ διὰ.τοῦτο ἠλεήθην, ἵνα ἐν ἐμοὶ
²am ¹I. But for this reason I was shewn mercy, that in me, [the]

πρώτῳ ἐνδείξηται ᵖἸησοῦς χριστὸς‖ τὴν ۹πᾶσαν‖ μακρο-
first, ³might ⁴shew ⁵forth ¹Jesus ²Christ the whole long-

θυμίαν, πρὸς ὑποτύπωσιν τῶν μελλόντων πιστεύειν ἐπ'
suffering, for a delineation of those being about to believe on

αὐτῷ εἰς ζωὴν αἰώνιον. 17 τῷ.δὲ βασιλεῖ τῶν αἰώνων,
him to life eternal. Now to the King of the ages, [the]

ἀφθάρτῳ, ἀοράτῳ, μόνῳ ʳσοφῷ‖ θεῷ, τιμὴ καὶ δόξα εἰς τοὺς
incorruptible, invisible, only wise God, honour and glory to the

αἰῶνας τῶν αἰώνων. ἀμήν. 18 ταύτην τὴν παραγγελίαν
ages of the ages. Amen. This charge

παρατίθεμαί σοι, τέκνον Τιμόθεε, κατὰ τὰς προ-
I commit to thee, [my] child Timotheus, according to the ⁵going

---

ʰ χρήσηται L. ⁱ πατρολῴαις LTTrA. ᵏ μητρολῴαις LTTrA. ˡ — καὶ LTTrA. ᵐ τὸ LTTrA. ⁿ + με me (being) L. ᵒ ἀλλὰ LTTrAW. ᵖ χριστὸς Ἰησοῦς LTrA. ۹ ἅπασαν LTTrAW. ʳ — σοφῷ GLTTrAW.

αγούσας ἐπί σε προφητείας, ἵνα *στρατεύῃ* ἐν αὐταῖς τὴν
before ²as ³to ⁴thee ¹prophecies, that thou mightest war by them the

καλὴν στρατείαν, 19 ἔχων πίστιν καὶ ἀγαθὴν συνείδησιν,
good   warfare,   holding faith and ²good ¹a conscience;

ἥν   τινες ἀπωσάμενοι, περὶ τὴν πίστιν ἐναυάγησαν·
which [conscience] some, having cast away, as to   faith   made shipwreck;

20 ὧν ἐστιν Ὑμέναιος καὶ Ἀλέξανδρος, οὓς παρέδωκα τῷ
of whom are Hymenæus and Alexander, whom I delivered up

σατανᾷ, ἵνα παιδευθῶσιν μὴ βλασφημεῖν.
to Satan, that they may be disciplined not to blaspheme.

2 Παρακαλῶ οὖν πρῶτον πάντων . ποιεῖσθαι δεήσεις,
  I exhort therefore, first of all, to be made   supplications,

προσευχάς, ἐντεύξεις, εὐχαριστίας, ὑπὲρ πάντων ἀνθρώ-
prayers, intercessions, thanksgivings, for all   men;

πων, 2 ὑπὲρ βασιλέων καὶ πάντων τῶν ἐν ὑπεροχῇ ὄντων,
       for kings   and   all   that in dignity   are,

ἵνα ἤρεμον καὶ ἡσύχιον βίον διάγωμεν ἐν πάσῃ εὐσεβείᾳ καὶ
that a tranquil and quiet   life we may lead in all   piety   and

σεμνότητι· 3 τοῦτο· γὰρ καλὸν καὶ ἀποδεκτὸν ἐνώπιον τοῦ
gravity;   for this [is] good and acceptable   before

σωτῆρος ἡμῶν θεοῦ, 4 ὃς πάντας ἀνθρώπους θέλει σωθῆναι
our Saviour   God, who ²all   ³men   ¹wishes to be saved

καὶ εἰς ἐπίγνωσιν ἀληθείας ἐλθεῖν. 5 εἷς γὰρ θεός, εἷς καὶ
and ⁴to ⁵knowledge ⁶of [⁶the] ⁷truth ¹to ²come. For ³one ¹God [²is], and one

μεσίτης θεοῦ καὶ ἀνθρώπων,   ἄνθρωπος χριστὸς Ἰη-
[the] mediator of God and men,   [the] man   Christ   Je-

σοῦς, 6 ὁ δοὺς ἑαυτὸν ἀντίλυτρον ὑπὲρ πάντων, ᵗτὸ μαρ-
sus, who gave himself a ransom   for   all,   the   tes-

τύριον καιροῖς ἰδίοις, 7 εἰς ὃ ἐτέθην ἐγὼ
timony [to be rendered] in ²times ¹its ²own, to which ²was ³appointed ¹I

κήρυξ καὶ ἀπόστολος· ἀλήθειαν λέγω ʷἐν χριστῷ, οὐ
a herald and apostle, ([the] truth I speak in Christ, ²not

ψεύδομαι· διδάσκαλος ἐθνῶν, ἐν πίστει καὶ ἀληθείᾳ.
¹I ²do lie,) a teacher of [the] nations, in faith and truth.

8 Βούλομαι οὖν προσεύχεσθαι τοὺς ἄνδρας ἐν παντὶ τόπῳ,
  I will   therefore ³to ⁴pray   ¹the ²men in every   place,

ἐπαίροντας ὁσίους χεῖρας χωρὶς ὀργῆς καὶ διαλογισμοῦ·
lifting up holy   hands apart from wrath and reasoning.

9 ὡσαύτως ˣκαὶ ʸτὰς γυναῖκας ἐν καταστολῇ κοσμίῳ μετὰ
In like manner also the   women in ²guise   ¹seemly with

αἰδοῦς καὶ σωφροσύνης κοσμεῖν ἑαυτάς, μὴ ἐν πλέγμασιν,
modesty and discreetness to adorn themselves, not with plaitings,

ᶻῇ ᵃχρυσῷ, ἢ μαργαρίταις, ἢ ἱματισμῷ πολυτελεῖ, 10 ᵇἀλλ'
or gold, or pearls, or ²clothing ¹costly,   but

ὃ πρέπει γυναιξὶν ἐπαγγελλομέναις θεοσέβειαν, δι'
what is becoming to women   professing [the] fear of God, by

ἔργων ἀγαθῶν. 11 Γυνὴ ἐν ἡσυχίᾳ μανθανέτω ἐν πάσῃ
²works good. ⁴A ³woman ⁷in ⁸quietness ³let ⁶learn in all

ὑποταγῇ· 12 ᶜγυναικὶ δὲ διδάσκειν οὐκ ἐπιτρέπω, οὐδὲ αὐ-
subjection; but a woman to teach I do not allow, nor to exercise

θεντεῖν ἀνδρός, ᵈἀλλ' εἶναι ἐν ἡσυχίᾳ. 13 Ἀδὰμ γὰρ
authority over man, but to be in quietness;   for Adam

πρῶτος ἐπλάσθη, εἶτα Εὖα. 14 καὶ Ἀδὰμ οὐκ ἠπατήθη· ἡ δὲ
first   was formed, then Eve·   and Adam was not deceived; but the

mit unto thee, son Timothy, according to the prophecies which went before on thee, that thou by them mightest war a good warfare; 19 holding faith, and a good conscience; which some having put away concerning faith have made shipwreck : 20 of whom is Hymenæus and Alexander; whom I have delivered unto Satan, that they may learn not to blaspheme.

II. I exhort therefore, that, first of all, supplications, prayers, intercessions, and giving of thanks, be made for all men; 2 for kings, and for all that are in authority; that we may lead a quiet and peaceable life in all godliness and honesty. 3 For this is good and acceptable in the sight of God our Saviour; 4 who will have all men to be saved, and to come unto the knowledge of the truth. 5 For there is one God, and one mediator between God and men, the man Christ Jesus; 6 who gave himself a ransom for all, to be testified in due time. 7 Whereunto I am ordained a preacher, and an apostle, (I speak the truth in Christ, and lie not;) a teacher of the Gentiles in faith and verity.

8 I will therefore that men pray every where, lifting up holy hands, without wrath and doubting. 9 In like manner also, that women adorn themselves in modest apparel, with shamefacedness and sobriety; not with broided hair, or gold, or pearls, or costly array; 10 but (which becometh women professing godliness) with good works. 11 Let the woman learn in silence with all subjection. 12 But I suffer not a woman to teach, nor to usurp authority over the man, but to be in silence. 13 For Adam was first formed, then Eve. 14 And Adam was not deceived, but

---

ˢ στρατεύσῃ TTr.   ᵗ — γὰρ for LTTr.   ᵛ — τὸ μαρτύριον L.   ʷ — ἐν χριστῷ GLTTrAW.
ˣ — καὶ LT[Tr].   ʸ — τὰς LTTrAW.   ᶻ καὶ and LTTrA.   ᵃ χρυσίῳ L.   ᵇ ἀλλὰ W.
ᶜ διδάσκειν δὲ γυναικὶ LTTrA.   ᵈ ἀλλὰ LTr.

the woman being deceived. was in the transgression. 15 Notwithstanding she shall be saved in childbearing, if they continue in faith and charity and holiness with sobriety.

III. This is a true saying, If a man desire the office of a bishop, he desireth a good work. 2 A bishop then must be blameless, the husband of one wife, vigilant, sober, of good behaviour, given to hospitality, apt to teach ; 3 not given to wine, no striker, not greedy of filthy lucre; but patient, not a brawler, not covetous ; 4 one that ruleth well his own house, having his children in subjection with all gravity ; 5 (for if a man know not how to rule his own house, how shall he take care of the church of God ?) 6 not a novice, lest being lifted up with pride he fall into the condemnation of the devil. 7 Moreover he must have a good report of them which are without ; lest he fall into reproach and the snare of the devil. 8 Likewise must the deacons be grave, not doubletongued, not given to much wine, not greedy of filthy lucre ; 9 holding the mystery of the faith in a pure conscience. 10 And let these also first be proved ; then let them use the office of a deacon, being found blameless. 11 Even so must their wives be grave, not slanderers, sober, faithful in all things. 12 Let the deacons be the husbands of one wife, ruling their children and their own houses well. 13 For they that have used the office of a deacon well purchase to themselves a good degree, and great boldness in the faith which is in Christ Jesus.

14 These things write I unto thee, hoping to come unto thee shortly : 15 but if I tarry long, that thou mayest

γυνὴ ᵉἀπατηθεῖσα‖ ἐν παραβάσει γέγονεν· 15 σωθήσεται.δὲ
woman, having been deceived, in transgression has become. But she shall be saved

διὰ τῆς τεκνογονίας, ἐὰν μείνωσιν ἐν πίστει καὶ ἀγάπῃ
through the childbearing, if they abide in faith · and love

καὶ ἁγιασμῷ μετὰ σωφροσύνης.
and sanctification with discreetness.

3 Πιστὸς ὁ λόγος· εἴ τις ἐπισκοπῆς ὀρέγεται,
Faithful [is] the word : if any ⁴overseership ¹stretches ²forward ³to

καλοῦ ἔργου ἐπιθυμεῖ. 2 δεῖ οὖν τὸν ἐπίσκοπον ᶠἀνεπί-
of ²good ¹a work he is desirous. It behoves then the overseer irreproach-

ληπτον‖ εἶναι, μιᾶς γυναικὸς ἄνδρα, ᵍνηφάλεον,‖ σώφρονα,
able to be, ²of ³one ⁴wife ¹husband, sober, discreet,

κόσμιον, φιλόξενον, διδακτικόν· 3 μὴ πάροινον, μὴ πλήκτην,
decorous, hospitable, apt to teach ; not given to wine, not a striker,

ʰμὴ αἰσχροκερδῆ,‖ ἀλλ᾽‖ ἐπιεικῆ, ἄμαχον, ἀφιλάργυρον·
not greedy of base gain, but gentle, not contentious, not loving money;

4 τοῦ.ἰδίου.οἴκου καλῶς προϊστάμενον, τέκνα ἔχοντα ἐν
his own house well ruling, [his] children having in

ὑποταγῇ μετὰ πάσης σεμνότητος· 5 εἰ.δέ τις τοῦ.ἰδίου.οἴκου
subjection with all gravity ; (but if one his own house

προστῆναι οὐκ.οἶδεν, πῶς ἐκκλησίας θεοῦ ἐπιμελήσεται ;
[how] to rule knows not, how [the] assembly of God shall he take care of ?)

6 μὴ νεόφυτον, ἵνα.μὴ τυφωθεὶς εἰς κρίμα ἐμπέσῃ
not a novice, lest being puffed up, into [the] crime ⁴he ⁵may ⁶fall

τοῦ διαβόλου. 7 δεῖ.δὲ ᵏαὐτὸν‖ καὶ μαρτυρίαν καλὴν
¹of ²the ³devil. But it behoves ʰim also a ²testimony ¹good

ἔχειν ἀπὸ τῶν ἔξωθεν, ἵνα.μὴ εἰς ὀνειδισμὸν ἐμπέσῃ καὶ
to have from those without, lest into reproach he may fall and [the]

παγίδα τοῦ διαβόλου. 8 Διακόνους ὡσαύτως σεμνούς, μὴ
snare of the devil. ·Those who serve, in like manner, grave, not

διλόγους, μὴ οἴνῳ πολλῷ προσέχοντας, μὴ αἰσχροκερδεῖς,
double-tongued, not to ²wine ¹much given, not greedy of base gain,

9 ἔχοντας τὸ μυστήριον τῆς πίστεως ἐν καθαρᾷ συνειδήσει.
holding the mystery of the faith in ²pure ¹a conscience.

10 καὶ.οὗτοι.δὲ δοκιμαζέσθωσαν πρῶτον, εἶτα διακονείτωσαν,
And these also let them be proved first, then let them serve,

ἀνέγκλητοι ὄντες. 11 γυναῖκας ὡσαύτως σεμνάς, μὴ δια-
²unimpeachable ¹being. Women in like manner grave, not slan-

βόλους, ᶦνηφαλέους,‖ πιστὰς ἐν πᾶσιν. 12 διάκονοι ἔστω-
derers, sober, faithful in all things. ²Those ³who ⁴serve ¹let

σαν μιᾶς γυναικὸς ἄνδρες, τέκνων καλῶς προϊστάμενοι
⁵be ⁷of ⁸one ⁹wife ⁶husbands, [¹²their] ¹³children ¹¹well ¹⁰ruling

καὶ τῶν.ἰδίων οἴκων. 13 οἱ.γὰρ καλῶς διακονήσαντες, βαθμὸν
and their own houses. For those well having served, a ²degree

ἑαυτοῖς καλὸν περιποιοῦνται, καὶ πολλὴν παρρησίαν ἐν
³for ⁴themselves ¹good acquire, and much boldness in

πίστει τῇ ἐν χριστῷ Ἰησοῦ.
faith which [is] in Christ Jesus.

14 Ταῦτά σοι γράφω, ἐλπίζων ἐλθεῖν πρός σε ᵐτάχιον·‖
These things to thee I write, hoping to come to thee more quickly ;

15 ἐὰν.δὲ βραδύνω, ἵνα εἰδῇς πῶς δεῖ ἐν
but if I should delay, that thou mayest know how it behoves [one] in [the]

οἴκῳ θεοῦ ἀναστρέφεσθαι, ἥτις ἐστὶν ἐκκλησία θεοῦ
house of God to conduct oneself, which is [the] assembly of ²God [¹the]

ᵉ ἐξαπατηθεῖσα LTTrAW.   ᶠ ἀνεπίλημπτον LTTrA.   ᵍ νηφάλιον EGLTTrAW.   ʰ — μὴ
αἰσχροκερδῆ GLTTrAW.   ᶦ ἀλλὰ LTTr.   ᵏ — αὐτὸν (read δεῖ it is necessary) LTTrA.
ᶦ νηφαλίους EGLTTrAW.   ᵐ ἐν τάχει quickly LTr.

ζῶντος, στῦλος καὶ ἑδραίωμα τῆς ἀληθείας. 16 καὶ ὁμολο-
³living,   pillar   and   base   of the truth.   And confes-

γουμένως μέγα ἐστὶν τὸ τῆς εὐσεβείας μυστήριον· ⁿθεὸς‖
sedly   great   is   the   ²of ²piety   ¹mystery: God

ἐφανερώθη ἐν σαρκί, ἐδικαιώθη ἐν πνεύματι, ὤφθη ἀγ-
was manifested in   flesh,   was justified in [the]   Spirit,   was seen   by

γέλοις,. ἐκηρύχθη ἐν ἔθνεσιν, ἐπιστεύθη ἐν κόσμῳ,
angels,   was proclaimed among [the] nations, was believed on in [the] world,

°ἀνελήφθη‖ ἐν δόξῃ.
was received up in glory.

4 Τὸ.δὲ πνεῦμα ῥητῶς λέγει, ὅτι ἐν ὑστέροις καιροῖς ἀπο-
   But the   Spirit   expressly speaks, that in   latter   times   ²shall

στήσονταί τινες τῆς πίστεως, προσέχοντες πνεύμασιν πλάνοις
³depart ⁴from ¹some the   faith,   giving heed   to ²spirits   ¹deceiving

καὶ διδασκαλίαις δαιμονίων 2 ἐν ὑποκρίσει ψευδολόγων,
and   teachings   of demons   in hypocrisy   of speakers of lies,

ᴾκεκαυτηριασμένων‖ τὴν.ἰδίαν συνείδησιν, 3 κωλυόντων
being cauterized   [as to] their own   conscience,   forbidding

γαμεῖν, ἀπέχεσθαι βρωμάτων, ἃ ὁ θεὸς ἔκτισεν εἰς
to marry, [bidding] to abstain   from meats,   which God   created ' for

ᑫμετάληψιν‖ μετὰ εὐχαριστίας τοῖς πιστοῖς καὶ ἐπεγνωκόσιν
reception   with   thanksgiving for the faithful and   who know

τὴν ἀλήθειαν. 4 ὅτι πᾶν κτίσμα θεοῦ καλόν, καὶ οὐδὲν
the   truth.   Because every creature of God [is] good,   and nothing

ἀπόβλητον, μετὰ εὐχαριστίας λαμβανόμενον· 5 ἁγιάζεται
to be rejected,   with   thanksgiving   being received ;   ²it ³is ⁴sanctified

γὰρ διὰ λόγου θεοῦ καὶ ἐντεύξεως. 6 Ταῦτα ὑποτι-
¹for   by   ²word ¹God's and intercourse [with him]. These things laying

θέμενος τοῖς ἀδελφοῖς, καλὸς ἔσῃ διάκονος ʳἸησοῦ
before   the   brethren,   ²good ⁴thou ⁵wilt ⁶be ¹a ³servant of Jesus

χριστοῦ,‖ ἐντρεφόμενος τοῖς λόγοις τῆς πίστεως, καὶ τῆς
Christ,   being nourished with the words of the   faith,   and of the

καλῆς διδασκαλίας ᾗ παρηκολούθηκας. 7 Τοὺς.δὲ βεβήλους
good   teaching   which thou hast closely followed. But the   profane

καὶ .γραώδεις μύθους παραιτοῦ· γύμναζε.δὲ σεαυτὸν πρὸς
and old wives'   fables   refuse;   but exercise   thyself   to

εὐσέβειαν·. 8 ἡ.γὰρ.σωματικὴ γυμνασία πρὸς ὀλίγον ἐστὶν
piety ;   for bodily   exercise   for · a little   is

ὠφέλιμος· ἡ.δὲ.εὐσέβεια πρὸς πάντα ὠφέλιμός ἐστιν, ἐπαγγε-
profitable,   but piety   for everything ²profitable ¹is,   pro-

λίαν ἔχουσα ζωῆς τῆς .νῦν.καὶ τῆς μελλούσης.
mise having of life, of that which [is] now and of that which [is] coming.

9 πιστὸς ὁ λόγος καὶ πάσης ἀποδοχῆς ἄξιος. 10 εἰς.τοῦτο.γὰρ
Faithful [is] the word and of all   acceptation worthy ;   for, for this

ˢκαὶ‖ κοπιῶμεν καὶ ᵗὀνειδιζόμεθα,‖ ὅτι ἠλπίκαμεν ἐπὶ θεῷ
both we labour   and   are reproached, because we have hope in a ²God

ζῶντι, ὅς ἐστιν σωτὴρ πάντων ἀνθρώπων, μάλιστα πιστῶν.
¹living, who is Preserver of all   men,   specially of believers.

11 Παράγγελλε ταῦτα καὶ δίδασκε. 12 μηδείς σου τῆς
   Charge   these things and   teach.   ²No ³one ⁵thy

νεότητος καταφρονείτω, ἀλλὰ τύπος γίνου τῶν πιστῶν ἐν
⁶youth   ¹let ⁴despise,   but a pattern be   of the believers   in

λόγῳ, ἐν ἀναστροφῇ, ἐν ἀγάπῃ, ᵛἐν πνεύματι,‖ ἐν πίστει,
word,   in conduct,   in love,   in [the] Spirit,   in faith,

know how thou oughtest to behave thyself in the house of God, which is the church of the living God, the pillar and ground of the truth. 16 And without controversy great is the mystery of godliness : God was manifest in the flesh, justified in the Spirit, seen of angels, preached unto the Gentiles, believed on in the world, received up into glory.

IV. Now the Spirit speaketh expressly, that in the latter times some shall depart from the faith, giving heed to seducing spirits, and doctrines of devils; 2 speaking lies in hypocrisy ; having their conscience seared with a hot iron; 3 forbidding to marry, *and commanding* to abstain from meats, which God hath created to be received with thanksgiving of them which believe and know the truth. 4 For every creature of God *is* good, and nothing to be refused, if it be received with thanksgiving : 5 for it is sanctified by the word of God and prayer. 6 If thou put the brethren in remembrance of these things, thou shalt be a good minister of Jesus Christ, nourished up in the words of faith and of good doctrine, whereunto thou hast attained. 7 But refuse profane and old wives' fables, and exercise thyself *rather* unto godliness. 8 For bodily exercise profiteth little: but godliness is profitable unto all things, having promise of the life that now is, and of that which is to come. 9 This *is* a faithful saying and worthy of all acceptation. 10 For therefore we both labour and suffer reproach, because we trust in the living God, who is the Saviour of all men, specially of those that believe. 11 These things command and teach. 12 Let no man despise thy youth; but be thou an example of the believers, in word, in

ⁿ ὃς who GLTTrAW.   ° ἀνελήμφθη LTTrA.   ᴾ κεκαυστηριασμένων TTr.   ᑫ μετάλημψιν
LTTrA.   ʳ χριστοῦ Ἰησοῦ LTTrAW.   ˢ — καὶ LTTr[A].   ᵗ ἀγωνιζόμεθα we combat LTTr.
ᵛ — ἐν πνεύματι GLTTrAW.

conversation, in charity, in spirit, in faith, in purity. 13 Till I come, give attendance to reading, to exhortation, to doctrine. 14 Neglect not the gift that is in thee, which was given thee by prophecy, with the laying on of the hands of the presbytery. 15 Meditate upon these things; give thyself wholly to them; that thy profiting may appear to all. 16 Take heed unto thyself, and unto the doctrine; continue in them : for in doing this thou shalt both save thyself, and them that hear thee.

V. Rebuke not an elder, but intreat *him* as a father; *and* the younger men as brethren; 2 the elder women as mothers; the younger as sisters, with all purity. 3 Honour widows that are widows indeed. 4 But if any widow have children or nephews, let them learn first to shew piety at home, and to requite their parents : for that is good and acceptable before God. 5 Now she that is a widow indeed, and desolate, trusteth in God, and continueth in supplications and prayers night and day. 6 But she that liveth in pleasure is dead while she liveth. 7 And these things give in charge, that they may be blameless. 8 But if any provide not for his own, and specially for those of his own house, he hath denied the faith, and is worse than an infidel. 9 Let not a widow be taken into the number under threescore years old, having been the wife of one man, 10 well reported of for good works; if she have brought up children, if she have lodged strangers, if she have washed the saints' feet. if she have relieved the afflicted, if she have diligently followed every good work. 11 But the younger widows refuse : for when they have begun to wax

ἐν ἁγνείᾳ. 13 ἕως ἔρχομαι, πρόσεχε τῇ ἀναγνώσει, τῇ παρα-
in purity. Till I come, give heed to reading, to exhor-

κλήσει, τῇ διδασκαλίᾳ. 14 μὴ ἀμέλει τοῦ ἐν σοὶ χαρίσματος,
tation, to teaching. Be not negligent of the ²in ³thee ¹gift,

ὃ ἐδόθη σοι διὰ´ προφητείας μετὰ ἐπιθέσεως τῶν χει-
which was given to thee through prophecy with laying on of the hands

ρῶν τοῦ πρεσβυτερίου. 15 ταῦτα μελέτα, ἐν τούτοις ἴσθι·
of the elderhood. These things meditate on, in them be,

ἵνα σου ἡ προκοπὴ φανερὰ ᾖ ͯἐν͔ πᾶσιν. 16 ἔπεχε
that thy advancement manifest may be among all. Give heed

σεαυτῷ καὶ τῇ διδασκαλίᾳ· ἐπίμενε αὐτοῖς· τοῦτο γὰρ
to thyself and to the teaching; continue in them; for this

ποιῶν, καὶ σεαυτὸν σώσεις καὶ τοὺς ἀκούοντάς σου.
doing, both thyself thou shalt save and those that hear thee.

5 Πρεσβυτέρῳ μὴ ἐπιπλήξῃς, ἀλλὰ παρακάλει ὡς
An elder do not sharply rebuke, but exhort [him] as

πατέρα· νεωτέρους ὡς ἀδελφούς· 2 πρεσβυτέρας ὡς
a father; younger [men] as brethren; elder [women] as

μητέρας· νεωτέρας ὡς ἀδελφάς, ἐν πάσῃ ἁγνείᾳ. 3 χήρας
mothers; younger as sisters, with all purity. ⁰Widows

τίμα τὰς ὄντως χήρας. 4 εἰ δέ τις χήρα τέκνα ἢ ἔκγονα
¹honour that [are] ²indeed ¹widows; but if any widow ²children ³or ³descendants

ἔχει, μανθανέτωσαν πρῶτον τὸν ἴδιον οἶκον εὐσεβεῖν, καὶ
¹have, let them learn first [as to] their own house to be pious, and

ἀμοιβὰς ἀποδιδόναι τοῖς προγόνοις· τοῦτο γάρ ἐστιν ˣκαλὸν
³recompense ¹to ²render to [their] parents; for this is good

καὶ͔ ἀπόδεκτον ἐνώπιον τοῦ θεοῦ. 5 ἡ δὲ ὄντως χήρα
and acceptable before God. Now she who [is] ³indeed ¹a ²widow,

καὶ μεμονωμένη ἤλπικεν ἐπὶ ᵞτὸν͔ θεόν, καὶ προσμένει ταῖς
and left alone, has [her] hope in God, and continues

δεήσεσιν καὶ ταῖς προσευχαῖς νυκτὸς καὶ ἡμέρας· 6 ἡ δὲ
in supplications and prayers night and day. But she that

σπαταλῶσα, ζῶσα τέθνηκεν. 7 καὶ ταῦτα παράγγελλε,
lives in self-gratification, living is dead. And these things charge,

ἵνα ᶻἀνεπίληπτοι͕ ὦσιν. 8 εἰ δέ τις τῶν ἰδίων καὶ μάλιστα
that irreproachable they may be. But if anyone his own and specially

ᵃτῶν͔ οἰκείων οὐ ᵇπρονοεῖ,͔ τὴν πίστιν ἤρνηται, καὶ
[his] household does not provide for, the faith he has denied, and

ἔστιν ἀπίστου χείρων. 9 Χήρα καταλεγέσθω μὴ
is ²than ³an ⁴unbeliever ¹worse. ⁶A ⁷widow ⁵let be put on the list ²not

ἔλαττον ἐτῶν ἑξήκοντα γεγονυῖα, ἑνὸς ἀνδρὸς γυνή, 10 ἐν
³less ⁴than ⁶years ⁵sixty ¹being, of one man wife, in

ἔργοις καλοῖς μαρτυρουμένη, εἰ ἐτεκνοτρόφησεν, εἰ ἐξενο-
²works ¹good being borne witness to, if she brought up children, if she enter-

δόχησεν, εἰ ἁγίων πόδας ἔνιψεν, εἰ θλιβομένοις ἐπήρ-
tained strangers, if saints' feet she washed, if to the oppressed she impart-

κεσεν, εἰ παντὶ ἔργῳ ἀγαθῷ ἐπηκολούθησεν. 11 Νεωτέρας δὲ
ed relief, if every ²work ¹good she followed after. But younger

χήρας παραιτοῦ· ὅταν γὰρ ᶜκαταστρηνιάσωσιν͔ τοῦ
widows refuse; for when they may have grown wanton against

χριστοῦ, γαμεῖν θέλουσιν, 12 ἔχουσαι κρίμα ὅτι τὴν
Christ, to marry they wish, having judgment because [their]

πρώτην πίστιν ἠθέτησαν. 13 ἅμα δὲ καὶ ἀργαὶ μανθά-
first faith they cast off. And withal also [to be] idle they

---

w ∽ ἐν (*read* πᾶσιν to all) LTTrAW. x ∽ καλὸν καὶ GLTTrAW. y ∽ τὸν [L]T.
z ἀνεπίλημπτοι LTTrA. a ∽ τῶν LTTr[A]. b προνοεῖται TTr. c καταστρηνιασουσιν
they shall grow wanton against A.

νουσιν, περιερχόμεναι τὰς οἰκίας· οὐ.μόνον.δὲ ἀργαί, ἀλλὰ
learn, going about to the houses; and not only idle, but

καὶ φλύαροι καὶ περίεργοι, λαλοῦσαι τὰ μὴ.δέοντα. 14 βού-
also tattlers and busy-bodies, speaking things [they] ought not. I

λομαι οὖν. νεωτέρας γαμεῖν, τεκνογονεῖν, οἰκοδεσποτεῖν,
will. therefore younger [ones] to marry, to bear children, to rule the house,

μηδεμίαν ἀφορμὴν διδόναι τῷ ἀντικειμένῳ λοιδορίας χάριν.
³no ⁴occasion· ¹to ²give to the adversary ³of ⁴reproach ¹on ²account.

15 ἤδη.γάρ τινες ἐξετράπησαν ὀπίσω τοῦ σατανᾶ. 16 Εἴ τις
For already some are turned aside after Satan. If any

ᵈπιστὸς ἢ‖ πιστὴ ἔχει χήρας, ᵉἐπαρκείτω‖ αὐ-
believing [man] or believing [woman] have widows, let him impart relief to

ταῖς. καὶ μὴ βαρείσθω ἡ ἐκκλησία, ἵνα ταῖς ὄντως χήραις
them, and not let be burdened the assembly, that to the ²indeed ¹widows

ἐπαρκέσῃ.
it may impart relief.

17 Οἱ καλῶς προεστῶτες πρεσβύτεροι διπλῆς τιμῆς
· The ⁶well ·²who ³take ⁴the ⁵lead ¹elders of double honour

ἀξιούσθωσαν, μάλιστα οἱ κοπιῶντες ἐν λόγῳ καὶ διδασ-
let be counted worthy, specially those labouring in word and teach-

καλίᾳ. 18 λέγει.γὰρ ἡ γραφή, ᶠΒοῦν ἀλοῶντα οὐ φι-
ing; for says the scripture, An ox treading out corn ³not ¹thou

μώσεις·‖ καί, Ἄξιος ὁ ἐργάτης τοῦ.μισθοῦ.αὐτοῦ. 19 Κατὰ
²shalt muzzle, and, Worthy [is] the workman of his hire. Against

πρεσβυτέρου κατηγορίαν μὴ.παραδέχου, ἐκτὸς εἰ.μὴ ἐπὶ
an elder an accusation receive not, unless on [the testi-

δύο ἢ τριῶν μαρτύρων. 20 Τοὺς ᵍ ἁμαρτάνοντας ἐνώπιον
mony of] two or three witnesses. Those that sin ²before

πάντων ἔλεγχε, ἵνα καὶ οἱ λοιποὶ φόβον ἔχωσιν. 21 Διαμαρ-
³all ¹convict, that also the rest ²fear ¹may ²have. I earnestly

τύρομαι ἐνώπιον τοῦ θεοῦ καὶ ʰκυρίου Ἰησοῦ χριστοῦ·‖ καὶ
testify before God and [the] Lord Jesus Christ and

τῶν ἐκλεκτῶν ἀγγέλων, ἵνα ταῦτα φυλάξῃς χωρὶς
the elect angels, that these things thou shouldest keep, apart from

προκρίματος, μηδὲν ποιῶν κατὰ ¹πρόσκλισιν.‖
prejudice, nothing doing by partiality.

22 Χεῖρας ταχέως μηδενὶ ἐπιτίθει, μηδὲ κοινώνει ἁμαρτίαις
Hands quickly on no one lay, nor share in sins

ἀλλοτρίαις. σεαυτὸν ἁγνὸν τήρει. 23 μηκέτι ὑδροπότει, ᵏἀλλ'‖
of others. Thyself pure keep. No longer drink water, but

οἴνῳ ὀλίγῳ χρῶ διὰ τὸν.στόμαχόν.¹σου‖ καὶ τὰς πυκνάς
⁴wine ²a ³little ¹use on account of thy stomach and ²frequent

σου ἀσθενείας. 24 Τινῶν ἀνθρώπων αἱ ἁμαρτίαι πρόδηλοί
¹thy · infirmities. Of some men the sins manifest

εἰσιν, προάγουσαι εἰς κρίσιν· τισὶν.δὲ καὶ ἐπακολουθοῦσιν.
are, going before to judgment; and some also they follow after.

25 ὡσαύτως ᵐ καὶ τὰ ⁿκαλὰ ἔργα‖ πρόδηλά ᵒἐστιν·‖ καὶ τὰ
In like manner also good works manifest are, and those that

ἄλλως ἔχοντα, κρυβῆναι οὐ.ᵖδύναται.‖
otherwise are, ²be ³hid ¹cannot.

6 Ὅσοι εἰσὶν ὑπὸ ζυγὸν δοῦλοι, τοὺς.ἰδίους δεσπότας
As many ²as ³are ⁴under ⁵yoke ¹bondmen, their own masters

---

d. — πιστὸς ἢ (read ἐπαρ. let her impart relief) LTTr[A].		e ἐπαρκείσθω LTTr.		f οὐ
φιμώσεις βοῦν ἀλοῶντα L.		g + δὲ but (those that) L[A].		h χριστοῦ Ἰησοῦ LTTrAW.
i πρόσκλησιν advocacy L.		k ἀλλὰ LTTrA.		l — σοῦ (read [thy]) LTTrA.		m + δὲ
but (in like manner) LW.		n ἔργα τὰ καλὰ LTTrAW.		o — ἐστιν LTTrA; εἰσιν W.
p δύνανται LTTrAW.

hand; and they that are otherwise cannot be hid.

VI. Let as many servants as are under the yoke count their own masters worthy of all honour, that the name of God and *his* doctrine be not blasphemed. 2 And they that have believing masters, let them not despise *them*, because they are brethren; but rather do *them* service, because they are faithful and beloved, partakers of the benefit. These things teach and exhort. 3 If any man teach otherwise, and consent not to wholesome words, *even* the words of our Lord Jesus Christ, and to the doctrine which is according to godliness; 4 he is proud, knowing nothing, but doting about questions and strifes of words, whereof cometh envy, strife, railings, evil surmisings, 5 perverse disputings of men of corrupt minds, and destitute of the truth, supposing that gain is godliness: from such withdraw thyself. 6 But godliness with contentment is great gain. 7 For we brought nothing into *this* world, *and it is* certain we can carry nothing out. 8 And having food and raiment let us be therewith content. 9 But they that will be rich fall into temptation and a snare, and *into* many foolish and hurtful lusts, which drown men in destruction and perdition. 10 For the love of money is the root of all evil: which while some coveted after, they have erred from the faith, and pierced themselves through with many sorrows. 11 But thou, O man of God, flee these things; and follow after righteousness, godliness, faith, love, patience, meekness. 12 Fight the good fight of faith, lay hold on eternal life, whereunto thou art also called, and hast professed a good profession before many witnesses. 13 I

πάσης τιμῆς ἀξίους ἡγείσθωσαν, ἵνα μὴ τὸ ὄνομα τοῦ θεοῦ
of all honour worthy let them esteem, that not the name of God

καὶ ἡ διδασκαλία βλασφημῆται. 2 οἱ.δὲ πιστοὺς ἔχοντες
and the teaching be blasphemed. And they that ²believing ¹have

δεσπότας, μὴ.καταφρονείτωσαν, ὅτι ἀδελφοί εἰσιν· ἀλλὰ
masters, let them not despise [them], because brethren they are; but

μᾶλλον δουλευέτωσαν, ὅτι πιστοί εἰσιν, καὶ ἀγα-
rather let them serve [them], because believing [ones] they are and be-

πητοὶ οἱ τῆς εὐεργεσίας ἀντιλαμβανόμενοι. ταῦτα δίδασκε
loved who ⁵the ⁶good ⁷service ¹are ²being ³helped ⁴by. These things teach

καὶ παρακάλει. 3 Εἴ τις ἑτεροδιδασκαλεῖ, καὶ ᵠμὴ.προσέρχεται∥
and exhort. If anyone teaches other doctrine, and draws not near

ὑγιαίνουσιν λόγοις τοῖς τοῦ.κυρίου.ἡμῶν Ἰησοῦ χριστοῦ, καὶ
²sound ¹to words, those of our Lord Jesus Christ, and

τῇ κατ εὐσέβειαν διδασκαλίᾳ, 4 τετύφωται, μηδὲν
the ²according ³to ⁴piety ¹teaching, he is puffed up, nothing

ἐπιστάμενος, ἀλλὰ νοσῶν περὶ ζητήσεις καὶ λογομαχίας,
knowing, but sick about questions and disputes of words,

ἐξ ὧν γίνεται φθόνος, ἔρις, βλασφημίαι, ὑπόνοιαι πονηραί,
out of which come envy, strife, evil speakings, ²suspicions ¹wicked,

5 ʳπαραδιατριβαὶ∥ διεφθαρμένων ἀνθρώπων τὸν νοῦν, καὶ
vain argumentations ³corrupted ¹of ²men in mind, and

ἀπεστερημένων τῆς ἀληθείας, νομιζόντων πορισμὸν εἶναι τὴν
destitute of the truth, holding ⁴gain ²to ³be

εὐσέβειαν· ˢἀφίστασο ἀπὸ τῶν τοιούτων.∥ 6 Ἔστιν.δὲ πορισμὸς
¹piety; withdraw from such. But ⁴is ⁵gain

μέγας ἡ εὐσέβεια μετὰ αὐταρκείας. 7 οὐδὲν.γὰρ εἰσηνέγκαμεν
⁶great ¹piety ²with ³contentment. For nothing we brought

εἰς τὸν κόσμον, ᵗδῆλον∥ ὅτι οὐδὲ ἐξενεγκεῖν τι δυνά-
into the world, [it is] manifest that neither to carry out anything are we

μεθα· 8 ἔχοντες.δὲ διατροφὰς καὶ σκεπάσματα, τούτοις ἀρ-
able. But having sustenance and coverings, with these we shall

κεσθησόμεθα. 9 Οἱ.δὲ βουλόμενοι πλουτεῖν, ἐμπίπτουσιν εἰς
be satisfied. But those desiring to be rich, fall into

πειρασμὸν καὶ παγίδα καὶ ἐπιθυμίας πολλὰς ἀνοήτους καὶ
temptation and a snare and ⁵desires ¹many ²unwise ³and

βλαβεράς, αἵτινες βυθίζουσιν τοὺς ἀνθρώπους εἰς ὄλεθρον
⁴hurtful, which sink men into destruction

καὶ ἀπώλειαν. 10 ῥίζα.γὰρ πάντων τῶν κακῶν ἐστιν ἡ φιλ-
and perdition. For a root of all evils is the love

αργυρία· ἧς τινες ὀρεγόμενοι ἀπεπλανήθησαν ἀπὸ τῆς
of money; which some stretching after were seduced from the

πίστεως, καὶ ἑαυτοὺς περιέπειραν ὀδύναις πολλαῖς. 11 Σὺ
faith, and themselves pierced with ²sorrows ¹many. ⁴Thou

δέ, ὦ ἄνθρωπε ᵘτοῦ∥ θεοῦ, ταῦτα φεῦγε· δίωκε.δὲ δικαιο-
³but, O man of God, these things flee, and pursue right-

σύνην, εὐσέβειαν, πίστιν, ἀγάπην, ὑπομονήν, ᵛπραότητα·
eousness, piety, faith, love, endurance, meekness.

12 ἀγωνίζου τὸν καλὸν ἀγῶνα τῆς πίστεως· ἐπιλαβοῦ τῆς
Combat the good comba of the faith. Lay hold

αἰωνίου ζωῆς, εἰς ἣν ʷκαὶ∥ ἐκλήθης, καὶ ὡμολόγησας
of eternal life, to which also thou wast called, and didst confess

τὴν καλὴν ὁμολογίαν ἐνώπιον πολλῶν μαρτύρων. 13 Παραγ-
the good confession before many witnesses. 13 I

ᵠ μὴ προσέχεται cleaves not T.   ʳ διαπαρατριβαὶ constant quarrellings GLTTrAW.
ˢ — ἀφίστασο ἀπὸ τῶν τοιούτων LTTrAW.   ᵗ — δῆλον (read ὅτι so that) LTTrA.   ᵘ — τοῦ
LTTr[A].   ᵛ πραϋπάθειαν meekness of spirit LTrAW; πραϋπαθίαν T.   ʷ —καὶ GLTTrAW.

γέλλω ˣσοι‖ ἐνώπιον ʸτοῦ‖ θεοῦ τοῦ ᶻζωοποιοῦντος‖ τὰ πάντα,
charge thee before God who quickens all things,

καὶ χριστοῦ Ἰησοῦ τοῦ μαρτυρήσαντος ἐπὶ Ποντίου ᵃΠι-
and Christ Jesus who witnessed before Pontius Pi-

λάτου‖ τὴν καλὴν ὁμολογίαν, 14 τηρῆσαί σε τὴν ἐντολὴν
late the good confession, that thou keep the commandment

ἄσπιλον, ᵇἀνεπίληπτον,‖ μέχρι τῆς ἐπιφανείας τοῦ κυρίου
spotless, irreproachable, until the appearing of ²Lord

ἡμῶν Ἰησοῦ χριστοῦ, 15 ἣν καιροῖς ἰδίοις δείξει ὁ
¹our Jesus Christ; which in its own times ⁶shall ⁷shew ¹the

μακάριος καὶ μόνος δυνάστης, ὁ βασιλεὺς τῶν βασιλευόν-
³blessed ³and ⁴only ⁵Ruler, the King of those being kings

των καὶ κύριος τῶν κυριευόντων, 16 ὁ μόνος ἔχων ἀθα-
and Lord of those being lords; who alone has im-

νασίαν, φῶς οἰκῶν ἀπρόσιτον, ὃν εἶδεν οὐδεὶς
mortality, ²in ⁴light ¹dwelling ³unapproachable, whom ⁵did ⁶see ¹no ²one

ἀνθρώπων οὐδὲ ἰδεῖν δύναται, ᾧ τιμὴ καὶ κράτος
³of ⁴men nor to see is able; to whom honour, and might

αἰώνιον. ἀμήν.
eternal. Amen.

17 Τοῖς πλουσίοις ἐν τῷ νῦν αἰῶνι παράγγελλε, μὴ
To the rich in the present age charge, not

ᶜὑψηλοφρονεῖν,‖ μηδὲ ἠλπικέναι ἐπὶ πλούτου ἀδηλότητι,
to be high-minded, nor to have hope in ³of ⁴riches [¹the] ²uncertainty;

ἀλλ' ᵈἐν‖ ᵉτῷ‖ θεῷ ᶠτῷ ζῶντι,‖ τῷ παρέχοντι ἡμῖν ᵍ ʰπλου-
but in ³God ¹the ²living, who gives us richly

σίως πάντα‖ εἰς ἀπόλαυσιν· 18 ἀγαθοεργεῖν, πλουτεῖν ἐν
all things for enjoyment; to do good, to be rich in

ἔργοις καλοῖς, εὐμεταδότους εἶναι, κοινωνικούς, 19 ἀπο-
²works ¹good, liberal in distributing to be, ready to communicate, trea-

θησαυρίζοντας ἑαυτοῖς θεμέλιον καλὸν εἰς τὸ μέλλον, ἵνα
suring up for themselves a ²foundation ¹good for the future, that

ἐπιλάβωνται τῆς ⁱαἰωνίου‖ ζωῆς.
they may lay hold of eternal life.

20 Ὦ Τιμόθεε, τὴν ᵏπαρακαταθήκην‖ φύλαξον,
O Timotheus, the deposit committed [to thee] keep,

ἐκτρεπόμενος τὰς βεβήλους κενοφωνίας, καὶ ἀντιθέσεις τῆς
avoiding profane empty babblings, and oppositions

ψευδωνύμου γνώσεως· 21 ἥν τινες ἐπαγγελλόμενοι, περὶ
of falsely-named knowledge, which some professing, in reference to

τὴν πίστιν ἠστόχησαν. Ἡ χάρις ˡμετὰ σοῦ.‖ ᵐἀμήν.‖
the faith missed the mark. Grace [be] with thee. Amen.

ⁿΠρὸς Τιμόθεον πρώτη ἐγράφη ἀπὸ Λαοδικείας, ἥτις
²To ³Timothy ¹first written from Laodicæa, which

ἐστιν μητρόπολις Φρυγίας τῆς Πακατιανῆς.‖
is the chief city of Phrygia Pacatiana.

give thee charge in the sight of God, who quickeneth all things, and *before* Christ Jesus, who before Pontius Pilate witnessed a good confession: 14 that thou keep *this* commandment without spot, unrebukable, until the appearing of our Lord Jesus Christ: 15 which in his times he shall shew, *who is* the blessed and only Potentate, the King of kings, and Lord of lords; 16 who only hath immortality, dwelling in the light which no man can approach unto; whom no man hath seen, nor can see: to whom *be* honour and power everlasting. Amen.

17 Charge them that are rich in this world, that they be not highminded, nor trust in uncertain riches, but in the living God, who giveth us richly all things to enjoy; 18 that they do good, that they be rich in good works, ready to distribute, willing to communicate; 19 laying up in store for themselves a good foundation against the time to come, that they may lay hold on eternal life.

20 O Timothy, keep that which is committed to thy trust, avoiding profane *and* vain babblings, and oppositions of science falsely so called: 21 which some professing have erred concerning the faith. Grace *be* with thee. Amen.

ˣ — σοι (*read* [thee]) T. ʸ — τοῦ T. ᶻ ζωογονοῦντος preserves alive LTTrA. ᵃ Πειλάτου T. ᵇ ἀνεπίλημπτον LTTrA. ᶜ ὑψηλὰ φρονεῖν to mind high things T. ᵈ ἐπὶ LTTr.
ᵉ — τῷ TTr. ᶠ — τῷ ζῶντι LTTrA. ᵍ + τὰ L. ʰ πάντα πλουσίως GLTTrAW. ⁱ ὄντως
(*read* of that which [is] truly life) GLTTrAW. ᵏ παραθήκην GLTTrAW. ˡ μεθ' ὑμῶν with
you LTTr. ᵐ — ἀμήν GLTTrAW. ⁿ — *the subscription* GLTW; Πρὸς Τιμόθεον α΄ TrA.

PAUL, an apostle of Jesus Christ by the will of God, according to the promise of life which is in Christ Jesus, 2 to Timothy, my dearly beloved son: Grace, mercy, and peace, from God the Father and Christ Jesus our Lord.

3 I thank God, whom I serve from my forefathers with pure conscience, that without ceasing I have remembrance of thee in my prayers night and day; 4 greatly desiring to see thee, being mindful of thy tears, that I may be filled with joy; 5 when I call to remembrance the unfeigned faith that is in thee, which dwelt first in thy grandmother Lois, and thy mother Eunice; and I am persuaded that in thee also. 6 Wherefore I put thee in remembrance that thou stir up the gift of God, which is in thee by the putting on of my hands. 7 For God hath not given us the spirit of fear; but of power, and of love, and of a sound mind. 8 Be not thou therefore ashamed of the testimony of our Lord, nor of me his prisoner: but be thou partaker of the afflictions of the gospel according to the power of God; 9 who hath saved us, and called us with an holy calling, not according to our works, but according to his own purpose and grace, which was given us in Christ Jesus before the world began, 10 but is now made manifest by the appearing of our Saviour Jesus Christ, who hath abolished death, and hath brought life and immortality to light through the gospel; 11 whereunto I am

ΠΑΥΛΟΣ ἀπόστολος ᵇἸησοῦ χριστοῦ‖ διὰ θελήματος θεοῦ
Paul, apostle of Jesus Christ by [the] will of God
κατ᾽ ἐπαγγελίαν ζωῆς τῆς ἐν χριστῷ Ἰησοῦ, 2 Τι-
according to promise of life which [is] in Christ Jesus, to Ti-
μοθέῳ ἀγαπητῷ τέκνῳ· χάρις, ἔλεος, εἰρήνη ἀπὸ θεοῦ
motheus [my] beloved child: Grace, mercy, peace from God [the]
πατρὸς καὶ χριστοῦ Ἰησοῦ τοῦ κυρίου ἡμῶν.
Father and Christ Jesus our Lord.

3 Χάριν ἔχω τῷ θεῷ, ᾧ λατρεύω ἀπὸ προγόνων ἐν
I am thankful to God, whom I serve from [my] forefathers with
καθαρᾷ συνειδήσει, ὡς ἀδιάλειπτον ἔχω τὴν περὶ σοῦ μνείαν
pure conscience, how unceasingly I have the ²of ³thee ¹remembrance
ἐν ταῖς δεήσεσίν μου ᶜνυκτὸς καὶ ἡμέρας,‖ 4 ἐπιποθῶν σε
in my supplications night and day, longing ³thee
ἰδεῖν, μεμνημένος σου τῶν δακρύων, ἵνα χαρᾶς πληρωθῶ·
¹to ²see, remembering thy tears, that with joy I may be filled;
5 ὑπόμνησιν ᵈλαμβάνων‖ τῆς ἐν σοὶ ἀνυποκρίτου πίστεως,
²remembrance ¹taking of the ³in ⁴thee ¹unfeigned ²faith,
ἥτις ἐνῴκησεν πρῶτον ἐν τῇ μάμμῃ σου Λωΐδι καὶ τῇ μητρί
which dwelt first in thy grandmother Lois and in ²mother
σου ᵉΕὐνείκῃ,‖ πέπεισμαι δὲ ὅτι καὶ ἐν σοί. 6 Δι᾽ ἣν αἰτίαν
¹thy Eunice, and I am persuaded that also in thee. For which cause
ἀναμιμνήσκω σε ἀναζωπυρεῖν τὸ χάρισμα τοῦ θεοῦ, ὅ ἐστιν
I remind thee to kindle up the gift of God which is
ἐν σοὶ διὰ τῆς ἐπιθέσεως τῶν χειρῶν μου. 7 οὐ γὰρ ἔδωκεν
in thee by the laying on of my hands. For ⁴not ²gave
ἡμῖν ὁ θεὸς πνεῦμα δειλίας, ἀλλὰ δυνάμεως καὶ ἀγάπης
³us ¹God a spirit of cowardice, but of power, and of love,
καὶ σωφρονισμοῦ. 8 μὴ οὖν ἐπαισχυνθῇς τὸ
and of wise discretion. ⁴Not ⁵therefore ²thou ³shouldest be ashamed of the
μαρτύριον τοῦ κυρίου ἡμῶν, μηδὲ ἐμὲ τὸν δέσμιον αὐτοῦ· ἀλλὰ
testimony of our Lord, nor me his prisoner; but
ᶠσυγκακοπάθησον‖ τῷ εὐαγγελίῳ κατὰ δύναμιν θεοῦ, 9 τοῦ
suffer evils along with the glad tidings according to ²power ¹God's; who
σώσαντος ἡμᾶς καὶ καλέσαντος κλήσει ἁγίᾳ, οὐ κατὰ
saved us and called [us] with a ²calling ¹holy, not according to
τὰ ἔργα ἡμῶν, ἀλλὰ ᵍκατ᾽‖ ἰδίαν πρόθεσιν καὶ χάριν τὴν
our works, but according to his own purpose and grace, which
δοθεῖσαν ἡμῖν ἐν χριστῷ Ἰησοῦ πρὸ χρόνων αἰωνίων,
[was] given us in Christ Jesus before the ages of time,
10 φανερωθεῖσαν δὲ νῦν διὰ τῆς ἐπιφανείας τοῦ σωτῆρος ἡμῶν
but made manifest now by the appearing of our Saviour
ʰἸησοῦ χριστοῦ,‖ καταργήσαντος μὲν τὸν θάνατον, φωτίσαν-
Jesus Christ, who annulled death, ²brought ³to
τος δὲ ζωὴν καὶ ἀφθαρσίαν διὰ τοῦ εὐαγγελίου, 11 εἰς ὃ
⁴light ¹and life and incorruptibility by the glad tidings; to which

ᵃ + Παύλου τοῦ Ἀποστόλου of the Apostle Paul Ε; + Παύλου G; Πρὸς Τιμόθεον β′
Ι.ΤΤrAW. ᵇ χριστοῦ Ἰησοῦ ΤΤrAW. ᶜ νυκτὸς καὶ ἡμέρας (read night and day longing
&c. LTr. ᵈ λαβὼν having taken LTTrA. ᵉ Εὐνίκη EGLTTrAW. ᶠ συν- T. ᵍ κατὰ
LTTr:A. ʰ χριστοῦ Ἰησοῦ LTTr.

ἐτέθην   ἐγὼ   κῆρυξ   καὶ   ἀπόστολος   καὶ   διδάσκαλος
²was ³appointed   ¹I   a herald   and   apostle   and   teacher
¹ἐθνῶν.‖   12 δι'. ἣν αἰτίαν καὶ ταῦτα πάσχω· ἀλλ' οὐκ
of [the] nations.   For which cause   also these things I suffer; but   ²not
ἐπαισχύνομαι, οἶδα.γὰρ ᾧ πεπίστευκα, καὶ πέπεισμαι ὅτι
¹I ¹am ashamed;   for I know whom I have believed, and am persuaded that
δυνατός ἐστιν τὴν παραθήκην   μου φυλάξαι εἰς ἐκείνην
able   he is   the deposit committed [to him] of me to keep   for   that
τὴν ἡμέραν. 13 ὑποτύπωσιν ἔχε ὑγιαινόντων λόγων, ὧν
day.   ²A ³delineation ¹have   of sound   words, which [words]
παρ' ἐμοῦ ἤκουσας, ἐν πίστει καὶ ἀγάπῃ τῇ ἐν χριστῷ
from   me thou didst hear, in   faith   and   love   which [are] in   Christ
Ἰησοῦ. 14 τὴν καλὴν ¹παρακαταθήκην‖   φύλαξον διὰ
Jesus.   The good   deposit committed [to thee]   keep   by [the]
πνεύματος ἁγίου τοῦ ἐνοικοῦντος ἐν ἡμῖν. 15 Οἶδας τοῦτο,
²Spirit   ¹Holy which   dwells   in   us.   Thou knowest this,
ὅτι ἀπεστράφησάν με πάντες οἱ   ἐν τῇ Ἀσίᾳ, ὧν ἐστιν
that turned away from me all   who [are]   in   Asia, of whom is
ᵏΦύγελλος‖ καὶ ¹ᵗἙρμογένης. 16 Δῴη ἔλεος ὁ κύριος τῷ
Phygellus   and Hermogenes.   May ³grant ⁴mercy ¹the ²Lord to the
Ὀνησιφόρου οἴκῳ· ὅτι πολλάκις με ἀνέψυξεν, καὶ τὴν
²of ³Onesiphorus ¹house, because   oft   me he refreshed, and
ἅλυσίν.μου οὐκ.ᵐἐπῃσχύνθη,‖ 17 ἀλλὰ γενόμενος ἐν Ῥώμῃ,
my chain   was not ashamed of;   but   having been   in   Rome,
ⁿσπουδαιότερον‖ ἐζήτησέν με καὶ εὗρεν· 18 δῴη αὐτῷ
more diligently   he sought out me and found [me]— may ³grant ⁴to ⁵him
ὁ κύριος εὑρεῖν ἔλεος παρὰ κυρίου ἐν ἐκείνῃ τῇ ἡμέρᾳ· καὶ
¹the ²Lord   to find mercy from [the] Lord in   that   day:— and
ὅσα ἐν Ἐφέσῳ διηκόνησεν βέλτιον   σὺ γινώσκεις.
how much in Ephesus he served   ³better [⁴than ⁵I ⁶need ⁷say] ¹thou ²knowest.

2 Σὺ οὖν, τέκνον.μου, ἐνδυναμοῦ ἐν τῇ χάριτι τῇ
  Thou therefore,   my child,   be strong   in   the   grace which [is]
ἐν χριστῷ Ἰησοῦ· 2 καὶ   ἃ   ἤκουσας παρ' ἐμοῦ
in   Christ   Jesus.   And the things which thou didst hear   of   me
διὰ πολλῶν μαρτύρων, ταῦτα παράθου πιστοῖς ἀνθρώποις,
with   many   witnesses,   these   commit to faithful   men,
οἵτινες ἱκανοὶ ἔσονται καὶ ἑτέρους διδάξαι. 3 °σὺ οὖν
such as competent shall be   also   others   to teach.   Thou therefore
κακοπάθησον‖ ὡς καλὸς στρατιώτης ᴾΙησοῦ χριστοῦ.‖ 4 οὐδεὶς
¹suffer hardship as ²good   ¹a soldier   of Jesus   Christ.   No one
στρατευόμενος ἐμπλέκεται ταῖς τοῦ βίου ᵠπραγματείαις,‖
serving as a soldier entangles himself with the   ²of ³life   ¹affairs,
ἵνα τῷ στρατολογήσαντι ἀρέσῃ. 5 ἐὰν.δὲ καὶ ἀθλῇ
that him who enrolled him as a soldier he may please.   And if also ²contend
τις, οὐ.στεφανοῦται ἐὰν.μὴ νομίμως ἀ-
[²in ⁴the ⁵games] ¹anyone, he is not crowned   unless   lawfully he shall
θλήσῃ. 6 τὸν κοπιῶντα γεωργὸν δεῖ πρῶτον τῶν
have contended.   The   ³labour ¹husbandman ²must before of the
καρπῶν μεταλαμβάνειν.
fruits   partaking.

7 Νόει ʳἃ‖ λέγω· ˢδῴη‖ γάρ σοι ὁ κύριος σύνεσιν
  Consider the things I say, ²may ⁵give ¹for ⁶thee ³the ⁴Lord understanding

¹ — ἐθνῶν T.   ¹ παραθήκην GLTTrAW.   ᵏ Φύγελος Phygelus LTTrAW.   ¹ Ἑρμογενης Ermogenes T.   ᵐ ἐπαισχύνθη LTTrA.   ⁿ σπουδαίως diligently LTTr.   ° συγκακοπάθησον (συνκ– T) suffer hardship with [me] LTTrAW.   ᴾ χριστοῦ Ἰησοῦ LTTrAW.   ᵠ πραγματίαις T.   ʳ ἃ what LTTrAW.   ˢ δώσει will give LTTrAW.

appointed a preacher, and an apostle, and a teacher of the Gentiles. 12 For the which cause I also suffer these things: nevertheless I am not ashamed: for I know whom I have believed, and am persuaded that he is able to keep that which I have committed unto him against that day. 13 Hold fast the form of sound words, which thou hast heard of me, in faith and love which is in Christ Jesus. 14 That good thing which was committed unto thee keep by the Holy Ghost which dwelleth in us. 15 This thou knowest, that all they which are in Asia be turned away from me; of whom are Phygellus and Hermogenes. 16 The Lord give mercy unto the house of Onesiphorus; for he oft refreshed me, and was not ashamed of my chain: 17 but, when he was in Rome, he sought me out very diligently, and found me. 18 The Lord grant unto him that he may find mercy of the Lord in that day: and in how many things he ministered unto me at Ephesus, thou knowest very well.

II. Thou therefore, my son, be strong in the grace that is in Christ Jesus. 2 And the things that thou hast heard of me among many witnesses, the same commit thou to faithful men, who shall be able to teach others also. 3 Thou therefore endure hardness, as a good soldier of Jesus Christ. 4 No man that warreth entangleth himself with the affairs of this life; that he may please him who hath chosen him to be a soldier. 5 And if a man also strive for masteries, yet is he not crowned, except he strive lawfully. 6 The husbandman that laboureth must be first partaker of the fruits.

7 Consider what I

ay; and the Lord give thee understanding in all things. 8 Remember that Jesus Christ of the seed of David was raised from the dead according to my gospel ; 9 wherein I suffer trouble, as an evildoer, even unto bonds ; but the word of God is not bound. 10 Therefore I endure all things for the elect's sakes, that they may also obtain the salvation which is in Christ Jesus with eternal glory. 11 *It is* a faithful saying : For if we be dead with *him*, we shall also live with *him*: 12 if we suffer, we shall also reign with *him*: if we deny *him*, he also will deny us: 13 if we believe not, *yet* he abideth faithful : he cannot deny himself.

14 Of these things put *them* in remembrance, charging *them* before the Lord that they strive not about words to no profit, *but* to the subverting of the hearers. 15 Study to shew thyself approved unto God, a workman that needeth not to be ashamed, rightly dividing the word of truth. 16 But shun profane *and* vain babblings ; for they will increase unto more ungodliness. 17 And their word will eat as doth a canker : of whom is Hymenæus and Philetus ; 18 who concerning the truth have erred, saying that the resurrection is past already ; and overthrow the faith of some. 19 Nevertheless the foundation of God standeth sure, having this seal, The Lord knoweth them that are his. And, Let every one that nameth the name of Christ depart from iniquity. 20 But in a great house there are not only vessels of gold and of silver, but also of wood and of earth ; and some to honour, and some to dishonour. 21 If a man therefore purge himself from these, he

ἐν πᾶσιν. 8 Μνημόνευε Ἰησοῦν χριστὸν ἐγηγερμένον ἐκ
in all things. Remember Jesus Christ raised from among

νεκρῶν, ἐκ σπέρματος 'Δαβίδ,'' κατὰ τὸ εὐαγγέλιόν
[the] dead, of [the] seed of David, according to ²glad ³tidings

μου· 9 ἐν ᾧ κακοπαθῶ μέχρι δεσμῶν ὡς κακοῦργος· ˇἀλλ''
¹my, in which I suffer hardship unto bonds as an evil doer : but

ὁ λόγος τοῦ θεοῦ οὐ.δέδεται. 10 διὰ τοῦτο πάντα ὑπο-
the word of God is not bound. Because of this all things I en-

μένω διὰ τοὺς ἐκλεκτούς, ἵνα καὶ αὐτοὶ σωτηρίας τύ-
dure for sake of the elect, that also they [the] salvation may

χωσιν τῆς ἐν χριστῷ Ἰησοῦ μετὰ δόξης αἰωνίου. 11 πιστὸς
obtain which [is] in Christ Jesus with ²glory ¹eternal. Faithful

ὁ λόγος· εἰ.γὰρ συναπεθάνομεν, καὶ ʷσυζήσομεν·''
[is] the word ; for if we died together with [him], also we shall live together ;

12 εἰ ὑπομένομεν, καὶ ˣσυμβασιλεύσομεν·'' εἰ ʸἀρνούμεθα,''
if we endure, also we shall reign together ; if we deny

κἀκεῖνος ἀρνήσεται ἡμᾶς· 13 εἰ ἀπιστοῦμεν, ἐκεῖνος
[him], he also will deny us ; if we are unfaithful, he

πιστὸς μένει· ἀρνήσασθαι ᶻ ἑαυτὸν οὐ.ʒύναται.
faithful abides ; to deny himself he is not able.

14 Ταῦτα ὑπομίμνησκε, διαμαρτυρόμενος ἐνώπιον
²These ³things ⁴put ⁵in ⁶remembrance ¹of, testifying earnestly before

ᵃτοῦ κυρίου'' ᵇμὴ λογομαχεῖν'' ᶜεἰς'' οὐδὲν χρήσιμον, ἐπὶ
the Lord not to dispute about words ²for ³nothing ¹profitable, to

καταστροφῇ τῶν ἀκουόντων. 15 σπούδασον σεαυτὸν
subversion of those who hear. Be diligent ³thyself

δόκιμον παραστῆσαι τῷ θεῷ, ἐργάτην ἀνεπαίσχυντον, ὀρθο-
⁴approved ¹to ²present to God, a workman not ashamed, straight-

τομοῦντα τὸν λόγον τῆς ἀληθείας· 16 τὰς.δὲ.βεβήλους κενο-
ly cutting the word of truth ; but profane empty

φωνίας περιΐστασο· ἐπὶ πλεῖον γὰρ προκόψουσιν ἀσεβείας,
babblings stand aloof from, ²to ³more ¹for they will advance of ungodliness,

17 καὶ ὁ.λόγος.αὐτῶν ὡς γάγγραινα νομὴν ἕξει· ὧν ἐστιν
and their word as a gangrene pasture will have ; of whom is

Ὑμέναιος καὶ Φιλητός, 18 οἵτινες περὶ τὴν ἀλήθειαν
Hymenæus and Philetus ; who concerning the truth

ἠστόχησαν, λέγοντες ᵈτὴν'' ἀνάστασιν ἤδη γεγονέναι.
missed the mark, asserting the resurrection already to have taken place ;

καὶ ἀνατρέπουσιν τὴν τινων πίστιν. 19 ὁ ᵉμέντοι'' στερεὸς
and are overthrowing the ²of ³some ¹faith. Nevertheless ²firm

θεμέλιος τοῦ θεοῦ ἕστηκεν, ἔχων τὴν.σφραγῖδα.ταύτην, Ἔγνω
³foundation ¹God's stands, having this seal, ²Knows

κύριος τοὺς ὄντας αὐτοῦ, καὶ Ἀποστήτω ἀπὸ ἀδι-
¹[the] ²Lord those that are his, and Let depart from unright-

κίας πᾶς ὁ ὀνομάζων τὸ ὄνομα ᶠχριστοῦ.'' 20 ἐν μεγάλῃ
eousness everyone who names the name of Christ. ²In ⁴great

δὲ οἰκίᾳ· οὐκ.ἔστιν μόνον σκεύη χρυσᾶ καὶ ἀργυρᾶ, ἀλλὰ
¹but ³a house there are not only vessels golden and silver, but

καὶ ξύλινα καὶ ὀστράκινα, καὶ ἃ μὲν εἰς τιμήν, ἃ.δὲ εἰς
also wooden and earthen, and some to honour, others to

ἀτιμίαν. 21 ἐὰν οὖν τις ἐκκαθάρῃ ἑαυτὸν ἀπὸ τούτων,
dishonour. If therefore one shall have purged himself from these,

---

ᵗ Δαυείδ LTTrA ; Δαυίδ GW. ᵛ ἀλλὰ LTTrAW. ʷ συν- LTTrA. ˣ συν- T. ʸ ἀρνησόμεθα we shall deny LTTrA. ᶻ + γὰρ for (to deny) LTTrAW. ᵃ τοῦ θεοῦ God TTr. ᵇ μὴ λογομάχει Dispute thou not about words L. ᶜ ἐπ' LTTrA. ᵈ τὴν (read [the]) TTr[A] ᵉ μέν τοι Tr. ᶠ κυρίου of [the] Lord GLTTrAW.

ἔσται σκεῦος εἰς τιμήν, ἡγιασμένον, ᵍκαι‖ εὔχρηστον
he shall be a vessel   to honour, having been sanctified, and   serviceable

τῷ δεσπότῃ, εἰς πᾶν ἔργον ἀγαθὸν ἡτοιμασμένον.
to the master,   for every ²work ¹good having been prepared.

22 τὰς.δὲ.νεωτερικὰς ἐπιθυμίας φεῦγε· δίωκε.δὲ δικαιοσύνην,
   But youthful   lusts   flee·   and pursue righteousness,

πίστιν, ἀγάπην, εἰρήνην μετὰ ʰ τῶν ἐπικαλουμένων τὸν
faith,   love,   peace with those that   call on   the

κύριον ἐκ καθαρᾶς καρδίας. 23 τὰς.δὲ.μωρὰς καὶ ἀπαι-
Lord out of ²pure ¹a heart.   But foolish   and   undis-

δεύτους ζητήσεις παραιτοῦ, εἰδὼς ὅτι γεννῶσιν μάχας·
ciplined questionings refuse, knowing that they beget contentions.

24 δοῦλον.δὲ κυρίου οὐ.δεῖ μάχεσθαι, ¹ἀλλ'‖ ἤπιον
And ³a ¹bondman ⁵of [⁶the] ⁷Lord ¹it ²behoves not to contend, but gentle

εἶναι πρὸς πάντας, διδακτικόν, ἀνεξίκακον, 25 ἐν ᵏπραότητι‖
to be towards all ;   apt to teach ;   forbearing ;   in   meekness

παιδεύοντα τοὺς ἀντιδιατιθεμένους, μήποτε ¹δῷ‖ αὐτοῖς
disciplining those that oppose,   if perhaps ²may ³give ⁴them

ὁ θεὸς μετάνοιαν εἰς ἐπίγνωσιν ἀληθείας, 26 καὶ ἀνα-
¹God repentance to acknowledgment of [the] truth,   and they may

νήψωσιν ἐκ τῆς τοῦ διαβόλου παγίδος, ἐζωγρημένοι ὑπ'
awake up out of the ²of ³the ⁴devil ¹snare, having been taken by

αὐτοῦ εἰς τὸ ἐκείνου θέλημα.
him for his   will.

3 Τοῦτο.δὲ ᵐγίνωσκε,‖ ὅτι ἐν ἐσχάταις ἡμέραις ἐνστή-
  But this   know thou, that in [the] last   days   ³will ⁴be

σονται καιροὶ χαλεποί. 2 ἔσονται.γὰρ οἱ ἄνθρωποι φίλαυτοι,
²present ²times ¹difficult ;   for ¹will ⁵be   ¹men   lovers of self,

φιλάργυροι, ἀλαζόνες, ὑπερήφανοι, βλάσφημοι, γονεῦσιν
lovers of money, vaunting, proud,   evil speakers. to parents

ἀπειθεῖς, ἀχάριστοι, ἀνόσιοι, 3 ἄστοργοι, ἄσπονδοι,
disobedient, unthankful, unholy, without natural affection, implacable,

διάβολοι, ἀκρατεῖς, ἀνήμεροι, ἀφιλάγαθοι, 4 προδόται,
slanderers, incontinent, savage, not lovers of good,   betrayers,

προπετεῖς, τετυφωμένοι, φιλήδονοι μᾶλλον ἢ φιλόθεοι,
headlong,   puffed up, lovers of pleasure rather than lovers of God ;

5 ἔχοντες μόρφωσιν εὐσεβείας, τὴν.δὲ δύναμιν αὐτῆς ἠρνη-
having   a form   of piety, but the power of it deny-

μένοι. καὶ τούτους ἀποτρέπου. 6 ἐκ.τούτων.γὰρ εἰσιν οἱ
ing :   and these turn away from.   For of these   are   those who

ἐνδύνοντες εἰς τὰς οἰκίας καὶ ⁿαἰχμαλωτεύοντες τὰ‖ γυναικάρια
[are] entering into houses and   leading captive   silly women

σεσωρευμένα ἁμαρτίαις, ἀγόμενα ἐπιθυμίαις ποικίλαις, 7 πάν-
laden   with sins, led away by ²lusts ¹various,   al-

τοτε μανθάνοντα καὶ μηδέποτε εἰς ἐπίγνωσιν ἀληθείας
ways learning and never to [the] knowledge of [the] truth

ἐλθεῖν δυνάμενα. 8 ὃν.τρόπον.δὲ Ἰαννῆς καὶ Ἰαμβρῆς ἀντέ-
²to ³come ¹able.   Now in the way Jannes and Jambres with-

στησαν Μωϋσεῖ, οὕτως καὶ οὗτοι ἀνθίστανται τῇ ἀληθείᾳ,
stood Moses,   thus also these   withstand   the truth,

ἄνθρωποι κατεφθαρμένοι τὸν.νοῦν, ἀδόκιμοι περὶ
men   utterly corrupted in mind, found worthless as regards

τὴν πίστιν. 9 ἀλλ' οὐ.προκόψουσιν ἐπὶ.πλεῖον· ἡ.γὰρ ἄνοια
the faith.   But they shall not advance farther,   ¹for ²folly

shall be a vessel unto honour, sanctified, and meet for the master's use, *and* prepared unto every good work. 22 Flee also youthful lusts : but follow righteousness, faith, charity, peace, with them that call on the Lord out of a pure heart. 23 But foolish and unlearned questions avoid, knowing that they do gender strifes. 24 And the servant of the Lord must not strive ; but be gentle unto all *men*, apt to teach, patient, 25 in meekness instructing those that oppose themselves ; if God peradventure will give them repentance to the acknowledging of the truth ; 26 and *that* they may recover themselves out of the snare of the devil, who are taken captive by him at his will.

III. This know also, that in the last days perilous times shall come. 2 For men shall be lovers of their own selves, covetous, boasters, proud, blasphemers, disobedient to parents, unthankful, unholy, 3 without natural affection, trucebreakers, false accusers, incontinent, fierce, despisers of those that are good, 4 traitors, heady, highminded, lovers of pleasures more than lovers of God ; 5 having a form of godliness, but denying the power thereof : from such turn away. 6 For of this sort are they which creep into houses, and lead captive silly women laden with sins, led away with divers lusts, 7 ever learning, and never able to come to the knowledge of the truth. 8 Now as Jannes and Jambres withstood Moses, so do these also resist the truth : men of corrupt minds, reprobate concerning the faith. 9 But they shall proceed no further : for their folly

---

shall be manifest unto all *men*, as theirs also was. 10 But thou hast fully known my doctrine, manner of life, purpose, faith, long-suffering, charity, patience, 11 persecutions, afflictions, which came unto me at Antioch, at Iconium, at Lystra; what persecutions I endured: but out of *them* all the Lord delivered me. 12 Yea, and all that will live godly in Christ Jesus shall suffer persecution. 13 But evil men and seducers shall wax worse and worse, deceiving, and being deceived. 14 But continue thou in the things which thou hast learned and hast been assured of, knowing of whom thou hast learned *them*; 15 and that from a child thou hast known the holy scriptures, which are able to make thee wise unto salvation through faith which is in Christ Jesus. 16 All scripture *is* given by inspiration of God, and *is* profitable for doctrine, for reproof, for correction, for instruction in righteousness: 17 that the man of God may be perfect, throughly furnished unto all good works.

IV. 1 charge *thee* therefore before God, and the Lord Jesus Christ, who shall judge the quick and the dead at his appearing and his kingdom; 2 preach the word; be instant in season, out of season; reprove, rebuke, exhort with all longsuffering and doctrine. 3 For the time will come when they will not endure sound doctrine; but after their own lusts shall they heap to themselves teachers, having itching ears; 4 and they shall turn away *their* ears from the truth, and shall be

αὐτῶν ἔκδηλος ἔσται πᾶσιν, ὡς καὶ ἡ ἐκείνων ἐγένετο.
[1]their fully manifest shall be to all, as also that of those became.

10 σὺ δὲ °παρηκολούθηκάς∥ μου τῇ διδασκαλίᾳ, τῇ ἀγωγῇ,
But thou hast closely followed my teaching, conduct,

τῇ προθέσει, τῇ πίστει, τῇ μακροθυμίᾳ, τῇ ἀγάπῃ, τῇ ὑπομονῇ,
purpose, faith, patience, love, endurance,

11 τοῖς διωγμοῖς, τοῖς παθήμασιν, οἷά μοι ἐγένετο ἐν Ἀν-
persecutions, sufferings: such as to me happened in An-

τιοχείᾳ, ἐν Ἰκονίῳ, ἐν Λύστροις· οἵους διωγμοὺς ὑπ-
tioch, in Iconium, in Lystra; what manner of persecutions I en-

ήνεγκα, καὶ ἐκ πάντων με ᴾἐρρύσατο∥ ὁ κύριος. 12 καὶ
dured; and out of all [4]me [5]delivered [1]the [2]Lord. And

πάντες δὲ οἱ θέλοντες ᵠεὐσεβῶς ζῆν∥ ἐν χριστῷ Ἰησοῦ
all indeed who wish piously to live in Christ Jesus

διωχθήσονται· 13 πονηροὶ δὲ ἄνθρωποι καὶ γόητες προ-
will be persecuted. But wicked men and impostors shall

κόψουσιν ἐπὶ τὸ χεῖρον, πλανῶντες καὶ πλανώμενοι. 14 σὺ δὲ
advance to worse, misleading and being misled. But thou

μένε ἐν οἷς ἔμαθες, καὶ ἐπιστώθης, εἰδὼς παρὰ
abide in the things thou didst learn, and wast assured of, having known from

ʳτίνος∥ ἔμαθες, 15 καὶ ὅτι ἀπὸ βρέφους ˢτὰ∥ ἱερὰ
whom thou didst learn [them]; and that from a babe the sacred

γράμματα οἶδας, τὰ δυνάμενά σε σοφίσαι εἰς
letters thou hast known, which [are] able [3]thee [1]to [2]make wise to

σωτηρίαν, διὰ πίστεως τῆς ἐν χριστῷ Ἰησοῦ. 16 πᾶσα
salvation, through faith which [is] in Christ Jesus. Every

γραφὴ θεόπνευστος καὶ ὠφέλιμος πρὸς διδασκαλίαν, πρὸς
scripture [is] God-inspired and profitable for teaching, for

ᵗἔλεγχον,∥ πρὸς ἐπανόρθωσιν, πρὸς ᵛπαιδείαν∥ τὴν ἐν
conviction, for correction, for discipline which [is] in

δικαιοσύνῃ· 17 ἵνα ἄρτιος ᾖ ὁ τοῦ θεοῦ ἄνθρωπος, πρὸς
righteousness; that complete may be the [2]of [3]God [1]man, to

πᾶν ἔργον ἀγαθὸν ἐξηρτισμένος.
every [2]work [1]good fully fitted.

4 Διαμαρτύρομαι ʷοὖν ἐγὼ∥ ἐνώπιον τοῦ θεοῦ καὶ ˣτοῦ
[2]Earnestly [3]testify [4]therefore [1]I before God and the

κυρίου∥ ʸἸησοῦ χριστοῦ,∥ τοῦ μέλλοντος κρίνειν ζῶντας καὶ
Lord Jesus Christ, who is about to judge living and

νεκροὺς ᶻκατὰ∥ τὴν ἐπιφάνειαν αὐτοῦ καὶ τὴν βασιλείαν
dead according to his appearing and [2]kingdom

αὐτοῦ, 2 κήρυξον τὸν λόγον, ἐπίστηθι εὐκαίρως ἀκαίρως,
[1]his, proclaim the word; be urgent in season, out of season,

ἔλεγξον, ᵃἐπιτίμησον, παρακάλεσον,∥ ἐν πάσῃ μακροθυμίᾳ
convict, rebuke, encourage, with all patience

καὶ διδαχῇ. 3 ἔσται γὰρ καιρὸς ὅτε τῆς ὑγιαινούσης δι-
and teaching. For there will be a time when sound teach-

δασκαλίας οὐκ ἀνέξονται, ἀλλὰ κατὰ τὰς ᵇἐπιθυμίας
ing they will not bear; but according to [3]desires

τὰς ἰδίας∥ ἑαυτοῖς ἐπισωρεύσουσιν διδασκάλους, κνηθό-
[1]their [2]own to themselves will heap up teachers,

μενοι τὴν ἀκοήν· 4 καὶ ἀπὸ μὲν τῆς ἀληθείας τὴν ἀκοὴν ἀπο-
having an itching ear; and from the truth the ear they will

° παρηκολούθησάς didst closely follow LTTrA. ᴾ ἐρύσατο LTTr. ᵠ ζῆν εὐσεβῶς TTr.
ʳ τίνων what [persons] LTTrA. ˢ — τὰ [L]TTrA. ᵗ ἐλεγμόν LTTrA. ᵛ παιδίαν T.
ʷ — οὖν ἐγὼ GLTTrAW. ˣ — τοῦ κυρίου GLTTrAW. ʸ χριστοῦ Ἰησοῦ LTTrAW. ᶻ , καὶ
and [by] GLTTrAW. ᵃ παρακαλεσον. ἐπιτίμησον T. ᵇ ἰδίας ἐπιθυμίας GLTTrAW.

στρέψουσιν, ἐπὶ δὲ τοὺς μύθους ἐκτραπήσονται. 5 σὺ δὲ
turn away, and to fables will be turned aside. But thou,

νῆφε ἐν πᾶσιν, κακοπάθησον, ἔργον ποίησον εὐαγ-
be sober in all things, suffer hardships, [the] work do of an

γελιστοῦ, τὴν διακονίαν σου πληροφόρησον. 6 Ἐγὼ γὰρ ἤδη
evangelist, thy service fully carry out. For I already

σπένδομαι, καὶ ὁ καιρὸς τῆς ᶜἐμῆς ἀναλύσεως‖ ἐφ-
am being poured out, and the time of my release is

έστηκεν. 7 τὸν ᵈἀγῶνα τὸν καλὸν‖ ἠγώνισμαι, τὸν δρόμον
come. The ²combat ¹good I have combated, the course

τετέλεκα, τὴν πίστιν τετήρηκα· 8 λοιπὸν ἀπόκειταί μοι
I have finished, the faith I have kept. Henceforth is laid up for me

ὁ τῆς δικαιοσύνης στέφανος, ὃν ἀποδώσει μοι ὁ κύριος
the ⁴²of ³righteousness ¹crown, which ⁶will ⁷render ⁸to ⁹me ¹the ²Lord

ἐν ἐκείνῃ τῇ ἡμέρᾳ, ὁ δίκαιος κριτής· οὐ μόνον δὲ ἐμοί,
¹⁰in ¹¹that ¹²day ³the ⁴righteous ⁵judge; and not only to me,

ἀλλὰ καὶ πᾶσιν τοῖς ἠγαπηκόσιν τὴν ἐπιφάνειαν αὐτοῦ.
but also to all who ¹love his appearing.

9 Σπούδασον ἐλθεῖν πρός με ταχέως. 10 Δημᾶς γάρ με
Be diligent to come to me quickly; for Demas ²me

ἐγκατέλιπεν, ἀγαπήσας τὸν νῦν αἰῶνα, καὶ ἐπορεύθη εἰς
¹forsook, having loved the present age, and is gone to

Θεσσαλονίκην· Κρήσκης εἰς ᵉΓαλατίαν,‖ Τίτος εἰς ᶠΔαλματίαν·‖
Thessalonica; Crescens to Galatia, Titus to Dalmatia.

11 Λουκᾶς ἐστιν μόνος μετ᾽ ἐμοῦ. Μάρκον ἀναλαβὼν ἄγε
Luke ²is ¹alone with me. Mark having taken bring

μετὰ σεαυτοῦ· ἔστιν γάρ μοι εὔχρηστος εἰς διακονίαν. 12 Τυ-
with thyself· for he is ²to ¹me ⁴useful for service. ²Ty-

χικὸν δὲ ἀπέστειλα εἰς Ἔφεσον. 13 Τὸν ᵍφαιλόνην‖ ὃν
chicus ¹but I sent to Ephesus. The cloak which

ἀπέλιπον ἐν ʰΤρωάδι‖ παρὰ Κάρπῳ, ἐρχόμενος φέρε, καὶ τὰ
I left in Troas with Carpus, [when] coming bring, and the

βιβλία, μάλιστα τὰς μεμβράνας. 14 Ἀλέξανδρος ὁ χαλκεὺς
books, especially the parchments. Alexander the smith

πολλά μοι κακὰ ἐνεδείξατο· ¹ἀποδώῃ‖ αὐτῷ ὁ
²many ⁵against ⁶me ³evil ⁴things ¹did. May ³render ⁴to ⁵him ¹the

κύριος κατὰ τὰ ἔργα αὐτοῦ· 15 ὃν καὶ σὺ φυλάσσου,
²Lord according to his works. Whom also thou be ware of,

λίαν γὰρ ᵏἀνθέστηκεν‖ τοῖς ἡμετέροις λόγοις. 16 Ἐν τῇ
for exceedingly he has withstood our words. In

πρώτῃ μου ἀπολογίᾳ οὐδείς μοι ¹συμπαρεγένετο,‖ ἀλλὰ πάντες
my first defence no one ²me ¹stood ⁴with, but all

με ἐγκατέλιπον· μὴ αὐτοῖς λογισθείη· 17 ὁ δὲ κύριός
me forsook. Not to them may it be reckoned. But the Lord

μοι παρέστη, καὶ ἐνεδυνάμωσέν με, ἵνα δι᾽ ἐμοῦ τὸ κή-
²me ¹stood ²by, and strengthened me, that through me the ·pro-

ρυγμα πληροφορηθῇ, καὶ ᵐἀκούσῃ‖ πάντα τὰ ἔθνη· καὶ
clamation might be fully made, and ⁴should ⁵hear ¹all ²the ³nations; and.

ⁿἐῤῥύσθην‖ ἐκ στόματος λέοντος. 18 ᵒκαὶ‖ ῥύσεταί με
I was delivered out of [the] ²mouth ¹lion's. And ⁴will ⁵deliver ⁶me

ὁ κύριος ἀπὸ παντὸς ἔργου πονηροῦ, καὶ σώσει εἰς τὴν
¹the ²Lord from every ⁴work ³wicked, and will preserve [me] for

ᶜ ἀναλύσεώς μου LTTr.   ᵈ καλὸν ἀγῶνα LTTr.   ᵉ Γαλλίαν Gallia T.   ᶠ Δελματίαν L.
ᵍ φελόνην EᵤLTTrAW.   ʰ Τρωάδι LT.   ¹ ἀποδώσει shall render LTTrAW.   ᵏ ἀντέστη
he withstood LTTrAW.   συν- A; παρεγένετο stood by LTTr.   ᵐ ἀκούσωσιν LTTrAWⱼ
ⁿ ἐρύσθην LTTrA.   ᵒ — καὶ LTTrA.

heavenly kingdom: to whom be glory for ever and ever. Amen.

βασιλείαν.αὐτοῦ τὴν ἐπουράνιον· ᾧ ἡ δόξα εἰς τοὺς
his kingdom   the   heavenly;   to whom [be] glory unto the

αἰῶνας τῶν αἰώνων. ἀμήν.
ages   of the   ages.   Amen.

19 Salute Prisca and Aquila, and the household of Onesiphorus. 20 Erastus abode at Corinth: but Trophimus have I left at Miletum sick. 21 Do thy diligence to come before winter. Eubulus greeteth thee, and Pudens, and Linus, and Claudia, and all the brethren. 22 The Lord Jesus Christ be with thy spirit. Grace be with you. Amen.

19 Ἄσπασαι Πρίσκαν καὶ Ἀκύλαν, καὶ τὸν Ὀνησιφόρου
   Salute   Prisca   and   Aquila,   and the [2]of [3]Onesiphorus

οἶκον. 20 Ἔραστος ἔμεινεν ἐν Κορίνθῳ· Τρόφιμον.δὲ ἀπέλιπον
[1]house.   Erastus   remained in Corinth, but Trophimus   I left

ἐν Μιλήτῳ ἀσθενοῦντα. 21 Σπούδασον πρὸ χειμῶνος ἐλθεῖν.
in Miletus   sick.   Be diligent   before   winter   to come.

Ἀσπάζεταί σε Εὔβουλος, καὶ Πούδης, καὶ �q Λῖνος,‖ καὶ
[2]Salutes [3]thee [1]Eubulus,   and   Pudens,   and   Linus,   and

Κλαυδία, καὶ οἱ ἀδελφοὶ πάντες. 22 Ὁ κύριος ʳ Ἰησοῦς‖
Claudia,   and [2]the [3]brethren [1]all.   The Lord   Jesus

ˢ χριστὸς‖ μετὰ τοῦ.πνεύματός.σου. ἡ χάρις μεθ' ὑμῶν.
Christ [be] with   thy spirit.   Grace [be] with you.

ᵗ ἀμήν.‖
Amen.

ᵛ Πρὸς Τιμόθεον δευτέρα, τῆς Ἐφεσίων ἐκκλη-
[2]To [3]Timotheus [1]second, [8]of [9]the [11]of [[12]the] [13]Ephesians [10]assem-

σίας πρῶτον ἐπίσκοπον χειροτονηθέντα, ἐγράφη ἀπὸ
bly [[a]the] [6]first [7]overseer [4]chosen,   written   from

Ῥώμης, ὅτε ἐκ.δευτέρου παρέστη Παῦλος τῷ Καίσαρι
Rome,   when a second time [2]was [3]placed [4]before [1]Paul   Cæsar

Νέρωνι.‖
Nero.

ᵃ Η ΠΡΟΣ ΤΙΤΟΝ ΕΠΙΣΤΟΛΗ ΠΑΥΛΟΥ.‖
THE   ⁴TO   ⁵TITUS   [1]EPISTLE   [2]OF [3]PAUL.

PAUL, a servant of God, and an apostle of Jesus Christ, according to the faith of God's elect, and the acknowledging of the truth which is after godliness; 2 in hope of eternal life, which God, that cannot lie, promised before the world began: 3 but hath in due times manifested his word through preaching, which is committed unto me according to the commandment of God our Saviour; 4 to Titus, mine own son after the common faith: Grace, mercy, and peace, from God the Father and the Lord Jesus Christ our Saviour.

ΠΑΥΛΟΣ δοῦλος θεοῦ, ἀπόστολος.δὲ Ἰησοῦ χριστοῦ κατὰ
Paul   bondman of God,   and apostle   of Jesus   Christ according to

πίστιν ἐκλεκτῶν θεοῦ καὶ ἐπίγνωσιν ἀληθείας τῆς
[the] faith [3]elect [1]of [2]God's and knowledge of [the] truth which [is]

κατ' εὐσέβειαν, 2 ἐπ' ἐλπίδι ζωῆς αἰωνίου, ἣν ἐπηγ-
according to   piety;   in [the] hope of life eternal,   which [2]pro-

γείλατο ὁ ἀψευδὴς θεὸς πρὸ χρόνων.αἰωνίων, 3 ἐ-
mised [1]the [3]who [4]cannot [5]lie [2]God before   the ages of time,

φανέρωσεν.δὲ καιροῖς.ἰδίοις τὸν.λόγον.αὐτοῦ, ἐν κηρύγματι
but manifested   in its own seasons   his word   in [the] proclamation

ὃ ἐπιστεύθην ἐγὼ κατ' ἐπιταγὴν τοῦ σωτῆρος
which [2]was [3]entrusted [4]with [1]I according to [the] commandment of [2]Saviour

ἡμῶν θεοῦ, 4 Τίτῳ γνησίῳ τέκνῳ κατὰ κοινὴν
[1]our   God;   to Titus [my] true   child according to [our] common

πίστιν, χάρις, ᵇ ἔλεος,‖ εἰρήνη ἀπὸ θεοῦ πατρός, καὶ
faith: Grace,   mercy   peace. from God [the] Father, and [the]

ᶜ κυρίου Ἰησοῦ χριστοῦ‖ τοῦ.σωτῆρος.ἡμῶν
Lord   Jesus   Christ   our Saviour.

5 For this cause left I thee in Crete, that

5 Τούτου.χάριν ᵈ κατέλιπόν‖ σε ἐν Κρήτῃ, ἵνα τὰ.λείποντα
For this cause   I left   thee in Crete,   that the things lacking

---

�q — Λίνος LTW.   ʳ — Ἰησοῦς TTr[A].   ˢ — χριστὸς LTTr[A].   ᵗ — ἀμήν GLTTrAW.
ᵛ — the subscription GLTW; Πρὸς Τιμόθεον β΄ (— β΄ A) TrA.
ᵃ + τοῦ Ἀποστόλου the apostle E; Πρὸς Τίτον LTTrAW.   ᵇ καὶ and TTrAW.   ᶜ χριστοῦ
Ἰησοῦ LTTrA.   ᵈ ἀπέλιπόν LTTrAW.

ᵉἐπιδιορθώσῃ,‖	καὶ καταστήσῃς κατὰ.πόλιν πρεσ-
thou mightest go on to set right,	and mightest appoint	in every city

βυτέρους, ὡς ἐγώ σοι διεταξάμην· 6 εἴ τις ἐστὶν ἀνέγ-
elders,	as I ²thee ¹ordered:	if anyone is	unim-

κλητος, μιᾶς γυναικὸς ἀνήρ, τέκνα ἔχων πιστά, μὴ ἐν
peachable, ²of ¹one ⁴wife ¹husband, ⁷children ⁵having ⁶believing, not under

κατηγορίᾳ ἀσωτίας ἢ ἀνυπότακτα. 7 δεῖ.γὰρ τὸν ἐπί-
accusation of dissoluteness or insubordinate.	For it behoves the over-

σκοπον ἀνέγκλητον εἶναι, ὡς θεοῦ οἰκονόμον· μὴ αὐθάδη,
seer	unimpeachable to be, as God's steward;	no: selfwilled,

μὴ ὀργίλον, μὴ πάροινον, μὴ πλήκτην, μὴ αἰσχροκερδῆ,
not passionate, not given to wine, not a striker, not greedy of base gain,

8 ἀλλὰ φιλόξενον, φιλάγαθον, σώφρονα, δίκαιον, ὅσιον, ἐγ-
but	hospitable, a lover of good, discreet,	just,	holy,	tem-

κρατῆ, 9 ἀντεχόμενον τοῦ κατὰ τὴν διδαχὴν πιστοῦ
perate,	holding to	the ²according ⁴to ³the ⁵teaching ¹faithful

λόγου, ἵνα δυνατὸς ᾖ καὶ παρακαλεῖν ἐν τῇ διδασκαλίᾳ
²word,	that able he may be both to encourage with	²teaching

τῇ ὑγιαινούσῃ, καὶ τοὺς ἀντιλέγοντας ἐλέγχειν. 10 εἰσὶν.γὰρ
¹sound,	and those who gainsay	to convict.	For there are

πολλοὶ ᶠκαὶ‖ ἀνυπότακτοι ματαιολόγοι καὶ φρεναπάται, μά-
many	and insubordinate	vain talkers and mind-deceivers, espe-

λιστα ᵍ οἱ ἐκ ʰ περιτομῆς, 11 οὓς δεῖ ἐπιστο-
cially those of [the] circumcision,	whom it is necessary to stop the

μίζειν· οἵτινες ὅλους οἴκους ἀνατρέπουσιν, διδάσκοντες
mouths of, who whole houses	overthrow,	teaching

ἃ μὴ.δεῖ, αἰσχροῦ κέρδους χάριν· 12 εἶπέν
things which [they] ought not, ⁴base ⁵gain ¹for ²sake ³of.	¹⁴Said

τις ἐξ αὐτῶν ἴδιος.αὐτῶν προφήτης, Κρῆτες ἀεὶ
⁶one ⁷of ⁸themselves ¹¹of ¹²their ¹³own ⁹a ¹⁰prophet,	Cretans always [are]

ψεῦσται, κακὰ θηρία, γαστέρες ἀργαί. 13 ἡ.μαρτυρία.αὕτη
liars,	evil wild beasts, ²gluttons ¹lazy.	This testimony

ἐστὶν ἀληθής· δι' ἣν αἰτίαν ἔλεγχε αὐτοὺς ἀποτόμως, ἵνα
is	true;	for which cause convict them	with severity, that

ὑγιαίνωσιν ἐν τῇ πίστει, 14 μὴ προσέχοντες Ἰουδαϊκοῖς
they may be sound in the faith,	not giving heed	to Jewish

μύθοις καὶ ἐντολαῖς ἀνθρώπων ἀποστρεφομένων τὴν ἀλή-
fables	and commandments of men,	turning away from	the truth.

θειαν. 15 πάντα ⁱμὲν‖ καθαρὰ τοῖς καθαροῖς· τοῖς.δὲ
All things [are]	pure to the pure;	but to those who

ᵏμεμιασμένοις‖ καὶ ἀπίστοις οὐδὲν καθαρόν, ἀλλὰ μεμίαν-
are defiled	and unbelieving nothing [is] pure;	but are de-

ται αὐτῶν καὶ ὁ νοῦς καὶ ἡ.συνείδησις. 16 θεὸν ὁμολογοῦσιν
filed ²their ¹both mind and _[their] conscience.	God they profess

εἰδέναι, τοῖς.δὲ.ἔργοις ἀρνοῦνται, βδελυκτοὶ ὄντες καὶ
to know, but in works	deny	[him], ²abominable ¹being and

ἀπειθεῖς, καὶ πρὸς πᾶν ἔργον ἀγαθὸν ἀδόκιμοι.
disobedient, and as to every ²work ¹good	found worthless.

2 Σὺ.δὲ λάλει ἃ πρέπει τῇ ὑγιαινούσῃ διδασ-
But ²thou ¹speak the things that become	sound	teach-

καλίᾳ· 2 πρεσβύτας νηφαλίους εἶναι, σεμνούς, σώ-
ing:	[the] aged [men] ²sober	¹to ²be,	grave,	dis-

φρονας, ὑγιαίνοντας τῇ πίστει. τῇ ἀγάπῃ, τῇ ὑπομονῇ·
creet,	sound	in faith,	in love,	in endurance;

| thou shouldest set in order the things that are wanting, and ordain elders in every city, as I had appointed thee: 6 if any be blameless, the husband of one wife, having faithful children not accused of riot or unruly. 7 For a bishop must be blameless, as the steward of God; not selfwilled, not soon angry, not given to wine, no striker, not given to filthy lucre ; 8 but a lover of hospitality, a lover of good men, sober, just. holy, temperate; 9 holding fast the faithful word as he hath been taught, that he may be able by sound doctrine both to exhort and to convince the gainsayers. 10 For there are many unruly and vain talkers and deceivers, specially they of the circumcision : 11 whose mouths must be stopped, who subvert whole houses, teaching things which they ought not, for filthy lucre's sake. 12 One of themselves, even a prophet of their own, said, The Cretians are alway liars, evil beasts, slow bellies. 13 This witness is true. Wherefore rebuke them sharply, that they may be sound in the faith ; 14 not giving heed to Jewish fables, and commandments of men, that turn from the truth. 15 Unto the pure all things are pure : but unto them that are defiled and unbelieving is nothing pure ; but even their mind and conscience is defiled. 16 They profess that they know God; but in works they deny him, being abominable, and disobedient, and unto every good work reprobate. II. But speak thou the things which become sound doctrine : 2 that the aged men be sober, grave, temperate, sound in faith, in charity, in patience. 3 The |

ᵉ ἐπιδιορθώσῃς L.	ᶠ — καὶ LTTr[A].	ᵍ + [δὲ] but (especially) L.	ʰ + τῆς the ΤΤ
ⁱ — μὲν LTTrAW.	ᵏ μεμιαμμένοις LTTr ; μεμιαμένοις A.

aged women likewise, that *they be* in behaviour as becometh holiness, not false accusers, not given to much wine, teachers of good things ; 4 that they may teach the young women to be sober, to love their husbands, to love their children, 5 *to be* discreet, chaste, keepers at home. good, obedient to their own husbands, that the word of God be not blasphemed. 6 Young men likewise exhort to be sober minded. 7 In all things shewing thyself a pattern of good works : in doctrine *shewing* uncorruptness, gravity, sincerity, 8 sound speech, that cannot be condemned ; that he that is of the contrary part may be ashamed, having no evil thing to say of you. 9 *Exhort* servants to be obedient unto their own masters, *and* to please *them* well in all *things;* not answering again ; 10 not purloining, but shewing all good fidelity ; that they may adorn the doctrine of God our Saviour in all things. 11 For the grace of God that bringeth salvation hath appeared to all men, 12 teaching us that, denying ungodliness and worldly lusts, we should live soberly, righteously, and godly. in this present world ; 13 looking for that blessed hope, and the glorious appearing of the great God and our Saviour Jesus Christ ; 14 who gave himself for us, that he might redeem us from all iniquity, and purify unto himself a peculiar people, zealous of good works. 15 These things speak, and exhort, and rebuke with all authority. Let no man despise thee.

III. Put them in mind to be subject to principalities and

---

3 πρεσβύτιδας   ὡσαύτως ἐν καταστήματι ἱερο-
[the] aged   [women] in like manner in   deportment   as becomes

πρεπεῖς, μὴ διαβόλους, ¹μὴ‖ οἴνῳ πολλῷ δεδουλωμένας,
sacred ones, not slanderers,   not ²to ⁴wine ³much   ¹enslaved,

καλοδιδασκάλους, 4 ἵνα ᵐσωφρονίζωσιν‖ τὰς νέας
teachers of what is right ;   that   they may school   the young [women]

φιλάνδρους   εἶναι,   φιλοτέκνους, 5 σώφρονας,
lovers of [their] husbands to be, lovers of [their] children,   discreet,

ἁγνάς, ⁿοἰκουρούς,‖ ἀγαθάς, ὑποτασσομένας τοῖς ἰδίοις ἀν-
chaste, keepers at home, good,   subject   to their own hus-

δράσιν, ἵνα μὴ ὁ λόγος τοῦ θεοῦ βλασφημῆται. 6 Τοὺς
bands, that not the word   of God may be evil spoken of. The

νεωτέρους   ὡσαύτως   παρακάλει σωφρονεῖν, ᵒ 7 περὶ
younger [men] in like manner   exhort   to be discreet ;   in

πάντα σεαυτὸν παρεχόμενος τύπον καλῶν ἔργων, ἐν τῇ
all things thyself   holding forth   a pattern of good works ; in

διδασκαλίᾳ ᴾἀδιαφθορίαν,‖ σεμνότητα, ᑫἀφθαρσίαν,‖ 8 λόγον
teaching   uncorruptness,   gravity,   incorruption,   ²speech

ὑγιῆ, ἀκατάγνωστον, ἵνα ὁ ἐξ ἐναντίας ἐντραπῇ, μηδὲν
¹sound, not to be condemned ; that he who is opposed may be ashamed, ²nothing

ἔχων ʳπερὶ ὑμῶν λέγειν‖ φαῦλον. 9 Δούλους ⁵ἰδίοις
¹having ⁶concerning ⁷you ⁴to ⁵say   ³evil.   Bondmen to their own

δεσπόταις‖ ὑποτάσσεσθαι, ἐν πᾶσιν εὐαρέστους εἶναι, μὴ
masters   to be subject,   in everything well-pleasing   to be, not

ἀντιλέγοντας, 10 μὴ νοσφιζομένους, ἀλλὰ ᵗπίστιν πᾶσαν‖
contradicting ;   not   purloining,   but   ²fidelity ³all

ἐνδεικνυμένους ἀγαθήν· ἵνα τὴν διδασκαλίαν ᵛ τοῦ σωτῆρος
¹shewing   ³good,   that the   teaching   ²Saviour

ʷὑμῶν‖ θεοῦ κοσμῶσιν ἐν πᾶσιν. 11 Ἐπεφάνη γὰρ ἡ
¹of ²your God they may adorn in all things.   For ¹¹appeared ¹the

χάρις τοῦ θεοῦ ˣἡ‖   σωτήριος πᾶσιν ἀνθρώποις,
²grace ³of ⁴God ⁵which ⁶brings ⁷salvation ⁸for ⁹all ¹⁰men,

12 παιδεύουσα ἡμᾶς ἵνα ἀρνησάμενοι τὴν ἀσέβειαν καὶ τὰς
instructing   us that, having denied   ungodliness and

κοσμικὰς ἐπιθυμίας, σωφρόνως καὶ δικαίως καὶ εὐσεβῶς ζή-
worldly desires,   discreetly   and righteously and piously we

σωμεν ἐν τῷ νῦν αἰῶνι, 13 προσδεχόμενοι τὴν μακαρίαν
should live in the present age,   awaiting   the blessed

ἐλπίδα καὶ ἐπιφάνειαν τῆς δόξης τοῦ μεγάλου θεοῦ καὶ σωτῆ-
hope and appearing of the glory   ³great ⁴God ⁵and ⁶Sa-

ρος ἡμῶν ᵞἸησοῦ χριστοῦ,‖ 14 ὃς ἔδωκεν ἑαυτὸν ὑπὲρ ἡμῶν,
viour ¹of ²our Jesus   Christ ;   who gave   himself for   us,

ἵνα λυτρώσηται ἡμᾶς ἀπὸ πάσης ἀνομίας, καὶ καθαρίσῃ
that he might redeem us from all   lawlessness, and might purify

ἑαυτῷ λαὸν περιούσιον, ζηλωτὴν καλῶν ἔργων. 15 Ταῦτα
to himself a people peculiar,   zealous of good works.   These things

λάλει, καὶ παρακάλει, καὶ ἔλεγχε μετὰ πάσης ἐπιταγῆς.
speak,   and   exhort,   and convict with   all   command.

μηδείς σου περιφρονείτω.
²No ⁵one ³thee   ¹let ⁴despise.

3 Ὑπομίμνησκε αὐτοὺς ἀρχαῖς ᶻκαὶ‖ ἐξουσίαις ὑποτάσ-
Put ²in ³remembrance ¹them   to rulers and to authorities   to be

---

¹ μηδὲ ΠΟΓ TTrA.   ᵐ σωφρονίζουσιν they school TTrA.   ⁿ οἰκουργούς workers at home LTTrA.   ᵒ Read to be discreet in all things, T.   ᴾ ἀφθορίαν incorruption LTTɾAW.   ᑫ — ἀφθαρσίαν EGLTTɾAW.   ʳ λέγειν περὶ ἡμῶν (us) LTTɾA ; περὶ ἡμῶν λέγειν GW.   ⁵ δεσπόταις ἰδίοις L.   ᵗ πᾶσαν πίστιν LTTɾA.   ᵛ + τὴν which [is] LTTɾAW.   ʷ ἡμῶν of our EGLTT.AW.   ˣ — ἡ (read σωτη. bringing salvation) LTTɾA.   ᵞ χριστοῦ Ἰησοῦ TTɾ.   ᶻ — καὶ LTTɾA.

σεσθαι, πειθαρχεῖν, πρὸς πᾶν ἔργον ἀγαθὸν ἑτοίμους εἶναι,
subject, to be obedient, · 'to ⁵every ⁷work ⁶good ³ready ¹to ²be,

2 μηδένα βλασφημεῖν, ἀμάχους εἶναι, ἐπιεικεῖς,
no one to speak evil of, not ³contentious ¹to ²be, [to be] gentle,

πᾶσαν ἐνδεικνυμένους ªπραότητα‖ πρὸς πάντας ἀνθρώπους.
²all ¹shewing meekness towards all men.

3 ἦμεν.γάρ ποτε καὶ ἡμεῖς ἀνόητοι, ἀπειθεῖς, πλανώ-
For ²were ³once ⁴also ¹we without intelligence, disobedient, led

μενοι, δουλεύοντες ἐπιθυμίαις καὶ ἡδοναῖς ποικίλαις, ἐν κακίᾳ
astray, serving ²lusts ³and ⁴pleasures ¹various, in malice

καὶ φθόνῳ διάγοντες, στυγητοί, μισοῦντες ἀλλήλους· 4 ὅτε.δὲ
and envy living, hateful, hating one another. But when

ἡ χρηστότης καὶ ἡ φιλανθρωπία ἐπεφάνη τοῦ.σωτῆρος.ἡμῶν
the kindness and the love to man ⁵appeared ¹of ²our ³Saviour

θεοῦ, 5 οὐκ ἐξ ἔργων τῶν ἐν δικαιοσύνῃ ᵇὧν‖ ἐποιήσαμεν
⁴God, not by works which [were] in righteousness which ²practised

ἡμεῖς, ἀλλὰ κατὰ ᶜτὸν.αὐτοῦ.ἔλεον‖ ἔσωσεν ἡμᾶς, διὰ
¹we, but according to his mercy he ²saved us, through [the]

λουτροῦ ᵈπαλιγγενεσίας‖ καὶ ἀνακαινώσεως πνεύματος ἁγίου,
washing of regeneration and renewing of [the] ²Spirit ¹Holy,

6 οὗ ἐξέχεεν ἐφ' ἡμᾶς πλουσίως διὰ Ἰησοῦ χριστοῦ τοῦ
which he poured out on us richly through Jesus Christ

σωτῆρος.ἡμῶν· 7 ἵνα δικαιωθέντες τῇ ἐκείνου.χάριτι, κληρο-
our Saviour ; that having been justified by his grace, heirs

νόμοι ᵉγενώμεθα‖ κατ' ἐλπίδα ζωῆς ᶠαἰωνίου.
we should become according to [the] hope of life eternal.

8 Πιστὸς ὁ λόγος, καὶ περὶ τούτων βούλομαί σε δια-
Faithful [is] the word, and concerning these ²things I desire thee to

βεβαιοῦσθαι, ἵνα φροντίζωσιν καλῶν ἔργων προΐστασθαι
affirm strongly, that ⁶may ⁷take ⁸care ¹³good ¹⁴works ⁹to ¹⁰be ¹¹forward ¹²in

οἱ πεπιστευκότες ᵍτῷ‖ θεῷ. ταῦτά ἐστιν ᵍτὰ‖ καλὰ καὶ
¹they ²who ³have ⁴believed ⁵God. These things are good and

ὠφέλιμα τοῖς ἀνθρώποις· 9 μωρὰς.δὲ ζητήσεις καὶ γενεαλο-
profitable to men ; but foolish questions and genealo-

γίας καὶ ᵇἔρεις‖ καὶ μάχας νομικὰς περιΐστασο· εἰσὶν
gies and strifes and contentions about [the] law stand aloof from; ²they ³are

γὰρ ἀνωφελεῖς καὶ μάταιοι. 10 Αἱρετικὸν ἄνθρωπον μετὰ
¹for unprofitable and vain. A sectarian man after

μίαν καὶ δευτέραν νουθεσίαν παραιτοῦ, 11 εἰδὼς ὅτι ἐξέ-
one and a second admonition reject, knowing that is

στραπται ὁ τοιοῦτος, καὶ ἁμαρτάνει, ὢν αὐτοκατάκριτος.
perverted such a one, .and sins, being self-condemned.

12 Ὅταν πέμψω Ἀρτεμᾶν πρός σε ἢ Τυχικόν, σπούδα-
When I shall send Artemas to thee, or Tychicus, be dili-

σον ἐλθεῖν πρός με εἰς Νικόπολιν· ἐκεῖ.γὰρ κέκρικα
gent to come to' me to Nicopolis ; for there ·I have decided

παραχειμάσαι. 13 Ζηνᾶν τὸν νομικὸν καὶ ⁱἈπολλῶ‖ σπου-
to winter. Zenas the lawyer and Apollos dili-

δαίως πρόπεμψον, ἵνα μηδὲν αὐτοῖς ᵏλείπῃ.‖ 14 μαν-
gently set forward, that nothing to them may be lacking; ²let

θανέτωσαν δὲ καὶ οἱ ἡμέτεροι καλῶν ἔργων προΐστασθαι
⁵learn ¹and ⁴also ³ours ¹⁰good ¹¹works ⁶to ⁷be ⁸forward ⁹in

εἰς τὰς ἀναγκαίας χρείας, ἵνα μὴ.ὦσιν ἄκαρποι. 15 Ἀσ-
for necessary wants, that they may not be unfruitful. ⁵Sa-

---

powers, to obey magistrates, to be ready to every good work, 2 to speak evil of no man, to be no brawlers, *but* gentle, shewing all meekness unto all men. 3 For we ourselves also were sometimes foolish, disobedient, deceived, serving divers lusts and pleasures, living in malice and envy, hateful, *and* hating one another. 4 But after that the kindness and love of God our Saviour toward man appeared, 5 not by works of righteousness which we have done, but according to his mercy he saved us, by the washing of regeneration, and renewing of the Holy Ghost; 6 which he shed on us abundantly through Jesus Christ our Saviour; 7 that being justified by his grace, we should be made heirs according to the hope of eternal life. 8 *This is* a faithful saying, and these things I will that thou affirm constantly, that they which have believed in God might be careful to maintain good works. These things are good and profitable unto men. 9 But avoid foolish questions, and genealogies, and contentions, and strivings about the law; for they are unprofitable and vain. 10 A man that is an heretick after the first and second admonition reject; 11 knowing that he that is such is subverted, and sinneth, being condemned of himself.

12 When I shall send Artemas unto thee, or Tychicus, be diligent to come unto me to Nicopolis: for I have determined there to winter. 13 Bring Zenas the lawyer and Apollos on their journey diligently, that nothing be wanting unto them. 14 And let ours also learn to maintain good works for necessary uses, that they be not unfruitful. 15 All that are with

---

ª πραΰτητα LTTrA.   ᵇ ἃ LTTrA.   ᶜ τὸ αὐτοῦ ἔλεος LTTrAW.   ᵈ παλιγενεσίας T.
ᵉ γενηθῶμεν LTTrAW.   ᶠ — τῷ LTTrAW.   ᵍ — τὰ LTTrAW.   ʰ ἔριν strife T.   ⁱ Ἀπολ-
λῶν T.   ᵏ λίπῃ T.

me salute thee. Greet them that love us in the faith. Grace be with you all. Amen.

πάζονταί σε οἱ μετ᾽ ἐμοῦ πάντες. ἄσπασαι τοὺς φι-
lute   "thee   ²those ³with ⁴me   ¹all.   Salute   those who

λοῦντας ἡμᾶς ἐν πίστει. ἡ χάρις μετὰ πάντων ὑμῶν.
love   us¹ in [the] faith.   Grace [be] with   ²all   ¹you.

ἀμήν.ꞈ
Amen.

ᵐΠρὸς Τίτον, τῆς Κρητῶν ἐκκλησίας πρῶτον ἐπί-
To   Titus   ⁴of ⁵the ²of [⁵the] ³Cretans ⁶assembly   ²first   ³over-

σκοπον χειροτονηθέντα, ἐγράφη ἀπὸ Νικοπόλεως τῆς Μακε-
seer   ¹chosen.   written from   Nicopolis   of Mace-

δονίας.ꞈ
donia.

Ἡ ΠΡΟΣ ΦΙΛΗΜΟΝΑ ΕΠΙΣΤΟΛΗ ΠΑΥΛΟΥ.ꞈ
THE   ⁴TO   ⁵PHILEMON   ¹EPISTLE   ²OF ³PAUL.

PAUL, a prisoner of Jesus Christ, and Timothy our brother, unto Philemon our dearly beloved, and fellowlabourer, 2 and to our beloved Apphia, and Archippus our fellowsoldier, and to the church in thy house : 3 Grace to you, and peace, from God our Father and the Lord Jesus Christ.

ΠΑΥΛΟΣ δέσμιος χριστοῦ Ἰησοῦ, καὶ Τιμόθεος ὁ ἀδελφός,
Paul,   prisoner   of Christ   Jesus,   and Timotheus the brother,

Φιλήμονι τῷ ἀγαπητῷ καὶ συνεργῷ.ἡμῶν, 2 καὶ Ἀπφίᾳ τῇ
to Philemon the   beloved   and our fellow-worker,   and to Apphia the

ᵇἀγαπητῇ,ꞈ καὶ Ἀρχίππῳ τῷ ᶜσυστρατιώτῃꞈ.ἡμῶν, καὶ τῇ
ᵇbeloved,   and to Archippus   our fellow-soldier,   and to the

κατ᾽ οἶκόν.σου ἐκκλησίᾳ· 3 χάρις ὑμῖν καὶ εἰρήνη ἀπὸ θεοῦ
²in ³thy ⁴house   ¹assembly: Grace to you and   peace   from God

πατρὸς.ἡμῶν καὶ κυρίου Ἰησοῦ χριστοῦ.
our Father   and [the] Lord   Jesus   Christ.

4 I thank my God, making mention of thee always in my prayers, 5 hearing of thy love and faith, which thou hast toward the Lord Jesus, and toward all saints ; 6 that the communication of thy faith may become effectual by the acknowledging of every good thing which is in you in Christ Jesus. 7 For we have great joy and consolation in thy love, because the bowels of the saints are refreshed by thee, brother.

4 Εὐχαριστῶ τῷ.θεῷ.μου, πάντοτε μνείαν σου ποιούμενος
I thank   my God,   always   mention of thee   making

ἐπὶ τῶν.προσευχῶν.μου, 5 ἀκούων σου τὴν ἀγάπην καὶ τὴν
at   my prayers,   · hearing of thy   love   and

πίστιν ἣν ἔχεις ᵃπρὸςꞈ τὸν κύριον Ἰησοῦν καὶ εἰς πάν-
faith   which thou hast towards the   Lord   Jesus,   and towards all

τας τοὺς ἁγίους, 6 ὅπως ἡ κοινωνία τῆς.πίστεώς.σου ἐνεργὴς
the   saints,   so that the fellowship   of thy faith   efficient

γένηται ἐν ἐπιγνώσει παντὸς ἀγαθοῦ ᵉτοῦꞈ ἐν
may become in [the] acknowledgment of every   good [thing] which [is] in

ᶠὑμῖνꞈ εἰς χριστὸν ᵍἸησοῦν.ꞈ 7 ʰχάρινꞈ γὰρ ἔχομεν πολλὴνꞈ
you towards Christ   Jesus.   ⁵Thankfulness ¹for ²we ³have ⁴great

καὶ παράκλησιν ἐπὶ τῇ.ἀγάπῃ.σου, ὅτι τὰ σπλάγχνα
and encouragement by occasion of   thy love,   because the bowels

τῶν ἁγίων ἀναπέπαυται· διὰ σοῦ, ἀδελφέ.
of the saints   have been refreshed by thee, brother.

8 Wherefore, though I might be much bold in Christ to enjoin thee that which is convenient, 9 yet for love's sake I rather beseech thee, being such an one as Paul the aged, and now also a prisoner of Jesus Christ. 10 I beseech thee for my son One-

8 Διὸ πολλὴν ἐν χριστῷ παῤῥησίαν ἔχων ἐπιτάσσειν σοι
Wherefore much \ ²in ³Christ ¹boldness having to order   thee

τὸ ἀνῆκον, 9 διὰ τὴν ἀγάπην μᾶλλον παρακαλῶ·
what [is] becoming, for the sake of   love   rather   I exhort,

τοιοῦτος ὢν ὡς Παῦλος πρεσβύτης, νυνὶ.δὲ καὶ δέσμιος
such a one being as   Paul   [the] aged,   and now also prisoner

ᵏἸησοῦ χριστοῦ·ꞈ 10 παρακαλῶ σε περὶ τοῦ ἐμοῦ τέκνου, ὃν
of Jesus Christ.   I exhort thee for   my   child,   whom

---

¹ — ἀμήν G[L]TTrAW.   ᵐ — the subscription GLTw ; Πρὸς Τίτον TrA.
ᵃ + τοῦ Ἀποστόλου the Apostle E ; Πρὸς Φιλήμονα LTTrAW.   ᵇ ἀδελφῇ sister LTTrA
ᶜ συνσ- LTTrA.   ᵈ εἰς LTrA.   ᵉ — τοῦ LTr.   ᶠ ἡμῖν US GLTrAW.   ᵍ — Ἰησοῦν LTTr[A].
ʰ χαρὰν joy EGLTTrAW.   ¹ πολλὴν ἔσχον I had great LTTrAW.   ᵏ χριστοῦ Ἰησοῦ LTTrA.

ἐγέννησα ἐν τοῖς δεσμοῖς ¹μου,‖ Ὀνήσιμον, 11 τόν ποτέ σοι
I begot in ᵃbonds ¹my, Onesimus, once to thee

ἄχρηστον. νυνὶ.δὲ ᵐ σοι καὶ ἐμοὶ εὔχρηστον, ὃν ἀνέπεμ-
unserviceable, but now to thee and to me serviceable : whom I sent

ψαⁿ· 12 ᵒσὺ.δὲ‖ αὐτόν, ᵖτουτέστιν‖ τὰ ἐμὰ σπλάγχνα,
back [to thee]: but thou him, (that is, my bowels,)

�q προσλαβοῦ·‖ 13 ὃν ἐγὼ ἐβουλόμην πρὸς ἐμαυτὸν κατέχειν,
receive : whom I was desiring with myself to keep,

ἵνα ὑπὲρ σοῦ ʳδιακονῇ μοι‖ ἐν τοῖς δεσμοῖς τοῦ εὐαγγελίου·
that for thee he might serve me in the bonds of the glad tidings ;

14 χωρὶς.δὲ τῆς.σῆς.γνώμης οὐδὲν ἠθέλησα ποιῆσαι, ἵνα μὴ
but apart from thy mind nothing I wished to do, that not

ὡς κατὰ.ἀνάγκην τὸ.ἀγαθόν.σου ᾖ, ἀλλὰ κατὰ.ἑκούσιον.
as of necessity thy good might be, but of willingness :

15 τάχα.γὰρ διὰ τοῦτο ἐχωρίσθη πρὸς ὥραν,
for perhaps because of this he was separated [from thee] for a time,

ἵνα αἰώνιον αὐτὸν ἀπέχῃς· 16 οὐκέτι ὡς δοῦλον,
that eternally him thou mightest possess ; no longer as a bondman,

ˢἀλλʼ‖ ὑπὲρ δοῦλον, ἀδελφὸν ἀγαπητόν, μάλιστα ἐμοί,
but above a bondman, a brother beloved, specially to me,

πόσῳ.δὲ μᾶλλόν σοι καὶ ἐν σαρκὶ καὶ ἐν κυρίῳ;
and how much rather to thee both in [the] flesh and in [the] Lord?

17 εἰ οὖν ᵗἐμὲ‖ ἔχεις κοινωνόν, προσλαβοῦ αὐτὸν ὡς
If therefore me thou holdest a partner, receive him as

ἐμέ· 18 εἰ.δὲ τι ἠδίκησέν σε ἢ ὀφείλει, τοῦτο ἐμοὶ.ᵛἐλλόγει.‖
me ; but if anything he wronged thee, or owes, this put to my account.

19 ἐγὼ Παῦλος ἔγραψα τῇ.ἐμῇ χειρί, ἐγὼ ἀποτίσω· ἵνα
I Paul wrote [it] with my [own] hand ; I will repay ; that

μὴ.λέγω σοι ὅτι καὶ σεαυτόν μοι προσοφείλεις. 20 Ναί,
I may not say to thee that even thyself to me thou owest also. Yea,

ἀδελφέ, ἐγώ σου ὀναίμην ἐν κυρίῳ· ἀνάπαυσόν μου
brother, ⁴I ³of ⁴thee ¹may have profit in [the] Lord : refresh my

τὰ σπλάγχνα ἐν ʷκυρίῳ.‖ 21 πεποιθὼς τῇ.ὑπακοῇ.σου
bowels in [the] Lord. Being persuaded of thy obedience

ἔγραψά σοι, εἰδὼς ὅτι καὶ ὑπὲρ ˣὃ‖ λέγω ποιήσεις.
I wrote to thee, knowing that even above what I may say thou wilt do.

22 ‖Ἅμα.δὲ καὶ ἑτοίμαζέ μοι ξενίαν· ἐλπίζω.γὰρ ὅτι διὰ
But withal also prepare me a lodging ; for I hope that through

τῶν.προσευχῶν.ὑμῶν χαρισθήσομαι ὑμῖν. 23 ʸἈσπάζονταί‖
your prayers I shall be granted to you. ¹³Salute

σε Ἐπαφρᾶς ὁ συναιχμάλωτός μου ἐν χριστῷ Ἰησοῦ,
¹⁴thee ¹Epaphras ³fellow-prisoner ²my ⁴in ⁵Christ ⁶Jesus ;

24 Μάρκος, Ἀρίσταρχος, Δημᾶς, Λουκᾶς, οἱ.συνεργοί.μου.
⁷Mark, ⁸Aristarchus, ⁹Demas, ¹⁰Luke, ¹¹my ¹²fellow-workers.

25 ἡ χάρις τοῦ.κυρίου.ᶻἡμῶν‖ Ἰησοῦ χριστοῦ μετὰ τοῦ
The grace of our Lord Jesus Christ [be] with

πνεύματος.ὑμῶν. ᵃἀμήν.‖
your spirit. Amen.

ᵇΠρὸς Φιλήμονα ἐγράφη ἀπὸ Ῥώμης, διὰ Ὀνησίμου
To Philemon written from Rome, by Onesimus

οἰκέτου.‖
a servant.

simus, whom I have begotten in my bonds: 11 which in time past was to thee unprofitable, but now profitable to thee and to me: 12 whom I have sent again: thou therefore receive him, that is, mine own bowels : 13 whom I would have retained with me, that in thy stead he might have ministered unto me in the bonds of the gospel : 14 but without thy mind would I do nothing; that thy benefit should not be as it were of necessity, but willingly. 15 For perhaps he therefore departed for a season, that thou shouldest receive him for ever; 16 not now as a servant, but above a servant, a brother beloved, specially to me, but how much more unto thee, both in the flesh, and in the Lord? 17 If thou count me therefore a partner, receive him as myself. 18 If he hath wronged thee, or oweth *thee* ought, put that on mine account ; 19 I Paul have written *it* with mine own hand, I will repay *it*: albeit I do not say to thee how thou owest unto me even thine own self besides. 20 Yea, brother, let me have joy of thee in the Lord: refresh my bowels in the Lord. 21 Having confidence in thy obedience I wrote unto thee, knowing that thou wilt also do more than I say. 22 But withal prepare me also a lodging: for I trust that through your prayers I shall be given unto you. 23 There salute thee Epaphras, my fellowprisoner in Christ Jesus ; 24 Marcus, Aristarchus, Demas, Lucas, my fellowlabourers. 25 The grace of our Lord Jesus Christ *be* with your spirit. Amen.

¹ — μου LTTrA. ᵐ + καὶ also T. ⁿ + σοι to thee LTTrAW. ᵒ — σὺ δὲ LTTrA.
ᵖ τοῦτ' ἔστιν GT. �q — προσλαβοῦ LTTrA. ʳ μοι διακονῇ GLTTrAW. ˢ ἀλλὰ TTr.
ᵗ με GLTTrAW. ᵛ ἐλλόγα LTTrA. ʷ χριστῷ Christ GLTTrAW. ˣ ἃ the things which LTTrA.
ʸ ἀσπάζεταί (*read* Epaphras my fellow-prisoner salutes thee) GLTTrAW. ᶻ — ἡμῶν (*read*
of the Lord) T. ᵃ — ἀμήν GLTTrAW. ᵇ — *the subscription* GLTW ; Πρὸς Φιλήμονα TrA.

ᴬΗ ΠΡΟΣ ΕΒΡΑΙΟΥΣ ΕΠΙΣΤΟΛΗ ΠΑΥΛΟΥ.ᵃ
THE ⁴TO [⁵THE] ⁶HEBREWS ¹⁺¹EPISTLE ²OF ³PAUL.

GOD, who at sundry times and in divers manners spake in time past unto the fathers by the prophets, 2 hath in these last days spoken unto us by his Son, whom he hath appointed heir of all things, by whom also he made the worlds; 3 who being the brightness of his glory, and the express image of his person, and upholding all things by the word of his power, when he had by himself purged our sins, sat down on the right hand of the Majesty on high; 4 being made so much better than the angels, as he hath by inheritance obtained a more excellent name than they. 5 For unto which of the angels said he at any time, Thou art my Son, this day have I begotten thee? And again, I will be to him a Father, and he shall be to me a Son? 6 And again, when he bringeth in the firstbegotten into the world, he saith, And let all the angels of God worship him. 7 And of the angels he saith, Who maketh his angels spirits, and his ministers a flame of fire. 8 But unto the Son he saith, Thy throne, O God, is for ever and ever: a sceptre of righteousness is the sceptre of thy kingdom. 9 Thou hast loved righteousness, and hated iniquity; therefore God, even thy God, hath anointed thee with the oil of gladness above thy fellows. 10 And, Thou, Lord, in the beginning hast laid the foundation of the earth; and the heavens are the works of thine hands: 11 they shall perish;

ΠΟΛΥΜΕΡΩΣ καὶ πολυτρόπως πάλαι ὁ θεὸς λαλήσας
In many parts and in many ways of old God having spoken
τοῖς πατράσιν ἐν τοῖς προφήταις, ἐπ᾽ ᵇἐσχάτων¹¹ τῶν ἡμερῶν
to the fathers in the prophets, in ¹last ³days
τούτων, ἐλάλησεν ἡμῖν ἐν‿υἱῷ, 2 ὃν ἔθηκεν κληρονό-
¹these spoke to us in Son, whom he appointed heir
μον πάντων, δι᾽ οὗ καὶ ᶜτοὺς αἰῶνας ἐποίησεν,¹¹ 3 ὃς ὢν
of all things, by whom also the worlds he made: who being
ἀπαύγασμα τῆς‿δόξης καὶ χαρακτὴρ τῆς ὑποστάσεως
[the] effulgence of [his] glory and [the] exact expression of ²substance
αὐτοῦ, φέρων‿τε τὰ‿πάντα τῷ ῥήματι τῆς‿δυνάμεως‿αὐτοῦ,
¹his, and upholding all things by the word of his power,
ᵈδι᾽ ἑαυτοῦ¹¹ καθαρισμὸν ᵉποιησάμενος τῶν ἁμαρτιῶν¹¹
by himself [the] purification having made ,of ⁴sins
ᶠἡμῶν,¹¹ ἐκάθισεν ἐν δεξιᾷ τῆς μεγαλωσύνης ἐν ὑψηλοῖς,
¹our, sat down on [the] right hand of the greatness on high,
4 τοσούτῳ κρείττων γενόμενος τῶν ἀγγέλων, ὅσῳ
by so much better having become than the angels, as much as
διαφορώτερον παρ᾽ αὐτοὺς κεκληρονόμηκεν ὄνομα. 5 Τίνι‿γὰρ
³more ⁴excellent ⁵beyond ⁶them ⁷he ⁸has ⁹inherited ¹a ²name. For to which
εἶπέν ποτε τῶν ἀγγέλων, Υἱός μου εἶ σύ, ἐγὼ σήμερον
⁴said ⁵he ⁶ever ¹of ²the ³angels, ⁸Son ⁷my art thou: I to-day
γεγέννηκά σε; καὶ πάλιν, Ἐγὼ ἔσομαι αὐτῷ εἰς πατέρα,
have begotten thee? and again, I will be to him for Father,
καὶ αὐτὸς ἔσται μοι εἰς υἱόν; 6 ὅταν‿δὲ πάλιν εἰσαγάγῃ
and he shall be to me for Son? and ²when ¹again he brings in
τὸν πρωτότοκον εἰς τὴν οἰκουμένην, λέγει, Καὶ προσκυνη-
the first-born into the habitable world, he says, And let wor-
σάτωσαν αὐτῷ πάντες ἄγγελοι θεοῦ. 7 Καὶ πρὸς μὲν
ship him all [the] angels of God. And as to
τοὺς ἀγγέλους λέγει, Ὁ ποιῶν τοὺς‿ἀγγέλους‿αὐτοῦ πνεύ-
the angels he says, Who makes his angels spi-
ματα, καὶ τοὺς‿λειτουργοὺς‿αὐτοῦ πυρὸς φλόγα· 8 πρὸς‿δὲ
rits, and his ministers ³of ⁴fire ¹a ²flame; but as to
τὸν υἱόν, Ὁ‿θρόνος‿σου, ὁ θεός. εἰς τὸν αἰῶνα τοῦ αἰῶνος·
the Son, Thy throne, O God, [is] to the age of the age.
ᵍῥάβδος ʰ εὐθύτητος ᶦἡ¹¹ ῥάβδος τῆς‿βασιλείας‿σου. 9 ἠγά-
a sceptre of uprightness [is] the sceptre of thy kingdom. Thou
πησας δικαιοσύνην καὶ ἐμίσησας ᵏἀνομίαν.¹¹ διὰ τοῦτο
didst love righteousness and didst hate lawlessness; because of this
ἔχρισέν σε ὁ θεὸς ὁ‿θεός‿σου ἔλαιον ἀγαλλιάσεως παρὰ τοὺς
⁴anointed ⁵thee ¹God ²thy ³God with [the] oil of exultation above
μετόχους‿σου. 10 Καί, Σὺ κατ᾽‿ἀρχάς, κύριε, τὴν γῆν ἐθε-
thy companions. And, Thou, in the beginning, Lord, the earth didst
μελίωσας, καὶ ἔργα τῶν‿χειρῶν‿σου εἰσὶν οἱ οὐρανοί· 11 αὐτοὶ
found, and works of thy hands are the heavens. They

ᵃ — Παύλου EG ; Πρὸς Ἑβραίους LTTrAW. ᵇ ἐσχάτου (read at the end of these days)
GLTTrAW. ᶜ ἐποίησεν τοὺς αἰῶνας LTTrAW. ᵈ — δι᾽ ἑαυτοῦ LTTrA. ᵉ τῶν ἁμαρτιῶν
ποιησάμενος LTTrA. ᶠ — ἡμῶν LTTrAW. ᵍ + καὶ and L ; + καὶ ἡ and the (sceptre) TTrA.
ʰ + τῆς LTTr. ᶦ — ἡ (read [the]) LTTr. ᵏ ἀδικίαν unrighteousness T.

ἀπολοῦνται, σὺ.δὲ διαμένεις· καὶ　πάντες ὡς ἱμάτιον παλαιω-
shall perish,　but thou continuest; and [they] all　as a garment shall grow

θήσονται, 12 καὶ ὡσεὶ περιβόλαιον ¹ἑλίξεις‖ αὐτοὺς^m, καὶ
old,　　and as　a covering thou shalt roll up them,　and

ἀλλαγήσονται· σὺ.δὲ ὁ αὐτὸς εἶ, καὶ τὰ.ἔτη.σου οὐκ ἐκλεί-
they shall be changed; but thou the same art, and　thy years ²not ¹shall

ψουσιν. 13 Πρὸς.τίνα.δὲ τῶν ἀγγέλων εἴρηκέν ποτε, Κάθου ἐκ
fail.　　But as to which of the angels　said he ever,　Sit　at

δεξιῶν.μου, ἕως.ἂν.θῶ τοὺς.ἐχθρούς.σου　ὑποπόδιον τῶν
my right hand　until I place　thine enemies　[as] a footstool.　¹for

ποδῶν σου; 14 οὐχὶ πάντες εἰσὶν λειτουργικὰ πνεύματα, εἰς
³feet ²thy?　⁶Not　⁷all ⁴are ⁵they ministering　spirits,　for

διακονίαν ἀποστελλόμενα διὰ τοὺς μέλλοντας κληρονο-
service　　being sent forth on account of those　being about　to inherit

μεῖν σωτηρίαν;
salvation?

2 Διὰ τοῦτο δεῖ περισσοτέρως ⁿἡμᾶς · προσέχειν‖
On account of this it behoves more abundantly　us　to give heed

τοῖς　ἀκουσθεῖσιν, μήποτε °παραρρυῶμεν.‖ 2 εἰ.γὰρ
to the things　heard,　lest at any time we should slip away.　For if

ὁ δι᾽ ἀγγέλων λαληθεὶς λόγος ἐγένετο βέβαιος, καὶ πᾶσα
the ³by　²angels ¹spoken ¹word　was　confirmed, and every

παράβασις καὶ παρακοὴ ἔλαβεν ἔνδικον μισθαποδοσίαν, 3 πῶς
transgression and disobedience received　just　recompense,　how

ἡμεῖς ἐκφευξόμεθα τηλικαύτης ἀμελήσαντες σωτηρίας; ἥτις
²we　¹shall escape　⁵so ⁶great [⁷if ²we] ³have ⁴neglected a salvation? which

ἀρχὴν　λαβοῦσα λαλεῖσθαι διὰ τοῦ κυρίου, ὑπὸ
³a ⁴commencement ¹having ²received to be spoken [of] by the Lord,　⁵by

τῶν　ἀκουσάντων εἰς ἡμᾶς ἐβεβαιώθη, 4 συνεπιμαρτυ-
⁶those ⁷that　⁸heard ³to ⁴us　¹was ²confirmed; ¹⁰bearing ¹¹witness

ροῦντος　τοῦ θεοῦ σημείοις τε καὶ τέρασιν, καὶ ποικίλαις
¹² with [¹³them]　⁹God ¹⁵by ¹⁶signs ¹⁴both and wonders,　and　various

δυνάμεσιν, καὶ πνεύματος ἁγίου μερισμοῖς, κατὰ τὴν
acts of power,　and ²of [³the] ⁵Spirit ⁴Holy ¹distributions, according to

αὐτοῦ θέλησιν.
his　　will.

5 Οὐ.γὰρ ἀγγέλοις ὑπέταξεν τὴν οἰκουμένην τὴν μέλ-
For not　to angels did he subject　the habitable world which is to

λουσαν, περὶ ἧς λαλοῦμεν· 6 διεμαρτύρατο.δέ που τὶς
come,　of which we speak;　but ²fully ³testified ⁴somewhere ¹one

λέγων, Τί ἐστιν ἄνθρωπος, ὅτι μιμνήσκῃ αὐτοῦ· ἢ υἱὸς
saying, What is　man,　that thou art mindful of him,　or son

ἀνθρώπου, ὅτι ἐπισκέπτῃ ᴾαὐτόν;‖ 7 ἠλάττωσας αὐτὸν
of man,　that thou visitest　him?　Thou didst make ⁴lower ¹him

βραχύ τι παρ᾽ ἀγγέλους· δόξῃ καὶ τιμῇ ἐστεφάνωσας
³little ²some than [the] angels;　with glory and honour thou didst crown
(or for a little)

αὐτόν, ᑫκαὶ κατέστησας αὐτὸν ἐπὶ τὰ ἔργα τῶν.χειρῶν.σου·‖
him,　and　didst set　him　over the works　of thy hands;

8 πάντα ὑπέταξας ὑποκάτω τῶν.ποδῶν.αὐτοῦ. Ἐν.γὰρ
all things thou didst subject　under　his feet.　For in

τῷ‖ ὑποτάξαι ˢαὐτῷ‖ τὰ.πάντα, οὐδὲν ἀφῆκεν αὐτῷ ἀνυπότακ-
subjecting to him all things, nothing he left to him　unsubject.

τον· νῦν.δὲ οὔπω ὁρῶμεν αὐτῷ τὰ.πάντα ὑποτεταγμένα·
But now not yet do we see to him　all things　subjected;

---

but thou remainest; and they all shall wax old as doth a garment; 12 and as a vesture shalt thou fold them up, and they shall be changed: but thou art the same, and thy years shall not fail. 13 But to which of the angels said he at any time, Sit on my right hand, until I make thine enemies thy footstool? 14 Are they not all ministering spirits, sent forth to minister for them who shall be heirs of salvation?

II. Therefore we ought to give the more earnest heed to the things which we have heard, lest at any time we should let *them* slip. 2 For if the word spoken by angels was stedfast, and every transgression and disobedience received a just recompence of reward; 3 how shall we escape, if we neglect so great salvation; which at the first began to be spoken by the Lord, and was confirmed unto us by them that heard *him;* 4 God also bearing *them* witness, both with signs and wonders, and with divers miracles, and gifts of the Holy Ghost, according to his own will?

5 For unto the angels hath he not put in subjection the world to come, whereof we speak. 6 But one in a certain place testified, saying, What is man, that thou art mindful of him? or the son of man, that thou visitest him? 7 Thou madest him a little lower than the angels; thou crownedst him with glory and honour, and didst set him over the works of thy hands: 8 thou hast put all things in subjection under his feet. For in that he put all in subjection under him, he left nothing *that is* not put under him. But now we see not yet all things put un-

---

¹ ἀλλάξεις thou shalt change ᴛ.　　ᵐ + ὡς ἱμάτιον as a garment ʟ.[ᴛ·].　　ⁿ προσέχειν
ἡμᾶς ʟᴛᴛʳᴀᴡ.　° παραρυῶμεν ʟᴛᴛʳᴀ.　ᴾ αὐτοῦ ᴡ.　ᑫ — καὶ κατέστησας to end of verse
G[ʟ]ᴛ[ᴛʳ]ᴀ.　ʳ τῷ γὰρ ʟᴛᴛʳᴀᴡ.　ˢ [αὐτῷ] ʟ.

der him. 9 But we see Jesus, who was made a little lower than the angels for the suffering of death, crowned with glory and honour; that he by the grace of God should taste death for every man. 10 For it became him, for whom *are* all things, and by whom *are* all things, in bringing many sons unto glory, to make the captain of their salvation perfect through sufferings. 11 For both he that sanctifieth and they who are sanctified *are* all of one : for which cause he is not ashamed to call them brethren, 12 saying, I will declare thy name unto my brethren, in the midst of the church will I sing praise unto thee. 13 And again, I will put my trust in him. And again, Behold I and the children which God hath given me. 14 Forasmuch then as the children are partakers of flesh and ·blood, he also himself likewise took part of the same; that through death he might destroy him that had the power of death, that is, the devil; 15 and deliver them who through fear of death were all their lifetime subject to bondage. 16 For verily he took not on *him the nature of* angels; but he took on *him* the seed of Abraham. 17 Wherefore in all things it behoved him to be made like unto *his* brethren, that he might be a merciful and faithful high priest in things *pertaining* to God, to make reconciliation for the sins of the people. 18 For in that he himself hath suffered being tempted, he is able to succour them that are tempted.

III. Wherefore, holy brethren, partakers of the heavenly calling, consider the Apostle and High Priest of our profession, Christ Jesus; 2 who was faithful to him that appointed him, as also Moses *was faithful* in all his house. 3 For

9 τὸν.δὲ βραχύ τι παρ' ἀγγέλους ἠλαττωμένον βλέπομεν
but ⁴who ³little ⁷some ¹⁰than [¹¹the] ¹²angels [²was] ⁶made ⁹lower ¹we ²see
(or for a little)
Ἰησοῦν .διὰ τὸ πάθημα τοῦ θανάτου δόξῃ καὶ τιμῇ
³Jesus on account of the suffering of death with glory and with honour
ἐστεφανωμένον, ὅπως χάριτι θεοῦ ὑπὲρ παντὸς γεύσηται
crowned; so that by [the] grace of God for every one he might taste
(or every thing)
θανάτου. 10 Ἔπρεπεν.γὰρ αὐτῷ, δι' ὃν τὰ.πάντα καὶ δι'
death. For it was becoming to him, for whom [are] all things and by
οὗ τὰ.πάντα, πολλοὺς υἱοὺς εἰς δόξαν ἀγαγόντα, τὸν
whom [are] all things, many sons to glory bringing, the
ἀρχηγὸν τῆς.σωτηρίας.αὐτῶν διὰ παθημάτων τελειῶσαι.
leader of their salvation through sufferings to make perfect.
11 ὅ.τε.γὰρ ἁγιάζων καὶ οἱ ἁγιαζόμενοι, ἐξ ἑνὸς πάντες·
For both he who sanctifies and those sanctified of one [are] all;
δι' ἣν αἰτίαν οὐκ.ἐπαισχύνεται ἀδελφοὺς αὐτοὺς καλεῖν, 12 λέ-
for which cause he is not ashamed ⁴brethren ³them ¹to ²call, say-
γων, Ἀπαγγελῶ τὸ.ὄνομά.σου τοῖς.ἀδελφοῖς.μου,.ἐν μέσῳ
ing, I will declare thy name to my brethren; in [the] midst
ἐκκλησίας ὑμνήσω.σε. 13 Καὶ πάλιν, Ἐγὼ ἔσομαι
of [the] assembly I will sing praise to thee. And again, I will be
πεποιθὼς ἐπ' αὐτῷ. Καὶ πάλιν, Ἰδοὺ ἐγὼ καὶ τὰ παιδία ἅ
trusting in him. And again, Behold I and the children which
μοι ἔδωκεν ὁ θεός. 14 Ἐπεὶ οὖν τὰ παιδία κεκοινώνηκεν
¹me ²gave ¹God. Since therefore the children have partaken
ᵛσαρκὸς καὶ αἵματος,ǁ καὶ αὐτὸς παραπλησίως μετέσχεν
of flesh and blood, also he in like manner took part in
τῶν.αὐτῶν, ἵνα διὰ τοῦ θανάτου καταργήσῃ τὸν τὸ κράτος
the same, that through death he might annul him who ²the ³might
ἔχοντα τοῦ θανάτου, ʷτουτέστινǁ τὸν διάβολον, 15 καὶ ἀπαλ-
¹has of death, that is, the devil; and might set
λάξῃ τούτους ὅσοι φόβῳ θανάτου διὰ παντὸς τοῦ.ζῆν
free those whosoever by fear of death through all their lifetime
ἔνοχοι ἦσαν ˣδουλείας.ǁ 16 οὐ.γὰρ δήπου ἀγγέλων ἐπιλαμ-
²subject ¹were to bondage. For not indeed of angels takes he
βάνεται, ἀλλὰ σπέρματος Ἀβραὰμ ἐπιλαμβάνεται. 17 ὅθεν
hold, but of [the] seed of Abraham he takes hold. Wherefore
ὤφειλεν κατὰ πάντα τοῖς.ἀδελφοῖς ὁμοιωθῆναι, ἵνα ἐλεή-
it behoved [him] in all things to [his] brethren to be made like, that a merci-
μων γένηται καὶ πιστὸς ἀρχιερεὺς τὰ πρὸς τὸν θεόν,
ful ⁵he ⁶might ⁷be ¹and ²faithful ³high ⁴priest [in] things relating to God,
εἰς τὸ ἱλάσκεσθαι τὰς ἁμαρτίας τοῦ λαοῦ. 18 ἐν.ᾧ.γὰρ
for to make propitiation for the sins of the people; for in that
πέπονθεν αὐτὸς πειρασθείς, δύναται τοῖς πειραζομένοις
he ²has ³suffered ¹himself having been tempted, he is able those who are tempted
βοηθῆσαι.
to help.

3 Ὅθεν, ἀδελφοὶ ἅγιοι, κλήσεως ἐπουρανίου μέτοχοι,
Wherefore, ²brethren ¹holy, of [the] ²calling ¹heavenly partakers,
κατανοήσατε τὸν ἀπόστολον καὶ ἀρχιερέα τῆς.ὁμολογίας.ἡμῶν
consider the apostle and high priest of our confession,
ʸχριστὸνǁ Ἰησοῦνǁ 2 πιστὸν ὄντα τῷ ποιήσαντι αὐτόν, ὡς
Christ Jesus, ²faithful ¹being to him who appointed him, as
καὶ ᶻΜωσῆςǁ ἐν ὅλῳ τῷ.οἴκῳ.αὐτοῦ. 3 πλείονος.γὰρ ᵃδόξης
also Moses in all his house. For ²of ³more ⁴glory

ᵛ αἵματος καὶ σαρκός LTTrAW. ʷ τοῦτ' ἔστιν GT. ˣ δουλίας T. ʸ — χριστὸν GLTTrAW.
ᶻ Μωϋσῆς GLTTrAW.· ᵃ οὗτος δόξης GLTTrAW.

οὗτος[a] παρὰ[b]Μωσῆν[n] ἠξίωται, καθ᾽.ὅσον πλείονα τιμὴν
ᵃhe than Moses has been counted worthy, by how much more honour

ἔχει τοῦ οἴκου ὁ κατασκευάσας αὐτόν· 4 πᾶς.γὰρ οἶκος
has �="5"than ᵉthe ⁷house ᵃhe ²who ³built ⁴it. For every house

κατασκευάζεται ὑπό τινος· ὁ.δὲ ᶜτὰ[c].πάντα κατασκευάσας
is built by some one; but he who all things built [is]

θεός. 5 καὶ ᵈΜωσῆς[d] μὲν πιστὸς ἐν ὅλῳ τῷ.οἴκῳ.αὐτοῦ ὡς
God. And Moses indeed [was] faithful in all his house as

θεράπων, εἰς μαρτύριον τῶν λαληθησομένων·
a ministering servant, for a testimony of the things going to be spoken;

6 χριστὸς.δὲ ὡς υἱὸς ἐπὶ τὸν.οἶκον.αὐτοῦ, οὗ οἶκός ἐσμεν
but Christ as Son over his house, whose house are

ἡμεῖς, ᵉἐάνπερ[e] τὴν παῤῥησίαν καὶ τὸ καύχημα τῆς ἐλπίδος
we, if indeed the boldness and the boasting of the hope

ᶠμέχρι τέλους βεβαίαν[n] κατάσχωμεν.
unto [the] end firm we should hold.

7 Διό, καθὼς λέγει.τὸ πνεῦμα τὸ ἅγιον, Σήμερον ἐὰν τῆς
Wherefore, even as says the Spirit the Holy, To-day if

φωνῆς.αὐτοῦ ἀκούσητε, 8 μὴ.σκληρύνητε τὰς.καρδίας.ὑμῶν,
his voice ye will hear, harden not your hearts,

ὡς.ἐν τῷ παραπικρασμῷ, κατὰ τὴν ἡμέραν τοῦ πειρασμοῦ ἐν
as in the provocation, in the day of temptation, in

τῇ ἐρήμῳ, 9 οὗ ἐπείρασάν ᵍμε[n] οἱ.πατέρες.ὑμῶν, ʰἐδοκίμασάν
the wilderness, where ²tempted ⁴me ¹your ³fathers, proved

με,[n] καὶ εἶδον τὰ.ἔργα.μου ⁱτεσσαράκοντα᾽ ἔτη· 10 διὸ προσ-
me, and saw my works forty years. Wherefore I was

ὤχθισα τῇ γενεᾷ ʲἐκείνῃ,[n] καὶ ᵏεἶπον,[n] Ἀεὶ πλανῶνται τῇ
indignant . with ²generation ¹that, and said, Always they err in

καρδίᾳ· αὐτοὶ.δὲ οὐκ.ἔγνωσαν τὰς.ὁδούς.μου· 11 ὡς ὤμοσα ἐν
in heart; and they did not know my ways; so I swore in

τῇ.ὀργῇ.μου, Εἰ εἰσελεύσονται εἰς τὴν.κατάπαυσίν.μου. 12 Βλέ-
my wrath, If they shall enter into my rest. Take

πετε, ἀδελφοί, μήποτε ἔσται ἔν τινι ὑμῶν καρδία πονηρὰ
heed, brethren, lest perhaps shall be in anyone of you a ᵃheart ¹wicked

ἀπιστίας ἐν τῷ ἀποστῆναι ἀπὸ θεοῦ ζῶντος· 13 ἀλλὰ
of unbelief in departing from ²God [¹the] ³living. But

παρακαλεῖτε ἑαυτοὺς καθ᾽.ἑκάστην.ἡμέραν, ἄχρις.οὗ τὸ σήμερον
encourage yourselves every day as long as ⁴to-day

ᵐκαλεῖται, ἵνα μὴ σκληρυνθῇ ˡτις ἐξ ὑμῶν[n] ἀπάτῃ τῆς
ᵐit is ³called, that not may be hardened any of you by [the] deceitfulness

ἁμαρτίας· 14 μέτοχοι.γὰρ ᵐγεγόναμεν τοῦ χριστοῦ, ⁿἐάνπερ[n]
of sin. For companions we have become of the Christ, if indeed

τὴν ἀρχὴν τῆς ὑποστάσεως μέχρι τέλους βεβαίαν κατά-
ᵃthe beginning of the assurance unto [the] end firm we

σχωμεν· 15 ἐν τῷ.λέγεσθαι, Σήμερον ἐὰν τῆς.φωνῆς.αὐτοῦ
should hold; in ᵃits being said, To-day if his voice

ἀκούσητε, μὴ.σκληρύνητε τὰς.καρδίας.ὑμῶν, ὡς ἐν τῷ παραπι-
ye will hear, harden not your hearts, as in the provoca-

κρασμῷ. 16 ᵒτινὲς.γὰρ ἀκούσαντες παρεπίκραναν,[n] ἀλλ᾽ οὐ
tion. For some having heard provoked, but not

πάντες οἱ ἐξελθόντες.ἐξ Αἰγύπτου διὰ ᴾΜωσέως.[q] 17 τίσιν.δὲ
all who came out from Egypt by Moses. And with whom

---

this man was counted worthy of more glory than Moses, inasmuch as he who hath builded the house hath more honour than the house. 4 For every house is builded by some man; but he that built all things is God. 5 And Moses verily was faithful in all his house, as a servant, for a testimony of those things which were to be spoken after; 6 but Christ as a son over his own house; whose house are we, if we hold fast the confidence and the rejoicing of the hope firm unto the end.

7 Wherefore (as the Holy Ghost saith, To day if.ye will hear his voice, 8 harden not your hearts, as in the provocation, in the day of temptation in the wilderness: 9 when your fathers tempted me, proved me, and saw my works forty years. 10 Wherefore I was grieved with that generation, and said, They do alway err in their heart ; and they have ·not known my ways. 11 So I sware in my wrath, They shall not enter into my rest.) 12 Take heed, brethren, lest there be in any of you an evil heart of unbelief, in departing from the living God. 13 But exhort one another daily, while it is called To day ; lest any of you be hardened through the deceitfulness of sin. 14 For we are made partakers of Christ, if we hold the beginning of our confidence. stedfast unto the end; 15 while it is said, To day·if ye will hear his voice, harden not your hearts, as in the provocation. 16 For some, when they had heard, did provoke: howbeit not all that came out of Egypt by Moses. 17 But with

---

ᵇ Μωσῆν GLTTrAW. ᶜ — τὰ LTTrAW. ᵈ Μωσῆς GLTTrAW. ᵉ ἐάν[περ] L ; ἐὰν if TTrA.
ᶠ — μέχρι τέλους βεβαίαν A. ᵍ — με LTTrAW. ʰ ἐν δοκιμασίᾳ by proving [me]
LTTrAW. ⁱ τεσσεράκοντα TTrA. ʲ ταύτῃ this LTTrAW. ᵏ εἶπα L ⁱ ἐξ ὑμῶν τις
GLAW. ᵐ τοῦ χριστοῦ γεγόναμεν GLTTrAW. ⁿ ἐάν περ LTr. ᵒ τίνες γὰρ ἀκού. παρεπί-
κρᾶβαν; For who, having heard, provoked? GLTTrAW. ᴾ Μωϋσέως GLTTrAW. ᑫ ; (read
as a question but [was it] not all, &c. ?) GLTTrAW. ʳ + [καὶ] also L.

whom was he grieved forty years? *was it* not with them that had sinned, whose carcases fell in the wilderness? 18 And to whom sware he that they should not enter into his rest, but· to them that believed not? 19 So we see that they could not enter in because of unbelief. IV. Let us therefore fear, lest, a promi-e being left *us* of entering into his rest, any of you should seem to come short of it. 2 For unto us was the gospel preached, as well as unto them: but the word preached did not profit them, not being mixed with faith in them that heard *it.* 3 For we which have believed do enter into rest, as he said, As I have sworn in my wrath, if they shall enter into my rest: although the works were finished from the foundation of the world. 4 For he spake in a certain place of the seventh *day* on this wise, And God did rest the seventh day from all his works. 5 And in this *place* again, If they shall enter into my rest. 6 Seeing therefore it remaineth that some must enter therein, and they to whom it was first preached entered not in because of unbelief: 7 again, he limiteth a certain day, saying in David, To day, after so long a time; as it is said, To day if ye will hear his voice, harden not your hearts. 8 For if Jesus had given them rest, then would he not afterward have spoken of another day. 9 There remaineth therefore a rest to the people of God. 10 For he that is entered into his rest, he also hath ceased from his own works, as God *did* from his. 11 Let us labour therefore to enter into that rest, lest any man fall after the same example of un-

προσώχθισεν ⁸τεσσαράκοντα‖ ἔτη; οὐχὶ τοῖς ἁμαρ-
was he indignant forty years? [Was it] not with those who

τήσασιν, ὧν τὰ κῶλα ἔπεσεν ἐν τῇ ἐρήμῳ; 18 τίσιν.δὲ
sinned, of whom the carcases fell in the wilderness? And to whom

ὤμοσεν μὴ.εἰσελεύσεσθαι εἰς τὴν.κατάπαυσιν.αὐτοῦ, εἰ.μὴ
swore he [that they] shall not enter into his rest, except

τοῖς ἀπειθήσασιν; 19 καὶ βλέπομεν ὅτι οὐκ.ἠδυνήθησαν
to those who disobeyed? And we see that they were not able

εἰσελθεῖν δι' ἀπιστίαν. 4 Φοβηθῶμεν οὖν μήποτε
to enter in on account of unbelief. We should fear therefore lest perhaps

καταλειπομένης ἐπαγγελίας εἰσελθεῖν εἰς τὴν.κατάπαυσιν.αὐ-
³being ⁴left ¹a ²promise to enter into his rest,

τοῦ, δοκῇ τις ἐξ ὑμῶν ὑστερηκέναι. 2 καὶ.γὰρ ἐσμεν.εὐηγ-
⁴might ⁵seem ¹any ²of ³you to come short. For indeed we have had

γελισμένοι, καθάπερ κἀκεῖνοι· ἀλλ' οὐκ ὠφέλησεν ὁ
glad tidings announced [to us] even as also they; but not did profit ²the

λόγος τῆς ἀκοῆς ἐκείνους, μὴ ⁰συγκεκραμένος‖ τῇ πίστει
³word ⁴of ⁵the ⁶report ¹them, not having been mixed with faith

τοῖς ἀκούσασιν. 3 εἰσερχόμεθα.γὰρ εἰς ᵛτὴν‖ κατάπαυσιν
in those who heard. For we enter into the rest,

οἱ πιστεύσαντες, καθὼς εἴρηκεν, Ὡς ὤμοσα ἐν τῇ.ὀργῇ.μου,
who believed; as he has said, So I swore in my wrath,

Εἰ εἰσελεύσονται εἰς τὴν.κατάπαυσίν.μου· καίτοι τῶν ἔργων
If they shall enter into my rest; though verily the works

ἀπὸ καταβολῆς κόσμου γενηθέντων. 4 Εἴρηκεν.γάρ που
from [the] foundation of [the] world were done. For he has said somewhere

περὶ τῆς ἑβδόμης οὕτως, Καὶ κατέπαυσεν ὁ θεὸς ἐν τῇ
concerning the seventh [day] thus, And ²rested ¹God on the

ἡμέρᾳ τῇ ἑβδόμῃ ἀπὸ πάντων τῶν.ἔργων.αὐτοῦ· 5 καὶ ἐν τού-
²day ¹seventh from all his works; and in this

τῳ πάλιν, Εἰ εἰσελεύσονται εἰς τὴν.κατάπαυσίν.μου. 6 Ἐπεὶ
[place] again, If they shall enter into my rest. Since

οὖν ᵛἀπολείπεταί τινας εἰσελθεῖν εἰς αὐτήν, καὶ οἱ πρό-
therefore it remains [for] some to enter into it, and those who

τερον εὐαγγελισθέντες οὐκ.εἰσῆλθον ᵂδι'‖ ἀπείθειαν, 7 πά-
formerly heard glad tidings did not enter in on account of disobedience, again

λιν τινὰ ὁρίζει ἡμέραν, Σήμερον, ἐν ˣΔαβὶδ‖ λέγων, μετὰ
a certain ²he ³determines ¹day, To-day, in David saying, after

τοσοῦτον χρόνον, καθὼς ᵞεἴρηται,‖ Σήμερον ἐὰν τῆς φωνῆς
so long a time, (according as it has been said,) To-day, if ²voice

αὐτοῦ ἀκούσητε, μὴ.σκληρύνητε τὰς.καρδίας.ὑμῶν. 8 Εἰ.γὰρ
¹his ye will hear, harden not your hearts. For if

αὐτοὺς Ἰησοῦς κατέπαυσεν, οὐκ ἂν περὶ ἄλλης ἐλά-
³them ¹Jesus ²gave ⁴rest, not concerning another ²would ³he ⁴have
(i.e. Joshua)

λει μετὰ.ταῦτα ἡμέρας· 9 ἄρα ἀπολείπεται σαββατισμὸς τῷ
⁵spoken ⁶afterwards ¹day. Then remains a sabbatism to the

λαῷ τοῦ.θεοῦ. 10 ὁ.γὰρ εἰσελθὼν εἰς τὴν.κατάπαυσιν.αὐτοῦ,
people of God. For he that entered into his rest,

καὶ αὐτὸς κατέπαυσεν ἀπὸ τῶν.ἔργων.αὐτοῦ, ὥσπερ ἀπὸ
also he rested from his works, as from

τῶν.ἰδίων ὁ θεός. 11 Σπουδάσωμεν οὖν εἰσελθεῖν εἰς
⁴his ⁵own ¹God [²did]. We should be diligent therefore to enter into

ἐκείνην τὴν κατάπαυσιν, ἵνα.μὴ ἐν τῷ αὐτῷ τις ὑποδείγ-
that rest, lest ⁴after ⁵the ⁶same ¹anyone ⁷example

ˢ τεσσεράκοντα ΤΤrΑ.   ᵗ συγκεκερασμένους LΤΤΑ, συγκεκραμένους w, (*read* them not united in faith with those, &c.); συνκεκερασμένος.Τ.   ᵛ [τὴν] Τr.   ᵂ διὰ Α.   ˣ Δανεὶδ LΤΤrΑ; Δαυὶδ GW.   ᵞ προείρηται it has.been said before LΤΤrΑw.

ματι πέσῃ τῆς ἀπειθείας. 12 ζῶν.γὰρ ὁ λόγος τοῦ θεοῦ καὶ
²may ³fall of disobedience. For living [is] the word of God and

ἐνεργής, καὶ τομώτερος ὑπὲρ πᾶσαν μάχαιραν δίστομον, καὶ
efficient, and sharper than every ²sword ¹two-edged, even

διϊκνούμενος ἄχρι μερισμοῦ ψυχῆς.ᶻτε‖ καὶ πνεύματος, ἁρ-
penetrating to [the] division both of soul and spirit, ²of

μῶν τε καὶ μυελῶν, καὶ κριτικὸς ἐνθυμήσεων καὶ ἐννοιῶν
³joints ¹both and marrows, and [is] a discerner of [the] thoughts and intents

καρδίας· 13 καὶ οὐκ.ἔστιν κτίσις ἀφανὴς ἐνώπιον αὐτοῦ·
of [the] heart. And there is not a created thing unapparent before him;

πάντα.δὲ γυμνὰ καὶ τετραχηλισμένα τοῖς ὀφθαλμοῖς αὐτοῦ,
but all things [are] naked and laid bare to the eyes of him,

πρὸς ὃν ἡμῖν ὁ λόγος.
with whom [is] our account.

14 Ἔχοντες.οὖν ἀρχιερέα μέγαν διεληλυθότα τοὺς
Having therefore a ²high ³priest ¹great [who] has passed through the

οὐρανούς, Ἰησοῦν τὸν υἱὸν τοῦ θεοῦ, κρατῶμεν τῆς ὁμο-
heavens, Jesus the Son of God, we should hold fast the con-

λογίας. 15 οὐ.γὰρ ἔχομεν ἀρχιερέα μὴ δυνάμενον ᵃσυμπα-
fession. For not have we a high priest not able to sym-

θῆσαι‖ ταῖς.ἀσθενείαις.ἡμῶν, ᵇπεπειραμένον‖.δὲ κατὰ πάντα
pathise with our infirmities, but [who] has been tempted in all things

καθ᾽.ὁμοιότητα χωρὶς ἁμαρτίας. 16 προσερχώμεθα οὖν
according to [our] likeness, apart from sin. We should come therefore

μετὰ παρρησίας τῷ θρόνῳ τῆς χάριτος, ἵνα λάβωμεν ᶜἔλεον,‖
with boldness to the throne of grace, that we may receive mercy,

καὶ χάριν εὕρωμεν εἰς εὔκαιρον βοήθειαν.
and ᵍgrace ¹may ²find for opportune help.

5 Πᾶς.γὰρ ἀρχιερεὺς ἐξ ἀνθρώπων λαμβανόμενος, ὑπὲρ
For every high priest from among men being taken for

ἀνθρώπων καθίσταται τὰ πρὸς τὸν θεόν, ἵνα προσφέρῃ
men is constituted in things relating to God, that he may offer

δῶρά.ᵈτε‖ καὶ θυσίας ὑπὲρ ἁμαρτιῶν, 2 μετριοπαθεῖν δυνά-
both gifts, and sacrifices for sins; ³to ⁴exercise ⁵forbearance ¹being

μενος τοῖς ἀγνοοῦσιν καὶ πλανωμένοις, ἐπεὶ καὶ αὐτὸς
²able with those being ignorant and erring, since also himself

περίκειται ἀσθένειαν· 3 καὶ ᵉδιὰ ταύτην‖ ὀφείλει,
is encompassed with infirmity; and on account of this [infirmity] he ought,

καθὼς περὶ τοῦ λαοῦ, οὕτως καὶ περὶ ᶠἑαυτοῦ‖ προσφέρειν
even as for the people, so also for himself to offer

ᵍὑπὲρ‖ ἁμαρτιῶν. 4 Καὶ οὐχ ἑαυτῷ τις λαμβάνει τὴν τιμήν,
for sins. And not to himself anyone takes the honour,

ἀλλὰ ʰὁ‖ καλούμενος ὑπὸ τοῦ θεοῦ, ⁱκαθάπερ‖ καὶ ʰὁ‖ Ἀαρών.
but ʰhe being called by God, even as also Aaron.

5 οὕτως καὶ ὁ χριστὸς οὐχ ἑαυτὸν ἐδόξασεν. γενηθῆναι ἀρχ-
Thus also the Christ not himself did glorify to become a high

ιερέα, ἀλλ᾽ ὁ λαλήσας πρὸς αὐτόν, Υἱός.μου εἶ.σύ, ἐγὼ σή-
priest; but he who said to him, ²Son ¹my art thou, I to-

μερον γεγέννηκά σε. 6 καθὼς καὶ ἐν ἑτέρῳ λέγει, Σὺ
day have begotten thee. Even as also in another [place] he says, Thou [art]

ἱερεὺς εἰς.τὸν.αἰῶνα κατὰ τὴν τάξιν Μελχισεδέκ. 7 Ὃς ἐν
a priest for ever according to the order of Melchisedec. Who in

---

belief. 12 For the word of God is quick, and powerful, and sharper than any twoedged sword, piercing even to the dividing asunder of soul and spirit, and of the joints and marrow, and is a discerner of the thoughts and intents of the heart. 13 Neither is there any creature that is not manifest in his sight: but all things are naked and opened unto the eyes of him with whom we have to do.

14 Seeing then that we have a great high priest, that is passed into the heavens, Jesus the Son of God, let us hold fast our profession. 15 For we have not an high priest which cannot be touched with the feeling of our infirmities; but was in all points tempted like as we are, yet without sin. 16 Let us therefore come boldly unto the throne of grace, that we may obtain mercy, and find grace to help in time of need.

V. For every high priest taken from among men is ordained for men in things pertaining to God, that he may offer both gifts and sacrifices for sins: 2 who can have compassion on the ignorant, and on them that are out of the way; for that he himself also is compassed with infirmity. 3 And by reason hereof he ought, as for the people, so also for himself, to offer for sins. 4 And no man taketh this honour unto himself, but he that is called of God, as was Aaron. 5 So also Christ glorified not himself to be made an high priest; but he that said unto him, Thou art my Son, to day have I begotten thee. 6 As he saith also in another place, Thou art a priest for ever after the order of Melchisedec. 7 Who in

---

the days of his flesh, when he had offered up prayers and supplications with strong crying and tears unto him that was able to save him from death, and was heard in that he feared ; 8 though he were a Son, yet learned he obedience by the things which he suffered ; 9 and being made perfect, he became the author of eternal salvation unto all them that obey him ; 10 called of God an high priest after the order of Melchisedec. 11 Of whom we have many things to say, and hard to be uttered, seeing ye are dull of hearing. 12 For when for the time ye ought to be teachers, ye have need that one teach you again which *be* the first principles of the oracles of God ; and are become such as have need of milk, and not of strong meat. 13 For every one that useth milk *is* unskilful in the word *of* righteousness : for he is a babe. 14 But strong meat belongeth to them that are of full age, *even* those who by reason of use have their senses exercised to discern both good and evil.

ταῖς ἡμέραις τῆς σαρκὸς αὐτοῦ δεήσεις τε καὶ ἱκετηρίας πρὸς
the days　　of his flesh　both supplications and entreaties　[2]to
τὸν δυνάμενον σώζειν αὐτὸν ἐκ θανάτου, μετὰ κραυ-
[4]him [5]who [6]was　[7]able [8]to [9]save [10]him [11]from [12]death, [13]with [13']cry-
γῆς ἰσχυρᾶς καὶ δακρύων προσενέγκας, καὶ εἰσακουσθεὶς ἀπὸ
ing [14]strong [16]and [17]tears [1]having [2]offered, and having been heard in
τῆς εὐλαβείας, 8 καίπερ ὢν υἱός, ἔμαθεν ἀφ' ὧν
that [he] feared ;　　though being a son, he learned, from the things which
ἔπαθεν τὴν ὑπακοήν, 9 καὶ τελειωθεὶς ἐγένετο [k]τοῖς
he suffered,　　obedience ;　　and having been perfected became to [2]those [3]that
ὑπακούουσιν αὐτῷ πᾶσιν|| αἴτιος σωτηρίας αἰωνίου· 10 προσ-
[4]obey　　[5]him　[1]all, author of [2]salvation [1]eternal ;　　having
αγορευθεὶς ὑπὸ τοῦ θεοῦ ἀρχιερεὺς κατὰ τὴν τάξιν Μελ-
been saluted ` by　　God [as] high priest according to the order of Mel-
χισεδέκ. 11 Περὶ οὗ ` πολὺς ἡμῖν ὁ λόγος καὶ δυσερμή-
chisedec.　Concerning whom [3]is] [4]much [1]our [2]discourse and difficult in inter-
νευτος λέγειν, ἐπεὶ νωθροὶ γεγόνατε ταῖς ἀκοαῖς. 12 καὶ γὰρ
pretation to speak, since sluggish ye have become in hearing.　　For truly
ὀφείλοντες εἶναι διδάσκαλοι διὰ τὸν χρόνον, πάλιν
[when ye] ought to be teachers because of the time, again
χρείαν ἔχετε τοῦ διδάσκειν ὑμᾶς τίνα τὰ στοιχεῖα τῆς
need ye have of [one] to teach you what [are] the elements of the
ἀρχῆς τῶν λογίων τοῦ θεοῦ· καὶ γεγόνατε χρείαν ἔχοντες
beginning of the oracles of God, and have become [2]need [1]having
γάλακτος, [l]καὶ|| οὐ στερεᾶς τροφῆς. 13 πᾶς γὰρ ὁ μετέχων
of milk, and not of solid food ;　for everyone that partakes
γάλακτος ἄπειρος λόγου δικαιοσύνης· νήπιος γάρ ἐστιν·
of milk [is] unskilled in [the] word of righteousness, for an infant he is ;
14 τελείων δὲ ἐστιν ἡ στερεὰ τροφή, τῶν διὰ τὴν
but [4]for [5]the] [6]fully [2]grown [3]is [1]solid [2]food, who on account of
ἕξιν τὰ αἰσθητήρια γεγυμνασμένα ἐχόντων πρὸς διάκρισιν
habit [2]the [3]senses [4]exercised [1]have for distinguishing
καλοῦ τε καὶ κακοῦ.
[2]good [1]both and· evil.

VI. Therefore leaving the principles of the doctrine of Christ, let us go on unto perfection ; not laying again the foundation of repentance from dead works, and of faith toward God, 2 of the doctrine of baptisms, and of laying on of hands, and of resurrection of the dead, and of eternal judgment. 3 And this will we do, if God permit. 4 For *it is* impossible for those who were once enlightened, and have tasted of the heavenly gift, and were made partakers of the Holy Ghost, 5 and have tasted the good word of God, and the powers of the world to come, 6 if they shall fall away, to renew them again unto repentance ;

6 Διὸ ἀφέντες τὸν τῆς ἀρχῆς τοῦ χριστοῦ λόγον, ἐπὶ
Wherefore, having left the [2]of [3]the [4]beginning [5]of [6]the [7]Christ [1]discourse, to
τὴν τελειότητα φερώμεθα· μὴ πάλιν θεμέλιον καταβαλλόμενοι
the full growth we should go on ; not again a foundation laying
μετανοίας ἀπὸ νεκρῶν ἔργων, καὶ πίστεως ἐπὶ θεόν, 2 βαπ-
of repentance from dead works, and faith in God, [of] [1]wash-
τισμῶν [m]διδαχῆς,|| ἐπιθέσεώς τε χειρῶν, ἀναστάσεώς [n]τε||　νε-
ings [1]of [2]the] [3]doctrine, and of laying on of hands, and of resurrection of [the]
κρῶν, καὶ κρίματος αἰωνίου. 3 καὶ τοῦτο ποιήσομεν, [o]ἐάνπερ||
dead, and of [2]judgment [1]eternal ;　• and this will we do,　if indeed
ἐπιτρέπῃ ὁ θεός. 4 ἀδύνατον γὰρ τοὺς ἅπαξ φωτισθέντας,
[2]permit [1]God.　　For [it is] impossible, those once enlightened,
γευσαμένους τε τῆς δωρεᾶς τῆς ἐπουρανίου, καὶ μετόχους
and [who] tasted of the [2]gift [1]heavenly,　and· partakers
γενηθέντας πνεύματος ἁγίου, 5 καὶ καλὸν γευσαμένους
became of [the] [2]Spirit [1]Holy, and [2the] [3]good [1]tasted
θεοῦ ῥῆμα δυνάμεις τε μέλλοντος αἰῶνος, 6 καὶ
[5]of [6]God [4]word and [the] works of power of [the] [2]to [3]come [1]age, and
παραπεσόντας, πάλιν ἀνακαινίζειν εἰς μετάνοιαν, ἀνασταυ-
[who] fell away, again to renew to repentance, crucify-

---

k πᾶσιν τοῖς ὑπακούουσιν αὐτῷ LTTrA　　　l — καὶ T[Tr].　　m διδαχήν [the] doctrine L
n [τε] Tr.　　　o ἐάν περ LTrW.

ρο̃υντας ἑαυτοῖς τὸν υἱὸν τοῦ θεοῦ καὶ παραδειγ-
ing for themselves [as they do] the Son of God, and exposing

ματίζοντας. 7 γῆ.γὰρ ἡ πιοῦσα τὸν ἐπ' αὐτῆς ᴾπολλάκις
[him] publicly. For ground which drank the ⁴upon ⁵it ³often

ἐρχόμενον‖ ὑετόν, καὶ τίκτουσα βοτάνην εὔθετον ἐκείνοις
²coming ¹rain, and produces ¹herbage ¹fit for those

δι' οὓς καὶ γεωργεῖται, μεταλαμβάνει εὐλογίας ἀπὸ τοῦ
for sake of whom also it is tilled, partakes of blessing from

θεοῦ· 8 ἐκφέρουσα.δὲ ἀκάνθας καὶ τριβόλους, ἀδόκιμος καὶ
God; but [that] bringing forth thorns and thistles [is] rejected and

κατάρας ἐγγύς, ἧς τὸ τέλος εἰς καῦσιν. 9 Πεπείσμεθα.δὲ
³a ⁴curse ¹near ²to, of which the end [is] for burning. But we are persuaded

περὶ ὑμῶν, ἀγαπητοί, τὰ.ᑫκρείττονα‖ καὶ ἐχόμενα
concerning you, beloved, better things, and [things] connected with

σωτηρίας, εἰ καὶ οὕτως λαλοῦμεν. 10 οὐ.γὰρ ἄδικος ὁ θεὸς
salvation, if ¹even thus we speak. For not unrighteous [is] God

ἐπιλαθέσθαι τοῦ.ἔργου.ὑμῶν καὶ ʳτοῦ κόπου‖ τῆς ἀγάπης ἧς
to forget your work and the labour of love which

ἐνεδείξασθε εἰς τὸ.ὄνομα.αὐτοῦ, διακονήσαντες τοῖς ἁγίοις καὶ
ye did shew to his name, having served to the saints and

διακονοῦντες. 11 ἐπιθυμοῦμεν.δὲ ἕκαστον ὑμῶν τὴν αὐτὴν
[still] serving. But we desire each of you the same

ἐνδείκνυσθαι σπουδὴν πρὸς τὴν πληροφορίαν τῆς ἐλπίδος ἄχρι
²to ³shew ¹diligence to the full assurance of the hope unto

τέλους· 12 ἵνα μὴ νωθροὶ γένησθε, μιμηταὶ.δὲ τῶν διὰ
[the] end; that ²not ⁴sluggish ¹ye ²be, but imitators of those who through

πίστεως καὶ μακροθυμίας κληρονομούντων τὰς ἐπαγγελίας.
faith and long patience inherit the promises.

13 Τῷ.γὰρ.Ἀβραὰμ ἐπαγγειλάμενος ὁ θεός, ἐπεὶ κατ' οὐδενὸς
For ⁴to ⁵Abraham ²having ³promised ¹God, since by no one

εἶχεν μείζονος ὀμόσαι, ὤμοσεν καθ' ἑαυτοῦ, 14 λέγων, sʳΗ‖.μὴν
he had greater to swear, swore by himself, saying, Surely

εὐλογῶν εὐλογήσω σε, καὶ πληθύνων πληθυνῶ σε· 15 καὶ
blessing I will bless thee, and multiplying I will multiply thee; and

οὕτως μακροθυμήσας ἐπέτυχεν τῆς ἐπαγγελίας. 16 ἄνθρω-
thus having had long patience he obtained the promise. ²Men

ποι ᵗμὲν‖ γὰρ κατὰ τοῦ μείζονος ὀμνύουσιν, καὶ πάσης αὐτοῖς
³indeed ¹for ⁵by ⁶the ⁷greater ⁴swear, and of all ²to ³them

ἀντιλογίας πέρας εἰς βεβαίωσιν ὁ ὅρκος· 17 ἐν.ᾧ περισσό-
¹gainsaying an end for confirmation [is] the oath. Wherein ³more ⁴a-

τερον βουλόμενος ὁ θεὸς ἐπιδεῖξαι τοῖς κληρονόμοις τῆς ἐπαγ-
bundantly ²desiring ¹God to shew to the heirs of pro-

γελίας τὸ ἀμετάθετον τῆς.βουλῆς.αὐτοῦ, ἐμεσίτευσεν ὅρκῳ,
mise the unchangeableness of his counsel, interposed by an oath,

18 ἵνα διὰ δύο πραγμάτων ἀμεταθέτων, ἐν οἷς ἀδύνατον
that by two ²things ¹unchangeable, in which [it was] impossible

ψεύσασθαι ᵛθεόν, ἰσχυρὰν παράκλησιν ἔχωμεν οἱ κατα-
³to ⁴lie [¹for] ²God, strong encouragement we might have who fled

φυγόντες κρατῆσαι τῆς προκειμένης ἐλπίδος· 19 ἣν ὡς
for refuge to lay hold on the ²set ³before [⁴us] ¹hope, which as

ἄγκυραν ἔχομεν τῆς ψυχῆς ᵂἀσφαλῆ‖.τε καὶ βεβαίαν, καὶ εἰσ-
an anchor we have of the soul both certain and firm, and en-

ερχομένην εἰς τὸ ἐσώτερον τοῦ καταπετάσματος, 20 ὅπου
tering into that within the veil; where

seeing they crucify to themselves the Son of God afresh, and put him to an open shame. 7 For the earth which drinketh in the rain that cometh oft upon it, and bringeth forth herbs meet for them by whom it is dressed, receiveth blessing from God : 8 but that which beareth thorns and briers is rejected, and is nigh unto cursing; whose end is. to be burned. 9 But, beloved, we are persuaded better things of you, and things that accompany salvation, though we thus speak. 10 For God is not unrighteous to forget your work and labour of love, which ye have shewed toward his name, in that ye have ministered to the saints, and do minister. 11 And we desire that every one of you do shew the same diligence to the full assurance of hope unto the end : 12 that ye be not slothful, but followers of them who through faith and patience inherit the promises. 13 For when God made promise to Abraham, because he could sware by no greater, he sware by himself, 14 saying, Surely blessing I will bless thee, and multiplying I will multiply thee. 15 And so, after he had patiently endured, he obtained the promise. 16 For men verily swear by the greater : and an oath for confirmation is to them an end of all strife. 17 Wherein God, willing more abundantly to shew unto the heirs of promise the immutability of his counsel, confirmed it by an oath : 18 that by two immutable things, in which it was impossible for God to lie, we might have a strong consolation, who have fled for refuge to lay hold upon the hope set before us : 19 which hope we have as an anchor of the soul, both sure and stedfast, and which entereth into that within the veil; 20 whither the forerunner is for us entered, *even* Jesus, made an high priest for ever after the order of Melchisedec.

VII. For this Melchisedec, king of Salem, priest of the most high God, who met Abraham returning from the slaughter of the kings, and blessed him; 2 to whom also Abraham gave a tenth part of all; first being by interpretation King of righteousness, and after that also King of Salem, which is, King of peace; 3 without father, without mother, without descent, having neither beginning of days, nor end of life; but made like unto the Son of God; abideth a priest continually. 4 Now consider how great this man *was*, unto whom even the patriarch Abraham gave the tenth of the spoils. 5 And verily they that are of the sons of Levi, who receive the office of the priesthood, have a commandment to take tithes of the people according to the law, that is, of their brethren, though they come out of the loins of Abraham: 6 but he whose descent is not counted from them received tithes of Abraham, and blessed him that had the promises. 7 And without all contradiction the less is blessed of the better. 8 And here men that die receive tithes; but there he *receiveth them*, of whom it is witnessed that he liveth. 9 And as I may so say, Levi also, who receiveth tithes, payed tithes in Abraham. 10 For he was yet in the loins of his father, when Melchisedec met him. 11 If therefore perfection were by the Levitical priesthood, (for under it the people received the law,) what further need *was there* that another priest should rise after the order of Melchisedec, and not be called

πρόδρομος ὑπὲρ ἡμῶν εἰσῆλθεν Ἰησοῦς, κατὰ τὴν τάξιν
[as] forerunner for us ²entered ¹Jesus, according to the order

Μελχισεδὲκ ἀρχιερεὺς γενόμενος εἰς.τὸν.αἰῶνα.
of Melchisedec   a high priest having become   for ever.

7 Οὗτος.γὰρ ὁ Μελχισεδέκ, βασιλεὺς Σαλήμ, ἱερεὺς τοῦ θεοῦ
For this   Melchisedec,   king   of Salem, priest of God

ˣτοῦ‖ ὑψίστου, ˢὁ‖ συναντήσας Ἀβραὰμ ὑποστρέφοντι ἀπὸ τῆς
the most high, who met Abraham returning from the

κοπῆς τῶν βασιλέων, καὶ εὐλογήσας αὐτόν· 2 ᾧ καὶ δεκάτην
smiting of the kings, and having blessed him; to whom also ³a ⁴tenth

ἀπὸ πάντων ἐμέρισεν Ἀβραάμ· πρῶτον μὲν ἑρμηνευόμενος
⁵of ⁶all ²divided ¹Abraham; first being interpreted

βασιλεὺς δικαιοσύνης, ἔπειτα.δὲ καὶ βασιλεὺς Σαλήμ, ὅ. ἐστιν
king of righteousness, and then also king of Salem, which is

βασιλεὺς εἰρήνης· 3 ἀπάτωρ, ἀμήτωρ, ἀγενεαλόγητος·
king of peace; without father, without mother, without genealogy;

μήτε ἀρχὴν ἡμερῶν, μήτε ζωῆς τέλος ἔχων· ἀφωμοιωμένος.δὲ
neither beginning of days, nor ²of ³life ¹end having, but assimilated

τῷ υἱῷ τοῦ θεοῦ. μένει ἱερεὺς εἰς.τὸ.διηνεκές. 4 Θεωρεῖτε.δὲ
to the Son of God, abides a priest in perpetuity. Now consider

πηλίκος οὗτος, ᾧ ᶻκαὶ‖ δεκάτην Ἀβραὰμ ἔδωκεν ἐκ
how great this [one was], to whom ⁶even ⁵a ⁷tenth ¹Abraham ²gave ³out ⁴of

τῶν ἀκροθινίων ὁ πατριάρχης. 5 καὶ οἱ μὲν ἐκ τῶν
¹⁰the ¹¹spoils ²the ¹patriarch. And they indeed from among the

ᵃυἱῶν‖ ᵇΛευΐ‖ τὴν ἱερατείαν λαμβανοντες, ἐντολὴν ἔχουσιν
sons of Levi, ³the ⁴priesthood [¹who] ²receive, commandment have

ᶜἀποδεκατοῦν‖ τὸν λαὸν κατὰ τὸν νόμον, ᵈτουτέστιν,‖
to take tithes from the people according to the law, that is [from]

τοὺς.ἀδελφοὺς.αὐτῶν, καίπερ ἐξεληλυθότας ἐκ τῆς ὀσφύος
their brethren though having come out of the loins

Ἀβραάμ· 6 ὁ.δὲ μὴ.γενεαλογούμενος ἐξ αὐτῶν δεδεκάτω-
of Abraham; but he [who] reckons no genealogy from them has tithed

κεν·ᵉτὸν‖ Ἀβραάμ, καὶ τὸν ἔχοντα τὰς ἐπαγγελίας ᶠεὐλό-
Abraham, and ³him ⁴who ²had ⁶the ⁷promises ¹has

γηκεν·‖ 7 χωρὶς.δὲ πάσης ἀντιλογίας τὸ ἔλαττον ὑπὸ τοῦ
⁵blessed. But apart from all gainsaying the inferior by the

κρείττονος εὐλογεῖται. 8 καὶ ὧδε μὲν δεκάτας ἀποθνήσκοντες
superior is blessed. And here ⁵tithes [²that] ³die

ἄνθρωποι λαμβάνουσιν· ἐκεῖ.δὲ, μαρτυρούμενος ὅτι ζῇ.
¹men ⁴receive; but there [one] witnessed of that he lives.

9 καί, ὡς.ἔπος.εἰπεῖν, ᵍδιὰ‖ Ἀβραὰμ· καὶ ʰΛευΐ‖ ὁ δεκάτας
and, so to speak, through Abraham, also Levi, who ²tithes

λαμβάνων δεδεκάτωται· 10 ἔτι.γὰρ ἐν τῇ ὀσφύϊ τοῦ.πατρὸς
¹receives, has been tithed. For yet in the loins of [his] father

ἦν, ὅτε συνήντησεν αὐτῷ ⁱὁ· Μελχισεδέκ. 11 Εἰ μὲν ρῦν
he was when ²met ³him ¹Melchisedec. If indeed then

τελείωσις διὰ τῆς ᵏΛευϊτικῆς‖ ἱερωσύνης ἦν, ὁ.λαὸς.γὰρ
perfection by the Levitical priesthood were, for the people [²based]

ἐπ ¹αὐτῇ‖ ᵐνενομοθέτητο,‖ τίς ἔτι χρεία κατὰ
⁴upon ⁷it ¹had ²received [³the] ¹law, what still need [was there] according to

τὴν τάξιν Μελχισεδὲκ ἕτερον ἀνίστασθαι ἱερέα, καὶ οὐ
the order of Melchisedec [for] another ²to ³arise ¹priest; and not

---

ˣ — τοῦ E.   ʸ ὅς (*read* who, having met) LTТrA.   ᶻ — καὶ LTr.   ᵃ — υἱῶν (*read*
[sons]) L.   ᵇ Λευεὶ ТТrA.   ᶜ ἀποδεκατοῖν ТТrA.   ᵈ τοῦτ' ἐστιν GT.   ᵉ — τὸν LТТrA.
ᶠ ηὐλόγηκεν L.   ᵍ δι' LTТrA.   ʰ Λευὶς L; Λευεὶς ТТrA.   ⁱ — ὁ LTТrA.   ᵏ Λευειτικῆς TA.
ˡ αὐτῆς (*read* on the ground of it) LТТrAW.   ᵐ νενομοθέτηται has received [the] law LTТrAW.

κατὰ τὴν τάξιν Ἀαρὼν ˈλέγεσθαι; 12 μετατιθεμένης·γὰρ
according to the order of Aaron to be named? For ³being ⁴changed

τῆς ἱερωσύνης, ἐξ ἀνάγκης καὶ νόμου μετάθεσις γίνεται.
¹the ²priesthood, from necessity also of law a change takes place.

13 ἐφ᾽·ὃν·γὰρ λέγεται ταῦτα, φυλῆς ἑτέρας μετέσχηκεν, ἀφ᾽·ἧς
For he of whom are said these things, a ²tribe ¹different has part in, of which

οὐδεὶς προσέσχηκεν τῷ θυσιαστηρίῳ· 14 πρόδηλον·γὰρ ὅτι
no one has given attendance at the altar. For [it is] manifest that

ἐξ Ἰούδα ἀνατέταλκεν ὁ·κύριος·ἡμῶν, εἰς ἣν φυλὴν ⁿοὐδὲν
out of Juda has sprung our Lord, as to which tribe ³nothing

περὶ ἱερωσύνης⁰ᵘ ᵒΜωσῆς⁰ ἐλάλησεν. 15 Καὶ περισσότερον
⁴concerning ⁵priesthood ¹Moses ²spoke. And more abundantly

ἔτι κατάδηλόν ἐστιν, εἰ κατὰ τὴν ὁμοιότητα Μελχισεδὲκ
yet quite manifest it is, since according to the similitude of Melchisedec

ἀνίσταται ἱερεὺς ἕτερος, 16 ὃς οὐ κατὰ νόμον ²ἐντο-
arises a ²priest ¹different, who not according to law of ²command-

λῆς Ρσαρκικῆς⁰ᵖ γέγονεν, ἀλλὰ κατὰ δύναμιν ζωῆς
ment ¹fleshly has been constituted, but according to power of ³life

ἀκαταλύτου· 17 ᵠμαρτυρεῖᵘ·γὰρ, "Ὅτι σὺ ἱερεὺς εἰς τὸν
¹indissoluble. For he testifies, Thou [art] a priest for

αἰῶνα κατὰ τὴν τάξιν Μελχισεδέκ. 18 Ἀθέτησις μὲν γὰρ
ever after the order of Melchisedec. ²A ³putting ⁴away ¹for

γίνεται προαγούσης ἐντολῆς, διὰ τὸ·αὐτῆς·ἀσθενὲς
there is of the ³going ²before ¹commandment, because of its weakness

καὶ ἀνωφελές, 19 οὐδὲν·γὰρ ἐτελείωσεν ὁ νόμος, [ἐπεισ-
and unprofitableness, (for ⁴nothing ³perfected ¹the ²law,) [ᶜthe] ⁷intro-

αγωγὴ δὲ κρείττονος ἐλπίδος, δι᾽ ἧς ἐγγίζομεν τῷ θεῷ. 20 Καὶ
duction ⁸and of a better hope by which we draw near to God. And

καθ᾽·ὅσον οὐ χωρὶς ὁρκωμοσίας· οἱ μὲν γὰρ,
by how much [it was] not apart from [the] swearing of an oath, (²they ¹for

χωρὶς ὁρκωμοσίας εἰσὶν ἱερεῖς γεγονότες, 21 ὁ·δέ,
without [the] swearing of an oath are ²priests ¹become, but he

ʳμετὰᵘ ὁρκωμοσίας, διὰ τοῦ λέγοντος πρὸς αὐτόν,
with [the] swearing of an oath, by him who says, as to him,

Ὤμοσεν κύριος καὶ οὐ·μεταμεληθήσεται, Σὺ ἱερεὺς εἰς τὸν
²sware [¹the] ²Lord, and will not repent, Thou [art] a priest for

αἰῶνα ˢκατὰ τὴν τάξιν Μελχισεδέκ·ᵘ 22 κατὰ·ᵗτοσοῦτονᵘᵘ
ever according to the order of Melchisedec,) by so much

κρείττονος διαθήκης γέγονεν ἔγγυος Ἰησοῦς. 23 Καὶ οἱ
of a better covenant ²has become ¹surety ¹Jesus. And they

μὲν πλειονές εἰσιν·γεγονότες ἱερεῖςᵘ διὰ τὸ θανάτῳ κω-
²many ¹are priests on account of by death being

λύεσθαι παραμένειν· 24 ὁ·δὲ, διὰ τὸ·μένειν·αὐτὸν εἰς
hindered from continuing; but he, because of his abiding for

τὸν αἰῶνα, ἀπαράβατον ἔχει τὴν ἱερωσύνην· 25 ὅθεν καὶ
ever, ⁴intransmissible ¹has ²the ³priesthood. Whence also

σώζειν εἰς·τὸ·παντελὲς δύναται τοὺς προσερχομένους δι᾽
to save completely he is able those who approach by

αὐτοῦ τῷ θεῷ, πάντοτε ζῶν εἰς·τὸ·ἐντυγχάνειν ὑπὲρ αὐτῶν.
him to God, always living to intercede for them.

26 τοιοῦτος·γὰρ ἡμῖν ʷἔπρεπεν ἀρχιερεύς, ὅσιος, ἄκακος,
For such ⁶us ⁴became ¹a ²high ³priest, holy, harmless,

after the order of Aaron? 12 For the priesthood being changed, there is made of necessity a change also of the law. 13 For he of whom these things are spoken pertaineth to another tribe, of which no man gave attendance at the altar. 14 For it is evident that our Lord sprang out of Juda; of which tribe Moses spake nothing concerning priesthood. 15 And it is yet far more evident: for that after the similitude of Melchisedec there ariseth another priest, 16 who is made, not after the law of a carnal commandment, but after the power of an endless life. 17 For he testifieth, Thou art a priest for ever after the order of Melchisedec. 18 For there is verily a disannulling of the commandment going before for the weakness and unprofitableness thereof. 19 For the law made nothing perfect, but the bringing in of a better hope did; by the which we draw nigh unto God. 20 And inasmuch as not without an oath he was made priest: 21 (for those priests were made without an oath; but this with an oath by him that said unto him, The Lord sware and will not repent, Thou art a priest for ever after the order of Melchisedec :) 22 by so much was Jesus made a surety of a better testament. 23 And they truly were many priests, because they were not suffered to continue by reason of death: 24 but this man, because he continueth ever, hath an unchangeable priesthood. 25 Wherefore he is able also to save them to the uttermost that come unto God by him, seeing he ever liveth to make intercession for them. 26 For such an high priest became us, who

---

is holy, harmless, undefiled, separate from sinners, and made higher than the heavens ; 27 who needeth not daily, as those high priests, to offer up sacrifice, first for his own sins, and then for the people's : for this he did once, when he offered up himself. 28 For the law maketh men high priests which have infirmity ; but the word of the oath, which was since the law, maketh the Son, who is consecrated for evermore.

ἀμίαντος, κεχωρισμένος ἀπὸ τῶν ἁμαρτωλῶν, καὶ ὑψηλότερος
undefiled,   separated   from   sinners,   and   [2]higher

τῶν οὐρανῶν γενόμενος· 27 ὃς οὐκ.ἔχει καθ'.ἡμέραν ἀνάγ-
[3]than [4]the [5]heavens [1]become :   who has not   day by day   neces-

κην, ὥσπερ οἱ ἀρχιερεῖς, πρότερον ὑπὲρ τῶν.ἰδίων ἁμαρτιῶν
sity,   as   the high priests,   first   for   his own   sins

θυσίας ἀναφέρειν, ἔπειτα τῶν τοῦ λαοῦ· τοῦτο.γὰρ
[4]sacrifices [1]to [2]offer [3]up,   then   for those of the people ;   for this

ἐποίησεν ˣἐφάπαξ,ǁ ἑαυτὸν ʸἀνενέγκας.ǁ 28 ὁ.νόμος.γὰρ ἀν-
he did   once for all, [4]himself [1]having [2]offered [3]up.   For the law

θρώπους καθίστησιν ἀρχιερεῖς, ἔχοντας ἀσθένειαν· ὁ.λόγος.δὲ
[2]men   [1]constitutes high priests, [who] have   infirmity ;   but the word

τῆς ὁρκωμοσίας τῆς μετὰ τὸν νόμον, υἱὸν εἰς τὸν
of the swearing of the oath, which [is]   after   the   law,   a Son for

αἰῶνα τετελειωμένον.
ever   has perfected.

VIII. Now of the things which we have spoken this is the sum : We have such an high priest, who is set on the right hand of the throne of the Majesty in the heavens ; 2 a minister of the sanctuary, and of the true tabernacle, which the Lord pitched, and not man.

8 Κεφάλαιον.δὲ ἐπὶ τοῖς λεγομένοις, τοιοῦτον
Now a summary   of   the things being spoken of [is],   [3]such

ἔχομεν ἀρχιερέα, ὃς ἐκάθισεν ἐν δεξιᾷ τοῦ θρόνου τῆς
[1]we [2]have a high priest, who sat down on [the] right hand of the throne of the

μεγαλωσύνης ἐν τοῖς οὐρανοῖς, 2 τῶν ἁγίων λειτουργός, καὶ
greatness   in the heavens ;   [2]of [3]the [4]holies [1]minister,   and

τῆς σκηνῆς τῆς ἀληθινῆς, ἣν ἔπηξεν ὁ κύριος, ᶻκαὶǁ οὐκ
of the [2]tabernacle [1]true   which [3]pitched [1]the [2]Lord   and not

ἄνθρωπος.
man.

3 For every high priest is ordained to offer gifts and sacrifices : wherefore it is of necessity that this man have somewhat also to offer. 4 For if he were on earth, he should not be a priest, seeing that there are priests that offer gifts according to the law : 5 who serve unto the example and shadow of heavenly things, as Moses was admonished of God when he was about to make the tabernacle : for, See, saith he, that thou make all things according to the pattern shewed to thee in the mount. 6 But now hath he obtained a more excellent ministry, by how much also he is the mediator of a better covenant, which was established upon better promises. 7 For if that first covenant had been faultless, then should no place have been sought for the second. 8 For finding fault with

3 Πᾶς.γὰρ ἀρχιερεὺς εἰς τὸ προσφέρειν δῶρά.τε καὶ θυσίας
For every high priest for   to offer   both gifts and sacrifices

καθίσταται· ὅθεν ἀναγκαῖον ἔχειν τι καὶ τοῦ-
is constituted ; whence [it is] necessary [4]to [5]have [6]something [3]also [1]for] [2]this

τον ὃ προσενέγκῃ. 4 εἰ.μὲν ᵃγὰρǁ ἦν ἐπὶ γῆς, οὐδ'
[3]one which he may offer.   [2]If [3]indeed [1]for   he were on earth, not even

ἂν.ἦν ἱερεύς, ὄντων ᵇτῶν ἱερέωνǁ τῶν προσφερόντων
would he be a priest, there being   the   priests   who   offer

κατὰ ᶜτὸνǁ νόμον τὰ δῶρα, 5 οἵτινες ὑποδείγματι καὶ
according to the law   the gifts,   5 who   [the] representation and

σκιᾷ λατρεύουσιν τῶν ἐπουρανίων, καθὼς κεχρημάτισ-
shadow   serve   of the heavenlies,   according as [2]was [4]divinely [4]in-

ται ᵈΜωσῆςǁ μέλλων ἐπιτελεῖν τὴν σκηνήν, Ὅρα.γάρ,
structed [1]Moses   being about to construct the tabernacle ;   for, see,

φησιν, ᵉποιήσῃςǁ πάντα κατὰ τὸν τύπον τὸν δειχθέντα
says he, thou make   all things according to   the   pattern which was shewn

σοι ἐν τῷ ὄρει. 6 ᵍνυνὶˠ.δὲ διαφορωτέρας ᵍτέτευχενǁ
thee in the mountain.   But now   a more excellent   [2]he [3]has [4]obtained

λειτουργίας, ὅσῳ καὶ κρείττόνός ἐστιν διαθήκης μεσίτης,
[1]ministry,   by so much as also   of a better [4]he [3]is [1]covenant [2]mediator,

ἥτις ἐπὶ κρείττοσιν ἐπαγγελίαις νενομοθέτηται. 7 Εἰ.γὰρ
which upon   better   promises   has been established.   For if

ἡ.πρώτη.ἐκείνη ἦν ἄμεμπτος, οὐκ ἂν δευτέρας ἐζητεῖτο
that first   [one] were faultless,   not   for a second would [2]be [3]sought

τόπος. 8 μεμφόμενος.γὰρ ʰαὐτοῖςǁ λέγει, Ἰδού, ἡμέραι ἔρ-
[1]place.   For finding fault,   [3]to [4]them [1]he [2]says,   Lo,   days   are

---

χονται, λέγει κύριος, καὶ συντελέσω ἐπὶ τὸν ' οἶκον
coming, saith [the] Lord, and I will ratify as regards the house

'Ισραὴλ καὶ ἐπὶ τὸν οἶκον 'Ιούδα διαθήκην καινήν' 9 οὐ
of Israel and as regards the house of Juda a ²covenant ¹new; not

κατὰ τὴν'.διαθήκην ἣν ἐποίησα τοῖς.πατράσιν.αὐτῶν,
according to the covenant which I made with their fathers,

ἐν ἡμέρᾳ ἐπιλαβομένου'.μου‖ τῆς.χειρὸς.αὐτῶν ἐξαγαγεῖν
in [the] day of my taking hold of their hand to lead

αὐτοὺς ἐκ γῆς Αἰγύπτου' ὅτι αὐτοὶ οὐκ.ἐνέμειναν ἐν
them out of [the] land of Egypt; because they did not continue in

τῇ.διαθήκῃ.μου, κἀγὼ ἠμέλησα αὐτῶν, λέγει κύριος. 10 ὅτι
my covenant, and I disregarded them, saith [the] Lord. Because

αὕτη ἡ διαθήκη ᵏ ἣν διαθήσομαι τῷ οἴκῳ 'Ισραὴλ μετὰ
this [is] the covenant which I will covenant with the house of Israel after

τὰς.ἡμέρας.ἐκείνας, λέγει κύριος, διδοὺς νόμους.μου εἰς
those days, says [the] Lord, giving my laws into

τὴν.διάνοιαν.αὐτῶν καὶ ἐπὶ ᶦκαρδίας‖ αὐτῶν ἐπιγράψω αὐτούς'
their mind, also upon ²hearts ¹their I will inscribe them;

καὶ ἔσομαι αὐτοῖς εἰς θεόν, καὶ αὐτοὶ ἔσονταί μοι εἰς λαόν.
and I will be to them for God, and they shall be to me for people.

11 καὶ οὐ.μὴ διδάξωσιν ἕκαστος τὸν ᵐπλησίον‖ αὐτοῦ, καὶ
And not at all shall they teach each ²neighbour ¹his, and

ἕκαστος τὸν.ἀδελφὸν.αὐτοῦ, λέγων, Γνῶθι τὸν κύριον' ὅτι
each his brother, saying, Know the Lord; because

πάντες εἰδήσουσίν με, ἀπὸ μικροῦ ⁿαὐτῶν‖ ἕως
all shall know me, from [the] little [one] of them to [the]

μεγάλου αὐτῶν' 12 ὅτι ἵλεως ἔσομαι ταῖς.ἀδικίαις.αὐτῶν,
great [one] of them. Because merciful I will be to their unrighteousnesses,

καὶ τῶν.ἁμαρτιῶν.αὐτῶν ᵒκαὶ τῶν.ἀνομιῶν.αὐτῶν‖ οὐ.μὴ
and their sins and their lawlessnesses in no wise

μνησθῶ ἔτι. 13 'Εν τῷ λέγειν καινήν, πεπαλαίωκεν
will I remember more. In the saying New, he has made old

τὴν πρώτην' τὸ.δὲ παλαιούμενον καὶ γηράσκον ἐγγὺς
the first; but that which grows old and aged [is] near

ἀφανισμοῦ.
disappearing.

9 ᵖΕἶχεν‖ μὲν οὖν ᑫκαὶ‖ ἡ πρώτη ʳσκηνὴ‖ δικαιώματα
⁴Had ⁷indeed ⁵therefore ⁶also ¹the ²first ³tabernacle ordinances

λατρείας, τό.τε ἅγιον κοσμικόν. 2 σκηνὴ.γὰρ κατε-
of service, and the sanctuary, a worldly [one]. For a tabernacle was

σκευάσθη ἡ πρώτη, ἐν ᾗ ἥ.τε λυχνία καὶ ἡ τρά-
prepared, the first, in which [were] both the lampstand and the ta-

πεζα καὶ ἡ πρόθεσις τῶν ἄρτων, ἥτις λέγεται ˢἅγια.‖ 3 μετὰ
ble and the presentation of the loaves, which is called holy; ²after

δὲ τὸ δεύτερον καταπέτασμα σκηνὴ ἡ λεγομένη ᵗἅγια‖
¹but the second veil a tabernacle which [is] called holy

ἁγίων, 4 χρυσοῦν ἔχουσα θυμιατήριον, καὶ τὴν κιβωτὸν τῆς
of holies, · ²a ³golden ¹having censer, and the ark of the

διαθήκης περικεκαλυμμένην πάντοθεν χρυσίῳ, ἐν ᾗ
covenant, having been covered round ³in ⁴every ⁵part ¹with ²gold, in which

στάμνος χρυσῆ ἔχουσα τὸ μάννα, καὶ ἡ ῥάβδος 'Ααρὼν
[was the] ²pot ¹golden having the manna, and the rod of Aaron

them, he saith, Be-
hold, the days come,
saith the Lord, when I
will make a new cove-
nant with the house of
Israel and with the
house of Judah: 9 not
according to the cove-
nant that I made with
their fathers in the
day when I took them
by the hand to lead
them out of the land of
Egypt; because they
continued not in my
covenant, and I re-
garded them not, saith
the Lord. 10 For this
is the covenant that I
will make with the
house of Israel after
those days, saith the
Lord; I will put my
laws into their mind,
and write them in
their hearts: and I
will be to them a God,
and they shall be to me
a people: 11 and they
shall not teach every
man his neighbour,
and every man his
brother, saying, Know
the Lord: for all shall
know me, from the
least to the greatest.
12 For I will be merci-
ful to their unright-
eousness, and their
sins and their iniqui-
ties will I remember
no more. 13 In that he
saith, A new covenant,
he hath made the first
old. Now that which
decayeth and waxeth
old is ready to vanish
away.

IX. Then verily the
first covenant had also
ordinances of divine
service, and a worldly
sanctuary. 2 For there
was a tabernacle made;
the first, wherein was
the candlestick, and
the table, and the
shewbread; which is
called the sanctuary.
3 And after the second
veil, the tabernacle
which is called the Ho-
liest of all; 4 which
had the golden censer,
and the ark of the cove-
nant overlaid round a-
bout with gold, where-
in was the golden pot
that had manna, and

ⁱ — μου my E.　　ᵏ + [μου] (read my covenant) L.　　ˡ καρδίαν heart τ.　　ᵐ πολίτην
(read his [fellow] citizen) GLTTrAW.　　ⁿ — αὐτῶν LTTrA.　　ᵒ — καὶ τῶν ἀνομιῶν αὐτῶν
TTrA.　　ᵖ Εἶχε τ.　　ᑫ [καὶ] Tr.　　ʳ — σκηνὴ GLTTrAW.　　ˢ ἅγια holy place EGTTrAW ;
ἅγια ἁγίων holy of holies L.　　ᵗ τὰ ἅγια τῶν (read the holy of holies) Tr.

Aaron's rod that budded, and the tables of the covenant; 5 and over it the cherubins of glory shadowing the mercyseat; of which we cannot now speak particularly. 6 Now when these things were thus ordained, the priests went always into the first tabernacle, accomplishing the service *of God.* 7 But into the second *went* the high priest alone once every year, not without blood, which he offered for himself, and *for* the errors of the people: 8 the Holy Ghost this signifying, that the way into the holiest of all was not yet made manifest, while as the first tabernacle was yet standing: 9 which *was* a figure for the time then present, in which were offered both gifts and sacrifices, that could not make him that did the service perfect, as pertaining to the conscience; 10 *which stood* only in meats and drinks, and divers washings, and carnal ordinances, imposed *on them* until the time of reformation. 11 But Christ being come an high priest of good things to come, by a greater and more perfect tabernacle, not made with hands, that is to say, not of this building; 12 neither by the blood of goats and calves, but by his own blood he entered in once into the holy place, having obtained eternal redemption *for us.* 13 For if the blood of bulls and of goats, and the ashes of an heifer sprinkling the unclean, sanctifieth to the purifying of the flesh: 14 how much more shall the blood of Christ, who through the eternal Spirit offered himself without spot to God, purge your conscience from dead works to serve the living God? 15 And for this cause he is the mediator of

---

ἡ βλαστήσασα, καὶ αἱ πλάκες τῆς διαθήκης· 5 ὑπεράνω.δὲ
that sprouted, and the tablets of the covenant; and above

αὐτῆς *'χερουβὶμ"* δόξης κατασκιάζοντα τὸ ἱλαστήριον·
it [the] cherubim of glory overshadowing the mercy seat;

περὶ ὧν οὐκ.ἔστιν νῦν λέγειν κατὰ.μέρος.
concerning which it is not now [the time] to speak in detail.

6 Τούτων.δὲ οὕτως κατεσκευασμένων, εἰς μὲν τὴν πρώτην
Now these things thus having been prepared, into the first

σκηνὴν *'διαπαντὸς"* εἰσίασιν οἱ ἱερεῖς τὰς λατρείας ἐπιτελοῦν-
tabernacle at all times enter the priests, the services accomplish-

τες· 7 εἰς.δὲ τὴν δευτέραν ἅπαξ τοῦ.ἐνιαυτοῦ μόνος ὁ ἀρχιε-
ing; but into the second once in the year alone the high

ρεύς, οὐ χωρὶς αἵματος, ὃ προσφέρει ὑπὲρ ἑαυτοῦ καὶ
priest, not apart from blood, which he offers for himself and

τῶν τοῦ λαοῦ ἀγνοημάτων· 8 τοῦτο δηλοῦντος τοῦ πνεύ-
the of the people sins of ignorance: this signifying the Spirit

ματος τοῦ ἁγίου, μήπω πεφανερῶσθαι τὴν τῶν ἁγίων
the Holy, [that] not yet has been made manifest the of the holies

ὁδὸν ἔτι τῆς πρώτης σκηνῆς ἐχούσης στάσιν· 9 ἥτις
way, still the first tabernacle having a standing; which [is]

παραβολὴ εἰς τὸν καιρὸν τὸν ἐνεστηκότα, καθ' *ὃν* δῶρά.τε
a simile for the time present, in which both gifts

καὶ θυσίαι προσφέρονται, μὴ δυνάμεναι κατὰ συνείδησιν τε-
and sacrifices are offered, not being able as to conscience to

λειῶσαι τὸν λατρεύοντα, 10 μόνον ἐπὶ βρώμασιν καὶ
perfect him who serves, [consisting] only in meats and

πόμασιν καὶ διαφόροις βαπτισμοῖς, *καὶ* *δικαιώμασιν"* σαρκός,
drinks and divers washings, and ordinances of flesh,

μέχρι καιροῦ διορθώσεως ἐπικείμενα. 11 Χριστὸς.δὲ
until the time of setting things right imposed. But Christ

παραγενόμενος ἀρχιερεὺς τῶν *μελλόντων"* ἀγαθῶν, διὰ τῆς
being come high priest of the coming good things, by the

μείζονος καὶ τελειοτέρας σκηνῆς, οὐ χειροποιήτου, *τουτέστιν"*
greater and more perfect tabernacle, not made by hand, (that is,

οὐ ταύτης τῆς κτίσεως, 12 οὐδὲ δι' αἵματος τράγων καὶ
not of this creation,) nor by blood of goats and

μόσχων, διὰ.δὲ τοῦ.ἰδίου.αἵματος εἰσῆλθεν *ἐφάπαξ"* εἰς
calves, but by his own blood, entered once for all into

τὰ ἅγια, αἰωνίαν λύτρωσιν *εὑράμενος."* 13 εἰ.γὰρ τὸ αἷμα
the holies, eternal redemption having found. For if the blood

ταύρων καὶ τράγων", καὶ σποδὸς δαμάλεως ῥαντίζουσα τοὺς
of bulls and of goats, and ashes of a heifer sprinkling

κεκοινωμένους, ἁγιάζει πρὸς τὴν τῆς σαρκὸς καθαρότητα,
defiled, sanctifies for the of the flesh purity,

14 πόσῳ μᾶλλον τὸ αἷμα τοῦ χριστοῦ, ὃς διὰ πνεύματος
how much rather the blood of the Christ who through [the] Spirit

αἰωνίου ἑαυτὸν προσήνεγκεν ἄμωμον τῷ θεῷ, καθαριεῖ τὴν
eternal himself offered spotless to God, shall purify the

συνείδησιν *ὑμῶν"* ἀπὸ νεκρῶν ἔργων, εἰς τὸ λατρεύειν θεῷ
conscience your from dead works for to serve God [the]

ζῶντι; 15 Καὶ διὰ.τοῦτο διαθήκης καινῆς μεσίτης ἐστίν,
living! And for this reason of a covenant new mediator he is,

---

t χερουβεὶν LTTr; χερουβὶν A.   v διὰ παντὸς LTrA.   w ἦν (read according to which [simile]) LTTrAW.   x — καὶ GLT[Tr]AW.   y δικαιώματα LTTrAW.   z γενομένων L.   a τοῦτ' ἔστιν GT.   b ἐφ' ἅπαξ Tr.   c εὑρόμενος E.   d τράγων καὶ ταύρων LTTrAW.   ἡμῶν our LAW.   f + καὶ ἀληθινῷ and true L.

ὅπως θανάτου γενομένου, εἰς ἀπολύτρωσιν τῶν ἐπὶ τῇ
so that,   death having taken place for   redemption   of the ²under ³the

πρώτῃ διαθήκῃ παραβάσεων, τὴν ἐπαγγελίαν λάβωσιν
⁴first ⁵covenant ¹transgressions,   the   promise   ¹⁰might ¹¹receive

οἱ κεκλημένοι τῆς αἰωνίου κληρονομίας. 16 ὅπου.γὰρ
⁸they ⁶who ⁷have ⁸been ⁹called ¹of ²the ²eternal   ⁴inheritance.   (For where

διαθήκη,   θάνατον   ἀνάγκη   φέρεσθαι   τοῦ
[there is] a testament, [⁴for ⁵the] ⁶death [¹it ²is] ³necessary ¹⁰to ¹¹come ¹²in ⁷of ⁸the

διαθεμένου· 17 διαθήκη.γὰρ ἐπὶ.νεκροῖς βεβαία, ἐπεὶ
⁹testator.   For a testament in the case of [the] dead [is] affirmed, since

μήποτε ἰσχύει ὅτε ζῇ ὁ διαθέμενος.ᵍ 18 ὅθεν ʰοὐδ'ⁱⁱ
in no way it is of force when ²is ⁴living ¹the ²testator.)   Whence neither

ἡ πρώτη χωρὶς αἵματος ¹ἐγκεκαίνισται.ⁱⁱ 19 λαληθείσης
the first apart from blood has been inaugurated. ⁴Having ⁵been ⁶spoken

γὰρ πάσης ἐντολῆς κατὰ ᵏνόμον ὑπὸ Μωϋσέως παντὶ
¹for ²every ³commandment according to law by Moses to all

τῷ λαῷ, λαβὼν τὸ αἷμα τῶν μόσχων καὶ ¹τράγων, μετὰ
the people, having taken the blood of calves and of goats, with

ὕδατος καὶ ἐρίου κοκκίνου καὶ ὑσσώπου, αὐτό.τε τὸ βιβλίον
water and ²wool ¹scarlet and hyssop, both ³itself ¹the ²book

καὶ πάντα τὸν λαὸν ᵐἐρράντισεν,ⁱⁱ 20 λέγων, Τοῦτο τὸ
and all the people he sprinkled, saying, This [is] the

αἷμα τῆς διαθήκης ἧς ἐνετείλατο πρὸς ὑμᾶς ὁ θεός. 21 καὶ
blood of the covenant which ²enjoined ²to ¹you ¹God. And

τὴν σκηνὴν δὲ καὶ πάντα τὰ σκεύη τῆς λειτουργίας τῷ
the tabernacle too and all the vessels of the ministration with

αἵματι ὁμοίως ᵐἐρράντισεν,ⁱⁱ 22 καὶ ὑχεδὸν ἐν αἵματι
blood in like manner he sprinkled; and almost ³with ⁴blood

πάντα καθαρίζεται κατὰ τὸν νόμον, καὶ χωρὶς αἱματ-
¹all ²things are purified according to the law, and apart from blood-

εκχυσίας οὐ.γίνεται ἄφεσις. 23 Ἀνάγκη οὖν τὰ μὲν
shedding there is no remission. [It was] necessary then [for] the

ὑποδείγματα τῶν ἐν τοῖς οὐρανοῖς τούτοις καθαρίζεσθαι,
representations of the things in the heavens with these to be purified,

αὐτὰ.δὲ τὰ ἐπουράνια κρείττοσιν θυσίαις παρὰ ταύτας.
but ³themselves ¹the ²heavenlies with better sacrifices than these.

24 οὐ.γὰρ εἰς χειροποίητα ⁿἅγια εἰσῆλθενⁿ ⁰ὁⁱ χριστός, ἀντί-
For not into ²made ³by ⁴hands ¹holies entered the Christ, fi-

τυπα τῶν ἀληθινῶν, ἀλλ' εἰς αὐτὸν τὸν οὐρανόν, νῦν ἐμφα-
gures of the true [ones], but into ²itself ¹heaven, now to

νισθῆναι τῷ.προσώπῳ τοῦ θεοῦ ὑπὲρ ἡμῶν· 25 οὐδ' ἵνα
appear before the face of God for us: nor that

πολλάκις προσφέρῃ ἑαυτόν, ὥσπερ ὁ ἀρχιερεὺς εἰσέρχεται εἰς
often he should offer himself, even as the high priest enters into

τὰ ἅγια κατ'.ἐνιαυτὸν ἐν αἵματι ἀλλοτρίῳ· 26 ἐπεὶ ἔ-
the holies year by year with ²blood ¹another's; since it was neces-

δει αὐτὸν πολλάκις παθεῖν ἀπὸ καταβολῆς κόσμου·
sary for him often to have suffered from [the] foundation of [the] world.

ᵖνῦν.δὲ ἅπαξ ἐπὶ συντελείᾳ τῶν αἰώνων, εἰς ἀθέτη-
But now once in [the] consummation of the ages, for [the] putting

σινᵠ ἁμαρτίας, διὰ τῆς.θυσίας.αὐτοῦ πεφανέρωται. 27 καὶ
away of sin by his sacrifice he has been manifested. And

καθ'.ὅσον ἀπόκειται τοῖς ἀνθρώποις ἅπαξ ἀποθανεῖν, μετὰ
for as much as it is apportioned to men once to die, ²after

the new testament, that by means of death, for the redemption of the transgressions *that were* under the first testament, they which are called might receive the promise of eternal inheritance. 16 For where a testament *is*, there must also of necessity be the death of the testator. 17 For a testament *is* of force after men are dead: otherwise it is of no strength at all while the testator liveth. 18 Whereupon neither the first *testament* was dedicated without blood. 19 For when Moses had spoken every precept to all the people according to the law, he took the blood of calves and of goats, with water, and scarlet wool, and hyssop, and sprinkled both the book, and all the people, 20 saying, This *is* the blood of the testament which God hath enjoined unto you. 21 Moreover he sprinkled with blood both the tabernacle, and all the vessels of the ministry. 22 And almost all things are by the law purged with blood; and without shedding of blood is no remission. 23 *It was* therefore necessary that the patterns of things in the heavens should be purified with these; but the heavenly things themselves with better sacrifices than these. 24 For Christ is not entered into the holy places made with hands, *which are* the figures of the true; but into heaven itself, now to appear in the presence of God for us: 25 nor yet that he should offer himself often, as the high priest entereth into the holy place every year with blood of others; 26 for then must he often have suffered since the foundation of the world: but now once in the end of the world hath he appeared to put away sin by the sacrifice of himself. 27 And as it is appointed unto

---

ᵍ *Read the sentence as a question* L.   ʰ οὐδὲ LTrAW.   ⁱ ἐν- T.   ᵏ + τὸν the LTrAW.
ˡ + τῶν LTTrAW.   ᵐ ἐράντισεν LTTrA.   ⁿ εἰσῆλθεν ἅγια TTₗA.   ⁰ — ὁ LTTrAW.
ᵖ νυνὶ LTTrA.   ᵠ + τῆς LTTr.

men once to die, but after this the judgment: 28 so Christ was once offered to bear the sins of many; and unto them that look for him shall he appear the second time without sin unto salvation.

X. For the law having a shadow of good things to come, *and* not the very image of the things, can never with those sacrifices which they offered year by year continually make the comers thereunto perfect. 2 For then would they not have ceased to be offered? because that the worshippers once purged should have had no more conscience of sins. 3 But in those *sacrifices there is a* remembrance again *made* of sins every year. 4 For *it is* not possible that the blood of bulls and of goats should take away sins. 5 Wherefore when he cometh into the world, he saith, Sacrifice and offering thou wouldest not, but a body hast thou prepared me: 6 in burnt offerings and *sacrifices* for sin thou hast had no pleasure. 7 Then said I, Lo, I come (in the volume of the book it is written of me,) to do thy will, O God. 8 Above when he said, Sacrifice and offering and burnt offerings and *offering* for sin thou wouldest not, neither hadst pleasure *therein;* which are offered by the law; 9 then said he, Lo, I come to do thy will, O God. He taketh away the first, that he may establish the second. 10 By the which will we are sanctified through the offering of the body of Jesus Christ once *for all.* 11 And every priest standeth daily ministering and offering oftentimes the same sacrifices, which can never take away sins:

δὲ τοῦτο κρίσις· 28 οὕτως ᵀ ὁ χριστὸς ἅπαξ προσενεχθεὶς
¹and this, judgment;   thus the Christ,   once having been offered
εἰς τὸ πολλῶν ἀνενεγκεῖν ἁμαρτίας, ἐκ.δευτέρου χωρὶς
for ⁵of ⁶many ¹to ²bear [³the] ⁴sins,   a second time ⁸apart ⁹from
ἁμαρτίας ὀφθήσεται τοῖς αὐτὸν ἀπεκδεχομένοις εἰς
¹⁰sin   ¹shall ²appear ³to ⁴those ⁵that ⁷him   ⁶await   for
σωτηρίαν.
salvation.

10 Σκιὰν.γὰρ ἔχων ὁ νόμος τῶν μελλόντων ἀγαθῶν, οὐκ
For ⁴a ⁵ shadow ³having ¹the ²law of the   coming   good things, not
αὐτὴν τὴν εἰκόνα τῶν πραγμάτων, κατ᾽.ἐνιαυτὸν ταῖς.αὐταῖς
³itself ¹the ²image of the   things,   year by year   with the same
θυσίαις ˢἃς‖ προσφέρουσιν εἰς.τὸ.διηνεκὲς οὐδέποτε ᵗδύναται‖
sacrifices which   they offer   in perpetuity   never   is able
τοὺς προσερχομένους τελειῶσαι. 2 ἐπεὶ ᵛοὐκ.ἀν.ἐπαύσαντο
³those ⁴who   ²approach   ¹to ²perfect. Since would they not have ceased
προσφερόμεναι, διὰ τὸ μηδεμίαν ἔχειν ἔτι συνείδησιν
to be offered,   on account of ⁷no ⁹any ⁶having ⁸longer ¹⁰conscience
ἁμαρτιῶν τοὺς λατρεύοντας, ἅπαξ ʷκεκαθαρμένους‖; 3 ἀλλ᾽
¹¹of ¹²sins ¹those ²who   ⁴serve   ⁴once   ⁵purged?   But
ἐν αὐταῖς ἀνάμνησις ἁμαρτιῶν κατ᾽.ἐνιαυτόν. 4 ἀδύ-
in these a remembrance of sins   year by year [there is]. ⁴Impos-
νατον γὰρ αἷμα ταύρων καὶ τράγων ἀφαιρεῖν ἁμαρ-
sible [²it ³is] ¹for [for the] blood of bulls and of goats to take away sins.
τίας. 5 Διὸ εἰσερχόμενος εἰς τὸν κόσμον λέγει, ˣθυσίαν καὶ
  Wherefore coming   into the world he says, Sacrifice and
προσφορὰν‖ οὐκ.ἠθέλησας, σῶμα.δὲ κατηρτίσω μοι· 6 ὁλο-
offering   thou willedst not, but a body thou didst prepare me. Burnt
καυτώματα καὶ περὶ ἁμαρτίας οὐκ.ᵞεὐδόκησας.‖
offerings   and [sacrifices] for   sin   thou delightedst not in.
7 τότε εἶπον, Ἰδοὺ ἥκω, ἐν κεφαλίδι βιβλίου γέγραπται
Then I said, Lo, I come, (in [the] roll of [the] book it is written
περὶ ἐμοῦ, τοῦ ποιῆσαι, ὁ θεός, τὸ.θέλημά.σου. 8 Ἀνώτερον
of me,) to do, O God, thy.will.   Above
λέγων, Ὅτι ᶻθυσίαν‖ καὶ ᵃπροσφορὰν‖ καὶ ὁλοκαυτώματα
saying, Sacrifice and offering and burnt offerings
καὶ περὶ ἁμαρτίας οὐκ.ἠθέλησας, οὐδὲ ᵇεὐδόκησας,‖
and [sacrifices] for sin thou willedst not, nor delightedst in,
αἵτινες κατὰ ᶜτὸν‖ νόμον προσφέρονται, 9 τότε εἴρηκεν,
(which according to the law are offered); then he said,
Ἰδοὺ ἥκω τοῦ ποιῆσαι, ᵈὁ θεός.‖ τὸ.θέλημά.σου. ἀναιρεῖ τὸ
Lo, I come, to do, O God, thy will. He takes away the
πρῶτον, ἵνα τὸ δεύτερον στήσῃ· 10 ἐν ᾧ θελήματι
first, that the second he may establish; by which will
ἡγιασμένοι ἐσμὲν ᵉοἱ· διὰ τῆς προσφορᾶς τοῦ σώματος ᶠτοῦ‖
⁵sanctified ¹we ²are   through the offering of the body
Ἰησοῦ χριστοῦ ᵍἐφάπαξ.‖ 11 Καὶ πᾶς μὲν ʰἱερεὺς‖ ἕστηκεν
of Jesus Christ once for all. And every priest stands
καθ᾽.ἡμέραν λειτουργῶν, καὶ τὰς αὐτὰς πολλάκις προσφέρων
day by day ministering, and the same ²often ⁴offering
θυσίας, αἵτινες οὐδέποτε δύνανται περιελεῖν ἁμαρτίας·
¹sacrifices, which   never   are able to take away sins.

ᵀ + καὶ also GLTTrAW.   ˢ αἷς TA.   ᵗ δύνανται they are able LTr.   ᵛ — οὐκ not (read *the sentence not as a question*) E.   ʷ κεκαθερισμένους L; κεκαθαρισμένους TTrAW.   ˣ προσφορὰν καὶ θυσίαν W.   ᵞ ηὐδόκησας LTTrA.   ᶻ θυσίας sacrifices LTTⁱAW.   ᵃ προσφορὰς offerings LTTrAW.   ᵇ ηὐδόκησας LTTr.   ᶜ — τὸν LTTr[A].   ᵈ — ὁ θεός GLTTrAW.   ᵉ — οἱ EGLTTrAW.   ᶠ — τοῦ GLTTrAW.   ᵍ ἐφ᾽ ἅπαξ Tr.   ʰ ἀρχιερεὺς high priest LA.

12 [1]αὐτὸς[11].δὲ μίαν ὑπὲρ ἁμαρτιῶν προσενέγκας θυσίαν, εἰς
But he, [3]one [5]for [6]sins [1]having [2]offered [4]sacrifice, in

τὸ διηνεκὲς ἐκάθισεν ἐν δεξιᾷ τοῦ θεοῦ, 13 τὸ.λοιπὸν
perpetuity sat down at [the] right hand of God, henceforth

ἐκδεχόμενος ἕως τεθῶσιν οἱ.ἐχθροί.αὐτοῦ ὑποπόδιον τῶν
awaiting until be placed his enemies [as] a footstool

ποδῶν αὐτοῦ. 14 μιᾷ.γὰρ προσφορᾷ τετελείωκεν ' εἰς.τὸ.διη-
for [2]feet [1]his. For by one offering he has perfected in perpe-

νεκὲς τοὺς ἁγιαζομένους. 15 Μαρτυρεῖ.δὲ ἡμῖν καὶ τὸ πνεῦμα
tuity the sanctified. And bears witness to us also the Spirit

τὸ ἅγιον· μετὰ.γὰρ τὸ [k]προειρηκέναι,[||] 16 Αὕτη ἡ δια-
the Holy; for after the having said before, This [is] the cove-

θήκη ἣν διαθήσομαι πρὸς αὐτοὺς μετὰ τὰς.ἡμέρας.ἐκείνας,
nant which I will covenant towards them after those days,

λέγει κύριος, διδοὺς νόμους.μου ἐπὶ καρδίας.αὐτῶν, καὶ ἐπὶ
says [the] Lord: giving my laws into their hearts, also into

[l]τῶν.διανοιῶν[||] αὐτῶν ἐπιγράψω αὐτούς· 17 καὶ τῶν ἁμαρτιῶν
[2]minds [1]their I will inscribe them; and [2]sins

αὐτῶν καὶ τῶν.ἀνομιῶν.αὐτῶν οὐ.μὴ [m]μνησθῶ[1] ἔτι.
[1]their and their lawlessnesses in no wise will I remember any more.

18 ὅπου.δὲ ἄφεσις τούτων, οὐκέτι προσφορὰ περὶ
But where remission of these [is], no longer [is there] an offering for

ἁμαρτίας.
sin.

19 Ἔχοντες οὖν, ἀδελφοί, παρρησίαν εἰς τὴν.εἴσοδον
Having therefore, brethren, boldness for entrance into

τῶν ἁγίων ἐν τῷ αἵματι Ἰησοῦ, 20 ἣν ἐνεκαίνισεν ἡμῖν
the holies by the blood of Jesus, [7]which [9]he [9]dedicated [10]for [11]us

ὁδὸν πρόσφατον καὶ.ζῶσαν διὰ τοῦ καταπετάσματος, [n]τουτ-
[a] [2]way [3]newly [1]made [8]and [6]living through the veil, that

ἔστιν[1] τῆς.σαρκὸς.αὐτοῦ, 21 καὶ ἱερέα μέγαν ἐπὶ τὸν οἶκον
is, his flesh; and a [2]priest [1]great over the house

τοῦ θεοῦ, 22 προσερχώμεθα μετὰ ἀληθινῆς καρδίας ἐν
of God [having], we should approach with a true heart, in

πληροφορίᾳ πίστεως, [o]ἐρραντισμένοι[||] τὰς καρδίας ἀπὸ συν-
full assurance of faith, having been sprinkled [as to] the hearts from a [2]con-

ειδήσεως πονηρᾶς, καὶ [p]λελουμένοι[||] τὸ σῶμα ὕδατι
science [1]wicked, and having been washed [as to] the body with [2]water

καθαρῷ· [q] 23 κατέχωμεν τὴν ὁμολογίαν τῆς ἐλπίδος ἀκλινῆ,
[1]pure. We should hold fast the confession of the hope unwavering,

πιστὸς.γὰρ ὁ ἐπαγγειλάμενος· 24 καὶ κατανοῶμεν ἀλ-
for [is] faithful he who promised; and we should consider one

λήλους εἰς παροξυσμὸν ἀγάπης καὶ καλῶν ἔργων, 25 μὴ
another for provoking to love and to good works; not

ἐγκαταλείποντες τὴν ἐπισυναγωγὴν ἑαυτῶν, καθὼς
forsaking the assembling together of ourselves, even as [the]

ἔθος τισίν, ἀλλὰ παρακαλοῦντες· καὶ τοσούτῳ
custom [is] with some; but encouraging [one another], and by so much

μᾶλλον ὅσῳ βλέπετε ἐγγίζουσαν τὴν ἡμέραν. 26 ἑκου-
[the] more as ye see drawing near the day. [2]Where] [3]will-

σίως γὰρ ἁμαρτανόντων ἡμῶν μετὰ τὸ.λαβεῖν τὴν ἐπίγνωσιν
ingly [1]for [5]sin [4]we after receiving the knowledge

τῆς ἀληθείας, οὐκέτι περὶ ἁμαρτιῶν ἀπολείπεται θυσία·
of the truth, no longer [2]for [3]sins [1]remains [1a]sacrifice.

12 but this man, after he had offered one sacrifice for sins for ever, sat down on the right hand of God; 13 from henceforth expecting till his enemies be made his footstool. 14 For by one offering he hath perfected for ever them that are sanctified. 15 *Whereof* the Holy Ghost also is a witness to us : for after that he had said before, 16 This *is* the covenant that I will make with them after those days, saith the Lord, I will put my laws into their hearts, and in their minds will I write them; 17 and their sins and iniquities will I remember no more. 18 Now where remission of these *is, there is* no more offering for sin.

19 Having therefore, brethren, boldness to enter into the holiest by the blood of Jesus, 20 by a new and living way, which he hath consecrated for us, through the veil, that is to say, his flesh; 21 and *having* an high priest over the house of God; 22 let us draw near with a true heart in full assurance of faith, having our hearts sprinkled from an evil conscience, and our bodies washed with pure water. 23 Let us hold fast the profession of *our* faith without wavering; (for he *is* faithful that promised;) 24 and let us consider one another to provoke unto love and to good works : 25 not forsaking the assembling of ourselves together, as the manner of some *is*; but exhorting *one another*: and so much the more, as ye see the day approaching. 26 For if we sin wilfully after that we have received the knowledge of the truth, there remaineth no more sacrifice for sins, 27 but a certain fearful looking for of

---

[i] οὗτος (*read* But this one LTTrAW. [k] εἰρηκέναι having said LTTrAW. [l] τὴν διάνοιαν mind LTTrAW. [m] μνησθήσομαι LTTrA. [n] τοῦτ' ἐστιν GT. [o] ῥεραντισμένοι LTTrA. [p] λελουσμένοι ᴛ. [q] *Punctuate so as to join* we should hold fast *with what precedes* GLTTr.

judgment and fiery indignation, which shall devour the adversaries. 28 He that despised Moses' law died without mercy under two or three witnesses: 29 of how much sorer punishment, suppose ye, shall he be thought worthy, who hath trodden under foot the Son of God, and hath counted the blood of the covenant, wherewith he was sanctified, an unholy thing, and hath done despite unto the Spirit of grace? 30 For we know him that hath said, Vengeance *belongeth* unto me, I will recompense, saith the Lord. And again, The Lord shall judge his people. 31 *It is* a fearful thing to fall into the hands of the living God.

32 But call to remembrance the former days, in which, after ye were illuminated, ye endured a great fight of afflictions; 33 partly, whilst ye were made a gazing-stock both by reproaches and afflictions; and partly, whilst ye became companions of them that were so used. 34 For ye had compassion of me in my bonds, and took joyfully the spoiling of your goods, knowing in yourselves that ye have in heaven a better and an enduring substance. 35 Cast not away therefore your confidence, which hath great recompence of reward. 36 For ye have need of patience, that, after ye have done the will of God, ye might receive the promise. 37 For yet a little while, and he that shall come will come, and will not tarry. 38 Now the just shall live by faith: but if *any man* draw back, my soul shall have no pleasure in him. 39 But we are not of them who draw back unto perdition; but of them that believe to the saving of the soul.

27 φοβερὰ.δέ τις ἐκδοχὴ κρίσεως, καὶ πυρὸς ζῆλος ἐσ-
but a ²fearful ¹certain expectation of judgment, and ²of ³fire ¹fervour ⁵to
θίειν μέλλοντος τοὺς ὑπεναντίους. 28 ἀθετήσας τις
⁴devour ⁴about the adversaries. ³Having ⁴set ⁵aside ¹any ²one
νόμον ʳΜωσέως¹¹ χωρὶς οἰκτιρμῶν ἐπὶ   δυσὶν
[the] law of Moses, ²without ³compassions ⁴on [⁵the ⁶testimony ⁷of] ⁵two
ἢ τρισὶν μάρτυσιν ἀποθνήσκει· 29 πόσῳ δοκεῖτε χείρονος
⁸or ¹⁰three ¹¹witnesses ¹dies: how much ³think ⁴ye ¹worse
ἀξιωθήσεται τιμωρίας ὁ τὸν υἱὸν τοῦ θεοῦ
⁵shall ⁶he ⁷be ⁸counted ⁹worthy ¹⁰of ²punishment who the Son of God
καταπατήσας, καὶ τὸ αἷμα τῆς διαθήκης κοινὸν ἡγησά-
trampled upon, and ²the ⁴blood ⁵of ⁶the ⁷covenant ²common ¹esteem-
μενος ἐν.ᾧ ἡγιάσθη, καὶ τὸ πνεῦμα τῆς χάριτος
ed wherewith he was sanctified, and the Spirit of grace
ἐνυβρίσας; 30 οἴδαμεν.γὰρ τὸν εἰπόντα, Ἐμοὶ ἐκδίκησις,
insulted! For we know him who said, To me ²vengeance
ἐγὼ ἀνταποδώσω, ˢλέγει κύριος·¹¹ καὶ πάλιν,
[¹belongs]; I will recompense, says [the] Lord: and again, [The]
ᵗΚύριος κρινεῖ¹¹ τὸν.λαὸν.αὐτοῦ. 31 Φοβερὸν τὸ ἐμπεσεῖν
Lord will judge his people. [It is] a fearful thing to fall
εἰς χεῖρας θεοῦ ζῶντος.
into [the] hands of ³God [¹the] ²living.
32 Ἀναμιμνήσκεσθε.δὲ τὰς πρότερον ἡμέρας, ἐν αἷς φωτισ-
But call to remembrance the former days in which, having
θέντες πολλὴν ἄθλησιν ὑπεμείνατε παθημάτων· 33 τοῦτο
been enlightened, ²much ⁴conflict ¹ye ³endured of sufferings; partly,
μέν, ὀνειδισμοῖς.τε καὶ θλίψεσιν θεατριζόμενοι· τοῦτο.δέ,
both in reproaches and tribulations being made a spectacle; and partly,
κοινωνοὶ τῶν οὕτως ἀναστρεφομένων γενηθέντες·
³partners ⁴of ⁵those ⁶thus ⁷passing [⁹them] ¹having ²become.
34 καὶ.γὰρ τοῖς·ᵛδεσμοῖς.μου¹ συνεπαθήσατε, καὶ τὴν ἁρπαγὴν
For both with my bonds ye sympathized, and the plunder
τῶν.ὑπαρχόντων.ὑμῶν μετὰ χαρᾶς προσεδέξασθε, γινώσκοντες
of your possessions with joy ye received, knowing
ἔχειν ʷἐν ˣἑαυτοῖς κρείττονα¹¹ ὕπαρξιν ʸἐν οὐρανοῖς¹¹ καὶ
to have in yourselves a better ³possession ⁴in [⁵the] ⁶heavens ¹and
μένουσαν. 35 μὴ.ἀποβάλητε οὖν τὴν.παρρησίαν.ὑμῶν,
²abiding. Cast not away therefore your boldness
ἥτις ἔχει ᶻμισθαποδοσίαν μεγάλην.¹¹ 36 ὑπομονῆς.γὰρ ἔχετε
which has ²recompense ¹great. For of endurance ye have
χρείαν, ἵνα τὸ θέλημα τοῦ θεοῦ ποιήσαντες κομίσησθε τὴν
need, that the will of God having done ye may receive the
ἐπαγγελίαν. 37 ἔτι.γὰρ ᵃμικρὸν.ὅσον.ὅσον, ὁ ἐρχόμενος
promise. For yet a very little while, he.who comes
ἥξει, καὶ οὐ.ᵃχρονιεῖ.¹¹ 38 ὁ.δὲ ᵇδίκαιος¹¹ ἐκ πίστεως ζήσε-
will come, and will not delay. But the just by faith shall
ται· καὶ ἐὰν ὑποστείληται, οὐκ.εὐδοκεῖ ἡ.ψυχή.μου ἐν αὐτῷ.
live; and if he draw back, ³delights ⁴not ¹my.²soul in him.
39 ἡμεῖς.δὲ οὐκ.ἐσμὲν ὑποστολῆς εἰς ἀπώλειαν, ἀλλὰ
But we are not of [those] drawing back to destruction, but
πίστεως εἰς περιποίησιν ψυχῆς.
of faith to saving [the] soul.

ʳ Μωῦσέως GLTTrAW.   ˢ — λέγει κύριος TTr.   ᵗ κρινεῖ κύριος LTTrAW.   ᵛ δεσ-
μίοις (*read* with prisoners) GLTTrAW.   ʷ — ἐν GLTTrAW.   ˣ ἑαυτοὺς κρείσσονα
LTTr; ἑαυτοῖς (for yourselves) κρείσσονα A.   ʸ — ἐν οὐρανοῖς LTTrAW.   ᶻ μεγάλην
μισθαποδοσίαν LTTrAW.   ᵃ χρονίσει TTr.   ᵇ δίκαιός μου (*read* my just [one]) LTTrA.

11 Ἔστιν.δὲ πίστις ἐλπιζομένων   ὑπόστασις, πραγμά-
　　Now ²is   ¹faith of [things] hoped for [the] assurance,   of things
τῶν   ἔλεγχος οὐ βλεπομένων. 2 ἐν.ταύτῃ.γὰρ ἐμαρτυ-
[²the] ⁴conviction ¹not   ²seen.   For by this   ³were ⁴borne
ρήθησαν οἱ πρεσβύτεροι. 3 Πίστει νοοῦμεν   κατηρτίσθαι
¹witness ⁶to ¹the   ²elders.   By faith we apprehend to have been framed
τοὺς αἰῶνας ῥήματι θεοῦ, εἰς.τὸ μὴ ἐκ   φαινομένων
the   worlds by [the] word of God, so that ²not ⁷from [⁸things] ⁹appearing
ᶜτὰ   βλεπόμενα‖ γεγονέναι. 4 Πίστει   πλείονα   θυσίαν
¹the ²things   ³seen   ⁴have ⁶being.   By faith ²a ³more ⁴excellent ⁵sacrifice
Ἀβελ παρὰ Κάϊν προσήνεγκεν τῷ θεῷ, δι᾽ ἧς   ἐμαρτυ-
¹Abel thau Cain   offered   to God, by which he was borne wit-
ρήθη εἶναι δίκαιος, μαρτυροῦντος ἐπὶ τοῖς.δώροις.αὐτοῦ ᵈτοῦ
ness to as being righteous, ²bearing ³witness ⁴to   ⁵his ⁶gifts
θεοῦ.‖ καὶ δι᾽ αὐτῆς ἀποθανὼν ἔτι ᵉλαλεῖται.‖ 5 Πίστει Ἐνὼχ
¹God, and through it,   having died, yet   speaks.   By faith Enoch
μετετέθη   τοῦ μὴ ἰδεῖν θάνατον, καὶ οὐχ.ᶠεὑρίσκετο,‖ διότι
was translated   not to see   death,   and   was not found,   because
μετέθηκεν αὐτὸν ὁ θεός· πρὸ.γὰρ τῆς.μεταθέσεως.ᵍαὐτοῦ‖ με-
²translated ³him   ¹God;   for before   his translation   he has
μαρτύρηται ʰεὐηρεστηκέναι‖ τῷ θεῷ. 6 χωρὶς.δὲ πίστεω.
been borne witness to to have well pleased   God.   But apart from faith
ἀδύνατον εὐαρεστῆσαι· πιστεῦσαι.γὰρ δεῖ   τὸν
[it is] impossible to well please [him]. For ⁸to ⁹believe ¹it ²behoves ³him ⁴who
προσερχόμενον ᶦτῷ‖ θεῷ. ὅτι.ἐστίν, καὶ   τοῖς ἐκζητοῦσιν
⁵approaches   ⁶to ⁷God, that he is, and [that] for those who seek ²out
αὐτὸν μισθαποδότης γίνεται. 7 Πίστει   χρηματισ-
¹him   a ᵏrewarder he becomes.   By faith ²having ³been ⁴divinely ⁵in-
θεὶς Νῶε περὶ   τῶν μηδέπω βλεπομένων,   εὐλαβη-
structed ¹Noah concerning the things not yet   seen,   having been moved
θεὶς   κατεσκεύασεν κιβωτὸν εἰς   σωτηρίαν τοῦ οἴκου
with fear,   prepared   an ark for [the] salvation of ²house
αὐτοῦ· δι᾽ ἧς κατέκρινεν τὸν κόσμον, καὶ τῆς   κατὰ πίστιν
¹his ;   by which he condemned the world,   and of the ³according ³to ⁴faith
δικαιοσύνης ἐγένετο κληρονόμος. 8 Πίστει ᵏ καλούμενος Ἀ-
¹righteousness became   heir.   By faith   being called A-
βραὰμ ὑπήκουσεν ἐξελθεῖν εἰς ᶦτὸν‖ τόπον ὃν ᵐἤμελλεν‖
braham   obeyed to go out into the   place which he was about
λαμβάνειν εἰς κληρονομίαν, καὶ ἐξῆλθεν, μὴ ἐπιστάμενος ποῦ
to receive for an inheritance, and went out, not knowing where
ἔρχεται. 9 Πίστει παρῴκησεν εἰς ⁿτὴν‖ γῆν τῆς ἐπαγγελίας,
he is going.   By faith he sojourned in the   land of the promise,
ὡς ἀλλοτρίαν,   ἐν σκηναῖς κατοικήσας μετὰ Ἰσαὰκ καὶ
as [in] a strange [country], in tents having dwelt with Isaac and
Ἰακὼβ τῶν ᵒσυγκληρονόμων‖ τῆς ἐπαγγελίας τῆς αὐτῆς·
Jacob,   the   joint-heirs   of the ²promise   ¹same ;
10 ἐξεδέχετο.γὰρ τὴν τοὺς θεμελίους ἔχουσαν πόλιν, ἧς
for he was waiting for the   ²foundations ¹having ¹city, of which [the]
τεχνίτης καὶ δημιουργὸς ὁ θεός. 11 Πίστει καὶ αὐτὴ Σάρρα
artificer and constructor [is] God.   By faith also ²herself ¹Sarah
δύναμιν εἰς   καταβολὴν σπέρματος ἔλαβεν, καὶ παρὰ καιρὸν
power for [the] conception of seed received, and beyond ²age

XI. Now faith is the sub-stance of things hoped for, the evidence of things not seen. 2 For by it the elders obtained a good report. 3 Through faith we understand that the worlds were framed by the word of God, so that things which are seen were not made of things which do appear. 4 By faith Abel offered unto God a more excellent sacrifice than Cain, by which he obtained witness that he was righteous. God testifying of his gifts: and by it he being dead yet speaketh. 5 By faith Enoch was translated that he should not see death; and was not found, because God had translated him: for before his translation he had this testimony, that he pleased God. 6 But without faith it is impossible to please him: for he that cometh to God must believe that he is, and that he is a rewarder of them that diligently seek him. 7 By faith Noah, being warned of God of things not seen as yet, moved with fear, prepared an ark to the saving of his house; by the which he condemned the world, and became heir of the righteousness which is by faith. 8 By faith Abraham, when he was called to go out into a place which he should after receive for an inheritance, obeyed; and he went out, not knowing whither he went. 9 By faith he sojourned in the land of promise, as in a strange country, dwelling in tabernacles with Isaac and Jacob, the heirs with him of the same promise: 10 for he looked for a city which hath foundations, whose builder and maker is God. 11 Through faith also Sara herself received strength to conceive seed, and was delivered of a child when she

---

ᶜ τὸ βλεπόμενον that seen (read γεγ. ᵉhas ᵉbeing) LTTrA.   ᵈ τῷ θεῷ (read bearing witness by his gifts to God) LTr.   ᵉ λαλεῖ GLTTrAW.   ᶠ ηὑρίσκετο LTTrAW.   ᵍ — αὐτοῦ (read the translation) LTTrA.   ʰ εὐηρεστηκέναι LA.   ᶦ - τῷ T[Tr].   ᵏ + ὁ the [one] L[Tr].
ˡ — τον (read a place) LTTrA.   ᵐ ἔμελλεν LA.   ⁿ — τὴν (read [the]) LTTrA.   ᵒ συν- T.

was past age, because she judged him faithful who had promised. 12 Therefore sprang there even of one, and him as good as dead, so many as the stars of the sky in multitude. and as the sand which is by the sea shore innumerable.

ἡλικίας Pἔτεκεν,‖ ἐπεὶ πιστὸν ἡγήσατο τὸν ἐπαγγειλάμενον.
[1]seasonable gave birth; since faithful she esteemed him who promised.
12 διὸ καὶ ἀφ᾽ ἑνὸς ᵠἐγεννήθησαν,‖ καὶ.ταῦτα νενεκρω-
Wherefore also from one were born, and that too of [one] having
μένου, καθὼς τὰ ἄστρα τοῦ οὐρανοῦ τῷ πλήθει, καὶ ʳὡσεὶ‖
become dead, even as the stars of the heaven in multitude, and as
ἄμμος ἡ παρὰ τὸ χεῖλος τῆς θαλάσσης ἡ ἀναρίθμητος.
[2]sand [4]which[[5]is] [6]by [7]the [8]shore [9]of [10]the [11]sea [1]the [2]countless.

13 These all died in faith, not having received the promises, but having seen them afar off, and were persuaded of them, and embraced them, and confessed that they were strangers and pilgrims on the earth. 14 For they that say such things declare plainly that they seek a country. 15 And truly, if they had been mindful of that country from whence they came out, they might have had opportunity to have returned. 16 But now they desire a better country, that is, an heavenly: wherefore God is not ashamed to be called their God: for he hath prepared for them a city.

13 Κατὰ πίστιν ἀπέθανον οὗτοι πάντες, μὴ ˢλαβόντες‖ τὰς
In faith [3]died [2]these [1]all, not having received the
ἐπαγγελίας, ἀλλὰ πόρρωθεν αὐτὰς ἰδόντες, ᵗκαὶ πεισθέν-
promises, but from afar them having seen, and having been per-
τες,‖ καὶ ἀσπασάμενοι, καὶ ὁμολογήσαντες ὅτι ξένοι καὶ
suaded, and having embraced [them], and having confessed that strangers and
παρεπίδημοί εἰσιν ἐπὶ τῆς γῆς. 14 οἱ.γὰρ τοιαῦτα λέ-
sojourners they are on the earth. For they who such things
γοντες, ἐμφανίζουσιν ὅτι πατρίδα ἐπιζητοῦσιν. 15 καὶ.εἰ
say, make manifest that [their] own country they are seeking. And if
μὲν ἐκείνης ᵛἐμνημόνευον‖ ἀφ᾽ ἧς ᵂἐξῆλθον,‖ εἶ-
indeed ᵗthat [1]they [2]were [3]remembering from whence they came out, they might
χον.ἂν καιρὸν ἀνακάμψαι· 16 ˣνυνὶ‖.δὲ κρείττονος ὀρέ-
have had opportunity to have returned; but now a better they stretch
γονται, ᵞτουτέστιν,‖ ἐπουρανίου· διὸ οὐκ.ἐπαισχύνεται
forward to, that is, a heavenly; wherefore ²is ³not ⁴ashamed ⁵of
αὐτοὺς ὁ θεός, θεὸς ἐπικαλεῖσθαι αὐτῶν· ἡτοίμασεν.γὰρ αὐτοῖς
⁶them [1]God. [11]God ⁷to ⁸be ⁹called [10]their; for he prepared for them
πόλιν.
a city.

17 By faith Abraham, when he was tried, offered up Isaac: and he that had received the promises offered up his only begotten son, 18 of whom it was said, That in Isaac shall thy seed be called: 19 accounting that God was able to raise him up, even from the dead; from whence also he received him in a figure. 20 By faith Isaac blessed Jacob and Esau concerning things to come. 21 By faith Jacob, when he was a dying, blessed both the sons of Joseph; and worshipped, leaning upon the top of his staff. 22 By faith Joseph, when he died, made mention of the departing of the children of Israel; and gave commandment concerning his bones. 23 By faith Moses, when he was born, was

17 Πίστει προσενήνοχεν Ἀβραὰμ τὸν Ἰσαὰκ πειραζόμενος,
By faith ⁴has ⁵offered ⁶up ¹Abraham ⁷Isaac ²being ³tried,
καὶ τὸν.μονογενῆ προσέφερεν ὁ τὰς ἐπαγγελίας ἀνα-
and [⁹his] ¹⁰only-begotten ⁶was ⁷offering ⁸up ¹he ²who ⁴the ⁵promises ³ac-
δεξάμενος, 18 πρὸς ὃν ἐλαλήθη, Ὅτι ἐν Ἰσαὰκ κληθήσεταί
cepted, as to whom it was said, In Isaac shall be called
σοι σπέρμα· 19 λογισάμενος ὅτι καὶ ἐκ νεκρῶν
thy seed; reckoning that even from among [the] dead
ᶻἐγείρειν δυνατὸς‖ ὁ θεός, ὅθεν αὐτὸν καὶ ἐν παραβολῇ
⁴to ⁵raise ³able [²was] ¹God, whence him also in a simile
ἐκομίσατο. 20 Πίστει ᵃ περὶ μελλόντων ᵇεὐλόγησεν‖ Ἰσαὰκ
he received. By faith concerning things coming ²blessed ¹Isaac
τὸν Ἰακὼβ καὶ τὸν Ἠσαῦ. 21 Πίστει Ἰακὼβ ἀποθνήσκων
Jacob and Esau. By faith Jacob dying
ἕκαστον τῶν υἱῶν Ἰωσὴφ ᵇεὐλόγησεν‖ καὶ προσεκύνησεν
²each ³of ⁴the ⁵sons ⁶of ⁷Joseph ¹blessed and worshipped
ἐπὶ τὸ ἄκρον τῆς.ράβδου.αὐτοῦ. 22 Πίστει Ἰωσὴφ τελευτῶν
on the top of his staff. By faith Joseph dying,
περὶ τῆς ἐξόδου τῶν υἱῶν Ἰσραὴλ ἐμνημόνευσεν, καὶ
concerning the going forth of the sons of Israel made mention, and
περὶ τῶν.ὀστέων.αὐτοῦ ἐνετείλατο.
concerning his bones gave command.
23 Πίστει ᶜΜωσῆς‖ γεννηθεὶς ἐκρύβη τρίμηνον ὑπὸ
By faith Moses, having been born, was laid three months by

ᴾ — ἔτεκεν (read and [that] beyond a seasonable age) GLTTrA.   ᵠ ἐγεννήθησαν LA.
ʳ ὡς ἡ GLTTrAW.   ˢ προσδεξάμενοι L; κομισάμενοι TTr.   ᵗ — καὶ πεισθέντες GLTTrAW.
ᵛ μνημονεύουσιν they are mindful TTr.   ᵂ ἐξέβησαν they went out LTTrAW.   ˣ νῦν
GLTTrAW.   ᵞ τοῦτ᾽ ἔστιν GT.   ᶻ ἐγεῖραι δύναται is able to raise L.   ᵃ + καὶ also
L[Tr]AW.   ᵇ ηὐλόνησεν LA.   ᶜ Μωϋσῆς GLTTrAW.

τῶν.πατέρων.αὐτοῦ διότι εἶδον ἀστεῖον τὸ παιδίον· καὶ
his parents because they saw ⁴beautiful ¹the ²little ³child; and

οὐκ.ἐφοβήθησαν τὸ ᵈδιάταγμα‖ τοῦ βασιλέως. 24 Πίστει
did not fear the injunction of the king. By faith

ᵉΜωσῆς‖ μέγας γενόμενος ἠρνήσατο λέγεσθαι υἱὸς θυγατρὸς
Moses, great having become, refused to be called son of ²daughter

Φαραώ, 25 μᾶλλον ἑλόμενος ᶠσυγκακουχεῖσθαι‖ τῷ λαῷ
¹Pharaoh's; ³rather ³having ⁴chosen to suffer affliction with the people

τοῦ θεοῦ, ἢ πρόσκαιρον ἔχειν ἁμαρτίας ἀπόλαυσιν·
of God, than [³the] ⁴temporary ¹to ²have ⁶of ⁷sin ⁵enjoyment;

26 μείζονα πλοῦτον ἡγησάμενος τῶν ᵍἐν‖ ʰΑἰγύπτῳ θη-
greater riches having esteemed ⁶than ⁷the ⁹in ¹⁰Egypt ⁸trea-

σαυρῶν τὸν ὀνειδισμὸν τοῦ χριστοῦ· ἀπέβλεπεν.γὰρ εἰς τὴν
sures ¹the ²reproach ³of ⁴the ⁵Christ; for he had respect to the

μισθαποδοσίαν. 27 Πίστει κατέλιπεν Αἴγυπτον, μὴ φοβηθεὶς
recompense. By faith he left Egypt, not having feared

τὸν θυμὸν τοῦ βασιλέως· τὸν.γὰρ ἀόρατον ὡς ὁρῶν
the indignation of the king; for ³the ⁴invisible [⁵one] ¹as ²seeing

ἐκαρτέρησεν. 28 Πίστει πεποίηκεν τὸ πάσχα καὶ τὴν πρόσ-
he persevered. By faith he has kept the passover and the affu-

χυσιν τοῦ αἵματος, ἵνα.μὴ ὁ.ⁱὀλοθρεύων‖ τὰ πρωτότοκα θί-
sion of the blood, lest the destroyer of the firstborn [ones] might

γῃ αὐτῶν. 29 Πίστει διέβησαν τὴν ἐρυθρὰν θάλασσαν
touch them. By faith they passed through the Red Sea

ὡς διὰ ξηρᾶςᵏ· ἧς πεῖραν.λαβόντες οἱ Αἰγύπτιοι
as through dry [land]; of which ³having ⁴made ⁵trial ¹the ²Egyptians

κατεπόθησαν. 30 Πίστει τὰ τείχη Ἱεριχὼ ᵐἔπεσεν‖, κυ-
were swallowed up. By faith the walls of Jericho fell, having

κλωθέντα ἐπὶ ἑπτὰ ἡμέρας. 31 Πίστει Ῥαὰβ ἡ πόρνη οὐ
been encircled for seven days. By faith Rahab the harlot ²not

συναπώλετο τοῖς ἀπειθήσασιν, δεξαμένη τοὺς κατασκό-
¹did ³perish ⁴with those who disobeyed, having received the spies

πους μετ' εἰρήνης.
with peace.

32 Καὶ τί ἔτι λέγω; ἐπιλείψει.ⁿγάρ μεⁿ διηγούμενον ὁ
And what more do I say? For ³will ⁴fail ⁵me ⁶relating ¹the

χρόνος περὶ Γεδεών, ᵒΒαράκ ᴾτε καὶ‖ Σαμψὼν ᑫκαὶ‖ Ἰεφθάε,
²time of Gedeon, Barak also and Sampson and Jephthae,

ʳΔαβὶδ‖ τε καὶ Σαμουὴλ καὶ τῶν προφητῶν· 33 οἳ διὰ πίστεως
David also and Samuel and of the prophets· who by faith

κατηγωνίσαντο βασιλείας, ˢεἰργάσαντο‖ δικαιοσύνην, ἐπέτυχον
overcame kingdoms, wrought righteousness, obtained

ἐπαγγελιῶν, ἔφραξαν στόματα λεόντων, 34 ἔσβεσαν δύναμιν
promises, stopped mouths of lions, quenched [the] power

πυρός, ἔφυγον στόματα ᵗμαχαίρας,‖ ᵛἐνεδυναμώθησαν‖ ἀπὸ
of fire, escaped [the] mouths of [the] sword, acquired strength out of

ἀσθενείας, ἐγενήθησαν ἰσχυροὶ ἐν πολέμῳ, παρεμβολὰς
weakness, became mighty in war, [²the] ²armies

ἔκλιναν ἀλλοτρίων· 35 ἔλαβον ʷγυναῖκες‖ ἐξ ἀνα-
¹made ⁴to ⁷give ⁸way ⁴of ⁵strangers· ¹⁰Received ⁹women by resur-

στάσεως τοὺς.νεκροὺς.αὐτῶν· ἄλλοι.δὲ ἐτυμπανίσθησαν, οὐ
rection their dead; and others were tortured, not

ᵈ δόγμα decree L. ᵉ Μωϋσῆς GLTTrAW. ᶠ συν- T. ᵍ — ἐν GTTrAW. ʰ Αἰγύπτου
of Egypt GLTTrAW. ⁱ ὀλεθρεύων LA. ᵏ + γῆς land LTTrAW. ˡ Ἱερειχὼ T.
ᵐ ἔπεσαν LTTrA. ⁿ με γὰρ LTTrA. ᵒ + καὶ and W. ᴾ — τε καὶ LTTrW. ᑫ — καὶ LTTr.
ʳ Δαυείδ LTTrA; Δαυὶδ GW. ˢ ἠργάσαντο TTr. ᵗ μαχαίρης LTTrA. ᵛ ἐδυναμώθησαν were
strengthened LTTr. ʷ γυναικας (read they received by resurrection women [that is]
their dead L.

hid three months of his
parents, because they
saw *he was* a proper
child; and they were
not afraid of the king's
commandment. 24 By
faith Moses, when he
was come to years, re-
fused to be called
the son of Pharaoh's
daughter; 25 choosing
rather to suffer afflic-
tion with the people of
God, than to enjoy the
pleasures of sin for a
season; 26 esteeming
the reproach of Christ
greater riches than the
treasures in Egypt: for
he had respect unto
the recompence of the
reward. 27 By faith
he forsook Egypt, not
fearing the wrath of
the king: for he en-
dured, as seeing
him who is invisible.
28 Through faith he
kept the passover, and
the sprinkling of blood,
lest he that destroyed
the firstborn should
touch them. 29 By faith
they passed through
the Red sea as by dry
land: which the Egyp-
tians assaying to do
were drowned. 30 By
faith the walls of Je-
richo fell down, after
they were compassed
about seven days.
31 By faith the harlot
Rahab perished not
with them that believ-
ed not, when she had
received the spies with
peace.

32 And what shall I
more say? for the time
would fail me to tell
of Gedeon, and of Ba-
rak, and of Samson,
and of Jephthae; of
David also, and Sam-
uel, and of the pro-
phets: 33 who through
faith subdued king-
doms, wrought right-
eousness, obtained
promises, stopped the
mouths of lions,
34 quenched the vio-
lence of fire, escaped
the edge of the sword,
out of weakness were
made strong, waxed
valiant in fight, turn-
ed to flight the armies
of the aliens. 35 Wo-
men received their
dead raised to life a-

gain : and others were tortured, not accepting deliverance ; that they might obtain a better resurrection : 36 and others had trial of cruel mockings and scourgings, yea, moreover of bonds and imprisonment : 37 they were stoned, they were sawn asunder, were tempted, were slain with the sword : they wandered about in sheepskins and goatskins ; being destitute, afflicted, tormented ; 38 (of whom the world was not worthy:) they wandered in deserts, and in mountains, and in dens and caves of the earth. 39 And these all, having obtained a good report through faith, received not the promise : 40 God having provided some better thing for us, that they without us should not be made perfect.

προσδεξάμενοι τὴν ἀπολύτρωσιν, ἵνα κρείττονος ἀναστάσεως
having accepted redemption, that a better resurrection
τύχωσιν· 36 ἕτεροι.δὲ ἐμπαιγμῶν καὶ μαστίγων πεῖραν
they might obtain ; and others ²of ³mockings ⁴and ⁵of ⁶scourgings ¹trial
ἔλαβον, ἔτι.δὲ δεσμῶν καὶ φυλακῆς· 37 ἐλιθάσθησαν,
received, yea, moreover, of bonds and of imprisonment. They were stoned,
ˣἐπρίσθησαν, ἐπειράσθησαν,‖ ἐν φόνῳ ʸμαχαίρας‖ ἀπέθα-
were sawn asunder, were tempted, by slaughter of [the] sword they
νον· περιῆλθον ἐν μηλωταῖς, ἐν αἰγείοις δέρμασιν, ὑστερού-
died ; they wandered in sheep-skins, in goats' skins, being des-
μενοι, θλιβόμενοι, κακουχούμενοι, 38 ὧν οὐκ.ἦν ἄξιος ὁ
titute, being oppressed, being evil treated, (of whom ³was ⁴not ⁵worthy ¹the
κόσμος· ᶻἐν‖ ἐρημίαις πλανώμενοι καὶ ὄρεσιν καὶ σπηλαίοις
²world,) in deserts wandering and in mountains and in caves
καὶ ταῖς ὀπαῖς τῆς γῆς. 39 Καὶ οὗτοι πάντες μαρτυρη-
and in the holes of the earth. And these all, having been born
θέντες διὰ τῆς πίστεως, οὐκ.ἐκομίσαντο ªτὴν ἐπαγγελίαν,‖
witness to through faith, did not receive the promise,
40 τοῦ θεοῦ περὶ ἡμῶν κρεῖττόν τι προβλεψαμένου, ἵνα.μὴ
God for us ²better ¹something having foreseen, that not
χωρὶς ἡμῶν τελειωθῶσιν.
apart from us they should be made perfect.

XII. Wherefore seeing we also are compassed about with so great a cloud of witnesses, let us lay aside every weight, and the sin which doth so easily beset us, and let us run with patience the race that is set before us, 2 looking unto Jesus the author and finisher of our faith ; who for the joy that was set before him endured the cross, despising the shame, and is set down at the right hand of the throne of God. 3 For consider him that endured such contradiction of sinners against himself, lest ye be wearied and faint in your minds. 4 Ye have not yet resisted unto blood, striving against sin. 5 And ye have forgotten the exhortation which speaketh unto you as unto children, My son, despise not thou the chastening of the Lord, nor faint when thou art rebuked of him : 6 for whom the Lord loveth he chasteneth, and scourgeth every son whom he receiveth. 7 If ye endure chastening, God dealeth

12 Τοιγαροῦν καὶ ἡμεῖς τοσοῦτον ἔχοντες περικείμενον
Therefore also we ²so ³great having ⁸encompassing
ἡμῖν νέφος μαρτύρων, ὄγκον ἀποθέμενοι πάντα καὶ
⁹us ⁴a ⁵cloud ⁶of ⁷witnesses, ¹⁴weight ¹⁰having ¹¹laid ¹²aside ¹³every and
τὴν εὐπερίστατον ἁμαρτίαν, δι᾽ ὑπομονῆς τρέχωμεν τὸν
the easily-surrounding sin, with endurance we should run the
προκείμενον ἡμῖν ἀγῶνα, 2 ἀφορῶντες εἰς τὸν τῆς πίστεως
²lying ³before ⁴us ¹race, looking away to ²the ⁶of ⁷faith
ἀρχηγὸν καὶ τελειωτὴν Ἰησοῦν, ὃς ἀντὶ τῆς προκει-
³leader ⁴and ⁵completer ¹Jesus : who in view of the ª⁻ly-
μένης αὐτῷ χαρᾶς ὑπέμεινεν σταυρόν, αἰσχύνης
ing ²before ⁴him ¹joy endured [the] cross, [the] shame
καταφρονήσας, ἐν.δεξιᾷ.τε τοῦ θρόνου τοῦ θεοῦ ᵇἐκάθι-
having despised, and at [the] right hand of the throne of God sat
σεν.‖ 3 ἀναλογίσασθε.γὰρ τὸν τοιαύτην ὑπομεμενηκότα
down. For consider well him who ²so ⁴great ¹has ³endured
ὑπὸ τῶν ἁμαρτωλῶν εἰς ᶜαὐτὸν‖ ἀντιλογίαν, ἵνα μὴ κά-
⁶from ⁷sinners ⁹against ⁸himself. ⁵gainsaying, that ¹⁰not ¹ye ¹¹be
μητε, ταῖς.ψυχαῖς.ὑμῶν ἐκλυόμενοι. 4 Οὔπω μέχρις αἵματος
¹³wearied, ¹²in ¹your ¹⁴souls ¹²fainting. Not yet unto blood
ἀντικατέστητε πρὸς τὴν ἁμαρτίαν ἀνταγωνιζόμενοι, 5 καὶ
resisted ye ²against ³sin ¹wrestling, and
ἐκλέλησθε τῆς παρακλήσεως, ἥτις ὑμῖν ὡς υἱοῖς διαλέ-
ye have quite forgotten the exhortation, which to you, as to sons, he ad-
γεται·ᵈ Υἱέ.μου, μὴ.ὀλιγώρει ᵉπαιδείας‖ κυρίου, μηδὲ ἐκ-
dresses : My son, despise not [the] discipline of [the] Lord, nor
λύου ὑπ᾽ αὐτοῦ ἐλεγχόμενος. 6 ὃν.γὰρ ἀγαπᾷ κύριος
faint, by him being reproved ; for whom ³loves [¹the] ²Lord
παιδεύει· μαστιγοῖ.δὲ πάντα υἱὸν ὃν παραδέχεται· 7 ᶠΕἰ‖
he disciplines, and scourges every son whom he receives. If
ᵍπαιδείαν‖ ὑπομένετε, ὡς υἱοῖς ὑμῖν προσφέρεται
discipline ye endure, ⁶as ⁷with ⁸sons ⁴with ⁵you ¹is ³dealing

---

ˣ ἐπειράσθησαν, ἐπρίσθησαν T.   ʸ μαχαίρης LTTrA.   ᶻ ἐπὶ LTTrA.   ª τὰς ἐπαγγελίας the
promises L.   ᵇ κεκάθικεν has sat down GLTTrAW.   ᶜ ἑαυτὸν LTTrA.   ᵈ Read the sentence
as a question L.   ᵉ παιδίας T.   ᶠ εἰς (read ye endure for discipline) LTTrA.   ᵍ παιδίαν T.

ὁ θεός· τίς.γὰρ ʰἐστιν‖ υἱὸς ὃν οὐ.παιδεύει πατήρ;
¹God; ˙for who is [the] son whom ²disciplines ⁴not [¹the] ²Father?

8 εἰ.δὲ χωρίς ἐστε ¹παιδείας,‖ ἧς μέτοχοι γεγόνασιν πάν-
But if ²without ¹ye ²are discipline, of which ⁴partakers ²have ³become ¹all,

τες, ἄρα νόθοι ʲἐστὲ καὶ οὐχ υἱοί.‖ 9 εἶτα τοὺς μὲν τῆς σαρκὸς
then bastards ye are and not sons. Moreover the ⁴flesh

ἡμῶν πατέρας εἴχομεν παιδευτάς, καὶ · ᵏἐνετρε-
²of ³our ¹fathers we have had [as] those who discipline [us], and we respected

πόμεθα·‖ οὐ ¹πολλῷ‖ μᾶλλον ὑποταγησόμεθα τῷ πατρὶ
[them]; ²not ⁴much ⁵rather ¹shall ³we be in subjection to the Father

τῶν πνευμάτων, καὶ ζήσομεν; 10 οἱ.μὲν.γὰρ πρὸς ὀλίγας
of spirits, and shall live? For they indeed for a few

ἡμέρας κατὰ τὸ δοκοῦν αὐτοῖς ἐπαίδευον· ὁ.δὲ ἐπὶ
days according to that which seemed good to them disciplined; but he for

τὸ συμφέρον, εἰς τὸ μεταλαβεῖν τῆς.ἁγιότητος.αὐτοῦ. 11 πᾶσα
profit, for [us] ¹ to partake of his holiness. ²Any
(lit. every)

ᵐδὲ παιδεία‖ πρὸς μὲν τὸ.παρὸν οὐ.δοκεῖ χαρᾶς εἶναι,
¹but discipline for the present seems not [²matter] ⁴of ⁵joy ¹to ²be,

ἀλλὰ λύπης· ὕστερον.δὲ καρπὸν εἰρηνικὸν τοῖς δι᾽ αὐτῆς
but of grief; but afterwards ³fruit ²peaceable ⁶to ⁷those ¹¹by ¹²it

γεγυμνασμένοις ἀποδίδωσιν δικαιοσύνης.
⁸having ¹⁰exercised ¹renders ⁴of ⁵righteousness.

12 Διὸ τὰς παρειμένας χεῖρας καὶ τὰ παραλελυμένα γόνατα
Wherefore the ²hanging ³down ¹hands and the enfeebled knees

ἀνορθώσατε 13 καὶ τροχιὰς ὀρθὰς ⁿποιήσατε‖ τοῖς.ποσὶν.ὑμῶν,
lift up; and ²paths ¹straight make for your feet,

ἵνα μὴ τὸ χωλὸν ἐκτραπῇ, ἰαθῇ.δὲ
lest that which [is] lame be turned aside; but that ⁷it ²may ⁴be ³healed

μᾶλλον. 14 εἰρήνην διώκετε μετὰ πάντων, καὶ τὸν ἁγιασμόν,
¹rather. Peace pursue with all, and sanctification,

οὐ χωρὶς οὐδεὶς ὄψεται τὸν κύριον· 15 ἐπισκοποῦντες μή
³which ¹apart ²from no one shall see the Lord; looking diligently lest

τις ὑστερῶν ἀπὸ τῆς χάριτος τοῦ θεοῦ· μή τις ῥίζα πικρίας
any lack the grace of God; lest any root of bitterness

ἄνω φύουσα ἐνοχλῇ, καὶ °διὰ ταύτης‖ μιανθῶσιν ᴾ
²up ¹springing should trouble [you], and by this be defiled

πολλοί· 16 μή τις πόρνος ἢ βέβηλος, ὡς Ἡσαῦ, ὃς
many; lest [there be] any fornicator or profane person, as Esau, who

ἀντὶ βρώσεως μιᾶς qἀπέδοτο‖ τὰ πρωτοτόκια ʳαὐτοῦ.‖ 17 ἴστε
for ²meal ¹one sold ⁴birthright ³his; ⁷ye ⁶know

γὰρ ὅτι καὶ μετέπειτα θέλων κληρονομῆσαι τὴν εὐλογίαν ἀπε-
⁵for that also afterwards, wishing to inherit the blessing, he was

δοκιμάσθη· μετανοίας.γὰρ τόπον οὐχ.εὗρεν, καίπερ μετὰ δακ-
rejected, for ²of ³repentance ¹place he found not, although with

ρύων ἐκζητήσας αὐτήν.
tears having earnestly sought it.

18 Οὐ.γὰρ προσεληλύθατε ψηλαφωμένῳ ˢὄρει,‖ καὶ
For ³not ¹ye ²have come to ³being ⁴touched [¹the] ²mount and

κεκαυμένῳ πυρί, καὶ γνόφῳ, καὶ ᵗσκότῳ,‖ καὶ θυέλλῃ,
having been kindled with fire, and to obscurity, and to darkness, and to tempest,

19 καὶ σάλπιγγος ἤχῳ, καὶ φωνῇ ῥημάτων, ἧς οἱ
and ²trumpet's ¹to sound, and to voice of words; which [voice] they that

with you as with sons;
for what son is he
whom the father chas-
teneth not? 8 But if
ye be without chastise-
ment, whereof all are
partakers, then are ye
bastards, and not sons.
9 Furthermore we have
had fathers of our
flesh which corrected
us, and we gave them
reverence : shall we
not much rather be in
subjection unto the
Father of spirits, and
live? 10 For they ve-
rily for a few days
chastened us after
their own pleasure;
but he for our profit,
that we might be par-
takers of his holiness.
11 Now no chastening
for the present seem-
eth to be joyous, but
grievous : nevertheless
afterward it yieldeth
the peaceable fruit of
righteousness unto
them which are ex-
ercised thereby.

12 Wherefore lift up
the hands which hang
down, and the feeble
knees ; 13 and make
straight paths for your
feet, lest that which is
lame be turned out
of the way; but let
it rather be healed.
14 Follow peace with
all men, and holiness,
without which no man
shall see the Lord :
15 looking diligently
lest any man fail of
the grace of God ; lest
any root of bitterness
springing up trouble
you, and thereby many
be defiled ; 16 lest there
be any fornicator, or
profane person, as E-
sau, who for one mor-
sel of meat sold his
birthright. 17 For ye
know how that after-
ward, when he would
have inherited the
blessing, he was re-
jected : for he found
no place of repentance,
though he sought it
carefully with tears.

18 For ye are not
come unto the mount
that might be touched,
and that burned with
fire, nor unto black-
ness, and darkness,
and tempest, 19 and
the sound of a trumpet,
and the voice of words;

ʰ — ἐστιν LTTr[A]. ⁱ παιδίας T. ʲ καὶ οὐχ υἱοί ἐστε LTTrA. ᵏ ἐντρεπόμεθα we
respect E. ˡ πολὺ LTTrA. ᵐ μὲν παιδία discipline indeed T. ⁿ ποιεῖτε TTr. ° δι᾽
αὐτῆς through it L. ᴾ + οἱ the LTTrAW. q ἀπέδετο LA. ʳ ἑαυτοῦ his own LTTrA.
ˢ — ὄρει (read [that] being touched) LTTrA. ᵗ ζόφῳ LTTrAW.

which voice they that heard intreated that the word should not be spoken to them any more : 20 (for they could not endure that which was commanded. And if so much as a beast touch the mountain, it shall be stoned, or thrust through with a dart : 21 and so terrible was the sight, that Moses said, I exceedingly fear and quake :) 22 but ye are come unto mount Sion, and unto the city of the living God, the heavenly Jerusalem, and to an innumerable company of angels, 23 to the general assembly and church of the firstborn, which are written in heaven, and to God the Judge of all, and to the spirits of just men made perfect, 24 and to Jesus the mediator of the new covenant, and to the blood of sprinkling, that speaketh better things than that of Abel. 25 See that ye refuse not him that speaketh. For if they escaped not who refused him that spake on earth, much more shall not we escape, if we turn away from him that speaketh from heaven : 26 whose voice then shook the earth : but now he hath promised, saying, Yet once more I shake not the earth only, but also heaven. 27 And this word, Yet once more, signifieth the removing of those things that are shaken, as of things that are made, that those things which cannot be shaken may remain. 28 Wherefore we receiving a kingdom which cannot be moved, let us have grace, whereby we may serve God acceptably with reverence and godly fear : 29 for our God is a consuming fire.

XIII. Let brotherly love continue. 2 Be not forgetful to entertain strangers : for thereby some have entertained angels una-

ἀκούσαντες παρῃτήσαντο   μὴ προστεθῆναι αὐτοῖς
heard   excused themselves [asking] ³not ⁴to ⁵be ⁶addressed ⁷to ⁸them [¹the]

λόγον· 20 οὐκ.ἔφερον.γὰρ τὸ   διαστελλόμενον, Κἂν θηρίον
²word ;   (for they could not bear that [which] was commanded : And if a beast

θίγῃ τοῦ ὄρους λιθοβοληθήσεται, ⁿἢ βολίδι κατατοξευ-
should touch the mountain,   it shall be stoned,   or   with a dart   shot

θήσεται·‖ 21 καί, οὕτως φοβερὸν ἦν τὸ φανταζόμενον,
through ;   and,   so   fearful   was   the   spectacle   [that]

ᵛΜωσῆς‖ εἶπεν, Ἔκφοβός εἰμι καὶ ἔντρομος· 22 ἀλλὰ προσ-
Moses   said,   ³greatly ⁴afraid ¹I ²am and trembling:)   but   ye have

ἐληλύθατε Σιὼν ὄρει, καὶ   πόλει θεοῦ   ζῶντος, Ἱερου-
come to   ²Sion ¹mount; and [the] city of ³God [¹the] ²living,   ³Jeru-

σαλὴμ ἐπουρανίῳ, καὶ μυριάσιν ʷἀγγέλων   23 πανηγύρει,
salem   ⁴heavenly ;   and to myriads of angels,   [the] universal gathering ;

καὶ ἐκκλησίᾳ πρωτοτόκων ˣἐν   οὐρανοῖς ἀπογεγραμ-
and to [the] assembly of [the] firstborn [ones] in [the] heavens   regis-

μένων,‖ καὶ   κριτῇ θεῷ πάντων, καὶ πνεύμασιν δικαίων
tered ;   and to [²the] ³judge ¹God   of all ;   and to [the] spirits of [the] just

τετελειωμένων, 24 καὶ διαθήκης νέας μεσίτῃ Ἰησοῦ, καὶ
[who] have been perfected;   and ⁴of ⁵a ²covenant ³fresh ⁶mediator ¹to ²Jesus; and

αἵματι ῥαντισμοῦ ʸκρείττονα‖ λαλοῦντι παρὰ τὸν Ἄβελ
to [the] blood of sprinkling, ²better ³things ¹speaking   than   Abel.

25 Βλέπετε μὴ.παραιτήσησθε τὸν λαλοῦντα. εἰ.γὰρ ἐκεῖνοι
  Take heed   ye refuse not   him who   speaks.   For if   they

οὐκ.ᶻἔφυγον,‖ ᵃτὸν‖ ἐπὶ ᵇτῆς‖ γῆς   παραιτησάμενοι χρη-
escaped not,   ³him ⁴that ⁵on ⁶the   ⁷earth [¹who]   ²refused   divine-

ματίζοντα, ᶜπολλῷ‖.μᾶλλον ἡμεῖς οἱ τὸν ἀπ᾽   οὐρανῶν
ly instructed [them],   much more   we   who ⁴him ⁵from [⁶the] ⁷heavens

ἀποστρεφόμενοι, 26 οὗ ἡ φωνὴ τὴν γῆν ἐσάλευσεν τότε,
¹turn   ²away ³from ¹   whose   voice   ²the   ³earth   ¹shook   then ;

νῦν.δὲ ἐπήγγελται, λέγων, Ἔτι ἅπαξ ἐγὼ ᵈσείω‖ οὐ μόνον
but now he has promised,   saying,   Yet   once   I   shake   not   only

τὴν γῆν, ἀλλὰ καὶ τὸν οὐρανόν. 27 Τὸ.δὲ Ἔτι.ἅπαξ, δηλοῖ
the   earth,   but also   the   heaven.   But the   Yet   once, signifies

ᵉτῶν   σαλευομένων τὴν‖ μετάθεσιν, ὡς πεποιημένων,
³of ⁴the [⁵things]   ⁶shaken   ¹the   ²removing,   as   having been made,

ἵνα   μείνῃ τὰ   μὴ.σαλευόμενα. 28 διὸ βασιλείαν
that ⁵may ⁶remain ¹the [²things]   ³not ⁴shaken.   Wherefore a kingdom

ἀσάλευτον παραλαμβάνοντες, ἔχωμεν χάριν, δι᾽ ἧς
not to be shaken   receiving,   may we have grace,   by which

λατρεύωμεν εὐαρέστως τῷ θεῷ μετὰ ᶠαἰδοῦς καὶ εὐλαβείας.‖
we may serve   ²well ³pleasingly ¹God   with   reverence and   fear.

29 καὶ.γὰρ ὁ.θεὸς.ἡμῶν   πῦρ καταναλίσκον.
  For also   our God   [is] a ²fire   ¹consuming.

13 Ἡ φιλαδελφία μενέτω. 2 τῆς φιλοξενίας μὴ ἐπιλαν-
  ²Brotherly ³love ¹let abide ;   of hospitality ²not ¹be for-

θάνεσθε· διὰ.ταύτης.γὰρ ἔλαθόν τινες ξενίσαντες ἀγγέλους.
getful ;   for by this   unawares some   entertained   angels.

3 μιμνήσκεσθε τῶν δεσμίων, ὡς συνδεδεμένοι·   τῶν κακου-
  Be mindful   of prisoners,   as   bound with [them]; those   being

χουμένων, ὡς καὶ αὐτοὶ ὄντες ἐν   σώματι. 4 τίμιος
evil-treated,   as also yourselves being in [the] body. Honourable [let]

ᵘ — ἢ βολίδι κατατοξευθήσεται GLTTrAW.   ᵛ Μωϋσῆς GLTTrAW.   ʷ Separate myriads from of angels by a comma GLTrA.   ˣ ἀπογεγραμμένων ἐν οὐρανοῖς GLTTrAW.   ʸ κρείττον a better thing GLTTrAW.   ᶻ ἐξέφυγον LTTrA.   ᵃ τὸν placed after παραιτησάμενοι LTTrA. ᵇ — τῆς GLTTrAW.   ᶜ πολὺ LTTrA.   ᵈ σείσω will shake LTTrA.   ᵉ τὴν τῶν σαλευομένων LTTrA.   ᶠ εὐλαβείας καὶ δέους fear and awe LTTrA.

ὁ γάμος ἐν πᾶσιν, καὶ ἡ κοίτη ἀμίαντος· πόρ-
marriage [be held] in every [way], and the bed [be] undefiled ; ²for-

νους ᵍδὲ‖ καὶ μοιχοὺς κρινεῖ ὁ θεός. 5 ἀφιλάργυρος
nicators ¹but and adulterers ²will ³judge ¹God. Without love of money [let

ὁ τρόπος· ἀρκούμενοι τοῖς.παροῦσιν· αὐτὸς
your] manner of life [be], satisfied with present [circumstances] ; ²he

γὰρ εἴρηκεν, Οὐ.μή σε ἀνῶ, οὐδ᾽.οὐ.μή σε ʰἐγκαταλίπω.‖
¹for has said, In no wise thee will I leave, nor in any wise thee will I forsake.

6 ὥστε θαρρῦντας.ἡμᾶς.λέγειν, Κύριος ἐμοὶ βοηθός,
So that we may boldly say, [The] Lord [is] to me a helper,

ⁱκαὶ‖ οὐ.φοβηθήσομαι·ᵏ τί ποιήσει μοι ἄνθρωπος ;
and I will not be afraid : what shall ᵈdo ³to ⁴me ¹man ?

7 Μνημονεύετε τῶν.ἡγουμένων.ὑμῶν, οἵτινες ἐλάλησαν
Remember your leaders, who spoke

ὑμῖν τὸν λόγον τοῦ θεοῦ· ὧν ἀναθεωροῦντες τὴν ἔκβασιν
to you the word of God ; of whom, considering the issue

τῆς.ἀναστροφῆς, μιμεῖσθε τὴν.πίστιν. 8 Ἰησοῦς χριστὸς
of [their] conduct, imitate [their] faith. Jesus Christ

ˡχθὲς‖ καὶ σήμερον ὁ αὐτός, καὶ εἰς τοὺς αἰῶνας.· 9 διδα-
yesterday and to-day [is] the same, and to the ages. With

χαῖς ποικίλαις καὶ ξέναις μὴ.ᵐπεριφέρεσθε·‖ καλὸν.γὰρ
teachings ¹various ²and ³strange be not carried about ; for [it is] good [for]

χάριτι βεβαιοῦσθαι τὴν καρδίαν, οὐ βρώμασιν, ἐν οἷς οὐκ
⁶with ⁷grace ³to ⁴be ⁵confirmed ¹the ²heart. not meats ; in which ²not

ὠφελήθησαν οἱ ⁿπεριπατήσαντες.‖ 10 Ἔχομεν θυσια-
¹were ³profited those who walked [therein]. We have an al-

στήριον ἐξ·ὓδ ψυγεῖν οὐκ.ἔχουσιν ἐξουσίαν οἱ τῇ σκηνῇ
tar of which to eat they have not authority who the tabernacle

λατρεύοντες. 11 ὧν.γὰρ εἰσφέρεται ζώων τὸ αἷμα
serve ; for of those ²whose ⁴is ⁵brought ¹animals ³blood [as sacri-

ᵒπερὶ ἁμαρτίας‖ εἰς τὰ ἅγιαᵖ διὰ τοῦ ἀρχιερέως, τούτων
fices] for sin into the holies by the high priest, of these

τὰ σώματα κατακαίεται ἔξω τῆς παρεμβολῆς· 12 διὸ καὶ
the bodies are burned outside the camp. Wherefore also

Ἰησοῦς, ἵνα ἁγιάσῃ διὰ τοῦ.ἰδίου αἵματος τὸν λαόν,
Jesus, that he might sanctify by his own blood the people,

ἔξω τῆς πύλης ἔπαθεν. 13 τοίνυν ἐξερχώμεθα πρὸς αὐτὸν
outside the gate suffered : therefore we should go forth to him

ἔξω τῆς παρεμβολῆς, τὸν.ὀνειδισμὸν.αὐτοῦ φέροντες· 14 οὐ
outside the camp, his reproach bearing ; ⁴not

γὰρ ἔχομεν ὧδε μένουσαν πόλιν, ἀλλὰ τὴν μέλλουσαν ἐπι-
¹for ²we ³have here an abiding city, but the coming one we are

ζητοῦμεν. 15 Δι᾽ αὐτοῦ �vᵒὖν‖ ἀναφέρωμεν θυσίαν αἰνέσεως
seeking for. By him therefore we should offer [the] sacrifice of praise

ʳδιαπαντὸς‖ τῷ θεῷ, ˢτουτέστιν,‖ καρπὸν χειλέων ὁμολογούν-
continually to God, that is, fruit of [the] lips confess-

των τῷ.ὀνόματι.αὐτοῦ. 16 τῆς.δὲ.εὐποιίας καὶ κοινωνίας
ing to his name. But of doing good and of communicating

μὴ.ἐπιλανθάνεσθε· τοιαύταις.γὰρ θυσίαις εὐαρεστεῖται ὁ θεός.
be not forgetful, for with such sacrifices is ²well ³pleased ¹God.

17 Πείθεσθε τοῖς.ἡγουμένοις.ὑμῶν, καὶ ὑπείκετε· αὐτοὶ.γὰρ
Obey your leaders, and be submissive : for they

wares, 3 Remember them that are in bonds, as bound with them ; and them which suffer adversity, as being yourselves also in the body. 4 Marriage is honourable in all, and the bed undefiled : but whoremongers and a-dulterers God will judge. 5 Let your conversation be without covetousness ; and be content with such things as ye have : for he hath said, I will never leave thee, nor forsake thee. 6 So that we may boldly say, The Lord is my helper, and I will not fear what man shall do un-to me.

7 Remember them which have the rule over you, who have spoken unto you the word of God : whose faith follow, consider-ing the end of their conversation. 8 Jesus Christ the same yester-day, and to day, and for ever. 9 Be not carried about with di-vers and strange doc-trines. For it is a good thing that the heart be established with grace ; not with meats, which have not profit-ed them that have been occupied therein. 10 We have an altar, where-of they have no right to eat which serve the tabernacle. 11 For the bodies of those beasts, whose blood is brought into the sanctuary by the high priest for sin, are burned without the camp. 12 Where-fore Jesus also, that he might sanctify the people with his own blood, suffered with-out the gate. 13 Let us go forth therefore unto him without the camp, bearing his re-proach. 14 For here have we no continuing city, but we seek one to come. 15 By him therefore let us offer the sacrifice of praise to God continually, that is, the fruit of our lips giving thanks to his name. 16 But to do good and to com-municate forget not : for with such sacrifices

---

ᵍ γὰρ for LTTrA. ʰ ἐγκαταλείπω do I forsake TA. ⁱ — καὶ [L]T[TrA]. ᵏ Textus
Receptus is punctuated as in Authorized version. ˡ ἐχθὲς LTTrAW. ᵐ παραφέρεσθε carried
away GLTTrAW. ⁿ περιπατοῦντες walk LTTr. ᵒ — περὶ ἁμαρτίας LA. ᵖ + περὶ
ἁμαρτίας for sin L. ᑫ [οὖν] Tr. ʳ διὰ παντὸς LTrA. ˢ τοῦτ᾽ ἐστιν GT.

38

God is well pleased. 17 Obey them that have the rule over you, and submit yourselves: for they watch for your souls, as they that must give account, that they may do it with joy, and not with grief: for that is unprofitable for you. 18 Pray for us: for we trust we have a good conscience, in all things willing to live honestly. 19 But I beseech *you* the rather to do this, that I may be restored to you the sooner. 20 Now the God of peace, that brought again from the dead our Lord Jesus, that great Shepherd of the sheep, through the blood of the everlasting covenant, 21 make you perfect in every good work to do his will, working in you that which is well-pleasing in his sight, through Jesus Christ; to whom *be* glory for ever and ever. Amen. 22 And I beseech you, brethren, suffer the word of exhortation: for I have written a letter unto you in few words.

23 Know ye that *our* brother Timothy is set at liberty; with whom, if he come shortly, I will see you. 24 Salute all them that have the rule over you, and all the saints. They of Italy salute you. 25 Grace *be* with you all. Amen.

Interlinear (main):

ἀγρυπνοῦσιν ὑπὲρ τῶν.ψυχῶν.ὑμῶν, ὡς λόγον ἀποδώσον-
watch   for   your souls,   as [4]account [1]about [2]to [3]ren-
τες· ἵνα μετὰ χαρᾶς τοῦτο ποιῶσιν, καὶ μὴ στενάζοντες·
der; that with joy   this   they may do, and not groaning,
ἀλυσιτελὲς.γὰρ ὑμῖν   τοῦτο. 18 Προσεύχεσθε περὶ
for unprofitable for you [would|be], this.   Pray   for
ἡμῶν· [1]πεποίθαμεν[||].γάρ, ὅτι καλὴν συνείδησιν ἔχομεν, ἐν
us: for we are persuaded, that a good conscience we have, in
πᾶσιν καλῶς [5]θέλοντες ἀναστρέφεσθαι· 19 περισσοτέρως.δὲ
all things [5]well [1]wishing [2]to [3]conduct [4]ourselves. But more abundantly
παρακαλῶ τοῦτο ποιῆσαι, ἵνα τάχιον ἀποκατασταθῶ
I exhort [you] this   to do, that more quickly I may be restored
ὑμῖν. 20 Ὁ.δὲ θεὸς τῆς εἰρήνης, ὁ ἀναγαγὼν ἐκ
to you.   And the God   of peace, who brought again from among [the]
νεκρῶν τὸν ποιμένα τῶν προβάτων τὸν μέγαν ἐν
dead the Shepherd of the sheep   the great [one] in [the power of
αἵματι διαθήκης αἰωνίου, τὸν.κύριον.ἡμῶν Ἰησοῦν,
the] blood of [the] [2]covenant [1]eternal,   our Lord   Jesus,
21 καταρτίσαι ὑμᾶς ἐν παντὶ [v]ἔργῳ[||] ἀγαθῷ, εἰς τὸ ποιῆσαι
perfect   you in every [2]work [1]good, for to do
τὸ.θέλημα.αὐτοῦ, [w]ποιῶν ἐν [x]ὑμῖν[||] τὸ εὐάρεστον ἐνώ-
his will,   doing in you that which [is] well pleasing be-
πιον αὐτοῦ, διὰ Ἰησοῦ χριστοῦ· ᾧ ἡ δόξα εἰς τοὺς
fore him, through Jesus Christ; to whom [be] glory to the
αἰῶνας τῶν αἰώνων. ἀμήν. 22 Παρακαλῶ.δὲ ὑμᾶς, ἀδελ-
ages of the ages.   Amen.   But I exhort you, breth-
φοί, [y]ἀνέχεσθε[||] τοῦ λόγου τῆς παρακλήσεως· καὶ.γὰρ διὰ
ren, bear   the word   of exhortation, for also in
βραχέων ἐπέστειλα ὑμῖν.
few words I wrote to you.

23 Γινώσκετε τὸν ἀδελφὸν [z] Τιμόθεον ἀπολελυμένον, μεθ'
Know ye the brother Timotheus has been released; with
οὗ, ἐὰν τάχιον ἔρχηται, ὄψομαι ὑμᾶς. 24 Ἀσπάσασθε
whom, if sooner he should come, I will see you.   Salute
πάντας τοὺς.ἡγουμένους.ὑμῶν, καὶ πάντας τοὺς ἁγίους.
all   your leaders,   and all the saints.
ἀσπάζονται ὑμᾶς οἱ ἀπὸ τῆς Ἰταλίας. 25 ἡ χάρις μετὰ
[4]Salute [5]you [3]they [2]from [3]Italy.   Grace [be] with
πάντων ὑμῶν. [a]ἀμήν.[||]
[2]all [1]you. Amen.

[b]Πρὸς Ἑβραίους ἐγράφη ἀπὸ τῆς Ἰταλίας, διὰ Τιμοθέου.[||]
To [the] Hebrews written from   Italy, by Timotheus.

---

[c]ΙΑΚΩΒΟΥ ΕΠΙΣΤΟΛΗ ΚΑΘΟΛΙΚΗ.[||]
[4]OF [5]JAMES [1]THE] [3]EPISTLE [2]GENERAL.

JAMES, a servant of God and of the Lord Jesus Christ, to the twelve tribes which are scattered abroad, greeting.

ΙΑΚΩΒΟΣ θεοῦ καὶ κυρίου Ἰησοῦ χριστοῦ δοῦλος, ταῖς
James [2]of [3]God [4]and [5]of [6]the] [7]Lord [8]Jesus [9]Christ [1]bondman, to the
δώδεκα φυλαῖς ταῖς ἐν τῇ διασπορᾷ χαίρειν.
twelve tribes which [are] in the dispersion, greeting.

---

t πειθόμεθα we persuade ourselves LTTrAW.   v — ἔργῳ T.   w + αὑτῷ to himself L.
z ἡμῖν us T.   y ἀνέχεσθαι to bear L.   x + ἡμῶν (read our brother) LTTrAW.   a — ἀμήν T.
b — *the subscription* GLTW; Πρὸς Ἑβραίους TrA.
c + τοῦ ἀποστόλου the Apostle E; Ἐπιστολαὶ (— Ἐπιστ. L) καθολικαί. Ἰακώβου ἐπι-
στολή General Epistles. Epistle of James GLW; Ἰακώβου ἐπιστολή TTrA.

2 Πᾶσαν χαρὰν ἡγήσασθε, ἀδελφοί.μου, ὅταν πειρασμοῖς
All joy esteem [it], my brethren, when ⁶temptations

περιπέσητε ποικίλοις, 3 γινώσκοντες ὅτι τὸ δοκίμιον ὑμῶν
¹ye ²may ³fall ⁴into ⁵various, knowing that the proving of your

τῆς πίστεως κατεργάζεται ὑπομονήν· 4 ἡ.δὲ.ὑπομονὴ ἔργον
faith works out ²endurance. But ²endurance [¹its] ⁵work

τέλειον ἐχέτω, ἵνα ἦτε τέλειοι καὶ ὁλόκληροι, ἐν μηδενὶ λει-
²perfect ¹let ³have, that ye may be perfect and complete, in nothing lack-

πόμενοι. 5 εἰ.δέ τις ὑμῶν λείπεται σοφίας, αἰτείτω παρὰ τοῦ
ing. But if anyone of you lack wisdom, let him ask from ²who

διδόντος θεοῦ πᾶσιν ἁπλῶς, καὶ μὴ.ὀνειδίζοντος, καὶ δοθήσε-
²gives ¹God to all freely, and reproaches not, and it shall be

ται αὐτῷ. 6 αἰτείτω.δὲ ἐν πίστει, μηδὲν διακρινόμενος· ὁ.γὰρ
given to him: but let him ask in faith, nothing doubting. For he that

διακρινόμενος ἔοικεν κλύδωνι θαλάσσης ἀνεμιζομένῳ καὶ
doubts is like a wave of [the] sea being driven by the wind and

ῥιπιζομένῳ. 7 μὴ.γὰρ οἰέσθω ὁ.ἄνθρωπος.ἐκεῖνος, ὅτι ᵈλή-
being tossed; for ²not ¹let ³suppose ³that ⁴man that he

ψεταί‖ τι παρὰ τοῦ κυρίου· 8 ἀνὴρ δίψυχος,
shall receive anything from the Lord; [he is] a ²man ¹double-minded,

ἀκατάστατος ἐν πάσαις ταῖς.ὁδοῖς.αὐτοῦ. 9 Καυχάσθω.δὲ
unstable in all his ways. But let ²boast

ὁ ἀδελφὸς ὁ ταπεινὸς ἐν τῷ.ὕψει.αὐτοῦ· 10 ὁ.δὲ πλούσιος
¹the ²brother ³of ⁴low ⁵degree in his elevation, and the rich

ἐν τῇ.ταπεινώσει.αὐτοῦ, ὅτι ὡς ἄνθος χόρτου παρελεύ-
in his humiliation, because as ²flower [¹the] ²grass's he will pass

σεται, 11 ἀνέτειλεν.γὰρ ὁ ἥλιος σὺν τῷ.καύσωνι, καὶ ἐξή-
away. For ³rose ¹the ²sun with [its] burning heat, and dried

ρανεν τὸν χόρτον, καὶ τὸ ἄνθος αὐτοῦ ἐξέπεσεν, καὶ ἡ εὐ-
up the grass, and the flower of it fell, and the

πρέπεια τοῦ.προσώπου.αὐτοῦ ἀπώλετο· οὕτως καὶ ὁ πλούσιος
comeliness of its appearance perished: thus also the rich

ἐν ταῖς.πορείαις.αὐτοῦ μαρανθήσεται. 12 Μακάριος ἀνὴρ
in his goings shall wither. Blessed [is the] man

ὃς ὑπομένει πειρασμόν· ὅτι δόκιμος γενόμενος ᵉλήψεται‖
who endures temptation; because ³proved ¹having ²been he shall receive

τὸν στέφανον τῆς ζωῆς, ὃν ἐπηγγείλατο ᶠὁ κύριος‖ τοῖς
the crown of life, which ³promised ¹the ²Lord to those that

ἀγαπῶσιν αὐτόν.
love him.

13 Μηδεὶς πειραζόμενος λεγέτω, Ὅτι ἀπὸ ᵍτοῦ‖ θεοῦ πειρά-
²No ³one ⁴being ⁵tempted ¹let say, From God I am

ζομαι· ὁ.γὰρ.θεὸς ἀπείραστός ἐστιν κακῶν, πειράζει.δὲ αὐτὸς
tempted. For God ²not ³to ⁴be ⁵tempted ¹is by evils, and ²tempts ¹himself

οὐδένα. 14 ἕκαστος.δὲ πειράζεται, ʰὑπὸ τῆς.ἰδίας ἐπιθυμίας
no one. But each one is tempted, by his own lust

ἐξελκόμενος καὶ δελεαζόμενος· 15 εἶτα ἡ ἐπιθυμία συλλαβοῦσα
being drawn away and being allured; then lust having conceived

τίκτει ἁμαρτίαν· ἡ.δὲ.ἁμαρτία ἀποτελεσθεῖσα ἀποκύει
gives birth to sin; but sin having been completed brings forth

θάνατον. 16 Μὴ.πλανᾶσθε, ἀδελφοί μου ἀγαπητοί· 17 πᾶσα
death. Be not misled, ³brethren ¹my ²beloved. Every

δόσις ἀγαθὴ καὶ πᾶν δώρημα τέλειον ἄνωθέν ἐστιν
²act ³of ⁴giving ¹good and every ²gift ¹perfect ⁴from ⁷above ³is

2 My brethren, count it all joy when ye fall into divers temptations; 3 knowing *this,* that the trying of your faith worketh patience. 4 But let patience have *her* perfect work, that ye may be perfect and entire, wanting nothing. 5 If any of you lack wisdom, let him ask of God, that giveth to all *men* liberally, and upbraideth not; and it shall be given him. 6 But let him ask in faith, nothing wavering. For he that wavereth is like a wave of the sea driven with the wind and tossed. 7 For let not that man think that he shall receive any thing of the Lord. 8 A double minded man *is* unstable in all his ways. 9 Let the brother of low degree rejoice in that he is exalted: 10 but the rich, in that he is made low: because as the flower of the grass he shall pass away. 11 For the sun is no sooner risen with a burning heat, but it withereth the grass, and the flower thereof falleth, and the grace of the fashion of it perisheth: so also shall the rich man fade away in his ways. 12 Blessed *is* the man that endureth temptation: for when he is tried, he shall receive the crown of life, which the Lord hath promised to them that love him.

13 Let no man say when he is tempted, I am tempted of God: for God cannot be tempted with evil, neither tempteth he any man: 14 but every man is tempted, when he is drawn away of his own lust, and enticed. 15 Then when lust hath conceived, it bringeth forth sin: and sin, when it is finished, bringeth forth death. 16 Do not err, my beloved brethren. 17 Every good gift and every perfect gift is from above, and cometh down from the Father of lights, with

---

ᵈ λήμψεταί LTTrA. ᵉ λήμψεται LTTrA. ᶠ — ὁ κύριος (*read* ἐπηγ. he promised) LTTrA.
ᵍ — τοῦ GLTTrAW. ʰ ἀπὸ A.

whom is no variableness, neither shadow of turning. 18 Of his own will begat he us with the word of truth, that we should be a kind of firstfruits of his creatures.

καταβαῖνον ἀπὸ τοῦ πατρὸς τῶν φώτων, παρ' ᾧ οὐκ.ἔνι
⁴coming ⁵down from the Father of lights, with whom there is not

παραλλαγή, ἢ τροπῆς ἀποσκίασμα. 18 βουληθεὶς ἀπε-
variation, or ²of ³turning ¹shadow. Having willed [it] he be-

κύησεν ἡμᾶς λόγῳ ἀληθείας, εἰς τὸ εἶναι ἡμᾶς ἀπαρχήν
gat us by [the] word of truth, for ²to ³be ¹us ⁷first-fruits

τινα τῶν.αὐτοῦ.κτισμάτων.
⁴a ⁵sort ⁶of of his creatures.

19 Wherefore, my beloved brethren, let every man be swift to hear, slow to speak, slow to wrath: 20 for the wrath of man worketh not the righteousness of God. 21 Wherefore lay apart all filthiness and superfluity of naughtiness, and receive with meekness the engrafted word, which is able to save your souls. 22 But be ye doers of the word, and not hearers only, deceiving your own selves. 23 For if any be a hearer of the word, and not a doer, he is like unto a man beholding his natural face in a glass: 24 for he beholdeth himself, and goeth his way, and straightway forgetteth what manner of man he was. 25 But whoso looketh into the perfect law of liberty, and continueth *therein*, he being not a forgetful hearer, but a doer of the work, this man shall be blessed in his deed. 26 If any man among you seem to be religious, and bridleth not his tongue, but deceiveth his own heart, this man's religion *is* vain. 27 Pure religion and undefiled before God and the Father is this, To visit the fatherless and widows in their affliction, *and* to keep himself unspotted from the world.

19 ⁱ"Ὥστε," ἀδελφοί μου ἀγαπητοί, ἔστω ᵏ πᾶς ἄνθρωπος
So that, ³brethren ¹my ²beloved, let ³be ¹every ²man

ταχὺς εἰς τὸ ἀκοῦσαι, βραδὺς εἰς τὸ λαλῆσαι, βραδὺς εἰς ὀργήν.
swift to hear, slow to speak, slow to wrath;

20 ὀργὴ.γὰρ ἀνδρὸς δικαιοσύνην θεοῦ ¹οὐ.κατεργάζεται."
for ²wrath ¹man's ⁷righteousness ⁶God's ³works ⁴not ⁵out.

21 Διὸ ἀποθέμενοι πᾶσαν ῥυπαρίαν καὶ περισσείαν κα-
Wherefore, having laid aside all filthiness and abounding of wick-

κίας, ἐν πραΰτητι δέξασθε τὸν ἔμφυτον λόγον, τὸν δυνά-
edness, in meekness accept the implanted word, which [is]

μενον σῶσαι τὰς.ψυχὰς.ὑμῶν. 22 γίνεσθε.δὲ ποιηταὶ λόγου,
able to save your souls. But be ye doers of [the] word,

καὶ μὴ ᵐμόνον ἀκροαταί," παραλογιζόμενοι ἑαυτούς. 23 ὅτι
and not only hearers, beguiling yourselves. Because

εἴ τις ἀκροατὴς λόγου ἐστὶν καὶ οὐ ποιητής, οὗτος
if any man a hearer of [the] word is and not a doer, this one

ἔοικεν.ἀνδρὶ κατανοοῦντι τὸ πρόσωπον τῆς γενέσεως αὐτοῦ
is like to a man considering ²face ²natural ¹his

ἐν ἐσόπτρῳ· 24 κατενόησεν.γὰρ ἑαυτὸν καὶ ἀπελήλυθεν, καὶ
in a mirror: for he considered himself and has gone away, and

εὐθέως ἐπελάθετο ὁποῖος ἦν. 25 ὁ.δὲ παρακύψας εἰς
immediately forgot what ³like ¹he ²was. But he that looked into

νόμον τέλειον τὸν τῆς ἐλευθερίας, καὶ παραμείνας,
[the] ²law ¹perfect, that of freedom, and continued in [it],

ⁿοὗτος" οὐκ ἀκροατὴς ἐπιλησμονῆς γενόμενος, ἀλλὰ ποιητὴς
this one not a ⁴hearer ³forgetful having been, but a doer

ἔργου, οὗτος μακάριος ἐν τῇ.ποιήσει.αὐτοῦ ἔσται. 26 Εἰ
of [the] work, this one blessed in his doing shall be. If

ᵒτις δοκεῖ θρῆσκος εἶναι ᴾἐν ὑμῖν," μὴ χαλιναγωγῶν
anyone ³seems ⁶religious ⁴to ⁵be ¹among ²you, not bridling

γλῶσσαν.αὐτοῦ, ᑫἀλλ'" ἀπατῶν καρδίαν.ʳαὐτοῦ," τούτου
his tongue, but deceiving his heart, of this one

μάταιος ἡ ˢθρησκεία." 27 ˢθρησκεία" καθαρὰ καὶ ἀμίαντος
vain [is] the religion. Religion pure and undefiled

παρὰ ᵗτῷ" θεῷ καὶ πατρὶ αὕτη ἐστίν, ἐπισκέπτεσθαι ὀρ-
before God and [the] Father ²this ¹is: to visit or-

φανοὺς καὶ χήρας ἐν τῇ.θλίψει.αὐτῶν, ἄσπιλον ἑαυτὸν τηρεῖν
phans and widows in their tribulation, unspotted ³oneself ¹to ²keep

ἀπὸ τοῦ κόσμου.
from the world.

II. My brethren, have not the faith of our Lord Jesus Christ, *the Lord* of glory, with respect of persons. 2 For if there come un-

2 Ἀδελφοί.μου, μὴ ἐν ᵛπροσωποληψίαις" ἔχετε τὴν πίστιν
My brethren, not ⁴with ⁵respect ⁶of ⁷persons ¹do ³have the faith

τοῦ.κυρίου.ἡμῶν Ἰησοῦ χριστοῦ τῆς δόξης· 2 ἐάν.γὰρ
of our Lord Jesus Christ, [Lord] of glory; for if

ⁱ"Ἴστε Ye know [it] LTTrA.   ᵏ + δὲ but (let) LTTrA.   ˡ οὐκ ἐργάζεται works not LTTrA.
ᵐ ἀκροαταὶ μόνον LTrAW.   ⁿ — οὗτος LTTrA.   ᵒ + δὲ but (if) L.   ᵖ — ἐν ὑμῖν
GLTTrAW.   ᑫ ἀλλὰ LTTrAW.   ʳ ἑαυτοῦ (*read* his own heart) L.   ˢ θρησκία T.
ᵗ — τῷ TW.   ᵛ προσωπολημψίαις LTTrA.

εἰσέλθῃ εἰς ᵂτὴνᶥᶥ.συναγωγὴν.ὑμῶν ἀνὴρ χρυσοδακτύλιος
may have come into   your ·ynagogue   a man   with gold rings

ἐν ἐσθῆτι λαμπρᾷ, εἰσέλθῃ.δὲ καὶ πτωχὸς ἐν ῥυπαρᾷ
in ²apparel ¹splendid, and may have come in also   a poor [man] in   vile

ἐσθῆτι, 3 ˣκαὶ ἐπιβλέψητε᷾ ἐπὶ τὸν φοροῦντα τὴν ἐσθῆτα
apparel,   and ye may have looked upon him who   wears   the ²apparel

τὴν λαμπράν, καὶ εἴπητε ʸαὐτῷ,ᶥᶥ Σὺ κάθου ὧδε καλῶς, καὶ
¹splendid,   and may have said to him, Thou sit thou here well,   and

τῷ πτωχῷ εἴπητε, Σὺ στῆθι ἐκεῖ, ἢ κάθου ᶻὧδεᶥᶥ ὑπὸ
to the poor may have said, Thou stand thou there, or sit thou here under

τὸ.ὑποπόδιόν.μου· 4 ᵃκαὶ³ οὐ διεκρίθητε ἐν ἑαυτοῖς,
my footstool :   ⁴also ³not ¹did ²ye make a difference among yourselves,

καὶ ἐγένεσθε κριταὶ διαλογισμῶν πονηρῶν; 5 Ἀκούσατε,
and   became judges [having] ²reasonings ¹evil?   Hear,

ἀδελφοί μου ἀγαπητοί, οὐχ ὁ θεὸς ἐξελέξατο τοὺς πτωχοὺς
³brethren ¹my ²beloved: ³not ⁶God ⁴did choose the poor

ᵇτοῦ κόσμου ᶥᶥ ᶜτούτου,ᶥᶥ πλουσίους ἐν πίστει, καὶ κληρονόμους
³world ¹of ²this,   rich   in faith, and   heirs

τῆς βασιλείας ἧς ἐπηγγείλατο τοῖς ἀγαπῶσιν αὐτόν;
of the kingdom which he promised to those that love   him?

6 ὑμεῖς.δὲ ἠτιμάσατε τὸν πτωχόν. ᵈοὐχᶥᶥ οἱ πλούσιοι
But ye   dishonoured the   poor [man]. ²Not ³the ⁴rich

καταδυναστεύουσιν ᵉἡμῶν,ᶥᶥ καὶ αὐτοὶ ἕλκουσιν ὑμᾶς
¹do oppress   you,   and [²not] ³they ¹do drag   you

εἰς κριτήρια; 7 οὐκ αὐτοὶ βλασφημοῦσιν τὸ καλὸν
before [the] tribunals? ²not ³they   ¹do blaspheme the good

ὄνομα τὸ ἐπικληθὲν ἐφ' ὑμᾶς; 8 Εἰ μέντοι νόμον τελεῖτε
name which was called upon you?   If indeed [the] ²law ³ye ⁴keep

βασιλικόν, κατὰ τὴν γραφήν, Ἀγαπήσεις τὸν.πλησίον.σου
¹royal according to the scripture, Thou shalt love   thy neighbour

ὡς σεαυτόν, καλῶς ποιεῖτε· 9 εἰ.δὲ ᶠπροσωποληπτεῖτε,ᶥᶥ ἁμαρ-
as thyself, ·³well ¹ye ²do.   But if ye have respect of persons, ³sin

τίαν ἐργάζεσθε, ἐλεγχόμενοι ὑπὸ τοῦ νόμου ὡς παραβάται.
¹ye ²work, being convicted by the law   as transgressors.

10 ὅστις.γὰρ ὅλον τὸν νόμον ᵍτηρήσει, πταίσει³ δὲ ἐν ἑνί,
For whosoever ²whole ¹the law shall keep, ²shall ³stumble ¹but in one

γέγονεν πάντων ἔνοχος. 11 ὁ.γὰρ εἰπών, Μὴ μοι-
[point], he has become ²of ³all ¹guilty.   For he who said, ³not ¹Thou

χεύσῃς, εἶπεν καί, Μὴ.φονεύσῃς· εἰ.δὲ
²mayest commit adultery, said also, Thou mayest not commit murder. Now if

οὐ.ʰμοιχεύσεις, φονεύσειςᶥᶥ δέ, γέγονας
thou shalt not commit adultery, ²shalt ³commit ⁴murder ¹but, thou hast become

παραβάτης νόμου. 12 Οὕτως λαλεῖτε καὶ οὕτως ποιεῖτε, ὡς
a transgressor of [the] law. So speak ye and so   do, · as

διὰ νόμου ἐλευθερίας μέλλοντες κρίνεσθαι· 13 ἡ.γὰρ.κρίσις
by [the] law of freedom being about to be judged ;   for judgment

ⁱἀνίλεωςᶥᶥ τῷ μὴ.ποιήσαντι ἔλεος· ᵏκαὶᶥᶥ κατα-
[will be] without mercy to him that wrought not mercy. And ²boasts

καυχᾶται ἔλεος κρίσεως.
³over   ¹mercy judgment.

14 Τί ¹τὸᶥᶥ ὄφελος, ἀδελφοί.μου, ἐὰν πίστιν ᵐλέγῃ τιςᶥᶥ
What [is] the profit, my brethren, if ⁵faith ²say ¹anyone

to your assembly a
man with a gold ring,
in goodly apparel, and
there come in also a
poor man in vile rai-
ment; 3 and ye have
respect to him that
weareth the gay cloth-
ing, and say unto him,
Sit thou here in a good
place ; and say to the
poor, Stand thou there,
or sit here under my
footstool : 4 are ye not
then partial in your-
selves, and are be-
come judges of evil
thoughts? 5 Hearken,
my beloved brethren,
Hath not God chosen
the · poor of this
world rich in faith,
and heirs of the king-
dom which he hath
promised to them that
love him ? 6 But ye
have despised the poor.
Do not rich men op-
press you, and draw
you before the judg-
ment seats ? 7 Do not
they blaspheme that
worthy name by the
which ye are call-
ed ? 8 If ye fulfil the
royal law according to
the scripture, Thou
shalt love thy neigh-
bour as thyself, ye do
well : 9 but if ye have
respect to persons, ye
commit sin, and are
convinced of the law
as transgressors. 10 For
whosoever shall keep
the whole law, and yet
offend in one point, he
is guilty of all. 11 For
he that said, Do not
commit adultery, said
also, Do not kill. Now
if thou commit no
adultery, yet if thou
kill, thou art become a
transgressor of the law.
12 So speak ye, and so
do, as they that shall
be judged by the law
of liberty. 13 For he
shall have judgment
without mercy, that
hath shewed no mercy;
and mercy rejoiceth
against judgment.

14 What doth it
profit, my brethren,

ᵂ — τὴν LTTrA.   ˣ ἐπιβλέψητε δὲ A.   ʸ — αὐτῷ GLTTrA.   ᶻ — ὧδε LTTrA.   ᵃ — καὶ LTTrA.
ᵇ τῷ κόσμῳ (as regards the world) LTTrAW.   ᶜ — τούτου GLTTrAW.   ᵈ οὐχὶ LW.   ᵉ ὑμᾶς T.
ᶠ προσωπολημπτεῖτε LTTrA.   ᵍ τηρήσῃ, πταίσῃ (read shall have kept, but shall have stumbled) LTTrAW.   ʰ μοιχεύεις, φονεύεις (read if thou committest not adultery but committest
murder) LTT ·A.   ⁱ ἀνέλεος pitiless LTTrAW.   ᵏ — καὶ GLTTrAW.   ˡ — τὸ L.   ᵐ τις λέγῃ L.

though a man say he hath faith, and have not works? can faith save him? 15 If a brother or sister be naked, and destitute of daily food, 16 and one of you say unto them, Depart in peace, be ye warmed and filled; notwithtanding ye give them not those things which are needful to the body; what *doth it* profit? 17 Even so faith, if it hath not works, is dead, being alone. 18 Yea, a man may say, Thou hast faith, and I have works: shew me thy faith without thy works, and I will shew thee my faith by my works. 19 Thou believest that there is one God; thou doest well: the devils also believe, and tremble. 20 But wilt thou know, O vain man, that faith without works is dead? 21 Was not Abraham our father justified by works, when he had offered Isaac his son upon the altar? 22 Seest thou how faith wrought with his works, and by works was faith made perfect? 23 And the scripture was fulfilled which saith, Abraham believed God, and it was imputed unto him for righteousness: and he was called the Friend of God. 24 Ye see then how that by works a man is justified, and not by faith only. 25 Likewise also was not Rahab the harlot justified by works, when she had received the messengers, and had sent *them* out another way? 26 For as the body without the spirit is dead, so faith without works is dead also.

III. My brethren, be not many masters, knowing that we shall receive the greater condemnation. 2 For in many things we offend all. If any man

ἔχειν, ἔργα.δὲ μὴ.ἔχῃ; μὴ δύναται ἡ πίστις σῶσαι αὐτόν;
[³he] ⁴has, but works have not? is ²able ¹faith to save him?

15 ἐὰν.ⁿδὲ‖ ἀδελφὸς ἢ ἀδελφὴ γυμνοὶ ὑπάρχωσιν, καὶ λειπό-
Now if a brother or a sister ²naked ¹be, and desti-

μενοι °ὦσιν‖ τῆς ἐφημέρου τροφῆς, 16 εἴπῃ.δὲ τις αὐτοῖς
tute may be of daily food, and ᵃsay ¹anyone ᵇto ⁷them

ἐξ ὑμῶν, Ὑπάγετε ἐν εἰρήνῃ, θερμαίνεσθε καὶ χορτά-
²from ³amongst ⁴you, Go in peace; be warmed and be fill-

ζεσθε, μὴ.δῶτε.δὲ αὐτοῖς τὰ ἐπιτήδεια τοῦ σώματος, τί
ed; but give not to them the needful things for the body, what [is]

Ρτὸ‖ ὄφελος; 17 οὕτως καὶ ἡ πίστις ἐὰν μὴ ᵠἔργα ἔχῃ‖ νεκρά
the profit? So also faith, if ²not ⁴works ¹it ³have, ⁶dead

ἐστιν καθ᾽ ἑαυτήν. 18 ἀλλ᾽ ἐρεῖ τις Σὺ πίστιν ἔχεις,
⁵is by itself. But ³will ⁴say ¹some²one, Thou ²faith ¹hast

κἀγὼ ἔργα ἔχω· δεῖξόν μοι τὴν.πίστιν.σου ʳἐκ‖ τῶν.ἔργων
and I ²works ¹have. Shew me thy faith from ²works

ˢσου,‖ κἀγὼ ᵗδείξω σοι‖ ἐκ τῶν.ἔργων.μου τὴν.πίστιν ᵘμου.‖
¹thy, and I will shew thee from my works ²faith ¹my.

19 σὺ πιστεύεις ὅτι ˅ὁ θεὸς εἷς ἐστιν.‖ καλῶς ποιεῖς· καὶ τὰ
Thou believest that God ²one ¹is. ⁵Well ³thou ⁴doest; even the

δαιμόνια πιστεύουσιν, καὶ φρίσσουσιν. 20 θέλεις.δὲ γνῶναι,
demons believe, and shudder. But wilt thou know,

ὦ ἄνθρωπε κενέ, ὅτι ἡ πίστις χωρὶς τῶν.ἔργων ʷνεκρά‖ ἐστιν;
O ²man ¹empty, that faith apart from works dead is?

21 Ἀβραὰμ ὁ.πατὴρ.ἡμῶν οὐκ ἐξ ἔργων ἐδικαιώθη, ἀνε-
³Abraham ⁴our ⁵father ²not ⁷by ⁸works ¹was ⁶justified, having

νέγκας Ἰσαὰκ τὸν.υἱὸν.αὐτοῦ ἐπὶ τὸ θυσιαστήριον; 22 βλέ-
offered Isaac his son upon the altar? Thou

πεις ὅτι ἡ πίστις ˣσυνήργει‖ τοῖς.ἔργοις.αὐτοῦ, καὶ ἐκ τῶν
seest that faith was working with his works, and by the

ἔργων ἡ πίστις ἐτελειώθη; ʸ 23 καὶ ἐπληρώθη ἡ γραφὴ ἡ
works faith was perfected. And was fulfilled the scripture which

λέγουσα, Ἐπίστευσεν.δὲ Ἀβραὰμ τῷ.θεῷ, καὶ ἐλογίσθη
says, Now ²believed ¹Abraham God, and it was reckoned

αὐτῷ εἰς δικαιοσύνην, καὶ φίλος θεοῦ ἐκλήθη. 24 Ὁρᾶτε
to him for righteousness, and friend of God he was called. Ye see

ᶻτοίνυν‖ ὅτι ἐξ ἔργων δικαιοῦται ἄνθρωπος, καὶ οὐκ ἐκ πίστεως
then that by works is justified a man, and not by faith

μόνον.ᵃ 25 ὁμοίως.δὲ καὶ Ῥαὰβ ἡ πόρνη οὐκ ἐξ ἔργων
only. But in like manner also ³Rahab ⁴the ⁵harlot ²not ⁷by ⁸works

ἐδικαιώθη, ὑποδεξαμένη τοὺς ἀγγέλους, καὶ ἑτέρᾳ ὁδῷ
¹was ⁶justified, having received the messengers, and by another way

ἐκβαλοῦσα; 26 ὥσπερ.γὰρ τὸ σῶμα χωρὶς πνεύματος
having put [them] forth? For as the body apart from spirit

νεκρόν ἐστιν, οὕτως καὶ ἡ πίστις χωρὶς ᵇτῶν‖ ἔργων νεκρά
²dead ¹is, so also faith apart from works ²dead

ἐστιν.
¹is.

3 Μὴ πολλοὶ διδάσκαλοι γίνεσθε, ἀδελφοί.μου, εἰδότες ὅτι
²Not ³many ⁴teachers ¹be, my brethren, knowing that

μεῖζον κρίμα ᶜληψόμεθα.ᵈ 2 πολλὰ.γὰρ πταίομεν ἅπαντες.
greater judgment we shall receive. For ²often ¹we ³stumble ⁴all.

ⁿ — δὲ now TTr.   ° — ὦσιν TTrA.   ᴾ — τὸ L.   ᵠ ἔχῃ ἔργα GLTTrAW.   ʳ χωρὶς apart
from GLTTrAW.   ˢ — σου LTTrAW.   ᵗ σοι δείξω TTr.   ᵘ — μου TTrAW.   ˅ εἷς ἐστιν
ὁ θεός LTTr ; εἷς ὁ θεός ἐστιν AW.   ʷ ἀργή idle LTTrA.   ˣ συνεργεῖ works with TTr.
ʸ *Read verse* 22 *interrogatively, as pointed in the Greek.* EGLTrW.   ᶻ — τοίνυν GLTTrAW.
ᵃ *Read verse* 24 *as a question* GLTr.   ᵇ — τῶν T[Tr].   ᶜ λημψόμεθα LTTrA.

εἰ τις ἐν λόγῳ οὐ πταίει. οὖτος τέλειος ἀνήρ, δυνατὸς
If anyone in word stumble not, this one [is] a perfect man, able ·

χαλιναγωγῆσαι καὶ ὅλον τὸ σῶμα. 3 ᵈ'Ἰδοὺ‖ τῶν ἵππων
to bridle also ²whole ¹the body. Lo, ⁶of ⁷the ⁸horses

τοὺς χαλινοὺς εἰς τὰ στόματα βάλλομεν ᵉπρὸς‖ τὸ πείθεσθαι
¹the ²bits ³in ⁴the ⁵mouths we put, for ²to ³obey

αὐτοὺς ἡμῖν,‖ καὶ ὅλον τὸ σῶμα αὐτῶν μετάγομεν. 4 Ἰδοὺ
¹them us, and ²whole ¹their body we turn about. Lo,

καὶ τὰ πλοῖα τηλικαῦτα ὄντα, καὶ ὑπὸ ᵍσκληρῶν ἀνέμων‖
also the ships, ²so ³great ¹being, and by violent winds

ἐλαυνόμενα, μετάγεται ὑπὸ ἐλαχίστου πηδαλίου, ὅπου
being driven, are turned about by a very small rudder, wherever

ʰἂν‖ ἡ ὁρμὴ τοῦ εὐθύνοντος ⁱβούληται.‖ 5 οὕτως καὶ
the impulse of him who steers may will. Thus also

ἡ γλῶσσα μικρὸν μέλος ἐστίν, καὶ ᵏμεγαλαυχεῖ.‖ Ἰδού,
the tongue a little member is, and boasts great things. Lo,

ˡὀλίγον· πῦρ ἡλίκην ὕλην ἀνάπτει· 6 ᵐκαὶ‖ ἡ γλῶσσα
a little fire how large a wood it kindles; and the tongue [is]

πῦρ, ὁ κόσμος τῆς ἀδικίας. ⁿοὕτως‖ ἡ γλῶσσα καθίσταται
fire, the world of unrighteousness. Thus the tongue is set

ἐν τοῖς μέλεσιν ἡμῶν, ᵒἡ‖ σπιλοῦσα ὅλον τὸ σῶμα, καὶ φλο-
in our members, the defiler [of] ²whole ¹the body, and setting

γίζουσα τὸν τροχὸν τῆς γενέσεως, καὶ φλογιζομένη ὑπὸ τῆς
on fire the course of nature, and being set on fire by

γεέννης· 7 πᾶσα γὰρ φύσις θηρίων τε καὶ πετεινῶν, ἑρπε-
gehenna. For every species both of beasts and of birds, ²of ³creeping

τῶν τε καὶ ἐναλίων, δαμάζεται καὶ ᵒδεδάμασται τῇ
⁴things ¹both and things of the sea, is subdued and has been subdued by

φύσει τῇ ἀνθρωπίνῃ· 8 τὴν δὲ γλῶσσαν οὐδεὶς ᴾδύναται
²species ¹the ²human; but the tongue no one ³is ⁴able

ἀνθρώπων δαμάσαι·‖ �q ἀκατάσχετον ⁴ κακόν, μεστὴ ἰοῦ
¹of ²men to subdue; [it is] an unrestrainable evil, full of ²poison

θανατηφόρου. 9 ἐν αὐτῇ εὐλογοῦμεν ʳτὸν θεὸν‖ καὶ πατέρα,
¹death-bringing. Therewith we bless God and [the] Father,

καὶ ἐν αὐτῇ καταρώμεθα τοὺς ἀνθρώπους τοὺς καθ'
and therewith we curse ¹men who according to [the]

ὁμοίωσιν θεοῦ γεγονότας· 10 ἐκ τοῦ αὐτοῦ στόματος ἐξέρ-
likeness of God are made. Out of the same mouth goes

χεται εὐλογία καὶ κατάρα. οὐ χρή, ἀδελφοί μου, ταῦτα
forth blessing and cursing. ²Not ⁵ought, ¹my ²brethren, ²these ³things

οὕτως γίνεσθαι. 11 μήτι ἡ πηγὴ ἐκ τῆς αὐτῆς ὀπῆς
thus to be. ²The ⁴fountain ⁵out ⁶of ⁷the ⁸same ⁹opening

βρύει τὸ γλυκὺ καὶ τὸ πικρόν; 12 μὴ δύναται, ἀδελφοί
¹pours ²forth sweet and bitter? Is able, ²brethren

μου, συκῆ ἐλαίας ποιῆσαι, ἢ ἄμπελος σῦκα; ˢοὕτως‖ ᵗοὐδεμία
¹my, a fig-tree olives to produce, or a vine figs? Thus no

πηγὴ ἁλυκὸν καὶ‖ γλυκὺ ποιῆσαι ὕδωρ.
fountain [is able] salt and sweet ²to ³produce ¹water.

13 Τίς σοφὸς καὶ ἐπιστήμων ἐν ὑμῖν; δειξάτω ἐκ τῆς
Who [is] wise and understanding among you; let him shew out of

offend not in word, the same *is* a perfect man, *and* able also to bridle the whole body. 3 Behold, we put bits in the horses' mouths, that they may obey us; and we turn about their whole body. 4 Behold also the ships, which though *they be* so great, and *are* driven of fierce winds, yet are they turned about with a very small helm, whithersoever the governor listeth. 5 Even so the tongue is a little member, and boasteth great things. Behold, how great a matter a little fire kindleth ! 6 And the tongue *is* a fire, a world of iniquity : so is the tongue among our members, that it defileth the whole body, and setteth on fire the course of nature ; and it is set on fire of hell. 7 For every kind of beasts, and of birds, and of serpents, and of things in the sea, is tamed, and hath been tamed of mankind · 8 but the tongue can no man tame ; *it is* an unruly evil, full of deadly poison. 9 Therewith bless we God, even the Father; and therewith curse we men, which are made after the similitude of God. 10 Out of the same mouth proceedeth blessing and cursing. My brethren, these things ought not so to be. 11 Doth a fountain send forth at the same place sweet *water* and bitter? 12 Can the fig tree, my brethren, bear olive berries? either a vine, figs? so *can* no fountain both yield salt water and fresh.

13 Who *is* a wise man and endued with knowledge among you?

ᵈ ἴδε G ; εἰ δὲ but if (*read* καὶ also) LTTrAW.　　ᵉ εἰς LTTrA.　　ᶠ ἡμῖν αὐτούς A.
ᵍ ἀνέμων σκληρῶν LTTrAW.　　ʰ — ἂν (*read* where) TTr.　　ⁱ βούλεται wills TTr.
ᵏ μεγάλα αὐχεῖ LTTrA.　　ˡ ἡλίκον *literally* how great (*some translate* how small) LTTrAW.
ᵐ — καὶ (*read* the tongue kindles. A fire, &c.) T.　　ⁿ — οὕτως LTTrAW.　　ᵒ καὶ
(*read* both defiling) T.　　ᴾ δαμάσαι δύναται ἀνθρώπων LTrA.　　q ἀκατάστατον an unsettled
LTTrAW.　　ʳ τὸν κύριον the Lord LTTrA.　　ˢ — οὕτως LTTrAW.　　ᵗ οὔτε ἁλυκὸν neither
salt [water is able] GLTTrAW.

let him shew out of a good conversation his works with meekness of wisdom. 14 But if ye have bitter envying and strife in your hearts, glory not, and lie not against the truth. 15 This wisdom descendeth not from above, but is earthly, sensual, devilish. 16 For where envying and strife is, there is confusion and every evil work. 17 But the wisdom that is from above is first pure, then peaceable, gentle, and easy to be intreated, full of mercy and good fruits, without partiality, and without hypocrisy. 18 And the fruit of righteousness is sown in peace of them that make peace. IV. From whence come wars and fightings among you? come they not hence, even of your lusts that war in your members? 2 Ye lust, and have not: ye kill, and desire to have, and cannot obtain: ye fight and war, yet ye have not, because ye ask not. 3 Ye ask, and receive not, because ye ask amiss, that ye may consume it upon your lusts. 4 Ye adulterers and adulteresses, know ye not that the friendship of the world is enmity with God? Whosoever therefore will be a friend of the world is the enemy of God. 5 Do ye think that the scripture saith in vain, The spirit that dwelleth in us lusteth to envy? 6 But he giveth more grace. Wherefore he saith, God resisteth the proud, but giveth grace unto the humble. 7 Submit yourselves therefore to God. Resist the devil, and he will flee from you. 8 Draw nigh to God, and he will draw nigh to you. Cleanse your hands, ye sinners; and purify your hearts, ye double minded. 9 Be afflicted, and mourn, and weep: let your

καλῆς ἀναστροφῆς τὰ.ἔργα.αὐτοῦ ἐν πραΰτητι σοφίας. 14 εἰ.δὲ
good   conduct   his works   in meekness of wisdom;   but if

ζῆλον   πικρὸν ἔχετε καὶ ἐριθείαν ἐν τῇ.καρδίᾳ.ὑμῶν, μὴ κατα-
²emulation ¹bitter ye have and contention in   your heart,   ²not ¹do

καυχᾶσθε ⁰καὶ ψεύδεσθε κατὰ τῆς ἀληθείας.‖ 15 Οὐκ ἔστιν
boast against and lie   against the   truth.   ³Not ²is

αὕτη ἡ σοφία ἄνωθεν κατερχομένη, ᵛἀλλ᾽‖ ἐπίγειος, ψυ-
¹this the wisdom from above coming down, but   earthly, na-

χική, δαιμονιώδης. 16 ὅπου.γὰρ ζῆλος καὶ ἐριθεία, ἐκεῖ
tural, devilish.   For where emulation and contention [are]; there

ἀκαταστασία καὶ πᾶν φαῦλον πρᾶγμα. 17 ἡ.δὲ ἄνωθεν
[is] commotion and every evil   thing.   But the ²from ³above

σοφία πρῶτον μὲν ἁγνή ἐστιν, ἔπειτα εἰρηνική, ἐπιεικής,
¹wisdom ⁵first   ⁶pure ⁴is,   then   peaceable, gentle,

εὐπειθής, μεστὴ ἐλέους καὶ καρπῶν ἀγαθῶν, ἀδιάκριτος ʷκαὶ‖
yielding, full of mercy and of ²fruits ¹good, impartial   and

ἀνυπόκριτος. 18 καρπὸς.δὲ ˣτῆς‖ δικαιοσύνης ἐν εἰρήνῃ σπεί-
unfeigned.   But [the] fruit   of righteousness in peace   is

ρεται τοῖς ποιοῦσιν εἰρήνην. 4 Πόθεν πόλεμοι καὶ ʸ
sown for those that make peace.   Whence [come] wars and

μάχαι ἐν ὑμῖν; οὐκ ἐντεῦθεν, ἐκ τῶν.ἡδονῶν.ὑμῶν
fightings among you? [Is it] not thence, from your pleasures,

τῶν στρατευομένων ἐν τοῖς.μέλεσιν.ὑμῶν; 2 ἐπιθυμεῖτε, καὶ
which war   in   your members?   Ye desire,   and

οὐκ.ἔχετε· φονεύετε καὶ ζηλοῦτε, καὶ οὐ.δύνασθε ἐπιτυχεῖν·
have not ; ye kill and are emulous, and are not able to obtain ;

μάχεσθε καὶ πολεμεῖτε, ᶻοὐκ.ἔχετε ᵃδέ,‖ διὰ τὸ μὴ αἰτεῖσθαι
ye fight and war,   ²ye ³have ⁴not ¹but because ⁵not ²ask

ὑμᾶς· 3 αἰτεῖτε, καὶ οὐ.λαμβάνετε, διότι κακῶς αἰτεῖσθε ἵνα
¹you.   Ye ask, and receive not, because evilly ye ask, that

ἐν ταῖς.ἡδοναῖς.ὑμῶν δαπανήσητε. 4 ᵇΜοιχοὶ καὶ‖ μοιχα-
in   your pleasures ye may spend [it]. Adulterers and adulte-

λίδες, οὐκ.οἴδατε ὅτι ἡ φιλία τοῦ κόσμου, ἔχθρα ᶜτοῦ
resses, know ye not that the friendship of the world enmity [with]

θεοῦ ἐστιν;‖ ὃς.ᵈἄν‖ οὖν βουληθῇ φίλος εἶναι τοῦ κόσμου,
God is?   Whosoever therefore be minded a friend to be of the world,

ἐχθρὸς τοῦ θεοῦ καθίσταται. 5 ἢ δοκεῖτε ὅτι κενῶς ἡ γρα-
an enemy of God is constituted. Or think ye that in vain the scrip-

φὴ λέγει;ᵉ πρὸς φθόνον ἐπιποθεῖ τὸ πνεῦμα ὃ ᶠκατῴκησεν
ture speaks? with envy does ³long ¹the ²Spirit which took up [his] abode

ἐν ἡμῖν;ᵍ 6 μείζονα.δὲ δίδωσιν χάριν· διὸ λέγει, Ὁ θεὸς
in us?   But ²greater ¹he ²gives grace. Wherefore he says,   God

ὑπερηφάνοις ἀντιτάσσεται, ταπεινοῖς.δὲ δίδωσιν χάριν.
[⁴the] ⁵proud ¹sets ²himself ³against, but to [the] lowly he gives grace.

7 Ὑποτάγητε οὖν τῷ θεῷ. ἀντίστητε ʰ τῷ διαβόλῳ, καὶ
Subject yourselves therefore to God. Resist the devil,   and

φεύξεται ἀφ᾽ ὑμῶν· 8 ἐγγίσατε τῷ θεῷ, καὶ ἐγγιεῖ ὑμῖν.
he will flee from you. Draw near to God, and he will draw near to you.

καθαρίσατε χεῖρας, ἁμαρτωλοί, καὶ ἁγνίσατε καρδίας,
Have cleansed [your] hands, sinners,   and have purified [your] hearts,

δίψυχοι. 9 ταλαιπωρήσατε καὶ πενθήσατε ⁱκαὶ‖ κλαύσατε.
ye double minded. Be wretched, and mourn,   and weep.

ᵘ τῆς ἀληθείας καὶ ψεύδεσθε T.   ᵛ ἀλλὰ TTr.   ʷ — καὶ LTTrA.   ˣ — τῆς GLTTrAW.
ʸ + πόθεν whence LTTrAW.   ᶻ + καὶ and T.   ᵃ — δέ GLTTrA.   ᵇ — Μοιχοὶ καὶ
LTTrAW ; join adulteresses to what precedes T.   ᶜ ἐστὶν τῷ θεῷ is with God T.   ᵈ ἐὰν LT.
ᵉ — ; Text. Rec. and LA.   ᶠ κατῴκισεν he made to dwell LTTrA.   ᵍ — ; T.   ʰ + δὲ but
(resist) LTTrA.   ⁱ — καὶ T.

ὁ.γέλως.ὑμῶν εἰς πένθος μεταστραφήτω, καὶ　　ἡ.χαρὰ εἰς
²Your ³laughter ⁴to ³mourning　¹let be turned,　and　[your] joy　to

κατήφειαν. 10 ταπεινώθητε ἐνώπιον ᵏτοῦ‖ κυρίου, καὶ ὑψώ-
heaviness.　10 Humble yourselves before　　the　Lord,　and he will

σει ὑμᾶς.
exalt you.

11 Μὴ.καταλαλεῖτε ἀλλήλων, ἀδελφοί·　ὁ　καταλαλῶν
Speak not against　one another,　brethren.　He that speaks against

ἀδελφοῦ, ¹καὶ‖ κρίνων τὸν.ἀδελφὸν.αὐτοῦ, καταλαλεῖ
[his] brother,　and　judges　his brother,　　speaks against [the]

νόμου, καὶ κρίνει　νόμον· εἰ.δὲ νόμον κρίνεις, οὐκ
law,　and　judges [the] law.　But if [the] law thou judgest, ³not

εἶ　ποιητὴς νόμου, ἀλλὰ κριτής. 12 εἷς ἐστιν ὁ νομο-
¹thou ²art　a doer　of [the] law,　but a judge.　One is　the　law-

θέτηςᵐ, ὁ δυνάμενος σῶσαι καὶ ἀπολέσαι· σὺ ⁿ τίς εἶ ᵒὃς
giver,　who　is able　to save　and to destroy: ³thou ¹who ²art that

κρίνεις‖ τὸν ᵖἕτερον‖;
judgest　the　other?

13 Ἄγε νῦν οἱ λέγοντες, Σήμερον ᑫκαὶ‖ αὔριον ʳπορευ-
Go to now, ye who　say,　To-day　and to-morrow we may

σώμεθα‖ εἰς τήνδε.τὴν.πόλιν, καὶ ˢποιήσωμεν‖ ἐκεῖ ἐνιαυτὸν
go　into　such a city　· and　may spend　there ²year

¹ἕνα‖ καὶ ᵛἐμπορευσώμεθα,‖ καὶ ʷκερδήσωμεν·‖ 14 οἵτινες οὐκ
¹one and　may traffic,　and　may make gain,　ye who ²not

ἐπίστασθε ˣτὸ‖ τῆς αὔριον·　ποία.ʸγὰρ‖ η.ζωὴ.ὑμῶν;
¹know　what on the morrow [will be], (for what [is]　your life?

ἀτμὶς ᶻγὰρ‖ ᵃἐστιν‖ ἡ πρὸς ὀλίγον　φαινομένη, ἔπειτα
A vapour even　it is, which for　a little [while]　appears,　²then

ᵇδὲ‖ ἀφανιζομένη· 15 ἀντὶ τοῦ λέγειν.ὑμᾶς, Ἐὰν ὁ κύριος
¹and　disappears,)　instead of　your saying,　If the Lord

θελήσῃ, καὶ ᶜζήσωμεν,‖ καὶ ᵈποιήσωμεν‖ τοῦτο ἢ ἐκεῖνο.
should will　and we should live, also　we may do　this　or　that.

16 νῦν.δὲ καυχᾶσθε ἐν ταῖς.ᵉἀλαζονείαις‖.ὑμῶν· πᾶσα καύχη-
But now　ye boast in　your vauntings :　　all　²boasting

σις τοιαύτη πονηρά ἐστιν. 17 εἰδότι　οὖν καλὸν ποιεῖν,
¹such　evil　is.　To [him] knowing therefore good　to do,

καὶ μὴ ποιοῦντι,　ἁμαρτία αὐτῷ ἐστιν.
and not doing [it],　sin　to him it is.

5 Ἄγε νῦν οἱ.πλούσιοι, κλαύσατε ὀλολύζοντες ἐπὶ ταῖς
Go to now,　[ye] rich,　weep,　howling　over

ταλαιπωρίαις ὑμῶν ταῖς　ἐπερχομέναις. 2 ὁ.πλοῦτος
²miseries　¹your　that [are]　coming upon [you].　²Riches

ὑμῶν σέσηπεν, καὶ τὰ.ἱμάτια.ὑμῶν σητόβρωτα γέγονεν·
¹your　have rotted, and　your garments　moth-eaten　have become.

3 ὁ.χρυσὸς.ὑμῶν καὶ ὁ.ἄργυρος　κατίωται,　καὶ ὁ.ἰὸς.αὐτῶν
Your gold　and　silver　has been eaten away, and　their canker

εἰς μαρτύριον ὑμῖν ἔσται, καὶ φάγεται τὰς.σάρκας.ὑμῶν ὡς
for a testimony against you shall be, and　shall eat　your flesh　as

πῦρ· ἐθησαυρίσατε ἐν　ἐσχάταις ἡμέραις. 4 ἰδού, ὁ μισθὸς
fire.　Ye treasured up　in [the]　last　days.　Lo,　the　hire

---

laughter be turned to mourning, and your joy to heaviness. 10 Humble yourselves in the sight of the Lord, and he shall lift you up.

11 Speak not evil one of another, brethren. He that speaketh evil of his brother, and judgeth his brother, speaketh evil of the law, and judgeth the law : but if thou judge the law, thou art not a doer of the law, but a judge. 12 There is one lawgiver, who is able to save and to destroy : who art thou that judgest another?

13 Go to now, ye that say, To day or to morrow we will go into such a city, and continue there a year, and buy and sell, and get gain : 14 whereas ye know not what shall be on the morrow. For what is your life? It is even a vapour, that appeareth for a little time, and then vanisheth away. 15 For that ye ought to say, If the Lord will, we shall live, and do this, or that. 16 But now ye rejoice in your boastings : all such rejoicing is evil. 17 Therefore to him that knoweth to do good, and doeth it not, to him it is sin.

V. Go to now, ye rich men, weep and howl for your miseries that shall come upon you. 2 Your riches are corrupted, and your garments are moth-eaten. 3 Your gold and silver is cankered ; and the rust of them shall be a witness against you, and shall eat your flesh as it were fire. Ye have heaped treasure together for the last days. 4 Behold, the

---

ᵏ — τοῦ (read [the]) LTTrA.　　¹ ἢ or LTTrA.　　ᵐ + καὶ κριτής and judge, GLTTrA.　ⁿ + δὲ but (who) GLTTrA.　ᵒ ὁ κρίνων LTTrA.　ᵖ πλησίον (read [thy] neighbour) LTTrA.　ᑫ ἢ or ELTTr.　ʳ πορευσόμεθα we will go ELTTrAW.　ˢ ποιήσομεν will spend ELTAW.　ᵗ — ἕνα (read a year) LTTr.　ᵛ ἐμπορευσόμεθα will traffic ELTTrAW.　ʷ κερδήσομεν will make gain ELTTrAW.　ˣ τὰ L.　ʸ [γὰρ] Tr.　ᶻ — γάρ L.　ᵃ ἐστε ye are LTTrAW.　ᵇ καὶ LTTrA ;　— δὲ W.　ᶜ ζήσομεν we shall live LTTrAW.　ᵈ ποιήσομεν we shall do ELTTrAW.　ᵉ ἀλαζονίαις T.

hire of the labourers who have reaped down your fields, which is of you kept back by fraud, crieth : 'and the cries of them which have reaped are entered into the ears of the Lord of sabaoth. 5 Ye have lived in pleasure on the earth, and been wanton ; ye have nourished your hearts, as in a day of slaughter. 6 Ye have condemned *and* killed the just ; *and* he doth not resist you.

7 Be patient therefore, brethren, unto the coming of the Lord. Behold, the husbandman waiteth for the precious fruit of the earth, and hath long patience for it, until he receive the early and latter rain. 8 Be ye also patient ; stablish your hearts : for the coming of the Lord draweth nigh. 9 Grudge not one against another, brethren, lest ye be condemned : behold, the judge standeth before the door. 10 Take, my brethren, the prophets, who have spoken in the name of the Lord, for an example of suffering affliction, and of patience. 11 Behold, we count them happy which endure. Ye have heard of the patience of Job, and have seen the end of the Lord ; that the Lord is very pitiful, and of tender mercy. 12 But above all things, my brethren, swear not, neither by heaven, neither by the earth, neither by any other oath : but let your yea be yea ; and *your* nay, nay, lest ye fall into condemnation. 13 Is any among you afflicted? let him pray. Is any merry? let him sing psalms. 14 Is any sick among you? let him call for the elders of the church ; and let them pray over him, anointing him with oil in the name of the

τῶν ἐργατῶν τῶν ἀμησάντων τὰς χώρας ὑμῶν, ὁ ᶠἀπεστερη-
of the workmen who harvested your fields, which has been

μένος,� ἀφ᾽ ὑμῶν κράζει, καὶ αἱ βοαὶ τῶν θερισάιτων εἰς
kept back by you, cries out, and the cries of those who reaped, into

τὰ ὦτα κυρίου Σαβαὼθ ᵍεἰσεληλύθασιν.‖ 5 ἐτρυφήσατε
the ears of [the] Lord of Hosts have entered. Ye lived in indulgence

ἐπὶ τῆς γῆς, καὶ ἐσπαταλήσατε. ἐθρέψατε τὰς καρδίας ὑμῶν
upon the earth, and lived in self-gratification; ye nourished your hearts

ʰὡς‖ ἐν ἡμέρᾳ σφαγῆς. 6 κατεδικάσατε, ἐφονεύσατε τὸν δί-
as in a day of slaughter; ye condemned, ye killed, the

καιον· οὐκ ἀντιτάσσεται ὑμῖν.
just; he does not resist you.

7 Μακροθυμήσατε οὖν, ἀδελφοί, ἕως τῆς παρουσίας τοῦ
Be patient therefore, brethren, till the coming of the

κυρίου. ἰδού, ὁ γεωργὸς ἐκδέχεται τὸν τίμιον καρπὸν τῆς
Lord. Lo, the husbandman awaits the precious fruit of the

γῆς, μακροθυμῶν ἐπ᾽ αὐτῷ ἕως ⁱἂν‖ λάβῃ ʲὑετὸν‖ ᵏπρώ-
earth, being patient for it until it receive [the] ʳrain ʲear-

ιμον‖ καὶ ὄψιμον· 8 μακροθυμήσατε καὶ ὑμεῖς, στηρίξατε
ly ³and ³latter. Be patient also ye: establish

τὰς καρδίας ὑμῶν, ὅτι ʰἡ παρουσία τοῦ κυρίου ἤγγικεν.
your hearts, because the coming of the Lord has drawn near.

9 Μὴ στενάζετε ˡκατ᾽ ἀλλήλων, ἀδελφοί,‖ ἵνα μὴ ᵐκατακρι-
Groan not against one another, brethren, that not ¹ye ²be con-

θῆτε·‖ ἰδού, ⁿ κριτὴς πρὸ τῶν θυρῶν ἕστηκεν. 10 Ὑπό-
demned. Lo, [the] judge before the door stands. [As] an ex-

δειγμα λάβετε ᵒτῆς κακοπαθείας, ἀδελφοί μου,‖ καὶ τῆς
ample ²take ¹of ²suffering ³evils, ⁷my ⁶brethren, ⁴and

μακροθυμίας, τοὺς προφήτας οἳ ἐλάλησαν ᵖ τῷ ὀνόματι κυ-
⁵of ⁶patience, the prophets who spoke in the name of [the]

ρίου. 11 ἰδού, μακαρίζομεν τοὺς ᑫὑπομένοντας.‖ τὴν ὑπο-
Lord. Lo, we call blessed those who endure. The en-

μονὴν Ἰὼβ ἠκούσατε, καὶ τὸ τέλος κυρίου ʳεἴδετε,‖ ὅτι
durance of Job ye have heard of, and the end of [the] Lord ye saw; that

πολύσπλαγχνός ἐστιν ὁ κύριος καὶ οἰκτίρμων. 12 Πρὸ
full of tender pity is the Lord and compassionate. ²Before

πάντων δέ, ἀδελφοί μου, μὴ ὀμνύετε, μήτε τὸν οὐρανόν,
³all ⁴things ¹but my brethren, swear not, neither [by] heaven,

μήτε τὴν γῆν, μήτε ἄλλον τινὰ ὅρκον· ἤτω δὲ ὑμῶν τὸ ναί,
nor the earth; nor any other oath; but let be of you the yea,

ναί, καὶ τὸ οὔ, οὔ· ἵνα μὴ ˢεἰς ὑπόκρισιν‖ πέσητε. 13 κακο-
yea, and the nay, nay, that not into hypocrisy ye may fall. Does ²suf-

παθεῖ τις ἐν ὑμῖν; προσευχέσθω· εὐθυμεῖ τις;
fer ⁵hardships ¹anyone ²among ³you? let him pray: is ²cheerful ¹anyone?

ψαλλέτω. 14 ἀσθενεῖ τις ἐν ὑμῖν; προσκαλεσάσθω
let him praise; is ²sick ¹anyone among you? let him call to [him]

τοὺς πρεσβυτέρους τῆς ἐκκλησίας, καὶ προσευξάσθωσαν ἐπ᾽
the elders of the assembly, and let them pray over

αὐτόν, ἀλείψαντες ᵗαὐτὸν‖ ἐλαίῳ ἐν τῷ ὀνόματι ᵛτοῦ‖ κυρίου·
him, having anointed him with oil in the name of the Lord;

ᶠ ἀφυστερημένος ᴛᴛʳ.   ᵍ εἰσελήλυθαν ʟᴛᴛʳᴀ́ᴡ.   ʰ — ὡς ʟᴛᴛʳᴀᴡ.   ⁱ — ἂν ᴛᴛʳᴀ.
ʲ — ὑετὸν (*read* [rain]) ʟᴛᴛʳᴀ.   ᵏ πρόϊμον ᴛᴛʳ.   ˡ ἀδελφοί, κατ᾽ ἀλλήλων ʟᴛʳᴀ.   ᵐ κρι-
θῆτε ¹ye ²be judged ɢʟᴛᴛʳᴀᴡ.   ⁿ + ὁ τῆς ɢʟᴛᴛʳᴀᴡ.   ᵒ , ἀδελφοί μου, τῆς κακοπαθείας
(— μου my ʟᴛᴛʳᴀᴡ) ɢʟᴛᴛʳᴀᴡ.   ᵖ + ἐν (the) ʟᴛᴛʳ.   ᑫ ὑπομείναντας endured ʟᴛᴛʳᴀ.
ʳ ἴδετε see ye ᴀ.   ˢ ὑπὸ κρίσιν under judgment ᴇɢʟᴛᴛʳᴀᴡ.   ᵗ — αὐτὸν (*read* [him]) ᴛ.
ᵛ — τοῦ (*read* of [the]) ʟ[ᴛʳ]ᴀ.

15 καὶ ἡ εὐχὴ τῆς πίστεως σώσει τὸν κάμνοντα, καὶ ἐγε-
and the prayer · of faith shall save the exhausted one, and ²will

ρεῖ αὐτὸν ὁ κύριος· κἂν ἁμαρτίας ᾖ.πεποιηκώς,
¹raise²up ⁶him ¹the ²Lord; and if ⁷sins ¹he ²be[³one ⁴who] ⁵has ⁶committed,

ἀφεθήσεται αὐτῷ. 16 ἐξομολογεῖσθε ʷ ἀλλήλοις
it shall be forgiven him.   Confess   to one another [your]

ˣτὰ παραπτώματα,ǁ καὶ ʸεὔχεσθεǁ ὑπὲρ ἀλλήλων, ὅπως ἰαθῆ-
offences,   and pray   for one another, that ye may be

τε. πολὺ ἰσχύει δέησις δικαίου ἐνεργουμένη.
healed. ²Much ⁵prevails [¹the] ³supplication ⁴of ²a ³righteous [⁷man] ⁶operative.

17 ᶻἩλίαςǁ ἄνθρωπος ἦν ὁμοιοπαθὴς ἡμῖν, καὶ προσευχῇ
Elias   ²a ³man   ¹was of like feelings to us, and with prayer

προσηύξατο τοῦ μὴ βρέξαι· καὶ οὐκ.ἔβρεξεν ἐπὶ τῆς γῆς
he prayed [for it]   not to rain; and it did not rain upon the earth

ἐνιαυτοὺς τρεῖς καὶ μῆνας ἕξ. 18 καὶ πάλιν προσηύξατο, καὶ
²years ¹three and ²months ¹six;   and again he prayed, and

ὁ οὐρανὸς ᵃὑετὸν ἔδωκεν,ǁ καὶ ἡ γῆ ἐβλάστησεν τὸν
the heaven ²rain ¹gave,   and the earth caused ³to ⁴sprout

καρπὸν αὐτῆς.
²fruit ¹its.

19. Ἀδελφοὶ, ᵇ ἐάν τις ἐν ὑμῖν πλανηθῇ ἀπὸ τῆς ἀλη-
Brethren,   if anyone among you   err   from the truth,

θείας, καὶ ἐπιστρέψῃ τις αὐτόν, 20 ᶜγινωσκέτωǁ ὅτι ὁ
and ²bring ³back ¹anyone him,   let him know that he who

ἐπιστρέψας ἁμαρτωλὸν ἐκ πλάνης ὁδοῦ.αὐτοῦ, σώσει
brings back   a sinner   from [the] error   of his way, shall save

ψυχὴν ᵈ ἐκ θανάτου, καὶ καλύψει πλῆθος ἁμαρτιῶν.
a soul   from death,   and shall cover a multitude of sins.

ᵉἸακώβου ἐπιστολή.ǁ
²Of ³James ¹epistle.

ᶠΠΕΤΡΟΥ ΚΑΘΟΛΙΚΗ ΕΠΙΣΤΟΛΗ ΠΡΩΤΗ.ǁ
⁴OF ⁵PETER   ²GENERAL   ³EPISTLE   ¹FIRST.

ΠΕΤΡΟΣ ἀπόστολος Ἰησοῦ χριστοῦ, ἐκλεκτοῖς παρεπιδήμοις
Peter,   apostle of Jesus   Christ, to [the] elect   sojourners

διασπορᾶς Πόντου, Γαλατίας, Καππαδοκίας, Ἀσίας, καὶ
of [the] dispersion of Pontus, of Galatia,   of Cappadocia,   of Asia, and

Βιθυνίας, 2 κατὰ πρόγνωσιν θεοῦ πατρός, ἐν ἁγιασ-
Bithynia,   according to [the] foreknowledge of God [the] Father, by sanctifi-

μῷ πνεύματος, εἰς ὑπακοὴν καὶ ῥαντισμὸν αἵματος
cation of [the] Spirit, unto [the] obedience and   sprinkling of [the] blood

Ἰησοῦ χριστοῦ· χάρις ὑμῖν καὶ εἰρήνη πληθυνθείη.
of Jesus Christ: Grace to you and   peace   be multiplied.

3 Εὐλογητὸς ὁ θεὸς καὶ πατὴρ τοῦ.κυρίου.ἡμῶν Ἰησοῦ
Blessed [be] the God and Father   of our Lord   Jesus

χριστοῦ, ὁ κατὰ τὸ.πολὺ.αὐτοῦ ἔλεος ἀναγεννήσας ᵍἡμᾶςǁ
Christ, who according to   his great   mercy begat ²again   ¹us

---

Lord: 15 and the prayer of faith shall save the sick, and the Lord shall raise him up; and if he have committed sins, they shall be forgiven him. 16 Confess *your* faults one to another, and pray one for another, that ye may be healed. The effectual fervent prayer of a righteous man availeth much. 17 Elias was a man subject to like passions as we are, and he prayed earnestly that it might not rain: and it rained not on the earth by the space of three years and six months. 18 And he prayed again, and the heaven gave rain, and the earth brought forth her fruit.

19 Brethren, if any of you do err from the truth, and one convert him ; 20 let him know, that he which converteth the sinner from the error of his way shall save a soul from death, and shall hide a multitude of sins.

PETER, an apostle of Jesus Christ, to the strangers scattered throughout Pontus, Galatia, Cappadocia, Asia, and Bithynia, 2 elect according to the foreknowledge of God the Father, through sanctification of the Spirit, unto obedience and sprinkling of the blood of Jesus Christ : Grace unto you, and peace, be multiplied.

3 Blessed *be* the God and Father of our Lord Jesus Christ, which according to

---

ʷ + οὖν therefore LTTrA.   ˣ τὰς ἁμαρτίας sins LTTr.   ʸ προσεύχεσθε L.   ᶻ Ἡλείας T.
ᵃ ἔδωκεν ὑετὸν LTTr.   ᵇ + μου my (brethren) LTTrA.   ᶜ γινώσκετε know ye A.
ᵈ + αὐτοῦ (read his soul) LT.   ᵉ — the subscription EGLTW; Ἰακώβου TrA.
ᶠ + τοῦ ἀποστόλου the apostle E; — καθολικη G; Πέτρου ἐπιστολὴ αʹ Tr; Πέτρου α LTAW.
ᵍ ὑμᾶς you E.

his abundant mercy hath begotten us again unto a lively hope by the resurrection of Jesus Christ from the dead, 4 to an inheritance incorruptible, and undefiled, and that fadeth not away, reserved in heaven for you, 5 who are kept by the power of God through faith unto salvation ready to be revealed in the last time. 6 Wherein ye greatly rejoice, though now for a season, if need be, ye are in heaviness through manifold temptations: 7 that the trial of your faith, being much more precious than of gold that perisheth, though it be tried with fire, might be found unto praise and honour and glory at the appearing of Jesus Christ: 8 whom having not seen, ye love; in whom, though now ye see *him* not, yet believing, ye rejoice with joy unspeakable and full of glory: 9 receiving the end of your faith, *even* the salvation of *your* souls. 10 Of which salvation the prophets have inquired and searched diligently, who prophesied of the grace *that should come* unto you: 11 searching what, or what manner of time the Spirit of Christ which was in them did signify, when it testified beforehand the sufferings of Christ, and the glory that should follow. 12 Unto whom it was revealed, that not unto themselves, but unto us they did minister the things, which are now reported unto you by them that have preached the gospel unto you with the Holy Ghost sent down from heaven; which things the angels desire to look into. 13 Wherefore gird up the loins of your mind, be sober, and hope to the end for the grace that is to be brought unto you at the revelation of Jesus Christ ; 14 as obedient children, not fashioning yourselves

εἰς ἐλπίδα ζῶσαν δι' ἀναστάσεως Ἰησοῦ χριστοῦ ἐκ
to a [2]hope [1]living through [the] resurrection of Jesus Christ from among

νεκρῶν, 4 εἰς κληρονομίαν ἄφθαρτον καὶ ἀμίαντον καὶ
[the] dead, to an inheritance incorruptible and undefiled and

ἀμάραντον, τετηρημένην ἐν οὐρανοῖς εἰς ʰἡμᾶς,‖ 5 τοὺς ἐν
unfading, reserved in [the] heavens for us, who by

δυνάμει θεοῦ φρουρουμένους διὰ πίστεως, εἰς σωτηρίαν
[the] power of God [are] being guarded through faith, for salvation

ἑτοίμην ἀποκαλυφθῆναι ἐν καιρῷ ἐσχάτῳ· 6 ἐν ᾧ ἀγαλ-
ready to be revealed in [the] [2]time [1]last. Wherein ye ex-

λιᾶσθε, ὀλίγον ἄρτι, εἰ δέον ⁱἐστίν,‖ λυπηθέντες
ult, for a little while at present, if necessary it is, having been put to grief

ἐν ποικίλοις πειρασμοῖς, 7 ἵνα τὸ δοκίμιον ὑμῶν τῆς πίστεως
in various trials, that the proving of your faith,

ᵏπολὺ τιμιώτερον‖ χρυσίου τοῦ ἀπολλυμένου, διὰ πυρὸς δὲ
(much more precious than gold that perishes,) [2]by [3]fire [1]though

δοκιμαζομένου, εὑρεθῇ εἰς ἔπαινον καὶ ˡτιμὴν καὶ δόξαν,‖ ἐν
being proved, be found to praise and honour and glory, in

ἀποκαλύψει Ἰησοῦ χριστοῦ· 8 ὃν οὐκ ᵐεἰδότες‖ ἀγαπᾶτε,
[the] revelation of Jesus Christ, whom not having seen ye love ;

εἰς ὃν ἄρτι μὴ ὁρῶντες, πιστεύοντες δέ, ἀγαλλιᾶσθε
on whom now [though] not looking, but believing, ye exult

χαρᾷ ἀνεκλαλήτῳ καὶ δεδοξασμένῃ, 9 κομιζόμενοι τὸ τέλος
with joy unspeakable and glorified, receiving the end .

τῆς πίστεως ὑμῶν, σωτηρίαν ψυχῶν· 10 περὶ ἧς
of your faith, [the] salvation of [your] souls ; concerning which

σωτηρίας ἐξεζήτησαν καὶ ⁿἐξηρεύνησαν‖ προφῆται οἱ περὶ
salvation [3]sought [10]out [11]and [12]searched [13]out [1]prophets, [2]who [4]of

τῆς εἰς ὑμᾶς χάριτος προφητεύσαντες, 11 ᵒἐρευνῶντες‖ εἰς
[5]the [7]towards [8]you [6]grace [3]prophesied ; searching to

τίνα ἢ ποῖον καιρὸν ἐδήλου τὸ ἐν αὐτοῖς πνεῦμα
what or what manner of time [7]was [8]signifying [1]the [5]in [6]them [2]Spirit

χριστοῦ, προμαρτυρόμενον τὰ εἰς χριστὸν παθήματα, καὶ
[3]of [4]Christ, testifying beforehand of the [2]belonging] [3]to [4]Christ [1]sufferings, and

τὰς μετὰ ταῦτα δόξας· 12 οἷς ἀπεκαλύφθη ὅτι οὐχ ἑαυτοῖς,
the [2]after [3]these [1]glories ; to whom it was revealed, that not to themselves

Pἡμῖν‖ δὲ διηκόνουν αὐτά, ἃ νῦν ἀνηγγέλη ὑμῖν διὰ
[2]to [3]us [1]but were serving those things, which now were announced to you by

τῶν εὐαγγελισαμένων ὑμᾶς ᵠἐν‖ πνεύματι ἁγίῳ ἀπο-
those who announced the glad tidings to you in [the] [2]Spirit [1]Holy

σταλέντι ἀπ' οὐρανοῦ, εἰς ἃ ἐπιθυμοῦσιν ἄγγελοι παρακύψαι.
sent from heaven, into which [2]desire [1]angels to look.

13 Διὸ ἀναζωσάμενοι τὰς ὀσφύας τῆς διανοίας ὑμῶν, νή-
Wherefore having girded up the loins of your mind, be-

φοντες, τελείως ἐλπίσατε ἐπὶ τὴν φερομένην ὑμῖν χάριν ἐν
ing sober, perfectly hope in the [2]being [3]brought [4]to [5]you [1]grace at

ἀποκαλύψει Ἰησοῦ χριστοῦ. 14 ὡς τέκνα ὑπακοῆς, μὴ
[the] revelation of Jesus Christ ; as children of obedience, not

ʳσυσχηματιζόμενοι‖ ταῖς πρότερον ἐν τῇ ἀγνοίᾳ ὑμῶν ἐπιθυ-
fashioning yourselves to the former [2]in [3]your [4]ignorance [1]de-

μίαις, 15 ἀλλὰ κατὰ τὸν καλέσαντα ὑμᾶς ἅγιον καὶ
sires ; but according as he who called you [is] holy, also

αὐτοὶ ἅγιοι ἐν πάσῃ ἀναστροφῇ γενήθητε· 16 διότι
[3]yourselves [4]holy [5]in [2]all [7]your] [8]conduct [1]be [6]ye ; because

---

ʰ ὑμᾶς you GLTTrAW. ⁱ — ἐστίν TTr. ᵏ πολυτιμότερον GLTTrA. ˡ δόξαν καὶ
τιμήν LTTrAW. ᵐ ἰδόντες LTTrAW. ⁿ ἐξηραύνησαν TTrA. ᵒ ἐραννῶντες TTrA.
ᴾ ὑμῖν to you GLTTrAW. ᵠ — ἐν (read ἁγίῳ by [the] Holy) LTrA. ʳ συνσ- TrA.

γέγραπται, Αγιοι ˢγένεσθε,‖ ᵗὅτι‖ ἐγὼ ἅγιός ᵛεἰμι.‖ 17 Καὶ
it has been written, ³Holy ¹be ²ye, because ¹ ²holy ¹am. And

εἰ πατέρα ἐπικαλεῖσθε τὸν ʷἀπροσωπολήπτως‖ κρίνοντα
if [as] Father ye call on him who without regard of persons judges

κατὰ τὸ ἑκάστου ἔργον, ἐν φόβῳ τὸν τῆς-παροικίας-ὑμῶν
according to the ²of ³each work, in fear the ²of ³your ˢsojourn

χρόνον ἀναστράφητε· 18 εἰδότες ὅτι οὐ φθαρτοῖς, ἀρ-
¹time pass ye, knowing that not by corruptible things, by

γυρίῳ ἢ χρυσίῳ, ἐλυτρώθητε ἐκ τῆς-ματαίας-ὑμῶν ἀναστροφῆς
silver or by gold, ye were redeemed from your vain manner of life

πατροπαραδότου, 19 ἀλλὰ τιμίῳ αἵματι ὡς ἀμνοῦ
handed down from [your] fathers, but by precious blood as of a lamb

ἀμώμου καὶ ἀσπίλου χριστοῦ· 20 προεγνωσ-
without blemish and without spot [the blood] of Christ: having been fore-

μένου μὲν πρὸ καταβολῆς κόσμου, φανερωθέντος-δὲ ἐπ'
known indeed before [the] foundation of [the] world, but manifested at

ˣἐσχάτων‖ τῶν χρόνων δι' ὑμᾶς, 21 τοὺς δι' αὐτοῦ
[the] last times for the sake of you, who by him

ʸπιστεύοντας‖ εἰς θεόν, τὸν ἐγείραντα αὐτὸν ἐκ νεκρῶν,
believe in God, who raised up him from among [the] dead,

καὶ δόξαν αὐτῷ δόντα, ὥστε τὴν-πίστιν-ὑμῶν καὶ ἐλπίδα εἶναι
and glory to him gave, so as for your faith and hope to be

εἰς θεόν. 22 Τὰς-ψυχὰς-ὑμῶν ἡγνικότες ἐν τῇ ὑπακοῇ τῆς
in God. Your souls having purified by obedience to the

ἀληθείας ᶻδιὰ‖ πνεύματος‖ εἰς φιλαδελφίαν ἀνυπόκριτον, ἐκ
truth through [the] Spirit to brotherly love unfeigned, out of

ᵃκαθαρᾶς‖ καρδίας ἀλλήλους ἀγαπήσατε ἐκτενῶς· 23 ἀναγε-
²pure ¹a heart one another love ye fervently. Having been

γεννημένοι οὐκ ἐκ σπορᾶς φθαρτῆς, ἀλλὰ ἀφθάρτου, διὰ
begotten again, not of ²seed ¹corruptible, but of incorruptible, by

λόγου ζῶντος θεοῦ καὶ μένοντος ᵇεἰς-τὸν-αἰῶνα.‖ 24 διότι
[the] word ³living ¹of ²God and abiding for ever. Because

πᾶσα σὰρξ ᶜὡς‖ χόρτος, καὶ πᾶσα δόξα ᵈἀνθρώπου‖ ὡς
all flesh [is] as grass, and all [the] glory of man as [the]

ἄνθος χόρτου. ἐξηράνθη ὁ χόρτος, καὶ τὸ ἄνθος ᵉαὐτοῦ‖
flower of grass. ³Withered ¹the ²grass, and the flower of it

ἐξέπεσεν· 25 τὸ-δὲ ῥῆμα κυρίου μένει εἰς-τὸν-αἰῶνα. Τοῦτο-δέ
fell away; but the word of [the] Lord abides for ever. But this

ἐστιν τὸ ῥῆμα τὸ εὐαγγελισθὲν εἰς ὑμᾶς.
is the word which was announced to you.

2 Ἀποθέμενοι οὖν πᾶσαν κακίαν καὶ πάντα δόλον καὶ
Having laid aside therefore all malice and all guile and

ὑποκρίσεις καὶ φθόνους καὶ πάσας καταλαλιάς, 2 ὡς ἀρτιγέν-
hypocrisies and envyings and all evil speakings, as new-

νητα βρέφη, τὸ λογικὸν ἄδολον γάλα ἐπιποθήσατε, ἵνα ἐν
born babes, the ²mental ¹genuine milk long ye after, that by

αὐτῷ αὐξηθῆτε, 3 ᵍεἴπερ‖ ἐγεύσασθε ὅτι χρηστὸς ὁ κύριος.
it ye may grow, if indeed ye did taste that [³is] ⁴good ¹the ²Lord.

4 πρὸς ὃν προσερχόμενοι, λίθον ζῶντα, ὑπὸ ἀνθρώπων μὲν
To whom coming, a ²-stone ¹living, by men indeed

ἀποδεδοκιμασμένον, παρὰ-δὲ θεῷ ἐκλεκτόν, ἔντιμον, 5 καὶ αὐ-
rejected, but with God chosen, precious, also your-

according to the form-
er lusts in your ignor-
ance: 15 but as he
which hath called you
is holy, so be ye holy
in all manner of con-
versation ; 16 because
it is written, Be ye
holy ; for I am holy.
17 And if ye call on
the Father, who with-
out respect of persons
judgeth according to
every man's work pass
the time of your so-
journing here in fear:
18 forasmuch as ye
know that ye were hot
redeemed with cor-
ruptible things, as
silver and gold, from
your vain conversa-
tion received by tradi-
tion from your fathers;
19 but with the pre-
cious blood of Christ,
as of a lamb without
blemish and without
spot : 20 who verily
was foreordained be-
fore the foundation of
the world, but was
manifest in these last
times for you, 21 who
by him do believe in
God, that raised him
up from the dead, and
gave him glory ; that
your faith and hope
might be in God.
22 Seeing ye have puri-
fied your souls in
obeying the truth
through the Spirit un-
to unfeigned love of
the brethren, see that
ye love one another
with a pure heart fer-
vently : 23 being born
again, not of corrupti-
ble seed, but of incor-
ruptible, by the word
of God, which liveth
and abideth for ever.
24 For all flesh is as
grass, and all the
glory of man as the
flower of grass. The
grass withereth, and
the flower thereof
falleth away : 25 but
the word of the Lord
endureth for ever. And
this is the word which
by the gospel is preach-
ed unto you.
II. Wherefore lay-
ing aside all malice,
and all guile, and hy-
pocrisies, and envies,
and all evil speakings,
2 as new born babes,
desire the sincere milk
of the word, that ye
may grow thereby :

ˢ ἔσεσθε ye shall be LTTrAW.   ᵗ διότι T.   ᵛ — εἰμι (read [am]) LTTrAW.   ʷ ἀπροσ-
ωπολήμπτως LTTrA.   ˣ ἐσχάτου (read end of the times) LTTrA.   ʸ πιστοὺς [are] believers LTTrA.   ᶻ διὰ πνεύματος LTTrAW.   ᵃ — καθαρᾶς (read from [the] heart) LTTrA.
ᵇ — εἰς τὸν αἰῶνα GLTTrAW.   ᶜ — ὡς L.   ᵈ αὐτῆς (read its glory) GLTTrAW.   ᵉ — αὐτοῦ LTTᵢ[A]W.   ᶠ + εἰς σωτηρίαν unto salvation GLTTrAW.   ᵍ εἰ if LTTᵣ.

3 if so be ye have tasted that the Lord is gracious. 4 To whom coming, *as unto* a living stone, disallowed indeed of men, but chosen of God, *and* precious, 5 ye also, as lively stones, are built up a spiritual house, an holy priesthood, to offer up spiritual sacrifices, acceptable to God by Jesus Christ. 6 Wherefore also it is contained in the scripture, Behold, I lay in Sion a chief corner stone, elect, precious: and he that believeth on him shall not be confounded. 7 Unto you therefore which believe *he is* precious: but unto them which be disobedient, the stone which the builders disallowed, the same is made the head of the corner, 8 and a stone of stumbling, and a rock of offence, *even to them* which stumble at the word, being disobedient: whereunto also they were appointed. 9 But ye *are* a chosen generation, a royal priesthood, an holy nation, a peculiar people; that ye should shew forth the praises of him who hath called you out of darkness into his marvellous light: 10 which in time past *were* not a people, but *are* now the people of God: which had not obtained mercy, but now have obtained mercy.

11 Dearly beloved, I beseech *you* as strangers and pilgrims, abstain from fleshly lusts, which war against the soul; 12 having your conversation honest among the Gentiles: that, whereas they speak against you as evildoers, they may by *your* good works, which they shall behold, glorify God in the day of visitation.

13 Submit yourselves to every ordinance of man for the Lord's sake: whether it be to the king, as supreme; 14 or unto governors, as unto them that are

τοὶ ὡς λίθοι ζῶντες ᵃοἰκοδομεῖσθε,‖ οἶκος πνευματικός, ᵏ
selves, as ²stones ¹living, are being built up, a ²house ¹spiritual,

ἱεράτευμα ἅγιον, ἀνενέγκαι πνευματικὰς θυσίας εὐπροσδέκτους
a ²priesthood ¹holy to offer spiritual sacrifices acceptable

ˡτῷ θεῷ διὰ Ἰησοῦ χριστοῦ. 6 ᵐΔιὸ καὶ‖ περιέχει ⁿἐν τῇ
to God by Jesus Christ. Wherefore also it is contained in the

γραφῇ,‖ Ἰδοὺ τίθημι ἐν Σιὼν λίθον ἀκρογωνιαῖον, ἐκλεκτόν,
scripture: Behold, I place in Sion a ²stone ¹corner, chosen,

ἔντιμον· καὶ ὁ πιστεύων ἐπʼ αὐτῷ οὐ.μὴ καταισχυνθῇ.
precious: and he that believes on him in no wise should be put to shame.

7 Ὑμῖν οὖν ἡ τιμὴ τοῖς πιστεύουσιν· ᵒἀπει-
To you therefore [³is] ⁴the ⁵preciousness ¹who ²believe; ⁷to[⁸those]⁹dis-

θοῦσιν‖ δέ, ᴾλίθον‖ ὃν ἀπεδοκίμασαν οἱ οἰκοδομοῦντες,
obeying ⁶but, [the] stone which ³rejected ¹those ²building,

οὗτος ἐγενήθη εἰς κεφαλὴν γωνίας, 8 καὶ λίθος προσκόμ-
this became head of [the] corner, and a stone of stum-

ματος καὶ πέτρα σκανδάλου· οἳ προσκόπτουσιν τῷ λόγῳ
bling and a rock of offence; who stumble at the word,

ἀπειθοῦντες, εἰς ὃ καὶ ἐτέθησαν· 9 ὑμεῖς.δὲ γένος ἐκ-
being disobedient, to which also they were appointed. But ye [are] a ²race

λεκτόν, βασίλειον ἱεράτευμα, ἔθνος ἅγιον, λαὸς εἰς|περι-
¹chosen, a kingly priesthood, a ²nation ¹holy, a people for¹ a pos-

ποίησιν, ὅπως τὰς ἀρετὰς ἐξαγγείλητε τοῦ ἐκ σκότους
session, that the virtues ye might set forth of him who out of darkness

ὑμᾶς καλέσαντος εἰς τὸ.θαυμαστὸν.αὐτοῦ φῶς· 10 οἱ ποτὲ
²you ¹called to his wonderful light; who once

οὐ λαός, νῦν.δὲ λαὸς θεοῦ· οἱ οὐκ.ἠλεημένοι,
[were] not a people, but now [are] ²people ¹God's; who had not received mercy,

νῦν.δὲ ἐλεηθέντες.
but now received mercy

11 Ἀγαπητοί, παρακαλῶ ὡς παροίκους καὶ παρεπιδή-
Beloved, I exhort [you] as strangers and sojourners,

μους, ἀπέχεσθαι�q τῶν σαρκικῶν ἐπιθυμιῶν, αἵτινες στρατεύον-
to abstain from fleshly desires, which war

ται κατὰ τῆς ψυχῆς· 12 τὴν.ἀναστροφὴν.ὑμῶν ἐν τοῖς
against the soul; ²your ²manner ⁶of ⁷life ¹among ⁸the

ἔθνεσιν ἔχοντες καλήν, ἵνα ἐν.ῷ καταλαλοῦσιν ὑμῶν ὡς
⁹nations ⁴having ⁵right that wherein they speak against you as

κακοποιῶν, ἐκ τῶν καλῶν ἔργων ʳἐποπτεύσαντες‖ δοξά-
evil doers, through [your] good works having witnessed they

σωσιν τὸν θεὸν ἐν ἡμέρᾳ ἐπισκοπῆς·
may glorify God in [the] day of visitation.

13 Ὑποτάγητε ˢοὖν‖ πάσῃ ἀνθρωπίνῃ κτίσει, διὰ
Be in subjection therefore to every human institution for the sake of

τὸν κύριον· εἴτε βασιλεῖ, ὡς ὑπερέχοντι· 14 εἴτε ἡγεμόσιν,
the Lord; whether to [the] king as supreme, or to governors

ὡς δἰ αὐτοῦ πεμπομένοις εἰς ἐκδίκησιν ᵗμὲν‖ κακοποιῶν,
as by him sent, for vengeance [on] evil doers,

ἔπαινον.δὲ ἀγαθοποιῶν· 15 ὅτι οὕτως ἐστὶν τὸ θέλημα
and praise [to] well doers; (because so is the will

τοῦ θεοῦ, ἀγαθοποιοῦντας φιμοῦν τὴν τῶν ἀφρόνων
of God, [by] well doing to put to silence the ²of ³senseless

ⁱ ἐποικοδομεῖσθε T.   ᵏ + εἰς for LTTrA.   ˡ — τῷ LTTrA.   ᵐ διότι because GLTTrAW.
ⁿ — τῇ TTrA ; ἡ γραφή (*read* the scripture contains) L.   ᵒ ἀπιστοῦσιν (*read* but to [those] unbelieving) TTr.   ᴾ λίθος LTrA.   q + ὑμᾶς (*read* that ye abstain) L.   ʳ ἐποπτεύ-οντες witnessing LTTrAW.   ˢ — οὖν LTTrA.   ᵗ — μὲν GLTTrAW.

ἀνθρώπων ἀγνωσίαν· 16 ὡς ἐλεύθεροι, καὶ μὴ ὡς ἐπικά-
of men [the] ignorance;) as free, and not as a

λυμμα ἔχοντες τῆς κακίας τὴν ἐλευθερίαν, ἀλλ᾽ ὡς ᵛδοῦλοι
cloak having of malice freedom, but as bondmen

θεοῦ.‖ 17 πάντας τιμήσατε, τὴν ἀδελφότητα ἀγαπᾶτε, τὸν
of God. All shew honour to, the brotherhood love,

θεὸν φοβεῖσθε, τὸν βασιλέα τιμᾶτε.
God fear, the king honour.

18 Οἱ οἰκέται, ὑποτασσόμενοι ἐν παντὶ φόβῳ τοῖς δεσ-
Servants, being subject with all fear to [your]

πόταις, οὐ μόνον τοῖς ἀγαθοῖς καὶ ἐπιεικέσιν, ἀλλὰ καὶ
masters, not only to the good and gentle, but also

τοῖς σκολιοῖς. 19 τοῦτο γὰρ χάρις, εἰ διὰ συνείδησιν
to the crooked. For this [is] acceptable if for sake of conscience

θεοῦ ὑποφέρει τις λύπας, πάσχων ἀδίκως. 20 ποῖον γὰρ
towards God endures anyone griefs, suffering unjustly. For what

κλέος, εἰ ἁμαρτάνοντες καὶ κολαφιζόμενοι ὑπομενεῖτε;
glory [is it], if sinning and being buffeted ye endure it?

ἀλλ᾽ εἰ ἀγαθοποιοῦντες καὶ πάσχοντες ὑπομενεῖτε, τοῦτο ʷ
but if doing good and suffering ye endure [it], this [is]

χάρις παρὰ θεῷ. 21 εἰς τοῦτο γὰρ ἐκλήθητε, ὅτι καὶ
acceptable with God. For to this ye were called; because also

χριστὸς ἔπαθεν ὑπὲρ ˣἡμῶν,‖ ʸἡμῖν‖ ὑπολιμπάνων ὑπογραμ-
Christ, suffered for us, us leaving a model

μόν, ἵνα ἐπακολουθήσητε τοῖς ἴχνεσιν αὐτοῦ· 22 ὃς ἁμαρτίαν
that ye should follow after in his steps; who sin

οὐκ ἐποίησεν, οὐδὲ εὑρέθη δόλος ἐν τῷ στόματι αὐτοῦ· 23 ὃς
did no, neither was found guile in his mouth; who,

λοιδορούμενος οὐκ ἀντελοιδόρει, πάσχων οὐκ ἠπείλει,
being railed at, railed not in return; [when] suffering threatened not;

παρεδίδου δὲ τῷ κρίνοντι δικαίως· 24 ὃς τὰς
but gave [himself] over to him who judges righteously; who

ἁμαρτίας ἡμῶν αὐτὸς ἀνήνεγκεν ἐν τῷ σώματι αὐτοῦ ἐπὶ τὸ
our sins himself bore in his body on the

ξύλον, ἵνα ταῖς ἁμαρτίαις ἀπογενόμενοι, τῇ δικαιοσύνῃ ζή-
tree, that, to sins [we] being dead, to righteousness we

σωμεν· οὗ τῷ μώλωπι αὐτοῦ‖ ἰάθητε. 25 ἦτε γὰρ ὡς πρό-
may live; by whose bruise ye were healed. For ye were as

βατα ᵃπλανώμενα·‖ ἀλλ᾽ ἐπεστράφητε νῦν ἐπὶ τὸν ποιμένα
sheep going astray, but are returned now to the shepherd

καὶ ἐπίσκοπον τῶν ψυχῶν ὑμῶν.
and overseer of your souls.

3 Ὁμοίως, ᵇαἱ‖ γυναῖκες, ὑποτασσόμεναι τοῖς ἰδίοις ἀν-
Likewise, wives, being subject to your own hus-

δράσιν, ἵνα καὶ εἴ τινες ἀπειθοῦσιν τῷ λόγῳ, διὰ τῆς τῶν
bands, that, even if any are disobedient to the word, by the of the

γυναικῶν ἀναστροφῆς ἄνευ λόγου ᶜκερδηθήσωνται,‖ 2 ἐπο-
wives conduct without [the] word they may be gained, hav-

πτεύσαντες τὴν ἐν φόβῳ ἁγνὴν ἀναστροφὴν ὑμῶν·
ing witnessed [carried out] in fear chaste conduct your;

3 ὧν ἔστω οὐχ ὁ ἔξωθεν ἐμπλοκῆς ᵈτριχῶν,‖ ᵉκαὶ‖
whose let it not be the outward [one] of braiding of hair, and

περιθέσεως χρυσίων, ἢ ἐνδύσεως ἱματίων κόσμος·
putting around of gold, or putting on of garments adorning;

---

sent by him for the punishment of evil-doers, and for the praise of them that do well. 15 For so is the will of God, that with well doing ye may put to silence the ignorance of foolish men: 16 as free, and not using your liberty for a cloke of malicious-ness, but as the ser-vants of God. 17 Ho-nour all men. Love the brotherhood. Fear God. Honour the king.

18 Servants, be sub-ject to your own masters with all fear; not only to the good and gentle, but also to the froward. 19 For this is thankworthy, if a man for conscience to-ward God endure grief, suffering wrongfully. 20 For what glory is it, if, when ye be buffeted for your faults, ye shall take it patiently? but if, when ye do well, and suffer for it, ye take it patient-ly, this is acceptable with God. 21 For even hereunto were ye called: because Christ also suffered for us, leaving us an ex-ample, that ye should follow his steps: 22 who did no sin, neither was guile found in his mouth: 23 who, when he was reviled, reviled not again; when he suffered, he threatened not; but committed himself to him that judgeth righteously: 24 who his own self bare our sins in his own body on the tree, that we, being dead to sins, should live un-to righteousness: by whose stripes ye were healed. 25 For ye were as sheep going astray; but are now returned unto the Shepherd and Bishop of your souls.

III. Likewise, ye wives, be in subjection to your own husbands; that, if any obey not the word, they also may without the word be won by the conver-sation of the wives; 2 while they behold your chaste conversa-tion coupled with fear. 3 Whose adorning let it not be that outward adorning of plaiting the hair, and of wear-

---

ᵛ θεοῦ δοῦλοι TTrA.   ʷ + γὰρ for (this) LA.   ˣ ὑμῶν you EGLTTrA.   ʸ ὑμῖν you
EGLTTrAW.   ᶻ — αὐτοῦ LTr[A].   ᵃ πλανώμενοι (read ye were going astray as sheep) LTTrA.
ᵇ — αἱ LTTr[A].   ᶜ κερδηθήσονται they will be gained LTTrA.   ᵈ — τριχῶν L.   ᵉ ἢ or L.

ing of gold, or of putting on of apparel; 4 but *let it be* the hidden man of the heart, in that which is not corruptible, *even the ornament* of a meek and quiet spirit, which is in the sight of God of great price. 5 For after this manner in the old time the holy women also, who trusted in God, adorned themselves, being in subjection unto their own husbands: 6 even as Sara obeyed Abraham, calling him lord: whose daughters ye are, as long as ye do well, and are not afraid with any amazement. 7 Likewise, ye husbands, dwell with *them* according to knowledge, giving honour unto the wife, as unto the weaker vessel, and as being heirs together of the grace of life; that your prayers be not hindered.

8 Finally, *be ye* all of one mind, having compassion one of another, love as brethren, *be* pitiful, *be* courteous: 9 not rendering evil for evil, or railing for railing: but contrariwise blessing; knowing that ye are thereunto called, that ye should inherit a blessing. 10 For he that will love life, and see good days, let him refrain his tongue from evil, and his lips that they speak no guile: 11 let him eschew evil, and do good; let him seek peace, and ensue it. 12 For the eyes of the Lord *are* over the righteous, and his ears *are* open unto their prayers: but the face of the Lord is against them that do evil. 13 And who is he that will harm you, if ye be followers of that which is good? 14 But and if ye suffer for righteousness' sake, happy *are ye*: and be not afraid of their terror, neither be troubled: 15 but sanctify the Lord God in your hearts: and *be*

4 ἀλλ' ὁ κρυπτὸς τῆς καρδίας ἄνθρωπος, ἐν τῷ ἀφθάρτῳ
but the hidden of the heart man, in the incorruptible

τοῦ ᶠπρᾳέος καὶ ἡσυχίου‖ πνεύματος, ὅ ἐστιν ἐνώπιον
[ornament] of the meek and quiet spirit, which is before

τοῦ θεοῦ πολυτελές. 5 οὕτως·γάρ ποτε καὶ αἱ ἅγιαι γυναῖκες
God of great price. For thus formerly also the holy women

αἱ ἐλπίζουσαι ᵍἐπὶ τὸν‖ θεὸν ἐκόσμουν ἑαυτάς, ὑποτασσό-
those hoping in God adorned themselves, being sub-

μεναι τοῖς·ἰδίοις ἀνδράσιν· 6 ὡς Σάῤῥα ʰὑπήκουσεν‖ τῷ
ject to their own husbands; as Sarah obeyed

Ἀβραάμ, ³κύριον αὐτὸν ²καλοῦσα, ἧς ἐγενήθητε τέκνα· ἀγα-
Abraham, ³lord ²him ¹calling; of whom ye became children, do-

θοποιοῦσαι καὶ μὴ·φοβούμεναι μηδεμίαν πτόησιν. 7 Οἱ
ing good and not fearing [with] any consternation.
(*lit.* no)

ἄνδρες ὁμοίως, συνοικοῦντες κατὰ γνῶσιν, ὡς ἀσθε-
Husbands likewise, dwelling with [them] according to knowledge, as with a

νεστέρῳ σκεύει τῷ γυναικείῳ ἀπονέμοντες τιμήν, ὡς
weaker ·[even] ⁴vessel ¹with ²the ³female, rendering [them] honour, as

καὶ ⁱσυγκληρονόμοι‖ χάριτος ζωῆς. εἰς τὸ μὴ ᵏἐκκόπτεσ-
also [being] joint-heirs of [the] grace of life, so as ³not ⁴to ⁵be ⁶cut

θαι‖ τὰς·προσευχὰς·ὑμῶν.
³off ¹your ²prayers.

8 Τὸ·δὲ·τέλος, πάντες ὁμόφρονες, συμπαθεῖς, φιλ-
Finally, all [being] of one mind, sympathizing, loving

άδελφοι, εὔσπλαγχνοι, ˡφιλόφρονες·‖ 9 μὴ ἀποδιδόντες
the brethren, tender hearted, friendly, not rendering

κακὸν ἀντὶ κακοῦ, ἢ λοιδορίαν ἀντὶ λοιδορίας· τοὐναντίον·δὲ
evil for evil, or railing for railing; but on the contrary,

εὐλογοῦντες, ᵐεἰδότες‖ ὅτι εἰς τοῦτο ἐκλήθητε, ἵνα εὐλογίαν
blessing, knowing that to this ye were called, that blessing

κληρονομήσητε. 10 ὁ·γὰρ θέλων ζωὴν ἀγαπᾶν, καὶ ἰδεῖν
ye should inherit. For he that wills ²life ¹to ²love, and to see

ἡμέρας ἀγαθάς, παυσάτω τὴν·γλῶσσαν·ᵃαὐτοῦ‖ ἀπὸ
²days ¹good, let him cause to cease his tongue from

κακοῦ, καὶ χείλη ⁿαὐτοῦ‖ τοῦ μὴ λαλῆσαι δόλον. 11 ἐκκλι-
evil, and ²lips ¹his not to speak guile. Let him turn

νάτω ᵒ ἀπὸ κακοῦ, καὶ ποιησάτω ἀγαθόν· ζητησάτω εἰρήνην,
aside from evil, and let him do good. Let him seek peace

καὶ διωξάτω αὐτήν. 12 ὅτι ᴾοἱ‖ ὀφθαλμοὶ κυρίου ἐπὶ
and let him pursue it: because the eyes of [the] Lord [are] on

δικαίους, καὶ ὦτα·αὐτοῦ εἰς δέησιν·αὐτῶν· πρόσωπον·δὲ
[the] righteous, and his ears towards their supplication. But [the] face

κυρίου ἐπὶ ποιοῦντας κακά. 13 καὶ τίς ὁ κακώ-
of [the] Lord [is] against those doing evil. And who [is] he that shall in-

σων ὑμᾶς, ἐὰν τοῦ ἀγαθοῦ ᑫμιμηταὶ‖ γένησθε;
jure you, if ²of ³that ⁴which [⁵is] ¹good ᶦimitators ye should be?

14 ἀλλ' εἰ καὶ πάσχοιτε διὰ δικαιοσύνην, μακάριοι.
But if also ye should suffer on account of righteousness, blessed [are ye]:

τὸν·δὲ·φόβον·αὐτῶν μὴ·φοβηθῆτε, μηδὲ ταραχθῆτε·
but their fear ye should not be afraid of, neither should ye be troubled;

15 κύριον·δὲ τὸν ʳθεὸν‖ ἁγιάσατε ἐν ταῖς·καρδίαις·ὑμῶν·
but ³Lord ²the ⁴God ¹sanctify in your hearts,

ᶠ ἡσυχίου καὶ πραέος L; πραέως (πραέος A) καὶ ἡσυχίου TTrA. ᵍ εἰς LTTrAW. ʰ ὑπήκουεν L. ⁱ συνκληρονόμοις T; συγκληρονόμοις to joint-heirs TrA. ᵏ ἐγκόπτεσθαι to be hindered GLTrAW; ἐν- T. ˡ ταπεινόφρονες humble minded GLTTrAW. ᵐ — εἰδότες (*read* ὅτι because) LTTrA. ⁿ — αὐτοῦ (*read* [his]) LTTrA. ᵒ + δὲ and (let him turn aside) LTrA. ᴾ — οἱ (*read* [the] Lord's eyes) LTTrA. ᑫ ζηλωταὶ zealous LTTrAW. ʳ χριστὸν Christ LTTrAW.

ἔτοιμοι.ˢδὲ‖ ἀεὶ πρὸς ἀπολογίαν παντὶ τῷ αἰτοῦντι ὑμᾶς
and ready [be] always for   a defence   to everyone   that asks you
λόγον   περὶ τῆς ἐν ὑμῖν ἐλπίδος, ᵗμετὰ πραΰτητος καὶ
an account concerning the ²in ³you ¹hope,   with   meekness and
φόβου· 16 συνείδησιν ἔχοντες ἀγαθήν, ἵνα ἐν.ᾧ ᵛκαταλαλῶ-
fear ;   ²a ⁴conscience ¹having   ³good, that whereas they may speak
σιν‖ ʷὑμῶν ὡς κακοποιῶν,‖ καταισχυνθῶσιν οἱ ἐπηρεάζοντες
against you as   evil doers,   they may be ashamed who calumniate
ὑμῶν τὴν ἀγαθὴν ἐν χριστῷ ἀναστροφήν. 17 κρεῖττον.γὰρ
your   good ⁴in ⁵Christ ¹manner ²of ³life.   For [it is] better,
ἀγαθοποιοῦντας, εἰ ˣθέλει‖ τὸ θέλημα τοῦ θεοῦ, πάσχειν,
[²for ⁹you] ¹⁰doing ¹¹good, ¹if ⁶wills [⁷it] the ³will   ⁴of ⁵God, to suffer,
ἢ κακοποιοῦντας· 18 ὅτι καὶ χριστὸς ἅπαξ περὶ ἁμαρ-
than doing evil;   because ²indeed ¹Christ once for sins
τιῶν ᵞἔπαθεν‖ δίκαιος ὑπὲρ ἀδίκων, ἵνα ἡμᾶς προσαγάγῃ
suffered, [the] just for [the] unjust, that us he might bring
ᶻτῷ‖ θεῷ, θανατωθεὶς μὲν σαρκί, ζωοποιηθεὶς.δὲ ᵃτῷ‖
to God ; having been put to death in flesh, but made alive by the
πνεύματι, 19 ἐν ᾧ καὶ τοῖς ἐν φυλακῇ πνεύμασιν πορευθεὶς
Spirit,   in which also to the ²in ³prison ¹spirits having gone
ἐκήρυξεν, 20 ἀπειθήσασίν ποτε, ὅτε ᵇἅπαξ ἐξεδέχετο‖ ἡ
he preached, [who] disobeyed sometime, when once was waiting the
τοῦ θεοῦ μακροθυμία ἐν ἡμέραις Νῶε,   κατασκευα-
²of ³God ¹longsuffering in [the] days of Noe, [while was] being pre-
ζομένης κιβωτοῦ, εἰς ἣν ᶜὀλίγαι,‖ ᵈτουτέστιν‖ ὀκτώ, ψυχαὶ
pared [the] ark, into which few,   that is   eight   souls
διεσώθησαν δι' ὕδατος, 21 ᵉὃ‖ καὶ ᶠἡμᾶς‖ ἀντίτυπον νῦν
were saved through water,   which ²also ¹us   ¹figure   ²now
σώζει βάπτισμα, οὐ σαρκὸς ἀπόθεσις ῥύπου, ἀλλὰ
⁴saves [even] baptism, not of flesh a putting away of [the] filth, but
συνειδήσεως ἀγαθῆς ἐπερώτημα εἰς θεόν, δι' ἀνα-
⁵of ⁶a.⁸conscience ¹good [¹the] ²demand ³towards ⁹God, by [the] re-
στάσεως Ἰησοῦ χριστοῦ, 22 ὅς ἐστιν ἐν δεξιᾷ ᵍτοῦ‖ θεοῦ,
surrection of Jesus Christ, who is at [the] right hand of God,
πορευθεὶς εἰς οὐρανόν, ὑποταγέντων αὐτῷ ἀγγέλων καὶ
gone into heaven, ⁸having ⁷been ⁶subjected ⁹to ¹⁰him ¹angels ²and
ἐξουσιῶν καὶ δυνάμεων.
²authorities ⁴and ⁵powers.

4 Χριστοῦ οὖν παθόντος ʰὑπὲρ ἡμῶν‖ σαρκί, καὶ ὑμεῖς τὴν
  Christ then having suffered for us in [the] flesh, also ye ⁴the
αὐτὴν ἔννοιαν ὁπλίσασθε· ὅτι ὁ παθὼν ⁱἐν‖ σαρκί,
⁵same   ⁶mind ¹arm ²yourselves ³with; for he that suffered in [the] flesh
πέπαυται ἁμαρτίας· 2 εἰς τὸ μηκέτι ἀνθρώπων ἐπιθυμίαις,
has done with sin ;   no longer ¹⁰men's   ²to ¹¹lusts,
ἀλλὰ θελήματι θεοῦ τὸν ἐπίλοιπον ἐν σαρκὶ βιῶσαι χρόνον.
¹²but ¹³to ¹⁵will ¹⁴God's ³the ⁴remaining ⁶in [⁷the] ⁵flesh ¹to ²live ⁸time.
3 ἀρκετὸς.γὰρ ᵏἡμῖν‖ ὁ παρεληλυθὼς χρόνος ˡτοῦ βίου,‖ τὸ
For [is] sufficient for us the   past   time   of life the
ᵐθέλημα‖ τῶν ἐθνῶν ⁿκατεργάσασθαι,‖ πεπορευμένους ἐν
will of the nations to have worked out,   having walked in

ready always to give
an answer to every
man that asketh you
a reason of the hope
that is in you with
meekness and fear:
16 having a good con-
science; that, where-
as they speak evil of
you, as of evildoers,
they may be ashamed
that falsely accuse
your good conversa-
tion in Christ. 17 For
it is better, if the will
of God be so, that ye
suffer for well doing,
than for evil doing.
18 For Christ also hath
once suffered for sins,
the just for the un-
just, that he might
bring us to God, being
put to death in the
flesh, but quickened by
the Spirit : 19 by which
also he went and
preached unto the spi-
rits in prison; 20 which
sometime were disobe-
dient, when once the
longsuffering of God
waited in the days
of Noah, while the
ark was a preparing,
wherein few, that is,
eight souls were saved
by water. 21 The like
figure whereunto even
baptism doth also now
save us (not the put-
ting away of the filth
of the flesh, but the
answer of a good con-
science toward God,)
by the resurrection of
Jesus Christ: 22 who is
gone into heaven, and
is on the right hand of
God; angels and au-
thorities and powers
being made subject un-
to him.

IV. Forasmuch then
as Christ hath suffered
for us in the flesh, arm
yourselves likewise
with the same mind :
for he that hath suf-
fered in the flesh hath
ceased from sin ; 2 that
he no longer should
live the rest of his time
in the flesh to the lusts
of men, but to the will
of God. 3 For the time
past of our life may
suffice us to have
wrought the will of
the Gentiles, when we

ˢ — δὲ and LTTr[A].   ᵗ + ἀλλὰ but LTTrAW.   ᵛ καταλαλοῦσιν they speak against
LTrW ; καταλαλεῖσθε ye are spoken against TA.   ʷ — ὑμῶν ὡς κακοποιῶν TA.   ˣ θέλοι
may will GLTTrAW.   ᵞ ἀπέθανεν died LTTr.   ᶻ — τῷ W.   ᵃ — τῷ (read [in the]) GLTTrAW.
ᵇ ἀπεξεδέχετο (omit once) GLTTrAW.   ᶜ ὀλίγοι few [persons] LTTrAW.   ᵈ τοῦτ' ἔστιν GT.
ᵉ ᾧ to which E.   ᶠ ὑμᾶς you LTTrA.   ᵍ — τοῦ TTr[A].   ʰ — ὑπὲρ ἡμῶν LTTrA.
ⁱ — ἐν (read [in]) LTTrA.   ᵏ — ἡμῖν LTTrA.   ˡ — τοῦ βίου LTTrAW.   ᵐ βούλημα LTTrAW.
ⁿ κατειργάσθαι LTTrAW.

walked in lasciviousness, lusts, excess of wine, revellings, banquetings, and abominable idolatries: 4 wherein the think it strange that ye run not with *them* to the same excess of riot, speaking evil of you: 5 who shall give account to him that is ready to judge the quick and the dead. 6 For for this cause was the gospel preached also to them that are dead, that they might be judged according to men in the flesh, but live according to God in the spirit.

7 But the end of all things is at hand : be ye therefore sober, and watch unto prayer. 8 And above all things have fervent charity among yourselves : for charity shall cover the multitude of sins. 9 Use hospitality one to another without grudging. 10 As every man hath received the gift, *even so* minister the same one to another, as good stewards of the manifold grace of God. 11 If any man speak, *let him speak* as the oracles of God ; if any man minister, *let him do it* as of the ability which God giveth : that God in all things may be glorified through Jesus Christ, to whom be praise and dominion for ever and ever. Amen.

12 Beloved, think it not strange concerning the fiery trial which is to try you, as though some strange thing happened unto you : 13 but rejoice, inasmuch as ye are partakers of Christ's sufferings; that, when his glory shall be revealed, ye may be glad also with exceeding joy. 14 If ye be reproached for the name of Christ, happy *are ye;* for the spirit of glory and of God resteth upon you: on their part he is evil spoken of, but on your part he is glorified. 15 But let none of you suffer as a murderer, or *as* a thief, or *as* an evildoer, or as a busybody in other men's matters. 16 Yet if *any*

ἀσελγείαις,　ἐπιθυμίαις,　οἰνοφλυγίαις,　κώμοις,　πότοις, και
licentiousness,　lusts,　wine-drinking,　revels,　drinkings, and
ἀθεμίτοις εἰδωλολατρείαις· 4 ἐν.ᾧ　ξενίζονται,　μὴ συν-
unhallowed idolatries.　Wherein they think it strange ²not　³run-
τρεχόντων　ὑμῶν εἰς τὴν αὐτὴν τῆς ἀσωτίας ἀνάχυσιν,
ning ⁴with [⁵them] ¹your to the　same　²of ³dissoluteness ¹overflow,
βλασφημοῦντες·　5 οἳ ἀποδώσουσιν λόγον τῷ ἑτοίμως
speaking evil　[of you]; who shall render　account to him ²ready
ἔχοντι κρῖναι　ζῶντας καὶ　νεκρούς. 6 εἰς.τοῦτο.γὰρ　καὶ
¹who ²is to judge [the] living　and [the] dead.　For.to this [end] also
νεκροῖς　εὐηγγελίσθη,　ἵνα　κριθῶσιν　μὲν
to [the] dead were the glad tidings announced, that they might be judged indeed
κατὰ ἀνθρώπους σαρκί,　ζῶσιν.δὲ κατὰ θεὸν πνεύματι.
as regards　men　in [the] flesh; but might live as regards God in [the] Spirit.

7 Πάντων.δὲ　τὸ τέλος　ἤγγικεν·　σωφρονήσατε　οὖν
But of all things the　end　has drawn near: be sober-minded therefore,
καὶ νήψατε εἰς ᵒτὰς‖ προσευχάς· 8 πρὸ πάντων ᴾδὲ‖ τὴν
and be watchful unto　prayers ;　²before ³all ⁴things ¹but
εἰς ἑαυτοὺς ἀγάπην ἐκτενῆ ἔχοντες, ὅτι ᑫ ἀγάπη ᵏκαλύψει‖
among yourselves ³love ²fervent ¹having, because love　will cover
πλῆθος ἁμαρτιῶν. 9 φιλόξενοι εἰς ἀλλήλους ἄνευ ˢγογγυσ-
a multitude of sins;　ho·pitable ·to one another, without murmur-
μῶν·‖ 10 ἕκαστος καθὼς　ἔλαβεν χάρισμα, εἰς ἑαυτοὺς
ings ;　each　according as he received　a gift,　to each other
αὐτὸ διακονοῦντες, ὡς καλοὶ οἰκονόμοι ποικίλης χάριτος
²it　¹serving,　as　good　stewards of [the] various　grace
θεοῦ· 11 εἴ τις λαλεῖ, ὡς λόγια θεοῦ· εἴ τις διακονεῖ, ὡς
of God.　If anyone speaks— as oracles of God ; if anyone serves—　as
ἐξ ἰσχύος ἧς χορηγεῖ ὁ θεός· ἵνα ἐν πᾶσιν δοξάζηται ὁ
of strength which ²supplies　¹God; that in all things may be glorified
θεὸς διὰ Ἰησοῦ χριστοῦ, ᾧ ἐστιν ἡ δόξα καὶ τὸ κράτος
God through Jesus　Christ, to whom is　the glory and the　might
εἰς τοὺς αἰῶνας τῶν αἰώνων. ἀμήν.
to the . ages of the ages.　Amen.

12 Ἀγαπητοί, μὴ.ξενίζεσθε τῇ ἐν ὑμῖν πυρώσει
Beloved, take not as strange the ⁴amongst ⁵you ¹fire [²of ³persecution]
πρὸς πειρασμὸν ὑμῖν　γινομένῃ, ὡς ξένου ὑμῖν
for　trial　to you [which is] taking place, as if a strange thing to you
συμβαίνοντος· 13 ἀλλὰ ᵏκαθὸ‖　κοινωνεῖτε τοῖς τοῦ χρισ-
[is]　happening;　but according as ye have share in the　²of
τοῦ παθήμασιν, χαίρετε, ἵνα καὶ ἐν τῇ ἀποκαλύψει τῆς δόξης
³Christ ¹sufferings,　rejoice, that also in the　revelation　of ²glory
αὐτοῦ　χαρῆτε ἀγαλλιώμενοι. 14 εἰ ὀνειδίζεσθε ἐν
¹his ye may rejoice　exulting.　If ye are reproached in [the]
ὀνόματι χριστοῦ, μακάριοι·　ὅτι τὸ　τῆς δόξηςᵛ καὶ
name　of Christ,　blessed [are ye]; because the [spirit]　of glory and
τὸ τοῦ θεοῦ πνεῦμα ἐφ᾽ ὑμᾶς ἀναπαύεται· ᵂκατὰ.μὲν.αὐτοὺς
the ²of ³God ¹Spirit upon you　rests;　on their part
βλασφημεῖται, κατὰ.δὲ.ὑμᾶς δοξάζεται.‖ 15 μὴ.γὰρ τις
he is blasphemed,　but on your part he is glorified.　Assuredly ²not ³anyone
ὑμῶν πασχέτω ὡς φονεύς, ἢ κλέπτης, ἢ κακοποιός, ἢ ὡς
⁴of ⁵you ¹let suffer as a murderer, or　thief,　or evil doer,　or as
ˣἀλλοτριοεπίσκοπος.‖ 16 εἰ.δὲ ὡς χριστιανός, μὴ αἰσχυ-
overlooker of other people's matters; but if as　a christian, ³not ¹let ²him

ᵒ — τὰς LTTrAW.　ᴾ — δὲ TTrA.　ᑫ + ἡ EG.　ʳ καλύπτει covers LTTrAW.　ˢ γογ-
γυσμοῦ murmuring LTTrAW.　ᵗ καθὼς E.　ᵛ + καὶ δυνάμεως and of power L.　ᵂ — κατὰ
μὲν to end of verse LTTrA.　ˣ ἀλλοτριεπίσκοπος LTTr.

νέσθω,   δοξαζέτω.δὲ τὸν θεὸν ἐν τῷ ʸμέρει‖ τούτῳ. 17 ὅτι
be ashamed, but let him glorify God in ²respect ¹this.   Because

ὁ καιρὸς τοῦ ἄρξασθαι τὸ κρίμα ἀπὸ τοῦ οἴκου τοῦ θεοῦ·
the time [for] ³to ⁴have ⁵begun ¹the ²judgment from the house of God

εἰ.δὲ πρῶτον ἀφ᾽ ἡμῶν, τί τὸ τέλος τῶν ἀπειθούντων
[is come]; but if first from us, what the end of those disobeying

τῷ τοῦ θεοῦ εὐαγγελίῳ; 18 καὶ εἰ ὁ δίκαιος μόλις σώζεται,
the ³of ⁴God ¹glad ²tidings? And if the righteous with difficulty is saved,

ὁ ἀσεβὴς καὶ ᶻἁμαρτωλὸς ποῦ φανεῖται; 19 ὥστε καὶ
³the ⁴ungodly ⁵and ⁶sinner ¹where ²shall appear?   Wherefore also

οἱ πάσχοντες κατὰ τὸ θέλημα τοῦ θεοῦ, ᵃὡς‖ πιστῷ
they who suffer according to the will of God as to a faithful

κτίστῃ παρατιθέσθωσαν τὰς.ψυχὰς.ᵇἑαυτῶν‖ ἐν ᶜἀγαθοποιΐᾳ.‖
Creator let them commit their souls in well doing.

5 Πρεσβυτέρους ᵈ ᵉτοὺς‖ ἐν ὑμῖν παρακαλῶ ὁ ᶠσυμ-
Elders who [are] among you I exhort who [am] fellow

πρεσβύτερος‖ καὶ μάρτυς τῶν τοῦ χριστοῦ παθημάτων, ὁ
elder and witness of the ²of ³the ⁴Christ ¹sufferings, who

καὶ τῆς μελλούσης ἀποκαλύπτεσθαι δόξης κοινωνός, 2 ποι-
also of the ²about ³to ⁴be ⁵revealed ¹glory [am] partaker: shep-

μάνατε τὸ ἐν ὑμῖν ποίμνιον τοῦ θεοῦ, ᵍἐπισκοποῦντες‖ μὴ
herd the ⁴among ⁵you ¹flock ²of ³God, exercising oversight not

ἀναγκαστῶς, ʰἀλλ᾽‖ ἑκουσίως·ⁱ μηδὲ αἰσχροκερδῶς, ἀλλὰ προ-
by constraint, but willingly; not for base gain, but. readi-

θύμως· 3 μηδ᾽ ὡς κατακυριεύοντες τῶν κλήρων, ἀλλὰ
ly ; not as exercising lordship over [your] possessions, but

τύποι γινόμενοι τοῦ ποιμνίου· 4 καὶ φανερωθέντος
patterns being of the flock. And ⁴having ⁵been ⁶manifested

τοῦ ἀρχιποίμενος, κομιεῖσθε τὸν ἀμαράντινον τῆς δόξης
¹the ²chief ³shepherd, ye shall receive the unfading ²of ³glory

στέφανον.
¹crown.

5 Ὁμοίως, νεώτεροι, ὑποτάγητε πρεσβυτέροις· πάντες
Likewise, [ye] younger [ones], be subject to [the] elder [ones], ²all

δὲ ἀλλήλοις ᵏὑποτασσόμενοι‖ τὴν ταπεινοφροσύνην ἐγκομβώ-
¹and one to another being subject ²humility ¹bind

σασθε· ὅτι ὁ θεὸς ὑπερηφάνοις ἀντιτάσσεται, ταπεινοῖς
²on ; because God [the] proud sets himself against, ²to [³the] ⁴humble

δὲ δίδωσιν χάριν. 6 ταπεινώθητε οὖν ὑπὸ τὴν κραταιὰν
¹but gives grace. Be humbled therefore under the mighty

¹χεῖρα‖ τοῦ θεοῦ, ἵνα ὑμᾶς ὑψώσῃ ἐν καιρῷᵐ· 7 πᾶσαν
hand of God, that you he may exalt in [due] time ; all

τὴν.μέριμναν.ὑμῶν ⁿἐπιρρίψαντες‖ ἐπ᾽ αὐτόν, ὅτι αὐτῷ
your care having cast upon him, because with him

μέλει περὶ ὑμῶν. 8 νήψατε, γρηγορήσατε, ᵒὅτι‖ ὁ ἀντίδικος
there is care about you. Be sober, watch, because ²adversary

ὑμῶν διάβολος, ὡς λέων ὠρυόμενος, περιπατεῖ, ζητῶν ᵖτίνα‖
¹your [the] · devil, as a ²lion ¹roaring, goes about, seeking whom

ᑫκαταπίῃ·‖ 9 ᾧ ἀντίστητε στερεοὶ τῇ πίστει, εἰδότες τὰ
he may swallow up. Whom resist, firm in faith, knowing the

αὐτὰ τῶν παθημάτων τῇ ἐν ʳκόσμῳ ὑμῶν.ἀδελφότητι
same sufferings ⁷which [⁸is] ⁹in [¹⁰the] ¹¹world ⁴in ⁵your ⁶brotherhood

ʸ ὀνόματι name LTTrAW. ᵃ — ὡς LTTrA. ᵇ αὐτῶν LTTrAW.
ᶜ ἀγαθοποιΐαις LW. ᵈ + οὖν then LTTrA. ᵉ — τοὺς LTrA. ᶠ συν- T. ᵍ — ἐπισκοποῦντες T[A]. ʰ ἀλλὰ TTrA. ⁱ + κατὰ θεόν according to God LTTr. ᵏ — ὑποτασσόμενοι LTTrAW. ˡ χεῖραν T. ᵐ + ἐπισκοπῆς (read in time of visitation) L. ⁿ ἐπιρίψαντες LTTrA. ᵒ — ὅτι GLTTrAW. ᵖ τινὰ some one L. ᑫ καταπιεῖν to swallow up LTA ;
καταπίειν Tr. ʳ + τῷ the TTr.

accomplished in your brethren that are in the world. 10 But the God of all grace, who hath called us unto his eternal glory by Christ Jesus, after that ye have suffered a while, make you perfect, stablish, strengthen, settle *you*. 11 To him *be* glory and dominion for ever and ever. Amen.

ἐπιτελεῖσθαι. 10 ὁ.δὲ θεὸς πάσης χάριτος, ὁ καλέσας
¹are ²being ³accomplished. But the God of all grace, who called
ˢἡμᾶς⸗ εἰς τὴν αἰώνιον αὐτοῦ δόξαν ἐν χριστῷ ᵗ'Ιησοῦ,‖ ὀλίγον
us to ²eternal ¹his glory in Christ Jesus, a little while
παθόντας, αὐτὸς ᵛκαταρτίσαι ὑμᾶς,‖ ʷστηρίξαι, σθενώ-
[ye] having suffered, ²himself ¹may perfect you, may he establish, may he
σαι,‖ ˣθεμελιώσαι⸗ 11 αὐτῷ ʸἡ δόξα καὶ‖ τὸ κράτος εἰς
strengthen, may he found [you]: to him [be] the glory and the might, to
τοὺς αἰῶνας τῶν αἰώνων. ἀμήν.
the ages of the ages. Amen.

12 By Silvanus, a faithful brother unto you, as I suppose, I have written briefly, exhorting, and testifying that this is the true grace of God wherein ye stand. 13 The *church* that is at Babylon, elected together with *you*, saluteth you; and *so doth* Marcus my son. 14 Greet ye one another with a kiss of charity. Peace *be* with you all that are in Christ Jesus. Amen.

12 Διὰ Σιλουανοῦ ὑμῖν ᶻτοῦ‖ πιστοῦ ἀδελφοῦ, ὡς λογίζο-
By Silvanus, ⁴to⁵you ¹the ²faithful ³brother, as I reckon,
μαι, δι'.ὀλίγων ἔγραψα, παρακαλῶν καὶ ἐπιμαρτυρῶν ταύτην
briefly I wrote, exhorting and testifying this
εἶναι ἀληθῆ χάριν τοῦ θεοῦ, εἰς ἣν ᵃἑστήκατε.‖ 13 'Ασπά-
to be [the] true grace of God, in which ye stand. ⁷Sa-
ζεται ὑμᾶς ἡ ἐν Βαβυλῶνι συνεκλεκτή, καὶ Μάρκος
lutes ⁴you ¹she ⁵in ⁶Babylon ²elected ³with [⁴you], and Mark
ὁ.υἱός.μου. 14 ἀσπάσασθε ἀλλήλους ἐν φιλήματι ἀγάπης.
my son. Salute one another with a kiss of love.
εἰρήνη ὑμῖν πᾶσιν τοῖς ἐν χριστῷ ᵇ'Ιησοῦ.‖ ᶜἀμήν.‖
Peace [be] with you all who [are] in Christ Jesus. Amen.

ᵈΠέτρου ἐπιστολὴ καθολικὴ πρώτη.‖
⁴Of ⁵Peter ³Epistle ²General ¹First.

ᵉΕΠΙΣΤΟΛΗ ΠΕΤΡΟΥ ΚΑΘΟΛΙΚΗ ΔΕΥΤΕΡΑ.‖
³EPISTLE ⁴OF ⁵PETER ²GENERAL ¹SECOND.

SIMON Peter, a servant and an apostle of Jesus Christ, to them that have obtained like precious faith with us through the righteousness of God and our Saviour Jesus Christ: 2 Grace and peace be multiplied unto you through the knowledge of God, and of Jesus our Lord,

ᶠΣΥΜΕΩΝ‖ Πέτρος δοῦλος καὶ ἀπόστολος 'Ιησοῦ χριστοῦ,
Simeon Peter, bondman and apostle of Jesus Christ,
τοῖς ἰσότιμον ἡμῖν λαχοῦσιν πίστιν ἐν δικαιο-
to those who ²like ³precious ⁵with ⁶us ¹obtained ⁴faith through [the] right-
σύνῃ τοῦ.θεοῦ.ἡμῶν καὶ σωτῆρος ᵍ 'Ιησοῦ χριστοῦ· 2 χάρις
eousness of our God and Saviour Jesus Christ: Grace
ὑμῖν καὶ εἰρήνη πληθυνθείη ἐν ἐπιγνώσει τοῦ θεοῦ, καὶ
to you and peace be multiplied in [the] knowledge of God, and
'Ιησοῦ τοῦ.κυρίου.ἡμῶν.
of Jesus our Lord.

3 According as his divine power hath given unto us all things that *pertain* unto life and godliness, through the knowledge of him that hath called us to glory and virtue: 4 whereby are given unto us exceeding great and precious promises: that by these ye might be partakers of the divine nature, having escaped the

3 'Ωςʰ πάντα ἡμῖν τῆς θείας.δυνάμεως αὐτοῦ τὰ
As ⁸all ⁹things ⁶to ⁷us ²divine ³power ¹his ¹⁰which [¹¹pertain]
πρὸς ζωὴν καὶ εὐσέβειαν δεδωρημένης, διὰ τῆς ἐπιγνώσεως
¹²to ¹³life ¹⁴and ¹⁵piety ⁴has ⁵given, through the knowledge
τοῦ καλέσαντος ἡμᾶς ¹διὰ δόξης καὶ ἀρετῆς,‖ 4 δι' ὧν
of him who called us by glory and virtue, through which
τὰ ᵏμέγιστα ἡμῖν καὶ τίμια‖ ἐπαγγέλματα δεδώρηται, ἵνα
⁶the ⁷greatest ⁴to ⁵us ⁸and ⁹precious ¹⁰promises ¹has ²given, that
διὰ τούτων γένησθε θείας κοινωνοὶ φύσεως, ἀπο-
through these ye may become ²of [³the] ⁴divine ¹partakers nature, hav-

---

ˢ ὑμᾶς you LTTrAW. ᵗ — 'Ιησοῦ T[Tr].⸗ ᵛ καταρτίσει will perfect [you] LTTrAW.
ʷ στηρίξει, σθενώσει will establish, will strengthen GLTTrAW. ˣ θεμελιώσει will found
GTAW; — θεμελιώσαι LT. ʸ — ἡ δόξα καὶ LTTrA. ᶻ — τοῦ L. ᵃ στῆτε stand
ye LTTrA. ᵇ — 'Ιησοῦ LTTrA. ᶜ — ἀμήν GLTTrA. ᵈ — *the subscription* EGLTW;
Πέτρου α' TrA.
ᵉ + τοῦ ἀποστόλου the apostle E; — καθολικὴ G; Πέτρου β' LTAW; Πέτρου ἐπιστολὴ β' Tr.
ᶠ Σίμων Simon L. ᵍ + ἡμῶν our (Saviour) E. ʰ + τὰ T. ¹ ἰδίᾳ δόξῃ καὶ ἀρετῇ by [his]
own glory and virtue LTTrAW./ ᵏ μέγιστα καὶ τίμια ἡμῖν LTrA ; τίμια ἡμῖν καὶ μέγιστα T.

φυγόντες τῆς ἐν ¹κόσμῳ ἐν ἐπιθυμίᾳ φθορᾶς. 5 καὶ
ing escaped the ²in [³the] ⁴world ⁵through ⁶lust ¹corruption. ¹²also

ᵐαὐτὸ.τοῦτο‖ δέ, σπουδὴν πᾶσαν παρεισενέγκαν-
⁸for ⁹this ¹⁰very ¹¹reason ⁷but, ¹³diligence. ¹⁷all ¹³having ¹⁴brought ¹⁵in ¹⁶be-

τες, ἐπιχορηγήσατε ἐν τῇ.πίστει.ὑμῶν τὴν ἀρετήν, ἐν.δὲ τῇ ἀρετῇ
sides, supply ye in your faith virtue, and in virtue

τὴν γνῶσιν, 6 ἐν.δὲ τῇ γνώσει τὴν ἐγκράτειαν, ἐν.δὲ τῇ ἐγκρα-
knowledge, and in knowledge self-control, and in self-con-

τείᾳ τὴν ὑπομονήν, ἐν.δὲ τῇ ὑπομονῇ τὴν εὐσέβειαν, 7 ἐν.δὲ
trol endurance, and in endurance piety, and in

τῇ εὐσεβείᾳ τὴν φιλαδελφίαν, ἐν.δὲ τῇ φιλαδελφίᾳ τὴν ἀγάπην.
piety brotherly love, and in brotherly love love :

8 ταῦτα.γὰρ ὑμῖν ⁿὑπάρχοντα‖ καὶ πλεονάζοντα, οὐκ
for these things ³in ³you ¹being and abounding [³to ⁴be] ⁵neither

ἀργοὺς οὐδὲ ἀκάρπους καθίστησιν εἰς τὴν τοῦ.κυρίου.ἡμῶν
⁶idle ⁷nor ⁸unfruitful ¹make [²you] as to the ²of ³our ⁴Lord

Ἰησοῦ χριστοῦ ἐπίγνωσιν· 9 ᾧ.γὰρ μὴ.πάρεστιν ταῦτα
⁵Jesus ⁶Christ ¹knowledge; for with whom are not present these things

τυφλός ἐστιν, μυωπάζων, λήθην.λαβὼν τοῦ καθαρισμοῦ τῶν
blind · he is, short sighted, having forgotten the purification

πάλαι αὐτοῦ °ἁμαρτιῶν.‖ 10· Διὸ μᾶλλον, ἀδελφοί, σπου-
⁴of ⁵old ¹of ²his ³sins. Wherefore rather, brethren, be dili-

δάσατε ᵖ βεβαίαν ὑμῶν τὴν κλῆσιν καὶ ἐκλογὴν ᵠποιεῖσθαι·‖
gent ⁷sure ³your ⁴calling ⁵and ⁶election ¹to ²make,

ταῦτα.γὰρ ποιοῦντες οὐ.μὴ πταίσητέ ποτε. 11 οὕτως
for these things doing in no wise shall ye stumble at any time. Thus

γὰρ πλουσίως ἐπιχορηγηθήσεται ὑμῖν ἡ εἴσοδος εἰς τὴν αἰώ-
for ³richly ¹shall ²be supplied to you the entrance into the eter-

νιον βασιλείαν τοῦ.κυρίου.ἡμῶν καὶ σωτῆρος Ἰησοῦ χριστοῦ.
nal kingdom of our Lord and Saviour Jesus Christ.

12 Διὸ ʳοὐκ.ἀμελήσω‖ ˢὑμᾶς ἀεὶ‖ ὑπομιμνήσκειν
Wherefore I will not neglect ³you ⁴always ¹to ²put in remembrance

περὶ τούτων, καίπερ εἰδότας, καὶ ἐστηριγμένους ἐν
concerning these things, although knowing [them] and having been established in

τῇ παρούσῃ ἀληθείᾳ. 13 δίκαιον.δὲ ἡγοῦμαι, ἐφ'.ὅσον εἰμὶ ἐν
the present truth. But right I esteem it, as long as I am in

τούτῳ τῷ σκηνώματι, διεγείρειν ὑμᾶς ἐν ὑπομνήσει·
this tabernacle, to stir up you by putting [you] in remembrance,

14 εἰδὼς ὅτι ταχινή ἐστιν ἡ ἀπόθεσις τοῦ.σκηνώματός.μου,
knowing that speedily is the putting off of my tabernacle

καθὼς καὶ ὁ.κύριος.ἡμῶν Ἰησοῦς χριστὸς ἐδήλωσέν μοι.
[to be], as also our Lord Jesus Christ signified to me;

15 σπουδάσω.δὲ καὶ ἑκάστοτε ἔχειν.ὑμᾶς μετὰ
but I will be diligent also at every time for you to have [it in your power] after

τὴν.ἐμὴν ἔξοδον τὴν τούτων μνήμην.ποιεῖσθαι. 16 οὐ.γὰρ
my departure ⁵these ⁶things ¹to ²have ³in ⁴remembrance. For not

σεσοφισμένοις μύθοις ἐξακολουθήσαντες ἐγνωρίσαμεν ὑμῖν τὴν
⁴cleverly-imagined ⁵fables ¹having ²followed ³out we made known to you the

τοῦ.κυρίου.ἡμῶν Ἰησοῦ χριστοῦ δύναμιν καὶ παρουσίαν, ἀλλ'
⁴of ⁵our ⁶Lord ⁷Jesus ⁸Christ ¹power ²and ³coming, but

ἐπόπται γενηθέντες τῆς.ἐκείνου μεγαλειότητος. 17 λαβὼν
eye-witnesses having been of his majesty. ²Having ³received

γὰρ παρὰ θεοῦ πατρὸς τιμὴν καὶ δόξαν, φωνῆς ἐνεχθεί-
¹for from God [the] Father honour and glory, ²a ³voice ¹having ⁴been

corruption that is in the world through lust. 5 And beside this, giving all diligence, add to your faith virtue ; and to virtue knowledge ; 6 and to knowledge temperance ; and to temperance patience ; and to patience godliness ; 7 and to godliness brotherly kindness ; and to brotherly kindness charity. 8 For if these things be in you, and abound, they make you that ye shall neither be barren nor unfruitful in the knowledge of our Lord Jesus Christ. 9 But he that lacketh these things is blind, and cannot see afar off, and hath forgotten that he was purged from his old sins. 10 Wherefore the rather, brethren, give diligence to make your calling and election sure: for if ye do these things, ye shall never fall : 11 for so an entrance shall be ministered unto you abundantly into the everlasting kingdom of our Lord and Saviour Jesus Christ.

12 Wherefore I will not be negligent to put you always in remembrance of these things, though ye know them, and be established in the present truth. 13 Yea, I think it meet, as long as I am in this tabernacle, to stir you up by putting you in remembrance ; 14 knowing that shortly I must put off this my tabernacle, even as our Lord Jesus Christ hath shewed me. 15 Moreover I will endeavour that ye may be able after my decease to have these things always in remembrance. 16 For we have not followed cunningly devised fables, when we made known unto you the power and coming of our Lord Jesus Christ, but were eyewitnesses of his majesty. 17 For he received from God the Father honour and glory when there came such a voice to him from the excellent glory; This is my be-

¹ + τῷ the LTTr. ᵐ αὐτοὶ (read but ye also) L ⁿ παρόντα being present L.
° ἁμαρτημάτων GTTr. ᵖ + ἵνα διὰ τῶν καλῶν ὑμῶν ἔργων that by your good works L.
ᵠ ποιεῖσθε ye make L. ʳ μελλήσω I will take care LTTrAW. ˢ ἀεὶ ὑμᾶς GTTrAW.

loved Son, in whom I am well pleased. 18And this voice which came from heaven we heard, when we were with him in the holy mount. 19 We have also a more sure word of prophecy; whereunto ye do well that ye take heed, as unto a light that shineth in a dark place, until the day dawn, and the day star arise in your hearts: 20 knowing this first, that no prophecy of the scripture is of any private interpretation. 21 For the prophecy came not in old time by the will of man: but holy men of God spake as they were moved by the Holy Ghost.

II. But there were false prophets also among the people, even as there shall be false teachers among you, who privily shall bring in damnable heresies, even denying the Lord that bought them, and bring upon themselves swift destruction. 2 And many shall follow their pernicious ways; by reason of whom the way of truth shall be evil spoken of. 3 And through covetousness shall they with feigned words make merchandise of you: whose judgment now of a long time lingereth not, and their damnation slumbereth not. 4 For if God spared not the angels that sinned, but cast *them* down to hell, and delivered *them* into chains of darkness, to be reserved unto judgment; 5 and spared not the old world, but saved Noah the eighth *person*, a preacher of righteousness, bringing in the flood upon the world of the ungodly; 6 and turning the cities of Sodom and Gomorrha into ashes condemned *them* with an overthrow, making *them* an ensample unto those that after should live ungodly; 7 and delivered just Lot, vexed with the filthy conversation of the

σης   αὐτῷ τοιᾶσδε ὑπὸ τῆς μεγαλοπρεποῦς δόξης, Ὁὗτός
[6]brought [7]to [8]him [1]such by the   very excellent   glory :   This

ἐστιν ὁ.υἱός.μου ὁ ἀγαπητός,‖ εἰς ὃν ἐγὼ εὐδόκησα. 18 καὶ
is   my Son the beloved,   in whom I have found delight. And

ταύτην τὴν φωνὴν ἡμεῖς ἠκούσαμεν ἐξ οὐρανοῦ ἐνεχθεῖσαν,
this   voice   we   heard   [2]from [3]heaven [1]brought,

σὺν αὐτῷ ὄντες ἐν τῷ ᵛὄρει τῷ ἁγίῳ.‖ 19 καὶ ἔχομεν βεβαι-
with [6]him [4]being on the [2]mount [1]holy.   and we have   more

ότερον τὸν προφητικὸν λόγον, ᾧ καλῶς ποιεῖτε προσέχοντες,
sure   the prophetic word, to which [3]well [1]ye [2]do taking heed,

ὡς λύχνῳ φαίνοντι ἐν αὐχμηρῷ τόπῳ, ἕως.οὗ ἡμέρα διαυγάσῃ,
as to a lamp shining in an obscure place, until day should dawn,

καὶ φωσφόρος ἀνατείλῃ ἐν ταῖς.καρδίαις.ὑμῶν· 20 τοῦτο
and [the] morning star should arise in   your hearts;   this

πρῶτον γινώσκοντες, ὅτι πᾶσα προφητεία γραφῆς ἰδίας
first   knowing,   that [2]any [3]prophecy [4]of [5]scripture [6]of [8]its [9]own
(lit. every)

ἐπιλύσεως οὐ.γίνεται. 21 οὐ.γὰρ θελήματι ἀνθρώπου ἠνέχθη
[10]interpretation [6]is [1]not,   for not by [the] will of man was [2]brought

ʷποτὲ   προφητεία,‖ ˣἀλλ᾽‖ ὑπὸ   πνεύματος ἁγίου φερό-
[5]at [4]any [5]time [1]prophecy, but, [3]by [the] [2]Spirit [3]Holy [1]being

μενοι ἐλάλησαν ʸοἱ‖ ᶻἅγιοι‖ ᵃ θεοῦ ἄνθρωποι.
[2]borne, [12]spoke [7]the [8]holy [10]of [11]God [9]men.

2 Ἐγένοντο.δὲ καὶ ψευδοπροφῆται ἐν τῷ λαῷ, ὡς καὶ
But there were also   false prophets   among the people, as also

ἐν ὑμῖν ἔσονται ψευδοδιδάσκαλοι, οἵτινες παρεισάξουσιν
among you will be   false teachers,   who   will bring in stealthily

αἱρέσεις ἀπωλείας, καὶ τὸν ἀγοράσαντα αὐτοὺς δεσπότην ἀρ-
[2]sects [1]destructive, and [2]the [4]who [5]bought [6]them [3]Master [1]de-

νούμενοι, ἐπάγοντες ἑαυτοῖς ταχινὴν ἀπώλειαν· 2 καὶ πολλοὶ
nying,   bringing upon themselves swift destruction ; and many

ἐξακολουθήσουσιν αὐτῶν ταῖς ᵇἀπωλείαις,‖ δι᾽ οὓς ἡ ὁδὸς
will follow out   their   destructive ways, through whom the way

τῆς ἀληθείας βλασφημηθήσεται· 3 καὶ ἐν πλεονεξίᾳ πλασ-
of the truth   will be evil spoken of. And through covetousness with

τοῖς   λόγοις ὑμᾶς ἐμπορεύσονται· οἷς τὸ κρίμα ἔκπαλαι
well-turned words you they will make gain of : for whom judgment of old

οὐκ.ἀργεῖ, καὶ ἡ.ἀπώλεια.αὐτῶν οὐ.νυστάζει. 4 Εἰ.γὰρ ὁ θεὸς
is not idle, and their destruction slumbers not.   For if   God

ἀγγέλων ἁμαρτησάντων οὐκ.ἐφείσατο, ἀλλὰ ᶜσειραῖς‖
[the] angels who sinned   spared not, but [2]to [3]chains

ζόφου   ταρταρώσας   παρέδωκεν
[10]of [11]darkness [1]having [2]cast [[3]them] [4]to [5]the [6]deepest [7]abyss delivered [them]

εἰς κρίσιν ᵈτετηρημένους·‖ 5 καὶ ἀρχαίου κόσμου οὐκ
for judgment having been kept ; and [the] ancient world [1]not

ἐφείσατο, ᵉἀλλ᾽‖ ὄγδοον Νῶε δικαιοσύνης κήρυκα ἐφύ-
[1]spared, but [[3]the],[e]ighth [2]Noe [7]of [8]righteousness [5]a [6]herald [1]pre-

λαξεν, κατακλυσμὸν κόσμῳ ἀσεβῶν ἐπάξας· 6 καὶ
served, [the] flood upon [the] world of [the] ungodly having brought in; and

πόλεις Σοδόμων καὶ Γομόρρας τεφρώσας   κατα-
[the] cities of Sodom and Gomorrha having reduced to ashes with an

στροφῇ κατέκρινεν, ὑπόδειγμα   μελλόντων ἀσε-
overthrow condemned [them], [3]an [4]example [[5]to [6]those] [7]being [8]about [9]to [10]live

---

ᵗ Ὁ υἱός μου ὁ ἀγαπητός μου οὗτός ἐστιν my Son my beloved this is A.   ᵛ ἁγίῳ
ὄρει TᵣA.   ʷ προφητεία ποτέ TᵣA.   ˣ ἀλλὰ TTᵣAW.   ʸ — οἱ GLTTᵣAW.   ᶻ ἀπὸ
(read men from God) TA.   ᵃ + τοῦ L.   ᵇ ἀσελγείαις licentiousnesses GLTTᵣAW.   ᶜ σιροῖς
to dens LT ; σειροῖς to dens TᵣA.   ᵈ τηρουμένους to be kept GTTᵣAW ; κολαζομένους τηρεῖν
to keep, to be punished L.   ᵉ ἀλλὰ TTᵣA.

ρ̇ειν τεθεικώς· 7 καὶ δίκαιον Λώτ, καταπονούμενον ὑπὸ τῆς
[1]ungodly [1]having [2]set; and righteous Lot, oppressed by the

τῶν ἀθέσμων ἐν ἀσελγείᾳ ἀναστροφῆς, ᶠἐῤῥύσατο‖ 8 βλέμ-
[4]of [5]the [6]lawless [2]in [3]licentiousness [1]conduct he delivered, ([7]through

ματι γὰρ καὶ ἀκοῇ ᵍὁ‖ δίκαιος, ʰἐγκατοικῶν‖ ἐν αὐτοῖς,
[3]seeing [4]for and hearing, the righteous [man], dwelling among them,

ἡμέραν ἐξ ἡμέρας ψυχὴν δικαίαν ἀνόμοις ἔργοις
day by day [²his] [4]soul [3]righteous [5]with [6]their] [7]lawless [8]works

ἐβασάνιζεν· 9 οἶδεν κύριος εὐσεβεῖς ἐκ ᶦπειρασμοῦ‖
[1]tormented,) [11]knows [9]the][10]Lord [how the] pious out of temptation

ῥύεσθαι, ἀδίκους.δὲ εἰς ἡμέραν κρίσεως κολαζομένους
[1]to deliver, and [the] unrighteous to a day of judgment [3]to [4]be [5]punished

τηρεῖν· 10 μάλιστα.δὲ τοὺς ὀπίσω σαρκὸς ἐν ἐπιθυμίᾳ
[1]to [2]keep; and specially those who after [the] flesh in [the] lust

μιασμοῦ πορευομένους, καὶ κυριότητος καταφρονοῦντας.
of pollution walk, and lordship despise. [They

Τολμηταί, αὐθάδεις, δόξας οὐ.τρέμουσιν βλασφημοῦντες·
are] daring, self-willed; [7]glories [1]they [2]tremble [3]not [4]speaking [5]evil [6]of;

11 ὅπου ἄγγελοι ἰσχύϊ καὶ δυνάμει μείζονες ὄντες, οὐ φέ-
where angels [3]in [4]strength [5]and [6]power [2]greater [1]being, [8]not [7]do

ρουσιν κατ' αὐτῶν ᵏπαρὰ κυρίῳ‖ βλάσφημον κρίσιν.
bring against them, before [the] Lord, a railing charge.

12 οὗτοι.δέ, ὡς ἄλογα ζῶα ᶦφυσικὰ γεγενημένα‖ εἰς ἅλω-
But these, as [2]irrational [3]animals [1]natural born for cap-

σιν καὶ φθοράν, ἐν οἷς ἀγνοοῦσιν βλασφημοῦντες, ἐν
ture and corruption, [3]in [4]what [5]they [6]are [7]ignorant [8]of [1]speaking [2]evil, in

τῇ.φθορᾷ.αὐτῶν ᵐκαταφθαρήσονται,‖ 13 κομιούμενοι
their corruption shall utterly perish, being about to receive [the]

μισθὸν ἀδικίας, ἡδονὴν ἡγούμενοι τὴν ἐν.ἡμέρᾳ τρυφήν,
reward of unrighteousness; [4]pleasure [1]esteeming [2]ephemeral [3]indulgence;

σπίλοι καὶ μῶμοι, ἐντρυφῶντες ἐν ταῖς ⁿἀπάταις‖ αὐτῶν, συν-
spots and blemishes, luxuriating in [2]deceits [1]their, feast-

ευωχούμενοι ὑμῖν, 14 ὀφθαλμοὺς ἔχοντες μεστοὺς μοιχαλίδος
ing with you; eyes having full of an adulteress,

καὶ ᵒἀκαταπαύστους‖ ἁμαρτίας, δελεάζοντες ψυχὰς ἀστηρίκ-
and that cease not from sin, alluring souls unestablish-

τους, καρδίαν γεγυμνασμένην ᴾπλεονεξίαις‖ ἔχοντες, κατάρας
ed; [²a] [³heart] [⁴exercised] [⁵in] [⁶craving] [¹having], [⁸of·⁹curse

τέκνα, 15 ᑫκαταλιπόντες‖ ʳτὴν‖ εὐθεῖαν ὁδόν, ἐπλανήθησαν,
[⁴children], having left [³the] straight way, they went astray,

ἐξακολουθήσαντες τῇ ὁδῷ τοῦ Βαλαὰμ τοῦ Βοσόρ, ὃς
having followed in the way of Balaam, [son] of Bosor, who [the]

μισθὸν ἀδικίας ἠγάπησεν, 16 ἔλεγξιν.δὲ ἔσχεν ἰδίας
reward of unrighteousness loved; but reproof had of his own

παρανομίας· ὑποζύγιον ἄφωνον, ἐν ἀνθρώπου φωνῇ
wickedness, [the] [²beast [³of ⁴burden [¹dumb, in man's voice

φθεγξάμενον, ἐκώλυσεν τὴν τοῦ προφήτου παραφρονίαν.
speaking, forbade the [²of ³the [⁴prophet [¹madness.

17 οὗτοί εἰσιν πηγαὶ ἄνυδροι, ˢνεφέλαι‖ ὑπὸ λαίλαπος ἐλαυ-
These are fountains without water, clouds by storm being

νόμεναι, οἷς ὁ ζόφος τοῦ σκότους ᵗεἰς.αἰῶνα‖ τετήρηται.
driven, to whom the gloom of darkness for ever is kept.

wicked : 8 (for that
righteous man dwell-
ing among them, in
seeing and hearing,
vexed his righteous
soul from day to day
with their unlawful
deeds ;) 9 the Lord
knoweth how to de-
liver the godly out of
temptations, and to
reserve the unjust un-
to the day of judgment
to be punished : 10 but
chiefly them that walk
after the flesh in the
lust of uncleanness,
and despise govern-
ment. Presumptuous
are they, selfwilled,
they are not afraid to
speak evil of dignities.
11 Whereas angels,
which are greater in
power and might
bring not railing ac-
cusation against them
before the Lord. 12 But
these, as natural
brute beasts, made to
be taken and destroy-
ed, speak evil of the
things that they un-
derstand not ; and
shall utterly perish in
their own corruption ;
13 and shall receive the
reward of unright-
eousness, as they that
count it pleasure to
riot in the daytime.
Spots they are and
blemishes, sporting
themselves with their
own deceivings while
they feast with you ;
14 having eyes full of
adultery, and that
cannot cease from
sin ; beguiling unsta-
ble souls : an heart
they have exercised
with covetous practi-
ces ; cursed children :
15 which have forsaken
the right way, and are
gone astray, following
the way of Balaam the
son of Bosor, who lov-
ed the wages of un-
righteousness ; 16 but
was rebuked for his in-
iquity : the dumb ass
speaking with man's
voice forbad the mad-
ness of the prophet.
17 These are wells
without water, clouds
that are carried with
a tempest ; to whom
the mist of darkness
is reserved for ever.
18 For when they
speak great swelling
words of vanity, they

ᶠ ἐρύσατο TrA. ᵍ — ὁ (read [the]) L. ʰ ἐν- T. ᶦ πειρασμῶν temptations T.
ᵏ — παρὰ·κυρίῳ L[Tr]. ᶦ φυσικὰ γεγενημένα EG ; γεγεννημ. (γεγενημ. T) φυσικὰ (read irrational animals, born naturally) LTTrAW. ᵐ καὶ φθαρήσονται shall even perish LTTrAW.
ⁿ ἀγάπαις [²love [³feasts LTr. ᵒ ἀκαταπάστους insatiable (for sin) L. ᴾ πλεονεξίας GLTTrAW.
ᑫ καταλείποντες leaving T. ʳ — τὴν (read [the]) GLTTrAW. ˢ καὶ ὁμίχλαι and mists
GLTTrAW. ᵗ — εἰς αἰῶνα LTTrA.

allure through the lusts of the flesh, *through much* wantonness, those that were clean escaped from them who live in error. 19 While they promise them liberty, they themselves are the servants of corruption: for of whom a man is overcome, of the same is he brought in bondage. 20 For if after they have escaped the pollutions of the world through the knowledge of the Lord and Saviour Jesus Christ, they are again entangled therein, and overcome, the latter end is worse with them than the beginning. 21 For it had been better for them not to have known the way of righteousness, than, after they have known *it*, to turn from the holy commandment delivered unto them. 22 But it is happened unto them according to the true proverb, The dog *is* turned to his own vomit again; and the sow that was washed to her wallowing in the mire.

III. This second epistle, beloved, I now write unto you; in *both* which I stir up your pure minds by way of remembrance: 2 that ye may be mindful of the words which were spoken before by the holy prophets, and of the commandment of us the apostles of the Lord and Saviour: 3 knowing this first, that there shall come in the last days scoffers, walking after their own lusts, 4 and saying, Where is the promise of his coming? for since the fathers fell asleep, all things continue as *they were* from the beginning of the creation. 5 For this they willingly are ignorant of, that by the word of God the heavens were of old, and the earth standing out of the water and in the water: 6 whereby the world that then was, being overflowed with water, perished:

18 ὑπέρογκα.γὰρ   ματαιότητος φθεγγόμενοι, δελεάζουσιν
For great swelling [words] of vanity   speaking,   they allure

ἐν   ἐπιθυμίαις σαρκός, ᵛἀσελγείαις, τοὺς ᵂὄντως⁴
with [the] desires of [the] flesh, by licentiousnesses, those who indeed

ˣἀποφυγόντας‖ τοὺς ἐν ³πλάνῃ ἀναστρεφομένους, 19 ἐλευ-
escaped from   those who ²in ³error   ⁴walk,   ⁴free-

θερίαν αὐτοῖς ἐπαγγελλόμενοι, αὐτοὶ   δοῦλοι ὑπάρχοντες
dom   ⁵them   ²promising,   themselves ²bondmen ¹being

τῆς φθορᾶς·   ᾧ.γάρ τις   ἥττηται, τούτῳ ʸκαὶ‖ δε-
of corruption; for by whom anyone has been subdued, by him also he is

δούλωται.   20 εἰ.γὰρ ἀποφυγόντες τὰ μιάσματα τοῦ κόσμου
held in bondage.   For if having escaped the pollutions of the world

ἐν   ἐπιγνώσει τοῦ κυρίου ᶻ καὶ σωτῆρος Ἰησοῦ χριστοῦ,
through [the] knowledge of the Lord   and Saviour Jesus Christ,

τούτοις.δὲ πάλιν ἐμπλακέντες   ἡττῶνται, γέγονεν
but ⁸by ⁹these ⁴again ⁵having ³been ⁶entangled ⁵they ⁶are ⁷subdued, has become

αὐτοῖς τὰ ἔσχατα   χείρονα τῶν πρώτων. 21 ᵃκρεῖττον‖
to them the last [state] worse than the first.   ²Better

γὰρ ἦν αὐτοῖς μὴ ἐπεγνωκέναι τὴν ὁδὸν τῆς δικαιοσύνης,
¹for it were for them not to have known the way of righteousness,

ἢ ἐπιγνοῦσιν ᵇ ᶜἐπιστρέψαι‖ ᵈἐκ‖ τῆς παραδοθείσης αὐ-
than having known [it] to have turned from the ³delivered ⁴to

τοῖς ἁγίας ἐντολῆς. 22 συμβέβηκεν.ᵉδὲ‖ αὐτοῖς τὸ   τῆς
⁵them ¹holy ²commandment.   But has happened   to them the [word] of the

ἀληθοῦς παροιμίας,   Κύων ἐπιστρέψας ἐπὶ τὸ.ἴδιον ἐξέραμα·
true proverb: [The] dog having returned to his own   vomit;

καί, ᵛὙς λουσαμένη, εἰς ᶠκύλισμα‖ βορβόρου.
and, [The] ²sow ¹washed, to [her] rolling place in [the] mire.

3 Ταύτην ἤδη, ἀγαπητοί, δευτέραν ὑμῖν γράφω ἐπιστολήν,
This now, beloved, a second ²to ³you ⁴I ¹write ¹epistle,

ἐν   αἷς διεγείρω ὑμῶν ἐν   ὑπομνήσει   τὴν εἰλικρι-
in [both] which I stir up your ³in ⁴putting [⁵you] ⁶in ⁷remembrance ¹pure

νῆ διάνοιαν, 2 μνησθῆναι τῶν προειρημένων ῥημάτων ὑπὸ τῶν
²mind,   to be mindful of the ²spoken ³before ¹words by the

ἁγίων προφητῶν, καὶ τῆς τῶν ἀποστόλων ᵍἡμῶν‖ ἐντολῆς,
holy prophets, and of the ⁹the ¹⁰apostles ⁷by ⁸us ¹commandment

τοῦ κυρίου καὶ σωτῆρος· 3 τοῦτο πρῶτον γινώσκοντες, ὅτι
²of ³the ⁴Lord ⁵and ⁶Saviour; this first knowing, that

ἐλεύσονται ἐπʼ ʰἐσχάτου‖ τῶν ἡμερῶν ⁱ ἐμπαῖκται, κατὰ
will come at the close of the days mockers, according to

τὰς.ἰδίας.ᵏαὐτῶν ἐπιθυμίας‖ πορευόμενοι, 4 καὶ λέγοντες, Ποῦ
their own lusts walking, and saying, Where

ἐστιν ἡ ἐπαγγελία τῆς.παρουσίας.αὐτοῦ; ἀφʼ.ἧς.γὰρ οἱ πατέ-
is the promise of his coming? for since the fa-

ρες ἐκοιμήθησαν, πάντα οὕτως διαμένει ἀπʼ ἀρχῆς κτί-
thers fell asleep, all things thus continue from [the] beginning of [the]

σεως. 5 λανθάνει.γὰρ αὐτοὺς τοῦτο θέλοντας, ὅτι
creation. For ²is ³hidden ⁴from ⁵them ¹this, [they] willing [it], that

οὐρανοὶ ἦσαν ἔκπαλαι, καὶ γῆ ἐξ ὕδατος καὶ διʼ ὕδατος
heavens were of old, and an earth out of water and in water

συνεστῶσα, τῷ τοῦ θεοῦ λόγῳ, 6 διʼ ὧν   ὁ τότε
subsisting, by the ²of ³God ¹word, through which [waters] the then

---

ᵛ + ἐν E.   ᵂ ὀλίγως scarcely GLTTrAW.   ˣ ἀποφεύγοντας are escaping from LTTrAW.
ʸ — καὶ ϯ[Tr].   ᶻ + ἡμῶν (*read* our Lord) LT.   ᵃ κρεῖσσον T.   ᵇ + εἰς τὰ ὀπίσω to the
[things] behind L.   ᶜ ὑποστρέψαι to have turned.back LTTrA.   ᵈ ἀπὸ L.   ᵉ — δὲ but
LTTrA.   ᶠ κυλισμὸν rolling TTrA.   ᵍ ὑμῶν (*read* by your apostles) LTTrAW.   ʰ ἐσχάτων
(*read* in the last days) LTTrAW.   ⁱ + ἐν ἐμπαιγμονῇ (*read* mockers, with mocking)
GLTTrAW.   ᵏ ἐπιθυμίας αὐτῶν ƷLTTrA.

κόσμος ὕδατι κατακλυσθεὶς ἀπώλετο· 7 οἱ.δὲ νῦν οὐρανοὶ
world with water having been deluged perished. But the now heavens

καὶ ἡ γῆ ¹αὐτοῦ‖ λόγῳ τεθησαυρισμένοι εἰσίν, πυρὶ τηρού-
and the earth by his word ²treasured ³up ¹are, for fire being·

μενοι εἰς ἡμέραν κρίσεως καὶ ἀπωλείας τῶν ἀσεβῶν ἀνθρώπων.
kept to a day of judgment and destruction of ungodly men.

8 ἕν.δὲ.τοῦτο μὴ.λανθανέτω ὑμᾶς, ἀγαπητοί, ὅτι μία ἡμέρα
But this one thing let not be hidden from you, beloved, that one day

παρὰ κυρίῳ ὡς χίλια ἔτη, καὶ χίλια ἔτη ὡς ἡμέρα
with [the] Lord [is] as a thousand years, and a thousand years as ²day

μία. 9 οὐ.βραδύνει ᵐὁ‖ κύριος τῆς ἐπαγγελίας, ὥς τινες βρα-
¹one. ⁵Does ²not ⁷delay ³the ⁴Lord the promise, as some ⁵de-

δυτῆτα ἡγοῦνται· ἀλλὰ μακροθυμεῖ ⁿεἰς‖ ᵒἡμᾶς,‖ μὴ βουλό-
lay ¹esteem, but is longsuffering towards us, not will-

μενός τινας ἀπολέσθαι, ἀλλὰ πάντας εἰς μετάνοιαν χωρῆ-
ing [for] any to perish, but all to repentance to

σαι. 10 ἥξει.δὲ ᴾἡ‖ ἡμέρα κυρίου ὡς κλέπτης ᑫἐν‖ νυκτί,‖
come. But shall come the day of [the] Lord as a thief in [the] night,

ἐν ᾗ ʳοἱ‖ οὐρανοὶ ῥοιζηδὸν παρελεύσονται, στοιχεῖα.δὲ
in which the heavens with rushing noise shall pass away, and [the] elements

καυσούμενα ˢλυθήσονται,‖ καὶ γῆ καὶ τὰ ἐν αὐτῇ ἔργα
burning with heat shall be dissolved, and [the]earth and the ²in ³it ¹works

ᵗκατακαήσεται.‖
shall be burnt up.

11 Τούτων ᵗοὖν‖ πάντων λυομένων, ποταποὺς
These things then all being to be dissolved, what kind of [persons]

δεῖ ὑπάρχειν ὑμᾶς ἐν ἁγίαις ἀναστροφαῖς καὶ εὐσεβείαις,
ought ²to ³be ¹ye in holy conduct and piety,

12 προσδοκῶντας καὶ σπεύδοντας τὴν παρουσίαν τῆς τοῦ
expecting and hastening the coming of the

θεοῦ ἡμέρας δι᾽ ἣν οὐρανοὶ πυρούμενοι λυθή-
²of ³God ¹day by reason of which [the] heavens, being on fire, shall be dis-

σονται, καὶ στοιχεῖα καυσούμενα ʷτήκεται;‖ 13 καινοὺς
solved, and [the] elements burning with heat shall melt? ²New

δὲ οὐρανοὺς καὶ ˣγῆν καινὴν‖ ʸκατὰ‖ ᶻτὸ ἐπάγγελμα‖ αὐτοῦ
¹but heavens and ²earth ¹a ²new according to ²promise ³his,

προσδοκῶμεν, ἐν οἷς δικαιοσύνη κατοικεῖ. 14 διό, ἀγαπη-
we expect, in which righteousness dwells. Wherefore, belov-

τοί, ταῦτα προσδοκῶντες, σπουδάσατε ἄσπιλοι καὶ ἀμώ-
ed, these things expecting be diligent without spot and unblam-

μητοι αὐτῷ εὑρεθῆναι ἐν εἰρήνῃ, 15 καὶ τὴν τοῦ.κυρίου.ἡμῶν
able by him to be found in peace; and the ²of ³our ⁴Lord

μακροθυμιαν, σωτηρίαν ἡγεῖσθε· καθὼς καὶ ὁ ἀγαπητὸς
¹longsuffering, ²salvation ⁵esteem ⁴ye; according as also ²beloved

ἡμῶν ἀδελφὸς Παῦλος κατὰ τὴν ᵃαὐτῷ δοθεῖσαν‖ σοφίαν
¹our brother Paul according to the ²to ³him ²given ¹wisdom

ἔγραψεν ὑμῖν, 16 ὡς καὶ ἐν πάσαις ᵇταῖς‖ ἐπιστολαῖς, λαλῶν
wrote to you, as also in all [his] epistles, speaking

ἐν αὐταῖς περὶ τούτων· ἐν ᶜοἷς‖ ἐστιν δυσνόητά
in them concerning these things, among which are ³hard ⁴to ⁵be ⁶understood

7 but the heavens and the earth, which are now, by the same word are kept in store, reserved unto fire against the day of judgment and perdition of ungodly men. 8 But, beloved, be not ignorant of this one thing, that one day is with the Lord as a thousand years, and a thousand years as one day. 9 The Lord is not slack concerning his promise, as some men count slackness; but is longsuffering to us-ward, not willing that any should perish, but that all should come to repentance. 10 But the day of the Lord will come as a thief in the night; in the which the heavens shall pass away with a great noise, and the elements shall melt with fervent heat, the earth also and the works that are therein shall be burned up. 11 Seeing then that all these things shall be dissolved, what manner of persons ought ye to be in all holy conversation and godliness, 12 looking for and hasting unto the coming of the day of God, wherein the heavens being on fire shall be dissolved, and the elements shall melt with fervent heat? 13 Nevertheless we, according to his promise, look for new heavens and a new earth, wherein dwelleth righteousness. 14 Wherefore, beloved, seeing that ye look for such things, be diligent that ye may be found of him in peace, without spot, and blameless. 15 And account that the longsuffering of our Lord is salvation; even as our beloved brother Paul also according to the wisdom given unto him hath written unto you; 16 as also in all his epistles, speaking in them of these things; in which are some things hard to be

understood, which they that are unlearned and unstable wrest, as *they do* also the other scriptures, unto their own destruction.

17 Ye therefore, beloved, seeing ye know *these things* before, beware lest ye also, being led away with the error of the wicked, fall from your own stedfastness. 18 But grow in grace, and *in* the knowledge of our Lord and Saviour Jesus Christ. To him *be* glory both now and for ever. Amen.

τινα,   ἃ οἱ ἀμαθεῖς καὶ ἀστήρικτοι στρεβλοῦσιν, ὡς
¹some ²things, which the untaught and unestablished   wrest,   ᵃas
καὶ τὰς λοιπὰς γραφάς, πρὸς τὴν.ἰδίαν.αὐτῶν ἀπώλειαν.
also the other scriptures, to   their own   destruction.
17 Ὑμεῖς οὖν, ἀγαπητοί, προγινώσκοντες φυλάσσεσθε,
Ye therefore, beloved,   knowing beforehand,   beware,
ἵνα.μὴ τῇ τῶν ἀθέσμων πλάνῃ συναπαχθέντες, ἐκπέ-
lest with the ²of ³the ⁴lawless [⁵ones] ¹error having been led away, ye should
σητε τοῦ.ἰδίου στηριγμοῦ· 18 αὐξάνετε.δὲ ἐν χάριτι καὶ
fall from your own steadfastness :   but grow in   grace, and
γνώσει τοῦ.κυρίου.ἡμῶν καὶ σωτῆρος Ἰησοῦ χριστοῦ.
in [the] knowledge of our Lord   and Saviour Jesus   Christ.
αὐτῷ ἡ δόξα καὶ νῦν καὶ εἰς ἡμέραν αἰῶνος. ᵈἀμήν.‖ ᵉ
To him [be] glory both now and to [the] day of eternity.   Amen.

ΕΠΙΣΤΟΛΗ ΙΩΑΝΝΟΥ ΚΑΘΟΛΙΚΗ ΠΡΩΤΗ.‖
³EPISTLE   ⁴OF ⁵JOHN   ⁷GENERAL   ¹FIRST.

THAT which was from the beginning, which we have heard, which we have seen with our eyes, which we have looked upon, and our hands have handled, of the Word of life; 2 (for the life was manifested, and we have seen *it*, and bear witness, and shew unto you that eternal life, which was with the Father, and was manifested unto us;) 3 that which we have seen and heard declare we unto you, that ye also may have fellowship with us: and truly our fellowship *is* with the Father, and with his Son Jesus Christ. 4 And these things write we unto you, that your joy may be full.

Ὃ   ἦν ἀπ'   ἀρχῆς,   ὃ   ἀκηκόαμεν,   ὃ   ἑω-
That which was from [the] beginning, that which we have heard, that which we
ράκαμεν τοῖς.ὀφθαλμοῖς.ἡμῶν, ὃ   ἐθεασάμεθα καὶ αἱ χεῖρες
have seen   with our eyes,   that which we gazed upon and ²hands
ἡμῶν ἐψηλάφησαν περὶ τοῦ λόγου τῆς ζωῆς· 2 καὶ ἡ ζωὴ
¹our   handled   concerning the Word of life; (and the life
ἐφανερώθη, καὶ ἑωράκαμεν, καὶ μαρτυροῦμεν, καὶ ἀπαγγέλ-
was manifested, and we have seen, and   bear witness,   and   re-
λομεν ὑμῖν τὴν ζωὴν τὴν αἰώνιον, ἥτις ἦν πρὸς τὸν πατέρα,
port to you the ²life   ¹eternal, which was with the Father,
καὶ ἐφανερώθη ἡμῖν· 3 ὃ   ἑωράκαμεν καὶ ἀκηκόαμεν,
and was manifested to us :)   that which we have seen and have heard
ἀπαγγέλλομενᵍ ὑμῖν, ἵνα καὶ ὑμεῖς κοινωνίαν ἔχητε μεθ'
we report   to you, that also ye   fellowship may have with
ἡμῶν· καὶ ἡ κοινωνία δὲ ἡ ἡμετέρα μετὰ τοῦ πατρὸς καὶ
us ;   and ²fellowship ³indeed   ¹our [is] with the Father, and
μετὰ τοῦ.υἱοῦ.αὐτοῦ Ἰησοῦ χριστοῦ· 4 καὶ ταῦτα ʰγράφο-
with   his Son   Jesus   Christ.   And these things   we
μεν ὑμῖν,‖ ἵνα ἡ χαρὰ ¹ἡμῶν‖ ᾖ πεπληρωμένη.
write to you that ²joy   ¹our may be   full.

5 This then is the message which we have heard of him, and declare unto you, that God is light, and in him is no darkness at all. 6 If we say that we have fellowship with him, and walk in darkness, we lie, and do not the truth : 7 but if we walk in the light, as he is in the light, we have fellowship one

5 Καὶ ᵏαὕτη ἐστὶν‖ ἡ ¹ἐπαγγελία‖ ἣν ἀκηκόαμεν ἀπ'
And this   is   the   message   which we have heard from
αὐτοῦ, καὶ ἀναγγέλλομεν ὑμῖν, ὅτι ὁ θεὸς φῶς ἐστιν, καὶ
him, and announce   to you, that God ²light ¹is,   and
σκοτία ᵐἐν αὐτῷ οὐκ.ἔστιν‖.οὐδεμία. 6 ἐὰν εἴπωμεν ὅτι
darkness in him   is not any at all.   If we should say that
κοινωνίαν ἔχομεν μετ' αὐτοῦ, καὶ ἐν τῷ σκότει περιπατῶμεν,
fellowship we have with him, and in darkness should walk,
ψευδόμεθα, καὶ οὐ.ποιοῦμεν τὴν ἀλήθειαν· 7 ἐὰν.δὲ ἐν τῷ
we lie,   and do not practise the   truth.   But if in the
φωτὶ περιπατῶμεν, ὡς αὐτός ἐστιν ἐν τῷ φωτί, κοινωνίαν
light   we should walk, as he   is in the light, fellowship

ᵈ — ἀμήν τ[ΤΓΑ].   ᵉ + Πέτρου β' 2 Peter ΤΓΑ.
ᶠ + τοῦ ἀποστόλου the apostle E ; — καθολικη G ; Ἰωάννου α' LTAW ; Ἰωάνου ἐπιστολὴ
α' Tr.   ᵍ + καὶ also LTTΓΑW.   ʰ γράφομεν ἡμεῖς we write ΤΤΓΑ.   ⁱ ὑμῶν 'your EGW.
ᵏ ἐστιν αὕτη ΤΤΓΑW.   ¹ ἀγγελία GLTTΓΑW.   ᵐ οὐκ ἔστιν ἐν αὐτῷ Tr.

ἔχομεν μετ' ἀλλήλων, καὶ τὸ αἷμα Ἰησοῦ ⁿχριστοῦ‖ τοῦ υἱοῦ
we have with one another, and the blood of Jesus Christ ²Son

αὐτοῦ καθαρίζει ἡμᾶς ἀπὸ πάσης ἁμαρτίας. 8 ἐὰν εἴπωμεν
¹his cleanses us from every sin. If we should say

ὅτι ἁμαρτίαν οὐκ.ἔχομεν, ἑαυτοὺς πλανῶμεν καὶ ἡ ἀλήθεια
that sin we have not, ourselves we deceive, and the truth

°οὐκ.ἔστιν ἐν ἡμῖν.‖ 9 ἐὰν ὁμολογῶμεν τὰς.ἁμαρτίας.ἡμῶν,
is not in us. If we should confess our sins,

πιστός ἐστιν καὶ δίκαιος, ἵνα ἀφῇ ᴾἡμῖν‖ τὰς.ἁμαρτίας,
faithful he is and righteous, that he may forgive us the sins,

καὶ καθαρίσῃ ἡμᾶς ἀπὸ πάσης ἀδικίας. 10 ἐὰν εἴπωμεν
and may cleanse us from all unrighteousness. If we should say

ὅτι οὐχ.ἡμαρτήκαμεν, ψεύστην ποιοῦμεν αὐτόν, καὶ ὁ λόγος
that we have not sinned, a liar we make him, and ²word

αὐτοῦ οὐκ.ἔστιν ἐν ἡμῖν.
¹his is not in us.

2 Τεκνία μου, ταῦτα γράφω ὑμῖν, ἵνα μὴ.ἁμάρτητε·
²Little ³children ¹my, these things I write to you, that ye may not sin;

καὶ ἐάν τις ἁμάρτῃ, παράκλητον ἔχομεν πρὸς τὸν πατέρα,
and if anyone should sin, a Paraclete we have with the Father,

Ἰησοῦν χριστὸν δίκαιον 2 καὶ αὐτὸς ᵠἱλασμός ἐστιν‖
Jesus Christ [the] righteous; and he [the] propitiation is

περὶ τῶν.ἁμαρτιῶν.ἡμῶν· οὐ περὶ τῶν.ἡμετέρων δὲ μόνον,
for our sins ; ²not ³for ⁴ours ¹but only,

ἀλλὰ καὶ περὶ ὅλου τοῦ κόσμου.
but also for ²whole ¹the world.

3 Καὶ ἐν τούτῳ γινώσκομεν ὅτι ἐγνώκαμεν αὐτόν, ἐὰν
And by this we know that we have known him, if

τὰς.ἐντολὰς.αὐτοῦ τηρῶμεν. 4 ὁ λέγων, ʳἜγνωκα αὐτόν,
his commandments we keep. He that says, I have known him,

καὶ τὰς.ἐντολὰς.αὐτοῦ μὴ.τηρῶν, ψεύστης ἐστίν, καὶ ἐν τούτῳ
and his commandments is not keeping, a liar is, and in him

ἡ ἀλήθεια οὐκ.ἔστιν· 5 ὃς.δ'.ἂν τηρῇ αὐτοῦ τὸν λόγον,
the truth is not; but whoever may keep his word,

ἀληθῶς ἐν τούτῳ ἡ ἀγάπη τοῦ θεοῦ τετελείωται. ἐν τούτῳ
truly in him the love of God has been perfected. By this

γινώσκομεν ὅτι ἐν αὐτῷ ἐσμεν. 6 ὁ λέγων ἐν αὐτῷ
we know that in him we are. He that says in him [he]

μένειν, ὀφείλει, καθὼς ἐκεῖνος περιεπάτησεν, ϛαὶ αὐτὸς °οὕτως‖
abides, ought, even as he walked, also himself so

περιπατεῖν. 7 ᵗἀδελφοί,‖ οὐκ ἐντολὴν καινὴν γράφω ὑμῖν,
to walk. Brethren, not a ²commandment ¹new I write to you,

ἀλλ' ἐντολὴν παλαιάν, ἣν εἴχετε ἀπ' ἀρχῆς· ἡ
but ²commandment ¹an ²old, which ye had from [the] beginning: the

ἐντολὴ ἡ παλαιά ἐστιν ὁ λόγος ὃν ἠκούσατε ᵛἀπ'
²commandment ¹old is the word which ye heard from [the]

ἀρχῆς.‖ 8 πάλιν ἐντολὴν καινὴν γράφω ὑμῖν, ὅ ἐστιν
beginning. Again a ²commandment ¹new I write to you, which is

ἀληθὲς ἐν αὐτῷ καὶ ἐν ὑμῖν, ὅτι ἡ σκοτία παράγεται,
true in him and in you, because the darkness is passing away,

καὶ τὸ φῶς τὸ ἀληθινὸν ἤδη φαίνει. 9 ὁ λέγων ἐν τῷ
and the ²light ¹true already shines. He that says in the

φωτὶ εἶναι, καὶ τὸν.ἀδελφὸν.αὐτοῦ μισῶν, ἐν τῇ σκοτίᾳ ἐστὶν
light [he] is, and ²his ³brother ¹hates, in the darkness is

with another, and the blood of Jesus Christ his Son cleanseth us from all sin. 8 If we say that we have no sin, we deceive ourselves, and the truth is not in us. 9 If we confess our sins, he is faithful and just to forgive us our sins, and to cleanse us from all unrighteousness. 10 If we say that we have not sinned, we make him a liar, and his word is not in us.

II. My little children, these things write I unto you, that ye sin not. And if any man sin, we have an advocate with the Father, Jesus Christ the righteous: 2 and he is the propitiation for our sins: and not for ours only, but also for the sins of the whole world.

3 And hereby we do know that we know him, if we keep his commandments. 4 He that saith, I know him, and keepeth not his commandments, is a liar, and the truth is not in him. 5 But whoso keepeth his word, in him verily is the love of God perfected: hereby know we that we are in him. 6 He that saith he abideth in him ought himself also so to walk, even as he walked. 7 Brethren, I write no new commandment unto you, but an old commandment which ye had from the beginning. The old commandment is the word which ye have heard from the beginning. 8 Again, a new commandment I write unto you, which thing is true in him and in you: because the darkness is past, and the true light now shineth. 9 He that saith he is in the light, and hateth his brother, is in darkness even until

---

ⁿ — χριστοῦ LTTrA. ° ἐν ἡμῖν οὐκ ἔστιν LTrW. ᴾ ἡμῶν our (sins) w. ᵠ ἐστιν
ἱλασμός L. ʳ + ὅτι [L]TTrA. ˢ — οὕτως LTr[A]. ᵗ ἀγαπητοί beloved GLTTrAW.
ᵛ—ἀπ' ἀρχῆς LTTrA.

now. 10 He that loveth his brother abideth in the light, and there is none occasion of stumbling in him. 11 But he that hateth his brother is in darkness, and walketh in darkness, and knoweth not whither he goeth, because that darkness hath blinded his eyes.

ἕως ἄρτι. 10 ὁ ἀγαπῶν τὸν ἀδελφὸν αὐτοῦ, ἐν τῷ φωτι
until now.　He that loves　his brother,　in the light

μένει, καὶ σκάνδαλον ʷἐν αὐτῷ οὐκ.ἔστιν.‖ 11 ὁ.δὲ
abides, and ⁴'cause ⁵of ⁶offence　⁷in　⁸him　¹there ²is ³not.　But he that

μισῶν τὸν ἀδελφὸν αὐτοῦ, ἐν τῇ σκοτίᾳ ἐστίν, καὶ ἐν τῇ σκοτίᾳ
hates　his brother,　in the darkuess is,　and in the darkness

περιπατεῖ, καὶ οὐκ.οἶδεν ποῦ ὑπάγει, ὅτι ἡ σκοτία ἐτύφ-
walks,　and knows not where　he goes, because the darkness blind-

λωσεν τοὺς.ὀφθαλμοὺς.αὐτοῦ.
ed　his eyes.

12 I write unto you, little children, because your sins are forgiven you for his name's sake.

12 Γράφω ὑμῖν, τεκνία, ὅτι ἀφέωνται ὑμῖν
I write to you, little children, because have been forgiven you [your]

αἱ ἁμαρτίαι διὰ τὸ.ὄνομα.αὐτοῦ.
sins　for the sake of　his name.

13 I write unto you, fathers, because ye have known him that is from the beginning. I write unto you, young men, because ye have overcome the wicked one. I write unto you, little children, because ye have known the Father.

13 Γράφω ὑμῖν, πατέρες, ὅτι ἐγνώκατε τὸν ἀπ'
I write to you, fathers, because ye have known him who [is] from

ἀρχῆς. Γράφω ὑμῖν, νεανίσκοι, ὅτι νενικήκατε τὸν
[the] beginning. I write to you, young men, because ye have overcome the

πονηρόν. ˣΓράφω‖ ὑμῖν, παιδία, ὅτι ἐγνώκατε τὸν
wicked [one]. I write to you, little children, because ye have known the

πατέρα.
Father.

14 I have written unto you, fathers, because ye have known him that is from the beginning. I have written unto you, young men, because ye are strong, and the word of God abideth in you, and ye have overcome the wicked one. 15 Love not the world, neither the things that are in the world. If any man love the world, the love of the Father is not in him. 16 For all that is in the world, the lust of the flesh, and the lust of the eyes, and the pride of life, is not of the Father, but is of the world. 17 And the world passeth away, and the lust thereof: but he that doeth the will of God abideth for ever. 18 Little children, it is the last time: and as ye have heard that antichrist shall come, even now are there many antichrists; whereby we know that it is the last time. 19 They went out from us, but they were not of us; for if they had been of us, they would no doubt have continued with us: but they went out, that they might be made manifest that they were not all of

14 Ἔγραψα ὑμῖν, πατέρες, ὅτι ἐγνώκατε τὸν
I wrote to you, fathers, because ye have known him who [is]

ἀπ' ἀρχῆς. Ἔγραψα ὑμῖν, νεανίσκοι, ὅτι ἰσχυροί ἐστε,
from [the] beginning. I wrote to you, young men, because strong ye are

καὶ ὁ λόγος τοῦ θεοῦ ἐν ὑμῖν μένει, καὶ νενικήκατε τὸν
and the word of God in you abides, and ye have overcome the

πονηρόν. 15 μὴ.ἀγαπᾶτε τὸν κόσμον, μηδὲ τὰ ἐν τῷ
wicked [one]. Love not the world, nor the things in the

κόσμῳ· ἐάν τις ἀγαπᾷ τὸν κόσμον, οὐκ ἔστιν ἡ ἀγάπη
world. If anyone should love the world, ⁷not ⁸is ¹the ²love

τοῦ πατρὸς ἐν αὐτῷ· 16 ὅτι πᾶν τὸ ἐν τῷ κόσμῳ,
³of ⁴the ⁵Father in him; because all that which [is] in the world,

ἡ ἐπιθυμία τῆς σαρκός, καὶ ἡ ἐπιθυμία τῶν ὀφθαλμῶν, καὶ
the desire of the flesh, and the desire of the eyes, and

ἡ ʸἀλαζονεία‖ τοῦ βίου, οὐκ.ἔστιν ἐκ τοῦ πατρός, ᶻαλλ'‖ ἐκ
the vaunting of life, is not of the Father, but of

τοῦ κόσμου ἐστίν. 17 καὶ ὁ κόσμος παράγεται, καὶ ἡ ἐπι-
the world is;　and the world is passing away, and the

θυμία αὐτοῦ· ὁ.δὲ ποιῶν τὸ θέλημα τοῦ θεοῦ μένει εἰς τὸν
lust of it, but he that does the will of God abides for

αἰῶνα. 18 Παιδία, ἐσχάτη ὥρα ἐστίν· καὶ καθὼς
ever.　Little children, [the] last hour it is, and according as

ἠκούσατε ὅτι ᵃὁ‖ ἀντίχριστος ἔρχεται, καὶ νῦν ἀντίχριστοι
ye heard that the antichrist is coming, even now ᶻantichrists

πολλοὶ γεγόνασιν· ὅθεν γινώσκομεν ὅτι ἐσχάτη ὥρα ἐστίν.
¹many have arisen, whence we know that [the] last hour it is.

19 ἐξ ἡμῶν ᵇἐξῆλθον,‖ ἀλλ' οὐκ.ἦσαν ἐξ ἡμῶν· εἰ.γὰρ
From among us they went out, but they were not of us; for if

ᶜἦσαν ἐξ ἡμῶν,‖ μεμενήκεισαν.ἂν μεθ' ἡμῶν· ἀλλ' ἵνα φανε-
they were of us, they would have remained with us, but that they

ρωθῶσιν ὅτι οὐκ.εἰσὶν πάντες ἐξ ἡμῶν. 20 καὶ ὑμεῖς
might be made manifest that ⁴are ³not ¹all of us. And ye

ʷ οὐκ ἔστιν ἐν αὐτῷ LTA.　ˣ ἔγραψα I wrote LTTrAW.　ʸ ἀλαζονία T.　ᶻ ἀλλὰ TTrW.
ᵃ — ὁ LTTrAW.　ᵇ ἐξῆλθαν LTTrAW.　ᶜ ἐξ ἡμῶν ἦσαν Tr.

χρῖσμα ἔχετε ἀπὸ τοῦ ἁγίου, καὶ οἴδατε ᵈπάντα.‖
[the] anointing have from the holy [one], and ye know all things.

21 οὐκ.ἔγραψα ὑμῖν ὅτι οὐκ.οἴδατε τὴν ἀλήθειαν, ἀλλ' ὅτι
I wrote not to you because ye know not the truth, but because

οἴδατε αὐτήν, καὶ ὅτι πᾶν ψεῦδος ἐκ τῆς ἀληθείας οὐκ ἔστιν.
ye know it, and that ²any ³lie ⁵of ⁶the ⁷truth ¹not ⁴is.
(lit. every)

22 Τίς ἐστιν ὁ ψεύστης εἰ.μὴ ὁ ἀρνούμενος ὅτι Ἰησοῦς οὐκ
Who is the liar but he that denies that Jesus not

ἔστιν ὁ χριστός; οὗτός ἐστιν ὁ ἀντίχριστος ὁ ἀρνούμενος
is the Christ? He is the antichrist who denies

τὸν πατέρα καὶ τὸν υἱόν. 23 πᾶς ὁ ἀρνούμενος τὸν υἱόν,
the Father and the Son. Everyone that denies the Son,

οὐδὲ τὸν πατέρα ἔχει. ᵉ 24 Ὑμεῖς ᶠοῦν‖ ὃ ἠκούσατε ἀπ'
neither ³the ⁴Father ¹has ²he. Ye therefore what ye heard from

ἀρχῆς, ἐν ὑμῖν μενέτω. ἐὰν ἐν ὑμῖν μείνῃ ὃ ἀπ'
[the] beginning, in you let it abide: if in you should abide what from

ἀρχῆς ἠκούσατε, καὶ ὑμεῖς ἐν τῷ υἱῷ καὶ ᵍἐν‖ τῷ πατρὶ
[the] beginning ye heard, also ye in the Son and in the Father

μενεῖτε. 25 καὶ αὕτη ἐστὶν ἡ ἐπαγγελία, ἣν αὐτὸς ἐπηγ-
shall abide. And this is the promise which he pro-

γείλατο ἡμῖν, τὴν ᶦζωὴν τὴν αἰώνιον. 26 ταῦτα ἔγραψα ὑμῖν
mised us, life eternal. These things I wrote to you

περὶ τῶν πλανώντων ὑμᾶς. 27 καὶ ὑμεῖς τὸ χρῖσμα
concerning those who lead ²astray ¹you: and you the anointing

ὃ ἐλάβετε ἀπ' αὐτοῦ, ʰἐν ὑμῖν μένει,‖ καὶ οὐ χρείαν ἔχετε
which ye received from him, in you abides, and not need ye have

ἵνα τις διδάσκῃ ὑμᾶς· ἀλλ' ὡς τὸ ᶦαὐτὸ χρῖσμα διδάσκει
that anyone should teach you; but as the same anointing teaches

ὑμᾶς περὶ πάντων, καὶ ἀληθές ἐστιν, καὶ οὐκ.ἔστιν ψεῦ-
you concerning all things, and true is, and is not a

δος· καὶ καθὼς ἐδίδαξεν ὑμᾶς, ʲμενεῖτε‖ ἐν αὐτῷ.
lie; and even as it taught you, ye shall abide in him.

28 Καὶ νῦν, τεκνία, μένετε ἐν αὐτῷ· ἵνα ᵏὅταν‖ φανερω-
And now, little children, abide in him, that when he be mani-

θῇ, ˡἔχωμεν‖ παρρησίαν, καὶ μὴ αἰσχυνθῶμεν ἀπ'.αὐτοῦ,
fested we may have boldness, and not be put to shame from before him

ἐν τῇ.παρουσίᾳ.αὐτοῦ.
at his coming.

29 Ἐὰν εἰδῆτε ὅτι δίκαιός ἐστιν, γινώσκετε ὅτι ᵐ πᾶς ὁ
If ye know that righteous he is, ye know that everyone who

ποιῶν τὴν δικαιοσύνην, ἐξ αὐτοῦ, ⁿγεγέννηται.‖ 3 Ἴδετε πο-
practises righteousness, of him has been begotten. See

ταπὴν ἀγάπην δέδωκεν ἡμῖν ὁ πατήρ, ἵνα τέκνα θεοῦ
what love ³has ⁴given ⁵to ⁶us ¹the ²Father, that children of God

κληθῶμεν·ᵒ διὰ τοῦτο ὁ κόσμος οὐ.γινώσκει ἡμᾶς,
we should be called. On account of this the world knows not us,

ὅτι οὐκ.ἔγνω αὐτόν. 2 ἀγαπητοί, νῦν τέκνα θεοῦ ἐσμεν,
because it knew not him. Beloved, now children of God are we,

καὶ οὔπω ἐφανερώθη τί ἐσόμεθα· οἴδαμεν.ᴾδὲ ὅτι ἐὰν
and not yet was it manifested what we shall be; but we know that if

φανερωθῇ, ὅμοιοι αὐτῷ ἐσόμεθα, ὅτι ὀψόμεθα αὐτὸν καθώς
he be manifested, like him we shall be, for we shall see him as

us. 20 But ye have an unction from the Holy One, and ye know all things. 21 I have not written unto you because ye know not the truth, but because ye know it, and that no lie is of the truth. 22 Who is a liar but he that denieth that Jesus is the Christ? He is antichrist, that denieth the Father and the Son. 23 Whosoever denieth the Son, the same hath not the Father: [but] he that acknowledgeth the Son hath the Father also. 24 Let that therefore abide in you, which ye have heard from the beginning. If that which ye have heard from the beginning shall remain in you, ye also shall continue in the Son, and in the Father. 25 And this is the promise that he hath promised us, even eternal life. 26 These things have I written unto you concerning them that seduce you. 27 But the anointing which ye have received of him abideth in you, and ye need not that any man teach you : but as the same anointing teacheth you of all things, and is truth, and is no lie, and even as it hath taught you, ye shall abide in him.

28 And now, little children, abide in him; that, when he shall appear, we may have confidence, and not be ashamed before him at his coming.

29 If ye know that he is righteous, ye know that every one that doeth righteousness is born of him. III. Behold, what manner of love the Father hath bestowed upon us, that we should be called the sons of God: therefore the world knoweth us not, because it knew him not. 2 Beloved, now are we the sons of God, and it doth not yet appear what we shall be: but we know that, when he shall appear, we shall be like him; for we shall see him ;

ᵈ πάντες (read ye all know) ᴛ. ᵉ + ὁ ὁμολογῶν τὸν υἱὸν καὶ τὸν πατέρα ἔχει he that confesses the Son has the Father also ɢʟᴛᴛ ʀᴀ ᴡ. ᶠ — οὖν ʟᴛᴛʀᴀ. ᵍ — ἐν ʟ. ʰ μένει ἐν ὑμῖν ʟᴛᴛʀᴀ. ᶦ αὐτοῦ (read as his anointing) ᴛᴛʀᴀ. ʲ.μένετε abide ʟᴛᴛʀᴀᴡ. ᵏ ἐὰν ʟᴛᴛʀᴀ. ˡ σχῶμεν ʟᴛᴛʀᴀ. ⁿ γεγένηται in Stephens. ᵒ + καὶ ἐσμέν and we are [such] ʟᴛᴛʀᴀ. ᴾ — δὲ but ʟᴛᴛʀᴀᴡ.

as he is. 3 And every man that hath this hope in him purifieth himself, even as he is pure.

ἐστιν. 3 καὶ πᾶς ὁ ἔχων τὴν.ἐλπίδα.ταύτην ἐπ᾽ αὐτῷ,
he is. And everyone that has this hope in him,
ἁγνίζει ἑαυτόν, καθὼς ἐκεῖνος ἁγνός ἐστιν.
purifies himself, even as he ²pure ¹is.

4 Whosoever committeth sin transgresseth also the law : for sin is the transgression of the law. 5 And ye know that he was manifested to take away our sins; and in him is no sin. 6 Whosoever abideth in him sinneth not : whosoever sinneth hath not seen him, neither known him.

4 Πᾶς ὁ ποιῶν τὴν ἁμαρτίαν, καὶ τὴν ἀνομίαν ποιεῖ,
Everyone that practises sin, also lawlessness practises;
καὶ ᵠ ἡ¹ ἁμαρτία ἐστὶν ἡ ἀνομία. 5 καὶ οἴδατε ὅτι ἐκεῖνος
and sin is lawlessness. And ye know that he
ἐφανερώθη, ἵνα τὰς ἁμαρτίας ʳἡμῶν‖ ἄρῃ καὶ
was manifested, that ²sins ¹our he might take away ; and
ἁμαρτία ἐν αὐτῷ οὐκ.ἔστιν. 6 πᾶς ὁ ἐν αὐτῷ μένων οὐχ
sin in him is not. ²Anyone ³that ⁵in ⁶him ⁴abides ¹not
(lit. everyone)
ἁμαρτάνει· πᾶς ὁ ἁμαρτάνων οὐχ ἑώρακεν αὐτόν, οὐδὲ
sins : ²anyone ³that ⁴sins ¹not has seen him, nor
(lit. everyone)
ἔγνωκεν αὐτόν.
has known him.

7 Little children, let no man deceive you : he that doeth righteousness is righteous, even as he is righteous. 8 He that committeth sin is of the devil : for the devil sinneth from the beginning. For this purpose the Son of God was manifested, that he might destroy the works of the devil. 9 Whosoever is born of God doth not commit sin ; for his seed remaineth in him : and he cannot sin, because he is born of God. 10 In this the children of God are manifest, and the children of the devil : whosoever doeth not righteousness is not of God, neither he that loveth not his brother. 11 For this is the message that ye heard from the beginning, that we should love one another. 12 Not as Cain, who was of that wicked one, and slew his brother. And wherefore slew he him ? Because his own works were evil, and his brother's righteous.

7 Τεκνία, μηδεὶς πλανάτω ὑμᾶς· ὁ ποιῶν τὴν
Little children, ²no ³one ¹let ⁴lead ⁵astray ⁵you ; he that practises
δικαιοσύνην, δίκαιός ἐστιν, καθὼς ἐκεῖνος δίκαιός ἐστιν. 8 ὁ
righteousness, righteous is, even as he righteous is. He that
ποιῶν τὴν ἁμαρτίαν, ἐκ τοῦ διαβόλου ἐστίν· ὅτι ἀπ᾽
practises sin, of the devil is ; because from [the]
ἀρχῆς ὁ διάβολος ἁμαρτάνει. εἰς τοῦτο ἐφανερώθη ὁ υἱὸς
beginning the devil sins. For this was manifested the Son
τοῦ θεοῦ, ἵνα λύσῃ τὰ ἔργα τοῦ διαβόλου. 9 πᾶς ὁ
of God, that he might undo the works of the devil. ²Anyone ³that
(lit. everyone)
γεγεννημένος ἐκ τοῦ θεοῦ ἁμαρτίαν οὐ ποιεῖ, ὅτι σπέρμα
⁴has ⁵been ⁶begotten ⁷of ⁸God, ¹⁰sin ¹not ⁹practises, because ²seed
αὐτοῦ ἐν αὐτῷ μένει· καὶ οὐ.δύναται ἁμαρτάνειν, ὅτι ἐκ τοῦ
¹his in him abides, and he is not able to sin, because of
θεοῦ γεγέννηται. 10 ἐν τούτῳ φανερά ἐστιν τὰ τέκνα τοῦ
God he has been begotten. In this manifest are the children
θεοῦ καὶ τὰ τέκνα τοῦ διαβόλου. πᾶς ὁ μὴ ˢποιῶν
of God and the children of the devil. ²Anyone ³that ¹not ⁴practises
(lit. everyone)
δικαιοσύνην‖ οὐκ ἔστιν ἐκ τοῦ θεοῦ, καὶ ὁ μὴ.ἀγαπῶν τὸν
⁵righteousness ¹not is of God, and he that loves not
ἀδελφὸν αὐτοῦ. 11 ὅτι αὕτη ἐστὶν ἡ ἀγγελία ἣν ἠκούσατε
²brother ¹his. Because this is the message which ye heard
ἀπ᾽ ἀρχῆς, ἵνα ἀγαπῶμεν ἀλλήλους· 12 οὐ καθὼς
from [the] beginning ; that we should love one another : not as
Κάϊν ἐκ τοῦ πονηροῦ ἦν, καὶ ἔσφαξεν τὸν ἀδελφὸν
Cain [who] of the wicked [one] was, and slew ²brother
αὐτοῦ· καὶ χάριν τίνος ἔσφαξεν αὐτόν; ὅτι τὰ.ἔργα.αὐτοῦ
¹his ; and on account of what slew he him ? because his works
πονηρὰ ἦν, τὰ.δὲ τοῦ.ἀδελφοῦ.αὐτοῦ δίκαια.
²wicked ¹were, and those of his brother righteous.

13 Marvel not, my brethren, if the world hate you. 14 We know that we have passed from death unto life, because we love the brethren. He that loveth not his brother abideth in death. 15 Whosoever hateth

13 ᵗΜὴ.θαυμάζετε, ἀδελφοί ᵛμου,‖ εἰ μισεῖ ὑμᾶς ὁ κόσμος.
Wonder not, ²brethren ¹my, if ³hates ⁴you ¹the ²world.
14 ἡμεῖς οἴδαμεν ὅτι μεταβεβήκαμεν ἐκ τοῦ θανάτου εἰς τὴν
We know that we have passed from death to
ζωήν, ὅτι ἀγαπῶμεν τοὺς ἀδελφούς· ὁ μὴ.ἀγαπῶν
life, because we love the brethren. He that loves not [his]
ʷτὸν ἀδελφόν,‖ μένει ἐν τῷ θανάτῳ. 15 πᾶς ὁ μισῶν τὸν
brother, abides in death. Everyone that hates

ἀδελφὸν αὐτοῦ, ἀνθρωποκτόνος εστίν, καὶ οἴδατε ὅτι πᾶς
²brother ¹his   a murderer   is,   and ye know that ²any
(lit. every)
ἀνθρωποκτόνος οὐκ ἔχει ζωὴν αἰώνιον ἐν ˣαὐτῷ‖ μένουσαν.
³murderer   ¹not has life eternal ²in ³him ¹abiding.

his brother is a murderer : and ye know that no murderer hath eternal life abiding in him.

16 Ἐν τούτῳ ἐγνώκαμεν τὴν ἀγάπην, ὅτι ἐκεῖνος ὑπὲρ
   By this we have known   love,   because he   for
ἡμῶν τὴν.ψυχὴν.αὐτοῦ ἔθηκεν· καὶ ἡμεῖς ὀφείλομεν ὑπὲρ τῶν
us   his life   laid down ; and we   ought   for the
ἀδελφῶν τὰς ψυχὰς ʸτιθέναι.‖ 17 ὃς.δ᾽.ἂν ἔχῃ τὸν
brethren [our] lives   to lay down.   But whoever may have
βίον   τοῦ κόσμου, καὶ θεωρῇ τὸν.ἀδελφὸν.αὐτοῦ χρείαν
²means ⁴of ³life ¹the ²world's, and may see his brother ²need
ἔχοντα, καὶ κλείσῃ τὰ.σπλάγχνα.αὐτοῦ ἀπ᾽ αὐτοῦ, πῶς ἡ
¹having, and may shut up his bowels   from him, how ²the
ἀγάπη τοῦ θεοῦ μένει ἐν αὐτῷ;
³love ⁴of ⁵God ¹abides in him?

16 Hereby perceive we the love of God, because he laid down his life for us : and we ought to lay down our lives for the brethren. 17 But whoso hath this world's good, and seeth his brother have need, and shutteth up his bowels of compassion from him, how dwelleth the love of God in him?

18 Τεκνία ²μου,‖ μὴ.ἀγαπῶμεν λόγῳ μηδὲ ᵃ γλώσσῃ,
   ²Little ³children ¹my, we should not love in word, nor with tongue,
ᵇἀλλ᾽‖ ᶜἔργῳ καὶ ἀληθείᾳ. 19 ᵈκαὶ‖ ἐν τούτῳ ᵉγινώσκομεν‖
but in work and in truth.   And by this   we know
ὅτι ἐκ τῆς ἀληθείας ἐσμέν, καὶ ἔμπροσθεν αὐτοῦ πείσομεν
that of the truth   we are, and before   him   shall persuade
τὰς.καρδίας.ἡμῶν· 20 ᶠὅτι‖ ἐὰν καταγινώσκῃ ἡμῶν ἡ καρδία,
our hearts,   that if ³should ⁴condemn ¹our ²heart,
ὅτι μείζων ἐστὶν ὁ θεὸς τῆς.καρδίας.ἡμῶν καὶ γινώσκει πάντα.
that greater is God than our heart   and knows all things
21 ἀγαπητοί, ἐὰν ἡ καρδία ᵍἡμῶν‖ μὴ.καταγινώσκῃ ἡμῶν,
   Beloved, if ¹heart ²our   should not condemn us,
παρρησίαν ἔχομεν πρὸς τὸν θεόν, 22 καὶ ὃ.ἐὰν αἰτῶμεν,
boldness we have towards God,   and whatsoever we may ask,
λαμβάνομεν ʰπαρ᾽‖ αὐτοῦ, ὅτι τὰς.ἐντολὰς.αὐτοῦ τηροῦμεν,
we receive from him, because his commandments we keep,
καὶ τὰ ἀρεστὰ ἐνώπιον αὐτοῦ ποιοῦμεν. 23 καὶ αὕτη
and the things pleasing before him   we practise.   And this
ἐστὶν ἡ.ἐντολὴ.αὐτοῦ, ἵνα ⁱπιστεύσωμεν‖ τῷ ὀνόματι τοῦ
is his commandment, that we should believe on the name
υἱοῦ.αὐτοῦ Ἰησοῦ χριστοῦ, καὶ ἀγαπῶμεν ἀλλήλους, καθὼς
of his Son   Jesus Christ, and should love one another, even as
ἔδωκεν ἐντολὴν ἡμῖν. 24 καὶ ὁ τηρῶν τὰς.ἐντολὰς.αὐτοῦ,
he gave commandment to us.   And he that keeps his commandments,
ἐν αὐτῷ μένει, καὶ αὐτὸς ἐν αὐτῷ· καὶ ἐν τούτῳ γινώσκομεν
in him abides, and he in ᵛhim· and by this   we know
ὅτι μένει ἐν ἡμῖν, ἐκ τοῦ πνεύματος οὗ ἡμῖν ἔδωκεν.
that he abides in us, by the Spirit   which to us he gave.

18 My little children, let us not love in word, neither in tongue; but in deed and in truth. 19 And hereby we know that we are of the truth, and shall assure our hearts before him, 20 For if our heart condemn us, God is greater than our heart, and knoweth all things. 21 Beloved, if our heart condemn us not, then have we confidence toward God. 22 And whatsoever we ask, we receive of him, because we keep his commandments, and do those things that are pleasing in his sight. 23 And this is his commandment, That we should believe on the name of his Son Jesus Christ, and love one another, as he gave us commandment. 24 And he that keepeth his commandments dwelleth in him, and he in him. And hereby we know that he abideth in us, by the Spirit which he hath given us.

4 Ἀγαπητοί, μὴ παντὶ πνεύματι πιστεύετε, ἀλλὰ δοκιμά-
  Beloved, ²not ³every ⁴spirit ¹believe,   but   prove
ζετε τὰ πνεύματα, εἰ ἐκ τοῦ θεοῦ ἐστιν· ὅτι πολλοὶ ψευδο-
the spirits,   if of God   they are ; because many   false
προφῆται ἐξεληλύθασιν εἰς τὸν κόσμον. 2 ἐν τούτῳ γινώσκετε
prophets   have gone out into the world.   By this   ye know
τὸ πνεῦμα τοῦ θεοῦ· πᾶν πνεῦμα ὃ ὁμολογεῖ Ἰησοῦν χριστὸν
the Spirit   of God : every spirit which confesses Jesus   Christ

IV. Beloved, believe not every spirit, but try the spirits whether they are of God : because many false prophets are gone out into the world. 2 Hereby know ye the Spirit of God : Every spirit that confesseth that Jesus Christ is come

---

ˣ ἑαυτῷ himself LT.   ʸ θεῖναι LTTrAW   ᶻ — μου LTTrAW.   ᵃ + τῇ (read with the tongue) GLTTrAW.   ᵇ ἀλλὰ TTr.   ᶜ + ἐν in (work) GLTTrAW.   ᵈ — καὶ L[Tr].   ᵉ γνωσό-μεθα we shall know LTTrAW.   ᶠ ὅτι (read whatever our heart) L.   ᵍ — ἡμῶν (read the heart) LTr[A].   ʰ ἀπ᾽ LTTrA.   ⁱ πιστεύωμεν we believe LTTr ; πιστεύ[σ]ωμεν A.

in the flesh is of God: 3 and every spirit that confesseth not that Jesus Christ is come in the flesh is not of God: and this is that *spirit* of antichrist, whereof ye have heard that it should come; and even now already is it in the world. 4 Ye are of God, little children, and have overcome them: because greater is he that is in you, than he that is in the world. 5 They are of the world: therefore speak they of the world, and the world heareth them. 6 We are of God: he that knoweth God heareth us; he that is not of God heareth not us. Hereby know we the spirit of truth, and the spirit of error.

7 Beloved, let us love one another: for love is of God; and every one that loveth is born of God, and knoweth God. 8 He that loveth not knoweth not God; for God is love. 9 In this was manifested the love of God toward us, because that God sent his only begotten Son into the world, that we might live through him. 10 Herein is love, not that we loved God, but that he loved us, and sent his Son to *be* the propitiation for our sins. 11 Beloved, if God so loved us, we ought also to love one another. 12 No man hath seen God at any time. If we love one another, God dwelleth in us, and his love is perfected in us. 13 Hereby know we that we dwell in him, and he in us, because he hath given us of his Spirit. 14 And we have seen and do testify that the Father sent the Son *to be* the Saviour of the world.

ἐν σαρκὶ ἐληλυθότα, ἐκ τοῦ θεοῦ ἐστιν. 3 καὶ πᾶν πνεῦμα
[2]in [3]flesh [1]come, of God is; and [2]any [3]spirit
(*lit.* every)

ὃ μὴ ὁμολογεῖ τὸν Ἰησοῦν [k]χριστὸν ἐν σαρκὶ ἐληλυθότα,‖ ἐκ
[4]which [5]confesses [6]not [7]Jesus [8]Christ [10]in [11]flesh [9]come, [12]of

τοῦ θεοῦ οὐκ ἔστιν· καὶ τοῦτό ἐστιν τὸ τοῦ ἀντιχρίστου,
[14]God [1]not [12]is: and this is that [power] of the antichrist,

ὃ ἀκηκόατε ὅτι ἔρχεται, καὶ νῦν ἐν τῷ κόσμῳ ἐστὶν ἤδη.
[of] which ye heard that it comes, and now in the world is it already.

4 Ὑμεῖς ἐκ τοῦ θεοῦ ἐστε, τεκνία, καὶ νενικήκατε αὐτούς·
Ye of God are, little children, and have overcome them,

ὅτι μείζων ἐστὶν ὁ ἐν ὑμῖν ἢ ὁ ἐν τῷ κόσμῳ.
because greater is he who [is] in you than he who [is] in the world.

5 αὐτοὶ ἐκ τοῦ κόσμου εἰσίν, διὰ τοῦτο ἐκ τοῦ κόσμου λα-
They of the world are; because of this of the world they

λοῦσιν, καὶ ὁ κόσμος αὐτῶν ἀκούει. 6 ἡμεῖς ἐκ τοῦ θεοῦ
talk, and the world [2]them [1]hears. We of God

ἐσμεν· ὁ γινώσκων τὸν θεόν, ἀκούει ἡμῶν· ὃς οὐκ ἔστιν
are; he that knows God, hears us; he that is not

ἐκ τοῦ θεοῦ, οὐκ ἀκούει ἡμῶν. ἐκ τούτου γινώσκομεν τὸ πνεῦμα
of God, hears not us. By this we know the spirit

τῆς ἀληθείας καὶ τὸ πνεῦμα τῆς πλάνης.
of truth and the spirit of error.

7 Ἀγαπητοί, ἀγαπῶμεν ἀλλήλους· ὅτι ἡ ἀγάπη ἐκ τοῦ
Beloved, we should love one another; because love [2]of

θεοῦ ἐστιν, καὶ πᾶς ὁ ἀγαπῶν, ἐκ τοῦ θεοῦ γεγέννηται,
[3]God [1]is, and everyone that loves, of God has been begotten,

καὶ γινώσκει τὸν θεόν. 8 ὁ μὴ ἀγαπῶν, οὐκ ἔγνω τὸν θεόν·
and knows God. He that loves not, knew not God;

ὅτι ὁ θεὸς ἀγάπη ἐστίν. 9 ἐν τούτῳ ἐφανερώθη ἡ ἀγάπη
because God [2]love [1]is. In this was manifested the love

τοῦ θεοῦ ἐν ἡμῖν, ὅτι τὸν υἱὸν αὐτοῦ μονογενῆ ἀπέ-
of God as to us, that his Son the only-begotten [2]has

σταλκεν ὁ θεὸς εἰς τὸν κόσμον, ἵνα ζήσωμεν δι᾽ αὐτοῦ.
[3]sent [1]God into the world, that we might live through him.

10 ἐν τούτῳ ἐστὶν ἡ ἀγάπη, οὐχ ὅτι ἡμεῖς ἠγαπήσαμεν τὸν
In this is love, not that we loved

θεόν, ἀλλ᾽ ὅτι αὐτὸς ἠγάπησεν ἡμᾶς, καὶ ἀπέστειλεν τὸν υἱὸν
God, but that he loved us, and sent [2]Son

αὐτοῦ ἱλασμὸν περὶ τῶν ἁμαρτιῶν ἡμῶν. 11 ἀγαπητοί, εἰ
[1]his a propitiation for our sins. Beloved, if

οὕτως ὁ θεὸς ἠγάπησεν ἡμᾶς, καὶ ἡμεῖς ὀφείλομεν ἀλλήλους
[2]so [1]God loved us, also we ought one another

ἀγαπᾶν. 12 θεὸν οὐδεὶς πώποτε τεθέαται· ἐὰν ἀγαπῶμεν
to love. [5]God [1]no [2]one [6]at [7]any [8]time [3]has [4]seen; if we should love

ἀλλήλους, ὁ θεὸς ἐν ἡμῖν μένει, καὶ ἡ ἀγάπη αὐτοῦ [1]τετελειω-
one another, God in us abides, and his love [2]perfect-

μένη ἐστὶν ἐν ἡμῖν.‖ 13 ἐν τούτῳ γινώσκομεν ὅτι ἐν αὐτῷ
ed [1]is in us. By this we know that in him

μένομεν, καὶ αὐτὸς ἐν ἡμῖν, ὅτι ἐκ τοῦ πνεύματος αὐτοῦ
we abide, and he in us, because of his Spirit

δέδωκεν ἡμῖν. 14 καὶ ἡμεῖς τεθεάμεθα καὶ μαρτυροῦμεν ὅτι
he has given to us. And we have seen and bear witness that

ὁ πατὴρ ἀπέσταλκεν τὸν υἱὸν σωτῆρα τοῦ κόσμου.
the Father has sent the Son [as] Saviour of the world.

---

k — χριστὸν w; — χριστὸν ἐν σαρκὶ ἐληλυθότα (*read* the Jesus) GLTTrA.   [1] ἐν ἡμῖν
τετελειωμένα ἐστίν L; τετελ. ἐν ἡμῖν ἐστίν TTrA.

15 Ὅς.ἂν ὁμολογήσῃ ὅτι Ἰησοῦς ἐστιν ὁ υἱὸς τοῦ θεοῦ, ὁ
　　Whosoever may confess that Jesus is the Son of God,
θεὸς ἐν αὐτῷ μένει, καὶ αὐτὸς ἐν τῷ θεῷ. 16 καὶ ἡμεῖς ἐγνώ-
God in him abides, and he in God. And we have
καμεν καὶ πεπιστεύκαμεν τὴν ἀγάπην ἣν ἔχει ὁ θεὸς ἐν ἡμῖν.
known and have believed the love which ²has ¹God as to us.
ὁ ὑὸς ἀγάπη ἐστίν, καὶ ὁ μένων ἐν τῇ ἀγάπῃ, ἐν τῷ θεῷ
G d ²love ¹is, and he that abides in love, in God
μένει, καὶ ὁ θεὸς ἐν αὐτῷ^m. 17 ἐν τούτῳ τετελείωται ἡ ἀγάπη
abides, and God in him. In this has been perfected love
μεθ᾽ ἡμῶν, ἵνα παρρησίαν ἔχωμεν ἐν τῇ ἡμέρᾳ τῆς κρίσεως,
with us, that boldness we may have in the day of judgment,
ὅτι καθὼς ἐκεῖνός ἐστιν, καὶ ἡμεῖς ἐσμεν ἐν τῷ.κόσμῳ.τούτῳ.
that even as he is, also we are in this world.
18 φόβος οὐκ.ἔστιν ἐν τῇ ἀγάπῃ, ⁿἀλλ᾽^ǁ ἡ τελεία ἀγάπη ἔξω
⁴Fear ¹there ²is ³not in love, but perfect love ²out
βάλλει τὸν φόβον, ὅτι ὁ φόβος κόλασιν ἔχει· ὁ.δὲ φοβού-
¹casts fear; because fear ²torment ¹has, and he that fears
μενος οὐ.τετελείωται ἐν τῇ ἀγάπῃ. 19 ἡμεῖς ^o ἀγαπῶμεν
has not been made perfect in love. We love
Ραὐτὸν^ǁ ὅτι ^qαὐτὸς^ǁ πρῶτος ἠγάπησεν ἡμᾶς.
him because he first loved us.

20 Ἐάν τις εἴπῃ, Ὅτι ἀγαπῶ τὸν θεόν, καὶ τὸν ἀδελ-
If anyone should say, I love God, and ⁴bro-
φὸν αὐτοῦ μισῇ, ψεύστης ἐστίν· ὁ.γὰρ μὴ.ἀγαπῶν τὸν
ther ³his ¹should ²hate, a liar he is. For he that loves not
ἀδελφὸν.αὐτοῦ ὃν ἑώρακεν, τὸν θεὸν ὃν οὐχ.ἑώρακεν,
his brother whom he has seen, ⁷God ⁸whom ⁹he ¹⁰has ¹¹not ¹²seen,
ʳπῶς^ǁ δύναται ἀγαπᾶν; 21 καὶ ταύτην τὴν ἐντολὴν ἔχο-
¹how ²is ³he ⁴able ⁵to ⁶love? And this commandment we
μεν ἀπ᾽ αὐτοῦ, ἵνα ὁ ἀγαπῶν τὸν θεὸν ἀγαπᾷ καὶ τὸν
have from him, that he that loves God should love also
ἀδελφὸν αὐτοῦ. 5 Πᾶς ὁ πιστεύων ὅτι Ἰησοῦς ἐστιν ὁ
ⁱbrother ¹his. Everyone that believes that Jesus is the
χριστὸς ἐκ τοῦ θεοῦ γεγέννηται· καὶ πᾶς ὁ ἀγαπῶν τὸν
Christ, of God has been begotten; and everyone that loves him that
γεννήσαντα ἀγαπᾷ ^sκαὶ^ǁ τὸν γεγεννημένον ἐξ αὐτοῦ. 2 ἐν
begat, loves also him that has been begotten of him. By
τούτῳ γινώσκομεν ὅτι ἀγαπῶμεν τὰ τέκνα τοῦ θεοῦ, ὅταν τὸν
this we know that we love the children of God, when
θεὸν ἀγαπῶμεν καὶ τὰς.ἐντολὰς.αὐτοῦ ᵗτηρῶμεν.^ǁ 3 αὕτη.γὰρ
God we love and his commandments keep. For this
ἐστιν ἡ ἀγάπη τοῦ θεοῦ, ἵνα τὰς.ἐντολὰς.αὐτοῦ τηρῶμεν·
is the love of God, that his commandments we should keep;
καὶ αἱ.ἐντολαὶ.αὐτοῦ βαρεῖαι οὐκ.εἰσίν. 4 ὅτι πᾶν τὸ γε-
and his commandments burdensome are not. Because all that has
γεννημένον ἐκ τοῦ θεοῦ νικᾷ τὸν κόσμον· καὶ αὕτη ἐστὶν
been begotten of God overcomes the world; and this is
ἡ νίκη ἡ νικήσασα τὸν κόσμον, ἡ.πίστις.ἡμῶν· 5 τίς^v
the victory which overcame the world, our faith. Who
ἐστιν ὁ νικῶν τὸν κόσμον, εἰ.μὴ ὁ πιστεύων ὅτι Ἰησοῦς
is he that overcomes the world, but he that believes that Jesus
ἐστιν ὁ υἱὸς τοῦ θεοῦ;
is the Son of God?

15 Whosoever shall confess that Jesus is the Son of God, God dwelleth in him, and he in God. 16 And we have known and believed the love that God hath to us. God is love; and he that dwelleth in love dwelleth in God, and God in him. 17 Herein is our love made perfect, that we may have boldness in the day of judgment: because as he is, so are we in this world. 18 There is no fear in love; but perfect love casteth out fear: because fear hath torment. He that feareth is not made perfect in love. 19 We love him, because he first loved us.

20 If a man say, I love God, and hateth his brother, he is a liar: for he that loveth not his brother whom he hath seen, how can he love God whom he hath not seen? 21 And this commandment have we from him, That he who loveth God love his brother also. V. Whosoever believeth that Jesus is the Christ is born of God; and every one that loveth him that begat loveth him also that is begotten of him. 2 By this we know that we love the children of God,. when we love God, and keep his commandments. 3 For this is the love of God, that we keep his commandments: and his commandments are not grievous. 4 For whatsoever is born of God overcometh the world: and this is the victory that overcometh the world, even our faith. 5 Who is he that overcometh the world, but he that believeth that Jesus is the Son of God?

---

^m + μένει abides [L]ΤΑ. 　　ⁿ ἀλλὰ Τr. 　　^o + οὖν therefore ι. 　　^p — αὐτὸν LTTrAW.
^q ὁ θεὸς God L. 　^r οὐ (read he is not able) LTTrA. 　^s [καὶ] LTr. 　^t ποιῶμεν may do LTTrAW,
^v + [δέ] but (who) Τr.
4U

6 This is he that came by water and blood, even Jesus Christ ; not by water only, but by water and blood. And it is the Spirit that beareth witness, because the Spirit is truth. 7 For there are three that bear record in heaven, the Father, the Word, and the Holy Ghost : and these three are one. 8 And there are three that bear witness in earth, the Spirit, and the water, and the blood : and these three agree in one. 9 If we receive the witness of men, the witness of God is greater : for this is the witness of God which he hath testified of his Son. 10 He that believeth on the Son of God hath the witness in himself : he that believeth not God hath made him a liar ; because he believeth not the record that God gave of his Son. 11 And this is the record, that God hath given to us eternal life, and this life is in his Son. 12 He that hath the Son hath life ; and he that hath not the Son of God hath not life.

6 Οὗτός ἐστιν ὁ ἐλθὼν δι' ὕδατος καὶ αἵματος, Ἰησοῦς
This　　is he who came　　by　water　　and blood,　　Jesus
ῶ ‖ χριστός· οὐκ ἐν τῷ ὕδατι μόνον, ᵡἀλλ'‖ ἐν τῷ ὕδατι καὶ ʸ
the Christ ;　not　by　water　　only,　　but　by　water　and
τῷ αἵματι· καὶ τὸ πνεῦμά ἐστιν τὸ μαρτυροῦν ὅτι τὸ πνεῦμά
blood.　And the Spirit　it is that bears witness, because the Spirit
ἐστιν ἡ ἀλήθεια. 7 ὅτι τρεῖς εἰσιν οἱ μαρτυροῦντες ᶻἐν τῷ
is　the truth.　　Because three there are who bear witness　in
οὐρανῷ, ὁ πατήρ, ὁ λόγος, καὶ τὸ ἅγιον πνεῦμα· καὶ οὗτοι
heaven, the Father, the Word, and the Holy　Ghost ; and these
οἱ τρεῖς ἕν εἰσιν. 8 καὶ τρεῖς εἰσιν οἱ μαρτυροῦντες ἐν τῇ
three one are.　　And three there are who　bear witness　on
γῇ,‖ τὸ πνεῦμα, καὶ τὸ ὕδωρ, καὶ τὸ αἷμα, καὶ οἱ τρεῖς εἰς τὸ
earth, the Spirit, and the water, and the blood ; and the three to the
ἕν　　εἰσιν. 9 εἰ τὴν μαρτυρίαν τῶν ἀνθρώπων λαμβάνο-
one [point] are.　　If the　witness　　of men　　we re-
μεν, ἡ μαρτυρία τοῦ θεοῦ μείζων ἐστίν· ὅτι αὕτη ἐστὶν
ceive, the　witness　of God ²greater ¹is.　Because this　　is
ἡ μαρτυρία τοῦ θεοῦ, ᵃἣν‖ μεμαρτύρηκεν περὶ τοῦ.υἱοῦ.αὐτοῦ.
the witness　of God which he has witnessed concerning　his Son.
10 ὁ πιστεύων εἰς τὸν υἱὸν τοῦ θεοῦ ἔχει τὴν μαρτυρίαν ᵇ ἐν
He that believes on the Son　of God has the　witness　　in
ᶜἑαυτῷ·‖ ὁ μὴ.πιστεύων ᵈτῷ θεῷ‖ ψεύστην πεποίηκεν αὐτόν,
himself ; he that believes not　God　⁴a ⁵liar ¹has ²made ³him.
ὅτι οὐ.πεπίστευκεν εἰς τὴν μαρτυρίαν, ἣν μεμαρτύρηκεν ᴼ
because he has not believed in the　witness　which ²has ³witnessed
θεὸς περὶ τοῦ.υἱοῦ.αὐτοῦ. 11 καὶ αὕτη ἐστὶν ἡ μαρτυρία
¹God concerning　his Son.　　And this　　is the witness,
ὅτι ζωὴν αἰώνιον ἔδωκεν ἡμῖν ὁ θεός· καὶ αὕτη ἡ ζωὴ ἐν τῷ
that life eternal　²gave ³to ⁴us ¹God; and this　life ²in
υἱῷ αὐτοῦ ἐστιν. 12 ὁ ἔχων τὸν υἱόν, ἔχει τὴν ζωήν· ὁ
⁴Son ³his ¹is :　he that has the Son, has　　life : he that
μὴ.ἔχων τὸν υἱὸν τοῦ θεοῦ, τὴν ζωὴν οὐκ.ἔχει.
has not the Son of God,　life　has not.

13 These things have I written unto you that believe on the name of the Son of God ; that ye may know that ye have eternal life, and that ye may believe on the name of the Son of God. 14 And this is the confidence that we have in him, that, if we ask any thing according to his will, he heareth us : 15 And if we know :hat he hear us, whatsoever we ask, we know that we have the petitions that we desired of him.

16 If any man see his brother sin a sin which is not unto death, he shall ask, and he shall give him life for them that

13 Ταῦτα ἔγραψα ὑμῖν ᵉτοῖς πιστεύουσιν εἰς τὸ ὄνομα
These things I wrote to you who　　believe　　on the name
τοῦ υἱοῦ τοῦ θεοῦ,‖ ἵνα εἰδῆτε ὅτι ζωὴν ᶠἔχετε αἰώνιον,‖ ᵍκαὶ
of the Son　of　God, that ye may know that ⁴life ¹ye ²have ³eternal,　and
ἵνα πιστεύητε‖ εἰς τὸ ὄνομα τοῦ υἱοῦ τοῦ θεοῦ. 14 καὶ αὕτη
that ye may believe on the name of the Son　of God.　　And this
ἐστὶν ἡ παρρησία ἣν ἔχομεν πρὸς αὐτόν, ʰὅτι ἐάν τι‖
is　the boldness which we have towards　him,　that if anything
αἰτώμεθα κατὰ τὸ.θέλημα.αὐτοῦ, ἀκούει ἡμῶν· 15 καὶ
we may ask according to　his will,　he hears　us.　And
ᶦἐὰν‖ οἴδαμεν ὅτι ἀκούει ἡμῶν, ὅ.ᵏἂν‖ αἰτώμεθα, οἴδαμεν ὅτι
if　we know that he hears　us,　whatsoever we may ask, we know that
ἔχομεν τὰ αἰτήματα ἃ ᾐτήκαμεν ˡπαρ'‖ αὐτοῦ.
we have the　requests which we have asked from　him.

16 Ἐάν τις ᵐἴδῃ‖ τὸν.ἀδελφὸν.αὐτοῦ ἁμαρτάνοντα
If anyone should see　his brother　　sinning
ἁμαρτίαν μὴ πρὸς θάνατον, αἰτήσει, καὶ δώσει αὐτῷ ζωήν,
a sin　not to　death,　he shall ask, and he shall give him　life

ʷ — ὁ ΤΤrΑW.　ˣ ἀλλὰ Τr　ʸ + ἐν by LΤΤrΑW.　ᶻ — ἐν τῷ οὐρανῷ . . . . τῇ γῇ
verse 8 GLΤΤrΑW.　ᵃ ὅτι that LΤΤrΑW.　ᵇ + τοῦ θεοῦ of God L.　ᶜ αὐτῷ him ΤΤrΑ.　ᵈ τῷ
υἱῷ the Son L.　ᵉ — τοῖς πιστεύουσιν εἰς τὸ ὄνομα τοῦ υἱοῦ τοῦ θεοῦ GLΤΤrΑW.　ᶠ αἰώνιον
ἔχετε G.　ᵍ οἱ πιστεύοντες [ye] believers GLW ; τοῖς πιστεύουσιν to [you] who believe ΤΤrΑ.
ʰ ὅτι ἂν whatever L.　ᶦ ἂν L.　ᵏ ἐὰν Τ.　ˡ ἀπ' LΤΤr.　ᵐ εἰδῇ L.

τοῖς ἁμαρτάνουσιν μὴ πρὸς θάνατον. ἔστιν ἁμαρτία
for those that sin not to death. There is a sin

πρὸς θάνατον· οὐ περὶ ἐκείνης λέγω ἵνα ἐρωτήσῃ·
to death; not concerning that do I say that he should beseech.

17 πᾶσα ἀδικία ἁμαρτία ἐστίν, καὶ ἔστιν ἁμαρτία οὐ πρὸς
Every unrighteousness ²sin ¹is; and there is a sin not to

θάνατον. 18 οἴδαμεν ὅτι πᾶς ὁ γεγεννημένος ἐκ τοῦ θεοῦ
death. We know that ²anyone ³that ⁴has ⁵been ⁶begotten ⁷of ⁸God
(lit. everyone)

οὐχ ἁμαρτάνει· ⁿἀλλ'ᴵᴵ ὁ γεννηθεὶς ἐκ τοῦ θεοῦ τηρεῖ °ἑαυ-
¹not sins, but he that was begotten of God keeps him-

τόν,ᴵᴵ καὶ ὁ πονηρὸς οὐχ ἅπτεται αὐτοῦ. 19 οἴδαμεν ὅτι
self, and the wicked [one] does not touch him. We know that

ἐκ τοῦ θεοῦ ἐσμεν, καὶ ὁ κόσμος ὅλος ἐν τῷ πονηρῷ κεῖται.
of God we are, and the ²world ¹whole in the wicked [one] lies.

20 ᴾοἴδαμεν.δὲᴵᴵ ὅτι ὁ υἱὸς τοῦ θεοῦ ἥκει, καὶ δέδωκεν ἡμῖν
And we know that the Son of God is come, and has given us

διάνοιαν ἵνα ᵠγινώσκωμενᴵᴵ τὸν ἀληθινόν· καί ἐσμεν
an understanding that we might know him that [is] true; and we are

ἐν τῷ ἀληθινῷ, ἐν τῷ.υἱῷ.αὐτοῦ Ἰησοῦ χριστῷ. οὗτός
in him that [is] true, in his Son Jesus Christ. He

ἐστιν ὁ ἀληθινὸς θεός, καὶ ʳἡᴵᴵ ζωὴ αἰώνιος.
is the true God, and life eternal.

21 Τεκνία, φυλάξατε ˢἑαυτοὺςᴵᴵ ἀπὸ τῶν εἰδώλων. ᵗἀμήν.ᴵᴵ
Little children, keep yourselves from idols. Amen.

ᵛἸωάννου ἐπιστολὴ καθολικὴ πρώτη.ᴵᴵ
⁴Of ⁵John ³epistle ²general ¹first.

sin not unto death. There is a sin unto death : I do not say that he shall pray for it. 17 All unrighteousness is sin: and there is a sin not unto death. 18 We know that whosoever is born of God sinneth not ; but he that is begotten of God keepeth himself, and that wicked one toucheth him not. 19 And we know that we are of God, and the whole world lieth in wickedness. 20 And we know that the Son of God is come, and hath given us an understanding, that we may know him that is true, and we are in him that is true. This is the true God, and eternal life.

21 Little children, keep yourselves from idols. Amen.

ᵃΕΠΙΣΤΟΛΗ ΙΩΑΝΝΟΥ ΔΕΥΤΕΡΑ.ᴵᴵ
²EPISTLE ³OF ⁴JOHN ¹SECOND.

Ὁ πρεσβύτερος ᵇἐκλεκτῇᴵᴵ ᶜκυρίᾳᴵᴵ καὶ τοῖς.τέκνοις.αὐτῆς,
The elder to [the] elect lady and her children,

οὓς ἐγὼ ἀγαπῶ ἐν ἀληθείᾳ, καὶ οὐκ ἐγὼ μόνος, ἀλλὰ καὶ
whom I love in truth, and not I only, but also

πάντες οἱ ἐγνωκότες τὴν ἀλήθειαν, 2 διὰ τὴν ἀλή-
all those who have known the truth, for sake of the

θειαν τὴν μένουσαν ἐν ἡμῖν, καὶ μεθ' ἡμῶν ἔσται εἰς.τὸν.αἰῶνα·
truth which abides in us, and with us shall be for ever.

3 ἔσται μεθ' ᵈἡμῶνᴵᴵ χάρις, ἔλεος, εἰρήνη παρὰ θεοῦ πατρὸς
²Shall ³be ⁴with ⁵us ¹grace, mercy, peace, from God [the] Father,

καὶ παρὰ ᵉκυρίουᴵᴵ Ἰησοῦ χριστοῦ τοῦ υἱοῦ τοῦ πατρός, ἐν
and from [the] Lord Jesus Christ, the Son of the Father, in

ἀληθείᾳ καὶ ἀγάπῃ.
truth and love.

4 Ἐχάρην λίαν ὅτι εὕρηκα ἐκ τῶν.τέκνων.σου περιπα-
I rejoiced exceedingly that I have found of thy children walk-

τοῦντας ἐν ἀληθείᾳ, καθὼς ἐντολὴν ἐλάβομεν παρὰ τοῦ
ing in truth, as commandment we received from the

THE elder unto the elect lady and her children, whom I love in the truth ; and not I only, but also all they that have known the truth ; 2 for the truth's sake, which dwelleth in us, and shall be with us for ever. 3 Grace be with you, mercy, and peace, from God the Father, and from the Lord Jesus Christ, the Son of the Father, in truth and love.

4 I rejoiced greatly that I found of thy children walking in truth, as we have received a commandment from the Father.

ⁿ ἀλλὰ Tr. ° αὐτόν him TTrA. ᴾ καὶ οἴδαμεν GL. ᵠ γινώσκομεν we know TTrA.
ʳ — ἡ LTTrA. ˢ ἑαυτά LTTr. ᵗ — ἀμήν GLTTrAW. ᵛ — the subscription EGLTW ;
'Ιωάνου α' Tr ; 'Ιωάννου α' A.
ᵃ + τοῦ ἀποστόλου the apostle E ; + καθολικὴ general E ; 'Ιωάννου β' LTAW ; 'Ιωάνου
ἐπιστολὴ β' Tr. ᵇ Stephens puts a capital 'E, reading the word as a proper name.
ᶜ Κυρίᾳ Cyria (reading the word as a proper name) GLT. ᵈ ὑμῶν you EGLW. ᵉ — κυρίου LTTrAW.

5 And now I beseech thee, lady, not as though I wrote a new commandment unto thee, but that which we had from the beginning, that we love one another. 6 And this is love, that we walk after his commandments. This is the commandment, That, as ye have heard from the beginning, ye should walk in it. 7 For many deceivers are entered into the world, who confess not that Jesus Christ is come in the flesh. This is a deceiver and an antichrist. 8 Look to yourselves, that we lose not those things which we have wrought, but that we receive a full reward. 9 Whosoever transgresseth, and abideth not in the doctrine of Christ, hath not God. He that abideth in the doctrine of Christ, he hath both the Father and the Son. 10 If there come any unto you, and bring not this doctrine, receive him not into your house, neither bid him God speed : 11 for he that biddeth him God speed is partaker of his evil deeds.

12 Having many things to write unto you, I would not write with paper and ink: but I trust to come unto you, and speak face to face, that our joy may be full. 13 The children of thy elect sister greet thee. Amen.

πατρός. ὃ καὶ νῦν ἐρωτῶ σε, ᶠκυρία,ǁ οὐχ ὡς ἐντολὴν
Father   And now I beseech thee, lady,   not as a ²commandment
γράφω σοι καινήν,ǁ ἀλλὰ ἣν ʰεἴχομενǁ ἀπ᾽ ἀρ-
³I ⁴write ⁵to ⁶thee ¹new,   but that which we were having from [the] begin-
χῆς, ἵνα ᾽ ἀγαπῶμεν ἀλλήλους. 6 καὶ αὕτη ἐστὶν ἡ ἀγάπη,
ning, that we should love one another.   And this is love,
ἵνα περιπατῶμεν κατὰ τὰς ἐντολὰς αὐτοῦ. αὕτη ⁱἐστὶν ἡ
that we should walk according to his commandments. This is the
ἐντολή,ǁ ᵏκαθὼς ἠκούσατε ἀπ᾽ ἀρχῆς, ἵνα ἐν αὐτῇ
commandment, even as ye heard from [the] beginning, that in it
περιπατῆτε· 7 ὅτι πολλοὶ πλάνοι ˡεἰσῆλθονǁ εἰς τὸν
ye might walk. Because many deceivers entered into the
κόσμον, οἱ μὴ ὁμολογοῦντες Ἰησοῦν χριστὸν ἐρχόμενον ἐν
world, those who do not confess Jesus Christ coming in
σαρκί· οὗτός ἐστιν ὁ πλάνος καὶ ὁ ἀντίχριστος. 8 βλέπετε
flesh— this is the deceiver and the antichrist.   See to
ἑαυτούς, ἵνα μὴ ᵐἀπολέσωμενǁ ἃ ⁿεἰργασάμεθα,ǁ ἀλλὰ
yourselves, that ³not ¹we ²may lose what things we wrought, but
μισθὸν πλήρη ᵒἀπολάβωμεν.ǁ 9 πᾶς ὁ ᴾπαραβαίνων,ǁ καὶ
a ²reward ¹full we may receive. ²Anyone ³who ⁴transgresses, ⁵and
(lit. everyone)
μὴ μένων ἐν τῇ διδαχῇ τοῦ χριστοῦ, θεὸν οὐκ ἔχει· ὁ
⁶abides ⁷not ⁸in ⁹the ¹⁰teaching ¹¹of ¹²the ¹³Christ, ¹⁵God ¹⁴has. He that
μένων ἐν τῇ διδαχῇ �q τοῦ χριστοῦ,ǁ οὗτος καὶ τὸν πατέρα
⁹abides in the teaching of the Christ, this [one] both the Father
καὶ τὸν υἱὸν ἔχει. 10 εἴ τις ἔρχεται πρὸς ὑμᾶς, καὶ ταύτην
and the Son has. If anyone comes to you, and this
τὴν διδαχὴν οὐ φέρει, μὴ λαμβάνετε αὐτὸν εἰς οἰκίαν,
teaching does not bring, do not receive him into [the] house,
καὶ χαίρειν αὐτῷ μὴ λέγετε· 11 ὁ ʳγὰρ λέγωνǁ αὐτῷ χαίρειν,
and ³Hail! ⁴to ⁵him ¹say ²not ;   for he who says to him Hail !
κοινωνεῖ τοῖς ἔργοις αὐτοῦ τοῖς πονηροῖς·
partakes in ³works ¹his ²evil.

12 Πολλὰ ἔχων ὑμῖν γράφειν, οὐκ ˢἠβουλήθηνǁ διὰ χάρ-
Many things having ³to ⁴you ¹to ²write, I would not with pa-
του καὶ μέλανος· ᵗἀλλὰ ἐλπίζω· ᵛἐλθεῖνǁ πρὸς ὑμᾶς, καὶ στόμα
per and ink; but hope to come to you, and mouth
πρὸς στόμα λαλῆσαι, ἵνα ἡ χαρὰ ʷἡμῶνǁ ˣᾖ πεπληρωμένη.ǁ
to mouth to speak, that ²joy ¹our may be full.
13 ἀσπάζεταί σε τὰ τέκνα τῆς ἀδελφῆς σου τῆς ʸἐκλεκ-
⁷Salute ⁸thee ¹the ²children ⁶sister ³of ⁴thine ⁵elect
τῆς.ǁ ᶻἀμήν.ǁ
Amen.

ᵃἸωάννου ἐπιστολὴ δευτέρα.ǁ
³Of ⁴John ²epistle ¹second.

ᶠ Κυρία Cyria (see verse 1) GLT.   g γράφων (writing) σοι καινὴν EGAW; καινὴν γράφων
σοι LTTr.   ʰ εἴχαμεν TTr.   ⁱ ἡ ἐντολή ἐστιν LTTʳAW.   ᵏ + ἵνα that T.   ˡ ἐξῆλθαν (-θον TAW) went forth LTr.   ᵐ ἀπολέσητε ye may lose LTTʳAW.   ⁿ εἰργάσασθε
ye wrought LTTʳW.   ᵒ ἀπολάβητε ye may receive LTTʳAW.   ᴾ προάγων goes forward
LTTʳAW.   q — τοῦ χριστοῦ LTTʳA.   ʳ λέγων γὰρ LTTʳA.   ˢ ἐβουλήθην LTTʳAW.
ᵗ ἐλπίζω γὰρ for I hope GL.   ᵛ γενέσθαι LTTʳAW.   ʷ ὑμῶν your LTTʳA.   ˣ πεπληρωμένη ᾖ LT.   ʸ See note b verse 1.   ᶻ — ἀμήν GLTTʳAW.   ᵃ — the subscription EGLTW ;
Ἰωάνου β´ Tr ; Ἰωάννου β´ A.

ᵇΕΠΙΣΤΟΛΗ ΙΩΆΝΝΟΥ ΤΡΙΤΗ.ᵈ
²EPISTLE   ³OF ⁴JOHN   ¹THIRD.

'Ο πρεσβύτερος Γαίῳ τῷ ἀγαπητῷ, ὃν ἐγὼ ἀγαπῶ ἐν
The   elder   to Gaius the   beloved,   whom I   love in
ἀληθείᾳ.
truth.

THE elder unto the wellbeloved Gaius, whom I love in the truth.

2 Ἀγαπητέ, περὶ πάντων εὔχομαί σε εὐοδοῦσθαι καὶ
Beloved. concerning all things I wi-h thee to prosper aud
ὑγιαίνειν, καθὼς εὐοδοῦταί σου ἡ ψυχή. 3 ἐχάρην °γὰρᵈ
be in health, even as prospers thy   soul.   For I rejoiced
λίαν ἐρχομένων   ἀδελφῶν καὶ μαρτυρούντων σου τῇ
exceedingly, ᶜcoming ['the] ²brethren and bearing witness of thy
ἀληθείᾳ, καθὼς σὺ ἐν ἀληθείᾳ περιπατεῖς. 4 μειζοτέραν τού-
truth,   even as thou in truth walkest. ⁵Greater ⁶than
των   οὐκ.ἔχω χαράν, ἵνα ἀκούω τὰ.ἐμὰ.τέκνα ἐν ᵈ
⁷these ⁸things ¹I ²have ³not ⁴joy, that I should hear of my children in
ἀληθείᾳ περιπατοῦντα. 5 Ἀγαπητέ, πιστὸν ποιεῖς ὃ.ἐὰν
truth   walking.   Beloved, faithfully thou doest whatever
ᵉἐργάσῃᵈ   εἰς τοὺς ἀδελφοὺς καὶ ᶠεἰς τοὺςᵈ
thou mayest have wrought towards the brethren and towards
ξένους, 6 οἳ ἐμαρτύρησάν σοι τῇ ἀγάπῃ ἐνώπιον ἐκ-
strangers, (who witnessed of thy love before [the] as-
κλησίας· οὓς καλῶς ποιήσεις προπέμψας ἀξίως τοῦ θεοῦ·
sembly) whom ⁹well ⁸thou ⁷wilt ⁶do ¹setting ²forward ³worthily ⁴of ⁵God;
7 ὑπὲρ γὰρ τοῦ ὀνόματος ᵍ ʰἐξῆλθον ¹ μηδὲν λαμβάνοντες
for. for the   name   they went forth, ²nothing ¹taking
ἀπὸ τῶν ⁱἐθνῶν.ᵈ 8 ἡμεῖς οὖν ὀφείλομεν ᵏἀπολαμβάνεινᵈ
from the nations.   We therefore ought   to receive
τοὺς τοιούτους, ἵνα συνεργοὶ γινώμεθα τῇ ἀληθείᾳ. 9 *Ἐ-
such,   that fellow-workers we may be with the truth.   I
γοαψα¹ τῇ ἐκκλησίᾳ· ἀλλ' ὁ φιλοπρωτεύων αὐτῶν
wrote to the assembly; but ²who ³loves ⁴to ⁵be ⁶first ⁷among ⁸them
ᵐΔιοτρεφὴςᵈ οὐκ.ἐπιδέχεται ἡμᾶς. 10 διὰ τοῦτο, ἐὰν ἔλθω,
¹Diotrephes, receives not   us.   On account of this, if I come,
ὑπομνήσω   αὐτοῦ τὰ ἔργα ἃ ποιεῖ, λόγοις
I will bring to remembrance of him the works which he does, with ²words
πονηροῖς φλυαρῶν ἡμᾶς· καὶ μὴ ἀρκούμενος ἐπὶ τούτοις,
¹evil prating against us; and not satisfied with these,
οὔτε αὐτὸς ἐπιδέχεται τοὺς ἀδελφούς, καὶ τοὺς βουλομέ-
neither himself receives the brethren, and those who would
νους κωλύει, καὶ ⁿἐκᵈ τῆς ἐκκλησίας ἐκβάλλει. 11 Ἀγα-
he forbids, and from the assembly casts [them] out. Be-
πητέ, μὴ.μιμοῦ τὸ κακόν, ἀλλὰ τὸ ἀγαθόν. He that
loved, do not imitate that which [is] evil, but what [is] good.
ἀγαθοποιῶν, ἐκ τοῦ θεοῦ ἐστιν· ὁ.°δὲᵈ κακοποιῶν οὐχ ἑώ-
does good, of   God is; but he that does evil ²not ¹has
ρακεν τὸν θεόν. 12 Δημητρίῳ μεμαρτύρηται ὑπὸ πάντων, καὶ
seen   God.   To Demetrius witness is borne by all, and

2 Beloved, I wish above all things that thou mayest prosper and be in health, even as thy soul prospereth. 3 For I rejoiced greatly, when the brethren came and testified of the truth that is in thee, even as thou walkest in the truth. 4 I have no greater joy than to hear that my children walk in truth. 5 Beloved, thou doest faithfully whatsoever thou doest to the brethren, and to strangers; 6 which have borne witness of thy charity before the church: whom if thou bring forward on their journey after a godly sort, thou shalt do well: 7 because that for his name's sake they went forth, taking nothing of the Gentiles. 8 We therefore ought to receive such, that we might be fellowhelpers to the truth. 9 I wrote unto the church: but Diotrephes, who loveth to have the preeminence among them, receiveth us not. 10 Wherefore, if I come, I will remember his deeds which he doeth, prating against us with malicious words: and not content therewith, neither doth he himself receive the brethren, and forbiddeth them that would, and casteth them out of the church. 11 Beloved, follow not that which is evil, but that which is good. He that doeth good is of God: but he that doeth evil hath not seen God. 12 Demetrius hath good report of all men, and

---

ᵇ + τοῦ ἀποστόλου the apostle E; + καθολικὴ general E; Ἰωάννου γ' LTAW; Ἰωάνου ἐπιστολὴ γ' Tr. ᶜ — γὰρ τ[Tr]. ᵈ + τῇ the LTTrAW. ᵉ ἐργάξῃ thou workest L. ᶠ τοῦτο that LTTrAW. ᵍ + αὐτοῦ (read his name) E. ʰ ἐξῆλθαν LTTr. ⁱ ἐθνικῶν (read those of the nations) LTTrAW. ᵏ ὑπολαμβάνειν to sustain LTTrAW. ¹ + τι somewhat LTTrAW. ᵐ Διοτρέφης LA. ⁿ — ἐκ (read [from]) T. ° — δὲ but GLTTrAW.

and of the truth itself: yea, and we *also* bear record; and ye know that our record is true.

pῦπ'‖ αὐτῆς τῆς ἀληθείας· καὶ ἡμεῖς δὲ μαρτυροῦμεν, καὶ
by ³itself ¹the ²truth; and we also bear witness, and

ⁱοἴδατε‖ ὅτι ἡ.μαρτυρία.ἡμῶν ἀληθής ἐστιν.
ye know that our witness ²true ¹is.

13 I had many things to write, but I will not with ink and pen write unto thee: 14 but I trust I shall shortly see thee, and we shall speak face to face. Peace *be* to thee. *Our* friends salute thee. Greet the friends by name.

13 Πολλὰ εἶχον ʳγράφειν,‖ ἀλλ' οὐ.θέλω διὰ μέλανος καὶ
Many things I had to write, but I will not with ink and

καλάμου ˢσοι γράψαι·‖ 14 ἐλπίζω.δὲ εὐθέως ᵗἰδεῖν σε,‖
pen ³to ⁴thee ¹to ²write; but I hope immediately to see thee,

καὶ στόμα πρὸς στόμα λαλήσομεν. 15 Εἰρήνη σοι. ἀσπά-
and mouth to mouth we shall speak. Peace to thee. ³Sa-

ζονταί σε οἱ φίλοι. ἀσπάζου τοὺς φίλους κατ' ὄνομα.
lute ⁴thee ¹the ²friends. Salute the friends by name.

ᵛἸωάννου ἐπιστολὴ καθολικὴ τρίτη.‖
⁴Of ⁵John ³epistle ²general ¹third.

ᵃΕΠΙΣΤΟΛΗ ΤΟΥ ΙΟΥΔΑ ΚΑΘΟΛΙΚΗ.‖
²EPISTLE　　³OF ⁴JUDE　　¹GENERAL.

JUDE, the servant of Jesus Christ, and brother of James, to them that are sanctified by God the Father, and preserved in Jesus Christ, *and* called: 2 Mercy unto you, and peace, and love, be multiplied.

ΙΟΥΔΑΣ Ἰησοῦ χριστοῦ δοῦλος, ἀδελφὸς.δὲ Ἰακώβου, τοῖς
Jude, of Jesus Christ bondman, and brother of James, to the

ἐν θεῷ πατρὶ ᵇἡγιασμένοις‖ καὶ Ἰησοῦ χριστῷ τετηρη-
⁴in ⁵God [⁶the] ⁷Father ⁸sanctified ⁹and ¹⁰in ¹¹Jesus ¹²Christ ⁹kept

μένοις κλητοῖς· 2 ἔλεος ὑμῖν καὶ εἰρήνη καὶ ἀγάπη
¹called [²ones]. Mercy to you and peace, and love

πληθυνθείη.
be multiplied.

3 Beloved, when I gave all diligence to write unto you of the common salvation, it was needful for me to write unto you, and exhort *you* that ye should earnestly contend for the faith which was once delivered unto the saints. 4 For there are certain men crept in unawares, who were before of old ordained to this condemnation, ungodly men, turning the grace of our God into lasciviousness, and denying the only Lord God, and our Lord Jesus Christ.

3 Ἀγαπητοί, πᾶσαν σπουδὴν ποιούμενος γράφειν ὑμῖν
Beloved, ²all ³diligence ¹using to write to you

περὶ τῆς κοινῆς ᶜ σωτηρίας, ἀνάγκην ἔσχον γράψαι ὑμῖν,
concerning the common salvation, necessity I had to write to you,

παρακαλῶν ἐπαγωνίζεσθαι τῇ ἅπαξ παραδοθείσῃ τοῖς
exhorting [you] to contend earnestly for the ²once ³delivered ⁴to ⁵the

ἁγίοις πίστει. 4 παρεισέδυσαν.γάρ τινες ἄνθρωποι, οἱ
⁶saints ¹faith. For came in stealthily certain men, they who

πάλαι προγεγραμμένοι εἰς τοῦτο τὸ κρίμα, ἀσεβεῖς
of old have been before marked out to this sentence, ungodly [persons]

τὴν τοῦ.θεοῦ.ἡμῶν ᵈχάριν‖ μετατιθέντες εἰς ἀσέλγειαν καὶ τὸν
²the ⁴of ⁵our ⁶God ³grace ¹changing into licentiousness and ⁷the

μόνον δεσπότην ᵉθεὸν‖ καὶ κύριον.ἡμῶν Ἰησοῦν χριστὸν
⁸only ⁹master— ⁵God ⁶and ⁷our ⁸Lord ⁹Jesus ¹⁰Christ

ἀρνούμενοι.
¹denying.

5 I will therefore put you in remembrance, though ye once knew this, how that the Lord, having saved the people out of the land of Egypt, afterward destroyed them that believed

5 Ὑπομνῆσαι.δὲ ὑμᾶς βούλομαι, εἰδότας ᶠὑμᾶς‖ ἅπαξ
But ³put ⁵in ⁶remembrance ⁴you ¹I ²would, ⁸knowing ⁷you once

ᵍτοῦτο,‖ ὅτι ʰὁ‖ ⁱκύριος‖ λαὸν ἐκ γῆς Αἰγύπτου σώ-
this, that the Lord a people out of [the] land of Egypt having

σας, τὸ.δεύτερον τοὺς μὴ.πιστεύσαντας ἀπώλεσεν. 6 ἀγ-
saved, in the second place those who believed not he destroyed.

ᵖ ὑπὸ T.　　�q οἶδας thou knowest LTTrA.　　ʳ γράψαι σοι to write to thee LTTrAW.
ˢ γράφειν σοι L; σοι γράφειν TTrAW.　　ᵗ σε ἰδεῖν LTTrA.　　ᵛ —the subscription EGLTW;
Ἰωάνου γ' Tr; Ἰωάννου γ' A.　　ᵃ + ἀποστόλου apostle E; Ἰούδα ἐπιστολὴ GLTrW; Ἰούδα TA.　　ᵇ ἠγαπημένοις beloved
LTTrAW.　　ᶜ + ἡμῶν (read our common) LTTrA.　　ᵈ χάριτα LTTrAW.　　ᵉ θεὸν GLTrAW.
ᶠ — ὑμᾶς LTTrAW.　　ᵍ πάντα all things LTTrAW.　　ʰ ὁ TTrA.　　ⁱ Ἰησοῦς Jesus LA.

γέλους τε τοὺς μὴ.τηρήσαντας τὴν.ἑαυτῶν ἀρχήν, ἀλλὰ
Angels [1]and who kept not their own first-state, but

ἀπολιπόντας τὸ.ἴδιον οἰκητήριον, εἰς κρίσιν μεγάλης
left their own dwelling, unto [the] judgment of [the] great

ἡμέρας δεσμοῖς ἀϊδίοις ὑπὸ ζόφον τετήρηκεν· 7 ὡς Σόδομα
day in [2]bonds [1]eternal under darkness he keeps; as Sodom

καὶ Γόμοῤῥα, καὶ αἱ περὶ αὐτὰς πόλεις, τὸν ὅμοιον [1]τού-
and Gomorrha, and the [2]around [3]them [1]cities, in like [2]with

τοις τρόπον‖ ἐκπορνεύσασαι, καὶ ἀπελθοῦσαι
[2]them [1]manner having given themselves to fornication and having gone

ὀπίσω σαρκὸς ἑτέρας, πρόκεινται δεῖγμα, πυρὸς αἰωνίου
after [2]flesh [1]other, are set forth as an example, [4]of [6]fire [5]eternal

δίκην ὑπέχουσαι. 8 ὁμοίως.μέντοι καὶ οὗτοι ἐνυπνια-
[2the] [3]penalty [1]undergoing. Yet in like manner also these dream-

ζόμενοι, σάρκα μὲν μιαίνουσιν, κυριότητα.δὲ ἀθετοῦσιν,
ers [2the] [3]flesh [1]defile, and [2]lordship [1]set [3]aside,

δόξας.δὲ βλασφημοῦσιν. 9 m ὁ.δὲ‖.Μιχαὴλ ὁ ἀρχάγγελος,
and [4]glories [1]speak [2]evil [3]of. But Michael the archangel,

n ὅτε‖ τῷ διαβόλῳ διακρινόμενος διελέγετο περὶ τοῦ o Μω-
when with the devil disputing he reasoned about the [2]of

σέως‖ σώματος, οὐκ.ἐτόλμησεν κρίσιν ἐπενεγκεῖν βλασ-
[3]Moses [1]body, did not dare [5]a [7]charge [1]to [2]bring [3]against [4him] [6]rail-

φημίας, p ἀλλ'‖ εἶπεν, Ἐπιτιμήσαι σοι κύριος. 10 οὗτοι.δὲ
ing, but said, [3]Rebuke [4]thee [1the] [2]Lord. But these,

ὅσα μὲν οὐκ.οἴδασιν βλασφημοῦσιν· ὅσα.δὲ
whatever things they know not they speak evil of; but whatever things

φυσικῶς, ὡς τὰ ἄλογα ζῶα, ἐπίστανται, ἐν τούτοις
naturally, as the irrational animals, they understand, in these things

φθείρονται. 11 οὐαὶ αὐτοῖς· ὅτι τῇ ὁδῷ τοῦ Κάϊν
they corrupt themselves. Woe to them! because in the way of Cain

ἐπορεύθησαν, καὶ τῇ πλάνῃ τοῦ Βαλαὰμ μισθοῦ ἐξεχύθησαν,
they went, and to the error of Balaam for reward rushed,

καὶ τῇ ἀντιλογίᾳ τοῦ Κορὲ ἀπώλοντο. 12 οὗτοί εἰσιν q ἐν
and in the gainsaying of Korah perished. These are in

ταῖς.ἀγάπαις.ὑμῶν σπιλάδες, συνευωχούμενοι r ἀφόβως,
your love feasts sunken rocks, feasting together [with you] fearlessly,

ἑαυτοὺς ποιμαίνοντες· νεφέλαι ἄνυδροι, ὑπὸ ἀνέμων
[2]themselves [1]pasturing; clouds without water, by winds

s περιφερόμεναι·‖ δένδρα φθινοπωρινὰ ἄκαρπα δὶς ἀποθα-
being carried about, [2]trees [1]autumnal, without fruit, twice dead,

νόντα ἐκριζωθέντα· 13 κύματα ἄγρια θαλάσσης ἐπαφρίζοντα
rooted up; [2]waves [1]wild of [the] sea, foaming out

τὰς.ἑαυτῶν αἰσχύνας· ἀστέρες πλανῆται, οἷς ὁ ζόφος τοῦ
their own shames; [2]stars [1]wandering, to whom the gloom

σκότους εἰς.τὸν‖.αἰῶνα τετήρηται. 14 t προεφήτευσεν‖.δὲ καὶ
of darkness for ever has been kept. And [6]prophesied [7]also

τούτοις ἔβδομος ἀπὸ Ἀδὰμ Ἐνώχ, λέγων, Ἰδού,
[8]as [9]to [10]these [2the] [3]seventh [4]from [5]Adam, [1]Enoch, . saying, Behold,

ἦλθεν κύριος ἐν w μυριάσιν ἁγίαις‖ αὐτοῦ, 15 ποιῆσαι
[3]came [1the] [2]Lord amidst [3]myriads [4]holy [1]his, to execute

κρίσιν κατὰ πάντων, καὶ x ἐξελέγξαι‖ πάντας τοὺς ἀσεβεῖς
judgment against all, and to convict all the ungodly

not. 6 And the angels which kept not their first estate, but left their own habitation, he hath reserved in everlasting chains under darkness unto the judgment of the great day. 7 Even as Sodom and Gomorrha, and the cities about them in like manner, giving themselves over to fornication, and going after strange flesh, are set forth for an example, suffering the vengeance of eternal fire. 8 Likewise also these filthy dreamers defile the flesh, despise dominion, and speak evil of dignities. 9 Yet Michael the archangel, when contending with the devil he disputed about the body of Moses, durst not bring against him a railing accusation, but said, The Lord rebuke thee. 10 But these speak evil of those things which they know not: but what they know naturally, as brute beasts, in those things they corrupt themselves. 11 Woe unto them! for they have gone in the way of Cain, and ran greedily after the error of Balaam for reward, and perished in the gainsaying of Core. 12 These are spots in your feasts of charity, when they feast with you, feeding themselves without fear: clouds they are without water, carried about of winds; trees whose fruit withereth, without fruit, twice dead, plucked up by the roots; 13 raging waves of the sea, foaming out their own shame; wandering stars, to whom is reserved the blackness of darkness for ever. 14 And Enoch also, the seventh from Adam, prophesied of these, saying, Behold, the Lord cometh with ten thousands of his saints, 15 to execute judgment upon all, and to convince all

---

[1] τρόπον τούτοις LTTrAW.   m ὅτε when L.   n τότε at that time L.   o Μωϋσέως
LTTrAW.   p ἀλλὰ LTTrAW.   q + οἱ (read the sunken rocks) LTTrA.   r Text. Rec. and
Tr place the comma after συνευ-   s παραφέρομεναι being carried along GLTTrAW.   t — τὸν
GLTTrAW.   t ἐπροφήτευσεν TTr.   w ἁγίαις μυριάσιν GLTTrAW.   x ἐλέγξαι LTTrA.

that are ungodly a-
mong them of all
their ungodly deeds
which they have un-
godly committed, and
of all their hard
speeches which ungod-
ly sinners have spoken
against him. 16 These
are murmurers, com-
plainers, walking af-
ter their own lusts ;
and their mouth speak-
eth great swelling
words, having men's
persons in admiration
because of advantage.
17 But, beloved, re-
member ye the words
which were spoken be-
fore of the apostles
of our Lord Jesus
Christ ; 18 how that
they told you there
should be mockers
in the last time, who
should walk after
their own ungodly
lusts. 19 These be they
who separate them-
selves, sensual, hav-
ing not the Spirit.
20 But ye, beloved,
building up yourselves
on your most holy
faith, praying in the
Holy Ghost, 21 keep
yourselves in the love
of God, looking for the
mercy of our Lord Je-
sus Christ unto eternal
life. 22 And of some
have compassion, mak-
ing a difference : 23 and
others save with fear,
pulling *them* out of
the fire ; hating even
the garment spotted
by the flesh.

24 Now unto him
that is able to keep you
from falling, and to
present *you* faultless
before the presence of
his glory with exceed-
ing joy, 25 to the only
wise God our Saviour,
be glory and majesty,
dominion and power,
both now and ever. A-
men.

ʸαὐτῶν‖ περὶ πάντων τῶν ἔργων ᶻἀσεβείας‖ αὐτῶν ὧν
of them concerning all ²works ³of ⁴ungodliness ¹their which
ἠσέβησαν, καὶ περὶ πάντων τῶν σκληρῶνᵃ ὧν
they did ungodlily, and concerning all the hard [things] which
ἐλάλησαν κατ' αὐτοῦ ἁμαρτωλοὶ ἀσεβεῖς. 16 οὗτοί εἰσιν
³spoke ⁴against ⁵him ²sinners ¹ungodly. These are
γογγυσταί, μεμψίμοιροι, κατὰ τὰς ἐπιθυμίας αὐτῶν πορευό-
murmurers, complainers, ²after ³their ⁴lusts ¹walk-
μενοι· καὶ τὸ στόμα αὐτῶν λαλεῖ ὑπέρογκα, θαυμάζοντες
ing ; and their mouth speaks great swelling [words], admiring
πρόσωπα ὠφελείας χάριν. 17 ὑμεῖς δέ, ἀγαπητοί, μνή-
persons ²profit ¹for ²the ³sake ⁴of. But ye, beloved, re-
σθητε τῶν ᵇῥημάτων τῶν προειρημένων‖ ὑπὸ τῶν ἀπο-
member the words which have been spoken before by the apo-
στόλων τοῦ κυρίου ἡμῶν Ἰησοῦ χριστοῦ· 18 ὅτι ἔλεγον ὑμῖν,
stles of our Lord Jesus Christ, that they said to you,
ᶜὅτι‖ ᵈἐν ἐσχάτῳ χρόνῳ‖ ἔσονται ἐμπαῖκται, κατὰ τὰς
that in [the] last time there will be mockers, ²after
ἑαυτῶν ἐπιθυμίας πορευόμενοι τῶν ἀσεβειῶν. 19 οὗτοί εἰσιν
³their ⁴own ¹walking of ungodlinesses. These are
οἱ ἀποδιορίζοντεςᵉ, ψυχικοί, πνεῦμα μὴ
they who set apart [themselves], natural [men], [³the] ⁴Spirit ¹not
ἔχοντες. 20 ὑμεῖς δέ, ἀγαπητοί, ᶠτῇ ἁγιωτάτῃ ὑμῶν πίστει
²having. ¹ But ye, beloved, on your most holy faith
ἐποικοδομοῦντες ἑαυτούς, ἐν πνεύματι ἁγίῳ προσευχό-
building up yourselves, in [the] ²Spirit ¹Holy pray-
μενοι, 21 ἑαυτοὺς ἐν ἀγάπῃ θεοῦ τηρήσατε, προσδεχό-
ing, ²yourselves ³in [⁴the] ⁵love ⁶of ⁷God ¹keep, await-
μενοι τὸ ἔλεος τοῦ κυρίου ἡμῶν Ἰησοῦ χριστοῦ, εἰς ζωὴν
ing the mercy of our Lord Jesus Christ unto life
αἰώνιον. 22 καὶ οὓς μὲν ᵍἐλεεῖτε διακρινόμενοι·‖ 23 ʰοὓς δὲ
eternal. And ²some ¹pity, making a difference but others
ἐν φόβῳ σώζετε, ἐκ τοῦ πυρὸς ἁρπάζοντες,‖ μισοῦντες
with fear save, out of the fire snatching [them] ; hating
καὶ τὸν ἀπὸ τῆς σαρκὸς ἐσπιλωμένον χιτῶνα.
even the ³by ⁴the ⁵flesh ²spotted ¹garment.

24 Τῷ δὲ δυναμένῳ φυλάξαι ¹αὐτοὺς‖ ἀπταίστους, καὶ
But to him who is able to keep them without stumbling, and
στῆσαι κατενώπιον τῆς δόξης αὐτοῦ ἀμώμους ἐν ἀγαλ-
to set [them] before his glory blameless with exul-
λιάσει, 25 μόνῳ ᵏσοφῷ‖ θεῷ σωτῆρι ἡμῶν, ¹ δόξα ᵐκαὶ‖
tation, to [the] only wise God our Saviour, [be] glory and
μεγαλωσύνη, κράτος καὶ ἐξουσία, ⁿκαὶ νῦν καὶ εἰς πάντας
greatness, might and authority, both now, and to all
τοὺς αἰῶνας. ἀμήν.
the ages. Amen.

ᵒἘπιστολὴ Ἰούδα καθολική.‖
²Epistle ³of ⁴Jude ¹general.

ʸ — αὐτῶν LTTrA. ᶻ [ἀσεβείας] Tr. ᵃ + λόγων speeches T. ᵇ προειρημένων ῥημάτων words having been spoken before L. ᶜ — ὅτι LT[Tr]. ᵈ ἐπ' ἐσχάτου τοῦ (— τοῦ
Tr[A]w) χρόνου at the end of the time LTTrAW. ᵉ + ἑαυτοὺς themselves EG ᶠ ἐποικοδομοῦντες ἑαυτοὺς τῇ ἁγιωτάτῃ ὑμῶν πίστει LTTrAW. ᵍ ἐλέγχετε διακρινομένους [who]
dispute, convict LTTrAW. ʰ οὓς δὲ σώζετε ἐκ πυρὸς ἁρπάζοντες, οὓς δὲ ἐλεᾶτε (ἐλεεῖτε w)
ἐν φόβῳ but others save, from [the] fire snatching [them], and others pity in fear
LTTrAW. ¹ ὑμᾶς you (and read set [you] before) EGLTTrW. ᵏ — σοφῷ GLTTrAW.
ˡ + διὰ Ἰησοῦ χριστοῦ τοῦ κυρίου ἡμῶν through Jesus Christ our Lord GLTTrAW. ᵐ — καὶ
LTTrAW. ⁿ + πρὸ παντὸς τοῦ αἰῶνος before the whole age (read καὶ and) LTTrAW. ᵒ — the
subscription EGLTW ; Ἰούδα TrA.

^aΑΠΟΚΑΛΥΨΙΣ ΙΩΑΝΝΟΥ ΤΟΥ ΘΕΟΛΟΓΟΥ.^b
REVELATION   OF JOHN   THE   DIVINE

ΑΠΟΚΑΛΥΨΙΣ Ἰησοῦ χριστοῦ, ἢν ἔδωκεν αὐτῷ ὁ θεός,
Revelation   of Jesus   Christ,   which ²gave ³to ⁴him ¹God,
δεῖξαι τοῖς δούλοις αὐτοῦ ἃ δεῖ γενέσθαι ἐν τάχει, καὶ
to shew   to his bondmen⁻   what things must take place   shortly: and
ἐσήμανεν ἀποστείλας διὰ τοῦ ἀγγέλου αὐτοῦ τῷ δούλῳ αὐτοῦ
he signified [it], having sent   by   his angel   to his bondman
^bἸωάννῃ,^{||} 2 ὃς ἐμαρτύρησεν τὸν λόγον τοῦ θεοῦ καὶ τὴν
John,   who   testified   the   word   of God and the
μαρτυρίαν Ἰησοῦ χριστοῦ, ὅσα ^cτε^{||} ^dεἶδεν.^{||} 3 μακά-
testimony of Jesus   Christ, ²whatsoever³things ¹and he saw.   Bless-
ριος ὁ ἀναγινώσκων, καὶ οἱ ἀκούοντες ^eτοὺς λόγους^{||}
ed [is] he that   reads,   and they that hear   the   words
τῆς προφητείας, καὶ τηροῦντες τὰ ἐν αὐτῇ γεγραμμένα·
of the   prophecy,   and   keep   the things ²in ³it ¹written;
ὁ γὰρ καιρὸς ἐγγύς.
for the   time [is] near.

4 ^fἸωάννης^{||} ταῖς ἑπτὰ ἐκκλησίαις ταῖς ἐν τῇ Ἀσίᾳ·
John   to the seven   assemblies which [are] in   Asia:
χάρις ὑμῖν καὶ εἰρήνη ἀπὸ ^gτοῦ^{||} ὁ ὢν καὶ ὁ ἦν καὶ ὁ
Grace to you and peace   from   him who is and who was and who [is]
ἐρχόμενος· καὶ ἀπὸ τῶν ἑπτὰ πνευμάτων ^hἃ^{||} ⁱἐστιν^{||} ἐνώπιον
to come;   and from the seven   Spirits   which are   before
τοῦ θρόνου αὐτοῦ· 5 καὶ ἀπὸ Ἰησοῦ χριστοῦ, ὁ μάρτυς ὁ
his throne;   and from   Jesus   Christ,   the ²witness ¹
πιστός, ὁ πρωτότοκος ^kἐκ^{||} τῶν νεκρῶν. καὶ ὁ ἄρχων τῶν
faithful, the firstborn from among the dead.   and the ruler of the
βασιλέων τῆς γῆς· τῷ ^lἀγαπήσαντι^{||} ἡμᾶς, καὶ ^mλού-
kings   of the earth. To him who   loved   us,   and wash-
σαντι ἡμᾶς ⁿἀπὸ^{||} τῶν ἁμαρτιῶν ἡμῶν^{||} ἐν τῷ αἵματι αὐτοῦ·
ed   us   from   our sins   in   his blood,
6 καὶ ἐποίησεν ^pἡμᾶς^{||} ^qβασιλεῖς καὶ^{||} ἱερεῖς τῷ θεῷ καὶ πατρὶ
and made   us   kings   and priests to ²God ³and ⁴Father
αὐτοῦ· αὐτῷ ἡ δόξα καὶ τὸ κράτος εἰς τοὺς αἰῶνας ^rτῶν
¹his: to him [be] the glory and the   might to   the   ages   of the
αἰώνων.^{||} ἀμήν.
ages.   Amen.

7 Ἰδού, ἔρχεται μετὰ τῶν νεφελῶν, καὶ ὄψεται αὐτὸν πᾶς
Behold, he comes with   the   clouds,   and shall see him   every
ὀφθαλμός, καὶ οἵτινες αὐτὸν ἐξεκέντησαν· καὶ κόψονται
eye,   and they which ²him   ¹pierced,   and ³shall ⁴wail
ἐπ' αὐτὸν πᾶσαι αἱ φυλαὶ τῆς γῆς. ναί, ἀμήν.
⁵on ¹⁰account¹¹of ¹²him ¹all ²the ³tribes ⁴of ⁵the ⁶earth. Yea, amen.

8 Ἐγώ εἰμι τὸ ^sΑ^{||} καὶ τὸ ^tΩ,^{||} ^vἀρχὴ καὶ τέλος^{||} λέγει
I   am   the   A   and the   Ω,   beginning and ending,   says

THE Revelation of Je-
sus Christ, which God
gave unto him, to shew
unto his servants
things which must
shortly come to pass;
and he sent and signi-
fied *it* by his angel unto his servant John:
2 who bare record of
the word of God, and
of the testimony of
Jesus Christ, and of
all things that he saw.
3 Blessed *is* he that
readeth, and they that
hear the words of this
prophecy, and keep
those things which are
written therein: for
the time *is* at hand.

4 JOHN to the seven
churches which are in
Asia: Grace *be* unto
you, and peace, from
him which is, and
which was, and which
is to come; and from
the seven Spirits which
are before his throne;
5 and from Jesus
Christ, *who is* the
faithful witness, *and*
the firstbegotten of
the dead, and the
prince of the kings of
the earth. Unto him
that loved us, and
washed us from our
sins in his own blood,
6 and hath made us
kings and priests unto
God and his Father;
to him *be* glory and do-
minion for ever and
ever. Amen.

7 Behold, he cometh
with clouds; and every
eye shall see him, and
they *also* which pierc-
ed him : and all kin-
dreds of the earth shall
wail because of him.
Even so, Amen.

8 I am Alpha and
Omega, the beginning
and the ending, saith

---

^a Ἀποκάλυψις G ; Ἀποκάλυψις Ἰωάννου (Ἰωάνου Tr) LTTrAW.   ^b Ἰωάνη Tr.   ^c — τε
GLTTrAW.   ^d ἴδεν T.   ^e τὸν λόγον the word T.   ^f Ἰωάνης Tr.   ^g — τοῦ (*read* [him])
GLTTrAW.   ^h τῶν Tr.   ⁱ — ἐστιν (*read* [are]) LTTrAW.   ^k — ἐκ (*read* τῶν of the)
GLTTrAW.   ^l ἀγαπῶντι loves GLTTrAW.   ^m λύσαντι freed LTTr ; λ[ο]ύσαντι A.   ⁿ ἐκ LTTrA.
^o [ἡμῶν] A.   ^p ἡμῶν L ; ἡμῖν for us Tr.   ^q βασιλείαν, a kingdom, GLTTrAW.   ^r — τῶν
αἰώνων A.   ^s ἄλφα Alpha LTTrAW.   ^t ὦ LA.   ^v — ἀρχὴ καὶ τέλος GLTTrAW.

the Lord, which is,
and which was, and
which is to come, the
Almighty.

9 I John, who also
am your brother, and
companion in tribula-
tion, and in the king-
dom and patience of
Jesus Christ, was in
the isle that is called
Patmos, for the word
of God, and for the
testimony of Jesus
Christ. 10 I was in the
Spirit on the Lord's
day, and heard behind
me a great voice, as of
a trumpet, 11 saying,
I am Alpha and Ome-
ga, the first and the
last: and, What thou
seest, write in a book;
and send it unto the
seven churches which
are in Asia; unto Eph-
esus, and unto Smyr-
na, and unto Perga-
mos, and unto Thya-
tira, and unto Sardis,
and unto Philadelphia,
and unto Laodicea.
12 And I turned to see
the voice that spake
with me. And being
turned, I saw seven
golden candlesticks;
13 and in the midst of
the seven candlesticks
one like unto the Son
of man, clothed with
a garment down to
the foot, and girt a-
bout the paps with a
golden girdle. 14 His
head and his hairs
were white like wool,
as white as snow; and
his eyes were as a
flame of fire; 15 and
his feet like unto fine
brass, as if they burn-
ed in a furnace; and
his voice as the sound
of many waters. 16 And
he had in his right
hand seven stars: and
out of his mouth went
a sharp two-edged
sword: and his coun-
tenance was as the
sun shineth in his
strength. 17 And when
I saw him, I fell at his
feet as dead. And he

ʷὁ κύριος,‖ ὁ ὢν καὶ ὁ ἦν καὶ ο ἐρχόμενος, ὁ παντο-
the Lord, who is and who was and who [is] to come, the Al-
κράτωρ.
mighty.

9 Ἐγὼ ˣἸωάννης,‖ ὁ ˣκαὶ‖ ἀδελφὸς ὑμῶν καὶ ᶻσυγκοινωνὸς ᴿ
I John, also ²brother ¹your and fellow-partaker
ἐν τῇ θλίψει καὶ ᵃἐν τῇ‖ βασιλείᾳ καὶ ὑπομονῇ ᵇ ᶜἸησοῦ χρισ-
in the tribulation and in the kingdom and endurance of Jesus Christ,
τοῦ,‖ ἐγενόμην ἐν τῇ νήσῳ τῇ καλουμένῃ Πάτμῳ, διὰ
was in the island which [is] called Patmos, because of
τὸν λόγον τοῦ θεοῦ καὶ ᵈδιὰ‖ τὴν μαρτυρίαν Ἰησοῦ ᵉχρισ-
the word of God and because of the testimony of Jesus Christ.
τοῦ.‖ 10 ἐγενόμην ἐν πνεύματι ἐν τῇ κυριακῇ ἡμέρᾳ· καὶ
I became in [the] Spirit on the Lord's day, and
ἤκουσα ὀπίσω μου φωνὴν μεγάλην ὡς σάλπιγγος, 11 λεγού-
I heard behind me a ²voice ¹loud as of a trumpet, say-
σης, ᶠἘγώ εἰμι τὸ Α καὶ τὸ Ω, ὁ πρῶτος καὶ ὁ ἔσχατος· καί,‖
ing, I am the Α and the Ω, the first and the last; and,
ᴼ βλέπεις γράψον εἰς βιβλίον, καὶ πέμψον ταῖς ᵍἐκκλησίαις
What thou seest write in a book, and send to the assemblies
ᵸταῖς ἐν Ἀσίᾳ,‖ εἰς Ἔφεσον, καὶ εἰς ⁱΣμύρναν,‖ καὶ εἰς
which [are] in Asia: to Ephesus, and to Smyrna, and to
Πέργαμον, καὶ εἰς ᵏΘυάτειρα,‖ καὶ εἰς Σάρδεις, καὶ εἰς ˡΦιλα-
Pergamos, and to Thyatira, and to Sardis, and to Phila-
δέλφειαν,‖ καὶ εἰς ᵐΛαοδίκειαν.‖ 12 καὶ ἐπέστρεψα βλέπειν
delphia, and to Laodicea. And I turned to see
τὴν φωνὴν ἥτις ⁿἐλάλησεν‖ μετ᾿ ἐμοῦ· καὶ ἐπιστρέψας εἶδον
the voice which spoke with me, and having turned I saw
ἑπτὰ λυχνίας χρυσᾶς, 13 καὶ ἐν μέσῳ τῶν ᵒἑπτὰ‖ λυχ-
seven ²lampstands ¹golden, and in [the] midst of the seven lamp-
νιῶν ὅμοιον ᴾυἱῷ‖ ἀνθρώπου, ἐνδεδυμένον
stands [one] like [the] Son of man, clothed in [a garment]
ποδήρη, καὶ περιεζωσμένον προς τοῖς ᑫμαστοῖς‖ ζώνην
reaching to the feet, and ⁴girt ⁵about ⁶with ¹at ²the ³breasts ⁷a ⁹girdle
ʳχρυσῆν·‖ 14 ἡ.δὲ.κεφαλὴ.αὐτοῦ καὶ αἱ τρίχες λευκαὶ ˢὡσεὶ‖
⁸golden: and his head and hair white as if
ἔριον λευκόν, ὡς χιών· καὶ οἱ.ὀφθαλμοὶ.αὐτοῦ ὡς φλὸξ πυρός·
²wool ¹white, as snow; and his eyes as a flame of fire;
15 καὶ οἱ.πόδες.αὐτοῦ ὅμοιοι χαλκολιβάνῳ ὡς ἐν καμίνῳ
and his feet like fine brass, as if ³in ⁴a ⁵furnace [¹they]
ᵗπεπυρωμένοι·‖ καὶ ἡ.φωνὴ.αὐτοῦ ὡς φωνὴ ὑδάτων πολλῶν·
²glowed; and his voice as [the] voice of ²waters ¹many,
16 καὶ ἔχων ἐν τῇ δεξιᾷ ⱽαὐτοῦ χειρὶ‖ ἀστέρας ἑπτά· καὶ ἐκ
and having in ⁷right ¹his hand ²stars ⁷seven, and out of
τοῦ.στόματος.αὐτοῦ ῥομφαία δίστομος ὀξεῖα ἐκπορευομένη· καὶ
his mouth a ³sword ²two-edged ¹sharp going forth, and
ἡ.ὄψις.αὐτοῦ ὡς ὁ ἥλιος φαίνει ἐν τῇ.δυνάμει.αὐτοῦ. 17 καὶ
his countenance as the sun shines in its power. And
ὅτε εἶδον αὐτόν, ἔπεσα πρὸς τοὺς.πόδας.αὐτοῦ ὡς νεκρός· καὶ
when I saw him, I fell at his feet as dead: and

ʷ κυριος ὁ θεός [the] Lord God GLTTrAW.   ˣ Ἰωάνης Tr.   ʸ — καὶ GLTTrAW.   ᶻ συν T.
ᵃ — ἐν τῇ GLTTrAW.   ᵇ + ἐν in (Jesus) LTTrAW.   ᶜ χριστῷ Ἰησοῦ W; — χριστοῦ
LTTrA.   ᵈ — διὰ LTr[A].   ᵉ — χριστοῦ LTTrA.   ᶠ — Ἐγώ εἰμι... ἔσχατος· καὶ
GLTTrAW.   ᵍ + ἑπτὰ seven GLTTrAW.   ᵸ — ταῖς ἐν Ἀσίᾳ GLTTrAW.   ⁱ Ζμύρναν T.
ᵏ Θυάτειραν LAW.   ˡ Φιλαδελφίαν T.   ᵐ Λαοδικίαν T.   ⁿ ἐλάλει was speaking LTTrAW.
ᵒ — ἑπτὰ LT[TrA].   ᴾ υἱὸν T.   ᑫ μαζοῖς L; μασθοῖς T.   ʳ χρυσᾶν LTTrA.   ˢ ὡς
ᴬˢ GLTTrAW.   ᵗ πεπυρωμένης (-ένῳ T) [it] glowed LTr.   ⱽ χειρὶ αὐτοῦ LTTrA.

ᵂἐπέθηκεν‖ τὴν.δεξιὰν.αὐτοῦ ˣχεῖρα‖ ἐπ' ἐμέ, λέγων ʸμοι,‖
he laid   his right   ¹hand   upon me,   saying   to me,

Μὴ.φοβοῦ· ἐγώ εἰμι ὁ πρῶτος καὶ ὁ ἔσχατος, 18 καὶ ὁ
Fear not;   ι   am the   first   and the   last,   and the

ζῶν, καὶ ἐγενόμην νεκρός, καὶ ἰδοὺ ζῶν εἰμι εἰς.τοὺς
living [one]: and I became   dead,   and behold ³alive ¹I ⁴am to the

αἰῶνας τῶν αἰώνων· ᶻἀμήν·‖ καὶ ἔχω τὰς κλεῖς τοῦ ᵃᾅδου καὶ
ages of the   ages,   Amen; and have the keys   of hades and

τοῦ θανάτου.‖ 19 γράψον ᵇ ἃ εἶδες, καὶ ἅ
of death.   Write   the things which thou sawest and the things

εἰσιν, καὶ ἃ μέλλει ᶜγίνεσθαι‖ μετὰ ταῦτα· 20 τὸ
which are, and the things which are about to take place after these.   The

μυστήριον τῶν ἑπτὰ ἀστέρων ᵈὧν‖ εἶδες ᵉἐπὶ τῆς δεξιᾶς‖
mystery of the seven   stars   which thou sawest on ²right ³hand

μου, καὶ τὰς ἑπτὰ λυχνίας τὰς χρυσᾶς. οἱ ἑπτὰ ἀστέρες
¹my. and the seven ²lampstands   ¹golden. · The seven   stars

ἄγγελοι τῶν ἑπτὰ ἐκκλησιῶν εἰσιν· καὶ ᶠαἱⁱ ᵍἑπτὰ λυχνίαι‖
²angels ³of ⁴the ⁵seven ⁶assemblies ¹are; and the   seven lampstands

ᵇἃς εἶδες‖ ἑπτὰ ἐκκλησίαι εἰσίν.
which thou sawest ²seven ³assemblies ¹are.

2 Τῷ ἀγγέλῳ ⁱτῆς‖ ᵏἘφεσίνης‖ ἐκκλησίας γράψον, Τάδε
To the angel of the Ephesian   assembly write: These things

λέγει ὁ κρατῶν τοὺς ἑπτὰ ἀστέρας ἐν τῇ.δεξιᾷ.αὐτοῦ, ὁ
says he who holds   the seven stars   in   his right hand, who

περιπατῶν ἐν μέσῳ ᾽ τῶν ἑπτὰ λυχνιῶν τῶν ˡχρυσῶν·‖
walks   in [the] midst of the seven ²lampstands   ¹golden.

2 Οἶδα τὰ.ἔργα σου, καὶ τὸν κόπον ᵐσου,‖ καὶ τὴν ὑπομονήν
I know   thy works, and   ²labour ¹thy,   and ²endurance

σου, καὶ ὅτι οὐ.δύνῃ βαστάσαι κακούς,. καὶ ⁿἐπειράσω‖
¹thy, and that thou canst not   bear   evil [ones]; and thou didst try

τοὺς ᵒφάσκοντας εἶναι ἀποστόλους‖ καὶ οὐκ.εἰσίν,
those who declare [themselves] to be   apostles   and are not,

καὶ εὗρες αὐτοὺς ψευδεῖς, 3 καὶ ᴾἐβάστασας καὶ ὑπομονὴν
and didst find them   liars;   and   didst bear   and ²endurance

ἔχεις, καὶ‖ διὰ τὸ.ὄνομά.μου ᵠκεκοπίακας καὶ οὐ.κέκμηκας.‖
¹hast, and for the sake of my name   hast laboured and hast not wearied:

4 ʳἀλλ'‖ ἔχω κατὰ σοῦ, ὅτι τὴν.ἀγάπην.σου τὴν πρώτην
but I have against thee, that   thy ²love   ¹first

ˢἀφῆκας.‖ 5 μνημόνευε οὖν πόθεν ᵗἐκπέπτωκας,‖ καὶ
thou didst leave.   Remember therefore whence thou hast fallen from, and

μετανόησον, καὶ τὰ πρῶτα ἔργα ποίησον· εἰ.δὲ μή, ἔρχομαι
repent,   and the first works   do: but if not, I am coming

σοι ᵛτάχει,‖ καὶ κινήσω τὴν.λυχνίαν.σου ἐκ τοῦ τόπου
to thee quickly, and I will remove thy lampstand out of ²place

αὐτῆς, ἐὰν.μὴ μετανοήσῃς. 6 ἀλλὰ τοῦτο ἔχεις, ὅτι
¹its, except thou shouldest repent. But   this thou hast, that

μισεῖς τὰ ἔργα τῶν Νικολαϊτῶν, ἃ κἀγὼ μισῶ. 7 ὁ
thou hatest the works of the Nicolaitanes, which I also hate.   He that

---

laid his right hand up-
on me, saying unto
me, Fear not; I am
the first and the last:
18 *I am* he that liveth,
and was dead; and,
behold, I am alive for
evermore, Amen; and
have the keys of hell
and of death. 19 Write
the things which thou
hast seen, and the
things which are, and
the things which shall
be hereafter; 20 the
mystery of the seven
stars which thou saw-
est in my right hand,
and the seven golden
candlesticks. The se-
ven stars are the an-
gels of the seven
churches: and the se-
ven candlesticks which
thou sawest are the
seven churches.

II. Unto the angel of
the church of Ephesus
write; These things
saith he that holdeth
the seven stars in his
right hand, who walk-
eth in the midst of the
seven golden candle-
sticks; 2 I know thy
works, and thy labour,
and thy patience, and
how thou canst not
bear them which are
evil: and thou hast
tried them which say
they are apostles, and
are not, and hast found
them liars: 3 and hast
borne, and hast pa-
tience, and for my
name's sake hast la-
boured, and hast not
fainted. 4 Neverthe-
less I have somewhat
against thee, because
thou hast left thy first
love. 5 Remember
therefore from whence
thou art fallen, and
repent, and do the first
works; or else I will
come unto thee quick-
ly, and will remove
thy candlestick out of
his place, except thou
repent. 6 But this thou
hast, that thou hatest
the deeds of the Nico-
laitanes, which I also
hate. 7 He that hath

ᵂ ἔθηκεν GLTTrAW.   ˣ — χεῖρα (read δεξιὰν right hand) GLTTrAW.   ʸ — μοι GLTTrAW.
ᶻ — ἀμήν GLTTrAW.   ᵃ θανάτου καὶ τοῦ ᾅδου GLTTrAW   ᵇ + οὖν therefore GLTTrAW.
ᶜ γενέσθαι TA.   ᵈ οὓς LTTrA.   ᵉ ἐν (in) τῇ δεξιᾷ L.   ᶠ — αἱ W.   ᵍ λυχνίαι αἱ ἑπτὰ
GLTTrAW.   ʰ — ἃς εἶδες GLTTrAW.   ⁱ τῷ (read ἐκκλ. of the assembly) LTr.   ᵏ ἐν
Ἐφέσῳ in Ephesus GLTTrAW.   ˡ χρυσέων LTrA.   ᵐ — σου LTTrA.   ⁿ ἐπείρασας GLTTrAW.
ᵒ λέγοντας ἑαυτοὺς ἀποστόλους εἶναι declare themselves to be apostles (— εἶναι LTTrA)
GLTTrAW.   ᴾ ὑπομονὴν ἔχεις καὶ ἐβάστασας GLTTrAW.   ᵠ καὶ οὐ κεκοπίακες and hast not
wearied LTTrA; καὶ οὐκ ἐκοπίασας and didst not weary GW.   ʳ ἀλλὰ TTrW.   ˢ ἀφῆκες TTr.
ᵗ πέπτωκας thou hast fallen GLTrAW; πέπτωκες T.   ᵛ ταχὺ EGW; τάνει LTTrA.

an ear, let him hear what the Spirit saith unto the churches; To him that overcometh will I give to eat of the tree of life, which is in the midst of the paradise of God.

8 And unto the angel of the church in Smyrna write; These things saith the first and the last, which was dead, and is alive; 9 I know thy works, and tribulation, and poverty, (but thou art rich) and *I know* the blasphemy of them which say they are Jews, and are not, but *are* the synagogue of Satan. 10 Fear none of those things which thou shalt suffer: behold, the devil shall cast *some* of you into prison, that ye may be tried; and ye shall have tribulation ten days: be thou faithful unto death, and I will give thee a crown of life. 11 He that hath an ear, let him hear what the Spirit saith unto the churches; He that overcometh shall not be hurt of the second death.

12 And to the angel of the church in Pergamos write; These things saith he which hath the sharp sword with two edges; 13 I know thy works, and where thou dwellest, *even* where Satan's seat *is*: and thou holdest fast my name, and hast not denied my faith, even in those days wherein Antipas *was* my faithful martyr, who was slain among you, where Satan dwelleth. 14 But I have a few things against thee, because thou hast there them that hold the doctrine of Balaam, who taught Balac to cast a stumblingblock before the children of Israel, to eat things sacrificed unto idols, and to commit fornication. 15 So

ἔχων οὓς ἀκουσάτω τί τὸ πνεῦμα λέγει ταῖς[w] ἐκκλησίαις·
has an ear, let him hear what the Spirit says to the assemblies.

τῷ [x]νικῶντι‖ δώσω αὐτῷ φαγεῖν ἐκ τοῦ ξύλου τῆς ζωῆς
To him that overcomes, I will give to him to eat of the tree of life

ὅ ἐστιν ἐν [y]μέσῳ τοῦ παραδείσου‖ τοῦ Θεοῦ[z].
which is in [the] midst of the paradise of God.

8 Καὶ τῷ ἀγγέλῳ [a]τῆς‖ [b]ἐκκλησίας Σμυρναίων‖ γράψον,
And to the angel of the assembly of Smyrneans write,

Τάδε λέγει ὁ πρῶτος καὶ ὁ ἔσχατος, ὃς ἐγένετο νεκρὸς
These things says the first and the last, who became dead

καὶ ἔζησεν· 9 Οἶδά σου [c]τὰ ἔργα καὶ‖ τὴν θλίψιν καὶ τὴν
and lived. 9 I know thy works and tribulation and the

πτωχείαν· [d]πλούσιος δὲ‖ εἶ· καὶ τὴν βλασφημίαν[e] τῶν·
poverty; but rich thou art; and the calumny of those who

λεγόντων Ἰουδαίους εἶναι ἑαυτούς, καὶ οὐκ εἰσίν, ἀλλὰ συν-
declare Jews to be themselves, and are not, but a syn-

αγωγὴ τοῦ σατανᾶ. 10 [f]μηδὲν‖ φοβοῦ ἃ μέλλεις
agogue of Satan. 10 Not at all fear the things which thou art about

πάσχειν. ἰδού,[g] μέλλει [h]βαλεῖν[i] [i]ἐξ ὑμῶν ὁ διάβολος‖
to suffer. Lo, is about to cast [some] of you the devil

εἰς φυλακήν, ἵνα πειρασθῆτε· καὶ [k]ἕξετε[e] θλίψιν ἡμερῶν
into prison, that ye may be tried; and ye shall have tribulation days

δέκα. γίνου πιστὸς ἄχρι θανάτου, καὶ δώσω σοι τὸν στέ-
ten. Be thou faithful unto death, and I will give to thee the

φανον τῆς ζωῆς. 11 ὁ ἔχων οὓς ἀκουσάτω τί τὸ πνεῦμα
crown of life. He that has an ear, let him hear what the Spirit

λέγει ταῖς ἐκκλησίαις· ὁ νικῶν οὐ μὴ ἀδικηθῇ ἐκ
says to the assemblies. He that overcomes in no wise shall be injured of

τοῦ θανάτου τοῦ δευτέρου.
the death second.

12 Καὶ τῷ ἀγγέλῳ τῆς ἐν Περγάμῳ ἐκκλησίας γράψον,
And to the angel of the in Pergamos assembly write:

Τάδε λέγει ὁ ἔχων τὴν ῥομφαίαν τὴν δίστομον τὴν
These things says he who has the sword two-edged the

ὀξεῖαν· 13 Οἶδα [l]τὰ ἔργα σου καὶ‖ ποῦ κατοικεῖς, ὅπου
sharp, I know thy works and where thou dwellest, where the

θρόνος τοῦ σατανᾶ, καὶ κρατεῖς τὸ ὄνομά μου, καὶ οὐκ
throne of Satan [is]; and thou holdest fast my name, and not

ἠρνήσω τὴν πίστιν μου [m]καὶ‖ ἐν ταῖς ἡμέραις [n]ἐν‖ [o]αἷς‖ [p]Ἀν-
didst deny my faith even in the days in which An-

τίπας‖ ὁ μάρτυς μου ὁ πιστός[q], ὃς ἀπεκτάνθη παρ' ὑμῖν,
tipas my witness faithful [was], who was killed among you,

ὅπου [r]κατοικεῖ ὁ σατανᾶς.‖ 14 [s]ἀλλ'‖ ἔχω κατὰ σοῦ ὀλίγα,
where dwells Satan. But I have against thee a few things;

[t]ὅτι‖ ἔχεις ἐκεῖ κρατοῦντας τὴν διδαχὴν Βαλαάμ, ὃς
because thou hast there [those] holding the teaching of Balaam, who

ἐδίδασκεν [v]ἐν‖ [wa]τῷ‖ Βαλὰκ βαλεῖν σκάνδαλον ἐνώπιον τῶν
taught Balak to cast a snare before the

υἱῶν Ἰσραήλ, φαγεῖν εἰδωλόθυτα καὶ πορνεῦσαι.
sons of Israel, to eat things sacrificed to idols and to commit fornication.

w + ἑπτὰ seven L. 　x νικοῦντι L. 　y τῷ παραδείσῳ the paradise GLTTrAW. 　z + μου (read of my God) G[A]w. 　a τῷ (read ἐκκλ. of the assembly) L. 　b ἐν Σμύρνῃ (Ζμύρνῃ T.) ἐκκλησίας assembly in Smyrna GLTTrAW. 　c — τὰ ἔργα καὶ LTTrA. 　d ἀλλὰ πλούσιος GLTTrAW. 　e — ἐκ of (those who) GLTTrAW. 　f μὴ Not LTrAW. 　g + δὴ indeed [A]w. 　h βάλλειν LTrA. 　i ὁ διάβολος ἐξ ὑμῶν GLTTrAW. 　k ἔχητε ye may have L. 　l — τὰ ἔργα σου καὶ LTTrA. 　m — καὶ T[TrA]. 　n — ἐν LTTrAW. 　o — αἷς (read in those days [was] Antipas) LTTr[A]. 　p Ἀντείπας T. 　q + μου (read my faithful [one]) LT[TrA]w. 　r ὁ σατανᾶς κατοικεῖ GLTTrAW. 　s ἀλλὰ W. 　t ἔτι L. 　v — ἐν EGLTTrAW. 　wa τὸν E.

15 οὕτως ἔχεις καὶ σὺ κρατοῦντας τὴν διδαχὴν ˣτῶν‖
So hast also thou [those] holding the teaching of the

Νικολαϊτῶν ʸὃ μισῶ.‖ 16 μετανόησον ᶻ· εἰ.δὲ μή, ἔρχομαί
Nicolaitanes, which thing I hate. Repent ! but if not, I am coming

σοι ταχύ, καὶ πολεμήσω μετ' αὐτῶν ἐν τῇ ῥομφαίᾳ τοῦ
to thee quickly, and will make war with them with the sword

στόματός.μου. 17 ὁ ἔχων οὖς ἀκουσάτω τί τὸ πνεῦμα
of my mouth. He that has an ear, let him hear what the Spirit

λέγει ταῖς ἐκκλησίαις· τῷ ᵃνικῶντι‖ δώσω αὐτῷ ᵇφαγεῖν
says to the assemblies. To him that overcomes, I will give to him to eat

ἀπὸ‖ τοῦ μάννα τοῦ κεκρυμμένου, καὶ δώσω αὐτῷ ψῆφον
of the ²manna ¹hidden; and I will give to him a ²pebble

λευκήν, καὶ ἐπὶ τὴν ψῆφον ὄνομα καινὸν γεγραμμένον, ὃ
¹white, and on the pebble a ²name ¹new written, which

οὐδεὶς ᶜἔγνω‖ εἰ.μὴ ὁ λαμβάνων.
no one knew except he who receives [it].

18 Καὶ τῷ ἀγγέλῳ ᵈτῆς‖ ἐν Θυατείροις ἐκκλησίας γράψον,
And to the angel of the ²in ³Thyatira ¹assembly write:

Τάδε λέγει ὁ υἱὸς τοῦ θεοῦ, ὁ ἔχων τοὺς ὀφθαλμοὺς
These things says the Son of God, he who has ²eyes

ᵉαὐτοῦ‖ ὡς ᶠφλόγα‖ πυρός, καὶ οἱ.πόδες.αὐτοῦ ὅμοιοι χαλκολι-
¹his as a flame of fire, and his feet like fine

βάνῳ· 19 Οἶδά σου τὰ ἔργα καὶ τὴν ᵍἀγάπην, καὶ τὴν δια-
brass. I know thy works, and love, and ser-

κονίαν, καὶ τὴν πίστιν‖ καὶ ʰτὴν‖ ὑπομονήν ⁱσου,‖ καὶ τὰ ἔργα
vice, and faith, and ²endurance ¹thy, and ²works

σου, ᵏκαὶ‖ τὰ ἔσχατα πλείονα τῶν πρώτων. 20 ¹ἀλλ'‖
¹thy, and the last [to be] more than the first. But

ἔχω κατὰ σοῦ ᵐὀλίγα,‖ ὅτι ⁿἐᾷς‖ τὴν γυναῖκαᵒ ᵖⁱἸεζα-
I have against thee a few things that thou sufferest the woman Jeze-

βήλ, ᵠτὴν λέγουσαν‖ ʳἑαυτὴν‖ προφῆτιν, ˢδιδάσκειν καὶ πλα-
bel, her who calls herself a prophetess, to teach and to

νᾶσθαι‖ ἐμοὺς δούλους, πορνεῦσαι καὶ ᵗεἰδωλό-
mislead my bondmen, to commit fornication and ³things ⁴sacrificed ⁵to

θυτα φαγεῖν.‖ 21 καὶ ἔδωκα αὐτῇ χρόνον ἵνα μετανοήσῃ ᵛἐκ
⁶idols ¹to ²eat. And I gave her time that she might repent of

τῆς.πορνείας.αὐτῆς, καὶ οὐ.μετενόησεν.‖ 22 ἰδού, ʷἐγὼ‖ βάλλω
her fornication; and she repented not. Lo, I cast

αὐτὴν εἰς κλίνην, καὶ τοὺς μοιχεύοντας μετ' αὐτῆς εἰς
her into a bed, and those who commit adultery with her into

θλῖψιν μεγάλην, ἐὰν.μὴ ˣᵃμετανοήσωσιν‖ ἐκ τῶν ἔργων
²tribulation ¹great, except they should repent of ²works

ʸᵃαὐτῶν.‖ 23 καὶ τὰ.τέκνα.αὐτῆς ἀποκτενῶ ἐν θανάτῳ· καὶ
¹their. And her children I will kill with death; and

γνώσονται.πᾶσαι αἱ ἐκκλησίαι ὅτι ἐγώ εἰμι ὁ ᶻᵃἐρευνῶν‖
⁴shall ²know ¹all ²the ³assemblies that I am he who searches

---

hast thou also them that hold the doctrine of the Nicolaitanes, which thing I hate. 16 Repent; or else I will come unto thee quickly, and will fight against them with the sword of my mouth. 17 He that hath an ear, let him hear what the Spirit saith unto the churches; To him that overcometh will I give to eat of the hidden manna, and will give him a white stone, and in the stone a new name written, which no man knoweth saving he that receiveth it.

18 And unto the angel of the church in Thyatira write; These things saith the Son of God, who hath his eyes like unto a flame of fire, and his feet are like fine brass; 19 I know thy works, and charity, and service, and faith, and thy patience, and thy works; and the last to be more than the first. 20 Notwithstanding I have a few things against thee, because thou sufferest that woman Jezebel, which calleth herself a prophetess, to teach and to seduce my servants to commit fornication, and to eat things sacrificed unto idols. 21 And I gave her space to repent of her fornication; and she repented not. 22 Behold, I will cast her into a bed, and them that commit adultery with her into great tribulation, except they repent of their deeds. 23 And I will kill her children with death; and all the churches shall know that I am he which searcheth the

---

ˣ — τῶν the ʟ[Tr]ᴀᴡ. ʸ ὁμοίως in like manner GLTTrAW. ᶻ + οὖν therefore GLTr[A]w. ᵃ νικοῦντι LTTr. ᵇ — φαγεῖν ἀπὸ GLTTrAW. ᶜ οἶδεν knows GLTTrAW. ᵈ τῷ (read ἐκκλ. of the assembly) L. ᵉ — αὐτοῦ L. ᶠ φλὸξ T. ᵍ ἀγάπην, καὶ τὴν πίστιν καὶ τὴν διακονίαν GLTA ; πίστιν καὶ τὴν ἀγάπην καὶ τὴν διακονίαν Tr. ʰ — τὴν L. ⁱ — σου T. ᵏ — καὶ (read thy last works) GLTTrAW. ¹ ἀλλὰ TrAW. ᵐ — ὀλίγα GLTTrAW. ⁿ ἀφεὶς thou lettest alone GLTTrAW. ᵒ + σου (read thy wife) GL[A]w. ᵖ τὴν Ἰεζάβελ L ; Ἰεζάβελ GT ; Ἰεζαβὲλ TrAW. ᵠ ἣ λέγουσα she who calls GLTTrAW. ʳ αὐτὴν T. ˢ καὶ διδάσκει καὶ πλανᾷ τοὺς and she teaches and misleads GLTTrAW. ᵗ φαγεῖν εἰδωλόθυτα GLTTrAW. ᵛ καὶ οὐ θέλει μετανοῆσαι ἐκ τῆς πορνείας αὐτῆς and she wills not to repent of her fornication GLTTrAW. ʷ — ἐγὼ (read βάλλω I cast) GLTTrAW. ˣᵃ μετανοήσουσιν they shall repent TTrA. ʸᵃ αὐτῆς her GLTTrAW. ᶻᵃ ἐραυνῶν LTTr.

reins and hearts : and I will give unto every one of you according to your works. 24 But unto you I say, and unto the rest in Thyatira, as many as have not this doctrine, and which have not known the depths of Satan, as they speak; I will put upon you none other burden. 25 But that which ye have *already* hold fast till I come. 26 And he that overcometh, and keepeth my works unto the end, to him will I give power over the nations : 27 and he shall rule them with a rod of iron ; as the vessels of a potter shall they be broken to shivers : even as I received of my Father. 28 And I will give him the morning 'star. 29 He that hath an ear, let him hear what the Spirit saith unto the churches.

III. And unto the angel of the church in Sardis write ; These things saith he that hath the seven Spirits of God, and the seven stars ; I know thy works, that thou hast a name that thou livest, and art dead. 2 Be watchful, and strengthen the things which remain, that are ready to die : for I have not found thy works perfect before God. 3 Remember therefore how thou hast received and heard, and hold fast, and repent. If therefore thou shalt not watch, I will come on thee as a thief, and thou shalt not know what hour I will come upon thee. 4 Thou hast a few names even in Sardis which have not defiled their garments ; and they shall walk with me in white : for they are worthy. 5 He that overcometh, the same shall be clothed in white raiment ; and I will not blot out his

νεφροὺς καὶ καρδίας· καὶ δώσω ὑμῖν ἑκάστῳ κατὰ τὰ
reins and hearts; and I will give to you each according to
ἔργα ὑμῶν. 24 ὑμῖν.δὲ λέγω [a]καὶ[/a] λοιποῖς τοῖς ἐν
[2]works [1]your.   But to you I say, and to [the] rest who [are] in
Θυατείροις, ὅσοι οὐκ.ἔχουσιν τὴν.διδαχὴν.ταύτην, [b]καὶ[/b]
Thyatira, as many as have not this teaching,   and
οἵτινες οὐκ.ἔγνωσαν τὰ [c]βάθη[/c] τοῦ σατανᾶ, ὡς λέγουσιν, Οὐ
who knew not the depths of Satan, as they say; [2]not
[d]βαλῶ[/d] ἐφ' ὑμᾶς ἄλλο βάρος· 25 πλὴν ὃ ἔχετε κρατή-
[1][4]will [4]cast upon you any other burden;   but what ye have 'hold
σατε, [e]ἄχρις[/e] οὗ.ἂν.ἥξω. 26 καὶ ὁ νικῶν καὶ ὁ
fast till I shall come.   And he that overcomes, and he that
τηρῶν ἄχρι τέλους τὰ.ἔργα.μου, δώσω αὐτῷ ἐξουσίαν
keeps until [the] end my works, I will give to him authority
ἐπὶ τῶν ἐθνῶν· 27 καὶ ποιμανεῖ αὐτοὺς ἐν ῥάβδῳ σι-
over the nations, and he shall shepherd them with [2]rod [1]an
δηρᾷ· ὡς τὰ σκεύη τὰ.κεραμικὰ συντρίβεται, ὡς κἀγὼ
[2]iron, as vessels of pottery · are broken in pieces; as I also
εἴληφα παρὰ τοῦ.πατρός.μου· 28 καὶ δώσω αὐτῷ τὸν
have received from my Father;   and I will give to him the
ἀστέρα τὸν πρωϊνόν. 29 ὁ ἔχων οὖς ἀκουσάτω τί τὸ
[2]star [1]morning.   He that has an ear, let him hear what the
πνεῦμα λέγει ταῖς ἐκκλησίαις.
Spirit says to the assemblies.

3 Καὶ τῷ ἀγγέλῳ τῆς ἐν Σάρδεσιν ἐκκλησίας γράψον,
And to the angel of the [2]in [3]Sardis [1]assembly write :
Τάδε λέγει ὁ ἔχων τὰ[f] πνεύματα τοῦ θεοῦ καὶ τοὺς
These things says he who has the Spirits of God and the
ἑπτὰ ἀστέρας· Οἶδά σου τὰ ἔργα, ὅτι [g]τὸ[/g] ὄνομα ἔχεις ὅτι
seven stars. I know thy works, that [3]the [4]name [1]thou [2]hast that
ζῇς, καὶ νεκρὸς εἶ. 2 γίνου γρηγορῶν, καὶ [h]στήριξον[/h]
thou livest, and [2]dead [1]art.   Be watchful, and strengthen
τὰ.λοιπὰ ἃ [i]μέλλει[/i] ἀποθανεῖν· οὐ.γὰρ.εὕρηκά
the things that remain, which are about to die, for I have not found
σου [j]τὰ[/j] ἔργα πεπληρωμένα ἐνώπιον τοῦ θεοῦ[k]. 3 μνημόνευε
thy works complete before God.   Remember
[l]οὖν[/l] πῶς εἴληφας καὶ ἤκουσας, καὶ τήρει, καὶ
therefore how thou hast received and heard, and keep [it] and
μετανόησον· ἐὰν οὖν μὴ.γρηγορήσῃς, ἥξω [m]ἐπὶ σὲ[/m]
repent.   If therefore thou shalt not watch I will come upon thee
ὡς κλέπτης, καὶ οὐ.μὴ [n]γνῷς[/n] ποίαν ὥραν ἥξω
as a thief, and in no wise shalt thou know what hour I shall come
ἐπὶ σέ. 4 [o]Ρἔχεις ὀλίγα[/o] ὀνόματα [q]καὶ[/q] ἐν Σάρδεσιν, ἃ οὐκ
upon thee. 4 Thou hast a few names also in Sardis which [2]not
ἐμόλυναν τὰ.ἱμάτια.αὐτῶν· καὶ περιπατήσουσιν μετ' ἐμοῦ ἐν
[1]defiled their garments; and they shall walk with me in
λευκοῖς, ὅτι ἄξιοί εἰσιν. 5 ὁ νικῶν, [r]οὗτος[/r] περι-
white, because worthy they are.   He that overcomes, he shall
βαλεῖται ἐν ἱματίοις λευκοῖς· καὶ οὐ.μὴ ἐξαλείψω τὸ ὄνομα
be clothed in [2]garments [1]white; and in no wise will I blot out [2]name

---

αὐτοῦ ἐκ τῆς βίβλου τῆς ζωῆς, καὶ ˢἐξομολογήσομαι‖ τὸ ὄνομα
¹his from the book of life, and will confess ²name

αὐτοῦ ἐνώπιον τοῦ.πατρός.μου καὶ ἐνώπιον τῶν ἀγγέλων
¹his before my Father and before ²angels

αὐτοῦ. 6 ὁ ἔχων οὖς ἀκουσάτω τί τὸ πνεῦμα λέγει
¹his. He that has an ear, let him hear what the Spirit says

ταῖς ἐκκλησίαις.
to the assemblies.

7 Καὶ τῷ ἀγγέλῳ τῆς ἐν ᵗΦιλαδελφείᾳ‖ ἐκκλησίας γράψον,
And to the angel of the ²in ³Philadelphia ¹assembly write:

Τάδε λέγει ᵛὁ ἅγιος, ὁ ἀληθινός,‖ ὁ ἔχων τὴν ᵂκλεῖδα‖
These things says the Holy, the True; he who has the key

ˣτοῦ‖ ʸΔαβίδ,‖ ὁ ἀνοίγων καὶ οὐδεὶς ᶻκλείει,‖ ᵃκαὶ‖ ᵇκλείει‖ καὶ
of David, who opens and no one shuts, and shuts and

οὐδεὶς ᶜἀνοίγει·‖ 8 Οἶδά σου τὰ ἔργα· ἰδού, δέδωκα ἐνώπιόν
no one opens. I know thy works. Lo, I have set before

σου θύραν ᵈἀνεῳγμένην,‖ ᵉκαὶ‖ οὐδεὶς δύναται κλεῖσαι αὐτήν
thee ³door ᵈan ²opened, and no one is able to shut it,

ὅτι μικρὰν ἔχεις δύναμιν, καὶ ἐτήρησάς μου τὸν λόγον,
because ²a ¹little ¹thou ²hast power, and didst keep my word,

καὶ οὐκ.ἠρνήσω τὸ.ὄνομά.μου. 9 ἰδού, ᶠδίδωμι‖ ἐκ τῆς συνα-
and didst not deny my name. Lo, I give of the syna-

γωγῆς τοῦ σατανᾶ τῶν λεγόντων ἑαυτοὺς Ἰουδαίους εἶναι,
gogue of Satan those that declare themselves ³Jews ¹to ²be,

καὶ οὐκ.εἰσίν, ἀλλὰ ψεύδονται· ἰδού, ποιήσω αὐτοὺς ἵνα
and are not, but do lie; lo, I will cause them that

ᵍἥξωσιν‖ καὶ ʰπροσκυνήσωσιν‖ ἐνώπιον τῶν.ποδῶν.σου,
they should come and should do homage before thy feet,

καὶ γνῶσιν ὅτι ἐγὼ ἠγάπησά σε. 10 ὅτι ἐτήρησας τὸν
and should know that I loved thee. Because thou didst keep the

λόγον τῆς.ὑπομονῆς.μου, κἀγώ σε τηρήσω ἐκ τῆς ὥρας τοῦ
word of my endurance, I also thee will keep out of the hour

πειρασμοῦ τῆς μελλούσης ἔρχεσθαι ἐπὶ τῆς οἰκουμένης
of trial which [is] about to come upon the ²habitable ³world

ὅλης, πειράσαι τοὺς κατοικοῦντας ἐπὶ τῆς γῆς. 11 ¹Ἰδού,‖
¹whole, to try them that dwell upon the earth. Behold,

ἔρχομαι ταχύ· κράτει ὃ ἔχεις, ἵνα μηδεὶς λάβῃ τὸν
I come quickly: hold fast what thou hast, that no one take

στέφανόν σου. 12 ὁ νικῶν, ποιήσω αὐτὸν στύλον ἐν τῷ
²crown ¹thy. He that overcomes, I will make him a pillar in the

ναῷ τοῦ.θεοῦ.μου, καὶ ἔξω οὐ.μὴ ἐξέλθῃ ἔτι, καὶ γράψω
temple of my God, and out not at all shall he go more; and I will write

ἐπ᾽ αὐτὸν τὸ ὄνομα τοῦ.θεοῦ.μου, καὶ τὸ ὄνομα τῆς πόλεως
upon him the name of my God, and the name of the city

τοῦ.θεοῦ.μου, τῆς καινῆς Ἰερουσαλήμ, ᵏἡ καταβαίνουσα‖
of my God, the new Jerusalem, which comes down

ἐκ τοῦ οὐρανοῦ ἀπὸ τοῦ.θεοῦ.μου, καὶ τὸ.ὄνομά.μου τὸ
out of heaven from my God, and my ²name

καινόν. 13 ὁ ἔχων οὖς ἀκουσάτω τί τὸ πνεῦμα λέγει
¹new. He that has an ear, let him hear what the Spirit says

ταῖς ἐκκλησίαις.
to the assemblies.

name out of the book of life, but I will confess his name before my Father, and before his angels. 6 He that hath an ear, let him hear what the Spirit saith unto the churches.

7 And to the angel of the church in Philadelphia write; These things saith he that is holy, he that is true, he that hath the key of David, he that openeth, and no man shutteth; and shutteth, and no man openeth; 8 I know thy works: behold, I have set before thee an open door, and no man can shut it: for thou hast a little strength, and hast kept my word, and hast not denied my name. 9 Behold, I will make them of the synagogue of Satan, which say they are Jews, and are not, but do lie; behold, I will make them to come and worship before thy feet, and to know that I have loved thee. 10 Because thou hast kept the word of my patience, I also will keep thee from the hour of temptation, which shall come upon all the world, to try them that dwell upon the earth. 11 Behold, I come quickly: hold that fast which thou hast, that no man take thy crown. 12 Him that overcometh will I make a pillar in the temple of my God, and he shall go no more out: and I will write upon him the name of my God, and the name of the city of my God, *which is* new Jerusalem, which cometh down out of heaven from my God: and *I will write upon him* my new name. 13 He that hath an ear, let him hear what the Spirit saith unto the churches.

ˢ ὁμολογήσω GLTTrAW.   ᵗ Φιλαδελφία T.   ᵛ ὁ ἀληθινός, ὁ ἅγιος A.   ᵂ κλεῖν GLTTrAW.
ˣ — τοῦ LTr[A.]   ʸ Δαυείδ LTTrA; Δαυΐδ GW.   ᶻ κλείσει shall shut LTTrAW.   ᵃ [καὶ] L.
ᵇ κλείων shutting LTTr.   ᶜ ἀνοίξει shall open TTrAW.   ᵈ ἠνεῳγμένη T.   ᵉ ἦν
which GLTTrAW.   ᶠ διδῶ I will give LTA; δίδω Tr.   ᵍ ἥξουσιν they shall come LTTrA.
ʰ προσκυνήσουσιν shall do homage LTTrA.   ¹ Ἰδού GLTTrAW.   ᵏ ἡ καταβαίνει Е.

14 And unto the angel of the church of the Laodiceans write; These things saith the Amen, the faithful and true witness, the beginning of the creation of God; 15 I know thy works, that thou art neither cold nor hot: I would thou wert cold or hot. 16 So then because thou art lukewarm, and neither cold nor hot, I will spue thee out of my mouth. 17 Because thou sayest, I am rich, and increased with goods, and have need of nothing; and knowest not that thou art wretched, and miserable, and poor, and blind, and naked: 18 I counsel thee to buy of me gold tried in the fire, that thou mayest be rich; and white raiment, that thou mayest be clothed, and that the shame of thy nakedness do not appear; and anoint thine eyes with eyesalve, that thou mayest see. 19 As many as I love, I rebuke and chasten: be zealous therefore, and repent. 20 Behold, I stand at the door, and knock: if any man hear my voice, and open the door, I will come in to him, and will sup with him, and he with me. 21 To him that overcometh will I grant to sit with me in my throne, even as I also overcame, and am set down with my Father in his throne. 22 He that hath an ear, let him hear what the Spirit saith unto the churches.

IV. After this I looked, and, behold, a door was opened in heaven: and the first voice which I heard was as it were of a trumpet talking with me; which said, Come up hither, and I will shew thee things which must be hereafter. 2 And imme-

14 Καὶ τῷ ἀγγέλῳ τῆς ¹ἐκκλησίας Λαοδικέων" γραψον,
And to the angel of the assembly of [the] Laodiceans write:
Τάδε λέγει ὁ ἀμήν, ὁ μάρτυς ὁ πιστὸς καὶ ἀληθινός, ἡ
These things says the Amen, the witness faithful and true, the
ἀρχὴ τῆς κτίσεως τοῦ θεοῦ· 15 Οἶδά σου τὰ ἔργα. ὅτι οὔτε
beginning of the creation of God. I know thy works, that neither
ψυχρὸς εἶ, οὔτε ζεστός· ὄφελον ψυχρὸς ᵐεἴης," ἢ ζεστός·
cold thou art, nor hot; I would cold thou wert or hot.
16 οὕτως ὅτι χλιαρὸς εἶ, καὶ οὔτε ⁿψυχρὸς οὔτε ζεστός,"
Thus because lukewarm thou art, and neither cold nor hot,
μέλλω σε ἐμέσαι ἐκ τοῦ.στόματός.μου. 17 ὅτι λέγεις,
I am about ³thee ¹to ²spue out of my mouth. Because thou sayest,
ᵒ'Ὅτι πλούσιός εἰμι καὶ πεπλούτηκα καὶ ᴾοὐδενὸς" χρειαν ἔχω,
Rich I am, and have grown rich and ³of ⁴nothing ²need ¹have,
καὶ οὐκ.οἶδας ὅτι σὺ εἶ ὁ ταλαίπωρος καὶ ᑫ ʳἐλεεινός," καὶ
and knowest not that thou art the wretched, and miserable, and
πτωχὸς καὶ τυφλὸς καὶ γυμνός· 18 συμβουλεύω σοι ἀγοράσαι
poor, and blind, and naked; I counsel thee to buy
παρ' ἐμοῦ χρυσίον πεπυρωμένον ἐκ πυρός, ἵνα πλουτήσῃς,
from me gold purified by fire, that thou mayest be rich;
καὶ ἱμάτια λευκά, ἵνα περιβάλῃ καὶ μὴ.φανερωθῇ
and ²garments ¹white, that thou mayest be clothed, and may not be made manifest
ἡ αἰσχύνη τῆς.γυμνότητός.σου· καὶ ˢκολλούριον" ᵗἔγχρισον"
the shame of thy nakedness; and ⁴eye-salve ¹anoint ²thou ³with
τοὺς.ὀφθαλμούς.σου, ἵνα βλέπῃς. 19 ἐγὼ ὅσους ἐὰν φιλῶ,
thine eyes, that thou mayest see. I as many as I love,
ἐλέγχω καὶ παιδεύω· ᶻζήλωσον" οὖν καὶ μετανόησον.
I rebuke and discipline; be thou zealous therefore and repent.
20 ἰδού, ἕστηκα ἐπὶ τὴν θύραν καὶ κρούω· ἐάν τις ἀκούσῃ
Behold, I stand at the door and knock; if anyone hear
τῆς.φωνῆς.μου, καὶ ἀνοιξῃ τὴν θύραν, ʷ εἰσελεύσομαι πρὸς
my voice and open the door, I will come in to
αὐτόν, καὶ δειπνήσω μετ' αὐτοῦ, καὶ αὐτὸς μετ' ἐμοῦ. 21 ὁ
him, and will sup with him, and he with me. He that
νικῶν, δώσω αὐτῷ καθίσαι μετ' ἐμοῦ ἐν τῷ.θρόνῳ.μου, ὡς
overcomes, I will give to him to sit with me in my throne, as
κἀγὼ ἐνίκησα, καὶ ἐκάθισα μετὰ τοῦ.πατρός.μου ἐν τῷ θρόνῳ
I also overcame, and sat down with my Father in ²throne
αὐτοῦ. 22 ὁ ἔχων οὖς ἀκουσάτω τί τὸ πνεῦμα λέγει
¹his. He that has an ear, let him hear what the Spirit says
ταῖς ἐκκλησίαις.
to the assemblies.

4 Μετὰ ταῦτα ˣεἶδον," καὶ ἰδοὺ θύρα ʸἠνεῳγμένη" ἐν τῷ
After these things I saw, and behold a door opened in
οὐρανῷ, καὶ ἡ φωνὴ ἡ πρώτη ἣν ἤκουσα ὡς σάλπιγγος
heaven, and the ²voice ¹first which I heard [was] as of a trumpet
λαλούσης μετ' ἐμοῦ, ᶻλέγουσα," ᵃ'Ανάβα" ὧδε, καὶ δείξω
speaking with me, saying, Come up hither, and I will shew
σοι ᵇἅ" δεῖ γενέσθαι μετὰ ταῦτα.ᶜ 2 ᵈκαὶ" εὐθέως
to thee what things must take place after these things. And immediately

---

ˡ ἐν Λαοδικείᾳ (Λαοδικίᾳ Τ) ἐκκλησίας assembly in Laodicea GLTTrAW.   ᵐ ἧς GLTTrAW.
ⁿ ζεστὸς οὔτε ψυχρός GTTrAW.   ᵒ — ὅτι [A]w.   ᴾ οὐδὲν ³in ¹no ²wise LTTrA.   ᑫ + ὁ the
GL[A].   ʳ ἐλεινος A.   ˢ κολλύριον TTrA.   ᵗ ἐγχρίσαι GW; ἐγχρίσαι to anoint with LA;
ἐγχρίσαι anoint with TTr.   ᵛ ζήλευε LTTrAW.   ʷ + καὶ (read I will both come in) T[A]W.
ˣ ἰδοῦ T.   ʸ ἀνεῳγμένη GLW.   ᶻ λέγων GLTTrAW.   ᵃ 'Ανάβηθι L.   ᵇ ὅσα
whatsoever things L.   ᶜ Punctuate so as to read Immediately after these things L.
ᵈ — καὶ LTTrAW.

ἐγενόμην ἐν πνεύματι· καὶ ἰδού, θρόνος ἔκειτο ἐν τῷ
I became in [the] Spirit; and behold, a throne was set in the

οὐρανῷ, καὶ ἐπὶ ᵉτοῦ θρόνου‖ καθήμενος· 3 καὶ ὁ καθή-
heaven, and upon the throne [one] sitting, and he who [was] sit-

μενος ᶠἦν· ὅμοιος ὁράσει λίθῳ ἰάσπιδι καὶ ᵍσαρδίνῳ·· καὶ
ting was like in appearance to a ²stone ¹jasper and a sardius; and

ἶρις κυκλόθεν τοῦ θρόνου ʰὅμοιος‖ ὁράσει σμαραγ-
a rainbow [was] around the throne like in appearance to an eme-

δίνῳ. 4 καὶ κυκλόθεν τοῦ θρόνου ⁱθρόνοι‖ εἴκοσι ᵏκαὶ ‖ ˡτέσ-
rald. And around the throne ²thrones ¹twenty ²and

σαρες,‖ καὶ ἐπὶ τοὺς ᵐθρόνους εἶδον τοὺς εἴκοσι καὶ τέσσαρας‖
²four, and on the thrones I saw the twenty and four

πρεσβυτέρους καθημένους, περιβεβλημένους ⁿἐν‖ ἱματίοις
elders sitting, clothed in ²garments

λευκοῖς· καὶ ᵒἔσχον‖ ἐπὶ τὰς κεφαλὰς αὐτῶν στεφάνους ᵖχρυσ-
¹white; and they had on their heads ²crowns ¹gold-

οῦς.‖ 5 καὶ ἐκ τοῦ θρόνου ἐκπορεύονται ἀστραπαὶ καὶ
en. And out of the throne go forth lightnings and

ᑫβρονταὶ καὶ φωναί·‖ καὶ ἑπτὰ λαμπάδες πυρὸς καιόμεναι
thunders and voices; and seven lamps of fire burning

ἐνώπιον τοῦ θρόνου ʳ, ˢαἵ‖ ᵗεἰσιν‖ ᵗὰᵈ ἑπτὰ πνεύματα τοῦ
before the throne, which are the seven Spirits

θεοῦ· 6 καὶ ἐνώπιον τοῦ θρόνου ʷ θάλασσα ὑαλίνη, ὁμοία
of God; and before the throne a ²sea ¹glass, like

κρυστάλλῳ. καὶ ἐν μέσῳ τοῦ θρόνου καὶ κύκλῳ τοῦ θρόνου
crystal. And in [the] midst of the throne and around the throne

ˣτέσσαρα‖ ζῶα γέμοντα ὀφθαλμῶν ʸἔμπροσθεν‖ καὶ
four living creatures, full of eyes before and

ὄπισθεν. 7 καὶ τὸ ζῶον τὸ πρῶτον ὅμοιον λέοντι,
behind; and the ²living ³creature ¹first [was] like a lion,

καὶ τὸ δεύτερον ζῶον ὅμοιον μόσχῳ, καὶ τὸ τρίτον ζῶ-
and the second living creature like a calf, and the third living

ον ᶻἔχον‖ τὸ πρόσωπον ᵃὡς‖ ᵇἄνθρωπος,‖ καὶ τὸ τέταρτον
creature having the face as a man, and the fourth

ζῶον ὅμοιον ἀετῷ ᶜπετωμένῳ.‖ 8 καὶ ᵈ ᵉᵃτέσσαρα‖
living creature like ²eagle ¹a ³flying. And [the] four

ζῶα, ἐν ᶠᵃκαθ' ἑαυτό,‖ ᵍᵃεἶχον‖ ἀνὰ πτέρυγας ἕξ.
living creatures, each for itself had respectively ²wings ¹six;

κυκλόθεν καὶ ἔσωθεν ʰᵃγέμοντα‖ ὀφθαλμῶν, καὶ ἀνάπαυσιν οὐκ
around and within full of eyes; and ⁴cessation ³not

ἔχουσιν ἡμέρας καὶ νυκτός, ⁱᵃλέγοντα,‖ Ἅγιος, ἅγιος, ἅγιος
¹they ²have day and night, saying, Holy, holy, holy,

κύριος ὁ θεὸς ὁ παντοκράτωρ, ὁ ἦν καὶ ὁ ὢν καὶ ὁ
Lord God Almighty, who was, and who is, and who [is]

ἐρχόμενος. 9 καὶ ὅταν δώσουσιν τὰ ' ζῶα δόξαν καὶ
to come. And when ⁴shall ⁵give the ²living ³creatures glory and

τιμὴν καὶ εὐχαριστίαν τῷ καθημένῳ ἐπὶ ᵏᵃτοῦ θρόνου,‖ τῷ
honour and thanksgiving to him who sits upon the throne, who

---

diately I was in the Spirit: and. beho'd, a throne was set in heaven, and one sat on the throne. 3 And he that sat was to look upon like a jasper and a sardine stone: and there was a rainbow round about the throne, in sight like unto an emerald. 4 And round about the throne were four and twenty seats: and upon the seats I saw four and twenty elders sitting, clothed in white raiment; and they had on their heads crowns of gold. 5 And out of the throne proceeded lightnings and thunderings and voices: and there were seven lamps of fire burning before the throne, which are the seven Spirits of God. 6 And before the throne there was a sea of glass like unto crystal: and in the midst of the throne, and round about the throne, were four beasts full of eyes before and behind. 7 And the first beast was like a lion, and the second beast like a calf, and the third beast had a face as a man, and the fourth beast was like a flying eagle. 8 And the four beasts had each of them six wings about him; and they were full of eyes within: and they rest not day and night, saying, Holy, holy, holy, Lord God Almighty, which was, and is, and is to come. 9 And when those beasts give glory and honour and thanks to him that sat on the

---

ᵉ τὸν θρόνον LTTrAW. ᶠ — ἦν GLTTrAW. ᵍ σαρδίῳ GLTTrAW. ʰ ὁμοία E. ⁱ θρόνους LT.
ᵏ — καὶ GLTTrAW. ˡ τέσσερας L; τέσσαρας T. ᵐ θρόνους τοὺς (— τοὺς GTT) εἴκοσι
τέσσαρας GTTrW; εἴκοσι τέσσερας (τέσσαρας Α) θρόνους LA. ⁿ — ἐν (read ἱματίοις with
garments) L. ᵒ — ἔσχον GLTTrAW. ᵖ χρυσέους Tr. ᑫ φωναὶ καὶ βρονταί GLTTrAW.
ʳ + [αὐτοῦ] (read his throne) A. ˢ ἅ LT. ᵗ ἐστιν L. ᵛ [τὰ] A. ʷ + ὡς as
GLTTrAW. ˣ τέσσερα LTTr. ʸ ἔνπροσθεν T. ᶻ ἔχων TTrA. — ὡς G[A]W. ᵇ ἀνθρώπου of a man GLTTrAW. ᶜ πετομένῳ GLTTrAW. ᵈ + τὰ the GLTTrAW. ᵉᵃ τέσσερα
LTTr. ᶠᵃ καθ' ἓν αὐτῶν (ἕκαστον αὐτῶν Tr) (read each of them) GLTA. ᵍᵃ ἔχον (ἔχων
TTrA) having GLW. ʰᵃ γέμουσιν are full GLTTrAW. ⁱᵃ λέγοντες GLTTrAW. ᵏᵃ τῷ
θρόνῳ LTTrA.

throne, who liveth for ever and ever, 10 the four and twenty elders fall down before him that sat on the throne, and worship him that liveth for ever and ever, and cast their crowns before the throne, saying, 11 Thou art worthy, O Lord, to receive glory and honour and power: for thou hast created all things, and for thy pleasure they are and were created.

V. And I saw in the right hand of him that sat on the throne a book written within and on the backside, sealed with seven seals. 2 And I saw a strong angel proclaiming with a loud voice, Who is worthy to open the book, and to loose the seals thereof? 3 And no man in heaven, nor in earth, neither under the earth, was able to open the book, neither to look thereon. 4 And I wept much, because no man was found worthy to open and to read the book, neither to look thereon. 5 And one of the elders saith unto me, Weep not: behold, the Lion of the tribe of Juda, the Root of David, hath prevailed to open the book, and to loose the seven seals thereof. 6 And I beheld, and, lo, in the midst of the throne and of the four beasts, and in the midst of the elders, stood a Lamb as it had been slain, having seven horns and seven eyes, which are the seven Spirits of God sent forth into all the earth. 7 And he came and took the book out of the right hand of

ζῶντι εἰς τοὺς αἰῶνας τῶν αἰώνων, 10 πεσοῦνται οἱ εἴκοσι [1]καὶ‖
lives to the ages of the ages, shall fall the twenty and

τέσσαρες πρεσβύτεροι ἐνώπιον τοῦ καθημένου ἐπὶ τοῦ
four elders before him who sits upon the

θρόνου, καὶ [m]προσκυνοῦσιν‖ τῷ ζῶντι εἰς τοὺς αἰῶνας τῶν
throne, and they worship him who lives to the ages of the

αἰώνων, καὶ [n]βάλλουσιν‖ τοὺς στεφάνους αὐτῶν ἐνώπιον τοῦ
ages; and cast their crowns before the

θρόνου, λέγοντες, 11 Ἄξιος εἶ, [o]κύριε,‖ λαβεῖν τὴν δόξαν
throne, saying, Worthy art thou, O Lord, to receive glory

καὶ τὴν τιμὴν καὶ [p]τὴν‖ δύναμιν· ὅτι σὺ ἔκτισας τὰ
and honour and power: because thou didst create

πάντα, καὶ διὰ τὸ θέλημά σου [q]εἰσὶν‖ καὶ ἐκτίσθησαν.
all things, and for thy will they are, and were created.

5 Καὶ εἶδον ἐπὶ τὴν δεξιὰν τοῦ καθημένου ἐπὶ τοῦ
And I saw on the right hand of him who sits upon the

θρόνου βιβλίον γεγραμμένον ἔσωθεν καὶ ὄπισθεν, κατεσφρα-
throne a book, written within and on [the] back, having been

γισμένον σφραγῖσιν ἑπτά. 2 καὶ εἶδον ἄγγελον ἰσχυρὸν κη-
sealed with [2]seals [1]seven. And I saw [3]angel [1]a [2]strong pro-

ρύσσοντα[r] φωνῇ μεγάλῃ, Τίς [s]ἐστιν‖ ἄξιος ἀνοῖξαι τὸ
claiming with a [2]voice [1]loud, Who is worthy to open the

βιβλίον, καὶ λῦσαι τὰς σφραγῖδας αὐτοῦ; 3 καὶ οὐδεὶς [t]ἠδύ-
book, and to loose the seals of it? And no one was

νατο‖ ἐν τῷ οὐρανῷ, [v]οὐδὲ‖ ἐπὶ τῆς γῆς, [v]οὐδὲ‖ ὑποκάτω τῆς
able in the heaven, nor upon the earth, nor under the

γῆς, ἀνοῖξαι τὸ βιβλίον, [w]οὐδὲ‖ βλέπειν αὐτό. 4 καὶ [x]ἐγὼ‖
earth, to open the book, nor to look at it. And I

ἔκλαιον [y]πολλά,‖ ὅτι οὐδεὶς ἄξιος εὑρέθη ἀνοῖξαι [z]καὶ ἀνα-
was weeping much, because no one worthy was found to open and to

γνῶναι‖ τὸ βιβλίον, οὔτε βλέπειν αὐτό. 5 καὶ εἷς ἐκ τῶν
read the book, nor to look at it. And one of the

πρεσβυτέρων λέγει μοι, Μὴ κλαῖε· ἰδού, ἐνίκησεν ὁ λέων
elders says to me, Do not weep. Behold, [3]overcame [1]the [2]Lion

ὁ [a]ὢν‖ ἐκ τῆς φυλῆς Ἰούδα, ἡ ῥίζα [b]Δαβίδ,‖ ἀνοῖξαι
which is of the tribe of Juda, the root of David, [so as] to open

τὸ βιβλίον, καὶ [c]λῦσαι‖ τὰς ἑπτὰ σφραγῖδας αὐτοῦ. 6 καὶ
the book, and to loose the seven seals of it. And

εἶδον [d]καὶ‖ [e]ἰδού,‖ ἐν μέσῳ τοῦ θρόνου καὶ τῶν τεσσάρων
I saw, and behold, in [the] midst of the throne and the four

ζώων, καὶ ἐν μέσῳ τῶν πρεσβυτέρων, ἀρνίον [f]ἑστη-
living creatures, and in [the] midst of the elders, a Lamb stand-

κὸς‖ ὡς ἐσφαγμένον, [g]ἔχον‖ κέρατα ἑπτὰ καὶ ὀφθαλμοὺς
ing as having been slain, having [2]horns [1]seven and [2]eyes

ἑπτά, [h]οἳ‖ εἰσιν τὰ [i]ἑπτὰ‖ [k]τοῦ θεοῦ πνεύματα‖ [la]τὰ‖ [ma]ἀπε-
[1]seven, which are the seven [2]of [3]God [1]Spirits which have

σταλμένα‖ εἰς πᾶσαν τὴν γῆν. 7 καὶ ἦλθεν, καὶ εἴληφεν [na]τὸ
been sent into all the earth: and he came and took the

---

[1] — καὶ GLTTrAW.   [m] προσκυνήσουσιν shall worship EGLTTrAW.   [n] βαλοῦσιν shall cast EGLTTrAW.   [o] ὁ κύριος καὶ ὁ θεὸς ἡμῶν O Lord and our God LTTrAW.   [p] — τὴν L.   [q] ἦσαν they were GLTTrAW.   [r] + ἐν in (a loud voice) GLTTrAW.   [s] — ἐστιν (read [is]) LTTrAW.   [t] ἐδύνατο T.   [v] οὔτε T.   [w] οὔτε LTTr.   [x] — ἐγὼ (read ἔκλαιον I was weeping) T[Tr].   [y] πολύ LTTrAW.   [z] — καὶ ἀναγνῶναι GLTTrAW.   [a] — ὢν (read [is]) GLTTrAW.   [b] Δαυείδ LTTrA; Δαυὶδ GW.   [c] — λῦσαι GLTTrAW.   [d] — καὶ GTTrAW.   [e] — ἰδού GLTTrAW.   [f] ἑστηκὼς TTr.   [g] ἔχων TTrA.   [h] ἃ W.   [i] — ἑπτὰ L.   [k] πνεύματα τοῦ θεοῦ GLTTrAW.   [la] — τὰ (read ἀπεστ. having been sent) LTTrA.   [ma] ἀπεσταλμένοι LTr; ἀποστελλόμενα [are] being sent w.   [na] — τὸ βιβλίον (read [it]) LTTrA.

βιβλίον‖ ἐκ τῆς δεξιᾶς τοῦ καθημένου ἐπὶ τοῦ θρόνου.
book   out of the   right hand of him who sits   on the throne.

8 καὶ ὅτε ἔλαβεν τὸ βιβλίον τὰ ᵒτέσσαρα‖ ζῶα καὶ οἱ
And when he took the book the four living creatures and the

ᴾεἰκοσιτέσσαρες‖ πρεσβύτεροι ᑫἔπεσον‖ ἐνώπιον τοῦ ἀρνίου,
four-and-twenty   elders   fell   before the Lamb,

ἔχοντες ἕκαστος ʳκιθάρας‖ καὶ φιάλας ˢχρυσᾶς‖ γεμούσας θυ-
having each   harps   and ²bowls ¹golden full   of in-

μιαμάτων, αἵ εἰσιν αἱ προσευχαὶ τῶν ἁγίων· 9 καὶ ᾄδουσιν
cences, which are the prayers of the saints. And they sing

ᾠδὴν καινήν, λέγοντες, ᵀἌξιος εἶ λαβεῖν τὸ βιβλίον, καὶ
a ²song ¹new, saying, Worthy art thou to take the book, and

ἀνοῖξαι τὰς σφραγῖδας αὐτοῦ· ὅτι ἐσφάγης καὶ ἠγόρασας
to open its seals ;   because thou wast slain, and didst purchase

τῷ θεῷ ᵛἡμᾶς‖ ἐν τῷ αἵματί σου, ἐκ πάσης φυλῆς καὶ γλώσ-
²to ³God ¹us by   thy blood, out of every tribe and tongue

σης καὶ λαοῦ καὶ ἔθνους, 10 καὶ ἐποίησας ᵛἡμᾶς‖ ᵂτῷ θεῷ ἡμῶν‖
and people and nation, and didst make us   to our God

ˣβασιλεῖς‖ καὶ ἱερεῖς· καὶ ʸβασιλεύσομεν‖ ἐπὶ τῆς γῆς. 11 Καὶ
kings   and priests; and we shall reign over the earth. And

εἶδον, καὶ ἤκουσα ᶻ φωνὴν ἀγγέλων πολλῶν ᵃκυκλόθεν‖ τοῦ
I saw, and I heard [the] voice ²of ³angels ¹many around the

θρόνου καὶ τῶν ζώων καὶ τῶν πρεσβυτέρων·ᵇ καὶ χιλι-
throne and of the living creatures and of the   elders ; and thou-

άδες χιλιάδων, 12 λέγοντες φωνῇ μεγάλῃ, ᶜἌξιόν‖ ἐστιν
sands of thousands, saying with a ²voice ¹loud, Worthy is

τὸ ἀρνίον τὸ ἐσφαγμένον λαβεῖν τὴν δύναμιν καὶ ᵈ πλοῦτον
the Lamb that has been slain to receive power, and riches,

καὶ σοφίαν καὶ ἰσχὺν καὶ τιμὴν καὶ δόξαν καὶ εὐλογίαν.
and wisdom, and strength, and honour, and glory, and blessing.

13 Καὶ πᾶν κτίσμα ὃ ᵉἐστιν‖ ἐν τῷ οὐρανῷ, καὶ ᶠἐν τῇ γῇ,‖
And every creature which is in the heaven and in the earth

καὶ ὑποκάτω τῆς γῆς, καὶ ἐπὶ τῆς θαλάσσης ᵍᾅ‖ ʰἐστιν,‖
and under   the earth, and ⁴on ⁵the   ⁶sea ¹those ²that ³are,

καὶ τὰ ἐν αὐτοῖς ⁱπάντα,‖ ᵏἤκουσα ˡλέγοντας,‖ Τῷ
and ²the ³things ⁴in ⁵them ¹all, heard I saying, To him who

καθημένῳ ἐπὶ ᵐτοῦ θρόνου‖ καὶ τῷ ἀρνίῳ ἡ εὐλογία καὶ ἡ
sits   on the throne, and to the Lamb, Blessing, and

τιμὴ καὶ ἡ δόξα καὶ τὸ κράτος εἰς τοὺς αἰῶνας τῶν αἰώνων.
honour, and glory, and might, to the ages of the ages.

14 Καὶ τὰ ⁿτέσσαρα‖ ζῶα ἔλεγον, ᵒᵃἈμήν· καὶ οἱ ᵖᵃεἰκοσι-
And the four living creatures said, Amen ; and the four-and-

τέσσαρες‖ πρεσβύτεροι ἔπεσαν, καὶ προσεκύνησαν
twenty   elders   fell down and   worshipped   [him who]

ᵍᵃζῶντι εἰς τοὺς αἰῶνας τῶν αἰώνων.‖
lives to the ages of the ages.

6 Καὶ ʳᵃεἶδον‖ ὅτε ἤνοιξεν τὸ ἀρνίον μίαν ἐκ τῶν ˢᵃ σφρα-
And I saw when ³opened ¹the ²Lamb one of the   seals,

---

him that sat upon the throne. 8 And when he had taken the book, the four beasts and four *and* twenty elders fell down before the Lamb, having every one of them harps, and golden vials full of odours, which are the prayers of saints. 9 And they sung a new song, saying, Thou art worthy to take the book, and to open the seals thereof: for thou wast slain, and hast redeemed us to God by thy blood out of every kindred, and tongue, and people, and nation; 10 and hast made us unto our God kings and priests: and we shall reign on the earth. 11 And I beheld, and I heard the voice of many angels round about the throne and the beasts and the elders: and the number of them was ten thousand times ten thousand, and thousands of thousands; 12 saying with a loud voice, Worthy is the Lamb that was slain to receive power, and riches, and wisdom, and strength, and honour, and glory, and blessing. 13 And every creature which is in heaven, and on the earth, and under the earth, and such as are in the sea, and all that are in them, heard I saying, Blessing, and honour, and glory, and power, *be* unto him that sitteth upon the throne, and unto the Lamb for ever and ever. 14 And the four beasts said, Amen. And the four *and* twenty elders fell down and worshipped him that liveth for ever and ever.

VI. And I saw when the Lamb opened one

ᵒ τέσσερα LTTr.   ᵖ εἴκοσι τέσσαρες LTA.   ᑫ ἔπεσαν LTTrAW.   ʳ κιθάραν a harp LTTᵀAW.
ˢ χρυσέας Tr.   ᵗ — ἡμᾶς LTAW.   ᵛ αὐτοὺς them GLTTrAW.   ʷ — τῷ θεῷ ἡμῶν A.
ˣ βασιλείαν a kingdom LTTrA.   ʸ βασιλεύουσιν they reign LTrAW; βασιλεύσουσιν they
shall reign GT.   ᶻ + ὡς as TTr[A].   ᵃ κύκλῳ GLTTrAW.   ᵇ + καὶ ἦν ὁ ἀριθμὸς αὐτῶν μυριάδες μυριάδων and the number of them was myriads of myriads EGLTTrAW.   ᶜ Ἄξιός T.
ᵈ + τὸν W.   ᵉ — ἐστιν (read [is]) LTTᵀAW.   ᶠ ἐπὶ τῆς γῆς on the earth GLTTrAW.
ᵍ — ᾅ LTTrA.   ʰ — ἐστιν TTr.   ⁱ , πάντας (read I heard all) W.   ᵏ + καὶ also T.
ˡ λέγοντα L.   ᵐ τῷ θρόνῳ LTA.   ⁿ τέσσερα LTTr.   ᵒᵃ + τὸ W.   ᵖᵃ — εἴκοσι-
τέσσαρες GLTTrAW.   ᑫᵃ — ζῶντι to end of verse GLTTrAW.   ʳᵃ ἴδον T.   ˢᵃ + ἐπτὰ
seven GLTTrAW.

of the seals, and I heard, as it were the noise of thunder, one of the four beasts saying, Come and see. 2 And I saw, and behold a white horse: and he that sat on him had a bow; and a crown was given unto him: and he went forth conquering, and to conquer.

γίδων, καὶ ἤκουσα ἑνὸς ἐκ τῶν τεσσάρων ζώων λέγον-
and I heard ⁿone ⁷of ᵗʰᵉ °four ¹⁰living ¹¹creatures ¹²say-
τος, ὡς ʳφωνῆς᾽ βροντῆς, Ἔρχου ᵛκαὶ βλέπε.‖ 2 Καὶ ʷεἶδον,‖
ing, ¹as ²a ²voice ᵗof ²thunder, Come and see. And I saw,
καὶ ἰδού, ᵢἵππος λευκός, καὶ ὁ καθήμενος ἐπ᾽ ˣαὐτῷ‖ ἔχων
and behold, a ᵃhorse ¹white, and he sitting on it having
τόξον· καὶ ἐδόθη αὐτῷ στέφανος, καὶ ἐξῆλθεν νικῶν, καὶ
a bow; and was given to him a crown, and he went forth overcoming and
ἵνα νικήσῃ.
that he might overcome.

3 And when he had opened the second seal, I heard the second beast say, Come and see. 4 And there went out another horse that was red: and power was given to him that sat thereon to take peace from the earth, and that they should kill one another: and there was given unto him a great sword.

3 Καὶ ὅτε ἤνοιξεν τὴν ʸδευτέραν σφραγῖδα‖ ἤκουσα τοῦ
And when he opened the second seal I heard the
δευτέρου ζώου λέγοντος, Ἔρχου ᶻκαὶ βλέπε.‖ 4 Καὶ
second living creature saying, Come and see. And
ἐξῆλθεν ἄλλος ἵππος πυρρός· καὶ τῷ καθημένῳ ἐπ᾽ ˣαὐτῷ‖
went forth another horse red; and to him sitting on it
ἐδόθη ᵃαὐτῷ‖ λαβεῖν τὴν εἰρήνην ᵇἀπὸ᾽ τῆς γῆς, καὶ ἵνα
was given to him to take the peace from the earth, and that
ἀλλήλους ᶜσφάξωσιν·‖ καὶ ἐδόθη αὐτῷ μάχαιρα μεγάλη.
one another they should slay; and was given to him a ²sword ¹great.

5 And when he had opened the third seal, I heard the third beast say, Come and see. And I beheld, and lo a black horse; and he that sat on him had a pair of balances in his hand. 6 And I heard a voice in the midst of the four beasts say, A measure of wheat for a penny, and three measures of barley for a penny; and see thou hurt not the oil and the wine.

5 Καὶ ὅτε ἤνοιξεν τὴν ᵈτρίτην σφραγῖδα‖ ἤκουσα τοῦ τρίτου
And when he opened the third seal I heard the third
ζώου λέγοντος, Ἔρχου ᵛκαὶ βλέπε.‖ Καὶ ʷεἶδον,‖ καὶ
living creature saying, Come and see. And I saw, and
ἰδού, ἵππος μέλας, καὶ ὁ καθήμενος ἐπ᾽ ˣαὐτῷ‖ ἔχων ζυγὸν
behold, a ²horse ¹black, and he sitting on it having a balance
ἐν τῇ χειρὶ αὐτοῦ. 6 καὶ ἤκουσα ᵉ φωνὴν ἐν μέσῳ τῶν
in his hand. And I heard a voice in [the] midst of the
τεσσάρων ζώων λέγουσαν, Χοῖνιξ σίτου δηναρίου,
four living creatures, saying, A chœnix of wheat for a denarius,
καὶ τρεῖς χοίνικες ᶠκριθῆς᾽ δηναρίου· καὶ τὸ ἔλαιον καὶ τὸν
and three chœnixes of barley for a denarius: and the oil and the
οἶνον μὴ ἀδικήσῃς.
wine thou mayest not injure.

7 And when he had opened the fourth seal, I heard the voice of the fourth beast say, Come and see. 8 And I looked, and behold a pale horse: and his name that sat on him was Death, and Hell followed with him. And power was given unto them over the fourth part of the earth, to kill with sword, and with hunger, and with death, and with the beasts of the earth.

7 Καὶ ὅτε ἤνοιξεν τὴν σφραγῖδα τὴν τετάρτην, ἤκουσα
And when he opened the ᶻseal ¹fourth, I heard [the]
ᵍφωνὴν‖ τοῦ τετάρτου ζώου ʰλέγουσαν,‖ Ἔρχου ᵛκαὶ
voice of the fourth living creature saying, Come and
βλέπε.‖ 8 Καὶ ʷεἶδον,‖ καὶ ἰδού, ἵππος χλωρός, καὶ ὁ καθήμενος
see. And I saw, and behold, a ²horse ¹pale, and he sitting
ἐπάνω αὐτοῦ, ὄνομα αὐτῷ ᶦὁᶦ Θάνατος, καὶ ὁ ᾅδης ᵏἀκο-
on it, ²name ¹his [was] Death, and hades fol-
λουθεῖ‖ μετ᾽ αὐτοῦ· καὶ ἐδόθη ¹αὐτοῖς᾽ ἐξουσία ᵐἀποκτεῖναι
lows with him; and was given to them authority to kill
ἐπὶ τὸ τέταρτον τῆς γῆς‖ ἐν ῥομφαίᾳ καὶ ἐν λιμῷ καὶ ἐν
over the fourth of the earth with sword and with famine and with
θανάτῳ, καὶ ὑπὸ τῶν θηρίων τῆς γῆς.
death, and by the beasts of the earth.

9 And when he had opened the fifth seal,

9 Καὶ ὅτε ἤνοιξεν τὴν πέμπτην σφραγῖδα ʷεἶδον‖ ὑποκάτω
And when he opened the fifth seal I saw under

ᵗ φωνή (read without the numerals) GLTTrAW.   ᵛ καὶ ἴδε and behold ɢᴡ; — καὶ βλέπε LTTrA.   ʷ ἴδον T.   ˣ αὐτὸν GLTTrAW.   ʸ σφραγῖδα τὴν δευτέραν GLTTrAW.   ᶻ — καὶ βλέπε GLTTrAW.   ᵃ [αὐτῷ] L.   ᵇ ἐκ GLTTrAW.   ᶜ σφάξουσιν they shall slay LTTrA.   ᵈ σφραγῖδα τὴν τρίτην GLTTrAW.   ᵉ + ὡς as LTTrA.   ᶠ κριθῶν LTTrAW.   ᵍ — φωνὴν (read I heard the fourth) ɢ[Tr]ᴡ.   ʰ λέγοντος (connect λέγουσαν with φωνὴν; λέγοντος with ζώον) GLTTrAW.   ᶦ — ὁ T[A].   ᵏ ἠκολούθει followed GLTTrAW.   ¹ αὐτῷ to him ɢ.   ᵐ ἐπὶ τὸ τέταρτον τῆς γῆς, ἀποκτεῖναι GLTTrAW.

τοῦ θυσιαστηρίου·τὰς ψυχὰς τῶν ἐσφαγμένων διὰ τὸν
the　　altar　　the souls　of those having been slain　because of the

λόγον τοῦ θεοῦ, καὶ °διὰ‖ τὴν μαρτυρίαν ἣν εἶχον, 10 καὶ
word　　of God, and because of the　testimony　which they held ;　and

Pἔκραζον‖　φωνῇ μεγάλῃ, λέγοντες, "Ἔως πότε, ὁ δεσ-
they were crying with a ²voice ¹loud,　saying,　Until when, O Mas-

πότης ὁ ἅγιος καὶ ᵠὁ‖ ἀληθινός,　οὐ·κρίνεις　καὶ ἐκδικεῖς
ter,　the holy and the　true,　dost thou not judge and　avenge

τὸ·αἶμα·ἡμῶν ʳἀπὸ‖ τῶν κατοικούντων ἐπὶ τῆς γῆς; 11 Καὶ
our blood　on those who　dwell　on the earth?　And

ˢἐδόθησαν‖ ᵗ ᵛἑκάστοις‖·ᵂστολαὶ λευκαί,‖ καὶ ἐῤῥέθη αὐτοῖς ἵνα
were given　to each ²robes ¹white ; and it was said to them that

ἀναπαύσωνται ˣἔτι χρόνον‖ ʸμικρόν,‖ ἕως ᶻοὗ‖ ᵃπληρώσονται‖
they should rest　yet a ²time ¹little,　until　shall be fulfilled

καὶ οἱ·σύνδουλοι·αὐτῶν καὶ οἱ·ἀδελφοὶ·αὐτῶν, οἱ μέλλοντες
both　their fellow-bondmen and　their brethren,　those being about

ᵇἀποκτείνεσθαι‖ ὡς καὶ αὐτοί.
to be killed　as also they.

12 Καὶ ᶜεἶδον‖ ὅτε ἤνοιξεν τὴν σφραγῖδα τὴν ἕκτην· καὶ
And　I saw　when he opened the ²seal ¹sixth, and

ᵈἰδού,‖ σεισμὸς μέγας ἐγένετο, καὶ ὁ ἥλιος ᵉἐγένετο μέλας‖
behold, ⁵earthquake ²a ⁴great ¹there ³was, and the sun　became black

ὡς σάκκος τρίχινος, καὶ ἡ σελήνη ᶠ ἐγένετο ὡς αἷμα, 13 καὶ
as ²sackcloth ¹hair,　and the moon　became as blood,　and

οἱ ἀστέρες τοῦ οὐρανοῦ ἔπεσαν εἰς τὴν γῆν, ὡς συκῆ ᵍβάλλει‖
the stars of the heaven　fell　unto the earth, as a fig-tree casts

τοὺς·ὀλύνθους·αὐτῆς, ὑπὸ ʰμεγάλου ἀνέμου‖ σειομένη· 14 καὶ
its untimely figs,　by　a great　wind　being shaken.　And

ⁱ οὐρανὸς ἀπεχωρίσθη ὡς βιβλίον ᵏεἱλισσόμενον,‖ καὶ πᾶν
heaven　departed　as a book　being rolled up,　and every

ὄρος καὶ νῆσος ἐκ τῶν·τόπων·αὐτῶν ἐκινήθησαν· 15 καὶ
mountain and island out of　their places　were moved.　And

οἱ βασιλεῖς τῆς γῆς, καὶ οἱ μεγιστᾶνες, καὶ οἱ ¹πλούσιοι, καὶ
the kings of the earth, and the great,　and the rich,　and

οἱ χιλίαρχοι,‖ καὶ οἱ ᵐδυνατοί,‖ καὶ πᾶς δοῦλος καὶ ⁿπᾶς‖
the chief captains, and the　powerful,　and every bondman, and every

ἐλεύθερος　ἔκρυψαν ἑαυτοὺς εἰς τὰ σπήλαια καὶ εἰς τὰς
free　[man] hid　themselves in the　caves　and in the

πέτρας τῶν ὀρέων, 16 καὶ λέγουσιν τοῖς ὄρεσιν καὶ ταῖς
rocks　of the mountains ;　and they say to the mountains and to the

πέτραις, ᵒᵃΠέσετε‖ ἐφ᾽ ἡμᾶς, καὶ κρύψατε ἡμᾶς ἀπὸ　προσ-
rocks,　Fall on us, and hide　us　from [the]　face

ώπου τοῦ　καθημένου ἐπὶ Pᵃτοῦ θρόνου,‖ καὶ ἀπὸ τῆς ὀργῆς
of him who　sits　on the throne,　and from the wrath

τοῦ ἀρνίου· 17 ὅτι ἦλθεν ἡ ἡμέρα ἡ μεγάλη τῆς ὀργῆς
of the Lamb ;　because is come the ²day ¹great　⁵wrath

ᵠᵃαὐτοῦ,‖ καὶ τίς δύναται σταθῆναι ;
³of ⁴his, and who is able to stand?

I saw under the altar the souls of them that were slain for the word of God, and for the testimony which they held : 10 and they cried with a loud voice, saying, How long, O Lord, holy and true, dost thou not judge and avenge our blood on them that dwell on the earth? 11 And white robes were given unto every one of them ; and it was said unto them, that they should rest yet for a little season, until their fellowservants also and their brethren, that should be killed as they were, should be fulfilled.

12 And I beheld when he had opened the sixth seal, and, lo, there was a great earthquake ; and the sun became black as sackcloth of hair, and the moon became as blood ; 13 and the stars of heaven fell unto the earth, even as a fig tree casteth her untimely figs, when she is shaken of a mighty wind. 14 And the heaven departed as a scroll when it is rolled together ; and every mountain and island were moved out of their places. 15 And the kings of the earth, and the great men, and the rich men, and the chief captains, and the mighty men, and every bondman, and every free man, hid themselves in the dens and in the rocks of the mountains ; 16 and said to the mountains and rocks, Fall on us, and hide us from the face of him that sitteth on the throne, and from the wrath of the Lamb : 17 for the great day of his wrath is come ; and who shall be able to stand?

° — διὰ L[A].　P ἔκραξαν they cried GLTTrAW.　ᵠ — ὁ GLTTrAW.　ʳ ἐκ from LTTrAW.
ˢ ἐδόθη was given GLTTrAW.　ᵗ + αὐτοῖς to them GLTTrAW.　ᵛ — ἑκάστοις GW ; ἑκάστῳ each LTTᵢ[A].　ᵂ στολὴ λευκή a white robe GLTTrAW.　ˣ χρόνον ἔτι L.　ʸ — μικρόν G.　ᶻ — οὗ GLTTrAW.　ᵃ πληρωθῶσιν should be fulfilled LW ; πληρώσωσιν should fulfil [it] GTTrA.　ᵇ ἀποκτέννεσθαι GLTTrA.　ᶜ ἴδον T.　ᵈ — ἰδού GLTTrAW.　ᵉ μέλας ἐγένετο GT.　ᶠ + ὅλη whole (moon) GLTTrAW.　ᵍ βάλλουσα casting T.　ʰ ἀνέμου μεγάλου GLTTrAW.　ⁱ + ὁ the GLTTrAW.　ᵏ ἑλισσόμενον LTTrAW.　¹ χιλίαρχοι, καὶ οἱ πλούσιοι GLTTrAW.　ᵐ ἰσχυροὶ strong GLTTrAW.　ⁿ — πᾶς LTTrAW.　ᵒᵃ Πέσατε LAW.　Pᵃ τῷ θρόνῳ TA.　ᵠᵃ αὐτῶν ³of ⁴their TTr.

VII. And after these things I saw four angels standing on the four corners of the earth, holding the four winds of the earth, that the wind should not blow on the earth, nor on the sea, nor on any tree. 2 And I saw another angel ascending from the east, having the seal of the living God: and he cried with a loud voice to the four angels, to whom it was given to hurt the earth and the sea, 3 saying, Hurt not the earth, neither the sea, nor the trees, till we have sealed the servants of our God in their foreheads. 4 And I heard the number of them which were sealed: *and there were* sealed an hundred *and* forty *and* four thousand of all the tribes of the children of Israel. 5 Of the tribe of Juda *were* sealed twelve thousand. Of the tribe of Reuben *were* sealed twelve thousand. Of the tribe of Gad *were* sealed twelve thousand. 6 Of the tribe of Aser *were* sealed twelve thousand. Of the tribe of Nephthalim *were* sealed twelve thousand. Of the tribe of Manasses *were* sealed twelve thousand. 7 Of the tribe of Simeon *were* sealed twelve thousand. Of the tribe of Levi *were* sealed twelve thousand. Of the tribe of Issachar *were* sealed twelve thousand. 8 Of the tribe of Zabulon *were* sealed twelve thousand. Of the tribe of Joseph *were* sealed twelve thousand. Of the tribe of Benjamin *were* sealed twelve thousand.

7 ʳΚαὶʱ μετὰ ˢταῦταʱ ᵗεἶδονʱ τέσσαρας ἀγγέλους ἑστῶτας
And　after these things　I saw　four　angels　standing

ἐπὶ τὰς τέσσαρας γωνίας τῆς γῆς, κρατοῦντας τοὺς τέσσαρας
upon the　four　corners of the earth,　holding　the　four

ἀνέμους τῆς γῆς, ἵνα μὴ　πνέῃ　ἄνεμος ἐπὶ τῆς γῆς, μήτε
winds　of the earth, that no ²might ³blow ¹wind　on the earth,　nor

ἐπὶ τῆς θαλάσσης, μήτε ἐπὶ ᵛπᾶνʱ δένδρον. 2 Καὶ ᵗεἶδονʱ ἄλ-
on the　sea,　nor upon any　tree.　And I saw　an-
　　　　　　　　　　　　(*lit.* every)

λον ἄγγελον ʷἀναβάνταʱ ἀπὸ ˣἀνατολῆςʱ ἡλίου, ἔχοντα
other　angel　having ascended from [the] rising of [the] sun, having

σφραγῖδα θεοῦ　ζῶντος· καὶ ἔκραξεν　φωνῇ μεγάλῃ
[the]　seal　of ³God [¹the] ²living; and he cried with a ²voice· ¹loud

τοῖς τέσσαρσιν ἀγγέλοις, οἷς　ἐδόθη　αὐτοῖς ἀδικῆσαι τὴν
to the　four　angels to whom it was given to them to injure　the

γῆν καὶ τὴν θάλασσαν, 3 λέγων, Μὴ ἀδικήσητε τὴν γῆν,
earth and the　sea,　saying,　Injure not　the　earth,

μήτε τὴν θάλασσαν, μήτε τὰ δένδρα, ʸἄχριςʱ ᶻοῦʱ ˢσφραγίζω-
nor the　sea,　nor the trees,　until　we

μενʱ τοὺς δούλους τοῦ θεοῦ ἡμῶν ἐπὶ τῶν μετώπων αὐτῶν.
seal　the　bondmen　of our God　on　their foreheads.

4 Καὶ ἤκουσα τὸν ἀριθμὸν τῶν ἐσφραγισμένων· ᵇρμδʹʱ χιλιάδες,
And I heard the number of the　sealed,　144　thousand,

ἐσφραγισμένοι ἐκ πάσης φυλῆς υἱῶν Ἰσραήλ· 5 ἐκ
sealed　out of every　tribe of [the] sons of Israel;　out of [the]

φυλῆς Ἰούδα, ᶜιβʹʱ χιλιάδες ἐσφραγισμένοι· ἐκ　φυλῆς
tribe of Judah, 12　thousand　sealed;　out of [the] tribe

Ῥουβήν, ᶜιβʹʱ χιλιάδες ᵈἐσφραγισμένοιʱ ἐκ　φυλῆς Γάδ,
of Reuben, 12　thousand　sealed;　out of [the] tribe of Gad,

ᶜιβʹʱ χιλιάδες ᵈἐσφραγισμένοιʱ 6 ἐκ　φυλῆς Ἀσήρ, ᶜιβʹʱ
12　thousand　sealed;　out of [the] tribe of Aser, 12

χιλιάδες ᵈἐσφραγισμένοιʱ ἐκ　φυλῆς ᵉΝεφθαλείμ,ʱ ᶜιβʹʱ
thousand　sealed;　out of [the] tribe of Nephthalim, 12

χιλιάδες ᵈἐσφραγισμένοιʱ ἐκ　φυλῆς ᶠΜανασσῆ,ʱ ᶜιβʹʱ
thousand　sealed;　out of [the] tribe of Manasses, 12

χιλιάδες ᵈἐσφραγισμένοιʱ 7 ἐκ　φυλῆς Συμεών, ᶜιβʹʱ χιλι-
thousand　sealed;　out of [the] tribe of Simeon, 12　thou-

άδες ᵈἐσφραγισμένοιʱ ἐκ　φυλῆς ᵍΛευΐ,ʱ ᶜιβʹʱ χιλιάδες
sand　sealed;　out of [the] tribe of Levi, 12　thousand·

ᵈἐσφραγισμένοιʱ ἐκ　φυλῆς ʰἸσαχάρ,ʱ ᶜιβʹʱ χιλιάδες ᵈἐσφρα-
sealed;　out of [the] tribe of Issachar, 12　thousand　seal-

γισμένοιʱ 8 ἐκ　φυλῆς Ζαβουλών, ᶜιβʹʱ χιλιάδες ᵈἐσφρα-
ed;　out of [the] tribe of Zabulon, 12　thousand　seal-

γισμένοιʱ ἐκ　φυλῆς Ἰωσήφ, ᶜιβʹʱ χιλιάδες ᵈἐσφραγισμένοιʱ
ed;　out of [the] tribe of Joseph, 12　thousand　sealed;

ἐκ　φυλῆς ᵢΒενιαμίν,ʱ ᶜιβʹʱ χιλιάδες ἐσφραγισμένοι.
out of [the] tribe of Benjamin, 12　thousand　sealed.

9 After this I beheld, and, lo, a great multitude, which no man could number, of all nations, and

9 Μετὰ ταῦτα ᵗεἶδον,ʱ ᵏκαὶʱ ˡἰδού,ʱ ᵐὄχλος πολύς,ʱ ὃν
After these things I saw,　and behold, a ²crowd ¹great, which

ἀριθμῆσαι αὐτὸν οὐδεὶς ⁿἠδύνατο,ʱ ἐκ παντὸς ἔθνους καὶ
³to ⁶number ⁷it ¹no ²one ³was ⁴able,　out of every　nation and

ʳ — καὶ ʟ[ᴛʀ ᴀ].　ˢ τοῦτο this ʟᴛᴛʀᴀᴡ.　ᵗ ἴδον ᴛ.　ᵛ τι any ʟᴛʀ[ᴀ]ᴡ.　ʷ ἀναβαί-
βοντα ascending ɢʟᴛᴛʀᴀᴡ.　ˣ ἀνατολῶν ʟ.　ʸ ἄχρι ʟᴛᴀ.　ᶻ — οὗ ʟᴛᴛʀᴀ.　ᵃ σφρα-
γίσωμεν we may have sealed ᴇɢʟᴛᴛʀᴀᴡ.　ᵇ ἑκατὸν τεσσεράκοντα (τεσσαρ- ɢᴡ) τέσσαρας
a hundred and forty-four ɢʟᴛᴛʀᴀᴡ.　ᶜ δώδεκα twelve ʟᴛᴛʀᴀᴡ.　ᵈ — ἐσφραγισμέν-
ʟᴛᴛʀᴀᴡ.　ᵉ Νεφθαλὶμ ᴀ.　ᶠ Μαννασσῆ ᴛʀ.　ᵍ Λευεὶ ᴛᴛʀ.　ʰ Ἰσασχὰρ ᴇ; Ἰσσαχὰρ
ᴛʀᴀ; Ἰσάχαρ ᴛ.　ᵢ Βενιαμεὶν ʟᴛᴛʀ.　ᵏ — καὶ ʟ.　ˡ — ἰδού ʟ.　ᵐ ὄχλον πολὺν ᴇ.
ⁿ ἐδύνατο ʟᴛᴛʀᴀᴡ.

φυλῶν καὶ λαῶν καὶ γλωσσῶν, °ἑστῶτες ἐνώπιον τοῦ θρόνου
tribes, and peoples, and tongues.   standing before the throne
καὶ ἐνώπιον τοῦ ἀρνίου, ᵖπεριβεβλημένοι‖ στολὰς λευκάς, καὶ
and before the Lamb,   clothed with   ²robes ¹white, and
ᑫφοίνικες ἐν ταῖς χερσὶν αὐτῶν· 10 καὶ ᶜκράζοντες‖ φωνῇ
palms in   their hands;   and crying with a ²voice
μεγάλῃ, λέγοντες, Ἡ σωτηρία ˢτῷ καθημένῳ ἐπὶ τοῦ
¹loud, saying,   Salvation to him who sits   on the
θρόνου τοῦ θεοῦ ἡμῶν,‖ καὶ τῷ ἀρνίῳ. 11 Καὶ πάντες οἱ ἄγ-
throne of our God, and to the Lamb. And all the an-
γελοι ᵗἑστήκεσαν‖ κύκλῳ τοῦ θρόνου καὶ τῶν πρεσβυτέρων καὶ
gels stood around the throne and the elders and
τῶν τεσσάρων ζώων, καὶ ᵂἔπεσον‖ ἐνώπιον τοῦ θρόνου
the four living creatures, and fell before the throne
ἐπὶ ᵂπρόσωπον‖ αὐτῶν, καὶ προσεκύνησαν τῷ θεῷ, 12 λέγον-
²face ¹their, and worshipped God,   say-
τες, Ἀμήν· ἡ εὐλογία καὶ ἡ δόξα καὶ ἡ σοφία καὶ ἡ εὐχαριστία
ing, Amen Blessing, and glory, and wisdom, and thanksgiving,
καὶ ἡ τιμὴ καὶ ἡ δύναμις καὶ ἡ ἰσχὺς τῷ θεῷ ἡμῶν εἰς τοὺς
and honour, and power, and strength, to our God to the
αἰῶνας τῶν αἰώνων. ˣἀμήν.‖
ages of the ages.   Amen.

13 Καὶ ἀπεκρίθη εἷς ἐκ τῶν πρεσβυτέρων, λέγων μοι, Οὗτοι
And ²answered ¹one ²of ³the ⁴elders,   saying to me, These
οἱ περιβεβλημένοι τὰς στολὰς τὰς λευκάς, τίνες εἰσίν, καὶ
who are clothed with the ²robes ¹white, who are they, and
πόθεν ἦλθον; 14 Καὶ εἴρηκα αὐτῷ, Κύριε, σὺ οἶδας. Καὶ
whence came they? And I said to him, [My] lord, thou knowest. And
εἶπέν μοι, Οὗτοί εἰσιν οἱ ἐρχόμενοι ᶻἐκ τῆς θλίψεως τῆς‖
he said to me, These are they who come out of the ²tribulation
μεγάλης, καὶ ἔπλυναν τὰς στολὰς αὐτῶν, καὶ ἐλεύκαναν
¹great, and they washed their robes, and made white
ᵃστολὰς‖ ᵇαὐτῶν‖ ἐν τῷ αἵματι τοῦ ἀρνίου. 15 διὰ τοῦτό
²robes ¹their in the blood of the Lamb. Because of this
εἰσιν ἐνώπιον τοῦ θρόνου τοῦ θεοῦ, καὶ λατρεύουσιν αὐτῷ
are they before the throne of God, and serve him
ἡμέρας καὶ νυκτὸς ἐν τῷ ναῷ αὐτοῦ· καὶ ὁ καθήμενος ἐπὶ
day and night in his temple; and he who sits on
ᶜτοῦ θρόνου‖ σκηνώσει ἐπ' αὐτούς. 16 οὐ πεινάσουσιν
the throne shall tabernacle over them.   They shall not hunger
ἔτι, οὐδὲ ᵈδιψήσουσιν ἔτι, ᵉοὐδὲ‖ μὴ πέσῃ ἐπ' αὐ-
any more, neither shall they thirst any more, nor at all shall fall upon
τοὺς ὁ ἥλιος, οὐδὲ πᾶν καῦμα· 17 ὅτι τὸ ἀρνίον τὸ
them the sun, nor any heat ; because the Lamb which [is]
ᶠἀνάμεσον‖ τοῦ θρόνου ποιμανεῖ αὐτούς, καὶ ὁδηγήσει αὐτοὺς
in [the] midst of the throne will shepherd them, and will lead them
ἐπὶ ᵍζώσας‖ πηγὰς ὑδάτων, καὶ ἐξαλείφει ὁ θεὸς πᾶν
to living fountains of waters, and ²will ¹wipe ⁴away ¹God every
δάκρυον ʰἀπὸ‖ τῶν ὀφθαλμῶν αὐτῶν.
tear from their eyes.

kindreds, and peo-
ple, and tongues, stood
before the throne, and
before the Lamb,
clothed with white
robes, and palms in
their hands ; 10 and
cried with a loud voice,
saying, Salvation to
our God which sitteth
upon the throne, and
unto the Lamb. 11 And
all the angels stood
round about the
throne, and about the
elders and the four
beasts, and fell before
the throne on their
faces, and worshipped
God, 12 saying, Amen:
Blessing, and glory,
and wisdom, and
thanksgiving, and
honour, and power,
and might, be unto
our God for ever and
ever. Amen.

13 And one of the
elders answered, say-
ing unto me, What
are these which are
arrayed in white robes?
and whence came
they? 14 And I said
unto him, Sir, thou
knowest. And he
said to me, These are
they which came out
of great tribulation,
and have washed their
robes, and made them
white in the blood of
the Lamb. 15 There-
fore are they be-
fore the throne of God,
and serve him day and
night in his temple :
and he that sitteth on
the throne shall dwell
among them. 16 They
shall hunger no more,
neither thirst any
more ; neither shall
the sun light on them,
nor any heat. 17 For
the Lamb which is in
the midst of the
throne shall feed them,
and shall lead them
unto living fountains
of waters : and God
shall wipe away all
tears from their eyes.

ᵒ ἑστῶτας AW. ᵖ περιβεβλημένους GLTTrAW. ᑫ φοίνικας T. ʳ κράζουσιν they cry
GLTTrAW. ˢ τῷ θεῷ ἡμῶν τῷ καθημένῳ ἐπὶ τῷ θρόνῳ (τοῦ θρόνου EG) to our God who sits
on the throne EGLTTrAW. ᵗ εἱστήκεισαν LTTrA ; ἑστήκεισαν W. ᵛ ἔπεσαν LTTrAW.
ᵂ τὰ πρόσωπα faces GLTTrAW. ˣ — ἀμήν L. ʸ + μου my (lord) G[L]TTrAW. ᶻ ἀπὸ
θλίψεως from ²tribulation L. ᵃ — στολὰς GLTTrAW. ᵇ αὐτὰς them GLTTr[A]W. ᶜ τῷ
θρόνῳ T. ᵈ + μὴ (read neither at all) L. ᵉ οὐδ' οὐ A. ᶠ ἀνὰ μέσον EGLTAW.
ᵍ ζωῆς (read to fountains of waters of life) GLTTrAW. ʰ ἐκ GLTTrAW.

VIII. And when he had opened the seventh seal, there was silence in heaven about the space of half an hour. 2 And I saw the seven angels which stood before God; and to them were given seven trumpets. 3 And another angel came and stood at the altar, having a golden censer; and there was given unto him much incense, that he should offer *it* with the prayers of all saints upon the golden altar which was before the throne. 4 And the smoke of the incense, *which came* with the prayers of the saints, ascended up before God out of the angel's hand. 5 And the angel took the censer, and filled it with fire of the altar, and cast *it* into the earth: and there were voices, and thunderings, and lightnings, and an earthquake.

8 Καὶ ¹ὅτε‖ ἤνοιξεν τὴν σφραγῖδα τὴν ἑβδόμην, ἐγένετε
And when he opened the ²seal ¹seventh, ⁴was
σιγὴ ἐν τῷ οὐρανῷ ὡς ᵏἡμιώριον.‖ 2 Καὶ ¹εἶδον‖ τοὺς ἑπτὰ
³silence in the heaven about half-an-hour. And I saw the seven
ἀγγέλους, οἳ ἐνώπιον τοῦ θεοῦ ἑστήκασιν, καὶ ἐδόθησαν
angels, who ²before ³God ¹stand, and were given
αὐτοῖς ἑπτὰ σάλπιγγες. 3 καὶ ἄλλος ἄγγελος ἦλθεν, καὶ
to them seven trumpets. And another angel came and
ἐστάθη ἐπὶ ᵐτὸ θυσιαστήριον,‖ ἔχων λιβανωτὸν χρυσοῦν‖ καὶ
stood at the altar, having a ²censer ¹golden; and
ἐδόθη αὐτῷ θυμιάματα πολλά, ἵνα ⁿδώσῃ‖ ταῖς
³was ⁴given ⁵to ⁶him ⁴incense ¹much, that he might give [it] to the
προσευχαῖς τῶν ἁγίων πάντων ἐπὶ τὸ θυσιαστήριον τὸ
prayers of ²the ³saints ¹all upon the ²altar
χρυσοῦν τὸ ἐνώπιον τοῦ θρόνου. 4 καὶ ἀνέβη ὁ καπνὸς
¹golden which [was] before the throne. And went up the smoke
τῶν θυμιαμάτων ταῖς προσευχαῖς τῶν ἁγίων, ἐκ χειρὸς
of the incense with the prayers of the saints, out of [the] hand
τοῦ ἀγγέλου, ἐνώπιον τοῦ θεοῦ. 5 καὶ εἴληφεν ὁ ἄγγελος ᵒτὸ‖
of the angel, before God. And ³took ¹the ²angel the
λιβανωτόν, καὶ ἐγέμισεν ᴾαὐτὸ‖ ἐκ τοῦ πυρὸς τοῦ θυσιαστη-
censer, and filled it from the fire of the altar,
ριου, καὶ ἔβαλεν εἰς τὴν γῆν· καὶ ἐγένοντο ᑫφωναὶ καὶ
and cast [it] into the earth: and there were voices, and
βρονταὶ καὶ ἀστραπαὶ καὶ σεισμός.
thunders, and lightnings, and an earthquake.

6 And the seven angels which had the seven trumpets prepared themselves to sound.

6 Καὶ οἱ ἑπτὰ ἄγγελοι ʳἔχοντες τὰς ἑπτὰ σάλπιγγας ἡτοί-
And the seven angels having the seven trumpets pre-
μασαν ˢἑαυτοὺς‖ ἵνα σαλπίσωσιν.
pared themselves that they might sound [their] trumpets.

7 The first angel sounded, and there followed hail and fire mingled with blood, and they were cast upon the earth: and the third part of trees was burnt up, and all green grass was burnt up.

7 Καὶ ὁ πρῶτος ᵗἄγγελος‖ ἐσάλπισεν, καὶ ἐγένετο
And the first angel sounded [his] trumpet; and there was
χάλαζα καὶ πῦρ ᵛμεμιγμένα‖ ʷ αἵματι, καὶ ἐβλήθη εἰς τὴν
hail and fire mingled with blood, and it was cast upon the
γῆν· ˣ καὶ τὸ τρίτον τῶν δένδρων κατεκάη, καὶ πᾶς χόρτος
earth: and the third of the trees was burnt up, and all ²grass
χλωρὸς κατεκάη.
¹green was burnt up.

8 And the second angel sounded, and as it were a great mountain burning with fire was cast into the sea: and the third part of the sea became blood; 9 and the third part of the creatures which were in the sea, and had life, died; and the third part of the ships were destroyed.

8 Καὶ ὁ δεύτερος ἄγγελος ἐσάλπισεν, καὶ ὡς
And the second angel sounded [his] trumpet; and as [it were]
ὄρος μέγα πυρὶ καιόμενον ἐβλήθη εἰς τὴν θάλασσαν· καὶ
a ²mountain ¹great ⁴with ⁵fire ³burning was cast into the sea, and
ἐγένετο τὸ τρίτον τῆς θαλάσσης αἷμα. 9 καὶ ἀπέθανεν τὸ
⁶became ¹the ²third ³of ⁴the ⁵sea blood. And ¹⁴died ¹the
τρίτον τῶν κτισμάτων τῶν ἐν τῇ θαλάσσῃ τὰ ἔχοντα
²third ³of ⁴the ⁵creatures ⁶which [⁷were] ⁸in ⁹the ¹⁰sea ¹¹which ¹²have
ψυχάς, καὶ τὸ τρίτον τῶν πλοίων ʸδιεφθάρη.‖
¹³life; and the third of the ships was destroyed.

10 And the third angel sounded, and there

10 Καὶ ὁ τρίτος ἄγγελος ἐσάλπισεν, καὶ ἔπεσεν ἐκ
And the third angel sounded [his] trumpet; and ⁶fell ⁵out ⁶of

<hr/>

ⁱ ὅταν LTTrA.   ᵏ ἡμίωρον LTTrA.   ˡ ἴδον T.   ᵐ τοῦ θυσιαστηρίου TTrA.   ⁿ δώσει he shall give LTTrA.   ᵒ τὸν EGLTTrAW.   ᴾ αὐτὸν EGLTTrAW.   ᑫ βρονταὶ καὶ
ἀστραπαὶ καὶ φωναὶ L; βρονταὶ καὶ φωναὶ καὶ ἀστραπαὶ TTrA.   ʳ + οἱ (read who have)
GLTTrAW.   ˢ αὐτοὺς LTTr.   ᵗ — ἄγγελος GLTTrAW.   ᵛ μεμιγμένον T.   ʷ + ἐν
with (blood) GLTTrAW.   ˣ + καὶ τὸ τρίτον τῆς γῆς κατεκάη, and the third of the earth was
burnt up GLTTrAW.   ʸ διεφθάρησαν were destroyed LTTrA.

τοῦ οὐρανοῦ ἀστὴρ μέγας καιόμενος ὡς λαμπάς, καὶ ἔπεσεν
[7]the [8]heaven ¹a ³star ²great, burning as a lamp, and it fell

ἐπὶ τὸ τρίτον τῶν ποταμῶν, καὶ ἐπὶ τὰς πηγὰς ᶻ ὑδάτων.
upon the third of the rivers, and upon the fountains of waters.

11 καὶ τὸ ὄνομα τοῦ ἀστέρος λέγεται ᵃ Ἄψινθος· καὶ ᵇγίνεται
And the name of the star is called Wormwood; and ³becomes

τὸ τρίτον ᶜ εἰς ἄψινθον, καὶ πολλοὶ ᵈ ἀνθρώπων ἀπέθανον
¹the ²third into wormwood, and many ¹of ²men died

ἐκ τῶν ὑδάτων, ὅτι ἐπικράνθησαν.
of the waters, because they were made bitter.

12 Καὶ ὁ τέταρτος ἄγγελος ἐσάλπισεν, καὶ ἐπλήγη
And the fourth angel sounded [his] trumpet; and was ʼsmitten

τὸ τρίτον τοῦ ἡλίου καὶ τὸ τρίτον τῆς σελήνης καὶ τὸ τρίτον
the third of the sun, and the third of the moon, and the third

τῶν ἀστέρων, ἵνα σκοτισθῇ τὸ τρίτον αὐτῶν, καὶ ἡ
of the stars; that should be darkened the third of them, and the

ἡμέρα μὴ ᵉφαίνῃ‖ τὸ τρίτον αὐτῆς, καὶ ἡ νὺξ ὁμοίως.
day ³not ¹should appear [for] the third of it, and the night likewise.

13 Καὶ ᶠεἶδον,‖ καὶ ἤκουσα ἑνὸς ᵍἀγγέλου πετωμένου‖ ἐν
And I saw, and heard one angel flying in

μεσουρανήματι, λέγοντος φωνῇ μεγάλῃ, Οὐαί, οὐαί, οὐαί,
mid-heaven, saying with a ¹voice ¹loud, Woe, woe, woe,

ʰτοῖς κατοικοῦσιν‖ ἐπὶ τῆς γῆς, ἐκ τῶν λοιπῶν φωνῶν
to those who dwell on the earth, from the remaining voices

τῆς σάλπιγγος τῶν τριῶν ἀγγέλων τῶν μελλόντων σαλ-
of the trumpet of the three angels who [are] about to sound

πίζειν.
[their] trumpets.

9 Καὶ ὁ πέμπτος ἄγγελος ἐσάλπισεν, καὶ ἱεἶδον‖
And the fifth angel sounded [his] trumpet; and I saw

ἀστέρα ἐκ τοῦ οὐρανοῦ πεπτωκότα εἰς τὴν γῆν, καὶ ἐδό-
a star out of the heaven fallen to the earth, and there was

θη αὐτῷ ἡ κλεὶς τοῦ φρέατος τῆς ἀβύσσου. 2 καὶ ἤνοιξεν
given to it the key of the pit of the abyss. And it opened

τὸ φρέαρ τῆς ἀβύσσου. καὶ ἀνέβη καπνὸς ἐκ τοῦ φρέατος
the pit of the abyss; and there went up smoke out of the pit

ὡς καπνὸς καμίνου μεγάλης, καὶ ᵏἐσκοτίσθη‖ ὁ ἥλιος
as [the] smoke of a ²furnace ¹great; and ³was ⁴darkened ¹the ²sun

καὶ ὁ ἀὴρ ἐκ τοῦ καπνοῦ τοῦ φρέατος. 3 καὶ ἐκ τοῦ καπνοῦ
and the air by the smoke of the pit. And out of the smoke

ἐξῆλθον ἀκρίδες εἰς τὴν γῆν, καὶ ἐδόθη ¹αὐταῖς‖ ἐξουσία,
came forth locusts unto the earth, and was given ¹to them power,

ὡς ἔχουσιν ἐξουσίαν οἱ σκορπίοι τῆς γῆς· 4 καὶ ἐρρέθη
as ²have ⁷power ¹the ²scorpions ³of ⁴the ⁵earth; and it was said

¹αὐταῖς‖ ἵνα μὴ ᵐἀδικήσωσιν‖ τὸν χόρτον τῆς γῆς, οὐδὲ πᾶν
to them, that ³not ¹they ²should injure the grass of the earth, nor any

χλωρόν, οὐδὲ πᾶν δένδρον, εἰ μὴ τοὺς ἀνθρώπους ⁿμόνους‖.
green thing, nor any tree, but the men only

οἵτινες οὐκ ἔχουσιν τὴν σφραγῖδα τοῦ θεοῦ ἐπὶ τῶν μετώπων
who have not the seal of God on ²foreheads

ᵒαὐτῶν.‖ 5 καὶ ἐδόθη ᵖαὐταῖς‖ ἵνα μὴ ἀποκτείνωσιν αὐτούς,
¹their. And it was given to them that they should not kill them,

---

fell a great star from heaven, burning as it were a lamp, and it fell upon the third part of the rivers, and upon the fountains of waters; 11 and the name of the star is called Wormwood: and the third part of the waters became wormwood; and many men died of the waters, because they were made bitter.

12 And the fourth angel sounded, and the third part of the sun was smitten, and the third part of the moon, and the third part of the stars; so as the third part of them was darkened, and the day shone not for a third part of it, and the night likewise.

13 And I beheld, and heard an angel flying through the midst of heaven, saying with a loud voice, Woe, woe, woe, to the inhabiters of the earth by reason of the other voices of the trumpet of the three angels which are yet to sound!

IX. And the fifth angel sounded, and I saw a star fall from heaven unto the earth: and to him was given the key of the bottomless pit. 2 And he opened the bottomless pit; and there arose a smoke out of the pit, as the smoke of a great furnace; and the sun and the air were darkened by reason of the smoke of the pit. 3 And there came out of the smoke locusts upon the earth: and unto them was given power, as the scorpions of the earth have power. 4 And it was commanded them that they should not hurt the grass of the earth, neither any green thing, neither any tree; but only those men which have not the seal of God in their foreheads. 5 And to them it was given

---

ᶻ + τῶν of the (waters) GLTTᵣAW.   ᵃ + ὁ GLTAW.   ᵇ ἐγένετο became LTTᵣAW.
ᶜ + τῶν ὑδάτων of the waters EGLTTᵣAW.   ᵈ + τῶν of the (men) GLTTᵣAW.   ᵉ φάνῃ
LTW; φανῇ TᵣA.   ᶠ ἴδον T.   ᵍ ἀετοῦ πετομένου eagle flying GLTTᵣAW.   ʰ τοὺς
κατοικοῦντας TTᵣA.   ⁱ ἴδον T.   ᵏ ἐσκοτώθη LTA.   ¹ αὐτοῖς T.   ᵐ ἀδικήσουσιν ¹they
²shall injure LTA.   ⁿ — μόνους GLTTᵣAW.   ᵒ — αὐτῶν (read on the foreheads) LTTᴴ.
ᵖ αὐτοῖς LT.

that they should not kill them, but that they should be tormented five months : and their torment *was* as the torment of a scorpion, when he striketh a man. 6 And in those days shall men seek death, and shall not find it ; and shall desire to die, and death shall flee from them. 7 And the shapes of the locusts *were* like unto horses prepared unto battle ; and on their heads *were* as it were crowns like gold, and their faces *were* as the faces of men. 8 And they had hair as the hair of women, and their teeth were as *the teeth* of lions. 9 And they had breastplates, as it were breastplates of iron ; and the sound of their wings *was* as the sound of chariots of many horses running to battle. 10 And they had tails like unto scorpions, and there were stings in their tails : and their power *was* to hurt men five months. 11 And they had 'a king over them, *which is* the angel of the bottomless pit, whose name *is* in the Hebrew tongue *is* Abaddon, but in the Greek tongue hath *his* name Apollyon.

12 One woe is past ; *and*, behold, there come two woes more hereafter.

13 And the sixth angel sounded, and I heard a voice from the four horns of the golden altar which is before God, 14 saying to the sixth angel which had the trumpet, Loose the four angels which are bound in the great river Euphrates. 15 And the four angels were loosed, which were prepared for an hour,

ἀλλ' ἵνα ᵠβασανισθῶσιν‖ μῆνας πέντε· καὶ ὁ βασανισμὸς
but   that they should be tormented ²months ¹five ;   and   ²torment
αὐτῶν   ὡς   βασανισμὸς σκορπίου, ὅταν παίσῃ ἄν-
¹their [was] as [the]   torment   of a scorpion, when it may strike a
θρωπον· 6 καὶ ἐν ταῖς.ἡμέραις.ἐκείναις ζητήσουσιν οἱ ἄνθρω-
man.   And in   those days   ³shall ²seek   ¹men
ποι τὸν θάνατον, καὶ ʳοὐχ‖ ˢεὑρήσουσιν‖ αὐτόν· καὶ ἐπιθυμή-
    death, and ²not   ¹shall find it ;   and   ¹desire
σουσιν ἀποθανεῖν, καὶ ᵗφεύξεται‖ ᵛὁ θάνατος ἀπ' αὐτῶν.‖
        to die,   and ²shall ³flee ¹death   from them.
7 καὶ τὰ ὁμοιώματα τῶν ἀκρίδων ʷὅμοια‖ ἵπποις ἡτοι-
And the likenesses of the locusts [were] like to horses pre-
μασμένοις εἰς πόλεμον, καὶ ἐπὶ τὰς.κεφαλὰς.αὐτῶν ὡς στέφανοι
pared   for war, and upon   their heads   as   crowns
ὅμοιοι ˣχρυσῷ,‖ καὶ τὰ.πρόσωπα.αὐτῶν ὡς πρόσωπα ἀνθρώ-
like   gold ;   and   their faces   as faces   of
πων· 8 καὶ ʸεἶχον‖ τρίχας ὡς τρίχας γυναικῶν· καὶ οἱ ὀδόντες
men ;   and they had hair as ²hair ¹women's ; and   ²teeth
αὐτῶν ὡς λεόντων ἦσαν· 9 καὶ εἶχον θώρακας ὡς θώρακας
¹their ⁴as ⁵of⁶lions ³were ;   and they had breastplates as ²breastplates
σιδηροῦς· καὶ ἡ φωνὴ τῶν.πτερύγων.αὐτῶν   ὡς   ᶻφωνὴ
¹iron ;   and the sound of their wings   [was] as [the] sound
ἁρμάτων ἵππων πολλῶν τρεχόντων εἰς πόλεμον. 10 καὶ
of chariots of ²horses ¹many   running   to   war ;   and
ἔχουσιν οὐρὰς ᶻὁμοίας‖ σκορπίοις, καὶ κέντρα·ᵃ ᵇἦν‖ ἐν ταῖς
they have tails like   scorpions, and stings ; ⁴was ⁵in
οὐραῖς αὐτῶν ᶜκαὶ‖ ἡ.ἐξουσία.αὐτῶν ἀδικῆσαι τοὺς ἀνθρώπους
⁷tails ⁶their ¹and ²their ³power   to injure   men
μῆνας πέντε. 11 ᵈκαὶ‖ ἔχουσιν ᵉἐφ' αὐτῶν‖ βασιλέα ᶠτὸν‖
²months ¹five.   And they have over them   a king,   the
ἄγγελον τῆς ἀβύσσου· ᵍ ὄνομα αὐτῷ Ἑβραϊστὶ Ἀβαδδών, καὶ
angel   of the abyss :   his name   in Hebrew Abaddon, and
ἐν τῇ Ἑλληνικῇ   ὄνομα ἔχει Ἀπολλύων.
in the   Greek   [for] name he has Apollyon.
12 Ἡ οὐαὶ ἡ μία ἀπῆλθεν· ἰδού, ʰἔρχονται‖ ἔτι δύο οὐαὶ
³Woe ¹the ²first is past. Lo, ⁴come   ¹yet ²two ³woes
μετὰ ταῦτα.
after these things.
13 Καὶ ὁ ἕκτος ἄγγελος ἐσάλπισεν, καὶ ἤκουσα φωνὴν
And the sixth angel sounded [his] trumpet ; and I heard ²voice
μίαν ἐκ τῶν ⁱτεσσάρων‖ κεράτων τοῦ θυσιαστηρίου τοῦ χρυσοῦ
¹one from the four   horns of the   ²altar   ¹golden
τοῦ ἐνώπιον τοῦ θεοῦ, 14 ᵏλέγουσαν‖ τῷ ἕκτῳ ἀγγέλῳ
which [is] before God,   saying   to the sixth angel
ˡὃς εἶχε‖ τὴν σάλπιγγα, Λῦσον τοὺς τέσσαρας ἀγγέλους τοὺς
who had   the trumpet, Loose the four   angels   who
δεδεμένους ἐπὶ τῷ ποταμῷ τῷ μεγάλῳ Εὐφράτῃ. 15 Καὶ ἐλύ-
are bound at the ²river   ¹great Euphrates.   And were
θησαν οἱ τέσσαρες ἄγγελοι οἱ ἡτοιμασμένοι εἰς τὴν ὥραν καὶ
loosed the four   angels   who had been prepared for the hour and

---

ᵠ βασανισθήσονται they shall be tormented LTTrA.   ʳ οὐ μὴ in no wise GLTTrAW.
ˢ εὑρωσιν should find L.   ᵗ φεύγει ²flees LTTrA.   ᵛ ἀπ' αὐτῶν ὁ θάνατος G.   ʷ ὁμοιοι T.
ˣ χρυσοῖ golden G.   ʸ εἶχαν LTTrA.   ᶻ ὁμοίοις Tr.   ᵃ *Punctuate so as to read* and
stings were in their tails *Text. Rec. and* G.   ᵇ καὶ and LTTrAW.   ᶜ — καὶ LTTrAW.
ᵈ — καὶ GLTTrAW.   ᵉ ἐπ' αὐτῶν LTTrA.   ᶠ — τὸν (*read* an angel) A.   ᵍ + ῷ ᵍ̲ο
whom T.   ʰ ἔρχεται LTTrA.   ⁱ — τεσσάρων LTr[A].   ᵏ λέγοντα LTTrAW.   ˡ ὁ ἔχων
who has GLTTrAW.

ἡμέραν καὶ μῆνα καὶ ἐνιαυτόν, ἵνα ἀποκτείνωσιν τὸ τρίτον
day and month and year, that they might kill the third

τῶν ἀνθρώπων. 16 καὶ ὁ ἀριθμὸς ⁿ στρατευμάτων τοῦ ἱππι-
of men; and the ' number of [the] armies of the caval-

κοῦ ᵒδύο μυριάδες‖ μυριάδων· ᴾκαὶ‖ ἤκουσα τὸν ἀριθμὸν
ry [was] two myriads of myriads, and I heard the number

αὐτῶν. 17 καὶ οὕτως �q εἶδον‖ τοὺς ἵππους ἐν τῇ ὁράσει, καὶ
of them. And thus I saw the horses in the vision, and

τοὺς καθημένους ἐπ' αὐτῶν, ἔχοντας θώρακας πυρίνους καὶ
those sitting on them, having breastplates fiery, and

ὑακινθίνους καὶ θειώδεις· καὶ αἱ κεφαλαὶ τῶν ἵππων
hyacinthine, and brimstone-like; and the heads of the horses [were]

ὡς κεφαλαὶ λεόντων, καὶ ἐκ τῶν στομάτων αὐτῶν ἐκπορεύε-
as heads of lions, and out of their mouths goes

ται πῦρ καὶ καπνὸς καὶ θεῖον· 18 ʳὑπὸ‖ τῶν τριῶν ˢ τούτων
out fire and smoke and brimstone. By ²three ¹these

ἀπεκτάνθησαν τὸ τρίτον τῶν ἀνθρώπων, ἐκ τοῦ πυρὸς καὶ
were killed the third of the men, by the fire and

ᵗἐκ‖ τοῦ καπνοῦ καὶ ᵗἐκ‖ τοῦ θείου, τοῦ ἐκπορευομένου ἐκ
by the smoke and by the brimstone, which goes forth out of

τῶν στομάτων αὐτῶν. 19 ᵛαἱ γὰρ ἐξουσίαι αὐτῶν ἐν τῷ
their mouths. For the powers of them ³in

στόματι αὐτῶν εἰσιν·‖ αἱ γὰρ οὐραὶ αὐτῶν ὅμοιαι ὄφεσιν,
'mouth ²their ¹are; for their tails [are] like serpents,

ἔχουσαι κεφαλάς, καὶ ἐν αὐταῖς ἀδικοῦσιν. 20 καὶ οἱ λοιποὶ
having heads, and with them they injure. And the rest

τῶν ἀνθρώπων οἳ οὐκ ἀπεκτάνθησαν ἐν ταῖς πληγαῖς ταύταις,
of the men who were not killed by these plagues,

ʷοὔτε‖ μετενόησαν ἐκ τῶν ἔργων τῶν χειρῶν αὐτῶν, ἵνα μὴ
²not ²even ¹repented of the works of their hands, that ²not

ˣπροσκυνήσωσιν‖ τὰ δαιμόνια, καὶ εἴδωλα τὰ χρυσᾶ καὶ
¹they ²should do homage to the demons, and ˣidols ¹the golden and

τὰ ἀργυρᾶ καὶ τὰ χαλκᾶ καὶ τὰ λίθινα καὶ τὰ ξύλινα,
silver and brazen and stone and wooden,

ἃ οὔτε βλέπειν ᶻδύναται,‖ οὔτε ἀκούειν, οὔτε περιπατεῖν·
which neither ³to ⁴see ¹are ²able, nor to hear, nor to walk.

21 καὶ οὐ μετενόησαν ἐκ τῶν φόνων αὐτῶν, οὔτε ἐκ τῶν
And they repented not of their murders, nor of

ᵃφαρμακειῶν‖ αὐτῶν, οὔτε ἐκ τῆς πορνείας αὐτῶν, οὔτε ἐκ
²sorceries ¹their, nor of their fornications, nor of

τῶν κλεμμάτων αὐτῶν.
their thefts.

10 Καὶ εἶδον ἄλλον ἄγγελον ἰσχυρὸν καταβαίνοντα ἐκ τοῦ
And I saw another ²angel ¹strong coming down out of the

οὐρανοῦ, περιβεβλημένον νεφέλην, καὶ ᵇ ἶρις ἐπὶ ᶜτῆς κεφ-
heaven, clothed with a cloud, and a rainbow on the

αλῆςᵈ, καὶ τὸ πρόσωπον αὐτοῦ ὡς ὁ ἥλιος, καὶ οἱ πόδες αὐτοῦ
head, and his face as the sun, and his feet

ὡς στύλοι πυρός· 2 καὶ ᵉεἶχεν‖ ἐν τῇ χειρὶ αὐτοῦ βιβλαρίδιον
as pillars of fire, and he had in his hand a little book

and a day, and a month, and a year, for to slay the third part of men. 16 And the number of the army of the horsemen *were* two hundred thousand thousand: and I heard the number of them. 17 And thus I saw the horses in the vision, and them that sat on them, having breastplates of fire, and of jacinth, and brimstone: and the heads of the horses *were* as the heads of lions; and out of their mouths issued fire and smoke and brimstone. 18 By these three was the third part of men killed, by the fire, and by the smoke, and by the brimstone, which issued out of their mouths. 19 For their power is in their mouth, and in their tails: for their tails *were* like unto serpents, and had heads, and with them they do hurt. 20 And the rest of the men which were not killed by these plagues yet repented not of the works of their hands, that they should not worship devils, and idols of gold, and silver, and brass, and stone, and of wood: which neither can see, nor hear, nor walk: 21 neither repented they of their murders, nor of their sorceries, nor of their fornication, nor of their thefts.

X. And I saw another mighty angel come down from heaven, clothed with a cloud: and a rainbow *was* upon his head, and his face *was* as it were the sun, and his feet as pillars of fire: 2 and he had in his hand a little book

---
ⁿ + τῶν of the (armies) GLTTrAW.   ᵒ δισμυριάδες LTA.   ᴾ — καὶ GLTTrAW.
q ἴδον T.   ʳ ἀπὸ from GLTTrAW.   ˢ + πληγῶν ²plagues GLTTrAW.   ᵗ — ἐκ
GLTTrAW.   ᵛ ἡ γὰρ ἐξουσία τῶν ἵππων For the power of the horses (αὐτῶν for τῶν ἵππων
W) ἐν τῷ στόματι αὐτῶν ἐστιν καὶ ἐν ταῖς οὐραῖς αὐτῶν is in their mouth and in their tails
GLTTrAW.   ʷ οὐ not GW; οὐδὲ TA.   ˣ προσκυνήσουσιν they shall do homage to LTTrAW.
y + τὰ GLTTrAW.   ᶻ δύνανται LTTrA.   ᵃ φαρμακιῶν T; φαρμάκων Aʹ.   ᵇ + ἡ the
(rainbow) GLTTrAW.   ᶜ τὴν κεφαλὴν LTTrAW.   ᵈ + αὐτοῦ (read his head) GLTTrAW.
ᵉ ἔχων having GLTTrAW.

open : and he set his right foot upon the sea, and *his* left *foot* on the earth, 3 and cried with a loud voice, as *when* a lion roareth : and when he had cried, seven thunders uttered their voices. 4 And when the seven thunders had uttered their voices, I was about to write : and I heard a voice from heaven saying unto me, Seal up those things which the seven thunders uttered, and write them not. 5 And the angel which I saw stand upon the sea and upon the earth lifted up his hand to heaven, 6 and sware by him that liveth for ever and ever, who created heaven, and the things that therein are, and the earth, and the things that therein are, and the sea, and the things which are therein, that there should be time no longer : 7 but in the days of the voice of the seventh angel, when he shall begin to sound, the mystery of God should be finished, as he hath declared to his servants the prophets.

f ἀνεῳγμένον·‖ καὶ ἔθηκεν τὸν.πόδα.αὐτοῦ τὸν δεξιὸν ἐπὶ ᵍτὴν
open.　　　And he placed　　　his ²foot　　　　¹right upon ᵗhe

θάλασσαν,‖ τὸν.δὲ εὐώνυμον ἐπὶ ʰτὴν γῆν,‖ 3 καὶ ἔκραξεν
sea,　　　and the　left　upon the earth,　　and　cried

φωνῇ μεγάλῃ ὥσπερ λέων μυκᾶται· καὶ ὅτε ἔκραξεν,
with a ²voice ¹loud　as　a lion　roars.　And when he cried,

ἐλάλησαν αἱ ἑπτὰ βρονταὶ τὰς.ἑαυτῶν.φωνάς· 4 καὶ ὅτε
⁴spoke ¹the ²seven ³thunders　　their voices.　　And when

ἐλάλησαν αἱ ἑπτὰ βρονταὶ ⁱτὰς.φωνὰς.ἑαυτῶν,‖ ᵏἔμελλον‖
⁴spoke ¹the ²seven ³thunders　　their voices,　　I was about

γράφειν· καὶ ἤκουσα φωνὴν ἐκ τοῦ οὐρανοῦ, λέγουσάν ˡμοι,‖
to write :　And I heard a voice out of the heaven,　saying　to me,

Σφράγισον ἃ　　ἐλάλησαν αἱ ἑπτὰ βρονταί, καὶ μὴ ᵐταῦτα‖
Seal　what [things] ⁴spoke ¹the ²seven ³thunders, and ³not ²them

γράψῃς. 5 Καὶ ὁ ἄγγελος. ὃν εἶδον ἑστῶτα ἐπὶ τῆς θαλάσσης
¹write.　And the angel whom I saw standing on the　sea

καὶ ἐπὶ τῆς γῆς, ἦρεν τὴν.χεῖρα.αὐτοῦ ⁿ εἰς τὸν οὐρανόν,
and on　the earth, lifted up　his hand　　to　the　heaven,

6 καὶ ὤμοσεν ἐν τῷ ζῶντι εἰς τοὺς αἰῶνας τῶν αἰώνων, ὃς
and　sware by him who lives to the ages of the ages, who

ἔκτισεν τὸν οὐρανὸν καὶ　τὰ ἐν αὐτῷ, καὶ τὴν γῆν καὶ
created the　heaven　and the things in　it,　and the earth and

τὰ ἐν αὐτῇ, ᵒκαὶ τὴν θάλασσαν καὶ τὰ ἐν αὐτῇ,‖
the things in　it,　and the　sea　　and the things in it,

Ὅτι χρόνος ᵖοὐκ ἔσται ἔτι·‖ 7 ᵠἀλλὰ‖ ἐν ταῖς ἡμέραις τῆς
Delay ³no ¹shall ²be longer ;　but　in the days of the

φωνῆς τοῦ ἑβδόμου ἀγγέλου, ὅταν μέλλῃ σαλπίζειν,
voice of the seventh　angel,　when he is about to sound [the] trumpet,

καὶ ʳτελεσθῇ‖　τὸ μυστήριον τοῦ θεοῦ, ὡς εὐηγ-
also should be completed the mystery of God,　as he did announce

γέλισεν ˢτοῖς.ἑαυτοῦ.δούλοις τοῖς προφήταις.‖
the glad tidings to　his boudmen　the prophets.

8 And the voice which I heard from heaven spake unto me again, and said, Go *and* take the little book which is open in the hand of the angel which standeth upon the sea and upon the earth. 9 And I went unto the angel, and said unto him, Give me the little book. And he said unto me, Take *it*, and eat it up ; and it shall make thy belly bitter, but it shall be in thy mouth sweet as honey. 10 And I took the little book out of the angel's hand, and ate it up ; and it was in my mouth sweet as honey : and as soon

8 Καὶ ἡ φωνὴ ἣν ἤκουσα ἐκ τοῦ οὐρανοῦ,　πάλιν
And the voice which I heard out of the heaven [was] again

ᵗλαλοῦσα‖ μετ᾽ ἐμοῦ, καὶ ᵛλέγουσα,‖ Ὕπαγε λάβε τὸ ʷβιβλα-
speaking with me, and saying,　Go,　take the little

ρίδιον‖ τὸ ἠνεῳγμένον ἐν τῇ χειρὶ ˣ ἀγγέλου τοῦ ἑστῶτος
book which is open in the hand of [the] angel who is standing

ἐπὶ τῆς θαλάσσης καὶ ἐπὶ τῆς γῆς. 9 Καὶ ʸἀπῆλθον‖ πρὸς τὸν
on　the　sea　and on the earth.　And I went　to the

ἄγγελον, λέγων αὐτῷ, ᶻΔός‖ μοι τὸ βιβλαρίδιον. Καὶ λέγει
angel,　saying to him,　Give me the little book.　And he says

μοι, Λάβε καὶ κατάφαγε αὐτό· καὶ πικρανεῖ σου τὴν
to me,　Take　and eat ²up　¹it :　and it shall make bitter thy

κοιλίαν, ἀλλ᾽ ἐν τῷ.στόματί.σου ἔσται γλυκὺ ὡς μέλι. 10 Καὶ
belly,　but in thy mouth　it shall be sweet as honey.　And

ἔλαβον τὸ βιβλαρίδιον ἐκ τῆς χειρὸς τοῦ ἀγγέλου, καὶ κατέ-
I took the little book out of the hand of the angel,　and ate

φαγον αὐτό· καὶ ἦν ἐν τῷ.στόματί.μου ὡς μέλι γλυκύ· καὶ
²up　¹it ; and it was in　my mouth　²as ³honey ¹sweet ; and

---

f ἠνεῳγμένον LTTrA.　ᵍ τῆς θαλάσσης GLTTrAW.　ʰ τῆς γῆς GLTTrAW.　ⁱ — τὰς φωνὰς ἑαυτῶι GLTTrAW.　ᵏ ἤμελλον LTTrAW.　ˡ — μοι GLTTrAW.　ᵐ αὐτὰ LTTrAW. ⁿ + τὴν δεξιὰν the right GLTTrAW.　ᵒ [καὶ τὴν θάλασσαν καὶ τὰ ἐν αὐτῇ] L.　ᵖ οὐκέτι ἔσται GLTTrAW.　ᵠ ἀλλ᾽ LTTrA.　ʳ ἐτελέσθη was completed GLTTrAW.　ˢ τοὺς ἑαυτοῦ δούλους τοὺς προφήτας GLTTrAW.　ᵗ λαλοῦσαν LTTrAW.　ᵛ λέγουσαν LTTrAW.　ʷ βιβλίον book LTᵣA.　ˣ + τοῦ of the GLTTrAW.　ʸ ἀπῆλθα LT.　ᶻ δοῦνα᾽ (read telling him to give) GLTTrAW.

ὅτε εφαγον αὐτό, ἐπικράνθη ἡ.κοιλία.μου. 11 καὶ ᶜλέγει‖
when I did eat　it,　³was ⁴made ⁵bitter　¹my ²belly.　　And, he says

μοι, Δεῖ.σε πάλιν προφητεῦσαι ἐπὶ λαοῖς καὶ ᵈ ἔθνεσιν καὶ
to me, Thou must again　　prophesy　as to peoples, and　nations, and

γλώσσαις καὶ βασιλεῦσιν πολλοῖς.
tongues,　and　²kings　¹many.

11 Καὶ ἐδόθη μοι κάλαμος ὅμοιος ῥάβδῳ, ᵉ λέγων, ᶠＥγει-
And was given to me　a reed　like　a staff,　saying,　¹Rise,

ραι,‖ καὶ μέτρησον τὸν ναὸν τοῦ θεοῦ, καὶ τὸ θυσιαστήριον,
and　measure　the temple　of God, and the　altar,

καὶ τοὺς προσκυνοῦντας ἐν αὐτῷ. 2 καὶ τὴν αὐλὴν τὴν
and those who　worship　in it.　　And the　court which

ᵍἔσωθεν‖ τοῦ ναοῦ ἔκβαλε ʰἔξω,‖ καὶ μὴ αὐτὴν μετρήσῃς,
[is] within　the temple　cast out, and ³not ²it　¹measure;

ὅτι ἐδόθη τοῖς ἔθνεσιν· καὶ τὴν πόλιν τὴν ἁγίαν
because it was given [up] to the nations,　and the　²city　¹holy

πατήσουσιν μῆνας ¹τεσσαράκοντα‖ ᵏ δύο. 3 καὶ δώσω
shall they trample upon ²months　¹forty　²two.　　And I will give

τοῖς.δυσὶν.μάρτυσίν.μου, καὶ προφητεύσουσιν ἡμέρας
[power]　to my two witnesses,　and they shall prophesy　⁷days

χιλίας διακοσίας ἑξήκοντα, ¹περιβεβλημένοι‖ σάκ-
¹a²thousand ³two ⁴hundred [⁵and]　⁶sixty,　clothed in　sack-

κους. 4 οὗτοί εἰσιν αἱ δύο ἐλαῖαι, καὶ ᵐ δύο λυχνίαι
cloth.　These are　ᵗthe two olive trees, and [the] two lampstands

αἱ ἐνώπιον ⁿτοῦ ᵒθεοῦ‖ τῆς γῆς ᴾἑστῶσαι.‖ 5 καὶ εἴ τις
which　²before　³the　⁴God ⁵of ⁶the ⁷earth　¹stand.　　And if anyone

αὐτοὺς ᑫθέλῃ‖ ἀδικῆσαι, πῦρ ἐκπορεύεται ἐκ τοῦ στόματος
⁵them　¹should ²will ³to ⁴injure, fire　goes out　of　⁶mouth

αὐτῶν, καὶ κατεσθίει τοὺς.ἐχθροὺς.αὐτῶν· καὶ εἴ τις ʳαὐτοὺς
¹their, and devours　their enemies.　And if anyone　⁵them

θέλῃ‖ ἀδικῆσαι, οὕτως δεῖ.αὐτὸν ἀποκτανθῆναι. 6 οὗτοι
¹should ²will ³to ⁴injure,　thus　must he　be killed.　　These

ἔχουσιν ˢ ¹ἐξουσίαν κλεῖσαι τὸν οὐρανόν,‖ ἵνα μὴ ᵛβρέχῃ
have　authority　to shut　the heaven,　that no　²may ³fall

ὑετὸς ἐν ἡμέραις αὐτῶν τῆς προφητείας·‖ καὶ ἐξουσίαν
¹rain in [the]　days　of their　prophecy;　and authority

ἔχουσιν ἐπὶ τῶν ὑδάτων, στρέφειν αὐτὰ εἰς αἷμα, καὶ πατά-
they have over　the waters,　to turn　them into blood; and　to

ξαι τὴν γῆν ʷ ˣπάσῃ πληγῇ, ὁσάκις ἐὰν θελήσωσιν.‖ 7 καὶ
smite the earth with every plague, as often as　they may will.　And

ὅταν τελέσωσιν τὴν.μαρτυρίαν.αὐτῶν, τὸ θηρίον τὸ
when they shall have completed　their testimony,　the beast who

ἀναβαῖνον ἐκ τῆς ἀβύσσου ποιήσει ʸπόλεμον μετ' αὐτῶν,‖
comes up out of the abyss　will make　war　with them,

καὶ νικήσει αὐτούς, καὶ ἀποκτενεῖ αὐτούς. 8 καὶ ᶻτὰ
and will overcome them,　and will kill　them:　and

πτώματα‖ αὐτῶν ἐπὶ τῆς πλατείας ᵃᵃπόλεως τῆς με-
²bodies　¹their [will be] on the　street　of ³city　¹the

as I had eaten it, my
belly was bitter.
11 And he said unto
me, Thou must pro-
phesy again before
many peoples, and na-
tions, and tongues,
and kings.

XI. And there was
given me a reed like
unto a rod : and the
angel stood, saying,
Rise, and measure the
temple of God, and the
altar, and them that
worship therein. 2 But
the court which is
without the temple
leave out, and measure
it not ; for it is given
unto the Gentiles : and
the holy city shall
they tread under foot
forty and two months.
3 And I will give
power unto my two
witnesses, and they
shall prophesy a thou-
sand two hundred and
threescore days, cloth-
ed in sackcloth. 4 These
are the two olive trees,
and the two candle-
sticks standing before
the God of the earth.
5 And if any man
will hurt them, fire
proceedeth out of their
mouth, and devoureth
their enemies : and if
any man will hurt
them, he must in this
manner be killed.
6 These have power to
shut heaven, that it
rain not in the days
of their prophecy : and
have power over wa-
ters to turn them to
blood, and to smite
the earth with all
plagues, as often as
they will. 7 And when
they shall have finish-
ed their testimony, the
beast that ascend-
eth out of the bottom-
less pit shall make
war against them, and
shall overcome them,
and kill them. 8 And
their dead bodies *shall*
lie in the street of
the great city, which

ᶜ λέγουσίν they say LTTrA.　ᵈ + ἐπὶ as to T.　ᵉ + καὶ ὁ ἄγγελος εἰστήκει and
the angel stood E.　ᶠＥγειρε LTTrAW.　ᵍ ἔξωθεν outside EGLTTrAW.　ʰ ἔξωθεν
outside LTTr.　ⁱ τεσσεράκοντα LTTrA.　ᵏ + καὶ and LAW.　ˡ περιβεβλημένους Tr.
ᵐ + αἱ the GLTTrAW.　ⁿ — τοῦ L.　ᵒ κυρίου Lord GLTTrAW.　ᴾ ἑστῶτες GLTTrAW.
ᑫ θέλει wills GLTTrAW.　ʳ αὐτοὺς.θέλει them wills G ; θέλει αὐτοὺς LAW ; θελήσῃ αὐτοὺς
should have willed them T; αὐτοὺς θελήσῃ Tr.　ˢ + τὴν the LTr[A]w.　ᵗ τὸν οὐρανὸν
ἐξουσίαν κλεῖσαι G.　ᵛ ὑετὸς βρέχῃ τὰς ἡμέρας τῆς προφητείας αὐτῶν (αὐτῶν τῆς προφ. w)
(read [during] the days) GLTTrAW.　ʷ ἐν with (every) LTTrA.　ˣ ὁσάκις ἐὰν θελήσωσιν ἐν πάσῃ πληγῇ GW.　ʸ μετ' αὐτῶν πόλεμον GLTTrA.　ᶻ τὸ πτῶμα body GLTTrAW.
ᵃᵃ + τῆς LTTrAW.

spiritually is called Sodom and Egypt, where also our Lord was crucified. 9 And they of the people and kindreds and tongues and nations shall see their dead bodies three days and an half, and shall not suffer their dead bodies to be put in graves. 10 And they that dwell upon the earth shall rejoice over them, and make merry, and shall send gifts one to another; because these two prophets tormented them that dwelt on the earth. 11 And after three days and an half the Spirit of life from God entered into them, and they stood upon their feet; and great fear fell upon them which saw them. 12 And they heard a great voice from heaven saying unto them, Come up hither. And they ascended up to heaven in a cloud; and their enemies beheld them. 13 And the same hour was there a great earthquake, and the tenth part of the city fell, and in the earthquake were slain of men seven thousand: and the remnant were affrighted, and gave glory to the God of heaven.

14 The second woe is past; and, behold, the third woe cometh quickly.

15 And the seventh angel sounded; and there were great voices in heaven, saying, The kingdoms of this world are become the kingdoms of our Lord, and of his Christ; and he shall reign for ever and ever. 16 And the four and twenty elders, which sat before

γάλης, ἥτις καλεῖται πνευματικῶς Σόδομα καὶ Αἴγυπτος,
great, which is called spiritually Sodom and Egypt,
ὅπου καὶ ὁ κύριος ᵇἡμῶν‖ ἐσταυρώθη. 9 καὶ ᶜβλέψουσιν‖
where also ²Lord ¹our was crucified. And ¹¹shall ¹²see [ᶜsome]
ἐκ τῶν λαῶν καὶ φυλῶν καὶ γλωσσῶν καὶ ἐθνῶν ᵈτὰ πτώ-
²of ³the ⁴peoples ⁵and ⁶tribes ⁷and ⁸tongues ⁹and ¹⁰nations ¹⁴bodies
ματα‖ αὐτῶν ἡμέρας τρεῖς ᵉκαὶ‖ ἥμισυ, καὶ τὰ πτώματα αὐτῶν
¹³their ¹⁶days ¹⁵three and a half, and their bodies
οὐκ ᶠἀφήσουσιν‖ τεθῆναι εἰς ᵍμνήματα.‖ 10 καὶ‑ οἱ κατ-
³not ¹they ²will suffer to be put into tombs. And they that
οἰκοῦντες ἐπὶ τῆς γῆς ʰχαροῦσιν‖ ἐπ᾽ αὐτοῖς, καὶ ⁱεὐφρανθή-
dwell on the earth will rejoice over them, and will make
σονται‖ καὶ δῶρα ᵏπέμψουσιν‖ ἀλλήλοις, ὅτι οὗτοι οἱ δύο
merry, and gifts will send to one another, because these, the two
προφῆται ἐβασάνισαν τοὺς κατοικοῦντας ἐπὶ τῆς γῆς.
prophets, tormented them that dwell upon the earth.

11 καὶ μετὰ τὰς τρεῖς ἡμέρας καὶ ἥμισυ, πνεῦμα ζωῆς
And after the three days and a half, [the] spirit of life
ἐκ τοῦ θεοῦ εἰσῆλθεν ˡἐπ᾽ αὐτούς,‖ καὶ ἔστησαν ἐπὶ τοὺς
from God did enter into them, and they stood upon
πόδας αὐτῶν, καὶ φόβος μέγας ᵐἔπεσεν‖ ἐπὶ τοὺς θεωροῦντας
²feet ¹their; and ²fear ¹great fell upon those beholding
αὐτούς. 12 καὶ ἤκουσαν ⁿφωνὴν μεγάλην‖ ἐκ τοῦ οὐρανοῦ,
them: and they heard a ²voice ¹great out of the heaven,
ᵒλέγουσαν‖ αὐτοῖς, ᴾΑνάβητε‖ ὧδε. Καὶ ἀνέβησαν εἰς τὸν
saying to them, Come up hither. And they went up to the
οὐρανὸν ἐν τῇ νεφέλῃ, καὶ ἐθεώρησαν αὐτοὺς οἱ ἐχθροὶ αὐτῶν.
heaven in the cloud; and ³beheld ⁴them ¹their ²enemies.

13 Καὶ ἐν ἐκείνῃ τῇ ὥρᾳ ἐγένετο σεισμὸς μέγας, καὶ τὸ
And in that hour there was ²earthquake ¹a ³great, and the
δέκατον τῆς πόλεως ἔπεσεν, καὶ ἀπεκτάνθησαν ἐν τῷ σεισμῷ
tenth of the city fell, and there were killed in the earthquake
ὀνόματα ἀνθρώπων χιλιάδες ἑπτά· καὶ οἱ λοιποὶ ἔμφοβοι
³names ⁴of ⁵men ²thousand ¹seven. And the rest ²afraid
ἐγένοντο, καὶ ἔδωκαν δόξαν τῷ θεῷ τοῦ οὐρανοῦ.
¹became, and gave glory to the God of the heaven.

14 Ἡ οὐαὶ ᑫἡ‖ δευτέρα ἀπῆλθεν· ἰδού, ἡ οὐαὶ ἡ τρίτη
³Woe ¹the ²second is past: lo, the ²woe ¹third
ἔρχεται ταχύ.
comes quickly.

15 Καὶ ὁ ἕβδομος ἄγγελος ἐσάλπισεν, καὶ ἐγένοντο
And the seventh angel sounded [his] trumpet; and ³were
φωναὶ μεγάλαι ἐν τῷ οὐρανῷ, ʳλέγουσαι,‖ ˢἘγένοντο αἱ
²voices ¹great in the heaven, saying, ⁶Are ⁷become ¹the
βασιλεῖαι‖ τοῦ κόσμου τοῦ κυρίου ἡμῶν, καὶ τοῦ χριστοῦ αὐτοῦ,
²kingdoms ³of ⁴the ⁵world our Lord's, and his Christ's,
καὶ βασιλεύσει εἰς τοὺς αἰῶνας τῶν αἰώνων. 16 Καὶ ᵗοἱ‖
and he shall reign to the ages of the ages. And the
εἴκοσι ᵛκαὶ‖ τέσσαρες πρεσβύτεροι ᵂοἱ‖ ἐνώπιον τοῦ θεοῦ ˣκαθή-
twenty and four elders, who before God sit

ᵇ αὐτῶν their GLTTrAW.   ᶜ βλέπουσιν see GLTTrAW.   ᵈ τὸ πτῶμα body GLTTrAW.
ᵉ [καὶ] A.   ᶠ ἀφίουσιν they suffer LTTrA; ἀφιοῦσιν W.   ᵍ μνῆμα a tomb GLTTrAW.
ʰ χαίρουσιν rejoice GLTTrAW.   ⁱ εὐφραίνονται make merry LTTrAW.   ᵏ πέμπουσιν send T.
ˡ ἐν (— ἐν Tr[A]) αὐτοῖς GLTTrAW.   ᵐ ἐπέπεσεν LTTrAW.   ⁿ φωνῆς μεγάλης TrA.   ᵒ λεγούσης TrA.   ᴾ Ἀνάβατε LTTrAW.   ᑫ — ἡ W.   ʳ λέγοντες GLTAW.   ˢ Ἐγένετο ἡ
βασιλεία ᵉis ⁷become ⁵the ᵗkingdom GLTTrAW.   ᵗ — οἱ L[A].   ᵛ — καὶ GLTTrAW,
ᵂ — οἱ (read καθή. sitting) L[A].   ˣ οἱ κάθηνται (read who [are] before God who sit) TTr.

μενοι‖ ἐπὶ τοὺς.θρόνους.αὐτῶν, ἔπεσαν ἐπὶ τὰ.πρόσωπα.αὐτῶν,
on   their thrones,   fell   upon   their faces,

καὶ προσεκύνησαν τῷ θεῷ, 17 λέγοντες, Εὐχαριστοῦμέν σοι,
and   worshipped   God,   saying,   We give thanks to thee,

κύριε ὁ θεὸς ὁ παντοκράτωρ,   ὁ ὢν καὶ ὁ ἦν ʸκαὶ ὁ
Lord God   Almighty,   [He] who is, and who was, and who [is]

ἐρχόμενος,‖ ᶻὅτι   εἴληφας   τὴν δύναμίν σου τὴν μεγάλην,
coming,   that thou hast taken   ²power ¹thy   ²great,

καὶ ἐβασίλευσας. 18 καὶ τὰ ἔθνη ὠργίσθησαν, καὶ ἦλθεν ἡ
and   reigned.   And the nations were angry, and is come

ὀργή σου, καὶ ὁ καιρὸς τῶν νεκρῶν, κριθῆναι, καὶ δοῦναι τὸν
²wrath ¹thy, and the time of the dead to be judged, and to give the

μισθὸν τοῖς.δούλοις.σου τοῖς προφήταις, καὶ τοῖς ἁγίοις καὶ
reward to thy bondmen   the prophets,   and to the saints, and

τοῖς   φοβουμένοις τὸ.ὄνομά.σου, ᵃτοῖς μικροῖς καὶ τοῖς
to those who fear   thy name,   the   small   and the

μεγάλοις,‖ καὶ   διαφθεῖραι   τοὺς ᵇδιαφθείροντας‖ τὴν γῆν.
great ;   and to bring to corruption those who corrupt   the earth.

19 Καὶ ἠνοίγη ὁ ναὸς τοῦ θεοῦ ᶜἐν τῷ οὐρανῷ, καὶ ὤφ-
And was opened the temple of God in the heaven,   and was

θη ἡ κιβωτὸς τῆς.διαθήκης.ᵈαὐτοῦ‖ ἐν τῷ.ναῷ.αὐτοῦ· καὶ
seen the ark   of his covenant   in   his temple :   and

ἐγένοντο ἀστραπαὶ καὶ φωναὶ καὶ βρονταὶ καὶ σεισμὸς καὶ
there were lightnings and voices and thunders and an earthquake and

χάλαζα μεγάλη.
²hail ¹great.

12 Καὶ σημεῖον μέγα ὤφθη ἐν τῷ οὐρανῷ, γυνὴ περι-
And a ²sign ¹great was seen in the heaven; a woman cloth-

βεβλημένη τὸν ἥλιον, καὶ ἡ σελήνη ὑποκάτω τῶν.ποδῶν.αὐτῆς,
ed with   the sun, and the moon   under   her feet,

καὶ ἐπὶ τῆς.κεφαλῆς.αὐτῆς στέφανος ἀστέρων δώδεκα· 2 καὶ
and on   her head   a crown of ²stars ¹twelve ;   and

ἐν.γαστρὶ.ἔχουσα, ᵉ ᶠκράζει‖ ὠδίνουσα καὶ βασανιζομένη
being with child   she cries being in travail, and   being in pain

τεκεῖν.
to bring forth.

3 Καὶ ὤφθη ἄλλο σημεῖον ἐν τῷ οὐρανῷ, καὶ ἰδού, δρά-
And was seen another sign   in the heaven, and behold, a ²dra-

κων ᵍμέγας πυῤῥός,‖ ἔχων κεφαλὰς ἑπτὰ καὶ κέρατα δέκα· καὶ
gon ¹great ²red,   having ²heads ¹seven and ²horns ¹ten, and

ἐπὶ τὰς.κεφαλὰς.αὐτοῦ ʰδιαδήματα ἑπτά·‖ 4 καὶ ἡ.οὐρὰ.αὐτοῦ
upon his heads   ²diadems ¹seven ;   and   his tail

σύρει τὸ τρίτον τῶν ἀστέρων τοῦ οὐρανοῦ, καὶ ἔβαλεν αὐτοὺς
drags the third of the stars of the heaven, and he cast   them

εἰς τὴν γῆν. καὶ ὁ δράκων ἕστηκεν ἐνώπιον τῆς γυναικὸς τῆς
to the earth. And the dragon stands before   the   woman   who

μελλούσης τεκεῖν, ἵνα ὅταν τέκῃ,   τὸ.τέκνον.αὐτῆς
is about to bring forth, that when she should bring forth, her child

καταφάγῃ. 5 καὶ   ἔτεκεν   υἱὸν ⁱἄῤῥενα,‖ ὃς μέλλει ποι-
he might devour. And she brought forth a ²son ¹male, who is about. to

μαίνειν πάντα τὰ ἔθνη ἐν ῥάβδῳ σιδηρᾷ· καὶ ἡρπάσθη
shepherd   all   the nations with ²rod ¹an ²iron : and was caught away

God on their seats, fell upon their faces, and worshipped God, 17 saying, We give thee thanks, O Lord God Almighty, which art, and wast, and art to come ; because thou hast taken to thee thy great power, and hast reigned. 18 And the nations were angry, and thy wrath is come, and the time of the dead, that they should be judged, and that thou shouldest give reward unto thy servants the prophets, and to the saints, and them that fear thy name, small and great ; and shouldest destroy them which destroy the earth.

19 And the temple of God was opened in heaven, and there was seen in his temple the ark of his testament : and there were lightnings, and voices, and thunderings, and an earthquake, and great hail.

XII. And there appeared a great wonder in heaven ; a woman clothed with the sun, and the moon under her feet, and upon her head a crown of twelve stars : 2 and she being with child cried, travailing in birth, and pained to be delivered.

3 And there appeared another wonder in heaven ; and behold a great red dragon, having seven heads and ten horns, and seven crowns upon his heads. 4 And his tail drew the third part of the stars of heaven, and did cast them to the earth : and the dragon stood before the woman which was ready to be delivered, for to devour her child as soon as it was born. 5 And she brought forth a man child, who was to rule all nations with a rod of iron : and her

---

ʸ — καὶ ὁ ἐρχόμενος GLTTrAW. ᶻ + καὶ and T. ᵃ τοὺς μικροὺς καὶ τοὺς μεγάλους LTrA. ᵇ διαφθείραντας corrupted L. ᶜ + ὁ which [is] LTTr. ᵈ τοῦ κυρίου (read the covenant of the Lord) G. ᵉ + καὶ and LT[A]. ᶠ ἔκραζεν was crying L. ᵍ πυῤῥὸς μέγας LTTrA. ʰ ἑπτὰ διαδήματα GLTTrAW. ⁱ ἄρσεν LTTrAW.

child was caught up unto God, and *to* his throne. 6 And the woman fled into the wilderness, where she hath a place prepared of God, that they should feed her there a thousand two hundred *and* threescore days.

7 And there was war in heaven: Michael and his angels fought against the dragon; and the dragon fought and his angels, 8 and prevailed not; neither was their place found any more in heaven. 9 And the great dragon was cast out, that old serpent, called the Devil, and Satan, which deceiveth the whole world: he was cast out into the earth, and his angels were cast out with him. 10 And I heard a loud voice saying in heaven, Now is come salvation, and strength, and the kingdom of our God, and the power of his Christ: for the accuser of our brethren is cast down, which accused them before our God day and night. 11 And they overcame him by the blood of the Lamb, and by the word of their testimony; and they loved not their lives unto the death. 12 Therefore rejoice, ye heavens, and ye that dwell in them. Woe to the inhabiters of the earth and of the sea! for the devil is come down unto you, having great wrath, because he knoweth that he hath but a short time.

13 And when the dragon saw that he was cast unto the earth, he persecuted the woman which brought forth the man *child*. 14 And to

---

τὸ.τέκνον.αὐτῆς πρὸς τὸν θεὸν καὶ [k] τὸν.θρόνον.αὐτοῦ. 6 καὶ
her child   to   God   and   his throne.   And

ἡ γυνὴ ἔφυγεν εἰς τὴν ἔρημον, ὅπου ἔχει [l] τόπον ἡτοιμασ-
the woman fled into the wilderness, where she has a place   pre-

μένον ἀπὸ τοῦ θεοῦ, ἵνα ἐκεῖ [m]τρέφωσιν[ll] αὐτὴν ἡμέρας
pared of   God, that there they should nourish her   [7]days

χιλίας διακοσίας ἑξήκοντα.
[1]a [2]thousand [3]two [4]hundred [[5]and] [6]sixty.

7 Καὶ ἐγένετο πόλεμος ἐν τῷ οὐρανῷ· [n]ὁ[ll] Μιχαὴλ καὶ
And there was war in the heaven: Michael and

οἱ.ἄγγελοι.αὐτοῦ [o]ἐπολέμησαν κατὰ[ll] τοῦ δράκοντος, καὶ ὁ
his angels   warred   against   the   dragon,   and the

δράκων ἐπολέμησεν, καὶ οἱ.ἄγγελοι.αὐτοῦ· 8 καὶ οὐκ [p]ἴσχυ-
dragon   warred,   and   his angels;   and [3]not [1]they [2]pre-

σαν,[ll] [q]οὔτε[ll] τόπος εὑρέθη αὐτῶν ἔτι ἐν τῷ οὐρανῷ. 9 καὶ
vailed,   nor   [3]place [1]was [4]found [2]their any more in the heaven.   And

ἐβλήθη ὁ δράκων ὁ μέγας, ὁ ὄφις ὁ ἀρχαῖος, ὁ καλού-
was cast [out] the [2]dragon [1]great, the [2]serpent [1]ancient, who   is

μενος διάβολος, καὶ ὁ σατανᾶς, ὁ πλανῶν τὴν οἰκουμένην
called   Devil,   and the   Satan,   who misleads the   [2]habitable

ὅλην, ἐβλήθη εἰς τὴν γῆν, καὶ οἱ.ἄγγελοι.αὐτοῦ
[3]world] [1]whole, he was cast into the earth, and   his angels

μετ' αὐτοῦ ἐβλήθησαν. 10 Καὶ ἤκουσα φωνὴν μεγάλην [r]λέ-
with [4]him [2]were [3]cast.   And I heard a [2]voice [1]great   saying

γουσαν ἐν τῷ οὐρανῷ,[ll] [s]Ἄρτι ἐγένετο ἡ σωτηρία καὶ ἡ δύνα-
saying   in the heaven,   Now is come the salvation and the ·power

μις καὶ ἡ βασιλεία τοῦ.θεοῦ.ἡμῶν, καὶ ἡ ἐξουσία τοῦ χριστοῦ
and the kingdom of our God,   and the authority   [5]Christ

αὐτοῦ· ὅτι [s]κατεβλήθη[ll] ὁ [t]κατήγορος[ll] τῶν.ἀδελφῶν.ἡμῶν,
[1]of [2]his; because is cast down the   accuser   of our brethren,

ὁ κατηγορῶν [v]αὐτῶν[ll] ἐνώπιον τοῦ.θεοῦ.ἡμῶν ἡμέρας καὶ
who ' accuses   them   before   our God   day , and

νυκτός. 11 καὶ αὐτοὶ ἐνίκησαν αὐτὸν διὰ τὸ αἷμα τοῦ
night.   And they overcame   him by reason of the blood of the

ἀρνίου, καὶ διὰ τὸν λόγον τῆς.μαρτυρίας.αὐτῶν, καὶ
Lamb,   and by reason of the   word   of their testimony,   and

[w]οὐκ[ll] ἠγάπησαν τὴν.ψυχὴν.αὐτῶν ἄχρι θανάτου. 12 διὰ
[2]not [1]loved   their life   unto death.   Because of

τοῦτο εὐφραίνεσθε [x]οἱ[ll] οὐρανοὶ καὶ οἱ ἐν αὐτοῖς σκηνοῦντες.
this   rejoice ye   heavens and [ye] who in them   tabernacle.

οὐαὶ [y]τοῖς κατοικοῦσιν[ll] [z]τὴν γῆν καὶ τὴν θάλασσαν,[ll] ὅτι
Woe to those who inhabit   the earth and the   sea,   because

κατέβη ὁ διάβολος πρὸς ὑμᾶς ἔχων θυμὸν μέγαν, εἰ-
is come down the devil   to you having [2]fury [1]great, know-

δὼς ὅτι ὀλίγον καιρὸν ἔχει.
ing that a short time he has.

13 Καὶ ὅτε εἶδεν ὁ δράκων ὅτι ἐβλήθη εἰς τὴν γῆν,
And when [3]saw [1]the [2]dragon that he was cast into the earth,

ἐδίωξεν τὴν γυναῖκα ἥτις ἔτεκεν τὸν [a]ἄῤῥενα.[ll] 14 καὶ
he persecuted ·the   woman   which brought forth the   male [child].   And

---

[k] + πρὸς to GLTTrAW.   [l] + ἐκεῖ there GTAW.   [m] τρέφουσιν they nourish TTr; ἐκτρέφωσιν W.   [n] ὅ τε both L.   [o] τοῦ (— τοῦ T[A]) πολεμῆσαι μετὰ warred with GLTTrAW.   [p] ἴσχυσεν he prevailed G.   [q] οὐδὲ GLTTrAW.   [r] ἐν τῷ οὐρανῷ λέγουσαν GLTTrAW.   [s] ἐβλήθη is cast [out] LTTrA.   [t] κατήγωρ GLTA.   [v] αὐτοὺς LTrA. [w] οὐχ L.   [x] — οἱ TTrA.   [y] — τοῖς κατοικοῦσιν GLTTrAW.   [z] τῇ γῇ καὶ τῇ θαλάσσῃ GW. [a] ἄρσεναν L; ἄρσενα TTrA.

ἐδόθησαν τῇ γυναικὶ [b] δύο πτέρυγες τοῦ ἀετοῦ τοῦ μεγάλου,
were given to the woman two wings of the ²eagle¹ ¹great,

ἵνα πέτηται εἰς τὴν ἔρημον εἰς τὸν.τόπον.αὐτῆς, ὅπου· τρέ-
that she might fly into the wilderness into her place, where she is

φεται ἐκεῖ καιρόν, καὶ καιρούς, καὶ ἥμισυ καιροῦ, ἀπὸ
nourished there a time, and times, and half a time, from [the]

προσώπου τοῦ ὄφεως. 15 καὶ ἔβαλεν ὁ ὄφις [c]ὀπίσω τῆς
face of the serpent. And ³cast ¹the ²serpent ³after ¹the

γυναικὸς ἐκ τοῦ.στόματος.αὐτοῦ¹ ὕδωρ ὡς ποταμόν, ἵνα
¹⁰woman ⁶out ⁵of ¹his ⁷mouth water as a river, that

[d]ταύτην‖ ποταμοφόρητον· ποιήσῃ. .16 καὶ
⁴her [⁵as ⁶one] ⁷carried ⁸away ⁹by ¹⁰a ¹¹river ¹he ²might ³make. And

ἐβοήθησεν ἡ γῆ τῇ γυναικί, καὶ ἤνοιξεν ἡ γῆ τὸ στόμα
³helped ¹the ²earth the woman, and ³opened ¹the ²earth mouth

αὐτῆς, καὶ κατέπιεν τὸν ποταμὸν ὃν ἔβαλεν ὁ δράκων·
⁴its, and swallowed up the river which ³cast ¹the ²dragon

ἐκ τοῦ.στόματος.αὐτοῦ. 17 καὶ ὠργίσθη ὁ δράκων [e]ἐπὶ‖
out of his mouth. And ³was ⁴angry ¹the ²dragon with

τῇ γυναικί, καὶ ἀπῆλθεν ποιῆσαι πόλεμον μετὰ τῶν λοιπῶν
the woman, and went to make war with the rest

τοῦ.σπέρματος.αὐτῆς, τῶν τηρούντων τὰς ἐντολὰς τοῦ
of her seed, who keep the commandments

θεοῦ, καὶ ἐχόντων τὴν μαρτυρίαν [f]τοῦ‖ Ἰησοῦ [g]χριστοῦ.‖
of God, and have the testimony of Jesus Christ.

18 Καὶ [h]ἐστάθην‖ ἐπὶ τὴν ἄμμον τῆς θαλάσσης· 13 καὶ
And I stood upon the sand of the sea; and

εἶδον ἐκ τῆς θαλάσσης θηρίον ἀναβαῖνον, ἔχον ¹κεφαλὰς
I saw out of the sea a beast rising, having ²heads

ἑπτὰ καὶ κέρατα δέκα·‖ καὶ ἐπὶ τῶν.κεράτων.αὐτοῦ δέκα δια-
¹seven and ²horns ¹ten, and on ¹its horns ten dia-

δήματα, καὶ ἐπὶ τὰς.κεφαλὰς.αὐτοῦ [k]ὄνομα‖ βλασφημίας.
dems, and upon its heads [the] name of blasphemy.

2 καὶ τὸ θηρίον ὃ εἶδον ἦν ὅμοιον παρδάλει, καὶ οἱ πόδες
And the beast which I saw was like to a leopard, and ²feet

αὐτοῦ ὡς ¹ἄρκτου,‖ καὶ τὸ.στόμα.αὐτοῦ ὡς στόμα [m]λέοντος.‖
¹its as of a bear, and its mouth as [the] mouth of a lion;

καὶ ἔδωκεν αὐτῷ ὁ δράκων τὴν.δύναμιν.αὐτοῦ, καὶ τὸν θρόνον
and ³gave ⁴to ⁵it ¹the ²dragon his power, and ³throne

αὐτοῦ, καὶ ἐξουσίαν μεγάλην. 3 καὶ [n]εἶδον‖ μίαν [o] τῶν κεφα-
¹his, and ²authority ¹great. And I saw one ³heads

λῶν αὐτοῦ ὡς ἐσφαγμένην εἰς θάνατον· καὶ ἡ πληγὴ τοῦ
¹of ²its as slain to death; and the wound

θανάτου αὐτοῦ ἐθεραπεύθη, καὶ [p]ἐθαυμάσθη‖ [q]ἐν‖ [r]ὅλῃ τῇ
³death ¹of ²its was healed: and there was wonder in ²whole ¹the

γῇ‖ ὀπίσω τοῦ θηρίου. 4 καὶ προσεκύνησαν [s]τὸν δράκοντα‖
earth after the beast. And they did homage to the dragon,

[t]ὃς‖ ἔδωκεν [v]ἐξουσίαν τῷ θηρίῳ, καὶ προσεκύνησαν [w]τὸ
who gave authority to the beast; and they did homage to the

θηρίον,‖ λέγοντες, Τίς ὅμοιος τῷ θηρίῳ; [x]τίς δύναται
beast, saying, Who [is] like to the beast? who is able

---

the woman were given two wings of a great eagle, that she might fly into the wilderness, into her place, where she is nourished for a time, and times, and half a time, from the face of the serpent. 15 And the serpent cast out of his mouth water as a flood after the woman, that he might cause her to be carried away of the flood. 16 And the earth helped the woman, and the earth opened her mouth, and swallowed up the flood which the dragon cast out of his mouth. 17 And the dragon was wroth with the woman, and went to make war with the remnant of her seed, which keep the commandments of God, and have the testimony of Jesus Christ.

XIII. And I stood upon the sand of the sea, and saw a beast rise up out of the sea, having seven heads and ten horns, and upon his horns ten crowns, and upon his heads the name of blasphemy. 2 And the beast which I saw was like unto a leopard, and his feet were as the feet of a bear, and his mouth as the mouth of a lion: and the dragon gave him his power, and his seat, and great authority. 3 And I saw one of his heads as it were wounded to death; and his deadly wound was healed: and all the world wondered after the beast. 4 And they worshipped the dragon which gave power unto the beast: and they worshipped the beast, saying, Who is like unto the beast? who is able

---

[b] + αἱ the LTTᵣ[A]W. [c] ἐκ τοῦ στόματος αὐτοῦ ὀπίσω τῆς γυναικὸς GLTTᵣAW. [d] αὐτὴν GLTTᵣAW. [e] — ἐπὶ (read τῇ with the) L. [f] — τοῦ GLTTᵣAW. [g] — χριστοῦ GLTTᵣAW. [h] ἐστάθη it stood LTᵣA. [i] κέρατα δέκα καὶ κεφαλὰς ἑπτά GLTTᵣAW. [k] ὀνόματα names GLTTᵣW. [l] ἄρκου GLTTᵣAW. [m] λεόντων of lions T. [n] — εἶδον GLTTᵣAW. [o] + ἐκ of (its) GLTTᵣAW. [p] ἐθαύμασεν (read the whole earth wondered) EGTAW. [q] + ἐν EGLTAW. [r] ὅλη ἡ γῆ EGLTAW. [s] τῷ δράκοντι GLTTᵣAW. [t] ὅτι (read because he gave) GLTTᵣAW. [v] + τὴν the GLTTᵣAW. [w] τῷ θηρίῳ GLTTᵣAW. [x] + καὶ and GLTTᵣAW.

to make war with him? 5 And there was given unto him a mouth speaking great things and blasphemies; and power was given unto him to continue forty and two months. 6 And he opened his mouth in blasphemy against God, to blaspheme his name, and his tabernacle, and them that dwell in heaven. 7 And it was given unto him to make war with the saints, and to overcome them: and power was given him over all kindreds, and tongues, and nations. 8 And all that dwell upon the earth shall worship him, whose names are not written in the book of life of the Lamb slain from the foundation of the world. 9 If any man have an ear, let him hear. 10 He that leadeth into captivity shall go into captivity: he that killeth with the sword must be killed with the sword. Here is the patience and the faith of the saints.

πολεμῆσαι μετ᾽ αὐτοῦ; 5 καὶ ἐδόθη αὐτῷ στόμα λαλοῦν
to make war with it? And was given to it a mouth speaking

μεγάλα καὶ ᵞβλασφημίας᾿ καὶ ἐδόθη αὐτῷ ἐξουσία ᵃ ποιῆ-
great things and blasphemy; and was given to it authority to

σαι μῆνας ᵃτεσσαράκοντα ᵇ δύο·᾿ 6 καὶ ἤνοιξεν τὸ στόμα αὐτοῦ
act ²months ¹forty ²two. And it opened its mouth

εἰς ᶜβλασφημίαν᾿ πρὸς τὸν θεόν, βλασφημῆσαι τὸ ᵒνομα
for blasphemy against God, to blaspheme ²name

αὐτοῦ, καὶ τὴν σκηνὴν αὐτοῦ, ᵈκαὶ᾿ τοὺς ἐν τῷ οὐρανῷ
¹his, and his tabernacle, and those who ²in ³the ⁴heaven

σκηνοῦντας. 7 ᵉκαὶ ἐδόθη αὐτῷ ᶠπόλεμον ποιῆσαι᾿ μετὰ τῶν
¹tabernacle. And was given to it ³war ¹to ²make with the

ἁγίων, καὶ νικῆσαι αὐτούς·᾿ καὶ ἐδόθη αὐτῷ ἐξουσία ἐπὶ
saints, and to overcome them; and was given to it authority over

πᾶσαν φυλὴν ᵍ καὶ γλῶσσαν καὶ ἔθνος. 8 καὶ προσκυνήσου-
every tribe, and tongue, and nation; and shall do homage

σιν ʰαὐτῷ᾿ πάντες οἱ κατοικοῦντες ἐπὶ τῆς γῆς ⁱὧν᾿ οὐ
to it all who dwell on the earth of whom ²not

γέγραπται ᵏτὰ ὀνόματα᾿ ἐν ˡτῇ βίβλῳ᾿ τῆς ζωῆς τοῦ
¹have been written the names ⁷in ⁸the ⁹book ¹⁰of ¹¹life ¹²of ¹³the

ἀρνίου ᵐἐσφαγμένου ἀπὸ καταβολῆς κόσμου. 9 Εἰ
¹⁶Lamb ¹⁴slain ¹from [²the] ³founding ⁴of [⁵the] ⁶world. If

τις ἔχει οὖς, ἀκουσάτω. 10 Εἴ τις ⁿ ᵒαἰχμαλωσίαν᾿
anyone has an ear, let him hear. If anyone [²into] ³captivity

Ρσυνάγει,᾿ εἰς αἰχμαλωσίαν ὑπάγει· εἴ τις ἐν ᑫμαχαίρᾳ᾿
¹gathers, into captivity he goes. If anyone with [the] sword

ʳἀποκτενεῖ,᾿ ˢδεῖ᾿ αὐτὸν ἐν ᑫμαχαίρᾳ᾿ ἀποκτανθῆναι· ὧδέ
will kill, ²must ¹he with [the] sword be killed. Here

ἐστιν ἡ ὑπομονὴ καὶ ἡ πίστις τῶν ἁγίων.
is the endurance and the faith of the saints.

11 And I beheld another beast coming up out of the earth; and he had two horns like a lamb, and he spake as a dragon. 12 And he exerciseth all the power of the first beast before him, and causeth the earth and them which dwell therein to worship the first beast, whose deadly wound was healed. 13 And he doeth great wonders, so that he maketh fire come down from heaven on the earth in the sight of men, 14 and deceiveth them that dwell on the earth by the means of those miracles which

11 Καὶ εἶδον ἄλλο θηρίον ἀναβαῖνον ἐκ τῆς γῆς, καὶ
And I saw another beast rising out of the earth, and

εἶχεν κέρατα δύο ὅμοια ἀρνίῳ, καὶ ἐλάλει ὡς δράκων. 12 καὶ
it had ²horns ¹two like to a lamb, and spoke as a dragon; and

τὴν ἐξουσίαν τοῦ πρώτου θηρίου πᾶσαν ποιεῖ ἐνώπιον
²the ³authority ⁴of ⁵the ⁶first ⁷beast ¹all it exercises before

αὐτοῦ· καὶ ποιεῖ τὴν γῆν καὶ τοὺς ᵗκατοικοῦντας ἐν αὐτῇ᾿
it, and causes the earth and those who dwell in it

ἵνα ᵛπροσκυνήσωσιν᾿ τὸ θηρίον τὸ πρῶτον, οὗ ἐθερα-
that they should do homage to the ²beast ¹first, of whom was

πεύθη ἡ πληγὴ τοῦ θανάτου αὐτοῦ· 13 καὶ ποιεῖ σημεῖα
healed the wound of its death. And it works ²signs

μεγάλα, ʷἵνα καὶ πῦρ ποιῇ᾿ ˣκαταβαίνειν ἐκ τοῦ οὐ-
¹great, that even fire it should cause to come down out of the hea-

ρανοῦ᾿ εἰς τὴν γῆν ἐνώπιον τῶν ἀνθρώπων. 14 καὶ πλανᾷ
ven to the earth before men. And it misleads

τοὺς κατοικοῦντας ἐπὶ τῆς γῆς, διὰ τὰ σημεῖα ἃ
those who dwell on the earth, by reason of the signs which

ʸ βλάσφημα blasphemous [things] LA. ᶻ + πόλεμον war (read ποιῇ. to make) Ε. ᵃ τεσ-
σαρακονταδύο Ε; τεσσεράκοντα δύο LTTrA. ᵇ + [καὶ] and L. ᶜ βλασφημίας LTTrAW.
ᵈ — καὶ LTTrAW. ᵉ — καὶ ἐδόθη... νικῆσαι αὐτούς L. ᶠ ποιῆσαι πόλεμον TTrA. ᵍ +. καὶ
λαὸν and people GLTTrAW. ʰ αὐτὸν GLTTrAW. ⁱ οὗ (read [everyone] of whom has
not been written) LTTrA. ᵏ τὸ ὄνομα αὐτοῦ his name LTTrA; τὸ ὄνομα the name GW.
ˡ τῷ βιβλίῳ GLTTrAW. ᵐ + τοῦ (read which was slain) GLTTrAW. ⁿ + εἰς [is]
for LTAW. ᵒ — αἰχμαλωσίαν (read εἰς for) Tr. ᵖ — συνάγει LTTrAW. ᑫ μαχαίρῃ
LTTrA. ʳ ἀποκτείνει kills L; ἀποκτανθῆναι to be killed A. ˢ — δεῖ Α. ᵗ ἐν αὐτῇ
κατοικοῦντας GTTrA. ᵛ προσκυνήσουσιν they shall do homage LTTrA. ʷ καὶ πῦρ ἵνα
GW. ˣ ἐκ τοῦ οὐρανοῦ καταβαίνειν (καταβῇ G; καταβαίνῃ should come down W) GLTrA

ἐδόθη αὐτῷ ποιῆσαι ἐνώπιον τοῦ θηρίου, λέγων τοῖς
it was given to it to work before the beast, saying to those who

κατοικοῦσιν ἐπὶ τῆς γῆς, ποιῆσαι ᶻεἰκόνα‖ τῷ θηρίῳ ᵃᵈ‖
dwell on the earth, to make an image to the beast, which

ἔχει τὴν πληγὴν τῆς ᵇμαχαίρας‖ καὶ ἔζησεν. 15 καὶ ἐδόθη
has the wound of the sword, and lived. And it was given

ᶜαὐτῷ ᵈδοῦναι πνεῦμα‖ τῇ εἰκόνι τοῦ θηρίου, ἵνα καὶ λα-
to it to give breath to the image of the beast, that also should

λήσῃ ἡ εἰκὼν τοῦ θηρίου, καὶ ποιήσῃ, ᵉ ὅσοι ᶠἂν‖ μὴ
speak the image of the beast, and should cause as many as not

ᵍπροσκυνήσωσιν‖ ʰτὴν εἰκόνα‖ τοῦ θηρίου ⁱἵνα‖ ἀποκτανθῶσιν.
would do homage to the image of the beast that they should be killed.

16 καὶ ποιεῖ πάντας, τοὺς μικροὺς καὶ τοὺς μεγάλους, καὶ
And it causes all, the small and the great, and

τοὺς πλουσίους καὶ τοὺς πτωχούς, καὶ τοὺς ἐλευθέρους καὶ
the rich and the poor, and the free and

τοὺς δούλους, ἵνα ᵏδώσῃ‖ αὐτοῖς χάραγμα ἐπὶ τῆς χειρὸς
the bondmen, that it should give them a mark on hand

αὐτῶν τῆς δεξιᾶς, ἢ ἐπὶ ˡτῶν μετώπων‖ αὐτῶν, 17 ᵐκαὶ‖ ἵνα
their right, or on foreheads their; and that

μή.τις δύνηται ἀγοράσαι ἢ πωλῆσαι, εἰ.μὴ ὁ ἔχων τὸ
no one should be able to buy or to sell, except he who has the

χάραγμα ⁿἢ‖ ᵒτὸ ὄνομα‖ τοῦ θηρίου, ἢ τὸν ἀριθμὸν τοῦ
mark or the name of the beast, or the number

ὀνόματος αὐτοῦ. 18 ᵖὯδε ἡ σοφία ἐστίν. ὁ ἔχων Pτὸν‖
name of its. Here wisdom is. He who has

νοῦν, ψηφισάτω τὸν ἀριθμὸν τοῦ θηρίου· ἀριθμὸς.γὰρ
understanding let him count the number of the beast: for number

ἀνθρώπου ἐστίν, καὶ ὁ.ἀριθμὸς.αὐτοῦ ᑫ ᵡξϛʹ.‖
a man's it is; and its number [is] 666.

14 Καὶ ˢεἶδον,‖ καὶ ἰδού, ᵗ ἀρνίον ᵛἑστηκὸς‖ ἐπὶ τὸ ὄρος
And I saw, and behold, [the] Lamb standing upon mount

Σιών, καὶ μετ' αὐτοῦ ἑκατὸν ʷτεσσαράκοντα τέσσαρες‖
Sion, and with him a hundred [and] forty four

χιλιάδες, ἔχουσαι τὸ ὄνομα ˣ τοῦ.πατρὸς.αὐτοῦ γεγραμμένον
thousand, having the name of his Father written

ἐπὶ τῶν.μετώπων.αὐτῶν. 2 καὶ ἤκουσα φωνὴν ἐκ τοῦ οὐ-
on their foreheads. And I heard a voice out of the hea-

ρανοῦ ὡς φωνὴν ὑδάτων πολλῶν, καὶ ὡς φωνὴν βροντῆς
ven as a voice of waters many, and as a voice of thunder

μεγάλης· καὶ ʸφωνὴν ἤκουσα‖ ᶻᵃκιθαρῳδῶν κιθαριζόντων ἐν
great: and a voice I heard of harpers harping with

ταῖς.κιθάραις.αὐτῶν. 3 καὶ ᾄδουσιν ᵃᵃὡς‖ ᾠδὴν καινὴν ἐνώ-
their harps. And they sing as a song new

πιον τοῦ θρόνου, καὶ ἐνώπιον τῶν τεσσάρων ζώων καὶ
fore the throne, and before the four living creatures and

τῶν πρεσβυτέρων· καὶ οὐδεὶς ᵇᵃἠδύνατο‖ μαθεῖν τὴν ᾠδήν,
the elders. And no one was able to learn the song

ᶻ εἰκόναν L.   ᵃ ὃς who LTTrAW.   ᵇ μαχαίρης LTTrA.   ᶜ αὐτῇ (that is, the image) L.
ᵈ πνεῦμα δοῦναι W.   ᵉ + ἵνα that LTr[A]W.   ᶠ ἐὰν LTTrA.   ᵍ προσκυνήσωσιν shall do
homage T.   ʰ τῇ εἰκόνι GTTrW.   ⁱ — ἵνα (omit that they) LTTrAW.   ᵏ δῶσιν they should
give GLTTrAW.   ˡ τὸ μέτωπον forehead GLTTrAW.   ᵐ — καὶ LT[A].   ⁿ — ἢ GLTTrAW.
ᵒ τοῦ ὀνόματος of the name L.   ᵖ — τὸν GLTTrAW.   ᑫ + ἐστιν is Tr.   ʳ ἑξακόσιοι ἑξήκοντα
ἓξ six hundred [and] sixty-six LA.   ˢ ἴδον T.   ᵗ + τὸ the GLTTrAW.   ᵛ ἑστὸς LTTrAW.
ʷ τεσσαρακοντατέσσαρες EGW ; τεσσεράκοντα τέσσαρες LTTrA.   ˣ + αὐτοῦ καὶ τὸ ὄνομα
(read his name and the name) GLTTrAW.   ʸ ἡ φωνὴ ἣν ἤκουσα the voice which I heard
[was] GLTTrAW.   ᶻᵃ + ὡς as GLTTrAW.   ᵃᵃ — ὡς GT[Tra].   ᵇᵃ ἐδύνατο LTT.A.

he had power to do in the sight of the beast; saying to those that dwell on the earth, that they should make an image to the beast, which had the wound by a sword, and did live. 15 And he had power to give life unto the image of the beast, that the image of the beast should both speak, and cause that as many as would not worship the image of the beast should be killed. 16 And he causeth all, both small and great, rich and poor, free and bond, to receive a mark in their right hand, or in their foreheads : 17 and that no man might buy or sell, save he that had the mark, or the name of the beast, or the number of his name. 18 Here is wisdom. Let him that hath understanding count the number of the beast: for it is the number of a man; and his number is six hundred threescore and six.

XIV. And I looked, and, lo, a Lamb stood on the mount Sion, and with him an hundred forty and four thousand, having his Father's name written in their foreheads. 2 And I heard a voice from heaven, as the voice of many waters, and as the voice of a great thunder: and I heard the voice of harpers harping with their harps: 3 and they sung as it were a new song before the throne, and before the four beasts, and the elders: and no man could learn that song but the hundred and

forty *and* four thousand, which were redeemed from the earth.
4 These are they which were not defiled with women ; for they are virgins. These are they which follow the Lamb whithersoever he goeth. These were redeemed from among men, *being* the firstfruits unto God and to the Lamb. 5 And in their mouth was found no guile : for they are without fault before the throne of God.

εἰ.μὴ αἱ ἑκατὸν ᶜτεσσαράκοντα τέσσαρες‖ χιλιάδες, οἱ
except the hundred [and] forty four thousand, who

ἠγορασμένοι ἀπὸ τῆς γῆς. 4 οὗτοί εἰσιν οἳ μετὰ
have been purchased from the earth. These are they who with

γυναικῶν οὐκ.ἐμολύνθησαν· παρθένοι.γάρ εἰσιν· οὗτοί ᵈεἰσιν‖
women were not defiled, for virgins they are : these are

οἱ ἀκολουθοῦντες τῷ ἀρνίῳ ὅπου ἂν ᵉὑπάγῃ.‖ οὗτοι
they who follow the Lamb wheresoever he may go. These

ἠγοράσθησαν ἀπὸ τῶν ἀνθρώπων, ἀπαρχὴ τῷ θεῷ καὶ
were purchased from among men [as] firstfruits to God and

τῷ ἀρνίῳ. 5 καὶ ἐν τῷ.στόματι.αὐτῶν οὐχ.εὑρέθη ᶠδόλος·‖
to the Lamb : and in their mouth was not found guile ;

ἄμωμοι.ᵍγάρ‖ εἰσιν ʰἐνώπιον τοῦ θρόνου τοῦ θεοῦ.‖
for blameless they are before the throne of God.

6 And I saw another angel fly in the midst of heaven, having the everlasting gospel to preach unto them that dwell on the earth, and to every nation, and kindred, and tongue, and people, 7 saying with a loud voice, Fear God, and give glory to him ; for the hour of his judgment is come : and worship him that made heaven, and earth, and the sea, and the fountains of waters.

6 Καὶ εἶδον ⁱἄλλον‖ ἄγγελον ʲπετώμενον‖ ἐν μεσου-
And I saw another angel flying in mid-

ρανήματι, ἔχοντα εὐαγγέλιον αἰώνιον εὐαγγελίσαιᵏ
heaven, having [the] ²glad ³tidings ¹everlasting to announce [to]

τοὺς ¹κατοικοῦντας‖ ἐπὶ τῆς γῆς, καὶ ᵐ πᾶν ἔθνος καὶ φυλὴν
those who dwell on the earth, and every nation and tribe

καὶ γλῶσσαν καὶ λαόν, 7 ⁿλέγοντα‖ °ἐν‖ φωνῇ μεγάλῃ,
and tongue and people, saying with a ²voice ¹loud,

Φοβήθητε τὸν θεόν, καὶ δότε αὐτῷ δόξαν, ὅτι ἦλθεν ἡ ὥρα
Fear God, and give to him glory, because is come the hour

τῆς.κρίσεως.αὐτοῦ· καὶ προσκυνήσατε τῷ ποιήσαντι τὸν
of his judgment ; and do homage to him who made the

οὐρανὸν καὶ τὴν γῆν καὶ ᴾ θάλασσαν καὶ πηγὰς ὑδάτων.
heaven and the earth and sea and fountains of waters.

8 And there followed another angel, saying, Babylon is fallen, is fallen, that great city, because she made all nations drink of the wine of the wrath of her fornication.

8 Καὶ ἄλλος ᑫἄγγελος‖ ἠκολούθησεν, λέγων, Ἔπεσεν ʳἔπε-
And another angel followed, saying, Is fallen, is

σεν‖ ˢΒαβυλὼν‖ ᵗἡ πόλις‖ ἡ μεγάλη ᵛὅτι‖ ἐκ τοῦ οἴνου τοῦ
fallen Babylon ³city ¹the ²great, because of the wine of the

θυμοῦ τῆς.πορνείας.αὐτῆς πεπότικεν πάντα ᵂ ἔθνη.
fury of her fornication she has given ⁴to ³drink ¹all ²nations.

9 And the third angel followed them, saying with a loud voice, If any man worship the beast and his image, and receive *his* mark in his forehead, or in his hand, 10 the same shall drink of the wine of the wrath of God, which is poured out without mixture into the cup of his indignation ; and he shall be tormented with fire and brimstone in the presence of the holy angels, and in the presence of the Lamb :

9 Καὶ ˣ ᔆτριτος ἄγγελος‖ ἠκολούθησεν αὐτοῖς, λέγων ἐν
And a third angel followed them, saying with

φωνῇ μεγάλῃ, Εἴ τις ᶻτὸ θηρίον προσκυνεῖ‖ καὶ τὴν
a ²voice ¹loud, If anyone ⁴the beast ¹does ²homage ³to and

εἰκόνα αὐτοῦ, καὶ λαμβάνει χάραγμα ἐπὶ τοῦ.μετώπου.αὐτοῦ,
²image ¹its, and receives a mark on his forehead

ἢ ἐπὶ τὴν.χεῖρα.αὐτοῦ, 10 καὶ αὐτὸς πίεται ἐκ τοῦ οἴνου
or upon his hand, also he shall drink of the wine

τοῦ θυμοῦ τοῦ θεοῦ, τοῦ κεκερασμένου ἀκράτου ἐν τῷ
of the fury of God which is mixed undiluted in the

ποτηρίῳ τῆς.ὀργῆς.αὐτοῦ, καὶ βασανισθήσεται ἐν πυρὶ καὶ
cup of his wrath, and he shall be tormented in fire and

θείῳ. ἐνώπιον ᵃτῶν‖ ᵇἁγίων ἀγγέλων,‖ καὶ ἐνώπιον τοῦ
brimstone, before the holy angels, and before the

ᶜ τεσσαρακοντατέσσαρες EGW ; τεσσεράκοντα τέσσαρες LTTrA.   ᵈ — εἰσιν (*read* [are])
LTTrA.   ᵉ ὑπάγει he goes LTrA.   ᶠ ψεῦδος falsehood GLTTrAW.   ᵍ — γάρ for LA.
ʰ — ἐνώπιον τοῦ θρόνου τοῦ θεοῦ GLTTrAW.   ⁱ [ἄλλον] A.   ʲ πετόμενον GLTTrAW.
ᵏ + ἐπὶ unto LTTrAW.   ¹ καθημένους sit GLTTrAW.   ᵐ + ἐπὶ unto GLTTrAW.   ⁿ λέγων
GLTTrAW.   ° — ἐν (*read* φωνῇ with a voice) L.   ᴾ + τὴν the GTW.   ᑫ δεύτερος
ἄγγελος a second angel LTrAW ; ἄγ. δεύ. T.   ʳ [ἔπεσεν] A.   ˢ Βαβυλὼν E.   ᵗ — ἡ
πόλις GLTTrAW.   ᵛ ἣ which (*read* πεπ. has given to drink) LTTrAW.   ᵂ + τὰ the
LTTrAW.   ˣ + ἄλλος another GLTTrAW.   ʸ ἄγγελος τρίτος GLTTrAW.   ᶻ προσκυνεῖ
τὸ θηρίον GLTTrAW.   ᵃ — τῶν LTTr.   ᵇ ἀγγέλων ἁγίων LTTr ; — ἁγίων A.

ἀρνίου· 11 καὶ ὁ καπνὸς τοῦ.βασανισμοῦ.αὐτῶν °ἀναβαίνει
Lamb.   And the   smoke   of their torment   goes up

εἰς αἰῶνας αἰώνων·‖ καὶ οὐκ.ἔχουσιν ἀνάπαυσιν ἡμέρας καὶ
to   ages   of ages,   and they have no   respite   day   and

νυκτὸς οἱ προσκυνοῦντες τὸ θηρίον καὶ τὴν.εἰκόνα.αὐτοῦ, καὶ
night who do homage to   the beast   and   its image,   and

εἴ τις λαμβάνει τὸ χάραγμα τοῦ.ὀνόματος.αὐτοῦ. 12 ʳὮδε d
if anyone receives the mark   of its name.   Here [²the]

ὑπομονὴ τῶν ἁγίων ἐστίν· ᵉὧδε‖ οἱ τηροῦντες τὰς ἐν-
³endurance ⁴of ⁵the ⁶saints ¹is,   here they who   keep   the command-

τολὰς τοῦ θεοῦ καὶ τὴν πιστιν Ἰησοῦ.
ments   of God and the   faith   of Jesus.

13 Καὶ ἤκουσα φωνῆς ἐκ τοῦ οὐρανοῦ, λεγούσης ᶠμοι,‖
   And I heard a voice out of the heaven,   saying   to me,

Γράψον, Μακάριοι οἱ νεκροὶ οἱ ἐν   κυρίῳ ἀποθνήσκοντες
Write,   Blessed   the dead   who in [the] Lord   die

ᵍἀπάρτι.‖ Ναί, λέγει τὸ πνεῦμα, ἵνα ʰἀναπαύσωνται‖ ἐκ
from henceforth. Yea, saith the Spirit, that they may rest   from

τῶν.κόπων.αὐτῶν· τὰ ⁱδὲ‖ ἔργα αὐτῶν ἀκολουθεῖ μετ' αὐτῶν.
  their labours ;   and ²works ¹their   follow   with them.

14 Καὶ ᵏεἶδον,‖ καὶ ἰδού, νεφέλη λευκή, καὶ ἐπὶ τὴν νεφέλην
   And I saw, and behold, a ²cloud ¹white, and upon the   cloud

¹καθήμενος ὅμοιος‖ ᵐυἱῷ‖ ἀνθρώπου, ἔχων ἐπὶ ⁿτῆς‖
[one]   sitting   like [the] Son   of man,   having on

κεφαλῆς‖ αὐτοῦ στέφανον χρυσοῦν, καὶ ἐν τῇ.χειρὶ.αὐτοῦ δρέ-
²head   ¹his   a ²crown   ¹golden;   and in   his hand   a sic-

πανον ὀξύ. 15 καὶ ἄλλος ἄγγελος ἐξῆλθεν ἐκ τοῦ ναοῦ,
²sickle ¹sharp.   And another   angel   came out of the   temple,

κράζων ἐν °μεγάλῃ φωνῇ‖ τῷ καθημένῳ ἐπὶ τῆς νεφέλης,
crying with a   loud   voice to him   sitting   on   the   cloud,

Πέμψον τὸ.δρέπανόν.σου,.καὶ θέρισον, ὅτι ἦλθέν ᵖσοι‖ ἡ
Send   thy sickle   and reap; because is come to thee the

ὥρα ᑫτοῦᵈ θερίσαι, ὅτι ἐξηράνθη ὁ θερισμὸς τῆς γῆς. 16 Καὶ
hour   to reap, because is dried the harvest of the earth.   And

ἔβαλεν ὁ καθήμενος ἐπὶ ʳτὴν νεφέλην‖ τὸ.δρέπανον.αὐτοῦ
ᵉput ⁷forth ¹he   ²sitting ³upon ⁴the   ⁵cloud   his sickle

ἐπὶ τὴν γῆν, καὶ ἐθερίσθη ἡ γῆ.
upon the   earth, and was reaped the earth.

17 Καὶ ἄλλος ἄγγελος ἐξῆλθεν ἐκ τοῦ ναοῦ τοῦ ἐν τῷ
   And another   angel   came   out of the temple which [is] in the

οὐρανῷ, ἔχων καὶ αὐτὸς δρέπανον ὀξύ. 18 καὶ ἄλλος ἄγ-
heaven, ³having ²also ¹he   a ²sickle ¹sharp.   And another an-

γελος ˢἐξῆλθεν‖ ἐκ τοῦ θυσιαστηρίου, ᵗἔχων ἐξουσίαν ἐπὶ τοῦ
gel   came   out of the   altar,   having authority over

πυρός, καὶ ἐφώνησεν ᵛκραυγῇ‖ μεγάλῃ τῷ ἔχοντι τὸ δρέπανον
fire,   and he called   with a ²cry ¹loud   to him having   ³sickle

τὸ ὀξύ, λέγων, Πέμψον σου τὸ δρέπανον τὸ ὀξύ, καὶ τρύγη-
⁴the ²sharp, saying,   Send   thy   ²sickle   ¹sharp, and gather

σον τοὺς βότρυας ᵂ τῆς γῆς, ὅτι ἤκμασαν · αἱ σταφυλαὶ
the   bunches   of the earth; because are fully ripe   ²grapes

---

ᶜ εἰς αἰῶνας αἰώνων ἀναβαίνει GLTTrAW.   ᵈ + ἡ τὴν LTTrAW.   ᵉ — ὧδε GLTTrAW.
ᶠ — μοι GLTTrAW.   ᵍ ἀπ᾽ ἄρτι GLA.   ʰ ἀναπαήσονται they shall rest LTTrA ; ἀναπαύσονται
they shall rest W.   ⁱ γὰρ for LTTrA.   ᵏ ἴδον T.   ¹ καθήμενον ὅμοιον GLTTrAW.
ᵐ υἱὸν T.   ⁿ τὴν κεφαλὴν LT.   ° φωνῇ μεγάλῃ GLTTrAW.   ᵖ — σοι GLTTrAW.
ᑫ — τοῦ LTTrAW.   ʳ τῆς νεφέλης LTTrA.   ˢ — ἐξῆλθεν L.   ᵗ + ὁ who (read ἔχων
has) LAW.   ᵛ φωνῇ with a voice LTTr.   ᵂ + τῆς ἀμπέλου of the vine EGLTTrAW.

11 and the smoke of their torment ascendeth up, for ever and ever: and they have no rest day nor night, who worship the beast and his image, and whosoever receiveth the mark of his name. 12 Here is the patience of the saints : here are they that keep the commandments of God, and the faith of Jesus.

13 And I heard a voice from heaven saying unto me, Write, Blessed are the dead which die in the Lord from henceforth: Yea, saith the Spirit, that they may rest from their labours ; and their works do follow them.

14 And I looked, and behold a white cloud, and upon the cloud one sat like unto the Son of man, having on his head a golden crown, and in his hand a sharp sickle. 15 And another angel came out of the temple, crying with a loud voice to him that sat on the cloud, Thrust in thy sickle, and reap : for the time is come for thee to reap ; for the harvest of the earth is ripe. 16 And he that sat on the cloud thrust in his sickle on the earth; and the earth was reaped.

17 And another angel came out of the temple which is in heaven, he also having a sharp sickle. 18 And another angel came out from the altar, which had power over fire ; and cried with a loud cry to him that had the sharp sickle, saying, Thrust in thy sharp sickle, and gather the clusters of the vine of the earth ; for her grapes

are fully ripe. 19 And the angel thrust in his sickle into the earth, and gathered the vine of the earth, and cast *it* into the great winepress of the wrath of God. 20 And the winepress was trodden without the city, and blood came out of the winepress, even unto the horse bridles, by the space of a thousand *and* six hundred furlongs.

αὐτῆς. 19 Καὶ ἔβαλεν ὁ ἄγγελος τὸ.δρέπανον.αὐτοῦ εἰς
¹her.   And ⁴put ⁵forth ¹the ²angel   his sickle   to

τὴν γῆν, καὶ ἐτρύγησεν τὴν ἄμπελον τῆς γῆς, καὶ ἔβαλεν
the earth, and gathered the   vine of the earth, and cast [the fruit]

εἰς τὴν ληνὸν τοῦ. θυμοῦ τοῦ θεοῦ ˣτὴν μεγάλην.‖ 20 καὶ
into   ³winepress ⁴of ⁵the ⁶fury   ⁷of ⁸God ¹the   ²great ;   and

ἐπατήθη ἡ ληνὸς ʸἔξω‖ τῆς πόλεως, καὶ ἐξῆλθεν αἷμα
was trodden the winepress outside the   city,   and ²came ³forth ¹blood

ἐκ τῆς ληνοῦ ἄχρι τῶν χαλινῶν τῶν ἵππων, ἀπὸ
out of the winepress as far as the   bits   of the horses, to the distance of

σταδίων χιλίων ἐξακοσίων.
⁵furlongs ¹a ²thousand ³six ⁴hundred.

XV. And I saw another sign in heaven, great and marvellous, seven angels having the seven last plagues; for in them is filled up the wrath of God.

15 Καὶ ᵃεἶδον‖ ἄλλο σημεῖον ἐν τῷ οὐρανῷ μέγα καὶ θαυ-
   And I saw another   sign   in the heaven, great and won-

μαστόν, ἀγγέλους ἑπτά, ἔχοντας πληγὰς ἑπτὰ τὰς ἐσχάτας,
derful :   ²angels ¹seven, having   ²plagues ¹seven, the   last ;

ὅτι ἐν αὐταῖς ἐτελέσθη ὁ θυμὸς τοῦ θεοῦ.
because in them was completed the fury   of God.

2 And I saw as it were a sea of glass mingled with fire: and them that had gotten the victory over the beast, and over his image, and over his mark, *and* over the number of his name, stand on the sea of glass, having the harps of God. 3 And they sing the song of Moses the servant of God, and the song of the Lamb, saying, Great and marvellous *are* thy works, Lord God Almighty; just and true *are* thy ways, thou King of saints. 4 Who shall not fear thee, O Lord, and glorify thy name? for *thou* only *art* holy : for all nations shall come and worship before thee; for thy judgments are made manifest.

2 Καὶ ᵃεἶδον‖ ὡς θάλασσαν ὑαλίνην μεμιγμένην πυρί,
   And I saw as a ²sea   ¹glass   mingled with fire,

καὶ τοὺς νικῶντας ἐκ τοῦ θηρίου καὶ ἐκ τῆς.εἰκόνος.αὐτοῦ
and the overcomers of the   beast, and of   its image,

καὶ ᵇἐκ τοῦ.χαράγματος.αὐτοῦ,‖ ἐκ τοῦ ἀριθμοῦ τοῦ ὀνόματος
and of   its mark,   of the number of the ⁷name

αὐτοῦ, ἑστῶτας ἐπὶ τὴν θάλασσαν τὴν ὑαλίνην, ἔχοντας
¹of ²its, standing upon the ²sea   ¹glass,   having

κιθάρας τοῦ θεοῦ. 3 καὶ ᾄδουσιν τὴν ᾠδὴν ᶜΜωσέως‖ ᵈ δού-
harps   of God.   And they sing the song of Moses,   bond-

λου τοῦ θεοῦ, καὶ τὴν ᾠδὴν τοῦ ἀρνίου, λέγοντες, Μεγάλα καὶ
man   of God, and the song of the Lamb,   saying,   Great   and

θαυμαστὰ τὰ.ἔργα.σου, κύριε ὁ θεὸς ὁ παντοκράτωρ· δί-
wonderful [are] thy works, Lord   God   Almighty ;   right-

καιαι καὶ ἀληθιναὶ αἱ.ὁδοί.σου, ὁ βασιλεὺς τῶν ᵉἁγίων.‖
eous and true [are] thy ways, [thou]   King   of saints.

4 τίς οὐ μὴ φοβηθῇ ᶠσε,‖ κύριε, καὶ ᵍδοξάσῃ‖ τὸ.ὄνομά.σου;
Who ²not ¹should fear thee, O Lord, and glorify   thy name ?

ὅτι μόνος ὅσιος· ὅτι πάντα τὰ ἔθνη ἥξουσιν καὶ
for [thou] only [art] holy ; for all   the nations shall come and

προσκυνήσουσιν ἐνώπιόν σου· ὅτι τὰ.δικαιώματά.σου
do homage   before   thee ; for   thy righteous   [acts]
                             (*lit.* righteousnesses)

ἐφανερώθησαν.
were manifested.

5 And after that I looked, and, behold, the temple of the tabernacle of the testimony in heaven was opened : 6 and the seven angels came out of the temple, having the seven plagues, clothed in pure and white linen, and having their breasts girded with golden girdles. 7 And one of the

5 Καὶ μετὰ ταῦτα ᵃεἶδον,‖ καὶ ʰἰδού,‖ ἠνοίγη ὁ ναὸς
   And after these things I saw, and behold, was opened the temple

τῆς σκηνῆς τοῦ μαρτυρίου ἐν τῷ οὐρανῷ· 6 καὶ ἐξῆλθον οἱ
of the tabernacle of the testimony in the heaven ;   and came forth the

ἑπτὰ ἄγγελοι ⁱ ἔχοντες τὰς ἑπτὰ πληγάς, ἐκ τοῦ ναοῦ,
seven angels   ²having ⁶the ⁷seven ⁸plagues ¹out ²of ³the ⁴temple,

ἐνδεδυμένοι ᵏλίνον‖ καθαρὸν ˡκαὶ‖ λαμπρόν, καὶ περιεζωσμένοι
clothed in   linen   pure   and   bright,   and   girt with

περὶ τὰ στήθη ζώνας χρυσᾶς. 7 καὶ ἓν ἐκ τῶν τεσσάρων
³about ⁴the ⁵breasts ²girdles ¹golden.   And one of the   four

---

ˣ τὸν μέγαν GLTTrAW.   ʸ ἔξωθεν GLTTrAW.   ᵃ ἴδον T.   ᵇ — ἐκ τοῦ χαράγματος
αὐτοῦ GLTTrAW.   ᶜ Μωϋσέως GLTTrAW.   ᵈ + τοῦ the LTTrA.   ᵉ ἐθνῶν of nations
GLTTrAW.   ᶠ σε LTTrA.   ᵍ δοξάσει shall glorify LTTrAW.   ʰ — ἰδού GLTTrAW.
ⁱ + οἱ those GLTTr[A]W.   ᵏ λίθον stone LTr.   ˡ — καὶ GLTTrAW.

ζώων   ἔδωκεν τοῖς ἑπτὰ ἀγγέλοις ἑπτὰ φιάλας χρυσᾶς,
living creatures gave to the seven angels seven ²bowls ˈgolden,

γεμούσας τοῦ θυμοῦ τοῦ θεοῦ τοῦ ζῶντος εἰς τοὺς αἰῶνας
full of the fury of God, who lives to the ages

τῶν αἰώνων. 8 καὶ ἐγεμίσθη ὁ ναὸς καπνοῦ ἐκ τῆς δόξης
of the ages. And ³was.⁴filled ¹the ²temple with smoke from the glory

τοῦ θεοῦ, καὶ ἐκ τῆς.δυνάμεως.αὐτοῦ· καὶ οὐδεὶς ᵐἠδύνατο‖
of God, and from his power: and no one ʷas able

εἰσελθεῖν εἰς τὸν ναόν, ἄχρι τελεσθῶσιν αἱ ἑπτὰ πληγαὶ τῶν
to enter into the temple until were completed the seven plagues of the

ἑπτὰ ἀγγέλων.
seven angels.

16 Καὶ ἤκουσα ⁿφωνῆς μεγάλης‖ ἐκ τοῦ ναοῦ, λεγούσης
And I heard a ²voice ˈloud out of the temple, saying

τοῖς ἑπτὰ ἀγγέλοις, Ὑπάγετε, καὶ ᵒἐκχέατε‖ τὰς ᵖ φιάλας τοῦ
to the seven angels, Go, and pour out the bowls of the

θυμοῦ τοῦ θεοῦ εἰς τὴν γῆν.
fury of God into the earth.

2 Καὶ ἀπῆλθεν ὁ πρῶτος, καὶ ἐξέχεεν τὴν.φιάλην.αὐτοῦ
And ³departed ¹the ²first, and poured out his bowl

�qἐπὶ‖ τὴν γῆν· καὶ ἐγένετο ἕλκος κακὸν καὶ πονηρὸν ʳεἰς‖ τοὺς
on to the ²earth; and came a sore, evil and grievous, upon the

ἀνθρώπους τοὺς ἔχοντας τὸ χάραγμα τοῦ θηρίου, καὶ τοὺς
men who had the mark of the beast, and those

ˢτῇ.εἰκόνι.αὐτοῦ προσκυνοῦντας.‖
ˢto ⁴his ⁵image ¹doing ²homage.

3 Καὶ ὁ δεύτερος ᵗἄγγελος‖ ἐξέχεεν τὴν.φιάλην.αὐτοῦ εἰς
And the second angel poured out his bowl into

τὴν θάλασσαν· καὶ ἐγένετο αἷμα ὡς νεκροῦ, καὶ πᾶσα ψυχὴ
the sea; and it became blood, as of [one] dead; and every ²soul

ᵛζῶσα‖ ἀπέθανεν ʷ ἐν τῇ θαλάσσῃ.
¹living died in the sea.

4 Καὶ ὁ τρίτος ˣἄγγελος‖ ἐξέχεεν τὴν.φιάλην.αὐτοῦ εἰς
And the third angel poured out his bowl into

τοὺς ποταμοὺς καὶ ʸεἰς‖ τὰς πηγὰς τῶν ὑδάτων· καὶ ᶻἐγένετο‖
the rivers, and into the fountains of waters; and they became

αἷμα. 5 καὶ ἤκουσα τοῦ ἀγγέλου τῶν ὑδάτων λέγοντος,
blood. And I heard the angel of the waters saying,

Δίκαιος, ᵃκύριε,‖ εἶ, ὁ ὢν καὶ ὁ ἦν ᵇκαὶ ὁ‖ ὅσιος, ὅτι
Righteous, O Lord, art thou, who art and who wast and the holy one, that

ταῦτα ἔκρινας· 6 ὅτι ᶜαἷμα‖ ἁγίων καὶ προ-
these things thou didst judge; because [the] blood of saints and of pro-

φητῶν ἐξέχεαν, καὶ αἷμα αὐτοῖς ᵈἔδωκας‖ ᵉπιεῖν·‖ ἄξιοι
phets they poured out, and blood to them thou didst give to drink; ²worthy

ᶠγάρ‖ εἰσιν. 7 Καὶ ἤκουσα ᵍἄλλου ἐκ‖ τοῦ θυσιαστηρίου λέ-
for they are. And I heard another out of the altar say-

γοντος, Ναί, κύριε ὁ θεὸς ὁ παντοκράτωρ, ἀληθιναὶ καὶ δίκαιαι
ing, Yea, Lord God Almighty, true and righteous

αἱ.κρίσεις.σου.
[are] thy judgments.

8 Καὶ ὁ τέταρτος ˣἄγγελος‖ ἐξέχεεν τὴν.φιάλην.αὐτοῦ ἐπὶ
And the fourth angel poured out his bowl upon

four beasts gave unto the seven angels seven golden vials full of the wrath of God, who liveth for ever and ever. 8 And the temple was filled with smoke from the glory of God, and from his power; and no man was able to enter into the temple, till the seven plagues of the seven angels were fulfilled.

XVI. And I heard a great voice out of the temple saying to the seven angels, Go your ways, and pour out the vials of the wrath of God upon the earth.

2 And the first went, and poured out his vial upon the earth; and there fell a noisome and grievous sore upon the men which had the mark of the beast, and upon them which worshipped his image.

3 And the second angel poured out his vial upon the sea; and it became as the blood of a dead man: and every living soul died in the sea.

4 And the third angel poured out his vial upon the rivers and fountains of waters; and they became blood. 5 And I heard the angel of the waters say, Thou art righteous, O Lord, which art, and wast, and shalt be, because thou hast judged thus. 6 For they have shed the blood of saints and prophets, and thou hast given them blood to drink; for they are worthy. 7 And I heard another out of the altar say, Even so, Lord God Almighty, true and righteous are thy judgments.

8 And the fourth angel poured out his

ᵐ ἐδύνατο LTTrA. ⁿ μεγάλης φωνῆς LTAW. ᵒ ἐκχέετε LTA. ᵖ + ἑπτὰ seven GLTTrAW. q εἰς into LTTrAW. ʳ ἐπὶ upon LTTrAW. ˢ προσκυνοῦντας τῇ εἰκόνι αὐτοῦ GLTTrAW. ᵗ ἄγγελος LTTrAW. ᵛ ζωῆς (read soul of life) GLTTrA. ʷ + τὰ the [things] LTTrAW. ˣ — ἄγγελος GLTTrAW. ʸ — εἰς LTTrA. ᶻ ἐγένοντο L. ᵃ — κύριε GLTTrAW. ᵇ + καὶ GT; — καὶ ὁ (read ὅσιος holy) LTrAW. ᶜ αἷματα bloods T. ᵈ δέδωκας thou hast given LT.AW. ᵉ πὶν L; πεῖν TA. ᶠ — γάρ GLTTrAW. ᵍ — ἄλλου ἐκ GLTTrAW.

vial upon the sun; and power was given unto him to scorch men with fire. 9 And men were scorched with great heat, and blasphemed the name of God, which hath power over these plagues: and they repented not to give him glory.

τὸν ἥλιον· καὶ ἐδόθη αὐτῷ καυματίσαι τοὺς ἀνθρώπους ἐν
the   sun;   and it was given to it   to scorch   men   wi

πυρί· 9 καὶ ἐκαυματίσθησαν οἱ ἄνθρωποι καῦμα μέγα, κα
fire.   And ²were ³scorched   ¹men   with ²heat ¹great, a

ἐβλασφήμησαν τὸ ὄνομα τοῦ θεοῦ τοῦ.ἔχοντος ʰ ἐξουσίαν ἐπ
they blasphemed the name   of God,   who has   authority over

τὰς.πληγὰς.ταύτας, καὶ οὐ.μετενόησαν δοῦναι αὐτῷ δόξαν.
these plagues,   and   did not repent   to give him   glory.

10 And the fifth angel poured out his vial upon the seat of the beast; and his kingdom was full of darkness; and they gnawed their tongues for pain, 11 and blasphemed the God of heaven because of their pains and their sores, and repented not of their deeds.

10 Καὶ ὁ πέμπτος ¹ἄγγελος‖ ἐξέχεεν τὴν.φιάλην.αὐτοῦ ἐπ
And the   fifth   angel   poured out   his bowl   upon

τὸν θρόνον τοῦ θηρίου· καὶ ἐγένετο ἡ.βασιλεία.αὐτοῦ ἐσκοτω-
the throne of the beast;   and became ¹its ²kingdom   dark-

μένη· καὶ ᵏἐμασσῶντο‖ τὰς.γλώσσας.αὐτῶν ἐκ τοῦ πόνου,
ened;   and they were gnawing   their tongues   for the distress,

11 καὶ ἐβλασφήμησαν τὸν θεὸν τοῦ οὐρανοῦ ἐκ τῶν πόνων
and   blasphemed   the God of the heaven for ²distresses

αὐτῶν καὶ ἐκ τῶν.ἑλκῶν.αὐτῶν, καὶ οὐ.μετενόησαν ἐκ τῶν
¹their and for   their sores,   and   did not repent   of

ἔργων αὐτῶν.
²works ¹their.

12 And the sixth angel poured out his vial upon the great river Euphrates; and the water thereof was dried up, that the way of the kings of the east might be prepared. 13 And I saw three unclean spirits like frogs come out of the mouth of the dragon, and out of the mouth of the beast, and out of the mouth of the false prophet. 14 For they are the spirits of devils, which work miracles, which go forth unto the kings of the earth and of the whole world, to gather them to the battle of that great day of God Almighty. 15 Behold, I come as a thief. Blessed is he that watcheth, and keepeth his garments, lest he walk naked, and they see his shame. 16 And he gathered them together into a place called in the Hebrew tongue Armageddon.

12 Καὶ ὁ ἕκτος ¹ἄγγελος‖ ἐξέχεεν τὴν.φιάλην.αὐτοῦ ἐπὶ τὸν
And the sixth   angel   poured out   his bowl   upon the

ποταμὸν τὸν μέγαν ¹τὸν‖ Εὐφράτην· καὶ ἐξηράνθη τὸ ὕδωρ
²river   ¹great, • the   Euphrates;   and was dried up ²water

αὐτοῦ. ἵνα ἑτοιμασθῇ ἡ ὁδὸς τῶν· βασιλέων τῶν ἀπ
¹its,   that might be prepared the way of the kings ²the ¹from

ᵐἀνατολῶν‖ ἡλίου. 13 Καὶ ⁿεἶδον‖ ἐκ τοῦ στόματος τοῦ
rising   of [the] sun.   And   I saw   out of the mouth of the

δράκοντος, καὶ ἐκ τοῦ στόματος τοῦ θηρίου, καὶ ἐκ τοῦ
dragon,   and out of the   mouth of the beast,   and out of the

στόματος τοῦ ψευδοπροφήτου, πνεύματα τρία ἀκάθαρτα
mouth   of the   false prophet,   ³spirits ¹three ²unclean

ᵒὅμοια βατράχοις·‖ 14 εἰσὶν.γὰρ πνεύματα ᴾδαιμόνων‖ ποι-
like   frogs;   for they are   spirits   of demons   do-

οῦντα �q σημεῖα ἐκπορεύεσθαι‖ ἐπὶ τοὺς βασιλεῖς ʳτῆς γῆς καὶ
ing   signs,   to go forth   to   the kings   of the earth and

τῆς οἰκουμένης ὅλης, συναγαγεῖν αὐτοὺς εἰς ˢ πόλεμον
of the   ²habitable [²world] ¹whole to gather together them unto   battle

τῆς ᵗἡμέρας ἐκείνης τῆς μεγάλης‖ τοῦ θεοῦ τοῦ παντοκράτορος.
of ³day   ¹that   ²great   of God the   Almighty.

15 Ἰδού, ἔρχομαι ὡς κλέπτης. μακάριος ὁ γρηγορῶν,
Behold,   I come as   a thief.   Blessed   [is] he that   watches,

καὶ τηρῶν τὰ.ἱμάτια.αὐτοῦ, ἵνα μὴ γυμνὸς περιπατῇ, καὶ
and keeps   his garments,   that not   naked   he may walk, and

βλέπωσιν τὴν.ἀσχημοσύνην.αὐτοῦ. 16 καὶ συνήγαγεν
they see   his shame.   And he gathered together

αὐτοὺς εἰς τὸν τόπον τὸν καλούμενον Ἑβραϊστὶ ᵛἈρμα-
them   to the place   which   is called   in Hebrew   Arma-

γεδδών.‖
geddon.

17 And the seventh angel poured out his

17 Καὶ ὁ ἕβδομος ʷἄγγελος‖ ἐξέχεεν τὴν.φιάλην.αὐτοῦ
And the   seventh   angel   poured out   his bowl

ʰ + τὴν LTTrW.   ⁱ — ἄγγελος GLTTrAW.   ᵏ ἐμασῶντο LTTrAW.   ˡ — τὸν GT[Tr]
ᵐ ἀνατολῆς TTrA.   ⁿ ἴδον T.   ᵒ ὡς (as) βάτραχοι GLTTrAW.   ᴾ δαιμονίων GLTTrAW
q σημεῖα ἃ ἐκπορεύεται signs which go forth EGTTrAW; σημεῖα· ἐκπορεύεται signs: they g
forth L.   ʳ — τῆς γῆς καὶ GLTTrAW.   ˢ + τὸν the GLTTrAW.   ᵗ μεγάλης ἡμέρας ι.
ἡμέρας τῆς μεγάλης TTrA.   ᵛ Ἀρμαγεδών GLTTrAW.   ʷ — ἄγγελος GLTTrAW.

ˣεἰς‖ τὸν ἀέρα· καὶ ἐξῆλθεν φωνὴ ʸμεγάλη‖ ᶻἀπὸ‖ τοῦ ναοῦ
into the air; and came out a ᶻvoice ¹loud from the temple

ᵃτοῦ οὐρανοῦ,‖ ἀπὸ τοῦ θρόνου, λέγουσα, Γέγονεν. 18 Καὶ
of the heaven, from the throne, saying, It is done.   And

ἐγένοντο ᵇφωναὶ καὶ βρονταὶ καὶ ἀστραπαί,‖ καὶ ˢσεισμὸς
there were voices and thunders and lightnings; and ᵉearthquake

ἐγένετο μέγας, οἷος οὐκ.ἐγένετο ἀφ᾽ οὗ ᶜοἱ ἄνθρωποι ἐγέ-
ᵈthere ²was ³a ⁴great, such as was not since   men

νοντο‖ ἐπὶ τῆς γῆς, τηλικοῦτος σεισμὸς οὕτως μέγας. 19 καὶ
were on the earth, so mighty an earthquake, so great.   And

ἐγένετο ἡ πόλις ἡ μεγάλη εἰς τρία μέρη, καὶ αἱ πόλεις τῶν
⁵became ¹the ³city ²great into three parts; and the cities of the

ἐθνῶν ᵈἔπεσον·‖ καὶ Βαβυλὼν ἡ μεγάλη ἐμνήσθη ἐνώπιον
nations fell; and Babylon the great was remembered before

τοῦ θεοῦ, δοῦναι αὐτῇ τὸ ποτήριον τοῦ οἴνου τοῦ θυμοῦ τῆς
God, to give her the cup of the wine of the fury

ὀργῆς αὐτοῦ. 20 καὶ πᾶσα νῆσος ἔφυγεν, καὶ ὄρη οὐχ
³wrath ¹of ²his.   And every island fled; and ²mountains ¹no

εὑρέθησαν. 21 καὶ χάλαζα μεγάλη ὡς.ταλαντιαία καταβαίνει
were found; and a ²hail ¹great as of a talent weight comes down

ἐκ τοῦ οὐρανοῦ ἐπὶ τοὺς ἀνθρώπους· καὶ ἐβλασφήμησαν οἱ
out of the heaven upon   men;   and ²blasphemed

ἄνθρωποι τὸν θεόν, ἐκ τῆς πληγῆς τῆς χαλάζης· ὅτι με-
¹men   God, because of the plague of the hail, for

γάλη ἐστὶν ἡ.πληγὴ.αὐτῆς σφόδρα.
³great ²is ⁴its ⁵plague ¹exceeding.

17 Καὶ ἦλθεν εἷς ἐκ τῶν ἑπτὰ ἀγγέλων τῶν ἐχόντων τὰς
And came one of the seven angels of those having the

ἑπτὰ φιάλας, καὶ ἐλάλησεν μετ᾽ ἐμοῦ, λέγων ᵉμοι,‖ Δεῦρο,
seven bowls, and spoke with me, saying to me, Come here,

δείξω σοι τὸ κρίμα τῆς πόρνης τῆς μεγάλης, τῆς καθη-
I will shew thee the sentence of the ²harlot ¹great, who sits

μένης ἐπὶ ᶠτῶν‖ ὑδάτων ᶠτῶν‖ πολλῶν· 2 μεθ᾽ ἧς ἐπόρνευ-
upon the ²waters ¹many; with whom ⁶committed ⁷for-

σαν οἱ βασιλεῖς τῆς γῆς, καὶ ἐμεθύσθησαν ᵍἐκ τοῦ οἴνου
nication ¹the ²kings ³of ⁴the ⁵earth; and were made drunk with the wine

τῆς.πορνείας.αὐτῆς οἱ κατοικοῦντες τὴν γῆν.‖ 3 Καὶ
of her fornication those.that dwell on the earth. And

ἀπήνεγκέν με εἰς ἔρημον ἐν πνεύματι· καὶ ʰεἶδον‖ γυναῖκα
he carried away me ⁴to ⁵a ⁶wilderness ¹in [²the] ³Spirit; and I saw a woman

καθημένην ἐπὶ θηρίον κόκκινον, ⁱγέμον ὀνομάτων‖ βλασφημίας,
sitting upon a ²beast ¹scarlet, full of names of blasphemy,

ᵏἔχον‖ κεφαλὰς ἑπτὰ καὶ κέρατα δέκα. 4 καὶ ἡ γυνὴ ˡἦ‖
having ¹heads ¹seven and ²horns ¹ten. And the woman

περιβεβλημένη ᵐπορφύρᾳ‖ καὶ ⁿκοκκίνῳ,‖ ᵒκαὶ‖ κεχρυσωμένη
clothed in purple   and scarlet, and decked
                                       (lit. gilded)

ᴾχρυσῷ‖ καὶ λίθῳ τιμίῳ καὶ μαργαρίταις, ἔχουσα ᑫχρυσοῦν
with gold and ²stone ¹precious and pearls, having a golden

ποτήριον‖ ἐν τῇ.χειρὶ.αὐτῆς, ʳγέμον‖ βδελυγμάτων καὶ ˢἀκαθ-
cup   in her hand, full of abominations and of unclean-

vial into the air; and
there came a great
voice out of the
temple of heaven,
from the throne,
saying, It is done.
18 And there were
voices, and thunders,
and lightnings; and
there was a great
earthquake, such as
was not since men
were upon the earth,
so mighty an earth-
quake, *and* so great.
19 And the great city
was divided into three
parts, and the cities of
the nations fell: and
great Babylon came
in remembrance be-
fore God, to give unto
her the cup of the wine
of the fierceness of his
wrath. 20 And every
island fled away, and
the mountains were
not found. 21 And
there fell upon men a
great hail out of hea-
ven, *every stone* about
the weight of a talent:
and men blasphemed
God because of the
plague of the hail;
for the plague thereof
was exceeding great.

XVII. And there
came one of the seven
angels which had the
seven vials, and talked
with me, saying unto
me, Come hither; I
will shew unto thee the
judgment of the great
whore that sitteth
upon many waters :
2 with whom the kings
of the earth have com-
mitted fornication,
and the inhabitants
of the earth have been
made drunk with the
wine of her fornica-
tion. 3 So he carried
me away in the spirit
into the wilderness:
and I saw a woman
sit upon a scarlet
coloured beast, full of
names of blasphemy,
having seven heads
and ten horns. 4 And
the woman was array-
ed in purple and scar-
let colour, and decked
with gold and pre-
cious stones and
pearls, having a gold-
en cup in her hand full
of abominations and

ˣ ἐπὶ upon GLTTrAW.   ʸ — μεγάλη LA.   ᶻ ἐκ out of LTTrA.   ᵃ — τοῦ οὐρανοῦ
LTTrAW.   ᵇ ἀστραπαὶ καὶ φωναὶ καὶ βρονταί GLTTrAW.   ᶜ ἄνθρωπος ἐγένετο man was
LTTrAW.   ᵈ ἔπεσαν LTTrAW.   ᵉ — μοι GLTTrAW.   ᶠ — τῶν LTTr[A].   ᵍ οἱ κατοικοῦντες τὴν γῆν ἐκ τοῦ οἴνου τῆς πορνείας αὐτῆς GLTTrAW.   ʰ εἶδα L.   ⁱ γέμοντα ὀνόματα
LTA : γέμον τὰ (— τα W) ὀνόματα T W.   ᵏ ἔχοντα TA.   ˡ ἦν was GLTTrAW.   ᵐ πορφυροῦν GLTTrAW.   ⁿ κόκκινον GLTTrAW.   ᵒ [καὶ] A.   ᴾ χρυσίῳ GLAW.   ᑫ ποιή-
ριον χρυσοῦν LTTrAW.   ʳ γέμων T.   ˢ τὰ ἀκάθαρτα τῆς the unclean things GLTTrAW.

filthiness of her forni- cation: 5 and upon her forehead was a name written, MYS- TERY, BABYLON THE GREAT, THE MOTHER OF HAR- LOTS AND ABOMI- NATIONS OF THE EARTH. 6 And I saw the woman drunken with the blood of the saints, and with the blood of the mar- tyrs of Jesus: and when I saw her, I wondered with great admiration. 7 And the angel said unto me, Wherefore didst thou marvel? I will tell thee the mystery of the woman, and of the beast that carrieth her, which hath the seven heads and ten horns. 8 The beast that thou sawest was, and is not; and shall ascend out of the bot- tomless pit, and go into perdition: and they that dwell on the earth shall wonder, whose names were not written in the book of life from the foundation of the world, when they be- hold the beast that was, and is not, and yet is. 9 And here is the mind which hath wisdom. The seven heads are seven moun- tains, on which the woman sitteth. 10 And there are seven kings: five are fallen, and one is, and the other is not yet come; and when he cometh, he must continue a short space. 11 And the beast that was, and is not, even he is the eighth, and is of the seven, and goeth into perdition. 12 And the ten horns which thou sawest are ten kings, which have received no kingdom as yet; but receive power as kings one hour with the beast. 13 These have one mind, and shall give their power and strength unto the beast. 14 These shall

ἄρτητος‖ πορνείας.αὐτῆς, 5 καὶ ἐπὶ τὸ.μέτωπον.αὐτῆς
ness of her fornication; and upon her forehead

ὄνομα γεγραμμένον, Μυστήριον, Βαβυλὼν ἡ μεγάλη, ἡ
a name written, Mystery, Babylon the Great, the

μήτηρ τῶν πορνῶν καὶ τῶν βδελυγμάτων τῆς γῆς. 6 Καὶ
mother of the harlots and of the abominations of the earth. And

ᵗεἶδον‖ τὴν γυναῖκα μεθύουσαν ἐκ τοῦ αἵματος τῶν ἁγίων, καὶ
I saw the woman drunk with the blood of the saints, and

ἐκ τοῦ αἵματος τῶν μαρτύρων Ἰησοῦ· καὶ ἐθαύμασα, ἰδὼν
with the blood of the witnesses of Jesus. And I wondered, having seen

αὐτήν, θαῦμα μέγα. 7 Καὶ εἶπέν μοι ὁ ἄγγελος, ᵛΔιατί‖
her, with ²wonder ¹great. And ³said ⁴to ⁵me ¹the ²angel, Why

ἐθαύμασας; ἐγὼ ʷσοὶ ἐρῶ‖ τὸ μυστήριον τῆς γυναικός,
didst thou wonder? I thee will tell the mystery of the woman,

καὶ τοῦ θηρίου τοῦ βαστάζοντος αὐτήν, τοῦ ἔχοντος τὰς
and of the beast which carries her, which has the

ἑπτὰ κεφαλὰς καὶ τὰ δέκα κέρατα. 8 ˣθηρίον ὃ εἶδες,
seven heads and the ten horns. [The] beast which thou sawest,

ἦν, καὶ οὐκ.ἔστιν, καὶ μέλλει ἀναβαίνειν ἐκ τῆς ἀβύσσου,
was, and is not, and is about to come up out of the abyss,

καὶ εἰς ἀπώλειαν ʸὑπάγειν·‖ καὶ ᶻθαυμάσονται‖ οἱ κατοι-
and into destruction to go; and shall wonder they who dwell

κοῦντες ἐπὶ τῆς γῆς, ὧν ᵃοὐ.γέγραπται‖ ᵇτὰ ὀνόματα‖ ἐπὶ
on the earth, of whom are not written the names in

τὸ βιβλίον τῆς ζωῆς ἀπὸ καταβολῆς κόσμου, ᶜβλέ-
the book of life from [the] foundation of [the] world, see-

ποντες‖ τὸ θηρίον ᵈὃ τι‖ ἦν, καὶ οὐκ ἔστιν, ᵉκαίπερ ἐστίν.‖
ing the beast which was and ²not ¹is, and yet is.

9 ὧδε ὁ νοῦς ὁ ἔχων σοφίαν. αἱ ἑπτὰ κεφαλαί, ᶠὄρη
Here [is] the mind which has wisdom. The seven heads ²mountains

εἰσὶν ἑπτά, ὅπου ἡ γυνὴ κάθηται ἐπ᾽ αὐτῶν. 10 καὶ βα-
¹are ²seven, where the woman sits on them. And

σιλεῖς ἑπτά εἰσιν· οἱ πέντε ἔπεσαν, ᵍκαὶ‖ ὁ εἷς ἐστιν, ο
kings ²seven ¹there ²are: the five are fallen, and the one is; the

ἄλλος οὔπω ἦλθεν· καὶ ὅταν ἔλθῃ, ὀλίγον αὐτὸν.δεῖ
other ²not ³yet ¹is come: and when he shall have come, a little while he must

μεῖναι. 11 καὶ τὸ θηρίον ὃ ἦν, καὶ οὐκ ἔστιν, καὶ ʰαὐτὸς‖
remain. And the beast which was, and ²not ¹is, ⁴also ³he

ὄγδοός ἐστιν, καὶ ἐκ τῶν ἑπτά ἐστιν, καὶ εἰς ἀπώλεια
²an ⁷eighth ⁵is, and of the seven is, and into destruction

ὑπάγει. 12 καὶ τὰ δέκα κέρατα ἃ εἶδες, δέκα βασιλεῖς
goes. And the ten horns which thou sawest ten kings

εἰσιν, οἵτινες βασιλείαν ⁱοὔπω‖ ἔλαβον, ᵏἀλλ᾽‖ ἐξουσίαν ὡς
are, which ⁴a ⁵kingdom ²not ³yet ¹received, but authority as

βασιλεῖς μίαν ὥραν λαμβάνουσιν μετὰ τοῦ θηρίου. 13 οὗτοι
kings one hour receive with the beast. These

μίαν ˡγνώμην ἔχουσιν,‖ καὶ τὴν δύναμιν καὶ ᵐτὴν‖ ἐξουσίαν
one mind have, and the power and the authority

ⁿἑαυτῶν‖ τῷ θηρίῳ ᵒδιαδιδώσουσιν.‖ 14 οὗτοι μετὰ τοῦ
of themselves to the beast they shall give up. These with the

---

ᵗ εἶδα LTTrA. ᵛ Διὰ τί LTrA. ʷ ἐρῶ σοι LTrA. ˣ + τὸ The GLTTrA. ʸ ὑπάγει goes LAW. ᶻ θαυμασθήσονται L. ᵃ οὐκ ἐγέγραπτο was not written L. ᵇ τὸ ὄνομα (read the name is not written) LTTrA. ᶜ βλεπόντων GLTTrAW. ᵈ ὅτι (read that it was) GLTTrAW. ᵉ καὶ παρέσται and shall be present GLTTrAW. ᶠ ἑπτὰ ὄρη εἰσὶν GLTTrA. ᵍ — καὶ GLTTrAW. ʰ οὗτος this Tr. ⁱ οὐκ not L. ᵏ ἀλλὰ LTTrA. ˡ ἔχουσιν γνώμην G. ᵐ — τὴν LTrA. ⁿ αὐτῶν (read their authority) LTTrAW. ᵒ διδόασιν they give GLTTrAW.

ἀρνίου πολεμήσουσιν, καὶ τὸ ἀρνίον νικήσει αὐτούς, ὅτι
Lamb   war will make, and the Lamb will overcome them because

κύριος κυρίων ἐστὶν καὶ βασιλεὺς βασιλέων· καὶ οἱ
Lord of lords he is and King   of kings : and those that [are]

μετ᾽ αὐτοῦ, κλητοὶ καὶ ἐκλεκτοὶ καὶ πιστοί. 15 Καὶ ᴾλέγει‖
with him, called, and chosen, and faithful. And he says

μοι, Τὰ ὕδατα ἃ εἶδες, οὗ ἡ πόρνη κάθηται, λαοὶ καὶ
to me, The waters which thou sawest, where the harlot sits, ²peoples ³and

ὄχλοι εἰσίν, καὶ ἔθνη καὶ γλῶσσαι. 16 καὶ τὰ δέκα κέρατα
⁴multitudes ¹are, and nations and tongues. And the ten horns

ἃ εἶδες ᵠἐπὶ‖ τὸ θηρίον, οὗτοι μισήσουσιν τὴν πόρνην,
which thou sawest upon the beast, these shall hate the harlot,

καὶ ἠρημωμένην ποιήσουσιν αὐτὴν καὶ γυμνήν, καὶ τὰς
and desolate shall make her and naked, and

σάρκας αὐτῆς φάγονται, καὶ αὐτὴν κατακαύσουσιν ʳἐν‖ πυρί.
⁴flesh ³her ¹shall ²eat, and ³her ¹shall ²burn with fire ;

17 ὁ γὰρ θεὸς ἔδωκεν εἰς τὰς καρδίας αὐτῶν ποιῆσαι τὴν
for God gave to their hearts to do

γνώμην αὐτοῦ, ˢκαὶ ποιῆσαι μίαν γνώμην,‖ καὶ δοῦναι τὴν
²mind ¹his, and to do one mind, and to give

βασιλείαν αὐτῶν τῷ θηρίῳ, ἄχρι ᵗτελεσθῇ τὰ ῥήματα‖
²kingdom ¹their to the beast, until should be fulfilled the sayings

τοῦ θεοῦ. 18 καὶ ἡ γυνὴ ἣν εἶδες, ἔστιν ἡ πόλις ἡ
of God. And the woman whom thou sawest is the ²city

μεγάλη, ἡ ἔχουσα βασιλείαν ἐπὶ τῶν βασιλέων τῆς γῆς.
¹great, which has kingship over the kings of the earth.

18 ᵛΚαὶ‖ μετὰ ταῦτα εἶδον ʷ ἄγγελον καταβαίνοντα· ἐκ
And after these things I saw an angel descending out of

τοῦ οὐρανοῦ, ἔχοντα ἐξουσίαν μεγάλην· καὶ ἡ γῆ ἐφω-
the heaven, having ²authority ¹great: and the earth was enlight-

τίσθη ἐκ τῆς δόξης αὐτοῦ. 2 καὶ ἔκραξεν ˣἐν ἰσχύϊ, φωνῇ
ened with his glory. And he cried mightily with a ²voice

μεγάλῃ,‖ λέγων, Ἔπεσεν ʸἔπεσεν‖ Βαβυλὼν ἡ μεγάλη, καὶ
¹loud, saying, Is fallen, is fallen Babylon the great, and

ἐγένετο κατοικητήριον ᶻδαιμόνων,‖ καὶ φυλακὴ παντὸς πνεύ-
is become a habitation of demons, and a hold of every ³spi-

ματος ἀκαθάρτουᵃ, καὶ φυλακὴ παντὸς ὀρνέου ἀκαθάρτου καὶ
rit ¹unclean, and a hold of every ⁴bird ¹unclean ²and

μεμισημένου· 3 ὅτι ἐκ ᵇτοῦ οἴνου‖ τοῦ θυμοῦ τῆς πορ-
³hated : because of the wine of the fury of the ²forni-

νείας αὐτῆς ᶜπέπωκεν‖ πάντα τὰ ἔθνη, καὶ οἱ βασιλεῖς
cation ¹of ²her ⁷have ⁶drunk ⁴all ⁵the ⁸nations; and the kings

τῆς γῆς μετ᾽ αὐτῆς ἐπόρνευσαν, καὶ οἱ ἔμποροι τῆς
of the earth with her did commit fornication, and the merchants of the

γῆς ἐκ τῆς δυνάμεως τοῦ στρήνους αὐτῆς ἐπλούτησαν.
earth through the power of her luxury were enriched.

4 Καὶ ἤκουσα ἄλλην φωνὴν ἐκ τοῦ οὐρανοῦ, λέγουσαν,
And I heard another voice out of the heaven, saying,

ᵈ Ἐξέλθετε‖ ᵉ ἐξ αὐτῆς ὁ λαός μου,‖ ἵνα μὴ ᶠσυγκοινωνήσητε‖
Come ye out of her, my people, that ye may not have fellowship

Right column (translation)

make war with the Lamb, and the Lamb shall overcome them : for he is Lord of lords, and King of kings : and they that are with him are called, and chosen, and faithful. 15 And he saith unto me, The waters which thou sawest, where the whore sitteth, are peoples, and multitudes, and nations, and tongues. 16 And the ten horns which thou sawest upon the beast, these shall hate the whore, and shall make her desolate and naked, and shall eat her flesh, and burn her with fire. 17 For God hath put in their hearts to fulfil his will, and to agree, and give their kingdom unto the beast, until the words of God shall be fulfilled. 18 And the woman which thou sawest is that great city, which reigneth over the kings of the earth.

XVIII. And after these things I saw another angel come down from heaven, having great power; and the earth was lightened with his glory. 2 And he cried mightily with a strong voice, saying, Babylon the great is fallen, is fallen, and is become the habitation of devils, and the hold of every foul spirit, and a cage of every unclean and hateful bird. 3 For all nations have drunk of the wine of the wrath of her fornication, and the kings of the earth have committed fornication with her, and the merchants of the earth are waxed rich through the abundance of her delicacies. 4 And I heard another voice from heaven, saying, Come out of her, my people,

---

ᴾ εἶπεν L. ᵠ καὶ and GLTTrAW. ʳ — ἐν (read πυρί with fire) T[A]. ˢ — καὶ ποιῆσαι μίαν γνώμην L ; καὶ ποιήσαι γνώμην μίαν G[A]. ᵗ τελεσθήσονται (shall be fulfilled) οἱ λόγοι GLTTrAW. ᵛ — καὶ LTTrAW. ʷ + ἄλλον (read another angel) GLTTrAW. ˣ ἐν ([ἐν] A) ἰσχυρᾷ φωνῇ with a strong voice GLTTrAW. ʸ — ἔπεσεν Tr[A]. LTTrA. ᶻ δαιμονίων LTTrA. ᵃ + καὶ μεμισημένου and hated (spirit) L. ᵇ — τοῦ οἴνου L[Tr]A. ᶜ πέπωκαν LTW ; πέπτωκαν have fallen (read ἐκ by) Tr ; πέπ[τ]ωκαν A. ᵈ Ἐξέλθατε TTrAW ; Ἔξελθε Come thou L. ᵉ ὁ λαός μου ἐξ αὐτῆς T. ᶠ συν- T.

that ye be not partakers of her sins, and that ye receive not of her plagues. 5 For her sins have reached unto heaven, and God hath remembered her iniquities. 6 Reward her even as she rewarded you, and double unto her double according to her works: in the cup which she hath filled fill to her double. 7 How much she hath glorified herself, and lived deliciously, so much torment and sorrow give her: for she saith in her heart, I sit a queen, and am no widow, and shall see no sorrow. 8 Therefore shall her plagues come in one day, death, and mourning, and famine; and she shall be utterly burned with fire: for strong *is* the Lord God who judgeth her. 9 And the kings of the earth, who have committed fornication and lived deliciously with her, shall bewail her, and lament for her, when they shall see the smoke of her burning, 10 standing afar off for the fear of her torment, saying, Alas, alas that great city Babylon, that mighty city! for in one hour is thy judgment come. 11 And the merchants of the earth shall weep and mourn over her ; for no man buyeth their merchandise any more: 12 the merchandise of gold, and silver, and precious stones, and of pearls, and fine linen, and purple, and silk, and scarlet, and all thyine wood, and all manner vessels of ivory, and all manner vessels of most precious wood, and of brass, and iron, and marble, 13 and cinnamon, and odours, and ointments, and frankincense, and wine, and oil, and fine flour,

ταῖς.ἁμαρτίαις.αὐτῆς, καὶ ^gἵνα μὴ.λάβητε ἐκ τῶν πληγῶν
in her sins,   and that ye may not receive of   ²plagues

αὐτῆς·‖ 5 ὅτι ^hἠκολούθησαν‖ αὐτῆς αἱ ἁμαρτίαι ἄχρι τοῦ
¹her: for   ³followed   ¹her   ²sins   as far as the

οὐρανοῦ, καὶ ἐμνημόνευσεν ὁ θεὸς τὰ.ἀδικήματα.αὐτῆς. 6 ἀπό-
heaven, and ²remembered   ¹God   her unrighteousnesses.   Ren-

δοτε αὐτῇ ὡς καὶ αὐτὴ ἀπέδωκεν ⁱὑμῖν,‖ καὶ διπλώσατε ^kαὐτῇ‖
der to her as also she   rendered   to you ; and double ye   to her

^lδιπλᾶ κατὰ τὰ.ἔργα.αὐτῆς· ἐν τῷ ποτηρίῳ ᾧ ἐκέρασεν,
double, according to   her works.   In the   cup   which she mixed,

κεράσατε αὐτῇ διπλοῦν. 7 ὅσα ἐδόξασεν ^mἑαυτὴν‖ καὶ
mix ye   to her   double.   So much as she glorified   herself   and

ἐστρηνίασεν, τοσοῦτον δότε αὐτῇ βασανισμὸν καὶ πένθος·
lived luxuriously, so much   give to her   torment   and mourning.

ὅτι ἐν τῇ.καρδίᾳ.αὐτῆς λέγει, ⁿΚάθημαι βασίλισσα, καὶ
Because in   her heart   she says,   I sit   a queen,   and

χήρα οὐκ.εἰμί, καὶ πένθος οὐ.μὴ ἴδω. 8 Διὰ τοῦτο
a widow I am not : and mourning in no wise may I see.   On account of this

ἐν μιᾷ ἡμέρᾳ ἥξουσιν αἱ.πληγαί.αὐτῆς, θάνατος καὶ πένθος
in one   day   shall come   her plagues,   death   and mourning

καὶ λιμός· καὶ ἐν πυρὶ κατακαυθήσεται· ὅτι ἰσχυρὸς ^oκύριος‖
and famine, and with fire   she shall be burnt ; for strong [is the] Lord

ὁ θεὸς ὁ ^pκρίνων‖ αὐτήν. 9 καὶ ^qκλαύσονται‖ ^rαὐτήν,‖ καὶ
God who judges   her.   And shall weep for   her,   and

κόψονται ἐπ᾽ ^sαὐτῇ‖ οἱ βασιλεῖς τῆς γῆς, οἱ μετ᾽ αὐτῆς πορ-
shall bewail for   her, the kings of the earth, who with her commit-

νεύσαντες καὶ στρηνιάσαντες, ὅταν βλέπωσιν τὸν καπνὸν
ted fornication and lived luxuriously,   when   they see   the   smoke

τῆς.πυρώσεως.αὐτῆς, 10 ἀπὸ μακρόθεν ἑστηκότες διὰ
of her burning,   ²from   ³afar   ¹standing on account of

τὸν φόβον τοῦ.βασανισμοῦ.αὐτῆς, λέγοντες, Οὐαί, οὐαί, ἡ
the   fear   of her torment,   saying,   Woe, woe, the

πόλις ἡ μεγάλη Βαβυλών, ἡ πόλις ἡ ἰσχυρά, ὅτι ^tἐν‖ μιᾷ ὥρᾳ
²city   ¹great,   Babylon, the ²city   ¹strong ! for in one hour

ἦλθεν ἡ.κρίσις.σου. 11 Καὶ οἱ ἔμποροι τῆς γῆς κλαίουσιν καὶ
is come thy judgment.   And the merchants of the earth   weep   and

πενθοῦσιν ἐπ᾽ ^vαὐτῇ,‖ ὅτι τὸν.γόμον.αὐτῶν οὐδεὶς ἀγοράζει
mourn   for   her, because   their lading   no one   buys

οὐκέτι· 12 γόμον χρυσοῦ, καὶ ἀργύρου, καὶ λίθου τιμίου,
any more;   lading   of gold, and   of silver, and of ²stone ¹precious,
(*lit.* no more)

καὶ ^wμαργαρίτου,‖ καὶ ^xβύσσου,‖ καὶ πορφύρας, καὶ ^yσηρικοῦ,‖
and   of pearl,   and of fine linen, and of purple, and   of silk,

καὶ κοκκίνου· καὶ πᾶν ξύλον θύινον, καὶ πᾶν σκεῦος ἐλεφάν-
and of scarlet, and all ²wood ¹thyine, and every article   of

τινον, καὶ πᾶν σκεῦος ἐκ ξύλου τιμιωτάτου, καὶ χαλκοῦ, καὶ
ivory, and every article of ³wood ¹most ²precious, and of brass, and

σιδήρου, καὶ μαρμάρου, 13 καὶ ^zκινάμωμον,‖ ^aκαὶ θυμιάματα
of iron, and of marble,   and   cinnamon,   and   incense,

καὶ μύρον, καὶ λίβανον, καὶ οἶνον, καὶ ἔλαιον, καὶ σεμίδαλιν,
and ointment, and frankincense, and wine, and   oil,   and finest flour,

---

^g ἐκ τῶν πληγῶν αὐτῆς ἵνα μὴ λάβητε GLTTrAW.   ^h ἐκολλήθησαν were joined together GLTTrAW.   ⁱ — ὑμῖν GLTTrAW.   ^k — αὐτῇ LTTrAW.   ^l + τὰ the TTr[A].   ^m αὐτὴν LTTrAW.   ⁿ + ὅτι LTTrA.   ^o [κύριος] A.   ^p κρίνας judged GLTTrAW.   ^q κλαύσουσιν TTrAW.   ^r — αὐτὴν GLTTrAW.   ^s — αὐτὴν TTrAW.   ^t — ἐν (read [in]) GLTTrAW.   ^v αὐτὴν TTrA.   ^w μαργαρίτας pearls L ; μαργαριτῶν of pearls TTrA.   ^x βυσσίνου GLTTrAW.   ^y σιρικοῦ LT.   ^z κιννάμωμον LTTrA.   ^a + καὶ ἄμωμον and amomum GLTTrAW.

καὶ σῖτον, καὶ κτήνη, καὶ πρόβατα, καὶ ἵππων, καὶ ῥεδῶν,
and wheat, and cattle, and sheep, and of horses, and of chariots,

καὶ σωμάτων, καὶ ψυχὰς ἀνθρώπων. 14 καὶ ἡ ὀπώρα ᶜτῆς
and of slaves, and souls of men.   And the ripe fruits of the
        (lit. of bodies)

ἐπιθυμίας τῆς ψυχῆς.σου‖ ᵈἀπῆλθεν‖ ἀπὸ σοῦ, καὶ πάντα τὰ
desire   of thy soul   are departed   from thee,   and   all   the

λιπαρὰ καὶ ᶜτα‖ λαμπρὰ ᶠἀπῆλθεν‖ ἀπὸ σοῦ, καὶ ᵍοὐκέτι‖
fat things and   the   bright things   are departed   from thee, and ⁴any ⁵more
                                                            (lit. no more)

ʰοὐ.μὴ   εὑρήσῃς   αὐτά.‖ 15 οἱ ἔμποροι τούτων οἱ
⁴in ²no ³wise shouldst thou find them.   The merchants of these things, who

πλουτήσαντες ἀπ᾽ αὐτῆς, ἀπὸ μακρόθεν στήσονται διὰ
were enriched from her, from afar shall stand because of

τὸν φόβον τοῦ.βασανισμοῦ.αὐτῆς, κλαίοντες καὶ πενθοῦντες,
the   fear   of her torment,   weeping   and   mourning,

16 ⁱκαὶ‖ λέγοντες, Οὐαί, οὐαί, ἡ πόλις ἡ μεγάλη, ἡ περι-
and saying, Woe, woe, the ²city   ¹great,   which [was] cloth-

βεβλημένη ᵏβύσσινον‖ καὶ πορφυροῦν καὶ ᵏκόκκινον,‖ καὶ
ed with   fine linen   and   purple   and   scarlet,   and

κεχρυσωμένη ˡἐν‖ ᵐχρυσῷ‖ καὶ λίθῳ τιμίῳ καὶ ⁿμαργαρί-
decked   with   gold   and ²stone ¹precious and   pearls !
(lit. gilded)

ταις·‖ 17 ὅτι μιᾷ ὥρᾳ ἠρημώθη ὁ τοσοῦτος πλοῦτος. Καὶ
        for in one hour was made desolate so great wealth.   And

πᾶς κυβερνήτης, καὶ °πᾶς ἐπὶ τῶν πλοίων ὁ ὅμιλος,‖ καὶ
every steersman, and all ³in   ⁴ships ¹the ²company, and

ναῦται, καὶ ὅσοι τὴν θάλασσαν.ἐργάζονται, ἀπὸ.μακρόθεν
sailors, and as many as   trade by sea,   afar off

ἔστησαν, 18 καὶ ᵖἔκραζον,‖ ᑫὁρῶντες‖ τὸν καπνὸν τῆς πυρώ-
stood,   and   cried,   seeing   the   smoke   ²burn-

σεως αὐτῆς, λέγοντες, Τίς   ὁμοία τῇ πόλει ʳ τῇ μεγάλῃ;
ing ¹of ²her, saying, What [city is] like to the ²city   ¹great ?

19 Καὶ ˢἔβαλον‖ χοῦν ἐπὶ τὰς.κεφαλὰς.αὐτῶν, καὶ ᵗἔκραζον‖
And they cast   dust upon   their heads,   and   cried,

κλαίοντες καὶ πενθοῦντες, λέγοντες, Οὐαί, οὐαί, ἡ πόλις ἡ
weeping   and   mourning,   saying, Woe, woe, the ²city

μεγάλη, ἐν ᾗ ἐπλούτησαν πάντες οἱ ἔχοντες ᵛ πλοῖα ἐν τῇ
¹great, in which were enriched all   who had   ships in the

θαλάσσῃ ἐκ τῆς.τιμιότητος.αὐτῆς, ὅτι μιᾷ ὥρᾳ ἠρημώ-
sea   through   her costliness !   for in one hour she was made

θη. 20 Εὐφραίνου ἐπ᾽ ᵂαὐτήν,‖ οὐρανέ, καὶ οἱ ἅγιοι ˣ ἀπό-
desolate. Rejoice over   her, O heaven, and [ye] holy   apo-

στολοι καὶ οἱ προφῆται, ὅτι ἔκρινεν ὁ θεὸς τὸ.κρίμα.ὑμῶν ἐξ
stles and [ye] prophets; for ²did ³judge ¹God your judgment upon

αὐτῆς. 21 Καὶ ἦρεν εἷς ἄγγελος ἰσχυρὸς λίθον ὡς ʸμύλον‖
her.   And ⁴took ⁵up ¹one ³angel   ²strong a stone, as a ⁶millstone

μέγαν, καὶ ἔβαλεν εἰς τὴν θάλασσαν, λέγων, Οὕτως ὁρμή-
¹great, and cast [it] into the sea,   saying, Thus   with

ματι βληθήσεται Βαβυλὼν ἡ μεγάλη πόλις, καὶ οὐ.μὴ
violence shall be cast down Babylon   the   great   city,   and not at all

and wheat, and beasts, and sheep, and horses, and chariots, and slaves, and souls of men. 14 And the fruits that thy soul lusted after are departed from thee, and all things which were dainty and goodly are departed from thee, and thou shalt find them no more at all. 15 The merchants of these things, which were made rich by her, shall stand afar off for the fear of her torment, weeping and wailing, 16 and saying, Alas, alas that great city, that was clothed in fine linen, and purple, and scarlet, and decked with gold, and precious stones, and pearls ! 17 for in one hour so great riches is come to nought. And every shipmaster, and all the company in ships, and sailors, and as many as trade by sea, stood afar off, 18 and cried when they saw the smoke of her burning, saying, What city is like unto this great city ! 19 And they cast dust on their heads, and cried, weeping and wailing, saying, Alas, alas that great city, wherein were made rich all that had ships in the sea by reason of her costliness ! for in one hour is she made desolate. 20 Rejoice over her, thou heaven, and ye holy apostles and prophets; for God hath avenged you on her. 21 And a mighty angel took up a stone like a great millstone, and cast it into the sea, saying, Thus with violence shall that great city Babylon be thrown down, and shall be found no more

ᶜ σου τῆς ἐπιθυμίας τῆς ψυχῆς LTTrAW.   ᵈ ἀπώλετο are destroyed ᵂ.   ᵉ [τὰ] ᴀ.
ᶠ ἀπώλετο (-λοντο T) are destroyed GLTTrAW.   ᵍ — οὐκέτι Tr.   ʰ αὐτὰ οὐ μὴ εὑρήσουσιν (shall they find) (εὕρῃς ᵂ) LᴀW ; οὐ μὴ αὐτὰ εὑρήσουσιν TTr.   ⁱ — καὶ LTTrAW.
ᵏ βύσσινον and κόκκινον transposed L.   ˡ — ἐν (read [with]) LTr[ᴀ].   ᵐ χρυσίῳ GLTrAW.
ᵐ μαργαρίτῃ pearl LTTrᴀ.   ° πᾶς ὁ ἐπὶ τόπον πλέων every one who sails to [any] place
GLTTrAW.   ᵖ ἔκραξαν LTrᴀ.   ᑫ βλέποντες GLTTrAW.   ʳ + ταύτῃ (read this great
city) L.   ˢ ἔβαλαν L ; [ἐπ]έβαλον ᴀ.   ᵗ ἔκραξαν Lᴀ.   ᵛ + τὰ LTTrᴀ.   ᵂ αὐτῇ GLTTrAW
ˣ + καὶ οἱ (read [ye] saints and [ye] apostles) GLTTrAW.   ʸ μύλινον Lᴀ.

at all. 22 And the voice of harpers, and musicians, and of pipers, and trumpeters, shall be heard no more at all in thee; and no craftsman, of whatsoever craft *he be*, shall be found any more in thee; and the sound of a millstone shall be heard no more at all in thee; 23 and the light of a candle shall shine no more at all in thee; and the voice of the bridegroom and of the bride shall be heard no more at all in thee: for thy merchants were the great men of the earth; for by thy sorceries were all nations deceived. 24 And in her was found the blood of prophets, and of saints, and of all that were slain upon the earth.

εὑρεθῇ ἔτι. 22 καὶ φωνὴ κιθαρῳδῶν καὶ μουσικῶν καὶ
may be found longer: and   voice   of harpers   and   musicians   and
αὐλητῶν καὶ σαλπιστῶν οὐ.μὴ ἀκουσθῇ ἐν σοὶ ἔτι, καὶ
flute-players and   trumpeters   not at all may be heard   in thee longer, and
πᾶς τεχνίτης πάσης τέχνης οὐ.μὴ   εὑρεθῇ   ἐν σοὶ ἔτι, καὶ
any artificer of any   art   not at all may be found in thee longer, and
(*lit.* every)   (*lit.* of every)
φωνὴ μύλου οὐ.μὴ ἀκουσθῇ ἐν σοὶ ἔτι, 23 καὶ φῶς
sound of millstone not at all may be heard in the longer,   and light
λύχνου οὐ.μὴ ᶻφανῇ ᵃἐν σοὶ ἔτι, καὶ φωνὴ νυμφίου καὶ
of lamp not at all may shine in   thee longer, and   voice of bridegroom and
νύμφης οὐ.μὴ   ἀκουσθῇ ἐν σοὶ ἔτι· ὅτι ᵇοἱ.ἔμποροί.σου
of bride not at all   may be heard   in thee longer; for   thy merchants
ἦσαν οἱ μεγιστᾶνες τῆς γῆς, ὅτι ἐν τῇ.φαρμακείᾳ.σου ἐπλα-
were the great ones of the earth, for by   thy sorcery   were
νήθησαν πάντα τὰ ἔθνη. 24 καὶ ἐν αὐτῇ   ᵈαἷμα προφη-
misled   all   the nations.   And in her [the] blood   of pro-
τῶν καὶ ἁγίων εὑρέθη, καὶ πάντων τῶν ἐσφαγμένων ἐπὶ τῆς
phets and saints was found, and   of all   the   slain   on the
γῆς.
earth.

XIX. And after these things I heard a great voice of much people in heaven, saying, Alleluia; Salvation, and glory, and honour, and power, unto the Lord our God: 2 for true and righteous *are* his judgments: for he hath judged the great whore, which did corrupt the earth with her fornication, and hath avenged the blood of his servants at her hand. 3 And again they said, Alleluia. And her smoke rose up for ever and ever. 4 And the four and twenty elders and the four beasts fell down and worshipped God that sat on the throne, saying, Amen; Alleluia. 5 And a voice came out of the throne, saying, Praise our God, all ye his servants, and ye that fear him, both small and great. 6 And I heard as it were the voice of a great multitude, and as the voice of many waters, and as the voice of

19 ᵉΚαὶ μετὰ ταῦτα ἤκουσα ᶠ φωνὴν ᵍὄχλου
  And   after these things I heard   a ²voice ³of ⁴a ⁵multitude
πολλοῦ μεγάλην ἐν τῷ οὐρανῷ, ʰλέγοντος, Ἀλληλούϊα· ἡ
¹great   ⁵loud   in the heaven,   saying,   Hallelujah: the
σωτηρία καὶ ἡ δόξα ⁱκαὶ ἡ τιμὴ καὶ ἡ δύναμις ᵏκυρίῳ
salvation and the glory and the honour and the   power to the Lord
τῷ.θεῷ.ἡμῶν· 2. ὅτι ἀληθιναὶ καὶ δίκαιαι αἱ.κρίσεις.αὐτοῦ·
our God: for   true and righteous [are] his judgments;
ὅτι ἔκρινεν τὴν πόρνην τὴν μεγάλην, ἥτις ἔφθειρεν τὴν γῆν
for he judged the ²harlot   ¹great,   who corrupted the earth
ἐν τῇ.πορνείᾳ.αὐτῆς, καὶ ἐξεδίκησεν τὸ αἷμα τῶν δούλων
with her fornication,   and he did avenge the blood   ³bondmen
αὐτοῦ ἐκ ¹τῆς.χειρὸς.αὐτῆς. 3 Καὶ δεύτερον εἴρηκαν, Ἀλλη-
¹of ²his at   her hand.   And a second time they said, Halle-
λούϊα· Καὶ ὁ.καπνὸς.αὐτῆς ἀναβαίνει εἰς τοὺς αἰῶνας τῶν
lujah. And   her smoke   goes up   to the   ages of the
αἰώνων. 4 Καὶ ᵐἔπεσαν οἱ ⁿπρεσβύτεροι οἱ εἴκοσι καὶ τέσ-
ages.   And fell down the ⁴elders   ¹twenty ²and
σαρες, καὶ τὰ °τέσσαρα   ζῷα, καὶ προσεκύνησαν τῷ
³four,   and the   four   living creatures and   worshipped
θεῷ τῷ καθημένῳ ἐπὶ ᵖτοῦ θρόνου, λέγοντες, Ἀμήν· Ἀλλη-
God who   sits   on the throne,   saying,   Amen,   Halle-
λούϊα. 5 Καὶ φωνὴ ᑫἐκ τοῦ θρόνου ἐξῆλθεν λέγουσα, Αἰνεῖτε
lujah.   And a voice out of the throne came forth, saying,   Praise
ʳτὸν.θεὸν.ἡμῶν πάντες οἱ.δοῦλοι.αὐτοῦ, ˢκαὶ οἱ.φοβούμενοι
our God   all [ye] his bondmen,   and [ye]   who fear
αὐτὸν ᵗκαὶ αἱ μικροὶ καὶ οἱ μεγάλοι. 6 Καὶ ἤκουσα ὡς φωνὴν
him, both the small and the   great.   And I heard as   a voice
ὄχλου πολλοῦ, καὶ ᵛὡς φωνὴν ὑδάτων πολλῶν, καὶ ὡς
of a ²multitude ¹great,   and as   a voice of ²waters   ¹many,   and as

---

ᶻ φάνῃ LT.   ᵃ — ἐν (*read* σοι upon thee) L[A].   ᵇ — οἱ L.   ᶜ φαρμακίᾳ TA.   ᵈ αἵματα
bloods GTW.   ᵉ — καὶ GLTTrAW.   ᶠ + ὡς as EGLTTrAW.   ᵍμεγάλην ὄχλου πολλοῦ GLTTrA.
ʰ λεγόντων GLTTrAW.   ⁱ — καὶ ἡ τιμὴ GLTTrAW.   ᵏ τοῦ θεοῦ ἡμῶν of our God GLTTrAW.
ˡ — τῆς GLTTrAW.   ᵐ ἔπεσον EG.   ⁿ — καὶ GTTrAW ; εἴκοσι τέσσαρες πρεσβύτεροι L.
° τέσσερα LTTrA.   ᵖ τῷ θρόνῳ LTTrA.   ᑫ ἀπὸ from LTrAW.   ʳ τῷ θεῷ LTTrAW.
ˢ — καὶ T[TrA].   ᵗ — καὶ GLTTrAW.   ᵛ — ὡς L

φωνὴν βροντῶν ἰσχυρῶν, ʷλέγοντας,‖ Ἀλληλούϊα· ὅτι ἐβασί-
a voice of ʷthunders ¹strong, saying, Hallelujah, for has

λευσεν κύριος ὁ θεὸς ˣ ὁ παντοκράτωρ.· 7 χαίρωμεν καὶ
reigned [the] Lord God the Almighty. We should rejoice and

ʸἀγαλλιώμεθα,‖ καὶ ᶻδῶμεν‖ τὴν δόξαν αὐτῷ· ὅτι ἦλθεν ὁ
should exult; and should give glory to him; for is come the

γάμος τοῦ ἀρνίου, καὶ ἡ.γυνὴ.αὐτοῦ ἡτοίμασεν ἑαυτήν. 8 Καὶ
marriage of the Lamb, and his wife did make ²ready ¹herself. And

ἐδόθη αὐτῇ ἵνα περιβάληται βύσσινον ᵃκαθαρὸν καὶ
it was given to her that she should be clothed in fine linen, pure and

λαμπρόν·‖ τὸ.γὰρ βύσσινον ⁻τὰ δικαιώματά ᵇἐστιν τῶν
bright; for the fine linen ²the ³righteousnesses ¹is of the

ἁγίων.‖ 9 Καὶ λέγει μοι, Γράψον, Μακάριοι οἱ εἰς τὸ
saints. And he says to me, Write, Blessed [are] they who to the

δεῖπνον τοῦ γάμου τοῦ ἀρνίου κεκλημένοι. Καὶ λέγει μοι,
supper of the marriage of the Lamb are called. And he says to me,

Οὗτοι οἱ λόγοι ᶜ ἀληθινοί ᵈεἰσιν τοῦ θεοῦ.‖ 10 Καὶ ᵉἔπεσον‖
These ²the ⁴words ³true ¹are of God. And I fell

ἔμπροσθεν τῶν.ποδῶν.αὐτοῦ προσκυνῆσαι αὐτῷ· καὶ λέγει
before his feet to do homage to him. And he says

μοι, Ὅρα μή· σύνδουλός σου εἰμὶ καὶ τῶν ἀδελ-
to me, See [thou do it] not. Fellow-bondman of thee I am and ⁴breth-

φῶν σου τῶν ἐχόντων τὴν μαρτυρίαν ᶠτοῦ‖ Ἰησοῦ· τῷ θεῷ
ren ¹of ²thy who have the testimony of Jesus. To God

προσκύνησον· ἡ.γὰρ μαρτυρία ᶠτοῦ‖ Ἰησοῦ ἐστιν τὸ πνεῦμα
do homage. For ⁶the ⁷testimony ⁸of ⁹Jesus ⁵is ¹the ⁴spirit

τῆς προφητείας.
³of ⁴prophecy.

11 Καὶ εἶδον τὸν οὐρανὸν ᵍἀνεῳγμένον,‖ καὶ ἰδού, ἵππος
And I saw the heaven opened, and behold, a ²horse

λευκός, καὶ ὁ καθήμενος ἐπʼ αὐτόν, ʰκαλούμενος πιστὸς‖
¹white, and he who sits upon it, called Faithful

καὶ ἀληθινός, καὶ ἐν δικαιοσύνῃ κρίνει καὶ πολεμεῖ· 12 οἱ
and True, and in righteousness he judges and makes war.

δὲ ὀφθαλμοὶ αὐτοῦ ⁱὡς‖ φλὸξ πυράς, καὶ ἐπὶ τὴν κεφαλὴν
And ²eyes ¹his [were] as a flame of fire, and upon ²head

αὐτοῦ διαδήματα πολλά, ἔχων ᵏ ὄνομα γεγραμμένον ὃ οὐδεὶς
¹his ⁴diadems ³many, having a name written which no one

οἶδεν εἰ.μὴ αὐτός· 13 καὶ περιβεβλημένος ἱμάτιον ˡβεβαμ-
knows but himself, and clothed with a garment dip-

μένον‖ αἵματι· καὶ ᵐκαλεῖται‖ τὸ.ὄνομα.αὐτοῦ, Ὁ λόγος τοῦ
ped in blood; and ³is ⁴called ¹his ²name, The Word of

θεοῦ. 14 Καὶ τὰ στρατεύματα ⁿ ἐν τῷ οὐρανῷ ἠκολούθει αὐτῷ
God. And the armies in the heaven were following him

ἐφʼ ἵπποις λευκοῖς, ἐνδεδυμένοι βύσσινον λευκὸν ᵒκαὶ‖ καθαρόν.
upon ²horses ¹white, clothed in fine linen, white and clean.

15 καὶ ἐκ τοῦ.στόματος.αὐτοῦ ἐκπορεύεται ῥομφαία ὀξεῖα,
And out of his mouth goes forth a ²sword ¹sharp,

ἵνα ἐν αὐτῇ ᵖπατάσσῃ‖ τὰ ἔθνη· καὶ αὐτὸς ποιμανεῖ
that with it he might smite the nations; and he shall shepherd

Right column (KJV):

mighty thunderings, saying, Alleluia : for the Lord God omnipotent reigneth. 7 Let us be glad and rejoice, and give honour to him : for the marriage of the Lamb is come, and his wife hath made herself ready. 8 And to her was granted that she should be arrayed in fine linen, clean and white : for the fine linen is the righteousness of saints. 9 And he saith unto me, Write, Blessed are they which are called unto the marriage supper of the Lamb. And he saith unto me, These are the true sayings of God. 10 And I fell at his feet to worship him. And he said unto me, See thou do it not : I am thy fellowservant, and of thy brethren that have the testimony of Jesus : worship God : for the testimony of Jesus is the spirit of prophecy.

11 And I saw heaven opened, and behold a white horse ; and he that sat upon him was called Faithful and True, and in righteousness he doth judge and make war. 12 His eyes were as a flame of fire, and on his head were many crowns ; and he had a name written, that no man knew, but he himself. 13 And he was clothed with a vesture dipped in blood : and his name is called The Word of God. 14 And the armies which were in heaven followed him upon white horses, clothed in fine linen, white and clean. 15 And out of his mouth goeth a sharp sword, that with it he should

---

ʷ λεγόντων ELTTrW ; λέγοντες GA.   ˣ + ἡμῶν (read our God) GTTrW.   ʸ ἀγαλλιῶμεν
LTTrA.   ᶻ δώσομεν shall give LA.   ᵃ λαμπρὸν καὶ (— καὶ LTTrA) καθαρόν GLTTrA.
ᵇ τῶν ἁγίων ἐστίν LTTrA.   ᶜ + οἱ LAW.   ᵈ τοῦ θεοῦ εἰσιν LTTrA.   ᵉ ἔπεσα LTTrAW.
ᶠ —τοῦ LTTrAW.   ᵍ ἠνεῳγμένον LTTrA.   ʰ πιστὸς καλούμενος Tr ; [καλούμενος] πιστὸς A.
ⁱ — ὡς TT[A].   ᵏ + [ὀνόματα γεγραμμένα, καὶ] names written and A.   ˡ περιρεραμ-
μένον sprinkled round T.   ᵐ κέκληται LTTrAW.   ⁿ + τὰ which [are] EGL[A]W.   ᵒ — καὶ
GLTTrAW.   ᵖ πατάξῃ GLTTrAW.

smite the nations:
and he shall rule
them with a rod of
iron: and he treadeth
the winepress of the
fierceness and wrath of
Almighty God. 16And
he hath on *his* ves-
ture and on his thigh
a name written, KING
OF KINGS, AND
LORD OF LORDS.

αὐτοὺς ἐν ῥάβδῳ σιδηρᾷ· καὶ αὐτὸς πατεῖ τὴν ληνὸν τοῦ
them with ³rod ¹an ²iron; and he treads the press of the
οἴνου τοῦ θυμοῦ �q καὶ‖ τῆς ὀργῆς τοῦ θεοῦ τοῦ παντοκρά-
wine of the fury and of the wrath of God the Almighty.
τορος. 16 καὶ ἔχει ἐπὶ   τὸ ἱμάτιον καὶ ἐπὶ τὸν μηρὸν αὐτοῦ
And he has upon [his] garment and upon his thigh
ʳτὸ‖ ὄνομα γεγραμμένον, Βασιλεὺς βασιλέων καὶ κύριος
the name written, King of kings and Lord
κυρίων.
of lords.

17 And I saw an an-
gel standing in the
sun; and he cried with
a loud voice, saying to
all the fowls that fly
in the midst of hea-
ven, Come and gather
yourselves together
unto the supper of
the great God; 18 that
ye may eat the flesh
of kings, and the flesh
of captains, and the
flesh of mighty men,
and the flesh of horses,
and of them that sit
on them, and the flesh
of all *men, both* free
and bond, both small
and great.

17 Καὶ εἶδον ἕνα ἄγγελον ἑστῶτα ἐν τῷ ἡλίῳ· καὶ
And I saw one angel standing in the sun; and
ἔκραξεν ˢ φωνῇ μεγάλῃ λέγων πᾶσιν τοῖς ὀρνέοις τοῖς
he cried with a ²voice ¹loud, saying to all the ' birds which
ᵗπετωμένοις‖ ἐν μεσουρανήματι, Δεῦτε ᵛκαὶ συνάγεσθε‖ εἰς
fly in mid-heaven, Come and gather yourselves to
τὸ δεῖπνον ʷτοῦ μεγάλου‖ θεοῦ, 18 ἵνα φάγητε σάρκας βα-
the supper of the great God, that ye may eat flesh of
σιλέων, καὶ σάρκας χιλιάρχων, καὶ σάρκας ἰσχυρῶν,
kings, and flesh of chief captains, and flesh of strong [men],
καὶ σάρκας ἵππων καὶ τῶν καθημένων ἐπ' ˣαὐτῶν,‖ καὶ
and flesh of horses and of those who sit on them, and
σάρκας πάντων, ἐλευθέρων ʸ καὶ δούλων, καὶ μικρῶν ᶻ καὶ
flesh of all, free and bond, and small and
μεγάλων.
great.

19 And I saw the
beast, and the kings
of the earth, and their
armies, gathered to-
gether to make war
against him that sat
on the horse, and
against his army.
20 And the beast was
taken, and with him
the false prophet that
wrought miracles be-
fore him, with which
he deceived them that
had received the mark
of the beast, and them
that worshipped his
image. These both
were cast alive into a
lake of fire burning
with brimstone. 21And
the remnant were
slain with the sword
of him that sat upon
the horse, which
sword proceeded out
of his mouth: and all
the fowls were filled
with their flesh.

19 Καὶ ᵃεἶδον‖ τὸ θηρίον, καὶ τοὺς βασιλεῖς τῆς γῆς,
And I saw the beast, and the kings of the earth,
καὶ τὰ στρατεύματα ᵇαὐτῶν‖ συνηγμένα ποιῆσαι ᶜ πόλε-
and ²armies ¹their gathered together to make
μον μετὰ τοῦ καθημένου ἐπὶ τοῦ ἵππου, καὶ μετὰ τοῦ
war with him who sits on the horse, and with
στρατεύματος αὐτοῦ. 20 καὶ ἐπιάσθη τὸ θηρίον, καὶ ᵈ ᵉμετὰ
²army ¹his. And was taken the beast, and with
τούτου ὁ‖ ψευδοπροφήτης ὁ ποιήσας τὰ σημεῖα ἐνώπιον
him the false prophet who wrought the signs before
αὐτοῦ, ἐν οἷς ἐπλάνησεν τοὺς λαβόντας τὸ χάραγμα τοῦ
him, by which he misled those who received the mark of the
θηρίου, καὶ τοὺς προσκυνοῦντας τῇ εἰκόνι αὐτοῦ· ζῶντες
beast, and those who do homage to his image. Alive
ἐβλήθησαν οἱ δύο εἰς τὴν λίμνην τοῦ πυρὸς ᶠτὴν καιομένην ᵛ
were cast the two into the lake of fire which burns
ἐν ᵍτῷ‖ θείῳ. 21 καὶ οἱ λοιποὶ ἀπεκτάνθησαν ἐν τῇ
with brimstone; and the rest were killed with the
ῥομφαίᾳ τοῦ καθημένου ἐπὶ τοῦ ἵππου, τῇ ʰἐκπο-
sword of him who sits on the horse, [the sword] which goes
ρευομένῃ‖ ἐκ τοῦ στόματος αὐτοῦ· καὶ πάντα τὰ ὄρνεα ἐχορ-
forth out of his mouth; and all the birds were
τάσθησαν ἐκ τῶν σαρκῶν αὐτῶν.
filled with their flesh.

�q — καὶ GLTTrA.   ʳ — τὸ (*read* a name) GLTTrAW.   ˢ + ἐν in (a loud voice) T[A].
ᵗ πετομένοις GLTTrAW.   ᵛ συνάχθητε GLTTrAW.   ʷ τὸ μέγα τοῦ (*read* the great supper
of) GLTTrAW.   ˣ αὐτούς LTrA.   ʸ + τε both (free) GLTTrAW.   ᶻ + τε both (small) w.
ᵃ ἴδον T.   ᵇ αὐτοῦ its L.   ᶜ + τὸν LTTrAW.   ᵈ + [οἱ] those A.   ᵉ μετ' αὐτοῦ ὁ
LTTrA; ὁ μετ' αὐτοῦ GW.   ᶠ τῆς καιομένης LTTrA.   ᵍ — τῷ GLTTrAW.   ʰ ἐξελθούσῃ
came forth GLTTrAW.

20 Καὶ ⁱεἶδον‖ ἄγγελον καταβαίνοντα ἐκ τοῦ οὐρανοῦ,
And I saw   an angel   descending   out of the   heaven,

ἔχοντα τὴν ʲκλεῖδα‖ τῆς ἀβύσσου, καὶ ἅλυσιν μεγάλην ἐπὶ
having the   key   of the abyss,   and a ²chain ¹great in

τὴν.χεῖρα.αὐτοῦ. 2 καὶ ἐκράτησεν τὸν δράκοντα, ᵏτὸν ὄφιν
his hand.   And he laid hold of the   dragon,   the ²serpent

τὸν ἀρχαῖον,‖ ˡὅς ἐστιν‖ διάβολος καὶ ᵐ σατανᾶς, καὶ ἔδησεν
¹ancient,   who is [the]   devil   and   Satan,   and bound

αὐτὸν χίλια ἔτη, 3 καὶ ἔβαλεν αὐτὸν εἰς τὴν ἄβυσσον, καὶ
him a thousand years,   and cast   him   into the   abyss,   and

ἔκλεισεν ⁿαὐτόν,‖ καὶ ἐσφράγισεν ἐπάνω αὐτοῦ, ἵνα μὴ
shut   him [up], and   sealed   over   him,   that ²not

ᵒπλανήσῃ‖ ᵖτὰ ἔθνη ἔτι,‖ ἄχρι τελεσθῇ τὰ χίλια
¹he ²should mislead the nations longer, until were completed the thousand

ἔτη· ᑫκαὶ‖ μετὰ ταῦτα δεῖ.ᵣαὐτὸν λυθῆναι‖ μικρὸν
years;   and after these things   he must   be loosed   a little

χρόνον.
time.

4 Καὶ ⁱεἶδον‖ θρόνους, καὶ ἐκάθισαν ἐπ᾽ αὐτούς, καὶ κρίμα
And I saw   thrones,   and they sat upon them,   and judgment

ἐδόθη αὐτοῖς· καὶ τὰς ψυχὰς τῶν πεπελεκισμένων διὰ
was given to them; and the   souls of those   beheaded   on account of

τὴν μαρτυρίαν Ἰησοῦ, καὶ διὰ τὸν λόγον τοῦ θεοῦ, καὶ
the   testimony   of Jesus, and on account of the word   of God, and

οἵτινες οὐ.προσεκύνησαν ˢτῷ θηρίῳ,‖ ᵗοὔτε‖ ᵛτὴν.εἰκόνα⌐.αὐτοῦ,
those who did not do homage to the   beast,   nor   his image,

καὶ οὐκ.ἔλαβον τὸ χάραγμα ἐπὶ τὸ.μέτωπον.ʷαὐτῶν,‖ καὶ ἐπὶ
and did not receive the   mark upon   their forehead,   and upon

τὴν.χεῖρα.αὐτῶν· καὶ ἔζησαν, καὶ ἐβασίλευσαν μετὰ ˣ χριστοῦ
their hand;   and they lived, and   reigned   with   Christ

ʸτὰ‖ χίλια ἔτη· 5 ᶻ οἱ.ᵃδὲ‖ λοιποὶ τῶν νεκρῶν οὐκ ᵇἀνέζησαν
the thousand years: but the   rest   of the dead ²not ¹lived again

ἕως‖ τελεσθῇ τὰ χίλια ἔτη. αὕτη ἡ ἀνάστασις
till   have been completed the thousand years. This [is] the ²resurrection

ἡ πρώτη. 6 μακάριος καὶ ἅγιος ὁ ἔχων μέρος ἐν τῇ ἀνα-
¹first.   Blessed   and holy he who has   part in the ²resur-

στάσει τῇ πρώτῃ· ἐπὶ τούτων ὁ ᶜθάνατος ὁ δεύτερος‖ οὐκ.ἔχει
rection ¹first: over these the ²death ¹second   has no

ἐξουσίαν, ᵈἀλλ᾽‖ ἔσονται ἱερεῖς τοῦ θεοῦ καὶ τοῦ χριστοῦ,
authority;   but   they shall be priests   of God and of the   Christ,

καὶ ᵉβασιλεύσουσιν‖ μετ᾽ αὐτοῦ ᶠ χίλια ἔτη. 7 Καὶ ὅταν τε-
and   shall reign   with him   a thousand years.   And when may

λεσθῇ τὰ χίλια ἔτη, λυθήσεται ὁ σατανᾶς ἐκ τῆς
have been completed the thousand years, will be loosed   Satan   out of

φυλακῆς αὐτοῦ, 8 καὶ ἐξελεύσεται πλανῆσαι τὰ ἔθνη τὰ
²prison ¹his,   and will go out   to mislead the nations which [are]

ἐν ταῖς τέσσαρσιν γωνίαις τῆς γῆς, τὸν Γὼγ καὶ ᵍτὸν‖ Μαγώγ,
in the   four   corners of the earth,   Gog and   Magog,

XX. And I saw an angel come down from heaven, having the key of the bottomless pit and a great chain in his hand. 2 And he laid hold on the dragon, that old serpent, which is the Devil, and Satan, and bound him a thousand years, 3 and cast him into the bottomless pit, and shut him up, and set a seal upon him, that he should deceive the nations no more, till the thousand years should be fulfilled: and after that he must be loosed a little season.

4 And I saw thrones, and they sat upon them, and judgment was given unto them: and I saw the souls of them that were beheaded for the witness of Jesus, and for the word of God, and which had not worshipped the beast, neither his image, neither had received his mark upon their foreheads, or in their hands; and they lived and reigned with Christ a thousand years. 5 But the rest of the dead lived not again until the thousand years were finished. This is the first resurrection. 6 Blessed and holy is he that hath part in the first resurrection: on such the second death hath no power, but they shall be priests of God and of Christ, and shall reign with him a thousand years. 7 And when the thousand years are expired, Satan shall be loosed out of his prison, 8 and shall go out to deceive the nations which are in the four quarters of the earth, Gog and Magog, to

---

¹ ἴδον T.   ʲ κλεῖν GLTTrAW.   ᵏ ὁ ὄφις ὁ ἀρχαῖος LTTrA.   ˡ ὅ ἐστιν ὁ which is the T.
ᵐ + ὁ LTTrAW.   ⁿ — αὐτὸν GLTTrAW.   ᵒ πλανᾷ G.   ᵖ ἔτι τὰ ἔθνη GLTTrA.   ᑫ — καὶ
LTTrAW.   ʳ λυθῆναι αὐτὸν LA.   ˢ τὸ θηρίον GLTTrAW.   ᵗ οὐδὲ LTTrAW.   ᵛ τῇ εἰκόνι EG.
ʷ — αὐτῶν (read [their]) GLTTrAW.   ˣ + τοῦ the EGLTTrAW.   ʸ — τὰ (read a thousand) LTTrAW.   ᶻ + καὶ (read and the rest) Tr.   ᵃ — δὲ but LTTrAW.   ᵇ ἔζησαν ἄχρι
ªlived till GLTTrAW.   ᶜ δεύτερος θάνατος GLTTrA.   ᵈ ἀλλὰ TTrW.   ᵉ βασιλεύ[σ]ουσιν A
ᶠ + τὰ the (thousand) TTr[A].   ᵍ — τὸν LT[Tr]A.
43

gather them together to battle: the number of whom *is* as the sand of the sea. 9 And they went up on the breadth of the earth, and compassed the camp of the saints about, and the beloved city : and fire came down from God out of heaven, and devoured them. 10 And the devil that deceived them was cast into the lake of fire and brimstone, where the beast and the false prophet *are*, and shall be tormented day and night for ever and ever.

συναγαγεῖν αὐτοὺς εἰς ʰ πόλεμον, ὧν ὁ ἀριθμὸς ⁱ ὡς
to gather together them unto war, of whom the number [is] as
ἡ ἄμμος τῆς θαλάσσης. 9 καὶ ἀνέβησαν ἐπὶ τὸ πλάτος τῆς
the sand of the sea. And they went up upon the breadth of the
γῆς, καὶ ᵏἐκύκλωσαν∥ τὴν παρεμβολὴν τῶν ἁγίων, καὶ τὴν
earth, and encircled the camp of the saints, and the
πόλιν τὴν ἠγαπημένην· καὶ κατέβη πῦρ ˡἀπὸ τοῦ θεοῦ ἐκ
²city ¹beloved: and ²came ʼdown ¹fire from God out of
τοῦ οὐρανοῦ,∥ καὶ κατέφαγεν αὐτούς· 10 καὶ ὁ διάβολος ὁ
the heaven and devoured them: and the devil who
πλανῶν αὐτοὺς ἐβλήθη εἰς τὴν λίμνην τοῦ πυρὸς καὶ ᵐ
misleads them was cast into the lake of fire and
θείου, ὅπου ⁿ τὸ θηρίον καὶ ὁ ψευδοπροφήτης· καὶ
of brimstone, where [are] the beast and the false prophet; and
βασανισθήσονται ἡμέρας καὶ νυκτὸς εἰς τοὺς αἰῶνας τῶν
they shall be tormented day and night for the ages of the
αἰώνων.
ages.

11 And I saw a great white throne, and him that sat on it, from whose face the earth and the heaven fled away; and there was found no place for them. 12 And I saw the dead, small and great, stand before God; and the books were opened: and another book was opened, which is *the book* of life: and the dead were judged out of those things which were written in the books, according to their works. 13 And the sea gave up the dead which were in it; and death and hell delivered up the dead which were in them: and they were judged every man according to their works. 14 And death and hell were cast into the lake of fire. This is the second death. 15 And whosoever was not found written in the book of life was cast into the lake of fire.

11 Καὶ εἶδον θρόνον ᵒλευκὸν μέγαν,∥ καὶ τὸν καθήμενον
And I saw a ³throne ²white ¹great and him who sits
Ρἐπ'∥ ᵠαὐτοῦ,∥ οὗ ἀπὸ ʳ προσώπου ἔφυγεν ἡ γῆ καὶ ὁ οὐ-
on it, ²whose ¹from face fled the earth and the hea-
ρανός, καὶ τόπος οὐχ εὑρέθη αὐτοῖς. 12 καὶ εἶδον τοὺς
ven, and place was not found for them. And I saw the
νεκρούς, ˢμικροὺς καὶ μεγάλους.∥ ἑστῶτας ἐνώπιον ᵗτοῦ θεοῦ,∥
dead, small and great, standing before God,
καὶ βιβλία ᵛἠνεῴχθησαν·∥ καὶ ʷβιβλίον ἄλλο∥ ˣἠνεῴχθη,∥
and books were opened; and ²book ¹another was opened,
ὅ ἐστιν τῆς ζωῆς· καὶ ἐκρίθησαν οἱ νεκροὶ ἐκ τῶν
which is [that] of life. And were judged the dead out of the things
γεγραμμένων ἐν τοῖς βιβλίοις, κατὰ τὰ ἔργα αὐτῶν.
written in the books according to their works.
13 καὶ ἔδωκεν ἡ θάλασσα τοὺς ʸἐν αὐτῇ νεκρούς,∥ καὶ ὁ
And ³gave ⁴up ¹the ²sea the ²in ³it ¹dead, and
θάνατος καὶ ὁ ἅδης ᶻἔδωκαν∥ τοὺς ᵃἐν αὐτοῖς νεκρούς·∥ καὶ ἐ-
death and hades gave up the ²in ¹them ¹dead; and they
κρίθησαν ἕκαστος κατὰ τὰ ἔργα αὐτῶν. 14 καὶ ὁ θάνατος
were judged each according to their works: and death
καὶ ὁ ἅδης ἐβλήθησαν εἰς τὴν λίμνην τοῦ πυρός· οὗτός ᵇἐστιν
and hades were cast into the lake of fire. This is
ὁ δεύτερος θάνατος.∥ ᶜ 15 καὶ εἴ τις οὐχ εὑρέθη ἐν τῇ
the second death. And if anyone was not found in the
βίβλῳ τῆς ζωῆς γεγραμμένος, ἐβλήθη εἰς τὴν λίμνην τοῦ
book of life written, he was cast into the lake
πυρός.
of fire.

XXI. And I saw a new heaven and a new earth: for the first

21 Καὶ εἶδον οὐρανὸν καινὸν καὶ γῆν καινήν· ὁ γὰρ
And I saw a ²heaven ¹new and ²earth ¹a ²new; for the

ʰ + τὸν LTTrAW. ⁱ + αὐτῶν of them GLTTrAW. ᵏ ἐκύκλευσαν LTAW. ˡ ἐκ τοῦ
οὐρανοῦ ἀπὸ τοῦ θεοῦ G; — ἀπὸ τοῦ θεοῦ LTAW. ᵐ + τοῦ T. ⁿ + καὶ both GLTTrAW.
ᵒ μέγαν λευκόν GLTTrAW. Ρ ἐπάνω Tr. ᵠ αὐτόν GT. ʳ + τοῦ (*read* from the face
of whom) LTTrAW. ˢ τοὺς μεγάλους καὶ τοὺς μικρούς the great and the small LTTrAW.
ᵗ τοῦ θρόνου the throne GLTTrAW. ᵛ ἠνοίχθησαν GLTTrAW. ʷ ἄλλο βιβλίον GLTTrAW.
ˣ ἠνοίχθη LTTrAW. ʸ νεκροὺς τοὺς ἐν αὐτῇ dead which [were] in it GLTTrAW. ᶻ ἔδωκεν L. ᵃ νεκροὺς τοὺς ἐν αὐτοῖς dead which [were] in them GLTTrAW. ᵇ θάνατος ὁ
δεύτερός ἐστιν GLTAW ; ὁ δεύτερος θάνατός ἐστιν Tr. ᶜ + , ἡ λίμνη τοῦ πυρός the lake
of fire I.TTrAW.

πρῶτος οὐρανὸς καὶ ἡ πρώτη γῆ ᵈπαρῆλθεν,‖ καὶ ἡ θά-
¹first　　heaven　and the　first　earth were passed away, and the

λασσα οὐκ ἔστιν ἔτι.
sea　　²no　¹is　longer.

2 Καὶ ᵉἐγὼ Ἰωάννης‖ ᶠεἶδον‖ τὴν πόλιν τὴν ἁγίανᶠ, Ἱερ-
And　I　　John　　saw　the　²city　　¹holy,　⁴Jer-

ουσαλὴμ καινήνᶠ, καταβαίνουσαν ᵍἀπὸ τοῦ θεοῦ ἐκ τοῦ οὐ-
usalem　³new,　　coming down　from　　God out of　hea-

ρανοῦ,‖ ἡτοιμασμένην ὡς νύμφην κεκοσμημένην τῷ ἀνδρὶ
ven,‖　prepared　　as　a bride　　adorned　　for ²husband

αὐτῆς. 3 καὶ ἤκουσα φωνῆς μεγάλης ἐκ τοῦ ʰοὐρανοῦ,‖
¹her.　And　I heard　a ²voice　¹great　out of the　heaven,

λεγούσης, Ἰδού, ἡ σκηνὴ τοῦ θεοῦ μετὰ τῶν ἀνθρώπων,
saying,　Behold, the tabernacle　of God [is] with　　men,

καὶ σκηνώσει μετ᾽ αὐτῶν· καὶ αὐτοὶ ⁱλαοὶ‖ αὐτοῦ ἔσονται,
and he shall tabernacle with　them, and they ²peoples ³his　¹shall ²be,

καὶ αὐτὸς ὁ θεὸς ᵏἔσται μετ᾽ αὐτῶν‖ ⁱθεὸς.αὐτῶν.‖ 4 καὶ ἐξα-
and ²himself ¹God shall be with　them　　their God.　　And ²shall

λείψει ᵐὁ θεὸς‖ πᾶν δάκρυον ⁿἀπὸ‖ τῶν.ὀφθαλμῶν.αὐτῶν,
³wipe ⁴away ¹God every tear　　from　　their eyes;

καὶ °ὁ‖ θάνατος οὐκ.ἔσται ἔτι· οὔτε πένθος, οὔτε κραυγή,
and　　death　shall be no longer, nor　mourning, nor　crying,

οὔτε πόνος οὐκ ἔσται ἔτι· Pὅτι‖ τὰ πρῶτα ᑫἀπῆλθον.‖
nor distress ³any ¹shall ⁴be longer, because the former things are passed away.
(lit. not)

5 Καὶ εἶπεν ὁ καθήμενος ἐπὶ ʳτοῦ θρόνου,‖ Ἰδού, καινὰ
And said he who sits　on the throne,　　Lo,　new

ˢπάντα ποιῶ.‖ Καὶ λέγει ᵗμοι,‖ Γράψον· ὅτι οὗτοι οἱ λόγοι
all things I make. And he says to me, Write, because these　words

ᵛἀληθινοὶ καὶ πιστοί‖ εἰσιν. 6 Καὶ εἶπέν μοι, ʷΓέγονεν.‖ ἐγώ
true　and faithful　are.　And he said to me, It is done.　I

ˣεἰμι‖ τὸ ʸΑ‖ καὶ τὸ ᶻΩ,‖ ἡ ἀρχὴ καὶ τὸ τέλος. ἐγὼ τῷ
am the A and the Ω, the beginning and the end.　I to him that

διψῶντι δώσω ª ἐκ τῆς πηγῆς τοῦ ὕδατος τῆς ζωῆς δωρεάν.
thirsts will give of the fountain of the water　of life gratuitously.

7 ὁ νικῶν κληρονομήσει ᵇπάντα,‖ καὶ ἔσομαι αὐτῷ θεός,
He that overcomes shall inherit　all things, and I will be to him God,

καὶ αὐτὸς ἔσται μοι ᶜὁ‖ υἱός. 8 ᵈªδειλοῖς.δὲ‖ καὶ ἀπίστοις ᵉª
and　he shall be to me　son:　but to [the] fearful, and unbelieving,

καὶ ἐβδελυγμένοις καὶ φονεῦσιν καὶ πόρνοις καὶ ᶠªφαρμακεῦσιν‖
and　abominable,　and murderers, and fornicators, and　sorcerers,

καὶ.εἰδωλολάτραις, καὶ πᾶσιν τοῖς ᵍªψευδέσιν,‖ τὸ.μέρος.αὐτῶν
and　idolaters,　and　all　liars,　their part

ἐν τῇ λίμνῃ τῇ καιομένῃ πυρὶ καὶ θείῳ, ὅ ἐστιν
[is] in the lake which burns with fire and brimstone; which is [the]

ʰªδεύτερος θάνατος.‖
second　death.

heaven and the first
earth were passed a-
way; and there was
no more sea.

2 And I John saw
the holy city, new
Jerusalem, coming
down from God out
of heaven, prepared as
a bride adorned for
her husband. 3 And I
heard a great voice
out of heaven saying,
Behold, the tabernacle
of God is with men,
and he will dwell with
them, and they shall
be his people, and God
himself shall be with
them, and be their
God. 4 And God shall
wipe away all tears
from their eyes; and
there shall be no more
death, neither sorrow,
nor crying, neither
shall there be any
more pain: for the
former things are
passed away. 5 And
he that sat upon the
throne said, Behold, I
make all things new.
And he said unto me,
Write: for these words
are true and faithful.
6 And he said unto me,
It is done. I am Alpha
and Omega, the be-
ginning and the end.
I will give unto him
that is athirst of the
fountain of the water
of life freely. 7 He
that overcometh shall
inherit all things; and
I will be his God, and
he shall be my son.
8 But the fearful, and
unbelieving, and the
abominable, and mur-
derers, and whore-
mongers, and sorcer-
ers, and idolaters, and
all liars, shall have
their part in the lake
which burneth with
fire and brimstone:
which is the second
death.

ᵈ ἀπῆλθον GW; ἀπῆλθαν LTTrA.　ᵉ — ἐγὼ Ἰωάννης GLTTrW.　ᶠ εἶδον I saw placed after
καινήν GLTTrW; after ἁγίαν A.　ᵍ ἐκ τοῦ οὐρανοῦ ἀπὸ τοῦ θεοῦ GLTTrAW.　ʰ θρόνου
throne LTA.　ⁱ λαὸς people GW.　ᵏ μετ᾽ αὐτῶν ἔσται GLTrAW.　ⁱ — θεὸς αὐτῶν
TTr; αὐτῶν θεός LAW.　ᵐ — ὁ θεὸς (read ἐξαλείψει he shall wipe away) GTTr[A]W.
ⁿ ἐκ LTTrA.　° — ὁ T.　P — ὅτι L[TrA].　ᑫ ἀπῆλθαν LTTrA; ἀπῆλθεν W.　ʳ τῷ
θρόνῳ GLTTrAW.　ˢ ποιῶ πάντα LTTrAW.　ᵗ — μοι LT[Tr]AW.　ᵛ πιστοὶ καὶ ἀληθινοί
GLTTrAW.　ʷ Γέγοναν They are done LTTrW; Γέγονα[ν] (read Γέγονα ἐγώ I am become) A.
ˣ — εἰμι (read [am] T)[A].　ʸ ἄλφα Alpha LTTrAW.　ᶻ Ω̄ L.　ª + αὐτῷ to him T[A]W.
ᵇ ταῦτα these things GLTTrAW.　ᶜ — ὁ LTTrAW.　ᵈª τοῖς (the) δὲ δειλοῖς GLTTrAW.
ᵉª + καὶ ἁμαρτωλοῖς and sinners W.　ᶠª φαρμακοῖς GLTTrAW.　ᵍª ψεύσταις L.　ʰª ὁ
θάνατος ὁ δεύτερος GLTTrAW.

9 And there came unto me one of the seven angels which had the seven vials full of the seven last plagues, and talked with me, saying, Come hither, I will shew thee the bride, the Lamb's wife. 10 And he carried me away in the spirit to a great and high mountain, and shewed me that great city, the holy Jerusalem, descending out of heaven from God, 11 having the glory of God: and her light was like unto a stone most precious, even like a jasper stone, clear as crystal; 12 and had a wall great and high, and had twelve gates, and at the gates twelve angels, and names written thereon, which are the names of the twelve tribes of the children of Israel: 13 on the east three gates; on the north three gates; on the south three gates; and on the west three gates. 14 And the wall of the city had twelve foundations, and in them the names of the twelve apostles of the Lamb. 15 And he that talked with me had a golden reed to measure the city, and the gates thereof, and the wall thereof. 16 And the city lieth foursquare, and the length is as large as the breadth: and he measured the city with the reed, twelve thousand furlongs. The length and the breadth and the height of it are equal. 17 And he measured the wall thereof, an hundred and forty and four cubits, according to the measure of a man, that is, of the an-

9 Καὶ ἦλθεν ¹πρός με‖ εἷς ᵏ τῶν ἑπτὰ ἀγγέλων τῶν ἐχόν-
And came　to me　one of the seven　angels　which　had
των τὰς ἑπτὰ φιάλας ¹τὰς γεμούσας‖ τῶν ἑπτὰ πληγῶν τῶν
the seven bowls　full　of the seven ²plagues
ἐσχάτων, καὶ ἐλάλησεν μετ᾽ ἐμοῦ, λέγων, Δεῦρο, δείξω
¹last,　and spoke　with me,　saying,　Come hither, I will shew
σοι τὴν νύμφην ᵐτοῦ ἀρνίου τὴν γυναῖκα.‖ 10 Καὶ ἀπήνεγκέν
thee the bride　²Lamb's ¹the　wife.　And he carried away
με ἐν πνεύματι ⁿἐπ᾽‖ ὄρος μέγα καὶ ὑψηλόν, καὶ ἔδειξέν
me in [the] Spirit　to a mountain great and　high,　and shewed
μοι τὴν πόλιν ᵒτὴν μεγάλην,ᵏ τὴν ἁγίαν Ἱερουσαλήμ, κατα-
me the ²city ¹great,　the holy　Jerusalem,　de-
βαίνουσαν ἐκ τοῦ οὐρανοῦ ἀπὸ τοῦ θεοῦ, 11 ἔχουσαν τὴν
scending out of the heaven from　God,　11 having the
δόξαν τοῦ θεοῦ· ᵖκαὶ‖ ὁ.φωστὴρ.αὐτῆς ὅμοιος λίθῳ τιμιω-
glory of God, and　her radiance [was] like a stone most pre-
　　　　　　　　　　　　　　　　　　(lit. her luminary)
τάτῳ, ὡς λίθῳ ἰάσπιδι κρυσταλλίζοντι· 12 ᑫἔχουσάν τε‖
cious,　as a ²stone ²jasper ¹crystal-like;　having also
τεῖχος μέγα καὶ ὑψηλόν, ʳἔχουσαν‖ πυλῶνας δώδεκα, ˢκαὶ᛫ ἐπὶ
a wall great and high;　having ²gates ¹twelve, and at
ᵗτοῖς πυλῶσιν‖ ἀγγέλους δώδεκα,‖ καὶ ὀνόματα ἐπιγεγραμ-
the gates　²angels ¹twelve,　and names　inscrib-
μένα, ἅ ἐστιν ᵛ τῶν δώδεκα φυλῶν ʷτῶν‖ υἱῶν Ἰσραήλ·
ed,　which are [those] of the twelve tribes of the sons of Israel.
13 ˣἀπ᾽‖ ʸἀνατολῆς‖ πυλῶνες τρεῖς· ᶻ ἀπὸ βορρᾶ
On [the]　east　²gates ¹three;　on [the] north
πυλῶνες τρεῖς· ᶻ ἀπὸ νότου πυλῶνες τρεῖς· ᶻ ἀπὸ
²gates ¹three;　on [the] south ²gates ¹three,　on [the]
δυσμῶν πυλῶνες τρεῖς. 14 καὶ τὸ τεῖχος τῆς πόλεως ᵃἔχον‖
west ²gates ¹three.　And the wall of the city having
θεμελίους δώδεκα, καὶ ᵇἐν αὐτοῖς‖ ὀνόματα τῶν δώδεκα
²foundations ¹twelve, and in them　names　of the twelve
ἀποστόλων τοῦ ἀρνίου. 15 καὶ ὁ λαλῶν μετ᾽ ἐμοῦ εἶχεν ᶜ
apostles of the Lamb.　And he speaking with me had
κάλαμον χρυσοῦν, ἵνα μετρήσῃ τὴν πόλιν, καὶ τοὺς πυ-
a ²reed ¹golden, that he might measure the city, and
λῶνας αὐτῆς, καὶ τὸ.τεῖχος.αὐτῆς. 16 καὶ ἡ πόλις τετράγωνος
²gates ¹its, and its wall.　And the city ²four-square
κεῖται, καὶ τὸ.μῆκος.αὐτῆς ᵈτοσοῦτόν ἐστιν‖ ὅσον ᵉκαὶ‖ τὸ
¹lies, and its length so much is as also the
πλάτος. καὶ ἐμέτρησεν τὴν πόλιν τῷ καλάμῳ ἐπὶ ᶠσταδίων‖
breadth. And he measured the city with the reed— ²furlongs
δώδεκα χιλιάδων· τὸ μῆκος καὶ τὸ πλάτος καὶ τὸ ὕψος αὐτῆς
¹twelve ²thousand; the length and the breadth and the height of it
ἴσα ἐστίν. 17 καὶ ἐμέτρησεν τὸ.τεῖχος.αὐτῆς ἑκατὸν
²equal ¹are.　And he measured　its wall,　a hundred [and]
ᵍτεσσαράκοντα τεσσάρων‖ πηχῶν μέτρον ἀνθρώπου, ὅ ἐστιν
forty　four　cubits, ²measure ¹a ²man's, which is,

i — πρός με GLTTrAW.
[angels] were full LTTrA. ᵐ τὴν γυναῖκα τοῦ ἀρνίου LTTrAW. ⁿ ἐπὶ LTTrAW. ᵒ — τὴν
μεγάλην (read the holy city) GLTTrAW. ᵖ — καὶ GLTTrAW. ᑫ ἔχουσα (omit
also) GLTTrAW. ʳ ἔχουσα GLTTrA. ˢ — καὶ ἐπὶ τοῖς πυλῶσιν ἀγγέλους δώδεκα L.
ᵗ τοὺς πυλῶνας Tr. ᵛ + τὰ ὀνόματα the names L[TrA]. ʷ — τῶν (read of [the]) LTTrAW.
ˣ ἀπὸ GLTTrAW. ʸ ἀνατολῶν GW. ᶻ + καὶ and LTTrAW. ᵃ ἔχων TTrA. ᵇ ἐπ᾽
αὐτῶν δώδεκα on them twelve GLTTrAW. ᶜ + μέτρον a measure GLTTrA. ᵈ — τοσοῦ-
τόν ἐστιν (read [is]) GLTTrAW. ᵉ — καὶ TTr[A]. ᶠ σταδίους EGLTrA. ᵍ τεσσεράκοντα τεσσάρων LT; τεσσαρακοντατεσσάρων (τεσσε- A) EAW.

ἀγγέλου. 18 καὶ ¹ἦν‖·ἡ ᵏἐνδόμησις‖ τοῦ.τείχους.αὐτῆς
[the] angel's.   And ⁶was ¹the ²structure ³of ⁴its ⁴wall

ᾔασπις· καὶ ἡ πόλις χρυσίον καθαρόν, ¹ὁμοία‖ ὑάλῳ καθαρῷ,
jasper ; and the city ²gold ¹pure, like ²glass ³pure :

19 ᵐκαὶ‖ οἱ θεμέλιοι τοῦ τείχους τῆς πόλεως παντὶ λίθῳ
and the foundations of the wall of the city with every ²stone

τιμίῳ κεκοσμημένοι. ὁ θεμέλιος ὁ πρῶτος ἴασπις· ὁ
¹precious [were] adorned : the ²foundation ¹first, jasper ; the

δεύτερος σάπφειρος· ὁ τρίτος ⁿχαλκηδών·‖ ὁ τέταρτος σμά-
¹second, sapphire ; the third, ·chalcedony ; the fourth, eme-

ραγδος· 20 ὁ πέμπτος °σαρδόνυξ·‖ ὁ ἕκτος ᴾσάρδιος·‖ ὁ
rald ; the fifth, sardonyx ; the sixth, sardius ; the

ἕβδομος χρυσόλιθος· ὁ ὄγδοος βήρυλλος· ὁ ᑫἔνατος‖ τοπά-
⁵seventh, chrysolite ; the eighth, beryl ; the ninth, to-

ζιον· ὁ δέκατος ʳχρυσόπρασος·‖ ὁ ἑνδέκατος ὑάκινθος· ὁ
paz ; the tenth, chrysoprasus ; the eleventh, jacinth ; the

δωδέκατος ἀμέθυστος. 21 καὶ οἱ δώδεκα πυλῶνες, δώδεκα
twelfth, amethyst. And the twelve gates, twelve

μαργαρῖται· ἀνὰ εἷς ἕκαστος τῶν πυλώνων ἦν ἐξ ἑνὸς
pearls ; ²respectively ²one ¹each of the gates was of one

μαργαρίτου· καὶ ἡ πλατεῖα τῆς πόλεως, χρυσίον καθαρόν, ὡς
pearl ; and the street of the city ²gold ¹pure, as

ὕαλος ˢδιαφανής.‖ 22 Καὶ ναὸν οὐκ εἶδον· ἐν αὐτῇ· ὁ.γὰρ
²glass ¹transparent. And ⁴temple ²no ¹I ³saw in it ; for the

κύριος ὁ θεὸς ὁ παντοκράτωρ ᵗ ναὸς.αὐτῆς ἐστιν, καὶ τὸ
Lord God Almighty its temple is, and the

ἀρνίον. 23 καὶ ἡ πόλις οὐ χρείαν ἔχει τοῦ ἡλίου, οὐδὲ τῆς
Lamb. And the city ²no ³need ¹has of the sun, nor of the

σελήνης, ἵνα φαίνωσιν ᵛἐν‖ αὐτῇ· ἡ.γὰρ δόξα τοῦ θεοῦ ἐφώ-
moon, that they should shine in it ; for the glory of God en-

τισεν αὐτήν, καὶ ὁ λύχνος αὐτῆς τὸ ἀρνίον. 24 καὶ ʷτὰ
lightened it, and the lamp of it [is] the Lamb. And the

ἔθνη τῶν σωζομένων ἐν τῷ.φωτὶ.αὐτῆς περιπατήσουσιν·‖ καὶ
nations of the saved in its light shall walk ; and

οἱ βασιλεῖς τῆς γῆς φέρουσιν τὴν δόξαν ˣκαὶ τὴν τιμὴν‖ αὐτῶν
the kings · of the earth bring ²glory ³and ⁴honour ¹their

εἰς αὐτήν. 25 καὶ οἱ.πυλῶνες.αὐτῆς οὐ.μὴ κλεισθῶσιν ἡμέρας·
unto it. And its gates not at all shall be shut by day ;

νὺξ γὰρ οὐκ ἔσται ἐκεῖ. 26 καὶ οἴσουσιν τὴν δόξαν καὶ
²night ¹for ²no shall be there. And they shall bring the glory and

τὴν τιμὴν τῶν ἐθνῶν εἰς αὐτήν. 27 καὶ οὐ.μὴ εἰσέλθῃ εἰς
the honour of the nations unto it. And in no wise may enter into

αὐτὴν πᾶν ʸκοινοῦν,‖ καὶ ᶻποιοῦν‖ βδέλυγμα καὶ ψεῦ-
it anything defiling, and practising abomination and a
(lit. everything)

δος· εἰ.μὴ οἱ γεγραμμένοι ἐν τῷ βιβλίῳ τῆς ζωῆς τοῦ
lie ; but those who are written in the book of life of the

ἀρνίου.
Lamb.

22 Καὶ ἔδειξέν μοι ᵃκαθαρὸν‖ ποταμὸν ὕδατος ζωῆς,
And he shewed me ²pure ¹a river of water of life,

---

gel. 18 And the build-
ing of the wall of it
was of jasper : and the
city was pure gold,
like unto clear glass.
19 And the founda-
tions of the wall of the
city were garnished
with all manner of
precious stones. The
first foundation was
jasper ; the second,
sapphire ; the third,
a chalcedony ; the
fourth, an emerald ;
20 the fifth, sardonyx ;
the sixth, sardius ; the
seventh chrysolite ;
the eighth, beryl ; the
ninth, a topaz ; the
tenth, a chrysoprasus ;
the eleventh, a jacinth ;
the twelfth, an ame-
thyst. 21 And the
twelve gates were
twelve pearls ; every
several gate was of
one pearl : and the
street of the city was
pure gold, as it were
transparent glass.
22 And I saw no tem-
ple therein : for the
Lord God Almighty
and the Lamb are the
temple of it. 23 And
the city had no need
of the sun, neither of
the moon, to shine in
it : for the glory of
God did lighten it,
and the Lamb is the
light thereof. 24 And
the nations of them
which are saved shall
walk in the light of
it : and the kings of the
earth do bring their
glory and honour into
it. 25 And the gates
of it shall not be shut
at all by day : for
there shall be no night
there. 26 And they
shall bring the glory
and honour of the na-
tions into it. 27 And
there shall in no wise
enter into it any
thing that defileth,
neither whatsoever
worketh abomination,
or maketh a lie : but
they which are written
in the Lamb's book of
life.

XXII. And he shew-
ed me a pure river of
water of life, clear as

ⁱ — ἦν (read [was]) LTA. ᵏ ἐνδώμησις TTr. ˡ ὅμοιον LTTrAW. ᵐ — καὶ LTA. ⁿ χαλ-
κεδών T. ° σαρδιόνυξ L. ᴾ σάρδιον LTTrAW. ᑫ ἔννατος EGW. ʳ χρυσόπρασον L.
ˢ διαυγής GLTTrAW. ᵗ + ὁ L[A]W. ᵛ — ἐν (read αὐτῇ for it) GLTTrAW. ʷ περιπατήσουσιν τὰ ἔθνη.διὰ τοῦ φωτὸς αὐτῆς the nations shall walk by means of its light
GLTTrAW. ˣ — τὴν W ; — καὶ τὴν τιμὴν LTTrA. ʸ κοινὸν common GLTTrAW. ᶻ (+ ὁ
he who TTr) ποιῶν ([he who] LAW) practises LTTrAW. ᵃ — καθαρὸν GLTTrAW.

crystal, proceeding out of the throne of God and of the Lamb. 2 In the midst of the street of it, and on either side of the river, *was there* the tree of life, which bare twelve *manner of* fruits, *and* yielded her fruit every month; and the leaves of the tree *were* for the healing of the nations. 3 And there shall be no more curse : but the throne of God and of the Lamb shall be in it ; and his servants shall serve him : 4 and they shall see his face ; and his name *shall be* in their foreheads. 5 And there shall be no night there; and they need no candle, neither light of the sun ; for the Lord God giveth them light : and they shall reign for ever and ever.

λαμπρὸν ὡς κρύσταλλον, ἐκπορευόμενον ἐκ τοῦ θρόνου τοῦ
bright   as   crystal,   going forth   out of the   throne
θεοῦ καὶ τοῦ ἀρνίου. 2 ἐν μέσῳ τῆς.πλατείας.αὐτῆς, καὶ τοῦ
of God and of the   Lamb.   In the midst   of its street,   and of the
ποταμοῦ, ἐντεῦθεν καὶ [b]ἐντεῦθεν,[|] ξύλον ζωῆς, [c]ποιοῦν[|]
river,   on this side and   on that side,   [the] tree   of life, producing
καρποὺς δώδεκα, κατὰ [d]μῆνα[|] [e]ἕνα[|] ἕκαστον [f]ἀποδιδοῦν[|] τὸν
[2]fruits   [1]twelve,   [4]month   [3]each   yielding
καρπὸν αὐτοῦ· καὶ τὰ φύλλα τοῦ ξύλου εἰς θεραπείαν τῶν
[2]fruit   [1]its ;   and the leaves of the tree   for   healing   of the
ἐθνῶν. 3 Καὶ πᾶν [g]κατανάθεμα[|] οὐκ ἔσται ἔτι· καὶ ὁ θρόνος
nations.   And [2]any   [3]curse   [1]not shall be longer; and the throne
       (*lit.* every)
τοῦ θεοῦ καὶ τοῦ ἀρνίου ἐν αὐτῇ ἔσται· καὶ οἱ.δοῦλοι.αὐτοῦ
of God and of the Lamb   in   it   shall be ; and   his bondmen
λατρεύσουσιν αὐτῷ· 4 καὶ ὄψονται τὸ.πρόσωπον.αὐτοῦ, καὶ
shall serve   him,   and they shall see   his face ;   and
τὸ.ὄνομα.αὐτοῦ ἐπὶ τῶν.μετώπων.αὐτῶν. 5 καὶ νὺξ οὐκ ἔσται
his name   on   their foreheads   [is]. And [2]night [1]no shall be
[h]ἐκεῖ[|] καὶ [i]χρείαν οὐκ ἔχουσιν[|] [k]λύχνου καὶ φωτὸς ἡλίου,[|]
there, and   [4]need   [3]no [1]they [2]have   of a lamp and of light of [the] sun,
ὅτι   κύριος ὁ θεὸς [m]φωτίζει[|] αὐτούς· καὶ βασιλεύσουσιν
because [the] Lord   God   enlightens   them,   and   they shall reign
εἰς τοὺς αἰῶνας τῶν αἰώνων.
to   the   ages   of the   ages.

6 Καὶ εἶπέν μοι, Οὗτοι οἱ λόγοι   πιστοὶ καὶ ἀληθινοί·
And he said to me, These   words [are] faithful and   true;

6 And he said unto me, These sayings *are* faithful and true: and the Lord God of the holy prophets sent his angel to shew unto his servants the things which must shortly be done. 7 Behold, I come quickly : blessed *is* he that keepeth the sayings of the prophecy of this book. 8 And I John saw these things, and heard *them*. And when I had heard and seen, I fell down to worship before the feet of the angel which shewed me these things. 9 Then saith he unto me, See *thou do it* not: for I am thy fellowservant, and of *thy* brethren the prophets, and of them which keep the sayings of this book: worship God. 10 And he saith unto me, Seal not the sayings of the prophecy of this book: for the time is at hand. 11 He that is unjust,

καὶ [n]κύριος ὁ θεὸς τῶν [o]ἁγίων[|] προφητῶν ἀπέστειλεν τὸν
and [the] Lord   God of the   holy   prophets   sent
ἄγγελον αὐτοῦ δεῖξαι τοῖς.δούλοις.αὐτοῦ   ἃ   δεῖ γε-
[2]angel   [1]his to shew   his bondmen   the things which must come
νέσθαι ἐν.τάχει. 7 [p]Ἰδού,[|] ἔρχομαι ταχύ. μακάριος ὁ
to pass   soon.   Behold, I am coming quickly. Blessed [is] he who
τηρῶν τοὺς λόγους τῆς προφητείας τοῦ.βιβλίου.τούτου. 8 [q]Καὶ[|]
keeps   the words of the   prophecy   of this book.   And
ἐγὼ[|] Ἰωάννης ὁ [r]βλέπων ταῦτα καὶ ἀκούων·[|]
I   John   [was] he who [was]   seeing [3]these [4]things [1]and [2]hearing.
καὶ ὅτε ἤκουσα καὶ [s]ἔβλεψα[|] [t]ἔπεσα[|] προσκυνῆσαι ἔμπροσθεν
And when I heard and   saw   I fell down   to do homage   before
τῶν ποδῶν τοῦ ἀγγέλου τοῦ [u]δεικνύοντός[|] μοι ταῦτα. 9 καὶ
the   feet of the   angel   who [was]   shewing   me these things. And
λέγει μοι, Ὅρα   μή· σύνδουλός σου [v]γάρ[|] εἰμι, καὶ
he says to me, See [thou do it] not : [4]fellowbondman [5]of [6]thee [1]for [2]I [3]am, and
τῶν.ἀδελφῶν.σου τῶν προφητῶν, καὶ τῶν τηρούντων τοὺς
of thy brethren   the   prophets,   and of those who   keep   the
λόγους τοῦ.βιβλίου.τούτου· τῷ θεῷ προσκύνησον. 10 Καὶ
words   of this book ·   to God   do homage.   And
λέγει μοι, Μή.σφραγίσῃς τοὺς λόγους τῆς προφητείας τοῦ
he says to me, Seal not   the   words of the   prophecy   of
βιβλίου τούτου· [w]ὅτι[|] ὁ καιρὸς [x]ἐγγύς ἐστιν. 11 ὁ ἀδι-
[1]book   [1]of [2]this ;   because the time   [2]near [1]is.   He that is un-

---

[b] ἐκεῖθεν LTTrAW.   [c] ποιῶν T.   [d] μῆναν L.   [e] — ἕνα GLTTrAW.   [f] ἀποδιδοὺς TTrA.
[g] κατάθεμα GLTTrAW.   [h] ἔτι longer GLTTrAW.   [i] οὐχ ἕξουσιν they shall have no (οὐκ
ἔχουσιν TTr) χρείαν LTTrAW ; οὐ χρεία G.   [k] + φωτὸς of light LTTrA.   [l] — ἡλίου W.
[m] φωτιεῖ (φωτίσει L) ἐπ' shall enlighten GLTTrAW.   [n] + ὁ the LTTrA.   [o] πνευμάτων τῶν
spirits of the GLTTrAW.   [p] + καὶ and. GLTTrAW.   [q] κἀγὼ LTTrAW.   [r] ἀκούων καὶ βλέπων
ταῦτα GLTTrAW ; βλέπων καὶ ἀκούων ταῦτα T.   [s] ἔβλεπον W.   [t] ἔπεσον EG.   [u] δεικνύν-
τος T.   [v] — γάρ GLTTrAW.   [w] — ὅτι GLTTrAW.   [x] + γὰρ for (the time) LTTrAW.

κῶν ἀδικησάτω ἔτι· καὶ ʲὸ ῥυπῶν‖ ᶻῥυπωσάτω‖
righteous let him be unrighteous still; and he that is filthy   let him be filthy

ἔτι· καὶ ὁ δίκαιος ᵃδικαιωθήτω‖ ἔτι· καὶ ὁ ἅγιος
still; and he that [is] righteous let him be righteous still; and he that [is] holy

ἁγιασθήτω ἔτι. 12 ᵇΚαὶ‖ ἰδού, ἔρχομαι ταχύ, καὶ ὁ
let him be sanctified still. And, behold, I am coming quickly, and

μισθός μου μετ᾽ ἐμοῦ, ἀποδοῦναι· ἑκάστῳ ὡς τὸ ἔργον ᶜαὐτοῦ
reward ¹my with me, to render to each as ²work ¹his

ἔσται.‖ 13 ἐγώ ᵈεἰμι‖ τὸ ᵉΑ‖ καὶ τὸ ᶠΩ,‖ ᵍἀρχὴ καὶ τέλος,
shall be. I am the A and the Ω, [the] beginning and end,

ὁ πρῶτος καὶ ὁ ἔσχατος.‖ 14 Μακάριοι   οἱ ᵇποιοῦν-
the first and the last. Blessed [are] they that do

τες τὰς ἐντολὰς αὐτοῦ,‖ ἵνα ἔσται ἡ ἐξουσία αὐτῶν ἐπὶ τὸ
his commandments, that ³shall ⁴be ¹their ²authority to the

ξύλον τῆς ζωῆς, καὶ τοῖς πυλῶσιν εἰσέλθωσιν εἰς τὴν πόλιν.
tree of life, and by the gates they should go in to the city.

15 ἔξω ⁱδὲ‖ οἱ κύνες καὶ οἱ φαρμακοὶ καὶ οἱ πόρνοι καὶ
But without [are] the dogs, and the sorcerers, and the fornicators, and

οἱ φονεῖς καὶ οἱ εἰδωλολάτραι, καὶ πᾶς ᵏὁ‖ ˡφιλῶν καὶ
the murderers, and the idolaters, and everyone that loves and

ποιῶν‖ ᶦψεῦδος.
practises a lie.

16 Ἐγὼ Ἰησοῦς ἔπεμψα τὸν ἄγγελόν μου μαρτυρῆσαι
I   Jesus sent mine angel to testify

ὑμῖν ταῦτα ᵐἐπὶ‖ ταῖς ἐκκλησίαις· ἐγώ εἰμι ἡ ῥίζα καὶ
to you these things in the assemblies. I am the root and

τὸ γένος ⁿτοῦ‖ ᵒΔαυΐδ,‖ ὁ ἀστὴρ ὁ λαμπρὸς ᵖκαὶ‖ ᑫὀρθρι-
the offspring of David, the ⁴star ¹bright ²and ³morn-

νός.‖ 17 Καὶ τὸ πνεῦμα καὶ ἡ νύμφη λέγουσιν, ʳΕλθέ·‖
ing. And the Spirit and the bride say, Come.

καὶ ὁ ἀκούων εἰπάτω, ʳἘλθέ.‖ καὶ ὁ διψῶν ˢἐλθέτω,‖
And he that hears let him say, Come. And he that thirsts let him come;

ᵗκαὶ‖ ὁ θέλων ᵛλαμβανέτω τὸ‖ ὕδωρ ζωῆς δωρεάν.
and he that wills, let him take the water of life gratuitously.

18 ʷΣυμμαρτυροῦμαι γὰρ‖ παντὶ ˣ ἀκούοντι τοὺς λόγους
For I jointly testify to everyone hearing the words

τῆς προφητείας τοῦ βιβλίου τούτου· ἐάν τις ʸᵃἐπιτιθῇ πρὸς
of the prophecy of this book, If anyone should add to

ταῦτα,‖ ἐπιθήσει ᶻᵃὁ θεὸς ἐπ᾽ αὐτὸν‖ τὰς πληγὰς τὰς γε-
these things, ²shall ³add ¹God unto him the plagues which are

γραμμένας ⁱἐν ᵃᵃ βιβλίῳ τούτῳ· 19 καὶ ἐάν τις ᵇᵃἀφαιρῇ‖
written in this book. And if anyone should take

ἀπὸ τῶν λόγων ᶜᵃβίβλου‖ τῆς προφητείας ταύτης, ᵈᵃἀφαιρή-
from the words of [the] book of this prophecy, ²shall ²take

σει‖ ὁ θεὸς τὸ μέρος αὐτοῦ ἀπὸ ᵉᵃβίβλου‖ τῆς ζωῆς, καὶ
away ¹God his part from [the] book of life, and

(right margin KJV text)
let him be unjust still: and he which is filthy, let him be filthy still: and he that is righteous, let him be righteous still: and he that is holy, let him be holy still. 12 And, behold, I come quickly; and my reward is with me, to give every man according as his work shall be. 13 I am Alpha and Omega, the beginning and the end, the first and the last. 14 Blessed are they that do his commandments, that they may have right to the tree of life, and may enter in through the gates into the city. 15 For without are dogs, and sorcerers, and whoremongers, and murderers, and idolaters, and whosoever loveth and maketh a lie.

16 I Jesus have sent mine angel to testify unto you these things in the churches. I am the root and the offspring of David, and the bright and morning star. 17 And the Spirit and the bride say, Come. And let him that heareth say, Come. And let him that is athirst come. And whosoever will, let him take the water of life freely.

18 For I testify unto every man that heareth the words of the prophecy of this book, If any man shall add unto these things, God shall add unto him the plagues that are written in this book: 19 and if any man shall take away from the words of the book of this prophecy, God shall take away his part out of the book of life,

---

ʲ ὁ ῥυπαρὸς the filthy [one] GLTTrAW. ᶻ ῥυπανθήτω LTTrA ; ῥυπαρευθήτω GW. ᵃ δικαιοσύνην ποιησάτω let him practise righteousness GLTTrAW. ᵇ — καὶ GLTTrAW. ᶜ ἐστιν
αὐτοῦ (read his work is) LTTrA. ᵈ — εἰμι (read [am]) GLTTrAW. ᵉ ἄλφα Alpha LTTrAW.
ᶠ ὦ L. ᵍ ὁ (— ὁ L[A]) πρῶτος καὶ ὁ (— ὁ L[A]) ἔσχατος, (+ ἡ the GLTA) ἀρχὴ καὶ (+ τὸ the
GLTA) τέλος GLTTrA. ʰ πλύνοντες τὰς στολὰς αὐτῶν wash their robes LTTrA. ⁱ — δὲ
but GLTTrAW. ᵏ — ὁ (read loving and practising) LTTrAW. ˡ ποιῶν καὶ φιλῶν T.
ᵐ — ἐπὶ (read ταῖς to the) W ; ἐν L. ⁿ — τοῦ GLTTrAW. ᵒ Δαυείδ LTTrA ; Δαυΐδ GW.
ᵖ — καὶ GTTrAW. ᑫ ὁ πρωϊνός the morning GLTTrAW. ʳ Ἔρχου GLTTrAW. ʳ ἐρχέσθω
GLTTrAW. ᵗ — καὶ GLTTrAW. ᵛ λαβέτω GLTTrAW. ʷ Μαρτυρῶ ἐγὼ I testify GLTTrAW.
ˣ + τῷ who (hears) GLTTrAW. ʸᵃ ἐπιθῇ ἐπ᾽ αὐτά GLTTrAW. ᶻᵃ ἐπ᾽ αὐτὸν ὁ θεὸς T.
ᵃᵃ + τῷ GLTTrAW. ᵇᵃ ἀφέλῃ GLTTrAW. ᶜᵃ τοῦ βιβλίου GLTTrAW. ᵈᵃ ἀφελεῖ GLTTrAW.
ᵉᵃ τοῦ ξύλου the tree GLTTrAW.

and out of the holy city, and *from* the things which are written in this book.

f^{ἐκ}‖ τῆς πόλεως τῆς ἁγίας, ^gκαὶ‖ τῶν γεγραμμένων
out of the ²city ¹holy, and of those who are written
ἐν ^h βιβλίῳ τούτῳ.
in ²book ¹this.

20 He which testifieth these things saith, Surely I come quickly. Amen. Even so, come, Lord Jesus.

20 Λέγει ὁ μαρτυρῶν ταῦτα, Ναὶ ἔρχομαι ταχύ.
⁶Says ¹he ²who ³testifies ⁴these ⁵things, Yea, I am coming quickly.
Ἀμήν. ⁱΝαί,‖ ἔρχου, κύριε Ἰησοῦ.
Amen; yea, come, Lord Jesus.

21 The grace of our Lord Jesus Christ *be* with you all. Amen.

21 Ἡ χάρις τοῦ κυρίου.^kἡμῶν‖ Ἰησοῦ ¹χριστοῦ‖ μετὰ
The grace of our Lord Jesus Christ [be] with
^mπάντων‖ ⁿὑμῶν.‖ ^o ᵖΑμήν.‖ ^q
²all ¹you. Amen.

---

f — ἐκ L[TrA]. g — καὶ (*read* τῶν which) GLTTrAW. h + τῷ GLTTrAW. i — Ναι
GLTTrAW ; (*join* Amen *with* quickly ETr). k — ἡμῶν (*read* of the Lord) GLTTrAW.
l — χριστοῦ LTTrA. m — πάντων TrA. n — ὑμῶν GLTTrAW. o + τῶν ἁγίων the
saints GTrAW. p — Ἀμήν GLTTrA. q + ἀποκάλυψις Ἰωάννου Revelation of John A.

ΤΕΛΟΣ.

A NEW

Greek-English Lexicon

TO THE

New Testament

SUPPLEMENTED BY A CHAPTER ELUCIDATING THE SYNONYMS OF
THE NEW TESTAMENT WITH A COMPLETE INDEX
TO THE SYNONYMS

BY

THE LATE GEORGE RICKER BERRY, Ph.D.

OF THE UNIVERSITY OF CHICAGO AND COLGATE UNIVERSITY
DEPARTMENT OF SEMITIC LANGUAGES

EDITOR OF

THE INTERLINEAR HEBREW-ENGLISH OLD TESTAMENT

Chicago, WILCOX & FOLLETT *Company*
1952

INTRODUCTION TO NEW TESTAMENT LEXICON.

AS a result of their wide experience as sellers of text-books of all kinds, extending over many years, the publishers have become aware that clergymen, theological students, and New Testament students generally, possess the conviction that none of the smaller New Testament Lexicons is entirely satisfactory. There are several essential and entirely practical features, not embodied in any of the smaller New Testament Lexicons, which should be incorporated in a work intended to fulfill all necessary require- ments. It is with the definite intention of supplying this need that the publishers have undertaken the preparation of this new Lexicon. It aims to retain all the desirable features of the best small Lexicons in use, and also to present the several additional points demanded, while keeping within the compass of a volume of convenient size.

This Lexicon endeavors to put into a brief and compact form as much as possible of the material found in the larger New Testament Lexicons. The fact has been remembered that in nine cases out of ten the object in consulting a Lexicon is to refer quickly to the standard meanings of a word, rather than to study an exhaustive treatment of it. Hence, while every clergyman would like to possess one of the larger New Testament Lexicons, he still needs the small one for convenience in ordinary use. So it is assumed that this small New Testament Lexicon will be needed both for use independently, and also by those who have one of the larger Lexicons. It is hoped that in this volume the publishers' intention has been realized of producing a volume that better than any other so far published will serve this purpose quickly and well.

It may be desirable to point out a few features which have been made prominent. It will be at once apparent that some of these are not ordinarily found in the smaller New Testament Lexicons:

The inflection of nouns, adjectives, and verbs has been indicated with all the fullness which was considered practically necessary. In nouns, the ending of the genitive case has regularly been given, being omitted only with indeclinable nouns. The article indicating the gender regularly follows the genitive ending. Other cases have been given only rarely, when they are irregular or peculiar. In adjectives, the endings of the nominative have been given. In verbs, a different form for the present tense, such as a contracted form, has regularly been given, and ordinarily the ending of the future. The endings of the other tenses have only been given in some special cases when they are peculiar, or irregular. Of course the inflection in general has considered only the forms occurring in the New Testament; it is only rarely that classical forms not occurring in the New Testament have been given, since they would be of little practical value in ordinary New Testament study.

The hyphen, to separate the parts of compound words, has been used with considerable freedom, but in general accordance with the following principles. It has been used of course to separate the parts of words which are actually compounded of the two or more portions which appear in the word. Words derived from a compound word would not usually have the hyphen, but sometimes it has been inserted, especially when otherwise the derivation would not be obvious. So, too, the hyphen has been used with derivatives of a compound word, in cases where the original compound word does not occur in the New Testament, as otherwise the character of the word would not appear. The hyphen has also been used in many cases where the compound word is slightly changed in form from the parts of which it is composed, where this variation is not very great. Such a wide use of the hyphen has been for the purpose of increasing the practical value of this feature.

The original plan in reference to Synonyms was to give in the Lexicon itself definitions of a few of the most important ones. After most of the Lexicon was in type, however, it was decided, in view of the importance of the subject, that a very helpful feature would be a special section devoted to Synonyms. This has accordingly been prepared. The result is, of course, that a few words already treated in the Lexicon have here been given a fuller treatment.

The Index to the Synonyms includes all the nouns treated in the Lexicon proper, as well as those in the Synonyms, and this double treatment will always be found to be expressly indicated by its appropriate sign.

Some indications of the history of a word will surely be serviceable to the average student. Consequently, the words whose first known occurrence is in the Septuagint, in the Apocrypha, and in the New Testament, are indicated by the respective abbreviations at the end of the articles. Where the usage is in doubt, no indication has been given. The material for this has been drawn chiefly from Thayer. The other classifications which Thayer gives, it was thought would not be of sufficient practical use to the average student to be incorporated.

In the case of words from foreign languages, the language has been indicated in every instance, except with a part of the proper names, chiefly from the Hebrew, where the origin would be readily inferred. It has been the aim to make this feature accurate and up to date. In this matter, considerable help has been received from E. Kautzsch, *Grammatik des Biblisch-Aramäischen.*

The grammatical references given are to the three grammars which are probably in the most common use, viz.: S. G. Green, *Handbook to the Grammar of the Greek Testament,* Revised and Improved Edition; G. B. Winer, *A Grammar of the Idiom of the New Testament,* Seventh Edition, Translated by J. H. Thayer; and Alexander Buttman, *A Grammar of the New Testament Greek,* Translated by J. H. Thayer. These have been indicated respectively by the abbreviations Gr., Wi., and Bu., the references in the first two being by sections, in the last, for convenience, by pages.

The usual custom has been followed of making the received text, the so-called *Textus Receptus,* the basis of this Lexicon, except that sometimes another accentuation has been adopted, which seemed preferable. All the variations of any importance of the text of Westcott and Hort have been given. This does not include all the minor variations in spelling and accentuation. It was thought that to indicate the variants of other editors would occupy more space than it would be profitable to give. For the same reason no mention has been made of variant readings of the *Textus Receptus* itself.

The asterisk * at the end of many articles indicates that all the passages in which the word occurs in the New Testament have been given.

Besides other works which have already been mentioned, much material has been drawn from R. C. Trench, *Synonyms of the New Testament,* and from the New Testament Lexicons of Thayer and Cremer, as well as from the small ones of Green and Hickie.

The New Testament books have been indicated by the shortest abbreviations that would be easily intelligible. It is thought that they will be understood without explanation. The list of other abbreviations which is here added includes only those which might not be recognized without express indication.

ABBREVIATIONS.

Ap.	= Apocrypha (of the Old Testament).	**O. T.**	= Old Testament.
A. V.	= Authorized Version.	**Rec.**	= Textus Receptus.
Bu.	= Alexander Buttman (*Grammar of New Testament Greek*).	**R. V.**	= Revised Version.
		S.	= Septuagint.
dim.	= diminutive.	**sc.**	= namely, to wit.
fig.	= figurative.	**sq.**	= following.
Gr.	= S. G. Green (*Handbook to the Grammar of the Greek Testament*).	**W. H.**	= Westcott and Hort (*The New Testament in the Original Greek*).
i.e.	= that is.	**Wi.**	= G. B. Winer (*Grammar of the Idiom of the New Testament*).
lit.	= literally.		
met.	= metaphorically.		- hyphen, see Introduction.
mrg.	= margin.		* indicates that all the passages in which a
N. T.	= New Testament.		word occurs in the New Testament
orig.	= originally.		have been given.

Concerning the abbreviations for the Books of the New Testament, see last paragraph of
Introduction.

GREEK-ENGLISH NEW TESTAMENT LEXICON.

Ἀ, α, ἄλφα, *alpha*, *a*, the first letter. Numerally, α' = 1; ‚α = 1000. For α in composition, see Gr. § 147*b*, *c*. Fig., τὸ Α, or τὸ Ἄλφα (W. H.), *the first principle of all things;* of the Father, Rev. i. 8, xxi. 6; the Son, i. 11 (W. H. omit), xxii. 13.*

Ἀαρών (Heb.), *Aaron*, Lu. i. 5; Ac. vii. 40; Heb. v. 4, vii. 11, ix. 4.*

Ἀβαδδών, ὁ (Heb. "destruction"), *Abaddon*, Rev. ix. 11. (S.)*

ἀ-βαρής, ές (from βάρος), *without weight;* hence, *not burdensome*, 2 Cor. xi. 9.*

Ἀββᾶ, or Ἀββά (W. H.), (Aram.), *Father!* only as an invocation, Mar. xiv. 36; Ro. viii. 15; Gal. iv. 6. (N. T.)*

Ἄβελ, ὁ (W. H. Ἅβελ), (Heb.), *Abel*, Mat. xxiii. 35; Lu. xi. 51; Heb. xi. 4, xii. 24.*

Ἀβιά, ὁ (Heb.), *Abia* or *Abijah*, the king, Mat. i. 7; the priest, Lu. i. 5.*

Ἀβιάθαρ, ὁ (Heb.), *Abiathar*, Mar. ii. 26.*

Ἀβιληνή, ῆς, ἡ, *Abilene*, a district between Lebanon and Hermon towards Phœnicia, named from Abila, its chief city, Lu. iii. 1.*

Ἀβιούδ, ὁ (Heb.), *Abiud*, Mat. i. 13.*

Ἀβραάμ, ὁ (Heb.), *Abraham*, Mat. i. 1, 2; Ro. iv. 1, 2, 3.

ἄ-βυσσος, ου, ἡ (originally adj. *bottomless*), *abyss*, Lu. viii. 31; Ro. x. 7; Rev. ix. 1, 2, 11, xi. 7, xvii. 8, xx. 1, 3.*

Ἄγαβος, ου, ὁ, *Agabus*, Ac. xi. 28, xxi. 10.*

ἀγαθο-εργέω, ῶ (or ἀγαθουργέω), *to be beneficent*, 1 Tim. vi. 18; Ac. xiv. 17 (W. H.). (N. T.)*

ἀγαθο-ποιέω, ῶ, (1) *to do good to*, acc. of pers., Lu. vi. 33; (2) *to act well*, 1 Pet. ii. 15, 20. (S.)

ἀγαθο-ποιΐα, ας, ἡ, *well-doing*, in sense (2) of preceding, 1 Pet. iv. 19. (N. T.)*

ἀγαθο-ποιός, οῦ, ὁ (originally adj.), *well doer*, 1 Pet. ii. 14.*

ἀγαθός, ή, όν (κρείσσων, κράτιστος), *good* in general, in various senses, in itself or its effects, physically or morally, used of both persons and things, Mat. vii. 18; Lu. vi. 45; 1 Pet. ii. 18; Phil. i. 6. τὸ ἀγαθόν, *the Good*, Mat. xix. 17 (W. H.); τὰ ἀγαθά, *goods, wealth, blessings*, Lu. i. 53; Ro. x. 15.

ἀγαθωσύνη, ης, ἡ, *goodness*, 2 Th. i. 11. (S.) *Syn.*: ἀγαθωσύνη emphasizes the *zeal for goodness;* χρηστότης, *kindness, benignity.*

ἀγαλλίασις, εως, ἡ, *exultation, gladness*, Lu. i. 14, 44. (S.)

ἀγαλλιάω, ῶ, ασω, *to leap for joy;* hence, *exult, rejoice;* generally deponent. Followed by ἵνα (subj.), Jn. viii. 56; ἐπί (dat.), Lu. i. 47; or ἐν (dat.), Jn. v. 35. (S.)

ἄ-γαμος, ον, adj., *unmarried*, 1 Cor. vii. 8, 11, 32, 34.*

ἀγανακτέω, ῶ, ήσω, *to be indignant, angry.* With περί (gen.), Mat. xx. 24; or ὅτι, Lu. xiii. 14.

ἀγανάκτησις, εως, ἡ, *indignation*, 2 Cor. vii. 11.*

ἀγαπάω, ῶ, ήσω, *to love*, Lu. vii. 47; *to wish well to*, Mat. v.

43, xix. 19; *to take pleasure in*, Heb. i. 9; *to long for*, 2 Tim. iv. 8. *Syn.*: ἀγαπάω denotes the love of the reason, esteem; φιλέω, the love of the feelings, warm instinctive affection.

ἀγάπη, ης, ἡ, *love, benevolence.* Object with εἰς, ἐν, or genitive, Gr. § 269, Wi. § 30*a*, Bu. 329. ἀγάπαι (Ju. 12), *love-feasts.* (S.)

ἀγαπητός, ή, όν, *beloved*, Mat. iii. 17.

Ἅγαρ, ἡ (W. H. Ἄγαρ), (Heb.), *Hagar*, Gal. iv. 24, 25 (W. H.).*

ἀγγαρεύω, σω (from the Persian), *to impress* into the public service; hence, *to compel to perform any service*, Mat. v. 41, xxvii. 32; Mar. xv. 21.*

ἀγγεῖον, ου, τό, *vessel, utensil*, Mat. xiii. 48 (Rec.), xxv. 4.*

ἀγγελία, ας, ἡ, *message*, 1 Jn. i. 5 (W. H.), iii. 11.*

ἄγγελος, ου, ὁ, *messenger*, Mat. xi. 10; spec. of God's messengers to men, *angel*, Mat. iv. 6. So of fallen spirits, Ju. 6. "Angel of a church" (Rev. i. 20, ii., iii.), either *messenger*, or *elder*, or *an angel* who watches over the church.

ἄγγος, εος, τό, *vessel*, Mat. xiii. 48 (W. H.).*

ἄγε, interj. (properly impv. of ἄγω), *come now!* Ja. iv. 13, v. 1.*

ἀγέλη, ης, ἡ, *a flock* or *herd*, Mat. viii. 30.

ἀ-γενεα-λόγητος, ου, adj., *of unrecorded genealogy*, Heb. vii. 3. (N. T.)*

ἀ-γενής, ές (from γένος), low-born, base, 1 Cor. i. 28.*

ἁγιάζω, σω (from ἅγιος), to set apart from common use. Hence, to hallow, or regard with religious reverence, Mat. vi. 9; to consecrate to religious service, whether persons or things, Mat. xxiii. 17; Jn. xvii. 19; to cleanse for such consecration, Heb. ix. 13; so to purify, sanctify, 1 Cor. vi. 11. οἱ ἁγιαζόμενοι, those who are being sanctified; οἱ ἡγιασμένοι, those who are sanctified, Ac. xx. 32.

ἁγιασμός, οῦ, ὁ, sanctification, holiness, 1 Cor. i. 30; 1 Th. iv. 7. (S.)

ἅγιος, α, ον, hallowed, worthy of veneration, holy, consecrated, whether persons, places, or things. οἱ ἅγιοι, "the Saints"; τὸ ἅγιον, the Temple; τὰ ἅγια, the Sanctuary; ἅγια ἁγίων, the Holy of Holies; πνεῦμα ἅγιον, the Holy Spirit. Syn.: see Trench, § lxxxviii.

ἁγιότης, τητος, ἡ, holiness, Heb. xii. 10; 2 Cor. i. 12 (W. H.). (Ap.)*

ἁγιωσύνη, ης, ἡ, holiness, Ro. i. 4; 2 Cor. vii. 1; 1 Th. iii. 13. (S.)*

ἀγκάλη, ης, ἡ, the (curve of the) arm, Lu. ii. 28.*

ἄγκιστρον, ου, τό, fishhook, Mat. xvii. 27.*

ἄγκυρα, ας, ἡ, an anchor, Ac. xxvii. 29, 30, 40; Heb. vi. 19.

ἄ-γναφος, ον, adj., unfulled, undressed, Mat. ix. 16; Mar. ii. 21. (N. T.)*

ἁγνεία, ας, ἡ, purity, 1 Tim. iv. 12, v. 2.*

ἁγνίζω, σω, to cleanse, purify; ceremonially, Jn. xi. 55; morally, Ja. iv. 8.

ἁγνισμός, οῦ, ὁ, ceremonial purification, Ac. xxi. 26.*

ἀ-γνοέω, ῶ, ἥσω (see γιγνώσκω), (1) not to know, to be ignorant, 1 Tim. i. 13; ἀγνοῶν, ignorant; ἀγνοούμενος, unknown, Gal. i. 22; ignored, disregarded, 1 Cor. xiv. 38 (W. H.); (2) not to understand, Mar. ix. 32; Lu. ix. 45.

ἀγνόημα, ατος, τό, a sin of ignorance, error, Heb. ix. 7.* Syn.: see Trench, § lxvi.

ἄγνοια, ας, ἡ, ignorance Ac. iii.

17, xvii. 30; Ep. iv. 18; 1 Pet. i. 14.*

ἁγνός, ή, όν, pure, 2 Cor. vii. 11; chaste, Tit. ii. 5. Syn.: see ἅγιος.

ἁγνότης, τητος, ἡ, purity, 2 Cor. vi. 6, xi. 3 (W. H.).*

ἁγνῶς, adv., purely, sincerely, Phil. i. 17.*

ἀγνωσία, ας, ἡ, ignorance, spec. willful ignorance, 1 Cor. xv. 34; 1 Pet. ii. 15.*

ἄγνωστος, ον, unknown, Ac. xvii. 23.*

ἀγορά, ᾶς, ἡ (ἀγείρω), a place of public resort, forum, market place, Ac. xvii. 17; used for the market, Mar. vii. 4; as the place of public assemblies, trials, etc., Ac. xvi. 19.

ἀγοράζω, σω, to purchase, buy, with gen. of price, Mar. vi. 37, or ἐκ, Mat. xxvii. 7, once ἐν, Rev. v. 9; fig., to redeem, ransom, Rev. v. 9, xiv. 3.

ἀγοραῖος, ον, belonging to the forum; hence (sc. ἡμέραι) court days, Ac. xix. 38; (sc. ἄνθρωποι) idlers, xvii. 5.*

ἄγρα, ας, ἡ, a catching, Lu. v. 4; the thing caught, a catch of fish, v. 9.*

ἀ-γράμματος, ον, unlearned, i.e., in Rabbinical lore, Ac. iv. 13.* Syn.: ἀγράμματος means illiterate, without knowledge gained by study; ἰδιώτης, not a specialist, or without knowledge gained by mingling in public life.

ἀγρ-αυλέω, ῶ, to live in the fields, Lu. ii. 8.*

ἀγρεύω, σω (to take in hunting), fig., to ensnare, Mar. xii. 13.*

ἀγρι-έλαιος, ον, ἡ, wild olive, Ro. xi. 17, 24.*

ἄγριος, ία, ιον, wild, of honey, Mat. iii. 4; Mar. i. 6; fierce, of waves, Ju. 13.*

Ἀγρίππας, α, ὁ, Agrippa, i.e., Herod Agrippa II. See Ἡρῴδης.

ἀγρός, οῦ, ὁ, field, spec. the country, Mat. vi. 28; plur., country districts, hamlets, Mar. v. 14.

ἀγρυπνέω, ῶ (ὕπνος), to be sleepless; hence, met., to watch, to be vigilant, Mar. xiii. 33; Lu. xxi. 36; Ep. vi. 18; Heb. xiii. 17.*

ἀγρυπνία, ας, ἡ, sleeplessness,

watching, 2 Cor. vi. 5, xi. 27.*

ἄγω, ξω, 2 a., ἤγαγον, trans., to lead, bring; with πρός (acc.), ἕως, εἰς, of destination; with ἐπί (acc.)., of purpose, as Ac. viii. 32; to bring before, for trial, Ac. xxv. 17. Also to spend, as of time; to keep, as a particular day, Mat. xiv. 6 (not W. H.); Lu. xxiv. 21 (impers.). Fig., to lead the inclination, induce, Lu. iv. 1. Mid., to go, depart; subj., ἄγωμεν, let us go! Mat. xxvi. 46.

ἀγωγή, ῆς, ἡ (ἄγω), a leading, course of life, 2 Tim. iii. 10.*

ἀγών, ῶνος, ὁ, contest, conflict; fig., of the Christian life, as Heb. xii. 1; solicitude, anxiety, Col. ii. 1.

ἀγωνία, ας, ἡ, contest, agony, Lu. xxii. 44 (not W. H.).*

ἀγωνίζομαι, to strive, as in the public games, 1 Cor. ix. 25; to contend with an adversary, Jn. xviii. 36; fig., of Christian effort and endurance, Col. i. 29.

Ἀδάμ, ὁ (Heb.), Adam.*

ἀ-δάπανος, ον, free of charge, gratuitous, 1 Cor. ix. 18.*

Ἀδδί, ὁ, Addi, Lu. iii. 28 (not mentioned in O. T.).*

ἀδελφή, ῆς, ἡ, a sister, (1) lit., Mat. xix. 29; (2) fig. of Christian friendship, 1 Cor. vii. 15.

ἀδελφός, οῦ, ὁ, a brother, (1) lit. (see Gr. § 256), Mat. i. 2; (2) of more general relations, a fellow-countryman, Mat. v. 47; a fellow-Christian, Mat. xxiii. 8; a fellow-man, Mat. v. 22–24; also expressing the relation between Christ and believers, Mat. xxv. 40. The "brethren of Jesus" (Mat. xiii. 55; Jn. vii. 3; Ac. i. 14; Gal. i. 19) are probably to be understood literally.

ἀδελφότης, τητος, ἡ, the brotherhood, i.e., the Christian community, 1 Pet. ii. 17, v. 9. (Ap.)*

ἄ-δηλος, ον, not manifest, uncertain, Lu. xi. 44; 1 Cor. xiv. 8.*

ἀ-δηλότης, τητος, uncertainty, 1 Tim. vi. 17.*

ἀδήλως, adv., uncertainly, 1 Cor. ix. 26.*

ἀδημονέω, ῶ, *to be troubled, distressed*, Mar. xiv. 33.

ᾅδης, ου, ὁ (ἀ priv. and ἰδεῖν), *the invisible world, Hades*, Lu. xvi. 23; fig., of deep degradation, Mat. xi. 23. See πύλη.

ἀ-διά-κριτος, ον, *without uncertainty, unambiguous*, Ja. iii. 17.*

ἀ-διά-λειπτος, ον, *without intermission, unceasing*, Ro. ix. 2; 2 Tim. i. 3.*

ἀδιαλείπτως, adv., *without intermission, incessantly*, Ro. i. 9; 1 Th. i. 2, ii. 13, v. 17.*

ἀ-δια-φθορία, ας, ἡ, *incorruptibility, soundness*, Tit. ii. 7 (not W. H.). (N. T.)*

ἀδικέω, ῶ, ἤσω (ἄδικος), intrans., *to act unjustly, commit a crime*, Ac. xxv. 11; trans., *to wrong, injure*, Mat. xx. 13; hence, *to hurt*, without any notion of wrong, Lu. x. 19, and Rev. often; pass., *to be wronged*, 2 Cor. vii. 12; mid., *to suffer wrong*, 1 Cor. vi. 7.

ἀδίκημα, ατος, τό, *a wrong, misdeed*, Ac. xviii. 14, xxiv. 20; Rev. xviii. 5.*

ἀδικία, ας, ἡ, *wrong* (towards man or God); hence, *injustice*, Lu. xviii. 6; Ro. ix. 14; *unrighteousness*, Ro. i. 18, 29; *act of unrighteousness*, 1 Jn. v. 17; Heb. viii. 12.

ἄ-δικος, ον, *unjust, unrighteous*, generally, opposed to δίκαιος, as Mat. v. 45, to εὐσεβής, as 2 Pet. ii. 9, or to πιστός, as Lu. xvi. 10.

ἀδίκως, adv., *unjustly, undeservedly*, 1 Pet. ii. 19.*

ἀ-δόκιμος, ον (tested, but not approved), *reprobate, rejected*, Ro. i. 28; 1 Cor. ix. 27; 2 Cor. xiii. 5, 6, 7; 2 Tim. iii. 8; Tit. i. 16; Heb. vi. 8.*

ἄ-δολος, ον, *without fraud, unadulterated*, 1 Pet. ii. 2.* *Syn.*: see Trench, § lvi.

Ἀδραμυττηνός, ή, όν, *of Adramyttium*, a seaport of Mysia, Ac. xxvii. 2.*

Ἀδρίας, ου, ὁ, *the Adriatic*, the sea between Greece and Italy, Ac. xxvii. 27.*

ἀδρότης, τητος, ἡ, *abundance, liberality*, 2 Cor. viii. 20.*

ἀδυνατέω, ῶ, ἤσω, *to be impossible*, with dat. of pers., Mat. xvii. 20; or παρά (dat., W. H. gen.), Lu. i. 37.*

ἀ-δύνατος, ον, (1) of persons, act., *powerless*, Ac. xiv. 8; (2) of things, pass., *impossible*, Ro. viii. 3.

ᾄδω, ᾄσω (contr. from ἀείδω), *to sing*, with cognate acc., ᾠδήν, *a song*, Rev. v. 9, xiv. 3, xv. 3; with dat., *to sing* (praise) *to*, Ep. v. 19; Col. iii. 16.*

ἀεί, adv., *always;* of continuous time, *unceasingly*, Ac. vii. 51; of successive intervals, *from time to time, on every occasion*, 1 Pet. iii. 15.

ἀετός, οῦ, ὁ, *an eagle*, Rev. iv. 7; gen. *bird of prey*, as Mat. xxiv. 28.

ἄ-ζυμος, ον, *unleavened*, only in plur., sc. λάγανα, *cakes*, or ἄρτοι, *loaves;* met., *the paschal feast*, Lu. xxii. 1; fig., *uncorrupted, sincere*, 1 Cor. v. 7, 8.

Ἀζώρ, indecl. (Heb.), *Azor*, Mat. i. 13, 14; not mentioned in O. T.*

Ἄζωτος, ου, ἡ, *Azotus* or *Ashdod*, Ac. viii. 40.*

ἀήρ, ἀέρος, ὁ, *the air, atmosphere*, Ac. xxii. 23; Ep. ii. 2.

ἀ-θανασία, ας, ἡ (see θάνατος), *immortality*, 1 Cor. xv. 53, 54; 1 Tim. vi. 16.*

ἀ-θέμιτος, ον (θέμις, *law*), *unlawful, criminal*, Ac. x. 28; 1 Pet. iv. 3.*

ἄ-θεος, ον, *without God*, Ep. ii. 12.*

ἄ-θεσμος, ον (θεσμός, *statute*), *lawless*, 2 Pet. ii. 7, iii. 17.*

ἀ-θετέω, ῶ, ἤσω (θε- as in τίθημι), *to make void, invalid;* of things, *to nullify*, Lu. vii. 30; chiefly of persons, *to slight, reject*, Lu. x. 16.

ἀ-θέτησις, εως, ἡ, *nullification, abrogation*, Heb. vii. 18, ix. 26.*

Ἀθῆναι, ῶν, αἱ, *Athens*, Ac. xvii. 15.

Ἀθηναῖος, α, ον, *Athenian*, Ac. xvii. 21, 22.*

ἀθλέω, ῶ (ἆθλος, *a contest*), *to contend* in the public games, 2 Tim. ii. 5.*

ἄθλησις, εως, ἡ, *contest*, as in the public games; only fig. Heb. x. 32.*

ἀθροίζω, *to gather together*, Lu. xxiv. 33 (W. H.).*

ἀ-θυμέω, ω, *to lose heart, despond*, Col. iii. 21.*

ἀθῷος, ον, *unpunished, innocent*, Mat. xxvii. 4 (not W. H.); with ἀπό, of the crime, ver. 24.*

αἴγειος, η, ον (αἴξ, *goat*), *of* or *belonging to a goat*, Heb. xi. 37.*

αἰγιαλός, οῦ, ὁ, *the shore, beach;* used of Gennesaret, Mat. xiii. 2, 48; Jn. xxi. 4; of the Mediterranean, Ac. xxi. 5, xxvii. 39, 40.*

Αἰγύπτιος, α, ον, *Egyptian*, Ac. vii. 22.

Αἴγυπτος, ου, ἡ, *Egypt*, Mat. ii. 13.

ἀΐδιος, ον, adj. (ἀεί), *eternal, everlasting*, Ro. i. 20; Ju. 6.*

αἰδώς, οῦς, ἡ, *modesty*, 1 Tim. ii. 9; *reverence*, Heb. xii. 28 (not W. H.).* *Syn.*: see Trench, § xix; Thayer, p. 14.

Αἰθίοψ, οπος, ὁ, *an Ethiopian*, Ac. viii. 27.*

αἷμα, ατος, τό, *blood*, (1) in general, Jn. xix. 34; (2) *natural life*, which was believed to reside in the blood, especially with σάρξ, 1 Cor. xv. 20; so *human nature* generally; hence, (3) *natural relationship*, Jn. i. 13; (4) blood *shed* of sacrificial victims, Heb. ix. 7, 12; (5) hence, *the blood of Christ, his atoning death*, 1 Cor. x. 16; Rev. vii. 14; (6) *violent death, bloodshed, murder*, Lu. xiii. 1; Mat. xxiii. 30, 35; (7) in Ac. ii. 20, etc., the reference is to the *color of blood*.

αἱματ-εκ-χυσία, ας, ἡ, *shedding of blood*, Heb. ix. 22. (N. T.)*

αἱμορροέω, ῶ, *to suffer from a flow of blood*, Mat. ix. 20.*

Αἰνέας, α, ὁ, *Aeneas*, Ac. ix. 33, 34.*

αἴνεσις, εως, ἡ, *praise*, Heb. xiii. 15. (S.)*

αἰνέω, ῶ, ἔσω and ἤσω, *to praise*, only of praise to God, Lu. ii. 13, 20.

αἴνιγμα, ατος, τό, *an enigma, an obscure thing*, 1 Cor. xiii. 12.*

αἶνος, ου, ὁ, *praise* to God, Mat. xxi. 16; Lu. xviii. 43.*

Αἰνών, ἡ (Heb.), *Aenon*, Jn. iii. 23.*

αἵρεσις, εως, ἡ (αἱρέω), *choice*, its act or result; hence, *a tenet, heresy,* 2 Pet. ii. 1; *a sect,* Ac. v. 17; *dissension,* Gal. v. 20.

αἱρετίζω, σω, *to choose,* Mat. xii. 18.*

αἱρετικός, ή, όν, *schismatic, factious,* Tit. iii. 10.*

αἱρέω (irreg., Gr. § 103, 1, Wi. § 15, Bu. 53), *to take,* only in mid. in N. T., *to choose, prefer,* Phil. i. 22 ; 2 Th. ii. 13; Heb. xi. 25.*

αἴρω (Gr. § 92), (1) *to raise, lift up,* Mar. xvi. 18; Jn. xi. 41 ; (2) *to bear, carry,* Mat. iv. 6; Lu. ix. 23; (3) *to bear away, carry off,* in general, Mat. xxi. 21 ; Jn. xix. 31; *to take away* sin, of the redeeming work of Christ, Jn. i. 29; 1 Jn. iii. 5; *to remove by death,* Jn. xvii. 15; Mat. xxiv. 39.

αἰσθάνομαι, 2 a. ᾐσθόμην, dep., *to perceive, understand,* Lu. ix. 45.*

αἴσθησις, εως, ή, *perception, discernment,* Phil. i. 9.*

αἰσθητήριον, ου, τό, *organ of perception, faculty of judgment,* Heb. v. 14.*

αἰσχρο-κερδής, ες, *eager for base gain, sordid,* 1 Tim. iii. 3 (not W. H.), 8; Tit. i. 7.*

αἰσχροκερδῶς, *from eagerness for base gain,* 1 Pet. v. 2. (N. T.)*

αἰσχρο-λογία, ας, ή, *foul language, scurrility,* Col. iii. 8.*

αἰσχρός, ά, όν, *base, disgraceful,* 1 Cor. xi. 6.

αἰσχρότης, τητος, ή, *baseness, dishonor,* Ep. v. 4.*

αἰσχύνη, ης, ή, *shame,* in personal feeling, Lu. xiv. 9; or in the estimation of others, Heb. xii. 2; *a shameful thing,* Ju. 13. *Syn.:* see αἰδώς.

αἰσχύνομαι, οῦμαι, in N. T. only pass., *to be put to shame, made ashamed,* 2 Cor. x. 8; Phil. i. 20.

αἰτέω, ῶ, ήσω, *to ask, pray, require,* Ja. i. 6; usually with two accs., or acc. of thing and ἀπό or παρά (gen.) of person; mid., *to ask for one's self, beg,* Jn. xvi. 26. *Syn.:* αἰτέω is to ask a favor, as a suppliant; ἐρωτάω, to ask a question, or as an equal; πυνθάνομαι, to ask for infor-

mation. But see Thayer, p. 18.

αἴτημα, ατος, τό, *petition, request,* Lu. xxiii. 24; Phil. iv. 6; 1 Jn. v. 15. *Syn.:* see Trench, § li.

αἰτία, ας, ή, *cause,* (1) as the *reason* or *ground* of anything, Ac. x. 21; (2) in Mat. xix. 10, *the state of the case;* (3) forensically, *a crime,* Ac. xiii. 28; *a charge of crime, accusation,* Ac. xxv. 18, 27.

αἰτίαμα, ατος, τό, *accusation, charge,* Ac. xxv. 7 (W. H. read αἰτίωμα).*

αἴτιος, ία, ιον, *causative of,* used as subst., in masc., *the cause, author,* only Heb. v. 9; in neut., *a cause, reason,* espec. of punishment, Ac. xix. 40; *a fault, crime,* like αἰτία, Lu. xxiii. 4, 14, 22.*

αἰτίωμα. See αἰτίαμα. (N. T.)*

αἰφνίδιος, ον, *unexpected, sudden,* Lu. xxi. 34 (W. H. ἐφνίδιος); 1 Th. v. 3.*

αἰχμ-αλωσία, ας, ή, *captivity,* Rev. xiii. 10; abstract for concrete, Ep. iv. 8.*

αἰχμ-αλωτεύω, σω, *to make prisoners of, to take captive,* Ep. iv. 8; 2 Tim. iii. 6 (W. H. read the following). (S.)*

αἰχμ-αλωτίζω, σω, *to lead captive,* Lu. xxi. 24.

αἰχμ-άλωτος, ου, ὁ, ή, *captive,* Lu. iv. 18 (from Is. lxi. 1).*

αἰών, ῶνος, ὁ (ἀεί), originally *an indefinitely long period of time, an age;* hence, (1) *an unbroken age, eternity,* past, as Ac. xv. 18; future, 2 Pet. iii. 18, especially in the following phrases: εἰς τὸν αἰῶνα, *for ever,* with negative adv. *never;* εἰς τοὺς αἰῶνας, a stronger expression, *for evermore;* εἰς τοὺς αἰῶνας τῶν αἰώνων, stronger still (see Gr. § 327, ii, Wi. § 36, 2), *for ever and ever.* Phrase slightly varied, Ep. iii. 21; Heb. i. 8; 2 Pet. iii. 18; Ju. 25; Rev. xiv. 11; (2) in plur., *the worlds, the universe,* Heb. i. 2, xi. 3; (3) *the present age* (ὁ αἰὼν οὗτος, ὁ ἐνεστὼς αἰών, ὁ νῦν αἰών), Gal. i. 4; 1 Tim. vi. 17, in contrast with the time after the second coming of Christ, *the coming age* (ὁ αἰὼν ἐκεῖνος, αἰὼν μέλλων, ὁ

αἰὼν ὁ ἐρχόμενος, οἱ αἰῶνες οἱ ἐπερχόμενοι), Lu. xx. 35, xviii. 30; Ep. ii. 7; Mat. xii. 32. *Syn.:* αἰών is the world under the aspect of *time;* κόσμος, under that of *space.* See Thayer, p. 19.

αἰώνιος (ία, only in 2 Th. ii. 16; Heb. ix. 12; or ιος), ιον, (1) *without beginning or end, eternal,* Ro. xvi. 26; Heb. ix. 14; (2) *without beginning,* Ro. xvi. 25; 2 Tim. i. 9; (3) *without end, everlasting;* often with ζωή, *eternal life,* denoting life which in its character is essentially eternal, see Jn. v. 24, vi. 47, xvii. 3. Neut., used as adv., *for ever,* Philem. 15.

ἀ-καθαρσία, ας, ή (καθαίρω), *uncleanness, impurity,* usually in a moral sense, Ro. i. 24; 2 Cor. xii. 21.

ἀ-καθάρτης, τητος, ή, *impurity,* Rev. xvii. 4 (W. H. read the following). (N. T.)*

ἀ-κάθαρτος, ον, *unclean, impure,* (1) of ceremonial defilement, Ac. x. 14; 1 Cor. vii. 14; (2) of evil spirits, with πνεῦμα, Gospels, Acts, Rev.; (3) of human beings, *impure, lewd,* Ep. v. 5.

ἀ-καιρέομαι, οῦμαι, dep., *to lack opportunity,* Phil. iv. 10.*

ἀ-καίρως, adv., *unseasonably,* 2 Tim. iv. 2, opp. to εὐκαίρως.*

ἄ-κακος, ον, *guileless,* Ro. xvi. 18; Heb. vii. 26.*

ἄκανθα, ης, ή, *thorn, briar,* Mat. vii. 16.

ἀκάνθινος, ον, *made of thorns,* Mar. xv. 17; Jn. xix. 5.*

ἄ-καρπος, ον, *unfruitful, barren,* generally fig., Mat. xiii. 22; Tit. iii. 14.

ἀ-κατά-γνωστος, ον, *not to be condemned,* Tit. ii. 8.*

ἀ-κατα-κάλυπτος, ον, *unveiled,* 1 Cor. xi. 5, 13.*

ἀ-κατά-κριτος, ον, *uncondemned,* Ac. xvi. 37, xxii. 25. (N. T.)*

ἀ-κατά-λυτος, ον, *indissoluble,* Heb. vii. 16.*

ἀ-κατά-παστος, ον, *unfed, hungry for* (gen.), 2 Pet. ii. 14 (W. H. for the following). (N. T.)*

ἀ-κατά-παυστος, ον, *not to be restrained,* with gen., 2 Pet. ii. 14 (see preceding).*

ἀ-κατα-στασία, ας, ή, *instabil-*

ity; hence, *sedition, tumult, disorder,* Ja. iii. 16, 2 Cor. vi. 5.

ἀ-κατά-στατος, ον, *inconstant, unstable,* Ja. i. 8, iii. 8 (W. H.).*

ἀ-κατά-σχετος, ον, *that cannot be restrained,* Ja. iii. 8 (W. H. read preceding). (S.)*

Ἀκελ-δαμά (Aram., *field of blood*), *Aceldama,* Ac. i. 19 (W. H. read Ἀκελδαμάχ). (N. T.)*

ἀ-κέραιος, ον (κεράννυμι), *unmixed;* hence, fig., *simple, innocent, guileless,* Mat. x. 16; Ro. xvi. 19; Phil. ii. 15.*

ἀ-κλινής, ές, *unbending;* hence, *firm, steadfast,* Heb. x. 23.*

ἀκμάζω, σω, *to reach the point of perfection;* so, of fruit, *to be fully ripe,* Rev. xiv. 18.*

ἀκμήν, acc. of ἀκμή as adv., *even now, even yet,* Mat. xv. 16.*

ἀκοή, ῆς, ἡ (ἀκούω), *hearing,* (1) *the sense of hearing,* 2 Pet. ii. 8; (2) *the organ of hearing, the ear,* 2 Tim. iv. 3, 4; (3) *the thing heard, a report, speech, doctrine,* Jn. xii. 38; Mar. i. 28. ἀκοῇ ἀκούειν, "to hear with hearing," *i.e, attentively* (a Hebraism), Mat. xiii. 14.

ἀκολουθέω, ῶ, ήσω, (1) *to accompany, follow,* or *attend,* with dat., or μετά (gen.), or ὀπίσω (gen.), espec. of the disciples of Christ; so, met., *to obey* and *imitate,* Mat. iv. 25; Mar. ix. 38.

ἀκούω, σω or σομαι, pf., ἀκήκοα, *to hear,* (1) without object, Mar. iv. 3, vii. 37; (2) with object (acc. or gen., Gr. § 249a, 1, Wi. § 30, 7 c, Bu. 165 sq., 301), *to hear, listen to, heed, understand,* Mat. xii. 19; Lu. i. 41. οἱ ἀκούοντες, *hearers* or *disciples.* In pass., *to be noised abroad,* Ac. xi. 22.

ἀ-κρασία, as, ἡ, *intemperance, incontinence,* Mat. xxiii. 25; 1 Cor. vii. 5.*

ἀ-κρατής, ές (κράτος), *powerless, without self-control,* 2 Tim. iii. 3.*

ἄ-κρατος, ον (κεράννυμι), *unmixed, undiluted* (of strong wine), Rev. xiv. 10.*

ἀκρίβεια, as, ἡ, *exactness, strictness,* Ac. xxii. 3.*

ἀκριβής, ές, *exact, strict,* Ac. xxvi. 5.

ἀκριβόω, ῶ, ώσω, *to inquire closely, learn carefully* (R. V.), Mat. ii. 7, 16.*

ἀκριβῶς, adv., *exactly, diligently,* Ac. xviii. 25.

ἀκρίς, ίδος, ἡ, *a locust,* Mat. iii. 4.

ἀκροατήριον, ίου, τό (ἀκροάομαι, *to hear*), *the place of* (judicial) *hearing,* Ac. xxv. 23.*

ἀκροατής, οῦ, ὁ, *a hearer,* Ro. ii. 13; Ja. i. 22, 23, 25.*

ἀκροβυστία, as, ἡ, *the foreskin,* Ac. xi. 3; *uncircumcision,* Ro. iv. 10; met., *an uncircumcised Gentile,* Ep. ii. 11. (S.)

ἀκρο-γωνιαῖος, α, ον (with λίθος expressed or understood), *a corner foundation stone,* ref. to Christ, Ep. ii. 20; 1 Pet. ii. 6. (S.)*

ἀκρο-θίνιον, ίου, τό, *first-fruits, i.e.,* the best of the produce, applied (plur.) to spoils taken in battle, Heb. vii. 4.*

ἄκρος, a, ον, *outermost, pointed;* neut., τὸ ἄκρον, *the end, extremity,* Lu. xvi. 24.

Ἀκύλας, ου, ὁ (Latin), *Aquila,* Ac. xviii. 2.

ἀ-κυρόω, ῶ, *to deprive of power, set aside* (a law), Mat. xv. 6; Mar. vii. 13; Gal. iii. 17.

ἀ-κωλύτως, adv., *freely, without hindrance,* Ac. xxviii. 31.*

ἄκων, ουσα, ον (ἀ, ἕκων), *unwilling,* 1 Cor. ix. 17.*

ἀλάβαστρον, ου, τό, *a box made of alabaster, a vessel for perfume,* Mat. xxvi. 7; Mar. xiv. 3; Lu. vii. 37.*

ἀλαζονία, as, ἡ, *boasting, show, ostentation,* Ja. iv. 16; 1 Jn. ii. 16.*

ἀλαζών, όνος, ὁ, *a boaster,* Ro. i. 30; 2 Tim. iii. 2.*

ἀλαλάζω, άσω, *to raise a cry* or *loud sound;* in mourning, Mar. v. 38; of cymbals, 1 Cor. xiii. 1.*

ἀ-λάλητος, ον, *not to be uttered in words,* Ro. viii. 26.*

ἄ-λαλος, ον, *dumb, making dumb,* Mar. vii. 37, ix. 17, 25.*

ἅλας, ατος, τό, *salt,* lit. and fig., as Mat. v. 13.

ἀλείφω, ψω, *to anoint,* festally, or in homage, also medicinally, or in embalming the

dead, Mar. xvi. 1, Lu. vii. 46. *Syn.:* χρίω has always a religious and symbolical force, which is absent in ἀλείφω.

ἀλεκτορο-φωνία, as, ἡ, *the cock-crowing,* the third watch of the night, between midnight and dawn, Mar. xiii. 35.*

ἀλέκτωρ, ορος, ὁ, *a cock,* Mat. xxvi. 34; Jn. xiii. 38.

Ἀλεξανδρεύς, έως, ὁ, *an Alexandrian,* Ac. vi. 9, xviii. 24.*

Ἀλεξανδρινός, ή, όν, *Alexandrian,* Ac. xxvii. 6, xxviii. 11.*

Ἀλέξανδρος, ου, ὁ, *Alexander.* Four of this name are mentioned, Mar. xv. 21; Ac. iv. 6; Ac. xix. 33; 1 Tim. i. 20; 2 Tim. iv. 14.*

ἄλευρον, ου, τό, *wheaten flour,* Mat. xiii. 33; Lu. xiii. 21.*

ἀλήθεια, as, ἡ, *truth;* generally, as Mar. v. 33; espec., (1) *freedom from error, exactness,* as (2) the Truth, or *Word of God;* Jesus is called *the Truth,* Jn. xiv. 6; (3) *truthfulness, veracity, sincerity, integrity,* opposed to ἀδικία, Ro. ii. 8; 1 Cor. xiii. 6.

ἀληθεύω, *to speak the truth,* Gal. iv. 16; Ep. iv. 15.*

ἀληθής, ές (ἀ, λαθ- in λανθάνω), *unconcealed, true,* Ac. xii. 9; Jn. iv. 18; *truthful,* Mat. xxii. 16; Mar. xii. 14. *Syn.:* ἀληθής means true *morally,* faithful; ἀληθινός, *genuine,* in contrast either with the *false* or the *imperfect.*

ἀληθινός, ή, όν, *real, genuine,* contrasted with the fictitious, as Lu. xvi. 11; Jn. i. 9; with the typical, as Jn. vi. 32; Heb. viii. 2, ix. 24. *Syn.:* see ἀληθής.

ἀλήθω, ήσω, *to grind* with a handmill, Mat. xxiv. 41; Lu. xvii. 35.*

ἀληθῶς, adv., *truly, really, certainly,* Ac. xii. 11.

ἁλιεύς (W. H. ἁλεεύς), έως, ὁ, *a fisherman,* Mat. iv. 18.

ἁλιεύω, εύσω, *to fish,* Jn. xxi. 3. (S.)*

ἁλίζω, ίσω, *to salt, season with salt,* Mat. v. 13; Mar. ix. 49.

ἁλίσγημα, ατος, τό, *pollution,* Ac. xv. 20. (N. T.)*

ἀλλά (prop. n. plur. of ἄλλος), *but,* an adversative particle.

See Gr. § 404, Wi. § 53, 7, Bu. 369 sq.

ἀλλάσσω, άξω, to change, Ac. vi. 14; to exchange, Ro. i. 23; to transform, 1 Cor. xv. 51.

ἀλλαχόθεν, adv., from elsewhere, Jn. x. 1.*

ἀλλαχοῦ, adv., elsewhere, Mar. i. 38 (W. H.).*

ἀλλ-ηγορέω, ῶ, to speak allegorically; pass. part., Gal. iv. 24.*

Ἀλληλούϊα (W. H. Ἀλ-), (Heb.), Hallelujah, Praise ye Jehovah, Rev. xix, 1, 3, 4, 6. (S.)*

ἀλλήλων, reciprocal pron., gen. plur. (Gr. § 61c), one another, each other, Ro. i. 12.

ἀλλο-γενής, ές, of another nation, a foreigner, Lu. xvii. 18. (S.)*

ἅλλομαι (dep.), ἁλοῦμαι, ἡλάμην, to leap, Ac. iii. 8, xiv. 10; to bubble up, as water, Jn. iv. 14.*

ἄλλος, η, ο, other, another, Mar. vi. 15; ὁ ἄλλος, the other, Mat. v. 39; οἱ ἄλλοι, the others, the rest. Syn.: ἄλλος indicates that which is simply numerically distinct; ἕτερος, that which is generically distinct, different.

ἀλλοτριο-επίσκοπος, ου, ὁ, one who looks at or busies himself in the things of another, a busybody, 1 Pet. iv. 15 (W. H. ἀλλοτριεπίσκοπος). (N. T.)*

ἀλλότριος, ια, ιον, belonging to another, Heb. ix. 25; foreign, strange, Ac. vii. 6; not of one's own family, Mat. xvii. 25; hostile, Heb. xi. 34.

ἀλλό-φυλος, ου, adj., foreign, of another tribe or race, Ac. x. 28.*

ἄλλως, adv., otherwise, 1 Tim. v. 25.*

ἀλοάω, ῶ, ήσω, to beat or thresh, as grain, 1 Cor. ix. 9, 10; 1 Tim. v. 18.*

ἄ-λογος, ον, (1) without speech or reason, irrational, 2 Pet. ii. 12, Ju. 10; (2) unreasonable, absurd, Ac. xxv. 27.*

ἀλόη, ης, ἡ, the aloe, Jn. xix. 39. (S.)*

ἅλς, ἁλός, ὁ, salt. Rec. only in Mar. ix. 49 (dat.), W. H. only in ix. 50 (acc.). See ἅλας.*

ἁλυκός, ἡ, όν (ἅλς), salt, brackish, Ja. iii. 12.*

ἄ-λυπος, ον, free from sorrow, Phil. ii. 28.*

ἅλυσις, εως, ἡ, a chain or manacle, Mar. v. 3; Ac. xxi. 33.

ἀ-λυσιτελής, ές, without gain, unprofitable, Heb. xiii. 17.*

ἄλφα, το, see A.

Ἀλφαῖος, ου, ὁ, Alphæus. Two of the name are mentioned, Mar. ii. 14, iii. 18 (the latter being called Κλωπάς, Jn. xix. 25; another form of the orig. Hebrew name).

ἅλων, ωνος, ὁ, ἡ, a threshing-floor; met., the grain of the threshing-floor, Mat. iii. 12; Lu. iii. 17.

ἀλώπηξ, εκος, ἡ, a fox, Mat. viii. 20; Lu. ix. 58; applied to Herod, Lu. xiii. 32.*

ἅλωσις, εως, ἡ, a taking or catching, 2 Pet. ii. 12.*

ἅμα, adv., at the same time, Ac. xxiv. 26; prep., with or together with (dat.), Mat. xiii. 29; ἅμα πρωΐ, with the dawn, Mat. xx. 1.

ἀ-μαθής, ές, unlearned, ignorant, 2 Pet. iii. 16.*

ἀμαράντινος, ου, adj., composed of amaranth, i.e., everlasting, 1 Pet. v. 4.*

ἀ-μάραντος, ου, adj. (μαραίνομαι), unfading, 1 Pet. i. 4.*

ἁμαρτάνω, τήσω, to miss a mark, to err, to sin, Mat. xxvii. 4; Jn. v. 14; with cogn. acc., ἁμαρτίαν, to sin a sin, 1 Jn. v. 16; with εἰς, to sin against, Lu. xv. 18, 21.

ἁμάρτημα, ατος, τό, a sin, evil deed. Syn.: see ἀγνόημα.

ἁμαρτία, as, ἡ, (1) a sinning (= τὸ ἁμαρτάνειν), Ro. v. 12, 13; 2 Cor. v. 21; (2) a sin, sing., as Ac. vii. 60; plur. (more freq.), spec. in the phrase ἀφιέναι τὰς ἁμαρτίας, to forgive sins, Mat. ix. 2, 5, 6. In Heb. x. 6, 8, 18, περὶ ἁμαρτίας is sin-offering. Syn.: see ἀγνόημα.

ἀ-μάρτυρος, ον, without witness, Ac. xiv. 17.*

ἁμαρτωλός, ον, sinful, or substantively, a sinner, espec. habitually and notoriously, 1 Tim. i. 19; Lu. xv. 2. The Jews used the word for

idolaters, i.e., Gentiles, Mar. xiv. 41.

ἄ-μαχος, ον, not quarrelsome, 1 Tim. iii. 3; Tit. iii. 2.*

ἀμάω, ῶ, ήσω, to reap, Ja. v. 4.*

ἀμέθυστος, ου, ἡ, an amethyst (supposed to be an antidote against drunkenness. Hence the name, from ἀ, μεθύω), Rev. xxi. 20.*

ἀμελέω, ῶ, ήσω, not to care for, to disregard, neglect, with gen. or inf., Heb. ii. 3; 2 Pet. i. 12 (not W. H.).

ἄ-μεμπτος, ον, blameless, Phil. ii. 15; Heb. viii. 7.

ἀ-μέμπτως, adv., blamelessly, 1 Th. ii. 10, iii. 13 (W. H. mrg.).

ἀ-μέριμνος, ον, free from solicitude or anxiety, Mat. xxviii. 14; 1 Cor. vii. 32.*

ἀ-μετά-θετος, ον, unchangeable, Heb. vi. 18; τὸ ἀμετάθετον, immutability, Heb. vi. 17.*

ἀ-μετα-κίνητος, ου, adj., immovable, firm, 1 Cor. xv. 58.*

ἀ-μετα-μέλητος, ον, not to be regretted or repented of, Ro. xi. 29; hence, unchangeable, 2 Cor. vii. 10.*

ἀ-μετα-νόητος, ου, adj., unrepentant, impenitent, Ro. ii. 5.*

ἄ-μετρος, ον, beyond measure, immoderate 2 Cor. x. 13, 15.*

ἀμήν, Amen, a Hebrew adjective, true, faithful, used (1) as an adverb, at the beginning of a sentence, verily, truly, indeed; (2) at the end of ascriptions of praise, etc., optatively, as γένοιτο, so be it; (3) substantively, 2 Cor. i. 20, as a name of Christ, the Amen, the faithful witness, Rev. iii. 14. (S.)

ἀ-μήτωρ, ορος, ὁ, ἡ (μήτηρ), without mother, i.e., in the genealogies, Heb. vii. 3.*

ἀ-μίαντος, ον (μιαίνω), undefiled, sincere, pure, Heb. vii. 26, xiii. 4; 1 Pet. i. 4; Ja. i. 27.*

Ἀμιναδάβ, ὁ (Heb.), Aminadab, Mat. i. 4; Lu. iii. 33 (not W. H.).*

ἄμμος, ου, ἡ, sand, Ro. ix. 27; Heb. xi. 12.

ἀμνός, οῦ, ὁ, a lamb; fig., of Christ, Jn. i. 29, 36; Ac. viii. 32; 1 Pet. i. 19.*

ἐμοιβή, ῆς, ἡ (ἀμείβω), requital,
1 Tim. v. 4.*

ἔμπελος, ου, ἡ, a vine, (1) lit.,
Mat. xxvi. 29; (2) fig., as Jn.
xv. 1.

ἀμπελ-ουργός, οῦ, ὁ, ἡ, a vine-
dresser, Lu. xiii. 7.*

ἀμπελών, ῶνος, ὁ, a vineyard,
Lu. xx. 9; 1 Cor. ix. 7.

Ἀμπλίας, ίου, ὁ, Amplias, Ro.
xvi. 8.*

ἀμύνω, ῶ, in N. T. only in mid.,
to defend from, take vengeance on, Ac. vii. 24.*

ἀμφιάζω, to clothe, Lu. xii. 28
(W. H.).*

ἀμφιβάλλω, to cast around,
Mar. i. 16 (W. H.).*

ἀμφί-βληστρον, ου, τό, a fishing
net, Mat. iv. 18; Mar. i. 16
(not W. H.).* Syn.: σαγήνη
is the drag-net, much larger
than ἀμφίβληστρον, the casting net; δίκτυον is general,
a net of any kind.

ἀμφι-έννυμι, έσω, to put on, to
clothe, Lu. vii. 25.

Ἀμφίπολις, εως, ἡ, Amphipolis,
a city in the S. of Macedonia,
Ac. xvii. 1.*

ἄμφ-οδον, ου, τό, a street, Mar.
xi. 4.*

ἀμφότεροι, αι, α, both, Ac. xxiii.
8.

ἀ-μώμητος, ον, without blame or
fault, Phil. ii. 15 (W. H.
ἄμεμπτοι); 2 Pet. iii. 14.*

ἄμωμον, ου, τό, amomum, a
spice plant, Rev. xviii. 13
(not Rec.).*

ἄ-μωμος, ον, without blemish,
1 Pet. i. 19; Heb. ix. 14;
fig., blameless, Eph. i. 4; Ju.
24.

Ἀμών, ὁ (Heb.), Amon, Mat. i.
10 (W. H. Ἀμώς).*

Ἀμώς, ὁ (Heb.), Amos, Lu. iii.
25.*

ἄν, a particle, expressing possi-
bility, uncertainty, or condi-
tionality. At the beginning
of a sentence it is a contrac-
tion of ἐάν. See Gr. §§ 378 b,
380, 383 δ, Wi. § 42, Bu. 216
sq.

ἀνά, prep., lit., upon (acc.); in
composition, up, again; used
in many phrases. See Gr.
§§ 297 and 147a, Wi. §§ 49 b,
52, 4, 2), Bu. 331, 332.

ἀνα-βαθμός, οῦ, ὁ (βαίνω), means
of ascent, steps, stairs, Ac.
xxi. 35, 40.*

ἀνα-βαίνω, βήσομαι, 2 a. ἀνέβην,
(1) to ascend, espec. to Jerusalem, Mat. xx. 17; on board
ship, Mar. vi. 51; to heaven,
Ro. x. 6; (2) to spring up, as
plants, etc., used of a rumor,
Ac. xxi. 31; of thoughts coming into mind, Lu. xxiv. 38.

ἀνα-βάλλω, mid., to postpone,
defer, Ac. xxiv. 22.*

ἀνα-βιβάζω, to draw up, as a
net to shore, Mat. xiii. 48.*

ἀνα-βλέπω, (1) to look up, as
Mar. viii. 24; (2) to look
again, to recover sight, as
Mat. xi. 5.

ἀνά-βλεψις, εως, ἡ, recovery of
sight, Lu. iv. 18.*

ἀνα-βοάω, ῶ, to exclaim, cry
aloud (not in W. H.), Mat.
xxvii. 46, Mar. xv. 8, Lu. ix.
38.*

ἀνα-βολή, ῆς, ἡ, putting off, delay, Ac. xxv. 17.*

ἀνάγαιον, ου, τό, upper room,
W. H. in Mar. xiv. 15; Lu.
xxii. 12, for Rec. ἀνώγεον.*

ἀν-αγγέλλω, to announce, make
known, Ac. xiv. 27, xix. 18;
to report, 2 Cor. vii. 7.

ἀνα-γεννάω, ῶ, to beget again,
1 Pet. i. 3, 23.*

ἀνα-γινώσκω, to know again, to
know well. N. T., to read,
Jn. xix. 20; 2 Cor. iii. 15.

ἀναγκάζω, ἄσω, to force, to compel by force or persuasion,
Ac. xxvi. 11; 2 Cor. xii. 11.

ἀναγκαῖος, αία, αῖον, necessary,
fit, Tit. iii. 14; Phil. i. 24;
also close or near, as friends,
Ac. x. 24.

ἀναγκαστῶς, adv., necessarily
or by constraint, 1 Pet. v. 2.*

ἀνάγκη, ης, ἡ, (1) necessity,
Philem. 14; 1 Cor. vii. 37;
followed by inf. (with ἐστι
understood), there is need to,
Mat. xviii. 7; (2) distress,
Lu. xxi. 23.

ἀνα-γνωρίζω, to make known,
aor. pass., Ac. vii. 13 (Rec.).*

ἀνά-γνωσις, εως, ἡ, reading, Ac.
xiii. 15; 2 Cor. iii. 14; 1 Tim.
iv. 13.*

ἀν-άγω, to bring, lead, or take
up, Lu. ii. 22; Ac. ix. 39;
to offer up, as sacrifices, Ac.
vii. 41; pass., to put to sea, to
set sail, Lu. viii. 22; Ac. xiii.
13.

ἀνα-δείκνυμι, to show, as by up-
lifting, to show plainly, Ac.

i. 24; to appoint, announce,
Lu. x. 1.*

ἀνά-δειξις, εως, ἡ, a showing or
public announcing, Lu. i.
80.*

ἀνα-δέχομαι, dep., to receive
with a welcome, guests, Ac.
xxviii. 7; promises, Heb. xi.
17.*

ἀνα-δίδωμι, to give up, deliver,
as by messengers, Ac. xxiii.
33.*

ἀνα-ζάω, ῶ, to live again, revive
(W. H. only in Ro. vii. 9,
and doubtfully Lu. xv. 24).

ἀνα-ζητέω, ῶ, to seek with diligence, Lu. ii. 44, 45 (W. H.);
Ac. xi. 25.*

ἀνα-ζώννυμι, to gird or bind up,
as a loose dress is girded
about the loins; mid. fig.,
1 Pet. i. 13. (S.)*

ἀνα-ζωπυρέω, ῶ (πῦρ), to re-
kindle or rouse up; fig., 2
Tim. i. 6.*

ἀνα-θάλλω, to thrive or flourish
again, Phil. iv. 10.*

ἀνά-θεμα, ατος, τό, a person or
thing accursed, Gal. i. 8;
1 Cor. xvi. 22; an execration
or curse, Ac. xxiii. 14. Syn.:
ἀνάθημα is a thing devoted in
honor of God, consecrated;
ἀνάθεμα, simply a later form
of ἀνάθημα, has come to
mean a thing devoted to destruction.

ἀναθεματίζω, ίσω, to bind (one's
self) by a curse, Ac. xxiii. 12,
14, 21; to affirm with curses,
Mar. xiv. 71.*

ἀνα-θεωρέω, ῶ, to look at attentively, to consider, Ac. xvi.
23; Heb. xiii. 7.*

ἀνά-θημα, ατος, τό, anything
consecrated and laid by, a
votive offering, Lu. xxi. 5
(W. H.).* Syn.: see ἀνά-
θεμα.

ἀν-αιδεία, ας, ἡ, shamelessness,
impudence, Lu. xi. 8.*

ἀναίρεσις, εως, ἡ, a taking away,
i.e., by a violent death, Ac.
viii. 1, xxii. 20 (Rec.).*

ἀν-αιρέω, ῶ (see Gr. § 103, 1,
Wi. § 15, Bu. 53), to take
away, to abolish, Heb. x. 9;
to take off, to kill, Mat. ii. 16;
mid., to take up, Ac. vii. 21.

ἀν-αίτιος, ον, guiltless, Mat. xii.
5, 7.*

ἀνα-καθίζω, to sit up (properly
trans. with ἑαυτόν under

stooα), Lu. vii. 15; Ac. ix. 40.*

ἀνα-καινίζω, to renew, restore to a former condition, Heb. vi. 6.*

ἀνα-καινόω, ῶ, to renew, amend, to change the life, 2 Cor. iv. 16; Col. iii. 10. (N. T.)*

ἀνα-καίνωσις, εως, ἡ, a renewal or change of heart and life, Ro. xii. 2 : Tit. iii. 5. (N. T.)* Syn.: see Trench, § xviii.

ἀνα-καλύπτω, to unveil, make manifest; pass., 2 Cor. iii. 14, 18.*

ἀνα-κάμπτω, to bend or turn back, return, Heb. xi. 15.

ἀνά-κειμαι, dep., to recline at a meal, Mat. ix. 10; ὁ ἀνακείμενος, one who reclines at table, a guest, Mat. xxii. 10, 11 (W. H. omit in Mar. v. 40).

ἀνα-κεφαλαιόω, ῶ, to gather together into one, to sum up under one head; pass., Ro. xiii. 9; mid., Ep. i. 10.*

ἀνα-κλίνω, to lay down an infant, Lu. ii. 7; to make to recline at table, Mar. vi. 39; pass., to recline, as at a feast, like ἀνάκειμαι, Lu. xiii. 29.

ἀνα-κόπτω, to check (lit., beat back), Gal. v. 7 (W. H. ἐγκόπτω).*

ἀνα-κράζω, to cry out, to shout aloud, Mar. i. 23, vi. 49.

ἀνα-κρίνω, to investigate, inquire, examine (judicially), to judge of. Only in Lu., Ac., and 1 Cor.

ἀνά-κρισις, εως, ἡ, judicial examination, Ac. xxv. 26.*

ἀνα-κυλίω, to roll back, Mar. xvi. 4 (W. H. for ἀποκ-).*

ἀνα-κύπτω, to raise one's self up, Lu. xiii. 11; Jn. viii. 7, 10; fig., to be elated, Lu. xxi. 28.*

ἀνα-λαμβάνω, to take up, Ac. vii. 43; pass., of Christ's being taken up to heaven, Mar. xvi. 19.

ἀνά-λημψις (W. H. -λημψις), εως, ἡ, a being taken up, i.e., into heaven, Lu. ix. 51.*

ἀν-αλίσκω, λώσω, to consume, destroy, Lu. ix. 54; Gal. v. 15; 2 Th. ii. 8 (not W. H.).*

ἀνα-λογία, ας, ἡ, proportion, analogy, Ro. xii. 6.*

ἀνα-λογίζομαι, to think upon, consider attentively, Heb. xii. 3.*

ἄν-αλος, ον, without saltness, insipid, Mar. ix. 50.*

ἀνά-λυσις, εως, ἡ, a loosening of a ship from her moorings, departure, 2 Tim. iv. 6.*

ἀνα-λύω, to depart, Phil. i. 23; to return, Lu. xii. 36.*

ἀν-αμάρτητος, ον, without blame, faultless, Jn. viii. 7 (W. H. omit).*

ἀνα-μένω, to await, 1 Th. i. 10.*

ἀνα-μιμνήσκω, to remind, admonish, two accs., or acc. and inf., 1 Cor. iv. 17; pass., to remember, to call to mind, gen. or acc., 2 Cor. vii. 15.

ἀνά-μνησις, εως, ἡ, remembrance, a memorial, Heb. x. 3.

ἀνα-νεόω, ῶ, to renew; mid., to renew one's self, to be renewed, Ep. iv. 23.*

ἀνα-νήφω, to recover soberness, 2 Tim. ii. 26.*

Ἀνανίας, α, ὁ (from Heb.), Ananias. Three of the name are mentioned, Ac. v. 1–5, ix. 10, xxiii. 2.

ἀν-αντι-ρρήτος, ον, indisputable, not to be contradicted, Ac. xix. 36.*

ἀναντιρρήτως, adv., without contradiction, Ac. x. 29.*

ἀν-άξιος, ον, unworthy, inadequate, 1 Cor. vi. 2.*

ἀναξίως, adv., unworthily, unbecomingly, 1 Cor. xi. 27 (not in ver. 29, W. H.).*

ἀνά-παυσις, εως, ἡ, rest, cessation from labor, refreshment, Rev. iv. 8; Mat. xii. 43.

ἀνα-παύω, to give rest or refreshment, Mat. xi. 28; mid., to take rest, Mar. vi. 31 (W. H. read in Rev. xiv. 13, ἀναπαήσονται, 2 fut. pass.).

ἀνα-πείθω, σω, to persuade, in a bad sense, seduce, mislead, Ac. xviii. 13.*

ἀνα-πέμπω, to remit, send back, Lu. xxiii. 11.

ἀνα-πηδάω, leap up (W. H., in Mar. x. 50, for Rec. ἀνίστημι).*

ἀνά-πηρος, ον, maimed, having lost a member, Lu. xiv. 13, 21 (W. H. ἀνάπειρος).*

ἀνα-πίπτω, to fall down, lie down, Mat. xv. 35; N. T., to recline at table, Lu. xi. 37, xiv. 10.

ἀνα-πληρόω, ῶ, to fill up, 1 Th. ii. 16; to fulfill, as a prophecy,

Mat. xiii. 14; to perform, as a precept, Gal. vi. 2; to occupy or fill a place, 1 Cor. xiv. 16; to supply a deficiency, Phil. ii. 30.

ἀν-απο-λόγητος, ου, adj., inexcusable, Ro. i. 20, ii. 1.*

ἀνα-πτύσσω, to unroll, as a volume, Lu. iv. 17 (not W. H.).*

ἀν-άπτω, to kindle, set on fire, Lu. xii. 49; Ac. xxviii. 2 (not W. H.); Ja. iii. 5.*

ἀν-αρίθμητος, ον, innumerable, Heb. xi. 12.*

ἀνα-σείω, to stir up, move, instigate, Mar. xv. 11; Lu. xxiii. 5.*

ἀνα-σκευάζω, to pervert, unsettle, destroy, Ac. xv. 24.*

ἀνα-σπάω, to draw up, Lu. xiv. 5; Ac. xi. 10.*

ἀνά-στασις, εως, ἡ, a rising up, as opposed to falling, Lu. ii. 34; rising, as from death or the grave, resurrection, the future state, Ro. i. 4, vi. 5.

ἀνα-στατόω, ῶ, to unsettle, put in commotion, Ac. xvii. 6, xxi. 38; Gal. v. 12.*

ἀνα-σταυρόω, ῶ, to crucify afresh, Heb. vi. 6.*

ἀνα-στενάζω, to groan or sigh deeply, Mar. viii. 12.*

ἀνα-στρέφω, to turn up, overturn, Jn. ii. 15; intrans., to return, Ac. v. 22; mid. (as Lat. versari), to be or to live in a place or state, to move among, to pass one's time or be conversant with persons; generally, to conduct one's self, 2 Cor. i. 12; 1 Tim. iii. 15.

ἀνα-στροφή, ῆς, ἡ, behavior, manner of life, Gal. i. 13; Ep. iv. 22.

ἀνα-τάσσομαι, to arrange, compose a narrative, Lu. i. 1.*

ἀνα-τέλλω, to spring up or rise, as the sun, a star, a cloud, Mat. xiii. 6; Lu. xii. 54; of the Messiah, Heb. vii. 14; trans., to cause to rise, Mat. v. 45.

ἀνα-τίθημι, mid., to set forth, declare, Ac. xxv. 14; Gal. ii. 2.*

ἀνατολή, ῆς, ἡ, the dawn, dayspring, Lu. i. 78; generally, the east, where the sun rises, Mat. ii. 2, 9; sing. and plur, see Gr. § 240a.

ἀνα-τρέπω, to subvert, overthrow, 2 Tim. ii. 18; Tit. i. 11.*

ἀνα-τρέφω, to nurse, bring up, educate, Lu. iv. 16 (W. H. mrg.); Ac. vii. 20, 21, xxii. 3.*

ἀνα-φαίνω, mid., to appear, Lu. xix. 11; pass., to be shown a thing (acc.), Ac. xxi. 3 (W. H. read act., in sense to come in sight of).*

ἀνα-φέρω, οἴσω, to bear or lead, to offer, as sacrifice, Heb. vii. 27; to bear, as sin, 1 Pet. ii. 24.

ἀνα-φωνέω, ῶ, to cry out aloud, Lu. i. 42.*

ἀνά-χυσις, εως, ἡ, a pouring out; hence, excess, 1 Pet. iv. 4.*

ἀνα-χωρέω, ῶ, to depart, withdraw, Mat. ix. 24; Mar. iii. 7.

ἀνά-ψυξις, εως, ἡ, a refreshing, Ac. iii. 20.*

ἀνα-ψύχω, to refresh, to revive, 2 Tim. i. 16.*

ἀνδραποδιστής, οῦ, ὁ, a man-stealer, 1 Tim. i. 10.*

Ἀνδρέας, ου, ὁ, Andrew, Jn i 40.

ἀνδρίζω, ίσω, mid., to act like a man, to be brave, 1 Cor. xvi. 13.*

Ἀνδρόνικος, ου, ὁ, Andronicus, Ro. xvi. 7.*

ἀνδρό-φονος, ου, ὁ, a man-slayer, 1 Tim. i. 9.*

ἀν-έγκλητος, ον, not open to accusation, unblamable, 1 Cor. i. 8; Col. i. 22.

ἀν-εκ-διήγητος, ον, not to be spoken, inexpressible, 2 Cor. ix. 15. (N. T.)*

ἀν-εκ-λάλητος, unspeakable, 1 Pet. i. 8. (N.T.)*

ἀν-έκ-λειπτος, ον, unfailing, Lu. xii. 33.*

ἀνεκτός, ή, όν, tolerable, supportable; only in comp., Mat. x. 15, xi. 22, 24.

ἀν-ελεήμων, ον, without compassion, cruel, Ro. i. 31.*

ἀνεμίζω, to agitate or drive with wind; pass., Ja. i. 6. (N.T.)*

ἄνεμος, ου, ὁ, the wind, Mat. xi. 7, fig., applied to empty doctrines, Ep. iv. 14.

ἀν-ένδεκτος, ον (ἐνδέχομαι), adj., impossible, Lu. xvii. 1. (N. T.)*

ἀν-εξ-ερεύνητος (W. H. -ραύ-), ον, adj., unsearchable, Ro. xi. 33.*

ἀνεξί-κακος, ον, patient of injury, 2 Tim. ii. 24. (N. T.)*

ἀν-εξ-ιχνίαστος, ον, that cannot be explored, incomprehensible, Ro. xi. 33; Ep. iii. 8. (S.)*

ἀν-επ-αίσχυντος, ον, having no cause to be ashamed, 2 Tim. ii. 15.*

ἀν-επί-ληπτος (W. H. -λημπ-), ον, adj., never caught doing wrong, irreproachable, 1 Tim. iii. 2, v. 7, vi. 14.*

ἀν-έρχομαι, to come or go up, Jn. vi. 3; Gal. i. 17, 18.*

ἄνεσις, εως, ἡ (ἀνίημι), relaxation, remission, as from bonds, burden, etc., Ac. xxiv. 23; 2 Th. i. 7.

ἀν-ετάζω, to examine judicially, Ac. xxii. 24, 29. (S.)*

ἄνευ, adv. as prep., with gen., without, 1 Pet. iii. 1.

ἀν-εύθετος, ον, inconvenient, Ac. xxvii. 12. (N. T.)*

ἀν-ευρίσκω, to find by searching for, Lu. ii. 16; Ac. xxi. 4.*

ἀν-έχω, mid., to bear with, forbear, have patience with, endure, Mat. xvii. 17; Lu. ix. 41; gen. of pers. or thing.

ἀνεψιός, οῦ, ὁ, a cousin, Col. iv. 10.*

ἄνηθον, ου, τό, anise, dill, Mat. xxiii. 23.*

ἀνήκει, impers., it is fit or proper; part., τὸ ἀνῆκον, τὰ ἀνήκοντα, the becoming, Philem. 8.

ἀν-ήμερος, ον, adj., not tame, fierce, 2 Tim. iii. 3.*

ἀνήρ, ἀνδρός, ὁ, (1) a man, in sex and age (Lat. vir), Ac. viii. 12; hence, (2) a husband, Ro. vii. 2, 3; (3) a person generally, Lu. vii. 41; plur. voc., ἄνδρες, Sirs!; often in apposition with adjectives and nouns, as ἀνὴρ ἁμαρτωλός, ἀνὴρ προφήτης, Lu. v. 8, xxiv. 19.

ἀνθ-ίστημι, to oppose, withstand, resist, with dat., Ro. ix. 19, Mat. v. 39.

ἀνθ-ομολογέομαι, οῦμαι, to confess, give thanks to, dat., Lu. ii. 38.*

ἄνθος, ους, τό, a flower, Ja. i. 10, 11; 1 Pet. i. 24.*

ἀνθρακιά, ᾶς, ἡ, a heap of burning coals, Jn. xviii. 18, xxi. 9.*

ἄνθραξ, ακος, ὁ, a coal, Ro. xii. 20.*

ἀνθρωπ-άρεσκος, ον, desirous of pleasing men, Ep. vi. 6; Col iii. 22. (S.)*

ἀνθρώπινος, ίνη, ινον, human, belonging to man, Ja. iii. 7; 1 Cor. x. 13.

ἀνθρωπο-κτόνος, ου, ὁ, ἡ, a homicide, a manslayer, Jn. viii. 44; 1 Jn. iii. 15.*

ἄνθρωπος, ου, ὁ, a man, one of the human race (Lat. homo). Like ἀνήρ, joined in apposition with substantives, as Mat. xviii. 23, xxi. 33.

ἀνθ-υπατεύω, to be proconsul, Ac. xviii. 12 (not W. H.).*

ἀνθ-ύπατος, ου, ὁ, a proconsul, Ac. xiii. 7, 8, 12.

ἀν-ίημι, to unloose, let go, Ac. xvi. 26, xxvii. 40; to give up, Ep. vi. 9; to leave, neglect, Heb. xiii. 5.*

ἀν-ίλεως, ων, without mercy, Ja. ii. 13 (W. H. read ἀνέλεος). (N. T.)*

ἄ-νιπτος, ον, adj., unwashed, Mat. xv. 20; Mar. vii. 2, 5 (Rec.).*

ἀν-ίστημι, to raise up one lying or dead, Ac. ix. 41; Jn. vi. 39, 40; intrans. (in 2 a., pf. and mid.), to rise from a recumbent posture, Mar. i. 35; to rise again from the dead, Lu. xvi. 31; aor. part., often combined with other verbs, as "rising (ἀναστάς) he went."

Ἄννα, ας, ἡ, Anna, Lu. ii. 36.*

Ἄννας, α, ὁ, Annas, Lu. iii. 2; Jn. xviii. 13, 24; Ac. iv. 6.*

ἀ-νόητος, ον, foolish, thoughtless, Ro. i. 14; 1 Tim. vi. 9.

ἄνοια, ας, ἡ, folly, madness, Lu. vi. 11; 2 Tim. iii. 9.*

ἀνοίγω, ξω, to open, Ac. v 19, xii. 10, 14; intrans. in 2 perf., ἀνέῳγα, to be open, 2 Cor. vi. 11; 1 Cor. xvi. 9.

ἀν-οικο-δομέω, ῶ, to build up again, Ac. xv. 16.*

ἄνοιξις, εως, ἡ, opening (the act of), Ep. vi. 19.*

ἀ-νομία, ας, ἡ, lawlessness, iniquity, Mat. xxiii. 28; Tit. ii. 14; αἱ ἀνομίαι, iniquities, evil deeds, Ro. iv. 7. Syn.: see ἁγνόημα.

ἄ-νομος, ον, (1) without law, not subject to the law, used of Gentiles, 1 Cor. ix. 21; (2) 'awless; as subst., a male-

factor; ὁ ἄνομος, *the lawless one,* 2 Th. ii. 8.

ἀνόμως, adv., *without law,* Ro. ii. 12.

ἀν-ορθόω, ῶ, *to make upright* or *straight again, to rebuild, make strong,* Lu. xiii. 13; Ac. xv. 16; Heb. xii. 12.*

ἀν-όσιος, ον, *unholy,* 1 Tim. i. 9; 2 Tim. iii. 2.*

ἀνοχή, ῆς, ἡ, *forbearance, toleration,* Ro. ii. 4, iii. 25.* *Syn.:* ὑπομονή is patience under trials, referring to *things;* μακροθυμία, patience under provocation, referring to *persons;* ἀνοχή is a forbearance *temporary* in its nature.

ἀντ-αγωνίζομαι, *to resist, strive against,* Heb. xii. 4.*

ἀντ-άλλαγμα, ατος,τό,*an equivalent, price,* Mat. xvi. 26; Mar. viii. 37.*

ἀντ-ανα-πληρόω, ῶ, *to fill up in turn,* Col. i. 24.*

ἀντ-απο-δίδωμι, *to recompense, requite,* Lu. xiv. 14; Ro. xii. 19.

ἀντ-από-δομα, ατος, τό, *a recompense, requital,* Lu. xiv. 12; Ro. xi. 9. (S.)*

ἀντ-από-δοσις, εως, ἡ, *a reward, recompense,* Col. iii. 24.*

ἀντ-απο-κρίνομαι, *to reply against, contradict,* Lu. xiv. 6; Ro. ix. 20.*

ἀντ-εῖπον (used as 2 aor. of ἀντιλέγω, see φημί), *to contradict, to gainsay,* Lu. xxi. 15; Ac. iv. 14.*

ἀντ-έχω, mid., *to hold fast, to adhere to* (gen.), Mat. vi. 24; Lu. xvi. 13; 1 Th. v. 14; Tit. i. 9.*

ἀντί, prep., gen., *instead of, for.* See Gr. §§ 291, 147 a, Wi. §§ 47 a, 52, 4, 3), Bu. 321.

ἀντι-βάλλω, *to throw in turn, exchange words,* Lu. xxiv. 17.*

ἀντι-δια-τίθημι, mid.,*to set one's self against, oppose,* 2 Tim. ii. 25.*

ἀντί-δικος, ου, ὁ (orig. adj.), *an opponent at law,* Mat. v. 25; Lu. xii. 58, xviii. 3; *an adversary,* 1 Pet. v. 8.*

ἀντί-θεσις, εως, ἡ, *opposition,* 1 Tim. vi. 20.*

ἀντι-καθ-ίστημι, *to resist,* Heb. xii. 4.*

ἀντι-καλέω, *to call* or *invite in turn,* Lu. xiv. 12.*

ἀντί-κειμαι, *to oppose, resist*

(dat.), Lu. xiii. 17, xxi. 15; ὁ ἀντικείμενος, *an adversary,* 1 Cor. xvi. 9; Phil. i. 28.

ἀντικρύ (W. H. ἄντικρυς), adv., *over against,* Ac. xx. 15.*

ἀντι-λαμβάνω, mid.,*to take hold of, help, share in* (gen.), Lu. i. 54; Ac. xx. 35; 1 Tim. vi. 2.

ἀντι-λέγω, *to speak against, contradict* (dat.), Ac. xiii. 45; *to oppose, deny,* Jn. xix. 12.

ἀντί-ληψις (W. H. -λημψ-), εως, *help, ministration,* 1 Cor. xii. 28.*

ἀντι-λογία, ας, ἡ, *contradiction, contention, rebellion,* Heb. vi. 16, vii. 7, xii. 3; Ju. 11.*

ἀντι-λοιδορέω, *to revile* or *reproach again,* 1 Pet. ii. 23.*

ἀντί-λυτρον, ου, τό, *a ransom-price,* 1 Tim. ii. 16.*

ἀντι-μετρέω, ῶ, *to measure in return,* Mat. vii. 2 (not W. H.); Lu. vi. 38. (N. T.)*

ἀντι-μισθία, ας, ἡ, *recompense,* Ro. i. 27; 2 Cor. vi. 13. (N. T.)*

Ἀντιόχεια, ας, ἡ, *Antioch.* Two places of the name are mentioned, Ac. xi. 26, xiii. 14.

Ἀντιοχεύς, έως, ὁ, *a citizen of Antioch,* Ac. vi. 5.*

ἀντι-παρ-έρχομαι, *to pass by opposite to,* Lu. x. 31, 32.*

Ἀντίπας, α, ὁ, *Antipas,* Rev. ii. 13.*

Ἀντιπατρίς, ίδος, ἡ, *Antipatris,* Ac. xxiii. 31.*

ἀντι-πέραν (W. H. ἀντίπερα), adv., *on the opposite side* or *shore,* Lu. viii. 26.*

ἀντι-πίπτω, *to fall against, resist,* Ac. vii. 51.*

ἀντι-στρατεύομαι, dep., *to make war against,* Ro. vii. 23.*

ἀντι-τάσσω, mid., *to set one's self against, resist* (dat.), Ro. xiii. 2; Ja. iv. 6, v. 6; 1 Pet. v. 5; Ac. xviii. 6.*

ἀντί-τυπος, ον, *like in pattern,* Heb. ix. 24; τὸ ἀντίτυπον, *corresponding in form,* as wax to the seal, *antitype,* 1 Pet. iii. 21.*

Ἀντί-χριστος, ου, ὁ, *opposer of Christ, Antichrist,* 1 Jn. ii. 18, 22, iv. 3; 2 Jn. 7. (N. T.)*

ἀντλέω, ῶ, *to draw* from a vessel, Jn. ii. 8, 9, iv. 7, 15.*

ἄντλημα, ατος, τό, *a bucket,* Jn. iv. 11.*

ἀντ-οφθαλμέω, ῶ, *to look in the face;* so *to meet the wind,* Ac. xxvii. 15.*

ἄν-υδρος, ον, *without water, dry,* Mat. xii. 43; Lu. xi. 24.

ἀν-υπό-κριτος, ον, adj., *without hypocrisy, unfeigned,* Ro. xii. 9; 2 Cor. vi. 6. (Ap.)

ἀν-υπό-τακτος, ον, *not subject to rule,* of things, Heb. ii. 8; *unruly,* of persons, 1 Tim. i. 9; Tit. i. 6, 10.*

ἄνω, adv. (ἀνά), *up, above, upwards;* τὰ ἄνω, *heaven* or *heavenly things,* as Jn. viii. 23.

ἀνώγεον, ου, τό, *an upper chamber.* See ἀνάγαιον.*

ἄνωθεν, adv. (ἄνω), (1) of place, *from above,* as Jn. iii. 31, xix. 11; with prepp. ἀπό, ἐκ, *from the top,* as Mar. xv. 38; Jn. xix. 23; (2) of time, *from the first,* only Lu. i. 3; Ac. xxvi. 5. In Jn. iii. 4, 7, *again* (see Gal. iv. 9); or, perhaps here also, *from above.*

ἀνωτερικός, ή, όν, *upper, higher,* Ac. xix. 1.*

ἀνώτερος, α, ον (compar. of ἄνω; only neut. as adv.), *higher, to a higher place,* Lu. xiv. 10; *above, before,* Heb. x. 8.*

ἀν-ωφελής, ές, *unprofitable,* Tit iii. 9; Heb. vii. 18.*

ἀξίνη, ης, ἡ, *an axe,* Mat. iii. 10; Lu. iii. 9.*

ἄξιος, ία, ιον, adj., *worthy, deserving of, suitable to* (gen.), Heb. xi. 38; Lu. xii. 48; Ac. xxvi. 20.

ἀξιόω, ῶ, *to deem worthy* (acc. and gen., or inf.), Lu. vii. 7; 2 Th. i. 11; *think fit,* Ac. xv. 38, xxviii. 22.

ἀξίως, adv., *worthily, suitably* (with gen.), Ro. xvi. 2; Phil. i. 27.

ἀ-όρατος, ον. *invisible, unseen,* Col. i. 16; 1 Tim. i. 17.

ἀπ-αγγέλλω, *to report, relate, make known, declare,* Ac. iv. 23; 1 Th. i. 9.

ἀπ-άγχω, mid., *to hang* or *strangle one's self,* Mat. xxvii. 5.*

ἀπ-άγω, *to lead, carry,* or *take away,* Lu. xiii. 15; *to lead away* to execution, Mat. xxvi. 57; Mar. xiv. 44, 53; *to lead* or *tend,* as a way, Mat. vii. 13, 14.

ἀ-παίδευτος, ον, adj., *uninstructed, ignorant,* 2 Tim. ii. 23.*

ἀπ-αίρω, *to take away;* in N.T. only 1 a. pass., Mat. ix. 15; Mar. ii. 20; Lu. v. 35.*

ἀπ-αιτέω, *to ask back, require, reclaim,* Lu. vi. 30, xii. 20.*

ἀπ-αλγέω, *to be past feeling,* Ep. iv. 19.*

ἀπ-αλλάσσω, pass., *to be removed from, to depart,* Ac. xix. 12; pass., *to be set free* (with ἀπό), Lu. xii. 58; *to deliver,* Heb. ii. 15.*

ἀπ-αλλοτριόω, *to estrange, alienate* (gen.), Ep. ii. 12, iv. 18; Col. i. 21.*

ἀπαλός, ή, όν, *tender,* as a shoot of a tree, Mat. xxiv. 32; Mar. xiii. 28.*

ἀπ-αντάω, ῶ, *to meet, to encounter* (dat.), Mar. xiv. 13.

ἀπ-άντησις, εως, ἡ, *a meeting, an encountering; εἰς ἀπάντησιν* (gen. or dat.), *to meet* any one, Ac. xxviii. 15.

ἅπαξ, adv., of time, *once,* 1 Th. ii. 18; *once for all,* Heb. vi. 4, x. 2.

ἀ-παρά-βατος, ον, *inviolable, unchangeable,* Heb. vii. 24.*

ἀ-παρα-σκεύαστος, ον, adj., *unprepared,* 2 Cor. ix. 4.*

ἀπ-αρνέομαι, οῦμαι, *to deny, disown,* Mat. xxvi. 34, 35; *to disregard,* Mar. viii. 34.

ἀπ-άρτι, adv., of time (see ἄρτι), *henceforth,* Rev. xiv. 13. (W. H. read ἀπ' ἄρτι.)*

ἀπ-αρτισμός, οῦ, ὁ, *completion,* Lu. xiv. 28.*

ἀπ-αρχή, ῆς, ἡ, *the first-fruits,* consecrated to God (see W H., 2 Th. ii. 13).

ἅ-πας, ασα, αν (like πᾶς, Gr. § 37), *all, all together, the whole.*

ἀπασπάζομαι, see ἀσπάζομαι. (N. T.)*

ἀπατάω, ῶ, ήσω, *to deceive, lead into error,* Ja. i. 26; Ep. v. 6; 1 Tim. ii. 14 (W. H. ἐξαπ-).* (The stronger form ἐξαπατάω is more freq.)

ἀπάτη, ης, ἡ, *deceit, deceitfulness,* Col. ii. 8; Heb. iii. 13.

ἀ-πάτωρ, ορος, ὁ, ἡ (πατήρ), *without father, i.e.,* in the genealogies, Heb. vii. 3.*

ἀπ-αύγασμα, ατος, τό, *reflected brightness,* Heb. i. 3.*

ἀπ-εῖδον (W. H. ἀφεῖδον), 2 aor. οἱ ἀφοράω, which see.

ἀ-πείθεια, ας, ἡ, *willful unbelief,* *obstinacy, disobedience,* Heb. iv. 6, 11.

ἀ-πειθέω ῶ, *to refuse belief, be disobedient,* Jn. iii. 36; Ro. ii. 8.

ἀ-πειθής, ές, *unbelieving, disobedient,* Lu. i. 17; 2 Tim. iii. 2.

ἀπειλέω, ῶ, ήσω, *to threaten, forbid by threatening,* Ac. iv. 17; 1 Pet. ii. 23.*

ἀπειλή, ῆς, ἡ, *a threatening, threat,* Ac. iv. 17 (W. H. omit), 29, ix. 1; Ep. vi. 9.*

ἄπ-ειμι (εἰμί, *to be*), *to be absent,* as 1 Cor. v. 3.

ἄπ-ειμι (εἶμι, *to go*), *to go away, to depart,* Ac. xvii. 10.*

ἀπ-εῖπον (see εἶπον), mid., *to renounce, disown,* 2 Cor. iv. 2.*

ἀ-πείραστος, ον, adj., *incapable of being tempted,* Ja. i. 13.*

ἄ-πειρος, ον, adj., *inexperienced, unskillful* in (gen.), Heb. v. 13.*

ἀπ-εκ-δέχομαι, *to wait for, expect earnestly* or *patiently,* Ro. viii. 19, 23, 25; Heb. ix. 28. (N. T.)

ἀπ-εκ-δύομαι, *to strip, divest, renounce,* Col. ii. 15, iii. 9.*

ἀπέκδυσις, εως, ἡ, *a putting* or *stripping off, renouncing,* Col. ii. 11. (N. T.)*

ἀπ-ελαύνω, *to drive away,* Ac. xviii. 16.*

ἀπ-ελεγμός, οῦ, ὁ (ἐλέγχω), *repudiation, censure, disrepute,* Ac. xix. 27. (N. T.)*

ἀπ-ελεύθερος, ον, ὁ, ἡ, *a freedman,* 1 Cor. vii. 22.*

Ἀπελλῆς, οῦ, ὁ, *Apelles,* Ro. xvi. 10.*

ἀπ-ελπίζω, σω, *to despair,* Lu. vi. 35; R. V. "never despairing" (see R. V. mrg.).*

ἀπ-έναντι, adv. (gen.), *over against, in the presence of, in opposition to.*

ἀ-πέραντος, ον (περαίνω), *interminable,* 1 Tim. i. 4.*

ἀ-περισπάστως, adv. (περισπάω), *without distraction,* 1 Cor. vii. 35.*

ἀ-περί-τμητος, ον, *uncircumcised;* fig., Ac. vii. 51. (S.)*

ἀπ-έρχομαι, *to go* or *come from* one place to another, *to go away, depart; to go apart; to go back, to return; to go forth,* as a rumor.

ἀπ-έχω, *to have in full,* Mat. vi. 2; *to be far* (abs., or ἀπό). Lu. vii. 6; impers., ἀπέχει, *it is enough,* Mar. xiv. 41; mid., *to abstain from* (gen., or ἀπό), 1 Th. iv. 3.

ἀπιστέω, ῶ, *to disbelieve* (dat.), Mar. xvi. 11; *to be unfaithful,* Ro. iii. 3.

ἀπιστία, ας, ἡ, *unbelief, distrust, a state of unbelief,* 1 Tim. i. 13; Heb. iii. 12, 19; *unfaithfulness,* Ro. iii. 3.

ἄ-πιστος, ον, *not believing, incredulous,* Jn. xx. 27; hence, *an unbeliever* or *infidel,* 2 Cor. iv. 4; *unfaithful,* Lu. xii. 46; Rev. xxi. 8; pass., *incredible,* only Ac. xxvi. 8.

ἁπλόος, οῦς, ῆ, οῦν, *simple, sound,* Mat. vi. 22; Lu. xi. 34.*

ἁπλότης, τητος, ἡ, *simplicity, sincerity, purity,* 2 Cor. i. 12; Col. iii. 22.

ἁπλῶς, adv., *simply, sincerely,* Ja. i. 5.*

ἀπό, prep. gen., *from.* See Gr. § 292, Wi. § 47 b, Bu. 321 sq.; and for the force of the prep. in composition, Gr. § 147 a, Wi. § 52, 4, Bu. 344.

ἀπο-βαίνω, see Gr. § 94, I., 6 d; fut., -βήσομαι), *to go* or *come out of,* as from a ship, Lu. v. 2; Jn. xxi. 9; *to turn out, result,* Lu. xxi. 13; Phil. i. 19.*

ἀπο-βάλλω, *to throw away,* Mar. x. 50; Heb. x. 35.*

ἀπο-βλέπω, *to look away from* all besides; hence, *to look earnestly at* (εἰς), Heb. xi. 26.*

ἀπό-βλητος, ον, verbal adj., *to be thrown away, rejected,* 1 Tim. iv. 4.*

ἀπο-βολή, ῆς, ἡ, *a casting away, rejection, loss,* Ac. xxvii. 22; Ro. xi. 15.*

ἀπο-γίνομαι, *to die,* 1 Pet. ii. 24.*

ἀπο-γραφή, ῆς, ἡ, *a record, register, enrolment,* Lu. ii. 2; Ac. v. 37.*

ἀπο-γράφω, *to enrol, inscribe in a register,* Lu. ii. 1, 3, 5; Heb. xii. 23.*

ἀπο-δείκνυμι, *to show by proof, demonstrate, set forth,* Ac. ii. 22, xxv. 7; 1 Cor. iv. 9; 2 Th. ii. 4.*

ἀπο-δειξις, εως, ἡ, *demonstration, proof,* 1 Cor. ii. 4.*

ἀπο-δεκατόω, ῶ, (1) *to pay the tenth* or *tithe*, Mat. xxiii. 23; (2) *to levy tithes on*, acc., Heb. vii. 5. (S.)

ἀπό-δεκτος, ον, verbal adj., *acceptable*, 1 Tim. ii. 3, v. 4.*

ἀπο-δέχομαι, *to receive with pleasure, to welcome*, Ac. xviii. 27, xxviii. 30.

ἀπο-δημέω, ῶ, *to go from one's own people, to go into another country;* only in the parables of our Lord, as Mat. xxi. 33; Lu. xv. 13.

ἀπό-δημος, ον, *gone abroad, sojourning in another country* (R. V.), Mar. xiii. 34.*

ἀπο-δίδωμι, *to give from one's self, to deliver*, Mat. xxvii. 58; in mid., *to sell*, Ac. v. 8; *to pay off, discharge* what is due, Mat. v. 26; Lu. xvi. 2; *to restore*, Lu. iv. 20; *to requite, recompense*, Ro. ii. 6; Rev. xviii. 6.

ἀπο-δι-ορίζω, *to separate off, i.e.*, into parties, Ju. 19.*

ἀπο-δοκιμάζω, *to reject*, as disapproved or worthless, Mar. viii. 31; Heb. xii. 17.

ἀπο-δοχή, ῆς, ἡ, *acceptance, approbation*, 1 Tim. i. 15, iv. 9.*

ἀπό-θεσις, εως, ἡ, *a putting away*, 1 Pet. iii. 21; 2 Pet. i. 14.*

ἀπο-θήκη, ης, ἡ, *a repository, granary, storehouse*, Mat. iii. 12; Lu. iii. 17.

ἀπο-θησαυρίζω, *to treasure up, lay by in store*, 1 Tim. vi. 19.*

ἀπο-θλίβω, *to press closely*, Lu. viii. 45.*

ἀπο-θνήσκω (ἀπό, intensive; the simple θνήσκω is rare), *to die*, (1) of natural death, human, animal, or vegetable, Mat. ix. 24; (2) of spiritual death, Ro. vii. 10; Rev. iii. 2; (3) in Epp. of Paul, *to die to* (dat.), as Ro. vi. 2; also in other shades of meaning. For tenses see θνήσκω.

ἀπο-καθ-ίστημι, ἀποκαταστήσω (also -καθιστάω and -άνω, see Mar. ix. 12; Ac. i. 6), *to restore, e.g.*, to health, or as a state or kingdom, Lu. vi. 10, Ac. i. 6.

ἀπο-καλύπτω, *to uncover, bring to light, reveal*, Mat. x. 26; Lu. x. 21; 1 Cor. ii. 10. See Thayer, p. 62.

ἀπο-κάλυψις, εως, ἡ, *revelation, manifestation, enlightenment*, 1 Cor. xiv. 26; Ep. iii. 3; 2 Th. i. 7. (S.) *Syn.:* see Trench, § xciv.

ἀπο-καρα-δοκία, ας, ἡ, (κάρα, *head;* ἀπό, intensive), *earnest expectation*, as if looking for with the head outstretched, Ro. viii. 19; Phil. i. 20.*

ἀπο-κατ-αλλάσσω, *to reconcile, change from one state of feeling to another*, Ep. ii. 16; Col. i. 20, 22. (N. T.)*

ἀπο-κατά-στασις, εως, ἡ, *restitution, restoration*, Ac. iii. 21.*

ἀπό-κειμαι, *to be laid away, to be reserved for* (dat.), Lu. xix. 20; Col. i. 5; 2 Tim. iv. 8; Heb. ix. 27.*

ἀπο-κεφαλίζω (κεφαλή), *to behead*, Mat. xiv. 10; Mar. vi. 16, 27; Lu. ix. 9. (S.)*

ἀπο-κλείω, *to shut close*, as a door, Lu. xiii. 25.*

ἀπο-κόπτω, *to smite* or *cut off*, Mar. ix. 43, 45; Jn. xviii. 10, 26; Ac. xxvii. 32; mid., Gal. v. 12 (see R. V.).*

ἀπό-κριμα, ατος, τό, *an answer*, 2 Cor. i. 9.*

ἀπο-κρίνομαι (for aor., see Gr. § 100, Wi. § 39, 2), *to answer*, Mar. xii. 28; Col. iv. 6; often used (like the corresponding Hebrew verb) where the "answer" is not to a distinct question, but to some suggestion of the accompanying circumstances; so especially in the phrase ἀποκριθεὶς εἶπεν, *answered and said*, as Mat. xi. 25; Lu. i. 60.

ἀπό-κρισις, εως, ἡ, *an answer, reply*, Lu. ii. 47.

ἀπο-κρύπτω, *to hide, conceal*, 1 Cor. ii. 7; Ep. iii. 9.

ἀπό-κρυφος, ον, *hidden, concealed*, Mar. iv. 22; Lu. viii. 17; *stored up*, Col. ii. 3.

ἀπο-κτείνω, ενῶ, *to put to death, kill*, Mat. xvi. 21; Rev. ii. 13; fig., *to abolish*, Ep. ii. 16.

ἀπο-κυέω, ῶ, *to bring forth;* fig., Ja. i. 15, 18.*

ἀπο-κυλίω, ίσω, *to roll away*, Mat. xxviii. 2; Mar. xvi. 3; Lu. xxiv. 2. (S.)*

ἀπο-λαμβάνω, *to receive from* any one, Gal. iv. 5· *to receive back, recover*, Lu. xv. 27;

mid., *to take aside* with one's self, Mar. vii. 33.

ἀπό-λαυσις, εως, ἡ (λαύω, *to enjoy*), *enjoyment*, 1 Tim. vi. 17; Heb. xi. 25.*

ἀπο-λείπω, *to leave, to leave behind*, 2 Tim. iv. 13, 20; *to desert*, Ju. 6; pass., *to be reserved*, Heb. iv. 9.

ἀπο-λείχω, *to lick*, as a dog, Lu. xvi. 21 (W. H. ἐπιλείχω).*

ἀπ-όλλυμι (see Gr. § 116, 2, Wi. § 15, Bu. 64), *to destroy, to bring to nought, to put to death*, Mar. i. 24; Ro. xiv. 15; *to lose*, Mat. x. 42; Jn. vi. 39; mid., pass. (and 2d perf.), *to perish, die*, Mat. viii. 25; *to be lost*, Lu. xxi. 18.

Ἀπολλύων, οντος, ὁ (prop. part of ἀπολλύω, *Destroyer*), *Apollyon*, Rev. ix. 11. (N. T.)*

Ἀπολλωνία, ας, ἡ, *Apollonia*, a city of Macedonia, Ac. xvii. 1.*

Ἀπολλώς, ώ, ὁ, *Apollos*, Ac. xviii. 24.

ἀπο-λογέομαι, οῦμαι (λόγος), *to defend one's self by speech*, Lu. xxi. 14; Ac. xxvi. 24; *to defend, excuse*, Ro. ii. 15.

ἀπο-λογία, ας, ἡ, *a verbal defense*, "apology," Ac. xxv. 16; 1 Cor. ix. 3.

ἀπο-λούω, mid., *to wash away*, as sins, Ac. xxii. 16; 1 Cor. vi. 11.*

ἀπο-λύτρωσις, εως, ἡ, *redemption, deliverance*, Ro. iii. 24; Heb. ix. 15, xi. 35. *Syn.:* see Trench, § lxxvii.

ἀπο-λύω, *to release, let go, to send away*, Ac. xxviii. 18; Mat. xv. 23; spec., *to put away* a wife, *divorce*, Mat. i. 19; Lu. xvi. 18; mid., *to depart*, Ac. xxviii. 25.

ἀπο-μάσσω, ξω, *to wipe off*, as dust from the feet; mid., Lu. x. 11.*

ἀπο-νέμω, *to assign to, apportion*, 1 Pet. iii. 7.*

ἀπο-νίπτω, mid., *to wash one's self*, Mat. xxvii. 24.*

ἀπο-πίπτω, *to fall from*, Ac. ix. 18.*

ἀπο-πλανάω, ῶ, *to lead astray*, Mar. xiii. 22; 1 Tim. vi. 10.*

ἀπο-πλέω, εύσω, *to sail away*, Ac. xiii. 4, xiv. 26, xx. 15, xxvii. 1.*

ἀπο-πλύνω, to wash or rinse, as nets, Lu. v. 2 (W. H. πλύνω).*

ἀπο-πνίγω, to suffocate, choke, Mat. xiii. 7; Lu. viii. 7, 33.*

ἀ-πορέω, ῶ (πόρος, resource), except Mar. vi. 20 (W. H.), only mid. in N. T., to be in doubt, to be perplexed, Jn. xiii. 22; 2 Cor. iv. 8.

ἀπορία, as, ἡ, perplexity, disquiet, Lu. xxi. 25.*

ἀπο-ρρίπτω, to throw or cast down or off, Ac. xxvii. 43; ἑαυτούς understood.*

ἀπ-ορφανίζω (ὀρφανος), "to make orphans of"; to bereave, pass., 1 Th. ii. 17.*

ἀπο-σκευάζομαι, to pack away, pack up, Ac. xxi. 15 (W. H. ἐπισκευάζομαι).*

ἀπο-σκίασμα, ατος, τό (σκιάζω), a shade, a shadow, Ja. i. 17. (N. T.)*

ἀπο-σπάω, ῶ, άσω, to draw out, unsheathe, Mat. xxvi. 51; to withdraw, to draw away, Ac. xxi. 1.

ἀπο-στασία, as, ἡ, defection, apostasy, Ac. xxi. 21; 2 Th. ii. 3.*

ἀπο-στάσιον, ου, τό, repudiation, divorce, Mat. xix. 7; Mar. x. 4; met., bill of divorce, as Mat. v. 31.*

ἀπο-στεγάζω (στέγη), to unroof, Mar. ii. 4.*

ἀπο-στέλλω, to send forth, send, as a messenger, commission, etc., spoken of prophets, teachers, and other messengers, Mat. x. 40; Lu. vii. 3; Ac. x. 36; to send away, dismiss, Lu. iv. 18; Mar. v. 10, viii. 26.

ἀπο-στερέω, ῶ, ήσω, to defraud, abs., as Mar. x. 19; deprive of by fraud, acc. and gen., 1 Tim. vi. 5.

ἀπο-στολή, ῆς, ἡ, apostleship, Ac. i. 25; Ro. i. 5; 1 Cor. ix. 2; Gal. ii. 8.*

ἀπό-στολος, ου, ὁ, (1) a messenger, 2 Cor. viii. 23; Heb. iii. 1; (2) an apostle, i.e., a messenger of Christ to the world, Lu. vi. 13; Gal. i. 1; used of others besides Paul and the Twelve, Ac. xiv. 14; 1 Th. ii. 6; 2 Cor. viii. 23.

ἀπο-στοματίζω (στόμα), to entice to speak off-hand, Lu. xi. 53.*

ἀπο-στρέφω, to turn away, trans.

(with ἀπό, as Ac. iii. 26); restore, replace, Mat. xxvi. 52; mid., to desert, reject, acc., Mat. v. 42.

ἀπο-στυγέω, ῶ, to detest, to abhor, Ro. xii. 9.*

ἀπο-συνάγωγος, ον, excluded from the synagogue, excommunicated, Jn. ix. 22, xii. 42, xvi. 2. (N. T.)*

ἀπο-τάσσω, ξω, mid., to separate one's self from, withdraw from (dat.), Mar. vi. 46; to take leave of, renounce, send away (dat.), Lu. xiv. 33.

ἀπο-τελέω, ῶ, έσω, to perfect, Ja. i. 15; Lu. xiii. 32 (W. H.).*

ἀπο-τίθημι, mid., to lay off or aside, Ac. vii. 58; to renounce, Ro. xiii. 12.

ἀπο-τίνασσω, to shake off, Lu. ix. 5; Ac. xxviii. 5.*

ἀπο-τίνω (or -τίω), τίσω, to repay, Philem. 19.*

ἀπο-τολμάω, ῶ, to assume boldness, Ro. x. 20.*

ἀπο-τομία, as, ἡ (τέμνω, to cut), severity, Ro. xi. 22.*

ἀπο-τόμως, adv., severely, sharply, 2 Cor. xiii. 10; Tit. i. 13.*

ἀπο-τρέπω, mid., to turn away from, shun, acc., 2 Tim. iii. 5.*

ἀπ-ουσία, as (ἄπειμι), absence, Phil. ii. 12.*

ἀπο-φέρω, to bear away from one place to another, Mar. xv. 1; Rev. xvii. 3.

ἀπο-φεύγω, to escape, 2 Pet. i. 4, ii. 18, 20.*

ἀπο-φθέγγομαι, to speak out, declare, Ac. ii. 4, 14, xxvi. 25. (S.)*

ἀπο-φορτίζομαι (φόρτος, a burden), to unload, discharge, Ac. xxi. 3.*

ἀπό-χρησις, εως, ἡ (ἀπό, intens.), abuse, misuse, Col. ii. 22.*

ἀπο-χωρέω, ῶ, to go away, depart, Mat. vii. 23; Lu. ix. 39; Ac. xiii. 13.*

ἀπο-χωρίζω, to part asunder, Ac. xv. 39; Rev. vi. 14.*

ἀπο-ψύχω, to breathe out life, to faint, Lu. xxi. 26.*

Ἄππιος, ου, ὁ, Appius; Ἀππιου φόρον, the Forum of Appius, a town in Italy, situated on the Appian Way, Ac. xxviii. 15.*

ἀ-πρός-ιτος, ον (προς, εἶμι), not to be approached, 1 Tim. vi. 16.*

ἀ-πρός-κοπος, ον (κόπτω), act., not causing to stumble, 1 Cor. x. 32; pass., not caused to stumble, blameless, without offense, Ac. xxiv. 16; Phil. i. 10. (Ap.)*

ἀ-προσωπο-λήπτως (W. H. -λήμπτ-), adv., without respect of persons, impartially, 1 Pet. i. 17. (N. T.)*

ἄ-πταιστος, ον (πταίω, to fall), without stumbling or falling, Ju. 24.*

ἅπτω, ψω, to kindle, as light or fire, Lu. viii. 16, xi. 33; mid., to touch, Mat viii. 3; 1 Cor. vii. 1. Syn.: ἅπτομαι is to touch or handle; θιγγάνω, a lighter touch; ψηλαφάω, to feel or feel after.

Ἀπφία, as, ἡ, Apphia, Philem. 2.*

ἀπ-ωθέω, ῶ, ἀπώσω, mid., to repulse, to reject, Ac. vii. 27, 39.

ἀπώλεια, as, ἡ (ἀπόλλυμι), destroying, waste, of things, Ro. ix. 22; Mar. xiv. 4; destruction, in general, Ac. viii. 20; perdition, 2 Th. ii. 3; Rev. xvii. 8, 11.

ἀρά, ᾶς, ἡ, curse, imprecation, Ro. iii. 14.*

ἄρα, conj., illative, therefore, thence, since. See Gr. § 406, Wi. § 53, 8, Bu. 371.

ἆρα, adv. interrogative, usually where the answer is negative, Lu. xviii. 8; Ac. viii. 30; Gal. ii. 17.*

Ἀραβία, as, ἡ, Arabia, Gal. i 17, iv. 25.*

Ἀράμ, ὁ (Heb.), Aram, Mat. i. 3, 4; Lu. iii. 33 (not W. H.).*

Ἄραψ, αβος, ὁ, an Arabian, Ac. ii. 11.*

ἀργέω, ῶ, to linger, to delay, 2 Pet. ii. 3.*

ἀργός, όν (ἀ, ἔργον), idle, lazy, Mat. xx. 3; Tit. i. 12.

ἀργύρεος, οῦς, ᾶ, οῦν, made of silver, Ac. xix. 24; 2 Tim. ii. 20; Rev. ix. 20.*

ἀργύριον, ου, τό, silver, Ac. iii. 6; a piece of silver, a shekel, Mat. xvi. 15; money in general, Mar. xiv. 11.

ἀργυρο-κόπος, ου, ὁ, a silversmith, Ac. xix. 24.*

ἄργυρος, ου, ὁ, silver, Ac. xvii 29; Ja. v. 3.

Ἄρειος πάγος, ου, ὁ, Areopagus, or Mars' Hill, an open space on a hill in Athens, where the supreme court was held, Ac. xvii. 19, 22.* ("Αρειος is an adj. from "Αρης, Mars.)

Ἀρεοπαγίτης, ου, ὁ, *a judge of the Areopagite court*, Ac. xvii. 34.*

ἀρέσκεια, ας, ἡ, *a pleasing, a desire of pleasing*, Col. i. 10.*

ἀρέσκω, ἀρέσω, *to be pleasing to*, Mat. xiv. 6; Gal. i. 10; *to seek to please* or *gratify, to accommodate one's self to* (dat.), 1 Cor. x. 33; 1 Th. ii. 4.

ἀρεστός, ή, όν, *acceptable, pleasing to*, Jn. viii. 29; Ac. xii. 3.

Ἀρέτας, α, ὁ, *Aretas*, a king of Arabia Petræa, 2 Cor. xi. 32.*

ἀρετή, ῆς, ἡ, *virtue*, 2 Pet. i. 5; *any moral excellence, perfection*, Phil. iv. 8; 1 Pet. ii. 9; 2 Pet. i. 3.*

(**ἄρην**), gen. ἀρνός, *a lamb*, Lu. x. 3.*

ἀριθμέω, ῶ, *to number*, Mat. x. 30; Lu. xii. 7; Rev. vii. 9.*

ἀριθμός, οῦ, ὁ, *a number*, Jn. vi. 10; Ac. vi. 7.

Ἀριμαθαία, ας, ἡ, *Arimathæa*, a city of Palestine, Mat. xxvii. 57; Mar. xv. 43.

Ἀρίσταρχος, ου, ὁ, *Aristarchus*, Ac. xix. 29; Col. iv. 10.

ἀριστάω, ῶ, ἤσω (ἄριστον), *to breakfast*, Jn. xxi. 12, 15; *to dine*, Lu xi. 37.

ἀριστερός, ά, όν, *left*; ἡ ἀριστερά (χείρ), *the left hand*, Mat. vi. 3; ἐξ ἀριστερῶν, *on the left*, Mar. x. 37 (W. H.); Lu. xxiii. 33, without ἐξ; 2 Cor. vi. 7. (The more common word is εὐώνυμος.)*

Ἀριστόβουλος, ου, ὁ, *Aristobulus*, Ro. xvi. 10.*

ἄριστον, ου, τό, *dinner*, Mat. xxii. 4; Lu. xi. 38, xiv. 12.* See δεῖπνον.

ἀρκετός, ή, όν, *sufficient*, Mat. vi. 34, x. 25; 1 Pet. iv. 3.*

ἀρκέω, ῶ, *to be sufficient for*, Mat. xxv. 9; 2 Cor. xii. 9; pass., *to be satisfied with*, Lu. iii. 14; Heb. xiii. 5.

ἄρκτος (W. H. ἄρκος), ου, ὁ, ἡ, *a bear*, Rev. xiii. 2.*

ἅρμα, ατος, τό, *a chariot*, Ac. viii. 28, 29, 38; Rev. ix. 9.*

Ἁρμαγεδδών (Heb. or Aram., der. disputed), (W. H. Ἁρ Μαγεδών), *Harmageddon*, Rev. xvi. 16. (N. T.)*

ἁρμόζω, σω, *to fit together*; mid., *to espouse, to betroth*, 2 Cor. xi. 2.*

ἁρμός, οῦ, ὁ, *a joint*, i.e., of limbs in a body, Heb. iv. 12.*

ἀρνέομαι, οῦμαι, *to deny*, Mat. xxvi. 70; Jn. i. 20; 2 Tim. ii. 12; *to renounce*, Tit. ii. 12; *to reject*, Ac. iii. 14.*

ἀρνίον, ου, τό (dimin. of ἀρήν), *a little lamb*, Jn. xxi. 15; freq. in Rev., of Christ.

ἀροτριάω, ῶ, άσω, *to plow*, Lu. xvii. 7; 1 Cor. ix. 10.*

ἄροτρον, ου, τό, *a plow*, Lu. ix. 62.*

ἁρπαγή, ῆς, ἡ (ἁρπάζω), *the act of plundering*, Heb. x. 34; *plunder, spoil*, Mat. xxiii. 25; Lu. xi. 39.*

ἁρπαγμός, οῦ, ὁ, *spoil, an object of eager desire, a prize*, Phil. ii. 6.*

ἁρπάζω, άσω (2 aor. pass., ἡρπάγην), *to snatch, seize violently, take by force*, Jn. x. 12; *to carry off suddenly*, Jn. vi. 15; Ac. xxiii. 10.*

ἅρπαξ, αγος, adj., *rapacious, ravenous*, Mat. vii. 15; Lu. xviii. 11; *a robber, an extortioner*, 1 Cor. v. 10, 11, vi. 10.*

ἀρραβών, ῶνος, ὁ (from Heb.), *a pledge, an earnest*, ratifying a contract, 2 Cor. i. 22, v. 5; Ep. i. 14.*

ἄρραφος (W. H. ἄραφος), ον, *not seamed* or *sewn*, Jn. xix. 23. (N. T.)*

ἄρρην, εν (W. H. ἄρσην, εν), *of the male sex*, Ro. i. 27; Rev. xii. 5, 13.*

ἄρρητος, ον, adj., *unspoken, unspeakable*, 2 Cor. xii. 4.*

ἄρρωστος, ον, adj. (ῥώννυμι), *infirm, sick*, Mat. xiv. 14; 1 Cor. xi. 30.

ἀρσενο-κοίτης, ου, ὁ (ἄρσην κοίτη), *a sodomite*, 1 Cor. vi. 9; 1 Tim. i. 10.*

ἄρσην, εν, *male*, Mat. xix. 4; Gal. iii. 28.

Ἀρτεμᾶς, ᾶ, ὁ, *Artemas*, Tit. iii. 12.*

Ἄρτεμις, ιδος or ιος, ἡ, *Artemis*, the Persian or Ephesian Artemis, to be distinguished from the Artemis of the Greeks, the sister of Apollo, Ac. xix. 24, 27, 28, 34, 35.*

ἀρτέμων, ονος, ὁ (ἀρτάω, *to sus-*

pend), prob. *the foresail*, Ac. xxvii. 40.*

ἄρτι, adv. of time, *now, just now, at this moment*; with other particles, as ἕως ἄρτι, *till now*; ἀπ' ἄρτι, *from now* or *henceforward*.

ἀρτι-γέννητος, ον, *newly* or *recently born*, 1 Pet. ii. 2. (N. T.)*

ἄρτιος, ου, adj., *perfect, complete*, wanting in nothing, 2 Tim. iii. 17.* *Syn.:* ἄρτιος means fully adapted for its purpose; ὁλόκληρος, entire, having lost nothing; τέλειος, fully developed, complete.

ἄρτος, ου, ὁ, *bread, loaf, food;* fig., *spiritual nutriment;* ἄρτοι τῆς προθέσεως, *show-bread*, Mat. xii. 4; Mar. ii. 26.

ἀρτύω (ἄρω, *to fit*), *to season, to flavor*, as with salt, Mar. ix. 50; Lu. xiv. 34; fig., Col. iv. 6.*

Ἀρφαξάδ, ὁ (Heb.), *Arphaxad*, Lu. iii. 36.*

ἀρχ-άγγελος, ου, ὁ, *an arch-* or *chief-angel*, 1 Th. iv. 16; Ju. 9. (N. T.)*

ἀρχαῖος, α, ον, *old, ancient*, Lu. ix. 8, 19; 2 Pet. ii. 5.

Ἀρχέλαος, ου, ὁ, *Archelaus*, Mat. ii. 22.*

ἀρχή, ῆς, ἡ, (1) *a beginning*, of time, space, or series, Jn. i. 1; 2 Pet. iii. 4; *the outermost point*, Ac. x. 11. Used of Christ, *the leader*, Col. i. 18; Rev. iii. 14, xxi. 6, xxii. 13. Adv. phrases: ἀπ' ἀρχῆς, *from the beginning*; ἐν ἀρχῇ, *in the beginning*; ἐξ ἀρχῆς, *from the beginning* or *from the first*; κατ' ἀρχάς, *at the beginning*; τὴν ἀρχήν, *originally*. (2) *rule, pre-eminence, principality* (see ἄρχω): espec. in pl., ἀρχαί, *rulers, magistrates*, as Lu. xii. 11; of supramundane powers, *principalities*, as Ep. iii. 10.

ἀρχ-ηγός, οῦ, ὁ (ἀρχή, ἄγω), *the beginner, author, prince*, Ac. iii. 15, v. 31; Heb. ii. 10, xii. 2.*

ἀρχ-ιερατικός, ή, όν, *belonging to the office of the high-priest, pontifical*, Ac. iv. 6.*

ἀρχ-ιερεύς, έως, ὁ, (1) *the high-priest*, Mat. xxvi. 3; Heb. ix. 7, 25; so of Christ only in

Heb., as ii. 17, iii. 1, etc.;
(2) in pl. used more widely to include high-priestly
families and deposed high-
priests, Mat. ii. 4; Lu. xix.
47; Ac. iv. 23.

ἀρχι-ποίμην, ενος, ὁ, *the chief
shepherd*, a title of Christ,
1 Pet. v. 4. (N.T.)*

Ἄρχιππος, ου, ὁ, *Archippus*,
Col. iv. 17; Philem. 2.*

ἀρχι-συνάγωγος, ου, ὁ, *presid-
ing officer* or *ruler of a synagogue*, Lu. viii. 49; Ac. xiii.
15.

ἀρχι-τέκτων, ονος, ὁ, *a masterbuilder, an architect*, 1 Cor.
iii. 10.*

ἀρχι-τελώνης, ου, ὁ, *a chief collector of taxes, a chief publican*, Lu. xix. 2. (N.T.)*

ἀρχι-τρίκλινος, ου, ὁ, *a superintendent of a dining room*,
Jn. ii. 8, 9. (N.T.)*

ἄρχω, *to reign, to rule* (gen.),
only Mar. x. 42; Ro. xv. 12;
mid., *to begin*, often with
infin.; ἀρξάμενος ἀπὸ, *beginning from* (see Gr. § 287).

ἄρχων, οντος, ὁ, prop. particip.,
ruler, prince, leader, Ac. xvi.
19; Ro. xiii. 3.

ἄρωμα, ατος, τό, *spice, perfume*,
Mar. xvi. 1; Lu. xxiii. 56,
xxiv. 1; Jn. xix. 40.*

Ἀσά, ὁ (Heb.), *Asa*, Mat. i. 7, 8.*

ἀ-σάλευτος, ον, *unshaken, immovable*, Ac. xxvii. 41; Heb.
xii. 28.*

ἄ-σβεστος, ον, adj. (σβέννυμι),
*not to be quenched, inextin-
guishable*, Mat. iii. 12; Lu.
iii. 17; Mar. ix. 43, 45 (W.
H. omit).*

ἀσέβεια, ας, ἡ, *impiety, ungodliness, wickedness*, Ro. i. 18;
Ju. 15, 18. *Syn.:* see ἀγνόημα.

ἀσεβέω, ῶ, ήσω, *to be ungodly,
act impiously*, 2 Pet. ii. 6;
Ju. 15.*

ἀ-σεβής, ές (σέβομαι), *impious,
ungodly, wicked*, Ro. iv. 5;
Ju. 4, 15.

ἀ-σέλγεια, ας, ἡ, *excess, wantonness, lasciviousness*, Mar. vii.
22; Ep. iv. 19.

ἄ-σημος, ον, *not remarkable, obscure, ignoble*, Ac. xxi. 39.*

Ἀσήρ, ὁ, *Asher*, Lu. ii. 36;
Rev. vii. 6.*

ἀσθένεια, ας, ἡ, *weakness, bodily
infirmity, sickness*, 1 Cor. xv.
43; Heb. xi. 34; fig., *mental

weakness, distress, Ro. vi. 19;
Heb. v. 2.

ἀσθενέω, ῶ, *to be weak*, Ro. viii.
3; 2 Cor. xiii. 4; *to be sick*,
Lu. iv. 40; Ac. ix. 37.

ἀσθένημα, ατος, τό, *weakness,
infirmity*; fig., Ro. xv. 1.*

ἀ-σθενής, ές (σθένος, *strength*)
"without strength," *weak,
infirm*, Mat. xxvi. 41; Ro.
v. 6; 1 Cor. iv. 10; *sick*, Lu.
x. 9; Ac. iv. 9; 1 Cor. xi.
30.

Ἀσία, ας, ἡ, *Asia proper* or
Proconsular Asia, a district
in the west of Asia Minor,
Ac. vi. 9; 1 Pet. i. 1; Rev. i.
4; *a part of Proconsular Asia*,
Ac. ii. 9.

Ἀσιανός, οῦ, ὁ, *belonging to
Asia*, Ac. xx. 4.*

Ἀσιάρχης, ου, ὁ, *an Asiarch,
a president of Asia*, a citizen
appointed annually to preside over the worship and
celebrations in honor of the
gods, Ac. xix. 31.*

ἀσιτία, ας, ἡ (σῖτος, *corn*), *abstinence, a fast*, Ac. xxvii.
21.*

ἄ-σιτος, ον, *fasting*, Ac. xxvii.
33.*

ἀσκέω, ῶ, ήσω, *to exercise one's
self, use diligence in*, Ac.
xxiv. 16.*

ἀσκός, οῦ, ὁ, *a bottle* of skin,
Mat. ix. 17; Mar. ii. 22; Lu.
v. 37, 38.*

ἀσμένως, adv. (from part. of
ἥδομαι), *with joy, gladly*, Ac.
ii. 41 (W. H. omit); Ac. xxi.
17.*

ἄ-σοφος, ον, *not wise*, Ep. v.
15.*

ἀσπάζομαι, dep., *to embrace,
salute, to greet* (actually or
by letter), Mat. x. 2; 1 Cor.
xvi. 19, 20; always of persons, except Heb. xi. 13,
"having embraced (R. V.
greeted) the promises"; *to
take leave of* (only Ac. xx. 1;
in xxi. 6, W. H. read ἀπασπάζομαι).

ἀσπασμός, οῦ, ὁ, *salutation,
greeting*, Mat. xxiii. 7; Col.
iv. 18.

ἄ-σπιλος, ον (σπῖλος), *without
spot, unblemished*, 1 Tim. vi.
14; 1 Pet. i. 19.

ἀσπίς, ίδος, ἡ, *an asp, a venomous serpent*, Ro. iii. 13.*

ἄ-σπονδος, ον (σπονδή), "not

to be bound by truce," *implacable*, 2 Tim. iii. 3; Ro. i.
31 (not W. H.).*

ἀσσάριον, ιου, τό, *a small coin*
equal to the tenth part of a
drachma, *an assarium*, Mat.
x. 29; Lu. xii. 6. See Gr.
§ 154 a.

ἆσσον, adv. (compar. of ἄγχι),
nearer, close by, Ac. xxvii. 13.*

Ἄσσος, ου, ἡ, *Assos*, Ac. xx.
13, 14.*

ἀ-στατέω, ῶ, ήσω, *to be unsettled, to have no fixed abode*,
1 Cor. iv. 11.*

ἀστεῖος, ον (ἄστυ, *city*, see urbane), *fair, beautiful*, Ac.
vii. 20; Heb. xi. 23.*

ἀστήρ, έρος, ὁ, *a star*, Mar. xiii.
25; 1 Cor. xv. 41; Rev. vi.
13.

ἀ-στήρικτος, ον (στηρίζω), *unsettled, unstable*, 2 Pet. ii. 14,
iii. 16.*

ἄ-στοργος, ον (στοργή), *without
natural affection*, Ro. i. 31;
2 Tim. iii. 3.*

ἀ-στοχέω, ῶ (στόχος), *to miss
in aim, swerve from*, 1 Tim.
i. 6, vi. 21; 2 Tim. ii. 18.*

ἀστραπή, ῆς, ἡ, *lightning*, Lu.
x. 18; Rev. iv. 5; vivid
brightness, lustre, Lu. xi. 36.

ἀστράπτω, *to flash*, as lightning, Lu. xvii. 24; *to be lus-
trous*, xxiv. 4.*

ἄστρον, ου, τό, *a star* (orig. *con-
stellation*), Lu. xxi. 25; Ac.
vii. 43, xxvii. 20; Heb. xi.
12.*

Ἀσύγκριτος, ου, ὁ, *Asyncritus*,
Ro. xvi. 14.*

ἀ-σύμφωνος, ον, *dissonant, dis-
cordant*, Ac. xxviii. 25.*

ἀ-σύνετος, ον, *without understanding, foolish*, Mat. xv.
16; Ro. x. 19.

ἀ-σύνθετος, ον, *covenant-break-
ing, treacherous*, Ro. i. 31.*

ἀσφάλεια, ας, ἡ, *security*, Ac.
v. 23; 1 Th. v. 3; *certainty*,
Lu. i. 4.*

ἀ-σφαλής, ές (σφάλλω, *fallo*),
safe, Phil. iii. 1; *secure, firm*,
Heb. vi. 19; *certain*, Ac. xxv.
26; τὸ ἀσφαλές, *the certainty*,
Ac. xxi. 34, xxii. 30.*

ἀσφαλίζω, σω (mid.), *to make
fast, to secure*, Mat. xxvii.
65, 66; Ac. xvi. 24; pass., *to
be made secure*, Mat. xxvii.
64.*

ἀσφαλῶς, adv., *safely*, Mar. xiv.

44; Ac. xvi. 23; *assuredly*, Ac. ii. 36.*

ἀσχημονέω, ῶ, *to act improperly* or *unseemly*, I Cor. vii. 36, xiii. 5.*

ἀσχημοσύνη, ης, ἡ, *unseemliness*, Ro. i. 27; *shame, nakedness*, Rev. xvi. 15.*

ἀ-σχήμων, ον (σχῆμα), *uncomely, unseemly*, I Cor. xii. 23.*

ἀ-σωτία, ας, ἡ (σώζω), *an abandoned course, profligacy*, Ep. v. 18; Tit. i. 6; I Pet. iv. 4.*

ἀ-σώτως, adv., *profligately, dissolutely*, Lu. xv. 13.*

ἀτακτέω, ῶ, *to behave disorderly*, 2 Th. iii. 7.*

ἄ-τακτος, ον (τάσσω), *irregular, disorderly*, I Th. v. 14.*

ἀτάκτως, adv., *disorderly, irregularly*, 2 Th. iii. 6, 11.*

ἄ-τεκνος, ον, ὁ, ἡ (τέκνον), *childless*, Lu. xx. 28, 29.*

ἀτενίζω, σω, *to look intently upon* (dat. or εἰς), Lu. iv. 20; Ac. i. 10; 2 Cor. iii. 7, 13.

ἄτερ, adv., as prep. with gen., *without, in the absence of*, Lu. xxii. 6, 35.*

ἀτιμάζω, σω, *to dishonor, contemn*, whether persons or things, by word or by deed, Lu. xx. 11; Jn. viii. 49; Ja. ii. 6.

ἀτιμία, ας, ἡ, *dishonor, ignominy, disgrace, ignoble use*, I Cor. xi. 14; Ro. i. 26, ix. 21.

ἄ-τιμος, ον (τιμή), *without honor, despised*, Mat. xiii. 57; Mar. vi. 4; I Cor. iv. 10, xii. 23.*

ἀτιμόω, ῶ, *to dishonor, treat with indignity*, Mar. xii. 4 (not W. H.).*

ἀτμίς, ίδος, ἡ, *a vapor*, Ac. ii. 19; Ja. iv. 14.

ἄ-τομον, ου, τό (τέμνω), *an atom* of time, *moment*, I Cor. xv. 52.*

ἄ-τοπος, ον (τόπος), *misplaced, unbecoming, mischievous*, Lu. xxiii. 41; Ac. xxviii. 6.

Ἀττάλεια, ας, ἡ, *Attalia*, Ac. xiv. 25.*

αὐγάζω, *to shine forth*, 2 Cor. iv. 4.*

αὐγή, ῆς, ἡ, *brightness, daylight*, Ac. xx. 11.*

Αὔγουστος, ου, ὁ (Lat.), *Augustus*, Lu. ii. 1.* Compare Σεβαστός.

αὐθάδης, ες (αὐτός, ἥδομαι), *self-pleasing, arrogant*, Tit. i. 7; 2 Pet. ii. 10.*

αὐθαίρετος, ον (αὐτός, αἱρέομαι), *of one's own accord*, 2 Cor. viii. 3, 17.*

αὐθεντέω, ῶ, *to exercise authority over* (gen.), I Tim. ii. 12. (N. T.)*

αὐλέω, ῶ, ήσω, *to play on a flute, to pipe*, Mat. xi. 17; Lu. vii. 32; I Cor. xiv. 7.

αὐλή, ῆς, ἡ (ἄω, *to blow*), *an open space, uncovered court* or *hall* of a house, as Lu. xi. 21, xxii. 55; *a sheepfold*, Jn. x. 1, 16.

αὐλητής, οῦ, ὁ, *a flute-player*, Mat. ix. 23; Rev. xviii. 22.*

αὐλίζομαι (to lodge in the open air), *to lodge, pass the night*, Mat. xxi. 17; Lu. xxi. 37.*

αὐλός, οῦ, ὁ (ἄω), *a flute, pipe*, I Cor. xiv. 7.*

αὐξάνω (also αὔξω), αὐξήσω, trans., *to make to grow*, as I Cor. iii. 6, 7; pass., *to grow, increase, become greater*, Mat. xiii. 32; Col. i. 10; generally intrans., *to grow, increase*, as Mat. vi. 28.

αὔξησις, εως, ἡ, *growth, increase*, Ep. iv. 16; Col. ii. 19.*

αὔριον, adv. (αὔρα, *morning breeze*, ἄω), *to-morrow*, Mat. vi. 30; Lu. xiii. 32, 33; ἡ (sc. ἡμέρα) αὔριον, *the morrow*, Mat. vi. 34; Ac. iv. 3.

αὐστηρός, ά, όν (dry), *harsh, austere*, Lu. xix. 21, 22.*

αὐτάρκεια, ας, ἡ, *sufficiency*, 2 Cor. ix. 8; *contentment*, I Tim. vi. 6.*

αὐτ-άρκης, ες (ἀρκέω, sufficient for self), *content, satisfied*, Phil. iv. 11.*

αὐτο-κατά-κριτος, ον, *self-condemned*, Tit. iii. 11. (N. T.)*

αὐτόματος, ον, *spontaneous, of its own accord*, Mar. iv. 28; Ac. xii. 10.*

αὐτ-όπτης, ου, ὁ, *an eye-witness*, Lu. i. 2.*

αὐτός, ή, ό, pron., *he, she, it*; in nom. nearly always emphatic. Properly demonstrative, *self, very*; joined with each of the persons of the verb, with or without a pers. pron., *I myself, thou thyself*, etc.; with the article, *the same; the same* with (dat.), I Cor. xi. 5; ἐπὶ τὸ αὐτό, *at the same place* or *time, together*;

κατὰ τὸ αὐτό, *together*, only Ac. xiv. 1. See Gr. § 335, Wi. § 22, 3, 4, Bu. 105 sq.

αὐτοῦ, adv. of place, *here, there*, Mat. xxvi. 36; Ac. xviii. 19, xxi. 4.

αὐτοῦ, ῆς, οῦ, pron. reflex. (contr. for ἑαυτοῦ), *of himself, herself*, etc. (W. H. in the majority of cases read αὐτοῦ, αὐτῷ, etc., but retain αὑτοῦ, etc., in some, as Mat. vi. 34; Jn. ii. 24; Ac. xiv. 17, etc.).

αὐτό-φωρος, ον (φώρ, *a thief*), *in the very act*, Jn. viii. 4, neut. dat. with ἐπί (W. H. omit).*

αὐτό-χειρ, ρος, ὁ, *with one's own hand*, Ac. xxvii. 19.*

αὐχμηρός, ά, όν, *dark, dismal*, 2 Pet. i. 19.*

ἀφ-αιρέω, *to take away*, as Lu. x. 42; *to take away* sin, only Ro. xi. 27; Heb. x. 4; *to smite off*, as Mat. xxvi. 51, and parallel passages.

ἀ-φανής, ές (φαίνω), *not appearing, hidden*, Heb. iv. 13.*

ἀ-φανίζω, *to put out of sight, destroy*, Mat. vi. 19, 20; *to disfigure*, Mat. vi. 16; pass., *to vanish, perish*, Ac. xiii. 41; Ja. iv. 14.*

ἀ-φανισμός, οῦ, ὁ, *a disappearing, destruction*, Heb. viii. 13.*

ἄ-φαντος, ον, *disappearing, not seen*, Lu. xxiv. 31.*

ἀφεδρών, ῶνος, ὁ, *draught, privy*, Mat. xv. 17· Mar. vii. 19. (N. T.)*

ἀ-φειδία, ας, ἡ (φείδομαι), *severity*, Col. ii. 23.*

ἀφελότης, τητος, ἡ, *simplicity, sincerity*, Ac. ii. 46. (N. T.)*

ἄφ-εσις, εως, ἡ (ἀφίημι), *deliverance;* lit., only Lu. iv. 18; elsewhere always of *deliverance* from sin, remission, forgiveness, Mat. xxvi. 28; Lu. i. 77; Ep. i. 7. *Syn.:* πάρεσις is a simple *suspension of punishment* for sin, in contrast with ἄφεσις, *complete forgiveness*.

ἀφή, ῆς, ἡ (ἅπτω, *to fit*), *that which connects, a joint*, Ep. iv. 16; Col. ii. 19.*

ἀφθαρσία, ας, ἡ, *incorruption, immortality*, I Cor. xv.; Ro. ii. 7; 2 Tim. i. 10; Ep. vi. 24; *incorruptness*, Tit. ii. 7 (W. H. ἀφθορία).*

ἄ-φθαρτος, ον (φθείρω), incorruptible, imperishable, Ro. i. 23; 1 Cor. ix. 25, xv. 52; 1 Tim. i. 17; 1 Pet. i. 4, 23, iii. 4.*

ἀ-φθορία, as, ἡ, incorruptness, Tit. ii. 7 (W. H.). (N. T.)*

ἀφ-ίημι (see Gr. § 112, Wi. § 14, 3), to send away, as (1) to let go, emit, Mat. xxvii. 50; Mar. xv. 37; dismiss, in senses varying according to the obj.; spec., to disregard, pass by, send away, divorce, Mat. xv. 14; Heb. vi. 1; 1 Cor. vii. 11, 12, 13; hence, (2) to forgive (dat. pers.), very often, Mat. xviii. 27; Mar. ii. 5, 7; (3) to permit, concede, abs., or with inf., as Mar. x. 14; or acc., as Mat. iii. 15 (dat., Mat. v. 40); or ἵνα, subj., Mar. xi. 6; or subj. alone, Lu. v. 42; (4) to leave, depart from, abandon, leave behind, Mat. xxii. 22; Mar. i. 31; Lu. v. 11, xvii. 34, 35.

ἀφικνέομαι, οῦμαι (2 aor., ἀφικόμην), to arrive at, to reach, Ro. xvi. 19.*

ἀ-φιλ-άγαθος, ον, not loving goodness and good men, 2 Tim. iii. 3. (N. T.)*

ἀ-φιλ-άργυρος, ον, not loving money, not avaricious, 1 Tim. iii. 3; Heb. xiii. 5. (N. T.)*

ἄφιξις, εως, ἡ, orig. arrival; departure, Ac. xx. 29.*

ἀφ-ίστημι, ἀποστήσω, trans. in pres., imperf., 1 aor., fut., to lead away, to seduce; intrans. in perf., plup., 2 aor., to go away, depart, avoid, withdraw from (often with ἀπό); mid., to fail, abstain from, absent one's self.

ἄφνω, adv., suddenly, Ac. ii. 2, xvi. 26, xxviii. 6.*

ἀ-φόβως, adv., without fear, Lu. i. 74; Phil. i. 14; 1 Cor. xvi. 10; Ju. 12.*

ἀφ-ομοιόω, ῶ, to make like, in pass., Heb. vii. 3.*

ἀφ-οράω, ῶ (2 a., ἀπ- or ἀφ-εῖδον), to look away from others at (εἰς) one, to regard earnestly, Heb. xii. 2; to see, Phil. ii. 23.*

ἀφ-ορίζω, fut. ιῶ, trans., to separate from (ἐκ or ἀπό), Mat. xiii. 49, xxv. 32; to separate for a purpose (εἰς, Ac. xiii. 2; Ro. i. 1; or inf.,

Gal. i. 15); to excommunicate, Lu. vi. 22.

ἀφ-ορμή, ῆς, ἡ, an occasion, opportunity, Ro. vii. 8, 11; 2 Cor. v. 12.

ἀφρίζω, to foam at the mouth, Mar. ix. 18, 20.*

ἀφρός, οῦ, ὁ, foam, froth, Lu. ix. 39.*

ἀ-φροσύνη, ης, ἡ, foolishness, Mar. vii. 22; 2 Cor. xi. 1, 17, 22.*

ἄ-φρων, ονος, ὁ, ἡ (φρήν), inconsiderate, foolish, rash, Lu. xi. 40; Ro. ii. 20.

ἀφ-υπνόω, ῶ (ἀπό, intensive), to fall asleep, Lu. viii. 23.*

ἀφυστερέω, ῶ, to keep back by fraud, Ja. v. 4 (W. H.).*

ἄ-φωνος, ον, dumb, without the faculty of speech: of animals, Ac. viii. 32; 2 Pet. ii. 16; of idols, 1 Cor. xii. 2. In 1 Cor. xiv. 10 the R. V. mrg. is probably the correct rendering.*

Ἄχαζ, ὁ (Heb.), Ahaz, Mat. i. 9.*

Ἀχαΐα, as, ἡ, Achaia, a Roman province including all Greece except Thessaly, Ac. xix. 21; 1 Cor. xvi. 15.

Ἀχαϊκός, οῦ, ὁ, Achaicus, 1 Cor. xvi. 17.*

ἀ-χάριστος, ον, unthankful, Lu. vi. 35; 2 Tim. iii. 2.*

Ἀχείμ, ὁ (Heb.), Achim, Mat. i. 14.*

ἀ-χειρο-ποίητος, ον, not made with hands, Mar. xiv. 58; 2 Cor. v. 1; Col. ii. 11. (N. T.)*

ἀχλύς, ύος, ἡ, a mist, dimness, Ac. xiii. 11.*

ἀ-χρεῖος, ον, useless, good for nothing, unprofitable, Mat. xxv. 30; Lu. xvii. 10.*

ἀ-χρειόω (W. H. ἀχρεόω), pass., to be made useless, Ro. iii. 12.*

ἄ-χρηστος, ον, useless, unprofitable, Philem. 11.*

ἄχρι and ἄχρις, adv. as prep., with gen., even to, until, as far as, whether of place, time, or degree; ἄχρις οὗ or ἄχρις alone, with the force of a conjunction, until. See μέχρι.

ἄχυρον, ου, τό, chaff, Mat. iii. 12; Lu. iii. 17.*

ἀ-ψευδής, ές, free from falsehood, truthful, Tit. i. 2.*

ἄψινθος, ου, ὁ and ἡ, wormwood, Rev. viii. 11.*

ἄ-ψυχος, ον, without life, inanimate, 1 Cor. xiv. 7.*

B

Β, β, βῆτα, beta, b, the second letter. Numerally, β' = 2; ͵β = 2000.

Βαάλ (W. H. Βάαλ), ὁ, ἡ (Heb. Master), Baal, chief deity of the Phœnicians and other Semitic nations, Ro. xi. 4 (fem.), from 1 Kings xix. 18 (S.)*

Βαβυλών, ῶνος, ἡ, Babylon, lit., Mat. i. 11, 12, 17; Ac. vii. 43, and prob. 1 Pet. v. 13; mystically, in Rev. xiv. 8, xvi. 19, xvii. 5, xviii. 2, 10, 21.*

βαθμός, οῦ, ὁ (βαίνω, to step), a step or degree in dignity, 1 Tim. iii. 13. (S.)*

βάθος, ους, τό, depth, lit. or fig., Mat. xiii. 5; 1 Cor. ii. 10; 2 Cor. viii. 2 (ἡ κατὰ βάθους πτωχεία, their deep poverty).

βαθύνω, υνῶ, to make deep, Lu. vi. 48.*

βαθύς, εῖα, ύ, deep, Jn. iv. 11; in Lu. xxiv. 1, ὄρθρου βαθέος, in the early dawn (W. H. βαθέως, probably a genit. form).

βαΐον, ου, τό (Egyptian), a palm branch, Jn. xii. 13.*

Βαλαάμ, ὁ (Heb.), Balaam. A name emblematic of seducing teachers, 2 Pet. ii. 15; Ju. 11; Rev. ii. 14.*

Βαλάκ, ὁ (Heb.), Balak, Rev. ii. 14.*

βαλάντιον (W. H. -λλ-), ου, τό, a money-bag, purse, Lu. x. 4, xii. 33, xxii. 35, 36.*

βάλλω, βαλῶ, βέβληκα, ἔβαλον, to throw, cast, put (with more or less force, as modified by the context); of liquids, to pour. Pass. perf., with intrans. force, as Mat. viii. 6 ("has been cast"), lies. The verb is intrans., Ac. xxvii. 14, rushed. In Mar. xiv. 65 the true reading is prob. ἔλαβον. Generally trans. with acc. and dat., or ἐπί (acc., sometimes gen.), εἰς, ἀπό, ἐκ, and other prepp. or advv.

βαπτίζω, σω (in form a frequentative of βάπτω, see Gr.

§ 144 b), (1) mid. or pass.,
reflex., *to bathe* one's self,
only in Mar. vii. 4; Lu. xi.
38; (2) of the Christian ordinance, *to immerse, submerge,
to baptize*. The material (water, fire, the Holy Spirit) is
expressed by dat., εἰς or ἐν;
the purpose or result by εἰς.
Pass. or. mid., *to be baptized,
to receive baptism;* (3) fig., of
overwhelming woe, Mar. x.
38, 39; Lu. xii. 50.

βάπτισμα, ατος, τό, *the rite* or
ceremony of baptism, Mat.
iii. 7; Ep. iv. 5; fig., for overwhelming afflictions, Mar. x.
38, 39; Lu. xii. 50. (N. T.)

βαπτισμός, οῦ, ὁ, *the act of
cleansing*, as vessels, Mar.
vii. 4, 8 (W. H. omit); of
Jewish lustrations, *washings*
(pl.), Heb. ix. 10. For Heb.
vi. 2, see Gr. § 260 b, 2 (b).*

βαπτιστής, οῦ, ὁ, *one who baptizes;* the surname of John,
Christ's forerunner, Mat. iii.
1; Mar. viii. 28.

βάπτω, βάψω, *to dip*, Lu. xvi.
24; Jn. xiii. 26; *to dye, color*,
Rev. xix. 13.*

βάρ (Aram.), *son*, only Mat.
xvi. 17 (βὰρ Ἰωνᾶ, W. H.
βαριωνᾶ). Also prefix to
many surnames, meaning
son of. (N. T.)

Βαρ-αββᾶς, ᾶ, ὁ, *Barabbas*, Mat.
xxvii. 16, 17; Jn. xviii. 40.

Βαράκ, ὁ, *Barak*, Heb. xi. 32.*

Βαραχίας, ου, ὁ, *Barachiah*,
Mat. xxiii. 35.*

βάρβαρος, ου, ὁ (prob. onoma-
top., descriptive of unintel-
ligible sounds), properly adj.,
a foreigner, barbarian, as 1
Cor. xiv. 11; used of all
foreigners not Greeks, Ac.
xxviii. 2, 4; Col. iii. 11; Ro.
i. 14.*

βαρέω, ῶ (see βάρος), in N. T.
only pass. βαρέομαι, οῦμαι, *to
be weighed down, to be oppressed*, as by sleep, Lu. ix.
32; mental troubles, 2 Cor.
i. 8, v. 4.

βαρέως, adv., *heavily, with difficulty*, Mat. xiii. 15; Ac.
xxviii. 27.*

Βαρ-θολομαῖος, ου, ὁ, *Bartholomew*, surname (prob.) of
Nathanael, Mat. x. 3.

Βαρ-ιησοῦς, οῦ, ὁ, *Bar-Jesus*,
Ac. xiii. 6.*

Βαρ-ιωνᾶς, ᾶ, ὁ, *Bar-Jonas*, surname of Peter, Mat. xvi. 17
(W. H.).*

Βαρ-νάβας, α, ὁ, *Barnabas* (perhaps "son of comfort," see
παράκλησις), Ac. ix. 27; Col.
iv. 10.

βάρος, ους, τό, *weight, burden*,
only fig., Ac. xv. 28; Rev.
ii. 24.

Βαρ-σαβᾶς, ᾶ, ὁ, *Barsabas*.
Two are mentioned, Ac. i.
23, xv. 22.*

Βαρ-τίμαιος, ου, ὁ, *Bartimæus*,
Mar. x. 46.*

βαρύνω, *to weigh down*, Lu.
xxi. 34 (Rec.).*

βαρύς, εῖα, ύ (see βάρος), (1)
heavy, Mat. xxiii. 4; (2)
weighty, important, Mat.
xxiii. 23; Ac. xxv. 7; 2 Cor.
x. 10; (3) *oppressive* or *grievous*, Ac. xx. 29; 1 Jn. v.
3.*

βαρύ-τιμος, ον, *of great price*,
Mat. xxvi. 7.*

βασανίζω (see βάσανος), *to examine*, as by torture; hence,
to torment, vex, Mar. v. 7;
Rev. xi. 10, xii. 2; of waves,
to buffet, Mat. xiv. 24; Mar.
vi. 48.

βασανισμός, οῦ, ὁ, *torture, torment*, Rev. ix. 5, xiv. 11,
xviii. 7, 10, 15.*

βασανιστής, οῦ, ὁ, *one who tor-
tures, a tormentor, jailer*, Mat.
xviii. 34.*

βάσανος, ου, ἡ (lit., *a touch-
stone*), *torture, torment*, Mat.
iv. 24; Lu. xvi. 23, 28.*

βασιλεία, ας, ἡ, *a kingdom, royal
power* or *dignity, reign;* ἡ
βασιλεία τοῦ Θεοῦ, τοῦ χριστοῦ, τῶν οὐρανῶν (the last
form only in Mat.), *the divine, spiritual kingdom*, or
reign of Messiah, in the
world, in the individual, or
in the future state; υἱοὶ τῆς
βασιλείας, *sons of the kingdom*, Jews, its original possessors, Mat. viii. 12; true
believers, Mat. xiii. 38. In
Rev. i. 6, v. 10, for βασιλεῖς
καί, W. H. read βασιλείαν, *a
kingdom* consisting of priests
(R. V.).

βασίλειος, ον, *royal, regal*, 1 Pet.
ii. 9, from Exod. xix. 6; τὰ
βασίλεια, as subst., *a regal
mansion, palace*, Lu. vii. 25.*

βασιλεύς, έως, ὁ, *a leader, ruler,*

king, sometimes subordinate
to higher authority, as the
Herods. Applied to God,
always with distinguishing
epithets, Mat. v. 35; 1 Tim.
i. 17, vi. 15; Rev. xv. 3;
to Christ, Mat. ii. 2; Jn. i.
49, etc.; to Christians, Rev.
i. 6, v. 10 (Rec., but see
under βασιλεία).

βασιλεύω, εύσω, *to have authority, to reign*, or *to possess*
or *exercise dominion; to be
βασιλεύς* generally. With
gen. or ἐπί (gen.), of the kingdom; ἐπί (acc.), of the persons governed.

βασιλικός, ή, όν, *belonging to a
king, royal*, Jn. iv. 46, 49;
Ac. xii. 20, 21; Ja. ii. 8.*

βασίλισσα, ης, ἡ, *a queen*, Mat.
xii. 42; Lu. xi. 31; Ac. viii.
27; Rev. xviii. 7.*

βάσις, εως, ἡ (βαίνω), prop. *a
going*, hence, *the foot*, Ac. iii.
7.*

βασκαίνω, ανῶ, *to bewitch, bring
under malign influence*, Gal.
iii. 1.*

βαστάζω, άσω, *to lift, lift up;*
often with the sense of bearing away. Thus, (1) *to carry*,
a burden, as Lu. xiv. 27;
tidings, as Ac. ix. 15; (2)
to take on one's self, as disease or weaknesses, Ro. xv.
1; condemnation, Gal. v. 10;
reproach, Gal. vi. 17; (3) *to
bear with* or *endure*, Rev. ii.
2; (4) *to take away*, Mat. viii.
17; Jn. xii. 6.

βάτος, ου, ὁ, ἡ, *a thorn-bush* or
bramble, Lu. vi. 44; Ac. vii.
30, 35. "The Bush," Mar.
xii. 26; Lu. xx. 37 denotes
the section of the O. T. so
called (Exod. iii.).*

βάτος, ου, ὁ (Heb.), *a bath*, or
Jewish measure for liquids
containing 8 or 9 gallons,
Lu. xvi. 6. (Ap.)*

βάτραχος, ου, ὁ, *a frog*, Rev.
xvi. 13.*

βαττο-λογέω, ῶ (prob. from
βατ, an unmeaning sound;
see βάρβαρος), *to babble, talk
to no purpose*, Mat. vi. 7. (N.
T.)*

βδέλυγμα, ατος, τό (see βδελύσσω), *something unclean* and
*abominable, an object of mor-
al repugnance*, Lu. xvi. 15;
spec. (as often in O.T.) *idol-*

atry, Rev. xvii. 4, 5, xxi. 27.
"Abomination of desola-
tion," Mat. xxiv. 15; Mar.
xiii. 14 (from Dan. ix. 27)
refers to the pollution of
the temple by some idola-
trous symbol. (S.)*

βδελυκτός, ή, όν, disgusting,
abominable, Tit. i. 16. (S.)*

βδελύσσω, ξω, to defile, only
mid.; to loathe, Ro. ii. 22;
and pass. perf. part., defiled,
Rev. xxi. 8.*

βέβαιος, a, ον, steadfast, constant,
firm, Heb. vi. 19; Ro. iv. 16.

βεβαιόω, ῶ, to confirm, to establish, whether of persons or
things, Mar. xvi. 20; Ro.
xv. 8; Heb. xiii. 9.

βεβαίωσις, εως, ή, confirmation,
Phil. i. 7; Heb. vi. 16.*

βέβηλος, ον (βα- in βαίνω,
"that on which any one
may step"), common, un-
sanctified, profane, of things
or persons, 1 Tim. iv. 7;
Heb. xii. 16.

βεβηλόω, ῶ, to make common,
to profane, the Sabbath, Mat.
xii. 5; the temple, Ac. xxiv.
6. (S.)*

Βεελ-ζεβούλ (W. H. Βεεζεβούλ),
ὁ (Heb.), Beelzebul, a name
of Satan, Mat. x. 25; Lu. xi.
15, 18, 19. (N. T.)

Βελίαλ, ὁ (Heb. worthlessness),
or Βελίαρ (W. H.), derivation
doubtful, a name for Satan,
2 Cor. vi. 15. (N. T.)*

βελόνη, ης, ή, a needle, Lu.
xviii. 25 (W. H.).*

βέλος, ους, τό (βάλλω), a missile,
such as a javelin or dart, Ep.
vi. 16.*

βελτίων, ον, ονος (a compar. of
ἀγαθός), better; neut. as adv.,
2 Tim. i. 18.*

Βεν-ιαμίν, ὁ (Heb. Ben = son),
Benjamin, Ac. xiii. 21; Rev.
vii. 8.

Βερνίκη, ης, ή, Bernice, Ac.
xxv. 13, 23, xxvi. 30.*

Βέροια, ας, ή, Berœa, Ac. xvii.
10, 13.*

Βεροιαῖος, α, ον, Berœan, Ac.
xx. 4.*

Βηθ-, a Hebrew and Aramaic
prefix to many local names,
meaning house or abode of.

Βηθ-αβαρά, ᾶς, ή, Bethabara,
"house of the ford," Jn. i.
28 (W. H. read Βηθανία).*

Βηθ-ανία, ας, ή, Bethany, "house

of misery." There were two
places of the name: (1) Jn.
xi. 1, etc.; (2) on the Jordan,
Jn. i. 28 (W. H.). See Βηθα-
βαρά.

Βηθ-εσδά, ή, Bethesda, "house
of compassion," Jn. v. 2 (W.
H. Βηθζαθά).*

Βηθ-λεέμ, ή, Bethlehem, "house
of bread," Lu. ii. 4, 15.

Βηθ-σαϊδά, ή, Bethsaida, "house
of hunting" or "fishing."
There were two places of
the name: one in Galilee,
Jn. xii. 21; the other on the
east of the Jordan, Lu. ix.
10.

Βηθ-φαγή, ή, Bethphage, "house
of figs," Mat. xxi. 1; Mar.
xi. 1; Lu. xix. 29.*

βῆμα, ατος, τό (βα- in βαίνω), a
step, a space; βῆμα ποδός, a
space for the foot, Ac. vii. 5;
a raised space or bench, tribunal, judgment-seat, Jn. xix.
13; 2 Cor. v. 10.

βήρυλλος, ου, ὁ, ή, a beryl, a
gem of greenish hue, Rev.
xxi. 20.*

βία, ας, ή, force, violence, Ac.
v. 26, xxi. 35, xxiv. 7 (W. H.
omit), xxvii. 41.*

βιάζω, to use violence; mid., to
enter forcibly, with εἰς, Lu.
xvi. 16; pass., to suffer violence, to be assaulted, Mat. xi.
12.*

βίαιος, α, ον, violent, Ac. ii. 2.*

βιαστής, οῦ, ὁ, one who employs
force, a man of violence, Mat.
xi. 12.*

βιβλαρίδιον, ου, τό, a little book,
Rev. x. 2, 8 (not W. H.), 9,
10. (N. T.)*

βιβλίον, ου, τό (dim. of following), a small book, a scroll,
as Lu. iv. 17; Rev. v. 1;
βιβλίον ἀποστασίου, a bill of
divorcement, Mat. xix. 7;
Mar. x. 4.

βίβλος, ου, ὁ, a written book,
roll or volume, Mat. i. 1;
Phil. iv. 3. The word means
papyrus, from which ancient
books were made.

βιβρώσκω (βρο-), perf. βέβρωκα,
to eat, Jn. vi. 13.*

Βιθυνία, ας, ή, Bithynia, Ac.
xvi. 7; 1 Pet. i. 1.*

βίος, ου, ὁ, (1) life, as Lu. viii.
14; (2) means of life, livelihood, as Lu. viii. 43; (3)
goods or property, as Lu. xv.

12; 1 Jn. iii. 17. Syn.: ζωή
is life in its principle, and
used for spiritual and immortal life; βίος is life in its
manifestations, denoting the
manner of life.

βιόω, ῶ, to pass one's life, 1 Pet.
iv. 2.*

βίωσις, εως, ή, manner or habit
of life, Ac. xxvi. 4. (Ap.)*

βιωτικός, ή, όν, of or belonging
to (this) life, Lu. xxi. 34;
1 Cor. vi. 3, 4.*

βλαβερός, ά, όν, hurtful, 1 Tim.
vi. 9.*

βλάπτω (βλαβ-), βλάψω, to hurt
or injure, Mar. xvi. 18 (W.
H. omit); Lu. iv. 35.*

βλαστάνω (or βλαστάω, Mar.
iv. 27, W. H.), βλαστήσω,
intrans., to sprout, to spring
up, to put forth buds, Mat.
xiii. 26; Mar. iv. 27; Heb.
ix. 4; trans., to bring forth
(καρπόν), Ja. v. 18.*

Βλάστος, ου, ὁ, Blastus, Ac.
xii. 20.*

βλασφημέω, ῶ, to speak abusively, to rail, abs., as Ac. xiii.
45; to calumniate, speak evil
of, blaspheme, with acc., rarely εἰς; often of men or things.
Spec. of God, Rev. xvi. 11;
the Holy Spirit, Lu. xii. 10;
the divine name or doctrine,
1 Tim. vi. 1.

βλασφημία, ας, ή, evil-speaking,
reviling, blasphemy, Mat. xii.
31; Mar. xiv. 64.

βλάσφημος, ον, slanderous, Ac.
vi. 11; subst., a blasphemer,
1 Tim. i. 13; 2 Tim. iii. 2.

βλέμμα, ατος, τό, a look, glance,
2 Pet. ii. 8.*

βλέπω, ψω, to see, to have the
power of seeing, to look at,
behold; with εἰς, to look to,
Mat. xxii. 16; Mar. xii. 14;
with ἵνα or μή, to take care
(once without, Mar. xiii. 9);
with ἀπό, to beware of; once
with κατά (acc.), geograph-
ically, to look towards, Ac.
xxvii. 12.

βλητέος, έα, έον, a verbal adj.
(βάλλω), that ought to be put,
Mar. ii. 22 (W. H. omit);
Lu. v. 38. (N. T.)*

Βοανεργές (W. H. -ηρ-), (Heb.),
Boanerges, "sons of thun-
der," Mar. iii. 17. (N. T.)*

βοάω, ῶ (βοή), to shout for joy,
Gal. iv. 27; to cry for grief,

Ac. viii. 7; *to publish openly,
to cry aloud,* Mar. xv. 34; Ac.
xvii. 6; with πρός (acc.), *to
appeal to,* Lu. xviii. 7, 38.

βοή, ῆς, ἡ, *a loud cry,* Ja. v. 4.*

βοήθεια, ας, ἡ, *help,* Ac. xxvii.
17; Heb. iv. 16.*

βοηθέω, ῶ, *to go to the help of,
to succor* (dat.), Mat. xv. 25;
Rev. xii. 16.

βοηθός, οῦ, ὁ, ἡ (properly adj.),
a helper, Heb. xiii. 6.*

βόθυνος, ου, ὁ, *a pit, ditch,* Mat.
xii. 11, xv. 14; Lu. vi. 39.*

βολή, ῆς, ἡ, *a throwing;* λίθου
βολή, *a stone's throw,* Lu.
xxii. 41.*

βολίζω, σω, *to heave the lead,
take soundings,* Ac. xxvii. 28.
(N. T.)*

βολίς, ίδος, ἡ, *a weapon thrown,*
as *a dart* or *javelin,* Heb. xii.
20 (W. H. omit).*

Βοόζ, ὁ (Heb.), *Booz* or *Boaz,*
Mat. i. 5 (W. H. Βοές); Lu.
iii. 32 (W. H. Βοός).*

βόρβορος, ου, ὁ, *mire, filth,* 2 Pet.
ii. 22.*

Βορρᾶς, ᾶ, ὁ (*Boreas,* the north
wind), *the North,* Lu. xiii. 29;
Rev. xxi. 13.*

βόσκω, ήσω, *to feed,* as Mat.
viii. 33; Jn. xxi. 15, 17; mid.,
to feed, graze, as Mar. v. 11.
Syn.: ποιμαίνω is the broader
word, to act as shepherd,
literally or spiritually; βόσκω, simply to *feed* the flock.

Βοσόρ, ὁ (Heb. *Beor*), *Bosor,* 2
Pet. ii. 15 (W. H. Βεώρ).*

βοτάνη, ης, ἡ (βόσκω), *herbage,
pasturage,* Heb. vi. 7.*

βότρυς, υος, ὁ, *a cluster of grapes,*
Rev. xiv. 18.*

βουλευτής, οῦ, ὁ, *a councilor, a
senator,* Mar. xv. 43; Lu.
xxiii. 50.*

βουλεύω, σω, *to advise,* N. T.
mid. only; (1) *to consult, to
deliberate,* with εἰ, Lu. xiv.
31; (2) *to resolve on* or *purpose,* with inf., Ac v. 33, xv.
37 (W. H. in both passages
read βούλομαι), xxvii. 39; ἵνα,
Jn. xi. 53 (W. H.), xii. 10;
acc., 2 Cor. i. 17.*

βουλή, ῆς, ἡ, *a design, purpose,
plan,* Lu. xxiii. 51; Ac. v. 38;
Ep. i. 11.

βούλημα, ατος, τό (βούλομαι),
will, counsel, purpose, Ac.
xxvii. 43; Ro. ix. 19; 1 Pet.
iv. 3 (W. H.).*

βούλομαι, 2d pers. sing. βούλει,
aug. with ἐ or ἠ, *to will,* as
(1) *to be willing, to incline to,*
Mar. xv. 15; (2) *to intend,*
Mat. i. 19; (3) *to desire,* 1
Tim. vi. 9. Generally with
inf., sometimes understood,
as Ja. i. 18; with subj., Jn.
xviii. 39.

βουνός, οῦ, ὁ, *a hill, rising
ground,* Lu. iii. 5; xxiii.
30.*

βοῦς, βοός, ὁ, ἡ, *an animal of
the ox kind,* male or female,
Lu. xiii. 15; 1 Tim. v. 18.

βραβεῖον, ου, τό, *the prize,* in
the games, 1 Cor. ix. 24;
Phil. iii. 14.*

βραβεύω (lit., to act as arbiter
in the games), *to rule, arbi-
trate,* Col. iii. 15.*

βραδύνω, νῶ (βραδύς), *to be slow,
to linger,* 1 Tim. iii. 15; 2 Pet.
iii. 9 (gen.).*

βραδυ-πλοέω, ῶ, *to sail slowly,*
Ac. xxvii. 7. (N. T.)*

βραδύς, εῖα, ύ, *slow;* dat. of
sphere, Lu. xxiv. 25; εἰς, Ja.
i. 19.*

βραδυτής, τῆτος, ἡ, *slowness,* 2
Pet. iii. 9.*

βραχίων, ονος, ὁ, *the arm;* met.,
strength, Lu. i. 51; Jn. xii.
38; Ac. xiii. 17.*

βραχύς, εῖα, ύ, *short, little,* only
neut.; of time, Lu. xxii. 58;
Ac. v. 34; Heb. ii. 7, 9; place,
Ac. xxvii. 28; διὰ βραχέων,
Heb. xiii. 22, *in few words;*
βραχύ τι, Jn. vi. 7, of quantity, *a little.**

βρέφος, ους, τό, *a child unborn,*
Lu. i. 41, 44; *a babe,* as Lu.
ii. 12, 16; 2 Tim. iii. 15.

βρέχω, ξω, *to moisten,* Lu. vii.
38, 44; *to rain, to send rain,*
Mat. v. 45; Lu. xvii. 29;
impers., Ja. v. 17; intrans.,
Rev. xi. 6.*

βροντή, ῆς, ἡ, *thunder,* Jn. xii.
29; Rev. iv. 5.

βροχή, ῆς, ἡ (βρέχω), *a heavy
rain,* Mat. vii. 25, 27. (S.)*

βρόχος, ου, ὁ, *a noose* or *snare,*
1 Cor. vii. 35.*

βρυγμός, οῦ, ὁ, *a grinding* or
gnashing, as Mat. viii. 12.

βρύχω, ξω, *to grind* or *gnash,*
as the teeth, for rage or pain,
Ac. vii. 54.*

βρύω, σω, *to send forth abundantly,* as a fountain, Ja. iii.
11.*

βρῶμα, ατος, τό (see βιβρώσκω),
food of any kind, Mat. xiv.
15; Jn. iv. 34; 1 Cor. viii. 8,
13.

βρώσιμος, ον, *eatable,* Lu. xxiv.
41.*

βρῶσις, εως, ἡ, (1) *the act of
eating,* as 1 Cor. viii. 4; (2)
corrosion, Mat. vi. 19, 20;
(3) *food,* Jn. iv. 32; Heb. xii.
16.

βυθίζω, σω, *to cause to sink,* fig.,
1 Tim. vi. 9; mid., *to sink,*
Lu. v. 7.*

βυθός, οῦ, ὁ, *the deep, the sea,*
2 Cor. xi. 25.*

βυρσεύς, έως, ὁ, *a tanner,* Ac.
ix. 43, x. 6, 32.*

βύσσινος, η, ον, *made of byssus,
fine linen,* Rev. xviii. 12 (W.
H.), 16, xix. 8, 14.*

βύσσος, ου, ἡ, *byssus,* a species
of flax, and of linen manu-
factured from it, highly priz-
ed for its softness, whiteness,
and delicacy, Lu. xvi. 19;
Rev. xviii. 12 (Rec.).*

βωμός, οῦ, ὁ, *an altar,* Ac. xvii.
23.* *Syn.:* βωμός is a heathen
altar; θυσιαστήριον, the altar
of the true God.

Γ

Γ, γ, γάμμα, *gamma,* *g* hard,
the third letter of the Greek
alphabet. In numeral value,
γ′ = 3; ,γ = 3000.

Γαββαθά (W. H. -θά), ἡ (Aram.),
Gabbatha ; an elevated place
or *tribunal,* Jn. xix. 13. See
λιθόστρωτον. (N. T.)*

Γαβριήλ, ὁ (Heb. *man of God*),
the archangel *Gabriel,* Lu.
i. 19, 26.*

γάγγραινα, ης, ἡ, *a gangrene,
mortification,* 2 Tim. ii. 17.*

Γάδ, ὁ (Heb.), *Gad,* Rev. vii.
5.*

Γαδαρηνός, ή, όν, *belonging to
Gadara,* Mar. v. 1 (Rec.);
Mat. viii. 28 (W. H.). See
Γεργεσηνός.

γάζα, ης, ἡ (Persian), *treasure,*
as of a government, Ac. viii.
27.*

Γάζα, ης, ἡ (Heb.), *Gaza,* a
strong city of the ancient
Philistines in the W. of
Palestine, Ac. viii. 26. (The
adj., ἔρημος, *desert,* refers to
ὁδός.)*

γαζο-φυλάκιον, ου, τό, *a place*

for the guardianship of treasure, treasury; a part of the temple so called, Mar. xii. 41, 43; Lu. xxi. 1; Jn. viii. 20. (S.)*

Γάϊος, ου, ὁ (Lat.), *Gaius,* or *Caius.* There are four of the name in N. T., Ac. xix. 29, xx. 4; 1 Cor. i. 14, and Ro. xvi. 23; 3 Jn. 1.*

γάλα, ακτος, τό, *milk,* lit., 1 Cor. ix. 7; fig., for the elements of Christian knowledge, 1 Cor. iii. 2; Heb. v. 12, 13; 1 Pet. ii. 2.*

Γαλάτης, ου, ὁ, *a Galatian,* Gal. iii. 1.*

Γαλατία, ας, ἡ, *Galatia,* or *Gallogræcia,* a province of Asia Minor, Gal. i. 2; 1 Cor. xvi. 1; 2 Tim. iv. 10; 1 Pet. i. 1.*

Γαλατικός, ή, όν, *belonging to Galatia,* Ac. xvi. 6, xviii. 23.*

γαλήνη, ης, ἡ, *a calm,* Mat. viii. 26; Mar. iv. 39; Lu. viii. 24.*

Γαλιλαία, ας, ἡ (from Heb.), *Galilee,* the N. division of Palestine, Mat. iv. 15.

Γαλιλαῖος, αία, αῖον, *of* or *belonging to Galilee,* Mat. xxvi. 69; Ac. i. 11.

Γαλλίων, ωνος, ὁ, *Gallio,* a proconsul of Achaia, Ac. xviii. 12, 14, 17.*

Γαμαλιήλ, ὁ (Heb.), *Gamaliel,* Ac. v. 34, xxii. 3.*

γαμέω, ῶ, ήσω, 1st aor. ἐγάμησα and ἔγημα, abs. or trans. (with acc.), *to marry;* active properly of the man; pass. and mid. of the woman, with dat., 1 Cor. vii. 39; Mar. x. 12 (W. H. ἄλλον for Rec. ἄλλῳ); but in N. T. the act. also is used of the woman, as 1 Cor. vii. 28, 34.

γαμίζω, *to give in marriage* (a daughter), Rec. only Mar. xii. 25; Lu. xvii. 27, xx. 35; W. H. add Mat. xxii. 30, xxiv. 38; 1 Cor. vii. 38. (N. T.)*

γαμίσκω = γαμίζω, Mar. xii. 25 (Rec.); Lu. xx. 34 (W. H.).*

γάμος, ου, ὁ, *marriage,* spec. *a marriage feast,* sing. or plur., Heb. xiii. 4; Rev. xix. 7. See Gr. § 240, Wi. § 27, 3, Bu. 23.

γάρ (γε ἄρα), "truly then," a causal postpositive particle

or conjunction, *for,* introducing a reason for the thing previously said. Used in questions to intensify the inquiry; often with other particles. For the special uses of γάρ, see Gr. § 407, Wi. § 53, 8, Bu. 370.

γαστήρ, τρός (sync.), ἡ, (1) *the womb,* as Mat. i. 18; (2) *the stomach,* only Tit. i. 12, from Epimenides, "idle bellies," *gluttons.*

γέ, an enclitic particle indicating emphasis, *at least, indeed.* Sometimes used alone, as Ro. viii. 32; 1 Cor. iv. 8; generally in connection with other particles, as ἀλλά, ἄρα, εἴ; εἰ δὲ μήγε, stronger than εἰ δὲ μή, *if otherwise indeed;* καίγε, *and at least, and even;* καίτοιγε, *though indeed;* μενοῦνγε, *yea, indeed;* μήτιγε, "*to say nothing of,*" 1 Cor. vi. 3.

Γεδεών, ὁ (Heb.), *Gideon,* Heb. xi. 32.*

γέ-εννα, ης, ἡ (Heb. *valley of Hinnom*), met., *Gehenna, place of punishment* in the future world, Mat. x. 28, etc. Sometimes with τοῦ πυρός, as Mat. v. 22. Compare 2 Kings xxiii. 10. (S.)

Γεθ-σημανῆ, or -νεί (W. H.), ἡ (Heb. *oil-press*), *Gethsemane,* a small field at the foot of the Mount of Olives, over the brook Kidron, Mat. xxvi. 36; Mar. xiv. 32.*

γείτων, ονος, ὁ, ἡ, *a neighbor,* Lu. xiv. 12, xv. 6, 9; Jn. ix. 8.*

γελάω, ῶ, άσω, *to laugh,* Lu. vi. 21, 25.*

γέλως, ωτος, ὁ, *laughter,* Ja. iv. 9.*

γεμίζω, σω, *to fill,* with acc. and gen. (also ἀπό or ἐκ), Mar. xv. 36; Rev. viii. 5; pass. abs., *to be full,* Mat. iv. 37; Lu. xiv. 23.

γέμω, *to be full of,* with gen. (ἐκ, Mat. xxiii. 25; perhaps acc., Rev. xvii. 3).

γενεά, ᾶς, ἡ, *generation,* as (1) *offspring, race, descent,* Mat. i. 17; Lu. ix. 41; (2) *the people of any given time;* (3) *an age of the world's duration,* Mat. xxiv. 34; Ac. xiii. 36; εἰς γενεὰς καὶ γενεάς (W.

H.), *unto generations and generations* (R. V.), Lu. i. 50.

γενεα-λογέω, ῶ, *to reckon a genealogy* or *pedigree,* pass. with ἐκ, Heb. vii. 6.*

γενεα-λογία, ας, ἡ, *genealogy,* N. T. plur., 1 Tim. i. 4; Tit. iii. 9; prob. of Gnostic speculations on the origin of being.*

γενέσια, ων, τά, *a birthday celebration,* Mat. xiv. 6; Mar. vi. 21.*

γένεσις, εως, ἡ, *birth, lineage,* Mat. i. 1 (W. H. add Mat. i. 18; Lu. i. 14, for Rec. γέννησις); Ja. i. 23, τὸ πρόσωπον τῆς γενέσεως αὐτοῦ, *the countenance of his birth,* or, as A. V., R. V., "his natural face"; Ja. iii. 6, τὸν τροχὸν τῆς γενέσεως, *the wheel of nature* (R. V.).*

γενετή, ῆς, ἡ, *birth,* Jn. ix. 1.*

γένημα, ατος, τό. See γέννημα.

γεννάω, ῶ, ήσω, *to beget, give birth to, produce, effect,* Mat. i. 3, 5, 6; Lu. i. 13, 57; Ac. vii. 8, 29; pass., *to be begotten, born* (often in John, of spiritual renewal), Mat. i. 20; Jn. i. 13; 1 Jn. v. 1.

γέννημα, ατος, τό, (1) *progeny, generation,* as Mat. iii. 7; (2) *produce* generally, as Mat. xxvi. 29; fig., *fruit, result,* as 2 Cor. ix. 10. In sense (2) W. H. always read γένημα, and sometimes elsewhere.

Γεννησαρέτ (Aram.), *Gennesaret* (*Chinnereth* or Chinneroth, in O. T.), a region of Galilee, with village or town of the same name, Mat. xiv. 34. Used of the adjacent lake, as Lu. v. 1.

γέννησις, εως, ἡ. See γένεσις.*

γεννητός, ή, όν, verb. adj., *begotten, born,* Mat. xi. 11; Lu. vii. 28.*

γένος, ους, τό, (1) *offspring,* Ac. xvii. 28, 29; (2) *family,* Ac. xiii. 26; (3) *stock, race,* Ac. vii. 19; Gal. i. 14; (4) *nation,* Mar. vii. 26; (5) *kind* or *species,* Mar. ix. 29; 1 Cor. xiv. 10.

Γεργεσηνός, ή, όν, or Γερασηνός, *Gergesene, belonging to Gergesa* or *Gerasa.* The copies vary between these forms and Γαδαρηνός, Mat. viii. 28; Mar. v. 1; Lu. viii. 26, 37.*

γερουσία, as, ἡ (γέρων), *an assembly of elders, senate,* Ac. v. 21.*

γέρων, οντος, ὁ, *an old man,* Jn. iii. 4.*

γεύω, *to make to taste,* only mid. in N. T.; *to taste,* as abs., *to take food,* Ac. x. 10; or with obj. gen., or acc. See Gr. § 249 a, (2), Wi. §§ 3, p. 33, 30, 7 c, Bu. 167. Fig., *to experience,* as Mat. xvi. 28; once with ὅτι, 2 Pet. ii. 3.

γεωργέω, ῶ, *to cultivate* or *till the earth,* Heb. vi. 7.*

γεώργιον, ου, τό, *a tilled field,* fig., 1 Cor. iii. 9. (S.)*

γεωργός, οῦ, ὁ, *one who tills the ground, a husbandman,* 2 Tim. ii. 6; Ja. v. 7: *a vine-dresser,* Lu. xx. 9, 10, 14, 16.

γῆ, γῆς, ἡ, contr. for γέα or γαῖα, *land* or *earth,* as (1) *the material soil;* (2) *the producing soil, the ground;* (3) *land,* as opposed to sea; (4) *earth,* as opposed to heaven, often involving suggestions of human weakness and sin; (5) *region* or *territory.*

γῆρας, (αος) ως, τό, *old age,* Lu. i. 36 (dat., Rec. γήρᾳ, W. H. γήρει).*

γηράσκω, or γηράω, άσω, *to become old,* Jn. xxi. 18; Heb. viii. 13.*

γίνομαι, for γίγνομαι. See Gr. § 94, 8 a. γενήσομαι, ἐγενόμην and ἐγενήθην, γέγονα (with pres. force) and γεγένημαι, *to become,* as (1) *to begin to be,* used of persons, *to be born,* Jn. viii. 58; of the works of creation, *to be made,* Jn. i. 3, 10; and of other works, *to be wrought* or *performed;* so, to pass out of one state into another, *to grow into, to be changed into,* Jn. ii. 9; often with εἰς, Lu. xiii. 19; (2) of ordinary or extraordinary occurrences, *to happen, to take place, to be done;* of the day, the night, Mar. vi. 2; of thunder, earthquake, calm, etc.; of feasts or public solemnities, *to be held* or *celebrated;* frequently in the phrase καὶ ἐγένετο, *and it came to pass* (with καί, or following verb, or inf.); also, μὴ γένοιτο, *let it never happen!* or *God forbid!;* (3) with

adj. or predicative subst., *to become,* where quality, character, or condition is specified; often in prohibitions, μὴ γίνου, μὴ γίνεσθε, *become not,* as Mat. vi. 16; (4) with the cases of substantives and the prepositions, the verb forms many phrases, to be interpreted according to the meaning of the case or prep.

γινώσκω, or γιγνώσκω (see Gr. § 94, 8 b, Wi. § 39, 3, note 2, Bu. 55), γνώσομαι, 2d aor. ἔγνων (imper. γνῶθι), perf. ἔγνωκα, (1) *to become aware of, to perceive,* with acc.; (2) *to know, to perceive, understand,* with acc. or ὅτι, or acc. and inf., or τί interrog.; Ἑλληνιστὶ γ., *to understand* Greek, Ac. xxi. 37; *to be conscious of,* by experience, as 2 Cor. v. 21; (3) *to know carnally* (a Hebraistic euphemism), Mat. i. 25; Lu. i. 34; (4) specially of the fellowship between Christians and God or Christ, 1 Cor. viii. 3; Mat. vii. 23 (negatively); Jn. xvii. 3; Heb. viii. 11; Phil. iii. 10, etc.

γλεῦκος, ους, τό, *sweet* or *new wine,* Ac. ii. 13.*

γλυκύς, εῖα, ύ, *sweet,* Ja. iii. 11, 12; Rev. x. 9, 10.*

γλῶσσα, ης, ἡ, (1) *the tongue,* Mar. vii. 33, 35; 1 Jn. iii. 18 (2) *a language,* Ac. ii. 11; (3) *a nation* or *people* distinguished by their language, Rev. v. 9, vii. 9.

γλωσσό-κομον, ου, τό, *a little box* or *case for money,* Jn. xii. 6, xiii. 29 (orig. from holding the "tongue-pieces" of flutes, etc.).*

γναφεύς, έως, ὁ, *a fuller, cloth-dresser,* Mar. ix. 3.*

γνήσιος, α, ον (sync. from γενήσιος), *legitimate, genuine, true,* 1 Tim. i. 2; Tit. i. 4; Phil. iv. 3; τὸ γνήσιον, *sincerity,* 2 Cor. viii. 8.*

γνησίως, adv., *genuinely, sincerely,* Phil. ii. 20.*

γνόφος, ου, ὁ, *darkness, gloom,* Heb. xii. 18.*

γνώμη, ης, ἡ, (γνο- in γινώσκω), *opinion, judgment, intention,* 1 Cor. i. 10; 2 Cor. viii. 10.

γνωρίζω, ίσω, or ιῶ, (1) *to make known, to declare* (with acc.

and dat., ὅτι or τί, interrog., Col. i. 27); (2) intrans., *to know,* only Phil. i. 22.

γνῶσις, εως, ἡ, (1) subj., *knowledge,* with gen. of obj. (gen. subj., Ro. xi. 33); (2) obj., *science, doctrine, wisdom,* as Lu. xi. 52. *Syn.:* see Trench, § lxxv.

γνώστης, ου, ὁ, *one who knows, an expert,* Ac. xxvi. 3. (S.)*

γνωστός, ή, όν, verb. adj., *known,* as Ac. ii. 14, iv. 10; *knowable,* Ro. i. 19; *notable,* Ac. iv. 16; οἱ γνωστοί, *one's acquaintance,* Lu. ii. 44.

γογγύζω, ύσω, *to murmur* in a low voice, Jn. vii. 32; discontentedly, *to grumble,* as 1 Cor. x. 10, with acc., or περί, gen., πρός, acc., κατά, gen. (S.)

γογγυσμός, οῦ, ὁ, *muttering,* Jn. vii. 12; *murmuring,* Ac. vi. 1; Phil. ii. 14; 1 Pet. iv. 9. (S.)*

γογγυστής, οῦ, ὁ, *a murmurer, complainer,* Ju. 16. (N. T.)*

γόης, ητος, ὁ (γοάω, *to moan*), *an enchanter, an impostor,* 2 Tim. iii. 13.*

Γολγοθά (W. H., some -θᾶ), (Aram.), *Golgotha,* "the place of a skull" (prob. from its shape), *Calvary,* Mat. xxvii. 33; Mar. xv. 22; Jn. xix. 17. See κρανίον. (N. T.)*

Γόμορρα, ας, ἡ, or, ων, τά, *Gomorrha,* Ro. ix. 29.

γόμος, ου, ὁ (γέμω), (1) *a burden, e.g.,* of a ship, Ac. xxi. 3; (2) *wares* or *merchandise,* Rev. xviii. 11, 12.*

γονεύς, έως, ὁ (γεν- in γίγνομαι), *a parent,* only in plural, Lu. ii. 41; Ep. vi. 1.

γόνυ, ατος, τό, *the knee;* often in plur. after τιθέναι or κάμπτειν, *to put* or *bend the knees, to kneel,* in devotion, Lu. xxii. 41; Ro. xi. 4.

γονυ-πετέω, ῶ (πίπτω), *to fall on the knees, to kneel to* (acc.), Mar. x. 17.

γράμμα, ατος, τό (γράφω), (1) *a letter of the alphabet,* Gal. vi. 11, *in what large letters,* perhaps noting emphasis; *letter,* as opposed to spirit, Ro. ii. 29, etc.; (2) *a writing,* such as *a bill* or *an epistle,* as Lu. xvi. 6, 7; Ac. xxviii. 21; τὰ ἱερὰ γράμματα, 2 Tim.

iii. 15, *the holy writings*, or *the Scriptures ;* (3) plur., *literature, learning* generally, Jn. vii. 15.

γραμματεύς, έως, ό, (1) *a clerk, secretary, a scribe*, Ac. xix. 35 ; (2) one of that class among the Jews who copied and interpreted the O. T. Scriptures (see *νομικός*), Mat. xxiii. 34 ; (3) met., *a man of learning generally*, Mat. xiii. 52.

γραπτός, ή, όν, verb. adj., *written*, Ro. ii. 15.*

γραφή, ῆς, ή, (1) *a writing ;* (2) spec., ή γραφή or αί γραφαί, *the Scriptures, writings* of the O. T., 2 Pet. iii. 16 ; (3) a particular *passage*, Mar. xii. 10.

γράφω, ψω, γέγραφα, *to grave, write, inscribe ;* έγράφη, γέγραπται, or γεγραμμένον έστί, a formula of quotation, *It is written ;* often with dat. of pers., as Mar. x. 5.

γραώδης, ες (γραῦς, εἶδος), *old-womanish, foolish*, 1 Tim. iv. 7.*

γρηγορέω, ῶ (from έγρήγορα, perf. of έγείρω), *to keep awake, watch, be vigilant*, Mar. xiii. 35, 37 ; Rev. xvi. 15.

γυμνάζω (γυμνός), *to exercise, train*, 1 Tim. iv. 7 ; Heb. v. 14, xii. 11 ; 2 Pet. ii. 14.*

γυμνασία, ας, ή, *exercise, training*, 1 Tim. iv. 8.*

γυμνητεύω, or ιτεύω (W. H.), *to be naked* or *poorly clad*, 1 Cor. iv. 11.*

γυμνός, ή, όν, (1) *naked*, Mar. xiv. 52 ; Rev. iii. 17 ; *ill-clad*, Mat. xxv. 36, 48 ; *having only an inner garment*, Jn. xxi. 7 ; (2) *bare, i.e., open* or *manifest*, Heb. iv. 13 ; (3) *mere*, 1 Cor. xv. 37.

γυμνότης, τητος, ή, (1) *nakedness*, Rev. iii. 18 ; (2) *scanty clothing*, Ro. viii. 35 ; 2 Cor. xi. 27. (N. T.)*

γυναικάριον, ου, τό (dim.), *a silly woman*, 2 Tim. iii. 6.*

γυναικεῖος, α, ον, *womanish, female ;* 1 Pet. iii. 7, the *weaker* vessel.*

γυνή, γυναικός, voc. γύναι, ή, (1) *a woman*, Mat. ix. 20 ; Ro. vii. 2 ; (2) *a wife*, Ac. v. 1, 7 ; Ep. v. 28. The voc. is the form of ordinary address,

often used in reverence and honor ; compare Jn. ii. 4 and xix. 26.

Γώγ, ό, a proper name, *Gog*. In Ezek. xxxviii. 2, king of Magog, a land of the remote north ; hence, in Rev. xx. 8, of a people far remote from Palestine.*

γωνία, ας, ή, *a corner*, as Mat. vi. 5, xxi. 42 (from S.) ; met., *a secret place*, Ac. xxvi. 26.

Δ

Δ, δ, δέλτα, *delta, d*, the fourth letter of the Greek alphabet. As a numeral, δ' = 4 ; ,δ = 4000.

Δαβίδ, also Δαυΐδ, Δαυείδ (W. H.), ό (Heb.), *David*, king of Israel ; ό υἱὸς Δ., *the Son of David*, an appellation of the Messiah ; έν Δ., *in David, i.e.*, in the Psalms, Heb. iv. 7.

δαιμονίζομαι (see δαίμων), 1st aor. part., δαιμονισθείς, *to be possessed by a demon*, Mat. iv. 24 ; Mar. i. 32.

δαιμόνιον, ου, τό (orig. adj.), *a deity*, Ac. xvii. 18 ; *a demon* or *evil spirit ;* δαιμόνιον ἔχειν, *to have a demon* or *to be a demoniac*, Lu. iv. 33 ; Jn. vii. 20.

δαιμονιώδης, ες, *resembling a demon, demoniacal*, Ja. iii. 15. (N. T.)*

δαίμων, ονος, ό, ή, in classic Greek, any spirit superior to man ; hence often of the inferior deities ; in N. T., *an evil spirit, a demon* (W. H. have the word only in one passage, Mat. viii. 31) ; δαιμόνιον is generally used.

δάκνω, *to bite*, met., Gal. v. 15.*

δάκρυ, υος, or δάκρυον, ου, τό, *a tear*, Ac. xx. 19, 31 : Heb. v. 7.

δακρύω, σω, *to weep*, Jn. xi. 35.*

δακτύλιος, ου, ό (δάκτυλος), *a ring*, Lu. xv. 22.*

δάκτυλος, ου, ό, *a finger ;* έν δακτύλῳ θεοῦ, met., *by the power of God*, Lu. xi. 20, comp. Mat. xii. 28.

Δαλμανουθά, ή, *Dalmanutha*, a town or village near Magdala, Mar. viii. 10.*

Δαλματία, ας, ή, *Dalmatia*, a

part of Illyricum near Macedonia, 2 Tim. iv. 10.*

δαμάζω, σω, *to subdue, tame*, Mar. v. 4 ; Ja. iii. 7, 8.*

δάμαλις, εως, ή, *a heifer*, Heb. ix. 13.*

Δάμαρις, ιδος, ή, *Damaris*, Ac. xvii. 34.*

Δαμασκηνός, ή, όν, *belonging to Damascus*, 2 Cor. xi. 32.*

Δαμασκός, οῦ, ή, *Damascus*, Ac. ix. 2, 3.

δανείζω, *to lend* money, Lu. vi. 34, 35 ; mid., *to borrow*, Mat. v. 42.*

δάνειον, ου, τό, *a loan, a debt*, Mat. xviii. 27.*

δανειστής, οῦ, ό, *a money-lender, a creditor*, Lu. vii. 41.*

Δανιήλ, ό (Heb.), *Daniel*, Mat. xxiv. 15 ; Mar. xiii. 14 (not W. H.).*

δαπανάω, ῶ, ήσω, *to spend*, Mar. v. 26 ; trans., *to bear expense* for (έπί, dat.), Ac. xxi. 24 ; (ὑπέρ, gen.), 2 Cor. xii. 15 ; *to consume in luxury, to waste*, Lu. xv. 14 ; Ja. iv. 3.*

δαπάνη, ης, ή, *expense, cost*, Lu. xiv. 28.*

δέ, an adversative and distinctive particle, *but, now, moreover*, etc. See Gr. § 404, ii, Wi. § 53, 7, Bu. 364 sq., and μέν.

δέησις, εως, ή, *supplication, prayer*, Ep. vi. 18 ; Ja. v. 16. *Syn.:* see αἴτημα.

δεῖ, impers., see Gr. § 101, Wi. § 58, 9 b, Bu. 147, 164, *it is necessary, one must, it ought, it is right* or *proper*, with inf. (expressed or implied), as Mat. xvi. 21 ; Ac. iv. 12 ; Mar. xiii. 14.

δεῖγμα, ατος, τό (δείκνυμι), *an example, a specimen*, Ju. 7.*

δειγματίζω, σω, *to make an example* or *spectacle* (as disgrace), Col. ii. 15 ; Mat. i. 19 (W. H.). (N. T.)*

δείκνυμι and **δεικνύω** (see Gr. § 114, Bu. 45), (1) *to present to sight, to show, to teach* (acc. and dat.), Mat. iv. 18 ; 1 Cor xii. 31 ; Rev. xvii. 1 ; (2) *to prove* (acc. and έκ), Ja. ii. 18, iii. 13 ; *to show by words* (ὅτι), Mat. xvi. 21 ; inf., Ac. x. 28.

δειλία, ας, ή, *timidity, cowardice*, 2 Tim. i. 7.* *Syn.:* δειλία is always used in a bad sense ; εὐλάβεια, regularly in a good sense, *pious* fear; φόβος is general, denoting either bad or good.

δειλιάω, ῶ, *to be timid, fearful*, Jn. xiv. 27. (S.)*

δειλός, ή, όν, *timid, cowardly*, Mat. viii. 26; Mar. iv. 40; Rev. xxi. 8.*

δεῖνα, ὁ, ἡ, τό, gen. δεῖνος, pron., *a certain person, such a one*, Mat. xxvi. 18.*

δεινῶς, adv. (δεινός, *vehement*), *vehemently, terribly*, Mat. viii. 6; Lu. xi. 53.*

δειπνέω, ῶ, *to take the* δεῖπνον, *to sup*, Lu. xvii. 8, xxii. 20; 1 Cor. xi. 25; met., of familiar intercourse, Rev. iii. 20.*

δεῖπνον, ου, τό, *the chief or evening meal, supper* (see ἀριστον), Lu. xiv. 17, 24; Jn. xiii. 2, 4; κυριακὸν δεῖπνον, *the Lord's Supper*, 1 Cor. xi. 20.

δεισιδαιμονία, ας, ἡ, *religion*, in general, Ac. xxv. 19.*

δεισι-δαίμων, ον (δείδω, *to fear*), *devoutly disposed, addicted to worship*, Ac. xvii. 22. See Gr. § 323 c.* *Syn.:* see Trench, § xlviii.

δέκα, οἱ, αἱ, τά, *ten*; in Rev. ii. 10, *a ten days tribulation*, *i.e.*, brief.

δεκα-δύο (W. H. δώδεκα), *twelve*, Ac. xix. 7, xxiv. 11. (S.)*

δεκα-πέντε, *fifteen*, Jn. xi. 18; Ac. xxvii. 28, Gal. i. 18.*

Δεκά-πολις, εως, ἡ, *Decapolis*, a district E. of Jordan comprising ten towns. It is uncertain what they all were, but they included Gadara, Hippo, Pella, and Scythopolis, Mat. iv. 25; Mar. v. 20, vii. 31.*

δεκα-τέσσαρες, ων, οἱ, αἱ, -σαρα, τά, *fourteen*, Mat. i. 17; 2 Cor. xii. 2; Gal. ii. 1.*

δεκάτη, ης, ἡ, *a tenth part, a tithe*, Heb. vii. 2, 4, 8, 9.*

δέκατος, η, ον, ordinal, *tenth*, Jn. i. 39; Rev. xxi. 20; τὸ δέκατον, Rev. xi. 13, *the tenth part.*

δεκατόω, ῶ, *to receive tithe of*, acc., Heb. vii. 6; pass., *to pay tithe*, Heb. vii. 9. (S.)*

δεκτός, ή, όν (verbal adj. from δέχομαι), *accepted, acceptable*, Lu. iv. 19, 24; Ac. x. 35; 2 Cor. vi. 2; Phil. iv. 18. (S.)*

δελεάζω (δέλεαρ, *a bait*), *to take*

or *entice*, as with a bait, Ja. i. 14; 2 Pet. ii. 14, 18.*

δένδρον, ου, τό, *a tree*, Mat. vii. 17; Lu. xiii. 19.

δεξιό-λαβος, ου, ὁ, "*holding in the right hand*"; plur., *spearmen*, Ac. xxiii. 23. (N. T.)*

δεξιός, ά, όν, *the right*, opp. to ἀριστερός, *the left;* ἡ δεξιά, *the right hand;* τὰ δεξιά, *the right-hand side;* ἐκ δεξιῶν, *on the right* (see Gr. § 293, 1, Wi. § 19, 1 a); δεξιὰς διδόναι, *to give the right hand, i.e., to receive to friendship or fellowship.*

δέομαι, 1st aor. ἐδεήθην, *to have need of* (gen.), as mid. of δέω (see δεῖ); *to make request of* (gen.); *to beseech, pray*, abs., or with εἰ, ἵνα, or ὅπως, of purpose.

δέον, οντος, τό (particip. of δεῖ, as subst.), *the becoming or needful;* with ἐστί = δεῖ, 1 Pet. i. 6; Ac. xix. 36; plur., 1 Tim. v. 13.*

δέος, ους, τό (W. H.), *fear, awe*, Heb. xii. 28.*

Δερβαῖος, ου, ὁ, *of Derbe*, Ac. xx. 4.*

Δέρβη, ης, ἡ, *Derbe*, a city of Lycaonia, Ac. xiv. 6, 20, xvi. 1.*

δέρμα, ατος, τό (δέρω), *an animal's skin*, Heb. xi. 37.*

δερμάτινος, η, ον, *made of skin, leathern*, Mat. iii. 4; Mar. i. 6.*

δέρω, 1st aor. ἔδειρα, 2d fut. pass. δαρήσομαι, *to scourge, to beat*, so as to flay off the skin; ἀέρα δέρων, 1 Cor. ix. 26, *beating air.*

δεσμεύω, σω, *to bind, put in chains* as a prisoner, Lu. viii. 29 (W. H.); Ac. xxii. 4; *to bind* as a bundle, Mat. xxiii. 4.*

δεσμέω, ῶ, *to bind*, Lu. viii. 29 (Rec.).*

δέσμη, ης, ἡ, *a bundle*, Mat. xiii. 30.*

δέσμιος, ιου, ὁ, *one bound, a prisoner*, Ac. xvi. 25, 27; Ep. iii. 1.

δεσμός, οῦ, ὁ (δέω), *a bond*, sing. only in Mar. vii. 35, ὁ δεσμὸς τῆς γλώσσης, and Lu. xiii. 16; plur., δεσμοί or (τὰ) δεσμά, *bonds* or *imprisonment*, Lu. viii. 29; Phil. i. 13.

δεσμο-φύλαξ, ακος, ὁ, *a jailer*, Ac. xvi. 23, 27, 36.*

δεσμωτήριον, ίου, τό, *a prison*, Mat. xi. 2; Ac. v. 21, 23, xvi. 26.*

δεσμώτης, ου, ὁ, *a prisoner*, Ac. xxvii. 1, 42.

δεσπότης, ου, ὁ, *a lord* or *prince, a master*, as 1 Tim. vi. 1; applied to God, Lu. ii. 29; Ac. iv. 24; Ju. 4; to Christ, 2 Pet. ii. 1; Rev. vi. 10. *Syn.:* δεσπότης indicates more absolute and unlimited authority than κύριος.

δεῦρο, adv., (1) of place, *here, hither;* used only as an imperative, *come hither*, as Mat. xix. 21; (2) of time, *hitherto*, only Ro. i. 13.

δεῦτε, adv., as if plur. of δεῦρο (or contr. from δεῦρ' ἴτε), *come, come hither*, as Mat iv. 19, xi. 28.

δευτεραῖος, αία, αῖον, *on the second day*, Ac. xxviii. 13. See Gr. § 319.*

δευτερό-πρωτος, ον, *the second-first*, Lu. vi. 1 (W. H. omit). See Gr. § 148, Wi. § 16, 4, and note. (N. T.)*

δεύτερος, α, ον, ordinal, *second* in number, as Mat. xxii. 26; in order, Mat. xxii. 39; τὸ δεύτερον or δεύτερον, adverbially, *the second time, again*, as 2 Cor. xiii. 2; so ἐκ δευτέρου, as Mar. xiv. 72; ἐν τῷ δευτέρῳ, Ac. vii. 13.

δέχομαι, 1st aor. ἐδεξάμην, dep., *to take, receive, accept, to receive* kindly, *to welcome*, persons, as Mar. vi. 11; things (a doctrine, the kingdom of heaven), as Mar. x. 15; 2 Cor. xi. 4.

δέω, *to want*. See δεῖ and δέομαι.

δέω, 1st aor., ἔδησα; perf., δέδεκα; pass., δέδεμαι; 1st aor. pass. inf., δεθῆναι, *to bind together*, bundles, as Ac. x. 11; *to swathe* dead bodies for burial, as Jn. xi. 44; *to bind* persons in bondage, as Mat. xxii. 13; Mar. vi. 17; 2 Tim. ii. 9; fig., Mat. xviii. 18; δεδεμένος τῷ πνεύματι, Ac. xx. 22, *bound in the spirit*, under an irresistible impulse.

δή, a particle indicating *certainty* or *reality*, and so augmenting the vivacity of a clause or sentence; *truly, indeed, by all means, therefore.* Used with other particles, δήποτε, δήπου, which see.

δῆλος, η, ον, *manifest, evident,* Mat. xxvi. 73; neut., sc. ἐστί, *it is evident,* with ὅτι, 1 Cor. xv. 27; Gal. iii. 11; 1 Tim. vi. 7 (W. H., R. V. omit).*

δηλόω, ῶ, *to manifest, to reveal, to bring to light, to imply* or *signify,* 1 Cor. i. 11, iii. 13; Col. i. 8; Heb. ix. 8, xii. 27; 1 Pet. i. 11; 2 Pet. i. 14.*

Δημᾶς, ᾶ, ὁ, *Demas,* Col. iv. 14; Philem. 24; 2 Tim. iv. 10.*

δημ-ηγορέω, ῶ, *to deliver a public oration;* with πρός, Ac. xii. 21.*

Δημήτριος, ου, ὁ, *Demetrius.* Two of the name are mentioned, Ac. xix. 24, 38; 3 Jn. 12.*

δημι-ουργός, οῦ, ὁ ("a public worker"), *an artisan, a builder,* Heb. xi. 10.* *Syn.:* δημιουργός emphasizes more the idea of *power;* τεχνίτης, that of *wisdom.*

δῆμος, ου, ὁ, *the people,* an organized multitude publicly convened, Ac. xii. 22, xvii. 5, xix. 30, 33.*

δημόσιος, α, ον, *belonging to the people, public,* Ac. v. 18; dat. fem., as adv., δημοσίᾳ, *publicly,* Ac. xvi. 37, xviii. 28, xx. 20.*

δηνάριον, ίου, τό, properly a Latin word (see Gr. § 154 a), *denarius,* Mat. xviii. 28; Rev. vi. 6.

δή-ποτε, adv. with ᾧ, *whatsoever,* giving a generalizing force, Jn. v. 4 (W. H. omit).*

δή-που, adv., *indeed, perhaps, verily,* Heb. ii. 16.*

διά, prep. (cognate with δύο, *two;* δίς, *twice*), *through;* (1) with gen., *through, during, by means of;* (2) with acc., *through, on account of, for the sake of.* See Gr. §§ 147 a, 299, Wi. § 47 i, Bu. 182, 183, 187.

δια-βαίνω, *to pass through,* trans., Heb. xi. 29; or intrans., with πρός (person), Lu. xvi. 26; εἰς (place), Ac. xvi. 9.*

δια-βάλλω, *to slander, accuse,* Lu. xvi. 1.*

δια-βεβαιόω, ῶ, in mid., *to affirm, assert strongly,* 1 Tim. i. 7; Tit. iii. 8.*

δια-βλέπω, *to see through, to see clearly,* Mat. vii. 5; Lu. vi. 42; Mar. viii. 25 (W. H.).*

διάβολος, ον (διαβάλλω), *prone to slander, slanderous,* 1 Tim. iii. 11; 2 Tim. iii. 3; Tit. ii. 3; ὁ διάβολος, *the accuser, the devil,* equivalent to the Hebrew *Satan,* Mat. iv. 1, 5; 2 Tim. ii. 26.

δι-αγγέλλω, *to announce everywhere, publish abroad,* Lu. ix. 60; Ac. xxi. 26; Ro. ix. 17.*

διά-γε, or διά γε (W. H.), *yet on account of,* Lu. xi. 8.*

δια-γίνομαι, *to pass, elapse,* of time; in N. T. only 2d aor. part., gen. abs., *having elapsed,* Mar. xvi. 1; Ac. xxv. 13, xxvii. 9.*

δια-γινώσκω, *to distinguish, know accurately,* Ac. xxiii. 15; *to examine, decide,* Ac. xxiv. 22.*

δια-γνωρίζω, *to publish abroad,* Lu. ii. 17 (W. H. γνωρίζω).*

διά-γνωσις, εως, ἡ, *judicial examination, decision,* Ac. xxv. 21.*

δια-γογγύζω, *to murmur greatly,* Lu. xv. 2, xix. 7. (S.)*

δια-γρηγορέω, ῶ, *to remain awake* or *to be fully awake,* Lu. ix. 32. (N. T.)*

δι-άγω, *to lead* or *pass,* as time, life, 1 Tim. ii. 2 (βίον); Tit. iii. 3 (βίον omitted).*

δια-δέχομαι, *to succeed to,* Ac. vii. 45.*

διά-δημα, ατος, τό (δέω), a *diadem, crown,* Rev. xii. 3, xiii. 1, xix. 12.* *Syn.:* διάδημα always indicates the fillet, the symbol of royalty; στέφανος is the festal *garland* of victory.

δια-δίδωμι, *to distribute, divide,* Lu. xi. 22, xviii. 22; Jn. vi. 11; Ac. iv. 35; Rev. xvii. 13 (W. H. δίδωμι).*

διά-δοχος, ου, ὁ, ἡ, *a successor,* Ac. xxiv. 27.*

δια-ζώννυμι, *to gird,* Jn. xiii. 4, 5, xxi. 7.*

δια-θήκη, ης, ἡ (διατίθημι), (1) *a will* or *testament, a disposition,* as of property, Gal. iii. 15; Heb. ix. 16, 17; (2) a *compact* or *covenant* between God and man (see Gen. vi,

ix, xv, xvii; Exod. xxiv; Deut. v, xxviii). The two covenants mentioned, Gal. iv. 24; that of the O. T. is termed ἡ πρώτη δ., Heb. ix. 15; that of the N. T., ἡ καινὴ δ., Lu. xxii. 20. The O. T. itself (ἡ παλαιὰ δ., 2 Cor. iii. 14) as containing the first, and the N. T. as containing the second, are each called διαθήκη.

δι-αίρεσις, εως, ἡ, *difference, distinction,* as the result of distribution, 1 Cor. xii. 4, 5, 6.*

δι-αιρέω, ῶ, *to divide, distribute,* Lu. xv. 12; 1 Cor. xii. 11.*

δια-καθαρίζω, ιῶ, *to cleanse thoroughly,* Mat. iii. 12; Lu. iii. 17 (W. H. διακαθαίρω). (N. T.)*

δια-κατ-ελέγχομαι, *to confute entirely,* Ac. xviii. 28. (N. T.)*

δια-κονέω, ῶ, *to serve* or *wait upon,* especially at table, Jn. xii. 26; Lu. iv. 39; *to supply wants, to administer* or *distribute alms,* etc. (dat., person; acc., thing; occasionally abs.), Mat. xxv. 44; Ro. xv. 25; specially, *to serve as a deacon,* 1 Tim. iii. 10, 13; of prophets and apostles who ministered the divine will, 1 Pet. i. 12; 2 Cor. iii. 3.

δια-κονία, ας, ἡ, *service, ministry,* in various senses, especially for Christ, 2 Cor. iii. 7; Ro. xi. 13; Ac. vi. 4; *relief,* Ac. xi. 29; *a serving,* Lu. x. 40, *the office of deacon,* Ro. xii 7.

διά-κονος, ου, ὁ, ἡ, *a servant,* viewed in relation to his *work,* specially at table, as Mat. xxiii. 11; Mar. x. 43; one in God's service, *a minister,* as Ro. xiii. 4, xv. 8; *one who serves in the church, deacon* or *deaconess,* Phil. i. 1; 1 Tim. iii. 8, 12; Ro. xvi. 1.

διακόσιοι, αι, α, card. num., *two hundred,* Mar. vi. 37; Jn. vi. 7.

δι-ακούω, *to hear thoroughly,* Ac. xxiii. 35.*

δια-κρίνω, *to discern, to distinguish, make a distinction,* as Ac. xv. 9; 1 Cor. xi. 29. Mid. (aor pass.), (1) *to doubt, to hesitate*, as Mat. xxi. 21; Ja. i. 6; (2) *to dispute with*, Ac. xi. 2; Ju. 9.

διά-κρισις, εως, ἡ, *the act of distinction, discrimination*, Ro. xiv. 1; 1 Cor. xii. 10; Heb. v. 14.*

δια-κωλύω, *to hinder*, Mat. iii. 14.*

δια-λαλέω, ῶ, *to converse together*, Lu. vi. 11; *to talk of*, Lu. i. 65.*

δια-λέγω, in mid., *to reason, to discuss, to dispute*, as Mar. ix. 34; Ac. xx. 7; Ju. 9.

δια-λείπω, *to leave off, to cease*, Lu. vii. 45.*

διά-λεκτος, ου, ἡ, *speech, dialect, language*, Ac. i. 19, ii. 6, 8, xxi. 40, xxii. 2, xxvi. 14.*

δι-αλλάσσω, *to change*, as the disposition; pass., *to be reconciled to*, Mat. v. 24.*

δια-λογίζομαι, *to reason, to deliberate, to debate*, as Mar. ii. 6, 8, viii. 16, ix. 33.

διαλογισμός, οῦ, ὁ, *reflection, thought*, as Lu. ii. 35; *reasoning, opinion*, as Ro. i. 21; *hesitation, doubt*, Lu. xxiv. 38; *dispute, debate*, as Phil. ii. 14; 1 Tim. ii. 8.

δια-λύω, *to disperse, to break up*, Ac. v. 36.*

δια-μαρτύρομαι, dep. mid., *to testify, solemnly charge*, as Ac. ii. 40; 1 Tim. v. 21; *to testify to, solemnly affirm*, Ac. viii. 25; Heb. ii. 6.

δια-μάχομαι, dep. mid., *to contend* or *dispute fiercely*, Ac. xxiii. 9.*

δια-μένω, *to remain, continue*, Lu. i. 22, xxii. 28; Gal. ii. 5; Heb. i. 11; 2 Pet. iii. 4.*

δια-μερίζω, (1) *to divide* or *separate into parts*, as Mat. xxvii. 35, etc.; *to distribute*, as Lu. xxii. 17; (2) pass. with ἐπί, *to be divided* against, *be at discord* with; acc., Lu. xi. 17; dat., xii. 52.

δια-μερισμός, οῦ, ὁ, *dissension*, Lu. xii. 51.*

δια-νέμω, *to disseminate, to spread abroad*, Ac. iv. 17.*

δια-νεύω, *to make signs*, prob. by nodding, Lu. i. 22.*

δια-νόημα, ατος, τό, *a thought*, Lu. xi. 17.*

διά-νοια, ας, ἡ, *the mind, the intellect*, or *thinking faculty*,

as Mar. xii. 30; *the understanding*, 1 Jn. v. 20; *the feelings, disposition, affections*, as Col. i. 21; plur., *the thoughts*, as willful, depraved, Ep. ii. 3 (in Ep. i. 18, A. V., *the eyes of your understanding* (διανοίας), W. H. and R. V. read καρδίας, *the eyes of your heart*).

δι-αν-οίγω, *to open fully, i.e.,* the ears, Mar. vii. 34; the eyes, Lu. xxiv. 31; the heart, Ac. xvi. 14; the Scriptures, Lu. xxiv. 32.

δια-νυκτερεύω, *to pass the whole night*, Lu. vi. 12.*

δι-ανύω, *to perform to the end, complete*, Ac. xxi. 7.*

δια-παντός, adv., *always, continually* (W. H. always read διὰ παντός).

δια-παρα-τριβή, ῆς, ἡ, *contention, incessant wrangling*, 1 Tim. vi. 5 (W. H., Rec. has παραδιατριβή). (N. T.)*

δια-περάω, ῶ, άσω, *to cross over*, as Mat. ix. 1.

δια-πλέω, εύσω, *to sail across*, Ac. xxvii. 5.*

δια-πονέω, ῶ, mid., aor. pass., *to grieve one's self, to be vexed*, Ac. iv. 2, xvi. 18.*

δια-πορεύομαι, pass., *to go* or *pass through*, as Lu. xiii. 22.

δι-απορέω, ῶ, *to be in great doubt* or *perplexity*, Lu. ix. 7, xxiv. 4 (W. H. ἀπορέω); Ac. ii. 12, v. 24, x. 17.*

δια-πραγματεύομαι, *to gain by business* or *trading*, Lu. xix. 15.*

δια-πρίω (πρίω, *to saw*), in pass., *to be sawn through;* fig., *to be greatly moved with anger*, Ac. v. 33, vii. 54.*

δι-αρπάζω, άσω, *to plunder*, Mat. xii. 29; Mar. iii. 27.*

δια-ρρήγνυμι and διαρρήσσω, ξω, *to tear*, as garments, in grief or indignation, Mat. xxvi. 65; Mar. xiv. 63; Ac. xiv. 14; *to break asunder*, as a net, Lu. v. 6; as bonds, Lu. viii. 29.*

δια-σαφέω, ῶ, *to make clear, to declare*, Mat. xiii. 36 (W. H.), xviii. 31.

δια-σείω, *to treat with violence*, so as to extort anything, Lu. iii. 14.*

δια-σκορπίζω, *to scatter, to winnow*, as Mat. xxv. 24; *to dis-*

perse in conquest, as Lu. i. 51; *to waste* or *squander*, Lu. xv. 13, xvi. 1.

δια-σπάω, 1st aor. pass. διεσπάσθην, *to break asunder*, Mar. v. 4; *to tear in pieces*, Ac. xxiii. 10.*

δια-σπείρω, 2d aor. pass. διεσπάρην, *to scatter abroad, disperse*, Ac. viii. 1, 4, xi. 19.*

δια-σπορά, ᾶς, ἡ, *dispersion, state of being dispersed;* used of the Jews as scattered among the Gentiles, Jn. vii. 35; Ja. i. 1; 1 Pet. i. 1. (Ap.)*

δια-στέλλω, in mid., *to give a command* or *injunction*, Mar. viii. 15; Ac. xv. 24; foll. by ἵνα, Mat. xvi. 20 (W. H. mrg.); Mar. v. 43, vii. 36, ix. 9; pass. part., τὸ διαστελλόμενον, Heb. xii. 20, *the command.*

διά-στημα, ατος, τό, *an interval* of time, Ac. v. 7.*

δια-στολή, ῆς, ἡ, *distinction, difference*, Ro. iii. 22, x. 12; 1 Cor. xiv. 7.*

δια-στρέφω, *to seduce, turn away*, Lu. xxiii. 2; Ac. xiii. 8; *to pervert, oppose*, Ac. xiii. 10; perf. part. pass., διεστραμμένος, *perverse, corrupt*, Mat. xvii. 17; Lu. ix. 41; Ac. xx. 30; Phil. ii. 15.*

δια-σώζω, σω, *to save, to convey safe through*, Ac. xxiii. 24, xxvii. 43; 1 Pet. iii. 20; pass., *to reach a place in safety*, Ac. xxvii. 44, xxviii. 1, 4; *to heal perfectly*, Mat. xiv. 36; Lu. vii. 3.*

δια-ταγή, ῆς, ἡ, *a disposition, arrangement, ordinance*, Ac. vii. 53; Ro. xiii. 2.*

διά-ταγμα, ατος, τό, *a mandate, a decree*, Heb. xi. 23.*

δια-ταράσσω, *to trouble greatly, to agitate*, Lu. i. 29.*

δια-τάσσω, *to give orders to* (dat.), *arrange, prescribe*, Mat. xi. 1; Lu. viii. 55; 1 Cor. xvi. 1; mid., *to appoint, to ordain*, as 1 Cor. vii. 17 (also with dat. person; acc., thing).

δια-τελέω, ῶ, *to continue*, Ac. xxvii. 33.*

δια-τηρέω, ῶ, *to guard* or *keep with care*, Lu. ii. 51; with ἑαυτόν, etc., *to guard one's self from, to abstain* (ἐκ or ἀπό), Ac. xv. 29.*

δια-τί or διὰ τί (W. H.), *where-fore?*

δια-τίθημι, only mid. in N. T., *to dispose,* as (1) *to assign,* Lu. xxii. 29; (2) with cog. acc., διαθήκην, *make* a cove-nant with (dat. or πρός, acc.), Ac. iii. 25; Heb. viii. 10, x. 16; *make* a will, Heb. ix. 16, 17. See διαθήκη.*

δια-τρίβω, *to spend* or *pass* (χρόνον or ἡμέρας), as Ac. xiv. 3, 28; abs., *to stay,* as Jn. iii. 22.

δια-τροφή, ῆς, ἡ, *food, nourish-ment,* 1 Tim. vi. 8.*

δι-αυγάζω, *to shine through, to dawn,* 2 Pet. i. 19.*

δια-φανής, ές, *transparent,* Rev. xxi. 21 (W. H. διαυγής in same signif.).*

δια-φέρω, (1) *to carry through,* Mar. xi. 16; (2) *to spread abroad,* Ac. xiii. 49; (3) *to carry hither and thither,* Ac. xxvii. 27; (4) *to differ from* (gen.), 1 Cor. xv. 41; Gal. iv. 1; hence, (5) *to excel, sur-pass,* as Mat. vi. 26; (6) im-pers., διαφέρει, with οὐδέν, *it makes no difference* to (dat.), *matters nothing* to, Gal. ii. 6.

δια-φεύγω, *to escape by flight,* Ac. xxvii. 42.*

δια-φημίζω, *to report, publish abroad,* Mat. ix. 31, xxviii. 15; Mar. i. 45.*

δια-φθείρω, *to corrupt,* 1 Tim. vi. 5; Rev. xi. 18; *to destroy utterly,* Lu. xii. 33; Rev. viii. 9, xi. 18; pass., *to decay. to perish,* 2 Cor. iv. 16; opp. to ἀνακαινόω, *to renew.*

δια-φθορά, ᾶς, ἡ, *decay, corrup-tion, i.e.,* of the grave, Ac. ii. 27, 31, xiii. 34–37 (from S.).*

διά-φορος, ον, (1) *diverse, of different kinds,* Ro. xii. 6; Heb. ix. 10; (2) compar., *more excellent* than, Heb. i. 4, viii. 6.*

δια-φυλάσσω, *to guard care-fully, protect, defend,* Lu. iv. 10 (from S.).*

δια-χειρίζω, mid. N. T., *to lay hands on, put to death,* Ac. v. 30, xxvi. 21.*

δια-χλευάζω, see χλευάζω.

δια-χωρίζω, pass. N. T., "to be separated," *to depart from* (ἀπό), Lu. ix. 33.*

διδακτικός, ἡ, όν, *apt in teach*

ing, 1 Tim. iii. 2; 2 Tim. ii. 24.*

διδακτός, ἡ, όν, *taught, in-structed,* Jn. vi. 45; 1 Cor. ii. 13.*

διδασκαλία, ας, ἡ, *instruction, teaching,* as Ro. xii. 7; *the doctrine taught, precept, in-struction,* as Mat. xv. 9, etc.

διδάσκαλος, ου, ὁ, *a teacher,* especially of the Jewish law, *master, doctor,* as Lu. ii. 46; often in voc. as a title of address to Christ, *Master, Teacher.*

διδάσκω, διδάξω, *to teach, to be a teacher,* abs., Ro. xii. 7; *to teach,* with acc. of person, generally also acc. of thing; also with inf. or ὅτι, Mat. v. 2; Ac. iv. 2.

διδαχή, ῆς, ἡ, *the act of teach-ing,* Ac. ii. 42; 2 Tim. iv. 2; *that which is taught,* doctrine, Mar. i. 27; Ac. xvii. 19; Rev. ii. 24; with obj. gen., per-haps in Heb. vi. 2, see Gr. § 260 b, note, Wi. § 30, 1 a.

δί δραχμον, ου, τό (ριορ. adj., sc. νόμισμα, *coin*), *a double drachma,* or silver half-shek-el (in S. often *the shekel*), Mat. xvii. 24. (S.)*

Δίδυμος, η, ον, *double,* or *twin;* a surname of *Thomas* the apostle, Jn. xi. 16, xx. 24, xxi. 2.*

δίδωμι, *to give* (acc. and dat.); hence, in various connec-tions, *to yield, deliver, supply, commit,* etc. When used in a general sense, the dat. of person may be omitted, as Mat. xiii. 8. The thing given may be expressed by ἐκ or ἀπό, with gen. in a partitive sense instead of acc.; so Mat. xxv. 8; Lu. xx. 10. The purpose of a gift may be ex-pressed by inf., as Mat. xiv. 16; Jn. iv. 7; Lu. i. 73.

δι-εγείρω, *to wake up thorough-ly,* as Lu. viii. 24; *to excite,* Jn. vi. 18; fig., *to stir up, arouse,* 2 Pet. i. 13.

δι-ενθυμέομαι, οῦμαι (W. H.), *to reflect,* Ac. x. 19. (N. T.)*

δι-έξ-οδος, ου, ἡ, *a meeting-place of roads, a public spot* in a city, Mat. xxii. 9.*

δι-ερμηνευτής, οῦ, ὁ, *an inter-preter,* 1 Cor. xiv. 28. (N. T.)*

δι-ερμηνεύω, *to interpret,* Lu. xxiv. 27; 1 Cor. xii. 30, xiv. 5, 13, 27; *to translate,* Ac. ix. 36.*

δι-έρχομαι, *to pass through,* acc. or διά (gen.), destination ex-pressed by εἰς or ἕως; *to pass over* or *travel,* abs., Ac. viii. 4; *to spread,* as a report, Lu. v. 15.

δι-ερωτάω, ῶ, *to find by inquiry,* Ac. x. 17.*

δι-ετής, ές (δίς), *of two years,* Mat. ii. 16.*

διετία, ας, ἡ, *the space of two years,* Ac. xxiv. 27, xxviii. 30.*

δι-ηγέομαι, οῦμαι, *to relate in full, describe,* Mar. v. 16; Ac. viii. 33, ix. 27.

διήγησις, εως, ἡ, *a narrative,* Lu. i. 1.*

δι-ηνεκής, ές, *continuous;* εἰς τὸ διηνεκές, *continually,* Heb. vii. 3, x. 1, 12, 14.*

δι-θάλασσος, ον (δίς), *lying be-tween two seas,* Ac. xxvii. 41.*

δι-ϊκνέομαι, οῦμαι, *to pass through, pierce,* Heb. iv. 12.*

δι-ΐστημι, *to put apart, proceed,* Ac. xxvii. 28; 2 aor., intrans., Lu. xxii. 59, *one hour hav-ing intervened;* xxiv. 51, *he parted* from them.*

δι-ϊσχυρίζομαι, *to affirm con fidently,* Lu. xxii. 59; Ac. xii.

δικαιο-κρισία, ας, ἡ, *just judg-ment,* Ro. ii. 5. (S.)*

δίκαιος, α, ον, *just, right, up-right, righteous, impartial;* applied to things, to persons, to Christ, to God, Mat. i. 19; Heb. xi. 4; Ac. x. 22.

δικαιοσύνη, ης, ἡ, *righteousness, justice, rectitude,* Mat. iii. 15; Jn. xvi. 8, 10; Ro. v. 17, 21.

δικαιόω, ῶ, *to show to be right-eous,* 1 Tim. iii. 16; Ro. iii. 4; usually in N. T. in the de-clarative sense, *to hold guilt-less, to justify, to pronounce* or *treat as righteous,* as Mat. xii. 37; 1 Cor. iv. 4.

δικαίωμα, ατος, τό, *a righteous statute, an ordinance,* Lu. i. 6; Ro. i. 32, ii. 26; Heb. ix. 1, 10; especially *a judicial decree, of acquittal* (opp. to κατάκριμα, *condemnation*), Ro. v. 16; *of condemnation,*

Rev. xv. 4; *a righteous act*, Ro. v. 18; Rev. xix. 8.*

δικαίως, adv., *justly*, 1 Pet. ii. 23; Lu. xxiii. 41; *properly*, 1 Cor. xv. 34; *uprightly*, 1 Th. ii. 10; Tit. ii. 12.*

δικαίωσις, εως, ἡ, *acquittal, justification*, Ro. iv. 25, v. 18.*

δικαστής, οῦ, ὁ, *a judge*, Lu. xii. 14 (W. H. κριτής); Ac. vii. 27, 35.*

δίκη, ης, ἡ, *a judicial sentence*, Ac. xxv. 15 (W. H. καταδίκη); τίνω or ὑπέχω δίκην, *to suffer punishment*, 2 Th. i. 9; Ju. 7; *Justice, the name of a heathen deity*, Ac. xxviii. 4.*

δίκτυον, ου, τό, *a fishing-net*, Jn. xxi. 6, 8, 11. *Syn.*: see ἀμφίβληστρον.

δι-λόγος, ον (δίς), *double-tongued, deceitful*, 1 Tim. iii. 8. (N.T.)*

διό, conj. (διά and ὅ), *on which account, wherefore.*

δι-οδεύω, *to journey through*, Ac. xvii. 1; *to go about*, Lu. viii. 1.*

Διονύσιος, ου, ὁ, *Dionysius*, Ac. xvii. 34.*

διό-περ, conj., *for which very reason*, 1 Cor. viii. 13, x. 14, xiv. 13 (W. H. διό).*

Διο-πετής, ές, *fallen from Zeus, i.e.*, from heaven, Ac. xix. 35.*

δι-όρθωμα, see κατόρθωμα.

δι-όρθωσις, εως, ἡ, *reformation*, Heb. ix. 10.*

δι-ορύσσω, ξω, *to dig through*, Mat. vi. 19, 20, xxiv. 43; Lu. xii. 39.*

Διόσ-κουροι, ων, οἱ (children of Zeus), *Castor* and *Pollux*, Ac. xxviii. 11.*

δι-ότι, conj. (= διὰ τοῦτο, ὅτι), *on this account, because, for.*

Διο-τρεφής, οῦς, ὁ, *Diotrephes*, 3 Jn. 9.*

διπλόος, οῦς, ῆ, οῦν, *double, twofold*, 1 Tim. v. 17; Rev. xviii. 6; comp., διπλότερος with gen., *twofold more than*, Mat. xxiii. 15.*

διπλόω, ῶ, *to double*, Rev. xviii. 6.*

δίς, adv., *twice*, Lu. xviii. 12.

(Δίς), obsolete nom. for Ζεύς, gen. Διός, acc. Δία, *Zeus or Jupiter*, see Ζεύς.

δισ-τάζω, σω (δίς), *to waver, to doubt*, Mat. xiv. 31, xxviii. 17.*

δί-στομος, ον (δίς), *two-edged*, Heb. iv. 12; Rev. i. 16, ii. 12.*

δισ-χίλιοι, αι, α, num., *two thousand*, Mar. v. 13.

δι-υλίζω, *to strain off, filter through*, Mat. xxiii. 24.*

διχάζω, σω, *to set at variance, divide*, Mat. x. 35.*

διχο-στασία, ας, ἡ, *division, dissension*, Ro. xvi. 17; 1 Cor. iii. 3 (not W. H.); Gal. v. 20.*

διχο-τομέω, ῶ, ήσω, *to cut in two*, perhaps meaning *to scourge severely*, Mat. xxiv. 51; Lu. xii. 46.*

διψάω, ῶ, ήσω, *to thirst for, to desire earnestly*, acc., Mat. v. 6; or abs., *to thirst*, Jn. iv. 15; 1 Cor. iv. 11.

δίψος, ους, τό, *thirst*, 2 Cor. xi. 27.*

δί-ψυχος, ον (δίς), *double-minded*, Ja. i. 8, iv. 8.*

διωγμός, οῦ, ὁ, *persecution*, Mat. xiii. 21; Ro. viii. 35.

διώκτης, ου, ὁ, *a persecutor*, 1 Tim. i. 13. (N. T.)*

διώκω, ξω, *to pursue*, in various senses according to context; *to follow, follow after, press forward, to persecute.*

δόγμα, ατος, τό (δοκέω), *a decree, edict, ordinance*, Lu. ii. 1; Ac. xvi. 4, xvii. 7; Ep. ii. 15; Col. ii. 14.*

δογματίζω, σω, *to impose an ordinance*; mid., *to submit to ordinances*, Col. ii. 20.*

δοκέω, ῶ, δόξω, (1) *to think*, acc. and inf., Lu. viii. 18; 2 Cor. xi. 16; (2) *to seem, appear*, Lu. x. 36; Ac. xvii. 18; (3) δοκεῖ, impers., *it seems*, Mat. xvii. 25; *it seems good to* or *pleases*, dat., Lu. i. 3; Ac. xv. 22. *Syn.*: φαίνομαι means to appear *on the outside*; δοκέω, to appear *to an individual* to be true.

δοκιμάζω, σω, *to try, scrutinize, prove*, as 2 Cor. viii. 22; Lu. xii. 56; *to judge fit, approve*, as 1 Cor. xvi. 3. *Syn.*: δοκιμάζω means to test anything with the expectation of finding it good; πειράζω, either with no expectation, or of finding it bad.

δοκιμασία, ας, ἡ, the act of *proving*, Heb. iii. 9 (W. H.).*

δοκιμή, ῆς, ἡ, *a trial*, 2 Cor. viii. 2; *a proof*, 2 Cor. xiii. 3; *tried, approved character*, Ro. v. 4; 2 Cor. ix. 13. (N. T.)

δοκίμιον, ου, τό, *a test, trial*, 1 Pet. i. 7; Ja. i. 3.*

δόκιμος, ον (δέχομαι), *approved, acceptable*, as Ro. xiv. 18, xvi. 10.

δοκός, οῦ, ἡ, *a beam*, Mat. vii. 3, 4, 5; Lu. vi. 41, 42.*

δόλιος, ία, ιον, *deceitful*, 2 Cor. xi. 13.*

δολιόω, ῶ, *to deceive*, impf., 3d pers. plur., ἐδολιοῦσαν, an Alexandrian form from S., Ro. iii. 13. (S.)*

δόλος, ου, ὁ, *fraud, deceit, craft*, Mat. xxvi. 4; 2 Cor. xii. 16.

δολόω, ῶ, *to adulterate, corrupt*, 2 Cor. iv. 2.*

δόμα, ατος, τό (δίδωμι), *a gift*, Mat vii. 11; Lu. xi. 13; Ep. iv. 8; Phil. iv. 17.*

δόξα, ης, ἡ, from δοκέω, in two main significations: (1) *favorable recognition* or *estimation, honor, renown*, as Jn. v. 41, 44; 2 Cor. vi. 8; Lu. xvii. 18; and very frequently (2) *the appearance, the manifestation of that which calls forth praise*; so especially in the freq. phrase ἡ δόξα τοῦ θεοῦ, *glory, splendor.* Concrete plur. δόξαι, in 2 Pet. ii. 10; Ju. 8, *dignities*, angelic powers.

δοξάζω, σω, *to ascribe glory to, to honor, glorify*, Ro. xi. 13; 1 Cor. vi. 20.

Δορκάς, άδος, ἡ, *Dorcas*, Ac. iⱴ. 36, 39.*

δόσις, εως, ἡ, *a giving*, Phil. iv. 15; *a gift*, Ja. i. 17.*

δότης, ου, ὁ, *a giver*, 2 Cor. ix. 7. (S.)*

δουλ-αγωγέω, ῶ, *to bring into subjection*, 1 Cor. ix. 27.*

δουλεία, ας, ἡ, *slavery, bondage*, Ro. viii. 15, 21; Heb. ii. 15.

δουλεύω, σω, (1) *to be a slave*, absolutely, Ep. vi. 7; Ro. ix. 12; (2) *to be subject to, to obey*, dat., Ro. vii. 6; Gal. iv. 8.

δοῦλος, η, ον, adj. only Ro. vi. 19; as subst. ἡ δούλη, *a female slave*, Lu. i. 38, 48; ὁ δοῦλος, *a slave, bondman*, the lowest word for this idea (opp. to ἐλεύθερος); *a servant* (opp. to κύριος, δεσπότης), so in the freq. phrases δοῦλος τοῦ θεοῦ, δοῦλος Χριστοῦ.

δουλόω, ῶ, ώσω, *to reduce to*

bondage (acc. and dat.), Ac.
vii. 6; 1 Cor. ix. 19; pass.,
*to be held subject to, be in
bondage,* 1 Cor. vii. 15.

δοχή, *ῆς, ἡ (δέχομαι), a receiving* of guests, *a banquet,* Lu.
v. 29, xiv. 13.*

δράκων, *οντος, ὁ, a dragon* or
huge serpent; symb. for Satan, Rev.

δράμω, obs., *to run,* see τρέχω.

δράσσομαι, dep., *to grasp, take;*
acc., 1 Cor. iii. 19.*

δραχμή, *ῆς, ἡ, a drachma,*
an Attic silver coin nearly
equal to the Roman dena-
rius, or worth about sixteen
cents of our money, Lu. xv.
8, 9.*

δρέπανον, *ου, τό, a sickle* or
pruning-hook, Mar. iv. 29;
Rev. xiv. 14-19.*

δρόμος, *ου, ὁ, a running;* fig.,
course, career, Ac. xiii. 25,
xx. 24; 2 Tim. iv. 7.*

Δρουσίλλα, *ης, ἡ, Drusilla,* Ac.
xxiv. 24.*

δύναμαι, dep. (see Gr. § 109*b,*
1), *to be able,* abs., or with
inf. (sometimes omitted) or
acc.: *to have a capacity for;
to be strong,* as 1 Cor. iii. 2;
to have power to do, whether
through ability, disposition,
permission, or opportunity.

δύναμις, *εως, ἡ,* (1) *power, might,*
absolutely or as an attribute,
Lu. i. 17; Ac. iii. 12; (2)
power over, expressed by εἰς
or ἐπί (acc.), *ability to do;*
(3) *exercise of power, mighty
work, miracle,* as Mat. xi. 20;
(4) *forces,* as of an army,
spoken of the heavenly hosts,
as Mat. xxiv. 29; (5) *force,*
as of a word, *i.e., significance,*
1 Cor. xiv. 11. *Syn.:* τέρας
indicates a miracle as a
wonderful portent or prod-
igy; σημεῖον, as a sign, au-
thenticating the divine mission of the doer; δύναμις,
as an exhibition of divine
power.

δυναμόω, *ῶ, to strengthen, confirm,* Col. i. 11; Heb. xi. 34
(W. H.). (S.)*

δυνάστης, *ου, ὁ,* (1) *a potentate,
prince,* Lu. i. 52; 1 Tim. vi.
15; (2) *one in authority,* Ac.
viii. 27.*

δυνατέω, *ῶ, to be powerful, have
power,* 2 Cor. xiii. 3; (inf.),

Ro. xiv. 4 (W. H.); 2 Cor. ix.
8 (W. H.). (N. T.)*

δυνατός, *ή, όν, able, having
power, mighty,* Lu. xiv. 31;
1 Cor. i. 26; ὁ δυνατός, *the
Almighty,* Lu. i. 49; δυνατόν,
possible, Ro. xii. 18; Gal. iv.
15.

δύνω or **δύω,** 2d aor. ἔδυν, *to
sink; to set,* as the sun, Mar.
i. 32; Lu. iv. 40.*

δύο, indecl. num., except dat.
δυσί, *two.*

δυς-, an inseparable prefix, implying *adverse, difficult,* or
grievous.

δυσ-βάστακτος, *ον, hard to be
borne,* Mat. xxiii. 4 (not W.
H.); Lu. xi. 46. (S.)*

δυσ-εντερία, *ας, ἡ* (W. H. *ιον,
τό), dysentery,* Ac. xxviii.
8.*

δυσ-ερμήνευτος, *ον, hard to explain,* Heb. v. 11.*

δύσ-κολος, *ον* (lit., "difficult
about food "), *difficult,* Mar.
x. 24.*

δυσκόλως, adv., *with difficulty,
hardly,* Mat. xix. 23; Mar. x.
23; Lu. xviii. 24.*

δυσμή, *ῆς, ἡ* (only plur., δυσμαί),
the setting of the sun, the west,
Rev. xxi. 13; Mat. viii. 11.

δυσ-νόητος, *ον, hard* or *difficult
to be understood,* 2 Pet. iii.
16.*

δυσ-φημέω, *ῶ, to speak evil, de-
fame,* 1 Cor. iv. 13 (W. H.).*

δυσ-φημία, *ας, ἡ, evil report,
defamation,* 2 Cor. vi. 8.*

δώδεκα, indecl. num., *twelve;*
οἱ δώδεκα, *the twelve, i.e.,* the
Apostles.

δωδέκατος, *η, ον,* ord. num.,
twelfth, Rev. xxi. 20.*

δωδεκά-φυλον, *ου, τό, the twelve
tribes, Israel,* Ac. xxvi. 7.*

δῶμα, *ατος, τό, a house, a housetop,* Mat. xxiv. 17; Ac. x.
9.

δωρεά, *ᾶς, ἡ, a gift,* Jn. iv. 10;
Ro. v. 15; Ep. iv. 7.

δωρεάν, accus. of preced., as an
adv., *freely,* as 2 Cor. xi. 7;
without cause, groundlessly,
Jn. xv. 25; Gal. ii. 21.

δωρέομαι, *οῦμαι, to present, bestow,* Mar. xv. 45; pass., 2
Pet. i. 3, 4.*

δώρημα, *ατος, τό, a gift, bounty,*
Ro. v. 16; Ja. i. 17.*

δῶρον, *ου, τό, a gift, present,*
Ep. ii. 8; Rev. xi. 10.

E

E, ε, ἐψῑλον, *epsilon, e,* the fifth
letter. As a numeral, έ = 5;
/ε = 5000.

ἔα, interj., expressing surprise
or indignation, *ha! ah!* Mar.
i. 24 (W. H. omit); Lu. iv.
34.*

ἐάν or **ἄν,** conj. (for εἰ ἄν), *if,*
usually construed with sub-
junctive verb. See Gr. § 383,
Wi. § 41 *b,* 2, Bu. 221 sq.
W. H. have the indic. fut.
in Lu. xix. 40; Ac. viii. 31;
pres. in 1 Th. iii. 8; 1 Jn. v.
15 (Rec. also). Sometimes
equivalent to a particle of
time, *when,* Jn. xii. 32; after
the relative, with an indefinite force, ὃς ἐάν, who*soever,*
as Mat. v. 19, viii. 19; 1 Cor.
xvi. 6; ἐὰν δὲ καί, *and if also;*
ἐὰν μή, *except, unless,* Mat.
v. 20; *but that,* Mar. iv. 22,
ἐὰν περ, *if indeed,* Heb. vi. 3.

ἑαυτοῦ, *ῆς, οῦ,* pron., reflex., 3d
pers., *of one's self;* used also
in 1st and 2d persons. See
Gr. § 335, Wi. §§ 22, 5, 38, 6,
Bu. 111 sq. Genitive often
for possess. pron. λέγειν or
εἰπεῖν ἐν ἑαυτῷ, *to say within
one's self;* γίνεσθαι or ἔρχεσθαι ἐν ἑαυτῷ, *to come to
one's self;* πρὸς ἑαυτόν, *to
one's home,* Jn. xx. 10, or
privately, as Lu. xviii. 11; ἐν
ἑαυτοῖς, *among yourselves,
i.e.,* one with another; καθ'
ἑαυτόν, *apart;* παρ' ἑαυτόν,
at home.

ἐάω, *ῶ, ἐάσω;* impf., εἴων; 1st
aor., εἴασα, (1) *to permit,* inf.,
or acc. and inf., Mat. xxiv.
33; Lu. iv. 41; (2) *to leave,*
Ac. xxvii. 40.

ἑβδομήκοντα, indecl. num., *seventy;* οἱ ἑβδομήκοντα, *the seventy* disciples, Lu. x. 1, 17.

ἑβδομηκοντάκις, num. adv., *seventy times,* Mat. xviii. 22.
(S.)*

ἕβδομος, *η, ον,* ord. num., *seventh,*
Jn. iv. 52; Heb. iv. 4.

Ἔβερ, *ὁ, Eber* or *Heber,* Lu. iii.
35.*

Ἑβραϊκός, *ή, όν* (from Heb.),
Hebrew, Lu. xxiii. 38 (W. H.
omit). (N. T.)*

Ἑβραῖος (W. H. 'E-), *αία, αῖον*
(from Heb.), also subst., *ὁ, ἡ, a
Hebrew;* designating (1) any

Jew, 2 Cor. xi. 22; Phil. iii. 5; (2) a Jew of Palestine, in distinction from οἱ Ἑλληνισταί, or Jews born out of Palestine, and using the Greek language, Ac. vi. 1; (3) any Jewish Christian, Heb. (heading). (S.)* Syn.: Ἑβραῖος denotes a Jew who spoke Aramaic or Hebrew, in distinction from Ἑλληνιστής, a Greek-speaking Jew; Ἰουδαῖος, a Jew in distinction from other nations; Ἰσραηλίτης, one of the chosen people.

Ἑβραΐς (W. H. Ἑ-), (from Heb.), ίδος, ἡ, Hebrew, i.e., the Aramaic language, vernacular in the time of Christ and the Apostles, Ac. xxi. 40, xxii. 2, xxvi. 14. See Gr. § 150, Wi. § 3a. (Ap.)*

Ἑβραϊστί (W. H. Ἑ-), (from Heb.), adv., in the Hebrew language, i.e., in Aramaic, Jn. v. 2; Rev. ix. 11. (Ap.)

ἐγγίζω, fut. att., ἐγγιῶ; pf., ἤγγικα, to approach, to draw near, to be near, abs., or with dat. or εἰς, or ἐπί (acc.), Lu. xviii. 40; Ac. ix. 3; Mar. xi. 1.

ἐγ-γράφω (W. H. ἐνγ-), to inscribe, engrave, 2 Cor. iii. 2; Lu. x. 20 (W. H.).*

ἔγγυος, ου, ὁ, ἡ, a surety, Heb. vii. 22.*

ἐγγύς, adv., near; used of both place and time, with gen. or dat.

ἐγγύτερον, comp. of preceding, nearer, Ro. xiii. 11.*

ἐγείρω, ἐγερῶ, pass. perf., ἐγήγερμαι, to arouse, to awaken, Ac. xii. 7; to raise up, as a Savior, Ac. xiii. 23 (Rec.); to erect, as a building, Jn. ii. 19, 20; mid., to rise up, as from sleep, or from a recumbent posture, as at table, Jn. xi. 29, xiii. 4; applied to raising the dead, Jn. v. 21; used also of rising up against, as an adversary, or in judgment, Mat. xxiv. 7.

ἔγερσις, εως, ἡ, a rousing up; of the resurrection, Mat. xxvii. 53.*

ἐγκ-. In words beginning thus, W. H. generally write ἐνκ-.

ἐγ-κάθ-ετος, ου, ὁ, ἡ (ἐγκαθίημι), a spy, Lu. xx. 20.*

ἐγκαίνια, ίων, τά, a dedication, Jn. x. 22; of the feast commemorating the dedicating or purifying of the temple, after its pollution by Antiochus Epiphanes, 25 Chisleu, answering to mid-December. (S.)*

ἐγ-καινίζω, to dedicate, Heb. ix. 18, x. 20. (S.)*

ἐγ-κακέω, ῶ, and ἐνκακέω, to grow weary, to faint (W. H. in many passages for Rec. ἐκκακέω).

ἐγ-καλέω, ῶ, ἔσω, impf., ἐνεκάλουν, to bring a charge against, accuse, pers. dat., or κατά (gen.), crime in gen., Ac. xix. 38, 40; Ro. viii. 33.

ἐγ-κατα-λείπω, ψω, (1) to desert, to abandon, Mat. xxvii. 46; 2 Tim. iv. 10, 16; (2) to leave remaining, Ro. ix. 29.

ἐγ-κατ-οικέω, ῶ, to dwell among (ἐν), 2 Pet. ii. 8.*

ἐγ-καυχάομαι, to boast in, 2 Th. i. 4 (W. H.).*

ἐγ-κεντρίζω, to insert, as a bud or graft, to graft in; fig., Ro. xi. 17, 19, 23, 24.*

ἔγ-κλημα, ατος, τό, a charge or accusation, Ac. xxiii. 29, xxv. 16.*

ἐγ-κομβόομαι, οῦμαι, to gird on, as an outer garment, the badge of slavery, 1 Pet. v. 5. (N. T.)*

ἐγ-κοπή, ῆς, ἡ (W. H. ἐνκ-), a hindrance, 1 Cor. ix. 12.*

ἐγ-κόπτω, ψω, to impede, to hinder (acc., or inf. with τοῦ), Ro. xv. 22; 1 Th. ii. 18.

ἐγκράτεια, ας, ἡ, self-control, continence, Ac. xxiv. 25; Gal. v. 23; 2 Pet. i. 6.*

ἐγκρατεύομαι, dep., to be self-controlled, continent, especially in sensual pleasures, 1 Cor. vii. 9, ix. 25.*

ἐγ-κρατής, ές, self-controlled, continent, Tit. i. 8.*

ἐγ-κρίνω, to adjudge or reckon, to a particular rank (acc. and dat.), 2 Cor. x. 12.*

ἐγ-κρύπτω, to hide in, to mix with, Mat. xiii. 33; Lu. xiii. 21 (W. H. κρύπτω).*

ἔγ-κυος, ον, pregnant, Lu. ii. 5.*

ἐγ-χρίω, to rub in, anoint, Rev. iii. 18.*

ἐγώ, pers. pron., I; plur., ἡμεῖς, we. See Gr. § 53.

ἐδαφίζω, fut. (attic), ιῶ, to throw to the ground, to raze, Lu. xix. 44.*

ἔδαφος, ους, τό, the base, the ground, Ac. xxii. 7.*

ἑδραῖος, αία, αῖον, steadfast, firm, 1 Cor. vii. 37, xv. 58; Col. i. 23.*

ἑδραίωμα, ατος, τό, a stay, support, 1 Tim. iii. 15. (N. T.)*

Ἑζεκίας, ου, ὁ, Hezekiah, Mat. i. 9, 10.*

ἐθελο-θρησκεία, ας, ἡ, voluntary, arbitrary worship, Col. ii. 23. (N. T.)*

ἐθέλω, see θέλω.

ἐθίζω, to accustom; pass., perf. part., neut., τὸ εἰθισμένον, the custom, Lu. ii. 27.*

ἐθνάρχης, ου, ὁ, a prefect, ethnarch, 2 Cor. xi. 32.*

ἐθνικός, ή, όν, of Gentile race, heathen, as subst. ὁ ἐθνικός, the pagan, the Gentile, Mat. v. 47 (W. H.), vi. 7, xviii. 17; 3 Jn. 7 (W. H.).*

ἐθνικῶς, adv., like the Gentiles, Gal. ii. 14. (N. T.)*

ἔθνος, ους, τό, a race, a nation, Lu. xxii. 25; Ac. x. 35; τὰ ἔθνη, the nations, the heathen world, the Gentiles, Mat. iv. 15; Ro. iii. 29; by Paul, even Gentile Christians, Ro. xi. 13; Gal. ii. 12.

ἔθος, ους, τό, a usage, custom, Lu. i. 9; Ac. xxv. 16.

ἔθω, obs., pf. εἴωθα in pres. signif., to be accustomed, Mat. xxvii. 15; Mar. x. 1; τὸ εἰωθὸς αὐτῷ, his custom, Lu. iv. 16; Ac. xvii. 2.*

εἰ, a conditional conjunction (see Gr. § 383), if, since, though. After verbs indicating emotion, εἰ is equivalent to ὅτι, Mar. xv. 44. As an interrogative particle, εἰ occurs in both indirect and direct questions, Mar. xv. 45; Ac. i. 6. In oaths and solemn assertions, it may be rendered by that ... not. εἰ μή and εἰ μήτι, unless, except; εἰ δὲ μή, but if not, otherwise, Jn. xiv. 2; εἰ περ, if so be; εἰ πως, if possibly; εἴτε ... εἴτε, whether ... or.

εἶδον, see ὁράω, οἶδα.

εἶδος, ους, τό, outward appearance, form, Lu. iii. 22, ix. 29; Jn. v. 37; 2 Cor. v. 7; species, kind, 1 Th. v. 22.*

εἰδωλεῖον, ου, τό, an idol-temple, 1 Cor. viii. 10. (Ap.)*

εἰδωλό-θυτος, ον, sacrificed to idols ; used of meats, as Ac. xv. 29. (Ap.)

εἰδωλο-λατρεία, ας, ἡ, idolatry, 1 Cor. x. 14; Gal. v. 20; Col. iii. 5; 1 Pet. iv. 3. (N. T.)*

εἰδωλο-λάτρης, ου, ὁ, an idolater, 1 Cor. x. 7; Rev. xxi. 8. (N. T.)

εἴδωλον, ου, τό, an idol, a false god worshipped in an image, Ac. vii. 41; Ro. ii. 22.

εἰκῆ or εἰκῇ (W. H.), adv., without purpose, as Ro. xiii. 4; in vain, 1 Cor. xv. 2 (W. H. and R. V. omit in Mat. v. 22).

εἴκοσι, indecl. num., twenty.

εἴκω, to give way, to yield, Gal. ii. 5.*

εἴκω, obs., whence 2d perf. ἔοικα, to be like ; with dat., Ja. i. 6, 23.*

εἰκών, όνος, ἡ, an image, likeness, Mat. xii. 16; 1 Cor. xi. 7. Syn.: see Trench, § xv.

εἰλικρίνεια, ας, ἡ, clearness, sincerity, 1 Cor. v. 8; 2 Cor. i. 12, ii. 17.*

εἰλικρινής, ές (derivation doubtful), sincere, pure, Phil. i. 10; 2 Pet. iii. 1.*

εἰλίσσω (W. H. ἑλίσσω), to roll together, as a scroll, Rev. vi. 14.*

εἰμί (see Gr. § 110, Wi. § 14, 2, Bu. 49, 50), a verb of existence, (1) used as a predicate, to be, to exist, to happen, to come to pass ; with an infin. following, ἔστι, it is convenient, proper, etc., as Heb. ix. 5; (2) as the copula of subject and predicate, simply to be, or in the sense of to be like, to represent, Jn. vi. 35; Mat. xxvi. 26; 1 Cor. x. 4. With participles, it is used to form the periphrastic tenses, Lu. i. 22, iv. 16; Mat. xvi. 19, etc. With gen., as predicate, it marks quality, possession, participation, etc.; with dat., property, possession, destination, etc. The verb, when copula, is often omitted. Participle, ὤν, being ; τὸ ὄν, that which is ; οἱ ὄντες, τὰ ὄντα, persons or things that are.

εἶμι, to go, in some copies for

εἰμί, in Jn. vii. 34, 36 (not W. H.).*

ἕνεκα, εν, see ἕνεκα, εν.

εἴπερ, εἴπως, see under εἰ.

εἶπον (see Gr. § 103, 7, Wi. § 15, Bu. 57), (W. H. εἶπα), from obs. ἔπω, or εἴπω, to say ; in reply, to answer ; in narration, to tell ; in authoritative directions, to bid or command, as Lu. vii. 7.

εἰρηνεύω, to have peace, to be at peace, Mar. ix. 50; Ro. xii. 18; 2 Cor. xiii. 11; 1 Th. v. 13.*

εἰρήνη, ης, ἡ, peace, the opposite of strife; peace of mind, arising from reconciliation with God. In N. T. (like the corresponding Heb. word in O. T.), εἰρήνη generally denotes a perfect well-being. Often employed in salutations, as in Hebrew.

εἰρηνικός, ή, όν, peaceable, Ja. iii. 17; peaceful, Heb. xii. 11.*

εἰρηνο-ποιέω, ῶ, to make peace, reconcile, Col. i. 20. (S.)*

εἰρηνο-ποιός, όν, pacific, loving peace, Mat. v. 9.*

εἰς, prep. governing acc., into, to (the interior). See Gr. §§ 124, 298. In composition, it implies motion into or towards.

εἷς, μία, ἕν, a card. num., one ; used distributively, as Mat. xx. 21; by way of emphasis, as Mar. ii. 7; and indefinitely, as Mat. viii. 19; Mar. xii. 42. As an ordinal, the first, Mat. xxviii. 1; Rev. ix. 12.

εἰσ-άγω, 2d aor. εἰσήγαγον, to lead in, bring in, Lu. xxii. 54; Ac. viii. 45.

εἰσ-ακούω, to listen to, to hear prayer, Mat. vi. 7; Lu. i. 13; Ac. x. 31; Heb. v. 7; to hear so as to obey (gen.), 1 Cor. xiv. 21.*

εἰσ-δέχομαι, ἔξομαι, to receive with favor (acc.), 2 Cor. vi. 17, from S.*

εἴσ-ειμι, impf. εἰσῄειν, inf. εἰσιέναι (εἶμι), to go in, to enter (with εἰς), Ac. iii. 3, xxi. 18, 26; Heb. ix. 6.*

εἰσ-έρχομαι, 2d aor. εἰσῆλθον, to come in, to enter (chiefly with εἰς), Ac. xxiii. 16, 33; εἰσέρχομαι καὶ ἐξέρχομαι, to come and go in and out,

spoken of daily life and intercourse, Ac. i. 21; fig., of entrance into any state or condition, Mat. xix. 17; Heb. iii. 11, 18.

εἰσ-καλέω, ῶ, only mid. in N.T., to call or invite in, Ac. x. 23.*

εἴσ-οδος, ου, ἡ, an entrance, the act of entering, Heb. x. 19; 2 Pet. i. 11.

εἰσ-πηδάω, ῶ, to spring in, Ac xiv. 14 (W. H. ἐκπ-), xvi. 29.*

εἰσ-πορεύομαι, dep., to go in, to enter ; spoken of persons, as Mar. i. 21; of things, as Mat. xv. 17; εἰσπορεύομαι καὶ ἐκπορεύομαι, to go in and out in daily duties, Ac. ix. 28.

εἰσ-τρέχω, 2d aor. εἰσέδραμον, to run in, Ac. xii. 14.*

εἰσ-φέρω (see Gr. § 103, 6, Wi. § 15, Bu. 68), to lead into (with εἰς), e.g., temptation, as Lu. xi. 4; to bring in, Ac xvii. 20; 1 Tim. vi. 7.

εἶτα, adv., then, afterwards.

εἴτε, conj., see εἰ.

ἐκ, or, before a vowel, ἐξ, a prep. gov. gen., from, out of (the interior), used of place, time, and source. See Gr. § 293, Wi. § 47 b, Bu. 326 sq. In composition, ἐκ implies egress, removal, origin, publicity, unfolding, or is of intensive force.

ἕκαστος, η, ον, each, every one (with partitive gen.); εἷς ἕκαστος, every one.

ἑκάστοτε, adv., at every time, always, 2 Pet. i. 15.*

ἑκατόν, card. num., a hundred, Mat. xiii. 8, xviii. 12.

ἑκατοντα-έτης, ες, a hundred years old, Ro. iv. 9.*

ἑκατονταπλασίων, ον, acc. ονα, a hundredfold, Mat. xix. 29 (not W. H.); Mar. x. 30; Lu. viii. 8.*

ἑκατοντάρχης, ου, ὁ, captain over a hundred men, a centurion Ac. x. 1, 22, xxiv. 23.

ἑκατόνταρχος, ου, ὁ = preceding. Mat. viii. 5, 8, 13. In many passages a variant for preceding.

ἐκ-βαίνω, 2d aor. ἐξέβην, to go out, Heb. xi. 15 (W. H.).*

ἐκ-βάλλω, βαλῶ, to cast out, Jn. vi. 37; to drive out, Mat. xxi. 12; to expel, Gal. iv. 30; to send away, dismiss, reject,

Mar. i. 43; Lu. vi. 22; *to extract, draw out,* Lu. vi. 42; Mat. xii. 35.

ἔκ-βασις, εως, ἡ, *a way of escape,* 1 Cor. x. 13; *end, issue,* Heb. xiii. 7.*

ἐκ-βολή, ῆς, ἡ, *a throwing out,* Ac. xxvii. 18.*

ἐκ-γαμίζω (W. H. γαμίζω), *to give in marriage,* Mat. xxiv. 38 (Rec.); 1 Cor. vii. 38 (Rec.). (N. T.)

ἐκ-γαμίσκω = preceding, Lu. xx. 34, 35 (Rec.). (N. T.)*

ἔκ-γονος, ον, *sprung from;* neut. plur., *descendants,* 1 Tim. v. 4.*

ἐκ-δαπανάω, ῶ, *to spend entirely;* pass. reflex., *to expend one's energies* for (ὑπέρ), 2 Cor. xii. 15.*

ἐκ-δέχομαι, *to expect* (ἕως), *to wait for* (acc. or ἕως), Ja. v. 7; Heb. x. 13.

ἔκ-δηλος, ον, *conspicuous, manifest,* 2 Tim. iii. 9.*

ἐκ-δημέω, ῶ, *to go abroad, to be absent,* 2 Cor. v. 6, 8, 9.*

ἐκ-δίδωμι, N. T. mid., *to let out for one's advantage,* Mat. xxi. 33, 41; Mar. xii. 1; Lu. xx. 9.*

ἐκ-δι-ηγέομαι, οῦμαι, dep. mid., *to narrate at length, to declare,* Ac. xiii. 41, xv. 3.*

ἐκ-δικέω, ῶ, *to do justice to, defend, avenge* a person (acc. and ἀπό), Lu. xviii. 3, 5; Ro. xii. 19; *to demand requital for, avenge* a deed (acc.), 2 Cor. x. 6; Rev. vi. 10, xix. 2.*

ἐκ-δίκησις, εως, ἡ, *an avenging, vindication, punishment,* Ac. vii. 24; Ro. xii. 19; 1 Pet. ii. 14.

ἔκ-δικος, ου, ὁ, ἡ, *an avenger, one who adjudges* a culprit (dat.) *to punishment* for(περί) a crime, Ro. xiii. 4; 1 Th. iv. 6.*

ἐκ-διώκω, ώξω, *to persecute, to expel by persecuting,* Lu. xi. 49 (not W. H.); 1 Th. ii. 15.*

ἔκ-δοτος, ον, *delivered up,* Ac. ii. 23.*

ἐκ-δοχή, ῆς, ἡ, *a waiting for, expectation,* Heb. x. 27.*

ἐκ-δύω, *to unclothe, to strip off* (two accs.), Mat. xxvii. 31; 2 Cor. v. 4.

ἐκεῖ, adv., *there, thither.*

ἐκεῖθεν, adv., *from that place, thence.*

ἐκεῖνος, η, ο, pron., demonst., *that, that one there;* used antithetically, Mar. xvi. 20; and by way of emphasis, Mat. xxii. 23. See Gr. §§ 338, 340, Wi. §§ 18, 4, 23, 1, Bu. 104, 120.

ἐκεῖσε, adv., *thither,* Ac. xxi. 3; in const. præg., Ac. xxii. 5.*

ἐκ-ζητέω, ῶ, *to seek out* with diligence, Heb. xii. 17; 1 Pet. i. 10; *to seek after* God, Ac. xv. 17; Ro. iii. 11; Heb. xi. 6; *to require,* judicially, Lu. xi. 50, 51. (S.)*

ἐκ-ζήτησις, εως, ἡ, *a subject of inquiry,* 1 Tim. i. 4 (W. H.).*

ἐκ-θαμβέω, ῶ, N. T. pass., *to be amazed, greatly astonished,* Mar. ix. 15, xiv. 33, xvi. 5, 6.*

ἔκ-θαμβος, ον, *greatly astonished, amazed,* Ac. iii. 11.*

ἐκ-θαυμάζω, *to wonder greatly,* Mar. xii. 17 (W. H.).*

ἔκ-θετος, ον, *cast out, exposed* to perish, Ac. vii. 19.*

ἐκ-καθαίρω, 1st aor. ἐξεκάθαρα, *to cleanse thoroughly,* 1 Cor. v. 7; 2 Tim. ii. 4.*

ἐκ-καίω, N. T. pass., *to burn vehemently,* as with lust, Ro. i. 27.*

ἐκ-κακέω, ῶ, *to faint, to despond through fear* (Rec., for which W. H. have ἐγκ- and ἐνκ-).

ἐκ-κεντέω, ῶ, *to pierce through, to transfix,* Jn. xix. 37; Rev. i. 7.*

ἐκ-κλάω, *to break off,* Ro. xi. 17, 19, 20 (W. H.).*

ἐκ-κλείω, σω, *to shut out,* Gal. iv. 17; *to exclude,* Ro. iii. 27.*

ἐκκλησία, ας, ἡ (ἐκκαλέω), *an assembly,* Ac. xix. 32, 39, 41; usually legally, sometimes tumultuously gathered. Espec. in N. T., *an assembly of Christian believers, a church* in one place, Ac. xi. 26; often plural, as Ac. xv. 41; *the whole body of believers* on earth, 1 Cor. xii. 28; Ep. i. 22; or in heaven, Heb. xii. 23. *Syn.:* see Trench, § 1.

ἐκ-κλίνω, *to turn away from* (ἀπό), Ro. iii. 12, xvi. 17; 1 Pet. iii. 11.*

ἐκ-κολυμβάω, ῶ, *to swim out,* Ac. xxvii. 42.*

ἐκ-κομίζω, *to carry out* for burial, Lu. vii. 12.*

ἐκ-κόπτω, κόψω, *to cut off,* Mat. iii. 10, v. 30; 2 Cor. xi. 12 (in 1 Pet. iii. 7, W. H. read ἐνκόπτω, *to hinder*).

ἐκ-κρέμαμαι (mid. of ἐκκρεμάννυμι), *to hang upon,* of earnest attention, Lu. xix. 48.*

ἐκ-λαλέω, ῶ, *to speak out, to disclose,* Ac. xxiii. 22.*

ἐκ-λάμπω, *to shine forth,* Mat. xiii. 43.*

ἐκ-λανθάνω, in mid., *to forget entirely,* Heb. xii. 5.*

ἐκ-λέγω, mid. in N. T., 1st aor. ἐξελεξάμην, *to choose out for one's self, to elect,* Lu. x. 42; Ac. vi. 5, xiii. 17; 1 Cor. i. 27, 28.

ἐκ-λείπω, 2d aor. ἐξέλιπον, *to fail, to cease, to die,* Lu. xvi. 9, xxii. 32, xxiii. 45 (W. H.); Heb. i. 12.*

ἐκλεκτός, ή, όν, (1) *chosen, elect,* Lu. xviii. 7, xxiii. 35; 1 Tim. v. 21; Ro. viii. 33; Rev. xvii. 14; (2) *choice, select,* 2 Jn. i. 13; 1 Pet. ii. 4.

ἐκλογή, ῆς, ἡ, *a choice, selection,* Ro. ix. 11; 1 Th. i. 4; Ac. ix. 15 (*a vessel of choice, i.e., a chosen vessel*); concr., *the chosen ones,* Ro. xi. 7.

ἐκ-λύω, in pass., *to become weary* in body, or *despondent* in mind, Mar. viii. 3; Gal. vi. 9; Heb. xii. 5.

ἐκ-μάσσω, ξω, *to wipe, to wipe off,* Lu. vii. 38, 44; Jn. xi. 2, xii. 3, xiii. 5.*

ἐκ-μυκτηρίζω, *to deride, scoff at* (acc.), Lu. xvi. 14, xxiii. 35. (S.)*

ἐκ-νέω (lit., swim out), or ἐκνεύω (lit., turn by a side motion), *to withdraw,* Jn. v. 13.*

ἐκ-νήφω, *to return to soberness* of mind, 1 Cor. xv. 34.*

ἑκούσιος, ον (ἑκών), *voluntary, spontaneous,* Philem. 14.*

ἑκουσίως, adv., *voluntarily, of one's own accord,* Heb. x. 26; 1 Pet. v. 2.*

ἔκ-παλαι, adv., *from of old,* 2 Pet. ii. 3, iii. 5.*

ἐκ-πειράζω, σω, *to put to the test, to make trial of, to tempt,* Mat. iv. 7; Lu. iv. 12, x. 25; 1 Cor. x. 9. (S.)*

ἐκ-πέμπω, to send forth, Ac. xiii. 4, xvii. 10.*

ἐκ-περισσῶς, adv., exceedingly, Mar. xiv. 31 (W. H.). (N.T.)*

ἐκ-πετάννυμι, 1st aor. ἐξεπέτασα, to stretch forth, Ro. x. 21.*

ἐκ-πηδάω, ῶ, 1st aor. ἐξεπήδησα (W. H.), to spring forth, Ac. xiv. 14.*

ἐκ-πίπτω, to fall from (ἐκ), Ac. xii. 7; abs., to fall, Ja. i. 11; of a ship driven from its course, Ac. xxvii. 17; of love, to fail, 1 Cor. xiii. 8; of moral lapse, Gal. v. 4.

ἐκ-πλέω, εύσω, to sail away, Ac. xv. 39, xviii. 18, xx. 6.*

ἐκ-πληρόω, ῶ, to fill entirely, fulfill, Ac. xiii. 32.*

ἐκ-πλήρωσις, εως, ἡ, fulfillment, Ac. xxi. 26.*

ἐκ-πλήσσω, 2d aor. pass. ἐξεπλάγην, to strike with astonishment, Mat. xiii. 54; Ac. xiii. 12.

ἐκ-πνέω, εύσω, to breathe out, to expire, Mar. xv. 37, 39; Lu. xxiii. 46.*

ἐκ-πορεύομαι, dep., to go out (ἀπό, ἐκ, παρά, and εἰς, ἐπί, πρός); to proceed from, as from the heart; or as a river from its source, etc.

ἐκ-πορνεύω, to be given up to fornication, Ju. 7. (S.)*

ἐκ-πτύω, to reject, to loathe, Gal. iv. 14.*

ἐκ-ριζόω, ῶ, to root out, root up, Mat. xiii. 29, xv. 13; Lu. xvii. 6; Ju. 12.*

ἔκ-στασις, εως, ἡ, trance, Ac. x. 10; amazement, Mar. v. 42.

ἐκ-στρέφω, perf. pass. ἐξέστραμμαι, to change for the worse, to corrupt, Tit. iii. 11.*

ἐκ-ταράσσω, ξω, to agitate greatly, Ac. xvi. 20.*

ἐκ-τείνω, ω, 1st aor. ἐξέτεινα, to stretch out the hand, as Lu. v. 13; to cast out, as anchors, Ac. xxvii. 30.

ἐκ-τελέω, ῶ, έσω, to complete, Lu. xiv. 29, 30.*

ἐκτένεια, ας, ἡ, intentness, Ac. xxvi. 7.*

ἐκ-τενής, ές, intense, fervent, intent, 1 Pet. iv. 8; Ac. xii. 5 (W. H. -ώς); ἐκτενέστερον, comp. as adv., more earnestly, Lu. xxii. 44 (W.H. omit).*

ἐκτενῶς, adv., intently, earnest-

ly, 1 Pet. i. 22; Ac. xii. 5 (W. H.).*

ἐκ-τίθημι (see Gr. § 107, Wi. § 14, 1 b, Bu. 45 sq.), (1) to put out, expose an infant, Ac. vii. 21; (2) to expound, Ac. xi. 4, xviii. 26, xxviii. 23.*

ἐκ-τινάσσω, ξω, to shake off, Mat. x. 14; Mar. vi. 11; Ac. xiii. 51; to shake out, Ac. xviii. 6.*

ἕκτος, η, ον, ord. num., sixth.

ἐκτός, adv., generally as prep., with gen., without, besides, except, 1 Cor. vi. 18; Ac. xxvi. 22; ἐκτὸς εἰ μή, except, 1 Cor. xiv. 5; τὸ ἐκτός, the outside, Mat. xxiii. 26.

ἐκ-τρέπω, pass. in mid. sense, to turn from, to forsake, 1 Tim. i. 6, v. 15, vi. 20; 2 Tim. iv. 4; Heb. xii. 13.*

ἐκ-τρέφω, to nourish, Ep. v. 29; to bring up, Ep. vi. 4.*

ἔκ-τρωμα, ατος, τό, an abortive birth, an abortion, 1 Cor. xv. 8.*

ἐκ-φέρω, ἐξοίσω, to bring forth, carry out; espec. to burial, Ac. v. 6, 9; to produce, of the earth, Heb. vi. 8.

ἐκ-φεύγω, to flee out (abs., or with ἐκ), Ac. xvi. 27, xix. 16; to escape, 1 Th. v. 3; Ro. ii. 3.

ἐκ-φοβέω, ῶ, to terrify greatly, 2 Cor. x. 9.*

ἔκ-φοβος, ον, greatly terrified, Mar. ix. 6; Heb. xii. 21.*

ἐκ-φύω, 2d aor. pass. ἐξεφύην, to put forth, as a tree its leaves, Mat. xxiv. 32; Mar. xiii. 28.*

ἐκ-χέω, also ἐκχύνω; fut. ἐκχεῶ, 1st aor. ἐξέχεα (see Gr. § 96 c, Wi. § 13, 3 a, Bu. 68), to pour out, as Rev. xvi. 1–17; money, Jn. ii. 15; to shed blood, Lu. xi. 50; fig., to shed abroad, love, Ro. v. 5; pass., to be wholly given up to, Ju. 11.

ἐκ-χωρέω, ῶ, to depart from, Lu. xxi. 21.*

ἐκ-ψύχω, to expire, Ac. v. 5, 10, xii. 23.*

ἑκών, οῦσα, όν, voluntary, willing; used adverbially, Ro. viii. 20; 1 Cor. ix. 17.*

ἐλαία, ας, ἡ, an olive tree, Ro. xi. 17, 24; its fruit, the olive, Ja. iii. 12; τὸ ὅρος τῶν ἐλαιῶν, the Mount of Olives, Mar. xi. 1.

ἔλαιον, ου, τό, olive oil, Mat xxv. 3; Rev. vi. 6.

ἐλαιών, ῶνος, ὁ, an olive orchard, i.e., the Mount of Olives, Ac. i. 12. (S.)*

Ἐλαμίτης, ου, ὁ, an Elamite, i.e., inhabitant of the province of Elymais, Ac. ii. 9.*

ἐλάσσων or -ττων, ον, compar. of ἐλαχύς for μικρός, less; in excellence, Jn. ii. 10; in age, Ro. ix. 12; in rank, Heb. vii. 7; ἔλαττον, as adv., less, 1 Tim. v. 9.*

ἐλαττονέω, ῶ, to have less, to lack, 2 Cor. viii. 15.*

ἐλαττόω, ῶ, to make less or inferior, Heb. ii. 7, 9; pass., to decrease, Jn. iii. 30.*

ἐλαύνω, perf. part. ἐληλακώς, to drive, Lu. viii. 29; Ja. iii. 4; 2 Pet. ii. 17; to drive a ship, to row, Mar. vi. 48; Jn. vi. 19.*

ἐλαφρία, ας, ἡ, levity, inconstancy, 2 Cor. i. 17.*

ἐλαφρός, ά, όν, light, as a burden, Mat. xi. 30; 2 Cor. iv. 17.*

ἐλάχιστος, η, ον (superl. of ἐλαχύς for μικρός), smallest, least, in size, amount, or importance, Ja. iii. 4; Lu. xvi. 10; 1 Cor. vi. 2.

ἐλαχιστότερος, α, ον, a double comparison, less than the least, Ep. iii. 8. (N. T.)*

ἐλάω, see ἐλαύνω.

Ἐλεάζαρ, ὁ, Eleazar, Mat. i. 15.*

ἐλεάω (W. H., Rec. ἐλεέω), Ro. ix. 16; Ju. 22, 23.*

ἐλεγμός, οῦ, ὁ, reproof, 2 Tim iii. 16 (W. H.). (S.)*

ἔλεγξις, εως, ἡ, refutation, rebuke, 2 Pet. ii. 16. (S.)*

ἔλεγχος, ου, ὁ, evident demonstration, proof, Heb. xi. 1; 2 Tim. iii. 16 (not W. H.).*

ἐλέγχω, ω, to convict, refute, reprove, 1 Cor. xiv. 24; Jn. iii. 20; 1 Tim. v. 20.

ἐλεεινός, ή, όν, pitiable, miserable, 1 Cor. xv. 19; Rev. iii. 17.*

ἐλεέω, ῶ, to have mercy on, succor (acc.), Mat. ix. 27; Lu. xvi. 24; pass., to obtain mercy, Mat. v. 7.

ἐλεημοσύνη, ης, ἡ, mercy, pity; in N. T., alms, sometimes plur., Mat. vi. 4; Lu. xi. 41; Ac. ix. 36.

ἐλεήμων, ον, *full of pity, merciful,* Mat. v. 7; Heb. ii. 17.*

ἔλεος, ους, τό (and ον, ὁ, see Gr. § 32 a, Wi. § 9, note 2, Bu. 22), *mercy, pity,* especially on account of misery, Tit. iii. 5; Mat. ix. 13.

ἐλευθερία, ας, ἡ, *liberty, freedom,* from the Mosaic yoke, as 1 Cor. x. 29; Gal. ii. 4; from evil, as Ja. ii. 12; Ro. viii. 21; *license,* 2 Pet. ii. 19.

ἐλεύθερος, α, ον, *free,* as opposed to the condition of a slave; *delivered from obligation* (often with ἐκ, ἀπό); *at liberty to* (inf.); once with dat. of reference, Ro. vi. 20.

ἐλευθερόω, ῶ, *to set free* (generally with acc. and ἀπό); with modal dative, Gal. v. 1.

ἔλευσις, εως, ἡ (ἔρχομαι), *a coming, an advent,* Ac. vii. 52.*

ἐλεφάντινος, η, ον, *made of ivory,* Rev. xviii. 12.*

Ἐλιακείμ, ὁ (Heb.), *Eliakim,* Mat. i. 13; Lu. iii. 30.*

ἕλιγμα, ατος, τό, *a roll,* Jn. xix. 39 (W. H. for Rec. μίγμα).*

Ἐλιέζερ, ὁ (Heb.), *Eliezer,* Lu. iii. 29.*

Ἐλιούδ, ὁ (Heb.), *Eliud,* Mat. i. 14, 15.*

Ἐλισάβετ, ἡ (Heb. *Elisheba*), *Elisabeth,* Lu. i. 5, etc.

Ἐλισσαῖος, ου, ὁ, *Elisha,* Lu. iv. 27.*

ἐλίσσω, ίξω, as εἰλίσσω, *to roll up,* Heb. i. 12; Rev. vi. 14 (W. H.).*

ἕλκος, ους, τό, *a wound, an ulcer, a sore,* Lu. xvi. 21; Rev. xvi. 2, 11.*

ἑλκόω, ῶ, *to make a sore;* pass., *to be full of sores,* Lu. xvi. 20.*

ἑλκύω, σω, *to drag,* Ac. xvi. 19; *to draw,* a net, Jn. xxi. 6, 11; a sword, Jn. xviii. 10; *to draw over, to persuade,* Jn. vi. 44, xii. 32.* Syn.: σύρω always means to drag *by force;* ἑλκύω only *sometimes* involves force, often not.

ἕλκω (old form of foregoing), impf. εἷλκον, Ja. ii. 6; Ac. xxi. 30.*

Ἑλλάς, άδος, ἡ, *Hellas, Greece,* = Ἀχαῖα, Ac. xx. 2.*

Ἕλλην, ηνος, ὁ, *a Greek,* as distinguished (1) from βάρβαρος, *barbarian,* Ro. i. 14, and (2)

from Ἰουδαῖος, *Jew,* as Jn. vii. 35. Used for Greek proselytes to Judaism, Jn. xii. 20; Ac. xvii. 4.

Ἑλληνικός, ή, όν, *Grecian,* Lu. xxiii. 38 (W. H. omit); Rev. ix. 11.*

Ἑλληνίς, ίδος, ἡ, *a Greek* or *Gentile woman,* Mar. vii. 26; Ac. xvii. 12.*

Ἑλληνιστής, οῦ, ὁ (ἑλληνίζω, to *Hellenize,* or *adopt Greek manners and language*), *a Hellenist, Grecian Jew* (R. V.); a Jew by parentage and religion, but born in a Gentile country and speaking Greek, Ac. vi. 1, ix. 29, xi. 20.*

Ἑλληνιστί, adv., *in the Greek language,* Jn. xix. 20; Ac. xxi. 37.*

ἐλ-λογέω (ἐν; W. H. -άω), *to charge to, to put to one's account,* Ro. v. 13; Philem. 18. (N. T.)*

Ἐλμωδάμ (W. H. -μα-), ὁ, *Elmodam,* Lu. iii. 28.*

ἐλπίζω, att. fut. ἐλπιῶ, 1st aor. ἤλπισα, *to expect* (acc. or inf., or ὅτι); *to hope for* (acc.); *to trust in* (ἐπί, dat.; ἐν, once dat. only); *to direct hope towards* (εἰς, ἐπί, acc.).

ἐλπίς, ίδος, ἡ, *expectation, hope;* especially of the Christian hope. Met., (1) *the author,* as 1 Tim. i. 1; (2) *the object of hope,* as Tit. ii. 13 (in Ro. viii. 20 W. H. read ἐφ᾽ ἐλπίδι).

Ἐλύμας, α, ὁ (from Aram.), *Elymas,* Ac. xiii. 8.*

ἐλωΐ (prob. Aram. = Heb. ἠλί), *my God!* Mar. xv. 34; Mat. xxvii. 46 (W. H.); see ἠλί. (N. T.)*

ἐμαυτοῦ, ῆς, οῦ, *of myself,* a reflexive pron., found only in the gen., dat., and acc. cases; ἀπ᾽ ἐμαυτοῦ, *from myself,* Jn. v. 30.

ἐμ-βαίνω, 2d aor. ἐνέβην, part. ἐμβάς, *to go upon, into* (εἰς), always of entering a ship except Jn. v. 4 (W. H. omit).

ἐμ-βάλλω, *to cast into,* Lu. xii. 5.*

ἐμ-βάπτω, *to dip into,* Mat. xxvi. 23; Mar. xiv. 20; Jn. xiii. 26 (W. H. βάπτω).*

ἐμ-βατεύω, *to enter, to intrude, to pry into,* Col. ii. 18.*

ἐμ-βιβάζω, *to cause to enter, to put on board,* Ac. xxviι. 6.*

ἐμ-βλέπω, *to direct the eyes to anything, to look fixedly, to consider, to know by inspection* (acc., dat., or εἰς), Mar. viii. 25; Mat. xix. 26; Ac. xxii. 11.

ἐμ-βριμάομαι, ῶμαι, dep., *to snort, to be very angry,* Mar. xiv. 5; Jn. xi. 33, 38; *to charge sternly* (dat.), Mat. ix. 30; Mar. i. 43.*

ἐμέω, ῶ, 1st aor. inf. ἐμέσαι, *to vomit forth,* Rev. iii. 16.*

ἐμ-μαίνομαι, *to rage against* (dat.), Ac. xxvi. 11.*

Ἐμμανουήλ, ὁ (Heb. *God with us*), *Immanuel,* a name of Christ, Mat. i. 23. (S.)*

Ἐμμαούς, ἡ, *Emmaus,* a village a short distance from Jerusalem, Lu. xxiv. 13.*

ἐμ-μένω, *to remain* or *persevere in* (dat. or ἐν), Ac. xxviii. 30 (W. H.); Gal. iii. 10.

Ἐμμόρ, ὁ, *Emmor,* or *Hamor,* Ac. vii. 16.*

ἐμός, ή, όν, *mine,* denoting possession, power over, authorship, right, etc. See Gr. § 336, Wi. § 22, 7, Bu. 115 sq.

ἐμπαιγμονή, ῆς, ἡ, *mockery,* 2 Pet. iii. 3 (W. H.). (N. T.)*

ἐμπαιγμός, οῦ, ὁ, *a mocking, scoffing,* Heb. xi. 36. (S.)*

ἐμ-παίζω, ξω, *to mock* (abs. or dat.), Mar. x. 34, xv. 20; *to delude,* Mat. ii. 16.

ἐμπαίκτης, ου, ὁ, *a mocker,* 2 Pet. iii. 13; Ju. 18. (S.)*

ἐμ-περιπατέω, ῶ, ήσω, *to walk about in* (ἐν), 2 Cor. vi. 16. (S.)*

ἐμ-πίπλημι and -πλάω, ἐμπλήσω, ἐνέπλησα, part. pres. ἐμπιπλῶν, *to fill up, to satisfy,* as with food, etc. (gen.), Lu. i. 53; Ro. xv. 24.

ἐμ-πίπτω, *to fall into* or *among* (εἰς), Lu. x. 36; fig., *to incur,* as condemnation or punishment, 1 Tim. iii. 6; Heb. x. 31.

ἐμ-πλέκω, 2d aor. pass. ἐνεπλάκην, *to entangle, involve in,* 2 Tim. ii. 4; 2 Pet. ii. 20 (dat. of thing).*

ἐμ-πλοκή, ῆς, ἡ, *a plaiting, braiding,* of hair, 1 Pet. iii. 3.*

ἐμ-πνέω (W. H. ἐνπ-), *to breathe in, inhale* (gen.), Ac. ix. 1.*

ἐμ-πορεύομαι, dep., *to go about;* hence, *to trade, to traffic,* abs., Ja. iv. 13; *to use for gain* (acc.), 2 Pet. ii. 3.*

ἐμ-πορία, ας, ἡ, *trade, merchandise,* Mat. xxii. 5.*

ἐμ-πόριον, ου, τό, *emporium, a place for trading,* Jn. ii. 16.*

ἔμ-πορος, ου, ὁ, *a traveler, merchant, trader,* Mat. xiii. 45; Rev. xviii. 3, 11, 15, 23.*

ἐμ-πρήθω, σω, *to set on fire, to burn,* Mat. xxii. 7.*

ἔμ-προσθεν, adv., *before* (ἔμπροσθεν καὶ ὄπισθεν, *in front and behind,* Rev. iv. 6); as prep. (gen.), *before,* in presence of, Mat. x. 32; *before,* in rank, Jn. i. 15, 30.

ἐμ-πτύω, σω, *to spit upon* (dat. or εἰς), Mat. xxvii. 30; Mar. x. 34.

ἐμ-φανής, ές, *manifest* (dat.), Ac. x. 40; Ro. x. 20.*

ἐμφανίζω, ίσω, *to make manifest* (acc. and dat.), Jn. xiv. 22; Heb. ix. 24; *to disclose, make known* (ὅτι, or prepp. πρός, περί, etc.), Heb. xi. 14; Ac. xxv. 15.

ἔμ-φοβος, ον, *terrified, afraid,* Ac. x. 4, xxiv. 25.

ἐμ-φυσάω, ῶ, *to breathe upon,* acc., Jn. xx. 22.*

ἔμ-φυτος, ον, *implanted,* Ja. i. 21.*

ἐν, prep. gov. dat., *in,* generally as being or resting in; *within, among.* See Gr. § 295, Wi. § 48 a, Bu. 328 sq. ἐν- in composition has the force of *in, upon, into.* It is changed before γ, κ, ξ, and χ, into ἐγ-; before β, π, φ, ψ, and μ, into ἐμ-; and before λ, into ἐλ- (but W. H. prefer the unassimilated forms). The ν is, however, restored before the augment in verbs.

ἐν-αγκαλίζομαι, *to take into the arms,* Mar. ix. 36, x. 16.*

ἐν-άλιος, ον (ἅλς), *marine,* plur., *marine* animals, Ja. iii. 7.*

ἔν-αντι, adv., as prep. with gen., *in the presence of, before,* Lu. i. 8; Ac. viii. 21 (W. H.). (S.)*

ἐν-αντίος, α, ον, *over against, contrary,* of the wind, as Ac. xxvii. 4; *adverse, hostile,* as Ac. xxvi. 9; ἐξ ἐναντίας, *over against,* Mar. xv. 39. Neut., ἐναντίον, adv. as prep. with

gen., *in the presence of,* as Lu. xx. 26; Ac. vii. 10.

ἐν-άρχομαι, *to begin,* Gal. iii. 3; Phil. i. 6.*

ἔνατος, see ἔννατος.

ἐν-δεής, ές, *in want, destitute,* Ac. iv. 34.*

ἔν-δειγμα, ατος, τό, *proof, token,* 2 Th. i. 5.*

ἐν-δείκνυμι, N. T. mid., *to show, to manifest,* Ro. ix. 22; 2 Tim. iv. 14.

ἔνδειξις, εως, ἡ, *a proof, manifestation,* Ro. iii. 25, 26; 2 Cor. viii. 24; *a sign, token,* Phil. i. 28.*

ἕν-δεκα, οἱ, αἱ, τά, *eleven;* οἱ ἕνδεκα, *the eleven, i.e.,* apostles, Mat. xxviii. 16; Ac. i. 26.

ἐν-δέκατος, η, ον, *eleventh,* Mat. xx. 6, 9; Rev. xxi. 20.*

ἐν-δέχομαι, dep., *to allow;* only impersonally, οὐκ ἐνδέχεται, *it is not admissible* or *possible,* Lu. xiii. 33.*

ἐν-δημέω, ῶ, *to be at home,* 2 Cor. v. 6, 8, 9.*

ἐν-διδύσκω, *to put on, clothe,* Mar. xv. 17 (W. H.); mid., *to clothe one's self with* (acc.), Lu. viii. 27 (not W. H.), xvi. 19; Mar. xv. 17 (W. H.); see ἐνδύνω. (S.)*

ἔν-δικος, ον, *righteous, just,* Ro. iii. 8; Heb. ii. 2.*

ἐν-δόμησις, εως, ἡ, *the material of a building, a structure,* Rev. xxi. 18.*

ἐν-δοξάζω, σω, N. T. pass., *to be glorified in,* 2 Th. i. 10, 12. (S.)*

ἔν-δοξος, ον, *highly esteemed,* 1 Cor. iv. 10; *splendid, glorious,* Lu. xiii. 17; *of external appearance, splendid,* Lu. vii. 25; fig., *free from sin,* Ep. v. 27.*

ἔνδυμα, ατος, τό, *a garment, raiment,* Mat. iii. 4, xxviii. 3. (S.)

ἐν-δυναμόω, ῶ, *to strengthen,* Phil. iv. 13; 1 Tim. i. 12; pass., *to acquire strength, be strengthened,* Ac. ix. 22; Ro. iv. 20. (S.)

ἐν-δύνω (2 Tim. iii. 6) and ἐνδύω, *to clothe* or *to invest with* (two accs.); mid., *to enter, insinuate one's self into* (2 Tim. iii. 6), *to put on, clothe one's self with* (acc.); often fig., *to invest with.*

ἔν-δυσις, εως, ἡ, *a putting on of clothing,* 1 Pet. iii. 3.*

ἐν-έδρα, ας, ἡ, *an ambush,* Ac. xxiii. 16 (W. H.), xxv. 3.*

ἐν-εδρεύω, *to lie in ambush for* (acc.), Lu. xi. 54; Ac. xxiii. 21.*

ἐν-ειλέω, ῶ, 1st aor. ἐνείλησα, *to roll up, wrap in* (acc. and dat.), Mar. xv. 46.*

ἔν-ειμι, *to be in,* Lu. xi. 41, τὰ ἐνόντα, *such things as are in* (the platter, ver. 39), or *the things within your power.* For ἔνεστι, impers., see ἔνι.*

ἕνεκα or ἕνεκεν, sometimes εἵνεκεν, prep. with gen., *because of, by reason of, on account of; οὗ ἕνεκεν, because,* Lu. iv. 18; τίνος ἕνεκεν, *for what cause?* Ac. xix. 32.

ἐν-έργεια, ας, ἡ, *working, efficiency,* Ep. i. 19, 20, iv. 16; 2 Th. ii. 9.

ἐν-εργέω, ῶ, *to be operative, to work,* as Gal. ii. 8; trans., *to accomplish,* as 1 Cor. xii. 11; mid., *to work, to display activity,* 2 Cor. i. 6; 1 Th. ii. 13; part., ἐνεργουμένη, Ja. v. 16 (see R. V.).

ἐν-έργημα, ατος, τό, *working, effect;* plur., 1 Cor. xii. 6, 10.*

ἐν-εργής, ές, *active, effectual,* 1 Cor. xvi. 9; Heb. iv. 12; Philem. 6.*

ἐν-εστώς, perf. participle of ἐνίστημι.

ἐν-ευ-λογέω, ῶ, *to bless, to confer benefits on,* Ac. iii. 25 (W. H. εὐλ-); Gal. iii. 8. (S.)*

ἐν-έχω, (1) *to hold in, entangle,* only in pass. (dat.), Gal. v. 1; (2) *to set one's self against* (dat.), Mar. vi. 19; Lu. xi. 53.*

ἐνθά-δε, adv., *here,* Lu. xxiv. 41; Ac. xvii. 6; *hither,* Jn. iv. 15; Ac. xxv. 17.

ἐν-θυμέομαι, οῦμαι, dep. pass., *to revolve in mind, to think upon,* Mat. i. 20, ix. 4; Ac. x. 19 (W. H. διεν-).*

ἐν-θύμησις, εως, ἡ, *thought, reflection,* Mat. ix. 4, xii. 15; Ac. xvii. 29; Heb. iv. 12.*

ἔνι, perhaps contracted from ἔνεστι, impers., *there is in, is present,* 1 Cor. vi. 5 (W. H.); Gal. iii. 28; Col. iii. 11; Ja. i. 17.*

ἐνιαυτός, οῦ, ὁ, *a year,* Ac. xi. 26; Ja. iv. 13.

ἐν-ίστημι, to place in; in pf., plpf., and 2d aor., to be at hand, to threaten, 2 Th. ii. 2; 2 Tim. iii. 1; perf. part. ἐνεστηκώς, sync. ἐνεστώς, impending, or present, 1 Cor. vii. 26; Gal. i. 4; Heb. ix. 9; τὰ ἐνεστῶτα, present things, opp. to τὰ μέλλοντα, things to come, Ro. viii. 38; 1 Cor. iii. 22.*

ἐν-ισχύω, to invigorate, to strengthen, Lu. xxii. 43 (W. H. omit); Ac. ix. 19 (see W. H.).*

ἔννατος, η, ον (W. H. ἔνατος), ninth, Lu. xxiii. 44; Rev. xxi. 20.

ἐννέα, οἱ, αἱ, τά, nine, Lu. xvii. 17.*

ἐννενήκοντα-εννέα (W. H. as two words), ninety-nine, Mat. xviii. 12, 13; Lu. xv. 4, 7. (N. T.)*

ἐννεός, ά, όν (W. H. ἐνεός), dumb, speechless, as with amazement, Ac. ix. 7.*

ἐν-νεύω, to signify by a nod or sign (dat.), Lu. i. 62.*

ἔν-νοια, ας, ἡ (νοῦς), way of thinking, purpose, Heb. iv. 12; 1 Pet. iv. 1.*

ἔν-νομος, ον, bound by the law, 1 Cor. ix. 21; lawful, regular, Ac. xix. 39.*

ἔν-νυχος, ον (νύξ), in the night, neut. as adv., Mar. i. 35 (W. H. ἔννυχα).*

ἐν-οικέω, ῶ, ήσω, to dwell in (ἐν), Ro. viii. 11; Col. iii. 16.

ἑνότης, τητος, ἡ (εἷς), unity, unanimity, Ep. iv. 3, 13.*

ἐν-οχλέω, ῶ, to disturb, to occasion tumult, Heb. xii. 15; Lu. vi. 18 (W. H.).*

ἔν-οχος, ον, guilty of (gen. of the crime, or of that which is violated), 1 Cor. xi. 27; Mar. iii. 29; liable to (dat. of court, gen. of punishment), εἰς of the place of punishment), Mat. v. 21, 22; Mar. xiv. 64.

ἔν-ταλμα, ατος, τό, a precept, Mat. xv. 9; Mar. vii. 7; Col. ii. 22. (S.)*

ἐν-ταφιάζω, to prepare for burial, as by washing, swathing, adorning, anointing the body, Mat. xxvi. 12; Jn. xix. 40.*

ἐνταφιασμός, οῦ, ὁ, preparation

of a body for burial, Mar. xiv. 8; Jn. xii. 7. (N. T.)*

ἐν-τέλλω, in N. T. only mid. and pass.; fut. mid., ἐντελοῦμαι; perf., ἐντέταλμαι, to command, to enjoin (dat. of pers., or πρός with acc.), Ac. i. 2; Heb. ix 20.

ἐντεῦθεν, adv., hence; from this place or cause; repeated Jn. xix. 18, on this side and that.

ἔν-τευξις, εως, ἡ, prayer, intercession, 1 Tim. ii. 1, iv. 5.* Syn.: see αἴτημα.

ἔν-τιμος, ον, held in honor; precious, highly esteemed, Lu. vii. 2, xiv. 8; Phil. ii. 29; 1 Pet. ii. 4, 6.*

ἐντολή, ῆς, ἡ, a command or prohibition: of God's commands, 1 Cor. vii. 19; Christ's precepts or teachings, 1 Cor. xiv. 37; 1 Tim. vi. 14; traditions of the Rabbis, Tit. i. 14; αἱ ἐντολαί, the commandments, i.e., the ten.

ἐν-τόπιος, ον, ὁ (prop. adj.), a resident, Ac. xxi. 12.*

ἐντός, adv. as prep., with gen., within, Lu. xvii. 21; τὸ ἐντός, the inside, Mat. xxiii. 26.*

ἐν-τρέπω, ψω, 2d fut. pass., ἐντραπήσομαι; 2d aor. pass., ἐνετράπην; to put to shame, as 1 Cor. iv. 14; Tit. ii. 8; mid., to reverence, as Mat. xxi. 37.

ἐν-τρέφω, to nourish in (dat.); pass., fig., to be educated in, 1 Tim. iv. 6.*

ἔν-τρομος, ον, trembling through fear, Ac. vii. 32, xvi. 29; Heb. xii. 21.*

ἐν-τροπή, ῆς, η, shame, 1 Cor. vi. 5, xv. 34.* Syn.: see αἰδώς.

ἐν-τρυφάω, ῶ, to live luxuriously, to revel (with ἐν), 2 Pet. ii. 13.*

ἐν-τυγχάνω, to meet with, to address, Ac. xxv. 24; with ὑπέρ (gen.), to intercede for, Ro. viii. 27, 34; Heb. vii. 25; with κατά (gen.), to plead against, Ro. xi. 2.*

ἐν-τυλίσσω, ξω, to wrap in, to wrap up, Mat. xxvii. 59; Lu. xxiii. 53; Jn. xx. 7.*

ἐν-τυπόω, ῶ, to engrave, 2 Cor. iii. 7.*

ἐν-υβρίζω, σω, to treat contemptuously, Heb. x. 29.*

ἐν-υπνιάζομαι, dep. pass., to

dream (cognate acc.), Ac. ii. 17; to conceive impure thoughts, Ju. 8.*

ἐν-ύπνιον, ου, τό, a dream, Ac. ii. 17.*

ἐνώπιον (neut. of ἐνώπιος, from ἐν ὠπί, in view), as prep., with gen., before, in sight or presence of, Lu. i. 17; Rev. iii. 9; ἐνώπιον τοῦ θεοῦ, in the sight of God, Ro. xiv. 22; used in adjuration, 1 Tim. v. 21; χάρις ἐνώπιον τοῦ θεοῦ (Ac. vii. 4), favor with God.

Ἐνώς, ὁ, Enos, Lu. iii. 38.*

ἐν-ωτίζομαι, dep. mid. (ἐν ὠτίοις, in the ears), to listen to, Ac. ii. 14. (S.)*

Ἐνώχ, ὁ, Enoch, Lu. iii. 37; Ju. 14.*

ἐξ, prep., see ἐκ.

ἕξ, οἱ, αἱ, τά, card. num., six.

ἐξ-αγγέλλω, to declare abroad, celebrate, 1 Pet. ii. 9.*

ἐξ-αγοράζω, to redeem, Gal. iii. 13 (ἐκ), iv. 5; τὸν καιρόν, to buy up, redeem the opportunity from being lost, Ep. v. 16; Col. iv. 5.*

ἐξ-άγω, 2d aor. ἐξήγαγον, tr lead out (with ἔξω, ἐκ, εἰς).

ἐξ-αιρέω, ῶ (see Gr. § 103, 1 Wi. § 15, Bu. 53), to take out, pluck out, Mat. v. 29, xviii. 9; mid., to rescue, deliver, Ac. vii. 10, 34, xii. 11, xxiii. 27, xxvi. 17; Gal. i. 4.*

ἐξ-αίρω (see Gr. § 92), to lift up; to remove, 1 Cor. v. 2 (W. H. αἴρω), 13.*

ἐξ-αιτέω, ῶ, N. T., mid., to demand of; to ask for, Lu. xxii. 31.*

ἐξ-αίφνης (W. H. ἐξέφ-, except in Ac. xxii. 6), adv., suddenly, unexpectedly, Mar. xiii. 36.

ἐξ-ακολουθέω, ῶ, to follow after, to imitate, 2 Pet. i. 16, ii. 2, 15.*

ἑξακόσιοι, αι, α, six hundred, Rev. xiii. 18, xiv. 20.*

ἐξ-αλείφω, to wipe out, obliterate, Rev. iii. 5; Col. ii. 14; Ac. iii. 19; to wipe away (ἀπό or ἐκ), Rev. vii. 17, xxi. 4.*

ἐξ-άλλομαι, to leap up, Ac. iii. 8.*

ἐξ-ανά-στασις, εως, ἡ, a resurrection, Phil. iii. 11 (followed by ἐκ, W. H.).*

ἐξ-ανα-τέλλω, to spring up, as plants or corn, Mat. xiii. 5; Mar. iv. 5.*

ἐξ-αν-ίστημι, (1) trans. to raise

up offspring, Mar. xii. 19; Lu xx. 28; (2) 2d aor. intrans., *to rise up*, Ac. xv. 5.*

ἐξ-απατάω, ῶ, *to deceive thoroughly*, Ro. vii. 11; 2 Th. ii. 3.

ἐξάπινα, adv. (= ἐξαίφνης), *suddenly*, Mar. ix. 8. (S.)*

ἐξ-απορέομαι, οῦμαι, dep., *to be utterly without resource, to be in despair*, 2 Cor. i. 8, iv. 8.*

ἐξ-απο-στέλλω, *to send forth, send away*, Ac. vii. 12, xi. 12, xvii. 14.

ἐξ-αρτίζω, (1) *to completely furnish* (πρός, acc.), 2 Tim. iii. 17; (2) *to complete*, Ac. xxi. 5.*

ἐξ-αστράπτω, *to shine*, as lightning; of raiment, Lu. ix. 29. (S.)*

ἐξ-αυτῆς, adv. (sc. ὥρας), *from that very time, instantly*, as Mar. vi. 25; Ac. x. 33.

ἐξ-εγείρω, *to raise up*, Ro. ix. 17; 1 Cor. vi. 14.*

ἔξ-ειμι (εἶμι, see Gr. § 111, Bu. 50), *to go out*, Ac. xiii. 42, xvii. 15, xx. 7, xxvii. 43.*

ἔξ-ειμι (εἰμί), see ἔξεστι.

ἐξ-ελέγχω, *to convict, to rebuke sternly, to punish*, Ju. 15 (W. H. ἐλέγχω).*

ἐξ-έλκω, *to draw out* from the right way, Ja. i. 14.*

ἐξ-έραμα, ατος, τό, *vomit*, 2 Pet. ii. 22.*

ἐξερευνάω (W. H. -ραυ-), ῶ, *to search diligently*, 1 Pet. i. 10.*

ἐξ-έρχομαι (see Gr. § 103, 2, Wi. p. 33, § 15, Bu. 58), *to go* or *to come out of* (with gen. or ἐκ, ἀπό, ἔξω, παρά), *to go away, to depart, to issue* or *to spring from; to go forth;* of a rumor, *to be divulged* or *spread abroad; to emanate*, as thoughts from the heart, healing power from the Savior; *to go out*, i.e., *vanish*, as expiring hope, Ac. xvi. 19.

ἔξ-εστι, part. neut. ἐξόν (impers. from ἔξειμι), *it is lawful*, as Mat. xiv. 4; *it is becoming*, as Ac. xvi. 21; *it is possible*, as Mat. xx. 15. The part. is used in the same sense, with or without subst. verb, Mat. xii. 4; 2 Cor. xii. 4 (dat. and inf.).

ἐξ-ετάζω, *to search out, to examine strictly*, Mat. ii. 8, x. 11; Jn. xxi. 12.*

ἐξ-ηγέομαι, οῦμαι, dep. mid., *to narrate fully*, as Lu. xxiv. 35; *to declare*, as a teacher, as Jn. i. 18.

ἐξήκοντα, οἱ, αἱ, τά, *sixty*.

ἑξῆς, adv. (sc. ἔχω), *next in order*, only in the phrase τῇ ἑξῆς (sc. ἡμέρᾳ), *on the next day* (ἡμέρᾳ is expressed, Lu. ix. 37).

ἐξ-ηχέω, ῶ, N. T. only in pass., *to be sounded forth, promulgated widely*, 1 Th. i. 8.*

ἕξις, εως, ἡ (ἔχω), *habit, use*, Heb. v. 14.*

ἐξ-ίστημι, -ιστάω and -ιστάνω (see Gr. § 107, Wi. § 14, 1, Bu. 44 sq.), *to displace;* (1) trans., *to astonish*, Lu. xxiv. 22; Ac. viii. 9, 11; (2) 2d aor., perf. and mid., intrans., *to be astonished*, Mat. xii. 23; *to be insane*, 2 Cor. v. 13.

ἐξ-ισχύω, *to be perfectly able*, Ep. iii. 18.*

ἔξ-οδος, ου, ἡ, *an exit, departure*, Heb. xi. 22; *departure*, as from life, Lu. ix. 31; 2 Pet. i. 15.*

ἐξ-ολοθρεύω, *to destroy utterly*, Ac, iii. 23. (S)*

ἐξ-ομολογέω, ῶ, *to confess fully, to make acknowledgment of*, as of sins, etc.; in mid., *to acknowledge benefits conferred, to praise* (with dat.). Once, *to promise*, Lu. xxii. 6. (S.)

ἐξ-ορκίζω, *to adjure, put to oath*, Mat. xxvi. 63.*

ἐξ-ορκιστής, οῦ, ὁ, *an exorcist*, one who expels demons by conjuration, Ac. xix. 13.*

ἐξ-ορύσσω, ξω, *to dig out*, Gal. iv. 15; *to dig through*, Mar. ii. 4.*

ἐξ-ουδενέω=ἐξουθενέω, ῶ (οὐδείς), Mar. ix. 12 (W. H.).*

ἐξ-ουδενόω, ῶ = preceding, Mar. ix. 12 (Rec.).*

ἐξουθενέω, ῶ, *to make of no account, to despise utterly*, Lu. xviii. 9; Gal. iv. 14; perf. pass. part. ἐξουθενημένος, *contemned, despised*, 1 Cor. i. 28, vi. 4. (S.)

ἐξ-ουσία, ας, ἡ (ἔξεστι), (1) *power, ability*, as Jn. xix. 11; (2) *liberty, license, privilege, right*, as Ro. ix. 21; (3) *commission, authority*, as Mat. xxi. 23; (4) αἱ ἐξουσίαι, *the powers, i.e., rulers, magis-*

trates, Lu. xii. 11; *angels*, good and bad, Ep. i. 21, vi. 12. In 1 Cor. xi. 10, ἐξουσίαν, *a sign of the authority of a husband over his wife, i.e., the veil*.

ἐξ-ουσιάζω, *to exercise authority over* (gen.), Lu. xxii. 25; 1 Cor. vii. 4; pass., *to be under the power of* (ὑπό), 1 Cor. vi. 12.*

ἐξ-οχή, ῆς, ἡ, *eminence, distinction;* only in the phrase κατ' ἐξοχήν, *by way of distinction*, Ac. xxv. 23 (Gr. § 300β, 5).*

ἐξ-υπνίζω, σω, *to wake from sleep*, Jn. xi. 11. (S.)*

ἔξ-υπνος, ον, *roused out of sleep*, Ac. xvi. 27.*

ἔξω, adv., abs., or as prep. with gen., *without, outside;* οἱ ἔξω, *those without*, as Mar. iv. 11; 1 Cor. v. 12, 13. Used often after verbs of motion compounded with ἐκ.

ἔξωθεν, adv. of place, *from without;* τὸ ἔξωθεν, *the outside*, as Lu. xi. 39; οἱ ἔξωθεν, *those from without*, as 1 Tim. iii. 7, as prep. gen., Mar. vii. 15; Rev. xi. 2.

ἐξ-ωθέω, ῶ, *to drive out, expel*, Ac. vii. 45; *to propel*, as a vessel, Ac. xxvii. 39 (not W. H. text).*

ἐξώτερος, α, ον (comp of ἔξω), *outer*, in the phrase "outer darkness," Mat. viii. 12, xxii. 13, xxv. 30. (S.)*

ἔοικα, see εἴκω.

ἑορτάζω, *to keep* or *celebrate a feast*, 1 Cor. v. 8.*

ἑορτή, ῆς, ἡ, *a feast, a festival*, used of Jewish feasts, especially of the Passover, as Lu. ii. 41, xxii. 1.

ἐπ-αγγελία, ας, ἡ, (1) *a promise*, as 2 Cor. i. 20; Ac. xxiii. 21, generally plur.; *the promises*, specially, e.g., to Abraham, or those of the Gospel, as 2 Tim. i. 1; (2) met., *the thing promised*, as Ac. ii. 33; Heb. xi. 13, 33, 39.

ἐπ-αγγέλλω, mid. in N. T., except pass., Gal. iii. 19, (1) *to promise*, with dat., or acc. and dat., or inf., once cognate acc., 1 Jn. ii. 25; (2) *to make profession* or *avowal of* (acc.), 1 Tim. ii. 10, vi. 21.

ἐπ-άγγελμα, ατος, τό, *a promise,*
2 Pet. i. 4, iii. 13.*

ἐπ-άγω, *to bring upon,* Ac. v.
28; 2 Pet. ii. 1, 5.*

ἐπ-αγωνίζομαι, *to contend earnestly for* (dat.), Ju. 3.*

ἐπ-αθροίζω, pass., *to gather together,* Lu. xi. 29.*

Ἐπ-αίνετος, ου, ὁ, *Epænetus,*
Ro. xvi. 5.*

ἐπ-αινέω, ῶ, έσω, 1st aor. ἐπῄνεσα, *to commend, to praise,*
Lu. xvi. 8; Ro. xv. 11; 1 Cor.
xi. 2, 17, 22.*

ἔπ-αινος, ου, ὁ, *commendation,
praise,* Ro. ii. 29; Ep. i. 6,
12, 14; Phil. i. 11.

ἐπ-αίρω (see Gr. § 92), *to raise
up,* as hoisting a sail, Ac.
xxvii. 40; *to lift up,* as the
eyes, the hands in prayer,
the head in courage, the
heel against, or in opposition; pass., *to be lifted up*
2 Cor. xi. 20, of the ascension of Christ, Ac. i. 9.

ἐπ-αισχύνομαι, *to be ashamed,*
abs., 2 Tim. i. 12; *to be ashamed of* (acc. or ἐπί, dat.),
Mar. viii. 38; Ro. vi. 21.

ἐπ-αιτέω, ῶ, *to beg, to ask alms,*
Lu. xvi. 3, xviii. 35 (W. H.).*

ἐπ-ακολουθέω, ῶ, *to follow after*
(dat.); fig., 1 Tim. v. 10, 24;
1 Pet. ii. 21; Mar. xvi. 20
(see W. H.).*

ἐπ-ακούω, *to hearken to favorably* (gen. pers.), 2 Cor. vi.
2.*

ἐπ-ακροάομαι, ῶμαι, *to hear,
listen to* (gen. pers.), Ac. xvi.
25.*

ἐπάν, conj. (ἐπεὶ ἄν), *after, when*
(subj.), Mat. ii. 8; Lu. xi. 22,
34.*

ἐπ-άναγκες, adv., *necessarily*
(with art.), Ac. xv. 28.*

ἐπ-αν-άγω, trans., *to put* a vessel
out to sea, Lu. v. 3, 4; intrans., *to return,* Mat. xxi.
18.*

ἐν-ανα-μιμνήσκω, *to remind* one
again (acc.), Ro. xv. 15.*

ἐπ-ανα-παύομαι, *to rest upon*
(ἐπί, acc.), Lu. x. 6; *to rely,
to trust in* (dat.), Ro. ii. 17.
(S.)*

ἐπ-αν-έρχομαι, *to come back
again,* Lu. x. 35, xix. 15.*

ἐπ-αν-ίστημι, N. T. mid., *to rise
up against* (ἐπί, acc.), Mat.
x. 21; Mar. xiii. 12.*

ἐπ-αν-όρθωσις, εως, ἡ, *correction, reformation,* 2 Tim. iii.
16.*

ἐπ-άνω, adv., also used as prep.
gen., *above, upon; more than,*
in price or number; *superior
to,* in authority.

ἐπ-άρατος, ον, *accursed,* Jn. vii.
49 (W. H.).*

ἐπ-αρκέω, ῶ, έσω, *to aid, to relieve* (dat.), 1 Tim. v. 10, 16.*

ἐπ-αρχία, ας, ἡ, *a province,* a
region subject to a prefect,
Ac. xxiii. 34, xxv. 1.*

ἔπ-αυλις, εως, ἡ, *a dwelling,* Ac.
i. 20.*

ἐπ-αύριον, adv., *on the morrow,*
τῇ ἐπαύριον (ἡμέρᾳ), *on the
next day,* Mar. xi. 12. (S.)

ἐπ-αυτο-φώρῳ = ἐπ᾽ αὐτό-φώρῳ.

Ἐπαφρᾶς, ᾶ, ὁ, *Epaphras* of
Colossæ, Col. i. 7, iv. 12;
Philem. 23.*

ἐπ-αφρίζω, *to foam up* or *out*
(acc.), Ju. 13.*

Ἐπαφρόδιτος, ου, ὁ, *Epaphroditus,* a Macedonian, Phil. ii.
25, iv. 18.*

ἐπ-εγείρω, *to raise up, to excite
against* (ἐπί, acc., or κατά,
gen.), Ac. xiii. 50, xiv. 2.*

ἐπεί, conj., (1) of time, *after,*
only Lu. vii. 1 (W. H. ἐπειδή);
(2) of reason, *since, because,
seeing that,* Lu. i. 34; Jn. xiii.
29.

ἐπει-δή, conj., *since, inasmuch
as,* Lu. xi. 6; Phil. ii. 26; of
time, *after that,* only Lu. vii.
1 (W. H.).

ἐπει-δή-περ, conj., *since verily,
forasmuch as,* Lu. i. 1.*

ἐπ-εῖδον, see ἐφοράω.

ἔπ-ειμι (εἶμι, Gr. § 111, Bu. 50),
to come after, to follow; only
in part., ἐπιών, οὖσα, όν, *following,* Ac. vii. 26, xxiii. 11;
τῇ ἐπιούσῃ (sc. ἡμέρᾳ), *on the
following day,* Ac. xvi. 11,
xx. 15, xxi. 18.*

ἐπεί-περ, conj., *since indeed,*
Ro. iii. 30 (W. H. εἴπερ).*

ἐπ-εισ-αγωγή, ῆς, ἡ, *a bringing
in besides,* Heb. vii. 19.*

ἔπ-ειτα, adv., *thereupon, thereafter;* marking succession of
time, as Gal. i. 18; also of
order, as 1 Cor. xv. 46; 1
Th. iv. 17.

ἐπ-έκεινα (sc. μέρη), adv. with
gen., *beyond,* Ac. vii. 43.*

ἐπ-εκ-τείνω, in mid., *to stretch
forward to* (dat.), Phil. iii.
14.*

ἐπεν-δύτης, ου, ὁ, *an upper garment,* Jn. xxi. 7.*

ἐπ-εν-δύω, in mid., *to put on
over,* as an upper garment,
2 Cor. v. 2, 4.*

ἐπ-έρχομαι, *to come on, approach,
overtake, impend,* Ep. ii. 7;
Ac. viii. 24; *to attack,* Lu. xi.
22; τὰ ἐπερχόμενα, *the things
that are coming on* (dat.), Lu.
xxi. 26.

ἐπ-ερωτάω, ῶ, (1) *to interrogate,
to question* (two accs., or acc.
and περί, gen., or with εἰ,
τίς, etc.), Mat. xii. 10; Lu.
ii. 46; Ac. xxiii. 34; *to inquire after* God, Ro. x. 20;
(2) *to demand of* (acc. and
inf.), Mat. xvi. 1.

ἐπ-ερώτημα, ατος, τό, probably
inquiry, or *earnest desire,* 1
Pet. iii. 21; see R. V.*

ἐπ-έχω, (1) *to apply* (the mind)
to (dat.), *give attention to,* Lu.
xiv. 7; Ac. iii. 5; 1 Tim. iv.
16; (2) *to hold out, to exhibit,*
Phil. ii. 16; (3) *to delay, tarry,*
Ac. xix. 22.*

ἐπηρεάζω, *to insult, to treat
abusively,* Mat. v. 44 (not W.
H.); Lu. vi. 28; *to accuse
falsely* (acc. of charge), 1 Pet.
iii. 16.*

ἐπί, a preposition governing
gen., dat., or acc.; general
signification, *upon.* For its
various applications, see Gr.
§ 305, Wi. §§ 47g, 48c, 49l,
52, 4, 7), Bu. 336 sq. ἐπί-,
in composition, signifies *motion upon, towards,* or *against;
rest on, over,* or *at; addition,
succession, repetition, renewal;* and it is often intensive.

ἐπι-βαίνω, *to go upon* a ship, *to
mount* a horse or ass, *to come
to* or *into* a country (ἐπί, acc.,
εἰς, or simple dat.), Mat. xxi.
5; Ac. xx. 18, xxi. 2, 4 (W.
H.), 6 (W. H. ἐμβ-), xxv. 1,
xxvii. 2.*

ἐπι-βάλλω, (1) trans., *to cast
upon,* as Mar. xi. 7; *to put
on,* as a patch on a garment,
Lu. v. 36; *to lay upon,* Lu.
xx. 19; Jn. vii. 30; (2) intrans., *to rush upon,* Mar. iv.
37; *to fix the mind steadfastly
on* (dat.), Mar. xiv. 72; (3)
part., ἐπιβάλλων, *falling to*
his share, Lu. xv. 12.

ἐπι-βαρέω, ῶ. *to burden;* fig., 2

Cor. ii. 5; 1 Th. ii. 9; 2 Th. iii. 8.*

ἐπι-βιβάζω, *to cause to mount, to place upon*, Lu. x. 34, xix. 35; Ac. xxiii. 24.*

ἐπι-βλέπω, *to look upon* with favor (with ἐπί), Lu. i. 48, ix. 38; Ja. ii. 3.*

ἐπί-βλημα, ατος, τό, *a patch* on a garment, Mat. ix. 16; Mar. ii. 21; Lu. v. 36.*

ἐπι-βοάω, ῶ, *to cry out*, Ac. xxv. 24 (W. H. βοάω).*

ἐπι-βουλή, ῆς, ἡ, *a design against, a plot*, Ac. ix. 24, xx. 3, 19 (plur.), xxiii. 30.*

ἐπι-γαμβρεύω, *to marry a deceased brother's wife* (acc.), Mat. xxii. 24. (S.)*

ἐπί-γειος, ον, *earthly, belonging to the earth*, 2 Cor. v. 1; Phil. ii. 10; τὰ ἐπίγεια, *earthly things*, Phil. iii. 19.

ἐπι-γίνομαι, *to arise, spring up*, as a wind, Ac. xxviii. 13.*

ἐπι-γινώσκω, (1) *to know clearly, understand, discern;* (2) *to acknowledge;* (3) *to recognize;* (4) *to learn* (ὅτι), *become acquainted with* (acc.).

ἐπί-γνωσις, εως, ἡ, *accurate knowledge*, Ro. x. 2, Ep. i. 17; Heb. x. 26. *Syn.:* see γνῶσις.

ἐπι-γραφή, ῆς, ἡ, *an inscription, a title*, as Lu. xx. 24, xxiii. 38.

ἐπι-γράφω, ψω, *to inscribe, write upon*, as Mar. xv. 26; Rev. xxi. 12.

ἐπι-δείκνυμι (see Gr. § 114, Bu. 45), (1) *to show, exhibit*, Mat. xxiv. 1; Lu. xvii. 14; (2) *to demonstrate, prove* by argument, Ac. xviii. 28; Heb. vi. 17.

ἐπι-δέχομαι, *to receive hospitably*, 3 Jn. 10; *to accept, admit*, 3 Jn. 9.*

ἐπι-δημέω, ῶ, *to sojourn*, as foreigners in a country, Ac. ii. 10, xvii. 21.*

ἐπι-δια-τάσσομαι, *to ordain besides*, Gal. iii. 15. (N.T.)*

ἐπι-δίδωμι, *to deliver, to give up* (acc. and dat.), as Mat. vii. 9; Ac. xv. 30; *to give way* to the wind, Ac. xxvii. 15.

ἐπι-δι-ορθόω, *to set in order besides*, Tit. i. 5.*

ἐπι-δύω, *to set*, as the sun, Ep. iv. 26.*

ἐπιείκεια, ας, ἡ, *clemency, gen-* tleness, Ac. xxiv. 4; 2 Cor. x. 1.*

ἐπι-εικής, ές, *gentle, mild*, Phil. iv. 5; 1 Tim. iii. 3; Tit. iii. 2; Ja. iii. 17; 1 Pet. ii. 18.*

ἐπι-ζητέω, ῶ, *to seek for, search for*, Ac. xii. 19; *to desire*, Mat. vi. 32; Ac. xiii. 7; *to demand*, Mat. xii. 39, xvi. 4.

ἐπι-θανάτιος, ον, *condemned to death*, 1 Cor. iv. 9.*

ἐπί-θεσις, εως, ἡ, *a laying on* of hands, Ac. viii. 18; 1 Tim. iv. 14; 2 Tim. i. 6; Heb. vi. 2.*

ἐπι-θυμέω, ῶ, *to long for, to covet, to lust after*, Ja. iv. 2; Ro. vii. 7; Ac. xx. 33. (On Lu. xxii. 15, see Gr. § 280b, Wi. § 54, 3, Bu. 184.)

ἐπι-θυμητής, οῦ, ὁ, *an eager desirer of*, 1 Cor. x. 6.*

ἐπι-θυμία, ας, ἡ, *desire, eagerness for*, 1 Th. ii. 17; generally in a bad sense, *inordinate desire, lust, cupidity*, Ja. i. 14, 15; 2 Pet. ii. 10.

ἐπι-καθίζω, *to sit upon*, Mat. xxi. 7.*

ἐπι-καλέω, ῶ, ἐσω, *to call upon, to call by name, to invoke* in prayer, Ac. vii. 59 (abs.); Ro. x. 12, 14 (acc.); mid., *to appeal to* (acc.), Ac. xxv. 11; pass., *to be called* or *surnamed*, Lu. xxii. 3; Ac. xv. 17.

ἐπι-κάλυμμα, ατος, τό, *a covering, a cloak, a pretext*, 1 Pet. ii. 16.*

ἐπι-καλύπτω, *to cover over*, of sins, *i.e., to pardon*, Ro. iv. 7 (from S.).*

ἐπι-κατ-άρατος, ον, *accursed, doomed to punishment* or *destruction*, Jn. vii. 49 (W. H. ἐπάρατος); Gal. iii. 10, 13 (from S.).*

ἐπί-κειμαι, *to lie upon* (dat.), Jn. xi. 38, xxi. 9; so *to press upon*, as the multitude upon Christ, Lu. v. 1; as a tempest on a ship, Ac. xxvii. 20; fig., *to be laid on*, as necessity, 1 Cor. ix. 16; *to be laid* or *imposed upon*, as by a law, Heb. ix. 10; *to be urgent with entreaties*, Lu. xxiii. 23.*

'Επικούρειος, ου, ὁ, *an Epicurean*, a follower of Epicurus, Ac. xvii. 18.*

ἐπι-κουρία, ας, ἡ (κοῦρος, *help*), *help, aid*, Ac. xxvi. 22.*

ἐπι-κρίνω, *to decree, to give sentence* (acc. and inf.), Lu. xxiii. 24.*

ἐπι-λαμβάνω, N. T. mid., *to take hold of* (gen.), in kindness, as Lu. ix. 47; Ac. ix. 27; Heb. ii. 16; *to seize*, as a prisoner, Ac. xxi. 30, 33; met., *to lay hold of*, so as to possess, 1 Tim. vi. 12, 19.

ἐπι-λανθάνομαι, dep., *to forget, neglect* (inf., gen. or acc.), Mat. xvi. 5; Heb. vi. 10; part. perf. pass., ἐπιλελησμένος, *forgotten*, Lu. xii. 6.

ἐπι-λέγω, in pass., *to be named*, Jn. v. 2; mid., *to choose*, Ac. xv. 40.*

ἐπι-λείπω, λείψω, *not to suffice, to fail*, Heb. xi. 32.*

ἐπι-λείχω, *to lick over*, Lu. xvi. 21 (W. H.). (N. T.)*

ἐπι-λησμονή, ῆς, ἡ, *forgetfulness*, Ja. i. 25; see Gr. § 257. (Ap.)*

ἐπί-λοιπος, ον, *remaining over*, 1 Pet. iv. 2.*

ἐπί-λυσις, εως, ἡ, *an unloosing, interpretation*, 2 Pet. i. 20. (See ἴδιος.)*

ἐπι-λύω, *to explain, interpret*, Mar. iv. 34; *to decide*, as a debated question, Ac. xix. 39.*

ἐπι-μαρτυρέω, ῶ, *to testify earnestly*, 1 Pet. v. 12.*

ἐπι-μέλεια, ας, ἡ, *care, attention*, Ac. xxvii. 3.*

ἐπι-μέλομαι and έομαι, οῦμαι, fut. ήσομαι, *to take care of* (gen.), Lu. x. 34, 35; 1 Tim. iii. 5.*

ἐπι-μελῶς, adv., *carefully, diligently*, Lu. xv. 8.*

ἐπι-μένω, μενῶ, (1) *to remain, continue*, 1 Cor. xvi. 8; Gal. i. 18; (2) met., *to be constant, to persevere* (dat.), Ro. vi. 1; 1 Tim. iv. 16.

ἐπι-νεύω, *to nod to, to assent*, Ac. xviii. 20.*

ἐπί-νοια, ας, ἡ, *thought, purpose*, Ac. viii. 22.*

ἐπι-ορκέω, ῶ, ήσω, *to swear falsely*, Mat. v. 33.*

ἐπί-ορκος, ον, *perjured*, 1 Tim. i. 10.*

ἐπιούσιος, ον, probably from ἐπιοῦσα (ἔπειμι), *for the morrow, i.e., necessary* or *sufficient*, Mat. vi. 11; Lu. xi. 3. (N.T.)*

ἐπι-πίπτω, to fall upon (ἐπί, acc.), rush upon, Mar. iii. 10 (dat.); fig., to come upon (dat., or ἐπί, acc. or dat.), as an emotion, etc., Lu. i. 12; Ac. viii. 16.

ἐπι-πλήσσω, to rebuke, to chide, 1 Tim. v. 1.*

ἐπι-ποθέω, ῶ, to desire earnestly, to long for or after (inf. or acc.), as 2 Cor v. 2; to lust, abs., Ja. iv. 5.

ἐπι-πόθησις, εως, ἡ, longing, 2 Cor. vii. 7, 11. (N. T.)*

ἐπι-πόθητος, ον, longed for, Phil. iv. 1. (N. T.)*

ἐπι-ποθία, ας, ἡ, like ἐπιπόθησις, longing, Ro. xv. 23. (N. T.)*

ἐπι-πορεύομαι, dep., mid., to journey to (πρός), Lu. viii. 4.*

ἐπι-ρράπτω, to sew to, or upon, Mar. ii. 21 (ἐπί, dat.). (N. T.)*

ἐπι-ρρίπτω, to cast, or throw upon, Lu. xix. 35; of care cast upon God, 1 Pet. v. 7 (ἐπί, acc.).*

ἐπί-σημος, ον, remarkable, distinguished, in either a bad or good sense, Mat. xxvii. 16; Ro. xvi. 7.*

ἐπι-σιτισμός, οῦ, ὁ, food, provisions, Lu. ix. 12.*

ἐπι-σκέπτομαι, σκέψομαι, dep., to look upon, to visit, as Ac. vii. 23; Mat. xxv. 36, 43; of God, Ac. xv. 14; to look out, to select, Ac. vi. 3.

ἐπι-σκευάζομαι, see ἀποσκ-.

ἐπι-σκηνόω, ῶ, to fix a tent upon, to dwell, or remain on (ἐπί, acc.), 2 Cor. xii. 9.*

ἐπι-σκιάζω, άσω, to overshadow (acc. or dat.), Mat. xvii. 5; Mar. ix. 7; Lu. i. 35, ix. 34; Ac. v. 15.*

ἐπι-σκοπέω, ῶ, to act as ἐπίσκοπος, to oversee, to care for, 1 Pet. v. 2 (W. H. omit); μή, lest, Heb. xii. 15.*

ἐπι-σκοπή, ῆς, ἡ, (1) visitation for kind and gracious purposes, Lu. xix. 44; 1 Pet. ii. 12; (2) office, charge, Ac. i. 20 (from S.); (3) the office of a bishop, 1 Tim. iii. 1. (S.)*

ἐπί-σκοπος, ου, ὁ, (1) one who inspects, or superintends, of Christ, 1 Pet. ii. 25; (2) an overseer of a church, bishop, Ac. xx. 28; Phil. i. 1; 1 Tim. iii. 2· Tit. i. 7.*

ἐπι-σπάω, ῶ, to become uncircumcised, 1 Cor. vii. 18.*

ἐπι-σπείρω, to sow in addition, Mat. xiii. 25 (W. H.).*

ἐπ-ίσταμαι, dep., to know well, to understand (acc.), to know, with ὅτι, ὡς, etc.

ἐπί-στασις, εως, ἡ (W. H.), approach, onset, Ac. xxiv. 12; 2 Cor. xi. 28.*

ἐπι-στάτης, ου, ὁ, superintendent, master; only in Lu., in voc., ἐπιστάτα, addressed to Jesus, Master, v. 5, viii. 24, 45, ix. 33, 49, xvii. 13.*

ἐπι-στέλλω, to send by letter to, to write, Ac. xv. 20, xxi. 25 (W. H. ἀποστ-); Heb. xiii. 22.*

ἐπι-στήμων, ον, skillful, experienced, Ja. iii. 13.*

ἐπι-στηρίζω, to establish besides, confirm, Ac. xiv. 22, xv. 32, 41, xviii. 23 (not W. H.).*

ἐπι-στολή, ῆς, ἡ, an epistle, a letter, Ac. xv. 30; 2 Cor. x. 10.

ἐπι-στομίζω, to stop the mouth of, Tit. i. 11.*

ἐπι-στρέφω, ψω, (1) trans., to cause to turn (acc. and ἐπί), as to God, or to the worship of God, Ac. ix. 35; (2) intrans., to return, to turn back, either to good or evil, Ac. xxvi. 18; 2 Pet. ii. 21; to return upon, as a refused salutation, Mat. x. 13 (ἐπί, εἰς, πρός).

ἐπι-στροφή, ῆς, ἡ, a turning, conversion, Ac. xv. 3.*

ἐπι-συν-άγω, άξω, to gather together, into one place, as Mat. xxiii. 37.

ἐπι-συν-αγωγή, ῆς, ἡ, a gathering together, in one place, 2 Th. ii. 1; Heb. x. 25. (Ap.)*

ἐπι-συν-τρέχω, to run together besides, Mar. ix. 25. (N. T.)*

ἐπι-σύ-στασις, εως, ἡ (W. H. ἐπίστασις), (1) a seditious concourse, Ac. xxiv. 12; (2) a troublesome throng, 2 Cor. xi. 28. (S.)*

ἐπι-σφαλής, ές, likely to fall, dangerous, Ac. xxvii. 9.*

ἐπ-ισχύω, to be more urgent, Lu. xxiii. 5.*

ἐπι-σωρεύω, εύσω, to heap up, to obtain a multitude of, 2 Tim. iv. 3.*

ἐπι-ταγή, ῆς, ἡ, a command, an injunction, 2 Cor. viii. 8; Tit. ii. 15.

ἐπι-τάσσω, ξω, to command (abs.), Lu. xiv. 22; enjoin upon (dat. of pers., thing in acc. or inf.), Mar. ix. 25.

ἐπι-τελέω, ῶ, έσω, to bring to an end, to perform, as a service, Heb. ix. 6; mid., to come to an end, to leave off, Gal. iii. 3; pass., of sufferings, to be imposed upon, 1 Pet. v. 9.

ἐπιτήδειος, α, ον, fit, needful, Ja. ii. 16.*

ἐπι-τίθημι, θήσω, to put, place, or lay upon (with acc. and dat., or ἐπί, acc. or gen.), as the hands (to heal), as stripes, etc.; of gifts, to load with, Ac. xxviii. 10; mid., to rush upon in hostility, to oppose, Ac. xviii. 10.

ἐπι-τιμάω, ῶ, to rebuke (dat.), Lu. xvii. 3; to admonish (ἵνα), Mat. xii. 16.

ἐπι-τιμία, ας, ἡ, punishment, 2 Cor. ii. 6.*

ἐπι-τρέπω, to allow, permit, Mat. viii. 21; Heb. vi. 3.

ἐπι-τροπή, ῆς, ἡ, commission, full power, Ac. xxvi. 12.*

ἐπί-τροπος, ου, ὁ, one who is intrusted with; (1) a steward, Mat. xx. 8; Lu. viii. 3; (2) a tutor, Gal. iv. 2.*

ἐπι-τυγχάνω, to attain, acquire, (gen. or acc.), Ro. xi. 7; Heb. vi. 15, xi. 33; Ja. iv. 2.*

ἐπι-φαίνω, 1st aor. inf. ἐπιφᾶναι, 2d aor. pass. ἐπεφάνην, (1) to appear, as stars, Ac. xxvii. 20; (2) to shine upon (dat.), Lu. i. 79; (3) met., to be clearly known, Tit. ii. 11, iii. 4.*

ἐπιφάνεια, ας, ἡ, appearance, the advent of Christ, past and future, 1 Tim. vi. 14; 2 Tim. i. 10, iv. 1, 8; Tit. ii. 13; manifestation, 2 Th. ii. 8.* Syn.: see ἀποκάλυψις.

ἐπιφανής, ές, glorious, illustrious, Ac. ii. 20.*

ἐπι-φαύω, or -φαύσκω, fut. σω, to shine upon, give light to (dat.), Ep. v. 14. (S.)*

ἐπι-φέρω (see Gr. § 103, 6), to bring to (ἐπί, acc.), Ac. xix. 12 (not W. H.); to superadd, Phil. i. 16; to bring upon, inflict, as punishment, Ro. iii. 5; to bring against, as an accusation, Ac. xxv. 18 (not W. H.); Ju. 9.*

ἐπι-φωνέω, ῶ, to cry out, to shout, Lu. xxiii. 21; Ac. xii. 22, xxi. 34, xxii. 24 (W. H.).*

ἐπι-φώσκω, to grow light, to dawn, Mat. xxviii. 1; Lu. xxiii. 54.*

ἐπι-χειρέω, ῶ, to take in hand, undertake, Lu. i. 1; Ac. ix. 29, xix. 13.*

ἐπι-χέω, to pour upon, Lu. x. 34.*

ἐπι-χορηγέω, ῶ, to supply, 2 Pet. i. 5; 2 Cor. ix. 10; Gal. iii. 5; pass., to be furnished or supplied, Col. ii. 19; 2 Pet. i. 11.*

ἐπι-χορηγία, as, ἡ, a supply, Phil. i. 19; Ep. iv. 16. (N. T.)*

ἐπι-χρίω, to spread on, anoint (ἐπί, acc.), Jn. ix. 6 (not W. H.), 11.*

ἐπ-οικοδομέω, ῶ, to build upon (ἐπί, acc. or dat.), fig., 1 Cor. iii. 10–14; Ep. ii. 20; to build up, edify, Ac. xx. 32 (not W. H.); Col. ii. 7; Ju. 20.*

ἐπ-οκέλλω, to force forward, to run (a ship) aground, Ac. xxvii. 41 (ἐπικέλλω, W. H.).*

ἐπ-ονομάζω, to name, or call by a name of honor, pass. only, Ro. ii. 17.*

ἐπ-οπτεύω, to look upon, view attentively, 1 Pet. ii. 12, iii. 2.*

ἐπ-όπτης, ου, ὁ, an eye-witness, 2 Pet. i. 16.*

ἔπος, ους, τό, a word; ὡς ἔπος εἰπεῖν, so to speak, Heb. vii. 9.*

ἐπ-ουράνιος, ον, heavenly, celestial, of God, Mat. xviii. 35 (W. H. οὐράνιος); of intelligent beings, Phil. ii. 10; of the starry bodies, 1 Cor. xv. 40; so of kingdom, country, etc.; neut. plur., τὰ ἐπουράνια, heavenly things, or places, Jn. iii. 12; Ep. i. 3, 20, ii. 6, iii. 10; Heb. viii. 5, ix. 23.

ἑπτά, οἱ, αἱ, τά, card. num., seven, Lu. ii. 36; Ac. vi. 3; often symbol. in Revelation; οἱ ἑπτά, the seven deacons, Ac. xxi. 8.

ἑπτάκις, num. adv., seven times, Mat. xviii. 21, 22; Lu. xvii. 4.*

ἑπτακισ-χίλιοι, αι, α, card.num., seven thousand, Ro. xi. 4.*

ἔπω, see εἶπον.

Ἔραστος, ου, ὁ, Erastus, (1) Ac. xix. 22; (2) Ro. xvi. 23. Which is meant in 2 Tim. iv. 20 is uncertain.*

ἐργάζομαι, σομαι, dep., perf. in pass. sense, εἰργασμαι; (1) abs., to work, to trade, Lu. xiii. 14; Mat. xxv. 16; (2) to perform, do, Col. iii. 23; Jn. vi. 28; (3) to practice, as virtues, to commit, as sin, Ac. x. 35; Ja. ii. 9; (4) to acquire by labor, Jn. vi. 27.

ἐργασία, as, ἡ, (1) a working, performing, Ep. iv. 9; (2) effort, diligent labor, Lu. xii. 58; (3) work, gain by work, Ac. xvi. 16, 19; Ac. xix. 24; (4) occupation, business, Ac. xix. 25.*

ἐργάτης, ου, ὁ, a worker, laborer, Mat. ix. 37; applied to workers in the church, 2 Tim. ii. 15; a doer, of iniquity, Lu. xiii. 27.

ἔργον, ου, τό, work, employment, Mat. xiii. 34; Jn. xvii. 4; 1 Cor. xv. 58, anything accomplished, Ac. vii. 41; Heb. i. 10; an act, deed, in various senses, Jn. ix. 3; Rev. ii. 6; Ja. ii. 14; 1 Pet. i. 17.

ἐρεθίζω, to stimulate, to provoke, 2 Cor. ix. 2; Col. iii. 21.*

ἐρείδω, σω, to stick fast, Ac. xxvii. 41.*

ἐρεύγομαι, ξομαι, to utter, Mat. xiii. 35.*

ἐρευνάω, ῶ, ήσω (W. H. ἐραυνάω), to search diligently, Jn. v. 39; Ro. viii. 27; Rev. ii. 23.

ἐρέω, obsolete, see φημί and εἶπον.

ἐρημία, as, ἡ, a solitude, a wilderness, Mat. xv. 33; Mar. viii. 4; Heb. xi. 38; 2 Cor. xi. 26.*

ἔρημος, ον, deserted, desolate, waste, Ac. i. 20; Gal. iv. 27; used in the fem., as a subst., for a wilderness, Lu. i. 80· ἔρημος τῆς Ἰουδαίας, the wilderness of Judæa, the tract west of the Dead Sea, Mat. iii. 1; ἡ ἔρημος, the wilderness in which the Israelites wandered, Ac. vii. 30, 36, 38.

ἐρημόω, ῶ, to make desolate, Mat. xii. 25; Lu. xi. 17; to

reduce to naught, Rev. xvii. 16, xviii. 17, 19.*

ἐρήμωσις, εως, ἡ, desolation, Mat. xxiv. 15; Lu. xxi. 20; Mar. xiii. 14. (S.)*

ἐρίζω, ίσω (ἔρις), to contend, dispute, Mat. xii. 19.*

ἐριθεία, as, ἡ (W. H. ἐριθία), self-seeking, a partisan and factious spirit, Ro. ii. 8; Phil. i. 16, ii. 3; Ja. iii. 14, 16; plur. in 2 Cor. xii. 20; Gal. v. 20.*

ἔριον, ου, τό, wool, Heb. ix. 19; Rev. i. 14.*

ἔρις, ιδος, ἡ, contention, strife, Ro. i. 29; Gal. v. 20.

ἐρίφιον, ου, τό, and ἔριφος, ου, ὁ, a goat, kid, Mat. xxv. 32, 33; Lu. xv. 29.*

Ἑρμᾶς, ᾶ, ὁ, Doric for Ἑρμῆς, Hermas, Ro. xvi. 14.*

ἑρμηνεία, as, ἡ, interpretation 1 Cor. xii. 10, xiv. 26.*

ἑρμηνεύω, to interpret, translate, Jn. i. 38 (not W. H.), 42, ix. 7; Heb. vii. 2.*

Ἑρμῆς, οῦ, ὁ, (1) the Greek deity Hermes (in Latin, Mercury), Ac. xiv. 12; (2) Hermes, Ro. xvi. 14.*

Ἑρμογένης, ους, ὁ, Hermogenes, 2 Tim. i. 15.*

ἑρπετόν, οῦ, τό, a creeping creature, a reptile, Ac. x. 12, xi. 6; Ro. i. 23; Ja. iii. 7.

ἐρυθρός, ά, όν, red; ἡ ἐρυθρὰ θάλασσα, the Red Sea, Ac. vii. 36; Heb. xi. 29.*

ἔρχομαι, ἐλεύσομαι (see Gr. § 103, 2, Wi. § 15, Bu. 58), to come, to go, of persons or of things; ὁ ἐρχόμενος, the coming one, i.e., the Messiah, Mat. xi. 3; Heb. x. 37; Rev. i. 4, 8, iv. 8; to come, after, before, to, against, etc., as determined by the preposition which follows; to come forth, as from the grave, 1 Cor. xv. 35; to come back, as the prodigal, Lu. xv. 30.

ἐρωτάω, ῶ, ήσω, to question, Mat. xxi. 24; to ask, to beseech, Lu. vii. 36; Phil. iv. 3. Syn.: see αἰτέω.

ἐσθής, ῆτος, ἡ (ἕννυμι, 1st aor ἔσθην), clothing, raiment, Lu. xxiii. 11; Ac. xii. 21.

ἔσθησις, εως, ἡ, clothing, Lu. xxiv. 4 (ἐσθής, W. H.).*

ἐσθίω, 2d aor. ἔφαγον (see Gr. § 103, 3, Wi. § 15, Bu. 58)

to eat, to partake of food, used abs. or with acc. of food, or ἐκ, a word like *some* being understood; with μετά, gen., *to eat with;* with dat. (as Ro. xiv. 6), *to eat to the honor of;* met., *to devour, to consume,* as rust does, Ja. v. 3; or fire, Heb. x. 27.

ἔσθω (W. H.) = ἐσθίω, Mar. i. 6; Lu. xxii. 30.

Ἐσλί (W. H. -εί), ὁ, *Esli,* Lu. iii. 25.*

ἔσ-οπτρον, ου, τό, *a mirror* (of polished metal), Ja. i. 23; 1 Cor. xiii. 12.*

ἑσπέρα, ας, ἡ (prop. adj. with ὥρα), *evening,* Lu. xxiv. 29; Ac. iv. 3, xxviii. 23.*

Ἐσρώμ, ὁ, *Esrom,* Mat. i. 3; Lu. iii. 33.*

ἔσχατος, η, ον, (1) *the last, remotest,* in situation, dignity, or time, τὸ ἔσχατον, τὰ ἔσχατα, as subst., *the extremity, last state;* (2) used predicatively as an adverb, Mar. xii. 6, 22; absolutely, 1 Cor. xv. 8; (3) *the end* of what is spoken of, *e.g.,* the feast, Jn. vii. 37; the world, Jn. vi. 39, 40; (4) spec. of the Christian dispensation as *the last,* or *latter* (days), Heb. i. 2; (5) the *last* (day), *i.e.,* the day of judgment; (6) the phrase ὁ πρῶτος καὶ ὁ ἔσχατος, Rev. i. 11, 17, ii. 8, *the first and the last,* describes the *eternity* of God.

ἐσχάτως, adv., *extremely,* ἐσχάτως ἔχει, *is at the last extremity,* Mar. v. 23.*

ἔσω, adv. of place, *within,* abs., Mat. xxvi. 58; with gen., Mar. xv. 16; with an article preced., *the inner,* Ro. vii. 22; οἱ ἔσω, *those within the* Christian fold, opp. to οἱ ἔξω, 1 Cor. v. 12.

ἔσωθεν, adv. of place, *from within, within,* Lu. xi. 7; Rev. iv. 8; τὸ ἔσωθεν, the *interior, i.e.,* the mind or soul, Lu. xi. 39.

ἐσώτερος, α, ον (comp. of ἔσω), *inner,* Ac. xvi. 24; Heb. vi. 19.*

ἑταῖρος, ου, ὁ, *a companion, comrade,* Mat. xi. 16 (ἕτερος, W. H.); ἑταῖρε, voc., *friend,* Mat. xx. 13, xxii. 12, xxvi. 50.*

ἑτερό-γλωσσος, ου, ὁ, *one of another tongue* or *language,* 1 Cor. xiv. 21.*

ἑτερο-διδασκαλέω, ῶ, *to teach a different doctrine,* 1 Tim. i. 3, vi. 3. (N. T.)*

ἑτερο-ζυγέω, ῶ, *to be unequally yoked,* fig., 2 Cor. vi. 14. (N. T.)*

ἕτερος, α, ον, *other, another;* indefinitely, *any other;* definitely, *the other; diverse, different from. Syn.:* see ἄλλος.

ἑτέρως, adv., *otherwise, differently,* Phil. iii. 15.*

ἔτι, adv., *yet, still, even,* Lu. i. 15; *also,* Heb. xi. 36; implying accession or addition, *besides.*

ἑτοιμάζω, άσω, *to prepare, make ready,* Lu. xii. 47; Rev. xix. 7.

ἑτοιμασία, ας, ἡ, *preparation, readiness,* Ep. vi. 15.*

ἕτοιμος, η, ον, and -ος, ον, *prepared, ready,* of things or persons, Mat. xxii. 4, 8; Lu. xii. 40; ἐν ἑτοίμῳ ἔχειν, *to be in readiness,* 2 Cor. x. 6.

ἑτοίμως, adv., *readily, in readiness,* usually with ἔχω, Ac. xxi. 13; 2 Cor. xii. 14; 1 Pet. iv. 5.*

ἔτος, ους, τό, *a year,* Lu. iv. 25; κατ᾿ ἔτος, *yearly,* Lu. ii. 41.

εὖ, adv. (old neuter from εὖς), *well,* Ep. vi. 3; εὖ ποιεῖν (acc.), Mar. xiv. 7, *to do good to;* εὖ πράσσειν, *to fare well, to prosper,* Ac. xv. 29; used in commendation, *well! well done!* Mat. xxv. 21, 23; Lu. xix. 17.*

Εὖα, ας, ἡ, *Eve,* 2 Cor. xi. 3; 1 Tim. ii. 13.*

εὐ-αγγελίζω, σω, εὐηγγέλισα, εὐηγγέλισμαι, (1) act., *to bring glad tidings to* (acc. or dat.), Rev. x. 7, xiv. 6; (2) mid., *to announce, to publish* (acc. of message), *to announce the gospel* (abs.), *to preach to, evangelize* (acc. pers.); pass., *to be announced, to have glad tidings announced to* one. See Mat. xi. 5; Heb. iv. 2.

εὐαγγέλιον, ου, τό, *good tidings, the gospel,* Mar. i. 15; Ac. xv. 7; Ep. i. 13.

εὐαγγελιστής, οῦ, ὁ, *a messenger of good tidings, an evangelist,* Ac. xxi. 8; Ep. iv. 11; 2 Tim. iv. 5. (N. T.)*

εὐ-αρεστέω, ῶ, *to be well-pleasing to* (dat.), Heb. xi. 5, 6; pass., *to be pleased with,* Heb. xiii. 16.*

εὐ-άρεστος, ον, *acceptable, well-pleasing,* Ro. xii. 12. (Ap.)

εὐαρέστως, adv., *acceptably,* Heb. xii. 28.*

Εὔβουλος, ου, ὁ, *Eubulus,* 2 Tim. iv. 21.*

εὖ-γε, *well done!* Lu. xix. 17 (W. H.).*

εὐγενής, ές, *well-born, noble, noble-minded,* Lu. xix. 12; Ac. xvii. 11; 1 Cor. i. 26.*

εὐδία, ας, ἡ (from εὖ and Ζεύς, gen. Διός), *fair weather,* Mat. xvi. 2.*

εὐ-δοκέω, ῶ, ήσω, εὐδόκησα and ηὐδόκησα, *to think it good, decide,* Lu. xii. 32; 1 Th. iii. 1; *to be well pleased with,* Mat. xvii. 5; 2 Pet. i. 17.

εὐδοκία, ας, ἡ, *pleasure, goodwill,* Phil. ii. 13; 2 Th. i. 11; Mat. xi. 26.

εὐεργεσία, ας, ἡ, *a good deed to* (gen.), *a benefit,* Ac. iv. 9; 1 Tim. vi. 2.*

εὐεργετέω, ῶ, *to do good, to bestow benefits,* Ac. x. 38.*

εὐ-εργέτης, ου, ὁ, *a benefactor,* Lu. xxii. 25.*

εὔ-θετος, ον, *well-placed, fit, useful,* Lu. ix. 62, xiv. 35; Heb. vi. 7.*

εὐθέως, adv., *immediately, soon,* Mat. iv. 20; Gal. i. 16; 3 Jn.14.

εὐθυ-δρομέω, ῶ, *to run in a straight course,* Ac. xvi. 11, xxi. 1.*

εὐ-θυμέω, ῶ, *to be cheerful,* Ac. xxvii. 22, 25; Ja. v. 13.*

εὔ-θυμος, ον, *cheerful, having good courage,* Ac. xxiv. 10 (Rec.), xxvii. 36.*

εὐθύμως, *cheerfully,* Ac. xxiv. 10 (W. H.).*

εὐθύνω, *to make straight,* Jn. i. 23; *to guide, to steer,* as a ship, Ja. iii. 4.*

εὐθύς, εῖα, ύ, *straight;* met., *right, true;* also adv., of time, *straight, i.e., immediately, forthwith,* as εὐθέως (W. H. often εὐθύς for Rec. εὐθέως).

εὐθύτης, τητος, ἡ, *rectitude, uprightness,* Heb. i. 8 (from S.).*

εὐ-καιρέω, ῶ, *to have leisure* or *opportunity,* Mar. vi. 31; Ac. xvii. 21; 1 Cor. xvi. 12.*

εὐκαιρία, as, ἡ, convenient time, opportunity, Mat. xxvi. 16; Lu. xxii. 6.*

εὔ-καιρος, ον, well-timed, opportune, Mar. vi. 21; Heb. iv. 16.*

εὐκαίρως, adv., opportunely, Mar. xiv. 11; opposed to ἀκαίρως, 2 Tim. iv. 2.*

εὔ-κοπος, ον, easy, neut. comp. only, εὐκοπώτερον, easier, as Mat. ix. 5. (N. T.)

εὐ-λάβεια, as, ἡ, reverence, fear of God, piety, Heb. v. 7, xii. 28.* Syn.: see δειλία.

εὐ-λαβέομαι, οῦμαι, dep. pass., to fear, Ac. xxiii. 10 (W. H. φοβέω); with μή, to take precaution, Heb. xi. 7.*

εὐ-λαβής, ές, cautious, God-fearing, religious, Lu. ii. 25; Ac. ii. 5, viii. 2, xxii. 12 (W. H.).* Syn.: see δεισιδαίμων.

εὐ-λογέω, ῶ, ήσω, to praise, i.e., God, Lu. i. 64; to invoke blessings on, i.e., men, Ro. xii. 14; to bless or to ask blessing on, i.e., food, Lu. ix. 16; so of the Lord's Supper, Mat. xxvi. 26; 1 Cor. x. 16; used of what God does, to bless, to cause to prosper, Ac. iii. 26; hence, perf. pass. part. εὐλογημένος, blessed, favored of God, Mat. xxv. 34.

εὐλογητός, όν (verbal adj. from preced.), worthy of praise, of blessing, used only of God, Mar. xiv. 61; Lu. i. 68; Ro. i. 25, ix. 5; 2 Cor. i. 3, xi. 31; Ep. i. 3; 1 Pet. i. 3. (S.)*

εὐ-λογία, as, ἡ, adulation, flattery, Ro. xvi. 18; blessing, praise, to God, Rev. vii. 12; an invocation of blessings, benediction, Heb. xii. 17; blessing, benefit, 2 Cor. ix. 5; 1 Pet. iii. 9.

εὐ-μετά-δοτος, ον, ready to give, liberal, 1 Tim. vi. 18. (N.T.)*

Εὐνίκη, ης, ἡ, Eunice, 2 Tim. i. 5.*

εὐ-νοέω, ῶ, to be well disposed to, Mat. v. 25.*

εὔ-νοια, as, ἡ, good-will, 1 Cor. vii. 3 (not W. H.); Ep. vi. 7.*

εὐνουχίζω, σω, εὐνουχίσθην, to emasculate, make a eunuch, pass., Mat. xix. 12.*

εὐνοῦχος, ου, ὁ, a eunuch, Mat. xix. 12; Ac. viii. 27–39.*

Εὐοδία, as, ἡ, Euodia, Phil. iv. 2.*

εὐ-οδόω, ῶ, in N. T. pass. only, to be led in a good way, to prosper, Ro. i. 10; 1 Cor. xvi. 2; 3 Jn. 2.*

εὐ-πάρεδρος, ον, see εὐπρόσεδρος. (N. T.)

εὐ-πειθής, ές, easily obeying, compliant, Ja. iii. 17.*

εὐ-περί-στατος, ον, skillfully surrounding, i.e., besetting, Heb. xii. 1.*

εὐ-ποιΐα, as, ἡ, well-doing, beneficence, Heb. xiii. 16.*

εὐ-πορέω, ῶ, mid., to have means, to be prosperous, Ac. xi. 29.*

εὐ-πορία, as, ἡ, wealth, Ac. xix. 25.*

εὐ-πρέπεια, as, ἡ, beauty, gracefulness, Ja. i. 11.*

εὐ-πρόσ-δεκτος, ον, acceptable, Ro. xv. 16, 31; 2 Cor. vi. 2, viii. 12; 1 Pet. ii. 5.*

εὐ-πρόσ-εδρος, ον, assiduous, constantly attending on, 1 Cor. vii. 35 (εὐπάρεδρος, W. H.). (N. T.)*

εὐ-προσωπέω, ῶ, to make a fair appearance, Gal vi 12. (N. T.)*

εὐρ-ακύλων, ωνος, ὁ, the Euraquilo, a N.E. wind, Ac. xxvii. 14 (W. H.). (N. T.)*

εὑρίσκω, εὑρήσω, εὕρηκα, εὗρον, εὑρέθην, (1) to find, to discover, Lu. ii. 45; (2) to ascertain, to find by computation, or by examination, as a judge, Ac. xiii. 28; (3) to obtain, Heb. ix. 12; (4) to contrive, find out how, Lu. xix. 48.

εὐρο-κλύδων, ωνος, ὁ (from εὖρος, the S.E. wind, and κλύδων, wave), Euroclydon, a stormy wind, a hurricane, Ac. xxvii. 14. (N. T.)*

εὐρύ-χωρος, ον, broad, spacious, Mat. vii. 13.*

εὐσέβεια, as, ἡ, piety, godliness, Ac. iii. 12; 2 Tim. iii. 5.

εὐσεβέω, ῶ, to show piety, to worship, Ac. xvii. 23; 1 Tim. v. 4.*

εὐ-σεβής, ές, religious, pious, Ac. x. 2, 7, xxii. 12 (W. H. εὐλαβής); 2 Pet. ii. 9.* Syn.: see δεισιδαίμων.

εὐσεβῶς, adv., piously, religiously, 2 Tim. iii. 12; Tit. ii. 12.*

εὔ-σημος, ον, distinct, intelligible, 1 Cor. xiv. 9.*

εὔ-σπλαγχνος, ον, full of pity,

tender-hearted, Ep. iv. 32; 1 Pet. iii. 8.*

εὐ-σχημόνως, adv., in a seemly manner, decently, Ro. xiii. 13; 1 Cor. xiv. 40; 1 Th. iv. 12.*

εὐ-σχημοσύνη, ης, ἡ, decorum, becomingness, 1 Cor. ii. 23.*

εὐ-σχήμων, ον, reputable, decorous, Mar. xv. 43; Ac. xiii. 50, xvii. 12; τὸ εὐσχῆμον, seemliness, 1 Cor. vii. 35, xii. 24.*

εὐ-τόνως, adv., vehemently, forcibly, Lu. xxiii. 10; Ac. xviii. 28.*

εὐ-τραπελία, as, ἡ, low jesting, ribaldry, Ep. v. 4.*

Εὔτυχος, ου, ὁ, Eutychus, Ac. xx. 9.*

εὐ-φημία, as, ἡ, commendation, good report, 2 Cor. vi. 8.*

εὔ-φημος, ον, sounding well, spoken in a kindly spirit, Phil. iv. 8.*

εὐ-φορέω, ῶ, to bear plentifully, Lu. xii. 16.*

εὐ-φραίνω, νῶ, εὐφράνθην and ηὐφράνθην, act., to make glad, 2 Cor. ii. 2; pass., to be glad, to rejoice, Lu. xii. 19; Ac. ii. 26; Rev. xviii. 20.

Εὐφράτης, ου, ὁ, the Euphrates, Rev. ix. 14, xvi. 12.*

εὐφροσύνη, ης, ἡ, joy, gladness, Ac. ii. 28, xiv. 17.*

εὐ-χαριστέω, ῶ, to thank, give thanks, Ac. xxvii. 35; Ro. i. 8.

εὐχαριστία, as, ἡ, gratitude, thanksgiving, as 2 Cor. ix. 11, 12. Syn.: see αἴτημα.

εὐ-χάριστος, ον, thankful, grateful, Col. iii. 15.*

εὐχή, ῆς, ἡ, (1) prayer, Ja. v. 15; (2) a vow, Ac. xviii. 18, xxi. 23.* Syn.: see αἴτημα.

εὔχομαι, to pray, Ac. xxvi. 29; 2 Cor. xiii. 7; Ja. v. 16 (for with ὑπέρ or περί, gen.); to wish, Ac. xxvii. 29; Ro. ix. 3; 2 Cor. xiii. 9; 3 Jn. 2.*

εὔ-χρηστος, ον, useful, 2 Tim. ii. 21, iv. 11; Philem. 11.*

εὐ-ψυχέω, ῶ, to be in good spirits, to be cheerful, Phil. ii. 19.*

εὐ-ωδία, as, ἡ, fragrance, good odor, 2 Cor. ii. 15; Ep. v. 2; Phil. iv. 18.*

εὐ-ώνυμος, ον, left, hand, Ac. xxi. 3; foot, Rev. x. 2; ἐξ εὐωνύμων (neut. plur.), on the left, Mat. xx. 21, 23.

43

4

ἐφ-άλλομαι, *to leap upon*, ἐπί, acc., Ac. xix. 16.*

ἐφ-άπαξ, adv., *once for all*, Ro. vi. 10; Heb. vii. 27, ix. 12, x. 10; *at once*, 1 Cor. xv. 6.*

Ἐφεσῖνος, η, ον, *Ephesian, i.e.,* church, Rev. ii. 1 (not W. H.).*

Ἐφέσιος, α, ον, *Ephesian, belonging to Ephesus*, Ac. xix. 28, 34, 35, xxi. 29.*

Ἔφεσος, ου, ἡ, *Ephesus*, Ac. xviii. 19, 21, 24.

ἐφ-ευρετής, οῦ, ὁ, *an inventor, contriver*, Ro. i. 30.*

ἐφ-ημερία, ας, ἡ, *a course*, a division of priests for interchange of service, Lu. i. ͻ, 8. (S.)*

ἐφ-ήμερος, ον, *daily*, Ja. ii. 15.*

ἐφ-ικνέομαι, dep., 2d aor. inf. ἐφικέσθαι, *to come to, reach*, ἄχρι or εἰς, 2 Cor. x. 13, 14.*

ἐφ-ίστημι, 2d aor. ἐπέστην; perf. part. ἐφεστώς; always intrans. or mid. in N. T., (1) *to stand by*, Lu. ii. 38; Ac. xii. 7; (2) *to be urgent*, 2 Tim. iv. 2; (3) *to befall one*, as evil, Lu. xxi. 34; (4) *to be at hand, to impend*, 2 Tim. iv. 6.

ἐφνίδιος, see αἰφνίδιος.

ἐφ-οράω, ῶ, 2d aor. ἐπεῖδον, *to look upon*, Lu. i. 25; Ac. iv. 29.*

Ἐφραΐμ, ὁ, *Ephraim*, a city, Jn. xi. 54.*

ἐφφαθά, an Aramaic verb, imperative, *be thou opened*, Mar. vii. 34. (N. T.)*

ἐχθές, see χθές.

ἔχθρα, ας, ἡ, *enmity*, Gal. v. 20; Ep. ii. 15, 16.

ἐχθρός, ά, όν, *hated*, Ro. xi. 28; *hostile*, 1 Cor. xv. 25; used as subst., *an enemy*, Mat. x. 36; ὁ ἐχθρός, Lu. x. 19, *the enemy, i.e.*, Satan.

ἔχιδνα, ης, ἡ, *a viper*, lit., Ac. xxviii. 3; fig., as Mat. iii. 7.

ἔχω, ἕξω, impf. εἶχον, 2d aor. ἔσχον, perf. ἔσχηκα; (1) *to have or possess*, in general, physically or mentally, temporarily or permanently; μὴ ἔχειν, *to lack, to be poor*, Lu. viii. 6; 1 Cor. xi. 22; (2) *to be able*, Mar. xiv. 8; Heb. vi. 13; 2 Pet. i. 15; (3) with adverbs, or adverbial phrases, elliptically, "to have

(one's self) in any manner," *to be*, as κακῶς ἔχειν, *to be ill*; ἐσχάτως ἔχειν, *to be at the last extremity*; (4) *to hold*, 1 Tim. iii. 9; 2 Tim. i. 13; *to esteem*, Mat. xiv. 5; Phil. ii. 29; (5) mid., ἔχομαι, *to be near or next to*, Mar. i. 38; used of time, Ac. xxi. 26, *the day coming, the next day*; τὰ ἐχόμενα σωτηρίας, *things joined to or pertaining to salvation*, Heb. vi. 9.

ἕως, conj. and adv., (1) of time, *till, until*, used also as prep. with gen. ἕως οὗ, or ἕως ὅτου, *until when*, Lu. xiii. 8; (2) of place, *up to*, or *as far as*, also with gen., sometimes with εἰς or πρός (acc.), Mat. xxvi. 58; Lu. xxiv. 50; Ac. xxvi. 11; (3) spoken of a limit or term to anything, *up to the point of*, Mat. xxvi. 38; Lu. xxii. 51; Ro. ii. 12; (4) with particles, ἕως ἄρτι, ἕως τοῦ νῦν, *until now*; ἕως ὧδε, *to this place*; ἕως πότε, *how long?*; ἕως ἑπτάκις, *until seven times*; ἕως ἄνω, *up to the brim*, etc.

Z

Z, ζ, ζῆτα, *zeta, z*, the sixth letter, orig. of a mixed or compound sound, as if δς, now generally pronounced *z* or *ts*. As a numeral, ζ´ = 7; ͵ζ = 7000.

Ζαβουλών, ὁ (Heb.), *Zebulon*, Mat. iv. 13, 15; Rev. vii. 8.*

Ζακχαῖος, ου, ὁ, *Zacchæus*, Lu. xix. 2, 5, 8.*

Ζαρά, ὁ (Heb.), *Zara or Zerah*, Mat. i. 3.*

Ζαχαρίας, ου, ὁ, *Zacharias or Zachariah*, (1) the father of John the Baptist, Lu. i.; (2) the son of Barachiah, slain in the temple, Mat. xxiii. 35; Lu. xi. 51 (in 2 Chron. xxiv. 20 the son of Jehoiada).*

ζάω, ῶ, ζῇς, ζῇ, inf. ζῆν (W. H. ζῆν), fut. ζήσω or -ομαι, 1st aor. ἔζησα, *to live*, as (1) *to be alive*; part. ὁ ζῶν, *the Living One*, a description of God, as Mat. xvi. 16; (2) *to receive or regain life*, Jn. iv. 50; Mar. xvi. 11; (3) *to spend life* in any way, Gal. ii. 14; 2 Tim. iii. 12; (4) *to live*, in

the highest sense, to possess spiritual and eternal life, Lu. x. 28; Heb. x. 38; (5) met., as of water, *living* or *fresh*, opposed to stagnant, as Jn. iv. 10.

Ζεβεδαῖος, ου, ὁ, *Zebedee*, Mat. iv. 21, x. 2.

ζεστός, ή, όν (ζέω), *boiling, hot*, fig., Rev. iii. 15, 16.*

ζεῦγος, ους, τό, (1) *a yoke* (ζεύγνυμι, *to join*), Lu. xiv. 19; (2) *a pair*, Lu. ii. 24.*

ζευκτηρία, ας, ἡ, *a band, a fastening*, Ac. xxvii. 40. (N.T.)*

Ζεύς, Διός, acc. Δία, *Zeus* (Lat. *Jupiter*), the chief of the heathen deities, Ac. xiv. 12, 13.*

ζέω, part. ζέων, *to boil*; fig., *to be fervent*, Ac. xviii. 25; Ro xii. 11.*

ζηλεύω, *to be zealous*, Rev. iii. 19 (W. H.).*

ζῆλος, ου, ὁ, (1) *fervor, zeal*, Jn. ii. 17; (2) *rivalry, jealousy*, Ac. v. 17, xiii. 45; *fierceness*, Heb. x. 27.

ζηλόω, ῶ, ώσω, (1) *to have zeal for, to desire earnestly* (acc.), 1 Cor. xii. 31; 2 Cor. xi. 2; Gal. iv. 17; (2) *to be envious or jealous*, Ac. vii. 9; 1 Cor. xiii. 4; Ja. iv. 2.

ζηλωτής, οῦ, ὁ, (1) *one very zealous for* (gen.), Ac. xxi. 20; (2) *a Zealot*, one of a class of Jews very zealous for the Mosaic law, only Lu. vi. 15; Ac. i. 13. See Κανανίτης.

ζημία, ας, ἡ, *damage, loss*, Ac. xxvii. 10, 21; Phil. iii. 7, 8.*

ζημιόω, ῶ, pass., *to be damaged, to suffer loss of* (acc.), Mat. xvi. 26; Phil. iii. 8.

Ζηνᾶς, ᾶ, ὁ, *Zenas*, Tit. iii. 13.*

ζητέω, ῶ, ήσω, (1) *to seek*, absolutely, as Mat. vii. 7; (2) *to seek for* (acc.), Mat. vi. 33; Jn. v. 30; (3) *to desire, to wish for*, Mat. xii. 46; Col. iii. 1; *to inquire into*, Lu. xii. 29; Jn. xvi. 19.

ζήτημα, ατος, τό, *a question, dispute* (gen., or περί, gen.); Ac. xv. 2, xviii. 15, xxiii. 29, xxv. 19, xxvi. 3.*

ζήτησις, εως, ἡ, *question, debate, controversy*, Jn. iii. 25; Ac. xxv. 20.

ζιζάνιον, ου, τό (perh. Syriac), *zizanium, darnel*, a kind of bastard wheat, Mat. xiii. 25–40. (N. T.)*

Ζοροβάβελ, ὁ (Heb.), *Zerubbabel,* Mat. i. 12, 13; Lu. iii. 27.*

ζόφος, ου, ὁ, *darkness, thick gloom,* 2 Pet. ii. 4, 17; Ju. 6, 13; Heb. xii. 18 (W. H.).*

ζυγός, οῦ, ὁ, *a yoke,* (1) met., of servitude, 1 Tim. vi. 1; (2) fig., of any imposition by authority, Mat. xi. 29, 30; Ac. xv. 10; Gal. v. 1; (3) *a balance, pair of scales,* Rev. vi. 5.*

ζύμη, ης, ἡ, *leaven,* Mat. xvi. 6; fig., *corruptness,* 1 Cor. v. 6, 7, 8.

ζυμόω, ῶ, *to ferment, to leaven,* Mat. xiii. 33; Lu. xiii. 21; 1 Cor. v. 6; Gal. v. 9.*

ζωγρέω, ῶ (ζωός, ἀγρέω), *to take alive, to catch, capture,* Lu. v. 10; 2 Tim. ii. 26.*

ζωή, ῆς, ἡ (ζάω), *life,* literal, spiritual, eternal; ζωὴ αἰώνιος, *eternal life,* used of Christ, as *the source of life,* Jn. v. 26. *Syn.:* see βίος.

ζώνη, ης, ἡ, *a girdle,* Ac. xxi. 11; used as *a purse,* Mar. vi. 8.

ζώννυμι or **-ννύω,** see Gr. § 114, Bu. 45, *to gird,* Jn. xxi. 18; Ac. xii. 8 (W. H.).*

ζωο-γονέω, ῶ, ήσω, *to preserve alive,* Lu. xvii. 33; Ac. vii. 19; *to give life to,* 1 Tim. vi. 13 (W. H.).*

ζῶον, ου, τό, *a living creature, animal,* Heb. xiii. 11; 2 Pet. ii. 12.

ζωο-ποιέω, ῶ, ήσω, *to make alive, to give life to,* Jn. v. 21, vi. 63; 1 Cor. xv. 22, 36, 45; 2 Cor. iii. 6; Gal. iii. 21; Ro. iv. 17, viii. 11; 1 Pet. iii. 18.*

H

H, η, ἦτα, *eta, e,* the seventh letter. As a numeral, η′ = 8; ,η = 8000.

ἤ, a particle, disjunctive, *or;* interrogative, *whether* (see Gr. § 405, Wi. § 57, 1 b, Bu. 249); or comparative, *than* (see Gr. § 320, Wi. § 35, 1, 2, Bu. 360). With other particles, ἀλλ' ἤ, *except;* ἢ καί, *or else;* ἤπερ, *than at all,* Jn. xii. 43; ἤτοι ... ἤ, *whether*

... or (excluding any other alternative), Ro. vi. 16.

ἦ, affirmative particle with μήν, *surely,* Heb. vi. 14 (W. H. el).*

ἡγεμονεύω, *to be governor,* as proconsul, Lu. ii. 2; procurator, Lu. iii. 1.*

ἡγεμονία, ας, ἡ, *rule,* as of an emperor, Lu. iii. 1.*

ἡγεμών, όνος, ὁ, *governor,* as the head of a district, Mat. x. 18; especially the procurator of Judæa, as Pilate, Felix, Festus, Lu. xx. 20; *a chief town,* Mat. ii. 6.

ἡγέομαι, οῦμαι, dep. mid., (1) *to be leader,* in N. T. only part., ὁ ἡγούμενος, *the leader* or *chief* (gen.), as Ac. xiv. 12; Heb. xiii. 7, 17, 24; (2) *to consider, reckon, count,* as Phil. iii. 7, 8.

ἡδέως, adv. (ἡδύς, *sweet*), *gladly,* Mar. vi. 20, xii. 37; 2 Cor. xi. 19.*

ἤδη, adv. of time, *now, already,* as Mat. iii. 10; of the immediate future, Ro. i. 10.

ἥδιστα, adv., *most gladly,* 2 Cor. xii. 9, 15.*

ἡδονή, ῆς, ἡ, *pleasure, i.e.,* sensual, *lust, strong desire,* Lu. viii. 14; Tit. iii. 3; Ja. iv. 3; 2 Pet. ii. 13; *lust,* Ja. iv. 1.*

ἡδύ-οσμον, ου, τό (ἡδύς, ὀσμή), *mint,* Mat. xxiii. 23; Lu. xi. 42.*

ἦθος, ους, τό, as ἔθος, *manner, custom;* plur. ἤθη, *morals,* 1 Cor. xv. 33.*

ἥκω, ξω (perf. ἧκα, only Mar. viii. 3), *to have come,* or *to be present* (see Gr. § 361 d, note, Wi. § 40, 4 b, Bu. 203).

Ἠλί, ὁ (Heb.), *Heli,* Lu. iii. 23.*

ἠλί (W. H. ἐλωΐ), (Heb.), *my God,* Mat. xxvii. 46 (from Ps. xxii. 2). (N. T.)*

Ἠλίας, ου, ὁ, *Elias, i.e., Elijah,* Mat. xi. 14, xvi. 14.

ἡλικία, ας, ἡ, (1) *age, adult age;* ἡλικίαν ἔχει, *he is of age,* Jn. ix. 21; so, prob., Mat. vi. 27 (R. V. mrg.); (2) *stature, size,* Lu. xix. 3.

ἡλίκος, η, ον, *how great, how small,* Col. ii. 1; Ja. iii. 5.*

ἥλιος, ου, ὁ, *the sun, the light of the sun,* Mat. v. 45; Ac. xiii. 11.

ἧλος, ου, ὁ, *a nail,* Jn. xx. 25.*

ἡμεῖς, gen. ἡμῶν, dat. ἡμῖν, acc ἡμᾶς, plur. of ἐγώ.

ἡμέρα, ας, ἡ, *a day, i.e.,* from sunrise to sunset, Lu. xviii. 7; Ac. ix. 24; *a day* of twenty-four hours, Mat. vi. 34; fig. in various senses.

ἡμέτερος, α, ον, *our, our own,* Ac. ii. 11, xxvi. 5.

ἡμιθανής, ές, *half dead,* Lu. x. 30.*

ἥμισυς, εια, υ, gen., ἡμίσους, *half;* in neut. only, *half* of, (gen.) plur. (ἡμίση, W. H. ἡμίσια), Lu. xix. 8; sing., Mar. vi. 23; Rev. xi. 9, 11, xii. 14.*

ἡμιώριον, ου, τό, *a half-hour,* Rev. viii. 1.*

ἡνίκα, adv., *when, whenever,* 2 Cor. iii. 15, 16.*

ἤπερ, see ἤ.

ἤπιος, α, ον, *placid, gentle,* 1 Th. ii. 7 (W. H. νήπιος); 2 Tim. ii. 24.*

Ἤρ, ὁ (Heb.), *Er,* Lu. iii. 28.*

ἤρεμος, ον, *quiet, tranquil,* 1 Tim. ii. 2.*

Ἡρώδης (W. H. -ῴ-), ου, ὁ, *Herod.* Four of the name are mentioned: (1) *Herod the Great,* Mat. ii. 1; (2) *Herod Antipas,* or *H. the tetrarch,* Mat. xiv. 1, 3, 6; Lu. xxiii.; (3) *H. Agrippa,* Ac. xii.; (4) *H. Agrippa* the younger, called only *Agrippa,* Ac. xxv.

Ἡρωδιανοί (W. H. -ῴ-), ῶν, οἱ, *Herodians,* partisans of Herod Antipas, Mat. xxii. 16; Mar. iii. 6, xii. 13.*

Ἡρωδιάς (W. H. -ῴ-), άδος, ἡ, *Herodias,* Mat. xiv. 3, 6.

Ἡρωδίων (W. H. -ῴ-), ωνος, ὁ, *Herodion,* Ro. xvi. 11.*

Ἡσαΐας, ου, ὁ, *Esaias, i.e., Isaiah,* Mat. iii. 3, iv. 14.

Ἠσαῦ, ὁ, *Esau,* Ro. ix. 13; Heb. xi. 20, xii. 16.*

ἡσυχάζω, σω, (1) *to rest from work,* Lu. xxiii. 56; (2) *to cease from altercation, to be silent,* Lu. xiv. 4; Ac. xi. 18, xxi. 4; (3) *to live quietly,* 1 Th. iv. 11.*

ἡσυχία, ας, ἡ, (1) *silence,* Ac. xxii. 2; 1 Tim. ii. 11; (2) *tranquillity, quietness,* 2 Th. iii. 12.*

ἡσύχιος, α, ον, *quiet, tranquil,* 1 Tim. ii. 2; 1 Pet. iii. 4.*

ἤτοι, see ἤ.

ἡττάομαι, pass., (1) *to be made inferior* (abs.), 2 Cor. xii. 13; (2) *to be overcome by* (dat.), 2 Pet. ii. 19, 20.*

ἥττημα, ατος, τό, *inferiority, diminution*, Ro. xi. 12; *loss*, 1 Cor. vi. 7. (S.)* *Syn.:* see ἀγνόημα.

ἥττων or ἥσσων (W. H.), ον, compar. of κακός, *inferior*, neut. as adv., 2 Cor. xii. 15; τὸ ἧττον, as subst., *the worse*, 1 Cor. xi. 17.*

ἠχέω, ῶ, *to sound*, as the sea, Lu. xxi. 25 (not W. H.); as brass, 1 Cor. xiii. 1.*

ἦχος, ου, ὁ, and ους, τό, *sound, noise*, Lu. xxi. 25 (W. H.); Heb. xii. 19; Ac. ii. 2; *rumor, report*, Lu. iv. 37.*

Θ

Θ, θ, θῆτα, *theta, th*, the eighth letter. As a numeral, θ′ = 9; ͵θ = 9000.

Θαδδαῖος, ου, ὁ, *Thaddæus*, a surname of the apostle Jude (also called *Lebbæus*), Mat. x. 3; Mar. iii. 18.*

θάλασσα, ης, ἡ, (1) *the sea*, Ro. ix. 27; (2) *sea*, as the Mediterranean, the Red Sea, Ac. vii. 36, x. 6, 32; (3) Hebraistically, for the *lake* Gennesaret, Mat. viii. 24.

θάλπω, *to cherish, nourish*, Ep. v. 29; 1 Th. ii. 7.*

Θάμαρ, ἡ, *Tamar*, Mat. i. 3.*

θαμβέω, ῶ, *to be astonished, amazed*, Ac. ix. 6 (W. H. omit); so pass., Mar. i. 27, x. 32; with ἐπί (dat.), Mar. x. 24.*

θάμβος, ους, τό, *amazement*, Lu. iv. 36, v. 9; Ac. iii. 10.*

θανάσιμος, ον, *deadly, mortal*, Mar. xvi. 18.*

θανατη-φόρος, ον, *death-bringing*, Ja. iii. 8.*

θάνατος, ου, ὁ, *death*, lit. or fig., Jn. xi. 4; 2 Cor. iii. 7; Ro. i. 32; *the cause of death*, Ro. vii. 13.

θανατόω, ῶ, ώσω, *to put to death*, pass., *to be in danger of death*, Ro. viii. 36; fig., *to destroy, subdue*, as evil passions, Ro. viii. 13; pass., *to become dead to* (dat.), Ro. vii. 4.

θάπτω, ψω, 2d aor. ἔταφον, *to bury*, Mat. viii. 21, 22.

Θάρα, ὁ, *Terah*, Lu. iii. 34.*

θαρρέω, ῶ, ήσω, *to be of good courage, to have confidence*, εἰς or ἐν, 2 Cor. v. 6, 8, x. 1. In imperative, forms from θαρσέω are used, θάρσει, θαρσεῖτε, *take courage*.

θάρσος, ους, τό, *courage*, Ac. xxviii. 15.*

θαῦμα, ατος, τό, *a wonder*, 2 Cor. xi. 14 (W. H.); *wonder, amazement*, Rev. xvii. 6.*

θαυμάζω, σω, or σομαι, *to wonder*, abs., with διά, acc., ἐπί, dat., περί, gen., or ὅτι, εἰ; *to wonder at, admire*, acc.; pass., *to be admired* or *honored*.

θαυμάσιος, α, ον, *wonderful*, Mat. xxi. 15.*

θαυμαστός, ή, όν, *wonderful, marvelous*, Mat. xxi. 42; Mar. xii. 11; Jn. ix. 30; 2 Cor. xi. 14 (Rec.); 1 Pet. ii. 9; Rev. xv. 1, 3.*

θεά, ᾶς, ἡ, *a goddess*, Ac. xix. 27, and Rec. in 35, 37.*

θεάομαι, ῶμαι, dep., 1st aor. ἐθεασάμην, pass. ἐθεάθην, *to behold, to contemplate, to visit*, Mat. xi. 7; Ro. xv. 24.

θεατρίζω, *to make a spectacle of, expose to contempt*, Heb. x. 33. (N. T.)*

θέατρον, ου, τό, (1) *a place for public shows, a theatre*, Ac. xix. 29, 31; (2) *a spectacle*, 1 Cor. iv. 9.*

θεῖον, ου, τό, *sulphur* (from the following, *a divine incense*), Rev. ix. 17, 18.

θεῖος, εία, εῖον, *divine*, 2 Pet. i. 3, 4; τὸ θεῖον, *the deity*, Ac. xvii. 29.*

θειότης, τητος, ἡ, *deity, divine nature*, Ro. i. 20.* *Syn.:* θειότης is deity, *abstractly;* θεότης, *personally*.

θειώδης, ες, *sulphurous*, Rev. ix. 17. (N. T.)*

θέλημα, ατος, τό, *will*, Lu. xii. 47; Ep. i. 9; plur., *commands*, Ac. xiii. 22; *desire*, Ep. ii. 3.

θέλησις, εως, ἡ, *a willing, will*, Heb. ii. 4. (S.)*

θέλω, impf. ἤθελον, 1st aor. ἠθέλησα (ἐθέλω is not found in N. T.), *to wish, delight in, prefer, to will*, in the sense of assent, determination, or requirement.

θεμέλιος, ον, *belonging to a foundation;* hence, masc. (sc. λίθος), *a foundation*, or τὸ θεμέλιον (Lu.), in the same

sense, 2 Tim. ii. 9; Lu. vi. 49; fig., for the elements of doctrine or life, 1 Cor. iii. 10, 12; Heb. vi. 1.

θεμελιόω, ῶ, ώσω, *to lay a foundation, to found*, Heb. i. 10; fig., *to make stable*, Col. i. 23.

θεο-δίδακτος, ον, *taught of God*, 1 Th. iv. 9. (N. T.)*

θεο-λόγος, ου, ὁ, *one who treats of divine things*, of the apostle John in the title to Rev. (W. H. omit).*

θεο-μαχέω, ῶ, *to fight against God*, Ac. xxiii. 9 (W. H. omit).*

θεο-μάχος, ου, ὁ, *a fighter against God*, Ac. v. 39.*

θεό-πνευστος, ον (πνέω), *God-breathed, inspired by God*, 2 Tim. iii. 16.*

θεός, οῦ, ὁ, voc. once θεέ, Mat. xxvii. 46; (1) *a god*, generically, Ac. vii. 43, xii. 22; 2 Cor. iv. 4; Phil. iii. 19; Jn. x. 34 (quoted from S.); (2) *God;* ὁ θεός, *the revealed God*, Jn. i. 1; Ac. xvii. 24, etc.; (3) applied to Christ, Jn. i. 1, xx. 28.

θεο-σέβεια, ας, ἡ, *fear of God, piety*, 1 Tim. ii. 10.*

θεο-σεβής, ές, *God-worshipping, pious*, Jn. ix. 31.* *Syn.:* see δεισιδαίμων.

θεο-στυγής, ές, *hateful to God*, Ro. i. 30.*

θεότης, τητος, ἡ, *deity, Godhead*, Col. ii. 9.* *Syn.:* see θειότης.

Θεό-φιλος, ου, ὁ, *Theophilus*, Lu. i. 3; Ac. i. 1.*

θεραπεία, ας, ἡ, (1) *service;* hence (abs. for concrete), *servants, household*, Lu. xii. 42; Mat. xxiv. 45 (not W. H.); (2) *medical service, healing*, Lu. ix. 11; Rev. xxii. 2.*

θεραπεύω, εύσω, (1) *to serve, minister to*, only Ac. xvii. 25; (2) *to heal*, acc. of pers., and ἀπό or acc. of disease, Mat. xii. 10; Mar. vi. 5.

θεράπων, οντος, ὁ, *a servant, an attendant*, Heb. iii. 5.*

θερίζω, ίσω, *to reap* or *gather*, as grain, lit. or fig., Mat. vi. 26; Jn. iv. 37, 38.

θερισμός, οῦ, ὁ, *harvest*, lit. or fig., Jn. iv. 35; Lu. x. 2.

θεριστής, οῦ, ὁ, *a reaper*, Mat. xiii. 30, 39.*

θερμαίνω, ανῶ, only mid. in N. T., *to warm one's self*, Mar.

xiv. 54, 67; Jn. xviii. 18, 25;
Ja. ii. 16.*

θέρμη, ης, ἡ, *heat*, Ac. xxviii.
3.*

θέρος, ους, τό, *summer*, Mat.
xxiv. 32; Mar. xiii. 28; Lu.
xxi. 30.*

Θεσσαλονικεύς, έως, ὁ, *a Thes-
salonian*, Ac. xx. 4.

Θεσσαλονίκη, ης, ἡ, *Thessalonica*, Ac. xvii. 1, 11, 13.

Θευδᾶς, ᾶ, ὁ, *Theudas*, Ac. v.
36.*

θεωρέω, ῶ, *to be a spectator of,
to behold, to see, to know by
seeing, to experience;* abs.,
or with acc. or obj. clause.

θεωρία, ας, ἡ, *a sight, a spectacle*,
Lu. xxiii. 48.*

θήκη, ης, ἡ (τίθημι), *a receptacle*,
as a scabbard, Jn. xviii. 11.*

θηλάζω, (1) *to give suck*, Mat.
xxiv. 19; (2) *to suck*, Mat.
xxi. 16.

θῆλυς, εια, υ, *female*, fem., Ro.
i. 26, 27; neut., Mat. xix. 4;
Mar. x. 6; Gal. iii. 28.*

θήρα, ας, ἡ, *hunting*, hence, *a
trap*, Ro. xi. 9.*

θηρεύω, σω, *to hunt, to catch*,
Lu. xi. 54.*

θηριο-μαχέω, ῶ, *to fight with
wild beasts*, 1 Cor. xv. 32.*

θηρίον, ου, τό (prop. *a little
beast*), *a wild beast*, as Ac.
xi. 6; freq. in Rev.

θησαυρίζω, σω, *to store up, reserve*, lit. and fig., Lu. xii.
21; 2 Pet. iii. 7.

θησαυρός, οῦ, ὁ, *a treasure receptacle, treasure*, Lu. xii. 33,
34.

θιγγάνω, 2d aor. ἔθιγον, *to touch,
handle*, abs., Col. ii. 21; with
gen., Heb. xii. 20; *to injure*,
Heb. xi. 28.* *Syn.:* see
ἅπτω.

θλίβω, ψω, *to press upon*, Mar.
iii. 9; fig., *to afflict*, 2 Cor. i.
6; pass. perf. part. τεθλιμμέ-
νος, contracted, *narrow*, Mat.
vii. 14.

θλῖψις, εως, ἡ, *pressure, affliction, tribulation*, Ac. vii. 11;
2 Th. i. 6.

θνήσκω, 2d aor. ἔθανον, *to die;*
in N. T. only perf. τέθνηκα,
to be dead, Lu. viii. 49; 1 Tim.
v. 6.

θνητός, ή, όν, *liable to death,
mortal*, Ro. vi. 12, viii. 11;
1 Cor. xv. 53, 54; 2 Cor. iv.
11, v. 4.*

θορυβάζω, *to disturb, trouble*, Lu.
x. 41 (W. H.). (N. T.)*

θορυβέω, ῶ, *to disturb*, Ac. xvii.
5; pass., *to be troubled, to
wail*, Mat. ix. 23; Mar. v. 39;
Ac. xx. 10.*

θόρυβος, ου, ὁ, *noise, uproar*,
Mar. v. 38; Ac. xx. 1.

θραύω, σω, *to break, shatter*, Lu.
iv. 18.*

θρέμμα, ατος, το (τρέφω), *the
young of cattle, sheep*, etc.,
Jn. iv. 12.*

θρηνέω, ῶ, ήσω, abs., *to wail, lament*, Mat. xi. 17; Lu. vii.
32; Jn. xvi. 20; *to bewail*,
acc., Lu. xxiii. 27.*

θρῆνος, ου, ὁ, *a wailing*, Mat. ii.
18 (not W. H.).*

θρησκεία, ας, ἡ, *external worship, religious worship*, Ac.
xxvi. 5; Col. ii. 18; Ja. i. 26,
27.*

θρῆσκος, ου, ὁ (prop. adj.), *a
devotee, religious person*, Ja.
i. 26. (N. T.)* *Syn.:* see
δεισιδαίμων.

θριαμβεύω, σω, *to triumph over,
to lead in triumph*, 2 Cor. ii.
14; Col. ii. 15.*

θρίξ, τριχός, dat. plur. θριξί, ἡ,
a hair, human or animal, Jn.
xi. 2; Rev. ix. 8.

θροέω, ῶ, *to disturb, terrify by
clamor;* only pass. in N. T.,
Mat. xxiv. 6; Mar. xiii. 7;
2 Th. ii. 2.*

θρόμβος, ου, ὁ, *a clot, large drop*,
as of blood, Lu. xxii. 44.*

θρόνος, ου, ὁ, *a seat*, as of judgment, Mat. xix. 28; *a throne*,
or seat of power, Rev. iii.
21; met., of *kingly power*,
Rev. xiii. 2; concrete, of *the
ruler*, or occupant of the
throne, Col. i. 16.

Θυάτειρα, ων, τά, *Thyatira*, Ac.
xvi. 14; Rev. i. 11, ii. 18,
24.*

θυγάτηρ, τρός, ἡ, *a daughter*,
Mat. ix. 18; *a female descendant*, Lu. xiii. 16; met.,
of the inhabitants of a place,
collectively, Mat. xxi. 5.

θυγάτριον, ου, τὸ (dim. of θυγάτηρ), *a little daughter*, Mar.
v. 23, vii. 25.*

θύελλα, ης, ἡ, *a tempest*, Heb.
xii. 18.*

θύϊνος, η, ον, *made of the citrus
tree*, a strongly aromatic tree
of Africa, Rev. xviii. 12.*

θυμίαμα, ατος, τό, *incense*, Lu.

i. 10, 11; Rev. v. 8, viii. 3, 4,
xviii. 13.*

θυμιατήριον, ου, τό, *a censer*, or
an altar of incense, Heb. ix.
4.*

θυμιάω, ῶ, *to burn incense*, Lu.
i. 9.*

θυμομαχέω, ῶ, *to be very angry
with* (dat.), Ac. xii. 20.*

θυμός, οῦ, ὁ, *passion, great anger,
wrath*, Lu. iv. 28; Rev. xiv. 19.
Syn.: θυμός is *impulsive, tur-
bulent* anger; ὀργή is anger
as a *settled habit*, both may
be right or wrong; παροργισ-
μός is the bitterness of anger,
always wrong.

θυμόω, ῶ, *to provoke to great
anger;* pass., *to be very angry
with*, Mat. ii. 16.*

θύρα, ας, ἡ, *a door*, Lu. xi. 7;
Mat. xxvii. 60; met., Jn. x.
7, 9.

θυρεός, οῦ, ὁ, *a large* (door
shaped) *shield*, Ep. vi. 16.*

θυρίς, ίδος, ἡ (prop. *a little door*),
a window, Ac. xx. 9; 2 Cor.
xi. 33.*

θυρωρός, οῦ, ὁ, ἡ, *a door-keeper,
porter*, Mar. xiii. 34; Jn. x.
3, xviii. 16, 17.*

θυσία, ας, ἡ, *a sacrifice*, lit.
and fig., Ep. v. 2; 1 Pet.
ii. 5.

θυσιαστήριον, ου, τό, *an altar*,
for sacrifices, Lu. i. 11, ii.
51; Ja. ii. 21. (S.) *Syn.:* see
βωμός.

θύω, σω, (1) *to slay in sacrifice*,
Ac. xiv. 13; (2) *to kill animals*, for feasting, Mat. xxii.
4; (3) *to slay*, generally, Jn.
x. 10.

Θωμᾶς, ᾶ, ὁ (from Heb. = δίδυμος), *Thomas*, Mat. x. 3.

θώραξ, ακος, ὁ, *a breast-plate*,
Ep. vi. 14; 1 Th. v. 8; Rev.
ix. 9, 17.*

I

Ι, ι, Ἰῶτα, *iota, i*, the ninth letter.
As a numeral, ι′ = 10; ͺι =
10,000.

Ἰάειρος, ου, ὁ, *Jairus*, Mar. v.
22; Lu. viii. 41.*

Ἰακώβ, ὁ (Heb.), *Jacob*, (1) the
patriarch, Ac. vii. 8; (2) the
father-in-law of Mary, Mat.
i. 15.

Ἰάκωβος, ου, ὁ, Greek form of
preced., *James*, (1) the son
of Zebedee, Mat. iv. 21; (2)

47

the son of Alphæus, Mat. x.
3; (3) the Lord's brother,
Mat. xiii. 55. Some identify
(2) and (3).

ἴαμα, ατος, τό, *healing, cure,*
plur., 1 Cor. xii. 9, 28, 30.*

Ἰαμβρῆς, ὁ, *Jambres,* 2 Tim.
iii. 8.*

Ἰαννά, ὁ (W. H. -αἱ), (Heb.),
Jannai, Lu. iii. 24.*

Ἰαννῆς, ὁ, *Jannes,* 2 Tim. iii.
8.*

ἰάομαι, ῶμαι, ἰάσομαι, dep., mid.
aor., but passive in aor.,
perf. and fut., *to heal, to
restore to health,* of body or
mind; with ἀπό, of malady,
Mar. v. 29; Jn. xii. 40.

Ἰαρέδ, ὁ (Heb.), *Jared,* Lu. iii.
37.*

ἴασις, εως, ἡ, *a cure, healing,*
Lu. xiii. 32; Ac. iv. 22, 30.*

ἴασπις, ιδος, ἡ, *jasper,* a precious stone, Rev. iv. 3, xxi.
11, 18, 19.*

Ἰάσων, ονος, ὁ, *Jason,* Ac. xvii.
5, 6, 7, 9; Ro. xvi. 21; perhaps two persons.*

ἰατρός, οῦ, ὁ, *a physician,* Lu.
iv. 23; Col. iv. 14.

ἴδε, or ἰδέ (εἶδον), imper. act.
as interj., *behold!* often followed by nominative.

ἰδέα (W. H. εἰ-), ας, ἡ, *form,
outward appearance,* Mat.
xxviii. 3.* *Syn.:* see Trench,
§ lxx.

ἴδιος, α, ον, (1) *one's own,* denoting ownership, Mat. xxii.
5; Jn. x. 12; also what is
peculiar to, Ac. i. 19 (W. H.
omit); hence, τὰ ἴδια, *one's
own things, home, nation*
or *people, business* or *duty;*
οἱ ἴδιοι, *one's own people,
friends, companions,* neut.
and masc. contrasted in Jn.
i. 11; (2) *that which specially
pertains to, and is proper for,*
as 1 Cor. iii. 8; Gal. vi. 9;
(3) adverbially, κατ' ἴδιαν,
privately; ἰδίᾳ, *individually.*

ἰδιώτης, ου, ὁ, *a private person,
one unskilled in anything,*
Ac. iv. 13; 1 Cor. xiv. 16, 23,
24; 2 Cor. xi. 6.* *Syn.:* see
ἀγράμματος.

ἰδού (see ἴδε), imper. mid. as
interj., *lo! behold!* used to
call attention not only to
that which may be seen, but
also heard, or apprehended
in any way.

Ἰδουμαία, ας, ἡ, *Idumæa,* the
O. T. Edom, Mar. iii. 8.*

ἱδρώς, ῶτος, ὁ, *sweat,* Lu. xxii.
44.*

Ἰεζαβήλ, ἡ (Heb.), *Jezebel,* sym-
bolically used, Rev. ii. 20.*

Ἱεράπολις, εως, ἡ, *Hierapolis,*
in Phrygia, Col. iv. 13.*

ἱερατεία (W. H. -τία), ας, ἡ, *the
office of a priest, priesthood,*
Lu. i. 9; Heb. vii. 5.*

ἱεράτευμα, ατος, τό, *the order
of priests, priesthood,* applied
to Christians, 1 Pet. ii. 5, 9.
(S.)*

ἱερατεύω, σω, *to officiate as a
priest,* Lu. i. 8.*

Ἰερεμίας, ου, ὁ, *Jeremiah,* Mat.
ii. 17, xvi. 14, xxvii. 9 (this
quotation is from *Zecha-
riah*).*

ἱερεύς, έως, ὁ, *a priest,* Mat. viii.
4; sometimes *the High Priest,*
Ac. v. 24 (not W. H.); of
Christ, Heb. v. 6 (Ps. cx. 4);
of Christians generally, Rev.
i. 6, v. 10.

Ἰεριχώ, ἡ (Heb.), *Jericho,* Lu.
x. 30.

ἱερόθυτος, ον, *offered in sacrifice,*
1 Cor. x. 28 (W. H.).*

ἱερόν, οῦ, τό (prop. neut. of
ἱερός), *a temple,* used of a
heathen temple, as Ac. xix.
27; of the temple at Jerusalem, as Mat. xxiv. 1; and
of parts of the temple, as
Mat. xii. 5. *Syn.:* ἱερόν is
the whole sacred enclosure;
ναός, the *shrine* itself, the
holy place and the holy of
holies.

ἱεροπρεπής, ές, *suitable to a
sacred character* (*reverent,*
R. V.), Tit. ii. 3.*

ἱερός, ά, όν, *sacred, holy,* of the
Scriptures, 2 Tim. iii. 15;
τὰ ἱερά, *sacred things,* 1 Cor.
ix. 13.* *Syn.:* see ἅγιος.

Ἱεροσόλυμα (W. H. Ἱ-), ων,
τά, the usual form in Mat.,
Mar., and Jn.; see Ἱερου-
σαλήμ.

Ἱεροσολυμίτης, ου, ὁ, *one of
Jerusalem,* Mar. i. 5; Jn. vii.
25.*

ἱεροσυλέω, ῶ, *to commit sacrilege,* Ro. ii. 22.*

ἱερόσυλος, ον, *robbing temples,
sacrilegious,* Ac. xix. 37.*

ἱερουργέω, ῶ (ἱερός, ἔργον), *to
minister in holy things,* Ro.
xv. 16.*

Ἱερουσαλήμ (W. H. Ἱ-), ἡ
(Heb.), (for form, see Gr.
§ 156, Wi. § 10, 2, Bu. 6, 16,
18, 21), *Jerusalem,* (1) the
city; (2) the inhabitants.
In Gal. iv. 25, 26, ἡ νῦν Ἱ.
is the *Jewish dispensation,*
and is contrasted with ἡ
ἄνω Ἱ., the ideal *Christian
community;* also called Ἱ.
ἐπουράνιος, Heb. xii. 22; ἡ
καινὴ Ἱ., Rev. iii. 12, xxi. 2.

ἱερωσύνη, ης, ἡ, *the priestly
office,* Heb. vii. 11, 12, 14
(not W. H.), 24.*

Ἰεσσαί, ὁ (Heb.), *Jesse,* Mat. i.
5, 6.

Ἰεφθάε, ὁ (Heb.), *Jephthah,*
Heb. xi. 32.*

Ἰεχονίας, ου, ὁ, *Jechoniah,* or
Jehoiachin, Mat. i. 11, 12.*

Ἰησοῦς, οῦ, ὁ (Heb.), (see Gr.
§ 25, Wi. § 10, 1, Bu. 21),
(1) *Jesus,* the Savior, Mat.
i. 21, 25; (2) *Joshua,* Ac. vii.
45; Heb. iv. 8; (3) *a fellow-
laborer of Paul,* so named,
Col. iv. 11; (4) *Barabbas* is
so named in some early
MSS., Mat. xxvii. 16; (5)
an ancestor of Joseph, Lu. iii.
29 (W. H.).

ἱκανός, ή, όν, (1) *sufficient, competent* to, inf.; πρός (acc.) or
ἵνα; (2) *many, much,* of
number or time.

ἱκανότης, τητος, ἡ, *sufficiency,
ability,* 2 Cor. iii. 5.*

ἱκανόω, ῶ, *to make competent,*
2 Cor. iii. 6; Col. i. 12. (S.)*

ἱκετηρία, ας, ἡ, *supplication,*
Heb. v. 7.* *Syn.:* see αἴτημα.

ἱκμάς, άδος, ἡ, *moisture,* Lu.
viii. 6.*

Ἰκόνιον, ου, τό, *Iconium,* Ac.
xiv. 1, 19, 21.

ἱλαρός, ά, όν, *joyous, cheerful,*
2 Cor. ix. 7.*

ἱλαρότης, τητος, ἡ, *cheerfulness,*
Ro. xii. 8. (S.)*

ἱλάσκομαι, ἄσομαι, 1st aor. ἱλά-
σθην, (1) *to be propitious to,*
dat., Lu. xviii. 13; (2) *to
make atonement for, expiate,*
acc., Heb. ii. 17.*

ἱλασμός, οῦ, ὁ, *a propitiation,
atoning sacrifice,* 1 Jn. ii. 2,
iv. 10. (S.)* *Syn.:* see ἀπο-
λύτρωσις.

ἱλαστήριος, α, ον, *atoning,* neut.,
propitiation, Ro. iii. 25; (sc.
ἐπίθεμα, *covering*), *the mercy-
seat,* Heb. ix. 5. (S.)*

ἵλεως, ων (Attic for ἵλαος), *propitious, merciful,* Heb. viii. 12; ἵλεώς σοι, (God be) merciful to thee! *God forbid!* Mat. xvi. 22.*

Ἰλλυρικόν, οὐ, τό, *Illyricum,* Ro. xv. 19.*

ἱμάς, άντος, ὁ, *a thong* for scourging, Ac. xxii. 25; *thong, latchet* of a shoe, Mar. i. 7; Lu. iii. 16; Jn. i. 27.*

ἱματίζω, perf. pass. part. ἱματισμένος, *to clothe,* Mar. v. 15; Lu. viii. 35. (N. T.)*

ἱμάτιον, ου, τό (dim. of ἵμα = εἷμα, from ἔννυμι), (1) *clothing,* Mat. ix. 16; (2) *the outer garment,* worn over the χιτών, Jn. xix. 2. *Syn.:* see Trench, § 1.

ἱματισμός, οῦ, ὁ, *clothing, raiment,* Lu. vii. 25. *Syn.:* see ἱμάτιον.

ἱμείρομαι, *to long for, to love earnestly,* 1 Th. ii. 8 (W. H. ὁμειρομαι).*

ἵνα, conj., *that, to the end that; ἵνα μή, that not, lest.* See Gr. § 384, Wi. § 53, 9, Bu. 229 sq.

ἱνα-τί, or ἵνα τί (W. H.), conj., *in order that what* (may happen? sc. γένηται), *to what end?*

Ἰόππη, ης, ἡ, *Joppa,* Ac. xi. 5, 13.

Ἰορδάνης, ου, ὁ, *the Jordan,* Mar. i. 5, 9.

ἱός, οῦ, ὁ, (1) *poison,* Ro. iii. 13; Ja. iii. 8; (2) *rust,* Ja. v. 3.*

Ἰουδαία, ας, ἡ (really adj., fem., sc. γῆ), *Judæa,* Mat. ii. 1; including all Palestine, Lu. vii. 17.

Ἰουδαΐζω (from Heb.), *to conform to Jewish practice,* to "Judaize," in life or ritual, Gal. ii. 14. (S.)*

Ἰουδαϊκός, ή, όν (from Heb.), *Jewish,* or *Judaical,* Tit. i. 14.*

Ἰουδαϊκῶς, adv., *Jewishly,* in Jewish style, Gal. ii. 14.*

Ἰουδαῖος, αία, αῖον, *Jewish,* Jn. iv. 9; Ac. x. 28. Often in plur., with subst. understood, οἱ Ἰουδαῖοι, *the Jews. Syn.:* see Ἑβραῖος.

Ἰουδαϊσμός, οῦ, ὁ (from Heb.), *Judaism, the religion of the Jews,* Gal. i. 13, 14. (Ap.)*

Ἰούδας, α, ὁ, and Ἰούδα, ὁ, indecl., *Judah,* (1) son of Jacob; (2, 3) other unknown ancestors of Christ, Lu. iii. 26, 30; (4) *Jude,* an apostle; (5) *Judas* Iscariot; (6) *Judas* Barsabas, Ac. xv. 22; (7) *Judas,* a Jew living in Damascus, Ac. ix. 11; (8) *Judas,* a leader of sedition, Ac. v. 37; (9) *Judas,* a brother of our Lord, Mat. xiii. 55. See Ἰάκωβος.

Ἰουλία, ας, ἡ, *Julia,* Ro. xvi. 15.*

Ἰούλιος, ου, ὁ, *Julius,* Ac. xxvii. 1, 3.*

Ἰουνίας, α, ὁ, *Junias,* Ro. xvi. 7.*

Ἰοῦστος, ου, ὁ, *Justus.* Three of the name are mentioned, Ac. i. 23, xviii. 7; Col. iv. 11.*

ἱππεύς, έως, ὁ, *a horseman,* Ac. xxiii. 23, 32.*

ἱππικόν (prop. neut. adj.), οῦ, τό, *cavalry,* Rev. ix. 16.*

ἵππος, ου, ὁ, *a horse,* Ja. iii. 3.

ἶρις, ιδος, ἡ, *a rainbow,* Rev. iv. 3, x. 1.*

Ἰσαάκ, ὁ (Heb.), *Isaac,* Ro. ix. 7, 10.

ἰσ-άγγελος, ον, *like angels,* Lu. xx. 36. (N. T.)*

ἴσασι, see οἶδα.

Ἰσαχάρ, or Ἰσασχάρ, or Ἰσσαχάρ (W.H.), (Heb.), *Issachar,* Rev. vii. 7.*

Ἰσκαριώτης, ου, ὁ, a man *of Kerioth,* Mat. xxvi. 14, 25. See Josh. xv. 25.

ἴσος, η, ον (or ἶσος), *equal* (dat.), Mat. xx. 12; Lu. vi. 34; Jn. v. 18; Ac. xi. 17; *alike, consistent,* as truthful witnesses, Mar. xiv. 56, 59; ἴσα, adverbially, *on an equality* Phil. ii. 6; Rev. xxi. 16.*

ἰσότης, τητος, ἡ, *equality,* 2 Cor. viii. 13, 14; *equity,* Col. iv. 1.*

ἰσό-τιμος, ον, *equally precious,* 2 Pet. i. 1.*

ἰσό-ψυχος, ον *like-minded,* Phil. ii. 20.*

Ἰσραήλ, ὁ (Heb.), *Israel,* Ac. vii. 42, met., for the whole nation of the Israelites, Ro. xi. 2, 7, 26.

Ἰσραηλίτης, ου, ὁ, *an Israelite,* Ro. ix. 4. *Syn.:* see Ἑβραῖος.

ἴστε, see οἶδα.

ἵστημι (in Ro. iii. 31, Rec. has ἱστάω, W. H. ἱστάνω, see

Gr. § 107, Wi. § 15, Bu. 44), trans. in pres., imperf., fut., 1st aor.; *to cause to stand, to set up, to place, to fix* a time, *to confirm, to establish, to put in the balance, to weigh;* intrans. in perf., plup., and 2d aor., *to stand, to stand still* or *firm, to endure, to be confirmed* or *established, to come to a stand, to cease.*

ἱστορέω, ῶ, *to become personally acquainted with,* Gal. i. 18.*

ἰσχυρός, ά, όν, *strong, mighty, powerful, vehement,* Mar. iii. 27; 1 Cor. i. 25; Rev. xix. 6.

ἰσχύς, ύος, ἡ, *strength, power,* 2 Pet. ii. 11; Ep. i. 19.

ἰσχύω, ύσω, *to be strong, sound. to prevail, to be able* (inf.), *to have ability* for (acc.), Mar. ii. 17; Rev. xii. 8.

ἴσως (ἴσος), adv., *perhaps,* Lu. xx. 13.*

Ἰταλία, ας, ἡ, *Italy,* Ac. xviii. 2.

Ἰταλικός, ή, όν, *Italian,* Ac. x. 1.*

Ἰτουραία, ας, ἡ, *Ituræa,* Lu. iii. 1.*

ἰχθύδιον, ου, τό (dim. of ἰχθύς), *a little fish,* Mat. xv. 34; Mar. viii. 7.*

ἰχθύς, ύος, ὁ, *a fish,* Lu. v. 6; Jn. xxi. 11.

ἴχνος, ους, τό, *a footstep,* fig., Ro. iv. 12; 2 Cor. xii. 18; 1 Pet. ii. 21.*

Ἰωάθαμ, ὁ (Heb.), *Jotham,* Mat. i. 9.*

Ἰωάννα, ης, ἡ, *Joanna,* Lu. viii. 3, xxiv. 10.*

Ἰωαννᾶς, ᾶ, ὁ, *Joannas,* Lu. iii. 27.*

Ἰωάννης, ου, ὁ, *John,* (1) the Baptist; (2) the apostle; (3) a member of the Sanhedrin, Ac. iv. 6; (4) John Mark, Ac. xii. 12.

Ἰώβ, ὁ (Heb.), *Job,* Ja. v. 11.*

Ἰωβήδ, see Ὠβήδ.

Ἰωήλ, ὁ (Heb.), *Joel,* the prophet, Ac. ii. 16.*

Ἰωνάν, ὁ (Heb.), *Jonan,* Lu. iii. 30.*

Ἰωνᾶς, ᾶ, ὁ, *Jonas,* or *Jonah,* (1) the prophet, Mat. xii. 39–41; (2) the father of Peter, Jn. i. 42.

Ἰωράμ, ὁ (Heb.), *Joram,* or *Jehoram,* son of Jehoshaphat, Mat. i. 8.*

Ἰωρείμ, ὁ (Heb.), *Jorim,* Lu. iii. 29.*

'Ιωσαφάτ, ὁ (Heb.), *Jehosha-phat*, Mat. i. 8.*

'Ιωσῆς, ῆ (or ῆτος, W. H.), ὁ, *Joses*. Four are mentioned: (1) Lu. iii. 29 (W. H. 'Ιη-σοῦ); (2) Mar. vi. 3; Mat. xiii. 55 (W. H. 'Ιωσήφ); (3) Mat. xxvii. 56 (W. H. mrg.), Mar. xv. 40, 47; (4) Ac. iv. 36 (W. H. 'Ιωσήφ). Some think (2) and (3) identical.*

'Ιωσήφ, ὁ (Heb.), *Joseph*, (1) the patriarch, Jn. iv. 5; (2, 3, 4) three among the ancestors of Jesus, Lu. iii. 24, 26 (W. H. 'Ιωσήχ), 30; (5) the husband of Mary, the mother of Jesus, Mat. ii. 13, 19; (6) Joseph of Arimathæa, Mar. xv. 43, 45; (7) Joseph, called also Barsabas, Ac. i. 23. See also under 'Ιωσῆς.

Ιωσίας, ου, ὁ, *Josiah*, Mat. i. 10, 11.*

ἰῶτα, τό, *iota, yod*, the smallest letter of the Hebrew alphabet, Mat. v. 18.*

K

Κ, κ, κάππα, *kappa, k*, the tenth letter. As a numeral, κ' = 20; ,κ = 20,000.

κἀγώ (κἀμοί, κἀμέ), contr. for καὶ ἐγώ (καὶ ἐμοί, καὶ ἐμέ), *and I, I also, even I*.

καθά, adv., contr. from καθ' ἅ, *according as*, Mat. xxvii. 10.*

καθ-αίρεσις, εως, ἡ, *demolition, destruction* (opp. to οἰκοδομή, which see), 2 Cor. x. 4, 8, xiii. 10.*

καθ-αιρέω, καθελῶ, καθεῖλον, (1) *to take down*, Ac. xiii. 29; (2) *to demolish, destroy*, lit., Lu. xii. 18, or fig., 2 Cor. x. 5.

καθαίρω, αρῶ, *to cleanse, to prune*, Jn. xv. 2; Heb. x. 2 (W. H. καθαρίζω).*

καθ-άπερ, adv., *even as, just as*, 1 Th. ii. 11.

καθ-άπτω, άψω, *to fasten on*, intrans., Ac. xxviii. 3 (gen.).*

καθαρίζω, att. fut. καθαριῶ, *to cleanse*, lit., Lu. xi. 39; a leper, by healing his disease, Mat. viii. 2, 3; *from moral pollution*, Heb. ix. 22, 23; *to declare clean, i.e., from ceremonial pollution*, Ac. x. 15.

καθαρισμός, οῦ, ὁ, *cleansing*, physical, moral, or ceremonial, Mar. i. 44; Lu. ii. 22, v. 14; Jn. ii. 6, iii. 25; Heb. i. 3; 2 Pet. i. 9. (S.)*

καθαρός, ά, όν, *clean, pure*, physically, morally, or ceremonially, Mat. xxiii. 26; Tit. i. 15; Ro. xiv. 20.

καθαρότης, τητος, ἡ, *purity, i.e.*, ceremonial, Heb. ix. 13.*

καθ-έδρα, ας, ἡ, *a seat*, lit., Mat. xxi. 12; Mar. xi. 15; met., *a chair* of authority, Mat. xxiii. 2.*

καθ-έζομαι, *to sit down*, ἐν or ἐπί, dat., Lu. ii. 46; Jn. iv. 6.

καθ-εῖς (W. H. καθ' εἷς), adv. (see Gr. § 300β, 4, Wi. § 37, 3, Bu. 30), *one by one*, Jn. viii. 9.

καθ-εξῆς, adv. (see Gr. § 126d), *in orderly succession*, Lu. i. 3; Ac. xi. 4, xviii. 23. With art., Lu. viii. 1, ἐν τῷ κ., *soon afterwards;* Ac. iii. 24, οἱ κ., *those that come after.*

καθ-εύδω, *to sleep*, lit., Mat. viii. 24; fig., 1 Th. v. 6.

καθηγητής, οῦ, ὁ, *a guide, master*, Mat. xxiii. 8 (not W. H.), 10.*

καθ-ήκω, used only impers., *it is fit, it is becoming* (acc., inf.), Ac. xxii. 22; τὸ καθῆ-κον, *the becoming*, Ro. i. 28.*

κάθ-ημαι, 2d pers. κάθη for κά-θησαι, imper., κάθου (see Gr. § 367, Wi. § 15, 4, Bu. 49), *to be seated, to sit down, to sit, to be settled, to abide;* with εἰς, ἐν, ἐπί (gen., dat., acc.).

καθ-ημερινός, ή, όν, *daily*, Ac. vi. 1.*

καθ-ίζω, ίσω, (1) trans., *to cause to sit down, to set;* (2) intrans., *to seat one's self*, preps. as κάθημαι; *to sit down, to be sitting, to tarry;* mid. in Mat. xix. 28; Lu. xxii. 30.

καθ-ίημι, 1st aor. καθῆκα (see Gr. § 112, Bu. 46), *to send* or *let down*, Lu. v. 19; Ac. ix. 25, x. 11, xi. 5.*

καθ-ίστημι (and καθιστάω or -ανω), *to appoint, constitute, make, ordain, to conduct*, Ac. xvii. 15; *to appoint as ruler* over (ἐπί, gen., dat., acc.).

καθ-ό, adv. (for καθ' ὅ), *as, according as*, Ro. viii. 26; 2

Cor. viii. 12; 1 Pet. iv. 13.*

καθολικός, ή, όν, *general, universal* (found in the inscriptions of the seven Epistles of James, Peter, John and Jude, but omitted by W. H.).*

καθ-όλου, adv., *entirely; καθόλου μή*, Ac. iv. 18, *not at all.*

καθ-οπλίζω, *to arm fully*, pass., Lu. xi. 21.*

καθ-οράω, ῶ, *to see clearly*, pass., Ro. i. 20.*

καθ-ότι, adv., *as, according as*, Ac. ii. 45, iv. 35; *because that, for*, Lu. i. 7, xix. 9, Ac. ii. 24, xvii. 31 (W. H.).*

καθ-ώς, adv., *according as, even as*.

καθώσ-περ, adv., *just as*, Heb. v. 4 (W. H.).*

καί, conj., *and, also, even*. For the various uses of this conjunction, see Gr. § 403, Wi. § 53, 1-4, Bu. 360 sq.

Καϊάφας, α, ὁ, *Caiaphas*, Jn xi. 49.

Κάϊν, ὁ (Heb.), *Cain*, Heb. xi. 4

Καϊνάν, ὁ (Heb.), *Cainan*. Two are mentioned, Lu. iii. 36, 37.*

καινός, ή, όν, *new*, Lu. v. 38; Ac. xvii. 19. *Syn.: νέος* is new under the aspect of *time; καινός*, new in quality, of different character.

καινότης, τητος, ἡ, *newness* (moral and spiritual), Ro. vi. 4, vii. 6.*

καί-περ, conj., *although*, Phil. iii. 4; Heb. v. 8.

καιρός, οῦ, ὁ, *a fixed time, season, opportunity*, Lu. viii. 13; Heb. xi. 15; Ac. xiv. 17; Ro. viii. 18. *Syn.: χρόνος* is time in general, viewed simply as such; *καιρός*, definite, suitable time, the time of some decisive event, *crisis, opportunity*.

Καῖσαρ, αρος, ὁ, *Cæsar*, a title assumed by Roman emperors, after Julius Cæsar, as Lu. ii. 1, xx. 22; Ac. xvii. 7; Phil. iv. 22.

Καισάρεια, ας, ἡ, *Cæsarea*. Two cities of Palestine, one in Galilee (*Cæsarea Philippi*), Mat. xvi. 13; the other on the coast of the Mediterranean, Ac. viii. 40.

καί-τοι, conj., *and yet, although*, Heb. iv. 3; so καίτοιγε.

καίω, perf. pass. κέκαυμαι, *to kindle, light*, Mat. v. 15; pass., *to burn*, Lu. xii. 35; *to burn, consume*, Jn. xv. 6; fig., Lu. xxiv. 32.

κἀκεῖ (καὶ ἐκεῖ), *and there*, Ac. xiv. 7.

κἀκεῖθεν (καὶ ἐκεῖθεν), *and thence*, Ac. vii. 4, xx. 15.

κἀκεῖνος, η, ο (καὶ ἐκεῖνος), *and he, she, it*, Lu. xi. 7; Ac. xv. 11.

κακία, ας, ἡ, *badness*, (1) of character, *wickedness*, Ac. viii. 22; (2) of disposition, *malice, ill-will*, Col. iii. 8; (3) of condition, *affliction, evil*, Mat. vi. 34.

κακο-ήθεια, ας, ἡ, *malignity*, Ro. i. 29.*

κακο-λογέω, ῶ, *to speak evil of* (acc.), Mar. ix. 39; Ac. xix. 9; *to curse*, Mat. xv. 4; Mar. vii. 10.*

κακο-πάθεια, ας, ἡ, *a suffering of evil, affliction*, Ja. v. 10.*

κακο-παθέω, ῶ, *to suffer evil, to endure affliction*, 2 Tim. ii. 3 (W. H. συνκακ-), 9, iv. 5; Ja. v. 13.*

κακοποιέω, ῶ, abs., *to do harm*, Mar. iii. 4; Lu. vi. 9; *to do wrong*, 1 Pet. iii. 17; 3 Jn. 11.*

κακο-ποιός, όν, as subst., *an evil-doer*, Jn. xviii. 30 (not W. H.); 1 Pet. ii. 12, 14, iii. 16 (W. H. omit), iv. 15.*

κακός, ή, όν, *evil, wicked; τὸ κακόν, wickedness*, Mat.xxvii. 23: also *affliction*, Lu. xvi. 35.

κακ-οῦργος, ον, as subst., *a malefactor*, Lu. xxiii. 32, 33, 39; 2 Tim. ii. 9.*

κακ-ουχέω, ῶ, only in pass., part., *treated ill, harassed*, Heb. xi. 37, xiii. 3.*

κακόω, ῶ, ώσω, *to ill-treat, oppress*, Ac. vii. 6, 19, xii. 1, xviii. 10; 1 Pet. iii. 13; *to embitter*, Ac. xiv. 2.*

κακῶς, adv., *badly, wickedly*, Jn. xviii. 23; κακῶς ἔχειν, *to be sick*, or *in trouble*, Mat. iv. 24; Lu. v. 31.

κάκωσις, εως, ἡ, *affliction, ill-treatment*, Ac. vii. 34.*

καλάμη, ης, ἡ, *stubble*, 1 Cor. iii. 12.*

κάλαμος, ου, ὁ, *a stalk*, as (1) *a reed*, growing, Mat. xi. 7; (2) *a reed*, as a mock sceptre, Mat. xxvii. 29; (3) *a pen*, 3 Jn. 13; (4) *a measuring-rod*, Rev. xxi. 15.

καλέω, ῶ, έσω, κέκληκα, *to call;* hence, (1) *to summon*, Lu. xix. 13; (2) *to name*, Mat. i. 21, x. 25; (3) *to invite*, Jn. ii. 2; (4) *to appoint*, or *select*, for an office, Heb. v. 4; (5) pass., *to be called*, or *accounted, i.e., to be*, Mat. v. 9, 19; Ja. ii. 23.

καλλι-έλαιος, ου, ἡ, *a cultivated olive tree*, Ro. xi. 24.*

καλλίων (compar. of καλός), *better;* adv., κάλλιον, Ac. xxv. 10.*

καλο-διδάσκαλος, ου, ὁ, ἡ, *a teacher of what is good*, Tit. ii. 3. (N.T.)*

Καλοὶ Λιμένες, *Fair Havens*, a harbor in the island of Crete, Ac. xxvii. 8.*

καλο-ποιέω, ῶ, *to act uprightly*, 2 Th. iii. 13. (S.)*

καλός, ή, όν, *beautiful;* (1) physically, Lu. xxi. 25; (2) morally *beautiful, good, noble*, Mat. v. 16; Heb. xiii. 18; (3) *excellent, advantageous*, Lu. vi. 43; 1 Cor. vii. 1.

κάλυμμα, ατος, τό, *a covering, veil*, 2 Cor. iii. 13–16.*

καλύπτω, ψω, *to cover, veil*, Lu. xxiii. 30; 2 Cor. iv. 3.

καλῶς, adv., *well, rightly, nobly*, Jn. iv. 17; 1 Cor. xiv. 17.

κἀμέ, see κἀγώ.

κάμηλος, ου, ὁ, ἡ, *a camel*, Mar. i. 6, x. 25.

κάμινος, ου, ἡ, *a furnace*, Mat. xiii. 42, 50; Rev. i. 15, ix. 2.*

καμ-μύω (κατά and μύω), *to shut, close the eyes*, Mat. xiii. 15; Ac. xxviii. 27.*

κάμνω, καμῶ, perf. κέκμηκα, *to be weary, to be sick*, Heb. xii. 3; Ja. v. 15; Rev. ii. 3 (W. H. omit).*

κἀμοί, see κἀγώ.

κάμπτω, ψω, *to bend* the knee, *bow*, Ro. xi. 4, xiv. 11; Ep. iii. 14; Phil. ii. 10.*

κἄν (καὶ ἐάν), *and if*, Lu. xiii. 9; *even if, though*, Mat.xxvi. 35; *if even*, Heb. xii. 20; elliptically, *if only*, Mar. v. 28; Ac. v. 15.

Κανᾶ, ἡ, *Cana*, Jn. ii. 1, 11.

Κανανίτης, ου, ὁ, *a Zealot* (from the Aramaic, meaning the same as ζηλωτής), Mat. x. 4; Mar. iii. 18 (W. H. read Κα-ναναῖος, which has the same meaning). (N. T.)*

Κανδάκη, ης, ἡ, *Candace*, Ac. viii. 27.*

κανών, όνος, ὁ, prop. *a rod;* hence, (1) *a rule of conduct*, Gal. vi. 16; Phil. iii. 16 (W. H. omit); (2) *a limit* or *sphere of duty, province* (R. V.), 2 Cor. x. 13, 15, 16.*

Καπερ-ναούμ, or Καφαρ-ναούμ (W. H.), ἡ (Heb.), *Capernaum*, Jn. vi. 17, 24.

καπηλεύω, *to be a petty trader;* hence (with acc.), *to make merchandise of*, or *adulterate, corrupt*, 2 Cor. ii. 17.*

καπνός, οῦ, ὁ, *smoke*, Ac. ii. 19; Rev. viii. 4.

Καππαδοκία, ας, ἡ, *Cappadocia*, Ac. ii. 9; 1 Pet. i. 1.*

καρδία, ας, ἡ, *the heart*, met., as the seat of the affections, but chiefly of the understanding; fig., *the heart* of the earth, Mat. xii. 40.

καρδιο-γνώστης, ου, ὁ, *a knower of hearts*, Ac. i. 24, xv. 8. (N. T.)*

καρπός, οῦ, ὁ, *fruit, produce*, Lu. xii. 17; met., for *children*, Ac. ii. 30; *deeds, conduct*, the fruit of the hands, Mat. iii. 8; *effect, result*, Ro. vi. 21. Praise is called *the fruit of the lips*, Heb. xiii. 15.

Κάρπος, ου, ὁ, *Carpus*, 2 Tim. iv. 13.*

καρποφορέω, ῶ, ήσω, *to bring forth fruit*, Mar. iv. 28; mid., *to bear fruit of one's self*, Col. i. 6.

καρπο-φόρος, ον, *fruitful*, Ac. xiv. 17.*

καρτερέω, ῶ, ήσω, *to be strong, steadfast*, Heb. xi. 27.*

κάρφος, ους, τό, *a dry twig, a straw*, Mat. vii. 3, 4, 5; Lu. vi. 41, 42.*

κατά, prep., gov. the gen. and acc. cases, *down;* hence, gen., *down from, against*, etc.; acc., *according to, against*, etc. (see Gr. §§ 124, 147 a, Wi. §§ 47 k, 49 d, Bu. 334 sq.). In composition, κατά may import *descent, subjection, opposition, distribution*, and with certain verbs (as of destruction, diminu-

tion, and the like) is *intensive* = "utterly."

κατα-βαίνω, βήσομαι, βέβηκα,
2ὁ aor. κατέβην, *to go* or *come
down, descend,* used of persons and of things, as gifts
from heaven, of the clouds,
storms, lightnings; also of
anything that falls, Lu. xxii.
44; Rev. xvi. 21.

κατα-βάλλω, 1st aor. pass. κα-
τεβλήθην, *to cast down,* Rev.
xii. 10 (W. H. βάλλω); 2
Cor. iv. 9　mid., *to lay,* as a
foundation, Heb. vi. 1.*

κατα-βαρέω, ῶ, *to weigh down,
to burden,* 2 Cor. xii. 16.*

κατα-βαρύνω=καταβαρέω, Mar.
xiv. 40 (W. H.).*

κατά-βασις, εως, ἡ, *descent,
place of descent,* Lu. xix. 37.*

κατα-βιβάζω, *to bring down,
cast down,* Mat. xi. 23 (W.
H. καταβαίνω), Lu. x. 15
(Rec., W. H. mrg.).*

κατα-βολή, ῆς, ἡ, *a founding,
laying the foundation of,* Mat.
xiii. 35; Heb. xi. 11.

κατα-βραβεύω, *to give judgment
against as umpire of the
games, to deprive of reward,*
Col. ii. 18.*

κατ-αγγελεύς, έως, ὁ, *a proclaimer, a herald,* Ac. xvii.
18. (N. T.)*

κατ-αγγέλλω, *to declare openly,
to proclaim, to preach,* Ac.
xiii. 5, xv. 36.

κατα-γελάω, ῶ, *to laugh at,
deride,* gen., Mat. ix. 24;
Mar. v. 40; Lu. viii. 53.*

κατα-γινώσκω, *to condemn,
blame,* gen. of persons, Gal.
ii. 11; 1 Jn. iii. 20, 21.*

κατ-άγνυμι, fut. κατεάξω, *to
break down, to break in pieces,*
Mat. xii. 20; Jn. xix. 31–33.*

κατ-άγω, *to bring down,* as Ac.
ix. 30; Ro. x. 6; as a nautical
term, *to bring to land,* Lu. v.
11; pass., *to come to land,*
Ac. xxvii. 3, xxviii. 12.

κατ-αγωνίζομαι, dep., *to contend against, subdue* (acc.),
Heb. xi. 33.*

κατα-δέω, ῶ, *to bind up,* as
wounds, Lu. x. 34.*

κατά-δηλος, ον, *thoroughly evident,* Heb. vii. 15.*

κατα-δικάζω, *to condemn, to pronounce sentence against,* Mat.
xii. 7, 37; Lu. vi. 37; Ja. v.
6.*

κατα-δίκη, ης, ἡ, *a sentence of
condemnation,* Ac. xxv. 15
(W. H.).*

κατα-διώκω, *to follow closely,*
Mar. i. 36.*

κατα-δουλόω, ῶ, ὠσω, *to enslave,*
2 Cor. xi. 20; Gal. ii. 4.*

κατα-δυναστεύω, *to exercise
power over, to oppress,* Ac.
x. 38; Ja. ii. 6.*

κατά-θεμα, W. H. for κατανά-
θεμα, Rev. xxii. 3. (N T.)*

κατα-θεματίζω, W. H. for κα-
ταναθ-, Mat. xxvi. 74. (N.
T.)*

κατ-αισχύνω, *to make ashamed,*
1 Cor. i. 27; *to dishonor,* 1
Cor. xi. 4, 5; *to shame,* as
with disappointed expectation, 1 Pet. ii. 6; pass., *to be
ashamed,* as Lu. xiii. 17.

κατα-καίω, αὑσω, *to burn up, to
consume entirely,* as Mat. iii.
12; Heb. xiii. 11.

κατα-καλύπτω, in mid., *to wear
a veil,* 1 Cor. xi. 6, 7.*

κατα-καυχάομαι, ῶμαι, *to rejoice against, to glory over*
(gen.), Ro. xi. 18; Ja. ii. 13,
iii. 14. (S.)*

κατά-κειμαι, *to lie down,* as the
sick, Mar. i. 30; *to recline* at
table, Mar. xiv. 3.

κατα-κλάω, ῶ, *to break in pieces,*
Mar. vi. 41; Lu. ix. 16.*

κατα-κλείω, *to shut up, confine,* Lu. iii. 20; Ac. xxvi.
10.*

κατα-κληρο-δοτέω, ῶ, *to dis-
tribute by lot,* Ac. xiii. 19
(W. H. read the following).
(S.)*

κατα-κληρο-νομέω, ῶ, *to distribute by lot,* Ac. xiii. 19 (W.
H.). (S.)*

κατα-κλίνω, νῶ, *to cause to recline* at table, Lu. ix. 14, 15
(W. H.); mid., *to recline* at
table, Lu. vii. 36 (W. H.),
xiv. 8, xxiv. 30.*

κατα-κλύζω, σω, *to inundate,
deluge,* pass., 2 Pet. iii. 6.*

κατα-κλυσμός, οῦ, ὁ, *a deluge,
flood,* Mat. xxiv. 38, 39; Lu.
xvii. 27; 2 Pet. ii. 5.*

κατ-ακολουθέω, ῶ, *to follow
after* (abs. or dat.), Lu. xxiii.
55; Ac. xvi. 17.*

κατα-κόπτω, ψω, *to wound,* Mar.
v. 5.*

κατα-κρημνίζω, σω, *to cast down
headlong,* Lu. iv. 29.*

κατά-κριμα, ατος, τό, *con-*

demnation, Ro. v. 16, 18,
viii. 1.*

κατα-κρίνω, νῶ, *to judge worthy
of punishment* (gen. and dat.),
to condemn, as Mat. xx. 18;
Ro. ii. 1, viii. 3; in a more
general sense, Lu. xi. 31,
32.

κατά-κρισις, εως, ἡ, *the act of
condemnation,* 2 Cor. iii. 9,
vii. 3. (N. T.)*

κατα-κυριεύω, *to exercise authority over,* Mat. xx. 25; Mar.
x. 42; 1 Pet. v. 3; *to get the
mastery of,* Ac. xix. 16 (gen.).

κατα-λαλέω, ῶ, *to speak against*
(gen.), Ja. iv. 11; 1 Pet. ii.
12, iii. 16.*

κατα-λαλιά, ᾶς, ἡ, *evil-speaking,
defamation,* 2 Cor. xii. 20,
1 Pet. ii. 1. (N. T.)*

κατά-λαλος, ον, ὁ, ἡ, *an evil-
speaker, a defamer,* Ro. i. 30.
(N. T.)*

κατα-λαμβάνω, λήψομαι, *to seize*
or *lay hold of,* as Mar. ix. 18;
to grasp, to obtain, as the
prize in public games, Phil.
iii. 12, 13; *to overtake,* 1 Th.
v. 4; mid., *to comprehend, to
perceive,* ὅτι, or acc. and inf.,
Ep. iii. 18.

κατα-λέγω, *to register, to enrol,*
pass., 1 Tim. v. 9.*

κατά-λειμμα, ατος, τό, *a remnant, a residue,* Ro. ix. 27
(W. H. ὑπόλιμμα). (S.)*

κατα-λείπω, ψω, *to leave utterly,
to forsake,* Mar. x. 7; *to depart from,* Heb. xi. 27; *to
leave remaining, to reserve,*
Ro. xi. 4.

κατα-λιθάζω, σω, *to stone, to destroy by stoning,* Lu. xx. 6.
(N. T.)*

καταλλαγή, ῆς, ἡ, *reconciliation,*
Ro. v. 11, xi. 15; 2 Cor. v.
18, 19.* *Syn.:* see ἀπολύ-
τρωσις.

κατ-αλλάσσω, ξω, *to reconcile*
(acc. and dat.), Ro. v. 10; 1
Cor. vii. 11; 2 Cor. v. 18, 19,
20.*

κατά-λοιπος, ον, plur., *the rest,
the residue,* Ac. xv. 17.*

κατάλυμα, ατος, τό, *a lodging-
place, an inn,* Lu. ii. 7; *a
guest-chamber,* Mar. xiv. 14;
Lu. xxii. 11.*

κατα-λύω, ύσω, *to unloose,* (1)
lit., of a building, *to destroy,*
Mar. xiv. 58; (2) fig., of
law or command, *to render*

void, Mat. v. 17; (3) *to pass the night, to lodge,* Lu. ix. 12, xix. 7.

κατα-μανθάνω, 2d aor. κατέμαθον, *to consider carefully,* Mat. vi. 28.*

κατα-μαρτυρέω, ῶ, *to bear testimony against* (acc. of thing, gen. of pers.), Mat. xxvi. 62, xxvii. 13; Mar. xiv. 60, xv. 4 (not W. H.).*

κατα-μένω, *to remain, abide,* Ac. i. 13.*

κατα-μόνας (W. H. κατὰ μόνας), adv., *privately, alone,* Mar. iv. 10; Lu. ix. 18.*

κατ-ανά-θεμα, ατος, τό, *a curse,* Rev. xxii. 3; see κατάθεμα. (N. T.)*

κατ-ανα-θεματίζω, *to curse, devote to destruction,* Mat. xxvi. 74; see καταθεματίζω. (N. T.)*

κατ-αν-αλίσκω, *to consume,* as fire, Heb. xii. 29.*

κατα-ναρκάω, ῶ, ήσω, *to be burdensome to* (gen.), 2 Cor. xi. 9, xii. 13, 14.*

κατα-νεύω, *to nod, to make signs* ῳ, dat., Lu. v. 7.*

κατα-νοέω, ῶ, (1) *to observe carefully, perceive,* Lu. vi. 41; (2) *to consider* (acc.), Ac. xi. 6.

κατ-αντάω, ῶ, *to come to, to arrive at,* with εἰς, as Ac. xvi. 1; once with ἀντικρύ, Ac. xx. 15; met., *to attain to,* Phil. iii. 11.

κατάνυξις, εως, ή, *stupor,* Ro. xi. 8. (S.)*

κατα-νύσσω, ξω, 2d aor., pass. κατενύγην, *to prick through, to agitate greatly,* pass., Ac. ii. 37. (S.)*

κατ-αξιόω, ῶ, ώσω, *to judge worthy of* (gen.), pass., Lu. xx. 35, xxi. 36; Ac. v. 41; 2 Th. i. 5.*

κατα-πατέω, ῶ, *to trample on, to tread under foot* (acc.), as Lu. viii. 5.

κατάπαυσις, εως, ή, *a resting, rest,* Ac. vii. 49; Heb. iii. 11, 18, iv. 1, 3, 5, 10, 11.*

κατα-παύω, (1) trans., *to restrain,* acc. (also τοῦ μή, and inf.), Ac. xiv. 18; *to give rest,* Heb. iv. 8; (2) intrans., *to rest,* ἀπό, Heb. iv. 4, 10.*

κατα-πέτασμα (πετάννυμι), ατος, τό, *a veil, curtain,* separating the holy place and the

holy of holies, as Lu. xxiii. 45. (S.)

κατα-πίνω, 2d aor. κατέπιον, 1st aor. pass. κατεπόθην, *to drink down, swallow,* Mat. xxiii. 24; Rev. xii. 16; fig., *to devour, destroy,* 1 Cor. xv. 54; 2 Cor. ii. 7, v. 4; Heb. xi. 29; 1 Pet. v. 8.*

κατα-πίπτω, 2d aor. κατέπεσον, *to fall down,* Lu. viii. 6 (W. H.); Ac. xxvi. 14, xxviii. 6.*

κατα-πλέω, εύσομαι, 1st aor. κατέπλευσα, *to sail* to land, Lu. viii. 26.*

κατα-πονέω, ῶ, in pass., *to be oppressed, distressed,* Ac. vii. 24; 2 Pet. ii. 7.*

κατα-ποντίζω, pass., *to sink down,* Mat. xiv. 30; *to be drowned,* Mat. xviii. 6.*

κατ-άρα, ας, ή, *a curse, cursing,* Gal. iii. 10, 13; Heb. vi. 8; 2 Pet. ii. 14; Ja. iii. 10.*

κατ-αράομαι, ῶμαι, *to curse,* Mat. v. 44 (W. H. omit); Mar. xi. 21; Lu. vi. 28; Ro. xii. 14; Ja. iii. 9; pass., perf. part., *accursed,* Mat. xxv. 41.*

κατ-αργέω, ῶ, ήσω, *to render useless,* Lu. xiii. 7; *to cause to cease, abolish,* as Ro. iii. 3, 31, and frequently in Paul; *to sever* from (ἀπό), Ro. vii. 2; Gal. v. 4.

κατ-αριθμέω, ῶ, *to number among,* Ac. i. 17.*

κατ-αρτίζω, ίσω, *to refit, to repair,* Mat. iv. 21; *to restore* from error or sin, Gal. vi. 1; *to perfect, to complete,* 1 Th. iii. 10; 1 Pet. v. 10; pass., *to be restored* to harmony, 1 Cor. i. 10.

κατάρτισις, εως, ή, *a perfecting,* 2 Cor. xiii. 9.*

καταρτισμός, οῦ, ὁ, *a perfecting,* Ep. iv. 12. (N. T.)*

κατα-σείω, σω, *to shake* the hand, *to beckon,* Ac. xii. 17, xiii. 16, xix. 33, xxi. 40.*

κατα-σκάπτω, ψω, *to dig under, to demolish,* Ro. xi. 3; perf. part., pass., *ruins,* Ac. xv. 16 (not W. H.).*

κατα-σκευάζω, άσω, *to prepare, to build, to equip,* as Mat. xi. 10; Lu. i. 17; Heb. iii. 3, 4.

κατα-σκηνόω, ῶ, ώσω, *to pitch one's tent, to dwell,* Mat. xiii.

32; Mar. iv. 32; Lu. xiii. 19; Ac. ii. 26.*

κατα-σκήνωσις, εως, ή, *a dwelling-place, a haunt,* as of birds, Mat. viii. 20; Lu. ix. 58.*

κατα-σκιάζω, σω, *to overshadow,* Heb. ix. 5.*

κατα-σκοπέω, ῶ, *to spy out, to plot against,* Gal. ii. 4.*

κατά-σκοπος, ου, ὁ, *a spy,* Heb. xi. 31.*

κατα-σοφίζομαι, σομαι, *to deal deceitfully with,* Ac. vii. 19.*

κατα-στέλλω, λῶ, 1st aor. κατέστειλα, *to appease, restrain,* Ac. xix. 35, 36.*

κατά-στημα, ατος, τό, *behavior, conduct,* Tit. ii. 3.*

κατα-στολή, ῆς, ή, *dress, attire,* 1 Tim. ii. 9.*

κατα-στρέφω, ψω, *to overthrow,* Mat. xxi. 12; Mar. xi. 15; Ac. xv. 16 (W. H.).*

κατα-στρηνιάω, ῶ, άσω, *to grow wanton* to the loss of (gen.), 1 Tim. v. 11. (N. T.)*

κατα-στροφή, ῆς, ή, *overthrow, destruction,* 2 Tim. ii. 14; 2 Pet. ii. 6 (W. H. omit).*

κατα-στρώννυμι, στρώσω, *to prostrate, slay,* 1 Cor. x. 5.*

κατα-σύρω *to drag along* by force, 1 u. xii. 58.*

κατα-σφάζω, ξω, *to slay,* Lu. xix. 27.*

κατα-σφραγίζω, σω, *to seal up,* as a book, Rev. v. 1.*

κατά-σχεσις, εως, ή, *a possession,* Ac. vii. 5, 45. (S.)*

κατα-τίθημι, θήσω, 1st aor. κατέθηκα, *to deposit,* as a body in a tomb, Mar. xv. 46 (W. H. τίθημι); mid. κατατίθεσθαι χάριν, *to gain favor* with (dat.), Ac. xxiv. 27 xxv. 9.

κατα-τομή, ῆς, ή, *mutilation,* paronomasia with περιτομή Phil. iii. 2.*

κατα-τοξεύω, *to transfix,* Heb xii. 20 (W. H. omit).*

κατα-τρέχω, 2d aor. κατέδραμον, *to run down* (ἐπί, acc.), Ac. xxi. 32.*

κατα-φάγω, see κατεσθίω.

κατα-φέρω, κατοίσω, 1st aor. κατήνεγκα, pass. κατηνέχθην, *to cast down,* as an adverse vote, Ac. xxv. 7, xxvi. 10 (W. H.); pass., *to be borne down, to be overcome,* Ac. xx. 9.*

κατα-φεύγω, 2d aor. κατέφυγον, to flee for refuge, with εἰς, Ac. xiv. 6; with inf., Heb. vi. 18.*

κατα-φθείρω, pass., perf. κατέφθαρμαι, 2d aor. κατεφθάρην, to corrupt, 2 Tim. iii. 8; to destroy, 2 Pet. ii. 12 (W. H. φθείρω).*

κατα-φιλέω, ῶ, to kiss affectionately, or repeatedly (acc.), as Mat. xxvi. 49; Lu. xv. 20.

κατα-φρονέω, ῶ, ήσω, to despise (gen.), as Mat. vi. 24.

καταφρονητής, οῦ, ὁ, a despiser, Ac. xiii. 41. (S.)*

κατα-χέω, εύσω, 1st aor. κατέχεα, to pour down upon, Mat. xxvi. 7; Mar. xiv. 3.*

κατα-χθόνιος, ον, subterranean, Phil. ii. 10.*

κατα-χράομαι, ῶμαι, to use fully, 1 Cor. vii. 31, ix. 18 (dat.).*

κατα-ψύχω, to cool, to refresh, Lu. xvi. 24.*

κατ-είδωλος, ον, full of idols (R. V.), Ac. xvii. 16. (N.T.)*

κατ-έναντι, adv., or as prep. with gen., over against, before, in presence or in sight of.

κατ-ενώπιον, adv., in the presence of (gen.). (S.)

κατ-εξουσιάζω, to exercise authority over (gen.), Mat. xx. 25; Mar. x. 42. (N. T.)*

κατ-εργάζομαι, άσομαι, with mid. and pass. aor. (augm. ει-), to accomplish, achieve, Ro. xv. 18; Ep. vi. 13; to work out, result in, Ro. iv. 15, vii. 8.

κατ-έρχομαι, 2d aor. κατῆλθον, to come down, Lu. iv. 31, ix. 37.

κατ-εσθίω and -έσθω (Mar. xii. 40, W. H.), fut. καταφάγομαι (Jn. ii. 17, W. H.), 2d aor. κατέφαγον, to eat up, to devour entirely, lit. or fig., Mat. xiii. 4; Jn. ii. 17; Gal. v. 15.

κατ-ευθύνω, νῶ, to direct, to guide, Lu. i. 79; 1 Th. iii. 11; 2 Th. iii. 5.*

κατ-ευλογέω, to bless greatly, Mar. x. 16 (W. H.).*

κατ-εφ-ίστημι, 2d aor. κατεπέστην, to rise up against, Ac. xviii. 12. (N. T.)*

κατ-έχω, κατασχήσω, to seize on, to hold fast, to retain, possess, to prevent from doing

a thing (τοῦ μή, with inf.), to repress, Ro. i. 18; τὸ κατέχον, the hindrance, 2 Th. ii. 6; κατεῖχον εἰς τὸν αἰγιαλόν, they held for the shore, Ac. xxvii. 40.

κατ-ηγορέω, ῶ, ήσω, to accuse, to speak against, abs., or with person in gen.; charge in gen. alone or after περί or κατά; pass., to be accused; with ὑπό or παρά, of the accuser.

κατηγορία, ας, ἡ, an accusation, a charge, pers. in gen. alone, or after κατά; charge also in gen., 1 Tim. v. 19; Tit. i. 6.

κατήγορος, ου, ὁ, an accuser, Ac. xxiii. 30, 35.

κατήγωρ, ὁ (Heb.?), an accuser, Rev. xii. 10 (W.H.). (N.T.)*

κατήφεια, ας, ἡ, dejection, gloom, Ja. iv. 9.*

κατ-ηχέω, ῶ, ήσω, perf., pass. κατήχημαι (ἦχος), to instruct orally, to teach, inform, Lu. i. 4; Ac. xviii. 25, xxi. 21, 24; Ro. ii. 18; 1 Cor. xiv. 19; Gal. vi. 6.*

κατ' ἰδίαν, separately, privately, by one's self (see ἴδιος).

κατ-ιόω, ῶ (ἰός), to cover with rust, Ja. v. 3. (Ap.)*

κατ-ισχύω, to prevail against, overpower (gen.), Mat. xvi. 18; Lu. xxi. 36 (W.H.), xxiii. 23.*

κατ-οικέω, ῶ, (1) intrans., to dwell, with ἐν, εἰς (const. praeg.), ἐπί, gen., or adverbs of place, Ac. i. 20, vii. 4; fig., of qualities or attributes, to abide, Col. ii. 9; (2) trans. to dwell in, to inhabit (acc.), Mat. xxiii. 21; Ac. i. 19.

κατοίκησις, εως, ἡ, a dwelling, habitation, Mar. v. 3.*

κατοικητήριον, ου, τό, a dwelling-place, Ep. ii. 22; Rev. xviii. 2. (S.)*

κατοικία, ας, ἡ, a dwelling, habitation, Ac. xvii. 26.*

κατ-οικίζω, to cause to dwell, Ja. iv. 5 (W.H.).*

κατοπτρίζω, mid., to behold, as in a mirror, 2 Cor. iii. 18.*

κατ-όρθωμα, ατος, τό, an honorable or successful achievement, Ac. xxiv. 2 (W. H. διόρθωμα).*

κάτω, adv., downwards, down,

Mat. iv. 6, beneath, Mat. xiv. 66; of age, comp., κατωτέρω, under, Mat. ii. 16.

κατώτερος, α, ον (κάτω), lower, Ep. iv. 9 (on which see Gr. § 259, Wi. § 11, 2c, Bu. 28).*

καῦμα, ατος, τό (καίω), heat, scorching heat, Rev. vii. 16, xvi. 9.*

καυματίζω, σω, to scorch, burn, Mat. xiii. 6; Mar. iv. 6; Rev. xvi. 8, 9.*

καῦσις, εως, ἡ, a burning, burning up, Heb. vi. 8.*

καυσόω, ῶ, to burn up, pass., 2 Pet. iii. 10, 12. (N. T.)*

καύσων, ωνος, ὁ, scorching heat; perhaps a hot wind from the E., Mat. xx. 12; Lu. xii. 55; Ja. i. 11 (see Hos. xii. 1, etc.). (S.)*

καυτηριάζω (W. H. καυστ-), to brand, as with a hot iron; fig., pass., 1 Tim. iv. 2.*

καυχάομαι, ῶμαι, 2d pers. καυχᾶσαι, fut. ήσομαι, to glory, to boast, both in a good sense and in a bad, 1 Cor. i. 29; Ep. ii. 9; followed with prep., ἐν, περί, gen.; ὑπέρ, gen.; ἐπί, dat.

καύχημα, ατος, τό, the ground of glorying, as Ro. iv. 2; a glorying, 1 Cor. v. 6.

καύχησις, εως, ἡ, the act of boasting, glorying, Ro. xv. 17; Ja. iv. 16. (S.)

Καφαρναούμ (see Καπερναούμ), Capernaum.

Κεγχρεαί, ῶν, αἱ, Cenchreae, a port of Corinth, Ac. xviii. 18; Ro. xvi. 1.*

κέδρος, ου, ἡ, a cedar, Jn. xviii. 1; perhaps a mistaken reading for following.*

Κεδρών, ὁ (Heb. dark or turbid), Cedron, a turbid brook between the Mount of Olives and Jerusalem, a variant reading in Jn. xviii. 1.*

κεῖμαι, σαι, ται; impf. ἐκείμην, σο, το; to lie, to recline, to be laid, Lu. xxiii. 53; 1 Jn. v. 19; met., to be enacted, as laws, 1 Tim. i. 9.

κειρία, ας, ἡ, a band or bandage of linen, Jn. xi. 44.*

κείρω, κερῶ, to shear, as sheep, Ac. viii. 32; mid., to have the head shorn, Ac. xviii. 18; 1 Cor. xi. 6.*

κέλευσμα, ατος, τό, a command, a loud cry, 1 Th. iv. 16.*

κελεύω, σω, *to command, to order*, Ac. iv. 15, v. 34.

κενοδοξία, ας, ἡ, *vainglory, empty pride*, Phil. ii. 3.*

κενό-δοξος, ον, *vainglorious*, Gal. v. 26.*

κενός, ή, όν, *empty, vain*, Ep. v. 6; Col. ii. 8; *empty-handed*, Lu. i. 53; Ja. ii. 20; *fruitless, ineffectual*, 1 Cor. xv. 10, 58. *Syn. :* κενός, *empty*, refers to the contents; μάταιος, *aimless, purposeless*, to the result.

κενο-φωνία, ας, ἡ, *empty disputing, useless babbling*, 1 Tim. vi. 20; 2 Tim. ii. 16. (N. T.)*

κενόω, ῶ, ώσω, with ἑαυτόν, *to empty* one's self, *divest* one's self *of rightful dignity*, Phil. ii. 7; *to make useless or false*, Ro. iv. 14; 1 Cor. i. 17, ix. 15; 2 Cor. ix. 3.*

κέντρον, ου, τό, *a sting*, Rev. ix. 10; 1 Cor. xv. 55, 56; *a goad*, Ac. ix. 5 (W. H. omit), xxvi. 14.*

κεντυρίων, ωνος, ὁ, Latin (see Gr. § 154c), *a centurion*, the commander of a hundred foot-soldiers, Mar. xv. 39, 44, 45.*

κενῶς, adv., *in vain*, Ja. iv. 5.*

κεραία, or κερέα (W. H.), ας, ἡ, *a little horn* (the small projecting stroke by which certain similar Hebrew letters are distinguished, as ר and ד); met., *the minutest part*, Mat. v. 18; Lu. xvi. 17.*

κεραμεύς, έως, ὁ, *a potter*, Mat. xxvii. 7, 10; Ro. ix. 21.*

κεραμικός, ή, όν, *made of clay, earthen*, Rev. ii. 27.*

κεράμιον, ου, τό, *an earthen vessel, a pitcher*, Mar. xiv. 13; Lu. xxii. 10.*

κέραμος, ου, ὁ, *a roofing tile*, Lu. v. 19.*

κεράννυμι (see Gr. §§ 113, 114, Wi. § 15, Bu. 60), *to mix, to pour out for drinking*, Rev. xiv. 10, xviii. 6.*

κέρας, ατος, τό, *a horn*, as Rev. v. 6; fig., for *strength*, only Lu. i. 69; *a projecting point, horn* of the altar, only Rev. ix. 13.

κεράτιον, ου, τό, *a little horn*, the name of the fruit of the *carob tree*, Lu. xv. 16.*

κερδαίνω, ανῶ, 1st aor. ἐκέρδησα,

to gain, acquire, Mat. xxv. 16 (W. H.), 22; Ja. iv. 13; *to gain, win*, Phil. iii. 8; *to gain over* to a cause, 1 Cor. ix. 19–22.

κέρδος, ους, τό, *gain, advantage*, Phil. i. 21, iii. 7; Tit. i. 11.*

κέρμα, ατος, τό (κείρω), *a small piece of money*, Jn. ii. 15.*

κερματιστής, οῦ, ὁ, *a money-changer*, Jn. ii. 14.*

κεφάλαιον, ου, τό, *a sum of money*, Ac. xxii. 28; *the sum, main point* of an argument, Heb. viii. 1 (see R. V. and mrg.).*

κεφαλαιόω (W. H. -λιόω), ῶ, ώσω, *to smite on the head*, Mar. xii. 4.*

κεφαλή, ῆς, ἡ, *the head*, of human beings or animals; for the whole person, Ac. xviii. 6; *the head* of a corner (with γωνία), *corner-stone*, Lu. xx. 17; met., implying authority, *head, lord*, 1 Cor. xi. 3; Ep. i. 22; Col. i. 18.

κεφαλίς, ίδος, ἡ (prop. *top*), *a roll, a volume*, Heb. x. 7.*

κημόω, *to muzzle*, 1 Cor. ix. 9 (W. H. mrg.).*

κῆνσος, ου, ὁ, Latin (Gr. § 154d, Bu. 16), *a tax, a poll-tax*, Mat. xvii. 25, xxii. 17, 19; Mar. xii. 14.*

κῆπος, ου, ὁ, *a garden*, Lu. xiii. 19; Jn. xviii. 1, 26, xix. 41.*

κηπ-ουρός, οῦ, ὁ, *a gardener*, Jn. xx. 15.*

κηρίον, ου, τό, *a honeycomb*, Lu. xxiv. 42 (W. H. omit).*

κήρυγμα, ατος, τό, *a proclaiming, preaching*, as Mat. xii. 41; 1 Cor. i. 21; 2 Tim. iv. 17.

κῆρυξ, υκος, ὁ, *a herald, a preacher*, 1 Tim. ii. 7; 2 Tim. i. 11; 2 Pet. ii. 5.*

κηρύσσω, ξω, (1) *to proclaim, to publish*, Mar. vii. 36; (2) specially, *to preach* the Gospel, abs., or acc. and dat., Mar. i. 38; Lu. xii. 3; 1 Pet. iii. 19.

κῆτος, ους, τό, *a sea monster, a whale*, Mat. xii. 40.*

Κηφᾶς, ᾶ, ὁ (Aramaic, *a rock*), *Cephas, i.e.*, Peter, 1 Cor. i. 12, iii. 22.

κιβωτός, οῦ, ἡ, *a wooden chest*, used of the ark of the covenant, Heb. ix. 4; Rev. xi. 19;

of Noah's ark, Lu. xvii. 27; Heb. xi. 7.

κιθάρα, ας, ἡ, *a harp*, 1 Cor. xiv. 7; Rev. xv. 2.

κιθαρίζω, *to play upon a harp*, 1 Cor. xiv. 7; Rev. xiv. 2.*

κιθαρ-ῳδός, οῦ, ὁ, *a harper, singer to the harp*, Rev. xiv. 2, xviii. 22.*

Κιλικία, ας, ἡ, *Cilicia*, Ac. vi. 9, xxi. 39.

κινάμωμον (W. H. κιννά-), ου, τό, *cinnamon*, Rev. xviii. 13.*

κινδυνεύω, σω, *to be in danger*, Lu. viii. 23; Ac. xix. 27, 40; 1 Cor. xv. 30.*

κίνδυνος, ου, ὁ, *danger, peril*, Ro. viii. 35; 2 Cor. xi. 26.*

κινέω, ῶ, ήσω, *to move, to stir*, Mat. xxiii. 4; Ac. xvii. 28; *to shake* the head in mockery, Mat. xxvii. 39; Mar. xv. 29; *to remove*, Rev. ii. 5, vi. 14; *to excite*, Ac. xvii. 28, xxi. 30, xxiv. 5.*

κίνησις, εως, ἡ, *a moving, agitation*, Jn. v. 3 (W. H. omit).*

Κίς (W. H. Κείς), ὁ (Heb.), *Kish*, father of Saul, Ac. xiii. 21.*

κίχρημι, *to lend*, Lu. xi. 5.*

κλάδος, ου, ὁ, *a branch*, as Mat. xiii. 32; met., Ro. xi. 16–19.

κλαίω, αύσω, (1) abs., *to wail, to lament*, Lu. xix. 41; (2) trans., *to weep for* (acc.), Mat. ii. 18.

κλάσις, εως, ἡ, *a breaking*, Lu. xxiv. 35; Ac. ii. 42.*

κλάσμα, ατος, τό, *a broken piece, a fragment*, as Mat. xiv. 20

Κλαύδη (W. H. Καῦδα), ης, ἡ, *Clauda* or *Cauda*, a small island near Crete, Ac. xxvii. 16.*

Κλαυδία, ας, ἡ, *Claudia*, 2 Tim. iv. 21.*

Κλαύδιος, ου, ὁ, *Claudius*, the Roman emperor, Ac. xi. 28, xviii. 2; a military tribune (Lysias), Ac. xxiii. 26.*

κλαυθμός, οῦ, ὁ (κλαίω), *weeping, lamentation*, as Mat. ii. 18.

κλάω, άσω, only with ἄρτον, *to break* bread, in the ordinary meal, Mat. xiv. 19; or in the Lord's Supper, xxvi. 26; fig., of the body of Christ, 1 Cor. xi. 24 (W. H. omit).

κλείς, κλειδός, acc. sing. κλεῖδα

or κλεῖν, acc. plur. κλεῖδας or κλεῖς, ἡ, a key, as a symbol of power and authority, Mat. xvi. 19; Rev. i. 18, iii. 7, ix. 1, xx. 1; met., Lu. xi. 52.*

κλείω, σω, to shut, shut up, Mat. vi. 6; Lu. iv. 25.

κλέμμα, ατος, τό'(κλέπτω), theft, Rev. xi. 21.*

Κλεόπας, α, ὁ, Cleopas, Lu. xxiv. 18.*

κλέος, ους, τό, glory, praise, 1 Pet. ii. 20.*

κλέπτης, ου, ὁ, a thief, as Mat. vi. 19; met., of false teachers, Jn. x. 8. Syn.: κλέπτης, a thief, who steals secretly; λῃστής, a robber, who plunders openly, by violence.

κλέπτω, ψω, to steal, abs., Mat. xix. 18; or trans. (acc.), Mat. xxvii. 64.

κλῆμα, ατος, τό (κλάω), a tender branch, a shoot, of a vine, etc., Jn. xv. 2, 4, 5, 6.*

Κλήμης, εντος, ὁ, Clement, Phil. iv. 3.*

κληρονομέω, ῶ, ήσω, to inherit, Gal. iv. 30; to obtain, generally, Lu. x. 25.

κληρονομία, ας, ἡ, an inheritance, Lu. xii. 13; a possession, Gal. iii. 18.

κληρο-νόμος, ου, ὁ, an heir, Mat. xxi. 38; applied to Christ, Heb. i. 2; in general, one who obtains a possession, Heb. vi. 17.

κλῆρος, ου, ὁ, (1) a lot, Mat. xxvii. 35; hence, (2) that which is allotted, a portion, Ac. i. 17, 25, viii. 21, xxvi. 18; Col. i. 12; plur., persons assigned to one's care, 1 Pet. v. 3.*

κληρόω, ῶ, to make a heritage, Ep. i. 11.*

κλῆσις, εως, ἡ, a calling, invitation, in N. T. always of the divine call, as Ro. xi. 29; Ep. iv. 4.

κλητός, ή, όν, verb. adj. (καλέω), called, invited, Mat. xxii. 14; of Christians, the called, Ro. i. 6, 7, viii. 28; called to an office, Ro. i. 1; 1 Cor. i. 1.

κλίβανος, ου, ὁ, an oven, a furnace, Mat. vi. 30; Lu. xii. 28.*

κλίμα, ατος, τό, a tract of country, a region, Ro. xv. 23; 2 Cor. xi. 10; Gal. i. 21.*

κλινάριον, ου, τό, a small bed, Ac. v. 15 (W. H.).*

κλίνη, ης, ἡ, a bed, Mar. vii. 30; a portable bed, Mat. ix. 2, 6; a couch for reclining at meals, Mar. iv. 21.

κλινίδιον, ου, τό (dim.), a small bed, a couch, Lu. v. 19, 24.*

κλίνω, νῶ, perf. κέκλικα, (1) trans., to bow, in reverence, Lu. xxiv. 5; in death, Jn. xix. 30; to recline the head for rest, Mat. viii. 20; to turn to flight, Heb. xi. 34; (2) intrans., to decline, as the day, Lu. ix. 12.

κλισία, ας, ἡ, a company reclining at a meal, Lu. ix. 14.*

κλοπή, ῆς, ἡ, theft, Mat. xv. 19; Mar. vii. 21.*

κλύδων, ωνος, ὁ, a violent agitation of the sea, a wave, Lu. viii. 24; Ja. i. 6.*

κλυδωνίζομαι, to be agitated, as waves by the wind, Ep. iv. 14. (S.)*

Κλωπᾶς, ᾶ, ὁ, Clopas, Jn. xix. 25.*

κνήθω, to tickle; pass., to be tickled, to itch, 2 Tim. iv. 3.*

Κνίδος, ου, ἡ, Cnidus, Ac. xxvii. 7.*

κοδράντης, ου, ὁ, Lat. (see Gr. § 154a, Bu. 17), a quadrans, farthing, the fourth part of the Roman as, Mat. v. 26; Mar. xii. 42. (N. T.)*

κοιλία, ας, ἡ, (1) the belly, Mat. xv. 17; (2) the womb, Mat. xix. 12; (3) fig., the inner man, the heart, Jn. vii. 38.

κοιμάω, ῶ, pass., to fall asleep, Lu. xxii. 45; met., to die, Jn. xi. 12.

κοίμησις, εως, ἡ, repose, taking rest, Jn. xi. 13.*

κοινός, ή, όν, common, i.e., shared by many, Ac. iv. 32; unclean, ceremonially, Ac. x. 15; Heb. x. 29.

κοινόω, ῶ, ώσω, to make common or unclean, to profane, Mat. xv. 11; Ac. xxi. 28.

κοινωνέω, ῶ, ήσω, to have common share in, to partake in, Ro. xv. 27; to be associated in, Gal. vi. 6.

κοινωνία, ας, ἡ, participation, communion, fellowship, as 1 Cor. x. 16; 2 Cor. xiii. 13; 1 Jn. i. 3, 6, 7; a contribution, Ro. xv. 26; Heb. xiii. 16.

κοινωνικός, ή, όν, ready to communicate, liberal, 1 Tim. vi. 18.*

κοινωνός, ή, όν, as subst., a partner, Lu. v. 10; a sharer with, gen. obj., 2 Cor. i. 7.

κοίτη, ης, ἡ, a bed, Lu. xi. 7; met., marriage bed, Heb. xiii. 4; sexual intercourse (as illicit), Ro. xiii. 13; κοίτην ἔχειν, to conceive, Ro. ix. 10.*

κοιτών, ῶνος, ὁ, a bed-chamber, Ac. xii. 20.*

κόκκινος, η, ον, dyed from the κόκκος, crimson, Heb. ix. 19; Rev. xvii. 4. (S.)

κόκκος, ου, ὁ, a kernel, a grain, Lu. xiii. 19, xvii. 6.

κολάζω, σω, mid., to chastise, to punish, Ac. iv. 21; pass., 2 Pet. ii. 9.*

κολακεία (W. H. -κία), ας, ἡ, flattery, 1 Th. ii. 5.*

κόλασις, εως, ἡ, chastisement, punishment, Mat. xxv. 46; 1 Jn. iv. 18.*

Κολασσαί, ῶν, αἱ, see Κολοσσαί.

κολαφίζω, σω, to strike with the fist, to maltreat, Mar. xiv. 65. (N. T.)

κολλάω, ῶ, ήσω, pass., to cleave to, to join one's self to, Lu. x. 11; Ac. viii. 29.

κολλούριον, or κολλύριον, ου, τό, collyrium, eye-salve, Rev. iii. 18.*

κολλυβιστής, οῦ, ὁ (κόλλυβος, small coin), a money-changer, Mat. xxi. 12; Mar. xi. 15; Jn. ii. 15.*

κολοβόω, ῶ, ώσω, to cut off, to shorten, Mat. xxiv. 22; Mar. xiii. 20.*

Κολοσσαεύς, έως, ὁ, plur. Κολοσσαεῖς (W. H. Κολασσαεῖς), Colossians, only in the heading and subscription (Rec.) to the Epistle.

Κολοσσαί, or Κολασσαί, ῶν, αἱ, Colossæ, Col. i. 2.*

κόλπος, ου, ὁ, the bosom, the chest, (1) of the body; ἐν τῷ κόλπῳ (or τοῖς κόλποις) εἶναι, ἀνακεῖσθαι, to be in the bosom of, i.e., recline next to, at table; Lu. xvi. 22, 23 (of the heavenly banquet); Jn. xiii. 23; the phrase in Jn. i. 18 implies a still closer fellowship; (2) of the dress, used as a bag or pocket, Lu. vi.

38; (3) *a bay, a gulf of the sea,* Ac. xxvii. 39.*

κολυμβάω, ῶ, ήσω, *to swim,* Ac. xxvii. 43.*

κολυμβήθρα, ας, ἡ, *a swimming-place, a pool,* Jn. v. 2, 4 (Rec.), 7, ix. 7, 11 (Rec.).*

κολώνια, or κολωνία (W. H.), ας, ἡ (Lat.), *a colony;* Philippi is so called, Ac. xvi. 12. (N. T.)*

κομάω, ῶ, *to wear the hair long,* 1 Cor. xi. 14, 15.*

κόμη, ης, ἡ, *hair* of the head, 1 Cor. xi. 15.*

κομίζω, σω, mid. fut. κομίσομαι or κομιοῦμαι, *to bear, to bring,* Lu. vii. 37; mid., *to bring for one's self, i.e., to obtain,* Heb. x. 36; *to receive again, to recover,* Heb. xi. 19.

κομψότερον (comp. of κομψός), *better,* of convalescence, adverbially with ἔχω, Jn. iv. 52.*

κονιάω, ῶ, *to whitewash,* Mat. xxiii. 27; pass., Ac. xxiii. 3.*

κονι-ορτός, οῦ, ὁ (ὄρνυμι), *dust,* Mat. x. 14.

κοπάζω, υω, *to grow weary, to cease,* of the wind, Mat. xiv. 32; Mar. iv. 39, vi. 51.*

κοπετός, οῦ, ὁ (κόπτω), *vehement lamentation,* Ac. viii. 2.*

κοπή, ῆς, ἡ, *cutting, slaughter,* Heb. vii. 1.*

κοπιάω, ῶ, άσω, *to be weary,* Mat. xi. 28; *to labor, to toil,* Lu. v. 5; in the Gospel, Ro. xvi. 6, 12; 1 Cor. xv. 10.

κόπος, ου, ὁ, *labor, toil, trouble,* Lu. xi. 7; 2 Th. iii. 8.

κοπρία, ας, ἡ, *dung, manure,* Lu. xiii. 8 (not W. H.), xiv. 35.*

κόπριον, ου, τό, *dung,* Lu. xiii. 8 (W. H.).*

κόπτω, mid. fut. κόψομαι, *to cut off,* as branches, trees, etc., Mat. xxi. 8; mid., *to beat or cut one's self in grief, to bewail,* as Mat. xi. 17.

κόραξ, ακος, ὁ, *a raven,* Lu. xii. 24.*

κοράσιον, ου, τό (prop. dim. from κόρη), *a girl,* as Mar. vi. 22, 28.

κορβάν (W. H. κορβάν), (indecl.), and κορβανᾶς, ᾶ, ὁ (from Heb.), (1) *a gift, an offering* to God, Mar. vii. 11; (2) *the sacred treasury,* Mat. xxvii. 6.*

Κορέ, ὁ (Heb.), *Korah,* Ju. 11.*

κορέννυμι, έσω, pass. perf. κεκόρεσμαι, *to satiate, satisfy,* Ac. xxvii. 38; 1 Cor. iv. 8.*

Κορίνθιος, ου, ὁ, *a Corinthian,* Ac. xviii. 8; 2 Cor. vi. 11.*

Κόρινθος, ου, ἡ, *Corinth,* Ac. xviii. 1, xix. 1.

Κορνήλιος, ου, ὁ, *Cornelius,* Ac. x.*

κόρος, ου, ὁ (from Heb.), *a cor,* the largest dry measure, equal to ten βάτοι, or ten Attic medimni, Lu. xvi. 7. (S.)*

κοσμέω, ῶ, ήσω, *to put in order, to prepare,* Mat. xxv. 7; *to adorn,* Mat. xxiii. 29; 1 Tim. ii. 9; met., with honor, Tit. ii. 10; 1 Pet. iii. 5.

κοσμικός, ή, όν, (1) *earthly,* opp. to ἐπουράνιος, Heb. ix. 1; (2) *worldly, i.e., corrupt,* Tit. ii. 12.*

κόσμιος, ου, *orderly, modest,* 1 Tim. ii. 9, iii. 2.*

κοσμο-κράτωρ, ορος, ὁ, *lord of this world, world-ruler* (R V.), Ep. vi. 12.*

κόσμος, ου, ὁ, (1) *ornament, decoration,* only 1 Pet. iii. 3; hence, (2) *the material universe,* Lu. xi. 50, as well ordered and beautiful; (3) *the world,* Jn. xi. 9; *worldly affairs,* Gal. vi. 14; (4) *the inhabitants of the world,* 1 Cor. iv. 9; as opposed to God, Jn. viii. 23; (5) *a vast collection,* of anything, Ja. iii. 6. *Syn.:* see αἰών.

Κούαρτος, ου, ὁ (Latin, see Gr. § 159), *Quartus,* Ro. xvi. 23.*

κοῦμι (a Hebrew imperative fem.), *arise,* Mar. v. 41 (W. H. read κούμ, the masculine form). (N. T.)*

κουστωδία, ας, ἡ (Latin, see Gr. § 154 c, Bu. 17), *a guard,* Mat. xxvii. 65, 66, xxviii. 11. (N. T.)*

κουφίζω, *to lighten,* as a ship, Ac. xxvii. 38.*

κόφινος, ου, ὁ, *a basket,* as Mat. xiv. 20.

κράββατος (W. H. κράβαττος), ου, ὁ, *a couch, a light bed,* as Mar. ii. 12.

κράζω, ξω, *to cry out,* hoarsely, or urgently, or in anguish, Mar. v. 5; Ac. xix. 32.

κραιπάλη, ης, ἡ, *surfeiting,* caused by excessive drinking, Lu. xxi. 34.*

κρανίον, ου, τό, *a skull,* Lu. xxiii. 33; Κρανίου Τόπος. Greek for Γολγοθά, which see, Mat. xxvii. 33; Mar. xv. 22; Jn. xix. 17.*

κράσπεδον, ου, τό, *the fringe, tassel,* of a garment, as Mat. xxiii. 5.

κραταιός, ά, όν, *strong, mighty,* 1 Pet. v. 6.*

κραταιόω, ῶ, in pass. only, *to be strong, to grow strong,* Lu. i. 80, ii. 40; 1 Cor. xvi. 13; Ep. iii. 16. (S.)*

κρατέω, ῶ, ήσω, with acc., or gen., or acc. and gen. (see Gr. § 264, Wi. § 30, 8 d, Bu. 161), *to get possession of, obtain,* Ac. xxvii. 13; *to take hold of,* Mar. i. 31; Ac. iii. 11; *to seize,* Mat. xiv. 3; *to hold,* Rev. ii. 1; *to hold fast,* Rev. ii. 25, iii. 11; *to retain,* of sins, Jn. xx. 23.

κράτιστος, η, ον (prop. superlative of κρατύς, see κράτος), *most excellent, most noble,* a title of honor, Lu. i. 3; Ac. xxiii. 26, xxiv. 3, xxvi. 25.*

κράτος, ους, τό, *strength, power, dominion,* Ep. i. 19; 1 Pet. iv. 11; Heb. ii. 14; κατὰ κράτος, Ac. xix. 20, *greatly, mightily.*

κραυγάζω, σω, *to cry out, to shout,* as Mat. xii. 19.

κραυγή, ῆς, ἡ, *a crying, outcry,* as Heb. v. 7.

κρέας (ατος, αος, contr. κρέως), τό, plur. κρέατα, κρέα, *flesh, flesh-meat,* Ro. xiv. 21; 1 Cor. viii. 13.*

κρείσσων (or -ττ-), ον (prop. compar. of κρατύς, see κράτος), *stronger, more excellent,* as Heb. vii. 7, xii. 24.

κρεμάννυμι, or κρεμάω, ῶ, fut. άσω, *to hang up,* trans., Ac. v. 30; mid., *to be suspended, to hang,* Mat. xxii. 40; Ac. xxviii. 4.

κρημνός, οῦ, ὁ (κρεμάννυμι), *a precipice,* from its overhanging, Mat. viii. 32; Mar. v. 13; Lu. viii. 33.*

Κρής, ητός, ὁ, *a Cretan,* Ac. ii. 11; Tit. i. 12.*

Κρήσκης, ὁ (Latin), *Crescens,* 2 Tim. iv. 10.*

Κρήτη, ης, ἡ, *Crete,* now Candia, Ac. xxvii. 7.

κριθή, ῆς, ἡ, barley, Rev. vi.
6.*

κρίθινος, η, ον, made of barley;
ἄρτοι κρίθινοι, barley loaves,
Jn. vi. 9, 13.*

κρίμα, ατος, τό, a judgment, a
sentence, condemnation, as 1
Cor. xi. 29.

κρίνον, ου, τό, a lily, Mat. vi.
28; Lu. xii. 27.*

κρίνω, νῶ, κέκρικα, 1st aor. pass.
ἐκρίθην, (1) to have an opinion,
to think, Ac. xiii. 46, xv. 19;
(2) to approve, prefer, Ro.
xiv. 5; (3) to resolve, determine, 1 Cor. vii. 37; Tit. iii.
12; (4) to try, to sit in judgment on, Jn. xviii. 31; pass.
and mid., to appeal to trial,
i.e., to have a lawsuit, 1 Cor.
vi. 6.

κρίσις, εως, ἡ, (1) opinion,
formed and expressed, Jn.
viii. 16; Ju. 9; (2) judgment,
the act or result of, Ja. ii.
13; Lu. x. 14; (3) condemnation and punishment, Heb. x.
27; Rev. xviii. 10; (4) a tribunal, Mat. v. 21, 22; (5)
justice, Mat. xxiii. 23.

Κρίσπος, ου, ὁ, Crispus, Ac.
xviii. 8; 1 Cor. i. 14.*

κριτήριον, ου, τό, (1) a tribunal,
a court of justice, 1 Cor. vi.
2, 4 (see R. V.); Ja. ii. 6.*

κριτής, οῦ, ὁ, a judge, Mat. v.
25; Ac. xviii. 15; of the
O. T. "Judges," Ac. xiii.
20.

κριτικός, ή, όν, skilled in judging, gen. obj., Heb. iv. 12.*

κρούω, σω, to knock at a door,
Lu. xiii. 25.

κρύπτη, ης, ἡ, a cellar, a vault,
Lu. xi. 33.*

κρυπτός, ή, όν, verbal adj.
(κρύπτω), hidden, secret, Mat.
x. 26; Ro. ii. 16.

κρύπτω, ψω, 2d aor. pass. ἐκρύ-
βην, to hide, conceal, to lay up,
as Col. iii. 3.

κρυσταλλίζω, to be clear, like
crystal, Rev. xxi. 11. (N.T.)*

κρύσταλλος, ου, ὁ, crystal, Rev.
iv. 6, xxii. 1.*

κρυφαῖος, α, ον, hidden, secret,
Mat. vi. 18 (W. H.).*

κρυφῇ (W. H. -ῇ), adv., in
secret, secretly, Ep. v. 12.*

κτάομαι, ῶμαι, fut. ἤσομαι, ἐκτησάμην, dep., to acquire,
procure (price, gen., or ἐκ),
(see Gr. § 273, Wi. §§ 38, 7,

40, 4 b), Mat. x. 9; Lu. xviii.
12, xxi. 19; Ac. i. 18, viii.
20, xxii. 28; 1 Th. iv. 4.*

κτῆμα, ατος, τό, anything acquired, a possession, Mat.
xix. 22; Mar. x. 22; Ac. ii.
45, v. 1.

κτῆνος, ους, τό, a beast of burden (as representing property), Lu. x. 34; Ac. xxiii. 24;
1 Cor. xv. 39; Rev. xviii.
13.*

κτήτωρ, ορος, ὁ, a possessor, Ac.
iv. 34.*

κτίζω, σω, perf. pass. ἔκτισμαι,
to create, form, shape, physically or spiritually, as Ro.
i. 25; Ep. ii. 10.

κτίσις, εως, ἡ, creation, (1) the
act, Ro. i. 20; (2) the thing
created, creature, Ro. i. 25;
creation, generally, Ro. viii.
19–22; (3) met., an ordi-
nance, 1 Pet. ii. 13.

κτίσμα, ατος, τό, a thing created, a creature, 1 Tim. iv. 4;
Ja. i. 18; Rev. v. 13, viii.
9.*

κτίστης, ου, ὁ, a founder; a
creator, 1 Pet. iv. 19.*

κυβεία, ας, ἡ, dice-playing, fraud,
Ep. iv. 14.*

κυβέρνησις, εως, ἡ, governing,
direction, 1 Cor. xii. 28.*

κυβερνήτης, ου, ὁ, a steersman,
a pilot, Ac. xxvii. 11; Rev.
xviii. 17.*

κυκλεύω, to encircle, surround,
Rev. xx. 9 (W. H.).*

κυκλόθεν, adv. (κύκλος), round
about, gen., Rev. iv. 3, 4, 8,
v. 11 (not W. H.).*

κύκλος, ου, ὁ, a circle; only
in dat., κύκλῳ, as adv., abs.,
or with gen., round about,
around, Mar. iii. 34; vi. 6.

κυκλόω, ῶ, to encircle, surround, besiege, Lu. xxi. 20;
Jn. x. 24; Ac. xiv. 20; Heb.
xi. 30; Rev. xx. 9 (Rec.).*

κύλισμα, ατος, τό, a place for
wallowing, 2 Pet. ii. 22 (not
W. H.). (N.T.)*

κυλισμός, οῦ, ὁ, a rolling, wallowing, 2 Pet. ii. 22 (W. H.).*

κυλίω (for κυλίνδω), pass., to be
rolled, to wallow, Mar. ix.
20.*

κυλλός, ή, όν, crippled, lame,
especially in the hands, Mat.
xv. 30 (not W. H.), 31 (not
W. H.), xviii. 8; Mar. ix.
43.*

κῦμα, ατος, τό, a wave, as Mat.
viii. 24; Mar. iv. 37; Ju. 13.

κύμβαλον, ου, τό (κύμβος, hollow), a cymbal, 1 Cor. xiii.
1.*

κύμινον, ου, τό (from Heb.),
cumin, Mat. xxiii. 23.*

κυνάριον, ου, τό (dim. of κύων),
a little dog, Mat. xv. 26, 27;
Mar. vii. 27, 28.*

Κύπριος, ου, ὁ, a Cyprian or
Cypriote, Ac. iv. 36.

Κύπρος, ου, ἡ, Cyprus, Ac. xi.
19, xiii. 4.

κύπτω, ψω, to bend, to stoop
down, Mar. i. 7; Jn. viii. 6,
8 (W. H. omit).

Κυρηναῖος, ου, ὁ, a Cyrenæan,
Ac. vi. 9, xi. 20.

Κυρήνη, ης, ἡ, Cyrene, a city
of Africa, Ac. ii. 10.*

Κυρήνιος, ου, ὁ, Cyrenius or
Quirinius, Lu. ii. 2.*

κυρία, ας, ἡ, a lady, 2 Jn. i. 5
(some read Κυρία, Cyria, a
proper name).*

κυριακός, ή, όν, of or pertaining to the Lord, as the supper, 1 Cor. xi. 20; the day,
Rev. i. 10.*

κυριεύω, εύσω, to have authority,
abs., 1 Tim. vi. 15; to rule
over (gen.), Lu. xxii. 25.

κύριος, ου, ὁ, (1) lord, master,
Lu. xx. 15; Ac. xvi. 16; a
title of honor, Mat. xiii. 27,
xvi. 22; (2) the Lord, applied
to God, Mar. v. 19; Ac. vii.
33; (3) the Lord, employed
in the Epp. constantly of
Christ (see Gr. § 217 b, Wi.
§ 19, 1 a, p. 124, Bu. 89),
Ac. ix. 1; Ro. xiv. 8. Syn.:
see δεσπότης.

κυριότης, τητος, ἡ, lordship, dominion; collective concr.,
lords, Ep. i. 21; Col. i. 16; 2
Pet. ii. 10; Ju. 8. (N.T.)*

κυρόω, ῶ, to confirm, ratify, 2
Cor. ii. 8; Gal. iii. 15.*

κύων, κυνός, ὁ, ἡ, a dog, Lu. xvi.
21; fig., of shameless persons,
Phil. iii. 2.

κῶλον, ου, τό, a limb, a carcase,
N.T. plur. only, Heb. iii. 17.*

κωλύω, σω, to restrain, forbid,
hinder, Mar. ix. 38.

κώμη, ης, ἡ, a village, unwalled,
Mat. ix. 35.

κωμό-πολις, εως, ἡ, a large, city-
like village, without walls,
Mar. i. 38.*

κῶμος, ου, ὁ, a feasting, revel-

ing, Ro. xiii. 13; Gal. v. 21; 1 Pet. iv. 3.*

κώνωψ, ωπος, ὁ, *a gnat*, Mat. xxiii. 24.*

Κῶς, ῶ, ἡ, *Cos*, Ac. xxi. 1.*

Κωσάμ, ὁ (Heb.), *Cosam*, Lu. iii. 28.*

κωφός, ή, όν (κόπτω, lit., *blunted*), *dumb*, Mat. ix. 32, 33; *deaf*, Mat. xi. 5.

Δ

Δ, λ, λάμβδα, *lambda, l*, the eleventh letter. As a numeral, λ′ = 30; ͵λ = 30,000.

λαγχάνω, 2d aor. ἔλαχον, trans., *to obtain by lot, to obtain*, acc. or gen., Lu. i. 9; Ac. i. 17; 2 Pet. i. 1; abs., *to cast lots*, περί, gen., Jn. xix. 24.*

Λάζαρος, ου, ὁ, *Lazarus*, (1) of Bethany, Jn. xi. 1, 2; (2) in the parable, Lu. xvi. 20–25.

λάθρα (W. H. λάθρᾳ), (λανθάνω), adv., *secretly*, Jn. xi. 28.

λαῖλαψ απος, ἡ, *a whirlwind, a violent storm*, Mar. iv. 37; Lu. viii. 23; 2 Pet. ii. 17.*

λακτίζω (λάξ, adv., *with the heel*), *to kick*, Ac. ix. 5 (W. H. omit), xxvi. 14.*

λαλέω, ῶ, ήσω, (1) *to utter a sound, to speak*, absolutely, Rev. x. 4; Heb. xii. 24; Ja. ii. 12; (2) *to speak, to talk*, with acc. of thing spoken, also with modal dat. and dat. of person addressed. Hence, according to the nature of the case, met., *to declare*, by other methods than *vivâ voce*, as Ro. vii. 1; *to preach, to publish, to announce. Syn.: λέγω* has reference to the *thought* uttered; λαλέω simply to the *fact* of utterance.

λαλιά, ᾶς, ἡ, (1) *speech, report*, Jn. iv. 42; (2) *manner of speech, dialect*, Mat. xxvi. 73; Mar. xiv. 70 (W. H. omit); Jn. viii. 43.*

λαμά, or λαμμᾶ (perh. Heb.), and λεμά (Aram.), *why*, Mat. xxvii. 46; Mar. xv. 34 (Ps. xxii. 1). (N. T.)*

λαμβάνω, λήψομαι (W. H. λήμψομαι), εἴληφα, ἔλαβον, (1) *to take*, as in the hand, Mat. xiv. 19; hence, (2) *to claim, procure*, Lu. xix. 12; (3) *to take by force, seize*, Mat. xxi. 35; (4) *to take away*, by violence or fraud, Mat. v. 40; (5) *to choose*, Ac. xv. 14; (6) *to receive, accept, obtain*, Jn. xvi. 24; Ja. iii. 1; Rev. xviii. 4; (7) in certain periphrastic expressions — λαμβάνειν ἀρχήν, *to begin;* λ. λήθην, *to forget;* λ. ὑπόμνησιν, *to remember;* λ. πεῖραν, *to experience;* λ. πρόσωπον, "*to accept the person*," *i.e., to be partial.* The preposition "from," after this verb, is expressed by ἐκ, ἀπό, παρά (ὑπό, 2 Cor. xi. 24).

Λάμεχ, ὁ (Heb.), *Lamech*, Lu. iii. 36.*

λαμπάς, άδος, ἡ, prop. *a torch*, Rev. iv. 5, viii. 10; also *a lamp*, Jn. xviii. 3. *Syn.: φῶς* is light in general; φέγγος, radiance; φωστήρ, a heavenly body, luminary; λαμπάς, a torch; λύχνος, a lamp.

λαμπρός, ά, όν, *shining, magnificent*, Rev. xxii. 16; Lu. xxiii. 11.

λαμπρότης, τητος, ἡ, *splendor, brightness*, Ac. xxvi. 13.*

λαμπρῶς, adv., *magnificently*, Lu. xvi. 19.*

λάμπω, ψω, *to shine*, Mat. v. 15, 16, xvii. 2.

λανθάνω, 2d aor. ἔλαθον, (1) *to be hidden*, abs., Mar. vii. 24; Lu. viii. 47; (2) *to be hidden from* (acc.), Ac. xxvi. 26; 2 Pet. iii. 5, 8; (3) for part. constr., see Gr. § 394, 2, Wi. § 54, 4, Bu. 299; Heb. xiii. 2.*

λαξευτός, ή, όν, *hewn out of a rock*, Lu. xxiii. 53. (S.)*

Λαοδικεία, ας, ἡ, *Laodicea*, Col. ii. 1, iv. 13.

Λαοδικεύς, έως, ὁ, *a Laodicean*, Col. iv. 16; Rev. iii. 14 (not W. H.).*

λαός, οῦ, ὁ, (1) *a people*, spec. of *the people* of God, Lu. ii. 31; Ac. iv. 10; (2) *the common people*, Mat. xxvi. 5.

λάρυγξ, υγγος, ὁ, *the throat*, Ro. iii. 13.*

Λασαία (W. H. Λασέα), ας, ἡ, *Lasæa*, Ac. xxvii. 8.*

λάσκω, 1st aor. ἐλάκησα, *to burst asunder*, Ac. i. 18.*

λατομέω, ῶ, *to hew stones, to cut stones*, Mat. xxvii. 60; Mar. xv. 46. (S.)*

λατρεία, ας, ἡ, *worship, service rendered to God*, Jn. xvi. 2; Ro. ix. 4, xii. 1; Heb. ix. 1, 6.*

λατρεύω, σω, (1) *to worship, to serve*, Ac. vii. 7; (2) *to officiate as a priest*, Heb. xiii. 10. *Syn.: λατρεύω* is to worship God, as any one may do; λειτουργέω, to serve him in a special office or ministry.

λάχανον, ου, τό, *an herb, a garden plant*, Mat. xiii. 32.

Λεββαῖος, ου, ὁ, *Lebbæus*, Mat. x. 3 (not W. H.). See Θαδδαῖος.*

λεγεών (W. H. λεγιών), ῶνος, ὁ (Lat., see Gr. § 154e, Bu. 16), *a legion*, Mat. xxvi. 53; Mar. v. 9, 15; Lu. viii. 30; in N.T. times containing probably 6826 men. (N. T.)*

λέγω, only pres. and impf. in N. T., (1) *to speak, to say*, Ac. xiii. 15; Jn. i. 29, used also of writings, as Jn. xix. 37; (2) *to relate, to tell*, Lu. ix. 31, xviii. 1; (3) *to call*, pass., *to be called* or *named;* (4) pass., *to be chosen* or *appointed.* Dat. of person addressed. *Syn.:* see λαλέω.

λεῖμμα, ατος, τό (λείπω), *a remnant*, Ro. xi. 5.*

λεῖος, εία, εῖον, *smooth, level*, Lu. iii. 5 (from S.).*

λείπω, ψω, *to leave, to be wanting*, Lu. xviii. 22; Tit. i. 5, iii. 13; pass., *to be lacking, to be destitute of*, Ja. i. 4, 5, ii. 15.*

λειτουργέω, ῶ, (1) *to serve publicly in sacred things*, Ac. xiii. 2; Heb. x. 11; (2) *to minister to charitably*, Ro. xv. 27.* *Syn.:* see λατρεύω.

λειτουργία, ας, ἡ, (1) *a public ministration* or *service*, Lu. i. 23; Phil. ii. 17; Heb. viii. 6, ix. 21; (2) *a charitable gift*, Phil. ii. 30; 2 Cor. ix. 12.*

λειτουργικός, ή, όν, *employed in ministering*, Heb. i. 14 (S.)*

λειτουργός, οῦ, ὁ, *a minister* or *servant* to, gen. obj., Ro. xiii. 6, xv. 16; Phil. ii. 25; Heb. i. 7, viii. 2.*

λέντιον, ου, τό (Lat., see Gr. § 154e), *a towel, apron*, Jn. xiii. 4, 5. (N. T.)*

λεπίς, ίδος, ἡ, *a scale*, Ac. ix. 18.*

λέπρα, ας, ἡ, *the leprosy*, Mat. viii. 3; Mar. i. 42; Lu. v. 12, 13.*

λεπρός, οῦ, ὁ, *a leper*, Lu. iv. 27, vii. 22.

λεπτόν, οῦ, τό, prop. verb. adj. (sc. νόμισμα), from λέπω (*to strip off, pare down*), *a mite*, a small brass coin, one eighth of an *as*, the smallest Jewish coin, Mar. xii. 42; Lu. xii. 59, xxi. 2.*

Λευΐ, or Λευΐς (W. H. Λευείς), gen. Λευΐ, ὁ, *Levi*. Four are mentioned : (1) son of Jacob, ancestor of the priestly tribe; (2, 3) ancestors of Jesus, Lu. iii. 24, 29; (4) the apostle, also called *Matthew*, Lu. v. 27, 29.

Λευΐτης, ου, ὁ, *a Levite*, Lu. x. 32; Jn. i. 19; Ac. iv. 36.*

Λευϊτικός, ή, όν, *Levitical*, Heb. vii. 11.*

λευκαίνω, ανῶ, 1st aor. ἐλεύκανα, *to make white*, Mar. ix. 3; Rev. vii. 14.*

λευκός, ή, όν, (1) *white*, as Mat. v. 36; Jn. iv. 35; (2) *bright*, as Mat. xvii. 2.

λέων, οντος, ὁ, *a lion*, Heb. xi. 33; fig., 2 Tim. iv. 17; of Christ, Rev. v. 5.

λήθη, ης, ἡ, *forgetfulness*, 2 Pet. i. 9.*

ληνός, οῦ, ἡ, *a wine-press*, Mat. xxi. 33; fig. in Rev. xiv. 19, 20, xix. 15.*

λῆρος, ου, ὁ, *idle talk*, Lu. xxiv. 11.*

λῃστής, οῦ, ὁ, *a robber*, Mar. xi. 17; Jn. x. 1, 8. *Syn.:* see κλέπτης.

λῆψις (W. H. λῆμψις), εως, ἡ (λαμβάνω), *a receiving*, Phil. iv. 15.*

λίαν, adv., *very much;* with adj. or adv., *very*, Mat. iv. 8; Mar. xvi. 2.

λίβανος, ου, ὁ, *frankincense*, Mat. ii. 11; Rev. xviii. 13.*

λιβανωτός, οῦ, ὁ, *a censer for burning frankincense*, Rev. viii. 3, 5.*

λιβερτῖνος, ου, ὁ (Lat. *libertinus*), *a freedman*, Ac. vi. 9. Probably Jews who had been slaves at Rome under Pompey, and afterwards freed.*

Λιβύη, ης, ἡ, *Libya*, Ac. ii. 10.*

λιθάζω, σω, *to stone*, Jn. xi. 8; Ac. xiv. 19.

λίθινος, η, ον, *made of stone*, Jn. ii. 6; 2 Cor. iii. 3; Rev. ix. 20.*

λιθο-βολέω, ῶ, ήσω, *to throw stones at, to stone*, Mat. xxiii. 37; Mar. xii. 4 (W. H. omit). (S.)

λίθος, ου, ὁ, *a stone, i.e.*, (1) loose and lying about, Mat. iv. 3, 6; (2) built into a wall, etc., Mar. xiii. 2; (3) *a precious stone*, Rev. iv. 3, xvii. 4; (4) *a statue* or *idol* of stone, Ac. xvii. 29.

λιθό-στρωτον, ου, τό (prop. adj., *spread with stones*), *a mosaic pavement*, as name of a place near the prætorium or palace at Jerusalem, Jn. xix. 13.*

λικμάω, ῶ, ήσω, *to scatter*, as grain in winnowing, *to grind to powder* that may be scattered, Mat. xxi. 44; Lu. xx. 18.*

λιμήν, ένος, ὁ, *a harbor*, Ac. xxvii. 8, 12.*

λίμνη, ης, ἡ, *a lake, e.g.*, Gennesaret, Lu. v. 1.

λιμός, οῦ, ὁ, (1) *hunger*, 2 Cor. xi. 27; (2) *a famine*, Mat. xxiv. 7.

λίνον, ου, τό, *flax, linen made of flax*, Rev. xv. 6 (W. H. λίθος); *a lamp-wick*, Mat. xii. 20.*

Λίνος (W. H. Λίνος), ου, ὁ, *Linus*, 2 Tim. iv. 21.*

λιπαρός, ά, όν, *fat, dainty*, Rev. xviii. 14.*

λίτρα, ας, ἡ, *a pound*, a weight of twelve ounces, Jn. xii. 3, xix. 39.*

λίψ, λιβός, ὁ, *the S.W. wind;* used for the S.W. quarter of the heavens, Ac. xxvii. 12.*

λογία, ας, ἡ, *a collection, i.e.*, of money, 1 Cor. xvi. 1, 2. (N.T.)*

λογίζομαι, σομαι, dep. with mid. and pass., (1) *to reckon;* (2) *to place to the account of, to charge with*, acc. and dat., or with εἰς (see Gr. § 298, 6, Wi. § 32, 4 *b*, Bu. 151); (3) *to reason, argue, to infer, conclude*, from reasoning ; (4) *to think, suppose.*

λογικός, ή, όν, *rational, i.e.*, belonging to the sphere of

the reason, Ro. xii. 1; 1 Pet. ii. 2.*

λόγιον, ου, τό, *something spoken*, in N. T., *a divine communication, e.g.*, the Old Testament, Ac. vii. 38; Ro. iii. 2; and the doctrines of Christ, Heb. v. 12; 1 Pet. iv. 11.*

λόγιος, ον, *eloquent*, Ac. xviii. 24.*

λογισμός, οῦ, ὁ, *a reasoning, decision*, Ro. ii. 15; 2 Cor. x. 5.*

λογο-μαχέω, ῶ, *to contend about words*, 2 Tim. ii. 14. (N.T.)*

λογομαχία, ας, ἡ, *contention about words*, 1 Tim. vi 4. (N. T.)*

λόγος, ου, ὁ, (1) *a speaking, a saying, a word*, as the expression of thought (whereas ἔπος, ὄνομα, ῥῆμα refer to words in their outward form, as parts of speech), Mat. viii. 8; (2) the thing spoken, Mat. vii. 24, 26 — whether *doctrine*, 1 Tim. iv. 6; *prophecy*, 2 Pet. i. 19; *question*, Mat. xxi. 24; *a common saying* or *proverb*, Jn. iv. 37; *a precept, a command*, Jn. viii. 55; *the truth*, Mar. viii. 38; *conversation*, Lu. xxiv. 17; *teaching*, 1 Cor. ii. 4; *a narrative*, Ac. i. 1; *a public rumor*, Mat. xxviii. 15; *an argument*, Ac. ii. 40; *a charge* or *accusation*, Ac. xix. 38; (3) *reason*, Ac. xviii. 14; (4) *account, reckoning*, Heb. iv. 13; Ac. xx. 24; Mat. xviii. 23; Ac. x. 29; λόγος is used by John as a name of Christ, the Word of God, *i.e.*, the expression or manifestation of his thoughts to man, Jn. i. 1, etc.

λόγχη, ης, ἡ, *a lance, a spear*, Jn. xix. 34.*

λοιδορέω, ῶ, *to rail at, revile*, Jn. ix. 28; Ac. xxiii. 4; 1 Cor. iv. 12; 1 Pet. ii. 23.*

λοιδορία, ας, ἡ, *reviling*, 1 Tim. v. 14; 1 Pet. iii. 9.*

λοίδορος, ου, ὁ, *a reviler*, 1 Cor. v. 11, vi. 10.*

λοιμός, οῦ, ὁ, *a pestilence*, Mat. xxiv. 7 (W. H. omit), Lu. xxi. 11; Paul so called, Ac. xxiv. 5.*

λοιπός, ή, όν, *remaining, the rest*, Mat. xxv. 11; adv. τὸ λοιπόν, *as for the rest, more-*

over, finally, henceforth, 1
Cor. i. 16; Heb. x. 13; τοῦ
λοιποῦ, from henceforth, Gal.
vi. 17.

Δουκᾶς, ᾶ, ὁ (from Λουκανός,
see Gr. § 159 d, Wi. § 16, 4,
note 1, Bu. 20), Luke, Ac.
xvi. 10, xx. 5.

Δούκιος, ου, ὁ (Lat.), Lucius,
Ac. xiii. 1; Ro. xvi. 21.*

λουτρόν, οῦ, τό, a bath; in N.T.
baptism, Ep. v. 26; Tit. iii.
5.*

λούω, σω, to bathe, to wash, Ac.
ix. 37, xvi. 33; to cleanse, to
purify, Rev. i. 5 (W. H. λύω).
Syn.: πλύνω is to wash inanimate things; λούω, to
bathe the whole body; νίπτω,
to wash a part of the body.

Λύδδα, ης, ἡ, also Λύδδα, ων,
τά (W. H.), Lydda, Ac. ix.
32, 35, 38.*

Λυδία, as, ἡ, Lydia, Ac. xvi. 14,
40.*

Λυκαονία, as, ἡ, Lycaonia, Ac.
xiv. 6.*

Λυκαονιστί, adv., in the speech
of Lycaonia, Ac. xiv. 11.*

Λυκία, as, ἡ, Lycia, Ac. xxvii. 5.*

λύκος, ου, ὁ, a wolf, Jn. x. 12;
fig., Ac. xx. 29.

λυμαίνομαι, to ravage, to de-
vastate, Ac. viii. 3.*

λυπέω, ῶ, to grieve, a general
word, 2 Cor. ii. 2, 5; pass.,
to be grieved, saddened, Mat.
xxvi. 22, 37; 1 Pet. i. 6; to
aggrieve or offend, Ro. xiv.
15; Ep. iv. 30.

λύπη, ης, ἡ, grief, sorrow, 2
Cor. ix. 7; cause of grief,
annoyance, 1 Pet. ii. 19.

Λυσανίας, ου, ὁ, Lysanias, Lu.
iii. 1.*

Λυσίας, ου, ὁ, Lysias, Ac. xxiii.
26.

λύσις, εως, ἡ, a loosing, divorce,
1 Cor. vii. 27.*

λυσι-τελέω, ῶ (lit., to pay taxes),
impers., -εῖ, it is profitable or
preferable (dat. and ἤ), Lu.
xvii. 2.*

Λύστρα, as, ἡ, or ων, τά, Lystra,
Ac. xiv. 6, 8.

λύτρον, ου, τό, a ransom, Mat.
xx. 28; Mar. x. 45.*

λυτρόω, ῶ, ώσω, in N. T. only
mid. and pass., to ransom, to
deliver by paying a ransom,
Lu. xxiv. 21; Tit. ii. 14; 1
Pet. i. 18 (acc., pers.; dat.,
price, and ἀπό or ἐκ).*

λύτρωσις, εως, ἡ, deliverance,
redemption, Lu. i. 68, ii. 38;
Heb. ix. 12.*

λυτρωτής, οῦ, ὁ, a redeemer, a
deliverer, Ac. vii. 35.*

λυχνία, as, ἡ, a lampstand,
Mat. v. 15; fig., of a church,
Rev. ii. 1, 5; of a Christian
teacher, Rev. xi. 4.

λύχνος, ου, ὁ, a lamp, Mat. v.
15, vi. 22; used of John
the Baptist, Jn. v. 35; of
Christ, Rev. xxi. 23. Syn.:
see λαμπάς.

λύω, σω, to loose, as (1) lit., to
unbind, Mar. i. 7; Rev. v. 2;
(2) to set at liberty, Jn. xi. 44;
Ac. xxii. 30; (3) to pronounce
not binding, e.g., a law, Mat.
xviii. 18; (4) to disobey or
nullify the divine word, Jn.
vii. 23, x. 35; (5) to destroy,
e.g., the temple, Jn. ii. 19;
(6) to dismiss, i.e., an assembly, Ac. xiii. 43.

Λωΐς, ΐδος, ἡ, Lois, 2 Tim. i.
5.*

Λώτ, ὁ (Heb.), Lot, Lu. xvii.
28–32; 2 Pet. ii. 7.*

M

M, μ, μῦ, mu, m, the twelfth
letter. As a numeral, μ′ = 40;
͵μ = 40,000.

Μαάθ, ὁ (Heb.), Maath, Lu. iii.
26.*

Μαγδαλά, ἡ (Heb.), Magdala,
Mat. xv. 39 (W. H. and R.V.
Μαγαδάν).*

Μαγδαληνή, ῆς, ἡ, Magdalene,
i.e., a woman of Magdala, as
Mat. xxvii. 56, 61.

μαγεία (W. H. μαγία), as, ἡ,
magic, plur., magical arts,
Ac. viii. 11.*

μαγεύω, σω, to practice magical
arts, Ac. viii. 9.*

μάγος, ου, ὁ, (1) a magus, a
Persian astrologer, Mat. ii.
1, 7, 16; (2) a sorcerer, Ac.
xiii. 6, 8.*

Μαγώγ, ὁ (Heb.), Magog, Rev.
xx. 8; see Γώγ.*

Μαδιάμ, ἡ (Heb.), Midian, Ac.
vii. 29.*

μαθητεύω, σω, (1) trans., to
make a disciple of (acc.), to
instruct, Mat. xiii. 52, xxviii.
19; Ac. xiv. 21; (2) intrans.,
to be a disciple, Mat. xxvii.
57 (Rec., W. H. read pass.,
W. H. with active in mrg.).*

μαθητής, οῦ, ὁ (μανθάνω), a disciple, Mat. ix. 14, x. 24, xxii.
16; οἱ μαθηταί, specially, the
twelve, Mat. ix. 19.

μαθήτρια, as, ἡ, a female disciple, Ac. ix. 36.*

Μαθουσάλα, ὁ (Heb.), Methu-
selah, Lu. iii. 37.*

Μαϊνάν, ὁ (W. H. Μεννά),
(Heb.), Mainan or Menna,
Lu. iii. 31.*

μαίνομαι, dep., to be mad, to
rave, Jn. x. 20; Ac. xii. 15,
xxvi. 24, 25; 1 Cor. xiv.
23.*

μακαρίζω, fut. ιῶ, to pronounce
happy or blessed, Lu. i. 48;
Ja. v. 11.*

μακάριος, a, ον, happy, blessed,
Mat. v. 3–11; Lu. i. 45, vi.
20; 1 Cor. vii. 40.

μακαρισμός, οῦ, ὁ, a declaring
blessed, a pronouncing happy,
Ro. iv. 6, 9; Gal. iv. 15.*

Μακεδονία, as, ἡ, Macedonia,
Ac. xvi. 9, 10, 12.

Μακεδών, όνος, ὁ, a Macedonian,
Ac. xix. 29, xxvii. 2.

μάκελλον, ου, τό (Lat.), a meat
market, 1 Cor. x. 25.*

μακράν, adv. (acc. of μακρός,
sc. ὁδόν), afar, afar off, Lu.
xv. 20; εἰς preceding, Ac. ii.
39; ἀπό following, Ac. xvii.
27.

μακρόθεν, adv., from afar, Mar.
viii. 3; with ἀπό, as Mat.
xxvii. 55.

μακρο-θυμέω, ῶ, ήσω, to suffer
long, to have patience, to be
forbearing, 1 Cor. xiii. 4; to
delay, Lu. xviii. 7; to wait
patiently, Heb. vi. 15. (S.)

μακρο-θυμία, as, ἡ, forbearance, long-suffering, patience,
Ro. ii. 4, ix. 22. Syn.: see
ἀνοχή.

μακρο-θύμως, adv., patiently,
Ac. xxvi. 3. (N. T.)*

μακρός, ά, όν, long; of place,
distant, Lu. xv. 13, xix. 12;
of time, long, only in the
phrase μακρὰ προσεύχεσθαι,
to make long prayers, Mat.
xxiii. 14 (W. H. omit); Mar.
xii. 40; Lu. xx. 47.*

μακρο-χρόνιος, ον, long-lived,
Ep. vi. 3.*

μαλακία, as, ἡ, weakness, infirmity, Mat. iv. 23, ix. 35,
x. 1.*

μαλακός, ή, όν, soft, of garments, Mat. xi. 8; Lu. vii

25; *disgracefully effeminate*, 1 Cor. vi. 9.*

Μαλελεήλ, ὁ (Heb.), *Maleleel* or *Mahalaleel*, Lu. iii. 37.*

μάλιστα, adv. (superl. of μάλα, *very*), *most of all, especially*, Gal. vi. 10; 2 Tim. iv. 13.

μᾶλλον, adv. (comp. of μάλα), *more, rather;* πολλῷ μᾶλλον, *much more*, Mat. vi. 30; πόσῳ μᾶλλον, *how much more*, Mat. vii. 11; μᾶλλον ἤ, *more than*, Mat. xviii. 13; μᾶλλον is often of intensive force, *e.g.*, Mat. xxvii. 24; Ro. viii. 34. See Gr. § 321, Wi. §§ 35, 1, 65, 2, Bu. 83.

Μάλχος, ου, ὁ (Heb.), *Malchus*, Jn. xviii. 10.*

μάμμη, ης, ἡ, *a grandmother*, 2 Tim. i. 5.*

μαμμωνᾶς (W. H. μαμωνᾶς), ᾶ, ὁ (Aram.), *mammon, gain, wealth*, Mat. vi. 24; Lu. xvi. 9, 11, 13. (N. T.)*

Μαναήν, ὁ (Heb.), *Manaen*, Ac. xiii. 1.*

Μανασσῆς, gen. and acc. ῆ, ὁ, *Manasseh*, (1) son of Joseph, Rev. vii. 6; (2) Mat. i. 10.*

μανθάνω, μαθήσομαι, 2d aor. ἔμαθον, perf. μεμάθηκα, *to learn, to understand, to know, to be informed, to comprehend*. Used abs., or with acc. (ἀπό or παρά with gen. of the teacher, ἐν with example, 1 Cor. iv. 6).

μανία, ας, ἡ, *madness*, Ac. xxvi. 24.*

μάννα, τό (Heb., deriv. uncertain), *manna*, the food of the Israelites in the desert, Jn. vi. 31, 49; Heb. ix. 4. (S.)

μαντεύομαι, dep., *to utter responses, practice divination*, Ac. xvi. 16.*

μαραίνω, ανῶ, fut. pass. μαρανθήσομαι, *to wither, to fade away*, Ja. i. 11.*

μαρὰν ἀθά (two Aram. words), *our Lord cometh* (R.V. mrg.), 1 Cor. xvi. 22. (N. T.)*

μαργαρίτης, ου, ὁ, *a pearl*, Mat. xiii. 45, 46.

Μάρθα, ας, ἡ, *Martha*, Lu. x. 38, 40, 41.

Μαρία, ας, or **Μαριάμ**, indecl. (Heb. *Miriam*), ἡ, *Mary*. Six of the name are mentioned: (1) the mother of Jesus, Lu. i. 27; (2) the Magdalene, Mar. xv. 40, 47;

(3) the sister of Martha and Lazarus, Lu. x. 39, 42; (4) the wife of Cleopas, Mat. xxvii. 56, 61; (5) the mother of John Mark, Ac. xii. 12; (6) a Christian woman in Rome, Ro. xvi. 6.

Μάρκος, ου, ὁ, *Mark*, Ac. xii. 12, 25.

μάρμαρος, ου, ὁ, ἡ, *marble*, Rev. xviii. 12.*

μαρτυρέω, ῶ, ήσω, *to be a witness*, abs., *to testify* (περί, gen.), *to give testimony* (*to*, dat. of pers. or thing), *to commend;* pass., *to be attested*, *i.e.*, *honorably, to be of good report*.

μαρτυρία, ας, ἡ, *testimony, i.e.*, *legal*, Mar. xiv. 56, 59; or *general*, Jn. v. 34; with obj. gen., as Rev. xix. 10.

μαρτύριον, ου, τό, *testimony*, Mat. viii. 4 (*to*, dat.; *against*, ἐπί, acc.).

μαρτύρομαι, dep., *to call to witness*, Ac. xx. 26; Gal. v. 3; *to exhort solemnly*, Ac. xxvi. 22 (W. H.); Ep. iv. 17; 1 Th. ii. 11 (W. H.).*

μάρτυς, υρος, dat. plur. μάρτυσι, ὁ, *a witness, i.e.*, *judicially*, Mat. xviii. 16; *one who testifies* from what he has seen or experienced, 1 Th. ii. 10, Lu. xxiv. 48; *a martyr*, witnessing by his death, Ac. xxii. 20; Rev. ii. 13, xvii. 6.

μασσάομαι (W. H. -ασά-), ῶμαι, *to bite, to gnaw*, Rev. xvi. 10.*

μαστιγόω, ῶ, ώσω, *to scourge*, Mat. x. 17; fig., Heb. xii. 6.

μαστίζω, *to scourge*, Ac. xxii. 25.*

μάστιξ, ιγος, ἡ, *a whip, a scourge*, Ac. xxii. 24; Heb. xi. 36; fig., *calamity, disease*, Mar. iii. 10, v. 29, 34; Lu. vii. 21.*

μαστός, οῦ, ὁ, *the breast*, pl., Lu. xi. 27, xxiii. 29; Rev. i. 13.*

ματαιολογία, ας, ἡ, *vain, fruitless talk*, 1 Tim. i. 6.*

ματαιο-λόγος, ου, ὁ, *a vain, empty talker*, Tit. i. 10.*

μάταιος (αία), αιον, *vain, useless, empty*, 1 Cor. xv. 17; Ja. i. 26; τὰ μάταια, *vanities*, spec. of heathen deities, Ac. xiv. 15 (and O.T.). *Syn.:* see κενός.

ματαιότης, τητος, ἡ, (1) *vanity*,

2 Pet. ii. 18; (2) *perverseness*, Ep. iv. 17; (3) *frailty*, Ro. viii. 20.*

ματαιόω, ῶ, *to make vain* or *foolish;* pass., Ro. i. 21. (S.)*

μάτην, adv., *in vain, fruitlessly*, Mat. xv. 9; Mar. vii. 7.*

Ματθαῖος (W. H. Μαθθαῖος), ου, ὁ, *Matthew*, the apostle and evangelist, Mat. ix. 9, 10; also called Λευΐ.

Ματθάν (W. H. Μαθθάν), ὁ (Heb.), *Matthan*, Mat. i. 15.*

Ματθάτ, ὁ (Heb.), *Matthat*, Lu. iii. 24, 29 (W. H. Μαθθάτ).*

Ματθίας (W. H. Μαθθίας), α, ὁ, *Matthias*, Ac. i. 23, 26.*

Ματταθά, ὁ (Heb.), *Mattatha*, Lu. iii. 31.*

Ματταθίας, ου, ὁ, *Mattathias*, Lu. iii. 25, 26.*

μάχαιρα, ας and ης, ἡ, *a sword*, Jn. xviii. 10, 11; met., for *strife*, Mat. x. 34; fig., of spiritual weapons, Ep. vi. 17.

μάχη, ης, ἡ, *battle; contention, strife*, 2 Cor. vii. 5; 2 Tim. ii. 23; Tit. iii. 9; Ja. iv. 1.*

μάχομαι, *to fight, contend, dispute*, Jn. vi. 52; Ac. vii. 26; 2 Tim. ii. 24; Ja. iv. 2.*

μεγαλ-αυχέω, ῶ, *to boast great things, to be arrogant*, Ja. iii. 5 (W. H. μεγάλα αὐχεῖ).*

μεγαλεῖος, εία, εῖον, *grand, magnificent*, Lu. i. 49 (W. H. μεγάλα); Ac. ii. 11.*

μεγαλειότης, τητος, ἡ, *majesty, magnificence*, Lu. ix. 43; Ac. xix. 27; 2 Pet. i. 16.*

μεγαλο-πρεπής, ές, gen. οῦς, *fitting for a great man, magnificent, majestic*, 2 Pet. i. 17.*

μεγαλύνω, νῶ, (1) *to make great*, Mat. xxiii. 5; (2) *to magnify, extol, celebrate with praise*, Lu. i. 46; Ac. v. 13.

μεγάλως, adv., *greatly*, Phil. iv. 10.*

μεγαλωσύνη, ης, ἡ, *majesty*, Heb. i. 3, viii. 1; Ju. 25. (S.)*

μέγας, μεγάλη, μέγα (see Gr. § 39), comp. μείζων, sup. μέγιστος, *great*, in size, *full-grown, intense*, Mat. ii. 10, xxviii. 8; *wonderful*, 2 Cor. xi. 15; *noble, of high rank*, Rev. xi. 18, xiii. 16; applied to age, ὁ μείζων, *the elder*, Ro. ix. 12; μέγας indicates the *size* of things, their *meas-*

ure, number, cost, and *esti-mation* ; μεγάλη ἡμέρα, *a solemn, sacred day,* Jn. xix. 31.

μέγεθος, ους, τό, *greatness,* Ep. i. 19.*

μεγιστᾶνες, άνων, οἱ (sing. μεγι-στάν, only in Ap., Sirach iv. 7), *princes, great men, nobles,* Mar. vi. 21; Rev. vi. 15, xviii. 23. (S.)*

μεθ-ερμηνεύω, *to translate, to interpret,* pass. only, Mar. v. 41; Jn. i. 41.

μέθη, ης, ἡ, *drunkenness,* Lu. xxi. 34; Ro. xiii. 13; Gal. v. 21.*

μεθ-ίστημι (and μεθιστάνω, 1 Cor. xiii. 2), μεταστήσω, 1st aor., pass., μετεστάθην, lit., *to change the place of;* hence, *to remove,* 1 Cor. xiii. 2; Col. i. 13; *to lead astray,* Ac. xix. 26; *to re-move* from life, Ac. xiii. 22; *to remove* from office, Lu. xvi. 4.*

μεθ-οδεία (-οδία, W. H.), ας, ἡ, *a fraudulent artifice, a trick,* Ep. iv. 14, vi. 11. (N.T.)*

μεθ-όριος, α, ον, *bordering on;* τὰ μεθόρια, *borders, frontiers,* Mar. vii. 24 (W. H. ὅρια).*

μεθύσκω, *to make drunk;* pass., *to be drunk,* Lu. xii. 45; Jn. ii. 10; Ep. v. 18; 1 Th. v. 7.*

μέθυσος, ου, ὁ (prop. adj.), *a drunkard,* 1 Cor. v. 11, vi. 10.*

μεθύω, *to be drunken,* Mat. xxiv. 49; Ac. ii. 15; met., Rev. xvii. 6.

μείζων, comp. of μέγας, which see. It has itself a com-parative, μειζότερος, 3 Jn. 4 (see Gr. § 47, Wi. § 11, 2 b, Bu. 28).

μέλαν, ανος, τό (μέλας), *ink,* 2 Cor. iii. 3; 2 Jn. 12; 3 Jn. 13.*

μέλας, αινα, αν, *black,* Mat. v. 36; Rev. vi. 5, 12.*

Μελεᾶς, ᾶ, ὁ, *Melea,* Lu. iii. 31.*

μέλει, impers. (see Gr. § 101, Wi. § 30, 10d, Bu. 164), *it concerns,* dat. of pers., with gen. of object, as 1 Cor. ix. 9; or περί, as Jn. x. 13; or ὅτι, as Mar. iv. 38.

μελετάω, ῶ, ἤσω, *to practice,* 1 Tim. iv. 15; *to devise,* Ac. iv.

25; *to meditate,* Mar. xiii. 11 (not W. H.).*

μέλι, ιτος, τό, *honey,* Mat. iii. 4; Mar. i. 6; Rev. x. 9, 10.*

μελίσσιος, α, ον, *made by bees,* Lu. xxiv. 42 (W. H. omit). (N. T.)*

Μελίτη, ης, ἡ, *Melita,* now Malta, Ac. xxviii. 1 (W. H. Μελιτήνη).*

μέλλω, ἤσω, *to be about to do, to be on the point of doing,* with infin., generally the present infin., rarely aor.; the fut. infin. (the regular classical use) occurs only in the phrase μέλλειν ἔσεσθαι (only in Ac.); the verb may often be adequately rendered by our auxiliaries, *will, shall, must; to delay,* only Ac. xxii. 16. The participle is used absolutely: τὸ μέλλον, *the future,* Lu. xiii. 9; τὰ μέλ-λοντα, *things to come,* Ro. viii. 38. See Gr. § 363f, Wi. § 44, 7 c, Bu. 259.

μέλος, ους, τό, *a member* of the body, *a limb,* as Mat. v. 29, 30; Ro. xii. 4; fig., 1 Cor. vi. 15.

Μελχί (W. H. -εί), ὁ (Heb.), *Melchi.* Two are mentioned, Lu. iii. 24, 28.*

Μελχισεδέκ, ὁ (Heb. *king of righteousness*), *Melchizedek,* Heb. v., vi., vii.*

μεμβράνα, ης, ἡ (Lat.), *parch-ment,* 2 Tim. iv. 13. (N.T.)*

μέμφομαι, ψομαι, dep., *to blame, to censure,* abs., Mar. vii. 2 (W. H. omit); Ro. ix. 19; abs. or dat., Heb. viii. 8 (W. H. acc., with dat. mrg.).*

μεμψί-μοιρος, ον, *discontented, complaining,* Ju. 16.*

μέν, antithetic particle, *truly, indeed* (see Gr. § 136, Wi. § 53, 7 b), Bu. 364 sq.).

μεν-οῦν, conj., *moreover, there-fore, but.*

μεν-οῦν-γε, conj., *nay rather, nay truly,* Lu. xi. 28 (W. H. μενοῦν); Ro. ix. 20, x. 18; Phil. iii. 8 (W. H. μὲν οὖν γε). See Gr. § 406, Wi. § 61, 6, Bu. 370 sq.*

μέν-τοι, conj., *yet truly, never-theless, however,* Jn. iv. 27.

μένω, μενῶ, ἔμεινα, (1) intrans., *to remain, to abide;* so (a) of place, *to dwell,* Mat. x. 11; *to lodge,* Lu. xix. 5; (b) of

state, as Ac. v. 4; *to continue firm* and *constant in,* Jn. xv. 4; *to endure, to last, to be permanent,* 1 Cor. iii. 14; (2) trans., *to await, wait for,* only Ac. xx. 5, 23.

μερίζω, σω, (1) *to divide, sepa-rate,* mid., *to share* (μετά, gen.), Lu. xii. 13; pass., *to be divided, to be at variance,* Mat. xii. 25, 26; 1 Cor. i. 13; (2) *to distribute,* Mar. vi. 41, acc. and dat.

μέριμνα, ης, ἡ, *care, anxiety,* as dividing, distracting the mind, Mat. xiii. 22; Lu. viii. 14.

μεριμνάω, ῶ, ἤσω, *to be anxious, distracted, to care for;* abs., with dat., περί (gen.), acc. The various constructions may be illustrated from Mat. vi.: abs., vers. 27, 31; acc., ver. 34 (Rec.; see also 1 Cor. vii. 32–34); gen., ver. 34 (W. H.); dat., ver. 25; εἰς, ver. 34; περί, ver. 28.

μερίς, ίδος, ἡ, *a part* or *division* of a country, Ac. xvi. 12; *a share, portion,* Lu. x. 42; Ac. viii. 21, 2 Cor. vi. 15; Col. i. 12.*

μερισμός, οῦ, ὁ, *a dividing* or *division,* Heb. iv. 12; *dis-tribution, gifts distributed,* Heb. ii. 4.*

μεριστής, οῦ, ὁ, *a divider,* Lu. xii. 14. (N.T.)*

μέρος, ους, τό, *a part;* hence, (1) *a share,* Rev. xxii. 19; *fellowship,* Jn. xiii. 8; *a business* or *calling,* Ac. xix. 27; (2) *a part,* as the result of division, Jn. xix. 23. In adverbial phrases, μέρος τι, *partly, in some part;* ἀνὰ μέ-ρος, *alternately;* ἀπὸ μέρους, *partly; ἐκ μέρους, individual-ly,* of persons, *partially, im-perfectly,* of things; κατὰ μέρος, *particularly, in detail,* Heb. ix. 5.

μεσημβρία, ας, ἡ, *midday, noon,* Ac. xxii. 6; *the south,* Ac. viii. 26.

μεσιτεύω, σω, *to mediate, to give surety,* Heb. vi. 17.*

μεσίτης, ου, ὁ, *a mediator, i.e.,* one who interposes between parties and reconciles them, Gal. iii. 19, 20; 1 Tim. ii. 5; in the phrase μεσίτης διαθή-κης, *mediator of a covenant,* Heb. viii. 6, ix. 15, xii. 24.*

μεσο-νύκτιον, ου, τό, *midnight*, as Lu. xi. 5.

Μεσο-ποταμία, ας, ἡ, *Mesopotamia*, the region between the Euphrates and the Tigris, Ac. ii. 9, vii. 2.*

μέσος, η, ον, *middle*, of time or place, *in the midst* of (gen.), as Mat. xxv. 6; Jn. i. 26, xix. 18; Ac. i. 18, xxvi. 13; neut., τὸ μέσον, *the middle part*, used chiefly in adverbial phrases, with prepositions (art. generally omit.), ἐκ μέσου, *from among, away;* ἐν μέσῳ, *among;* ἀνὰ μέσον, *through the midst, among, between;* also with διά and εἰς.

μεσό-τοιχον, ου, τό, *a partition-wall*, Ep. ii. 14. (N. T.)*

μεσ-ουράνημα, ατος, τό, *mid-heaven*, Rev. viii. 13, xiv. 6, xix. 17.*

μεσόω, ῶ, *to be in the middle*, Jn. vii. 14.*

Μεσσίας, ου, ὁ (from Heb. *anointed*), *Messiah*, the same as Greek Χριστός, Jn. i. 41, iv. 25. (N. T.)*

μεστός, ή, όν, *full*, gen., Jn. xix. 29; Ro. i. 29.

μεστόω, ῶ, *to fill*, gen., Ac. ii. 13.*

μετά (akin to μέσος), prep., gov. the gen. and acc.; gen., *with, among;* acc., *after* (see Gr. § 301, Wi. §§ 47 h, 49 f, 52, 4, 10), Bu. 338 sq.). In composition, μετά denotes *participation, nearness, change,* or *succession* (often like the Latin prefix *trans-,* as in the words *transfer, translate*).

μετα-βαίνω, βήσομαι, *to pass over, to depart*, Lu. x. 7; Mat. xi. 1.

μετα-βάλλω, in mid., *to change one's mind*, Ac. xxviii. 6.*

μετ-άγω, *to turn about, to direct*, as horses, ships, Ja. iii. 3, 4.*

μετα-δίδωμι, *to share with, to impart*, Lu. iii. 11; Ro. i. 11; 1 Th. ii. 8; Ep. iv. 28; ὁ μεταδιδούς, *a distributor* of alms, Ro. xii. 8.*

μετά-θεσις, εως, ἡ, (1) *a transfer, a translation*, Heb. xi. 5; *a removal*, Heb. xii. 27; (2) *a change*, Heb. vii. 12.*

μετ-αίρω, *to remove*, intrans., *to depart*, Mat. xiii. 53, xix. 1.*

μετα-καλέω, ῶ, in mid., *to call to one's self, to send for*, Ac. vii. 14, x. 32, xx. 17, xxiv. 25.*

μετα-κινέω, ῶ, *to move away*, pass., *to be moved away*, Col. i. 23.*

μετα-λαμβάνω, *to take a share of*, Ac. ii. 46; *partake*, gen., 2 Tim. ii. 6; *to obtain* (acc.), Ac. xxiv. 25.

μετά-ληψις (W. H.-λημψις), εως, ἡ, *participation;* εἰς μ., *to be received*, 1 Tim. iv. 3.*

μετ-αλλάσσω, *to change* one thing (acc.) for (ἐν, εἰς) another, Ro. i. 25, 26.*

μετα-μέλομαι, μελήσομαι, 1st aor. μετεμελήθην, dep., pass., *to change one's mind*, Mat. xxi. 30, 32; Heb. vii. 21; *to repent, to feel sorrow for, regret*, Mat. xxvii. 3; 2 Cor. vii. 8. *Syn.:* μετανοέω is the nobler word, the regular expression for thorough repentance; μεταμέλομαι is more loosely used, generally expressing sorrow, regret or remorse.

μετα-μορφόω, ῶ, *to change the form, to transform*, Mat. xvii. 2; Mar. ix. 2; 2 Cor. iii. 18; Ro. xii. 2.*

μετα-νοέω, ῶ, ήσω, *to change one's views* and *purpose, to repent*, as Mat. iii. 2; Ac. viii. 22. *Syn.:* see μεταμέλομαι.

μετάνοια, ας, ἡ, *change of mind, repentance*, as Mat. iii. 8, 11.

μετα-ξύ (σύν or ξύν), adv. of time, *meanwhile*, Jn. iv. 31; *afterwards*, perh., Ac. xiii. 42 (see Gr. § 298, 7 b); as prep. with gen., *between*, of place, Mat. xxiii. 35.

μετα-πέμπω, in mid., *to send for to one's self, to summon*, Ac. x. 5, 22, 29, xi. 13, xxiv. 24, 26, xxv. 3; pass., x. 29.*

μετα-στρέφω (with 2d fut. and 2d aor. pass.), *to turn about, to change*, Ja. iv. 9; Ac. ii. 20; *to pervert, to corrupt*, Gal. i. 7.*

μετα-σχηματίζω, ίσω, *to change the figure of, transfigure*, Phil. iii. 21; mid., *to assume the appearance of any one*, 2 Cor. xi. 13, 14, 15; fig., *to transfer, i.e., to speak by way of illustration*, 1 Cor. iv. 6.*

μετα-τίθημι, *to transpose, to transfer*, Ac. vii. 16; Heb. xi. 5; *to change*, Heb. vii. 12; mid., *to transfer one's self, i.e., to fall away, to desert*, Gal. i. 6; *to pervert*, Ju. 4.*

μετ-έπειτα, adv., *afterwards*, Heb. xii. 17.*

μετ-έχω, μετασχήσω, 2d aor. μετέσχον, *to be partaker of, to share in*, 1 Cor. ix. 10, 12, x. 17, 21, 30; Heb. ii. 14, v. 13, vii. 13.*

μετεωρίζω, in pass., *to be troubled with anxiety, to be in suspense*, Lu. xii. 29.*

μετ-οικεσία, ας, ἡ, *change of abode, migration* (of the Babylonian exile), Mat. i. 11, 12, 17.*

μετ-οικίζω, ιῶ, *to cause to change one's habitation, to cause to migrate*, Ac. vii. 4, 43.*

μετοχή, ῆς, ἡ, *a sharing, a fellowship*, 2 Cor. vi. 14.*

μέτοχος, ου, ὁ (prop. adj.), *a partaker*, Heb. iii. 1, 14, vi. 4, xii. 8; *a partner, an associate*, Heb. i. 9; Lu. v. 7.*

μετρέω, ῶ, *to measure*, Rev. xi. 2; Lu. vi. 38; met., *to estimate, to judge of*, 2 Cor. x. 12.

μετρητής, οῦ, ὁ, prop. *a measurer; an amphora*, a liquid measure containing 72 sextarii, or somewhat less than 9 English gallons, Jn. ii. 6.*

μετριο-παθέω, ῶ, *to treat with moderation, bear gently with* (R. V.), Heb. v. 2.*

μετρίως, adv., *moderately*, Ac. xx. 12.*

μέτρον, ου, τό, *a measure*, Mat. xxiii. 32; Mar. iv. 24; *a measuring-rod*, Rev. xxi. 15; *a definite portion* or *measure*, Ro. xii. 3; Ep. iv. 16; adv. phrases, ἐκ μέτρου, *by measure, sparingly*, Jn. iii. 34; ἐν μέτρῳ, *in due measure*, Ep. iv. 16.

μέτωπον, ου, τό (ὤψ), *the forehead*, Rev. vii. 3, ix. 4 (only in Rev.).

μέχρι, or μέχρις, adv., as prep. with gen., *unto*, time, Mat. xiii. 30; Mar. xiii. 30; place, Ro. xv. 19; degree, 2 Tim. ii 9; Heb. iii. 4; as conj., *until*, Ep. iv. 13.

μή, a negative particle, *not;* for

distinction between μή and οὐ, see Gr. § 401, Wi. § 55, 1, Bu. 351 ; elliptically, *lest*, see Gr. § 384, Wi. § 56, 2 *b*, Bu. 241 sq.; interrogatively, see Gr. § 369, Wi. § 57, 3 *b*, Bu. 248 ; for the combination οὐ μή, see Gr. § 377, Wi. § 57, 3 *b*, Bu. 211 sq.

μή-γε, in the phrase εἰ δὲ μήγε, *but if not*, emphatic.

μηδαμῶς, adv., *by no means*, Ac. x. 14, xi. 8.*

μηδέ, compare οὐδέ, and see Gr. § 401, Wi. § 55, 6, Bu. 366 sq.; *not even*, Mar. ii. 2 ; 1 Cor. v. 11 ; generally used after a preceding μή, *and not, neither, but not, nor yet*, as Mat. vi. 25, vii. 6.

μηδείς, μηδεμία, μηδέν (εἷς), differing from οὐδείς as μή from οὐ (see Gr. § 401, Wi. § 55, 1, Bu. 351); *not one, no one, no person* or *thing, nothing*, Mat. viii. 4; Mar. v. 26; Gal. vi. 3.

μηδέ-ποτε, adv., *never*, 2 Tim. iii. 7.*

μηδέ-πω, adv., *not yet*, Heb. xi. 7.*

Μῆδος, ου, ὁ, *a Mede*, Ac. ii. 9.*

μηκέτι, adv. (ἔτι) *no more, no longer*, Mar. ix. 25, xi. 14; Ac. iv. 17.

μῆκος, ους, τό, *length*, Ep. iii. 18; Rev. xxi. 16.*

μηκύνω, *to make long;* pass., *to grow up*, as plants, Mar. iv. 27.*

μηλωτή, ῆς, ἡ, *a sheepskin*, Heb. xi. 37.*

μήν, a part. of strong affirmation, N. T. only in the combination ἦ μήν, *assuredly, certainly*, Heb. vi. 14 (W. H. εἰ μήν).*

μήν, μηνός, ὁ, (1) *a month*, as Ac. vii. 20; (2) *the new moon*, as a festival, Gal. iv. 10.

μηνύω, *to show, declare*, Lu. xx. 37; Jn. xi. 57; Ac. xxiii. 30; 1 Cor. x. 28.*

μὴ οὐκ, an interrogative formula, expecting the answer "yes," Ro. x. 18, 19; 1 Cor. ix. 4, 5.

μή-ποτε, adv., *never*, Heb. ix. 17; as conj., *lest ever, lest perhaps, lest at any time*, Lu. xii. 58; Ac. v. 39; interrog. part., *whether indeed,* Jn. vii. 26; Lu. iii. 15.

μή που, *lest anywhere*, Ac. xxvii. 29 (W. H., for Rec. μήπως).

μή-πω, adv., *not yet*, Ro. ix. 11; Heb. ix. 8.*

μή-πως, conj., *lest in any way, lest perhaps*, as Ac. xxvii. 29 (W. H. μή που), 1 Th. iii. 5.

μηρός, οῦ, ὁ, *the thigh*, Rev. xix. 16.*

μήτε, conj., differing from οὔτε as μή from οὐ (see Gr. § 401); *and not*, used after a preceding μή or μήτε, *neither ... nor;* in Mar. iii. 20, *not even*, W. H. read μηδέ.

μήτηρ, τρός, ἡ, *a mother*, Mat. i. 18, ii. 11 ; met., *a mother city*, Gal. iv. 26.

μήτι, adv., interrogatively used, *is it? whether at all?* generally expecting a negative answer; μήτιγε (W. H., Rec. μήτι γε), *not to say then?* 1 Cor. vi. 3.

μήτις (W. H. μή τις), pron. interrog., *has* or *is any one? whether any one?* Jn. iv. 33.*

μήτρα, ας, ἡ, *the womb*, Lu. ii. 23; Ro. iv. 19.*

μητρ-αλῷας (W. H. -ολῷας), ου, ὁ, *a matricide*, 1 Tim. i. 9.*

μία, fem. of εἷς, *one*.

μιαίνω, ανῶ, perf. pass. μεμίασμαι, *to stain, pollute, defile*, Jn. xviii. 28; Tit. i. 15, Heb. xii. 15; Ju. 8.*

μίασμα, ατος, τό, *pollution, defilement*, 2 Pet. ii. 20.*

μιασμός, οῦ, ὁ, *the act of defilement, pollution*, 2 Pet. ii. 10.*

μίγμα, ατος, τό, *a mixture*, Jn. xix. 39 (W. H. text ἔλιγμα).*

μίγνυμι, μίξω, ἔμιξα, perf. pass. μέμιγμαι, *to mix, to mingle*, Mat. xxvii. 34; Lu. xiii. 1; Rev. viii. 7, xv. 2.*

μικρός, ά, όν, *little, small, i.e.*, in size, Mat. xiii. 32 ; quantity, 1 Cor. v. 6; number, Lu. xii. 32; time, Jn. vii. 33; dignity, Mat. x. 42; age, Mat. xviii. 6, 10, 14.

Μίλητος, ου, ἡ, *Miletus*, Ac. xx. 15, 17 ; 2 Tim. iv. 20.*

μίλιον, ου, τό (Lat. *miliarium*), *a mile* (somewhat .ess than our mile), Mat. v. 41.*

μιμέομαι, οῦμαι, dep. mid., *to imitate*, 2 Th. iii. 7, 9; Heb. xiii. 7; 3 Jn. 11.*

μιμητής, οῦ, ὁ, *an imitator*, as 1 Cor. iv. 16.

μιμνήσκω (μνα-), mid., with fut. in pass. form μνησθήσομαι, 1st aor. ἐμνήσθην, perf. μέμνημαι, *to call to mind, to remember*, gen. pers. or thing, Mat. xxvi. 75; Lu. xxiii. 42; pass., *to be remembered, to be had in mind*, only Ac. x. 31; Rev. xvi. 16.

μισέω, ῶ, ήσω, *to hate, to detest*, Mat. v. 43; Jn. vii. 7; Ro. ix. 13.

μισθ-απο-δοσία, ας, ἡ, *recompense*, as (1) *reward*, Heb. x. 35, xi. 26; (2) *punishment*, Heb. ii. 2. (N. T.)*

μισθ-απο-δότης, ου, ὁ, *a rewarder*, Heb. xi. 6. (N. T.)*

μίσθιος, α, ον, *hired*, as subst., *a hired servant*, Lu. xv. 17, 19, 21 (W. H. in br.).*

μισθός, οῦ, ὁ, *hire, wages, recompense*, Mat. xx. 8; used of *reward*, Mat. v. 12, 46; of *punishment*, 2 Pet. ii. 13.

μισθόω, ῶ, ώσω, mid., *to hire*, Mat. xx. 1, 7.*

μίσθωμα, ατος, τό, *hire, rent;* anything rented, as a house, Ac. xxviii. 30.*

μισθωτός, οῦ, ὁ, *a hired servant*, Mar. i. 20; Jn. x. 12, 13.*

Μιτυλήνη, ης, ἡ, *Mitylene*, the capital of Lesbos, Ac. xx. 14.*

Μιχαήλ, ὁ (Heb. *who is like God?*), *Michael*, an archangel, Ju. 9; Rev. xii. 7.*

μνᾶ, ᾶς, ἡ, *a mina*, silver money = 100 δραχμαί, or about sixteen or seventeen dollars, Lu. xix. 13–25.*

μνάομαι, see μιμνήσκω.

Μνάσων, ωνος, ὁ, *Mnason*, Ac. xxi. 16.*

μνεία, ας, ἡ, *remembrance, recollection*, Phil. i. 3; 1 Th. iii. 6; μνείαν ποιεῖσθαι, *to mention*, Ro. i. 9.

μνῆμα, ατος, τό, *a monument, a tomb*, Mar. v. 5; Lu. xxiii. 53; less frequent than the following.

μνημεῖον, ου, τό, *a tomb, a sepulchre*, Mat. viii. 28; Jn. xi. 31.

μνήμη, ης, ἡ, *remembrance, mention;* μνήμην ποιεῖσθαι, *to make mention*, 2 Pet. i. 15.*

μνημονεύω, *to remember* (ὅτι)

recollect, call to mind (gen. or acc.), Mat. xvi. 9; Ac. xx. 31; to be mindful of, Heb. xi. 15; to make mention of (περί, gen.), Heb. xi. 22.

μνημόσυνον, ου, τό, a memorial, honorable remembrance, Mat. xxvi. 13; Mar. xiv. 9; Ac. x. 4.*

μνηστεύω, to ask in marriage; pass., to be betrothed, Mat. i. 18; Lu. i. 27, ii. 5.*

μογι-λάλος, ου, ὁ (prop. adj.), one speaking with difficulty, a stammerer, Mar. vii. 32.*

μόγις, adv., with difficulty, hardly, Lu. ix. 39 (W. H. μόλις).*

μόδιος, ου, ὁ (Lat.), a dry measure (16 sextarii), containing about a peck; a modius, Mat. v. 15; Mar. iv. 21; Lu. xi. 33. (N. T.)*

μοιχαλίς, ίδος, ἡ, an adulteress, Ro. vii. 3; fig., for departure from God, Mat. xvi. 4; Ja. iv. 4. (S.)

μοιχάομαι, ῶμαι, to commit adultery, Mat. v. 32.

μοιχεία, ας, ἡ, adultery, Mat. xv. 19.

μοιχεύω, σω, to commit adultery, abs. (acc., Mat. v. 28); fig., of forsaking God, Rev. ii. 22.

μοιχός, οῦ, ὁ, an adulterer, Lu. xviii. 11; 1 Cor. vi. 9; Heb. xiii. 4; Ja. iv. 4 (not W. H.).*

μόλις, adv., with difficulty, hardly, Lu. ix. 39 (W. H.); Ac. xiv. 18, xxvii. 7, 8, 16; Ro. v. 7; 1 Pet. iv. 18.*

Μολόχ, ὁ (Heb.), Moloch, Ac. vii. 43 (from S.).*

μολύνω, υνῶ, to pollute, to defile, 1 Cor. viii. 7; Rev. iii. 4, xiv. 4.*

μολυσμός, οῦ, ὁ, pollution, defilement, 2 Cor. vii. 1. (S.)*

μομφή, ῆς, ἡ, complaint, ground of complaint, Col. iii. 13.*

μονή, ῆς, ἡ, an abode, a dwelling-place, Jn. xiv. 2, 23.*

μονο-γενής, ές, gen. οῦς, only begotten, Lu. vii. 12, viii. 42, ix. 38; Heb. xi. 17; of Christ, Jn. i. 14, 18, iii. 16, 18; 1 Jn. iv. 9.*

μόνος, η, ον, only, alone, single, Lu. xxiv. 18; solitary, without company, Mar. vi. 47; forsaken, desolate, Jn. viii. 29; adv., μόνον, only.

μον-όφθαλμος, ον, having but one eye, Mat. xviii. 9; Mar. ix. 47.*

μονόω, ῶ, to leave alone; pass., to be left alone or desolate, 1 Tim. v. 5.*

μορφή, ῆς, ἡ, outward appearance, form, shape, Mar. xvi. 12; Phil. ii. 6, 7.* Syn.: see ἰδέα.

μορφόω, ῶ, ώσω, to form, to fashion, Gal. iv. 19.*

μόρφωσις, εως, ἡ, form, semblance, 2 Tim. iii. 5; form, system, Ro. ii. 20.*

μοσχο-ποιέω, ῶ, to make an image of a calf, Ac. vii. 41. (N. T.)*

μόσχος, ου, ὁ, ἡ, a calf, a young bullock, Lu. xv. 23, 27, 30; Heb. ix. 12, 19; Rev. iv. 7.*

μουσικός, ἡ, όν, skilled in music, a musician, Rev. xviii. 22.*

μόχθος, ου, ὁ, wearisome labor, toil, 2 Cor. xi. 27; 1 Th. ii. 9; 2 Th. iii. 8.*

μυελός, οῦ, ὁ, marrow, Heb. iv. 12.*

μυέω, ῶ, to initiate into, to instruct, Phil. iv. 12.*

μῦθος, ου, ὁ, a word; hence, a fiction, a fable, a falsehood, 1 Tim. i. 4, iv. 7; 2 Tim. iv. 4; Tit. i. 14; 2 Pet. i. 16.*

μυκάομαι, ῶμαι, to bellow, to roar, as a lion, Rev. x. 3.*

μυκτηρίζω, to turn up the nose; to mock, deride, Gal. vi. 7.*

μυλικός, ἡ, όν, pertaining to a mill; with λίθος, millstone, Mar. ix. 42 (not W. H.); Lu. xvii. 2 (W. H.). (N. T.)*

μύλινος, η, ον, in sense of foregoing, Rev. xviii. 21 (W. H.).*

μύλος, ου, ὁ, a millstone, as Mat. xviii. 6.

μυλών, ῶνος, ὁ, a mill-house, the place where grain was ground, Mat. xxiv. 41 (W. H. μύλος).*

Μύρα (W. H. Μύρρα), ων, τά, Myra, a city near the coast of Lycia, Ac. xxvii. 5.*

μυριάς, άδος, ἡ, a myriad, ten thousand, Ac. xix. 19; a vast multitude, Lu. xii. 1; Ac. xxi. 20; Heb. xii. 22; Ju. 14; Rev. v. 11, ix. 16.*

μυρίζω, σω, to anoint, Mar. xiv. 8.*

μυρίοι, ιαι, ια, innumerable, 1 Cor. iv. 15, xiv. 19; μύριοι,

ιαι, ια, ten thousand, Mat. xviii. 24.*

μύρον, ου, τό, ointment, Mat. xxvi. 7.

Μυσία, ας, ἡ, Mysia, Ac. xvi. 7, 8.*

μυστήριον, ου, τό, a mystery, anything hidden, a secret, Mat. xiii. 11; Ro. xi. 25. In classical Greek, τὰ μυστήρια are hidden religious rites and knowledge, revealed only to the initiated; hence, the word is used in N. T. of the truths of the Gospel as mysteries partly hidden, partly revealed, Ep. iii. 9; Col. i. 26, iv. 3; 1 Tim. iii. 16; a hidden meaning, Ep. v. 32; Rev. i. 20.

μυωπάζω, to see dimly, 2 Pet. i. 9.*

μώλωψ, ωπος, ὁ, a bruise, a stripe, 1 Pet. ii. 24.*

μωμάομαι, ῶμαι, dep., aor. mid. and pass., to blame, to find fault with, 2 Cor. vi. 3, viii. 20.*

μῶμος, ου, ὁ, a blemish; met., disgrace, 2 Pet. ii. 13.*

μωραίνω, ανῶ, to make foolish, 1 Cor. i. 20; pass., to become foolish, Ro. i. 22; to become insipid, tasteless, like spoiled salt, Mat. v. 13; Lu. xiv. 34.*

μωρία, ας, ἡ, folly, absurdity, 1 Cor. i. 18, 21, 23, ii. 14, iii. 19.*

μωρο-λογία, ας, ἡ, foolish talking, Ep. v. 4.*

μωρός, ά, όν, stupid, foolish, Mat. vii. 26, xxiii. 17, 19, (on Mat. v. 22, see Gr. § 153, ii.); τὸ μωρόν, foolishness, 1 Cor. i. 25, 27.

Μωσῆς (W. H. Μωυσῆς), έως, dat. εῖ or ῇ; acc. ῆν (once έα, Lu. xvi. 29), ὁ, Moses, met., the books of Moses, the Pentateuch, Lu. xvi. 29; 2 Cor. iii. 15.

N

N, ν, νῦ, nu, n, the thirteenth letter. As a numeral, ν′ = 50; ͵ν = 50,000.

Ναασσών, ὁ (Heb.), Naasson, Mat. i. 4; Lu. iii. 32.*

Ναγγαί, ὁ (Heb.), Naggai, Lu. iii. 25.*

Ναζαρέτ, -ρέθ or -ρά (W. H.

66

have all the forms), ἡ, *Naza-reth*, Mat. ii. 23; Lu. ii. 4, 39, 51.

Ναζαρηνός, οῦ, ὁ, *a Nazarene*, as Mar. i. 24.

Ναζωραῖος, ου, ὁ, *a Nazarene*, an appellation of Christ, Mat. ii. 23, xxvi. 71; Christians are called οἱ Ναζωραῖοι, Ac. xxiv. 5.

Ναθάν (W. H. -άμ), ὁ (Heb.), *Nathan*, Lu. iii. 31.*

Ναθαναήλ, ὁ, *Nathanael*, perhaps the same as *Bartholomew*, Jn. i. 45–49, xxi. 2.*

ναί, adv., affirming, *yes*, Mat. ix. 28; *even so*, Mat. xi. 26; Lu. x. 21; Rev. xxii. 20; *yea*, strongly affirming, Lu. vii. 26.

Ναΐν, ἡ, *Nain*, Lu. vii. 11.*

ναός, οῦ, ὁ (ναίω), *a temple, a shrine*, in general, Ac. xix. 24; *the temple*, Mat. xxiii. 16; met., used of Jesus Christ, Jn. ii. 19, 20; of Christians generally, I Cor. iii. 16; 2 Cor. vi. 16. *Syn.:* see ἱερόν.

Ναούμ, ὁ (Heb.), *Nahum*, Lu. iii. 25 (not the prophet).*

νάρδος, ου, ἡ, *nard, oil* or *ointment*, Mar. xiv. 3; Jn. xii. 3.*

Νάρκισσος, ου, ὁ, *Narcissus*, Ro. xvi. 11.*

ναυαγέω, ῶ (ἄγνυμι), *to suffer shipwreck*, 2 Cor. xi. 25; fig., I Tim. i. 19.*

ναύ-κληρος, ου, ὁ, *a ship-master*, or *owner*, Ac. xxvii. 11.*

ναῦς, acc. ναῦν, ἡ, *a ship*, Ac. xxvii. 41.*

ναύτης, ου, ὁ, *a sailor*, Ac. xxvii. 27, 30; Rev. xviii. 17.*

Ναχώρ, ὁ (Heb.), *Nachor*, Lu. iii. 34.*

νεανίας, ου, ὁ, *a young man, a youth*, Ac. vii. 58, xx. 9, xxiii. 17, 18, 22 (not W. H.).*

νεανίσκος, ου, ὁ, *a young man*, Mat. xix. 20; plur., of soldiers, Mar. xiv. 51; I Jn. ii. 13, 14; *an attendant*, Ac. v. 10.

Νεάπολις, εως, ἡ, *Neapolis*, Ac. xvi. 11.*

Νεεμάν (W. H. Ναιμάν), ὁ (Heb.), *Naaman*, Lu. iv. 27.*

νεκρός, ά, όν, *dead*, (1) lit., as Mat. xi. 5; οἱ νεκροί, *the dead*, generally, I Pet. iv. 6; (2) fig., *dead*, spiritually, Ep. ii. I; *dead* to (dat.), Ro. vi. 11;

inactive, inoperative, Ro. vii. 8.

νεκρόω, ῶ, *to put to death ;* fig., *to deprive of power, to render weak* and *impotent*, Ro. iv. 19; Col. iii. 5; Heb. xi. 12.*

νέκρωσις, εως, ἡ, *death, a being put to death*, 2 Cor. iv. 10; *deadness, impotency*, Ro. iv. 19.*

νεο-μηνία, see νουμηνία.

νέος, α, ον, (1) *new, fresh*, Mat. ix. 17; I Cor. v. 7; Col. iii. 10; (2) *young*, of persons, Tit. ii. 4. *Syn.:* see καινός.

νεοσσός (W. H. νοσσός), οῦ, ὁ, *a young bird*, Lu. ii. 24.*

νεότης, τητος, ἡ, *youth*, Lu. xviii. 21; I Tim. iv. 12.

νεό-φυτος, ον, *newly planted;* fig., *a recent convert*, I Tim. iii. 6.*

Νέρων, ωνος, ὁ, *Nero*, the Roman emperor, 2 Tim. iv. 23 (Rec).*

νεύω, σω, *to nod ;* so, *to beckon, to signify*, Jn. xiii. 24; Ac. xxiv. 10.*

νεφέλη, ης, ἡ, *a cloud*, Mar. ix. 7, xiii. 26.

Νεφθαλείμ, ὁ (Heb.), *Naphtali*, Mat. iv. 13, 15; Rev. vii. 6.*

νέφος, ους, τό, *a cloud ;* met., *a multitude, a great company*, Heb. xii. I.*

νεφρός, οῦ, ὁ, *a kidney*, plur., *the kidneys, the loins*, used (as Heb.) for the secret thoughts, desires, and purposes, Rev. ii. 23.*

νεω-κόρος, ου, ὁ (ναός and κορέω, *to sweep*), *a temple-keeper*, a designation of the people of Ephesus, Ac. xix. 35.*

νεωτερικός, ή, όν, *youthful, juvenile*, 2 Tim. ii. 22.*

νεώτερος, α, ον (comp. of νέος, which see), *younger, inferior in rank*, Lu. xv. 12, 13, xxii. 26; I Tim. v. 11, 14.

νή, adv., of affirmative swearing, *by*, with acc., I Cor. xv. 31.*

νήθω, *to spin*, Mat. vi. 28; Lu. xii. 27.*

νηπιάζω, *to be an infant*, I Cor. xiv. 20.*

νήπιος, α, ον, *infantile ;* as subst., *an infant, a babe*, Mat. xxi. 16; I Cor. xiii. 11; used of an age below manhood, Gal. iv. I; fig., of *un-*

learned, unenlightened persons, Mat. xi. 25; Ro. ii. 20; I Th. ii. 7 (W. H.).

Νηρεύς, έως, ὁ, *Nereus*, Ro. xvi. 15.*

Νηρί, ὁ (Heb.), *Neri*, Lu. iii. 27.*

νησίον, ου, τό (dim. of νῆσος), *a small island*, Ac. xxvii. 16.*

νῆσος, ου, ἡ (νέω, *to swim*), *an island*, Ac. xiii. 6, xxvii. 26.

νηστεία, ας, ἡ, *a fasting, a fast*, Mat. xvii. 21 (W. H. omit); Ac. xiv. 23; *the day of atonement, the chief Jewish fast-day*, Ac. xxvii. 9; *want of food*, 2 Cor. vi. 5, xi. 27.

νηστεύω, σω, *to abstain from food, to fast*, Mat. iv. 2, vi. 16–18.

νῆστις, ιος, plur. νήστεις, ὁ, ἡ, *fasting*, Mat. xv. 32; Mar. viii. 3.*

νηφάλιος or νηφάλεος, ου, *sober, tem*perate, I Tim. iii. 2, 11; Tit. ii. 2.*

νήφω, ψω, *to be sober, temperate*, fig., I Th. v. 6, 8.

Νίγερ, ὁ (Lat.), *Niger*, Ac. xiii. 1.*

Νικάνωρ, ορος, ὁ, *Nicanor*, Ac. vi. 5.*

νικάω, ῶ, ήσω, *to be victorious*, abs., Rev. iii. 21; *to conquer, overcome* (acc.), Lu. xi. 22, Jn. xvi. 33.

νίκη, ης, ἡ, *victory*, I Jn. v. 4.*

Νικό-δημος, ου, ὁ, *Nicodemus*, Jn. iii. I.

Νικολαΐτης, ου, ὁ, *a follower of Nicolaus* (probably a Greek equivalent for *Balaam*), *a Nicolaitan*, Rev. ii. 6, 15.*

Νικό-λαος, ου, ὁ, *Nicolaus*, Ac. vi. 5 (not to be confounded with preced.).*

Νικό-πολις, εως, ἡ, *Nicopolis*, Tit. iii. 12. Several cities of the name existed; this was probably on the promontory of Epirus.*

νῖκος, ους, τό, *victory*, I Cor. xv. 55, 57; εἰς νῖκος, from S., *to a victorious consummation, utterly*, Mat. xii. 20; I Cor. xv. 54.*

Νινευΐ, ἡ (Heb.), *Nineveh*, Lu. xi. 32 (W. H. read following).*

Νινευΐτης (W. H. -είτης), ου, ὁ, *a Ninevite*, Mat. xii. 41; Lu. xi. 30, 32 (W. H.).*

νιπτήρ, ῆρος, ὁ, a basin, for washing hands and feet, Jn. xiii. 5. (N. T.)*

νίπτω, ψω, to wash (acc.), Jn. xiii. 8; mid., to wash one's self, acc. of part, as Mar. vii. 3. Syn.: see λούω.

νοέω, ῶ, ήσω, to understand, to consider, abs., or with acc., or ὅτι, Jn. xii. 40; Ep. iii. 4; Mar. xiii. 14.

νόημα, ατος, τό, (1) a thought, purpose, device, 2 Cor. ii. 11, x. 5; Phil. iv. 7; (2) the mind, i.e., the understanding or intellect, 2 Cor. iii. 14, iv. 4, xi. 3.*

νόθος, η, ον, illegitimate, bastard, Heb. xii. 8.*

νομή, ῆς, ἡ (νέμω, to pasture), (1) pasturage, Jn. x. 9; (2) met., growth, increase, as of a gangrene, 2 Tim. ii. 17.*

νομίζω, σω (νόμος), (1) to think, to suppose, to expect, as the result of thinking, Mat. v. 17, xx. 10; (2) pass., to be customary, only Ac. xvi. 13 (but see W. H. and R. V.).

νομικός, ή, όν, pertaining to (the) law, Tit. iii. 9; as subst., a person learned in or teacher of the Mosaic law, Mat. xxii. 35; Tit. iii. 13.

νομίμως, adv., lawfully, 1 Tim. i. 8; 2 Tim. ii. 5.*

νόμισμα, ατος, τό, (lawful) money, coin, Mat. xxii. 19.*

νομο-διδάσκαλος, ου, ὁ, a teacher and interpreter of the Mosaic law, Lu v. 17; Ac. v. 34; 1 Tim. i. 7. (N. T.)*

νομο-θεσία, ας, ἡ, lawgiving, legislation, Ro. ix. 4.*

νομο-θετέω, ῶ, to enact laws; pass., to be enacted, Heb. viii. 6; to be furnished with laws, Heb. vii. 11.*

νομο-θέτης, ου, ὁ (τίθημι), a lawgiver, legislator, Ja. iv. 12.*

νόμος, ου, ὁ (νέμω, to apportion), a law, an edict, a statute, Lu. ii. 22; a standard of acting or judging, Ro. iii. 27; a written law, Ro. ii. 14; the Mosaic economy, Mat. v. 18; Ro. x. 4; the Christian dispensation or doctrines, Gal. vi. 2; Ro. xiii. 8; met., for the books containing the Mosaic law, i.e., the five books of Moses, Mat. xii. 5;

anά for the Old Testament generally, Jn. x. 34. On the article with νόμος, see Gr. § 234, Wi. § 19, 1 a, Bu. 89.

νόος, see νοῦς.

νοσέω, ῶ, to be sick; fig., to have a diseased appetite or craving for, περί (acc.), 1 Tim. vi. 4.*

νόσημα, ατος, τό, disease, sickness, Jn. v. 4 (W. H. omit).*

νόσος, ου, ἡ, disease, sickness, Mat. iv. 23, 24.

νοσσιά, ᾶς, ἡ, a brood of young birds, Lu. xiii. 34. (S.)*

νοσσίον, ου, τό, a brood of young birds, Mat. xxiii. 37.*

νοσσός, see νεοσσός.

νοσφίζω, in mid., to remove for one's self, to purloin, Ac. v. 2, 3; Tit. ii. 10.*

νότος, ου, ὁ, the south wind, Lu. xii. 55; the South, Lu. xi. 31.

νου-θεσία, ας, ἡ, admonition, counsel, 1 Cor. x. 11; Ep. vi. 4; Tit. iii. 10.*

νου-θετέω, ῶ, to admonish, to counsel, Ac. xx. 31.

νου-μηνία (W. H. νεο-), ας, ἡ, the new moon, as a festival, Col. ii. 16.*

νουν-εχῶς, adv., wisely, judiciously, Mar. xii. 34.*

νοῦς (orig. νόος), νοός, νοΐ, νοῦν, ὁ, the mind, i.e., the understanding or intellect, Lu.xxiv. 45; Phil. iv. 7; the reason, Ro. vii. 25, xii. 2; hence, any affection of the mind — as modes of thought — inclinations or dispositions, Ro. xiv. 5; 1 Cor. i. 10.

Νυμφᾶς, ᾶ, ὁ, Nymphas, Col. iv. 15.*

νύμφη, ης, ἡ, a betrothed woman, a bride, Rev. xviii. 23; a daughter-in-law, Mat. x. 35.

νυμφίος, ου, ὁ, a bridegroom, Jn. iii. 29.

νυμφών, ῶνος, ὁ, a bridal chamber; οἱ υἱοὶ τοῦ νυμφῶνος, the sons of the bridal chamber, friends of the bridegroom, Mat. ix. 15; Mar. ii. 19; Lu. v. 34; a room in which the marriage ceremonies were held, Mat. xxii. 10 (W. H.). (Ap.)*

νῦν and νυνί, adv., (1) of time, now, i.e., the actually present; now, in relation to time

just past, just now, even now; now, in relation to future time, just at hand, even now, immediately; ὁ, ἡ, τὸ νῦν, the present, with subst or (neut.) without; (2) of logical connection, now, 2 Cor. vii. 9; now then, i.e., implying the rise of one thing from another, 1 Cor. xiv. 6; (3) in commands and appeals, νῦν is emphatic, at this instant, Mat. xxvii. 42; Ja. iv. 13.

νύξ, νυκτός, ἡ, the night, night-time, lit., Ac. xvi. 33; often fig., a time of darkness and ignorance, Ro. xiii. 12; 1 Th. v. 5; death, Jn. ix. 4.

νύσσω, ξω, to stab, to pierce, Jn. xix. 34.*

νυστάζω, ξω, to nod in sleep, to be drowsy, Mat. xxv. 5; fig., to delay, 2 Pet. ii. 3.*

νυχθ-ήμερον, ου, τό, a night and a day, twenty-four hours, 2 Cor. xi. 25.*

Νῶε, ὁ (Heb.), Noah, Lu. iii. 36, xvii. 26, 27.

νωθρός, ά, όν, sluggish, dull, stupid, Heb. v. 11, vi. 12.*

νῶτος, ου, ὁ, the back of men or animals, Ro. xi. 10.*

Ξ

Ξ, ξ, ξί, xi, the double letter x (= γς, κς, or χς), the fourteenth letter of the alphabet. As numeral, ξ' = 60; ͵ξ = 60,000.

ξενία, ας, ἡ, hospitality; a lodging, Ac. xxviii. 23; Philem. 22.*

ξενίζω, σω, (1) to receive as a guest (acc.), Ac. x. 23, xxviii. 7; Heb. xiii. 2; pass., to be entertained, to lodge, Ac. x. 6, 18, 32, xxi. 16; (2) to astonish by strangeness, Ac. xvii. 20; pass., to think strangely of, to be surprised at (dat.), 1 Pet. iv. 4, 12.*

ξενο-δοχέω, ῶ, to entertain guests, to practice hospitality, 1 Tim. v. 10.*

ξένος, η, ον, masc., a guest-friend; as subst., a stranger, foreigner, Mat. xxv. 35, 38, 43, 44; a host, Ro. xvi. 23; alien, Ep. ii. 12; new, novel, Heb. xiii. 9; 1 Pet. iv. 12.

ξέστης, ου, ὁ (the Latin sextarius), a sextarius, a vessel

for measuring liquids, holding about a pint; *a pitcher*, of any size, Mar. vii. 4, 8 (W. H. omit).*

ξηραίνω, ανῶ, 1st aor., act., ἐξήρανα, 1st aor., pass., ἐξηράνθην, perf., pass., ἐξήραμμαι (3 s., ἐξήρανται, Mar. xi. 21), *to make dry, to wither*, Ja. i. 11; pass., *to become dry, be withered*, Mat. xiii. 6; *to be dried up*, Rev. xvi. 12; *to be ripened*, as corn, Rev. xiv. 15; *to pine away*, Mar. ix. 18.

ξηρός, ά, όν, *dry, withered*, of a tree, Lu. xxiii. 31; of a useless limb, Mat. xii. 10; Mar. iii. 3 (W. H.); Lu. vi. 6, 8; Jn. v. 3; of land, Heb. xi. 29; ἡ ξηρά (sc. γῆ), *dry land*, Mat. xxiii. 15.*

ξύλινος, ίνη, ινον, *wooden*, 2 Tim. ii. 20; Rev. ix. 20.*

ξύλον, ου, τό, *wood, e.g., timber* in building, 1 Cor. iii. 12; *anything made of wood, e.g., the stocks*, Ac. xvi. 24; *a staff*, Mat. xxvi. 47, 55; *a cross*, Ac. xiii. 29; Gal. iii. 13; *a living tree*, Rev. ii. 7.

ξυράω, ῶ, ήσω, perf. pass. ἐξύρημαι, *to shave*, Ac. xxi. 24; 1 Cor. xi. 5, 6.*

O

Ο, ο, ὃ μικρόν, *omicron*, short *o*, the fifteenth letter. As a numeral, ο′ = 70; ‚ο = 70,000.

ὁ, ἡ, τό, the definite article, *the*, originally demonstrative. For its uses, see Gr. §§ 193–234, Wi. §§ 17–20, Bu. 85–103.

ὀγδοήκοντα, num., indeclin., *eighty*, Lu. ii. 37, xvi. 7.*

ὄγδοος, η, ον, ord., *eighth*; on 2 Pet. ii. 5, see Gr. § 331, Wi. § 37, 2, Bu. 30.

ὄγκος, ου, ὁ, *a weight, an encumbrance*, Heb. xii. 1.*

ὅδε, ἥδε, τόδε, demon. pron., *this, that* (here). See Gr. § 339, Wi. § 23, 5, Bu. 103.

ὁδεύω, *to pass along a way, to journey*, Lu. x. 33.*

ὁδηγέω, ῶ, ήσω, *to lead along a way, to conduct, to guide*, Mat. xv. 14; Lu. vi. 39; Jn. xvi. 13; Ac. viii. 31; Rev. vii. 17.*

ὁδ-ηγός, οῦ, ὁ, *a leader, a guide*,

Ac. i. 16; fig., of instructors, Mat. xv. 14, xxiii. 16, 24; Ro. ii. 19.*

ὁδοι-πορέω, ῶ, *to travel, to pursue a way*, Ac. x. 9.*

ὁδοι-πορία, ας, ἡ, *a journey, a journeying*, Jn. iv. 6; 2 Cor. xi. 26.*

ὁδός, οῦ, ἡ, (1) *a way, a road*, Mat. ii. 12; (2) *a going, a progress*, Mar. vi. 8; (3) *a journey*, a day's or a Sabbath day's, Lu. ii. 44; Ac. i. 12; (4) fig., *manner of action, method of proceeding*, Ac. xiii. 10; Mat. xxi. 32; especially (5) *the Christian way*, Ac. ix. 2; 2 Pet. ii. 2; (6) used of Christ himself, *the Way*, Jn. xiv. 6.

ὁδούς, ὀδόντος, ὁ, *a tooth*, Mat. v. 38.

ὀδυνάω, ῶ, in mid. and pass., *to be tormented, to be greatly distressed*, Lu. ii. 48, xvi. 24, 25; Ac. xx. 38.*

ὀδύνη, ης, ἡ, *pain, distress*, of body or mind, Ro. ix. 2; 1 Tim. vi. 10.*

ὀδυρμός, οῦ, ὁ, *lamentation, wailing*, Mat. ii. 18; 2 Cor. vii. 7.*

Ὀζίας, ου, ὁ, *Uzziah*, Mat. i. 8, 9.*

ὄζω, *to stink, be offensive*, Jn. xi. 39.*

ὅθεν, adv., *whence*, of place, source, or cause, Mat. xii. 44; 1 Jn. ii. 18; Heb. ii. 17.

ὀθόνη, ης, ἡ, *a linen cloth*; hence, *a sheet*, Ac. x. 11, xi. 5.*

ὀθόνιον, ου, τό (dim. of ὀθόνη), *a linen bandage*, Jn. xix. 40.

οἶδα, plur. οἴδαμεν (for Attic ἴσμεν), οἴδατε (and Attic ἴστε, Heb. xii. 17), οἴδασι (and Attic ἴσασι, only Ac. xxvi. 4), *I know* (see Gr. § 103, 4, Wi. § 40, 4 b).

οἰκειακός, ή, όν, see οἰκιακός.

οἰκεῖος, α, ον, *domestic, belonging to a household*, Gal. vi. 10; Ep. ii. 19; 1 Tim. v. 8.*

οἰκέτεια, ας, ἡ, *household, body of servants*, Mat. xxiv. 45 (W. H.).*

οἰκέτης, ου, ὁ, *a domestic, a household servant*, Lu. xvi. 13; Ac. x. 7; Ro. xiv. 4; 1 Pet. ii. 18.

οἰκέω, ῶ, ήσω, trans., *to inhabit*, 1 Tim. vi. 16; intrans., *to*

dwell, Ro. viii. 9; 1 Cor. vii. 12, 13.

οἴκημα, ατος, τό, *a dwelling*, used of *a prison*, Ac. xii. 7.*

οἰκητήριον, ου, τό, *a dwelling-place, a habitation*, 2 Cor. v. 2; Ju. 6.*

οἰκία, ας, ἡ, (1) *a house*, Lu. xv. 8; (2) met., *a household, a family, goods, i.e.*, a house and all that is in it, Jn. iv. 53; Mar. xii. 40.

οἰκιακός, οῦ, ὁ, *one of a family*, whether child, or servant, Mat. x. 25, 36.*

οἰκοδεσποτέω, ῶ, *to manage a household*, 1 Tim. v. 14.*

οἰκο-δεσπότης, ου, ὁ, *a householder, a master of a house*, Mat. x. 25.

οἰκοδομέω, ῶ, *to erect a building, build*, Lu. xiv. 30; fig., of the building up of character, *to build up, edify*, 1 Cor. x. 23; *to encourage*, 1 Cor. viii. 10.

οἰκο-δομή, ῆς, ἡ (δέμω), *the act of building; a building*, lit., Mat. xxiv. 1; of the spiritual body, 2 Cor. v. 1; of the church, Ep. ii. 21; met., *edification, spiritual advancement*, Ro. xiv. 19, xv. 2.

οἰκοδομία, ας, ἡ, *edification*, 1 Tim. i. 4 (W. H. οἰκονομία).*

οἰκο-δόμος, ου, ὁ, *a builder*, Ac. iv. 11 (W. H.).*

οἰκονομέω, ῶ, *to be a steward*, Lu. xvi. 2.*

οἰκονομία, ας, ἡ, *management of household affairs, stewardship*, Lu. xvi. 2–4; *a dispensation*, 1 Cor. x. 17.

οἰκο-νόμος, ου, ὁ (νέμω), *a house-manager, a steward*, Lu. xvi. 1, 3, 8; of the Christian stewardship, 1 Cor. iv. 1; 1 Pet. iv. 10; Tit. i. 7.

οἶκος, ου, ὁ, *a house, a building*, for any purpose (gen.); met., *a family* resident in one house, *a family* perpetuated by succession; *the house of* God, *i.e.*, the temple; *the family* of God, *i.e.*, the church.

οἰκουμένη, ης, ἡ, pres. part. pass. fem. of οἰκέω (sc. γῆ), *the inhabited land*, or *world*; (1) *the Roman empire*, Lu. ii. 1; (2) *the world at large*, Lu. iv. 5, xxi. 26; (3) met., *the inhabitants of the world*

Ac. xvii. 6, 31 ; (4) *the universe*, Heb. ii. 5.

οἰκ-ουρός, οῦ, ὁ, ἡ (οὖρος, *keeper*), *attending to household affairs*, *domestic*, Tit. ii. 5 (W. H. οἰκουργός, with same meaning).*

οἰκτείρω, ήσω, *to pity, to have compassion on*, Ro. ix. 15 (from S.).*

οἰκτιρμός, οῦ, ὁ, *compassion*, *pity*, Ro. xii. 1 ; 2 Cor. i. 3; Phil. ii. 1 ; Col. iii. 12 ; Heb. x. 28.*

οἰκτίρμων, ον, *pitiful*, *merciful*, Lu. vi. 36 ; Ja. v. 11.*

οἶμαι, see οἴομαι.

οἰνο-πότης, ου, ὁ, *one given to wine-drinking*, Mat. xi. 19; Lu. vii. 34.*

οἶνος, ου, ὁ, *wine*, Mar. ii. 22 ; met., *a vine*, Rev. vi. 6; fig., of that which excites or inflames, Rev. xiv. 10, xvii. 2.

οἰνο-φλυγία, ας, ἡ (φλύω, *to overflow*), *drunkenness*, 1 Pet. iv. 3.*

οἴομαι and **οἶμαι**, *to think, to suppose*, acc. and inf., or ὅτι, Jn. xxi. 25 ; Phil. i. 16; Ja. i. 7.*

οἷος, α, ον, rel. pron., correl. to τοιοῦτος, *of what kind, such as.*

οἴσω, see φέρω.

ὀκνέω, ῶ, ήσω, *to be slothful, to delay, to hesitate*, Ac. ix. 38.*

ὀκνηρός, ά, όν, *slothful, backward*, Mat. xxv. 26; Ro. xii. 11; Phil. iii. 1.*

ὀκτα-ήμερος, ον, *of or belonging to the eighth day*, Phil. iii. 5.*

ὀκτώ, num., indecl., *eight*, Lu. ii. 21.

ὄλεθρος, ου, ὁ, *destruction, perdition*, 1 Cor. v. 5 ; 1 Th. v. 3 ; 2 Th. i. 9 ; 1 Tim. vi. 9.*

ὀλιγο-πιστία, ας, ἡ, *little faith*, Mat. xvii. 20 (W. H.). (N. T.)*

ὀλιγό-πιστος, ον, *of little faith*, Mat. vi. 30. (N. T.)

ὀλίγος, η, ον, (1) *little, small, brief*, Lu. x. 2; Ac. xiv. 28; (2) in plur., *few*, sometimes with gen., Mat. vii. 14; Ac. xvii. 4; (3) neut. as adv., ὀλίγον, of time, *soon*, Lu. v. 3; of space, *a little way*, Mar. vi. 31; (4) with prepositions preced. in various phrases,

as ἐν ὀλίγῳ, *with little trouble*, Ac. xxvi. 28.

ὀλιγό-ψυχος, ον, *faint-hearted*, 1 Th. v. 14. (S.)*

ὀλιγωρέω, ῶ, *to care little for, to despise* (gen.), Heb. xii. 5 (from S.).*

ὀλίγως, adv., *a little, scarcely*, 2 Pet. ii. 18 (W. H.).*

ὀλοθρευτής, οῦ, ὁ, *a destroyer*, 1 Cor. x. 10. (N. T.)*

ὀλοθρεύω, *to destroy*, Heb. xi. 28.*

ὁλο-καύτωμα, ατος, τό (καίω), *a whole burnt-offering*, the whole being consumed, Mar. xii. 33 ; Heb. x. 6, 8. (S.)*

ὁλοκληρία, ας, ἡ, *perfect soundness*, Ac. iii. 16. (S.)*

ὁλό-κληρος, ον, *complete in every part, sound, perfect*, 1 Th. v. 23; Ja. i. 4. *Syn.:* see ἄρτιος.

ὀλολύζω, as from the cry ολ-ολ, *to howl, to lament aloud*, Ja. v. 1.*

ὅλος, η, ον, *all, the whole* (see Gr. § 225, Wi. § 20, 1 *b*, a, Bu. 94), Jn. vii. 23 ; Ja. iii. 2 ; 1 Jn. v. 19.

ὁλο-τελής, ές, *perfect, complete*, 1 Th. v. 23.*

Ὀλυμπᾶς, ᾶ, ὁ, *Olympas*, Ro. xvi. 15.*

ὄλυνθος, ου, ὁ, *an unripe fig*, one which, not ripening in due time, grows through the winter and falls off in the spring, Rev. vi. 13.*

ὅλως (ὅλος), adv., *wholly, altogether*, 1 Cor. v. 1, vi. 7; with neg., *not at all*, Mat. v. 34; 1 Cor. xv. 29.*

ὄμβρος, ου, ὁ, *a violent rain*, Lu. xii. 54.*

ὀμείρομαι, *to long for*, 1 Th. ii. 8 (W. H., Rec. ἱμείρομαι).*

ὁμιλέω, ῶ, ήσω, *to associate with* (dat.), *to talk with* (πρός, acc.), Lu. xxiv. 14, 15 ; Ac. xx. 11, xxiv. 26.*

ὁμιλία, ας, ἡ, *intercourse, companionship*, 1 Cor. xv. 33.*

ὅμιλος, ου, ὁ, *a crowd, company*, Rev. xviii. 17 (not W. H.).*

ὁμίχλη, ης, ἡ, *a mist*, 2 Pet. ii. 17 (W. H.).*

ὄμμα, ατος, τό, *an eye*, Mat. xx. 34 (W. H.) ; Mar. viii. 23.*

ὄμνυμι and ὀμνύω, ὀμόσω (see Gr. § 116, 3, Wi. § 15, Bu.

45), *to swear, to take an oath*, Mar. xiv. 71 ; *to promise with an oath*, Mar. vi. 23.

ὁμο-θυμαδόν, adv., *with one mind, unanimously*, only in Ac. and Ro. xv. 6.

ὁμοιάζω, σω, *to be like*, Mat. xxiii. 27 (W. H. mrg.) ; Mar. xiv. 70 (not W. H.). (N. T.)*

ὁμοιο-παθής, ές, *being affected like another* (dat.), *having like passions* or *feelings*, Ac. xiv. 15; Ja. v. 17.*

ὅμοιος, οία, οιον, *like, similar to, resembling* (dat.), Jn. ix. 9; Rev. iv. 3; *of equal rank*, Mat. xxii. 39.

ὁμοιότης, τητος, ἡ, *likeness*, Heb. iv. 15, vii. 15.*

ὁμοιόω, ῶ, ώσω, (1) *to make like; pass., to be like*, or *to resemble*, Mat. vi. 8, xiii. 24; Ac. xiv. 11 ; (2) *to liken, to compare*, Mat. vii. 24 ; Mar. iv. 30; with acc. and dat.

ὁμοίωμα, ατος, τό, *likeness, similitude*, Ro. i. 23, v. 14, vi. 5, viii. 3 ; Phil. ii. 7; Rev. ix. 7.* *Syn.:* see εἰκών.

ὁμοίως, adv., *in like manner*, Lu. iii. 11 ; Jn. v. 19.

ὁμοίωσις, εως, ἡ, *likeness*, Ja. iii. 9.* *Syn.:* see εἰκών.

ὁμο-λογέω, ῶ, ήσω, 1st aor. ὡμολόγησα, *to speak the same thing;* hence, (1) *to confess*, in the sense of conceding or admitting, generally with ὅτι, Mat. xiv. 7; Heb. xi. 13; (2) *to profess*, or *acknowledge openly*, acc., or with ἐν, Mat. x. 32; Lu. xii. 8; Jn. ix. 22; (3) as ἐξομολογέω, *to praise* (dat.), Heb. xiii. 15.

ὁμολογία, ας, ἡ, *a profession*, or *a confession*, 2 Cor. ix. 13; 1 Tim. vi. 12, 13; Heb. iii. 1, iv. 14, x. 23.*

ὁμολογουμένως, adv., *confessedly, by assent of all*, 1 Tim. iii. 16.*

ὁμό-τεχνος, ον, *of the same trade* or *craft*, Ac. xviii. 3.*

ὁμοῦ, adv., *together, at the same place* or *time*, Jn. iv. 36.

ὁμό-φρων, ον (φρήν), *of one mind*, 1 Pet. iii. 8.*

ὁμόω, see ὄμνυμι.

ὅμως, adv., *yet*, 1 Cor. xiv. 7; Gal. iii. 15 ; with μέντοι, *nevertheless*, Jn. xii. 42.*

όναρ, τό, indecl., *a dream;* κατ' όναρ, *in a dream*, Mat. i. 20, ii. 12, 13, 19, 22, xxvii. 19.*

ονάριον, ου, τό (dim. of όνος), *a young ass*, Jn. xii. 14.*

όνειδίζω, σω, *to reproach, revile, upbraid*, Mat. xi. 20; Mar. xvi. 14; Lu. vi. 22.

όνειδισμός, ού, ό, *reproach, reviling*, Ro. xv. 3; 1 Tim. iii. 7; Heb. x. 33, xi. 26, xiii. 13. (S.)*

όνειδος, ους, τό, *reproach, disgrace*, Lu. i. 25.*

'Ονήσιμος, ου, ό (*profitable*), *Onesimus*, Col. iv. 9; Philem. 10.*

'Ονησί-φορος, ου, ό, *Onesiphorus*, 2 Tim. i. 16, iv. 19.*

όνικός, ή, όν, *pertaining to an ass;* μύλος όνικός, *a millstone turned by an ass, i.e.*, the large upper millstone, Mat. xviii. 6; Lu. xvii. 2 (not W. H.); Mar. ix. 42 (W. H.). (N. T.)*

όνίνημι, *to be useful, to help;* mid. aor., opt., όναίμην, *may I have help* or *joy from*, Philem. 20.*

όνομα, ατος, τό, *a name*, almost always of persons; in N. T., as in O. T., the *name* of a person is a mark of what he himself is, the name expresses the character, Mat. i. 21; Mar. iii. 16, v. 9; Lu. i. 31; hence the expressions ποιεῖν τι ἐπὶ τῷ ὀνόματι, ἐν τῷ ὀνόματι, διὰ τοῦ ὀνόματος; the name is often introduced by ὀνόματι, *by name*, once by τοὔνομα (τὸ ὄνομα), Mat. xxvii. 57; *fame, reputation*, Ep. i. 21; Phil. ii. 9.

όνομάζω, σω, *to give a name to*, Lu. vi. 13, 14; *to mention*, Ep. v. 3; *to call upon the name of*, 2 Tim. ii. 19.

όνος, ου, ό, ή, *an ass*, Mat. xxi. 2, 7; Lu. xiii. 15.

όντως, adv. (όν, neut. part. of εἰμί), *really, truly*, 1 Cor. xiv. 25; 1 Tim. v. 3, 5.

όξος, ους, τό, *vinegar;* in N. T., *sour wine*, mixed with water, a common drink of Roman soldiers, Jn. xix. 29, 30.

όξύς, εῖα, ύ, (1) *sharp*, as a weapon, Rev. i. 16, ii. 12; (2) *swift, eager*, Ro. iii. 15.

όπή, ῆς, ἡ, *an opening, a cavern*, Ja. iii. 11; Heb. xi. 38.*

όπισθεν, adv. of place, *from behind, after*, Mat. ix. 20, xv. 23.

όπίσω, adv., *behind, after*, of place, Lu. vii. 38; of time, Mat. iii. 11; abs., or with gen.; τὰ ὀπίσω, *those things that are behind*, Phil. iii. 14; εἰς τὰ ὀπίσω, *backward*, Jn. xviii. 6.

όπλίζω, σω, N. T., mid., *to arm one's self* with, acc., fig., 1 Pet. iv. 1.*

όπλον, ου, τό, *an instrument*, Ro. vi. 13; hence, plur., *arms, weapons*, Jn. xviii. 3; Ro. xiii. 12; 2 Cor. vi. 7, x. 4.*

όποῖος, οία, οῖον, relat. pron., *of what kind* or *manner*, correl. to τοιοῦτος, Ac. xxvi. 29; 1 Cor. iii. 13; Gal. ii. 6; 1 Th i. 9; Ja. i. 24.*

όπότε, adv. of time, *when*, Lu. vi. 3 (W. H. ὅτε).*

όπου, adv. of place, *where, whither; where*, referring to state, Col. iii. 11; *in case that*, 1 Cor. iii. 3.

όπτάνω, *to behold;* in pass., *to appear*, Ac. i. 3; see όράω. (S.)*

όπτασία, ας, ἡ, *a vision, a supernatural appearance*, Lu. i. 22, xxiv. 23; Ac. xxvi. 19; 2 Cor. xii. 1.*

όπτός, ή, όν, *roasted, broiled*, Lu. xxiv. 42.*

όπτω, όπτομαι, see όράω.

όπώρα, ας, ἡ, *autumn, autumnal fruits*, Rev. xviii. 14.*

όπως, rel. adv., *how*, Lu. xxiv. 20; as conj., *in order that, so that;* with ἄν, Ac. iii. 19 (see Gr. § 384, 2, Wi. § 42, 6, Bu. 234); after verbs of beseeching, and the like, *that*, Mat. ix. 38; Mar. iii. 6.

όραμα, ατος, τό, (1) *a spectacle*, Ac. vii. 31; (2) *a vision*, Ac. ix. 10, 12.

όρασις, εως, ἡ, *appearance*, Rev. iv. 3; *a vision*, Ac. ii. 17; Rev. ix. 17.

όρατός, ή, όν, *visible*, plur., neut., Col. i. 16.*

όράω, ῶ, ὄψομαι, ἑώρακα, εἶδον (see Gr. § 103, 4, Wi. § 15, Bu. 64), (1) *to see*, generally; (2) *to look upon* or *contemplate;* (3) *to see*, and so *to*

participate *in*, Lu. xvii. 22; Jn. iii. 36; (4) *to take heed*, Heb. viii. 5; Mat. viii. 4; with μή or equiv., *to beware*, Mat. xvi. 6; (5) pass., *to be seen, to appear to, to present one's self to* (dat.).

όργή, ῆς, ἡ, *anger, indignation*, Ep. iv. 31; often of the *wrath* of God, and its manifestation, Ro. i. 18. *Syn.:* see θυμός.

όργίζω, σω, *to irritate, to provoke;* pass., *to be angry*, abs., Mat. xviii. 34; *to be enraged with*, dat., or ἐπί, dat., Mat. v. 22; Rev. xii. 17.

όργίλος, η, ον, *prone to anger*, Tit. i. 7.*

όργυιά, ᾶς, ἡ, *a fathom*, about five or six feet, Ac. xxvii. 28.*

όρέγω, *to stretch forth;* mid., *to reach after, to desire* or *long eagerly for*, gen., 1 Tim. iii. 1, vi. 10; Heb. xi. 16.*

όρεινός, ή, όν, *mountainous, hilly* (sc. χώρα), Lu. i. 39, 65.*

όρεξις, εως, ἡ, *strong desire, lust*, Ro. i. 27.*

όρθο-ποδέω, ῶ, *to walk in a straight course*, fig., *to act uprightly*, Gal. ii. 14. (N.T.)*

όρθός, ή, όν, *upright*, Ac. xiv. 10; *straight*, Heb. xii. 13.*

όρθο-τομέω, ῶ (τέμνω), *to cut straight;* met., *to handle rightly, i.e., to teach correctly*, 2 Tim. ii. 15. (S.)*

όρθρίζω, *to rise early in the morning, to come early in the morning*, Lu. xxi. 38. (S.)*

όρθρινός, ή, όν, *early in the morning*, Lu. xxiv. 22 (W. H.); Rev. xxii. 16 (not W. H.).*

όρθριος, α, ον, *early in the morning*, Lu. xxiv. 22 (W. H. read preceding).*

όρθρος, ου, ό, *early dawn, daybreak*, Lu. xxiv. 1; Jn. viii. 2 (W. H. omit); Ac. v. 21.*

όρθῶς, adv., *rightly*, Mar. vii. 35; Lu. vii. 43, x. 28, xx. 21.*

όρίζω, σω, *to define; to determine*, Ac. xvii. 26; Heb. iv. 7; *to appoint, to decree*, Ac. x. 42, xi. 29; pass., perf. part., ὡρισμένος, *decreed*, Ac. ii. 23; neut., *decree*, Lu. xxii. 22.

όριον, ου, τό, plur., *the bound-*

aries of a place; hence, *districts, territory*, Mat. ii. 6, iv. 13.

ὁρκίζω, *to adjure by, to charge solemnly by*, with double acc., Mar. v. 7; Ac. xix. 13; 1 Th. v. 27 (W. H. ἐνορκίζω).*

ὅρκος, ου, ὁ, *an oath*, Mat. xiv. 1, 9; *a promise with an oath, a vow*, Mat. v. 33.

ὁρκ-ωμοσία, ας, ἡ, *the taking of an oath, an oath*, Heb. vii. 20, 21, 28. (S.)*

ὁρμάω, ῶ, ήσω, N. T., intrans., *to rush*, Mat. viii. 32; Ac. vii. 57 (εἰς, or ἐπί, acc.).

ὁρμή, ῆς, ἡ, *a rush, a violent assault*, Ac. xiv. 5; Ja. iii. 4.*

ὅρμημα, ατος, τό, *a rushing on, impulse*, Rev. xviii. 21.*

ὄρνεον, ου, τό, *a bird*, Rev. xviii. 2, xix. 17, 21.*

ὄρνις, ιθος, ὁ, ἡ, *a bird, a hen*, Mat. xxiii. 37; Lu. xiii. 34.*

ὁρο-θεσία, ας, ἡ, *a setting of boundaries, a definite limit*, Ac. xvii. 26. (N. T.)*

ὄρος, ους, τό, *a mountain*, Lu. iii. 5, ix. 28.

ὀρύσσω, ξω, *to dig, to dig out*, Mat. xxi. 33, xxv. 18; Mar. xii. 1.*

ὀρφανός, ή, όν, *bereaved, an orphan*, Jn. xiv. 18; as subst., Ja. i. 27.*

ὀρχέομαι, οῦμαι, ήσομαι, dep., mid., *to dance*, Mat. xi. 17, riv. 6; Mar. vi. 22; Lu. vii. 32.*

ὅς, ἥ, ὅ, relative pronoun, *who, which* (see Gr. §§ 58, 343–348, Wi. § 24, Bu. 281 sq.; for ὅς ἄν, ὅς ἐάν, *whoever*, see Gr. § 380, Wi. § 42, 3, Bu. 288) ; as demonst. in the phrase, ὅς μέν ... ὅς δέ, *that one ... this one*, as 2 Cor. ii. 16.

ὁσάκις, rel. adv., *as often as*, always with ἄν or ἐάν, 1 Cor. xi. 25, 26; Rev. xi. 6.*

ὅσιος (a), ον, *holy, pious*, of human beings, of Christ, and of God; τὰ ὅσια, *the holy promises*, Ac. xiii. 34. *Syn.*: see ἅγιος.

ὁσιότης, τητος, ἡ, *holiness, godliness*, Lu. i. 75; Ep. iv. 24.*

ὁσίως, adv., *holily*, 1 Th. ii. 10.*

ὀσμή, ῆς, ἡ, *a smell, an odor*, lit., Jn. xii. 3; fig., 2 Cor. ii. 14, 16; Ep. v. 2; Phil. iv. 18.*

ὅσος, η, ον, relat. pron., *how much, how great*, (1) of time, *how long, as long as*, Ro. vii. 1; repeated, the meaning is intensified, Heb. x. 37: ἔτι μικρὸν ὅσον ὅσον, *yet a little, a very, very little*; (2) of quantity, of number, *how much*, plur., *how many*, Mar. iii. 8; Jn. vi. 11; Ac. ix. 13; *as many as*, Mat. xiv. 36; with ἄν, ἐάν, *as many as, whatsoever*, Mat. vii. 12, xxi. 22; (3) of measure, degree, Heb. vii. 20.

ὅσ-περ, ἥ-περ, ὅ-περ, *the very one who*, Mar. xv. 6 (not W. H.).*

ὀστέον, contr. ὀστοῦν, οῦ, τό, *a bone*, Jn. xix. 36.

ὅσ-τις, ἥ-τις, ὅ, τι, compound relat., *whosoever, whichsoever, whatsoever* (see Gr. §§ 58 c, 349, Wi. § 42, 3, Bu. 115) ; the addition of ἄν, ἐάν, gives indefiniteness.

ὀστράκινος, η, ον, *made of earth, earthen*, 2 Cor. iv. 7; 2 Tim. ii. 20.*

ὄσφρησις, εως, ἡ, *the sense of smell, smelling*, 1 Cor. xii. 17.*

ὀσφύς, ύος, ἡ, *the loins*, Mat. iii. 4; Lu. xii. 35; Ac. ii. 30; 1 Pet. i. 13.

ὅταν (ὅτε, ἄν), rel. adv., *when, whensoever*; always with subj. except Mar. iii. 11, xi. 19 (W.H.), 25 (W.H.); Rev. iv. 9, viii. 1 (W. H.).

ὅτε, rel. adv., *when*, Mar. xiv. 12.

ὅτι, conj., (1) *that*, after verbs of declaring, etc., introducing the object-sentence; sometimes as a mere quotation mark, Mat. ii. 23; (2) *because* (see Gr. § 136, 6, Wi. § 53, 8 b, Bu. 357 sq.).

ὅτου (gen. of ὅστις), ἕως ὅτου, *until*, Lu. xxii. 16.

οὗ, adv. (gen. of ὅς), *where, whither; οὗ ἐάν, whithersoever*; also used of time, *when*, in the phrases, ἀφ᾽ οὗ, *since*, ἄχρις, ἕως, μέχρις οὗ, *until*.

οὐ (οὐκ before a vowel, οὐχ if the vowel is aspirated), *no,*

not (see Gr. §§ 134, 401, Wi. §§ 55, 56, Bu. 344 sq.).

οὐά, interj., *ah! aha!* derisive, Mar. xv. 29. (N. T.)*

οὐαί, interj., *woe! alas!* uttered in grief or denunciation, Mat. xi. 21; 1 Cor. ix. 16; ἡ οὐαί, as subst., Rev. ix. 12, *the woe, the calamity*. (S.)

οὐδαμῶς, adv., *by no means*, Mat. ii. 6.*

οὐ-δέ, conj., disj. neg., *but not, nor yet* (cf. μηδέ), *neither, nor, not even* (see Gr. § 401, Wi. § 55, 6, Bu. 366 sq.).

οὐδ-είς, οὐδεμία, οὐδέν (οὐδὲ εἷς), neg. adj., *not one, no one, none, nothing, of no moment, of no value, vain.*

οὐδέ-ποτε, adv., *never*, 1 Cor. xiii. 8; Mat. vii. 23.

οὐδέ-πω, adv., *not yet, never*, Jn. xix. 41.

οὐθείς, οὐθέν (οὔτε εἷς), *no one, nothing*, Ac. xxvi. 26 (W. H.); 1 Cor. xiii. 2, 2 Cor. xi. 8 (W. H.).*

οὐκ-έτι, adv., *no further, no more, no longer.*

οὐκ-οῦν, adv., *not therefore;* hence, in ordinary classic usage, an affirmative adverb, *therefore* (whereas οὔκουν retains its negative force, *not therefore*), Jn. xviii. 37.*

οὐ μή, an emphatic negative (see Gr. § 377, Wi. § 56, 3, Bu. 211 sq.).

οὖν, conj., *therefore, then*, Mat. xii. 12; employed espec. (1) in arguing, 1 Cor. iv. 16; (2) in exhortation, Mat. xxii. 9, 17, 21; (3) in interrogation, Mat. xiii. 27; Gal. iii. 19, 21; (4) to resume an interrupted subject, Mar. iii. 31; Jn. xi. 6; (5) to indicate mere transition from one point to another, most frequently in John, as viii. 13.

οὔ-πω, adv., *not yet.*

οὐρά, ᾶς, ἡ, *a tail* of an animal, Rev. ix. 10, 19, xii. 4.*

οὐράνιος, ον, *heavenly, in* or *pertaining to heaven*, as Lu. ii. 13; Ac. xxvi. 19.

οὐρανόθεν, adv., *from heaven*, Ac. xiv. 17, xxvi. 13.*

οὐρανός, οῦ, ὁ, *heaven*, (1) *the visible heavens* (both sing. and plural), through their whole extent, *the atmosphere, the sky, the starry heavens;*

72

(2) *the spiritual heavens,* the abode of God and holy beings, Mat. vi. 10; 2 Cor. xii. 2; "the third heaven," above the atmospheric and the sidereal; met., for the inhabitants of heaven, Rev. xviii. 20; especially for God, Lu. xv. 18.

Οὐρβανός, οῦ, ὁ, *Urbanus,* Ro. xvi. 9.*

Οὐρίας, ου, ὁ, *Uriah,* Mat. i. 6.*

οὖς, ὠτός, τό, (1) *the ear,* Mat. x. 27; (2) met., *the faculty of perception,* Mat. xi. 15.

οὐσία, ας, ἡ (ὤν, part. εἰμί), *property, wealth,* Lu. xv. 12, 13.*

οὔ-τε, conj., *and not; neither, nor,* with a negative preced.; οὔτε ... οὔτε, *neither ... nor.* (The readings often vary between οὔτε and οὐδέ.)

οὗτος, αὕτη, τοῦτο, demonstr. pron., *this* (near), appl. to persons and things, sometimes emphatic, Mat. v. 19; sometimes comtemptuous, *this fellow,* Mat. xiii. 55 (see Gr. §§ 338–342, Wi. § 23, Bu. 103 sq.; also ἐκεῖνος and ὅδε.)

οὕτως (and before a consonant sometimes οὕτω), adv., *thus, in this wise, so,* (1) in reference to antecedent or following statement; (2) correlative with ὡς or καθώς, *so ... as;* (3) qualifying adjectives, adverbs, or verbs, *so,* Heb. xii. 21; Mat. ix. 33; οὕτως ... οὕτως, 1 Cor. vii. 7, *in this manner ... in that.*

οὐχί, adv., (1) an intensive form of οὐ, Jn. xiii. 10, *by no means, not at all,* (2) mostly interrog., as Mat. v. 46, expecting an affirmative answer.

ὀφειλέτης, ου, ὁ, *a debtor,* Mat. xviii. 24; *one bound to some duty, e.g.,* obedience to the law, Gal. v. 3; *a delinquent, sinner,* Lu. xiii. 4.

ὀφειλή, ῆς, ἡ, *a debt, a duty,* Mat. xviii. 32; Ro. xiii. 7; 1 Cor. vii. 3 (W. H.). (N. T.)*

ὀφείλημα, ατος, τό, *a debt, what is justly due,* Ro. iv. 4; fig., *an offense, a sin,* Mat. vi. 12.*

ὀφείλω, (1) *to owe* money (acc.

and dat.), Mat. xviii. 28; τὸ ὀφειλόμενον, *the due,* Mat. xviii. 30; (2) *to be under obligation,* Mat. xxiii. 16; *to sin against,* Lu. xi. 4.

ὄφελον (see Gr. § 378, Wi. § 41 b, 5, note 2, Bu. 214 sq.), interjection, *O that! I wish! would that!* followed by indicative, 1 Cor. iv. 8; 2 Cor. xi. 1; Gal. v. 12; Rev. iii. 15.*

ὄφελος, ους, τό (ὀφέλλω, *to increase*), *profit, advantage,* 1 Cor. xv. 32; Ja. ii. 14, 16.*

ὀφθαλμο-δουλεία, ας, ἡ, *eye-service,* Ep. vi. 6; Col. iii. 22. (N. T.)*

ὀφθαλμός, οῦ, ὁ, *an eye;* fig., of the eye as the receptive channel into mind and heart, Mat. vi. 23 (see Mar. vii. 22; Mat. xx. 15); fig., *the eye of the mind, i.e., the understanding,* Mat. xxvi. 18.

ὄφις, εως, ὁ, *a serpent,* Mat. vii. 10; an emblem of wisdom, Mat. x. 16; of cunning, Mat. xxiii. 33; used symbol. for Satan, Rev. xii. 9, 14.

ὀφρύς, ύος, ἡ, *the eyebrow; the brow* of a mountain or hill, Lu. iv. 29.*

ὀχλέω, ῶ, *to disturb, to vex,* only in pass., Lu. vi. 18 (W. H. ἐνοχλέω), Ac. v. 16.*

ὀχλο-ποιέω, ῶ, *to gather a crowd,* Ac. xvii. 5. (N. T.)*

ὄχλος, ου, ὁ, *a crowd, an unorganized multitude,* Mat. ix. 23, 25; *the multitude, the common people,* Mar. xii. 12.

ὀχύρωμα, ατος, τό, *a fortress, a strong defense,* 2 Cor. x. 4.*

ὀψάριον, ου, τό (a relish with bread), *a little fish,* Jn. vi. 9, 11, xxi. 9, 10, 13. (N. T.)*

ὀψέ, adv., *late, in the evening,* Mar. xi. 11 (W. H.), 19, xiii. 35; *late in,* gen., Mat. xxviii. 1.*

ὄψιμος, ον, *latter,* of the rain, Ja. v. 7.*

ὄψιος, α, ον, *late,* Mar. xi. 11 (not W. H., see mrg.); as subst., ἡ ὀψία, *evening,* either the former of the two evenings reckoned among the Jews, Mat. viii. 16; or the latter, Mat. xiv. 23; see ver. 15.

ὄψις, εως, ἡ, *sight; the countenance,* Jn. xi. 44; Rev. i.

16; *external appearance,* Jn vii. 24.*

ὀψώνιον, ου, τό, lit., *relish, sauce,* like ὀψάριον, (1) plur., the *rations* of soldiers, their *wages,* Lu. iii. 14; 1 Cor. ix. 7; hence, (2) *wages,* generally, Ro. vi. 23; 2 Cor. xi. 8.*

Π

Π, π, πῖ, *pi, p,* the sixteenth letter. As a numeral, π′ = 80; ͵π = 80,000.

παγιδεύω, σω, *to ensnare, to entrap,* fig., Mat. xxii. 15. (S.)*

παγίς, ίδος, ἡ, *a snare, a trap,* Lu. xxi. 35; fig., Ro. xi. 9; 1 Tim. iii. 7, vi. 9; 2 Tim. ii. 26.*

πάγος, ου, ὁ, *a hill;* only with the adj. Ἄρειος, *Mars' Hill, Areopagus,* Ac. xvii. 19, 22.*

πάθημα, ατος, τό, (1) *suffering, affliction,* Ro. viii. 18; (2) *affection of mind, passion,* Ro. vii. 5; Gal. v. 24; (3) *an undergoing, an enduring,* Heb. ii. 9.

παθητός, ή, όν, *destined to suffer,* Ac. xxvi. 23.*

πάθος, ους, τό, *suffering, emotion,* in N.T., of an evil kind, *depraved passion, lust,* Ro. i. 26; 1 Th. iv. 5; Col. iii. 5.*

παιδ-αγωγός, οῦ, ὁ, *a boys' guardian* or *tutor,* "pædagogue," a slave who had the charge of the life and morals of the boys of a family, not strictly a teacher, 1 Cor. iv. 15; Gal. iii. 24, 25.*

παιδάριον, ου, τό (dim. of παῖς), *a little boy, a lad,* Mat. xi. 16 (W. H. παιδίον); Jn. vi. 9.*

παιδεία, ας, ἡ, *training and education* of children, Ep. vi. 4; hence, *instruction,* 2 Tim. iii. 16; *chastisement, correction,* Heb. xii. 5–11.*

παιδευτής, οῦ, ὁ, (1) *an instructor,* Ro. ii. 20; (2) *a chastiser,* Heb. xii. 9.*

παιδεύω, σω, *to train a child,* Ac. xxii. 3; hence, (1) *to instruct,* 1 Tim. i. 20; (2) *to correct, to chasten,* 2 Tim. ii. 25; Heb. xii. 7.

παιδιόθεν, adv., *from childhood,* Mar. ix. 21. (N. T.)*

παιδίον, ου, τό (dim. of παῖς),

a little child, an infant, Mat. ii. 8; *a child* more advanced, Mat. xiv. 21; fig., 1 Cor. xiv. 20.

παιδίσκη, ης, ἡ (fem. dim. of παῖς), *a young girl; a young female slave*, Lu. xii. 45, xxii. 56.

παίζω, *to play*, as a child, *to sport, to jest*, 1 Cor. x. 7.*

παῖς, παιδός, ὁ, ἡ, (1) *a child, a boy* or *girl*, Lu. ii. 43, viii. 51, 54; (2) *a servant, a slave*, as Mat. viii. 6, 8; ὁ παῖς τοῦ θεοῦ, *the servant of God*, used of any servant, Lu. i. 69; *of the Messiah*, Mat. xii. 18.

παίω, σω, *to strike, to smite*, with the fist, Mat. xxvi. 68; Lu. xxii. 64; with a sword, Mar. xiv. 47; Jn. xviii. 10; as a scorpion with its sting, Rev. ix. 5.*

Πακατιανή, ῆς, ἡ, *Pacatiana*, a part of Phrygia, 1 Tim. vi. 22 (Rec.).*

πάλαι, adv., *of old*, Heb. i. 1; *long ago*, Mat. xi. 21.

παλαιός, ά, όν, (1) *old, ancient*, 2 Cor. iii. 14; ὁ παλαιὸς ἄνθρωπος, *the old* or *former man, i.e.*, man in his old, unrenewed nature, Ro. vi. 6; (2) *worn out*, as a garment, Mat. ix. 16.

παλαιότης, τητος, ἡ, *oldness, obsoleteness*, Ro. vii. 6.*

παλαιόω, ῶ, *to make old, to declare obsolete*, Heb. viii. 13; pass., *to grow old, to become obsolete*, Lu. xii. 33; Heb. i. 11, viii. 13.*

πάλη, ης, ἡ, *a wrestling*, Ep. vi. 12.*

παλιγ-γενεσία (W. H. παλινγ-), ας, ἡ, *a new birth, regeneration*, Tit. iii. 5; *a renovation* of all things, Mat. xix. 28.* *Syn.*: see ἀνακαίνωσις.

πάλιν, adv., *again, back*, used of place or of time; a particle of continuation, *again, once more, further;* and of antithesis, as 2 Cor. x. 7, *on the other hand.*

παμ-πληθεί, adv., *all at once, all together*, Lu. xxiii. 18. (N. T.)*

πάμ-πολυς, παμπόλλη, πάμπολυ, *very great*, Mar. viii. 1 (not W. H.).*

Παμφυλία, ας, ἡ, *Pamphylia*, Ac. xiii. 13.

παν-δοχεῖον, ου, τό, *a khan*, or *Eastern inn*, Lu. x. 34.*

παν-δοχεύς, έως, ὁ (δέχομαι), *the keeper of a khan, a host*, Lu. x. 35.*

παν-ήγυρις, εως, ἡ (ἀγείρω), *a general festal assembly*, Heb. xii. 23.* *Syn.*: see ἐκκλησία.

παν-οικί, adv., *with one's whole household* or *family*, Ac. xvi. 34.*

παν-οπλία, ας, ἡ, *complete armor*, Lu. xi. 22; Ep. vi. 11, 13.*

πανουργία, ας, ἡ, *shrewdness, skill;* hence, *cunning, craftiness*, Lu. xx. 23; 1 Cor. iii. 19; 2 Cor. iv. 2, xi. 3; Ep. iv. 14.*

παν-οῦργος, ον (ἔργον), *doing everything; cunning, crafty*, 2 Cor. xii. 16.*

πανταχῇ, adv., *everywhere*, Ac. xxi. 28 (W. H.).*

πανταχόθεν, adv., *from all sides*, Mar. i. 45 (W. H. πάντοθεν).*

πανταχοῦ, adv., *everywhere*, Mar. xvi. 20; Lu. ix. 6.

παντελής, ές, *complete;* εἰς τὸ παντελές, *completely, perfectly*, Heb. vii. 25; the same phrase, with μή, *not at all*, Lu. xiii. 11.*

πάντη, adv., *in every way*, Ac. xxiv. 3.*

πάντοθεν, adv., *from all sides*, Mar. i. 45 (W. H.); Lu. xix. 43; Heb. ix. 4.*

παντο-κράτωρ, ορος, ὁ, *the almighty*, used of God, Rev. i. 8, iv. 8.

πάντοτε, adv., *always, at all times*, Mat. xxvi. 11.

πάντως, adv., *wholly, entirely*, 1 Cor. v. 10; *in every way, by all means*, Ro. iii. 9; *assuredly, certainly*, Ac. xxi. 22.

παρά, prep., gov. the gen., the dat., and accus., *beside;* with a gen. (of person), it indicates *source* or *origin;* with a dat., it denotes *presence with;* with an accus., it indicates motion *towards*, or *alongside*, and is employed in comparisons, *beyond;* for details see Gr. § 306, Wi. §§ 47 *b*, 48 *d*, 49*g*, Bu. 339 sq. In composition, παρά retains its general meaning, *besides*, sometimes denoting *nearness*, sometimes *motion by* or

past, so as to miss or fail; occasionally also stealthiness (*by the way*), as in παρεισάγω.

παρα-βαίνω, 2d aor. παρέβην, *to transgress*, Mat. xv. 2, 3; 2 Jn. 9 (W. H. προάγω); *to depart, desert*, Ac. i. 25.*

παρα-βάλλω, (1) *to compare*, Mar. iv. 30 (not W. H.); (2) *to betake one's self, arrive*, Ac. xx. 15.*

παρά-βασις, εως, ἡ, *a transgression*, Ro. ii. 23. *Syn.*: see ἀγνόημα.

παρα-βάτης, ου, ὁ, *a transgressor*, Ro. ii. 25, 27; Gal. ii. 18; Ja. ii. 9, 11.*

παρα-βιάζομαι, *to constrain by entreaties*, Lu. xxiv. 29; Ac. xvi. 15.*

παρα-βολεύομαι, *to expose one's self to peril, to be venturesome*, Phil. ii. 30 (W. H.). (N. T.)*

παρα-βολή, ῆς, ἡ, (1) *a comparison*, Heb. ix. 9; (2) *a parable*, often of those uttered by our Lord, Mar. iv. 2, 10; (3) *a proverb, an adage*, Lu. iv. 23; (4) perhaps in Heb. xi. 19, *a venture, a risk* (see παραβολεύομαι).

παραβουλεύομαι, *to consult amiss, be reckless*, Phil. ii. 30 (Rec.). (N. T.)*

παραγγελία, ας, ἡ, *a command, a charge*, Ac. v. 28, xvi. 24; 1 Th. iv. 2; 1 Tim. i. 5, 18.*

παρ-αγγέλλω, *to notify, to command, to charge*, Lu. viii. 29; 2 Th. iii. 4; dat. of person, acc. of thing, or ὅτι, ἵνα or inf., 1 Tim. vi. 13.

παρα-γίνομαι, *to come near, come forth, come against* (ἐπί, πρός), Lu. xii. 51, xxii. 52; Jn. iii. 23; Heb. ix. 11.

παρ-άγω, *to pass by*, Mat. xx. 30; *to depart*, Mat. ix. 27; *to pass away*, act., 1 Cor. vii. 31; pass., only 1 Jn. ii. 8, 17.

παρα-δειγματίζω, *to make a public example of, to expose to disgrace*, Mat. i. 19 (W. H. δειγματίζω); Heb. vi. 6.*

παράδεισος, ου, ὁ (probably a Persian word, " garden," "park "), *Paradise*, Lu. xxiii. 43; 2 Cor. xii. 4; Rev. ii. 7.*

παρα-δέχομαι, dep., mid., *to receive, accept, acknowledge*, Mar. iv. 20; Ac. xv. 4 (W

Ĥ.), xvi. 21, xxii. 18; 1 Tim. v. 19; Heb. xii. 6.*

παρα-δια-τριβή, ῆς, ἡ, *useless occupation,* 1 Tim. vi. 5 (W. H. διαπαρατριβή). (N. T.)*

παρα-δίδωμι, acc. and dat., (1) *to deliver over,* as to prison, judgment, or punishment, Mat. iv. 12; *to betray,* spec. of the betrayal by Judas; (2) *to surrender, abandon* one's self, Ep. iv. 19; (3) *to hand over, entrust, commit, deliver,* as Mat. xxv. 14; Lu. i. 2; Ac. vi. 14; (4) *to commend* to kindness, Ac. xiv. 26; (5) *to give* or *prescribe,* as laws, etc., Ac. vi. 14; (6) prob. *to permit,* in Mar. iv. 29, *when the fruit permits* or *allows.*

παρά-δοξος, ον, *strange, wonderful,* Lu. v. 26.*

παρά-δοσις, εως, ἡ, *an instruction,* or *tradition,* Mat. xv. 2; 1 Cor. xi. 2; 2 Th. ii. 15, iii. 6.

παρα-ζηλόω, ῶ, ώσω, *to provoke to rivalry,* Ro. xii. 11, 14; *to jealousy,* Ro. x. 19; *to anger,* 1 Cor. x. 22. (S.)*

παρα-θαλάσσιος, α, ον, *by the sea,* Mat. iv. 13.*

παρα-θεωρέω, ῶ, *to overlook, neglect,* Ac. vi. 1.*

παρα-θήκη, ης, ἡ, *a deposit, anything committed to one's charge,* 1 Tim. vi. 20 (W. H.); 2 Tim. i. 12, 14 (W. H.).*

παρ-αινέω, ῶ, *to exhort, admonish,* Ac. xxvii. 9, 22.*

παρ-αιτέομαι, οῦμαι, dep., mid., *to entreat for, to beg off, make excuse, refuse, reject,* Mar. xv. 6 (W. H.); Lu. xiv. 18, 19; Ac. xxv. 11; 1 Tim. iv. 7, v. 11; 2 Tim. ii. 23; Tit. iii. 10; Heb. xii. 19, 25.*

παρα-καθέζομαι, *to seat one's self,* Lu. x. 39 (W. H.).*

παρα-καθίζω, intrans., *to sit down beside,* Lu. x. 39 (Rec.).*

παρα-καλέω, ῶ, έσω, (1) *to send for, summon,* Ac. xxviii. 20; (2) *to beseech, entreat,* Mar. i. 40; (3) *to exhort, admonish,* Ac. xv. 32; 1 Tim. vi. 2; (4) *to comfort,* 2 Cor. i. 4; pass., *to be comforted,* Lu. xvi. 25.

παρα-καλύπτω, *to hide, to conceal,* Lu. ix. 45.*

παρα-κατα-θήκη, ης, ἡ, *a trust, a deposit,* 1 Tim. vi. 20; 2 Tim. i. 14 (in both passages W. H. read παραθήκη).*

παρά-κειμαι, *to be at hand, be present with* (dat.), Ro. vii. 18, 21.*

παρά-κλησις, εως, ἡ, *a calling for, a summons;* hence, (1) *exhortation,* Heb. xii. 5; (2) *entreaty,* 2 Cor. viii. 4; (3) *encouragement,* Phil. ii. 1; (4) *consolation, comfort,* Ro. xv. 4; met., of the Consoler, Lu. ii. 25; (5) generally, of the power of imparting all these, Ac. iv. 36.

παρά-κλητος, ου, ὁ, (1) *an advocate, intercessor,* 1 Jn. ii. 1; (2) *a consoler, comforter, helper,* of the Holy Spirit, Jn. xiv. 16, 26, xv. 26, xvi. 7.*

παρ-ακοή, ῆς, ἡ, *disobedience,* Ro. v. 19; 2 Cor. x. 6; Heb. ii. 2.* *Syn.:* see ἀγνόημα.

παρ-ακολουθέω, ῶ, ήσω, *to follow closely, to accompany* (dat.), Mar. xvi. 17 (not W. H., see mrg.); *to follow so as to trace out, to examine,* Lu. i. 3; *to follow* teaching, 1 Tim. iv. 6; 2 Tim. iii. 10.*

παρ-ακούω, *to hear negligently, to disregard,* Mat. xviii. 17; Mar. v. 36 (W. H.).*

παρα-κύπτω, ψω, *to stoop,* Lu. xxiv. 12; Jn. xx. 5, 11; fig., with εἰς, *to search into,* Ja. i. 25; 1 Pet. i. 12.*

παρα-λαμβάνω, λήψομαι (W. H. -λήμψ-), (1) *to take to one's self, to take with one,* Lu. ix. 10, 28, xi. 26; *to lead off* a prisoner, Jn. xix. 16; Ac. xxiii. 18; (2) *to receive by transmission,* Col. iv. 17; Heb. xii. 28; fig., *to receive by instruction,* Mar. vii. 4.

παρα-λέγω, N.T. in mid., *to lay one's course near,* in sailing, *to coast along,* Ac. xxvii. 8, 13.*

παρ-άλιος, ον, *adjacent to the sea, on the coast,* Lu. vi. 17.*

παρ-αλλαγή, ῆς, ἡ, *change, variation,* Ja. i. 17.*

παρα-λογίζομαι, dep., *to impose upon, to delude,* acc., Col. ii. 4; Ja. i. 22.*

παρα-λυτικός, ή, όν, *afflicted with paralysis,* in the whole

or a part of the body, Mat. iv. 24, viii. 6. (N. T.)

παρα-λύω, *to relax, to enfeeble,* only perf. part., pass., παραλελυμένος, *paralyzed, enfeebled.*

παρα-μένω, μενῶ, *to remain by* (dat., or πρός, acc.), *to abide with,* 1 Cor. xvi. 6 (W. H. καταμένω); Phil. i. 25 (W. H.); *to continue,* Ja. i. 25; Heb. vii. 23.*

παρα-μυθέομαι, οῦμαι, *to speak to, to cheer, to comfort,* Jn. xi. 19, 31; 1 Th. ii. 11, v. 14.*

παρα-μυθία, ας, ἡ, *encouragement, comfort,* 1 Cor. xiv. 3.*

παρα-μύθιον, ου, τό, *comfort,* Phil. ii. 1.*

παρα-νομέω, ῶ, *to act contrary to law,* Ac. xxiii. 3.*

παρα-νομία, ας, ἡ, *violation of law, transgression,* 2 Pet. ii. 16.* *Syn.:* see ἀγνόημα.

παρα-πικραίνω, ανῶ, 1st aor. παρεπίκρανα, *to provoke* God *to anger,* Heb. iii. 16. (S.)*

παρα-πικρασμός, οῦ, ὁ, *provocation* of God, Heb. iii. 8, 15. (S.)*

παρα-πίπτω, 2d aor. παρέπεσον, *to fall away,* Heb. vi. 6.*

παρα-πλέω, ῶ. εὔσομαι, *to sail past,* acc., Ac. xx. 16.*

παρα-πλήσιον, adv., *near to* (gen.), Phil. ii. 27.*

παραπλησίως, adv., *similarly, in like manner,* Heb. ii. 14.*

παρα-πορεύομαι, dep., mid., *to pass by, to pass along by,* Mar. xi. 20, xv. 29.

παρά-πτωμα, ατος, τό (παραπίπτω), *a falling away* or *aside, a sin,* Ep. i. 7, ii. 1, 5. *Syn.:* see ἀγνόημα.

παρα-ρρέω, 2d aor., pass., παρερρύην, pass., *to be carried past, to lose,* Heb. ii. 1.*

παρά-σημος, ον, *marked with* (dat.), Ac. xxviii. 11.*

παρα-σκευάζω, σω, *to prepare,* Ac. x. 10; mid., *to prepare one's self,* 1 Cor. xiv. 8; pass., *to be in readiness,* 2 Cor. ix. 2, 3.*

παρα-σκευή, ῆς, ἡ, *a preparation, i.e.,* the day immediately before a sabbath or other festival, Mat. xxvii. 62; Mar. xv. 42; Lu. xxiii. 54; Jn. xix. 14, 31, 42.*

παρα-τείνω, to extend, to prolong, Ac. xx. 7.*

παρα-τηρέω, ῶ, ήσω, (1) to watch, Mar. iii. 2; (2) to observe scrupulously, Gal. iv. 10.

παρα-τήρησις, εως, ἡ, observation, Lu. xvii. 20.*

παρα-τίθημι, θήσω (see Gr. § 107), (1) to place near or by the side of, as food, Lu. xi. 6; (2) to set or lay before, as instruction, Mat. xiii. 24; mid., to give in charge to, to entrust, Lu. xii. 48· to commend, to recommend (acc. and dat., or εἰς), Ac. xiv. 23.

παρα-τυγχάνω, to fall in with, chance to meet, Ac. xvii. 17.*

παρ-αυτίκα, adv., for the moment, 2 Cor. iv. 17.*

παρα-φέρω (see Gr. § 103, 6, Wi. § 52, 4, 11)), to remove (acc. and ἀπό), Mar. xiv. 36; Lu. xxii. 42; pass., to be led aside, carried away, Heb. xiii. 9 (W. H.); Ju. 12 (W. H.).*

παρα-φρονέω, ῶ, to be beside one's self, 2 Cor. xi. 23.*

παρα-φρονία, ας, ἡ, being beside one's self, madness, folly, 2 Pet. ii. 16. (N. T.)*

παρα-χειμάζω, άσω, to pass the winter, Ac. xxvii. 12, xxviij 11; 1 Cor. xvi. 6; Tit. iii. 12.*

παρα-χειμασία, ας, ἡ, a passing the winter, Ac. xxvii. 12.*

παρα-χρῆμα, adv., instantly, immediately, Lu. i. 64, iv. 39.

πάρδαλις, εως, ἡ, a leopard, a panther, Rev. xiii. 2.*

παρ-εδρεύω, to wait upon, to attend to (dat.), 1 Cor. ix. 13 (W. H.).*

πάρ-ειμι (εἰμί), to be near, to be present; part., παρών, present; τὸ παρόν, the present time; τὰ παρόντα, possessions.

παρ-εισ-άγω, ξω, to bring in secretly, 2 Pet. ii. 1.*

παρ-είσ-ακτος, ον, brought in secretly, surreptitious, Gal. ii. 4.*

παρ-εισ-δύω, or -ύνω, ύσω, to come in by stealth, to enter secretly, Ju. 4.*

παρ-εισ-έρχομαι (see Gr. § 103, 2), (1) to enter secretly, Gal.

ii. 4; (2) to enter in addition, Ro. v. 20.*

παρ-εισ-φέρω, to contribute besides, 2 Pet. i. 5.*

παρ-εκτός, adv., besides; τὰ παρεκτός, the things that occur besides, 2 Cor. xi. 28 (see R.V. mrg.); prep. with gen., except, Mat. v. 32; Ac. xxvi. 29; also Mat. xix. 9, W. H. mrg.*

παρ-εμ-βάλλω, βαλῶ, to cast up a bank about a city, Lu. xix. 43 (W. H.).*

παρ-εμ-βολή, ῆς, ἡ, (1) a camp, Heb. xiii. 11, 13; (2) soldiers' barracks, Ac. xxi. 34, 37; (3) an army in battle array, Heb. xi. 34.

παρ-εν-οχλέω, ῶ, to cause disturbance to, to disquiet (dat.), Ac. xv. 19.*

παρ-επί-δημος, ον, residing in a strange country; as subst., a stranger, foreigner, Heb. xi. 13; 1 Pet. i. 1, ii. 11.*

παρ-έρχομαι, ελεύσομαι (see Gr. § 103, 2, Wi. § 52, 4, 11)), (1) to pass by, with acc. of person or place; (2) to pass, elapse, as time; (3) to pass away or perish; (4) to pass from any one; (5) to pass carelessly, i.e., to disregard, neglect.

πάρ-εσις, εως, ἡ (ἵημι), passing over, prætermission, Ro. iii. 25.* Syn.: see ἄφεσις.

παρ-έχω, έξω, 2d aor. παρέσχον (dat. and acc.), (1) to offer, to supply, Lu. vi. 29; Ac. xxii. 2; espec. the phrase παρέχω κόπους, to cause trouble, Mat. xxvi. 10; (2) in mid., to present, manifest, Tit. ii. 7; to bestow, Col. iv. 1.

παρ-ηγορία, ας, ἡ, solace, Col. iv. 11.*

παρθενία, ας, ἡ, virginity, Lu. ii. 36.*

παρθένος, ον, ἡ, a virgin, a maid, Mat. xxv. 1, 7, 11; hence one who is chaste, Rev. xiv. 4, applied to the male sex.

Πάρθος, ον, ὁ, a Parthian, Ac. ii. 9.*

παρ-ίημι, to pass by or over, to relax; pass., perf. part., παρειμένος, weary, Heb. xii. 12.*

παρ-ίστημι, or παριστάνω (Ro. vi. 13, 16; see Gr. § 107),

στήσω, (1) trans. in act., pres., imp., fut., and 1st aor., to place near or at hand, to provide, Ac. xxiii. 24; to present, to offer, Ro. vi. 13, 16; specially, to dedicate, to consecrate, Lu. ii. 22; to cause to appear, to demonstrate, Ac. xxiv. 13; (2) intrans., perf., plup., 2d aor., and mid., to stand by, Mar. xiv. 47, 69, 70; Lu. xix. 24; to have come, Mar. iv. 29; to stand by, i.e., for aid or support, Ro. xvi. 2; to stand in hostile array, Ac. iv. 26.

Παρμενᾶς, acc. ᾶν, ὁ, Parmenas, Ac. vi. 5.*

πάρ-οδος, ου, ἡ, a passing by or through, 1 Cor. xvi. 7.*

παρ-οικέω, ῶ, to dwell in (ἐν or εἰς, const. præg.) as a stranger, Lu. xxiv. 18; Heb. xi. 9.*

παρ-οικία, ας, ἡ, a sojourning, a dwelling in a strange land, Ac. xiii. 17; 1 Pet. i. 17. (S.)*

πάρ-οικος, ον, generally as substantive, a stranger, a foreigner, Ac. vii. 6, 29; Ep. ii. 19; 1 Pet. ii. 11.*

παρ-οιμία, ας, ἡ (οἶμος, a way), (1) a current or trite saying, a proverb, 2 Pet. ii. 22; (2) an obscure saying, a symbolic saying, Jn. xvi. 25, 29; (3) a comparative discourse, an allegory, Jn. x. 6.

πάρ-οινος, ον, given to wine, drunken, 1 Tim. iii. 3; Tit. i. 7.*

παρ-οίχομαι, to pass away, of time, Ac. xiv. 16.*

παρ-ομοιάζω, to resemble, Mat. xxiii. 27. (N. T.)*

παρ-όμοιος, ον, similar, Mar. vii. 8 (W. H. omit), 13.*

παρ-οξύνω, to provoke, to irritate, in pass., Ac. xvii. 16; 1 Cor. xiii. 5.*

παρ-οξυσμός, οῦ, ὁ, (1) incitement, Heb. x. 24; (2) contention, irritation, Ac. xv. 39.*

παρ-οργίζω, ιῶ, to provoke greatly, exasperate, Ro. x. 19; Ep. vi. 4.*

παρ-οργισμός, οῦ, ὁ, exasperation, wrath, Ep. iv. 26. (S.)* Syn.: see θυμός.

παρ-οτρύνω, to stir up, to incite, Ac. xiii. 50.*

παρ-ουσία, as, ἡ (εἰμί), (1) *presence*, 2 Cor. x. 10; Phil. ii. 20; (2) *a coming, an arrival, advent,* often of the second coming of Christ, 2 Cor. vii. 6, 7; 1 Th. iii. 13.

παρ-οψίς, ίδος, ἡ, *a dish for delicacies,* Mat. xxiii. 25, 26.*

παρρησία, as, ἡ, *freedom, openness,* especially in speaking, *boldness, confidence,* Ac. iv. 13; Heb. x. 19; παρρησίᾳ, ἐν παρρησίᾳ, or μετὰ παρρησίας, *boldly, openly.*

παρρησιάζομαι, dep., mid., 1st aor. ἐπαρρησιασάμην, *to speak freely, boldly, to be confident,* Ac. xviii. 26, xxvi. 26.

πᾶς, πᾶσα, πᾶν (see Gr. § 37), *all, the whole, every kind of* (see Gr. § 224, Wi. § 18, 4, Bu. 119 sq., and for negative in phrases, Gr. § 328, iii., Wi. § 26, 1, Bu. 121 sq.); adverbial phrases are διαπαντός (which see), *always;* ἐν παντί, ἐν πᾶσιν, *in everything;* and πάντα (neut. plur. acc.), *altogether.*

πάσχα, τό (Aram.), *the paschal lamb,* Mar. xiv. 12; applied to Christ, 1 Cor. v. 7; *the paschal supper,* Mar. xiv. 16; *the passover feast,* Mat. xxvi. 2. (S.)

πάσχω (παθ-, see Gr. § 94, i. 7), *to be affected with* anything, good or bad; so, *to enjoy good,* Gal. iii. 4; more commonly, *to endure suffering,* Mat. xvii. 15; *to suffer* (acc. of that suffered, ἀπό or ὑπό, gen., of person inflicting).

Πάταρα, άρων, τά, *Patara,* Ac. xxi. 1.*

πατάσσω, ξω, *to smite, to strike, to smite to death, to afflict,* Mat. xxvi. 31; Ac. xii. 23.

πατέω, ῶ, ήσω, *to tread upon,* Lu. x. 19; *to press by treading,* as grapes, Rev. xiv. 20, xix. 15; fig., *to tread down, to trample upon,* Lu. xxi. 24; Rev. xi. 2.*

πατήρ, τρός, ὁ (see Gr. § 30, ii., Wi. §§ 19, 1 a, 30, 3, Bu. 94), *a father;* often of God as the father of men, Mat. v. 16, 45; as the father of the Lord Jesus Christ, Mat. vii. 21; as the first person in the Trinity, Mat. xxviii. 19; as the source of manifold bless-

ings, 2 Cor. i. 3. Secondary meanings are: (1) *a founder of a race, an ancestor;* (2) *a senior, a father in age,* 1 Jn. ii. 13, 14; (3) *the author,* or *cause,* or *source of anything,* Jn. viii. 44; Heb. xii. 9; (4) *a spiritual father,* or means of converting any one to Christ, 1 Cor. iv. 15; (5) *one to whom resemblance is borne,* Jn. viii. 38, 41, 44.

Πάτμος, ου, ἡ, *Patmos,* Rev. i. 9.*

πατρ-αλώας (W. H. -ολώας), ου, ὁ, *a parricide,* 1 Tim. i. 9.*

πατριά, ᾶς, ἡ, *a family* (in O. T. a division between the tribe and the household), Lu. ii. 4; Ac. iii. 25; Ep. iii. 15 (on which see Gr. § 224).*

πατρι-άρχης, ου, ὁ, *head* or *founder of a family, a patriarch,* Ac. ii. 29, vii. 8, 9; Heb. vii. 4. (S.)*

πατρικός, ἡ, όν, *paternal, ancestral,* Gal. i. 14.*

πατρίς, ίδος, ἡ, *one's native place, fatherland,* Heb. xi. 14; *one's native place, i.e., city,* Mat. xiii. 54, 57.

Πατρόβας, acc. αν, ὁ, *Patrobas,* Ro. xvi. 14.*

πατρο-πará-δοτος, ον, *handed down from ancestors,* 1 Pet. i. 18.*

πατρῷος, α, ον, *received from the fathers, hereditary,* Ac. xxii. 3, xxiv. 14, xxviii. 17.*

Παῦλος, ου, ὁ, *Paul,* (1) Sergius Paulus, Ac. xiii. 7; (2) the apostle of the Gentiles, Ac. xxi. 40 (see Gr. § 159 c, Wi. § 18, 6).

παύω, σω, *to cause to cease, to restrain,* 1 Pet. iii. 10; generally mid., *to cease, desist,* Lu. v. 4, viii. 24.

Πάφος, ου, ἡ, *Paphos,* Ac. xiii. 6, 13.*

παχύνω (παχύς), *to make fat, to fatten;* pass., fig., *to become stupid,* Mat. xiii. 15; Ac. xxviii. 27.*

πέδη, ης, ἡ, *a shackle, a fetter for the feet,* Mar. v. 4; Lu. viii. 29.*

πεδινός, ἡ, όν, *level,* Lu. vi. 17.*

πεζεύω (πεζός), *to travel on foot* or *by land,* Ac. xx. 13.*

πεζῇ, adv., *on foot,* or *by land,* Mat. xiv. 13; Mar. vi. 33.*

πειθ-αρχέω, ῶ, (1) *to obey a ruler* or *one in authority,* Ac. v. 29, 32; Tit. iii. 1; (2) *to obey,* or *conform to advice,* Ac. xxvii. 21.*

πειθός (W. H. πιθός), ἡ, όν, *persuasive,* 1 Cor. ii. 4. (N.T.)*

πείθω, πείσω, *to persuade,* Ac. xviii. 4; *to influence by persuasion,* Mat. xxvii. 20; *to seek to please, to conciliate,* Ac. xiv. 29; 2 Cor. v. 11; *to appease, to render tranquil,* 1 Jn. iii. 19; *to conciliate, to aspire to the favor of,* Gal. i. 10; pass., *to yield to persuasion, to assent, to listen to, to obey,* Ac. v. 36, 37; the 2d perf., πέποιθα, is intrans., *to trust, to rely on, to have confidence in,* Mat. xxvii. 43; Ro. ii. 19.

πεινάω, ῶ, inf. πεινᾶν, άσω, (1) *to be hungry,* Mat. iv. 2, xii. 1, 3; hence, (2) *to be needy,* Lu. i. 53; (3) *to desire earnestly, to long for,* acc., Mat. v. 6.

πεῖρα, as, ἡ, *trial, experiment;* with λαμβάνω, *to make trial of, to experience,* Heb. xi. 29, 36.*

πειράζω, σω, (1) *to attempt* (inf.), Ac. xvi. 7; (2) *to make trial of, to test* (acc.), Jn. vi. 6; (3) *to tempt to sin,* Ja. i. 13, 14; ὁ πειράζων, *the tempter, i.e., the devil,* Mat. iv. 3. *Syn.:* see δοκιμάζω.

πειρασμός, οῦ, ὁ, *a trying, proving,* 1 Pet. iv. 12; Heb. iii. 8; *a tempting to sin,* Mat. vi. 13; *calamity, adversity,* as trying men, Ac. xx. 19. (S.)

πειράω, ῶ, only in mid., *to attempt,* Ac. ix. 26 (W. H. πειράζω), xxvi. 21.*

πεισμονή, ῆς, ἡ, *persuasion, conviction,* Gal. v. 8. (N.T.)*

πέλαγος, ους, τό, *the sea, the deep,* Mat. xviii. 6; Ac. xxvii. 5.*

πελεκίζω (πέλεκυς, *an axe*), *to behead,* Rev. xx. 4.*

πέμπτος, η, ον, ord. num., *the fifth,* Rev. vi. 9.

πέμπω, ψω, (1) *to send,* of persons, *to send forth,* spoken of teachers, as John Baptist, Jn. i. 33; of Jesus, Jn. iv. 34; of the Spirit, Jn. xiv. 26; of apostles, Jn. xiii. 20; (2) *to send,* of things, *to transmit*, Rev. xi. 10; *to send among* or *upon*, 2 Th. ii. 11; *to thrust in* the sickle, Rev. xiv. 15, 18.

πένης, ητος, ὁ, *poor*, 2 Cor. ix. 9.* *Syn.*: πτωχός implies utter destitution, usually beggary; πένης, simply poverty, scanty livelihood.

πενθερά, ᾶς, ἡ, *a mother-in-law*, a wife's mother, Mar. i. 30.

πενθερός, οῦ, ὁ, *a father-in-law*, a wife's father, Jn. xviii. 13.*

πενθέω, ῶ, ήσω, (1) *to mourn*, intrans., Ja. iv. 9; (2) *to mourn passionately for, to lament*, trans., 2 Cor. xii. 21.

πένθος, ους, τό, *mourning*, Ja. iv. 9; Rev. xviii. 7, 8, xxi. 4.*

πενιχρός, ά, όν, *poor, needy*, Lu. xxi. 2.*

πεντάκις, num. adv., *five times*, 2 Cor. xi. 24.*

πεντακισ-χίλιοι, αι, α, num., *five thousand*, Mat. xiv. 21.

πεντακόσιοι, αι, α, num., *five hundred*, Lu. vii. 41; 1 Cor. xv. 6.*

πέντε, οἱ, αἱ, τά, num. indecl., *five*, Mat. xiv. 17.

πεντε-και-δέκατος, η, ον, ord. num., *fifteenth*, Lu. iii. 1. (S.)*

πεντήκοντα, οἱ, αἱ, τά, num. indecl., *fifty*, Lu. vii. 41.

πεντηκοστή, ῆς, ἡ (lit. *fiftieth*), *Pentecost*, the feast beginning the fiftieth day after the second day of the Passover, *i.e.*, from the sixteenth day of the month Nisan, Ac. ii. 1, xx. 16; 1 Cor. xvi. 8.*

πέποιθα, see πείθω.

πεποίθησις, εως, ἡ, *trust, confidence*, with εἰς or ἐν, 2 Cor. viii. 22; Phil. iii. 4. (S.)

πέρ, an enclitic particle, cognate with περί, only found joined to pronouns or particles for intensity of meaning, as ἐάνπερ, εἴπερ, *if indeed*; ἐπείπερ, *since indeed*, καίπερ, *and really*; ὅσπερ, *the very one who*.

περαιτέρω (πέρα), adv., *further, besides*, Ac. xix. 39 (W. H.).*

πέραν, adv., *over, on the other side, beyond*, with article prefixed or genitive following, Mat. viii. 18, 28, xix. 1.

πέρας, ατος. τό, *a limit, the ex-*

tremity, in space, as Mat. xii. 42; or time, Heb. vi. 16.

Πέργαμος, ου, ἡ, *Pergamus* or *Pergamum*, Rev. i. 11, ii. 12.*

Πέργη, ης, ἡ, *Perga*, Ac. xiii. 13.

περί, a prep., governing the gen. and acc.; with gen., *about*, *i.e.*, concerning or respecting a thing; with acc., *about, around*, in reference to (see Gr. § 302, Wi. §§ 47 e, 49 i, Bu. 335). In composition, περί denotes *round about, on account of, above, beyond*.

περι-άγω, trans., *to lead* or *take about*, 1 Cor. ix. 5; intrans., *to go about* (acc. of place), Mat. iv. 23, ix. 35, xxiii. 15; Mar. vi. 6; Ac. xiii. 11.*

περι-αιρέω, ῶ (see Gr. § 103, 2, Wi. § 15, Bu. 53), *to take from around, take entirely away*, lit., Ac. xxvii. 40 (*to cast off* anchors, R. V.); fig., of the removal of sin, Heb. x. 11.

περι-άπτω, *to kindle*, Lu. xxii. 55 (W. H.).*

περι-αστράπτω, *to lighten around, to flash around* (acc., or περί, acc.), Ac. ix. 3, xxii. 6. (Ap.)*

περι-βάλλω, βαλῶ, βέβληκα, *to cast around* (acc. and dat.), Lu. xix. 43; *to clothe*, Mat. xxv. 36; for const., see Gr. § 284, Wi. § 53, 4, 12), Bu. 149; mid., *to clothe one's self, to be clothed*, Mat. vi. 29.

περι-βλέπω, N. T., in mid., *to look around*, abs., Mar. v. 32, ix. 8, x. 23; *to look round upon*, acc., Mar. iii. 5, 34, xi. 11; Lu. vi. 10.*

περι-βόλαιον, ου, τό, (1) *a mantle*, Heb. i. 12; (2) *a veil*, 1 Cor. xi. 15.*

περι-δέω, *to bind round about*, pass., plup., Jn. xi. 44.*

περι-δρέμω, see περιτρέχω.

περι-εργάζομαι, *to overdo, to be a busybody*, 2 Th. iii. 11.*

περί-εργος, ον, act., *overdoing, intermeddling*, 1 Tim. v. 13; pass., τὰ περίεργα, *superfluous arts, sorcery*, Ac. xix. 19.*

περι-έρχομαι (see Gr. § 103, 2, Wi. § 53, 4, 12)), *to go about*,

Ac. xix. 13; 1 Tim. v. 13; Heb. xi. 37; *to tack*, as a ship, Ac. xxviii. 13 (not W. H.).*

περι-έχω, *to encompass*; so, *to contain*, as a writing, Ac. xxiii. 25 (W. H. ἔχω); intrans., *to be contained*, 1 Pet. ii. 6; *to seize*, as astonishment, Lu. v. 9.*

περι-ζώννυμι, or -ζωννύω (see Gr. § 114, Wi. § 53, 4, 12), Bu. 191), *to gird one's self around*, mid. or pass., Ep. vi. 14; Lu. xii. 35, 37.

περί-θεσις, εως, ἡ, *a putting around*, as ornaments, 1 Pet. iii. 3. (N. T.)*

περι-ΐστημι (see Gr. § 107, Wi. § 14, 1), in intrans. tenses of act., *to stand around*, Jn. xi. 42; Ac. xxv. 7; mid., *to avoid, shun* (acc.), 2 Tim. ii. 16; Tit. iii. 9.*

περι-κάθαρμα, ατος, τό, *refuse, offscouring*, 1 Cor. iv. 13. (S.)*

περι-καλύπτω, *to cover round about, to cover up*, as the face, Mar. xiv. 65; Lu. xxii. 64; Heb. ix. 4.*

περί-κειμαι, *to lie about, surround*, dat., or περί, acc., Mar. ix. 42; Lu. xvii. 2; Heb. xii. 1; *to be encompassed* or *surrounded with*, acc., Ac. xxviii. 20; Heb. v. 2.*

περι-κεφαλαία, ας, ἡ, *a helmet*, Ep. vi. 17; 1 Th. v. 8.*

περι-κρατής, ές, *having full power over* (gen.), Ac. xxvii. 16. (Ap.)*

περι-κρύπτω, *to hide entirely*, Lu. i. 24. (N. T.)*

περι-κυκλόω, ῶ, ώσω, *to encircle, surround*, Lu. xix. 43.*

περι-λάμπω, *to shine around*, Lu. ii. 9; Ac. xxvi. 13.*

περι-λείπω, *to leave remaining*; pass., *to be left*, 1 Th. iv. 15, 17.*

περί-λυπος, ον, *very sorrowful*, Mat. xxvi. 38; Mar. vi. 26, xiv. 34; Lu. xviii. 23, 24 (W. H. omit).*

περι-μένω, *to wait for* (acc.), Ac. i. 4.*

πέριξ, adv., *round about*, Ac. v. 16.*

περι-οικέω, ῶ, *to dwell around, to be neighboring to* (acc.), Lu. i. 65.*

78

περί-οικος, ος, *dwelling around, a neighbor,* Lu. i. 58.*

περι-ούσιος, ον, *costly, treasured, select;* hence, *specially chosen,* Tit. ii. 14 (S.). (S.)*

περι-οχή, ῆς, ἡ (περιέχω), *a section* or *passage* of Scripture, Ac. viii. 32.*

περι-πατέω, ῶ, ήσω, *to walk, to walk about;* fig., as Hebrew, *to pass one's life, to conduct one's self* (adv. or nom. pred.), *to live according to* (ἐν, dat.; κατά, acc.).

περι-πείρω, *to pierce through,* fig., 1 Tim. vi. 10.*

περι-πίπτω, *to fall into the midst of* (dat.), *robbers,* Lu. x. 30; *temptations,* Ja. i. 2; *to happen upon* a place, Ac. xxvii. 41.*

περι-ποιέω, ῶ, N. T. in mid., *to preserve for one's self,* Lu. xvii. 33 (W. H.); *to get for one's self, purchase,* Ac. xx. 28; 1 Tim. iii. 13.*

περι-ποίησις, εως, ἡ, (1) *a preserving,* Heb. x. 39; (2) *an obtaining, a possessing,* 1 Th. v. 9; 2 Th. ii. 14; (3) *a possession,* Ep. i. 14; 1 Pet. ii. 9.

περι-ρρήγνυμι, *to tear off,* as garments, Ac. xvi. 22.*

περι-σπάω, ῶ, *to drag around;* hence, fig., pass., *to be distracted in mind,* Lu. x. 40.*

περισσεία, ας, ἡ, *abundance, superfluity,* Ro. v. 17; 2 Cor. viii. 2; Ja. i. 21; εἰς περισσείαν, as adv., *abundantly,* 2 Cor. x. 15.*

περίσσευμα, ατος, τό, *abundance,* Mat. xii. 34; Lu. vi. 45; 2 Cor. viii. 14; pl. *a residue,* Mar. viii. 8.*

περισσεύω, εύσω, *to be more than enough, to remain over, to be in abundance,* Lu. xii. 15; Jn. vi. 12; τὸ περισσεῦον, *the residue,* Mat. xiv. 20; *to redound to,* εἰς, 2 Cor. viii. 2; *to make to abound,* Mat. xiii. 12; 2 Cor. iv. 15.

περισσός, ή, όν, *abundant, more than is necessary,* Mat. v. 37; Mar. vii. 36; *superior,* Mat. v. 47; τὸ περισσόν, *excellence, pre-eminence,* Ro. iii. 1.

περισσοτέρως, adv. (compar. of περισσῶς), *more abundantly, more earnestly,* 2 Cor. vii. 13, 15.

περισσῶς, adv., *greatly, exceedingly,* Mar. x. 26.

περιστερά, ᾶς, ἡ, *a dove,* Mat. iii. 16, x. 16.

περι-τέμνω, *to cut around, to circumcise,* Lu. i. 59; pass. and mid., *to undergo circumcision, to cause one's self to be circumcised,* 1 Cor. vii. 18.

περι-τίθημι, *to place,* or *put about* or *around* (dat. and acc.), Mat. xxi. 33; fig., *to bestow, to confer,* 1 Cor. xii. 23.

περι-τομή, ῆς, ἡ, *circumcision,* the act, the custom, or state, Jn. v. 22, 23; Gal. v. 6; with art., *the circumcision, i.e.,* the Jews, Ro. iii. 30, iv. 9, 12; fig., for *spiritual purity,* Ro. ii. 29; Col. ii. 11. (S.)

περι-τρέπω, *to turn about, to turn* into (εἰς) *madness,* Ac. xxvi. 24.*

περι-τρέχω, 2d aor. περιέδραμον, *to run around* (acc.), Mar. vi. 55.*

περι-φέρω, *to bear* or *carry around,* Mar. vi. 55; 2 Cor. iv. 10; pass., fig., *to be carried about, carried away* by false teaching, Ep. iv. 14; Heb. xiii. 9; Ju. 12 (W. H., in last two, παραφέρω).

περι-φρονέω, ῶ, *to look down upon, to despise,* Tit. ii. 15.*

περί-χωρος, ον, *lying round about;* only as subst., ἡ περίχωρος (sc. γῆ), *the region round about,* Lu. iii. 3, iv. 14; *the inhabitants of such a region,* Mat. iii. 5.

περί-ψημα, ατος, τό, *scrapings, offscourings,* 1 Cor. iv. 13.*

περπερεύομαι, dep., intrans., *to boast,* 1 Cor. xiii. 4.*

Περσίς, ίδος, ἡ, *Persis,* Ro. xvi. 12.*

πέρυσι, adv., *last year;* ἀπὸ πέρυσι, *a year ago,* 2 Cor. viii. 10, ix. 2.*

πετάομαι, ῶμαι, or πέτομαι (W. H.), *to fly,* as a bird, Rev.*

πετεινόν, οῦ, τό, *a bird;* only in plur., *birds,* Mat. vi. 26, xiii. 4.

πέτομαι, see πετάομαι.

πέτρα, ας, ἡ, *a rock, a ledge, cliff,* Mat. vii. 24, 25, xxvii. 51; with art., *the rock, i.e.,* the rocky substratum of the soil, Lu. viii. 6, 13; *a large*

detached *rock,* fig., Ro. ix. 33; see also Mat. xvi. 18.

Πέτρος, ου, ὁ, *Peter* (prop., a rock = Κηφᾶς), Lu. iv. 38; Jn. i. 42.

πετρώδης, ες, *rocky, stony,* Mat. xiii. 5, 20; Mar. iv. 5, 16.*

πήγανον, ου, τό, *rue,* Lu. xi. 42.*

πηγή, ῆς, ἡ, *a fountain, spring,* Jn. iv. 14; Ja. iii. 11; fig., Rev. vii. 17; *a flow* of blood, Mar. v. 29.

πήγνυμι, *to fasten, to pitch* a tent, Heb. viii. 2.*

πηδάλιον, ου, τό, *the rudder* of a ship, Ac. xxvii. 40; Ja. iii. 4.*

πηλίκος, η, ον, *how large,* Gal. vi. 11 (see γράμμα); *how distinguished,* Heb. vii. 4.*

πηλός, οῦ, ὁ, *clay, mud,* Jn. ix. 6–15; Ro. ix. 21.*

πήρα, ας, ἡ, *a sack, a wallet,* for carrying provisions, Mat. x. 10; Mar. vi. 8; Lu. ix. 3, x. 4, xxii. 35, 36.*

πῆχυς, εως, ὁ, *a cubit,* the length from the elbow to the tip of the middle finger, *about a foot and a half,* Mat. vi. 27; Lu. xii. 25; Jn. xxi. 8; Rev. xxi. 17.*

πιάζω, σω, *to lay hold of,* Ac. iii. 7; *to take,* as in fishing or in hunting, Jn. xxi. 3, 10; Rev. xix. 20; *to arrest,* Jn. vii. 30.

πιέζω, *to press together,* as in a measure, Lu. vi. 38.*

πιθανο-λογία, ας, ἡ, *persuasive* or *plausible speech,* Col. ii. 4.*

πικραίνω, ανῶ, *to render bitter,* lit., Rev. viii. 11, x. 9, 10; *to embitter,* fig., Col. iii. 19.*

πικρία, ας, ἡ, *bitterness,* fig., Ac. viii. 23; Ro. iii. 14; Ep. iv. 31; Heb. xii. 15.*

πικρός, ά, όν, *bitter, acrid, malignant,* Ja. iii. 11, 14.*

πικρῶς, adv., *bitterly,* of weeping, Mat. xxvi. 75; Lu. xxii. 12.*

Πιλᾶτος, or Πιλᾶτος (W. H. Πειλᾶτος), ου, ὁ (Lat. *pilatus,* "armed with a javelin"), *Pilate,* Mar. xv. 1, 2.

πίμπλημι, πλήσω, 1st aorist pass., ἐπλήσθην, (1) *to fill* with (gen.), Mat. xxvii. 48; fig., of emotions, Lu. iv. 28; or of the Holy Spirit, Ac. ii.

4; (2) pass., *to be fulfilled* or *completed*, of time, Lu. i. 23, 57.

πίμπρημι (πρα-), and **πιμπράω**, pass., inf., πίμπρασθαι, *to be inflamed*, *to swell*, Ac. xxviii. 6.*

πινακίδιον, ου, τό (dim. of πίναξ), *a tablet for writing*, Lu. i. 63.*

πίναξ, ακος, ὁ, *a plate*, *platter*, Lu. xi. 39.

πίνω, fut. πίομαι, perf. πέπωκα, 2d aor. ἔπιον (inf. πεῖν, W. H.), *to drink*, abs., or with acc. of thing drunk (sometimes ἐκ or ἀπό), Lu. xii. 19, 29; *to imbibe*, as the earth imbibes rain, Heb. vi. 7; fig., *to receive into the soul*, *to partake of*, Jn. vii. 37.

πιότης, τητος, ἡ, *fatness*, as of the olive, Ro. xi. 17.*

πιπράσκω (πρα-), perf. πέπρακα, 1st aor. pass. ἐπράθην, perf. pass. πέπραμαι, *to sell*, Mat. xiii. 46; pass., with ὑπό, *to be sold under*, *to be a slave to*, Ro. vii. 14.

πίπτω (πετ-, see Gr. § 94, i. 8 d, Wi. § 13, 1 a, Bu. 167), πεσοῦμαι, (1) *to fall* (whence, by ἀπό or ἐκ; whither, by ἐπί or εἰς, acc.), Mat. xv. 27; Mar. iv. 5, 7, 8; hence, (2) *to fall prostrate*, as of persons, *to die*, *to perish*, Jn. xviii. 6; Rev. i. 17; of structures, *to fall in ruins*, Mat. vii. 25, 27; of institutions, *to fail*; (3) *to fall to*, as a lot, Ac. i. 26; (4) *to fall into* or *under*, as condemnation.

Πισιδία, ας, ἡ, *Pisidia*, Ac. xiv. 24, xiii. 14, where W. H. have adj. form.*

πιστεύω (see Gr. § 74, Wi. §§ 31, 5, 32, 5, 33 d, 39, 1 a, Bu. 173 sq., 337), εύσω, *to believe*, *be persuaded* of a thing (acc. or ὅτι); *to give credit to*, dat.; *to have confidence in*, *to trust*, *believe*, dat., εἰς, ἐν, ἐπί (dat.) or ἐπί (acc.), often of Christian faith, in God, in Christ; *to entrust* something (acc.) to any one (dat.); pass., *to be entrusted with* (acc.).

πιστικός, ή, όν, *genuine*, *pure*, of ointment, Mar. xiv. 3; Jn. xii. 3.*

πίστις, εως, ἡ, (1) *faith*, generally, as 2 Th. ii. 13; Heb. xi.

1; the object of the faith is expressed by obj. gen., or by εἰς, ἐν, πρός (acc.); (2) *fidelity*, *good faith*, Ro. iii. 3; 2 Tim. ii. 22; (3) *a pledge*, *a promise given*, 2 Tim. iv. 7; (4) met., for the whole of the *Christian character*, and (generally with art.) for the *Christian religion*.

πιστός, ή, όν, (1) *trustworthy*, *faithful*, in any relation or to any promise, of things or (generally) persons; (2) *believing*, abs., as οἱ πιστοί, *the followers of Christ*, or with dat.

πιστόω, ῶ, *to make faithful*; N. T., only in pass., *to be assured of*, 2 Tim. iii. 14.*

πλανάω, ῶ, ήσω, *to lead astray*, *to cause to wander*, Heb. xi. 38; fig., *to deceive*, Jn. vii. 12; pass., *to be misled*, *to err*, Mar. xii. 24, 27; Lu. xxi. 8.

πλάνη, ης, ἡ, *a wandering*; only fig., *deceit*, *delusion*, *error*, Mat. xxvii. 64; Ep. iv. 14.

πλανήτης, ου, ὁ, *a wanderer*; ἀστὴρ πλανήτης, *a wandering star*, Ju. 13.*

πλάνος, ον, *causing to wander*, *misleading*, 1 Tim. iv. 1; as subst., *a deceiver*, Mat. xxvii. 63; 2 Cor. vi. 8; 2 Jn. 7.*

πλάξ, ακός, ἡ, *a tablet* to write on, 2 Cor. iii. 3; Heb. ix. 4.*

πλάσμα, ατος, τό, *a thing formed* or *fashioned*, Ro. ix. 20.*

πλάσσω, άσω, *to form*, *mould*, as a potter his clay, Ro. ix. 20; 1 Tim. ii. 13.*

πλαστός, ή, όν, *formed*, *moulded*; fig., *feigned*, 2 Pet. ii. 3.*

πλατεῖα, ας, ἡ (fem. of πλατύς, *broad*, sc. ὁδός), *a street*, Mat. vi. 5, xii. 19.

πλάτος, ους, τό, *breadth*, Ep. iii. 18; Rev. xx. 9, xxi. 16.*

πλατύνω, *to make broad*, *to enlarge*, Mat. xxiii. 5; pass., fig., *to be enlarged*, in mind or heart, 2 Cor. vi. 11, 13.*

πλατύς, εῖα, ύ, *broad*, Mat. vii. 13.*

πλέγμα, ατος, τό (πλέκω), *anything interwoven*, *braided hair*, 1 Tim. ii. 9.*

πλεῖστος, η, ον, superl. of πολύς,

the greatest, *the most*, *very great*; τὸ πλεῖστον, adv., *mostly*, *at most*, 1 Cor. xiv. 27.

πλείων, εῖον (for declension see Gr. § 44, Bu. 127), compar. of πολύς, *more*, *greater*, in number, magnitude, comparison; οἱ πλείονες, οἱ πλείους, *the more*, *the most*, *the many*, *majority*, 2 Cor. ii. 6; πλεῖον or πλέον, as adv., *more*, Jn. xxi. 15; ἐπὶ πλεῖον, *further*, *longer*, Ac. iv. 17.

πλέκω, ξω, *to weave together*, *to plait*, Mat. xxvii. 29; Mar. xv. 17; Jn. xix. 2.*

πλέον, see πλείων.

πλεονάζω, σω, intrans., *to have more than enough*, 2 Cor. viii. 15; *to abound*, *to increase*, Ro. v. 20; 2 Cor. iv. 15; trans., *to cause to increase*, 1 Th. iii. 12.

πλεονεκτέω, ῶ, *to have more than another*; hence, *to overreach*, *take advantage of* (R. V.), 2 Cor. vii. 2, xii. 17, 18; 1 Th. iv. 6; pass., 2 Cor. ii. 11.*

πλεον-έκτης, ου, ὁ, *a covetous* or *avaricious person*, 1 Cor. v. 10, 11, vi. 10; Ep. v. 5.*

πλεονεξία, ας, ἡ, *covetousness*, *avarice*, Lu. xii. 15; 2 Pet. ii. 3. *Syn.*: πλεονεξία is more active, seeking to grasp the things it has not; φιλαργυρία, more passive, seeking to retain and multiply what it has.

πλευρά, ᾶς, ἡ, *the side* of the body, Jn. xix. 34.

πλέω, see πίμπλημι.

πλέω, impf. ἔπλεον, *to sail*, Lu. viii. 23; Ac. xxi. 3, xxvii. 6, 24; Rev. xviii. 17 (W. H.); with acc. of direction, Ac. xxvii. 2 (but W. H. read εἰς).*

πληγή, ῆς, ἡ (πλήσσω), *a blow*, *a stripe*, *a wound*, Ac. xvi. 33; Rev. xiii. 14; *an affliction*, Rev. ix. 20.

πλῆθος, ους, τό, *a multitude*, *a great number*, Mar. iii. 7, 8; Heb. xi. 12; with art., *the multitude*, *the whole number*, *the assemblage*, Ac. xiv. 4; *a quantity*, Ac. xxviii. 3.

πληθύνω, νῶ, (1) intrans., *to increase*, Ac. vi. 1; (2) trans., *to multiply*, *augment*, 2 Cor.

ix. 10; pass., *to be increased,* Mat. xxiv. 12.

πλήθω, see πίμπλημι.

πλήκτης, ου, ὁ, *a striker, a contentious person,* 1 Tim. iii. 3; Tit. i. 7.*

πλημμύρα, ας (W. H. ης), ἡ, *a flood,* Lu. vi. 48.*

πλήν, adv. (akin to πλέον, hence it *adds* a thought, generally adversative, sometimes partly confirmatory), *besides, but, nevertheless, of a truth,* Mat. xi. 22, xviii. 7, xxvi. 39, 64; πλὴν ὅτι, *except that,* Ac. xx. 23; as prep. with gen., *besides, excepting,* Mar. xii. 32; Ac. viii. 1.

πλήρης, ες, (1) *full,* abs., Mar. iv. 28; (2) *full of* (gen.), *abounding in,* Mar. viii. 19; Lu. iv. 1.

πληρο-φορέω, ῶ (φέρω), *to bring to the full, to fulfill,* 2 Tim. iv. 5, 17; pass., of things, *to be fully accomplished,* Lu. i. 1; of persons, *to be fully convinced,* Ro. iv. 21, xiv. 5; Col. iv. 12 (W. H.).*

πληρο-φορία, ας, ἡ, *fullness, entire possession, full assurance,* Col. ii. 2; 1 Th. i. 5; Heb. vi. 11, x. 22. (N. T.)*

πληρόω, ῶ, ώσω, *to fill* with (gen.), *to fill up, to pervade, to complete,* either time or number; *to bestow abundantly, to furnish liberally,* Phil. iv. 18; Ep. iii. 19; *to accomplish, to perform fully,* as prophecies, etc.; pass., *to be full of,* 2 Cor. vii. 4; Ep. v. 18; *to be made full, complete,* or *perfect,* Jn. iii. 29; Col. iv. 12 (W. H. read πληρο-φορέω).

πλήρωμα, ατος, τό, *fullness, plenitude, i.e.,* that which fills, 1 Cor. x. 26, 28; so, *the full number,* Ro. xi. 25; *the completion, i.e.,* that which makes full, *the fulfillment,* Mat. ix. 16; Ro. xiii. 10; *the fullness of time,* Gal. iv. 4, is the completion of an era; *the fullness of Christ,* Ep. i. 23, that which is filled by Christ, *i.e.,* the Church; *the fullness of the Godhead,* Col. ii. 9, all divine attributes.

πλησίον, adv., *near, near by,* with gen., Jn. iv. 5; with the art., ὁ πλησίον, *a neighbor,* Ac. vii. 27.

πλησμονή, ῆς, ἡ, *full satisfying, indulgence,* Col. ii. 23.*

πλήσσω, 2d aor. pass. ἐπλήγην, *to smite,* Rev. viii. 12.*

πλοιάριον, ου, τό (dim. of πλοῖον), *a small vessel, a boat,* Mar. iii. 9; Jn. xxi. 8.

πλοῖον, ου, τό, *a ship, a vessel,* Mat. iv. 21, 22; Mar. i. 19.

πλόος, οῦς, gen. οῦ or οός, ὁ, *a voyage,* Ac. xxi. 7, xxvii. 9, 10.*

πλούσιος, α, ον, *rich, abounding in* (ἐν), Lu. xii. 16; Ep. ii. 4.

πλουσίως, adv., *richly, abundantly,* Col. iii. 16.

πλουτέω, ῶ, ήσω, *to become rich, to be rich, to abound in,* Lu. i. 53; Ro. x. 12; Rev. xviii. 15.

πλουτίζω, *to make rich, to cause to abound in,* 1 Cor. i. 5; 2 Cor. vi. 10, ix. 11.*

πλοῦτος, ου, ὁ (see Gr. § 32 *a,* Wi. § 9 *e,* note 2, Bu. 22), *riches, wealth, abundance,* Ja. v. 2; Col. i. 27; spiritually, *enrichment,* Ro. xi. 12.

πλύνω, νῶ, *to wash,* Lu. v. 2 (W. H.); Rev. vii. 14, xxii. 14 (W. H.). *Syn.:* see λούω.

πνεῦμα, ατος, τό, (1) properly, *the wind,* or *the air in motion,* Jn. iii. 8; hence, (2) *the human spirit,* dist. from σῶμα and ψυχή, 1 Th. v. 23; (3) *a temper* or *disposition* of the soul, Lu. ix. 55; Ro. viii. 15; (4) *any intelligent, incorporeal being,* as (*a*) *the human spirit,* separated from the body, *the undying soul;* (*b*) *angels,* good and bad; (*c*) *God,* Jn. iv. 24; (*d*) *the Holy Spirit,* the third person of the Trinity (see Gr. § 217 *f,* Wi. § 19, 1 *a,* Bu. 89), in relation to Jesus, Lu. iv. 1; Ac. x. 38; in relation to prophets and apostles, Ac. xxi. 11; Jn. xx. 22; and in relation to saints generally, Gal. iii. 2.

πνευματικός, ή, όν, *spiritual,* relating to the human spirit, or belonging to a spirit, or imparted by the divine Spirit, 1 Cor. ii. 13 (see Gr. § 316, Wi. § 64, 5), 15, xv. 44; τὰ πνευματικά, *spiritual things,* Ro. xv. 27; *spiritual gifts,* 1 Cor. xii. 1.

πνευματικῶς, adv., *spiritually, i.e.,* by the aid of the Holy Spirit, 1 Cor. ii. 14; in a mystical sense, Rev. xi. 8. (N. T.)*

πνέω, εύσω, *to blow,* as the wind, Mat. vii. 25, 27.

πνίγω, *to choke, to seize by the throat,* Mat. xviii. 28; Mar. v. 13.*

πνικτός, ή, όν, *strangled,* Ac. xv. 20, 29; xxi. 25.

πνοή, ῆς, ἡ, (1) *breath,* Ac. xvii. 25; (2) *wind,* Ac. ii. 2.*

ποδήρης, ες, *reaching to the feet;* as subst. (sc. χιτών or ἐσθής), *a long robe,* Rev. i. 13.* *Syn..* see ἱμάτιον.

πόθεν, adv., interrog., *whence?* of place, Mat. xv. 33; *from what source?* Mat. xiii. 27; of cause, *how?* Lu. i. 43; Mar. xii. 37.

ποία, ας, ἡ, *grass, herbage,* according to some, in Ja. iv. 14; but more probably the word here is the fem. of ποῖος, *of what sort?* *

ποιέω, ῶ, ήσω, (1) *to make, i.e., to form, to bring about, to cause;* spoken of religious festivals, etc., *to observe, to celebrate;* of trees and plants, *to germinate, to produce; to cause to be* or *to become,* Mat. xxi. 13; *to declare to be,* Jn. viii. 53; *to assume,* Mat. xii. 33; (2) *to do,* generally; *to do, i.e.,* habitually, *to perform, to execute, to exercise, to practice, i.e., to pursue a course of action, to be active, to work, to spend, to pass, i.e.,* time or life, Ac. xv. 33. *Syn.:* see Trench, § xcvi.

ποίημα, ατος, τό, *a thing made, a work,* Ro. i. 20; Ep. ii. 10.*

ποίησις, εως, ἡ, *a doing,* Ja. i. 25.*

ποιητής, οῦ, ὁ, (1) *a doer, performer,* Ro. ii. 13; Ja. i. 22, 23, 25, iv. 11; (2) *a poet,* Ac. xvii. 28.*

ποικίλος, η, ον, *various, of different colors, diverse,* Lu. iv. 40.

ποιμαίνω, ανῶ, (1) *to feed a flock,* Lu. xvii. 7; 1 Cor. ix. 7; hence, fig., (2) *to be shepherd of, to tend, to cherish,* Mat. ii. 6; Jn. xxi. 16; Ac. xx. 28; 1 Pet. v. 2; Ju. 12;

Rev. vii. 17; (3) *to rule, govern*, Rev. ii. 27, xii. 5, xix. 15.* *Syn.:* see βόσκω.

ποιμήν, ένος, ὁ, (1) *a shepherd*, Mat. ix. 36, xxv. 32; (2) fig., of Christ as the *Shepherd*, Heb. xiii. 20; 1 Pet. ii. 25; and of his ministers as *pastors*, Ep. iv. 11

ποίμνη, ης, ἡ, (1) *a flock* of sheep or goats, Lu. ii. 8; 1 Cor. ix. 7; (2) fig., of Christ's followers, Mat. xxvi. 31; Jn. x. 16.*

ποίμνιον, ου, τό (= ποίμνη), *a flock;* only fig., Lu. xii. 32; Ac. xx. 28, 29; 1 Pet. v. 2, 3.*

ποῖος, ποία, ποῖον, an interrog. pronoun corresponding to οἶος and τοῖος, *of what kind, sort, species? what? what one?* In Lu. v. 19, sc. ὁδοῦ.

πολεμέω, ῶ, ήσω, *to make war, to contend* with (μετά, gen.), Rev. ii. 16, xiii. 4.

πόλεμος, ου, ὁ, (1) *war, a war*, Lu. xix. 31; (2) *a battle*, Rev. ix. 7, 9; (3) *strife*, Ja. iv. 1.

πόλις, εως, ἡ, *a city*, Ac. v. 16; met., *the inhabitants of a city*, Mar. i. 33; with art., *the city Jerusalem, the heavenly city*, of which Jerusalem was a symbol, Heb. xiii. 14; Rev. iii. 12.

πολιτ-άρχης, ου, ὁ, *a ruler of a city, a city magistrate*, Ac. xvii. 6, 8.*

πολιτεία, ας, ἡ, (1) *citizenship*, Ac. xxii. 28; (2) *a state, commonwealth*, Ep. ii. 12.*

πολίτευμα, ατος, τό, *a state, a commonwealth*, Phil. iii. 20.*

πολιτεύω, in mid., *to behave as a citizen;* hence, *to live, i.e., to order one's life*, Ac. xxiii. 1; Phil. i. 27.*

πολίτης, ου, ὁ, *a citizen*, Lu. xv. 15; Ac. xxi. 39; with gen., αὐτοῦ, *a fellow-citizen*, Lu. xix. 14; Heb. viii. 11 (W. H.).*

πολλάκις, adv., *many times, often*, Mar. v. 4, ix. 22.

πολλα-πλασίων, ον, gen. ονος, *manifold, many times more*, Mat. xix. 29 (W. H.); Lu. xviii. 30.*

πολυ-λογία, ας, ἡ, *much speaking*, Mat. vi. 7.*

πολυ-μερῶς, adv., *in many*

parts, by many portions, Heb. i. 1.*

πολυ-ποίκιλος, ον, *much varied, manifold*, Ep. iii. 10.*

πολύς, πολλή, πολύ (see Gr. § 39, 2), *many, numerous;* πολύ, *much, greatly*, as adv.; πολλοί, *many*, often with partitive genitive, or ἐκ; οἱ πολλοί, *the many* (see Gr. § 227, Wi. § 18, 3); πολλά, in like manner, *much, very much, often, many times;* πολλῷ, *by much*, joined with comparatives; ἐπὶ πολύ, *for a great while*, Ac. xxviii. 6; ἐν πολλῷ, *altogether*, Ac. xxvi. 29 (not W. H.).

πολύ-σπλαγχνος, ον, *very compassionate, of great mercy*, Ja. v. 11. (N. T.)*

πολυ-τελής, ές, *very costly, very precious*, Mar. xiv. 3; 1 Tim. ii. 9; 1 Pet. iii. 4.*

πολύ-τιμος, ον, *of great value, very costly*, Mat. xiii. 46; Jn. xii. 3; compar., 1 Pet. i. 7 (W. H.).*

πολυ-τρόπως, adv., *in many ways*, Heb. i. 1.*

πόμα, ατος, τό, *drink*, 1 Cor. x. 4; Heb. ix. 10.*

πονηρία, ας, ἡ, *evil disposition, wickedness*, Mat. xxii. 18; Lu. xi. 39; Ro. i. 29; 1 Cor. v. 8; Ep. vi. 12; plur., *malignant passions, iniquities*, Mar. vii. 22; Ac. iii. 26.*

πονηρός, ά, όν (πόνος), *evil, bad*, actively, of things or persons; *wicked, depraved*, spec. *malignant*, opp. to ἀγαθός; ὁ πονηρός, *the wicked one, i.e., Satan;* τὸ πονηρόν, *evil*.

πόνος, ου, ὁ, (1) *labor*, Col. iv. 13 (W. H.); (2) *pain, anguish*, Rev. xvi. 10, 11, xxi. 4.*

Ποντικός, ή, όν, *belonging to Pontus*, Ac. xviii. 2.*

Πόντιος, ου, ὁ, *Pontius*, the praenomen of Pilate, Lu. iii. 1.

Πόντος, ου, ὁ, *Pontus*, Ac. ii. 9; 1 Pet. i. 1.*

Πόπλιος, ου, ὁ, *Publius*, Ac. xxviii. 7, 8.*

πορεία, ας, ἡ, *a journey*, Lu. xiii. 22; *a pursuit, undertaking*, Ja. i. 11.*

πορεύομαι, σομαι, dep., with pass. aor., ἐπορεύθην, *to go, to go away, to depart, to journey,*

to travel, often (as Hebrew) *to take a course in life.*

πορθέω, ήσω, *to lay waste, to destroy*, Ac. ix. 21; Gal. i. 13, 23.*

πορισμός, οῦ, ὁ, *a source of gain*, 1 Tim. vi. 5, 6.*

Πόρκιος, ου, ὁ, *Porcius*, the praenomen of *Festus*, Ac. xxiv. 27.*

πορνεία, ας, ἡ, *fornication*, Ac. xv. 20, 29; fig. in Rev., *idolatry*, xiv. 8, xvii. 2, 4.

πορνεύω, σω, *to commit fornication*, 1 Cor. vi. 18; fig. in Rev., *to worship idols*, xviii. 3, 9.

πόρνη, ης, ἡ, *a harlot, a prostitute*, Mat. xxi. 31, 32; fig. in Rev., *an idolatrous community*, xvii. 1, 5.

πόρνος, ου, ὁ, *a man who prostitutes himself; a fornicator*, Ep. v. 5.

πόρρω, adv., *far, far off*, Mat. xv. 8; Mar. vii. 6; Lu. xiv. 32; comp., πορρωτέρω (or -τέρον, W. H.), Lu. xxiv. 28.*

πόρρωθεν, adv., *from afar, far off*, Lu. xvii. 12; Heb. xi. 13.*

πορφύρα, ας, ἡ, *a purple garment*, indicating wealth or rank, Mar. xv. 17, 20; Lu. xvi. 19; Rev. xvii. 4 (W. H. read following), with xviii. 12.*

πορφύρεος, οῦς, ᾶ, οῦν, *purple*, Jn. xix. 2, 5; Rev. xvii. 4 (W. H.), xviii. 16.*

πορφυρό-πωλις, ιδος, ἡ, *a female seller of purple cloth*, Ac. xvi. 14. (N. T.)*

ποσάκις, interrog. adv., *how often?* Mat. xviii. 21, xxiii. 37; Lu. xiii. 34.*

πόσις, εως, ἡ, *drink*, Jn. vi. 55; Ro. xiv. 17; Col. ii. 16.*

πόσος, η, ον, *how much? how great?* plur., *how many?* πόσῳ, as adv. with comparatives, *by how much?*

ποταμός, οῦ, ὁ, *a river, a torrent*, Mar. i. 5; Lu. vi. 48, 49.

ποταμο-φόρητος, ον, *carried away by a stream*, Rev. xii. 15. (N. T.)*

ποταπός, ή, όν, interrog. adj., *of what kind? of what manner?* Lu. i. 29, vii. 39.

πότε, interrog. adv., *when? at what time?* with ἕως, *how long?*

ποτέ, enclitic particle, *at some*

time, at one time or other
(see Gr. § 129, Wi. § 57, 2).
πότερος, α, ον, *which of two?*
N. T. neut. as adv., *whether,*
correlating with ἤ, *or*, Jn. vii.
17.*
ποτήριον, ου, τό, *a drinking-
cup*, Mar. vii. 4, xiv. 23; *the
contents of the cup*, 1 Cor. xi.
25; fig., *the portion which
God allots*, whether of good
or ill, commonly of the latter, Mat. xx. 22, 23, xxvi. 39.
ποτίζω, σω, *to cause to drink*
(two accs.); *to give drink to*
(acc.); fig., 1 Cor. iii. 2; *to
water* or *irrigate*, as plants,
1 Cor. iii. 6–8.
Ποτίολοι, ων, οἱ, *Puteoli*, Ac.
xxviii. 13.*
πότος, ου, ὁ (πίνω), *a drinking,
carousing*, 1 Pet. iv. 3.*
ποῦ, interrog. adv., *where?
whither?* Mat. ii. 4; Jn. vii.
35.
πού, an enclitic particle of
place or degree, *somewhere,
somewhere about*, Heb. ii. 6,
16 (W. H., see δήπου), iv 4;
Ro. iv. 19 (see Gr. § 129, Bu.
71).*
Πούδης, δεντος, ὁ, *Pudens*, 2
Tim. iv. 21.*
πούς, ποδός, ὁ, *the foot*, Lu. i.
79; ὑπὸ τοὺς πόδας, *under
the feet, i.e., entirely subdued,*
as Ro. xvi. 20.
πρᾶγμα, ατος, τό, *a thing done,
a fact, a thing, a business, a
suit*, as at law, Lu. i. 1; 1 Th.
iv. 6; Ro. xvi. 2; Heb. x. 1.
πραγματεία (W. H. -τία), ας, ἡ,
a business, occupation, 2 Tim.
ii. 4.*
πραγματεύομαι, σομαι, dep., *to
transact business, to trade,*
Lu. xix. 13.*
πραιτώριον, ου, τό (Lat. *prætorium*), *the palace* at Jerusalem occupied by the Ro-
man governor, Mat. xxvii.
27; Mar. xv. 16; Jn. xviii.
28, 33, xix. 9; so at Cæsarea,
Ac. xxiii. 35; *the quarters of
the prætorian army* in Rome,
Phil. i. 13.*
πράκτωρ, ορος, ὁ, *an officer employed to execute judicial sen-
tences*, Lu. xii. 58.*
πρᾶξις, εως, ἡ, (1) *a doing,
action, mode of action*, Mat.
xvi. 27; Lu. xxiii. 51; plur.,
deeds, acts, Ac. xix. 18; Ro.

viii. 13; Col. iii. 9; and in
inscription to the Acts of
the Apostles; (2) *function,
business*, Ro. xii. 4.*
πρᾶος, α, ον, Rec. in Mat. xi.
29 for πραΰς (W. H.).*
πραότης, τητος, ἡ, Rec. for
πραΰτης (W. H.) in 1 Cor.
iv. 21; 2 Cor. x. 1; Gal. v.
23, vi. 1; Ep. iv. 2; Col. iii.
12; 1 Tim. vi. 11 (W. H.
πραϋπάθια); 2 Tim. ii. 25;
Tit. iii. 2.*
πρασιά, ᾶς, ἡ, *a company
formed into divisions* like
garden-beds, Mar. vi. 40.*
For constr., see Gr. § 242,
Wi. § 37, 3, Bu. 30, 139.
πράσσω, or πράττω, ξω, pf.
πέπραχα, πέπραγμαι, (1) *to
do, perform, accomplish*, with
acc., 1 Th. iv. 11; 2 Cor. v.
10; (2) with advs., *to be in
any condition*, i.e., *to fare,*
Ac. xv. 29; Ep. vi. 21; (3) *to
exact, to require*, Lu. iii. 13.
Syn.: see ποιέω.
πραϋ-πάθεια (or ία), ας, ἡ (W.
H.), *mildness*, 1 Tim. vi. 11.*
πραΰς, εῖα, ύ, gen. έος or έως
(W. H.), pl. εῖς, *mild, gentle,*
Mat. v. 5, xi. 29 (see πρᾶος),
xxi. 5; 1 Pet. iii. 4.*
πραΰτης, τητος, ἡ, *mildness,
gentleness*, Ja. i. 21, iii. 13;
1 Pet. iii. 15; and W. H.
(πραΰτης) in the passages
quoted under πραότης.*
πρέπω, *to become, be fitting to*
(dat.), 1 Tim. ii. 10; Tit. ii.
1; Heb. vii. 26; impers. (see
Gr. § 101, Bu. 278), *it becomes, it is fitting to*, Mat. iii.
15; 1 Cor. xi. 13; Ep. v. 3;
Heb. ii. 10.*
πρεσβεία, ας, ἡ, *an embassy,
ambassadors*, Lu. xiv. 32,
xix. 14.*
πρεσβεύω, from πρέσβυς (lit.,
to be aged, old men being
usually chosen for the office), *to act as ambassador,*
2 Cor. v. 20; Ep. vi. 20.*
πρεσβυτέριον, ου, τό, *an assembly of elders, the Sanhedrin,*
Lu. xxii. 66; Ac. xxii. 5;
*officers of the church assem-
bled, presbytery*, 1 Tim. iv.
14.*
πρεσβύτερος, τέρα, τερον (compar. of πρέσβυς, *old*), generally used as subst., *elder,*
(1) in age, Ac. ii. 17; 1 Tim.

v. 1; plur., often, *ancestors,*
as Heb. xi. 2; (2) as subst.,
an elder, in dignity and office, *a member of the Jewish
Sanhedrin*, Mat. xvi. 21; *an
elder* of a Christian church,
Ac. xx. 17, 28; in Rev., of
the twenty-four *members of
the heavenly Sanhedrin*, iv.
4, 10.
πρεσβύτης, ου, ὁ, *an old man,*
Lu. i. 18; Tit. ii. 2; Philem.
9.*
πρεσβῦτις, ιδος, ἡ, *an old woman,*
Tit. ii. 3.*
πρηνής, ές, *falling headlong,*
Ac i. 18.*
πρίζω, or πρίω, 1st aor. pass.
ἐπρίσθην, *to saw, to saw
asunder*, Heb. xi. 37.*
πρίν, adv., of time, *formerly;*
as conj. in N. T., with or
without ἤ, *before that;* generally with acc. and inf.,
Mat. xxvi. 34; but after a
negative we find πρὶν ἄν
with subj. where the principal verb is in a primary
tense, Lu. 11. 26; πρίν with
opt. where it is in a histor-
ical tense, Ac. xxv. 16.
Πρίσκα, ης, ἡ, and dim. Πρισ-
κίλλα, ης, ἡ, a proper name,
Prisca or *Priscilla*, Ro. xvi.
3; 2 Tim. iv. 19.
πρό, prep. with gen., *before*, i.e.,
of place, time, or superiority
(see Gr. § 294, Wi. § 47 d,
Bu. 153). In composition,
it retains the same mean-
ings.
προ-άγω, άξω, *to bring out*, Ac.
xvi. 30; gen. intrans., *to go
before, to lead the way, to
precede*, in place, Mat. ii. 9;
in time, Mar. vi. 45; part.
προάγων, *preceding, previous,*
1 Tim. i. 18; Heb. vii. 18.
προ-αιρέω, ῶ, N. T., in mid., *to
propose to one's self, to purpose*, 2 Cor. ix. 7.*
προ-αιτιάομαι, ῶμαι, *to lay to
one's charge beforehand*, Ro.
iii. 9. (N. T.)*
προ-ακούω, *to hear before*, Col.
i. 5.*
προ-αμαρτάνω, *to sin before*, 2
Cor xii. 21, xiii. 2. (N. T.)*
προ-αύλιον, ου, τό, *a court before a building, a porch*, Mar.
xiv. 68.*
προ-βαίνω, *to go forward*, Mat.
iv. 21; Mar. i. 19; pf. part

προβεβηκὼς ἐν ἡμέραις, advanced in age, Lu. i. 7, 18, ii. 36.*

προ-βάλλω, to put forth, as trees their leaves, Lu. xxi. 30; to thrust forward, Ac. xix. 33.*

προβατικός, ή, όν, pertaining to sheep, Jn. v. 2.*

προβάτιον, ου, τό, dim. of following, a little sheep, a lamb, Jn. xxi. 16, 17 (W. H.).*

πρόβατον, ου, τό (προβαίνω), a sheep, Mat. vii. 15; fig., a follower of Christ, Jn. x. 7, 8.

προ-βιβάζω, σω, to drag forward, to urge forward, Mat. xiv. 8; Ac. xix. 33 (not W. H.).*

προ-βλέπω, N. T., in mid., to foresee or provide, Heb. xi. 40. (S.)*

προ-γίνομαι, to happen before, Ro. iii. 25.*

προ-γινώσκω, to know beforehand, Ac. xxvi. 5; 2 Pet. iii. 17; of the divine foreknowledge, Ro. viii. 29, xi. 2; 1 Pet. i. 20.*

πρόγνωσις, εως, ή, foreknowledge, Ac. ii. 23; 1 Pet. i. 2.*

πρό-γονος, ου, ὁ, a progenitor, plur., ancestors, 1 Tim. v. 4; 2 Tim. i. 3.*

προ-γράφω, ψω, to write before, in time, Ro. xv. 4; Ep. iii. 3; to depict or portray openly, Gal. iii. 1; to designate beforehand, Ju. 4.*

πρό-δηλος, ον, manifest to all, evident, 1 Tim. v. 24, 25; Heb. vii. 14.*

προ-δίδωμι, (1) to give before, Ro. xi. 35; (2) to give forth, betray; see following word.*

προδότης, ου, ὁ, a betrayer, Lu. vi. 16; Ac. vii. 52; 2 Tim. iii. 4.*

πρό-δρομος, ου, ὁ, ἡ (προτρέχω), a precursor, a forerunner, Heb. vi. 20.*

προ-εῖδον, 2d aor. of προοράω.

προ-εῖπον, 2d aor. of πρόφημι, perf. προείρηκα.

προ-ελπίζω, to hope before, Ep. i. 12.*

προ-εν-άρχομαι, to begin before, 2 Cor. viii. 6, 10. (N. T.)*

προ-επ-αγγέλλω, in mid., to promise before, Ro. i. 2; 2 Cor. ix. 5 (W. H.). (N. T.)*

προ-έρχομαι (see Gr. § 103, 2,

Bu. 144), (1) to go forward, advance, Ac. xii. 10; (2) to go before, precede, in time or place (gen. or acc.), Lu. xxii. 47; 2 Cor. ix. 5.

προ-ετοιμάζω, σω, to prepare beforehand, to predestine, Ro. ix. 23; Ep. ii. 10.*

προ-ευ-αγγελίζομαι, to foretell good tidings, preach the gospel beforehand, Gal. iii. 8.*

προ-έχω, in mid., to hold one's self before, to be superior, Ro. iii. 9 (see Gr. § 358, Wi. § 39, 3, note 3).*

προ-ηγέομαι, οῦμαι, to lead onward by example, Ro. xii. 10.*

πρόθεσις, εως, ἡ (προτίθημι), (1) a setting forth; οἱ ἄρτοι τῆς προθέσεως, the loaves of the presentation, or the showbread, Mat. xii. 4, compare Heb. ix. 2; (2) a predetermination, purpose, Ac. xi. 23.

προ-θέσμιος, α, ον, set beforehand, appointed before, Gal. iv. 2.*

προ-θυμία, ας, ἡ, inclination, readiness, Ac. xvii. 11; 2 Cor. viii. 11, 12, 19, ix. 2.*

πρό-θυμος, ον, eager, ready, willing, Mat. xxvi. 41; Mar. xiv. 38; τὸ πρόθυμον, readiness, Ro. i. 15.*

προθύμως, adv., readily, with alacrity, 1 Pet. v. 2.*

πρόϊμος, W. H., for πρώϊμος.

προ-ΐστημι, N.T. only intrans., act., 2d aor. and perf., and mid., (1) to preside over, to rule, gen., Ro. xii. 8; 1 Th. v. 12; 1 Tim. iii. 4, 5, 12, v. 17; (2) to give attention to, gen., Tit. iii. 8.*

προ-καλέω, ῶ, in mid., to provoke, stimulate, Gal. v. 26.*

προ-κατ-αγγέλλω, to announce beforehand, to promise, Ac. iii. 18, 24 (not W. H.), vii. 52; 2 Cor. ix. 5 (not W. H.).*

προ-κατ-αρτίζω, to prepare beforehand, 2 Cor. ix. 5.*

πρό-κειμαι, to lie or be placed before, to be appointed, as duty, example, reward, etc., Heb. vi. 18, xii. 1, 2; Ju. 7; to be at hand, to be present, 2 Cor. viii. 12.*

προ-κηρύσσω, ξω, to announce or preach beforehand, Ac. iii. 20 (not W. H.), xiii. 24.*

προ-κοπή, ῆς, ἡ, progress, ad-

vancement, Phil. i. 12, 25; 1 Tim. iv. 15.*

προ-κόπτω, to make progress in (dat. or ἐν), Lu. ii. 52; to advance to (ἐπί, acc.), 2 Tim. iii. 9; of time, to be advanced or far spent, Ro. xiii. 12.

πρό-κριμα, ατος, τό, a prejudgment, a prejudice, 1 Tim. v 21. (N. T.)*

προ-κυρόω, ῶ, to establish or ratify before, Gal. iii. 17. (N. T.)*

προ-λαμβάνω, to take before, anticipate, Mar. xiv. 8 ("she hath anticipated the anointing," i.e., hath anointed beforehand); 1 Cor. xi. 21; pass., to be overtaken or caught, Gal. vi. 1.*

προ-λέγω, to tell beforehand. forewarn, 2 Cor. xiii. 2; Gal. v. 21; 1 Th. iii. 4.*

προ-μαρτύρομαι, to testify beforehand, to predict, 1 Pet. i. 11. (N. T.)*

προ-μελετάω, ῶ, to meditate beforehand, Lu. xxi. 14.*

προ-μεριμνάω, ῶ, to be anxious beforehand, Mar. xiii. 11. (N. T.)*

προ-νοέω, ῶ, to perceive beforehand, to provide for, gen., 1 Tim. v. 8; in mid., to take thought for, acc., Ro. xii. 17; 2 Cor. viii. 21.*

πρό-νοια, ας, ἡ, forethought, Ac. xxiv. 3; provision for (gen.), Ro. xiii. 14.*

προ-οράω, ῶ, 2d aor. προεῖδον, to see beforehand, Ac. ii. 31, xxi. 29; Gal. iii. 8; mid., to have before one's eyes, Ac. ii. 25 (S.).*

προ-ορίζω, to predetermine, to foreordain, Ac. iv. 28; Ro. viii. 29, 30; 1 Cor. ii. 7; Ep. i. 5, 11. (N. T.)*

προ-πάσχω, to suffer beforehand, 1 Th. ii. 2.*

προ-πάτωρ, ορος, ὁ, a forefather, Ro. iv. 1 (W. H.).*

προ-πέμπω, to send forward, to accompany, Ro. xv. 24; to equip for a journey, Tit. iii. 13.

προ-πετής, ές (πίπτω), precipitate, rash, Ac. xix. 36; 2 Tim. iii. 4.*

προ-πορεύομαι, σομαι, in mid., to precede, to pass on before (gen.), Lu. i. 76; Ac. vii. 40.*

πρός (see Gr. § 307, Wi. §§ 47 f,

48 e, 49 h, Bu. 340), prep., gov. gen., dat., and accus. cases, general signif., towards. In composition, it denotes motion, direction, reference, nearness, addition.

προ-σάββατον, ου, τό, the day before the sabbath, Mar. xv. 42. (S.)*

προσ-αγορεύω, to address by name, to designate, Heb. v. 10.*

προσ-άγω, (1) trans., to bring to, to bring near, Mat. xviii. 24 (W. H.); Lu. ix. 41; Ac. xii 6 (W. H.), xvi. 20; 1 Pet. iii. 18; (2) intrans., to come to or towards, to approach, Ac. xxvii. 27.*

προσ-αγωγή, ῆς, ἡ, approach, access (εἰς, πρός, acc.), Ro. v. 2; Ep. ii. 18, iii. 12.*

προσ-αιτέω, ῶ, to beg, to ask earnestly, Mar. x. 46 (not W. H.); Lu. xviii. 35 (not W. H.); Jn. ix. 8.*

προσαίτης, ου, ὁ, a beggar, Mar. x. 46 (W. H.); Jn. ix. 8 (W. H.).*

προσ-ανα-βαίνω, to go up farther, Lu. xiv. 10.*

προσ-αναλίσκω, to spend in addition, Lu. viii. 43 (W. H. omit).*

προσ-ανα-πληρόω, ῶ, to fill up by adding to, to supply, 2 Cor. ix. 12, xi. 9.*

προσ-ανα-τίθημι, to lay up in addition; in mid., (1) to communicate or impart (acc. and dat.), Gal. ii. 6; (2) to consult with (dat.), Gal. i. 16.*

προσ-απειλέω, ῶ, to utter additional threats, Ac. iv. 21.*

προσ-δαπανάω, ῶ, ήσω, to spend in addition, Lu. x. 35.*

προσ-δέομαι, to want more, to need in addition (gen.), Ac. xvii. 25.*

προσ-δέχομαι, dep. mid., (1) to receive to companionship, Lu. xv. 2; (2) to admit, accept, Heb. xi. 35; (3) to await, to expect (acc.), Mar. xv. 43.

προσ-δοκάω, ῶ, to look for, expect, anticipate, whether with hope or fear, Lu. iii. 15, vii. 19, 20.

προσδοκία, ας, ἡ, a looking for, expectation, Lu. xxi. 26; Ac. xii. 11.*

προσ-εάω, ῶ, to permit one to approach, Ac. xxvii. 7. (N. T.)*

προσ-εγγίζω, to approach, to come near to (dat.), Mar. ii. 4 (not W. H.).*

προσεδρεύω, to wait upon, to minister to (dat.), 1 Cor. ix. 13 (W. H. παρεδρεύω).*

προσ-εργάζομαι, dep. mid., to gain by labor in addition, Lu. xix. 16.*

προσ-έρχομαι (see Gr. § 103, 2, Wi. § 52, 3, 4, 14)), (1) generally, to come or to go to, to approach, abs., or dat. of place or person, Mat. iv. 11, ix. 20, xxiv. 1; (2) specially, to approach, to draw near to, God or Christ, Heb. vii. 25; (3) to assent to, concur in, 1 Tim. vi. 3.

προσ-ευχή, ῆς, ἡ, (1) prayer to God, 1 Cor. vii. 5; Col. iv. 2; (2) a place where prayer is offered, only Ac. xvi. 13, 16 (see Gr. § 268, note). Syn.: see αἴτημα.

προσ-εύχομαι, dep. mid., to pray to God (dat.), to offer prayer, to pray for (acc. of thing, ὑπέρ or περί, of person, ἵνα or ὅπως, of object, occasionally inf.).

προσ-έχω, to apply, with νοῦν expressed or understood, to apply the mind, to attend to, dat.; with ἀπό, to beware of; also, to give heed to, inf. with μή.

προσ-ηλόω, ῶ, to fasten with nails, nail to, Col. ii. 14.*

προσ-ήλυτος, ου, ὁ (from προσέρχομαι, orig. adj.), a newcomer; a convert to Judaism, a proselyte, Mat. xxiii. 15; Ac. ii. 10, vi. 5, xiii. 43. (S.)*

πρόσ-καιρος, ου, for a season, temporary, Mat. xiii. 21; Mar. iv. 17; 2 Cor. iv. 18; Heb. xi. 25.*

προσ-καλέω, ῶ, N. T., mid., to call to one's self, to call for, to summon, Mar. iii. 13, 23, vi. 7; fig., to call to an office, to call to the Christian faith, Ac. ii. 39, xiii. 2.

προσ-καρτερέω, ῶ, ήσω, to persevere in, to continue steadfast in (dat.), Ac. i. 14, ii. 42; to wait upon (dat.), Mar. iii. 9; Ac. x. 7.

προσ-καρτέρησις, εως, ἡ, per-

severance, Ep. vi. 18. (N. T.)*

προσ-κεφάλαιον, ου, τό, a cushion for the head, a pillow, Mar. iv. 38.*

προσ-κληρόω, ῶ, to assign by lot, to allot; pass. (dat.), Ac. xvii. 4.*

προσ-κλίνω, to incline towards, Ac. v. 36 (W. H.).*

πρόσκλισις, εως, ἡ, an inclination towards, partiality, 1 Tim. v. 21.*

προσ-κολλάω, ῶ, pass., to join one's self to (dat.), as a companion, Ac. v. 36 (W. H. προσκλίνω); to cleave to (πρός, acc.), as husband to wife, Mat. xix. 5 (W. H. κολλάω); Mar. x. 7; Ep. v. 31.*

πρόσ-κομμα, ατος, τό, a stumbling-block, an occasion of falling, Ro. xiv. 13, 20; 1 Cor. viii. 9; with λίθος, a stone of stumbling (R. V.), 1 Pet. ii. 8; Ro. ix. 32, 33 (S.)*

προσ-κοπή, ῆς, ἡ, an occasion of stumbling, 2 Cor. vi. 3.*

προσ-κόπτω, to strike the foot against, Mat. iv. 6; so, to stumble, 1 Pet. ii. 8.

προσ-κυλίω, to roll to (dat., or ἐπί, acc.), Mat. xxvii. 60; Mar. xv. 46.*

προσ-κυνέω, ῶ, to bow down, to prostrate one's self to, to worship, God or inferior beings, to adore (dat. or acc.).

προσ-κυνητής, οῦ, ὁ, a worshipper, Jn. iv. 23.*

προσ-λαλέω, ῶ, to speak to (dat.), Ac. xiii. 43, xxviii. 20.*

προσ-λαμβάνω, N. T., mid., to take to one's self, i.e., food, companions, Ac. xxvii. 33, xxviii. 2; to receive to fellowship, Ro. xiv. 1.

πρόσ-ληψις (W. H. -λημψις), εως, ἡ, a taking to one's self, a receiving, Ro. xi. 15.*

προσ-μένω, to continue with or in, to adhere to (dat.), to stay in (ἐν) a place, Mat. xv. 32; 1 Tim. i. 3, v. 5.

προσ-ορμίζω (ὅρμος), mid., to come to anchor, Mar. vi. 53.*

προσ-οφείλω, to owe besides, Philem. 19.*

προσ-οχθίζω (ὀχθέω or ὀχθίζω), to be displeased or offended

with (dat.), Heb. iii. 10, 17 (S.).*

πρόσ-πεινος, ον (πεῖνα), *very hungry*, Ac. x. 10. (N. T.)*

προσ-πήγνυμι, *to fasten to*, applied to Christ's being fastened to the cross, Ac. ii. 23.*

προσ-πίπτω, (1) *to fall down before* (dat., or πρός, acc.), Mar. vii. 25; Lu. v. 8; (2) *to beat against* (dat.), Mat. vii. 25.

προσ-ποιέω, ῶ, in mid., *to conform one's self to ; hence, to pretend* (inf.), Lu. xxiv. 28; in Jn. viii. 6, perhaps, *to regard* (W. H. omit).*

προσ-πορεύομαι, *to come to, approach* (dat.), Mar. x. 35.*

προσ-ρήγνυμι, *to dash against*, as waves, Lu. vi. 48, 49.*

προσ-τάσσω, ξω, abs., or acc. and inf., *to enjoin* (acc.) *upon* (dat.), Lu. v. 14; Ac. x. 33.

προ-στάτις, ιδος, ἡ, *a female guardian, a protector*, Ro. xvi. 2.*

προσ-τίθημι, *to place near* or *by the side of, to add to* (dat., or ἐπί, dat. or acc.), Lu. iii. 20; Ac. xi. 24; mid., with inf., *to go on to do* a thing, *i.e., to do again*, Ac. xii. 3; Lu. xx. 11, 12; so 1st aor. pass., part., Lu. xix. 11, προσθεὶς εἶπεν, *he spoke again* (see Gr. § 399 d, Wi. § 54, 5, Bu. 299 sq.).

προσ-τρέχω, 2d aor. προσέδραμον, *to run to*, Mar. ix. 15, x. 17; Ac. viii. 30.*

προσ-φάγιον, ου, τό, *anything eaten with bread*, as fish, meat, etc., Jn. xxi. 5.*

πρό-σφατος, ον (from σφάζω, *to slaughter, just slaughtered*), *recent, new*, Heb. x. 20.*

προσφάτως, adv., *recently*, Ac. xviii. 2.*

προσ-φέρω, *to bring to*, dat., Mat. iv. 24, viii. 16; *to offer, to present*, as money, Ac. viii. 18; specially, *to offer sacrifice*, Ac. vii. 42; pass., *to bear one's self towards, to deal with*, Heb. xii. 7.

προσ-φιλής, ές, *pleasing, acceptable*, Phil. iv. 8.*

προσ-φορά, ᾶς, ἡ, *an offering, a sacrifice*, Ac. xxi. 26; Heb. x. 18.

προσ-φωνέω, ῶ, *to call to* (dat.),

Mat. xi. 16; *to call to one's self* (acc.), Lu. vi. 13.

πρόσ-χυσις, εως, ἡ (προσχέω), *an affusion, a sprinkling*, Heb. xi. 28. (N. T.)*

προσ-ψαύω, *to touch lightly*, Lu. xi. 46.*

προσωπολημπτέω (W. H. προσωπολημπτέω), ῶ, *to respect the person of any one, to show partiality*, Ja. ii. 9. (N. T.)*

προσωπο-λήμπτης (W. H. προσωπολήμπτης), ου, ὁ, *a respecter of persons, a partial one*, Ac. x. 34. (N. T.)*

προσωπολημψία (W. H. -λημψ-), ας, ἡ, *respect of persons, partiality*, Ro. ii. 11; Ep. vi. 9; Col. iii. 25; Ja. ii. 1. (N. T.)*

πρόσωπον, ου, τό (ὤψ), (1) *the face, the countenance*, Ja. i. 23; in antithesis with καρδία, *mere appearance*, 2 Cor. v. 12; (2) *the surface*, as of the earth, Lu. xxi. 35; of the heaven, Lu. xii. 56.

προ-τάσσω, *to appoint before*, Ac. xvii. 26 (W. H. προστάσσω).*

προ-τείνω, *to stretch out, to tie up* for scourging, Ac. xxii. 25.*

πρότερος, έρα, ερον (comparative of πρό), *former*, Ep. iv. 22; πρότερον or τὸ πρότερον, as adv., *before, formerly*, Heb. iv. 6.

προ-τίθημι, N. T. mid., *to set forth*, Ro. iii. 25; *to purpose, to design beforehand*, Ro. i. 13; Ep. i. 9.*

προ-τρέπω, in mid., *to exhort*, Ac. xviii. 27.*

προ-τρέχω, 2d aor. προέδραμον, *to run before, to outrun*, Lu. xix. 4; Jn. xx. 4.*

προ-ϋπ-άρχω, *to be previously*, with participle, Lu. xxiii. 12; Ac. viii. 9.*

πρό-φασις, εως, ἡ, *a pretext, an excuse*, 1 Th. ii. 5; dat. adverbially, *in appearance, ostensibly*, Mar. xii. 40.

προ-φέρω, *to bring forth*, Lu. vi. 45.*

πρό-φημι, fut. προερῶ, perf. προείρηκα, 2d aor. προεῖπον, *to say before, i.e., at an earlier time*, Gal. i. 9; in an earlier part of the discourse, 2 Cor. vii. 3; or prophetically, Mar. xiii. 23.

προ-φητεία, ας, ἡ, *prophecy*, as a gift, or in exercise, Ro. xii. 6; Rev. xix. 10; plur., *prophecies*, 1 Cor. xiii. 8.

προ-φητεύω, σω, *to be a prophet, to prophesy, to forth-tell*, or speak of divine things (the meaning *foretell* is secondary and incidental), Lu. i. 67; Ac. ii. 17, 18; of false prophets, Mat. vii. 22; *to divine*, used in mockery, Mat. xxvi. 68.

προ-φήτης, ου, ὁ, (1) *a prophet, i.e.*, one who has insight into divine things and speaks them forth to others, Mat. v. 12, xxi. 46; plur., *the prophetic books of the O. T.*, Lu. xxiv. 27, 44; (2) *a poet*, Tit. i. 12.

προ-φητικός, ή, όν, *prophetic, uttered by a prophet*, Ro. xvi. 26; 2 Pet. i. 19.*

προ-φῆτις, ιδος, ἡ, *a prophetess*, Lu. ii. 36; Rev. ii. 20.*

προ-φθάνω, *to anticipate, to be beforehand*, with participle, Mat. xvii. 25.*

προ-χειρίζομαι, *to appoint, to choose*, Ac. iii. 20 (W. H.), xxii. 14, xxvi. 16.*

προ-χειρο-τονέω, ῶ, *to designate beforehand*, Ac. x. 41.*

Πρόχορος, ου, ὁ, *Prochorus*, Ac. vi. 5.*

πρύμνα, ης, ἡ, *the hindmost part of a ship, the stern*, Mar. iv. 38; Ac. xxvii. 29, 41.*

πρωΐ, adv., *early in the morning, at dawn*, Mar. i. 35, xi. 20; with advs., ἅμα πρωΐ, λίαν πρωΐ, *very early in the morning*, Mat. xx. 1; Mar. xvi. 2.

πρώϊμος (W. H. πρό-), η, ον, *early, of the early rain*, Ja. v. 7.*

πρωϊνός, ή, όν, *belonging to the morning*, of the morning star, Rev. ii. 28, xxii. 16. (S.)*

πρώϊος, α, ον, *of the morning;* fem. (sc. ὥρα), *morning*, Mat. xxi. 18 (W. H. πρωΐ), xxvii. 1; Jn. xviii. 28 (W. H. πρωΐ), xxi. 4.*

πρῴρα, ας, ἡ, *the forward part of a ship, the prow*, Ac. xxvii. 30, 41.*

πρωτεύω, *to have pre-eminence, to be chief*, Col. i. 18.*

πρωτο-καθεδρία, ας, ἡ, a chief seat, Lu. xi. 43. (N. T.)

πρωτο-κλισία, ας, ἡ, the chief place at a banquet, Mar. xii. 39. (Ap.)

πρῶτος, η, ον (superlative of πρό), first, in place, time, or order; like πρότερος with following gen., before, only Jn. i. 15, 30; πρῶτον, as adverb, first, Mar. iv. 28; with gen., before, Jn. xv. 18; τὸ πρῶτον, at the first, Jn. x. 40.

πρωτο-στάτης, ου, ὁ, a leader, a chief, Ac. xxiv. 5.*

πρωτοτόκια, ων, τά, the right of the first-born, the birthright, Heb. xii. 16. (S.)*

πρωτό-τοκος, ον, first-born; ὁ πρωτότοκος, specially a title of Christ, Lu. ii. 7; plur., the first-born, Heb. xii. 23, of saints already dead.

πρώτως, adv., first, Ac. xi. 26 (W. H.).*

πταίω, σω, to stumble, to fall, to sin, Ro. xi. 11; 2 Pet. i. 10; Ja. ii. 10, iii. 2.*

πτέρνα, ης, ἡ, the heel, Jn. xiii. 18.*

πτερύγιον, ου, τό (dim. of πτέρυξ), an extremity, as a battlement or parapet, Mat. iv. 5; Lu. iv. 9.*

πτέρυξ, υγος, ἡ, a wing, Rev. iv. 8, xii. 14.

πτηνός, ή, όν (πέτομαι), winged, τὰ πτηνά, birds, 1 Cor. xv. 39.*

πτοέω, ῶ, to terrify, Lu. xxi. 9, xxiv. 37.*

πτόησις, εως, ἡ, terror, consternation, 1 Pet. iii. 6.*

Πτολεμαΐς, ΐδος, ἡ, Ptolemais, Ac. xxi. 7.*

πτύον, ου, τό, a winnowing-shovel, Mat. iii. 12; Lu. iii. 17.*

πτύρω, to frighten, Phil. i. 28.*

πτύσμα, ατος, τό, spittle, Jn. ix. 6.*

πτύσσω, ξω, to fold, to roll up, as a scroll, Lu. iv. 20.*

πτύω, σω, to spit, Mar. vii. 33, viii. 23; Jn. ix. 6.*

πτῶμα, ατος, τό (πίπτω), a body fallen in death, a carcase, Mat. xxiv. 28.

πτῶσις, εως, ἡ, a falling, a fall, lit. or fig., Mat. vii. 27; Lu. ii. 34.*

πτωχεία, ας, ἡ, beggary, poverty, 2 Cor. viii. 2, 9; Rev. ii. 9.*

πτωχεύω, σω, to be in poverty, 2 Cor. viii. 9.*

πτωχός, ή, όν, reduced to beggary, poor, destitute, Lu. xiv. 13, 21, xviii. 22; Ja. ii. 5; spiritually poor, in a good sense, Mat. v. 3; in a bad sense, Rev. iii. 17. Syn.: see πένης.

πυγμή, ῆς, ἡ (πύξ), the fist, Mar. vii. 3 (see R. V. and mrg.).*

Πύθων, ωνος, ὁ, Python; in N.T. a divining spirit; called after the Pythian serpent said to have guarded the oracle at Delphi and been slain by Apollo, Ac. xvi. 16 (see R. V.).*

πυκνός, ή, όν, frequent, 1 Tim. v. 23; neut. plur. πυκνά, as adverb, often, Lu. v. 33; so πυκνότερον, more frequently, Ac. xxiv. 26.*

πυκτεύω (πύκτης), to be a boxer, to box, 1 Cor. ix. 26.*

πύλη, ης, ἡ, a door or gate; πύλαι ᾅδου, the gates of Hades, i.e., the powers of the unseen world, Mat. xvi. 18.

πυλών, ῶνος, ὁ, a large gate, Ac. x. 17; a gateway, porch, Mat. xxvi. 71.

πυνθάνομαι, 2d aor. ἐπυθόμην, (1) to ask, ask from (παρά, gen.), to inquire, Mat. ii. 4; Lu. xv. 26; (2) to ascertain by inquiry, only Ac. xxiii. 34.

πῦρ, πυρός, τό, fire generally; of the heat of the sun, Rev. xvi. 8; of lightning, Lu. ix. 54; God is so called, Heb. xii. 29; fig. for strife, Lu. xii. 49; trials, 1 Cor. iii. 13; of the eternal fire, or future punishment, Mat. xviii. 8.

πυρά, ᾶς, ἡ, a fire, a pile of burning fuel, Ac. xxviii. 2, 3.*

πύργος, ου, ὁ, a tower, fortified structure, Lu. xiii. 4, xiv. 28.

πυρέσσω, to be sick with a fever, Mat. viii. 14; Mar. i. 30.*

πυρετός, οῦ, ὁ, a fever, Lu. iv. 38, 39.

πύρινος, η, ον, fiery, glittering, Rev. ix. 17.*

πυρόω, ῶ, N. T., pass., to be set on fire, to burn, to be inflamed, 2 Pet. iii. 12; 1 Cor. vii. 9; to glow with heat, as

metal in a furnace, to be purified by fire, Rev. iii. 18.

πυρράζω, to be fire-colored, to be red, Mat. xvi. 2, 3 (W. H. omit both). (S. πυρρίζω.)*

πυρρός, ά, όν, fire-colored, red, Rev. vi. 4, xii. 3.*

Πύρρος, ου, ὁ, Pyrrhus, Ac. xx. 4 (W. H.).*

πύρωσις, εως, ἡ, a burning, a conflagration, Rev. xviii. 9, 18; severe trial, as by fire, 1 Pet. iv. 12.*

πώ, an enclitic particle, even, yet, used only in composition; see μήπω, μηδέπω, οὔπω, οὐδέπω.

πωλέω, ῶ, ήσω, to sell, Mat. xxi. 12.

πῶλος, ου, ὁ, a colt, a young ass, as Mat. xxi. 2.

πώ-ποτε, adv., at any time, used only after a negative, not at any time, never, Jn. i. 18, v. 37.

πωρόω, ῶ, to harden, to render callous, fig., Jn. xii. 40; Ro. xi. 7.

πώρωσις, εως, ἡ, hardness of heart, obtuseness, Mar. iii. 5; Ro. xi. 25; Ep. iv. 18.*

πῶς, adv., interrog., how? in what manner? by what means? Also in exclamations, as Lu. xii. 50; Jn. xi. 36; with subj. or opt. (ἄν), implying a strong negative, Mat. xxvi. 54; Ac. viii. 31; often (N. T.) in indirect interrogations (classical ὅπως), Mat. vi. 28, etc.

πώς, an enclitic particle, in a manner, by any means.

P

Ρ, ρ, ῥῶ, rho, r, and as an initial always ῥ, rh, the seventeenth letter. As a numeral, ρ´ = 100; ͵ρ = 100,000.

Ῥαάβ, or Ῥαχάβ, ἡ (Heb.), Rahab, Heb. xi. 31.

ῥαββί (W. H. ῥαββεί), (Heb.), Rabbi, my master, a title of respect in Jewish schools of learning, often applied to Christ, Jn. iii. 26, iv. 31. (N. T.)

ῥαββονί, or ῥαββουνί (W. H. ῥαββουνεί), (Aram.), similar to ῥαββί, my master, Mar. x. 51; Jn. xx. 16. (N. T.)*

ῥαβδίζω, ίσω, to scourge, to beat

with rods, Ac. xvi. 22; 2 Cor. xi. 25.*

ῥάβδος, ου, ἡ, *a rod, staff*, Mat. x. 10; 1 Cor. iv. 21; Rev. xi. 1; *a rod of authority, a sceptre*, Heb. i. 8.

ῥαβδ-οῦχος, ου, ὁ (ἔχω), *a holder of the rods, a lictor*, a Roman officer, Ac. xvi. 35, 38.*

Ῥαγαῦ, ὁ (Heb.), *Ragau*, Lu. iii. 35.*

ῥᾳδι-ούργημα, ατος, τό, *a careless action, an act of villainy*, Ac. xviii. 14.*

ῥᾳδι-ουργία, ας, ἡ, *craftiness, villainy*, Ac. xiii. 10.*

ῥακά (Aram.), *an empty, i.e., senseless man*, Mat. v. 22 (see Gr. § 153, ii.). (N. T.)*

ῥάκος, ους, τό (ῥήγνυμι), *a remnant torn off, a piece of cloth*, Mat. ix. 16; Mar. ii. 21.*

Ῥαμᾶ, ἡ (Heb.), *Ramah*, Mat. ii. 18.*

ῥαντίζω, ίσω, *to sprinkle, to cleanse ceremonially* (acc.) *by sprinkling, to purify from* (ἀπό), Mar. vii. 4 (W. H.); Heb. ix. 13, 19, 21, x. 22. (S.)*

ῥαντισμός, οῦ, ὁ, *sprinkling, purification*, Heb. xii. 24; 1 Pet. i. 2. (S.)*

ῥαπίζω, ίσω, *to smite with the hand*, Mat. v. 39, xxvi. 67.*

ῥάπισμα, ατος, τό, *a blow with the open hand*, Mar. xiv. 65; Jn. xviii. 22, xix. 3.*

ῥαφίς, ίδος, ἡ, *a needle*, Mat. xix. 24; Mar. x. 25; Lu. xviii. 25 (W. H. βελόνη).*

Ῥαχάβ, see Ῥαάβ.

Ῥαχήλ, ἡ (Heb.), *Rachel*, Mat. ii. 18.*

Ῥεβέκκα, ης, ἡ, *Rebecca*, Ro. ix. 10.*

ῥέδα, or ῥέδη, ης, ἡ (Gallic), *a chariot*, Rev. xviii. 13. (N. T.)*

Ῥεμφάν, or Ῥεφάν (W. H. Ῥομφά), ὁ (prob. Coptic), *Remphan*, the *Saturn* of later mythology, Ac. vii. 43 (Heb., *Chiun*, Amos v. 26).*

ῥέω, ῥεύσω, *to flow*, Jn. vii. 38.*

ῥέω (see φημί, εἶπον). From this obs. root, *to say*, are derived: act. perf., εἴρηκα; pass., εἴρημαι; 1st aor. pass., ἐρρέθην or ἐρρήθην; part., ῥηθείς; espec. the neut. τό ῥηθέν, *that which was spoken* by (ὑπό, gen.).

Ῥήγιον, ου, τό, *Rhegium*, now Reggio, Ac. xxviii. 13.*

ῥῆγμα, ατος, τό (ῥήγνυμι), *what is broken, a ruin*, Lu. vi. 49.*

ῥήγνυμι (or ῥήσσω, as Mar. ix. 18), ῥήξω, *to break, to rend, to burst, to dash down, to break forth*, as into praise, Mat. vii. 6, ix. 17; Mar. ii. 22, ix. 18; Lu. v. 37, ix. 42; Gal. iv. 27.*

ῥῆμα, ατος, τό, *a thing spoken;* (1) *a word* or *saying* of any kind, as *command, report, promise*, Lu. vii. 1, ix. 45; Ro. x. 8; (2) *a thing, a matter, a business*, Lu. ii. 15; 2 Cor. xiii. 1.

Ῥησά, ὁ (Heb.), *Rhesa*, Lu. iii. 27.*

ῥήσσω, see ῥήγνυμι.

ῥήτωρ, ορος, ὁ, *an orator*, Ac. xxiv. 1.*

ῥητῶς, adv., *expressly, in so many words*, 1 Tim. iv. 1.*

ῥίζα, ης, ἡ, (1) *a root of a tree* or *a plant*, Mar. xi. 20; met., *the origin* or *source of anything*, 1 Tim. vi. 10; fig., *constancy, perseverance*, Mat. xiii. 21; (2) *that which comes from the root, a descendant*, Ro. xv. 12; Rev. v. 5.

ῥιζόω, ῶ, *to root;* perf. pass., participle, ἐρριζωμένος, *firmly rooted*, fig., Ep. iii. 17; Col. ii. 7.*

ῥιπή, ῆς, ἡ (ῥίπτω), *a stroke, a twinkle*, as of the eye, 1 Cor. xv. 52.*

ῥιπίζω, *to toss to and fro*, as waves by the wind, Ja. i. 6.*

ῥιπτέω, ῶ, *to throw off* or *away*, Ac. xxii. 23.*

ῥίπτω, ψω, 1st aor. ἔρριψα; part. ῥῖψας; *to throw, throw down, throw out, prostrate*, Mat. ix. 36, xv. 30, xxvii. 5; Lu. iv. 35, xvii. 2; Ac. xxvii. 19, 29.*

Ῥοβοάμ, ὁ (Heb.), *Rehoboam*, Mat. i. 7.*

Ῥόδη, ης, ἡ (*rose*), *Rhoda*, Ac. xii. 13.*

Ῥόδος, ου, ἡ, *Rhodes*, Ac. xxi. 1.*

ῥοιζηδόν, adv. (ῥοιζέω), *with a great noise*, 2 Pet. iii. 10.*

ῥομφαία, ας, ἡ, *a large sword*, as Rev. i. 16; fig., *piercing grief*, Lu. ii. 35.

Ῥουβήν, ὁ (Heb.), *Reuben*, Rev. vii. 5.*

Ῥούθ, ἡ (Heb.), *Ruth*, Mar. i. 5.*

Ῥοῦφος, ου, ὁ (Lat.), *Rufus*, Mar. xv. 21; Ro. xvi. 13.*

ῥύμη, ης, ἡ, *a street, a lane*, Mat. vi. 2; Lu. xiv. 21; Ac. ix. 11, xii. 10.*

ῥύομαι, σομαι, dep. mid., 1st aor., pass., ἐρρύσθην, *to draw* or *snatch from danger, to deliver*, 2 Pet. ii. 7; ὁ ῥυόμενος, *the deliverer*, Ro. xi. 26.

ῥυπαίνω, *to defile*, Rev. xxii. 11 (W. H.).*

ῥυπαρεύομαι, *to be filthy*, Rev. xxii. 11 (W. H. mrg.). (N. T.)*

ῥυπαρία, ας, ἡ, *filth, pollution*, Ja. i. 21.*

ῥυπαρός, ά, όν, *filthy, defiled*, Ja. ii. 2; Rev. xxii. 11 (W. H.).*

ῥύπος, ου, ὁ, *filth, filthiness*, 1 Pet. iii. 21.*

ῥυπόω, ῶ, *to be filthy*, Rev. xxii. 11 (not W. H.).*

ῥύσις, εως, ἡ (ῥέω), *a flowing, an issue*, Mar. v. 25; Lu. viii. 43, 44.*

ῥυτίς, ίδος, ἡ, *a wrinkle;* fig., *a spiritual defect*, Ep. v. 27.*

Ῥωμαϊκός, ή, όν, *Roman*, Lu. xxiii. 38 (W. H. omit).*

Ῥωμαῖος, ου, ὁ, *a Roman*, Jn. xi. 48.

Ῥωμαϊστί, adv., *in the Latin language*, Jn. xix. 10.*

Ῥώμη, ης, ἡ, *Rome*, Ac. xviii. 2; 2 Tim. i. 17.

ῥώννυμι, *to strengthen;* only perf., pass., impv., ἔρρωσο, ἔρρωσθε, *farewell*, Ac. xv. 29, xxiii. 30 (W. H. omit).*

Σ

Σ, σ, final ς, *sigma*, s, the eighteenth letter. As a numeral, σ'=200; ͵σ=200,000.

σαβαχθανί (W. H. -εί), (Aram.), *sabachthani, thou hast forsaken me*, Mat. xxvii. 46; Mar. xv. 34; from the Aramaic rendering of Ps. xxii. 1. (N. T.)*

σαβαώθ (Heb.), *sabaoth, hosts, armies*, Ro. ix. 29; Ja. v. 4. (S.)*

σαββατισμός, οῦ, ὁ, *a keeping of sabbath, a sabbath rest* (R. V.), Heb. iv. 9.*

σάββατον, ου, τό (from Heb.),

dat. plur. σάββασι(ν), (1) the sabbath, Mat. xii. 8, xxviii. 1; (2) a period of seven days, a week, Mar. xvi. 2, 9; in both senses the plural is also used. (S.)

σαγήνη, ης, ή, a drag-net, Mat. xiii. 47. (S.)* Syn.: see ἀμφίβληστρον.

Σαδδουκαῖος, ου, ό, a Sadducee; plur., of the sect in general; prob. derived from the Heb. name Zadok.

Σαδώκ, ό (Heb.), Sadok, Mat. i. 13.*

σαίνω, to move, disturb, pass., 1 Th. iii. 3.*

σάκκος, ου, ό, hair-cloth, sack-cloth, a sign of mourning, Mat. xi. 21; Lu. x. 13; Rev. vi. 12, xi. 3.*

Σαλά, ό (Heb.), Sala, Lu. iii. 35.*

Σαλαθιήλ, ό (Heb.), Salathiel, Mat. i. 12; Lu. iii. 27.*

Σαλαμίς, ῖνος, ή, Salamis, Ac. xiii. 5.*

Σαλείμ, τό, Salim, Jn. iii. 23.*

σαλεύω, σω, to shake, to cause to shake, as Mat. xi. 7; Heb. xii. 27; so, to excite, as the populace, Ac. xvii. 13; to disturb in mind, 2 Th. ii. 2.

Σαλήμ, ή (Heb.), Salem, Heb. vii. 1.*

Σαλμών, ό (Heb.), Salmon, Mat. i. 4, 5, Lu. iii. 32 (W. H. Σαλά).*

Σαλμώνη, ης, ή, Salmone, Ac. xxvii. 7.*

σάλος, ου, ό, the tossing of the sea in a tempest, Lu. xxi. 25.*

σάλπιγξ, ιγγος, ή, a trumpet, 1 Cor. xiv. 8; 1 Th. iv. 16.

σαλπίζω, ίσω (class. ίγξω), to sound a trumpet, Rev. ix. 1, 13; for impers. use, 1 Cor. xv. 52 (see Gr. § 171, Wi. § 58, 9 b, β), Bu. 134).

σαλπιστής, οῦ, ό (class. -ιγκτής), a trumpeter, Rev. xviii. 22.*

Σαλώμη, ης, ή, Salome, wife of Zebedee, Mar. xv. 40, xvi. 1.*

Σαμάρεια, ας, ή, Samaria, either (1) the district, Lu. xvii. 11; Jn. iv. 4; or (2) the city, afterwards called Sebaste, only Ac. viii. 5 (W. H.).

Σαμαρείτης, ου, ό, a Samaritan, Mat. x. 5; Lu. ix. 52.

Σαμαρεῖτις, ιδος, ή, a Samaritan woman, Jn. iv. 9.*

Σαμο-θράκη, ης, ή, Samothrace, Ac. xvi. 11.*

Σάμος, ου, ή, Samos, Ac. xx. 15.*

Σαμουήλ, ό (Heb.), Samuel, Ac. iii. 24.

Σαμψών, ό (Heb.), Samson, Heb. xi. 32.*

σανδάλιον, ου, τό, a sandal, Mar. vi. 9; Ac. xii. 8.*

σανίς, ίδος, ή, a plank, a board, Ac. xxvii. 44.*

Σαούλ, ό (Heb.), Saul, (1) the king of Israel, Ac. xiii. 21; (2) the apostle, only in direct address (elsewhere Σαῦλος), Ac. ix. 4, 17.

σαπρός, ά, όν, rotten, hence, useless, Mat. vii. 17, 18; fig., corrupt, Ep. iv. 29.

Σαπφείρη, ης, ή, Sapphira, Ac. v. 1.*

σάπφειρος, ου, ή, a sapphire, Rev. xxi. 19.*

σαργάνη, ης, ή, a basket, generally of twisted cords, 2 Cor. xi. 33.*

Σάρδεις, ων, dat. εσι(ν), αί, Sardis, Rev. i. 11, iii. 1, 4.*

σάρδινος, ου, ό (Rec. in Rev. iv. 3 for following). (N. T.)*

σάρδιον, ου, τό, a precious stone, sardius or carnelian, Rev. iv. 3 (W. H.), xxi. 20.*

σαρδ-όνυξ, υχος, ό, a sardonyx, a precious stone, white streaked with red, Rev. xxi. 20.*

Σάρεπτα, ων, τά, Sarepta, Lu. iv. 26.*

σαρκικός, ή, όν, fleshly, carnal, whether (1) belonging to human nature in its bodily manifestation, or (2) belonging to human nature as sinful, Ro. xv. 27; 1 Cor. iii. 3, ix. 11; 2 Cor. i. 12, x. 4; 1 Pet. ii. 11; for Rec. σαρκικός, W. H. substitute σάρκινος, in Ro. vii. 14; 1 Cor. iii. 1; Heb. vii. 16; and ἄνθρωπος in 1 Cor. iii. 4.*

σάρκινος, η, ον, (1) fleshy, consisting of flesh, opp. to λίθινος, 2 Cor. iii. 3; (2) fleshy, carnal (W.H. in the passages quoted under σαρκικός).*

σάρξ, σαρκός, ή, flesh, sing. Lu. xxiv. 39; plur., Ja. v. 3; the human body, man; the

human nature of man as distinguished from his divine nature (πνεῦμα); human nature, as sinful; πᾶσα σάρξ, every man. all men; κατὰ σάρκα, as a man; σὰρξ καὶ αἷμα, flesh and blood, i.e, man as frail and fallible; ζῆν, περιπατεῖν κατὰ σάρκα, to live, to walk after flesh, cf a carnal, unspiritual life. The word also denotes kinship, Ro. xi. 14.

Σαρούχ, ό (Heb.), (W. H. Σερούχ), Saruch or Serug, Lu iii. 35.*

σαρόω, ῶ, to sweep, to cleanse by sweeping, Mat. xii. 44; Lu. xi. 25, xv. 8.*

Σάρρα, ας, ή, Sarah, Ro. iv. 19, ix. 9.

Σάρων, ωνος, ό, Sharon, Ac. ix. 35.*

σατᾶν, ό (Heb.), and σατανᾶς, ᾶ, ό, an adversary, i.e., Satan, the Heb. proper name for the devil, διάβολος, Mat. iv 10, 15; Ac. xxvi. 18; met., for one who does the work of Satan, Mat. xvi. 23; Mar viii. 33. (S.)

σάτον, ου, τό (Aram.), a seah, a measure equal to about a peck and a half, Mat. xiii. 33; Lu. xiii. 21. (S.)*

Σαῦλος, ου, ό, Saul, the apostle, generally in this form (see Σαούλ), Ac. vii. 58, viii. 1, 3.

σβέννυμι, σβέσω, (1) to extinguish, to quench, Ep. vi. 16; (2) fig., to suppress, 1 Th. v. 19.

σεατοῦ, ῆς, οῦ (only masc. in N. T.), a reflex. pron., of thyself; dat., σεαυτῷ, to thyself; acc., σεαυτόν, thyself.

σεβάζομαι, dep., pass., to stand in awe of, to worship, Ro. i. 25.*

σέβασμα, ατος, τό, an object of religious worship, Ac. xvii. 23; 2 Th. ii. 4.*

σεβαστός, ή, όν, venerated, august, a title of the Roman emperors (= Lat. augustus), Ac. xxv. 21, 25. Hence, secondarily, Augustan, imperial, Ac. xxvii. 1.*

σέβομαι, dep., to reverence, to worship God, Mar. vii. 7· οἱ σεβόμενοι, the devout, i.e, proselytes of the gate, Ac. xvii. 17.

σειρά, âς, ἡ, a chain, 2 Pet. ii.
4 (W. H. read following).*
σειρός, οῦ, ὁ, a pit, 2 Pet. ii. 4
(W. H.).*
σεισμός, οῦ, ὁ, a shaking, as an
earthquake, Mat. xxiv. 7; a
storm at sea, Mat. viii. 24.
σείω, σω, to shake, Heb. xii.
26; fig., to agitate, Mat. xxi.
10.
Σεκοῦνδος, ου, ὁ (Lat.), Secundus, Ac. xx. 4.*
Σελεύκεια, ας, ἡ, Seleucia, Ac.
xiii. 4.*
σελήνη, ης, ἡ, the moon, Mar.
xiii. 24.
σεληνιάζομαι, io be epileptic,
Mat. iv. 24, xvii. 15. (N. T.)*
Σεμεΐ, ὁ (Heb.), (W. H. Σεμεείν),
Semei or Semein, Lu. iii. 26.*
σεμίδαλις, acc. ιν, ἡ, the finest
wheaten flour, Rev. xviii.
13.*
σεμνός, ἡ, όν, venerable, honorable, of men, 1 Tim. iii. 8,
11; Tit. ii. 2; of acts, Phil.
iv. 8.*
σεμνότης, τητος, ἡ, dignity,
honor, 1 Tim. ii. 2, iii. 4;
Tit. ii. 7.*
Σέργιος, ου, ὁ, Sergius, Ac. xiii.
7.*
Σήθ, ὁ (Heb.), Seth, Lu. iii.
38.*
Σήμ, ὁ (Heb.), Shem, Lu. iii.
36.*
σημαίνω, 1st aor. ἐσήμανα, to
signify, indicate, Jn. xii. 33;
Ac. xxv. 27.
σημεῖον, ου, τό, a sign, that by
which a thing is known, a
token, an indication, of divine
presence and power, 1 Cor.
xiv. 22; Lu. xxi. 7, 11; hence,
especially, a miracle, whether
real or unreal, Lu. xi. 16, 29;
2 Th. ii. 9. Syn.: see δύναμις.
σημειόω, ῶ, in mid., to mark
for one's self, to note, 2 Th.
iii. 14.*
σήμερον, adv., to-day, at this
time, now, Mat. vi. 11; Lu.
ii. 11; ἡ σήμερον (ἡμέρα), this
very day, Ac. xix. 40.
σήπω, to make rotten; 2d perf.
σέσηπα, to become rotten, perish, Ja. v. 2.*
σηρικός, ἡ, όν (W. H. σιρικός),
silken; neut. as subst., sil`,
Rev. xviii. 12.*
σής, σητός, ὁ, a moth, Mat. vi.
19, 20; Lu. xii. 33.*

σητό-βρωτος, ον, moth-erten, Ja.
v. 2.*
σθενόω, ῶ, to strengthen, 1 Pet.
v. 10. (N. T.)*
σιαγών, όνος, ἡ, the jawbone,
Mat. v. 39; Lu. vi. 29.*
σιγάω, ῶ, to keep silence, Lu.
ix. 36; pass., to be concealed,
Ro. xvi. 25.
σιγή, ῆς, ἡ, silence, Ac. xxi. 40;
Rev. viii. 1.*
σιδήρεος, έα, εον, contr., οῦς, ᾶ,
οῦν, made of iron, Ac. xii.
10; Rev. ii. 27.
σίδηρος, ου, ὁ, iron, Rev. xviii.
12.*
Σιδών, ῶνος, ἡ, Sidon, Mat. xi.
21, 22.
Σιδώνιος, α, ον, Sidonian, inhabitant of Sidon, Lu. iv. 26
(W. H.); Ac. xii. 20.
σικάριος, ου, ὁ (Lat.), an assassin, Ac. xxi. 38.*
σίκερα, τό (Aram.), intoxicating
drink, Lu. i. 15. (S.)*
Σίλας, dat. ᾳ, acc. αν, ὁ, Silas,
contr. from Σιλουανός, Ac.
xv. 22, 27.
Σιλουανός, οῦ, ὁ, Silvanus, 2
Cor. i. 9.
Σιλωάμ, ὁ, Siloam, Lu. xiii. 4;
Jn. ix. 7, 11.*
σιμικίνθιον, ου, τό (Lat. semi-
cinctium), an apron, worn
by artisans, Ac. xix. 12. (N.
T.)*
Σίμων, ωνος, ὁ, Simon; nine
persons of the name are
mentioned: (1) Peter, the
apostle, Mat. xvii. 25; (2)
the Zealot, an apostle, Lu.
vi. 15; (3) a brother of Jesus,
Mar. vi. 3; (4) a certain Cyrenian, Mar. xv. 21; (5) the
father of Judas Iscariot, Jn.
vi. 71; (6) a certain Pharisee,
Lu. vii. 40; (7) a leper, Mat.
xxvi. 6; (8) Simon Magus,
Ac. viii. 9; (9) a certain
tanner, Ac. ix. 43.
Σινᾶ, τό (Heb.), Sinai, Ac. vii.
30, 38; Gal. iv. 24, 25.*
σίναπι, εως, τό, mustard, Lu.
xiii. 19, xvii. 6.
σινδών, όνος, ἡ, fine linen, a
linen cloth, Mar. xiv. 51, 52,
xv. 46.
σινιάζω, to sift, as grain, to
prove by trials, Lu. xxii. 31.
(N. T.)*
σιρικός, see σηρικός.
σιτευτός, ἡ, όν, fattened, fatted,
Lu. xv. 23, 27, 30.*

σιτίον, ου, τό, grain, Ac. vii.
12 (W. H.).*
σιτιστός, ἡ, όν, fattened; τὰ
σιτιστά, fatlings, Mat. xxii.
4.*
σιτο-μέτριον, ου, τό, a measured
portion of grain or food, Lu.
xii. 42. (N. T.)*
σῖτος, ου, ὁ, wheat, grain, Jn.
xii. 24; 1 Cor. xv. 37.
Σιχάρ, see Συχάρ.
Σιών, ἡ, τό, Zion, the hill; used
for the city of Jerusalem,
Ro. xi. 26; fig., for heaven,
the spiritual Jerusalem, Heb.
xii. 22; Rev. xiv. 1.
σιωπάω, ῶ, ήσω, to be silent,
whether voluntarily or from
dumbness, Mar. iii. 4; Lu. i.
20; to become still, as the
sea, Mar. iv. 39.
σκανδαλίζω, ίσω, to cause to
stumble; met., to entice to sin,
Mat. xviii. 6, 8, 9; to cause
to fall away, Jn. vi. 61; pass.,
to be indignant, Mat. xv. 12.
σκάνδαλον, ου, τό, a snare, a
stumbling-block; fig., a cause
of error or sin, Mat. xiii. 41;
Ro. xiv. 13. (S.)
σκάπτω, ψω, to dig, Lu. vi. 48,
xiii. 8, xvi. 3.*
σκάφη, ης, ἡ, any hollow vessel;
a boat, Ac. xxvii. 16, 30, 32.*
σκέλος, ους, τό, the leg, Jn. xix.
31, 32, 33.*
σκέπασμα, ατος, τό, clothing,
1 Tim. vi. 8.*
Σκευᾶς, ᾶ, ὁ, Sceva, Ac. xix.
14.*
σκευή, ῆς, ἡ, furniture, fittings,
Ac. xxvii. 19.*
σκεῦος, ους, τό, (1) a vessel, to
contain a liquid, or for any
other purpose, Heb. ix. 21;
2 Tim. ii. 20; fig., of recip-
ients generally, a vessel of
mercy, of wrath, Ro. ix. 22,
23; an instrument by which
anything is done; household
utensils, plur., Mat. xii. 29;
of a ship, the tackling, Ac.
xxvii. 17; fig., of God's servants, Ac. ix. 15; 2 Cor. iv. 7.
σκηνή, ῆς, ἡ, a tent, a tabernacle,
an abode or dwelling, Mat.
xvii. 4; Ac. vii. 43, xv. 16;
Heb. viii. 5, xiii. 10.
σκηνο-πηγία, ας, ἡ, the feast of
tabernacles, Jn. vii. 2.*
σκηνο-ποιός, οῦ, ὁ, a tent-maker,
Ac. xviii. 3. (N. T.)*
σκῆνος, ους, τό, a tent; fig., of

the human body, 2 Cor. v. 1, 4.*

σκηνόω, ῶ, ώσω, to spread a tent, Rev. vii. 15; met., to dwell, Jn. i. 14; Rev. xii. 12, xiii. 6, xxi. 3.*

σκήνωμα, ατος, τό, a tent pitched, a dwelling, Ac. vii. 46; fig., of the body, 2 Pet. i. 13, 14.*

σκιά, ᾶς, ἡ, (1) a shadow, a thick darkness, Mat. iv. 16 (S.); (2) a shadow, an outline, Col. ii. 17.

σκιρτάω, ῶ, ήσω, to leap for joy, Lu. i. 41, 44, vi. 23.*

σκληρο-καρδία, ας, ἡ, hardness of heart, perverseness, Mat. xix. 8; Mar. x. 5, xvi. 14. (S.)*

σκληρός, ά, όν, hard, violent, as the wind, Ja. iii. 4; fig., grievous, painful, Ac. ix. 5 (W. H. omit), xxvi. 14; Ju. 15; harsh, stern, Mat. xxv. 24; Jn. vi. 60.*

σκληρότης, τητος, ἡ, fig., hardness of heart, obstinacy, Ro. ii. 5.*

σκληρο-τράχηλος, ον, stiffnecked; fig., obstinate, Ac. vii. 51. (S.)*

σκληρύνω, fig., to make hard, to harden, as the heart, Ro. ix. 18; Heb. iii. 8, 15, iv. 7; pass., to be hardened, to become obstinate, Ac. xix. 9; Heb. iii. 13.*

σκολιός, ά, όν, crooked, Lu. iii. 5; fig., perverse, Ac. ii. 40; Phil. ii. 15; unfair, 1 Pet. ii. 18.*

σκόλοψ, οπος, ὁ, a stake or thorn; fig., a sharp infliction, 2 Cor. xii. 7.*

σκοπέω, ῶ, (1) to look at, to regard attentively, Ro. xvi. 17; (2) to take heed (acc.), beware (μή), Gal. vi. 1.

σκοπός, οῦ, ὁ, a mark aimed at, a goal; κατὰ σκοπόν, towards the goal, i.e., aiming straight at it, Phil. iii. 14.*

σκορπίζω, σω, to disperse, to scatter abroad, as frightened sheep, Jn. x. 12; to distribute alms, 2 Cor. ix. 9.

σκορπίος, ου, ὁ, a scorpion, Lu. x. 19.

σκοτεινός, ή, όν, full of darkness, dark, Mar. vi. 23; Lu. xi. 34, 36.*

σκοτία, ας, ἡ, darkness, Mat. x.

27; fig., spiritual darkness, Jn. i. 5, vi. 17.

σκοτίζω, σω, in pass., to be darkened, as the sun, Mar. xiii. 24; fig., as the mind, Ro. i. 21.

σκότος, ους, τό (σκότος, ου, ὁ, only in Heb. xii. 18, where W. H. read ζόφος), darkness, physical, Mat. xxvii. 45; moral, Jn. iii. 19.

σκοτόω, ῶ, pass. only, to be darkened, Ep. iv. 18 (W.H.); Rev. ix. 2 (W. H.), xvi. 10.*

σκύβαλον, ου, τό, refuse, dregs, Phil. iii. 8.*

Σκύθης, ου, ὁ, a Scythian, as typical of the uncivilized, Col. iii. 11.*

σκυθρ-ωπός, όν, sad-countenanced, gloomy, Mat. vi. 16; Lu. xxiv. 17.*

σκύλλω, pass. perf. part. ἐσκυλμένος, to flay; to trouble, annoy, Mat. ix. 36 (W. H.); Mar. v. 35; Lu. vii. 6, viii. 29.*

σκῦλον, ου, τό, spoil taken from a foe, Lu. xi. 22.*

σκωληκό-βρωτος, ον, eaten by worms, Ac. xii. 23.*

σκώληξ, ηκος, ὁ, a gnawing worm, Mar. ix. 44 (W. H. omit)- 46 (W. H. omit), 48.*

σμαράγδινος, η, ον, made of emerald, Rev. iv. 3. (N.T.)*

σμάραγδος, ου, ὁ, an emerald, Rev. xxi. 19.*

σμύρνα, ης, ἡ, myrrh, Mat. ii. 11; Jn. xix. 39.*

Σμύρνα, ης, ἡ, Smyrna. Rev. i. 11, ii. 8 (W. H.).*

Σμυρναῖος, ου, ὁ, ἡ, one of Smyrna, a Smyrnæan, Rev. ii. 8 (not W. H.).*

σμυρνίζω, to mingle with myrrh, Mar. xv. 23. (N. T.)*

Σόδομα, ων, τά, Sodom, Mat. x. 15, xi. 23, 24.

Σολομών or -μῶν, ῶντος or ῶνος, ὁ, Solomon, Mat. vi. 29, xii. 42.

σορός, οῦ, ἡ, a bier, an open coffin, Lu. vii. 14.*

σός, σή, σόν, poss. pron., thy, thine (see Gr. §§ 56, 255, Bu. 115).

σουδάριον, ου, τό (Lat.), a handkerchief, Lu. xix. 20; Jn. xi. 44. (N. T.)

Σουσάννα, ης, ἡ, Susanna, Lu. viii. 3.*

σοφία, ας, ἡ, wisdom, insight, skill, human, Lu. xi. 31; or divine, 1 Cor. i. 21, 24. Syn.: see γνῶσις.

σοφίζω, to make wise, 2 Tim. iii. 15; pass., to be devised skillfully, 2 Pet. i. 16.*

σοφός, ή, όν, wise, either (1) in action, expert, Ro. xvi. 19; (2) in acquirement, learned, cultivated, 1 Cor. i. 19, 20; (3) philosophically, profound, Ju. 25; (4) practically, Ep. v. 15.

Σπανία, ας, ἡ, Spain, Ro. xv. 24, 28.*

σπαράσσω, ξω, to convulse, to throw into spasms, Mar. i. 26, ix. 20 (not W. H.), 26; Lu. ix. 39.*

σπαργανόω, ῶ, perf. pass. part. ἐσπαργανωμένος, to swathe, to wrap in swaddling clothes, Lu. ii. 7, 12.*

σπαταλάω, ῶ, ήσω, to live extravagantly or luxuriously, 1 Tim. v. 6; Ja. v. 5.* Syn.: The fundamental thought of στρηνιάω is of insolence and voluptuousness which spring from abundance; of τρυφάω, effeminate self-indulgence; of σπαταλάω, is effeminacy and wasteful extravagance.

σπάω, ῶ, mid., to draw, as a sword, Mar. xiv. 47; Ac. xvi. 27.*

σπεῖρα, ης, ἡ, (1) a cohort of soldiers, the tenth part of a legion, Ac. x. 1; (2) a military guard, Jn. xviii. 3, 12.

σπείρω, σπερῶ, 1st aor. ἔσπειρα, perf. pass. part. ἐσπαρμένος, 2d aor. pass. ἐσπάρην, to sow or scatter, as seed, Lu. xii. 24; to spread or scatter, as the word of God, Mat. xiii. 19; applied to giving alms, 2 Cor. ix. 6; to burial, 1 Cor. xv. 42, 43; and to spiritual effort generally, Gal. vi. 8.

σπεκουλάτωρ, ορος, ὁ (Lat.), a body-guardsman, a soldier in attendance upon royalty, Mar. vi. 27 (see Gr. § 154c). (N. T.)*

σπένδω, to pour out, as a libation, fig., Phil. ii. 17; 2 Tim. iv. 6.*

σπέρμα, ατος, τό, seed, produce, Mat. xiii. 24–38; children, offspring, posterity, Jn. vii. 42; a remnant, Ro. ix. 29.

σπερμο-λόγος, ου, ὁ, *a babbler,*
i.e., one who picks up trifles,
as birds do seed, Ac. xvii.
18.*

σπεύδω, σω, (1) *to hasten,* intrans., usually adding to another verb the notion of
speed, Lu. xix. 5, 6; (2) *to*
desire earnestly (acc.), 2 Pet.
iii. 12.

σπήλαιον, ου, τό, *a cave, a den,*
Heb. xi. 38.*

σπιλάς, άδος, ἡ, *a rock in the*
sea, a reef; fig., of false
teachers, *a hidden rock* (R.
V.), Ju. 12.*

σπῖλος, ου, ὁ, *a spot;* fig., *a*
fault, Ep. v. 27; 2 Pet. ii.
13.*

σπιλόω, ῶ, *to defile, to spot,* Ja.
iii. 6; Ju. 23.*

σπλάγχνα, ων, τά, *bowels,* only
Ac. i. 18; elsewhere, fig., *the*
affections, compassion, the
heart, as Col. iii. 12; 1 Jn.
iii. 17.

σπλαγχνίζομαι, dep., with 1st
aor. pass. ἐσπλαγχνίσθην, *to*
feel compassion, to have pity
on (gen., or ἐπί, dat. or acc.,
once περί, Mat. ix. 36).

σπόγγος, ου, ὁ, *a sponge,* Mat.
xxvii. 48; Mar. xv. 36; Jn.
xix. 29.*

σποδός, οῦ, ἡ, *ashes,* Mat. xi.
21; Lu. x. 13; Heb. ix. 13.*

σπορά, ᾶς, ἡ, *seed,* 1 Pet. i.
23.*

σπόριμος, ον, *sown;* neut. plur.
τὰ σπόριμα, *sown fields,* Mat.
xii. 1; Mar. ii. 23; Lu. vi. 1.*

σπόρος, ου, ὁ, *seed,* for sowing,
Lu. viii. 5, 11.

σπουδάζω, άσω, *to hasten, to*
give diligence (with inf.),
Heb. iv. 11; 2 Tim. iv. 9, 21.

σπουδαῖος, αία, αῖον, *diligent,*
earnest, 2 Cor. viii. 17, 22;
compar. neut. as adv., σπουδαιότερον, 2 Tim. i. 17 (not
W. H.).*

σπουδαίως, adv., *diligently, ear-*
nestly, Lu. vii. 4; 2 Tim. i.
17 (W. H.); Tit. iii. 13; *has-*
tily, compar., Phil. ii. 28.*

σπουδή, ῆς, ἡ, (1) *speed, haste,*
Mar. vi. 25; (2) *diligence,*
earnestness, Ro. xii. 11.

σπυρίς (W. H. σφυρίς), ίδος, ἡ,
a plaited basket, Mar. viii. 8,
20.

στάδιον, ου, τό, plur. οἱ στάδιοι,
(1) *a stadium,* one eighth of

a Roman mile, Jn. xi. 18;
(2) *a race-course,* for public
games, 1 Cor. ix. 24.

στάμνος, ου, ὁ, ἡ, *a jar* or *vase,*
for the manna, Heb. ix. 4.*

στασιαστής, οῦ, ὁ, *an insurgent,*
Mar. xv. 7 (W. H.).*

στάσις, εως, ἡ (ἵστημι), *a stand-*
ing, lit. only Heb. ix. 8; *an*
insurrection, Mar. xv. 7; *dis-*
sension, Ac. xv. 2.

στατήρ, ῆρος, ὁ, *a stater,* a silver
coin equal to two of the
δίδραχμον (which see), a
Jewish shekel, Mat. xvii.
27.*

σταυρός, οῦ, ὁ, *a cross,* Mat.
xxvii. 32, 40; met., often of
Christ's death, Gal. vi. 14;
Ep. ii. 16.

σταυρόω, ῶ, ώσω, *to fix to the*
cross, to crucify, Lu. xxiii.
21, 23; fig., *to destroy,* the
corrupt nature, Gal. v. 24.

σταφυλή, ῆς, ἡ, *a grape, a*
cluster of grapes, Mat. vii.
16; Lu. vi. 44; Rev. xiv.
18.*

στάχυς, υος, ὁ, *an ear of corn,*
Mat. xii. 1; Mar. ii. 23, iv.
28; Lu. vi. 1.*

Στάχυς, υος, ὁ, *Stachys,* Ro. xvi.
9.*

στέγη, ης, ἡ (lit. *a cover*), *a* flat
roof of a house, Mat. viii. 8;
Mar. ii. 4; Lu. vii. 6.*

στέγω, *to cover, to conceal, to*
bear with, 1 Cor. ix. 12, xiii.
7; 1 Th. iii. 1, 5.*

στεῖρος, α, ον, *barren,* Lu. i. 7,
36, xxiii. 29; Gal. iv. 27.*

στέλλω, *to set, arrange;* in mid.,
to provide for, take care, 2
Cor. viii. 20; *to withdraw*
from (ἀπό), 2 Th. iii. 6.*

στέμμα, ατος, τό, *a garland,* Ac.
xiv. 13.*

στεναγμός, οῦ, ὁ, *a groaning,*
Ac. vii. 34; Ro. viii. 26.*

στενάζω, ξω, *to groan,* expressing grief, anger, or desire,
Mar. vii. 34; Heb. xiii.
17.

στενός, ή, όν, *narrow,* Mat. vii.
13, 14; Lu. xiii. 24.*

στενο-χωρέω, ῶ, *to be narrow;*
in pass., *to be distressed,* 2
Cor. iv. 8, vi. 12.*

στενο-χωρία, as, ἡ, *a narrow*
space; great distress, Ro. ii.
9, viii. 35; 2 Cor. vi. 4, xii.
10.*

στερεός, ά, όν, *solid,* as food,

Heb. v. 12, 14; fig., *firm,*
steadfast, 1 Pet. v. 9; 2 Tim.
ii. 19.*

στερεόω, ῶ, ώσω, *to strengthen,*
confirm, establish, Ac. iii. 7,
16, xvi. 5.*

στερέωμα, ατος, τό, *firmness,*
steadfastness, Col. ii. 5.*

Στεφανᾶς, ᾶ, ὁ, *Stephanas,* 1
Cor. i. 16, xvi. 15, 17.

στέφανος, ου, ὁ, *a crown, a*
garland, of royalty, of victory in the games, of festal
joy, Jn. xix. 2, 5; 1 Cor. ix.
25; often used fig., 2 Tim.
iv. 8; Rev. ii. 10. *Syn.:* see
διάδημα.

Στέφανος, ου, ὁ, *Stephen,* Ac.
vi., vii.

στεφανόω, ῶ, ώσω, *to crown, to*
adorn, 2 Tim. ii. 5; Heb. ii.
7, 9.*

στῆθος, ους, τό, *the breast,* Lu.
xviii. 13.

στήκω (ἵστημι, ἕστηκα), *to stand,*
in the attitude of prayer,
Mar. xi. 25; generally, *to*
stand firm, persevere, as Ro.
xiv. 4; 1 Cor. xvi. 13; Gal.
v. 1. (S.)

στηριγμός, οῦ, ὁ, *firmness,*
steadfastness, 2 Pet. iii. 17.*

στηρίζω, ίξω or ίσω, pass. perf.
ἐστήριγμαι, (1) *to fix, to set*
firmly, Lu. ix. 51, xvi. 26;
(2) *to strengthen, to confirm,*
to support, as Lu. xxii. 32;
Ro. i. 11.

στιβάς, see στοιβάς.

στίγμα, ατος, τό, *a mark* or
brand, used of the traces of
the apostle's sufferings for
Christ, Gal. vi. 17.*

στιγμή, ῆς, ἡ, *a point of time,*
an instant, Lu. iv. 5.*

στίλβω, *to shine, to glisten,* Mar.
ix. 3.*

στοά, ᾶς, ἡ, *a colonnade, a*
portico, Jn. v. 2, x. 23; Ac.
iii. 11, v. 12.*

στοιβάς, άδος, ἡ (W.H. στιβάς),
a bough, a branch of a tree,
Mar. xi. 8.*

στοιχεῖα, ων, τά, *elements, ru*
diments, Gal. iv. 3, 9; Col.
ii. 8, 20; Heb. v. 12; 2 Pet.
iii. 10, 12.*

στοιχέω, ῶ, ήσω, *to walk,* always fig. of conduct; *to*
walk in (local dat.), Ac. xxi.
24; Ro. iv. 12; Gal. v. 25,
vi. 16; Phil. iii. 16.*

στολή, ῆς, ἡ, *a robe, i.e.,* the

ιong outer garment which was a mark of distinction, Lu. xv. 22. *Syn.:* see ἱμάτιον.

στόμα, ατος, τό, (1) *the mouth,* generally; hence, (2) *speech, speaking;* used of *testimony,* Mat. xviii. 16; *eloquence* or *power in speaking,* Lu. xxi. 15; (3) applied to an opening in the earth, Rev. xii. 16; (4) *the edge* or *point* of a sword, Lu. xxi. 24.

στόμαχος, ου, ὁ, *the stomach,* I Tim. v. 23.*

στρατεία, ας, ἡ, *warfare, military service;* of Christian warfare, 2 Cor. x. 4; I Tim. i. 18.*

στράτευμα, ατος, τό, (1) *an army,* Rev. ix. 16; (2) *a detachment of troops,* Ac. xxiii. 10, 27; plur., Lu. xxiii. 11.

στρατεύομαι, dep. mid., *to wage war, to fight,* Lu. iii. 14; fig., of the warring of lusts against the soul, Ja. iv. 1; *to serve as a soldier,* of Christian work, I Tim. i. 18; 2 Cor. x. 3.

στρατηγός, οῦ, ὁ (ἄγω), (1) *a leader of an army, a general;* (2) *a magistrate* or *governor,* Ac. xvi. 20–38; (3) *the captain* of the temple, Lu. xxii. 4, 52; Ac. iv. 1, v. 24, 26.*

στρατιά, ᾶς, ἡ, *an army;* met., *a host* of angels, Lu. ii. 13; *the host* of heaven, *i.e.,* the stars, Ac. vii. 42.*

στρατιώτης, ου, ὁ, *a soldier,* as Mat. viii. 9; fig., of a Christian, 2 Tim. ii. 3.

στρατολογέω, ῶ, ήσω, *to collect an army, to enlist troops,* 2 Tim. ii. 4.*

στρατοπεδ-άρχης, ου, ὁ, *the prætorian prefect, i.e.,* commander of the Roman emperor's body-guard, Ac. xxviii. 16 (W. H. omit).*

στρατόπεδον, ου, τό, *an encamped army,* Lu. xxi. 20.*

στρεβλόω, ῶ, *to rack, to pervert, to twist,* as words from their proper meaning, 2 Pet. iii. 16.*

στρέφω, ψω, 2d aor. pass. ἐστράφην, *to turn,* trans., Mat. v. 39; Rev. xi. 6 (*to change* into, εἰς); intrans., Ac. vii. 42; mostly in pass., *to turn one's self,* Jn. xx. 14; *to be con-*

verted, to be changed in mind and conduct, Mat. xviii. 3.

στρηνιάω, ῶ, άσω, *to live voluptuously,* Rev. xviii. 7, 9.* *Syn.:* see σπαταλάω.

στρῆνος, ους, τό, *profligate luxury, voluptuousness,* Rev. xviii. 3.*

στρουθίον, ου, τό (dim. of στρουθός), *a small bird, a sparrow,* Mat. x. 29, 31; Lu. xii. 6, 7.*

στρωννύω, or -ώννυμι, στρώσω, pass. perf. part. ἐστρωμένος ἔστρωμαι, *to spread,* Mat. xxi. 8; *to make a bed,* Ac. ix. 34; pass., *to be spread with couches,* ἀνάγαιον ἐστρωμένον, *an upper room furnished,* Mar. xiv. 15; Lu. xxii. 12.

στυγητός, όν, *hateful, detestable,* Tit. iii. 3.*

στυγνάζω, άσω, *to be gloomy,* Mar. x. 22; of the sky, Mat. xvi. 3.*

στύλος, ου, ὁ, *a pillar,* Gal. ii. 9; I Tim. iii. 15; Rev. iii. 12, x. 1.*

Στωϊκός, ή, όν (στοά, portico), *Stoic,* Ac. xvii. 18.*

σύ, σοῦ, σοί, σέ, plur. ὑμεῖς, *thou, ye,* the pers. pron. of second person (see Gr. § 53).

συγγ-. In some words commencing thus, W. H. prefer the unassimilated form συνγ-.

συγ-γένεια, ας, ἡ, *kindred, family,* Lu. i. 61; Ac. vii. 3, 14.*

συγ-γενής, ές, *akin,* as subst., *a relative,* Mar. vi. 4; Lu. xiv. 12; *a fellow-countryman,* Ro. ix. 3.

συγ-γενίς, ίδος, ἡ, *a kinswoman,* Lu. i. 36 (W. H.).*

συγ-γνώμη, ης, ἡ, *permission, indulgence,* I Cor. vii. 6.*

συγκ-. In words commencing thus, W. H. prefer the unassimilated form συνκ-.

συγ-κάθημαι, *to sit with* (dat. or μετά, gen.), Mar. xiv. 54; Ac. xxvi. 30.*

συγ-καθίζω, σω, (1) *to cause to sit down with,* Ep. ii. 6; (2) *to sit down together,* Lu. xxii. 55.*

συγ-κακο-παθέω, ῶ, *to suffer hardships together with,* 2 Tim. i. 8, ii. 3 (W. H.). (N. T.)*

συγ-κακουχέω, ῶ, pass., *to suffer*

ill-treatment with, Heb. xi 25. (N. T.)*

συγ-καλέω, ῶ, έσω, *to call together,* Lu. xv. 6; mid., *to call together to one's self,* Lu. ix. 1.

συγ-καλύπτω, *to conceal closely, to cover up wholly,* Lu. xii. 2.*

συγ-κάμπτω, ψω, *to bend together; to oppress,* Ro. xi. 10. (S.)*

συγ-κατα-βαίνω, *to go down with* any one, Ac. xxv. 5.*

συγ-κατά-θεσις, εως, ἡ, *assent, agreement,* 2 Cor. vi. 16.*

συγ-κατα-τίθημι, in mid., *to give a vote with, to assent to* (dat.), Lu. xxiii. 51.*

συγ-κατα-ψηφίζω, in pass., *to be voted* or *classed with* (μετά), Ac. i. 26.*

συγ-κεράννυμι, Ist aor. συνεκέρασα, pass. perf. συγκέκραμαι, *to mix with, to unite,* I Cor. xii. 24; pass., *to be united with,* Heb. iv. 2.*

συγ-κινέω, ῶ, ήσω, *to move together, stir up,* Ac. vi. 12.*

συγ-κλείω, ω, *to inclose, to shut in,* as fishes in a net, Lu. v. 6; *to shut* one *up* into (εἰς) or under (ὑπό, acc.) something, *to make subject to,* Ro. xi. 32; Gal. iii. 22, 23.*

συγ-κληρο-νόμος, ου, ὁ, ἡ, *a joint heir, a joint participant,* Ro. viii. 17; Ep. iii. 6; Heb. xi. 9; I Pet. iii. 7.*

συγ-κοινωνέω, ῶ, *to be a partaker with, have fellowship with,* Ep. v. 11; Phil. iv. 14; Rev. xviii. 4.*

συγ-κοινωνός, ου, ὁ, ἡ, *a partaker with, a co-partner,* Ro. xi. 17. (N. T.)

συγ-κομίζω, *to bear away together,* as in burying a corpse, Ac. viii. 2.*

συγ-κρίνω, *to join together, to combine,* I Cor. ii. 13; *to compare* (acc., dat.), 2 Cor. x. 12.*

συγ-κύπτω, *to be bowed together* or *bent double,* Lu. xiii. 11.*

συγ-κυρία, ας, ἡ, *a coincidence, an accident; κατὰ συγκυρίαν, by chance,* Lu. x. 31.*

συγ-χαίρω, 2d aor. in pass form συνεχάρην, *to rejoice with* (dat.), Lu. i. 58, xv. 6, 9; I Cor. xii. 26, xiii. 6; Phil. ii. 17, 18.*

συγ-χέω, also συγχύνω and

συγχύννω, perf. pass. συγκέχυμαι, to mingle together; (1) to bewilder, Ac. ii. 6, ix. 22; (2) to stir up, to throw into confusion, Ac. xix. 32, xxi. 27, 31.*

συγ-χράομαι, ῶμαι, to have dealings with (dat.), Jn. iv. 9.*

σύγ-χυσις, εως, ἡ, confusion, disturbance, Ac. xix. 29.*

συ-ζάω (W. H. συνζ-), ῶ, ήσω, to live together with (dat.), Ro. vi. 8; 2 Cor. vii. 3; 2 Tim. ii. 11.*

συ-ζεύγνυμι, 1st aor. συνέζευξα, to yoke together; to unite (acc.), as man and wife, Mat. xix. 6; Mar. x. 9.*

συ-ζητέω, ῶ, to seek together, to discuss, dispute, with dat., or πρός, acc., Mar. viii. 11, ix. 16.

συ-ζήτησις, εως, ἡ, mutual questioning, disputation, Ac. xv. 2 (W. H. ζήτησις), 7 (W. H. ζήτησις), xxviii. 29 (W. H. omit).*

συ-ζητητής, οῦ, ὁ, a disputer, as the Greek sophists, 1 Cor. i. 20. (N. T.)*

σύ-ζυγος, ου, ὁ, a yoke-fellow, a colleague, Phil. iv. 3 (prob. a proper name, Syzygus).*

συ-ζωο-ποιέω, ῶ, 1st aor. συνεζωοποίησα, to make alive together with, Ep. ii. 5; Col. ii. 13. (N. T.)*

συκάμινος, ου, ἡ, a sycamine-tree, Lu. xvii. 6.*

συκῆ, ῆς, ἡ (contr. from -έα), a fig-tree, Mar. xi. 13, 20, 21.

συκο-μωραία, ας, ἡ (W. H. -μορέα), a sycamore-tree, Lu. xix. 4.*

σῦκον, ου, τό, a fig, Ja. iii. 12.

συκο-φαντέω, ῶ, ήσω, to accuse falsely, to defraud, Lu. iii. 14, xix. 8 (gen. person, acc. thing).*

συλ-αγωγέω, ῶ, to plunder, Col. ii. 8. (N. T.)*

συλάω, ῶ, to rob, to plunder, 2 Cor. xi. 8.*

συλλ-. In words commencing thus, W. H. prefer the unassimilated form συνλ-.

συλ-λαλέω, 1st aor. συνελάλησα, to talk with (dat.), μετά (gen.), πρός (acc.), Mat. xvii. 3; Mar. ix. 4; Lu. iv. 36, ix. 30, xxii. 4; Ac. xxv. 12.*

συλ-λαμβάνω, συλλήψομαι, συ-

νείληφα, συνέλαβον, (1) to take together, to seize, Mat. xxvi. 55; (2) to conceive, of a woman, Lu. i. 24, 31; (3) mid., to apprehend (acc.), to help (dat.), Ac. xxvi. 21; Phil. iv. 3.

συλ-λέγω, ξω, to collect, to gather, Mat. xiii. 28, 29, 30.

συλ-λογίζομαι, σομαι, to reckon with one's self, to reason, Lu. xx. 5.*

συλ-λυπέομαι, οῦμαι, pass., to be grieved (ἐπί, dat.), Mar. iii. 5.*

συμβ-, συμμ-, συμπ-, συμφ-. In some words commencing thus, W. H. prefer the unassimilated form συνβ-, συνμ-, συνπ-, συνφ-.

συμ-βαίνω, 2d aor. συνέβην, to happen, to occur, Mar. x. 32; Ac. xx. 19; perf. part. τὸ συμβεβηκός, an event, Lu. xxiv. 14.

συμ-βάλλω, 2d aor. συνέβαλον, to throw together, hence, to ponder, Lu. ii. 19; to come up with, to encounter, with or without hostile intent (dat.), Lu. xiv. 31; Ac. xx. 14; to dispute with, Ac. xvii. 18; mid., to confer, consult with, Ac. iv. 15; to contribute (dat.), Ac. xviii. 27.*

συμ-βασιλεύω, σω, to reign together with, 1 Cor. iv. 8; 2 Tim. ii. 12.*

συμ-βιβάζω, άσω, (1) to unite, or knit together, Col. ii. 2, 19; (2) to put together in reasoning, and so, to conclude, prove, Ac. ix. 22; (3) to teach, instruct, 1 Cor. ii. 16.

συμ-βουλεύω, to give advice (dat.), Jn. xviii. 14; Rev. iii. 18; mid., to take counsel together (ἵνα or inf.), Mat. xxvi. 4; Jn. xi. 53 (W. H. βουλεύομαι); Ac. ix. 23.*

συμ-βούλιον, ου, τό, (1) mutual consultation, counsel; λαμβάνω, ποιέω συμβούλιον, to take counsel together, Mat. xii. 14, xxii. 15, xxvii. 1, 7, xxviii. 12; Mar. iii. 6, xv. 1; (2) a council, a gathering of counselors, Ac. xxv. 12.*

σύμ-βουλος, ου, ὁ, an adviser, a counselor, Ro. xi. 34.*

Συμεών, ὁ (Heb.), Simeon or

Simon (see Σίμων); the apostle Peter is so called, Ac. xv. 14; 2 Pet. i. 1; and four others are mentioned: (1) Lu. ii. 25, 34; (2) Lu. iii. 30; (3) Ac. xiii. 1; (4) Rev. vii. 7.*

συμ-μαθητής, οῦ, ὁ, a fellow-disciple, Jn. xi. 16.*

συμ-μαρτυρέω, ῶ, to bear witness together with, Ro. ii. 15, viii. 16, ix. 1; Rev. xxii. 18 (not W. H.).*

συμ-μερίζω, in mid., to divide together with, partake with (dat.), 1 Cor. ix. 13.*

συμ-μέτοχος, ον, jointly partaking, Ep. iii. 6, v. 7.*

συμ-μιμητής, οῦ, ὁ, a joint-imitator, Phil. iii. 17. (N. T.)*

συμ-μορφίζω, see συμμορφόω. (N. T.)

σύμ-μορφος, ον, similar, conformed to, gen., Ro. viii. 29; dat., Phil. iii. 21.*

συμ-μορφόω, ῶ, to bring to the same form with (dat.), Phil. iii. 10 (W. H. συμμορφίζω, in same sense). (N. T.)*

συμ-παθέω, ῶ, to sympathize with, to have compassion on (dat.), Heb. iv. 15, x. 34.*

συμ-παθής, ές, sympathizing, compassionate, 1 Pet. iii. 8.*

συμ-παρα-γίνομαι, to come together to (ἐπί, acc.), Lu. xxiii. 48; to stand by one, to help (dat.), 2 Tim. iv. 16 (W. H. παραγίνομαι).*

συμ-παρα-καλέω, ῶ, in pass., to be strengthened together, Ro. i. 12.*

συμ-παρα-λαμβάνω, 2d aor. συμπαρέλαβον, to take with one's self, as companion, Ac. xii. 25, xv. 37, 38; Gal. ii. 1.*

συμ-παρα-μένω, μενῶ, to remain or continue together with (dat.), Phil. i. 25 (W. H. παραμένω).*

συμ-πάρειμι, to be present together with, Ac. xxv. 24.*

συμ-πάσχω, to suffer together with, Ro. viii. 17; 1 Cor. xii. 26.*

συμ-πέμπω, to send together with, 2 Cor. viii. 18, 22.*

συμ-περι-λαμβάνω, to embrace completely, Ac. xx. 10.*

συμ-πίνω, 2d aor. συνέπιον, to drink together with, Ac. x. 41.*

συμ-πίπτω, *to fall together*, Lu. vi. 49 (W. H.).*

συμ-πληρόω, ῶ, *to fill completely*, Lu. viii. 23; pass., *to be completed, to be fully come*, Lu. ix. 51; Ac. ii. 1.*

συμ-πνίγω, *to choke utterly*, as weeds do plants, Mat. xiii. 22; Mar. iv. 7, 19; Lu. viii. 14; *to crowd upon* (acc.), Lu. viii. 42.*

συμ-πολίτης, ου, ὁ, *a fellow-citizen*, Ep. ii. 19.*

συμ-πορεύομαι, (1) *to journey together with* (dat.), Lu. vii. 11, xiv. 25, xxiv. 15; (2) intrans., *to come together, to assemble*, Mar. x. 1.*

συμπόσιον, ου, τό (συμπίνω), *a drinking party, a festive company*, συμπόσια συμπόσια, *by companies*, Mar. vi. 39.*

συμ-πρεσβύτερος, ου, ὁ, *a fellow-elder*, 1 Pet. v. 1. (N. T.)*

συμ-φάγω, see συνεσθίω.

συμ-φέρω, 1st aor. συνήνεγκα, *to bring together, to collect*, only Ac. xix. 19; generally intrans., and often impers., *to conduce to, to be profitable to*, 1 Cor. x. 23; 2 Cor. xii. 1; part. τὸ συμφέρον, *profit, advantage*, 1 Cor. vii. 35.

σύμ-φημι, *to assent to*, Ro. vii. 16.*

σύμ-φορος, ον, *profitable*, 1 Cor. vii. 35, x. 33 (W. H. for Rec. συμφέρον).*

συμ-φυλέτης, ου, ὁ, *one of the same tribe, a fellow-countryman*, 1 Th. ii. 14. (N. T.)*

σύμ-φυτος, ον, *grown together, united with* (R. V.), Ro. vi. 5.*

συμ-φύω, 2d aor. pass. part. συμφυείς, pass., *to grow at the same time*, Lu. viii. 7.*

συμ-φωνέω, ῶ, ήσω, *to agree with, agree together, arrange with* (dat., or μετά, gen.), of persons, Mat. xviii. 19, xx. 2, 13; Ac. v. 9; of things, *to be in accord with*, Lu. v. 36; Ac. xv. 15.*

συμ-φώνησις, εως, ἡ, *concord, agreement*, 2 Cor. vi. 15. (N. T.)*

συμ-φωνία, ας, ἡ, *harmony*, of instruments, *music*, Lu. xv. 25.*

σύμ-φωνος, ον, *harmonious, agreeing with; ἐκ συμφώνου, by agreement*, 1 Cor. vii. 5.*

συμ-ψηφίζω, *to compute, reckon up*, Ac. xix. 19.*

σύμ-ψυχος, ον, *of one accord*, Phil. ii. 2. (N. T.)*

σύν, a prep. gov. dative, *with* (see Gr. § 296, Wi. § 48b, Bu. 331). In composition, σύν denotes association with, or is intensive. The final ν changes to γ, λ, or μ, or is dropped, according to the initial letter of the word with which it is compounded (see Gr. § 4d, 5, Bu. 8); but W. H. usually prefer the unassimilated forms.

συν-άγω, ἄξω, (1) *to bring together, to gather, to assemble*, Lu. xv. 13; Jn. xi. 47; pass., *to be assembled, to come together*, Ac. iv. 5, xiii. 44; (2) *to receive hospitably*, only Mat. xxv. 35, 38, 43.

συναγωγή, ῆς, ἡ, *an assembly, a congregation, synagogue*, either the place, or the people gathered in the place, Lu. xii. 11, xxi. 12. *Syn.:* see ἐκκλησία.

συν-αγωνίζομαι, *to strive together with* another, *to aid* (dat.), Ro. xv. 30.*

συν-αθλέω, ῶ, ήσω, *to strive together for* (dat. of thing), Phil. i. 27; *or with* (dat. of person), Phil. iv. 3.*

συν-αθροίζω, σω, *to gather or collect together*, Ac. xix. 25; pass., *to be assembled together*, Lu. xxiv. 33 (W. H. ἀθροίζω); Ac. xii. 12.*

συν-αίρω, *to reckon together, to make a reckoning with*, Mat. xviii. 23, 24, xxv. 19.*

συν-αιχμάλωτος, ου, ὁ, *a fellow-captive or prisoner*, Ro. xvi. 7; Col. iv. 10; Philem. 23. (N. T.)*

συν-ακολουθέω, ῶ, ήσω, *to follow together with, to accompany*, Mar. v. 37, xiv. 51 (W. H.); Lu. xxiii. 49.*

συν-αλίζω, in pass., *to be assembled together with* (dat.), Ac. i. 4.*

συν-αλλάσσω, *to reconcile*, see συνελαύνω.

συν-ανα-βαίνω, *to go up together with* (dat.), Mar. xv. 41; Ac. xiii. 31.*

συν-ανά-κειμαι, *to recline together with*, as at a meal, *to feast with* (dat.), Mat. ix. 10; part. οἱ συνανακείμενοι, *the guests*, Mar. vi. 22, 26. (Ap.)

συν-ανα-μίγνυμι, pass., *to mingle together with, to keep company with* (dat.), 1 Cor. v. 9, 11; 2 Th. iii. 14.*

συν-ανα-παύομαι, σομαι, *to find rest or refreshment together with* (dat.), Ro. xv. 32. (S.)*

συν-αντάω, ῶ, ήσω, (1) *to meet with* (dat.), Lu. ix. 37, xxii. 10; Ac. x. 25; Heb. vii. 1, 10; (2) of things, *to happen to, to befall;* τὰ συναντήσοντα, *the things that shall happen*, Ac. xx. 22.*

συν-άντησις, εως, ἡ, *a meeting with*, Mat. viii. 34 (W. H. ὑπάντησις).*

συν-αντι-λαμβάνω, mid., lit., *to take hold together with; to assist, help* (dat.), Lu. x. 40; Ro. viii. 26.*

συν-απ-άγω, *to lead away along with;* in pass., *to be led or carried away in mind*, Ro. xii. 16 (see R. V. mrg.); Gal. ii. 13; 2 Pet. iii. 17.*

συν-απο-θνήσκω, *to die together with* (dat.), Mar. xiv. 31; 2 Cor. vii. 3; 2 Tim. ii. 11.*

συν-απ-όλλυμι, in mid., *to perish together with* (dat.), Heb. xi. 31.*

συν-απο-στέλλω, *to send together with* (acc.), 2 Cor. xii. 18.*

συν-αρμολογέω, ῶ, in pass., *to be framed together*, Ep. ii. 21, iv. 16. (N. T.)*

συν-αρπάζω, σω, *to seize, or drag by force* (dat.), Lu. viii. 29; Ac. vi. 12, xix. 29, xxvii. 15.*

συν-αυξάνω, in pass., *to grow together*, Mat. xiii. 30.*

σύν-δεσμος, ου, ὁ, *that which binds together, a band, a bond*, Ac. viii. 23; Ep. iv. 3; Col. ii. 19, iii. 14.*

συν-δέω, in pass., *to be bound together with* any one, as fellow-prisoners, Heb. xiii. 3.*

συν-δοξάζω, *to glorify together with* (σύν), pass., Ro. viii. 17.*

σύν-δουλος, ου, ὁ, *a fellow-slave, a fellow-servant*, Mat. xviii. 28–33; of Christians, *a fellow-worker, a colleague*, Col. i. 7.

συν-δρομή, ῆς, ἡ, *a running together, a concourse,* Ac. xxi. 30.*

συν-εγείρω, 1st aor. συνήγειρα, pass. συνηγέρθην; *to raise together, to raise with,* Ep. ii. 6; Col. ii. 12, iii. 1. (S.)*

συνέδριον, ου, τό, *a council, a tribunal,* Mat. x. 17; specially, *the Sanhedrin,* the Jewish council of seventy-one members, usually presided over by the high priest, Mat. v. 22, xxvi. 59; *the council-hall,* where the Sanhedrin met, Ac. iv. 15.

συνείδησις, εως, ἡ, *consciousness,* Heb. x. 2; *the conscience,* Ro. ii. 15; 2 Cor. iv. 2, v. 11; 1 Pet. ii. 19.

συν-είδον, 2d aor. of obs. pres., *to be conscious* or *aware of, to understand,* Ac. xii. 12, xiv. 6; perf. σύνοιδα, part. συνειδώς, *to be privy* to a design, Ac. v. 2; *to be conscious* to one's self (dat.) of guilt (acc.), 1 Cor. iv. 4.*

σύν-ειμι, *to be with* (dat.), Lu. ix. 18; Ac. xxii. 11.*

σύν-ειμι (εἶμι), part. συνιών, *to go* or *come with, to assemble,* Lu. viii. 4.*

συν-εισ-έρχομαι, *to enter together with* (dat.), Jn. vi. 22, xviii. 15.*

συν-έκδημος, ου, ὁ, ἡ, *a fellow-traveler,* Ac. xix. 29; 2 Cor. viii. 19.*

συν-εκλεκτός, ή, όν, *elected together with,* 1 Pet. v. 13. (N. T.)*

συν-ελαύνω, ελάσω, *to compel, to urge* (acc. and εἰς), Ac. vii. 26 (W. H. συναλλάσσω).*

συν-επι-μαρτυρέω, ῶ, *to unite in bearing witness,* Heb. ii. 4.*

συν-επι-τίθημι, mid., *to join in assailing,* Ac. xxiv. 9 (W. H. for συντίθημι).*

συν-έπομαι, *to follow with, to accompany* (dat.), Ac. xx. 4.*

συν-εργέω, ῶ, *to co-operate with* (dat.), *to work together,* 1 Cor. xvi. 16; Ro. viii. 28.

συν-εργός, όν, *co-working, helping;* as a subst., *a companion in work, a fellow-worker,* gen. of person, obj. with εἰς, or dat., or (met.) gen., 2 Cor. i. 24.

συν-έρχομαι (see Gr. § 103, 2, Wi. § 15, Bu. 58), *to come* or *go with, to accompany,* Ac. i. 21; *to come together, to assemble,* Ac. i. 6, v. 16; used also of conjugal intercourse, *to come* or *live together,* Mat. i. 18.

συν-εσθίω, 2d aor. συνέφαγον, *to eat with* (dat., or μετά, gen.), Lu. xv. 2; Ac. x. 41, xi. 3; 1 Cor. v. 11; Gal. ii. 12.*

σύνεσις, εως, ἡ (συνίημι), *a putting together,* in mind; hence, *understanding,* Lu. ii. 47; *the understanding,* the source of discernment, Mar. xii. 33.

συνετός, ή, όν (συνίημι), *intelligent, prudent, wise,* Mat. xi. 25; Lu. x. 21; Ac. xiii. 7; 1 Cor. i. 19.*

συν-ευδοκέω, ῶ, *to be pleased together with, to approve together* (dat.), Lu. xi. 48; Ac. viii. 1, xxii. 20; *to be of one mind with* (dat.), Ro. i. 32; *to consent, agree to* (inf.), 1 Cor. vii. 12, 13.*

συν-ευωχέω, ῶ, in pass., *to feast sumptuously with,* 2 Pet. ii. 13; Ju. 12.*

συν-εφ-ίστημι, *to rise up together against* (κατά), Ac. xvi. 22.*

συν-έχω, ξω, (1) *to press together, to close,* Ac. vii. 57; (2) *to press on every side, to confine,* Lu. viii. 45; (3) *to hold fast,* Lu. xxii. 63; (4) *to urge, impel,* Lu. xii. 50; 2 Cor. v. 14; (5) in pass., *to be afflicted with* sickness, Lu. iv. 38.

συν-ήδομαι, *to delight inwardly in* (dat.), Ro. vii. 22.*

συν-ήθεια, ας, ἡ, *a custom,* Jn. xviii. 39; 1 Cor. viii. 7 (W. H.), xi. 16.*

συν-ηλικιώτης, ου, ὁ, *one of the same age,* Gal. i. 14.*

συν-θάπτω, 2d aor. pass. συνετάφην, in pass., *to be buried together with,* Ro. vi. 4; Col. ii. 12.*

συν-θλάω, ῶ, fut. pass. συνθλασθήσομαι, *to break, to break in pieces,* Mat. xxi. 44; Lu. xx. 18.*

συν-θλίβω, *to press on all sides, to crowd upon,* Mar. v. 24, 31.*

συν-θρύπτω, *to break in pieces, to crush,* fig., Ac. xxi. 13. (N. T.)*

συν-ίημι, inf. συνιέναι, part. συνιῶν or συνιείς, fut. συνήσω, 1st aor. συνῆκα, *to put together,* in mind; hence, *to consider, understand* (acc.), *to be aware* (ὅτι), *to attend to* (ἐπί, dat.), Mat. xiii. 23, 51, xvi. 12; Mar. vi. 52.

συν-ίστημι, also συνιστάνω and συνιστάω, *to place together; to commend,* 2 Cor. iii. 1, vi. 4; *to prove, exhibit,* Gal. ii. 18; Ro. iii. 5, v. 8; perf. and 2d aor., intrans., *to stand with,* Lu. ix. 32; *to be composed of, to cohere,* Col. i. 17; 2 Pet. iii. 5.

συν-οδεύω, *to journey with, to accompany* (dat.), Ac. ix. 7.*

συν-οδία, ας, ἡ, *a company traveling together, a caravan,* Lu. ii. 44.*

συν-οικέω, ῶ, *to dwell together,* as in marriage, 1 Pet. iii. 7.*

συν-οικοδομέω, ῶ, in pass., *to be built up together,* Ep. ii. 22.*

συν-ομιλέω, ῶ, *to talk with* (dat.), Ac. x. 27.*

συν-ομορέω, ῶ, *to be contiguous to* (dat.), Ac. xviii. 7. (N. T.)*

συν-οχή, ῆς, ἡ, *constraint* of mind; hence, *distress, anguish,* Lu. xxi. 25; 2 Cor. ii. 4.*

συν-τάσσω, ξω, *to arrange with, prescribe, appoint,* Mat. xxi. 6 (W. H.), xxvi. 19, xxvii. 10.*

συν-τέλεια, ας, ἡ, *a completion, a consummation, an end,* Mat. xiii. 39, 40, 49, xxiv. 3, xxviii. 20; Heb. ix. 26.*

συν-τελέω, ῶ, έσω, (1) *to bring completely to an end,* Mat. vii. 28 (W. H. τελέω); Lu. iv. 2, 13; Ac. xxi. 27; (2) *to fulfill, to accomplish,* Ro. ix. 28; Mar. xiii. 4; *to make, to conclude,* Heb. viii. 8.*

συν-τέμνω, *to cut short, to bring to swift accomplishment,* Ro. ix. 28.*

συν-τηρέω, ῶ, (1) *to preserve, to keep safe,* Mat. ix. 17; Mar. vi. 20; Lu. v. 38 (W. H. omit); (2) *to keep in mind,* Lu. ii. 19.*

συν-τίθημι, in mid., *to place together, to make an agreement,* Lu. xxii. 5; Jn. ix. 22; Ac. xxiii. 20; *to assent,* Ac.

xxiv. 9 (W. H. συνεπιτί-θημι).*

συν-τόμως, adv., concisely, briefly, Ac. xxiv. 4.*

συν-τρέχω, 2d aor. συνέδραμον, to run together, as a multitude, Mar. vi. 33; Ac. iii. 11; to run with (fig.), 1 Pet. iv. 4.*

συν-τρίβω, ψω, to break by crushing, to break in pieces, Lu. ix. 39; Ro. xvi. 20; perf. pass. part. συντετριμμένος, bruised, Mat. xii. 20.

σύν-τριμμα, ατος, τό, crushing; fig., destruction, Ro. iii. 16. (S.)

σύν-τροφος, ου, ὁ, one brought up with, a foster-brother, Ac. xiii. 1.*

συν-τυγχάνω, 2d aor. inf. συντυχεῖν, to meet with, come to (dat.), Lu. viii. 19.*

Συντύχη, acc. ην, ἡ, Syntyche, Phil. iv. 2.*

συν-υπο-κρίνομαι, dep. pass., 1st aorist συνυπεκρίθην, to dissemble with, Gal. ii. 13.*

συν-υπουργέω, ῶ, to help together, 2 Cor. i. 11.*

συν-ωδίνω, to be in travail together, Ro. viii. 22.*

συν-ωμοσία, ας, ἡ, a swearing together, a conspiracy, Ac. xxiii. 13.*

Συράκουσαι, ῶν, αἱ, Syracuse, Ac. xxviii. 12.*

Συρία, ας, ἡ, Syria, Lu. ii. 2.

Σύρος, ου, ὁ, a Syrian, Lu. iv. 27.*

Συρο-φοίνισσα (W. H. Συροφοινίκισσα, mrg., Σύρα Φοινίκισσα), ης, ἡ, an appellative, a Syrophenician woman, Mar. vii. 26.*

Σύρτις, εως, acc. ιν, ἡ, (a quicksand), the Syrtis major, Ac. xxvii. 17.*

σύρω, to draw, to drag, Jn. xxi. 8; Ac. viii. 3, xiv. 19, xvii. 6; Rev. xii. 4.* Syn.: see ἕλκω.

συσ-. In some words commencing thus, W. H. prefer the uncontracted form συνσ-.

συ-σπαράσσω, ξω, to convulse completely (acc.), Mar. ix. 20 (W. H.); Lu. ix. 42.*

σύσ-σημον, ου, τό, a concerted signal, a sign agreed upon, Mar. xiv. 44.*

σύσ-σωμος (W. H. σύνσωμος),

ον, belonging to the same body; fig., of Jews and Gentiles, in one church, Ep. iii. 6. (N. T.)*

συ-στασιαστής, οῦ, ὁ, a fellow-insurgent (W. H. στασιαστής), Mar. xv. 7.*

συ-στατικός, ή, όν, commendatory, 2 Cor. iii. 1.*

συ-σταυρόω, ῶ, to crucify together with (acc. and dat.); lit., Mat. xxvii. 44; fig., Gal. ii. 19. (N. T.)

συ-στέλλω, (1) to contract, perf. pass. part., contracted, shortened, 1 Cor. vii. 29; (2) to wrap round, to swathe, as a dead body, Ac. v. 6.*

συ-στενάζω, to groan together, Ro. viii. 22.*

συ-στοιχέω, ῶ, to be in the same rank with; to answer to, to correspond to (dat.), Gal. iv. 25.*

συ-στρατιώτης, ου, ὁ, a fellow-soldier, i.e., in the Christian service, Phil. ii. 25; Philem. 2.*

συ-στρέφω, ψω, to roll or gather together, Mat. xvii. 22 (W. H.); Ac. xxviii. 3.*

συ-στροφή, ῆς, ἡ, a gathering together, a riotous concourse, Ac. xix. 40; a conspiracy, Ac. xxiii. 12.*

συ-σχηματίζω, in pass., to conform one's self, to be assimilated to (dat.), Ro. xii. 2; 1 Pet. i. 14.*

Συχάρ (W. H.), or Σιχάρ, ἡ, Sychar, Jn. iv. 5.*

Συχέμ, Shechem, (1) ὁ, the prince, Ac. vii. 16 (Rec., W. H. the city); (2) ἡ, the city, Ac. vii. 16.*

σφαγή, ῆς, ἡ, (1) slaughter, Ac. viii. 32; Ro. viii. 36 (S.); Ja. v. 5.*

σφάγιον, ου, τό, a slaughtered victim, Ac. vii. 42.*

σφάζω, ξω, pass., perf. part. ἐσφαγμένος, 2d aor. ἐσφάγην, to kill by violence, to slay, 1 Jn. iii. 12; Rev. v. 9, vi. 4.

σφόδρα, adv., exceedingly, greatly, Mat. ii. 10.

σφοδρῶς, adv., exceedingly, Ac. xxvii. 18.*

σφραγίζω, ίσω, to seal, to set a seal upon, (1) for security, Mat. xxvii. 66; (2) for secrecy, Rev. xxii. 10; (3) for designation, Ep. i. 13; or

(4) for authentication, Ro. xv. 28.

σφραγίς, ῖδος, ἡ, (1) a seal, a signet-ring, Rev. vii. 2; (2) the impression of a seal whether for security and secrecy, as Rev. v. 1; or for designation, Rev. ix. 4; (3) that which the seal attests, the proof, 1 Cor. ix. 2.

σφυρίς, see σπυρίς.

σφυρόν (W. H. σφυδρόν), οῦ, τό, the ankle-bone, Ac. iii. 7.*

σχεδόν, adv., nearly, almost, Ac. xiii. 44, xix. 26; Heb. ix. 22.*

σχῆμα, ατος, τό, fashion, habit, 1 Cor. vii. 31; form, appearance, Phil. ii. 7.* Syn.: see ἰδέα.

σχίζω, ίσω, to rend, to divide asunder, Mat. xxvii. 51; pass., to be divided into factions, Ac. xiv. 4.

σχίσμα, ατος, τό, a rent, as in a garment, Mar. ii. 21; a division, a dissension, 1 Cor. i. 10.

σχοινίον, ου, τό (dim. of σχοῖνος, a rush), a cord, a rope, Jn. ii. 15; Ac. xxvii. 32.*

σχολάζω, άσω, to be at leisure; to be empty or unoccupied, Mat. xii. 44; to have leisure for (dat.), give one's self to, 1 Cor. vii. 5.*

σχολή, ῆς, ἡ, leisure; a place where there is leisure for anything, a school, Ac. xix. 9.*

σώζω, σώσω, perf. σέσωκα, pass. σέσωσμαι, 1st aor. pass. ἐσώθην; (1) to save, from evil or danger, Mat. viii. 25, xvi. 25; (2) to heal, Mat. ix. 21, 22; Jn. xi. 12; (3) to save, i.e., from eternal death, 1 Tim. i. 15; part. pass. οἱ σωζόμενοι, those who are being saved, i.e., who are in the way of salvation, Ac. ii. 47.

σῶμα, ατος, τό, a body, i.e., (1) the living body of an animal, Ja. iii. 3; or of a man, as 1 Cor. xii. 12, espec. as the medium of human life, and of human life as sinful; the body of Christ, as the medium and witness of his humanity; σώματα, Rev. xviii. 13, slaves; (2) a dead body, a corpse, Ac. ix. 40; (3) fig.,

a community, the church,
the mystic body of Christ,
Col. i. 24; (4) *any material
body*, plants, sun, moon, etc.,
I Cor. xv. 37, 38, 40; (5) *substance*, opp. to shadow, Col.
ii. 17.

σωματικός, ή, όν, *of or pertaining to the body*, I Tim. iv. 8;
bodily, corporeal, Lu. iii. 22.*

σωματικῶς, adv., *bodily, cor-
poreally*, Col. ii. 9.*

Σώπατρος, ου, ὁ, *Sopater*, Ac.
xx. 4; (perh. = Σωσίπατρος,
see Ro. xvi. 21).*

σωρεύω, σω, *to heap up, to load*,
Ro. xii. 20; 2 Tim. iii. 16.*

Σωσθένης, ου, ὁ, *Sosthenes*, (1)
Ac. xviii. 17; (2) I Cor. i.
1.*

Σωσίπατρος, ου, ὁ, *Sosipater*,
Ro. xvi. 21 (see Ac. xx. 4).*

σωτήρ, ῆρος, ὁ, *a savior, deliverer, preserver*; a name
given to God, Lu. i. 47; I
Tim. i. 1, ii. 3, iv. 10; Tit. i.
3, ii. 10, iii. 4; Ju. 25; elsewhere always of Christ, Lu.
ii. 11; Jn. iv. 42.

σωτηρία, as, ἡ, *welfare, pros-
perity, deliverance, preserva-
tion*, from temporal evils,
Ac. vii. 25, xxvii. 34; Heb.
xi. 7; 2 Pet. iii. 15; specially
salvation, i.e., deliverance
from eternal death, viewed
either as present or future,
2 Cor. i. 6; I Th. v. 9.

σωτήριος, ον, *saving, bringing
salvation*, Tit. ii. 11; neut.
τὸ σωτήριον, *salvation*, Lu.
ii. 30, iii. 6; Ac. xxviii. 28;
Ep. vi. 17.*

σωφρονέω, ῶ, ήσω, (1) *to be of
sound mind*, Mar. v. 15; (2)
to be sober-minded, Ro. xii.
3; (3) *to exercise self-control*,
Tit. ii. 6.

σωφρονίζω, *to make sober-
minded, to admonish*, Tit. ii.
4.*

σωφρονισμός, οῦ, ὁ, *self-control*,
or *discipline*, 2 Tim. i. 7.*

σωφρόνως, adv., *soberly, with
moderation*, Tit. ii. 12.*

σωφροσύνη, ης, ἡ, *soundness of
mind, sanity*, Ac. xxvi. 25;
self-control, sobriety, I Tim.
ii. 9, 15.*

σώ-φρων, ον (σάος, σῶς, *sound*,
and φρήν), *of sound mind,
self-controlled, temperate*, I
Tim. iii. 2; Tit. i. 8, ii. 2, 5.*

T

Τ, τ, ταῦ, *tau, t*, the nineteenth
letter. As a numeral, τ' =
300; ,τ = 300,000.

ταβέρναι, ῶν, αἱ (Lat.), *taverns;*
Ac. xxviii. 15, Τρεῖς Ταβέρ-
ναι, *Three Taverns*, a place
on the Appian Way. (N.T.)*

Ταβθά, ἡ (Aram.), *Tabitha*,
Ac. ix. 36, 40.*

τάγμα, ατος, τό, *an order* or
series, a class, I Cor. xv.
23.*

τακτός, ή, όν, *appointed, fixed*,
Ac. xii. 21.*

ταλαιπωρέω, ῶ, ήσω, *to be distressed, to be miserable*, Ja.
iv. 9.*

ταλαιπωρία, as, ἡ, *hardship,
misery*, Ro. iii. 16; Ja. v.
1.*

ταλαί-πωρος, ον, *afflicted, miserable*, Ro. vii. 24; Rev. iii.
17.*

ταλαντιαῖος, αία, αῖον, *of the
weight of a talent*, Rev. xvi.
21.*

τάλαντον, ου, τό, *a talent*, of
silver or gold, Mat. xviii.
24. The N. T. talent is
probably the Syrian silver
talent, worth about 237 dollars, rather than the Attic,
worth about 1000 dollars.

ταλιθά, ἡ (Aram.), *a damsel*,
Mar. v. 41. (N.T.)*

ταμεῖον (or -μεῖ-), ου, τό, *a store-
chamber*, Lu. xii. 24; *a secret
chamber*, Mat. vi. 6, xxiv. 26;
Lu. xii. 3.*

τανῦν, adv. (τὰ νῦν, *the things
that now are*), *as respects the
present, at present, now*, only
in Ac. (W. H. always write
τὰ νῦν).

τάξις, εως, ἡ, *order, i.e.*, (1)
regular arrangement, Col. ii.
5; (2) *appointed succession*,
Lu. i. 8; (3) *position, rank*,
Heb. v. 6.

ταπεινός, ή, όν, *humble, lowly*,
in condition or in spirit; in
N. T. in a good sense, Ja. i.
9, iv. 6.

ταπεινοφροσύνη, ης, ἡ, *lowliness of mind, humility*, real,
as Phil. ii. 3; or affected, as
Col. ii. 18.

ταπεινό-φρων, ον, *humble*, I Pet.
iii. 8 (W. H. for φιλόφρων).
(S.)*

ταπεινόω, ῶ, ώσω, *to make* or

bring low, Lu. iii. 5; *to
humble, humiliate*, 2 Cor.
xii. 21; pass., *to be humbled*,
Lu. xviii. 14; pass., in mid.
sense, *to humble one's self*,
Ja. iv. 10.

ταπείνωσις, εως, ἡ, *low condition*, in circumstances, Lu. i.
48; *abasement*, in spirit, Ja.
i. 10.

ταράσσω, ξω, *to agitate*, as
water in a pool, Jn. v. 4
(W. H. omit), 7; *to stir
up, to disturb in mind*, with
fear, grief, anxiety, doubt,
Ac. xviii. 8; I Pet. iii.
14.

ταραχή, ῆς, ἡ, *a disturbance*,
Jn. v. 4 (W. H. omit); *a
tumult, sedition*, Mar. xiii. 8
(W. H. omit).*

τάραχος, ου, ὁ, *a disturbance*,
Ac. xix. 23; *commotion*, Ac.
xii. 18.*

Ταρσεύς, έως, ὁ, *one of Tarsus*,
Ac. ix. 11, xxi. 39.*

Ταρσός, οῦ, ἡ, *Tarsus*, Ac. ix.
30.

ταρταρόω, ῶ, ώσω, *to thrust
down to Tartarus (Gehenna)*,
2 Pet. ii. 4. (N.T.)*

τάσσω, ξω, (1) *to assign, arrange*, Ro. xiii. 1; (2) *to determine;* mid., *to appoint*,
Mat. xxviii. 16.

ταῦρος, ου, ὁ, *a bull*, Ac. xiv.
13.

ταὐτά, by crasis for τὰ αὐτά,
the same things.

ταῦτα, see οὗτος.

ταφή, ῆς, ἡ (θάπτω), *a burial*,
Mat. xxvii. 7.*

τάφος, ου, ὁ, *a burial-place, a
sepulchre*, as Mat. xxiii. 27.

τάχα, adv., *quickly; perhaps*,
Ro. v. 7; Philem. 15.*

ταχέως, adv. (ταχύς), *soon,
quickly*, Gal. i. 6; *hastily*,
2 Th. ii. 2; I Tim. v. 22.

ταχινός, ή, όν, *swift, quick*, 2
Pet. i. 14; ii. 1.*

τάχος, ους, τό, *quickness, speed*,
only in the phrase ἐν τάχει,
quickly, speedily, Lu. xviii.
8.

ταχύς, εῖα, ύ, *quick, swift*, only
Ja. i. 19; ταχύ, compar. τά-
χιον (W. H. τάχειον), superl.
τάχιστα, adverbially, *swift-
ly; more, most quickly.*

τέ, conj. of annexation, *and,
both* (see Gr. § 403, Wi. § 53,
2, Bu. 360 sq.).

τεῖχος, ους, τό, *a wall* of a city, Ac. ix. 25.

τεκμήριον, ου, τό, *a sign, a certain proof*, Ac. i. 3.*

τεκνίον, ου, τό (dim. of τέκνον), *a little child*, Jn. xiii. 33; Gal. iv. 19; 1 Jn. ii. 1, 12, 28, iii. 7, 18, iv. 4, v. 21.*

τεκνο-γονέω, ῶ, *to bear children*, 1 Tim. v. 14.*

τεκνο-γονία, ας, ἡ, *child-bearing*, 1 Tim. ii. 15.*

τέκνον, ου, τό (τίκτω), *a child, a descendant; an inhabitant*, Lu. xiii. 34; fig. of various forms of intimate union and relationship, *a disciple, a follower*, Philem. 10; hence, such phrases as τέκνα τῆς σοφίας, τέκνα ὑπακοῆς, τέκνα τοῦ φωτός, *children of wisdom, obedience, the light*, and espec. τέκνα τοῦ θεοῦ, *children of God*, Ro. viii. 16, 17, 21; 1 Jn.

τεκνο-τροφέω, ῶ, *to bring up children*, 1 Tim. v. 10.*

τέκτων, ονος, ὁ, *a carpenter*, Mat. xiii. 55; Mar. vi. 3.*

τέλειος, α, ον, *perfect*, as (1) *complete* in all its parts, Ja. i. 4; (2) *full grown of full age*, Heb. v. 14; (3) specially of the completeness of Christian character, *perfect*, Mat. v. 48. *Syn.:* see ἄρτιος.

τελειότης, τητος, ἡ, *perfectness, perfection*, Col. iii. 14; Heb. vi. 1.*

τελειόω, ῶ, ώσω, (1) *to complete, to finish*, as a course, a race, or the like, Jn. iv. 34; (2) *to accomplish*, as time, or prediction, Lu. ii. 43; Jn. xix. 28; (3) *to make perfect*, Heb. vii. 19; pass., *to be perfected*, Lu. xiii. 32.

τελείως (τέλειος), adv., *perfectly*, 1 Pet. i. 13.*

τελείωσις, εως, ἡ, *completion, fulfillment*, Lu. i. 45; *perfection*, Heb. vii. 11.*

τελειωτής, οῦ, ὁ, *a perfecter*, Heb. xii. 2. (N.T.)*

τελεσ-φορέω, ῶ, *to bring to maturity*, Lu. viii. 14.*

τελευτάω, ῶ, *to end, to finish*, e.g., life; so, *to die*, Mat. ix. 18; Mar. vii. 10.

τελευτή, ῆς, ἡ, *end* of life, *death*, Mat. ii. 15.*

τελέω, ῶ, έσω, τετέλεκα, τετέ-λεσμαι, ἐτελέσθην, (1) *to end, to finish*, Rev. xx. 3, 5, 7; (2) *to fulfill, to accomplish*, Lu. ii. 39; Ja. ii. 8; (3) *to pay*, Mat. xvii. 24.

τέλος, ους, τό, (1) *an end*, Lu. i. 33; (2) *event* or *issue*, Mat. xxvi. 58; (3) *the principal end, aim, purpose*, 1 Tim. i. 5; (4) *a tax*, Mat. xvii. 25; Ro. xiii. 7.

τελώνης, ου, ὁ, *a collector of taxes*, Lu. iii. 12, v. 27.

τελώνιον, ου, τό, *a toll-house, a tax-collector's office*, Mat. ix. 9; Mar. ii. 14; Lu. v. 27.*

τέρας, ατος, τό, *a wonder, a portent;* in N. T. only in plur., and joined with σημεῖα, *signs and wonders*, Ac. vii. 36; Jn. iv. 48. *Syn.:* see δύναμις.

Τέρτιος, ου, ὁ (Lat.), *Tertius*, Ro. xvi. 22.*

Τέρτυλλος, ου, ὁ, *Tertullus*, Ac. xxiv. 1, 2.*

τεσσαράκοντα, *forty*, Mat. iv. 2; Mar. i. 13.

τεσσαρακοντα-ετής, ές, *of forty years*, age or time, Ac. vii. 23, xiii. 18.*

τέσσαρες, τέσσαρα, gen. ων, *four*, Lu. ii. 37; Jn. xi. 17.

τεσσαρες-και-δέκατος, η, ον, ord. num., *fourteenth*, Ac. xxvii. 27, 33.*

τεταρταῖος, αια, αἶον, *of the fourth* (day); τεταρταῖός ἐστιν, *he has been dead four days*, Jn. xi. 39.*

τέταρτος, η, ον, ord. num., *fourth*, Mat. xiv. 25.

τετρά-γωνος, ον, *four-cornered, square*, Rev. xxi. 16.*

τετράδιον, ου, τό, *a quaternion*, or *guard of four soldiers*, Ac. xii. 4.*

τετρακισ-χίλιοι, αι, α, *four thousand*, Mar. viii. 9, 20.

τετρακόσιοι, αι, α, *four hundred*, Ac. v. 36.

τετρά-μηνος, ον, *of four months;* sc. χρόνος, *a period of four months*, Jn. iv. 35.*

τετρα-πλόος, οῦς, ῆ, οῦν, *fourfold*, Lu. xix. 8.*

τετρά-πους, ουν, gen. οδος, *four-footed*, Ac. x. 12, xi. 6; Ro. i. 23.*

τετρ-αρχέω (W.H.τετρααρχέω), ῶ, *to rule over* as a tetrarch (gen.), Lu. iii. 1.*

τετρ-άρχης (W.H.τετρααρχης), ου, ὁ, *a ruler over a fourth part of a region, a tetrarch*, applied also to rulers over any small dominion, Mat. xiv. 1.

τεύχω, see τυγχάνω.

τεφρόω, ῶ, ώσω (τέφρα, *ashes*), *to reduce to ashes*, 2 Pet. ii. 6.*

τέχνη, ης, ἡ, (1) *art, skill*, Ac. xvii. 29; (2) *an art, a trade*, Ac. xviii. 3; Rev. xviii. 22.*

τεχνίτης, ου, ὁ, *an artificer, craftsman*, Ac. xix. 24, 38; Rev. xviii. 22; used of God, Heb. xi. 10.* *Syn.:* see δημιουργός.

τήκω, *to make liquid;* pass., *to melt*, 2 Pet. iii. 12.*

τηλ-αυγῶς, adv. (τῆλε, *afar*, αὐγή, *radiance*), *clearly, distinctly*, Mar. viii. 25.*

τηλικ-οῦτος, αύτη, οῦτο, *so great*, 2 Cor. i. 10; Heb. ii. 3; Ja. iii. 4; Rev. xvi. 18.*

τηρέω, ῶ, ήσω, *to watch carefully*, with good or evil design; (1) *to guard*, Mat. xxvii. 36, 54; (2) *to keep* or *reserve*, 1 Cor. vii. 37; (3) *to observe, keep*, enactments or ordinances, Jn. xiv. 15, 21.

τήρησις, εως, ἡ, (1) *a prison*, Ac. iv. 3, v. 18; (2) *observance*, as of precepts, 1 Cor. vii. 19.*

Τιβεριάς, άδος, ἡ, *Tiberias*, Jn. vi. 1, 23, xxi. 1.*

Τιβέριος, ου, ὁ, *Tiberius*, Lu. iii. 1.*

τίθημι, θήσω (see Gr. § 107, Wi. § 14, 1, Bu. 45 sq.), (1) *to place, set, lay, put forth, put down, put away, put aside;* mid., *to cause to put*, or *to put for one's self;* (2) *to constitute, to make, to render;* mid., *to assign, determine.*

τίκτω, τέξομαι, 2d aor. ἔτεκον, 1st aor. pass. ἐτέχθην, *to bear, to bring forth*, of women, Lu. i. 57, ii. 6, 7; *to produce*, of the earth, Heb. vi. 7.

τίλλω, *to pluck, to pluck off*, Mat. xii. 1; Mar. ii. 23; Lu. vi. 1.*

Τιμαῖος, ου, ὁ, *Timaeus*, Mar. x. 46.*

τιμάω, ῶ, ήσω, (1) *to estimate, to value at a price*, Mat. xxvii. 9; (2) *to honor, to reverence*, Mar. vii. 6, 10.

τιμή, ῆς, ἡ, (1) a price, Mat.
xxvii. 6, 9; (2) honor, Ro. ix.
21; Heb. v. 4; 2 Tim. ii. 20,
21; 1 Pet. ii. 7.

τίμιος, a, ov, of great price, precious, honored, Rev. xvii. 4;
Heb. xiii. 4.

τιμιότης, τητος, ἡ, preciousness,
costliness, Rev. xviii. 19.*

Τιμό-θεος, ου, ὁ, Timothy, Ac.
xvii. 14, 15.

Τίμων, ωνος, ὁ, Timon, Ac. vi.
5.*

τιμωρέω, ῶ, to punish (acc.), Ac.
xxii. 5, xxvi. 11.*

τιμωρία, ας, ἡ, punishment,
penalty, Heb. x. 29.*

τίνω, τίσω, to pay; with δίκην,
to pay penalty, suffer punishment, 2 Th. i. 9.*

τὶς, τὶ, gen. τινός (enclitic),
indef. pron., any one, some
one (see Gr. § 352, Wi. § 25,
2, Bu. 85, 93).

τίς, τί, gen. τίνος; interrogative pron., who? which?
what? (see Gr. § 350, Wi.
§ 25, 1, Bu. 115, 138).

Τίτιος, ου, ὁ, Titius, Ac. xviii.
7 (W. H.).*

τίτλος, ου, ὁ (Lat.), a title, an
inscription, Jn. xix. 19, 20.*

Τίτος, ου, ὁ, Titus, 2 Cor. vii.
6, 13, 14.

τοι, an enclitic part., truly, indeed; see καίτοιγε, μέντοι,
τοιγαροῦν, τοίνυν.

τοι-γαρ-οῦν, consequently, therefore, 1 Th. iv. 8; Heb. xii. 1.*

τοί-γε, although (in καίτοιγε).

τοί-νυν, indeed now, therefore,
Lu. xx. 25; 1 Cor. ix. 26;
Heb. xiii. 13; Ja. ii. 24 (not
W. H.).*

τοιόσ-δε, τοιάδε, τοιόνδε, demonst. pron., of this kind,
such, 2 Pet. i. 17.*

τοιοῦτος, τοιαύτη, τοιοῦτο, demonst. denoting quality (as
τοσοῦτος denotes quantity,
and οὗτος simply deter-
mines), of such a kind, such,
so, used either with or without a noun, the corresponding relative is οἷος, as, only
Mar. xiii. 19; 1 Cor. xv. 48;
2 Cor. x. 11; once ὁποῖος,
Ac. xxvi. 29. For τοιοῦτος
with the article, see Gr.
§ 220, Wi. § 18, 4, Bu. 87.

τοῖχος, ου, ὁ, a wall of a house,
Ac. xxiii. 3; disting. from
τεῖχος, a wall of a city.*

τόκος, ου, ὁ (a bringing forth),
interest, usury, Mat. xxv. 27;
Lu. xix. 23.*

τολμάω, ῶ, ήσω, (1) to dare
(inf.), Mar. xi. 34; (2) to endure, Ro. v. 7; (3) to be bold,
2 Cor. xi. 21.

τολμηρότερον (τολμηρός), neut.
compar. as adv., more boldly,
Ro. xv. 15 (W. H. τολμηροτέρως).*

τολμητής, οῦ, ὁ, a daring, presumptuous man, 2 Pet. ii.
10.*

τομός, ή, όν, sharp, keen, comp.
τομώτερος, Heb. iv. 12.*

τόξον, ου, τό, a bow, Rev. vi.
2.*

τοπάζιον, ου, τό, topaz, Rev.
xxi. 20. (N. T.)*

τόπος, ου, ὁ, (1) a place, i.e.,
a district or region, or a particular spot in a region; (2)
the place one occupies, the
room, an abode, a seat, a
sheath for a sword; (3) a
passage in a book; (4) state,
condition; (5) opportunity.

τοσοῦτος, τοσαύτη, τοσοῦτο, demonst. pron. denoting quantity (see τοιοῦτος), so great,
so much, so long; plur., so
many.

τότε, demonst. adv., then.

τοὐναντίον, for τὸ ἐναντίον, on
the contrary, 2 Cor. ii. 7;
Gal. ii. 7; 1 Pet. iii. 9.*

τοὔνομα, for τὸ ὄνομα, acc. ab-
sol., by name, Mat. xxvii.
57.*

τουτέστι, for τοῦτ᾽ ἔστι (W.
H. prefer the uncontracted
form), that is, Ac. i. 19; Ro.
x. 6, 7, 8.

τοῦτο, neut. of οὗτος, which
see.

τράγος, ου, ὁ, a he-goat, Heb.
ix. 12, 13, 19, x. 4.*

τράπεζα, ης, ἡ, a table, (1) for
food and banqueting, Mat.
xv. 27; met., food, Ac. xvi.
34; (2) for money-changing
or business, Mar. xi. 15.

τραπεζίτης, ον, ὁ, a money-
changer, a banker, Mat. xxv.
27.*

τραῦμα, ατος, τό, a wound, Lu.
x. 34.*

τραυματίζω, ίσω, to wound, Lu.
xx. 12; Ac. xix. 16.*

τραχηλίζω, in pass., to be laid
bare, to be laid open, Heb. iv.
13.*

τράχηλος, ου, ὁ, the neck, Lu.
xv. 20; Ro. xvi. 4.

τραχύς, εῖα, ύ, rough, as ways,
Lu. iii. 5; as rocks in the
sea, Ac. xxvii. 29.*

Τραχωνῖτις, ιδος, ἡ, Trachonitis, the N.E. of the territory beyond Jordan, Lu.
iii. 1.*

τρεῖς, τρία, three, Mat. xii. 40.

τρέμω, to tremble, Mar. v. 33;
Lu. viii. 47; Ac. ix. 6 (W. H.
omit); to be afraid, 2 Pet. ii.
10.*

τρέφω, θρέψω, perf. pass. part.
τεθραμμένος, to feed, to nourish, Mat. vi. 26; Ac. xii. 20;
Ja. v. 5; to bring up, rear,
Lu. iv. 16.

τρέχω, 2d aor. ἔδραμον, (1) to
run, in general, Lu. xv. 20;
(2) to exert one's self, Ro. ix
16; (3) to make progress, as
doctrine, 2 Th. iii. 1.

τρῆμα, ατος, τό, a perforation,
the eye of a needle, Mat. xix.
24 (W. H.); Lu. xviii. 25
(W. H.).*

τριάκοντα, οἱ, αἱ, τά, indecl.,
thirty, Mat. xiii. 8.

τριακόσιοι, αι, α, three hundred, Mar. xiv. 5; Jn. xii.
5.*

τρίβολος, ου, ὁ, a thistle, Mat.
vii. 16; Heb. vi. 8.*

τρίβος, ου, ἡ, a worn path, a
beaten way, Mat. iii. 3; Mar.
i. 3; Lu. iii. 4.*

τρι-ετία, ας, ἡ, a space of three
years, Ac. xx. 31.*

τρίζω, to grate, to gnash, as the
teeth, Mar. ix. 18.*

τρί-μηνος, ον, of three months,
neut. as subst., Heb. xi.
23.*

τρίς, num. adv., thrice, Mat.
xxvi. 34, 75.

τρί-στεγος, ον, having three
stories; neut., the third story,
Ac. xx. 9.*

τρισ-χίλιοι, αι, α, three thousand, Ac. ii. 41.*

τρίτος, η, ον, ord. num., third;
neut. τὸ τρίτον, the third
part, Rev. viii. 7; the third
time, Mar. xiv. 41; ἐκ τρίτου,
the third time, Mat. xxvi. 44;
τῇ τρίτῃ (sc. ἡμέρᾳ), on the
third day, Lu. xiii. 32.

τρίχες, plur. of θρίξ, which
see.

τρίχινος, η, ον, made of hair,
Rev. vi. 12.*

τρόμος, ου, ὁ, *a trembling,* from fear, Mar. xvi. 8.

τροπή, ῆς, ἡ, *a turning,* Ja. i. 17 (see R.V.).*

τρόπος, ου, ὁ, (1) *way, manner;* ὃν τρόπον, *in like manner as, as,* Mat. xxiii. 37; (2) *manner of life, character,* Heb. xiii. 5.

τροπο-φορέω, ῶ, ήσω, *to bear with the disposition* or *character* of others, Ac. xiii. 18 (Rec. W. H., some read ἐτροφοφόρησεν, *he bore them as a nurse*). (S.)*

τροφή, ῆς, ἡ, *food, nourishment,* Mat. iii. 4, vi. 25.

Τρόφιμος, ου, ὁ, *Trophimus,* Ac. xx. 4, xxi. 29; 2 Tim. iv. 20.*

τροφός, οῦ, ἡ, *a nurse,* 1 Th. ii. 7.*

τροφο-φορέω, ῶ, see τροποφορέω.

τροχιά, ᾶς, ἡ, *a track of a wheel, a path,* fig., Heb. xii. 13.*

τροχός, οῦ, ὁ, *a wheel,* Ja. iii. 6.*

τρύβλιον, ου, τό, *a deep dish, a platter,* Mat. xxvi. 23; Mar. xiv. 20.*

τρυγάω, ῶ, ήσω, *to gather,* as the vintage, Lu. vi. 44; Rev. xiv. 18, 19.*

τρυγών, όνος, ἡ (τρύζω), *a turtledove,* Lu. ii. 24.*

τρυμαλιά, ᾶς, ἡ, *the eye* of a needle, Mar. x. 25; Lu. xviii. 25 (W. H. τρῆμα).*

τρύπημα, ατος, τ᷍ὸ, *a hole, the eye* of a needle, Mat. xix. 24 (W. H. text τρῆμα).*

Τρύφαινα, ης, ἡ, *Tryphæna,* Ro. xvi. 12.*

τρυφάω, ῶ, ήσω, *to live luxuriously and effeminately,* Ja. v. 5.* *Syn.:* see σπαταλάω.

τρυφή, ῆς, ἡ, *effeminate luxury,* Lu. vii. 25; 2 Pet. ii. 13.*

Τρυφῶσα, ης, ἡ, *Tryphosa,* Ro. xvi. 12.*

Τρωάς, άδος, ἡ, *Troas,* a city of Mysia, properly *Alexandria Troas,* Ac. xvi. 8, 11.

Τρωγύλλιον, ου, τό, *Trogyllium,* Ac. xx. 15 (W. H. omit).*

τρώγω, *to eat,* Mat. xxiv. 38; Jn. vi. 54–58, xiii. 18.*

τυγχάνω, 2d aor. ἔτυχον, perf. τέτυχα, (1) *to obtain, to get possession of* (gen.), Lu. xx. 35; Ac. xxiv. 2; (2) *io fall*

out, to happen, to happen to be; εἰ τύχοι, *if it should chance, it may be, perhaps,* 1 Cor. xiv. 10; 2d aor., part., τυχών, *ordinary, commonplace,* Ac. xix. 11; neut. τυχόν, *it may be, perhaps,* 1 Cor. xvi. 6.

τυμπανίζω, *to beat to death when stretched on a wheel,* Heb. xi. 35.*

τυπικῶς, adv., *typically, by way of example,* 1 Cor. x. 11 (W. H.). (N. T.)*

τύπος, ου, ὁ, (1) *a mark, an impression,* produced by a blow, Jn. xx. 25; (2) *the figure of a thing, a pattern,* Ac. vii. 44; Heb. viii. 5; (3) *an emblem, an example,* 1 Cor. x. 6; Phil. iii. 17; (4) *the form* or *contents* of a letter, Ac. xxiii. 25; (5) *a type,* Ro. v. 14.

τύπτω, ψω, *to beat, to strike,* as the breast in grief, Lu. xviii. 13; *to inflict punishment,* Ac. xxiii. 3; *to wound* or *disquiet* the conscience, 1 Cor. viii. 12.

Τύραννος, ου, ὁ, *Tyrannus,* Ac. xix. 9.*

τυρβάζω, *to agitate* or *disturb in mind,* Lu. x. 41 (W. H. θορυβάζω).*

Τύριος, ου, ὁ, ἡ (prop. adj.), *a Tyrian,* an inhabitant of Tyre, Ac. xii. 20.*

Τύρος, ου, ἡ, *Tyre,* a city of Phœnicia, Mat. xi. 21, 22.

τυφλός, ή, όν, *blind,* (1) physically, Lu. xiv. 13, 21; (2) mentally, *i.e., stupid, dull of apprehension,* Ro. ii. 19; 2 Pet. i. 9.

τυφλόω, ῶ, ώσω, fig., *to make blind* or *dull of apprehension,* Jn. xii. 40; 2 Cor. iv. 4; 1 Jn. ii. 11.*

τυφόω, ῶ, *to raise a smoke;* pass., fig., *to be proud, to be arrogant* and *conceited,* 1 Tim. iii. 6, vi. 4; 2 Tim. iii. 4.*

τύφω, pres. pass. part. τυφόμενος, *smoking,* Mat. xii. 20.*

τυφωνικός, ή, όν, *violent, tempestuous,* Ac. xxvii. 14.*

Τυχικός, or **Τύχικος** (W. H.), ου, ὁ, *Tychichus,* 2 Tim. iv. 12.

τυχόν, see τυγχάνω.

Υ

Υ, υ, ὕψιλον, *upsilon, u,* the twentieth letter. As a numeral, υ′ = 400; ,υ = 400,000. At the commencement of a word, υ is always aspirated.

ὑακίνθινος, η, ον, *of the color of hyacinth, dark purple,* Rev. ix. 17.*

ὑάκινθος, ου, ὁ, a precious stone of the color of hyacinth, *jacinth,* Rev. xxi. 20.*

ὑάλινος, η, ον, *glassy, transparent,* Rev. iv. 6, xv. 2.*

ὕαλος, ου, ὁ, *glass,* Rev. xxi. 18, 21.*

ὑβρίζω, σω, *to treat with insolence, to insult,* Mat. xxii. 6; Lu. xi. 45.

ὕβρις, εως, ἡ, (1) *insolence, insult,* 2 Cor. xii. 10; (2) *damage, loss,* Ac. xxvii. 10, 21.*

ὑβριστής, οῦ, ὁ, *an insolent, insulting man,* Ro. i. 30; 1 Tim. i. 13.*

ὑγιαίνω, *to be well, to be in health,* Lu. v. 31, xv. 27; fig., *to be sound,* in (ἐν) *faith,* doctrine, etc., Tit. i. 13; part. ὑγιαίνων, *healthful, wholesome,* of instruction, 1 Tim. i. 10.

ὑγιής, ές, (1) *sound, whole,* in health, Mat. xii. 13; Jn. v. 11, 15; (2) fig., *wholesome,* of teaching, Tit. ii. 8.

ὑγρός, ά, όν, *moist, green, i.e.* full of sap, Lu. xxiii. 31.*

ὑδρία, ας, ἡ, *a water-pot,* Jn. ii. 6, 7, iv. 28.*

ὑδρο-ποτέω, ῶ, *to be a water-drinker,* 1 Tim. v. 23.*

ὑδρωπικός, ή, όν, *dropsical,* Lu. xiv. 2.*

ὕδωρ, ὕδατος, τό, *water;* ὕδατα, *waters, streams,* Jn. iii. 23; also *a body of water,* as Mat. xiv. 28; ὕδωρ ζῶν, *living* or *running water;* fig., of spiritual truth, Jn. iv. 14.

ὑετός, οῦ, ὁ (ὕω, *to rain*), *rain,* Heb. vi. 7.

υἱοθεσία, ας, ἡ, *adoption* as a son, into the divine family, Ro. viii. 15, 23, ix. 4: Gal. iv. 5; Ep. i. 5.*

υἱός, οῦ, ὁ, *a son,* Mat. x. 37; *a descendant,* Lu. xx. 41, 44; *the offspring* or *young* of an animal, Mat. xxi. 5; *an adopted son,* Heb. xi. 24 · of various forms of close union and relationship (see τέκνον) ; *a disciple* or *follower*, Mat. xii. 27 ; *one who resembles* (gen.), Mat. v. 45 ; *one who partakes of any quality* or *character*, Lu. x. 6 ; Jn. xii. 36 ; ὁ υἱὸς τοῦ ἀνθρώπου, *son of man* (once only without art., Jn. v. 27), very often used by our Lord of himself (only once by another of him, Ac. vii. 56) ; *sons of men* denote *men* generally, Mar. iii. 28 ; Ep. iii. 5 ; υἱὸς τοῦ θεοῦ, *son of God*, used of men, Lu. xx. 36 ; Heb. ii. 10 ; usually of Christ, Mat. viii. 29 ; Jn. ix. 35 ; see also Gr. § 217 c.

ὕλη, ης, ἡ, *wood, fuel*, Ja. iii. 5.*

ὑμεῖς, plur. of σύ, which see.

Ὑμέναιος, ου, ὁ, *Hymenæus*, 1 Tim. i. 20 ; 2 Tim. ii. 17.*

ὑμέτερος, α, ον, possess. pron., *your*, as belonging to, or as proceeding from ; for the use of the article with the word, see Gr. § 223.

ὑμνέω, ῶ, ήσω, *to sing hymns to* (acc.), Ac. xvi. 25 ; Heb. ii. 12 ; *to sing*, Mat. xxvi. 30 ; Mar. xiv. 26.*

ὕμνος, ου, ὁ, *a hymn, a sacred song*, Ep. v. 19 ; Col. iii. 16.* *Syn.*: ψαλμός is used of the Psalms of the O. T. ; ὕμνος designates a song of *praise* to God ; ᾠδή is a general expression for a song.

ὑπ-άγω, *to go away, to depart*, Mar. vi. 31 ; Jn. vi. 67 ; imperat., sometimes an expression of aversion, *begone*, Mat. iv. 10 ; sometimes a farewell only, Mat. viii. 13, 32 ; *to die*, Mat. xxvi. 24.

ὑπ-ακοή, ῆς, ἡ, *obedience*, Ro. vi. 16. (S.)

ὑπ-ακούω, σω, (1) *to listen*, as at a door, to find who seeks admission, only Ac. xii. 13 ; (2) *to hearken to ;* hence, *to obey* (dat.), Mat. viii. 27 ; Heb. xi. 8.

ὑπ-ανδρος, ον, *subject to a husband, married*, Ro. vii. 2.*

ὑπ-αντάω, ῶ, ήσω, *to meet* (dat.), Mat. viii. 28.

ὑπ-άντησις, εως, ἡ, *a meeting*, Mat. viii. 34 (W. H.), xxv. 1 (W. H.) ; Jn. xii. 13. (S.)*

ὕπαρξις, εως, ἡ, *goods, substance*,

property, Ac. ii. 45 ; Heb. x. 34.*

ὑπ-άρχω, *to begin to be ; to be originally, to subsist ;* hence generally, *to be*, Lu. viii. 41 ; Ac. xxi. 20 ; with dat. of pers., *to have, to possess*, Ac. iii. 6, iv. 37 ; part., neut. pl., τὰ ὑπάρχοντα, *things which one possesses, goods, property*, Mat. xix. 21.

ὑπ-είκω, *to yield, to submit to authority*, Heb. xiii. 17.*

ὑπ-εναντίος, α, ον, *opposite to, adverse*, Col. ii. 14 ; as subst., *an adversary*, Heb. x. 27.*

ὑπέρ, prep., gov. gen. and acc.: with gen., *over, for, on behalf of ;* with acc., *above, superior to* (see Gr. § 303, Wi. § 47 l, Bu. 335) ; adverbially, *above, more*, 2 Cor. xi. 23. In composition, ὑπέρ denotes *superiority* (above), or *aid* (on behalf of).

ὑπερ-αίρω, in mid., *to lift up one's self, to exalt one's self, to be arrogant*, 2 Cor. xii. 7 ; 2 Th. ii. 4.*

ὑπέρ-ακμος, ον, *past the bloom of youth*, 1 Cor. vii. 36.*

ὑπέρ-άνω, adv. (gen.), *above*, Ep. i. 21, iv. 10 ; Heb. ix. 5.*

ὑπερ-αυξάνω, *to increase exceedingly*, 2 Th. i. 3.*

ὑπερ-βαίνω, *to go beyond, to overreach, defraud*, 1 Th. iv. 6.*

ὑπερ-βαλλόντως, adv., *beyond measure*, 2 Cor. xi. 23.*

ὑπερ-βάλλω, intrans., *to surpass ;* N.T., only pres. part. ὑπερβάλλων, *surpassing, excelling*, 2 Cor. iii. 10, ix. 14 ; Ep. i. 19, ii. 7, iii. 19.*

ὑπερ-βολή, ῆς, ἡ, *excess, surpassing excellence, pre-eminence*, 2 Cor. iv. 7, xii. 7 ; καθ᾽ ὑπερβολήν, as adv., *exceedingly*, Ro. vii. 13 ; 1 Cor. xii. 31 ; 2 Cor. i. 8 ; Gal. i. 13 ; καθ᾽ ὑπερβολὴν εἰς ὑπερβολήν, *more and more exceedingly* (R. V.), 2 Cor. iv. 17.*

ὑπερ-εῖδον, *to overlook, to take no notice of*, Ac. xvii. 30.*

ὑπερ-έκεινα, adv., *beyond*, 2 Cor. x. 16. (N. T.)*

ὑπερ-εκ-περισσοῦ, adv., *beyond all measure, in the highest degree*, Ep. iii. 20 ; 1 Th. iii. 10, v. 13.*

ὑπερ-εκ-τείνω, *to stretch out be*-

yond *measure*, 2 Cor. x. 14.*

ὑπερ-εκ-χύνω, pass., *to be poured out, to overflow*, Lu. vi. 38.*

ὑπερ-εν-τυγχάνω, *to intercede for*, Ro. viii. 26. (N. T.)*

ὑπερ-έχω, *to excel, to surpass* (gen.), *to be supreme ;* N.T. only pres. part., Ro. xiii. 1 ; Phil. ii. 3, iv. 7 ; 1 Pet. ii. 13 ; part. neut. τὸ ὑπερέχον, *excellency, super-eminence*, Phil. iii. 8.*

ὑπερηφανία, ας, ἡ, *pride, arrogance*, Mar. vii. 22.*

ὑπερ-ήφανος, ον, *proud, arrogant*, Ja. iv. 6.

ὑπερ-λίαν, adv., *very much, pre-eminently*, 2 Cor. xi. 5, xii. 11.*

ὑπερ-νικάω, ῶ, *to be more than conqueror*, Ro. viii. 37. (N. T.)*

ὑπέρ-ογκος, ον, *immoderate, boastful*, of language, 2 Pet. ii. 18 ; Ju. 16.*

ὑπερ-οχή, ῆς, ἡ, *superiority, excellence*, 1 Cor. ii. 1 ; 1 Tim. ii. 2.*

ὑπερ-περισσεύω, *to superabound*, Ro. v. 20 ; pass., *to be very abundant in* (dat.), 2 Cor. vii. 4. (N. T.)*

ὑπερ-περισσῶς, adv., *superabundantly, beyond measure*, Mar. vii. 37. (N. T.)*

ὑπερ-πλεονάζω, *to be exceedingly abundant*, 1 Tim. i. 14.*

ὑπερ-υψόω, ῶ, *to highly exalt*, Phil. ii. 9. (S.)*

ὑπερ-φρονέω, ῶ, *to think too highly of one's self*, Ro. xii. 3.*

ὑπερῷον, ου, τό, *the upper part of a house, an upper chamber*, Ac. i. 13, ix. 37, 39, xx. 8.*

ὑπ-έχω, *to submit to, to undergo* (acc.), Ju. 7.*

ὑπ-ήκοος, ον, *listening to, obedient*, Ac. vii. 39 ; 2 Cor. ii. 9 ; Phil. ii. 8.*

ὑπηρετέω, ῶ, *to minister to, to serve* (dat.), Ac. xiii. 36, xx. 34, xxiv. 23.*

ὑπ-ηρέτης, ου, ὁ (ἐρέτης, *a rower*), *a servant, attendant*, specially (1) *an officer, a lictor*, Mat. v. 25 ; (2) *an attendant in a synagogue*, Lu. iv. 20 ; (3) *a minister of the gospel*, Ac. xxvi. 16.

ὕπνος, ου, ὁ, *sleep*, Lu. ix. 32 ;

fig., *spiritual sleep*, Ro. xiii. 11.

ὑπό, prep., gov. gen. and acc., *under:* with gen., *by,* generally signifying the agent; with acc., *under, beneath,* of place, of time, or of subjection to authority (see Gr. § 304, Wi. §§ 47 *b*, 49 *k*, Bu. 340 sq.). In composition, ὑπό denotes *subjection, diminution, concealment.*

ὑπο-βάλλω, *to suborn, to instruct privately,* Ac. vi. 11.*

ὑπο-γραμμός, οῦ, ὁ, *a writing-copy; an example,* 1 Pet. ii. 21.*

ὑπό-δειγμα, ατος, τό, (1) *a figure, copy,* Heb. viii. 5, ix. 23; (2) *an example* for imitation, or for warning, Jn. xiii. 15; Heb. iv. 11; 2 Pet. ii. 6; Ja. v. 10.*

ὑπο-δείκνυμι, δείξω, *to show plainly,* to *teach, to warn,* Mat. iii. 7; Lu. iii. 7, vi. 47, xii. 5; Ac. ix. 16, xx. 35.*

ὑπο-δέχομαι, *to receive as a guest* (acc.), Lu. x. 38, xix. 6; Ac. xvii. 7, Ja. ii. 25.*

ὑπο-δέω, ῶ, ήσω, in mid., *to bind on one's sandals, be shod with* (acc.), Mar. vi. 9; Ac. xii. 8; Ep. vi. 15 (lit., *shod as to your feet*).*

ὑπόδημα, ατος, τό, *a sandal,* Mat. iii. 11, x. 10.

ὑπό-δικος, ον, *subject to judgment, under penalty to* (dat.), Ro. iii. 19.*

ὑπο-ζύγιον, ου, τό, *an animal under yoke, an ass,* Mat. xxi. 5; 2 Pet. ii. 16.*

ὑπο-ζώννυμι, *to under-gird,* as a ship for strength against the waves, Ac. xxvii. 17.*

ὑπο-κάτω, adv., *underneath* (as prep. with gen.), Rev. v. 3, 13.

ὑπο-κρίνομαι, dep., *to act under a mask, to personate, to feign* (acc., inf.), Lu. xx. 20.*

ὑπό-κρισις, εως, ἡ, lit., *stage playing; hypocrisy, dissembling,* 1 Tim. iv. 2.

ὑπο-κριτής, οῦ, ὁ, lit., *a stage player; a hypocrite, a dissembler,* Mat. vi. 2, 5, 16.

ὑπο-λαμβάνω, 2d aor. ὑπέλαβον, (1) *to take from under, to receive up,* Ac. i. 9; (2) *to take up a discourse, to answer,* Lu. x. 30; (3) *to think, to*

suppose, Lu. vii. 43; Ac. ii. 15; (4) *to receive, welcome,* 3 Jn. 8 (W. H.).*

ὑπό-λειμμα (or -λιμμα), ατος, τό, *a remnant,* Ro. ix. 27 (W. H.).*

ὑπο-λείπω, *to leave behind,* pass., Ro. xi. 3.*

ὑπο-λήνιον, ου, τό (ληνός), *a wine-vat, a pit under the wine-press,* dug in the ground, Mar. xii. 1. (S.)*

ὑπο-λιμπάνω, *to leave behind,* 1 Pet. ii. 21.*

ὑπο-μένω, μενῶ, (1) *to remain, tarry behind,* Lu. ii. 43; (2) *to bear up under, to endure* (acc.), 1 Pet. ii. 20; (3) *to persevere, to remain constant,* Mat. x. 22.

ὑπο-μιμνήσκω, ὑπομνήσω, 1st aor. pass. ὑπεμνήσθην, *to remind* (acc. of pers.), Jn. xiv. 26; mid., *to be reminded, to remember,* only Lu. xxii. 61.

ὑπό-μνησις, εως, ἡ, (1) *remembrance, recollection,* 2 Tim. i. 5; (2) *a putting in mind,* 2 Pet. i. 13, iii. 1.*

ὑπο-μονή, ῆς, ἡ, *a bearing up under, endurance, steadfastness, patient waiting for* (gen.), Lu. viii. 15; 2 Th. iii. 5. *Syn.:* see ἀνοχή.

ὑπο-νοέω, ῶ, *to conjecture, to suppose,* Ac. xiii. 25, xxv. 18, xxvii. 27.*

ὑπό-νοια, ας, ἡ, *a surmising, suspicion,* 1 Tim. vi. 4.*

ὑπο-πλέω, 1st aor. ὑπέπλευσα, *to sail under, i.e., to leeward of* (acc.), Ac. xxvii. 4, 7.*

ὑπο-πνέω, 1st aor. ὑπέπνευσα, *to blow gently,* of the wind, Ac. xxvii. 13.*

ὑπο-πόδιον, ου, τό, *a footstool,* Lu. xx. 43; Ac. ii. 35.*

ὑπό-στασις, εως, ἡ, *that which underlies;* hence, (1) *the substance, the reality* underlying mere appearance, Heb. i. 3; (2) *confidence, assurance,* 2 Cor. ix. 4, xi. 17; Heb. iii. 14, xi. 1.*

ὑπο-στέλλω, 1st aor. ὑπέστειλα, *to draw back,* Gal. ii. 12; mid., *to shrink, to draw one's self back,* Ac. xx. 27; Heb. x. 38; *to withhold, conceal* (acc.), Ac. xx. 20.*

ὑπο-στολή, ῆς, ἡ, *a shrinking, a drawing back,* Heb. x. 39.*

ὑπο-στρέφω, ψω, *to turn back,*

to return, intrans., Lu. ii. 43, viii. 37, 40.

ὑπο-στρώννυμι, or -ννύω, *to spread under,* Lu. xix. 36. (S.)*

ὑπο-ταγή, ῆς, ἡ, *subjection, submission,* 2 Cor. ix. 13; Gal. ii. 5; 1 Tim. ii. 11, iii. 4.*

ὑπο-τάσσω, ξω, 2d aor. pass. ὑπετάγην, *to place under, to subject,* 1 Cor. xv. 27; mid., *to submit one's self, to be obedient,* Ro. xiii. 5; Ep. v. 21.

ὑπο-τίθημι, *to set* or *put under, to lay down,* Ro. xvi. 4; mid., *to suggest to, put in mind,* 1 Tim. iv. 6.*

ὑπο-τρέχω, 2d aor. ὑπέδραμον, *to run under* lee or shelter of, Ac. xxvii. 16.*

ὑπο-τύπωσις, εως, ἡ, *pattern, example,* 1 Tim. i. 16; 2 Tim. i. 13.*

ὑπο-φέρω, 1st aor. ὑπήνεγκα, *to bear up under, to sustain, to endure,* 1 Cor. x. 13; 2 Tim. iii. 11; 1 Pet. ii. 19.*

ὑπο-χωρέω, ῶ, ήσω, *to withdraw, to retire,* Lu. v. 16, ix. 10.*

ὑπωπιάζω, *to strike under the eye;* hence, (1) *to bruise;* fig., *to buffet,* 1 Cor. ix. 27; (2) *to weary out,* by repeated application, Lu. xviii. 5.*

ὗς, ὑός, ὁ, ἡ, *a hog, boar* or *sow,* 2 Pet. ii. 22.*

ὕσσωπος, ου, ἡ (from Heb.), *hyssop, a stalk* or *stem of hyssop,* Jn. xix. 29; *a bunch of hyssop* for sprinkling, Heb. ix. 19. (S.)*

ὑστερέω, ῶ, ήσω, *to be behind;* abs., *to be lacking, to fall short,* Jn. ii. 3; with obj., *to be lacking* in, acc., Mat. xix. 20; gen., Lu. xxii. 35; ἀπό, Heb. xii. 15; *to be lacking,* Mar. x. 21; pass., *to lack, to come short,* 1 Cor i. 7, viii. 8; *to suffer need,* Lu. xv. 14.

ὑστέρημα, ατος, τό, (1) *that which is lacking* from (gen.), Col. i. 24; 1 Th. iii. 10; (2) *poverty, destitution,* Lu. xxi. 4. (S.)

ὑστέρησις, εως, ἡ, *poverty, penury,* Mar. xii. 44; Phil. iv. 11. (N. T.)*

ὕστερος, α, ον, compar., *later,* only 1 Tim. iv. 1 and Mat. xxi. 31 (W. H.); neut. as an adv., *lastly, afterward,* with gen., Mat. xxii. 27; Lu. xx. 32.

ὑφαντός, ή, όν (ὑφαίνω, to weave), woven, Jn. xix. 23.*

ὑψηλός, ή, όν, high, lofty, lit. or fig., τὰ ὑψηλά, things that are high, Ro. xii. 16; ἐν ὑψηλοῖς, on high, Heb. i. 3.

ὑψηλο-φρονέω, ῶ, to be high-minded, proud, Ro. xi. 20 (W.H. ὑψηλὰ φρόνει); 1 Tim. vi. 17. (N. T.)*

ὕψιστος, η, ον (superlat. of ὕψι, highly), highest, most high; neut., plur., the highest places, the heights, i.e., heaven, Lu. ii. 14; ὁ ὕψιστος, the Most High, i.e., God, Ac. vii. 48, xvi. 17; Lu. i. 32, 35, 76.

ὕψος, ους, τό, height, opp. to βάθος, Ep. iii. 18; Rev. xxi. 16; ἐξ ὕψους, from on high, i.e., from heaven, Lu. i. 78, xxiv. 49; so εἰς ὕψος, to heaven, Ep. iv. 8; fig., high station, Ja. i. 9.*

ὑψόω, ῶ, ώσω, (1) to raise on high, to lift up, as the brazen serpent, and Jesus on the cross, Jn. iii. 14, viii. 28; (2) to exalt, to set on high, Ac. ii. 33; Mat. xxiii. 12.

ὕψωμα, ατος, τό, height, Ro. viii. 39; barrier, bulwark (fig.), 2 Cor. x. 5.*

Φ

Φ, φ, φῖ, phi, ph, the twenty-first letter. As a numeral, φ′ = 500; ͵φ = 500,000.

φάγος, ου, ὁ, a glutton, Mat. xi. 19; Lu. vii. 34. (N. T.)*

φάγω, only used in fut. φάγομαι, and 2d aor. ἔφαγον; see ἐσθίω.

φαιλόνης, ου, ὁ (W.H. φελόνης), (Lat. pænula), a traveling-cloak, 2 Tim. iv. 13. (N. T.)*

φαίνω, φανῶ, 2d aor. pass. ἐφάνην, (1) trans., to show, in N.T. only mid. or pass., to appear, to be seen, to seem; τὰ φαινόμενα, things which can be seen, Heb. xi. 3; (2) intrans., to shine, to give light, Jn. i. 5, v. 35. Syn.. see δοκέω.

Φάλεκ, ὁ (Heb.), Peleg, Lu. iii. 35.*

φανερός, ά, όν, apparent, manifest, Ac. iv. 16; Gal. v. 19;

ἐν τῷ φανερῷ, as adv., manifestly, openly, Ro. ii. 28.

φανερόω, ῶ, ώσω, to make apparent, to manifest, to disclose, Jn. vii. 4, xxi. 11; pass., to be manifested, made manifest, 1 Tim. iii. 16; 2 Cor. v. 11.

φανερῶς, adv., clearly, Ac. x. 3; openly, Mar. i. 45; Jn. vii. 10.*

φανέρωσις, εως, ἡ, a manifestation (gen. obj.), 1 Cor. xii. 7; 2 Cor. iv. 2.* Syn.: see ἀποκάλυψις.

φανός, οῦ, ὁ, a torch, a lantern, Jn. xviii. 3.*

Φανουήλ, ὁ (Heb.), Phanuel, Lu. ii. 36.*

φαντάζω, to cause to appear; pass. part. τὸ φανταζόμενον, the appearance, Heb. xii. 21.*

φαντασία, ας, ἡ, display, pomp, Ac. xxv. 23.*

φάντασμα, ατος, τό, an apparition, a spectre, Mat. xiv. 26; Mar. vi. 49.*

φάραγξ, αγγος, ἡ, a valley, ravine, Lu. iii. 5.*

Φαραώ, ὁ, Pharaoh, the title of ancient Egyptian kings, Ac. vii. 13, 21.

Φαρές, ὁ (Heb.), Phares, Mat. i. 3; Lu. iii. 33.*

Φαρισαῖος, ου, ὁ (from the Heb. verb, to separate), a Pharisee, one of the Jewish sect so called, Mar. ii. 16, 18, 24. (N. T.)

φαρμακεία (W. H. -κία), ας, ἡ, magic, sorcery, enchantment, Gal. v. 20; Rev. ix. 21 (W. H. φάρμακον), xviii. 23.*

φαρμακεύς, έως, ὁ, a magician, sorcerer, Rev. xxi. 8 (W. H. read following).*

φάρμακον, ου, τό, a drug; an enchantment, Rev. ix. 21 (W. H.).*

φαρμακός, οῦ, ὁ (prop. adj.), a magician, sorcerer, Rev. xxi. 8 (W. H.), xxii. 15.*

φάσις, εως, ἡ, report, tidings, Ac. xxi. 31.*

φάσκω (freq. of φημί), to assert, to affirm, to profess, Ac. xxiv. 9, xxv. 19; Ro. i. 22; Rev. ii. 2 (W. H. omit).*

φάτνη, ης, ἡ, a manger, a crib, Lu. ii. 7, 12, 16, xiii. 15.*

φαῦλος, η, ον, good for nothing, wicked, base, Jn. iii. 20, v. 29; Ro. ix. 11 (W. H.); 2

Cor. v. 10 (W. H.); Tit. ii. 8; Ja. iii. 16.*

φέγγος, ους, τό, brightness, light, Mat. xxiv. 29; Mar. xiii. 24; Lu. xi. 33 (W. H. φῶς). Syn.: see λαμπάς.

φείδομαι, φείσομαι, dep., (1) to spare (gen.), Ac. xx. 29; (2) to abstain (inf.), 2 Cor. xii. 6.

φειδομένως, adv., sparingly, 2 Cor. ix. 6.*

φελόνης, see φαιλόνης.

φέρω, οἴσω, ἤνεγκα, ἠνέχθην (see Gr. § 103, Wi. § 15, Bu. 68), to bear, as (1) to carry, as a burden, Lu. xxiii. 26; (2) to produce fruit, Jn. xii. 24; (3) to bring, Ac. v. 16; (4) to endure, to bear with, Ro. ix. 22; (5) to bring forward, as charges, Jn. xviii. 29; (6) to uphold, Heb. i. 3; (7) pass., as nautical term, to be borne along, Ac. xxvii. 15, 17; (8) mid., to rush (bear itself on), Ac. ii. 2; to go on or advance, in learning, Heb. vi. 1. Syn.: φορέω means to bear something habitually and continuously, while in φέρω it is temporary bearing, and on special occasions.

φεύγω, ξομαι, ἔφυγον, to flee, to escape, to shun (acc. or ἀπό), Mat. viii. 33; 1 Cor. vi. 18; Heb. xii. 34; Rev. xvi. 20.

Φῆλιξ, ικος, ὁ, Felix, Ac. xxv. 14.

φήμη, ης, ἡ, a report, fame, Mat. ix. 26; Lu. iv. 14.*

φημί, impf. ἔφην (for other tenses, see εἶπον), to say, with ὅτι, dat. of pers., πρός (acc.), with pers., acc. of thing (once acc., inf., Ro. iii. 8).

Φῆστος, ου, ὁ, Festus, Ac. xxv. 1, 4, 9.

φθάνω, φθάσω, perf. ἔφθακα, (1) to be before, to precede, 1 Th. iv. 15; (2) to arrive, attain to (εἰς, ἄχρι, ἐπί), Mat. xii. 28; Lu. xi. 20; Ro. ix. 31; 2 Cor. x. 14; Phil. iii. 16; 1 Th. ii. 16.*

φθαρτός, ή, όν (φθείρω), corruptible, perishable, Ro. i. 23; 1 Cor. ix. 25, xv. 53, 54; 1 Pet. i. 18, 23.*

φθέγγομαι, γξομαι, dep., to speak aloud, to utter, Ac. iv. 18; 2 Pet. ii. 16, 18.*

φθείρω, φθερῶ, 2d aor. pass. ἐφθάρην, to corrupt, physically or morally, to spoil, to destroy, 2 Cor. vii. 2; Rev. xix. 2.

φθιν-οπωρινός, ή, όν, autumnal, Ju. 12.*

φθόγγος, ου, ὁ (φθέγγομαι), a sound, Ro. x. 18; 1 Cor. xiv. 7.*

φθονέω, ῶ, to envy (dat.), Gal. v. 26.*

φθόνος, ου, ὁ, envy, Phil. i. 15; Tit. iii. 3.

φθορά, ᾶς, ἡ (φθείρω), corruption, destruction, physical or moral, 1 Cor. xv. 42, 2 Pet. i. 4.

φιάλη, ης, ἡ, a bowl, broad and flat, Rev. v. 8, xv. 7.

φιλ-άγαθος, ον, loving goodness, Tit. i. 8.*

Φιλαδέλφεια, ας, ἡ, Philadelphia, Rev. i. 11, iii. 7.*

φιλαδελφία, ας, ἡ, brotherly love, love of Christian brethren, Ro. xii. 10; 1 Th. iv. 9; Heb. xiii. 1; 1 Pet. i. 22; 2 Pet. i. 7.*

φιλ-άδελφος, ον, loving the brethren, 1 Pet. iii. 8.*

φίλ-ανδρος, ον, loving one's husband, Tit. ii. 4.*

φιλ-ανθρωπία, ας, ἡ, love of mankind, benevolence, Ac. xxviii. 2; Tit. iii. 4.*

φιλ-ανθρώπως, adv., humanely, kindly, Ac. xxvii. 3.*

φιλαργυρία, ας, ἡ, love of money, avarice, 1 Tim. vi. 10.* Syn.: see πλεονεξία.

φιλ-άργυρος, ον, money-loving, avaricious, Lu. xvi. 14; 2 Tim. iii. 2.*

φίλ-αυτος, ον, self-loving, selfish, 2 Tim. iii. 2.*

φιλέω, ῶ, ήσω, (1) to love, Mat. vi. 5, x. 37; Lu. xx. 46; (2) to kiss, Mat. xxvi. 48. Syn.: see ἀγαπάω.

φίλη, ἡ, see φίλος.

φιλ-ήδονος, ον, pleasure-loving, 2 Tim. iii. 4.*

φίλημα, ατος, τό, a kiss, Lu. vii. 45; Ro. xvi. 16.

Φιλήμων, ονος, ὁ, Philemon, Philem. 1.*

Φίλητος, or Φιλητός, ου, ὁ, Philetus, 2 Tim. ii. 17.*

φιλία, ας, ἡ, friendship, Ja. iv. 4 (gen. obj.).*

Φιλιππήσιος, ου, ὁ, a Philippian, Phil. iv. 15.*

Φίλιπποι, ων, οἱ, Philippi, Ac. xvi. 12, xx. 6.

Φίλιππος, ου, ὁ, Philip. Four of the name are mentioned: (1) Jn. i. 44–47 · (2) Ac. vi. 5; (3) Lu. iii. 1; (4) Mat. xiv. 3.

Φιλό-θεος, ον, loving God, 2 Tim. iii. 4.*

Φιλό-λογος, ου, ὁ, Philologus, Ro. xvi. 15.*

φιλονεικία, ας, ἡ, love of dispute, contention, Lu. xxii. 24.*

φιλό-νεικος, ον, strife-loving, contentious, 1 Cor. xi. 16.*

φιλοξενία, ας, ἡ, love to strangers, hospitality, Ro. xii. 13; Heb. xiii. 2.*

φιλό-ξενος, ον, hospitable, 1 Tim. iii. 2; Tit. i. 8; 1 Pet. iv. 9.*

φιλο-πρωτεύω, to love the first place, to desire pre-eminence, 3 Jn. 9. (N.T.)*

φίλος, η, ον, friendly; ὁ φίλος, as subst., a friend, Lu. vii. 6, xi. 5; an associate, Mat. xi. 19; ἡ φίλη, a female friend, only Lu. xv. 9.

φιλοσοφία, ας, ἡ, love of wisdom, philosophy, in N.T. of the Jewish traditional theology, Col. ii. 8.*

φιλό-σοφος, ου, ὁ (prop. adj., wisdom-loving), a philosopher, in N.T. of Greek philosophers, Ac. xvii. 18.*

φιλό-στοργος, ον, tenderly loving, kindly affectionate to (εἰς), Ro. xii. 10.*

φιλό-τεκνος, ον, loving one's children, Tit. ii. 4.*

φιλο-τιμέομαι, οῦμαι, dep., to make a thing one's ambition, to desire very strongly (inf.), Ro. xv. 20; 2 Cor. v. 9; 1 Th. iv. 11.*

φιλοφρόνως, adv., in a friendly manner, kindly, Ac. xxviii. 7.*

φιλό-φρων, ον, friendly, kindly, 1 Pet. iii. 8 (W. H. ταπεινόφρων).*

φιμόω, ῶ, ώσω, to muzzle, 1 Cor. ix. 9; to reduce to silence, Mat. xxii. 34; pass., to be reduced to silence, to be silent, Mat. xxii. 12; of a storm, Mar. iv. 39.

Φλέγων, οντος, ὁ, Phlegon, Ro. xvi. 14.*

φλογίζω, to inflame, to fire with passion, Ja. iii. 6.*

φλόξ, φλογός, ἡ, a flame, Lu. xvi. 24.

φλυαρέω, ῶ, to talk idly, to make empty charges against any one (acc.), 3 Jn. 10.*

φλύαρος, ον, prating; talking foolishly, 1 Tim. v. 13.*

φοβερός, ά, όν, fearful, dreadful, Heb. x. 27, 31, xii. 21.*

φοβέω, ῶ, ήσω, to make afraid, to terrify; in N.T. only passive, to be afraid, to be terrified, sometimes with cognate acc., Mar. iv. 41; to fear (acc.), Mat. x. 26; to reverence, Mar. vi. 20; Lu. i. 50.

φόβητρον (W. H. -θρον), ου, τό, a terrible sight, a cause of terror, Lu. xxi. 11.*

φόβος, ου, ὁ, (1) fear, terror, alarm, Mat. xiv. 26; (2) the object or cause of fear, Ro. xiii. 3; (3) reverence, respect, 1 Pet. ii. 18; towards God, Ro. iii. 18; 1 Pet. i. 17. Syn.: see δειλία.

Φοίβη, ης, ἡ, Phœbe, Ro. xvi. 1.*

Φοινίκη, ης, ἡ, Phenice or Phœnicia, Ac. xi. 19, xv. 3, xxi. 2.

φοῖνιξ, ικος, ὁ, a palm-tree, a palm branch, Jn. xii. 13; Rev. vii. 9.*

Φοῖνιξ, ικος, ὁ, a proper name, Phœnice, a city of Crete, Ac. xxvii. 12.*

φονεύς, έως, ὁ, a murderer, Ac. vii. 52, xxviii. 4.

φονεύω, σω, to murder, Mat. xxiii. 31, 35; Ja. iv. 2.

φόνος, ου, ὁ, murder, slaughter, Heb. xi. 37; Rev. ix. 21.

φορέω, ῶ, έσω, to bear about, to wear, Mat. xi. 8; Jn. xix. 5; Ro. xiii. 4; 1 Cor. xv. 49; Ja. ii. 3.* Syn.: see φέρω.

φόρον, ου, τό (Lat.), forum (see Ἄππιος), Ac. xxviii. 15. (N. T.)*

φόρος, ου, ὁ (φέρω), a tax, especially on persons, Lu. xx. 22, xxiii. 2; Ro. xiii. 6, 7.*

φορτίζω, perf. pass. part. πεφορτισμένος, to load, to burden, Mat. xi. 28; Lu. xi. 46.*

φορτίον, ου, τό, a burden, Mat. xi. 30; the freight of a ship, Ac. xxvii. 10 (W. H.); the burden of ceremonial observances, Mat. xxiii. 4; Lu. xi. 46; the burden of faults, Gal. vi. 5.*

φόρτος, ου, ὁ, load, a ship's cargo, Ac. xxvii. 10 (W. H. read φορτίον).*

Φορτουνᾶτος, ου, ὁ (Lat.), *Fortunatus*, 1 Cor. xvi. 17.*

φραγέλλιον, ου, τό (Lat.), *a scourge*, Jn. ii. 15. (N. T.)*

φραγελλόω, ῶ (Lat.), *to flagellate, to scourge*, Mat. xxvii. 26; Mar. xv. 15. (N. T.)*

φραγμός, οῦ, ὁ, *a hedge*, Mat. xxi. 33; Mar. xii. 1; Lu. xiv. 23; fig., *partition*, Ep. ii. 14.*

φράζω, άσω, *to declare, explain, interpret*, Mat. xiii. 36 (not W. H.), xv. 15.*

φράσσω, ξω, *to stop, to close up*, Ro. iii. 19; 2 Cor. xi. 10; Heb. xi. 33.*

φρέαρ, φρέατος, τό, *a pit, a well*, Jn. iv. 11, 12.

φρεναπατάω, ῶ, *to deceive the mind, to impose upon* (acc.), Gal. vi. 3. (N. T.)*

φρεν-απάτης, ου, ὁ, *a mind-deceiver*, Tit. i. 10. (N. T.)*

φρήν, φρενός, ἡ (lit. *diaphragm*), plur. αἱ φρένες, *the mind, the intellect*, 1 Cor. xiv. 20.

φρίσσω, *to shudder*, Ja. ii. 19.*

φρονέω, ῶ, ήσω (φρήν), (1) *to think* (abs.), 1 Cor. xiii. 11; (2) *to think, judge* (acc.), Gal. v. 10; (3) *to direct the mind io, to seek for* (acc.), Ro. viii. 5; (4) *to observe*, a time as sacred, Ro. xiv. 6; (5) with ὑπέρ, *to care for*, Phil. iv. 10.

φρόνημα, ατος, τό, *thought, purpose*, Ro. viii. 6, 7, 27.*

φρόνησις, εως, ἡ, *understanding*, Lu. i. 17; Ep. i. 8.* *Syn.:* see γνῶσις.

φρόνιμος, ον, *intelligent, prudent*, Lu. xii. 42; 1 Cor. x. 15.

φρονίμως, adv., *prudently*, Lu. xvi. 8.*

φροντίζω, *to be thoughtful, to be careful*, inf., Tit. iii. 8.*

φρουρέω, ῶ, *to guard, to keep*, as by a military guard, lit., 2 Cor. xi. 32; fig., Gal. iii. 23 (as if in custody); Phil. iv. 7 (in security); 1 Pet. i. 5 (in reserve).*

φρυάσσω, ξω, *to rage*, Ac. iv. 25. (S.)*

φρύγανον, ου, τό, *a dry stick*, for burning, Ac. xxviii. 3.*

Φρυγία, ας, ἡ, *Phrygia*, Ac. ii. 10, xvi. 6, xviii. 23.

Φύγελλος (W. H. -ελος), ου, ὁ, *Phygellus*, 2 Tim. i. 15.*

φυγή, ῆς, ἡ, *flight*, Mat. xxiv. 20; Mar. xiii. 18 (W. H. omit).*

φυλακή, ῆς, ἡ, (1) *a keeping guard, a watching*, Lu. ii. 8; espec. of the four *watches* into which the night was divided, Mat. xiv. 25, Lu. xii. 38; (2) *a guard, i.e.*, men on guard, *a watch*, Ac. xii. 10; (3) *a prison*, Mat. v. 25; (4) *an imprisonment*, 2 Cor. vi. 5.

φυλακίζω, *to imprison*, Ac. xxii. 19. (S.)*

φυλακτήρια, ων, τά (plur. of adj.), *a safeguard, an amulet, a phylactery*, a slip of parchment, with Scripture words thereon, worn by the Jews, Mat. xxiii. 5.*

φύλαξ, ακος, ὁ, *a keeper, sentinel*, Ac. v. 23, xii. 6, 19.*

φυλάσσω, ξω, (1) *to keep guard*, or *watch over*, Ac. xii. 4; (2) *to keep in safety*, Lu. xi. 21; (3) *to observe*, as a precept, Gal. vi. 13; (4) mid., *to keep one's self from* (acc. or ἀπό), Lu. xii. 15; Ac. xxi. 25.

φυλή, ῆς, ἡ, (1) *a tribe*, of Israel, Heb. vii. 13, 14; (2) *a race*, or *people*, Rev. xiii. 7, xiv. 6.

φύλλον, ου, τό, *a leaf*, Mar. xi. 13.

φύραμα, ατος, τό, *a mass kneaded, a lump*, as of dough or clay, Ro. ix. 21, xi. 16; 1 Cor. v. 6, 7; Gal. v. 9.*

φυσικός, ή, όν, *natural*, as (1) *according to nature*, Ro. i. 26, 27; (2) *merely animal*, 2 Pet. ii. 12.*

φυσικῶς, adv., *by nature*, Ju. 10.*

φυσιόω, ῶ, *to inflate, to puff up*, 1 Cor. viii. 1; pass., *to be inflated, arrogant*, 1 Cor. iv. 6, 18, 19, v. 2, xiii. 4; Col. ii. 18.*

φύσις, εως, ἡ, generally, *nature;* specially, (1) *natural birth*, Gal. ii. 15; (2) *natural disposition, propensity*, Ep. ii. 3; (3) *native qualities*, or *properties*, Ja. iii. 7; 2 Pet. i. 4.

φυσίωσις, εως, ἡ, *a puffing up, pride*, 2 Cor. xii. 20. (N. T.)*

φυτεία, ας, ἡ, *a plant*, Mat. xv. 13.*

φυτεύω, σω, *to plant*, abs., or with acc., Mat. xxi. 33; 1 Cor. iii. 6, 8.

φύω, σω, 2d aor. pass. ἐφύην, part. φυείς, *to produce;* pass., *to grow*, Lu. viii. 6, 8; in-trans., *to spring up*, Heb. xii. 15.*

φωλεός, οῦ, ὁ, *a burrow, a hole*, Mat. viii. 20; Lu. ix. 58.*

φωνέω, ῶ, ήσω, (1) *to sound, to utter a sound* or *cry*, Lu. viii. 8; espec. of cocks, *to crow*, Mar. xiv. 30; (2) *to call to, to invite* (acc.), Mat. xx. 32; Lu. xiv. 12; (3) *to address, to name*, acc. (nom. of title), Jn. xiii. 13.

φωνή, ῆς, ἡ, (1) *a sound*, musical or otherwise, 1 Cor. xiv. 7, 8; Rev. vi. 1, xiv. 2, xix. 1, 6; (2) *an articulate sound, a voice, a cry*, Lu. xvii. 13; Ac. iv. 24; (3) *a language*, 1 Cor. xiv. 10.

φῶς, φωτός, τό (contr. from φάος, from φάω, *to shine*), (1) lit., *light*, Mat. xvii. 2; Jn. xi. 9; *a source of light*, Lu. xxii. 56; Ja. i. 17; *brightness*, Rev. xxii. 5; ἐν τῷ φωτί, *publicly*, Mat. x. 27; (2) fig., *light*, as an appellation of God, 1 Jn. i. 5; as a symbol of truth and purity, espec. the truth of Christ, Jn. iii. 19, 20, 21; used of Christ, Jn. i. 7, 8. *Syn.:* see λαμπάς.

φωστήρ, ῆρος, ὁ, (1) *a luminary*, Phil. ii. 15; (2) *brightness, splendor*, Rev. xxi. 11.* *Syn.:* see λαμπάς.

φωσ-φόρος, ον, *light-bearing, radiant;* the name of the morning star (Lat. *Lucifer*), the planet Venus, 2 Pet. i. 19.*

φωτεινός (W. H. -τινός), ή, όν, *bright, luminous, full of light*, lit., Mat. xvii. 5; fig., Mat. vi. 22; Lu. xi. 34, 36.*

φωτίζω, ίσω, pass. perf. πεφώτισμαι, 1st aor. ἐφωτίσθην, (1) *to light up, illumine*, lit. or fig. (acc., but ἐπί in Rev. xxii. 5), Lu. xi. 36; (2) *to bring to light, make evident*, 1 Cor. iv. 5.

φωτισμός, οῦ, ὁ, *light, lustre, illumination*, 2 Cor. iv. 4, 6. (S.)*

X

Χ, χ; **χῖ**, *chi, ch,* guttural, the twenty-second letter. As a numeral, χ' = 600; ͵χ = 600,000.

χαίρω, χαρήσομαι, 2d aor. pass. as act. *ἐχάρην, to rejoice, to be glad,* Lu. xv. 5, 32; Jn. iii. 29; impv. *χαῖρε, χαίρετε, hail!* Mat. xxvi. 49; inf. *χαίρειν, greeting,* Ac. xv. 23.

χάλαζα, ης, ἡ, *hail,* Rev. viii. 7, xi. 19, xvi. 21.*

χαλάω, ῶ, άσω, 1st aor. pass. *ἐχαλάσθην, to let down, to lower,* Mar. ii. 4; Lu. v. 4, 5; Ac. ix. 25, xxvii. 17, 30; 2 Cor. xi. 33.*

Χαλδαῖος, ου, ὁ, *a Chaldæan,* Ac. vii. 4.*

χαλεπός, ή, όν, (1) *hard, troublesome,* 2 Tim. iii. 1; (2) *harsh, fierce,* Mat. viii. 28.*

χαλιν-αγωγέω, ῶ, *to bridle, to curb,* Ja. i. 26, iii. 2. (N.T.)*

χαλινός, οῦ, ὁ, *a bridle, a curb,* Ja. iii. 3; Rev. xiv. 20.*

χάλκεος, οῦς, ῆ, οῦν, *brazen,* Rev. ix. 20.*

χαλκεύς, έως, ὁ, *a worker in brass* or *copper,* 2 Tim. iv. 14.*

χαλκηδών, όνος, ὁ, *chalcedony,* a precious stone, Rev. xxi. 19.*

χαλκίον, ου, τό, *a brazen vessel,* Mar. vii. 4.*

χαλκο-λίβανον, ου, τό (or -*νος, ου, ἡ*), meaning uncertain, either *some precious metal,* or *frankincense* (λίβανος) *of a yellow color,* Rev. i. 15, ii. 8. (N.T.)*

χαλκός, οῦ, ὁ, *copper, brass, money,* Mar. vi. 8, 1 Cor. xiii. 1.

χαμαί, adv., *on* or *to the ground,* Jn. ix. 6, xviii. 6.*

Χαναάν, ἡ, *Canaan,* Ac. vii. 11, xiii. 19.*

Χαναναῖος, αία, αῖον, *Canaanite, i.e.,* Phœnician, Mat. xv. 22.*

χαρά, ᾶς, ἡ, *joy, gladness,* Gal. v. 22; Col. i. 11; *a source of joy,* 1 Th. ii. 19, 20.

χάραγμα, ατος, τό, *sculpture,* Ac. xvii. 29; *engraving, a stamp, a sign,* Rev. xiv. 9, 11, xvi. 2.

χαρακτήρ, ῆρος, ὁ, *an impres-*

sion, an exact reproduction, Heb. i. 3.*

χάραξ, ακος, ὁ, *a palisade, a mound for besieging,* Lu. xix. 43.*

χαρίζομαι, ίσομαι, dep. mid., fut. pass. *χαρισθήσομαι,* (1) *to show favor to* (dat.), Gal. iii. 18; (2) *to forgive* (dat. pers., acc. thing), 2 Cor. xii. 10; Ep. iv. 32; Col. ii. 13; (3) *to give freely, bestow,* Lu. vii. 21; 1 Cor. ii. 12.

χάρις, ιτος, acc. *χάριν* and *χάριτα* (W. H. χάριν in Ac. xxiv. 27; Ju. 4), ἡ, (1) objectively, *agreeableness, charm,* Lu. iv. 22; (2) subjectively, *inclination towards, favor, kindness, liberality, thanks,* Lu. i. 30, ii. 40, 52; Ac. ii. 47, xxiv. 27; *χάριν ἔχειν, to thank; χάριν ἔχειν πρός, to be in favor with;* especially of the undeserved favor of God or Christ, 2 Cor. iv. 15, xii. 9; *χάριν,* used as prep. with gen. (lit., *with inclination towards), for the sake of, on account of,* Ep. iii. 14; 1 Tim. v. 14; Tit. i. 11.

χάρισμα, ατος, τό, *a gift of grace, an undeserved favor* from God to man, Ro. i. 11, v. 15, 16, vi. 23, xi. 29, xii. 6; 1 Cor. i. 7, vii. 7, xii. 4, 9, 28, 30, 31; 2 Cor. i. 11; 1 Tim. iv. 14; 2 Tim. i. 6; 1 Pet. iv. 10.*

χαριτόω, ῶ, *to favor, bestow freely on* (acc.), Ep. i. 6; pass., *to be favored,* Lu. i. 28. (Ap.)*

Χαρράν, ἡ (Heb.), *Charran* or *Haran,* Ac. vii. 2, 4.*

χάρτης, ου, ὁ, *paper,* 2 Jn. 12.*

χάσμα, ατος, τό, *a gap, a gulf,* Lu. xvi. 26.*

χεῖλος, ους, τό, *a lip;* plur., *mouth,* Mat. xv. 8; 1 Cor. xiv. 21; fig., *shore,* Heb. xi. 12.

χειμάζω, in pass., *to be storm-beaten,* or *tempest-tossed,* Ac. xxvii. 18.*

χείμαρρος, ου, ὁ, *a storm-brook, a wintry torrent,* Jn. xviii. 1.*

χειμών, ῶνος, ὁ, (1) *a storm, a tempest,* Ac. xxvii. 20; (2) *winter, the rainy season,* Mat. xxiv. 20.

χείρ, χειρός, ἡ, *a hand,* Lu. vi. 6; 1 Tim. ii. 8; met., for any exertion of *power,* Mat. xvii. 22; Lu. ix. 44; espec. in the phrases *the hand* of God, *the hand* of the Lord, for help, Ac. iv. 30, xi. 21; for punishment, Heb. x. 31.

χειραγωγέω, ῶ, *to lead by the hand,* Ac. ix. 8, xxii. 11.*

χειρ-αγωγός, όν, *leading* one *by the hand,* Ac. xiii. 11.*

χειρό-γραφον, ου, τό, *a handwriting, a bond;* fig., of the Mosaic law, Col. ii. 14.*

χειρο-ποίητος, ον, *done* or *made with hands,* Mar. xiv. 58; Ac. vii. 48, xvii. 24; Ep. ii. 11; Heb. ix. 11, 24.*

χειρο-τονέω, ῶ, *to vote by stretching out the hand, to choose by vote,* 2 Cor. viii. 19; *to appoint,* Ac. xiv. 23.*

χείρων, ον, compar. of κακός (which see), *worse,* Mat. xii. 45; *worse, more severe,* Heb x. 29; *εἰς τὸ χεῖρον, worse,* Mar. v. 26; *ἐπὶ τὸ χεῖρον, worse and worse,* 2 Tim. iii. 13.

χερουβίμ (W. H. Χερουβείν), *τά, cherubim,* the Heb. plural of cherub, the golden figures on the mercy-seat, Heb. ix. 5. (S.)*

χήρα, ας, ἡ, *a widow,* Ac. vi. 1, ix. 39, 41; Ja. i. 27.

χθές (W. H. ἐχθές), adv., *yesterday,* Jn. iv. 52; Ac. vii. 28; Heb. xiii. 8.*

χιλί-αρχος, ου, ὁ, *a commander of a thousand men, a military tribune,* Ac. xxi-xxv.

χιλιάς, άδος, ἡ, *a thousand,* Lu. xiv. 31; 1 Cor. x. 8.

χίλιοι, αι, α, *a thousand,* 2 Pet. iii. 8; Rev. xi. 3.

Χίος, ου, ἡ, *Chios,* Ac. xx. 15.*

χιτών, ῶνος, ὁ, *a tunic,* an under-garment, Lu. iii. 11, vi. 29; *a garment,* Mar. xiv. 63. *Syn.:* see ἱμάτιον.

χιών, όνος, ἡ, *snow,* Mat. xxviii. 3; Mar. ix. 3 (W. H. omit); Rev. i. 14.*

χλαμύς, ύδος, ἡ, *a short cloak* worn by Roman officers and magistrates, Mat. xxvii. 28 31.* *Syn.:* see ἱμάτιον.

χλευάζω, to mock, scoff (abs.), Ac. ii. 13 (W. H. διαχλευάζω), xvii. 32.*

χλιαρός, ά, όν, lukewarm, Rev. iii. 16.*

Χλόη, ης, ή, Chloe, 1 Cor. i. 11.*

χλωρός, ά, όν, (1) green, Mar. vi. 39; Rev. viii. 7, ix. 4; (2) pale, Rev. vi. 8.*

χξϜ, six hundred and sixty-six, Rev. xiii. 18 (W. H. write the numbers in full).*

χοϊκός, ή, όν, earthy, made of earth, 1 Cor. xv. 47-49. (N. T.)*

χοῖνιξ, ικος, ή, a chœnix, a measure containing two sextarii (see ξέστης), Rev. vi. 6.*

χοῖρος, ου, ὁ, plur., swine, Lu. viii. 32, 33, xv. 15, 16.

χολάω, ῶ, to be angry (dat.), Jn. vii. 23.*

χολή, ῆς, ή, (1) gall, fig., Ac. viii. 23; (2) perh. bitter herbs, such as wormwood, Mat. xxvii. 34.*

χόος, see χοῦς.

Χοραζίν (W. H. Χοραζείν), ή, Chorazin, Mat. xi. 21; Lu. x. 13.*

χορ-ηγέω, ῶ, to lead or furnish a chorus; hence, to furnish abundantly, to supply, 2 Cor. ix. 10; 1 Pet. iv. 11.*

χορός, οῦ, ὁ, a dance, dancing, plur., Lu. xv. 25.*

χορτάζω, to feed, to satisfy with (gen. or ἀπό), Mat. v. 6, xv. 33; Mar. viii. 4; Lu. xvi. 21.

χόρτασμα, ατος, τό, food, sustenance, Ac. vii. 11.*

χόρτος, ου, ὁ, grass, herbage, Mat. vi. 30; growing grain, Mat. xiii. 26; hay, 1 Cor. iii. 12.

Χουζᾶς, ᾶ, ὁ, Chuzas, Lu. viii. 3.*

χοῦς, οός, acc. οῦν, ὁ, dust, Mar. vi. 11; Rev. xviii. 19.*

χράομαι, ῶμαι, dep. (prop. mid. of χράω), to use (dat.), to make use of, 1 Cor. ix. 12, 15; 2 Cor. xiii. 10 (dat. om.); to deal with, Ac. xxvii. 3.

χράω, see κίχρημι.

χρεία, ας, ή, (1) need, necessity, plur., necessities, Mar. xi. 3; Tit. iii. 14; ἔχω χρείαν, to need, Jn. xiii. 10; (2) business, Ac. vi. 3.

χρεωφειλέτης (W. H. χρεοφιλέτης), ου, ὁ, a debtor, Lu. vii. 41, xvi. 5.*

χρή, impers. (from χράω), it is necessary, it is proper (acc. and inf.), Ja. iii. 10.*

χρήζω, to have need of, to need (gen.), Lu. xi. 8, xii. 30.

χρῆμα, ατος, τό, a thing of use; money, sing., only Ac. iv. 37; plur., riches, money, Mar. x. 23; Ac. viii. 18, 20.

χρηματίζω, ίσω, to transact business; hence, (1) to utter an oracle, to give a divine warning, Lu. ii. 26; Heb. xii. 25; pass., to receive a divine response, be warned of God, Mat. ii. 12, 22; Ac. x. 22; Heb. viii. 5, xi. 7; (2) to receive a name, to be called, Ac. xi. 26; Ro. vii. 3.*

χρηματισμός, οῦ, ὁ, an oracle, Ro. xi. 4.*

χρήσιμος, η, ον, useful, profitable, 2 Tim. ii. 14.*

χρῆσις, εως, ή, use, Ro. i. 26, 27.*

χρηστεύομαι, dep., to be kind, 1 Cor. xiii. 4. (N. T.)*

χρηστο-λογία, ας, ή, a kind address; in a bad sense, plausible speaking, Ro. xvi. 18. (N. T.)*

χρηστός, ή, όν, useful, good, 1 Cor. xv. 33; gentle, pleasant, Lu. v. 39; kind, 1 Pet. ii. 3; τὸ χρηστόν, kindness, Ro. ii. 4.

χρηστότης, τητος, ή, (1) goodness, generally, Ro. iii. 12; (2) specially, benignity, kindness, Col. iii. 12. Syn.: see ἀγαθωσύνη.

χρῖσμα, ατος, τό, an anointing, 1 Jn. ii. 20, 27.*

Χριστιανός, οῦ, ὁ, a Christian, Ac. xi. 26, xxvi. 28; 1 Pet. iv. 16.*

χριστός, οῦ, ὁ (verbal adj. from χρίω), anointed; as a proper name, the Messiah, the Christ (see Gr. § 217 e, Wi. § 18, 9, note 1, Bu. 89), Mat. xxiii. 10, etc.

χρίω, σω, to anoint, to consecrate by anointing, as Jesus, the Christ, Lu. iv. 18; Ac. iv. 27, x. 38; Heb. i. 9; applied also to Christians, 2 Cor. i. 21. Syn.: see ἀλείφω.

χρονίζω, to delay, to tarry, Mat.

xxiv. 48, xxv. 5; Lu. i. 21, xii. 45; Heb. x. 37.*

χρόνος, ου, ὁ, (1) time, generally, Lu. iv. 5; Gal. iv. 4; (2) a particular time, or season, Mat. ii. 7; Ac. i. 7. Syn.: see καιρός.

χρονο-τριβέω, ῶ, to wear away time, to spend time, Ac. xx. 16.*

χρύσεος, οῦς, ῆ, οῦν, golden, 2 Tim. ii. 20; Heb. ix. 4.

χρυσίον, ου, τό (dim. of χρυσός), a piece of gold, a golden ornament, Ac. iii. 6; 1 Pet. iii. 3.

χρυσο-δακτύλιος, ον, adorned with a gold ring, Ja. ii. 2. (N. T.)*

χρυσό-λιθος, ου, ὁ (a golden stone), a gem of a bright yellow color, a topaz, Rev. xxi. 20. (S.)*

χρυσό-πρασος, ου, ὁ, a gem of a greenish-golden color, a chrysoprase, Rev. xxi. 20. (N. T.)*

χρυσός, οῦ, ὁ, gold, anything made of gold, gold coin, Mat. ii. 11, x. 9; Ja. v. 3.

χρυσόω, ῶ, to adorn with gold, to gild, Rev. xvii. 4, xviii. 16.*

χρώς, χρωτός, ὁ, the skin, Ac. xix. 12.*

χωλός, ή, όν, lame, Ac. iii. 2; deprived of a foot, Mar. ix. 45.

χώρα, ας, ή, (1) a country, or region, Jn. xi. 54; (2) the land, opposed to the sea, Ac. xxvii. 27; (3) the country, dist. from town, Lu. ii. 8; (4) plur., fields, Jn. iv. 35.

χωρέω, ῶ, ήσω, lit., to make room; hence, (1) to have room for, receive, contain, Mat. xix. 11, 12; Jn. ii. 6, xxi. 25; 2 Cor. vii. 2; impers., to be room for, Mar. ii. 2; (2) to make room by departing, to go, Mat. xv. 17; to make progress, Jn. viii. 37; to turn one's self, 2 Pet. iii. 9.*

χωρίζω, ίσω, to put apart, to separate, Mat. xix. 6; mid. (1st aor. pass.), to separate one's self, of divorce, 1 Cor. vii. 11, 15; to depart, to go away (ἀπό or ἐκ), Ac. i. 4, xviii. 1.

χωρίον, ου, τό, a place, a field,

Mar. xiv. 32; plur., *lands*, Ac. iv. 34; *a farm, estate*, Ac. xxviii. 7.

χωρίς, adv., *separately, by itself*, only Jn. xx. 7; as prep. gov. gen., *apart from, without*, Jn. xv. 5; Ro. iii. 21; *besides, exclusive of*, Mat. xiv. 21.

χῶρος, ου, ὁ (Lat. *Caurus*), *the N.W. wind;* used for the N.W. quarter of the heavens, Ac. xxvii. 12. (N. T.)*

Ψ

Ψ, ψ, ψῖ, *psi, ps*, the twenty-third letter. As a numeral, ψ′ = 700; ͵ψ = 700,000.

ψάλλω, ψαλῶ, *to sing*, accompanied with instruments, *to sing psalms*, Ro. xv. 9; 1 Cor. xiv. 15; Ep. v. 19; Ja. v. 13.*

ψαλμός, οῦ, ὁ, *a psalm, a song of praise*, Ep. v. 19; Col. iii. 16; plur., *the book of Psalms* in the O. T., Lu. xxiv. 44. *Syn.:* see ὕμνος.

ψευδ-άδελφος, ου, ὁ, *a false brother, a pretended Christian*, 2 Cor. xi. 26; Gal. ii. 4. (N. T.)*

ψευδ-απόστολος, ου, ὁ, *a false or pretended apostle*, 2 Cor. xi. 13. (N. T.)*

ψευδής, ές, *false, deceitful, lying*, Ac. vi. 13; Rev. ii. 2, xxi. 8.*

ψευδο-διδάσκαλος, ου, ὁ, *a false teacher, a teacher of false doctrines*, 2 Pet. ii. 1. (N. T.)*

ψευδο-λόγος, ον, *false-speaking, speaking lies*, 1 Tim. iv. 2.*

ψεύδομαι, dep., 1st aor. ἐψευσάμην, *to deceive, to lie, to speak falsely*, Heb. vi. 18; Rev. iii. 9; *to lie to* (acc.), Ac. v. 3.

ψευδο-μάρτυρ, or -υς, υρος, ὁ, *a false witness*, Mat. xxvi. 60; 1 Cor. xv. 15.*

ψευδο-μαρτυρέω, ῶ, ήσω, *to testify falsely*, Lu. xviii. 20.

ψευδο-μαρτυρία, as, ἡ, *false testimony*, Mat. xv. 19, xxvi. 59.*

ψευδο-προφήτης, ου, ὁ, *a false prophet*, one who in God's name teaches what is false, Mar. xiii. 22; 2 Pet. ii. 1. (S.)

ψεῦδος, ους, τό, *a falsehood, a lie*, Jn. viii. 44; 2 Th. ii. 11.

ψευδό-χριστος, ου, ὁ, *a false Christ, a pretended Messiah*, Mat. xxiv. 24; Mar. xiii. 22. (N. T.)*

ψευδ-ώνυμος, ον, *falsely named*, 1 Tim. vi. 20.*

ψεῦσμα, ατος, τό, *falsehood, perfidy*, Ro. iii. 7.*

ψεύστης, ου, ὁ, *a liar, a deceiver*, Jn. viii. 44, 55; Ro. iii. 4.

ψηλαφάω, ῶ, *to feel, to touch, to handle* (acc.), Lu. xxiv. 39; Heb. xii. 18; 1 Jn. i. 1; *to feel after, grope for*, fig., Ac. xvii. 27.* *Syn.:* see ἅπτω.

ψηφίζω, ίσω, *to reckon, to compute*, Lu. xiv. 28; Rev. xiii. 18.*

ψῆφος, ου, ἡ, *a small stone, a pebble*, Rev. ii. 17; used for voting, hence, *a vote*, Ac. xxvi. 10.*

ψιθυρισμός, οῦ, ὁ, *a whispering, a secret slandering*, 2 Cor. xii. 20. (S.)*

ψιθυριστής, οῦ, ὁ, *a whisperer, a secret slanderer*, Ro. i. 30.*

ψιχίον, ου, τό, *a crumb*, Mat. xv. 27; Mar. vii. 28; Lu. xvi. 21 (W. H. omit). (N. T.)*

ψυχή, ῆς, ἡ, (1) *the vital breath, the animal life*, of animals, Rev. viii. 9, xvi. 3, elsewhere only of man, Mat. vi. 25; (2) *the human soul*, as distinguished from the body, Mat. x. 28; (3) *the soul* as the seat of the affections, the will, etc., Ac. xiv. 2, 22; (4) *the self* (like Heb.), Mat. x. 39; (5) *a human person, an individual*, Ro. xiii. 1.

ψυχικός, ή, όν, *animal, natural, sensuous*, 1 Cor. ii. 14, xv. 44, 46; Ja. iii. 15; Ju. 19.*

ψῦχος, ους, τό, *cold*, Jn. xviii. 18.

ψυχρός, ά, όν, *cold*, Mat. x. 42 (sc. ὕδατος); fig., *cold-hearted*, Rev. iii. 15, 16.*

ψύχω, 2d fut. pass. ψυγήσομαι, *to cool;* pass., fig., *to be cooled, to grow cold*, Mat. xxiv. 12.*

ψωμίζω, *to feed*, Ro. xii. 20; *to spend in feeding*, 1 Cor. xiii. 3.*

ψωμίον, ου, τό, *a bit, a morsel*, Jn. xiii. 26, 27, 30. (S.)*

ψώχω, *to rub, to rub to pieces*, as ears of corn, Lu. vi. 1.*

Ω

Ω, ω, ὦ μέγα, *omega, o*, the twenty-fourth letter. As a numeral, ω′ = 800; ͵ω = 800,000. τὸ ᾿Ω, a name of God and Christ (see under A), Rev. i. 8, 11 (W. H. omit), xxi. 6, xxii. 13.*

ὦ, interj., *O*, used before the vocative in address, Ac. i. 1, xviii. 14; in exclamation, of admiration, Mat. xv. 28; Ro. xi. 33; or of reproof, Lu. xxiv. 25.

᾿Ωβήδ, ὁ, *Obed*, Mat. i. 5 (W. H. ᾿Ιωβήδ); Lu. iii. 32 (W. H. ᾿Ιωβήλ).*

ὧδε, adv., of place, *hither, here;* so, *in this life*, Heb. xiii. 14; *herein, in this matter*, Rev. xiii. 10; ὧδε ἢ ὧδε, *here or there*, Mat. xxiv. 23.

ᾠδή, ῆς, ἡ, *an ode, a song*, Rev. v. 9, xv. 3. *Syn.:* see ὕμνος.

ὠδίν, ῖνος, ἡ, *the pain of childbirth, acute pain, severe anguish*, Mat. xxiv. 8; Mar. xiii. 8; Ac. ii. 24; 1 Th. v. 3.*

ὠδίνω, *to feel the pains of childbirth, to travail*, Gal. iv. 27; Rev. xii. 2; fig., Gal. iv. 19.*

ὦμος, ου, ὁ, *a shoulder*, Mat. xxiii. 4; Lu. xv. 5.*

ὠνέομαι, οῦμαι, ήσομαι, *to buy* (gen. of price), Ac. vii. 16.*

ὠόν (W. H. ᾠόν), οῦ, τό, *an egg*, Lu. xii. 12.*

ὥρα, as, ἡ, (1) *a definite space of time, a season;* (2) *an hour*, Mar. xiii. 32; Ac. xvi. 33; (3) *the particular time for anything*, Lu. xiv. 17; Mat. xxvi. 45.

ὡραῖος, αία, αῖον, *fair, beautiful*, Mat. xxiii. 27; Ac. iii. 2, 10; Ro. x. 15.*

ὠρύομαι, dep. mid., *to roar, to howl*, as a beast, 1 Pet. v. 8.*

ὡς, an adv. of comparison, *as, like as, about, as it were, according as*, 2 Pet. i. 3; *how*, Lu. viii. 47; *how!* Ro. x. 15; as particle of time,

when, while, as soon as, Lu.
i. 23, xx. 37 ; Ro. xv. 24 ; as
consecutive particle, *so that*
(inf.), Ac. xx. 24 ; ὡς ἔπος
εἰπεῖν, *so to speak*, Heb. vii.
9.

ὡσαννά, interj., *hosanna!* (Heb.,
Ps. cxviii. 25, *save now!*),
Mat. xxi. 9, 15 ; Mar. xi. 9,
10 ; Jn. xii. 13. (N. T.)*

ὡσ-αύτως, adv., *in like manner,
likewise*, Mat. xx. 5, 1 Tim.
ii. 9.

ὡσ-εί, adv., *as if, as though,
like as*, with numerals, *about,*
Ac. ii. 3, 41.

Ὡσηέ, ὁ, *Hosea*, Ro. ix. 25.*

ὥσ-περ, adv., *just as, as*, Mat.
xii. 40 ; 1 Cor. viii. 5.

ὡσ-περ-εί, adv., *just as if, as it
were*, 1 Cor. xv. 8.*

ὥσ-τε, conj., *so that* (inf., see
Gr. § 391, Wi. §§ 41 *b*, 5,
note 1, 44, 1, Bu. 244), *therefore*, Mat. viii. 24 ; Gal. iii.
9, 24.

ὠτάριον, ου, τό (dim. of οὖς, see
παιδάριον), *an ear*, Mar. xiv.
47 (W. H.); Jn. xviii. 10
(W. H.).*

ὠτίον, ου, τό (dim. of οὖς, an
ear), *an ear*, Mat. xxvi. 51 ;

Lu. xxii. 51 ; Jn. xviii. 26 ;
also in the passages under
ὠτάριον (Rec.).*

ὠφέλεια, ας, ἡ, *usefulness, profit, advantage*, Ro. iii. 1 ; Ju.
16.*

ὠφελέω, ῶ, ήσω, *to be useful,
to profit, to benefit, to help*
(acc., also acc. of defini-
tion), Ro. ii. 25 ; 1 Cor. xiv.
6 ; pass., *to be profited, to be
helped*, Mat. xvi. 26.

ὠφέλιμος, ον, *profitable, bene-
ficial*, dat. of pers., Tit. iii.
8 ; πρός (acc.), of obj., 1
Tim. iv. 8 ; 2 Tim. iii. 16.*

NEW TESTAMENT SYNONYMS.

INTRODUCTION.

A *careful* discrimination between synonyms in the study of any language is a matter of the utmost importance, and also consequently of considerable difficulty. But there are some considerations which make a treatment of the synonyms of the New Testament especially difficult and especially necessary. The Greek language in classical times was one which was admirably adapted for expressing fine shades of meaning, and therefore one which abounded in synonyms. In later Greek, outside of the New Testament, some of these distinctions were changed or modified. The writers of the New Testament were men of Semitic habits of thought and expression. They also had theological and ethical teachings to impart which were far more profound and spiritual than had been conveyed by the Greek language previous to that time. These and other facts affecting the New Testament Greek necessarily modify the meaning of many of the synonyms there used, in some cases effecting a complete transformation.

The object in the present treatment is to consider the New Testament usage. Hence, the distinctions of classical Greek are stated only so far as they are also found in New Testament usage, or are of importance for determining the latter. For a discrimination of the distinctive meanings of New Testament synonyms, three things must usually be considered :

First, the etymological meaning of the words;
Second, the relations in which the words are found in classical Greek;
Third, the relations in which they are found in New Testament Greek, the last being often the chief factor.

The use of the words in the Septuagint is also important, for their connection with the Hebrew words which they are used to translate often throws light on their meaning.

The discussions here given aim to be brief, but yet to outline clearly the important and fundamental differences of meaning. Some words which are often given in works on this subject have been omitted, for the reason that the definitions as given in the Lexicon sufficiently indicate the important distinctions. There has been added, however, a consideration of some other words which are not so commonly included.

The chief works from which material and suggestions have been drawn are mentioned in the Introduction to the Lexicon.

The reason is stated in the Introduction to the Lexicon why in some cases the same word is treated both in the synonyms of the Lexicon itself, and also in this place. In every such instance the treatment here is to be regarded as supplementary to that in the Lexicon proper.

The synonyms here discussed do not belong exclusively nor chiefly to any one class of words. Both theological and non-theological terms are included. The aim has been to consider all the synonyms most likely to be confounded with one another, *i.e.*, all those most important, for practical use, to the average student of the New Testament.

INDEX TO SYNONYMS.

This Index includes all the synonyms discussed in any way, even those indicated by simply giving references to literature concerning them, both in the Lexicon itself and in this separate chapter. Where the same word is discussed in both, the treatment in this separate chapter, as previously stated, is to be considered as supplementary to that in the Lexicon proper.

The references BY PAGES *are in every case to the Lexicon itself;* BY SECTIONS, *to this separate chapter.*

113

§ 1. Holy, sacred, pure.

ἱερός, ὅσιος, ἅγιος, ἀγνός, σεμνός.

None of these words in classical Greek has necessarily any moral significance. Those which now have such a meaning have developed it in Biblical Greek. ἱερός means *sacred*, implying some special relation to God, so that it may not be violated. It refers, however, to formal relation rather than to character. It designates an external relation, which ordinarily is not an internal relation as well. It is used to describe persons or things. This is the commonest word for *holy* in classical Greek, and expresses their usual conception of holiness, but it is rare in the N.T. because it fails to express the fullness of the N.T. conception. ὅσιος, used of persons or things, describes that which is in harmony with the divine constitution of the moral universe. Hence, it is that which is in accordance with the general and instinctively felt idea of right, "what is consecrated and sanctioned by universal law and consent" (Passow), rather than what is in accordance with any system of revealed truth. As contrary to ὅσιος, *i.e.*, as ἀνοσία, the Greeks regarded, *e.g.*, a marriage between brother and sister such as was common in Egypt, or the omission of the rites of sepulture in connection with a relative. ἅγιος has probably as its fundamental meaning *separation*, *i.e.*, from the world to God's service. If not the original meaning, this at any rate is a meaning early in use. This separation, however, is not chiefly external, it is rather a separation from evil and defilement. The moral signification of the word is therefore the prominent one. This word, rare and of neutral meaning in classical Greek, has been developed in meaning, so that it expresses the full N.T. conception of holiness as no other does. ἀγνός is probably related to ἅγιος. It means specifically *pure*. But this may be only in a ceremonial sense, or it may have a moral signification. It sometimes describes freedom from impurities of the flesh. σεμνός is that which inspires *reverence* or *awe*. In classical Greek it was often applied to the gods. But frequently it has the lower idea of that which is humanly venerable, or even refers simply to externals, as to that which is magnificent, grand, or impressive.

§ 2. Sin.

ἁμαρτία, ἁμάρτημα, ἀσέβεια, παρακοή, ἀνομία, παρανομία, παράβασις, παράπτωμα, ἀγνόημα, ἥττημα.

ἁμαρτία meant originally *the missing of a mark*. When applied to moral things the idea is similar, it is missing the true end of life, and so it is used as a general term for *sin.*　It means both the act of sinning and the result, the sin itself.　ἁμάρτημα means only the sin itself, not the act, in its particular manifestations as separate deeds of disobedience to a divine law. ἀσέβεια is *ungodliness,* positive and active irreligion, a condition of direct opposition to God.　παρακοή is strictly *failing to hear,* or hearing carelessly and inattentively.　The sin is in this failure to hear when God speaks, and also in the active disobedience which ordinarily follows.　ἀνομία is *lawlessness,* contempt of law, a condition or action not simply without law, as the etymology might indicate, but contrary to law.　The law is usually by implication the Mosaic law.　παρανομία occurs only once, 2 Pet. ii. 16, and is practically equivalent to ἀνομία.　παράβασις is *transgression,* the passing beyond some assigned limit.　It is the breaking of a distinctly recognized commandment.　It consequently means more than ἁμαρτία.　παράπτωμα is used in different senses, sometimes in a milder sense, denoting an error, a mistake, a fault; and sometimes meaning a trespass, a willful sin.　ἀγνόημα occurs only once, Heb. ix. 7.　It indicates *error,* sin which to a certain extent is the result of ignorance.　ἥττημα denotes *being worsted, defeated.* In an ethical sense it means *a failure in duty, a fault.* — All these different words may occasionally but not usually be used simply to describe the same act from different points of view.　The fundamental meanings of these words may well be summed up in the language of Trench : Sin "may be regarded as the missing of a mark or aim : it is then ἁμαρτία or ἁμάρτημα ; the overpassing or transgressing of a line : it is then παράβασις ; the disobedience to a voice : in which case it is παρακοή ; the falling where one should have stood upright : this will be παράπτωμα ; ignorance of what one ought to have known : this will be ἀγνόημα ; diminishing of that which should have been rendered in full measure, which is ἥττημα ; non-observance of a law, which is ἀνομία or παρανομία."

§ 3. Sincere.

ἁπλοῦς, ἀκέραιος, ἄκακος, ἄδολος.

ἁπλοῦς is literally *spread out without folds,* and hence means single, simple, without complexity of character and motive.　In the N.T. this idea of simplicity is always favorable ; in classical Greek the word is also occasionally used in an unfavorable sense, denoting foolish simplicity.　ἀκέραιος also means *simple,* literally *free from any foreign admixture, unadulterated, free from disturbing elements.*　ἄκακος in Heb. vii. 26 means one in whom exists absence of all evil, and so by implication the presence of all good.　It passes also through the merely negative meaning of absence of evil, found in S., to the unfavorable meaning of simple, easily deceived, credulous, which is found in Ro. xvi. 18. ἄδολος, occurring only in 1 Pet. ii. 2, means *sincere, unmixed, without guile.*

§ 4. Sins of the tongue.

μωρολογία, αἰσχρολογία, εὐτραπελία.

μωρολογία, used only once in the N.T., is *foolish talking*, but this in the Biblical sense of the word foolish, which implies that it is also sinful. It is conversation which is first insipid, then corrupt. It is random talk, which naturally reveals the vanity and sin of the heart. αἰσχρολογία, also used once, means any kind of disgraceful language, especially abuse of others. In classical Greek it sometimes means distinctively language which leads to lewdness. εὐτραπελία, occurring once, originally meant *versatility in conversation*. It acquires, however, an unfavorable meaning, since polished, refined conversation has a tendency to become evil in many ways. The word denotes, then, a subtle form of evil-speaking, sinful conversation without the coarseness which frequently accompanies it, but not without its malignity.

§ 5. Shame, disgrace.

αἰδώς, αἰσχύνη, ἐντροπή, (σωφροσύνη).

αἰδώς is the feeling of *innate moral repugnance* to doing a dishonorable act. This moral repugnance is not found in αἰσχύνη, which is rather the feeling of *disgrace* which results from doing an unworthy thing, or the fear of such disgrace which serves to prevent its being done. αἰδώς is thus the nobler word, αἰσχύνη having regard chiefly to the opinions of others. αἰδώς is the fear of doing a shameful thing, αἰσχύνη is chiefly the fear of being found out. "αἰδώς would always restrain a good man from an unworthy act, while αἰσχύνη might sometimes restrain a bad one" (Trench). ἐντροπή stands somewhat between the other two words in meaning, but in the N.T. leans to the nobler side, indicating that *wholesome shame* which leads a man to consideration of his condition if it is unworthy, and to a change of conduct for the better. σωφροσύνη, *self-command*, may not seem to have much in common with these three words. As a matter of fact, however, it expresses positively that which αἰδώς expresses negatively.

§ 6. Prayer.

εὐχή, προσευχή, δέησις, ἔντευξις, εὐχαριστία, αἴτημα, ἱκετηρία.

εὐχή, when it means *prayer*, has apparently a general signification. **προσευχή** and **δέησις** are often used together. προσευχή is restricted to prayer to God, while δέησις has no such restriction. δέησις also refers chiefly to prayer *for particular benefits*, while προσευχή is more general. The prominent thought in **ἔντευξις** is that of boldness and freedom in approach to God. **εὐχαριστία** is *thanksgiving*, the grateful acknowledgment of God's mercies, chiefly in prayer. **αἴτημα,** much like δέησις, denotes a specific petition for a particular thing. In **ἱκετηρία** the attitude of humility and deprecation in prayer is specially emphasized. All these words may indicate at times not different kinds of prayer, but the same prayer viewed from different stand-points.

§ 7. To rebuke ; rebuke, accusation.

ἐπιτιμάω, ἐλέγχω ; αἰτία, ἔλεγχος.

ἐπιτιμάω means simply *to rebuke*, in any sense. It may be justly or unjustly, and, if justly, the rebuke may be heeded or it may not. **ἐλέγχω,** on the other hand, means to rebuke with sufficient cause, and also effectually, so as to bring the one rebuked to a confession or at least a conviction of sin. In other words, it means *to convince.* A similar distinction exists between the nouns **αἰτία** and **ἔλεγχος.** αἰτία is an accusation, whether false or true. ἔλεγχος is a charge which is shown to be true, and often is so confessed by the accused. It has both a judicial and a moral meaning.

§ 8. Boaster, proud, insolent.

ἀλαζών, ὑπερήφανος, ὑβριστής.

ἀλαζών is properly *a boaster*, who tells great things concerning his own prowess and achievements, with the implied idea that many of his claims are false. This word naturally describes a trait which manifests itself in contact with one's fellow-men, not one which exists simply within the heart. **ὑπερή-φανος** describes one who thinks too highly of himself, describing a trait which is simply internal, not referring primarily to external manifestation, although this is implied. It means one who is *proud,* the external manifestation when it appears being in the form of *arrogance* in dealing with others. **ὑβριστής** describes one who delights in *insolent wrong-doing* toward others, finds pleasure in such acts. Cruelty and lust are two of the many forms which this quality assumes. These three words occur together in Ro. i. 30. They are never used in a good sense. They may be said to move in a certain sense in an ascending scale of guilt, designating respectively "the boastful *in words*, the proud and overbearing *in thoughts*, the insolent and injurious *in acts*" (Cremer).

§ 9. Incorruptible, unfading.

ἄφθαρτος, ἀμάραντος, ἀμαράντινος.

ἄφθαρτος is properly *incorruptible*, unaffected by corruption and decay. It is applied to God, and to that which is connected with him. **ἀμάραντος** expresses the same idea in another way. It means *unfading*, the root idea being that it is unaffected by the withering which is common in the case of flowers. **ἀμαράντινος,** derived from *ἀμάραντος*, means *composed of amaranths, i.e.*, of unfading flowers.

§ 10. Faultless, unblamed.

ἄμωμος, ἄμεμπτος, ἀνέγκλητος, ἀνεπίληπτος.

ἄμωμος is *faultless, without blemish, free from imperfections.* It refers especially to character. **ἄμεμπτος** is strictly *unblamed*, one with whom no fault is found. This of course refers particularly to the verdict of others upon one. **ἀνέγκλητος** designates one against whom there is no accusation, implying not acquittal of a charge, but that no charge has been made. **ἀνεπίληπτος** means *irreprehensible*, designating one who affords nothing upon which an adversary might seize, in order to make a charge against him.

§ 11. Regeneration, renovation.

παλιγγενεσία, ἀνακαίνωσις.

παλιγγενεσία means *new birth.* In classical Greek it was used in a weakened sense to denote a recovery, restoration, revival. In the N.T. it is used only twice, but in a higher sense. In Tit. iii. 5 it means *new birth, regeneration*, referring to God's act of causing the sinner to pass from the death of sin into spiritual life in Christ. It has a wider meaning in Mat. xix. 28, where it is used of the change which is ultimately to take place in all the universe, its regeneration, which is the full working out of the change involved in the regeneration of the individual. **ἀνακαίνωσις** is *renewal* or *renovation,* denoting a continuous process through which man becomes more fully Christ-like, in which process he is a worker together with God. Some, as *e.g.* Cremer, without sufficient reason, have thought that the early use of παλιγγενεσία as a somewhat technical term, to denote the Pythagorean doctrine of transmigration, gave to the word a permanent eschatological coloring, so that in the N.T. it has the meaning *resurrection,* especially in Mat. xix. 28.

§ 12. Murderer.

φονεύς, ἀνθρωποκτόνος, σικάριος.

Both in derivation and usage, **φονεύς** and **ἀνθρωποκτόνος** are distinguished from each other just as the English *murderer* from *manslayer* or *homicide.* **σικάριος,** used only in Ac. xxi. 38, is the Latin *sicarius,* and means *an assassin,* usually hired for the work, who furtively stabbed his enemy with a short sword, the Latin *sica.* φονεύς is a generic word and may denote a murderer of any kind, σικάριος being one of the specific varieties which it includes.

§ 13. Anti-Christ, false Christ.

ψευδόχριστος, ἀντίχριστος.

ψευδόχριστος means *a false Christ, a pretended Messiah,* who sets himself up instead of Christ, proclaiming that he is Christ. Some have given about the same meaning to **ἀντίχριστος.** But it is much more probable that it means one diametrically opposed to Christ, one who sets himself up against Christ, proclaiming that there is no Christ.

§ 14. Profligacy.

ἀσωτία, ἀσέλγεια.

The fundamental idea of **ἀσωτία** is "wastefulness and riotous excess; of **ἀσέλγεια,** lawless insolence and wanton caprice" (Trench). *ἀσωτία* means reckless and extravagant expenditure, chiefly for the gratification of one's sensual desires. It denotes a dissolute, profligate course of life. In *ἀσέλγεια* also there is included the idea of profligacy, often of lasciviousness, but the fundamental thought is the acknowledging of no restraints, the insolent doing of whatever one's caprice may suggest.

§ 15. Covenant-breaker, implacable.

ἀσύνθετος, ἄσπονδος.

These words are quite similar in their effects, but opposite in their conception. **ἀσύνθετος,** occurring only in Ro. i. 31, is *covenant-breaker*, one who interrupts a state of peace and brings on war by disregarding an agreement by which peace is maintained. **ἄσπονδος** is *implacable*, one who refuses to agree to any terms or suggestions of peace. It implies a state of war, and a refusal of covenant or even of armistice to end it permanently or temporarily. In the N.T. use both words probably refer not to war in the strict sense so much as to discord and strife.

§ 16. Beautiful, graceful.

ἀστεῖος, ὡραῖος, καλός.

ἀστεῖος is properly one living in a city, urban. It soon acquires the meaning *urbane, polite, elegant.* Then it obtains to a limited extent the meaning *beautiful*, although never in the highest degree. **ὡραῖος,** from *ὥρα,* hour, period, means properly *timely.* From that comes the idea of being beautiful, since nearly everything is beautiful in its hour of fullest perfection. **καλός** is a much higher word. It means *beautiful*, physically or morally. It is, however, distinctly the beauty which comes from harmony, the beauty which arises from a symmetrical adjustment in right proportion, in other words, from the harmonious completeness of the object concerned.

§ 17. Wisdom, knowledge.

σοφία, φρόνησις, γνῶσις, ἐπίγνωσις.

σοφία is certainly the highest word of all these. It is properly *wisdom.* It denotes mental excellence in the highest and fullest sense, expressing an *attitude* as well as an *act* of the mind. It comprehends knowledge and implies goodness, including the striving after the highest ends, as well as the using of the best means for their attainment. It is never ascribed to any one but God and good men, except in a plainly ironical sense. **φρόνησις** is a middle term, sometimes having a meaning nearly as high as *σοφία,* sometimes much lower. It means *prudence, intelligence,* a skillful adaptation of the means to the end desired, the end, however, not being necessarily a good one. **γνῶσις** is *knowledge, cognition,* the understanding of facts or truths,

9

or else *insight, discernment.* ἐπίγνωσις has an intensive meaning as compared with γνῶσις, it is a fuller, clearer, more thorough knowledge.   The
verb ἐπιγινώσκω has the same intensive force as compared with γινώσκω.

§ 18. Religious.

θεοσεβής, εὐσεβής, εὐλαβής, θρῆσκος, δεισιδαίμων.

θεοσεβής, according to derivation and usage, means *worship of God* (or
of the gods), a fulfillment of one's duty towards God.   It is a general term,
meaning *religious* in a good sense.   **εὐσεβής** is distinguished from θεοσεβής
in two ways.   It is used to include the fulfillment of obligations of all kinds,
both towards God and man.   It is thus applied to the fulfillment of the
duties involved in human relations, as towards one's parents.   Furthermore,
when used in the higher sense, it means not any kind of worship, but, as the
etymology indicates, the worshipping of God *aright.*   **εὐλαβής,** meaning
originally *careful in handling,* in its religious application means careful in
handling divine things.   It characterizes the anxious and scrupulous worshipper, careful not to change anything that should be observed in worship,
and fearful of offending.   It means *devout,* and may be applied to an adherent
of any religion, being especially appropriate to describe the best of the Jewish
worshippers.   **θρῆσκος** is one who is diligent in the performance of the
outward service of God.   It applies especially to ceremonial worship.
δεισιδαίμων, in accordance with its derivation, makes prominent the element
of *fear.*   It emphasizes strongly the ideas of dependence and of anxiety for
divine favor.   It may be used as practically equivalent to θεοσεβής.   Often,
however, it implies that the fear which it makes prominent is an unworthy
fear, so that it comes to have the meaning *superstitious.*   In the N.T. it is
used, as is also the noun δεισιδαιμονία, in a purposely neutral sense, meaning
simply *religious,* neither conveying the highest meaning, nor plainly implying a lower meaning.

§ 19. Pure.

εἰλικρινής, καθαρός, ἀμίαντος.

εἰλικρινής denotes chiefly that which is pure as being *sincere,* free from
foreign admixture.   **καθαρός** is that which is pure as being *clean,* free
from soil or stain.   The meaning of both in the N.T. is distinctly ethical.
ἀμίαντος is *unspotted,* describing that which is far removed from every kind
of contamination.

§ 20. Assembly, church.

συναγωγή, ἐκκλησία, πανήγυρις.

Accordîng to their derivation, συναγωγή is simply *an assembly*, a mass of people gathered together; ἐκκλησία is a narrower word, also *an assembly*, but including only those specially *called together out of* a larger multitude, for the transaction of business. ἐκκλησία usually denotes a somewhat more select company than συναγωγή. A significant use of ἐκκλησία in strict harmony with its derivation was common among the Greeks. It was their common word for the lawful assembly in a free Greek city of all those possessing the rights of citizenship, for the transaction of public affairs. They were *summoned out of* the whole population, "a select portion of it, including neither the populace, nor strangers, nor yet those who had forfeited their civic rights" (Trench). συναγωγή had been, before N.T. times, appropriated to designate *a synagogue*, a Jewish assembly for worship, distinct from the Temple, in which sense it is used in the N.T. Probably for that reason, and also for its greater inherent etymological fitness, ἐκκλησία is the word taken to designate *a Christian church*, a company of believers who meet for worship. Both these words, however, are sometimes used in the N.T. in a non-technical sense. πανήγυρις, occurring only in Heb. xii. 23, differs from both, denoting a solemn assembly for festal rejoicing.

§ 21. Humility, gentleness.

ταπεινοφροσύνη, πραότης.

ταπεινοφροσύνη is *humility*, not the making of one's self small when he is really great, but thinking little of one's self, because this is in a sense the right estimate for any human being, however great. πραότης is founded upon this idea, and goes beyond it. It is the attitude of mind and behavior which, arising from humility, disposes one to receive with *gentleness and meekness* whatever may come to him from others or from God.

§ 22. Gentleness.

πραότης, ἐπιείκεια.

Both words may be translated *gentleness*, yet there are marked differences in meaning. πραότης is rather passive, denoting, as has been said above, see § 21, one's attitude toward others in view of their acts, bad or good. ἐπιείκεια is distinctly active, it is seen in one's deeds toward others, and it usually implies the relation of superior to inferior. It is fundamentally a relaxing of strict legal requirements concerning others, yet doing this in order more fully to carry out the real spirit of the law. It is *clemency* in which there is no element of weakness or injustice.

§ 23. Desire, lust.

ἐπιθυμία, πάθος, ὁρμή, ὄρεξις.

ἐπιθυμία is the broadest of these words. Its meaning may be good, but it is usually bad. It denotes any natural desire or appetite, usually with the implication that it is a depraved desire. πάθος has not as broad a meaning as in classical Greek, but denotes evil desire, chiefly, however, as a condition of the soul rather than in active operation. ὁρμή indicates *hostile* motion toward an object, either for seizing or repelling. ὄρεξις is a desire or appetite, especially seeking the object of gratification in order to make it one's own.

§ 24. Affliction.

θλῖψις, στενοχωρία.

θλῖψις according to its derivation means *pressure.* In its figurative sense it is that which presses upon the spirit, *affliction.* στενοχωρία meant originally *a narrow, confined space.* It denotes affliction as arising from cramping circumstances. In use it cannot always be distinguished from θλῖψις, but it is ordinarily a stronger word.

§ 25. Bad, evil.

κακός, πονηρός, φαῦλος.

These words may be used with very little distinction of meaning, but often the difference is marked. κακός frequently means *evil* rather negatively, referring to the absence of the qualities which constitute a person or thing what it should be or what it claims to be. It is also used meaning *evil* in a moral sense. It is a general antithesis to ἀγαθός. πονηρός is a word at once stronger and more active, it means *mischief-making*, delighting in injury, doing evil to others, dangerous, destructive. κακός describes the quality according to its nature, πονηρός, according to its effects. φαῦλος is the bad chiefly as the *worthless,* the good for nothing.

§ 26. Punishment.

τιμωρία, κόλασις

τιμωρία in classical and N.T. usage denotes especially the vindicative character of punishment, it is the punishment in relation to the *punisher*. **κόλασις** in classical Greek meant usually punishment which aimed at the reformation of the offender. But sometimes in later Greek, and always in the N.T., the idea of reformation seems to disappear, so that there remains simply the idea of punishment, but viewed in relation to the *punished*.

§ 27. To pollute.

μιαίνω, μολύνω.

μιαίνω meant originally *to stain*, as with color. **μολύνω** meant originally *to smear over*, as with mud or filth, always having a bad meaning, while the meaning of *μιαίνω* might be either good or bad. According to classical Greek, *μιαίνω* has a religious meaning, *to profane*, while *μολύνω* is simply *to spoil, disgrace*. As ethically applied in the N.T. they have both practically the same meaning, *to pollute, defile*. It is, however, true that *μιαίνω*, to judge from classical usage, refers chiefly to the effect of the act not on the individual, but on others, on the community.

§ 28. To do.

ποιέω, πράσσω.

These words are often used interchangeably, but in many cases a distinction can be drawn. **ποιέω** refers more to the object and end of an act, **πράσσω** rather to the means by which the object is attained. Hence, while *ποιέω* means *to accomplish*, *πράσσω* may mean nothing more than merely *to busy one's self about*. *ποιέω* often means to do a thing once for all, *πράσσω*, to do continually or repeatedly. From these distinctions it follows that *ποιέω*, being on the whole the higher word, is more often used of doing good, *πράσσω* more frequently of doing evil.

§ 29. Fleshly, fleshy, sensual.

σαρκικός, σάρκινος, ψυχικός.

σαρκικός means *fleshly*, that which is controlled by the wrong desires which rule in the flesh, flesh often being understood in its broad sense, see σάρξ.   It describes a man who gives the flesh the dominion in his life, a place which does not belong to it by right.   It means distinctly opposed to the Spirit of God, anti-spiritual.   σάρκινος properly means *fleshy*, made of flesh, flesh being the material of which it is composed.   When given a bad meaning, however, it is plainly similar to σαρκικός, but according to Trench not so strong, denoting one as unspiritual, undeveloped, rather than anti-spiritual.   Others, as Cremer and Thayer, with more probability make σάρκινος the stronger, it describes one who is flesh, wholly given up to the flesh, rooted in the flesh, rather than one who simply acts according to the flesh (σαρκικός).   There is much confusion between the two in the N.T. manuscripts.   ψυχικός has a meaning somewhat similar to σαρκικός.   Both are used in contrast with πνευματικός.   But ψυχικός has really a distinct meaning, describing the life which is controlled by the ψυχή.   It denotes, therefore, that which belongs to the animal life, or that which is controlled simply by the appetites and passions of the sensuous nature.

§ 30. Mercy, compassion.

ἔλεος, οἰκτιρμός.

Both words denote sympathy, fellow-feeling with misery, mercy, compassion.   ἔλεος, however, manifests itself chiefly in acts rather than words, while οἰκτιρμός is used rather of the inward feeling of compassion which abides in the heart.   A criminal might ask for ἔλεος, *mercy*, from his judge; but hopeless suffering may be the object of οἰκτιρμός, *compassion*.

§ 31. To love.

ἀγαπάω, φιλέω.

ἀγαπάω, and not φιλέω, is the word used of God's love to men, φιλανθροπία is, however, once used with this meaning, Tit. iii. 4.   ἀγαπάω is also the word ordinarily used of men's love to God, but φιλέω is once so used, 1 Cor. xvi. 22.   ἀγαπάω is the word used of love to one's enemies. The interchange of the words in Jn. xxi. 15–17 is very interesting and instructive.

§ 32. To will, to wish.

βούλομαι, θέλω.

In many cases these two words are used without appreciable distinction, meaning *conscious willing, purpose*.   But frequently it is evident that a difference is intended, although there is much difference of opinion as to the exact distinction. Thayer says that βούλομαι "seems to designate the will which follows deliberation," θέλω, "the will which proceeds from inclination." Grimm, on the other hand, says that θέλω gives prominence to the emotive element, βούλομαι to the rational and volitive; θέλω signifies the choice, while βούλομαι marks the choice as deliberate and intelligent. The view of Cremer on the whole seems preferable to any other. According to this view, βούλομαι has the wider range of meaning, but θέλω is the stronger word, θέλω denotes the active resolution, the will urging on to action, see Ro. vii. 15, while βούλομαι is rather to have in thought, to intend, to be determined. βούλομαι sometimes means no more than to have an inclination, see Ac. xxiii. 15. Instructive examples of the use of the two words in close proximity are found in Mar. xv. 9, 15, and especially Mat. i. 19.

§ 33. Schism.

σχίσμα, αἵρεσις.

σχίσμα is *actual division, separation.* αἵρεσις is rather *the separating tendency,* so it is really more fundamental than σχίσμα.

§ 34. Mind, understanding.

νοῦς, διάνοια.

νοῦς is distinctly *the reflective consciousness,* "the organ of moral thinking and knowing, the intellectual organ of moral sentiment" (Cremer). διάνοια meant originally *activity of thinking,* but has borrowed from νοῦς its common meaning of *faculty of thought.* It is more common than νοῦς, and has largely replaced it in its usual meanings.

§ 35. Law.

νόμος, θεσμός, ἐντολή, δόγμα.

νόμος is the common word meaning *law.* It may mean law in general. In the N.T., however, it usually means the law of God, and most frequently the Mosaic law. θεσμός is law considered with special reference to the authority on which it rests. ἐντολή is more specific, being used of a particular command. δόγμα is an authoritative conclusion, a proposition which it is expected that all will recognize as universally binding.

§ 36. Type, image.

τύπος, ἀντίτυπος.

τύπος has many meanings, among the most common being *image*, *pattern* or *model*, and *type*.   In the last sense it means a person or thing prefiguring a future person or thing, *e.g.*, Adam as a type of Christ, Ro. v. 14.   ἀντί-τυπος, as used in 1 Pet. iii. 21, is by Thayer and many others thought to correspond to τύπος as its counterpart, in the sense which the English word antitype suggests.   By Cremer it is rather given the meaning *image*.

§ 37. To ask.

αἰτέω, ἐρωτάω.

Thayer, as opposed to Trench and others, would make the distinction between these two words to be this : " αἰτέω signifies to ask for something to be given, not done, giving prominence to the thing asked for rather than the person, and hence is rarely used in exhortation.   ἐρωτάω, on the other hand, is to request a person to do (rarely to give) something ; referring more directly to the person, it is naturally used in exhortation, etc."

§ 38. World, age.

αἰών, κόσμος.

It is only in a part of their meanings that these two words are in any real sense synonymous, and it is that part which is here considered.   Both A. V. and R. V. often translate αἰών by *world*, thus obscuring the distinction between it and κόσμος.   αἰών is usually better expressed by *age*, it is the world at a given time, a particular period in the world's history.   κόσμος has very frequently an unfavorable meaning, denoting the inhabitants of the world, mankind in general, as opposed to God.   A similar meaning is often attached to αἰών, it means the spirit of the age, often in an unfavorable sense.   See Ep. ii. 2, where both words occur together.   An exceptional meaning for the plural of αἰών is found in Heb. i. 2 and xi. 3, where it denotes the worlds, apparently in reference to space rather than time.

§ 39. Rest.

ἀνάπαυσις, ἄνεσις.

Both words in a certain sense mean *rest*, but from different stand-points.   ἀνάπαυσις is rest which comes by cessation from labor, which may be simply temporary. ἄνεσις means literally the relaxation of strings which have been drawn tight. Hence, it is used to designate ease, especially that which comes by relaxation of unfavorable conditions of any kind, such as affliction.

§ 40. Wind.

πνεῦμα, πνοή, ἄνεμος, λαῖλαψ, θύελλα.

πνεῦμα when used in its lower meaning to denote wind means simply *an ordinary wind*, a regularly blowing current of air of considerable force. πνοή is distinguished from it as being a gentler motion of the air. ἄνεμος, on the other hand, is more forcible than πνεῦμα, it is the strong, often the tempestuous, wind. λαῖλαψ is the violent fitful wind which accompanies a heavy shower. θύελλα is more violent than any of the others, and often implies a conflict of opposing winds.

§ 41. Old.

παλαιός, ἀρχαῖος.

According to their derivation, παλαιός is that which has been in existence for a long time, ἀρχαῖος that which has been from the beginning. In use, at times no distinction can be drawn. Often, however, ἀρχαῖος does denote distinctively that which has been from the beginning, and so it reaches back to a point of time beyond παλαιός. παλαιός has often the secondary meaning of that which is old and so worn out, having suffered more or less from the injuries and ravages of time, its opposite in this sense being καινός.

§ 42. Harsh, austere.

αὐστηρός, σκληρός.

αὐστηρός has not necessarily an unfavorable meaning. It is well represented by the word *austere*, it means one who is earnest and severe, strict in his ways, opposed to all levity. By implication it may have the unfavorable meaning of harshness or moroseness. σκληρός has always an unfavorable meaning. It indicates one who is uncivil, intractable, rough and harsh. There is in it the implication of inhumanity.

§ 43. Darkness.

σκότος, γνόφος, ζόφος, ἀχλύς.

σκότος is a general word, meaning *darkness* in any sense.   **γνόφος** usually refers to darkness that accompanies a storm.   **ζόφος** meant originally *the gloom* of twilight.   It was then applied in classical Greek to the darkness of the underworld, the gloom of a sunless region.   The latter meaning seems to be practically the one which the word has in the N.T.   **ἀχλύς** is specifically a misty darkness.

§ 44. People, nation.

λαός, ἔθνος, δῆμος, ὄχλος.

λαός is a word which is usually limited in use to the chosen people, Israel.   **ἔθνος** in the singular is a general term for nation, applied to any nation, even to the Jews.   In the plural it ordinarily denotes all mankind aside from the Jews and in contrast with them, the Gentiles.   **δῆμος** is a people, especially organized and convened together, and exercising their rights as citizens.   **ὄχλος** is *a crowd*, an unorganized multitude, especially composed of those who have not the rights and privileges of free citizens.

§ 45. Servant, slave.

δοῦλος, θεράπων, διάκονος, οἰκέτης, ὑπηρέτης.

δοῦλος is the usual word for *slave*, one who is permanently in servitude, in subjection to a master.   **θεράπων** is simply one who renders service at a particular time, sometimes as a slave, more often as a freeman, who renders voluntary service prompted by duty or love.   It denotes one who serves, *in his relation to a person.*   **διάκονος** also may designate either a slave or a freeman, it denotes a servant viewed *in relation to his work.*   **οἰκέτης** designates a slave, sometimes being practically equivalent to δοῦλος. Usually, however, as the etymology of the term indicates, it means a slave as a member of the household, not emphasizing the servile idea, but rather the relation which would tend to mitigate the severity of his condition.   **ὑπηρέτης** means literally *an under-rower,* and was used to describe an ordinary rower on a war-galley.   It is then used, as in the N.T., to indicate any man, not a slave, who served in a subordinate position under a superior.

§ 46. To adulterate.

καπηλεύω, δολόω.

Both these words mean *to adulterate*, and some maintain that they are practically identical. But it is more probable that δολόω means simply to adulterate, while καπηλεύω conveys the idea of adulterating for the sake of making an unjust profit by the process.

§ 47. Animal.

ζῶον, θηρίον.

ζῶον is a general term, meaning *living creature*, which may include all living beings, in classical Greek even including man. In the N.T. it means ordinarily *animal*. θηρίον is *beast*, usually wild beast. It implies perhaps not necessarily wildness and ferocity, but at least a certain amount of brutality which is wanting in ζῶον. ζῶον emphasizes the qualities in which animals are akin to man, θηρίον, those in which they are inferior.

§ 48. Sea.

θάλασσα, πέλαγος.

θάλασσα is the more general word, indicating *the sea* or *ocean* as contrasted with the land or shore. It may be applied to small bodies of water. πέλαγος is *the open sea*, the uninterrupted expanse of water, in contrast with the portions broken by islands or with partly inclosed bays. The prominent thought is said by Trench to be breadth rather than depth. Noteworthy is the distinction between the two words in Mat. xviii. 6.

§ 49. To grieve.

λυπέομαι, πενθέω, θρηνέω, κόπτομαι.

λυπέομαι is the most general word, meaning simply *to grieve*, outwardly or inwardly. πενθέω means properly *to lament for the dead*. It is also applied to passionate lamentation of any kind, so great that it cannot be hid. θρηνέω is *to give utterance to a dirge* over the dead, either in unstudied words, or in a more elaborate poem. This word is used by S. in describing David's lament over Saul and Jonathan. κόπτομαι is *to beat the breast in grief*, ordinarily for the dead.

§ 50. Form, appearance.

ἰδέα, μορφή, σχῆμα.

ἰδέα denotes merely *outward appearance*. Both **μορφή** and **σχῆμα** express something more than that. They too denote outward form, but as including one's habits, activities and modes of action in general. In *μορφή* it is also implied that the outward form expresses the inner essence, an idea which is absent from *σχῆμα*. *μορφή* expresses the form as that which is intrinsic and essential, *σχῆμα* signifies the figure, shape, as that which is more outward and accidental. Both *σχῆμα* and *ἰδέα* therefore deal with externals, *σχῆμα* being more comprehensive than *ἰδέα*, while *μορφή* deals with externals as expressing that which is internal.

§ 51. Clothing.

ἱμάτιον, χιτών, ἱματισμός, χλαμύς, στολή, ποδήρης.

ἱμάτιον is used in a general sense to mean *clothing*, and may thus be applied to any garment when it is not desired to express its exact nature. In a more specific use, however, it denotes the large loose outer garment, *a cloak*, which ordinarily was worn, but in working was laid aside.   **χιτών** is best expressed by the word *tunic*.   It was a closely fitting under-garment, usually worn next the skin.   At times, especially in working, it was the only garment worn.   A person clothed only in the *χιτών* was often called *γυμνός* (Jn. xxi. 7).   *ἱμάτιον* and *χιτών* are often found associated as the upper and under garment respectively.   **ἱματισμός** does not denote a specific garment, but means *clothing*, being used, however, ordinarily only of garments more or less stately or costly.   **χλαμύς** is *a robe* or *cloak*, it is a technical expression for a garment of dignity or office.   **στολή** is any stately robe, ordinarily long, reaching to the feet or sweeping the ground, often worn by women. **ποδήρης** was originally an adjective meaning *reaching to the feet*.   It can hardly be distinguished in use from *στολή*.   It occurs only in Rev. i. 13.

§ 52. New.

νέος, καινός.

νέος is *the new* as contemplated under the aspect of time, that which has recently come into existence.   **καινός** is *the new* under the aspect of quality, that which has not seen service.   *καινός* therefore often means new as contrasted with that which has decayed with age, or is worn out, its opposite then being παλαιός. It sometimes suggests that which is unusual. It often implies praise, the new as superior to the old. Occasionally, on the other hand, it implies the opposite, the new as inferior to that which is old, because the old is familiar or because it has improved with age. Of course it is evident that both νέος and καινός may sometimes be applied to the same object, but from different points of view.

§ 53. Labor.

μόχθος, πόνος, κόπος.

μόχθος is *labor*, hard and often painful. It is the ordinary word for common labor which is the usual lot of humanity. πόνος is *labor* which demands one's whole strength. It is therefore applied to labors of an unusual kind, specially wearing or painful. In classical Greek it was the usual word employed to describe the labors of Hercules. κόπος denotes *the weariness* which results from labor, or labor considered from the stand-point of the resulting weariness.

§ 54. Drunkenness, drinking.

μέθη, πότος, οἰνοφλυγία, κῶμος, κραιπάλη.

μέθη is the ordinary word for *drunkenness*. πότος is rather concrete, *a drinking, carousing*. οἰνοφλυγία is a prolonged condition of drunkenness, *a debauch*. κῶμος includes *riot* and *revelry*, usually as arising from drunkenness. κραιπάλη denotes *the sickness* and *discomfort* resulting from drunkenness.

§ 55. War, battle.

πόλεμος, μάχη.

πόλεμος ordinarily means *war*, *i.e.*, the whole course of hostilities; μάχη, *battle*, a single engagement. It is also true that μάχη has often the weaker force of *strife* or *contention*, which is very seldom found in πόλεμος.

§ 56. Basket.

σπυρίς, κόφινος.

These words in the N.T. are used with an evident purpose to discriminate between them. The distinction, however, does not seem to have been chiefly one of size, as some have thought, but of use. σπυρίς is usually a basket for food, *a lunch-basket, a hamper*, while κόφινος is a more general term for *basket*. The descriptions of the two miracles of feeding the multitude use always different words in the two cases, see *e.g.* Mar. viii. 19, 20.

§ 57. It is necessary.

δεῖ, ὀφείλει.

δεῖ, the third person of δέω, is commonly used impersonally in classical Greek. This usage is less common, but frequent, in the N.T. δεῖ indicates a necessity in the nature of things rather than a personal obligation, it describes that which *must* be done. ὀφείλει indicates rather the personal obligation, it is that which is proper, something that *ought* to be done.

§ 58. Tax.

φόρος, τέλος, κῆνσος, δίδραχμον.

φόρος indicates *a direct tax* which was levied annually on houses, lands, and persons, and paid usually in produce. τέλος is *an indirect tax* on merchandise, which was collected at piers, harbors, and gates of cities. It was similar to modern import duties. κῆνσος, originally an enrollment of property and persons, came to mean *a poll-tax*, levied annually on individuals by the Roman government. δίδραχμον was the coin used to pay an annual tax levied by the religious leaders of Israel for the purpose of defraying the general expenses of the Temple.

§ 59. Tax-collector.

τελώνης, ἀρχιτελώνης.

The Roman system of collecting taxes, especially the τέλοι, in their provinces, included ordinarily three grades of officials. There was the highest, called in Latin *publicanus*, who paid a sum of money for the taxes of a certain province, and then exacted that and as much more as he could from the province. This man lived in Rome. Then there were the *sub-magistri*, who had charge each of a certain portion of territory, and who lived in the provinces. Then there were the *portitores*, the actual custom-house officers, who did the real work of collecting the taxes. The N.T. word τελώνης is used to describe one of the *portitores*, it is the lowest of these three grades. It does not correspond to the Latin *publicanus*, and the word *publican* used to translate it in A. V. and R. V. is apt to be misleading, *tax-collector* would be better. ἀρχιτελώνης, only occurring in Lu. xix. 2, evidently describes a higher official than τελώνης, and is probably one of the *submagistri*, the next higher grade.

§ 60. Child.

τέκνον, υἱός, παῖς, παιδίον, παιδάριον, παιδίσκη.

τέκνον and υἱός both point to parentage. τέκνον, however, emphasizes the idea of descent, giving prominence to the physical and outward aspects; while υἱός emphasizes the idea of relationship, and considers especially the inward, ethical, and legal aspects. παῖς as well as τέκνον emphasizes the idea of descent, but gives especial prominence to age, denoting a child as one who is young. παῖς is also often used of a servant. The number of years covered by the term παῖς is quite indefinite. Its diminutives παιδίον and παιδάριον are used without appreciable difference to denote a young child. (παιδίσκος in classical Greek and) παιδίσκη, in which the diminutive force is largely lost, cover the years of late childhood and early youth.

§ 61. Tribe, family, household.

φυλή, πατριά, οἶκος.

These words form a series. φυλή is sometimes *a race, nation,* but usually *a tribe,* such as one of the twelve tribes of Israel, descended from the twelve sons of Jacob. πατριά is a smaller division within the tribe, it is an association of families closely related, in the N.T. generally used of those descended from a particular one of the sons of Jacob's sons. οἶκος is yet narrower, *household,* including all the inmates of a single house, being the unit of organization.

Mackenzie's Manual of Ethics

THIRD EDITION, ENLARGED—ONE VOLUME, CLOTH—PRICE $2.00 POSTPAID

CONTENTS.

PART I. THE THEORY OF MORALS.

*The Scope of Ethics—The Relation of Ethics to Other Sciences—The Moral Judgment—Duty—
Will and Desire—Happiness—Perfection—The Freedom of the Will—The Individual and Society.*

PART II. THE MORAL LIFE.

*Moral Order—The Commandments—The Virtues—The Inner Life—Moral Pathology—Moral
Progress—The Relation of Art to Ethics—The Relation of Ethics to Religion.*

Mackenzie's Ethics has interested me more than any other discussion of the subject I have ever examined. It seems the product of an acute and scholarly mind, both critical and eclectic, finding the good and the evil in all beliefs; it is remarkably comprehensive, suggestive, and calculated to stimulate beneficially the thoughtful student.—*Rev. Jas. A. Quarles, Prof. of Ethics, Washington and Lee Univ'y, Lexington, Va.* (*Apr. 2, 97.*)

Mackenzie's Manual of Ethics is a work of a high order of scientific and literary excellence. The fundamental idea concerning right is sound; the order of discussion logical; the terminology free from unnecessary technicalities; and the style throughout is lucid and forcible.—*Rev. Eml. V. Gerhart, Theological Seminary, Lancaster, Pa.* (*May 24, 1897.*)

It gives me pleasure to state that in my judgment Mackenzie's Ethics will prove a most useful addition to the literature of the subject. The plan of the book is a good one, and the author succeeds in making his points very clear. I am glad to have such a work by me, and expect to consult it frequently.—*Rev. T. R. English, Prof. Eng. Bible and Pastoral Theol., Union Theol. Sem., Hampden-Sidney, Va.* (*May 14, 1897.*)

I have made considerable use of Mackenzie's Ethics. Professor Mackenzie's treatment is characterized by lucidity and freshness in an unusual degree. There is abundant evidence of mature knowledge and of a thorough mastery of his material—two qualifications which go very far toward making the best book for students. I shall make a larger use of this work in the future.—*John E. Russell, Prof. of Philosophy, Williams College, Williamstown, Mass.* (*March 31, 1897.*)

Prof. Mackenzie's Manual seems to me the most thoroughly interesting work on ethics that I know.—*Rev. N. P. Gilman, Professor of Ethics, Meadville Theological School, Meadville, Pa.* (*March 17, 1897.*)

I have examined with a great deal of interest Mackenzie's Manual of Ethics in the University Tutorial Series. I must say I am very highly pleased with the work.—*Rev. L. H. Murlin, Pres., Prof. of Philos. and Biblical Lit., Baker University, Baldwin, Kan.* (*September 17, 1896.*)

Fine presentation of the subject—both in matter and style.—*Rev. J. W. Flinn, Prof. of Philos. and Religion, South Carolina College, Columbia, S. C.* (*June 5, 1897.*)

The author has read widely, and his comments are bright and stimulating. The tone of ethical discussion is healthful and ennobling. To whatever chapter you open you find a brilliant essay, and are carried forward as upon a strong current without any effort upon the part of the reader.—*Rev. D. B. Perry, Pres., Prof. of Philos., Doane College, Crete, Nebraska.* (*May 21, 1897.*)

A careful reading of Mackenzie's Manual of Ethics convinces me that he has produced a scholarly and most suggestive treatise on this important and difficult science. His treatment is fresh, comprehensive, and inspiring. It is a highly creditable addition to Ethical literature, and will be welcomed by all thoughtful students of the subject.—*Rev. Wm. Willett Harsha, Prof. of Systematic Theol., Omaha Theological Seminary, Omaha, Neb.* (*May 3, 1897.*)

Mackenzie's Ethics has been adopted for use in:

Yale College	Bates College	Meadville Theological School
Brown University	Bowdoin College	Ouachita Baptist College
Boston University	Western Md. College	University of Minnesota
Columbian University	Geneva College	University of Kansas
Ohio State University	Eureka College	Bangor Theological Seminary
Smith College	Iowa College	Atlanta University
Mt. Holyoke College	Vanderbilt Univ., Nashville	Yankton College
Lafayette College	Montana College	Kenyon College
Washington and Lee University	Iowa Wesleyan University	Southwest Kansas College
Union College	Marietta College	Wake Forest College
Wesleyan Female College, Macon, Ga.	Nevada State University	Washburn College
Cumberland University	Howard University	Western College
Heidelberg College	Louisiana State University	Ogden College
Roanoke College	Middlebury College	Dakota University
University of California	University of Tennessee	Coates College for Women
Iowa State College	University of Buffalo	Greenville Female College
John B. Stetson University	Amity College	Furman University

Psychology Simplified for Teachers

By JOHN P. GORDY, Ph.D., LL.D.,

Head of the Pedagogical Department of the Ohio State University.

Professor Gordy's successful career having been pre-eminently that of a sympathetic teacher of teachers, this work fulfills the expressed wish of thousands of teachers to possess in book form for daily reference the simple methods of mind study that he has made so helpful in his familiar talks with teachers and parents.

The author's one aim is to guide the teacher to a finer success, and to help the parent as well, by setting them to studying their own minds and the minds of their pupils, or their children. Professor Gordy rightly believes that the very best elementary text-book in Psychology is — *the mind of a little child!* With this truth as a ground work, the question was how to present it in book form so as to stimulate the reader to think the subject out, and at the same time render the teacher's work rational by inging to view the laws of mind. The book itself best answers this question.

The writer's surprisingly simple presentation robs Psychology of whatever mystery or difficulty some young teachers have invested it. Gifted with a remarkable lucidity of style, he has produced a book that teachers like to get together and read aloud. It has been much read and talked over by reading circles and neighborhood clubs. Mothers read it aloud to their friends. In fact not only does this book envelop the subject of child-study with a new and fascinating interest for the teacher in the schools and the parent at home, but it is full of interest and instruction for all whose vocation or avocation brings them into any serious relationship with children —— the teacher in the Sunday school, the superintendent in the Bible class, the preacher in the pulpit, and the pastor in his social rounds; indeed everyone who comes into that contact with the child mind which implies influence toward the higher development.

As an added stimulus to self-study, and further to emphasize the value, to the teacher, of child-observation, a set of suggestive questions has been introduced at the end of each chapter, inviting comparison and discussion.

All these features make this the best handbook on the subject for teachers of whatever grade or degree of experience, for beginners in Psychology, and also for parents.

Prof. L. W. Hoffman, *Principal, WARWICK INSTITUTE, Warwick, N.Y.:* It is with some degree of pleasure I note that Gordy's " Lessons in Psychology " is to be brought to the wider attention of the teaching public through the medium of a firm of publishers so well and favorably known as is yours. The book readily commends itself wherever it becomes known as the most inspiring and usable one on the market covering the psychological topics of especial interest to teachers. I have used it with several teachers' classes always with the best results. Special merits of the work are clear explanations, accurate definitions, apt and pertinent illustrations from every-day experience, and a judicious selection and arrangement of the topics to be treated. The book is itself an excellent example of a correct method in teaching. The chapters on attention ought to be read and treasured by every teacher throughout the land. Aside from being an excellent text-book for class use it is far and above the best possible book to put into the hands of those who wish to study without the help of an instructor.

May 27, 1897.

ON APPROVAL — **Price $1.80 Postpaid** — ON APPROVAL

Money to be refunded if not perfectly satisfactory.

HANDY LITERAL TRANSLATIONS
(75 cents each)

"To one who is reading the Classics, a literal translation is a convenient and legitimate help; ...and every well-informed person will read the Classics either in the original or in a translation."

Latin

Cæsar's Gallic War. *The 7 Books*
Cæsar's Civil War
Catullus
Cicero's Brutus
Cicero's Defense of Roscius
Cicero De Officiis
Cicero On Old Age and Friendship
Cicero On Oratory
Cicero On the Nature of the Gods
Cicero's Select Orations
Cicero's Select Letters, *2 vols.*
Cicero's Tusculan Disputations
Cornelius Nepos, *complete*
Eutropius
Horace, *complete*
Juvenal's Satires, *complete*
Livy, Books I and II
Livy, Books XXI and XXII
Ovid's Metamorphoses, *2 vols.*
Phædrus' Fables
Plautus' Captivi, and Mostelaria
Plautus' Pseudolus; Miles Gloriosus
Plautus' Trinummus, and Menæchmi
Pliny's Select Letters, *2 vols.*
Quintilian, Books X and XII
Roman Life in Lat. Prose and Verse
Sallust: Catiline, and Jugurth. War
Seneca On Benefits
Tacitus' Annals, *1st Six Books*
Tacitus' Germany and Agricola
Tacitus On Oratory
Terence: Andria, Adelphi, Phormio
Terence: Heautontimorumenos
Virgil's Æneid, *the 1st Six Books*
Virgil's Eclogues and Georgics
Viri Romæ

Greek

Æschines Against Ctesiphon
Æschylus' Prometheus Bound, and Seven Against Thebes
Æschylus' Agamemnon
Aristophanes' Birds, and Frogs
Aristophanes' Clouds
Demosthenes On the Crown
Demosthenes' Olynthiacs, Philippics
Euripides' Alcestis, and Electra
Juripides' Bacchantes, Herc. Furens
Euripides' Hecuba, and Andromache
Euripides' Iphig. In Aulis, In Tauris
Euripides' Medea
Herodotus, Books VI and VII
Herodotus, Book VIII
Homer's Iliad, *the 1st Six Books*
Homer's Odyssey, *1st 12 Books*
Lucian's Select Dialogues, *2 vols.*
Lysias' Orations
Plato's Apology, Crito, and Phaedo
Plato's Gorgias
Plato's Laches *(paper)*
Plato's Protagoras, Euthyphron
Plato's Republic
Sophocles' Œd. Tyr. Elec., Antig.
Thucydides, Books I-IV
Thucydides, Books V-VIII
Xenophon's Anabasis, *1st 4 Books*
Xenophon's Cyropædia, *2 vols.*
Xenophon's Hellenica, Symposium
Xenophon's Memorabilia, *complete*

German

Corneille's Le Cid
Freytag's Die Journalisten
Goethe's Egmont
Goethe's Faust
Goethe's Iphigenia in Tauris
Goethe's Hermann and Dorothea
Hillern's Higher Than The Church
Lessing's Emilia Galotti
Lessing's Minna von Barnhelm
Lessing's Nathan the Wise
Schiller's Ballads
Schiller's Maid of Orleans
Schiller's Maria Stuart
Schiller's The Nephew as Uncle
Schiller's Wallenstein's Death
Schiller's William Tell
Storm's Immensee

French

Racine's Athalie

FOR INTERLINEARS, AND "COMPLETELY PARSED," SEE OTHER PAGES

INTERLINEAR TRANSLATIONS

Translations for both students and teachers is the recommendation of authorities today. They deplore that a classic reader's time should be wasted in eternal thumbing to vocabulary and grammar.

Part Page of Interlinear Cæsar

1. Omnis Gallia est divisa in tres partes
   All Gaul is divided into three parts
quarum Belgæ incŏlumt; aliam Aquitani;
of which the Belgæ inhabit; another the Aquitani;

List of Interlinear Translations

LATIN CLASSICS

Cæsar's Gallic War. Seven Books, $2.00.
Cicero's Orations. Enlarged Edition, $2.00.
Cicero on Old Age and Friendship, $2.00.
Cornelius Nepos, $2.00.
Horace, complete, $2.00.
Livy, Books XXI and XXII, $2.00.
Ovid's Metamorphoses, complete, $2.00.
Sallust's Catiline, and Jugurthine War, $2.00.
Tacitus' Germania and Agricola, $1.50.
Virgil's Æneid, First 6 Books. Revised, $2.00.
Virgil's Æneid, complete, the 12 Books, $2.00.
Virgil's Eclogues, Georgics and Last Six Books
   Æneid, $2.00.

GREEK CLASSICS

Demosthenes On the Crown, $2.00.
Homer's Iliad. First Six Books. Revised, $2.00
Xenophon's Anabasis. Xenophon's Memorabilia,
   $2.00.

GERMAN CLASSICS

Baumbach's Der Schwiegersohn, $1.50.
Gerstacker's Germelhausen, $1.50.
Heyse's L'Arrabiata, $1.50.

INTERLINEAR TESTAMENT TRANSLATIONS

New New Testament, entire with notes, Lexicon,
   etc. $4.00
New New Testament, entire, without notes, etc. $2.50
New Old Testament, Genesis and Exodus, with
   notes $4.00

COMPLETELY PARSED TRANSLATIONS

Contain Interlinear and Literal translations, Complete Parsing and Grammatical References. All at a glance without turning a leaf.

Parsed Translations

Cæsar's Gallic War. Book One only. Long vowels indicated throughout.

Cicero's First Oration Against Cataline.

Virgil's Æneid. Book One only.

INTERLINEAR TRANSLATIONS

The original text translated word for word and line for line with a Literal English translation.

LATIN CLASSICS

Cæsar's Gallic War. Seven Books, $2.00.

Cicero's Orations. Enlarged Edition, $2.00.

Cicero on Old Age and Friendship, $2.00.

Cornelius Nepos, $2.00.

Horace, complete, $2.00.

Livy, Books XXI and XXII, $2.00.

Ovid's Metamorphoses, complete, $2.00.

Sallust's Catiline, and Jugurthine War, $2.00.

Tacitus' Germania and Agricola, $1.50.

Virgil's Æneid, first 6 Books. Revised, $2.00.

Virgil's Æneid, complete, the 12 Books, $2.00.

Virgil's Eclogues, Georgics and Last Six Books
    Æneid, $2.00.

GREEK CLASSICS

Demosthenes On the Crown, $2.00.

Homer's Iliad. First Six Books. Revised, $2.00.

Xenophon's Anabasis. Xenophon's Memorabilia,
    $2.00.

GERMAN CLASSICS

Baumbach's Der Schwiegersohn, $1.50.

Gerstacker's Germelhausen, $1.50.

Heyse's L'Arrabiata, $1.50.

INTERLINEAR TESTAMENT TRANS-
LATIONS

New New Testament, entire with notes, Lexicon,
    etc. $4.00

New New Testament, entire, without notes, etc. $2.50

New Old Testament, Genesis and Exodus, with
    notes $4.00

COMPLETELY PARSED TRANSLATIONS

The most helpful of all translations.

Contains Interlinear and Literal translations, Complete Parsing and Grammatical References. All at a glance without turning the page.

Part Page of Parsed Cæsar

BOOK I.

omnis	dīvīsa	in	partēs	I. Gaul, as a whole,
all	*divided*	*into*	*parts*	is divided into three
liam	incolunt		Belgæ,	parts: the Belgæ in-
the	*inhabit*	*the Belgæ,*		habit one of these;
artiam		quī	ipsōrum	the Aquitani another;
one third	*(those)*	*who*	*of themselves*	and those who in their own language are call-

ing. f., subj. of *est dīvīsa (dīvīsa est);* the generic term ca, Celtica and Aquitania — conceived as a totality.
—— est, 3d pers. sing. pres. ind. of the irr.
o supine; compare A.S. is, GER. ist, GK.   ; *est* in copula, or as a part of the compound *dīvīsa est,* perf.

List of Parsed Translations

Cloth, $2.00 each, postpaid.

Cæsar's Gallic War. Book 1 only. Long vowels indicated throughout.

Cicero's 1st (First) Oration Against Catiline only.
Virgil's Æneid. Book 1 only.

The value of the INTERLINEAR IDEA under the test of use.

Rev. Amory H. Bradford, *(of "The Outlook,")* *Montclair, N. J. :* It seems to be eminently scholarly, and is the best thing of the kind that I have ever seen. The source from which it emanates is enough to guarantee its excellence. For those who are beginning the study of Hebrew or who desire to continue that study it seems to me singularly valuable. (Interlinear Old Testament, Volume One.) *November 2,* 1897.

Rev. R. S. MacArthur, *Calvary Baptist Church, New York City :* No preacher in the last decade of the nineteenth century can afford to be without some knowledge of the Hebrew and Greek originals of the Word of God. It is unfortunate that men are found in the ministry whose knowledge of the Word of God is limited to an English translation; but it is a wonderful gain to such men that there are now Interlinear editions both of the Old and the New Testaments. The publishers of such volumes make Bible students who are familiar with Hebrew and Greek their debtors; and they confer an inestimable benefit on those who have no knowledge of the languages in which the Scriptures were originally written. With these Interlinear Scriptures and appropriate lexicons and grammars, any diligent pastor, even though he may be earnestly engaged in daily pastoral service, may acquire such a knowledge of Hebrew and Greek as will enable him intelligently to examine the critical commentaries on the Scriptures. With such aids available few pastors are excusable for not making an earnest study of the Scriptures in their original tongues and acquiring at least a usable knowledge of crucial Hebrew and Greek words that appear in the best commentaries. All pastors who are graduates of colleges and theological seminaries ought to make heroic efforts to keep up their knowledge of the languages in which God's Word was originally written; and even those who have not had the advantages of the schools, may acquire such a knowledge of these languages as greatly to aid them in discovering and declaring the thought of God as revealed in Holy Scripture. The publishers of these volumes have made the entire ministry their debtors. They are doing a genuinely religious work, and these volumes may rightly be regarded as among the missionary forces of our time. They have conferred a great benefit upon good Hebrew and Greek scholars by publishing volumes which save time and labor. In these busy days these are considerations of great value. They also have made it possible for those who have not had the training of the schools to acquire a working knowledge of the languages in which the Scriptures were originally written. The editorship of these Interlinear volumes is scholarly; and the typography is legible and beautiful. The mechanical arrangement is labor saving, and the Synonyms and Lexicon furnish valuable helps to the most important of all studies. *October 6,* 1897.

Rev. Franklin Gaylord, *Pastor of Trinity Congregational Church, New York City,:* I have just purchased the first volume of your Interlinear Old Testament, (Genesis and Exodus). I consider the work simply invaluable and hope nothing will prevent its completion. Aside from its linguistic value this volume is a superb specimen of book-making. I am only too happy to add my unsought testimony to that of many others. *November 12,* 1897.

Dr. Chas. H. Davis, *Editor "Biblia," Meriden, Conn. :* It saves much time when one desires to look up the meaning of the Hebrew text. *October 14,* 1897.

Rev. F. P. Lewis, *Kansas City, Mo. :* I am well pleased with the books and you may book me for the subsequent volumes of the Interlinear Old Testament. *October 14,* 1897.

Rev. Robert Whitaker, *1264 24th Ave., Oakland, Cal. :* A year or two ago I bought a copy (cloth bound) of your Interlinear New Testament. It has proven to be of great assistance in my work. I herewith order a copy of the first volume of your Old Testament edition. I hope to possess myself of the other volumes as they are issued. You are doing a good work in the interest of better Bible study. *September 29,* 1897.

Rev. C. H. Sommer, *Lapeer, Mich.:* I have received the two books, and you may put me down for the complete set of Interlinear Old Testament volumes. *November 8,* 1897.

Rev. R. F. Adair, *Huntingdon, Tenn.:* I am in receipt of my "New Old-Testament" and am delighted with it. It is by far the best Hebrew type I have ever seen. So clear and plain. The paper so beautiful, and the mechanical work so neatly done. Put me down for the remaining volumes of this invaluable work. *Nov. 9, '97.*

Rev. J. M. Cochran, *Marietta, Ohio :* The greatest invention of the 19th century. *November 5,* 1897.

Rev. K. Spannuth, *649 Wayne St., Defiance, Ohio :* The finest and most useful Hebrew Old Testament. Paper and get-up beautiful. *October 25,* 1897.

Rev. C. C. Thorne, *Windham, N. Y. :* The Interlinear Old Testament, Vol. I., came last evening. It is a valuable addition to my library,—better as a help, in some respects, than a commentary. *October 15,* 1897.

Rev. G. B. Titus, *Everett, Mass. :* I am very much pleased with Vol. I. Interlinear Old Testament— It is one of the best working tools that I have. *October 20,* 1897.

The Interlinear Scriptures.

Old Testament, Volume I, Genesis and Exodus. *Hebrew-English Interlinear.* The Hebrew text is that of Baer and Delitzsch for Genesis; for Exodus that of Theile; and these texts have been retained unchanged. The interlined translation is strictly *literal*, even to the retention of the Hebrew idioms. In the left-hand margin of the pages is the King James Version; in the right-hand margin the Revised Version, enabling instant comparison of all four renderings. Footnotes on every page present the variorum readings of all the important *Versions* — — the Septuagint, the Peshitto, the Vulgate, the Targum of Onkelos, and others. This volume also contains the Hebrew alphabet with the English equivalents; and Tables showing the variations of the Hebrew verb.

> **Price:** Cloth, $4.00 ; Half-leather, $5.00 ; Divinity Circuit, $6.00.

The publishers propose to complete the Interlinear OLD Testament, within a reasonable time, in three additional volumes. Although each of the subsequent volumes must of necessity contain noticeably more pages than Volume I, nevertheless it is our intention, dependent upon the support given the undertaking by clergymen purchasers, to place a lower price upon each successive volume, bringing the price of the complete set down to *twelve dollars* instead of *sixteen dollars* for the cloth binding, and a proportional price for the other bindings. In fact all patrons who actually subscribe for the complete Old Testament when ordering Volume I, may do so upon that express stipulation, *the price of each subsequent volume not to be paid until publication.* A prompt and generous response to this really liberal offer *will encourage us to hasten materially the completion of the other volumes of this extremely expensive undertaking.*

New Testament, Complete. *New Edition* with Lexicon and Synonyms. *Greek-English Interlinear.* The Greek text is the standard. The interlined translation is strictly literal. The King James version is presented in parallel columns in the margins. Footnotes present the various readings of the text of the editions of Elzevir–1624, Griesbach, Lachmann, Tischendorf, Tregelles, Alford, and Wordsworth. The GREEK-ENGLISH NEW-TESTAMENT LEXICON, which makes its first bow in this volume, is entirely new. It is the work of Professor Berry, the editor of the Interlinear Old Testament, and produced under our auspices for this volume with the definite and well-accomplished purpose of supplying clergymen and Bible students with the very best ready-reference New-Testament Lexicon ever designed for their special needs. It contains also a lucid presentation of the SYNONYMS OF THE GREEK TESTAMENT with a complete INDEX.

> **Price** of the *Interlinear New Testament, Complete, with Lexicon and Synonyms:* Cloth, $4.00; Half-leather, $5.00 ; Divinity Circuit, $6.00.